1999
BASEBALL
CARD

PRICE GUIDE

•13TH EDITION•

PRICE GUIDE
EDITORS OF

Published by

 **krause
publications**

700 E. State Street • Iola, WI 54990-0001
Telephone: 715/445-2214

Please call or write for our free catalog of sports publications.
Our toll-free number to place an order or obtain a free catalog is 800-258-0929
or please use our regular business telephone 715-445-2214
for editorial comment and further information.

Library of Congress Catalog Number: 87-80033
ISBN: 0-87341-743-7

Printed in the United States of America

HOW TO USE THIS CATALOG

This catalog has been uniquely designed to serve the needs of collectors and dealers at all levels from beginning to advanced. It provides a comprehensive guide to nearly 20 years of baseball card issues, arranged so that even the most novice hobbyist can consult it with confidence and ease.

The following explanations summarize the general practices used in preparing this catalog's listings. However, because of specialized requirements which may vary from card set to card set, these must not be considered ironclad. Where these standards have been set aside, appropriate notations are usually incorporated.

ARRANGEMENT

The most important feature in identifying and pricing a baseball card is its set of origin. Therefore, the main body of this catalog, covering cards issued from 1981-date, has been alphabetically arranged according to the name by which the set is most popularly known to collectors, or by which it can be most easily identified by a person examining a card.

Among those card issuers who produced sets for more than a single year, their sets are then listed chronologically, from earliest to most recent, again within specific eras.

Within each set, the cards are listed by their designated card number, or in the absence of card numbers, alphabetically according to the last name of the player pictured. Listing numbers found in parentheses indicate the number does not appear on the card. Certain cards which fall outside the parameters of the normal card numbering for a specific set may be found at the beginning or end of the listings for that set.

IDENTIFICATION

While most modern baseball cards are well identified on front, back or both, as to date and issue, such has not always been the case. In general, the back of the card is more useful in identifying the set of origin than the front. The issuer or sponsor's name will usually appear on the back since, after all, baseball cards were first produced as a promotional item to stimulate sales of other products. As often as not, that issuer's name is the name by which the set is known to collectors and under which it will be found listed in this catalog.

In some difficult cases, identifying a baseball card's general age, if not specific year of issue, can usually be accomplished by studying the biological or statistical information on the back of the card. The last year mentioned in either the biography or stats is usually the year which preceded the year of issue.

PHOTOGRAPHS

A photograph of the front of at least one representative card from virtually every set listed in this catalog has been incorporated into the listings to aid in identification.

Photographs have been printed in reduced size. The actual size of cards in each set is given in the introductory text preceding its listing, unless the card is the standard size (2.5" by 3.5").

DATING

The dating of baseball cards by year of issue on the front or back of the card itself is a relatively new phenomenon. In most cases, to accurately determine a date of issue for an unidentified card, it must be studied for clues. As mentioned, the biography, career summary or statistics on the back of the card are the best way to pinpoint a year of issue. In most cases, the year of issue will be the year after the last season mentioned on the card.

In some cases, particular card sets were issued over a period of more than one calendar year, but since they are collected together as a single set, their specific year of issue is not important. Such sets will be listed with their complete known range of issue years.

NUMBERING

While many baseball card issues as far back as the 1880s have contained card numbers assigned by the issuer to facilitate the collecting of a complete set, the practice has by no means been universal. Even today, not every set bears card numbers.

Logically, those baseball cards which were numbered by their manufacturer are presented in that numerical order within the listings of this catalog whenever possible. In a few cases, complete player checklists were obtained from earlier published sources which did not note card numbers, and so numbers have been arbitrarily assigned. Many other unnumbered issues have been assigned catalog numbers to facilitate their universal identification within the hobby, especially when buying and selling by mail.

In all cases, numbers which have been assigned, or which otherwise do not appear on the card through error or by design, are shown in this catalog within parentheses. In virtually all cases, unless a more natural system suggested itself by the unique matter of a particular set, the assignment of numbers by the cataloging staff has been done by alphabetical arrangement of the players' last names or the card's principal title.

Significant collectible variations for any particular card are noted within the listings by the application of a suffix letter. In instances of variations, the suffix "a" is assigned to the variation which was created first, when it can be so identified.

NAMES

The identification of a player by full name on the front of his baseball card has been a common practice only since the 1920s. Prior to that, the player's last name and team were the usual information found on the card front.

As a general—though not universally applied—practice, the listings in this volume present the player's name exactly as it appears on the front of the card. If the player's full name only appears on the back, rather than on the front of the card, the listing may correspond to that designation.

A player's name checklisted in italic type indicates a rookie card.

Cards which contain misspelled first or last names, or even wrong initials, will have included in their listings the incorrect information, with a correction accompanying in parentheses. This extends, also, to cases where the name on the card does not correspond to the player actually pictured.

In some cases, to facilitate efficient presentations, to maintain ease of use for the reader, or to allow for proper computer sorting of data, a player's name or card title may be listed other than as it appears on the card.

GRADING

It is necessary that some sort of card grading standard be used so that buyer and seller (especially when dealing by mail) may reach an informed agreement on the value of a card.

Modern issues, which have been preserved in top condition in considerable number, are listed only in grade of Mint (MT), reflective of the fact that there exists in the current market little or no demand for cards of the recent past in lower grades.

Values for low-grade cards form 1981-date may be generally figured by using a figure of 75% of the Mint price for Near Mint specimens, and 40% of the Mint price for Excellent cards.

For the benefit of the reader, we present herewith the grading guide which was originally formulated in 1981 by Baseball Cards magazine (now SportsCards magazine) and Sports Collectors Digest, and has been continually refined since that time.

These grading definitions have been used in the pricing of cards in this book, but they are by no means a universally-accepted grading standard.

The potential buyer of a baseball card should keep that in mind when encountering cards of nominally the same grade, but at a price which differs widely from that quoted in this book.

Ultimately, the collector himself must formulate his own personal grading standards in deciding whether cards available for purchase meet the needs of his own collection.

No collector is required to adhere to the grading standards presented herewith—or to any other published grading standards—but all are invited to do so. The editors of Krause Publications' sports books and price guides are eager to work toward the development of a standardized system of card grading that will be consistent with the realities of the hobby marketplace. Contact the editor.

Mint (MT): A perfect card. Well-centered, with parallel borders which appear equal to the naked eye. Four sharp, square corners. No creases, edge dents, surface scratches, paper flaws, loss of luster, yellowing or fading, regardless of age. No imperfectly printed card—out of register, badly cut or ink flawed—or card stained by contact with gum, wax or other substances can be considered truly Mint, even if new out of the pack. Generally, to be considered in Mint condition, a card's borders must exist in a ratio of 60/40 side to side and top to bottom.

Near Mint (NR MT): A nearly perfectly card. At first glance, a Near Mint card appears perfect; upon closer examination, however, a minor flaw will be discovered. On well-centered cards, three of the four corners must be perfectly sharp; only one corner shows a minor imperfection upon close inspection. A slightly off-center card with one or more borders being noticeably unequal—but no worse than in a ratio of 70/30 S/S or T/B—would also fit this grade.

Excellent (EX): Corners are still fairly sharp with only moderate wear. Card borders may be off center as much as 80/20. No creases. May have very minor gum, wax or product stains, front or back. Surfaces may show slight loss of luster from rubbing across other cards.

ROOKIE CARDS

While the status (and automatic premium value) which a player's rookie card used to carry has diminished in recent years, and though the hobby still has not reached a universal definition of a rookie card, many significant rookie cards are noted in this catalog's listings by the use of italic type. For purposes of this catalog, a player's rookie card is considered to be any card in a licensed set from a major manufacturer in the first year in which that player appears on a card.

VALUATIONS

Values quoted in this book represent the current retail market at the time of compilation (December, 1998). The quoted values are the result of a unique system of evaluation and verification created by the catalog's editors. Utilizing specialized computer analysis and drawing upon recommendations provided through their daily involvement in the publication of the hobby's leading sports collectors' periodicals, as well as the input of consultants, dealers and collectors, each listing is, in the final analysis, the interpretation of that data by one or more of the editors.

It should be stressed, however, that this book is intended to serve only as an aid in evaluating cards; actual market conditions are constantly changing. This is especially true of the cards of current players, whose on-field performance during the course of a season can greatly affect the value of their cards—upwards or downwards. Because of the extremely volatile nature of new card prices, especially high-end issues, we have chosen not to include the very latest releases such as premium-price brands from the major companies, feeling it is better to have no listings at all for those cards than to have inaccurate values in print.

Because this volume is intended to reflect the national market, users will find regional price variances caused by demand differences. Cards of Astros slugger Jeff Bagwell will, for instance, often sell at prices greater than quoted herein at shops and shows in the Houston area. Conversely, his cards may be acquired at a discount from these valuations when purchased on the East or West Coast.

Publication of this book is not intended as a solicitation to buy or sell the listed cards by the editors, publishers or contributors.

Again, the values here are retail prices—what a collector can expect to pay when buying a card from a dealer. The wholesale price, that which a collector can expect to receive from a dealer when selling cards, will be significantly lower.

Most dealers operate on a 100 percent mark-up, generally paying about 50 percent of a card's retail value for cards which they are purchasing for inventory. On some high-demand cards, dealers will pay up to 75 percent or even 100 percent or more of retail value, anticipating continued price increases. Conversely, for many low-demand cards, such as common players' cards, dealers may pay as little as 10 percent or even less of retail with many base-brand cards of recent years having no resale value at all.

SETS

Collectors may note that the complete set prices for newer issues quoted in these listings are usually significantly lower than the total of the value of the individual cards which comprise the set. This reflects two factors in the baseball card market. First, a seller is often willing to take a lower composite price for a complete set as a "volume discount" and to avoid carrying in inventory a large number of common player or other lower-demand cards.

Second, to a degree, the value of common cards can be said to be inflated as a result of having a built-in overhead charge to justify the dealer's time in sorting cards, carrying them in stock and filling orders. This accounts for the fact that even brand new base-brand baseball cards, which cost the dealer around one cent each when bought in bulk, carry individual price tags of five cents or higher.

Some set prices shown, especially for old cards in top condition, are merely theoretical in that it is unlikely that a complete set exists in that condition. In general among older cards the range of conditions found in even the most painstakingly assembled complete set make the set values quoted useful only as a starting point for price negotiations.

ERRORS/VARIATIONS

It is often hard for the beginning collector to understand that an error on a baseball card, in and of itself, does not usually add premium value to that card. It is usually only when the correcting of an error in the subsequent printing creates a variation that premium value attaches to an error.

Minor errors, such as wrong stats or personal data, misspellings, inconsistencies, etc.—usually affecting the back of the card—are very common, especially in recent years. Unless a corrected variation was also printed, these errors are not noted in the listings of this book because they are not generally perceived by collectors to have premium value.

On the other hand, major effort has been expended to include the most complete listings ever for collectible variation cards. Many scarce and valuable variations are included in these listings because they are widely collected and often have significant premium value.

Beginning in the early 1990s, some card companies began production of their basic sets at more than one printing facility. This frequently resulted in numerous minor variations in photo cropping and back data presentation. Combined with a general decline in quality control from the mid-1980s through the early 1990s, which allowed unprecedented numbers of uncorrected error cards to be released, this caused a general softening of collector interest in errors and variations. Despite the fact most of these modern variations have no premium value, they are listed here as a matter of record.

COUNTERFEITS/REPRINTS

As the value of baseball cards has risen in the past 10-20 years, certain cards and sets have become too expensive for the average collector to obtain. This, along with changes in the technology of color printing, has given rise to increasing numbers of counterfeit and reprint cards.

While both terms describe essentially the same thing—a modern day copy which attempts to duplicate as closely as possible an original baseball card—there are differences which are important to the collector.

Generally, a counterfeit is made with the intention of deceiving somebody into believing it is genuine, and thus paying large amounts of money for it. The counterfeiter takes every pain to try to make his fakes look as authentic as possible. In recent years, the 1963 Pete Rose, 1984 Donruss Don Mattingly and more than 100 superstar cards of the late 1960s-early 1990s have been counterfeited - many of which were quickly detected because of the differences in quality of cardboard on which they were printed.

A reprint, on the other hand, while it may have been made to look as close as possible to an original card, is made with the intention of allowing collectors to buy them as substitutes for cards they may never be otherwise able to afford. The big difference is that a reprint is generally marked as such, usually on the back of the card.

In other cases, like the Topps 1952 reprint set and 1953-54 Archives issues, the replicas are printed in a size markedly different from the originals. Collectors should be aware, however, that unscrupulous persons will sometimes cut off or otherwise obliterate the distinguishing word— "Reprint," "Copy,"—or modern copyright date on the back of a reprint card in an attempt to pass it as genuine.

A collector's best defense against reprints and counterfeits is to acquire a knowledge of the look and feel of genuine baseball cards of various eras and issues.

NEW ISSUES

Because new baseball cards are being issued all the time, the cataloging of them remains an on-going challenge. The editor will attempt to keep abreast of new issues so that they may be added to future editions of this book. Readers are invited to submit news of new issues, especially limited-edition or regionally issued cards, to the editor. Address: Bob Lemke, Catalog Co-ordinator, 700 E. State St., Iola, Wis. 54990.

Late 1998-Early 1999 Issues

1998 Leaf Rookies & Stars

		MT
Complete Set (339):		250.00
Common Player:		.15
Shortprints (131-230, 301-339):		
Common SPs:		.40
Inserted 1:2		
True Blues: 10x to 20x		
SP True Blues: 3x to 5x		
Production 500 sets		
Longevities: 60x to 100x		
SP Longevities: 15x to 25x		
Production 50 sets		
1	Andy Pettitte	.50
2	Roberto Alomar	.50
3	Randy Johnson	.50
4	Manny Ramirez	.75
5	Paul Molitor	.50
6	Mike Mussina	.50
7	Jim Thome	.40
8	Tino Martinez	.30
9	Gary Sheffield	.25
10	Chuck Knoblauch	.30
11	Bernie Williams	.50
12	Tim Salmon	.25
13	Sammy Sosa	2.00
14	Wade Boggs	.25
15	Andres Galarraga	.50
16	Pedro Martinez	.50
17	David Justice	.30
18	Chan Ho Park	.30
19	Jay Buhner	.25
20	Ryan Klesko	.25
21	Barry Larkin	.25
22	Will Clark	.30
23	Raul Mondesi	.25
24	Rickey Henderson	.20
25	Jim Edmonds	.15
26	Ken Griffey Jr.	3.00
27	Frank Thomas	2.00
28	Cal Ripken Jr.	2.50
29	Alex Rodriguez	2.00
30	Mike Piazza	2.00
31	Greg Maddux	2.00
32	Chipper Jones	1.50
33	Tony Gwynn	1.50
34	Derek Jeter	1.50
35	Jeff Bagwell	.75
36	Juan Gonzalez	1.50
37	Nomar Garciaparra	2.00
38	Andruw Jones	.75
39	Hideo Nomo	.40
40	Roger Clemens	1.25
41	Mark McGwire	4.00
42	Scott Rolen	.75
43	Vladimir Guerrero	1.00
44	Barry Bonds	.75
45	Darin Erstad	.75
46	Albert Belle	.75
47	Kenny Lofton	.75
48	Mo Vaughn	.75
49	Ivan Rodriguez	.75
50	Jose Cruz Jr.	.50
51	Tony Clark	.50
52	Larry Walker	.40
53	Mark Grace	.25
54	Edgar Martinez	.15
55	Fred McGriff	.25
56	Rafael Palmeiro	.25
57	Matt Williams	.25
58	Craig Biggio	.25
59	Ken Caminiti	.20
60	Jose Canseco	.30
61	Brady Anderson	.15
62	Moises Alou	.25
63	Justin Thompson	.15
64	John Smoltz	.20
65	Carlos Delgado	.15
66	J.T. Snow	.15
67	Jason Giambi	.15
68	Garret Anderson	.15
69	Rondell White	.25
70	Eric Karros	.15
71	Javier Lopez	.25
72	Pat Hentgen	.15
73	Dante Bichette	.25
74	Charles Johnson	.15
75	Tom Glavine	.25
76	Rusty Greer	.15
77	Travis Fryman	.15
78	Todd Hundley	.15
79	Ray Lankford	.15
80	Denny Neagle	.15
81	Henry Rodriguez	.15
82	Sandy Alomar Jr.	.15
83	Robin Ventura	.15
84	John Olerud	.25
85	Omar Vizquel	.15
86	Darren Dreifort	.15
87	Kevin Brown	.25
88	Curt Schilling	.25
89	Francisco Cordova	.15
90	Brad Radke	.15
91	David Cone	.25
92	Paul O'Neill	.25
93	Vinny Castilla	.15
94	Marquis Grissom	.15
95	Brian Hunter	.15
96	Kevin Appier	.15
97	Bobby Bonilla	.15
98	Eric Young	.15
99	Jason Kendall	.25
100	Shawn Green	.15
101	Edgardo Alfonzo	.15
102	Alan Benes	.15
103	Bobby Higginson	.15
104	Todd Greene	.15
105	Jose Guillen	.25
106	Neifi Perez	.15
107	Edgar Renteria	.15
108	Chris Stynes	.15
109	Todd Walker	.25
110	Brian Jordan	.15
111	Joe Carter	.25
112	Ellis Burks	.15
113	Brett Tomko	.15
114	Mike Cameron	.15
115	Shannon Stewart	.15
116	Kevin Orie	.15
117	Brian Giles	.15
118	Hideki Irabu	.30
119	Delino DeShields	.15
120	David Segui	.15
121	Dustin Hermanson	.15
122	Kevin Young	.15
123	Jay Bell	.15
124	Doug Glanville	.15
125	*John Roskos*	.15
126	*Damon Hollins*	.15
127	Matt Stairs	.15
128	Cliff Floyd	.15
129	Derek Bell	.15
130	Darryl Strawberry	.15
131	Ken Griffey Jr. (Power Tools)	12.00
132	Tim Salmon (Power Tools)	1.00
133	Manny Ramirez (Power Tools)	3.00
134	Paul Konerko (Power Tools)	.75
135	Frank Thomas (Power Tools)	8.00
136	Todd Helton (Power Tools)	3.00
137	Larry Walker (Power Tools)	1.50
138	Mo Vaughn (Power Tools)	3.00
139	Travis Lee (Power Tools)	3.00
140	Ivan Rodriguez (Power Tools)	3.00
141	Ben Grieve (Power Tools)	3.00
142	Brad Fullmer (Power Tools)	.75
143	Alex Rodriguez (Power Tools)	8.00
144	Mike Piazza (Power Tools)	8.00
145	Greg Maddux (Power Tools)	8.00
146	Chipper Jones (Power Tools)	6.00
147	Kenny Lofton (Power Tools)	3.00
148	Albert Belle (Power Tools)	3.00
149	Barry Bonds (Power Tools)	3.00
150	Vladimir Guerrero (Power Tools)	3.00
151	Tony Gwynn (Power Tools)	6.00
152	Derek Jeter (Power Tools)	6.00
153	Jeff Bagwell (Power Tools)	.15
154	Juan Gonzalez (Power Tools)	.15
155	Nomar Garciaparra (Power Tools)	.15
156	Andruw Jones (Power Tools)	.15
157	Hideo Nomo (Power Tools)	1.50
158	Roger Clemens (Power Tools)	5.00
159	Mark McGwire (Power Tools)	15.00
160	Scott Rolen (Power Tools)	3.00
161	Travis Lee (Team Line-Up)	3.00
162	Ben Grieve (Team Line-Up)	3.00
163	Jose Guillen (Team Line-Up)	.40
164	John Olerud (Team Line-Up)	.50
165	Kevin Appier (Team Line-Up)	.40
166	Marquis Grissom (Team Line-Up)	.40
167	Rusty Greer (Team Line-Up)	.40
168	Ken Caminiti (Team Line-Up)	.60
169	Craig Biggio (Team Line-Up)	.75
170	Ken Griffey Jr. (Team Line-Up)	12.00
171	Larry Walker (Team Line-Up)	1.50
172	Barry Larkin (Team Line-Up)	.75
173	Andres Galarraga (Team Line-Up)	2.00
174	Wade Boggs (Team Line-Up)	.75
175	Sammy Sosa (Team Line-Up)	10.00
176	Mike Piazza (Team Line-Up)	8.00
177	Jim Thome (Team Line-Up)	1.50
178	Paul Molitor (Team Line-Up)	2.00
179	Tony Clark (Team Line-Up)	1.50
180	Jose Cruz Jr. (Team Line-Up)	2.00
181	Darin Erstad (Team Line-Up)	3.00
182	Barry Bonds (Team Line-Up)	3.00
183	Vladimir Guerrero (Team Line-Up)	3.00
184	Scott Rolen (Team Line-Up)	3.00
185	Mark McGwire (Team Line-Up)	15.00
186	Nomar Garciaparra (Team Line-Up)	8.00
187	Gary Sheffield (Team Line-Up)	.75
188	Cal Ripken Jr. (Team Line-Up)	10.00
189	Frank Thomas (Team Line-Up)	8.00
190	Andy Petitte (Team Line-Up)	1.50
191	Paul Konerko	.75
192	Todd Helton	3.00
193	Mark Kotsay	.75

194	Brad Fullmer	.75
195	*Kevin Millwood*	12.00
196	David Ortiz	.15
197	Kerry Wood	10.00
198	Miguel Tejada	1.00
199	Fernando Tatis	.40
200	Jaret Wright	2.00
201	Ben Grieve	3.00
202	Travis Lee	3.00
203	Wes Helms	.40
204	Geoff Jenkins	.40
205	Russell Branyan	.40
206	*Esteban Yan*	.40
207	Ben Ford	.40
208	*Rich Butler*	3.00
209	*Ryan Jackson*	.40
210	A.J. Hinch	.40
211	*Magglio Ordonez*	5.00
212	*David Dellucci*	2.00
213	Billy McMillon	.40
214	Mike Lowell	5.00
215	*Todd Erdos*	.40
216	Carlos Mendoza	1.00
217	*Frank Catalanotto*	.40
218	*Julio Ramirez*	2.00
219	*John Halama*	.60
220	Wilson Delgado	.40
221	*Mike Judd*	.40
222	*Rolando Arrojo*	4.00
223	Jason LaRue	.40
224	*Manny Aybar*	.60
225	Jorge Velandia	.40
226	Mike Kinkade	.40
227	*Carlos Lee*	.60
228	Bobby Hughes	.40
229	*Ryan Christenson*	1.00
230	*Masato Yoshii*	1.00
231	Richard Hidalgo	.15
232	Rafael Medina	.15
233	Damian Jackson	.15
234	Derek Lowe	.15
235	Mario Valdez	.15
236	Eli Marrero	.15
237	Juan Encarnacion	.15
238	Livan Hernandez	.15
239	Bruce Chen	.25
240	Eric Milton	.15
241	Jason Varitek	.15
242	Scott Elarton	.15
243	*Manuel Barrios*	.30
244	Mike Caruso	.15
245	Tom Evans	.15
246	Pat Cline	.15
247	Matt Clement	.15
248	Karim Garcia	.15
249	Richie Sexson	.25
250	Sidney Ponson	.15
251	Randall Simon	.25
252	Tony Saunders	.15
253	Javier Valentin	.15
254	Danny Clyburn	.15
255	Michael Coleman	.15
256	*Hanley Frias*	.25
257	Miguel Cairo	.15
258	*Rob Stanifer*	.15
259	Lou Collier	.15
260	Abraham Nunez	.15
261	Ricky Ledee	.30
262	Carl Pavano	.15
263	Derrek Lee	.15
264	Jeff Abbott	.15
265	Bob Abreu	.15
266	Bartolo Colon	.15
267	Mike Drumright	.15
268	Daryle Ward	.15
269	Gabe Alvarez	.15
270	Josh Booty	.15
271	Damian Moss	.15
272	Brian Rose	.15
273	Jarrod Washburn	.15
274	Bobby Estalella	.15
275	Enrique Wilson	.15
276	Derrick Gibson	.15
277	Ken Cloude	.15
278	Kevin Witt	.15
279	Donnie Sadler	.15
280	Sean Casey	.25
281	Jacob Cruz	.15
282	Ron Wright	.15
283	Jeremi Gonzalez	.15
284	Desi Relaford	.15
285	Bobby Smith	.15
286	Javier Vazquez	.15
287	*Steve Woodard*	.25
288	Greg Norton	.15
289	Cliff Politte	.15

290	Felix Heredia	.15
291	Braden Looper	.15
292	Felix Martinez	.15
293	Brian Meadows	.15
294	Edwin Diaz	.15
295	Pat Watkins	.15
296	*Marc Pisciotta*	.15
297	Rick Gorecki	.15
298	DaRond Stovall	.15
299	Andy Larkin	.15
300	Felix Rodriguez	.15
301	Blake Stein	.40
302	*John Rocker*	2.50
303	*Justin Baughman*	1.50
304	*Jesus Sanchez*	1.50
305	Randy Winn	.40
306	Lou Merloni	.40
307	*Jim Parque*	2.00
308	Dennis Reyes	.40
309	*Orlando Hernandez*	25.00
310	Jason Johnson	.40
311	Torii Hunter	.40
312	Mike Piazza	8.00
313	*Mike Frank*	2.50
314	*Troy Glaus*	20.00
315	*Jin Cho*	.75
316	Ruben Mateo	8.00
317	*Ryan Minor*	6.00
318	Aramis Ramirez	.75
319	Adrian Beltre	1.50
320	*Matt Anderson*	3.00
321	Gabe Kapler	20.00
322	*Jeremy Giambi*	6.00
323	Carlos Beltran	.40
324	Dermal Brown	1.00
325	Ben Davis	.40
326	Eric Chavez	2.00
327	*Bob Howry*	1.00
328	Roy Halladay	.40
329	George Lombard	.40
330	Michael Barrett	.40
331	*Fernando Seguignol*	5.00
332	*J.D. Drew*	75.00
333	*Odalis Perez*	4.00
334	*Alex Cora*	1.50
335	*Placido Polanco*	1.50
336	*Armando Rios*	1.00
337	Sammy Sosa (HR commemorative)	10.00
338	Mark McGwire (HR commemorative)	15.00
339	Sammy Sosa, Mark McGwire (Checklist)	5.00

1998 Leaf Rookies & Stars Cross Training

		MT
Complete Set (10):		240.00
Common Player:		8.00
Production 1,000 sets		
1	Kenny Lofton	12.00
2	Ken Griffey Jr.	60.00
3	Alex Rodriguez	40.00
4	Greg Maddux	40.00
5	Barry Bonds	15.00
6	Ivan Rodriguez	15.00
7	Chipper Jones	30.00
8	Jeff Bagwell	15.00
9	Nomar Garciaparra	40.00
10	Derek Jeter	30.00

1998 Leaf Rookies & Stars Crusade

		MT
Complete Green Set (30):		500.00
Common Player:		8.00
Production 250 sets		
Purples: 1x to 2x		
Production 100 sets		
Reds: 2x to 4x		
Production 25 sets		
101	Richard Hidalgo	8.00
102	Paul Konerko	20.00
103	Miguel Tejada	25.00
104	Fernando Tatis	8.00
105	Travis Lee	50.00
106	Wes Helms	8.00
107	Rich Butler	20.00
108	Mark Kotsay	15.00
109	Eli Marrero	8.00
110	David Ortiz	8.00
111	Juan Encarnacion	8.00
112	Jaret Wright	40.00
113	Livan Hernandez	8.00
114	Ron Wright	15.00
115	Ryan Christenson	8.00
116	Eric Milton	8.00
117	Brad Fullmer	15.00
118	Karim Garcia	8.00
119	Abraham Nunez	8.00
120	Ricky Ledee	25.00
121	Carl Pavano	8.00
122	Derrek Lee	8.00
123	A.J. Hinch	8.00
124	Brian Rose	8.00
125	Bobby Estalella	8.00
126	Kevin Millwood	60.00
127	Kerry Wood	150.00
128	Sean Casey	20.00
129	Russell Branyan	8.00
130	Magglio Ordonez	40.00

1998 Leaf Rookies & Stars Donruss MVPs

		MT
Complete Set (20):		150.00
Common Player:		2.00
Production 4,500 sets		
Pennant Editions: 2x to 4x		
Production 500 sets		
1	Frank Thomas	12.00
2	Chuck Knoblauch	2.00
3	Cal Ripken Jr.	15.00
4	Alex Rodriguez	12.00
5	Ivan Rodriguez	5.00
6	Albert Belle	5.00
7	Ken Griffey Jr.	20.00
8	Juan Gonzalez	10.00
9	Roger Clemens	8.00
10	Mo Vaughn	5.00
11	Jeff Bagwell	5.00
12	Craig Biggio	2.00
13	Chipper Jones	10.00
14	Barry Larkin	2.00
15	Mike Piazza	12.00

16	Barry Bonds	5.00
17	Andruw Jones	5.00
18	Tony Gwynn	10.00
19	Greg Maddux	12.00
20	Mark McGwire	25.00

1998 Leaf Rookies & Stars Extreme Measures

		MT
Complete Set (10):		300.00
Common Player:		6.00
1	Ken Griffey Jr. (944)	60.00
2	Frank Thomas (653)	50.00
3	Tony Gwynn (628)	40.00
4	Mark McGwire (942)	75.00
5	Larry Walker (280)	20.00
6	Mike Piazza (960)	40.00
7	Roger Clemens (708)	30.00
8	Greg Maddux (980)	40.00
9	Jeff Bagwell (873)	20.00
10	Nomar Garciaparra (989)	40.00

1998 Leaf Rookies & Stars Freshman Orientation

		MT
Complete Set (20):		60.00
Common Player:		1.50
Production 5,000 sets		
1	Todd Helton	6.00
2	Ben Grieve	6.00
3	Travis Lee	6.00
4	Paul Konerko	2.50
5	Jaret Wright	4.00
6	Livan Hernandez	1.50
7	Brad Fullmer	2.50
8	Carl Pavano	1.50
9	Richard Hidalgo	1.50
10	Miguel Tejada	2.50
11	Mark Kotsay	2.00
12	David Ortiz	1.50
13	Juan Encarnacion	1.50
14	Fernando Tatis	1.50
15	Kevin Millwood	7.00
15s	Kevin Millwood ("SAMPLE" overprint on back)	3.00
16	Kerry Wood	20.00
17	Magglio Ordonez	4.00
18	Derek Lee	1.50
19	Jose Cruz Jr.	5.00
20	A.J. Hinch	1.50

1998 Leaf Rookies & Stars Great American Heroes

		MT
Complete Set (20):		250.00
Common Player:		4.00
Production 2,500 sets		
1	Frank Thomas	20.00
2	Cal Ripken Jr.	25.00
3	Ken Griffey Jr.	30.00
4	Alex Rodriguez	20.00
5	Greg Maddux	20.00
6	Mike Piazza	20.00
7	Chipper Jones	15.00
8	Tony Gwynn	15.00
9	Jeff Bagwell	8.00
10	Juan Gonzalez	15.00
11	Hideo Nomo	5.00
12	Roger Clemens	12.00
13	Mark McGwire	40.00
14	Barry Bonds	8.00
15	Kenny Lofton	8.00
16	Larry Walker	4.00
17	Paul Molitor	6.00
18	Wade Boggs	4.00
19	Barry Larkin	4.00
20	Andres Galarraga	6.00

1998 Leaf Rookies & Stars Home Run Derby

		MT
Complete Set (20):		200.00
Common Player:		4.00
Production 2,500 sets		
1	Tino Martinez	4.00
2	Jim Thome	6.00
3	Larry Walker	4.00
4	Tony Clark	6.00
5	Jose Cruz Jr.	6.00
6	Barry Bonds	8.00
7	Scott Rolen	8.00
8	Paul Konerko	4.00
9	Travis Lee	8.00
10	Todd Helton	8.00
11	Mark McGwire	40.00
12	Andruw Jones	8.00
13	Nomar Garciaparra	20.00
14	Juan Gonzalez	15.00
15	Jeff Bagwell	8.00
16	Chipper Jones	15.00
17	Mike Piazza	20.00
18	Frank Thomas	20.00
19	Ken Griffey Jr.	30.00
20	Albert Belle	8.00

1998 Leaf Rookies & Stars ML Hard Drives

		MT
Complete Set (20):		220.00
Common Player:		4.00
Production 2,500 sets		
1	Jeff Bagwell	8.00
2	Juan Gonzalez	15.00
3	Nomar Garciaparra	20.00
4	Ken Griffey Jr.	30.00
5	Frank Thomas	20.00
6	Cal Ripken Jr.	25.00
7	Alex Rodriguez	20.00
8	Mike Piazza	20.00

9	Chipper Jones	15.00
10	Tony Gwynn	15.00
11	Derek Jeter	15.00
12	Mo Vaughn	8.00
13	Ben Grieve	8.00
14	Manny Ramirez	8.00
15	Vladimir Guerrero	10.00
16	Scott Rolen	8.00
17	Darin Erstad	8.00
18	Kenny Lofton	6.00
19	Brad Fullmer	4.00
20	David Justice	4.00

1998 Leaf Rookies & Stars Standing Ovation

		MT
Complete Set (10):		90.00
Common Player:		2.00
Production 5,000 sets		
1	Barry Bonds	5.00
2	Mark McGwire	25.00
3	Ken Griffey Jr.	20.00
4	Frank Thomas	12.00
5	Tony Gwynn	10.00
6	Cal Ripken Jr.	15.00
7	Greg Maddux	12.00
8	Roger Clemens	8.00
9	Paul Molitor	4.00
10	Ivan Rodriguez	5.00

1998 Leaf Rookies & Stars Ticket Masters

		MT
Complete Set (20):		225.00
Common Player:		4.00
Production 2,250 sets		
Die-Cuts: 3x to 5x		
Production 250 sets		
1	Ken Griffey Jr., Alex Rodriguez	35.00
2	Frank Thomas, Albert Belle	20.00
3	Cal Ripken Jr., Roberto Alomar	25.00

4	Greg Maddux, Chipper Jones	20.00
5	Tony Gwynn, Ken Caminiti	15.00
6	Derek Jeter, Andy Pettitte	15.00
7	Jeff Bagwell, Craig Biggio	8.00
8	Juan Gonzalez, Ivan Rodriguez	15.00
9	Nomar Garciaparra, Mo Vaughn	20.00
10	Vladimir Guerrero, Brad Fullmer	10.00
11	Andruw Jones, Andres Galarraga	8.00
12	Tino Martinez, Chuck Knoblauch	4.00
13	Raul Mondesi, Paul Konerko	4.00
14	Roger Clemens, Jose Cruz Jr.	10.00
15	Mark McGwire, Brian Jordan	40.00
16	Kenny Lofton, Manny Ramirez	8.00
17	Larry Walker, Todd Helton	8.00
18	Darin Erstad, Tim Salmon	8.00
19	Travis Lee, Matt Williams	8.00
20	Ben Grieve, Jason Giambi	8.00

1999 Pacific

		MT
Complete Set (450):		40.00
Common Player:		.10
Platinum Blues: 75x to 120x		
Yng Stars & RCs: 40x to 75x		
Inserted 1:73		
1	Garret Anderson	.10
2	Jason Dickson	.10
3	Gary DiSarcina	.10
4	Jim Edmonds	.20
5	Darin Erstad	.75
6	Chuck Finley	.10
7	Shigetosi Hasegawa	.10
8	Ken Hill	.10
9	Dave Hollins	.10
10	Phil Nevin	.10
11	Troy Percival	.10
12	Tim Salmon	.25
13	Brian Anderson	.10
14	Tony Batista	.10
15	Jay Bell	.10
16	Andy Benes	.10
17	Yamil Benitez	.10
18	Omar Daal	.10
19	David Dellucci	.10
20	Karim Garcia	.10
21	Bernard Gilkey	.10
22	Travis Lee	.75
23	Aaron Small	.10
24	Kelly Stinnett	.10
25	Devon White	.10
26	Matt Williams	.25
27	Bruce Chen	.10
28	Andres Galarraga	.35
29	Tom Glavine	.20
30	Ozzie Guillen	.10
31	Andruw Jones	.75
32	Chipper Jones	1.50
33	Ryan Klesko	.25
34	George Lombard	.10
35	Javy Lopez	.10
36	Greg Maddux	2.00
37	Marty Malloy	.10
38	Dennis Martinez	.10

39	Kevin Millwood	.25
40	Alex Rodriguez	2.00
41	Denny Neagle	.10
42	John Smoltz	.20
43	Michael Tucker	.10
44	Walt Weiss	.10
45	Roberto Alomar	.50
46	Brady Anderson	.10
47	Harold Baines	.10
48	Mike Bordick	.10
49	Danny Clyburn	.10
50	Eric Davis	.10
51	Scott Erickson	.10
52	Chris Hoiles	.10
53	Jimmy Key	.10
54	Ryan Minor	.40
55	Mike Mussina	.50
56	Jesse Orosco	.10
57	Rafael Palmeiro	.25
58	Sidney Ponson	.10
59	Arthur Rhodes	.10
60	Cal Ripken Jr.	2.00
61	B.J. Surhoff	.10
62	Steve Avery	.10
63	Darren Bragg	.10
64	Dennis Eckersley	.10
65	Nomar Garciaparra	2.00
66	Sammy Sosa	2.50
67	Tom Gordon	.10
68	Reggie Jefferson	.10
69	Darren Lewis	.10
70	Mark McGwire	4.00
71	Pedro Martinez	.50
72	Troy O'Leary	.10
73	Bret Saberhagen	.10
74	Mike Stanley	.10
75	John Valentin	.10
76	Jason Varitek	.10
77	Mo Vaughn	.75
78	Tim Wakefield	.10
79	Manny Alexander	.10
80	Rod Beck	.10
81	Brant Brown	.10
82	Mark Clark	.10
83	Gary Gaetti	.10
84	Mark Grace	.25
85	Jose Hernandez	.10
86	Lance Johnson	.10
87	Jason Maxwell	.10
88	Mickey Morandini	.10
89	Terry Mulholland	.10
90	Henry Rodriguez	.10
91	Scott Servais	.10
92	Kevin Tapani	.10
93	Pedro Valdes	.10
94	Kerry Wood	2.50
95	Jeff Abbott	.10
96	James Baldwin	.10
97	Albert Belle	.75
98	Mike Cameron	.10
99	Mike Caruso	.10
100	Wil Cordero	.10
101	Ray Durham	.10
102	Jaime Navarro	.10
103	Greg Norton	.10
104	Magglio Ordonez	.20
105	Mike Sirotka	.10
106	Frank Thomas	2.00
107	Robin Ventura	.10
108	Craig Wilson	.10
109	Aaron Boone	.10
110	Bret Boone	.10
111	Sean Casey	.20
112	Pete Harnisch	.10
113	John Hudek	.10
114	Barry Larkin	.25
115	Eduardo Perez	.10
116	Mike Remlinger	.10
117	Reggie Sanders	.10
118	Chris Stynes	.10
119	Eddie Taubensee	.10
120	Brett Tomko	.10
121	Pat Watkins	.10
122	Dmitri Young	.10
123	Sandy Alomar Jr.	.10
124	Dave Burba	.10
125	Bartolo Colon	.10
126	Joey Cora	.10
127	Brian Giles	.10
128	Dwight Gooden	.10
129	Mike Jackson	.10
130	David Justice	.25
131	Kenny Lofton	.60
132	Charles Nagy	.10
133	Chad Ogea	.10
134	Manny Ramirez	.75

135	Richie Sexson	.20
136	Jim Thome	.40
137	Omar Vizquel	.10
138	Jaret Wright	.40
139	Pedro Astacio	.10
140	Jason Bates	.10
141	Dante Bichette	.25
142	Vinny Castilla	.10
143	Edgar Clemente	.10
144	Derrick Gibson	.10
145	Curtis Goodwin	.10
146	Todd Helton	.60
147	Bobby Jones	.10
148	Darryl Kile	.10
149	Mike Lansing	.10
150	Chuck McElroy	.10
151	Neifi Perez	.10
152	Jeff Reed	.10
153	John Thomson	.10
154	Larry Walker	.30
155	Jamey Wright	.10
156	Kimera Bartee	.10
157	Geronimo Berroa	.10
158	Raul Casanova	.10
159	Frank Catalanotto	.10
160	Tony Clark	.40
161	Deivi Cruz	.10
162	Damion Easley	.10
163	Juan Encarnacion	.10
164	Luis Gonzalez	.10
165	Seth Greisinger	.10
166	Bob Higginson	.10
167	Brian Hunter	.10
168	Todd Jones	.10
169	Justin Thompson	.10
170	Antonio Alfonseca	.10
171	Dave Berg	.10
172	John Cangelosi	.10
173	Craig Counsell	.10
174	Todd Dunwoody	.10
175	Cliff Floyd	.10
176	Alex Gonzalez	.10
177	Livan Hernandez	.10
178	Ryan Jackson	.10
179	Mark Kotsay	.20
180	Derrek Lee	.10
181	Matt Mantei	.10
182	Brian Meadows	.10
183	Edgar Renteria	.10
184	Moises Alou	.25
185	Brad Ausmus	.10
186	Jeff Bagwell	.75
187	Derek Bell	.10
188	Sean Berry	.10
189	Craig Biggio	.25
190	Carl Everett	.10
191	Ricky Gutierrez	.10
192	Mike Hampton	.10
193	Doug Henry	.10
194	Richard Hidalgo	.10
195	Randy Johnson	.50
196	Russ Johnson	.10
197	Shane Reynolds	.10
198	Bill Spiers	.10
199	Kevin Appier	.10
200	Tim Belcher	.10
201	Jeff Conine	.10
202	Johnny Damon	.10
203	Jermaine Dye	.10
204	Jeremy Giambi	.20
205	Jeff King	.10
206	Shane Mack	.10
207	Jeff Montgomery	.10
208	Hal Morris	.10
209	Jose Offerman	.10
210	Dean Palmer	.10
211	Jose Rosado	.10
212	Glendon Rusch	.10
213	Larry Sutton	.10
214	Mike Sweeney	.10
215	Bobby Bonilla	.20
216	Alex Cora	.10
217	Darren Dreifort	.10
218	Mark Grudzielanek	.10
219	Todd Hollandsworth	.10
220	Trenidad Hubbard	.10
221	Charles Johnson	.10
222	Eric Karros	.20
223	Matt Luke	.10
224	Ramon Martinez	.20
225	Raul Mondesi	.25
226	Chan Ho Park	.20
227	Jeff Shaw	.10
228	Gary Sheffield	.25
229	Eric Young	.10
230	Jeromy Burnitz	.10

231	Jeff Cirillo	.10
232	Marquis Grissom	.10
233	Bobby Hughes	.10
234	John Jaha	.10
235	Geoff Jenkins	.10
236	Scott Karl	.10
237	Mark Loretta	.10
238	Mike Matheny	.10
239	Mike Myers	.10
240	Dave Nilsson	.10
241	Bob Wickman	.10
242	Jose Valentin	.10
243	Fernando Vina	.10
244	Rick Aguilera	.10
245	Ron Coomer	.10
246	Marty Cordova	.10
247	Denny Hocking	.10
248	Matt Lawton	.10
249	Pat Meares	.10
250	Paul Molitor	.50
251	Otis Nixon	.10
252	Alex Ochoa	.10
253	David Ortiz	.20
254	A.J. Pierzynski	.10
255	Brad Radke	.10
256	Terry Steinbach	.10
257	Bob Tewksbury	.10
258	Todd Walker	.25
259	Shane Andrews	.10
260	Shayne Bennett	.10
261	Orlando Cabrera	.10
262	Brad Fullmer	.25
263	Vladimir Guerrero	1.00
264	Wilton Guerrero	.10
265	Dustin Hermanson	.10
266	Terry Jones	.10
267	Steve Kline	.10
268	Carl Pavano	.10
269	F.P. Santangelo	.10
270	Fernando Seguignol	.10
271	Ugueth Urbina	.10
272	Jose Vidro	.10
273	Chris Widger	.10
274	Edgardo Alfonzo	.10
275	Carlos Baerga	.10
276	John Franco	.10
277	Todd Hundley	.10
278	Butch Huskey	.10
279	Bobby Jones	.10
280	Al Leiter	.20
281	Greg McMichael	.10
282	Brian McRae	.10
283	Hideo Nomo	.40
284	John Olerud	.20
285	Rey Ordonez	.10
286	Mike Piazza	2.00
287	Turk Wendell	.10
288	Masato Yoshii	.10
289	David Cone	.20
290	Chad Curtis	.10
291	Joe Girardi	.10
292	Orlando Hernandez	1.50
293	Hideki Irabu	.20
294	Derek Jeter	1.50
295	Chuck Knoblauch	.25
296	Mike Lowell	.20
297	Tino Martinez	.25
298	Ramiro Mendoza	.20
299	Paul O'Neill	.25
300	Andy Pettitte	.40
301	Jorge Posada	.25
302	Tim Raines	.10
303	Mariano Rivera	.20
304	David Wells	.20
305	Bernie Williams	.50
306	Mike Blowers	.10
307	Tom Candiotti	.10
308	Eric Chavez	.30
309	Ryan Christenson	.10
310	Jason Giambi	.10
311	Ben Grieve	.75
312	Rickey Henderson	.20
313	A.J. Hinch	.10
314	Jason McDonald	.10
315	Bip Roberts	.10
316	Kenny Rogers	.10
317	Scott Spiezio	.10
318	Matt Stairs	.10
319	Miguel Tejada	.25
320	Bob Abreu	.10
321	Alex Arias	.10
322	*Gary Bennett*	.25
323	Ricky Bottalico	.10
324	Rico Brogna	.10
325	Bobby Estalella	.10
326	Doug Glanville	.10

327	Kevin Jordan	.10
328	Mark Leiter	.10
329	Wendell Magee	.10
330	Mark Portugal	.10
331	Desi Relaford	.10
332	Scott Rolen	.75
333	Curt Schilling	.20
334	Kevin Sefcik	.10
335	Adrian Brown	.10
336	Emil Brown	.10
337	Lou Collier	.10
338	Francisco Cordova	.10
339	Freddy Garcia	.10
340	Jose Guillen	.20
341	Jason Kendall	.20
342	Al Martin	.10
343	Abraham Nunez	.10
344	Aramis Ramirez	.20
345	Ricardo Rincon	.10
346	Jason Schmidt	.10
347	Turner Ward	.10
348	Tony Womack	.10
349	Kevin Young	.10
350	Juan Acevedo	.10
351	Delino DeShields	.10
352	J.D. Drew	6.00
353	Ron Gant	.20
354	Brian Jordan	.10
355	Ray Lankford	.20
356	Eli Marrero	.10
357	Kent Mercker	.10
358	Matt Morris	.10
359	Luis Ordaz	.10
360	Donovan Osborne	.10
361	Placido Polanco	.10
362	Fernando Tatis	.10
363	Andy Ashby	.10
364	Kevin Brown	.20
365	Ken Caminiti	.20
366	Steve Finley	.10
367	Chris Gomez	.10
368	Tony Gwynn	1.50
369	Joey Hamilton	.10
370	Carlos Hernandez	.10
371	Trevor Hoffman	.10
372	Wally Joyner	.10
373	Jim Leyritz	.10
374	Ruben Rivera	.10
375	Greg Vaughn	.20
376	Quilvio Veras	.10
377	Rich Aurilla	.10
378	Barry Bonds	.75
379	Ellis Burks	.10
380	Joe Carter	.20
381	Stan Javier	.10
382	Brian Johnson	.10
383	Jeff Kent	.10
384	Jose Mesa	.10
385	Bill Mueller	.10
386	Robb Nen	.10
387	Armando Rios	.10
388	Kirk Rueter	.10
389	Rey Sanchez	.10
390	J.T. Snow	.10
391	David Bell	.10
392	Jay Buhner	.25
393	Ken Cloude	.10
394	Russ Davis	.10
395	Jeff Fassero	.10
396	Ken Griffey Jr.	3.00
397	*Giomar Guevara*	.25
398	Carlos Guillen	.10
399	Edgar Martinez	.10
400	Shane Monahan	.10
401	Jamie Moyer	.10
402	David Segui	.10
403	Makoto Suzuki	.10
404	Mike Timlin	.10
405	Dan Wilson	.10
406	Wilson Alvarez	.10
407	Rolando Arrojo	.25
408	Wade Boggs	.25
409	Miguel Cairo	.10
410	Roberto Hernandez	.10
411	Mike Kelly	.10
412	Aaron Ledesma	.10
413	Albie Lopez	.10
414	Dave Martinez	.10
415	Quinton McCracken	.10
416	Fred McGriff	.25
417	Bryan Rekar	.10
418	Paul Sorrento	.10
419	Randy Winn	.10
420	John Burkett	.10
421	Will Clark	.25
422	Royce Clayton	.10

423	Juan Gonzalez	1.50
424	Tom Goodwin	.10
425	Rusty Greer	.10
426	Rick Helling	.10
427	Roberto Kelly	.10
428	Mark McLemore	.10
429	Ivan Rodriguez	.75
430	Aaron Sele	.10
431	Lee Stevens	.10
432	Todd Stottlemyre	.10
433	John Wetteland	.10
434	Todd Zeile	.10
435	Jose Canseco	.40
436	Roger Clemens	1.50
437	Felipe Crespo	.10
438	Jose Cruz Jr.	.50
439	Carlos Delgado	.10
440	Tom Evans	.10
441	Tony Fernandez	.10
442	Darrin Fletcher	.10
443	Alex Gonzalez	.10
444	Shawn Green	.10
445	Roy Halladay	.10
446	Pat Hentgen	.10
447	Juan Samuel	.10
448	Benito Santiago	.10
449	Shannon Stewart	.10
450	Woody Williams	.10

1999 Pacific Cramer's Choice

		MT
Complete Set (10):		1200.
Common Player:		40.00
Inserted 1:721		
1	Cal Ripken Jr.	140.00
2	Nomar Garciaparra	125.00
3	Frank Thomas	125.00
4	Ken Griffey Jr.	200.00
5	Alex Rodriguez	125.00
6	Greg Maddux	125.00
7	Sammy Sosa	150.00
8	Kerry Wood	125.00
9	Mark McGwire	250.00
10	Tony Gwynn	100.00

1999 Pacific Dynagon Diamond

		MT
Complete Set (20):		75.00
Common Player:		1.00
Inserted 1:9		
1	Cal Ripken Jr.	5.00
2	Nomar Garciaparra	5.00
3	Frank Thomas	5.00
4	Derek Jeter	4.00
5	Ben Grieve	2.00
6	Ken Griffey Jr.	8.00
7	Alex Rodriguez	5.00
8	Juan Gonzalez	4.00
9	Travis Lee	2.00
10	Chipper Jones	4.00
11	Greg Maddux	5.00
12	Sammy Sosa	6.00
13	Kerry Wood	5.00
14	Jeff Bagwell	2.00
15	Hideo Nomo	1.50
16	Mike Piazza	5.00

17	J.D. Drew	10.00
18	Mark McGwire	10.00
19	Tony Gwynn	4.00
20	Barry Bonds	2.00

1999 Pacific Dynagon Diamond Titanium

		MT
Complete Set (20):		2200.
Common Player:		25.00
Production 99 sets		
1	Cal Ripken Jr.	175.00
2	Nomar Garciaparra	150.00
3	Frank Thomas	150.00
4	Derek Jeter	125.00
5	Ben Grieve	60.00
6	Ken Griffey Jr.	250.00
7	Alex Rodriguez	150.00
8	Juan Gonzalez	125.00
9	Travis Lee	60.00
10	Chipper Jones	125.00
11	Greg Maddux	150.00
12	Sammy Sosa	200.00
13	Kerry Wood	150.00
14	Jeff Bagwell	60.00
15	Hideo Nomo	40.00
16	Mike Piazza	150.00
17	J.D. Drew	150.00
18	Mark McGwire	300.00
19	Tony Gwynn	125.00
20	Barry Bonds	60.00

1999 Pacific Gold Crown Die-Cuts

		MT
Complete Set (36):		500.00
Common Player:		4.00
Inserted 1:37		
1	Darin Erstad	10.00
2	Cal Ripken Jr.	25.00
3	Nomar Garciaparra	25.00
4	Pedro Martinez	8.00
5	Mo Vaughn	10.00
6	Frank Thomas	25.00
7	Kenny Lofton	8.00
8	Manny Ramirez	10.00
9	Jaret Wright	6.00
10	Paul Molitor	8.00
11	Derek Jeter	20.00
12	Bernie Williams	8.00
13	Ben Grieve	10.00
14	Ken Griffey Jr.	40.00
15	Alex Rodriguez	25.00
16	Rolando Arrojo	4.00
17	Wade Boggs	4.00
18	Juan Gonzalez	20.00
19	Ivan Rodriguez	10.00
20	Roger Clemens	20.00
21	Travis Lee	10.00
22	Chipper Jones	25.00
23	Greg Maddux	25.00
24	Sammy Sosa	30.00
25	Kerry Wood	30.00
26	Todd Helton	8.00
27	Jeff Bagwell	10.00
28	Craig Biggio	4.00
29	Vladimir Guerrero	12.00
30	Hideo Nomo	6.00
31	Mike Piazza	25.00
32	Scott Rolen	10.00
33	J.D. Drew	40.00
34	Mark McGwire	45.00
35	Tony Gwynn	20.00
36	Barry Bonds	10.00

Modern cards have little collector value in conditions lower than Mint. Figure NM cards at 75% of values shown; EX cards at 40%.

Values shown reflect the market as of January, 1999. On-field performances of current players in the 1999 baseball season are not factored in.

1999 Pacific Team Checklists

		MT
Complete Set (30):		100.00
Common Player:		1.50
Inserted 1:18		
1	Darin Erstad	3.00
2	Cal Ripken Jr.	8.00
3	Nomar Garciaparra	8.00
4	Frank Thomas	8.00
5	Manny Ramirez	3.00
6	Damion Easley	1.50
7	Jeff King	1.50
8	Paul Molitor	2.50
9	Derek Jeter	6.00
10	Ben Grieve	3.00
11	Ken Griffey Jr.	12.00
12	Wade Boggs	2.00
13	Juan Gonzalez	6.00
14	Roger Clemens	6.00
15	Travis Lee	3.00
16	Chipper Jones	6.00
17	Sammy Sosa	10.00
18	Barry Larkin	2.00
19	Todd Helton	2.50
20	Mark Kotsay	1.50
21	Jeff Bagwell	3.00
22	Raul Mondesi	2.00
23	Jeff Cirillo	1.50
24	Vladimir Guerrero	4.00
25	Mike Piazza	8.00
26	Scott Rolen	3.00
27	Jason Kendall	1.50
28	Mark McGwire	15.00
29	Tony Gwynn	6.00
30	Barry Bonds	3.00

1999 Pacific Timelines

		MT
Complete Set (20):		1200.
Common Player:		20.00
Inserted 1:181 H		
1	Cal Ripken Jr.	100.00
2	Frank Thomas	100.00
3	Jim Thome	20.00
4	Paul Molitor	30.00
5	Bernie Williams	30.00
6	Derek Jeter	80.00
7	Ken Griffey Jr.	140.00
8	Alex Rodriguez	100.00
9	Wade Boggs	20.00
10	Jose Canseco	20.00
11	Roger Clemens	80.00
12	Andres Galarraga	20.00
13	Chipper Jones	80.00
14	Greg Maddux	100.00
15	Sammy Sosa	120.00
16	Larry Walker	20.00
17	Randy Johnson	20.00
18	Mike Piazza	100.00
19	Mark McGwire	160.00
20	Tony Gwynn	80.00

1999 Pacific Private Stock

		MT
Complete Set (150):		45.00
Common Player:		.25
1	Jeff Bagwell	1.50
2	Roger Clemens	2.00
3	J.D. Drew	12.00
4	Nomar Garciaparra	4.00
5	Juan Gonzalez	2.50
6	Ken Griffey Jr.	5.00

7	Tony Gwynn	2.50
8	Derek Jeter	2.50
9	Chipper Jones	2.50
10	Travis Lee	1.25
11	Greg Maddux	3.00
12	Mark McGwire	6.00
13	Mike Piazza	3.00
14	Manny Ramirez	1.25
15	Cal Ripken Jr.	4.00
16	Alex Rodriguez	3.00
17	Ivan Rodriguez	1.25
18	Sammy Sosa	4.00
19	Frank Thomas	3.00
20	Kerry Wood	5.00
21	Roberto Alomar	.75
22	Moises Alou	.40
23	Albert Belle	1.25
24	Craig Biggio	.25
25	Wade Boggs	.40
26	Barry Bonds	1.25
27	Jose Canseco	.75
28	Jim Edmonds	.25
29	Darin Erstad	1.25
30	Andres Galarraga	.75
31	Tom Glavine	.40
32	Ben Grieve	1.25
33	Vladimir Guerrero	1.50
34	Wilton Guerrero	.25
35	Todd Helton	1.25
36	Andruw Jones	1.25
37	Ryan Klesko	.40
38	Kenny Lofton	1.00
39	Javy Lopez	.40
40	Pedro Martinez	1.00
41	Paul Molitor	1.00
42	Raul Mondesi	.40
43	Rafael Palmeiro	.40
44	Tim Salmon	.40
45	Jim Thome	.75
46	Mo Vaughn	1.25
47	Larry Walker	.75
48	David Wells	.25
49	Bernie Williams	.75
50	Jaret Wright	.75
51	Bobby Abreu	.25
52	Garret Anderson	.25
53	Rolando Arrojo	.25
54	Tony Batista	.25
55	Rod Beck	.25
56	Derek Bell	.25
57	Marvin Benard	.25
58	Dave Berg	.25
59	Dante Bichette	.50
60	Aaron Boone	.25
61	Bret Boone	.25
62	Scott Brosius	.25
63	Brant Brown	.25
64	Kevin Brown	.40
65	Jeromy Burnitz	.25
66	Ken Caminiti	.40
67	Mike Caruso	.25
68	Sean Casey	.40
69	Vinny Castilla	.25
70	Eric Chavez	.75
71	Ryan Christenson	.25
72	Jeff Cirillo	.25
73	Tony Clark	.75
74	Will Clark	.50
75	Edgard Clemente	.25
76	David Cone	.40
77	Marty Cordova	.25
78	Jose Cruz Jr.	1.00
79	Eric Davis	.25
80	Carlos Delgado	.25
81	David Dellucci	.25
82	Delino DeShields	.25
83	Gary DiSarcina	.25
84	Damion Easley	.25
85	Dennis Eckersley	.25
86	Cliff Floyd	.25
87	Jason Giambi	.25
88	Doug Glanville	.25
89	*Alex Gonzalez*	.25
90	Mark Grace	.50
91	Rusty Greer	.25
92	Jose Guillen	.40
93	Carlos Guillen	.25
94	Jeffrey Hammonds	.25
95	Rick Helling	.25
96	Bob Henley	.25
97	Livan Hernandez	.25
98	Orlando Hernandez	2.00
99	Bob Higginson	.25
100	Trevor Hoffman	.25
101	Randy Johnson	.75
102	Brian Jordan	.25

103	Wally Joyner	.25
104	Eric Karros	.25
105	Jason Kendall	.40
106	Jeff Kent	.25
107	Jeff King	.25
108	Mark Kotsay	.40
109	Ray Lankford	.25
110	Barry Larkin	.40
111	Mark Loretta	.25
112	Edgar Martinez	.25
113	Tino Martinez	.50
114	Quinton McCracken	.25
115	Fred McGriff	.40
116	Ryan Minor	.75
117	Hal Morris	.25
118	Bill Mueller	.25
119	Mike Mussina	1.00
120	Dave Nilsson	.25
121	Otis Nixon	.25
122	Hideo Nomo	.75
123	Paul O'Neill	.50
124	Jose Offerman	.25
125	John Olerud	.40
126	Rey Ordonez	.25
127	David Ortiz	.25
128	Dean Palmer	.25
129	Chan Ho Park	.50
130	Aramis Ramirez	.50
131	Edgar Renteria	.25
132	Armando Rios	.25
133	Henry Rodriguez	.25
134	Scott Rolen	1.25
135	Curt Schilling	.40
136	David Segui	.25
137	Richie Sexson	.25
138	Gary Sheffield	.50
139	John Smoltz	.40
140	Matt Stairs	.25
141	Justin Thompson	.25
142	Greg Vaughn	.40
143	Omar Vizquel	.25
144	Tim Wakefield	.25
145	Todd Walker	.40
146	Devon White	.25
147	Rondell White	.40
148	Matt Williams	.50
149	*Enrique Wilson*	.25
150	Kevin Young	.25

1999 Pacific Private Stock Exclusive Series

		MT
Complete Set (20):		1250.
Common Player:		8.00
Production 299 sets H		
1	Jeff Bagwell	30.00
2	Roger Clemens	50.00
3	J.D. Drew	75.00
4	Nomar Garciaparra	75.00
5	Juan Gonzalez	60.00
6	Ken Griffey Jr.	125.00
7	Tony Gwynn	60.00
8	Derek Jeter	60.00
9	Chipper Jones	60.00
10	Travis Lee	30.00
11	Greg Maddux	75.00
12	Mark McGwire	150.00
13	Mike Piazza	75.00
14	Manny Ramirez	30.00
15	Cal Ripken Jr.	100.00
16	Alex Rodriguez	75.00
17	Ivan Rodriguez	30.00
18	Sammy Sosa	100.00
19	Frank Thomas	75.00
20	Kerry Wood	75.00

1999 Pacific Private Stock Homerun History

		MT
Complete Set (22):		200.00
Common McGwire:		12.00
Common Sosa:		8.00
Inserted 1:12		
1	Home Run #61(Mark McGwire)	15.00
2	Home Run #59(Sammy Sosa)	10.00
3	Home Run #62(Mark McGwire)	15.00
4	Home Run #60(Sammy Sosa)	10.00
5	Home Run #63(Mark McGwire)	15.00
6	Home Run #61(Sammy Sosa)	10.00
7	Home Run #64(Mark McGwire)	15.00
8	Home Run #62(Sammy Sosa)	10.00
9	Home Run #65(Mark McGwire)	15.00
10	Home Run #63(Sammy Sosa)	10.00
11	Home Run #67(Mark McGwire)	15.00
12	Home Run #64(Sammy Sosa)	10.00
13	Home Run #68(Mark McGwire)	15.00
14	Home Run #65(Sammy Sosa)	10.00
15	Home Run #70(Mark McGwire)	15.00
16	Home Run #66(Sammy Sosa)	10.00
17	A Season of Celebration(Mark McGwire)	15.00
18	A Season of Celebration(Sammy Sosa)	10.00
19	Awesome Power(Sammy Sosa, Mark McGwire)	15.00
20	Transcending Sports(Mark McGwire, Sammy Sosa)	15.00
21	Crown Die-Cut(Mark McGwire)	15.00
22	Crown Die-Cut(Cal Ripken Jr.)	10.00

1999 Pacific Private Stock Platinum Series

		MT
Common Player:		2000.
Production 199 sets		
1	Jeff Bagwell	50.00
2	Roger Clemens	60.00
3	J.D. Drew	90.00
4	Nomar Garciaparra	90.00
5	Juan Gonzalez	75.00
6	Ken Griffey Jr.	150.00
7	Tony Gwynn	75.00
8	Derek Jeter	75.00
9	Chipper Jones	75.00
10	Travis Lee	40.00
11	Greg Maddux	90.00
12	Mark McGwire	200.00
13	Mike Piazza	90.00
14	Manny Ramirez	40.00
15	Cal Ripken Jr.	120.00
16	Alex Rodriguez	90.00
17	Ivan Rodriguez	40.00
18	Sammy Sosa	120.00
19	Frank Thomas	90.00
20	Kerry Wood	90.00
21	Roberto Alomar	30.00
22	Moises Alou	10.00
23	Albert Belle	40.00
24	Craig Biggio	15.00
25	Wade Boggs	20.00
26	Barry Bonds	40.00
27	Jose Canseco	25.00
28	Jim Edmonds	10.00
29	Darin Erstad	40.00
30	Andres Galarraga	30.00
31	Tom Glavine	15.00
32	Ben Grieve	40.00
33	Vladimir Guerrero	50.00
34	Wilton Guerrero	10.00
35	Todd Helton	40.00
36	Andruw Jones	40.00
37	Ryan Klesko	15.00
38	Kenny Lofton	15.00
39	Javy Lopez	15.00
40	Pedro Martinez	40.00
41	Paul Molitor	30.00
42	Raul Mondesi	15.00
43	Rafael Palmeiro	15.00
44	Tim Salmon	15.00
45	Jim Thome	30.00
46	Mo Vaughn	40.00
47	Larry Walker	20.00
48	David Wells	10.00
49	Bernie Williams	30.00
50	Jaret Wright	25.00

1999 Pacific Private Stock Preferred Series 0

		MT
Complete Set (20):		1000.
Common Player:		5.00
Production 399 sets		
1	Jeff Bagwell	25.00
2	Roger Clemens	35.00
3	J.D. Drew	60.00
4	Nomar Garciaparra	60.00
5	Juan Gonzalez	50.00
6	Ken Griffey Jr.	100.00
7	Tony Gwynn	50.00
8	Derek Jeter	50.00
9	Chipper Jones	50.00
10	Travis Lee	25.00
11	Greg Maddux	60.00
12	Mark McGwire	120.00
13	Mike Piazza	60.00
14	Manny Ramirez	25.00
15	Cal Ripken Jr.	75.00
16	Alex Rodriguez	60.00
17	Ivan Rodriguez	25.00
18	Sammy Sosa	75.00
19	Frank Thomas	60.00
20	Kerry Wood	60.00

1999 Pacific Private Stock PS-206

		MT
Complete Set (150):		25.00
Common Player:		.25
Inserted 1:1		
parallels: 8x to 15x		
Inserted 1:25		
1	Jeff Bagwell	.75
2	Roger Clemens	1.00
3	J.D. Drew	6.00
4	Nomar Garciaparra	2.00
5	Juan Gonzalez	1.50
6	Ken Griffey Jr.	3.00
7	Tony Gwynn	1.50
8	Derek Jeter	1.50
9	Chipper Jones	1.50
10	Travis Lee	.75
11	Greg Maddux	2.00
12	Mark McGwire	4.00
13	Mike Piazza	2.00
14	Manny Ramirez	.75
15	Cal Ripken Jr.	2.50
16	Alex Rodriguez	2.00
17	Ivan Rodriguez	.75
18	Sammy Sosa	2.50
19	Frank Thomas	2.00
20	Kerry Wood	2.50
21	Roberto Alomar	.50
22	Moises Alou	.25
23	Albert Belle	.75
24	Craig Biggio	.25
25	Wade Boggs	.25
26	Barry Bonds	.75
27	Jose Canseco	.40
28	Jim Edmonds	.25
29	Darin Erstad	.75
30	Andres Galarraga	.50
31	Tom Glavine	.40
32	Ben Grieve	.75
33	Vladimir Guerrero	1.00
34	Wilton Guerrero	.25
35	Todd Helton	.75
36	Andruw Jones	.75
37	Ryan Klesko	.25
38	Kenny Lofton	.75
39	Javy Lopez	.25
40	Pedro Martinez	.60
41	Paul Molitor	.50
42	Raul Mondesi	.35
43	Rafael Palmeiro	.35
44	Tim Salmon	.40
45	Jim Thome	.50
46	Mo Vaughn	.75
47	Larry Walker	.40
48	David Wells	.25

49	Bernie Williams	.60
50	Jaret Wright	.50
51	Bobby Abreu	.25
52	Garret Anderson	.25
53	Rolando Arrojo	.25
54	Tony Batista	.25
55	Rod Beck	.25
56	Derek Bell	.25
57	Marvin Benard	.25
58	Dave Berg	.25
59	Dante Bichette	.40
60	Aaron Boone	.25
61	Bret Boone	.25
62	Scott Brosius	.25
63	Brant Brown	.25
64	Kevin Brown	.35
65	Jeromy Burnitz	.25
66	Ken Caminiti	.25
67	Mike Caruso	.25
68	Sean Casey	.25
69	Vinny Castilla	.25
70	Eric Chavez	.50
71	Ryan Christenson	.25
72	Jeff Cirillo	.25
73	Tony Clark	.50
74	Will Clark	.40
75	Edgard Clemente	.25
76	David Cone	.25
77	Marty Cordova	.25
78	Jose Cruz Jr.	.60
79	Eric Davis	.25
80	Carlos Delgado	.25
81	David Dellucci	.25
82	Delino DeShields	.25
83	Gary DiSarcina	.25
84	Damion Easley	.25
85	Dennis Eckersley	.25
86	Cliff Floyd	.25
87	Jason Giambi	.25
88	Doug Glanville	.25
89	Alex Gonzalez	.25
90	Mark Grace	.40
91	Rusty Greer	.25
92	Jose Guillen	.25
93	Carlos Guillen	.25
94	Jeffrey Hammonds	.25
95	Rick Helling	.25
96	Bob Henley	.25
97	Livan Hernandez	.25
98	Orlando Hernandez	2.00
99	Bob Higginson	.25
100	Trevor Hoffman	.25
101	Randy Johnson	.50
102	Brian Jordan	.25
103	Wally Joyner	.25
104	Eric Karros	.25
105	Jason Kendall	.40
106	Jeff Kent	.25
107	Jeff King	.25
108	Mark Kotsay	.40
109	Ray Lankford	.25
110	Barry Larkin	.40
111	Mark Loretta	.25
112	Edgar Martinez	.25
113	Tino Martinez	.40
114	Quinton McCracken	.25
115	Fred McGriff	.40
116	Ryan Minor	.75
117	Hal Morris	.25
118	Bill Mueller	.25
119	Mike Mussina	.50
120	Dave Nilsson	.25
121	Otis Nixon	.25
122	Hideo Nomo	.40
123	Paul O'Neill	.40
124	Jose Offerman	.25
125	John Olerud	.40
126	Rey Ordonez	.25
127	David Ortiz	.25
128	Dean Palmer	.25
129	Chan Ho Park	.40
130	Aramis Ramirez	.40
131	Edgar Renteria	.25
132	Armando Rios	.25
133	Henry Rodriguez	.25
134	Scott Rolen	.75
135	Curt Schilling	.25
136	David Segui	.25
137	Richie Sexson	.25
138	Gary Sheffield	.40
139	John Smoltz	.25
140	Matt Stairs	.25
141	Justin Thompson	.25
142	Greg Vaughn	.40
143	Omar Vizquel	.25
144	Tim Wakefield	.25
145	Todd Walker	.40
146	Devon White	.25
147	Rondell White	.35
148	Matt Williams	.40
149	Enrique Wilson	.25
150	Kevin Young	.25

1999 Pacific Private Stock Vintage Series

		MT
Common Player:		15.00
Production 99 sets		
1	Jeff Bagwell	70.00
2	Roger Clemens	100.00
3	J.D. Drew	150.00
4	Nomar Garciaparra	150.00
5	Juan Gonzalez	125.00
6	Ken Griffey Jr.	250.00
7	Tony Gwynn	125.00
8	Derek Jeter	125.00
9	Chipper Jones	125.00
10	Travis Lee	60.00
11	Greg Maddux	150.00
12	Mark McGwire	300.00
13	Mike Piazza	150.00
14	Manny Ramirez	60.00
15	Cal Ripken Jr.	200.00
16	Alex Rodriguez	150.00
17	Ivan Rodriguez	60.00
18	Sammy Sosa	200.00
19	Frank Thomas	150.00
20	Kerry Wood	150.00
21	Roberto Alomar	40.00
22	Moises Alou	15.00
23	Albert Belle	60.00
24	Craig Biggio	20.00
25	Wade Boggs	30.00
26	Barry Bonds	60.00
27	Jose Canseco	40.00
28	Jim Edmonds	15.00
29	Darin Erstad	60.00
30	Andres Galarraga	40.00
31	Tom Glavine	25.00
32	Ben Grieve	60.00
33	Vladimir Guerrero	75.00
34	Wilton Guerrero	15.00
35	Todd Helton	60.00
36	Andruw Jones	60.00
37	Ryan Klesko	20.00
38	Kenny Lofton	50.00
39	Javy Lopez	20.00
40	Pedro Martinez	50.00
41	Paul Molitor	50.00
42	Raul Mondesi	25.00
43	Rafael Palmeiro	25.00
44	Tim Salmon	25.00
45	Jim Thome	40.00
46	Mo Vaughn	60.00
47	Larry Walker	30.00
48	David Wells	15.00
49	Bernie Williams	50.00
50	Jaret Wright	40.00

1999 Topps

	MT
Complete Set (242):	30.00
Common Player:	.10
MVP Stars: 60x to 100x	
Yng Stars & RCs: 30x to 60x	

Production 100 sets		
1	Roger Clemens	1.00
2	Andres Galarraga	.30
3	Scott Brosius	.10
4	John Flaherty	.10
5	Jim Leyritz	.10
6	Ray Durham	.10
7	Mickey Mantle (Retired)	.10
8	Joe Vizcaino	.10
9	Will Clark	.25
10	David Wells	.10
11	Jose Guillen	.20
12	Scott Hatteberg	.10
13	Edgardo Alfonzo	.10
14	Mike Bordick	.10
15	Manny Ramirez	.60
16	Greg Maddux	1.50
17	David Segui	.10
18	Darryl Strawberry	.10
19	Brad Radke	.10
20	Kerry Wood	2.50
21	Matt Anderson	.10
22	Derek Lee	.10
23	Mickey Morandini	.10
24	Paul Konerko	.20
25	Travis Lee	.60
26	Ken Hill	.10
27	Kenny Rogers	.10
28	Paul Sorrento	.10
29	Quilvio Veras	.10
30	Todd Walker	.20
31	Ryan Jackson	.10
32	John Olerud	.20
33	Doug Glanville	.10
34	Nolan Ryan	2.50
35	Ray Lankford	.10
36	Mark Loretta	.10
37	Jason Dickson	.10
38	Sean Bergman	.10
39	Quinton McCracken	.10
40	Bartolo Colon	.10
41	Brady Anderson	.10
42	Chris Stynes	.10
43	Jorge Posada	.10
44	Justin Thompson	.10
45	Johnny Damon	.10
46	Armando Benitez	.10
47	Brant Brown	.10
48	Charlie Hayes	.10
49	Darren Dreifort	.10
50	Juan Gonzalez	1.25
51	Chuck Knoblauch	.25
52	Todd Helton (Rookie All-Star)	.50
53	Rick Reed	.10
54	Chris Gomez	.10
55	Gary Sheffield	.25
56	Rod Beck	.10
57	Rey Sanchez	.10
58	Garret Anderson	.10
59	Jimmy Haynes	.10
60	Steve Woodard	.10
61	Rondell White	.20
62	Vladimir Guerrero	.75
63	Eric Karros	.20
64	Russ Davis	.10
65	Mo Vaughn	.60
66	Sammy Sosa	2.00
67	Troy Percival	.10
68	Kenny Lofton	.50
69	Bill Taylor	.10
70	Mark McGwire	3.00
71	Roger Cedeno	.10
72	Javy Lopez	.10
73	Damion Easley	.10
74	Andy Pettitte	.40
75	Tony Gwynn	1.25
76	Ricardo Rincon	.10
77	F.P. Santangelo	.10
78	Jay Bell	.10
79	Scott Servais	.10
80	Jose Canseco	.25
81	Roberto Hernandez	.10
82	Todd Dunwoody	.10
83	John Wetteland	.10
84	Mike Caruso (Rookie All-Star)	.10
85	Derek Jeter	1.25
86	Aaron Sele	.10
87	Jose Lima	.10
88	Ryan Christenson	.10
89	Jeff Cirillo	.10
90	Jose Hernandez	.10
91	Mark Kotsay (Rookie All-Star)	.20
92	Darren Bragg	.10

93	Albert Belle	.60
94	Matt Lawton	.10
95	Pedro Martinez	.50
96	Greg Vaughn	.20
97	Neifi Perez	.10
98	Gerald Williams	.10
99	Derek Bell	.10
100	Ken Griffey Jr.	2.50
101	David Cone	.20
102	Brian Johnson	.10
103	Dean Palmer	.10
104	Javier Valentin	.10
105	Trevor Hoffman	.10
106	Butch Huskey	.10
107	Dave Martinez	.10
108	Billy Wagner	.10
109	Shawn Green	.10
110	Ben Grieve (Rookie All-Star)	.60
111	Tom Goodwin	.10
112	Jaret Wright	.40
113	Aramis Ramirez	.25
114	Dmitri Young	.10
115	Hideki Irabu	.20
116	Roberto Kelly	.10
117	Jeff Fassero	.10
118	Mark Clark	.10
119	Jason McDonald	.10
120	Matt Williams	.25
121	Dave Burba	.10
122	Bret Saberhagen	.10
123	Deivi Cruz	.10
124	Chad Curtis	.10
125	Scott Rolen	.60
126	Lee Stevens	.10
127	J.T. Snow Jr.	.10
128	Rusty Greer	.10
129	Brian Meadows	.10
130	Jim Edmonds	.20
131	Ron Gant	.20
132	A.J. Hinch (Rookie All-Star)	.10
133	Shannon Stewart	.10
134	Brad Fullmer	.25
135	Cal Eldred	.10
136	Matt Walbeck	.10
137	Carl Everett	.10
138	Walt Weiss	.10
139	Fred McGriff	.20
140	Darin Erstad	.60
141	Dave Nilsson	.10
142	Eric Young	.10
143	Dan Wilson	.10
144	Jeff Reed	.10
145	Brett Tomko	.10
146	Terry Steinbach	.10
147	Seth Greisinger	.10
148	Pat Meares	.10
149	Livan Hernandez	.10
150	Jeff Bagwell	.75
151	Bob Wickman	.10
152	Omar Vizquel	.10
153	Eric Davis	.10
154	Larry Sutton	.10
155	Magglio Ordonez (Rookie All-Star)	.20
156	Eric Milton	.10
157	Darren Lewis	.10
158	Rick Aguilera	.10
159	Mike Lieberthal	.10
160	Robb Nen	.10
161	Brian Giles	.10
162	Jeff Brantley	.10
163	Gary DiSarcina	.10
164	John Valentin	.10
165	David Dellucci	.10
166	Chan Ho Park	.20
167	Masato Yoshii	.10
168	Jason Schmidt	.10
169	LaTroy Hawkins	.10
170	Bret Boone	.10
171	Jerry DiPoto	.10
172	Mariano Rivera	.20
173	Mike Cameron	.10
174	Scott Erickson	.10
175	Charles Johnson	.10
176	Bobby Jones	.10
177	Francisco Cordova	.10
178	Todd Jones	.10
179	Jeff Montgomery	.10
180	Mike Mussina	.50
181	Bob Abreu	.10
182	Ismael Valdes	.10
183	Andy Fox	.10
184	Woody Williams	.10
185	Denny Neagle	.10

186	Jose Valentin	.10
187	Darrin Fletcher	.10
188	Gabe Alvarez	.10
189	Eddie Taubensee	.10
190	Edgar Martinez	.10
191	Jason Kendall	.20
192	Darryl Kile	.10
193	Jeff King	.10
194	Rey Ordonez	.10
195	Andruw Jones	.60
196	Tony Fernandez	.10
197	Jamey Wright	.10
198	B.J. Surhoff	.10
199	Vinny Castilla	.10
200	David Wells (Season Highlight)	.10
201	Mark McGwire (Season Highlight)	1.50
202	Sammy Sosa (Season Highlight)	1.00
203	Roger Clemens (Season Highlight)	.50
204	Kerry Wood (Season Highlight)	1.00
205	Lance Berkman, Mike Frank, Gabe Kapler (Prospects)	1.50
206	Alex Escobar, Ricky Ledee, Mike Stoner (Prospects)	.50
207	Peter Bergeron, Jeremy Giambi, George Lombard (Prospects)	.50
208	Michael Barrett, Ben Davis, Robert Fick (Prospects)	.25
209	Pat Cline, Ramon Hernandez, Jayson Werth (Prospects)	.75
210	Bruce Chen, Chris Enochs, Ryan Anderson (Prospects)	1.50
211	Mike Lincoln, Octavio Dotel, Brad Penny (Prospects)	.20
212	Chuck Abbott, Brent Butler, Danny Klassen (Prospects)	.25
213	Chris Jones, Jeff Urban (Draft Pick)	.10
214	Arturo McDowell, Tony Torcato (Draft Pick)	.10
215	Josh McKinley, Jason Tyner (Draft Pick)	.10
216	Matt Burch, Seth Etherton (Draft Pick)	.10
217	Mamon Tucker, Rick Elder (Draft Pick)	.10
218	J.M. Gold, Ryan Mills (Draft Pick)	1.50
219	Adam Brown, Choo Freeman (Draft Pick)	.10
220	Mark McGwire 1-60	8.00
	McGwire 63-69	15.00
	McGwire 61-62, 70	25.00
221	Larry Walker	.25
222	Bernie Williams	.30
223	Mark McGwire	2.00
224	Ken Griffey Jr.	1.50
225	Sammy Sosa	1.00
226	Juan Gonzalez	.75
227	Dante Bichette	.25
228	Alex Rodriguez	.75
229	Sammy Sosa	1.00
230	Derek Jeter	.60
231	Greg Maddux	.75
232	Roger Clemens	.50
233	Ricky Ledee	.10
234	Chuck Knoblauch	.20
235	Bernie Williams	.40
236	Tino Martinez	.20
237	Orlando Hernandez	2.50
238	Scott Brosius	.10
239	Andy Pettitte	.25
240	Mariano Rivera	.20
241	Checklist	.10
242	Checklist	.10

1999 Topps Autographs

		MT
Complete Set (8):		450.00
Common Player:		25.00
Inserted 1:532 H		
A1	Roger Clemens	120.00
A2	Chipper Jones	70.00
A3	Scott Rolen	50.00
A4	Alex Rodriguez	120.00
A5	Andres Galarraga	35.00
A6	Rondell White	25.00
A7	Ben Grieve	50.00
A8	Troy Glaus	40.00

1999 Topps Hall of Fame

	MT
Complete Set (10):	20.00
Common Player:	1.00
Inserted 1:12	
HOF1 Mike Schmidt	4.00
HOF2 Brooks Robinson	2.50
HOF3 Stan Musial	3.00
HOF4 Willie McCovey	1.00
HOF5 Eddie Mathews	2.00
HOF6 Reggie Jackson	4.00
HOF7 Ernie Banks	3.00
HOF8 Whitey Ford	1.00
HOF9 Bob Feller	1.00
HOF10 Yogi Berra	3.00

1999 Topps Lords of the Diamond

	MT
Complete Set (15):	60.00
Common Player:	1.00
Inserted 1:18	
LD1 Ken Griffey Jr.	10.00
LD2 Chipper Jones	5.00
LD3 Sammy Sosa	8.00
LD4 Frank Thomas	6.00
LD5 Mark McGwire	12.00
LD6 Jeff Bagwell	2.50
LD7 Alex Rodriguez	6.00
LD8 Juan Gonzalez	5.00
LD9 Barry Bonds	2.50
LD10 Nomar Garciaparra	6.00
LD11 Darin Erstad	2.50
LD12 Tony Gwynn	5.00
LD13 Andres Galarraga	1.00
LD14 Mike Piazza	6.00
LD15 Greg Maddux	6.00

1999 Topps New Breed

	MT
Complete Set (15):	35.00
Common Player:	.50

Inserted 1:18

NB1	Darin Erstad	2.50
NB2	Brad Fullmer	1.00
NB3	Kerry Wood	8.00
NB4	Nomar Garciaparra	6.00
NB5	Travis Lee	2.50
NB6	Scott Rolen	2.50
NB7	Todd Helton	1.00
NB8	Vladimir Guerrero	3.00
NB9	Derek Jeter	5.00
NB10	Alex Rodriguez	6.00
NB11	Ben Grieve	2.50
NB12	Andruw Jones	2.50
NB13	Paul Konerko	.50
NB14	Aramis Ramirez	.50
NB15	Adrian Beltre	.75

1999 Topps Nolan Ryan Reprints

		MT
Complete Set (27):		220.00
Common Odd number:		6.00
Inserted 1:18		
Common Even number:		12.00
Inserted 1:72		
Refractors: 2x to 3x		
Inserted 1:288		
Nolan Ryan Autograph:		250.00
1	Nolan Ryan (1968)	15.00
2	Nolan Ryan (1969)	15.00
3	Nolan Ryan (1970)	6.00
4	Nolan Ryan (1971)	15.00
5	Nolan Ryan (1972)	6.00
6	Nolan Ryan (1973)	15.00
7	Nolan Ryan (1974)	6.00
8	Nolan Ryan (1975)	15.00
9	Nolan Ryan (1976)	6.00
10	Nolan Ryan (1977)	15.00
11	Nolan Ryan (1978)	6.00
12	Nolan Ryan (1979)	15.00
13	Nolan Ryan (1980)	6.00
14	Nolan Ryan (1981)	15.00
15	Nolan Ryan (1982)	6.00
16	Nolan Ryan (1983)	15.00
17	Nolan Ryan (1984)	6.00
18	Nolan Ryan (1985)	15.00
19	Nolan Ryan (1986)	6.00
20	Nolan Ryan (1987)	15.00
21	Nolan Ryan (1988)	6.00
22	Nolan Ryan (1989)	15.00
23	Nolan Ryan (1990)	6.00
24	Nolan Ryan (1991)	15.00
25	Nolan Ryan (1992)	6.00
26	Nolan Ryan (1993)	15.00
27	Nolan Ryan (1994)	6.00

1999 Topps Picture Perfect

		MT
Complete Set (10):		20.00
Common Player:		.50
Inserted 1:8		
P1	Ken Griffey Jr.	4.00
P2	Kerry Wood	3.00
P3	Pedro Martinez	1.00
P4	Mark McGwire	5.00
P5	Greg Maddux	2.50
P6	Sammy Sosa	3.00
P7	Greg Vaughn	.50
P8	Juan Gonzalez	2.00
P9	Jeff Bagwell	1.50
P10	Derek Jeter	2.00

1999 Topps Power Brokers

		MT
Complete Set (20):		180.00
Common Player:		2.00
Inserted 1:36		
Refractors: 2x to 3x		
Inserted 1:144		
PB1	Mark McGwire	30.00
PB2	Andres Galarraga	3.00
PB3	Ken Griffey Jr.	25.00
PB4	Sammy Sosa	20.00
PB5	Juan Gonzalez	12.00
PB6	Alex Rodriguez	15.00
PB7	Frank Thomas	15.00
PB8	Jeff Bagwell	6.00
PB9	Vinny Castilla	2.00
PB10	Mike Piazza	15.00
PB11	Greg Vaughn	2.00
PB12	Barry Bonds	6.00
PB13	Mo Vaughn	6.00
PB14	Jim Thome	4.00
PB15	Larry Walker	3.00
PB16	Chipper Jones	12.00
PB17	Nomar Garciaparra	15.00
PB18	Manny Ramirez	6.00
PB19	Roger Clemens	10.00
PB20	Kerry Wood	20.00

1999 Topps Stars 'N Steel

		MT
Complete Set (44):		150.00
Common Player:		2.00
Golds: 2x to 4x		
Inserted 1:12		
Holographics: 4x to 8x		
Inserted 1:24		
1	Kerry Wood	20.00
2	Ben Grieve	8.00
3	Chipper Jones	12.00
4	Alex Rodriguez	15.00
5	Mo Vaughn	6.00
6	Bernie Williams	5.00
7	Juan Gonzalez	12.00
8	Vinny Castilla	2.00
9	Tony Gwynn	12.00
10	Manny Ramirez	6.00
11	Raul Mondesi	3.00
12	Roger Clemens	10.00
13	Darin Erstad	6.00
14	Barry Bonds	6.00
15	Cal Ripken Jr.	20.00
16	Barry Larkin	3.00
17	Scott Rolen	6.00
18	Albert Belle	6.00
19	Craig Biggio	2.00
20	Tony Clark	4.00
21	Mark McGwire	30.00
22	Andres Galarraga	3.00
23	Kenny Lofton	6.00
24	Pedro Martinez	4.00
25	Paul O'Neill	3.00
26	Ken Griffey Jr.	25.00
27	Travis Lee	12.00
28	Tim Salmon	3.00
29	Frank Thomas	15.00
30	Larry Walker	3.00
31	Moises Alou	2.00
32	Vladimir Guerrero	8.00
33	Ivan Rodriguez	6.00
34	Derek Jeter	15.00
35	Greg Vaughn	3.00
36	Gary Sheffield	3.00
37	Carlos Delgado	2.00
38	Greg Maddux	15.00
39	Sammy Sosa	20.00
40	Mike Piazza	15.00
41	Nomar Garciaparra	15.00
42	Dante Bichette	3.00
43	Jeff Bagwell	8.00
44	Jim Thome	4.00

1999 Ultra

		MT
Complete Set (250):		100.00
Common Player:		.10
Common Season Crown:		.50
Inserted 1:8		
Common Prospect:		.25
Inserted 1:4		
Gold Medallion (1-215): 1.5x to 2x		
Inserted 1:1		
Gold Medall. Prospect: 5x to 10x		
Inserted 1:40		
Gold Medall. Season Crown: 3x to 6x		
Inserted 1:80		
Platinums (1-215): 60x to 100x		
Production 99 sets		
Platinum Prospects: 15x to 30x		
Production 65 sets		
Platinum Season Crowns: 40x to 60x		
Production 50 sets		
1	Greg Maddux	2.00
2	Greg Vaughn	.20
3	John Wetteland	.10
4	Tino Martinez	.25
5	Todd Walker	.25
6	Troy O'Leary	.10
7	Barry Larkin	.25
8	Mike Lansing	.10
9	Delino DeShields	.10
10	Brett Tomko	.10
11	Carlos Perez	.10
12	Mark Langston	.10
13	Jamie Moyer	.10
14	Jose Guillen	.20
15	Bartolo Colon	.10
16	Brady Anderson	.10
17	Walt Weiss	.10
18	Shane Reynolds	.10
19	David Segui	.10
20	Vladimir Guerrero	1.00
21	Freddy Garcia	.10
22	Carl Everett	.10
23	Jose Cruz Jr.	.50
24	David Ortiz	.10
25	Andruw Jones	.75
26	Darren Lewis	.10
27	Ray Lankford	.10
28	Wally Joyner	.10
29	Charles Johnson	.10
30	Derek Jeter	1.50
31	Sean Casey	.10
32	Bobby Bonilla	.20
33	Todd Zelle	.10
34	Todd Helton	.75
35	David Wells	.10
36	Darin Erstad	.75
37	Ivan Rodriguez	.75
38	Antonio Osuna	.10
39	Mickey Morandini	.10
40	Rusty Greer	.10
41	Rod Beck	.10

42	Larry Sutton	.10
43	Edgar Renteria	.10
44	Otis Nixon	.10
45	Eli Marrero	.10
46	Reggie Jefferson	.10
47	Trevor Hoffman	.10
48	Andres Galarraga	.40
49	Scott Brosius	.10
50	Vinny Castilla	.10
51	Bret Boone	.10
52	Masato Yoshii	.10
53	Matt Williams	.25
54	Robin Ventura	.10
55	Jay Powell	.10
56	Dean Palmer	.10
57	Eric Milton	.10
58	Willie McGee	.10
59	Tony Gwynn	1.50
60	Tom Gordon	.10
61	Dante Bichette	.25
62	Jaret Wright	.40
63	Devon White	.10
64	Frank Thomas	2.00
65	Mike Piazza	2.00
66	Jose Offerman	.10
67	Pat Meares	.10
68	Brian Meadows	.10
69	Nomar Garciaparra	2.00
70	Mark McGwire	4.00
71	Tony Graffanino	.10
72	Ken Griffey Jr.	3.00
73	Ken Caminiti	.20
74	Todd Jones	.10
75	A.J. Hinch	.10
76	Marquis Grissom	.10
77	Jay Buhner	.25
78	Albert Belle	.75
79	Brian Anderson	.10
80	Quinton McCracken	.10
81	Omar Vizquel	.10
82	Todd Stottlemyre	.10
83	Cal Ripken Jr.	2.00
84	Magglio Ordonez	.10
85	John Olerud	.10
86	Hal Morris	.10
87	Derrek Lee	.10
88	Doug Glanville	.10
89	Marty Cordova	.10
90	Kevin Brown	.10
91	Kevin Young	.10
92	Rico Brogna	.10
93	Wilson Alvarez	.10
94	Bob Wickman	.10
95	Jim Thome	.50
96	Mike Mussina	.50
97	Al Leiter	.10
98	Travis Lee	.75
99	Jeff King	.10
100	Kerry Wood	3.00
101	Cliff Floyd	.10
102	Jose Valentin	.10
103	Manny Ramirez	.75
104	Butch Huskey	.10
105	Scott Erickson	.10
106	Ray Durham	.10
107	Johnny Damon	.10
108	Craig Counsell	.10
109	Rolando Arrojo	.10
110	Bob Abreu	.10
111	Tony Womack	.10
112	Mike Stanley	.10
113	Kenny Lofton	.60
114	Eric Davis	.10
115	Jeff Conine	.10
116	Carlos Baerga	.10
117	Rondell White	.20
118	Billy Wagner	.10
119	Ed Sprague	.10
120	Jason Schmidt	.10
121	Edgar Martinez	.10
122	Travis Fryman	.10
123	Armando Benitez	.10
124	Matt Stairs	.10
125	Roberto Hernandez	.10
126	Jay Bell	.10
127	Justin Thompson	.10
128	John Jaha	.10
129	Mike Caruso	.10
130	Miguel Tejada	.25
131	Geoff Jenkins	.10
132	Wade Boggs	.25
133	Andy Benes	.10
134	Aaron Sele	.10
135	Bret Saberhagen	.10
136	Mariano Rivera	.20
137	Neifi Perez	.10

138	Paul Konerko	.25
139	Barry Bonds	.75
140	Garret Anderson	.10
141	Bernie Williams	.60
142	Gary Sheffield	.25
143	Rafael Palmeiro	.25
144	Orel Hershiser	.10
145	Craig Biggio	.20
146	Dmitri Young	.10
147	Damion Easley	.10
148	Henry Rodriguez	.10
149	Brad Radke	.10
150	Pedro Martinez	.50
151	Mike Lieberthal	.10
152	Jim Leyritz	.10
153	Chuck Knoblauch	.25
154	Darryl Kile	.10
155	Brian Jordan	.10
156	Chipper Jones	1.50
157	Pete Harnisch	.10
158	Moises Alou	.20
159	Ismael Valdes	.10
160	Stan Javier	.10
161	Mark Grace	.25
162	Jason Giambi	.10
163	Chuck Finley	.10
164	Juan Encarnacion	.10
165	Chan Ho Park	.10
166	Randy Johnson	.50
167	J.T. Snow	.10
168	Tim Salmon	.25
169	Brian Hunter	.10
170	Rickey Henderson	.10
171	Cal Eldred	.10
172	Curt Schilling	.20
173	Alex Rodriguez	2.00
174	Dustin Hermanson	.10
175	Mike Hampton	.10
176	Shawn Green	.10
177	Roberto Alomar	.50
178	Sandy Alomar Jr.	.20
179	Larry Walker	.40
180	Mo Vaughn	.75
181	Raul Mondesi	.25
182	Hideki Irabu	.20
183	Jim Edmonds	.20
184	Shawn Estes	.10
185	Tony Clark	.40
186	Dan Wilson	.10
187	Michael Tucker	.10
188	Jeff Shaw	.10
189	Mark Grudzielanek	.10
190	Roger Clemens	1.50
191	Juan Gonzalez	1.50
192	Sammy Sosa	2.00
193	Troy Percival	.10
194	Robb Nen	.10
195	Bill Mueller	.10
196	Ben Grieve	.75
197	Luis Gonzalez	.10
198	Will Clark	.25
199	Jeff Cirillo	.10
200	Scott Rolen	.75
201	Reggie Sanders	.10
202	Fred McGriff	.25
203	Denny Neagle	.10
204	Brad Fullmer	.25
205	Royce Clayton	.10
206	Jose Canseco	.40
207	Jeff Bagwell	1.00
208	Hideo Nomo	.40
209	Karim Garcia	.10
210	Kenny Rogers	.10
211	Checklist(Kerry Wood)	1.50
212	Checklist(Alex Rodriguez)	1.00
213	Checklist(Cal Ripken Jr.)	1.00
214	Checklist(Frank Thomas)	1.00
215	Checklist(Ken Griffey Jr.)	1.50
216	Alex Rodriguez (Season Crowns)	4.00
217	Greg Maddux (Season Crowns)	4.00
218	Juan Gonzalez (Season Crowns)	3.00
219	Ken Griffey Jr. (Season Crowns)	6.00
220	Kerry Wood (Season Crowns)	6.00
221	Mark McGwire (Season Crowns)	8.00
222	Mike Piazza (Season Crowns)	4.00
223	Rickey Henderson (Season Crowns)	.25
224	Sammy Sosa (Season Crowns)	4.00

225	Travis Lee (Season Crowns)	1.50
226	Gabe Alvarez (Prospects)	.25
227	Matt Anderson (Prospects)	1.00
228	Adrian Beltre (Prospects)	.75
229	Orlando Cabrera (Prospects)	.10
230	Orlando Hernandez (Prospects)	6.00
231	Aramis Ramirez (Prospects)	.75
232	Troy Glaus (Prospects)	6.00
233	Gabe Kapler (Prospects)	5.00
234	Jeremy Giambi (Prospects)	1.50
235	Derrick Gibson (Prospects)	.25
236	Carlton Loewer (Prospects)	.25
237	Mike Frank (Prospects)	.50
238	Carlos Guillen (Prospects)	.25
239	Alex Gonzalez (Prospects)	.25
240	Enrique Wilson (Prospects)	.25
241	J.D. Drew (Prospects)	15.00
242	Bruce Chen (Prospects)	.25
243	Ryan Minor (Prospects)	2.00
244	Preston Wilson (Prospects)	.25
245	Josh Booty (Prospects)	.25
246	Luis Ordaz (Prospects)	.25
247	George Lombard (Prospects)	1.00
248	Matt Clement (Prospects)	.25
249	Eric Chavez (Prospects)	3.00
250	Corey Koskie (Prospects)	.75

1999 Ultra Book On

		MT
Complete Set (20):		60.00
Common Player:		.50
Inserted 1:6		
1	Kerry Wood	6.00
2	Ken Griffey Jr.	8.00
3	Frank Thomas	5.00
4	Albert Belle	2.00
5	Juan Gonzalez	4.00
6	Jeff Bagwell	2.50
7	Mark McGwire	10.00
8	Barry Bonds	2.00
9	Andruw Jones	2.00
10	Mo Vaughn	2.00
11	Scott Rolen	2.00
12	Travis Lee	2.00
13	Tony Gwynn	4.00
14	Greg Maddux	5.00
15	Mike Piazza	5.00
16	Chipper Jones	4.00
17	Nomar Garciaparra	5.00
18	Cal Ripken Jr.	5.00
19	Derek Jeter	4.00
20	Alex Rodriguez	5.00

Modern cards have little collector value in conditions lower than Mint. Figure NM cards at 75% of values shown; EX cards at 40%.

Values shown reflect the market as of January, 1999. On-field performances of current players in the 1999 baseball season are not factored in.

1999 Ultra Damage Inc.

		MT
Complete Set (15):		300.00
Common Player:		5.00
Inserted 1:72		
1	Alex Rodriguez	25.00
2	Greg Maddux	25.00
3	Cal Ripken Jr.	25.00
4	Chipper Jones	20.00
5	Derek Jeter	20.00
6	Frank Thomas	25.00
7	Juan Gonzalez	20.00
8	Ken Griffey Jr.	40.00
9	Kerry Wood	30.00
10	Mark McGwire	50.00
11	Mike Piazza	25.00
12	Nomar Garciaparra	25.00
13	Scott Rolen	10.00
14	Tony Gwynn	20.00
15	Travis Lee	10.00

1999 Ultra Diamond Producers

		MT
Complete Set (10):		500.00
Common Player:		10.00
Inserted 1:288		
1	Ken Griffey Jr.	80.00
2	Frank Thomas	50.00
3	Alex Rodriguez	50.00
4	Cal Ripken Jr.	50.00
5	Mike Piazza	50.00
6	Mark McGwire	100.00
7	Greg Maddux	50.00
8	Kerry Wood	60.00
9	Chipper Jones	40.00
10	Derek Jeter	40.00

1999 Ultra RBI Kings

		MT
Complete Set (30):		25.00
Common Player:		.25
Inserted 1:1 R		
1	Rafael Palmeiro	.25
2	Mo Vaughn	1.00
3	Ivan Rodriguez	1.00
4	Barry Bonds	1.00
5	Albert Belle	1.00
6	Jeff Bagwell	1.50
7	Mark McGwire	5.00
8	Darin Erstad	1.00
9	Manny Ramirez	1.00
10	Chipper Jones	2.00
11	Jim Thome	.50
12	Scott Rolen	1.00
13	Tony Gwynn	2.00
14	Juan Gonzalez	2.00
15	Mike Piazza	2.50
16	Sammy Sosa	3.00
17	Andruw Jones	1.00
18	Derek Jeter	2.00
19	Nomar Garciaparra	2.50
20	Alex Rodriguez	2.50
21	Frank Thomas	2.50
22	Cal Ripken Jr.	2.50
23	Ken Griffey Jr.	4.00
24	Travis Lee	1.00
25	Paul O'Neill	.25
26	Greg Vaughn	.25
27	Andres Galarraga	.50
28	Tino Martinez	.40
29	Jose Canseco	.40
30	Ben Grieve	1.00

1999 Ultra Thunderclap

		MT
Complete Set (15):		160.00
Common Player:		4.00
Inserted 1:36		
1	Alex Rodriguez	15.00
2	Andruw Jones	6.00
3	Cal Ripken Jr.	15.00
4	Chipper Jones	12.00
5	Darin Erstad	6.00
6	Derek Jeter	12.00
7	Frank Thomas	15.00
8	Jeff Bagwell	8.00
9	Juan Gonzalez	12.00
10	Ken Griffey Jr.	25.00
11	Mark McGwire	30.00
12	Mike Piazza	15.00
13	Travis Lee	6.00
14	Nomar Garciaparra	15.00
15	Scott Rolen	6.00

1999 Ultra World Premiere

		MT
Complete Set (15):		40.00
Common Player:		1.00
Inserted 1:18		
1	Gabe Alvarez	1.00
2	Kerry Wood	12.00
3	Orlando Hernandez	8.00
4	Mike Caruso	1.00
5	Matt Anderson	2.50
6	Randall Simon	1.00
7	Adrian Beltre	2.00
8	Scott Elarton	1.00
9	Karim Garcia	1.00
10	Mike Frank	1.00
11	Richard Hidalgo	1.00
12	Paul Konerko	2.00
13	Travis Lee	4.00
14	J.D. Drew	20.00
15	Miguel Tejada	2.00

1999 Upper Deck

		MT
Complete Set (255):		35.00
Common Player:		.10
Exclusive Stars: 60x to 100x		

RC's & Yng Stars: 30x to 60x
Production 100 sets

1	Troy Glaus (Star Rookies)	1.50
2	Adrian Beltre (Star Rookies)	.20
3	Matt Anderson (Star Rookies)	.25
4	Eric Chavez (Star Rookies)	.40
5	Jin Cho (Star Rookies)	.25
6	*Robert Smith* (Star Rookies)	.25
7	George Lombard (Star Rookies)	.10
8	Mike Kinkade (Star Rookies)	.10
9	Seth Greisinger (Star Rookies)	.10
10	J.D. Drew (Star Rookies)	8.00
11	Aramis Ramirez (Star Rookies)	.10
12	Carlos Guillen (Star Rookies)	.10
13	Justin Baughman (Star Rookies)	.10
14	Jim Parque (Star Rookies)	.10
15	Ryan Jackson (Star Rookies)	.10
16	Ramon Martinez (Star Rookies)	.10
17	Orlando Hernandez (Star Rookies)	1.50
18	Jeremy Giambi (Star Rookies)	.25
19	Gary DiSarcina	.10
20	Darin Erstad	.75
21	Troy Glaus	1.00
22	Chuck Finley	.10
23	Dave Hollins	.10
24	Troy Percival	.10
25	Tim Salmon	.25
26	Brian Anderson	.10
27	Jay Bell	.10
28	Andy Benes	.10
29	Brent Brede	.10
30	David Dellucci	.10
31	Karim Garcia	.10
32	Travis Lee	.75
33	Andres Galarraga	.30
34	Ryan Klesko	.25
35	Keith Lockhart	.10
36	Kevin Millwood	.40
37	Denny Neagle	.10
38	John Smoltz	.25
39	Michael Tucker	.10
40	Walt Weiss	.10
41	Dennis Martinez	.10
42	Javy Lopez	.10
43	Brady Anderson	.10
44	Harold Baines	.10
45	Mike Bordick	.10
46	Roberto Alomar	.50
47	Scott Erickson	.10
48	Mike Mussina	.50
49	Cal Ripken Jr.	2.00
50	Darren Bragg	.10
51	Dennis Eckersley	.10
52	Nomar Garciaparra	2.00
53	Scott Hatteberg	.10
54	Troy O'Leary	.10
55	Bret Saberhagen	.10
56	John Valentin	.10
57	Rod Beck	.10
58	Jeff Blauser	.10
59	Brant Brown	.10
60	Mark Clark	.10
61	Mark Grace	.25
62	Kevin Tapani	.10
63	Henry Rodriguez	.10
64	Mike Cameron	.10
65	Mike Caruso	.10
66	Ray Durham	.10
67	Jaime Navarro	.10
68	Magglio Ordonez	.25
69	Mike Sirotka	.10
70	Sean Casey	.20
71	Barry Larkin	.25
72	Jon Nunnally	.10
73	Paul Konerko	.25
74	Chris Stynes	.10
75	Brett Tomko	.10
76	Dmitri Young	.10
77	Sandy Alomar	.10
78	Bartolo Colon	.10
79	Travis Fryman	.10
80	Brian Giles	.10
81	David Justice	.25
82	Omar Vizquel	.10
83	Jaret Wright	.50

84	Jim Thome	.40
85	Charles Nagy	.10
86	Pedro Astacio	.10
87	Todd Helton	.60
88	Darryl Kile	.10
89	Mike Lansing	.10
90	Neifi Perez	.10
91	John Thomson	.10
92	Larry Walker	.40
93	Tony Clark	.40
94	Deivi Cruz	.10
95	Damion Easley	.10
96	Brian L. Hunter	.10
97	Todd Jones	.10
98	Brian Moehler	.10
99	Gabe Alvarez	.10
100	Craig Counsell	.10
101	Cliff Floyd	.10
102	Livan Hernandez	.10
103	Andy Larkin	.10
104	Derrek Lee	.10
105	Brian Meadows	.10
106	Moises Alou	.25
107	Sean Berry	.10
108	Craig Biggio	.25
109	Ricky Gutierrez	.10
110	Mike Hampton	.10
111	Jose Lima	.10
112	Billy Wagner	.10
113	Hal Morris	.10
114	Johnny Damon	.10
115	Jeff King	.10
116	Jeff Montgomery	.10
117	Glendon Rusch	.10
118	Larry Sutton	.10
119	Bobby Bonilla	.20
120	Jim Eisenreich	.10
121	Eric Karros	.20
122	Matt Luke	.10
123	Ramon Martinez	.20
124	Gary Sheffield	.25
125	Eric Young	.10
126	Charles Johnson	.10
127	Jeff Cirillo	.10
128	Marquis Grissom	.10
129	Jeremy Burnitz	.10
130	Bob Wickman	.10
131	Scott Karl	.10
132	Mark Loretta	.10
133	Fernando Vina	.10
134	Matt Lawton	.10
135	Pat Meares	.10
136	Eric Milton	.10
137	Paul Molitor	.50
138	David Ortiz	.10
139	Todd Walker	.25
140	Shane Andrews	.10
141	Brad Fullmer	.25
142	Vladimir Guerrero	1.00
143	Dustin Hermanson	.10
144	Ryan McGuire	.10
145	Ugueth Urbina	.10
146	John Franco	.10
147	Butch Huskey	.10
148	Bobby Jones	.10
149	John Olerud	.25
150	Rey Ordonez	.10
151	Mike Piazza	2.00
152	Hideo Nomo	.40
153	Masato Yoshii	.10
154	Derek Jeter	1.50
155	Chuck Knoblauch	.25
156	Paul O'Neill	.25
157	Andy Pettitte	.50
158	Mariano Rivera	.20
159	Darryl Strawberry	.25
160	David Wells	.20
161	Jorge Posada	.20
162	Ramiro Mendoza	.20
163	Miguel Tejada	.25
164	Ryan Christenson	.10
165	Rickey Henderson	.20
166	A.J. Hinch	.10
167	Ben Grieve	.75
168	Kenny Rogers	.10
169	Matt Stairs	.10
170	Bob Abreu	.10
171	Rico Brogna	.10
172	Doug Glanville	.10
173	Mike Grace	.10
174	Desi Relaford	.10
175	Scott Rolen	.75
176	Jose Guillen	.20
177	Francisco Cordova	.10
178	Al Martin	.10

179	Jason Schmidt	.10
180	Turner Ward	.10
181	Kevin Young	.10
182	Mark McGwire	4.00
183	Delino DeShields	.10
184	Eli Marrero	.10
185	Tom Lampkin	.10
186	Ray Lankford	.10
187	Willie McGee	.10
188	Matt Morris	.10
189	Andy Ashby	.10
190	Kevin Brown	.20
191	Ken Caminiti	.20
192	Trevor Hoffman	.10
193	Wally Joyner	.10
194	Greg Vaughn	.20
195	Danny Darwin	.10
196	Shawn Estes	.10
197	Orel Hershiser	.10
198	Jeff Kent	.10
199	Bill Mueller	.10
200	Robb Nen	.10
201	J.T. Snow	.10
202	Ken Cloude	.10
203	Russ Davis	.10
204	Jeff Fassero	.10
205	Ken Griffey Jr.	3.00
206	Shane Monahan	.10
207	David Segui	.10
208	Dan Wilson	.10
209	Wilson Alvarez	.10
210	Wade Boggs	.25
211	Miguel Cairo	.10
212	Bubba Trammell	.10
213	Quinton McCracken	.10
214	Paul Sorrento	.10
215	Kevin Stocker	.10
216	Will Clark	.25
217	Rusty Greer	.10
218	Rick Helling	.10
219	Mike McLemore	.10
220	Ivan Rodriguez	.75
221	John Wetteland	.10
222	Jose Canseco	.40
223	Roger Clemens	1.50
224	Carlos Delgado	.10
225	Darrin Fletcher	.10
226	Alex Gonzalez	.10
227	Jose Cruz Jr.	.50
228	Shannon Stewart	.10
229	Rolando Arrojo (Foreign Focus)	.20
230	Livan Hernandez (Foreign Focus)	.10
231	Orlando Hernandez (Foreign Focus)	1.00
232	Raul Mondesi (Foreign Focus)	.20
233	Moises Alou (Foreign Focus)	.20
234	Pedro J. Martinez (Foreign Focus)	.40
235	Sammy Sosa (Foreign Focus)	1.25
236	Vladimir Guerrero (Foreign Focus)	.50
237	Bartolo Colon (Foreign Focus)	.10
238	Miguel Tejada (Foreign Focus)	.10
239	Ismael Valdes (Foreign Focus)	.10
240	Mariano Rivera (Foreign Focus)	.10
241	Jose Cruz Jr. (Foreign Focus)	.25
242	Juan Gonzalez (Foreign Focus)	.75
243	Ivan Rodriguez (Foreign Focus)	.40
244	Sandy Alomar (Foreign Focus)	.10
245	Roberto Alomar (Foreign Focus)	.25
246	Magglio Ordonez (Foreign Focus)	.20
247	Kerry Wood (Highlights Checklist)	1.50
248	Mark McGwire (Highlights Checklist)	2.00
249	David Wells (Highlights Checklist)	.10
250	Rolando Arrojo (Highlights Checklist)	.20

251	Ken Griffey Jr. (Highlights Checklist)	1.50
252	Trevor Hoffman (Highlights Checklist)	.10
253	Travis Lee (Highlights Checklist)	.40
254	Roberto Alomar (Highlights Checklist)	.25
255	Sammy Sosa (Highlights Checklist)	1.25

1999 Upper Deck Crowning Glory

		MT
Complete Set (3):		25.00
Common Player:		8.00
Inserted 1:23		
Doubles: 4x to 8x		
Production 1,000 sets		
CG1	Roger Clemens, Kerry Wood	8.00
CG2	Mark McGwire, Barry Bonds	10.00
CG3	Ken Griffey Jr., Mark McGwire	12.00

1999 Upper Deck Game Jersey

		MT
Complete Set (5):		1200.
Common Player:		100.00
Inserted 1:2,500		
GJKW	Kerry Wood	350.00
GJCJ	Charles Johnson	100.00
GJMP	Mike Piazza	350.00
GJAR	Alex Rodriguez	375.00
GJJG	Juan Gonzalez	275.00
GJKWs	Kerry Wood Auto.	1500.

1999 Upper Deck Game Jersey-Hobby

		MT
Complete Set (6):		500.00
Common Player:		50.00
Inserted 1:288		
GJKG	Ken Griffey Jr.	250.00
GJAB	Adrian Beltre	50.00
GJBG	Ben Grieve	80.00
GJTL	Travis Lee	80.00
GJIV	Ivan Rodriguez	90.00
GJDE	Darin Erstad	70.00
GJKGs	Ken Griffey Jr. (Auto.)	

1999 Upper Deck Immaculate Perception

		MT
Complete Set (27):		220.00
Common Player:		3.00
Inserted 1:23		
Doubles: 2x to 3x		
Production 1,000 sets		
101	Jeff Bagwell	6.00
102	Craig Biggio	3.00
103	Barry Bonds	6.00
104	Roger Clemens	12.00
105	Jose Cruz Jr.	5.00
106	Nomar Garciaparra	15.00
107	Tony Clark	4.00
108	Ben Grieve	6.00
109	Ken Griffey Jr.	25.00
110	Tony Gwynn	12.00
111	Randy Johnson	5.00
112	Chipper Jones	12.00

113	Travis Lee	6.00
114	Kenny Lofton	5.00
115	Greg Maddux	15.00
116	Mark McGwire	30.00
117	Hideo Nomo	4.00
118	Mike Piazza	15.00
119	Manny Ramirez	6.00
120	Cal Ripken Jr.	15.00
121	Alex Rodriguez	15.00
122	Scott Rolen	6.00
123	Frank Thomas	15.00
124	Kerry Wood	20.00
125	Larry Walker	4.00
126	Vinny Castilla	3.00
127	Derek Jeter	12.00

1999 Upper Deck 10th Anniversary Team

	MT
Complete Set (30):	70.00
Common Player:	.50
Inserted 1:4	
Doubles: 2x to 3x	
Production 4,000 sets	
Triples: 20x to 40x	
Production 100 sets	
X1	Mike Piazza	5.00
X2	Mark McGwire	10.00
X3	Roberto Alomar	1.00
X4	Chipper Jones	4.00
X5	Cal Ripken Jr.	5.00
X6	Ken Griffey Jr.	8.00
X7	Barry Bonds	2.00
X8	Tony Gwynn	4.00
X9	Nolan Ryan	8.00
X10	Randy Johnson	1.50
X11	Dennis Eckersley	.50
X12	Ivan Rodriguez	2.00
X13	Frank Thomas	5.00
X14	Craig Biggio	.75
X15	Wade Boggs	.75
X16	Alex Rodriguez	5.00
X17	Albert Belle	2.00
X18	Juan Gonzalez	4.00
X19	Rickey Henderson	.75
X20	Greg Maddux	5.00
X21	Tom Glavine	.75
X22	Randy Myers	.50
X23	Sandy Alomar	.75
X24	Jeff Bagwell	2.00
X25	Derek Jeter	4.00
X26	Matt Williams	.75
X27	Kenny Lofton	1.50
X28	Sammy Sosa	6.00
X29	Larry Walker	.75
X30	Roger Clemens	4.00

1999 Upper Deck Wonder Years

	MT
Complete Set (30):	120.00
Common Player:	1.00
Inserted 1:7	
Doubles: 2x to 3x	

	Production 2,000 sets	
	Triples: 20x to 40x	
	Production 50 sets	
W01	Kerry Wood	10.00
W02	Travis Lee	3.00
W03	Jeff Bagwell	3.00
W04	Barry Bonds	3.00
W05	Roger Clemens	6.00
W06	Jose Cruz Jr.	2.00
W07	Andres Galarraga	1.50
W08	Nomar Garciaparra	8.00
W09	Juan Gonzalez	6.00
W10	Ken Griffey Jr.	12.00
W11	Tony Gwynn	6.00
W12	Derek Jeter	6.00
W13	Randy Johnson	2.00
W14	Andruw Jones	3.00
W15	Chipper Jones	6.00
W16	Kenny Lofton	2.50
W17	Greg Maddux	8.00
W18	Tino Martinez	1.50
W19	Mark McGwire	15.00
W20	Paul Molitor	2.00
W21	Mike Piazza	8.00
W22	Manny Ramirez	3.00
W23	Cal Ripken Jr.	8.00
W24	Alex Rodriguez	8.00
W25	Sammy Sosa	10.00
W26	Frank Thomas	8.00
W27	Mo Vaughn	3.00
W28	Larry Walker	1.50
W29	Scott Rolen	3.00
W30	Ben Grieve	3.00

1999 Upper Deck Black Diamond

	MT
Complete Set (120):	120.00
Common Player:	.25
Common Diamond Debut (91-120):	1.00
Inserted 1:4	
Double Diamonds: 3x to 5x	
Production 3,000 sets	
Double Diamond Debuts: 1.5x to 3x	
Production 2,500 sets	
Triple Diamonds: 6x to 10x	
Production 1,500 sets	
Triple Diamond Debuts: 3x to 5x	
Production 1,000 sets	
1	Darin Erstad	1.25
2	Tim Salmon	.50
3	Jim Edmonds	.40
4	Matt Williams	.50
5	David Dellucci	.25
6	Jay Bell	.25
7	Andres Galarraga	.75
8	Chipper Jones	2.50
9	Greg Maddux	3.00
10	Andruw Jones	1.25
11	Cal Ripken Jr.	3.00
12	Rafael Palmeiro	.50
13	Brady Anderson	.25
14	Mike Mussina	1.00
15	Nomar Garciaparra	3.00
16	Mo Vaughn	1.25
17	Pedro J. Martinez	.75
18	Sammy Sosa	4.00
19	Henry Rodriguez	.25
20	Frank Thomas	3.00
21	Magglio Ordonez	.40
22	Albert Belle	1.25
23	Paul Konerko	.40
24	Sean Casey	.40
25	Jim Thome	.75
26	Kenny Lofton	1.25
27	Sandy Alomar Jr.	.25
28	Jaret Wright	.75
29	Larry Walker	.75
30	Todd Helton	1.25
31	Vinny Castilla	.25
32	Tony Clark	.75
33	Damion Easley	.25
34	Mark Kotsay	.25
35	Derrek Lee	.25
36	Moises Alou	.40
37	Jeff Bagwell	1.50
38	Craig Biggio	.50
39	Randy Johnson	.75
40	Dean Palmer	.25
41	Johnny Damon	.25
42	Chan Ho Park	.50
43	Raul Mondesi	.50
44	Gary Sheffield	.50
45	Jeromy Burnitz	.25

46	Marquis Grissom	.25
47	Jeff Cirillo	.25
48	Paul Molitor	1.00
49	Todd Walker	.50
50	Vladimir Guerrero	1.50
51	Brad Fullmer	.50
52	Mike Piazza	3.00
53	Hideo Nomo	.75
54	Carlos Baerga	.25
55	John Olerud	.40
56	Derek Jeter	2.50
57	Hideki Irabu	.50
58	Tino Martinez	.50
59	Bernie Williams	.75
60	Miguel Tejada	.50
61	Ben Grieve	1.50
62	Jason Giambi	.25
63	Scott Rolen	1.25
64	Doug Glanville	.25
65	Desi Relaford	.25
66	Tony Womack	.25
67	Jason Kendall	.25
68	Jose Guillen	.25
69	Tony Gwynn	2.50
70	Ken Caminiti	.40
71	Greg Vaughn	.40
72	Kevin Brown	.40
73	Barry Bonds	1.25
74	J.T. Snow	.25
75	Jeff Kent	.25
76	Ken Griffey Jr.	5.00
77	Alex Rodriguez	3.00
78	Edgar Martinez	.25
79	Jay Buhner	.50
80	Mark McGwire	6.00
81	Delino DeShields	.25
82	Brian Jordan	.25
83	Quinton McCracken	.25
84	Fred McGriff	.50
85	Juan Gonzalez	2.50
86	Ivan Rodriguez	1.25
87	Will Clark	.50
88	Roger Clemens	2.00
89	Jose Cruz Jr.	1.00
90	Babe Ruth	5.00
91	Troy Glaus (Diamond Debut)	6.00
92	Jarrod Washburn (Diamond Debut)	1.00
93	Travis Lee (Diamond Debut)	4.00
94	Bruce Chen (Diamond Debut)	1.00
95	Mike Caruso (Diamond Debut)	1.00
96	Jim Parque (Diamond Debut)	1.00
97	Kerry Wood (Diamond Debut)	8.00
98	Jeremy Giambi (Diamond Debut)	3.00
99	Matt Anderson (Diamond Debut)	2.00
100	Seth Greisinger (Diamond Debut)	1.00
101	Gabe Alvarez (Diamond Debut)	1.00
102	Rafael Medina (Diamond Debut)	1.00
103	Daryle Ward (Diamond Debut)	1.00
104	Alex Cora (Diamond Debut)	1.00
105	Adrian Beltre (Diamond Debut)	2.00
106	Geoff Jenkins (Diamond Debut)	1.50
107	Eric Milton (Diamond Debut)	1.00
108	Carl Pavano (Diamond Debut)	2.00
109	Eric Chavez (Diamond Debut)	4.00
110	Orlando Hernandez (Diamond Debut)	8.00
111	A.J. Hinch (Diamond Debut)	1.00
112	Carlton Loewer (Diamond Debut)	1.00
113	Aramis Ramirez (Diamond Debut)	1.50
114	Cliff Politte (Diamond Debut)	1.00
115	Matt Clement (Diamond Debut)	1.00
116	Alex Gonzalez (Diamond Debut)	3.00
117	J.D. Drew (Diamond Debut)	30.00
118	Shane Monahan (Diamond Debut)	1.00

119	Rolando Arrojo (Diamond Debut)	3.00
120	George Lombard (Diamond Debut)	1.00

1999 Upper Deck Black Diamond Diamond Dominance

		, MT
Complete Set (30):		450.00
Common Player:		4.00
Production 1,500 sets		
D01	Kerry Wood	30.00
D02	Derek Jeter	20.00
D03	Alex Rodriguez	25.00
D04	Frank Thomas	25.00
D05	Jeff Bagwell	10.00
D06	Mo Vaughn	10.00
D07	Ivan Rodriguez	10.00
D08	Cal Ripken Jr.	30.00
D09	Rolando Arrojo	4.00
D10	Chipper Jones	20.00
D11	Kenny Lofton	10.00
D12	Paul Konerko	4.00
D13	Mike Piazza	25.00
D14	Ben Grieve	10.00
D15	Nomar Garciaparra	25.00
D16	Travis Lee	10.00
D17	Scott Rolen	10.00
D18	Juan Gonzalez	20.00
D19	Tony Gwynn	20.00
D20	Tony Clark	6.00
D21	Roger Clemens	18.00
D22	Sammy Sosa	30.00
D23	Larry Walker	6.00
D24	Ken Griffey Jr.	40.00
D25	Mark McGwire	50.00
D26	Barry Bonds	10.00
D27	Vladimir Guerrero	15.00
D28	Tino Martinez	6.00
D29	Greg Maddux	25.00
D30	Babe Ruth	50.00

1999 Upper Deck Black Diamond Game Used Bat

		MT
Complete Set (6):		1200.
Common Player:		100.00
JG	Juan Gonzalez	250.00
TG	Tony Gwynn	250.00
BW	Bernie Williams	100.00
MM	Mark McGwire	500.00
MV	Mo Vaughn	140.00
SS	Sammy Sosa	300.00

1999 Upper Deck Black Diamond Mystery Numbers

		MT
Complete Set (30):		1000.
Common Player:		4.00
M01	Babe Ruth (100)	250.00
M02	Ken Griffey Jr. (200)	200.00
M03	Kerry Wood (300)	90.00
M04	Mark McGwire (400)	100.00
M05	Alex Rodriguez (500)	60.00
M06	Chipper Jones (600)	40.00
M07	Nomar Garciaparra (700)	50.00
M08	Derek Jeter (800)	30.00
M09	Mike Piazza (900)	40.00
M10	Roger Clemens (1,000)	30.00
M11	Greg Maddux (1,100)	35.00
M12	Scott Rolen (1,200)	15.00
M13	Cal Ripken Jr. (1,300)	35.00
M14	Ben Grieve (1,400)	12.00
M15	Troy Glaus (1,500)	20.00
M16	Sammy Sosa (1,600)	30.00
M17	Darin Erstad (1,700)	10.00
M18	Juan Gonzalez (1,800)	20.00
M19	Pedro J. Martinez (1,900)	8.00
M20	Larry Walker (2,000)	8.00
M21	Vladimir Guerrero (2,100)	10.00
M22	Jeff Bagwell (2,200)	10.00
M23	Jaret Wright (2,300)	6.00
M24	Travis Lee (2,400)	8.00
M25	Barry Bonds (2,500)	8.00
M26	Orlando Hernandez (2,600)	20.00
M27	Frank Thomas (2,700)	15.00
M28	Tony Gwynn (2,800)	10.00
M29	Andres Galarraga (2,900)	6.00
M30	Craig Biggio (3,000)	4.00

1999 Upper Deck Black Diamond Quadruple Diamond

		MT
Common Player (1-90):		8.00
Production 150 sets		
Common Diamond Debut (91-120):		10.00
Production 100 sets		
1	Darin Erstad	60.00
2	Tim Salmon	30.00
3	Jim Edmonds	20.00
4	Matt Williams	25.00
5	David Dellucci	8.00
6	Jay Bell	8.00
7	Andres Galarraga	50.00
8	Chipper Jones	125.00
9	Greg Maddux	160.00
10	Andruw Jones	60.00
11	Cal Ripken Jr.	200.00
12	Rafael Palmeiro	25.00
13	Brady Anderson	10.00
14	Mike Mussina	50.00
15	Nomar Garciaparra	160.00
16	Mo Vaughn	60.00
17	Pedro J. Martinez	40.00
18	Sammy Sosa	200.00
19	Henry Rodriguez	10.00
20	Frank Thomas	160.00
21	Magglio Ordonez	20.00
22	Albert Belle	60.00
23	Paul Konerko	15.00
24	Sean Casey	15.00
25	Jim Thome	30.00
26	Kenny Lofton	60.00
27	Sandy Alomar Jr.	10.00
28	Jaret Wright	30.00
29	Larry Walker	30.00
30	Todd Helton	50.00
31	Vinny Castilla	10.00
32	Tony Clark	30.00
33	Damion Easley	8.00
34	Mark Kotsay	10.00
35	Derrek Lee	8.00
36	Moises Alou	15.00
37	Jeff Bagwell	60.00
38	Craig Biggio	20.00
39	Randy Johnson	40.00
40	Dean Palmer	8.00
41	Johnny Damon	8.00
42	Chan Ho Park	20.00
43	Raul Mondesi	20.00
44	Gary Sheffield	20.00
45	Jeromy Burnitz	8.00
46	Marquis Grissom	8.00
47	Jeff Cirillo	8.00
48	Paul Molitor	50.00
49	Todd Walker	20.00
50	Vladimir Guerrero	60.00
51	Brad Fullmer	20.00
52	Mike Piazza	160.00
53	Hideo Nomo	30.00
54	Carlos Baerga	8.00
55	John Olerud	15.00
56	Derek Jeter	125.00
57	Hideki Irabu	20.00
58	Tino Martinez	25.00
59	Bernie Williams	40.00
60	Miguel Tejada	20.00
61	Ben Grieve	60.00
62	Jason Giambi	8.00
63	Scott Rolen	60.00
64	Doug Glanville	8.00
65	Desi Relaford	8.00
66	Tony Womack	8.00
67	Jason Kendall	10.00
68	Jose Guillen	10.00
69	Tony Gwynn	125.00
70	Ken Caminiti	15.00
71	Greg Vaughn	15.00
72	Kevin Brown	15.00
73	Barry Bonds	60.00
74	J.T. Snow	8.00
75	Jeff Kent	10.00
76	Ken Griffey Jr.	250.00
77	Alex Rodriguez	160.00
78	Edgar Martinez	10.00
79	Jay Buhner	20.00
80	Mark McGwire	300.00
81	Delino DeShields	8.00
82	Brian Jordan	10.00
83	Quinton McCracken	8.00
84	Fred McGriff	20.00
85	Juan Gonzalez	125.00
86	Ivan Rodriguez	60.00
87	Will Clark	25.00
88	Roger Clemens	100.00
89	Jose Cruz Jr.	50.00
90	Babe Ruth	150.00
91	Troy Glaus (Diamond Debut)	100.00
92	Jarrod Washburn (Diamond Debut)	10.00
93	Travis Lee (Diamond Debut)	60.00
94	Bruce Chen (Diamond Debut)	15.00
95	Mike Caruso (Diamond Debut)	20.00
96	Jim Parque (Diamond Debut)	10.00
97	Kerry Wood (Diamond Debut)	125.00
98	Jeremy Giambi (Diamond Debut)	40.00
99	Matt Anderson (Diamond Debut)	25.00
100	Seth Greisinger (Diamond Debut)	10.00
101	Gabe Alvarez (Diamond Debut)	10.00
102	Rafael Medina (Diamond Debut)	10.00
103	Daryle Ward (Diamond Debut)	10.00
104	Alex Cora (Diamond Debut)	10.00
105	Adrian Beltre (Diamond Debut)	20.00
106	Geoff Jenkins (Diamond Debut)	15.00
107	Eric Milton (Diamond Debut)	10.00
108	Carl Pavano (Diamond Debut)	15.00
109	Eric Chavez (Diamond Debut)	50.00
110	Orlando Hernandez (Diamond Debut)	120.00
111	A.J. Hinch (Diamond Debut)	10.00
112	Carlton Loewer (Diamond Debut)	10.00
113	Aramis Ramirez (Diamond Debut)	20.00
114	Cliff Politte (Diamond Debut)	10.00
115	Matt Clement (Diamond Debut)	10.00
116	Alex Gonzalez (Diamond Debut)	30.00
117	J.D. Drew (Diamond Debut)	200.00
118	Shane Monahan (Diamond Debut)	10.00
119	Rolando Arrojo (Diamond Debut)	20.00
120	George Lombard (Diamond Debut)	10.00

A player's name in *italic* type indicates a rookie card.

MODERN MAJOR LEAGUE CARDS (1981-1998)

The vast majority of cards listed in this section were issued between 1981 and late-1998 and feature major league players only. The term "card" is used rather loosely as in this context it is construed to include virtually any series of cardboard or paper product, of whatever size and/or shape, depicting baseball players. Further, "cards" printed on wood, metal, plastic and other materials are either by their association with other issues or by their compatibility in size with the current 2-1/2" x 3-1/2" card standard also listed here.

Because modern cards are generally not popularly collected in lower grades, cards in this section carry only a Mint (MT) value quote. In general, post-1980 cards which grade Near Mint (NM) will retail at about 75% of the Mint price, while Excellent (EX) condition cards bring 40%.

B

1989 Bowman

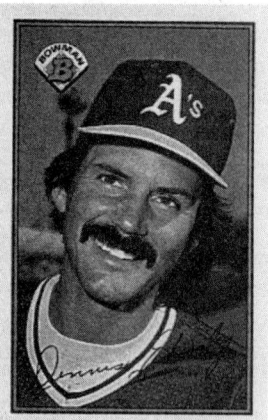

Topps, which purchased Bowman in 1955, revived the brand name in 1989, issuing a 484-card set. The 2-1/2" x 3-3/4" cards are slightly taller than current standard. Fronts contain a full-color player photo, with facsimile autograph and the Bowman logo in an upper corner. Backs include a breakdown of the player's stats against each team in his league. A series of "Hot Rookie Stars" highlights the set. The cards were distributed in both wax packs and rack packs. Each pack included a special reproduction of a classic Bowman card with a sweepstakes on the back.

		MT
Complete Set (484):		12.00
Common Player:		.05
Wax Box:		10.00
1	Oswald Peraza	.05
2	Brian Holton	.05
3	Jose Bautista	.05
4	*Pete Harnisch*	.20
5	Dave Schmidt	.05
6	Gregg Olson	.05
7	Jeff Ballard	.05
8	Bob Melvin	.05
9	Cal Ripken, Jr.	.75
10	Randy Milligan	.05
11	*Juan Bell*	.10
12	Billy Ripken	.05
13	Jim Trabor	.05
14	Pete Stanicek	.05
15	*Steve Finley*	.25
16	Larry Sheets	.05
17	Phil Bradley	.05
18	*Brady Anderson*	.40
19	Lee Smith	.09
20	Tom Fischer	.05
21	Mike Boddicker	.05
22	Rob Murphy	.05
23	Wes Gardner	.05
24	John Dopson	.05
25	Bob Stanley	.05
26	Roger Clemens	.40
27	Rich Gedman	.05
28	Marty Barrett	.05
29	Luis Rivera	.05
30	Jody Reed	.05
31	Nick Esasky	.05
32	Wade Boggs	.20
33	Jim Rice	.10
34	Mike Greenwell	.05
35	Dwight Evans	.08
36	Ellis Burks	.12
37	Chuck Finley	.05
38	Kirk McCaskill	.05
39	Jim Abbott	.10
40	*Bryan Harvey*	.08
41	Bert Blyleven	.08
42	Mike Witt	.05
43	Bob McClure	.05
44	Bill Schroeder	.05
45	Lance Parrish	.08
46	Dick Schofield	.05
47	Wally Joyner	.10
48	Jack Howell	.05
49	Johnny Ray	.05
50	Chili Davis	.08
51	Tony Armas	.05
52	Claudell Washington	.05
53	Brian Downing	.05
54	Devon White	.08
55	Bobby Thigpen	.05
56	Bill Long	.05
57	Jerry Reuss	.05
58	Shawn Hillegas	.05
59	Melido Perez	.05
60	Jeff Bittiger	.05
61	Jack McDowell	.08
62	Carlton Fisk	.10
63	Steve Lyons	.05
64	Ozzie Guillen	.05
65	Robin Ventura	.20
66	Fred Manrique	.05
67	Dan Pasqua	.05
68	Ivan Calderon	.05
69	Ron Kittle	.05
70	Daryl Boston	.05
71	Dave Gallagher	.05
72	Harold Baines	.08
73	*Charles Nagy*	.25
74	John Farrell	.05
75	Kevin Wickander	.05
76	Greg Swindell	.05
77	Mike Walker	.05
78	Doug Jones	.05
79	Rich Yett	.05
80	Tom Candiotti	.05
81	Jesse Orosco	.05
82	Bud Black	.05
83	Andy Allanson	.05
84	Pete O'Brien	.05
85	Jerry Browne	.05
86	Brook Jacoby	.05
87	*Mark Lewis*	.15
88	Luis Aguayo	.05
89	Cory Snyder	.05
90	Oddibe McDowell	.05
91	Joe Carter	.15
92	Frank Tanana	.05
93	Jack Morris	.08
94	Doyle Alexander	.05
95	Steve Searcy	.05
96	Randy Bockus	.05
97	Jeff Robinson	.05
98	Mike Henneman	.05
99	Paul Gibson	.05
100	Frank Williams	.05
101	Matt Nokes	.05
102	Rico Brogna	.05
103	Lou Whitaker	.08
104	Al Pedrique	.05
105	Alan Trammell	.10
106	Chris Brown	.05
107	Pat Sheridan	.05
108	Gary Pettis	.05
109	Keith Moreland	.05
110	Mel Stottlemyre, Jr.	.05
111	Bret Saberhagen	.08
112	Floyd Bannister	.05
113	Jeff Montgomery	.05
114	Steve Farr	.05
115	Tom Gordon	.05
116	Charlie Leibrandt	.05
117	Mark Gubicza	.05
118	Mike MacFarlane	.05
119	Bob Boone	.05
120	Kurt Stillwell	.05
121	George Brett	.40
122	Frank White	.05

#	Player	Price	#	Player	Price	#	Player	Price
123	Kevin Seitzer	.05	219	Jay Buhner	.15	314	Kal Daniels	.05
124	Willie Wilson	.05	220	*Ken Griffey, Jr.*	5.00	315	Joel Youngblood	.05
125	Pat Tabler	.05	221	Drew Hall	.05	316	Eric Davis	.10
126	Bo Jackson	.20	222	Bobby Witt	.05	317	Dave Smith	.05
127	Hugh Walker	.05	223	Jamie Moyer	.05	318	Mark Portugal	.05
128	Danny Tartabull	.05	224	Charlie Hough	.05	319	Brian Meyer	.05
129	Teddy Higuera	.05	225	Nolan Ryan	.75	320	Jim Deshaies	.05
130	Don August	.05	226	Jeff Russell	.05	321	Juan Agosto	.05
131	Juan Nieves	.05	227	Jim Sundberg	.05	322	Mike Scott	.05
132	Mike Birkbeck	.05	228	Julio Franco	.08	323	Rick Rhoden	.05
133	Dan Plesac	.05	229	Buddy Bell	.05	324	Jim Clancy	.05
134	Chris Bosio	.05	230	Scott Fletcher	.05	325	Larry Andersen	.05
135	Bill Wegman	.05	231	Jeff Kunkel	.05	326	Alex Trevino	.05
136	Chuck Crim	.05	232	Steve Buechele	.05	327	Alan Ashby	.05
137	B.J. Surhoff	.05	233	Monty Fariss	.05	328	Craig Reynolds	.05
138	Joey Meyer	.05	234	Rick Leach	.05	329	Bill Doran	.05
139	Dale Sveum	.05	235	Ruben Sierra	.10	330	Rafael Ramirez	.05
140	Paul Molitor	.35	236	Cecil Espy	.05	331	Glenn Davis	.05
141	Jim Gantner	.05	237	Rafael Palmeiro	.15	332	*Willie Ansley*	.08
142	Gary Sheffield	.50	238	Pete Incaviglia	.05	333	Gerald Young	.05
143	Greg Brock	.05	239	Dave Steib	.05	334	Cameron Drew	.05
144	Robin Yount	.25	240	Jeff Musselman	.05	335	Jay Howell	.05
145	Glenn Braggs	.05	241	Mike Flanagan	.05	336	Tim Belcher	.05
146	Rob Deer	.05	242	Todd Stottlemyre	.08	337	Fernando Valenzuela	.07
147	Fred Toliver	.05	243	Jimmy Key	.05	338	Ricky Horton	.05
148	Jeff Reardon	.05	244	Tony Castillo	.05	339	Tim Leary	.05
149	Allan Anderson	.05	245	Alex Sanchez	.05	340	Bill Bene	.05
150	Frank Viola	.05	246	Tom Henke	.05	341	Orel Hershiser	.08
151	Shane Rawley	.05	247	John Cerutti	.05	342	Mike Scioscia	.05
152	Juan Berenguer	.05	248	Ernie Whitt	.05	343	Rick Dempsey	.05
153	Johnny Ard	.05	249	Bob Brenly	.05	344	Willie Randolph	.05
154	Tim Laudner	.05	250	Rance Mulliniks	.05	345	Alfredo Griffin	.05
155	Brian Harper	.05	251	Kelly Gruber	.05	346	Eddie Murray	.20
156	Al Newman	.05	252	Ed Sprague	.10	347	Mickey Hatcher	.05
157	Kent Hrbek	.08	253	Fred McGriff	.15	348	Mike Sharperson	.05
158	Gary Gaetti	.08	254	Tony Fernandez	.08	349	John Shelby	.05
159	Wally Backman	.05	255	Tom Lawless	.05	350	Mike Marshall	.05
160	Gene Larkin	.05	256	George Bell	.08	351	Kirk Gibson	.07
161	Greg Gagne	.05	257	Jesse Barfield	.05	352	Mike Davis	.05
162	Kirby Puckett	.50	258	Sandy Alomar, Sr.	.09	353	Bryn Smith	.05
163	Danny Gladden	.05	259	Ken Griffey (with Ken Griffey, Jr.)	.50	354	Pascual Perez	.05
164	Randy Bush	.05				355	Kevin Gross	.05
165	Dave LaPoint	.05	260	Cal Ripken, Sr.	.15	356	Andy McGaffigan	.05
166	Andy Hawkins	.05	261	Mel Stottlemyre, Sr.	.10	357	Brian Holman	.05
167	Dave Righetti	.05	262	Zane Smith	.05	358	Dave Wainhouse	.05
168	Lance McCullers	.05	263	Charlie Puleo	.05	359	Denny Martinez	.09
169	Jimmy Jones	.05	264	Derek Lilliquist	.05	360	Tim Burke	.05
170	Al Leiter	.05	265	Paul Assenmacher	.05	361	Nelson Santovenia	.05
171	John Candelaria	.05	266	John Smoltz	.15	362	Tim Wallach	.05
172	Don Slaught	.05	267	Tom Glavine	.15	363	Spike Owen	.05
173	Jamie Quirk	.05	268	*Steve Avery*	.15	364	Rex Hudler	.05
174	Rafael Santana	.05	269	*Pete Smith*	.09	365	Andres Galarraga	.20
175	Mike Pagliarulo	.05	270	Jody Davis	.05	366	Otis Nixon	.05
176	Don Mattingly	.40	271	Bruce Benedict	.05	367	Hubie Brooks	.05
177	Ken Phelps	.05	272	Andres Thomas	.05	368	Mike Aldrete	.05
178	Steve Sax	.05	273	Gerald Perry	.05	369	Rock Raines	.08
179	Dave Winfield	.10	274	Ron Gant	.15	370	Dave Martinez	.05
180	Stan Jefferson	.05	275	Darrell Evans	.08	371	Bob Ojeda	.05
181	Rickey Henderson	.10	276	Dale Murphy	.10	372	Ron Darling	.05
182	Bob Brower	.05	277	Dion James	.05	373	Wally Whitehurst	.05
183	Roberto Kelly	.05	278	Lonnie Smith	.05	374	Randy Myers	.05
184	Curt Young	.05	279	Geronimo Berroa	.05	375	David Cone	.15
185	Gene Nelson	.05	280	Steve Wilson	.05	376	Dwight Gooden	.10
186	Bob Welch	.05	281	Rick Suctcliffe	.05	377	Sid Fernandez	.05
187	Rick Honeycutt	.05	282	Kevin Coffman	.05	378	Dave Proctor	.05
188	Dave Stewart	.05	283	Mitch Williams	.05	379	Gary Carter	.10
189	Mike Moore	.05	284	Greg Maddux	.70	380	Keith Miller	.05
190	Dennis Eckersley	.08	285	Paul Kilgus	.05	381	Gregg Jefferies	.10
191	Eric Plunk	.05	286	Mike Harkey	.05	382	Tim Teufel	.05
192	Storm Davis	.05	287	Lloyd McClendon	.05	383	Kevin Elster	.05
193	Terry Steinbach	.05	288	Damon Berryhill	.05	384	Dave Magadan	.05
194	Ron Hassey	.05	289	Ty Griffin	.05	385	Keith Hernandez	.08
195	Stan Royer	.10	290	Ryne Sandberg	.50	386	Mookie Wilson	.05
196	Walt Weiss	.05	291	Mark Grace	.35	387	Darryl Strawberry	.10
197	Mark McGwire	1.50	292	Curt Wilkerson	.05	388	Kevin McReynolds	.05
198	Carney Lansford	.05	293	Vance Law	.05	389	Mark Carreon	.05
199	Glenn Hubbard	.05	294	Shawon Dunston	.12	390	Jeff Parrett	.05
200	Dave Henderson	.05	295	Jerome Walton	.05	391	Mike Maddux	.05
201	Jose Canseco	.15	296	Mitch Webster	.05	392	Don Carman	.05
202	Dave Parker	.09	297	Dwight Smith	.05	393	Bruce Ruffin	.05
203	Scott Bankhead	.05	298	Andre Dawson	.15	394	Ken Howell	.05
204	Tom Niedenfuer	.05	299	Jeff Sellers	.05	395	Steve Bedrosian	.05
205	Mark Langston	.08	300	Jose Rijo	.05	396	Floyd Youmans	.05
206	*Erik Hanson*	.12	301	John Franco	.05	397	Larry McWilliams	.05
207	Mike Jackson	.05	302	Rick Mahler	.05	398	Pat Combs	.07
208	Dave Valle	.05	303	Ron Robinson	.05	399	Steve Lake	.05
209	Scott Bradley	.05	304	Danny Jackson	.05	400	Dickie Thon	.05
210	Harold Reynolds	.08	305	Rob Dibble	.05	401	Ricky Jordan	.05
211	Tino Martinez	.50	306	Tom Browning	.05	402	Mike Schmidt	.30
212	Rich Renteria	.05	307	Bo Diaz	.05	403	Tom Herr	.05
213	Rey Quinones	.05	308	Manny Trillo	.05	404	Chris James	.05
214	Jim Presley	.05	309	Chris Sabo	.05	405	Juan Samuel	.05
215	Alvin Davis	.05	310	Ron Oester	.05	406	Von Hayes	.05
216	Edgar Martinez	.10	311	Barry Larkin	.15	407	Ron Jones	.05
217	Darnell Coles	.05	312	Todd Benzinger	.05	408	Curt Ford	.05
218	Jeffrey Leonard	.05	313	Paul O'Neill	.20	409	Bob Walk	.05

410	Jeff Robinson	.05
411	Jim Gott	.05
412	Scott Medvin	.05
413	John Smiley	.05
414	Bob Kipper	.05
415	Brian Fisher	.05
416	Doug Drabek	.05
417	Mike Lavalliere	.05
418	Ken Oberkfell	.05
419	Sid Bream	.05
420	Austin Manahan	.05
421	Jose Lind	.05
422	Bobby Bonilla	.10
423	Glenn Wilson	.05
424	Andy Van Slyke	.05
425	Gary Redus	.05
426	Barry Bonds	.50
427	Don Heinkel	.05
428	Ken Dayley	.05
429	Todd Worrell	.05
430	Brad DuVall	.08
431	Jose DeLeon	.05
432	Joe Magrane	.05
433	John Ericks	.05
434	Frank DiPino	.05
435	Tony Pena	.05
436	Ozzie Smith	.35
437	Terry Pendleton	.05
438	Jose Oquendo	.05
439	Tim Jones	.05
440	Pedro Guerrero	.05
441	Milt Thompson	.05
442	Willie McGee	.08
443	Vince Coleman	.05
444	Tom Brunansky	.05
445	Walt Terrell	.05
446	Eric Show	.05
447	Mark Davis	.05
448	*Andy Benes*	.25
449	Eddie Whitson	.05
450	Dennis Rasmussen	.05
451	Bruce Hurst	.05
452	Pat Clements	.05
453	Benito Santiago	.08
454	Sandy Alomar, Jr.	.12
455	Garry Templeton	.05
456	Jack Clark	.05
457	Tim Flannery	.05
458	Roberto Alomar	.30
459	Camelo Martinez	.05
460	John Kruk	.05
461	Tony Gwynn	.40
462	Jerald Clark	.05
463	Don Robinson	.05
464	Craig Lefferts	.05
465	Kelly Downs	.05
466	Rick Rueschel	.05
467	Scott Garrelts	.05
468	Wil Tejada	.05
469	Kirt Manwaring	.05
470	Terry Kennedy	.05
471	Jose Uribe	.05
472	*Royce Clayton*	.15
473	Robby Thompson	.05
474	Kevin Mitchell	.08
475	Ernie Riles	.05
476	Will Clark	.20
477	Donnell Nixon	.05
478	Candy Maldonado	.05
479	Tracy Jones	.05
480	Brett Butler	.09
481	Checklist 1-121	.05
482	Checklist 122-242	.05
483	Checklist 243-363	.05
484	Checklist 364-484	.05

1989 Bowman Glossy

A special collectors' version of the revitalized Bowman cards was produced in 1989, differing from the regular-issue cards in the application of a high-gloss finish to the front and the use of a white cardboard stock. The "Tiffany" version (as the glossies are known to collectors, was sold only in complete boxed sets, with an estimated production of 5,000 to 10,000 sets.

	MT
Complete Set (495):	85.00
Common Player:	.25
(Single cards valued at 4-5X regular-issue 1989 Bowman.)	

1989 Bowman Inserts

Bowman inserted sweepstakes cards in its 1989 packs. Each sweepstakes card reproduces a classic Bowman card on the front, with a prominent "REPRINT" notice. With one card in each pack, they are by no means scarce. A "Tiffany" version of the reprints was produced for inclusion in the factory set of 1989 Bowman cards. The glossy-front inserts are valued at 10X the standard version.

		MT
Complete Set (11):		5.00
Common Player:		.10
(1)	Richie Ashburn	.10
(2)	Yogi Berra	.15
(3)	Whitey Ford	.10
(4)	Gil Hodges	.10
(5)	Mickey Mantle (1951)	2.00
(6)	Mickey Mantle (1953)	1.00
(7)	Willie Mays	.50
(8)	Satchel Paige	.25
(9)	Jackie Robinson	.75
(10)	Duke Snider	.15
(11)	Ted Williams	.75

1990 Bowman

BLUE JAYS • GLENALLEN HILL

Bowman followed its 1989 rebirth with a 528-card set in 1990. The 1990 cards follow the classic Bowman style featuring a full-color photo bordered in white. The Bowman logo appears in the upper-left corner. The player's team nickname and name appear on the bottom border of the card photo. Unlike the 1989 set, the 1990 cards are standard 2-1/2" x 3-1/2". Backs are horizontal and display the player's statistics against the teams in his league. Included in the set are special insert cards featuring a painted image of a modern-day superstar done in the style of the 1951 Bowman cards. The paintings were produced for Bowman by artist Craig Pursley. Insert backs contain

a sweepstakes offer with a chance to win a complete set of 11 lithographs made from these paintings.

	MT
Complete Set (528):	15.00
Common Player:	.05
Wax Box:	10.00

1	*Tommy Greene*	.20
2	Tom Glavine	.15
3	Andy Nezelek	.05
4	Mike Stanton	.05
5	Rick Lueken	.05
6	Kent Mercker	.05
7	Derek Lilliquist	.05
8	Charlie Liebrandt	.05
9	Steve Avery	.10
10	John Smoltz	.15
11	Mark Lemke	.05
12	Lonnie Smith	.05
13	Oddibe McDowell	.05
14	*Tyler Houston*	.10
15	Jeff Blauser	.05
16	Ernie Whitt	.05
17	Alexis Infante	.05
18	Jim Presley	.05
19	Dale Murphy	.15
20	Nick Esasky	.05
21	Rick Sutcliffe	.05
22	Mike Bielecki	.05
23	Steve Wilson	.05
24	Kevin Blankenship	.05
25	Mitch Williams	.05
26	Dean Wilkins	.05
27	Greg Maddux	.75
28	Mike Harkey	.05
29	Mark Grace	.30
30	Ryne Sandberg	.40
31	Greg Smith	.05
32	Dwight Smith	.05
33	Damon Berryhill	.05
34	Earl Cunningham	.05
35	Jerome Walton	.05
36	Lloyd McClendon	.05
37	Ty Griffin	.05
38	Shawon Dunston	.10
39	Andre Dawson	.15
40	Luis Salazar	.05
41	Tim Layana	.05
42	Rob Dibble	.05
43	Tom Browning	.05
44	Danny Jackson	.05
45	Jose Rijo	.05
46	Scott Scudder	.05
47	Randy Myers	.08
48	Brian Lane	.05
49	Paul O'Neill	.08
50	Barry Larkin	.10
51	Reggie Jefferson	.10
52	Jeff Branson	.05
53	Chris Sabo	.05
54	Joe Oliver	.05
55	Todd Benzinger	.05
56	Rolando Roomes	.05
57	Hal Morris	.05
58	Eric Davis	.12
59	Scott Bryant	.05
60	Ken Griffey	.08
61	*Darryl Kile*	.30
62	Dave Smith	.05
63	Mark Portugal	.05
64	*Jeff Juden*	.20
65	Bill Gullickson	.05
66	Danny Darwin	.05
67	Larry Andersen	.05
68	Jose Cano	.05
69	Dan Schatzeder	.05
70	Jim Deshaies	.05
71	Mike Scott	.05
72	Gerald Young	.05
73	Ken Caminiti	.10
74	Ken Oberkfell	.05
75	Dave Rhode	.05
76	Bill Doran	.05
77	Andujar Cedeno	.05
78	Craig Biggio	.08
79	Karl Rhodes	.05
80	Glenn Davis	.05
81	*Eric Anthony*	.15
82	John Wetteland	.15
83	Jay Howell	.05
84	Orel Hershiser	.10
85	Tim Belcher	.05
86	Kiki Jones	.05
87	Mike Hartley	.08
88	Ramon Martinez	.08

#	Player	Value
89	Mike Scioscia	.05
90	Willie Randolph	.05
91	Juan Samuel	.05
92	*Jose Offerman*	.15
93	Dave Hansen	.05
94	Jeff Hamilton	.05
95	Alfredo Griffin	.05
96	Tom Goodwin	.05
97	Kirk Gibson	.05
98	Jose Vizcaino	.05
99	Kal Daniels	.05
100	Hubie Brooks	.05
101	Eddie Murray	.15
102	Dennis Boyd	.05
103	Tim Burke	.05
104	Bill Sampen	.05
105	Brett Gideon	.05
106	Mark Gardner	.05
107	Howard Farmer	.05
108	Mel Rojas	.08
109	Kevin Gross	.05
110	Dave Schmidt	.05
111	Denny Martinez	.08
112	Jerry Goff	.05
113	Andres Galarraga	.10
114	Tim Welch	.05
115	*Marquis Grissom*	.50
116	Spike Owen	.05
117	*Larry Walker*	1.50
118	Rock Raines	.08
119	*Delino DeShields*	.20
120	Tom Foley	.05
121	Dave Martinez	.05
122	Frank Viola	.05
123	Julio Valera	.05
124	Alejandro Pena	.05
125	David Cone	.08
126	Dwight Gooden	.10
127	Kevin Brown	.20
128	John Franco	.05
129	Terry Bross	.05
130	Blaine Beatty	.05
131	Sid Fernandez	.05
132	Mike Marshall	.05
133	Howard Johnson	.05
134	Jaime Roseboro	.05
135	Alan Zinter	.05
136	Keith Miller	.05
137	Kevin Elster	.05
138	Kevin McReynolds	.05
139	Barry Lyons	.05
140	Gregg Jefferies	.15
141	Darryl Strawberry	.12
142	*Todd Hundley*	.25
143	Scott Service	.05
144	Chuck Malone	.05
145	Steve Ontiveros	.05
146	Roger McDowell	.05
147	Ken Howell	.05
148	Pat Combs	.10
149	Jeff Parrett	.05
150	Chuck McElroy	.05
151	Jason Grimsley	.10
152	Len Dykstra	.08
153	Mickey Morandini	.05
154	John Kruk	.05
155	Dickie Thon	.05
156	Ricky Jordan	.05
157	Jeff Jackson	.05
158	Darren Daulton	.08
159	Tom Herr	.05
160	Von Hayes	.05
161	*Dave Hollins*	.20
162	Carmelo Martinez	.05
163	Bob Walk	.05
164	Doug Drabek	.05
165	Walt Terrell	.05
166	Bill Landrum	.05
167	Scott Ruskin	.05
168	Bob Patterson	.05
169	Bobby Bonilla	.12
170	Jose Lind	.05
171	Andy Van Slyke	.05
172	Mike LaValliere	.05
173	*Willie Greene*	.20
174	Jay Bell	.05
175	Sid Bream	.05
176	Tom Prince	.05
177	Wally Backman	.05
178	*Moises Alou*	.25
179	Steve Carter	.05
180	Gary Redus	.05
181	Barry Bonds	.50
182	Don Slaught	.05
183	Joe Magrane	.05
184	Bryn Smith	.05
185	Todd Worrell	.05
186	Jose Deleon	.05
187	Frank DiPino	.05
188	John Tudor	.05
189	Howard Hilton	.05
190	John Ericks	.05
191	Ken Dayley	.05
192	*Ray Lankford*	.40
193	Todd Zeile	.10
194	Willie McGee	.08
195	Ozzie Smith	.40
196	Milt Thompson	.05
197	Terry Pendleton	.05
198	Vince Coleman	.05
199	Paul Coleman	.05
200	Jose Oquendo	.05
201	Pedro Guerrero	.05
202	Tom Brunansky	.05
203	Roger Smithberg	.05
204	Eddie Whitson	.05
205	Dennis Rasmussen	.05
206	Craig Lefferts	.05
207	Andy Benes	.10
208	Bruce Hurst	.05
209	Eric Show	.05
210	Rafael Valdez	.05
211	Joey Cora	.05
212	Thomas Howard	.10
213	Rob Nelson	.05
214	Jack Clark	.05
215	Garry Templeton	.05
216	Fred Lynn	.08
217	Tony Gwynn	.40
218	Benny Santiago	.05
219	Mike Pagliarulo	.05
220	Joe Carter	.15
221	Roberto Alomar	.30
222	Bip Roberts	.05
223	Rick Reuschel	.05
224	Russ Swan	.05
225	Eric Gunderson	.05
226	Steve Bedrosian	.05
227	Mike Remlinger	.05
228	Scott Garrelts	.05
229	Ernie Camacho	.05
230	Andres Santana	.05
231	Will Clark	.20
232	Kevin Mitchell	.08
233	Robby Thompson	.05
234	Bill Bathe	.05
235	Tony Perezchica	.05
236	Gary Carter	.10
237	Brett Butler	.10
238	Matt Williams	.20
239	Ernie Riles	.05
240	Kevin Bass	.05
241	Terry Kennedy	.05
242	*Steve Hosey*	.15
243	Ben McDonald	.20
244	Jeff Ballard	.05
245	Joe Price	.05
246	Curt Schilling	.05
247	Pete Harnisch	.05
248	Mark Williamson	.05
249	Gregg Olson	.05
250	Chris Myers	.05
251	David Segui	.08
252	Joe Orsulak	.05
253	Craig Worthington	.05
254	Mickey Tettleton	.05
255	Cal Ripken, Jr.	.90
256	Billy Ripken	.05
257	Randy Milligan	.05
258	Brady Anderson	.20
259	*Chris Hoiles*	.20
260	Mike Devereaux	.05
261	Phil Bradley	.05
262	*Leo Gomez*	.15
263	Lee Smith	.08
264	Mike Rochford	.05
265	Jeff Reardon	.05
266	Wes Gardner	.05
267	Mike Boddicker	.05
268	Roger Clemens	.40
269	Rob Murphy	.05
270	Mickey Pina	.05
271	Tony Pena	.05
272	Jody Reed	.05
273	Kevin Romine	.05
274	Mike Greenwell	.08
275	*Mo Vaughn*	1.50
276	Danny Heep	.05
277	Scott Cooper	.05
278	*Greg Blosser*	.10
279	Dwight Evans	.05
280	Ellis Burks	.10
281	Wade Boggs	.20
282	Marty Barrett	.05
283	Kirk McCaskill	.05
284	Mark Langston	.05
285	Bert Blyleven	.08
286	Mike Fetters	.05
287	Kyle Abbott	.08
288	Jim Abbott	.12
289	Chuck Finley	.05
290	Gary DiSarcina	.05
291	Dick Schofield	.05
292	Devon White	.08
293	Bobby Rose	.05
294	Brian Downing	.05
295	Lance Parrish	.08
296	Jack Howell	.05
297	Claudell Washington	.05
298	John Orton	.05
299	Wally Joyner	.08
300	Lee Stevens	.05
301	Chili Davis	.08
302	Johnny Ray	.05
303	Greg Hibbard	.05
304	Eric King	.05
305	Jack McDowell	.10
306	Bobby Thigpen	.05
307	Adam Peterson	.05
308	*Scott Radinsky*	.10
309	Wayne Edwards	.05
310	Melido Perez	.05
311	Robin Ventura	.20
312	*Sammy Sosa*	4.00
313	Dan Pasqua	.05
314	Carlton Fisk	.15
315	Ozzie Guillen	.05
316	Ivan Calderon	.05
317	Daryl Boston	.05
318	Craig Grebeck	.05
319	Scott Fletcher	.05
320	*Frank Thomas*	3.00
321	Steve Lyons	.05
322	Carlos Martinez	.05
323	Joe Skalski	.05
324	Tom Candiotti	.05
325	Greg Swindell	.05
326	Steve Olin	.05
327	Kevin Wickander	.05
328	Doug Jones	.05
329	Jeff Shaw	.05
330	Kevin Bearse	.05
331	Dion James	.05
332	Jerry Browne	.05
333	Albert Belle	.75
334	Felix Fermin	.05
335	Candy Maldonado	.05
336	Cory Snyder	.05
337	Sandy Alomar	.12
338	Mark Lewis	.08
339	*Carlos Baerga*	.20
340	Chris James	.05
341	Brook Jacoby	.05
342	Keith Hernandez	.05
343	Frank Tanana	.05
344	Scott Aldred	.05
345	Mike Henneman	.05
346	Steve Wapnick	.05
347	Greg Gohr	.05
348	Eric Stone	.05
349	Brian DuBois	.05
350	Kevin Ritz	.05
351	Rico Brogna	.08
352	Mike Heath	.05
353	Alan Trammell	.10
354	Chet Lemon	.05
355	Dave Bergman	.05
356	Lou Whitaker	.08
357	Cecil Fielder	.20
358	Milt Cuyler	.05
359	Tony Phillips	.05
360	*Travis Fryman*	.35
361	Ed Romero	.05
362	Lloyd Moseby	.05
363	Mark Gubicza	.08
364	Bret Saberhagen	.08
365	Tom Gordon	.05
366	Steve Farr	.05
367	Kevin Appier	.08
368	Storm Davis	.05
369	Mark Davis	.05
370	Jeff Montgomery	.05
371	Frank White	.05
372	Brent Mayne	.05
373	Bob Boone	.05
374	Jim Eisenreich	.05
375	Danny Tartabull	.05
376	Kurt Stillwell	.05

377	Bill Pecota	.05
378	Bo Jackson	.20
379	*Bob Hamelin*	.15
380	Kevin Seitzer	.05
381	Rey Palacios	.05
382	George Brett	.50
383	Gerald Perry	.05
384	Teddy Higuera	.05
385	Tom Filer	.05
386	Dan Plesac	.05
387	*Cal Eldred*	.15
388	Jaime Navarro	.05
389	Chris Bosio	.05
390	Randy Veres	.05
391	Gary Sheffield	.12
392	George Canale	.05
393	B.J. Surhoff	.05
394	Tim McIntosh	.05
395	Greg Brock	.05
396	Greg Vaughn	.12
397	Darryl Hamilton	.05
398	Dave Parker	.10
399	Paul Molitor	.30
400	Jim Gantner	.05
401	Rob Deer	.05
402	Billy Spiers	.05
403	Glenn Braggs	.05
404	Robin Yount	.25
405	Rick Aguilera	.05
406	Johnny Ard	.05
407	*Kevin Tapani*	.20
408	Park Pittman	.05
409	Allan Anderson	.05
410	Juan Berenguer	.05
411	Willie Banks	.05
412	Rich Yett	.05
413	Dave West	.05
414	Greg Gagne	.05
415	*Chuck Knoblauch*	.75
416	Randy Bush	.05
417	Gary Gaetti	.08
418	Kent Hrbek	.08
419	Al Newman	.05
420	Danny Gladden	.05
421	Paul Sorrento	.08
422	Derek Parks	.05
423	Scott Leius	.08
424	Kirby Puckett	.60
425	Willie Smith	.05
426	Dave Righetti	.05
427	Jeff Robinson	.05
428	Alan Mills	.05
429	Tim Leary	.05
430	Pascual Perez	.05
431	Alvaro Espinoza	.05
432	Dave Winfield	.15
433	Jesse Barfield	.05
434	Randy Velarde	.05
435	Rick Cerone	.05
436	Steve Balboni	.05
437	Mel Hall	.05
438	Bob Geren	.05
439	*Bernie Williams*	1.00
440	Kevin Maas	.05
441	Mike Blowers	.05
442	Steve Sax	.05
443	Don Mattingly	.60
444	Roberto Kelly	.05
445	Mike Moore	.05
446	Reggie Harris	.05
447	Scott Sanderson	.05
448	Dave Otto	.05
449	Dave Stewart	.08
450	Rick Honeycutt	.05
451	Dennis Eckersley	.10
452	Carney Lansford	.05
453	Scott Hemond	.05
454	Mark McGwire	1.50
455	Felix Jose	.05
456	Terry Steinbach	.05
457	Rickey Henderson	.15
458	Dave Henderson	.05
459	Mike Gallego	.05
460	Jose Canseco	.15
461	Walt Weiss	.05
462	Ken Phelps	.05
463	*Darren Lewis*	.25
464	Ron Hassey	.05
465	*Roger Salkeld*	.15
466	Scott Bankhead	.05
467	Keith Comstock	.05
468	Randy Johnson	.35
469	Erik Hanson	.05
470	Mike Schooler	.05
471	Gary Eave	.05
472	Jeffrey Leonard	.05

473	Dave Valle	.05
474	Omar Vizquel	.05
475	Pete O'Brien	.05
476	Henry Cotto	.05
477	Jay Buhner	.12
478	Harold Reynolds	.08
479	Alvin Davis	.05
480	Darnell Coles	.05
481	Ken Griffey, Jr.	2.00
482	Greg Briley	.05
483	Scott Bradley	.05
484	Tino Martinez	.25
485	Jeff Russell	.05
486	Nolan Ryan	.75
487	Robb Nen	.10
488	Kevin Brown	.08
489	Brian Bohanon	.05
490	Ruben Sierra	.08
491	Pete Incaviglia	.05
492	*Juan Gonzalez*	2.00
493	Steve Buechele	.05
494	Scott Coolbaugh	.05
495	Geno Petralli	.05
496	Rafael Palmeiro	.12
497	Julio Franco	.08
498	Gary Pettis	.05
499	Donald Harris	.05
500	Monty Fariss	.05
501	Harold Baines	.08
502	Cecil Espy	.05
503	Jack Daugherty	.05
504	Willie Blair	.05
505	Dave Steib	.05
506	Tom Henke	.05
507	John Cerutti	.05
508	Paul Kilgus	.05
509	Jimmy Key	.08
510	*John Olerud*	.40
511	Ed Sprague	.10
512	Manny Lee	.05
513	Fred McGriff	.15
514	Glenallen Hill	.08
515	George Bell	.05
516	Mookie Wilson	.05
517	Luis Sojo	.05
518	Nelson Liriano	.05
519	Kelly Gruber	.05
520	Greg Myers	.05
521	Pat Borders	.05
522	Junior Felix	.05
523	Eddie Zosky	.12
524	Tony Fernandez	.05
525	Checklist	.05
526	Checklist	.05
527	Checklist	.05
528	Checklist	.05

1990 Bowman Glossy

Reported production of fewer than 10,000 sets has created a significant premium for these glossy "Tiffany" versions of Bowman's 1990 baseball card set. The use of white cardboard stock and high-gloss front finish distinguishes theese cards from regular-issue Bowmans.

	MT
Complete Set (539):	75.00
Common Player:	.25

(Single cards valued at 4-5X regular-issue 1990 Bowman.)

Modern cards have little collector value in conditions lower than Mint. Figure NM cards at 75% of values shown; EX cards at 40%.

Values shown reflect the market as of January, 1999. On-field performances of current players in the 1999 baseball season are not factored in.

1990 Bowman Inserts

Bowman inserted sweepstakes cards in its 1990 packs, much like in 1989. This 11-card set features current players displayed in drawings by Craig Pursley.

			MT
Complete Set (11):			1.25
Common Player:			.05
(1)	Will Clark		.15
(2)	Mark Davis		.05
(3)	Dwight Gooden		.10
(4)	Bo Jackson		.10
(5)	Don Mattingly		.25
(6)	Kevin Mitchell		.05
(7)	Gregg Olson		.05
(8)	Nolan Ryan		.50
(9)	Bret Saberhagen		.05
(10)	Jerome Walton		.05
(11)	Robin Yount		.10

1991 Bowman

The 1991 Bowman set features 704 cards compared to 528 cards in the 1990 issue. The cards imitate the 1953 Bowman style. Special Rod Carew cards and gold foil-stamped cards are included. The set is numbered by teams. Like the 1989 and 1990 issues, the card backs feature a breakdown of performance against each other team in the league.

	MT
Complete Set (704):	17.50
Common Player:	.05
Wax Box:	25.00

#	Player	Price
1	Rod Carew-I	.08
2	Rod Carew-II	.08
3	Rod Carew-III	.08
4	Rod Carew-IV	.08
5	Rod Carew-V	.08
6	Willie Fraser	.05
7	John Olerud	.12
8	William Suero	.05
9	Roberto Alomar	.25
10	Todd Stottlemyre	.08
11	Joe Carter	.15
12	*Steve Karsay*	.15
13	Mark Whiten	.05
14	Pat Borders	.05
15	Mike Timlin	.05
16	Tom Henke	.05
17	Eddie Zosky	.05
18	Kelly Gruber	.05
19	Jimmy Key	.08
20	Jerry Schunk	.05
21	Manny Lee	.05
22	Dave Steib	.05
23	Pat Hentgen	.08
24	Glenallen Hill	.05
25	Rene Gonzales	.05
26	Ed Sprague	.10
27	Ken Dayley	.05
28	Pat Tabler	.05
29	*Denis Boucher*	.08
30	Devon White	.08
31	Dante Bichette	.15
32	Paul Molitor	.25
33	Greg Vaughn	.08
34	Dan Plesac	.05
35	Chris George	.05
36	Tim McIntosh	.05
37	Franklin Stubbs	.05
38	Bo Dodson	.05
39	Ron Robinson	.05
40	Ed Nunez	.05
41	Greg Brock	.05
42	Jaime Navarro	.05
43	Chris Bosio	.05
44	B.J. Surhoff	.05
45	Chris Johnson	.05
46	Willie Randolph	.05
47	Narciso Elvira	.05
48	Jim Gantner	.05
49	Kevin Brown	.05
50	Julio Machado	.05
51	Chuck Crim	.05
52	Gary Sheffield	.20
53	Angel Miranda	.08
54	Teddy Higuera	.05
55	Robin Yount	.25
56	Cal Eldred	.05
57	Sandy Alomar	.12
58	Greg Swindell	.05
59	Brook Jacoby	.05
60	Efrain Valdez	.05
61	Ever Magallanes	.05
62	Tom Candiotti	.05
63	Eric King	.05
64	Alex Cole	.05
65	Charles Nagy	.08
66	Mitch Webster	.05
67	Chris James	.05
68	*Jim Thome*	1.50
69	Carlos Baerga	.15
70	Mark Lewis	.08
71	Jerry Browne	.05
72	Jesse Orosco	.05
73	Mike Huff	.05
74	Jose Escobar	.05
75	Jeff Manto	.05
76	*Turner Ward*	.10
77	Doug Jones	.05
78	*Bruce Egloff*	.05
79	Tim Costo	.05
80	Beau Allred	.05
81	Albert Belle	.40
82	John Farrell	.05
83	Glenn Davis	.05
84	Joe Orsulak	.05
85	Mark Williamson	.05
86	Ben McDonald	.07
87	Billy Ripken	.05
88	Leo Gomez	.05
89	Bob Melvin	.05
90	Jeff Robinson	.05
91	Jose Mesa	.08
92	Gregg Olson	.05
93	Mike Devereaux	.05
94	Luis Mercedes	.05
95	*Arthur Rhodes*	.20
96	Juan Bell	.05
97	*Mike Mussina*	1.25
98	Jeff Ballard	.05
99	Chris Hoiles	.05
100	Brady Anderson	.15
101	Bob Milacki	.05
102	David Segui	.05
103	Dwight Evans	.05
104	Cal Ripken, Jr.	1.25
105	Mike Linskey	.05
106	*Jeff Tackett*	.05
107	Jeff Reardon	.05
108	Dana Kiecker	.05
109	Ellis Burks	.10
110	Dave Owen	.05
111	Danny Darwin	.05
112	Mo Vaughn	.40
113	Jeff McNeely	.05
114	Tom Bolton	.05
115	Greg Blosser	.07
116	Mike Greenwell	.05
117	*Phil Plantier*	.15
118	Roger Clemens	.35
119	John Marzano	.05
120	Jody Reed	.05
121	Scott Taylor	.05
122	Jack Clark	.05
123	Derek Livernois	.05
124	Tony Pena	.05
125	Tom Brunansky	.05
126	Carlos Quintana	.05
127	Tim Naehring	.05
128	Matt Young	.05
129	Wade Boggs	.30
130	Kevin Morton	.05
131	Pete Incaviglia	.05
132	Rob Deer	.05
133	Bill Gullickson	.05
134	Rico Brogna	.05
135	Lloyd Moseby	.05
136	Cecil Fielder	.15
137	Tony Phillips	.05
138	Mark Leiter	.05
139	John Cerutti	.05
140	Mickey Tettleton	.05
141	Milt Cuyler	.05
142	Greg Gohr	.05
143	Tony Bernazard	.05
144	Dan Gakeler	.05
145	Travis Fryman	.10
146	Dan Petry	.05
147	Scott Aldred	.05
148	John DeSilva	.05
149	Rusty Meacham	.05
150	Lou Whitaker	.08
151	Dave Haas	.05
152	Luis de los Santos	.05
153	Ivan Cruz	.05
154	Alan Trammell	.12
155	Pat Kelly	.05
156	Carl Everett	.07
157	Greg Cadaret	.05
158	Kevin Maas	.05
159	Jeff Johnson	.05
160	Willie Smith	.05
161	Gerald Williams	.05
162	Mike Humphreys	.05
163	Alvaro Espinoza	.05
164	Matt Nokes	.05
165	Wade Taylor	.10
166	Roberto Kelly	.05
167	John Habyan	.05
168	Steve Farr	.05
169	Jesse Barfield	.05
170	Steve Sax	.05
171	Jim Leyritz	.07
172	Robert Eenhoorn	.05
173	Bernie Williams	.25
174	Scott Lusader	.05
175	Torey Lovullo	.05
176	Chuck Cary	.05
177	Scott Sanderson	.05
178	Don Mattingly	.50
179	Mel Hall	.05
180	Juan Gonzalez	.60
181	Hensley Meulens	.05
182	Jose Offerman	.05
183	*Jeff Bagwell*	2.50
184	*Jeff Conine*	.35
185	*Henry Rodriguez*	.35
186	Jimmie Reese	.10
187	Kyle Abbott	.07
188	Lance Parrish	.07
189	Rafael Montalvo	.05
190	Floyd Bannister	.05
191	Dick Schofield	.05
192	Scott Lewis	.05
193	Jeff Robinson	.05
194	Kent Anderson	.05
195	Wally Joyner	.08
196	Chuck Finley	.05
197	Luis Sojo	.05
198	Jeff Richardson	.05
199	Dave Parker	.10
200	Jim Abbott	.12
201	Junior Felix	.05
202	Mark Langston	.08
203	*Tim Salmon*	1.50
204	Cliff Young	.05
205	Scott Bailes	.05
206	Bobby Rose	.05
207	Gary Gaetti	.07
208	Ruben Amaro	.05
209	Luis Polonia	.05
210	Dave Winfield	.25
211	Bryan Harvey	.05
212	Mike Moore	.05
213	Rickey Henderson	.15
214	Steve Chitren	.05
215	Bob Welch	.05
216	Terry Steinbach	.05
217	Ernie Riles	.05
218	*Todd Van Poppel*	.10
219	Mike Gallego	.05
220	Curt Young	.05
221	Todd Burns	.05
222	Vance Law	.05
223	Eric Show	.05
224	*Don Peters*	.05
225	Dave Stewart	.08
226	Dave Henderson	.05
227	Jose Canseco	.30
228	Walt Weiss	.05
229	Dann Howitt	.05
230	Willie Wilson	.05
231	Harold Baines	.07
232	Scott Hemond	.05
233	Joe Slusarski	.05
234	Mark McGwire	1.50
235	*Kirk Dressendorfer*	.12
236	*Craig Paquette*	.08
237	Dennis Eckersley	.10
238	Dana Allison	.05
239	Scott Bradley	.05
240	Brian Holman	.05
241	Mike Schooler	.05
242	Rich Delucia	.05
243	Edgar Martinez	.07
244	Henry Cotto	.05
245	Omar Vizquel	.05
246a	Ken Griffey, Jr.	2.00
246b	Ken Griffey Sr. (should be #255)	.10
247	Jay Buhner	.08
248	Bill Krueger	.05
249	*Dave Fleming*	.15
250	*Patrick Lennon*	.10
251	Dave Valle	.05
252	Harold Reynolds	.07
253	Randy Johnson	.20
254	Scott Bankhead	.05
255	See #246b (Not issued, see #246b)	
256	Greg Briley	.05
257	Tino Martinez	.20
258	Alvin Davis	.05
259	Pete O'Brien	.05
260	Erik Hanson	.05
261	*Bret Boone*	.50
262	Roger Salkeld	.10
263	Dave Burba	.08
264	*Kerry Woodson*	.12
265	Julio Franco	.08
266	Dan Peltier	.05
267	Jeff Russell	.05
268	Steve Buechele	.05
269	Donald Harris	.08
270	Robb Nen	.08
271	Rich Gossage	.07
272	*Ivan Rodriguez*	1.50
273	Jeff Huson	.05
274	Kevin Brown	.10
275	*Dan Smith*	.10
276	Gary Pettis	.05
277	Jack Daugherty	.05
278	Mike Jeffcoat	.05
279	Brad Arnsberg	.05
280	Nolan Ryan	.75
281	Eric McCray	.05

#	Name	Value	#	Name	Value	#	Name	Value
282	Scott Chiamparino	.05	378	Matt Williams	.12	472	Dwight Gooden	.10
283	Ruben Sierra	.10	379	Barry Larkin	.08	473	Charlie O'Brien	.05
284	Geno Petralli	.05	380	Barry Bonds	.40	474	Jeromy Burnitz	.20
285	Monty Fariss	.05	381	Bobby Bonilla	.12	475	John Franco	.05
286	Rafael Palmeiro	.15	382	Darryl Strawberry	.08	476	Daryl Boston	.05
287	Bobby Witt	.05	383	Benny Santiago	.07	477	Frank Viola	.05
288	Dean Palmer	.10	384	Don Robinson	.05	478	D.J. Dozier	.08
289	Tony Scruggs	.05	385	Paul Coleman	.05	479	Kevin McReynolds	.05
290	Kenny Rogers	.05	386	Milt Thompson	.05	480	Tom Herr	.05
291	Bret Saberhagen	.08	387	Lee Smith	.07	481	Gregg Jefferies	.08
292	*Brian McRae*	.20	388	Ray Lankford	.15	482	Pete Schourek	.08
293	Storm Davis	.05	389	Tom Pagnozzi	.05	483	Ron Darling	.05
294	Danny Tartabull	.05	390	Ken Hill	.05	484	Dave Magadan	.05
295	David Howard	.05	391	Jamie Moyer	.05	485	*Andy Ashby*	.10
296	Mike Boddicker	.05	392	*Greg Carmona*	.05	486	Dale Murphy	.12
297	Joel Johnston	.05	393	John Ericks	.05	487	Von Hayes	.05
298	Tim Spehr	.10	394	Bob Tewksbury	.05	488	*Kim Batiste*	.07
299	Hector Wagner	.05	395	Jose Oquendo	.05	489	*Tony Longmire*	.10
300	George Brett	.40	396	Rheal Cormier	.05	490	Wally Backman	.05
301	Mike Macfarlane	.05	397	*Mike Milchin*	.05	491	Jeff Jackson	.05
302	Kirk Gibson	.05	398	Ozzie Smith	.40	492	Mickey Morandini	.05
303	Harvey Pulliam	.05	399	*Aaron Holbert*	.10	493	Darrel Akerfelds	.05
304	Jim Eisenreich	.05	400	Jose DeLeon	.05	494	Ricky Jordan	.05
305	Kevin Seitzer	.05	401	Felix Jose	.05	495	Randy Ready	.05
306	Mark Davis	.05	402	Juan Agosto	.05	496	Darrin Fletcher	.05
307	Kurt Stillwell	.05	403	Pedro Guerrero	.05	497	Chuck Malone	.05
308	Jeff Montgomery	.05	404	Todd Zeile	.08	498	Pat Combs	.05
309	Kevin Appier	.07	405	Gerald Perry	.05	499	Dickie Thon	.05
310	Bob Hamelin	.08	406	Not issued		500	Roger McDowell	.05
311	Tom Gordon	.05	407	Bryn Smith	.05	501	Len Dykstra	.08
312	*Kerwin Moore*	.05	408	Bernard Gilkey	.15	502	Joe Boever	.05
313	Hugh Walker	.05	409	Rex Hudler	.05	503	John Kruk	.05
314	Terry Shumpert	.05	410a	Ralph Branca, Bobby	.10	504	Terry Mulholland	.07
315	Warren Cromartie	.05		Thomson		505	Wes Chamberlain	.05
316	Gary Thurman	.05	410b	Donovan Osborne	.08	506	*Mike Lieberthal*	.10
317	Steve Bedrosian	.05	411	Lance Dickson	.05	507	Darren Daulton	.07
318	Danny Gladden	.05	412	Danny Jackson	.05	508	Charlie Hayes	.05
319	Jack Morris	.08	413	Jerome Walton	.05	509	John Smiley	.05
320	Kirby Puckett	.45	414	Sean Cheetham	.05	510	Gary Varsho	.05
321	Kent Hrbek	.08	415	Joe Girardi	.05	511	Curt Wilkerson	.05
322	Kevin Tapani	.08	416	Ryne Sandberg	.25	512	*Orlando Merced*	.20
323	Denny Neagle	.12	417	Mike Harkey	.05	513	Barry Bonds	.40
324	Rich Garces	.05	418	George Bell	.05	514	Mike Lavalliere	.05
325	Larry Casian	.05	419	*Rick Wilkins*	.25	515	Doug Drabek	.05
326	Shane Mack	.05	420	Earl Cunningham	.05	516	Gary Redus	.05
327	Allan Anderson	.05	421	Heathcliff Slocumb	.05	517	*William Pennyfeather*	.05
328	Junior Ortiz	.05	422	Mike Bielecki	.05	518	Randy Tomlin	.05
329	*Paul Abbott*	.10	423	*Jessie Hollins*	.08	519	*Mike Zimmerman*	.05
330	Chuck Knoblauch	.20	424	Shawon Dunston	.12	520	Jeff King	.05
331	Chili Davis	.08	425	Dave Smith	.05	521	*Kurt Miller*	.10
332	*Todd Ritchie*	.05	426	Greg Maddux	.60	522	Jay Bell	.05
333	Brian Harper	.05	427	Jose Vizcaino	.05	523	Bill Landrum	.05
334	Rick Aguilera	.05	428	Luis Salazar	.05	524	Zane Smith	.05
335	Scott Erickson	.08	429	Andre Dawson	.10	525	Bobby Bonilla	.10
336	Pedro Munoz	.05	430	Rick Sutcliffe	.05	526	Bob Walk	.05
337	Scott Leuis	.05	431	Paul Assenmacher	.05	527	Austin Manahan	.05
338	Greg Gagne	.05	432	Erik Pappas	.05	528	*Joe Ausanio*	.05
339	Mike Pagliarulo	.05	433	Mark Grace	.20	529	Andy Van Slyke	.05
340	Terry Leach	.05	434	Denny Martinez	.07	530	Jose Lind	.05
341	Willie Banks	.05	435	Marquis Grissom	.12	531	*Carlos Garcia*	.25
342	Bobby Thigpen	.05	436	*Wil Cordero*	.40	532	Don Slaught	.05
343	*Roberto Hernandez*	.20	437	Tim Wallach	.05	533	Colin Powell	.25
344	Melido Perez	.05	438	*Brian Barnes*	.05	534	Frank Bolick	.05
345	Carlton Fisk	.15	439	Barry Jones	.05	535	*Gary Scott*	.05
346	Norberto Martin	.12	440	Ivan Calderon	.05	536	Nikco Riesgo	.05
347	*Johnny Ruffin*	.05	441	*Stan Spencer*	.05	537	*Reggie Sanders*	.50
348	*Jeff Carter*	.08	442	Larry Walker	.25	538	*Tim Howard*	.05
349	Lance Johnson	.05	443	*Chris Haney*	.08	539	*Ryan Bowen*	.10
350	Sammy Sosa	.75	444	Hector Rivera	.05	540	Eric Anthony	.05
351	Alex Fernandez	.15	445	Delino DeShields	.08	541	Jim Deshaies	.05
352	Jack McDowell	.08	446	Andres Galarraga	.10	542	Tom Nevers	.05
353	Bob Wickman	.05	447	Gilberto Reyes	.05	543	Ken Caminiti	.10
354	Wilson Alvarez	.10	448	Willie Greene	.07	544	Karl Rhodes	.05
355	Charlie Hough	.05	449	Greg Colbrunn	.07	545	Xavier Hernandez	.08
356	Ozzie Guillen	.05	450	*Rondell White*	.60	546	Mike Scott	.05
357	Cory Snyder	.05	451	Steve Frey	.05	547	Jeff Juden	.08
358	Robin Ventura	.15	452	*Shane Andrews*	.12	548	Darryl Kile	.07
359	Scott Fletcher	.05	453	Mike Fitzgerald	.05	549	Willie Ansley	.05
360	Cesar Bernhardt	.05	454	Spike Owen	.05	550	*Luis Gonzalez*	.35
361	Dan Pasqua	.05	455	Dave Martinez	.05	551	*Mike Simms*	.08
362	Tim Raines	.08	456	Dennis Boyd	.05	552	Mark Portugal	.05
363	Brian Drahman	.05	457	Eric Bullock	.05	553	Jimmy Jones	.05
364	Wayne Edwards	.05	458	*Reid Cornelius*	.10	554	Jim Clancy	.05
365	Scott Radinsky	.05	459	Chris Nabholz	.05	555	Pete Harnisch	.05
366	Frank Thomas	2.00	460	David Cone	.08	556	Craig Biggio	.10
367	Cecil Fielder	.10	461	Hubie Brooks	.05	557	Eric Yelding	.05
368	Julio Franco	.08	462	Sid Fernandez	.05	558	Dave Rohde	.05
369	Kelly Gruber	.05	463	*Doug Simons*	.08	559	Casey Candaele	.05
370	Alan Trammell	.12	464	Howard Johnson	.05	560	Curt Schilling	.08
371	Rickey Henderson	.20	465	Chris Donnels	.08	561	Steve Finley	.05
372	Jose Canseco	.20	466	Anthony Young	.10	562	Javier Ortiz	.05
373	Ellis Burks	.10	467	Todd Hundley	.10	563	Andujar Cedeno	.05
374	Lance Parrish	.07	468	Rick Cerone	.05	564	Rafael Ramirez	.05
375	Dave Parker	.08	469	Kevin Elster	.05	565	*Kenny Lofton*	2.00
376	Eddie Murray	.25	470	Wally Whitehurst	.05	566	Steve Avery	.08
377	Ryne Sandberg	.25	471	Vince Coleman	.05	567	Lonnie Smith	.05

568	Kent Mercker	.05
569	*Chipper Jones*	4.00
570	Terry Pendleton	.05
571	Otis Nixon	.05
572	Juan Berenguer	.05
573	Charlie Leibrandt	.05
574	Dave Justice	.20
575	Keith Mitchell	.05
576	Tom Glavine	.15
577	Greg Olson	.05
578	Rafael Belliard	.05
579	Ben Rivera	.05
580	John Smoltz	.10
581	Tyler Houston	.05
582	*Mark Wohlers*	.15
583	Ron Gant	.10
584	Ramon Caraballo	.05
585	Sid Bream	.05
586	Jeff Treadway	.05
587	*Javier Lopez*	1.00
588	Deion Sanders	.25
589	Mike Heath	.05
590	*Ryan Klesko*	2.00
591	Bob Ojeda	.05
592	Alfredo Griffin	.05
593	*Raul Mondesi*	.90
594	Greg Smith	.05
595	Orel Hershiser	.08
596	Juan Samuel	.05
597	Brett Butler	.10
598	Gary Carter	.10
599	Stan Javier	.05
600	Kal Daniels	.05
601	*Jamie McAndrew*	.10
602	Mike Sharperson	.05
603	Jay Howell	.05
604	*Eric Karros*	.40
605	Tim Belcher	.05
606	Dan Opperman	.05
607	Lenny Harris	.05
608	Tom Goodwin	.08
609	Darryl Strawberry	.10
610	Ramon Martinez	.08
611	Kevin Gross	.05
612	Zakary Shinall	.05
613	Mike Scioscia	.05
614	Eddie Murray	.30
615	Ronnie Walden	.05
616	Will Clark	.25
617	Adam Hyzdu	.05
618	Matt Williams	.15
619	Don Robinson	.05
620	Jeff Brantley	.05
621	Greg Litton	.05
622	Steve Decker	.05
623	Robby Thompson	.05
624	*Mark Leonard*	.09
625	Kevin Bass	.05
626	Scott Garrelts	.05
627	Jose Uribe	.05
628	Eric Gunderson	.05
629	Steve Hosey	.05
630	Trevor Wilson	.05
631	Terry Kennedy	.05
632	Dave Righetti	.05
633	Kelly Downs	.05
634	Johnny Ard	.05
635	*Eric Christopherson*	.10
636	Kevin Mitchell	.08
637	John Burkett	.05
638	*Kevin Rogers*	.10
639	Bud Black	.05
640	Willie McGee	.07
641	Royce Clayton	.07
642	Tony Fernandez	.05
643	Ricky Bones	.07
644	Thomas Howard	.05
645	Dave Staton	.15
646	Jim Presley	.05
647	Tony Gwynn	.40
648	Marty Barrett	.05
649	Scott Coolbaugh	.05
650	Craig Lefferts	.05
651	Eddie Whitson	.05
652	Oscar Azocar	.05
653	Wes Gardner	.05
654	Bip Roberts	.05
655	*Robbie Beckett*	.08
656	Benny Santiago	.06
657	Greg W. Harris	.05
658	Jerald Clark	.05
659	Fred McGriff	.20
660	Larry Andersen	.05
661	Bruce Hurst	.05
662	Steve Martin	.05
663	Rafael Valdez	.05

664	*Paul Faries*	.05
665	Andy Benes	.08
666	Randy Myers	.06
667	Rob Dibble	.05
668	Glenn Sutko	.05
669	Glenn Braggs	.05
670	Billy Hatcher	.05
671	Joe Oliver	.05
672	Freddie Benavides	.05
673	Barry Larkin	.10
674	Chris Sabo	.05
675	Mariano Duncan	.05
676	*Chris Jones*	.10
677	*Gino Minutelli*	.05
678	Reggie Jefferson	.10
679	Jack Armstrong	.05
680	Chris Hammond	.05
681	Jose Rijo	.05
682	Bill Doran	.05
683	Terry Lee	.05
684	Tom Browning	.05
685	Paul O'Neill	.10
686	Eric Davis	.12
687	*Dan Wilson*	.15
688	Ted Power	.05
689	Tim Layana	.05
690	Norm Charlton	.05
691	Hal Morris	.05
692	Rickey Henderson	.15
693	*Sam Militello*	.08
694	*Matt Mieske*	.10
695	*Paul Russo*	.05
696	*Domingo Mota*	.05
697	*Todd Guggiana*	.05
698	Marc Newfield	.08
699	Checklist	.05
700	Checklist	.05
701	Checklist	.05
702	Checklist	.05
703	Checklist	.05
704	Checklist	.05

1992 Bowman

FRED McGRIFF

Topps introduced several changes with the release of its 1992 Bowman set. The 705-card set features 45 special insert cards stamped with gold foil. The cards are printed with a premium UV coated glossy card stock. Several players without major league experience are featured in the set. Included in this group are 1991 MVP's of the minor leagues and first round draft choices. Eighteen of the gold-foil enchanced cards have been identified as short-prints (designated SP in the listings), printed in quantities one-half the other foils.

		MT
Complete Set (705):		325.00
Common Player:		.20
Wax Box:		240.00
1	Ivan Rodriguez	3.00
2	Kirk McCaskill	.20

3	Scott Livingstone	.25
4	*Salomon Torres*	.20
5	Carlos Hernandez	.20
6	Dave Hollins	.40
7	Scott Fletcher	.20
8	Jorge Fabregas	.25
9	Andujar Cedeno	.25
10	Howard Johnson	.20
11	*Trevor Hoffman*	1.50
12	Roberto Kelly	.20
13	Gregg Jefferies	.35
14	Marquis Grissom	.40
15	Mike Ignasiak	.20
16	Jack Morris	.25
17	William Pennyfeather	.20
18	Todd Stottlemyre	.25
19	Chito Martinez	.20
20	Roberto Alomar	2.50
21	Sam Militello	.25
22	Hector Fajardo	.20
23	*Paul Quantrill*	.40
24	Chuck Knoblauch	.40
25	Reggie Jefferson	.35
26	Jeremy McGarity	.25
27	Jerome Walton	.20
28	Chipper Jones	45.00
29	*Brian Barber*	.50
30	Ron Darling	.20
31	*Roberto Petagine*	.20
32	Chuck Finley	.20
33	Edgar Martinez	.50
34	Napolean Robinson	.25
35	Andy Van Slyke	.20
36	Bobby Thigpen	.20
37	Travis Fryman	.40
38	Eric Christopherson	.20
39	Terry Mulholland	.20
40	Darryl Strawberry	.35
41	*Manny Alexander*	.60
42	*Tracey Sanders*	.50
43	Pete Incaviglia	.20
44	Kim Batiste	.20
45	Frank Rodriguez	.40
46	Greg Swindell	.20
47	Delino DeShields	.20
48	John Ericks	.20
49	Franklin Stubbs	.20
50	Tony Gwynn	2.50
51	*Clifton Garrett*	.40
52	Mike Gardella	.20
53	Scott Erickson	.25
54	Gary Caballo	.25
55	*Jose Oliva*	.30
56	Brook Fordyce	.25
57	Mark Whiten	.25
58	Joe Slusarski	.20
59	*J.R. Phillips*	.50
60	Barry Bonds	3.00
61	Bob Milacki	.20
62	Keith Mitchell	.25
63	Angel Miranda	.20
64	Raul Mondesi	10.00
65	Brian Koelling	.25
66	Brian McRae	.30
67	John Patterson	.20
68	John Wetteland	.20
69	Wilson Alvarez	.25
70	Wade Boggs	.60
71	Darryl Ratliff	.20
72	Jeff Jackson	.20
73	Jeremy Hernandez	.30
74	Darryl Hamilton	.20
75	Rafael Belliard	.20
76	Ricky Trilcek	.20
77	*Felipe Crespo*	.45
78	Carney Lansford	.20
79	Ryan Long	.25
80	Kirby Puckett	3.00
81	Earl Cunningham	.20
82	Pedro Martinez	15.00
83	Scott Hatteberg	.50
84	Juan Gonzalez	5.00
85	Robert Nutting	.30
86	*Calvin Reese*	2.00
87	Dave Silvestri	.30
88	*Scott Ruffcorn*	1.00
89	Rick Aguilera	.20
90	Cecil Fielder	.40
91	Kirk Dressendorfer	.20
92	Jerry DiPoto	.20
93	Mike Felder	.20
94	Craig Paquette	.30
95	Elvin Paulino	.25
96	Donovan Osborne	.25
97	Hubie Brooks	.20
98	*Derek Lowe*	.25

No.	Name	Value	No.	Name	Value	No.	Name	Value
99	David Zancanaro	.30	195	Chili Davis	.25	291	Orlando Merced	.20
100	Ken Griffey, Jr.	12.00	196	Milt Cuyler	.20	292	Peter Hoy	.20
101	Todd Hundley	1.50	197	Von Hayes	.20	293	Tony Fernandez	.20
102	Mike Trombley	.50	198	Todd Revening	.30	294	Juan Guzman	.20
103	*Ricky Gutierrez*	.50	199	Joel Johnson	.20	295	Jesse Barfield	.20
104	Braulio Castillo	.20	200	Jeff Bagwell	6.00	296	Sid Fernandez	.20
105	Craig Lefferts	.20	201	Alex Fernandez	.50	297	Scott Cepicky	.30
106	Rick Sutcliffe	.20	202	Todd Jones	.30	298	*Garret Anderson*	4.00
107	Dean Palmer	.40	203	Charles Nagy	.30	299	Cal Eldred	.20
108	Henry Rodriguez	.75	204	Tim Raines	.30	300	Ryne Sandberg	1.25
109	*Mark Clark*	2.00	205	Kevin Maas	.20	301	Jim Gantner	.20
110	Kenny Lofton	9.00	206	Julio Franco	.25	302	*Mariano Rivera*	8.00
111	Mark Carreon	.20	207	Randy Velarde	.20	303	Ron Lockett	.35
112	*J.T. Bruett*	.20	208	Lance Johnson	.20	304	Jose Offerman	.20
113	Gerald Williams	.25	209	Scott Leius	.20	305	Denny Martinez	.25
114	Frank Thomas	7.00	210	Derek Lee	.30	306	*Luis Ortiz*	.40
115	Kevin Reimer	.20	211	Joe Sondrini	.20	307	David Howard	.20
116	Sammy Sosa	5.00	212	Royce Clayton	.25	308	Russ Springer	.40
117	Mickey Tettleton	.20	213	Chris George	.20	309	Chris Howard	.30
118	Reggie Sanders	.40	214	Gary Sheffield	1.00	310	Kyle Abbott	.25
119	Trevor Wilson	.20	215	Mark Gubicza	.20	311	*Aaron Sele*	4.00
120	Cliff Brantley	.20	216	Mike Moore	.20	312	Dave Justice	.60
121	Spike Owen	.20	217	Rick Huisman	.20	313	Pete O'Brien	.20
122	Jeff Montgomery	.20	218	Jeff Russell	.20	314	Greg Hansell	.30
123	Alex Sutherland	.20	219	D.J. Dozier	.20	315	Dave Winfield	.60
124	*Brien Taylor*	.35	220	Dave Martinez	.20	316	Lance Dickson	.20
125	Brian Williams	.30	221	Al Newman	.20	317	Eric King	.20
126	Kevin Seitzer	.20	222	Nolan Ryan	9.00	318	Vaughn Eshelman	.25
127	*Carlos Delgado*	8.00	223	Teddy Higuera	.20	319	Tim Belcher	.20
128	Gary Scott	.20	224	*Damon Buford*	.45	320	Andres Galarraga	.45
129	Scott Cooper	.20	225	Ruben Sierra	.30	321	Scott Bullett	.25
130	*Domingo Jean*	.20	226	Tom Nevers	.30	322	Doug Strange	.20
131	*Pat Mahomes*	.50	227	Tommy Greene	.30	323	Jerald Clark	.20
132	Mike Boddicker	.20	228	*Nigel Wilson*	.40	324	Dave Righetti	.20
133	Roberto Hernandez	.35	229	John DeSilva	.20	325	Greg Hibbard	.20
134	Dave Valle	.20	230	Bobby Witt	.20	326	Eric Dillman	.20
135	Kurt Stillwell	.20	231	Greg Cadaret	.20	327	*Shane Reynolds*	2.50
136	*Brad Pennington*	.50	232	John VanderWal	.20	328	Chris Hammond	.20
137	Jermaine Swifton	.30	233	Jack Clark	.20	329	Albert Belle	3.00
138	Ryan Hawblitzel	.40	234	Bill Doran	.20	330	*Rich Becker*	.50
139	Tito Navarro	.20	235	Bobby Bonilla	.35	331	Eddie Williams	.20
140	Sandy Alomar	.35	236	Steve Olin	.20	332	Donald Harris	.20
141	Todd Benzinger	.20	237	Derek Bell	.35	333	Dave Smith	.20
142	Danny Jackson	.20	238	David Cone	.30	334	Steve Fireovid	.20
143	*Melvin Nieves*	1.50	239	Victor Cole	.20	335	Steve Buechele	.20
144	Jim Campanis	.30	240	Rod Bolton	.20	336	Mike Schooler	.20
145	Luis Gonzalez	.20	241	Tom Pagnozzi	.20	337	Kevin McReynolds	.20
146	Dave Doorneweerd	.20	242	Rob Dibble	.20	338	Hensley Meulens	.20
147	Charlie Hayes	.20	243	Michael Carter	.20	339	*Benji Gil*	.90
148	Greg Maddux	7.00	244	Don Peters	.20	340	Don Mattingly	2.50
149	Brian Harper	.20	245	Mike LaValliere	.20	341	Alvin Davis	.20
150	Brent Miller	.20	246	Joe Perona	.20	342	Alan Mills	.20
151	*Shawn Estes*	2.50	247	Mitch Williams	.20	343	Kelly Downs	.20
152	Mike Williams	.20	248	Jay Buhner	.50	344	Leo Gomez	.20
153	Charlie Hough	.20	249	Andy Benes	.30	345	*Tarrik Brock*	.30
154	Randy Myers	.20	250	*Alex Ochoa*	3.00	346	Ryan Turner	.65
155	*Kevin Young*	.40	251	Greg Blosser	.30	347	John Smoltz	.50
156	Rick Wilkins	.20	252	Jack Armstrong	.20	348	Bill Sampen	.20
157	Terry Schumpert	.20	253	Juan Samuel	.20	349	Paul Byrd	.25
158	Steve Karsay	.40	254	Terry Pendleton	.20	350	Mike Bordick	.20
159	Gary DiSarcina	.20	255	Ramon Martinez	.25	351	Jose Lind	.20
160	Deion Sanders	2.00	256	Rico Brogna	.25	352	David Wells	.20
161	Tom Browning	.20	257	John Smiley	.20	353	Barry Larkin	.40
162	Dickie Thon	.20	258	Carl Everett	.20	354	Bruce Ruffin	.20
163	Luis Mercedes	.20	259	Tim Salmon	7.00	355	Luis Rivera	.20
164	Ricardo Ingram	.40	260	Will Clark	.75	356	Sid Bream	.20
165	*Tavo Alavarez*	.60	261	*Ugueth Urbina*	1.00	357	Julian Vasquez	.20
166	Rickey Henderson	.40	262	Jason Wood	.20	358	*Jason Bere*	.75
167	Jaime Navarro	.20	263	Dave Magadan	.20	359	Ben McDonald	.25
168	*Billy Ashley*	1.00	264	Dante Bichette	.90	360	Scott Stahoviak	.20
169	Phil Dauphin	.20	265	Jose DeLeon	.20	361	Kirt Manwaring	.20
170	Ivan Cruz	.20	266	*Mike Neill*	.30	362	Jeff Johnson	.25
171	Harold Baines	.25	267	Paul O'Neill	.35	363	Rob Deer	.20
172	Bryan Harvey	.20	268	Anthony Young	.20	364	Tony Pena	.20
173	Alex Cole	.20	269	Greg Harris	.20	365	Melido Perez	.20
174	Curtis Shaw	.30	270	Todd Van Poppel	.25	366	Clay Parker	.20
175	Matt Williams	1.50	271	Pete Castellano	.30	367	Dale Sveum	.20
176	Felix Jose	.20	272	Tony Phillips	.25	368	Mike Scioscia	.20
177	Sam Horn	.20	273	Mike Gallego	.20	369	Roger Salkeld	.25
178	Randy Johnson	1.50	274	*Steve Cooke*	.50	370	Mike Stanley	.20
179	Ivan Calderon	.20	275	Robin Ventura	.35	371	Jack McDowell	.25
180	Steve Avery	.25	276	Kevin Mitchell	.25	372	Tim Wallach	.20
181	William Suero	.20	277	Doug Linton	.20	373	Billy Ripken	.20
182	Bill Swift	.20	278	Robert Eenhorn	.20	374	Mike Christopher	.20
183	*Howard Battle*	.80	279	*Gabe White*	.50	375	Paul Molitor	.90
184	Ruben Amaro	.20	280	Dave Stewart	.30	376	Dave Stieb	.20
185	Jim Abbott	.40	281	Mo Sanford	.20	377	Pedro Guerrero	.20
186	Mike Fitzgerald	.20	282	Greg Perschke	.20	378	Russ Swan	.20
187	Bruce Hurst	.20	283	Kevin Flora	.30	379	Bob Ojeda	.20
188	Jeff Juden	.75	284	Jeff Williams	.20	380	Donn Pall	.20
189	Jeromy Burnitz	1.50	285	Keith Miller	.20	381	Eddie Zosky	.30
190	Dave Burba	.20	286	Andy Ashby	.20	382	Darnell Coles	.20
191	Kevin Brown	.20	287	Doug Dascenzo	.20	383	Tom Smith	.25
192	Patrick Lennon	.20	288	Eric Karros	.60	384	Mark McGwire	8.00
193	Jeffrey McNeely	.20	289	*Glenn Murray*	.40	385	Gary Carter	.35
194	Wil Cordero	.25	290	*Troy Percival*	1.00	386	Rich Amaral	.20

387	Alan Embree	.30
388	Jonathan Hurst	.30
389	*Bobby Jones*	4.00
390	Rico Rossy	.35
391	Dan Smith	.35
392	Terry Steinbach	.20
393	Jon Farrell	.20
394	Dave Anderson	.20
395	Benito Santiago	.30
396	Mark Wohlers	.20
397	Mo Vaughn	3.50
398	Randy Kramer	.25
399	*John Jaha*	2.00
400	Cal Ripken, Jr.	7.50
401	Ryan Bowen	.50
402	Tim McIntosh	.20
403	Bernard Gilkey	.30
404	Junior Felix	.20
405	Cris Colon	.25
406	Marc Newfield	.50
407	Bernie Williams	3.00
408	Jay Howell	.20
409	Zane Smith	.20
410	Jeff Shaw	.20
411	Kerry Woodson	.20
412	Wes Chamberlain	.20
413	Dave Mlicki	.20
414	Benny Distefano	.20
415	Kevin Rogers	.25
416	Tim Naehring	.20
417	Clemente Nunez	.30
418	Luis Sojo	.20
419	Kevin Ritz	.20
420	Omar Oliveras	.20
421	Manuel Lee	.20
422	Julio Valera	.20
423	Omar Vizquel	.20
424	Darren Burton	.25
425	Mel Hall	.20
426	Dennis Powell	.20
427	Lee Stevens	.20
428	Glenn Davis	.20
429	Willie Greene	.30
430	Kevin Wickander	.20
431	Dennis Eckersley	.30
432	Joe Orsulak	.20
433	Eddie Murray	.75
434	Matt Stairs	.20
435	Wally Joyner	.30
436	Rondell White	6.00
437	Rob Mauer	.20
438	Joe Redfield	.20
439	Mark Lewis	.20
440	Darren Daulton	.25
441	Mike Henneman	.20
442	John Cangelosi	.20
443	*Vince Moore*	.40
444	John Wehner	.20
445	Kent Hrbek	.30
446	Mark McLemore	.20
447	Bill Wegman	.20
448	Robby Thompson	.20
449	Mark Anthony	.30
450	Archi Cianfrocco	.20
451	Johnny Ruffin	.20
452	Javier Lopez	8.00
453	Greg Gohr	.25
454	Tim Scott	.25
455	Stan Belinda	.20
456	Darrin Jackson	.20
457	Chris Gardner	.20
458	Esteban Beltre	.20
459	Phil Plantier	.20
460	Jim Thome	15.00
461	*Mike Piazza*	50.00
462	Matt Sinatro	.20
463	Scott Servais	.30
464	*Brian Jordan*	4.00
465	Doug Drabek	.30
466	Carl Willis	.20
467	Bret Barbarie	.20
468	Hal Morris	.25
469	Steve Sax	.20
470	Jerry Willard	.20
471	Dan Wilson	.25
472	Chris Hoiles	.20
473	Rheal Cormier	.20
474	John Morris	.20
475	Jeff Reardon	.20
476	Mark Leiter	.20
477	Tom Gordon	.20
478	Kent Bottenfield	.25
479	Gene Larkin	.20
480	Dwight Gooden	.45
481	B.J. Surhoff	.20
482	Andy Stankiewicz	.20

483	Tino Martinez	1.50
484	Craig Biggio	.50
485	Denny Neagle	.30
486	Rusty Meacham	.20
487	Kal Daniels	.20
488	Dave Henderson	.20
489	Tim Costo	.20
490	Doug Davis	.20
491	Frank Viola	.20
492	Cory Snyder	.20
493	Chris Martin	.20
494	Dion James	.20
495	Randy Tomlin	.20
496	Greg Vaughn	.25
497	Dennis Cook	.20
498	Rosario Rodriguez	.20
499	Dave Staton	.20
500	George Brett	3.00
501	Brian Barnes	.20
502	Butch Henry	.20
503	Harold Reynolds	.25
504	*David Nied*	.25
505	Lee Smith	.30
506	Steve Chitren	.20
507	Ken Hill	.25
508	Robbie Beckett	.20
509	Troy Afenir	.20
510	Kelly Gruber	.20
511	Bret Boone	.30
512	Jeff Branson	.25
513	Mike Jackson	.20
514	Pete Harnisch	.20
515	Chad Kreuter	.20
516	Joe Vitko	.20
517	Orel Hershiser	.25
518	*John Doherty*	.30
519	Jay Bell	.20
520	Mark Langston	.25
521	Dann Howitt	.20
522	Bobby Reed	.25
523	Roberto Munoz	.30
524	Todd Ritchie	.20
525	Bip Roberts	.20
526	*Pat Listach*	.40
527	Scott Brosius	3.00
528	*John Roper*	.35
529	*Phil Hiatt*	.40
530	Denny Walling	.20
531	Carlos Baerga	.40
532	*Manny Ramirez*	30.00
533	Pat Clements	.20
534	Ron Gant	.30
535	Pat Kelly	.20
536	Billy Spiers	.20
537	Darren Reed	.30
538	Ken Caminiti	.30
539	*Butch Huskey*	2.50
540	Matt Nokes	.20
541	John Kruk	.20
542	John Jaha (Foil, SP)	1.00
543	*Justin Thompson*	4.00
544	Steve Hosey	.35
545	Joe Kmak	.20
546	John Franco	.20
547	Devon White	.20
548	Elston Hansen (Foil, SP)	.35
549	Ryan Klesko	20.00
550	Danny Tartabull	.20
551	Frank Thomas (Foil, SP)	10.00
552	Kevin Tapani	.20
553a	Willie Banks	.20
553b	Pat Clements	.20
554	*B.J. Wallace* (Foil, SP)	.50
555	*Orlando Miller*	.35
556	*Mark Smith*	.50
557	Tim Wallach (Foil)	.30
558	Bill Gullickson	.20
559	Derek Bell (Foil)	1.50
560	Joe Randa (Foil)	.65
561	Frank Seminara	.20
562	Mark Gardner	.20
563	Rick Greene (Foil)	.60
564	Gary Gaetti	.25
565	Ozzie Guillen	.20
566	Charles Nagy (Foil)	.40
567	Mike Milchin	.20
568	Ben Shelton (Foil)	.40
569	Chris Roberts (Foil)	.50
570	Ellis Burks	.25
571	Scott Scudder	.20
572	Jim Abbott (Foil)	.45
573	Joe Carter	.30
574	Steve Finley	.20
575	Jim Olander (Foil)	.35
576	Carlos Garcia	.20
577	Greg Olson	.20

578	Greg Swindell (Foil)	.35
579	Matt Williams (Foil)	1.00
580	Mark Grace	.40
581	Howard House (Foil)	.30
582	Luis Polonia	.20
583	Erik Hanson	.20
584	Salomon Torres (Foil)	.25
585	Carlton Fisk	.40
586	Bret Saberhagen	.25
587	*Chad McDonnell* (Foil)	.40
588	Jimmy Key	.25
589	Mike MacFarlane	.20
590	Barry Bonds (Foil)	3.00
591	Jamie McAndrew	.40
592	Shane Mack	.25
593	Kerwin Moore	.25
594	Joe Oliver	.20
595	Chris Sabo	.20
596	*Alex Gonzalez*	5.00
597	Brett Butler	.30
598	Mark Hutton	.20
599	Andy Benes (Foil)	.80
600	Jose Canseco	.60
601	Darryl Kile	.50
602	Matt Stairs (Foil, SP)	.40
603	Rob Butler (Foil)	.25
604	Willie McGee	.25
605	Jack McDowell	.25
606	Tom Candiotti	.20
607	Ed Martel	.20
608	Matt Mieske (Foil)	.50
609	Darrin Fletcher	.20
610	Rafael Palmeiro	.35
611	Bill Swift (Foil)	.35
612	Mike Mussina	4.00
613	Vince Coleman	.20
614	Scott Cepicky (Foil)	.40
615	Mike Greenwell	.20
616	Kevin McGehee	.20
617	Jeffrey Hammonds (Foil)	2.00
618	Scott Taylor	.30
619	Dave Otto	.20
620	Mark McGwire (Foil)	8.00
621	Kevin Tatar	.25
622	Steve Farr	.20
623	Ryan Klesko (Foil)	6.00
625	Andre Dawson	.60
626	Tino Martinez (Foil, SP)	1.00
627	*Chad Curtis*	.75
628	Mickey Morandini	.20
629	Gregg Olson (Foil, SP)	.60
630	Lou Whitaker	.25
631	Arthur Rhodes	.25
632	Brandon Wilson	.25
633	*Lance Jennings*	.30
634	*Allen Watson*	.45
635	Len Dykstra	.25
636	Joe Girardi	.20
637	Kiki Hernandez (Foil, SP)	.40
638	Mike Hampton	.30
639	Al Osuna	.20
640	Kevin Appier	.25
641	Rick Helling (Foil, SP)	.40
642	Jody Reed	.20
643	Ray Lankford	.35
644	John Olerud	.50
645	Paul Molitor (Foil, SP)	1.50
646	Pat Borders	.20
647	Mike Morgan	.20
648	Larry Walker	2.00
649	Pete Castellano (Foil, SP)	.40
650	Fred McGriff	.60
651	Walt Weiss	.20
652	Calvin Murray (Foil, SP)	.40
653	Dave Nilsson	.20
654	Greg Pirkl	.20
655	Robin Ventura (Foil, SP)	.50
656	Mark Portugal	.20
657	Roger McDowell	.20
658	Rick Hirtensteiner (Foil, SP)	.20
659	Glenallen Hill	.20
660	Greg Gagne	.20
661	Charles Johnson (Foil, SP)	5.00
662	Brian Hunter	.40
663	Mark Lemke	.20
664	Tim Belcher (Foil, SP)	.40
665	Rich DeLucia	.20
666	Bob Walk	.20
667	Joe Carter (Foil, SP)	1.00
668	Jose Guzman	.20
669	Otis Nixon	.20
670	Phil Nevin (Foil)	.40
671	Eric Davis	.30
672	*Damion Easley*	2.00
673	Will Clark (Foil)	.75
674	Mark Kiefer	.20

675	Ozzie Smith	1.25
676	Manny Ramirez (Foil)	8.00
677	Gregg Olson	.20
678	*Cliff Floyd*	3.00
679	Duane Singleton	.35
680	Jose Rijo	.20
681	Willie Randolph	.20
682	*Michael Tucker* (Foil)	4.00
683	Darren Lewis	.20
684	Dale Murphy	.35
685	Mike Pagliarulo	.20
686	Paul Miller	.25
687	Mike Robertson	.20
688	Mike Devereaux	.20
689	Pedro Astacio	.75
690	Alan Trammell	.40
691	Roger Clemens	3.00
692	Bud Black	.20
693	Turk Wendell	.30
694	Barry Larkin (Foil, SP)	1.50
695	Todd Zeile	.20
696	Pat Hentgen	.45
697	*Eddie Taubensee*	.40
698	Guillermo Vasquez	.20
699	Tom Glavine	.35
700	Robin Yount	1.00
701	Checklist	.20
702	Checklist	.20
703	Checklist	.20
704	Checklist	.20
705	Checklist	.20

1993 Bowman

CHIPPER JONES

Bowman's 708-card 1993 set once again features a premium UV-coated glossy stock. There are also 48 special insert cards, with gold foil stamping, randomly inserted one per pack or two per jumbo pack. The foil cards, numbered 339-374 and 693-704, feature top prospects and rookie-of-the-year candidates, as do several regular cards in the set. Cards are standard size.

		MT
Complete Set (708):		95.00
Common Player:		.10
Wax Box:		40.00
1	Glenn Davis	.10
2	*Hector Roa*	.15
3	*Ken Ryan*	.25
4	*Derek Wallace*	.20
5	Jorge Fabregas	.10
6	Joe Oliver	.10
7	Brandon Wilson	.15
8	*Mark Thompson*	.40
9	Tracy Sanders	.10
10	Rich Renteria	.10
11	Lou Whitaker	.15
12	*Brian Hunter*	2.50
13	Joe Vitiello	.20
14	Eric Karros	.25
15	Joe Kmak	.10

16	Tavo Alvarez	.15
17	*Steve Dunn*	.30
18	Tony Fernandez	.10
19	Melido Perez	.10
20	Mike Lieberthal	.10
21	Terry Steinbach	.10
22	Stan Belinda	.10
23	Jay Buhner	.15
24	Allen Watson	.10
25	*Daryl Henderson*	.25
26	*Ray McDavid*	.40
27	Shawn Green	1.00
28	Bud Black	.10
29	*Sherman Obando*	.35
30	*Mike Hostetler*	.10
31	*Nate Hinchey*	.20
32	Randy Myers	.10
33	*Brian Grebeck*	.20
34	John Roper	.10
35	Larry Thomas	.15
36	Alex Cole	.10
37	*Tom Kramer*	.15
38	*Matt Whisenant*	.25
39	*Chris Gomez*	.40
40	Luis Gonzalez	.10
41	Kevin Appier	.12
42	*Omar Daal*	.20
43	Duane Singleton	.10
44	Bill Risley	.10
45	*Pat Meares*	.25
46	Butch Huskey	.15
47	Bobby Munoz	.10
48	Juan Bell	.10
49	*Scott Lydy*	.25
50	Dennis Moeller	.10
51	Marc Newfield	.15
52	*Tripp Cromer*	.20
53	Kurt Miller	.10
54	Jim Pena	.10
55	Juan Guzman	.15
56	Matt Williams	.40
57	Harold Reynolds	.12
58	*Donnie Elliott*	.15
59	*Jon Shave*	.30
60	*Kevin Roberson*	.20
61	*Hilly Hathaway*	.15
62	Jose Rijo	.10
63	*Kerry Taylor*	.20
64	Ryan Hawblitzel	.10
65	Glenallen Hill	.10
66	*Ramon D. Martinez*	.20
67	Travis Fryman	.15
68	Tom Nevers	.10
69	Phil Hiatt	.10
70	Tim Wallach	.10
71	B.J. Surhoff	.10
72	Rondell White	.65
73	*Denny Hocking*	.20
74	*Mike Oquist*	.25
75	Paul O'Neill	.12
76	Willie Banks	.10
77	Bob Welch	.10
78	*Jose Sandoval*	.20
79	Bill Haselman	.10
80	Rheal Cormier	.10
81	Dean Palmer	.15
82	*Pat Gomez*	.25
83	Steve Karsay	.15
84	*Carl Hanselman*	.20
85	T.R. Lewis	.25
86	Chipper Jones	4.00
87	Scott Hatteberg	.20
88	Greg Hibbard	.10
89	*Lance Painter*	.20
90	*Chad Mottola*	.40
91	Jason Bere	.25
92	Dante Bichette	.35
93	Sandy Alomar	.15
94	Carl Everett	.10
95	*Danny Bautista*	.30
96	Steve Finley	.10
97	David Cone	.10
98	Todd Hollandsworth	1.50
99	Matt Mieske	.10
100	Larry Walker	.75
101	Shane Mack	.10
102	Aaron Ledesma	.20
103	*Andy Pettitte*	6.00
104	Kevin Stocker	.10
105	Mike Mobler	.10
106	Tony Menedez	.10
107	Derek Lowe	.15
108	Basil Shabazz	.10
109	Dan Smith	.10
110	*Scott Sanders*	.25
111	Todd Stottlemyre	.10

112	*Benji Sikonton*	.30
113	Rick Sutcliffe	.10
114	*Lee Heath*	.15
115	Jeff Russell	.10
116	*Dave Stevens*	.20
117	*Mark Holzemer*	.20
118	Tim Belcher	.10
119	Bobby Thigpen	.10
120	*Roger Bailey*	.20
121	*Tony Mitchell*	.25
122	Junior Felix	.10
123	*Rich Robertson*	.20
124	*Andy Cook*	.20
125	*Brian Bevil*	.25
126	Darryl Strawberry	.25
127	Cal Eldred	.10
128	Cliff Floyd	.20
129	Alan Newman	.10
130	Howard Johnson	.10
131	Jim Abbott	.15
132	Chad McConnell	.15
133	*Miguel Jimenez*	.20
134	Brett Backlund	.20
135	*John Cummings*	.30
136	Brian Barber	.15
137	Rafael Palmeiro	.20
138	*Tim Worrell*	.20
139	*Jose Pett*	.50
140	Barry Bonds	1.00
141	Damon Buford	.10
142	Jeff Blauser	.10
143	Frankie Rodriguez	.25
144	Mike Morgan	.10
145	Gary DeSarcina	.10
146	Calvin Reese	.10
147	Johnny Ruffin	.10
148	David Nied	.10
149	Charles Nagy	.12
150	*Mike Myers*	.20
151	*Kenny Carlyle*	.20
152	Eric Anthony	.10
153	Jose Lind	.10
154	Pedro Martinez	1.50
155	Mark Kiefer	.10
156	*Tim Laker*	.20
157	Pat Mahomes	.10
158	Bobby Bonilla	.15
159	Domingo Jean	.10
160	Darren Daulton	.12
161	Mark McGwire	6.00
162	*Jason Kendall*	4.00
163	Desi Relaford	.25
164	Ozzie Canseco	.10
165	Rick Helling	.10
166	*Steve Pegues*	.20
167	Paul Molitor	.35
168	*Larry Carter*	.20
169	Arthur Rhodes	.10
170	*Damon Hollins*	.40
171	Frank Viola	.10
172	*Steve Trachsel*	1.50
173	*J.T. Snow*	1.50
174	*Keith Gordon*	.20
175	Carlton Fisk	.15
176	*Jason Bates*	.20
177	*Mike Crosby*	.20
178	Benny Santiago	.10
179	Mike Moore	.10
180	Jeff Juden	.20
181	Darren Burton	.10
182	*Todd Williams*	.20
183	John Jaha	.10
184	*Mike Lansing*	.75
185	*Pedro Grifol*	.20
186	Vince Coleman	.10
187	Pat Kelly	.10
188	*Clemente Alvarez*	.20
189	Ron Darling	.10
190	Orlando Merced	.10
191	Chris Bosio	.10
192	*Steve Dixon*	.20
193	Doug Dascenzo	.10
194	*Ray Holbert*	.35
195	Howard Battle	.15
196	Willie McGee	.12
197	*John O'Donoghue*	.20
198	Steve Avery	.15
199	Greg Blosser	.15
200	Ryne Sandberg	.75
201	Joe Grahe	.10
202	Dan Wilson	.10
203	*Domingo Martinez*	.20
204	Andres Galarraga	.20
205	*Jamie Taylor*	.20
206	*Darrell Whitmore*	.25
207	*Ben Blomdahl*	.20

#	Name	Price		#	Name	Price		#	Name	Price
208	Doug Drabek	.10		304	Aaron Holbert	.10		400	Tyler Green	.10
209	Keith Miller	.10		305	Juan Gonzalez	1.50		401	Mike Bordick	.10
210	Billy Ashley	.15		306	*Billy Hall*	.25		402	Scott Bullett	.10
211	*Mike Farrell*	.20		307	Duane Ward	.10		403	*Lagrande Russell*	.20
212	John Wetteland	.10		308	Rod Beck	.10		404	Ray Lankford	.15
213	Randy Tomlin	.10		309	*Jose Mercedes*	.25		405	Nolan Ryan	3.00
214	Sid Fernandez	.10		310	Otis Nixon	.10		406	Robbie Beckett	.10
215	*Quilvio Veras*	.25		311	*Gettys Glaze*	.25		407	*Brent Bowers*	.20
216	Dave Hollins	.15		312	Candy Maldonado	.10		408	*Adell Davenport*	.20
217	Mike Neill	.10		313	Chad Curtis	.15		409	Brady Anderson	.25
218	Andy Van Slyke	.10		314	Tim Costo	.10		410	Tom Glavine	.15
219	Bret Boone	.20		315	Mike Robertson	.10		411	*Doug Hecker*	.30
220	Tom Pagnozzi	.10		316	Nigel Wilson	.12		412	Jose Guzman	.10
221	*Mike Welch*	.20		317	*Greg McMichael*	.25		413	Luis Polonia	.10
222	Frank Seminara	.10		318	*Scott Pose*	.20		414	Brian Williams	.10
223	Ron Villone	.10		319	Ivan Cruz	.10		415	Bo Jackson	.20
224	*D.J. Thielen*	.25		320	Greg Swindell	.10		416	Eric Young	.15
225	Cal Ripken, Jr.	4.00		321	Kevin McReynolds	.10		417	Kenny Lofton	.90
226	*Pedro Borbon*	.20		322	Tom Candiotti	.10		418	Orestes Destrade	.10
227	Carlos Quintana	.10		323	*Bob Wishnevski*	.20		419	Tony Phillips	.15
228	*Tommy Shields*	.20		324	Ken Hill	.10		420	Jeff Bagwell	1.00
229	Tim Salmon	.60		325	Kirby Puckett	1.00		421	Hark Gardner	.10
230	John Smiley	.10		326	*Tim Bogar*	.20		422	Brett Butler	.15
231	Ellis Burks	.15		327	Mariano Rivera	.40		423	*Graeme Lloyd*	.15
232	Pedro Castellano	.10		328	Mitch Williams	.10		424	Delino DeShields	.10
233	Paul Byrd	.10		329	Craig Paquette	.10		425	Scott Erickson	.10
234	Bryan Harvey	.10		330	Jay Bell	.10		426	Jeff Kent	.10
235	Scott Livingstone	.10		331	*Jose Martinez*	.35		427	Jimmy Key	.10
236	*James Mouton*	.50		332	Rob Deer	.10		428	Mickey Morandini	.10
237	Joe Randa	.15		333	Brook Fordyce	.10		429	*Marcos Arkas*	.25
238	Pedro Astacio	.15		334	Matt Nokes	.10		430	Don Slaught	.10
239	Darryl Hamilton	.10		335	Derek Lee	.15		431	Randy Johnson	.45
240	*Joey Eischen*	.40		336	*Paul Ellis*	.20		432	Omar Olivares	.10
241	*Edgar Herrera*	.20		337	*Desi Wilson*	.15		433	Charlie Leibrandt	.10
242	Dwight Gooden	.15		338	Roberto Alomar	.75		434	Kurt Stillwell	.10
243	Sam Militello	.10		339	Jim Tatum (Foil)	.20		435	*Scott Brow*	.15
244	*Ron Blazier*	.20		340	J.T. Snow (Foil)	.30		436	Robby Thompson	.10
245	Ruben Sierra	.12		341	Tim Salmon (Foil)	.75		437	Ben McDonald	.15
246	Al Martin	.10		342	*Russ Davis* (Foil)	1.00		438	Deion Sanders	.50
247	Mike Felder	.10		343	Javier Lopez (Foil)	.60		439	Tony Pena	.10
248	Bob Tewksbury	.10		344	*Troy O'Leary* (Foil)	.75		440	Mark Grace	.30
249	Craig Lefferts	.10		345	*Marty Cordova* (Foil)	2.50		441	Eduardo Perez	.15
250	Luis Lopez	.10		346	*Bubba Smith* (Foil)	.35		442	*Tim Pugh*	.30
251	Devon White	.10		347	Chipper Jones (Foil)	4.00		443	Scott Ruffcorn	.15
252	Will Clark	.35		348	Jessie Hollins (Foil)	.20		444	*Jay Gainer*	.20
253	Mark Smith	.15		349	Willie Greene (Foil)	.25		445	Albert Belle	1.00
254	Terry Pendleton	.10		350	Mark Thompson (Foil)	.30		446	Bret Barberie	.10
255	Aaron Sele	.25		351	Nigel Wilson (Foil)	.25		447	Justin Mashore	.10
256	*Jose Viera*	.15		352	Todd Jones (Foil)	.20		448	Pete Harnisch	.10
257	Damion Easley	.15		353	Raul Mondesi (Foil)	.90		449	Greg Gagne	.10
258	*Rod Lofton*	.20		354	Cliff Floyd (Foil)	.40		450	Eric Davis	.15
259	*Chris Snopek*	.40		355	Bobby Jones (Foil)	.30		451	Dave Mlicki	.10
260	*Quinton McCracken*	1.00		356	Kevin Stocker (Foil)	.20		452	Moises Alou	.15
261	*Mike Matthews*	.30		357	Midre Cummings (Foil)	.35		453	Rick Aguilera	.10
262	*Hector Carrasco*	.40		358	Allen Watson (Foil)	.20		454	Eddie Murray	.50
263	Rick Greene	.20		359	Ray McDavid (Foil)	.40		455	Bob Wickman	.10
264	*Chris Bolt*	.25		360	Steve Hosey (Foil)	.25		456	Wes Chamberlain	.10
265	George Brett	1.00		361	Brad Pennington (Foil)	.25		457	Brent Gates	.10
266	*Rick Gorecki*	.25		362	Frankie Rodriguez (Foil)	.25		458	Paul Weber	.10
267	Francisco Gamez	.15		363	Troy Percival (Foil)	.25		459	Mike Hampton	.10
268	Marquis Grissom	.15		364	Jason Bere (Foil)	.25		460	Ozzie Smith	.40
269	Kevin Tapani	.10		365	Manny Ramirez (Foil)	2.50		461	Tom Henke	.10
270	Ryan Thompson	.15		366	Justin Thompson (Foil)	.50		462	Ricky Gutuerrez	.10
271	Gerald Williams	.10		367	Joe Vitello (Foil)	.25		463	Jack Morris	.12
272	*Paul Fletcher*	.20		368	Tyrone Hill (Foil)	.20		464	*Joel Chimelis*	.20
273	Lance Blankenship	.10		369	David McCarty (Foil)	.15		465	Gregg Olson	.10
274	*Marty Heff*	.20		370	Brien Taylor (Foil)	.20		466	Javier Lopez	.40
275	Shawn Estes	.50		371	Todd Van Poppel (Foil)	.15		467	Scott Cooper	.10
276	Rene Arocha	.25		372	Marc Newfield (Foil)	.25		468	Willie Wilson	.10
277	*Scott Evre*	.30		373	*Terrell Lowery* (Foil)	.60		469	Mark Langston	.10
278	Phil Plantier	.10		374	Alex Gonzalez (Foil)	.40		470	Barry Larkin	.20
279	*Paul Spoljaric*	.40		375	Ken Griffey, Jr.	5.00		471	Rod Bolton	.10
280	Chris Gahbs	.15		376	Donovan Osborne	.10		472	Freddie Benavides	.10
281	Harold Baines	.12		377	*Ritchie Moody*	.15		473	*Ken Ramos*	.20
282	*Jose Oliva*	.15		378	Shane Andrews	.30		474	Chuck Carr	.10
283	Matt Whiteside	.20		379	Carlos Delgado	.65		475	Cecil Fielder	.25
284	*Brant Brown*	2.50		380	Bill Swift	.10		476	Eddie Taubensee	.10
285	Russ Springer	.10		381	Leo Gomez	.10		477	*Chris Eddy*	.25
286	Chris Sabo	.10		382	Ron Gant	.15		478	Greg Hansell	.10
287	Ozzie Guillen	.10		383	Scott Fletcher	.10		479	Kevin Reimer	.10
288	*Marcus Moore*	.40		384	*Matt Walbeck*	.15		480	Denny Martinez	.12
289	Chad Ogea	.25		385	Chuck Finley	.10		481	Chuck Knoblauch	.20
290	Walt Weiss	.10		386	Kevin Mitchell	.12		482	Mike Draper	.10
291	Brian Edmondson	.10		387	Wilson Alvarez	.10		483	Spike Owen	.10
292	Jimmy Gonzalez	.10		388	*John Burke*	.25		484	Terry Mulholland	.10
293	*Danny Miceli*	.30		389	Alan Embree	.10		485	Dennis Eckersley	.12
294	Jose Offerman	.10		390	Trevor Hoffman	.15		486	Blas Minor	.10
295	Greg Vaughn	.10		391	Alan Trammell	.15		487	Dave Fleming	.10
296	Frank Bolick	.10		392	Todd Jones	.10		488	Dan Cholonsky	.15
297	*Mike Maksudian*	.25		393	Felix Jose	.10		489	Ivan Rodriguez	.75
298	John Franco	.10		394	Orel Hershiser	.15		490	Gary Sheffield	.25
299	Danny Tartabull	.10		395	Pat Listach	.10		491	Ed Sprague	.10
300	Len Dykstra	.12		396	Gabe White	.10		492	Steve Hosey	.15
301	Bobby Witt	.10		397	*Dan Serafini*	.60		493	*Jimmy Haynes*	1.00
302	*Trey Beamon*	.90		398	Todd Hundley	.15		494	John Smoltz	.25
303	Tino Martinez	.25		399	Wade Boggs	.35		495	Andre Dawson	.25

496	Rey Sanchez	.10
497	*Ty Van Burkleo*	.20
498	*Bobby Ayala*	.40
499	Tim Raines	.15
500	Charlie Hayes	.10
501	Paul Sorrento	.10
502	*Richie Lewis*	.30
503	*Jason Pfaff*	.15
504	Ken Caminiti	.20
505	Mike Macfarlane	.10
506	Jody Reed	.10
507	*Bobby Hughes*	.75
508	Wil Cordero	.10
509	*George Tsanis*	.20
510	Bret Saberhagen	.12
511	*Derek Jeter*	12.00
512	Gene Schall	.30
513	Curtis Shaw	.10
514	Steve Cooke	.15
515	Edgar Martinez	.15
516	Mike Milchin	.10
517	Billy Ripken	.10
518	Andy Benes	.12
519	*Juan de la Rosa*	.20
520	John Burkett	.10
521	Alex Ochoa	.30
522	*Tony Tarasco*	.25
523	Luis Ortiz	.15
524	Rick Williams	.10
525	*Chris Turner*	.20
526	Rob Dibble	.10
527	Jack McDowell	.12
528	Daryl Boston	.10
529	*Bill Wertz*	.20
530	Charlie Hough	.10
531	Sean Bergman	.15
532	Doug Jones	.10
533	Jeff Montgomery	.10
534	*Roger Cedeno*	1.00
535	Robin Yount	.40
536	Mo Vaughn	.75
537	Brian Harper	.10
538	Juan Castillo	.10
539	Steve Farr	.10
540	John Kruk	.10
541	Troy Neel	.15
542	*Danny Clyburn*	.60
543	*Jim Converse*	.30
544	Gregg Jefferies	.15
545	Jose Canseco	.40
546	*Julio Bruno*	.25
547	Rob Butler	.10
548	Royce Clayton	.12
549	Chris Hoiles	.10
550	Greg Maddux	2.50
551	*Joe Ciccarella*	.25
552	Ozzie Timmons	.10
553	Chili Davis	.12
554	Brian Koelling	.10
555	Frank Thomas	4.00
556	Vinny Castilla	1.50
557	Reggie Jefferson	.10
558	Rob Natal	.10
559	Mike Henneman	.10
560	Craig Biggio	.20
561	*Billy Brewer*	.20
562	Dan Melendez	.20
563	*Kenny Felder*	.40
564	*Miguel Batista*	.25
565	Dave Winfield	.20
566	Al Shirley	.10
567	Robert Eenhoorn	.10
568	Mike Williams	.10
569	*Tanyon Sturtze*	.30
570	Tim Wakefield	.10
571	Greg Pirkl	.10
572	*Sean Lowe*	.40
573	*Terry Burows*	.15
574	*Kevin Higgins*	.30
575	Joe Carter	.20
576	Kevin Rogers	.10
577	Manny Alexander	.10
578	Dave Justice	.30
579	*Brian Conroy*	.15
580	*Jessie Hollins*	.20
581	*Ron Watson*	.20
582	Bip Roberts	.10
583	*Tom Urbani*	.15
584	*Jason Hutchins*	.30
585	Carlos Baerga	.20
586	Jeff Mutis	.25
587	Justin Thompson	.30
588	Orlando Miller	.15
589	Brian McRae	.15
590	Ramon Martinez	.12
591	Dave Nilsson	.10
592	*Jose Vidro*	.35
593	Rich Becker	.10
594	*Preston Wilson*	.50
595	Don Mattingly	1.25
596	Tony Longmire	.10
597	Kevin Seitzer	.10
598	*Midre Cummings*	.60
599	Omar Vizquel	.10
600	Lee Smith	.12
601	*David Hulse*	.15
602	*Darrell Sherman*	.20
603	Alex Gonzalez	.25
604	Geronimo Pena	.10
605	Mike Devereaux	.10
606	*Sterling Hitchcock*	.30
607	Mike Greenwell	.10
608	Steve Buechele	.10
609	Troy Percival	.10
610	Bobby Kelly	.10
611	*James Baldwin*	.75
612	Jerald Clark	.10
613	*Albie Lopez*	.40
614	Dave Magadan	.10
615	Mickey Tettleton	.10
616	*Sean Runyan*	.35
617	Bob Hamelin	.10
618	Raul Mondesi	1.00
619	Tyrone Hill	.25
620	Darrin Fletcher	.10
621	Mike Trombley	.10
622	Jeromy Burnitz	.10
623	Bernie Williams	.60
624	*Mike Farmer*	.20
625	Rickey Henderson	.35
626	Carlos Garcia	.10
627	*Jeff Darwin*	.40
628	Todd Zeile	.15
629	Benji Gil	.10
630	Tony Gwynn	2.00
631	*Aaron Small*	.25
632	*Joe Rosselli*	.30
633	Mike Mussina	.50
634	Ryan Klesko	2.00
635	Roger Clemens	1.50
636	Sammy Sosa	3.00
637	*Orlando Palmeiro*	.20
638	Willie Greene	.10
639	George Bell	.10
640	*Garvin Alston*	.30
641	*Pete Janicki*	.40
642	*Chris Sheff*	.25
643	*Felipe Lira*	.40
644	Roberto Petagine	.10
645	Wally Joyner	.12
646	Mike Piazza	3.00
647	Jaime Navarro	.10
648	*Jeff Hartsock*	.25
649	David McCarty	.15
650	Bobby Jones	.20
651	Mark Hutton	.10
652	Kyle Abbott	.10
653	*Steve Cox*	.25
654	Jeff King	.10
655	Norm Charlton	.10
656	*Mike Gulan*	.30
657	Julio Franco	.12
658	*Cameron Cairncross*	.30
659	John Olerud	.25
660	Salomon Torres	.10
661	Brad Pennington	.10
662	Melvin Nieves	.10
663	Ivan Calderon	.10
664	Turk Wendell	.10
665	Chris Pritchett	.10
666	Reggie Sanders	.15
667	Robin Ventura	.15
668	Joe Girardi	.10
669	Manny Ramirez	2.50
670	Jeff Conine	.15
671	Greg Gohr	.10
672	Andujar Cedeno	.10
673	*Les Norman*	.15
674	*Mike James*	.20
675	*Marshall Boze*	.40
676	B.J. Wallace	.15
677	Kent Hrbek	.12
678	Jack Voight	.10
679	Brien Taylor	.15
680	Curt Schilling	.10
681	Todd Van Poppel	.12
682	Kevin Young	.15
683	Tommy Adams	.10
684	Bernard Gilkey	.10
685	Kevin Brown	.10
686	Fred McGriff	.30
687	Pat Borders	.10
688	Kirt Manwaring	.10
689	Sid Bream	.10
690	John Valentin	.15
691	*Steve Olsen*	.20
692	*Roberto Mejia*	.25
693	*Carlos Delgado* (Foil)	1.00
694	*Steve Gibralter* (Foil)	.40
695	Gary Mota (Foil)	.25
696	*Jose Malave* (Foil)	1.00
697	*Larry Sutton* (Foil)	1.00
698	*Dan Frye* (Foil)	.35
699	*Tim Clark* (Foil)	.40
700	*Brian Rupp* (Foil)	.40
701	Felipe Alou, Moises Alou (Foil)	.25
702	Bobby Bonds, Barry Bonds (Foil)	.75
703	Ken Griffey Sr., Ken Griffey Jr. (Foil)	1.00
704	Hal McRae, Brian McRae (Foil)	.25
705	Checklist 1	.10
706	Checklist 2	.10
707	Checklist 3	.10
708	Checklist 4	.10

1994 Bowman

Bowman baseball for 1994 was a 682-card set issued all in one series, including a 52-card foil subset. There were 11 regular cards plus one foil card in each pack, with a suggested retail price of $2. The cards have a full-bleed design, with gold-foil stamping on every card. As in the past, the set includes numerous rookies and propects, along with the game's biggest stars. The 52-card foil subset features 28 Top Prospects, with the player's team logo in the background; 17 Minor League MVPs, with a stadium in the background; and seven Diamonds in the Rough, with, you guessed it, a diamond as a backdrop.

		MT
Complete Set (682):		120.00
Common Player:		.10
Wax Box:		30.00
1	Joe Carter	.25
2	Marcus Moore	.10
3	*Doug Creek*	.15
4	Pedro Martinez	.75
5	Ken Griffey, Jr.	5.00
6	Greg Swindell	.10
7	J.J. Johnson	.10
8	*Homer Bush*	.15
9	*Arquimedez Pozo*	.40
10	Bryan Harvey	.10
11	J.T. Snow	.20
12	*Alan Benes*	3.00
13	Chad Kreuter	.10

#	Name	Price
14	Eric Karros	.15
15	Frank Thomas	3.00
16	Bret Saberhagen	.12
17	Terrell Lowery	.10
18	Rod Bolton	.10
19	Harold Baines	.12
20	Matt Walbeck	.10
21	Tom Glavine	.15
22	Todd Jones	.10
23	Alberto Castillo	.10
24	Ruben Sierra	.12
25	Don Mattingly	1.00
26	Mike Morgan	.10
27	*Jim Musselwhite*	.20
28	Matt Brunson	.25
29	*Adam Meinershagen*	.25
30	Joe Girardi	.10
31	Shane Halter	.10
32	*Jose Paniagua*	.25
33	Paul Perkins	.12
34	*John Hudek*	.40
35	Frank Viola	.10
36	*David Lamb*	.15
37	Marshall Boze	.10
38	*Jorge Posada*	4.00
39	*Brian Anderson*	1.00
40	Mark Whiten	.10
41	Sean Bergman	.10
42	*Jose Parra*	.20
43	Mike Robertson	.10
44	Pete Walker	.15
45	Juan Gonzalez	1.50
46	*Cleveland Ladell*	.25
47	Mark Smith	.10
48	*Kevin Jarvis*	.25
49	*Amaury Telemaco*	.25
50	Andy Van Slyke	.10
51	*Rikkert Faneyte*	.20
52	Curtis Shaw	.10
53	*Matt Drews*	.40
54	Wilson Alvarez	.10
55	Manny Ramirez	1.50
56	Bobby Munoz	.10
57	Ed Sprague	.10
58	*Jamey Wright*	1.50
59	Jeff Montgomery	.10
60	Kirk Rueter	.10
61	Edgar Martinez	.15
62	Luis Gonzalez	.10
63	*Tim Vanegmond*	.15
64	Bip Roberts	.10
65	John Jaha	.10
66	Chuck Carr	.10
67	Chuck Finley	.10
68	Aaron Holbert	.10
69	Cecil Fielder	.25
70	*Tom Engle*	.15
71	Ron Karkovice	.10
72	Joe Orsulak	.10
73	*Duff Brumley*	.25
74	*Craig Clayton*	.15
75	Cal Ripken, Jr.	2.50
76	*Brad Fullmer*	8.00
77	Tony Tarasco	.10
78	*Terry Farrar*	.15
79	Matt Williams	.25
80	Rickey Henderson	.20
81	Terry Mulholland	.10
82	Sammy Sosa	3.00
83	Paul Sorrento	.10
84	Pete Incaviglia	.10
85	*Darren Hall*	.40
86	Scott Klingenbeck	.10
87	*Dario Perez*	.15
88	Ugueth Urbina	.10
89	*Dave Vanhof*	.15
90	Domingo Jean	.10
91	Otis Nixon	.10
92	Andres Berumen	.10
93	Jose Valentin	.10
94	*Edgar Renteria*	4.00
95	Chris Turner	.10
96	Ray Lankford	.15
97	Danny Bautista	.10
98	*Chan Ho Park*	5.00
99	*Glenn DiSarcina*	.15
100	Butch Huskey	.12
101	Ivan Rodriguez	.75
102	Johnny Ruffin	.10
103	Alex Ochoa	.20
104	*Torii Hunter*	.60
105	Ryan Klesko	1.00
106	Jay Bell	.10
107	*Kurt Peltzer*	.15
108	Miguel Jimenez	.10
109	Russ Davis	.15
110	Derek Wallace	.10
111	*Keith Lockhart*	.25
112	Mike Lieberthal	.10
113	Dave Stewart	.12
114	Tom Schmidt	.10
115	Brian McRae	.12
116	Moises Alou	.15
117	Dave Fleming	.10
118	Jeff Bagwell	1.00
119	Luis Ortiz	.10
120	Tony Gwynn	1.50
121	Jaime Navarro	.10
122	Benny Santiago	.10
123	Darrel Whitmore	.10
124	*John Mabry*	.25
125	Mickey Tettleton	.10
126	Tom Candiotti	.10
127	Tim Raines	.15
128	Bobby Bonilla	.15
129	John Dettmer	.10
130	Hector Carrasco	.10
131	Chris Hoiles	.10
132	Rick Aguilera	.10
133	Dave Justice	.40
134	Esteban Loaiza	.25
135	Barry Bonds	.75
136	Bob Welch	.10
137	Mike Stanley	.10
138	Roberto Hernandez	.10
139	Sandy Alomar	.15
140	Darren Daulton	.12
141	*Angel Martinez*	.25
142	Howard Johnson	.10
143	Bob Hamelin	.10
144	*J.J. Thobe*	.25
145	Roger Salkeld	.10
146	Orlando Miller	.10
147	Dmitri Young	.10
148	*Tim Hyers*	.25
149	*Mark Loretta*	.25
150	Chris Hammond	.10
151	*Joel Moore*	.25
152	Todd Zeile	.15
153	Wil Cordero	.10
154	Chris Smith	.10
155	James Baldwin	.20
156	*Edgardo Alfonzo*	3.00
157	*Kym Ashworth*	.50
158	*Paul Bako*	.25
159	*Rick Krivda*	.40
160	Pat Mahomes	.10
161	Damon Hollins	.15
162	*Felix Martinez*	.15
163	*Jason Myers*	.25
164	*Izzy Molina*	.25
165	Brien Taylor	.10
166	*Kevin Orie*	2.00
167	*Casey Whitten*	.25
168	Tony Longmire	.10
169	John Olerud	.25
170	Mark Thompson	.10
171	Jorge Fabregas	.10
172	John Wetteland	.10
173	Dan Wilson	.10
174	Doug Drabek	.10
175	Jeffrey McNeely	.10
176	Melvin Nieves	.10
177	*Doug Glanville*	.75
178	*Javier De La Hoya*	.25
179	Chad Curtis	.10
180	Brian Barber	.10
181	Mike Henneman	.10
182	Jose Offerman	.10
183	*Robert Ellis*	.35
184	John Franco	.10
185	Benji Gil	.10
186	Hal Morris	.10
187	Chris Sabo	.10
188	*Blaise Ilsley*	.15
189	Steve Avery	.15
190	*Rick White*	.25
191	Rod Beck	.10
(192)	Mark McGwire (no card number)	6.00
193	Jim Abbott	.15
194	Randy Myers	.10
195	Kenny Lofton	.75
196	Mariano Duncan	.10
197	*Lee Daniels*	.15
198	Armando Reynoso	.10
199	Joe Randa	.10
200	Cliff Floyd	.30
201	*Tim Harkrider*	.25
202	*Kevin Gallaher*	.15
203	Scott Cooper	.10
204	*Phil Stidham*	.20
205	*Jeff D'Amico*	.75
206	Matt Whisenant	.10
207	De Shawn Warren	.10
208	Rene Arocha	.10
209	*Tony Clark*	15.00
210	*Jason Jacome*	1.00
211	*Scott Christman*	.25
212	Bill Pulsipher	.30
213	Dean Palmer	.12
214	Chad Mottola	.15
215	Manny Alexander	.10
216	Rich Becker	.15
217	*Andre King*	.40
218	Carlos Garcia	.10
219	*Ron Pezzoni*	.15
220	Steve Karsay	.10
221	*Jose Musset*	.25
222	Karl Rhodes	.10
223	*Frank Cimorelli*	.15
224	Kevin Jordan	.25
225	Duane Ward	.10
226	John Burke	.10
227	Mike MacFarlane	.10
228	Mike Lansing	.10
229	Chuck Knoblauch	.30
230	Ken Caminiti	.25
231	*Gar Finnvold*	.15
232	*Derrek Lee*	8.00
233	Brady Anderson	.25
234	*Vic Darensbourg*	.15
235	Mark Langston	.10
236	*T.J. Mathews*	.25
237	Lou Whitaker	.12
238	Roger Cedeno	.15
239	Alex Fernandez	.15
240	Ryan Thompson	.10
241	*Kerry Lacy*	.15
242	Reggie Sanders	.15
243	Brad Pennington	.10
244	*Bryan Eversgerd*	.15
245	Greg Maddux	2.50
246	Jason Kendall	.25
247	J.R. Phillips	.25
248	Bobby Witt	.10
249	Paul O'Neill	.20
250	Ryne Sandberg	.50
251	Charles Nagy	.12
252	Kevin Stocker	.10
253	Shawn Green	.40
254	Charlie Hayes	.10
255	Donnie Elliott	.10
256	*Rob Fitzpatrick*	.15
257	Tim Davis	.10
258	James Mouton	.15
259	Mike Greenwell	.10
260	Ray McDavid	.12
261	Mike Kelly	.10
262	*Andy Larkin*	.60
(263)	Marquis Riley (no card number)	.10
264	Bob Tewksbury	.10
265	Brian Edmondson	.10
266	*Eduardo Lantigua*	.15
267	Brandon Wilson	.10
268	Mike Welch	.10
269	Tom Henke	.10
270	Calvin Reese	.10
271	*Greg Zaun*	.25
272	Todd Ritchie	.10
273	Javier Lopez	.30
274	Kevin Young	.10
275	Kirt Manwaring	.10
276	*Bill Taylor*	.15
277	Robert Eenhoorn	.10
278	Jessie Hollins	.10
279	Julian Tavarez	.50
280	Gene Schall	.10
281	Paul Molitor	.50
282	*Neifi Perez*	3.00
283	Greg Gagne	.10
284	Marquis Grissom	.15
285	Randy Johnson	.50
286	Pete Harnisch	.10
287	*Joel Bennett*	.40
288	Derek Bell	.15
289	Darryl Hamilton	.10
290	Gary Sheffield	.25
291	Eduardo Perez	.10
292	Basil Shabazz	.10
293	Eric Davis	.15
294	Pedro Astacio	.10
295	Robin Ventura	.15
296	Jeff Kent	.12
297	Rick Helling	.10
298	Joe Oliver	.10
299	Lee Smith	.12

No.	Name	Price		No.	Name	Price		No.	Name	Price
300	Dave Winfield	.25		396	*Ray Suplee*	.25		492	*Carlos Reyes*	.20
301	Deion Sanders	.50		397	Tony Phillips	.12		493	Andy Pettitte	2.00
302	*Ravelo Manzanillo*	.15		398	Ramon Martinez	.12		494	Brant Brown	.15
303	Mark Portugal	.10		399	Julio Franco	.12		495	Daron Kirkreit	.15
304	Brent Gates	.10		400	Dwight Gooden	.15		496	*Ricky Bottalico*	.40
305	Wade Boggs	.30		401	*Kevin Lomon*	.15		497	Devon White	.10
306	Rick Wilkins	.10		402	Jose Rijo	.10		498	*Jason Johnson*	.25
307	Carlos Baerga	.20		403	Mike Devereaux	.10		499	Vince Coleman	.10
308	Curt Schilling	.10		404	*Mike Zolecki*	.25		500	Larry Walker	.50
309	Shannon Stewart	.10		405	Fred McGriff	.25		501	Bobby Ayala	.10
310	Darren Holmes	.10		406	Danny Clyburn	.15		502	Steve Finley	.10
311	*Robert Toth*	.25		407	Robby Thompson	.10		503	Scott Fletcher	.10
312	Gabe White	.10		408	Terry Steinbach	.10		504	Brad Ausmus	.10
313	*Mac Suzuki*	.45		409	Luis Polonia	.10		505	*Scott Talanoa*	.40
314	*Alvin Morman*	.15		410	Mark Grace	.25		506	Orestes Destrade	.10
315	Mo Vaughn	.75		411	Albert Belle	1.25		507	Gary DiSarcina	.10
316	*Bryce Florie*	.15		412	John Kruk	.10		508	*Willie Smith*	.25
317	*Gabby Martinez*	.25		413	*Scott Spiezio*	2.00		509	Alan Trammell	.15
318	Carl Everett	.10		414	Ellis Burks	.15		510	Mike Piazza	2.00
319	Kerwin Moore	.10		415	Joe Vitiello	.15		511	Ozzie Guillen	.10
320	Tom Pagnozzi	.10		416	Tim Costo	.10		512	Jeromy Burnitz	.10
321	Chris Gomez	.15		417	Marc Newfield	.15		513	Darren Oliver	.10
322	Todd Williams	.10		418	*Oscar Henriquez*	.40		514	Kevin Mitchell	.12
323	Pat Hentgen	.10		419	*Matt Perisho*	.25		515	Rafael Palmeiro	.20
324	*Kirk Presley*	.75		420	Julio Bruno	.10		516	David McCarty	.10
325	Kevin Brown	.10		421	Kenny Felder	.10		517	Jeff Blauser	.10
326	*Jason Isringhausen*	1.50		422	Tyler Green	.10		518	Trey Beamon	.20
327	*Rick Forney*	.25		423	Jim Edmonds	.50		519	Royce Clayton	.10
328	*Carlos Pulido*	.25		424	Ozzie Smith	.40		520	Dennis Eckersley	.12
329	*Terrell Wade*	.75		425	Rick Greene	.10		521	Bernie Williams	.60
330	Al Martin	.10		426	Todd Hollandsworth	.40		522	Steve Buechele	.10
331	*Dan Carlson*	.25		427	*Eddie Pearson*	.35		523	Denny Martinez	.12
332	*Mark Acre*	.15		428	Quilvio Veras	.10		524	Dave Hollins	.10
333	Sterling Hitchcock	.10		429	Kenny Rogers	.10		525	Joey Hamilton	.30
334	*Jon Ratliff*	.50		430	Willie Greene	.10		526	Andres Galarraga	.25
335	*Alex Ramirez*	2.00		431	Vaughn Eshelman	.20		527	Jeff Granger	.10
336	*Phil Geisler*	.25		432	Pat Meares	.10		528	Joey Eischen	.10
337	*Eddie Zambrano* (Foil)	.25		433	*Jermaine Dye*	1.50		529	Desi Relaford	.10
338	Jim Thome (Foil)	1.00		434	Steve Cooke	.10		530	Roberto Petagine	.10
339	James Mouton (Foil)	.25		435	Bill Swift	.10		531	Andre Dawson	.15
340	Cliff Floyd (Foil)	.40		436	*Fausto Cruz*	.25		532	Ray Holbert	.10
341	Carlos Delgado (Foil)	.50		437	Mark Hutton	.10		533	Duane Singleton	.10
342	Roberto Petagine (Foil)	.10		438	*Brooks Kieschnick*	2.00		534	*Kurt Abbott*	.30
343	Tim Clark (Foil)	.10		439	Yorkis Perez	.10		535	Bo Jackson	.15
344	Bubba Smith (Foil)	.15		440	Len Dykstra	.15		536	Gregg Jefferies	.15
345	Randy Curtis (Foil)	.20		441	Pat Borders	.10		537	David Mysel	.10
346	*Joe Biasucci* (Foil)	.20		442	*Doug Walls*	.20		538	Raul Mondesi	.75
347	*D.J. Boston* (Foil)	.10		443	Wally Joyner	.12		539	Chris Snopek	.15
348	Ruben Rivera (Foil)	4.00		444	Ken Hill	.10		540	Brook Fordyce	.15
349	*Bryan Link* (Foil)	.20		445	Eric Anthony	.10		541	*Ron Frazier*	.25
350	*Mike Bell* (Foil)	1.00		446	Mitch Williams	.10		542	Brian Koelling	.10
351	*Marty Watson* (Foil)	.20		447	Cory Bailey	.25		543	Jimmy Haynes	.75
352	*Jason Myers* (Foil)	.20		448	Dave Staton	.10		544	Marty Cordova	.75
353	Chipper Jones (Foil)	2.00		449	Greg Vaughn	.10		545	*Jason Green*	.30
354	Brooks Kieschnick (Foil)	1.25		450	Dave Magadan	.10		546	Orlando Merced	.10
355	Calvin Reese (Foil)	.10		451	Chili Davis	.10		547	*Lou Pote*	.20
356	John Burke (Foil)	.10		452	*Gerald Santos*	.25		548	Todd Van Poppel	.12
357	Kurt Miller (Foil)	.10		453	Joe Perona	.10		549	Pat Kelly	.10
358	Orlando Miller (Foil)	.10		454	Delino DeShields	.10		550	Turk Wendell	.10
359	Todd Hollandsworth (Foil)	1.00		455	Jack McDowell	.10		551	*Herb Perry*	.15
360	Rondell White (Foil)	.40		456	Todd Hundley	.15		552	*Ryan Karp*	.25
361	Bill Pulsipher (Foil)	.25		457	Ritchie Moody	.10		553	Juan Guzman	.10
362	Tyler Green (Foil)	.15		458	Bret Boone	.10		554	*Bryan Rekar*	.25
363	Midre Cummings (Foil)	.25		459	Ben McDonald	.10		555	Kevin Appier	.10
364	Brian Barber (Foil)	.10		460	Kirby Puckett	.75		556	*Chris Schwab*	.25
365	Melvin Nieves (Foil)	.10		461	Gregg Olson	.10		557	Jay Buhner	.20
366	Salomon Torres (Foil)	.10		462	*Rich Aude*	.50		558	Andujar Cedeno	.10
367	Alex Ochoa (Foil)	.20		463	John Burkett	.10		559	*Ryan McGuire*	.60
368	Frank Rodriguez (Foil)	.15		464	Troy Neel	.10		560	Ricky Gutierrez	.10
369	Brian Anderson (Foil)	.25		465	Jimmy Key	.12		561	*Keith Kimsey*	.20
370	James Baldwin (Foil)	.35		466	Ozzie Timmons	.10		562	Tim Clark	.10
371	Manny Ramirez (Foil)	1.50		467	Eddie Murray	.30		563	Damion Easley	.10
372	Justin Thompson (Foil)	.15		468	*Mark Tranberg*	.15		564	*Clint Davis*	.15
373	Johnny Damon (Foil)	1.00		469	Alex Gonzalez	.25		565	Mike Moore	.10
374	Jeff D'Amico (Foil)	1.00		470	David Nied	.10		566	Orel Hershiser	.15
375	Rich Becker (Foil)	.15		471	Barry Larkin	.20		567	Jason Bere	.15
376	Derek Jeter (Foil)	3.00		472	*Brian Looney*	.25		568	Kevin McReynolds	.10
377	Steve Karsay (Foil)	.20		473	Shawn Estes	.30		569	*Leland Macon*	.20
378	Mac Suzuki (Foil)	.30		474	*A.J. Sager*	.15		570	*John Courtright*	.20
379	Benji Gil (Foil)	.10		475	Roger Clemens	1.00		571	Sid Fernandez	.10
380	Alex Gonzalez (Foil)	.25		476	Vince Moore	.10		572	Chad Roper	.10
381	Jason Bere (Foil)	.25		477	*Scott Karl*	.15		573	Terry Pendleton	.10
382	Brett Butler (Foil)	.25		478	Kurt Miller	.10		574	Danny Miceli	.10
383	Jeff Conine (Foil)	.15		479	Garret Anderson	.60		575	Joe Rosselli	.10
384	Darren Daulton (Foil)	.12		480	Allen Watson	.10		576	Mike Bordick	.10
385	Jeff Kent (Foil)	.12		481	*Jose Lima*	.20		577	Danny Tartabull	.10
386	Don Mattingly (Foil)	1.00		482	Rick Gorecki	.10		578	Jose Guzman	.10
387	Mike Piazza (Foil)	2.00		483	*Jimmy Hurst*	.50		579	Omar Vizquel	.10
388	Ryne Sandberg (Foil)	.60		484	Preston Wilson	.25		580	Tommy Greene	.10
389	Rich Amaral	.10		485	Will Clark	.35		581	Paul Spoljaric	.10
390	Craig Biggio	.25		486	*Mike Ferry*	.15		582	Walt Weiss	.10
391	*Jeff Suppan*	1.50		487	*Curtis Goodwin*	.40		583	*Oscar Jimenez*	.40
392	Andy Benes	.10		488	Mike Myers	.10		584	Rod Henderson	.10
393	Cal Eldred	.10		489	Chipper Jones	2.00		585	Derek Lowe	.10
394	Jeff Conine	.15		490	Jeff King	.10		586	*Richard Hidalgo*	5.00
395	Tim Salmon	.30		491	*Bill Van Landingham*	.75		587	*Shayne Bennett*	.15

588	*Tim Belk*	.40
589	Matt Mieske	.10
590	Nigel Wilson	.15
591	*Jeff Knox*	.15
592	Bernard Gilkey	.12
593	David Cone	.15
594	*Paul LoDuca*	.25
595	Scott Ruffcorn	.12
596	Chris Roberts	.10
597	*Oscar Munoz*	.25
598	*Scott Sullivan*	.40
599	*Matt Jarvis*	.15
600	Jose Canseco	.40
601	*Tony Graffanino*	.20
602	Don Slaught	.10
603	*Brett King*	.25
604	*Jose Herrera*	.60
605	Melido Perez	.10
606	*Mike Hubbard*	.15
607	Chad Ogea	.15
608	*Wayne Gomes*	.35
609	Roberto Alomar	.50
610	*Angel Echevarria*	.20
611	Jose Lind	.10
612	Darrin Fletcher	.10
613	Chris Bosio	.10
614	Darryl Kile	.10
615	Frank Rodriguez	.15
616	Phil Plantier	.10
617	Pat Listach	.10
618	Charlie Hough	.10
619	*Ryan Hancock*	.30
620	*Darrel Deak*	.25
621	Travis Fryman	.15
622	Brett Butler	.15
623	Lance Johnson	.10
624	Pete Smith	.10
625	James Hurst	.10
626	Roberto Kelly	.10
627	Mike Mussina	.50
628	Kevin Tapani	.10
629	John Smoltz	.15
630	Midre Cummings	.15
631	Salomon Torres	.10
632	Willie Adams	.10
633	Derek Jeter	3.00
634	Steve Trachsel	.25
635	Albie Lopez	.25
636	Jason Moler	.10
637	Carlos Delgado	.40
638	Roberto Mejia	.10
639	Darren Burton	.10
640	B.J. Wallace	.10
641	*Brad Clontz*	.15
642	*Billy Wagner*	1.00
643	Aaron Sele	.25
644	Cameron Cairncross	.10
645	Brian Harper	.10
(646)	Marc Valdes (no card number)	.15
647	Mark Ratekin	.10
648	*Terry Bradshaw*	.35
649	Justin Thompson	.15
650	*Mike Busch*	.25
651	*Joe Hall*	.15
652	Bobby Jones	.15
653	*Kelly Stinnett*	.25
654	*Rod Steph*	.20
655	*Jay Powell*	.35
(656)	*Keith Garagozzo* (no card number)	.15
657	Todd Dunn	.20
658	*Charles Peterson*	.25
659	Darren Lewis	.10
660	*John Wasdin*	.50
661	*Tate Seefried*	.60
662	*Hector Trinidad*	.40
663	*John Carter*	.50
664	Larry Mitchell	.10
665	*David Catlett*	.20
666	Dante Bichette	.30
667	Felix Jose	.10
668	Rondell White	.30
669	Tino Martinez	.45
670	Brian Hunter	.35
671	Jose Malave	.20
672	Archi Cianfrocco	.10
673	*Mike Matheny*	.15
674	Bret Barberie	.10
675	*Andrew Lorraine*	.60
676	Brian Jordan	.15
677	Tim Belcher	.10
678	*Antonio Osuna*	.20
679	Checklist I	.10
680	Checklist II	.10
681	Checklist III	.10
682	Checklist IV	.10

1994 Bowman Previews

Bowman Preview cards were randomly inserted into Stadium Club 1994 Baseball Series II at a rate of one every 24 packs. This 10-card set featured several proven major league stars, as well as minor league players. Card number 10, James Mouton, is designed as a special MVP foil card.

		MT
Complete Set (10):		75.00
Common Player:		4.50
1	Frank Thomas	25.00
2	Mike Piazza	15.00
3	Albert Belle	10.00
4	Javier Lopez	8.00
5	Cliff Floyd	4.50
6	Alex Gonzalez	4.50
7	Ricky Bottalico	4.50
8	Tony Clark	10.00
9	Mac Suzuki	4.50
10	James Mouton (Foil)	4.50

1994 Bowman's Best

The first ever set of Bowman's Best consisted of 90 Blue cards, 90 Red cards and 20 Mirror Images, featuring a Red veteran and a Blue prospect player matched by position on each card. This 200-card

set utilized Topps Finest technology and includes full-color photos front and back with a high-gloss finish. Bowman's Best was available in eight-card wax packs, with each pack containing seven cards and a Mirror Image card. There is also a 200-card parallel set officially titled "Special Effects," which uses Topps' refractor technology. Both the Red and Blue set are numbered 1-90, with the Mirror Image cards numbered 91-110.

		MT
Complete Set (200):		95.00
Common Player:		.50
Wax Box:		
Red Set		100.00
1	Paul Molitor	1.25
2	Eddie Murray	1.25
3	Ozzie Smith	2.00
4	Rickey Henderson	.75
5	Lee Smith	.60
6	Dave Winfield	.75
7	Roberto Alomar	2.50
8	Matt Williams	1.25
9	Mark Grace	.75
10	Lance Johnson	.50
11	Darren Daulton	.50
12	Tom Glavine	.75
13	Gary Sheffield	.75
14	Rod Beck	.50
15	Fred McGriff	1.00
16	Joe Carter	.60
17	Dante Bichette	1.00
18	Danny Tartabull	.50
19	Juan Gonzalez	5.00
20	Steve Avery	.60
21	John Wetteland	.50
22	Ben McDonald	.50
23	Jack McDowell	.50
24	Jose Canseco	1.50
25	Tim Salmon	1.00
26	Wilson Alvarez	.50
27	Gregg Jefferies	.60
28	John Burkett	.50
29	Greg Vaughn	.50
30	Robin Ventura	.60
31	Paul O'Neill	.65
32	Cecil Fielder	.60
33	Kevin Mitchell	.50
34	Jeff Conine	.50
35	Carlos Baerga	.50
36	Greg Maddux	6.00
37	Roger Clemens	3.50
38	Deion Sanders	1.50
39	Delino DeShields	.50
40	Ken Griffey, Jr.	10.00
41	Albert Belle	3.00
42	Wade Boggs	1.00
43	Andres Galarraga	.75
44	Aaron Sele	.50
45	Don Mattingly	4.00
46	David Cone	.50
47	Len Dykstra	.50
48	Brett Butler	.55
49	Bill Swift	.50
50	Bobby Bonilla	.60
51	Rafael Palmeiro	1.00
52	Moises Alou	.55
53	Jeff Bagwell	3.50
54	Mike Mussina	2.00
55	Frank Thomas	8.00
56	Jose Rijo	.50
57	Ruben Sierra	.50
58	Randy Myers	.50
59	Barry Bonds	3.00
60	Jimmy Key	.50
61	Travis Fryman	.60
62	John Olerud	.75
63	Dave Justice	.75
64	Ray Lankford	.50
65	Bob Tewksbury	.50
66	Chuck Carr	.50
67	Jay Buhner	.50
68	Kenny Lofton	3.00
69	Marquis Grissom	.75
70	Sammy Sosa	6.00
71	Cal Ripken, Jr.	8.00
72	Ellis Burks	.75
73	Jeff Montgomery	.50
74	Julio Franco	.50
75	Kirby Puckett	4.00

#	Player	Price
76	Larry Walker	1.50
77	Andy Van Slyke	.50
78	Tony Gwynn	4.00
79	Will Clark	1.50
80	Mo Vaughn	2.00
81	Mike Piazza	6.00
82	James Mouton	.90
83	Carlos Delgado	.90
84	Ryan Klesko	1.50
85	Javier Lopez	1.00
86	Raul Mondesi	1.50
87	Cliff Floyd	1.00
88	Manny Ramirez	3.00
89	Hector Carrasco	.50
90	Jeff Granger	.50

Blue Set

#	Player	Price
1	Chipper Jones	6.00
2	Derek Jeter	6.00
3	Bill Pulsipher	1.00
4	James Baldwin	1.25
5	*Brooks Kieschnick*	1.50
6	Justin Thompson	1.50
7	Midre Cummings	.50
8	Joey Hamilton	1.00
9	Calvin Reese	1.00
10	Brian Barber	.50
11	John Burke	.50
12	De Shawn Warren	.50
13	*Edgardo Alfonzo*	3.00
14	*Eddie Pearson*	.50
15	Jimmy Haynes	.50
16	Danny Bautista	.65
17	Roger Cedeno	1.00
18	Jon Lieber	.50
19	*Billy Wagner*	1.00
20	*Tate Seefried*	.75
21	Chad Mottola	1.00
22	Jose Malave	.50
23	*Terrell Wade*	.75
24	Shane Andrews	1.00
25	*Chan Ho Park*	6.00
26	*Kirk Presley*	1.50
27	Robbie Beckett	.50
28	Orlando Miller	.50
29	*Jorge Posada*	4.00
30	Frank Rodriguez	1.50
31	Brian Hunter	2.50
32	Billy Ashley	1.00
33	Rondell White	2.00
34	John Roper	.50
35	Marc Valdes	.50
36	Scott Ruffcorn	1.00
37	Rod Henderson	.50
38	Curt Goodwin	.50
39	Russ Davis	1.25
40	Rick Gorecki	.50
41	Johnny Damon	2.50
42	Roberto Petagine	.75
43	Chris Snopek	.50
44	Mark Acre	.50
45	Todd Hollandsworth	1.50
46	Shawn Green	2.00
47	John Carter	.50
48	Jim Pittsley	1.00
49	*John Wasdin*	1.00
50	D.J. Boston	.50
51	Tim Clark	.75
52	Alex Ochoa	1.50
53	Chad Roper	1.00
54	Mike Kelly	.50
55	*Brad Fullmer*	8.00
56	Carl Everett	.75
57	*Tim Belk*	.50
58	*Jimmy Hurst*	.50
59	*Mac Suzuki*	1.00
60	Michael Moore	.50
61	Alan Benes	4.00
62	*Tony Clark*	15.00
63	*Edgar Renteria*	5.00
64	Trey Beamon	.50
65	*LaTroy Hawkins*	2.00
66	*Wayne Gomes*	1.50
67	Ray McDavid	.50
68	John Dettmer	.50
69	Willie Greene	.75
70	Dave Stevens	.50
71	*Kevin Orie*	3.00
72	Chad Ogea	1.00
73	Ben Van Ryn	.75
74	Kym Ashworth	1.00
75	*Dmitri Young*	.75
76	Herb Perry	.50
77	Joey Eischen	1.00
78	*Arquimedez Pozo*	1.00
79	Ugueth Urbina	.75
80	Keith Williams	.50
81	*John Frascatore*	.50
82	Garey Ingram	.75
83	Aaron Small	.50
84	*Olmedo Saenz*	.50
85	Jesus Tavarez	.75
86	*Jose Silva*	1.00
87	*Gerald Witasick, Jr.*	.50
88	Jay Maldonado	.75
89	Keith Heberling	.75
90	*Rusty Greer*	6.00

Mirror Images

#	Players	Price
91	Frank Thomas, Kevin Young	6.00
92	Fred McGriff, Brooks Kieschnick	2.00
93	Matt Williams, Shane Andrews	1.50
94	Cal Ripken, Jr., Kevin Orie	5.00
95	Barry Larkin, Derek Jeter	3.00
96	Ken Griffey, Jr., Johnny Damon	7.50
97	Barry Bonds, Rondell White	2.50
98	Albert Belle, Jimmy Hurst	1.50
99	Raul Mondesi, *Ruben Rivera*	3.00
100	Roger Clemens, Scott Ruffcorn	2.00
101	Greg Maddux, John Wasdin	3.00
102	Tim Salmon, Chad Mottola	1.50
103	Carlos Baerga, Arquimedez Pozo	2.00
104	Mike Piazza, Buddy Hughes	3.00
105	Carlos Delgado, Melvin Nieves	1.50
106	Javier Lopez, Jorge Posada	2.00
107	Manny Ramirez, Jose Malave	2.50
108	Travis Fryman, Chipper Jones	3.00
109	Steve Avery, Bill Pulsipher	1.00
110	John Olerud, Shawn Green	1.50

1994 Bowman's Best Refractors

This 200-card parallel set, officially titled "Special Effects," uses Topps' refractor technology. The refractors were packed at the rate of three per wax box of Bowman's Best, but are very difficult to differentiate from the regular high-tech cards.

#	Player	MT
	Complete Set (200):	1200.
	Common Player:	
	Red Set	2.00
1	Paul Molitor	12.00
2	Eddie Murray	10.00
3	Ozzie Smith	20.00
4	Rickey Henderson	6.00
5	Lee Smith	2.00
6	Dave Winfield	6.00
7	Roberto Alomar	35.00
8	Matt Williams	15.00
9	Mark Grace	6.00
10	Lance Johnson	2.00
11	Darren Daulton	2.00
12	Tom Glavine	5.00
13	Gary Sheffield	3.00
14	Rod Beck	2.00
15	Fred McGriff	15.00
16	Joe Carter	8.00
17	Dante Bichette	12.00
18	Danny Tartabull	2.00
19	Juan Gonzalez	50.00
20	Steve Avery	4.00
21	John Wetteland	2.00
22	Ben McDonald	2.00
23	Jack McDowell	4.00
24	Jose Canseco	20.00
25	Tim Salmon	10.00
26	Wilson Alvarez	2.00
27	Gregg Jefferies	4.00
28	John Burkett	2.00
29	Greg Vaughn	2.00
30	Robin Ventura	4.00
31	Paul O'Neill	4.00
32	Cecil Fielder	5.00
33	Kevin Mitchell	2.00
34	Jeff Conine	2.00
35	Carlos Baerga	20.00
36	Greg Maddux	60.00
37	Roger Clemens	25.00
38	Deion Sanders	15.00
39	Delino DeShields	2.00
40	Ken Griffey, Jr.	100.00
41	Albert Belle	30.00
42	Wade Boggs	10.00
43	Andres Galarraga	4.00
44	Aaron Sele	4.00
45	Don Mattingly	45.00
46	David Cone	2.00
47	Len Dykstra	3.00
48	Brett Butler	2.00
49	Bill Swift	2.00
50	Bobby Bonilla	3.00
51	Rafael Palmeiro	5.00
52	Moises Alou	2.00
53	Jeff Bagwell	40.00
54	Mike Mussina	15.00
55	Frank Thomas	75.00
56	Jose Rijo	2.00
57	Ruben Sierra	4.00
58	Randy Myers	2.00
59	Barry Bonds	40.00
60	Jimmy Key	2.00
61	Travis Fryman	4.00
62	John Olerud	5.00
63	Dave Justice	12.00
64	Ray Lankford	2.00
65	Bob Tewksbury	2.00
66	Chuck Carr	2.00
67	Jay Buhner	4.00
68	Kenny Lofton	35.00
69	Marquis Grissom	3.00
70	Sammy Sosa	50.00
71	Cal Ripken, Jr.	90.00
72	Ellis Burks	2.00
73	Jeff Montgomery	2.00
74	Julio Franco	2.00
75	Kirby Puckett	40.00
76	Larry Walker	15.00
77	Andy Van Slyke	2.00
78	Tony Gwynn	25.00
79	Will Clark	15.00
80	Mo Vaughn	30.00
81	Mike Piazza	60.00
82	James Mouton	3.00
83	Carlos Delgado	8.00
84	Ryan Klesko	25.00
85	Javier Lopez	6.00
86	Raul Mondesi	22.00
87	Cliff Floyd	4.00
88	Manny Ramirez	40.00
89	Hector Carrasco	2.00
90	Jeff Granger	2.00

Blue Set

#	Player	Price
1	Chipper Jones	60.00
2	Derek Jeter	70.00
3	Bill Pulsipher	15.00
4	James Baldwin	5.00
5	Brooks Kieschnick	20.00
6	Justin Thompson	2.00
7	Midre Cummings	2.00
8	Joey Hamilton	12.00
9	Calvin Reese	5.00
10	Brian Barber	2.00
11	John Burke	2.00
12	De Shawn Warren	2.00
13	Edgardo Alfonzo	4.00
14	Eddie Pearson	2.00
15	Jimmy Haynes	2.00
16	Danny Bautista	3.00
17	Roger Cedeno	6.00
18	Jon Lieber	2.00
19	Billy Wagner	8.00
20	Tate Seefried	3.00
21	Chad Mottola	5.00
22	Jose Malave	2.00
23	Terrell Wade	4.00
24	Shane Andrews	5.00
25	Chan Ho Park	4.00
26	Kirk Presley	4.00
27	Robbie Beckett	2.00
28	Orlando Miller	2.00
29	Jorge Posada	10.00
30	Frank Rodriguez	5.00
31	Brian Hunter	20.00
32	Billy Ashley	7.50
33	Rondell White	10.00
34	John Roper	2.00
35	Marc Valdes	2.00
36	Scott Ruffcorn	5.00
37	Rod Henderson	2.00
38	Curt Goodwin	4.00
39	Russ Davis	5.00
40	Rick Gorecki	2.00

41	Johnny Damon	20.00
42	Roberto Petagine	2.00
43	Chris Snopek	5.00
44	Mark Acre	2.00
45	Todd Hollandsworth	7.50
46	Shawn Green	5.00
47	John Carter	2.00
48	Jim Pittsley	2.00
49	John Wasdin	8.00
50	D.J. Boston	2.00
51	Tim Clark	3.00
52	Alex Ochoa	5.00
53	Chad Roper	4.00
54	Mike Kelly	2.00
55	Brad Fullmer	15.00
56	Carl Everett	4.00
57	Tim Belk	2.00
58	Jimmy Hurst	2.00
59	Mac Suzuki	4.00
60	Michael Moore	2.00
61	Alan Benes	20.00
62	Tony Clark	70.00
63	Edgar Renteria	30.00
64	Trey Beamon	2.00
65	LaTroy Hawkins	8.00
66	Wayne Gomes	5.00
67	Ray McDavid	2.00
68	John Dettmer	2.00
69	Willie Greene	3.00
70	Dave Stevens	2.00
71	Kevin Orie	20.00
72	Chad Ogea	4.00
73	Ben Van Ryn	4.00
74	Kym Ashworth	4.00
75	Dmitri Young	4.00
76	Herb Perry	2.00
77	Joey Eischen	6.00
78	Arquimedez Pozo	4.00
79	Ugueth Urbina	2.00
80	Keith Williams	2.00
81	John Frascatore	2.00
82	Garey Ingram	2.00
83	Aaron Small	2.00
84	Olmedo Saenz	2.00
85	Jesus Tavarez	8.00
86	Jose Silva	5.00
87	Gerald Witasick, Jr.	2.00
88	Jay Maldonado	5.00
89	Keith Heberling	5.00
90	Rusty Greer	5.00
Mirror Images		
91	Frank Thomas, Kevin Young	30.00
92	Fred McGriff, Brooks Kieschnick	6.00
93	Matt Williams, Shane Andrews	5.00
94	Cal Ripken, Jr., Kevin Orie	30.00
95	Barry Larkin, Derek Jeter	12.00
96	Ken Griffey, Jr., Johnny Damon	35.00
97	Barry Bonds, Rondell White	8.00
98	Albert Belle, Jimmy Hurst	12.00
99	Raul Mondesi, Ruben Rivera	25.00
100	Roger Clemens, Scott Ruffcorn	10.00
101	Greg Maddux, John Wasdin	25.00
102	Tim Salmon, Chad Mottola	6.00
103	Carlos Baerga, Arquimedez Pozo	6.00
104	Mike Piazza, Buddy Hughes	15.00
105	Carlos Delgado, Melvin Nieves	6.00
106	Javier Lopez, Jorge Posada	15.00
107	Manny Ramirez, Jose Malave	12.00
108	Travis Fryman, Chipper Jones	15.00
109	Steve Avery, Bill Pulsipher	5.00
110	John Olerud, Shawn Green	4.00

Cards before 1981 are priced Near Mint (NM), Excellent (EX), and Very Good (VG).

Cards 1981 to present are priced Mint (MT), Near Mint (NM), and Excellent (EX).

1995 Bowman

Large numbers of rookie cards and a lengthy run of etched-foil cards distinguishes the 1995 Bowman set. The set's basic cards share a design with a large color photo flanked at left by a severely horizontally compressed mirror image in green, and at bottom by a similar version in brown. Most of the bottom image is covered by the player's last name printed in silver (cards #1-220, rookies) or gold (cards #275-439, veterans) foil. A color team logo is in the lower-left corner of all cards, and the Bowman logo is in red foil at top. In-between are the foil-etched subsets of "Minor League MVPs," "1st Impressions," and "Prime Prospects." Each of these cards, seeded one per regular pack and two per jumbo, has the player photo set against a background of textured color foil, with a prismatic silver border. Each of the foil cards can also be found in a gold-toned version, in a ratio of six silver to one gold. Backs of the rookies' cards have a portrait photo at right and a scouting report at left. Veterans' cards have either a scouting report for younger players, or a chart of stats versus each team played in 1994. Backs of all the foil cards have a scouting report.

		MT
Complete Set (439):		175.00
Common Player:		.10
Wax Box:		220.00
1	Billy Wagner	.10
2	Chris Widger	.10
3	Brent Bowers	.10
4	Bob Abreu	4.00
5	Lou Collier	.30
6	Juan Acevedo	.35
7	Jason Kelley	.20
8	Brian Sackinsky	.10
9	Scott Christman	.10
10	Damon Hollins	.15
11	Willis Otanez	.25
12	Jason Ryan	.20
13	Jason Giambi	.75
14	Andy Taulbee	.30
15	Mark Thompson	.10
16	Hugo Pivaral	.25
17	Brien Taylor	.10
18	Antonio Osuna	.10
19	Edgardo Alfonzo	.12
20	Carl Everett	.10
21	Matt Drews	.15
22	Bartolo Colon	8.00
23	Andruw Jones	20.00
24	Robert Person	.40

25	Derrek Lee	2.00
26	John Ambrose	.20
27	Eric Knowles	.30
28	Chris Roberts	.10
29	Don Wengert	.10
30	Marcus Jensen	.30
31	Brian Barber	.10
32	Kevin Brown	.10
33	Benji Gil	.10
34	Mike Hubbard	.10
35	Bart Evans	.35
36	Enrique Wilson	2.00
37	Brian Buchanan	.20
38	Ken Ray	.25
39	Micah Franklin	.40
40	Ricky Otero	.30
41	Jason Kendall	.15
42	Jimmy Hurst	.10
43	Jerry Wolak	.20
44	Jayson Peterson	.30
45	Allen Battle	.20
46	Scott Stahoviak	.10
47	Steve Schrenk	.30
48	Travis Miller	.20
49	Eddie Rios	.25
50	Mike Hampton	.10
51	Chad Frontera	.30
52	Tom Evans	.50
53	C.J. Nitkowski	.10
54	Clay Caruthers	.25
55	Shannon Stewart	.10
56	Jorge Posada	.10
57	Aaron Holbert	.10
58	Harry Berrios	.20
59	Steve Rodriguez	.10
60	Shane Andrews	.15
61	Will Cunnane	.25
62	Richard Hidalgo	1.50
63	Bill Selby	.20
64	Jay Cranford	.20
65	Jeff Suppan	.15
66	Curtis Goodwin	.10
67	John Thomson	.30
68	Justin Thompson	.10
69	Troy Percival	.10
70	Matt Wagner	.25
71	Terry Bradshaw	.10
72	Greg Hansell	.10
73	John Burke	.10
74	Jeff D'Amico	.10
75	Ernie Young	.10
76	Jason Bates	.10
77	Chris Stynes	.10
78	Cade Gaspar	.25
79	Melvin Nieves	.10
80	Rick Gorecki	.10
81	Felix Rodriguez	.20
82	Ryan Hancock	.10
83	Chris Carpenter	1.50
84	Ray McDavid	.10
85	Chris Wimmer	.10
86	Doug Glanville	.15
87	DeShawn Warren	.10
88	Damian Moss	1.50
89	Rafael Orellano	.20
90	Vladimir Guerrero	40.00
91	Raul Casanova	.75
92	Karim Garcia	4.00
93	Bryce Florie	.10
94	Kevin Orie	1.00
95	Ryan Nye	.25
96	Matt Sachse	.30
97	Ivan Arteaga	.25
98	Glenn Murray	.10
99	Stacy Hollins	.20
100	Jim Pittsley	.10
101	Craig Mattson	.30
102	Neifi Perez	.40
103	Keith Williams	.10
104	Roger Cedeno	.10
105	Tony Terry	.25
106	Jose Malave	.10
107	Joe Rosselli	.10
108	Kevin Jordan	.10
109	Sid Roberson	.20
110	Alan Embree	.10
111	Terrell Wade	.10
112	Bob Wolcott	.10
113	Carlos Perez	.25
114	Mike Bovee	.50
115	Tommy Davis	.30
116	Jeremey Kendall	.25
117	Rich Aude	.10
118	Rick Huisman	.10
119	Tim Belk	.10
120	Edgar Renteria	.75

121	*Calvin Maduro*	.25
122	Jerry Martin	.35
123	*Ramon Fermin*	.20
124	*Kimera Bartee*	.35
125	Mark Farris	.10
126	Frank Rodriguez	.10
127	*Bobby Higginson*	5.00
128	Bret Wagner	.10
129	*Edwin Diaz*	.75
130	Jimmy Haynes	.10
131	Chris Weinke	.25
132	*Damian Jackson*	1.50
133	Felix Martinez	.10
134	*Edwin Hurtado*	.40
135	*Matt Raleigh*	.30
136	Paul Wilson	.40
137	Ron Villone	.10
138	*Eric Stuckenschneider*	.20
139	Tate Seefried	.10
140	*Rey Ordonez*	3.00
141	Eddie Pearson	.10
142	Kevin Gallaher	.10
143	Torii Hunter	.20
144	Daron Kirkreit	.10
145	Craig Wilson	.10
146	Ugueth Urbina	.10
147	Chris Snopek	.10
148	Kym Ashworth	.10
149	Wayne Gomes	.10
150	Mark Loretta	.10
151	*Ramon Morel*	.25
152	Trot Nixon	.10
153	Desi Relaford	.10
154	Scott Sullivan	.10
155	Marc Barcelo	.10
156	Willie Adams	.10
157	*Derrick Gibson*	8.00
158	*Brian Meadows*	.20
159	Julian Tavarez	.10
160	Bryan Rekar	.10
161	Steve Gibralter	.10
162	Esteban Loaiza	.10
163	John Wasdin	.10
164	Kirk Presley	.10
165	Mariano Rivera	.45
166	Andy Larkin	.10
167	*Sean Whiteside*	.20
168	*Matt Apana*	.25
169	*Shawn Senior*	.15
170	Scott Gentile	.10
171	Quilvio Veras	.10
172	*Elieser Marrero*	3.00
173	*Mendy Lopez*	.20
174	Homer Bush	.10
175	*Brian Stephenson*	.25
176	Jon Nunnally	.10
177	Jose Herrera	.10
178	*Corey Avrard*	.25
179	David Bell	.10
180	Jason Isringhausen	1.25
181	Jamey Wright	.10
182	*Lonell Roberts*	.15
183	Marty Cordova	.15
185	Amaury Telemaco	.10
185	John Mabry	.15
186	*Andrew Vessel*	.20
187	*Jim Cole*	.15
188	Marquis Riley	.10
189	Todd Dunn	.10
190	John Carter	.10
191	*Donnie Sadler*	1.00
192	Mike Bell	.10
193	*Chris Cumberland*	.20
194	Jason Schmidt	.20
195	Matt Brunson	.15
196	James Baldwin	.10
197	*Bill Simas*	.20
198	Gus Gandarillas	.10
199	Mac Suzuki	.15
200	*Rick Holifield*	.25
201	*Fernando Lunar*	.20
202	Kevin Jarvis	.10
203	*Everett Stull*	.20
204	Steve Wojciechowski	.10
205	Shawn Estes	.15
206	Jermaine Dye	.30
207	Marc Kroon	.12
208	*Peter Munro*	.30
209	Pat Watkins	.10
210	Matt Smith	.10
211	Joe Vitiello	.10
212	Gerald Witasick, Jr.	.10
213	*Freddy Garcia*	.25
214	*Glenn Dishman*	.20
215	*Jay Canizaro*	.20
216	Angel Martinez	.10

217	*Yamil Benitez*	.25
218	*Fausto Macey*	.20
219	Eric Owens	.10
220	Checklist	.10
221	Dwayne Hosey (Minor League MVPs)	.20
222	*Brad Woodall* (Minor League MVPs)	.25
223	Billy Ashley (Minor League MVPs)	.10
224	*Mark Grudzielanek* (Minor League MVPs)	1.25
• 225	*Mark Johnson* (Minor League MVPs)	.40
226	*Tim Unroe* (Minor League MVPs)	.30
227	Todd Greene (Minor League MVPs)	3.00
228	Larry Sutton (Minor League MVPs)	.10
229	Derek Jeter (Minor League MVPs)	4.00
230	*Sal Fasano* (Minor League MVPs)	.10
231	Ruben Rivera (Minor League MVPs)	2.00
232	*Chris Truby* (Minor League MVPs)	.15
233	John Donati (Minor League MVPs)	.10
234	*Decomba Conner* (Minor League MVPs)	.25
235	*Sergio Nunez* (Minor League MVPs)	.20
236	*Ray Brown* (Minor League MVPs)	.75
237	Juan Melo (Minor League MVPs)	1.00
238	Hideo Nomo (First Impressions)	12.00
239	*Jaime Bluma* (First Impressions)	.20
240	*Jay Payton* (First Impressions)	2.00
241	Paul Konerko (First Impressions)	10.00
242	Scott Elarton (First Impressions)	1.50
243	*Jeff Abbott* (First Impressions)	1.50
244	*Jim Brower* (First Impressions)	.30
245	*Geoff Blum* (First Impressions)	.30
246	Aaron Boone (First Impressions)	1.00
247	J.R. Phillips (Top Prospects)	.15
248	Alex Ochoa (Top Prospects)	.50
249	Nomar Garciaparra (Top Prospects)	25.00
250	Garret Anderson (Top Prospects)	.40
251	Ray Durham (Top Prospects)	.30
252	Paul Shuey (Top Prospects)	.10
253	Tony Clark (Top Prospects)	2.00
254	Johnny Damon (Top Prospects)	.65
255	Duane Singleton (Top Prospects)	.10
256	LaTroy Hawkins (Top Prospects)	.10
257	Andy Pettitte (Top Prospects)	1.50
258	Ben Grieve (Top Prospects)	25.00
259	Marc Newfield (Top Prospects)	.10
260	Terrell Lowery (Top Prospects)	.10
261	Shawn Green (Top Prospects)	.10
262	Chipper Jones (Top Prospects)	2.00
263	Brooks Kieschnick (Top Prospects)	.50
264	Calvin Reese (Top Prospects)	.10
265	Doug Million (Top Prospects)	.10
266	Marc Valdes (Top Prospects)	.10
267	Brian Hunter (Top Prospects)	.35
268	Todd Hollandsworth (Top Prospects)	.75

269	Rod Henderson (Top Prospects)	.20
270	Bill Pulsipher (Top Prospects)	.20
271	*Scott Rolen* (Top Prospects)	25.00
272	Trey Beamon (Top Prospects)	.10
273	Alan Benes (Top Prospects)	.40
274	Dustin Hermanson (Top Prospects)	.25
275	Ricky Bottalico	.10
276	Albert Belle	1.00
277	Deion Sanders	.40
278	Matt Williams	.50
279	Jeff Bagwell	1.50
280	Kirby Puckett	1.50
281	Dave Hollins	.10
282	Don Mattingly	1.50
283	Joey Hamilton	.25
284	Bobby Bonilla	.15
285	Moises Alou	.12
286	Tom Glavine	.15
287	Brett Butler	.15
288	Chris Hoiles	.10
289	Kenny Rogers	.10
290	Larry Walker	.60
291	Tim Raines	.12
292	Kevin Appier	.10
293	Roger Clemens	2.00
294a	Chuck Carr	.10
294b	Cliff Floyd (Wrong number, should be #394)	.20
295	Randy Myers	.10
296	Dave Nilsson	.10
297	Joe Carter	.20
298	Chuck Finley	.10
299	Ray Lankford	.15
300	Roberto Kelly	.10
301	Jon Lieber	.10
302	Travis Fryman	.10
303	Mark McGwire	5.00
304	Tony Gwynn	2.50
305	Kenny Lofton	1.25
306	Mark Whiten	.10
307	Doug Drabek	.10
308	Terry Steinbach	.10
309	Ryan Klesko	1.25
310	Mike Piazza	3.00
311	Ben McDonald	.10
312	Reggie Sanders	.15
313	Alex Fernandez	.10
314	Aaron Sele	.10
315	Gregg Jefferies	.15
316	Rickey Henderson	.25
317	Brian Anderson	.10
318	Jose Valentin	.10
319	Rod Beck	.10
320	Marquis Grissom	.15
321	Ken Griffey Jr.	4.00
322	Bret Saberhagen	.10
323	Juan Gonzalez	2.00
324	Paul Molitor	.40
325	Gary Sheffield	.60
326	Darren Daulton	.10
327	Bill Swift	.10
328	Brian McRae	.10
329	Robin Ventura	.12
330	Lee Smith	.10
331	Fred McGriff	.50
332	Delino DeShields	.10
333	Edgar Martinez	.15
334	Mike Mussina	1.00
335	Orlando Merced	.10
336	Carlos Baerga	.20
337	Wil Cordero	.10
338	Tom Pagnozzi	.10
339	Pat Hentgen	.10
340	Chad Curtis	.10
341	Darren Lewis	.10
342	Jeff Kent	.10
343	Bip Roberts	.10
344	Ivan Rodriguez	.75
345	Jeff Montgomery	.10
346	Hal Morris	.10
347	Danny Tartabull	.10
348	Raul Mondesi	.60
349	Ken Hill	.10
350	Pedro Martinez	.50
351	Frank Thomas	3.00
352	Manny Ramirez	1.25
353	Tim Salmon	.30
354	William Van Landingham	.10
355	Andres Galarraga	.20
356	Paul O'Neill	.15
357	Brady Anderson	.20
358	Ramon Martinez	.12

359	John Olerud	.15
360	Ruben Sierra	.10
361	Cal Eldred	.10
362	Jay Buhner	.15
363	Jay Bell	.10
364	Wally Joyner	.12
365	Chuck Knoblauch	.15
366	Len Dykstra	.10
367	John Wetteland	.10
368	Roberto Alomar	.75
369	Craig Biggio	.25
370	Ozzie Smith	.60
371	Terry Pendleton	.10
372	Sammy Sosa	3.00
373	Carlos Garcia	.10
374	Jose Rijo	.10
375	Chris Gomez	.10
376	Barry Bonds	1.00
377	Steve Avery	.10
378	Rick Wilkins	.10
379	Pete Harnisch	.10
380	Dean Palmer	.10
381	Bob Hamelin	.10
382	Jason Bere	.10
383	Jimmy Key	.10
384	Dante Bichette	.35
385	Rafael Palmeiro	.25
386	David Justice	.25
387	Chili Davis	.10
388	Mike Greenwell	.10
389	Todd Zeile	.10
390	Jeff Conine	.10
391	Rick Aguilera	.10
392	Eddie Murray	.40
393	Mike Stanley	.10
394	(Not issued - see #294)	
395	Randy Johnson	.50
396	David Nied	.10
397	Devon White	.10
398	Royce Clayton	.10
399	Andy Benes	.10
400	John Hudek	.10
401	Bobby Jones	.10
402	Eric Karros	.15
403	Will Clark	.30
404	Mark Langston	.10
405	Kevin Brown	.10
406	Greg Maddux	2.50
407	David Cone	.10
408	Wade Boggs	.25
409	Steve Trachsel	.10
410	Greg Vaughn	.10
411	Mo Vaughn	1.00
412	Wilson Alvarez	.10
413	Cal Ripken Jr.	4.00
414	Rico Brogna	.10
415	Barry Larkin	.30
416	Cecil Fielder	.20
417	Jose Canseco	.40
418	Jack McDowell	.10
419	Mike Lieberthal	.10
420	Andrew Lorraine	.10
421	Rich Becker	.10
422	Tony Phillips	.12
423	Scott Ruffcorn	.10
424	Jeff Granger	.10
425	Greg Pirkl	.10
426	Dennis Eckersley	.12
427	Jose Lima	.10
428	Russ Davis	.10
429	Armando Benitez	.10
430	Alex Gonzalez	.10
431	Carlos Delgado	.30
432	Chan Ho Park	.15
433	Mickey Tettleton	.10
434	Dave Winfield	.15
435	John Burkett	.10
436	Orlando Miller	.10
437	Rondell White	.25
438	Jose Oliva	.10
439	Checklist	.10

Modern cards have little collector value in conditions lower than Mint. Figure NM cards at 75% of values shown; EX cards at 40%.

Values shown reflect the market as of January, 1999. On-field performances of current players in the 1999 baseball season are not factored in.

1995 Bowman Gold

The only chase cards in the '95 Bowman set are gold versions of the foil-etched "Minor League MVPs," "1st Impressions" and "Prime Prospects." The gold cards are found in every 6th (regular) or 12th (jumbo) pack, on average, in place of the silver versions.

		MT
Complete Set (54):		150.00
Common Player:		1.50
221	Dwayne Hosey (Minor League MVPs)	1.50
222	Brad Woodall (Minor League MVPs)	2.50
223	Billy Ashley (Minor League MVPs)	1.50
224	Mark Grudzielanek (Minor League MVPs)	4.00
225	Mark Johnson (Minor League MVPs)	1.50
226	Tim Unroe (Minor League MVPs)	1.50
227	Todd Greene (Minor League MVPs)	4.00
228	Larry Sutton (Minor League MVPs)	1.50
229	Derek Jeter (Minor League MVPs)	10.00
230	Sal Fasano (Minor League MVPs)	1.50
231	Ruben Rivera (Minor League MVPs)	4.00
232	Chris Truby (Minor League MVPs)	1.50
233	John Donati (Minor League MVPs)	1.50
234	Decomba Conner (Minor League MVPs)	1.50
235	Sergio Nunez (Minor League MVPs)	1.50
236	Ray Brown (Minor League MVPs)	1.50
237	Juan Melo (Minor League MVPs)	2.00
238	Hideo Nomo (First Impressions)	10.00
239	Jamie Bluma (First Impressions)	1.50
240	Jay Payton (First Impressions)	2.00
241	Paul Konerko (First Impressions)	15.00
242	Scott Elarton (First Impressions)	1.50
243	Jeff Abbott (First Impressions)	1.50
244	Jim Brower (First Impressions)	1.50
245	Geoff Blum (First Impressions)	1.50
246	Aaron Boone (First Impressions)	2.50
247	J.R. Phillips (Top Prospects)	1.50
248	Alex Ochoa (Top Prospects)	2.00
249	Nomar Garciaparra (Top Prospects)	30.00
250	Garret Anderson (Top Prospects)	3.00
251	Ray Durham (Top Prospects)	1.50
252	Paul Shuey (Top Prospects)	1.50
253	Tony Clark (Top Prospects)	5.00
254	Johnny Damon (Top Prospects)	1.50
255	Duane Singleton (Top Prospects)	1.50
256	LaTroy Hawkins (Top Prospects)	1.50
257	Andy Pettitte (Top Prospects)	6.00
258	Ben Grieve (Top Prospects)	30.00
259	Marc Newfield (Top Prospects)	1.50
260	Terrell Lowery (Top Prospects)	1.50
261	Shawn Green (Top Prospects)	1.50
262	Chipper Jones (Top Prospects)	10.00
263	Brooks Kieschnick (Top Prospects)	2.00
264	Calvin Reese (Top Prospects)	1.50
265	Doug Million (Top Prospects)	1.50
266	Marc Valdes (Top Prospects)	1.50
267	Brian Hunter (Top Prospects)	2.00
268	Todd Hollandsworth (Top Prospects)	3.00
269	Rod Henderson (Top Prospects)	1.50
270	Bill Pulsipher (Top Prospects)	1.50
271	Scott Rolen (Top Prospects)	30.00
272	Trey Beamon (Top Prospects)	1.50
273	Alan Benes (Top Prospects)	4.00
274	Dustin Hermanson (Top Prospects)	3.00

1995 Bowman's Best

Actually made up of three sub-sets, all cards feature a player photo set against a silver foil background. The 90 veterans' cards have a broad red-foil stripe in the background beneath the team logo; the 90 rookies' cards have a similar stripe in tones of blue. All of those cards are printed in Topps' Finest technology. The 15 Mirror Image cards are in horizontal format, printed more conventionally on metallic foil, and have a rookie and veteran sharing the card. Backs of each card continue the color theme, have '94 and career stats and a highlight or two. Standard packaging was seven-card foil packs with inserts consisting of higher-tech parallel sets of the regular issue.

		MT
Complete Set (195):		225.00
Common Player:		.25
Wax Box:		250.00
Complete Set Red (90):		60.00
1	Randy Johnson	1.00
2	Joe Carter	.50
3	Chili Davis	.25
4	Moises Alou	.25
5	Gary Sheffield	.50
6	Kevin Appier	.25
7	Denny Neagle	.25
8	Ruben Sierra	.25
9	Darren Daulton	.25
10	Cal Ripken Jr.	6.00
11	Bobby Bonilla	.25
12	Manny Ramirez	1.50
13	Barry Bonds	2.00
14	Eric Karros	.25
15	Greg Maddux	4.50
16	Jeff Bagwell	2.50
17	Paul Molitor	.50
18	Ray Lankford	.25
19	Mark Grace	.50
20	Kenny Lofton	2.00
21	Tony Gwynn	2.00
22	Will Clark	.50
23	Roger Clemens	3.00
24	Dante Bichette	.75
25	Barry Larkin	.60
26	Wade Boggs	.50
27	Kirby Puckett	2.50
28	Cecil Fielder	.50
29	Jose Canseco	.75
30	Juan Gonzalez	3.00
31	David Cone	.40
32	Craig Biggio	.30
33	Tim Salmon	.75
34	David Justice	.50
35	Sammy Sosa	4.00
36	Mike Piazza	4.00
37	Carlos Baerga	.40
38	Jeff Conine	.25
39	Rafael Palmeiro	.50
40	Bret Saberhagen	.25
41	Len Dykstra	.25
42	Mo Vaughn	2.00
43	Wally Joyner	.25
44	Chuck Knoblauch	.25
45	Robin Ventura	.25
46	Don Mattingly	3.00
47	Dave Hollins	.25
48	Andy Benes	.25
49	Ken Griffey Jr.	8.00
50	Albert Belle	2.00
51	Matt Williams	.50
52	Rondell White	.40
53	Raul Mondesi	.50
54	Brian Jordan	.25
55	Greg Vaughn	.25
56	Fred McGriff	.75
57	Roberto Alomar	2.00
58	Dennis Eckersley	.25
59	Lee Smith	.25
60	Eddie Murray	.75
61	Kenny Rogers	.25
62	Ron Gant	.35
63	Larry Walker	1.00
64	Chad Curtis	.25
65	Frank Thomas	6.00
66	Paul O'Neill	.25
67	Kevin Seitzer	.25
68	Marquis Grissom	.25
69	Mark McGwire	7.00
70	Travis Fryman	.25
71	Andres Galarraga	.40
72	Carlos Perez	.40
73	Tyler Green	.25
74	Marty Cordova	.40
75	Shawn Green	.25
76	Vaughn Eshelman	.25
77	John Mabry	.25
78	Jason Bates	.25
79	Jon Nunnally	.25
80	Ray Durham	.40
81	Edgardo Alfonzo	.25

82	Esteban Loaiza	.25
83	Hideo Nomo	15.00
84	Orlando Miller	.25
85	Alex Gonzalez	.25
86	Mark Grudzielanek	1.25
87	Julian Tavarez	.25
88	Benji Gil	.25
89	Quilvio Veras	.25
90	Ricky Bottalico	.25
Complete Set Blue (90):		150.00
1	Derek Jeter	5.00
2	Vladimir Guerrero	45.00
3	Bob Abreu	5.00
4	Chan Ho Park	.40
5	Paul Wilson	1.00
6	Chad Ogea	.40
7	Andruw Jones	25.00
8	Brian Barber	.25
9	Andy Larkin	.25
10	Richie Sexson	15.00
11	Everett Stull	.25
12	Brooks Kieschnick	1.00
13	Matt Murray	.25
14	John Wasdin	.25
15	Shannon Stewart	.75
16	Luis Ortiz	.25
17	Marc Kroon	.40
18	Todd Greene	3.00
19	Juan Acevedo	.25
20	Tony Clark	4.00
21	Jermaine Dye	.75
22	Derrek Lee	3.00
23	Pat Watkins	.25
24	Calvin Reese	.25
25	Ben Grieve	25.00
26	Julio Santana	.25
27	Felix Rodriguez	.25
28	Paul Konerko	10.00
29	Nomar Garciaparra	30.00
30	Pat Ahearne	.25
31	Jason Schmidt	1.50
32	Billy Wagner	1.00
33	Rey Ordonez	3.00
34	Curtis Goodwin	.25
35	Sergio Nunez	1.00
36	Tim Belk	.25
37	Scott Elarton	1.00
38	Jason Isringhausen	1.50
39	Trot Nixon	1.00
40	Sid Roberson	.25
41	Ron Villone	.75
42	Ruben Rivera	1.50
43	Rick Huisman	.25
44	Todd Hollandsworth	.75
45	Johnny Damon	.50
46	Garret Anderson	.50
47	Jeff D'Amico	.25
48	Dustin Hermanson	.25
49	Juan Encarnacion	8.00
50	Andy Pettitte	4.00
51	Chris Stynes	.25
52	Troy Percival	.25
53	LaTroy Hawkins	.50
54	Roger Cedeno	.50
55	Alan Benes	1.00
56	Karim Garcia	6.00
57	Andrew Lorraine	.25
58	Gary Rath	.50
59	Bret Wagner	.25
60	Jeff Suppan	.25
61	Bill Pulsipher	.50
62	Jay Payton	2.00
63	Alex Ochoa	.50
64	Ugueth Urbina	.50
65	Armando Benitez	.25
66	George Arias	.25
67	Raul Casanova	1.00
68	Matt Drews	.50
69	Jimmy Haynes	.25
70	Jimmy Hurst	.25
71	C.J. Nitkowski	.25
72	Tommy Davis	.50
73	Bartolo Colon	10.00
74	Chris Carpenter	3.00
75	Trey Beamon	.25
76	Bryan Rekar	.50
77	James Baldwin	.25
78	Marc Valdes	.25
79	Tom Fordham	.75
80	Marc Newfield	.25
81	Angel Martinez	.25
82	Brian Hunter	.25
83	Jose Herrera	.25
84	Glenn Dishman	.50
85	Jacob Cruz	5.00
86	Paul Shuey	.25

87	Scott Rolen	30.00
88	Doug Million	.25
89	Desi Relaford	.25
90	Michael Tucker	.25
Common Mirror Image (15):		.50
1	Ben Davis, Ivan Rodriguez	2.00
2	Mark Redman, Manny Ramirez	1.50
3	Reggie Taylor, Deion Sanders	1.50
4	Ryan Jaroncyk, Shawn Green	.50
5	Juan LeBron, Juan Gonzalez	1.00
6	Toby McKnight, Craig Biggio	.50
7	Michael Barrett, Travis Fryman	.50
8	Corey Jenkins, Mo Vaughn	1.00
9	Ruben Rivera, Frank Thomas	4.00
10	Curtis Goodwin, Kenny Lofton	2.00
11	Brian Hunter, Tony Gwynn	1.00
12	Todd Greene, Ken Griffey Jr.	5.00
13	Karim Garcia, Matt Williams	1.75
14	Billy Wagner, Randy Johnson	1.00
15	Pat Watkins, Jeff Bagwell	1.50

1995 Bowman's Best Refractors

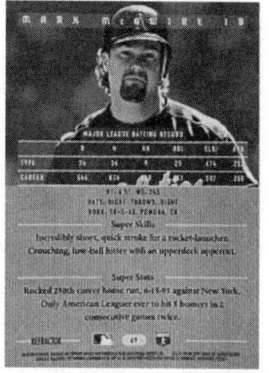

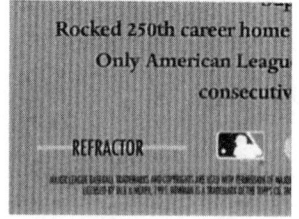

The large volume of silver foil in the background of the red and blue subsets in '95 Best make the Refractor technology much easier to see than in best issues. The chase cards, found one per six packs on average, also have a small "RE-FRACTOR" printed near the lower-left corner on back. The 15-card Mirror Image subset was not paralleled in Refractor technology, but in a process Topps calls "diffraction-foil" which creates a strong vertical-stripe rainbow effect in the background.

		MT
Complete Set (195):		2400.
Common Refractors:		3.00
Complete Set Red Refractors (90):		1000.
1	Randy Johnson	12.00
2	Joe Carter	6.00
3	Chili Davis	3.00
4	Moises Alou	5.00
5	Gary Sheffield	12.00
6	Kevin Appier	3.00
7	Denny Neagle	3.00
8	Ruben Sierra	3.00
9	Darren Daulton	3.00
10	Cal Ripken Jr.	60.00
11	Bobby Bonilla	3.00
12	Manny Ramirez	15.00
13	Barry Bonds	20.00
14	Eric Karros	3.00
15	Greg Maddux	50.00
16	Jeff Bagwell	30.00
17	Paul Molitor	15.00
18	Ray Lankford	3.00
19	Mark Grace	8.00
20	Kenny Lofton	20.00
21	Tony Gwynn	40.00
22	Will Clark	8.00
23	Roger Clemens	30.00
24	Dante Bichette	10.00
25	Barry Larkin	10.00
26	Wade Boggs	5.00
27	Kirby Puckett	30.00
28	Cecil Fielder	5.00
29	Jose Canseco	8.00
30	Juan Gonzalez	40.00
31	David Cone	5.00
32	Craig Biggio	5.00
33	Tim Salmon	8.00
34	David Justice	5.00
35	Sammy Sosa	50.00
36	Mike Piazza	50.00
37	Carlos Baerga	3.00
38	Jeff Conine	3.00
39	Rafael Palmeiro	8.00
40	Bret Saberhagen	3.00
41	Len Dykstra	3.00
42	Mo Vaughn	20.00
43	Wally Joyner	3.00
44	Chuck Knoblauch	8.00
45	Robin Ventura	3.00
46	Don Mattingly	30.00
47	Dave Hollins	3.00
48	Andy Benes	3.00
49	Ken Griffey Jr.	80.00
50	Albert Belle	20.00
51	Matt Williams	10.00
52	Rondell White	5.00
53	Raul Mondesi	8.00
54	Brian Jordan	3.00
55	Greg Vaughn	3.00
56	Fred McGriff	8.00
57	Roberto Alomar	15.00
58	Dennis Eckersley	3.00
59	Lee Smith	3.00
60	Eddie Murray	15.00
61	Kenny Rogers	3.00
62	Ron Gant	4.00
63	Larry Walker	15.00
64	Chad Curtis	3.00
65	Frank Thomas	60.00
66	Paul O'Neill	6.00
67	Kevin Seitzer	3.00
68	Marquis Grissom	3.00
69	Mark McGwire	90.00
70	Travis Fryman	3.00
71	Andres Galarraga	8.00
72a	Carlos Perez	5.00
72b	Carlos Perez (no "Refractor" on back)	5.00
73	Tyler Green	3.00
74	Marty Cordova	5.00
75	Shawn Green	3.00
76	Vaughn Eshelman	3.00
77	John Mabry	3.00
78	Jason Bates	3.00
79	Jon Nunnally	3.00
80	Ray Durham	3.00
81	Edgardo Alfonzo	3.00
82	Esteban Loaiza	3.00
83	Hideo Nomo	75.00
84a	Orlando Miller	3.00
84b	Orlando Miller (no "Refractor" on back)	3.00
85	Alex Gonzalez	3.00
86	Mark Grudzielanek	6.00
87	Julian Tavarez	3.00
88	Benji Gil	3.00
89	Quilvio Veras	3.00
90	Ricky Bottalico	3.00
Complete Set Blue Refractors (90):		1400.
1	Derek Jeter	50.00
2	Vladimir Guerrero	140.00
3	Bob Abreu	30.00
4	Chan Ho Park	5.00
5	Paul Wilson	20.00
6	Chad Ogea	5.00
7	Andruw Jones	100.00
8	Brian Barber	3.00
9	Andy Larkin	3.00
10	Richie Sexson	40.00
11	Everett Stull	3.00
12	Brooks Kieschnick	6.00
13	Matt Murray	3.00
14	John Wasdin	3.00
15	Shannon Stewart	3.00
16	Luis Ortiz	3.00
17	Marc Kroon	3.00
18	Todd Greene	8.00
19	Juan Acevedo	3.00
20	Tony Clark	30.00
21	Jermaine Dye	6.00
22	Derrek Lee	30.00
23	Pat Watkins	3.00
24	Calvin Reese	3.00
25	Ben Grieve	100.00
26	Julio Santana	3.00
27	Felix Rodriguez	3.00
28	Paul Konerko	40.00
29	Nomar Garciaparra	120.00
30	Pat Ahearne	3.00
31	Jason Schmidt	6.00
32	Billy Wagner	5.00
33	Rey Ordonez	15.00
34	Curtis Goodwin	3.00
35	Sergio Nunez	3.00
36	Tim Belk	3.00
37	Scott Elarton	3.00
38	Jason Isringhausen	6.00
39	Trot Nixon	4.00
40	Sid Roberson	3.00
41	Ron Villone	3.00
42	Ruben Rivera	20.00
43	Rick Huisman	3.00
44	Todd Hollandsworth	6.00
45	Johnny Damon	6.00
46	Garret Anderson	6.00
47	Jeff D'Amico	3.00
48	Dustin Hermanson	3.00
49	Juan Encarnacion	50.00
50	Andy Pettitte	30.00
51	Chris Stynes	3.00
52	Troy Percival	3.00
53	LaTroy Hawkins	3.00
54	Roger Cedeno	8.00
55	Alan Benes	6.00
56	Karim Garcia	25.00
57	Andrew Lorraine	3.00
58	Gary Rath	3.00
59	Bret Wagner	3.00
60	Jeff Suppan	3.00
61	Bill Pulsipher	10.00
62	Jay Payton	15.00
63	Alex Ochoa	8.00
64	Ugueth Urbina	3.00
65	Armando Benitez	3.00
66	George Arias	3.00
67	Raul Casanova	5.00
68	Matt Drews	3.00
69	Jimmy Haynes	3.00
70	Jimmy Hurst	3.00
71	C.J. Nitkowski	3.00
72	Tommy Davis	3.00
73	Bartolo Colon	50.00
74	Chris Carpenter	10.00
75	Trey Beamon	3.00
76	Bryan Rekar	3.00
77	James Baldwin	3.00
78	Marc Valdes	3.00
79	Tom Fordham	3.00
80	Marc Newfield	3.00
81	Angel Martinez	3.00
82	Brian Hunter	3.00
83	Jose Herrera	3.00
84	Glenn Dishman	3.00
85	Jacob Cruz	25.00
86	Paul Shuey	3.00
87	Scott Rolen	120.00
88	Desi Relaford	3.00
89	Michael Tucker	5.00
Common Mirror Image Foil:		3.00
1	Ben Davis, Ivan Rodriguez	10.00
2	Mark Redman, Manny Ramirez	10.00
3	Reggie Taylor, Deion Sanders	7.50
4	Ryan Jaroncyk, Shawn Green	3.00
5	Juan LeBron, Juan Gonzalez	6.00
6	Toby McKnight, Craig Biggio	4.00
7	Michael Barrett, Travis Fryman	3.00
8	Corey Jenkins, Mo Vaughn	8.00
9	Ruben Rivera, Frank Thomas	20.00
10	Curtis Goodwin, Kenny Lofton	10.00
11	Brian Hunter, Tony Gwynn	6.00
12	Todd Greene, Ken Griffey Jr.	25.00
13	Karim Garcia, Matt Williams	8.00
14	Billy Wagner, Randy Johnson	10.00
15	Pat Watkins, Jeff Bagwell	9.00

1995 Bowman's Best Refractors - Jumbo

These super-size versions of Bowman's Best Refractors were produced exclusively for inclusion as a one-per-box insert in retail boxes of the product distributed by ANCO to large retail chains. The 4-1/4" x 5-3/4" cards are identical in all ways except size to the regular refractors. The jumbo inserts were not produced in equal quantities, with the most popular players being printed in greater numbers.

		MT
Complete Set (10):		225.00
Common Player:		10.00
10	Cal Ripken Jr.	30.00
15	Greg Maddux	20.00
21	Tony Gwynn	20.00
35	Sammy Sosa	20.00
36	Mike Piazza	25.00
42	Mo Vaughn	10.00
49	Ken Griffey Jr.	40.00
50	Albert Belle	15.00
65	Frank Thomas	25.00
83	Hideo Nomo	20.00

1996 Bowman

As part of a Bowman Guaranteed Value Program, Topps stated it would pay $100 for this set in 1999, if collectors mail in a Guaranteed Certificate Request form (one per three packs), a $5 fee and the complete set in numerical order.

For each set which is sent in, Topps guaranteed it would send the collector $100 (only one per person). Every set which is redeemed would be destroyed. The 385-card set has 110 veteran stars and 275 prospects; the backs of the prospects' cards provide a detailed scouting report on the player pictured. In addition, a gold foil stamped logo (1st Bowman Card) will be included on the card front for those who are making their first appearance in a Bowman set (156 in all). Insert sets include Bowman's Best Previews, Bowman's Best Refractors, Bowman's Best Atomic Refractors, a 1952 Mickey Mantle Bowman reprint (1 in 48 packs) and Minor League Player of the Year candidates. A 385-card parallel version of the entire base set was also produced on 18-point foilboard. These cards were seeded one per pack.

	MT
Complete Set (385):	125.00
Common Player:	.15
Unlisted Rookies: .50 to .75	
Unlisted Stars: .50 to .75	
Mickey Mantle '52 Bowman Reprint	30.00
Wax Box:	140.00

#	Player	MT
1	Cal Ripken Jr.	3.50
2	Ray Durham	.15
3	Ivan Rodriguez	1.00
4	Fred McGriff	.35
5	Hideo Nomo	1.25
6	Troy Percival	.15
7	Moises Alou	.15
8	Mike Stanley	.15
9	Jay Buhner	.30
10	Shawn Green	.15
11	Ryan Klesko	1.00
12	Andres Galarraga	.30
13	Dean Palmer	.15
14	Jeff Conine	.15
15	Brian Hunter	.15
16	J.T. Snow	.15
17	Larry Walker	.60
18	Barry Larkin	.40
19	Alex Gonzalez	.15
20	Edgar Martinez	.20
21	Mo Vaughn	1.25
22	Mark McGwire	5.00
23	Jose Canseco	.40
24	Jack McDowell	.20
25	Dante Bichette	.30
26	Wade Boggs	.35
27	Mike Piazza	3.00
28	Ray Lankford	.15
29	Craig Biggio	.20
30	Rafael Palmeiro	.35
31	Ron Gant	.25
32	Javy Lopez	.25
33	Brian Jordan	.25
34	Paul O'Neill	.20
35	Mark Grace	.35
36	Matt Williams	.40
37	Pedro Martinez	.40
38	Rickey Henderson	.20
39	Bobby Bonilla	.20
40	Todd Hollandsworth	.35
41	Jim Thome	.60
42	Gary Sheffield	.75
43	Tim Salmon	.30
44	Gregg Jefferies	.15
45	Roberto Alomar	1.25
45p	Roberto Alomar (unmarked promo card, fielding photo on front)	20.00
46	Carlos Baerga	.20
47	Mark Grudzielanek	.15
48	Randy Johnson	.50
49	Tino Martinez	.15
50	Robin Ventura	.15
51	Ryne Sandberg	1.00
52	Jay Bell	.15
53	Jason Schmidt	.15
54	Frank Thomas	3.50
55	Kenny Lofton	1.25
56	Ariel Prieto	.15
57	David Cone	.25
58	Reggie Sanders	.15
59	Michael Tucker	.15
60	Vinny Castilla	.15
61	Lenny Dykstra	.15
62	Todd Hundley	.25
63	Brian McRae	.15
64	Dennis Eckersley	.15
65	Rondell White	.15
66	Eric Karros	.15
67	Greg Maddux	2.50
68	Kevin Appier	.15
69	Eddie Murray	.50
70	John Olerud	.15
71	Tony Gwynn	2.00
72	David Justice	.25
73	Ken Caminiti	.40
74	Terry Steinbach	.15
75	Alan Benes	.25
76	Chipper Jones	3.00
77	Jeff Bagwell	1.50
77p	Jeff Bagwell (unmarked promo card, name in gold)	15.00
78	Barry Bonds	1.00
79	Ken Griffey Jr.	4.00
80	Roger Cedeno	.15
81	Joe Carter	.25
82	Henry Rodriguez	.15
83	Jason Isringhausen	.25
84	Chuck Knoblauch	.25
85	Manny Ramirez	1.25
86	Tom Glavine	.25
87	Jeffrey Hammonds	.15
88	Paul Molitor	.50
89	Roger Clemens	1.50
90	Greg Vaughn	.15
91	Marty Cordova	.25
92	Albert Belle	1.00
93	Mike Mussina	.75
94	Garret Anderson	.15
95	Juan Gonzalez	2.00
96	John Valentin	.15
97	Jason Giambi	.30
98	Kirby Puckett	1.50
99	Jim Edmonds	.30
100	Cecil Fielder	.25
101	Mike Aldrete	.15
102	Marquis Grissom	.15
103	Derek Bell	.15
104	Raul Mondesi	.40
105	Sammy Sosa	2.50
106	Travis Fryman	.15
107	Rico Brogna	.15
108	Will Clark	.30
109	Bernie Williams	.75
110	Brady Anderson	.25
111	Torii Hunter	.15
112	Derek Jeter	2.50
113	*Mike Kusiewicz*	.15
114	Scott Rolen	4.00
115	Ramon Castro	.15
116	*Jose Guillen*	8.00
117	*Wade Walker*	.40
118	Shawn Senior	.15
119	*Onan Masaoka*	.40
120	*Marlon Anderson*	.40
121	*Katsuhiro Maeda*	1.00
122	*Garrett Stephenson*	.15
123	Butch Huskey	.15
124	D'Angelo Jimenez	1.50
125	*Tony Mounce*	.15
126	Jay Canizaro	.15
127	Juan Melo	.20
128	Steve Gibralter	.15
129	Freddy Garcia	.15
130	Julio Santana	.15
131	Richard Hidalgo	.25
132	Jermaine Dye	.75
133	Willie Adams	.15
134	Everett Stull	.15
135	Ramon Morel	.15
136	Chan Ho Park	.15
137	Jamey Wright	.15
138	*Luis Garcia*	.15
139	Dan Serafini	.15
140	*Ryan Dempster*	1.50
141	Tate Seefried	.15
142	Jimmy Hurst	.15
143	Travis Miller	.15
144	Curtis Goodwin	.15
145	*Rocky Coppinger*	1.00
146	Enrique Wilson	.40
147	Jaime Bluma	.15
148	Andrew Vessel	.15
149	Damian Moss	.75
150	*Shawn Gallagher*	.15
151	Pat Watkins	.15
152	Jose Paniagua	.15
153	Danny Graves	.15
154	*Bryon Gainey*	.15
155	Steve Soderstrom	.15
156	*Cliff Brumbaugh*	.15
157	*Eugene Kingsale*	.75
158	Lou Collier	.15
159	Todd Walker	4.00
160	Kris Detmers	1.00
161	*Josh Booty*	.75
162	*Greg Whiteman*	.15
163	Damian Jackson	.15
164	Tony Clark	1.00
165	Jeff D'Amico	.15
166	Johnny Damon	.40
167	Rafael Orellano	.15
168	Ruben Rivera	.40
169	Alex Ochoa	.30
170	Jay Powell	.15
171	Tom Evans	.15
172	Ron Villone	.15
173	Shawn Estes	.15
174	John Wasdin	.15
175	Bill Simas	.15
176	Kevin Brown	.15
177	Shannon Stewart	.15
178	Todd Greene	.15
179	Bob Wolcott	.15
180	Chris Snopek	.15
181	Nomar Garciaparra	4.00
182	*Cameron Smith*	.15
183	Matt Drews	.15
184	Jimmy Haynes	.15
185	Chris Carpenter	.40
186	Desi Relaford	.15
187	Ben Grieve	4.00
188	Mike Bell	.15
189	*Luis Castillo*	2.00
190	Ugueth Urbina	.15
191	Paul Wilson	.15
191p	Paul Wilson (unmarked promo card, name in gold)	5.00
192	Andruw Jones	4.00
193	Wayne Gomes	.15
194	*Craig Counsell*	1.00
195	Jim Cole	.15
196	Brooks Kieshnick	.15
197	Trey Beamon	.15
198	*Marino Santana*	.40
199	Bob Abreu	.40
200	Calvin Reese	.15
201	Dante Powell	2.00
202	George Arias	.15
202p	George Arias (unmarked promo card, name in gold)	5.00
203	*Jorge Velandia*	.40
204	*George Lombard*	4.00
205	*Byron Browne*	.40
206	John Frascatore	.15
207	Terry Adams	.15
208	*Wilson Delgado*	.40
209	Billy McMillon	.15
210	Jeff Abbott	.25
211	Trot Nixon	.15
212	Amaury Telemaco	.15
213	Scott Sullivan	.15
214	Justin Thompson	.15
215	Decomba Conner	.15
216	Ryan McGuire	.15
217	*Matt Luke*	.40
218	Doug Million	.15
219	*Jason Dickson*	1.50
220	*Ramon Hernandez*	4.00
221	Mark Bellhorn	2.00
222	Eric Ludwick	.40
223	*Luke Wilcox*	.40
224	*Marty Malloy*	.40
225	*Gary Coffee*	.40
226	Wendell Magee	.75
227	*Brett Tomko*	2.00
228	Derek Lowe	.15
229	*Jose Rosado*	2.00
230	*Steve Bourgeois*	.40
231	*Neil Weber*	.40
232	Jeff Ware	.15
233	Edwin Diaz	.20
234	Greg Norton	.15
235	Aaron Boone	.25
236	Jeff Suppan	.15
237	Bret Wagner	.15
238	Elieser Marrero	.15
239	Will Cunnane	.15
240	*Brian Barkley*	.40
241	Jay Payton	.75
242	Marcus Jensen	.15
243	Ryan Nye	.15

244	Chad Mottola	.15
245	*Scott McClain*	.40
246	*Jesse Ibarra*	.40
247	*Mike Darr*	1.00
248	*Bobby Estalella*	3.00
249	Michael Barrett	.15
250	*Jamie Lopiccolo*	.40
251	*Shane Spencer*	6.00
252	Ben Petrick	2.00
253	*Jason Bell*	.40
254	*Arnold Gooch*	.40
255	T.J. Mathews	.15
256	Jason Ryan	.15
257	Pat Cline	.40
258	*Rafael Carmona*	.40
259	Carl Pavano	6.00
260	Ben Davis	.15
261	Matt Lawton	.75
262	Kevin Sefcik	.40
263	Chris Fussell	.75
264	Mike Cameron	4.00
265	Marty Janzen	.40
266	Livan Hernandez	6.00
267	*Raul Ibanez*	.75
268	Juan Encarnacion	1.50
269	*David Yocum*	.40
270	*Jonathan Johnson*	.40
271	Reggie Taylor	.15
272	*Danny Buxbaum*	.40
273	Jacob Cruz	.50
274	*Bobby Morris*	.40
275	*Andy Fox*	.40
276	Greg Keagle	.15
277	Charles Peterson	.15
278	Derrek Lee	.35
279	*Bryant Nelson*	.40
280	Antone Williamson	.15
281	Scott Elarton	.15
282	*Shad Williams*	.40
283	Rich Hunter	.40
284	Chris Sheff	.15
285	Derrick Gibson	1.50
286	Felix Rodriguez	.15
287	*Brian Banks*	.40
288	Jason McDonald	.15
289	*Glendon Rusch*	1.00
290	Gary Rath	.15
291	Peter Munro	.15
292	Tom Fordham	.15
293	Jason Kendall	.15
294	Russ Johnson	.15
295	*Joe Long*	.40
296	*Robert Smith*	1.50
297	*Jarrod Washburn*	2.00
298	*Dave Coggin*	.40
299	*Jeff Yoder*	.40
300	*Jed Hansen*	.40
301	*Matt Morris*	3.00
302	*Josh Bishop*	.40
303	Dustin Hermanson	.15
304	Mike Gulan	.15
305	Felipe Crespo	.15
306	Quinton McCracken	.15
307	*Jim Bonnici*	.40
308	Sal Fasano	.15
309	*Gabe Alvarez*	2.00
310	Heath Murray	.40
311	*Jose Valentin*	2.00
312	Bartolo Colon	.75
313	Olmedo Saenz	.15
314	Norm Hutchins	2.00
315	Chris Holt	.40
316	*David Doster*	.40
317	Robert Person	.15
318	*Donne Wall*	.40
319	*Adam Riggs*	.40
320	Homer Bush	.15
321	*Brad Rigby*	.40
322	Lou Merloni	.40
323	Neifi Perez	.15
324	Chris Cumberland	.15
325	*Alvie Shepherd*	.40
326	*Jarrod Patterson*	.40
327	Ray Ricken	.40
328	*Danny Klassen*	.75
329	*David Miller*	.40
330	*Chad Alexander*	.40
331	Matt Beaumont	.15
332	Damon Hollins	.15
333	Todd Dunn	.15
334	*Mike Sweeney*	2.00
335	Richie Sexson	1.00
336	Billy Wagner	.25
337	*Ron Wright*	4.00
338	Paul Konerko	1.00
339	*Tommy Phelps*	.40

340	Karim Garcia	1.00
341	*Mike Grace*	.50
342	*Russell Branyan*	6.00
343	Randy Winn	.40
344	A.J. Pierzynski	.40
345	Mike Busby	.40
346	Matt Beech	.40
347	Jose Cepeda	.40
348	Brian Stephenson	.15
349	Rey Ordonez	.75
350	Rich Aurilia	.40
351	*Edgard Velazquez*	2.50
352	Raul Casanova	.15
353	*Carlos Guillen*	1.00
354	*Bruce Aven*	.40
355	*Ryan Jones*	1.00
356	*Derek Aucoin*	.40
357	*Brian Rose*	6.00
358	*Richard Almanzar*	.40
359	*Fletcher Bates*	.40
360	*Russ Ortiz*	.40
361	*Wilton Guerrero*	2.00
362	*Geoff Jenkins*	3.00
363	Pete Janicki	.15
364	Yamil Benitez	.15
365	Aaron Holbert	.15
366	Tim Belk	.15
367	Terrell Wade	.15
368	Terrence Long	.15
369	Brad Fullmer	.25
370	Matt Wagner	.15
371	Craig Wilson	.15
372	Mark Loretta	.15
373	Eric Owens	.15
374	Vladimir Guerrero	3.00
375	Tommy Davis	.15
376	Donnie Sadler	.15
377	Edgar Renteria	.60
378	Todd Helton	8.00
379	*Ralph Milliard*	.40
380	*Darin Blood*	1.50
381	Shayne Bennett	.15
382	Mark Redman	.15
383	Felix Martinez	.15
384	*Sean Watkins*	.40
385	Oscar Henriquez	.15

1996 Bowman Minor League Player of the Year

Fifteen prospects who were candidates for Minor League Player of the Year are featured in this 1996 Bowman baseball insert set. Cards were seeded one per every 12 packs.

		MT
Complete Set (15):		40.00
Common Player:		2.00
1	Andruw Jones	10.00
2	Derrick Gibson	3.00
3	Bob Abreu	2.00
4	Todd Walker	4.00
5	Jamey Wright	2.00
6	Wes Helms	4.00
7	Karim Garcia	4.00

8	Bartolo Colon	2.00
9	Alex Ochoa	2.00
10	Mike Sweeney	2.00
11	Ruben Rivera	2.00
12	Gabe Alvarez	2.00
13	Billy Wagner	3.00
14	Vladimir Guerrero	8.00
15	Edgard Velazquez	5.00

1996 Mickey Mantle Reprints

Reprints of Mickey Mantle's 1952 Bowman baseball card were created for insertion in Bowman and Bowman's Best products for 1996. The 2-1/2" x 3-1/2" card can be found in regular (gold seal on front), Finest, Finest Refractor and Atomic Refractor versions.

		MT
Complete Set (4):		60.00
Common Player:		10.00
20	Mickey Mantle (reprint)	10.00
20	Mickey Mantle (Finest)	10.00
20	Mickey Mantle (Refractor)	20.00
20	Mickey Mantle (Atomic Refractor)	30.00

1996 Bowman's Best Preview

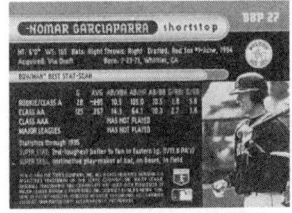

These cards use Topps' regular Finest technology. The cards were seeded one per every 12 packs of 1996 Bowman baseball. Fifteen veterans and 15 prospects are featured in the set.

		MT
Complete Set (30):		100.00
Common Player:		1.50
1	Chipper Jones	10.00
2	Alan Benes	2.00
3	Brooks Kieshnick	1.50
4	Barry Bonds	5.00
5	Rey Ordonez	2.00
6	Tim Salmon	2.50
7	Mike Piazza	10.00

8	Billy Wagner	1.50
9	Andruw Jones	6.00
10	Tony Gwynn	8.00
11	Paul Wilson	1.50
12	Calvin Reese	1.50
13	Frank Thomas	12.00
14	Greg Maddux	10.00
15	Derek Jeter	10.00
16	Jeff Bagwell	8.00
17	Barry Larkin	2.50
18	Todd Greene	1.50
19	Ruben Rivera	1.50
20	Richard Hidalgo	1.50
21	Larry Walker	2.50
22	Carlos Baerga	1.50
23	Derrick Gibson	1.50
24	Richie Sexson	2.00
25	Mo Vaughn	5.00
26	Hideo Nomo	4.00
27	Nomar Garciaparra	12.00
28	Cal Ripken Jr.	12.00
29	Karim Garcia	2.50
30	Ken Griffey Jr.	18.00

1996 Bowman's Best Preview Refractors

BROOKS KIESCHNICK

Bowman takes its hot technology of Refractors to a higher level with these Finest Atomic Refractors, cards with a "foil-patterned, starburst-like effect." The Finest Refractor cards are seeded one per every 24 packs of 1996 Bowman baseball; Atomic Refractors are seeded one per every 48 packs. Fifteen veterans and 15 prospects are featured.

		MT
Complete Set (30):		300.00
Common Player:		5.00
Atomic Refractors: 1.5x-2x		
1	Chipper Jones	20.00
2	Alan Benes	5.00
3	Brooks Kieshnick	5.00
4	Barry Bonds	10.00
5	Rey Ordonez	5.00
6	Tim Salmon	8.00
7	Mike Piazza	20.00
8	Billy Wagner	5.00
9	Andruw Jones	15.00
10	Tony Gwynn	18.00
11	Paul Wilson	5.00
12	Calvin Reese	5.00
13	Frank Thomas	25.00
14	Greg Maddux	20.00
15	Derek Jeter	20.00
16	Jeff Bagwell	15.00
17	Barry Larkin	8.00
18	Todd Greene	5.00
19	Ruben Rivera	5.00
20	Richard Hidalgo	5.00
21	Larry Walker	8.00
22	Carlos Baerga	5.00
23	Derrick Gibson	5.00
24	Richie Sexson	6.00
25	Mo Vaughn	10.00

26	Hideo Nomo	12.00
27	Nomar Garciaparra	20.00
28	Cal Ripken Jr.	25.00
29	Karim Garcia	5.00
30	Ken Griffey Jr.	35.00

1996 Bowman's Best

JERMAINE DYE

Bowman's Best returns in its traditional format of 180 cards, including 90 established stars and 90 up-and-coming prospects and rookies. There are three types of insert sets found in Bowman's Best - Mirror Image, Bowman's Best Cuts and the 1952 Bowman Mickey Mantle reprint. Mirror Image features four top players and 10 different positions, pairing an American League veteran and a prospect on one side, and a National League veteran and a prospect on the other. These cards are seeded one per 48 packs. Bowman's Best Cuts are die-cut chromium cards of 15 top stars; they are seeded one per 24 packs. There is also a 1952 Bowman Mickey Mantle chromium reprint found in every 24th pack. This is No. 20 in the Mantle reprint series from 1996 Topps Baseball. There are also Refractors and Atomic Refractors randomly seeded in packs. They form parallel sets. Regular issue Refractors are seeded one per every 12 packs; Atomic Refractors are seeded one per every 48 packs. Mirror Image Refractors are found one per every 96 packs, while Mirror Image Atomic Refractors are seeded one per every 192 packs. Bowman's Best Cuts Refractors are seeded in every 48th pack, while Bowman's Best Cuts Atomic Refractors are in every 96th pack. Refractor versions of the Mantle reprint are seeded one per every 96 packs; Atomic Refractor Mantle reprints are seeded in every 192nd pack.

Modern cards have little collector value in conditions lower than Mint.
Figure NM cards at 75% of values shown;
EX cards at 40%.

		MT
Complete Set (180):		100.00
Common Player:		.25
Unlisted Stars: .50 to .75		
Complete Refractor Set (180):		2000.
Veteran Star Refractors: 5x to 10x		
Young Stars and RCs: 4x to 8x		
Veteran Star Atomics: 25x to 35x		
Young Stars and RCs Atomics: 15x to 25x		
1952 Mickey Mantle:		8.00
1952 Mantle Refractor:		20.00
1952 Mantle Atomic Refractor:		40.00
Wax Box:		160.00
1	Hideo Nomo	1.25
2	Edgar Martinez	.25
3	Cal Ripken Jr.	5.00
4	Wade Boggs	.50
5	Cecil Fielder	.50
6	Albert Belle	1.50
7	Chipper Jones	4.00
8	Ryne Sandberg	1.50
9	Tim Salmon	.75
10	Barry Bonds	1.50
11	Ken Caminiti	.75
12	Ron Gant	.25
13	Frank Thomas	5.00
14	Dante Bichette	.75
15	Jason Kendall	.25
16	Mo Vaughn	1.50
17	Rey Ordonez	.40
18	Henry Rodriguez	.25
19	Ryan Klesko	.75
20	Jeff Bagwell	2.00
21	Randy Johnson	1.00
22	Jim Edmonds	.50
23	Kenny Lofton	1.50
24	Andy Pettitte	1.50
25	Brady Anderson	.40
26	Mike Piazza	4.00
27	Greg Vaughn	.25
28	Joe Carter	.40
29	Jason Giambi	.25
30	Ivan Rodriguez	1.25
31	Jeff Conine	.25
32	Rafael Palmeiro	.40
33	Roger Clemens	2.00
34	Chuck Knoblauch	.50
35	Reggie Sanders	.25
36	Andres Galarraga	.50
37	Paul O'Neill	.50
38	Tony Gwynn	3.00
39	Paul Wilson	.25
40	Garret Anderson	.25
41	David Justice	.40
42	Eddie Murray	.75
43	*Mike Grace*	.50
44	Marty Cordova	.40
45	Kevin Appier	.25
46	Raul Mondesi	.50
47	Jim Thome	.75
48	Sammy Sosa	3.00
49	Craig Biggio	.35
50	Marquis Grissom	.25
51	Alan Benes	.25
52	Manny Ramirez	1.50
53	Gary Sheffield	.75
54	Mike Mussina	1.00
55	Robin Ventura	.25
56	Johnny Damon	.25
57	Jose Canseco	.50
58	Juan Gonzalez	3.00
59	Tino Martinez	.65
60	Brian Hunter	.25
61	Fred McGriff	.60
62	Jay Buhner	.40
63	Carlos Delgado	.25
64	Moises Alou	.35
65	Roberto Alomar	1.00
66	Barry Larkin	.50
67	Vinny Castilla	.25
68	Ray Durham	.25
69	Travis Fryman	.25
70	Jason Isringhausen	.25
71	Ken Griffey Jr.	6.00
72	John Smoltz	.40
73	Matt Williams	.50
74	Chan Ho Park	.25
75	Mark McGwire	7.00
76	Jeffrey Hammonds	.25
77	Will Clark	.50
78	Kirby Puckett	2.00
79	Derek Jeter	4.00
80	Derek Bell	.25
81	Eric Karros	.25
82	Lenny Dykstra	.25
83	Larry Walker	.75

84	Mark Grudzielanek	.25
85	Greg Maddux	4.00
86	Carlos Baerga	.25
87	Paul Molitor	.50
88	John Valentin	.25
89	Mark Grace	.40
90	Ray Lankford	.25
91	Andruw Jones	4.00
92	Nomar Garciaparra	5.00
93	Alex Ochoa	.25
94	Derrick Gibson	.25
95	Jeff D'Amico	.25
96	Ruben Rivera	.50
97	Vladimir Guerrero	3.00
98	Calvin Reese	.25
99	Richard Hidalgo	.25
100	Bartolo Colon	1.00
101	Karim Garcia	1.00
102	Ben Davis	1.00
103	Jay Powell	.25
104	Chris Snopek	.25
105	*Glendon Rusch*	.40
106	Enrique Wilson	.50
107	*Antonio Alfonseca*	.25
108	*Wilton Guerrero*	2.00
109	*Jose Guillen*	10.00
110	*Miguel Mejia*	.25
111	Jay Payton	.75
112	Scott Elarton	.50
113	Brooks Kieschnick	.25
114	Dustin Hermanson	.25
115	Roger Cedeno	.25
116	Matt Wagner	.25
117	Lee Daniels	.25
118	Ben Grieve	4.00
119	Ugueth Urbina	.25
120	Danny Graves	.50
121	*Dan Donato*	.25
122	*Matt Ruebel*	.25
123	*Mark Sievert*	.25
124	Chris Stynes	.25
125	Jeff Abbott	.25
126	*Rocky Coppinger*	.75
127	Jermaine Dye	.50
128	Todd Greene	.25
129	Chris Carpenter	.25
130	Edgar Renteria	.75
131	Matt Drews	.25
132	*Edgard Velazquez*	3.00
133	Casey Whitten	.25
134	*Ryan Jones*	.75
135	Todd Walker	4.00
136	*Geoff Jenkins*	3.00
137	*Matt Morris*	4.00
138	Richie Sexson	1.50
139	*Todd Dunwoody*	4.00
140	*Gabe Alvarez*	3.00
141	J.J. Johnson	.25
142	Shannon Stewart	.25
143	Brad Fullmer	.50
144	Julio Santana	.25
145	Scott Rolen	4.00
146	Amaury Telemaco	.25
147	Trey Beamon	.25
148	Billy Wagner	.25
149	Todd Hollandsworth	.25
150	Doug Million	.25
151	*Jose Valentin*	2.00
152	Wes Helms	6.00
153	Jeff Suppan	.25
154	*Luis Castillo*	2.00
155	Bob Abreu	.25
156	Paul Konerko	1.50
157	Jamey Wright	.25
158	Eddie Pearson	.25
159	Jimmy Haynes	.25
160	Derrek Lee	.75
161	Damian Moss	.75
162	*Carlos Guillen*	1.50
163	*Chris Fussell*	1.00
164	*Mike Sweeney*	1.00
165	Donnie Sadler	.25
166	Desi Relaford	.25
167	Steve Gibralter	.25
168	Neifi Perez	.30
169	Antone Williamson	.25
170	*Marty Janzen*	.25
171	Todd Helton	8.00
172	*Raul Ibanez*	1.00
173	Bill Selby	.25
174	*Shane Monahan*	1.50
175	Robin Jennings	.25
176	*Bobby Chouinard*	.25
177	Einar Diaz	.25
178	Jason Thompson	.25
179	*Rafael Medina*	1.50
180	Kevin Orie	1.00

1996 Bowman's Best Refractors

Parallel sets of 180 Refractors and Atomic Refractors were randomly seeded in Bowman's Best packs. Regular-issue Refractors are seeded one per 12 packs; Atomic Refractors are seeded one per 48 packs. Mirror Image Refractors are found one per 96 packs, while Mirror Image Atomic Refractors are seeded one per 192 packs. Refractor versions of the Mantle reprint are seeded one per every 96 packs; Atomic Refractor Mantle reprints are seeded in every 192nd pack.

	MT
Complete Set, Refractors (180):	2000.00
Common Refractor:	2.00
Common Atomic Refractor:	9.00
(Refractors: Veteran stars 5-10X regular Bowman's Best; young stars and rookies 4-8X. Atomic Refractors: Veteran stars 40-50X; young stars and rookies 25-35X.)	

Grading Guide

Mint (MT): A perfect card. Well-centered with all corners sharp and square. No creases, stains, edge nicks, surface marks, yellowing or fading.

Near Mint (NM): A nearly perfect card. At first glance, a NM card appears to be perfect. May be slightly off-center. No surface marks, creases or loss of gloss.

Excellent (EX): Corners are still fairly sharp with only moderate wear. Borders may be off-center. No creases or stains on fronts or backs, but may show slight loss of surface luster.

Very Good (VG): Shows obvious handling. May have rounded corners, minor creases, major gum or wax stains. No major creases, tape marks, writing, etc.

1996 Bowman's Best Cuts

Bowman's Best Cuts give collectors the first die-cut chromium cards in a 15-card set of top stars. The cards were seeded one per every 24 packs. Refractor versions were also made; they are seeded one per every 48 packs. Atomic Refractor versions were seeded one per every 96 packs.

		MT
Complete Set (15):		100.00
Common Player:		2.50
1	Ken Griffey Jr.	25.00
2	Jason Isringhausen	2.50
3	Derek Jeter	15.00
4	Andruw Jones	12.00
5	Chipper Jones	15.00
6	Ryan Klesko	4.00
7	Raul Mondesi	2.50
8	Hideo Nomo	5.00
9	Mike Piazza	15.00
10	Manny Ramirez	5.00
11	Cal Ripken Jr.	20.00
12	Ruben Rivera	2.50
13	Tim Salmon	3.00
14	Frank Thomas	20.00
15	Jim Thome	5.00

1996 Bowman's Best Cuts Refractors

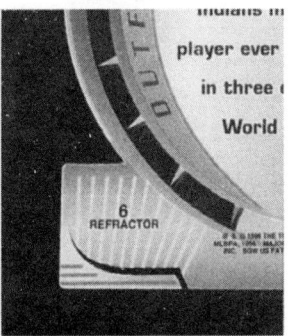

Two Refractor versions are made of these die-cut chromium cards - regular Refractors and Atomic Refractors. The regular versions are seeded one per every 48 packs; Atomic Refractors appear in every 96th pack.

	MT
Complete Set (15):	325.00
Common Player:	8.00
Atomics: 2x	
1 Ken Griffey Jr.	60.00
2 Jason Isringhausen	8.00
3 Derek Jeter	40.00
4 Andruw Jones	30.00
5 Chipper Jones	40.00
6 Ryan Klesko	10.00
7 Raul Mondesi	10.00
8 Hideo Nomo	15.00
9 Mike Piazza	40.00
10 Manny Ramirez	15.00
11 Cal Ripken Jr.	50.00
12 Ruben Rivera	10.00
13 Tim Salmon	10.00
14 Frank Thomas	50.00
15 Jim Thome	12.00

1996 Bowman's Best Mirror Image

Mirror Image inserts feature four top players at 10 different positions, pairing an American League veteran and a prospect on one side and a National League veteran and prospect on the other. These cards are seeded one per every 48 packs. Mirror Image Refractors (one in every 96 packs) and Mirror Image Atomic Refractors (one in every 192 packs) were also produced.

	MT
Complete Set (10):	160.00
Common Player:	8.00
Refractors: 1.5x to 2x	
Atomics: 2x to 4x	
1 Jeff Bagwell, Todd Helton, Frank Thomas, Richie Sexson	25.00
2 Craig Biggio, Luis Castillo, Roberto Alomar, Desi Relaford	10.00
3 Chipper Jones, Scott Rolen, Wade Boggs, George Arias	20.00
4 Barry Larkin, Neifi Perez, Cal Ripken Jr., Mark Bellhorn	20.00
5 Larry Walker, Karim Garcia, Albert Belle, Ruben Rivera	10.00
6 Barry Bonds, Andruw Jones, Kenny Lofton, Donnie Sadler	15.00
7 Tony Gwynn, Vladimir Guerrero, Ken Griffey Jr., Ben Grieve	40.00
8 Mike Piazza, Ben Davis, Ivan Rodriguez, Jose Valentin	20.00
9 Greg Maddux, Jamey Wright, Mike Mussina, Bartolo Colon	20.00

10	Tom Glavine, Billy Wagner, Randy Johnson, Jarrod Washburn	10.00

1997 Bowman Pre-production

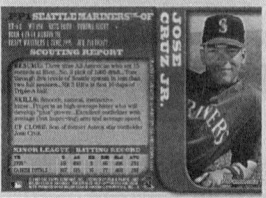

The format for 1997 Bowman's base set was previewed in this sample issue distributed to card dealers and the hobby press. The samples are virtually identical to the issued versions of the same players' cards, except they carry a "PP" prefix to the number on back.

		MT
Complete Set (4):		16.00
Common Player:		3.00
PP1	Jose Cruz, Jr.	3.00
PP2	Andruw Jones	5.00
PP3	Derek Jeter	7.50
PP4	Sammy Sosa	8.00

1997 Bowman

The 1997 Bowman set consists of 440 base cards, an increase of 55 cards from the '96 set. Card fronts have a player photo within a red or blue frame, with the player's name and team logo at the bottom of the frame. A black border surrounds the outside of the card. Card backs feature another color photo, along with the player's 1996 statistics broken down by opponent. Players making their first appearance in a Bowman set have a "1st Bowman Card" designation on the card. Cards of prospects contain either silver or red foil on the fronts. Inserts within the set include Certified Autographs (found in gold, blue and black ink versions), Scouts Honor Roll, and Bowman's Best Previews. Cards were sold in 10-card packs for a suggested retail

price of $2.50 each, and Topps offered collectors a $125 guarantee on the value of the set by the year 2000.

	MT
Complete Set (440):	150.00
Complete Series 1 Set (221):	80.00
Complete Series 2 Set (219):	70.00
Common Player:	.15
Foil Stars: 2x to 4x	
Foil Yng. Stars: 1.5x to 3x	
Series 1 Box:	110.00
Series 2 Box:	90.00
1 Derek Jeter	2.50
2 Edgar Renteria	.15
3 Chipper Jones	2.50
4 Hideo Nomo	.75
5 Tim Salmon	.25
6 Jason Giambi	.15
7 Robin Ventura	.15
8 Tony Clark	.75
9 Barry Larkin	.25
10 Paul Molitor	.50
11 Bernard Gilkey	.15
12 Jack McDowell	.15
13 Andy Benes	.15
14 Ryan Klesko	.75
15 Mark McGwire	5.00
16 Ken Griffey Jr.	4.00
17 Robb Nen	.15
18 Cal Ripken Jr.	3.00
19 John Valentin	.15
20 Ricky Bottalico	.15
21 Mike Lansing	.15
22 Ryne Sandberg	1.00
23 Carlos Delgado	.15
24 Craig Biggio	.20
25 Eric Karros	.15
26 Kevin Appier	.15
27 Mariano Rivera	.20
28 Vinny Castilla	.15
29 Juan Gonzalez	1.75
30 Al Martin	.15
31 Jeff Cirillo	.15
32 Eddie Murray	.50
33 Ray Lankford	.15
34 Manny Ramirez	1.00
35 Roberto Alomar	.75
36 Will Clark	.25
37 Chuck Knoblauch	.20
38 Harold Baines	.15
39 Trevor Hoffman	.15
40 Edgar Martinez	.15
41 Geronimo Berroa	.15
42 Rey Ordonez	.15
43 Mike Stanley	.15
44 Mike Mussina	.75
45 Kevin Brown	.15
46 Dennis Eckersley	.15
47 Henry Rodriguez	.15
48 Tino Martinez	.25
49 Eric Young	.15
50 Bret Boone	.15
51 Raul Mondesi	.25
52 Sammy Sosa	2.50
53 John Smoltz	.25
54 Billy Wagner	.15
55 Jeff D'Amico	.15
56 Ken Caminiti	.25
57 Jason Kendall	.15
58 Wade Boggs	.25
59 Andres Galarraga	.25
60 Jeff Brantley	.15
61 Mel Rojas	.15
62 Brian Hunter	.15
63 Bobby Bonilla	.15
64 Roger Clemens	1.50
65 Jeff Kent	.15
66 Matt Williams	.40
67 Albert Belle	1.00
68 Jeff King	.15
69 John Wetteland	.15
70 Deion Sanders	.40
71 Bubba Trammell	2.00
72 Felix Heredia	.60
73 Billy Koch	.40
74 Sidney Ponson	.40
75 Ricky Ledee	4.00
76 Brett Tomko	.15
77 Braden Looper	.50
78 Damian Jackson	.15
79 Jason Dickson	.40
80 Chad Green	1.00
81 R.A. Dickey	.40
82 Jeff Liefer	.40
83 Matt Wagner	.15

84	Richard Hidalgo	.15	180	Shane Monahan	.25	276	Cecil Fielder	.30
85	Adam Riggs	.15	181	*Jimmy Anderson*	.75	277	Mo Vaughn	1.00
86	Robert Smith	.15	182	Juan Melo	.15	278	Alex Fernandez	.15
87	*Chad Hermansen*	5.00	183	*Pablo Ortega*	1.00	279	Michael Tucker	.15
88	Felix Martinez	.15	184	*Calvin Pickering*	3.00	280	Jose Valentin	.15
89	J.J. Johnson	.15	185	Reggie Taylor	.15	281	Sandy Alomar	.15
90	Todd Dunwoody	1.00	186	*Jeff Farnsworth*	.40	282	Todd Hollandsworth	.15
91	Katsuhiro Maeda	.15	187	Terrence Long	.15	283	Rico Brogna	.15
92	Darin Erstad	2.00	188	Geoff Jenkins	.40	284	Rusty Greer	.15
93	Elieser Marrero	.15	189	*Steve Rain*	.40	285	Roberto Hernandez	.15
94	Bartolo Colon	.15	190	*Nerio Rodriguez*	1.00	286	Hal Morris	.15
95	Chris Fussell	.25	191	Derrick Gibson	.40	287	Johnny Damon	.15
96	Ugueth Urbina	.15	192	Darin Blood	.40	288	Todd Hundley	.30
97	*Josh Paul*	.50	193	Ben Davis	.15	289	Rondell White	.30
98	Jaime Bluma	.15	194	*Adrian Beltre*	8.00	290	Frank Thomas	3.00
99	*Seth Greisinger*	.40	195	*Damian Sapp*	2.00	291	*Don Denbow*	.15
100	*Jose Cruz*	6.00	196	*Kerry Wood*	20.00	292	Derrek Lee	.15
101	Todd Dunn	.15	197	Nate Rolison	1.50	293	Todd Walker	.50
102	*Joe Young*	.40	198	*Fernando Tatis*	4.00	294	Scott Rolen	1.50
103	Jonathan Johnson	.15	199	*Brad Penny*	.40	295	Wes Helms	1.50
104	*Justin Towle*	2.00	200	*Jake Westbrook*	.75	296	Bob Abreu	.15
105	Brian Rose	1.00	201	Edwin Diaz	.15	297	*John Patterson*	2.00
106	Jose Guillen	1.00	202	*Joe Fontenot*	.60	298	Alex Gonzalez	1.00
107	Andruw Jones	2.00	203	Matt Halloran	.75	299	Grant Roberts	3.00
108	*Mark Kotsay*	4.00	204	Blake Stein	.40	300	Jeff Suppan	.15
109	Wilton Guerrero	.15	205	Onan Masaoka	.15	301	Luke Wilcox	.15
110	Jacob Cruz	.15	206	Ben Petrick	.15	302	Marlon Anderson	.15
111	Mike Sweeney	.35	207	*Matt Clement*	1.50	303	Ray Brown	.15
112	Julio Mosquera	.15	208	Todd Greene	.15	304	*Mike Caruso*	1.50
113	Matt Morris	.40	209	Ray Ricken	.15	305	*Sam Marsonek*	.40
114	Wendell Magee	.15	210	*Eric Chavez*	5.00	306	*Brady Raggio*	.40
115	John Thomson	.15	211	Edgard Velazquez	.40	307	*Kevin McGlinchy*	.75
116	*Javier Valentin*	.30	212	*Bruce Chen*	2.00	308	*Roy Halladay*	1.00
117	Tom Fordham	.15	213	*Danny Patterson*	.40	309	*Jeremi Gonzalez*	1.50
118	Ruben Rivera	.15	214	Jeff Yoder	.15	310	*Aramis Ramirez*	6.00
119	*Mike Drumright*	.50	215	*Luis Ordaz*	.40	311	*Dermal Brown*	3.00
120	Chris Holt	.15	216	Chris Widger	.15	312	Justin Thompson	.15
121	*Sean Maloney*	.40	217	Jason Brester	.15	313	*Jay Tessmer*	.20
122	Michael Barrett	.15	218	Carlton Loewer	.15	314	Mike Johnson	.15
123	*Tony Saunders*	1.50	219	*Chris Reitsma*	1.50	315	Danny Clyburn	.15
124	Kevin Brown	.15	220	Neifi Perez	.15	316	Bruce Aven	.15
125	Richard Almanzar	.15	221	*Hideki Irabu*	6.00	317	*Keith Foulke*	.40
126	Mark Redman	.15	222	Ellis Burks	.15	318	*Jimmy Osting*	.40
127	*Anthony Sanders*	1.50	223	Pedro J. Martinez	.30	319	*Valerio DeLosSantos*	.40
128	Jeff Abbott	.15	224	Kenny Lofton	1.00	320	Shannon Stewart	.15
129	Eugene Kingsale	.15	225	Randy Johnson	.75	321	Willie Adams	.15
130	Paul Konerko	1.00	226	Terry Steinbach	.15	322	Larry Barnes	.15
131	*Randall Simon*	4.00	227	Bernie Williams	.75	323	Mark Johnson	.15
132	Andy Larkin	.15	228	Dean Palmer	.15	324	*Chris Stowers*	.40
133	Rafael Medina	.25	229	Alan Benes	.15	325	Brandon Reed	.15
134	Mendy Lopez	.15	230	Marquis Grissom	.15	326	Randy Winn	.15
135	Freddy Garcia	.15	231	Gary Sheffield	.40	327	Steven Chavez	.15
136	Karim Garcia	.40	232	Curt Schilling	.15	328	Nomar Garciaparra	1.50
137	*Larry Rodriguez*	.50	233	Reggie Sanders	.15	329	*Jacque Jones*	2.00
138	Carlos Guillen	.15	234	Bobby Higginson	.15	330	Chris Clemons	.15
139	Aaron Boone	.15	235	Moises Alou	.25	331	Todd Helton	1.50
140	Donnie Sadler	.15	236	Tom Glavine	.30	332	Ryan Brannan	.40
141	Brooks Kieschnick	.15	237	Mark Grace	.30	333	*Alex Sanchez*	1.00
142	Scott Spiezio	.15	238	Ramon Martinez	.15	334	Arnold Gooch	.15
143	Everett Stull	.15	239	Rafael Palmeiro	.30	335	Russell Branyan	1.00
144	Enrique Wilson	.15	240	John Olerud	.15	336	Daryle Ward	1.50
145	*Milton Bradley*	.40	241	Dante Bichette	.30	337	*John LeRoy*	.40
146	Kevin Orie	.20	242	Greg Vaughn	.15	338	Steve Cox	.15
147	Derek Wallace	.15	243	Jeff Bagwell	1.50	339	Kevin Witt	1.50
148	Russ Johnson	.15	244	Barry Bonds	1.00	340	Norm Hutchins	.15
149	*Joe Lagarde*	.40	245	Pat Hentgen	.15	341	Gabby Martinez	.15
150	Luis Castillo	.40	246	Jim Thome	.75	342	Kris Detmers	.15
151	Jay Payton	.25	247	Jermaine Allensworth	.15	343	*Mike Villano*	.50
152	Joe Long	.15	248	Andy Pettitte	1.00	344	Preston Wilson	.15
153	Livan Hernandez	.75	249	Jay Bell	.15	345	*Jim Manias*	.40
154	*Vladimir Nunez*	1.00	250	John Jaha	.15	346	*Deivi Cruz*	1.00
155	Calvin Reese	.15	251	Jim Edmonds	.15	347	*Donzell McDonald*	.50
156	George Arias	.15	252	Ron Gant	.15	348	*Rod Myers*	.40
157	Homer Bush	.15	253	David Cone	.30	349	*Shawn Chacon*	.75
158	Chris Carpenter	.15	254	Jose Canseco	.40	350	*Elvin Hernandez*	.40
159	*Eric Milton*	2.50	255	Jay Buhner	.30	351	*Orlando Cabrera*	1.00
160	Richie Sexson	.25	256	Greg Maddux	2.50	352	Brian Banks	.15
161	Carl Pavano	1.00	257	Brian McRae	.15	353	Robbie Bell	.75
162	*Chris Gissell*	.40	258	Lance Johnson	.15	354	Brad Rigby	.15
163	Mac Suzuki	.15	259	Travis Fryman	.15	355	Scott Elarton	.15
164	Pat Cline	.15	260	Paul O'Neill	.30	356	*Kevin Sweeney*	.75
165	Ron Wright	1.00	261	Ivan Rodriguez	.75	357	Steve Soderstrom	.15
166	Dante Powell	.40	262	Gregg Jefferies	.15	358	Ryan Nye	.15
167	Mark Bellhorn	.25	263	Fred McGriff	.30	359	*Marlon Allen*	.40
168	George Lombard	.75	264	Derek Bell	.15	360	*Donny Leon*	.40
169	*Pee Wee Lopez*	.40	265	Jeff Conine	.15	361	*Garrett Neubart*	.40
170	Paul Wilder	2.00	266	Mike Piazza	2.50	362	*Abraham Nunez*	1.50
171	Brad Fullmer	.15	267	Mark Grudzielanek	.15	363	*Adam Eaton*	.40
172	*Willie Martinez*	.75	268	Brady Anderson	.15	364	*Octavio Dotel*	.40
173	*Dario Veras*	.40	269	Marty Cordova	.15	365	*Dean Crow*	.40
174	Dave Coggin	.15	270	Ray Durham	.15	366	*Jason Baker*	.40
175	Kris Benson	3.00	271	Joe Carter	.15	367	Sean Casey	2.00
176	Torii Hunter	.15	272	Brian Jordan	.15	368	*Joe Lawrence*	.40
177	D.T. Cromer	.40	273	David Justice	.15	369	*Adam Johnson*	1.00
178	Nelson Figueroa	1.25	274	Tony Gwynn	2.00	370	Scott Schoeneweis	.40
179	*Hiram Bocachica*	1.50	275	Larry Walker	.40	371	Gerald Witasick, Jr.	.15

372	*Ronnie Belliard*	.40
373	Russ Ortiz	.15
374	*Robert Stratton*	.40
375	Bobby Estalella	.40
376	*Corey Lee*	.75
377	Carlos Beltran	.75
378	Mike Cameron	.50
379	*Scott Randall*	.40
380	*Corey Erickson*	1.50
381	Jay Canizaro	.15
382	*Kerry Robinson*	.40
383	*Todd Noel*	.50
384	*A.J. Zapp*	2.50
385	Jarrod Washburn	.15
386	Ben Grieve	1.50
387	*Javier Vazquez*	1.00
388	Tony Graffanino	.15
389	*Travis Lee*	15.00
390	DaRond Stovall	.15
391	*Dennis Reyes*	1.50
392	Danny Buxbaum	.15
393	*Marc Lewis*	1.50
394	*Kelvim Escobar*	1.00
395	Danny Klassen	.25
396	*Ken Cloude*	2.00
397	Gabe Alvarez	.15
398	*Jaret Wright*	10.00
399	Raul Casanova	.15
400	*Clayton Brunner*	.75
401	*Jason Marquis*	1.00
402	Marc Kroon	.15
403	Jamey Wright	.15
404	*Matt Snyder*	.40
405	*Josh Garrett*	1.00
406	Juan Encarnacion	.75
407	Heath Murray	.15
408	*Brett Herbison*	.50
409	*Brent Butler*	2.50
410	*Danny Peoples*	1.50
411	*Miguel Tejada*	4.00
412	Damian Moss	.15
413	Jim Pittsley	.15
414	Dmitri Young	.15
415	Glendon Rusch	.15
416	Vladimir Guerrero	1.50
417	*Cole Liniak*	1.50
418	Ramon Hernandez	.50
419	*Cliff Politte*	.75
420	*Mel Rosario*	.50
421	*Jorge Carrion*	.50
422	*John Barnes*	.40
423	*Chris Stowe*	.40
424	Vernon Wells	3.00
425	*Brett Caradonna*	1.00
426	Scott Hodges	1.00
427	*Jon Garland*	2.00
428	*Nathan Haynes*	.60
429	*Geoff Goetz*	.75
430	*Adam Kennedy*	1.00
431	*T.J. Tucker*	.50
432	*Aaron Akin*	.75
433	*Jayson Werth*	1.50
434	*Glenn Davis*	1.00
435	*Mark Mangum*	.50
436	*Troy Cameron*	2.00
437	*J.J. Davis*	2.50
438	*Lance Berkman*	6.00
439	*Jason Standridge*	.75
440	*Jason Dellaero*	1.00
441	Hideki Irabu	1.00

1997 Bowman Autographs

A total of 90 players signed autographs for inclusion in both Series I and II packs. Each autograph card is printed on 16-point stock and features a special Certified Autograph stamp. Every autograph card can be found in one of three versions. A blue ink version was inserted 1:96 packs; black ink 1:503 packs; gold ink 1:1,509 packs.

	MT
Complete Set (90):	2000.
Complete Series 1 Set (46):	900.00
Complete Series 2 Set (44):	1200.
Common Blue Ink:	15.00
Black Ink Autos: 1.5x to 2.5x	
Gold Ink Autos: 4x to 6x	
Multipliers doesn't apply to Jeter	

1	Jeff Abbott	15.00
2	Bob Abreu	20.00
3	Willie Adams	15.00
4	Brian Banks	15.00
5	Kris Benson	30.00
6	Darin Blood	15.00
7	Jaime Bluma	15.00
8	Kevin Brown	20.00
9	Ray Brown	15.00
10	Homer Bush	15.00
11	Mike Cameron	30.00
12	Jay Canizaro	15.00
13	Luis Castillo	15.00
14	Dave Coggin	20.00
15	Bartolo Colon	20.00
16	Rocky Coppinger	15.00
17	Jacob Cruz	25.00
18	Jose Cruz	60.00
19	Jeff D'Amico	20.00
20	Ben Davis	25.00
21	Mike Drumbright	15.00
22	Scott Elarton	15.00
23	Darin Erstad	50.00
24	Bobby Estalella	15.00
25	Joe Fontenot	15.00
26	Tom Fordham	15.00
27	Brad Fullmer	25.00
28	Chris Fussell	15.00
29	Karim Garcia	25.00
30	Kris Detmers	15.00
31	Todd Greene	25.00
32	Ben Grieve	60.00
33	Vladimir Guerrero	60.00
34	Jose Guillen	30.00
35	Roy Halladay	15.00
36	Wes Helms	30.00
37	Chad Hermansen	50.00
38	Richard Hidalgo	25.00
39	Todd Hollandsworth	20.00
40	Damian Jackson	15.00
41	Derek Jeter	75.00
42	Andruw Jones	50.00
43	Brooks Kieschnick	20.00
44	Eugene Kingsale	15.00
45	Paul Konerko	25.00
46	Marc Kroon	15.00
47	Derrek Lee	35.00
48	Travis Lee	110.00
49	Terrence Long	15.00
50	Curt Lyons	15.00
51	Elieser Marrero	20.00
52	Rafael Medina	15.00
53	Juan Melo	20.00
54	Shane Monahan	20.00
55	Julio Mosquera	15.00
56	Heath Murray	15.00
57	Ryan Nye	15.00
58	Kevin Orie	25.00
59	Russ Ortiz	15.00
60	Carl Pavano	35.00
61	Jay Payton	25.00
62	Neifi Perez	25.00
63	Sidney Ponson	15.00
64	Calvin Reese	15.00
65	Ray Ricken	15.00
66	Brad Rigby	15.00
67	Adam Riggs	15.00
68	Ruben Rivera	20.00
69	J.J. Johnson	15.00
70	Scott Rolen	60.00
71	Tony Saunders	20.00
72	Donnie Sadler	15.00
73	Richie Sexson	30.00
74	Scott Spiezio	25.00
75	Everett Stull	15.00
76	Mike Sweeney	15.00
77	Fernando Tatis	40.00
78	Miguel Tejada	25.00
79	Justin Thompson	25.00
80	Justin Towle	25.00
81	Billy Wagner	20.00
82	Todd Walker	25.00
83	Luke Wilcox	15.00
84	Paul Wilder	25.00
85	Enrique Wilson	15.00
86	Kerry Wood	125.00
87	Jamey Wright	20.00
88	Ron Wright	25.00
89	Dmitri Young	15.00
90	Nelson Figueroa	15.00

A player's name in *italic* type indicates a rookie card.

1997 Bowman International Best

This 20-card parallel set features a flag design on the background of each card front depicting the player's country of origin. On back is another color photo, player personal data, a record of his best season and colored flags representing 14 nations who have sent players to the major leagues. One International Best card was inserted in every pack.

	MT
Complete Set (20):	75.00
Common Player:	1.50
Refractors: 1.5x to 2x	
Atomic Refractors: 2x to 3x	

BBI1	Frank Thomas	12.00
BBI2	Ken Griffey Jr.	15.00
BBI3	Juan Gonzalez	7.00
BBI4	Bernie Williams	3.00
BBI5	Hideo Nomo	3.00
BBI6	Sammy Sosa	10.00
BBI7	Larry Walker	2.00
BBI8	Vinny Castilla	1.50
BBI9	Mariano Rivera	1.50
BBI10	Rafael Palmeiro	2.00
BBI11	Nomar Garciaparra	10.00
BBI12	Todd Walker	3.00
BBI13	Andruw Jones	6.00
BBI14	Vladimir Guerrero	5.00
BBI15	Ruben Rivera	1.50
BBI16	Bob Abreu	1.50
BBI17	Karim Garcia	2.00
BBI18	Katsuhiro Maeda	1.50
BBI19	Jose Cruz Jr.	6.00
BBI20	Damian Moss	1.50

1997 Bowman Rookie of the Year Candidates

This 15-card insert was inserted in one per 12 packs of Bowman Series II. Fronts featured a color shot of the player over a textured foil background, with the player's name across the bottom and the words "Rookie of the Year Favorites" across the top with the word "Rookie" in large script letters. Card numbers carried a "ROY" prefix.

	MT
Complete Set (15):	30.00
Common Player:	1.50
ROY1 Jeff Abbott	1.50
ROY2 Karim Garcia	2.50
ROY3 Todd Helton	4.00
ROY4 Richard Hidalgo	1.50
ROY5 Geoff Jenkins	2.00
ROY6 Russ Johnson	1.50
ROY7 Paul Konerko	4.00
ROY8 Mark Kotsay	5.00
ROY9 Ricky Ledee	5.00
ROY10 Travis Lee	12.00
ROY11 Derek Lee	2.00
ROY12 Elieser Marrero	1.50
ROY13 Juan Melo	1.50
ROY14 Brian Rose	2.00
ROY15 Fernando Tatis	3.00

1997 Bowman Scouts' Honor Roll

This insert features 15 prospects deemed to have the most potential by Topps' scouts. Each card features a double-etched foil design and is inserted 1:12 packs.

	MT
Complete Set (15):	60.00
Common Player:	1.50
1 Dmitri Young	1.50
2 Bob Abreu	1.50
3 Vladimir Guerrero	6.00
4 Paul Konerko	5.00
5 Kevin Orie	2.00
6 Todd Walker	2.50
7 Ben Grieve	4.00
8 Darin Erstad	6.00
9 Derek Lee	1.50
10 Jose Cruz	8.00
11 Scott Rolen	8.00
12 Travis Lee	15.00
13 Andruw Jones	6.00
14 Wilton Guerrero	1.50
15 Nomar Garciaparra	8.00

1997 Bowman's Best Preview

This 20-card set, featuring 10 veterans and 10 prospects, features a preview of the design used on the Bowman's Best product. Three different versions of the Preview cards were available: Regular version (1:12 packs), Refractors (1:48) and Atomic Refractors (1:96).

	MT
Complete Set (20):	100.00
Common Player:	1.50
Refractors: 2x to 3x	
Atomic Refractors: 3x to 5x	
1 Frank Thomas	10.00
2 Ken Griffey Jr.	15.00
3 Barry Bonds	4.00
4 Derek Jeter	10.00
5 Chipper Jones	10.00
6 Mark McGwire	15.00
7 Cal Ripken Jr.	12.00
8 Kenny Lofton	4.00
9 Gary Sheffield	2.00
10 Jeff Bagwell	7.00
11 Wilton Guerrero	1.50
12 Scott Rolen	6.00
13 Todd Walker	2.50
14 Ruben Rivera	1.50
15 Andruw Jones	8.00
16 Nomar Garciaparra	10.00
17 Vladimir Guerrero	5.00
18 Miguel Tejada	4.00
19 Bartolo Colon	1.50
20 Katsuhiro Maeda	1.50

1997 Bowman's Best

The 200-card base set is divided into a 100-card subset featuring current super-stars on a gold chromium stock, and 100 cards of top prospects on a silver chromium stock. Packs contained six cards each and carried a suggested retail price of $5 each. Autographed cards of 10 different players were randomly inserted into packs, with each player signing regular, Refractor and Atomic Refractor versions of their cards. Bowman's Best Laser Cuts and Mirror Image are the two other inserts, each with Refractor and Atomic Refractor editions.

	MT
Complete Set (200):	100.00
Common Player:	.25
Star Refractors: 6x to 10x	
Young Star & RC Refractors: 4x to 8x	
Star Atomics: 12x to 20x	
Yng Star & RC Atomics: 8x to 15x	
Wax Box:	150.00
1 Ken Griffey Jr.	5.00
2 Cecil Fielder	.40
3 Albert Belle	1.50
4 Todd Hundley	.40
5 Mike Piazza	3.00
6 Matt Williams	.75
7 Mo Vaughn	1.50
8 Ryne Sandberg	1.50
9 Chipper Jones	3.00
10 Edgar Martinez	.25
11 Kenny Lofton	1.50
12 Ron Gant	.25
13 Moises Alou	.35
14 Pat Hentgen	.25
15 Steve Finley	.25
16 Mark Grace	.50
17 Jay Buhner	.50
18 Jeff Conine	.25
19 Jim Edmonds	.25
20 Todd Hollandsworth	.25
21 Andy Petitte	1.25
22 Jim Thome	.75
23 Eric Young	.25
24 Ray Lankford	.25
25 Marquis Grissom	.25
26 Tony Clark	1.00
27 Jermaine Allensworth	.25
28 Ellis Burks	.25
29 Tony Gwynn	2.50
30 Barry Larkin	.50
31 John Olerud	.25
32 Mariano Rivera	.40
33 Paul Molitor	1.00
34 Ken Caminiti	.50
35 Gary Sheffield	.75
36 Al Martin	.25
37 John Valentin	.25
38 Frank Thomas	4.00
39 John Jaha	.25
40 Greg Maddux	3.00
41 Alex Fernandez	.25
42 Dean Palmer	.25
43 Bernie Williams	1.25
44 Deion Sanders	.50
45 Mark McGwire	6.00
46 Brian Jordan	.25
47 Bernard Gilkey	.25
48 Will Clark	.50
49 Kevin Appier	.25
50 Tom Glavine	.40
51 Chuck Knoblauch	.50
52 Rondell White	.25
53 Greg Vaughn	.25
54 Mike Mussina	1.25
55 Brian McRae	.25
56 Chili Davis	.25
57 Wade Boggs	.50
58 Jeff Bagwell	2.00
59 Roberto Alomar	1.25
60 Dennis Eckersley	.25
61 Ryan Klesko	.75
62 Manny Ramirez	1.25
63 John Wetteland	.25
64 Cal Ripken Jr.	4.00
65 Edgar Renteria	.25
66 Tino Martinez	.75
67 Larry Walker	.75
68 Gregg Jefferies	.25
69 Lance Johnson	.25
70 Carlos Delgado	.25
71 Craig Biggio	.40
72 Jose Canseco	.40
73 Barry Bonds	1.50
74 Juan Gonzalez	2.50
75 Eric Karros	.25
76 Reggie Sanders	.25
77 Robin Ventura	.25
78 Hideo Nomo	1.50
79 David Justice	.40
80 Vinny Castilla	.25
81 Travis Fryman	.25
82 Derek Jeter	2.50
83 Sammy Sosa	3.00
84 Ivan Rodriguez	1.50
85 Rafael Palmeiro	.40
86 Roger Clemens	2.00
87 Jason Giambi	.25
88 Andres Galarraga	.50
89 Jermaine Dye	.25
90 Joe Carter	.25
91 Brady Anderson	.25
92 Derek Bell	.25
93 Randy Johnson	1.00
94 Fred McGriff	.40
95 John Smoltz	.40
96 Harold Baines	.25
97 Raul Mondesi	.50
98 Tim Salmon	.50

99	Carlos Baerga	.25
100	Dante Bichette	.50
101	Vladimir Guerrero	2.00
102	Richard Hidalgo	.25
103	Paul Konerko	1.00
104	*Alex Gonzalez*	1.50
105	Jason Dickson	.40
106	Jose Rosado	.25
107	Todd Walker	.75
108	*Seth Greisinger*	.50
109	Todd Helton	2.00
110	Ben Davis	.25
111	Bartolo Colon	.25
112	Elieser Marrero	.25
113	Jeff D'Amico	.25
114	*Miguel Tejada*	4.00
115	Darin Erstad	1.50
116	*Kris Benson*	4.00
117	*Adrian Beltre*	10.00
118	Neifi Perez	.25
119	Calvin Reese	.25
120	Carl Pavano	1.25
121	Juan Melo	.25
122	*Kevin McGlinchy*	.25
123	Pat Cline	.25
124	*Felix Heredia*	.60
125	Aaron Boone	.25
126	Glendon Rusch	.25
127	Mike Cameron	.75
128	Justin Thompson	.25
129	*Chad Hermansen*	5.00
130	*Sidney Ponson*	.50
131	*Willie Martinez*	1.00
132	*Paul Wilder*	2.00
133	Geoff Jenkins	.30
134	*Roy Halladay*	1.00
135	Carlos Guillen	.25
136	Tony Batista	.25
137	Todd Greene	.25
138	Luis Castillo	.25
139	*Jimmy Anderson*	.75
140	Edgard Velazquez	.40
141	Chris Snopek	.25
142	Ruben Rivera	.25
143	*Javier Valentin*	.40
144	Brian Rose	1.50
145	*Fernando Tatis*	4.00
146	*Dean Crow*	.25
147	Karim Garcia	.40
148	Dante Powell	.25
149	*Hideki Irabu*	8.00
150	Matt Morris	.50
151	Wes Helms	1.00
152	Russ Johnson	.25
153	Jarrod Washburn	.25
154	*Kerry Wood*	25.00
155	*Joe Fontenot*	.60
156	Eugene Kingsale	.25
157	Terrence Long	.25
158	Calvin Maduro	.25
159	Jeff Suppan	.25
160	DaRond Stovall	.25
161	Mark Redman	.25
162	*Ken Cloude*	2.50
163	Bobby Estalella	.25
164	*Abraham Nunez*	2.00
165	Derrick Gibson	.40
166	*Mike Drumright*	.75
167	Katsuhiro Maeda	.25
168	Jeff Liefer	.40
169	Ben Grieve	1.50
170	Bob Abreu	.25
171	Shannon Stewart	.25
172	*Braden Looper*	.50
173	Brant Brown	.25
174	Marlon Anderson	.75
175	Brad Fullmer	.25
176	Carlos Beltran	.25
177	Nomar Garciaparra	3.00
178	Derrek Lee	.25
179	*Valerio DeLosSantos*	.25
180	Dmitri Young	.25
181	Jamey Wright	.25
182	*Hiram Bocachica*	1.50
183	Wilton Guerrero	.25
184	Chris Carpenter	.25
185	Scott Spiezio	.25
186	Andruw Jones	2.00
187	*Travis Lee*	20.00
188	*Jose Cruz Jr.*	8.00
189	Jose Guillen	1.00
190	Jeff Abbott	.25
191	*Ricky Ledee*	5.00
192	Mike Sweeney	.25
193	Donnie Sadler	.25
194	Scott Rolen	2.50

195	Kevin Orie	.25
196	*Jason Conti*	.75
197	*Mark Kotsay*	5.00
198	Eric Milton	2.50
199	Russell Branyan	1.50
200	*Alex Sanchez*	1.00

1997 Bowman's Best Autographs

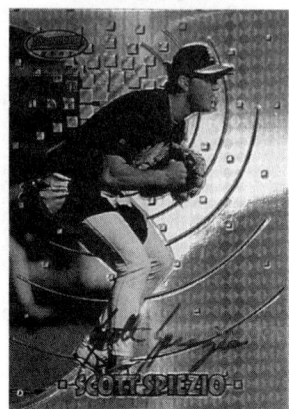

Ten different players each signed 10 regular versions of their respective Bowman's Best cards (1:170 packs), 10 of their Bowman's Best Refractors (1:2,036 packs) and 10 of their Bowman's Best Atomic Refractors (1:6,107 packs). Each autograph card features a special Certified Autograph stamp on the front.

		MT
Complete Set (10):		600.00
Common Player:		25.00
Refractors: 1.5x to 2x		
Atomics: 5x to 8x		
29	Tony Gwynn	125.00
33	Paul Molitor	40.00
82	Derek Jeter	140.00
91	Brady Anderson	30.00
98	Tim Salmon	35.00
107	Todd Walker	30.00
183	Wilton Guerrero	25.00
185	Scott Spiezio	25.00
188	Jose Cruz Jr.	60.00
194	Scott Rolen	65.00

1997 Bowman's Best Cuts

Each card in this 20-card insert features a laser-cut design on chromium stock. Backs have another color photo and list several of the player's career "Bests". Three different versions of each card are available: Regular (1:24 packs), Refractor (1:48 packs) and Atomic Refractor (1:96 packs).

		MT
Complete Set (20):		150.00
Common Player:		2.50
Refractors: 1.5x to 2x		
Atomic Refractors: 2x to 3x		
BC1	Derek Jeter	12.00
BC2	Chipper Jones	12.00
BC3	Frank Thomas	15.00
BC4	Cal Ripken Jr.	15.00
BC5	Mark McGwire	25.00
BC6	Ken Griffey Jr.	20.00
BC7	Jeff Bagwell	8.00
BC8	Mike Piazza	12.00
BC9	Ken Caminiti	3.00
BC10	Albert Belle	6.00
BC11	Jose Cruz Jr.	10.00
BC12	Wilton Guerrero	2.50
BC13	Darin Erstad	7.00
BC14	Andruw Jones	10.00
BC15	Scott Rolen	12.00
BC16	Jose Guillen	5.00
BC17	Bob Abreu	2.50
BC18	Vladimir Guerrero	8.00
BC19	Todd Walker	4.00
BC20	Nomar Garciaparra	12.00

1997 Bowman's Best Mirror Image

This 10-card insert features four players on each double-sided card - two veterans and two rookies - utilizing Finest technology. Regular Mirror Image cards are found 1:48 packs, while Refractor versions are seeded 1:96 packs and Atomic Refractors are found 1:192 packs.

		MT
Complete Set (10):		150.00
Common Card:		12.00
Refractors: 1.5x		
Atomic Refractors: 2x to 3x		
MI1	Nomar Garciaparra, Derek Jeter, Hiram Bocachica, Barry Larkin	20.00
MI2	Travis Lee, Frank Thomas, Derek Lee, Jeff Bagwell	20.00
MI3	Kerry Wood, Greg Maddux, Kris Benson, John Smoltz	25.00
MI4	Kevin Brown, Ivan Rodriguez, Elieser Marrero, Mike Piazza	20.00
MI5	Jose Cruz Jr., Ken Griffey Jr., Andruw Jones, Barry Bonds	25.00

MI6	Jose Guillen, Juan Gonzalez, Richard Hidalgo, Gary Sheffield	15.00
MI7	Paul Konerko, Mark McGwire, Todd Helton, Rafael Palmeiro	20.00
MI8	Wilton Guerrero, Craig Biggio, Donnie Sadler, Chuck Knoblauch	10.00
MI9	Russell Branyan, Matt Williams, Adrian Beltre, Chipper Jones	18.00
MI10	Bob Abreu, Kenny Lofton, Vladimir Guerrero, Albert Belle	15.00

1997 Bowman Chrome

Bowman Chrome was released in the winter after the conclusion of the 1997 season in one 300-card set. Packs contained four cards and carried an SRP of $3. Each card is simply a reprint of the regular Bowman set, with a chromium finish added to it. Key rookies include: Kerry Wood, Adrian Beltre, Travis Lee, Jose Cruz Jr., and Aramis Ramirez. Inserts include: International parallels (1:4 packs), Internation Refractors (1:24), Refractors (1:12), Rookie of the Year Favorites (1:24), ROY Favorites (1:72), Scout's Honor Roll (1:12) and Scout's Honor Roll Refractors (1:36).

	MT
Complete Set (300):	375.00
Common Player:	.25
Internationals: 1.5x to 2.5x	
Wax Box:	275.00
1 Derek Jeter	4.00
2 Chipper Jones	4.00
3 Hideo Nomo	1.25
4 Tim Salmon	.60
5 Robin Ventura	.40
6 Tony Clark	1.00
7 Barry Larkin	.75
8 Paul Molitor	1.00
9 Andy Benes	.25
10 Ryan Klesko	.50
11 Mark McGwire	8.00
12 Ken Griffey Jr.	7.00
13 Robb Nen	.25
14 Cal Ripken Jr.	5.00
15 John Valentin	.25
16 Ricky Bottalico	.25
17 Mike Lansing	.25
18 Ryne Sandberg	2.00
19 Carlos Delgado	.50
20 Craig Biggio	.50
21 Eric Karros	.40
22 Kevin Appier	.25

23	Mariano Rivera	.50
24	Vinny Castilla	.40
25	Juan Gonzalez	3.00
26	Al Martin	.25
27	Jeff Cirillo	.25
28	Ray Lankford	.25
29	Manny Ramirez	1.50
30	Roberto Alomar	1.25
31	Will Clark	.75
32	Chuck Knoblauch	.75
33	Harold Baines	.25
34	Edgar Martinez	.40
35	Mike Mussina	1.25
36	Kevin Brown	.40
37	Dennis Eckersley	.40
38	Tino Martinez	.75
39	Raul Mondesi	.50
40	Sammy Sosa	5.00
41	John Smoltz	.50
42	Billy Wagner	.25
43	Ken Caminiti	.50
44	Wade Boggs	.50
45	Andres Galarraga	.75
46	Roger Clemens	2.50
47	Matt Williams	.75
48	Albert Belle	1.50
49	Jeff King	.25
50	John Wetteland	.25
51	Deion Sanders	.75
52	Ellis Burks	.25
53	Pedro Martinez	.75
54	Kenny Lofton	1.50
55	Randy Johnson	1.00
56	Bernie Williams	1.00
57	Marquis Grissom	.40
58	Gary Sheffield	.75
59	Curt Schilling	.50
60	Reggie Sanders	.25
61	Bobby Higginson	.25
62	Moises Alou	.40
63	Tom Glavine	.50
64	Mark Grace	.75
65	Rafael Palmeiro	.60
66	John Olerud	.50
67	Dante Bichette	.50
68	Jeff Bagwell	2.50
69	Barry Bonds	1.50
70	Pat Hentgen	.25
71	Jim Thome	1.00
72	Andy Pettitte	1.00
73	Jay Bell	.25
74	Jim Edmonds	.40
75	Ron Gant	.40
76	David Cone	.40
77	Jose Canseco	.75
78	Jay Buhner	.50
79	Greg Maddux	4.00
80	Lance Johnson	.25
81	Travis Fryman	.40
82	Paul O'Neill	.50
83	Ivan Rodriguez	1.50
84	Fred McGriff	.50
85	Mike Piazza	4.00
86	Brady Anderson	.40
87	Marty Cordova	.25
88	Joe Carter	.40
89	Brian Jordan	.25
90	David Justice	.75
91	Tony Gwynn	3.50
92	Larry Walker	.75
93	Mo Vaughn	1.50
94	Sandy Alomar	.40
95	Rusty Greer	.40
96	Roberto Hernandez	.25
97	Hal Morris	.25
98	Todd Hundley	.25
99	Rondell White	.50
100	Frank Thomas	5.00
101	Bubba Trammell	2.50
102	Sidney Ponson	2.00
103	Ricky Ledee	8.00
104	Brett Tomko	.25
105	Braden Looper	1.00
106	Jason Dickson	.40
107	Chad Green	3.00
108	R.A. Dickey	.75
109	Jeff Liefer	.40
110	Richard Hidalgo	.25
111	Chad Hermansen	12.00
112	Felix Martinez	.25
113	J.J. Johnson	.25
114	Todd Dunwoody	1.50
115	Katsuhiro Maeda	.25
116	Darin Erstad	2.50
117	Elieser Marrero	.25
118	Bartolo Colon	.25

119	Ugueth Urbina	.25
120	Jaime Bluma	.25
121	Seth Greisinger	2.00
122	Jose Cruz Jr.	20.00
123	Todd Dunn	.25
124	Justin Towle	4.00
125	Brian Rose	1.50
126	Jose Guillen	1.50
127	Andruw Jones	3.50
128	Mark Kotsay	12.00
129	Wilton Guerrero	.25
130	Jacob Cruz	.25
131	Mike Sweeney	.25
132	Matt Morris	.50
133	John Thomson	.25
134	Javier Valentin	.40
135	Mike Drumright	1.50
136	Michael Barrett	.25
137	Tony Saunders	3.00
138	Kevin Brown	.25
139	Anthony Sanders	4.00
140	Jeff Abbott	.25
141	Eugene Kingsale	.25
142	Paul Konerko	2.00
143	Randall Simon	6.00
144	Freddy Garcia	.25
145	Karim Garcia	.40
146	Carlos Guillen	.25
147	Aaron Boone	.25
148	Donnie Sadler	.25
149	Brooks Kieschnick	.25
150	Scott Spiezio	.25
151	Kevin Orie	.25
152	Russ Johnson	.25
153	Livan Hernandez	.40
154	Vladimir Nunez	3.00
155	Calvin Reese	.25
156	Chris Carpenter	.25
157	Eric Milton	8.00
158	Richie Sexson	.40
159	Carl Pavano	1.50
160	Pat Cline	.25
161	Ron Wright	.25
162	Dante Powell	.25
163	Mark Bellhorn	.25
164	George Lombard	1.00
165	Paul Wilder	4.00
166	Brad Fullmer	.50
167	Kris Benson	7.00
168	Torii Hunter	.25
169	D.T. Cromer	.25
170	Nelson Figueroa	1.00
171	Hiram Bocachica	2.50
172	Shane Monahan	.25
173	Juan Melo	.25
174	Calvin Pickering	8.00
175	Reggie Taylor	.25
176	Geoff Jenkins	.50
177	Steve Rain	1.00
178	Nerio Rodriguez	1.00
179	Derrick Gibson	1.00
180	Darin Blood	.25
181	Ben Davis	.25
182	Adrian Beltre	30.00
183	Kerry Wood	75.00
184	Nate Rolison	3.00
185	Fernando Tatis	8.00
186	Jake Westbrook	2.00
187	Edwin Diaz	.25
188	Joe Fontenot	2.00
189	Matt Halloran	1.00
190	Matt Clement	8.00
191	Todd Greene	.25
192	Eric Chavez	18.00
193	Edgard Velazquez	.25
194	Bruce Chen	6.00
195	Jason Brester	.25
196	Chris Reitsma	1.50
197	Neifi Perez	.25
198	Hideki Irabu	15.00
199	Don Denbow	.25
200	Derrek Lee	.25
201	Todd Walker	.75
202	Scott Rolen	4.00
203	Wes Helms	2.00
204	Bob Abreu	.25
205	John Patterson	4.00
206	Alex Gonzalez	3.00
207	Grant Roberts	4.00
208	Jeff Suppan	.25
209	Luke Wilcox	.25
210	Marlon Anderson	.25
211	Mike Caruso	5.00
212	Roy Halladay	3.00
213	Jeremi Gonzalez	3.00
214	Aramis Ramirez	20.00

215	*Dermal Brown*	10.00
216	Justin Thompson	.25
217	Danny Clyburn	.25
218	Bruce Aven	.25
219	Keith Foulke	.25
220	Shannon Stewart	.25
221	Larry Barnes	.25
222	Mark Johnson	.75
223	Randy Winn	.25
224	Nomar Garciaparra	5.00
225	*Jacque Jones*	5.00
226	Chris Clemons	.25
227	Todd Helton	3.00
228	Ryan Brannan	1.50
229	*Alex Sanchez*	2.00
230	Russell Branyan	1.50
231	Daryle Ward	3.00
232	Kevin Witt	5.00
233	Gabby Martinez	.25
234	Preston Wilson	.25
235	*Donzell McDonald*	2.00
236	*Orlando Cabrera*	2.00
237	Brian Banks	.25
238	Robbie Bell	2.00
239	Brad Rigby	.25
240	Scott Elarton	.25
241	*Donny Leon*	.75
242	Abraham Nunez	3.00
243	*Adam Eaton*	.75
244	*Octavio Dotel*	.75
245	Sean Casey	6.00
246	*Joe Lawrence*	.75
247	*Adam Johnson*	2.50
248	*Ronnie Belliard*	1.00
249	Bobby Estalella	.25
250	*Corey Lee*	1.50
251	Mike Cameron	.75
252	*Kerry Robinson*	1.50
253	A.J. Zapp	6.00
254	Jarrod Washburn	.25
255	Ben Grieve	4.00
256	*Javier Vazquez*	2.00
257	*Travis Lee*	35.00
258	*Dennis Reyes*	3.00
259	Danny Buxbaum	.25
260	*Kelvim Escobar*	1.00
261	Danny Klassen	.35
262	*Ken Cloude*	5.00
263	Gabe Alvarez	.25
264	*Clayton Brunner*	1.50
265	*Jason Marquis*	3.00
266	Jamey Wright	.25
267	*Matt Snyder*	.75
268	*Josh Garrett*	3.00
269	Juan Encarnacion	1.00
270	Heath Murray	.25
271	*Brent Butler*	8.00
272	*Danny Peoples*	3.00
273	*Miguel Tejada*	10.00
274	Jim Pittsley	.25
275	Dmitri Young	.25
276	Vladimir Guerrero	2.50
277	Cole Liniak	6.00
278	Ramon Hernandez	.75
279	Cliff Politte	2.00
280	*Mel Rosario*	.75
281	*Jorge Carrion*	1.00
282	*John Barnes*	3.00
283	*Chris Stowe*	1.50
284	Vernon Wells	10.00
285	*Brett Caradonna*	5.00
286	Scott Hodges	2.00
287	*Jon Garland*	5.00
288	Nathan Haynes	2.00
289	*Geoff Goetz*	3.00
290	Adam Kennedy	3.00
291	*T.J. Tucker*	.75
292	*Aaron Akin*	1.50
293	*Jayson Werth*	10.00
294	*Glenn Davis*	3.00
295	*Mark Mangum*	1.50
296	*Troy Cameron*	5.00
297	*J.J. Davis*	7.00
298	Lance Berkman	20.00
299	*Jason Standridge*	3.00
300	*Jason Dellaero*	3.00

1997 Bowman Chrome Refractors

All 300 cards in Bowman Chrome were reprinted in Refractor versions and inserted one per 12 packs. The cards are very similar to the base cards, but feature a refractive foil finish.

		MT
Common Player:		5.00
Star Refractors: 6x to 12x		
Young Stars & RC's: 3x to 6x		
International Refractors: 1x to 1.5x		

1	Derek Jeter	50.00
2	Chipper Jones	60.00
3	Hideo Nomo	20.00
4	Tim Salmon	15.00
5	Robin Ventura	8.00
6	Tony Clark	15.00
7	Barry Larkin	15.00
8	Paul Molitor	20.00
9	Andy Benes	5.00
10	Ryan Klesko	15.00
11	Mark McGwire	125.00
12	Ken Griffey Jr.	100.00
13	Robb Nen	5.00
14	Cal Ripken Jr.	80.00
15	John Valentin	5.00
16	Ricky Bottalico	5.00
17	Mike Lansing	5.00
18	Ryne Sandberg	30.00
19	Carlos Delgado	10.00
20	Craig Biggio	10.00
21	Eric Karros	8.00
22	Kevin Appier	5.00
23	Mariano Rivera	8.00
24	Vinny Castilla	8.00
25	Juan Gonzalez	50.00
26	Al Martin	5.00
27	Jeff Cirillo	5.00
28	Ray Lankford	5.00
29	Manny Ramirez	25.00
30	Roberto Alomar	20.00
31	Will Clark	15.00
32	Chuck Knoblauch	15.00
33	Harold Baines	5.00
34	Edgar Martinez	8.00
35	Mike Mussina	20.00
36	Kevin Brown	8.00
37	Dennis Eckersley	8.00
38	Tino Martinez	15.00
39	Raul Mondesi	12.00
40	Sammy Sosa	60.00
41	John Smoltz	8.00
42	Billy Wagner	5.00
43	Ken Caminiti	8.00
44	Wade Boggs	12.00
45	Andres Galarraga	15.00
46	Roger Clemens	40.00
47	Matt Williams	15.00
48	Albert Belle	25.00
49	Jeff King	5.00
50	John Wetteland	5.00
51	Deion Sanders	10.00
52	Ellis Burks	5.00
53	Pedro Martinez	15.00
54	Kenny Lofton	25.00
55	Randy Johnson	20.00
56	Bernie Williams	20.00
57	Marquis Grissom	8.00
58	Gary Sheffield	15.00
59	Curt Schilling	10.00
60	Reggie Sanders	5.00
61	Bobby Higginson	5.00
62	Moises Alou	10.00
63	Tom Glavine	10.00
64	Mark Grace	15.00
65	Rafael Palmeiro	10.00
66	John Olerud	10.00
67	Dante Bichette	10.00
68	Jeff Bagwell	35.00
69	Barry Bonds	25.00
70	Pat Hentgen	5.00
71	Jim Thome	20.00
72	Andy Pettitte	20.00
73	Jay Bell	5.00
74	Jim Edmonds	5.00
75	Ron Gant	8.00
76	David Cone	8.00
77	Jose Canseco	15.00
78	Jay Buhner	12.00
79	Greg Maddux	60.00
80	Lance Johnson	5.00
81	Travis Fryman	8.00
82	Paul O'Neill	10.00
83	Ivan Rodriguez	25.00
84	Fred McGriff	10.00
85	Mike Piazza	60.00
86	Brady Anderson	8.00
87	Marty Cordova	5.00

88	Joe Carter	8.00
89	Brian Jordan	5.00
90	David Justice	15.00
91	Tony Gwynn	50.00
92	Larry Walker	15.00
93	Mo Vaughn	25.00
94	Sandy Alomar	8.00
95	Rusty Greer	8.00
96	Roberto Hernandez	5.00
97	Hal Morris	5.00
98	Todd Hundley	5.00
99	Rondell White	10.00
100	Frank Thomas	70.00
101	*Bubba Trammell*	25.00
102	*Sidney Ponson*	20.00
103	*Ricky Ledee*	40.00
104	Brett Tomko	5.00
105	*Braden Looper*	15.00
106	Jason Dickson	5.00
107	*Chad Green*	25.00
108	*R.A. Dickey*	10.00
109	Jeff Liefer	5.00
110	Richard Hidalgo	5.00
111	*Chad Hermansen*	50.00
112	Felix Martinez	5.00
113	J.J. Johnson	5.00
114	Todd Dunwoody	10.00
115	Katsuhiro Maeda	5.00
116	Darin Erstad	30.00
117	Elieser Marrero	5.00
118	Bartolo Colon	10.00
119	Ugueth Urbina	5.00
120	Jaime Bluma	5.00
121	Seth Greisinger	20.00
122	Jose Cruz Jr.	80.00
123	Todd Dunn	5.00
124	Justin Towle	25.00
125	Brian Rose	10.00
126	Jose Guillen	15.00
127	Andruw Jones	25.00
128	*Mark Kotsay*	40.00
129	Wilton Guerrero	5.00
130	Jacob Cruz	5.00
131	Mike Sweeney	5.00
132	Matt Morris	10.00
133	John Thomson	5.00
134	*Javier Valentin*	8.00
135	*Mike Drumright*	15.00
136	Michael Barrett	5.00
137	*Tony Saunders*	20.00
138	Kevin Brown	5.00
139	*Anthony Sanders*	20.00
140	Jeff Abbott	5.00
141	Eugene Kingsale	5.00
142	Paul Konerko	25.00
143	*Randall Simon*	40.00
144	Freddy Garcia	5.00
145	Karim Garcia	5.00
146	Carlos Guillen	5.00
147	Aaron Boone	5.00
148	Donnie Sadler	5.00
149	Brooks Kieschnick	5.00
150	Scott Spiezio	5.00
151	Kevin Orie	5.00
152	Russ Johnson	5.00
153	Livan Hernandez	8.00
154	Vladimir Nunez	20.00
155	Calvin Reese	5.00
156	Chris Carpenter	5.00
157	*Eric Milton*	30.00
158	Richie Sexson	5.00
159	Carl Pavano	15.00
160	Pat Cline	5.00
161	Ron Wright	8.00
162	Dante Powell	5.00
163	Mark Bellhorn	5.00
164	George Lombard	5.00
165	*Paul Wilder*	25.00
166	Brad Fullmer	10.00
167	*Kris Benson*	40.00
168	Torii Hunter	5.00
169	D.T. Cromer	5.00
170	Nelson Figueroa	10.00
171	*Hiram Bocachica*	20.00
172	Shane Monahan	5.00
173	Juan Melo	5.00
174	*Calvin Pickering*	50.00
175	Reggie Taylor	5.00
176	Geoff Jenkins	8.00
177	Steve Rain	8.00
178	Nerio Rodriguez	8.00
179	Derrick Gibson	8.00
180	Darin Blood	5.00
181	Ben Davis	5.00
182	Adrian Beltre	90.00
183	*Kerry Wood*	200.00

184	Nate Rolison	20.00
185	Fernando Tatis	40.00
186	Jake Westbrook	12.00
187	Edwin Diaz	5.00
188	Joe Fontenot	10.00
189	Matt Halloran	8.00
190	Matt Clement	25.00
191	Todd Greene	5.00
192	Eric Chavez	50.00
193	Edgard Velazquez	5.00
194	*Bruce Chen*	30.00
195	Jason Brester	5.00
196	*Chris Reitsma*	10.00
197	Neifi Perez	5.00
198	*Hideki Irabu*	50.00
199	*Don Denbow*	5.00
200	Derrek Lee	5.00
201	Todd Walker	12.00
202	Scott Rolen	40.00
203	Wes Helms	12.00
204	Bob Abreu	5.00
205	*John Patterson*	20.00
206	*Alex Gonzalez*	20.00
207	*Grant Roberts*	25.00
208	Jeff Suppan	5.00
209	Luke Wilcox	5.00
210	Marlon Anderson	5.00
211	*Mike Caruso*	30.00
212	*Roy Halladay*	20.00
213	*Jeremi Gonzalez*	20.00
214	Aramis Ramirez	75.00
215	*Dermal Brown*	40.00
216	Justin Thompson	5.00
217	Danny Clyburn	5.00
218	Bruce Aven	5.00
219	Keith Foulke	5.00
220	Shannon Stewart	5.00
221	Larry Barnes	5.00
222	Mark Johnson	8.00
223	Randy Winn	5.00
224	Nomar Garciaparra	60.00
225	*Jacque Jones*	25.00
226	Chris Clemons	5.00
227	Todd Helton	30.00
228	*Ryan Brannan*	10.00
229	*Alex Sanchez*	12.00
230	Russell Branyan	10.00
231	Daryle Ward	15.00
232	Kevin Witt	30.00
233	Gabby Martinez	5.00
234	Preston Wilson	5.00
235	*Donzell McDonald*	10.00
236	*Orlando Cabrera*	10.00
237	Brian Banks	5.00
238	Robbie Bell	10.00
239	Brad Rigby	5.00
240	Scott Elarton	5.00
241	*Donny Leon*	8.00
242	*Abraham Nunez*	20.00
243	*Adam Eaton*	8.00
244	*Octavio Dotel*	8.00
245	Sean Casey	40.00
246	*Joe Lawrence*	8.00
247	*Adam Johnson*	15.00
248	*Ronnie Belliard*	10.00
249	Bobby Estalella	5.00
250	Corey Lee	10.00
251	Mike Cameron	10.00
252	Kerry Robinson	10.00
253	*A.J. Zapp*	40.00
254	Jarrod Washburn	10.00
255	Ben Grieve	40.00
256	*Javier Vazquez*	10.00
257	Travis Lee	150.00
258	*Dennis Reyes*	20.00
259	Danny Buxbaum	5.00
260	Kelvim Escobar	8.00
261	Danny Klassen	5.00
262	Ken Cloude	30.00
263	Gabe Alvarez	5.00
264	*Clayton Brunner*	10.00
265	*Jason Marquis*	20.00
266	Jamey Wright	5.00
267	*Matt Snyder*	8.00
268	*Josh Garrett*	20.00
269	Juan Encarnacion	8.00
270	Heath Murray	5.00
271	*Brent Butler*	40.00
272	*Danny Peoples*	20.00
273	*Miguel Tejada*	50.00
274	Jim Pittsley	5.00
275	Dmitri Young	5.00
276	Vladimir Guerrero	25.00
277	*Cole Liniak*	40.00
278	Ramon Hernandez	5.00
279	*Cliff Politte*	10.00

280	*Mel Rosario*	5.00
281	*Jorge Carrion*	8.00
282	*John Barnes*	20.00
283	*Chris Stowe*	10.00
284	*Vernon Wells*	50.00
285	*Brett Caradonna*	30.00
286	*Scott Hodges*	10.00
287	*Jon Garland*	30.00
288	*Nathan Haynes*	15.00
289	*Geoff Goetz*	20.00
290	*Adam Kennedy*	20.00
291	*T.J. Tucker*	5.00
292	*Aaron Akin*	10.00
293	*Jayson Werth*	50.00
294	Glenn Davis	20.00
295	*Mark Mangum*	10.00
296	*Troy Cameron*	30.00
297	*J.J. Davis*	40.00
298	*Lance Berkman*	80.00
299	*Jason Standridge*	10.00
300	*Jason Dellaero*	12.00

1997 Bowman Chrome Scout's Honor Roll

This 15-card set featured top prospects and rookies as selected by the Bowman Scouts. These chromium cards are numbered with a "SHR" prefix and were inserted one per 12 packs, while Refractor versions are seeded one per 36 packs.

	MT
Complete Set (15):	70.00
Common Player:	1.50
Refractors: 1.5x to 2.5x	
SHR1 Dmitri Young	1.50
SHR2 Bob Abreu	1.50
SHR3 Vladimir Guerrero	5.00
SHR4 Paul Konerko	4.00
SHR5 Kevin Orie	1.50
SHR6 Todd Walker	2.00
SHR7 Ben Grieve	6.00
SHR8 Darin Erstad	4.00
SHR9 Derrek Lee	1.50
SHR10 Jose Cruz, Jr.	12.00
SHR11 Scott Rolen	8.00
SHR12 Travis Lee	20.00
SHR13 Andruw Jones	6.00
SHR14 Wilton Guerrero	1.50
SHR15 Nomar Garciaparra	10.00

1997 Bowman Chrome ROY Candidates

This 15-card insert set features color action photos of 1998 Rookie of the Year candidates printed on chromium finish cards. Card backs are numbered with a "ROY" prefix and were inserted one per 24 packs of Bowman Chrome. Refractor versions are seeded one per 72 packs.

	MT
Complete Set (15):	70.00
Common Player:	2.00
Refractors: 1.5x to 2.5x	
ROY1 Jeff Abbott	2.00
ROY2 Karim Garcia	2.50
ROY3 Todd Helton	7.00
ROY4 Richard Hidalgo	2.00
ROY5 Geoff Jenkins	2.00
ROY6 Russ Johnson	2.00
ROY7 Paul Konerko	8.00
ROY8 Mark Kotsay	10.00
ROY9 Ricky Ledee	8.00
ROY10 Travis Lee	30.00
ROY11 Derrek Lee	2.00
ROY12 Elieser Marrero	2.00
ROY13 Juan Melo	2.00
ROY14 Brian Rose	3.00
ROY15 Fernando Tatis	8.00

1998 Bowman

Bowman arrived in a 440-card set released in two, 220-card series in 1998. Within each series, there were 150 prospects printed on a silver and blue design and 70 veterans printed on a silver and red design. The cards feature a Bowman stamp, and in cases where is the player's first Bowman card a "Bowman Rookie Card" stamp is included. The player's facsimile signature from their first Bowman contract runs down the side. The entire set was paralleled twice in a Bowman International parallel (one per pack) and a Golden Anniversary parallel (numbered to 50). Inserts in Series I include Autographs, Scout's Choice, and Japanese Rookies. Inserts in Series II include: Autographs, 1999 Rookie of the Year Favorites, Minor League MVPs and Japanese Rookies.

		MT
Complete Set (441):		160.00
Complete Series I set (221):		90.00
Complete Series II set (220):		75.00
Common Player:		.20
Unlisted Stars: .50 to .75		
Internationals: 1.5x to 3x		
Inserted 1:1		
Wax Box:		85.00
1	Nomar Garciaparra	2.50
2	Scott Rolen	1.50
3	Andy Pettitte	.75
4	Ivan Rodriguez	1.00
5	Mark McGwire	5.00
6	Jason Dickson	.20
7	Jose Cruz Jr.	1.50
8	Jeff Kent	.20
9	Mike Mussina	.75
10	Jason Kendall	.20
11	Brett Tomko	.20
12	Jeff King	.20
13	Brad Radke	.20
14	Robin Ventura	.30
15	Jeff Bagwell	1.50
16	Greg Maddux	2.50
17	John Jaha	.20
18	Mike Piazza	2.50
19	Edgar Martinez	.20
20	David Justice	.40
21	Todd Hundley	.20
22	Tony Gwynn	2.00
23	Larry Walker	.60
24	Bernie Williams	.75
25	Edgar Renteria	.20
26	Rafael Palmeiro	.40
27	Tim Salmon	.50
28	Matt Morris	.40
29	Shawn Estes	.20
30	Vladimir Guerrero	1.00
31	Fernando Tatis	.20

#	Player	Value
32	Justin Thompson	.20
33	Ken Griffey Jr.	4.00
34	Edgardo Alfonzo	.20
35	Mo Vaughn	1.00
36	Marty Cordova	.20
37	Craig Biggio	.40
38	Roger Clemens	1.50
39	Mark Grace	.50
40	Ken Caminiti	.40
41	Tony Womack	.20
42	Albert Belle	1.00
43	Tino Martinez	.75
44	Sandy Alomar	.40
45	Jeff Cirillo	.20
46	Jason Giambi	.20
47	Darin Erstad	1.00
48	Livan Hernandez	.20
49	Mark Grudzielanek	.20
50	Sammy Sosa	2.00
51	Curt Schilling	.40
52	Brian Hunter	.20
53	Neifi Perez	.20
54	Todd Walker	.40
55	Jose Guillen	.40
56	Jim Thome	.75
57	Tom Glavine	.40
58	Todd Greene	.20
59	Rondell White	.40
60	Roberto Alomar	.75
61	Tony Clark	.60
62	Vinny Castilla	.40
63	Barry Larkin	.50
64	Hideki Irabu	1.00
65	Johnny Damon	.20
66	Juan Gonzalez	2.00
67	John Olerud	.40
68	Gary Sheffield	.50
69	Raul Mondesi	.40
70	Chipper Jones	2.50
71	David Ortiz	.75
72	*Warren Morris*	.50
73	Alex Gonzalez	.40
74	Nick Bierbrodt	.20
75	Roy Halladay	.40
76	Danny Buxbaum	.20
77	Adam Kennedy	.40
78	*Jared Sandberg*	1.50
79	Michael Barrett	.20
80	Gil Meche	.40
81	Jayson Werth	.50
82	Abraham Nunez	.50
83	Ben Petrick	.20
84	Brett Caradonna	.40
85	*Mike Lowell*	2.00
86	*Clay Bruner*	1.00
87	*John Curtice*	1.00
88	Bobby Estalella	.20
89	Juan Melo	.20
90	Arnold Gooch	.20
91	*Kevin Millwood*	6.00
92	Richie Sexson	.20
93	Orlando Cabrera	.40
94	Pat Cline	.20
95	Anthony Sanders	.50
96	Russ Johnson	.20
97	Ben Grieve	1.50
98	Kevin McGlinchy	.20
99	Paul Wilder	.20
100	Russ Ortiz	.20
101	*Ryan Jackson*	2.00
102	Heath Murray	.20
103	Brian Rose	.40
104	*Ryan Radmanovich*	1.00
105	Ricky Ledee	1.00
106	*Jeff Wallace*	.50
107	*Ryan Minor*	5.00
108	Dennis Reyes	.50
109	*James Manias*	1.00
110	Chris Carpenter	.20
111	Daryle Ward	.20
112	Vernon Wells	.75
113	Chad Green	.40
114	*Mike Stoner*	5.00
115	Brad Fullmer	.20
116	Adam Eaton	.20
117	Jeff Liefer	.20
118	*Corey Koskie*	2.00
119	Todd Helton	.75
120	*Jaime Jones*	1.00
121	Mel Rosario	.20
122	Geoff Goetz	.20
123	Adrian Beltre	3.00
124	Jason Dellaero	.50
125	*Gabe Kapler*	5.00
126	Scott Schoeneweis	.20
127	Ryan Brannan	.20
128	Aaron Akin	.20
129	*Ryan Anderson*	6.00
130	Brad Penny	.20
131	Bruce Chen	.50
132	Eli Marrero	.20
133	Eric Chavez	1.50
134	*Troy Glaus*	10.00
135	Troy Cameron	.50
136	*Brian Sikorski*	.75
137	*Mike Kinkade*	2.00
138	Braden Looper	.20
139	Mark Mangum	.20
140	Danny Peoples	.50
141	J.J. Davis	.75
142	Ben Davis	.20
143	Jacque Jones	.50
144	Derrick Gibson	.20
145	Bronson Arroyo	.50
146	*Cristian Guzman*	.50
147	Jeff Abbott	.20
148	*Mike Cuddyer*	6.00
149	Jason Romano	.75
150	Shane Monahan	.20
151	*Ntema Ndungidi*	1.00
152	Alex Sanchez	.40
153	*Jack Cust*	2.00
154	Brent Butler	1.00
155	Ramon Hernandez	.20
156	Norm Hutchins	.20
157	Jason Marquis	.20
158	Jacob Cruz	.20
159	*Rob Burger*	1.50
160	Eric Milton	.75
161	Preston Wilson	.20
162	*Jason Fitzgerald*	1.00
163	Dan Serafini	.20
164	Peter Munro	.20
165	Trot Nixon	.20
166	Homer Bush	.20
167	Dermal Brown	1.00
168	Chad Hermansen	1.50
169	*Julio Moreno*	.75
170	*John Roskos*	1.00
171	Grant Roberts	1.00
172	Ken Cloude	.50
173	Jason Brester	.20
174	Jason Conti	.20
175	Jon Garland	.50
176	Robbie Bell	.20
177	Nathan Haynes	.20
178	*Ramon Ortiz*	5.00
179	Shannon Stewart	.20
180	Pablo Ortega	.20
181	*Jimmy Rollins*	1.00
182	Sean Casey	.50
183	*Ted Lilly*	.50
184	Chris Enochs	2.50
185	*Magglio Ordonez*	3.00
186	Mike Drumright	.20
187	Aaron Boone	.20
188	Matt Clement	.20
189	Todd Dunwoody	.40
190	Larry Rodriguez	.20
191	Todd Noel	.20
192	Geoff Jenkins	.20
193	George Lombard	.20
194	Lance Berkman	2.00
195	*Marcus McCain*	.50
196	Ryan McGuire	.20
197	*Jhensy Sandoval*	2.00
198	Corey Lee	.20
199	Mario Valdez	.20
200	*Robert Fick*	1.00
201	Donnie Sadler	.20
202	Marc Kroon	.20
203	David Miller	.20
204	Jarrod Washburn	.20
205	Miguel Tejada	1.50
206	Raul Ibanez	.20
207	John Patterson	.50
208	Calvin Pickering	.75
209	Felix Martinez	.20
210	Mark Redman	.20
211	Scott Elarton	.20
212	*Jose Amado*	.75
213	Kerry Wood	8.00
214	Dante Powell	.20
215	Aramis Ramirez	2.50
216	A.J. Hinch	1.50
217	*Dustin Carr*	.50
218	Mark Kotsay	1.50
219	Jason Standridge	.20
220	Luis Ordaz	.20
221	*Orlando Hernandez*	8.00
222	Cal Ripken Jr.	3.00
223	Paul Molitor	.75
224	Derek Jeter	2.50
225	Barry Bonds	1.00
226	Jim Edmonds	.20
227	John Smoltz	.40
228	Eric Karros	.30
229	Ray Lankford	.20
230	Rey Ordonez	.20
231	Kenny Lofton	1.00
232	Alex Rodriguez	2.50
233	Dante Bichette	.40
234	Pedro Martinez	.75
235	Carlos Delgado	.20
236	Rod Beck	.20
237	Matt Williams	.50
238	Charles Johnson	.20
239	Rico Brogna	.20
240	Frank Thomas	2.50
241	Paul O'Neill	.50
242	Jaret Wright	1.00
243	Brant Brown	.20
244	Ryan Klesko	.40
245	Chuck Finley	.20
246	Derek Bell	.20
247	Delino DeShields	.20
248	Chan Ho Park	.40
249	Wade Boggs	.40
250	Jay Buhner	.50
251	Butch Huskey	.20
252	Steve Finley	.20
253	Will Clark	.50
254	John Valentin	.20
255	Bobby Higginson	.20
256	Darryl Strawberry	.40
257	Randy Johnson	.75
258	Al Martin	.20
259	Travis Fryman	.20
260	Fred McGriff	.40
261	Jose Valentin	.20
262	Andruw Jones	1.00
263	Kenny Rogers	.20
264	Moises Alou	.40
265	Denny Neagle	.20
266	Ugueth Urbina	.20
267	Derrek Lee	.20
268	Ellis Burks	.20
269	Mariano Rivera	.40
270	Dean Palmer	.20
271	Eddie Taubensee	.20
272	Brady Anderson	.20
273	Brian Giles	.20
274	Quinton McCracken	.20
275	Henry Rodriguez	.20
276	Andres Galarraga	.50
277	Jose Canseco	.60
278	David Segui	.20
279	Bret Saberhagen	.20
280	Kevin Brown	.40
281	Chuck Knoblauch	.60
282	Jeromy Burnitz	.20
283	Jay Bell	.20
284	Manny Ramirez	1.00
285	Rick Helling	.20
286	Francisco Cordova	.20
287	Bob Abreu	.20
288	J.T. Snow Jr.	.20
289	Hideo Nomo	.60
290	Brian Jordan	.20
291	Javy Lopez	.20
292	Travis Lee	2.00
293	Russell Branyan	.20
294	Paul Konerko	.40
295	*Masato Yoshii*	1.50
296	Kris Benson	.40
297	Juan Encarnacion	.20
298	Eric Milton	.20
299	Mike Caruso	.20
300	*Ricardo Arambolcs*	2.50
301	Bobby Smith	.20
302	Billy Koch	.20
303	Richard Hidalgo	.20
304	*Justin Baughman*	1.00
305	Chris Gissell	.20
306	*Donnie Bridges*	1.50
307	*Nelson Lara*	1.00
308	*Randy Wolf*	.75
309	*Jason LaRue*	1.00
310	*Jason Gooding*	.50
311	*Edgar Clemente*	.50
312	Andrew Vessel	.20
313	Chris Reitsma	.20
314	*Jesus Sanchez*	1.00
315	*Buddy Carlyle*	.75
316	Randy Winn	.20
317	Luis Rivera	2.50
318	*Marcus Thames*	1.50
319	A.J. Pierzynski	.20

320	Scott Randall	.20
321	Damian Sapp	.20
322	Eddie Yarnell	3.00
323	Luke Allen	1.50
324	J.D. Smart	.20
325	Willie Martinez	.20
326	Alex Ramirez	.20
327	Eric DuBose	1.00
328	Kevin Witt	.20
329	Dan McKinley	.75
330	Cliff Politte	.20
331	Vladimir Nunez	.20
332	John Halama	.50
333	Nerio Rodriguez	.20
334	Desi Relaford	.20
335	Robinson Checo	.20
336	John Nicholson	1.00
337	Tom LaRosa	.75
338	Kevin Nicholson	2.00
339	Javier Vazquez	.20
340	A.J. Zapp	.20
341	Tom Evans	.20
342	Kerry Robinson	.20
343	Gabe Gonzalez	.75
344	Ralph Milliard	.20
345	Enrique Wilson	.20
346	Elvin Hernandez	.20
347	Mike Lincoln	1.50
348	Cesar King	2.00
349	Cristian Guzman	1.00
350	Donzell McDonald	.20
351	Jim Parque	1.00
352	Mike Saipe	1.00
353	Carlos Febles	.75
354	Dernell Stenson	2.00
355	Mark Osborne	1.50
356	Odalis Perez	1.50
357	Jason Dewey	1.00
358	Joe Fontenot	.20
359	Jason Grilli	1.50
360	Kevin Haverbusch	1.50
361	Jay Yennaco	.50
362	Brian Buchanan	.20
363	John Barnes	.20
364	Chris Fussell	.20
365	Kevin Gibbs	.75
366	Joe Lawrence	.20
367	DaRond Stovall	.20
368	Brian Fuentes	2.00
369	Jimmy Anderson	.20
370	Laril Gonzalez	1.00
371	Scott Williamson	1.00
372	Milton Bradley	.20
373	Jason Halper	.75
374	Brent Billingsley	.75
375	Joe DePastino	.20
376	Jake Westbrook	.20
377	Octavio Dotel	.20
378	Jason Williams	.50
379	Julio Ramirez	1.50
380	Seth Greisinger	.20
381	Mike Judd	1.00
382	Ben Ford	.50
383	Tom Bennett	.20
384	Adam Butler	.50
385	Wade Miller	.75
386	Kyle Peterson	.75
387	Tommy Peterman	1.00
388	Onan Masaoka	.20
389	Jason Rakers	.75
390	Rafael Medina	.20
391	Luis Lopez	.20
392	Jeff Yoder	.20
393	Vance Wilson	.75
394	Fernando Seguignol	2.00
395	Ron Wright	.20
396	Ruben Mateo	4.00
397	Steve Lomasney	.75
398	Damian Jackson	.20
399	Mike Jerzembeck	.75
400	Luis Rivas	1.50
401	Kevin Burford	1.50
402	Glenn Davis	.20
403	Robert Luce	.75
404	Cole Liniak	.20
405	Matthew LeCroy	1.00
406	Jeremy Giambi	2.50
407	Shawn Chacon	.20
408	Dewayne Wise	1.50
409	Steve Woodard	.75
410	Francisco Cordero	.50
411	Damon Minor	.75
412	Lou Collier	.20
413	Justin Towle	.20
414	Juan LeBron	.20
415	Michael Coleman	.20

416	Felix Rodriguez	.20
417	Paul Ah Yat	.75
418	Kevin Barker	1.50
419	Brian Meadows	.20
420	Darnell McDonald	3.00
421	Matt Kinney	.75
422	Mike Vavrek	.75
423	Courtney Duncan	.75
424	Kevin Millar	.75
425	Ruben Rivera	.20
426	Steve Shoemaker	.50
427	Dan Reichert	.75
428	Carlos Lee	2.00
429	Rod Barajas	.75
430	Pablo Ozuna	2.00
431	Todd Belitz	.50
432	Sidney Ponson	.20
433	Steve Carver	1.00
434	Esteban Yan	1.50
435	Cedrick Bowers	.75
436	Marlon Anderson	.20
437	Carl Pavano	.20
438	Jae Weong Seo	1.00
439	Jose Taveras	1.50
440	Matt Anderson	2.50
441	Darron Ingram	1.00

1998 Bowman Autographs

Nomar Garciaparra

		MT
Complete Set (70):		
Common Player:		15.00
Inserted 1:149		
Silvers: 1.5x to 2.5x		
Inserted 1:992		
Golds: 2x to 3x		
Inserted 1:2,976		
1	Adrian Beltre	50.00
2	Brad Fullmer	25.00
3	Ricky Ledee	25.00
4	David Ortiz	25.00
5	Fernando Tatis	20.00
6	Kerry Wood	90.00
7	Mel Rosario	15.00
8	Cole Liniak	20.00
9	A.J. Hinch	25.00
10	Jhensy Sandoval	15.00
11	Jose Cruz Jr.	40.00
12	Richard Hidalgo	20.00
13	Geoff Jenkins	15.00
14	Carl Pavano	25.00
15	Richie Sexson	25.00
16	Tony Womack	20.00
17	Scott Rolen	60.00
18	Ryan Minor	50.00
19	Elieser Marrero	15.00
20	Jason Marquis	15.00
21	Mike Lowell	25.00
22	Todd Helton	35.00
23	Chad Green	15.00
24	Scott Elarton	15.00
25	Russell Branyan	20.00
26	Mike Drumright	15.00
27	Ben Grieve	60.00
28	Jacque Jones	25.00

29	Jared Sandberg	20.00
30	Grant Roberts	25.00
31	Mike Stoner	40.00
32	Brian Rose	15.00
33	Randy Winn	15.00
34	Justin Towle	25.00
35	Anthony Sanders	15.00
36	Rafael Medina	15.00
37	Corey Lee	15.00
38	Mike Kinkade	15.00
39	Norm Hutchins	15.00
40	Jason Brester	15.00
41	Ben Davis	15.00
42	Nomar Garciaparra	80.00
43	Jeff Liefer	15.00
44	Eric Milton	20.00
45	Preston Wilson	20.00
46	Miguel Tejada	30.00
47	Luis Ordaz	15.00
48	Travis Lee	80.00
49	Kris Benson	25.00
50	Jacob Cruz	20.00
51	Dermal Brown	25.00
52	Marc Kroon	15.00
53	Chad Hermansen	40.00
54	Roy Halladay	15.00
55	Eric Chavez	50.00
56	Jason Conti	15.00
57	Juan Encarnacion	20.00
58	Paul Wilder	25.00
59	Aramis Ramirez	50.00
60	Cliff Politte	15.00
61	Todd Dunwoody	15.00
62	Paul Konerko	30.00
63	Shane Monahan	15.00
64	Alex Sanchez	15.00
65	Jeff Abbott	25.00
66	John Patterson	15.00
67	Peter Munro	15.00
68	Jarrod Washburn	30.00
69	Derrek Lee	15.00
70	Ramon Hernandez	15.00

1998 Bowman Golden Anniversary

This 440-card parallel set celebrated Bowman's 50th anniversary with a gold-stamped facsimile autograph on each card. Golden Anniversary cards were inserted into both Series I (1:237) and Series II (1:194) packs and were sequentially numbered to 50.

		MT
Common Player:		15.00
Production 50 sets		
Stars: 25x to 50x		
Yng Stars: 15x to 30x		
Rookies: 6x to 12x		
1	Nomar Garciaparra	200.00
2	Scott Rolen	125.00
3	Andy Pettitte	60.00
4	Ivan Rodriguez	100.00
5	Mark McGwire	450.00
6	Jason Dickson	15.00
7	Jose Cruz Jr.	75.00
8	Jeff Kent	15.00
9	Mike Mussina	75.00
10	Jason Kendall	15.00
11	Brett Tomko	15.00
12	Jeff King	15.00
13	Brad Radke	15.00
14	Robin Ventura	25.00
15	Jeff Bagwell	125.00
16	Greg Maddux	250.00
17	John Jaha	15.00
18	Mike Piazza	250.00
19	Edgar Martinez	15.00
20	David Justice	40.00
21	Todd Hundley	15.00
22	Tony Gwynn	200.00
23	Larry Walker	60.00
24	Bernie Williams	60.00
25	Edgar Renteria	15.00
26	Rafael Palmeiro	40.00
27	Tim Salmon	40.00
28	Matt Morris	15.00
29	Shawn Estes	15.00
30	Vladimir Guerrero	100.00
31	Fernando Tatis	15.00

32	Justin Thompson	15.00
33	Ken Griffey Jr.	400.00
34	Edgardo Alfonzo	15.00
35	Mo Vaughn	100.00
36	Marty Cordova	15.00
37	Craig Biggio	30.00
38	Roger Clemens	150.00
39	Mark Grace	40.00
40	Ken Caminiti	30.00
41	Tony Womack	15.00
42	Albert Belle	100.00
43	Tino Martinez	60.00
44	Sandy Alomar	40.00
45	Jeff Cirillo	15.00
46	Jason Giambi	15.00
47	Darin Erstad	100.00
48	Livan Hernandez	15.00
49	Mark Grudzielanek	15.00
50	Sammy Sosa	200.00
51	Curt Schilling	40.00
52	Brian Hunter	15.00
53	Neifi Perez	15.00
54	Todd Walker	40.00
55	Jose Guillen	40.00
56	Jim Thome	60.00
57	Tom Glavine	40.00
58	Todd Greene	15.00
59	Rondell White	30.00
60	Roberto Alomar	75.00
61	Tony Clark	60.00
62	Vinny Castilla	25.00
63	Barry Larkin	40.00
64	Hideki Irabu	60.00
65	Johnny Damon	15.00
66	Juan Gonzalez	200.00
67	John Olerud	40.00
68	Gary Sheffield	50.00
69	Raul Mondesi	40.00
70	Chipper Jones	250.00
71	David Ortiz	25.00
72	*Warren Morris*	20.00
73	Alex Gonzalez	15.00
74	Nick Bierbrodt	15.00
75	Roy Halladay	20.00
76	Danny Buxbaum	15.00
77	Adam Kennedy	20.00
78	*Jared Sandberg*	30.00
79	Michael Barrett	15.00
80	Gil Meche	15.00
81	Jayson Werth	20.00
82	Abraham Nunez	20.00
83	Ben Petrick	15.00
84	Brett Caradonna	20.00
85	Mike Lowell	25.00
86	*Clay Bruner*	20.00
87	*John Curtice*	20.00
88	Bobby Estalella	15.00
89	Juan Melo	15.00
90	Arnold Gooch	15.00
91	Kevin Millwood	100.00
92	Richie Sexson	15.00
93	Orlando Cabrera	15.00
94	Pat Cline	15.00
95	Anthony Sanders	20.00
96	Russ Johnson	15.00
97	Ben Grieve	125.00
98	Kevin McGlinchy	15.00
99	Paul Wilder	15.00
100	Russ Ortiz	15.00
101	Ryan Jackson	35.00
102	Heath Murray	15.00
103	Brian Rose	20.00
104	*Ryan Radmanovich*	20.00
105	Ricky Ledee	25.00
106	*Jeff Wallace*	20.00
107	Ryan Minor	90.00
108	Dennis Reyes	15.00
109	*James Manias*	20.00
110	Chris Carpenter	15.00
111	Daryle Ward	15.00
112	Vernon Wells	20.00
113	Chad Green	15.00
114	*Mike Stoner*	80.00
115	Brad Fullmer	20.00
116	Adam Eaton	15.00
117	Jeff Liefer	15.00
118	Corey Koskie	20.00
119	Todd Helton	50.00
120	*Jaime Jones*	25.00
121	Mel Rosario	15.00
122	Geoff Goetz	15.00
123	Adrian Beltre	120.00
124	Jason Dellaero	20.00
125	Gabe Kapler	100.00
126	Scott Schoeneweis	15.00
127	Ryan Brannan	15.00

128	Aaron Akin	15.00
129	Ryan Anderson	100.00
130	Brad Penny	15.00
131	Bruce Chen	20.00
132	Eli Marrero	15.00
133	Eric Chavez	30.00
134	Troy Glaus	160.00
135	Troy Cameron	20.00
136	*Brian Sikorski*	20.00
137	Mike Kinkade	20.00
138	Braden Looper	15.00
139	Mark Mangum	15.00
140	Danny Peoples	15.00
141	J.J. Davis	20.00
142	Ben Davis	15.00
143	Jacque Jones	15.00
144	Derrick Gibson	15.00
145	Bronson Arroyo	15.00
146	*Cristian Guzman*	15.00
147	Jeff Abbott	15.00
148	*Mike Cuddyer*	30.00
149	Jason Romano	20.00
150	Shane Monahan	15.00
151	*Ntema Ndungidi*	20.00
152	Alex Sanchez	15.00
153	*Jack Cust*	35.00
154	Brent Butler	20.00
155	Ramon Hernandez	15.00
156	Norm Hutchins	15.00
157	Jason Marquis	15.00
158	Jacob Cruz	15.00
159	*Rob Burger*	30.00
160	Eric Milton	20.00
161	Preston Wilson	15.00
162	*Jason Fitzgerald*	20.00
163	Dan Serafini	15.00
164	Peter Munro	15.00
165	Trot Nixon	20.00
166	Homer Bush	15.00
167	Dermal Brown	20.00
168	Chad Hermansen	25.00
169	*Julio Moreno*	20.00
170	*John Roskos*	20.00
171	Grant Roberts	20.00
172	Ken Cloude	15.00
173	Jason Brester	15.00
174	Jason Conti	15.00
175	Jon Garland	15.00
176	Robbie Bell	15.00
177	Nathan Haynes	15.00
178	Ramon Ortiz	40.00
179	Shannon Stewart	15.00
180	Pablo Ortega	15.00
181	*Jimmy Rollins*	20.00
182	Sean Casey	20.00
183	*Ted Lilly*	15.00
184	*Chris Enochs*	40.00
185	*Magglio Ordonez*	60.00
186	Mike Drumright	15.00
187	Aaron Boone	15.00
188	Matt Clement	15.00
189	Todd Dunwoody	15.00
190	Larry Rodriguez	15.00
191	Todd Noel	15.00
192	Geoff Jenkins	15.00
193	George Lombard	15.00
194	Lance Berkman	60.00
195	*Marcus McCain*	20.00
196	Ryan McGuire	15.00
197	*Jhensy Sandoval*	20.00
198	Corey Lee	15.00
199	Mario Valdez	15.00
200	*Robert Fick*	20.00
201	Donnie Sadler	15.00
202	Marc Kroon	15.00
203	David Miller	15.00
204	Jarrod Washburn	15.00
205	Miguel Tejada	25.00
206	Raul Ibanez	15.00
207	John Patterson	15.00
208	Calvin Pickering	15.00
209	Felix Martinez	15.00
210	Mark Redman	15.00
211	Scott Elarton	15.00
212	*Jose Amado*	20.00
213	Kerry Wood	250.00
214	Dante Powell	15.00
215	Aramis Ramirez	100.00
216	A.J. Hinch	30.00
217	*Dustin Carr*	15.00
218	Mark Kotsay	25.00
219	Jason Standridge	15.00
220	Luis Ordaz	15.00
221	Orlando Hernandez	125.00

1998 Bowman Japanese Rookies

Bowman offered collectors a chance to receive original BBM Japanese rookie cards of three players. Series I had rookie cards of Hideo Nomo and Shigetoshi Hasegawa inserted in one per 2,685 packs, while Series II offered Hideki Irabu seeded one per 4,411 packs.

	MT
Complete Set (2):	50.00
Common Player:	10.00
BBM11 Hideo Nomo	40.00
BBM17 Shigetosi Hasegawa	10.00

1998 Bowman Minor League MVP's

This 10-card insert set features players who are former Minor League MVPs and are now playing in the majors. Minor League MVPs were seeded one per 12 packs of Series II.

	MT
Complete Set (11):	40.00
Common Player:	1.50
MVP1 Jeff Bagwell	6.00
MVP2 Andres Galarraga	2.50
MVP3 Juan Gonzalez	8.00
MVP4 Tony Gwynn	8.00
MVP5 Vladimir Guerrero	4.00
MVP6 Derek Jeter	8.00
MVP7 Andruw Jones	4.00
MVP8 Tino Martinez	2.50
MVP9 Manny Ramirez	4.00
MVP10 Gary Sheffield	1.50
MVP11 Jim Thome	2.50

Values quoted in this guide reflect the retail price of a card — the price a collector can expect to pay when buying a card from a dealer.

The wholesale price — that which a collector can expect to receive from a dealer when selling cards — will be significantly lower, depending on desirability and condition.

1998 Bowman ROY Favorites

Rookie of the Year Favorites displayed 20 players who had a legitimate shot at the 1999 Rookie of the Year award as selected by the Bowman Scouts. The insert was seeded per 12 packs of Series II.

	MT
Complete Set (10):	25.00
Common Player:	1.00
ROY1 Adrian Beltre	3.00
ROY2 Troy Glaus	10.00
ROY3 Chad Hermansen	1.00
ROY4 Matt Clement	2.50
ROY5 Eric Chavez	6.00
ROY6 Kris Benson	1.00
ROY7 Richie Sexson	2.00
ROY8 Randy Wolf	1.00
ROY9 Ryan Minor	5.00
ROY10 Alex Gonzalez	1.00

1998 Bowman Scout's Choice

This 20-card insert had players with major potential and could win the Rookie of the Year award. Scout's Choice inserts were seeded one per 12 packs of Series I.

	MT
Complete Set (21):	75.00
Common Player:	1.50
Inserted 1:12	
SC1 Paul Konerko	4.00
SC2 Richard Hidalgo	1.50

SC3	Mark Kotsay	3.00
SC4	Ben Grieve	6.00
SC5	Chad Hermansen	4.00
SC6	Matt Clement	1.50
SC7	Brad Fullmer	3.00
SC8	Eli Marrero	1.50
SC9	Kerry Wood	20.00
SC10	Adrian Beltre	5.00
SC11	Ricky Ledee	1.50
SC12	Travis Lee	10.00
SC13	Abraham Nunez	1.50
SC14	Ryan Anderson	10.00
SC15	Dermal Brown	1.50
SC16	Juan Encarnacion	1.50
SC17	Aramis Ramirez	10.00
SC18	Todd Helton	4.00
SC19	Kris Benson	5.00
SC20	Russell Branyan	1.50
SC21	Mike Stoner	5.00

1998 Bowman's Best

Bowman's Best was issued in a single 200-card series in 1998 and contained 100 prospects and 100 veterans. The prospects were shown on a silver design, while the veterans were shown on gold. The set was paralleled twice - once in a Refractor version seeded one per 20 packs and sequentially numbered to 400, and next in an Atomic Refractor version inserted one per 82 packs and numbered to 100 sets. Inserts include regular, Refractor and Atomic Refractor versions of: Autographs, Double-Sided Mirror Image Fusion and Performers.

	MT
Complete Set (200):	90.00
Common Player:	.25
Star Refractors: 15x to 25x	
Yng Stars & RC's: 8x to 15x	
Production 400 sets	
Star Atomic Refractors 60x to 100x	
Yng Stars & RC's 25x to 50x	
Production 100 sets	
Wax Box:	100.00
1 Mark McGwire	6.00
2 Hideo Nomo	.75
3 Barry Bonds	1.25
4 Dante Bichette	.50
5 Chipper Jones	3.00
6 Frank Thomas	4.00
7 Kevin Brown	.40
8 Juan Gonzalez	2.50
9 Jay Buhner	.50
10 Chuck Knoblauch	.50
11 Cal Ripken Jr.	4.00
12 Matt Williams	.50
13 Jim Edmonds	.25
14 Manny Ramirez	1.25

15	Tony Clark	.75
16	Mo Vaughn	1.25
17	Bernie Williams	1.00
18	Scott Rolen	1.50
19	Gary Sheffield	.60
20	Albert Belle	1.25
21	Mike Piazza	3.00
22	John Olerud	.50
23	Tony Gwynn	2.50
24	Jay Bell	.25
25	Jose Cruz Jr.	1.25
26	Justin Thompson	.25
27	Ken Griffey Jr.	5.00
28	Sandy Alomar	.40
29	Mark Grudzielanek	.25
30	Mark Grace	.50
31	Ron Gant	.40
32	Javy Lopez	.25
33	Jeff Bagwell	2.00
34	Fred McGriff	.50
35	Rafael Palmeiro	.50
36	Vinny Castilla	.40
37	Andy Benes	.25
38	Pedro Martinez	1.00
39	Andy Pettitte	.75
40	Marty Cordova	.25
41	Rusty Greer	.25
42	Kevin Orie	.25
43	Chan Ho Park	.75
44	Ryan Klesko	.50
45	Alex Rodriguez	3.00
46	Travis Fryman	.25
47	Jeff King	.25
48	Roger Clemens	2.00
49	Darin Erstad	1.25
50	Brady Anderson	.25
51	Jason Kendall	.25
52	John Valentin	.25
53	Ellis Burks	.25
54	Brian Hunter	.25
55	Paul O'Neill	.50
56	Ken Caminiti	.50
57	David Justice	.60
58	Eric Karros	.40
59	Pat Hentgen	.25
60	Greg Maddux	3.00
61	Craig Biggio	.50
62	Edgar Martinez	.25
63	Mike Mussina	1.00
64	Larry Walker	.75
65	Tino Martinez	.75
66	Jim Thome	1.00
67	Tom Glavine	.50
68	Raul Mondesi	.50
69	Marquis Grissom	.25
70	Randy Johnson	1.00
71	Steve Finley	.25
72	Jose Guillen	.50
73	Nomar Garciaparra	3.00
74	Wade Boggs	.75
75	Bobby Higginson	.25
76	Robin Ventura	.40
77	Derek Jeter	2.50
78	Andruw Jones	1.25
79	Ray Lankford	.25
80	Vladimir Guerrero	1.25
81	Kenny Lofton	1.25
82	Ivan Rodriguez	1.25
83	Neifi Perez	.25
84	John Smoltz	.40
85	Tim Salmon	.50
86	Carlos Delgado	.25
87	Sammy Sosa	4.00
88	Jaret Wright	1.25
89	Roberto Alomar	.75
90	Paul Molitor	.75
91	Dean Palmer	.25
92	Barry Larkin	.50
93	Jason Giambi	.25
94	Curt Schilling	.40
95	Eric Young	.25
96	Denny Neagle	.25
97	Moises Alou	.40
98	Livan Hernandez	.25
99	Todd Hundley	.25
100	Andres Galarraga	.50
101	Travis Lee	3.00
102	Lance Berkman	2.00
103	Orlando Cabrera	.40
104	*Mike Lowell*	2.50
105	Ben Grieve	2.00
106	*Jae Weong Seo*	.75
107	Richie Sexson	.25
108	Eli Marrero	.25
109	Aramis Ramirez	2.50
110	Paul Konerko	.50

111	Carl Pavano	.25
112	Brad Fullmer	.50
113	Matt Clement	.40
114	Donzell McDonald	.25
115	Todd Helton	1.25
116	Mike Caruso	.25
117	Donnie Sadler	.25
118	Bruce Chen	.50
119	Jarrod Washburn	.25
120	Adrian Beltre	3.00
121	Ryan Jackson	2.50
122	Kevin Millar	.50
123	Corey Koskie	2.50
124	Dermal Brown	1.00
125	Kerry Wood	6.00
126	Juan Melo	.25
127	Ramon Hernandez	.25
128	Roy Halladay	.25
129	Ron Wright	.25
130	Darnell McDonald	3.00
131	Odaliz Perez	2.00
132	Alex Cora	.75
133	Justin Towle	.50
134	Juan Encarnacion	.25
135	Brian Rose	.40
136	Russell Branyan	.25
137	Cesar King	.75
138	Ruben Rivera	.25
139	Ricky Ledee	.25
140	Vernon Wells	1.00
141	Luis Rivas	.75
142	Brent Butler	1.00
143	Karim Garcia	.25
144	George Lombard	.40
145	Masato Yoshii	1.50
146	Braden Looper	.25
147	Alex Sanchez	.40
148	Kris Benson	1.00
149	Mark Kotsay	1.50
150	Richard Hidalgo	.25
151	Scott Elarton	.25
152	Ryan Minor	6.00
153	Troy Glaus	15.00
154	Carlos Lee	3.00
155	Michael Coleman	.25
156	Jason Grilli	.75
157	Julio Ramirez	1.50
158	Preston Wilson	.25
159	Ryan Brannan	.25
160	Edgar Clemente	.50
161	Miguel Tejada	1.50
162	Chad Hermansen	1.50
163	Ryan Anderson	8.00
164	Ben Petrick	.25
165	Alex Gonzalez	.40
166	Ben Davis	.25
167	John Patterson	.50
168	Cliff Politte	.25
169	Randall Simon	1.50
170	Javier Vazquez	.25
171	Kevin Witt	.50
172	Geoff Jenkins	.25
173	David Ortiz	1.00
174	Derrick Gibson	.25
175	Abraham Nunez	.50
176	A.J. Hinch	1.50
177	Ruben Mateo	6.00
178	Magglio Ordonez	4.00
179	Todd Dunwoody	.25
180	Daryle Ward	.50
181	Mike Kinkade	2.50
182	Willie Martinez	.25
183	Orlando Hernandez	15.00
184	Eric Milton	.75
185	Eric Chavez	1.50
186	Damian Jackson	.25
187	Jim Parque	1.50
188	Dan Reichert	1.00
189	Mike Drumright	.25
190	Todd Walker	.50
191	Shane Monahan	.25
192	Derrek Lee	.25
193	Jeremy Giambi	3.00
194	Dan McKinley	.75
195	Tony Armas	1.50
196	Matt Anderson	3.00
197	Jim Chamblee	.75
198	Francisco Cordero	.75
199	Calvin Pickering	1.00
200	Reggie Taylor	.25

1998 Bowman's Best Autographs

This 10-card set included autographed cards from five prospects and five veterans. Each card contained the Topps "Certified Autograph Issue" logo for authentication. Regular versions were seeded one per 180 packs, Refractor versions were seeded one per 2,158 packs and Atomic Refractor versions were seeded one per 6,437 packs.

		MT
Complete Set (10):		450.00
Common Player:		25.00
Inserted 1:180		
Refractors: 1.5x to 2.5x		
Inserted 1:2,158		
Atomics: 2x to 4x		
Inserted 1:6,437		
5	Chipper Jones	90.00
10	Chuck Knoblauch	35.00
15	Tony Clark	35.00
20	Albert Belle	50.00
25	Jose Cruz Jr.	45.00
105	Ben Grieve	75.00
110	Paul Konerko	25.00
115	Todd Helton	40.00
120	Adrian Beltre	40.00
125	Kerry Wood	100.00

1998 Bowman's Best Mirror Image

This 20-card die-cut insert features a veteran star on one side and a young player of the same position on the other. Regular versions are seeded one per 12 packs, while Refractor versions are seeded one per 809 packs and numbered to 100 and Atomic Refractors were seeded one per 3,237 packs and numbered to 25.

		MT
Complete Set (20):		100.00
Common Player:		1.50
Inserted 1:12		
MI1	Frank Thomas, David Ortiz	12.00
MI2	Chuck Knoblauch, Enrique Wilson	1.50
MI3	Nomar Garciaparra, Miguel Tejada	8.00
MI4	Alex Rodriguez, Mike Caruso	8.00
MI5	Cal Ripken Jr., Ryan Minor	12.00
MI6	Ken Griffey Jr., Ben Grieve	15.00
MI7	Juan Gonzalez, Juan Encarnacion	8.00
MI8	Jose Cruz Jr., Ruben Mateo	4.00
MI9	Randy Johnson, Ryan Anderson	3.00
MI10	Ivan Rodriguez, A.J. Hinch	4.00
MI11	Jeff Bagwell, Paul Konerko	5.00
MI12	Mark McGwire, Travis Lee	15.00
MI13	Craig Biggio, Chad Hermanson	1.50
MI14	Mark Grudzielanek, Alex Gonzalez	1.50
MI15	Chipper Jones, Adrian Beltre	10.00
MI16	Larry Walker, Mark Kotsay	2.00
MI17	Tony Gwynn, Preston Wilson	7.00
MI18	Barry Bonds, Richard Hidalgo	4.00
MI19	Greg Maddux, Kerry Wood	15.00
MI20	Mike Piazza, Ben Petrick	10.00

1998 Bowman's Best Mirror Image Refractors

All 20 cards in the Mirror Image insert were reprinted in both Refractor and Atomic Refractor versions. Refractors were seeded one per 809 packs and numbered to 100 sets, while Atomic Refractors were seeded one per 3,237 packs and numbered to 25 sets.

		MT
Complete Set (20):		2500.
Common Player:		25.00
Production 100 sets		
Atomic Refractors: 1.5x to 2.5x		
Production 25 sets		
MI1	Frank Thomas, David Ortiz	250.00
MI2	Chuck Knoblauch, Enrique Wilson	40.00
MI3	Nomar Garciaparra, Miguel Tejada	200.00
MI4	Alex Rodriguez, Mike Caruso	200.00
MI5	Cal Ripken Jr., Ryan Minor	250.00
MI6	Ken Griffey Jr., Ben Grieve	350.00
MI7	Juan Gonzalez, Juan Encarnacion	180.00
MI8	Jose Cruz Jr., Ruben Mateo	75.00
MI9	Randy Johnson, Ryan Anderson	60.00
MI10	Ivan Rodriguez, A.J. Hinch	80.00
MI11	Jeff Bagwell, Paul Konerko	125.00
MI12	Mark McGwire, Travis Lee	300.00
MI13	Craig Biggio, Chad Hermanson	40.00
MI14	Mark Grudzielanek, Alex Gonzalez	25.00
MI15	Chipper Jones, Adrian Beltre	200.00
MI16	Larry Walker, Mark Kotsay	40.00
MI17	Tony Gwynn, Preston Wilson	180.00

		MT
MI18	Barry Bonds, Richard Hidalgo	75.00
MI19	Greg Maddux, Kerry Wood	300.00
MI20	Mike Piazza, Ben Petrick	200.00

1998 Bowman's Best Performers

Performers contained 10 players who had the best minor league stats in 1997. Regular versions were inserted one per six packs, while Refractors were seeded one per 809 packs and numbered to 200 and Atomic Refractors were inserted one per 3,237 and numbered to 50 sets.

		MT
Complete Set (10):		20.00
Common Player:		1.00
BP1	Ben Grieve	4.00
BP2	Travis Lee	8.00
BP3	Ryan Minor	3.00
BP4	Todd Helton	2.00
BP5	Brad Fullmer	1.50
BP6	Paul Konerko	1.00
BP7	Adrian Beltre	3.00
BP8	Richie Sexson	1.00
BP9	Aramis Ramirez	2.50
BP10	Russell Branyan	1.00

1998 Bowman's Best Performers Refractors

All 10 cards in the Performers insert also arrived in Refractor and Atomic Refractor versions. Refractors were seeded one per 809 packs and numbered to 200 sets, while Atomic Refractors are seeded one per 3,237 packs and numbered to 50 on the back.

		MT
Complete Set (10):		500.00
Common Player:		1.00
Production 200 sets		
Atomic Refractors: 1.5x to 2.5x		
Production 50 sets		
BP1	Ben Grieve	100.00
BP2	Travis Lee	150.00
BP3	Ryan Minor	100.00
BP4	Todd Helton	60.00
BP5	Brad Fullmer	15.00
BP6	Paul Konerko	25.00
BP7	Adrian Beltre	90.00
BP8	Richie Sexson	10.00
BP9	Aramis Ramirez	40.00
BP10	Russell Branyan	10.00

1998 Bowman Chrome

All 440 cards in Bowman I and II have been reprinted with a chromium finish for Bowman Chrome. Issue in two Series, it contained International and Golden Anniversary parallels, similar to Bowman. International parallels were seeded one per four packs, with Refractor versions every 24 packs. Golden Anniversary parallels were exclusive to hobby packs and inserted one per 164 packs and sequentially numbered to 50 sets. Refractor versions were seeded one per 1,279 packs and numbered to just five sets. In addition, 50 Bowman Chrome Reprints were inserted with 25 in each series.

		MT
Complete Set (441):		300.00
Complete Series I Set (221):		180.00
Complete Series II Set (220):		120.00
Common Player:		.20
Internationals: 1.5x to 2.5x		
Inserted 1:4		
Refractors: 5x to 10x		
Young Stars & RC's: 3x to 6x		
Inserted 1:12		
Intern. Refractors: 8x to 15x		
Young Stars & RC's: 4x to 10x		
Inserted 1:24		
Wax Box:		110.00
1	Nomar Garciaparra	5.00
2	Scott Rolen	3.00
3	Andy Pettitte	1.50
4	Ivan Rodriguez	2.00
5	Mark McGwire	10.00
6	Jason Dickson	.40
7	Jose Cruz Jr.	2.00
8	Jeff Kent	.40
9	Mike Mussina	1.50
10	Jason Kendall	.40
11	Brett Tomko	.40
12	Jeff King	.40
13	Brad Radke	.40
14	Robin Ventura	.50
15	Jeff Bagwell	3.00
16	Greg Maddux	5.00
17	John Jaha	.40
18	Mike Piazza	5.00
19	Edgar Martinez	.40
20	David Justice	.75
21	Todd Hundley	.40
22	Tony Gwynn	4.00
23	Larry Walker	1.00
24	Bernie Williams	1.50
25	Edgar Renteria	.40
26	Rafael Palmeiro	.75
27	Tim Salmon	1.00
28	Matt Morris	.50
29	Shawn Estes	.40

30	Vladimir Guerrero	2.00
31	Fernando Tatis	.60
32	Justin Thompson	.40
33	Ken Griffey Jr.	8.00
34	Edgardo Alfonzo	.40
35	Mo Vaughn	2.00
36	Marty Cordova	.40
37	Craig Biggio	.75
38	Roger Clemens	3.00
39	Mark Grace	.75
40	Ken Caminiti	.60
41	Tony Womack	.40
42	Albert Belle	2.00
43	Tino Martinez	1.00
44	Sandy Alomar	.60
45	Jeff Cirillo	.40
46	Jason Giambi	.40
47	Darin Erstad	2.00
48	Livan Hernandez	.40
49	Mark Grudzielanek	.40
50	Sammy Sosa	5.00
51	Curt Schilling	.60
52	Brian Hunter	.40
53	Neifi Perez	.40
54	Todd Walker	.60
55	Jose Guillen	.60
56	Jim Thome	1.00
57	Tom Glavine	.60
58	Todd Greene	.40
59	Rondell White	.50
60	Roberto Alomar	1.50
61	Tony Clark	1.25
62	Vinny Castilla	.50
63	Barry Larkin	.75
64	Hideki Irabu	1.50
65	Johnny Damon	.40
66	Juan Gonzalez	4.00
67	John Olerud	.60
68	Gary Sheffield	.75
69	Raul Mondesi	.60
70	Chipper Jones	5.00
71	David Ortiz	1.50
72	*Warren Morris*	3.00
73	Alex Gonzalez	.40
74	Nick Bierbrodt	.40
75	Roy Halladay	.40
76	Danny Buxbaum	.40
77	Adam Kennedy	.40
78	*Jared Sandberg*	5.00
79	Michael Barrett	.40
80	Gil Meche	.40
81	Jayson Werth	2.50
82	Abraham Nunez	.75
83	Ben Petrick	.40
84	Brett Caradonna	.40
85	*Mike Lowell*	4.00
86	Clay Bruner	2.00
87	*John Curtice*	4.00
88	Bobby Estalella	.40
89	Juan Melo	.40
90	Arnold Gooch	.40
91	*Kevin Millwood*	15.00
92	Richie Sexson	.40
93	Orlando Cabrera	.40
94	Pat Cline	.40
95	Anthony Sanders	.50
96	Russ Johnson	.40
97	Ben Grieve	3.00
98	Kevin McGlinchy	.40
99	Paul Wilder	.40
100	Russ Ortiz	.40
101	*Ryan Jackson*	4.00
102	Heath Murray	.40
103	Brian Rose	.40
104	*Ryan Radmanovich*	2.00
105	Ricky Ledee	1.50
106	*Jeff Wallace*	2.00
107	*Ryan Minor*	10.00
108	Dennis Reyes	.50
109	*James Manias*	2.00
110	Chris Carpenter	.40
111	Daryle Ward	.50
112	Vernon Wells	2.50
113	Chad Green	.40
114	*Mike Stoner*	10.00
115	Brad Fullmer	.60
116	Adam Eaton	.40
117	Jeff Liefer	.40
118	*Corey Koskie*	4.00
119	Todd Helton	2.00
120	*Jaime Jones*	2.00
121	Mel Rosario	.40
122	Geoff Goetz	.40
123	Adrian Beltre	3.00
124	Jason Dellaero	.50
125	*Gabe Kapler*	10.00

#	Name	Value		#	Name	Value		#	Name	Value
126	Scott Schoeneweis	.40		222	Cal Ripken Jr.	6.00		318	*Marcus Thames*	3.00
127	Ryan Brannan	.40		223	Paul Molitor	1.50		319	A.J. Pierzynski	.20
128	Aaron Akin	.40		224	Derek Jeter	5.00		320	Scott Randall	.20
129	*Ryan Anderson*	18.00		225	Barry Bonds	2.00		321	Damian Sapp	.20
130	Brad Penny	.40		226	Jim Edmonds	.40		322	*Eddie Yarnell*	6.00
131	Bruce Chen	.50		227	John Smoltz	.40		323	Luke Allen	3.00
132	Eli Marrero	.40		228	Eric Karros	.40		324	J.D. Smart	.20
133	Eric Chavez	3.00		229	Ray Lankford	.20		325	Willie Martinez	.20
134	*Troy Glaus*	30.00		230	Rey Ordonez	.20		326	Alex Ramirez	.20
135	Troy Cameron	.50		231	Kenny Lofton	2.00		327	*Eric DuBose*	2.00
136	*Brian Sikorski*	1.50		232	Alex Rodriguez	5.00		328	Kevin Witt	.20
137	*Mike Kinkade*	4.00		233	Dante Bichette	.50		329	*Dan McKinley*	1.50
138	Braden Looper	.40		234	Pedro Martinez	1.50		330	Cliff Politte	.20
139	Mark Mangum	.40		235	Carlos Delgado	.20		331	Vladimir Nunez	.20
140	Danny Peoples	.50		236	Rod Beck	.20		332	*John Halama*	1.00
141	J.J. Davis	1.50		237	Matt Williams	.50		333	Nerio Rodriguez	.20
142	Ben Davis	.40		238	Charles Johnson	.20		334	Desi Relaford	.20
143	Jacque Jones	.50		239	Rico Brogna	.20		335	Robinson Checo	.20
144	Derrick Gibson	.40		240	Frank Thomas	5.00		336	*John Nicholson*	2.00
145	Bronson Arroyo	.50		241	Paul O'Neill	.75		337	*Tom LaRosa*	1.50
146	*Luis DeLosSantos*	3.00		242	Jaret Wright	2.00		338	*Kevin Nicholson*	4.00
147	Jeff Abbott	.40		243	Brant Brown	.20		339	Javier Vazquez	.20
148	*Mike Cuddyer*	8.00		244	Ryan Klesko	.50		340	A.J. Zapp	.20
149	Jason Romano	1.50		245	Chuck Finley	.20		341	Tom Evans	.20
150	Shane Monahan	.40		246	Derek Bell	.20		342	Kerry Robinson	.20
151	*Ntema Ndungidi*	4.00		247	Delino DeShields	.20		343	*Gabe Gonzalez*	1.50
152	Alex Sanchez	.40		248	Chan Ho Park	.50		344	Ralph Milliard	.20
153	*Jack Cust*	6.00		249	Wade Boggs	.50		345	Enrique Wilson	.20
154	Brent Butler	2.00		250	Jay Buhner	.75		346	Elvin Hernandez	.20
155	Ramon Hernandez	.40		251	Butch Huskey	.20		347	*Mike Lincoln*	3.00
156	Norm Hutchins	.40		252	Steve Finley	.20		348	*Cesar King*	4.00
157	Jason Marquis	.40		253	Will Clark	.75		349	Cristian Guzman	2.00
158	Jacob Cruz	.40		254	John Valentin	.20		350	Donzell McDonald	.20
159	*Rob Burger*	2.50		255	Bobby Higginson	.20		351	*Jim Parque*	3.00
160	Eric Milton	1.50		256	Darryl Strawberry	.50		352	*Mike Saipe*	2.00
161	Preston Wilson	.40		257	Randy Johnson	1.50		353	*Carlos Febles*	2.00
162	*Jason Fitzgerald*	2.50		258	Al Martin	.20		354	*Dernell Stenson*	5.00
163	Dan Serafini	.40		259	Travis Fryman	.20		355	*Mark Osborne*	3.00
164	Peter Munro	.40		260	Fred McGriff	.50		356	*Odalis Perez*	4.00
165	Trot Nixon	.40		261	Jose Valentin	.20		357	*Jason Dewey*	2.00
166	Homer Bush	.40		262	Andruw Jones	2.00		358	Joe Fontenot	.20
167	Dermal Brown	2.00		263	Kenny Rogers	.20		359	*Jason Grilli*	3.00
168	Chad Hermansen	3.00		264	Moises Alou	.50		360	*Kevin Haverbusch*	3.00
169	*Julio Moreno*	2.00		265	Denny Neagle	.20		361	*Jay Yennaco*	1.00
170	*John Roskos*	2.00		266	Ugueth Urbina	.20		362	Brian Buchanan	.20
171	Grant Roberts	1.50		267	Derek Lee	.20		363	John Barnes	.20
172	Ken Cloude	.50		268	Ellis Burks	.20		364	Chris Fussell	.20
173	Jason Brester	.40		269	Mariano Rivera	.50		365	*Kevin Gibbs*	1.50
174	Jason Conti	.40		270	Dean Palmer	.20		366	Joe Lawrence	.20
175	Jon Garland	.50		271	Eddie Taubensee	.20		367	DaRond Stovall	.20
176	Robbie Bell	.40		272	Brady Anderson	.20		368	*Brian Fuentes*	2.00
177	Nathan Haynes	.40		273	Brian Giles	.20		369	Jimmy Anderson	.20
178	*Ramon Ortiz*	6.00		274	Quinton McCracken	.20		370	*Laril Gonzalez*	2.00
179	Shannon Stewart	.40		275	Henry Rodriguez	.20		371	*Scott Williamson*	2.00
180	Pablo Ortega	.40		276	Andres Galarraga	.75		372	Milton Bradley	.20
181	*Jimmy Rollins*	4.00		277	Jose Canseco	1.00		373	*Jason Halper*	1.50
182	Sean Casey	1.00		278	David Segui	.20		374	*Brent Billingsley*	1.50
183	*Ted Lilly*	.75		279	Bret Saberhagen	.20		375	*Joe DePastino*	.20
184	*Chris Enochs*	6.00		280	Kevin Brown	.50		376	Jake Westbrook	.20
185	*Magglio Ordonez*	8.00		281	Chuck Knoblauch	.75		377	Octavio Dotel	.20
186	Mike Drumright	.40		282	Jeromy Burnitz	.20		378	*Jason Williams*	1.00
187	Aaron Boone	.40		283	Jay Bell	.20		379	*Julio Ramirez*	3.00
188	Matt Clement	.40		284	Manny Ramirez	2.00		380	Seth Greisinger	.20
189	Todd Dunwoody	.40		285	Rick Helling	.20		381	*Mike Judd*	2.00
190	Larry Rodriguez	.40		286	Francisco Cordova	.20		382	*Ben Ford*	1.00
191	Todd Noel	.40		287	Bob Abreu	.20		383	Tom Bennett	.20
192	Geoff Jenkins	.40		288	J.T. Snow Jr.	.20		384	*Adam Butler*	1.00
193	George Lombard	.50		289	Hideo Nomo	1.50		385	*Wade Miller*	2.00
194	Lance Berkman	4.00		290	Brian Jordan	.20		386	*Kyle Peterson*	2.00
195	*Marcus McCain*	.75		291	Javy Lopez	.20		387	*Tommy Peterman*	2.00
196	Ryan McGuire	.40		292	Travis Lee	4.00		388	*Onan Masaoka*	.20
197	*Jhensy Sandoval*	7.00		293	Russell Branyan	.20		389	*Jason Rakers*	1.50
198	Corey Lee	.40		294	Paul Konerko	.50		390	Rafael Medina	.20
199	Mario Valdez	.40		295	*Masato Yoshii*	3.00		391	Luis Lopez	.20
200	*Robert Fick*	3.00		296	Kris Benson	.75		392	Jeff Yoder	.20
201	Donnie Sadler	.40		297	Juan Encarnacion	.20		393	*Vance Wilson*	1.50
202	Marc Kroon	.40		298	Eric Milton	.20		394	*Fernando Seguignol*	5.00
203	David Miller	.40		299	Mike Caruso	.20		395	Ron Wright	.20
204	Jarrod Washburn	.40		300	*Ricardo Aramboles*	6.00		396	*Ruben Mateo*	8.00
205	Miguel Tejada	3.00		301	Bobby Smith	.20		397	*Steve Lomasney*	2.00
206	Raul Ibanez	.40		302	Billy Koch	.20		398	Damian Jackson	.20
207	John Patterson	.60		303	Richard Hidalgo	.20		399	*Mike Jerzembeck*	1.50
208	Calvin Pickering	2.00		304	*Justin Baughman*	2.00		400	*Luis Rivas*	3.00
209	Felix Martinez	.40		305	Chris Gissell	.20		401	*Kevin Burford*	3.00
210	Mark Redman	.40		306	*Donnie Bridges*	3.00		402	Glenn Davis	.20
211	Scott Elarton	.40		307	*Nelson Lara*	2.00		403	*Robert Luce*	1.50
212	*Jose Amado*	1.50		308	Randy Wolf	2.00		404	Cole Liniak	.20
213	Kerry Wood	10.00		309	Jason LaRue	2.00		405	Matthew LeCroy	2.00
214	Dante Powell	.40		310	*Jason Gooding*	1.00		406	*Jeremy Giambi*	5.00
215	Aramis Ramirez	4.00		311	*Edgar Clemente*	1.00		407	Shawn Chacon	.20
216	A.J. Hinch	3.00		312	Andrew Vessel	.20		408	Dewayne Wise	3.00
217	Dustin Carr	2.00		313	Chris Reitsma	.20		409	Steve Woodard	1.50
218	Mark Kotsay	3.00		314	*Jesus Sanchez*	2.00		410	*Francisco Cordero*	1.00
219	Jason Standridge	.40		315	*Buddy Carlyle*	2.00		411	*Damon Minor*	2.00
220	Luis Ordaz	.40		316	Randy Winn	.20		412	Lou Collier	.20
221	*Orlando Hernandez*	30.00		317	Luis Rivera	5.00		413	Justin Towle	.20

414	Juan LeBron	.20
415	Michael Coleman	.20
416	Felix Rodriguez	.20
417	Paul Ah Yat	2.00
418	Kevin Barker	2.00
419	Brian Meadows	.20
420	Darnell McDonald	6.00
421	Matt Kinney	2.00
422	Mike Vavrek	2.00
423	Courtney Duncan	1.50
424	Kevin Millar	2.00
425	Ruben Rivera	.20
426	Steve Shoemaker	1.00
427	Dan Reichert	1.50
428	Carlos Lee	4.00
429	Rod Barajas	2.00
430	Pablo Ozuna	5.00
431	Todd Belitz	1.00
432	Sidney Ponson	.20
433	Steve Carver	2.00
434	Esteban Yan	2.00
435	Cedrick Bowers	2.00
436	Marlon Anderson	.20
437	Carl Pavano	.20
438	Jae Weong Seo	3.00
439	Jose Taveras	3.00
440	Matt Anderson	4.00
441	Darron Ingram	3.00

1998 Bowman Chrome Golden Anniversary

Golden Anniversary parallels were printed for all 440 cards in Bowman Chrome I and II. They were exclusive to hobby packs, seeded one per 164 packs and sequentially numbered to 50 sets. Refractor versions were also available, numbered to just five sets and inserted one per 1,279 packs.

		MT
Common Player:		15.00
Production 50 sets		
1	Nomar Garciaparra	200.00
2	Scott Rolen	125.00
3	Andy Pettitte	60.00
4	Ivan Rodriguez	100.00
5	Mark McGwire	450.00
6	Jason Dickson	15.00
7	Jose Cruz Jr.	75.00
8	Jeff Kent	15.00
9	Mike Mussina	75.00
10	Jason Kendall	15.00
11	Brett Tomko	15.00
12	Jeff King	15.00
13	Brad Radke	15.00
14	Robin Ventura	25.00
15	Jeff Bagwell	125.00
16	Greg Maddux	250.00
17	John Jaha	15.00
18	Mike Piazza	250.00
19	Edgar Martinez	15.00
20	David Justice	40.00
21	Todd Hundley	15.00
22	Tony Gwynn	200.00
23	Larry Walker	60.00
24	Bernie Williams	60.00
25	Edgar Renteria	15.00
26	Rafael Palmeiro	40.00
27	Tim Salmon	40.00
28	Matt Morris	15.00
29	Shawn Estes	15.00
30	Vladimir Guerrero	100.00
31	Fernando Tatis	15.00
32	Justin Thompson	15.00
33	Ken Griffey Jr.	400.00
34	Edgardo Alfonzo	15.00
35	Mo Vaughn	100.00
36	Marty Cordova	15.00
37	Craig Biggio	30.00
38	Roger Clemens	150.00
39	Mark Grace	40.00
40	Ken Caminiti	30.00
41	Tony Womack	15.00
42	Albert Belle	100.00
43	Tino Martinez	60.00
44	Sandy Alomar	40.00

45	Jeff Cirillo	15.00
46	Jason Giambi	15.00
47	Darin Erstad	100.00
48	Livan Hernandez	15.00
49	Mark Grudzielanek	15.00
50	Sammy Sosa	200.00
51	Curt Schilling	40.00
52	Brian Hunter	15.00
53	Neifi Perez	15.00
54	Todd Walker	40.00
55	Jose Guillen	40.00
56	Jim Thome	60.00
57	Tom Glavine	40.00
58	Todd Greene	15.00
59	Rondell White	30.00
60	Roberto Alomar	75.00
61	Tony Clark	60.00
62	Vinny Castilla	25.00
63	Barry Larkin	40.00
64	Hideki Irabu	60.00
65	Johnny Damon	15.00
66	Juan Gonzalez	200.00
67	John Olerud	40.00
68	Gary Sheffield	50.00
69	Raul Mondesi	40.00
70	Chipper Jones	250.00
71	David Ortiz	25.00
72	Warren Morris	20.00
73	Alex Gonzalez	15.00
74	Nick Bierbrodt	15.00
75	Roy Halladay	20.00
76	Danny Buxbaum	15.00
77	Adam Kennedy	20.00
78	Jared Sandberg	30.00
79	Michael Barrett	15.00
80	Gil Meche	15.00
81	Jayson Werth	20.00
82	Abraham Nunez	20.00
83	Ben Petrick	15.00
84	Brett Caradonna	20.00
85	Mike Lowell	25.00
86	Clay Bruner	20.00
87	John Curtice	20.00
88	Bobby Estalella	15.00
89	Juan Melo	15.00
90	Arnold Gooch	15.00
91	Kevin Millwood	100.00
92	Richie Sexson	15.00
93	Orlando Cabrera	15.00
94	Pat Cline	15.00
95	Anthony Sanders	20.00
96	Russ Johnson	15.00
97	Ben Grieve	125.00
98	Kevin McGlinchy	15.00
99	Paul Wilder	15.00
100	Russ Ortiz	15.00
101	Ryan Jackson	35.00
102	Heath Murray	15.00
103	Brian Rose	20.00
104	Ryan Radmanovich	20.00
105	Ricky Ledee	25.00
106	Jeff Wallace	20.00
107	Ryan Minor	90.00
108	Dennis Reyes	15.00
109	James Manias	20.00
110	Chris Carpenter	15.00
111	Daryle Ward	15.00
112	Vernon Wells	20.00
113	Chad Green	15.00
114	Mike Stoner	80.00
115	Brad Fullmer	20.00
116	Adam Eaton	15.00
117	Jeff Liefer	15.00
118	Corey Koskie	20.00
119	Todd Helton	50.00
120	Jaime Jones	25.00
121	Mel Rosario	15.00
122	Geoff Goetz	15.00
123	Adrian Beltre	120.00
124	Jason Dellaero	20.00
125	Gabe Kapler	100.00
126	Scott Schoeneweis	15.00
127	Ryan Brannan	15.00
128	Aaron Akin	15.00
129	Ryan Anderson	100.00
130	Brad Penny	15.00
131	Bruce Chen	20.00
132	Eli Marrero	15.00
133	Eric Chavez	30.00
134	Troy Glaus	180.00
135	Troy Cameron	20.00
136	Brian Sikorski	20.00
137	Mike Kinkade	20.00
138	Braden Looper	15.00
139	Mark Mangum	15.00
140	Danny Peoples	15.00

141	J.J. Davis	20.00
142	Ben Davis	15.00
143	Jacque Jones	15.00
144	Derrick Gibson	15.00
145	Bronson Arroyo	15.00
146	Cristian Guzman	15.00
147	Jeff Abbott	15.00
148	Mike Cuddyer	30.00
149	Jason Romano	20.00
150	Shane Monahan	15.00
151	Ntema Ndungidi	20.00
152	Alex Sanchez	15.00
153	Jack Cust	35.00
154	Brent Butler	20.00
155	Ramon Hernandez	15.00
156	Norm Hutchins	15.00
157	Jason Marquis	15.00
158	Jacob Cruz	15.00
159	Rob Burger	30.00
160	Eric Milton	20.00
161	Preston Wilson	15.00
162	Jason Fitzgerald	20.00
163	Dan Serafini	15.00
164	Peter Munro	15.00
165	Trot Nixon	20.00
166	Homer Bush	15.00
167	Dermal Brown	20.00
168	Chad Hermansen	25.00
169	Julio Moreno	20.00
170	John Roskos	20.00
171	Grant Roberts	20.00
172	Ken Cloude	15.00
173	Jason Brester	15.00
174	Jason Conti	15.00
175	Jon Garland	15.00
176	Robbie Bell	15.00
177	Nathan Haynes	15.00
178	Ramon Ortiz	40.00
179	Shannon Stewart	15.00
180	Pablo Ortega	15.00
181	Jimmy Rollins	20.00
182	Sean Casey	20.00
183	Ted Lilly	15.00
184	Chris Enochs	40.00
185	Magglio Ordonez	60.00
186	Mike Drumright	15.00
187	Aaron Boone	15.00
188	Matt Clement	15.00
189	Todd Dunwoody	15.00
190	Larry Rodriguez	15.00
191	Todd Noel	15.00
192	Geoff Jenkins	15.00
193	George Lombard	15.00
194	Lance Berkman	60.00
195	Marcus McCain	20.00
196	Ryan Bradley	15.00
197	Jhensy Sandoval	20.00
198	Corey Lee	15.00
199	Mario Valdez	15.00
200	Robert Fick	20.00
201	Donnie Sadler	15.00
202	Marc Kroon	15.00
203	David Miller	15.00
204	Jarrod Washburn	15.00
205	Miguel Tejada	25.00
206	Raul Ibanez	15.00
207	John Patterson	15.00
208	Calvin Pickering	15.00
209	Felix Martinez	15.00
210	Mark Redman	15.00
211	Scott Elarton	15.00
212	Jose Amado	20.00
213	Kerry Wood	250.00
214	Dante Powell	15.00
215	Aramis Ramirez	100.00
216	A.J. Hinch	30.00
217	Dustin Carr	15.00
218	Mark Kotsay	25.00
219	Jason Standridge	15.00
220	Luis Ordaz	15.00
221	Orlando Hernandez	125.00
222	Cal Ripken Jr.	300.00
223	Paul Molitor	50.00
224	Derek Jeter	225.00
225	Barry Bonds	100.00
226	Jim Edmonds	30.00
227	John Smoltz	30.00
228	Eric Karros	20.00
229	Ray Lankford	15.00
230	Rey Ordonez	15.00
231	Kenny Lofton	80.00
232	Alex Rodriguez	250.00
233	Dante Bichette	30.00
234	Pedro Martinez	75.00
235	Carlos Delgado	25.00
236	Rod Beck	15.00

237	Matt Williams	40.00
238	Charles Johnson	15.00
239	Rico Brogna	15.00
240	Frank Thomas	250.00
241	Paul O'Neill	40.00
242	Jaret Wright	75.00
243	Brant Brown	15.00
244	Ryan Klesko	30.00
245	Chuck Finley	15.00
246	Derek Bell	15.00
247	Delino DeShields	15.00
248	Chan Ho Park	30.00
249	Wade Boggs	50.00
250	Jay Buhner	30.00
251	Butch Huskey	15.00
252	Steve Finley	15.00
253	Will Clark	40.00
254	John Valentin	15.00
255	Bobby Higginson	15.00
256	Darryl Strawberry	25.00
257	Randy Johnson	75.00
258	Al Martin	15.00
259	Travis Fryman	15.00
260	Fred McGriff	30.00
261	Jose Valentin	15.00
262	Andruw Jones	100.00
263	Kenny Rogers	15.00
264	Moises Alou	25.00
265	Denny Neagle	15.00
266	Ugueth Urbina	15.00
267	Derrek Lee	15.00
268	Ellis Burks	15.00
269	Mariano Rivera	25.00
270	Dean Palmer	15.00
271	Eddie Taubensee	15.00
272	Brady Anderson	15.00
273	Brian Giles	15.00
274	Quinton McCracken	15.00
275	Henry Rodriguez	15.00
276	Andres Galarraga	50.00
277	Jose Canseco	40.00
278	David Segui	15.00
279	Bret Saberhagen	15.00
280	Kevin Brown	25.00
281	Chuck Knoblauch	40.00
282	Jeromy Burnitz	15.00
283	Jay Bell	15.00
284	Manny Ramirez	100.00
285	Rick Helling	15.00
286	Francisco Cordova	15.00
287	Bob Abreu	15.00
288	J.T. Snow Jr.	15.00
289	Hideo Nomo	60.00
290	Brian Jordan	15.00
291	Javy Lopez	25.00
292	Travis Lee	150.00
293	Russell Branyan	15.00
294	Paul Konerko	25.00
295	*Masato Yoshii*	40.00
296	Kris Benson	30.00
297	Juan Encarnacion	15.00
298	Eric Milton	15.00
299	Mike Caruso	15.00
300	*Ricardo Aramboles*	75.00
301	Bobby Smith	15.00
302	Billy Koch	15.00
303	Richard Hidalgo	15.00
304	Justin Baughman	25.00
305	Chris Gissell	15.00
306	*Donnie Bridges*	25.00
307	*Nelson Lara*	25.00
308	*Randy Wolf*	25.00
309	*Jason LaRue*	25.00
310	*Jason Gooding*	20.00
311	*Edgar Clemente*	20.00
312	Andrew Vessel	15.00
313	Chris Reitsma	15.00
314	*Jesus Sanchez*	25.00
315	*Buddy Carlyle*	25.00
316	Randy Winn	15.00
317	Luis Rivera	60.00
318	*Marcus Thames*	30.00
319	A.J. Pierzynski	15.00
320	Scott Randall	15.00
321	Damian Sapp	15.00
322	*Eddie Yarnell*	75.00
323	Luke Allen	30.00
324	J.D. Smart	15.00
325	Willie Martinez	15.00
326	Alex Ramirez	15.00
327	*Eric DuBose*	25.00
328	Kevin Witt	15.00
329	*Dan McKinley*	25.00
330	Cliff Politte	15.00
331	Vladimir Nunez	15.00
332	*John Halama*	20.00

333	Nerio Rodriguez	15.00
334	Desi Relaford	15.00
335	Robinson Checo	15.00
336	*John Nicholson*	25.00
337	*Tom LaRosa*	25.00
338	*Kevin Nicholson*	40.00
339	Javier Vazquez	15.00
340	A.J. Zapp	15.00
341	Tom Evans	15.00
342	Kerry Robinson	15.00
343	*Gabe Gonzalez*	25.00
344	Ralph Milliard	15.00
345	Enrique Wilson	15.00
346	Elvin Hernandez	15.00
347	*Mike Lincoln*	30.00
348	*Cesar King*	50.00
349	Cristian Guzman	25.00
350	Donzell McDonald	15.00
351	Jim Parque	30.00
352	*Mike Saipe*	25.00
353	*Carlos Febles*	60.00
354	*Dernell Stenson*	60.00
355	*Mark Osborne*	30.00
356	*Odalis Perez*	50.00
357	*Jason Dewey*	25.00
358	Joe Fontenot	15.00
359	*Jason Grilli*	35.00
360	*Kevin Haverbusch*	35.00
361	*Jay Yennaco*	20.00
362	Brian Buchanan	15.00
363	John Barnes	15.00
364	Chris Fussell	15.00
365	*Kevin Gibbs*	25.00
366	Joe Lawrence	15.00
367	DaRond Stovall	15.00
368	*Brian Fuentes*	25.00
369	Jimmy Anderson	15.00
370	*Laril Gonzalez*	25.00
371	*Scott Williamson*	25.00
372	Milton Bradley	15.00
373	*Jason Halper*	25.00
374	*Brent Billingsley*	25.00
375	*Joe DePastino*	15.00
376	Jake Westbrook	15.00
377	Octavio Dotel	15.00
378	*Jason Williams*	20.00
379	*Julio Ramirez*	30.00
380	Seth Greisinger	15.00
381	*Mike Judd*	25.00
382	Ben Ford	20.00
383	Tom Bennett	15.00
384	*Adam Butler*	20.00
385	Wade Miller	25.00
386	Kyle Peterson	25.00
387	*Tommy Peterman*	25.00
388	Onan Masaoka	15.00
389	*Jason Rakers*	25.00
390	Rafael Medina	15.00
391	Luis Lopez	15.00
392	Jeff Yoder	15.00
393	Vance Wilson	25.00
394	*Fernando Seguignol*	70.00
395	Ron Wright	15.00
396	Ruben Mateo	90.00
397	*Steve Lomasney*	25.00
398	Damian Jackson	15.00
399	*Mike Jerzembeck*	25.00
400	*Luis Rivas*	35.00
401	*Kevin Burford*	35.00
402	Glenn Davis	15.00
403	*Robert Luce*	25.00
404	Cole Liniak	15.00
405	*Matthew LeCroy*	25.00
406	Jeremy Giambi	60.00
407	Shawn Chacon	15.00
408	*Dewayne Wise*	35.00
409	*Steve Woodard*	25.00
410	*Francisco Cordero*	20.00
411	*Damon Minor*	25.00
412	Lou Collier	15.00
413	Justin Towle	15.00
414	Juan LeBron	15.00
415	Michael Coleman	15.00
416	Felix Rodriguez	15.00
417	*Paul Ah Yat*	25.00
418	*Kevin Barker*	25.00
419	Brian Meadows	15.00
420	*Darnell McDonald*	60.00
421	*Matt Kinney*	25.00
422	*Mike Vavrek*	25.00
423	*Courtney Duncan*	25.00
424	*Kevin Millar*	25.00
425	Ruben Rivera	15.00
426	*Steve Shoemaker*	20.00
427	*Dan Reichert*	25.00
428	Carlos Lee	40.00

429	Rod Barajas	25.00
430	*Pablo Ozuna*	50.00
431	*Todd Belitz*	20.00
432	Sidney Ponson	15.00
433	*Steve Carver*	25.00
434	Esteban Yan	25.00
435	*Cedrick Bowers*	25.00
436	Marlon Anderson	15.00
437	Carl Pavano	15.00
438	*Jae Weong Seo*	30.00
439	*Jose Taveras*	30.00
440	Matt Anderson	40.00
441	*Darron Ingram*	35.00

1998 Bowman Chrome Reprints

Bowman Chrome Reprints showcased 50 of the most popular Bowman rookie cards to appear in the brand. Regular versions were seeded one per 12, while Refractor versions were seeded one per 36. There were 25 cards from this set inserted into each series.

	MT
Complete Set (50):	130.00
Common Player:	1.00
Inserted 1:12	
Refractors: 1.5x to 2.5x	
Inserted 1:36	
BC1 Yogi Berra	6.00
BC2 Jackie Robinson	15.00
BC3 Don Newcombe	1.00
BC4 Don Newcombe	1.00
BC5 Willie Mays	8.00
BC6 Gil McDougald	1.00
BC7 Don Larsen	3.00
BC8 Elston Howard	1.50
BC9 Robin Ventura	1.00
BC10 Brady Anderson	1.00
BC11 Gary Sheffield	2.00
BC12 Tino Martinez	2.50
BC13 Ken Griffey Jr.	18.00
BC14 John Smoltz	1.00
BC15 Sandy Alomar Jr.	1.00
BC16 Larry Walker	2.50
BC17 Todd Hundley	1.00
BC18 Mo Vaughn	5.00
BC19 Sammy Sosa	10.00
BC20 Frank Thomas	12.00
BC21 Chuck Knoblauch	2.50
BC22 Bernie Williams	3.00
BC23 Juan Gonzalez	8.00
BC24 Mike Mussina	4.00
BC25 Mike Mussina	3.00
BC26 Tim Salmon	2.50
BC27 Ivan Rodriguez	5.00
BC28 Kenny Lofton	5.00
BC29 Chipper Jones	12.00
BC30 Javier Lopez	1.00
BC31 Ryan Klesko	2.00
BC32 Raul Mondesi	2.00
BC33 Raul Mondesi	2.00
BC34 Carlos Delgado	1.00

BC35	Mike Piazza	12.00
BC36	Manny Ramirez	5.00
BC37	Andy Pettitte	3.00
BC38	Derek Jeter	12.00
BC39	Brad Fullmer	2.00
BC40	Richard Hidalgo	1.00
BC41	Tony Clark	3.00
BC42	Andruw Jones	5.00
BC43	Vladimir Guerrero	6.00
BC44	Nomar Garciaparra	12.00
BC45	Paul Konerko	2.00
BC46	Ben Grieve	6.00
BC47	Hideo Nomo	4.00
BC48	Scott Rolen	5.00
BC49	Jose Guillen	1.00
BC50	Livan Hernandez	1.00

C

1995 Certified

The concepts of hobby-only distribution and limited production which were the hallmarks of Pinnacle's Select brand were carried a step further with the post-season release of Select Certified baseball. Printed on double-thich cardboard stock card fronts feature all metallic-foil printing protected by a double laminated gloss coat. Backs have key player stats against each team in the league. The final 44 cards in the set are distinguished with a special Rookie logo and with gold added to the silver foil in the photo background.

		MT
Complete Set (135):		40.00
Common Player:		.20
Wax Box:		80.00
1	Barry Bonds	1.00
2	Reggie Sanders	.20
3	Terry Steinbach	.20
4	Eduardo Perez	.20
5	Frank Thomas	3.00
6	Wil Cordero	.20
7	John Olerud	.40
8	Deion Sanders	.50
9	Mike Mussina	.75
10	Mo Vaughn	1.00
11	Will Clark	.50
12	Chili Davis	.20
13	Jimmy Key	.20
14	Eddie Murray	.50
15	Bernard Gilkey	.20
16	David Cone	.35
17	Tim Salmon	.40
18	(Not issued, replaced w/ #2131)	.20

19	Steve Ontiveros	.20
20	Andres Galarraga	.40
21	Don Mattingly	1.25
22	Kevin Appier	.20
23	Paul Molitor	.75
24	Edgar Martinez	.30
25	Andy Benes	.20
26	Rafael Palmeiro	.40
27	Barry Larkin	.50
28	Gary Sheffield	.75
29	Wally Joyner	.20
30	Wade Boggs	.40
31	Rico Brogna	.20
32	Eddie Murray (Murray Tribute)	.60
33	Kirby Puckett	1.50
34	Bobby Bonilla	.30
35	Hal Morris	.20
36	Moises Alou	.30
37	Javier Lopez	.30
38	Chuck Knoblauch	.40
39	Mike Piazza	2.50
40	Travis Fryman	.20
41	Rickey Henderson	.40
42	Jim Thome	.60
43	Carlos Baerga	.20
44	Dean Palmer	.20
45	Kirk Gibson	.20
46	Bret Saberhagen	.20
47	Cecil Fielder	.30
48	Manny Ramirez	1.00
49	Derek Bell	.20
50	Mark McGwire	5.00
51	Jim Edmonds	.40
52	Robin Ventura	.20
53	Ryan Klesko	.60
54	Jeff Bagwell	1.50
55	Ozzie Smith	.75
56	Albert Belle	1.00
57	Darren Daulton	.20
58	Jeff Conine	.20
59	Greg Maddux	2.50
60	Lenny Dykstra	.20
61	Randy Johnson	.75
62	Fred McGriff	.40
63	Ray Lankford	.20
64	Dave Justice	.40
65	Paul O'Neill	.40
66	Tony Gwynn	2.00
67	Matt Williams	.50
68	Dante Bichette	.40
69	Craig Biggio	.40
70	Ken Griffey Jr.	4.00
71	J.T. Snow	.20
72	Cal Ripken Jr.	3.00
73	Jay Bell	.20
74	Joe Carter	.40
75	Roberto Alomar	.75
76	Benji Gil	.20
77	Ivan Rodriguez	1.00
78	Raul Mondesi	.50
79	Cliff Floyd	.20
80	Eric Karros, Mike Piazza, Raul Mondesi (Dodger Dynasty)	.75
81	Royce Clayton	.20
82	Billy Ashley	.20
83	Joey Hamilton	.20
84	Sammy Sosa	2.50
85	Jason Bere	.20
86	Dennis Martinez	.20
87	Greg Vaughn	.20
88	Roger Clemens	1.50
89	Larry Walker	.50
90	Mark Grace	.50
91	Kenny Lofton	1.00
92	*Carlos Perez*	.40
93	Roger Cedeno	.20
94	Scott Ruffcorn	.20
95	Jim Pittsley	.20
96	Andy Pettitte	1.00
97	James Baldwin	.20
98	*Hideo Nomo*	6.00
99	Ismael Valdes	.20
100	Armando Benitez	.20
101	Jose Malave	.20
102	*Bobby Higginson*	1.50
103	LaTroy Hawkins	.35
104	Russ Davis	.20
105	Shawn Green	.35
106	Joe Vitiello	.20
107	Chipper Jones	2.50
108	Shane Andrews	.20
109	Jose Oliva	.20
110	Ray Durham	.40
111	Jon Nunnally	.20

112	Alex Gonzalez	.40
113	Vaughn Eshelman	.20
114	Marty Cordova	.50
115	*Mark Grudzielanek*	.75
116	Brian Hunter	.40
117	Charles Johnson	.40
118	Alex Rodriguez	4.00
119	David Bell	.20
120	Todd Hollandsworth	.40
121	Joe Randa	.20
122	Derek Jeter	2.50
123	Frank Rodriguez	.20
124	Curtis Goodwin	.20
125	Bill Pulsipher	.20
126	John Mabry	.20
127	Julian Tavarez	.20
128	Edgardo Alfonzo	.20
129	Orlando Miller	.20
130	Juan Acevedo	.20
131	Jeff Cirillo	.20
132	Roberto Petagine	.20
133	Antonio Osuna	.20
134	Michael Tucker	.20
135	Garret Anderson	.40
2131	Cal Ripken Jr. (Consecutive Game Record)	4.00

1995 Certified Mirror Gold

Inserted at an average rate of one per five packs, this parallel set is a gold-foil version of the 135 cards in the regular Select Certified set.

	MT
Complete Set (135):	600.00
Common Player:	2.00
Mirror Gold Stars: 5x to 10x	
Yng Stars & RC's: 4x to 8x	
(Mirror Gold single cards are valued at 4X-6X regular Select Certified cards.)	

1995 Certified Checklists

The seven checklists issued with Select Certified are not numbered as part of the set. They are found one per foil pack and are printed on much thinner card stock than the regular-issue cards.

		MT
Complete Set (7):		.75
Common Player:		.15
1	Ken Griffey Jr. (A.L., #3-41)	.25
2	Frank Thomas (A.L., #42-95)	.25
3	Cal Ripken Jr. (A.L., #96-135)	.25

4	Jeff Bagwell (N.L., #1-58)	.15
5	Mike Piazza (N.L., #59-92)	.15
6	Barry Bonds (N.L., #93-133)	.15
7	Manny Ramirez, Raul Mondesi (Chase cards)	.15

1995 Certified Future

A striking new all-metal, brushed-foil printing technology was used in the production of this chase set of 10 rookie players with "unlimited future potential." Stated odds of finding a Certified Future insert card were one in 19 packs.

		MT
Complete Set (10):		90.00
Common Player:		3.00
1	Chipper Jones	20.00
2	Curtis Goodwin	3.00
3	Hideo Nomo	12.00
4	Shawn Green	5.00
5	Ray Durham	5.00
6	Todd Hollandsworth	7.50
7	Brian Hunter	5.00
8	Carlos Delgado	7.50
9	Michael Tucker	5.00
10	Alex Rodriguez	35.00

1995 Certified Gold Team

A dozen of the top position players in the league were selected for appearance in this insert set. Cards are printed in a special double-sided,

all-gold Dufex technology. An action photo is featured on the front, a portrait on back. Odds of picking a Gold Team card were stated as one in 41 packs.

		MT
Complete Set (12):		220.00
Common Player:		8.00
1	Ken Griffey Jr.	50.00
2	Frank Thomas	40.00
3	Cal Ripken Jr.	40.00
4	Jeff Bagwell	20.00
5	Mike Piazza	30.00
6	Barry Bonds	12.00
7	Matt Williams	8.00
8	Don Mattingly	20.00
9	Will Clark	8.00
10	Tony Gwynn	25.00
11	Kirby Puckett	25.00
12	Jose Canseco	8.00

1995 Certified Potential Unlimited

Dufex printing with textured foil highlights and transparent inks is featured in this chase set which was produced in an edition of no more the 1,975 sets, as witnessed by the numbering on card backs. Approximate odds of finding a Potential Unlimited card are one per 29 packs. A super-scarce edition of 903 cards each featuring "micro-etch" foil printing technology was issued at the rate of one per 70 packs.

		MT
Complete Set (20):		200.00
Common Player:		5.00
Complete Numbered 903 Set		400.00
903's: 1.5X		
1	Cliff Floyd	5.00
2	Manny Ramirez	15.00
3	Raul Mondesi	8.00
4	Scott Ruffcorn	5.00
5	Billy Ashley	5.00
6	Alex Gonzalez	5.00
7	Midre Cummings	5.00
8	Charles Johnson	8.00
9	Garret Anderson	5.00
10	Hideo Nomo	35.00
11	Chipper Jones	35.00
12	Curtis Goodwin	5.00
13	Frank Rodriguez	5.00
14	Shawn Green	5.00
15	Ray Durham	5.00
16	Todd Hollandsworth	8.00
17	Brian Hunter	5.00
18	Carlos Delgado	8.00
19	Michael Tucker	5.00
20	Alex Rodriguez	75.00

1996 Certified

This hobby-exclusive set has 144 cards in its regular issue, plus six parallel versions and two insert sets. The parallel sets are: Certified Red (one per five packs), Certified Blue (one per 50), Artist's Proofs (one per 12), Mirror Red (one per 100), Mirror Blue (one per 200), and Mirror Gold (one per 300). Breaking down the numbers, there are 1,800 Certified Red sets, 180 Certified Blue, 500 Artist's Proofs, 90 Mirror Red 45 Mirror Blue and 30 Mirror Gold sets. The insert sets are Interleague Preview cards and Select Few. Cards #135-144 are a "Pastime Power" subset.

		MT
Complete Set (144):		40.00
Common Player:		.20
Unlisted Stars: .40 to .60		
Comp. Certified Red Set (144):		500.00
Common Red:		1.00
Reds: 4x to 6x		
Artist's Proofs: 10x to 15x		
Blues: 20x to 35x		
Wax Box:		200.00
1	Frank Thomas	4.00
2	Tino Martinez	.40
3	Gary Sheffield	.75
4	Kenny Lofton	1.50
5	Joe Carter	.40
6	Alex Rodriguez	4.00
7	Chipper Jones	3.00
8	Roger Clemens	1.50
9	Jay Bell	.20
10	Eddie Murray	.50
11	Will Clark	.50
12	Mike Mussina	1.25
13	Hideo Nomo	1.25
14	Andres Galarraga	.40
15	Marc Newfield	.20
16	Jason Isringhausen	.20
17	Randy Johnson	.75
18	Chuck Knoblauch	.40
19	J.T. Snow	.20
20	Mark McGwire	5.00
21	Tony Gwynn	2.00
22	Albert Belle	1.50
23	Gregg Jefferies	.20
24	Reggie Sanders	.20
25	Bernie Williams	1.00
26	Ray Lankford	.20
27	Johnny Damon	.20
28	Ryne Sandberg	1.25
29	Rondell White	.40
30	Mike Piazza	3.00
31	Barry Bonds	1.25
32	Greg Maddux	3.00
33	Craig Biggio	.20
34	John Valentin	.20
35	Ivan Rodriguez	1.25
36	Rico Brogna	.20

37	Tim Salmon	.40
38	Sterling Hitchcock	.20
39	Charles Johnson	.20
40	Travis Fryman	.20
41	Barry Larkin	.60
42	Tom Glavine	.40
43	Marty Cordova	.20
44	Shawn Green	.20
45	Ben McDonald	.20
46	Robin Ventura	.20
47	Ken Griffey Jr.	5.00
48	Orlando Merced	.20
49	Paul O'Neill	.40
50	Ozzie Smith	1.00
51	Manny Ramirez	1.25
52	Ismael Valdes	.20
53	Cal Ripken Jr.	4.00
54	Jeff Bagwell	2.00
55	Greg Vaughn	.20
56	Juan Gonzalez	2.00
57	Raul Mondesi	.50
58	Carlos Baerga	.20
59	Sammy Sosa	2.50
60	Mike Kelly	.20
61	Edgar Martinez	.20
62	Kirby Puckett	1.50
63	Cecil Fielder	.35
64	David Cone	.30
65	Moises Alou	.40
66	Fred McGriff	.50
67	Mo Vaughn	1.25
68	Edgardo Alfonzo	.20
69	Jim Thome	.75
70	Rickey Henderson	.20
71	Dante Bichette	.40
72	Lenny Dykstra	.20
73	Benji Gil	.20
74	Wade Boggs	.40
75	Jim Edmonds	.20
76	Michael Tucker	.20
77	Carlos Delgado	.20
78	Butch Huskey	.20
79	Billy Ashley	.20
80	Dean Palmer	.20
81	Paul Molitor	.50
82	Ryan Klesko	1.00
83	Brian Hunter	.20
84	Jay Buhner	.40
85	Larry Walker	.60
86	Mike Bordick	.20
87	Matt Williams	.40
88	Jack McDowell	.30
89	Hal Morris	.20
90	Brian Jordan	.20
91	Andy Pettitte	1.50
92	Melvin Nieves	.20
93	Pedro Martinez	.40
94	Mark Grace	.40
95	Garret Anderson	.20
96	Andre Dawson	.30
97	Ray Durham	.20
98	Jose Canseco	.50
99	Roberto Alomar	1.25
100	Derek Jeter	2.50
101	Alan Benes	.40
102	Karim Garcia	.60
103	*Robin Jennings*	.20
104	Bob Abreu	.20
105	Sal Fasano (Card front has Livan Hernandez' name)	.20
106	Steve Gibralter	.20
107	Jermaine Dye	.30
108	Jason Kendall	.20
109	*Mike Grace*	.50
110	Jason Schmidt	.20
111	Paul Wilson	.30
112	Rey Ordonez	.75
113	*Wilton Guerrero*	1.00
114	Brooks Kieschnick	.20
115	George Arias	.20
116	*Osvaldo Fernandez*	.20
117	Todd Hollandsworth	.30
118	John Wasdin	.20
119	Eric Owens	.20
120	Chan Ho Park	.20
121	Mark Loretta	.20
122	Richard Hidalgo	.20
123	Jeff Suppan	.20
124	Jim Pittsley	.20
125	LaTroy Hawkins	.20
126	Chris Snopek	.20
127	Justin Thompson	.20
128	Jay Powell	.20
129	Alex Ochoa	.20
130	Felipe Crespo	.20
131	*Matt Lawton*	.20

132	Jimmy Haynes	.20
133	Terrell Wade	.20
134	Ruben Rivera	.60
135	Frank Thomas (Pastime Power)	2.50
136	Ken Griffey Jr. (Pastime Power)	3.00
137	Greg Maddux (Pastime Power)	2.00
138	Mike Piazza (Pastime Power)	2.00
139	Cal Ripken Jr. (Pastime Power)	2.50
140	Albert Belle (Pastime Power)	1.00
141	Mo Vaughn (Pastime Power)	.75
142	Chipper Jones (Pastime Power)	2.00
143	Hideo Nomo (Pastime Power)	.60
144	Ryan Klesko (Pastime Power)	.60

1996 Certified Artist's Proofs

Only 500 cards each of this parallel issue were reported produced, seeded one in every dozen packs. The cards are identical to the regular-issue Select Certified except for the presence on front of a prismatic gold Artist's Proof logo.

	MT
Complete Set (144):	1800.
Common Player:	7.50
(Star cards valued at 8X-20X regular Select Certified edition)	

1996 Certified Red, Blue

These 1996 Select Certified insert cards were the most common of the parallel cards issued; they were seeded one per every five packs. There were 1,800 Certified Red sets produced, with the number of Certified Blue sets at 180. Cards are essentially the same as regular-issue Select Certified except for the color of the foil background on front.

	MT
Complete Set, Red (144):	800.00
Common Player, Red:	2.00
Artist's Proofs (144): 2.5x	
Certified Blue (144): 5x to 7x	

1	Frank Thomas	30.00
2	Tino Martinez	4.00
3	Gary Sheffield	6.00
4	Kenny Lofton	10.00
5	Joe Carter	3.00
6	Alex Rodriguez	30.00
7	Chipper Jones	25.00
8	Roger Clemens	12.00
9	Jay Bell	2.00
10	Eddie Murray	8.00
11	Will Clark	4.00
12	Mike Mussina	8.00
13	Hideo Nomo	8.00
14	Andres Galarraga	5.00
15	Marc Newfield	2.00
16	Jason Isringhausen	2.00
17	Randy Johnson	8.00
18	Chuck Knoblauch	5.00
19	J.T. Snow	2.00
20	Mark McGwire	20.00
21	Tony Gwynn	25.00
22	Albert Belle	12.00
23	Gregg Jefferies	2.00
24	Reggie Sanders	2.00
25	Bernie Williams	8.00
26	Ray Lankford	2.00
27	Johnny Damon	3.00
28	Ryne Sandberg	10.00
29	Rondell White	4.00
30	Mike Piazza	25.00
31	Barry Bonds	10.00
32	Greg Maddux	25.00
33	Craig Biggio	4.00
34	John Valentin	2.00
35	Ivan Rodriguez	8.00
36	Rico Brogna	2.00
37	Tim Salmon	5.00
38	Sterling Hitchcock	2.00
39	Charles Johnson	2.00
40	Travis Fryman	2.00
41	Barry Larkin	5.00
42	Tom Glavine	4.00
43	Marty Cordova	3.00
44	Shawn Green	2.00
45	Ben McDonald	2.00
46	Robin Ventura	2.00
47	Ken Griffey Jr.	45.00
48	Orlando Merced	2.00
49	Paul O'Neill	4.00
50	Ozzie Smith	8.00
51	Manny Ramirez	10.00
52	Ismael Valdes	2.00
53	Cal Ripken Jr.	30.00
54	Jeff Bagwell	20.00
55	Greg Vaughn	2.00
56	Juan Gonzalez	20.00
57	Raul Mondesi	5.00
58	Carlos Baerga	2.00
59	Sammy Sosa	20.00
60	Mike Kelly	2.00
61	Edgar Martinez	2.00
62	Kirby Puckett	12.00
63	Cecil Fielder	4.00
64	David Cone	3.00
65	Moises Alou	3.00
66	Fred McGriff	4.00
67	Mo Vaughn	10.00
68	Edgardo Alfonzo	2.00
69	Jim Thome	8.00
70	Rickey Henderson	2.00
71	Dante Bichette	4.00
72	Lenny Dykstra	2.00
73	Benji Gil	2.00
74	Wade Boggs	5.00
75	Jim Edmonds	4.00
76	Michael Tucker	2.00
77	Carlos Delgado	2.00
78	Butch Huskey	2.00
79	Billy Ashley	2.00
80	Dean Palmer	2.00
81	Paul Molitor	8.00
82	Ryan Klesko	8.00
83	Brian Hunter	2.00
84	Jay Buhner	5.00
85	Larry Walker	6.00
86	Mike Bordick	2.00
87	Matt Williams	5.00
88	Jack McDowell	2.00
89	Hal Morris	2.00
90	Brian Jordan	2.00
91	Andy Pettitte	8.00
92	Melvin Nieves	2.00
93	Pedro Martinez	4.00
94	Mark Grace	4.00
95	Garret Anderson	2.00
96	Andre Dawson	3.00
97	Ray Durham	2.00

98	Jose Canseco	4.00
99	Roberto Alomar	8.00
100	Derek Jeter	25.00
101	Alan Benes	4.00
102	Karim Garcia	6.00
103	Robin Jennings	2.00
104	Bob Abreu	2.00
105	Sal Fasano (Card front has Livan Hernandez' name)	2.00
106	Steve Gibralter	2.00
107	Jermaine Dye	2.00
108	Jason Kendall	2.00
109	Mike Grace	4.00
110	Jason Schmidt	2.00
111	Paul Wilson	3.00
112	Rey Ordonez	3.00
113	Wilton Guerrero	6.00
114	Brooks Kieschnick	2.00
115	George Arias	2.00
116	Osvaldo Fernandez	2.00
117	Todd Hollandsworth	3.00
118	John Wasdin	2.00
119	Eric Owens	2.00
120	Chan Ho Park	2.00
121	Mark Loretta	2.00
122	Richard Hidalgo	2.00
123	Jeff Suppan	2.00
124	Jim Pittsley	2.00
125	LaTroy Hawkins	2.00
126	Chris Snopek	2.00
127	Justin Thompson	2.00
128	Jay Powell	2.00
129	Alex Ochoa	2.00
130	Felipe Crespo	2.00
131	Matt Lawton	2.00
132	Jimmy Haynes	2.00
133	Terrell Wade	2.00
134	Ruben Rivera	3.00
135	Frank Thomas (Pastime Power)	15.00
136	Ken Griffey Jr. (Pastime Power)	25.00
137	Greg Maddux (Pastime Power)	12.00
138	Mike Piazza (Pastime Power)	12.00
139	Cal Ripken Jr. (Pastime Power)	20.00
140	Albert Belle (Pastime Power)	6.00
141	Mo Vaughn (Pastime Power)	5.00
142	Chipper Jones (Pastime Power)	12.00
143	Hideo Nomo (Pastime Power)	4.00
144	Ryan Klesko (Pastime Power)	3.00

1996 Certified Mirror Gold, Blue, Red

These 1996 Select Certified inserts are the scarcest of the set. Only 30 Mirror Gold sets were made, with 60 Mirror Blue sets and 90 Mirror Red. Due to the improbability of completing the collection, no complete set price is given.

		MT
Mirror Gold (144):		
Common Player, Gold:		100.00
Mirror Blue: (144): 35-40% of Gold		
Common Player, Blue:		35.00
Mirror Red (144): 20-25% of Gold		
Common Player, Red:		20.00
1	Frank Thomas	2000.
2	Tino Martinez	450.00
3	Gary Sheffield	425.00
4	Kenny Lofton	700.00
5	Joe Carter	250.00
6	Alex Rodriguez	2250.
7	Chipper Jones	1450.
8	Roger Clemens	1000.
9	Jay Bell	100.00
10	Eddie Murray	650.00
11	Will Clark	400.00
12	Mike Mussina	500.00
13	Hideo Nomo	1100.
14	Andres Galarraga	300.00

15	Marc Newfield	125.00
16	Jason Isringhausen	150.00
17	Randy Johnson	600.00
18	Chuck Knoblauch	400.00
19	J.T. Snow	175.00
20	Mark McGwire	2000.
21	Tony Gwynn	1400.
22	Albert Belle	1000.
23	Gregg Jefferies	100.00
24	Reggie Sanders	150.00
25	Bernie Williams	400.00
26	Ray Lankford	200.00
27	Johnny Damon	150.00
28	Ryne Sandberg	550.00
29	Rondell White	175.00
30	Mike Piazza	1800.
31	Barry Bonds	700.00
32	Greg Maddux	1750.
33	Craig Biggio	250.00
34	John Valentin	100.00
35	Ivan Rodriguez	750.00
36	Rico Brogna	125.00
37	Tim Salmon	300.00
38	Sterling Hitchcock	100.00
39	Charles Johnson	175.00
40	Travis Fryman	200.00
41	Barry Larkin	150.00
42	Tom Glavine	250.00
43	Marty Cordova	100.00
44	Shawn Green	100.00
45	Ben McDonald	100.00
46	Robin Ventura	175.00
47	Ken Griffey Jr.	3200.
48	Orlando Merced	100.00
49	Paul O'Neill	100.00
50	Ozzie Smith	550.00
51	Manny Ramirez	500.00
52	Ismael Valdes	100.00
53	Cal Ripken Jr.	2400.
54	Jeff Bagwell	1200.
55	Greg Vaughn	100.00
56	Juan Gonzalez	1600.
57	Raul Mondesi	200.00
58	Carlos Baerga	100.00
59	Sammy Sosa	750.00
60	Mike Kelly	100.00
61	Edgar Martinez	100.00
62	Kirby Puckett	1400.
63	Cecil Fielder	200.00
64	David Cone	100.00
65	Moises Alou	275.00
66	Fred McGriff	275.00
67	Mo Vaughn	500.00
68	Edgardo Alfonzo	125.00
69	Jim Thome	450.00
70	Rickey Henderson	300.00
71	Dante Bichette	200.00
72	Lenny Dykstra	100.00
73	Benji Gil	100.00
74	Wade Boggs	400.00
75	Jim Edmonds	250.00
76	Michael Tucker	200.00
77	Carlos Delgado	100.00
78	Butch Huskey	100.00
79	Billy Ashley	100.00
80	Dean Palmer	150.00
81	Paul Molitor	550.00
82	Ryan Klesko	350.00
83	Brian Hunter	160.00
84	Jay Buhner	250.00
85	Larry Walker	650.00
86	Mike Bordick	100.00
87	Matt Williams	350.00
88	Jack McDowell	100.00
89	Hal Morris	100.00
90	Brian Jordan	100.00
91	Andy Pettitte	400.00
92	Melvin Nieves	100.00
93	Pedro Martinez	350.00
94	Mark Grace	300.00
95	Garret Anderson	125.00
96	Andre Dawson	250.00
97	Ray Durham	100.00
98	Jose Canseco	325.00
99	Roberto Alomar	500.00
100	Derek Jeter	1200.
101	Alan Benes	100.00
102	Karim Garcia	275.00
103	Robin Jennings	100.00
104	Bob Abreu	150.00
105	Livan Hernandez (photo actually Sal Fasano)	125.00
106	Steve Gibralter	100.00
107	Jermaine Dye	125.00
108	Jason Kendall	100.00
109	Mike Grace	125.00

110	Jason Schmidt	100.00
111	Paul Wilson	150.00
112	Rey Ordonez	200.00
113	Wilton Guerrero	275.00
114	Brooks Kieschnick	100.00
115	George Arias	100.00
116	Osvaldo Fernandez	100.00
117	Todd Hollandsworth	100.00
118	John Wasdin	100.00
119	Eric Owens	100.00
120	Chan Ho Park	125.00
121	Mark Loretta	100.00
122	Richard Hidalgo	175.00
123	Jeff Suppan	100.00
124	Jim Pittsley	100.00
125	LaTroy Hawkins	100.00
126	Chris Snopek	100.00
127	Justin Thompson	125.00
128	Jay Powell	100.00
129	Alex Ochoa	125.00
130	Felipe Crespo	100.00
131	Matt Lawton	125.00
132	Jimmy Haynes	100.00
133	Terrell Wade	100.00
134	Ruben Rivera	200.00
135	Frank Thomas (Pastime Power)	1000.
136	Ken Griffey Jr. (Pastime Power)	2000.
137	Greg Maddux (Pastime Power)	700.00
138	Mike Piazza (Pastime Power)	700.00
139	Cal Ripken Jr. (Pastime Power)	1000.
140	Albert Belle (Pastime Power)	450.00
141	Mo Vaughn (Pastime Power)	200.00
142	Chipper Jones (Pastime Power)	575.00
143	Hideo Nomo (Pastime Power)	350.00
144	Ryan Klesko (Pastime Power)	175.00

1996 Certified Interleague Preview

These 1996 Select Certified insert cards feature 21 prospective matchups from when interleague play begins. The cards were seeded one per every 42 packs.

		MT
Complete Set (25):		475.00
Common Player:		8.00
1	Ken Griffey Jr., Hideo Nomo	60.00
2	Greg Maddux, Mo Vaughn	40.00
3	Frank Thomas, Sammy Sosa	60.00
4	Mike Piazza, Jim Edmonds	40.00
5	Ryan Klesko, Roger Clemens	15.00
6	Derek Jeter, Rey Ordonez	25.00
7	Johnny Damon, Ray Lankford	15.00
8	Manny Ramirez, Reggie Sanders	25.00
9	Barry Bonds, Jay Buhner	18.00
10	Jason Isringhausen, Wade Boggs	10.00
11	David Cone, Chipper Jones	40.00
12	Jeff Bagwell, Will Clark	30.00
13	Tony Gwynn, Randy Johnson	25.00
14	Cal Ripken Jr., Tom Glavine	50.00

15	Kirby Puckett, Alan Benes	20.00
16	Gary Sheffield, Mike Mussina	15.00
17	Raul Mondesi, Tim Salmon	12.00
18	Rondell White, Carlos Delgado	8.00
19	Cecil Fielder, Ryne Sandberg	20.00
20	Kenny Lofton, Brian Hunter	25.00
21	Paul Wilson, Paul O'Neill	8.00
22	Ismael Valdes, Edgar Martinez	8.00
23	Matt Williams, Mark McGwire	40.00
24	Albert Belle, Barry Larkin	15.00
25	Brady Anderson, Marquis Grissom	8.00

1996 Certified Select Few

Eighteen top players are featured on these 1996 Select Certified inserts, which utilize holographic technology with a dot matrix hologram. Cards were seeded one per every 60 packs.

		MT
Complete Set (18):		190.00
Common Player:		4.00
1	Sammy Sosa	20.00
2	Derek Jeter	20.00
3	Ken Griffey Jr.	30.00
4	Albert Belle	8.00
5	Cal Ripken Jr.	25.00
6	Greg Maddux	20.00
7	Frank Thomas	25.00
8	Mo Vaughn	8.00
9	Chipper Jones	20.00
10	Mike Piazza	20.00
11	Ryan Klesko	5.00
12	Hideo Nomo	8.00
13	Alan Benes	4.00
14	Manny Ramirez	8.00
15	Gary Sheffield	6.00
16	Barry Bonds	8.00
17	Matt Williams	4.00
18	Johnny Damon	4.00

1996 Circa

This hobby-exclusive product was limited to 2,000 sequentially numbered cases. The regular-issue set has 196 player cards, including 18 top prospects and four prospects. Circa also has a 200-card parallel set called Rave which is limited to 150 sets. Each Rave card is sequentially numbered from 1-150. Two other insert sets were also produced - Boss, and Access.

		MT
Complete Set (200):		25.00
Common Player:		.10
Wax Box:		40.00
1	Roberto Alomar	.75
2	Brady Anderson	.20
3	*Rocky Coppinger*	.10
4	Eddie Murray	.40
5	Mike Mussina	.75
6	Randy Myers	.10
7	Rafael Palmeiro	.25
8	Cal Ripken Jr.	2.50
9	Jose Canseco	.30
10	Roger Clemens	1.00
11	Mike Greenwell	.10
12	Tim Naehring	.10
13	John Valentin	.15
14	Mo Vaughn	1.00
15	Tim Wakefield	.10
16	Jim Abbott	.10
17	Garret Anderson	.10
18	Jim Edmonds	.25
19	*Darin Erstad*	2.50
20	Chuck Finley	.10
21	Troy Percival	.10
22	Tim Salmon	.20
23	J.T. Snow	.15
24	Wilson Alvarez	.10
25	Harold Baines	.12
26	Ray Durham	.10
27	Alex Fernandez	.20
28	Tony Phillips	.15
29	Frank Thomas	2.50
30	Robin Ventura	.15
31	Sandy Alomar Jr.	.15
32	Albert Belle	.75
33	Kenny Lofton	1.00
34	Dennis Martinez	.10
35	Jose Mesa	.10
36	Charles Nagy	.10
37	Manny Ramirez	.75
37p	Manny Ramirez (overprinted "PROMOTIONAL SAMPLE")	3.00
38	Jim Thome	.50
39	Travis Fryman	.10
40	Bob Higginson	.20
41	Melvin Nieves	.10
42	Alan Trammell	.10
43	Kevin Appier	.10
44	Johnny Damon	.10
45	Keith Lockhart	.10
46	Jeff Montgomery	.10
47	Joe Randa	.10
48	Bip Roberts	.10
49	Ricky Bones	.10
50	Jeff Cirillo	.10
51	Marc Newfield	.10
52	Dave Nilsson	.10
53	Kevin Seitzer	.10
54	Ron Coomer	.10
55	Marty Cordova	.20
56	Roberto Kelly	.10
57	Chuck Knoblauch	.30
58	Paul Molitor	.50
59	Kirby Puckett	1.00
60	Scott Stahoviak	.10
61	Wade Boggs	.25

62	David Cone	.20
63	Cecil Fielder	.20
64	Dwight Gooden	.15
65	Derek Jeter	1.50
66	Tino Martinez	.30
67	Paul O'Neill	.20
68	Andy Pettitte	1.00
69	Ruben Rivera	.30
70	Bernie Williams	.50
71	Geronimo Berroa	.10
72	Jason Giambi	.20
73	Mark McGwire	3.00
74	Terry Steinbach	.10
75	Todd Van Poppel	.10
76	Jay Payton	.20
77	Norm Charlton	.10
78	Ken Griffey Jr.	3.00
79	Randy Johnson	.50
80	Edgar Martinez	.10
81	Alex Rodriguez	3.00
82	Paul Sorrento	.10
83	Dan Wilson	.10
84	Will Clark	.30
85	Kevin Elster	.10
86	Juan Gonzalez	1.50
87	Rusty Greer	.10
88	Ken Hill	.10
89	Mark McLemore	.10
90	Dean Palmer	.10
91	Roger Pavlik	.10
92	Ivan Rodriguez	.75
93	Joe Carter	.20
94	Carlos Delgado	.15
95	Juan Guzman	.10
96	John Olerud	.15
97	Ed Sprague	.10
98	Jermaine Dye	.20
99	Tom Glavine	.20
100	Marquis Grissom	.10
101	Andruw Jones	1.50
102	Chipper Jones	2.00
103	David Justice	.25
104	Ryan Klesko	.50
105	Greg Maddux	2.00
106	Fred McGriff	.40
107	John Smoltz	.25
108	Brant Brown	.10
109	Mark Grace	.25
110	Brian McRae	.10
111	Ryne Sandberg	.75
112	Sammy Sosa	1.50
113	Steve Trachsel	.10
114	Bret Boone	.10
115	Eric Davis	.12
116	Steve Gibralter	.10
117	Barry Larkin	.25
118	Reggie Sanders	.15
119	John Smiley	.10
120	Dante Bichette	.25
121	Ellis Burks	.15
122	Vinny Castilla	.10
123	Andres Galarraga	.20
124	Larry Walker	.40
125	Eric Young	.10
126	Kevin Brown	.10
127	Greg Colbrunn	.10
128	Jeff Conine	.15
129	Charles Johnson	.15
130	Al Leiter	.10
131	Gary Sheffield	.40
132	Devon White	.10
133	Jeff Bagwell	1.25
134	Derek Bell	.15
135	Craig Biggio	.20
136	Doug Drabek	.10
137	Brian Hunter	.10
138	Darryl Kile	.10
139	Shane Reynolds	.10
140	Brett Butler	.10
141	Eric Karros	.15
142	Ramon Martinez	.10
143	Raul Mondesi	.25
144	Hideo Nomo	.75
145	Chan Ho Park	.12
146	Mike Piazza	2.00
147	Moises Alou	.20
148	Yamil Benitez	.10
149	Mark Grudzielanek	.10
150	Pedro Martinez	.20
151	Henry Rodriguez	.10
152	David Segui	.10
153	Rondell White	.20
154	Carlos Baerga	.10
155	John Franco	.10
156	Bernard Gilkey	.10
157	Todd Hundley	.20

158	Jason Isringhausen	.15
159	Lance Johnson	.10
160	Alex Ochoa	.10
161	Rey Ordonez	.25
162	Paul Wilson	.20
163	Ron Blazier	.10
164	Ricky Bottalico	.10
165	Jim Eisenreich	.10
166	Pete Incaviglia	.10
167	Mickey Morandini	.10
168	Ricky Otero	.10
169	Curt Schilling	.10
170	Jay Bell	.10
171	Charlie Hayes	.10
172	Jason Kendall	.15
173	Jeff King	.10
174	Al Martin	.10
175	Alan Benes	.20
176	Royce Clayton	.10
177	Brian Jordan	.10
178	Ray Lankford	.10
179	John Mabry	.10
180	Willie McGee	.10
181	Ozzie Smith	.50
182	Todd Stottlemyre	.10
183	Andy Ashby	.10
184	Ken Caminiti	.25
185	Steve Finley	.10
186	Tony Gwynn	1.50
187	Rickey Henderson	.10
188	Wally Joyner	.15
189	Fernando Valenzuela	.10
190	Greg Vaughn	.10
191	Rod Beck	.10
192	Barry Bonds	1.00
193	Shawon Dunston	.15
194	Chris Singleton	.10
195	Robby Thompson	.10
196	Matt Williams	.25
197	Checklist(Barry Bonds)	.30
198	Checklist(Ken Griffey Jr.)	1.00
199	Checklist(Cal Ripken Jr.)	.75
200	Checklist(Frank Thomas)	1.00

1996 Circa Access

This 1996 Fleer Circa insert set highlights 30 players on a three-panel design that includes multiple photographs, personal information and statistics. The cards were seeded one per every 12 packs.

		MT
Complete Set (30):		125.00
Common Player:		2.00
1	Cal Ripken Jr.	15.00
2	Mo Vaughn	5.00
3	Tim Salmon	2.50
4	Frank Thomas	15.00
5	Albert Belle	5.00
6	Kenny Lofton	5.00
7	Manny Ramirez	5.00
8	Paul Molitor	3.00
9	Kirby Puckett	8.00
10	Paul O'Neill	2.00
11	Mark McGwire	25.00

12	Ken Griffey Jr.	20.00
13	Randy Johnson	4.00
14	Greg Maddux	12.00
15	John Smoltz	3.00
16	Sammy Sosa	12.00
17	Barry Larkin	3.00
18	Gary Sheffield	4.00
19	Jeff Bagwell	8.00
20	Hideo Nomo	4.00
21	Mike Piazza	12.00
22	Moises Alou	2.00
23	Henry Rodriguez	2.00
24	Rey Ordonez	2.00
25	Jay Bell	2.00
26	Ozzie Smith	4.00
27	Tony Gwynn	8.00
28	Rickey Henderson	2.00
29	Barry Bonds	5.00
30	Matt Williams	3.00
30p	Matt Williams (overprinted "PROMOTIONAL SAMPLE")	3.00

1996 Circa Boss

This 1996 Fleer Circa insert set showcases the game's top stars on an embossed design. Cards were seeded one per every six packs.

		MT
Complete Set (50):		125.00
Common Player:		1.00
1	Roberto Alomar	3.00
2	Cal Ripken Jr.	12.00
2p	Cal Ripken Jr. (overprinted "PROMOTIONAL SAMPLE")	8.00
3	Jose Canseco	1.50
4	Mo Vaughn	4.00
5	Tim Salmon	1.50
6	Frank Thomas	12.00
7	Robin Ventura	1.00
8	Albert Belle	4.00
9	Kenny Lofton	4.00
10	Manny Ramirez	4.00
11	Dave Nilsson	1.00
12	Chuck Knoblauch	1.50
13	Paul Molitor	2.50
14	Kirby Puckett	6.00
15	Wade Boggs	1.50
16	Dwight Gooden	1.00
17	Paul O'Neill	1.00
18	Mark McGwire	20.00
19	Jay Buhner	1.50
20	Ken Griffey Jr.	15.00
21	Randy Johnson	2.50
22	Will Clark	1.50
23	Juan Gonzalez	8.00
24	Joe Carter	1.00
25	Tom Glavine	1.00
26	Ryan Klesko	2.50
27	Greg Maddux	10.00
28	John Smoltz	1.50
29	Ryne Sandberg	5.00
30	Sammy Sosa	8.00
31	Barry Larkin	2.00
32	Reggie Sanders	1.00
33	Dante Bichette	1.50

34	Andres Galarraga	1.50
35	Charles Johnson	1.00
36	Gary Sheffield	2.50
37	Jeff Bagwell	8.00
38	Hideo Nomo	3.00
39	Mike Piazza	10.00
40	Moises Alou	1.00
41	Henry Rodriguez	1.00
42	Rey Ordonez	1.00
43	Ricky Otero	1.00
44	Jay Bell	1.00
45	Royce Clayton	1.00
46	Ozzie Smith	2.50
47	Tony Gwynn	6.00
48	Rickey Henderson	1.00
49	Barry Bonds	4.00
50	Matt Williams	2.00

1996 Circa Rave

This hobby-exclusive product, limited to 2,000 sequentially numbered cases, featured a chase set called Rave which is limited to 150 sets. Each Rave card is sequentially numbered from 1-150. Announced insert rate for Raves was one per 60 packs.

		MT
Complete Set (200):		4150.
Common Player:		15.00
Semistars:		30.00
1	Roberto Alomar	50.00
2	Brady Anderson	20.00
3	*Rocky Coppinger*	15.00
4	Eddie Murray	30.00
5	Mike Mussina	50.00
6	Randy Myers	15.00
7	Rafael Palmeiro	30.00
8	Cal Ripken Jr.	200.00
9	Jose Canseco	30.00
10	Roger Clemens	100.00
11	Mike Greenwell	15.00
12	Tim Naehring	15.00
13	John Valentin	15.00
14	Mo Vaughn	60.00
15	Tim Wakefield	15.00
16	Jim Abbott	15.00
17	Garret Anderson	15.00
18	Jim Edmonds	25.00
19	Darin Erstad	125.00
20	Chuck Finley	15.00
21	Troy Percival	15.00
22	Tim Salmon	25.00
23	J.T. Snow	15.00
24	Wilson Alvarez	15.00
25	Harold Baines	15.00
26	Ray Durham	15.00
27	Alex Fernandez	15.00
28	Tony Phillips	15.00
29	Frank Thomas	150.00
30	Robin Ventura	15.00
31	Sandy Alomar Jr.	25.00
32	Albert Belle	60.00
33	Kenny Lofton	60.00
34	Dennis Martinez	15.00

35	Jose Mesa	15.00	131	Gary Sheffield	40.00	
36	Charles Nagy	15.00	132	Devon White	15.00	
37	Manny Ramirez	60.00	133	Jeff Bagwell	80.00	
38	Jim Thome	50.00	134	Derek Bell	15.00	
39	Travis Fryman	15.00	135	Craig Biggio	25.00	
40	Bob Higginson	15.00	136	Doug Drabek	15.00	
41	Melvin Nieves	15.00	137	Brian Hunter	15.00	
42	Alan Trammell	15.00	138	Darryl Kile	15.00	
43	Kevin Appier	15.00	139	Shane Reynolds	15.00	
44	Johnny Damon	15.00	140	Brett Butler	15.00	
45	Keith Lockhart	15.00	141	Eric Karros	15.00	
46	Jeff Montgomery	15.00	142	Ramon Martinez	20.00	
47	Joe Randa	15.00	143	Raul Mondesi	25.00	
48	Bip Roberts	15.00	144	Hideo Nomo	75.00	
49	Ricky Bones	15.00	145	Chan Ho Park	30.00	
50	Jeff Cirillo	15.00	146	Mike Piazza	150.00	
51	Marc Newfield	15.00	147	Moises Alou	20.00	
52	Dave Nilsson	15.00	148	Yamil Benitez	15.00	
53	Kevin Seitzer	15.00	149	Mark Grudzielanek	15.00	
54	Ron Coomer	15.00	150	Pedro Martinez	40.00	
55	Marty Cordova	15.00	151	Henry Rodriguez	15.00	
56	Roberto Kelly	15.00	152	David Segui	15.00	
57	Chuck Knoblauch	40.00	153	Rondell White	20.00	
58	Paul Molitor	60.00	154	Carlos Baerga	15.00	
59	Kirby Puckett	90.00	155	John Franco	15.00	
60	Scott Stahoviak	15.00	156	Bernard Gilkey	15.00	
61	Wade Boggs	30.00	157	Todd Hundley	20.00	
62	David Cone	25.00	158	Jason Isringhausen	15.00	
63	Cecil Fielder	25.00	159	Lance Johnson	15.00	
64	Dwight Gooden	15.00	160	Alex Ochoa	15.00	
65	Derek Jeter	140.00	161	Rey Ordonez	20.00	
66	Tino Martinez	40.00	162	Paul Wilson	15.00	
67	Paul O'Neill	30.00	163	Ron Blazier	15.00	
68	Andy Pettitte	50.00	164	Ricky Bottalico	15.00	
69	Ruben Rivera	20.00	165	Jim Eisenreich	15.00	
70	Bernie Williams	50.00	166	Pete Incaviglia	15.00	
71	Geronimo Berroa	15.00	167	Mickey Morandini	15.00	
72	Jason Giambi	20.00	168	Ricky Otero	15.00	
73	Mark McGwire	250.00	169	Curt Schilling	20.00	
74	Terry Steinbach	15.00	170	Jay Bell	15.00	
75	Todd Van Poppel	15.00	171	Charlie Hayes	15.00	
76	Jay Buhner	25.00	172	Jason Kendall	20.00	
77	Norm Charlton	15.00	173	Jeff King	15.00	
78	Ken Griffey Jr.	250.00	174	Al Martin	15.00	
79	Randy Johnson	50.00	175	Alan Benes	20.00	
80	Edgar Martinez	15.00	176	Royce Clayton	15.00	
81	Alex Rodriguez	150.00	177	Brian Jordan	15.00	
82	Paul Sorrento	15.00	178	Ray Lankford	15.00	
83	Dan Wilson	15.00	179	John Mabry	15.00	
84	Will Clark	30.00	180	Willie McGee	15.00	
85	Kevin Elster	15.00	181	Ozzie Smith	75.00	
86	Juan Gonzalez	125.00	182	Todd Stottlemyre	15.00	
87	Rusty Greer	15.00	183	Andy Ashby	15.00	
88	Ken Hill	15.00	184	Ken Caminiti	25.00	
89	Mark McLemore	15.00	185	Steve Finley	15.00	
90	Dean Palmer	15.00	186	Tony Gwynn	125.00	
91	Roger Pavlik	15.00	187	Rickey Henderson	15.00	
92	Ivan Rodriguez	60.00	188	Wally Joyner	15.00	
93	Joe Carter	20.00	189	Fernando Valenzuela	15.00	
94	Carlos Delgado	15.00	190	Greg Vaughn	15.00	
95	Juan Guzman	15.00	191	Rod Beck	15.00	
96	John Olerud	25.00	192	Barry Bonds	60.00	
97	Ed Sprague	15.00	193	Shawon Dunston	15.00	
98	Jermaine Dye	15.00	194	Chris Singleton	15.00	
99	Tom Glavine	25.00	195	Robby Thompson	15.00	
100	Marquis Grissom	15.00	196	Matt Williams	30.00	
101	Andruw Jones	80.00	197	Checklist(Barry Bonds)	25.00	
102	Chipper Jones	150.00	198	Checklist(Ken Griffey Jr.)	125.00	
103	David Justice	25.00	199	Checklist(Cal Ripken Jr.)	100.00	
104	Ryan Klesko	40.00	200	Checklist(Frank Thomas)	90.00	
105	Greg Maddux	150.00				
106	Fred McGriff	25.00				
107	John Smoltz	20.00				
108	Brant Brown	15.00				
109	Mark Grace	30.00				
110	Brian McRae	15.00				
111	Ryne Sandberg	75.00				
112	Sammy Sosa	150.00				
113	Steve Trachsel	15.00				
114	Bret Boone	15.00				
115	Eric Davis	15.00				
116	Steve Gibralter	15.00				
117	Barry Larkin	30.00				
118	Reggie Sanders	15.00				
119	John Smiley	15.00				
120	Dante Bichette	25.00				
121	Ellis Burks	15.00				
122	Vinny Castilla	15.00				
123	Andres Galarraga	25.00				
124	Larry Walker	50.00				
125	Eric Young	15.00				
126	Kevin Brown	15.00				
127	Greg Colbrunn	15.00				
128	Jeff Conine	15.00				
129	Charles Johnson	15.00				
130	Al Leiter	20.00				

1997 Circa

Circa baseball returned for the second year in 1997, with a 400-card set, including 393 player cards and seven checklists. The cards feature an art-type look, similar to Z-Force in basketball, and arrived in eight-card packs. The set was paralleled in a Rave insert and was accompanied by five inserts: Boss, Fast Track, Icons, Limited Access and Rave Reviews.

		MT
Complete Set (400):		40.00
Common Player:		.10
Hobby Box:		55.00
1	Kenny Lofton	.75
2	Ray Durham	.10
3	Mariano Rivera	.20
4	Jon Lieber	.10
5	Tim Salmon	.20
6	Mark Grudzielanek	.10
7	Neifi Perez	.10
8	Cal Ripken Jr.	2.50
9	John Olerud	.10
10	Edgar Renteria	.10
11	Jose Rosado	.10
12	Mickey Morandini	.10
13	Orlando Miller	.10
14	Ben McDonald	.10
15	Hideo Nomo	.75
16	Fred McGriff	.25
17	Sean Berry	.10
18	Roger Pavlik	.10
19	Aaron Sele	.10
20	Joey Hamilton	.10
21	Roger Clemens	1.00
22	Jose Herrera	.10
23	Ryne Sandberg	.75
24	Ken Griffey Jr.	3.00
25	Barry Bonds	.75
26	Dan Naulty	.10
27	Wade Boggs	.20
28	Ray Lankford	.10
29	Rico Brogna	.10
30	Wally Joyner	.10
31	F.P. Santangelo	.10
32	Vinny Castilla	.10
33	Eddie Murray	.40
34	Kevin Elster	.10
35	Mike Macfarlane	.10
36	Jeff Kent	.10
37	Orlando Merced	.10
38	Jason Isringhausen	.10
39	Chad Ogea	.10
40	Greg Gagne	.10
41	Curt Lyons	.25
42	Mo Vaughn	.75
43	Rusty Greer	.10
44	Shane Reynolds	.10
45	Frank Thomas	2.50
46	Chris Hoiles	.10
47	Scott Sanders	.10
48	Mark Lemke	.10
49	Fernando Vina	.10
50	Mark McGwire	3.00

Values quoted in this guide reflect the retail price of a card — the price a collector can expect to pay when buying a card from a dealer.

The wholesale price — that which a collector can expect to receive from a dealer when selling cards — will be significantly lower, depending on desirability and condition.

#	Name	Price	#	Name	Price	#	Name	Price
51	Bernie Williams	.50	144	Turk Wendell	.10	240	Dennis Eckersley	.10
52	Bobby Higginson	.10	145	Darrin Fletcher	.10	241	Darin Erstad	1.00
53	Kevin Tapani	.10	146	Marquis Grissom	.10	242	Lee Smith	.10
54	Rich Becker	.10	147	Andy Benes	.10	243	Cecil Fielder	.20
55	*Felix Heredia*	.40	148	Nomar Garciaparra	2.00	244	Tony Clark	.50
56	Delino DeShields	.10	149	Andy Pettitte	.75	245	Scott Erickson	.10
57	Rick Wilkins	.10	150	Tony Gwynn	1.50	246	Bob Abreu	.10
58	Edgardo Alfonzo	.10	151	Robb Nen	.10	247	Ruben Sierra	.10
59	Brett Butler	.10	152	Kevin Seitzer	.10	248	Chili Davis	.10
60	Ed Sprague	.10	153	Ariel Prieto	.10	249	Darryl Hamilton	.10
61	Joe Randa	.10	154	Scott Karl	.10	250	Albert Belle	.75
62	Ugueth Urbina	.10	155	Carlos Baerga	.10	251	Todd Hollandsworth	.10
63	Todd Greene	.10	156	Wilson Alvarez	.10	252	Terry Adams	.10
64	Devon White	.10	157	Thomas Howard	.10	253	Rey Ordonez	.10
65	Bruce Ruffin	.10	158	Kevin Appier	.10	254	Steve Finley	.10
66	Mark Gardner	.10	159	Russ Davis	.10	255	Jose Valentin	.10
67	Omar Vizquel	.10	160	Justin Thompson	.10	256	Royce Clayton	.10
68	Luis Gonzalez	.10	161	Pete Schourek	.10	257	Sandy Alomar	.10
69	Tom Glavine	.20	162	John Burkett	.10	258	Mike Lieberthal	.10
70	Cal Eldred	.10	163	Roberto Alomar	.75	259	Ivan Rodriguez	.50
71	William VanLandingham	.10	164	Darren Holmes	.10	260	Rod Beck	.10
72	Jay Buhner	.20	165	Travis Miller	.10	261	Ron Karkovice	.10
73	James Baldwin	.10	166	Mark Langston	.10	262	Mark Gubicza	.10
74	Robin Jennings	.10	167	Juan Guzman	.10	263	Chris Holt	.10
75	Terry Steinbach	.10	168	Pedro Astacio	.10	264	Jaime Bluma	.10
76	Billy Taylor	.10	169	Mark Johnson	.10	265	Francisco Cordova	.15
77	Armando Benitez	.10	170	Mark Leiter	.10	266	Javy Lopez	.20
78	Joe Girardi	.10	171	Heathcliff Slocumb	.10	267	Reggie Jefferson	.10
79	Jay Bell	.10	172	Dante Bichette	.20	268	Kevin Brown	.10
80	Damon Buford	.10	173	Brian Giles	.10	269	Scott Brosius	.10
81	Deion Sanders	.40	174	Paul Wilson	.10	270	Dwight Gooden	.10
82	Bill Haselman	.10	175	Eric Davis	.10	271	Marty Cordova	.10
83	John Flaherty	.10	176	Charles Johnson	.10	272	Jeff Brantley	.10
84	Todd Stottlemyre	.10	177	Willie Greene	.10	273	Joe Carter	.10
85	J.T. Snow	.10	178	Geronimo Berroa	.10	274	Todd Jones	.10
86	Felipe Lira	.10	179	Mariano Duncan	.10	275	Sammy Sosa	1.50
87	Steve Avery	.10	180	Robert Person	.10	276	Randy Johnson	.50
88	Trey Beamon	.10	181	David Segui	.10	277	B.J. Surhoff	.10
89	Alex Gonzalez	.10	182	Ozzie Guillen	.10	278	Chan Ho Park	.10
90	Mark Clark	.10	183	Osvaldo Fernandez	.10	279	Jamey Wright	.10
91	Shane Andrews	.10	184	Dean Palmer	.10	280	Manny Ramirez	.75
92	Randy Myers	.10	185	Bob Wickman	.10	281	John Franco	.10
93	Gary Gaetti	.10	186	Eric Karros	.10	282	Tim Worrell	.10
94	Jeff Blauser	.10	187	Travis Fryman	.10	283	Scott Rolen	1.25
95	Tony Batista	.10	188	Andy Ashby	.10	284	Reggie Sanders	.10
96	Todd Worrell	.10	189	Scott Stahoviak	.10	285	Mike Fetters	.10
97	Jim Edmonds	.10	190	Norm Charlton	.10	286	Tim Wakefield	.10
98	Eric Young	.10	191	Craig Paquette	.10	287	Trevor Hoffman	.10
99	Roberto Kelly	.10	192	John Smoltz	.25	288	Donovan Osborne	.10
100	Alex Rodriguez	3.00	193	Orel Hershiser	.10	289	Phil Nevin	.10
100p	Alex Rodriguez (overprinted "PROMOTIONAL SAMPLE")	5.00	194	Glenallen Hill	.10	290	Jermaine Allensworth	.10
			195	George Arias	.10	291	Rocky Coppinger	.10
			196	Brian Jordan	.10	292	Tim Raines	.10
101	Julio Franco	.10	197	Greg Vaughn	.10	293	Henry Rodriguez	.10
102	Jeff Bagwell	1.25	198	Rafael Palmeiro	.20	294	Paul Sorrento	.10
103	Bobby Witt	.10	199	Darryl Kile	.10	295	Tom Goodwin	.10
104	Tino Martinez	.25	200	Derek Jeter	2.00	296	Raul Mondesi	.25
105	Shannon Stewart	.10	201	Jose Vizcaino	.10	297	Allen Watson	.10
106	Brian Banks	.10	202	Rick Aguilera	.10	298	Derek Bell	.10
107	Eddie Taubensee	.10	203	Jason Schmidt	.10	299	Gary Sheffield	.40
108	Terry Mulholland	.10	204	Trot Nixon	.10	300	Paul Molitor	.40
109	Lyle Mouton	.10	205	Tom Pagnozzi	.10	301	Shawn Green	.10
110	Jeff Conine	.10	206	Mark Wohlers	.10	302	Darren Oliver	.10
111	Johnny Damon	.10	207	Lance Johnson	.10	303	Jack McDowell	.10
112	Quilvio Veras	.10	208	Carlos Delgado	.10	304	Denny Neagle	.10
113	Wilton Guerrero	.20	209	Cliff Floyd	.10	305	Doug Drabek	.10
114	Dmitri Young	.10	210	Kent Mercker	.10	306	Mel Rojas	.10
115	Garret Anderson	.10	211	Matt Mieske	.10	307	Andres Galarraga	.20
116	Bill Pulsipher	.10	212	Ismael Valdes	.10	308	Alex Ochoa	.10
117	Jacob Brumfield	.10	213	Shawon Dunston	.10	309	Gary DiSarcina	.10
118	Mike Lansing	.10	214	Melvin Nieves	.10	310	Ron Gant	.10
119	Jose Canseco	.30	215	Tony Phillips	.10	311	Gregg Jefferies	.10
120	Mike Bordick	.10	216	Scott Spiezio	.10	312	Ruben Rivera	.10
121	Kevin Stocker	.10	217	Michael Tucker	.10	313	Vladimir Guerrero	1.00
122	Frank Rodriguez	.10	218	Matt Williams	.25	314	Willie Adams	.10
123	Mike Cameron	.10	219	Ricky Otero	.10	315	Bip Roberts	.10
124	*Tony Womack*	.40	220	Kevin Ritz	.10	316	Mark Grace	.20
125	Bret Boone	.10	221	Darryl Strawberry	.10	317	Bernard Gilkey	.10
126	Moises Alou	.10	222	Troy Percival	.10	318	Marc Newfield	.10
127	Tim Naehring	.10	223	Eugene Kingsale	.10	319	Al Leiter	.10
128	Brant Brown	.20	224	Julian Tavarez	.10	320	Otis Nixon	.10
129	Todd Zeile	.10	225	Jermaine Dye	.10	321	Tom Candiotti	.10
130	Dave Nilsson	.10	226	Jason Kendall	.10	322	Mike Stanley	.10
131	Donne Wall	.10	227	Sterling Hitchcock	.10	323	Jeff Fassero	.10
132	Jose Mesa	.10	228	Jeff Cirillo	.10	324	Billy Wagner	.10
133	Mark McLemore	.10	229	Roberto Hernandez	.10	325	Todd Walker	.75
134	Mike Stanton	.10	230	Ricky Bottalico	.10	326	Chad Curtis	.10
135	Dan Wilson	.10	231	Bobby Bonilla	.10	327	Quinton McCracken	.10
136	Jose Offerman	.10	232	Edgar Martinez	.10	328	Will Clark	.25
137	David Justice	.30	233	John Valentin	.10	329	Andruw Jones	1.50
138	Kirt Manwaring	.10	234	Ellis Burks	.10	330	Robin Ventura	.10
139	Raul Casanova	.10	235	Benito Santiago	.10	331	Curtis Pride	.10
140	Ron Coomer	.10	236	Terrell Wade	.10	332	Barry Larkin	.30
141	Dave Hollins	.10	237	Armando Reynoso	.10	333	Jimmy Key	.10
142	Shawn Estes	.10	238	Danny Graves	.10	334	David Wells	.10
143	Darren Daulton	.10	239	Ken Hill	.10	335	Mike Holtz	.10

336	Paul Wagner	.10
337	Greg Maddux	2.00
338	Curt Schilling	.10
339	Steve Trachsel	.10
340	John Wetteland	.10
341	Rickey Henderson	.10
342	Ernie Young	.10
343	Harold Baines	.10
344	Bobby Jones	.10
345	Jeff D'Amico	.10
346	John Mabry	.10
347	Pedro Martinez	.10
348	Mark Lewis	.10
349	Dan Miceli	.10
350	Chuck Knoblauch	.10
351	John Smiley	.10
352	Brady Anderson	.10
353	Jim Leyritz	.10
354	Al Martin	.10
355	Pat Hentgen	.10
356	Mike Piazza	2.00
357	Charles Nagy	.10
358	Luis Castillo	.15
359	Paul O'Neill	.10
360	Steve Reed	.10
361	Tom Gordon	.10
362	Craig Biggio	.10
363	Jeff Montgomery	.10
364	Jamie Moyer	.10
365	Ryan Klesko	.40
366	Todd Hundley	.20
367	Bobby Estalella	.10
368	Jason Giambi	.10
369	Brian Hunter	.10
370	Ramon Martinez	.10
371	Carlos Garcia	.10
372	Hal Morris	.10
373	Juan Gonzalez	1.25
374	Brian McRae	.10
375	Mike Mussina	.60
376	John Ericks	.10
377	Larry Walker	.35
378	Chris Gomez	.10
379	John Jaha	.10
380	Rondell White	.20
381	Chipper Jones	2.00
382	David Cone	.20
383	Alan Benes	.20
384	Troy O'Leary	.10
385	Ken Caminiti	.30
386	Jeff King	.10
387	Mike Hampton	.10
388	Jaime Navarro	.10
389	Brad Radke	.10
390	Joey Cora	.10
391	Jim Thome	.40
392	Alex Fernandez	.20
393	Chuck Finley	.10
394	Andruw Jones CL	.75
395	Ken Griffey Jr. CL	1.50
396	Frank Thomas CL	1.25
397	Alex Rodriguez CL	1.50
398	Cal Ripken Jr. CL	1.25
399	Mike Piazza CL	1.00
400	Greg Maddux CL	1.00

1997 Circa Boss

Boss was the easiest insert to get in Circa. These 20 embossed cards were seeded one per six packs. The insert displayed some of baseball's best players. A Super Boss parallel insert set features metallic-foil background and graphics on front, and is inserted at a rate of one per 36 packs.

		MT
Complete Set (20):		50.00
Common Player:		1.00
Super Boss: 2x to 3x		
1	Jeff Bagwell	3.00
2	Albert Belle	2.00
3	Barry Bonds	2.00
4	Ken Caminiti	1.00
5	Juan Gonzalez	3.00
6	Ken Griffey Jr.	8.00
7	Tony Gwynn	3.00
8	Derek Jeter	5.00
9	Andruw Jones	4.00
10	Chipper Jones	5.00
11	Greg Maddux	5.00
12	Mark McGwire	10.00
13	Mike Piazza	5.00
14	Manny Ramirez	2.00
15	Cal Ripken Jr.	6.00
16	Alex Rodriguez	8.00
17	John Smoltz	1.00
18	Frank Thomas	6.00
19	Mo Vaughn	2.00
20	Bernie Williams	1.50

1997 Circa Emerald Autograph Redemption Cards

These box-topper cards were a hobby box exclusive and were redeemable (until May 31, 1998) for autographed special cards of six young stars. Fronts have a green-foil enhanced player action photo. Backs provide details of the redemption program.

		MT
Complete Set (6):		80.00
Common Player:		6.00
(1)	Darin Erstad	15.00
(2)	Todd Hollandsworth	6.00
(3)	Alex Ochoa	6.00
(4)	Alex Rodriguez	50.00
(5)	Scott Rolen	18.00
(6)	Todd Walker	8.00

A player's name in *italic* type indicates a rookie card.

1997 Circa Emerald Autographs

Special green-foil enhanced cards of six top young stars were available via a mail-in redemption. The cards feature authentic player signatures on front and an embossed authentication seal. Backs are identical to the regular card of each featured player.

		MT
Complete Set (6):		500.00
Common Player:		30.00
100	Alex Rodriguez	180.00
241	Darin Erstad	75.00
251	Todd Hollandsworth	30.00
283	Scott Rolen	90.00
308	Alex Ochoa	30.00
325	Todd Walker	40.00

1997 Circa Fast Track

Fast Track highlighted 10 top rookies and young stars on a flocked design that showed grass raised fabric. Cards featured the insert name in the top left corner and were inserted every 24 packs.

		MT
Complete Set (10):		50.00
Common Player:		2.50
1	Vladimir Guerrero	6.00
2	Todd Hollandsworth	2.50

3	Derek Jeter	8.00
4	Andruw Jones	6.00
5	Chipper Jones	8.00
6	Andy Pettitte	4.00
7	Mariano Rivera	3.00
8	Alex Rodriguez	12.00
9	Scott Rolen	8.00
10	Todd Walker	4.00

1997 Circa Icons

Twelve of baseball's top sluggers were displayed on 100-percent holofoil cards in Icons. Icons were found at a rate of one per 36 packs.

		MT
Complete Set (12):		100.00
Common Player:		3.00
1	Juan Gonzalez	10.00
2	Ken Griffey Jr.	20.00
3	Tony Gwynn	10.00
4	Derek Jeter	10.00
5	Chipper Jones	12.00
6	Greg Maddux	12.00
7	Mark McGwire	25.00
8	Mike Piazza	12.00
9	Cal Ripken Jr.	15.00
10	Alex Rodriguez	12.00
11	Frank Thomas	15.00
12	Matt Williams	4.00

1997 Circa Limited Access

Limited Access was a retail-only insert found every 18 packs. Cards featured an in-depth, statistical anal-

ysis including the player's favorite pitcher to hit and each pitcher's least favorite hitter to face. Limited Access contained a die-cut, bi-fold design resembling a book, and featured 15 different players.

		MT
Complete Set (15):		110.00
Common Player:		2.00
1	Jeff Bagwell	8.00
2	Albert Belle	5.00
3	Barry Bonds	5.00
4	Juan Gonzalez	8.00
5	Ken Griffey Jr.	20.00
6	Tony Gwynn	10.00
7	Derek Jeter	10.00
8	Chipper Jones	12.00
9	Greg Maddux	12.00
10	Mark McGwire	25.00
11	Mike Piazza	12.00
12	Cal Ripken Jr.	15.00
13	Alex Rodriguez	12.00
14	Frank Thomas	15.00
15	Mo Vaughn	5.00

1997 Circa Rave

In its second year, Rave parallel inserts for Circa baseball were limited to inclusion only in hobby packs. Stated insertion rate was one card per "30 to 40" packs. Rave cards are distinguished from regular-edition Circa cards by the use of purple metallic foil for the brand name and player identification on front. Rave backs also carry a silver-foil serial number detailing its position within a production of 150 for each card.

		MT
Complete Set (400):		30.00
Common Player:		15.00
Semistars:		30.00
1	Kenny Lofton	60.00
2	Ray Durham	15.00
3	Mariano Rivera	20.00
4	Jon Lieber	15.00
5	Tim Salmon	30.00
6	Mark Grudzielanek	15.00
7	Neifi Perez	15.00
8	Cal Ripken Jr.	200.00
9	John Olerud	20.00
10	Edgar Renteria	15.00
11	Jose Rosado	15.00
12	Mickey Morandini	15.00
13	Orlando Miller	15.00
14	Ben McDonald	15.00
15	Hideo Nomo	50.00
16	Fred McGriff	20.00
17	Sean Berry	15.00
18	Roger Pavlik	15.00
19	Aaron Sele	15.00
20	Joey Hamilton	15.00
21	Roger Clemens	90.00
22	Jose Herrera	15.00
23	Ryne Sandberg	60.00
24	Ken Griffey Jr.	250.00
25	Barry Bonds	60.00
26	Dan Naulty	15.00
27	Wade Boggs	25.00
28	Ray Lankford	15.00
29	Rico Brogna	15.00
30	Wally Joyner	15.00
31	F.P. Santangelo	15.00
32	Vinny Castilla	20.00
33	Eddie Murray	25.00
34	Kevin Elster	15.00
35	Mike Macfarlane	15.00
36	Jeff Kent	15.00
37	Orlando Merced	15.00
38	Jason Isringhausen	15.00
39	Chad Ogea	15.00
40	Greg Gagne	15.00
41	Curt Lyons	15.00
42	Mo Vaughn	60.00
43	Rusty Greer	15.00
44	Shane Reynolds	15.00
45	Frank Thomas	150.00
46	Chris Hoiles	15.00
47	Scott Sanders	15.00
48	Mark Lemke	15.00
49	Fernando Vina	15.00
50	Mark McGwire	250.00
51	Bernie Williams	50.00
52	Bobby Higginson	15.00
53	Kevin Tapani	15.00
54	Rich Becker	15.00
55	Felix Heredia	15.00
56	Delino DeShields	15.00
57	Rick Wilkins	15.00
58	Edgardo Alfonzo	15.00
59	Brett Butler	15.00
60	Ed Sprague	15.00
61	Joe Randa	15.00
62	Ugueth Urbina	15.00
63	Todd Greene	15.00
64	Devon White	15.00
65	Bruce Ruffin	15.00
66	Mark Gardner	15.00
67	Omar Vizquel	15.00
68	Luis Gonzalez	15.00
69	Tom Glavine	20.00
70	Cal Eldred	15.00
71	William VanLandingham	15.00
72	Jay Buhner	25.00
73	James Baldwin	15.00
74	Robin Jennings	15.00
75	Terry Steinbach	15.00
76	Billy Taylor	15.00
77	Armando Benitez	15.00
78	Joe Girardi	15.00
79	Jay Bell	15.00
80	Damon Buford	15.00
81	Deion Sanders	25.00
82	Bill Haselman	15.00
83	John Flaherty	15.00
84	Todd Stottlemyre	15.00
85	J.T. Snow	15.00
86	Felipe Lira	15.00
87	Steve Avery	15.00
88	Trey Beamon	15.00
89	Alex Gonzalez	15.00
90	Mark Clark	15.00
91	Shane Andrews	15.00
92	Randy Myers	15.00
93	Gary Gaetti	15.00
94	Jeff Blauser	15.00
95	Tony Batista	15.00
96	Todd Worrell	15.00
97	Jim Edmonds	15.00
98	Eric Young	15.00
99	Roberto Kelly	15.00
100	Alex Rodriguez	200.00
101	Julio Franco	15.00
102	Jeff Bagwell	100.00
103	Bobby Witt	15.00
104	Tino Martinez	30.00
105	Shannon Stewart	15.00
106	Brian Banks	15.00
107	Eddie Taubensee	15.00
108	Terry Mulholland	15.00
109	Lyle Mouton	15.00
110	Jeff Conine	15.00
111	Johnny Damon	15.00
112	Quilvio Veras	15.00
113	Wilton Guerrero	20.00
114	Dmitri Young	15.00
115	Garret Anderson	15.00

#	Name	Price	#	Name	Price	#	Name	Price
116	Bill Pulsipher	15.00	212	Ismael Valdes	15.00	308	Alex Ochoa	15.00
117	Jacob Brumfield	15.00	213	Shawon Dunston	15.00	309	Gary DiSarcina	15.00
118	Mike Lansing	15.00	214	Melvin Nieves	15.00	310	Ron Gant	20.00
119	Jose Canseco	30.00	215	Tony Phillips	15.00	311	Gregg Jefferies	15.00
120	Mike Bordick	15.00	216	Scott Spiezio	15.00	312	Ruben Rivera	15.00
121	Kevin Stocker	15.00	217	Michael Tucker	15.00	313	Vladimir Guerrero	60.00
122	Frank Rodriguez	15.00	218	Matt Williams	25.00	314	Willie Adams	15.00
123	Mike Cameron	15.00	219	Ricky Otero	15.00	315	Bip Roberts	15.00
124	Tony Womack	15.00	220	Kevin Ritz	15.00	316	Mark Grace	25.00
125	Bret Boone	15.00	221	Darryl Strawberry	15.00	317	Bernard Gilkey	15.00
126	Moises Alou	15.00	222	Troy Percival	15.00	318	Marc Newfield	15.00
127	Tim Naehring	15.00	223	Eugene Kingsale	15.00	319	Al Leiter	15.00
128	Brant Brown	20.00	224	Julian Tavarez	15.00	320	Otis Nixon	15.00
129	Todd Zeile	15.00	225	Jermaine Dye	15.00	321	Tom Candiotti	15.00
130	Dave Nilsson	15.00	226	Jason Kendall	15.00	322	Mike Stanley	15.00
131	Donne Wall	15.00	227	Sterling Hitchcock	15.00	323	Jeff Fassero	15.00
132	Jose Mesa	15.00	228	Jeff Cirillo	15.00	324	Billy Wagner	15.00
133	Mark McLemore	15.00	229	Roberto Hernandez	15.00	325	Todd Walker	40.00
134	Mike Stanton	15.00	230	Ricky Bottalico	15.00	326	Chad Curtis	15.00
135	Dan Wilson	15.00	231	Bobby Bonilla	20.00	327	Quinton McCracken	15.00
136	Jose Offerman	15.00	232	Edgar Martinez	20.00	328	Will Clark	25.00
137	David Justice	30.00	233	John Valentin	15.00	329	Andruw Jones	60.00
138	Kirt Manwaring	15.00	234	Ellis Burks	20.00	330	Robin Ventura	15.00
139	Raul Casanova	15.00	235	Benito Santiago	15.00	331	Curtis Pride	15.00
140	Ron Coomer	15.00	236	Terrell Wade	15.00	332	Barry Larkin	25.00
141	Dave Hollins	15.00	237	Armando Reynoso	15.00	333	Jimmy Key	15.00
142	Shawn Estes	15.00	238	Danny Graves	15.00	334	David Wells	15.00
143	Darren Daulton	15.00	239	Ken Hill	15.00	335	Mike Holtz	15.00
144	Turk Wendell	15.00	240	Dennis Eckersley	20.00	336	Paul Wagner	15.00
145	Darrin Fletcher	15.00	241	Darin Erstad	90.00	337	Greg Maddux	150.00
146	Marquis Grissom	15.00	242	Lee Smith	15.00	338	Curt Schilling	15.00
147	Andy Benes	15.00	243	Cecil Fielder	20.00	339	Steve Trachsel	15.00
148	Nomar Garciaparra	150.00	244	Tony Clark	50.00	340	John Wetteland	15.00
149	Andy Pettitte	50.00	245	Scott Erickson	15.00	341	Rickey Henderson	20.00
150	Tony Gwynn	125.00	246	Bob Abreu	15.00	342	Ernie Young	15.00
151	Robb Nen	15.00	247	Ruben Sierra	15.00	343	Harold Baines	15.00
152	Kevin Seitzer	15.00	248	Chili Davis	15.00	344	Bobby Jones	15.00
153	Ariel Prieto	15.00	249	Darryl Hamilton	15.00	345	Jeff D'Amico	15.00
154	Scott Karl	15.00	250	Albert Belle	60.00	346	John Mabry	15.00
155	Carlos Baerga	15.00	251	Todd Hollandsworth	15.00	347	Pedro Martinez	30.00
156	Wilson Alvarez	15.00	252	Terry Adams	15.00	348	Mark Lewis	15.00
157	Thomas Howard	15.00	253	Rey Ordonez	15.00	349	Dan Miceli	15.00
158	Kevin Appier	15.00	254	Steve Finley	15.00	350	Chuck Knoblauch	30.00
159	Russ Davis	15.00	255	Jose Valentin	15.00	351	John Smiley	15.00
160	Justin Thompson	15.00	256	Royce Clayton	15.00	352	Brady Anderson	20.00
161	Pete Schourek	15.00	257	Sandy Alomar	15.00	353	Jim Leyritz	15.00
162	John Burkett	15.00	258	Mike Lieberthal	15.00	354	Al Martin	15.00
163	Roberto Alomar	50.00	259	Ivan Rodriguez	60.00	355	Pat Hentgen	15.00
164	Darren Holmes	15.00	260	Rod Beck	15.00	356	Mike Piazza	150.00
165	Travis Miller	15.00	261	Ron Karkovice	15.00	357	Charles Nagy	15.00
166	Mark Langston	15.00	262	Mark Gubicza	15.00	358	Luis Castillo	15.00
167	Juan Guzman	15.00	263	Chris Holt	15.00	359	Paul O'Neill	25.00
168	Pedro Astacio	15.00	264	Jaime Bluma	15.00	360	Steve Reed	15.00
169	Mark Johnson	15.00	265	Francisco Cordova	15.00	361	Tom Gordon	15.00
170	Mark Leiter	15.00	266	Javy Lopez	20.00	362	Craig Biggio	25.00
171	Heathcliff Slocumb	15.00	267	Reggie Jefferson	15.00	363	Jeff Montgomery	15.00
172	Dante Bichette	25.00	268	Kevin Brown	15.00	364	Jamie Moyer	15.00
173	Brian Giles	15.00	269	Scott Brosius	15.00	365	Ryan Klesko	40.00
174	Paul Wilson	15.00	270	Dwight Gooden	20.00	366	Todd Hundley	20.00
175	Eric Davis	15.00	271	Marty Cordova	15.00	367	Bobby Estalella	15.00
176	Charles Johnson	15.00	272	Jeff Brantley	15.00	368	Jason Giambi	15.00
177	Willie Greene	15.00	273	Joe Carter	20.00	369	Brian Hunter	15.00
178	Geronimo Berroa	15.00	274	Todd Jones	15.00	370	Ramon Martinez	20.00
179	Mariano Duncan	15.00	275	Sammy Sosa	150.00	371	Carlos Garcia	15.00
180	Robert Person	15.00	276	Randy Johnson	50.00	372	Hal Morris	15.00
181	David Segui	15.00	277	B.J. Surhoff	15.00	373	Juan Gonzalez	125.00
182	Ozzie Guillen	15.00	278	Chan Ho Park	15.00	374	Brian McRae	15.00
183	Osvaldo Fernandez	15.00	279	Jamey Wright	15.00	375	Mike Mussina	50.00
184	Dean Palmer	15.00	280	Manny Ramirez	60.00	376	John Ericks	15.00
185	Bob Wickman	15.00	281	John Franco	15.00	377	Larry Walker	40.00
186	Eric Karros	15.00	282	Tim Worrell	15.00	378	Chris Gomez	15.00
187	Travis Fryman	20.00	283	Scott Rolen	90.00	379	John Jaha	15.00
188	Andy Ashby	15.00	284	Reggie Sanders	15.00	380	Rondell White	20.00
189	Scott Stahoviak	15.00	285	Mike Fetters	15.00	381	Chipper Jones	150.00
190	Norm Charlton	15.00	286	Tim Wakefield	15.00	382	David Cone	20.00
191	Craig Paquette	15.00	287	Trevor Hoffman	15.00	383	Alan Benes	20.00
192	John Smoltz	20.00	288	Donovan Osborne	15.00	384	Troy O'Leary	15.00
193	Orel Hershiser	15.00	289	Phil Nevin	15.00	385	Ken Caminiti	25.00
194	Glenallen Hill	15.00	290	Jermaine Allensworth	15.00	386	Jeff King	15.00
195	George Arias	15.00	291	Rocky Coppinger	15.00	387	Mike Hampton	15.00
196	Brian Jordan	20.00	292	Tim Raines	15.00	388	Jaime Navarro	15.00
197	Greg Vaughn	15.00	293	Henry Rodriguez	15.00	389	Brad Radke	15.00
198	Rafael Palmeiro	25.00	294	Paul Sorrento	15.00	390	Joey Cora	15.00
199	Darryl Kile	15.00	295	Tom Goodwin	15.00	391	Jim Thome	50.00
200	Derek Jeter	125.00	296	Raul Mondesi	25.00	392	Alex Fernandez	15.00
201	Jose Vizcaino	15.00	297	Allen Watson	15.00	393	Chuck Finley	15.00
202	Rick Aguilera	15.00	298	Derek Bell	15.00	394	Andruw Jones CL	30.00
203	Jason Schmidt	15.00	299	Gary Sheffield	40.00	395	Ken Griffey Jr. CL	125.00
204	Trot Nixon	15.00	300	Paul Molitor	50.00	396	Frank Thomas CL	90.00
205	Tom Pagnozzi	15.00	301	Shawn Green	15.00	397	Alex Rodriguez CL	80.00
206	Mark Wohlers	15.00	302	Darren Oliver	15.00	398	Cal Ripken Jr. CL	80.00
207	Lance Johnson	15.00	303	Jack McDowell	15.00	399	Mike Piazza CL	60.00
208	Carlos Delgado	15.00	304	Denny Neagle	15.00	400	Greg Maddux CL	60.00
209	Cliff Floyd	15.00	305	Doug Drabek	15.00			
210	Kent Mercker	15.00	306	Mel Rojas	15.00			
211	Matt Mieske	15.00	307	Andres Galarraga	25.00			

1997 Circa Rave Reviews

Hitters that continually put up great numbers were selected in Rave Reviews. The insert was found every 288 packs, contained 12 stars and was printed on 100-percent holofoil.

		MT
Complete Set (12):		300.00
Common Player:		15.00
1	Albert Belle	15.00
2	Barry Bonds	15.00
3	Juan Gonzalez	25.00
4	Ken Griffey Jr.	50.00
5	Tony Gwynn	25.00
6	Greg Maddux	30.00
7	Mark McGwire	50.00
8	Eddie Murray	10.00
9	Mike Piazza	30.00
10	Cal Ripken Jr.	40.00
11	Alex Rodriguez	30.00
12	Frank Thomas	40.00

1998 Circa Thunder

The 1998 Circa Thunder set was issued as one series of 300 cards and sold in eight-card packs for $1.59. This set marked Sky-Box's brand transition from Circa to Thunder so it named this product with both names. There are two card No. 8 in the set, but Marquis Grissom should be No. 280 (Cal Ripken is No. 8). There is also a Cal Ripken promo card that was sent to dealers and media. The card is identical to the base card, but has the words "Promotional Sample" written across the back. Inserts include: Rave and Super Rave parallels, Boss, Fast Track, Quick Strike, Limited Access, Rave Review and Thunder Boomers.

		MT
Complete Set (300):		25.00
Common Player:		.15
Wax Box:		50.00
1	Ben Grieve	1.25
2	Derek Jeter	2.00
3	Alex Rodriguez	2.00
4	Paul Molitor	.50
5	Nomar Garciaparra	2.00
6	Fred McGriff	.25
7	Kenny Lofton	.75
8	Cal Ripken Jr.	2.50
9	Matt Williams	.30

10	Chipper Jones	2.00
11	Barry Larkin	.25
12	Steve Finley	.15
13	Billy Wagner	.15
14	Rico Brogna	.15
15	Tim Salmon	.30
16	Hideo Nomo	.60
17	Tony Clark	.50
18	Jason Kendall	.15
19	Juan Gonzalez	1.50
20	Jeromy Burnitz	.15
21	Roger Clemens	1.00
22	Mark Grace	.30
23	Robin Ventura	.25
24	Manny Ramirez	.75
25	Mark McGwire	4.00
26	Gary Sheffield	.30
27	Vladimir Guerrero	.75
28	Butch Huskey	.15
29	Cecil Fielder	.25
30	Roderick Myers	.15
31	Greg Maddux	2.00
32	Bill Mueller	.15
33	Larry Walker	.30
34	Henry Rodriguez	.15
35	Mike Mussina	.60
36	Ricky Ledee	.25
37	Bobby Bonilla	.25
38	Curt Schilling	.30
39	Luis Gonzalez	.15
40	Troy Percival	.15
41	Eric Milton	.40
42	Mo Vaughn	.75
43	Raul Mondesi	.30
44	Kenny Rogers	.15
45	Frank Thomas	2.50
46	Jose Canseco	.30
47	Tom Glavine	.25
48	*Rich Butler*	.40
49	Jay Buhner	.25
50	Jose Cruz Jr.	1.00
51	Bernie Williams	.50
52	Doug Glanville	.15
53	Travis Fryman	.15
54	Rey Ordonez	.15
55	Jeff Conine	.15
56	Trevor Hoffman	.15
57	Kirk Rueter	.15
58	Ron Gant	.25
59	Carl Everett	.15
60	Joe Carter	.25
61	Livan Hernandez	.25
62	John Jaha	.15
63	Ivan Rodriguez	.75
64	Willie Blair	.15
65	Todd Helton	.75
66	Kevin Young	.15
67	Mike Caruso	.15
68	Steve Trachsel	.15
69	Marty Cordova	.15
70	Alex Fernandez	.15
71	Eric Karros	.25
72	Reggie Sanders	.15
73	Russ Davis	.15
74	Roberto Hernandez	.15
75	Barry Bonds	.75
76	Alex Gonzalez	.15
77	Roberto Alomar	.50
78	Troy O'Leary	.15
79	Bernard Gilkey	.15
80	Ismael Valdes	.15
81	Travis Lee	3.00
82	Brant Brown	.15
83	Gary DiSarcina	.15
84	Joe Randa	.15
85	Jaret Wright	1.50
86	Quilvio Veras	.15
87	Rickey Henderson	.15
88	Randall Simon	.25
89	Mariano Rivera	.25
90	Ugueth Urbina	.15
91	Fernando Vina	.15
92	Alan Benes	.25
93	Dante Bichette	.25
94	Karim Garcia	.15
95	A.J. Hinch	.75
96	Shane Reynolds	.15
97	Kevin Stocker	.15
98	John Wetteland	.15
99	Terry Steinbach	.15
100	Ken Griffey Jr.	3.00
101	Mike Cameron	.25
102	Damion Easley	.15
103	Randy Myers	.15
104	Jason Schmidt	.15
105	Jeff King	.15

106	Gregg Jefferies	.15
107	Sean Casey	.40
108	Mark Kotsay	.40
109	Brad Fullmer	.15
110	Wilson Alvarez	.15
111	Sandy Alomar Jr.	.25
112	Walt Weiss	.15
113	Doug Jones	.15
114	Andy Benes	.25
115	Paul O'Neill	.25
116	Dennis Eckersley	.15
117	Todd Greene	.15
118	Bobby Jones	.15
119	Darrin Fletcher	.15
120	Eric Young	.15
121	Jeffrey Hammonds	.15
122	Mickey Morandini	.15
123	Chuck Knoblauch	.40
124	Moises Alou	.25
125	Miguel Tejada	.50
126	Brian Anderson	.15
127	Edgar Renteria	.15
128	Mike Lansing	.15
129	Quinton McCracken	.15
130	Ray Lankford	.15
131	Andy Ashby	.15
132	Kelvim Escobar	.15
133	*Mike Lowell*	.25
134	Randy Johnson	.50
135	Andres Galarraga	.35
136	Armando Benitez	.15
137	Rusty Greer	.15
138	Jose Guillen	.25
139	Paul Konerko	.75
140	Edgardo Alfonzo	.15
141	Jim Leyritz	.15
142	Mark Clark	.15
143	Brian Johnson	.15
144	Scott Rolen	1.00
145	David Cone	.25
146	Jeff Shaw	.15
147	Shannon Stewart	.15
148	Brian Hunter	.15
149	Garret Anderson	.15
150	Jeff Bagwell	1.00
151	James Baldwin	.15
152	Devon White	.15
153	Jim Thome	.40
154	Wally Joyner	.15
155	Mark Wohlers	.15
156	Jeff Cirillo	.15
157	Jason Giambi	.15
158	Royce Clayton	.15
159	Dennis Reyes	.15
160	Raul Casanova	.15
161	Pedro Astacio	.15
162	Todd Dunwoody	.15
163	Sammy Sosa	1.50
164	Todd Hundley	.15
165	Wade Boggs	.25
166	Robb Nen	.15
167	Dan Wilson	.15
168	Hideki Irabu	.50
169	B.J. Surhoff	.15
170	Carlos Delgado	.15
171	Fernando Tatis	.15
172	Bob Abreu	.15
173	David Ortiz	.25
174	Tony Womack	.15
175	*Magglio Ordonez*	.75
176	Aaron Boone	.15
177	Brian Giles	.15
178	Kevin Appier	.15
179	Chuck Finley	.15
180	Brian Rose	.25
181	Ryan Klesko	.30
182	Mike Stanley	.15
183	Dave Nilsson	.15
184	Carlos Perez	.15
185	Jeff Blauser	.15
186	Richard Hidalgo	.15
187	Charles Johnson	.25
188	Vinny Castilla	.25
189	Joey Hamilton	.15
190	Bubba Trammell	.15
191	Eli Marrero	.15
192	Scott Erickson	.15
193	Pat Hentgen	.15
194	Jorge Fabregas	.15
195	Tino Martinez	.30
196	Bobby Higginson	.15
197	Dave Hollins	.15
198	*Rolando Arrojo*	.40
199	Joey Cora	.15
200	Mike Piazza	2.00
201	Reggie Jefferson	.15

202	John Smoltz	.25
203	Bobby Smith	.15
204	Tom Goodwin	.15
205	Omar Vizquel	.15
206	John Olerud	.25
207	Matt Stairs	.15
208	Bobby Estalella	.15
209	Miguel Cairo	.15
210	Shawn Green	.15
211	Jon Nunnally	.15
212	Al Leiter	.15
213	Matt Lawton	.15
214	Brady Anderson	.15
215	Jeff Kent	.15
216	Ray Durham	.15
217	Al Martin	.15
218	Jeff D'Amico	.15
219	Kevin Tapani	.15
220	Jim Edmonds	.25
221	Jose Vizcaino	.15
222	Jay Bell	.15
223	Ken Caminiti	.25
224	Craig Biggio	.30
225	Bartolo Colon	.25
226	Neifi Perez	.15
227	Delino DeShields	.15
228	Javier Lopez	.15
229	David Wells	.15
230	Brad Rigby	.15
231	John Franco	.15
232	Michael Coleman	.15
233	Edgar Martinez	.25
234	Francisco Cordova	.15
235	Johnny Damon	.15
236	Deivi Cruz	.15
237	J.T. Snow	.15
238	Enrique Wilson	.15
239	Rondell White	.25
240	Aaron Sele	.25
241	Tony Saunders	.15
242	Ricky Bottalico	.15
243	Cliff Floyd	.15
244	Chili Davis	.15
245	Brian McRae	.15
246	Brad Radke	.15
247	Chan Ho Park	.25
248	Lance Johnson	.15
249	Rafael Palmeiro	.25
250	Tony Gwynn	1.50
251	Denny Neagle	.15
252	Dean Palmer	.15
253	Jose Valentin	.15
254	Matt Morris	.15
255	Ellis Burks	.15
256	Jeff Suppan	.15
257	Jimmy Key	.15
258	Justin Thompson	.15
259	Brett Tomko	.15
260	Mark Grudzielanek	.15
261	Mike Hampton	.15
262	Jeff Fassero	.15
263	Charles Nagy	.15
264	Pedro Martinez	.40
265	Todd Zeile	.15
266	Will Clark	.30
267	Abraham Nunez	.15
268	Dave Martinez	.15
269	Jason Dickson	.15
270	Eric Davis	.15
271	Kevin Orie	.15
272	Derrek Lee	.25
273	Andruw Jones	.75
274	Juan Encarnacion	.15
275	Carlos Baerga	.15
276	Andy Pettitte	.50
277	Brent Brede	.15
278	Paul Sorrento	.15
279	Mike Lieberthal	.15
281	Darin Erstad	.75
282	Willie Greene	.15
283	Derek Bell	.15
284	Scott Spiezio	.15
285	David Segui	.15
286	Albert Belle	.75
287	Ramon Martinez	.15
288	Jeremi Gonzalez	.15
289	Shawn Estes	.15
290	Ron Coomer	.15
291	John Valentin	.15
292	Kevin Brown	.15
293	Michael Tucker	.15
294	Brian Jordan	.15
295	Darryl Kile	.15
296	David Justice	.30
297	Jose Cruz Jr. CL	.50
298	Ken Griffey Jr. CL	1.50

299	Alex Rodriguez CL	1.00
300	Frank Thomas CL	1.25

1998 Circa Thunder Boss

This 20-card insert set was seeded one per six packs of Circa Thunder. Cards are embossed with the player's last name printed in large letters across the top.

		MT
Complete Set (20):		50.00
Common Player:		1.00
1B	Jeff Bagwell	2.50
2B	Barry Bonds	1.50
3B	Roger Clemens	2.50
4B	Jose Cruz Jr.	2.00
5B	Nomar Garciaparra	4.00
6B	Juan Gonzalez	3.00
7B	Ken Griffey Jr.	6.00
8B	Tony Gwynn	3.00
9B	Derek Jeter	3.00
10B	Chipper Jones	4.00
11B	Travis Lee	4.00
12B	Greg Maddux	4.00
13B	Pedro Martinez	1.00
14B	Mark McGwire	8.00
15B	Mike Piazza	4.00
16B	Cal Ripken Jr.	5.00
17B	Alex Rodriguez	4.00
18B	Scott Rolen	2.00
19B	Frank Thomas	5.00
20B	Larry Walker	1.00

1998 Circa Thunder Fast Track

This 10-card insert showcases some of the top young stars in baseball and was seeded one per 24 packs of Circa. Card fronts picture the player over a closeup of a gold foil baseball on the left. The right side has smaller head shots of all 10 players with the featured player's head in gold foil.

		MT
Complete Set (10):		35.00
Common Player:		1.50
1FT	Jose Cruz Jr.	5.00
2FT	Juan Encarnacion	1.50
3FT	Brad Fullmer	3.00
4FT	Nomar Garciaparra	6.00
5FT	Todd Helton	3.00
6FT	Livan Hernandez	1.50
7FT	Travis Lee	10.00
8FT	Neifi Perez	1.50
9FT	Scott Rolen	4.00
10FT	Jaret Wright	5.00

1998 Circa Thunder Limited Access

This 15-card, retail exclusive insert was seeded one per 18 packs. The cards were bi-fold and die-cut with foil stamping on the front. The theme of the insert was to provide an in-depth statistical scouting analysis of each player..

		MT
Complete Set (15):		90.00
Common Player:		2.00
1LA	Jeff Bagwell	6.00
2LA	Roger Clemens	6.00
3LA	Jose Cruz Jr.	6.00
4LA	Nomar Garciaparra	10.00
5LA	Juan Gonzalez	8.00
6LA	Ken Griffey Jr.	15.00
7LA	Tony Gwynn	8.00
8LA	Derek Jeter	8.00
9LA	Greg Maddux	10.00
10LA	Pedro Martinez	2.00
11LA	Mark McGwire	20.00
12LA	Mike Piazza	10.00
13LA	Alex Rodriguez	10.00
14LA	Frank Thomas	12.00
15LA	Larry Walker	2.00

1998 Circa Thunder Quick Strike

This insert pictures 12 different players over a colorful foil-board front that is die-cut. Quick Strikes were seeded one per 36 packs of Circa Thunder.

		MT
Complete Set (12):		90.00
Common Player:		3.00
1QS	Jeff Bagwell	8.00
2QS	Roger Clemens	8.00
3QS	Jose Cruz Jr.	8.00
4QS	Nomar Garciaparra	12.00
5QS	Ken Griffey Jr.	20.00
6QS	Greg Maddux	12.00
7QS	Pedro Martinez	3.00
8QS	Mark McGwire	25.00
9QS	Mike Piazza	12.00
10QS	Alex Rodriguez	12.00
11QS	Frank Thomas	15.00
12QS	Larry Walker	3.00

1998 Circa Thunder Rave

Rave paralleled each card in Circa Thunder except for the four checklist cards. A special silver sparkling foil is used on the player's name and the Thunder logo on the card front. This 296-card set was inserted approximately one per 36 packs and sequentially numbered to 150 sets on the back.

		MT
Common Player:		10.00
Production 150 sets		
1	Ben Grieve	60.00
2	Derek Jeter	100.00
3	Alex Rodriguez	120.00
4	Paul Molitor	40.00
5	Nomar Garciaparra	120.00
6	Fred McGriff	25.00
7	Kenny Lofton	50.0
8	Cal Ripken Jr.	150.
9	Matt Williams	2
10	Chipper Jones	1
11	Barry Larkin	
12	Steve Finley	
13	Billy Wagner	

No.	Name	Price	No.	Name	Price	No.	Name	Price
14	Rico Brogna	10.00	110	Wilson Alvarez	10.00	206	John Olerud	20.00
15	Tim Salmon	25.00	111	Sandy Alomar Jr.	20.00	207	Matt Stairs	10.00
16	Hideo Nomo	40.00	112	Walt Weiss	10.00	208	Bobby Estalella	10.00
17	Tony Clark	40.00	113	Doug Jones	10.00	209	Miguel Cairo	10.00
18	Jason Kendall	10.00	114	Andy Benes	20.00	210	Shawn Green	10.00
19	Juan Gonzalez	100.00	115	Paul O'Neill	20.00	211	Jon Nunnally	10.00
20	Jeromy Burnitz	10.00	116	Dennis Eckersley	20.00	212	Al Leiter	10.00
21	Roger Clemens	80.00	117	Todd Greene	10.00	213	Matt Lawton	10.00
22	Mark Grace	25.00	118	Bobby Jones	10.00	214	Brady Anderson	10.00
23	Robin Ventura	20.00	119	Darrin Fletcher	10.00	215	Jeff Kent	10.00
24	Manny Ramirez	50.00	120	Eric Young	10.00	216	Ray Durham	10.00
25	Mark McGwire	200.00	121	Jeffrey Hammonds	10.00	217	Al Martin	10.00
26	Gary Sheffield	25.00	122	Mickey Morandini	10.00	218	Jeff D'Amico	10.00
27	Vladimir Guerrero	50.00	123	Chuck Knoblauch	25.00	219	Kevin Tapani	10.00
28	Butch Huskey	10.00	124	Moises Alou	20.00	220	Jim Edmonds	20.00
29	Cecil Fielder	20.00	125	Miguel Tejada	30.00	221	Jose Vizcaino	10.00
30	Roderick Myers	10.00	126	Brian Anderson	10.00	222	Jay Bell	10.00
31	Greg Maddux	120.00	127	Edgar Renteria	10.00	223	Ken Caminiti	20.00
32	Bill Mueller	10.00	128	Mike Lansing	10.00	224	Craig Biggio	25.00
33	Larry Walker	30.00	129	Quinton McCracken	10.00	225	Bartolo Colon	20.00
34	Henry Rodriguez	10.00	130	Ray Lankford	10.00	226	Neifi Perez	10.00
35	Mike Mussina	40.00	131	Andy Ashby	10.00	227	Delino DeShields	10.00
36	Ricky Ledee	20.00	132	Kelvim Escobar	10.00	228	Javier Lopez	20.00
37	Bobby Bonilla	20.00	133	Mike Lowell	10.00	229	David Wells	10.00
38	Curt Schilling	20.00	134	Randy Johnson	40.00	230	Brad Rigby	10.00
39	Luis Gonzalez	10.00	135	Andres Galarraga	25.00	231	John Franco	10.00
40	Troy Percival	10.00	136	Armando Benitez	10.00	232	Michael Coleman	10.00
41	Eric Milton	25.00	137	Rusty Greer	10.00	233	Edgar Martinez	20.00
42	Mo Vaughn	50.00	138	Jose Guillen	20.00	234	Francisco Cordova	10.00
43	Raul Mondesi	25.00	139	Paul Konerko	25.00	235	Johnny Damon	10.00
44	Kenny Rogers	10.00	140	Edgardo Alfonzo	10.00	236	Deivi Cruz	10.00
45	Frank Thomas	150.00	141	Jim Leyritz	10.00	237	J.T. Snow	10.00
46	Jose Canseco	25.00	142	Mark Clark	10.00	238	Enrique Wilson	10.00
47	Tom Glavine	20.00	143	Brian Johnson	10.00	239	Rondell White	20.00
48	Rich Butler	10.00	144	Scott Rolen	75.00	240	Aaron Sele	10.00
49	Jay Buhner	20.00	145	David Cone	20.00	241	Tony Saunders	10.00
50	Jose Cruz Jr.	50.00	146	Jeff Shaw	10.00	242	Ricky Bottalico	10.00
51	Bernie Williams	40.00	147	Shannon Stewart	10.00	243	Cliff Floyd	10.00
52	Doug Glanville	10.00	148	Brian Hunter	10.00	244	Chili Davis	10.00
53	Travis Fryman	10.00	149	Garret Anderson	10.00	245	Brian McRae	10.00
54	Rey Ordonez	10.00	150	Jeff Bagwell	80.00	246	Brad Radke	10.00
55	Jeff Conine	10.00	151	James Baldwin	10.00	247	Chan Ho Park	25.00
56	Trevor Hoffman	10.00	152	Devon White	10.00	248	Lance Johnson	10.00
57	Kirk Rueter	10.00	153	Jim Thome	40.00	249	Rafael Palmeiro	25.00
58	Ron Gant	20.00	154	Wally Joyner	10.00	250	Tony Gwynn	100.00
59	Carl Everett	10.00	155	Mark Wohlers	10.00	251	Denny Neagle	10.00
60	Joe Carter	20.00	156	Jeff Cirillo	10.00	252	Dean Palmer	10.00
61	Livan Hernandez	20.00	157	Jason Giambi	10.00	253	Jose Valentin	10.00
62	John Jaha	10.00	158	Royce Clayton	10.00	254	Matt Morris	10.00
63	Ivan Rodriguez	50.00	159	Dennis Reyes	10.00	255	Ellis Burks	10.00
64	Willie Blair	10.00	160	Raul Casanova	10.00	256	Jeff Suppan	10.00
65	Todd Helton	40.00	161	Pedro Astacio	10.00	257	Jimmy Key	10.00
66	Kevin Young	10.00	162	Todd Dunwoody	10.00	258	Justin Thompson	10.00
67	Mike Caruso	10.00	163	Sammy Sosa	100.00	259	Brett Tomko	10.00
68	Steve Trachsel	10.00	164	Todd Hundley	10.00	260	Mark Grudzielanek	10.00
69	Marty Cordova	10.00	165	Wade Boggs	20.00	261	Mike Hampton	10.00
70	Alex Fernandez	10.00	166	Robb Nen	10.00	262	Jeff Fassero	10.00
71	Eric Karros	20.00	167	Dan Wilson	10.00	263	Charles Nagy	10.00
72	Reggie Sanders	10.00	168	Hideki Irabu	40.00	264	Pedro Martinez	30.00
73	Russ Davis	10.00	169	B.J. Surhoff	10.00	265	Todd Zeile	10.00
74	Roberto Hernandez	10.00	170	Carlos Delgado	10.00	266	Will Clark	25.00
75	Barry Bonds	50.00	171	Fernando Tatis	10.00	267	Abraham Nunez	10.00
76	Alex Gonzalez	10.00	172	Bob Abreu	10.00	268	Dave Martinez	10.00
77	Roberto Alomar	40.00	173	David Ortiz	10.00	269	Jason Dickson	10.00
78	Troy O'Leary	10.00	174	Tony Womack	10.00	270	Eric Davis	10.00
79	Bernard Gilkey	10.00	175	Magglio Ordonez	25.00	271	Kevin Orie	10.00
80	Ismael Valdes	10.00	176	Aaron Boone	10.00	272	Derrek Lee	10.00
81	Travis Lee	125.00	177	Brian Giles	10.00	273	Andruw Jones	50.00
82	Brant Brown	10.00	178	Kevin Appier	10.00	274	Juan Encarnacion	10.00
83	Gary DiSarcina	10.00	179	Chuck Finley	10.00	275	Carlos Baerga	10.00
84	Joe Randa	10.00	180	Brian Rose	20.00	276	Andy Pettitte	40.00
85	Jaret Wright	75.00	181	Ryan Klesko	25.00	277	Brent Brede	10.00
86	Quilvio Veras	10.00	182	Mike Stanley	10.00	278	Paul Sorrento	10.00
87	Rickey Henderson	10.00	183	Dave Nilsson	10.00	279	Mike Lieberthal	10.00
88	Randall Simon	10.00	184	Carlos Perez	10.00	280	Marquis Grissom	10.00
89	Mariano Rivera	20.00	185	Jeff Blauser	10.00	281	Darin Erstad	50.00
90	Ugueth Urbina	10.00	186	Richard Hidalgo	10.00	282	Willie Greene	10.00
91	Fernando Vina	10.00	187	Charles Johnson	20.00	283	Derek Bell	10.00
92	Alan Benes	20.00	188	Vinny Castilla	20.00	284	Scott Spiezio	10.00
93	Dante Bichette	25.00	189	Joey Hamilton	10.00	285	David Segui	10.00
94	Karim Garcia	10.00	190	Bubba Trammell	10.00	286	Albert Belle	50.00
95	A.J. Hinch	25.00	191	Eli Marrero	10.00	287	Ramon Martinez	10.00
96	Shane Reynolds	10.00	192	Scott Erickson	10.00	288	Jeremi Gonzalez	10.00
97	Kevin Stocker	10.00	193	Pat Hentgen	10.00	289	Shawn Estes	10.00
	John Wetteland	10.00	194	Jorge Fabregas	10.00	290	Ron Coomer	10.00
	Steinbach	10.00	195	Tino Martinez	25.00	291	John Valentin	10.00
	Jr.	200.00	196	Bobby Higginson	10.00	292	Kevin Brown	10.00
		10.00	197	Dave Hollins	10.00	293	Michael Tucker	10.00
		10.00	198	Rolando Arrojo	10.00	294	Brian Jordan	10.00
		10.00	199	Joey Cora	10.00	295	Darryl Kile	10.00
		10.00	200	Mike Piazza	120.00	296	David Justice	25.00
		25.00	201	Reggie Jefferson	10.00	297	Jose Cruz Jr. CL	25.00
		30.00	202	John Smoltz	20.00	298	Ken Griffey Jr. CL	100.00
		20.00	203	Bobby Smith	10.00	299	Alex Rodriguez CL	60.00
			204	Tom Goodwin	10.00	300	Frank Thomas CL	75.00
			205	Omar Vizquel	10.00			

1998 Circa Thunder Rave Reviews

Rave Reviews were inserted at one per 288 packs of Circa Thunder. The cards were die-cut in a horizontal design with bronze foil etching and the image of a ball field in the background. This was the most difficult insert to pull from packs of Circa Thunder at one per 288 packs.

		MT
Complete Set (15):		500.00
Common Player:		15.00
1RR	Jeff Bagwell	25.00
2RR	Barry Bonds	20.00
3RR	Roger Clemens	35.00
4RR	Jose Cruz Jr.	20.00
5RR	Nomar Garciaparra	50.00
6RR	Juan Gonzalez	40.00
7RR	Ken Griffey Jr.	80.00
8RR	Tony Gwynn	40.00
9RR	Derek Jeter	50.00
10RR	Greg Maddux	50.00
11RR	Mark McGwire	100.00
12RR	Mike Piazza	50.00
13RR	Alex Rodriguez	50.00
14RR	Frank Thomas	50.00
15RR	Larry Walker	15.00

1998 Circa Thunder Super Rave

Only 25 Super Rave parallel sets were printed and they were inserted approximately one per 216 packs. The set contains 296 cards in total, which is 300 minus the four checklist cards. Fronts are identified by sparkling gold foil on the player's name and the Thunder logo, with sequential numbering on the back to 25.

		MT
Common Player:		40.00
Semistars:		80.00
1	Ben Grieve	250.00
2	Derek Jeter	500.00
3	Alex Rodriguez	500.00
4	Paul Molitor	150.00
5	Nomar Garciaparra	500.00
6	Fred McGriff	80.00
7	Kenny Lofton	200.00
8	Cal Ripken Jr.	600.00
9	Matt Williams	80.00
10	Chipper Jones	450.00
11	Barry Larkin	80.00
12	Steve Finley	40.00
13	Billy Wagner	40.00
14	Rico Brogna	40.00
15	Tim Salmon	125.00
16	Hideo Nomo	125.00
17	Tony Clark	125.00
18	Jason Kendall	40.00
19	Juan Gonzalez	400.00
20	Jeromy Burnitz	40.00
21	Roger Clemens	300.00
22	Mark Grace	80.00
23	Robin Ventura	60.00
24	Manny Ramirez	200.00
25	Mark McGwire	800.00
26	Gary Sheffield	70.00
27	Vladimir Guerrero	200.00
28	Butch Huskey	40.00
29	Cecil Fielder	60.00
30	Roderick Myers	40.00
31	Greg Maddux	500.00
32	Bill Mueller	40.00
33	Larry Walker	100.00
34	Henry Rodriguez	40.00
35	Mike Mussina	150.00
36	Ricky Ledee	60.00
37	Bobby Bonilla	60.00
38	Curt Schilling	60.00
39	Luis Gonzalez	40.00
40	Troy Percival	40.00
41	Eric Milton	60.00
42	Mo Vaughn	200.00
43	Raul Mondesi	80.00
44	Kenny Rogers	40.00
45	Frank Thomas	500.00
46	Jose Canseco	80.00
47	Tom Glavine	60.00
48	Rich Butler	40.00
49	Jay Buhner	80.00
50	Jose Cruz Jr.	200.00
51	Bernie Williams	150.00
52	Doug Glanville	40.00
53	Travis Fryman	60.00
54	Rey Ordonez	40.00
55	Jeff Conine	40.00
56	Trevor Hoffman	40.00
57	Kirk Rueter	40.00
58	Ron Gant	60.00
59	Carl Everett	40.00
60	Joe Carter	60.00
61	Livan Hernandez	60.00
62	John Jaha	40.00
63	Ivan Rodriguez	200.00
64	Willie Blair	40.00
65	Todd Helton	200.00
66	Kevin Young	40.00
67	Mike Caruso	40.00
68	Steve Trachsel	40.00
69	Marty Cordova	40.00
70	Alex Fernandez	40.00
71	Eric Karros	60.00
72	Reggie Sanders	40.00
73	Russ Davis	40.00
74	Roberto Hernandez	40.00
75	Barry Bonds	200.00
76	Alex Gonzalez	40.00
77	Roberto Alomar	150.00
78	Troy O'Leary	40.00
79	Bernard Gilkey	40.00
80	Ismael Valdes	40.00
81	Travis Lee	250.00
82	Brant Brown	40.00
83	Gary DiSarcina	40.00
84	Joe Randa	40.00
85	Jaret Wright	200.00
86	Quilvio Veras	40.00
87	Rickey Henderson	50.00
88	Randall Simon	40.00
89	Mariano Rivera	60.00
90	Ugueth Urbina	40.00
91	Fernando Vina	40.00
92	Alan Benes	60.00
93	Dante Bichette	80.00
94	Karim Garcia	60.00
95	A.J. Hinch	40.00
96	Shane Reynolds	40.00
97	Kevin Stocker	40.00
98	John Wetteland	40.00
99	Terry Steinbach	40.00
100	Ken Griffey Jr.	700.00
101	Mike Cameron	40.00
102	Damion Easley	40.00
103	Randy Myers	40.00
104	Jason Schmidt	40.00
105	Jeff King	40.00
106	Gregg Jefferies	40.00
107	Sean Casey	75.00
108	Mark Kotsay	75.00
109	Brad Fullmer	75.00
110	Wilson Alvarez	40.00
111	Sandy Alomar Jr.	60.00
112	Walt Weiss	40.00
113	Doug Jones	40.00
114	Andy Benes	50.00
115	Paul O'Neill	70.00
116	Dennis Eckersley	50.00
117	Todd Greene	40.00
118	Bobby Jones	40.00
119	Darrin Fletcher	40.00
120	Eric Young	40.00
121	Jeffrey Hammonds	40.00
122	Mickey Morandini	40.00
123	Chuck Knoblauch	80.00
124	Moises Alou	60.00
125	Miguel Tejada	80.00
126	Brian Anderson	40.00
127	Edgar Renteria	40.00
128	Mike Lansing	40.00
129	Quinton McCracken	40.00
130	Ray Lankford	40.00
131	Andy Ashby	40.00
132	Kelvim Escobar	40.00
133	Mike Lowell	40.00
134	Randy Johnson	150.00
135	Andres Galarraga	80.00
136	Armando Benitez	40.00
137	Rusty Greer	40.00
138	Jose Guillen	60.00
139	Paul Konerko	60.00
140	Edgardo Alfonzo	40.00
141	Jim Leyritz	40.00
142	Mark Clark	40.00
143	Brian Johnson	40.00
144	Scott Rolen	250.00
145	David Cone	60.00
146	Jeff Shaw	40.00
147	Shannon Stewart	40.00
148	Brian Hunter	40.00
149	Garret Anderson	40.00
150	Jeff Bagwell	250.00
151	James Baldwin	40.00
152	Devon White	40.00
153	Jim Thome	125.00
154	Wally Joyner	40.00
155	Mark Wohlers	40.00
156	Jeff Cirillo	40.00
157	Jason Giambi	40.00
158	Royce Clayton	40.00
159	Dennis Reyes	40.00
160	Raul Casanova	40.00
161	Pedro Astacio	40.00
162	Todd Dunwoody	40.00
163	Sammy Sosa	500.00
164	Todd Hundley	40.00
165	Wade Boggs	75.00
166	Robb Nen	40.00
167	Dan Wilson	40.00
168	Hideki Irabu	80.00
169	B.J. Surhoff	40.00
170	Carlos Delgado	40.00
171	Fernando Tatis	40.00
172	Bob Abreu	40.00
173	David Ortiz	40.00
174	Tony Womack	40.00
175	Magglio Ordonez	70.00
176	Aaron Boone	40.00
177	Brian Giles	40.00
178	Kevin Appier	40.00
179	Chuck Finley	40.00
180	Brian Rose	50.00
181	Ryan Klesko	70.00
182	Mike Stanley	40.00
183	Dave Nilsson	40.00
184	Carlos Perez	40.00
185	Jeff Blauser	40.00
186	Richard Hidalgo	40.00
187	Charles Johnson	50.00
188	Vinny Castilla	60.00
189	Joey Hamilton	40.00
190	Bubba Trammell	40.00
191	Eli Marrero	40.00
192	Scott Erickson	40.00
193	Pat Hentgen	40.00
194	Jorge Fabregas	40.00
195	Tino Martinez	80.00
196	Bobby Higginson	40.00
197	Dave Hollins	40.00
198	Rolando Arrojo	40.00
199	Joey Cora	40.00
200	Mike Piazza	500.00
201	Reggie Jefferson	40.00
202	John Smoltz	50.00
203	Bobby Smith	40.00
204	Tom Goodwin	40.00
205	Omar Vizquel	40.00
206	John Olerud	50.00
207	Matt Stairs	40.00
208	Bobby Estalella	40.00
209	Miguel Cairo	40.00
210	Shawn Green	40.00
211	Jon Nunnally	40.00
212	Al Leiter	40.00
213	Matt Lawton	40.00
214	Brady Anderson	50.00
215	Jeff Kent	40.00
216	Ray Durham	40.00
217	Al Martin	40.00
218	Jeff D'Amico	40.00
219	Kevin Tapani	40.00
220	Jim Edmonds	50.00
221	Jose Vizcaino	40.00
222	Jay Bell	40.00
223	Ken Caminiti	60.00
224	Craig Biggio	60.00
225	Bartolo Colon	50.00
226	Neifi Perez	40.00
227	Delino DeShields	40.00
228	Javier Lopez	50.00
229	David Wells	40.00

230	Brad Rigby	40.00
231	John Franco	40.00
232	Michael Coleman	40.00
233	Edgar Martinez	50.00
234	Francisco Cordova	40.00
235	Johnny Damon	40.00
236	Deivi Cruz	40.00
237	J.T. Snow	40.00
238	Enrique Wilson	40.00
239	Rondell White	60.00
240	Aaron Sele	40.00
241	Tony Saunders	40.00
242	Ricky Bottalico	40.00
243	Cliff Floyd	40.00
244	Chili Davis	40.00
245	Brian McRae	40.00
246	Brad Radke	40.00
247	Chan Ho Park	70.00
248	Lance Johnson	40.00
249	Rafael Palmeiro	80.00
250	Tony Gwynn	400.00
251	Denny Neagle	40.00
252	Dean Palmer	40.00
253	Jose Valentin	40.00
254	Matt Morris	40.00
255	Ellis Burks	40.00
256	Jeff Suppan	40.00
257	Jimmy Key	40.00
258	Justin Thompson	40.00
259	Brett Tomko	40.00
260	Mark Grudzielanek	40.00
261	Mike Hampton	40.00
262	Jeff Fassero	40.00
263	Charles Nagy	40.00
264	Pedro Martinez	120.00
265	Todd Zeile	40.00
266	Will Clark	80.00
267	Abraham Nunez	40.00
268	Dave Martinez	40.00
269	Jason Dickson	40.00
270	Eric Davis	40.00
271	Kevin Orie	40.00
272	Derrek Lee	40.00
273	Andruw Jones	200.00
274	Juan Encarnacion	40.00
275	Carlos Baerga	40.00
276	Andy Pettitte	150.00
277	Brent Brede	40.00
278	Paul Sorrento	40.00
279	Mike Lieberthal	40.00
280	Marquis Grissom	40.00
281	Darin Erstad	200.00
282	Willie Greene	40.00
283	Derek Bell	40.00
284	Scott Spiezio	40.00
285	David Segui	40.00
286	Albert Belle	200.00
287	Ramon Martinez	40.00
288	Jeremi Gonzalez	40.00
289	Shawn Estes	40.00
290	Ron Coomer	40.00
291	John Valentin	40.00
292	Kevin Brown	40.00
293	Michael Tucker	40.00
294	Brian Jordan	40.00
295	Darryl Kile	40.00
296	David Justice	80.00
297	Jose Cruz Jr. CL	100.00
298	Ken Griffey Jr. CL	350.00
299	Alex Rodriguez CL	250.00
300	Frank Thomas CL	250.00

Values quoted in this guide reflect the retail price of a card — the price a collector can expect to pay when buying a card from a dealer.

The wholesale price — that which a collector can expect to receive from a dealer when selling cards — will be significantly lower, depending on desirability and condition.

1994 Collector's Choice

This base-brand set, released in two series, is more widely available than the regular 1994 Upper Deck set. The cards feature the traditional UV coating and holograms and have large photos with a narrow pinstripe border. Backs have stats and a color photo. Series I has 320 cards and subsets titled Rookie Class, Draft Picks and Top Performers. Series II's subsets are Up Close and Personal, Future Foundation and Rookie Class. Each of the set's player cards can also be found with either a gold- (1 in 36 packs) or silver-foil replica-autograph card; one silver-signature card appears in every pack.

		MT
	Complete Set (670):	30.00
	Complete Series 1 (320):	12.00
	Complete Series 2 (350):	18.00
	Common Player:	.05
	Series 1 or 2 Wax Box:	25.00
1	Rich Becker	.05
2	Greg Blosser	.05
3	Midre Cummings	.05
4	Carlos Delgado	.20
5	Steve Dreyer	.05
6	Carl Everett	.10
7	Cliff Floyd	.10
8	Alex Gonzalez	.15
9	Shawn Green	.15
10	Butch Huskey	.10
11	Mark Hutton	.05
12	Miguel Jimenez	.05
13	Steve Karsay	.10
14	Marc Newfield	.10
15	Luis Ortiz	.05
16	Manny Ramirez	.65
17	Johnny Ruffin	.05
18	Scott Stahoviak	.10
19	Salomon Torres	.05
20	Gabe White	.10
21	Brian Anderson	.10
22	Wayne Gomes	.10
23	Jeff Granger	.10
24	Steve Soderstrom	.15
25	Trot Nixon	.15
26	Kirk Presley	.10
27	Matt Brunson	.05
28	Brooks Kieschnick	.55
29	Billy Wagner	.40
30	Matt Drews	.10
31	Kurt Abbott	.20
32	Luis Alicea	.05
33	Roberto Alomar	.40
34	Sandy Alomar Jr.	.10
35	Moises Alou	.10
36	Wilson Alvarez	.05
37	Rich Amaral	.05
38	Eric Anthony	.05
39	Luis Aquino	.05
40	Jack Armstrong	.05

41	Rene Arocha	.05
42	Rich Aude	.10
43	Brad Ausmus	.05
44	Steve Avery	.05
45	Bob Ayrault	.05
46	Willie Banks	.05
47	Bret Barberie	.05
48	Kim Batiste	.05
49	Rod Beck	.05
50	Jason Bere	.05
51	Sean Berry	.05
52	Dante Bichette	.25
53	Jeff Blauser	.05
54	Mike Blowers	.05
55	Tim Bogar	.05
56	Tom Bolton	.05
57	Ricky Bones	.05
58	Bobby Bonilla	.10
59	Bret Boone	.05
60	Pat Borders	.05
61	Mike Bordick	.05
62	Daryl Boston	.05
63	Ryan Bowen	.05
64	Jeff Branson	.05
65	George Brett	.35
66	Steve Buechele	.05
67	Dave Burba	.05
68	John Burkett	.05
69	Jeromy Burnitz	.10
70	Brett Butler	.08
71	Rob Butler	.05
72	Ken Caminiti	.20
73	Cris Carpenter	.05
74	Vinny Castilla	.10
75	Andujar Cedeno	.05
76	Wes Chamberlain	.05
77	Archi Cianfrocco	.05
78	Dave Clark	.05
79	Jerald Clark	.05
80	Royce Clayton	.05
81	David Cone	.10
82	Jeff Conine	.08
83	Steve Cooke	.05
84	Scott Cooper	.05
85	Joey Cora	.05
86	Tim Costa	.05
87	Chad Curtis	.05
88	Ron Darling	.05
89	Danny Darwin	.05
90	Rob Deer	.05
91	Jim Deshaies	.05
92	Delino DeShields	.05
93	Rob Dibble	.05
94	Gary DiSarcina	.05
95	Doug Drabek	.05
96	Scott Erickson	.05
97	Rikkert Faneyte	.10
98	Jeff Fassero	.05
99	Alex Fernandez	.10
100	Cecil Fielder	.15
101	Dave Fleming	.05
102	Darrin Fletcher	.05
103	Scott Fletcher	.05
104	Mike Gallego	.05
105	Carlos Garcia	.05
106	Jeff Gardner	.05
107	Brent Gates	.10
108	Benji Gil	.05
109	Bernard Gilkey	.05
110	Chris Gomez	.05
111	Luis Gonzalez	.05
112	Tom Gordon	.05
113	Jim Gott	.05
114	Mark Grace	.10
115	Tommy Greene	.05
116	Willie Greene	.05
117	Ken Griffey, Jr.	1.50
118	Bill Gullickson	.05
119	Ricky Gutierrez	.05
120	Juan Guzman	.05
121	Chris Gwynn	.05
122	Tony Gwynn	.50
123	Jeffrey Hammonds	.10
124	Erik Hanson	.05
125	Gene Harris	.05
126	Greg Harris	.05
127	Bryan Harvey	.05
128	Billy Hatcher	.05
129	Hilly Hathaway	.05
130	Charlie Hayes	.05
131	Rickey Henderson	.15
132	Mike Henneman	.05
133	Pat Hentgen	.10
134	Roberto Hernandez	.05
135	Orel Hershiser	.05
136	Phil Hiatt	.10

#	Player	Price
137	Glenallen Hill	.05
138	Ken Hill	.05
139	Eric Hillman	.05
140	Chris Hoiles	.05
141	Dave Hollins	.05
142	David Hulse	.05
143	Todd Hundley	.15
144	Pete Incaviglia	.05
145	Danny Jackson	.05
146	John Jaha	.05
147	Domingo Jean	.05
148	Gregg Jefferies	.05
149	Reggie Jefferson	.05
150	Lance Johnson	.05
151	Bobby Jones	.15
152	Chipper Jones	.75
153	Todd Jones	.05
154	Brian Jordan	.10
155	Wally Joyner	.05
156	Dave Justice	.15
157	Ron Karkovice	.05
158	Eric Karros	.10
159	Jeff Kent	.05
160	Jimmy Key	.10
161	Mark Kiefer	.05
162	Darryl Kile	.05
163	Jeff King	.05
164	Wayne Kirby	.05
165	Ryan Klesko	.45
166	Chuck Knoblauch	.15
167	Chad Kreuter	.05
168	John Kruk	.05
169	Mark Langston	.05
170	Mike Lansing	.05
171	Barry Larkin	.20
172	Manuel Lee	.05
173	*Phil Leftwich*	.10
174	Darren Lewis	.05
175	Derek Lilliquist	.05
176	Jose Lind	.05
177	Albie Lopez	.05
178	Javier Lopez	.20
179	Torey Lovullo	.05
180	Scott Lydy	.05
181	Mike Macfarlane	.05
182	Shane Mack	.05
183	Greg Maddux	1.00
184	Dave Magadan	.05
185	Joe Magrane	.05
186	Kirt Manwaring	.05
187	Al Martin	.05
188	*Pedro A. Martinez*	.15
189	Pedro J. Martinez	.15
190	Ramon Martinez	.10
191	Tino Martinez	.20
192	Don Mattingly	.50
193	Derrick May	.05
194	David McCarty	.05
195	Ben McDonald	.05
196	Roger McDowell	.05
197	Fred McGriff	.25
198	Mark McLemore	.05
199	Greg McMichael	.05
200	Jeff McNeely	.05
201	Brian McRae	.05
202	Pat Meares	.05
203	Roberto Mejia	.05
204	Orlando Merced	.05
205	Jose Mesa	.05
206	Blas Minor	.05
207	Angel Miranda	.05
208	Paul Molitor	.30
209	Raul Mondesi	.50
210	Jeff Montgomery	.05
211	Mickey Morandini	.05
212	Mike Morgan	.05
213	Jamie Moyer	.05
214	Bobby Munoz	.05
215	Troy Neel	.05
216	Dave Nilsson	.05
217	John O'Donoghue	.05
218	Paul O'Neill	.10
219	Jose Offerman	.05
220	Joe Oliver	.05
221	Greg Olson	.05
222	Donovan Osborne	.05
223	Jayhawk Owens	.05
224	Mike Pagliarulo	.05
225	Craig Paquette	.05
226	Roger Pavlik	.05
227	Brad Pennington	.05
228	Eduardo Perez	.05
229	Mike Perez	.05
230	Tony Phillips	.05
231	Hipolito Pichardo	.05
232	Phil Plantier	.05
233	*Curtis Pride*	.15
234	Tim Pugh	.05
235	Scott Radinsky	.05
236	Pat Rapp	.05
237	Kevin Reimer	.05
238	Armando Reynoso	.05
239	Jose Rijo	.05
240	Cal Ripken, Jr.	1.50
241	Kevin Roberson	.05
242	Kenny Rogers	.05
243	Kevin Rogers	.05
244	Mel Rojas	.05
245	John Roper	.05
246	Kirk Rueter	.05
247	Scott Ruffcorn	.10
248	Ken Ryan	.05
249	Nolan Ryan	.75
250	Bret Saberhagen	.05
251	Tim Salmon	.25
252	Reggie Sanders	.10
253	Curt Schilling	.10
254	David Segui	.05
255	Aaron Sele	.10
256	Scott Servais	.05
257	Gary Sheffield	.25
258	Ruben Sierra	.05
259	Don Slaught	.05
260	Lee Smith	.05
261	Cory Snyder	.05
262	Paul Sorrento	.05
263	Sammy Sosa	.75
264	Bill Spiers	.05
265	Mike Stanley	.05
266	Dave Staton	.05
267	Terry Steinbach	.05
268	Kevin Stocker	.05
269	Todd Stottlemyre	.10
270	Doug Strange	.05
271	Bill Swift	.05
272	Kevin Tapani	.05
273	Tony Tarasco	.05
274	*Julian Tavarez*	.20
275	Mickey Tettleton	.05
276	Ryan Thompson	.05
277	Chris Turner	.05
278	John Valentin	.05
279	Todd Van Poppel	.05
280	Andy Van Slyke	.05
281	Mo Vaughn	.40
282	Robin Ventura	.10
283	Frank Viola	.05
284	Jose Vizcaino	.05
285	Omar Vizquel	.05
286	Larry Walker	.20
287	Duane Ware	.05
288	Allen Watson	.10
289	Bill Wegman	.05
290	Turk Wendell	.05
291	Lou Whitaker	.05
292	Devon White	.05
293	Rondell White	.15
294	Mark Whiten	.05
295	Darrell Whitmore	.05
296	Bob Wickman	.05
297	Rick Wilkins	.05
298	Bernie Williams	.25
299	Matt Williams	.30
300	Woody Williams	.05
301	Nigel Wilson	.05
302	Dave Winfield	.10
303	Anthony Young	.05
304	Eric Young	.05
305	Todd Zeile	.05
306	Jack McDowell, John Burkett, Tom Glavine (Top Performers)	.10
307	Randy Johnson (Top Performers)	.15
308	Randy Myers (Top Performers)	.05
309	Jack McDowell (Top Performers)	.05
310	Mike Piazza (Top Performers)	.40
311	Barry Bonds (Top Performers)	.25
312	Andres Galarraga (Top Performers)	.10
313	Juan Gonzalez, Barry Bonds (Top Performers)	.35
314	Albert Belle (Top Performers)	.40
315	Kenny Lofton (Top Performers)	.15
316	Checklist 1-64(Barry Bonds)	.10
317	Checklist 65-128(Ken Griffey, Jr.)	.30
318	Checklist 129--192(Mike Piazza)	.15
319	Checklist 193-256(Kirby Puckett)	.10
320	Checklist 257-320(Nolan Ryan)	.15
321	Checklist 321-370(Roberto Alomar)	.15
322	Checklist 371-420(Roger Clemens)	.15
323	Checklist 421-470(Juan Gonzalez)	.15
324	Checklist 471-520(Ken Griffey, Jr.)	.30
325	Checklist 521-570(David Justice)	.10
326	Checklist 571-620(John Kruk)	.05
327	Checklist 621-670(Frank Thomas)	.30
328	California Angels Checklist(Tim Salmon)	.10
329	Houston Astros Checklist(Jeff Bagwell)	.15
330	Oakland Athletics Checklist(Mark McGwire)	.75
331	Toronto Blue Jays Checklist(Roberto Alomar)	.15
332	Atlanta Braves Checklist(David Justice)	.10
333	Milwaukee Brewers Checklist(Pat Listach)	.05
334	St. Louis Cardinals Checklist(Ozzie Smith)	.10
335	Chicago Cubs Checklist(Ryne Sandberg)	.10
336	Los Angeles Dodgers Checklist(Mike Piazza)	.25
337	Montreal Expos Checklist(Cliff Floyd)	.05
338	San Francisco Giants Checklist(Barry Bonds)	.15
339	Cleveland Indians Checklist(Albert Belle)	.20
340	Seattle Mariners Checklist(Ken Griffey, Jr.)	.50
341	Florida Marlins Checklist(Gary Sheffield)	.20
342	New York Mets Checklist(Dwight Gooden)	.05
343	Baltimore Orioles Checklist(Cal Ripken, Jr.)	.50
344	San Diego Padres Checklist(Tony Gwynn)	.20
345	Philadelphia Phillies Checklist(Lenny Dykstra)	.05
346	Pittsburgh Pirates Checklists(Andy Van Slyke)	.05
347	Texas Rangers Checklist(Juan Gonzalez)	.20
348	Boston Red Sox Checklist(Roger Clemens)	.15
349	Cincinnati Reds Checklist(Barry Larkin)	.10
350	Colorado Rockies Checklist(Andres Galarraga)	.10
351	Kansas City Royals Checklist(Kevin Appier)	.05
352	Detroit Tigers C?hecklist(Cecil Fielder)	.10
353	Minnesota Twins Checklist(Kirby Puckett)	.20
354	Chicago White Sox Checklist(Frank Thomas)	.50
355	New York Yankees Checklist(Don Mattingly)	.30
356	Bo Jackson	.10
357	Randy Johnson	.30
358	Darren Daulton	.05
359	Charlie Hough	.05
360	Andres Galarraga	.10
361	Mike Felder	.05
362	Chris Hammond	.05
363	Shawon Dunston	.05
364	Junior Felix	.05
365	Ray Lankford	.05
366	Darryl Strawberry	.05
367	Dave Magadan	.05
368	Gregg Olson	.05
369	Len Dykstra	.05
370	Darrin Jackson	.05
371	Dave Stewart	.05
372	Terry Pendleton	.05

No.	Player	Price	No.	Player	Price	No.	Player	Price
373	Arthur Rhodes	.05	469	B.J. Surhoff	.05	565	Kenny Lofton	.35
374	Benito Santiago	.05	470	Kevin Mitchell	.05	566	Gary Gaetti	.05
375	Travis Fryman	.10	471	Bobby Witt	.05	567	Todd Worrell	.05
376	Scott Brosius	.05	472	Milt Thompson	.05	568	Mark Portugal	.05
377	Stan Belinda	.05	473	John Smiley	.05	569	Dick Schofield	.05
378	Derek Parks	.05	474	Alan Trammell	.05	570	Andy Benes	.10
379	Kevin Seitzer	.05	475	Mike Mussina	.30	571	Zane Smith	.05
380	Wade Boggs	.15	476	Rick Aguilera	.05	572	Bobby Ayala	.05
381	Wally Whitehurst	.05	477	Jose Valentin	.05	573	Chip Hale	.05
382	Scott Leius	.05	478	Harold Baines	.05	574	Bob Welch	.05
383	Danny Tartabull	.05	479	Bip Roberts	.05	575	Deion Sanders	.25
384	Harold Reynolds	.05	480	Edgar Martinez	.10	576	Dave Nied	.05
385	Tim Raines	.05	481	Rheal Cormier	.05	577	Pat Mahomes	.05
386	Darryl Hamilton	.05	482	Hal Morris	.05	578	Charles Nagy	.05
387	Felix Fermin	.05	483	Pat Kelly	.05	579	Otis Nixon	.05
388	Jim Eisenreich	.05	484	Roberto Kelly	.05	580	Dean Palmer	.05
389	Kurt Abbott	.05	485	Chris Sabo	.05	581	Roberto Petagine	.05
390	Kevin Appier	.05	486	Kent Hrbek	.05	582	Dwight Smith	.05
391	Chris Bosio	.05	487	Scott Kamieniecki	.05	583	Jeff Russell	.05
392	Randy Tomlin	.05	488	Walt Weiss	.05	584	Mark Dewey	.05
393	Bob Hamelin	.05	489	Karl Rhodes	.05	585	Greg Vaughn	.05
394	Kevin Gross	.05	490	Derek Bell	.05	586	Brian Hunter	.05
395	Wil Cordero	.05	491	Chili Davis	.05	587	Willie McGee	.05
396	Joe Girardi	.05	492	Brian Harper	.05	588	Pedro J. Martinez	.10
397	Orestes Destrade	.05	493	Felix Jose	.05	589	Roger Salkeld	.05
398	Chris Haney	.05	494	Trevor Hoffman	.05	590	Jeff Bagwell	.50
399	Xavier Hernandez	.05	495	Dennis Eckersley	.05	591	Spike Owen	.05
400	Mike Piazza	.75	496	Pedro Astacio	.05	592	Jeff Reardon	.05
401	Alex Arias	.05	497	Jay Bell	.05	593	Erik Pappas	.05
402	Tom Candiotti	.05	498	Randy Velarde	.05	594	Brian Williams	.05
403	Kirk Gibson	.05	499	David Wells	.05	595	Eddie Murray	.25
404	Chuck Carr	.05	500	Frank Thomas	1.25	596	Henry Rodriguez	.08
405	Brady Anderson	.15	501	Mark Lemke	.05	597	Erik Hanson	.05
406	Greg Gagne	.05	502	Mike Devereaux	.05	598	Stan Javier	.05
407	Bruce Ruffin	.05	503	Chuck McElroy	.05	599	Mitch Williams	.05
408	Scott Hemond	.05	504	Luis Polonia	.05	600	John Olerud	.05
409	Keith Miller	.05	505	Damion Easley	.05	601	Vince Coleman	.05
410	John Wetteland	.05	506	Greg A. Harris	.05	602	Damon Berryhill	.05
411	Eric Anthony	.05	507	Chris James	.05	603	Tom Brunansky	.05
412	Andre Dawson	.05	508	Terry Mulholland	.05	604	Robb Nen	.05
413	Doug Henry	.05	509	Pete Smith	.05	605	Rafael Palmeiro	.10
414	John Franco	.05	510	Rickey Henderson	.15	606	Cal Eldred	.05
415	Julio Franco	.05	511	Sid Fernandez	.05	607	Jeff Brantley	.05
416	Dave Hansen	.05	512	Al Leiter	.05	608	Alan Mills	.05
417	Mike Harkey	.05	513	Doug Jones	.05	609	Jeff Nelson	.05
418	Jack Armstrong	.05	514	Steve Farr	.05	610	Barry Bonds	.40
419	Joe Orsulak	.05	515	Chuck Finley	.05	611	*Carlos Pulido*	.10
420	John Smoltz	.15	516	Bobby Thigpen	.05	612	*Tim Hyers*	.15
421	Scott Livingstone	.05	517	Jim Edmonds	.25	613	Steve Howe	.05
422	Darren Holmes	.05	518	Graeme Lloyd	.05	614	*Brian Turang*	.05
423	Ed Sprague	.05	519	Dwight Gooden	.10	615	Leo Gomez	.05
424	Jay Buhner	.15	520	Pat Listach	.05	616	Jesse Orosco	.05
425	Kirby Puckett	.60	521	Kevin Bass	.05	617	Dan Pasqua	.05
426	Phil Clark	.05	522	Willie Banks	.05	618	Marvin Freeman	.05
427	Anthony Young	.05	523	Steve Finley	.05	619	Tony Fernandez	.05
428	Reggie Jefferson	.05	524	Delino DeShields	.05	620	Albert Belle	.50
429	Mariano Duncan	.05	525	Mark McGwire	2.00	621	Eddie Taubensee	.05
430	Tom Glavine	.15	526	Greg Swindell	.05	622	Mike Jackson	.05
431	Dave Henderson	.05	527	Chris Nabholz	.05	623	Jose Bautista	.05
432	Melido Perez	.05	528	Scott Sanders	.05	624	Jim Thome	.30
433	Paul Wagner	.05	529	David Segui	.05	625	Ivan Rodriguez	.30
434	Tim Worrell	.05	530	Howard Johnson	.05	626	Ben Rivera	.05
435	Ozzie Guillen	.05	531	Jaime Navarro	.05	627	Dave Valle	.05
436	Mike Butcher	.05	532	Jose Vizcaino	.05	628	Tom Henke	.05
437	Jim Deshaies	.05	533	Mark Lewis	.05	629	Omar Vizquel	.05
438	Kevin Young	.05	534	Pete Harnisch	.05	630	Juan Gonzalez	.40
439	Tom Browning	.05	535	Robby Thompson	.05	631	Roberto Alomar (Up Close)	.15
440	Mike Greenwell	.05	536	Marcus Moore	.05	632	Barry Bonds (Up Close)	.20
441	Mike Stanton	.05	537	Kevin Brown	.10	633	Juan Gonzalez (Up Close)	.25
442	John Doherty	.05	538	Mark Clark	.05	634	Ken Griffey, Jr. (Up Close)	.75
443	John Dopson	.05	539	Sterling Hitchcock	.05	635	Michael Jordan (Up Close)	3.00
444	Carlos Baerga	.10	540	Will Clark	.20	636	Dave Justice (Up Close)	.10
445	Jack McDowell	.10	541	Denis Boucher	.05	637	Mike Piazza (Up Close)	.40
446	Kent Mercker	.05	542	Jack Morris	.05	638	Kirby Puckett (Up Close)	.25
447	Ricky Jordan	.05	543	Pedro Munoz	.05	639	Tim Salmon (Up Close)	.15
448	Jerry Browne	.05	544	Bret Boone	.05	640	Frank Thomas (Up Close)	.75
449	Fernando Vina	.05	545	Ozzie Smith	.25	641	*Alan Benes* (Future Foundation)	.60
450	Jim Abbott	.05	546	Dennis Martinez	.05	642	Johnny Damon (Future Foundation)	.10
451	Teddy Higuera	.05	547	Dan Wilson	.05	643	*Brad Fullmer* (Future Foundation)	1.00
452	Tim Naehring	.05	548	Rick Sutcliffe	.05	644	Derek Jeter (Future Foundation)	1.50
453	Jim Leyritz	.05	549	Kevin McReynolds	.05	645	*Derrek Lee* (Future Foundation)	1.25
454	Frank Castillo	.05	550	Roger Clemens	.35	646	Alex Ochoa (Future Foundation)	.20
455	Joe Carter	.15	551	Todd Benzinger	.05	647	*Alex Rodriguez* (Future Foundation)	5.00
456	Craig Biggio	.10	552	Bill Haselman	.05	648	*Jose Silva* (Future Foundation)	.15
457	Geronimo Pena	.05	553	Bobby Munoz	.05	649	*Terrell Wade* (Future Foundation)	.20
458	Alejandro Pena	.05	554	Ellis Burks	.10	650	Preston Wilson (Future Foundation)	.15
459	Mike Moore	.05	555	Ryne Sandberg	.25			
460	Randy Myers	.05	556	Lee Smith	.05			
461	Greg Myers	.05	557	Danny Bautista	.05			
462	Greg Hibbard	.05	558	Rey Sanchez	.05			
463	Jose Guzman	.05	559	Norm Charlton	.05			
464	Tom Pagnozzi	.05	560	Jose Canseco	.25			
465	Marquis Grissom	.05	561	Tim Belcher	.05			
466	Tim Wallach	.05	562	Denny Neagle	.10			
467	Joe Grahe	.05	563	Eric Davis	.05			
468	Bob Tewksbury	.05	564	Jody Reed	.05			

651	Shane Andrews (Rookie Class)	.05
652	James Baldwin (Rookie Class)	.10
653	*Ricky Bottalico* (Rookie Class)	.10
654	Tavo Alvarez (Rookie Class)	.05
655	Donnie Elliott (Rookie Class)	.10
656	Joey Eischen (Rookie Class)	.05
657	Jason Giambi (Rookie Class)	.35
658	Todd Hollandsworth (Rookie Class)	.20
659	Brian Hunter (Rookie Class)	.20
660	Charles Johnson (Rookie Class)	.20
661	*Michael Jordan* (Rookie Class)	7.50
662	Jeff Juden (Rookie Class)	.05
663	Mike Kelly (Rookie Class)	.05
664	James Mouton (Rookie Class)	.15
665	Ray Holbert (Rookie Class)	.10
666	Pokey Reese (Rookie Class)	.05
667	*Ruben Santana* (Rookie Class)	.10
668	Paul Spoljaric (Rookie Class)	.05
669	Luis Lopez (Rookie Class)	.05
670	Matt Walbeck (Rookie Class)	.10

1994 Collector's Choice Silver Signature

Each of the cards in the debut edition of Upper Deck's Collector's Choice brand was also issued in a parallel edition bearing a facsimile silver-foil signature on front. The silver-signature cards were inserted at a one-per-pack rate in the set's foil packs, and proportionally in other types of packaging.

	MT
Complete Set (670):	200.00
Complete Series 1 (1-320):	120.00
Complete Series 2 (321-670):	80.00
Common Player:	.25

(Star cards valued 1.5X-3X corresponding cards in regular Collector's Choice)

A player's name in *italic* type indicates a rookie card.

1994 Collector's Choice Gold Signature

A super-scarce parallel set of the premiere-issue Collector's Choice in 1994 was the gold-signature version found on average of only once per 36 foil packs. In addition to a gold-foil facsimile signature on the card front, this edition features gold-colored borders on the regular player cards.

	MT
Complete Set (670):	2750.
Complete Series 1 (1-320):	1650.
Complete Series 2 (321-670):	1350.
Common Player:	1.50

(Star cards valued at 20X to 40X same cards in regular Collector's Choice)

1994 Collector's Choice Home Run All-Stars

Among the most attractive of the 1994 chase cards, the perceived high production (over a million sets according to stated odds of winning) of this set keeps it affordable. Sets were available by a mail-in offer to persons who found a winner card in Series 1 foil packs (about one per box). Cards feature a combination of brick-bordered hologram and color player photo on front, along with a gold-foil facsimile autograph. On back the brick border is repeated, as is the photo on the hologram, though this time in full color. There is a stadium photo in the background, over which is printed a description of the player's home run prowess. A numbering error' resulted in two cards numbered HA4 and no card with the HA5 number.

	MT
Complete Set (8):	4.00
Common Player:	.25
1HA Juan Gonzalez	1.00
2HA Ken Griffey, Jr.	3.00
3HA Barry Bonds	.75

4HAa	Bobby Bonilla	.25
4HAb	Cecil Fielder	.35
6HA	Albert Belle	.75
7HA	David Justice	.40
8HA	Mike Piazza	1.50

1995 Collector's Choice

Issued in a single series of 530 cards, Upper Deck's base-brand baseball series features a number of subsets within the main body of the issue, as well as several insert sets. Basic cards feature large photos on front and back, with the back having full major league stats. The set opens with a 27-card Rookie Class subset featuring front photos on which the background has been rendered in hot pink tones. Backs have a lime-green box with a scouting report on the player and a box featuring 1994 minor and major league stats. The next 18 cards are Future Foundation cards which have the prospects pictured with a posterized background on front, with backs similar to the posterized background on front, with backs similar to the Rookie Class cards. Career finale cards of five retired superstars follow, then a run of Best of the '90s cards honoring specific record-setting achievements, followed by cards depicting major award winners of the previous season, and taking the place of a card within the regular series. Each of the last three named subsets features borderless color photos on front, with backs similar to the regular cards. Immediately preceding the regular cards, which are arranged in team-set order, is a five-card What's the Call subset featuring cartoon representations of the players. A set of five checklist cards marking career highlights ends the set.

	MT
Complete Set (530):	20.00
Common Player:	.05
Wax Box:	30.00
1 Charles Johnson (Rookie Class)	.15
2 Scott Ruffcorn (Rookie Class)	.05
3 Ray Durham (Rookie Class)	.15
4 Armando Benitez (Rookie Class)	.05

#	Player	Price
5	Alex Rodriguez (Rookie Class)	2.00
6	Julian Tavarez (Rookie Class)	.08
7	Chad Ogea (Rookie Class)	.05
8	Quilvio Veras (Rookie Class)	.10
9	Phil Nevin (Rookie Class)	.05
10	Michael Tucker (Rookie Class)	.10
11	Mark Thompson (Rookie Class)	.05
12	Rod Henderson (Rookie Class)	.05
13	Andrew Lorraine (Rookie Class)	.05
14	Joe Randa (Rookie Class)	.05
15	Derek Jeter (Rookie Class)	1.00
16	Tony Clark (Rookie Class)	.60
17	Juan Castillo (Rookie Class)	.05
18	Mark Acre (Rookie Class)	.05
19	Orlando Miller (Rookie Class)	.05
20	Paul Wilson (Rookie Class)	.15
21	John Mabry (Rookie Class)	.05
22	Garey Ingram (Rookie Class)	.05
23	*Garret Anderson* (Rookie Class)	.15
24	Dave Stevens (Rookie Class)	.05
25	Dustin Hermanson (Rookie Class)	.05
26	Paul Shuey (Rookie Class)	.05
27	J.R. Phillips (Rookie Class)	.05
28	Ruben Rivera (Future Foundation)	.40
29	Nomar Garciaparra (Future Foundation)	1.50
30	John Wasdin (Future Foundation)	.05
31	Jim Pittsley (Future Foundation)	.05
32	*Scott Elarton* (Future Foundation)	.20
33	*Raul Casanova* (Future Foundation)	.40
34	Todd Greene (Future Foundation)	.05
35	Bill Pulsipher (Future Foundation)	.15
36	Trey Beamon (Future Foundation)	.10
37	Curtis Goodwin (Future Foundation)	.05
38	Doug Million (Future Foundation)	.05
39	*Karim Garcia* (Future Foundation)	1.50
40	Ben Grieve (Future Foundation)	1.50
41	Mark Farris (Future Foundation)	.05
42	*Juan Acevedo* (Future Foundation)	.20
43	C.J. Nitkowski (Future Foundation)	.05
44	*Travis Miller* (Future Foundation)	.15
45	Reid Ryan (Future Foundation)	.10
46	Nolan Ryan	1.00
47	Robin Yount	.25
48	Ryne Sandberg	.40
49	George Brett	.60
50	Mike Schmidt	.40
51	Cecil Fielder (Best of the 90's)	.10
52	Nolan Ryan (Best of the 90's)	.60
53	Rickey Henderson (Best of the 90's)	.05
54	George Brett, Robin Yount, Dave Winfield (Best of the 90's)	.25
55	Sid Bream (Best of the 90's)	.05
56	Carlos Baerga (Best of the 90's)	.05
57	Lee Smith (Best of the 90's)	.05
58	Mark Whiten (Best of the 90's)	.05
59	Joe Carter (Best of the 90's)	.10
60	Barry Bonds (Best of the 90's)	.25
61	Tony Gwynn (Best of the 90's)	.35
62	Ken Griffey Jr. (Best of the 90's)	1.00
63	Greg Maddux (Best of the 90's)	.75
64	Frank Thomas (Best of the 90's)	.75
65	Dennis Martinez, Kenny Rogers (Best of the 90's)	.05
66	David Cone (Cy Young)	.10
67	Greg Maddux (Cy Young)	1.50
68	Jimmy Key (Most Victories)	.05
69	Fred McGriff (All-Star MVP)	.25
70	Ken Griffey Jr. (HR Champ)	2.00
71	Matt Williams (HR Champ)	.25
72	Paul O'Neill (Batting Title)	.05
73	Tony Gwynn (Batting Title)	.50
74	Randy Johnson (Ks Leader)	.35
75	Frank Thomas (MVP)	1.50
76	Jeff Bagwell (MVP)	.60
77	Kirby Puckett (RBI leader)	.60
78	Bob Hamelin (ROY)	.05
79	Raul Mondesi (ROY)	.25
80	Mike Piazza (All-Star)	.75
81	Kenny Lofton (SB Leader)	.40
82	Barry Bonds (Gold Glove)	.40
83	Albert Belle (All-Star)	.50
84	Juan Gonzalez (HR Champ)	.50
85	Cal Ripken Jr. (2,000 Straight Games)	2.00
86	Barry Bonds (What's the Call?)	.20
87	Mike Piazza (What's the Call?)	.40
88	Ken Griffey Jr. (What's the Call?)	1.00
89	Frank Thomas (What's the Call?)	.75
90	Juan Gonzalez (What's the Call?)	.30
91	Jorge Fabregas	.05
92	J.T. Snow	.10
93	Spike Owen	.05
94	Eduardo Perez	.05
95	Bo Jackson	.10
96	Damion Easley	.05
97	Gary DiSarcina	.05
98	Jim Edmonds	.15
99	Chad Curtis	.05
100	Tim Salmon	.15
101	Chili Davis	.05
102	Chuck Finley	.05
103	Mark Langston	.05
104	Brian Anderson	.05
105	Lee Smith	.05
106	Phil Leftwich	.05
107	Chris Donnels	.05
108	John Hudek	.05
109	Craig Biggio	.10
110	Luis Gonzalez	.05
111	Brian L. Hunter	.20
112	James Mouton	.05
113	Scott Servais	.05
114	Tony Eusebio	.05
115	Derek Bell	.05
116	Doug Drabek	.05
117	Shane Reynolds	.05
118	Darryl Kile	.05
119	Greg Swindell	.05
120	Phil Plantier	.05
121	Todd Jones	.05
122	Steve Ontiveros	.05
123	Bobby Witt	.05
124	Brent Gates	.05
125	Rickey Henderson	.05
126	Scott Brosius	.05
127	Mike Bordick	.05
128	Fausto Cruz	.05
129	Stan Javier	.05
130	Mark McGwire	2.00
131	Geronimo Berroa	.05
132	Terry Steinbach	.05
133	Steve Karsay	.05
134	Dennis Eckersley	.05
135	Ruben Sierra	.05
136	Ron Darling	.05
137	Todd Van Poppel	.05
138	Alex Gonzalez	.10
139	John Olerud	.10
140	Roberto Alomar	.50
141	Darren Hall	.05
142	Ed Sprague	.05
143	Devon White	.05
144	Shawn Green	.10
145	Paul Molitor	.25
146	Pat Borders	.05
147	Carlos Delgado	.15
148	Juan Guzman	.05
149	Pat Hentgen	.05
150	Joe Carter	.15
151	Dave Stewart	.05
152	Todd Stottlemyre	.05
153	Dick Schofield	.05
154	Chipper Jones	1.00
155	Ryan Klesko	.50
156	Dave Justice	.25
157	Mike Kelly	.05
158	Roberto Kelly	.05
159	Tony Tarasco	.05
160	Javier Lopez	.10
161	Steve Avery	.05
162	Greg McMichael	.05
163	Kent Mercker	.05
164	Mark Lemke	.05
165	Tom Glavine	.15
166	Jose Oliva	.05
167	John Smoltz	.15
168	Jeff Blauser	.05
169	Troy O'Leary	.05
170	Greg Vaughn	.05
171	Jody Reed	.05
172	Kevin Seitzer	.05
173	Jeff Cirillo	.05
174	B.J. Surhoff	.05
175	Cal Eldred	.05
176	Jose Valentin	.05
177	Turner Ward	.05
178	Darryl Hamilton	.05
179	Pat Listach	.05
180	Matt Mieske	.05
181	Brian Harper	.05
182	Dave Nilsson	.05
183	Mike Fetters	.05
184	John Jaha	.05
185	Ricky Bones	.05
186	Geronimo Pena	.05
187	Bob Tewksbury	.05
188	Todd Zeile	.05
189	Danny Jackson	.05
190	Ray Lankford	.05
191	Bernard Gilkey	.05
192	Brian Jordan	.05
193	Tom Pagnozzi	.05
194	Rick Sutcliffe	.05
195	Mark Whiten	.05
196	Tom Henke	.05
197	Rene Arocha	.05
198	Allen Watson	.05
199	Mike Perez	.05
200	Ozzie Smith	.25
201	Anthony Young	.05
202	Rey Sanchez	.05
203	Steve Buechele	.05
204	Shawon Dunston	.05
205	Mark Grace	.10
206	Glenallen Hill	.05
207	Eddie Zambrano	.05
208	Rick Wilkins	.05
209	Derrick May	.05
210	Sammy Sosa	.75
211	Kevin Roberson	.05
212	Steve Trachsel	.05
213	Willie Banks	.05
214	Kevin Foster	.05
215	Randy Myers	.05
216	Mike Morgan	.05
217	Rafael Bournigal	.05
218	Delino DeShields	.05
219	Tim Wallach	.05
220	Eric Karros	.10
221	Jose Offerman	.05
222	Tom Candiotti	.05
223	Ismael Valdes	.10
224	Henry Rodriguez	.05
225	Billy Ashley	.15
226	Darren Dreifort	.05
227	Ramon Martinez	.10
228	Pedro Astacio	.05
229	Orel Hershiser	.05
230	Brett Butler	.05
231	Todd Hollandsworth	.10
232	Chan Ho Park	.10
233	Mike Lansing	.05
234	Sean Berry	.05
235	Rondell White	.15
236	Ken Hill	.05
237	Marquis Grissom	.05
238	Larry Walker	.20
239	John Wetteland	.05
240	Cliff Floyd	.10
241	Joey Eischen	.05
242	Lou Frazier	.05
243	Darrin Fletcher	.05

#	Name	Price
244	Pedro J. Martinez	.15
245	Wil Cordero	.05
246	Jeff Fassero	.05
247	Butch Henry	.05
248	Mel Rojas	.05
249	Kirk Rueter	.10
250	Moises Alou	.05
251	Rod Beck	.05
252	John Patterson	.05
253	Robby Thompson	.05
254	Royce Clayton	.08
255	William Van Landingham	.05
256	Darren Lewis	.05
257	Kirt Manwaring	.05
258	Mark Portugal	.05
259	Bill Swift	.05
260	Rikkert Faneyte	.05
261	Mike Jackson	.05
262	Todd Benzinger	.05
263	Bud Black	.05
264	Salomon Torres	.25
265	Eddie Murray	.05
266	Mark Clark	.05
267	Paul Sorrento	.30
268	Jim Thome	.05
269	Omar Vizquel	.05
270	Carlos Baerga	.05
271	Jeff Russell	.05
272	Herbert Perry	.05
273	Sandy Alomar Jr.	.05
274	Dennis Martinez	.50
275	Manny Ramirez	.05
276	Wayne Kirby	.05
277	Charles Nagy	.05
278	Albie Lopez	.05
279	Jeromy Burnitz	.08
280	Dave Winfield	.08
281	Tim Davis	.08
282	Marc Newfield	.20
283	Tino Martinez	.05
284	Mike Blowers	.05
285	Goose Gossage	.05
286	Luis Sojo	.05
287	Edgar Martinez	.05
288	Rich Amaral	.05
289	Felix Fermin	.10
290	Jay Buhner	.05
291	Dan Wilson	.05
292	Bobby Ayala	.05
293	Dave Fleming	.05
294	Greg Pirkl	.05
295	Reggie Jefferson	.05
296	Greg Hibbard	.05
297	Yorkis Perez	.05
298	Kurt Miller	.05
299	Chuck Carr	.05
300	Gary Sheffield	.20
301	Jerry Browne	.05
302	Dave Magadan	.05
303	Kurt Abbott	.05
304	Pat Rapp	.05
305	Jeff Conine	.05
306	Benito Santiago	.05
307	Dave Weathers	.05
308	Robb Nen	.05
309	Chris Hammond	.05
310	Bryan Harvey	.05
311	Charlie Hough	.05
312	Greg Colbrunn	.05
313	David Segui	.05
314	Rico Brogna	.05
315	Jeff Kent	.05
316	Jose Vizcaino	.05
317	Jim Lindeman	.05
318	Carl Everett	.05
319	Ryan Thompson	.10
320	Bobby Bonilla	.05
321	Joe Orsulak	.05
322	Pete Harnisch	.05
323	Doug Linton	.15
324	Todd Hundley	.05
325	Bret Saberhagen	.05
326	Kelly Stinnett	.08
327	Jason Jacome	.05
328	Bobby Jones	.05
329	John Franco	.10
330	Rafael Palmeiro	.05
331	Chris Hoiles	.05
332	Leo Gomez	.05
333	Chris Sabo	.10
334	Brady Anderson	.10
335	Jeffrey Hammonds	.05
336	Dwight Smith	.05
337	Jack Voigt	.05
338	Harold Baines	.05
339	Ben McDonald	.05
340	Mike Mussina	.30
341	Bret Barberie	.05
342	Jamie Moyer	.05
343	Mike Oquist	.05
344	Sid Fernandez	.05
345	Eddie Williams	.05
346	Joey Hamilton	.05
347	Brian Williams	.05
348	Luis Lopez	.05
349	Steve Finley	.10
350	Andy Benes	.05
351	Andujar Cedeno	.05
352	Bip Roberts	.05
353	Ray McDavid	.05
354	Ken Caminiti	.15
355	Trevor Hoffman	.05
356	Mel Nieves	.05
357	Brad Ausmus	.05
358	Andy Ashby	.05
359	Scott Sanders	.05
360	Gregg Jefferies	.05
361	Mariano Duncan	.05
362	Dave Hollins	.05
363	Kevin Stocker	.05
364	Fernando Valenzuela	.05
365	Lenny Dykstra	.05
366	Jim Eisenreich	.05
367	Ricky Bottalico	.05
368	Doug Jones	.05
369	Ricky Jordan	.05
370	Darren Daulton	.05
371	Mike Lieberthal	.05
372	Bobby Munoz	.05
373	John Kruk	.05
374	Curt Schilling	.05
375	Orlando Merced	.05
376	Carlos Garcia	.05
377	Lance Parrish	.05
378	Steve Cooke	.05
379	Jeff King	.05
380	Jay Bell	.05
381	Al Martin	.05
382	Paul Wagner	.05
383	Rick White	.05
384	Midre Cummings	.05
385	Jon Lieber	.05
386	Dave Clark	.05
387	Don Slaught	.05
388	Denny Neagle	.05
389	Zane Smith	.05
390	Andy Van Slyke	.40
391	Ivan Rodriguez	.05
392	David Hulse	.05
393	John Burkett	.05
394	Kevin Brown	.05
395	Dean Palmer	.05
396	Otis Nixon	.05
397	Rick Helling	.05
398	Kenny Rogers	.05
399	Darren Oliver	.05
400	Will Clark	.25
401	Jeff Frye	.05
402	Kevin Gross	.05
403	John Dettmer	.05
404	Manny Lee	.05
405	Rusty Greer	.10
406	Aaron Sele	.05
407	Carlos Rodriguez	.05
408	Scott Cooper	.05
409	John Valentin	.50
410	Roger Clemens	.05
411	Mike Greenwell	.05
412	Tim Vanegmond	.05
413	Tom Brunansky	.05
414	Steve Farr	.30
415	Jose Canseco	.05
416	Joe Hesketh	.05
417	Ken Ryan	.05
418	Tim Naehring	.05
419	Frank Viola	.08
420	Andre Dawson	.50
421	Mo Vaughn	.05
422	Jeff Brantley	.05
423	Pete Schourek	.05
424	Hal Morris	.30
425	Deion Sanders	.15
426	Brian L. Hunter	.05
427	Bret Boone	.05
428	Willie Greene	.05
429	Ron Gant	.10
430	Barry Larkin	.10
431	Reggie Sanders	.05
432	Eddie Taubensee	.05
433	Jack Morris	.05
434	Jose Rijo	.05
435	Johnny Ruffin	.05
436	John Smiley	.05
437	John Roper	.05
438	David Nied	.05
439	Roberto Mejia	.05
440	Andres Galarraga	.10
441	Mike Kingery	.05
442	Curt Leskanic	.05
443	Walt Weiss	.05
444	Marvin Freeman	.05
445	Charlie Hayes	.05
446	Eric Young	.05
447	Ellis Burks	.05
448	Joe Girardi	.05
449	Lance Painter	.05
450	Dante Bichette	.10
451	Bruce Ruffin	.05
452	Jeff Granger	.05
453	Wally Joyner	.05
454	Jose Lind	.05
455	Jeff Montgomery	.05
456	Gary Gaetti	.05
457	Greg Gagne	.05
458	Vince Coleman	.05
459	Mike Macfarlane	.05
460	Brian McRae	.05
461	Tom Gordon	.05
462	Kevin Appier	.05
463	Billy Brewer	.05
464	Mark Gubicza	.05
465	Travis Fryman	.10
466	Danny Bautista	.05
467	Sean Bergman	.05
468	Mike Henneman	.05
469	Mike Moore	.05
470	Cecil Fielder	.20
471	Alan Trammell	.05
472	Kirk Gibson	.05
473	Tony Phillips	.05
474	Mickey Tettleton	.05
475	Lou Whitaker	.05
476	Chris Gomez	.05
477	John Doherty	.05
478	Greg Gohr	.05
479	Bill Gullickson	.05
480	Rick Aguilera	.05
481	Matt Walbeck	.05
482	Kevin Tapani	.05
483	Scott Erickson	.05
484	Steve Dunn	.05
485	David McCarty	.05
486	Scott Leius	.05
487	Pat Meares	.05
488	Jeff Reboulet	.05
489	Pedro Munoz	.05
490	Chuck Knoblauch	.10
491	Rich Becker	.05
492	Alex Cole	.05
493	Pat Mahomes	.05
494	Ozzie Guillen	.05
495	Tim Raines	.05
496	Kirk McCaskill	.05
497	Olmedo Saenz	.05
498	Scott Sanderson	.05
499	Lance Johnson	.05
500	Michael Jordan	2.50
501	Warren Newson	.05
502	Ron Karkovice	.05
503	Wilson Alvarez	.05
504	Jason Bere	.05
505	Robin Ventura	.05
506	Alex Fernandez	.05
507	Roberto Hernandez	.05
508	Norberto Martin	.05
509	Bob Wickman	.05
510	Don Mattingly	.75
511	Melido Perez	.05
512	Pat Kelly	.05
513	Randy Velarde	.05
514	Tony Fernandez	.05
515	Jack McDowell	.10
516	Luis Polonia	.05
517	Bernie Williams	.35
518	Danny Tartabull	.05
519	Mike Stanley	.05
520	Wade Boggs	.25
521	Jim Leyritz	.05
522	Steve Howe	.05
523	Scott Kamienecki	.05
524	Russ Davis	.05
525	Jim Abbott	.05
526	Checklist 1-106(Eddie Murray)	.10
527	Checklist 107-212(Alex Rodriguez)	.40
528	Checklist 213-318(Jeff Bagwell)	.15
529	Checklist 319-424(Joe Carter)	.05
530	Checklist 425-530(Fred McGriff)	.10
---	National Packtime offer card	.05

1995 Collector's Choice Silver Signature

A silver-foil facsimile autograph added to the card front is the only difference between these chase cards and regular-issue Collector's Choice cards. The silver-signature inserts are found one per pack in regular foil packs, and two per pack in retail jumbo packs.

	MT
Complete Set (530):	50.00
Common Player:	.10
Yng Stars & RC's: 1x to 2x	
(Star cards valued 1.5X-3X corresponding cards in regular-issue Collectors Choice)	

1995 Collector's Choice Gold Signature

The top-of-the-line chase card in 1995 Collectors Choice is the Gold Signature parallel set. Each card in the 530-card set was created in a special gold version that was found on average only one per box of foil packs. Other than the addition of a gold-foil facsimile autograph on front, the cards are identical to regular-issue Collectors Choice.

	MT
Complete Set (530):	800.00
Common Player:	2.00
Yng Stars & RC's: 4x to 8x	
(Star cards valued at 8X-15X same cards in regular Collectors Choice edition)	

1995 Collector's Choice Trade Cards

A series of five mail-in redemption cards was included as inserts into UD Collector's Choice, at the rate of approximately one per 11 packs. The cards could be sent in with $2 to receive 11 Collector's Choice Update cards, as specified on the front of the card. The trade offer expired on Feb. 1, 1996.

		MT
Complete Set (5):		2.50
Common Player:		.50
TC1	Larry Walker (#531-541)	.75
TC2	David Cone (#542-552)	.50
TC3	Marquis Grissom (#553-563)	.50
TC4	Terry Pendleton (#564-574)	.50
TC5	Fernando Valenzuela (#575-585)	.50

1995 Collector's Choice Redemption Cards

These update cards were available only via a mail-in offer involving trade cards found in foil packs. Each trade card was redeemable for a specific 11-card set of players shown in their new uniforms as a result of rookie call-ups, trades and free agent signings. The cards are in the same format as the regular 1995 Collector's Choice issue. The update redemption cards are numbered by team nickname from Angels through Yankees, the numbers running contiguously from the body of the CC set.

		MT
Complete Set (55):		12.00
Common Player:		.25
531	Tony Phillips	.35
532	Dave Magadan	.25
533	Mike Gallego	.25
534	Dave Stewart	.35
535	Todd Stottlemyre	.35
536	David Cone	.90
537	Marquis Grissom	.90
538	Derrick May	.25
539	Joe Oliver	.25
540	Scott Cooper	.25
541	Ken Hill	.25
542	Howard Johnson	.25
543	Brian McRae	.35
544	Jaime Navarro	.25
545	Ozzie Timmons	.25
546	Roberto Kelly	.30
547	Hideo Nomo	4.00
548	Shane Andrews	.60
549	Mark Grudzielanek	.30
550	Carlos Perez	.30
551	Henry Rodriguez	.40
552	Tony Tarasco	.25
553	Glenallen Hill	.30
554	Terry Mulholland	.25
555	Orel Hershiser	.90
556	Darren Bragg	.25
557	John Burkett	.25
558	Bobby Witt	.25
559	Terry Pendleton	.30
560	Andre Dawson	.50
561	Brett Butler	.45
562	Kevin Brown	.75
563	Doug Jones	.25
564	Andy Van Slyke	.25
565	Jody Reed	.25
566	Fernando Valenzuela	.35
567	Charlie Hayes	.25
568	Benji Gil	.25
569	Mark McLemore	.25
570	Mickey Tettleton	.25
571	Bob Tewksbury	.25
572	Rheal Cormier	.25
573	Vaughn Eshelman	.30
574	Mike Macfarlane	.25
575	Mark Whiten	.25
576	Benito Santiago	.35
577	Jason Bates	.25
578	Bill Swift	.25
579	Larry Walker	.60
580	Chad Curtis	.35
581	Bobby Higginson	.35
582	Marty Cordova	1.00
583	Mike Devereaux	.25
584	John Kruk	.25
585	John Wetteland	.25

1995 Collector's Choice "You Crash the Game"

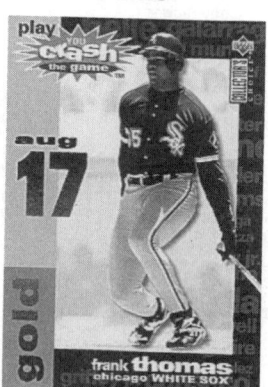

These insert cards gave collectors a reason to follow box scores around the major leagues between June 18-Oct. 1. Each of the 20 noted home run hitters can be found with three different dates foilstamped on the card front. If the player hit a home run on that day, the card could be redeemed for a set of 20 special prize cards. Stated odds of finding a You Crash the Game card were one in five packs.

Most of the inserts are silver-foil enhanced, with about one in eight being found with gold foil. Winning cards are much scarcer than the others since they had to be mailed in for redemption.

		MT
Complete Set, Silver (20):		7.00
Common Player, Silver:		.25
Complete Set, Gold (20):		18.00
Common Player, Gold:		.50
	Silver Set	7.00
CG1	Jeff Bagwell (July 30)	.25
CG1	Jeff Bagwell (Aug. 13)	.25
CG1	Jeff Bagwell (Sept. 28)	.25
CG2	Albert Belle (June 18)	.40
CG2	Albert Belle (Aug. 26)	.40
CG2	Albert Belle (Sept. 20)	.40
CG3	Barry Bonds (June 28)	.50
CG3	Barry Bonds (July 9)	.50
CG3	Barry Bonds (Sept. 6)	.50
CG4	Jose Canseco (June 30)(winner)	2.00
CG4	Jose Canseco (July 30)(winner)	2.00
CG4	Jose Canseco (Sept. 3)	.50
CG5	Joe Carter (July 14)	.25
CG5	Joe Carter (Aug. 9)	.25
CG5	Joe Carter (Sept. 23)	.25
CG6	Cecil Fielder (July 4)	.25
CG6	Cecil Fielder (Aug. 2)	.25
CG6	Cecil Fielder (Oct. 1)	.25
CG7	Juan Gonzalez (June 29)	.60
CG7	Juan Gonzalez (Aug. 13)	.60
CG7	Juan Gonzalez (Sept. 3)(winner)	3.00
CG8	Ken Griffey Jr. (July 2)	1.00
CG8	Ken Griffey Jr. (Aug. 24)(winner)	5.00
CG8	Ken Griffey Jr. (Sept. 15)	1.00
CG9	Bob Hamelin (July 23)	.25
CG9	Bob Hamelin (Aug. 1)	.25
CG9	Bob Hamelin (Sept. 29)	.25
CG10	David Justice (June 24)	.25
CG10	David Justice (July 25)	.25
CG10	David Justice (Sept. 17)	.25
CG11	Ryan Klesko (July 13)	.25
CG11	Ryan Klesko (Aug. 20)	.25
CG11	Ryan Klesko (Sept. 10)	.25
CG12	Fred McGriff (Aug. 25)	.25
CG12	Fred McGriff (Sept. 8)	.25
CG12	Fred McGriff (Sept. 24)	.25
CG13	Mark McGwire (July 23)	1.00
CG13	Mark McGwire (Aug. 3)(winner)	3.50
CG13	Mark McGwire (Sept. 27)	1.00
CG14	Raul Mondesi (July 27)(winner)	2.00
CG14	Raul Mondesi (Aug. 13)	.40
CG14	Raul Mondesi (Sept. 15)(winner)	2.00
CG15	Mike Piazza (July 23)(winner)	3.00
CG15	Mike Piazza (Aug. 27)(winner)	3.00
CG15	Mike Piazza (Sept. 19)	.65
CG16	Manny Ramirez (June 21)	.25
CG16	Manny Ramirez (Aug. 13)	.25
CG16	Manny Ramirez (Sept. 26)	.25
CG17	Alex Rodriguez (Sept. 10)	.50
CG17	Alex Rodriguez (Sept. 18)	.50
CG17	Alex Rodriguez (Sept. 24)	.50
CG18	Gary Sheffield (July 5)	.25
CG18	Gary Sheffield (Aug. 13)	.25
CG18	Gary Sheffield (Sept. 4)(winner)	2.00
CG19	Frank Thomas (July 26)	.75
CG19	Frank Thomas (Aug. 17)	.75
CG19	Frank Thomas (Sept. 23)	.75
CG20	Matt Williams (July 29)	.25
CG20	Matt Williams (Aug. 12)	.25
CG20	Matt Williams (Sept. 19)	.25
	Gold Set	18.00
CG1	Jeff Bagwell (July 30)	1.00
CG1	Jeff Bagwell (Aug. 13)	1.00
CG1	Jeff Bagwell (Sept. 28)	1.00
CG2	Albert Belle (June 18)	1.25
CG2	Albert Belle (Aug. 26)	1.25
CG2	Albert Belle (Sept. 20)	1.25
CG3	Barry Bonds (June 28)	1.50
CG3	Barry Bonds (July 9)	1.50
CG3	Barry Bonds (Sept. 6)	1.50
CG4	Jose Canseco (June 30)(winner)	3.00

CG4	Jose Canseco (July 30)(winner)	3.00
CG4	Jose Canseco (Sept. 3)	1.25
CG5	Joe Carter (July 14)	.75
CG5	Joe Carter (Aug. 9)	.75
CG5	Joe Carter (Sept. 23)	.75
CG6	Cecil Fielder (July 4)	.75
CG6	Cecil Fielder (Aug. 2)	.75
CG6	Cecil Fielder (Oct. 1)	.75
CG7	Juan Gonzalez (June 29)	1.50
CG7	Juan Gonzalez (Aug. 13)	1.50
CG7	Juan Gonzalez (Sept. 3)(winner)	4.00
CG8	Ken Griffey Jr. (July 2)	3.00
CG8	Ken Griffey Jr. (Aug. 24)(winner)	6.00
CG8	Ken Griffey Jr. (Sept. 15)	3.00
CG9	Bob Hamelin (July 23)	.50
CG9	Bob Hamelin (Aug. 1)	.50
CG9	Bob Hamelin (Sept. 29)	.50
CG10	David Justice (June 24)	.75
CG10	David Justice (July 25)	.75
CG10	David Justice (Sept. 17)	.75
CG11	Ryan Klesko (July 13)	.75
CG11	Ryan Klesko (Aug. 20)	.75
CG11	Ryan Klesko (Sept. 10)	.75
CG12	Fred McGriff (Aug. 25)	.75
CG12	Fred McGriff (Sept. 8)	.75
CG12	Fred McGriff (Sept. 24)	.75
CG13	Mark McGwire (July 23)	2.00
CG13	Mark McGwire (Aug. 3)(winner)	6.00
CG13	Mark McGwire (Sept. 27)	2.00
CG14	Raul Mondesi (July 27)(winner)	2.50
CG14	Raul Mondesi (Aug. 13)	.90
CG14	Raul Mondesi (Sept. 15)(winner)	2.50
CG15	Mike Piazza (July 23)(winner)	4.00
CG15	Mike Piazza (Aug. 27)(winner)	4.00
CG15	Mike Piazza (Sept. 19)	1.25
CG16	Manny Ramirez (June 21)	.75
CG16	Manny Ramirez (Aug. 13)	.75
CG16	Manny Ramirez (Sept. 26)	.75
CG17	Alex Rodriguez (Sept. 10)	1.25
CG17	Alex Rodriguez (Sept. 18)	1.25
CG17	Alex Rodriguez (Sept. 24)	1.25
CG18	Gary Sheffield (July 5)	.75
CG18	Gary Sheffield (Aug. 13)	.75
CG18	Gary Sheffield (Sept. 4)(winner)	2.50
CG19	Frank Thomas (July 26)	2.50
CG19	Frank Thomas (Aug. 17)	2.50
CG19	Frank Thomas (Sept. 23)	2.50
CG20	Matt Williams (July 29)	1.00
CG20	Matt Williams (Aug. 12)	1.00
CG20	Matt Williams (Sept. 19)	1.00

1995 Collector's Choice "Crash" Winners

These 20-card sets were awarded to collectors who redeemed "You Crash the Game" winners cards. A silver-foil enhanced set was sent to winners with silver redemption cards, a gold version was sent to gold winners. A $3 redemption fee was required. Fronts are similar to the game cards, except for the foil printing down the left side in the place of the game date. Instead of redemption rules on the back of award cards there are career highlights at left and a silver panel at right with the names of the players in the set.

		MT
Complete Set, Silver (20):		12.00
Complete Set, Gold (20):		45.00
Common Player, Silver:		.50
Common Player, Gold:		2.00
	SILVER SET	
CR1	Jeff Bagwell	1.50
CR2	Albert Belle	1.50
CR3	Barry Bonds	1.50
CR4	Jose Canseco	1.50
CR5	Joe Carter	1.00
CR6	Cecil Fielder	1.00
CR7	Juan Gonzalez	2.00
CR8	Ken Griffey Jr.	6.00
CR9	Bob Hamelin	.50
CR10	Dave Justice	1.50
CR11	Ryan Klesko	1.50
CR12	Fred McGriff	1.50
CR13	Mark McGwire	4.00
CR14	Raul Mondesi	1.00
CR15	Mike Piazza	3.00
CR16	Manny Ramirez	1.00
CR17	Alex Rodriguez	1.50
CR18	Gary Sheffield	1.00
CR19	Frank Thomas	5.00
CR20	Matt Williams	1.00
	GOLD SET	
CR1	Jeff Bagwell	5.00
CR2	Albert Belle	5.00
CR3	Barry Bonds	5.00
CR4	Jose Canseco	4.00
CR5	Joe Carter	3.00
CR6	Cecil Fielder	3.00
CR7	Juan Gonzalez	7.50
CR8	Ken Griffey Jr.	15.00
CR9	Bob Hamelin	2.00
CR10	Dave Justice	5.00
CR11	Ryan Klesko	5.00
CR12	Fred McGriff	5.00
CR13	Mark McGwire	10.00
CR14	Raul Mondesi	3.00
CR15	Mike Piazza	7.50
CR16	Manny Ramirez	4.00
CR17	Alex Rodriguez	5.00
CR18	Gary Sheffield	4.00
CR19	Frank Thomas	10.00
CR20	Matt Williams	4.00

1995 Collector's Choice/SE

The first Upper Deck baseball card issue for 1995 was this 265-card issue which uses blue borders and a blue foil "Special Edition" trapezoidal logo to impart a premium look. The set opens with a Rookie Class subset of 25 cards on which the background has been rendered in orange hues. A series of six Record Pace cards, horizontal with blue and yellow backgrounds, immediately precedes the regular cards. Base cards in the set are arranged in team-alpha order. Front and back have large color photos, while backs offer complete major league stats. Interspersed within the teams are special cards with borderless front designs honoring players who won significant awards in the 1994 season. In the middle of the set is another subset, Stat Leaders, which pictures various players in a silver dollar-sized circle at the center of the card and lists the 1994 leaders in that category on the back. A dozen-card Fantasy Team subset near the end of the set lists on back the top-rated players at each position, picturing one of them on front, with a giant blue baseball. The set closes with five checklists honoring career highlights from the '94 season.

		MT
Complete Set (265):		20.00
Common Player:		.05
Wax Box:		35.00
1	Alex Rodriguez	3.00
2	Derek Jeter	1.50
3	Dustin Hermanson	.15
4	Bill Pulsipher	.15
5	Terrell Wade	.05
6	Darren Dreifort	.05
7	LaTroy Hawkins	.15
8	Alex Ochoa	.10
9	Paul Wilson	.25
10	Ernie Young	.10
11	Alan Benes	.25
12	Garret Anderson	.15
13	Armando Benitez	.15
14	Robert Perez	.05
15	Herbert Perry	.05
16	Jose Silva	.05
17	Orlando Miller	.10
18	Russ Davis	.10
19	Jason Isringhausen	.25
20	Ray McDavid	.05
21	Duane Singleton	.05
22	Paul Shuey	.05
23	Steve Dunn	.05
24	Mike Lieberthal	.05
25	Chan Ho Park	.10
26	Ken Griffey Jr. (Record Pace)	1.00
27	Tony Gwynn (Record Pace)	.35
28	Chuck Knoblauch (Record Pace)	.10
29	Frank Thomas (Record Pace)	1.00
30	Matt Williams (Record Pace)	.10
31	Chili Davis	.05
32	Chad Curtis	.05
33	Brian Anderson	.05
34	Chuck Finley	.05
35	Tim Salmon	.25
36	Bo Jackson	.10
37	Doug Drabek	.05
38	Craig Biggio	.10
39	Ken Caminiti	.20
40	Jeff Bagwell	1.00
41	Darryl Kile	.05
42	John Hudek	.05
43	Brian L. Hunter	.10
44	Dennis Eckersley	.10
45	Mark McGwire	3.00
46	Brent Gates	.05
47	Steve Karsay	.05
48	Rickey Henderson	.10
49	Terry Steinbach	.05
50	Ruben Sierra	.05
51	Roberto Alomar	.60

52	Carlos Delgado	.15
53	Alex Gonzalez	.10
54	Joe Carter	.20
55	Paul Molitor	.25
56	Juan Guzman	.05
57	John Olerud	.10
58	Shawn Green	.05
59	Tom Glavine	.15
60	Greg Maddux	2.00
61	Roberto Kelly	.05
62	Ryan Klesko	.50
63	Javier Lopez	.15
64	Jose Oliva	.05
65	Fred McGriff	.25
66	Steve Avery	.05
67	Dave Justice	.15
68	Ricky Bones	.05
69	Cal Eldred	.05
70	Greg Vaughn	.10
71	Dave Nilsson	.05
72	Jose Valentin	.05
73	Matt Mieske	.05
74	Todd Zeile	.05
75	Ozzie Smith	.40
76	Bernard Gilkey	.05
77	Ray Lankford	.10
78	Bob Tewksbury	.05
79	Mark Whiten	.05
80	Gregg Jefferies	.05
81	Randy Myers	.05
82	Shawon Dunston	.10
83	Mark Grace	.15
84	Derrick May	.05
85	Sammy Sosa	.75
86	Steve Trachsel	.05
87	Brett Butler	.08
88	Delino DeShields	.05
89	Orel Hershiser	.10
90	Mike Piazza	1.50
91	Todd Hollandsworth	.15
92	Eric Karros	.10
93	Ramon Martinez	.10
94	Tim Wallach	.05
95	Raul Mondesi	.25
96	Larry Walker	.25
97	Wil Cordero	.05
98	Marquis Grissom	.05
99	Ken Hill	.05
100	Cliff Floyd	.10
101	Pedro J. Martinez	.15
102	John Wetteland	.05
103	Rondell White	.15
104	Moises Alou	.10
105	Barry Bonds	.75
106	Darren Lewis	.05
107	Mark Portugal	.05
108	Matt Williams	.25
109	William VanLandingham	.08
110	Bill Swift	.05
111	Robby Thompson	.05
112	Rod Beck	.05
113	Darryl Strawberry	.10
114	Jim Thome	.40
115	Dave Winfield	.10
116	Eddie Murray	.35
117	Manny Ramirez	.50
118	Carlos Baerga	.05
119	Kenny Lofton	.50
120	Albert Belle	.60
121	Mark Clark	.05
122	Dennis Martinez	.05
123	Randy Johnson	.40
124	Jay Buhner	.20
125	Ken Griffey Jr.	3.00
125a	Ken Griffey Jr. (overprinted "For Promotional Use Only")	3.00
126	Rich Gossage	.05
127	Tino Martinez	.20
128	Reggie Jefferson	.05
129	Edgar Martinez	.05
130	Gary Sheffield	.20
131	Pat Rapp	.05
132	Bret Barberie	.05
133	Chuck Carr	.05
134	Jeff Conine	.05
135	Charles Johnson	.15
136	Benito Santiago	.05
137	Matt Williams (Stat Leaders)	.15
138	Jeff Bagwell (Stat Leaders)	.35
139	Kenny Lofton (Stat Leaders)	.25
140	Tony Gwynn (Stat Leaders)	.35
141	Jimmy Key (Stat Leaders)	.05
142	Greg Maddux (Stat Leaders)	.60
143	Randy Johnson (Stat Leaders)	.20

144	Lee Smith (Stat Leaders)	.05
145	Bobby Bonilla	.05
146	Jason Jacome	.05
147	Jeff Kent	.05
148	Ryan Thompson	.05
149	Bobby Jones	.05
150	Bret Saberhagen	.05
151	John Franco	.05
152	Lee Smith	.05
153	Rafael Palmeiro	.15
154	Brady Anderson	.10
155	Cal Ripken Jr.	2.50
156	Jeffrey Hammonds	.10
157	Mike Mussina	.40
158	Chris Hoiles	.05
159	Ben McDonald	.05
160	Tony Gwynn	1.00
161	Joey Hamilton	.10
162	Andy Benes	.05
163	Trevor Hoffman	.05
164	Phil Plantier	.05
165	Derek Bell	.05
166	Bip Roberts	.05
167	Eddie Williams	.05
168	Fernando Valenzuela	.05
169	Mariano Duncan	.05
170	Lenny Dykstra	.05
171	Darren Daulton	.05
172	Danny Jackson	.05
173	Bobby Munoz	.05
174	Doug Jones	.05
175	Jay Bell	.05
176	Zane Smith	.05
177	Jon Lieber	.05
178	Carlos Garcia	.05
179	Orlando Merced	.05
180	Andy Van Slyke	.05
181	Rick Helling	.05
182	Rusty Greer	.05
183	Kenny Rogers	.05
184	Will Clark	.25
185	Jose Canseco	.30
186	Juan Gonzalez	1.00
187	Dean Palmer	.05
188	Ivan Rodriguez	.50
189	John Valentin	.10
190	Roger Clemens	1.00
191	Aaron Sele	.05
192	Scott Cooper	.05
193	Mike Greenwell	.05
194	Mo Vaughn	.75
195	Andre Dawson	.10
196	Ron Gant	.10
197	Jose Rijo	.05
198	Bret Boone	.05
199	Deion Sanders	.20
200	Barry Larkin	.20
201	Hal Morris	.05
202	Reggie Sanders	.05
203	Kevin Mitchell	.05
204	Marvin Freeman	.05
205	Andres Galarraga	.15
206	Walt Weiss	.05
207	Charlie Hayes	.05
208	David Nied	.05
209	Dante Bichette	.15
210	David Cone	.10
211	Jeff Montgomery	.05
212	Felix Jose	.05
213	Mike Macfarlane	.05
214	Wally Joyner	.05
215	Bob Hamelin	.05
216	Brian McRae	.05
217	Kirk Gibson	.05
218	Lou Whitaker	.05
219	Chris Gomez	.05
220	Cecil Fielder	.15
221	Mickey Tettleton	.05
222	Travis Fryman	.10
223	Tony Phillips	.05
224	Rick Aguilera	.05
225	Scott Erickson	.05
226	Chuck Knoblauch	.15
227	Kent Hrbek	.05
228	Shane Mack	.05
229	Kevin Tapani	.05
230	Kirby Puckett	1.00
231	Julio Franco	.05
232	Jack McDowell	.10
233	Jason Bere	.05
234	Alex Fernandez	.05
235	Frank Thomas	2.50
236	Ozzie Guillen	.05
237	Robin Ventura	.05
238	Michael Jordan	3.50
239	Wilson Alvarez	.05

240	Don Mattingly	.75
241	Jim Abbott	.05
242	Jim Leyritz	.05
243	Paul O'Neill	.05
244	Melido Perez	.05
245	Wade Boggs	.25
246	Mike Stanley	.05
247	Danny Tartabull	.05
248	Jimmy Key	.05
249	Greg Maddux (Fantasy Team)	.60
250	Randy Johnson (Fantasy Team)	.20
251	Bret Saberhagen (Fantasy Team)	.05
252	John Wetteland (Fantasy Team)	.05
253	Mike Piazza (Fantasy Team)	.50
254	Jeff Bagwell (Fantasy Team)	.30
255	Craig Biggio (Fantasy Team)	.05
256	Matt Williams (Fantasy Team)	.10
257	Wil Cordero (Fantasy Team)	.05
258	Kenny Lofton (Fantasy Team)	.25
259	Barry Bonds (Fantasy Team)	.30
260	Dante Bichette (Fantasy Team)	.10
261	Checklist 1-53	.05
262	Checklist 54-106	.05
263	Checklist 107-159	.05
264	Checklist 160-212	.05
265	Checklist 213-265	.05

1995 Collector's Choice/SE Silver

The cards in this parallel edition feature the addition of a silver-foil facsimile autograph on the card front. Also, the blue SE logo and card borders have been replaced with silver on the chase cards, which are found on average of one per pack.

	MT
Complete Set (265):	50.00
Common Player:	.15

Yng Stars & RC's: 1x to 2x
(Star cards valued at 2X-3X corresponding cards in regular Collectors Choice SE)

1995 Collector's Choice/SE Gold

Each of the cards in the CCSE issue can be found in a premium chase card version which replaces

the blue border and SE logo with gold, and adds a gold-foil facsimile autograph to the front of the card. The gold-version SE inserts are found on average of one per 36 packs.

	MT
Complete Set (265):	1200.
Common Player:	2.00

Yng Stars & RC's: 8x to 12x
(Star cards valued at 8X-20X same cards in regular Collectors Choice SE edition)

1996 Collector's Choice

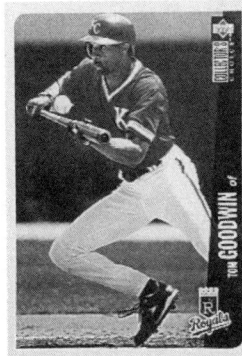

The third year for Collector's Choice includes 730 cards in two series with packs formatted in retail and hobby versions. The 280 regular player cards are joined by subsets of Rookie Class, International Flavor, Traditional Threads, Fantasy Team, Stat Leaders, Season Highlights, First Class, Arizona Fall League, Awards and Checklists. Packs feature a number of different insert sets including silver and gold signature parallel sets, interactive "You Make the Play" cards, four cards from the cross-brand Cal Ripken Collection and three postseason trade cards redeemable for 10-card sets recalling the League Championships and World Series. An additional 30 cards (#761-790) featuring traded players in their new uniforms was issued only in factory sets.

		MT
	Complete Series 1&2:	30.00
	Complete Series 1 (1-365):	15.00
	Complete Series 2 (396-760):	15.00
	Complete Factory Set (1-790):	40.00
	Trade Set (366T-395T):	6.00
	Common Player:	.05
	Wax Box:	28.00
1	Cal Ripken Jr.	1.75
2	Edgar Martinez, Tony Gwynn (1995 Stat Leaders)	.35
3	Albert Belle, Dante Bichette (1995 Stat Leaders)	.30
4	Albert Belle, Mo Vaughn, Dante Bichette (1995 Stat Leaders)	.30
5	Kenny Lofton, Quilvio Veras (1995 Stat Leaders)	.30
6	Mike Mussina, Greg Maddux (1995 Stat Leaders)	1.00
7	Randy Johnson, Hideo Nomo (1995 Stat Leaders)	.35
8	Randy Johnson, Greg Maddux (1995 Stat Leaders	1.00
9	Jose Mesa, Randy Myers (1995 Stat Leaders)	.05
10	Johnny Damon (Rookie Class)	.25
11	Rick Krivda (Rookie Class)	.05
12	Roger Cedeno (Rookie Class)	.05
13	Angel Martinez (Rookie Class)	.05
14	Ariel Prieto (Rookie Class)	.05
15	John Wasdin (Rookie Class)	.05
16	Edwin Hurtado (Rookie Class)	.05
17	Lyle Mouton (Rookie Class)	.05
18	Chris Snopek (Rookie Class)	.10
19	Mariano Rivera (Rookie Class)	.15
20	Ruben Rivera (Rookie Class)	.40
21	*Juan Castro* (Rookie Class)	.15
22	Jimmy Haynes (Rookie Class)	.05
23	Bob Wolcott (Rookie Class)	.05
24	Brian Barber (Rookie Class)	.05
25	Frank Rodriguez (Rookie Class)	.05
26	Jesus Tavarez (Rookie Class)	.05
27	Glenn Dishman (Rookie Class)	.05
28	Jose Herrera (Rookie Class)	.05
29	Chan Ho Park (Rookie Class)	.05
30	Jason Isringhausen (Rookie Class)	.15
31	Doug Johns (Rookie Class)	.05
32	Gene Schall (Rookie Class)	.05
33	Kevin Jordan (Rookie Class)	.05
34	*Matt Lawton* (Rookie Class)	.20
35	Karim Garcia (Rookie Class)	.30
36	George Williams (Rookie Class)	.05
37	Orlando Palmeiro (Rookie Class)	.05
38	Jamie Brewington (Rookie Class)	.05
39	Robert Person (Rookie Class)	.05
40	Greg Maddux	1.25
41	Marquis Grissom	.10
42	Chipper Jones	1.25
43	David Justice	.15
44	Mark Lemke	.05
45	Fred McGriff	.25
46	Javy Lopez	.15
47	Mark Wohlers	.05
48	Jason Schmidt	.10
49	John Smoltz	.15
50	Curtis Goodwin	.05
51	Greg Zaun	.05
52	Armando Benitez	.05
53	Manny Alexander	.05
54	Chris Hoiles	.05
55	Harold Baines	.05
56	Ben McDonald	.05
57	Scott Erickson	.05
58	Jeff Manto	.05
59	Luis Alicea	.05
60	Roger Clemens	.35
61	Rheal Cormier	.05
62	Vaughn Eshelman	.05
63	Zane Smith	.05
64	Mike Macfarlane	.05
65	Erik Hanson	.05
66	Tim Naehring	.05
67	Lee Tinsley	.05
68	Troy O'Leary	.05
69	Garret Anderson	.05
70	Chili Davis	.05
71	Jim Edmonds	.15
72	Troy Percival	.05
73	Mark Langston	.05
74	Spike Owen	.05
75	Tim Salmon	.25
76	Brian Anderson	.05
77	Lee Smith	.05
78	Jim Abbott	.05
79	Jim Bullinger	.05

No.	Player	Price
80	Mark Grace	.10
81	Todd Zeile	.05
82	Kevin Foster	.05
83	Howard Johnson	.05
84	Brian McRae	.05
85	Randy Myers	.05
86	Jaime Navarro	.05
87	Luis Gonzalez	.05
88	Ozzie Timmons	.05
89	Wilson Alvarez	.05
90	Frank Thomas	1.50
91	James Baldwin	.05
92	Ray Durham	.05
93	Alex Fernandez	.05
94	Ozzie Guillen	.05
95	Tim Raines	.05
96	Roberto Hernandez	.05
97	Lance Johnson	.05
98	John Kruk	.05
99	Mark Portugal	.05
100	Don Mattingly (Traditional Threads)	.50
101	Jose Canseco (Traditional Threads)	.20
102	Raul Mondesi (Traditional Threads)	.20
103	Cecil Fielder (Traditional Threads)	.05
104	Ozzie Smith (Traditional Threads)	.15
105	Frank Thomas (Traditional Threads)	.75
106	Sammy Sosa (Traditional Threads)	.50
107	Fred McGriff (Traditional Threads)	.20
108	Barry Bonds (Traditional Threads)	.25
109	Thomas Howard	.05
110	Ron Gant	.05
111	Eddie Taubensee	.05
112	Hal Morris	.05
113	Jose Rijo	.05
114	Pete Schourek	.05
115	Reggie Sanders	.05
116	Benito Santiago	.05
117	Jeff Brantley	.05
118	Julian Tavarez	.05
119	Carlos Baerga	.15
120	Jim Thome	.30
121	Jose Mesa	.05
122	Dennis Martinez	.05
123	Dave Winfield	.05
124	Eddie Murray	.25
125	Manny Ramirez	.60
126	Paul Sorrento	.05
127	Kenny Lofton	.60
128	Eric Young	.05
129	Jason Bates	.05
130	Bret Saberhagen	.05
131	Andres Galarraga	.10
132	Joe Girardi	.05
133	John Vander Wal	.05
134	David Nied	.05
135	Dante Bichette	.20
136	Vinny Castilla	.05
137	Kevin Ritz	.05
138	Felipe Lira	.05
139	Joe Boever	.05
140	Cecil Fielder	.15
141	John Flaherty	.05
142	Kirk Gibson	.05
143	Brian Maxcy	.05
144	Lou Whitaker	.05
145	Alan Trammell	.05
146	Bobby Higginson	.05
147	Chad Curtis	.05
148	Quilvio Veras	.05
149	Jerry Browne	.05
150	Andre Dawson	.05
151	Robb Nen	.05
152	Greg Colbrunn	.05
153	Chris Hammond	.05
154	Kurt Abbott	.05
155	Charles Johnson	.05
156	Terry Pendleton	.05
157	Dave Weathers	.05
158	Mike Hampton	.05
159	Craig Biggio	.75
160	Jeff Bagwell	.75
161	Brian L. Hunter	.10
162	Mike Henneman	.05
163	Dave Magadan	.05
164	Shane Reynolds	.05
165	Derek Bell	.05
166	Orlando Miller	.05
167	James Mouton	.05
168	Melvin Bunch	.05
169	Tom Gordon	.05
170	Kevin Appier	.05
171	Tom Goodwin	.05
172	Greg Gagne	.05
173	Gary Gaetti	.05
174	Jeff Montgomery	.05
175	Jon Nunnally	.05
176	Michael Tucker	.05
177	Joe Vitiello	.05
178	Billy Ashley	.05
179	Tom Candiotti	.05
180	Hideo Nomo	.50
181	Chad Fonville	.05
182	Todd Hollandsworth	.10
183	Eric Karros	.05
184	Roberto Kelly	.05
185	Mike Piazza	1.00
186	Ramon Martinez	.05
187	Tim Wallach	.05
188	Jeff Cirillo	.05
189	Sid Roberson	.05
190	Kevin Seitzer	.05
191	Mike Fetters	.05
192	Steve Sparks	.05
193	Matt Mieske	.05
194	Joe Oliver	.05
195	B.J. Surhoff	.05
196	Alberto Reyes	.05
197	Fernando Vina	.05
198	LaTroy Hawkins	.05
199	Marty Cordova	.10
200	Kirby Puckett	.75
201	Brad Radke	.05
202	(Pedro Munoz)	.05
203	Scott Klingenbeck	.05
204	Pat Meares	.05
205	Chuck Knoblauch	.05
206	Scott Stahoviak	.05
207	Dave Stevens	.05
208	Shane Andrews	.05
209	Moises Alou	.05
210	David Segui	.05
211	Cliff Floyd	.05
212	Carlos Perez	.05
213	Mark Grudzielanek	.05
214	Butch Henry	.05
215	Rondell White	.10
216	Mel Rojas	.05
217	Ugueth Urbina	.05
218	Edgardo Alfonzo	.05
219	Carl Everett	.05
220	John Franco	.05
221	Todd Hundley	.05
222	Bobby Jones	.05
223	Bill Pulsipher	.15
224	Rico Brogna	.05
225	Jeff Kent	.05
226	Chris Jones	.05
227	Butch Huskey	.05
228	Robert Eenhoorn	.05
229	Sterling Hitchcock	.05
230	Wade Boggs	.15
231	Derek Jeter	1.00
232	Tony Fernandez	.05
233	Jack McDowell	.10
234	Andy Pettitte	.50
235	David Cone	.10
236	Mike Stanley	.05
237	Don Mattingly	.75
238	Geronimo Berroa	.05
239	Scott Brosius	.05
240	Rickey Henderson	.10
241	Terry Steinbach	.05
242	Mike Gallego	.05
243	Jason Giambi	.05
244	Steve Ontiveros	.05
245	Dennis Eckersley	.05
246	Dave Stewart	.05
247	Don Wengert	.05
248	Paul Quantrill	.05
249	Ricky Bottalico	.05
250	Kevin Stocker	.05
251	Lenny Dykstra	.05
252	Tony Longmire	.05
253	Tyler Green	.05
254	Mike Mimbs	.05
255	Charlie Hayes	.05
256	Mickey Morandini	.05
257	Heathcliff Slocumb	.05
258	Jeff King	.05
259	Midre Cummings	.05
260	Mark Johnson	.05
261	Freddy Garcia	.05
262	Jon Lieber	.05
263	Esteban Loaiza	.10
264	Danny Miceli	.05
265	Orlando Merced	.05
266	Denny Neagle	.05
267	Steve Parris	.05
268	Fantasy Team '95(Greg Maddux)	.60
269	Fantasy Team '95(Randy Johnson)	.10
270	Fantasy Team '95(Hideo Nomo)	.25
271	Fantasy Team '95(Jose Mesa)	.05
272	Fantasy Team '95(Mike Piazza)	.50
273	Fantasy Team '95(Mo Vaughn)	.30
274	Fantasy Team '95(Craig Biggio)	.05
275	Fantasy Team '95(Edgar Martinez)	.05
276	Fantasy Team '95(Barry Larkin)	.15
277	Fantasy Team '95(Sammy Sosa)	.50
278	Fantasy Team '95(Dante Bichette)	.05
279	Fantasy Team '95(Albert Belle)	.40
280	Ozzie Smith	.30
281	Mark Sweeney	.05
282	Terry Bradshaw	.05
283	Allen Battle	.05
284	Danny Jackson	.05
285	Tom Henke	.05
286	Scott Cooper	.05
287	Tripp Cromer	.05
288	Bernard Gilkey	.05
289	Brian Jordan	.05
290	Tony Gwynn	.75
291	Brad Ausmus	.05
292	Bryce Florie	.05
293	Andres Berumen	.05
294	Ken Caminiti	.10
295	Bip Roberts	.05
296	Trevor Hoffman	.05
297	Roberto Petagine	.05
298	Jody Reed	.05
299	Fernando Valenzuela	.05
300	Barry Bonds	.50
301	Mark Leiter	.05
302	Mark Carreon	.05
303	Royce Clayton	.05
304	Kirt Manwaring	.05
305	Glenallen Hill	.05
306	Deion Sanders	.20
307	Joe Rosselli	.05
308	Robby Thompson	.05
309	William VanLandingham	.05
310	Ken Griffey Jr.	2.00
311	Bobby Ayala	.05
312	Joey Cora	.05
313	Mike Blowers	.05
314	Darren Bragg	.05
315	Randy Johnson	.25
316	Alex Rodriguez	2.00
317	Andy Benes	.05
318	Tino Martinez	.05
319	Dan Wilson	.05
320	Will Clark	.30
321	Jeff Frye	.05
322	Benji Gil	.05
323	Rick Helling	.05
324	Mark McLemore	.05
325	Dave Nilsson (International Flavor)	.05
326	Larry Walker (International Flavor)	.20
327	Jose Canseco (International Flavor)	.20
328	Raul Mondesi (International Flavor)	.25
329	Manny Ramirez (International Flavor)	.40
330	Robert Eenhoorn (International Flavor)	.05
331	Chili Davis (International Flavor)	.05
332	Hideo Nomo (International Flavor)	.25
333	Benji Gil (International Flavor)	.05
334	Fernando Valenzuela (International Flavor)	.05
335	Dennis Martinez (International Flavor)	.05

336	Roberto Kelly (International Flavor)	.05
337	Carlos Baerga (International Flavor)	.10
338	Juan Gonzalez (International Flavor)	.40
339	Roberto Alomar (International Flavor)	.25
340	Chan Ho Park (International Flavor)	.05
341	Andres Galarraga (International Flavor)	.10
342	Midre Cummings (International Flavor)	.05
343	Otis Nixon	.05
344	Jeff Russell	.05
345	Ivan Rodriguez	.25
346	Mickey Tettleton	.05
347	Bob Tewksbury	.05
348	Domingo Cedeno	.05
349	Lance Parrish	.05
350	Joe Carter	.15
351	Devon White	.05
352	Carlos Delgado	.05
353	Alex Gonzalez	.05
354	Darren Hall	.05
355	Paul Molitor	.25
356	Al Leiter	.05
357	Randy Knorr	.05
358	Checklist 1-46 (12-player Astros-Padres trade)	.05
359	Checklist 47-92(Hideo Nomo)	.10
360	Checklist 93-138(Ramon Martinez)	.05
361	Checklist 139-184(Robin Ventura)	.05
362	Checklist 185-230(Cal Ripken Jr.)	.30
363	Checklist 231-275(Ken Caminiti)	.05
364	Checklist 276-320(Eddie Murray)	.10
365	Checklist 321-365(Randy Johnson)	.10
366	A.L. Divisional Series(Tony Pena)	.10
367	A.L. Divisional Series(Jim Thome)	.10
368	A.L. Divisional Series(Don Mattingly)	.40
369	A.L. Divisional Series(Jim Leyritz)	.10
370	A.L. Divisional Series(Ken Griffey Jr.)	1.25
371	A.L. Divisional Series(Edgar Martinez)	.10
372	N.L. Divisional Series(Pete Schourek)	.10
373	N.L. Divisional Series(Mark Lewis)	.10
374	N.L. Divisonal Series(Chipper Jones)	1.00
375	N.L. Divisonal Series(Fred McGriff)	.25
376	N.L. Championship Series(Javy Lopez)	.15
377	N.L. Championship Series(Fred McGriff)	.25
378	N.L. Championship Series(Charlie O'Brien)	.10
379	N.L. Championship Series(Mike Devereaux)	.10
380	N.L. Championship Series(Mark Wohlers)	.10
381	A.L. Championship Series(Bob Wolcott)	.10
382	A.L. Championship Series(Manny Ramirez)	.25
383	A.L. Championship Series(Jay Buhner)	.15
384	A.L. Championship Series(Orel Hershiser)	.10
385	A.L. Championship Series(Kenny Lofton)	.25
386	World Series(Greg Maddux)	1.00
387	World Series(Javy Lopez)	.15
388	World Series(Kenny Lofton)	.25
389	World Series(Eddie Murray)	.30
390	World Series(Luis Polonia)	.10
391	World Series(Pedro Borbon)	.10
392	World Series(Jim Thome)	.20
393	World Series(Orel Hershiser)	.15
394	World Series(David Justice)	.20
395	World Series(Tom Glavine)	.20
396	Braves Team Checklist(Greg Maddux)	.25
397	Mets Team Checklist(Brett Butler)	.05
398	Phillies Team Checklist(Darren Daulton)	.05
399	Marlins Team Checklist(Gary Sheffield)	.10
400	Expos Team Checklist(Moises Alou)	.05
401	Reds Team Checklist(Barry Larkin)	.10
402	Astros Team Checklist(Jeff Bagwell)	.15
403	Cubs Team Checklist(Sammy Sosa)	.40
404	Cardinals Team Checklist(Ozzie Smith)	.10
405	Pirates Team Checklist(Jeff King)	.05
406	Dodgers Team Checklist(Mike Piazza)	.25
407	Rockies Team Checklist(Dante Bichette)	.10
408	Padres Team Checklist(Tony Gwynn)	.15
409	Giants Team Checklist(Barry Bonds)	.15
410	Indians Team Checklist(Kenny Lofton)	.15
411	Royals Team Checklist(Jon Nunnally)	.05
412	White Sox Team Checklist(Frank Thomas)	.40
413	Brewers Team Checklist(Greg Vaughn)	.05
414	Twins Team Checklist(Paul Molitor)	.10
415	Mariners Team Checklist(Ken Griffey Jr.)	.50
416	Angels Team Checklist(Jim Edmonds)	.05
417	Rangers Team Checklist(Juan Gonzalez)	.25
418	Athletics Team Checklist(Mark McGwire)	.75
419	Red Sox Team Checklist(Roger Clemens)	.15
420	Yankees Team Checklist(Wade Boggs)	.05
421	Orioles Team Checklist(Cal Ripken Jr.)	.40
422	Tigers Team Checklist(Cecil Fielder)	.05
423	Blue Jays Team Checklist(Joe Carter)	.05
424	*Osvaldo Fernandez* (Rookie Class)	.20
425	Billy Wagner (Rookie Class)	.10
426	George Arias (Rookie Class)	.05
427	Mendy Lopez (Rookie Class)	.05
428	Jeff Suppan (Rookie Class)	.05
429	Rey Ordonez (Rookie Class)	.25
430	Brooks Kieschnick (Rookie Class)	.10
431	*Raul Ibanez* (Rookie Class)	.10
432	*Livan Hernandez* (Rookie Class)	1.00
433	Shannon Stewart (Rookie Class)	.05
434	Steve Cox (Rookie Class)	.05
435	Trey Beamon (Rookie Class)	.05
436	Sergio Nunez (Rookie Class)	.05
437	Jermaine Dye (Rookie Class)	.15
438	*Mike Sweeney* (Rookie Class)	.15
439	Richard Hidalgo (Rookie Class)	.05
440	Todd Greene (Rookie Class)	.15
441	*Robert Smith* (Rookie Class)	.25
442	Rafael Orellano (Rookie Class)	.15
443	*Wilton Guerrero* (Rookie Class)	.35
444	*David Doster* (Rookie Class)	.05
445	Jason Kendall (Rookie Class)	.10
446	Edgar Renteria (Rookie Class)	.15
447	Scott Spiezio (Rookie Class)	.10
448	Jay Canizaro (Rookie Class)	.10
449	Enrique Wilson (Rookie Class)	.05
450	Bob Abreu (Rookie Class)	.15
451	Dwight Smith	.05
452	Jeff Blauser	.05
453	Steve Avery	.05
454	Brad Clontz	.05
455	Tom Glavine	.10
456	Mike Mordecai	.05
457	Rafael Belliard	.05
458	Greg McMichael	.05
459	Pedro Borbon	.05
460	Ryan Klesko	.40
461	Terrell Wade	.05
462	Brady Anderson	.10
463	Roberto Alomar	.40
464	Bobby Bonilla	.05
465	Mike Mussina	.35
466	*Cesar Devarez*	.05
467	Jeffrey Hammonds	.05
468	Mike Devereaux	.05
469	B.J. Surhoff	.05
470	Rafael Palmeiro	.15
471	John Valentin	.05
472	Mike Greenwell	.05
473	Dwayne Hosey	.05
474	Tim Wakefield	.05
475	Jose Canseco	.25
476	Aaron Sele	.05
477	Stan Belinda	.05
478	Mike Stanley	.05
479	Jamie Moyer	.05
480	Mo Vaughn	.60
481	Randy Velarde	.05
482	Gary DiSarcina	.05
483	Jorge Fabregas	.05
484	Rex Hudler	.05
485	Chuck Finley	.05
486	Tim Wallach	.05
487	Eduardo Perez	.05
488	Scott Sanderson	.05
489	J.T. Snow	.05
490	Sammy Sosa	.50
491	Terry Adams	.05
492	Matt Franco	.05
493	Scott Servais	.05
494	Frank Castillo	.05
495	Ryne Sandberg	.35
496	Rey Sanchez	.05
497	Steve Trachsel	.05
498	Jose Hernandez	.05
499	Dave Martinez	.05
500	Babe Ruth (First Class)	1.00
501	Ty Cobb (First Class)	.50
502	Walter Johnson (First Class)	.15
503	Christy Mathewson (First Class)	.05
504	Honus Wagner (First Class)	.25
505	Robin Ventura	.05
506	Jason Bere	.05
507	*Mike Cameron*	.50
508	Ron Karkovice	.05
509	Matt Karchner	.05
510	Harold Baines	.05
511	Kirk McCaskill	.05
512	Larry Thomas	.05
513	Danny Tartabull	.05
514	Steve Gibralter	.05
515	Bret Boone	.05
516	Jeff Branson	.05
517	Kevin Jarvis	.05
518	Xavier Hernandez	.05
519	Eric Owens	.05
520	Barry Larkin	.15
521	Dave Burba	.05
522	John Smiley	.05
523	Paul Assenmacher	.05
524	Chad Ogea	.05
525	Orel Hershiser	.05
526	Alan Embree	.05
527	Tony Pena	.05
528	Omar Vizquel	.05
529	Mark Clark	.05
530	Albert Belle	.60
531	Charles Nagy	.05
532	Herbert Perry	.05
533	Darren Holmes	.05
534	Ellis Burks	.05
535	Bill Swift	.05

#	Name	Value
536	Armando Reynoso	.05
537	Curtis Leskanic	.05
538	Quinton McCracken	.05
539	Steve Reed	.05
540	Larry Walker	.15
541	Walt Weiss	.05
542	Bryan Rekar	.05
543	Tony Clark	.50
544	Steve Rodriguez	.05
545	C.J. Nitkowski	.05
546	Todd Steverson	.05
547	Jose Lima	.05
548	Phil Nevin	.05
549	Chris Gomez	.05
550	Travis Fryman	.05
551	Mark Lewis	.05
552	Alex Arias	.05
553	Marc Valdes	.05
554	Kevin Brown	.05
555	Jeff Conine	.05
556	John Burkett	.05
557	Devon White	.05
558	Pat Rapp	.05
559	Jay Powell	.05
560	Gary Sheffield	.20
561	Jim Dougherty	.05
562	Todd Jones	.05
563	Tony Eusebio	.05
564	Darryl Kile	.05
565	Doug Drabek	.05
566	Mike Simms	.05
567	Derrick May	.05
568	*Donne Wall*	.05
569	Greg Swindell	.05
570	Jim Pittsley	.05
571	Bob Hamelin	.05
572	Mark Gubicza	.05
573	Chris Haney	.05
574	Keith Lockhart	.05
575	Mike Macfarlane	.05
576	Les Norman	.05
577	Joe Randa	.05
578	Chris Stynes	.05
579	Greg Gagne	.05
580	Raul Mondesi	.25
581	Delino DeShields	.05
582	Pedro Astacio	.05
583	Antonio Osuna	.05
584	Brett Butler	.05
585	Todd Worrell	.05
586	Mike Blowers	.05
587	Felix Rodriguez	.05
588	Ismael Valdes	.05
589	Ricky Bones	.05
590	Greg Vaughn	.05
591	Mark Loretta	.05
592	Cal Eldred	.05
593	Chuck Carr	.05
594	Dave Nilsson	.05
595	John Jaha	.05
596	Scott Karl	.05
597	Pat Listach	.05
598	*Jose Valentin*	.15
599	Mike Trombley	.05
600	Paul Molitor	.20
601	Dave Hollins	.05
602	Ron Coomer	.05
603	Matt Walbeck	.05
604	Roberto Kelly	.05
605	Rick Aguilera	.05
606	Pat Mahomes	.05
607	Jeff Reboulet	.05
608	Rich Becker	.05
609	Tim Scott	.05
610	Pedro J. Martinez	.05
611	Kirk Rueter	.05
612	Tavo Alvarez	.05
613	Yamil Benitez	.05
614	Darrin Fletcher	.05
615	Mike Lansing	.05
616	Henry Rodriguez	.05
617	Tony Tarasco	.05
618	Alex Ochoa	.05
619	Tim Bogar	.05
620	Bernard Gilkey	.05
621	Dave Mlicki	.05
622	Brent Mayne	.05
623	Ryan Thompson	.05
624	Pete Harnisch	.05
625	Lance Johnson	.05
626	Jose Vizcaino	.05
627	Doug Henry	.05
628	Scott Kamieniecki	.05
629	Jim Leyritz	.05
630	Ruben Sierra	.05
631	Pat Kelly	.05

#	Name	Value
632	Joe Girardi	.05
633	John Wetteland	.05
634	Melido Perez	.05
635	Paul O'Neill	.05
636	Jorge Posada	.10
637	Bernie Williams	.20
638	Mark Acre	.25
639	Mike Bordick	.05
640	Mark McGwire	2.50
641	Fausto Cruz	.05
642	Ernie Young	.05
643	Todd Van Poppel	.05
644	Craig Paquette	.05
645	Brent Gates	.05
646	Pedro Munoz	.05
647	Andrew Lorraine	.05
648	Sid Fernandez	.05
649	Jim Eisenreich	.05
650	Johnny Damon (Arizona Fall League)	.15
651	Dustin Hermanson (Arizona Fall League)	.05
652	Joe Randa (Arizona Fall League)	.05
653	Michael Tucker (Arizona Fall League)	.10
654	Alan Benes (Arizona Fall League)	.20
655	Chad Fonville (Arizona Fall League)	.05
656	David Bell (Arizona Fall League)	.05
657	Jon Nunnally (Arizona Fall League)	.05
658	Chan Ho Park (Arizona Fall League)	.05
659	LaTroy Hawkins (Arizona Fall League)	.05
660	Jamie Brewington (Arizona Fall League)	.05
661	Quinton McCracken (Arizona Fall League)	.05
662	Tim Unroe (Arizona Fall League)	.05
663	Jeff Ware (Arizona Fall League)	.05
664	Todd Greene (Arizona Fall League)	.15
665	Andrew Lorraine (Arizona Fall League)	.05
666	Ernie Young (Arizona Fall League)	.05
667	Toby Borland	.05
668	Lenny Webster	.05
669	Benito Santiago	.05
670	Gregg Jefferies	.05
671	Darren Daulton	.05
672	Curt Schilling	.05
673	Mark Whiten	.05
674	Todd Zeile	.05
675	Jay Bell	.05
676	Paul Wagner	.05
677	Dave Clark	.05
678	Nelson Liriano	.05
679	Ramon Morel	.10
680	Charlie Hayes	.05
681	Angelo Encaracion	.05
682	Al Martin	.05
683	Jacob Brumfield	.05
684	Mike Kingery	.05
685	Carlos Garcia	.05
686	Tom Pagnozzi	.05
687	David Bell	.05
688	Todd Stottlemyre	.05
689	Jose Oliva	.05
690	Ray Lankford	.05
691	Mike Morgan	.05
692	John Frascatore	.05
693	John Mabry	.05
694	Mark Petkovsek	.05
695	Alan Benes	.25
696	Steve Finley	.05
697	Marc Newfield	.05
698	Andy Ashby	.05
699	Marc Kroon	.05
700	Wally Joyner	.05
701	Joey Hamilton	.05
702	Dustin Hermanson	.05
703	Scott Sanders	.05
704	Marty Cordova (Award Win.-ROY)	.05
705	Hideo Nomo (Award Win.-ROY)	.20
706	Mo Vaughn (Award Win.-MVP)	.25

#	Name	Value
707	Barry Larkin (Award Win.-MVP)	.15
708	Randy Johnson (Award Win.-CY)	.15
709	Greg Maddux (Award Win.-CY)	.60
710	Mark McGwire (Award-Comeback)	.75
711	Ron Gant (Award-Comeback)	.05
712	Andujar Cedeno	.05
713	Brian Johnson	.05
714	J.R. Phillips	.05
715	Rod Beck	.05
716	Sergio Valdez	.05
717	*Marvin Benard*	.05
718	Steve Scarsone	.05
719	*Rich Aurilia*	.10
720	Matt Williams	.30
721	John Patterson	.05
722	Shawn Estes	.05
723	Russ Davis	.05
724	Rich Amaral	.05
725	Edgar Martinez	.05
726	Norm Charlton	.05
727	Paul Sorrento	.05
728	Luis Sojo	.05
729	Arquimedez Pozo	.05
730	Jay Buhner	.15
731	Chris Bosio	.05
732	Chris Widgor	.05
733	Kevin Gross	.05
734	Darren Oliver	.05
735	Dean Palmer	.05
736	Matt Whiteside	.05
737	Luis Ortiz	.05
738	Roger Pavlik	.05
739	Damon Buford	.05
740	Juan Gonzalez	.75
741	Rusty Greer	.05
742	Lou Frazier	.05
743	Pat Hentgen	.05
744	Tomas Perez	.05
745	Juan Guzman	.05
746	Otis Nixon	.05
747	Robert Perez	.05
748	Ed Sprague	.05
749	Tony Castillo	.05
750	John Olerud	.05
751	Shawn Green	.05
752	Jeff Ware	.05
753	Checklist 396-441/Blake St. Bombers(Dante Bichette, Larry Walker, Andres Galarraga, Vinny Castilla)	.10
754	Checklist 442-487(Greg Maddux)	.35
755	Checklist 488-533(Marty Cordova)	.05
756	Checklist 534-579(Ozzie Smith)	.15
757	Checklist 580-625(John Vander Wal)	.05
758	Checklist 626-670(Andres Galarraga)	.10
759	Checklist 671-715(Frank Thomas)	.40
760	Checklist 716-760(Tony Gwynn)	.30
761	Randy Myers	.10
762	Kent Mercker	.10
763	David Wells	.10
764	Tom Gordon	.10
765	Wil Cordero	.10
766	Dave Magadan	.10
767	Doug Jones	.10
768	Kevin Tapani	.10
769	Curtis Goodwin	.10
770	Julio Franco	.10
771	Jack McDowell	.15
772	Al Leiter	.10
773	Sean Berry	.10
774	Bip Roberts	.10
775	Jose Offerman	.10
776	Ben McDonald	.15
777	Dan Serafini	.25
778	Ryan McGuire	.25
779	Tim Raines	.10
780	Tino Martinez	.15
781	Kenny Rogers	.10
782	Bob Tewksbury	.10
783	Rickey Henderson	.15
784	Ron Gant	.20
785	Gary Gaetti	.10
786	Andy Benes	.15
787	Royce Clayton	.10

788	Darryl Hamilton	.10
789	Ken Hill	.10
790	Erik Hanson	.10

1996 Collector's Choice Silver Signature

A silver border instead of white, and a facsimile autograph in silver ink on the card front differentiate these parallel insert cards from the regular-issue Collector's Choice. The inserts are seeded at the rate of one per pack.

	MT
Complete Set (730):	50.00
Common Player:	.10

(Star cards valued at 1.5X-2X regular version)

1996 Collector's Choice Gold Signature

This insert set parallels each card in the regular Collector's Choice set. Found on average of one per 35 packs, the cards are nearly identical to the regular version except for the presence of a facsimile autograph in gold ink on the front and gold, instead of white, borders.

	MT
Complete Set (730):	1200.00
Common Player:	1.00
Yng Stars & RCs:	8x to 15x

(Star cards valued at 8X-20X regular version)

1996 Collector's Choice A Cut Above

This 10-card set highlights the career of Ken Griffey Jr. The front had a color photo with "The Griffey Years" printed in the left border and the year of his accomplishment in the right border. The backs have a headshot and description of his achievement. This set was inserted one per six-card retail pack.

	MT
Complete Set (10):	8.00
1-10 Ken Griffey Jr.	1.00

1996 Collector's Choice Crash the Game

For a second season, Upper Deck continued its interactive chase card series, "You Crash the Game." At a ratio of about one per five packs for a silver version and one per 49 packs for a gold version, cards of the game's top sluggers can be found bearing one of three date ranges representing a three- or four-game series in which that player was scheduled to play during the 1996 season. If the player hit a home run during the series shown on the card, the card could be redeemed (for $1.75) by mail for a "Super Premium" wood-and-plastic card of the player. Both silver and gold Crash cards feature silver and red prismatic foil behind the player action photo. Silver versions have the Crash logo, series dates and player ID in silver foil on front; those details are in gold foil on the gold cards. Backs have contest rules printed on a gray (silver) or yellow (gold) background. Card numbers are preceded by a "CG" prefix. Cards were redeemable only until Nov. 25, 1996. Winning cards are indicated with an asterisk; they would be in shorter supply than those which could not be redeemed.

		MT
Complete Silver Set (90):		40.00
Common Silver Player:		.50
Gold Version: 5-6X		
1a	Chipper Jones (July 11-14*)	3.00
1b	Chipper Jones (Aug. 27-29*)	3.00
1c	Chipper Jones (Sept. 19-23)	2.00
2a	Fred McGriff (July 1-3)	.50
2b	Fred McGriff (Aug. 30-Sept. 1)	.50
2c	Fred McGriff (Sept. 10-12*)	.90
3a	Rafael Palmeiro (July 4-7*)	.90
3b	Rafael Palmeiro (Aug. 29-Sept. 1)	.50
3c	Rafael Palmeiro (Sept. 26-29)	.50
4a	Cal Ripken Jr. (June 27-30)	3.00
4b	Cal Ripken Jr. (July 25-28*)	6.00
4c	Cal Ripken Jr. (Sept. 2-4)	3.00
5a	Jose Canseco (June 27-30)	.50
5b	Jose Canseco (July 11-14*)	.90
5c	Jose Canseco (Aug. 23-25)	.50
6a	Mo Vaughn (June 21-23*)	.90
6b	Mo Vaughn (July 18-21*)	.90
6c	Mo Vaughn (Sept. 20-22)	.50
7a	Jim Edmonds (July 18-21*)	.90
7b	Jim Edmonds (Aug. 16-18*)	.90
7c	Jim Edmonds (Sept. 20-22)	.50
8a	Tim Salmon (June 20-23)	.50
8b	Tim Salmon (July 30-Aug. 1)	.50
8c	Tim Salmon (Sept. 9-12)	.50
9a	Sammy Sosa (July 4-7*)	3.00
9b	Sammy Sosa (Aug. 1-4*)	3.00
9c	Sammy Sosa (Sept. 2-4)	1.50
10a	Frank Thomas (June 27-30)	2.00
10b	Frank Thomas (July 4-7)	2.00
10c	Frank Thomas (Sept. 2-4*)	4.00
11a	Albert Belle (June 25-26)	.75
11b	Albert Belle (Aug. 2-5*)	1.50
11c	Albert Belle (Sept. 6-8)	.75
12a	Manny Ramirez (July 18-21*)	.90
12b	Manny Ramirez (Aug. 26-28)	.50
12c	Manny Ramirez (Sept. 9-12*)	.90
13a	Jim Thome (June 27-30)	.50
13b	Jim Thome (July 4-7*)	.90
13c	Jim Thome (Sept. 23-25)	.50
14a	Dante Bichette (July 11-14*)	.90
14b	Dante Bichette (Aug. 9-11)	.50
14c	Dante Bichette (Sept. 9-12)	.50
15a	Vinny Castilla (July 1-3)	.50
15b	Vinny Castilla (Aug. 23-25*)	.50
15c	Vinny Castilla (Sept. 13-15*)	.90
16a	Larry Walker (June 24-26)	.65
16b	Larry Walker (July 18-21)	.65
16c	Larry Walker (Sept. 27-29)	.65
17a	Cecil Fielder (June 27-30)	.50
17b	Cecil Fielder (July 30-Aug. 1*)	.90
17c	Cecil Fielder (Sept. 17-19*)	.50
18a	Gary Sheffield (July 4-7)	.50
18b	Gary Sheffield (Aug. 2-4)	.50
18c	Gary Sheffield (Sept. 5-8*)	.90
19a	Jeff Bagwell (July 4-7*)	1.50
19b	Jeff Bagwell (Aug. 16-18)	.90
19c	Jeff Bagwell (Sept. 13-15)	.90
20a	Eric Karros (July 4-7*)	.90
20b	Eric Karros (Aug. 13-15*)	.90
20c	Eric Karros (Sept. 16-18)	.50
21a	Mike Piazza (June 27-30*)	4.00
21b	Mike Piazza (July 26-28)	2.50
21c	Mike Piazza (Sept. 12-15*)	4.00
22a	Ken Caminiti (July 11-14*)	.90
22b	Ken Caminiti (Aug. 16-18*)	.90
22c	Ken Caminiti (Sept. 19-22*)	.90
23a	Barry Bonds (June 27-30*)	3.00
23b	Barry Bonds (July 22-24)	1.50
23c	Barry Bonds (Sept. 24-26)	1.50
24a	Matt Williams (July 11-14*)	1.00
24b	Matt Williams (Aug. 19-21)	.55
24c	Matt Williams (Sept. 27-29)	.55
25a	Jay Buhner (June 20-23)	.50
25b	Jay Buhner (July 25-28)	.50
25c	Jay Buhner (Aug. 29-Sept. 1*)	.90
26a	Ken Griffey Jr. (July 18-21*)	6.00
26b	Ken Griffey Jr. (Aug. 16-18*)	6.00
26c	Ken Griffey Jr. (Sept. 20-22*)	6.00
27a	Ron Gant (June 24-27*)	.90
27b	Ron Gant (July 11-14*)	.90
27c	Ron Gant (Sept. 27-29*)	.90
28a	Juan Gonzalez (June 28-30*)	3.00
28b	Juan Gonzalez (July 15-17*)	3.00
28c	Juan Gonzalez (Aug. 6-8)	1.50
29a	Mickey Tettleton (July 4-7*)	.90
29b	Mickey Tettleton (Aug. 6-8)	.50
29c	Mickey Tettleton (Sept. 6-8*)	.90
30a	Joe Carter (June 25-27)	.50
30b	Joe Carter (Aug. 5-8)	.50
30c	Joe Carter (Sept. 23-25)	.50

Cards before 1981 are priced Near Mint (NM), Excellent (EX), and Very Good (VG).

Cards 1981 to present are priced Mint (MT), Near Mint (NM), and Excellent (EX).

1996 Collector's Choice Crash Winners

Collectors who held "You Crash The Game" insert cards with date ranges on which the pictured player hit a home run could redeem them (for $1.75 per card) for a premium card of that player. The redemption cards have a layer of clear plastic bonded to a wood-laminate front. Within a starburst cutout at center is the player photo with a red background. Cards have a Crash/Game logo in the lower-right corner, in either silver or gold, depending on which winning card was submitted for exchange. Backs have 1995 and career stats along with licensing and copyright data. There were no winning cards of Tim Salmon, Larry Walker or Joe Carter.

		MT
Complete Set (27):		140.00
Common Player:		3.00
Gold Version: 4-5X		
CR1	Chipper Jones	12.00
CR2	Fred McGriff	3.00
CR3	Rafael Palmeiro	4.00
CR4	Cal Ripken Jr.	12.50
CR5	Jose Canseco	4.00
CR6	Mo Vaughn	5.00
CR7	Jim Edmonds	3.00
CR9	Sammy Sosa	9.00
CR10	Frank Thomas	12.00
CR11	Albert Belle	6.00
CR12	Manny Ramirez	4.00
CR13	Jim Thome	3.00
CR14	Dante Bichette	3.00
CR15	Vinny Castilla	3.00
CR17	Cecil Fielder	3.00
CR18	Gary Sheffield	3.00
CR19	Jeff Bagwell	7.50
CR20	Eric Karros	3.00
CR21	Mike Piazza	10.00
CR22	Ken Caminiti	3.00
CR23	Barry Bonds	7.50
CR24	Matt Williams	4.00
CR25	Jay Buhner	3.00
CR26	Ken Griffey Jr.	15.00
CR27	Ron Gant	3.00
CR28	Juan Gonzalez	7.50
CR29	Mickey Tettleton	3.00

A player's name in *italic* type indicates a rookie card.

1996 Collector's Choice Nomo Scrapbook

The five-card, regular-sized set was randomly inserted in 1996 Upper Deck Collector's Choice baseball. The card fronts depict the Los Angeles pitcher in action with his name in atypical lower-case type down the right border. The card backs feature in-depth text below Nomo's name, both in atypical text.

		MT
Complete Set (5):		6.00
Common Player:		1.50
1	Hideo Nomo	1.50
2	Hideo Nomo	1.50
3	Hideo Nomo	1.50
4	Hideo Nomo	1.50
5	Hideo Nomo	1.50

1996 Collector's Choice Ripken Collection

The 23-card, regular-sized Cal Ripken Collection was randomly inserted in various Upper Deck baseball releases in 1996. Cards #1-4 were found in Series 1 Collector's Choice; cards 5-8 were found in Upper Deck Series 1; cards 9-12 in Collector's Choice Series 2; cards 13-17 in Upper Deck Series 2; cards 18-22 in SP baseball and the header card in Collector's Choice.

	MT
Complete Set (1-4, 9-12)	40.00
Common Card:	4.00
Header Card:	4.00
(See also Upper Deck Series 1 and 2, and Upper Deck/SP)	

1996 Collector's Choice "You Make the Play"

This insert series of interactive game cards was packaged with Series 1 Collector's Choice. Each player's card can be found with one of two play outcomes printed thereon, which are then used to play a baseball card game utilizing a playing field and scorecard found on box bottoms. Regular versions of the cards are seeded one per pack, while gold-signature versions are found one per 36 packs.

		MT
Complete Set (45):		11.00
Common Player:		.25
Gold version: 10X-15X regular		
1a	Kevin Appier (Strike out)	.25
1b	Kevin Appier (Pick off)	.25
2a	Carlos Baerga (Home run)	.25
2b	Carlos Baerga (Ground out)	.25
3a	Jeff Bagwell (Walk)	.40
3b	Jeff Bagwell (Strike out)	.40
4a	Jay Bell (Sacrifice)	.25
4b	Jay Bell (Walk)	.25
5a	Albert Belle (Fly out)	.75
5b	Albert Belle (Home run)	.75
6a	Craig Biggio (Single)	.35
6b	Craig Biggio (Strike out)	.35
7a	Wade Boggs (Single)	.35
7b	Wade Boggs (Ground out)	.35
8a	Barry Bonds (Strike out)	.60
8b	Barry Bonds (Reach on error)	.60
9a	Bobby Bonilla (Walk)	.25
9b	Bobby Bonilla (Strike out)	.25
10a	Jose Canseco (Strike out)	.35
10b	Jose Canseco (Double)	.35
11a	Joe Carter (Double)	.25
11b	Joe Carter (Fly out)	.25
12a	Darren Daulton (Ground out)	.25
12b	Darren Daulton (Catcher's interference)	.25
13a	Cecil Fielder (Stolen base)	.30
13b	Cecil Fielder (Home run)	.30
14a	Ron Gant (Home run)	.25
14b	Ron Gant (Fly out)	.25
15a	Juan Gonzalez (Double)	.60
15b	Juan Gonzalez (Fly out)	.60
16a	Ken Griffey Jr. (Home run)	2.00
16b	Ken Griffey Jr. (Hit by pitch)	2.00
17a	Tony Gwynn (Single)	.60
17b	Tony Gwynn (Ground out)	.60
18a	Randy Johnson (Strike out)	.45
18b	Randy Johnson (K - reach on wild pitch)	.45
19a	Chipper Jones (Walk)	.60
19b	Chipper Jones (Strike out)	.60
20a	Barry Larkin (Ground out)	.30
20b	Barry Larkin (Stolen base)	.30
21a	Kenny Lofton (Triple)	.30
21b	Kenny Lofton (Stolen base)	.30

Modern cards have little collector value in conditions lower than Mint. Figure NM cards at 75% of values shown; EX cards at 40%.

Values shown reflect the market as of January, 1999. On-field performances of current players in the 1999 baseball season are not factored in.

22a	Greg Maddux (Single)	.45
22b	Greg Maddux (Strike out)	.45
23a	Don Mattingly (Fly out)	.50
23b	Don Mattingly (Double)	.50
24a	Fred McGriff (Double)	.30
24b	Fred McGriff (Home run)	.30
25a	Mark McGwire (Strike out)	1.50
25b	Mark McGwire (Home run)	1.50
26a	Paul Molitor (Ground out)	.45
26b	Paul Molitor (Single)	.45
27a	Raul Mondesi (Single)	.35
27b	Raul Mondesi (Fly out)	.35
28a	Eddie Murray (Sacrifice fly)	.45
28b	Eddie Murray (Ground out)	.45
29a	Hideo Nomo (Strike out)	.90
29b	Hideo Nomo (Balk)	.90
30a	Jon Nunnally (Single)	.25
30b	Jon Nunnally (Error)	.25
31a	Mike Piazza (Strike out)	.45
31b	Mike Piazza (Single)	.45
32a	Kirby Puckett (Walk)	.45
32b	Kirby Puckett (Ground out)	.45
33a	Cal Ripken Jr. (Home run)	1.75
33b	Cal Ripken Jr. (Double)	1.75
34a	Alex Rodriguez (Strike out)	.65
34b	Alex Rodriguez (Triple)	.65
35a	Tim Salmon (Sacrifice fly)	.35
35b	Tim Salmon (Strike out)	.35
36a	Gary Sheffield (Fly out)	.25
36b	Gary Sheffield (Single)	.25
37a	Lee Smith (Strike out)	.25
37b	Lee Smith (Pick off of lead runner)	.25
38a	Ozzie Smith (Ground out)	.45
38b	Ozzie Smith (Single)	.45
39a	Sammy Sosa (Stolen base)	1.00
39b	Sammy Sosa (Single)	1.00
40a	Frank Thomas (Walk)	1.50
40b	Frank Thomas (Home run)	1.50
41a	Greg Vaughn (Sacrifice fly)	.35
41b	Greg Vaughn (Strike out)	.35
42a	Mo Vaughn (Hit by Pitch)	.50
42b	Mo Vaughn (Stolen base)	.50
43a	Larry Walker (Strike out)	.30
43b	Larry Walker (Walk)	.30
44a	Rondell White (Triple)	.25
44b	Rondell White (Fly out)	.25
45a	Matt Williams (Home run)	.35
45b	Matt Williams (Single)	.35

1997 Collector's Choice

Raul MONDESI OF

The 246-card, regular-sized set contained four subsets: Rookie Class (1-27), Leaders (56-63), Postseason (218-224) and Ken Griffey Jr. Checklists (244-246). Insert sets are: Stick'Ums, Premier Power, Clearly Dominant and The Big Show. The base card fronts feature a color action shot with the player's name appearing on the bottom edge. The team logo is located in the lower-left corner and each card features a white border.

Backs contain another action shot on the upper half portion with bio, stat and career/season information included. The cards came in 12-card packs retailing for 99 cents.

	MT
Complete Set (506):	30.00
Complete Series 1 Set (246):	15.00
Complete Series 2 Set (260):	18.00
Common Player:	.05
Series 1 Wax Box:	28.00
Series 2 Wax Box:	35.00

1	Andruw Jones (Rookie Class)	1.00
2	Rocky Coppinger (Rookie Class)	.05
3	Jeff D'Amico (Rookie Class)	.05
4	Dmitri Young (Rookie Class)	.05
5	Darin Erstad (Rookie Class)	.75
6	Jermaine Allensworth (Rookie Class)	.05
7	Damian Jackson (Rookie Class)	.05
8	Bill Mueller (Rookie Class)	.05
9	Jacob Cruz (Rookie Class)	.40
10	Vladimir Guerrero (Rookie Class)	.60
11	Marty Janzen (Rookie Class)	.05
12	Kevin L. Brown (Rookie Class)	.05
13	Willie Adams (Rookie Class)	.05
14	Wendell Magee (Rookie Class)	.05
15	Scott Rolen (Rookie Class)	1.00
16	Matt Beech (Rookie Class)	.05
17	Neifi Perez (Rookie Class)	.05
18	Jamey Wright (Rookie Class)	.05
19	Jose Paniagua (Rookie Class)	.05
20	Todd Walker (Rookie Class)	.40
21	Justin Thompson (Rookie Class)	.05
22	Robin Jennings (Rookie Class)	.05
23	*Dario Veras* (Rookie Class)	.05
24	Brian Lesher (Rookie Class)	.05
25	Nomar Garciaparra (Rookie Class)	1.25
26	Luis Castillo (Rookie Class)	.10
27	Brian Giles (Rookie Class)	.05
28	Jermaine Dye	.15
29	Terrell Wade	.05
30	Fred McGriff	.25
31	Marquis Grissom	.05
32	Ryan Klesko	.30
33	Javier Lopez	.10
34	Mark Wohlers	.05
35	Tom Glavine	.15
36	Denny Neagle	.05
37	Scott Erickson	.05
38	Chris Hoiles	.05
39	Roberto Alomar	.50
40	Eddie Murray	.30
41	Cal Ripken Jr.	1.50
42	Randy Myers	.05
43	B.J. Surhoff	.05
44	Rick Krivda	.05
45	Jose Canseco	.20
46	Heathcliff Slocumb	.05
47	Jeff Suppan	.05
48	Tom Gordon	.05
49	Aaron Sele	.05
50	Mo Vaughn	.75
51	Darren Bragg	.05
52	Wil Cordero	.05
53	Scott Bullett	.05
54	Terry Adams	.05
55	Jackie Robinson	.50
56	Tony Gwynn, Alex Rodriguez (Batting Leaders)	.50
57	Andres Galarraga, Mark McGwire (Homer Leaders)	.75
58	Andres Galarraga, Albert Belle (RBI Leaders)	.25
59	Eric Young, Kenny Lofton (SB Leaders)	.15
60	John Smoltz, Andy Pettitte (Victory Leaders)	.25
61	John Smoltz, Roger Clemens (Strikeout Leaders)	.30

62	Kevin Brown, Juan Guzman (ERA Leaders)	.05
63	John Wetteland, Todd Worrell, Jeff Brantley (Save Leaders)	.05
64	Scott Servais	.05
65	Sammy Sosa	.75
66	Ryne Sandberg	.60
67	Frank Castillo	.05
68	Rey Sanchez	.05
69	Steve Trachsel	.05
70	Robin Ventura	.05
71	Wilson Alvarez	.05
72	Tony Phillips	.05
73	Lyle Mouton	.05
74	Mike Cameron	.05
75	Harold Baines	.05
76	Albert Belle	.60
77	Chris Snopek	.05
78	Reggie Sanders	.05
79	Jeff Brantley	.05
80	Barry Larkin	.20
81	Kevin Jarvis	.05
82	John Smiley	.05
83	Pete Schourek	.05
84	Thomas Howard	.05
85	Lee Smith	.05
86	Omar Vizquel	.05
87	Julio Franco	.05
88	Orel Hershiser	.05
89	Charles Nagy	.05
90	Matt Williams	.20
91	Dennis Martinez	.05
92	Jose Mesa	.05
93	Sandy Alomar Jr.	.05
94	Jim Thome	.25
95	Vinny Castilla	.05
96	Armando Reynoso	.05
97	Kevin Ritz	.05
98	Larry Walker	.20
99	Eric Young	.05
100	Dante Bichette	.15
101	Quinton McCracken	.05
102	John Vander Wal	.05
103	Phil Nevin	.05
104	Tony Clark	.40
105	Alan Trammell	.05
106	Felipe Lira	.05
107	Curtis Pride	.05
108	Bobby Higginson	.05
109	Mark Lewis	.05
110	Travis Fryman	.05
111	Al Leiter	.05
112	Devon White	.05
113	Jeff Conine	.05
114	Charles Johnson	.05
115	Andre Dawson	.05
116	Edgar Renteria	.20
117	Robb Nen	.05
118	Kevin Brown	.05
119	Derek Bell	.05
120	Bob Abreu	.05
121	Mike Hampton	.05
122	Todd Jones	.05
123	Billy Wagner	.10
124	Shane Reynolds	.05
125	Jeff Bagwell	1.00
126	Brian L. Hunter	.05
127	Jeff Montgomery	.05
128	*Rod Myers*	.05
129	Tim Belcher	.05
130	Kevin Appier	.05
131	Mike Sweeney	.05
132	Craig Paquette	.05
133	Joe Randa	.05
134	Michael Tucker	.05
135	Raul Mondesi	.20
136	Tim Wallach	.05
137	Brett Butler	.05
138	Karim Garcia	.35
139	Todd Hollandsworth	.15
140	Eric Karros	.05
141	Hideo Nomo	.35
142	Ismael Valdes	.05
143	Cal Eldred	.05
144	Scott Karl	.05
145	Matt Mieske	.05
146	Mike Fetters	.05
147	Mark Loretta	.05
148	Fernando Vina	.05
149	Jeff Cirillo	.05
150	Dave Nilsson	.05
151	Kirby Puckett	1.00
152	Rich Becker	.05
153	Chuck Knoblauch	.15
154	Marty Cordova	.05

#	Player	Value
155	Paul Molitor	.25
156	Rick Aguilera	.05
157	Pat Meares	.05
158	Frank Rodriguez	.05
159	David Segui	.05
160	Henry Rodriguez	.05
161	Shane Andrews	.05
162	Pedro J. Martinez	.05
163	Mark Grudzielanek	.05
164	Mike Lansing	.05
165	Rondell White	.05
166	Ugueth Urbina	.05
167	Rey Ordonez	.20
168	Robert Person	.05
169	Carlos Baerga	.15
170	Bernard Gilkey	.05
171	John Franco	.05
172	Pete Harnisch	.05
173	Butch Huskey	.05
174	Paul Wilson	.15
175	Bernie Williams	.25
176	Dwight Gooden	.05
177	Wade Boggs	.15
178	Ruben Rivera	.20
179	Jim Leyritz	.05
180	Derek Jeter	1.00
181	Tino Martinez	.15
182	Tim Raines	.05
183	Scott Brosius	.05
184	Jason Giambi	.15
185	Geronimo Berroa	.05
186	Ariel Prieto	.05
187	Scott Spiezio	.05
188	John Wasdin	.05
189	Ernie Young	.05
190	Mark McGwire	2.50
191	Jim Eisenreich	.05
192	Ricky Bottalico	.05
193	Darren Daulton	.05
194	David Doster	.05
195	Gregg Jefferies	.05
196	Lenny Dykstra	.05
197	Curt Schilling	.05
198	Todd Stottlemyre	.05
199	Willie McGee	.05
200	Ozzie Smith	.35
201	Dennis Eckersley	.05
202	Ray Lankford	.05
203	John Mabry	.05
204	Alan Benes	.05
205	Ron Gant	.10
206	Archi Cianfrocco	.05
207	Fernando Valenzuela	.05
208	Greg Vaughn	.05
209	Steve Finley	.05
210	Tony Gwynn	.75
211	Rickey Henderson	.05
212	Trevor Hoffman	.05
213	Jason Thompson	.05
214	Osvaldo Fernandez	.05
215	Glenallen Hill	.05
216	William VanLandingham	.05
217	Marvin Benard	.05
218	Juan Gonzalez (Postseason)	.40
219	Roberto Alomar (Postseason)	.25
220	Brian Jordan (Postseason)	.05
221	John Smoltz (Postseason)	.15
222	Javy Lopez (Postseason)	.05
223	Bernie Williams (Postseason)	.20
224	Jim Leyritz, John Wetteland (Postseason)	.05
225	Barry Bonds	.60
226	Rich Aurilia	.05
227	Jay Canizaro	.05
228	Dan Wilson	.05
229	Bob Wolcott	.05
230	Ken Griffey Jr.	2.00
231	Sterling Hitchcock	.05
232	Edgar Martinez	.05
233	Joey Cora	.05
234	Norm Charlton	.05
235	Alex Rodriguez	2.00
236	Bobby Witt	.05
237	Darren Oliver	.05
238	Kevin Elster	.05
239	Rusty Greer	.05
240	Juan Gonzalez	1.00
241	Will Clark	.20
242	Dean Palmer	.05
243	Ivan Rodriguez	.30
244	Checklist(Ken Griffey Jr.)	.50
245	Checklist(Ken Griffey Jr.)	.50
246	Checklist(Ken Griffey Jr.)	.50
247	Ken Griffey Jr. CL	.50
248	Ken Griffey Jr. CL	.50
249	Ken Griffey Jr. CL	.50
250	Eddie Murray	.25
251	Troy Percival	.05
252	Garret Anderson	.05
253	Allen Watson	.05
254	Jason Dickson	.15
255	Jim Edmonds	.10
256	Chuck Finley	.05
257	Randy Velarde	.05
258	Shigetosi Hasegawa	.05
259	Todd Greene	.05
260	Tim Salmon	.20
261	Mark Langston	.05
262	Dave Hollins	.05
263	Gary DiSarcina	.05
264	Kenny Lofton	.50
265	John Smoltz	.15
266	Greg Maddux	1.25
267	Jeff Blauser	.05
268	Alan Embree	.05
269	Mark Lemke	.05
270	Chipper Jones	1.25
271	Mike Mussina	.35
272	Rafael Palmeiro	.15
273	Jimmy Key	.05
274	Mike Bordick	.05
275	Brady Anderson	.10
276	Eric Davis	.05
277	Jeffrey Hammonds	.05
278	Reggie Jefferson	.05
279	Tim Naehring	.05
280	John Valentin	.05
281	Troy O'Leary	.05
282	Shane Mack	.05
283	Mike Stanley	.05
284	Tim Wakefield	.05
285	Brian McRae	.05
286	Brooks Kieschnick	.05
287	Shawon Dunston	.05
288	Kevin Foster	.05
289	Mel Rojas	.05
290	Mark Grace	.15
291	Brant Brown	.05
292	Amaury Telemaco	.05
293	Dave Martinez	.05
294	Jaime Navarro	.05
295	Ray Durham	.05
296	Ozzie Guillen	.05
297	Roberto Hernandez	.05
298	Ron Karkovice	.05
299	James Baldwin	.05
300	Frank Thomas	1.50
301	Eddie Taubensee	.05
302	Bret Boone	.05
303	Willie Greene	.05
304	Dave Burba	.05
305	Deion Sanders	.20
306	Reggie Sanders	.05
307	Hal Morris	.05
308	Pokey Reese	.05
309	Tony Fernandez	.05
310	Manny Ramirez	.50
311	Chad Ogea	.05
312	Jack McDowell	.05
313	Kevin Mitchell	.05
314	Chad Curtis	.05
315	Steve Kline	.05
316	Kevin Seitzer	.05
317	Kirt Manwaring	.05
318	Bill Swift	.05
319	Ellis Burks	.05
320	Andres Galarraga	.15
321	Bruce Ruffin	.05
322	Mark Thompson	.05
323	Walt Weiss	.05
324	Todd Jones	.05
325	Andruw Jones (Griffey Hot List)	.50
326	Chipper Jones (Griffey Hot List)	.60
327	Mo Vaughn (Griffey Hot List)	.25
328	Frank Thomas (Griffey Hot List)	.75
329	Albert Belle (Griffey Hot List)	.30
330	Mark McGwire (Griffey Hot List)	1.00
331	Derek Jeter (Griffey Hot List)	.60
332	Alex Rodriguez (Griffey Hot List)	1.00
333	Juan Gonzalez (Griffey Hot List)	.50
334	Ken Griffey Jr. (Griffey Hot List)	1.00
335	Brian L. Hunter	.05
336	Brian Johnson	.05
337	Omar Olivares	.05
338	*Deivi Cruz*	.05
339	Damion Easley	.05
340	Melvin Nieves	.05
341	Moises Alou	.05
342	Jim Eisenreich	.05
343	Mark Hutton	.05
344	Alex Fernandez	.05
345	Gary Sheffield	.15
346	Pat Rapp	.05
347	Brad Ausmus	.05
348	Sean Berry	.05
349	Darryl Kile	.05
350	Craig Biggio	.10
351	Chris Holt	.05
352	Luis Gonzalez	.05
353	Pat Listach	.05
354	Jose Rosado	.05
355	Mike Macfarlane	.05
356	Tom Goodwin	.05
357	Chris Haney	.05
358	Chili Davis	.05
359	Jose Offerman	.05
360	Johnny Damon	.05
361	Bip Roberts	.05
362	Ramon Martinez	.05
363	Pedro Astacio	.05
364	Todd Zeile	.05
365	Mike Piazza	1.25
366	Greg Gagne	.05
367	Chan Ho Park	.05
368	Wilton Guerrero	.15
369	Todd Worrell	.05
370	John Jaha	.05
371	Steve Sparks	.05
372	Mike Matheny	.05
373	Marc Newfield	.05
374	Jeromy Burnitz	.05
375	Jose Valentin	.05
376	Ben McDonald	.05
377	Roberto Kelly	.05
378	Bob Tewksbury	.05
379	Ron Coomer	.05
380	Brad Radke	.05
381	Matt Lawton	.05
382	Dan Naulty	.05
383	Scott Stahoviak	.05
384	Matt Wagner	.05
385	Jim Bullinger	.05
386	Carlos Perez	.05
387	Darrin Fletcher	.05
388	Chris Widger	.05
389	F.P. Santangelo	.05
390	Lee Smith	.05
391	Bobby Jones	.05
392	John Olerud	.05
393	Mark Clark	.05
394	Jason Isringhausen	.05
395	Todd Hundley	.15
396	Lance Johnson	.05
397	Edgardo Alfonzo	.05
398	Alex Ochoa	.05
399	Darryl Strawberry	.05
400	David Cone	.15
401	Paul O'Neill	.05
402	Joe Girardi	.05
403	Charlie Hayes	.05
404	Andy Pettitte	.50
405	Mariano Rivera	.10
406	Mariano Duncan	.05
407	Kenny Rogers	.05
408	Cecil Fielder	.10
409	George Williams	.05
410	Jose Canseco	.20
411	Tony Batista	.05
412	Steve Karsay	.05
413	Dave Telgheder	.05
414	Billy Taylor	.05
415	Mickey Morandini	.05
416	Calvin Maduro	.05
417	Mark Leiter	.05
418	Kevin Stocker	.05
419	Mike Lieberthal	.05
420	Rico Brogna	.05
421	Mark Portugal	.05
422	Rex Hudler	.05
423	Mark Johnson	.05
424	Esteban Loiaza	.05
425	Lou Collier	.05
426	Kevin Elster	.05
427	Francisco Cordova	.05
428	Marc Wilkins	.05
429	Joe Randa	.05
430	Jason Kendall	.05

431	Jon Lieber	.05
432	Steve Cooke	.05
433	*Emil Brown*	.10
434	*Tony Womack*	.25
435	Al Martin	.05
436	Jason Schmidt	.05
437	Andy Benes	.05
438	Delino DeShields	.05
439	Royce Clayton	.05
440	Brian Jordan	.05
441	Donovan Osborne	.05
442	Gary Gaetti	.05
443	Tom Pagnozzi	.05
444	Joey Hamilton	.05
445	Wally Joyner	.05
446	John Flaherty	.05
447	Chris Gomez	.05
448	Sterling Hitchcock	.05
449	Andy Ashby	.05
450	Ken Caminiti	.15
451	Tim Worrell	.05
452	Jose Vizcaino	.05
453	Rod Beck	.05
454	Wilson Delgado	.05
455	Darryl Hamilton	.05
456	Mark Lewis	.05
457	Mark Gardner	.05
458	Rick Wilkins	.05
459	Scott Sanders	.05
460	Kevin Orie	.05
461	Glendon Rusch	.05
462	Juan Melo	.10
463	Richie Sexson	.10
464	Bartolo Colon	.05
465	Jose Guillen	.50
466	Heath Murray	.05
467	Aaron Boone	.05
468	*Bubba Trammell*	.50
469	Jeff Abbott	.05
470	Derrick Gibson	.15
471	Matt Morris	.15
472	Ryan Jones	.05
473	Pat Cline	.05
474	Adam Riggs	.05
475	Jay Payton	.05
476	Derrek Lee	.15
477	Elieser Marrero	.05
478	Lee Tinsley	.05
479	Jamie Moyer	.05
480	Jay Buhner	.15
481	Bob Wells	.05
482	Jeff Fassero	.05
483	Paul Sorrento	.05
484	Russ Davis	.05
485	Randy Johnson	.40
486	Roger Pavlik	.05
487	Damon Buford	.05
488	Julio Santana	.05
489	Mark McLemore	.05
490	Mickey Tettleton	.05
491	Ken Hill	.05
492	Benji Gil	.05
493	Ed Sprague	.05
494	Mike Timlin	.05
495	Pat Hentgen	.05
496	Orlando Merced	.05
497	Carlos Garcia	.05
498	Carlos Delgado	.15
499	Juan Guzman	.05
500	Roger Clemens	.75
501	Erik Hanson	.05
502	Otis Nixon	.05
503	Shawn Green	.05
504	Charlie O'Brien	.05
505	Joe Carter	.15
506	Alex Gonzalez	.05

1997 Collector's Choice All-Star Connection

This 45-card insert from Series 2 highlights All-Star caliber players. Cards feature a large starburst pattern behind the player's photo and were inserted one per pack.

A player's name in *italic* type indicates a rookie card.

		MT
Complete Set (45):		18.00
Common Player:		.15
1	Mark McGwire	3.00
2	Chuck Knoblauch	.20
3	Jim Thome	.35
4	Alex Rodriguez	2.50
5	Ken Griffey Jr.	2.50
6	Brady Anderson	.15
7	Albert Belle	.75
8	Ivan Rodriguez	.40
9	Pat Hentgen (new)	.15
10	Frank Thomas	2.00
11	Roberto Alomar	.40
12	Robin Ventura	.15
13	Cal Ripken Jr.	2.00
14	Juan Gonzalez	1.00
15	Manny Ramirez	.50
16	Bernie Williams	.40
17	Terry Steinbach	.15
18	Andy Pettitte (new)	.50
19	Jeff Bagwell	1.00
20	Craig Biggio	.15
21	Ken Caminiti	.15
22	Barry Larkin	.15
23	Tony Gwynn	.75
24	Barry Bonds	.50
25	Kenny Lofton	.50
26	Mike Piazza	1.50
27	John Smoltz	.25
28	Andres Galarraga	.15
29	Ryne Sandberg	.50
30	Chipper Jones	1.50
31	Mark Grudzielanek	.15
32	Sammy Sosa	1.00
33	Steve Finley	.15
34	Gary Sheffield	.25
35	Todd Hundley	.25
36	Greg Maddux	1.50
37	Mo Vaughn	.50
38	Eric Young	.15
39	Vinny Castilla	.15
40	Derek Jeter	1.50
41	Lance Johnson (new)	.15
42	Ellis Burks	.15
43	Bernard Gilkey	.15
44	Javy Lopez	.15
45	Hideo Nomo	.40

1997 Collector's Choice Big Shots

This 20-card insert depicts the game's top stars in unique photos. Cards were inserted 1:12 packs. Gold Signature Editions, featuring a gold foil-stamped facsimile autograph, were inserted 1:144 packs. Fronts are highlighted in silver foil. Backs repeat a portion of the front photo, have a picture of the photographer and his comments about the picture.

		MT
Complete Set (20):		60.00
Common Player:		.75
Gold Signature Edition: 3X-5X		
1	Ken Griffey Jr.	10.00
2	Nomar Garciaparra	6.00
3	Brian Jordan	.75
4	Scott Rolen	4.00
5	Alex Rodriguez	8.00
6	Larry Walker	1.00
7	Mariano Rivera	.75
8	Cal Ripken Jr.	8.00
9	Deion Sanders	1.00
10	Frank Thomas	6.00
11	Dean Palmer	.75
12	Ken Caminiti	1.00
13	Derek Jeter	6.00
14	Roger Clemens	3.00
15	Chipper Jones	6.00
16	Jay Buhner	.75
17	Jay Buhner	.75
18	Mike Piazza	6.00
19	Tony Gwynn	4.00
20	Barry Bonds	2.50

1997 Collector's Choice Big Show

The 45-card, regular-sized set was inserted one per pack of Series 1. Backs feature player comments written by ESPN SportsCenter hosts Keith Olbermann and Dan Patrick, whose portraits appear both front and back. On front, printed on metallic foil, is an action shot of the player, with his name printed along the left border of the horizontal cards. The cards are numbered "X/45." A parallel set to this chase-card series carries a gold-foil "World Headquarters Edition" seal at lower-right.

		MT
Complete Set (45):		30.00
Common Player:		.25
1	Greg Maddux	2.50
2	Chipper Jones	2.50
3	Andruw Jones	2.00
4	John Smoltz	.40
5	Cal Ripken Jr.	3.00

6	Roberto Alomar	.75
7	Rafael Palmeiro	.25
8	Eddie Murray	.50
9	Jose Canseco	.25
10	Roger Clemens	.60
11	Mo Vaughn	1.00
12	Jim Edmonds	.25
13	Tim Salmon	.25
14	Sammy Sosa	1.50
15	Albert Belle	1.00
16	Frank Thomas	3.00
17	Barry Larkin	.40
18	Kenny Lofton	.75
19	Manny Ramirez	.75
20	Matt Williams	.40
21	Dante Bichette	.25
22	Gary Sheffield	.40
23	Craig Biggio	.25
24	Jeff Bagwell	1.50
25	Todd Hollandsworth	.25
26	Raul Mondesi	.25
27	Hideo Nomo	.60
28	Mike Piazza	2.50
29	Paul Molitor	.75
30	Kirby Puckett	1.50
31	Rondell White	.25
32	Rey Ordonez	.25
33	Paul Wilson	.25
34	Derek Jeter	2.00
35	Andy Pettitte	.75
36	Mark McGwire	5.00
37	Jason Kendall	.25
38	Ozzie Smith	.75
39	Tony Gwynn	1.50
40	Barry Bonds	.75
41	Alex Rodriguez	4.00
42	Jay Buhner	.25
43	Ken Griffey Jr.	4.00
44	Randy Johnson	.40
45	Juan Gonzalez	1.50

1997 Collector's Choice Big Show World Headquarters

The 45-card chase set in Series 2 is also found in a special parallel version which carries a "World Headquarters Edition" gold-foil seal on front at the lower-right.

	MT
Complete Set (45):	150.00
Common Player:	1.00
(Star cards valued at 4X-8X regular Big Show version)	

A player's name in *italic* type indicates a rookie card.

1997 Collector's Choice Clearly Dominant

The five-card, regular-sized set features Seattle outfielder Ken Griffey Jr. on each card and was inserted every 144 packs of 1997 Collector's Choice baseball.

		MT
Complete Set (5):		50.00
Common Griffey Jr.:		12.00
CD1	Ken Griffey Jr.	12.00
CD2	Ken Griffey Jr.	12.00
CD3	Ken Griffey Jr.	12.00
CD4	Ken Griffey Jr.	12.00
CD5	Ken Griffey Jr.	12.00

Cards before 1981 are priced Near Mint (NM), Excellent (EX), and Very Good (VG).

Cards 1981 to present are priced Mint (MT), Near Mint (NM), and Excellent (EX).

1997 Collector's Choice Clearly Dominant Jumbos

Each of the five Ken Griffey Jr. cards from the Collector's Choice insert set was also produced in a special retail-only 5" x 3-1/2" jumbo version. The supersize Clearly Dominant cards were packaged in a special collectors' kit which also included a Griffey stand-up figure and eight packs of CC cards, retailing for about $15. The cards could also be purchased as a complete set for $10.

		MT
Complete Set (5):		10.00
Common Card:		2.00
CD1	Ken Griffey Jr.	2.00
CD2	Ken Griffey Jr.	2.00
CD3	Ken Griffey Jr.	2.00
CD4	Ken Griffey Jr.	2.00
CD5	Ken Griffey Jr.	2.00

1997 Collector's Choice Hot List Jumbos

These 5" x 7" versions of the "Ken Griffey Jr.'s Hot List" subset from Series 1 are an exclusive boxtopper in certain retail packaging of Series 2 Collector's Choice. Other than size, the jumbos are identical to the regular Hot List cards, including foil background printing on front.

		MT
Complete Set (10):		50.00
Common Player:		3.00
325	Andruw Jones	4.00
326	Chipper Jones	6.00
327	Mo Vaughn	3.00
328	Frank Thomas	6.00
329	Albert Belle	4.00
330	Mark McGwire	10.00
331	Derek Jeter	5.00
332	Alex Rodriguez	8.00
333	Juan Gonzalez	5.00
334	Ken Griffey Jr.	9.00

1997 Collector's Choice New Frontier

A 20-card insert in Series 2 highlighting anticipated interleague matchups. Cards were inserted 1:69 packs.

		MT
Complete Set (20):		250.00
Common Player:		3.00
NF1	Alex Rodriguez, Tony Gwynn	35.00
NF3	Jose Canseco, Hideo Nomo	7.00
NF5	Mark McGwire, Barry Bonds	30.00
NF7	Juan Gonzalez, Ken Caminiti	15.00
NF9	Tim Salmon, Mike Piazza	25.00
NF11	Ken Griffey Jr., Andres Galarraga	35.00
NF13	Jay Buhner, Dante Bichette	3.00
NF15	Frank Thomas, Ryne Sandberg	30.00
NF17	Roger Clemens, Andruw Jones	20.00

NF19	Jim Thome, Sammy Sosa	12.00
NF21	David Justice, Deion Sanders	3.00
NF23	Todd Walker, Kevin Orie	8.00
NF25	Albert Belle, Jeff Bagwell	12.00
NF27	Manny Ramirez, Brian Jordan	8.00
NF29	Derek Jeter, Chipper Jones	25.00
NF31	Mo Vaughn, Gary Sheffield	8.00
NF33	Carlos Delgado, Vladimir Guerrero	10.00
NF35	Cal Ripken Jr., Greg Maddux	30.00
NF37	Cecil Fielder, Todd Hundley	3.00
NF39	Mike Mussina, Scott Rolen	12.00

1997 Collector's Choice Premier Power

ALEX RODRIGUEZ Seattle Mariners™ - SS

The 20-card, regular-sized set was included one per 15 packs of 1997 Collector's Choice. Fronts feature an action shot with the player's name, team and position on the lower card edge. The "Premier Power" logo appears in silver foil in the lower half with spotlights aiming out toward the card sides, also in silver foil. The bottom portion of the card, below the spotlights, is transparent red. Backs are bordered in red with the same card front shot appearing in black-and-white above a brief description and "Power Facts." The cards are numbered with a "PP" prefix. A parallel gold-foil version was available every 69 packs.

		MT
Complete Set (20):		75.00
Common Player:		1.00
Golds: 2x to 3x		
PP1	Mark McGwire	20.00
PP2	Brady Anderson	1.50
PP3	Ken Griffey Jr.	15.00
PP4	Albert Belle	4.00
PP5	Juan Gonzalez	7.00
PP6	Andres Galarraga	1.50
PP7	Jay Buhner	1.00
PP8	Mo Vaughn	4.00
PP9	Barry Bonds	4.00
PP10	Gary Sheffield	2.50
PP11	Todd Hundley	1.50
PP12	Frank Thomas	12.00
PP13	Sammy Sosa	10.00
PP14	Ken Caminiti	2.00
PP15	Vinny Castilla	1.00
PP16	Ellis Burks	1.00
PP17	Rafael Palmeiro	1.00
PP18	Alex Rodriguez	12.00
PP19	Mike Piazza	10.00
PP20	Eddie Murray	2.50

1997 Collector's Choice Stick'Ums

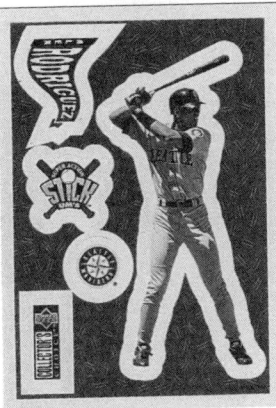

The 30-piece 2-1/2" x 3-1/2" sticker set was inserted one per three packs of 1997 Collector's Choice. Fronts feature a bright background color and include five different peel-off stickers: An action shot of the player, a pennant in team colors featuring the player's name, a team logo, an Upper Deck Collector's Choice logo and a "Super Action Stick'Ums" decal. Backs feature the 20-player checklist in black ink over a gray background. An unnumbered version of the stickers (without Smith and Puckett) was sold in a special retail-only package.

		MT
Complete Set (30):		25.00
Common Player:		.25
1	Ozzie Smith	.50
2	Andruw Jones	1.50
3	Alex Rodriguez	3.00
4	Paul Molitor	.50
5	Jeff Bagwell	1.00
6	Manny Ramirez	.75
7	Kenny Lofton	.75
8	Albert Belle	.75
9	Jay Buhner	.25
10	Chipper Jones	2.00
11	Barry Larkin	.40
12	Dante Bichette	.25
13	Mike Piazza	2.00
14	Andres Galarraga	.25
15	Barry Bonds	.75
16	Brady Anderson	.25
17	Gary Sheffield	.50
18	Jim Thome	.50
19	Tony Gwynn	1.25
20	Cal Ripken Jr.	2.50
21	Sammy Sosa	1.50
22	Juan Gonzalez	1.00
23	Greg Maddux	2.00
24	Ken Griffey Jr.	3.00
25	Mark McGwire	3.00
26	Kirby Puckett	1.00
27	Mo Vaughn	.75
28	Vladimir Guerrero	.75
29	Ken Caminiti	.40
30	Frank Thomas	2.50

1997 Collector's Choice Toast of the Town

This 30-card Series 2 insert features top stars on foil-enhanced cards. Odds of finding one of these inserts are 1:35 packs.

		MT
Complete Set (30):		240.00
Common Player:		2.50
T1	Andruw Jones	8.00
T2	Chipper Jones	15.00
T3	Greg Maddux	15.00
T4	John Smoltz	2.50
T5	Kenny Lofton	6.00
T6	Brady Anderson	2.50
T7	Cal Ripken Jr.	20.00
T8	Mo Vaughn	6.00
T9	Sammy Sosa	12.00
T10	Albert Belle	6.00
T11	Frank Thomas	15.00
T12	Barry Larkin	2.50
T13	Manny Ramirez	6.00
T14	Jeff Bagwell	10.00
T15	Mike Piazza	15.00
T16	Paul Molitor	4.00
T17	Vladimir Guerrero	6.00
T18	Todd Hundley	2.50
T19	Derek Jeter	15.00
T20	Andy Pettitte	4.00
T21	Bernie Williams	4.00
T22	Mark McGwire	30.00
T23	Scott Rolen	10.00
T24	Ken Caminiti	2.50
T25	Tony Gwynn	10.00
T26	Barry Bonds	6.00
T27	Ken Griffey Jr.	25.00
T28	Alex Rodriguez	25.00
T29	Juan Gonzalez	10.00
T30	Roger Clemens	6.00

1997 Collector's Choice You Crash the Game

A 30-card interactive set found in Series 2 packs features the game's top home run hitters. Cards were inserted 1:5 packs. Card fronts feature red-foil Crash logo and a range of game dates. Those holding cards of players who homered in that span could (for $2 per card handling fee, redeem them for high-tech versions. Instant winner cards (seeded 1:721) were redeemable for complete 30-card upgrade sets. Winning cards are marked with an asterisk; theoretically they would be scarcer than losing cards because many were redeemed. The contest cards expired on Sept. 8, 1997.

		MT
Complete Set (30):		40.00
Common Player:		.50
CG1	Ryan Klesko	
	July 28-30	.50
	August 8-11	.50
	Sept. 19-21	.50
CG2	Chipper Jones	
	August 15-17	3.00
	August 29-31	3.00
	Sept. 12-14	3.00
CG3	Andruw Jones	
	August 22-24*	3.00
	Sept. 1-3	1.50
	Sept. 19-22	1.50
CG4	Brady Anderson	
	July 31-Aug. 3*	1.00
	Sept. 4-7	.50
	Sept. 19-22	.50
CG5	Rafael Palmeiro	
	July 29-30	.50
	Aug. 29-31	.50
	Sept. 26-28	.50
CG6	Cal Ripken Jr.	
	August 8-10*	6.00
	Sept. 1-3*	6.00
	Sept. 11-14	4.00
CG7	Mo Vaughn	
	August 14-17	.75
	August 29-31*	1.50
	Sept. 23-25*	1.50
CG8	Sammy Sosa	
	August 1-3*	3.00
	August 29-31	1.50
	Sept. 19-21*	3.00
CG9	Albert Belle	
	August 7-10	.65
	Sept. 11-14	.65
	Sept. 19-21*	1.25
CG10	Frank Thomas	
	August 29-31	2.50
	Sept. 1-3	2.50
	Sept. 23-25*	5.00
CG11	Manny Ramirez	
	August 12-14*	1.00
	August 29-31	.50
	Sept. 11-14*	1.00
CG12	Jim Thome	
	July 28-30	.50
	August 15-18*	1.00
	Sept. 19-22	.50
CG13	Matt Williams	
	August 4-5	.50
	Sept. 1-3*	1.00
	Sept. 23-25	.50
CG14	Dante Bichette	
	July 24-27*	1.00
	August 28-29	.50
	Sept. 26-28*	1.00
CG15	Vinny Castilla	
	August 12-13	.50
	Sept. 4-7*	1.00
	Sept. 19-21	.50
CG16	Andres Galarraga	
	August 8-10*	1.00
	August 30-31	.50
	Sept. 12-14	.50
CG17	Gary Sheffield	
	August 1-3*	1.00
	Sept. 1-3*	1.00
	Sept. 12-14*	1.00
CG18	Jeff Bagwell	
	Sept. 9-10	.75
	Sept. 19-22*	1.50
	Sept. 23-25*	1.50
CG19	Eric Karros	
	August 1-3	.50
	August 15-17	.50
	Sept. 25-28*	1.00
CG20	Mike Piazza	
	August 11-12	2.00
	Sept. 5-8*	4.00
	Sept. 19-21*	4.00
CG21	Vladimir Guerrero	
	August 22-24	1.00
	August 29-31	1.00
	Sept. 19-22	1.00
CG22	Cecil Fielder	
	August 29-31	.50

	Sept. 4-7	.50
	Sept. 26-28*	1.00
CG23	Jose Canseco	
	August 22-24	.65
	Sept. 12-14	.65
	Sept. 26-28	.65
CG24	Mark McGwire	
	July 31-Aug. 3	2.50
	August 30-31	2.50
	Sept. 19-22*	5.00
CG25	Ken Caminiti	
	August 8-10	.50
	Sept. 4-7	.50
	Sept. 17-18*	1.00
CG26	Barry Bonds	
	August 5-7	.90
	Sept. 4-7*	2.00
	Sept. 23-24*	2.00
CG27	Jay Buhner	
	August 7-10	.50
	August 28-29	.50
	Sept. 1-3	.50
CG28	Ken Griffey Jr.	
	August 22-24*	5.00
	August 28-29	3.00
	Sept. 19-22	5.00
CG29	Alex Rodriguez	
	July 29-31	1.50
	August 30-31	1.50
	Sept. 12-15	1.50
CG30	Juan Gonzalez	
	August 11-13*	2.00
	August 30-31	1.00
	Sept. 19-21*	2.00

1997 Collector's Choice Crash Winners

These are the prize cards from CC's interactive "You Crash the Game" cards in Series 2. Persons who redeemed a Crash card with the correct date(s) on which the pictured player homered received (for a $2 handling fee) this high-end version of the Crash card. The redemption cards have the same basic design as the contest cards, but use different player photos with fronts printed on metallic-foil stock, and a team logo in place of the Crash foil logo. Where the contest cards have game rules on back, the redemption cards have another photo of the player and career highlights. Complete redemption sets were available upon redeeming an instant winner card, found on average of one per 721 packs. Because some cards were only available in complete redemption sets, and others might have been available for more than one date range, some cards will be scarcer than others.

		MT
Complete Set (30):		45.00
Common Player:		2.00
CG1	Ryan Klesko	2.50
CG2	Chipper Jones	6.00
CG3	Andruw Jones	3.00
CG4	Brady Anderson	2.00
CG5	Rafael Palmeiro	3.00
CG6	Cal Ripken Jr.	7.00

CG7	Mo Vaughn	2.50
CG8	Sammy Sosa	3.00
CG9	Albert Belle	2.50
CG10	Frank Thomas	6.00
CG11	Manny Ramirez	2.00
CG12	Jim Thome	2.00
CG13	Matt Williams	2.00
CG14	Dante Bichette	2.00
CG15	Vinny Castilla	2.00
CG16	Andres Galarraga	2.00
CG17	Gary Sheffield	2.00
CG18	Jeff Bagwell	2.50
CG19	Eric Karros	2.00
CG20	Mike Piazza	5.00
CG21	Vladimir Guerrero	4.00
CG22	Cecil Fielder	2.00
CG23	Jose Canseco	3.00
CG24	Mark McGwire	5.00
CG25	Ken Caminiti	2.00
CG26	Barry Bonds	2.50
CG27	Jay Buhner	3.00
CG28	Ken Griffey Jr.	7.50
CG29	Alex Rodriguez	6.00
CG30	Juan Gonzalez	2.50

1997 Collector's Choice Update

This update set was offered via a mail-in redemption offer. Traded players in their new uniforms and 1997 rookies are the focus of the set. Fronts are color photos which are borderless at top and sides. Beneath each photo the player's name and team logo appear in a red (A.L.) or blue (N.L.) baseball design. Backs have another photo, major and minor league career stats and a trvia question.

		MT
Complete Set (30):		8.00
Common Player:		.25
U1	Jim Leyritz	.25
U2	Matt Perisho	.25
U3	Michael Tucker	.25
U4	Mike Johnson	.25
U5	Jaime Navarro	.25
U6	Doug Drabek	.25
U7	Terry Mulholland	.35
U8	Brett Tomko	.25
U9	Marquis Grissom	.40
U10	David Justice	.40
U11	Brian Moehler	.25
U12	Bobby Bonilla	.40
U13	Todd Dunwoody	.40
U14	Tony Saunders	.25
U15	Jay Bell	.25
U16	Jeff King	.25
U17	Terry Steinbach	.25
U18	Steve Bieser	.25
U19	*Takashi Kashiwada*	.40
U20	Hideki Irabu	1.50
U21	Damon Mashore	.25
U22	Quilvio Veras	.25
U23	Will Cunnane	.25
U24	Jeff Kent	.35
U25	J.T. Snow	.40
U26	Dante Powell	.25
U27	Jose Cruz Jr.	1.50
U28	John Burkett	.25
U29	John Wetteland	.25
U30	Benito Santiago	.25

Figure values of lower-grade cards from 1981-date as:

Near Mint (NM) 75%
Excellent (EX) 40%
of the listed Mint price

For cards through 1980, values should be figured as:

Excellent (EX) 50%
Very Good (VG) 30%
of the listed Near Mint price

1997 Collector's Choice Team Sets

A special version of Collector's Choice cards for 12 popular major league teams was produced in two retail packages by Upper Deck. In one version, blister packs containing 13 player cards and a metallic-foil team logo/checklist card was sold for a suggested retail price of $1.99. The second version, exclusive to Wal-Mart, is a hard plastic blister pack containing two cello-wrapped packages. One holds a random assortment of 15 Series I Collector's Choice cards. The other has 13 player cards and a foil logo/checklist card for a specific team. The team-set cards are identical to the regular-issue cards, from either Series 1 or Series 2. Each of the team-set cards also has a number on back which differs from the regular edition. Packaged with the Wal-Mart version is a 3-1/2" x 5" "Home Team Heroes" card, listed seperately.

		MT
Common Player:		.10
	Atlanta Braves team set:	4.00
AB	Team logo/checklist	.10
AB1	Andruw Jones	1.00
AB2	Kenny Lofton	.45
AB3	Fred McGriff	.20
AB4	Michael Tucker	.10
AB5	Ryan Klesko	.35
AB6	Javy Lopez	.15
AB7	Mark Wohlers	.10
AB8	Tom Glavine	.20
AB9	Denny Neagle	.10
AB10	Chipper Jones	1.25

AB11	Jeff Blauser	.10
AB12	Greg Maddux	1.25
AB13	John Smoltz	.20
	Baltimore Orioles team set:	2.00
BO	Team logo/checklist	.10
BO1	Rocky Coppinger	.10
BO2	Scott Erickson	.10
BO3	Chris Hoiles	.10
BO4	Roberto Alomar	.40
BO5	Cal Ripken Jr.	1.50
BO6	Randy Myers	.10
BO7	B.J. Surhoff	.10
BO8	Mike Mussina	.40
BO9	Rafael Palmeiro	.25
BO10	Jimmy Key	.10
BO11	Mike Bordick	.10
BO12	Brady Anderson	.20
BO13	Eric Davis	.10
	Chicago White Sox team set:	2.50
CW	Team logo/checklist	.10
CW1	Robin Ventura	.10
CW2	Wilson Alvarez	.10
CW3	Tony Phillips	.10
CW4	Lyle Mouton	.10
CW5	James Baldwin	.10
CW6	Harold Baines	.10
CW7	Albert Belle	.75
CW8	Chris Snopek	.10
CW9	Ray Durham	.10
CW10	Frank Thomas	1.50
CW11	Ozzie Guillen	.10
CW12	Roberto Hernandez	.10
CW13	Jaime Navarro	.10
	Cleveland Indians team set:	1.50
CI	Team logo/checklist	.10
CI1	Brian Giles	.10
CI2	Omar Vizquel	.10
CI3	Julio Franco	.10
CI4	Orel Hershiser	.10
CI5	Charles Nagy	.10
CI6	Matt Williams	.20
CI7	Jose Mesa	.10
CI8	Sandy Alomar	.20
CI9	Jim Thome	.40
CI10	David Justice	.25
CI11	Marquis Grissom	.15
CI12	Chad Ogea	.10
CI13	Manny Ramirez	.50
	Colorado Rockies team set:	1.25
CR	Team logo/checklist	.10
CR1	Dante Bichette	.20
CR2	Vinny Castilla	.10
CR3	Kevin Ritz	.10
CR4	Larry Walker	.30
CR5	Eric Young	.10
CR6	Quinton McCracken	.10
CR7	John Vander Wal	.10
CR8	Jamey Wright	.10
CR9	Mark Thompson	.10
CR10	Andres Galarraga	.25
CR11	Ellis Burks	.10
CR12	Kirt Manwaring	.10
CR13	Walt Weiss	.10
	New York Yankees team set:	3.00
NY	Team logo/checklist	.10
NY1	Bernie Williams	.40
NY2	Dwight Gooden	.20
NY3	Wade Boggs	.25
NY4	Ruben Rivera	.20
NY5	Derek Jeter	1.25
NY6	Tino Martinez	.25
NY7	Tim Raines	.10
NY8	Joe Girardi	.10
NY9	Charlie Hayes	.10
NY10	Andy Pettitte	.40
NY11	Cecil Fielder	.20
NY12	Paul O'Neill	.20
NY13	David Cone	.20
	Seattle Mariners team set:	.10
SM	Team logo/checklist	.10
SM1	Dan Wilson	.10
SM2	Ken Griffey Jr.	2.00
SM3	Edgar Martinez	.10
SM4	Joey Cora	.10
SM5	Norm Charlton	.10
SM6	Alex Rodriguez	1.50
SM7	Randy Johnson	.40
SM8	Paul Sorrento	.10
SM9	Jamie Moyer	.10
SM10	Jay Buhner	.20
SM11	Russ Davis	.10
SM12	Jeff Fassero	.10
SM13	Bob Wells	.10

1998 Collector's Choice

The 530-card Collectors Choice set was issued in two 265-card series. Series One featured 197-regular cards, five checklists and four subsets. Cover Story features 18 of the league's top stars, Rookie Class has 27 young players, the nine-card Top of the Charts subset honors 1997's statistical leaders and Masked Marauders is a nine-card subset. The inserts in Series One are Super Action Stick-Ums, Evolution Revolution and StarQuest. Series Two has 233 regular cards, five checklists cards, an 18-card Rookie Class subset and the nine-card Golden Jubilee subset. Inserts in Series Two include Mini Bobbing Head Cards, You Crash the Game and Star-Quest.

		MT
Complete Set (530):		30.00
Complete Series I Set (265):		15.00
Complete Series II Set (265):		15.00
Common Player:		.05
Wax Box:		40.00
1	Nomar Garciaparra (Cover Glory)	.60
2	Roger Clemens (Cover Glory)	.30
3	Larry Walker (Cover Glory)	.10
4	Mike Piazza (Cover Glory)	.60
5	Mark McGwire (Cover Glory)	1.00
6	Tony Gwynn (Cover Glory)	.50
7	Jose Cruz Jr. (Cover Glory)	.50
8	Frank Thomas (Cover Glory)	.75
9	Tino Martinez (Cover Glory)	.10
10	Ken Griffey Jr. (Cover Glory)	1.00
11	Barry Bonds (Cover Glory)	.25
12	Scott Rolen (Cover Glory)	.50
13	Randy Johnson (Cover Glory)	.15
14	Ryne Sandberg (Cover Glory)	.25
15	Eddie Murray (Cover Glory)	.10
16	Kevin Brown (Cover Glory)	.05
17	Greg Maddux (Cover Glory)	.60
18	Sandy Alomar Jr. (Cover Glory)	.05
19	Checklist(Ken Griffey Jr., Adam Riggs)	.50
20	Checklist(Nomar Garciaparra, Charlie O'Brien)	.30
21	Checklist(Ben Grieve, Ken Griffey Jr., Larry Walker, Mark McGwire)	1.00

#	Player	Price
22	Checklist(Mark McGwire, Cal Ripken Jr.)	1.00
23	Checklist(Tino Martinez)	.05
24	Jason Dickson	.05
25	Darin Erstad	.60
26	Todd Greene	.15
27	Chuck Finley	.05
28	Garret Anderson	.05
29	Dave Hollins	.05
30	Rickey Henderson	.05
31	John Smoltz	.15
32	Michael Tucker	.05
33	Jeff Blauser	.05
34	Javier Lopez	.10
35	Andruw Jones	1.00
36	Denny Neagle	.05
37	Randall Simon	.15
38	Mark Wohlers	.05
39	Harold Baines	.05
40	Cal Ripken Jr.	1.50
41	Mike Bordick	.05
42	Jimmy Key	.05
43	Armando Benitez	.05
44	Scott Erickson	.05
45	Eric Davis	.05
46	Bret Saberhagen	.05
47	Darren Bragg	.05
48	Steve Avery	.05
49	Jeff Frye	.05
50	Aaron Sele	.05
51	Scott Hatteberg	.05
52	Tom Gordon	.05
53	Kevin Orie	.06
54	Kevin Foster	.05
55	Ryne Sandberg	.50
56	Doug Glanville	.05
57	Tyler Houston	.05
58	Steve Trachsel	.05
59	Mark Grace	.15
60	Frank Thomas	1.50
61	*Scott Eyre*	.15
62	Jeff Abbott	.05
63	Chris Clemons	.05
64	Jorge Fabregas	.05
65	Robin Ventura	.10
66	Matt Karchner	.05
67	Jon Nunnally	.05
68	Aaron Boone	.05
69	Pokey Reese	.05
70	Deion Sanders	.15
71	Jeff Shaw	.05
72	Eduardo Perez	.05
73	Brett Tomko	.05
74	Bartolo Colon	.05
75	Manny Ramirez	.40
76	Jose Mesa	.05
77	Brian Giles	.05
78	Richie Sexson	.05
79	Orel Hershiser	.05
80	Matt Williams	.20
81	Walt Weiss	.05
82	Jerry DiPoto	.05
83	Quinton McCracken	.05
84	Neifi Perez	.05
85	Vinny Castilla	.10
86	Ellis Burks	.05
87	John Thomson	.05
88	Willie Blair	.05
89	Bob Hamelin	.05
90	Tony Clark	.35
91	Todd Jones	.05
92	Deivi Cruz	.05
93	*Frank Catalanotto*	.15
94	Justin Thompson	.05
95	Gary Sheffield	.25
96	Kevin Brown	.15
97	Charles Johnson	.10
98	Bobby Bonilla	.10
99	Livan Hernandez	.05
100	Paul Konerko (Rookie Class)	.60
101	Craig Counsell (Rookie Class)	.05
102	*Magglio Ordonez* (Rookie Class)	.50
103	Garrett Stephenson (Rookie Class)	.05
104	Ken Cloude (Rookie Class)	.15
105	Miguel Tejada (Rookie Class)	.40
106	Juan Encarnacion (Rookie Class)	.20
107	Dennis Reyes (Rookie Class)	.15
108	Orlando Cabrera (Rookie Class)	.05
109	Kelvim Escobar (Rookie Class)	.05
110	Ben Grieve (Rookie Class)	.75
111	Brian Rose (Rookie Class)	.05
112	Fernando Tatis (Rookie Class)	.20
113	Tom Evans (Rookie Class)	.05
114	Tom Fordham (Rookie Class)	.05
115	Mark Kotsay (Rookie Class)	.40
116	Mario Valdez (Rookie Class)	.05
117	Jeremi Gonzalez (Rookie Class)	.05
118	Todd Dunwoody (Rookie Class)	.05
119	Javier Valentin (Rookie Class)	.05
120	Todd Helton (Rookie Class)	.50
121	Jason Varitek (Rookie Class)	.05
122	Chris Carpenter (Rookie Class)	.05
123	*Kevin Millwood* (Rookie Class)	.50
124	Brad Fullmer (Rookie Class)	.05
125	Jaret Wright (Rookie Class)	1.00
126	Brad Rigby (Rookie Class)	.05
127	Edgar Renteria	.05
128	Robb Nen	.05
129	Tony Pena	.05
130	Craig Biggio	.15
131	Brad Ausmus	.05
132	Shane Reynolds	.05
133	Mike Hampton	.05
134	Billy Wagner	.05
135	Richard Hidalgo	.05
136	Jose Rosado	.05
137	Yamil Benitez	.05
138	Felix Martinez	.05
139	Jeff King	.05
140	Jose Offerman	.05
141	Joe Vitiello	.05
142	Tim Belcher	.05
143	Brett Butler	.05
144	Greg Gagne	.05
145	Mike Piazza	1.25
146	Ramon Martinez	.10
147	Raul Mondesi	.20
148	Adam Riggs	.05
149	Eddie Murray	.20
150	Jeff Cirillo	.05
151	Scott Karl	.05
152	Mike Fetters	.05
153	Dave Nilsson	.05
154	Antone Williamson	.05
155	Jeff D'Amico	.05
156	Jose Valentin	.05
157	Brad Radke	.05
158	Torii Hunter	.05
159	Chuck Knoblauch	.15
160	Paul Molitor	.35
161	Travis Miller	.05
162	Rich Robertson	.05
163	Ron Coomer	.05
164	Mark Grudzielanek	.05
165	Lee Smith	.05
166	Vladimir Guerrero	.60
167	Dustin Hermanson	.05
168	Ugueth Urbina	.05
169	F.P. Santangelo	.05
170	Rondell White	.15
171	Bobby Jones	.05
172	Edgardo Alfonzo	.15
173	John Franco	.05
174	Carlos Baerga	.05
175	Butch Huskey	.05
176	Rey Ordonez	.10
177	Matt Franco	.05
178	Dwight Gooden	.15
179	Chad Curtis	.05
180	Tino Martinez	.15
181	Charlie O'Brien (Masked Marauders)	.05
182	Sandy Alomar Jr. (Masked Marauders)	.05
183	Raul Casanova (Masked Marauders)	.05
184	Jim Leyritz (Masked Marauders)	.05
185	Mike Piazza (Masked Marauders)	.60
186	Ivan Rodriguez (Masked Marauders)	.25
187	Charles Johnson (Masked Marauders)	.10
188	Brad Ausmus (Masked Marauders)	.05
189	Brian Johnson (Masked Marauders)	.05
190	Wade Boggs	.20
191	David Wells	.05
192	Tim Raines	.05
193	Ramiro Mendoza	.05
194	Willie Adams	.05
195	Matt Stairs	.05
196	Jason McDonald	.05
197	Dave Magadan	.05
198	Mark Bellhorn	.05
199	Ariel Prieto	.05
200	Jose Canseco	.20
201	Bobby Estalella	.05
202	*Tony Barron*	.05
203	Midre Cummings	.05
204	Ricky Bottalico	.05
205	Mike Grace	.05
206	Rico Brogna	.05
207	Mickey Morandini	.05
208	Lou Collier	.05
209	*Kevin Polcovich*	.05
210	Kevin Young	.05
211	Jose Guillen	.25
212	Esteban Loaiza	.05
213	Marc Wilkins	.05
214	Jason Schmidt	.05
215	Gary Gaetti	.05
216	Fernando Valenzuela	.05
217	Willie McGee	.05
218	Alan Benes	.15
219	Eli Marrero	.05
220	Mark McGwire	2.50
221	Matt Morris	.05
222	Trevor Hoffman	.05
223	Will Cunnane	.05
224	Joey Hamilton	.05
225	Ken Caminiti	.15
226	Derrek Lee	.15
227	Mark Sweeney	.05
228	Carlos Hernandez	.05
229	Brian Johnson	.05
230	Jeff Kent	.05
231	Kirk Rueter	.05
232	Bill Mueller	.05
233	Dante Powell	.05
234	J.T. Snow	.15
235	Shawn Estes	.05
236	Dennis Martinez	.05
237	Jamie Moyer	.05
238	Dan Wilson	.05
239	Joey Cora	.05
240	Ken Griffey Jr.	2.00
241	Paul Sorrento	.05
242	Jay Buhner	.20
243	*Hanley Frias*	.05
244	John Burkett	.05
245	Juan Gonzalez	1.00
246	Rick Helling	.05
247	Darren Oliver	.05
248	Mickey Tettleton	.05
249	Ivan Rodriguez	.50
250	Joe Carter	.15
251	Pat Hentgen	.05
252	Marty Janzen	.05
253	Frank Thomas, Tony Gwynn (Top of the Charts)	.50
254	Mark McGwire, Ken Griffey Jr., Larry Walker (Top of the Charts)	1.00
255	Ken Griffey Jr., Andres Galarraga (Top of the Charts)	.50
256	Brian Hunter, Tony Womack (Top of the Charts)	.05
257	Roger Clemens, Denny Neagle (Top of the Charts)	.20
258	Roger Clemens, Curt Schilling (Top of the Charts)	.20
259	Roger Clemens, Pedro J. Martinez (Top of the Charts)	.20
260	Randy Myers, Jeff Shaw (Top of the Charts)	.05
261	Nomar Garciaparra, Scott Rolen (Top of the Charts)	.30
262	Charlie O'Brien	.05
263	Shannon Stewart	.05
264	Robert Person	.05
265	Carlos Delgado	.05
266	Checklist(Matt Williams, Travis Lee)	.40
267	Checklist(Nomar Garciaparra, Cal Ripken Jr.)	.40

No.	Player	Price
268	Checklist(Mark McGwire, Mike Piazza)	.75
269	Checklist(Tony Gwynn, Ken Griffey Jr.)	.50
270	Checklist(Fred McGriff, Jose Cruz Jr.)	.15
271	Andruw Jones (Golden Jubilee)	.25
272	Alex Rodriguez (Golden Jubilee)	.60
273	Juan Gonzalez (Golden Jubilee)	.50
274	Nomar Garciaparra (Golden Jubilee)	.60
275	Ken Griffey Jr. (Golden Jubilee)	1.00
276	Tino Martinez (Golden Jubilee)	.15
277	Roger Clemens (Golden Jubilee)	.40
278	Barry Bonds (Golden Jubilee)	.25
279	Mike Piazza (Golden Jubilee)	.60
280	Tim Salmon (Golden Jubilee)	.15
281	Gary DiSarcina	.05
282	Cecil Fielder	.15
283	Ken Hill	.05
284	Troy Percival	.05
285	Jim Edmonds	.05
286	Allen Watson	.05
287	Brian Anderson	.05
288	Jay Bell	.05
289	Jorge Fabregas	.05
290	Devon White	.05
291	Yamil Benitez	.05
292	Jeff Suppan	.05
293	Tony Batista	.05
294	Brent Brede	.05
295	Andy Benes	.15
296	Felix Rodriguez	.05
297	Karim Garcia	.05
298	Omar Daal	.05
299	Andy Stankiewicz	.05
300	Matt Williams	.25
301	Willie Blair	.05
302	Ryan Klesko	.20
303	Tom Glavine	.15
304	Walt Weiss	.05
305	Greg Maddux	1.25
306	Chipper Jones	1.25
307	Keith Lockhart	.05
308	Andres Galarraga	.20
309	Chris Hoiles	.05
310	Roberto Alomar	.40
311	Joe Carter	.15
312	Doug Drabek	.05
313	Jeffrey Hammonds	.05
314	Rafael Palmeiro	.20
315	Mike Mussina	.40
316	Brady Anderson	.05
317	B.J. Surhoff	.05
318	Dennis Eckersley	.05
319	Jim Leyritz	.05
320	Mo Vaughn	.50
321	Nomar Garciaparra	1.25
322	Reggie Jefferson	.05
323	Tim Naehring	.05
324	Troy O'Leary	.05
325	Pedro J. Martinez	.25
326	John Valentin	.05
327	Mark Clark	.05
328	Rod Beck	.05
329	Mickey Morandini	.05
330	Sammy Sosa	1.00
331	Jeff Blauser	.05
332	Lance Johnson	.05
333	Scott Servais	.05
334	Kevin Tapani	.05
335	Henry Rodriguez	.05
336	Jaime Navarro	.05
337	Benji Gil	.05
338	James Baldwin	.05
339	Mike Cameron	.05
340	Ray Durham	.05
341	Chris Snopek	.05
342	Eddie Taubensee	.05
343	Bret Boone	.05
344	Willie Greene	.05
345	Barry Larkin	.15
346	Chris Stynes	.05
347	Pete Harnisch	.05
348	Dave Burba	.05
349	Sandy Alomar Jr.	.15
350	Kenny Lofton	.50
351	Geronimo Berroa	.05
352	Omar Vizquel	.05
353	Travis Fryman	.05
354	Dwight Gooden	.05
355	Jim Thome	.40
356	David Justice	.25
357	Charles Nagy	.05
358	Chad Ogea	.05
359	Pedro Astacio	.05
360	Larry Walker	.25
361	Mike Lansing	.05
362	Kirt Manwaring	.05
363	Dante Bichette	.15
364	Jamey Wright	.05
365	Darryl Kile	.05
366	Luis Gonzalez	.05
367	Joe Randa	.05
368	Raul Casanova	.05
369	Damion Easley	.05
370	Brian L. Hunter	.05
371	Bobby Higginson	.05
372	Brian Moehler	.05
373	Scott Sanders	.05
374	Jim Eisenreich	.05
375	Derrek Lee	.05
376	Jay Powell	.05
377	Cliff Floyd	.05
378	Alex Fernandez	.05
379	Felix Heredia	.05
380	Jeff Bagwell	.75
381	Bill Spiers	.05
382	Chris Holt	.05
383	Carl Everett	.05
384	Derek Bell	.05
385	Moises Alou	.15
386	Ramon Garcia	.05
387	Mike Sweeney	.05
388	Glendon Rusch	.05
389	Kevin Appier	.05
390	Dean Palmer	.05
391	Jeff Conine	.05
392	Johnny Damon	.05
393	Jose Vizcaino	.05
394	Todd Hollandsworth	.05
395	Eric Karros	.05
396	Todd Zeile	.05
397	Chan Ho Park	.15
398	Ismael Valdes	.05
399	Eric Young	.05
400	Hideo Nomo	.40
401	Mark Loretta	.05
402	Doug Jones	.05
403	Jeromy Burnitz	.05
404	John Jaha	.05
405	Marquis Grissom	.05
406	Mike Matheny	.05
407	Todd Walker	.05
408	Marty Cordova	.05
409	Matt Lawton	.05
410	Terry Steinbach	.05
411	Pat Meares	.05
412	Rick Aguilera	.05
413	Otis Nixon	.05
414	Derrick May	.05
415	Carl Pavano (Rookie Class)	.05
416	A.J. Hinch (Rookie Class)	.15
417	*David Dellucci* (Rookie Class)	.25
418	Bruce Chen (Rookie Class)	.05
419	*Darron Ingram* (Rookie Class)	.05
420	Sean Casey (Rookie Class)	.05
421	Mark L. Johnson (Rookie Class)	.05
422	Gabe Alvarez (Rookie Class)	.05
423	Alex Gonzalez (Rookie Class)	.05
424	Daryle Ward (Rookie Class)	.15
425	Russell Branyan (Rookie Class)	.05
426	Mike Caruso (Rookie Class)	.05
427	*Mike Kinkade* (Rookie Class)	.25
428	Ramon Hernandez (Rookie Class)	.05
429	Matt Clement (Rookie Class)	.10
430	Travis Lee (Rookie Class)	1.50
431	Shane Monahan (Rookie Class)	.05
432	*Rich Butler* (Rookie Class)	.25
433	Chris Widger	.05
434	Jose Vidro	.05
435	Carlos Perez	.05
436	Ryan McGuire	.05
437	Brian McRae	.05
438	Al Leiter	.05
439	Rich Becker	.05
440	Todd Hundley	.05
441	Dave Mlicki	.05
442	Bernard Gilkey	.05
443	John Olerud	.15
444	Paul O'Neill	.15
445	Andy Pettitte	.40
446	David Cone	.15
447	Chili Davis	.05
448	Bernie Williams	.40
449	Joe Girardi	.05
450	Derek Jeter	1.00
451	Mariano Rivera	.15
452	George Williams	.05
453	Kenny Rogers	.05
454	Tom Candiotti	.05
455	Rickey Henderson	.05
456	Jason Giambi	.05
457	Scott Spiezio	.05
458	Doug Glanville	.05
459	Desi Relaford	.05
460	Curt Schilling	.15
461	Bob Abreu	.05
462	Gregg Jefferies	.05
463	Scott Rolen	.75
464	Mike Lieberthal	.05
465	Tony Womack	.05
466	Jermaine Allensworth	.05
467	Francisco Cordova	.05
468	Jon Lieber	.05
469	Al Martin	.05
470	Jason Kendall	.05
471	Todd Stottlemyre	.05
472	Royce Clayton	.05
473	Brian Jordan	.05
474	John Mabry	.05
475	Ray Lankford	.05
476	Delino DeShields	.05
477	Ron Gant	.05
478	Mark Langston	.05
479	Steve Finley	.05
480	Tony Gwynn	1.00
481	Andy Ashby	.05
482	Wally Joyner	.05
483	Greg Vaughn	.05
484	Sterling Hitchcock	.05
485	J. Kevin Brown	.05
486	Orel Hershiser	.05
487	Charlie Hayes	.05
488	Darryl Hamilton	.05
489	Mark Gardner	.05
490	Barry Bonds	.50
491	Robb Nen	.05
492	Kirk Rueter	.05
493	Randy Johnson	.40
494	Jeff Fassero	.05
495	Alex Rodriguez	1.25
496	David Segui	.05
497	Rich Amaral	.05
498	Russ Davis	.05
499	Bubba Trammell	.05
500	Wade Boggs	.20
501	Roberto Hernandez	.05
502	Dave Martinez	.05
503	Dennis Springer	.05
504	Paul Sorrento	.05
505	Wilson Alvarez	.05
506	Mike Kelly	.05
507	Albie Lopez	.05
508	Tony Saunders	.05
509	John Flaherty	.05
510	Fred McGriff	.15
511	Quinton McCracken	.05
512	Terrell Wade	.05
513	Kevin Stocker	.05
514	Kevin Elster	.05
515	Will Clark	.20
516	Bobby Witt	.05
517	Tom Goodwin	.05
518	Aaron Sele	.05
519	Lee Stevens	.05
520	Rusty Greer	.05
521	John Wetteland	.05
522	Darrin Fletcher	.05
523	Jose Canseco	.25
524	Randy Myers	.05
525	Jose Cruz Jr.	.50
526	Shawn Green	.05
527	Tony Fernandez	.05
528	Alex Gonzalez	.05
529	Ed Sprague	.05
530	Roger Clemens	.75

1998 Collector's Choice Cover Glory 5x7

		MT
Complete Set (8):		12.00
Common Player:		1.00
1	Nomar Garciaparra	2.00
2	Roger Clemens	1.50
3	Larry Walker	1.00
4	Mike Piazza	2.00
5	Mark McGwire	3.00
6	Tony Gwynn	1.50
7	Jose Cruz Jr.	1.50
8	Frank Thomas	2.50
9	Tino Martinez	1.00
10	Ken Griffey Jr.	3.50

1998 Collector's Choice Evolution Revolution

This 28-card insert features one player from each Major League team. The fronts have the team jersey and fold out to reveal the player's top 1997 accomplishment. Evolution Revolution was inserted one per 13 Series One packs.

		MT
Complete Set (28):		60.00
Common Player:		.75
Inserted 1:13		
ER1	Tim Salmon	1.25
ER2	Greg Maddux	6.00
ER3	Cal Ripken Jr.	8.00
ER4	Mo Vaughn	2.50
ER5	Sammy Sosa	4.00
ER6	Frank Thomas	8.00
ER7	Barry Larkin	1.00
ER8	Jim Thome	1.50
ER9	Larry Walker	1.25
ER10	Travis Fryman	.75
ER11	Gary Sheffield	1.50
ER12	Jeff Bagwell	4.00
ER13	Johnny Damon	.75
ER14	Mike Piazza	6.00
ER15	Jeff Cirillo	.75
ER16	Paul Molitor	2.00
ER17	Vladimir Guerrero	3.00
ER18	Todd Hundley	.75
ER19	Tino Martinez	.75
ER20	Jose Canseco	1.00
ER21	Scott Rolen	5.00
ER22	Al Martin	.75
ER23	Mark McGwire	12.00
ER24	Tony Gwynn	5.00
ER25	Barry Bonds	2.50
ER26	Ken Griffey Jr.	10.00
ER27	Juan Gonzalez	5.00
ER28	Roger Clemens	4.00

1998 Collector's Choice Mini Bobbing Heads

The cards in this 30-card insert fold into a stand-up figure with a removable bobbing head. They were inserted 1:3 in Series Two packs.

		MT
Complete Set (30):		20.00
Common Player:		.25
1	Tim Salmon	.40
2	Travis Lee	2.00
3	Matt Williams	.25
4	Chipper Jones	1.50
5	Greg Maddux	1.50
6	Cal Ripken Jr.	2.00
7	Nomar Garciaparra	1.50
8	Mo Vaughn	.75
9	Sammy Sosa	1.00
10	Frank Thomas	2.00
11	Kenny Lofton	.75
12	Jaret Wright	.75
13	Larry Walker	.40
14	Tony Clark	.50
15	Edgar Renteria	.25
16	Jeff Bagwell	1.00
17	Mike Piazza	1.50
18	Vladimir Guerrero	.75
19	Derek Jeter	1.25
20	Ben Grieve	.75
21	Scott Rolen	.75
22	Mark McGwire	3.00
23	Tony Gwynn	1.25
24	Barry Bonds	.75
25	Ken Griffey Jr.	2.50
26	Alex Rodriguez	1.50
27	Fred McGriff	.40
28	Juan Gonzalez	1.25
29	Roger Clemens	1.00
30	Jose Cruz Jr.	.75

1998 Collector's Choice Rookie Class: Prime Choice

This 18-card set is a parallel of the Rookie Class subset. Each card is foil-stamped with the words "Prime Choice Reserve." This hobby-only set is sequentially numbered to 500 and was inserted in Series Two packs.

		MT
Complete Set (18):		200.00
Common Player:		5.00
415	Carl Pavano	15.00
416	A.J. Hinch	15.00
417	David Dellucci	25.00
418	Bruce Chen	20.00
419	Darron Ingram	5.00
420	Sean Casey	20.00
421	Mark L. Johnson	5.00
422	Gabe Alvarez	5.00
423	Alex Gonzalez	15.00
424	Daryle Ward	10.00
425	Russell Branyan	10.00
426	Mike Caruso	15.00
427	Mike Kinkade	5.00
428	Ramon Hernandez	5.00
429	Matt Clement	5.00
430	Travis Lee	60.00
431	Shane Monahan	5.00
432	Rich Butler	20.00

1998 Collector's Choice StarQuest

The StarQuest insert in Series One consisted of 90 cards with four tiers. Special Delivery (one star, 45 cards) was inserted 1:1, Students of the Game (two stars, 20 cards) 1:21, Super Powers (three stars, 15 cards) 1:71 and Super Star Domain (four stars, 10 cards) 1:145.

		MT
Complete Set (90):		500.00
Common Special Delivery (1-45)		.20
Inserted 1:1		
Common Student of the Game (46-65):		1.50
Inserted 1:21		
Common Super Power (66-80):		5.00
Inserted 1:71		
Common Superstar Domain (81-90):		10.00
Inserted 1:145		
SQ1	Nomar Garciaparra	2.00
SQ2	Scott Rolen	1.50
SQ3	Jason Dickson	.20
SQ4	Jaret Wright	1.50
SQ5	Kevin Orie	.20
SQ6	Jose Guillen	.50
SQ7	Matt Morris	.20
SQ8	Mike Cameron	.30
SQ9	Kevin Polcovich	.20
SQ10	Jose Cruz Jr.	1.50
SQ11	Miguel Tejada	.50
SQ12	Fernando Tatis	.40
SQ13	Todd Helton	.75
SQ14	Ken Cloude	.20
SQ15	Ben Grieve	1.00
SQ16	Dante Powell	.20
SQ17	Bubba Trammell	.30
SQ18	Juan Encarnacion	.40
SQ19	Derek Lee	.20
SQ20	Paul Konerko	1.00
SQ21	Richard Hidalgo	.20
SQ22	Denny Neagle	.20
SQ23	David Justice	.40
SQ24	Pedro J. Martinez	.40
SQ25	Greg Maddux	2.00
SQ26	Edgar Martinez	.20
SQ27	Cal Ripken Jr.	2.50
SQ28	Tim Salmon	.40
SQ29	Shawn Estes	.20
SQ30	Ken Griffey Jr.	3.00
SQ31	Brad Radke	.20
SQ32	Andy Pettitte	.50
SQ33	Curt Schilling	.20
SQ34	Raul Mondesi	.40
SQ35	Alex Rodriguez	2.00
SQ36	Jeff Kent	.20
SQ37	Jeff Bagwell	1.25
SQ38	Juan Gonzalez	1.50
SQ39	Barry Bonds	.75

SQ40	Mark McGwire	4.00
SQ41	Frank Thomas	2.50
SQ42	Ray Lankford	.20
SQ43	Tony Gwynn	1.50
SQ44	Mike Piazza	2.00
SQ45	Tino Martinez	.20
SQ46	Nomar Garciaparra	10.00
SQ47	Paul Molitor	3.00
SQ48	Chuck Knoblauch	2.00
SQ49	Rusty Greer	1.50
SQ50	Cal Ripken Jr.	12.00
SQ51	Roberto Alomar	3.00
SQ52	Scott Rolen	7.00
SQ53	Derek Jeter	10.00
SQ54	Mark Grace	2.00
SQ55	Randy Johnson	2.50
SQ56	Craig Biggio	1.50
SQ57	Kenny Lofton	4.00
SQ58	Eddie Murray	2.00
SQ59	Ryne Sandberg	4.00
SQ60	Rickey Henderson	1.50
SQ61	Darin Erstad	4.00
SQ62	Jim Edmonds	1.50
SQ63	Ken Caminiti	2.00
SQ64	Ivan Rodriguez	3.00
SQ65	Tony Gwynn	8.00
SQ66	Tony Clark	8.00
SQ67	Andres Galarraga	6.00
SQ68	Rafael Palmeiro	6.00
SQ69	Manny Ramirez	8.00
SQ70	Albert Belle	10.00
SQ71	Jay Buhner	5.00
SQ72	Mo Vaughn	10.00
SQ73	Barry Bonds	10.00
SQ74	Chipper Jones	25.00
SQ75	Jeff Bagwell	18.00
SQ76	Jim Thome	8.00
SQ77	Sammy Sosa	12.00
SQ78	Todd Hundley	5.00
SQ79	Matt Williams	6.00
SQ80	Vinny Castilla	5.00
SQ81	Jose Cruz Jr.	25.00
SQ82	Frank Thomas	50.00
SQ83	Juan Gonzalez	30.00
SQ84	Mike Piazza	40.00
SQ85	Alex Rodriguez	40.00
SQ86	Larry Walker	12.00
SQ87	Tino Martinez	10.00
SQ88	Greg Maddux	40.00
SQ89	Mark McGwire	70.00
SQ90	Ken Griffey Jr.	65.00

1998 Collector's Choice Star Quest

The 30-card StarQuest insert was included in Series Two packs. The insert has four 30-card tiers - Single, Double, Triple and Home Run. The tier is designated by the number of baseball diamond icons on the card front. Single cards were inserted 1:1, Doubles 1:21, Triples 1:71 and Home Runs are sequentially numbered to 100.

		MT
Complete Set (30):		18.00
Common Player:		.25
Singles 1:1		
Doubles 1:21 4x to 8x		
Triples 1:71 12x to 20x		
1	Ken Griffey Jr.	2.00
2	Jose Cruz Jr.	.50
3	Cal Ripken Jr.	1.50
4	Roger Clemens	.75
5	Frank Thomas	1.50
6	Derek Jeter	1.00
7	Alex Rodriguez	1.25
8	Andruw Jones	.50
9	Vladimir Guerrero	.50
10	Mark McGwire	3.00
11	Kenny Lofton	.50
12	Pedro J. Martinez	.25
13	Greg Maddux	1.25
14	Larry Walker	.25
15	Barry Bonds	.50
16	Chipper Jones	1.25
17	Jeff Bagwell	.75
18	Juan Gonzalez	1.00
19	Tony Gwynn	1.00
20	Mike Piazza	1.25
21	Tino Martinez	.25
22	Mo Vaughn	.50
23	Ben Grieve	.60
24	Scott Rolen	.60
25	Nomar Garciaparra	1.25
26	Paul Konerko	.25
27	Jaret Wright	.50
28	Gary Sheffield	.25
29	Travis Lee	1.50
30	Todd Helton	.50

1998 Collector's Choice Star Quest Home Run

StarQuest Home Run cards are the fourth tier of the insert in Series Two. The cards have four baseball diamond icons to designate their level. Home Run cards are sequentially numbered to 100.

		MT
Common Player:		10.00
Semistars:		25.00
1	Ken Griffey Jr.	150.00
2	Jose Cruz Jr.	40.00
3	Cal Ripken Jr.	120.00
4	Roger Clemens	60.00
5	Frank Thomas	120.00
6	Derek Jeter	75.00
7	Alex Rodriguez	100.00
8	Andruw Jones	40.00
9	Vladimir Guerrero	40.00
10	Mark McGwire	150.00
11	Kenny Lofton	40.00
12	Pedro J. Martinez	20.00
13	Greg Maddux	100.00
14	Larry Walker	25.00
15	Barry Bonds	40.00
16	Chipper Jones	90.00
17	Jeff Bagwell	60.00
18	Juan Gonzalez	75.00
19	Tony Gwynn	75.00
20	Mike Piazza	100.00
21	Tino Martinez	20.00
22	Mo Vaughn	40.00
23	Ben Grieve	50.00
24	Scott Rolen	50.00
25	Nomar Garciaparra	90.00
26	Paul Konerko	10.00
27	Jaret Wright	40.00
28	Gary Sheffield	20.00
29	Travis Lee	100.00
30	Todd Helton	40.00

1998 Collector's Choice Stickums

This 30-card insert was seeded 1:3 Series One packs. The stickers can be peeled off the card.

		MT
Complete Set (30):		20.00
Common Player:		.25
1	Andruw Jones	.60
2	Chipper Jones	1.50
3	Cal Ripken Jr.	2.00
4	Nomar Garciaparra	1.50
5	Mo Vaughn	.60
6	Ryne Sandberg	.60
7	Sammy Sosa	1.25
8	Frank Thomas	2.00
9	Albert Belle	.60
10	Jim Thome	.40
11	Manny Ramirez	.60
12	Larry Walker	.40
13	Gary Sheffield	.40
14	Jeff Bagwell	.75
15	Mike Piazza	1.50
16	Paul Molitor	.50
17	Pedro J. Martinez	.50
18	Todd Hundley	.25
19	Derek Jeter	1.25
20	Tino Martinez	.50
21	Curt Schilling	.25
22	Mark McGwire	3.00
23	Tony Gwynn	1.25
24	Barry Bonds	.60
25	Ken Griffey Jr.	2.50
26	Alex Rodriguez	1.50
27	Juan Gonzalez	1.25
28	Ivan Rodriguez	.60
29	Roger Clemens	1.25
30	Jose Cruz Jr.	.75

A player's name in *italic* type indicates a rookie card.

1998 Collector's Choice You Crash the Game

These 30 game cards were inserted one per five Series Two packs. Each card features a player and a list of dates. If the pictured player hit a home run on one of those days, collectors with the card won a prize.

		MT
Complete Set (30):		30.00
Common Player:		.50
Inserted 1:5		
CG1	Ken Griffey Jr.	4.00
CG2	Travis Lee	3.00
CG3	Larry Walker	.75
CG4	Tony Clark	.75
CG5	Cal Ripken Jr.	3.00
CG6	Tim Salmon	.50
CG7	Vinny Castilla	.50
CG8	Fred McGriff	.50
CG9	Matt Williams	.75
CG10	Mark McGwire	2.50
CG11	Albert Belle	1.00
CG12	Jay Buhner	.50
CG13	Vladimir Guerrero	1.00
CG14	Andruw Jones	1.00
CG15	Nomar Garciaparra	2.50
CG16	Ken Caminiti	.50
CG17	Sammy Sosa	1.00
CG18	Ben Grieve	1.00
CG19	Mo Vaughn	1.00
CG20	Frank Thomas	3.00
CG21	Manny Ramirez	1.00
CG22	Jeff Bagwell	1.50
CG23	Jose Cruz Jr.	1.00
CG24	Alex Rodriguez	2.50
CG25	Mike Piazza	2.50
CG26	Tino Martinez	.75
CG27	Chipper Jones	2.50
CG28	Juan Gonzalez	2.00
CG29	Jim Thome	.75
CG30	Barry Bonds	1.00

1998 Collector's Choice Crash Winners

Collectors who redeemed winning "Crash" cards prior to the Dec. 1, 1998, deadline received an upgraded version of that player's card. Similar in format, the winners' cards have an action photo on front (different than the game card), with a metallic foil background. Instead of dates in the three circles at bottom

are the letters "W I N". Backs hae a career summary and stats, instead of the redemption instructions found on the game cards. The cards are numbered with a "CG" prefix.

		MT
Complete Set (30):		90.00
Common Player:		1.50
CG1	Ken Griffey Jr.	12.00
CG2	Travis Lee	9.00
CG3	Larry Walker	2.25
CG4	Tony Clark	2.25
CG5	Cal Ripken Jr.	9.00
CG6	Tim Salmon	1.50
CG7	Vinny Castilla	1.50
CG8	Fred McGriff	1.50
CG9	Matt Williams	2.25
CG10	Mark McGwire	8.00
CG11	Albert Belle	3.00
CG12	Jay Buhner	1.50
CG13	Vladimir Guerrero	3.00
CG14	Andruw Jones	3.00
CG15	Nomar Garciaparra	7.50
CG16	Ken Caminiti	1.50
CG17	Sammy Sosa	3.00
CG18	Ben Grieve	3.00
CG19	Mo Vaughn	3.00
CG20	Frank Thomas	8.00
CG21	Manny Ramirez	3.00
CG22	Jeff Bagwell	4.50
CG23	Jose Cruz Jr.	3.00
CG24	Alex Hodriguez	7.50
CG25	Mike Piazza	7.50
CG26	Tino Martinez	2.25
CG27	Chipper Jones	7.50
CG28	Juan Gonzalez	6.00
CG29	Jim Thome	2.25
CG30	Barry Bonds	3.00

1981 Donruss

TOM SEAVER PITCHER

The Donruss Co. of Memphis, Tenn., produced its premiere baseball card issue in 1981 with a set that consisted of 600 numbered cards and five unnumbered checklists. The cards, which measure 2-1/2" x 3-1/2", are printed on thin stock. The card fronts contain the Donruss logo plus the year of issue. The card backs are designed on a vertical format and have black print on red and white. The set, entitled "First Edition Collector Series," contains nearly 40 variations, those being first-printing errors that were

corrected in a subsequent print run. The cards were issued in gum wax packs, with hobby dealer sales being coordinated by TCMA of Amawalk, N.Y. The complete set price does not include the higher priced variations.

		MT
Complete Set (605):		45.00
Common Player:		.08
Wax Box:		70.00
Eight-card promo sheet:		20.00
1	Ozzie Smith	4.00
2	Rollie Fingers	.75
3	Rick Wise	.08
4	Gene Richards	.08
5	Alan Trammell	.60
6	Tom Brookens	.08
7a	Duffy Dyer (1980 Avg. .185)	.50
7b	Duffy Dyer (1980 Avg. 185)	.10
8	Mark Fidrych	.10
9	Dave Rozema	.08
10	Ricky Peters	.08
11	Mike Schmidt	3.00
12	Willie Stargell	.80
13	Tim Foli	.08
14	Manny Sanguillen	.08
15	Grant Jackson	.08
16	Eddie Solomon	.08
17	Omar Moreno	.08
18	Joe Morgan	.60
19	Rafael Landestoy	.08
20	Bruce Bochy	.08
21	Joe Sambito	.08
22	Manny Trillo	.08
23a	*Dave Smith* (incomplete box around stats)	.50
23b	*Dave Smith* (complete box around stats)	.50
24	Terry Puhl	.08
25	Bump Wills	.08
26a	John Ellis (Danny Walton photo - with bat)	.60
26b	John Ellis (John Ellis photo - with glove)	.10
27	Jim Kern	.08
28	Richie Zisk	.08
29	John Mayberry	.08
30	Bob Davis	.08
31	Jackson Todd	.08
32	Al Woods	.08
33	Steve Carlton	1.50
34	Lee Mazzilli	.08
35	John Stearns	.08
36	Roy Jackson	.08
37	Mike Scott	.15
38	Lamar Johnson	.08
39	Kevin Bell	.08
40	Ed Farmer	.08
41	Ross Baumgarten	.08
42	Leo Sutherland	.08
43	Dan Meyer	.08
44	Ron Reed	.08
45	Mario Mendoza	.08
46	Rick Honeycutt	.08
47	Glenn Abbott	.08
48	Leon Roberts	.08
49	Rod Carew	1.50
50	Bert Campaneris	.10
51a	Tom Donahue (incorrect spelling)	.50
51b	Tom Donohue (Donohue on front)	.10
52	Dave Frost	.08
53	Ed Halicki	.08
54	Dan Ford	.08
55	Garry Maddox	.10
56a	Steve Garvey (Surpassed 25 HR..)	1.25
56b	Steve Garvey (Surpassed 21 HR..)	.60
57	Bill Russell	.10
58	Don Sutton	.45
59	Reggie Smith	.10
60	Rick Monday	.10
61	Ray Knight	.10
62	Johnny Bench	1.25
63	Mario Soto	.08
64	Doug Bair	.08
65	George Foster	.20
66	Jeff Burroughs	.08
67	Keith Hernandez	.20
68	Tom Herr	.08
69	Bob Forsch	.08

70	John Fulgham	.08
71a	Bobby Bonds (lifetime HR 986)	.50
71b	Bobby Bonds (lifetime HR 326)	.15
72a	Rennie Stennett ("...breaking broke leg..." on back)	.50
72b	Rennie Stennett ("...breaking leg..." on back)	.10
73	Joe Strain	.08
74	Ed Whitson	.08
75	Tom Griffin	.08
76	Bill North	.08
77	Gene Garber	.08
78	Mike Hargrove	.08
79	Dave Rosello	.08
80	Ron Hassey	.08
81	Sid Monge	.08
82a	Joe Charboneau ("For some reason, Phillies..." on back)	1.00
82b	Joe Charboneau ("Phillies..." on back)	.25
83	Cecil Cooper	.15
84	Sal Bando	.10
85	Moose Haas	.08
86	Mike Caldwell	.08
87a	Larry Hisle ("...Twins with 28 RBI." on back)	.50
87b	Larry Hisle ("...Twins with 28 HR" on back)	.10
88	Luis Gomez	.08
89	Larry Parrish	.08
90	Gary Carter	.60
91	Bill Gullickson	.15
92	Fred Norman	.08
93	Tommy Hutton	.08
94	Carl Yastrzemski	1.25
95	Glenn Hoffman	.08
96	Dennis Eckersley	1.00
97a	Tom Burgmeier (Throws: Right)	.50
97b	Tom Burgmeier (Throws: Left)	.10
98	Win Remmerswaal	.08
99	Bob Horner	.15
100	George Brett	6.00
101	Dave Chalk	.08
102	Dennis Leonard	.08
103	Renie Martin	.08
104	Amos Otis	.08
105	Graig Nettles	.15
106	Eric Soderholm	.08
107	Tommy John	.20
108	Tom Underwood	.08
109	Lou Piniella	.12
110	Mickey Klutts	.08
111	Bobby Murcer	.10
112	Eddie Murray	4.00
113	Rick Dempsey	.08
114	Scott McGregor	.08
115	Ken Singleton	.10
116	Gary Roenicke	.08
117	Dave Revering	.08
118	Mike Norris	.08
119	Rickey Henderson	4.00
120	Mike Heath	.08
121	Dave Cash	.08
122	Randy Jones	.08
123	Eric Rasmussen	.08
124	Jerry Mumphrey	.08
125	Richie Hebner	.08
126	Mark Wagner	.08
127	Jack Morris	.45
128	Dan Petry	.08
129	Bruce Robbins	.08
130	Champ Summers	.08
131a	Pete Rose ("see card 251" on back)	2.50
131b	Pete Rose ("see card 371" on back)	2.00
132	Willie Stargell	.80
133	Ed Ott	.08
134	Jim Bibby	.08
135	Bert Blyleven	.12
136	Dave Parker	.45
137	Bill Robinson	.08
138	Enos Cabell	.08
139	Dave Bergman	.08
140	J.R. Richard	.10
141	Ken Forsch	.08
142	Larry Bowa	.15
143	Frank LaCorte (photo actually Randy Niemann)	.08
144	Dennis Walling	.08
145	Buddy Bell	.12

146	Fergie Jenkins	.75
147	Danny Darwin	.08
148	John Grubb	.08
149	Alfredo Griffin	.08
150	Jerry Garvin	.08
151	Paul Mirabella	.08
152	Rick Bosetti	.08
153	Dick Ruthven	.08
154	Frank Taveras	.08
155	Craig Swan	.08
156	Jeff Reardon	1.50
157	Steve Henderson	.08
158	Jim Morrison	.08
159	Glenn Borgmann	.08
160	Lamarr Hoyt (LaMarr)	.10
161	Rich Wortham	.08
162	Thad Bosley	.08
163	Julio Cruz	.08
164a	Del Unser (no 3B in stat heads)	.50
164b	Del Unser (3B in stat heads)	.10
165	Jim Anderson	.08
166	Jim Beattie	.08
167	Shane Rawley	.08
168	Joe Simpson	.08
169	Rod Carew	1.50
170	Fred Patek	.08
171	Frank Tanana	.10
172	Alfredo Martinez	.08
173	Chris Knapp	.08
174	Joe Rudi	.10
175	Greg Luzinski	.15
176	Steve Garvey	.65
177	Joe Ferguson	.08
178	Bob Welch	.20
179	Dusty Baker	.10
180	Rudy Law	.08
181	Dave Concepcion	.15
182	Johnny Bench	1.25
183	Mike LaCoss	.08
184	Ken Griffey	.12
185	Dave Collins	.08
186	Brian Asselstine	.08
187	Garry Templeton	.10
188	Mike Phillips	.08
189	Pete Vukovich	.08
190	John Urrea	.08
191	Tony Scott	.08
192	Darrell Evans	.12
193	Milt May	.08
194	Bob Knepper	.08
195	Randy Moffitt	.08
196	Larry Herndon	.08
197	Rick Camp	.08
198	Andre Thornton	.10
199	Tom Veryzer	.08
200	Gary Alexander	.08
201	Rick Waits	.08
202	Rick Manning	.08
203	Paul Molitor	3.00
204	Jim Gantner	.08
205	Paul Mitchell	.08
206	Reggie Cleveland	.08
207	Sixto Lezcano	.08
208	Bruce Benedict	.08
209	Rodney Scott	.08
210	John Tamargo	.08
211	Bill Lee	.08
212	Andre Dawson	1.00
213	Rowland Office	.08
214	Carl Yastrzemski	1.25
215	Jerry Remy	.08
216	Mike Torrez	.08
217	Skip Lockwood	.08
218	Fred Lynn	.20
219	Chris Chambliss	.08
220	Willie Aikens	.08
221	John Wathan	.08
222	Dan Quisenberry	.15
223	Willie Wilson	.15
224	Clint Hurdle	.08
225	Bob Watson	.08
226	Jim Spencer	.08
227	Ron Guidry	.25
228	Reggie Jackson	2.50
229	Oscar Gamble	.08
230	Jeff Cox	.08
231	Luis Tiant	.12
232	Rich Dauer	.08
233	Dan Graham	.08
234	Mike Flanagan	.10
235	John Lowenstein	.08
236	Benny Ayala	.08
237	Wayne Gross	.08
238	Rick Langford	.08
239	Tony Armas	.10

240a	Bob Lacy (incorrect spelling)	.50
240b	Bob Lacey (correct spelling)	.10
241	Gene Tenace	.08
242	Bob Shirley	.08
243	Gary Lucas	.08
244	Jerry Turner	.08
245	John Wockenfuss	.08
246	Stan Papi	.08
247	Milt Wilcox	.08
248	Dan Schatzeder	.08
249	Steve Kemp	.08
250	Jim Lentine	.08
251	Pete Rose	2.50
252	Bill Madlock	.12
253	Dale Berra	.08
254	Kent Tekulve	.08
255	Enrique Romo	.08
256	Mike Easler	.08
257	Chuck Tanner	.08
258	Art Howe	.08
259	Alan Ashby	.08
260	Nolan Ryan	8.00
261a	Vern Ruhle (Ken Forsch photo - head shot)	.50
261b	Vern Ruhle (Vern Ruhle photo - waist to head shot)	.10
262	Bob Boone	.10
263	Cesar Cedeno	.12
264	Jeff Leonard	.08
265	Pat Putnam	.08
266	Jon Matlack	.08
267	Dave Rajsich	.08
268	Billy Sample	.08
269	Damaso Garcia	.10
270	Tom Buskey	.08
271	Joey McLaughlin	.08
272	Barry Bonnell	.08
273	Tug McGraw	.10
274	Mike Jorgensen	.08
275	Pat Zachry	.08
276	Neil Allen	.08
277	Joel Youngblood	.08
278	Greg Pryor	.08
279	Britt Burns	.10
280	Rich Dotson	.25
281	Chet Lemon	.08
282	Rusty Kuntz	.08
283	Ted Cox	.08
284	Sparky Lyle	.10
285	Larry Cox	.08
286	Floyd Bannister	.08
287	Byron McLaughlin	.08
288	Rodney Craig	.08
289	Bobby Grich	.10
290	Dickie Thon	.08
291	Mark Clear	.08
292	Dave Lemanczyk	.08
293	Jason Thompson	.08
294	Rick Miller	.08
295	Lonnie Smith	.08
296	Ron Cey	.12
297	Steve Yeager	.08
298	Bobby Castillo	.08
299	Manny Mota	.08
300	Jay Johnstone	.08
301	Dan Driessen	.08
302	Joe Nolan	.08
303	Paul Householder	.08
304	Harry Spilman	.08
305	Cesar Geronimo	.08
306a	Gary Mathews (Mathews on front)	.65
306b	Gary Matthews (Matthews on front)	.10
307	Ken Reitz	.08
308	Ted Simmons	.12
309	John Littlefield	.08
310	George Frazier	.08
311	Dane Iorg	.08
312	Mike Ivie	.08
313	Dennis Littlejohn	.08
314	Gary LaVelle (Lavelle)	.08
315	Jack Clark	.25
316	Jim Wohlford	.08
317	Rick Matula	.08
318	Toby Harrah	.08
319a	Dwane Kuiper (Dwane on front)	.50
319b	Duane Kuiper (Duane on front)	.10
320	Len Barker	.08
321	Victor Cruz	.08
322	Dell Alston	.08
323	Robin Yount	4.00
324	Charlie Moore	.08

#	Player	Price
325	Lary Sorensen	.08
326a	Gorman Thomas ("...30-HR mark 4th..." on back)	.65
326b	Gorman Thomas ("...30-HR mark 3rd..." on back)	.10
327	Bob Rodgers	.08
328	Phil Niekro	.75
329	Chris Speier	.08
330a	Steve Rodgers (Rodgers on front)	.50
330b	Steve Rogers (Rogers on front)	.10
331	Woodie Fryman	.08
332	Warren Cromartie	.08
333	Jerry White	.08
334	Tony Perez	.25
335	Carlton Fisk	1.50
336	Dick Drago	.08
337	Steve Renko	.08
338	Jim Rice	.30
339	Jerry Royster	.08
340	Frank White	.10
341	Jamie Quirk	.08
342a	Paul Spittorff (Spittorff on front)	.50
342b	Paul Splittorff (Splittorff on front)	.10
343	Marty Pattin	.08
344	Pete LaCock	.08
345	Willie Randolph	.10
346	Rick Cerone	.08
347	Rich Gossage	.20
348	Reggie Jackson	2.50
349	Ruppert Jones	.08
350	Dave McKay	.08
351	Yogi Berra	.25
352	Doug Decinces (DeCinces)	.10
353	Jim Palmer	1.00
354	Tippy Martinez	.08
355	Al Bumbry	.08
356	Earl Weaver	.50
357a	Bob Picciolo (Bob on front)	.50
357b	Rob Picciolo (Rob on front)	.10
358	Matt Keough	.08
359	Dwayne Murphy	.08
360	Brian Kingman	.08
361	Bill Fahey	.08
362	Steve Mura	.08
363	Dennis Kinney	.08
364	Dave Winfield	2.00
365	Lou Whitaker	.45
366	Lance Parrish	.20
367	Tim Corcoran	.08
368	Pat Underwood	.08
369	Al Cowens	.08
370	Sparky Anderson	.15
371	Pete Rose	2.50
372	Phil Garner	.08
373	Steve Nicosia	.08
374	John Candelaria	.10
375	Don Robinson	.08
376	Lee Lacy	.08
377	John Milner	.08
378	Craig Reynolds	.08
379a	Luis Pujols (Pujois on front)	.50
379b	Luis Pujols (Pujois on front)	.10
380	Joe Niekro	.12
381	Joaquin Andujar	.10
382	*Keith Moreland*	.20
383	Jose Cruz	.12
384	Bill Virdon	.08
385	Jim Sundberg	.08
386	Doc Medich	.08
387	Al Oliver	.15
388	Jim Norris	.08
389	Bob Bailor	.08
390	Ernie Whitt	.08
391	Otto Velez	.08
392	Roy Howell	.08
393	*Bob Walk*	.20
394	Doug Flynn	.08
395	Pete Falcone	.08
396	Tom Hausman	.08
397	Elliott Maddox	.08
398	Mike Squires	.08
399	Marvis Foley	.08
400	Steve Trout	.08
401	Wayne Nordhagen	.08
402	Tony Larussa (LaRussa)	.08
403	Bruce Bochte	.08
404	Bake McBride	.08
405	Jerry Narron	.08
406	Rob Dressler	.08
407	Dave Heaverlo	.08
408	Tom Paciorek	.08
409	Carney Lansford	.10
410	Brian Downing	.10
411	Don Aase	.08
412	Jim Barr	.08
413	Don Baylor	.15
414	Jim Fregosi	.08
415	Dallas Green	.08
416	Dave Lopes	.10
417	Jerry Reuss	.10
418	Rick Sutcliffe	.20
419	Derrel Thomas	.08
420	Tommy LaSorda (Lasorda)	.50
421	*Charlie Leibrandt*	.50
422	Tom Seaver	2.00
423	Ron Oester	.08
424	Junior Kennedy	.08
425	Tom Seaver	2.00
426	Bobby Cox	.10
427	*Leon Durham*	.20
428	Terry Kennedy	.08
429	Silvio Martinez	.08
430	George Hendrick	.08
431	Red Schoendienst	.25
432	John LeMaster	.08
433	Vida Blue	.12
434	John Montefusco	.08
435	Terry Whitfield	.08
436	Dave Bristol	.08
437	Dale Murphy	.75
438	Jerry Dybzinski	.08
439	Jorge Orta	.08
440	Wayne Garland	.08
441	Miguel Dilone	.08
442	Dave Garcia	.08
443	Don Money	.08
444a	Buck Martinez (photo reversed)	.50
444b	Buck Martinez (photo correct)	.10
445	Jerry Augustine	.08
446	Ben Oglivie	.08
447	Jim Slaton	.08
448	Doyle Alexander	.10
449	Tony Bernazard	.08
450	Scott Sanderson	.08
451	Dave Palmer	.08
452	Stan Bahnsen	.08
453	Dick Williams	.08
454	Rick Burleson	.08
455	Gary Allenson	.08
456	Bob Stanley	.08
457a	*John Tudor* (lifetime W/L 9.7)	.75
457b	*John Tudor* (lifetime W/L 9-7)	.50
458	Dwight Evans	.15
459	Glenn Hubbard	.08
460	U L Washington	.08
461	Larry Gura	.08
462	Rich Gale	.08
463	Hal McRae	.10
464	Jim Frey	.08
465	Bucky Dent	.10
466	Dennis Werth	.08
467	Ron Davis	.08
468	Reggie Jackson	2.50
469	Bobby Brown	.08
470	*Mike Davis*	.10
471	Gaylord Perry	.75
472	Mark Belanger	.08
473	Jim Palmer	1.00
474	Sammy Stewart	.08
475	Tim Stoddard	.08
476	Steve Stone	.08
477	Jeff Newman	.08
478	Steve McCatty	.08
479	Billy Martin	.12
480	Mitchell Page	.08
481	Steve Carlton (CY)	.40
482	Bill Buckner	.12
483a	Ivan DeJesus (lifetime hits 702)	.50
483b	Ivan DeJesus (lifetime hits 642)	.10
484	Cliff Johnson	.08
485	Lenny Randle	.08
486	Larry Milbourne	.08
487	Roy Smalley	.08
488	John Castino	.08
489	Ron Jackson	.08
490a	Dave Roberts (1980 highlights begins "Showed pop...")	.50
490b	Dave Roberts (1980 highlights begins "Declared himself...")	.10
491	George Brett (MVP)	3.00
492	Mike Cubbage	.08
493	Rob Wilfong	.08
494	Danny Goodwin	.08
495	Jose Morales	.08
496	Mickey Rivers	.08
497	Mike Edwards	.08
498	Mike Sadek	.08
499	Lenn Sakata	.08
500	Gene Michael	.08
501	Dave Roberts	.08
502	Steve Dillard	.08
503	Jim Essian	.08
504	Rance Mulliniks	.08
505	Darrell Porter	.08
506	Joe Torre	.15
507	Terry Crowley	.08
508	Bill Travers	.08
509	Nelson Norman	.08
510	Bob McClure	.08
511	*Steve Howe*	.15
512	Dave Rader	.08
513	Mick Kelleher	.08
514	Kiko Garcia	.08
515	Larry Biittner	.08
516a	Willie Norwood (1980 highlights begins "Spent most...")	.50
516b	Willie Norwood (1980 highlights begins "Traded to...")	.10
517	Bo Diaz	.08
518	Juan Beniquez	.08
519	Scot Thompson	.08
520	Jim Tracy	.08
521	Carlos Lezcano	.08
522	Joe Amalfitano	.08
523	Preston Hanna	.08
524a	Ray Burris (1980 highlights begins "Went on...")	.50
524b	Ray Burris (1980 highlights begins "Drafted by...")	.10
525	Broderick Perkins	.08
526	Mickey Hatcher	.08
527	John Goryl	.08
528	Dick Davis	.08
529	Butch Wynegar	.08
530	Sal Butera	.08
531	Jerry Koosman	.10
532a	Jeff (Geoff) Zahn (1980 highlights begins "Was 2nd in...")	.50
532b	Jeff (Geoff) Zahn (1980 highlights begins "Signed a 3 year ...")	.10
533	Dennis Martinez	.12
534	Gary Thomasson	.08
535	Steve Macko	.08
536	Jim Kaat	.20
537	Best Hitters(George Brett, Rod Carew)	1.50
538	*Tim Raines*	6.00
539	Keith Smith	.08
540	Ken Macha	.08
541	Burt Hooton	.08
542	Butch Hobson	.08
543	Bill Stein	.08
544	Dave Stapleton	.08
545	Bob Pate	.08
546	Doug Corbett	.08
547	Darrell Jackson	.08
548	Pete Redfern	.08
549	Roger Erickson	.08
550	Al Hrabosky	.08
551	Dick Tidrow	.08
552	Dave Ford	.08
553	Dave Kingman	.12
554a	Mike Vail (1980 highlights begins "After...")	.50
554b	Mike Vail (1980 highlights begins "Traded...")	.10
555a	Jerry Martin (1980 highlights begins "Overcame...")	.50
555b	Jerry Martin (1980 highlights begins "Traded...")	.10
556a	Jesus Figueroa (1980 highlights begins "Had...")	.50
556b	Jesus Figueroa (1980 highlights begins "Traded...")	.10
557	Don Stanhouse	.08
558	Barry Foote	.08
559	Tim Blackwell	.08
560	Bruce Sutter	.15
561	Rick Reuschel	.10
562	Lynn McGlothen	.08

563a	Bob Owchinko (1980 highlights begins "Traded...")	.50
563b	Bob Owchinko (1980 highlights begins "Involved...")	.10
564	John Verhoeven	.08
565	Ken Landreaux	.08
566a	Glen Adams (Glen on front)	.50
566b	Glenn Adams (Glenn on front)	.10
567	Hosken Powell	.08
568	Dick Noles	.08
569	*Danny Ainge*	4.00
570	Bobby Mattick	.08
571	Joe LeFebvre (Lefebvre)	.08
572	Bobby Clark	.08
573	Dennis Lamp	.08
574	Randy Lerch	.08
575	*Mookie Wilson*	.30
576	Ron LeFlore	.08
577	Jim Dwyer	.08
578	Bill Castro	.08
579	Greg Minton	.08
580	Mark Littell	.08
581	Andy Hassler	.08
582	Dave Stieb	.15
583	Ken Oberkfell	.08
584	Larry Bradford	.08
585	Fred Stanley	.08
586	Bill Caudill	.08
587	Doug Capilla	.08
588	George Riley	.08
589	Willie Hernandez	.10
590	Mike Schmidt (MVP)	1.00
591	Steve Stone ((Cy Young 1980))	.08
592	Rick Sofield	.08
593	Bombo Rivera	.08
594	Gary Ward	.08
595a	Dave Edwards (1980 highlights begins "Sidelined...")	.50
595b	Dave Edwards (1980 highlights begins "Traded...")	.10
596	Mike Proly	.08
597	Tommy Boggs	.08
598	Greg Gross	.08
599	Elias Sosa	.08
600	Pat Kelly	.08
----	Checklist 1-120 (51 Tom Donohue)	.50
----	Checklist 1-120 (51 Tom Donohue)	.10
----	Checklist 121-240	.10
----	Checklist 241-360 (306 Gary Mathews)	.50
----	Checklist 241-360 (306 Gary Matthews)	.10
----	Checklist 361-480 (379 Luis Pujols)	.50
----	Checklist 361-480 (379 Luis Pujols)	.10
----	Checklist 481-600 (566 Glen Adams)	.50
----	Checklist 481-600 (566 Glenn Adams)	.10

1982 Donruss

Using card stock thicker than the previous year, Donruss issued a 660-card set which includes 653 numbered cards and seven unnumbered checklists. The cards were sold with puzzle pieces rather than gum as a result of a lawsuit by Topps. The puzzle pieces (three pieces on one card per pack) feature Babe Ruth. The first 26 cards of the set, entitled Diamond Kings, showcase the artwork of Dick Perez. Card fronts display the Donruss logo and the year of issue. Backs have black and blue ink on white stock and include the player's career highlights. The complete set price does not include the higher priced variations.

Orioles CAL RIPKEN, JR 3b

		MT
	Complete Set (660):	85.00
	Common Player:	.08
	Babe Ruth Puzzle:	3.00
	Wax Box:	120.00
1	Pete Rose (Diamond King)	3.00
2	Gary Carter (DK)	.50
3	Steve Garvey (DK)	.30
4	Vida Blue (DK)	.12
5a	Alan Trammel (DK)(last name incorrect)	1.50
5b	Alan Trammell (DK)(corrected)	.40
6	Len Barker (DK)	.08
7	Dwight Evans (DK)	.15
8	Rod Carew (DK)	.60
9	George Hendrick (DK)	.08
10	Phil Niekro (DK)	.60
11	Richie Zisk (DK)	.08
12	Dave Parker (DK)	.30
13	Nolan Ryan (DK)	4.00
14	Ivan DeJesus (DK)	.08
15	George Brett (DK)	1.50
16	Tom Seaver (DK)	.90
17	Dave Kingman (DK)	.15
18	Dave Winfield (DK)	1.00
19	Mike Norris (DK)	.08
20	Carlton Fisk (DK)	.80
21	Ozzie Smith (DK)	1.50
22	Roy Smalley (DK)	.08
23	Buddy Bell (DK)	.12
24	Ken Singleton (DK)	.10
25	John Mayberry (DK)	.08
26	Gorman Thomas (DK)	.10
27	Earl Weaver	.45
28	Rollie Fingers	.60
29	Sparky Anderson	.10
30	Dennis Eckersley	.80
31	Dave Winfield	2.00
32	Burt Hooton	.08
33	Rick Waits	.08
34	George Brett	3.00
35	Steve McCatty	.08
36	Steve Rogers	.08
37	Bill Stein	.08
38	Steve Renko	.08
39	Mike Squires	.08
40	George Hendrick	.08
41	Bob Knepper	.08
42	Steve Carlton	1.00
43	Larry Biittner	.08
44	Chris Welsh	.08
45	Steve Nicosia	.08
46	Jack Clark	.25
47	Chris Chambliss	.08
48	Ivan DeJesus	.08
49	Lee Mazzilli	.08
50	Julio Cruz	.08
51	Pete Redfern	.08
52	Dave Stieb	.12
53	Doug Corbett	.08
54	*George Bell*	1.00
55	Joe Simpson	.08
56	Rusty Staub	.10
57	Hector Cruz	.08
58	Claudell Washington	.10
59	Enrique Romo	.08
60	Gary Lavelle	.08
61	Tim Flannery	.08

62	Joe Nolan	.08
63	Larry Bowa	.15
64	Sixto Lezcano	.08
65	Joe Sambito	.08
66	Bruce Kison	.08
67	Wayne Nordhagen	.08
68	Woodie Fryman	.08
69	Billy Sample	.08
70	Amos Otis	.08
71	Matt Keough	.08
72	Toby Harrah	.08
73	*Dave Righetti*	.30
74	Carl Yastrzemski	1.00
75	Bob Welch	.12
76a	Alan Trammel (last name misspelled)	2.00
76b	Alan Trammell (corrected)	.60
77	Rick Dempsey	.08
78	Paul Molitor	2.50
79	Dennis Martinez	.10
80	Jim Slaton	.08
81	Champ Summers	.08
82	Carney Lansford	.08
83	Barry Foote	.08
84	Steve Garvey	.45
85	Rick Manning	.08
86	John Wathan	.08
87	Brian Kingman	.08
88	Andre Dawson	1.25
89	Jim Kern	.08
90	Bobby Grich	.10
91	Bob Forsch	.08
92	Art Howe	.08
93	Marty Bystrom	.08
94	Ozzie Smith	2.50
95	Dave Parker	.30
96	Doyle Alexander	.10
97	Al Hrabosky	.08
98	Frank Taveras	.08
99	Tim Blackwell	.08
100	Floyd Bannister	.10
101	Alfredo Griffin	.08
102	Dave Engle	.08
103	Mario Soto	.08
104	Ross Baumgarten	.08
105	Ken Singleton	.10
106	Ted Simmons	.12
107	Jack Morris	.30
108	Bob Watson	.08
109	Dwight Evans	.15
110	Tom Lasorda	.40
111	Bert Blyleven	.12
112	Dan Quisenberry	.15
113	Rickey Henderson	2.00
114	Gary Carter	.50
115	Brian Downing	.10
116	Al Oliver	.15
117	LaMarr Hoyt	.08
118	Cesar Cedeno	.12
119	Keith Moreland	.10
120	Bob Shirley	.08
121	Terry Kennedy	.08
122	Frank Pastore	.08
123	Gene Garber	.08
124	Tony Pena	.25
125	Allen Ripley	.08
126	Randy Martz	.08
127	Richie Zisk	.08
128	Mike Scott	.15
129	Lloyd Moseby	.12
130	Rob Wilfong	.08
131	Tim Stoddard	.08
132	Gorman Thomas	.08
133	Dan Petry	.08
134	Bob Stanley	.08
135	Lou Piniella	.15
136	Pedro Guerrero	.30
137	Len Barker	.08
138	Richard Gale	.08
139	Wayne Gross	.08
140	*Tim Wallach*	1.00
141	Gene Mauch	.08
142	Doc Medich	.08
143	Tony Bernazard	.08
144	Bill Virdon	.08
145	John Littlefield	.08
146	Dave Bergman	.08
147	Dick Davis	.08
148	Tom Seaver	1.50
149	Matt Sinatro	.08
150	Chuck Tanner	.08
151	Leon Durham	.08
152	Gene Tenace	.08
153	Al Bumbry	.08
154	Mark Brouhard	.08
155	Rick Peters	.08

No.	Player	Value
156	Jerry Remy	.08
157	Rick Reuschel	.10
158	Steve Howe	.08
159	Alan Bannister	.08
160	U L Washington	.08
161	Rick Langford	.08
162	Bill Gullickson	.08
163	Mark Wagner	.08
164	Geoff Zahn	.08
165	Ron LeFlore	.08
166	Dane Iorg	.08
167	Joe Niekro	.12
168	Pete Rose	2.00
169	Dave Collins	.08
170	Rick Wise	.08
171	Jim Bibby	.08
172	Larry Herndon	.08
173	Bob Horner	.12
174	Steve Dillard	.08
175	Mookie Wilson	.12
176	Dan Meyer	.08
177	Fernando Arroyo	.08
178	Jackson Todd	.08
179	Darrell Jackson	.08
180	Al Woods	.08
181	Jim Anderson	.08
182	Dave Kingman	.12
183	Steve Henderson	.08
184	Brian Asselstine	.08
185	Rod Scurry	.08
186	Fred Breining	.08
187	Danny Boone	.08
188	Junior Kennedy	.08
189	Sparky Lyle	.10
190	Whitey Herzog	.08
191	Dave Smith	.08
192	Ed Ott	.08
193	Greg Luzinski	.15
194	Bill Lee	.08
195	Don Zimmer	.08
196	Hal McRae	.15
197	Mike Norris	.08
198	Duane Kuiper	.08
199	Rick Cerone	.08
200	Jim Rice	.30
201	Steve Yeager	.08
202	Tom Brookens	.08
203	Jose Morales	.08
204	Roy Howell	.08
205	Tippy Martinez	.08
206	Moose Haas	.08
207	Al Cowens	.08
208	Dave Stapleton	.08
209	Bucky Dent	.10
210	Ron Cey	.12
211	Jorge Orta	.08
212	Jamie Quirk	.08
213	Jeff Jones	.08
214	Tim Raines	1.00
215	Jon Matlack	.08
216	Rod Carew	1.50
217	Jim Kaat	.20
218	Joe Pittman	.08
219	Larry Christenson	.08
220	Juan Bonilla	.08
221	Mike Easler	.08
222	Vida Blue	.12
223	Rick Camp	.08
224	Mike Jorgensen	.08
225	*Jody Davis*	.15
226	Mike Parrott	.08
227	Jim Clancy	.08
228	Hosken Powell	.08
229	Tom Hume	.08
230	Britt Burns	.08
231	Jim Palmer	1.00
232	Bob Rodgers	.08
233	Milt Wilcox	.08
234	Dave Revering	.08
235	Mike Torrez	.08
236	Robert Castillo	.08
237	*Von Hayes*	.25
238	Renie Martin	.08
239	Dwayne Murphy	.08
240	Rodney Scott	.08
241	Fred Patek	.08
242	Mickey Rivers	.08
243	Steve Trout	.08
244	Jose Cruz	.12
245	Manny Trillo	.08
246	Lary Sorensen	.08
247	Dave Edwards	.08
248	Dan Driessen	.08
249	Tommy Boggs	.08
250	Dale Berra	.08
251	Ed Whitson	.08
252	*Lee Smith*	8.00
253	Tom Paciorek	.08
254	Pat Zachry	.08
255	Luis Leal	.08
256	John Castino	.08
257	Rich Dauer	.08
258	Cecil Cooper	.15
259	Dave Rozema	.08
260	John Tudor	.08
261	Jerry Mumphrey	.08
262	Jay Johnstone	.08
263	Bo Diaz	.08
264	Dennis Leonard	.08
265	Jim Spencer	.08
266	John Milner	.08
267	Don Aase	.08
268	Jim Sundberg	.08
269	Lamar Johnson	.08
270	Frank LaCorte	.08
271	Barry Evans	.08
272	Enos Cabell	.08
273	Del Unser	.08
274	George Foster	.20
275	*Brett Butler*	2.00
276	Lee Lacy	.08
277	Ken Reitz	.08
278	Keith Hernandez	.20
279	Doug DeCinces	.10
280	Charlie Moore	.08
281	Lance Parrish	.20
282	Ralph Houk	.08
283	Rich Gossage	.20
284	Jerry Reuss	.10
285	Mike Stanton	.08
286	Frank White	.10
287	Bob Owchinko	.08
288	Scott Sanderson	.08
289	Bump Wills	.08
290	Dave Frost	.08
291	Chet Lemon	.08
292	Tito Landrum	.08
293	Vern Ruhle	.08
294	Mike Schmidt	2.00
295	Sam Mejias	.08
296	Gary Lucas	.08
297	John Candelaria	.10
298	Jerry Martin	.08
299	Dale Murphy	.75
300	Mike Lum	.08
301	Tom Hausman	.08
302	Glenn Abbott	.08
303	Roger Erickson	.08
304	Otto Velez	.08
305	Danny Goodwin	.08
306	John Mayberry	.08
307	Lenny Randle	.08
308	Bob Bailor	.08
309	Jerry Morales	.08
310	Rufino Linares	.08
311	Kent Tekulve	.08
312	Joe Morgan	.75
313	John Urrea	.08
314	Paul Householder	.08
315	Garry Maddox	.08
316	Mike Ramsey	.08
317	Alan Ashby	.08
318	Bob Clark	.08
319	Tony LaRussa	.12
320	Charlie Lea	.08
321	Danny Darwin	.08
322	Cesar Geronimo	.08
323	Tom Underwood	.08
324	Andre Thornton	.10
325	Rudy May	.08
326	Frank Tanana	.08
327	Davey Lopes	.10
328	Richie Hebner	.08
329	Mike Flanagan	.10
330	Mike Caldwell	.08
331	Scott McGregor	.08
332	Jerry Augustine	.08
333	Stan Papi	.08
334	Rick Miller	.08
335	Graig Nettles	.15
336	Dusty Baker	.10
337	Dave Garcia	.08
338	Larry Gura	.08
339	Cliff Johnson	.08
340	Warren Cromartie	.08
341	Steve Comer	.08
342	Rick Burleson	.08
343	John Martin	.08
344	Craig Reynolds	.08
345	Mike Proly	.08
346	Ruppert Jones	.08
347	Omar Moreno	.08
348	Greg Minton	.08
349	*Rick Mahler*	.10
350	Alex Trevino	.08
351	Mike Krukow	.08
352a	Shane Rawley (Jim Anderson photo - shaking hands)	.75
352b	Shane Rawley (correct photo - kneeling)	.15
353	Garth Iorg	.08
354	Pete Mackanin	.08
355	Paul Moskau	.08
356	Richard Dotson	.10
357	Steve Stone	.08
358	Larry Hisle	.08
359	Aurelio Lopez	.08
360	Oscar Gamble	.08
361	Tom Burgmeier	.08
362	Terry Forster	.08
363	Joe Charboneau	.08
364	Ken Brett	.08
365	Tony Armas	.10
366	Chris Speier	.08
367	Fred Lynn	.20
368	Buddy Bell	.12
369	Jim Essian	.08
370	Terry Puhl	.08
371	Greg Gross	.08
372	Bruce Sutter	.15
373	Joe Lefebvre	.08
374	Ray Knight	.10
375	Bruce Benedict	.08
376	Tim Foli	.08
377	Al Holland	.08
378	Ken Kravec	.08
379	Jeff Burroughs	.08
380	Pete Falcone	.08
381	Ernie Whitt	.08
382	Brad Havens	.08
383	Terry Crowley	.08
384	Don Money	.08
385	Dan Schatzeder	.08
386	Gary Allenson	.08
387	Yogi Berra	.25
388	Ken Landreaux	.08
389	Mike Hargrove	.08
390	Darryl Motley	.08
391	Dave McKay	.08
392	Stan Bahnsen	.08
393	Ken Forsch	.08
394	Mario Mendoza	.08
395	Jim Morrison	.08
396	Mike Ivie	.08
397	Broderick Perkins	.08
398	Darrell Evans	.15
399	Ron Reed	.08
400	Johnny Bench	1.50
401	*Steve Bedrosian*	.20
402	Bill Robinson	.08
403	Bill Buckner	.12
404	Ken Oberkfell	.08
405	*Cal Ripken, Jr.*	50.00
406	Jim Gantner	.08
407	Kirk Gibson	.80
408	Tony Perez	.30
409	Tommy John	.20
410	*Dave Stewart*	2.50
411	Dan Spillner	.08
412	Willie Aikens	.08
413	Mike Heath	.08
414	Ray Burris	.08
415	Leon Roberts	.08
416	*Mike Witt*	.20
417	Bobby Molinaro	.08
418	Steve Braun	.08
419	Nolan Ryan	9.00
420	Tug McGraw	.12
421	Dave Concepcion	.12
422a	Juan Eichelberger (Gary Lucas photo - white player)	.75
422b	Juan Eichelberger (correct photo - black player)	.08
423	Rick Rhoden	.10
424	Frank Robinson	.25
425	Eddie Miller	.08
426	Bill Caudill	.08
427	Doug Flynn	.08
428	Larry Anderson (Andersen)	.08
429	Al Williams	.08
430	Jerry Garvin	.08
431	Glenn Adams	.08
432	Barry Bonnell	.08
433	Jerry Narron	.08
434	John Stearns	.08
435	Mike Tyson	.08
436	Glenn Hubbard	.08

437	Eddie Solomon	.08
438	Jeff Leonard	.10
439	Randy Bass	.08
440	Mike LaCoss	.08
441	Gary Matthews	.10
442	Mark Littell	.08
443	Don Sutton	.45
444	John Harris	.08
445	Vada Pinson	.08
446	Elias Sosa	.08
447	Charlie Hough	.10
448	Willie Wilson	.15
449	Fred Stanley	.08
450	Tom Veryzer	.08
451	Ron Davis	.08
452	Mark Clear	.08
453	Bill Russell	.10
454	Lou Whitaker	.45
455	Dan Graham	.08
456	Reggie Cleveland	.08
457	Sammy Stewart	.08
458	Pete Vuckovich	.08
459	John Wockenfuss	.08
460	Glenn Hoffman	.08
461	Willie Randolph	.10
462	Fernando Valenzuela	.25
463	Ron Hassey	.08
464	Paul Splittorff	.08
465	Rob Picciolo	.08
466	Larry Parrish	.10
467	Johnny Grubb	.08
468	Dan Ford	.08
469	Silvio Martinez	.08
470	Kiko Garcia	.08
471	Bob Boone	.10
472	Luis Salazar	.08
473	Randy Niemann	.08
474	Tom Griffin	.08
475	Phil Niekro	.60
476	Hubie Brooks	.25
477	Dick Tidrow	.08
478	Jim Beattie	.08
479	Damaso Garcia	.08
480	Mickey Hatcher	.08
481	Joe Price	.08
482	Ed Farmer	.08
483	Eddie Murray	2.50
484	Ben Oglivie	.08
485	Kevin Saucier	.08
486	Bobby Murcer	.10
487	Bill Campbell	.08
488	Reggie Smith	.10
489	Wayne Garland	.08
490	Jim Wright	.08
491	Billy Martin	.12
492	Jim Fanning	.08
493	Don Baylor	.12
494	Rick Honeycutt	.08
495	Carlton Fisk	1.50
496	Denny Walling	.08
497	Bake McBride	.08
498	Darrell Porter	.08
499	Gene Richards	.08
500	Ron Oester	.08
501	*Ken Dayley*	.12
502	Jason Thompson	.08
503	Milt May	.12
504	Doug Bird	.08
505	Bruce Bochte	.08
506	Neil Allen	.08
507	Joey McLaughlin	.08
508	Butch Wynegar	.08
509	Gary Roenicke	.08
510	Robin Yount	2.50
511	Dave Tobik	.08
512	*Rich Gedman*	.15
513	*Gene Nelson*	.08
514	Rick Monday	.10
515	Miguel Dilone	.08
516	Clint Hurdle	.08
517	Jeff Newman	.08
518	Grant Jackson	.08
519	Andy Hassler	.08
520	Pat Putnam	.08
521	Greg Pryor	.08
522	Tony Scott	.08
523	Steve Mura	.08
524	Johnnie LeMaster	.08
525	Dick Ruthven	.08
526	John McNamara	.08
527	Larry McWilliams	.08
528	*Johnny Ray*	.10
529	*Pat Tabler*	.10
530	Tom Herr	.10
531a	San Diego Chicken (w/trademark symbol)	.75

531b	San Diego Chicken (no trademark symbol)	.80
532	Sal Butera	.08
533	Mike Griffin	.08
534	Kelvin Moore	.08
535	Reggie Jackson	2.00
536	Ed Romero	.08
537	Derrel Thomas	.08
538	Mike O'Berry	.08
539	Jack O'Connor	.08
540	*Bob Ojeda*	.50
541	Roy Lee Jackson	.08
542	Lynn Jones	.08
543	Gaylord Perry	.60
544a	Phil Garner (photo reversed)	.75
544b	Phil Garner (photo correct)	.10
545	Garry Templeton	.10
546	Rafael Ramirez	.08
547	Jeff Reardon	.50
548	Ron Guidry	.25
549	*Tim Laudner*	.12
550	John Henry Johnson	.08
551	Chris Bando	.08
552	Bobby Brown	.08
553	Larry Bradford	.08
554	*Scott Fletcher*	.40
555	Jerry Royster	.08
556	Shooty Babbitt	.08
557	*Kent Hrbek*	2.00
558	Yankee Winners(Ron Guidry, Tommy John)	.15
559	Mark Bomback	.08
560	Julio Valdez	.08
561	Buck Martinez	.08
562	*Mike Marshall*	.15
563	Rennie Stennett	.08
564	Steve Crawford	.08
565	Bob Babcock	.08
566	Johnny Podres	.08
567	Paul Serna	.08
568	Harold Baines	.65
569	Dave LaRoche	.08
570	Lee May	.08
571	Gary Ward	.10
572	John Denny	.08
573	Roy Smalley	.08
574	*Bob Brenly*	.20
575	Bronx Bombers(Reggie Jackson, Dave Winfield)	2.00
576	Luis Pujols	.08
577	Butch Hobson	.08
578	Harvey Kuenn	.08
579	Cal Ripken, Sr.	.08
580	Juan Berenguer	.08
581	Benny Ayala	.08
582	Vance Law	.08
583	*Rick Leach*	.12
584	George Frazier	.08
585	Phillies Finest(Pete Rose, Mike Schmidt)	1.00
586	Joe Rudi	.10
587	Juan Beniquez	.08
588	*Luis DeLeon*	.08
589	Craig Swan	.08
590	Dave Chalk	.08
591	Billy Gardner	.08
592	Sal Bando	.08
593	Bert Campaneris	.10
594	Steve Kemp	.08
595a	Randy Lerch (Braves)	.75
595b	Randy Lerch (Brewers)	.08
596	Bryan Clark	.08
597	Dave Ford	.08
598	Mike Scioscia	.20
599	John Lowenstein	.08
600	Rene Lachmann (Lachemann)	.08
601	Mick Kelleher	.08
602	Ron Jackson	.08
603	Jerry Koosman	.10
604	Dave Goltz	.08
605	Ellis Valentine	.08
606	Lonnie Smith	.08
607	Joaquin Andujar	.08
608	Garry Hancock	.08
609	Jerry Turner	.08
610	Bob Bonner	.08
611	Jim Dwyer	.08
612	Terry Bulling	.08
613	Joel Youngblood	.08
614	Larry Milbourne	.08
615	Phil Roof (photo actually Gene Roof)	.08
616	Keith Drumright	.08
617	Dave Rosello	.08

618	Rickey Keeton	.08
619	Dennis Lamp	.08
620	Sid Monge	.08
621	Jerry White	.08
622	*Luis Aguayo*	.08
623	Jamie Easterly	.08
624	*Steve Sax*	.75
625	Dave Roberts	.08
626	Rick Bosetti	.08
627	*Terry Francona*	.12
628	Pride of the Reds(Johnny Bench, Tom Seaver)	.80
629	Paul Mirabella	.08
630	Rance Mulliniks	.08
631	Kevin Hickey	.08
632	Reid Nichols	.08
633	Dave Geisel	.08
634	Ken Griffey	.12
635	Bob Lemon	.20
636	Orlando Sanchez	.08
637	Bill Almon	.08
638	Danny Ainge	1.25
639	Willie Stargell	.75
640	Bob Sykes	.08
641	Ed Lynch	.08
642	John Ellis	.08
643	Fergie Jenkins	.50
644	Lenn Sakata	.08
645	Julio Gonzales	.08
646	Jesse Orosco	.10
647	Jerry Dybzinski	.08
648	Tommy Davis	.08
649	Ron Gardenhire	.08
650	Felipe Alou	.12
651	Harvey Haddix	.08
652	Willie Upshaw	.15
653	Bill Madlock	.12
----	Checklist 1-26 DK (5 Trammel)	.50
----	Checklist 1-26 DK (5 Trammell)	.08
----	Checklist 27-130	.08
----	Checklist 131-234	.08
----	Checklist 235-338	.08
----	Checklist 339-442	.08
----	Checklist 443-544	.08
----	Checklist 545-653	.08

1983 Donruss

The 1983 Donruss set consists of 653 numbered cards plus seven unnumbered checklists. The 2-1/2" x 3-1/2" cards were issued with puzzle pieces (three pieces on one card per pack) that feature Ty Cobb. The first 26 cards in the set were once again the Diamond Kings series. The card fronts display the Donruss logo and the year of issue. The card backs have black print on yellow and white and include statistics, career highlights, and the player's contract status. (DK) in the checklist below indicates cards which belong to the Diamond Kings series.

	MT
Complete Set (660):	110.00
Common Player:	.08
Ty Cobb Puzzle:	3.00
Wax Box:	180.00

#	Player	Price
1	Fernando Valenzuela (DK)	.20
2	Rollie Fingers (DK)	.25
3	Reggie Jackson (DK)	.50
4	Jim Palmer (DK)	.40
5	Jack Morris (DK)	.20
6	George Foster (DK)	.20
7	Jim Sundberg (DK)	.08
8	Willie Stargell (DK)	.30
9	Dave Stieb (DK)	.12
10	Joe Niekro (DK)	.12
11	Rickey Henderson (DK)	1.50
12	Dale Murphy (DK)	.30
13	Toby Harrah (DK)	.08
14	Bill Buckner (DK)	.12
15	Willie Wilson (DK)	.15
16	Steve Carlton (DK)	.40
17	Ron Guidry (DK)	.15
18	Steve Rogers (DK)	.08
19	Kent Hrbek (DK)	.20
20	Keith Hernandez (DK)	.15
21	Floyd Bannister (DK)	.08
22	Johnny Bench (DK)	.60
23	Britt Burns (DK)	.08
24	Joe Morgan (DK)	.30
25	Carl Yastrzemski (DK)	.80
26	Terry Kennedy (DK)	.08
27	Gary Roenicke	.08
28	Dwight Bernard	.08
29	Pat Underwood	.08
30	Gary Allenson	.08
31	Ron Guidry	.25
32	Burt Hooton	.08
33	Chris Bando	.08
34	Vida Blue	.12
35	Rickey Henderson	2.50
36	Ray Burris	.08
37	John Butcher	.08
38	Don Aase	.08
39	Jerry Koosman	.10
40	Bruce Sutter	.15
41	Jose Cruz	.12
42	Pete Rose	2.50
43	Cesar Cedeno	.12
44	Floyd Chiffer	.08
45	Larry McWilliams	.08
46	Alan Fowlkes	.08
47	Dale Murphy	.75
48	Doug Bird	.08
49	Hubie Brooks	.12
50	Floyd Bannister	.08
51	Jack O'Connor	.08
52	Steve Senteney	.08
53	*Gary Gaetti*	.75
54	Damaso Garcia	.08
55	Gene Nelson	.08
56	Mookie Wilson	.10
57	Allen Ripley	.08
58	Bob Horner	.12
59	Tony Pena	.10
60	Gary Lavelle	.08
61	Tim Lollar	.08
62	Frank Pastore	.08
63	Garry Maddox	.10
64	Bob Forsch	.08
65	Harry Spilman	.08
66	Geoff Zahn	.08
67	Salome Barojas	.08
68	David Palmer	.08
69	Charlie Hough	.10
70	Dan Quisenberry	.15
71	Tony Armas	.10
72	Rick Sutcliffe	.12
73	Steve Balboni	.08
74	Jerry Remy	.08
75	Mike Scioscia	.08
76	John Wockenfuss	.08
77	Jim Palmer	.80
78	Rollie Fingers	.60
79	Joe Nolan	.08
80	Pete Vuckovich	.08
81	Rick Leach	.08
82	Rick Miller	.08
83	Graig Nettles	.15
84	Ron Cey	.12
85	Miguel Dilone	.08
86	John Wathan	.08
87	Kelvin Moore	.08
88a	Byrn Smith (first name incorrect)	.70
88b	Bryn Smith (first name correct)	.08
89	Dave Hostetler	.08
90	Rod Carew	1.00
91	Lonnie Smith	.08
92	Bob Knepper	.08
93	Marty Bystrom	.08
94	Chris Welsh	.08
95	Jason Thompson	.08
96	Tom O'Malley	.08
97	Phil Niekro	.65
98	Neil Allen	.08
99	Bill Buckner	.12
100	*Ed Vande Berg*	.08
101	Jim Clancy	.08
102	Robert Castillo	.08
103	Bruce Berenyi	.08
104	Carlton Fisk	.75
105	Mike Flanagan	.10
106	Cecil Cooper	.10
107	Jack Morris	.45
108	Mike Morgan	.12
109	Luis Aponte	.08
110	Pedro Guerrero	.15
111	Len Barker	.08
112	Willie Wilson	.15
113	Dave Beard	.08
114	Mike Gates	.08
115	Reggie Jackson	1.50
116	George Wright	.08
117	Vance Law	.08
118	Nolan Ryan	8.50
119	Mike Krukow	.08
120	Ozzie Smith	2.00
121	Broderick Perkins	.08
122	Tom Seaver	1.50
123	Chris Chambliss	.08
124	Chuck Tanner	.08
125	Johnnie LeMaster	.08
126	*Mel Hall*	.15
127	Bruce Bochte	.08
128	*Charlie Puleo*	.08
129	Luis Leal	.08
130	John Pacella	.08
131	Glenn Gulliver	.08
132	Don Money	.08
133	Dave Rozema	.08
134	Bruce Hurst	.15
135	Rudy May	.08
136	Tom LaSorda (Lasorda)	.45
137	Dan Spillner (photo actually Ed Whitson)	.08
138	Jerry Martin	.08
139	Mike Norris	.08
140	Al Oliver	.15
141	Daryl Sconiers	.08
142	Lamar Johnson	.08
143	Harold Baines	.20
144	Alan Ashby	.08
145	Garry Templeton	.10
146	Al Holland	.08
147	Bo Diaz	.08
148	Dave Concepcion	.12
149	Rick Camp	.08
150	Jim Morrison	.08
151	Randy Martz	.08
152	Keith Hernandez	.20
153	John Lowenstein	.08
154	Mike Caldwell	.08
155	Milt Wilcox	.08
156	Rich Gedman	.08
157	Rich Gossage	.20
158	Jerry Reuss	.10
159	Ron Hassey	.08
160	Larry Gura	.08
161	Dwayne Murphy	.08
162	Woodie Fryman	.08
163	Steve Comer	.08
164	Ken Forsch	.08
165	Dennis Lamp	.08
166	David Green	.08
167	Terry Puhl	.08
168	Mike Schmidt	2.50
169	*Eddie Milner*	.08
170	John Curtis	.08
171	Don Robinson	.08
172	Richard Gale	.08
173	Steve Bedrosian	.08
174	Willie Hernandez	.08
175	Ron Gardenhire	.08
176	Jim Beattie	.08
177	Tim Laudner	.08
178	Buck Martinez	.08
179	Kent Hrbek	.75
180	Alfredo Griffin	.08
181	Larry Andersen	.08
182	Pete Falcone	.08
183	Jody Davis	.10
184	Glenn Hubbard	.08
185	Dale Berra	.08
186	Greg Minton	.08
187	Gary Lucas	.08
188	Dave Van Gorder	.08
189	Bob Dernier	.08
190	*Willie McGee*	1.50
191	Dickie Thon	.08
192	Bob Boone	.10
193	Britt Burns	.08
194	Jeff Reardon	.75
195	Jon Matlack	.08
196	*Don Slaught*	.20
197	Fred Stanley	.08
198	Rick Manning	.08
199	Dave Righetti	.25
200	Dave Stapleton	.08
201	Steve Yeager	.08
202	Enos Cabell	.08
203	Sammy Stewart	.08
204	Moose Haas	.08
205	Lenn Sakata	.08
206	Charlie Moore	.08
207	Alan Trammell	.40
208	Jim Rice	.25
209	Roy Smalley	.08
210	Bill Russell	.08
211	Andre Thornton	.10
212	Willie Aikens	.08
213	Dave McKay	.08
214	Tim Blackwell	.08
215	Buddy Bell	.12
216	Doug DeCinces	.10
217	Tom Herr	.10
218	Frank LaCorte	.08
219	Steve Carlton	1.00
220	Terry Kennedy	.08
221	Mike Easler	.08
222	Jack Clark	.25
223	Gene Garber	.08
224	Scott Holman	.08
225	Mike Proly	.08
226	Terry Bulling	.08
227	Jerry Garvin	.08
228	Ron Davis	.08
229	Tom Hume	.08
230	Marc Hill	.08
231	Dennis Martinez	.10
232	Jim Gantner	.08
233	Larry Pashnick	.08
234	Dave Collins	.08
235	Tom Burgmeier	.08
236	Ken Landreaux	.08
237	John Denny	.08
238	Hal McRae	.12
239	Matt Keough	.08
240	Doug Flynn	.08
241	Fred Lynn	.15
242	Billy Sample	.08
243	Tom Paciorek	.08
244	Joe Sambito	.08
245	Sid Monge	.08
246	Ken Oberkfell	.08
247	Joe Pittman (photo actually Juan Eichelberger)	.08
248	Mario Soto	.08
249	Claudell Washington	.08
250	Rick Rhoden	.10
251	Darrell Evans	.15
252	Steve Henderson	.08
253	Manny Castillo	.08
254	Craig Swan	.08
255	Joey McLaughlin	.08
256	Pete Redfern	.08
257	Ken Singleton	.10
258	Robin Yount	2.50
259	Elias Sosa	.08
260	Bob Ojeda	.12
261	Bobby Murcer	.10
262	*Candy Maldonado*	.20
263	Rick Waits	.08
264	Greg Pryor	.08
265	Bob Owchinko	.08
266	Chris Speier	.08
267	Bruce Kison	.08
268	Mark Wagner	.08
269	Steve Kemp	.10
270	Phil Garner	.08
271	Gene Richards	.08
272	Renie Martin	.08
273	Dave Roberts	.08
274	Dan Driessen	.08
275	Rufino Linares	.08
276	Lee Lacy	.08
277	*Ryne Sandberg*	14.00
278	Darrell Porter	.08

No.	Name	Price	No.	Name	Price	No.	Name	Price
279	Cal Ripken, Jr.	16.00	372	Doug Bair	.08	467	Larry Parrish	.08
280	Jamie Easterly	.08	373	Ruppert Jones	.08	468	Bobby Grich	.10
281	Bill Fahey	.08	374	Alex Trevino	.08	469	Dane Iorg	.08
282	Glenn Hoffman	.08	375	Ken Dayley	.08	470	Joe Niekro	.12
283	Willie Randolph	.10	376	Rod Scurry	.08	471	Ed Farmer	.08
284	Fernando Valenzuela	.25	377	Bob Brenly	.08	472	Tim Flannery	.08
285	Alan Bannister	.08	378	Scot Thompson	.08	473	Dave Parker	.35
286	Paul Splittorff	.08	379	Julio Cruz	.08	474	Jeff Leonard	.08
287	Joe Rudi	.10	380	John Stearns	.08	475	Al Hrabosky	.08
288	Bill Gullickson	.08	381	Dale Murray	.08	476	Ron Hodges	.08
289	Danny Darwin	.08	382	*Frank Viola*	1.50	477	Leon Durham	.08
290	Andy Hassler	.08	383	Al Bumbry	.08	478	Jim Essian	.08
291	Ernesto Escarrega	.08	384	Ben Oglivie	.08	479	Roy Lee Jackson	.08
292	Steve Mura	.08	385	Dave Tobik	.08	480	Brad Havens	.08
293	Tony Scott	.08	386	Bob Stanley	.08	481	Joe Price	.08
294	Manny Trillo	.08	387	Andre Robertson	.08	482	Tony Bernazard	.08
295	Greg Harris	.08	388	Jorge Orta	.08	483	Scott McGregor	.08
296	Luis DeLeon	.08	389	Ed Whitson	.08	484	Paul Molitor	1.50
297	Kent Tekulve	.08	390	Don Hood	.08	485	Mike Ivie	.08
298	Atlee Hammaker	.08	391	Tom Underwood	.08	486	Ken Griffey	.12
299	Bruce Benedict	.08	392	Tim Wallach	.20	487	Dennis Eckersley	1.00
300	Fergie Jenkins	.45	393	Steve Renko	.08	488	Steve Garvey	.45
301	Dave Kingman	.15	394	Mickey Rivers	.08	489	Mike Fischlin	.08
302	Bill Caudill	.08	395	Greg Luzinski	.15	490	U.L. Washington	.08
303	John Castino	.08	396	Art Howe	.08	491	Steve McCatty	.08
304	Ernie Whitt	.08	397	Alan Wiggins	.08	492	Roy Johnson	.08
305	Randy S. Johnson	.08	398	Jim Barr	.08	493	Don Baylor	.12
306	Garth Iorg	.08	399	Ivan DeJesus	.08	494	Bobby Johnson	.08
307	Gaylord Perry	.60	400	*Tom Lawless*	.08	495	Mike Squires	.08
308	Ed Lynch	.08	401	Bob Walk	.08	496	Bert Roberge	.08
309	Keith Moreland	.08	402	Jimmy Smith	.08	497	Dick Ruthven	.08
310	Rafael Ramirez	.08	403	Lee Smith	1.75	498	Tito Landrum	.08
311	Bill Madlock	.12	404	George Hendrick	.08	499	Sixto Lezcano	.08
312	Milt May	.08	405	Eddie Murray	2.50	500	Johnny Bench	1.00
313	John Montefusco	.08	406	Marshall Edwards	.08	501	Larry Whisenton	.08
314	Wayne Krenchicki	.08	407	Lance Parrish	.35	502	Manny Sarmiento	.08
315	George Vukovich	.08	408	Carney Lansford	.08	503	Fred Breining	.08
316	Joaquin Andujar	.08	409	Dave Winfield	2.50	504	Bill Campbell	.08
317	Craig Reynolds	.08	410	Bob Welch	.12	505	Todd Cruz	.08
318	Rick Burleson	.08	411	Larry Milbourne	.08	506	Bob Bailor	.08
319	Richard Dotson	.10	412	Dennis Leonard	.08	507	Dave Stieb	.12
320	Steve Rogers	.08	413	Dan Meyer	.08	508	Al Williams	.08
321	Dave Schmidt	.08	414	Charlie Lea	.08	509	Dan Ford	.08
322	*Bud Black*	.20	415	Rick Honeycutt	.08	510	Gorman Thomas	.08
323	Jeff Burroughs	.08	416	Mike Witt	.10	511	Chet Lemon	.08
324	Von Hayes	.10	417	Steve Trout	.08	512	Mike Torrez	.08
325	Butch Wynegar	.08	418	Glenn Brummer	.08	513	Shane Rawley	.08
326	Carl Yastrzemski	.80	419	Denny Walling	.08	514	Mark Belanger	.08
327	Ron Roenicke	.08	420	Gary Matthews	.10	515	Rodney Craig	.08
328	*Howard Johnson*	1.00	421	Charlie Liebrandt (Leibrandt)	.08	516	Onix Concepcion	.08
329	Rick Dempsey	.08	422	Juan Eichelberger	.08	517	Mike Heath	.08
330a	Jim Slaton (one yellow box on back)	.70	423	*Matt Guante (Cecilio)*	.08	518	Andre Dawson	1.25
330b	Jim Slaton (two yellow boxes on back)	.08	424	Bill Laskey	.08	519	Luis Sanchez	.08
331	Benny Ayala	.08	425	Jerry Royster	.08	520	Terry Bogener	.08
332	Ted Simmons	.12	426	Dickie Noles	.08	521	Rudy Law	.08
333	Lou Whitaker	.25	427	George Foster	.15	522	Ray Knight	.10
334	Chuck Rainey	.08	428	*Mike Moore*	.65	523	Joe Lefebvre	.08
335	Lou Piniella	.12	429	Gary Ward	.08	524	Jim Wohlford	.08
336	Steve Sax	.15	430	Barry Bonnell	.08	525	*Julio Franco*	5.00
337	Toby Harrah	.08	431	Ron Washington	.08	526	Ron Oester	.08
338	George Brett	3.50	432	Rance Mulliniks	.08	527	Rick Mahler	.08
339	Davey Lopes	.10	433	Mike Stanton	.08	528	Steve Nicosia	.08
340	Gary Carter	.40	434	Jesse Orosco	.10	529	Junior Kennedy	.08
341	John Grubb	.08	435	Larry Bowa	.10	530a	Whitey Herzog (one yellow box on back)	.70
342	Tim Foli	.08	436	Biff Pocoroba	.08	530b	Whitey Herzog (two yellow boxes on back)	.10
343	Jim Kaat	.15	437	Johnny Ray	.08	531a	Don Sutton (blue frame)	.45
344	Mike LaCoss	.08	438	Joe Morgan	.60	531b	Don Sutton (green frame)	.45
345	Larry Christenson	.08	439	*Eric Show*	.25	532	Mark Brouhard	.08
346	Juan Bonilla	.08	440	Larry Biittner	.08	533a	Sparky Anderson (one yellow box on back)	.70
347	Omar Moreno	.08	441	Greg Gross	.08	533b	Sparky Anderson (two yellow boxes on back)	.10
348	Chili Davis	.75	442	Gene Tenace	.08	534	Roger LaFrancois	.08
349	Tommy Boggs	.08	443	Danny Heep	.08	535	George Frazier	.08
350	Rusty Staub	.10	444	Bobby Clark	.08	536	Tom Niedenfuer	.08
351	Bump Wills	.08	445	Kevin Hickey	.08	537	Ed Glynn	.08
352	Rick Sweet	.08	446	Scott Sanderson	.08	538	Lee May	.08
353	*Jim Gott*	.20	447	Frank Tanana	.10	539	Bob Kearney	.08
354	Terry Felton	.08	448	Cesar Geronimo	.08	540	Tim Raines	.35
355	Jim Kern	.08	449	Jimmy Sexton	.08	541	Paul Mirabella	.08
356	Bill Almon	.08	450	Mike Hargrove	.08	542	Luis Tiant	.12
357	Tippy Martinez	.08	451	Doyle Alexander	.10	543	Ron LeFlore	.08
358	Roy Howell	.08	452	Dwight Evans	.15	544	*Dave LaPoint*	.12
359	Dan Petry	.08	453	Terry Forster	.08	545	Randy Moffitt	.08
360	Jerry Mumphrey	.08	454	Tom Brookens	.08	546	Luis Aguayo	.08
361	Mark Clear	.08	455	Rich Dauer	.08	547	Brad Lesley	.08
362	Mike Marshall	.10	456	Rob Picciolo	.08	548	Luis Salazar	.08
363	Lary Sorensen	.08	457	Terry Crowley	.08	549	John Candelaria	.10
364	Amos Otis	.08	458	Ned Yost	.08	550	Dave Bergman	.08
365	Rick Langford	.08	459	Kirk Gibson	.20	551	Bob Watson	.08
366	Brad Mills	.08	460	Reid Nichols	.08	552	Pat Tabler	.08
367	Brian Downing	.10	461	Oscar Gamble	.08	553	Brent Gaff	.08
368	Mike Richardt	.08	462	Dusty Baker	.12	554	Al Cowens	.08
369	Aurelio Rodriguez	.08	463	Jack Perconte	.08	555	Tom Brunansky	.10
370	Dave Smith	.08	464	Frank White	.10			
371	Tug McGraw	.12	465	Mickey Klutts	.08			
			466	Warren Cromartie	.08			

556	Lloyd Moseby	.08
557a	Pascual Perez (Twins)	.90
557b	Pascual Perez (Braves)	.15
558	Willie Upshaw	.08
559	Richie Zisk	.08
560	Pat Zachry	.08
561	Jay Johnstone	.08
562	Carlos Diaz	.08
563	John Tudor	.10
564	Frank Robinson	.15
565	Dave Edwards	.08
566	Paul Householder	.08
567	Ron Reed	.08
568	Mike Ramsey	.08
569	Kiko Garcia	.08
570	Tommy John	.20
571	Tony LaRussa	.12
572	Joel Youngblood	.08
573	*Wayne Tolleson*	.08
574	Keith Creel	.08
575	Billy Martin	.12
576	Jerry Dybzinski	.08
577	Rick Cerone	.08
578	Tony Perez	.25
579	*Greg Brock*	.15
580	Glen Wilson (Glenn)	.20
581	Tim Stoddard	.08
582	Bob McClure	.08
583	Jim Dwyer	.08
584	Ed Romero	.08
585	Larry Herndon	.08
586	*Wade Boggs*	14.00
587	Jay Howell	.10
588	Dave Stewart	.75
589	Bert Blyleven	.12
590	Dick Howser	.08
591	Wayne Gross	.08
592	Terry Francona	.08
593	Don Werner	.08
594	Bill Stein	.08
595	Jesse Barfield	.45
596	Bobby Molinaro	.08
597	Mike Vail	.08
598	*Tony Gwynn*	26.00
599	Gary Rajsich	.08
600	Jerry Ujdur	.08
601	Cliff Johnson	.08
602	Jerry White	.08
603	Bryan Clark	.08
604	Joe Ferguson	.08
605	Guy Sularz	.08
606a	Ozzie Virgil (green frame around photo)	.90
606b	Ozzie Virgil (orange frame around photo)	.08
607	Terry Harper	.08
608	Harvey Kuenn	.08
609	Jim Sundberg	.08
610	Willie Stargell	.75
611	Reggie Smith	.10
612	Rob Wilfong	.08
613	Niekro Brothers(Joe Niekro, Phil Niekro)	.25
614	Lee Elia	.08
615	Mickey Hatcher	.08
616	Jerry Hairston	.08
617	John Martin	.08
618	Wally Backman	.08
619	*Storm Davis*	.10
620	Alan Knicely	.08
621	John Stuper	.08
622	Matt Sinatro	.08
623	*Gene Petralli*	.10
624	Duane Walker	.08
625	Dick Williams	.08
626	Pat Corrales	.08
627	Vern Ruhle	.08
628	Joe Torre	.08
629	Anthony Johnson	.08
630	Steve Howe	.08
631	Gary Woods	.08
632	Lamarr Hoyt (LaMarr)	.08
633	Steve Swisher	.08
634	Terry Leach	.08
635	Jeff Newman	.08
636	Brett Butler	.10
637	Gary Gray	.08
638	Lee Mazzilli	.08
639a	Ron Jackson (A's)	6.00
639b	Ron Jackson (Angels - green frame around photo)	.90
639c	Ron Jackson (Angels - red frame around photo)	.20
640	Juan Beniquez	.08
641	Dave Rucker	.08
642	Luis Pujols	.08
643	Rick Monday	.10
644	Hosken Powell	.08
645	San Diego Chicken	.20
646	Dave Engle	.08
647	Dick Davis	.08
648	MVP's(Vida Blue, Joe Morgan, Frank Robinson)	.15
649	Al Chambers	.08
650	Jesus Vega	.08
651	Jeff Jones	.08
652	Marvis Foley	.08
653	Ty Cobb (puzzle)	.08
----	DK checklist(Dick Perez) (no word "Checklist" on back)	.70
----	DK Checklist(Dick Perez) (word "Checklist" on back)	.08
----	Checklist 27-130	.08
----	Checklist 131-234	.08
----	Checklist 235-338	.08
----	Checklist 339-442	.08
----	Checklist 443-546	.08
----	Checklist 547-653	.08

1983 Donruss Action All-Stars

Eddie Murray
FIRST BASE

The cards in this 60-card set are designed on a horizontal format and contain a large close-up photo of the player on the left and a smaller action photo on the right. The 5" x 3-1/2" cards have deep red borders and contain the Donruss logo and the year of issue. Backs are printed in black on red and white and contain statistical and biographical information. The cards were sold with puzzle pieces (three pieces on one card per pack) that feature Mickey Mantle.

		MT
Complete Set (60):		5.00
Common Player:		.05
Mickey Mantle puzzle:		12.50
1	Eddie Murray	.30
2	Dwight Evans	.05
3a	Reggie Jackson (red covers part of statistics on back)	.30
3b	Reggie Jackson (red does not cover any statistics on back)	.30
4	Greg Luzinski	.08
5	Larry Herndon	.05
6	Al Oliver	.05
7	Bill Buckner	.05
8	Jason Thompson	.05
9	Andre Dawson	.15
10	Greg Minton	.05
11	Terry Kennedy	.05
12	Phil Niekro	.20
13	Willie Wilson	.05
14	Johnny Bench	.30
15	Ron Guidry	.05
16	Hal McRae	.05
17	Damaso Garcia	.05
18	Gary Ward	.05
19	Cecil Cooper	.05
20	Keith Hernandez	.05
21	Ron Cey	.05
22	Rickey Henderson	.30
23	Nolan Ryan	2.00
24	Steve Carlton	.30
25	John Stearns	.05
26	Jim Sundberg	.05
27	Joaquin Andujar	.05
28	Gaylord Perry	.20
29	Jack Clark	.05
30	Bill Madlock	.05
31	Pete Rose	.75
32	Mookie Wilson	.05
33	Rollie Fingers	.20
34	Lonnie Smith	.05
35	Tony Pena	.05
36	Dave Winfield	.25
37	Tim Lollar	.05
38	Rod Carew	.30
39	Toby Harrah	.05
40	Buddy Bell	.05
41	Bruce Sutter	.05
42	George Brett	.90
43	Carlton Fisk	.30
44	Carl Yastrzemski	.50
45	Dale Murphy	.20
46	Bob Horner	.05
47	Dave Concepcion	.05
48	Dave Stieb	.05
49	Kent Hrbek	.08
50	Lance Parrish	.05
51	Joe Niekro	.05
52	Cal Ripken, Jr.	2.00
53	Fernando Valenzuela	.08
54	Rickie Zisk	.05
55	Leon Durham	.05
56	Robin Yount	.30
57	Mike Schmidt	.75
58	Gary Carter	.08
59	Fred Lynn	.05
60	Checklist	.03

1984 Donruss

ASTROS
JOE NIEKRO P

The 1984 Donruss set consists of 651 numbered cards, seven unnumbered checklists and two "Living Legends" cards (designated A and B). The A and B cards were issued only in wax packs and were not available to hobby dealers purchasing factory sets. The card fronts differ in style from the previous years, however the Donruss logo and year of issue are still included. Backs have black print on green and white and are identical in format to the preceding year. The 2-1/2" x 3-1/2" cards were issued in packs with three pieces of a 63-piece puzzle of Duke Snider. The complete set price in the checklist that follows does not include the higher priced variations. Cards marked with (DK) or (RR) in the checklist refer to the Diamond Kings and Rated Rookies subsets. Each of the Diamond Kings cards and the DK checklist can be found in two varieties. The more common has Frank Steele's name misspelled "Steel" in the credit line at the bottom-right corner on the back. The error was later corrected.

		MT
	Complete Set (660):	275.00
	Common Player:	.15
	Duke Snider Puzzle:	3.50
	Wax Box:	430.00
A	Living Legends(Rollie Fingers, Gaylord Perry)	5.00
B	Living Legends(Johnny Bench, Carl Yastrzemski)	7.00
1a	Robin Yount (DK) (Steele)	3.00
1b	Robin Yount (DK) (Steele)	5.00
2a	Dave Concepcion (DK) (Steel)	.30
2b	Dave Concepcion (DK) (Steele)	.60
3a	Dwayne Murphy (DK) (Steel)	.25
3b	Dwayne Murphy (DK) (Steele)	.60
4a	John Castino (DK) (Steel)	.20
4b	John Castino (DK) (Steele)	.60
5a	Leon Durham (DK) (Steel)	.25
5b	Leon Durham (DK) (Steele)	.60
6a	Rusty Staub (DK) (Steel)	.30
6b	Rusty Staub (DK) (Steele)	.60
7a	Jack Clark (DK) (Steel)	.25
7b	Jack Clark (DK) (Steele)	.60
8a	Dave Dravecky (DK) (Steel)	.25
8b	Dave Dravecky (DK) (Steele)	.60
9a	Al Oliver (DK) (Steel)	.35
9b	Al Oliver (DK) (Steele)	.70
10a	Dave Righetti (DK) (Steel)	.25
10b	Dave Righetti (DK) (Steele)	.60
11a	Hal McRae (DK) (Steel)	.30
11b	Hal McRae (DK) (Steele)	.60
12a	Ray Knight (DK) (Steel)	.25
12b	Ray Knight (DK) (Steele)	.60
13a	Bruce Sutter (DK) (Steel)	.25
13b	Bruce Sutter (DK) (Steele)	.60
14a	Bob Horner (DK) (Steel)	.25
14b	Bob Horner (DK) (Steele)	.60
15a	Lance Parrish ((DK) (Steel)	.25
15b	Lance Parrish (DK) (Steele)	.60
16a	Matt Young (DK) (Steel)	.25
16b	Matt Young (DK) (Steele)	.60
17a	Fred Lynn (DK) (Steel)	.35
17b	Fred Lynn (DK) (Steele)	.70
18a	Ron Kittle (DK) (Steel)	.25
18b	Ron Kittle (DK) (Steele)	.60
19a	Jim Clancy (DK) (Steel)	.25
19b	Jim Clancy (DK) (Steele)	.60
20a	Bill Madlock (DK) (Steel)	.30
20b	Bill Madlock (DK) (Steele)	.60
21a	Larry Parrish (DK) (Steel)	.25
21b	Larry Parrish (DK) (Steele)	.60
22a	Eddie Murray (DK) (Steel)	2.00
22b	Eddie Murray (DK) (Steele)	4.00
23a	Mike Schmidt (DK) (Steel)	4.00
23b	Mike Schmidt (DK) (Steele)	5.00
24a	Pedro Guerrero (DK) (Steel)	.25
24b	Pedro Guerrero (DK) (Steele)	.60
25a	Andre Thornton (DK) (Steel)	.25
25b	Andre Thornton (DK) (Steele)	.60
26a	Wade Boggs (DK) (Steel)	3.00
26b	Wade Boggs (DK) (Steele)	4.00
27	*Joel Skinner* (RR)	.15
28	Tom Dunbar (RR)	.15
29a	Mike Stenhouse (RR)(no number on back)	.15
29b	Mike Stenhouse (RR)(29 on back)	4.00
30a	*Ron Darling* (RR)(no number on back)	2.00
30b	*Ron Darling* (RR)(30 on back)	3.00
31	*Dion James* (RR)	.15
32	*Tony Fernandez* (RR)	1.00
33	Angel Salazar (RR)	.15
34	*Kevin McReynolds* (RR)	1.50
35	*Dick Schofield* (RR)	.20
36	*Brad Komminsk* (RR)	.15
37	*Tim Teufel* (RR)	.30
38	Doug Frobel (RR)	.15
39	*Greg Gagne* (RR)	.80
40	Mike Fuentes (RR)	.15
41	*Joe Carter* (RR)	50.00
42	Mike Brown (RR)	.15
43	Mike Jeffcoat (RR)	.15
44	*Sid Fernandez* (RR)	4.00
45	Brian Dayett (RR)	.15
46	Chris Smith (RR)	.15
47	Eddie Murray	8.00
48	Robin Yount	6.00

49	Lance Parrish	.40
50	Jim Rice	.50
51	Dave Winfield	6.00
52	Fernando Valenzuela	.40
53	George Brett	12.00
54	Rickey Henderson	5.00
55	Gary Carter	.65
56	Buddy Bell	.20
57	Reggie Jackson	6.00
58	Harold Baines	.30
59	Ozzie Smith	6.00
60	Nolan Ryan	30.00
61	Pete Rose	6.00
62	Ron Oester	.15
63	Steve Garvey	.75
64	Jason Thompson	.15
65	Jack Clark	.25
66	Dale Murphy	1.00
67	Leon Durham	.15
68	Darryl Strawberry	10.00
69	Richie Zisk	.15
70	Kent Hrbek	.40
71	Dave Stieb	.25
72	Ken Schrom	.15
73	George Bell	.50
74	John Moses	.15
75	Ed Lynch	.15
76	Chuck Rainey	.15
77	Biff Pocoroba	.15
78	Cecilio Guante	.15
79	Jim Barr	.15
80	Kurt Bevacqua	.15
81	Tom Foley	.15
82	Joe Lefebvre	.15
83	*Andy Van Slyke*	2.00
84	Bob Lillis	.15
85	Rick Adams	.15
86	Jerry Hairston	.15
87	Bob James	.15
88	Joe Altobelli	.15
89	Ed Romero	.15
90	John Grubb	.15
91	John Henry Johnson	.15
92	Juan Espino	.15
93	Candy Maldonado	.15
94	Andre Thornton	.20
95	Onix Concepcion	.15
96	*Don Hill*	.15
97	Andre Dawson	5.00
98	Frank Tanana	.15
99	*Curt Wilkerson*	.15
100	Larry Gura	.15
101	Dwayne Murphy	.15
102	Tom Brennan	.15
103	Dave Righetti	.40
104	Steve Sax	.30
105	Dan Petry	.15
106	Cal Ripken, Jr.	36.00
107	Paul Molitor	8.00
108	Fred Lynn	.35
109	Neil Allen	.15
110	Joe Niekro	.20
111	Steve Carlton	5.00
112	Terry Kennedy	.15
113	Bill Madlock	.20
114	Chili Davis	.20
115	Jim Gantner	.15
116	Tom Seaver	6.00
117	Bill Buckner	.20
118	Bill Caudill	.15
119	Jim Clancy	.15
120	John Castino	.15
121	Dave Concepcion	.20
122	Greg Luzinski	.20
123	Mike Boddicker	.20
124	Pete Ladd	.15
125	Juan Berenguer	.15
126	John Montefusco	.15
127	Ed Jurak	.15
128	Tom Niedenfuer	.15
129	Bert Blyleven	.30
130	Bud Black	.15
131	Gorman Heimueller	.15
132	Dan Schatzeder	.15
133	Ron Jackson	.15
134	*Tom Henke*	1.50
135	Kevin Hickey	.15
136	Mike Scott	.15
137	Bo Diaz	.15
138	Glenn Brummer	.15
139	Sid Monge	.15
140	Rich Gale	.15
141	Brett Butler	.20
142	Brian Harper	.35
143	John Rabb	.15
144	Gary Woods	.15

145	Pat Putnam	.15
146	*Jim Acker*	.15
147	Mickey Hatcher	.15
148	Todd Cruz	.15
149	Tom Tellmann	.15
150	John Wockenfuss	.15
151	Wade Boggs	10.00
152	Don Baylor	.20
153	Bob Welch	.20
154	Alan Bannister	.15
155	Willie Aikens	.15
156	Jeff Burroughs	.15
157	Bryan Little	.15
158	Bob Boone	.15
159	Dave Hostetler	.15
160	Jerry Dybzinski	.15
161	Mike Madden	.15
162	Luis DeLeon	.15
163	Willie Hernandez	.15
164	Frank Pastore	.15
165	Rick Camp	.15
166	Lee Mazzilli	.15
167	Scot Thompson	.15
168	Bob Forsch	.15
169	Mike Flanagan	.15
170	Rick Manning	.15
171	Chet Lemon	.15
172	Jerry Remy	.15
173	Ron Guidry	.20
174	Pedro Guerrero	.25
175	Willie Wilson	.25
176	Carney Lansford	.20
177	Al Oliver	.30
178	Jim Sundberg	.15
179	Bobby Grich	.20
180	Richard Dotson	.20
181	Joaquin Andujar	.15
182	Jose Cruz	.20
183	Mike Schmidt	12.00
184	*Gary Redus*	.25
185	Garry Templeton	.15
186	Tony Pena	.20
187	Greg Minton	.15
188	Phil Niekro	1.00
189	Fergie Jenkins	1.00
190	Mookie Wilson	.15
191	Jim Beattie	.15
192	Gary Ward	.15
193	Jesse Barfield	.20
194	Pete Filson	.15
195	Roy Lee Jackson	.15
196	Rick Sweet	.15
197	Jesse Orosco	.15
198	*Steve Lake*	.15
199	Ken Dayley	.15
200	Manny Sarmiento	.15
201	Mark Davis	.15
202	Tim Flannery	.15
203	Bill Scherrer	.15
204	Al Holland	.15
205	David Von Ohlen	.15
206	Mike LaCoss	.15
207	Juan Beniquez	.15
208	*Juan Agosto*	.15
209	Bobby Ramos	.15
210	Al Bumbry	.15
211	Mark Brouhard	.15
212	Howard Bailey	.15
213	Bruce Hurst	.20
214	Bob Shirley	.15
215	Pat Zachry	.15
216	Julio Franco	3.00
217	Mike Armstrong	.15
218	Dave Beard	.15
219	Steve Rogers	.15
220	John Butcher	.15
221	*Mike Smithson*	.15
222	Frank White	.20
223	Mike Heath	.15
224	Chris Bando	.15
225	Roy Smalley	.15
226	Dusty Baker	.20
227	Lou Whitaker	.50
228	John Lowenstein	.15
229	Ben Oglivie	.15
230	Doug DeCinces	.15
231	Lonnie Smith	.15
232	Ray Knight	.20
233	Gary Matthews	.20
234	Juan Bonilla	.15
235	Rod Scurry	.15
236	Atlee Hammaker	.15
237	Mike Caldwell	.15
238	Keith Hernandez	.25
239	Larry Bowa	.20
240	Tony Bernazard	.15

No.	Player	Price	No.	Player	Price	No.	Player	Price
241	Damaso Garcia	.15	337	Joe Beckwith	.15	433	Jody Davis	.15
242	Tom Brunansky	.15	338	Rick Sutcliffe	.25	434	Danny Heep	.15
243	Dan Driessen	.15	339	*Mark Huismann*	.15	435	*Ed Nunez*	.15
244	Ron Kittle	.15	340	*Tim Conroy*	.15	436	Bobby Castillo	.15
245	Tim Stoddard	.15	341	Scott Sanderson	.15	437	Ernie Whitt	.15
246	Bob L. Gibson	.15	342	Larry Biittner	.15	438	Scott Ullger	.15
247	Marty Castillo	.15	343	Dave Stewart	.50	439	Doyle Alexander	.15
248	*Don Mattingly*	55.00	344	Darryl Motley	.15	440	Domingo Ramos	.15
249	Jeff Newman	.15	345	*Chris Codiroli*	.15	441	Craig Swan	.15
250	*Alejandro Pena*	.25	346	Rick Behenna	.15	442	Warren Brusstar	.15
251	Toby Harrah	.15	347	Andre Robertson	.15	443	Len Barker	.15
252	Cesar Geronimo	.15	348	Mike Marshall	.25	444	Mike Easler	.15
253	Tom Underwood	.15	349	Larry Herndon	.15	445	Renie Martin	.15
254	Doug Flynn	.15	350	Rich Dauer	.15	446	*Dennis Rasmussen*	.30
255	Andy Hassler	.15	351	Cecil Cooper	.20	447	Ted Power	.15
256	Odell Jones	.15	352	Rod Carew	4.00	448	*Charlie Hudson*	.15
257	Rudy Law	.15	353	Willie McGee	.40	449	*Danny Cox*	.50
258	Harry Spilman	.15	354	Phil Garner	.15	450	Kevin Bass	.15
259	Marty Bystrom	.15	355	Joe Morgan	1.00	451	Daryl Sconiers	.15
260	Dave Rucker	.15	356	Luis Salazar	.15	452	Scott Fletcher	.15
261	Ruppert Jones	.15	357	John Candelaria	.20	453	Bryn Smith	.15
262	Jeff Jones	.15	358	Bill Laskey	.15	454	Jim Dwyer	.15
263	*Gerald Perry*	.25	359	Bob McClure	.15	455	Rob Picciolo	.15
264	Gene Tenace	.15	360	Dave Kingman	.20	456	Enos Cabell	.15
265	Brad Wellman	.15	361	Ron Cey	.20	457	*Dennis Boyd*	.20
266	Dickie Noles	.15	362	*Matt Young*	.15	458	Butch Wynegar	.15
267	Jamie Allen	.15	363	Lloyd Moseby	.20	459	Burt Hooton	.15
268	Jim Gott	.15	364	Frank Viola	.45	460	Ron Hassey	.15
269	Ron Davis	.15	365	Eddie Milner	.15	461	*Danny Jackson*	.50
270	Benny Ayala	.15	366	Floyd Bannister	.20	462	Bob Kearney	.15
271	Ned Yost	.15	367	Dan Ford	.15	463	Terry Francona	.15
272	Dave Rozema	.15	368	Moose Haas	.15	464	Wayne Tolleson	.15
273	Dave Stapleton	.15	369	Doug Bair	.15	465	Mickey Rivers	.15
274	Lou Piniella	.20	370	*Ray Fontenot*	.15	466	John Wathan	.15
275	José Morales	.15	371	Luis Aponte	.15	467	Bill Almon	.15
276	Brod Perkins	.15	372	Jack Fimple	.15	468	George Vukovich	.15
277	Butch Davis	.15	373	*Neal Heaton*	.20	469	Steve Kemp	.15
278	Tony Phillips	3.00	374	Greg Pryor	.15	470	Ken Landreaux	.15
279	Jeff Reardon	.25	375	Wayne Gross	.15	471	Milt Wilcox	.15
280	Ken Forsch	.15	376	Charlie Lea	.15	472	Tippy Martinez	.15
281	*Pete O'Brien*	.50	377	Steve Lubratich	.15	473	Ted Simmons	.20
282	Tom Paciorek	.15	378	Jon Matlack	.15	474	Tim Foli	.15
283	Frank LaCorte	.15	379	Julio Cruz	.15	475	George Hendrick	.15
284	Tim Lollar	.15	380	John Mizerock	.15	476	Terry Puhl	.15
285	Greg Gross	.15	381	*Kevin Gross*	.50	477	Von Hayes	.15
286	Alex Trevino	.15	382	Mike Ramsey	.15	478	Bobby Brown	.15
287	Gene Garber	.15	383	Doug Gwosdz	.15	479	Lee Lacy	.15
288	Dave Parker	.50	384	Kelly Paris	.15	480	Joel Youngblood	.15
289	Lee Smith	3.00	385	Pete Falcone	.15	481	Jim Slaton	.15
290	Dave LaPoint	.15	386	Milt May	.15	482	*Mike Fitzgerald*	.15
291	*John Shelby*	.15	387	Fred Breining	.15	483	Keith Moreland	.15
292	Charlie Moore	.15	388	*Craig Lefferts*	.25	484	Ron Roenicke	.15
293	Alan Trammell	2.00	389	Steve Henderson	.15	485	Luis Leal	.15
294	Tony Armas	.20	390	Randy Moffitt	.15	486	Bryan Oelkers	.15
295	Shane Rawley	.15	391	Ron Washington	.15	487	Bruce Berenyi	.15
296	Greg Brock	.15	392	Gary Roenicke	.15	488	LaMarr Hoyt	.15
297	Hal McRae	.20	393	*Tom Candiotti*	.75	489	Joe Nolan	.15
298	Mike Davis	.15	394	Larry Pashnick	.15	490	Marshall Edwards	.15
299	Tim Raines	1.00	395	Dwight Evans	.30	491	*Mike Laga*	.15
300	Bucky Dent	.15	396	Goose Gossage	.25	492	Rick Cerone	.15
301	Tommy John	.35	397	Derrel Thomas	.15	493	Mike Miller (Rick)	.15
302	Carlton Fisk	4.00	398	Juan Eichelberger	.15	494	Rick Honeycutt	.15
303	Darrell Porter	.15	399	Leon Roberts	.15	495	Mike Hargrove	.15
304	Dickie Thon	.15	400	Davey Lopes	.15	496	Joe Simpson	.15
305	Garry Maddox	.15	401	Bill Gullickson	.15	497	*Keith Atherton*	.15
306	Cesar Cedeno	.20	402	Geoff Zahn	.15	498	Chris Welsh	.15
307	Gary Lucas	.15	403	Billy Sample	.15	499	Bruce Kison	.15
308	Johnny Ray	.20	404	Mike Squires	.15	500	Bob Johnson	.15
309	Andy McGaffigan	.15	405	Craig Reynolds	.15	501	Jerry Koosman	.15
310	Claudell Washington	.15	406	Eric Show	.15	502	Frank DiPino	.15
311	Ryne Sandberg	18.00	407	John Denny	.15	503	Tony Perez	.75
312	George Foster	.30	408	Dann Bilardello	.15	504	Ken Oberkfell	.15
313	*Spike Owen*	.50	409	Bruce Benedict	.15	505	*Mark Thurmond*	.15
314	Gary Gaetti	.35	410	Kent Tekulve	.15	506	Joe Price	.15
315	Willie Upshaw	.15	411	Mel Hall	.15	507	Pascual Perez	.15
316	Al Williams	.15	412	John Stuper	.15	508	*Marvell Wynne*	.15
317	Jorge Orta	.15	413	Rick Dempsey	.15	509	Mike Krukow	.15
318	Orlando Mercado	.15	414	Don Sutton	.75	510	Dick Ruthven	.15
319	*Junior Ortiz*	.15	415	Jack Morris	.50	511	Al Cowens	.15
320	Mike Proly	.15	416	John Tudor	.20	512	Cliff Johnson	.15
321	Randy S. Johnson	.15	417	Willie Randolph	.20	513	*Randy Bush*	.20
322	Jim Morrison	.15	418	Jerry Reuss	.15	514	Sammy Stewart	.15
323	Max Venable	.15	419	Don Slaught	.15	515	*Bill Schroeder*	.15
324	Tony Gwynn	20.00	420	Steve McCatty	.15	516	Aurelio Lopez	.15
325	Duane Walker	.15	421	Tim Wallach	.25	517	Mike Brown	.15
326	Ozzie Virgil	.15	422	Larry Parrish	.15	518	Graig Nettles	.35
327	Jeff Lahti	.15	423	Brian Downing	.20	519	Dave Sax	.15
328	*Bill Dawley*	.15	424	Britt Burns	.15	520	Gerry Willard	.15
329	Rob Wilfong	.15	425	David Green	.15	521	Paul Splittorff	.15
330	Marc Hill	.15	426	Jerry Mumphrey	.15	522	Tom Burgmeier	.15
331	Ray Burris	.15	427	Ivan DeJesus	.15	523	Chris Speier	.15
332	Allan Ramirez	.15	428	Mario Soto	.15	524	Bobby Clark	.15
333	Chuck Porter	.15	429	Gene Richards	.15	525	George Wright	.15
334	Wayne Krenchicki	.15	430	Dale Berra	.15	526	Dennis Lamp	.15
335	Gary Allenson	.15	431	Darrell Evans	.25	527	Tony Scott	.15
336	*Bob Meacham*	.15	432	Glenn Hubbard	.15	528	Ed Whitson	.15

529	Ron Reed	.15
530	Charlie Puleo	.15
531	Jerry Royster	.15
532	Don Robinson	.15
533	Steve Trout	.15
534	Bruce Sutter	.30
535	Bob Horner	.20
536	Pat Tabler	.15
537	Chris Chambliss	.15
538	Bob Ojeda	.15
539	Alan Ashby	.15
540	Jay Johnstone	.15
541	Bob Dernier	.15
542	*Brook Jacoby*	.25
543	U.L. Washington	.15
544	Danny Darwin	.15
545	Kiko Garcia	.15
546	Vance Law	.15
547	Tug McGraw	.20
548	Dave Smith	.15
549	Len Matuszek	.15
550	Tom Hume	.15
551	Dave Dravecky	.15
552	Rick Rhoden	.15
553	Duane Kuiper	.15
554	Rusty Staub	.20
555	Bill Campbell	.15
556	Mike Torrez	.15
557	Dave Henderson	.15
558	Len Whitehouse	.15
559	Barry Bonnell	.15
560	Rick Lysander	.15
561	Garth Iorg	.15
562	Bryan Clark	.15
563	Brian Giles	.15
564	Vern Ruhle	.15
565	Steve Bedrosian	.20
566	Larry McWilliams	.15
567	Jeff Leonard	.15
568	Alan Wiggins	.15
569	*Jeff Russell*	.50
570	Salome Barojas	.15
571	Dane Iorg	.15
572	Bob Knepper	.15
573	Gary Lavelle	.15
574	Gorman Thomas	.15
575	Manny Trillo	.15
576	Jim Palmer	3.00
577	Dale Murray	.15
578	Tom Brookens	.15
579	Rich Gedman	.15
580	*Bill Doran*	.50
581	Steve Yeager	.15
582	Dan Spillner	.15
583	Dan Quisenberry	.15
584	Rance Mulliniks	.15
585	Storm Davis	.15
586	Dave Schmidt	.15
587	Bill Russell	.15
588	*Pat Sheridan*	.20
589	Rafael Ramirez	.15
590	Bud Anderson	.15
591	George Frazier	.15
592	*Lee Tunnell*	.15
593	Kirk Gibson	.50
594	Scott McGregor	.15
595	Bob Bailor	.15
596	Tom Herr	.20
597	Luis Sanchez	.15
598	Dave Engle	.15
599	*Craig McMurtry*	.15
600	Carlos Diaz	.15
601	Tom O'Malley	.15
602	*Nick Esasky*	.15
603	Ron Hodges	.15
604	Ed Vande Berg	.15
605	Alfredo Griffin	.15
606	Glenn Hoffman	.15
607	Hubie Brooks	.20
608	Richard Barnes (photo actually Neal Heaton)	.15
609	*Greg Walker*	.20
610	Ken Singleton	.20
611	Mark Clear	.15
612	Buck Martinez	.15
613	Ken Griffey	.15
614	Reid Nichols	.15
615	*Doug Sisk*	.15
616	Bob Brenly	.15
617	Joey McLaughlin	.15
618	Glenn Wilson	.15
619	Bob Stoddard	.15
620	Len Sakata (Lenn)	.15
621	*Mike Young*	.15
622	John Stefero	.15
623	*Carmelo Martinez*	.15

624	Dave Bergman	.15
625	Runnin' Reds(David Green, Willie McGee, Lonnie Smith, Ozzie Smith)	.75
626	Rudy May	.15
627	Matt Keough	.15
628	*Jose DeLeon*	.15
629	Jim Essian	.15
630	*Darnell Coles*	.15
631	Mike Warren	.15
632	Del Crandall	.15
633	Dennis Martinez	.20
634	Mike Moore	.15
635	Lary Sorensen	.15
636	Ricky Nelson	.15
637	Omar Moreno	.15
638	Charlie Hough	.15
639	Dennis Eckersley	2.00
640	*Walt Terrell*	.20
641	Denny Walling	.15
642	*Dave Anderson*	.15
643	*Jose Oquendo*	.25
644	Bob Stanley	.15
645	Dave Geisel	.15
646	*Scott Garrelts*	.25
647	*Gary Pettis*	.25
648	Duke Snider Puzzle Card	.15
649	Johnnie LeMaster	.15
650	Dave Collins	.15
651	San Diego Chicken	.25
----	Checklist 1-26 DK (Perez-Steel on back)	.15
----	Checklist 1-26 DK (Perez-Steele on back)	.40
----	Checklist 27-130	.15
----	Checklist 131-234	.15
----	Checklist 235-338	.15
----	Checklist 339-442	.15
----	Checklist 443-546	.15
----	Checklist 547-651	.15

1984 Donruss Action All-Stars

KEN GRIFFEY *outfield*

Full-color photos on the card fronts and backs make the 1984 Donruss Action All-Stars set somewhat unusual. Fronts contain a large action photo plus the Donruss logo and year of issue inside a deep red border. The top half of the backs features a close-up photo with the bottom portion containing biographical and statistical information. The 3-1/2" x 5" cards were sold with Ted Williams puzzle pieces.

	MT
Complete Set (60):	7.50
Common Player:	.10
Ted Williams Puzzle:	10.00
1	Gary Lavelle	.10
2	Willie McGee	.10
3	Tony Pena	.10
4	Lou Whitaker	.10

5	Robin Yount	.65
6	Doug DeCinces	.10
7	John Castino	.10
8	Terry Kennedy	.10
9	Rickey Henderson	.65
10	Bob Horner	.10
11	Harold Baines	.10
12	Buddy Bell	.10
13	Fernando Valenzuela	.15
14	Nolan Ryan	2.50
15	Andre Thornton	.10
16	Gary Redus	.10
17	Pedro Guerrero	.10
18	Andre Dawson	.20
19	Dave Stieb	.10
20	Cal Ripken, Jr.	3.00
21	Ken Griffey	.10
22	Wade Boggs	.70
23	Keith Hernandez	.10
24	Steve Carlton	.40
25	Hal McRae	.10
26	John Lowenstein	.10
27	Fred Lynn	.10
28	Bill Buckner	.10
29	Chris Chambliss	.10
30	Richie Zisk	.10
31	Jack Clark	.10
32	George Hendrick	.10
33	Bill Madlock	.10
34	Lance Parrish	.10
35	Paul Molitor	.60
36	Reggie Jackson	.75
37	Kent Hrbek	.15
38	Steve Garvey	.25
39	Carney Lansford	.10
40	Dale Murphy	.25
41	Greg Luzinski	.10
42	Larry Parrish	.10
43	Ryne Sandberg	.75
44	Dickie Thon	.10
45	Bert Blyleven	.10
46	Ron Oester	.10
47	Dusty Baker	.10
48	Steve Rogers	.10
49	Jim Clancy	.10
50	Eddie Murray	.60
51	Ron Guidry	.10
52	Jim Rice	.10
53	Tom Seaver	.60
54	Pete Rose	1.00
55	George Brett	.75
56	Dan Quisenberry	.10
57	Mike Schmidt	.75
58	Ted Simmons	.10
59	Dave Righetti	.10
60	Checklist	.05

1985 Donruss

CAL RIPKEN $5

The black-bordered 1985 Donruss set includes 653 numbered cards and seven unnumbered checklists. Displaying the artwork of Dick Perez for the fourth consecutive year, cards #1-26 feature the Diamond Kings series. Donruss, reacting to the hobby craze over rookie cards, included a Rated Rookies subset (cards #27-46).

The cards, in standard 2-1/2" x 3-1/2", were issued with a Lou Gehrig puzzle. Backs repeat the format of previous years with black print on yellow and white. The complete set price does not include the higher priced variations. (DK) and (RR) refer to the Diamond Kings and Rated Rookies subsets.

		MT
Complete Set (660):		150.00
Common Player:		.10
Lou Gehrig Puzzle:		3.00
Wax Box:		215.00
1	Ryne Sandberg (DK)	2.50
2	Doug DeCinces (DK)	.10
3	Rich Dotson (DK)	.10
4	Bert Blyleven (DK)	.15
5	Lou Whitaker (DK)	.15
6	Dan Quisenberry (DK)	.10
7	Don Mattingly (DK)	3.50
8	Carney Lansford (DK)	.10
9	Frank Tanana (DK)	.10
10	Willie Upshaw (DK)	.10
11	Claudell Washington (DK)	.10
12	Mike Marshall (DK)	.10
13	Joaquin Andujar (DK)	.10
14	Cal Ripken, Jr. (DK)	5.00
15	Jim Rice (DK)	.15
16	Don Sutton (DK)	.30
17	Frank Viola (DK)	.15
18	Alvin Davis (DK)	.10
19	Mario Soto (DK)	.10
20	Jose Cruz (DK)	.10
21	Charlie Lea (DK)	.10
22	Jesse Orosco (DK)	.10
23	Juan Samuel (DK)	.10
24	Tony Pena (DK)	.10
25	Tony Gwynn (DK)	2.50
26	Bob Brenly (DK)	.10
27	Danny Tartabull (RR)	2.50
28	Mike Bielecki (RR)	.15
29	Steve Lyons (RR)	.20
30	Jeff Reed (RR)	.15
31	Tony Brewer (RR)	.10
32	John Morris (RR)	.10
33	Daryl Boston (RR)	.15
34	Alfonso Pulido (RR)	.10
35	Steve Kiefer (RR)	.10
36	Larry Sheets (RR)	.10
37	Scott Bradley (RR)	.10
38	Calvin Schiraldi (RR)	.10
39	Shawon Dunston (RR)	1.50
40	Charlie Mitchell (RR)	.10
41	Billy Hatcher (RR)	.50
42	Russ Stephans (RR)	.10
43	Alejandro Sanchez (RR)	.10
44	Steve Jeltz (RR)	.10
45	Jim Traber (RR)	.10
46	Doug Loman (RR)	.10
47	Eddie Murray	2.50
48	Robin Yount	2.50
49	Lance Parrish	.15
50	Jim Rice	.15
51	Dave Winfield	1.00
52	Fernando Valenzuela	.15
53	George Brett	4.50
54	Dave Kingman	.15
55	Gary Carter	.40
56	Buddy Bell	.12
57	Reggie Jackson	1.50
58	Harold Baines	.20
59	Ozzie Smith	2.50
60	Nolan Ryan	10.00
61	Mike Schmidt	4.00
62	Dave Parker	.35
63	Tony Gwynn	6.00
64	Tony Pena	.12
65	Jack Clark	.15
66	Dale Murphy	.60
67	Ryne Sandberg	6.00
68	Keith Hernandez	.20
69	Alvin Davis	.25
70	Kent Hrbek	.30
71	Willie Upshaw	.10
72	Dave Engle	.10
73	Alfredo Griffin	.10
74a	Jack Perconte (last line of highlights begins "Batted .346...")	.10
74b	Jack Perconte (last line of highlights begins "Led the ...")	.75
75	Jesse Orosco	.10

76	Jody Davis	.10
77	Bob Horner	.12
78	Larry McWilliams	.10
79	Joel Youngblood	.10
80	Alan Wiggins	.10
81	Ron Oester	.10
82	Ozzie Virgil	.10
83	Ricky Horton	.10
84	Bill Doran	.12
85	Rod Carew	1.00
86	LaMarr Hoyt	.10
87	Tim Wallach	.15
88	Mike Flanagan	.12
89	Jim Sundberg	.10
90	Chet Lemon	.10
91	Bob Stanley	.10
92	Willie Randolph	.12
93	Bill Russell	.10
94	Julio Franco	.75
95	Dan Quisenberry	.12
96	Bill Caudill	.10
97	Bill Gullickson	.10
98	Danny Darwin	.10
99	Curtis Wilkerson	.10
100	Bud Black	.10
101	Tony Phillips	.25
102	Tony Bernazard	.10
103	Jay Howell	.10
104	Burt Hooton	.10
105	Milt Wilcox	.10
106	Rich Dauer	.10
107	Don Sutton	.45
108	Mike Witt	.12
109	Bruce Sutter	.15
110	Enos Cabell	.10
111	John Denny	.10
112	Dave Dravecky	.10
113	Marvell Wynne	.10
114	Johnnie LeMaster	.10
115	Chuck Porter	.10
116	John Gibbons	.10
117	Keith Moreland	.10
118	Darnell Coles	.10
119	Dennis Lamp	.10
120	Ron Davis	.10
121	Nick Esasky	.10
122	Vance Law	.10
123	Gary Roenicke	.10
124	Bill Schroeder	.10
125	Dave Rozema	.10
126	Bobby Meacham	.10
127	Marty Barrett	.15
128	R.J. Reynolds	.15
129	Ernie Camacho	.10
130	Jorge Orta	.10
131	Lary Sorensen	.10
132	Terry Francona	.10
133	Fred Lynn	.20
134	Bobby Jones	.10
135	Jerry Hairston	.10
136	Kevin Bass	.10
137	Garry Maddox	.10
138	Dave LaPoint	.10
139	Kevin McReynolds	.20
140	Wayne Krenchicki	.10
141	Rafael Ramirez	.10
142	Rod Scurry	.10
143	Greg Minton	.10
144	Tim Stoddard	.10
145	Steve Henderson	.10
146	George Bell	.20
147	Dave Meier	.10
148	Sammy Stewart	.10
149	Mark Brouhard	.10
150	Larry Herndon	.10
151	Oil Can Boyd	.10
152	Brian Dayett	.10
153	Tom Niedenfuer	.10
154	Brook Jacoby	.10
155	Onix Concepcion	.10
156	Tim Conroy	.10
157	Joe Hesketh	.12
158	Brian Downing	.10
159	Tommy Dunbar	.10
160	Marc Hill	.10
161	Phil Garner	.10
162	Jerry Davis	.10
163	Bill Campbell	.10
164	John Franco	1.00
165	Len Barker	.10
166	Benny Distefano	.10
167	George Frazier	.10
168	Tito Landrum	.10
169	Cal Ripken, Jr.	10.00
170	Cecil Cooper	.10
171	Alan Trammell	.40

172	Wade Boggs	3.00
173	Don Baylor	.15
174	Pedro Guerrero	.15
175	Frank White	.12
176	Rickey Henderson	2.00
177	Charlie Lea	.10
178	Pete O'Brien	.10
179	Doug DeCinces	.12
180	Ron Kittle	.10
181	George Hendrick	.10
182	Joe Niekro	.12
183	Juan Samuel	.10
184	Mario Soto	.10
185	Goose Gossage	.25
186	Johnny Ray	.10
187	Bob Brenly	.10
188	Craig McMurtry	.10
189	Leon Durham	.10
190	Dwight Gooden	2.00
191	Barry Bonnell	.10
192	Tim Teufel	.10
193	Dave Stieb	.15
194	Mickey Hatcher	.10
195	Jesse Barfield	.10
196	Al Cowens	.10
197	Hubie Brooks	.10
198	Steve Trout	.10
199	Glenn Hubbard	.10
200	Bill Madlock	.15
201	Jeff Robinson	.10
202	Eric Show	.10
203	Dave Concepcion	.15
204	Ivan DeJesus	.10
205	Neil Allen	.10
206	Jerry Mumphrey	.10
207	Mike Brown	.10
208	Carlton Fisk	.75
209	Bryn Smith	.10
210	Tippy Martinez	.10
211	Dion James	.10
212	Willie Hernandez	.10
213	Mike Easler	.10
214	Ron Guidry	.10
215	Rick Honeycutt	.10
216	Brett Butler	.15
217	Larry Gura	.10
218	Ray Burris	.10
219	Steve Rogers	.10
220	Frank Tanana	.12
221	Ned Yost	.10
222	Bret Saberhagen	2.00
223	Mike Davis	.10
224	Bert Blyleven	.15
225	Steve Kemp	.10
226	Jerry Reuss	.10
227	Darrell Evans	.15
228	Wayne Gross	.10
229	Jim Gantner	.10
230	Bob Boone	.10
231	Lonnie Smith	.10
232	Frank DiPino	.10
233	Jerry Koosman	.12
234	Graig Nettles	.12
235	John Tudor	.12
236	John Rabb	.10
237	Rick Manning	.10
238	Mike Fitzgerald	.10
239	Gary Matthews	.12
240	Jim Presley	.10
241	Dave Collins	.10
242	Gary Gaetti	.30
243	Dann Bilardello	.10
244	Rudy Law	.10
245	John Lowenstein	.10
246	Tom Tellmann	.10
247	Howard Johnson	.25
248	Ray Fontenot	.10
249	Tony Armas	.12
250	Candy Maldonado	.10
251	Mike Jeffcoat	.10
252	Dane Iorg	.10
253	Bruce Bochte	.10
254	Pete Rose	2.00
255	Don Aase	.10
256	George Wright	.10
257	Britt Burns	.10
258	Mike Scott	.15
259	Len Matuszek	.10
260	Dave Rucker	.10
261	Craig Lefferts	.10
262	Jay Tibbs	.10
263	Bruce Benedict	.10
264	Don Robinson	.10
265	Gary Lavelle	.10
266	Scott Sanderson	.10
267	Matt Young	.10

#	Player	Price		#	Player	Price		#	Player	Price
268	Ernie Whitt	.10		364	Tom Brunansky	.15		456	Barbaro Garbey	.10
269	Houston Jimenez	.10		365	Brad Gulden	.10		457	Rich Gedman	.10
270	*Ken Dixon*	.10		366	Greg Walker	.10		458	Phil Niekro	.40
271	Peter Ladd	.10		367	Mike Young	.10		459	Mike Scioscia	.10
272	Juan Berenguer	.10		368	Rick Waits	.10		460	Pat Tabler	.10
273	Roger Clemens	30.00		369	Doug Bair	.10		461	Darryl Motley	.10
274	Rick Cerone	.10		370	Bob Shirley	.10		462	Chris Codoroli (Codiroli)	.10
275	Dave Anderson	.10		371	Bob Ojeda	.10		463	Doug Flynn	.10
276	George Vukovich	.10		372	Bob Welch	.10		464	Billy Sample	.10
277	Greg Pryor	.10		373	Neal Heaton	.10		465	Mickey Rivers	.10
278	Mike Warren	.10		374	Danny Jackson (photo actually Steve Farr)	.80		466	John Wathan	.10
279	Bob James	.10						467	Bill Krueger	.10
280	Bobby Grich	.12		375	Donnie Hill	.10		468	Andre Thornton	.12
281	*Mike Mason*	.10		376	Mike Stenhouse	.10		469	Rex Hudler	.15
282	Ron Reed	.10		377	Bruce Kison	.10		470	*Sid Bream*	.60
283	Alan Ashby	.10		378	Wayne Tolleson	.10		471	Kirk Gibson	.20
284	Mark Thurmond	.10		379	Floyd Bannister	.10		472	John Shelby	.10
285	Joe Lefebvre	.10		380	Vern Ruhle	.10		473	Moose Haas	.10
286	Ted Power	.10		381	Tim Corcoran	.10		474	Doug Corbett	.10
287	Chris Chambliss	.10		382	Kurt Kepshire	.10		475	Willie McGee	.15
288	Lee Tunnell	.10		383	Bobby Brown	.10		476	Bob Knepper	.10
289	Rich Bordi	.10		384	Dave Van Gorder	.10		477	Kevin Gross	.10
290	Glenn Brummer	.10		385	Rick Mahler	.10		478	Carmelo Martinez	.10
291	Mike Boddicker	.10		386	Lee Mazzilli	.10		479	Kent Tekulve	.10
292	Rollie Fingers	.40		387	Bill Laskey	.10		480	Chili Davis	.12
293	Lou Whitaker	.25		388	Thad Bosley	.10		481	Bobby Clark	.10
294	Dwight Evans	.15		389	Al Chambers	.10		482	Mookie Wilson	.12
295	Don Mattingly	8.00		390	Tony Fernandez	.50		483	Dave Owen	.10
296	Mike Marshall	.15		391	Ron Washington	.10		484	Ed Nunez	.10
297	Willie Wilson	.12		392	Bill Swaggerty	.10		485	Rance Mulliniks	.10
298	Mike Heath	.10		393	Bob L. Gibson	.10		486	Ken Schrom	.10
299	Tim Raines	.45		394	Marty Castillo	.10		487	Jeff Russell	.10
300	Larry Parrish	.12		395	Steve Crawford	.10		488	Tom Paciorek	.10
301	Geoff Zahn	.10		396	Clay Christiansen	.10		489	Dan Ford	.10
302	Rich Dotson	.12		397	Bob Bailor	.10		490	Mike Caldwell	.10
303	David Green	.10		398	Mike Hargrove	.10		491	Scottie Earl	.10
304	Jose Cruz	.12		399	Charlie Leibrandt	.10		492	Jose Rijo	.75
305	Steve Carlton	1.25		400	Tom Burgmeier	.10		493	Bruce Hurst	.12
306	Gary Redus	.10		401	Razor Shines	.10		494	Ken Landreaux	.10
307	Steve Garvey	.40		402	Rob Wilfong	.10		495	Mike Fischlin	.10
308	Jose DeLeon	.10		403	Tom Henke	.12		496	Don Slaught	.10
309	Randy Lerch	.10		404	Al Jones	.10		497	Steve McCatty	.10
310	Claudell Washington	.10		405	Mike LaCoss	.10		498	Gary Lucas	.10
311	Lee Smith	1.00		406	Luis DeLeon	.10		499	Gary Pettis	.10
312	Darryl Strawberry	.75		407	Greg Gross	.10		500	Marvis Foley	.10
313	Jim Beattie	.10		408	Tom Hume	.10		501	Mike Squires	.10
314	John Butcher	.10		409	Rick Camp	.10		502	*Jim Pankovitz*	.10
315	Damaso Garcia	.10		410	Milt May	.10		503	Luis Aguayo	.10
316	Mike Smithson	.10		411	*Henry Cotto*	.10		504	Ralph Citarella	.10
317	Luis Leal	.10		412	Dave Von Ohlen	.10		505	Bruce Bochy	.10
318	Ken Phelps	.10		413	Scott McGregor	.10		506	Bob Owchinko	.10
319	Wally Backman	.10		414	Ted Simmons	.10		507	Pascual Perez	.10
320	Ron Cey	.12		415	Jack Morris	.25		508	Lee Lacy	.10
321	Brad Komminsk	.10		416	Bill Buckner	.15		509	Atlee Hammaker	.10
322	Jason Thompson	.10		417	Butch Wynegar	.10		510	Bob Dernier	.10
323	*Frank Williams*	.10		418	Steve Sax	.15		511	Ed Vande Berg	.10
324	Tim Lollar	.10		419	Steve Balboni	.10		512	Cliff Johnson	.10
325	*Eric Davis*	1.50		420	Dwayne Murphy	.10		513	Len Whitehouse	.10
326	Von Hayes	.10		421	Andre Dawson	1.00		514	Dennis Martinez	.12
327	Andy Van Slyke	.60		422	Charlie Hough	.10		515	Ed Romero	.10
328	Craig Reynolds	.10		423	Tommy John	.25		516	Rusty Kuntz	.10
329	Dick Schofield	.10		424a	Tom Seaver (Floyd Bannister photo, left-hander)	2.00		517	Rick Miller	.10
330	Scott Fletcher	.10						518	Dennis Rasmussen	.10
331	Jeff Reardon	.12						519	Steve Yeager	.10
332	Rick Dempsey	.10		424b	Tom Seaver (correct photo)	30.00		520	Chris Bando	.10
333	Ben Oglivie	.10		425	Tom Herr	.10		521	U.L. Washington	.10
334	Dan Petry	.10		426	Terry Puhl	.10		522	*Curt Young*	.10
335	Jackie Gutierrez	.10		427	Al Holland	.10		523	Angel Salazar	.10
336	Dave Righetti	.10		428	Eddie Milner	.10		524	Curt Kaufman	.10
337	Alejandro Pena	.10		429	Terry Kennedy	.10		525	Odell Jones	.10
338	Mel Hall	.10		430	John Candelaria	.10		526	Juan Agosto	.10
339	Pat Sheridan	.10		431	Manny Trillo	.10		527	Denny Walling	.10
340	Keith Atherton	.10		432	Ken Oberkfell	.10		528	Andy Hawkins	.15
341	David Palmer	.10		433	Rick Sutcliffe	.15		529	Sixto Lezcano	.10
342	Gary Ward	.10		434	Ron Darling	.25		530	Skeeter Barnes	.10
343	Dave Stewart	.15		435	Spike Owen	.10		531	Randy S. Johnson	.10
344	*Mark Gubicza*	.35		436	Frank Viola	.25		532	Jim Morrison	.10
345	Carney Lansford	.10		437	Lloyd Moseby	.10		533	Warren Brusstar	.10
346	Jerry Willard	.10		438	Kirby Puckett	35.00		534a	*Jeff Pendleton* (error)	3.00
347	Ken Griffey	.12		439	Jim Clancy	.10		534b	*Terry Pendleton* (correct)	12.00
348	*Franklin Stubbs*	.10		440	Mike Moore	.10		535	Vic Rodriguez	.10
349	Aurelio Lopez	.10		441	Doug Sisk	.10		536	Bob McClure	.10
350	Al Bumbry	.10		442	Dennis Eckersley	1.00		537	Dave Bergman	.10
351	Charlie Moore	.10		443	Gerald Perry	.10		538	Mark Clear	.10
352	Luis Sanchez	.10		444	Dale Berra	.10		539	*Mike Pagliarulo*	.35
353	Darrell Porter	.10		445	Dusty Baker	.12		540	Terry Whitfield	.10
354	Bill Dawley	.10		446	Ed Whitson	.10		541	Joe Beckwith	.10
355	Charlie Hudson	.10		447	Cesar Cedeno	.12		542	Jeff Burroughs	.10
356	Garry Templeton	.10		448	*Rick Schu*	.10		543	Dan Schatzeder	.10
357	Cecilio Guante	.10		449	Joaquin Andujar	.10		544	Donnie Scott	.10
358	Jeff Leonard	.10		450	*Mark Bailey*	.10		545	Jim Slaton	.10
359	Paul Molitor	3.00		451	*Ron Romanick*	.10		546	Greg Luzinski	.12
360	Ron Gardenhire	.10		452	Julio Cruz	.10		547	*Mark Salas*	.10
361	Larry Bowa	.12		453	Miguel Dilone	.10		548	Dave Smith	.10
362	Bob Kearney	.10		454	Storm Davis	.12		549	John Wockenfuss	.10
363	Garth Iorg	.10		455	Jaime Cocanower	.10		550	Frank Pastore	.10

551	Tim Flannery	.10
552	Rick Rhoden	.12
553	Mark Davis	.10
554	*Jeff Dedmon*	.12
555	Gary Woods	.10
556	Danny Heep	.10
557	Mark Langston	2.00
558	Darrell Brown	.10
559	Jimmy Key	2.00
560	Rick Lysander	.10
561	Doyle Alexander	.10
562	Mike Stanton	.10
563	Sid Fernandez	.25
564	Richie Hebner	.10
565	Alex Trevino	.10
566	Brian Harper	.10
567	*Dan Gladden*	.30
568	Luis Salazar	.10
569	Tom Foley	.10
570	Larry Andersen	.10
571	Danny Cox	.10
572	Joe Sambito	.10
573	Juan Beniquez	.10
574	Joel Skinner	.10
575	*Randy St. Claire*	.10
576	Floyd Rayford	.10
577	Roy Howell	.10
578	John Grubb	.10
579	Ed Jurak	.10
580	John Montefusco	.10
581	Orel Hershiser	3.50
582	*Tom Waddell*	.10
583	Mark Huisman	.10
584	Joe Morgan	.40
585	Jim Wohlford	.10
586	Dave Schmidt	.10
587	*Jeff Kunkel*	.10
588	Hal McRae	.12
589	Bill Almon	.10
590	Carmen Castillo	.10
591	Omar Moreno	.10
592	*Ken Howell*	.10
593	Tom Brookens	.10
594	Joe Nolan	.10
595	Willie Lozado	.10
596	*Tom Nieto*	.10
597	Walt Terrell	.10
598	Al Oliver	.15
599	Shane Rawley	.10
600	*Denny Gonzalez*	.10
601	*Mark Grant*	.10
602	Mike Armstrong	.10
603	George Foster	.15
604	Davey Lopes	.10
605	Salome Barojas	.10
606	Roy Lee Jackson	.10
607	Pete Filson	.10
608	Duane Walker	.10
609	Glenn Wilson	.10
610	*Rafael Santana*	.10
611	Roy Smith	.10
612	Ruppert Jones	.10
613	Joe Cowley	.10
614	*Al Nipper* (photo actually Mike Brown)	.15
615	Gene Nelson	.10
616	Joe Carter	6.00
617	Ray Knight	.12
618	Chuck Rainey	.10
619	Dan Driessen	.10
620	Daryl Sconiers	.10
621	Bill Stein	.10
622	Roy Smalley	.10
623	Ed Lynch	.10
624	*Jeff Stone*	.10
625	Bruce Berenyi	.10
626	Kelvin Chapman	.10
627	Joe Price	.10
628	Steve Bedrosian	.12
629	Vic Mata	.10
630	Mike Krukow	.10
631	*Phil Bradley*	.15
632	Jim Gott	.10
633	Randy Bush	.10
634	*Tom Browning*	.60
635	Lou Gehrig Puzzle Card	.10
636	Reid Nichols	.10
637	*Dan Pasqua*	.60
638	German Rivera	.10
639	*Don Schulze*	.10
640a	Mike Jones (last line of highlights begins "Was 11-7...")	.10
640b	Mike Jones (last line of highlights begins "Spent some ...")	.75

641	Pete Rose	2.00
642	*Wade Rowdon*	.10
643	Jerry Narron	.10
644	*Darrell Miller*	.10
645	*Tim Hulett*	.10
646	Andy McGaffigan	.10
647	Kurt Bevacqua	.10
648	*John Russell*	.10
649	*Ron Robinson*	.10
650	Donnie Moore	.10
651a	Two for the Title(Don Mattingly, Dave Winfield) (yellow letters)	4.00
651b	Two for the Title(Don Mattingly, Dave Winfield) (white letters)	6.00
652	Tim Laudner	.10
653	*Steve Farr*	.15
----	Checklist 1-26 DK	.10
----	Checklist 27-130	.10
----	Checklist 131-234	.10
----	Checklist 235-338	.10
----	Checklist 339-442	.10
----	Checklist 443-546	.10
----	Checklist 547-653	.10

1985 Donruss Box Panels

In 1985, Donruss placed on the bottoms of its wax pack boxes a four-card panel which included three player cards and a Lou Gehrig puzzle card. The player cards, numbered PC1 through PC3, have backs identical to the regular 1985 Donruss issue. The card fronts are identical in design to the regular issue, but carry different photos.

		MT
Complete Panel:		5.00
Complete Singles Set (4):		3.50
Common Player:		.10
PC1	Dwight Gooden	1.00
PC2	Ryne Sandberg	3.00
PC3	Ron Kittle	.10
---	Lou Gehrig (puzzle card)	.10
1	Dwight Gooden	1.50
2	Ryne Sandberg	3.00
3	Ron Kittle	.10
----	Lou Gehrig Puzzle Card	.05

1985 Donruss Action All-Stars

In 1985, Donruss issued an Action All-Stars set for the third consecutive year. Card fronts feature an action photo with an inset portrait of the player inside a black border with grey boxes through it. The card backs have black print on blue and white and include statistical

and biographical information. The cards were issued with a Lou Gehrig puzzle.

		MT
Complete Set (60):		8.00
Common Player:		.15
Lou Gehrig Puzzle:		3.00
1	Tim Raines	.25
2	Jim Gantner	.15
3	Mario Soto	.15
4	Spike Owen	.15
5	Lloyd Moseby	.15
6	Damaso Garcia	.15
7	Cal Ripken, Jr.	3.50
8	Dan Quisenberry	.15
9	Eddie Murray	.75
10	Tony Pena	.15
11	Buddy Bell	.15
12	Dave Winfield	.65
13	Ron Kittle	.15
14	Rich Gossage	.15
15	Dwight Evans	.15
16	Al Davis	.15
17	Mike Schmidt	.90
18	Pascual Perez	.15
19	Tony Gwynn	1.00
20	Nolan Ryan	3.00
21	Robin Yount	.75
22	Mike Marshall	.15
23	Brett Butler	.20
24	Ryne Sandberg	1.00
25	Dale Murphy	.35
26	George Brett	.90
27	Jim Rice	.15
28	Ozzie Smith	.75
29	Larry Parrish	.15
30	Jack Clark	.15
31	Manny Trillo	.15
32	Dave Kingman	.15
33	Geoff Zahn	.15
34	Pedro Guerrero	.15
35	Dave Parker	.15
36	Rollie Fingers	.25
37	Fernando Valenzuela	.20
38	Wade Boggs	.60
39	Reggie Jackson	.50
40	Kent Hrbek	.20
41	Keith Hernandez	.15
42	Lou Whitaker	.15
43	Tom Herr	.15
44	Alan Trammell	.20
45	Butch Wynegar	.15
46	Leon Durham	.15
47	Dwight Gooden	.30
48	Don Mattingly	1.00
49	Phil Niekro	.25
50	Johnny Ray	.15
51	Doug DeCinces	.15
52	Willie Upshaw	.15
53	Lance Parrish	.15
54	Jody Davis	.15
55	Steve Carlton	.40
56	Juan Samuel	.15
57	Gary Carter	.20
58	Harold Baines	.15
59	Eric Show	.15
60	Checklist	.05

1985 Donruss Diamond Kings Supers

The 1985 Donruss Diamond Kings Supers are enlarged versions of the Diamond Kings cards in the regular 1985 Donruss set. The cards measure 4-15/16" x 6-3/4". The Diamond Kings series features the artwork of Dick Perez. Twenty-eight cards make up the Super set - 26 DK cards, an unnumbered checklist, and an unnumbered Dick Perez card. The back of the Perez card contains a brief history of Dick Perez and the Perez-Steele Galleries. The set could be obtained through a mail-in offer found on wax pack wrappers.

		MT
	Complete Set (28):	15.00
	Common Player:	.50
1	Ryne Sandberg	4.00
2	Doug DeCinces	.50
3	Richard Dotson	.50
4	Bert Blyleven	.50
5	Lou Whitaker	.50
6	Dan Quisenberry	.50
7	Don Mattingly	5.00
8	Carney Lansford	.50
9	Frank Tanana	.50
10	Willie Upshaw	.50
11	Claudell Washington	.50
12	Mike Marshall	.50
13	Joaquin Andujar	.50
14	Cal Ripken, Jr.	8.00
15	Jim Rice	.50
16	Don Sutton	.75
17	Frank Viola	.50
18	Alvin Davis	.50
19	Mario Soto	.50
20	Jose Cruz	.50
21	Charlie Lea	.50
22	Jesse Orosco	.50
23	Juan Samuel	.50
24	Tony Pena	.50
25	Tony Gwynn	4.00
26	Bob Brenly	.50
----	Checklist	.05
----	Dick Perez (DK artist)	.50

1985 Donruss Highlights

Designed in the style of the regular 1985 Donruss set, this issue features the Player of the Month in the major leagues plus highlight cards of special baseball events and milestones of the 1985 season. Fifty-six cards, including an unnumbered checklist, comprise the set which was available only through hobby dealers. The cards measure 2-1/2" x 3-1/2" and have glossy fronts. The last two cards in the set feature Donruss' picks for the A.L. and N.L. Rookies of the Year. The set was issued in a specially designed box.

		MT
	Complete Set (56):	18.00
	Common Player:	.10
1	Sets Opening Day Record(Tom Seaver)	.40
2	Establishes A.L. Save Mark(Rollie Fingers)	.15
3	A.L. Player of the Month - April(Mike Davis)	.10
4	A.L. Pitcher of the Month - April(Charlie Leibrandt)	.10
5	N.L. Player of the Month - April(Dale Murphy)	.30
6	N.L. Pitcher of the Month - April(Fernando Valenzuela)	.15

7	N.L. Shortstop Record(Larry Bowa)	.10
8	Joins Reds 2000 Hit Club(Dave Concepcion)	.10
9	Eldest Grand Slammer(Tony Perez)	.15
10	N.L. Career Run Leader(Pete Rose)	1.25
11	A.L. Player of the Month - May(George Brett)	.90
12	A.L. Pitcher of the Month - May(Dave Stieb)	.10
13	N.L. Player of the Month - May(Dave Parker)	.10
14	N.L. Pitcher of the Month - May(Andy Hawkins)	.10
15	Records 11th Straight Win(Andy Hawkins)	.10
16	Two Homers In First Inning(Von Hayes)	.10
17	A.L. Player of the Month - June(Rickey Henderson)	.60
18	A.L. Pitcher of the Month - June(Jay Howell)	.10
19	N.L. Player of the Month - June(Pedro Guerrero)	.10
20	N.L. Pitcher of the Month - June(John Tudor)	.10
21	Marathon Game Iron Men(Gary Carter, Keith Hernandez)	.10
22	Records 4000th K(Nolan Ryan)	2.00
23	All-Star Game MVP(LaMarr Hoyt)	.10
24	1st Ranger To Hit For Cycle(Oddibe McDowell)	.10
25	A.L. Player of the Month - July(George Brett)	.90
26	A.L. Pitcher of the Month - July(Bret Saberhagen)	.15
27	N.L. Player of the Month - July(Keith Hernandez)	.10
28	N.L. Pitcher of the Month - July(Fernando Valenzuela)	.15
29	Record Setting Base Stealers(Vince Coleman, Willie McGee)	.20
30	Notches 300th Career Win(Tom Seaver)	.35
31	Strokes 3000th Hit(Rod Carew)	.35
32	Establishes Met Record(Dwight Gooden)	.25
33	Achieves Strikeout Milestone(Dwight Gooden)	.25
34	Explodes For 9 RBI(Eddie Murray)	.40
35	A.L. Career Hbp Leader(Don Baylor)	.10
36	A.L. Player of the Month - August(Don Mattingly)	1.50
37	A.L. Pitcher of the Month - August(Dave Righetti)	.10
38	N.L. Player of the Month(Willie McGee)	.10
39	N.L. Pitcher of the Month - August(Shane Rawley)	.10
40	Ty-Breaking Hit(Pete Rose)	2.00
41	Hits 3 HRs, Drives In 8 Runs(Andre Dawson)	.10
42	Sets Yankee Theft Mark(Rickey Henderson)	.60
43	20 Wins In Rookie Season(Tom Browning)	.10
44	Yankee Milestone For Hits(Don Mattingly)	1.50
45	A.L. Player of the Month - September(Don Mattingly)	1.50
46	A.L. Pitcher of the Month - September(Charlie Leibrandt)	.10
47	N.L. Player of the Month - September(Gary Carter)	.10
48	N.L. Pitcher of the Month - September(Dwight Gooden)	.25
49	Major League Record Setter(Wade Boggs)	1.25
50	Hurls Shutout For 300th Win(Phil Niekro)	.25
51	Venerable HR King(Darrell Evans)	.10
52	N.L. Switch-hitting Record(Willie McGee)	.10
53	Equals DiMaggio Feat(Dave Winfield)	.30
54	Donruss N.L. Rookie of the Year(Vince Coleman)	.50
55	Donruss A.L. Rookie of the Year(Ozzie Guillen)	.40
----	Checklist	.05

1986 Donruss

In 1986, Donruss issued a 660-card set which included 653 numbered cards and seven unnumbered checklists. The 2-1/2" x 3-1/2" cards have fronts that feature blue borders and backs that have black print on blue and white. For the fifth year in a row, the first 26 cards in the set are Diamond Kings. The Rated Rookies subset (#27-46) appears once again. The cards were distributed with a Hank Aaron puzzle. The complete set price does not include the higher priced variations. In the checklist that follows, (DK) and (RR) refer to the Diamond Kings and Rated Rookies series.

		MT
	Complete Set (660):	80.00
	Common Player:	.08
	Hank Aaron Puzzle:	5.00
	Wax Box:	120.00
1	Kirk Gibson (DK)	.15
2	Goose Gossage (DK)	.15
3	Willie McGee (DK)	.15
4	George Bell (DK)	.15
5	Tony Armas (DK)	.10
6	Chili Davis (DK)	.10
7	Cecil Cooper (DK)	.12
8	Mike Boddicker (DK)	.10
9	Davey Lopes (DK)	.10
10	Bill Doran (DK)	.12
11	Bret Saberhagen (DK)	.25
12	Brett Butler (DK)	.15
13	Harold Baines (DK)	.15
14	Mike Davis (DK)	.10
15	Tony Perez (DK)	.15
16	Willie Randolph (DK)	.12
17	Bob Boone (DK)	.10
18	Orel Hershiser (DK)	.20
19	Johnny Ray (DK)	.12
20	Gary Ward (DK)	.10
21	Rick Mahler (DK)	.08
22	Phil Bradley (DK)	.10
23	Jerry Koosman (DK)	.12
24	Tom Brunansky (DK)	.15
25	Andre Dawson (DK)	.40
26	Dwight Gooden (DK)	.35
27	Kal Daniels (RR)	.10
28	Fred McGriff (RR)	5.00
29	Cory Snyder (RR)	.20
30	Jose Guzman (RR)	.10
31	Ty Gainey (RR)	.08
32	Johnny Abrego (RR)	.08
33a	Andres Galarraga (RR) accent mark over e of Andres on back)	6.00

No.	Player	Price
33b	*Andres Galarraga* (RR) no accent mark)	6.00
34	*Dave Shipanoff* (RR)	.08
35	*Mark McLemore* (RR)	.30
36	*Marty Clary* (RR)	.08
37	*Paul O'Neill* (RR)	4.00
38	Danny Tartabull (RR)	.40
39	*Jose Canseco* (RR)	15.00
40	*Juan Nieves* (RR)	.10
41	*Lance McCullers* (RR)	.20
42	*Rick Surhoff* (RR)	.08
43	*Todd Worrell* (RR)	.40
44	Bob Kipper (RR)	.08
45	*John Habyan* (RR)	.15
46	*Mike Woodard* (RR)	.08
47	Mike Boddicker	.10
48	Robin Yount	1.00
49	Lou Whitaker	.20
50	Dennis Boyd	.08
51	Rickey Henderson	.75
52	Mike Marshall	.10
53	George Brett	2.50
54	Dave Kingman	.15
55	Hubie Brooks	.10
56	*Oddibe McDowell*	.10
57	Doug DeCinces	.10
58	Britt Burns	.08
59	Ozzie Smith	1.50
60	Jose Cruz	.10
61	Mike Schmidt	2.00
62	Pete Rose	1.50
63	Steve Garvey	.30
64	Tony Pena	.10
65	Chili Davis	.10
66	Dale Murphy	.35
67	Ryne Sandberg	2.50
68	Gary Carter	.35
69	Alvin Davis	.10
70	Kent Hrbek	.25
71	George Bell	.15
72	Kirby Puckett	6.00
73	Lloyd Moseby	.10
74	Bob Kearney	.08
75	Dwight Gooden	.50
76	Gary Matthews	.10
77	Rick Mahler	.08
78	Benny Distefano	.08
79	Jeff Leonard	.08
80	Kevin McReynolds	.30
81	Ron Oester	.08
82	John Russell	.08
83	Tommy Herr	.10
84	Jerry Mumphrey	.08
85	Ron Romanick	.08
86	Daryl Boston	.08
87	Andre Dawson	1.00
88	Eddie Murray	1.00
89	Dion James	.08
90	Chet Lemon	.08
91	Bob Stanley	.08
92	Willie Randolph	.10
93	Mike Scioscia	.08
94	Tom Waddell	.08
95	Danny Jackson	.15
96	Mike Davis	.08
97	Mike Fitzgerald	.08
98	Gary Ward	.08
99	Pete O'Brien	.08
100	Bret Saberhagen	.45
101	Alfredo Griffin	.08
102	Brett Butler	.12
103	Ron Guidry	.12
104	Jerry Reuss	.08
105	Jack Morris	.25
106	Rick Dempsey	.08
107	Ray Burris	.08
108	Brian Downing	.10
109	Willie McGee	.15
110	Bill Doran	.10
111	Kent Tekulve	.08
112	Tony Gwynn	3.00
113	Marvell Wynne	.08
114	David Green	.08
115	Jim Gantner	.08
116	George Foster	.15
117	Steve Trout	.08
118	Mark Langston	.30
119	Tony Fernandez	.15
120	John Butcher	.08
121	Ron Robinson	.08
122	Dan Spillner	.08
123	Mike Young	.08
124	Paul Molitor	1.75
125	Kirk Gibson	.25
126	Ken Griffey	.12
127	Tony Armas	.08
128	*Mariano Duncan*	.15
129	Pat Tabler (Mr. Clutch)	.08
130	Frank White	.10
131	Carney Lansford	.08
132	Vance Law	.08
133	Dick Schofield	.08
134	Wayne Tolleson	.08
135	Greg Walker	.08
136	Denny Walling	.08
137	Ozzie Virgil	.08
138	Ricky Horton	.08
139	LaMarr Hoyt	.08
140	Wayne Krenchicki	.08
141	Glenn Hubbard	.08
142	Cecilio Guante	.00
143	Mike Krukow	.08
144	Lee Smith	.12
145	Edwin Nunez	.08
146	Dave Stieb	.12
147	Mike Smithson	.08
148	Ken Dixon	.08
149	Danny Darwin	.08
150	Chris Pittaro	.08
151	Bill Buckner	.12
152	Mike Pagliarulo	.10
153	Bill Russell	.08
154	Brook Jacoby	.08
155	Pat Sheridan	.08
156	*Mike Gallego*	.15
157	Jim Wohlford	.08
158	Gary Pettis	.00
159	Toby Harrah	.08
160	Richard Dotson	.08
161	Bob Knepper	.08
162	Dave Dravecky	.08
163	Greg Gross	.08
164	Eric Davis	.40
165	Gerald Perry	.10
166	Rick Rhoden	.10
167	Keith Moreland	.08
168	Jack Clark	.10
169	Storm Davis	.10
170	Cecil Cooper	.10
171	Alan Trammell	.35
172	Roger Clemens	5.00
173	Don Mattingly	4.00
174	Pedro Guerrero	.20
175	Willie Wilson	.12
176	Dwayne Murphy	.08
177	Tim Raines	.40
178	Larry Parrish	.10
179	Mike Witt	.10
180	Harold Baines	.15
181	*Vince Coleman*	.35
182	*Jeff Heathcock*	.08
183	Steve Carlton	.60
184	Mario Soto	.08
185	Goose Gossage	.20
186	Johnny Ray	.10
187	Dan Gladden	.08
188	Bob Horner	.12
189	Rick Sutcliffe	.12
190	Keith Hernandez	.10
191	Phil Bradley	.10
192	Tom Brunansky	.10
193	Jesse Barfield	.10
194	Frank Viola	.10
195	Willie Upshaw	.08
196	Jim Beattie	.08
197	Darryl Strawberry	.35
198	Ron Cey	.10
199	Steve Bedrosian	.12
200	Steve Kemp	.08
201	Manny Trillo	.08
202	Garry Templeton	.08
203	Dave Parker	.15
204	John Denny	.08
205	Terry Pendleton	.08
206	Terry Puhl	.08
207	Bobby Grich	.10
208	*Ozzie Guillen*	.90
209	Jeff Reardon	.12
210	Cal Ripken, Jr.	6.00
211	Bill Schroeder	.08
212	Dan Petry	.08
213	Jim Rice	.15
214	Dave Righetti	.08
215	Fernando Valenzuela	.25
216	Julio Franco	.25
217	Darryl Motley	.08
218	Dave Collins	.08
219	Tim Wallach	.12
220	George Wright	.08
221	Tommy Dunbar	.08
222	Steve Balboni	.08
223	Jay Howell	.08
224	Joe Carter	1.50
225	Ed Whitson	.08
226	Orel Hershiser	.25
227	Willie Hernandez	.08
228	Lee Lacy	.08
229	Rollie Fingers	.20
230	Bob Boone	.08
231	Joaquin Andujar	.08
232	Craig Reynolds	.08
233	Shane Rawley	.08
234	Eric Show	.08
235	Jose DeLeon	.08
236	*Jose Uribe*	.00
237	Moose Haas	.08
238	Wally Backman	.08
239	Dennis Eckersley	.15
240	Mike Moore	.08
241	Damaso Garcia	.08
242	Tim Teufel	.08
243	Dave Concepcion	.12
244	Floyd Bannister	.08
245	Fred Lynn	.20
246	Charlie Moore	.08
247	Walt Terrell	.08
248	Dave Winfield	.75
249	Dwight Evans	.12
250	*Dennis Powell*	.08
251	Andre Thornton	.10
252	Onix Concepcion	.00
253	Mike Heath	.08
254a	David Palmer (2B on front)	.08
254b	David Palmer (P on front)	.50
255	Donnie Moore	.08
256	Curtis Wilkerson	.08
257	Julio Cruz	.08
258	Nolan Ryan	6.00
259	Jeff Stone	.08
260a	John Tudor (1981 Games is .18)	.10
260b	John Tudor (1981 Games is 18)	.50
261	Mark Thurmond	.08
262	Jay Tibbs	.08
263	Rafael Ramirez	.08
264	Larry McWilliams	.08
265	Mark Davis	.08
266	Bob Dernier	.08
267	Matt Young	.08
268	Jim Clancy	.08
269	Mickey Hatcher	.08
270	Sammy Stewart	.08
271	Bob L. Gibson	.08
272	Nelson Simmons	.08
273	Rich Gedman	.10
274	Butch Wynegar	.08
275	Ken Howell	.08
276	Mel Hall	.08
277	Jim Sundberg	.08
278	Chris Codiroli	.08
279	*Herman Winningham*	.10
280	Rod Carew	.70
281	Don Slaught	.08
282	Scott Fletcher	.08
283	Bill Dawley	.08
284	Andy Hawkins	.08
285	Glenn Wilson	.08
286	Nick Esasky	.08
287	Claudell Washington	.08
288	Lee Mazzilli	.08
289	Jody Davis	.10
290	Darrell Porter	.08
291	Scott McGregor	.08
292	Ted Simmons	.10
293	Aurelio Lopez	.08
294	Marty Barrett	.10
295	Dale Berra	.08
296	Greg Brock	.08
297	Charlie Leibrandt	.08
298	Bill Krueger	.08
299	Bryn Smith	.08
300	Burt Hooton	.08
301	*Stu Cliburn*	.08
302	Luis Salazar	.08
303	Ken Dayley	.08
304	Frank DiPino	.08
305	Von Hayes	.10
306a	Gary Redus (1983 2B is .20)	.08
306b	Gary Redus (1983 2B is 20)	1.00
307	Craig Lefferts	.08
308	Sam Khalifa	.08
309	Scott Garrelts	.08
310	Rick Cerone	.08
311	Shawon Dunston	.20
312	Howard Johnson	.12
313	Jim Presley	.08
314	Gary Gaetti	.25

#	Player	Price
315	Luis Leal	.08
316	Mark Salas	.08
317	Bill Caudill	.08
318	Dave Henderson	.10
319	Rafael Santana	.08
320	Leon Durham	.08
321	Bruce Sutter	.12
322	Jason Thompson	.08
323	Bob Brenly	.08
324	Carmelo Martinez	.08
325	Eddie Milner	.08
326	Juan Samuel	.10
327	Tom Nieto	.08
328	Dave Smith	.08
329	*Urbano Lugo*	.08
330	Joel Skinner	.08
331	Bill Gullickson	.08
332	Floyd Rayford	.08
333	Ben Oglivie	.08
334	Lance Parrish	.20
335	Jackie Gutierrez	.08
336	Dennis Rasmussen	.12
337	Terry Whitfield	.08
338	Neal Heaton	.08
339	Jorge Orta	.08
340	Donnie Hill	.08
341	Joe Hesketh	.08
342	Charlie Hough	.10
343	Dave Rozema	.08
344	Greg Pryor	.08
345	Mickey Tettleton	.75
346	George Vukovich	.08
347	Don Baylor	.15
348	Carlos Diaz	.08
349	Barbaro Garbey	.08
350	Larry Sheets	.08
351	*Ted Higuera*	.15
352	Juan Beniquez	.08
353	Bob Forsch	.08
354	Mark Bailey	.08
355	Larry Andersen	.08
356	Terry Kennedy	.08
357	Don Robinson	.08
358	Jim Gott	.08
359	*Earnest Riles*	.10
360	*John Christensen*	.08
361	Ray Fontenot	.08
362	Spike Owen	.08
363	Jim Acker	.08
364a	Ron Davis (last line in highlights ends with "...in May.")	.08
364b	Ron Davis (last line in highlights ends with "...relievers (9).")	.50
365	Tom Hume	.08
366	Carlton Fisk	.60
367	Nate Snell	.08
368	Rick Manning	.08
369	Darrell Evans	.15
370	Ron Hassey	.08
371	Wade Boggs	1.00
372	Rick Honeycutt	.08
373	Chris Bando	.08
374	Bud Black	.08
375	Steve Henderson	.08
376	Charlie Lea	.08
377	Reggie Jackson	1.00
378	Dave Schmidt	.08
379	Bob James	.08
380	Glenn Davis	.15
381	Tim Corcoran	.08
382	Danny Cox	.10
383	Tim Flannery	.08
384	Tom Browning	.10
385	Rick Camp	.08
386	Jim Morrison	.08
387	Dave LaPoint	.08
388	Davey Lopes	.08
389	Al Cowens	.08
390	Doyle Alexander	.10
391	Tim Laudner	.08
392	Don Aase	.08
393	Jaime Cocanower	.08
394	Randy O'Neal	.08
395	Mike Easler	.08
396	Scott Bradley	.08
397	Tom Niedenfuer	.08
398	Jerry Willard	.08
399	Lonnie Smith	.08
400	Bruce Bochte	.08
401	Terry Francona	.08
402	Jim Slaton	.08
403	Bill Stein	.08
404	Tim Hulett	.08
405	Alan Ashby	.08
406	Tim Stoddard	.08
407	Garry Maddox	.08
408	Ted Power	.08
409	Len Barker	.08
410	Denny Gonzalez	.08
411	George Frazier	.08
412	Andy Van Slyke	.15
413	Jim Dwyer	.08
414	Paul Householder	.08
415	Alejandro Sanchez	.08
416	Steve Crawford	.08
417	Dan Pasqua	.10
418	Enos Cabell	.08
419	Mike Jones	.08
420	Steve Kiefer	.08
421	*Tim Burke*	.10
422	Mike Mason	.08
423	Ruppert Jones	.08
424	Jerry Hairston	.08
425	Tito Landrum	.08
426	Jeff Calhoun	.08
427	*Don Carman*	.08
428	Tony Perez	.15
429	Jerry Davis	.08
430	Bob Walk	.08
431	Brad Wellman	.08
432	Terry Forster	.08
433	Billy Hatcher	.10
434	Clint Hurdle	.08
435	*Ivan Calderon*	.15
436	Pete Filson	.08
437	Tom Henke	.08
438	Dave Engle	.08
439	Tom Filer	.08
440	Gorman Thomas	.08
441	*Rick Aguilera*	.50
442	Scott Sanderson	.08
443	Jeff Dedmon	.08
444	*Joe Orsulak*	.15
445	Atlee Hammaker	.08
446	Jerry Royster	.08
447	Buddy Bell	.10
448	Dave Rucker	.08
449	Ivan DeJesus	.08
450	Jim Pankovits	.08
451	Jerry Narron	.08
452	Bryan Little	.08
453	Gary Lucas	.08
454	Dennis Martinez	.12
455	Ed Romero	.08
456	*Bob Melvin*	.08
457	Glenn Hoffman	.08
458	Bob Shirley	.08
459	Bob Welch	.10
460	Carmen Castillo	.08
461	Dave Leeper	.08
462	*Tim Birtsas*	.08
463	Randy St. Claire	.08
464	Chris Welsh	.08
465	Greg Harris	.08
466	Lynn Jones	.08
467	Dusty Baker	.12
468	Roy Smith	.08
469	Andre Robertson	.08
470	Ken Landreaux	.08
471	Dave Bergman	.08
472	Gary Roenicke	.08
473	Pete Vuckovich	.08
474	*Kirk McCaskill*	.40
475	Jeff Lahti	.08
476	Mike Scott	.15
477	*Darren Daulton*	2.00
478	Graig Nettles	.15
479	Bill Almon	.08
480	Greg Minton	.08
481	Randy Ready	.08
482	*Len Dykstra*	2.00
483	Thad Bosley	.08
484	*Harold Reynolds*	.40
485	Al Oliver	.12
486	Roy Smalley	.08
487	John Franco	.15
488	Juan Agosto	.08
489	Al Pardo	.08
490	*Bill Wegman*	.15
491	Frank Tanana	.10
492	*Brian Fisher*	.08
493	Mark Clear	.08
494	Len Matuszek	.08
495	Ramon Romero	.08
496	John Wathan	.08
497	Rob Picciolo	.08
498	U.L. Washington	.08
499	John Candelaria	.10
500	Duane Walker	.08
501	Gene Nelson	.08
502	John Mizerock	.08
503	Luis Aguayo	.08
504	Kurt Kepshire	.08
505	Ed Wojna	.08
506	Joe Price	.08
507	*Milt Thompson*	.20
508	Junior Ortiz	.08
509	Vida Blue	.10
510	Steve Engel	.08
511	Karl Best	.08
512	*Cecil Fielder*	3.00
513	Frank Eufemia	.08
514	Tippy Martinez	.08
515	*Billy Robidoux*	.08
516	Bill Scherrer	.08
517	Bruce Hurst	.10
518	Rich Bordi	.08
519	Steve Yeager	.08
520	Tony Bernazard	.08
521	Hal McRae	.10
522	Jose Rijo	.10
523	*Mitch Webster*	.08
524	*Jack Howell*	.08
525	Alan Bannister	.08
526	Ron Kittle	.08
527	Phil Garner	.08
528	Kurt Bevacqua	.08
529	Kevin Gross	.08
530	Bo Diaz	.08
531	Ken Oberkfell	.08
532	Rick Reuschel	.08
533	Ron Meridith	.08
534	Steve Braun	.08
535	Wayne Gross	.08
536	Ray Searage	.08
537	Tom Brookens	.08
538	Al Nipper	.08
539	Billy Sample	.08
540	Steve Sax	.12
541	Dan Quisenberry	.10
542	Tony Phillips	.12
543	*Floyd Youmans*	.10
544	*Steve Buechele*	.35
545	Craig Gerber	.08
546	Joe DeSa	.08
547	Brian Harper	.08
548	Kevin Bass	.10
549	Tom Foley	.08
550	Dave Van Gorder	.08
551	Bruce Bochy	.08
552	R.J. Reynolds	.08
553	*Chris Brown*	.12
554	Bruce Benedict	.08
555	Warren Brusstar	.08
556	Danny Heep	.08
557	Darnell Coles	.08
558	Greg Gagne	.08
559	Ernie Whitt	.08
560	Ron Washington	.08
561	Jimmy Key	.15
562	Billy Swift	.15
563	Ron Darling	.10
564	Dick Ruthven	.08
565	Zane Smith	.10
566	Sid Bream	.10
567a	Joel Youngblood (P on front)	.08
567b	Joel Youngblood (IF on front)	.50
568	Mario Ramirez	.08
569	Tom Runnells	.08
570	Rick Schu	.08
571	Bill Campbell	.08
572	Dickie Thon	.08
573	Al Holland	.08
574	Reid Nichols	.08
575	Bert Roberge	.08
576	Mike Flanagan	.10
577	Tim Leary	.10
578	Mike Laga	.08
579	Steve Lyons	.08
580	Phil Niekro	.45
581	Gilberto Reyes	.08
582	Jamie Easterly	.08
583	Mark Gubicza	.12
584	*Stan Javier*	.15
585	Bill Laskey	.08
586	Jeff Russell	.08
587	Dickie Noles	.08
588	Steve Farr	.08
589	*Steve Ontiveros*	.15
590	Mike Hargrove	.08
591	Marty Bystrom	.08
592	Franklin Stubbs	.08
593	Larry Herndon	.08
594	Bill Swaggerty	.08

595	Carlos Ponce	.08
596	*Pat Perry*	.08
597	Ray Knight	.08
598	*Steve Lombardozzi*	.10
599	Brad Havens	.08
600	Pat Clements	.08
601	Joe Niekro	.12
602	Hank Aaron Puzzle Card	.08
603	*Dwayne Henry*	.08
604	Mookie Wilson	.10
605	Buddy Biancalana	.08
606	Rance Mulliniks	.08
607	Alan Wiggins	.08
608	Joe Cowley	.08
609a	Tom Seaver (green stripes around name)	1.00
609b	Tom Seaver (yellow stripes around name)	3.00
610	Neil Allen	.08
611	Don Sutton	.25
612	*Fred Toliver*	.08
613	Jay Baller	.08
614	Marc Sullivan	.08
615	John Grubb	.08
616	Bruce Kison	.08
617	Bill Madlock	.12
618	Chris Chambliss	.08
619	Dave Stewart	.15
620	Tim Lollar	.08
621	Gary Lavelle	.08
622	Charles Hudson	.08
623	*Joel Davis*	.08
624	*Joe Johnson*	.08
025	Sid Fernandez	.12
626	Dennis Lamp	.08
627	Terry Harper	.08
628	Jack Lazorko	.08
629	*Roger McDowell*	.25
630	Mark Funderburk	.08
631	Ed Lynch	.08
632	Rudy Law	.08
633	*Roger Mason*	.08
634	*Mike Felder*	.08
635	Ken Schrom	.08
636	Bob Ojeda	.08
637	Ed Vande Berg	.08
638	Bobby Meacham	.08
639	Cliff Johnson	.08
640	Garth Iorg	.08
641	Dan Driessen	.08
642	Mike Brown	.08
643	John Shelby	.08
644	Pete Rose (RB)	.50
645	Knuckle Brothers(Joe Niekro, Phil Niekro)	.25
646	Jesse Orosco	.08
647	*Billy Beane*	.08
648	Cesar Cedeno	.10
649	Bert Blyleven	.15
650	Max Venable	.08
651	Fleet Feet(Vince Coleman, Willie McGee)	.35
652	Calvin Schiraldi	.08
653	King of Kings(Pete Rose)	1.50
----	Checklist 1-26 DK	.08
----	Checklist 27-130 (45 is Beane)	.08
----	Checklist 27-130 (45 is Habyan)	.30
----	Checklist 131-234	.08
----	Checklist 235-338	.08
----	Checklist 339-442	.08
----	Checklist 443-546	.08
----	Checklist 547-653	.08

1986 Donruss Box Panels

For the second year in a row, Donruss placed baseball cards on the bottom of its wax and cello pack boxes. The cards, printed four to a panel, are standard 2-1/2" x 3-1/2". With numbering that begins where Donruss left off in 1985, cards PC4 through PC6 were found on boxes of regular Donruss issue wax packs. Cards PC7 through PC9 were found on boxes of the 1986 All-Star/Pop-up packs. An unnumbered Hank Aaron puzzle card was included on each box.

		MT
Complete Panel Set (2):		3.00
Complete Singles Set (8):		2.00
Common Single Player:		.15
Panel		1.00
PC4	Kirk Gibson	.25
PC5	Willie Hernandez	.15
PC6	Doug DeCinces	.15
---	Aaron Puzzle Card	.04
Panel		2.00
PC7	Wade Boggs	.75
PC8	Lee Smith	.25
PC9	Cecil Cooper	.15
---	Aaron Puzzle Card	.04

1986 Donruss All-Stars

Issued in conjunction with the 1986 Donruss Pop-Ups set, the All-Stars consist of 60 cards in 3-1/2" x 5" format. Fifty-nine players involved in the 1985 All-Star game plus an unnumbered checklist comprise the set. Card fronts have the same blue border found on the regular 1986 Donruss issue. Retail packs included one Pop-up card, three All-Star cards and one Hank Aaron puzzle-piece card.

		MT
Complete Set (60):		8.00
Common Player:		.10
Hank Aaron puzzle:		5.00
1	Tony Gwynn	.90
2	Tommy Herr	.10
3	Steve Garvey	.30
4	Dale Murphy	.30
5	Darryl Strawberry	.30
6	Graig Nettles	.10
7	Terry Kennedy	.10
8	Ozzie Smith	.75
9	LaMarr Hoyt	.10
10	Rickey Henderson	.50
11	Lou Whitaker	.10
12	George Brett	.75
13	Eddie Murray	.50
14	Cal Ripken, Jr.	2.50
15	Dave Winfield	.50
16	Jim Rice	.10
17	Carlton Fisk	.35
18	Jack Morris	.10
19	Jose Cruz	.10
20	Tim Raines	.15
21	Nolan Ryan	2.00
22	Tony Pena	.10
23	Jack Clark	.10
24	Dave Parker	.10
25	Tim Wallach	.10
26	Ozzie Virgil	.10
27	Fernando Valenzuela	.15
28	Dwight Gooden	.20
29	Glenn Wilson	.10
30	Garry Templeton	.10
31	Goose Gossage	.10
32	Ryne Sandberg	.75
33	Jeff Reardon	.10
34	Pete Rose	1.50
35	Scott Garrelts	.10
36	Willie McGee	.10
37	Ron Darling	.10
38	Dick Williams	.10
39	Paul Molitor	.50
40	Damaso Garcia	.10
41	Phil Bradley	.10
42	Dan Petry	.10
43	Willie Hernandez	.10
44	Tom Brunansky	.10
45	Alan Trammell	.20
46	Donnie Moore	.10
47	Wade Boggs	.60
48	Ernie Whitt	.10
49	Harold Baines	.10
50	Don Mattingly	1.00
51	Gary Ward	.10
52	Bert Blyleven	.10
53	Jimmy Key	.10
54	Cecil Cooper	.10
55	Dave Stieb	.10
56	Rich Gedman	.10
57	Jay Howell	.10
58	Sparky Anderson	.10
59	Minneapolis Metrodome	.10
---	Checklist	.05

1986 Donruss Diamond Kings Supers

Donruss produced a set of large-format Diamond Kings in 1986 for the second year in a row. The 4-11/16" x 6-3/4" cards are enlarged versions of the 26 Diamond Kings cards found in the regular 1986 Donruss set, plus an unnumbered checklist and an unnumbered Pete Rose "King of Kings" card.

		MT
Complete Set (28):		12.00
Common Player:		.50
1	Kirk Gibson	.75
2	Goose Gossage	.60
3	Willie McGee	.75
4	George Bell	.50
5	Tony Armas	.50
6	Chili Davis	.60
7	Cecil Cooper	.50
8	Mike Boddicker	.50
9	Davey Lopes	.50
10	Bill Doran	.50
11	Bret Saberhagen	.75
12	Brett Butler	.60
13	Harold Baines	.60
14	Mike Davis	.50
15	Tony Perez	.75
16	Willie Randolph	.50
18	Orel Hershiser	.75
19	Johnny Ray	.50
20	Gary Ward	.50
21	Rick Mahler	.50
22	Phil Bradley	.50
23	Jerry Koosman	.50
24	Tom Brunansky	.50
25	Andre Dawson	.75
26	Dwight Gooden	.75
----	Checklist	.05
----	King of Kings(Pete Rose)	1.50

Cards before 1981 are priced Near Mint (NM), Excellent (EX), and Very Good (VG).

Cards 1981 to present are priced Mint (MT), Near Mint (NM), and Excellent (EX).

1986 Donruss Highlights

Donruss, for the second year in a row, issued a 56-card highlights set featuring cards of each league's Player of the Month plus significant events of the 1986 season. The cards, 2-1/2" x 3-1/2," are similar in design to the regular 1986 Donruss set but have a gold border instead of blue. A "Highlights" logo appears in the lower-left corner of each card front. Backs are designed on a vertical format and feature black print on a yellow background. As in 1985, the set includes Donruss' picks for the Rookies of the Year. A new feature was three cards honoring the 1986 Hall of Fame inductees. The set, available only through hobby dealers, was issued in a specially designed box.

		MT
Complete Set (56):		6.00
Common Player:		.10
1	Homers In First At-Bat(Will Clark)	1.00
2	Oakland Milestone For Strikeouts(Jose Rijo)	.10
3	Royals' All-Time Hit Man(George Brett)	.45
4	Phillies RBI Leader(Mike Schmidt)	.45
5	KKKKKKKKKKKKKKKKKKKK KK(Roger Clemens)	.75
6	A.L. Pitcher of the Month-April(Roger Clemens)	.35
7	A.L. Player of the Month-April(Kirby Puckett)	.60
8	N.L. Pitcher of the Month-April(Dwight Gooden)	.20
9	N.L. Player of the Month-April(Johnny Ray)	.10
10	Eclipses Mantle HR Record(Reggie Jackson)	.25
11	First Five Hit Game of Career(Wade Boggs)	.25
12	A.L. Pitcher of the Month-May(Don Aase)	.10
13	A.L. Player of the Month-May(Wade Boggs)	.25
14	N.L. Pitcher of the Month-May(Jeff Reardon)	.10
15	N.L. Player of the Month-May(Hubie Brooks)	.10
16	Notches 300th Career Win(Don Sutton)	.10
17	Starts Season 14-0(Roger Clemens)	.25
18	A.L. Pitcher of the Month-June(Roger Clemens)	.25
19	A.L. Player of the Month-June(Kent Hrbek)	.10
20	N.L. Pitcher of the Month-June(Rick Rhoden)	.10
21	N.L. Player of the Month-June(Kevin Bass)	.10
22	Blasts 4 HRS in 1 Game(Bob Horner)	.15
23	Starting All Star Rookie(Wally Joyner)	.10
24	Starts 3rd Straight All Star Game(Darryl Strawberry)	.15
25	Ties All Star Game Record(Fernando Valenzuela)	.15
26	All Star Game MVP(Roger Clemens)	.25
27	A.L. Pitcher of the Month-July(Jack Morris)	.10
28	A.L. Player of the Month-July(Scott Fletcher)	.10
29	N.L. Pitcher of the Month-July(Todd Worrell)	.10
30	N.L. PLayer of the Month-July(Eric Davis)	.10
31	Records 3000th Strikeout(Bert Blyleven)	.10
32	1986 Hall of Fame Inductee(Bobby Doerr)	.10
33	1986 Hall of Fame Inductee(Ernie Lombardi)	.10
34	1986 Hall of Fame Inductee(Willie McCovey)	.25
35	Notches 4000th K(Steve Carlton)	.25
36	Surpasses DiMaggio Record(Mike Schmidt)	.45
37	Records 3rd "Quadruple Double"(Juan Samuel)	.10
38	A.L. Pitcher of the Month-August(Mike Witt)	.10
39	A.L. Player of the Month-August(Doug DeCinces)	.10
40	N.L. Pitcher of the Month-August(Bill Gullickson)	.10
41	N.L. Player of the Month-August(Dale Murphy)	.15
42	Sets Tribe Offensive Record(Joe Carter)	.15
43	Longest HR In Royals Stadium(Bo Jackson)	.35
44	Majors 1st No-Hitter In 2 Years(Joe Cowley)	.10
45	Sets M.L. Strikeout Record(Jim Deshaies)	.10
46	No Hitter Clinches Division(Mike Scott)	.10
47	A.L. Pitcher of the Month-September(Bruce Hurst)	.10
48	A.L. Player of the Month-September(Don Mattingly)	.50
49	N.L. Pitcher of the Month-September(Mike Krukow)	.10
50	N.L. Player of the Month-September(Steve Sax)	.10
51	A.L. Record For Steals By A Rookie(John Cangelosi)	.10
52	Shatters M.L. Save Mark(Dave Righetti)	.10
53	Yankee Record For Hits & Doubles(Don Mattingly)	.50
54	Donruss N.L. Rookie of the Year(Todd Worrell)	.10
55	Donruss A.L. Rookie of the Year(Jose Canseco)	1.25
56	Highlight Checklist	.05

1986 Donruss Pop-Ups

Issued in conjunction with the 1986 Donruss All-Stars set, the Pop-Ups (18 unnumbered cards) feature the 1985 All-Star Game starting lineups. The cards, 2-1/2" x 5", are die-cut and fold out to form a three-dimensional stand-up card. The background for the cards is the Minneapolis Metrodome, site of the 1985 All-Star Game. Retail packs included one Pop-Up card, three All-Star cards and one Hank Aaron puzzle card.

		MT
Complete Set (18):		3.00
Common Player:		.10
Hank Aaron Puzzle:		5.00
(1)	George Brett	.50
(2)	Carlton Fisk	.30
(3)	Steve Garvey	.20
(4)	Tony Gwynn	.75
(5)	Rickey Henderson	.40
(6)	Tommy Herr	.10
(7)	LaMarr Hoyt	.10
(8)	Terry Kennedy	.10
(9)	Jack Morris	.10
(10)	Dale Murphy	.20
(11)	Eddie Murray	.40
(12)	Graig Nettles	.10
(13)	Jim Rice	.10
(14)	Cal Ripken, Jr.	.90
(15)	Ozzie Smith	.40
(16)	Darryl Strawberry	.30
(17)	Lou Whitaker	.10
(18)	Dave Winfield	.40

1986 Donruss Rookies

CORY SNYDER IF

Entitled "The Rookies," this 56-card set includes the top 55 rookies of 1986 plus an unnumbered checklist. The cards are similar in format to the 1986 Donruss regular issue, except that the borders are green rather than blue. Several of the rookies who had cards in the regular 1986 Donruss set appear again in "The Rookies" set. The sets, which were only available through hobby dealers, came in a specially designed box.

		MT
Complete Set (56):		20.00
Common Player:		.10
1	Wally Joyner	.75
2	Tracy Jones	.10
3	Allan Anderson	.10
4	Ed Correa	.10
5	Reggie Williams	.10
6	Charlie Kerfeld	.10
7	Andres Galarraga	2.50
8	Bob Tewksbury	.60
9	Al Newman	.10
10	Andres Thomas	.10
11	Barry Bonds	7.50
12	Juan Nieves	.10
13	Mark Eichhorn	.10
14	Dan Plesac	.15
15	Cory Snyder	.10
16	Kelly Gruber	.10
17	Kevin Mitchell	.30
18	Steve Lombardozzi	.10
19	Mitch Williams	.15
20	John Cerutti	.10
21	Todd Worrell	.15
22	Jose Canseco	4.00
23	Pete Incaviglia	.30
24	Jose Guzman	.10
25	Scott Bailes	.10
26	Greg Mathews	.10
27	Eric King	.10
28	Paul Assenmacher	.10
29	Jeff Sellers	.10
30	Bobby Bonilla	.90
31	Doug Drabek	.75
32	Will Clark	4.00
33	Bip Roberts	.15
34	Jim Deshaies	.10
35	Mike LaValliere	.10
36	Scott Bankhead	.10
37	Dale Sveum	.10
38	Bo Jackson	1.50
39	Rob Thompson	.15
40	Eric Plunk	.10
41	Bill Bathe	.10
42	John Kruk	.45
43	Andy Allanson	.10
44	Mark Portugal	.10
45	Danny Tartabull	.25
46	Bob Kipper	.10
47	Gene Walter	.10
48	Rey Quinonez	.10
49	Bobby Witt	.25
50	Bill Mooneyham	.10
51	John Cangelosi	.10
52	Ruben Sierra	.45
53	Rob Woodward	.10
54	Ed Hearn	.10
55	Joel McKeon	.10
56	Checklist 1-56	.05

1987 Donruss

LANCE McCULLERS P

The 1987 Donruss set consists of 660 numbered cards, each measuring 2-1/2" x 3-1/2". Color photos

are surrounded by a bold black border separated by two narrow bands of yellow which enclose a brown area filled with baseballs. The player's name, team and team logo appear on the card fronts along with the words "Donruss '87". The card backs are designed on a horizontal format and contain black print on a yellow and white background. The backs are very similar to those in previous years' sets. Backs of cards issued in wax and rack packs face to the left when turned over, while those issued in factory sets face to the right. Cards were sold with Roberto Clemente puzzle pieces in each pack. Cards checklisted with a (DK) suffix are Diamond Kings; cards with an (RR) suffix are Rated Rookies.

		MT
Complete Set (660):		60.00
Common Player:		.05
Roberto Clemente Puzzle:		9.00
Wax Box:		55.00
1	Wally Joyner (DK)	.25
2	Roger Clemens (DK)	.50
3	Dale Murphy (DK)	.12
4	Darryl Strawberry (DK)	.12
5	Ozzie Smith (DK)	.30
6	Jose Canseco (DK)	.40
7	Charlie Hough (DK)	.08
8	Brook Jacoby (DK)	.10
9	Fred Lynn (DK)	.12
10	Rick Rhoden (DK)	.10
11	Chris Brown (DK)	.10
12	Von Hayes (DK)	.10
13	Jack Morris (DK)	.10
14a	Kevin McReynolds (DK)(no yellow stripe on back)	.75
14b	Kevin McReynolds (DK)(yellow stripe on back)	.20
15	George Brett (DK)	.60
16	Ted Higuera (DK)	.05
17	Hubie Brooks (DK)	.10
18	Mike Scott (DK)	.08
19	Kirby Puckett (DK)	.60
20	Dave Winfield (DK)	.25
21	Lloyd Moseby (DK)	.10
22a	Eric Davis (DK)(no yellow stripe on back)	1.00
22b	Eric Davis (DK)(yellow stripe on back)	.15
23	Jim Presley (DK)	.08
24	Keith Moreland (DK)	.08
25a	Greg Walker (DK)(no yellow stripe on back)	.50
25b	Greg Walker (DK)(yellow stripe on back)	.10
26	Steve Sax (DK)	.12
27	Checklist 1-27	.05
28	B.J. Surhoff (RR)	.30
29	Randy Myers (RR)	.35
30	Ken Gerhart (RR)	.08
31	Benito Santiago (RR)	.40
32	Greg Swindell (RR)	.15
33	Mike Birkbeck (RR)	.10
34	Terry Steinbach (RR)	.50
35	Bo Jackson (RR)	2.00
36	Greg Maddux (RR)	25.00
37	Jim Lindeman (RR)	.05
38	Devon White (RR)	.75
39	Eric Bell (RR)	.08
40	Will Fraser (RR)	.10
41	Jerry Browne (RR)	.15
42	Chris James (RR)	.15
43	Rafael Palmeiro (RR)	3.00
44	Pat Dodson (RR)	.05
45	Duane Ward (RR)	.25
46	Mark McGwire (RR)	25.00
47	Bruce Fields (RR) (Photo actually Darnell Coles)	.10
48	Eddie Murray	.50
49	Ted Higuera	.05
50	Kirk Gibson	.15
51	Oil Can Boyd	.05
52	Don Mattingly	1.00
53	Pedro Guerrero	.15
54	George Brett	1.00
55	Jose Rijo	.08
56	Tim Raines	.30

57	Ed Correa	.05
58	Mike Witt	.10
59	Greg Walker	.10
60	Ozzie Smith	.50
61	Glenn Davis	.08
62	Glenn Wilson	.08
63	Tom Browning	.10
64	Tony Gwynn	1.00
65	R.J. Reynolds	.05
66	Will Clark	2.50
67	Ozzie Virgil	.05
68	Rick Sutcliffe	.12
69	Gary Carter	.12
70	Mike Moore	.05
71	Bert Blyleven	.12
72	Tony Fernandez	.08
73	Kent Hrbek	.15
74	Lloyd Moseby	.08
75	Alvin Davis	.05
76	Keith Hernandez	.15
77	Ryne Sandberg	.90
78	Dale Murphy	.20
79	Sid Bream	.05
80	Chris Brown	.05
81	Steve Garvey	.20
82	Mario Soto	.05
83	Shane Rawley	.05
84	Willie McGee	.12
85	Jose Cruz	.10
86	Brian Downing	.08
87	Ozzie Guillen	.10
88	Hubie Brooks	.10
89	Cal Ripken, Jr.	2.50
90	Juan Nieves	.05
91	Lance Parrish	.08
92	Jim Rice	.12
93	Ron Guidry	.15
94	Fernando Valenzuela	.08
95	Andy Allanson	.05
96	Willie Wilson	.12
97	Jose Canseco	.75
98	Jeff Reardon	.10
99	Bobby Witt	.20
100	Checklist 28-133	.05
101	Jose Guzman	.05
102	Steve Balboni	.05
103	Tony Phillips	.10
104	Brook Jacoby	.10
105	Dave Winfield	.30
106	Orel Hershiser	.15
107	Lou Whitaker	.15
108	Fred Lynn	.15
109	Bill Wegman	.05
110	Donnie Moore	.05
111	Jack Clark	.15
112	Bob Knepper	.05
113	Von Hayes	.10
114	Bip Roberts	.40
115	Tony Pena	.08
116	Scott Garrelts	.05
117	Paul Molitor	.60
118	Darryl Strawberry	.25
119	Shawon Dunston	.10
120	Jim Presley	.05
121	Jesse Barfield	.05
122	Gary Gaetti	.15
123	Kurt Stillwell	.10
124	Joel Davis	.05
125	Mike Boddicker	.05
126	Robin Yount	.60
127	Alan Trammell	.25
128	Dave Righetti	.08
129	Dwight Evans	.12
130	Mike Scioscia	.05
131	Julio Franco	.10
132	Bret Saberhagen	.12
133	Mike Davis	.05
134	Joe Hesketh	.05
135	Wally Joyner	.25
136	Don Slaught	.05
137	Daryl Boston	.05
138	Nolan Ryan	2.50
139	Mike Schmidt	1.00
140	Tommy Herr	.10
141	Garry Templeton	.05
142	Kal Daniels	.05
143	Billy Sample	.05
144	Johnny Ray	.05
145	Rob Thompson	.40
146	Bob Dernier	.05
147	Danny Tartabull	.08
148	Ernie Whitt	.05
149	Kirby Puckett	1.00
150	Mike Young	.05
151	Ernest Riles	.05
152	Frank Tanana	.08

No.	Player	Price
153	Rich Gedman	.05
154	Willie Randolph	.10
155a	Bill Madlock (name in brown band)	.12
155b	Bill Madlock (name in red band)	.50
156a	Joe Carter (name in brown band)	.15
156b	Joe Carter (name in red band)	.40
157	Danny Jackson	.08
158	Carney Lansford	.08
159	Bryn Smith	.05
160	Gary Pettis	.05
161	Oddibe McDowell	.05
162	*John Cangelosi*	.12
163	Mike Scott	.15
164	Eric Show	.08
165	Juan Samuel	.08
166	Nick Esasky	.05
167	Zane Smith	.05
168	Mike Brown	.05
169	Keith Moreland	.05
170	John Tudor	.05
171	Ken Dixon	.05
172	Jim Gantner	.05
173	Jack Morris	.15
174	Bruce Hurst	.08
175	Dennis Rasmussen	.08
176	Mike Marshall	.05
177	Dan Quisenberry	.08
178	Eric Plunk	.08
179	Tim Wallach	.12
180	Steve Buechele	.05
181	Don Sutton	.20
182	Dave Schmidt	.05
183	Terry Pendleton	.08
184	*Jim Deshaies*	.15
185	Steve Bedrosian	.12
186	Pete Rose	1.25
187	Dave Dravecky	.08
188	Rick Reuschel	.10
189	Dan Gladden	.05
190	Rick Mahler	.05
191	Thad Bosley	.05
192	Ron Darling	.10
193	Matt Young	.05
194	Tom Brunansky	.10
195	Dave Stieb	.12
196	Frank Viola	.15
197	Tom Henke	.08
198	Karl Best	.05
199	Dwight Gooden	.25
200	Checklist 134-239	.05
201	Steve Trout	.05
202	Rafael Ramirez	.05
203	Bob Walk	.05
204	Roger Mason	.05
205	Terry Kennedy	.05
206	Ron Oester	.05
207	John Russell	.10
208	*Greg Mathews*	.05
209	Charlie Kerfeld	.05
210	Reggie Jackson	.35
211	Floyd Bannister	.05
212	Vance Law	.05
213	Rich Bordi	.05
214	*Dan Plesac*	.10
215	Dave Collins	.05
216	Bob Stanley	.05
217	Joe Niekro	.10
218	Tom Niedenfuer	.05
219	Brett Butler	.12
220	Charlie Leibrandt	.05
221	Steve Ontiveros	.05
222	Tim Burke	.05
223	Curtis Wilkerson	.05
224	*Pete Incaviglia*	.25
225	Lonnie Smith	.05
226	Chris Codiroli	.05
227	*Scott Bailes*	.05
228	Rickey Henderson	.40
229	Ken Howell	.05
230	Darnell Coles	.05
231	Don Aase	.05
232	Tim Leary	.05
233	Bob Boone	.08
234	Ricky Horton	.05
235	Mark Bailey	.05
236	Kevin Gross	.05
237	Lance McCullers	.05
238	Cecilio Guante	.05
239	Bob Melvin	.05
240	Billy Jo Robidoux	.05
241	Roger McDowell	.12
242	Leon Durham	.05
243	Ed Nunez	.05
244	Jimmy Key	.12
245	Mike Smithson	.05
246	Bo Diaz	.05
247	Carlton Fisk	.25
248	Larry Sheets	.05
249	*Juan Castillo*	.05
250	Eric King	.08
251	Doug Drabek	.30
252	Wade Boggs	.65
253	Mariano Duncan	.05
254	Pat Tabler	.05
255	Frank White	.10
256	Alfredo Griffin	.05
257	Floyd Youmans	.05
258	Rob Wilfong	.05
259	Pete O'Brien	.05
260	Tim Hulett	.05
261	Dickie Thon	.05
262	Darren Daulton	.60
263	Vince Coleman	.10
264	Andy Hawkins	.05
265	Eric Davis	.20
266	*Andres Thomas*	.05
267	*Mike Diaz*	.05
268	Chili Davis	.08
269	Jody Davis	.05
270	Phil Bradley	.08
271	George Bell	.08
272	Keith Atherton	.05
273	Storm Davis	.10
274	Rob Deer	.10
275	Walt Terrell	.05
276	Roger Clemens	1.00
277	Mike Easler	.05
278	Steve Sax	.10
279	Andre Thornton	.08
280	Jim Sundberg	.05
281	Bill Bathe	.05
282	Jay Tibbs	.05
283	Dick Schofield	.05
284	Mike Mason	.05
285	Jerry Hairston	.05
286	Bill Doran	.08
287	Tim Flannery	.05
288	Gary Redus	.05
289	John Franco	.10
290	*Paul Assenmacher*	.15
291	Joe Orsulak	.05
292	Lee Smith	.20
293	Mike Laga	.05
294	Rick Dempsey	.08
295	Mike Felder	.05
296	Tom Brookens	.05
297	Al Nipper	.05
298	Mike Pagliarulo	.10
299	Franklin Stubbs	.05
300	Checklist 240-345	.05
301	Steve Farr	.05
302	*Bill Mooneyham*	.05
303	Andres Galarraga	.75
304	Scott Fletcher	.05
305	Jack Howell	.05
306	*Russ Morman*	.10
307	Todd Worrell	.20
308	Dave Smith	.05
309	Jeff Stone	.05
310	Ron Robinson	.05
311	Bruce Bochy	.05
312	Jim Winn	.05
313	Mark Davis	.05
314	Jeff Dedmon	.05
315	*Jamie Moyer*	.08
316	Wally Backman	.05
317	Ken Phelps	.05
318	Steve Lombardozzi	.05
319	Rance Mulliniks	.05
320	Tim Laudner	.05
321	*Mark Eichhorn*	.08
322	*Lee Guetterman*	.05
323	Sid Fernandez	.08
324	Jerry Mumphrey	.05
325	David Palmer	.05
326	Bill Almon	.05
327	Candy Maldonado	.05
328	John Kruk	.15
329	John Denny	.05
330	Milt Thompson	.05
331	*Mike LaValliere*	.15
332	Alan Ashby	.05
333	Doug Corbett	.05
334	*Ron Karkovice*	.10
335	Mitch Webster	.05
336	Lee Lacy	.05
337	*Glenn Braggs*	.15
338	Dwight Lowry	.05
339	Don Baylor	.15
340	Brian Fisher	.05
341	*Reggie Williams*	.05
342	Tom Candiotti	.05
343	Rudy Law	.05
344	Curt Young	.05
345	Mike Fitzgerald	.05
346	Ruben Sierra	.50
347	*Mitch Williams*	.25
348	Jorge Orta	.05
349	Mickey Tettleton	.10
350	Ernie Camacho	.05
351	Ron Kittle	.05
352	Ken Landreaux	.05
353	Chet Lemon	.05
354	John Shelby	.05
355	Mark Clear	.05
356	Doug DeCinces	.08
357	Ken Dayley	.05
358	Phil Garner	.05
359	Steve Jeltz	.05
360	Ed Whitson	.05
361	Barry Bonds	4.00
362	Vida Blue	.10
363	Cecil Cooper	.08
364	Bob Ojeda	.05
365	Dennis Eckersley	.20
366	Mike Morgan	.05
367	Willie Upshaw	.05
368	*Allan Anderson*	.05
369	Bill Gullickson	.05
370	*Bobby Thigpen*	.10
371	Juan Beniquez	.05
372	Charlie Moore	.05
373	Dan Petry	.05
374	Rod Scurry	.05
375	Tom Seaver	.40
376	Ed Vande Berg	.05
377	Tony Bernazard	.05
378	Greg Pryor	.05
379	Dwayne Murphy	.05
380	Andy McGaffigan	.05
381	Kirk McCaskill	.08
382	Greg Harris	.05
383	Rich Dotson	.05
384	Craig Reynolds	.05
385	Greg Gross	.05
386	Tito Landrum	.05
387	Craig Lefferts	.05
388	Dave Parker	.25
389	Bob Horner	.10
390	Pat Clements	.05
391	Jeff Leonard	.05
392	Chris Speier	.05
393	John Moses	.05
394	Garth Iorg	.05
395	Greg Gagne	.05
396	Nate Snell	.05
397	*Bryan Clutterbuck*	.05
398	Darrell Evans	.12
399	Steve Crawford	.05
400	Checklist 346-451	.05
401	*Phil Lombardi*	.05
402	Rick Honeycutt	.05
403	Ken Schrom	.05
404	Bud Black	.05
405	Donnie Hill	.05
406	Wayne Krenchicki	.05
407	*Chuck Finley*	.35
408	Toby Harrah	.08
409	Steve Lyons	.05
410	Kevin Bass	.08
411	Marvell Wynne	.05
412	Ron Roenicke	.05
413	*Tracy Jones*	.08
414	Gene Garber	.05
415	Mike Bielecki	.05
416	Frank DiPino	.05
417	Andy Van Slyke	.25
418	Jim Dwyer	.05
419	Ben Oglivie	.05
420	Dave Bergman	.05
421	Joe Sambito	.05
422	*Bob Tewksbury*	.30
423	Len Matuszek	.05
424	*Mike Kingery*	.05
425	Dave Kingman	.15
426	*Al Newman*	.05
427	Gary Ward	.05
428	Ruppert Jones	.05
429	Harold Baines	.15
430	Pat Perry	.05
431	Terry Puhl	.05
432	Don Carman	.05
433	Eddie Milner	.05
434	LaMarr Hoyt	.05

435	Rick Rhoden	.10	531	*Dale Mohorcic*	.05
436	Jose Uribe	.05	532	Ron Hassey	.05
437	Ken Oberkfell	.05	533	Ty Gainey	.05
438	Ron Davis	.05	534	Jerry Royster	.05
439	Jesse Orosco	.08	535	*Mike Maddux*	.05
440	Scott Bradley	.05	536	Ted Power	.05
441	Randy Bush	.05	537	Ted Simmons	.08
442	*John Cerutti*	.10	538	*Rafael Belliard*	.12
443	Roy Smalley	.05	539	Chico Walker	.05
444	Kelly Gruber	.10	540	Bob Forsch	.05
445	Bob Kearney	.05	541	John Stefero	.05
446	*Ed Hearn*	.05	542	*Dale Sveum*	.08
447	Scott Sanderson	.05	543	Mark Thurmond	.05
448	Bruce Benedict	.05	544	*Jeff Sellers*	.05
449	Junior Ortiz	.05	545	Joel Skinner	.05
450	*Mike Aldrete*	.05	546	Alex Trevino	.05
451	Kevin McReynolds	.10	547	*Randy Kutcher*	.10
452	*Rob Murphy*	.10	548	Joaquin Andujar	.05
453	Kent Tekulve	.05	549	*Casey Candaele*	.10
454	Curt Ford	.05	550	Jeff Russell	.05
455	Davey Lopes	.08	551	John Candelaria	.10
456	Bobby Grich	.10	552	Joe Cowley	.05
457	Jose DeLeon	.05	553	Danny Cox	.05
458	Andre Dawson	.30	554	Denny Walling	.05
459	Mike Flanagan	.05	555	*Bruce Ruffin*	.20
460	*Joey Meyer*	.08	556	Buddy Bell	.10
461	*Chuck Cary*	.05	557	*Jimmy Jones*	.10
462	Bill Buckner	.10	558	Bobby Bonilla	.75
463	Bob Shirley	.05	559	Jeff Robinson	.05
464	*Jeff Hamilton*	.08	560	Ed Olwine	.05
465	Phil Niekro	.25	561	*Glenallen Hill*	.75
466	Mark Gubicza	.12	562	Lee Mazzilli	.05
467	Jerry Willard	.05	563	Mike Brown	.05
468	*Bob Sebra*	.05	564	George Frazier	.05
469	Larry Parrish	.08	565	*Mike Sharperson*	.10
470	Charlie Hough	.08	566	*Mark Portugal*	.10
471	Hal McRae	.10	567	Rick Leach	.05
472	*Dave Leiper*	.05	568	Mark Langston	.12
473	Mel Hall	.05	569	Rafael Santana	.05
474	Dan Pasqua	.10	570	Manny Trillo	.05
475	Bob Welch	.10	571	Cliff Speck	.05
476	Johnny Grubb	.05	572	Bob Kipper	.05
477	Jim Traber	.05	573	Kelly Downs	.10
478	*Chris Bosio*	.25	574	*Randy Asadoor*	.05
479	Mark McLemore	.08	575	*Dave Magadan*	.25
480	John Morris	.05	576	*Marvin Freeman*	.08
481	Billy Hatcher	.08	577	Jeff Lahti	.05
482	Dan Schatzeder	.05	578	Jeff Calhoun	.05
483	Rich Gossage	.15	579	Gus Polidor	.05
484	Jim Morrison	.05	580	Gene Nelson	.05
485	Bob Brenly	.05	581	Tim Teufel	.05
486	Bill Schroeder	.05	582	Odell Jones	.05
487	Mookie Wilson	.10	583	Mark Ryal	.05
488	*Dave Martinez*	.15	584	Randy O'Neal	.05
489	Harold Reynolds	.10	585	*Mike Greenwell*	.50
490	Jeff Hearron	.05	586	Ray Knight	.05
491	Mickey Hatcher	.05	587	*Ralph Bryant*	.05
492	*Barry Larkin*	2.00	588	Carmen Castillo	.05
493	Bob James	.05	589	Ed Wojna	.05
494	John Habyan	.05	590	Stan Javier	.05
495	*Jim Adduci*	.05	591	*Jeff Musselman*	.10
496	Mike Heath	.05	592	*Mike Stanley*	.20
497	Tim Stoddard	.05	593	Darrell Porter	.05
498	Tony Armas	.08	594	*Drew Hall*	.05
499	Dennis Powell	.05	595	*Rob Nelson*	.05
500	Checklist 452-557	.05	596	Bryan Oelkers	.05
501	Chris Bando	.05	597	*Scott Nielsen*	.05
502	*David Cone*	2.50	598	*Brian Holton*	.10
503	Jay Howell	.08	599	Kevin Mitchell	.12
504	Tom Foley	.05	600	Checklist 558-660	.05
505	*Ray Chadwick*	.05	601	Jackie Gutierrez	.05
506	*Mike Loynd*	.05	602	*Barry Jones*	.12
507	Neil Allen	.05	603	Jerry Narron	.05
508	Danny Darwin	.05	604	Steve Lake	.05
509	Rick Schu	.05	605	Jim Pankovits	.05
510	Jose Oquendo	.05	606	Ed Romero	.05
511	Gene Walter	.05	607	Dave LaPoint	.05
512	*Terry McGriff*	.05	608	Don Robinson	.05
513	Ken Griffey	.10	609	Mike Krukow	.05
514	Benny Distefano	.05	610	*Dave Valle*	.12
515	*Terry Mulholland*	.40	611	Len Dykstra	.15
516	Ed Lynch	.05	612	Roberto Clemente Puzzle Card	.15
517	Bill Swift	.25			
518	Manny Lee	.05	613	Mike Trujillo	.05
519	Andre David	.05	614	Damaso Garcia	.05
520	Scott McGregor	.05	615	Neal Heaton	.05
521	Rick Manning	.05	616	Juan Berenguer	.05
522	Willie Hernandez	.05	617	Steve Carlton	.35
523	Marty Barrett	.05	618	Gary Lucas	.05
524	Wayne Tolleson	.05	619	Geno Petralli	.05
525	*Jose Gonzalez*	.05	620	Rick Aguilera	.20
526	Cory Snyder	.05	621	Fred McGriff	.75
527	Buddy Biancalana	.05	622	Dave Henderson	.10
528	Moose Haas	.05	623	*Dave Clark*	.08
529	*Wilfredo Tejada*	.05	624	Angel Salazar	.05
530	Stu Cliburn	.05	625	Randy Hunt	.05

626	John Gibbons	.05
627	*Kevin Brown*	1.00
628	Bill Dawley	.05
629	Aurelio Lopez	.05
630	Charlie Hudson	.05
631	Ray Soff	.05
632	*Ray Hayward*	.05
633	Spike Owen	.05
634	Glenn Hubbard	.05
635	*Kevin Elster*	.12
636	Mike LaCoss	.05
637	Dwayne Henry	.05
638	*Rey Quinones*	.08
639	Jim Clancy	.05
640	Larry Anderson	.05
641	Calvin Schiraldi	.05
642	*Stan Jefferson*	.10
643	Marc Sullivan	.05
644	Mark Grant	.05
645	Cliff Johnson	.05
646	Howard Johnson	.10
647	Dave Sax	.05
648	Dave Stewart	.15
649	Danny Heep	.05
650	Joe Johnson	.05
651	*Bob Brower*	.05
652	Rob Woodward	.05
653	John Mizerock	.05
654	*Tim Pyznarski*	.05
655	*Luis Aquino*	.08
656	Mickey Brantley	.10
657	Doyle Alexander	.05
658	Sammy Stewart	.05
659	Jim Acker	.05
660	Pete Ladd	.05

1987 Donruss Box Panels

Continuing with an idea they initiated in 1985, Donruss once again placed baseball cards on the bottoms of their retail boxes. The cards, which are 2-1/2" x 3-1/2" in size, come four to a panel with each panel containing an unnumbered Roberto Clemente puzzle card. With numbering that begins where Donruss left off in 1986, cards PC 10 through PC 12 were found on boxes of Donruss regular issue wax packs. Cards PC 13 through PC 15 were located on boxes of the 1987 All-Star/Pop-Up packs.

		MT
Complete Panel Set (2):		3.00
Complete Singles Set (8):		3.00
Common Single Player:		.15
Panel		2.00
10	Dale Murphy	.35
11	Jeff Reardon	.15
12	Jose Canseco	1.50
----	Roberto Clemente Puzzle Card	.15

Panel		1.00
13	Mike Scott	.15
14	Roger Clemens	1.00
15	Mike Krukow	.15
----	Roberto Clemente Puzzle Card	.15

1987 Donruss All-Stars

Issued in conjunction with the Donruss Pop-Ups set for the second consecutive year, the 1987 Donruss All-Stars consist of 59 players (plus a checklist) who were selected to the 1986 All-Star Game. Measuring 3-1/2" x 5" in size, the card fronts feature black borders and American or National League logos. Included on back are the player's career highlights and All-Star Game statistics. Retail packs included one Pop-Up card, three All-Star cards and one Roberto Clemente puzzle card.

		MT
Complete Set:		5.00
Common Player:		.10
Roberto Clemente Puzzle:		9.00
1	Wally Joyner	.15
2	Dave Winfield	.40
3	Lou Whitaker	.10
4	Kirby Puckett	.75
5	Cal Ripken, Jr.	2.00
6	Rickey Henderson	.65
7	Wade Boggs	.75
8	Roger Clemens	.75
9	Lance Parrish	.10
10	Dick Howser	.10
11	Keith Hernandez	.10
12	Darryl Strawberry	.15
13	Ryne Sandberg	.75
14	Dale Murphy	.25
15	Ozzie Smith	.45
16	Tony Gwynn	.75
17	Mike Schmidt	.75
18	Dwight Gooden	.15
19	Gary Carter	.15
20	Whitey Herzog	.10
21	Jose Canseco	.60
22	John Franco	.10
23	Jesse Barfield	.10
24	Rick Rhoden	.10
25	Harold Baines	.15
26	Sid Fernandez	.10
27	George Brett	.75
28	Steve Sax	.10
29	Jim Presley	.10
30	Dave Smith	.10
31	Eddie Murray	.40
32	Mike Scott	.10
33	Don Mattingly	.90
34	Dave Parker	.10
35	Tony Fernandez	.10

36	Tim Raines	.12
37	Brook Jacoby	.10
38	Chili Davis	.15
39	Rich Gedman	.10
40	Kevin Bass	.10
41	Frank White	.10
42	Glenn Davis	.10
43	Willie Hernandez	.10
44	Chris Brown	.10
45	Jim Rice	.10
46	Tony Pena	.10
47	Don Aase	.10
48	Hubie Brooks	.10
49	Charlie Hough	.10
50	Jody Davis	.10
51	Mike Witt	.10
52	Jeff Reardon	.10
53	Ken Schrom	.10
54	Fernando Valenzuela	.12
55	Dave Righetti	.10
56	Shane Rawley	.10
57	Ted Higuera	.10
58	Mike Krukow	.10
59	Lloyd Moseby	.10
60	Checklist	.05

1987 Donruss Diamond Kings Supers

For a third season, Donruss produced a set of enlarged Diamond Kings, measuring 4-11/16" x 6-3/4". The 28-cards feature the artwork of Dick Perez, and contain 26 player cards, a checklist and a Roberto Clemente puzzle card. The set was available through a mail-in offer for $9.50 plus three wrappers.

		MT
Complete Set (28):		10.00
Common Player:		.20
1	Wally Joyner	.30
2	Roger Clemens	1.00
3	Dale Murphy	.40
4	Darryl Strawberry	.30
5	Ozzie Smith	.60
6	Jose Canseco	1.00
7	Charlie Hough	.20
8	Brook Jacoby	.20
9	Fred Lynn	.20
10	Rick Rhoden	.20
11	Chris Brown	.20
12	Von Hayes	.20
13	Jack Morris	.20
14	Kevin McReynolds	.20
15	George Brett	1.00
16	Ted Higuera	.20
17	Hubie Brooks	.20
18	Mike Scott	.20
19	Kirby Puckett	1.00
20	Dave Winfield	.50
21	Lloyd Moseby	.20
22	Eric Davis	.30
23	Jim Presley	.20
24	Keith Moreland	.20
25	Greg Walker	.20
26	Steve Sax	.20
27	Checklist	.05
---	Roberto Clemente Puzzle Card	.25

Values quoted in this guide reflect the retail price of a card — the price a collector can expect to pay when buying a card from a dealer.

The wholesale price — that which a collector can expect to receive from a dealer when selling cards — will be significantly lower, depending on desirability and condition.

1987 Donruss Highlights

For a third consecutive year, Donruss produced a 56-card set which highlighted the special events of the 1987 baseball season. The 2-1/2" x 3-1/2" cards have a front design similar to the regular 1987 Donruss set. A blue border and the "Highlights" logo are the significant differences. The backs feature black print on a white background and include the date the event took place plus the particulars. As in the past, the set includes Donruss' picks for the A.L. and N.L. Rookies of the Year. The set was issued in a specially designed box and was available only through hobby dealers.

		MT
Complete Set (56):		3.00
Common Player:		.10
1	First No-Hitter For Brewers(Juan Nieves)	.10
2	Hits 500th Homer(Mike Schmidt)	.40
3	N.L. Player of the Month - April(Eric Davis)	.15
4	N.L. Pitcher of the Month - April(Sid Fernandez)	.10
5	A.L. Player of the Month - April(Brian Downing)	.10
6	A.L. Pitcher of the Month - April(Bret Saberhagen)	.10
7	Free Agent Holdout Returns(Tim Raines)	.10
8	N.L. Player of the Month - May(Eric Davis)	.15
9	N.L. Pitcher of the Month - May(Steve Bedrosian)	.10
10	A.L. Player of the Month - May(Larry Parrish)	.10
11	A.L. Pitcher of the Month - May(Jim Clancy)	.10
12	N.L. Player of the Month - June(Tony Gwynn)	.40
13	N.L. Pitcher of the Month - June(Orel Hershiser)	.15
14	A.L. Player of the Month - June(Wade Boggs)	.50
15	A.L. Pitcher of the Month - June(Steve Ontiveros)	.10
16	All Star Game Hero(Tim Raines)	.15
17	Consecutive Game Homer Streak(Don Mattingly)	.60
18	1987 Hall of Fame Inductee(Jim "Catfish" Hunter)	.20
19	1987 Hall of Fame Inductee(Ray Dandridge)	.20
20	1987 Hall of Fame Inductee(Billy Williams)	.20

21	N.L. Player of the Month - July(Bo Diaz)	.10
22	N.L. Pitcher of the Month - July(Floyd Youmans)	.10
23	A.L. Player of the Month - July(Don Mattingly)	.75
24	A.L. Pitcher of the Month - July(Frank Viola)	.10
25	Strikes Out 4 Batters In 1 Inning(Bobby Witt)	.10
26	Ties A.L. 9-Inning Game Hit Mark(Kevin Seitzer)	.10
27	Sets Rookie Home Run Record(Mark McGwire)	1.00
28	Sets Cubs' 1st Year Homer Mark(Andre Dawson)	.15
29	Hits In 39 Straight Games(Paul Molitor)	.15
30	Record Weekend(Kirby Puckett)	.50
31	N.L. Player of the Month - August(Andre Dawson)	.15
32	N.L. Pitcher of the Month - August(Doug Drabek)	.10
33	A.L. Player of the Month - August(Dwight Evans)	.10
34	A.L. Pitcher of the Month - August(Mark Langston)	.10
35	100 RBI In 1st 2 Major League Seasons(Wally Joyner)	.15
36	100 SB In 1st 3 Major League Seasons(Vince Coleman)	.10
37	Orioles' All Time Homer King(Eddie Murray)	.35
38	Ends Consecutive Innings Streak(Cal Ripken)	1.00
39	Blue Jays Hit Record 10 Homers In 1 Game(Rob Ducey, Fred McGriff, Ernie Whitt)	.15
40	Equal A's RBI Marks(Jose Canseco, Mark McGwire)	.75
41	Sets All-Time Catching Record(Bob Boone)	.10
42	Sets Mets' One-Season HR Mark(Darryl Strawberry)	.15
43	N.L.'s All-Time Switch Hit HR King(Howard Johnson)	.10
44	Five Straight 200-Hit Seasons(Wade Boggs)	.50
45	Eclipses Rookie Game Hitting Streak(Benito Santiago)	.10
46	Eclipses Jackson's A's HR Record(Mark McGwire)	.75
47	13th Rookie To Collect 200 Hits(Kevin Seitzer)	.10
48	Sets Slam Record(Don Mattingly)	.75
49	N.L. Player of the Month - September(Darryl Strawberry)	.15
50	N.L. Pitcher of the Month - September(Pascual Perez)	.10
51	A.L. Player of the Month - September(Alan Trammell)	.10
52	A.L. Pitcher of the Month - September(Doyle Alexander)	.10
53	Strikeout King - Again(Nolan Ryan)	1.00
54	Donruss A.L. Rookie of the Year(Mark McGwire)	1.00
55	Donruss N.L. Rookie of the Year(Benito Santiago)	.15
56	Highlight Checklist	.05

Modern cards have little collector value in conditions lower than Mint. Figure NM cards at 75% of values shown; EX cards at 40%.

Values shown reflect the market as of January, 1999. On-field performances of current players in the 1999 baseball season are not factored in.

1987 Donruss Opening Day

REGGIE JACKSON DH

The Donruss Opening Day set includes all players in major league baseball's starting lineups on the opening day of the 1987 baseball season. Cards in the 272-piece set measure 2-1/2" x 3-1/2" and have a glossy coating. The fronts are identical in design to the regular Donruss set, but new photos were utilized along with maroon borders as opposed to black. The backs carry black printing on white and yellow and offer a brief player biography plus the player's career statistics. The set was packaged in a sturdy 15" by 5" by 2" box with a clear acetate lid.

		MT
Complete Set (272):		12.00
Common Player:		.10
1	Doug DeCinces	.10
2	Mike Witt	.10
3	George Hendrick	.10
4	Dick Schofield	.10
5	Devon White	.15
6	Butch Wynegar	.10
7	Wally Joyner	.25
8	Mark McLemore	.10
9	Brian Downing	.10
10	Gary Pettis	.10
11	Bill Doran	.10
12	Phil Garner	.10
13	Jose Cruz	.10
14	Kevin Bass	.10
15	Mike Scott	.10
16	Glenn Davis	.10
17	Alan Ashby	.10
18	Billy Hatcher	.10
19	Craig Reynolds	.10
20	Carney Lansford	.10
21	Mike Davis	.10
22	Reggie Jackson	.30
23	Mickey Tettleton	.15
24	Jose Canseco	1.75
25	Rob Nelson	.10
26	Tony Phillips	.15
27	Dwayne Murphy	.10
28	Alfredo Griffin	.10
29	Curt Young	.10
30	Willie Upshaw	.10
31	Mike Sharperson	.10
32	Rance Mulliniks	.10
33	Ernie Whitt	.10
34	Jesse Barfield	.10
35	Tony Fernandez	.10
36	Lloyd Moseby	.10
37	Jimmy Key	.15
38	Fred McGriff	.65
39	George Bell	.12
40	Dale Murphy	.40
41	Rick Mahler	.10

42	Ken Griffey	.10
43	Andres Thomas	.10
44	Dion James	.10
45	Ozzie Virgil	.10
46	Ken Oberkfell	.10
47	Gary Roenicke	.10
48	Glenn Hubbard	.10
49	Bill Schroeder	.10
50	Greg Brock	.10
51	Billy Jo Robidoux	.10
52	Glenn Braggs	.10
53	Jim Gantner	.10
54	Paul Molitor	.35
55	Dale Sveum	.10
56	Ted Higuera	.10
57	Rob Deer	.10
58	Robin Yount	.65
59	Jim Lindeman	.10
60	Vince Coleman	.10
61	Tommy Herr	.10
62	Terry Pendleton	.10
63	John Tudor	.10
64	Tony Pena	.10
65	Ozzie Smith	.55
66	Tito Landrum	.10
67	Jack Clark	.10
68	Bob Dernier	.10
69	Rick Sutcliffe	.10
70	Andre Dawson	.25
71	Keith Moreland	.10
72	Jody Davis	.10
73	Brian Dayett	.10
74	Leon Durham	.10
75	Ryne Sandberg	.75
76	Shawon Dunston	.15
77	Mike Marshall	.10
78	Bill Madlock	.10
79	Orel Hershiser	.15
80	Mike Ramsey	.10
81	Ken Landreaux	.10
82	Mike Scioscia	.10
83	Franklin Stubbs	.10
84	Mariano Duncan	.10
85	Steve Sax	.10
86	Mitch Webster	.10
87	Reid Nichols	.10
88	Tim Wallach	.10
89	Floyd Youmans	.10
90	Andres Galarraga	.25
91	Hubie Brooks	.10
92	Jeff Reed	.10
93	Alonzo Powell	.10
94	Vance Law	.10
95	Bob Brenly	.10
96	Will Clark	1.50
97	Chili Davis	.10
98	Mike Krukow	.10
99	Jose Uribe	.10
100	Chris Brown	.10
101	Rob Thompson	.10
102	Candy Maldonado	.10
103	Jeff Leonard	.10
104	Tom Candiotti	.10
105	Chris Bando	.10
106	Cory Snyder	.10
107	Pat Tabler	.10
108	Andre Thornton	.10
109	Joe Carter	.25
110	Tony Bernazard	.10
111	Julio Franco	.12
112	Brook Jacoby	.10
113	Brett Butler	.15
114	Donnell Nixon	.10
115	Alvin Davis	.10
116	Mark Langston	.12
117	Harold Reynolds	.10
118	Ken Phelps	.10
119	Mike Kingery	.10
120	Dave Valle	.10
121	Rey Quinones	.10
122	Phil Bradley	.10
123	Jim Presley	.10
124	Keith Hernandez	.10
125	Kevin McReynolds	.10
126	Rafael Santana	.10
127	Bob Ojeda	.10
128	Darryl Strawberry	.25
129	Mookie Wilson	.10
130	Gary Carter	.15
131	Tim Teufel	.10
132	Howard Johnson	.10
133	Cal Ripken, Jr.	2.50
134	Rick Burleson	.10
135	Fred Lynn	.10
136	Eddie Murray	.40
137	Ray Knight	.10

138	Alan Wiggins	.10
139	John Shelby	.10
140	Mike Boddicker	.10
141	Ken Gerhart	.10
142	Terry Kennedy	.10
143	Steve Garvey	.25
144	Marvell Wynne	.10
145	Kevin Mitchell	.15
146	Tony Gwynn	.75
147	Joey Cora	.10
148	Benito Santiago	.15
149	Eric Show	.10
150	Garry Templeton	.10
151	Carmelo Martinez	.10
152	Von Hayes	.10
153	Lance Parrish	.12
154	Milt Thompson	.10
155	Mike Easler	.10
156	Juan Samuel	.10
157	Steve Jeltz	.10
158	Glenn Wilson	.10
159	Shane Rawley	.10
160	Mike Schmidt	.75
161	Andy Van Slyke	.10
162	Johnny Ray	.10
163a	Barry Bonds (dark jersey, photo actually Johnny Ray)	175.00
163b	Barry Bonds (white jersey, correct photo)	2.50
164	Junior Ortiz	.10
165	Rafael Belliard	.10
166	Bob Patterson	.10
167	Bobby Bonilla	.25
168	Sid Bream	.10
169	Jim Morrison	.10
170	Jerry Browne	.10
171	Scott Fletcher	.10
172	Ruben Sierra	.12
173	Larry Parrish	.10
174	Pete O'Brien	.10
175	Pete Incaviglia	.12
176	Don Slaught	.10
177	Oddibe McDowell	.10
178	Charlie Hough	.10
179	Steve Buechele	.10
180	Bob Stanley	.10
181	Wade Boggs	.75
182	Jim Rice	.10
183	Bill Buckner	.10
184	Dwight Evans	.10
185	Spike Owen	.10
186	Don Baylor	.12
187	Marc Sullivan	.10
188	Marty Barrett	.10
189	Dave Henderson	.10
190	Bo Diaz	.10
191	Barry Larkin	.35
192	Kal Daniels	.10
193	Terry Francona	.10
194	Tom Browning	.10
195	Ron Oester	.10
196	Buddy Bell	.10
197	Eric Davis	.15
198	Dave Parker	.12
199	Steve Balboni	.10
200	Danny Tartabull	.10
201	Ed Hearn	.10
202	Buddy Biancalana	.10
203	Danny Jackson	.10
204	Frank White	.10
205	Bo Jackson	.50
206	George Brett	.75
207	Kevin Seitzer	.10
208	Willie Wilson	.10
209	Orlando Mercado	.10
210	Darrell Evans	.10
211	Larry Herndon	.10
212	Jack Morris	.10
213	Chet Lemon	.10
214	Mike Heath	.10
215	Darnell Coles	.10
216	Alan Trammell	.15
217	Terry Harper	.10
218	Lou Whitaker	.10
219	Gary Gaetti	.15
220	Tom Nieto	.10
221	Kirby Puckett	.75
222	Tom Brunansky	.10
223	Greg Gagne	.10
224	Dan Gladden	.10
225	Mark Davidson	.10
226	Bert Blyleven	.10
227	Steve Lombardozzi	.10
228	Kent Hrbek	.12
229	Gary Redus	.10
230	Ivan Calderon	.10

231	Tim Hulett	.10
232	Carlton Fisk	.15
233	Greg Walker	.10
234	Ron Karkovice	.10
235	Ozzie Guillen	.10
236	Harold Baines	.10
237	Donnie Hill	.10
238	Rich Dotson	.10
239	Mike Pagliarulo	.10
240	Joel Skinner	.10
241	Don Mattingly	1.50
242	Gary Ward	.10
243	Dave Winfield	.40
244	Dan Pasqua	.10
245	Wayne Tolleson	.10
246	Willie Randolph	.10
247	Dennis Rasmussen	.10
248	Rickey Henderson	.40
249	Angels Checklist	.05
250	Astros Checklist	.05
251	Athletics Checklist	.05
252	Blue Jays Checklist	.05
253	Braves Checklist	.05
254	Brewers Checklist	.05
255	Cardinals Checklist	.05
256	Dodgers Checklist	.05
257	Expos Checklist	.05
258	Giants Checklist	.05
259	Indians Checklist	.05
260	Mariners Checklist	.05
261	Orioles Checklist	.05
262	Padres Checklist	.05
263	Phillies Checklist	.05
264	Pirates Checklist	.05
265	Rangers Checklist	.05
266	Red Sox Checklist	.05
267	Reds Checklist	.05
268	Royals Checklist	.05
269	Tigers Checklist	.05
270	Twins Checklist	.05
271	White Sox/Cubs Checklist	.05
272	Yankees/Mets Checklist	.05

1987 Donruss Pop-Ups

For the second straight year, Donruss released in conjunction with its All-Stars issue a set of cards designed to fold out to form a three-dimensional stand-up card. Consisting of 20 cards, as opposed to the previous year's 18, the 1987 Donruss Pop-Ups set contains players selected to the 1986 All-Star Game. Background for the 2-1/2" x 5" cards is the Houston Astrodome, site of the 1986 mid-summer classic. Retail packs included one Pop-Up card, three All-Star cards and one Roberto Clemente puzzle card.

		MT
Complete Set (20):		3.00
Common Player:		.20
Roberto Clemente Puzzle:		9.00
(1)	Wade Boggs	.70
(2)	Gary Carter	.25
(3)	Roger Clemens	.75
(4)	Dwight Gooden	.25
(5)	Tony Gwynn	.75
(6)	Rickey Henderson	.40
(7)	Keith Hernandez	.20
(8)	Whitey Herzog	.20
(9)	Dick Howser	.20
(10)	Wally Joyner	.25
(11)	Dale Murphy	.30
(12)	Lance Parrish	.20
(13)	Kirby Puckett	.75
(14)	Cal Ripken, Jr.	1.50
(15)	Ryne Sandberg	.75
(16)	Mike Schmidt	.90
(17)	Ozzie Smith	.40
(18)	Darryl Strawberry	.25
(19)	Lou Whitaker	.20
(20)	Dave Winfield	.35

1987 Donruss Rookies

As they did in 1986, Donruss issued a 56-card set highlighting the major leagues' most promising rookies. The cards are standard 2-1/2" x 3-1/2" and are identical in design to the regular Donruss issue. The card fronts have green borders as opposed to the black found in the regular issue and carry the words "The Rookies" in the lower-left portion of the card. The set came housed in a specially designed box and was available only through hobby dealers.

		MT
Complete Set (56):		30.00
Common Player:		.10
1	Mark McGwire	15.00
2	Eric Bell	.10
3	Mark Williamson	.10
4	Mike Greenwell	.12
5	Ellis Burks	1.00
6	DeWayne Buice	.10
7	Mark Mclemore (McLemore)	.12
8	Devon White	.20
9	Willie Fraser	.10
10	Lester Lancaster	.10
11	Ken Williams	.10
12	Matt Nokes	.10
13	Jeff Robinson	.10
14	Bo Jackson	.60
15	Kevin Seitzer	.10
16	Billy Ripken	.10
17	B.J. Surhoff	.12
18	Chuck Crim	.10

19	Mike Birbeck	.10
20	Chris Bosio	.10
21	Les Straker	.10
22	Mark Davidson	.10
23	Gene Larkin	.10
24	Ken Gerhart	.10
25	Luis Polonia	.10
26	Terry Steinbach	.15
27	Mickey Brantley	.10
28	Mike Stanley	.10
29	Jerry Browne	.10
30	Todd Benzinger	.10
31	Fred McGriff	1.50
32	Mike Henneman	.15
33	Casey Candaele	.10
34	Dave Magadan	.10
35	David Cone	1.50
36	Mike Jackson	.10
37	John Mitchell	.10
38	Mike Dunne	.10
39	John Smiley	.15
40	Joe Magrane	.10
41	Jim Lindeman	.10
42	Shane Mack	.15
43	Stan Jefferson	.10
44	Benito Santiago	.20
45	Matt Williams	2.50
46	Dave Meads	.10
47	Rafael Palmeiro	1.00
48	Bill Long	.10
49	Bob Brower	.10
50	James Steels	.10
51	Paul Noce	.10
52	Greg Maddux	15.00
53	Jeff Musselman	.10
54	Brian Holton	.10
55	Chuck Jackson	.10
56	Checklist 1-56	.05

1988 Donruss

Darryl Strawberry OF

The 1988 Donruss set consists of 660 cards, each measuring 2-1/2" x 3-1/2". Fronts feature a full-color photo surrounded by a colorful border - alternating stripes of black, red, black, blue, black, blue, black, red and black (in that order) - separated by soft-focus edges and airbrushed fades. The player's name and position appear in a red band at the bottom of the card. The Donruss logo is situated in the upper-left corner, while the team logo is located in the lower-right. For the seventh consecutive season, Donruss included a subset of "Diamond Kings" cards (#1-27) in the issue. And for the fifth straight year, Donruss incorporated the popular "Rated Rookies" (card #28-47) with the set. Twenty-six of the

cards between #603-660 were short-printed to accommodate the printing of the 26 MVP insert cards.

		MT
Complete Set (660):		12.00
Common Player:		.05
Stan Musial Puzzle:		1.00
Wax Box:		9.00
1	Mark McGwire (DK)	.75
2	Tim Raines (DK)	.08
3	Benito Santiago (DK)	.08
4	Alan Trammell (DK)	.08
5	Danny Tartabull (DK)	.05
6	Ron Darling (DK)	.08
7	Paul Molitor (DK)	.15
8	Devon White (DK)	.10
9	Andre Dawson (DK)	.10
10	Julio Franco (DK)	.10
11	Scott Fletcher (DK)	.08
12	Tony Fernandez (DK)	.10
13	Shane Rawley (DK)	.05
14	Kal Daniels (DK)	.05
15	Jack Clark (DK)	.08
16	Dwight Evans (DK)	.08
17	Tommy John (DK)	.08
18	Andy Van Slyke (DK)	.10
19	Gary Gaetti (DK)	.08
20	Mark Langston (DK)	.08
21	Will Clark (DK)	.25
22	Glenn Hubbard (DK)	.05
23	Billy Hatcher (DK)	.05
24	Bob Welch (DK)	.05
25	Ivan Calderon (DK)	.05
26	Cal Ripken, Jr. (DK)	.35
27	Checklist 1-27	.05
28	*Mackey Sasser* (RR)	.10
29	*Jeff Treadway* (RR)	.05
30	*Mike Campbell* (RR)	.05
31	*Lance Johnson* (RR)	.15
32	*Nelson Liriano* (RR)	.08
33	Shawn Abner (RR)	.05
34	*Roberto Alomar* (RR)	1.50
35	*Shawn Hillegas* (RR)	.05
36	Joey Meyer (RR)	.05
37	Kevin Elster (RR)	.10
38	*Jose Lind* (RR)	.12
39	*Kirt Manwaring* (RR)	.15
40	*Mark Grace* (RR)	.50
41	*Jody Reed* (RR)	.15
42	*John Farrell* (RR)	.05
43	*Al Leiter* (RR)	.15
44	*Gary Thurman* (RR)	.08
45	*Vicente Palacios* (RR)	.05
46	*Eddie Williams* (RR)	.10
47	*Jack McDowell* (RR)	.25
48	Ken Dixon	.05
49	Mike Birbeck	.05
50	Eric King	.05
51	Roger Clemens	.40
52	Pat Clements	.05
53	Fernando Valenzuela	.10
54	Mark Gubicza	.05
55	Jay Howell	.05
56	Floyd Youmans	.05
57	Ed Correa	.05
58	*DeWayne Buice*	.10
59	Jose DeLeon	.05
60	Danny Cox	.05
61	Nolan Ryan	.60
62	Steve Bedrosian	.08
63	Tom Browning	.10
64	Mark Davis	.05
65	R.J. Reynolds	.05
66	Kevin Mitchell	.10
67	Ken Oberkfell	.05
68	Rick Sutcliffe	.10
69	Dwight Gooden	.12
70	Scott Bankhead	.05
71	Bert Blyleven	.10
72	Jimmy Key	.10
73	*Les Straker*	.08
74	Jim Clancy	.05
75	Mike Moore	.05
76	Ron Darling	.08
77	Ed Lynch	.05
78	Dale Murphy	.15
79	Doug Drabek	.08
80	Scott Garrelts	.05
81	Ed Whitson	.05
82	Rob Murphy	.05
83	Shane Rawley	.05
84	Greg Mathews	.05
85	Jim Deshaies	.08
86	Mike Witt	.08
87	Donnie Hill	.05

88	Jeff Reed	.05
89	Mike Boddicker	.05
90	Ted Higuera	.05
91	Walt Terrell	.05
92	Bob Stanley	.05
93	Dave Righetti	.10
94	Orel Hershiser	.08
95	Chris Bando	.05
96	Bret Saberhagen	.08
97	Curt Young	.05
98	Tim Burke	.05
99	Charlie Hough	.08
100a	Checklist 28-137	.05
100b	Checklist 28-133	.10
101	Robby Witt	.10
102	George Brett	.40
103	Mickey Tettleton	.10
104	Scott Bailes	.05
105	Mike Pagliarulo	.08
106	Mike Scioscia	.05
107	Tom Brookens	.05
108	Ray Knight	.08
109	Dan Plesac	.05
110	Wally Joyner	.12
111	Bob Forsch	.05
112	Mike Scott	.08
113	Kevin Gross	.05
114	Benito Santiago	.10
115	Bob Kipper	.05
116	Mike Krukow	.05
117	Chris Bosio	.05
118	Sid Fernandez	.10
119	Jody Davis	.05
120	Mike Morgan	.05
121	Mark Eichhorn	.05
122	Jeff Reardon	.10
123	John Franco	.10
124	Richard Dotson	.05
125	Eric Bell	.05
126	Juan Nieves	.05
127	Jack Morris	.12
128	Rick Rhoden	.05
129	Rich Gedman	.05
130	Ken Howell	.05
131	Brook Jacoby	.05
132	Danny Jackson	.10
133	Gene Nelson	.05
134	Neal Heaton	.05
135	Willie Fraser	.05
136	Jose Guzman	.05
137	Ozzie Guillen	.08
138	Bob Knepper	.05
139	*Mike Jackson*	.10
140	*Joe Magrane*	.08
141	Jimmy Jones	.05
142	Ted Power	.05
143	Ozzie Virgil	.05
144	*Felix Fermin*	.08
145	Kelly Downs	.05
146	Shawon Dunston	.10
147	Scott Bradley	.05
148	Dave Stieb	.10
149	Frank Viola	.10
150	Terry Kennedy	.05
151	Bill Wegman	.05
152	*Matt Nokes*	.10
153	Wade Boggs	.25
154	Wayne Tolleson	.05
155	Mariano Duncan	.05
156	Julio Franco	.10
157	Charlie Leibrandt	.05
158	Terry Steinbach	.10
159	Mike Fitzgerald	.05
160	Jack Lazorko	.05
161	Mitch Williams	.08
162	Greg Walker	.05
163	Alan Ashby	.05
164	Tony Gwynn	.40
165	Bruce Ruffin	.05
166	Ron Robinson	.05
167	Zane Smith	.05
168	Junior Ortiz	.05
169	Jamie Moyer	.05
170	Tony Pena	.05
171	Cal Ripken, Jr.	.50
172	B.J. Surhoff	.08
173	Lou Whitaker	.10
174	*Ellis Burks*	.25
175	Ron Guidry	.10
176	Steve Sax	.05
177	Danny Tartabull	.05
178	Carney Lansford	.05
179	Casey Candaele	.05
180	Scott Fletcher	.08
181	Mark McLemore	.05
182	Ivan Calderon	.05

#	Player	Value	#	Player	Value	#	Player	Value
183	Jack Clark	.08	278	Pedro Guerrero	.08	373	Dave Bergman	.05
184	Glenn Davis	.05	279	Brett Butler	.12	374	Charles Hudson	.05
185	Luis Aguayo	.05	280	Kevin Seitzer	.08	375	Calvin Schiraldi	.05
186	Bo Diaz	.05	281	Mike Davis	.05	376	Alex Trevino	.05
187	Stan Jefferson	.05	282	Andres Galarraga	.20	377	Tom Candiotti	.05
188	Sid Bream	.05	283	Devon White	.12	378	Steve Farr	.05
189	Bob Brenly	.05	284	Pete O'Brien	.05	379	Mike Gallego	.05
190	Dion James	.05	285	Jerry Hairston	.05	380	Andy McGaffigan	.05
191	Leon Durham	.05	286	Kevin Bass	.05	381	Kirk McCaskill	.08
192	Jesse Orosco	.05	287	Carmelo Martinez	.08	382	Oddibe McDowell	.05
193	Alvin Davis	.05	288	Juan Samuel	.05	383	Floyd Bannister	.05
194	Gary Gaetti	.12	289	Kal Daniels	.05	384	Denny Walling	.05
195	Fred McGriff	.25	290	Albert Hall	.05	385	Don Carman	.05
196	Steve Lombardozzi	.05	291	Andy Van Slyke	.10	386	Todd Worrell	.10
197	Rance Mulliniks	.05	292	Lee Smith	.10	387	Eric Show	.05
198	Rey Quinones	.05	293	Vince Coleman	.08	388	Dave Parker	.08
199	Gary Carter	.10	294	Tom Niedenfuer	.05	389	Rick Mahler	.05
200a	Checklist 138-247	.05	295	Robin Yount	.20	390	*Mike Dunne*	.08
200b	Checklist 134-239	.10	296	*Jeff Robinson*	.05	391	Candy Maldonado	.05
201	Keith Moreland	.05	297	*Todd Benzinger*	.10	392	Bob Dernier	.05
202	Ken Griffey	.08	298	Dave Winfield	.15	393	Dave Valle	.05
203	*Tommy Gregg*	.05	299	Mickey Hatcher	.05	394	Ernie Whitt	.05
204	Will Clark	.25	300a	Checklist 248-357	.05	395	Juan Berenguer	.05
205	John Kruk	.10	300b	Checklist 240-345	.10	396	Mike Young	.05
206	Buddy Bell	.08	301	Bud Black	.05	397	Mike Felder	.05
207	Von Hayes	.05	302	Jose Canseco	.20	398	Willie Hernandez	.05
208	Tommy Herr	.05	303	Tom Foley	.05	399	Jim Rice	.08
209	Craig Reynolds	.05	304	Pete Incaviglia	.10	400a	Checklist 358-467	.05
210	Gary Pettis	.05	305	Bob Boone	.08	400b	Checklist 346-451	.10
211	Harold Baines	.10	306	*Bill Long*	.05	401	Tommy John	.15
212	Vance Law	.05	307	Willie McGee	.10	402	Brian Holton	.05
213	Ken Gerhart	.05	308	*Ken Caminiti*	.40	403	Carmen Castillo	.05
214	Jim Gantner	.05	309	Darren Daulton	.08	404	Jamie Quirk	.05
215	Chet Lemon	.08	310	Tracy Jones	.05	405	Dwayne Murphy	.05
216	Dwight Evans	.10	311	Greg Booker	.05	406	*Jeff Parrett*	.15
217	Don Mattingly	.35	312	Mike LaValliere	.08	407	Don Sutton	.15
218	Franklin Stubbs	.05	313	Chili Davis	.10	408	Jerry Browne	.05
219	Pat Tabler	.05	314	Glenn Hubbard	.05	409	Jim Winn	.05
220	Bo Jackson	.25	315	*Paul Noce*	.05	410	Dave Smith	.05
221	Tony Phillips	.10	316	Keith Hernandez	.08	411	*Shane Mack*	.15
222	Tim Wallach	.08	317	Mark Langston	.12	412	Greg Gross	.05
223	Ruben Sierra	.10	318	Keith Atherton	.05	413	Nick Esasky	.05
224	Steve Buechele	.05	319	Tony Fernandez	.10	414	Damaso Garcia	.05
225	Frank White	.05	320	Kent Hrbek	.15	415	Brian Fisher	.05
226	Alfredo Griffin	.05	321	John Cerutti	.05	416	Brian Dayett	.05
227	Greg Swindell	.05	322	Mike Kingery	.05	417	Curt Ford	.05
228	Willie Randolph	.08	323	Dave Magadan	.08	418	*Mark Williamson*	.05
229	Mike Marshall	.05	324	Rafael Palmeiro	.20	419	Bill Schroeder	.05
230	Alan Trammell	.15	325	Jeff Dedmon	.05	420	*Mike Henneman*	.15
231	Eddie Murray	.20	326	Barry Bonds	.50	421	*John Marzano*	.05
232	Dale Sveum	.05	327	Jeffrey Leonard	.05	422	Ron Kittle	.05
233	Dick Schofield	.05	328	Tim Flannery	.05	423	Matt Young	.05
234	Jose Oquendo	.05	329	Dave Concepcion	.05	424	Steve Balboni	.05
235	Bill Doran	.05	330	Mike Schmidt	.30	425	*Luis Polonia*	.10
236	Milt Thompson	.05	331	Bill Dawley	.05	426	Randy St. Claire	.05
237	Marvell Wynne	.05	332	Larry Andersen	.05	427	Greg Harris	.05
238	Bobby Bonilla	.15	333	Jack Howell	.05	428	Johnny Ray	.05
239	Chris Speier	.05	334	*Ken Williams*	.05	429	Ray Searage	.05
240	Glenn Braggs	.05	335	Bryn Smith	.05	430	Ricky Horton	.05
241	Wally Backman	.05	336	*Billy Ripken*	.08	431	*Gerald Young*	.05
242	Ryne Sandberg	.30	337	Greg Brock	.05	432	Rick Schu	.05
243	Phil Bradley	.05	338	Mike Heath	.05	433	Paul O'Neill	.25
244	Kelly Gruber	.05	339	Mike Greenwell	.08	434	Rich Gossage	.12
245	Tom Brunansky	.05	340	Claudell Washington	.05	435	John Cangelosi	.05
246	Ron Oester	.05	341	Jose Gonzalez	.05	436	Mike LaCoss	.05
247	Bobby Thigpen	.05	342	Mel Hall	.05	437	Gerald Perry	.05
248	Fred Lynn	.15	343	Jim Eisenreich	.05	438	Dave Martinez	.05
249	Paul Molitor	.30	344	Tony Bernazard	.05	439	Darryl Strawberry	.15
250	Darrell Evans	.10	345	Tim Raines	.08	440	John Moses	.05
251	Gary Ward	.05	346	Bob Brower	.05	441	Greg Gagne	.05
252	Bruce Hurst	.05	347	Larry Parrish	.05	442	Jesse Barfield	.05
253	Bob Welch	.08	348	Thad Bosley	.05	443	George Frazier	.05
254	Joe Carter	.15	349	Dennis Eckersley	.12	444	Garth Iorg	.05
255	Willie Wilson	.10	350	Cory Snyder	.05	445	Ed Nunez	.05
256	Mark McGwire	1.50	351	Rick Cerone	.05	446	Rick Aguilera	.05
257	Mitch Webster	.05	352	John Shelby	.05	447	Jerry Mumphrey	.05
258	Brian Downing	.05	353	Larry Herndon	.05	448	Rafael Ramirez	.05
259	Mike Stanley	.05	354	John Habyan	.05	449	*John Smiley*	.10
260	Carlton Fisk	.15	355	*Chuck Crim*	.05	450	Atlee Hammaker	.05
261	Billy Hatcher	.08	356	Gus Polidor	.05	451	Lance McCullers	.05
262	Glenn Wilson	.05	357	Ken Dayley	.05	452	Guy Hoffman	.05
263	Ozzie Smith	.25	358	Danny Darwin	.05	453	Chris James	.05
264	Randy Ready	.05	359	Lance Parrish	.10	454	Terry Pendleton	.05
265	Kurt Stillwell	.05	360	*James Steels*	.05	455	*Dave Meads*	.08
266	David Palmer	.05	361	*Al Pedrique*	.05	456	Bill Buckner	.05
267	Mike Diaz	.05	362	Mike Aldrete	.05	457	*John Pawlowski*	.05
268	Rob Thompson	.08	363	Juan Castillo	.05	458	Bob Sebra	.05
269	Andre Dawson	.15	364	Len Dykstra	.10	459	Jim Dwyer	.05
270	Lee Guetterman	.05	365	Luis Quinones	.05	460	*Jay Aldrich*	.05
271	Willie Upshaw	.05	366	Jim Presley	.05	461	Frank Tanana	.05
272	Randy Bush	.05	367	Lloyd Moseby	.05	462	Oil Can Boyd	.08
273	Larry Sheets	.05	368	Kirby Puckett	.50	463	Dan Pasqua	.05
274	Rob Deer	.05	369	Eric Davis	.12	464	*Tim Crews*	.10
275	Kirk Gibson	.08	370	Gary Redus	.05	465	Andy Allanson	.05
276	Marty Barrett	.05	371	Dave Schmidt	.05	466	*Bill Pecota*	.05
277	Rickey Henderson	.15	372	Mark Clear	.05	467	Steve Ontiveros	.05

468	Hubie Brooks	.05
469	*Paul Kilgus*	.05
470	Dale Mohorcic	.05
471	Dan Quisenberry	.08
472	Dave Stewart	.10
473	Dave Clark	.05
474	Joel Skinner	.05
475	Dave Anderson	.05
476	Dan Petry	.05
477	*Carl Nichols*	.05
478	Ernest Riles	.05
479	George Hendrick	.05
480	John Morris	.05
481	*Manny Hernandez*	.05
482	Jeff Stone	.05
483	Chris Brown	.05
484	Mike Bielecki	.05
485	Dave Dravecky	.08
486	Rick Manning	.05
487	Bill Almon	.05
488	Jim Sundberg	.05
489	Ken Phelps	.05
490	Tom Henke	.08
491	Dan Gladden	.05
492	Barry Larkin	.15
493	*Fred Manrique*	.05
494	Mike Griffin	.05
495	*Mark Knudson*	.05
496	Bill Madlock	.10
497	Tim Stoddard	.05
498	*Sam Horn*	.05
499	*Tracy Woodson*	.05
500a	Checklist 468-577	.05
500b	Checklist 452-557	.10
501	Ken Schrom	.05
502	Angel Salazar	.05
503	Eric Plunk	.05
504	Joe Hesketh	.05
505	Greg Minton	.05
506	Geno Petralli	.05
507	Bob James	.05
508	*Robbie Wine*	.05
509	Jeff Calhoun	.05
510	Steve Lake	.05
511	Mark Grant	.05
512	Frank Williams	.05
513	*Jeff Blauser*	.30
514	Bob Walk	.05
515	Craig Lefferts	.05
516	Manny Trillo	.05
517	Jerry Reed	.05
518	Rick Leach	.05
519	*Mark Davidson*	.08
520	*Jeff Ballard*	.08
521	*Dave Stapleton*	.05
522	Pat Sheridan	.05
523	Al Nipper	.05
524	Steve Trout	.05
525	Jeff Hamilton	.05
526	*Tommy Hinzo*	.05
527	Lonnie Smith	.05
528	*Greg Cadaret*	.05
529	Rob McClure (Bob)	.05
530	Chuck Finley	.10
531	Jeff Russell	.05
532	Steve Lyons	.05
533	Terry Puhl	.05
534	Eric Nolte	.05
535	Kent Tekulve	.05
536	*Pat Pacillo*	.05
537	Charlie Puleo	.05
538	*Tom Prince*	.05
539	Greg Maddux	1.00
540	Jim Lindeman	.05
541	*Pete Stanicek*	.08
542	Steve Kiefer	.05
543	Jim Morrison	.05
544	Spike Owen	.05
545	*Jay Buhner*	.75
546	*Mike Devereaux*	.15
547	Jerry Don Gleaton	.05
548	Jose Rijo	.08
549	Dennis Martinez	.10
550	Mike Loynd	.05
551	Darrell Miller	.05
552	Dave LaPoint	.05
553	John Tudor	.05
554	*Rocky Childress*	.05
555	*Wally Ritchie*	.05
556	Terry McGriff	.05
557	Dave Leiper	.05
558	Jeff Robinson	.05
559	Jose Uribe	.05
560	Ted Simmons	.05
561	*Lester Lancaster*	.10
562	*Keith Miller*	.05

563	Harold Reynolds	.08
564	*Gene Larkin*	.05
565	Cecil Fielder	.15
566	Roy Smalley	.05
567	Duane Ward	.08
568	*Bill Wilkinson*	.05
569	Howard Johnson	.08
570	Frank DiPino	.05
571	*Pete Smith*	.05
572	Darnell Coles	.05
573	Don Robinson	.05
574	Rob Nelson	.05
575	Dennis Rasmussen	.05
576	Steve Jeltz (photo actually Juan Samuel)	.05
577	*Tom Pagnozzi*	.08
578	Ty Gainey	.05
579	Gary Lucas	.05
580	Ron Hassey	.05
581	Herm Winningham	.05
582	*Rene Gonzales*	.05
583	Brad Komminsk	.05
584	Doyle Alexander	.05
585	Jeff Sellers	.05
586	Bill Gullickson	.05
587	Tim Belcher	.08
588	*Doug Jones*	.15
589	*Melido Perez*	.15
590	Rick Honeycutt	.05
591	Pascual Perez	.05
592	Curt Wilkerson	.05
593	Steve Howe	.05
594	*John Davis*	.05
595	Storm Davis	.05
596	Sammy Stewart	.05
597	Neil Allen	.05
598	Alejandro Pena	.05
599	Mark Thurmond	.05
600a	Checklist 578-BC26	.05
600b	Checklist 558-660	.10
601	*Jose Mesa*	.10
602	*Don August*	.05
603	Terry Leach (SP)	.10
604	*Tom Newell*	.05
605	*Randall Byers* (SP)	.10
606	Jim Gott	.05
607	Harry Spilman	.05
608	John Candelaria	.05
609	*Mike Brumley*	.05
610	Mickey Brantley	.05
611	*Jose Nunez* (SP)	.10
612	Tom Nieto	.05
613	Rick Reuschel	.05
614	Lee Mazzilli (SP)	.10
615	*Scott Lusader*	.05
616	Bobby Meacham	.05
617	Kevin McReynolds (SP)	.15
618	Gene Garber	.05
619	*Barry Lyons* (SP)	.10
620	Randy Myers	.10
621	Donnie Moore	.05
622	Domingo Ramos	.05
623	Ed Romero	.05
624	*Greg Myers*	.08
625	Ripken Baseball Family(Billy Ripken, Cal Ripken, Jr., Cal Ripken, Sr.)	.30
626	Pat Perry	.05
627	Andres Thomas (SP)	.10
628	Matt Williams (SP)	.75
629	*Dave Hengel*	.05
630	Jeff Musselman (SP)	.10
631	Tim Laudner	.05
632	Bob Ojeda (SP)	.12
633	Rafael Santana	.05
634	*Wes Gardner*	.05
635	*Roberto Kelly* (SP)	.25
636	Mike Flanagan (SP)	.10
637	*Jay Bell*	.25
638	Bob Melvin	.05
639	*Damon Berryhill*	.10
640	*David Wells* (SP)	.25
641	Stan Musial Puzzle Card	.05
642	Doug Sisk	.05
643	*Keith Hughes*	.05
644	*Tom Glavine*	.50
645	Al Newman	.05
646	Scott Sanderson	.05
647	Scott Terry	.05
648	Tim Teufel (SP)	.12
649	Garry Templeton (SP)	.10
650	Manny Lee (SP)	.10
651	Roger McDowell (SP)	.15
652	Mookie Wilson (SP)	.15
653	David Cone (SP)	.25
654	*Ron Gant* (SP)	.25

655	Joe Price (SP)	.10
656	George Bell (SP)	.15
657	Gregg Jefferies (SP)	.25
658	*Todd Stottlemyre* (SP)	.15
659	*Geronimo Berroa* (SP)	.30
660	Jerry Royster (SP)	.10

1988 Donruss MVP

Dale Murphy OF

This 26-card set of standard-size player cards replaced the Donruss box-bottom cards in 1988. The bonus cards (numbered BC1 - BC26) were randomly inserted in Donruss wax or rack packs. Cards feature the company's choice of Most Valuable Player for each major league team and are titled "Donruss MVP." The MVP cards were not included in the factory-collated sets. Fronts carry the same basic red-blue-black border design as the 1988 Donruss basic issue. Backs are the same as the regular issue, except for the numbering system.

		MT
Complete Set (26):		5.00
Common Player:		.15
1	Cal Ripken, Jr.	1.00
2	Eric Davis	.20
3	Paul Molitor	.35
4	Mike Schmidt	.45
5	Ivan Calderon	.15
6	Tony Gwynn	.40
7	Wade Boggs	.40
8	Andy Van Slyke	.15
9	Joe Carter	.25
10	Andre Dawson	.20
11	Alan Trammell	.20
12	Mike Scott	.15
13	Wally Joyner	.20
14	Dale Murphy	.20
15	Kirby Puckett	.60
16	Pedro Guerrero	.15
17	Kevin Seitzer	.15
18	Tim Raines	.20
19	George Bell	.15
20	Darryl Strawberry	.25
21	Don Mattingly	.60
22	Ozzie Smith	.35
23	Mark McGwire	1.00
24	Will Clark	.25
25	Alvin Davis	.15
26	Ruben Sierra	.15

A player's name in *italic* type indicates a rookie card.

1988 Donruss All-Stars

Keith Hernandez 1B

For the third consecutive year, this set of 64 cards was marketed in conjunction with Donruss Pop-Ups. The 1988 issue included a major change - the cards were reduced in size from 3-1/2" x 5" to a standard 2-1/2" x 3-1/2". The set features players from the 1987 All-Star Game starting lineup. Card fronts feature full-color photos, framed in blue, black and white, with a Donruss logo at upper-left. Player name and position appear in a red banner below the photo, along with the appropriate National or American League logo. Backs include player stats and All-Star Game record. In 1988, All-Stars cards were distributed in individual packages containing three All-Stars, one Pop-Up and three Stan Musial puzzle pieces.

		MT
Complete Set (64):		3.00
Common Player:		.10
Stan Musial Puzzle:		1.00
1	Don Mattingly	.90
2	Dave Winfield	.25
3	Willie Randolph	.10
4	Rickey Henderson	.40
5	Cal Ripken, Jr.	1.50
6	George Bell	.10
7	Wade Boggs	.75
8	Bret Saberhagen	.10
9	Terry Kennedy	.10
10	John McNamara	.10
11	Jay Howell	.10
12	Harold Baines	.10
13	Harold Reynolds	.10
14	Bruce Hurst	.10
15	Kirby Puckett	.75
16	Matt Nokes	.10
17	Pat Tabler	.10
18	Dan Plesac	.10
19	Mark McGwire	1.00
20	Mike Witt	.10
21	Larry Parrish	.10
22	Alan Trammell	.15
23	Dwight Evans	.10
24	Jack Morris	.10
25	Tony Fernandez	.10
26	Mark Langston	.10
27	Kevin Seitzer	.10
28	Tom Henke	.10
29	Dave Righetti	.10
30	Oakland Coliseum	.10
31	(Wade Boggs) (Top Vote Getter)	.25
32	Checklist 1-32	.05
33	Jack Clark	.10
34	Darryl Strawberry	.15
35	Ryne Sandberg	.75
36	Andre Dawson	.20
37	Ozzie Smith	.40
38	Eric Davis	.15
39	Mike Schmidt	.75
40	Mike Scott	.10
41	Gary Carter	.12
42	Davey Johnson	.10
43	Rick Sutcliffe	.10
44	Willie McGee	.10
45	Hubie Brooks	.10
46	Dale Murphy	.30
47	Bo Diaz	.10
48	Pedro Guerrero	.10
49	Keith Hernandez	.10
50	Ozzie Virgil	.10
51	Tony Gwynn	.60
52	Rick Reuschel	.10
53	John Franco	.10
54	Jeffrey Leonard	.10
55	Juan Samuel	.10
56	Orel Hershiser	.10
57	Tim Raines	.10
58	Sid Fernandez	.10
59	Tim Wallach	.10
60	Lee Smith	.10
61	Steve Bedrosian	.10
62	(Tim Raines) (MVP)	.15
63	(Ozzie Smith) (Top Vote Getter)	.15
64	Checklist 33-64	.05

1988 Donruss Baseball's Best

Don Mattingly 1B

The design of this 336-card set is similar to the regular 1988 Donruss issue with the exception of the borders which are orange, instead of blue. Player photos are framed by the Donruss logo upper-left, team logo lower-right and a bright red and white player name that spans the bottom margin. Backs are black and white, framed by a yellow border, and include personal information, year-by-year stats and major league totals. This set was packaged in a bright red cardboard box containing six individually shrink-wrapped packs of 56 cards. Donruss marketed the set via retail chain outlets.

		MT
Complete Set (336):		9.00
Common Player:		.05
1	Don Mattingly	.75
2	Ron Gant	.20
3	Bob Boone	.05
4	Mark Grace	.45
5	Andy Allanson	.05
6	Kal Daniels	.05
7	Floyd Bannister	.05
8	Alan Ashby	.05
9	Marty Barrett	.05
10	Tim Belcher	.05
11	Harold Baines	.05
12	Hubie Brooks	.05
13	Doyle Alexander	.05
14	Gary Carter	.10
15	Glenn Braggs	.05
16	Steve Bedrosian	.05
17	Barry Bonds	.75
18	Bert Blyleven	.08
19	Tom Brunansky	.05
20	John Candelaria	.05
21	Shawn Abner	.05
22	Jose Canseco	.45
23	Brett Butler	.10
24	Scott Bradley	.05
25	Ivan Calderon	.05
26	Rich Gossage	.08
27	Brian Downing	.05
28	Jim Rice	.05
29	Dion James	.05
30	Terry Kennedy	.05
31	George Bell	.05
32	Scott Fletcher	.05
33	Bobby Bonilla	.15
34	Tim Burke	.05
35	Darrell Evans	.05
36	Mike Davis	.05
37	Shawon Dunston	.10
38	Kevin Bass	.05
39	George Brett	.45
40	David Cone	.10
41	Ron Darling	.05
42	Roberto Alomar	.30
43	Dennis Eckersley	.10
44	Vince Coleman	.05
45	Sid Bream	.05
46	Gary Gaetti	.08
47	Phil Bradley	.05
48	Jim Clancy	.05
49	Jack Clark	.05
50	Mike Krukow	.05
51	Henry Cotto	.05
52	Rich Dotson	.05
53	Jim Gantner	.05
54	John Franco	.05
55	Pete Incaviglia	.15
56	Joe Carter	.75
57	Roger Clemens	.75
58	Gerald Perry	.05
59	Jack Howell	.05
60	Vance Law	.05
61	Jay Bell	.08
62	Eric Davis	.10
63	Gene Garber	.05
64	Glenn Davis	.05
65	Wade Boggs	.40
66	Kirk Gibson	.08
67	Carlton Fisk	.10
68	Casey Candaele	.05
69	Mike Heath	.05
70	Kevin Elster	.05
71	Greg Brock	.05
72	Don Carman	.05
73	Doug Drabek	.08
74	Greg Gagne	.05
75	Danny Cox	.05
76	Rickey Henderson	.30
77	Chris Brown	.05
78	Terry Steinbach	.05
79	Will Clark	.35
80	Mickey Brantley	.05
81	Ozzie Guillen	.05
82	Greg Maddux	.75
83	Kirk McCaskill	.05
84	Dwight Evans	.05
85	Ozzie Virgil	.05
86	Mike Morgan	.05
87	Tony Fernandez	.08
88	Jose Guzman	.05
89	Mike Dunne	.05
90	Andres Galarraga	.10
91	Mike Henneman	.05
92	Alfredo Griffin	.05
93	Rafael Palmeiro	.12
94	Jim Deshaies	.05
95	Mark Gubicza	.05
96	Dwight Gooden	.10
97	Howard Johnson	.05
98	Mark Davis	.05
99	Dave Stewart	.08
100	Joe Magrane	.05
101	Brian Fisher	.05
102	Kent Hrbek	.08
103	Kevin Gross	.05
104	Tom Henke	.05
105	Mike Pagliarulo	.05
106	Kelly Downs	.05
107	Alvin Davis	.05

#	Player	Price
108	Willie Randolph	.05
109	Rob Deer	.05
110	Bo Diaz	.05
111	Paul Kilgus	.05
112	Tom Candiotti	.05
113	Dale Murphy	.15
114	Rick Mahler	.05
115	Wally Joyner	.10
116	Ryne Sandberg	.50
117	John Farrell	.05
118	Nick Esasky	.05
119	Bo Jackson	.25
120	Bill Doran	.05
121	Ellis Burks	.10
122	Pedro Guerrero	.05
123	Dave LaPoint	.05
124	Neal Heaton	.05
125	Willie Hernandez	.05
126	Roger McDowell	.05
127	Ted Higuera	.05
128	Von Hayes	.05
129	Mike LaValliere	.05
130	Dan Gladden	.05
131	Willie McGee	.05
132	Al Lieter	.08
133	Mark Grant	.05
134	Bob Welch	.05
135	Dave Dravecky	.05
136	Mark Langston	.08
137	Dan Pasqua	.05
138	Rick Sutcliffe	.05
139	Dan Petry	.05
140	Rich Gedman	.05
141	Ken Griffey	.05
142	Eddie Murray	.25
143	Jimmy Key	.08
144	Dale Mohorcic	.05
145	Jose Lind	.05
146	Dennis Martinez	.08
147	Chet Lemon	.05
148	Orel Hershiser	.10
149	Dave Martinez	.05
150	Billy Hatcher	.05
151	Charlie Leibrandt	.05
152	Keith Hernandez	.05
153	Kevin McReynolds	.05
154	Tony Gwynn	.75
155	Stan Javier	.05
156	Tony Pena	.05
157	Andy Van Slyke	.05
158	Gene Larkin	.05
159	Chris James	.05
160	Fred McGriff	.20
161	Rick Rhoden	.05
162	Scott Garrelts	.05
163	Mike Campbell	.05
164	Dave Righetti	.05
165	Paul Molitor	.15
166	Danny Jackson	.05
167	Pete O'Brien	.05
168	Julio Franco	.05
169	Mark McGwire	1.00
170	Zane Smith	.05
171	Johnny Ray	.05
172	Lester Lancaster	.05
173	Mel Hall	.05
174	Tracy Jones	.05
175	Kevin Seitzer	.05
176	Bob Knepper	.05
177	Mike Greenwell	.08
178	Mike Marshall	.05
179	Melido Perez	.05
180	Tim Raines	.10
181	Jack Morris	.05
182	Darryl Strawberry	.10
183	Robin Yount	.25
184	Lance Parrish	.05
185	Darnell Coles	.05
186	Kirby Puckett	.45
187	Terry Pendleton	.05
188	Don Slaught	.05
189	Jimmy Jones	.05
190	Dave Parker	.10
191	Mike Aldrete	.05
192	Mike Moore	.05
193	Greg Walker	.05
194	Calvin Schiraldi	.05
195	Dick Schofield	.05
196	Jody Reed	.05
197	Pete Smith	.05
198	Cal Ripken, Jr.	1.00
199	Lloyd Moseby	.05
200	Ruben Sierra	.08
201	R.J. Reynolds	.05
202	Bryn Smith	.05
203	Gary Pettis	.05
204	Steve Sax	.05
205	Frank DiPino	.05
206	Mike Scott	.05
207	Kurt Stillwell	.05
208	Mookie Wilson	.05
209	Lee Mazzilli	.05
210	Lance McCullers	.05
211	Rick Honeycutt	.05
212	John Tudor	.05
213	Jim Gott	.05
214	Frank Viola	.05
215	Juan Samuel	.05
216	Jesse Barfield	.05
217	Claudell Washington	.05
218	Rick Reuschel	.05
219	Jim Presley	.05
220	Tommy John	.05
221	Dan Plesac	.05
222	Barry Larkin	.15
223	Mike Stanley	.05
224	Cory Snyder	.05
225	Andre Dawson	.15
226	Ken Oberkfell	.05
227	Devon White	.08
228	Jamie Moyer	.05
229	Brook Jacoby	.05
230	Rob Murphy	.05
231	Bret Saberhagen	.08
232	Nolan Ryan	.90
233	Bruce Hurst	.05
234	Jesse Orosco	.05
235	Bobby Thigpen	.05
236	Pascual Perez	.05
237	Matt Nokes	.05
238	Bob Ojeda	.05
239	Joey Meyer	.05
240	Shane Rawley	.05
241	Jeff Robinson	.05
242	Jeff Reardon	.05
243	Ozzie Smith	.15
244	Dave Winfield	.30
245	John Kruk	.05
246	Carney Lansford	.05
247	Candy Maldonado	.05
248	Ken Phelps	.05
249	Ken Williams	.05
250	Al Nipper	.05
251	Mark McLemore	.05
252	Lee Smith	.08
253	Albert Hall	.05
254	Billy Ripken	.05
255	Kelly Gruber	.05
256	Charlie Hough	.05
257	John Smiley	.05
258	Tim Wallach	.05
259	Frank Tanana	.05
260	Mike Scioscia	.05
261	Damon Berryhill	.05
262	Dave Smith	.05
263	Willie Wilson	.05
264	Len Dykstra	.08
265	Randy Myers	.08
266	Keith Moreland	.05
267	Eric Plunk	.05
268	Todd Worrell	.05
269	Bob Walk	.05
270	Keith Atherton	.05
271	Mike Schmidt	.50
272	Mike Flanagan	.05
273	Rafael Santana	.05
274	Rob Thompson	.05
275	Rey Quinones	.05
276	Cecilio Guante	.05
277	B.J. Surhoff	.05
278	Chris Sabo	.05
279	Mitch Williams	.05
280	Greg Swindell	.05
281	Alan Trammell	.10
282	Storm Davis	.05
283	Chuck Finley	.05
284	Dave Stieb	.05
285	Scott Bailes	.05
286	Larry Sheets	.05
287	Danny Tartabull	.05
288	Checklist	.05
289	Todd Benzinger	.05
290	John Shelby	.05
291	Steve Lyons	.05
292	Mitch Webster	.05
293	Walt Terrell	.05
294	Pete Stanicek	.05
295	Chris Bosio	.05
296	Milt Thompson	.05
297	Fred Lynn	.08
298	Juan Berenguer	.05
299	Ken Dayley	.05
300	Joel Skinner	.05
301	Benito Santiago	.08
302	Ron Hassey	.05
303	Jose Uribe	.05
304	Harold Reynolds	.05
305	Dale Sveum	.05
306	Glenn Wilson	.05
307	Mike Witt	.05
308	Ron Robinson	.05
309	Denny Walling	.05
310	Joe Orsulak	.05
311	David Wells	.05
312	Steve Buechele	.05
313	Jose Oquendo	.05
314	Floyd Youmans	.05
315	Lou Whitaker	.05
316	Fernando Valenzuela	.00
317	Mike Boddicker	.05
318	Gerald Young	.05
319	Frank White	.05
320	Bill Wegman	.05
321	Tom Niedenfuer	.05
322	Ed Whitson	.05
323	Curt Young	.05
324	Greg Mathews	.05
325	Doug Jones	.05
326	Tommy Herr	.05
327	Kent Tekulve	.05
328	Rance Mulliniks	.05
329	Checklist	.05
330	Craig Lefferts	.05
331	Franklin Stubbs	.05
332	Rick Cerone	.05
333	Dave Schmidt	.05
334	Larry Parrish	.05
335	Tom Browning	.05
336	Checklist	.05

1988 Donruss Diamond Kings Supers

This 28-card set (including the checklist) marks the fourth edition of Donruss' super-size (5" x 7") set. These cards are exact duplicates of the 1988 Diamond Kings that feature player portraits by Dick Perez. A 12-piece Stan Musial puzzle was also included with the purchase of the super-size set which was marketed via a mail-in offer printed on Donruss wrappers.

		MT
Complete Set (28):		10.00
Common Player:		.25
1	Mark McGwire	3.00
2	Tim Raines	.30
3	Benito Santiago	.25
4	Alan Trammell	.30
5	Danny Tartabull	.25
6	Ron Darling	.25
7	Paul Molitor	.50
8	Devon White	.30
9	Andre Dawson	.30
10	Julio Franco	.25
11	Scott Fletcher	.25
12	Tony Fernandez	.25
13	Shane Rawley	.25
14	Kal Daniels	.25
15	Jack Clark	.25
16	Dwight Evans	.25
17	Tommy John	.25
18	Andy Van Slyke	.25
19	Gary Gaetti	.30
20	Mark Langston	.25
21	Will Clark	1.00
22	Glenn Hubbard	.25
23	Billy Hatcher	.25
24	Bob Welch	.25
25	Ivan Calderon	.25
26	Cal Ripken, Jr.	4.00
27	Checklist	.10
641	Stan Musial Puzzle Card	.25

A player's name in *italic* type indicates a rookie card.

1988 Donruss Pop-Ups

Donruss' 1988 Pop-Up cards were reduced to the standard 2-1/2" x 3-1/2". The set includes 20 cards that fold out so that the upper portion of the player stands upright, giving a three-dimensional effect. Pop-Ups feature players from the All-Star Game starting lineup. Card fronts feature full-color photos, with the player's name, team and position printed in black on a yellow banner near the bottom. As in previous issues, the backs contain only the player's name, league and position. Pop-Ups were distributed in individual packages containing one Pop-Up, three Stan Musial puzzle pieces and three All-Star cards.

		MT
Complete Set (20):		2.00
Common Player:		.10
Stan Musial Puzzle:		1.00
(1)	George Bell	.10
(2)	Wade Boggs	.50
(3)	Gary Carter	.12
(4)	Jack Clark	.10
(5)	Eric Davis	.15
(6)	Andre Dawson	.15
(7)	Rickey Henderson	.35
(8)	Davey Johnson	.10
(9)	Don Mattingly	.75
(10)	Terry Kennedy	.10
(11)	John McNamara	.10
(12)	Willie Randolph	.10
(13)	Cal Ripken, Jr.	1.00
(14)	Bret Saberhagen	.15
(15)	Ryne Sandberg	.65
(16)	Mike Schmidt	.70
(17)	Mike Scott	.10
(18)	Ozzie Smith	.35
(19)	Darryl Strawberry	.15
(20)	Dave Winfield	.30

Values quoted in this guide reflect the retail price of a card — the price a collector can expect to pay when buying a card from a dealer.

The wholesale price — that which a collector can expect to receive from a dealer when selling cards — will be significantly lower, depending on desirability and condition.

1988 Donruss Rookies

Mark Grace 1B

For the third consecutive year, Donruss issued a 56-card boxed set highlighting current rookies. The complete set includes a checklist and a 15-piece Stan Musial Diamond Kings puzzle. As in previous years, the set is similar to the company's basic issue, with the exception of the logo and border color. Card fronts feature red, green and black-striped borders, with a red-and-white player name printed in the lower-left corner beneath the photo. "The Rookies" logo is printed in red, white and black in the lower-right corner. Backs are printed in black on bright aqua and include personal data, recent performance stats and major league totals, as well as 1984-88 minor league stats. The cards are the standard 2-1/2" x 3-1/2".

		MT
Complete Set (56):		12.00
Common Player:		.10
1	Mark Grace	2.50
2	Mike Campbell	.10
3	Todd Frowirth	.10
4	Dave Stapleton	.10
5	Shawn Abner	.10
6	Jose Cecena	.10
7	Dave Gallagher	.10
8	Mark Parent	.10
9	Cecil Espy	.10
10	Pete Smith	.10
11	Jay Buhner	1.50
12	Pat Borders	.20
13	Doug Jennings	.10
14	*Brady Anderson*	1.00
15	Pete Stanicek	.10
16	Roberto Kelly	.15
17	Jeff Treadway	.10
18	Walt Weiss	.25
19	Paul Gibson	.10
20	Tim Crews	.10
21	Melido Perez	.10
22	Steve Peters	.10
23	Craig Worthington	.10
24	John Trautwein	.10
25	DeWayne Vaughn	.10
26	David Wells	1.50
27	Al Leiter	.15
28	Tim Belcher	.15
29	Johnny Paredes	.10
30	Chris Sabo	.20
31	Damon Berryhill	.10
32	Randy Milligan	.10
33	Gary Thurman	.10
34	Kevin Elster	.15
35	Roberto Alomar	3.00
36	*Edgar Martinez* (photo actually Edwin Nunez)	1.25
37	Todd Stottlemyre	.15

38	Joey Meyer	.10
39	Carl Nichols	.10
40	Jack McDowell	.20
41	Jose Bautista	.10
42	Sil Campusano	.10
43	John Dopson	.10
44	Jody Reed	.15
45	Darrin Jackson	.20
46	Mike Capel	.10
47	Ron Gant	.40
48	John Davis	.10
49	Kevin Coffman	.10
50	Cris Carpenter	.10
51	Mackey Sasser	.10
52	Luis Alicea	.15
53	Bryan Harvey	.15
54	Steve Ellsworth	.10
55	Mike Macfarlane	.15
56	Checklist 1-56	.05

1989 Donruss

Fred McGriff 1B

This basic annual issue consists of 660 2-1/2" x 3-1/2" cards, including 26 Diamond Kings (DK) portrait cards and 20 Rated Rookies (RR) cards. Top and bottom borders of the cards are printed in a variety of colors that fade from dark to light. A white-lettered player name is printed across the top margin. The team logo appears upper-right and the Donruss logo lower-left. A black outer stripe varnish gives faintly visible filmstrip texture to the border. Backs are in orange and black, similar to the 1988 design, with personal info, recent stats and major league totals. Team logo sticker cards (22 total) and Warren Spahn puzzle cards (63 total) are included in individual wax packs of cards.

		MT
Complete Set (660):		12.00
Common Player:		.05
Warren Spahn Puzzle:		1.00
Wax Box:		8.00
1	Mike Greenwell (DK)	.05
2	Bobby Bonilla (DK)	.08
3	Pete Incaviglia (DK)	.05
4	Chris Sabo (DK)	.08
5	Robin Yount (DK)	.15
6	Tony Gwynn (DK)	.25
7	Carlton Fisk (DK)	.12
8	Cory Snyder (DK)	.05
9	David Cone (DK)	.08
10	Kevin Seitzer (DK)	.08
11	Rick Reuschel (DK)	.05
12	Johnny Ray (DK)	.05
13	Dave Schmidt (DK)	.05
14	Andres Galarraga (DK)	.15
15	Kirk Gibson (DK)	.08
16	Fred McGriff (DK)	.15
17	Mark Grace (DK)	.20

No.	Player	Price
18	Jeff Robinson (DK)	.05
19	Vince Coleman (DK)	.05
20	Dave Henderson (DK)	.08
21	Harold Reynolds (DK)	.08
22	Gerald Perry (DK)	.05
23	Frank Viola (DK)	.08
24	Steve Bedrosian (DK)	.08
25	Glenn Davis (DK)	.08
26	Don Mattingly (DK)	.30
27	Checklist 1-27	.05
28	*Sandy Alomar, Jr. (RR)*	.45
29	*Steve Searcy (RR)*	.08
30	*Cameron Drew (RR)*	.05
31	*Gary Sheffield (RR)*	.75
32	*Erik Hanson (RR)*	.25
33	*Ken Griffey, Jr. (RR)*	5.00
34	*Greg Harris (RR)*	.05
35	*Gregg Jefferies (RR)*	.35
36	*Luis Medina (RR)*	.05
37	*Carlos Quintana (RR)*	.05
38	*Felix Jose (RR)*	.15
39	*Cris Carpenter (RR)*	.05
40	*Ron Jones (RR)*	.05
41	*Dave West (RR)*	.08
42	*Randy Johnson (RR)*	1.00
43	*Mike Harkey (RR)*	.10
44	*Pete Harnisch (RR)*	.15
45	*Tom Gordon (RR)*	.12
46	*Gregg Olson (RR)*	.10
47	*Alex Sanchez (RR)*	.05
48	Ruben Sierra	.08
49	Rafael Palmeiro	.25
50	Ron Gant	.15
51	Cal Ripken, Jr.	.75
52	Wally Joyner	.10
53	Gary Carter	.10
54	Andy Van Slyke	.08
55	Robin Yount	.25
56	Pete Incaviglia	.08
57	Greg Brock	.05
58	Melido Perez	.05
59	Craig Lefferts	.05
60	Gary Pettis	.05
61	Danny Tartabull	.05
62	Guillermo Hernandez	.05
63	Ozzie Smith	.25
64	Gary Gaetti	.12
65	Mark Davis	.05
66	Lee Smith	.08
67	Dennis Eckersley	.10
68	Wade Boggs	.30
69	Mike Scott	.05
70	Fred McGriff	.30
71	Tom Browning	.08
72	Claudell Washington	.05
73	Mel Hall	.05
74	Don Mattingly	.45
75	Steve Bedrosian	.05
76	Juan Samuel	.05
77	Mike Scioscia	.05
78	Dave Righetti	.05
79	Alfredo Griffin	.05
80	Eric Davis	.10
81	Juan Berenguer	.05
82	Todd Worrell	.08
83	Joe Carter	.25
84	Steve Sax	.05
85	Frank White	.05
86	John Kruk	.08
87	Rance Mulliniks	.05
88	Alan Ashby	.05
89	Charlie Leibrandt	.05
90	Frank Tanana	.05
91	Jose Canseco	.35
92	Barry Bonds	.50
93	Harold Reynolds	.08
94	Mark McLemore	.05
95	Mark McGwire	1.00
96	Eddie Murray	.20
97	Tim Raines	.08
98	Rob Thompson	.05
99	Kevin McReynolds	.08
100	Checklist 28-137	.05
101	Carlton Fisk	.12
102	Dave Martinez	.05
103	Glenn Braggs	.05
104	Dale Murphy	.12
105	Ryne Sandberg	.40
106	Dennis Martinez	.10
107	Pete O'Brien	.05
108	Dick Schofield	.05
109	Henry Cotto	.05
110	Mike Marshall	.05
111	Keith Moreland	.05
112	Tom Brunansky	.05
113	Kelly Gruber	.05
114	Brook Jacoby	.05
115	*Keith Brown*	.05
116	Matt Nokes	.08
117	Keith Hernandez	.05
118	Bob Forsch	.05
119	Bert Blyleven	.10
120	Willie Wilson	.08
121	Tommy Gregg	.05
122	Jim Rice	.08
123	Bob Knepper	.05
124	Danny Jackson	.08
125	Eric Plunk	.05
126	Brian Fisher	.05
127	Mike Pagliarulo	.05
128	Tony Gwynn	.45
129	Lance McCullers	.05
130	Andres Galarraga	.20
131	Jose Uribe	.05
132	Kirk Gibson	.08
133	David Palmer	.05
134	R.J. Reynolds	.05
135	Greg Walker	.05
136	Kirk McCaskill	.05
137	Shawon Dunston	.08
138	Andy Allanson	.05
139	Rob Murphy	.05
140	Mike Aldrete	.05
141	Terry Kennedy	.05
142	Scott Fletcher	.05
143	Steve Balboni	.05
144	Bret Saberhagen	.12
145	Ozzie Virgil	.05
146	Dale Sveum	.05
147	Darryl Strawberry	.12
148	Harold Baines	.10
149	George Bell	.08
150	Dave Parker	.12
151	Bobby Bonilla	.10
152	Mookie Wilson	.05
153	Ted Power	.05
154	Nolan Ryan	.75
155	Jeff Reardon	.05
156	Tim Wallach	.08
157	Jamie Moyer	.05
158	Rich Gossage	.08
159	Dave Winfield	.25
160	Von Hayes	.05
161	Willie McGee	.10
162	Rich Gedman	.05
163	Tony Pena	.05
164	Mike Morgan	.05
165	Charlie Hough	.05
166	Mike Stanley	.05
167	Andre Dawson	.20
168	Joe Boever	.05
169	Pete Stanicek	.05
170	Bob Boone	.08
171	Ron Darling	.08
172	Bob Walk	.05
173	Rob Deer	.05
174	Steve Buechele	.05
175	Ted Higuera	.05
176	Ozzie Guillen	.05
177	Candy Maldonado	.05
178	Doyle Alexander	.05
179	Mark Gubicza	.10
180	Alan Trammell	.15
181	Vince Coleman	.08
182	Kirby Puckett	.45
183	Chris Brown	.05
184	Marty Barrett	.05
185	Stan Javier	.05
186	Mike Greenwell	.08
187	Billy Hatcher	.05
188	Jimmy Key	.08
189	Nick Esasky	.05
190	Don Slaught	.05
191	Cory Snyder	.05
192	John Candelaria	.05
193	Mike Schmidt	.35
194	Kevin Gross	.05
195	John Tudor	.05
196	Neil Allen	.05
197	Orel Hershiser	.08
198	Kal Daniels	.05
199	Kent Hrbek	.15
200	Checklist 138-247	.05
201	Joe Magrane	.05
202	Scott Bailes	.05
203	Tim Belcher	.10
204	George Brett	.40
205	Benito Santiago	.12
206	Tony Fernandez	.10
207	Gerald Young	.05
208	Bo Jackson	.25
209	Chet Lemon	.05
210	Storm Davis	.05
211	Doug Drabek	.05
212	Mickey Brantley (photo actually Nelson Simmons)	.05
213	Devon White	.08
214	Dave Stewart	.05
215	Dave Schmidt	.05
216	Bryn Smith	.05
217	Brett Butler	.08
218	Bob Ojeda	.05
219	*Steve Rosenberg*	.05
220	Hubie Brooks	.05
221	B.J. Surhoff	.05
222	Rick Mahler	.05
223	Rick Sutcliffe	.05
224	Neal Heaton	.05
225	Mitch Williams	.08
226	Chuck Finley	.08
227	Mark Langston	.10
228	Jesse Orosco	.05
229	Ed Whitson	.05
230	Terry Pendleton	.08
231	Lloyd Moseby	.05
232	Greg Swindell	.05
233	John Franco	.05
234	Jack Morris	.10
235	Howard Johnson	.08
236	Glenn Davis	.05
237	Frank Viola	.08
238	Kevin Seitzer	.05
239	Gerald Perry	.05
240	Dwight Evans	.10
241	Jim Deshaies	.05
242	Bo Diaz	.05
243	Carney Lansford	.05
244	Mike LaValliere	.05
245	Rickey Henderson	.20
246	Roberto Alomar	.60
247	Jimmy Jones	.05
248	Pascual Perez	.05
249	Will Clark	.35
250	Fernando Valenzuela	.10
251	Shane Rawley	.05
252	Sid Bream	.05
253	Steve Lyons	.05
254	Brian Downing	.05
255	Mark Grace	.30
256	Tom Candiotti	.05
257	Barry Larkin	.12
258	Mike Krukow	.05
259	Billy Ripken	.05
260	Cecilio Guante	.05
261	Scott Bradley	.05
262	Floyd Bannister	.05
263	Pete Smith	.05
264	Jim Gantner	.05
265	Roger McDowell	.05
266	Bobby Thigpen	.05
267	Jim Clancy	.05
268	Terry Steinbach	.08
269	Mike Dunne	.05
270	Dwight Gooden	.10
271	Mike Heath	.05
272	Dave Smith	.05
273	Keith Atherton	.05
274	Tim Burke	.05
275	Damon Berryhill	.05
276	Vance Law	.05
277	Rich Dotson	.05
278	Lance Parrish	.08
279	Geronimo Berroa	.08
280	Roger Clemens	.40
281	Greg Mathews	.05
282	Tom Niedenfuer	.05
283	Paul Kilgus	.05
284	Jose Guzman	.05
285	Calvin Schiraldi	.05
286	Charlie Puleo	.05
287	Joe Orsulak	.05
288	Jack Howell	.05
289	Kevin Elster	.05
290	Jose Lind	.08
291	Paul Molitor	.25
292	Cecil Espy	.05
293	Bill Wegman	.05
294	Dan Pasqua	.05
295	Scott Garrelts	.05
296	Walt Terrell	.05
297	Ed Hearn	.05
298	Lou Whitaker	.08
299	Ken Dayley	.05
300	Checklist 248-357	.05
301	Tommy Herr	.05
302	Mike Brumley	.05
303	Ellis Burks	.10
304	Curt Young	.05

#	Name	Price	#	Name	Price	#	Name	Price
305	Jody Reed	.10	401	Mickey Tettleton	.08	497	Mike Campbell	.05
306	Bill Doran	.05	402	Curtis Wilkerson	.05	498	Gary Thurman	.05
307	David Wells	.08	403	Jeff Russell	.05	499	Zane Smith	.05
308	Ron Robinson	.05	404	Pat Perry	.05	500	Checklist 468-577	.05
309	Rafael Santana	.05	405	*Jose Alvarez*	.05	501	Mike Birkbeck	.05
310	Julio Franco	.10	406	Rick Schu	.05	502	Terry Leach	.05
311	Jack Clark	.05	407	*Sherman Corbett*	.05	503	Shawn Hillegas	.05
312	Chris James	.05	408	Dave Magadan	.08	504	Manny Lee	.05
313	Milt Thompson	.05	409	Bob Kipper	.05	505	*Doug Jennings*	.08
314	John Shelby	.05	410	Don August	.05	506	Ken Oberkfell	.05
315	Al Leiter	.05	411	Bob Brower	.05	507	Tim Teufel	.05
316	Mike Davis	.05	412	Chris Bosio	.05	508	Tom Brookens	.05
317	*Chris Sabo*	.15	413	Jerry Reuss	.05	509	Rafael Ramirez	.05
318	Greg Gagne	.05	414	Atlee Hammaker	.05	510	Fred Toliver	.05
319	Jose Oquendo	.05	415	Jim Walewander	.05	511	*Brian Holman*	.05
320	John Farrell	.05	416	*Mike Macfarlane*	.08	512	Mike Bielecki	.05
321	Franklin Stubbs	.05	417	Pat Sheridan	.05	513	*Jeff Pico*	.05
322	Kurt Stillwell	.05	418	Pedro Guerrero	.05	514	Charles Hudson	.05
323	Shawn Abner	.05	419	Allan Anderson	.05	515	Bruce Ruffin	.05
324	Mike Flanagan	.05	420	*Mark Parent*	.08	516	Larry McWilliams	.05
325	Kevin Bass	.05	421	Bob Stanley	.05	517	Jeff Sellers	.05
326	Pat Tabler	.05	422	Mike Gallego	.05	518	*John Costello*	.05
327	Mike Henneman	.08	423	Bruce Hurst	.05	519	Brady Anderson	.25
328	Rick Honeycutt	.05	424	Dave Meads	.05	520	Craig McMurtry	.05
329	John Smiley	.10	425	Jesse Barfield	.05	521	Ray Hayward	.05
330	Rey Quinones	.05	426	*Rob Dibble*	.15	522	Drew Hall	.05
331	Johnny Ray	.05	427	Joel Skinner	.05	523	*Mark Lemke*	.05
332	Bob Welch	.08	428	Ron Kittle	.05	524	*Oswald Peraza*	.05
333	Larry Sheets	.05	429	Rick Rhoden	.05	525	*Bryan Harvey*	.10
334	Jeff Parrett	.05	430	Bob Dernier	.05	526	Rick Aguilera	.05
335	Rick Reuschel	.05	431	Steve Jeltz	.05	527	Tom Prince	.05
336	Randy Myers	.10	432	Rick Dempsey	.05	528	Mark Clear	.05
337	Ken Williams	.05	433	Roberto Kelly	.10	529	Jerry Browne	.05
338	Andy McGaffigan	.05	434	Dave Anderson	.05	530	Juan Castillo	.05
339	Joey Meyer	.05	435	Herm Winningham	.05	531	Jack McDowell	.15
340	Dion James	.05	436	Al Newman	.05	532	Chris Speier	.05
341	Les Lancaster	.05	437	Jose DeLeon	.05	533	Darrell Evans	.08
342	Tom Foley	.05	438	Doug Jones	.08	534	Luis Aquino	.05
343	Geno Petralli	.05	439	Brian Holton	.05	535	Eric King	.05
344	Dan Petry	.05	440	Jeff Montgomery	.10	536	*Ken Hill*	.40
345	Alvin Davis	.05	441	Dickie Thon	.05	537	Randy Bush	.05
346	Mickey Hatcher	.05	442	Cecil Fielder	.20	538	Shane Mack	.05
347	Marvell Wynne	.05	443	*John Fishel*	.05	539	Tom Bolton	.05
348	Danny Cox	.05	444	Jerry Don Gleaton	.05	540	Gene Nelson	.05
349	Dave Stieb	.08	445	*Paul Gibson*	.05	541	Wes Gardner	.05
350	Jay Bell	.08	446	Walt Weiss	.08	542	Ken Caminiti	.10
351	Jeff Treadway	.05	447	Glenn Wilson	.05	543	Duane Ward	.05
352	Luis Salazar	.05	448	Mike Moore	.05	544	*Norm Charlton*	.12
353	Len Dykstra	.15	449	Chili Davis	.10	545	*Hal Morris*	.40
354	Juan Agosto	.05	450	Dave Henderson	.05	546	Rich Yett	.05
355	Gene Larkin	.05	451	*Jose Bautista*	.05	547	*Hensley Meulens*	.10
356	Steve Farr	.05	452	Rex Hudler	.05	548	Greg Harris	.05
357	Paul Assenmacher	.05	453	Bob Brenly	.05	549	Darren Daulton	.08
358	Todd Benzinger	.05	454	Mackey Sasser	.05	550	Jeff Hamilton	.05
359	Larry Andersen	.05	455	Daryl Boston	.05	551	Luis Aguayo	.05
360	Paul O'Neill	.12	456	Mike Fitzgerald	.05	552	Tim Leary	.05
361	Ron Hassey	.05	457	Jeffery Leonard	.05	553	Ron Oester	.05
362	Jim Gott	.05	458	Bruce Sutter	.05	554	Steve Lombardozzi	.05
363	Ken Phelps	.05	459	Mitch Webster	.05	555	*Tim Jones*	.05
364	Tim Flannery	.05	460	Joe Hesketh	.05	556	Bud Black	.05
365	Randy Ready	.05	461	Bobby Witt	.05	557	Alejandro Pena	.05
366	*Nelson Santovenia*	.05	462	Stew Cliburn	.05	558	*Jose DeJesus*	.05
367	Kelly Downs	.05	463	Scott Bankhead	.05	559	Dennis Rasmussen	.05
368	Danny Heep	.05	464	*Ramon Martinez*	.40	560	Pat Borders	.08
369	Phil Bradley	.05	465	Dave Leiper	.05	561	*Craig Biggio*	.50
370	Jeff Robinson	.05	466	*Luis Alicea*	.08	562	Luis de los Santos	.05
371	Ivan Calderon	.05	467	John Cerutti	.05	563	Fred Lynn	.10
372	Mike Witt	.05	468	Ron Washington	.05	564	*Todd Burns*	.05
373	Greg Maddux	.75	469	Jeff Reed	.05	565	Felix Fermin	.05
374	Carmen Castillo	.05	470	Jeff Robinson	.05	566	Darnell Coles	.05
375	Jose Rijo	.05	471	Sid Fernandez	.05	567	Willie Fraser	.05
376	Joe Price	.05	472	Terry Puhl	.05	568	Glenn Hubbard	.05
377	R.C. Gonzalez	.05	473	Charlie Lea	.05	569	*Craig Worthington*	.05
378	Oddibe McDowell	.05	474	*Israel Sanchez*	.05	570	*Johnny Paredes*	.05
379	Jim Presley	.05	475	Bruce Benedict	.05	571	Don Robinson	.05
380	Brad Wellman	.05	476	Oil Can Boyd	.05	572	Barry Lyons	.05
381	Tom Glavine	.25	477	Craig Reynolds	.05	573	Bill Long	.05
382	Dan Plesac	.05	478	Frank Williams	.05	574	Tracy Jones	.05
383	Wally Backman	.05	479	Greg Cadaret	.05	575	Juan Nieves	.05
384	*Dave Gallagher*	.05	480	*Randy Kramer*	.05	576	Andres Thomas	.05
385	Tom Henke	.05	481	*Dave Eiland*	.05	577	*Rolando Roomes*	.05
386	Luis Polonia	.05	482	Eric Show	.05	578	Luis Rivera	.05
387	Junior Ortiz	.05	483	Garry Templeton	.05	579	*Chad Kreuter*	.15
388	David Cone	.12	484	Wallace Johnson	.05	580	Tony Armas	.08
389	Dave Bergman	.05	485	Kevin Mitchell	.08	581	Jay Buhner	.15
390	Danny Darwin	.05	486	Tim Crews	.05	582	Ricky Horton	.05
391	Dan Gladden	.05	487	Mike Maddux	.05	583	Andy Hawkins	.05
392	*John Dopson*	.05	488	Dave LaPoint	.05	584	*Sil Campusano*	.05
393	Frank DiPino	.05	489	Fred Manrique	.05	585	Dave Clark	.05
394	Al Nipper	.05	490	Greg Minton	.05	586	*Van Snider*	.05
395	Willie Randolph	.05	491	*Doug Dascenzo*	.08	587	Todd Frohwirth	.05
396	Don Carman	.05	492	Willie Upshaw	.05	588	Warren Spahn Puzzle Card	.05
397	Scott Terry	.05	493	*Jack Armstrong*	.10	589	*William Brennan*	.05
398	Rick Cerone	.05	494	Kirt Manwaring	.10	590	*German Gonzalez*	.05
399	Tom Pagnozzi	.05	495	Jeff Ballard	.05	591	Ernie Whitt	.05
400	Checklist 358-467	.05	496	Jeff Kunkel	.05	592	Jeff Blauser	.05

593	Spike Owen	.05
594	Matt Williams	.35
595	Lloyd McClendon	.05
596	Steve Ontiveros	.05
597	*Scott Medvin*	.05
598	*Hipolito Pena*	.05
599	*Jerald Clark*	.05
600a	Checklist 578-BC26 (#635 is Kurt Schilling)	.15
600b	Checklist 578-BC26 (#635 is Curt Schilling)	.05
601	Carmelo Martinez	.05
602	Mike LaCoss	.05
603	Mike Devereaux	.05
604	*Alex Madrid*	.05
605	Gary Redus	.05
606	Lance Johnson	.08
607	*Terry Clark*	.05
608	Manny Trillo	.05
609	*Scott Jordan*	.05
610	Jay Howell	.05
611	*Francisco Melendez*	.05
612	Mike Boddicker	.05
613	Kevin Brown	.10
614	Dave Valle	.05
615	Tim Laudner	.05
616	*Andy Nezelek*	.05
617	Chuck Crim	.05
618	Jack Savage	.05
619	Adam Peterson	.05
620	Todd Stottlemyre	.05
621	*Lance Blankenship*	.10
622	*Miguel Garcia*	.05
623	Keith Miller	.05
624	*Ricky Jordan*	.08
625	Ernest Riles	.05
626	John Moses	.05
627	Nelson Liriano	.05
628	Mike Smithson	.05
629	Scott Sanderson	.05
630	Dale Mohorcic	.05
631	Marvin Freeman	.05
632	Mike Young	.05
633	Dennis Lamp	.05
634	*Dante Bichette*	.75
635	*Curt Schilling*	.25
636	*Scott May*	.05
637	*Mike Schooler*	.05
638	Rick Leach	.05
639	*Tom Lampkin*	.05
640	*Brian Meyer*	.05
641	Brian Harper	.05
642	*John Smoltz*	.75
643	Jose Canseco (40/40)	.20
644	Bill Schroeder	.05
645	Edgar Martinez	.15
646	*Dennis Cook*	.08
647	Barry Jones	.05
648	(Orel Hershiser) (59 and Counting)	.15
649	*Rod Nichols*	.05
650	Jody Davis	.05
651	*Bob Milacki*	.05
652	Mike Jackson	.05
653	*Derek Lilliquist*	.10
654	Paul Mirabella	.05
655	Mike Diaz	.05
656	Jeff Musselman	.05
657	Jerry Reed	.05
658	*Kevin Blankenship*	.08
659	Wayne Tolleson	.05
660	*Eric Hetzel*	.05

1989 Donruss Grand Slammers

One card from this 12-card set was included in each Donruss cello pack. The complete insert set was included in factory sets. The featured players all hit grand slams in 1988. The 2-1/2" x 3-1/2" cards feature full color action photos. Backs tell the story of the player's grand slam. Border color variations on the front of the card have been discovered, but the prices are consistent with all forms of the cards.

Walt Weiss SS

		MT
Complete Set (12):		2.50
Common Player:		.25
1	Jose Canseco	.40
2	Mike Marshall	.25
3	Walt Weiss	.25
4	Kevin McReynolds	.25
5	Mike Greenwell	.25
6	Dave Winfield	.30
7	Mark McGwire	1.00
8	Keith Hernandez	.25
9	Franklin Stubbs	.25
10	Danny Tartabull	.25
11	Jesse Barfield	.25
12	Ellis Burks	.30

1989 Donruss MVP

Will Clark 1B   DONRUSS 89

This set, numbered BC1-BC26, was randomly inserted in Donruss wax packs, but not included in factory sets or other card packs. Players highlighted were selected by Donruss, one player per team. MVP cards feature a variation of the design in the basic Donruss issue, with multi-color upper and lower borders and black side borders. The "MVP" designation in large, bright letters serves as a backdrop for the full-color player photo. The cards measure 2-1/2" x 3-1/2".

		MT
Complete Set (26):		3.00
Common Player:		.10
1	Kirby Puckett	.50
2	Mike Scott	.10
3	Joe Carter	.15
4	Orel Hershiser	.10

5	Jose Canseco	.40
6	Darryl Strawberry	.15
7	George Brett	.45
8	Andre Dawson	.25
9	Paul Molitor	.45
10	Andy Van Slyke	.10
11	Dave Winfield	.30
12	Kevin Gross	.10
13	Mike Greenwell	.10
14	Ozzie Smith	.30
15	Cal Ripken	1.00
16	Andres Galarraga	.20
17	Alan Trammell	.15
18	Kal Daniels	.10
19	Fred McGriff	.25
20	Tony Gwynn	.45
21	Wally Joyner	.15
22	Will Clark	.30
23	Ozzie Guillen	.10
24	Gerald Perry	.10
25	Alvin Davis	.10
26	Ruben Sierra	.10

1989 Donruss Diamond King Supers

Once again for 1989, collectors could acquire a 4-3/4" x 6-3/4" version of the Diamond King subset via a wrapper mail-in offer. Other than size, cards are identical to the DKs in the regular issue.

		MT
Complete Set (27):		14.00
Common Player:		.25
1	Mike Greenwell	.25
2	Bobby Bonilla	.50
3	Pete Incaviglia	.25
4	Chris Sabo	.25
5	Robin Yount	1.50
6	Tony Gwynn	2.50
7	Carlton Fisk	1.00
8	Cory Snyder	.25
9	David Cone	.60
10	Kevin Seitzer	.25
11	Rick Reuschel	.25
12	Johnny Ray	.25
13	Dave Schmidt	.25
14	Andres Galarraga	1.00
15	Kirk Gibson	.30
16	Fred McGriff	1.00
17	Mark Grace	1.50
18	Jeff Robinson	.25
19	Vince Coleman	.25
20	Dave Henderson	.25
21	Harold Reynolds	.25
22	Gerald Perry	.25
23	Frank Viola	.25
24	Steve Bedrosian	.25
25	Glenn Davis	.25
26	Don Mattingly	4.00
27	Checklist	.05

1989 Donruss All-Stars

bp114

For the fourth consecutive year Donruss featured a 64-card set with players from the 1988 All-Star Game. The card fronts include a red-to-gold fade or gold-to-red fade border and blue vertical side borders. The top border features the player's name and position along with the "Donruss 89" logo. Each full-color player photo is highlighted by a thin white line and includes a league logo in the lower right corner. Card backs reveal an orange-gold border and black and white printing. The player's ID and personal information is displayed with a gold star on both sides. The star in the left corner includes the card number. 1988 All-Star game statistics and run totals follow along with a career highlights feature surrounded by the team, All-Star Game MLB, MLBPA, and Leaf Inc. logos. The All-Stars were distributed in wax packages containing five All-Stars, one Pop-Up, and one three-piece Warren Spahn puzzle card.

	MT
Complete Set (64):	5.00
Common Player:	.10
Warren Spahn Puzzle:	1.00
1 Mark McGwire	1.00
2 Jose Canseco	.60
3 Paul Molitor	.25
4 Rickey Henderson	.25
5 Cal Ripken, Jr.	1.50
6 Dave Winfield	.25
7 Wade Boggs	.50
8 Frank Viola	.10
9 Terry Steinbach	.10
10 Tom Kelly	.10
11 George Brett	.60
12 Doyle Alexander	.10
13 Gary Gaetti	.10
14 Roger Clemens	.65
15 Mike Greenwell	.10
16 Dennis Eckersley	.15
17 Carney Lansford	.10
18 Mark Gubicza	.10
19 Tim Laudner	.10
20 Doug Jones	.10
21 Don Mattingly	.75
22 Dan Plesac	.10
23 Kirby Puckett	.75
24 Jeff Reardon	.10
25 Johnny Ray	.10
26 Jeff Russell	.10
27 Harold Reynolds	.10
28 Dave Stieb	.10
29 Kurt Stillwell	.10
30 Jose Canseco	.60
31 Terry Steinbach	.10
32 A.L. Checklist	.05
33 Will Clark	.40
34 Darryl Strawberry	.20
35 Ryne Sandberg	.75
36 Andre Dawson	.12
37 Ozzie Smith	.25
38 Vince Coleman	.10
39 Bobby Bonilla	.12
40 Dwight Gooden	.10
41 Gary Carter	.12
42 Whitey Herzog	.10
43 Shawon Dunston	.10
44 David Cone	.12
45 Andres Galarraga	.15
46 Mark Davis	.10
47 Barry Larkin	.15
48 Kevin Gross	.10
49 Vance Law	.10
50 Orel Hershiser	.10
51 Willie McGee	.10
52 Danny Jackson	.10
53 Rafael Palmeiro	.25
54 Bob Knepper	.10
55 Lance Parrish	.10
56 Greg Maddux	.85
57 Gerald Perry	.10
58 Bob Walk	.10
59 Chris Sabo	.10
60 Todd Worrell	.10
61 Andy Van Slyke	.10
62 Ozzie Smith	.25
63 Riverfront Stadium	.10
64 N.L. Checklist	.05

1989 Donruss Baseball's Best

For the second consecutive year, Donruss issued a "Baseball's Best" set in 1989 to highlight the game's top players. The special 336-card set was packaged in a special box and was sold at various retail chains nationwide following the conclusion of the 1989 baseball season. The cards are styled after the regular 1989 Donruss set with green borders and a glossy finish. The set included a Warren Spahn puzzle.

	MT
Complete Set (336):	20.00
Common Player:	.05
1 Don Mattingly	.90
2 Tom Glavine	.15
3 Bert Blyleven	.05
4 Andre Dawson	.10
5 Pete O'Brien	.05
6 Eric Davis	.10
7 George Brett	.50
8 Glenn Davis	.05
9 Ellis Burks	.15
10 Kirk Gibson	.08
11 Carlton Fisk	.10
12 Andres Galarraga	.15
13 Alan Trammell	.15
14 Dwight Gooden	.15
15 Paul Molitor	.15
16 Roger McDowell	.05
17 Doug Drabek	.05
18 Kent Hrbek	.08
19 Vince Coleman	.05
20 Steve Sax	.05
21 Roberto Alomar	.35
22 Carney Lansford	.05
23 Will Clark	.50
24 Alvin Davis	.05
25 Bobby Thigpen	.05
26 Ryne Sandberg	.75
27 Devon White	.08
28 Mike Greenwell	.08
29 Dale Murphy	.20
30 Jeff Ballard	.05
31 Kelly Gruber	.05
32 Julio Franco	.08
33 Bobby Bonilla	.10
34 Tim Wallach	.05
35 Lou Whitaker	.08
36 Jay Howell	.05
37 Greg Maddux	.75
38 Bill Doran	.05
39 Danny Tartabull	.05
40 Darryl Strawberry	.10
41 Ron Darling	.05
42 Tony Gwynn	.50
43 Mark McGwire	1.50
44 Ozzie Smith	.25
45 Andy Van Slyke	.05
46 Juan Berenguer	.05
47 Von Hayes	.05
48 Tony Fernandez	.05
49 Eric Plunk	.05
50 Ernest Riles	.05
51 Harold Reynolds	.05
52 Andy Hawkins	.05
53 Robin Yount	.30
54 Danny Jackson	.05
55 Nolan Ryan	1.25
56 Joe Carter	.12
57 Jose Canseco	.75
58 Jody Davis	.05
59 Lance Parrish	.05
60 Mitch Williams	.05
61 Brook Jacoby	.05
62 Tom Browning	.05
63 Kurt Stillwell	.05
64 Rafael Ramirez	.05
65 Roger Clemens	.60
66 Mike Scioscia	.05
67 Dave Gallagher	.05
68 Mark Langston	.08
69 Chet Lemon	.05
70 Kevin McReynolds	.05
71 Rob Deer	.05
72 Tommy Herr	.05
73 Barry Bonds	.75
74 Frank Viola	.05
75 Pedro Guerrero	.05
76 Dave Righetti	.05
77 Bruce Hurst	.05
78 Rickey Henderson	.30
79 Robby Thompson	.05
80 Randy Johnson	.35
81 Harold Baines	.05
82 Calvin Schiraldi	.05
83 Kirk McCaskill	.05
84 Lee Smith	.08
85 John Smoltz	.15
86 Mickey Tettleton	.08
87 Jimmy Key	.08
88 Rafael Palmeiro	.15
89 Sid Bream	.05
90 Dennis Martinez	.08
91 Frank Tanana	.05
92 Eddie Murray	.30
93 Shawon Dunston	.10
94 Mike Scott	.05
95 Bret Saberhagen	.10
96 David Cone	.10
97 Kevin Elster	.08
98 Jack Clark	.05
99 Dave Stewart	.08
100 Jose Oquendo	.05
101 Jose Lind	.05
102 Gary Gaetti	.05
103 Ricky Jordan	.05
104 Fred McGriff	.30
105 Don Slaught	.05
106 Jose Uribe	.05
107 Jeffrey Leonard	.05
108 Lee Guetterman	.05
109 Chris Bosio	.05
110 Barry Larkin	.15
111 Ruben Sierra	.08
112 Greg Swindell	.05
113 Gary Sheffield	.35
114 Lonnie Smith	.05
115 Chili Davis	.05
116 Damon Berryhill	.05
117 Tom Candiotti	.05
118 Kal Daniels	.05
119 Mark Gubicza	.05
120 Jim Deshaies	.05
121 Dwight Evans	.05
122 Mike Morgan	.05
123 Dan Pasqua	.05
124 Bryn Smith	.05
125 Doyle Alexander	.05
126 Howard Johnson	.05
127 Chuck Crim	.05
128 Darren Daulton	.08
129 Jeff Robinson	.05
130 Kirby Puckett	.50
131 Joe Magrane	.05
132 Jesse Barfield	.05
133 Mark Davis (Photo actually Dave Leiper)	.05
134 Dennis Eckersley	.10
135 Mike Krukow	.05
136 Jay Buhner	.12

137	Ozzie Guillen	.05
138	Rick Sutcliffe	.05
139	Wally Joyner	.10
140	Wade Boggs	.50
141	Jeff Treadway	.05
142	Cal Ripken	1.50
143	Dave Steib	.05
144	Pete Incaviglia	.05
145	Bob Walk	.05
146	Nelson Santovenia	.05
147	Mike Heath	.05
148	Willie Randolph	.05
149	Paul Kilgus	.05
150	Billy Hatcher	.05
151	Steve Farr	.05
152	Gregg Jefferies	.10
153	Randy Myers	.05
154	Garry Templeton	.05
155	Walt Weiss	.08
156	Terry Pendleton	.05
157	John Smiley	.05
158	Greg Gagne	.05
159	Lenny Dykstra	.08
160	Nelson Liriano	.05
161	Alvaro Espinoza	.05
162	Rick Reuschel	.05
163	Omar Vizquel	.08
164	Clay Parker	.05
165	Dan Plesac	.05
166	John Franco	.05
167	Scott Fletcher	.05
168	Cory Snyder	.05
169	Bo Jackson	.25
170	Tommy Gregg	.05
171	Jim Abbott	.10
172	Jerome Walton	.05
173	Doug Jones	.05
174	Todd Benzinger	.05
175	Frank White	.05
176	Craig Biggio	.10
177	John Dopson	.05
178	Alfredo Griffin	.05
179	Melido Perez	.05
180	Tim Burke	.05
181	Matt Nokes	.05
182	Gary Carter	.12
183	Ted Higuera	.05
184	Ken Howell	.05
185	Rey Quinones	.05
186	Wally Backman	.05
187	Tom Brunansky	.05
188	Steve Balboni	.05
189	Marvell Wynne	.05
190	Dave Henderson	.05
191	Don Robinson	.05
192	Ken Griffey, Jr.	4.00
193	Ivan Calderon	.05
194	Mike Bielecki	.05
195	Johnny Ray	.05
196	Rob Murphy	.05
197	Andres Thomas	.05
198	Phil Bradley	.05
199	Junior Felix	.05
200	Jeff Russell	.05
201	Mike LaValliere	.05
202	Kevin Gross	.05
203	Keith Moreland	.05
204	Mike Marshall	.05
205	Dwight Smith	.05
206	Jim Clancy	.05
207	Kevin Seitzer	.05
208	Keith Hernandez	.05
209	Bob Ojeda	.05
210	Ed Whitson	.05
211	Tony Phillips	.08
212	Milt Thompson	.05
213	Randy Kramer	.05
214	Randy Bush	.05
215	Randy Ready	.05
216	Duane Ward	.05
217	Jimmy Jones	.05
218	Scott Garrelts	.05
219	Scott Bankhead	.05
220	Lance McCullers	.05
221	B.J. Surhoff	.05
222	Chris Sabo	.05
223	Steve Buechele	.05
224	Joel Skinner	.05
225	Orel Hershiser	.08
226	Derek Lilliquist	.05
227	Claudell Washington	.05
228	Lloyd McClendon	.05
229	Felix Fermin	.05
230	Paul O'Neill	.12
231	Charlie Leibrandt	.05
232	Dave Smith	.05

233	Bob Stanley	.05
234	Tim Belcher	.05
235	Eric King	.05
236	Spike Owen	.05
237	Mike Henneman	.05
238	Juan Samuel	.05
239	Greg Brock	.05
240	John Kruk	.08
241	Glenn Wilson	.05
242	Jeff Reardon	.05
243	Todd Worrell	.05
244	Dave LaPoint	.05
245	Walt Terrell	.05
246	Mike Moore	.05
247	Kelly Downs	.05
248	Dave Valle	.05
249	Ron Kittle	.05
250	Steve Wilson	.05
251	Dick Schofield	.05
252	Marty Barrett	.05
253	Dion James	.05
254	Bob Milacki	.05
255	Ernie Whitt	.05
256	Kevin Brown	.05
257	R.J. Reynolds	.05
258	Tim Raines	.10
259	Frank Williams	.05
260	Jose Gonzalez	.05
261	Mitch Webster	.05
262	Ken Caminiti	.12
263	Bob Boone	.05
264	Dave Magadan	.05
265	Rick Aguilera	.05
266	Chris James	.05
267	Bob Welch	.05
268	Ken Dayley	.05
269	Junior Ortiz	.05
270	Allan Anderson	.05
271	Steve Jeltz	.05
272	George Bell	.05
273	Roberto Kelly	.08
274	Brett Butler	.12
275	Mike Schooler	.05
276	Ken Phelps	.05
277	Glenn Braggs	.05
278	Jose Rijo	.05
279	Bobby Witt	.05
280	Jerry Browne	.05
281	Kevin Mitchell	.10
282	Craig Worthington	.05
283	Greg Minton	.05
284	Nick Esasky	.05
285	John Farrell	.05
286	Rick Mahler	.05
287	Tom Gordon	.05
288	Gerald Young	.05
289	Jody Reed	.05
290	Jeff Hamilton	.05
291	Gerald Perry	.05
292	Hubie Brooks	.05
293	Bo Diaz	.05
294	Terry Puhl	.05
295	Jim Gantner	.05
296	Jeff Parrett	.05
297	Mike Boddicker	.05
298	Dan Gladden	.05
299	Tony Pena	.05
300	Checklist	.05
301	Tom Henke	.05
302	Pascual Perez	.05
303	Steve Bedrosian	.05
304	Ken Hill	.05
305	Jerry Reuss	.05
306	Jim Eisenreich	.05
307	Jack Howell	.05
308	Rick Cerone	.05
309	Tim Leary	.05
310	Joe Orsulak	.05
311	Jim Dwyer	.05
312	Geno Petralli	.05
313	Rick Honeycutt	.05
314	Tom Foley	.05
315	Kenny Rogers	.08
316	Mike Flanagan	.05
317	Bryan Harvey	.05
318	Billy Ripken	.05
319	Jeff Montgomery	.05
320	Erik Hanson	.05
321	Brian Downing	.05
322	Gregg Olson	.05
323	Terry Steinbach	.08
324	Sammy Sosa	8.00
325	Gene Harris	.05
326	Mike Devereaux	.05
327	Dennis Cook	.05
328	David Wells	.08

329	Checklist	.05
330	Kirt Manwaring	.05
331	Jim Presley	.05
332	Checklist	.05
333	Chuck Finley	.05
334	Rob Dibble	.05
335	Cecil Espy	.05
336	Dave Parker	.08

1989 Donruss Pop-Ups

DWIGHT GOODEN
METS – P

This set features the eighteen starters from the 1988 Major League All-Star game. The cards are designed with a perforated outline so each player can be popped up to stand upright. The flip side features a red, white, and blue "Cincinnati Reds All-Star Game" logo at the top, a league designation, and the player's name and position. The lower portion displays instructions for creating the base of the Pop-Up. The Pop-Ups were marketed in conjunction with All-Star and Warren Spahn Puzzle Cards.

		MT
Complete Set (20):		3.00
Common Player:		.20
Warren Spahn Puzzle:		1.00
(1)	Mark McGwire	.75
(2)	Jose Canseco	.60
(3)	Paul Molitor	.30
(4)	Rickey Henderson	.35
(5)	Cal Ripken, Jr.	1.00
(6)	Dave Winfield	.25
(7)	Wade Boggs	.50
(8)	Frank Viola	.20
(9)	Terry Steinbach	.20
(10)	Tom Kelly	.20
(11)	Will Clark	.45
(12)	Darryl Strawberry	.25
(13)	Ryne Sandberg	.60
(14)	Andre Dawson	.25
(15)	Ozzie Smith	.30
(16)	Vince Coleman	.20
(17)	Bobby Bonilla	.30
(18)	Dwight Gooden	.25
(19)	Gary Carter	.20
(20)	Whitey Herzog	.20

1989 Donruss Rookies

For the fourth straight year, Donruss issued a 56-card "Rookies" set in 1989. As in previous years, the set is similar in design to the regular Donruss set, except for a new "The Rookies" logo and a green and black border.

1990 Donruss

Donruss marked its 10th anniversary in the baseball card hobby with a 715-card set in 1990, up from previous 660-card sets. The standard-size cards feature bright red borders with the player's name in script at the top. The set includes 26 "Diamond Kings" (DK) in the checklist, 20 "Rated Rookies" (RR) and a Carl Yastrzemski puzzle. Each All-Star card back has two variations. The more common has the stats box headed "All-Star Performance". Slightly scarcer versions say "Recent Major League Performance", and are worth about twice the value of the correct version.

		MT
Complete Set (716):		10.00
Common Player:		.05
Carl Yastrzemski Puzzle:		1.00
Wax Box:		8.00
1	Bo Jackson (Diamond King)	.15
2	Steve Sax (DK)	.08
3a	Ruben Sierra (DK) (no vertical black line at top-right on back)	.25
3b	Ruben Sierra (DK) (vertical line at top-right on back)	.10
4	Ken Griffey, Jr. (DK)	.50
5	Mickey Tettleton (DK)	.08
6	Dave Stewart (DK)	.10
7	Jim Deshaies (DK)	.05
8	John Smoltz (DK)	.10
9	Mike Bielecki (DK)	.05
10a	Brian Downing (DK) (reversed negative)	.50
10b	Brian Downing (DK) (corrected)	.15
11	Kevin Mitchell (DK)	.08
12	Kelly Gruber (DK)	.05
13	Joe Magrane (DK)	.05
14	John Franco (DK)	.05
15	Ozzie Guillen (DK)	.08
16	Lou Whitaker (DK)	.08
17	John Smiley (DK)	.08
18	Howard Johnson (DK)	.08
19	Willie Randolph (DK)	.08
20	Chris Bosio (DK)	.05
21	Tommy Herr (DK)	.05
22	Dan Gladden (DK)	.05
23	Ellis Burks (DK)	.08
24	Pete O'Brien (DK)	.08
25	Bryn Smith (DK)	.05
26	Ed Whitson (DK)	.05
27	Checklist 1-27	.05
28	Robin Ventura (Rated Rookie)	.20
29	Todd Zeile (RR)	.15
30	Sandy Alomar, Jr. (RR)	.15
31	Kent Mercker (RR)	.20
32	Ben McDonald (RR)	.25

		MT
Complete Set (56):		7.00
Common Player:		.10
1	Gary Sheffield	.75
2	Gregg Jefferies	.25
3	Ken Griffey, Jr.	6.00
4	Tom Gordon	.10
5	Billy Spiers	.10
6	Deion Sanders	1.00
7	Donn Pall	.10
8	Steve Carter	.10
9	Francisco Oliveras	.10
10	Steve Wilson	.10
11	Bob Geren	.10
12	Tony Castillo	.10
13	Kenny Rogers	.20
14	Carlos Martinez	.10
15	Edgar Martinez	.25
16	Jim Abbott	.15
17	Torey Lovullo	.10
18	Mark Carreon	.15
19	Geronimo Berroa	.15
20	Luis Medina	.10
21	Sandy Alomar, Jr.	.30
22	Bob Milacki	.10
23	Joe Girardi	.15
24	German Gonzalez	.10
25	Craig Worthington	.10
26	Jerome Walton	.10
27	Gary Wayne	.10
28	Tim Jones	.10
29	Dante Bichette	1.50
30	Alexis Infante	.10
31	Ken Hill	.25
32	Dwight Smith	.10
33	Luis de los Santos	.10
34	Eric Yelding	.10
35	Gregg Olson	.10
36	Phil Stephenson	.10
37	Ken Patterson	.10
38	Rick Wrona	.10
39	Mike Brumley	.10
40	Cris Carpenter	.10
41	Jeff Brantley	.10
42	Ron Jones	.10
43	Randy Johnson	.90
44	Kevin Brown	.10
45	Ramon Martinez	.40
46	Greg Harris	.10
47	Steve Finley	.20
48	Randy Kramer	.10
49	Erik Hanson	.10
50	Matt Merullo	.10
51	Mike Devereaux	.10
52	Clay Parker	.10
53	Omar Vizquel	.15
54	Derek Lilliquist	.10
55	Junior Felix	.10
56	Checklist	.05

1989 Donruss Traded

Donruss issued its first "Traded" set in 1989, releasing a 56-card boxed set designed in the same style as the regular 1989 Donruss set. The set included a Stan Musial puzzle card and a checklist.

		MT
Complete Set (56):		3.00
Common Player:		.10
1	Jeffrey Leonard	.10
2	Jack Clark	.10
3	Kevin Gross	.10
4	Tommy Herr	.10
5	Bob Boone	.10
6	Rafael Palmeiro	.40
7	John Dopson	.10
8	Willie Randolph	.10
9	Chris Brown	.10
10	Wally Backman	.10
11	Steve Ontiveros	.10
12	Eddie Murray	.30
13	Lance McCullers	.10
14	Spike Owen	.10
15	Rob Murphy	.10
16	Pete O'Brien	.10
17	Ken Williams	.10
18	Nick Esasky	.10
19	Nolan Ryan	1.50
20	Brian Holton	.10
21	Mike Moore	.10
22	Joel Skinner	.10
23	Steve Sax	.10
24	Rick Mahler	.10
25	Mike Aldrete	.10
26	Jesse Orosco	.10
27	Dave LaPoint	.10
28	Walt Terrell	.10
29	Eddie Williams	.10
30	Mike Devereaux	.10
31	Julio Franco	.15
32	Jim Clancy	.10
33	Felix Fermin	.10
34	Curtis Wilkerson	.10
35	Bert Blyleven	.10
36	Mel Hall	.10
37	Eric King	.10
38	Mitch Williams	.10
39	Jamie Moyer	.10
40	Rick Rhoden	.10
41	Phil Bradley	.10
42	Paul Kilgus	.10
43	Milt Thompson	.10
44	Jerry Browne	.10
45	Bruce Hurst	.10
46	Claudell Washington	.10
47	Todd Benzinger	.10
48	Steve Balboni	.10
49	Oddibe McDowell	.10
50	Charles Hudson	.10
51	Ron Kittle	.10
52	Andy Hawkins	.10
53	Tom Brookens	.10
54	Tom Niedenfuer	.10
55	Jeff Parrett	.10
56	Checklist	.10

Values shown reflect the market as of January, 1999. On-field performances of current players in the 1999 baseball season are not factored in.

#	Player	Price
33a	*Juan Gonzalez (reversed negative) (RR)*	4.00
33b	*Juan Gonzalez (RR) (corrected)*	2.00
34	*Eric Anthony (RR)*	.15
35	*Mike Fetters (RR)*	.10
36	*Marquis Grissom (RR)*	.50
37	*Greg Vaughn (RR)*	.20
38	*Brian Dubois (RR)*	.08
39	*Steve Avery (RR)*	.20
40	*Mark Gardner (RR)*	.15
41	Andy Benes (RR)	.20
42	*Delino DeShields (RR)*	.15
43	*Scott Coolbaugh (RR)*	.05
44	*Pat Combs (RR)*	.08
45	*Alex Sanchez (RR)*	.05
46	*Kelly Mann (RR)*	.05
47	*Julio Machado (RR)*	.08
48	Pete Incaviglia	.05
49	Shawon Dunston	.08
50	Jeff Treadway	.05
51	Jeff Ballard	.05
52	Claudell Washington	.05
53	Juan Samuel	.05
54	John Smiley	.05
55	Rob Deer	.05
56	Geno Petralli	.05
57	Chris Bosio	.08
58	Carlton Fisk	.12
59	Kirt Manwaring	.05
60	Chet Lemon	.05
61	Bo Jackson	.25
62	Doyle Alexander	.05
63	Pedro Guerrero	.05
64	Allan Anderson	.05
65	Greg Harris	.05
66	Mike Greenwell	.08
67	Walt Weiss	.05
68	Wade Boggs	.25
69	Jim Clancy	.05
70	*Junior Felix*	.08
71	Barry Larkin	.12
72	Dave LaPoint	.05
73	Joel Skinner	.05
74	Jesse Barfield	.05
75	Tommy Herr	.05
76	Ricky Jordan	.05
77	Eddie Murray	.20
78	Steve Sax	.05
79	Tim Belcher	.05
80	Danny Jackson	.05
81	Kent Hrbek	.10
82	Milt Thompson	.05
83	Brook Jacoby	.05
84	Mike Marshall	.05
85	Kevin Seitzer	.05
86	Tony Gwynn	.35
87	Dave Steib	.05
88	Dave Smith	.05
89	Bret Saberhagen	.08
90	Alan Trammell	.10
91	Tony Phillips	.08
92	Doug Drabek	.05
93	Jeffrey Leonard	.05
94	Wally Joyner	.10
95	Carney Lansford	.05
96	Cal Ripken, Jr.	.60
97	Andres Galarraga	.15
98	Kevin Mitchell	.08
99	Howard Johnson	.08
100a	Checklist 28-129	.05
100b	Checklist 28-125	.05
101	Melido Perez	.05
102	Spike Owen	.05
103	Paul Molitor	.25
104	Geronimo Berroa	.05
105	Ryne Sandberg	.25
106	Bryn Smith	.05
107	Steve Buechele	.05
108	Jim Abbott	.10
109	Alvin Davis	.05
110	Lee Smith	.08
111	Roberto Alomar	.25
112	Rick Reuschel	.05
113a	Kelly Gruber (Born 2/22)	.05
113b	Kelly Gruber (Born 2/26)	.25
114	Joe Carter	.10
115	Jose Rijo	.05
116	Greg Minton	.05
117	Bob Ojeda	.05
118	Glenn Davis	.05
119	Jeff Reardon	.05
120	Kurt Stillwell	.05
121	John Smoltz	.15
122	Dwight Evans	.08
123	Eric Yelding	.08
124	John Franco	.05
125	Jose Canseco	.20
126	Barry Bonds	.30
127	Lee Guetterman	.05
128	Jack Clark	.05
129	Dave Valle	.05
130	Hubie Brooks	.05
131	Ernest Riles	.05
132	Mike Morgan	.05
133	Steve Jeltz	.05
134	Jeff Robinson	.05
135	Ozzie Guillen	.05
136	Chili Davis	.08
137	Mitch Webster	.05
138	Jerry Browne	.05
139	Bo Diaz	.05
140	Robby Thompson	.05
141	Craig Worthington	.05
142	Julio Franco	.08
143	Brian Holman	.05
144	George Brett	.25
145	Tom Glavine	.20
146	Robin Yount	.20
147	Gary Carter	.10
148	Ron Kittle	.05
149	Tony Fernandez	.05
150	Dave Stewart	.08
151	Gary Gaetti	.08
152	Kevin Elster	.08
153	Gerald Perry	.05
154	Jesse Orosco	.05
155	Wally Backman	.05
156	Dennis Martinez	.08
157	Rick Sutcliffe	.05
158	Greg Maddux	.60
159	Andy Hawkins	.05
160	John Kruk	.08
161	Jose Oquendo	.05
162	John Dopson	.05
163	Joe Magrane	.05
164	Billy Ripken	.05
165	Fred Manrique	.05
166	Nolan Ryan	.60
167	Damon Berryhill	.05
168	Dale Murphy	.10
169	Mickey Tettleton	.08
170a	Kirk McCaskill (Born 4/19)	.05
170b	Kirk McCaskill (Born 4/9)	.25
171	Dwight Gooden	.10
172	Jose Lind	.05
173	B.J. Surhoff	.05
174	Ruben Sierra	.08
175	Dan Plesac	.05
176	Dan Pasqua	.05
177	Kelly Downs	.05
178	Matt Nokes	.05
179	Luis Aquino	.05
180	Frank Tanana	.05
181	Tony Pena	.05
182	Dan Gladden	.05
183	Bruce Hurst	.05
184	Roger Clemens	.35
185	Mark McGwire	1.00
186	Rob Murphy	.05
187	Jim Deshaies	.05
188	Fred McGriff	.15
189	Rob Dibble	.05
190	Don Mattingly	.35
191	Felix Fermin	.05
192	Roberto Kelly	.08
193	Dennis Cook	.05
194	Darren Daulton	.08
195	Alfredo Griffin	.05
196	Eric Plunk	.05
197	Orel Hershiser	.10
198	Paul O'Neill	.15
199	Randy Bush	.05
200a	Checklist 130-231	.05
200b	Checklist 126-223	.05
201	Ozzie Smith	.15
202	Pete O'Brien	.05
203	Jay Howell	.05
204	Mark Gubicza	.05
205	Ed Whitson	.05
206	George Bell	.08
207	Mike Scott	.05
208	Charlie Leibrandt	.05
209	Mike Heath	.05
210	Dennis Eckersley	.10
211	Mike LaValliere	.05
212	Darnell Coles	.05
213	Lance Parrish	.08
214	Mike Moore	.05
215	*Steve Finley*	.20
216	Tim Raines	.10
217a	Scott Garrelts (Born 10/20)	.05
217b	Scott Garrelts (Born 10/30)	.25
218	Kevin McReynolds	.05
219	Dave Gallagher	.05
220	Tim Wallach	.05
221	Chuck Crim	.05
222	Lonnie Smith	.05
223	Andre Dawson	.12
224	Nelson Santovenia	.05
225	Rafael Palmeiro	.12
226	Devon White	.05
227	Harold Reynolds	.05
228	Ellis Burks	.10
229	Mark Parent	.05
230	Will Clark	.25
231	Jimmy Key	.08
232	John Farrell	.05
233	Eric Davis	.10
234	Johnny Ray	.05
235	Darryl Strawberry	.12
236	Bill Doran	.05
237	Greg Gagne	.05
238	Jim Eisenreich	.05
239	Tommy Gregg	.05
240	Marty Barrett	.05
241	Rafael Ramirez	.05
242	Chris Sabo	.08
243	Dave Henderson	.05
244	Andy Van Slyke	.08
245	Alvaro Espinoza	.05
246	Garry Templeton	.05
247	Gene Harris	.05
248	Kevin Gross	.05
249	Brett Butler	.08
250	Willie Randolph	.05
251	Roger McDowell	.05
252	Rafael Belliard	.05
253	Steve Rosenberg	.05
254	Jack Howell	.05
255	Marvell Wynne	.05
256	Tom Candiotti	.05
257	Todd Benzinger	.05
258	Don Robinson	.05
259	Phil Bradley	.05
260	Cecil Espy	.05
261	Scott Bankhead	.05
262	Frank White	.05
263	Andres Thomas	.05
264	Glenn Braggs	.05
265	David Cone	.10
266	Bobby Thigpen	.05
267	Nelson Liriano	.05
268	Terry Steinbach	.05
269	Kirby Puckett	.35
270	Gregg Jefferies	.15
271	Jeff Blauser	.05
272	Cory Snyder	.05
273	Roy Smith	.05
274	Tom Foley	.05
275	Mitch Williams	.05
276	Paul Kilgus	.05
277	Don Slaught	.05
278	Von Hayes	.05
279	Vince Coleman	.05
280	Mike Boddicker	.05
281	Ken Dayley	.05
282	Mike Devereaux	.05
283	*Kenny Rogers*	.10
284	Jeff Russell	.05
285	*Jerome Walton*	.08
286	Derek Lilliquist	.05
287	Joe Orsulak	.05
288	Dick Schofield	.05
289	Ron Darling	.05
290	Bobby Bonilla	.15
291	Jim Gantner	.05
292	Bobby Witt	.05
293	Greg Brock	.05
294	Ivan Calderon	.05
295	Steve Bedrosian	.05
296	Mike Henneman	.05
297	Tom Gordon	.05
298	Lou Whitaker	.08
299	Terry Pendleton	.05
300a	Checklist 232-333	.05
300b	Checklist 224-321	.05
301	Juan Berenguer	.05
302	Mark Davis	.05
303	Nick Esasky	.05
304	Rickey Henderson	.15
305	Rick Cerone	.05
306	Craig Biggio	.15
307	Duane Ward	.05
308	Tom Browning	.05
309	Walt Terrell	.05
310	Greg Swindell	.05
311	Dave Righetti	.05

No.	Player	Price	No.	Player	Price	No.	Player	Price
312	Mike Maddux	.05	405b	Sergio Valdez (corrected)	.05	500b	Checklist 420-517	.05
313	Len Dykstra	.08	406	Mark Williamson	.05	501	Gary Sheffield	.25
314	Jose Gonzalez	.05	407	Glenn Hoffman	.05	502	*Terry Bross*	.05
315	Steve Balboni	.05	408	*Jeff Innis*	.05	503	*Jerry Kutzler*	.05
316	Mike Scioscia	.05	409	Randy Kramer	.05	504	Lloyd Moseby	.05
317	Ron Oester	.05	410	Charlie O'Brien	.05	505	Curt Young	.05
318	*Gary Wayne*	.05	411	Charlie Hough	.05	506	Al Newman	.05
319	Todd Worrell	.05	412	Gus Polidor	.05	507	Keith Miller	.05
320	Doug Jones	.05	413	Ron Karkovice	.05	508	*Mike Stanton*	.15
321	Jeff Hamilton	.05	414	Trevor Wilson	.08	509	Rich Yett	.05
322	Danny Tartabull	.05	415	*Kevin Ritz*	.10	510	*Tim Drummond*	.05
323	Chris James	.05	416	Gary Thurman	.05	511	Joe Hesketh	.05
324	Mike Flanagan	.05	417	Jeff Robinson	.05	512	*Rick Wrona*	.10
325	Gerald Young	.05	418	Scott Terry	.05	513	Luis Salazar	.05
326	Bob Boone	.08	419	Tim Laudner	.05	514	Hal Morris	.05
327	Frank Williams	.05	420	Dennis Rasmussen	.05	515	Terry Mulholland	.08
328	Dave Parker	.08	421	Luis Rivera	.05	516	John Morris	.05
329	Sid Bream	.05	422	Jim Corsi	.05	517	Carlos Quintana	.05
330	Mike Schooler	.05	423	Dennis Lamp	.05	518	Frank DiPino	.05
331	Bert Blyleven	.08	424	Ken Caminiti	.10	519	Randy Milligan	.05
332	Bob Welch	.05	425	David Wells	.08	520	Chad Kreuter	.05
333	Bob Milacki	.05	426	Norm Charlton	.05	521	Mike Jeffcoat	.05
334	Tim Burke	.05	427	Deion Sanders	.25	522	Mike Harkey	.05
335	Jose Uribe	.05	428	Dion James	.05	523a	Andy Nezelek (Born 1985)	.05
336	Randy Myers	.05	429	Chuck Cary	.05	523b	Andy Nezelek (Born 1965)	.25
337	Eric King	.05	430	Ken Howell	.05	524	Dave Schmidt	.05
338	Mark Langston	.10	431	Steve Lake	.05	525	Tony Armas	.05
339	Ted Higuera	.05	432	Kal Daniels	.05	526	Barry Lyons	.05
340	Oddibe McDowell	.05	433	Lance McCullers	.05	527	*Rick Reed*	.05
341	Lloyd McClendon	.05	434	Lenny Harris	.05	528	Jerry Reuss	.05
342	Pascual Perez	.05	435	*Scott Scudder*	.05	529	*Dean Palmer*	.25
343	Kevin Brown	.08	436	Gene Larkin	.05	530	*Jeff Peterek*	.05
344	Chuck Finley	.05	437	Dan Quisenberry	.05	531	*Carlos Martinez*	.08
345	Erik Hanson	.05	438	*Steve Olin*	.05	532	Atlee Hammaker	.05
346	Rich Gedman	.05	439	Mickey Hatcher	.05	533	Mike Brumley	.05
347	Bip Roberts	.05	440	Willie Wilson	.05	534	Terry Leach	.05
348	Matt Williams	.20	441	Mark Grant	.05	535	*Doug Strange*	.05
349	Tom Henke	.05	442	Mookie Wilson	.05	536	Jose DeLeon	.05
350	Brad Komminsk	.05	443	Alex Trevino	.05	537	Shane Rawley	.05
351	Jeff Reed	.05	444	Pat Tabler	.05	538	Joey Cora	.10
352	Brian Downing	.05	445	Dave Bergman	.05	539	Eric Hetzel	.05
353	Frank Viola	.05	446	Todd Burns	.05	540	Gene Nelson	.05
354	Terry Puhl	.05	447	R.J. Reynolds	.05	541	Wes Gardner	.05
355	Brian Harper	.05	448	Jay Buhner	.08	542	Mark Portugal	.05
356	Steve Farr	.05	449	*Lee Stevens*	.10	543	Al Leiter	.05
357	Joe Boever	.05	450	Ron Hassey	.05	544	Jack Armstrong	.05
358	Danny Heep	.05	451	Bob Melvin	.05	545	Greg Cadaret	.05
359	Larry Andersen	.05	452	Dave Martinez	.05	546	Rod Nichols	.05
360	Rolando Roomes	.05	453	*Greg Litton*	.05	547	Luis Polonia	.05
361	Mike Gallego	.05	454	Mark Carreon	.05	548	Charlie Hayes	.05
362	Bob Kipper	.05	455	Scott Fletcher	.05	549	Dickie Thon	.05
363	Clay Parker	.05	456	Otis Nixon	.05	550	Tim Crews	.05
364	Mike Pagliarulo	.05	457	*Tony Fossas*	.05	551	Dave Winfield	.20
365	Ken Griffey, Jr.	2.00	458	John Russell	.05	552	Mike Davis	.05
366	Rex Hudler	.05	459	Paul Assenmacher	.05	553	Ron Robinson	.05
367	Pat Sheridan	.05	460	Zane Smith	.05	554	Carmen Castillo	.05
368	Kirk Gibson	.08	461	*Jack Daugherty*	.05	555	John Costello	.05
369	Jeff Parrett	.05	462	*Rich Monteleone*	.05	556	Bud Black	.05
370	Bob Walk	.05	463	Greg Briley	.05	557	Rick Dempsey	.05
371	Ken Patterson	.05	464	Mike Smithson	.05	558	Jim Acker	.05
372	Bryan Harvey	.05	465	Benito Santiago	.08	559	Eric Show	.05
373	Mike Bielecki	.05	466	*Jeff Brantley*	.05	560	Pat Borders	.05
374	*Tom Magrann*	.05	467	Jose Nunez	.05	561	Danny Darwin	.05
375	Rick Mahler	.05	468	Scott Bailes	.05	562	*Rick Luecken*	.05
376	Craig Lefferts	.05	469	Ken Griffey	.08	563	Edwin Nunez	.05
377	Gregg Olson	.05	470	Bob McClure	.05	564	Felix Jose	.05
378	Jamie Moyer	.05	471	Mackey Sasser	.05	565	John Cangelosi	.05
379	Randy Johnson	.25	472	Glenn Wilson	.05	566	Billy Swift	.05
380	Jeff Montgomery	.05	473	*Kevin Tapani*	.25	567	Bill Schroeder	.05
381	Marty Clary	.05	474	Bill Buckner	.05	568	Stan Javier	.05
382	*Bill Spiers*	.05	475	Ron Gant	.10	569	Jim Traber	.05
383	Dave Magadan	.05	476	Kevin Romine	.05	570	Wallace Johnson	.05
384	*Greg Hibbard*	.05	477	Juan Agosto	.05	571	Donell Nixon	.05
385	Ernie Whitt	.05	478	Herm Winningham	.05	572	Sid Fernandez	.05
386	Rick Honeycutt	.05	479	Storm Davis	.05	573	Lance Johnson	.08
387	Dave West	.05	480	Jeff King	.10	574	Andy McGaffigan	.05
388	Keith Hernandez	.05	481	*Kevin Mmahat*	.05	575	Mark Knudson	.05
389	Jose Alvarez	.05	482	Carmelo Martinez	.05	576	*Tommy Greene*	.20
390	Albert Belle	.50	483	*Omar Vizquel*	.10	577	Mark Grace	.15
391	Rick Aguilera	.05	484	Jim Dwyer	.05	578	*Larry Walker*	1.50
392	Mike Fitzgerald	.05	485	Bob Knepper	.05	579	Mike Stanley	.05
393	*Dwight Smith*	.05	486	Dave Anderson	.05	580	Mike Witt	.05
394	*Steve Wilson*	.05	487	Ron Jones	.05	581	Scott Bradley	.05
395	*Bob Geren*	.05	488	Jay Bell	.05	582	Greg Harris	.05
396	Randy Ready	.05	489	*Sammy Sosa*	4.00	583a	Kevin Hickey (black stripe over top of "K" vertical stroke)	.05
397	Ken Hill	.08	490	*Kent Anderson*	.05			
398	Jody Reed	.05	491	Domingo Ramos	.05	583b	Kevin Hickey (black stripe under "K")	.05
399	Tom Brunansky	.05	492	Dave Clark	.05			
400a	Checklist 334-435	.05	493	Tim Birtsas	.05	584	Lee Mazzilli	.05
400b	Checklist 322-419	.05	494	Ken Oberkfell	.05	585	Jeff Pico	.05
401	Rene Gonzales	.05	495	Larry Sheets	.05	586	*Joe Oliver*	.05
402	Harold Baines	.08	496	Jeff Kunkel	.05	587	Willie Fraser	.05
403	Cecilio Guante	.05	497	Jim Presley	.05	588	Puzzle card(Carl Yastrzemski)	.05
404	Joe Girardi	.08	498	Mike Macfarlane	.05			
405a	*Sergio Valdez* (black line crosses S in Sergio)	.25	499	Pete Smith	.05	589	Kevin Bass	.05
			500a	Checklist 436-537	.05			

590	John Moses	.05
591	Tom Pagnozzi	.05
592	*Tony Castillo*	.05
593	Jerald Clark	.05
594	Dan Schatzeder	.05
595	Luis Quinones	.05
596	Pete Harnisch	.08
597	Gary Redus	.05
598	Mel Hall	.05
599	Rick Schu	.05
600a	Checklist 538-639	.05
600b	Checklist 518-617	.05
601	Mike Kingery	.05
602	Terry Kennedy	.05
603	Mike Sharperson	.05
604	Don Carman	.05
605	Jim Gott	.05
606	Dunn Pall	.05
607	Rance Mulliniks	.05
608	Curt Wilkerson	.05
609	Mike Felder	.05
610	Guillermo Hernandez	.05
611	Candy Maldonado	.05
612	Mark Thurmond	.05
613	Rick Leach	.05
614	Jerry Reed	.05
615	Franklin Stubbs	.05
616	Billy Hatcher	.05
617	Don August	.05
618	Tim Teufel	.05
619	Shawn Hillegas	.05
620	Manny Lee	.05
621	Gary Ward	.05
622	*Mark Guthrie*	.05
623	Jeff Musselman	.05
624	Mark Lemke	.05
625	Fernando Valenzuela	.08
626	*Paul Sorrento*	.20
627	Glenallen Hill	.08
628	Les Lancaster	.05
629	Vance Law	.05
630	Randy Velarde	.08
631	Todd Frohwirth	.05
632	Willie McGee	.08
633	Oil Can Boyd	.05
634	Cris Carpenter	.05
635	Brian Holton	.05
636	Tracy Jones	.05
637	Terry Steinbach (AS)	.08
638	Brady Anderson	.12
639a	Jack Morris (black line crosses J of Jack)	.25
639b	Jack Morris (corrected)	.08
640	*Jaime Navarro*	.05
641	Darrin Jackson	.05
642	*Mike Dyer*	.05
643	Mike Schmidt	.25
644	Henry Cotto	.05
645	John Cerutti	.05
646	*Francisco Cabrera*	.05
647	Scott Sanderson	.05
648	Brian Meyer	.05
649	Ray Searage	.05
650	Bo Jackson (AS)	.15
651	Steve Lyons	.05
652	Mike LaCoss	.05
653	Ted Power	.05
654	Howard Johnson (AS)	.05
655	*Mauro Gozzo*	.05
656	*Mike Blowers*	.15
657	Paul Gibson	.05
658	Neal Heaton	.05
659a	Nolan Ryan 5,000 K's (King of Kings (#665) back)	2.50
659b	Nolan Ryan 5,000 K's (correct back)	.50
660a	Harold Baines (AS) (black line through star on front, Recent Major League Performance on back)	.50
660b	Harold Baines (AS) (black line through star on front, All-Star Game Performance on back)	1.50
660c	Harold Baines (AS) (black line behind star on front, Recent Major League Performance on back)	.75
660d	Harold Baines (AS) (black line behind star on front, All-Star Game Performance on back)	.10
661	Gary Pettis	.05
662	*Clint Zavaras*	.05
663	Rick Reuschel (AS)	.05
664	Alejandro Pena	.05

665a	Nolan Ryan (King of Kings) 5,000 K's (#659) back)	2.50
665b	Nolan Ryan (King of Kings) (correct back)	.50
665c	Nolan Ryan (King of Kings) (no number on back)	1.00
666	Ricky Horton	.05
667	Curt Schilling	.05
668	Bill Landrum	.05
669	Todd Stottlemyre	.05
670	Tim Leary	.05
671	*John Wetteland*	.25
672	Calvin Schiraldi	.05
673	Ruben Sierra (AS)	.05
674	Pedro Guerrero (AS)	.05
675	Ken Phelps	.05
676	Cal Ripken (AS)	.25
677	Denny Walling	.05
678	Goose Gossage	.05
679	*Gary Mielke*	.05
680	Bill Bathe	.05
681	Tom Lawless	.05
682	*Xavier Hernandez*	.15
683	Kirby Puckett (AS)	.20
684	Mariano Duncan	.05
685	Ramon Martinez	.10
686	Tim Jones	.05
687	Tom Filer	.05
688	Steve Lombardozzi	.05
689	*Bernie Williams*	1.00
690	*Chip Hale*	.05
691	*Beau Allred*	.05
692	Ryne Sandberg (AS)	.25
693	*Jeff Huson*	.10
694	Curt Ford	.05
695	Eric Davis (AS)	.05
696	Scott Lusader	.05
697	Mark McGwire (AS)	.50
698	*Steve Cummings*	.05
699	*George Canale*	.05
700a	Checklist 640-715/BC1-BC26	.05
700b	Checklist 640-716/BC1-BC26	.05
700c	Checklist 618-716	.05
701	Julio Franco (AS)	.05
702	*Dave Johnson*	.05
703	Dave Stewart (AS)	.05
704	*Dave Justice*	.40
705	Tony Gwynn (AS)	.15
706	Greg Myers	.05
707	Will Clark (AS)	.10
708	Benito Santiago (AS)	.05
709	Larry McWilliams	.05
710	Ozzie Smith (AS)	.10
711	*John Olerud*	.25
712	Wade Boggs (AS)	.10
713	*Gary Eave*	.05
714	Bob Tewksbury	.05
715	Kevin Mitchell (AS)	.05
716	A. Bartlett Giamatti	.25

1990 Donruss Grand Slammers

For the second consecutive year Donruss produced a set in honor of players who hit grand slams in the previous season. The cards are styled after the 1990 Donruss regular issue. The cards were inserted into 1990 Donruss factory sets, and one card per cello pack.

		MT
Complete Set (12):		2.00
Common Player:		.10
1	Matt Williams	.30
2	Jeffrey Leonard	.10
3	Chris James	.10
4	Mark McGwire	1.00
5	Dwight Evans	.10
6	Will Clark	.25
7	Mike Scioscia	.10
8	Todd Benzinger	.10
9	Fred McGriff	.30
10	Kevin Bass	.10
11	Jack Clark	.10
12	Bo Jackson	.25

1990 Donruss MVP

This special 26-card set includes one player from each Major League team. Numbered BC-1 (the "BC" stands for "Bonus Card") through BC-26, the cards from this set were randomly packed in 1990 Donruss wax packs and were not available in factory sets or other types of packaging. The red-bordered cards are similar in design to the regular 1990 Donruss set, except the player photos are set against a special background made up of the "MVP" logo.

		MT
Complete Set (26):		1.25
Common Player:		.10
1	Bo Jackson	.25
2	Howard Johnson	.10
3	Dave Stewart	.10
4	Tony Gwynn	.35
5	Orel Hershiser	.10
6	Pedro Guerrero	.10
7	Tim Raines	.12
8	Kirby Puckett	.35
9	Alvin Davis	.10
10	Ryne Sandberg	.40
11	Kevin Mitchell	.10
12a	John Smoltz (photo of Tom Glavine)	2.00
12b	John Smoltz (corrected)	.40
13	George Bell	.10
14	Julio Franco	.10
15	Paul Molitor	.25
16	Bobby Bonilla	.15
17	Mike Greenwell	.10
18	Cal Ripken	.60
19	Carlton Fisk	.15
20	Chili Davis	.10
21	Glenn Davis	.10
22	Steve Sax	.10
23	Eric Davis	.15
24	Greg Swindell	.10
25	Von Hayes	.10
26	Alan Trammell	.12

1990 Donruss Diamond Kings Supers

Donruss made this set available through a mail-in offer. Three wrappers, $10 and $2 for postage were necessary to obtain this set. The cards are exactly the same design as the regular Donruss Diamond Kings except they measure approximately 5" x 6-3/4" in size. The artwork of Dick Perez is featured.

		MT
Complete Set (26):		6.00
Common Player:		.10
1	Bo Jackson	.50
2	Steve Sax	.10
3	Ruben Sierra	.10
4	Ken Griffey, Jr.	4.00
5	Mickey Tettleton	.10
6	Dave Stewart	.10
7	Jim Deshaies	.10
8	John Smoltz	.25
9	Mike Bielecki	.10
10	Brian Downing	.10
11	Kevin Mitchell	.10
12	Kelly Gruber	.10
13	Joe Magrane	.10
14	John Franco	.10
15	Ozzie Guillen	.10
16	Lou Whitaker	.10
17	John Smiley	.10
18	Howard Johnson	.10
19	Willie Randolph	.10
20	Chris Bosio	.10
21	Tommy Herr	.10
22	Dan Gladden	.10
23	Ellis Burks	.20
24	Pete O'Brien	.10
25	Bryn Smith	.10
26	Ed Whitson	.10

1990 Donruss Best A.L.

This 144-card set features the top players of the American League. The 2-1/2" x 3-1/2" cards feature the same front design as the regular Donruss set, exception with blue borders instead of red. Backs feature a yellow frame with complete statistics and biographical information provided. This marks the first year that Donruss divided its baseball-best issue into two sets designated by league.

		MT
Complete Set (144):		6.00
Common Player:		.05
1	Ken Griffey, Jr.	1.50
2	Bob Milacki	.05
3	Mike Boddicker	.05
4	Bert Blyleven	.05
5	Carlton Fisk	.10
6	Greg Swindell	.05
7	Alan Trammell	.10
8	Mark Davis	.05
9	Chris Bosio	.05
10	Gary Gaetti	.08
11	Matt Nokes	.05
12	Dennis Eckersley	.08
13	Kevin Brown	.05
14	Tom Henke	.05
15	Mickey Tettleton	.08
16	Jody Reed	.05
17	Mark Langston	.08
18	Melido Perez	.05

19	John Farrell	.05
20	Tony Phillips	.08
21	Bret Saberhagen	.08
22	Robin Yount	.10
23	Kirby Puckett	.25
24	Steve Sax	.05
25	Dave Stewart	.10
26	Alvin Davis	.05
27	Geno Petralli	.05
28	Mookie Wilson	.05
29	Jeff Ballard	.05
30	Ellis Burks	.10
31	Wally Joyner	.08
32	Bobby Thigpen	.05
33	Keith Hernandez	.05
34	Jack Morris	.05
35	George Brett	.20
36	Dan Plesac	.05
37	Brian Harper	.05
38	Don Mattingly	.45
39	Dave Henderson	.05
40	Scott Bankhead	.05
41	Rafael Palmeiro	.10
42	Jimmy Key	.05
43	Gregg Olson	.05
44	Tony Pena	.05
45	Jack Howell	.05
46	Eric King	.05
47	Cory Snyder	.05
48	Frank Tanana	.05
49	Nolan Ryan	.60
50	Bob Boone	.05
51	Dave Parker	.08
52	Allan Anderson	.05
53	Tim Leary	.05
54	Mark McGwire	1.50
55	Dave Valle	.05
56	Fred McGriff	.20
57	Cal Ripken	1.50
58	Roger Clemens	.25
59	Lance Parrish	.05
60	Robin Ventura	.10
61	Doug Jones	.05
62	Lloyd Moseby	.05
63	Bo Jackson	.15
64	Paul Molitor	.10
65	Kent Hrbek	.08
66	Mel Hall	.05
67	Bob Welch	.05
68	Erik Hanson	.05
69	Harold Baines	.05
70	Junior Felix	.05
71	Craig Worthington	.05
72	Jeff Reardon	.05
73	Johnny Ray	.05
74	Ozzie Guillen	.05
75	Brook Jacoby	.05
76	Chet Lemon	.05
77	Mark Gubicza	.05
78	B.J. Surhoff	.05
79	Rick Aguilera	.05
80	Pascual Perez	.05
81	Jose Canseco	.35
82	Mike Schooler	.05
83	Jeff Huson	.05
84	Kelly Gruber	.05
85	Randy Milligan	.05
86	Wade Boggs	.35
87	Dave Winfield	.15
88	Scott Fletcher	.05
89	Tom Candiotti	.05
90	Mike Heath	.05
91	Kevin Seitzer	.05
92	Ted Higuera	.05
93	Kevin Tapani	.05
94	Roberto Kelly	.05
95	Walt Weiss	.05
96	Checklist	.05
97	Sandy Alomar	.10
98	Pete O'Brien	.05
99	Jeff Russell	.05
100	John Olerud	.12
101	Pete Harnisch	.05
102	Dwight Evans	.05
103	Chuck Finley	.05
104	Sammy Sosa	1.00
105	Mike Henneman	.05
106	Kurt Stillwell	.05
107	Greg Vaughn	.08
108	Dan Gladden	.05
109	Jesse Barfield	.05
110	Willie Randolph	.05
111	Randy Johnson	.20
112	Julio Franco	.08
113	Tony Fernandez	.05
114	Ben McDonald	.05

115	Mike Greenwell	.08
116	Luis Polonia	.05
117	Carney Lansford	.05
118	Bud Black	.05
119	Lou Whitaker	.05
120	Jim Eisenreich	.05
121	Gary Sheffield	.10
122	Shane Mack	.05
123	Alvaro Espinoza	.05
124	Rickey Henderson	.15
125	Jeffrey Leonard	.05
126	Gary Pettis	.05
127	Dave Steib	.05
128	Danny Tartabull	.05
129	Joe Orsulak	.05
130	Tom Brunansky	.05
131	Dick Schofield	.05
132	Candy Maldonado	.05
133	Cecil Fielder	.10
134	Terry Shumpert	.05
135	Greg Gagne	.05
136	Dave Righetti	.05
137	Terry Steinbach	.05
138	Harold Reynolds	.05
139	George Bell	.05
140	Carlos Quintana	.05
141	Ivan Calderon	.05
142	Greg Brock	.05
143	Ruben Sierra	.08
144	Checklist	.05

1990 Donruss Best N.L.

This 144-card set features the top players in the National League for 1990. The 2-1/2" x 3-1/2" cards feature the same design as the regular 1990 Donruss cards, except they have blue, rather than red borders. Traded players are featured with their new teams. This set, along with the A.L. Best set, was available at select retail stores and within the hobby.

		MT
Complete Set (144):		6.00
Common Player:		.05
1	Eric Davis	.10
2	Tom Glavine	.08
3	Mike Bielecki	.05
4	Jim Deshaies	.05
5	Mike Scioscia	.05
6	Spike Owen	.05
7	Dwight Gooden	.12
8	Ricky Jordan	.05
9	Doug Drabek	.05
10	Bryn Smith	.05
11	Tony Gwynn	.40
12	John Burkett	.05
13	Nick Esasky	.05
14	Greg Maddux	.75
15	Joe Oliver	.05
16	Mike Scott	.05
17	Tim Belcher	.05
18	Kevin Gross	.05
19	Howard Johnson	.08
20	Darren Daulton	.08
21	John Smiley	.05
22	Ken Dayley	.05
23	Craig Lefferts	.05
24	Will Clark	.25
25	Greg Olson	.05
26	Ryne Sandberg	.45
27	Tom Browning	.05
28	Eric Anthony	.08
29	Juan Samuel	.05
30	Dennis Martinez	.08
31	Kevin Elster	.05
32	Tom Herr	.05
33	Sid Bream	.05
34	Terry Pendleton	.05
35	Roberto Alomar	.30
36	Kevin Bass	.05
37	Jim Presley	.05
38	Les Lancaster	.05
39	Paul O'Neill	.10
40	Dave Smith	.05
41	Kirk Gibson	.05
42	Tim Burke	.05
43	David Cone	.08

44	Ken Howell	.05
45	Barry Bonds	.50
46	Joe Magrane	.05
47	Andy Benes	.08
48	Gary Carter	.10
49	Pat Combs	.05
50	John Smoltz	.08
51	Mark Grace	.15
52	Barry Larkin	.15
53	Danny Darwin	.05
54	Orel Hershiser	.08
55	Tim Wallach	.05
56	Dave Magadan	.05
57	Roger McDowell	.05
58	Bill Landrum	.05
59	Jose DeLeon	.05
60	Bip Roberts	.05
61	Matt Williams	.12
62	Dale Murphy	.10
63	Dwight Smith	.05
64	Chris Sabo	.05
65	Glenn Davis	.05
66	Jay Howell	.05
67	Andres Galarraga	.08
68	Frank Viola	.05
69	John Kruk	.05
70	Bobby Bonilla	.10
71	Todd Zeile	.10
72	Joe Carter	.10
73	Robby Thompson	.05
74	Jeff Blauser	.05
75	Mitch Williams	.05
76	Rob Dibble	.05
77	Rafael Ramirez	.05
78	Eddie Murray	.20
79	Dave Martinez	.05
80	Darryl Strawberry	.10
81	Dickie Thon	.05
82	Jose Lind	.05
83	Ozzie Smith	.20
84	Bruce Hurst	.05
85	Kevin Mitchell	.08
86	Lonnie Smith	.05
87	Joe Girardi	.05
88	Randy Myers	.05
89	Craig Biggio	.08
90	Fernando Valenzuela	.08
91	Larry Walker	.15
92	John Franco	.05
93	Dennis Cook	.05
94	Bob Walk	.05
95	Pedro Guerrero	.05
96	Checklist	.05
97	Andre Dawson	.10
98	Ed Whitson	.05
99	Steve Bedrosian	.05
100	Oddibe McDowell	.05
101	Todd Benzinger	.05
102	Bill Doran	.05
103	Alfredo Griffin	.05
104	Tim Raines	.10
105	Sid Fernandez	.05
106	Charlie Hayes	.05
107	Mike LaValliere	.05
108	Jose Oquendo	.05
109	Jack Clark	.05
110	Scott Garrelts	.05
111	Ron Gant	.10
112	Shawon Dunston	.10
113	Mariano Duncan	.05
114	Eric Yelding	.05
115	Hubie Brooks	.05
116	Delino DeShields	.08
117	Gregg Jefferies	.10
118	Len Dykstra	.08
119	Andy Van Slyke	.05
120	Lee Smith	.08
121	Benito Santiago	.05
122	Jose Uribe	.05
123	Jeff Treadway	.05
124	Jerome Walton	.05
125	Billy Hatcher	.05
126	Ken Caminiti	.08
127	Kal Daniels	.05
128	Marquis Grissom	.12
129	Kevin McReynolds	.05
130	Wally Backman	.05
131	Willie McGee	.05
132	Terry Kennedy	.05
133	Garry Templeton	.05
134	Lloyd McClendon	.05
135	Daryl Boston	.05
136	Jay Bell	.05
137	Mike Pagliarulo	.05
138	Vince Coleman	.05
139	Brett Butler	.08
140	Von Hayes	.05
141	Ramon Martinez	.08
142	Jack Armstrong	.05
143	Franklin Stubbs	.05
144	Checklist	.05

1990 Donruss Learning Series

Cards from this 55-card set were released as part of an educational package available to schools. The cards are styled like the regular-issue 1990 Donruss cards, but feature a special "learning series" logo on the front. The backs feature career highlights, statistics and card numbers. The cards were not released directly to the hobby.

		MT
Complete Set (55):		20.00
Common Player:		.25
1	George Brett (DK)	2.00
2	Kevin Mitchell	.25
3	Andy Van Slyke	.25
4	Benito Santiago	.30
5	Gary Carter	.40
6	Jose Canseco	1.00
7	Rickey Henderson	.85
8	Ken Griffey, Jr.	9.00
9	Ozzie Smith	2.00
10	Dwight Gooden	.35
11	Ryne Sandberg (DK)	2.00
12	Don Mattingly	3.00
13	Ozzie Guillen	.25
14	Dave Righetti	.25
15	Rick Dempsey	.25
16	Tom Herr	.25
17	Julio Franco	.25
18	Von Hayes	.25
19	Cal Ripken	5.00
20	Alan Trammell	.35
21	Wade Boggs	1.50
22	Glenn Davis	.25
23	Will Clark	.75
24	Nolan Ryan	5.00
25	George Bell	.25
26	Cecil Fielder	.35
27	Gregg Olson	.25
28	Tim Wallach	.25
29	Ron Darling	.25
30	Kelly Gruber	.25
31	Shawn Boskie	.25
32	Mike Greenwell	.25
33	Dave Parker	.30
34	Joe Magrane	.25
35	Dave Stewart	.25
36	Kent Hrbek	.30
37	Robin Yount	1.00
38	Bo Jackson	.50
39	Fernando Valenzuela	.30
40	Sandy Alomar, Jr.	.35
41	Lance Parrish	.25
42	Candy Maldonado	.25
43	Mike LaValliere	.25
44	Jim Abbott	.25
45	Edgar Martinez	.30
46	Kirby Puckett	2.00
47	Delino DeShields	.25
48	Tony Gwynn	1.50
49	Carlton Fisk	.40
50	Mike Scott	.25
51	Barry Larkin	.30
52	Andre Dawson	.40
53	Tom Glavine	.35
54	Tom Browning	.25
55	Checklist	.05

1990 Donruss Rookies

For the fifth straight year, Donruss issued a 56-card "Rookies" set in 1990. As in previous years, the set is similar in design to the regular Donruss set, except for a new "The Rookies" logo and green borders instead of red. The set is packaged in a special box and includes a Carl Yastrzemski puzzle card.

		MT
Complete Set (56):		2.00
Common Player:		.10
1	Sandy Alomar	.25
2	John Olerud	.25
3	Pat Combs	.10
4	Brian Dubois	.10
5	Felix Jose	.10
6	Delino DeShields	.15
7	Mike Stanton	.10
8	Mike Munoz	.10
9	Craig Grebeck	.10
10	Joe Kraemer	.10
11	Jeff Huson	.10
12	Bill Sampen	.10
13	Brian Bohanon	.10
14	Dave Justice	.50
15	Robin Ventura	.20
16	Greg Vaughn	.20
17	Wayne Edwards	.10
18	Shawn Boskie	.10
19	*Carlos Baerga*	.20
20	Mark Gardner	.10
21	Kevin Appier	.30
22	Mike Harkey	.10
23	Tim Layana	.10
24	Glenallen Hill	.10
25	Jerry Kutzler	.10
26	Mike Blowers	.12
27	Scott Ruskin	.10
28	Dana Kiecker	.10
29	Willie Blair	.10
30	Ben McDonald	.15
31	Todd Zeile	.20
32	Scott Coolbaugh	.10
33	Xavier Hernandez	.10
34	Mike Hartley	.10
35	Kevin Tapani	.12
36	Kevin Wickander	.10
37	Carlos Hernandez	.10
38	Brian Traxler	.10
39	Marty Brown	.10
40	Scott Radinsky	.10
41	Julio Machado	.10

42	Steve Avery	.10
43	Mark Lemke	.10
44	Alan Mills	.10
45	Marquis Grissom	.50
46	Greg Olson	.10
47	Dave Hollins	.20
48	Jerald Clark	.10
49	Eric Anthony	.10
50	Tim Drummond	.10
51	John Burkett	.20
52	Brent Knackert	.10
53	Jeff Shaw	.10
54	John Orton	.10
55	Terry Shumpert	.10
56	Checklist	.05

1991 Donruss

Travis Fryman THIRD BASE

Donruss used a two-series format in 1991. The first series was released in December, 1990, and the second in February, 1991. The 1991 design is somewhat reminiscent of the 1986 set, with blue borders on Series I cards; green on Series II. Limited edition cards including an autographed Ryne Sandberg card (5,000) were randomly inserted in wax packs. Other features of the set include 40 Rated Rookies, (RR) in the checklist, Legends and Elite insert series, and another Diamond King (DK) subset. Cards were distributed in packs with Willie Stargell puzzle pieces.

	MT
Complete Set (792):	10.00
Common Player:	.05
Willie Stargell Puzzle:	1.00
Series 1 or 2 Wax Box:	9.00

1	Dave Steib (Diamond King)	.05
2	Craig Biggio (DK)	.05
3	Cecil Fielder (DK)	.12
4	Barry Bonds (DK)	.20
5	Barry Larkin (DK)	.10
6	Dave Parker (DK)	.05
7	Len Dykstra (DK)	.08
8	Bobby Thigpen (DK)	.05
9	Roger Clemens (DK)	.15
10	Ron Gant (DK)	.08
11	Delino DeShields (DK)	.08
12	Roberto Alomar (DK)	.15
13	Sandy Alomar (DK)	.08
14	Ryne Sandberg (DK)	.15
15	Ramon Martinez (DK)	.05
16	Edgar Martinez (DK)	.08
17	Dave Magadan (DK)	.05
18	Matt Williams (DK)	.12
19	Rafael Palmeiro (DK)	.08
20	Bob Welch (DK)	.05
21	Dave Righetti (DK)	.05
22	Brian Harper (DK)	.05
23	Gregg Olson (DK)	.05
24	Kurt Stillwell (DK)	.05
25	Pedro Guerrero (DK)	.05
26	Chuck Finley (DK)	.05

27	Diamond King checklist	.05
28	Tino Martinez (Rated Rookie)	.15
29	Mark Lewis (RR)	.10
30	*Bernard Gilkey* (RR)	.15
31	Hensley Meulens (RR)	.05
32	*Derek Bell* (RR)	.30
33	Jose Offerman (RR)	.08
34	Terry Bross (RR)	.10
35	*Leo Gomez* (RR)	.08
36	Derrick May (RR)	.08
37	*Kevin Morton* (RR)	.05
38	Moises Alou (RR)	.15
39	*Julio Valera* (RR)	.05
40	Milt Cuyler (RR)	.05
41	*Phil Plantier* (RR)	.10
42	*Scott Chiamparino* (RR)	.05
43	*Ray Lankford* (RR)	.20
44	*Mickey Morandini* (RR)	.08
45	Dave Hansen (RR)	.10
46	*Kevin Belcher* (RR)	.08
47	Darrin Fletcher (RR)	.10
48	Steve Sax (All Star)	.05
49	Ken Griffey, Jr. (AS)	.50
50a	Jose Canseco (AS)(A's in stat line on back)	.12
50b	Jose Canseco (AS)(AL in stat line on back)	.15
51	Sandy Alomar (AS)	.08
52	Cal Ripken, Jr. (AS)	.20
53	Rickey Henderson (AS)	.15
54	Bob Welch (AS)	.05
55	Wade Boggs (AS)	.10
56	Mark McGwire (AS)	.50
57	Jack McDowell	.08
58	Jose Lind	.05
59	Alex Fernandez	.20
60	Pat Combs	.05
61	*Mike Walker*	.05
62	Juan Samuel	.05
63	Mike Blowers	.05
64	Mark Guthrie	.05
65	Mark Salas	.05
66	Tim Jones	.05
67	Tim Leary	.05
68	Andres Galarraga	.10
69	Bob Milacki	.05
70	Tim Belcher	.05
71	Todd Zeile	.08
72	Jerome Walton	.05
73	Kevin Seitzer	.05
74	Jerald Clark	.05
75	John Smoltz	.10
76	Mike Henneman	.05
77	Ken Griffey, Jr.	1.50
78	Jim Abbott	.08
79	Gregg Jefferies	.10
80	Kevin Reimer	.05
81	Roger Clemens	.25
82	Mike Fitzgerald	.05
83	Bruce Hurst	.05
84	Eric Davis	.10
85	Paul Molitor	.15
86	Will Clark	.25
87	Mike Bielecki	.05
88	Bret Saberhagen	.10
89	Nolan Ryan	.50
90	Bobby Thigpen	.05
91	Dickie Thon	.05
92	Duane Ward	.05
93	Luis Polonia	.05
94	Terry Kennedy	.05
95	Kent Hrbek	.08
96	Danny Jackson	.05
97	Sid Fernandez	.05
98	Jimmy Key	.08
99	Franklin Stubbs	.05
100	Checklist 28-103	.05
101	R.J. Reynolds	.05
102	Dave Stewart	.08
103	Dan Pasqua	.05
104	Dan Plesac	.05
105	Mark McGwire	.75
106	John Farrell	.05
107	Don Mattingly	.30
108	Carlton Fisk	.10
109	Ken Oberkfell	.05
110	Darrel Akerfelds	.05
111	Gregg Olson	.05
112	Mike Scioscia	.05
113	Bryn Smith	.05
114	Bob Geren	.05
115	Tom Candiotti	.05
116	Kevin Tapani	.08
117	Jeff Treadway	.05
118	Alan Trammell	.10

119	Pete O'Brien	.05
120	Joel Skinner	.05
121	Mike LaValliere	.05
122	Dwight Evans	.08
123	Jody Reed	.05
124	Lee Guetterman	.05
125	Tim Burke	.05
126	Dave Johnson	.05
127	Fernando Valenzuela	.10
128	Jose DeLeon	.05
129	Andre Dawson	.10
130	Gerald Perry	.05
131	Greg Harris	.05
132	Tom Glavine	.10
133	Lance McCullers	.05
134	Randy Johnson	.25
135	Lance Parrish	.08
136	Mackey Sasser	.05
137	Geno Petralli	.05
138	Dennis Lamp	.05
139	Dennis Martinez	.08
140	Mike Pagliarulo	.05
141	Hal Morris	.08
142	Dave Parker	.10
143	Brett Butler	.08
144	Paul Assenmacher	.05
145	Mark Gubicza	.05
146	Charlie Hough	.05
147	Sammy Sosa	.75
148	Randy Ready	.05
149	Kelly Gruber	.05
150	Devon White	.08
151	Gary Carter	.12
152	Gene Larkin	.05
153	Chris Sabo	.05
154	David Cone	.08
155	Todd Stottlemyre	.08
156	Glenn Wilson	.05
157	Bob Walk	.05
158	Mike Gallego	.05
159	Greg Hibbard	.05
160	Chris Bosio	.05
161	Mike Moore	.05
162	Jerry Browne	.05
163	Steve Sax	.05
164	Melido Perez	.05
165	Danny Darwin	.05
166	Roger McDowell	.05
167	Bill Ripken	.05
168	Mike Sharperson	.05
169	Lee Smith	.08
170	Matt Nokes	.05
171	Jesse Orosco	.05
172	Rick Aguilera	.05
173	Jim Presley	.05
174	Lou Whitaker	.08
175	Harold Reynolds	.08
176	Brook Jacoby	.05
177	Wally Backman	.05
178	Wade Boggs	.20
179	Chuck Cary	.05
180	Tom Foley	.05
181	Pete Harnisch	.05
182	Mike Morgan	.05
183	Bob Tewksbury	.05
184	Joe Girardi	.05
185	Storm Davis	.05
186	Ed Whitson	.05
187	Steve Avery	.12
188	Lloyd Moseby	.05
189	Scott Bankhead	.05
190	Mark Langston	.08
191	Kevin McReynolds	.08
192	Julio Franco	.08
193	John Dopson	.05
194	Oil Can Boyd	.05
195	Bip Roberts	.05
196	Billy Hatcher	.05
197	Edgar Diaz	.05
198	Greg Litton	.05
199	Mark Grace	.15
200	Checklist 104-179	.05
201	George Brett	.25
202	Jeff Russell	.05
203	Ivan Calderon	.05
204	Ken Howell	.05
205	Tom Henke	.05
206	Bryan Harvey	.05
207	Steve Bedrosian	.05
208	Al Newman	.05
209	Randy Myers	.08
210	Daryl Boston	.05
211	Manny Lee	.05
212	Dave Smith	.05
213	Don Slaught	.05
214	Walt Weiss	.05

No.	Name	Value
215	Donn Pall	.05
216	Jamie Navarro	.05
217	Willie Randolph	.05
218	Rudy Seanez	.05
219	*Jim Leyritz*	.10
220	Ron Karkovice	.05
221	Ken Caminiti	.10
222a	Von Hayes (Traded players' first names included in How Acquired on back)	.05
222b	Von Hayes (No first names)	.05
223	Cal Ripken, Jr.	.75
224	Lenny Harris	.05
225	Milt Thompson	.05
226	Alvaro Espinoza	.05
227	Chris James	.05
228	Dan Gladden	.05
229	Jeff Blauser	.05
230	Mike Heath	.05
231	Omar Vizquel	.05
232	Doug Jones	.05
233	Jeff King	.05
234	Luis Rivera	.05
235	Ellis Burks	.08
236	Greg Cadaret	.05
237	Dave Martinez	.05
238	Mark Williamson	.05
239	Stan Javier	.05
240	Ozzie Smith	.20
241	*Shawn Boskie*	.08
242	Tom Gordon	.05
243	Tony Gwynn	.30
244	Tommy Gregg	.05
245	Jeff Robinson	.05
246	Keith Comstock	.05
247	Jack Howell	.05
248	Keith Miller	.05
249	Bobby Witt	.05
250	Rob Murphy	.05
251	Spike Owen	.05
252	Garry Templeton	.05
253	Glenn Braggs	.05
254	Ron Robinson	.05
255	Kevin Mitchell	.08
256	Les Lancaster	.05
257	*Mel Stottlemyre*	.10
258	Kenny Rogers	.05
259	Lance Johnson	.05
260	John Kruk	.08
261	Fred McGriff	.15
262	Dick Schofield	.05
263	Trevor Wilson	.05
264	David West	.05
265	Scott Scudder	.05
266	Dwight Gooden	.10
267	*Willie Blair*	.08
268	Mark Portugal	.05
269	Doug Drabek	.05
270	Dennis Eckersley	.10
271	Eric King	.05
272	Robin Yount	.15
273	Carney Lansford	.05
274	Carlos Baerga	.20
275	Dave Righetti	.05
276	Scott Fletcher	.05
277	Eric Yelding	.05
278	Charlie Hayes	.05
279	Jeff Ballard	.05
280	Orel Hershiser	.10
281	Jose Oquendo	.05
282	Mike Witt	.05
283	Mitch Webster	.05
284	Greg Gagne	.05
285	*Greg Olson*	.05
286	Tony Phillips	.08
287	Scott Bradley	.05
288	Cory Snyder	.05
289	Jay Bell	.08
290	Kevin Romine	.05
291	Jeff Robinson	.05
292	Steve Frey	.08
293	Craig Worthington	.05
294	Tim Crews	.05
295	Joe Magrane	.05
296	*Hector Villanueva*	.05
297	*Terry Shumpert*	.05
298	Joe Carter	.15
299	Kent Mercker	.05
300	Checklist 180-255	.05
301	Chet Lemon	.05
302	Mike Schooler	.05
303	Dante Bichette	.08
304	Kevin Elster	.05
305	Jeff Huson	.05
306	Greg Harris	.05
307	Marquis Grissom	.12
308	Calvin Schiraldi	.05
309	Mariano Duncan	.05
310	Bill Spiers	.05
311	Scott Garrelts	.05
312	Mitch Williams	.08
313	Mike Macfarlane	.05
314	Kevin Brown	.10
315	Robin Ventura	.15
316	Darren Daulton	.10
317	Pat Borders	.05
318	Mark Eichhorn	.05
319	Jeff Brantley	.05
320	Shane Mack	.05
321	Rob Dibble	.05
322	John Franco	.05
323	Junior Felix	.05
324	Casey Candaele	.05
325	Bobby Bonilla	.10
326	Dave Henderson	.05
327	Wayne Edwards	.05
328	Mark Knudson	.05
329	Terry Steinbach	.08
330	*Colby Ward*	.05
331	*Oscar Azocar*	.05
332	*Scott Radinsky*	.10
333	Eric Anthony	.05
334	Steve Lake	.05
335	Bob Melvin	.05
336	Kal Daniels	.05
337	Tom Pagnozzi	.05
338	*Alan Mills*	.08
339	Steve Olin	.05
340	Juan Berenguer	.05
341	Francisco Cabrera	.05
342	Dave Bergman	.05
343	Henry Cotto	.05
344	Sergio Valdez	.05
345	Bob Patterson	.05
346	John Marzano	.05
347	*Dana Kiecker*	.05
348	Dion James	.05
349	Hubie Brooks	.05
350	Bill Landrum	.05
351	*Bill Sampen*	.05
352	Greg Briley	.05
353	Paul Gibson	.05
354	Dave Eiland	.05
355	Steve Finley	.05
356	Bob Boone	.05
357	Steve Buechele	.05
358	Chris Hoiles	.08
359	Larry Walker	.25
360	Frank DiPino	.05
361	Mark Grant	.05
362	Dave Magadan	.05
363	Robby Thompson	.05
364	Lonnie Smith	.05
365	Steve Farr	.05
366	Dave Valle	.05
367	*Tim Naehring*	.08
368	Jim Acker	.05
369	Jeff Reardon	.05
370	Tim Teufel	.05
371	Juan Gonzalez	.60
372	Luis Salazar	.05
373	Rick Honeycutt	.05
374	Greg Maddux	.75
375	Jose Uribe	.05
376	Donnie Hill	.05
377	Don Carman	.05
378	*Craig Grebeck*	.05
379	Willie Fraser	.05
380	Glenallen Hill	.08
381	Joe Oliver	.05
382	Randy Bush	.05
383	Alex Cole	.05
384	Norm Charlton	.05
385	Gene Nelson	.05
386a	Checklist 256-331 (blue borders)	.05
386b	Checklist 256-331 (green borders)	.05
387	Rickey Henderson (MVP)	.15
388	Lance Parrish (MVP)	.05
389	Fred McGriff (MVP)	.15
390	Dave Parker (MVP)	.10
391	Candy Maldonado (MVP)	.05
392	Ken Griffey, Jr. (MVP)	.40
393	Gregg Olson (MVP)	.05
394	Rafael Palmeiro (MVP)	.10
395	Roger Clemens (MVP)	.20
396	George Brett (MVP)	.15
397	Cecil Fielder (MVP)	.15
398	Brian Harper (MVP)	.05
399	Bobby Thigpen (MVP)	.05
400	Roberto Kelly (MVP)	.08
401	Danny Darwin (MVP)	.05
402	Dave Justice (MVP)	.25
403	Lee Smith (MVP)	.05
404	Ryne Sandberg (MVP)	.15
405	Eddie Murray (MVP)	.15
406	Tim Wallach (MVP)	.05
407	Kevin Mitchell (MVP)	.05
408	Darryl Strawberry (MVP)	.05
409	Joe Carter (MVP)	.08
410	Len Dykstra (MVP)	.08
411	Doug Drabek (MVP)	.05
412	Chris Sabo (MVP)	.05
413	*Paul Marak* (RR)	.05
414	Tim McIntosh (RR)	.05
415	*Brian Barnes* (RR)	.05
416	*Eric Gunderson* (RR)	.05
417	*Mike Gardiner* (RR)	.10
418	Steve Carter (RR)	.08
419	*Gerald Alexander* (RR)	.05
420	Rich Garces (RR)	.05
421	*Chuck Knoblauch* (RR)	.30
422	*Scott Aldred* (RR)	.05
423	*Wes Chamberlain* (RR)	.10
424	Lance Dickson (RR)	.05
425	*Greg Colbrunn* (RR)	.15
426	*Rich Delucia* (RR)	.08
427	*Jeff Conine* (RR)	.40
428	*Steve Decker* (RR)	.10
429	*Turner Ward* (RR)	.10
430	Mo Vaughn (RR)	.75
431	*Steve Chitren* (RR)	.10
432	Mike Benjamin (RR)	.10
433	Ryne Sandberg (AS)	.10
434	Len Dykstra (AS)	.05
435	Andre Dawson (AS)	.10
436	Mike Scioscia (AS)	.05
437	Ozzie Smith (AS)	.10
438	Kevin Mitchell (AS)	.05
439	Jack Armstrong (AS)	.05
440	Chris Sabo (AS)	.05
441	Will Clark (AS)	.10
442	Mel Hall	.05
443	Mark Gardner	.05
444	Mike Devereaux	.05
445	Kirk Gibson	.05
446	Terry Pendleton	.05
447	Mike Harkey	.05
448	Jim Eisenreich	.05
449	Benito Santiago	.08
450	Oddibe McDowell	.05
451	Cecil Fielder	.15
452	Ken Griffey, Sr.	.08
453	Bert Blyleven	.08
454	Howard Johnson	.05
455	Monty Farris	.05
456	Tony Pena	.05
457	Tim Raines	.08
458	Dennis Rasmussen	.05
459	Luis Quinones	.05
460	B.J. Surhoff	.05
461	Ernest Riles	.05
462	Rick Sutcliffe	.05
463	Danny Tartabull	.05
464	Pete Incaviglia	.05
465	Carlos Martinez	.05
466	Ricky Jordan	.05
467	John Cerutti	.05
468	Dave Winfield	.12
469	Francisco Oliveras	.05
470	Roy Smith	.05
471	Barry Larkin	.12
472	Ron Darling	.05
473	David Wells	.05
474	Glenn Davis	.05
475	Neal Heaton	.05
476	Ron Hassey	.05
477	Frank Thomas	1.50
478	Greg Vaughn	.05
479	Todd Burns	.05
480	Candy Maldonado	.05
481	Dave LaPoint	.05
482	Alvin Davis	.05
483	Mike Scott	.05
484	Dale Murphy	.12
485	Ben McDonald	.10
486	Jay Howell	.05
487	Vince Coleman	.05
488	Alfredo Griffin	.05
489	Sandy Alomar	.12
490	Kirby Puckett	.30
491	Andres Thomas	.05
492	Jack Morris	.08
493	Matt Young	.05
494	Greg Myers	.05
495	Barry Bonds	.35
496	Scott Cooper	.05

497	Dan Schatzeder	.05
498	Jesse Barfield	.05
499	Jerry Goff	.05
500	Checklist 332-408	.05
501	*Anthony Telford*	.08
502	Eddie Murray	.20
503	*Omar Olivares*	.12
504	Ryne Sandberg	.20
505	Jeff Montgomery	.05
506	Mark Parent	.05
507	Ron Gant	.10
508	Frank Tanana	.05
509	Jay Buhner	.08
510	Max Venable	.05
511	Wally Whitehurst	.05
512	Gary Pettis	.05
513	Tom Brunansky	.05
514	Tim Wallach	.08
515	Craig Lefferts	.05
516	*Tim Layana*	.05
517	Darryl Hamilton	.05
518	Rick Reuschel	.05
519	Steve Wilson	.05
520	Kurt Stillwell	.05
521	Rafael Palmeiro	.15
522	Ken Patterson	.05
523	Len Dykstra	.12
524	Tony Fernandez	.05
525	Kent Anderson	.05
526	*Mark Leonard*	.08
527	Allan Anderson	.05
528	Tom Browning	.05
529	Frank Viola	.05
530	John Olerud	.20
531	Juan Agosto	.05
532	Zane Smith	.05
533	Scott Sanderson	.05
534	Barry Jones	.05
535	Mike Felder	.05
536	Jose Canseco	.20
537	Felix Fermin	.05
538	Roberto Kelly	.08
539	Brian Holman	.05
540	Mark Davidson	.05
541	Terry Mulholland	.08
542	Randy Milligan	.05
543	Jose Gonzalez	.05
544	*Craig Wilson*	.08
545	Mike Hartley	.05
546	Greg Swindell	.05
547	Gary Gaetti	.08
548	Dave Justice	.40
549	Steve Searcy	.05
550	Erik Hanson	.05
551	Dave Stieb	.08
552	Andy Van Slyke	.05
553	Mike Greenwell	.10
554	Kevin Maas	.05
555	Delino Deshields	.08
556	Curt Schilling	.05
557	Ramon Martinez	.08
558	Pedro Guerrero	.05
559	Dwight Smith	.05
560	Mark Davis	.05
561	Shawn Abner	.05
562	Charlie Leibrandt	.05
563	John Shelby	.05
564	Bill Swift	.05
565	Mike Fetters	.05
566	Alejandro Pena	.05
567	Ruben Sierra	.15
568	Carlos Quintana	.05
569	Kevin Gross	.05
570	Derek Lilliquist	.05
571	Jack Armstrong	.05
572	Greg Brock	.05
573	Mike Kingery	.05
574	Greg Smith	.05
575	*Brian McRae*	.25
576	Jack Daugherty	.05
577	Ozzie Guillen	.05
578	Joe Boever	.05
579	Luis Sojo	.05
580	Chili Davis	.08
581	Don Robinson	.05
582	Brian Harper	.05
583	Paul O'Neill	.10
584	Bob Ojeda	.05
585	Mookie Wilson	.05
586	Rafael Ramirez	.05
587	Gary Redus	.05
588	Jamie Quirk	.05
589	Shawn Hilligas	.05
590	*Tom Edens*	.05
591	Joe Klink	.05
592	Charles Nagy	.08

593	Eric Plunk	.05
594	Tracy Jones	.05
595	Craig Biggio	.10
596	Jose DeJesus	.05
597	Mickey Tettleton	.08
598	Chris Gwynn	.05
599	Rex Hudler	.05
600	Checklist 409-506	.05
601	Jim Gott	.05
602	Jeff Manto	.08
603	Nelson Liriano	.05
604	Mark Lemke	.05
605	Clay Parker	.05
606	Edgar Martinez	.08
607	*Mark Whiten*	.20
608	Ted Power	.05
609	Tom Bolton	.05
610	Tom Herr	.05
611	Andy Hawkins	.05
612	Scott Ruskin	.05
613	Ron Kittle	.05
614	John Wetteland	.08
615	*Mike Perez*	.10
616	Dave Clark	.05
617	Brent Mayne	.12
618	Jack Clark	.05
619	Marvin Freeman	.05
620	Edwin Nunez	.05
621	Russ Swan	.05
622	Johnny Ray	.05
623	Charlie O'Brien	.05
624	*Joe Bitker*	.05
625	Mike Marshall	.05
626	Otis Nixon	.05
627	Andy Benes	.10
628	Ron Oester	.05
629	Ted Higuera	.05
630	Kevin Bass	.05
631	Damon Berryhill	.05
632	Bo Jackson	.15
633	Brad Arnsberg	.05
634	Jerry Willard	.05
635	Tommy Greene	.05
636	*Bob MacDonald*	.05
637	Kirk McCaskill	.05
638	John Burkett	.05
639	*Paul Abbott*	.05
640	Todd Benzinger	.05
641	Todd Hundley	.08
642	George Bell	.08
643	*Javier Ortiz*	.05
644	Sid Bream	.05
645	Bob Welch	.05
646	Phil Bradley	.05
647	Bill Krueger	.05
648	Rickey Henderson	.15
649	Kevin Wickander	.05
650	Steve Balboni	.05
651	Gene Harris	.05
652	Jim Deshaies	.05
653	Jason Grimsley	.05
654	Joe Orsulak	.05
655	*Jimmy Poole*	.05
656	Felix Jose	.05
657	Dennis Cook	.05
658	Tom Brookens	.05
659	Junior Ortiz	.05
660	Jeff Parrett	.05
661	Jerry Don Gleaton	.05
662	Brent Knackert	.05
663	Rance Mulliniks	.05
664	John Smiley	.05
665	Larry Andersen	.05
666	Willie McGee	.08
667	*Chris Nabholz*	.08
668	Brady Anderson	.10
669	*Darren Holmes*	.12
670	Ken Hill	.05
671	Gary Varsho	.05
672	Bill Pecota	.05
673	Fred Lynn	.05
674	Kevin D. Brown	.05
675	Dan Petry	.05
676	Mike Jackson	.05
677	Wally Joyner	.08
678	Danny Jackson	.05
679	*Bill Haselman*	.05
680	Mike Boddicker	.05
681	*Mel Rojas*	.12
682	Roberto Alomar	.25
683	Dave Justice (R.O.Y.)	.25
684	Chuck Crim	.05
685a	Matt Williams (Last line of Career Highlights ends, "most DP's in")	.20

685b	Matt Williams (last line ends "8/24-27/87.")	.25
686	Shawon Dunston	.08
687	*Jeff Schulz*	.05
688	John Barfield	.05
689	Gerald Young	.05
690	*Luis Gonzalez*	.15
691	Frank Wills	.05
692	Chuck Finley	.05
693	Sandy Alomar (R.O.Y.)	.10
694	Tim Drummond	.05
695	Herm Winningham	.05
696	Darryl Strawberry	.10
697	Al Leiter	.05
698	*Karl Rhodes*	.08
699	Stan Belinda	.05
700	Checklist 507-604	.05
701	Lance Blankenship	.05
702	Willie Stargell (Puzzle Card)	.05
703	Jim Gantner	.05
704	*Reggie Harris*	.05
705	Rob Ducey	.05
706	Tim Hulett	.05
707	Atlee Hammaker	.05
708	Xavier Hernandez	.05
709	Chuck McElroy	.05
710	John Mitchell	.05
711	Carlos Hernandez	.05
712	Geronimo Pena	.05
713	*Jim Neidlinger*	.05
714	John Orton	.05
715	Terry Leach	.05
716	Mike Stanton	.05
717	Walt Terrell	.05
718	Luis Aquino	.05
719	Bud Black	.05
720	Bob Kipper	.05
721	*Jeff Gray*	.05
722	Jose Rijo	.05
723	Curt Young	.05
724	Jose Vizcaino	.08
725	*Randy Tomlin*	.05
726	Junior Noboa	.05
727	Bob Welch (Award Winner)	.05
728	Gary Ward	.05
729	Rob Deer	.05
730	*David Segui*	.08
731	Mark Carreon	.05
732	Vicente Palacios	.05
733	Sam Horn	.05
734	*Howard Farmer*	.08
735	Ken Dayley	.05
736	Kelly Mann	.05
737	*Joe Grahe*	.05
738	Kelly Downs	.05
739	*Jimmy Kremers*	.05
740	Kevin Appier	.12
741	Jeff Reed	.05
742	Jose Rijo (World Series)	.05
743	*Dave Rohde*	.08
744	Dr. Dirt/Mr. Clean(Len Dykstra, Dale Murphy)	.08
745	Paul Sorrento	.08
746	Thomas Howard	.08
747	*Matt Stark*	.05
748	Harold Baines	.08
749	Doug Dascenzo	.05
750	Doug Drabek (Award Winner)	.05
751	Gary Sheffield	.10
752	*Terry Lee*	.05
753	*Jim Vatcher*	.05
754	Lee Stevens	.05
755	Randy Veres	.05
756	Bill Doran	.05
757	Gary Wayne	.05
758	*Pedro Munoz*	.10
759	Chris Hammond	.05
760	Checklist 605-702	.05
761	Rickey Henderson (MVP)	.12
762	Barry Bonds (MVP)	.25
763	Billy Hatcher (World Series)	.05
764	Julio Machado	.05
765	Jose Mesa	.05
766	Willie Randolph (World Series)	.05
767	*Scott Erickson*	.10
768	Travis Fryman	.15
769	*Rich Rodriguez*	.12
770	Checklist 703-770; BC1-BC22	.05

1991 Donruss Elite

Donruss released a series of special inserts in 1991. Ten thousand of each Elite card was released, while 7,500 Legend cards and 5,000 Signature cards were issued. Cards were inserted in wax packs and feature marble borders. The Legend card features a Dick Perez drawing. Each card is designated with a serial number on the back.

		MT
Complete Set (10):		750.00
Common Player:		15.00
1	Barry Bonds	60.00
2	George Brett	90.00
3	Jose Canseco	45.00
4	Andre Dawson	30.00
5	Doug Drabek	20.00
6	Cecil Fielder	30.00
7	Rickey Henderson	30.00
8	Matt Williams	45.00
---	Nolan Ryan (Legend)	200.00
---	Ryne Sandberg (Signature)	275.00

1991 Donruss Grand Slammers

This set features players who hit grand slams in 1990. The cards are styled after the 1991 Donruss regular-issue cards. The featured player is showcased with a star in the background. The set was included in factory sets and randomly in jumbo packs.

		MT
Complete Set (14):		2.50
Common Player:		.10
1	Joe Carter	.15
2	Bobby Bonilla	.15
3	Kal Daniels	.10
4	Jose Canseco	.30
5	Barry Bonds	.35
6	Jay Buhner	.15
7	Cecil Fielder	.25
8	Matt Williams	.25
9	Andres Galarraga	.15
10	Luis Polonia	.10
11	Mark McGwire	.75
12	Ron Karkovice	.10
13	Darryl Strawberry	.15
14	Mike Greenwell	.10

1991 Donruss Highlights

This insert features highlights from the 1990 season. Cards have a "BC" prefix to the number and are styled after the 1991 regular-issue Donruss cards. Cards 1-10 feature blue borders due to their release with Series I cards. Cards 11-22 feature green borders and were released with Series II cards. A highlight logo appears on the front of the card. Each highlight is explained in depth on the card back.

		MT
Complete Set (22):		3.00
Common Player:		.10
1	Mark Langston, Mike Witt (No-Hit Mariners)	.10
2	Randy Johnson (No-Hits Tigers)	.20
3	Nolan Ryan (No-Hits A's)	.40
4	Dave Stewart (No-Hits Blue Jays)	.15
5	Cecil Fielder (50 Homer Club)	.15
6	Carlton Fisk (Record Home Run)	.20
7	Ryne Sandberg (Sets Fielding Records)	.25
8	Gary Carter (Breaks Catching Mark)	.10
9	Mark McGwire (Home Run Milestone)	.50
10	Bo Jackson (4 Consecutive HRs)	.25
11	Fernando Valenzuela (No-Hits Cardinals)	.10
12	Andy Hawkins (No-Hits White Sox)	.10
13	Melido Perez (No-Hits Yankees)	.10
14	Terry Mulholland (No-Hits Giants)	.10
15	Nolan Ryan (300th Win)	.40
16	Delino DeShields (4 Hits In Debut)	.10
17	Cal Ripken (Errorless Games)	.50
18	Eddie Murray (Switch Hit Homers)	.25
19	George Brett (3 Decade Champ)	.25
20	Bobby Thigpen (Shatters Save Mark)	.10
21	Dave Stieb (No-Hits Indians)	.10
22	Willie McGee (NL Batting Champ)	.12

A player's name in *italic* type indicates a rookie card.

1991 Donruss Rookies

Red borders highlight the 1991 Donruss Rookies cards. This set marks the sixth year that Donruss produced such an issue. As in past years, "The Rookies" logo appears on the card fronts. The set is packaged in a special box and includes a Willie Stargell puzzle card.

		MT
Complete Set (56):		4.00
Common Player:		.10
1	Pat Kelly	.15
2	Rich DeLucia	.10
3	Wes Chamberlain	.10
4	Scott Leius	.10
5	Darryl Kile	.15
6	Milt Cuyler	.10
7	Todd Van Poppel	.10
8	Ray Lankford	.30
9	Brian Hunter	.10
10	Tony Perezchica	.10
11	Ced Landrum	.10
12	Dave Burba	.10
13	Ramon Garcia	.10
14	Ed Sprague	.10
15	Warren Newson	.10
16	Paul Faries	.10
17	Luis Gonzalez	.15
18	Charles Nagy	.15
19	Chris Hammond	.10
20	Frank Castillo	.10
21	Pedro Munoz	.15
22	Orlando Merced	.15
23	Jose Melendez	.10
24	Kirk Dressendorfer	.10
25	Heathcliff Slocumb	.10
26	Doug Simons	.10
27	Mike Timlin	.15
28	Jeff Fassero	.12
29	Mark Leiter	.10
30	Jeff Bagwell	2.50
31	Brian McRae	.25
32	Mark Whiten	.15
33	Ivan Rodriguez	1.00
34	Wade Taylor	.10
35	Darren Lewis	.15
36	Mo Vaughn	1.00
37	Mike Remlinger	.10
38	Rick Wilkins	.15
39	Chuck Knoblauch	.60
40	Kevin Morton	.10
41	Carlos Rodriguez	.10
42	Mark Lewis	.15
43	Brent Mayne	.10
44	Chris Haney	.10
45	Denis Boucher	.10
46	Mike Gardiner	.10
47	Jeff Johnson	.10
48	Dean Palmer	.15
49	Chuck McElroy	.10
50	Chris Jones	.10
51	Scott Kamieniecki	.10
52	Al Osuna	.10
53	Rusty Meacham	.10

54	Chito Martinez	.10
55	Reggie Jefferson	.15
56	Checklist	.05

1992 Donruss

For the second consecutive year, Donruss released its card set in two series. The 1992 cards feature improved stock, an anti-counterfeit feature and include both front and back photos. Once again Rated Rookies and All-Stars are included in the set. Special highlight cards also can be found in the 1992 Donruss set. Production was reduced in 1992 compared to 1988-1991.

		MT
	Complete Set (784):	15.00
	Common Player:	.05
	Series 1 or 2 Wax Box:	15.00
1	*Mark Wohlers* (Rated Rookie)	.30
2	Wil Cordero (Rated Rookie)	.30
3	Kyle Abbott (Rated Rookie)	.08
4	*Dave Nilsson* (Rated Rookie)	.10
5	Kenny Lofton (Rated Rookie)	2.00
6	*Luis Mercedes* (Rated Rookie)	.10
7	*Roger Salkeld* (Rated Rookie)	.15
8	Eddie Zosky (Rated Rookie)	.25
9	*Todd Van Poppel* (Rated Rookie)	.15
10	*Frank Seminara* (Rated Rookie)	.10
11	*Andy Ashby* (Rated Rookie)	.20
12	Reggie Jefferson (Rated Rookie)	.10
13	Ryan Klesko (Rated Rookie)	1.25
14	*Carlos Garcia* (Rated Rookie)	.15
15	*John Ramos* (Rated Rookie)	.05
16	Eric Karros (Rated Rookie)	.25
17	Pat Lennon (Rated Rookie)	.10
18	*Eddie Taubensee* (Rated Rookie)	.10
19	*Roberto Hernandez* (Rated Rookie)	.10
20	D.J. Dozier (Rated Rookie)	.08
21	Dave Henderson (All-Star)	.05
22	Cal Ripken, Jr. (All-Star)	.20
23	Wade Boggs (All-Star)	.10
24	Ken Griffey, Jr. (All-Star)	.75
25	Jack Morris (All-Star)	.05
26	Danny Tartabull (All-Star)	.05
27	Cecil Fielder (All-Star)	.10
28	Roberto Alomar (All-Star)	.20
29	Sandy Alomar (All-Star)	.05
30	Rickey Henderson (All-Star)	.15
31	Ken Hill	.08
32	John Habyan	.05
33	Otis Nixon (Highlight)	.05
34	Tim Wallach	.05
35	Cal Ripken, Jr.	.75
36	Gary Carter	.10

37	Juan Agosto	.05
38	Doug Dascenzo	.05
39	Kirk Gibson	.08
40	Benito Santiago	.08
41	Otis Nixon	.05
42	Andy Allanson	.05
43	Brian Holman	.05
44	Dick Schofield	.05
45	Dave Magadan	.05
46	Rafael Palmeiro	.12
47	Jody Reed	.05
48	Ivan Calderon	.05
49	Greg Harris	.05
50	Chris Sabo	.05
51	Paul Molitor	.15
52	Robby Thompson	.05
53	Dave Smith	.05
54	Mark Davis	.05
55	Kevin Brown	.08
56	Donn Pall	.05
57	Len Dykstra	.15
58	Roberto Alomar	.30
59	Jeff Robinson	.05
60	Willie McGee	.08
61	Jay Buhner	.10
62	Mike Pagliarulo	.05
63	Paul O'Neill	.12
64	Hubie Brooks	.05
65	Kelly Gruber	.05
66	Ken Caminiti	.08
67	Gary Redus	.05
68	Harold Baines	.08
69	Charlie Hough	.05
70	B.J. Surhoff	.05
71	Walt Weiss	.05
72	Shawn Hillegas	.05
73	Roberto Kelly	.08
74	Jeff Ballard	.05
75	Craig Biggio	.10
76	Pat Combs	.05
77	Jeff Robinson	.05
78	Tim Belcher	.05
79	Cris Carpenter	.05
80	Checklist 1-79	.05
81	Steve Avery	.10
82	Chris James	.05
83	Brian Harper	.05
84	Charlie Leibrandt	.05
85	Mickey Tettleton	.08
86	Pete O'Brien	.05
87	Danny Darwin	.05
88	Bob Walk	.05
89	Jeff Reardon	.05
90	Bobby Rose	.05
91	Danny Jackson	.05
92	John Morris	.05
93	Bud Black	.05
94	Tommy Greene (Highlight)	.05
95	Rick Aguilera	.05
96	Gary Gaetti	.05
97	David Cone	.08
98	John Olerud	.20
99	Joel Skinner	.05
100	Jay Bell	.08
101	Bob Milacki	.05
102	Norm Charlton	.05
103	Chuck Crim	.05
104	Terry Steinbach	.05
105	Juan Samuel	.05
106	Steve Howe	.05
107	Rafael Belliard	.05
108	Joey Cora	.05
109	Tommy Greene	.08
110	Gregg Olson	.05
111	Frank Tanana	.05
112	Lee Smith	.08
113	Greg Harris	.05
114	Dwayne Henry	.05
115	Chili Davis	.08
116	Kent Mercker	.08
117	Brian Barnes	.05
118	Rich DeLucia	.05
119	Andre Dawson	.15
120	Carlos Baerga	.25
121	Mike LaValliere	.05
122	Jeff Gray	.05
123	Bruce Hurst	.05
124	Alvin Davis	.05
125	John Candelaria	.05
126	Matt Nokes	.05
127	George Bell	.10
128	Bret Saberhagen	.10
129	Jeff Russell	.05
130	Jim Abbott	.10
131	Bill Gullickson	.05
132	Todd Zeile	.10

133	Dave Winfield	.15
134	Wally Whitehurst	.05
135	Matt Williams	.15
136	Tom Browning	.05
137	Marquis Grissom	.15
138	Erik Hanson	.05
139	Rob Dibble	.05
140	Don August	.05
141	Tom Henke	.05
142	Dan Pasqua	.05
143	George Brett	.20
144	Jerald Clark	.05
145	Robin Ventura	.10
146	Dale Murphy	.10
147	Dennis Eckersley	.10
148	Eric Yelding	.05
149	Mario Diaz	.05
150	Casey Candaele	.05
151	Steve Olin	.05
152	Luis Salazar	.05
153	Kevin Maas	.05
154	Nolan Ryan (Highlight)	.40
155	Barry Jones	.05
156	Chris Hoiles	.10
157	Bobby Ojeda	.05
158	Pedro Guerrero	.05
159	Paul Assenmacher	.05
160	Checklist 80-157	.05
161	Mike Macfarlane	.05
162	Craig Lefferts	.05
163	*Brian Hunter*	.05
164	Alan Trammell	.10
165	Ken Griffey, Jr.	1.50
166	Lance Parrish	.08
167	Brian Downing	.05
168	John Barfield	.05
169	Jack Clark	.05
170	Chris Nabholz	.05
171	Tim Teufel	.05
172	Chris Hammond	.05
173	Robin Yount	.20
174	Dave Righetti	.05
175	Joe Girardi	.05
176	Mike Boddicker	.05
177	Dean Palmer	.10
178	Greg Hibbard	.05
179	Randy Ready	.05
180	Devon White	.08
181	Mark Eichhorn	.05
182	Mike Felder	.05
183	Joe Klink	.05
184	Steve Bedrosian	.05
185	Barry Larkin	.10
186	John Franco	.05
187	*Ed Sprague*	.15
188	Mark Portugal	.05
189	Jose Lind	.05
190	Bob Welch	.08
191	Alex Fernandez	.15
192	Gary Sheffield	.15
193	Rickey Henderson	.20
194	Rod Nichols	.05
195	*Scott Kamieniecki*	.10
196	Mike Flanagan	.05
197	Steve Finley	.05
198	Darren Daulton	.08
199	Leo Gomez	.05
200	Mike Morgan	.05
201	Bob Tewksbury	.05
202	Sid Bream	.05
203	Sandy Alomar	.10
204	Greg Gagne	.05
205	Juan Berenguer	.05
206	Cecil Fielder	.15
207	Randy Johnson	.25
208	Tony Pena	.05
209	Doug Drabek	.05
210	Wade Boggs	.20
211	Bryan Harvey	.05
212	Jose Vizcaino	.05
213	*Alonzo Powell*	.05
214	Will Clark	.20
215	Rickey Henderson (Highlight)	.10
216	Jack Morris	.08
217	Junior Felix	.05
218	Vince Coleman	.08
219	Jimmy Key	.08
220	Alex Cole	.05
221	Bill Landrum	.05
222	Randy Milligan	.05
223	Jose Rijo	.08
224	Greg Vaughn	.08
225	Dave Stewart	.08
226	Lenny Harris	.05
227	Scott Sanderson	.05

No.	Player	Price
228	Jeff Blauser	.05
229	Ozzie Guillen	.05
230	John Kruk	.08
231	Bob Melvin	.05
232	Milt Cuyler	.05
233	Felix Jose	.05
234	Ellis Burks	.10
235	Pete Harnisch	.05
236	Kevin Tapani	.08
237	Terry Pendleton	.05
238	Mark Gardner	.05
239	Harold Reynolds	.05
240	Checklist 158-237	.05
241	Mike Harkey	.05
242	Felix Fermin	.05
243	Barry Bonds	.35
244	Roger Clemens	.30
245	Dennis Rasmussen	.05
246	Jose DeLeon	.05
247	Orel Hershiser	.10
248	Mel Hall	.05
249	*Rick Wilkins*	.15
250	Tom Gordon	.05
251	Kevin Reimer	.05
252	Luis Polonia	.05
253	Mike Henneman	.05
254	Tom Pagnozzi	.05
255	Chuck Finley	.05
256	Mackey Sasser	.05
257	John Burkett	.05
258	Hal Morris	.08
259	Larry Walker	.20
260	Billy Swift	.05
261	Joe Oliver	.05
262	Julio Machado	.05
263	Todd Stottlemyre	.05
264	Matt Merullo	.05
265	Brent Mayne	.05
266	Thomas Howard	.05
267	Lance Johnson	.05
268	Terry Mulholland	.05
269	Rick Honeycutt	.05
270	Luis Gonzalez	.05
271	Jose Guzman	.05
272	Jimmy Jones	.05
273	Mark Lewis	.05
274	Rene Gonzales	.05
275	*Jeff Johnson*	.05
276	Dennis Martinez (Highlight)	.05
277	Delino DeShields	.08
278	Sam Horn	.05
279	Kevin Gross	.05
280	Jose Oquendo	.05
281	Mark Grace	.20
282	Mark Gubicza	.05
283	Fred McGriff	.15
284	Ron Gant	.10
285	Lou Whitaker	.08
286	Edgar Martinez	.08
287	Ron Tingley	.05
288	Kevin McReynolds	.05
289	Ivan Rodriguez	.25
290	Mike Gardiner	.05
291	*Chris Haney*	.05
292	Darrin Jackson	.05
293	Bill Doran	.05
294	Ted Higuera	.05
295	Jeff Brantley	.05
296	Les Lancaster	.05
297	Jim Eisenreich	.05
298	Ruben Sierra	.08
299	Scott Radinsky	.05
300	Jose DeJesus	.05
301	*Mike Timlin*	.12
302	Luis Sojo	.05
303	Kelly Downs	.05
304	Scott Bankhead	.05
305	Pedro Munoz	.08
306	Scott Scudder	.05
307	Kevin Elster	.05
308	Duane Ward	.05
309	*Darryl Kile*	.15
310	Orlando Merced	.05
311	Dave Henderson	.05
312	Tim Raines	.10
313	Mark Lee	.05
314	Mike Gallego	.05
315	Charles Nagy	.05
316	Jesse Barfield	.05
317	Todd Frohwirth	.05
318	Al Osuna	.05
319	Darrin Fletcher	.05
320	Checklist 238-316	.05
321	David Segui	.05
322	Stan Javier	.05
323	Bryn Smith	.05
324	Jeff Treadway	.05
325	Mark Whiten	.05
326	Kent Hrbek	.08
327	Dave Justice	.35
328	Tony Phillips	.08
329	Rob Murphy	.05
330	Kevin Morton	.05
331	John Smiley	.05
332	Luis Rivera	.05
333	Wally Joyner	.10
334	*Heathcliff Slocumb*	.10
335	Rick Cerone	.05
336	*Mike Remlinger*	.05
337	Mike Moore	.05
338	Lloyd McClendon	.05
339	Al Newman	.05
340	Kirk McCaskill	.05
341	Howard Johnson	.05
342	Greg Myers	.05
343	Kal Daniels	.05
344	Bernie Williams	.25
345	Shane Mack	.05
346	Gary Thurman	.05
347	Dante Bichette	.08
348	Mark McGwire	1.50
349	Travis Fryman	.15
350	Ray Lankford	.08
351	Mike Jeffcoat	.05
352	Jack McDowell	.10
353	Mitch Williams	.08
354	Mike Devereaux	.05
355	Andres Galarraga	.10
356	Henry Cotto	.05
357	Scott Bailes	.05
358	Jeff Bagwell	.60
359	Scott Leius	.05
360	Zane Smith	.05
361	Bill Pecota	.05
362	Tony Fernandez	.05
363	Glenn Braggs	.05
364	Bill Spiers	.05
365	Vicente Palacios	.05
366	Tim Burke	.05
367	Randy Tomlin	.05
368	Kenny Rogers	.05
369	Brett Butler	.08
370	Pat Kelly	.10
371	Bip Roberts	.05
372	Gregg Jefferies	.15
373	Kevin Bass	.05
374	Ron Karkovice	.05
375	Paul Gibson	.05
376	Bernard Gilkey	.08
377	Dave Gallagher	.05
378	Bill Wegman	.05
379	Pat Borders	.05
380	Ed Whitson	.05
381	Gilberto Reyes	.05
382	Russ Swan	.05
383	Andy Van Slyke	.08
384	Wes Chamberlain	.08
385	Steve Chitren	.05
386	Greg Olson	.05
387	Brian McRae	.10
388	Rich Rodriguez	.05
389	Steve Decker	.05
390	Chuck Knoblauch	.10
391	Bobby Witt	.05
392	Eddie Murray	.15
393	Juan Gonzalez	.60
394	Scott Ruskin	.05
395	Jay Howell	.05
396	Checklist 317-396	.05
397	Royce Clayton (Rated Rookie)	.20
398	John Jaha (Rated Rookie)	.15
399	Dan Wilson (Rated Rookie)	.15
400	*Archie Corbin* (Rated Rookie)	.08
401	*Barry Manuel* (Rated Rookie)	.05
402	Kim Batiste (Rated Rookie)	.08
403	*Pat Mahomes* (Rated Rookie)	.08
404	Dave Fleming (Rated Rookie)	.10
405	Jeff Juden (Rated Rookie)	.15
406	*Jim Thome* (Rated Rookie)	.30
407	Sam Militello (Rated Rookie)	.10
408	*Jeff Nelson* (Rated Rookie)	.05
409	Anthony Young (Rated Rookie)	.15
410	Tino Martinez (Rated Rookie)	.25
411	*Jeff Mutis* (Rated Rookie)	.08
412	*Rey Sanchez* (Rated Rookie)	.08
413	*Chris Gardner* (Rated Rookie)	.08
414	*John Vander Wal* (Rated Rookie)	.08
415	Reggie Sanders (Rated Rookie)	.15
416	*Brian Williams* (Rated Rookie)	.10
417	Mo Sanford (Rated Rookie)	.15
418	*David Weathers* (Rated Rookie)	.08
419	*Hector Fajardo* (Rated Rookie)	.08
420	*Steve Foster* (Rated Rookie)	.08
421	Lance Dickson (Rated Rookie)	.10
422	Andre Dawson (All-Star)	.10
423	Ozzie Smith (All-Star)	.10
424	Chris Sabo (All-Star)	.05
425	Tony Gwynn (All-Star)	.10
426	Tom Glavine (All-Star)	.05
427	Bobby Bonilla (All-Star)	.10
428	Will Clark (All-Star)	.15
429	Ryne Sandberg (All-Star)	.15
430	Benito Santiago (All-Star)	.08
431	Ivan Calderon (All-Star)	.05
432	Ozzie Smith	.15
433	Tim Leary	.05
434	Bret Saberhagen (Highlight)	.05
435	Mel Rojas	.08
436	Ben McDonald	.08
437	Tim Crews	.05
438	Rex Hudler	.05
439	Chico Walker	.05
440	Kurt Stillwell	.05
441	Tony Gwynn	.30
442	John Smoltz	.08
443	Lloyd Moseby	.05
444	Mike Schooler	.05
445	Joe Grahe	.05
446	Dwight Gooden	.10
447	Oil Can Boyd	.05
448	John Marzano	.05
449	Bret Barberie	.05
450	Mike Maddux	.05
451	Jeff Reed	.05
452	Dale Sveum	.05
453	Jose Uribe	.05
454	Bob Scanlan	.05
455	Kevin Appier	.08
456	Jeff Huson	.05
457	Ken Patterson	.05
458	Ricky Jordan	.05
459	Tom Candiotti	.05
460	Lee Stevens	.05
461	*Rod Beck*	.15
462	Dave Valle	.05
463	Scott Erickson	.10
464	Chris Jones	.05
465	Mark Carreon	.05
466	Rob Ducey	.05
467	Jim Corsi	.05
468	Jeff King	.05
469	Curt Young	.05
470	Bo Jackson	.15
471	Chris Bosio	.05
472	Jamie Quirk	.05
473	Jesse Orosco	.05
474	Alvaro Espinoza	.05
475	Joe Orsulak	.05
476	Checklist 397-477	.05
477	Gerald Young	.05
478	Wally Backman	.05
479	Juan Bell	.05
480	Mike Scioscia	.05
481	Omar Olivares	.05
482	Francisco Cabrera	.05
483	Greg Swindell	.05
484	Terry Leach	.05
485	Tommy Gregg	.05
486	Scott Aldred	.05
487	Greg Briley	.05
488	Phil Plantier	.10
489	Curtis Wilkerson	.05
490	Tom Brunansky	.05
491	Mike Fetters	.05
492	Frank Castillo	.05
493	Joe Boever	.05
494	Kirt Manwaring	.05
495	Wilson Alvarez (Highlight)	.05
496	Gene Larkin	.05
497	Gary DiSarcina	.05
498	Frank Viola	.05
499	Manuel Lee	.05
500	Albert Belle	.35
501	Stan Belinda	.05

#	Player	Value
502	Dwight Evans	.05
503	Eric Davis	.12
504	Darren Holmes	.05
505	Mike Bordick	.05
506	Dave Hansen	.05
507	Lee Guetterman	.05
508	*Keith Mitchell*	.05
509	Melido Perez	.05
510	Dickie Thon	.05
511	Mark Williamson	.05
512	Mark Salas	.05
513	Milt Thompson	.05
514	Mo Vaughn	.35
515	Jim Deshaies	.05
516	Rich Garces	.05
517	Lonnie Smith	.05
518	Spike Owen	.05
519	Tracy Jones	.05
520	Greg Maddux	.75
521	Carlos Martinez	.05
522	Neal Heaton	.05
523	Mike Greenwell	.08
524	Andy Benes	.08
525	Jeff Schaefer	.05
526	Mike Sharperson	.05
527	Wade Taylor	.05
528	Jerome Walton	.05
529	Storm Davis	.05
530	*Jose Hernandez*	.05
531	Mark Langston	.05
532	Rob Deer	.05
533	Geronimo Pena	.05
534	*Juan Guzman*	.12
535	Pete Schourek	.05
536	Todd Benzinger	.05
537	Billy Hatcher	.05
538	Tom Foley	.05
539	Dave Cochrane	.05
540	Mariano Duncan	.05
541	Edwin Nunez	.05
542	Rance Mulliniks	.05
543	Carlton Fisk	.10
544	Luis Aquino	.05
545	Ricky Bones	.08
546	Craig Grebeck	.05
547	Charlie Hayes	.05
548	Jose Canseco	.25
549	Andujar Cedeno	.05
550	Geno Petralli	.05
551	Javier Ortiz	.05
552	Rudy Seanez	.05
553	Rich Gedman	.05
554	Eric Plunk	.05
555	Nolan Ryan, Rich Gossage (Highlight)	.20
556	Checklist 478-555	.05
557	Greg Colbrunn	.05
558	*Chito Martinez*	.10
559	Darryl Strawberry	.10
560	Luis Alicea	.05
561	Dwight Smith	.05
562	Terry Shumpert	.05
563	Jim Vatcher	.05
564	Deion Sanders	.10
565	Walt Terrell	.05
566	Dave Burba	.05
567	Dave Howard	.05
568	Todd Hundley	.05
569	Jack Daugherty	.05
570	Scott Cooper	.05
571	Bill Sampen	.05
572	Jose Melendez	.05
573	Freddie Benavides	.05
574	Jim Gantner	.05
575	Trevor Wilson	.05
576	Ryne Sandberg	.20
577	Kevin Seitzer	.05
578	Gerald Alexander	.05
579	Mike Huff	.05
580	Von Hayes	.05
581	Derek Bell	.15
582	Mike Stanley	.05
583	Kevin Mitchell	.08
584	Mike Jackson	.05
585	Dan Gladden	.05
586	Ted Power	.05
587	Jeff Innis	.05
588	Bob MacDonald	.05
589	*Jose Tolentino*	.05
590	Bob Patterson	.05
591	*Scott Brosius*	.10
592	Frank Thomas	1.50
593	Darryl Hamilton	.05
594	Kirk Dressendorfer	.05
595	Jeff Shaw	.05
596	Don Mattingly	.30
597	Glenn Davis	.05
598	Andy Mota	.05
599	Jason Grimsley	.05
600	Jimmy Poole	.05
601	Jim Gott	.05
602	Stan Royer	.08
603	Marvin Freeman	.05
604	Denis Boucher	.08
605	Denny Neagle	.10
606	Mark Lemke	.05
607	Jerry Don Gleaton	.05
608	Brent Knackert	.05
609	Carlos Quintana	.05
610	Bobby Bonilla	.12
611	Joe Hesketh	.05
612	Daryl Boston	.05
613	Shawon Dunston	.08
614	Danny Cox	.05
615	Darren Lewis	.12
616	Alejandro Pena, Kent Mercker, Mark Wohlers (Highlight)	.10
617	Kirby Puckett	.30
618	Franklin Stubbs	.05
619	Chris Donnels	.10
620	David Wells	.05
621	Mike Aldrete	.05
622	Bob Kipper	.05
623	Anthony Telford	.05
624	Randy Myers	.05
625	Willie Randolph	.05
626	Joe Slusarski	.05
627	John Wetteland	.05
628	Greg Cadaret	.05
629	Tom Glavine	.10
630	Wilson Alvarez	.10
631	Wally Ritchie	.05
632	Mike Mussina	.30
633	Mark Leiter	.05
634	Gerald Perry	.05
635	Matt Young	.05
636	Checklist 556-635	.05
637	Scott Hemond	.05
638	David West	.05
639	Jim Clancy	.05
640	Doug Piatt	.05
641	Omar Vizquel	.05
642	Rick Sutcliffe	.05
643	Glenallen Hill	.08
644	Gary Varsho	.05
645	Tony Fossas	.05
646	Jack Howell	.05
647	*Jim Campanis*	.10
648	Chris Gwynn	.05
649	Jim Leyritz	.05
650	Chuck McElroy	.05
651	Sean Berry	.08
652	Donald Harris	.10
653	Don Slaught	.05
654	*Rusty Meacham*	.05
655	Scott Terry	.05
656	Ramon Martinez	.10
657	Keith Miller	.05
658	Ramon Garcia	.05
659	*Milt Hill*	.10
660	Steve Frey	.05
661	Bob McClure	.05
662	*Ced Landrum*	.05
663	*Doug Henry*	.05
664	Candy Maldonado	.05
665	Carl Willis	.05
666	Jeff Montgomery	.05
667	*Craig Shipley*	.10
668	*Warren Newson*	.05
669	Mickey Morandini	.05
670	Brook Jacoby	.05
671	*Ryan Bowen*	.10
672	Bill Krueger	.05
673	Rob Mallicoat	.05
674	Doug Jones	.05
675	Scott Livingstone	.05
676	Danny Tartabull	.05
677	Joe Carter (Highlight)	.05
678	Cecil Espy	.05
679	Randy Velarde	.05
680	Bruce Ruffin	.05
681	*Ted Wood*	.05
682	Dan Plesac	.05
683	Eric Bullock	.05
684	Junior Ortiz	.05
685	Dave Hollins	.08
686	Dennis Martinez	.08
687	Larry Andersen	.05
688	Doug Simons	.05
689	*Tim Spehr*	.05
690	*Calvin Jones*	.05
691	Mark Guthrie	.05
692	Alfredo Griffin	.05
693	Joe Carter	.20
694	*Terry Mathews*	.08
695	Pascual Perez	.05
696	Gene Nelson	.05
697	Gerald Williams	.08
698	*Chris Cron*	.08
699	Steve Buechele	.05
700	Paul McClellan	.05
701	Jim Lindeman	.05
702	Francisco Oliveras	.05
703	*Rob Maurer*	.05
704	*Pat Hentgen*	.25
705	Jaime Navarro	.05
706	*Mike Magnante*	.05
707	Nolan Ryan	.75
708	Bobby Thigpen	.05
709	John Cerutti	.05
710	Steve Wilson	.05
711	Hensley Meulens	.05
712	*Rheal Cormier*	.20
713	Scott Bradley	.05
714	Mitch Webster	.05
715	Roger Mason	.05
716	Checklist 636-716	.05
717	*Jeff Fassero*	.10
718	Cal Eldred	.08
719	Sid Fernandez	.05
720	*Bob Zupcic*	.05
721	Jose Offerman	.08
722	*Cliff Brantley*	.10
723	Ron Darling	.05
724	Dave Stieb	.05
725	Hector Villanueva	.05
726	Mike Hartley	.05
727	*Arthur Rhodes*	.15
728	Randy Bush	.05
729	Steve Sax	.05
730	Dave Otto	.05
731	*John Wehner*	.05
732	Dave Martinez	.05
733	*Ruben Amaro*	.05
734	Billy Ripken	.05
735	Steve Farr	.05
736	Shawn Abner	.05
737	*Gil Heredia*	.10
738	Ron Jones	.05
739	Tony Castillo	.05
740	Sammy Sosa	.75
741	Julio Franco	.05
742	Tim Naehring	.08
743	*Steve Wapnick*	.05
744	Craig Wilson	.05
745	*Darrin Chapin*	.08
746	Chris George	.08
747	Mike Simms	.05
748	Rosario Rodriguez	.05
749	Skeeter Barnes	.05
750	Roger McDowell	.05
751	Dann Howitt	.05
752	Paul Sorrento	.05
753	*Braulio Castillo*	.08
754	*Yorkis Perez*	.05
755	Willie Fraser	.05
756	*Jeremy Hernandez*	.05
757	Curt Schilling	.05
758	Steve Lyons	.05
759	Dave Anderson	.05
760	Willie Banks	.05
761	Mark Leonard	.05
762	Jack Armstrong	.05
763	Scott Servais	.05
764	Ray Stephens	.05
765	Junior Noboa	.05
766	*Jim Olander*	.05
767	Joe Magrane	.05
768	Lance Blankenship	.05
769	*Mike Humphreys*	.10
770	*Jarvis Brown*	.08
771	Damon Berryhill	.05
772	Alejandro Pena	.05
773	Jose Mesa	.05
774	*Gary Cooper*	.05
775	Carney Lansford	.05
776	Mike Bielecki	.05
777	Charlie O'Brien	.05
778	Carlos Hernandez	.05
779	Howard Farmer	.05
780	Mike Stanton	.05
781	Reggie Harris	.05
782	Xavier Hernandez	.05
783	*Bryan Hickerson*	.05
784	Checklist 717-BC8	.05

1992 Donruss Bonus Cards

The eight bonus cards were randomly inserted in 1992 foil packs and are numbered with a "BC" prefix. Both leagues' MVPs, Cy Young and Rookie of the Year award winners are featured, as are logo cards for the expansion Colorado Rockies and Florida Marlins. Cards are standard size in a format similar to the regular issue.

		MT
Complete Set (8):		3.00
Common Player:		.30
1	Cal Ripken, Jr. (MVP)	1.00
2	Terry Pendleton (MVP)	.30
3	Roger Clemens (Cy Young)	.75
4	Tom Glavine (Cy Young)	.40
5	Chuck Knoblauch (Rookie of the Year)	.60
6	Jeff Bagwell (Rookie of the Year)	1.00
7	Colorado Rockies	.50
8	Florida Marlins	.50

1992 Donruss Diamond Kings

FRED McGRIFF

Donruss changed its Diamond Kings style and distribution in 1992. The cards still feature the art of Dick Perez, but quality was improved from past years. The cards were randomly inserted in foil packs. One player from each team is featured. Card numbers have a "DK" prefix.

		MT
Complete Set (27):		35.00
Common Player:		.50
1	Paul Molitor	2.50
2	Will Clark	1.25
3	Joe Carter	.65
4	Julio Franco	.50
5	Cal Ripken, Jr.	9.00
6	Dave Justice	2.00
7	George Bell	.50
8	Frank Thomas	9.00
9	Wade Boggs	1.50
10	Scott Sanderson	.50
11	Jeff Bagwell	4.00
12	John Kruk	.50
13	Felix Jose	.50
14	Harold Baines	.50
15	Dwight Gooden	.75
16	Brian McRae	.50
17	Jay Bell	.50
18	Brett Butler	.65
19	Hal Morris	.50
20	Mark Langston	.50
21	Scott Erickson	.50
22	Randy Johnson	1.25
23	Greg Swindell	.50
24	Dennis Martinez	.50
25	Tony Phillips	.50
26	Fred McGriff	1.25
27	Checklist	.25

1992 Donruss Elite

HOWARD JOHNSON

Donruss continued its Elite series in 1992 by inserting cards in foil packs. Each card was released in the same quantity as the 1991 inserts - 10,000 Elite, 7,500 Legend and 5,000 Signature. The Elite cards, now featuring a prismatic border, are numbered as a continuation of the 1991 issue. Rickey Henderson and Cal Ripken are the subjects of the Legend card and Signature card, respectively.

		MT
Complete Set (12):		800.00
Common Player:		10.00
9	Wade Boggs	30.00
10	Joe Carter	15.00
11	Will Clark	25.00
12	Dwight Gooden	15.00
13	Ken Griffey, Jr.	160.00
14	Tony Gwynn	50.00
15	Howard Johnson	10.00
16	Terry Pendleton	10.00
17	Kirby Puckett	65.00
18	Frank Thomas	120.00
---	Rickey Henderson (Legend)	65.00
---	Cal Ripken, Jr. (Signature)	375.00

1992 Donruss Rookies

HARVEY PULLIAM
ROYALS • OUTFIELD

Donruss increased the size of its Rookies set in 1992 to include 132 cards. In the past the cards were released only in boxed set form, but the 1992 cards were available in packs. Special "Phenoms" cards were randomly inserted into Rookies packs. The Phenoms cards feature black borders, while the Rookies cards are styled after the regular 1992 Donruss issue. The cards are numbered alphabetically.

		MT
Complete Set (132):		5.00
Common Player:		.05
Wax Box:		25.00
1	Kyle Abbott	.05
2	Troy Afenir	.05
3	Rich Amaral	.05
4	Ruben Amaro	.05
5	Billy Ashley	.10
6	Pedro Astacio	.10
7	Jim Austin	.05
8	Robert Ayrault	.05
9	Kevin Baez	.05
10	Estaban Beltre	.05
11	Brian Bohanon	.05
12	Kent Bottenfield	.05
13	Jeff Branson	.10
14	Brad Brink	.05
15	John Briscoe	.05
16	Doug Brocail	.05
17	Rico Brogna	.15
18	J.T. Bruett	.05
19	Jacob Brumfield	.12
20	Jim Bullinger	.10
21	Kevin Campbell	.05
22	Pedro Castellano	.05
23	Mike Christopher	.05
24	Archi Cianfrocco	.05
25	Mark Clark	.10
26	Craig Colbert	.05
27	Victor Cole	.05
28	Steve Cooke	.10
29	Tim Costo	.10
30	Chad Curtis	.30
31	Doug Davis	.05
32	Gary DiSarcina	.10
33	John Doherty	.10
34	Mike Draper	.05
35	Monty Fariss	.05
36	Bien Figueroa	.10
37	John Flaherty	.10
38	Tim Fortugno	.05
39	Eric Fox	.10
40	*Jeff Frye*	.10
41	Ramon Garcia	.05
42	Brent Gates	.25
43	Tom Goodwin	.10
44	Buddy Groom	.05
45	Jeff Grotewold	.10
46	Juan Guerrero	.05

47	Johnny Guzman	.10
48	Shawn Hare	.10
49	Ryan Hawblitzel	.10
50	Bert Heffernan	.05
51	Butch Henry	.05
52	Cesar Hernandez	.05
53	Vince Horsman	.10
54	Steve Hosey	.10
55	Pat Howell	.10
56	Peter Hoy	.05
57	Jon Hurst	.05
58	Mark Hutton	.05
59	Shawn Jeter	.10
60	Joel Johnston	.05
61	Jeff Kent	.40
62	Kurt Knudsen	.05
63	Kevin Koslofski	.10
64	Danny Leon	.05
65	Jesse Levis	.05
66	Tom Marsh	.05
67	Ed Martel	.05
68	Al Martin	.25
69	Pedro Martinez	1.00
70	Derrick May	.10
71	Matt Maysey	.10
72	Russ McGinnis	.05
73	Tim McIntosh	.05
74	Jim McNamara	.05
75	Jeff McNeely	.15
76	Rusty Meacham	.10
77	Tony Melendez	.05
78	Henry Mercedes	.05
79	Paul Miller	.05
80	Joe Millette	.05
81	Blas Minor	.05
82	Dennis Moeller	.05
83	Raul Mondesi	1.50
84	Rob Natal	.15
85	Troy Neel	.15
86	David Nied	.05
87	Jerry Nielsen	.05
88	Donovan Osborne	.10
89	John Patterson	.12
90	Roger Pavlik	.10
91	Dan Peltier	.05
92	Jim Pena	.05
93	William Pennyfeather	.10
94	Mike Perez	.10
95	Hipolito Pichardo	.05
96	Greg Pirkl	.05
97	Harvey Pulliam	.05
98	Manny Ramirez	2.50
99	Pat Rapp	.12
100	Jeff Reboulet	.05
101	Darren Reed	.10
102	Shane Reynolds	.10
103	Bill Risley	.10
104	Ben Rivera	.05
105	Henry Rodriguez	.10
106	Rico Rossy	.10
107	Johnny Ruffin	.10
108	Steve Scarsone	.10
109	Tim Scott	.05
110	Steve Shifflett	.05
111	Dave Silvestri	.10
112	Matt Stairs	.05
113	William Suero	.05
114	Jeff Tackett	.10
115	Eddie Taubensee	.25
116	Rick Trlicek	.05
117	Scooter Tucker	.05
118	Shane Turner	.05
119	Julio Valera	.05
120	Paul Wagner	.05
121	Tim Wakefield	.15
122	Mike Walker	.05
123	Bruce Walton	.05
124	Lenny Webster	.05
125	Bob Wickman	.10
126	Mike Williams	.05
127	Kerry Woodson	.05
128	Eric Young	.25
129	Kevin Young	.10
130	Pete Young	.05
131	Checklist	.05
132	Checklist	.05

A player's name in *italic* type indicates a rookie card.

1992 Donruss Rookie Phenoms

BRET BOONE
SEATTLE MARINERS—SS/2B

The first 12 cards in this insert set were available in Donruss Rookies foil packs. Cards 13-20 were found randomly packed in jumbo packs. Predominantly black on both front and back, the borders are highlighted with gold. A gold-foil "Phenoms" appears at top front.

		MT
Complete Set (20):		35.00
Common Player:		.50
1	Moises Alou	2.50
2	Bret Boone	1.50
3	Jeff Conine	1.00
4	Dave Fleming	.50
5	Tyler Green	.50
6	Eric Karros	1.00
7	Pat Listach	.50
8	Kenny Lofton	14.00
9	Mike Piazza	20.00
10	Tim Salmon	7.50
11	Andy Stankiewicz	.50
12	Dan Walters	.50
13	Ramon Caraballo	.50
14	Brian Jordan	1.50
15	Ryan Klesko	10.00
16	Sam Militello	.50
17	Frank Seminara	.50
18	Salomon Torres	.50
19	John Valentin	2.00
20	Wil Cordero	.85

1992 Donruss Update

Each retail factory set of 1992 Donruss cards contained a cello-wrapped four-card selection from this 22-card Update set. The cards feature the same basic format as the regular '92 Donruss, except they carry a "U" prefix to the card number on back. The cards feature rookies, highlights and traded players from the 1992 season.

		MT
Complete Set (22):		65.00
Common Player:		1.00
U-1	Pat Listach (Rated Rookie)	1.00
U-2	Andy Stankiewicz (Rated Rookie)	1.00
U-3	Brian Jordan (Rated Rookie)	3.00
U-4	Dan Walters (Rated Rookie)	1.00
U-5	Chad Curtis (Rated Rookie)	2.50
U-6	Kenny Lofton (Rated Rookie)	30.00
U-7	Mark McGwire (Highlight)	30.00
U-8	Eddie Murray (Highlight)	4.00
U-9	Jeff Reardon (Highlight)	1.00

U-10	Frank Viola	1.00
U-11	Gary Sheffield	4.00
U-12	George Bell	1.00
U-13	Rick Sutcliffe	1.00
U-14	Wally Joyner	2.00
U-15	Kevin Seitzer	1.00
U-16	Bill Krueger	1.00
U-17	Danny Tartabull	1.00
U-18	Dave Winfield	5.00
U-19	Gary Carter	2.00
U-20	Bobby Bonilla	2.00
U-21	Cory Snyder	1.00
U-22	Bill Swift	1.00

1993 Donruss

ROBERTO ALOMAR 2B

Rated Rookies and a randomly inserted Diamond Kings subset once again are featured in the 1993 Donruss set. Series I of the set includes 396 cards. Card fronts feature white borders surrounding a full-color player photo. The flip sides feature an additional photo, biographical information and career statistics. The cards are numbered on the back and the card's series is given with the number. The cards are UV coated. Series II contains a subset of players labeled with an "Expansion Draft" headline over their Marlins or Rockies team logo on front, even though the player photos are in the uniform of their previous team.

		MT
Complete Set (792):		30.00
Common Player:		.05
Series 1 or 2 Wax Box:		24.00
1	Craig Lefferts	.05
2	Kent Mercker	.05
3	Phil Plantier	.08
4	*Alex Arias*	.15
5	Julio Valera	.05
6	Dan Wilson	.12
7	Frank Thomas	2.00
8	Eric Anthony	.05
9	Derek Lilliquist	.05
10	*Rafael Bournigal*	.12
11	*Manny Alexander* (Rated Rookie)	.12
12	Bret Barberie	.05
13	Mickey Tettleton	.05
14	Anthony Young	.08
15	Tim Spehr	.05
16	*Bob Ayrault*	.10
17	Bill Wegman	.05
18	Jay Bell	.05
19	Rick Aguilera	.05
20	Todd Zeile	.08
21	Steve Farr	.05
22	Andy Benes	.08
23	Lance Blankenship	.05
24	Ted Wood	.05
25	Omar Vizquel	.05
26	Steve Avery	.15

No.	Player		No.	Player		No.	Player	
27	Brian Bohanon	.05	122	Checklist 1-80	.05	217	Tino Martinez	.10
28	Rick Wilkins	.05	123	Steve Sax	.05	218	*Henry Rodriguez*	.12
29	Devon White	.05	124	Chuck Carr	.05	219	Ed Sprague	.05
30	*Bobby Ayala*	.12	125	Mark Lewis	.05	220	Ken Hill	.08
31	Leo Gomez	.05	126	Tony Gwynn	.40	221	Chito Martinez	.05
32	Mike Simms	.05	127	Travis Fryman	.10	222	Bret Saberhagen	.08
33	Ellis Burks	.08	128	Dave Burba	.05	223	Mike Greenwell	.05
34	Steve Wilson	.05	129	Wally Joyner	.08	224	Mickey Morandini	.05
35	Jim Abbott	.08	130	John Smoltz	.08	225	Chuck Finley	.05
36	Tim Wallach	.05	131	Cal Eldred	.05	226	Denny Neagle	.08
37	Wilson Alvarez	.05	132	Checklist 81-159	.05	227	Kirk McCaskill	.05
38	Daryl Boston	.05	133	Arthur Rhodes	.05	228	Rheal Cormier	.05
39	Sandy Alomar, Jr.	.10	134	Jeff Blauser	.05	229	Paul Sorrento	.05
40	Mitch Williams	.08	135	Scott Cooper	.05	230	Darrin Jackson	.05
41	Rico Brogna	.10	136	Doug Strange	.05	231	Rob Deer	.05
42	Gary Varsho	.05	137	Luis Sojo	.05	232	Bill Swift	.05
43	Kevin Appier	.08	138	*Jeff Branson*	.10	233	Kevin McReynolds	.05
44	Eric Wedge (Rated Rookie)	.12	139	Alex Fernandez	.08	234	Terry Pendleton	.05
45	Dante Bichette	.08	140	Ken Caminiti	.08	235	Dave Nilsson	.05
46	Jose Oquendo	.05	141	Charles Nagy	.05	236	Chuck McElroy	.05
47	*Mike Trombley*	.05	142	Tom Candiotti	.05	237	Derek Parks	.05
48	Dan Walters	.05	143	Willie Green (Rated Rookie)	.10	238	Norm Charlton	.05
49	Gerald Williams	.05	144	John Vander Wal	.05	239	Matt Nokes	.05
50	Bud Black	.05	145	*Kurt Knudsen*	.05	240	*Juan Guerrero*	.08
51	Bobby Witt	.05	146	John Franco	.05	241	Jeff Parrett	.05
52	Mark Davis	.05	147	*Eddie Pierce*	.05	242	Ryan Thompson (Rated Rookie)	.15
53	*Shawn Barton*	.10	148	Kim Batiste	.05	243	Dave Fleming	.05
54	Paul Assenmacher	.05	149	Darren Holmes	.05	244	Dave Hansen	.05
55	Kevin Reimer	.05	150	*Steve Cooke*	.15	245	Monty Fariss	.05
56	*Billy Ashley* (Rated Rookie)	.30	151	Terry Jorgensen	.05	246	*Archi Cianfrocco*	.05
57	Eddie Zosky	.05	152	*Mark Clark*	.10	247	*Pat Hentgen*	.15
58	Chris Sabo	.05	153	Randy Velarde	.05	248	Bill Pecota	.05
59	Billy Ripken	.05	154	Greg Harris	.05	249	Ben McDonald	.08
60	*Scooter Tucker*	.12	155	*Kevin Campbell*	.10	250	Cliff Brantley	.05
61	*Tim Wakefield* (Rated Rookie)	.10	156	John Burkett	.05	251	*John Valentin*	.15
62	Mitch Webster	.05	157	Kevin Mitchell	.05	252	Jeff King	.05
63	Jack Clark	.05	158	Deion Sanders	.20	253	*Reggie Williams*	.10
64	Mark Gardner	.05	159	Jose Canseco	.25	254	Checklist 160-238	.05
65	Lee Stevens	.05	160	*Jeff Hartsock*	.05	255	Ozzie Guillen	.05
66	Todd Hundley	.05	161	*Tom Quinlan*	.10	256	Mike Perez	.05
67	Bobby Thigpen	.05	162	*Tim Pugh*	.10	257	Thomas Howard	.05
68	Dave Hollins	.10	163	Glenn Davis	.05	258	Kurt Stillwell	.05
69	Jack Armstrong	.05	164	*Shane Reynolds*	.12	259	Mike Henneman	.05
70	Alex Cole	.05	165	Jody Reed	.05	260	Steve Decker	.05
71	Mark Carreon	.05	166	Mike Sharperson	.05	261	Brent Mayne	.05
72	Todd Worrell	.05	167	Scott Lewis	.05	262	Otis Nixon	.05
73	*Steve Shifflett*	.05	168	Dennis Martinez	.08	263	*Mark Keifer*	.05
74	Jerald Clark	.05	169	Scott Radinsky	.05	264	Checklist 239-317	.05
75	Paul Molitor	.25	170	Dave Gallagher	.05	265	*Richie Lewis*	.05
76	*Larry Carter*	.05	171	Jim Thome	.25	266	*Pat Gomez*	.12
77	Rich Rowland	.05	172	Terry Mulholland	.05	267	*Scott Taylor*	.15
78	Damon Berryhill	.05	173	Milt Cuyler	.05	268	Shawon Dunston	.08
79	Willie Banks	.05	174	Bob Patterson	.05	269	Greg Myers	.05
80	Hector Villanueva	.05	175	Jeff Montgomery	.05	270	Tim Costo	.05
81	Mike Gallego	.05	176	Tim Salmon (Rated Rookie)	.50	271	Greg Hibbard	.05
82	Tim Belcher	.05	177	Franklin Stubbs	.05	272	Pete Harnisch	.05
83	Mike Bordick	.05	178	Donovan Osborne	.05	273	*Dave Mlicki*	.08
84	Craig Biggio	.08	179	*Jeff Reboulet*	.05	274	Orel Hershiser	.08
85	Lance Parrish	.05	180	*Jeremy Hernandez*	.08	275	Sean Berry (Rated Rookie)	.08
86	Brett Butler	.08	181	Charlie Hayes	.05	276	Doug Simons	.05
87	Mike Timlin	.05	182	Matt Williams	.20	277	*John Doherty*	.10
88	Brian Barnes	.05	183	Mike Raczka	.05	278	Eddie Murray	.15
89	Brady Anderson	.10	184	Francisco Cabrera	.05	279	Chris Haney	.05
90	D.J. Dozier	.05	185	Rich DeLucia	.05	280	Stan Javier	.05
91	Frank Viola	.05	186	Sammy Sosa	1.00	281	Jaime Navarro	.05
92	Darren Daulton	.08	187	Ivan Rodriguez	.40	282	Orlando Merced	.05
93	Chad Curtis	.15	188	Bret Boone (Rated Rookie)	.15	283	Kent Hrbek	.08
94	Zane Smith	.05	189	Juan Guzman	.10	284	Bernard Gilkey	.08
95	George Bell	.08	190	Tom Browning	.05	285	Russ Springer	.05
96	Rex Hudler	.05	191	Randy Milligan	.05	286	Mike Maddux	.05
97	Mark Whiten	.08	192	Steve Finley	.05	287	*Eric Fox*	.10
98	Tim Teufel	.05	193	John Patterson (Rated Rookie)	.08	288	Mark Leonard	.05
99	Kevin Ritz	.05	194	Kip Gross	.05	289	Tim Leary	.05
100	Jeff Brantley	.05	195	Tony Fossas	.05	290	Brian Hunter	.08
101	Jeff Conine	.08	196	Ivan Calderon	.05	291	Donald Harris	.05
102	Vinny Castilla	.20	197	Junior Felix	.05	292	Bob Scanlan	.05
103	Greg Vaughn	.05	198	Pete Schourek	.05	293	Turner Ward	.05
104	Steve Buechele	.05	199	Craig Grebeck	.05	294	Hal Morris	.08
105	Darren Reed	.05	200	Juan Bell	.05	295	Jimmy Poole	.05
106	Bip Roberts	.05	201	Glenallen Hill	.08	296	Doug Jones	.05
107	John Habyan	.05	202	Danny Jackson	.05	297	Tony Pena	.05
108	Scott Servais	.05	203	John Kiely	.08	298	Ramon Martinez	.08
109	Walt Weiss	.05	204	Bob Tewksbury	.08	299	*Tim Fortugno*	.12
110	J.T. Snow (Rated Rookie)	.75	205	*Kevin Koslofski*	.15	300	Marquis Grissom	.10
111	Jay Buhner	.08	206	Craig Shipley	.05	301	Lance Johnson	.05
112	Darryl Strawberry	.08	207	John Jaha	.10	302	*Jeff Kent*	.15
113	*Roger Pavlik*	.12	208	Royce Clayton	.05	303	Reggie Jefferson	.05
114	Chris Nabholz	.05	209	Mike Piazza (Rated Rookie)	1.50	304	Wes Chamberlain	.05
115	Pat Borders	.05	210	Ron Gant	.08	305	*Shawn Hare*	.12
116	*Pat Howell*	.10	211	Scott Erickson	.05	306	Mike LaValliere	.05
117	Gregg Olson	.05	212	Doug Dascenzo	.05	307	Gregg Jefferies	.08
118	Curt Schilling	.05	213	Andy Stankiewicz	.08	308	*Troy Neel* (Rated Rookie)	.20
119	Roger Clemens	.40	214	Geronimo Berroa	.05	309	Pat Listach	.05
120	*Victor Cole*	.05	215	Dennis Eckersley	.08	310	Geronimo Pena	.05
121	Gary DiSarcina	.05	216	Al Osuna	.05	311	Pedro Munoz	.05

#	Player	Price	#	Player	Price	#	Player	Price
312	*Guillermo Velasquez*	.10	406	Carlos Hernandez	.05	499	Chris Bosio	.05
313	Roberto Kelly	.08	407	Pedro Astacio (Rated Rookie)	.15	500	Shawn Boskie	.05
314	Mike Jackson	.05				501	Dave West	.05
315	Rickey Henderson	.12	408	Mel Rojas	.05	502	Milt Hill	.05
316	Mark Lemke	.05	409	Scott Livingstone	.05	503	Pat Kelly	.05
317	Erik Hanson	.05	410	Chico Walker	.05	504	Joe Boever	.05
318	Derrick May	.05	411	Brian McRae	.05	505	Terry Steinbach	.05
319	Geno Petralli	.05	412	Ben Rivera	.05	506	Butch Huskey (Rated Rookie)	.15
320	Melvin Nieves (Rated Rookie)	.15	413	Ricky Bones	.05			
321	*Doug Linton*	.15	414	Andy Van Slyke	.05	507	David Valle	.05
322	Rob Dibble	.05	415	Chuck Knoblauch	.12	508	Mike Scioscia	.05
323	Chris Hoiles	.05	416	Luis Alicea	.05	509	Kenny Rogers	.05
324	Jimmy Jones	.05	417	Bob Wickman	.08	510	Moises Alou	.10
325	Dave Staton (Rated Rookie)	.08	418	Doug Brocail	.05	511	David Wells	.05
326	Pedro Martinez	.08	419	Scott Brosius	.05	512	Mackey Sasser	.05
327	*Paul Quantrill*	.10	420	Rod Beck	.05	513	Todd Frohwirth	.05
328	Greg Colbrunn	.05	421	Edgar Martinez	.05	514	Ricky Jordan	.05
329	*Hilly Hathaway*	.12	422	Ryan Klesko	.35	515	Mike Gardiner	.05
330	Jeff Innis	.05	423	Nolan Ryan	1.00	516	Gary Redus	.05
331	Ron Karkovice	.05	424	Rey Sanchez	.05	517	Gary Gaetti	.05
332	*Keith Shepherd*	.12	425	Roberto Alomar	.35	518	Checklist 397-476	.05
333	*Alan Embree*	.12	426	Barry Larkin	.10	519	Carlton Fisk	.08
334	*Paul Wagner*	.15	427	Mike Mussina	.35	520	Ozzie Smith	.25
335	*Dave Haas*	.10	428	Jeff Bagwell	.75	521	Rod Nichols	.05
336	Ozzie Canseco	.05	429	Mo Vaughn	.40	522	Benito Santiago	.05
337	Bill Sampen	.05	430	Eric Karros	.10	523	Bill Gullickson	.05
338	Rich Rodriguez	.05	431	John Orton	.05	524	Robby Thompson	.05
339	Dean Palmer	.08	432	Wil Cordero	.10	525	Mike Macfarlane	.05
340	Greg Litton	.05	433	Jack McDowell	.08	526	Sid Bream	.05
341	Jim Tatum (Rated Rookie)	.10	434	Howard Johnson	.05	527	Darryl Hamilton	.05
342	*Todd Haney*	.05	435	Albert Belle	.50	528	Checklist 477-555	.05
343	Larry Casian	.05	436	John Kruk	.05	529	Jeff Tackett	.05
344	Ryne Sandberg	.35	437	Skeeter Barnes	.05	530	Greg Olson	.05
345	Sterling Hitchcock	.15	438	Don Slaught	.05	531	Bob Zupcic	.05
346	Chris Hammond	.05	439	Rusty Meacham	.05	532	Mark Grace	.10
347	Vince Horsman	.12	440	Tim Laker (Rated Rookie)	.12	533	Steve Frey	.05
348	*Butch Henry*	.12	441	Robin Yount	.25	534	Dave Martinez	.05
349	Dann Howitt	.05	442	Brian Jordan	.10	535	Robin Ventura	.12
350	Roger McDowell	.05	443	Kevin Tapani	.05	536	Casey Candaele	.05
351	Jack Morris	.08	444	Gary Sheffield	.15	537	Kenny Lofton	.30
352	Bill Krueger	.05	445	Rich Monteleone	.05	538	Jay Howell	.05
353	*Cris Colon*	.12	446	Will Clark	.25	539	Fernando Ramsey (Rated Rookie)	.10
354	*Joe Vitko*	.12	447	Jerry Browne	.05			
355	Willie McGee	.08	448	Jeff Treadway	.05	540	Larry Walker	.25
356	Jay Baller	.05	449	Mike Schooler	.05	541	Cecil Fielder	.12
357	Pat Mahomes	.05	450	Mike Harkey	.05	542	Lee Guetterman	.05
358	Roger Mason	.05	451	Julio Franco	.05	543	Keith Miller	.05
359	*Jerry Nielsen*	.10	452	Kevin Young (Rated Rookie)	.12	544	Len Dykstra	.10
360	Tom Pagnozzi	.05				545	B.J. Surhoff	.05
361	*Kevin Baez*	.08	453	Kelly Gruber	.05	546	Bob Walk	.05
362	*Tim Scott*	.08	454	Jose Rijo	.05	547	Brian Harper	.05
363	*Domingo Martinez*	.10	455	Mike Devereaux	.05	548	Lee Smith	.05
364	Kirt Manwaring	.05	456	Andujar Cedeno	.05	549	Danny Tartabull	.05
365	Rafael Palmeiro	.15	457	Damion Easley (Rated Rookie)	.12	550	Frank Seminara	.05
366	Ray Lankford	.08				551	Henry Mercedes	.05
367	Tim McIntosh	.05	458	Kevin Gross	.05	552	Dave Righetti	.05
368	*Jessie Hollins*	.08	459	Matt Young	.05	553	Ken Griffey, Jr.	2.00
369	Scott Leius	.05	460	Matt Stairs	.05	554	Tom Glavine	.08
370	Bill Doran	.05	461	Luis Polonia	.05	555	Juan Gonzalez	.60
371	*Sam Militello*	.10	462	Dwight Gooden	.05	556	Jim Bullinger	.08
372	Ryan Bowen	.05	463	Warren Newson	.05	557	Derek Bell	.08
373	Dave Henderson	.05	464	Jose DeLeon	.05	558	Cesar Hernandez	.05
374	Dan Smith (Rated Rookie)	.12	465	Jose Mesa	.05	559	Cal Ripken, Jr.	2.00
375	*Steve Reed*	.12	466	Danny Cox	.05	560	Eddie Taubensee	.05
376	Jose Offerman	.05	467	Dan Gladden	.05	561	John Flaherty	.05
377	Kevin Brown	.05	468	Gerald Perry	.05	562	Todd Benzinger	.05
378	Darrin Fletcher	.05	469	Mike Boddicker	.05	563	Hubie Brooks	.05
379	Duane Ward	.05	470	Jeff Gardner	.05	564	Delino DeShields	.05
380	Wayne Kirby (Rated Rookie)	.12	471	Doug Henry	.05	565	Tim Raines	.05
			472	Mike Benajmin	.05	566	Sid Fernandez	.05
381	*Steve Scarsone*	.08	473	Dan Peltier (Rated Rookie)	.05	567	Steve Olin	.05
382	Mariano Duncan	.05	474	Mike Stanton	.05	568	Tommy Greene	.05
383	*Ken Ryan*	.15	475	John Smiley	.05	569	Buddy Groom	.05
384	Lloyd McClendon	.05	476	Dwight Smith	.05	570	Randy Tomlin	.05
385	Brian Holman	.05	477	Jim Leyritz	.05	571	Hipolito Pichardo	.05
386	Braulio Castillo	.05	478	Dwayne Henry	.05	572	Rene Arocha (Rated Rookie)	.25
387	*Danny Leon*	.08	479	Mark McGwire	2.00			
388	Omar Olivares	.05	480	Pete Incaviglia	.05	573	Mike Fetters	.05
389	Kevin Wickander	.05	481	Dave Cochrane	.05	574	Felix Jose	.05
390	Fred McGriff	.20	482	Eric Davis	.08	575	Gene Larkin	.05
391	Phil Clark	.12	483	John Olerud	.15	576	Bruce Hurst	.05
392	Darren Lewis	.08	484	Ken Bottenfield	.08	577	Bernie Williams	.40
393	*Phil Hiatt*	.10	485	Mark McLemore	.05	578	Trevor Wilson	.05
394	Mike Morgan	.05	486	Dave Magadan	.05	579	Bob Welch	.05
395	Shane Mack	.05	487	John Marzano	.05	580	Dave Justice	.20
396	Checklist 318-396	.05	488	Ruben Amaro	.05	581	Randy Johnson	.35
397	David Segui	.05	489	Rob Ducey	.05	582	Jose Vizcaino	.05
398	Rafael Belliard	.05	490	Stan Belinda	.05	583	Jeff Huson	.05
399	Tim Naehring	.05	491	Dan Pasqua	.05	584	Rob Maurer (Rated Rookie)	.05
400	Frank Castillo	.05	492	Joe Magrane	.05	585	Todd Stottlemyre	.05
401	Joe Grahe	.05	493	Brook Jacoby	.05	586	Joe Oliver	.05
402	Reggie Sanders	.10	494	Gene Harris	.05	587	Bob Milacki	.05
403	Roberto Hernandez	.05	495	Mark Leiter	.05	588	Rob Murphy	.05
404	Luis Gonzalez	.05	496	Bryan Hickerson	.05	589	Greg Pirkl (Rated Rookie)	.05
405	Carlos Baerga	.15	497	Tom Gordon	.05	590	Lenny Harris	.05
			498	Pete Smith	.05	591	Luis Rivera	.05

592	John Wetteland	.05
593	Mark Langston	.05
594	Bobby Bonilla	.05
595	Esteban Beltre	.05
596	Mike Hartley	.05
597	Felix Fermin	.05
598	Carlos Garcia	.05
599	Frank Tanana	.05
600	Pedro Guerrero	.05
601	Terry Shumpert	.05
602	Wally Whitehurst	.05
603	Kevin Seitzer	.05
604	Chris James	.05
605	Greg Gohr (Rated Rookie)	.05
606	Mark Wohlers	.05
607	Kirby Puckett	.40
608	Greg Maddux	1.25
609	Don Mattingly	.60
610	Greg Cadaret	.05
611	Dave Stewart	.05
612	Mark Portugal	.05
613	Pete O'Brien	.05
614	Bobby Ojeda	.05
615	Joe Carter	.25
616	Pete Young	.05
617	Sam Horn	.05
618	Vince Coleman	.05
619	Wade Boggs	.20
620	*Todd Pratt*	.10
621	Ron Tingley	.05
622	Doug Drabek	.05
623	Scott Hemond	.05
624	Tim Jones	.05
625	Dennis Cook	.05
626	Jose Melendez	.05
627	Mike Munoz	.05
628	Jim Pena	.05
629	Gary Thurman	.05
630	Charlie Leibrandt	.05
631	Scott Fletcher	.05
632	Andre Dawson	.10
633	Greg Gagne	.05
634	Greg Swindell	.05
635	Kevin Maas	.05
636	Xavier Hernandez	.05
637	Ruben Sierra	.08
638	Dimitri Young (Rated Rookie)	.15
639	Harold Reynolds	.05
640	Tom Goodwin	.05
641	Todd Burns	.05
642	Jeff Fassero	.05
643	Dave Winfield	.20
644	Willie Randolph	.05
645	Luis Mercedes	.05
646	Dale Murphy	.10
647	Danny Darwin	.05
648	Dennis Moeller	.05
649	Chuck Crim	.05
650	Checklist 556-634	.05
651	Shawn Abner	.05
652	Tracy Woodson	.05
653	Scott Scudder	.05
654	Tom Lampkin	.05
655	Alan Trammell	.10
656	Cory Snyder	.05
657	Chris Gwynn	.05
658	Lonnie Smith	.05
659	Jim Austin	.05
660	Checklist 635-713	.05
661	(Tim Hulett)	.05
662	Marvin Freeman	.05
663	Greg Harris	.05
664	Heathcliff Slocumb	.05
665	Mike Butcher	.05
666	Steve Foster	.05
667	Donn Pall	.05
668	Darryl Kile	.05
669	Jesse Levis	.10
670	Jim Gott	.05
671	*Mark Hutton*	.10
672	Brian Drahman	.05
673	Chad Kreuter	.05
674	Tony Fernandez	.05
675	Jose Lind	.05
676	Kyle Abbott	.05
677	Dan Plesac	.05
678	Barry Bonds	.60
679	Chili Davis	.05
680	Stan Royer	.05
681	Scott Kamieniecki	.05
682	Carlos Martinez	.05
683	Mike Moore	.05
684	Candy Maldonado	.05
685	Jeff Nelson	.05
686	Lou Whitaker	.05

687	Jose Guzman	.05
688	Manuel Lee	.05
689	Bob MacDonald	.05
690	Scott Bankhead	.05
691	Alan Mills	.05
692	Brian Williams	.05
693	Tom Brunansky	.05
694	Lenny Webster	.05
695	Greg Briley	.05
696	Paul O'Neill	.08
697	Joey Cora	.05
698	Charlie O'Brien	.05
699	Junior Ortiz	.05
700	Ron Darling	.05
701	Tony Phillips	.08
702	William Pennyfeather	.05
703	Mark Gubicza	.05
704	Steve Hosey (Rated Rookie)	.12
705	Henry Cotto	.05
706	*David Hulse* (Expansion Draft)	.15
707	Mike Pagliarulo	.05
708	Dave Stieb	.05
709	Melido Perez	.05
710	Jimmy Key	.05
711	Jeff Russell	.05
712	David Cone	.05
713	Russ Swan	.05
714	Mark Guthrie	.05
715	Checklist 714-792	.05
716	Al Martin (Rated Rookie)	.15
717	Randy Knorr	.05
718	Mike Stanley	.05
719	Rick Sutcliffe	.05
720	Terry Leach	.05
721	Chipper Jones (Rated Rookie)	1.50
722	Jim Eisenreich	.05
723	Tom Henke	.05
724	Jeff Frye	.05
725	Harold Baines	.05
726	Scott Sanderson	.05
727	Tom Foley	.05
728	Bryan Harvey (Expansion Draft)	.05
729	Tom Edens	.05
730	Eric Young (Expansion Draft)	.12
731	Dave Weathers (Expansion Draft)	.05
732	Spike Owen	.05
733	Scott Aldred (Expansion Draft)	.05
734	Cris Carpenter (Expansion Draft)	.05
735	Dion James	.05
736	Joe Girardi (Expansion Draft)	.05
737	Nigel Wilson (Expansion Draft)	.10
738	Scott Chiamparino (Expansion Draft)	.05
739	Jeff Reardon	.05
740	Willie Blair (Expansion Draft)	.05
741	Jim Corsi (Expansion Draft)	.05
742	Ken Patterson	.05
743	Andy Ashby (Expansion Draft)	.05
744	Rob Natal (Expansion Draft)	.05
745	Kevin Bass	.05
746	Freddie Benavides (Expansion Draft)	.05
747	Chris Donnels (Expansion Draft)	.05
748	*Kerry Woodson*	.10
749	Calvin Jones (Expansion Draft)	
750	Gary Scott	.05
751	Joe Orsulak	.05
752	Armando Reynoso (Expansion Draft)	.05
753	Monty Farriss (Expansion Draft)	.05
754	Billy Hatcher	.05
755	Denis Boucher (Expansion Draft)	.05
756	Walt Weiss	.05
757	Mike Fitzgerald	.05
758	Rudy Seanez	.05
759	Bret Barberie (Expansion Draft)	.05
760	Mo Sanford (Expansion Draft)	.05
761	*Pedro Castellano* (Expansion Draft)	.12

762	Chuck Carr (Expansion Draft)	.05
763	Steve Howe	.05
764	Andres Galarraga	.10
765	Jeff Conine (Expansion Draft)	.05
766	Ted Power	.05
767	Butch Henry (Expansion Draft)	.05
768	Steve Decker (Expansion Draft)	.05
769	Storm Davis	.05
770	Vinny Castilla (Expansion Draft)	.05
771	Junior Felix (Expansion Draft)	.05
772	Walt Terrell	.05
773	Brad Ausmus (Expansion Draft)	.08
774	Jamie McAndrew (Expansion Draft)	.05
775	Milt Thompson	.05
776	Charlie Hayes (Expansion Draft)	.05
777	Jack Armstrong (Expansion Draft)	.05
778	Dennis Rasmussen	.05
779	Darren Holmes (Expansion Draft)	.05
780	*Alex Arias*	.12
781	Randy Bush	.05
782	Javier Lopez (Rated Rookie)	.60
783	Dante Bichette	.10
784	John Johnstone (Expansion Draft)	.08
785	Rene Gonzales	.05
786	Alex Cole (Expansion Draft)	.05
787	Jeromy Burnitz (Rated Rookie)	.15
788	Michael Huff	.05
789	Anthony Telford	.05
790	Jerald Clark (Expansion Draft)	.05
791	Joel Johnston	.05
792	David Nied (Rated Rookie)	.08

1993 Donruss Diamond Kings

ROGER CLEMENS

The traditional Donruss Diamond Kings cards were again used as an insert in Series I and Series II foil packs in 1993. The first 15 cards were found in Series I packs, while cards 16-31 were available in the second series packs.

		MT
Complete Set (31):		32.50
Common Player:		.75
1	Ken Griffey, Jr.	10.00
2	Ryne Sandberg	4.00
3	Roger Clemens	3.00
4	Kirby Puckett	4.50
5	Bill Swift	.75

6	Larry Walker	1.50
7	Juan Gonzalez	3.00
8	Wally Joyner	.75
9	Andy Van Slyke	.75
10	Robin Ventura	1.00
11	Bip Roberts	.75
12	Roberto Kelly	.75
13	Carlos Baerga	.75
14	Orel Hershiser	.75
15	Cecil Fielder	.75
16	Robin Yount	1.50
17	Darren Daulton	.75
18	Mark McGwire	10.00
19	Tom Glavine	.75
20	Roberto Alomar	3.50
21	Gary Sheffield	1.00
22	Bob Tewksbury	.75
23	Brady Anderson	1.00
24	Craig Biggio	.75
25	Eddie Murray	1.50
26	Luis Polonia	.75
27	Nigel Wilson	.75
28	David Nied	.75
29	Pat Listach	.75
30	Eric Karros	1.00
31	Checklist	.05

1993 Donruss Elite

PAUL MOLITOR

Continuing the card numbering from the 1992 Elite set, the Elite '93 inserts utilized a silver-foil prismatic front border with blue back printing. Each card is serial numbered as one of 10,000; this identified production number helping to make the Elites among the more valuable of insert cards.

		MT
Complete Set (20):		500.00
Common Player:		10.00
19	Fred McGriff	10.00
20	Ryne Sandberg	30.00
21	Eddie Murray	30.00
22	Paul Molitor	30.00
23	Barry Larkin	20.00
24	Don Mattingly	55.00
25	Dennis Eckersley	10.00
26	Roberto Alomar	30.00
27	Edgar Martinez	10.00
28	Gary Sheffield	15.00
29	Darren Daulton	10.00
30	Larry Walker	25.00
31	Barry Bonds	30.00
32	Andy Van Slyke	10.00
33	Mark McGwire	60.00
34	Cecil Fielder	10.00
35	Dave Winfield	15.00
36	Juan Gonzalez	45.00
---	Robin Yount (Legend)	25.00
---	Will Clark (Signature)	125.00

1993 Donruss Long Ball Leaders

460 FEET

ALBERT BELLE • INDIANS

Carrying a prefix of "LL" before the card number, these inserts were released in Series I (LL1-9) and Series II (LL10-18) jumbo packs, detailing mammoth home runs of the previous season.

		MT
Complete Set (18):		75.00
Common Player:		1.00
1	Rob Deer	1.00
2	Fred McGriff	2.00
3	Albert Belle	5.00
4	Mark McGwire	20.00
5	Dave Justice	2.00
6	Jose Canseco	2.50
7	Kent Hrbek	1.00
8	Roberto Alomar	3.50
9	Ken Griffey, Jr.	20.00
10	Frank Thomas	15.00
11	Darryl Strawberry	1.50
12	Felix Jose	1.00
13	Cecil Fielder	2.00
14	Juan Gonzalez	5.00
15	Ryne Sandberg	4.00
16	Gary Sheffield	2.00
17	Jeff Bagwell	6.00
18	Larry Walker	2.50

1993 Donruss Masters of the Game

Masters of the Game

Juan Gonzalez

Donruss issued a series of "Masters of the Game" art cards that were available only at Wal-

Mart stores. The oversized cards (3-1/2" x 5") feature the artwork of Dick Perez, creator of the Diamond Kings cards for the same company. The cards came issued one to a pack, along with a foil pack of 1993 Donruss cards for a retail price of about $3.

		MT
Complete Set (16):		55.00
Common Player:		2.50
1	Frank Thomas	5.00
2	Nolan Ryan	6.00
3	Gary Sheffield	2.50
4	Fred McGriff	2.50
5	Ryne Sandberg	3.00
6	Cal Ripken, Jr.	6.00
7	Jose Canseco	2.50
8	Ken Griffey, Jr.	7.50
9	Will Clark	2.50
10	Roberto Alomar	2.50
11	Juan Gonzalez	4.00
12	David Justice	2.50
13	Kirby Puckett	4.00
14	Barry Bonds	4.00
15	Robin Yount	2.50
16	Deion Sanders	2.50

1993 Donruss MVP's

Paul Molitor   Brewers

MVP

This set was inserted in jumbo packs of both Series I and Series II. Cards carry a MVP prefix to the card number.

		MT
Complete Set (26):		30.00
Common Player:		.50
1	Luis Polonia	.50
2	Frank Thomas	5.00
3	George Brett	2.50
4	Paul Molitor	1.00
5	Don Mattingly	3.50
6	Roberto Alomar	2.00
7	Terry Pendleton	.50
8	Eric Karros	.75
9	Larry Walker	1.00
10	Eddie Murray	.75
11	Darren Daulton	.50
12	Ray Lankford	.50
13	Will Clark	1.00
14	Cal Ripken, Jr.	6.00
15	Roger Clemens	2.50
16	Carlos Baerga	.75
17	Cecil Fielder	.75
18	Kirby Puckett	3.50
19	Mark McGwire	6.00
20	Ken Griffey, Jr.	6.00
21	Juan Gonzalez	2.50
22	Ryne Sandberg	2.50
23	Bip Roberts	.50
24	Jeff Bagwell	3.00
25	Barry Bonds	2.00
26	Gary Sheffield	1.00

1993 Donruss Spirit of the Game

Series I and Series II foil and jumbo packs could be found with these cards randomly inserted. Several multi-player cards are included in the set. Card numbers bear an SG prefix.

		MT
Complete Set (20):		25.00
Common Player:		1.00
1	Turning Two(Dave Winfield, Mike Bordick)	1.00
2	Play at the Plate(David Justice)	2.00
3	In There(Roberto Alomar)	2.00
4	Pumped(Dennis Eckersley)	1.00
5	Dynamic Duo(Juan Gonzalez, Jose Canseco)	2.50
6	Gone(Frank Thomas, George Bell)	2.50
7	Safe or Out?(Wade Boggs)	1.50
8	The Thrill(Will Clark)	1.50
9	Safe at Home(Damon Berryhill, Bip Roberts, Glenn Braggs)	1.00
10	Thirty X 31(Cecil Fielder, Mickey Tettleton, Rob Deer)	1.00
11	Bag Bandit(Kenny Lofton)	2.00
12	Back to Back(Fred McGriff, Gary Sheffield)	1.50
13	Range Rovers(Greg Gagne, Barry Larkin)	1.00
14	The Ball Stops Here(Ryne Sandberg)	2.00
15	Over the Top(Carlos Baerga, Gary Gaetti)	1.00
16	At the Wall(Danny Tartabull)	1.00
17	Head First(Brady Anderson)	1.25
18	Big Hurt(Frank Thomas)	6.00
19	No-Hitter(Kevin Gross)	1.00
20	3,000(Robin Yount)	1.50

Values quoted in this guide reflect the retail price of a card — the price a collector can expect to pay when buying a card from a dealer.

The wholesale price — that which a collector can expect to receive from a dealer when selling cards — will be significantly lower, depending on desirability and condition.

1994 Donruss

Donruss released its 1994 set in two 330-card series. Each series also includes, 50 Special Edition gold cards and several insert sets. Regular cards have full-bleed photos and are UV coated and foil stamped. Special Edition cards are gold-foil stamped on both sides and are included in each pack. Insert sets titled Spirit of the Game and Decade Dominators were produced in regular and super (3-1/2" x 5") formats. Other inserts were MVPs and Long Ball Leaders in regular size and super-size Award Winners. An Elite series of cards, continuing from previous years with #37-48, was also issued as inserts. A 10th Anniversary insert set features 10 popular 1984 Donruss cards in gold-foil enhanced reprint versions.

		MT
Complete Set (660):		44.00
Common Player:		.05
Series 1 Wax Box:		45.00
Series 2 Wax Box:		40.00
1	Nolan Ryan (Career Salute 27 Years)	2.50
2	Mike Piazza	1.25
3	Moises Alou	.10
4	Ken Griffey, Jr.	3.00
5	Gary Sheffield	.15
6	Roberto Alomar	.75
7	John Kruk	.05
8	Gregg Olson	.05
9	Gregg Jefferies	.08
10	Tony Gwynn	1.00
11	Chad Curtis	.10
12	Craig Biggio	.12
13	John Burkett	.05
14	Carlos Baerga	.15
15	Robin Yount	.25
16	Dennis Eckersley	.08
17	Dwight Gooden	.08
18	Ryne Sandberg	.50
19	Rickey Henderson	.12
20	Jack McDowell	.08
21	Jay Bell	.05
22	Kevin Brown	.08
23	Robin Ventura	.10
24	Paul Molitor	.25
25	Dave Justice	.15
26	Rafael Palmeiro	.15
27	Cecil Fielder	.20
28	Chuck Knoblauch	.08
29	Dave Hollins	.08
30	Jimmy Key	.05
31	Mark Langston	.05
32	Darryl Kile	.05
33	Ruben Sierra	.05
34	Ron Gant	.08
35	Ozzie Smith	.20
36	Wade Boggs	.25

37	Marquis Grissom	.10
38	Will Clark	.25
39	Kenny Lofton	.75
40	Cal Ripken, Jr.	3.00
41	Steve Avery	.08
42	Mo Vaughn	.60
43	Brian McRae	.05
44	Mickey Tettleton	.05
45	Barry Larkin	.10
46	Charlie Hayes	.05
47	Kevin Appier	.05
48	Robby Thompson	.05
49	Juan Gonzalez	1.00
50	Paul O'Neill	.10
51	Marcos Armas	.05
52	Mike Butcher	.05
53	Ken Caminiti	.10
54	Pat Borders	.05
55	Pedro Munoz	.05
56	Tim Belcher	.05
57	Paul Assenmacher	.05
58	Damon Berryhill	.05
59	Ricky Bones	.05
60	Rene Arocha	.05
61	Shawn Boskie	.05
62	Pedro Astacio	.05
63	Frank Bolick	.05
64	Bud Black	.05
65	Sandy Alomar, Jr.	.10
66	Rich Amaral	.05
67	Luis Aquino	.05
68	Kevin Baez	.05
69	Mike Devereaux	.05
70	Andy Ashby	.05
71	Larry Andersen	.05
72	Steve Cooke	.05
73	Mario Daiz	.05
74	Rob Deer	.05
75	Bobby Ayala	.05
76	Freddie Benavides	.05
77	Stan Belinda	.05
78	John Doherty	.05
79	Willie Banks	.05
80	Spike Owen	.05
81	Mike Bordick	.05
82	Chili Davis	.08
83	Luis Gonzalez	.05
84	Ed Sprague	.05
85	Jeff Reboulet	.05
86	Jason Bere	.20
87	Mark Hutton	.05
88	Jeff Blauser	.05
89	Cal Eldred	.05
90	Bernard Gilkey	.05
91	Frank Castillo	.05
92	Jim Gott	.05
93	Greg Colbrunn	.05
94	Jeff Brantley	.05
95	Jeremy Hernandez	.05
96	Norm Charlton	.05
97	Alex Arias	.05
98	John Franco	.05
99	Chris Hoiles	.05
100	Brad Ausmus	.05
101	Wes Chamberlain	.05
102	Mark Dewey	.05
103	Benji Gil (Rated Rookie)	.15
104	John Dopson	.05
105	John Smiley	.05
106	David Nied	.08
107	George Brett (Career Salute 21 Years)	1.00
108	Kirk Gibson	.05
109	Larry Casian	.05
110	Checklist(Ryne Sandberg 2,000 Hits)	.15
111	Brent Gates	.08
112	Damion Easley	.08
113	Pete Harnisch	.05
114	Danny Cox	.05
115	Kevin Tapani	.05
116	Roberto Hernandez	.05
117	Domingo Jean	.05
118	Sid Bream	.05
119	Doug Henry	.05
120	Omar Olivares	.05
121	Mike Harkey	.05
122	Carlos Hernandez	.05
123	Jeff Fassero	.10
124	Dave Burba	.05
125	Wayne Kirby	.05
126	John Cummings	.05
127	Bret Barberie	.05
128	Todd Hundley	.08
129	Tim Hulett	.05
130	Phil Clark	.05

#	Player	Value
131	Danny Jackson	.05
132	Tom Foley	.05
133	Donald Harris	.10
134	Scott Fletcher	.05
135	Johnny Ruffin (Rated Rookie)	.05
136	Jerald Clark	.05
137	Billy Brewer	.05
138	Dan Gladden	.05
139	Eddie Guardado	.05
140	Checklist(Cal Ripken, Jr. 2,000 Hits)	.25
141	Scott Hemond	.05
142	Steve Frey	.05
143	Xavier Hernandez	.05
144	Mark Eichhorn	.05
145	Ellis Burks	.08
146	Jim Leyritz	.05
147	Mark Lemke	.05
148	Pat Listach	.05
149	Donovan Osborne	.05
150	Glenallen Hill	.08
151	Orel Hershiser	.08
152	Darrin Fletcher	.05
153	Royce Clayton	.05
154	Derek Lilliquist	.05
155	Mike Felder	.05
156	Jeff Conine	.08
157	Ryan Thompson	.05
158	Ben McDonald	.08
159	Ricky Gutierrez	.05
160	Terry Mulholland	.05
161	Carlos Garcia	.05
162	Tom Henke	.05
163	Mike Greenwell	.05
164	Thomas Howard	.05
165	Joe Girardi	.05
166	Hubie Brooks	.05
167	Greg Gohr	.05
168	Chip Hale	.05
169	Rick Honeycutt	.05
170	Hilly Hathaway	.05
171	Todd Jones	.05
172	Tony Fernandez	.05
173	Bo Jackson	.15
174	Bobby Munoz	.05
175	Greg McMichael	.05
176	Graeme Lloyd	.05
177	Tom Pagnozzi	.05
178	Derrick May	.05
179	Pedro Martinez	.08
180	Ken Hill	.05
181	Bryan Hickerson	.05
182	Jose Mesa	.05
183	Dave Fleming	.05
184	Henry Cotto	.05
185	Jeff Kent	.05
186	Mark McLemore	.05
187	Trevor Hoffman	.08
188	Todd Pratt	.08
189	Blas Minor	.05
190	Charlie Leibrandt	.05
191	Tony Pena	.05
192	*Larry Luebbers*	.08
193	Greg Harris	.05
194	David Cone	.05
195	Bill Gullickson	.05
196	Brian Harper	.05
197	Steve Karsay (Rated Rookie)	.20
198	Greg Myers	.05
199	Mark Portugal	.05
200	Pat Hentgen	.08
201	Mike La Valliere	.05
202	Mike Stanley	.05
203	Kent Mercker	.05
204	Dave Nilsson	.05
205	Erik Pappas	.05
206	Mike Morgan	.05
207	Roger McDowell	.05
208	Mike Lansing	.10
209	Kirt Manwaring	.05
210	Randy Milligan	.05
211	Erik Hanson	.05
212	Orestes Destrade	.05
213	Mike Maddux	.05
214	Alan Mills	.05
215	Tim Mauser	.05
216	Ben Rivera	.05
217	Don Slaught	.05
218	Bob Patterson	.05
219	Carlos Quintana	.05
220	Checklist(Tim Raines 2,000 Hits)	.05
221	Hal Morris	.05
222	Darren Holmes	.05
223	Chris Gwynn	.05
224	Chad Kreuter	.05
225	Mike Hartley	.05
226	Scott Lydy	.05
227	Eduardo Perez	.08
228	Greg Swindell	.05
229	Al Leiter	.05
230	Scott Radinsky	.05
231	Bob Wickman	.05
232	Otis Nixon	.05
233	Kevin Reimer	.05
234	Geronimo Pena	.05
235	Kevin Roberson (Rated Rookie)	.10
236	Jody Reed	.05
237	Kirk Rueter (Rated Rookie)	.15
238	Willie McGee	.05
239	Charles Nagy	.05
240	Tim Leary	.05
241	Carl Everett	.05
242	Charlie O'Brien	.05
243	Mike Pagliarulo	.05
244	Kerry Taylor	.05
245	Kevin Stocker	.05
246	Joel Johnston	.05
247	Geno Petralli	.05
248	Jeff Russell	.05
249	Joe Oliver	.05
250	Robert Mejia	.05
251	Chris Haney	.05
252	Bill Krueger	.05
253	Shane Mack	.05
254	Terry Steinbach	.05
255	Luis Polonia	.05
256	Eddie Taubensee	.05
257	Dave Stewart	.05
258	Tim Raines	.05
259	Bernie Williams	.40
260	John Smoltz	.10
261	Kevin Seitzer	.05
262	Bob Tewksbury	.05
263	Bob Scanlan	.05
264	Henry Rodriguez	.05
265	Tim Scott	.05
266	Scott Sanderson	.05
267	Eric Plunk	.05
268	Edgar Martinez	.10
269	Charlie Hough	.05
270	Joe Orsulak	.05
271	Harold Reynolds	.05
272	Tim Teufel	.05
273	Bobby Thigpen	.05
274	Randy Tomlin	.05
275	Gary Redus	.05
276	Ken Ryan	.05
277	Tim Pugh	.05
278	Jayhawk Owens	.05
279	Phil Hiatt (Rated Rookie)	.08
280	Alan Trammell	.08
281	Dave McCarty (Rated Rookie)	.08
282	Bob Welch	.05
283	J.T. Snow	.20
284	Brian Williams	.05
285	Devon White	.05
286	Steve Sax	.05
287	Tony Tarasco	.10
288	Bill Spiers	.05
289	Allen Watson	.10
290	Checklist(Rickey Henderson 2,000 Hits)	.05
291	Joe Vizcaino	.05
292	Darryl Strawberry	.08
293	John Wetteland	.05
294	Bill Swift	.05
295	Jeff Treadway	.05
296	Tino Martinez	.10
297	Richie Lewis	.05
298	Bret Saberhagen	.05
299	Arthur Rhodes	.05
300	Guillermo Velasquez	.05
301	Milt Thompson	.05
302	Doug Strange	.05
303	Aaron Sele	.12
304	Bip Roberts	.05
305	Bruce Ruffin	.05
306	Jose Lind	.05
307	David Wells	.05
308	Bobby Witt	.05
309	Mark Wohlers	.05
310	B.J. Surhoff	.05
311	Mark Whiten	.05
312	Turk Wendell	.05
313	Raul Mondesi	.60
314	*Brian Turang*	.08
315	Chris Hammond	.05
316	Tim Bogar	.05
317	Brad Pennington	.05
318	Tim Worrell	.05
319	Mitch Williams	.05
320	Rondell White (Rated Rookie)	.30
321	Frank Viola	.05
322	Manny Ramirez (Rated Rookie)	1.50
323	Gary Wayne	.05
324	Mike Macfarlane	.05
325	Russ Springer	.05
326	Tim Wallach	.05
327	Salomon Torres (Rated Rookie)	.08
328	Omar Vizquel	.05
329	*Andy Tomberlin*	.10
330	Chris Sabo	.05
331	Mike Mussina	.40
332	Andy Benes	.08
333	Darren Daulton	.08
334	Orlando Merced	.05
335	Mark McGwire	4.00
336	Dave Winfield	.20
337	Sammy Sosa	1.50
338	Eric Karros	.10
339	Greg Vaughn	.05
340	Don Mattingly	1.00
341	Frank Thomas	2.50
342	Fred McGriff	.30
343	Kirby Puckett	1.00
344	Roberto Kelly	.08
345	Wally Joyner	.08
346	Andres Galarraga	.12
347	Bobby Bonilla	.08
348	Benito Santiago	.05
349	Barry Bonds	.75
350	Delino DeShields	.08
351	Albert Belle	.75
352	Randy Johnson	.40
353	Tim Salmon	.30
354	John Olerud	.15
355	Dean Palmer	.05
356	Roger Clemens	1.00
357	Jim Abbott	.08
358	Mark Grace	.12
359	Ozzie Guillen	.05
360	Lou Whitaker	.05
361	Jose Rijo	.05
362	Jeff Montgomery	.05
363	Chuck Finley	.05
364	Tom Glavine	.08
365	Jeff Bagwell	1.00
366	Joe Carter	.20
367	Ray Lankford	.05
368	Ramon Martinez	.08
369	Jay Buhner	.08
370	Matt Williams	.30
371	Larry Walker	.25
372	Jose Canseco	.25
373	Len Dykstra	.08
374	Bryan Harvey	.05
375	Andy Van Slyke	.05
376	Ivan Rodriguez	.50
377	Kevin Mitchell	.05
378	Travis Fryman	.15
379	Duane Ward	.05
380	Greg Maddux	2.00
381	Scott Servais	.05
382	Greg Olson	.05
383	Rey Sanchez	.05
384	Tom Kramer	.05
385	David Valle	.05
386	Eddie Murray	.10
387	Kevin Higgins	.05
388	Dan Wilson	.05
389	Todd Frohwirth	.05
390	Gerald Williams	.05
391	Hipolito Pichardo	.05
392	Pat Meares	.05
393	Luis Lopez	.05
394	Ricky Jordan	.05
395	Bob Walk	.05
396	Sid Fernandez	.05
397	Todd Worrell	.05
398	Darryl Hamilton	.05
399	Randy Myers	.05
400	Rod Brewer	.05
401	Lance Blankenship	.05
402	Steve Finley	.05
403	*Phil Leftwich*	.08
404	Juan Guzman	.05
405	Anthony Young	.05
406	Jeff Gardner	.05
407	Ryan Bowen	.05
408	Fernando Valenzuela	.05

409	David West	.05
410	Kenny Rogers	.05
411	Bob Zupcic	.05
412	Eric Young	.05
413	Bret Boone	.08
414	Danny Tartabull	.05
415	Bob MacDonald	.05
416	Ron Karkovice	.05
417	Scott Cooper	.05
418	Dante Bichette	.25
419	Tripp Cromer	.05
420	Billy Ashley	.10
421	Roger Smithberg	.05
422	Dennis Martinez	.08
423	Mike Blowers	.05
424	Darren Lewis	.05
425	Junior Ortiz	.05
426	Butch Huskey	.10
427	Jimmy Poole	.05
428	Walt Weiss	.05
429	Scott Bankhead	.05
430	Deion Sanders	.25
431	Scott Bullett	.05
432	Jeff Huson	.05
433	Tyler Green	.05
434	Billy Hatcher	.05
435	Bob Hamelin	.05
436	Reggie Sanders	.12
437	Scott Erickson	.08
438	Steve Reed	.05
439	Randy Velarde	.05
440	Checklist (Tony Gwynn 2,000 Hits)	.15
441	Terry Leach	.05
442	Danny Bautista	.05
443	Kent Hrbek	.08
444	Rick Wilkins	.05
445	Tony Phillips	.08
446	Dion James	.05
447	Joey Cora	.05
448	Andre Dawson	.10
449	Pedro Castellano	.05
450	Tom Gordon	.05
451	Rob Dibble	.05
452	Ron Darling	.05
453	Chipper Jones	1.00
454	Joe Grahe	.05
455	Domingo Cedeno	.05
456	Tom Edens	.05
457	Mitch Webster	.05
458	Jose Bautista	.05
459	Troy O'Leary	.05
460	Todd Zeile	.08
461	Sean Berry	.05
462	Brad Holman	.08
463	Dave Martinez	.05
464	Mark Lewis	.05
465	Paul Carey	.05
466	Jack Armstrong	.05
467	David Telgheder	.05
468	Gene Harris	.05
469	Danny Darwin	.05
470	Kim Batiste	.05
471	Tim Wakefield	.08
472	Craig Lefferts	.05
473	Jacob Brumfield	.05
474	Lance Painter	.05
475	Milt Cuyler	.05
476	Melido Perez	.05
477	Derek Parks	.05
478	Gary DiSarcina	.05
479	Steve Bedrosian	.05
480	Eric Anthony	.05
481	Julio Franco	.08
482	Tommy Greene	.05
483	Pat Kelly	.05
484	Nate Minchey (Rated Rookie)	.08
485	William Pennyfeather	.05
486	Harold Baines	.08
487	Howard Johnson	.05
488	Angel Miranda	.05
489	Scott Sanders	.05
490	Shawon Dunston	.08
491	Mel Rojas	.08
492	Jeff Nelson	.05
493	Archi Cianfrocco	.05
494	Al Martin	.05
495	Mike Gallego	.05
496	Mike Henneman	.05
497	Armando Reynoso	.05
498	Mickey Morandini	.05
499	Rick Renteria	.05
500	Rick Sutcliffe	.05
501	Bobby Jones (Rated Rookie)	.25

502	Gary Gaetti	.08
503	Rick Aguilera	.05
504	Todd Stottlemyre	.05
505	Mike Mohler	.05
506	Mike Stanton	.05
507	Jose Guzman	.05
508	Kevin Rogers	.05
509	Chuck Carr	.05
510	Chris Jones	.05
511	Brent Mayne	.05
512	Greg Harris	.05
513	Dave Henderson	.05
514	Eric Hillman	.05
515	Dan Peltier	.05
516	Craig Shipley	.05
517	John Valentin	.08
518	Wilson Alvarez	.05
519	Andujar Cedeno	.05
520	Troy Neel	.05
521	Tom Candiotti	.05
522	Matt Mieske	.05
523	Jim Thome	.30
524	Lou Frazier	.05
525	Mike Jackson	.05
526	Pedro Martinez	.08
527	Roger Pavlik	.05
528	Kent Bottenfield	.05
529	Felix Jose	.05
530	Mark Guthrie	.05
531	Steve Farr	.05
532	Craig Paquette	.05
533	Doug Jones	.05
534	Luis Alicea	.05
535	Cory Snyder	.05
536	Paul Sorrento	.05
537	Nigel Wilson	.08
538	Jeff King	.05
539	Willie Green	.05
540	Kirk McCaskill	.05
541	Al Osuna	.05
542	Greg Hibbard	.05
543	Brett Butler	.08
544	Jose Valentin	.05
545	Wil Cordero	.08
546	Chris Bosio	.05
547	Jamie Moyer	.05
548	Jim Eisenreich	.05
549	Vinny Castilla	.08
550	Checklist (Dave Winfield 3,000 Hits)	.05
551	John Roper	.05
552	Lance Johnson	.05
553	Scott Kamieniecki	.05
554	Mike Moore	.05
555	Steve Buechele	.05
556	Terry Pendleton	.05
557	Todd Van Poppel	.05
558	Rob Butler	.05
559	Zane Smith	.05
560	David Hulse	.05
561	Tim Costo	.05
562	John Habyan	.05
563	Terry Jorgensen	.05
564	Matt Nokes	.05
565	Kevin McReynolds	.05
566	Phil Plantier	.05
567	Chris Turner	.05
568	Carlos Delgado	.25
569	John Jaha	.05
570	Dwight Smith	.05
571	John Vander Wal	.05
572	Trevor Wilson	.05
573	Felix Fermin	.05
574	Marc Newfield (Rated Rookie)	.20
575	Jeromy Burnitz	.08
576	Leo Gomez	.05
577	Curt Schilling	.05
578	Kevin Young	.08
579	Jerry Spradlin	.08
580	Curt Leskanic	.05
581	Carl Willis	.05
582	Alex Fernandez	.08
583	Mark Holzemer	.05
584	Domingo Martinez	.05
585	Pete Smith	.05
586	Brian Jordan	.05
587	Kevin Gross	.05
588	J.R. Phillips (Rated Rookie)	.15
589	Chris Nabholz	.05
590	Bill Wertz	.05
591	Derek Bell	.08
592	Brady Anderson	.10
593	Matt Turner	.05
594	Pete Incaviglia	.05
595	Greg Gagne	.05

596	John Flaherty	.05
597	Scott Livingstone	.05
598	Rod Bolton	.05
599	Mike Perez	.05
600	Checklist (Roger Clemens 2,000 Strikeouts)	.08
601	Tony Castillo	.05
602	Henry Mercedes	.05
603	Mike Fetters	.05
604	Rod Beck	.05
605	Damon Buford	.05
606	Matt Whiteside	.05
607	Shawn Green	.12
608	Midre Cummings (Rated Rookie)	.15
609	Jeff McNeeley	.05
610	Danny Sheaffer	.05
611	Paul Wagner	.05
612	Torey Lovullo	.05
613	Javier Lopez	.25
614	Mariano Duncan	.05
615	Doug Brocail	.05
616	Dave Hansen	.05
617	Ryan Klesko	.60
618	Eric Davis	.08
619	Scott Ruffcorn (Rated Rookie)	.25
620	Mike Trombley	.05
621	Jaime Navarro	.05
622	Rheal Cormier	.05
623	Jose Offerman	.05
624	David Segui	.05
625	Robb Nen (Rated Rookie)	.05
626	Dave Gallagher	.05
627	Julian Tavarez	.25
628	Chris Gomez	.08
629	Jeffrey Hammonds (Rated Rookie)	.25
630	Scott Brosius	.05
631	Willie Blair	.05
632	Doug Drabek	.05
633	Bill Wegman	.05
634	Jeff McKnight	.05
635	Rich Rodriguez	.05
636	Steve Trachsel	.20
637	Buddy Groom	.05
638	Sterling Hitchcock	.08
639	Chuck McElroy	.05
640	Rene Gonzales	.05
641	Dan Plesac	.05
642	Jeff Branson	.05
643	Darrell Whitmore	.05
644	Paul Quantrill	.05
645	Rich Rowland	.05
646	Curtis Pride	.25
647	Erik Plantenberg	.05
648	Albie Lopez	.08
649	Rich Batchelor	.08
650	Lee Smith	.08
651	Cliff Floyd	.20
652	Pete Schourek	.05
653	Reggie Jefferson	.05
654	Bill Haselman	.05
655	Steve Hosey	.05
656	Mark Clark	.05
657	Mark Davis	.05
658	Dave Magadan	.05
659	Candy Maldonado	.05
660	Checklist (Mark Langston 2,0000 Strikeouts)	.05

1994 Donruss Special Edition - Gold

In 1994 Donruss added a Special Edition subset of 100 of the game's top players. Fifty cards each were included one or two per pack in all types of Donruss' Series I and II packaging. The cards use the same photos and format as the regular-issue version, but have special gold-foil stamping on front in the area of the team logo and player name, and on back in a "Special Edition" number box in the upper-left corner.

		MT
Complete Set (100):		35.00
Common Player:		.25
1	Nolan Ryan	3.00
2	Mike Piazza	2.50
3	Moises Alou	.25
4	Ken Griffey, Jr.	5.00
5	Gary Sheffield	.50
6	Roberto Alomar	1.00
7	John Kruk	.25
8	Gregg Olson	.25
9	Gregg Jefferies	.30
10	Tony Gwynn	1.00
11	Chad Curtis	.25
12	Craig Biggio	.25
13	John Burkett	.25
14	Carlos Baerga	.30
15	Robin Yount	.60
16	Dennis Eckersley	.25
17	Dwight Gooden	.35
18	Ryne Sandberg	.90
19	Rickey Henderson	.35
20	Jack McDowell	.25
21	Jay Bell	.25
22	Kevin Brown	.25
23	Robin Ventura	.25
24	Paul Molitor	.50
25	David Justice	.50
26	Rafael Palmeiro	.30
27	Cecil Fielder	.30
28	Chuck Knoblauch	.40
29	Dave Hollins	.25
30	Jimmy Key	.25
31	Mark Langston	.25
32	Darryl Kile	.25
33	Ruben Sierra	.30
34	Ron Gant	.40
35	Ozzie Smith	.40
36	Wade Boggs	.45
37	Marquis Grissom	.30
38	Will Clark	.40
39	Kenny Lofton	.40
40	Cal Ripken, Jr.	4.00
41	Steve Avery	.25
42	Mo Vaughn	.85
43	Brian McRae	.25
44	Mickey Tettleton	.25
45	Barry Larkin	.35
46	Charlie Hayes	.25
47	Kevin Appier	.25
48	Robby Thompson	.25
49	Juan Gonzalez	1.00
50	Paul O'Neill	.30
51	Mike Mussina	.40
52	Andy Benes	.25
53	Darren Daulton	.25
54	Orlando Merced	.25
55	Mark McGwire	5.00
56	Dave Winfield	.35
57	Sammy Sosa	2.00
58	Eric Karros	.25
59	Greg Vaughn	.25
60	Don Mattingly	1.50
61	Frank Thomas	3.00
62	Fred McGriff	.40
63	Kirby Puckett	1.50
64	Roberto Kelly	.25
65	Wally Joyner	.25
66	Andres Galarraga	.30
67	Bobby Bonilla	.25
68	Benito Santiago	.25
69	Barry Bonds	1.50
70	Delino DeShields	.25
71	Albert Belle	1.00

72	Randy Johnson	.50
73	Tim Salmon	.50
74	John Olerud	.25
75	Dean Palmer	.25
76	Roger Clemens	1.00
77	Jim Abbott	.25
78	Mark Grace	.35
79	Ozzie Guillen	.25
80	Lou Whitaker	.25
81	Jose Rijo	.25
82	Jeff Montgomery	.25
83	Chuck Finley	.25
84	Tom Glavine	.25
85	Jeff Bagwell	1.50
86	Joe Carter	.35
87	Ray Lankford	.25
88	Ramon Martinez	.25
89	Jay Buhner	.25
90	Matt Williams	.35
91	Larry Walker	.50
92	Jose Canseco	.40
93	Len Dykstra	.25
94	Bryan Harvey	.25
95	Andy Van Slyke	.25
96	Ivan Rodriguez	1.00
97	Kevin Mitchell	.25
98	Travis Fryman	.25
99	Duane Ward	.25
100	Greg Maddux	3.00

1994 Donruss
Anniversary-1984

This set commemorates and features 10 of the most popular cards from Donruss' 1984 set. The cards, inserted in Series I hobby foil packs only, are "holographically enhanced" with foil stamping and UV coating.

		MT
Complete Set (10):		55.00
Common Player:		2.50
1	Joe Carter	3.00
2	Robin Yount	3.50
3	George Brett	5.00
4	Rickey Henderson	2.50
5	Nolan Ryan	15.00
6	Cal Ripken, Jr.	18.00
7	Wade Boggs	2.50
8	Don Mattingly	8.00
9	Ryne Sandberg	4.00
10	Tony Gwynn	5.00

Values shown reflect the market as of January, 1999. On-field performances of current players in the 1999 baseball season are not factored in.

1994 Donruss
Diamond Kings

The artwork of Dick Perez is again featured on this insert set included in foil packs. Player art is set against garish color backgrounds with a red-and-silver "Diamond Kings" foil logo above, and the player's name in script at bottom. Backs are printed in red on pale yellow and feature a 1993 season summary. Cards have a DK preface to the number. Cards #1-14 and #29, Dave Winfield, were included in Series I packs; cards #15-28 were found in Series II, along with the checklist card (#30), featuring a Dick Perez self-portrait.

		MT
Complete Set (30):		50.00
Common Player:		.75
1	Barry Bonds	3.00
2	Mo Vaughn	1.50
3	Steve Avery	.75
4	Tim Salmon	1.50
5	Rick Wilkins	.75
6	Brian Harper	.75
7	Andres Galarraga	1.00
8	Albert Belle	2.50
9	John Kruk	.75
10	Ivan Rodriguez	1.50
11	Tony Gwynn	4.00
12	Brian McRae	.75
13	Bobby Bonilla	.75
14	Ken Griffey, Jr.	9.00
15	Mike Piazza	6.00
16	Don Mattingly	4.00
17	Barry Larkin	1.00
18	Ruben Sierra	.75
19	Orlando Merced	.75
20	Greg Vaughn	.75
21	Gregg Jefferies	.75
22	Cecil Fielder	1.00
23	Moises Alou	.75
24	John Olerud	.75
25	Gary Sheffield	1.00
26	Mike Mussina	1.00
27	Jeff Bagwell	3.00
28	Frank Thomas	8.00
29	Dave Winfield (King of Kings)	2.00
30	Dick Perez (Checklist)	.75

1994 Donruss
Diamond Kings
Supers

Each retail box of 1994 Donruss foil packs contains one super-size (4-7/8" x 6-13/16") version of the Diamond Kings inserts. Series I boxes offer cards #1-14, while #15-28 are found in Series II boxes. A 29th card, honoring Dave Winfield, was also produced. Super DKs are identical in format to the regular-size inserts, with the exception of a white serial number strip on the back which identifies the card within an edition of 10,000.

		MT
Complete Set (29):		95.00
Common Player:		3.00
1	Barry Bonds	5.00
2	Mo Vaughn	4.00
3	Steve Avery	3.00
4	Tim Salmon	4.50
5	Rick Wilkins	3.00
6	Brian Harper	3.00
7	Andres Galarraga	4.50
8	Albert Belle	4.00
9	John Kruk	3.00
10	Ivan Rodriguez	4.00
11	Tony Gwynn	5.00
12	Brian McRae	3.00
13	Bobby Bonilla	3.00
14	Ken Griffey, Jr.	7.50
15	Mike Piazza	6.00
16	Don Mattingly	5.00
17	Barry Larkin	4.00
18	Ruben Sierra	3.00
19	Orlando Merced	3.00
20	Greg Vaughn	3.00
21	Gregg Jefferies	3.00
22	Cecil Fielder	3.00
23	Moises Alou	3.00
24	John Olerud	3.00
25	Gary Sheffield	4.00
26	Mike Mussina	3.00
27	Jeff Bagwell	5.00
28	Frank Thomas	6.00
29	Dave Winfield	4.00

1994 Donruss Elite

Donruss continued its popular Elite Series with 12 more players in 1994. The cards, numbered #37-48, were inserted in foil packs only. The cards feature the player in a diamond on the front; the back offers an opinion of why the player is considered an elite and is serially numbered from 1-10,000.

		MT
Complete Set (12):		225.00
Common Player:		8.00
37	Frank Thomas	50.00
38	Tony Gwynn	35.00
39	Tim Salmon	15.00
40	Albert Belle	15.00
41	John Kruk	8.00
42	Juan Gonzalez	30.00
43	John Olerud	12.00
44	Barry Bonds	25.00
45	Ken Griffey, Jr.	60.00
46	Mike Piazza	40.00
47	Jack McDowell	8.00
48	Andres Galarraga	8.00

1994 Donruss Long Ball Leaders

The "Tale of the Tape" for the 1993 season is chronicled in this Series II hobby-only foil-pack insert. Silver prismatic foil highlights the typography on the front of the card which includes the "Long Ball Leaders" logos (complete with embossed baseball), the player's last name and the distance of his blast. Cards backs have another player photo superimposed on the venue in which the home run was hit. The distance is repeated in silver over the ballpark photo. In a wide silver box at bottom are data about the home run.

		MT
Complete Set (10):		55.00
Common Player:		1.00
1	Cecil Fielder	1.00
2	Dean Palmer	1.00
3	Andres Galarraga	1.00
4	Bo Jackson	1.50
5	Ken Griffey, Jr.	12.00
6	Dave Justice	2.00
7	Mike Piazza	9.00
8	Frank Thomas	10.00
9	Barry Bonds	5.00
10	Juan Gonzalez	6.00

1994 Donruss MVP's

These inserts were included in 1994 jumbo packs only. The fronts have a large metallic blue MVP logo, beneath which is a red stripe with the player's name and position in white. Backs have a portrait photo, stats for 1993 and a summary of why the player was selected as team MVP.

		MT
Complete Set (28):		30.00
Common Player:		.25
1	Dave Justice	.40
2	Mark Grace	.50
3	Jose Rijo	.25
4	Andres Galarraga	.40
5	Bryan Harvey	.25
6	Jeff Bagwell	1.50
7	Mike Piazza	6.00
8	Moises Alou	.25
9	Bobby Bonilla	.25
10	Len Dykstra	.25
11	Jeff King	.25
12	Gregg Jefferies	.25
13	Tony Gwynn	2.00
14	Barry Bonds	2.00
15	Cal Ripken, Jr.	6.00
16	Mo Vaughn	1.00
17	Tim Salmon	.50
18	Frank Thomas	6.00
19	Albert Belle	2.50
20	Cecil Fielder	.40
21	Wally Joyner	.25
22	Greg Vaughn	.25
23	Kirby Puckett	3.00
24	Don Mattingly	2.00
25	Ruben Sierra	.25
26	Ken Griffey, Jr.	8.00
27	Juan Gonzalez	2.00
28	John Olerud	.25

1994 Donruss Spirit of the Game

Ten players are featured in this insert set, packaged exclusively in retail boxes. Horizontal in format, fronts feature a color player action photo set against a gold-tone background which has the appearance of a multiple-exposure photo. On back a player portrait photo is set against a backdrop of red, white and blue bunting. There is a short previous-season write-up at right. Cards #1-5 were included with Series I, cards 6-10 were in Series II packs.

		MT
Complete Set (10):		30.00
Common Player:		1.50
1	John Olerud	1.50
2	Barry Bonds	5.00
3	Ken Griffey, Jr.	8.00
4	Mike Piazza	6.00
5	Juan Gonzalez	3.00
6	Frank Thomas	6.00
7	Tim Salmon	2.00
8	Dave Justice	2.00
9	Don Mattingly	4.00
10	Len Dykstra	1.50

1994 Donruss Spirit of the Game Supers

Virtually identical in format to the regular-size "Spirit of the Game" cards, these 3-1/2" x 5" versions have gold-foil, rather than holographic printing on the front, and have a serial number on back identifying it from an edition of 10,000. One super card was inserted in each specially designated retail box.

		MT
Complete Set (10):		60.00
Common Player:		3.00
1	John Olerud	5.00
2	Barry Bonds	6.00
3	Ken Griffey, Jr.	9.00
4	Mike Piazza	7.50
5	Juan Gonzalez	6.00
6	Frank Thomas	8.00
7	Tim Salmon	5.00
8	Dave Justice	3.00
9	Don Mattingly	6.00
10	Len Dykstra	3.00

1994 Donruss Award Winners Supers

Major award winners of the 1993 season are honored in in this super-size (3-1/2" x 5") insert set. One card was packaged in each box of U.S. jumbo packs and in each Canadian foil-pack box. On a gold-tone background, the card backs have another player photo, a description of his award winning performance and a white strip with a serial number identifying the card's place in an edition of 10,000.

		MT
Complete Set (10):		70.00
Common Player:		4.00
1	Barry Bonds (N.L. MVP)	7.50
2	Greg Maddux (N.L. Cy Young)	8.00
3	Mike Piazza (N.L. ROY)	8.00
4	Barry Bonds (N.L. HR Champ)	7.50
5	Kirby Puckett (All-Star MVP)	7.50
6	Frank Thomas (A.L. MVP)	10.00
7	Jack McDowell (A.L. Cy Young)	4.00
8	Tim Salmon (A.L. ROY)	7.50
9	Juan Gonzalez (A.L. HR Champ)	7.00
10	Paul Molitor (World Series MVP)	5.00

1994 Donruss Decade Dominators

CECIL FIELDER
HOMERUNS

Donruss selected 10 top home run hitters (Series I) and 10 RBI leaders of the 1990s for this insert set. Cards were issued in all types of Series I and II packs. Full-bleed UV-coated cards were gold-foil enhanced on the front. Backs featured another full-color player photo and charted information on his 1990s home run or RBI output and ranking.

		MT
Complete Set (20):		50.00
Common Player:		.75
Series I		
1	Cecil Fielder	1.00
2	Barry Bonds	2.00
3	Fred McGriff	1.50
4	Matt Williams	1.00
5	Joe Carter	.75
6	Juan Gonzalez	4.00
7	Jose Canseco	1.50
8	Ron Gant	.75
9	Ken Griffey, Jr.	8.00
10	Mark McGwire	10.00
Series II		
1	Tony Gwynn	4.00
2	Frank Thomas	6.00
3	Paul Molitor	1.50
4	Edgar Martinez	.75
5	Kirby Puckett	3.00
6	Ken Griffey, Jr.	8.00
7	Barry Bonds	2.50
8	Willie McGee	.75
9	Len Dykstra	.75
10	John Kruk	.75

1994 Donruss Decade Dominators Supers

Super-size (3-1/2" x 5") versions of the 1994 Donruss Decade Dominators insert cards were produced as a premium, one card being packaged in a paper checklist envelope in each hobby box of Donruss foil packs. The supers are identical in format to the regular-size cards with the exception of a white serial number strip on the back, identifying each card's position in an edition of 10,000.

		MT
Complete Set (20):		70.00
Common Player:		4.00
Series I		
1	Cecil Fielder	3.00
2	Barry Bonds	7.50
3	Fred McGriff	4.00
4	Matt Williams	4.00
5	Joe Carter	3.00
6	Juan Gonzalez	7.00
7	Jose Canseco	4.00
8	Ron Gant	3.00
9	Ken Griffey, Jr.	8.00
10	Mark McGwire	10.00
Series II		
1	Tony Gwynn	5.00
2	Frank Thomas	6.00
3	Paul Molitor	4.00
4	Edgar Martinez	3.00
5	Kirby Puckett	5.00
6	Ken Griffey, Jr.	8.00
7	Barry Bonds	7.50
8	Willie McGee	3.00
9	Lenny Dykstra	3.00
10	John Kruk	3.00

1995 Donruss

A pair of player photos on the front of each card and silver-foil highlights are featured on the 1995 Donruss set. Besides the main action photo on front, each card has a second photo in a home plate frame at lower-left. A silver-foil ribbon beneath has the player's team and name embossed. Above the small photo is the player's position, with a half-circle of stars over all; both elements in silver foil. Completing the silver-foil highlights is the Donruss logo at upper-left. Full-bleed backs have yet another action photo at center, with a large team logo at left and five years' worth of stats plus career numbers at bottom. Donruss was issued in retail and hobby 12-card packs, magazine distributor packs of 16 and jumbo packs of 20 cards. New to Donruss in 1995 were Super

Packs. These were packs that contained complete insert sets and were seeded every 90 packs.

		MT
Complete Set (550):		35.00
Complete Series 1:		20.00
Complete Series 2:		15.00
Common Player:		.05

		MT
Series 1 or 2 Wax Box:		40.00
1	Dave Justice	.20
2	Rene Arocha	.10
3	Sandy Alomar Jr.	.15
4	Luis Lopez	.08
5	Mike Piazza	1.50
6	Bobby Jones	.15
7	Damion Easley	.10
8	Barry Bonds	.75
9	Mike Mussina	.35
10	Kevin Seitzer	.05
11	John Smiley	.05
12	W. VanLandingham	.10
13	Ron Darling	.05
14	Walt Weiss	.10
15	Mike Lansing	.10
16	Allen Watson	.15
17	Aaron Sele	.20
18	Randy Johnson	.40
19	Dean Palmer	.10
20	Jeff Bagwell	.75
21	Curt Schilling	.10
22	Darrell Whitmore	.08
23	Steve Trachsel	.15
24	Dan Wilson	.10
25	Steve Finley	.05
26	Bret Boone	.10
27	Charles Johnson	.20
28	Mike Stanton	.05
29	Ismael Valdes	.10
30	Salomon Torres	.05
31	Eric Anthony	.05
32	Spike Owen	.05
33	Joey Cora	.05
34	Robert Eenhoorn	.05
35	Rick White	.05
36	Omar Vizquel	.05
37	Carlos Delgado	.20
38	Eddie Williams	.05
39	Shawon Dunston	.10
40	Darrin Fletcher	.10
41	Leo Gomez	.05
42	Juan Gonzalez	1.50
43	Luis Alicea	.05
44	Ken Ryan	.08
45	Lou Whitaker	.05
46	Mike Blowers	.05
47	Willie Blair	.05
48	Todd Van Poppel	.05
49	Roberto Alomar	.60
50	Ozzie Smith	.40
51	Sterling Hitchcock	.08
52	Mo Vaughn	.60
53	Rick Aguilera	.05
54	Kent Mercker	.05
55	Don Mattingly	1.00
56	Bob Scanlan	.05
57	Wilson Alvarez	.08
58	Jose Mesa	.05
59	Scott Kamieniecki	.08
60	Todd Jones	.05
61	John Kruk	.05
62	Mike Stanley	.08
63	Tino Martinez	.15
64	Eddie Zambrano	.08
65	Todd Hundley	.15
66	Jamie Moyer	.05
67	Rich Amaral	.05
68	Jose Valentin	.05
69	Alex Gonzalez	.15
70	Kurt Abbott	.08
71	Delino DeShields	.08
72	Brian Anderson	.10
73	John Vander Wal	.05
74	Turner Ward	.05
75	Tim Raines	.08
76	Mark Acre	.05
77	Jose Offerman	.10
78	Jimmy Key	.10
79	Mark Whiten	.05
80	Mark Gubicza	.05
81	Darren Hall	.05
82	Travis Fryman	.15
83	Cal Ripken, Jr.	2.50
84	Geronimo Berroa	.05
85	Bret Barberie	.08

		MT
86	Andy Ashby	.08
87	Steve Avery	.08
88	Rich Becker	.10
89	John Valentin	.10
90	Glenallen Hill	.08
91	Carlos Garcia	.08
92	Dennis Martinez	.10
93	Pat Kelly	.05
94	Orlando Miller	.10
95	Felix Jose	.05
96	Mike Kingery	.05
97	Jeff Kent	.10
98	Pete Incaviglia	.05
99	Chad Curtis	.10
100	Thomas Howard	.10
101	Hector Carrasco	.10
102	Tom Pagnozzi	.05
103	Danny Tartabull	.05
104	Donnie Elliott	.05
105	Danny Jackson	.05
106	Steve Dunn	.05
107	Roger Salkeld	.05
108	Jeff King	.08
109	Cecil Fielder	.20
110	Checklist	.05
111	Denny Neagle	.10
112	Troy Neel	.10
113	Rod Beck	.05
114	Alex Rodriguez	3.00
115	Joey Eischen	.05
116	Tom Candiotti	.05
117	Ray McDavid	.05
118	Vince Coleman	.05
119	Pete Harnisch	.05
120	David Nied	.05
121	Pat Rapp	.08
122	Sammy Sosa	1.50
123	Steve Reed	.05
124	Jose Oliva	.05
125	Rick Bottalico	.08
126	Jose DeLeon	.05
127	Pat Hentgen	.08
128	Will Clark	.35
129	Mark Dewey	.05
130	Greg Vaughn	.05
131	Darren Dreifort	.05
132	Ed Sprague	.08
133	Lee Smith	.08
134	Charles Nagy	.08
135	Phil Plantier	.08
136	Jason Jacome	.05
137	Jose Lima	.05
138	J.R. Phillips	.08
139	J.T. Snow	.08
140	Mike Huff	.05
141	Billy Brewer	.05
142	Jeromy Burnitz	.08
143	Ricky Bones	.05
144	Carlos Rodriguez	.05
145	Luis Gonzalez	.05
146	Mark Lemke	.05
147	Al Martin	.05
148	Mike Bordick	.08
149	Robb Nen	.08
150	Wil Cordero	.08
151	Edgar Martinez	.08
152	Gerald Williams	.05
153	Esteban Beltre	.05
154	Mike Moore	.05
155	Mark Langston	.05
156	Mark Clark	.05
157	Bobby Ayala	.05
158	Rick Wilkins	.05
159	Bobby Munoz	.05
160	Checklist	.05
161	Scott Erickson	.05
162	Paul Molitor	.30
163	Jon Lieber	.05
164	Jason Grimsley	.05
165	Norberto Martin	.05
166	Javier Lopez	.20
167	Brian McRae	.08
168	Gary Sheffield	.35
169	Marcus Moore	.05
170	John Hudek	.15
171	Kelly Stinnett	.05
172	Chris Gomez	.05
173	Rey Sanchez	.05
174	Juan Guzman	.05
175	Chan Ho Park	.15
176	Terry Shumpert	.05
177	Steve Ontiveros	.05
178	Brad Ausmus	.05
179	Tim Davis	.05
180	Billy Ashley	.08
181	Vinny Castilla	.10

		MT
182	Bill Spiers	.05
183	Randy Knorr	.05
184	Brian Hunter	.15
185	Pat Meares	.05
186	Steve Buechele	.05
187	Kirt Manwaring	.05
188	Tim Naehring	.05
189	Matt Mieske	.05
190	Josias Manzanillo	.05
191	Greg McMichael	.05
192	Chuck Carr	.05
193	Midre Cummings	.08
194	Darryl Strawberry	.15
195	Greg Gagne	.05
196	Steve Cooke	.00
197	Woody Williams	.05
198	Ron Karkovice	.05
199	Phil Leftwich	.10
200	Jim Thome	.35
201	Brady Anderson	.15
202	Pedro Martinez	.15
203	Steve Karsay	.10
204	Reggie Sanders	.08
205	Bill Risley	.05
206	Jay Bell	.08
207	Kevin Brown	.10
208	Tim Scott	.05
209	Len Dykstra	.05
210	Willie Greene	.05
211	Jim Eisenreich	.05
212	Cliff Floyd	.10
213	Otis Nixon	.05
214	Eduardo Perez	.05
215	Manuel Lee	.05
216	*Armando Benitez*	.15
217	Dave McCarty	.08
218	Scott Livingstone	.05
219	Chad Kreuter	.05
220	Checklist	.05
221	Brian Jordan	.10
222	Matt Whiteside	.05
223	Jim Edmonds	.20
224	Tony Gwynn	.75
225	Jose Lind	.05
226	Marvin Freeman	.05
227	Ken Hill	.05
228	David Hulse	.05
229	Joe Hesketh	.05
230	Roberto Petagine	.05
231	Jeffrey Hammonds	.08
232	John Jaha	.05
233	John Burkett	.08
234	Hal Morris	.05
235	Tony Castillo	.05
236	Ryan Bowen	.08
237	Wayne Kirby	.05
238	Brent Mayne	.05
239	Jim Bullinger	.05
240	Mike Lieberthal	.08
241	Barry Larkin	.25
242	David Segui	.05
243	Jose Bautista	.10
244	Hector Fajardo	.05
245	Orel Hershiser	.08
246	James Mouton	.15
247	Scott Leius	.05
248	Tom Glavine	.20
249	Danny Bautista	.08
250	Jose Mercedes	.05
251	Marquis Grissom	.10
252	Charlie Hayes	.05
253	Ryan Klesko	.60
254	Vicente Palacios	.05
255	Matias Carrillo	.05
256	Gary DiSarcina	.05
257	Kirk Gibson	.05
258	Garey Ingram	.05
259	Alex Fernandez	.08
260	John Mabry	.05
261	Chris Howard	.05
262	Miguel Jimenez	.05
263	Heath Slocumb	.05
264	Albert Belle	.75
265	Dave Clark	.05
266	Joe Orsulak	.05
267	Joey Hamilton	.15
268	Mark Portugal	.05
269	Kevin Tapani	.05
270	Sid Fernandez	.05
271	Steve Dreyer	.05
272	Denny Hocking	.05
273	Troy O'Leary	.05
274	Milt Cuyler	.05
275	Frank Thomas	2.50
276	Jorge Fabregas	.08
277	Mike Gallego	.08

#	Player	Price
278	Mickey Morandini	.05
279	Roberto Hernandez	.08
280	Henry Rodriguez	.08
281	Garret Anderson	.15
282	Bob Wickman	.05
283	Gar Finnvold	.05
284	Paul O'Neill	.10
285	Royce Clayton	.05
286	Chuck Knoblauch	.20
287	Johnny Ruffin	.05
288	Dave Nilsson	.08
289	David Cone	.08
290	Chuck McElroy	.05
291	Kevin Stocker	.08
292	Jose Rijo	.05
293	Sean Berry	.08
294	Ozzie Guillen	.05
295	Chris Hoiles	.05
296	Kevin Foster	.05
297	Jeff Frye	.05
298	Lance Johnson	.05
299	Mike Kelly	.05
300	Ellis Burks	.10
301	Roberto Kelly	.05
302	Dante Bichette	.25
303	Alvaro Espinoza	.05
304	Alex Cole	.05
305	Rickey Henderson	.10
306	Dave Weathers	.05
307	Shane Reynolds	.08
308	Bobby Bonilla	.15
309	Junior Felix	.05
310	Jeff Fassero	.08
311	Darren Lewis	.08
312	John Doherty	.05
313	Scott Servais	.05
314	Rick Helling	.05
315	Pedro Martinez	.15
316	Wes Chamberlain	.05
317	Bryan Eversgerd	.05
318	Trevor Hoffman	.08
319	John Patterson	.05
320	Matt Walbeck	.05
321	Jeff Montgomery	.05
322	Mel Rojas	.05
323	Eddie Taubensee	.05
324	Ray Lankford	.08
325	Jose Vizcaino	.05
326	Carlos Baerga	.15
327	Jack Voigt	.05
328	Julio Franco	.08
329	Brent Gates	.08
330	Checklist	.05
331	Greg Maddux	2.00
332	Jason Bere	.08
333	Bill Wegman	.05
334	Tuffy Rhodes	.05
335	Kevin Young	.08
336	Andy Benes	.08
337	Pedro Astacio	.08
338	Reggie Jefferson	.05
339	Tim Belcher	.05
340	Ken Griffey Jr.	3.00
341	Mariano Duncan	.05
342	Andres Galarraga	.20
343	Rondell White	.15
344	Cory Bailey	.05
345	Bryan Harvey	.05
346	John Franco	.05
347	Greg Swindell	.05
348	David West	.05
349	Fred McGriff	.30
350	Jose Canseco	.25
351	Orlando Merced	.05
352	Rheal Cormier	.05
353	Carlos Pulido	.05
354	Terry Steinbach	.05
355	Wade Boggs	.15
356	B.J. Surhoff	.05
357	Rafael Palmeiro	.15
358	Anthony Young	.08
359	Tom Brunansky	.05
360	Todd Stottlemyre	.08
361	Chris Turner	.05
362	Joe Boever	.05
363	Jeff Blauser	.05
364	Derek Bell	.08
365	Matt Williams	.30
366	Jeremy Hernandez	.05
367	Joe Girardi	.05
368	Mike Devereaux	.08
369	Jim Abbott	.08
370	Manny Ramirez	.60
371	Kenny Lofton	.75
372	Mark Smith	.05
373	Dave Fleming	.05
374	Dave Stewart	.08
375	Roger Pavlik	.05
376	Hipolito Pichardo	.05
377	Bill Taylor	.05
378	Robin Ventura	.10
379	Bernard Gilkey	.10
380	Kirby Puckett	1.00
381	Steve Howe	.05
382	Devon White	.05
383	Roberto Mejia	.05
384	Darrin Jackson	.05
385	Mike Morgan	.05
386	Rusty Meacham	.05
387	Bill Swift	.05
388	Lou Frazier	.05
389	Andy Van Slyke	.08
390	Brett Butler	.08
391	Bobby Witt	.05
392	Jeff Conine	.08
393	Tim Hyers	.05
394	Terry Pendleton	.05
395	Ricky Jordan	.05
396	Eric Plunk	.05
397	Melido Perez	.05
398	Darryl Kile	.08
399	Mark McLemore	.05
400	Greg Harris	.05
401	Jim Leyritz	.05
402	Doug Strange	.05
403	Tim Salmon	.25
404	Terry Mulholland	.05
405	Robby Thompson	.05
406	Ruben Sierra	.05
407	Tony Phillips	.08
408	Moises Alou	.10
409	Felix Fermin	.05
410	Pat Listach	.05
411	Kevin Bass	.05
412	Ben McDonald	.08
413	Scott Cooper	.05
414	Jody Reed	.05
415	Deion Sanders	.30
416	Ricky Gutierrez	.05
417	Gregg Jefferies	.08
418	Jack McDowell	.12
419	Al Leiter	.08
420	Tony Longmire	.08
421	Paul Wagner	.10
422	Geronimo Pena	.05
423	Ivan Rodriguez	.60
424	Kevin Gross	.05
425	Kirk McCaskill	.05
426	Greg Myers	.05
427	Roger Clemens	1.00
428	Chris Hammond	.05
429	Randy Myers	.05
430	Roger Mason	.05
431	Bret Saberhagen	.08
432	Jeff Reboulet	.05
433	John Olerud	.15
434	Bill Gullickson	.05
435	Eddie Murray	.40
436	Pedro Munoz	.05
437	Charlie O'Brien	.05
438	Jeff Nelson	.05
439	Mike Macfarlane	.05
440	Checklist	.05
441	Derrick May	.05
442	John Roper	.05
443	Darryl Hamilton	.05
444	Dan Miceli	.05
445	Tony Eusebio	.05
446	Jerry Browne	.05
447	Wally Joyner	.08
448	Brian Harper	.05
449	Scott Fletcher	.05
450	Bip Roberts	.05
451	Pete Smith	.08
452	Chili Davis	.08
453	Dave Hollins	.08
454	Tony Pena	.05
455	Butch Henry	.05
456	Craig Biggio	.10
457	Zane Smith	.05
458	Ryan Thompson	.08
459	Mike Jackson	.05
460	Mark McGwire	4.00
461	John Smoltz	.20
462	Steve Scarsone	.05
463	Greg Colbrunn	.08
464	Shawn Green	.20
465	David Wells	.05
466	Jose Hernandez	.05
467	Chip Hale	.05
468	Tony Tarasco	.05
469	Kevin Mitchell	.05
470	Billy Hatcher	.05
471	Jay Buhner	.15
472	Ken Caminiti	.20
473	Tom Henke	.05
474	Todd Worrell	.05
475	Mark Eichhorn	.05
476	Bruce Ruffin	.05
477	Chuck Finley	.05
478	Marc Newfield	.05
479	Paul Shuey	.05
480	Bob Tewksbury	.05
481	Ramon Martinez	.08
482	Melvin Nieves	.05
483	Todd Zeile	.08
484	Benito Santiago	.08
485	Stan Javier	.05
486	Kirk Rueter	.05
487	Andre Dawson	.10
488	Eric Karros	.10
489	Dave Magadan	.05
490	Checklist	.05
491	Randy Velarde	.05
492	Larry Walker	.20
493	Cris Carpenter	.05
494	Tom Gordon	.05
495	Dave Burba	.05
496	Darren Bragg	.05
497	Darren Daulton	.08
498	Don Slaught	.05
499	Pat Borders	.05
500	Lenny Harris	.05
501	Joe Ausanio	.05
502	Alan Trammell	.08
503	Mike Fetters	.05
504	Scott Ruffcorn	.05
505	Rich Rowland	.05
506	Juan Samuel	.05
507	Bo Jackson	.15
508	Jeff Branson	.05
509	Bernie Williams	.40
510	Paul Sorrento	.05
511	Dennis Eckersley	.08
512	Pat Mahomes	.05
513	Rusty Greer	.08
514	Luis Polonia	.05
515	Willie Banks	.05
516	John Wetteland	.05
517	Mike LaVailiere	.05
518	Tommy Greene	.05
519	Mark Grace	.20
520	Bob Hamelin	.05
521	Scott Sanderson	.05
522	Joe Carter	.20
523	Jeff Brantley	.05
524	Andrew Lorraine	.05
525	Rico Brogna	.05
526	Shane Mack	.05
527	Mark Wohlers	.05
528	Scott Sanders	.05
529	Chris Bosio	.05
530	Andujar Cedeno	.05
531	Kenny Rogers	.05
532	Doug Drabek	.05
533	Curt Leskanic	.05
534	Craig Shipley	.05
535	Craig Grebeck	.05
536	Cal Eldred	.05
537	Mickey Tettleton	.05
538	Harold Baines	.08
539	Tim Wallach	.05
540	Damon Buford	.08
541	Lenny Webster	.05
542	Kevin Appier	.05
543	Raul Mondesi	.40
544	Eric Young	.08
545	Russ Davis	.08
546	Mike Benjamin	.05
547	Mike Greenwell	.05
548	Scott Brosius	.05
549	Brian Dorsett	.05
550	Checklist	.05

1995 Donruss All-Stars

Exclusive to Wal-Mart jumbo packs were Donruss All-Stars. Nine cards featuring American Leaguers were inserted into Series I, while nine National League All-Stars were inserted into Series II jumbos.

		MT
Complete Set (18):		160.00
Complete Series 1 (9):		100.00
Complete Series 2 (9):		60.00
Common Player:		2.00
AL1	Jimmy Key	2.00
AL2	Ivan Rodriguez	7.00
AL3	Frank Thomas	25.00
AL4	Roberto Alomar	6.00
AL5	Wade Boggs	4.00
AL6	Cal Ripken, Jr.	25.00
AL7	Joe Carter	4.00
AL8	Ken Griffey, Jr.	35.00
AL9	Kirby Puckett	12.00
NL1	Greg Maddux	20.00
NL2	Mike Piazza	20.00
NL3	Gregg Jefferies	2.00
NL4	Mariano Duncan	2.00
NL5	Matt Williams	4.00
NL6	Ozzie Smith	5.00
NL7	Barry Bonds	8.00
NL8	Tony Gwynn	15.00
NL9	Dave Justice	4.00

1995 Donruss Bomb Squad

Bomb Squad features the top six home run hitters in each league on double-sided cards. These cards were only inserted into Series I retail and magazine distributor packs at a rate of one per 24 retail packs and one per 16 magazine distributor packs.

		MT
Complete Set (6):		15.00
Common Player:		1.00
1	Ken Griffey, Jr., Matt Williams	5.00
2	Frank Thomas, Jeff Bagwell	4.00
3	Albert Belle, Barry Bonds	2.50
4	Jose Canseco, Fred McGriff	1.50
5	Cecil Fielder, Andres Galarraga	1.00
6	Joe Carter, Kevin Mitchell	1.00

A player's name in *italic* type indicates a rookie card.

1995 Donruss Diamond Kings

Continuing a tradition begun in 1982, artist Dick Perez painted a series of 28 water colors to produce insert cards of the game's best; 14 in each series. A portrait of the player appears on a party-colored background, with Diamond Kings in gold across the top. Diamond Kings were inserted in all packs at a rate of one per 10.

		MT
Complete Set (29):		45.00
Complete Series 1 (14):		20.00
Complete Series 2 (15):		25.00
Common Player:		1.00
1	Frank Thomas	8.00
2	Jeff Bagwell	5.00
3	Chili Davis	1.00
4	Dante Bichette	1.50
5	Ruben Sierra	1.00
6	Jeff Conine	1.25
7	Paul O'Neill	1.25
8	Bobby Bonilla	1.00
9	Joe Carter	1.25
10	Moises Alou	1.00
11	Kenny Lofton	2.50
12	Matt Williams	1.50
13	Kevin Seitzer	1.00
14	Sammy Sosa	6.00
15	Scott Cooper	1.00
16	Raul Mondesi	1.50
17	Will Clark	1.50
18	Lenny Dykstra	1.00
19	Kirby Puckett	5.00
20	Hal Morris	1.00
21	Travis Fryman	1.00
22	Greg Maddux	6.00
23	Rafael Palmeiro	1.25
24	Tony Gwynn	5.00
25	David Cone	1.00
26	Al Martin	1.00
27	Ken Griffey Jr.	10.00
28	Gregg Jefferies	1.00
29	Checklist	.25

1995 Donruss Elite

Another Donruss insert tradition continues with the fifth annual presentation of the Elite series. Each of the 12 Elite cards (six per series) is produced in an edition of 10,000 and inserted into all types of packaging at the rate of one per 210 packs.

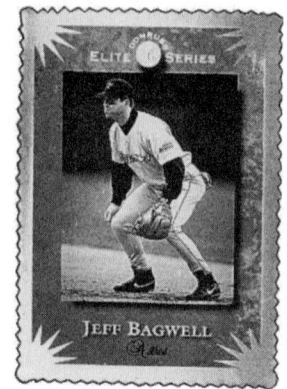

		MT
Complete Set (12):		300.00
Complete Series 1 (6):		160.00
Complete Series 2 (6):		140.00
Common Player:		8.00
49	Jeff Bagwell	30.00
50	Paul O'Neill	8.00
51	Greg Maddux	40.00
52	Mike Piazza	40.00
53	Matt Williams	10.00
54	Ken Griffey, Jr.	75.00
55	Frank Thomas	60.00
56	Barry Bonds	20.00
57	Kirby Puckett	25.00
58	Fred McGriff	10.00
59	Jose Canseco	10.00
60	Albert Belle	20.00

1995 Donruss Long Ball Leaders

Exclusive to Series 1 hobby packs, these eight cards feature the top long-distance home runs of 1994 in an eye-popping holographic foil presentation. Stated odds of picking one of these inserts from a hobby pack are one in 24.

		MT
Complete Set (8):		24.00
Common Player:		1.00
1	Frank Thomas	5.00
2	Fred McGriff	1.00
3	Ken Griffey, Jr.	6.00
4	Matt Williams	1.00
5	Mike Piazza	4.00
6	Jose Canseco	1.50
7	Barry Bonds	2.00
8	Jeff Bagwell	3.00

1995 Donruss Mound Marvels

Mound Marvels is an eight-card insert set containing some of the best pitchers in baseball. Cards were inserted into one per 18 retail and magazine packs of Donruss Series II. Each card features a two-way mirror that allows collectors to see the players' face through the mirror.

		MT
Complete Set (8):		20.00
Common Player:		1.50
1	Greg Maddux	8.00
2	David Cone	1.50
3	Mike Mussina	4.00
4	Bret Saberhagen	1.50
5	Jimmy Key	1.50
6	Doug Drabek	1.50
7	Randy Johnson	4.00
8	Jason Bere	1.50

1995 Donruss Dominators

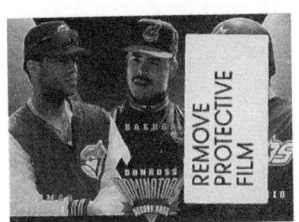

Dominators is a nine-card chase set inserted into hobby packs of Series II Donruss baseball at a rate of one per 24 packs. These acetate cards feature three of the top players at each position on a horizontal format.

		MT
Complete Set (9):		25.00
Common Player:		1.00
1	David Cone, Mike Mussina, Greg Maddux	3.00
2	Ivan Rodriguez, Mike Piazza, Darren Daulton	4.00
3	Fred McGriff, Frank Thomas, Jeff Bagwell	6.00
4	Roberto Alomar, Carlos Baerga, Craig Biggio	2.50
5	Robin Ventura, Travis Fryman, Matt Williams	2.00
6	Cal Ripken Jr., Barry Larkin, Wil Cordero	8.00
7	Albert Belle, Barry Bonds, Moises Alou	2.50
8	Ken Griffey Jr., Kenny Lofton, Marquis Grissom	8.00
9	Kirby Puckett, Paul O'Neill, Tony Gwynn	5.00

1995 Donruss Press Proofs

Designated as Press Proofs, the first 2,000 cards of each player in the '95 Donruss set were enhanced with gold, rather than silver, foil and inserted into packs at an average rate of one per 20 packs.

	MT
Complete Set (550):	1400.
Complete Series 1 (330):	800.00
Complete Series 2 (220):	600.00
Common Player:	2.00
Stars: 15x to 25x	
Yng Stars & RC's: 10x to 15x	
(Star cards valued at 20-	
35X regular 1995 Donruss.)	

1995 Donruss/ Top of the Order Card Game

In one of the earliest efforts to wed the play factor and collectibility that had made various fantasy card games so successful in 1994-95, Donruss created the interactive Top of the Order baseball card game. Printed on playing card stock with rounded corners and semi-gloss surface, the player cards feature color action photos and all manners of game-action indicators. Backs of each card are printed primarily in green with Don-russ logos. Cards were sold in several types of packaging, including 80- and 160-card boxed sets, and 12-card foil "booster" packs. Superstars' cards were printed in lesser quantities than those of journeyman players, resulting in values higher than would be the case based on player popularity alone if all cards were printed in equal quantities. The unnumbered cards are checklisted here in alphabetical order within team and league.

		MT
Complete Set:		175.00
Common Player:		.10
(1)	Brady Anderson	.10
(2)	Harold Baines	.10
(3)	Bret Barberie	.10
(4)	Armando Benitez	.10
(5)	Bobby Bonilla	.20
(6)	Scott Erickson	.15
(7)	Leo Gomez	.10
(8)	Curtis Goodwin	.10
(9)	Jeffrey Hammonds	.10
(10)	Chris Hoiles	.10
(11)	Doug Jones	.10
(12)	Ben McDonald	.10
(13)	Mike Mussina	1.00
(14)	Rafael Palmeiro	2.00
(15)	Cal Ripken Jr.	25.00
(16)	Rick Aguilera	.10
(17)	Luis Alicea	.10
(18)	Jose Canseco	.75
(19)	Roger Clemens	1.50
(20)	Mike Greenwell	.10
(21)	Erik Hanson	.10
(22)	Mike Macfarlane	.10
(23)	Tim Naehring	.10
(24)	Troy O'Leary	.10
(25)	Ken Ryan	.10
(26)	Aaron Sele	.15
(27)	Lee Tinsley	.10
(28)	John Valentin	.10
(29)	Mo Vaughn	3.50
(30)	Jim Abbott	.40
(31)	Mike Butcher	.10
(32)	Chili Davis	.10
(33)	Gary DiSarcina	.10
(34)	Damion Easley	.10
(35)	Jim Edmonds	1.50
(36)	Chuck Finley	.10
(37)	Mark Langston	.10
(38)	Greg Myers	.10
(39)	Spike Owen	.10
(40)	Troy Percival	.10
(41)	Tony Phillips	.10
(42)	Tim Salmon	2.25
(43)	Lee Smith	1.00
(44)	J.T. Snow	.15
(45)	Jason Bere	.10
(46)	Mike Devereaux	.10
(47)	Ray Durham	.20
(48)	Alex Fernandez	.15
(49)	Ozzie Guillen	1.00
(50)	Roberto Hernandez	.10
(51)	Lance Johnson	.10
(52)	Ron Karkovice	.10
(53)	Tim Raines	.20
(54)	Frank Thomas	20.00
(55)	Robin Ventura	.55
(56)	Sandy Alomar Jr.	.15
(57)	Carlos Baerga	3.50
(58)	Albert Belle	4.00
(59)	Kenny Lofton	5.00
(60)	Dennis Martinez	.15
(61)	Jose Mesa	.10
(62)	Eddie Murray	3.00
(63)	Charles Nagy	.10
(64)	Tony Pena	.10
(65)	Eric Plunk	.10
(66)	Manny Ramirez	4.50
(67)	Paul Sorrento	.10
(68)	Jim Thome	2.00
(69)	Omar Vizquel	.10
(70)	Danny Bautista	.10
(71)	Joe Boever	.10
(72)	Chad Curtis	.10
(73)	Cecil Fielder	.75
(74)	John Flaherty	.10
(75)	Travis Fryman	.40
(76)	Kirk Gibson	.10
(77)	Chris Gomez	.10

No.	Player	Price
(78)	Mike Henneman	.10
(79)	Bob Higginson	.25
(80)	Alan Trammell	.50
(81)	Lou Whitaker	1.50
(82)	Kevin Appier	.10
(83)	Billy Brewer	.10
(84)	Vince Coleman	.10
(85)	Gary Gaetti	.10
(86)	Greg Gagne	.10
(87)	Tom Goodwin	.10
(88)	Tom Gordon	.10
(89)	Mark Gubicza	.10
(90)	Bob Hamelin	.10
(91)	Phil Hiatt	.10
(92)	Wally Joyner	.15
(93)	Brent Mayne	.10
(94)	Jeff Montgomery	.10
(95)	Ricky Bones	.10
(96)	Mike Fetters	.10
(97)	Darryl Hamilton	.10
(98)	Pat Listach	.10
(99)	Matt Mieske	.10
(100)	Dave Nilsson	.10
(101)	Joe Oliver	.10
(102)	Kevin Seitzer	.10
(103)	B.J. Surhoff	.10
(104)	Jose Valentin	.10
(105)	Greg Vaughn	.10
(106)	Bill Wegman	.10
(107)	Alex Cole	.10
(108)	Marty Cordova	.50
(109)	Chuck Knoblauch	3.00
(110)	Scott Leius	.10
(111)	Pat Meares	.10
(112)	Pedro Munoz	.10
(113)	Kirby Puckett	15.00
(114)	Scott Stahoviak	.10
(115)	Mike Trombley	.10
(116)	Matt Walbeck	.10
(117)	Wade Boggs	11.00
(118)	David Cone	.10
(119)	Tony Fernandez	.10
(120)	Don Mattingly	15.00
(121)	Jack McDowell	.15
(122)	Paul O'Neill	.15
(123)	Melido Perez	.10
(124)	Luis Polonia	.10
(125)	Ruben Sierra	.10
(126)	Mike Stanley	.10
(127)	Randy Velarde	.10
(128)	John Wetteland	.10
(129)	Bob Wickman	.10
(130)	Bernie Williams	.20
(131)	Gerald Williams	.10
(132)	Geronimo Berroa	.10
(133)	Mike Bordick	.10
(134)	Scott Brosius	.10
(135)	Dennis Eckersley	.35
(136)	Brent Gates	.10
(137)	Rickey Henderson	.75
(138)	Stan Javier	.10
(139)	Mark McGwire	16.00
(140)	Steve Ontiveros	.10
(141)	Terry Steinbach	.10
(142)	Todd Stottlemyre	.10
(143)	Danny Tartabull	.10
(144)	Bobby Ayala	.10
(145)	Andy Benes	.15
(146)	Mike Blowers	.10
(147)	Jay Buhner	.20
(148)	Joey Cora	.10
(149)	Alex Diaz	.10
(150)	Ken Griffey Jr.	25.00
(151)	Randy Johnson	3.00
(152)	Edgar Martinez	2.00
(153)	Tino Martinez	.15
(154)	Bill Risley	.10
(155)	Alex Rodriguez	4.00
(156)	Dan Wilson	.10
(157)	Will Clark	7.00
(158)	Jeff Frye	.10
(159)	Benji Gil	.10
(160)	Juan Gonzalez	3.00
(161)	Rusty Greer	.10
(162)	Mark McLemore	.10
(163)	Otis Nixon	.10
(164)	Dean Palmer	.10
(165)	Ivan Rodriguez	2.50
(166)	Kenny Rogers	.10
(167)	Jeff Russell	.10
(168)	Mickey Tettleton	.10
(169)	Bob Tewksbury	.10
(170)	Bobby Witt	.10
(171)	Roberto Alomar	11.00
(172)	Joe Carter	7.00
(173)	Alex Gonzalez	.25
(174)	Candy Maldonado	.10
(175)	Paul Molitor	1.00
(176)	John Olerud	.15
(177)	Lance Parrish	.10
(178)	Ed Sprague	.10
(179)	Devon White	.10
(180)	Woody Williams	.10
(181)	Steve Avery	.35
(182)	Jeff Blauser	.10
(183)	Tom Glavine	.60
(184)	Marquis Grissom	.15
(185)	Chipper Jones	4.00
(186)	Dave Justice	7.00
(187)	Ryan Klesko	.50
(188)	Mark Lemke	.10
(189)	Javier Lopez	.20
(190)	Greg Maddux	17.50
(191)	Fred McGriff	2.50
(192)	Greg McMichael	.10
(193)	John Smoltz	4.00
(194)	Mark Wohlers	.10
(195)	Jim Bullinger	.10
(196)	Shawon Dunston	.10
(197)	Kevin Foster	.10
(198)	Luis Gonzalez	.10
(199)	Mark Grace	3.50
(200)	Brian McRae	.10
(201)	Randy Myers	.10
(202)	Jaime Navarro	.10
(203)	Rey Sanchez	.10
(204)	Scott Servais	.10
(205)	Sammy Sosa	4.00
(206)	Steve Trachsel	.10
(207)	Todd Zeile	.10
(208)	Bret Boone	1.00
(209)	Jeff Branson	.10
(210)	Jeff Brantley	.10
(211)	Hector Carrasco	.10
(212)	Ron Gant	.20
(213)	Lenny Harris	.10
(214)	Barry Larkin	2.50
(215)	Darren Lewis	.15
(216)	Hal Morris	.10
(217)	Mark Portugal	.10
(218)	Jose Rijo	.10
(219)	Reggie Sanders	1.50
(220)	Pete Schourek	.10
(221)	John Smiley	.10
(222)	Eddie Taubensee	.10
(223)	Dave Wells	.10
(224)	Jason Bates	.10
(225)	Dante Bichette	7.00
(226)	Vinny Castilla	.20
(227)	Andres Galarraga	6.00
(228)	Joe Girardi	.10
(229)	Mike Kingery	.10
(230)	Steve Reed	.10
(231)	Bruce Ruffin	.10
(232)	Bret Saberhagen	.15
(233)	Bill Swift	.10
(234)	Larry Walker	2.50
(235)	Walt Weiss	.10
(236)	Eric Young	.10
(237)	Kurt Abbott	.10
(238)	John Burkett	.10
(239)	Chuck Carr	.10
(240)	Greg Colbrunn	.10
(241)	Jeff Conine	1.00
(242)	Andre Dawson	.45
(243)	Chris Hammond	.10
(244)	Charles Johnson	.10
(245)	Robb Nen	.10
(246)	Terry Pendleton	.10
(247)	Gary Sheffield	2.50
(248)	Quilvio Veras	.10
(249)	Jeff Bagwell	3.00
(250)	Derek Bell	.20
(251)	Craig Biggio	.20
(252)	Doug Drabek	.10
(253)	Tony Eusebio	.10
(254)	John Hudek	.10
(255)	Brian Hunter	.15
(256)	Todd Jones	.10
(257)	Dave Magadan	.10
(258)	Orlando Miller	.10
(259)	James Mouton	.10
(260)	Shane Reynolds	.10
(261)	Greg Swindell	.10
(262)	Billy Ashley	.10
(263)	Tom Candiotti	.10
(264)	Delino DeShields	.10
(265)	Eric Karros	2.50
(266)	Roberto Kelly	.10
(267)	Ramon Martinez	.15
(268)	Raul Mondesi	2.50
(269)	Hideo Nomo	12.00
(270)	Jose Offerman	.10
(271)	Mike Piazza	16.00
(272)	Kevin Tapani	.10
(273)	Ismael Valdes	.15
(274)	Tim Wallach	.10
(275)	Todd Worrell	.10
(276)	Moises Alou	1.00
(277)	Sean Berry	.10
(278)	Wil Cordero	.10
(279)	Jeff Fassero	.10
(280)	Darrin Fletcher	.10
(281)	Mike Lansing	.10
(282)	Pedro J. Martinez	.10
(283)	Carlos Perez	.15
(284)	Mel Rojas	.10
(285)	Tim Scott	.10
(286)	David Segui	.10
(287)	Tony Tarasco	.10
(288)	Rondell White	.20
(289)	Rico Brogna	.10
(290)	Brett Butler	.10
(291)	John Franco	.10
(292)	Pete Harnisch	.10
(293)	Todd Hundley	.10
(294)	Bobby Jones	.10
(295)	Jeff Kent	.10
(296)	Joe Orsulak	.10
(297)	Ryan Thompson	.10
(298)	Jose Vizcaino	.10
(299)	Ricky Bottalico	.10
(300)	Darren Daulton	.35
(301)	Mariano Duncan	.10
(302)	Lenny Dykstra	.50
(303)	Jim Eisenreich	.10
(304)	Tyler Green	.10
(305)	Charlie Hayes	.10
(306)	Dave Hollins	.10
(307)	Gregg Jefferies	.50
(308)	Mickey Morandini	.10
(309)	Curt Schilling	.10
(310)	Heathcliff Slocumb	.10
(311)	Kevin Stocker	.10
(312)	Jay Bell	.10
(313)	Jacob Brumfield	.10
(314)	Dave Clark	.10
(315)	Carlos Garcia	.10
(316)	Mark Johnson	.10
(317)	Jeff King	.10
(318)	Nelson Liriano	.10
(319)	Al Martin	.10
(320)	Orlando Merced	.10
(321)	Dan Miceli	.10
(322)	Denny Neagle	.10
(323)	Mark Parent	.10
(324)	Dan Plesac	.10
(325)	Scott Cooper	.10
(326)	Bernard Gilkey	.10
(327)	Tom Henke	.10
(328)	Ken Hill	.10
(329)	Danny Jackson	.10
(330)	Brian Jordan	.15
(331)	Ray Lankford	.10
(332)	John Mabry	.10
(333)	Jose Oquendo	.10
(334)	Tom Pagnozzi	.10
(335)	Ozzie Smith	1.00
(336)	Andy Ashby	.10
(337)	Brad Ausmus	.10
(338)	Ken Caminiti	.10
(339)	Andujar Cedeno	.10
(340)	Steve Finley	.10
(341)	Tony Gwynn	12.00
(342)	Joey Hamilton	.10
(343)	Trevor Hoffman	.10
(344)	Jody Reed	.10
(345)	Bip Roberts	.10
(346)	Eddie Williams	.10
(347)	Rod Beck	.10
(348)	Mike Benjamin	.10
(349)	Barry Bonds	12.00
(350)	Royce Clayton	.20
(351)	Glenallen Hill	.10
(352)	Kirt Manwaring	.10
(353)	Terry Mulholland	.10
(354)	John Patterson	.10
(355)	J.R. Phillips	.10
(356)	Deion Sanders	6.00
(357)	Steve Scarsone	.10
(358)	Robby Thompson	.10
(359)	William VanLandingham	.10
(360)	Matt Williams	3.50

1996 Donruss

A clean, borderless look marks the 1996 Donruss regular-issue cards. Besides the player name in white inside a fading team-color stripe at top-right, the only other graphic enhancement on front is a 7/8" square foil box at bottom-center containing the company and team name, team logo and player position and uniform number. The foil box is enhanced with team colors, which are carried over to the horizontal backs. Backs also feature a color action photo at right, a large gray team logo and stats and career highlights. Basic packaging was 12-card foil packs with a suggested retail price of $1.79. Several types of insert cards were offered, each at a virtually unprecedented rate of scarcity. The set was issued in two series; Series 1 with 330 cards, Series 2 with 220 cards.

		MT
Complete Set (550):		45.00
Complete Series 1 (330):		25.00
Complete Series 2 (220):		20.00
Common Player:		.05
Series 1 Wax Box:		45.00
Series 2 Wax Box:		30.00
1	Frank Thomas	2.50
2	Jason Bates	.05
3	Steve Sparks	.05
4	Scott Servais	.05
5	Angelo Encarnacion	.05
6	Scott Sanders	.05
7	Billy Ashley	.05
8	Alex Rodriguez	3.00
9	Sean Bergman	.05
10	Brad Radke	.05
11	Andy Van Slyke	.05
12	Joe Girardi	.05
13	Mark Grudzielanek	.10
14	Rick Aguilera	.05
15	Randy Veres	.05
16	Tim Bogar	.05
17	Dave Veres	.05
18	Kevin Stocker	.05
19	Marquis Grissom	.08
20	Will Clark	.30
21	Jay Bell	.08
22	Allen Battle	.05
23	Frank Rodriguez	.05
24	Terry Steinbach	.05
25	Gerald Williams	.05
26	Sid Roberson	.05
27	Greg Zaun	.05
28	Ozzie Timmons	.05
29	Vaughn Eshelman	.05
30	Ed Sprague	.05
31	Gary DiSarcina	.05
32	Joe Boever	.05
33	Steve Avery	.05
34	Brad Ausmus	.05
35	Kirt Manwaring	.05

36	Gary Sheffield	.40
37	Jason Bere	.05
38	Jeff Manto	.05
39	David Cone	.10
40	Manny Ramirez	.75
41	Sandy Alomar	.08
42	Curtis Goodwin (Rated Rookie)	.05
43	Tino Martinez	.10
44	Woody Williams	.05
45	Dean Palmer	.08
46	Hipolito Pichardo	.05
47	Jason Giambi	.05
48	Lance Johnson	.08
49	Bernard Gilkey	.05
50	Kirby Puckett	1.00
51	Tony Fernandez	.05
52	Alex Gonzalez	.08
53	Bret Saberhagen	.05
54	Lyle Mouton (Rated Rookie)	.05
55	Brian McRae	.08
56	Mark Gubicza	.05
57	Sergio Valdez	.05
58	Darrin Fletcher	.05
59	Steve Parris	.05
60	Johnny Damon (Rated Rookie)	.20
61	Rickey Henderson	.10
62	Darrell Whitmore	.05
63	Roberto Petagine	.05
64	Trenidad Hubbard	.05
65	Heathcliff Slocumb	.05
66	Steve Finley	.05
67	Mariano Rivera	.25
68	Brian Hunter	.08
69	Jamie Moyer	.05
70	Ellis Burks	.08
71	Pat Kelly	.05
72	Mickey Tettleton	.05
73	Garret Anderson	.15
74	Andy Pettitte (Rated Rookie)	1.00
75	Glenallen Hill	.05
76	Brent Gates	.05
77	Lou Whitaker	.05
78	David Segui	.05
79	Dan Wilson	.08
80	Pat Listach	.05
81	Jeff Bagwell	1.00
82	Ben McDonald	.08
83	John Valentin	.05
84	John Jaha	.05
85	Pete Schourek	.05
86	Bryce Florie	.05
87	Brian Jordan	.15
88	Ron Karkovice	.05
89	Al Leiter	.08
90	Tony Longmire	.05
91	Nelson Liriano	.05
92	David Bell	.05
93	Kevin Gross	.05
94	Tom Candiotti	.05
95	Dave Martinez	.05
96	Greg Myers	.05
97	Rheal Cormier	.05
98	Chris Hammond	.05
99	Randy Myers	.05
100	Bill Pulsipher (Rated Rookie)	.15
101	Jason Isringhausen (Rated Rookie)	.20
102	Dave Stevens	.05
103	Roberto Alomar	.75
104	Bob Higginson (Rated Rookie)	.25
105	Eddie Murray	.35
106	Matt Walbeck	.05
107	Mark Wohlers	.05
108	Jeff Nelson	.05
109	Tom Goodwin	.05
110	Checklist 1-83 (Cal Ripken Jr.) (2,131 Consecutive Games)	1.50
111	Rey Sanchez	.05
112	Hector Carrasco	.05
113	B.J. Surhoff	.05
114	Dan Miceli	.05
115	Dean Hartgraves	.05
116	John Burkett	.05
117	Gary Gaetti	.05
118	Ricky Bones	.05
119	Mike Macfarlane	.05
120	Bip Roberts	.05
121	Dave Mlicki	.05
122	Chili Davis	.08
123	Mark Whiten	.05

124	Herbert Perry	.05
125	Butch Henry	.05
126	Derek Bell	.08
127	Al Martin	.05
128	John Franco	.05
129	William VanLandingham	.05
130	Mike Bordick	.05
131	Mike Mordecai	.05
132	Robby Thompson	.05
133	Greg Colbrunn	.05
134	Domingo Cedeno	.05
135	Chad Curtis	.08
136	Jose Hernandez	.05
137	Scott Klingenbeck	.05
138	Ryan Klesko	.75
139	John Smiley	.05
140	Charlie Hayes	.05
141	Jay Buhner	.20
142	Doug Drabek	.05
143	Roger Pavlik	.05
144	Todd Worrell	.05
145	Cal Ripken Jr.	2.50
146	Steve Reed	.05
147	Chuck Finley	.05
148	Mike Blowers	.05
149	Orel Hershiser	.08
150	Allen Watson	.05
151	Ramon Martinez	.08
152	Melvin Nieves	.05
153	Tripp Cromer	.05
154	Yorkis Perez	.05
155	Stan Javier	.05
156	Mel Rojas	.05
157	Aaron Sele	.05
158	Eric Karros	.15
159	Robb Nen	.05
160	Raul Mondesi	.30
161	John Wetteland	.05
162	Tim Scott	.05
163	Kenny Rogers	.05
164	Melvin Bunch	.05
165	Rod Beck	.05
166	Andy Benes	.05
167	Lenny Dykstra	.05
168	Orlando Merced	.05
169	Tomas Perez	.05
170	Xavier Hernandez	.05
171	Ruben Sierra	.08
172	Alan Trammell	.08
173	Mike Fetters	.05
174	Wilson Alvarez	.05
175	Erik Hanson	.05
176	Travis Fryman	.15
177	Jim Abbott	.05
178	Bret Boone	.08
179	Sterling Hitchcock	.05
180	Pat Mahomes	.05
181	Mark Acre	.05
182	Charles Nagy	.05
183	Rusty Greer	.15
184	Mike Stanley	.05
185	Jim Bullinger	.05
186	Shane Andrews	.05
187	Brian Keyser	.05
188	Tyler Green	.05
189	Mark Grace	.20
190	Bob Hamelin	.05
191	Luis Ortiz	.05
192	Joe Carter	.20
193	Eddie Taubensee	.05
194	Brian Anderson	.08
195	Edgardo Alfonzo	.08
196	Pedro Munoz	.05
197	David Justice	.25
198	Trevor Hoffman	.05
199	Bobby Ayala	.05
200	Tony Eusebio	.05
201	Jeff Russell	.05
202	Mike Hampton	.05
203	Walt Weiss	.05
204	Joey Hamilton	.05
205	Roberto Hernandez	.05
206	Greg Vaughn	.05
207	Felipe Lira	.05
208	Harold Baines	.08
209	Tim Wallach	.05
210	Manny Alexander	.05
211	Tim Laker	.05
212	Chris Haney	.05
213	Brian Maxcy	.05
214	Eric Young	.08
215	Darryl Strawberry	.08
216	Barry Bonds	.75
217	Tim Naehring	.05
218	Scott Brosius	.05
219	Reggie Sanders	.05

No.	Player	Price	No.	Player	Price	No.	Player	Price
220	Checklist 84-166(Eddie Murray) (3,000 Career Hits)	.20	312	Carl Everett	.05	405	Deion Sanders	.35
221	Luis Alicea	.05	313	Charles Johnson	.10	406	Dennis Eckersley	.08
222	Albert Belle	.75	314	Alex Diaz	.05	407	Tony Clark	.60
223	Benji Gil	.05	315	Jose Mesa	.05	408	Rondell White	.15
224	Dante Bichette	.25	316	Mark Carreon	.05	409	Luis Sojo	.05
225	Bobby Bonilla	.15	317	Carlos Perez (Rated Rookie)	.15	410	David Hulse	.05
226	Todd Stottlemyre	.05				411	Shane Reynolds	.05
227	Jim Edmonds	.15	318	Ismael Valdes	.08	412	Chris Hoiles	.05
228	Todd Jones	.05	319	Frank Castillo	.05	413	Lee Tinsley	.05
229	Shawn Green	.08	320	Tom Henke	.05	414	Scott Karl	.05
230	Javy Lopez	.20	321	Spike Owen	.05	415	Ron Gant	.15
231	Ariel Prieto	.05	322	Joe Orsulak	.05	416	Brian Johnson	.05
232	Tony Phillips	.08	323	Paul Menhart	.05	417	Jose Oliva	.05
233	James Mouton	.05	324	Pedro Borbon	.05	418	Jack McDowell	.15
234	Jose Oquendo	.05	325	Checklist 167-249(Paul Molitor) (1,000 Career RBI)	.25	419	Paul Molitor	.35
235	Royce Clayton	.05				420	Ricky Bottalico	.05
236	Chuck Carr	.05	326	Jeff Cirillo	.05	421	Paul Wagner	.05
237	Doug Jones	.05	327	Edwin Hurtado	.05	422	Terry Bradshaw	.05
238	Mark Mclemore (McLemore)	.05	328	Orlando Miller	.05	423	Bob Tewksbury	.05
			329	Steve Ontiveros	.05	424	Mike Piazza	2.00
239	Bill Swift	.05	330	Checklist 250-330(Kirby Puckett) (1,000 Career RBI)	.50	425	*Luis Andujar*	.05
240	Scott Leius	.05				426	Mark Langston	.05
241	Russ Davis	.05	331	Scott Bullett	.05	427	Stan Belinda	.05
242	Ray Durham (Rated Rookie)	.08	332	Andres Galarraga	.20	428	Kurt Abbott	.05
			333	Cal Eldred	.05	429	Shawon Dunston	.08
243	Matt Mieske	.05	334	Sammy Sosa	1.50	430	Bobby Jones	.05
244	Brent Mayne	.05	335	Don Slaught	.05	431	Jose Vizcaino	.05
245	Thomas Howard	.05	336	Jody Reed	.05	432	*Matt Lawton*	.05
246	Troy O'Leary	.05	337	Roger Cedeno	.05	433	Pat Hentgen	.05
247	Jacob Brumfield	.05	338	Ken Griffey Jr.	3.00	434	Cecil Fielder	.15
248	Mickey Morandini	.05	339	Todd Hollandsworth	.08	435	Carlos Baerga	.15
249	Todd Hundley	.20	340	Mike Trombley	.05	436	Rich Becker	.05
250	Chris Bosio	.05	341	Gregg Jefferies	.08	437	Chipper Jones	2.00
251	Omar Vizquel	.05	342	Larry Walker	.30	438	Bill Risley	.05
252	Mike Lansing	.08	343	Pedro Martinez	.08	439	Kevin Appier	.05
253	John Mabry	.05	344	Dwayne Hosey	.05	440	Checklist	.05
254	Mike Perez	.05	345	Terry Pendleton	.05	441	Jaime Navarro	.05
255	Delino DeShields	.05	346	Pete Harnisch	.05	442	Barry Larkin	.25
256	Wil Cordero	.05	347	Tony Castillo	.05	443	*Jose Valentin*	.15
257	Mike James	.05	348	Paul Quantrill	.05	444	Bryan Rekar	.05
258	Todd Van Poppel	.05	349	Fred McGriff	.40	445	Rick Wilkins	.05
259	Joey Cora	.05	350	Ivan Rodriguez	.50	446	Quilvio Veras	.05
260	Andre Dawson	.08	351	Butch Huskey	.05	447	Greg Gagne	.05
261	Jerry DiPoto	.05	352	Ozzie Smith	.50	448	Mark Kiefer	.05
262	Rick Krivda	.05	353	Marty Cordova	.20	449	Bobby Witt	.05
263	Glenn Dishman	.05	354	John Wasdin	.05	450	Andy Ashby	.05
264	Mike Mimbs	.05	355	Wade Boggs	.20	451	Alex Ochoa	.05
265	John Ericks	.05	356	Dave Nilsson	.05	452	Jorge Fabregas	.05
266	Jose Canseco	.35	357	Rafael Palmeiro	.20	453	Gene Schall	.05
267	Jeff Branson	.05	358	Luis Gonzalez	.05	454	Ken Hill	.05
268	Curt Leskanic	.05	359	Reggie Jefferson	.05	455	Tony Tarasco	.05
269	Jon Nunnally	.05	360	Carlos Delgado	.15	456	Donnie Wall	.05
270	Scott Stahoviak	.05	361	Orlando Palmeiro	.05	457	Carlos Garcia	.05
271	Jeff Montgomery	.05	362	Chris Gomez	.05	458	Ryan Thompson	.05
272	Hal Morris	.05	363	John Smoltz	.20	459	*Marvin Benard*	.08
273	Esteban Loaiza	.15	364	Marc Newfield	.05	460	Jose Herrera	.05
274	Rico Brogna	.05	365	Matt Williams	.30	461	Jeff Blauser	.05
275	Dave Winfield	.15	366	Jesus Tavarez	.05	462	Chris Hook	.05
276	J.R. Phillips	.05	367	Bruce Ruffin	.05	463	Jeff Conine	.08
277	Todd Zeile	.08	368	Sean Berry	.05	464	Devon White	.05
278	Tom Pagnozzi	.05	369	Randy Velarde	.05	465	Danny Bautista	.08
279	Mark Lemke	.05	370	Tony Pena	.05	466	Steve Trachsel	.05
280	Dave Magadan	.05	371	Jim Thome	.50	467	C.J. Nitkowski	.05
281	Greg McMichael	.05	372	Jeffrey Hammonds	.05	468	Mike Devereaux	.05
282	Mike Morgan	.05	373	Bob Wolcott	.05	469	David Wells	.05
283	Moises Alou	.15	374	Juan Guzman	.05	470	Jim Eisenreich	.05
284	Dennis Martinez	.08	375	Juan Gonzalez	1.50	471	Edgar Martinez	.08
285	Jeff Kent	.08	376	Michael Tucker	.08	472	Craig Biggio	.10
286	Mark Johnson	.05	377	Doug Johns	.05	473	Jeff Frye	.05
287	Darren Lewis	.08	378	*Mike Cameron*	1.00	474	Karim Garcia	.50
288	Brad Clontz	.05	379	Ray Lankford	.08	475	Jimmy Haynes	.05
289	Chad Fonville (Rated Rookie)	.20	380	Jose Parra	.05	476	Darren Holmes	.05
			381	Jimmy Key	.08	477	Tim Salmon	.25
290	Paul Sorrento	.05	382	John Olerud	.10	478	Randy Johnson	.35
291	Lee Smith	.08	383	Kevin Ritz	.05	479	Eric Plunk	.05
292	Tom Glavine	.20	384	Tim Raines	.08	480	Scott Cooper	.05
293	Antonio Osuna	.05	385	Rich Amaral	.05	481	Chan Ho Park	.08
294	Kevin Foster	.05	386	Keith Lockhart	.05	482	Ray McDavid	.05
295	*Sandy Martinez*	.05	387	Steve Scarsone	.05	483	Mark Petkovsek	.05
296	Mark Leiter	.05	388	Cliff Floyd	.08	484	Greg Swindell	.05
297	Julian Tavarez	.05	389	Rich Aude	.05	485	George Williams	.05
298	Mike Kelly	.05	390	Hideo Nomo	1.50	486	Yamil Benitez	.08
299	Joe Oliver	.05	391	Geronimo Berroa	.05	487	Tim Wakefield	.05
300	John Flaherty	.05	392	Pat Rapp	.05	488	Kevin Tapani	.05
301	Don Mattingly	.75	393	Dustin Hermanson	.05	489	Derrick May	.05
302	Pat Meares	.05	394	Greg Maddux	2.00	490	Checklist(Ken Griffey Jr.)	1.50
303	John Doherty	.05	395	Darren Daulton	.08	491	Derek Jeter	1.50
304	Joe Vitiello	.05	396	Kenny Lofton	.75	492	Jeff Fassero	.08
305	Vinny Castilla	.08	397	Ruben Rivera	.40	493	Benito Santiago	.05
306	Jeff Brantley	.05	398	Billy Wagner	.05	494	Tom Gordon	.05
307	Mike Greenwell	.05	399	Kevin Brown	.08	495	Jamie Brewington	.05
308	Midre Cummings	.05	400	Mike Kingery	.05	496	Vince Coleman	.05
309	Curt Shilling	.05	401	Bernie Williams	.50	497	Kevin Jordan	.05
310	Ken Caminiti	.25	402	Otis Nixon	.05	498	Jeff King	.05
311	Scott Erickson	.05	403	Damion Easley	.05	499	Mike Simms	.05
			404	Paul O'Neill	.10	500	Jose Rijo	.05

501	Denny Neagle	.08
502	Jose Lima	.05
503	Kevin Seitzer	.05
504	Alex Fernandez	.15
505	Mo Vaughn	.75
506	Phil Nevin	.08
507	J.T. Snow	.08
508	Andujar Cedeno	.05
509	Ozzie Guillen	.05
510	Mark Clark	.05
511	Mark McGwire	4.00
512	Jeff Reboulet	.05
513	Armando Benitez	.05
514	LaTroy Hawkins	.05
515	Brett Butler	.08
516	Tavo Alvarez	.05
517	Chris Snopek	.10
518	Mike Mussina	.35
519	Darryl Kile	.08
520	Wally Joyner	.08
521	Willie McGee	.08
522	Kent Mercker	.05
523	Mike Jackson	.05
524	Troy Percival	.05
525	Tony Gwynn	1.00
526	Ron Coomer	.05
527	Darryl Hamilton	.05
528	Phil Plantier	.05
529	Norm Charlton	.05
530	Craig Paquette	.05
531	Dave Burba	.05
532	Mike Henneman	.05
533	Terrell Wade	.08
534	Eddie Williams	.05
535	Robin Ventura	.10
536	Chuck Knoblauch	.20
537	Les Norman	.05
538	Brady Anderson	.15
539	Roger Clemens	.75
540	Mark Portugal	.05
541	Mike Matheny	.05
542	Jeff Parrett	.05
543	Roberto Kelly	.05
544	Damon Buford	.05
545	Chad Ogea	.05
546	Jose Offerman	.05
547	Brian Barber	.05
548	Danny Tartabull	.05
549	Duane Singleton	.05
550	Checklist(Tony Gwynn)	.50

1996 Donruss Diamond Kings

The most "common" of the '96 Donruss inserts are the popular Diamond Kings, featuring the portraits of Dick Perez on a black background within a mottled gold-foil frame. Once again, the DKs feature one player from each major league team; 14 were issued in each of Series 1 and 2. Like all '96 Donruss inserts, the DKs are numbered on back, within an edition of 10,000. Also on back are color action photos and career highlights.

Diamond Kings are inserted at the rate of one per 60 foil packs (Series 1), and one per 30 packs (Series 2), on average.

		MT
Complete Set (31):		320.00
Complete Series 1 (14):		160.00
Complete Series 2 (17):		160.00
Common Player Series 1:		6.00
Common Player Series 2:		4.00
1	Frank Thomas	25.00
2	Mo Vaughn	12.00
3	Manny Ramirez	10.00
4	Mark McGwire	40.00
5	Juan Gonzalez	20.00
6	Roberto Alomar	10.00
7	Tim Salmon	8.00
8	Barry Bonds	15.00
9	Tony Gwynn	20.00
10	Reggie Sanders	6.00
11	Larry Walker	10.00
12	Pedro Martinez	9.00
13	Jeff King	4.00
14	Mark Grace	8.00
15	Greg Maddux	25.00
16	Don Mattingly	15.00
17	Gregg Jefferies	4.00
18	Chad Curtis	4.00
19	Jason Isringhausen	6.00
20	B.J. Surhoff	4.00
21	Jeff Conine	4.00
22	Kirby Puckett	15.00
23	Derek Bell	4.00
24	Wally Joyner	4.00
25	Brian Jordan	4.00
26	Edgar Martinez	4.00
27	Hideo Nomo	8.00
28	Mike Mussina	8.00
29	Eddie Murray	6.00
30	Cal Ripken Jr.	25.00
31	Checklist	.50

1996 Donruss Elite

The Elite series continues as a Donruss insert in 1996, and they are the elite of the chase cards, being found, on average, only once per 140 packs (Series 1) or once per 75 packs (Series 2). The '96 Elite cards have a classic look bespeaking value. Player action photos at top center are framed in mottled silver foil and bordered in bright silver. Backs have another action photo, a few words about the player and a serial number from within an edition of 10,000 cards each. As usual, card numbering continues from the previous year.

		MT
Complete Set (12):		225.00
Complete Series 1 (6):		100.00
Complete Series 2 (6):		125.00
Common Player (61-66):		15.00
Common Player (67-72):		10.00
61	Cal Ripken Jr.	40.00
62	Hideo Nomo	15.00
63	Reggie Sanders	8.00
64	Mo Vaughn	15.00
65	Tim Salmon	10.00
66	Chipper Jones	30.00
67	Manny Ramirez	12.00
68	Greg Maddux	30.00
69	Frank Thomas	40.00
70	Ken Griffey Jr.	50.00
71	Dante Bichette	8.00
72	Tony Gwynn	25.00

1996 Donruss Freeze Frame

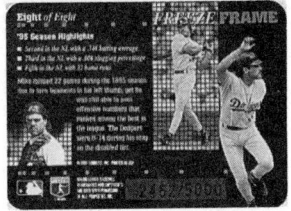

One of two insert sets exclusive to Series II Donruss is the Freeze Frame issue. Printed on heavy, round-cornered cardboard stock, the inserts feature multiple photos of the player on both front and back. Fronts combine matte and glossy finish plus a gold-foil Donruss logo. Backs are conventionally printed, include 1995 season highlights and a serial number from within the edition of 5,000. Stated odds of pulling a Freeze Frame insert are one per 60 packs.

		MT
Complete Set (8):		175.00
Common Player:		16.00
1	Frank Thomas	25.00
2	Ken Griffey Jr.	35.00
3	Cal Ripken Jr.	30.00
4	Hideo Nomo	10.00
5	Greg Maddux	24.00
6	Albert Belle	12.00
7	Chipper Jones	25.00
8	Mike Piazza	25.00

Cards before 1981 are priced Near Mint (NM), Excellent (EX), and Very Good (VG).

Cards 1981 to present are priced Mint (MT), Near Mint (NM), and Excellent (EX).

1996 Donruss Hit List

Printed on metallic foil with gold-foil graphic highlights, players who hit for high average with power or who collected milestone hits are featured in this insert set. Eight inserts were included in each of Series 1 and 2. Backs have another color action photo, a description of the player's batting prowess and a serial number from an edition of 10,000 cards each. The Hit List inserts are found at an average rate of once per 106 foil packs in Series 1 and once per 60 packs in Series 2.

		MT
Complete Set (16):		100.00
Complete Set Series 1 (8):		60.00
Complete Set Series 2 (8):		40.00
Common Player Series 1:		2.00
Common Player Series 2:		3.00
1	Tony Gwynn	10.00
2	Ken Griffey Jr.	20.00
3	Will Clark	3.00
4	Mike Piazza	12.00
5	Carlos Baerga	2.00
6	Mo Vaughn	5.00
7	Mark Grace	2.00
8	Kirby Puckett	5.00
9	Frank Thomas	12.00
10	Barry Bonds	5.00
11	Jeff Bagwell	6.00
12	Edgar Martinez	3.00
13	Tim Salmon	4.00
14	Wade Boggs	3.00
15	Don Mattingly	6.00
16	Eddie Murray	4.00

1996 Donruss Long Ball Leaders

Once again the previous season's longest home runs are recalled in this retail-only insert set, found at an average rate of once per 96 packs in Series 1 only. Fronts are bordered and trimmed in bright silver foil and feature the player in his home run stroke against a black background. The date, location and distance of his tape-measure shot are in an arc across the card front. Backs feature another batting action photo, further details of the home run and a serial number within an edition of 5,000.

		MT
Complete Set (8):		125.00
Common Player:		5.00
1	Barry Bonds	15.00
2	Ryan Klesko	8.00
3	Mark McGwire	60.00
4	Raul Mondesi	5.00
5	Cecil Fielder	5.00
6	Ken Griffey Jr.	50.00
7	Larry Walker	12.00
8	Frank Thomas	30.00

1996 Donruss Power Alley

Among the most visually dazzling of recent inserts in this hobby-only chase set featuring baseball's top sluggers. Action batting photos are found within several layers of prismatic foil in geometric patterns on front. Backs are horizontally formatted, feature portrait photos at left and power stats at right and bottom. In the lower-left corner is an individual serial number from within an edition of 5,000 cards each. The first 500 of each player's cards are specially die-cut at left- and right-center. Found only in Series 1 hobby foil packs, Power Alley inserts are a one per 92 pack pick.

		MT
Complete Set (10):		120.00
Common Player		4.00
1	Frank Thomas	30.00
2	Barry Bonds	10.00
3	Reggie Sanders	4.00
4	Albert Belle	10.00
5	Tim Salmon	6.00
6	Dante Bichette	6.00
7	Mo Vaughn	10.00
8	Jim Edmonds	4.00
9	Manny Ramirez	10.00
10	Ken Griffey Jr.	40.00

1996 Donruss Power Alley Die-Cuts

This chase set within a chase set features the first 500 in each player's numbered edition of 5,000 cards distinguished by special die-cutting at at left- and right-center. Found only in Series 1 hobby foil packs.

		MT
Complete Set (10):		450.00
Common Player:		15.00
1	Frank Thomas	90.00
2	Barry Bonds	30.00
3	Reggie Sanders	15.00
4	Albert Belle	30.00
5	Tim Salmon	20.00
6	Dante Bichette	20.00
7	Mo Vaughn	30.00
8	Jim Edmonds	15.00
9	Manny Ramirez	25.00
10	Ken Griffey Jr.	150.00

1996 Donruss Press Proofs

The first 2,000 of each regular card issued in the 1996 Donruss set are distinguished by the addition of a gold-foil "PRESS PROOF" stamped along the right side. As opposed to regular-issue cards which have silver-and-black card numbers and personal data strip at bottom, the Press Proof cards have those elements printed in black-on-gold. Stated odds of finding a Press Proof are one per 12 packs in Series 1, one per 10 packs in Series 2, on average.

	MT
Complete Set (550):	1700.
Complete Series 1 (330):	1000.
Complete Series 2 (220):	700.00
Common Player:	2.00
(Star cards valued 8X-15X corresponding regular-issue cards.)	

1996 Donruss Pure Power

These cards were random inserts found only in Series 2 retail packs. Fronts are printed on foil backgrounds and at bottom have a die-cut hole giving the impression a baseball has been batted through the card. On back the inserts are individually serial numbered within an edition of 5,000.

		MT
Complete Set (8):		150.00
Common Player:		6.00
1	Raul Mondesi	6.00
2	Barry Bonds	10.00
3	Albert Belle	10.00
4	Frank Thomas	30.00
5	Mike Piazza	30.00
6	Dante Bichette	8.00
7	Manny Ramirez	10.00
8	Mo Vaughn	10.00

1996 Donruss Round Trippers

An embossed white home plate design bearing the player's 1995 dinger output is featured on this Series II insert set. The entire background has been rendered in gold-flecked sepia tones. Typography on front is in bronze foil. Backs repeat the sepia background photo and include a month-by-month bar graph of the player's 1995 and career homers. Within the white home plate frame is the card's unique serial number from within an edition of

5,000. Odds of finding a Round Trippers card are stated at one per 55 packs, in hobby packs only.

		MT
Complete Set (10):		150.00
Common Player:		6.00
1	Albert Belle	10.00
2	Barry Bonds	10.00
3	Jeff Bagwell	15.00
4	Tim Salmon	6.00
5	Mo Vaughn	10.00
6	Ken Griffey Jr.	40.00
7	Mike Piazza	25.00
8	Cal Ripken Jr.	30.00
9	Frank Thomas	25.00
9p	Frank Thomas (Promo)	10.00
10	Dante Bichette	6.00

1996 Donruss Showdown

Baseball's top hitters and pitchers are matched on a silver and black foil background in this insert set. Gold-foil graphic highlights complete the horizontal front design. Backs are printed in on a black and gold background with color action photos and write-ups about each player. At top is a serial number from within an edition of 10,000 cards each. Show Down inserts are found at an average rate of one per Series 1 foil 105 packs.

		MT
Complete Set (8):		125.00
Common Player:		4.00
1	Frank Thomas, Hideo Nomo	25.00
2	Barry Bonds, Randy Johnson	10.00
3	Greg Maddux, Ken Griffey Jr.	40.00
4	Roger Clemens, Tony Gwynn	20.00
5	Mike Piazza, Mike Mussina	25.00
6	Cal Ripken Jr., Pedro Martinez	30.00
7	Tim Wakefield, Matt Williams	4.00
8	Manny Ramirez, Carlos Perez	8.00

Values quoted in this guide reflect the retail price of a card — the price a collector can expect to pay when buying a card from a dealer.

The wholesale price — that which a collector can expect to receive from a dealer when selling cards — will be significantly lower, depending on desirability and condition.

1997 Donruss

Donruss' 1997 regular-issue Series 1 set has 300 cards, including 30 Rated Rookies. Each regular card has a full-bleed color action photo on the front. Player identification is in the lower-left corner; the Donruss logo is at upper-left. Horizontal backs have a photo on one side; on the opposite side is a chart of career statistics and a brief player profile. The two sides are separated by five tilted capsules, each containing a biographical tidbit. Player identification is in the upper-right. A Press Proofs parallel set was made of 270 cards, excluding the 30 Rated Rookies. There were 2,000 of these sets made. Other Series 1 inserts include the annual Diamond Kings, 12 Elite inserts, 15 Armed and Dangerous cards, 15 Longball Leaders and 15 Rocket Launchers. A 180-card Donruss Update set was released later, designed as a follow-up to the regular '97 Donruss series. Regular cards are numbered #271-450. Like the first series, Press Proofs and Gold Press Proof parallel inserts were available. Other update inserts include Dominators, Franchise Futures, Power Alley, Rookie Diamond Kings and a special Cal Ripken Jr. set.

		MT
Complete Set (450):		45.00
Complete Series 1 Set (270):		25.00
Complete Series 2 Set (180):		20.00
Common Player:		.10
Wax Box:		45.00
Update Box:		35.00
1	Juan Gonzalez	1.25
2	Jim Edmonds	.15
3	Tony Gwynn	1.00
4	Andres Galarraga	.20
5	Joe Carter	.20
6	Raul Mondesi	.20
7	Greg Maddux	1.50
8	Travis Fryman	.10
9	Brian Jordan	.10
10	Henry Rodriguez	.10
11	Manny Ramirez	.75
12	Mark McGwire	3.00
13	Marc Newfield	.10
14	Craig Biggio	.10
15	Sammy Sosa	1.50
16	Brady Anderson	.10
17	Wade Boggs	.15
18	Charles Johnson	.10
19	Matt Williams	.20
20	Denny Neagle	.10

No.	Player	Value
21	Ken Griffey Jr.	2.50
22	Robin Ventura	.10
23	Barry Larkin	.20
24	Todd Zeile	.10
25	Chuck Knoblauch	.10
26	Todd Hundley	.10
27	Roger Clemens	.75
28	Michael Tucker	.10
29	Rondell White	.10
30	Osvaldo Fernandez	.10
31	Ivan Rodriguez	.50
32	Alex Fernandez	.10
33	Jason Isringhausen	.10
34	Chipper Jones	1.50
35	Paul O'Neill	.10
36	Hideo Nomo	.60
37	Roberto Alomar	.75
38	Derek Bell	.10
39	Paul Molitor	.30
40	Andy Benes	.10
41	Steve Trachsel	.10
42	J.T. Snow	.10
43	Jason Kendall	.10
44	Alex Rodriguez	2.50
45	Joey Hamilton	.10
46	Carlos Delgado	.10
47	Jason Giambi	.10
48	Larry Walker	.30
49	Derek Jeter	1.25
50	Kenny Lofton	.75
51	Devon White	.10
52	Matt Mieske	.10
53	Melvin Nieves	.10
54	Jose Canseco	.25
55	Tino Martinez	.30
56	Rafael Palmeiro	.15
57	Edgardo Alfonzo	.10
58	Jay Buhner	.15
59	Shane Reynolds	.10
60	Steve Finley	.10
61	Bobby Higginson	.10
62	Dean Palmer	.10
63	Terry Pendleton	.10
64	Marquis Grissom	.10
65	Mike Stanley	.10
66	Moises Alou	.10
67	Ray Lankford	.10
68	Marty Cordova	.15
69	John Olerud	.10
70	David Cone	.10
71	Benito Santiago	.10
72	Ryne Sandberg	.60
73	Rickey Henderson	.10
74	Roger Cedeno	.10
75	Wilson Alvarez	.10
76	Tim Salmon	.20
77	Orlando Merced	.10
78	Vinny Castilla	.10
79	Ismael Valdes	.10
80	Dante Bichette	.20
81	Kevin Brown	.10
82	Andy Pettitte	.60
83	Scott Stahoviak	.10
84	Mickey Tettleton	.10
85	Jack McDowell	.10
86	Tom Glavine	.10
87	Gregg Jefferies	.10
88	Chili Davis	.10
89	Randy Johnson	.35
90	John Mabry	.10
91	Billy Wagner	.10
92	Jeff Cirillo	.10
93	Trevor Hoffman	.10
94	Juan Guzman	.10
95	Geronimo Berroa	.10
96	Bernard Gilkey	.10
97	Danny Tartabull	.10
98	Johnny Damon	.20
99	Charlie Hayes	.10
100	Reggie Sanders	.10
101	Robby Thompson	.10
102	Bobby Bonilla	.10
103	Reggie Jefferson	.10
104	John Smoltz	.20
105	Jim Thome	.35
106	Ruben Rivera	.40
107	Darren Oliver	.10
108	Mo Vaughn	1.00
109	Roger Pavlik	.10
110	Terry Steinbach	.10
111	Jermaine Dye	.20
112	Mark Grudzielanek	.10
113	Rick Aguilera	.10
114	Jamey Wright	.10
115	Eddie Murray	.35
116	Brian Hunter	.10
117	Hal Morris	.10
118	Tom Pagnozzi	.10
119	Mike Mussina	.35
120	Mark Grace	.25
121	Cal Ripken Jr.	2.00
122	Tom Goodwin	.10
123	Paul Sorrento	.10
124	Jay Bell	.10
125	Todd Hollandsworth	.10
126	Edgar Martinez	.10
127	George Arias	.10
128	Greg Vaughn	.10
129	Roberto Hernandez	.10
130	Delino DeShields	.10
131	Bill Pulsipher	.10
132	Joey Cora	.10
133	Mariano Rivera	.25
134	Mike Piazza	1.50
135	Carlos Baerga	.15
136	Jose Mesa	.10
137	Will Clark	.25
138	Frank Thomas	2.00
139	John Wetteland	.10
140	Shawn Estes	.10
141	Garret Anderson	.10
142	Andre Dawson	.10
143	Eddie Taubensee	.10
144	Ryan Klesko	.50
145	Rocky Coppinger	.10
146	Jeff Bagwell	1.25
147	Donovan Osborne	.10
148	Greg Myers	.10
149	Brant Brown	.10
150	Kevin Elster	.10
151	Bob Wells	.10
152	Wally Joyner	.10
153	Rico Brogna	.10
154	Dwight Gooden	.10
155	Jermaine Allensworth	.10
156	Ray Durham	.10
157	Cecil Fielder	.20
158	Ryan Hancock	.10
159	Gary Sheffield	.20
160	Albert Belle	.75
161	Tomas Perez	.10
162	David Doster	.10
163	John Valentin	.10
164	Danny Graves	.10
165	Jose Paniagua	.10
166	Brian Giles	.10
167	Barry Bonds	.75
168	Sterling Hitchcock	.10
169	Bernie Williams	.50
170	Fred McGriff	.25
171	George Williams	.10
172	Amaury Telemaco	.10
173	Ken Caminiti	.10
174	Ron Gant	.10
175	David Justice	.15
176	James Baldwin	.10
177	Pat Hentgen	.10
178	Ben McDonald	.10
179	Tim Naehring	.10
180	Jim Eisenreich	.10
181	Ken Hill	.10
182	Paul Wilson	.10
183	Marvin Benard	.10
184	Alan Benes	.10
185	Ellis Burks	.10
186	Scott Servais	.10
187	David Segui	.10
188	Scott Brosius	.10
189	Jose Offerman	.10
190	Eric Davis	.10
191	Brett Butler	.10
192	Curtis Pride	.10
193	Yamil Benitez	.10
194	Chan Ho Park	.10
195	Bret Boone	.10
196	Omar Vizquel	.10
197	Orlando Miller	.10
198	Ramon Martinez	.10
199	Harold Baines	.10
200	Eric Young	.10
201	Fernando Vina	.10
202	Alex Gonzalez	.10
203	Fernando Valenzuela	.10
204	Steve Avery	.10
205	Ernie Young	.10
206	Kevin Appier	.10
207	Randy Myers	.10
208	Jeff Suppan	.10
209	James Mouton	.10
210	Russ Davis	.10
211	Al Martin	.10
212	Troy Percival	.10
213	Al Leiter	.10
214	Dennis Eckersley	.10
215	Mark Johnson	.10
216	Eric Karros	.10
217	Royce Clayton	.10
218	Tony Phillips	.10
219	Tim Wakefield	.10
220	Alan Trammell	.10
221	Eduardo Perez	.10
222	Butch Huskey	.10
223	Tim Belcher	.10
224	Jamie Moyer	.10
225	F.P. Santangelo	.10
226	Rusty Greer	.10
227	Jeff Brantley	.10
228	Mark Langston	.10
229	Ray Montgomery	.10
230	Rich Becker	.10
231	Ozzie Smith	.50
232	Rey Ordonez	.20
233	Ricky Otero	.10
234	Mike Cameron	.10
235	Mike Sweeney	.10
236	Mark Lewis	.10
237	Luis Gonzalez	.10
238	Marcus Jensen	.10
239	Ed Sprague	.10
240	Jose Valentin	.10
241	Jeff Frye	.10
242	Charles Nagy	.10
243	Carlos Garcia	.10
244	Mike Hampton	.10
245	B.J. Surhoff	.10
246	Wilton Guerrero	.10
247	Frank Rodriguez	.10
248	Gary Gaetti	.10
249	Lance Johnson	.10
250	Darren Bragg	.10
251	Darryl Hamilton	.10
252	John Jaha	.10
253	Craig Paquette	.10
254	Jaime Navarro	.10
255	Shawon Dunston	.10
256	Ron Wright	.75
257	Tim Belk	.10
258	Jeff Darwin	.10
259	Ruben Sierra	.10
260	Chuck Finley	.10
261	Darryl Strawberry	.10
262	Shannon Stewart	.10
263	Pedro Martinez	.10
264	Neifi Perez	.10
265	Jeff Conine	.10
266	Orel Hershiser	.10
267	Checklist 1-90(Eddie Murray) (500 Career HR)	.10
268	Checklist 91-180(Paul Molitor) (3,000 Career Hits)	.10
269	Checklist 181-270(Barry Bonds) (300 Career HR)	.30
270	Checklist - inserts(Mark McGwire) (300 Career HR)	.75
271	Matt Williams	.30
272	Todd Zeile	.10
273	Roger Clemens	.75
274	Michael Tucker	.10
275	J.T. Snow	.10
276	Kenny Lofton	.75
277	Jose Canseco	.25
278	Marquis Grissom	.10
279	Moises Alou	.10
280	Benito Santiago	.10
281	Willie McGee	.10
282	Chili Davis	.10
283	Ron Coomer	.10
284	Orlando Merced	.10
285	Delino DeShields	.10
286	John Wetteland	.10
287	Darren Daulton	.10
288	Lee Stevens	.10
289	Albert Belle	.75
290	Sterling Hitchcock	.10
291	David Justice	.20
292	Eric Davis	.10
293	Brian Hunter	.10
294	Darryl Hamilton	.10
295	Steve Avery	.10
296	Joe Vitiello	.10
297	Jaime Navarro	.10
298	Eddie Murray	.30
299	Randy Myers	.10
300	Francisco Cordova	.10
301	Javier Lopez	.15
302	Geronimo Berroa	.10
303	Jeffrey Hammonds	.10
304	Deion Sanders	.25

305	Jeff Fassero	.10
306	Curt Schilling	.10
307	Robb Nen	.10
308	Mark McLemore	.10
309	Jimmy Key	.10
310	Quilvio Veras	.10
311	Bip Roberts	.10
312	Esteban Loaiza	.10
313	Andy Ashby	.10
314	Sandy Alomar Jr.	.10
315	Shawn Green	.10
316	Luis Castillo	.10
317	Benji Gil	.10
318	Otis Nixon	.10
319	Aaron Sele	.10
320	Brad Ausmus	.10
321	Troy O'Leary	.10
322	Terrell Wade	.10
323	Jeff King	.10
324	Kevin Seitzer	.10
325	Mark Wohlers	.10
326	Edgar Renteria	.10
327	Dan Wilson	.10
328	Brian McRae	.10
329	Rod Beck	.10
330	Julio Franco	.10
331	Dave Nilsson	.10
332	Glenallen Hill	.10
333	Kevin Elster	.10
334	Joe Girardi	.10
335	David Wells	.10
336	Jeff Blauser	.10
337	Darryl Kile	.10
338	Jeff Kent	.10
339	Jim Leyritz	.10
340	Todd Stottlemyre	.10
341	Tony Clark	.50
342	Chris Hoiles	.10
343	Mike Lieberthal	.10
344	Matt Lawton	.10
345	Alex Ochoa	.10
346	Chris Snopek	.10
347	Rudy Pemberton	.10
348	Eric Owens	.10
349	Joe Randa	.10
350	John Olerud	.10
351	Steve Karsay	.10
352	Mark Whiten	.10
353	Bob Abreu	.10
354	Bartolo Colon	.10
355	Vladimir Guerrero	1.00
356	Darin Erstad	1.00
357	Scott Rolen	1.25
358	Andruw Jones	1.50
359	Scott Spiezio	.10
360	Karim Garcia	.10
361	*Hideki Irabu*	2.00
362	Nomar Garciaparra	1.25
363	Dmitri Young	.10
364	*Bubba Trammell*	1.00
365	Kevin Orie	.10
366	Jose Rosado	.10
367	Jose Guillen	.75
368	Brooks Kieschnick	.10
369	Pokey Reese	.10
370	Glendon Rusch	.10
371	Jason Dickson	.20
372	Todd Walker	.60
373	Justin Thompson	.10
374	Todd Greene	.10
375	Jeff Suppan	.10
376	Trey Beamon	.10
377	Damon Mashore	.10
378	Wendell Magee	.10
379	Shigetosi Hasegawa	.10
380	Bill Mueller	.10
381	Chris Widger	.10
382	Tony Grafannino	.10
383	Derrek Lee	.10
384	Brian Moehler	.10
385	Quinton McCracken	.10
386	Matt Morris	.20
387	Marvin Benard	.10
388	*Deivi Cruz*	.50
389	*Javier Valentin*	.20
390	Todd Dunwoody	.40
391	Derrick Gibson	.20
392	Raul Casanova	.10
393	George Arias	.10
394	*Tony Womack*	.25
395	Antone Williamson	.10
396	*Jose Cruz Jr.*	4.00
397	Desi Relaford	.10
398	Frank Thomas (Hit List)	1.25
399	Ken Griffey Jr. (Hit List)	1.50
400	Cal Ripken Jr. (Hit List)	1.25

401	Chipper Jones (Hit List)	1.00
402	Mike Piazza (Hit List)	1.00
403	Gary Sheffield (Hit List)	.15
404	Alex Rodriguez (Hit List)	1.50
405	Wade Boggs (Hit List)	.15
406	Juan Gonzalez (Hit List)	.60
407	Tony Gwynn (Hit List)	.60
408	Edgar Martinez (Hit List)	.10
409	Jeff Bagwell (Hit List)	.60
410	Larry Walker (Hit List)	.15
411	Kenny Lofton (Hit List)	.35
412	Manny Ramirez (Hit List)	.35
413	Mark McGwire (Hit List)	1.50
414	Roberto Alomar (Hit List)	.25
415	Derek Jeter (Hit List)	1.00
416	Brady Anderson (Hit List)	.10
417	Paul Molitor (Hit List)	.20
418	Dante Bichette (Hit List)	.15
419	Jim Edmonds (Hit List)	.10
420	Mo Vaughn (Hit List)	.35
421	Barry Bonds (Hit List)	.35
422	Rusty Greer (Hit List)	.10
423	Greg Maddux (King of the Hill)	1.00
424	Andy Pettitte (King of the Hill)	.35
425	John Smoltz (King of the Hill)	.10
426	Randy Johnson (King of the Hill)	.25
427	Hideo Nomo (King of the Hill)	.25
428	Roger Clemens (King of the Hill)	.35
429	Tom Glavine (King of the Hill)	.15
430	Pat Hentgen (King of the Hill)	.10
431	Kevin Brown (King of the Hill)	.10
432	Mike Mussina (King of the Hill)	.25
433	Alex Fernandez (King of the Hill)	.10
434	Kevin Appier (King of the Hill)	.10
435	David Cone (King of the Hill)	.15
436	Jeff Fassero (King of the Hill)	.10
437	John Wetteland (King of the Hill)	.10
438	Barry Bonds, Ivan Rodriguez (Interleague Showdown)	.25
439	Ken Griffey Jr., Andres Galarraga (Interleague Showdown)	1.00
440	Fred McGriff, Rafael Palmeiro (Interleague Showdown)	.15
441	Barry Larkin, Jim Thome (Interleague Showdown)	.20
442	Sammy Sosa, Albert Belle (Interleague Showdown)	1.50
443	Bernie Williams, Todd Hundley (Interleague Showdown)	.20
444	Chuck Knoblauch, Brian Jordan (Interleague Showdown)	.15
445	Mo Vaughn, Jeff Conine (Interleague Showdown)	.25
446	Ken Caminiti, Jason Giambi (Interleague Showdown)	.15
447	Raul Mondesi, Tim Salmon (Interleague Showdown)	.15
448	Checklist(Cal Ripken Jr.)	.75
449	Checklist(Greg Maddux)	.60
450	Checklist(Ken Griffey Jr.)	1.00

		MT
Complete Set (15):		140.00
Common Player:		3.00
1	Ken Griffey Jr.	30.00
2	Raul Mondesi	5.00
3	Chipper Jones	20.00
4	Ivan Rodriguez	8.00
5	Randy Johnson	6.00
6	Alex Rodriguez	25.00
7	Larry Walker	5.00
8	Cal Ripken Jr.	25.00
9	Kenny Lofton	8.00
10	Barry Bonds	8.00
11	Derek Jeter	18.00
12	Charles Johnson	4.00
13	Greg Maddux	20.00
14	Roberto Alomar	6.00
15	Barry Larkin	3.00

1997 Donruss Diamond Kings

Diamond Kings for 1997 are sequentially numbered from 1 to 10,000. To celebrate 15 years of this popular insert set, Donruss offered collectors a one-of-a-kind piece of artwork if they find one of the 10 cards with the serial number 1,982 (1982 was the first year of the Diamond Kings). Those who find these cards can redeem them for an original artwork provided by artist Dan Gardiner. In addition, Donruss printed the first 500 of each card on canvas stock.

1997 Donruss Armed and Dangerous

These 15 cards are numbered up to 5,000. They were inserted in 1997 Donruss Series 1 retail packs only.

		MT
Complete Set (10):		140.00
Common Player:		5.00
Canvas (1st 500): 5x to 10x		
1	Ken Griffey Jr.	30.00
2	Cal Ripken Jr.	25.00
3	Mo Vaughn	10.00
4	Chuck Knoblauch	7.50
5	Jeff Bagwell	12.00
6	Henry Rodriguez	5.00
7	Mike Piazza	20.00
8	Ivan Rodriguez	10.00
9	Frank Thomas	20.00
10	Chipper Jones	20.00

8	Juan Gonzalez	10.00
9	Mike Piazza	15.00
10	Jeff Bagwell	10.00
11	Sammy Sosa	15.00
12	Mark McGwire	30.00
13	Cecil Fielder	2.00
14	Ryan Klesko	4.00
15	Jose Canseco	4.00

1997 Donruss Elite Inserts

There were 2,500 sets of these insert cards made. The cards were randomly included in 1997 Donruss Series I packs. Fronts have a white marbled border and are graphically enhanced with silver foil, including a large script "E". On back is another photo, a career summary and a serial number from within the edition limit of 2,500.

		MT
Complete Set (12):		450.00
Common Player:		10.00
1	Frank Thomas	50.00
2	Paul Molitor	15.00
3	Sammy Sosa	40.00
4	Barry Bonds	20.00
5	Chipper Jones	50.00
6	Alex Rodriguez	65.00
7	Ken Griffey Jr.	80.00
8	Jeff Bagwell	30.00
9	Cal Ripken Jr.	65.00
10	Mo Vaughn	20.00
11	Mike Piazza	50.00
12	Juan Gonzalez	40.00

1997 Donruss Longball Leaders

These 1997 Donruss Series 1 inserts were limited to 5,000 each. They were seeded in retail packs only.

		MT
Complete Set (15):		90.00
Common Player:		2.00
1	Frank Thomas	15.00
2	Albert Belle	6.00
3	Mo Vaughn	6.00
4	Brady Anderson	2.00
5	Greg Vaughn	2.00
6	Ken Griffey Jr.	25.00
7	Jay Buhner	2.00

1997 Donruss Press Proofs

Each of the 450 cards in the Donruss base set was also produced in a Press Proof parallel edition of 2,000 cards. Virtually identical in design to the regular cards, the Press Proofs are printed on a metallic background with silver-foil highlights. Most Press Proof backs carry the notation "1 of 2000". Stated odds of finding a press proof are one per eight packs. A special "gold" press proof chase set features cards with gold-foil highlights, a die-cut at top and bottom and the note "1 of 500" on back. Gold press proofs are found on average of once per 32 packs.

	MT
Complete Set (270):	800.00
Common Player:	2.00
Complete Gold Set (270):	3200.
Common Gold Player:	7.50
Gold Stars/Rookies: 4X-6X	
(Press Proof star players' cards valued at 8-12X regular '97 Donruss version; Gold Press Proofs at 25-40X.)	

1997 Donruss Rated Rookies

Although numbered more like an insert set, Rated Rookies qre part of the regular-issue set. Cards are numbered 1-30, with no ratio given on packs. The cards are differentiated by a large silver-foil strip on the top right side with the words Rated Rookie.

		MT
Complete Set (30):		50.00
Common Player:		1.50
1	Jason Thompson	1.50
2	LaTroy Hawkins	1.50
3	Scott Rolen	10.00
4	Trey Beamon	1.50
5	Kimera Bartee	1.50
6	Nerio Rodriguez	1.50
7	Jeff D'Amico	1.50
8	Quinton McCracken	1.50
9	John Wasdin	1.50
10	Robin Jennings	1.50
11	Steve Gibralter	1.50
12	Tyler Houston	1.50
13	Tony Clark	4.00
14	Ugueth Urbina	1.50
15	Billy McMillon	1.50
16	Raul Casanova	1.50
17	Brooks Kieschnick	1.50
18	Luis Castillo	1.50
19	Edgar Renteria	2.50
20	Andruw Jones	10.00
21	Chad Mottola	1.50
22	Makoto Suzuki	1.50
23	Justin Thompson	1.50
24	Darin Erstad	8.00
25	Todd Walker	5.00
26	Todd Greene	1.50
27	Vladimir Guerrero	8.00
28	Darren Dreifort	1.50
29	John Burke	1.50
30	Damon Mashore	1.50

1997 Donruss Rocket Launchers

These 1997 Donruss Series 1 inserts are limited to 5,000 each. They were only included in magazine packs.

	MT
Complete Set (15):	100.00
Common Player:	3.00
1 Frank Thomas	15.00
2 Albert Belle	6.00
3 Chipper Jones	15.00
4 Mike Piazza	15.00
5 Mo Vaughn	6.00
6 Juan Gonzalez	12.00
7 Fred McGriff	4.00
8 Jeff Bagwell	8.00
9 Matt Williams	4.00
10 Gary Sheffield	3.00
11 Barry Bonds	6.00
12 Manny Ramirez	5.00
13 Henry Rodriguez	3.00
14 Jason Giambi	3.00
15 Cal Ripken Jr.	20.00

1997 Donruss Elite

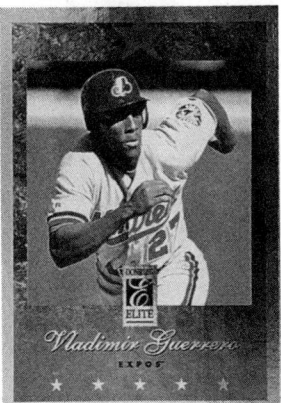

Donruss Elite Baseball is a 150-card, single-series set distributed as a hobby-only product. The regular-issue cards feature a silver border around the entire card, with a marblized frame around a color player photo at center. Backs feature a color player photo and minimal statistics and personal data. Elite was accompanied by an Elite Stars parallel set and three inserts: Leather and Lumber, Passing the Torch and Turn of the Century.

	MT
Complete Set (150):	40.00
Common Player:	.15
Wax Box:	75.00
1 Juan Gonzalez	1.75
2 Alex Rodriguez	4.00
3 Frank Thomas	3.00
4 Greg Maddux	2.50
5 Ken Griffey Jr.	4.00
6 Cal Ripken Jr.	3.00
7 Mike Piazza	2.50
8 Chipper Jones	2.50
9 Albert Belle	1.00
10 Andruw Jones	2.00
11 Vladimir Guerrero	1.50
12 Mo Vaughn	1.00
13 Ivan Rodriguez	.75
14 Andy Pettitte	1.00
15 Tony Gwynn	2.00
16 Barry Bonds	1.00
17 Jeff Bagwell	1.75
18 Manny Ramirez	1.00
19 Kenny Lofton	1.00
20 Roberto Alomar	.75
21 Mark McGwire	5.00
22 Ryan Klesko	.50
23 Tim Salmon	.30
24 Derek Jeter	2.00
25 Eddie Murray	.50

26 Jermaine Dye	.20
27 Ruben Rivera	.25
28 Jim Edmonds	.15
29 Mike Mussina	.75
30 Randy Johnson	.50
31 Sammy Sosa	2.00
32 Hideo Nomo	.75
33 Chuck Knoblauch	.35
34 Paul Molitor	.50
35 Rafael Palmeiro	.25
36 Brady Anderson	.20
37 Will Clark	.30
38 Craig Biggio	.25
39 Jason Giambi	.15
40 Roger Clemens	1.50
41 Jay Buhner	.25
42 Edgar Martinez	.15
43 Gary Sheffield	.40
44 Fred McGriff	.40
45 Bobby Bonilla	.15
46 Tom Glavine	.25
47 Wade Boggs	.25
48 Jeff Conine	.15
49 John Smoltz	.25
50 Jim Thome	.60
51 Billy Wagner	.15
52 Jose Canseco	.30
53 Javy Lopez	.15
54 Cecil Fielder	.25
55 Garret Anderson	.15
56 Alex Ochoa	.15
57 Scott Rolen	1.50
58 Darin Erstad	1.25
59 Rey Ordonez	.20
60 Dante Bichette	.25
61 Joe Carter	.25
62 Moises Alou	.25
63 Jason Isringhausen	.15
64 Karim Garcia	.50
65 Brian Jordan	.15
66 Ruben Sierra	.15
67 Todd Hollandsworth	.25
68 Paul Wilson	.15
69 Ernie Young	.15
70 Ryne Sandberg	1.25
71 Raul Mondesi	.30
72 George Arias	.15
73 Ray Durham	.15
74 Dean Palmer	.15
75 Shawn Green	.15
76 Eric Young	.15
77 Jason Kendall	.15
78 Greg Vaughn	.15
79 Terrell Wade	.15
80 Bill Pulsipher	.15
81 Bobby Higginson	.15
82 Mark Grudzielanek	.15
83 Ken Caminiti	.40
84 Todd Greene	.15
85 Carlos Delgado	.15
86 Mark Grace	.25
87 Rondell White	.25
88 Barry Larkin	.35
89 J.T. Snow	.15
90 Alex Gonzalez	.15
91 Raul Casanova	.15
92 Marc Newfield	.15
93 Jermaine Allensworth	.15
94 John Mabry	.15
95 Kirby Puckett	1.50
96 Travis Fryman	.15
97 Kevin Brown	.15
98 Andres Galarraga	.25
99 Marty Cordova	.15
100 Henry Rodriguez	.15
101 Sterling Hitchcock	.15
102 Trey Beamon	.15
103 Brett Butler	.15
104 Rickey Henderson	.15
105 Tino Martinez	.40
106 Kevin Appier	.15
107 Brian Hunter	.15
108 Eric Karros	.15
109 Andre Dawson	.15
110 Darryl Strawberry	.15
111 James Baldwin	.15
112 Chad Mottola	.15
113 Dave Nilsson	.15
114 Carlos Baerga	.15
115 Chan Ho Park	.15
116 John Jaha	.15
117 Alan Benes	.25
118 Mariano Rivera	.25
119 Ellis Burks	.15
120 Tony Clark	.75
121 Todd Walker	.75

122 Dwight Gooden	.15
123 Ugueth Urbina	.15
124 David Cone	.25
125 Ozzie Smith	.60
126 Kimera Bartee	.15
127 Rusty Greer	.15
128 Pat Hentgen	.15
129 Charles Johnson	.15
130 Quinton McCracken	.15
131 Troy Percival	.15
132 Shane Reynolds	.15
133 Charles Nagy	.15
134 Tom Goodwin	.15
135 Ron Gant	.15
136 Dan Wilson	.15
137 Matt Williams	.35
138 LaTroy Hawkins	.15
139 Kevin Seitzer	.15
140 Michael Tucker	.15
141 Todd Hundley	.25
142 Alex Fernandez	.15
143 Marquis Grissom	.15
144 Steve Finley	.15
145 Curtis Pride	.15
146 Derek Bell	.15
147 Butch Huskey	.15
148 Dwight Gooden	.15
149 Al Leiter	.15
150 Hideo Nomo	.50

1997 Donruss Elite Leather & Lumber

Leather and Lumber is a 10-card insert set filled with veterans. Genuine leather is featured on one side of the card, while wood card stock is on the other. There were 500 sequentially numbered sets produced.

	MT
Complete Set (10):	750.00
Common Player:	25.00
1 Ken Griffey Jr.	150.00
2 Alex Rodriguez	100.00
3 Frank Thomas	120.00
4 Chipper Jones	100.00
5 Ivan Rodriguez	40.00
6 Cal Ripken Jr.	120.00
7 Barry Bonds	40.00
8 Chuck Knoblauch	25.00
9 Manny Ramirez	30.00
10 Mark McGwire	150.00

1997 Donruss Elite Passing the Torch

Passing the Torch is a 12-card insert limited to 1,500 individually numbered sets. It features eight different stars, each with their own cards and then featured on a double-sided card with another player from the set.

	MT
Complete Set (12):	450.00
Common Player:	15.00
1 Cal Ripken Jr.	60.00
2 Alex Rodriguez	60.00
3 Cal Ripken Jr., Alex Rodriguez	80.00
4 Kirby Puckett	50.00
5 Andruw Jones	30.00
6 Kirby Puckett, Andruw Jones	30.00
7 Cecil Fielder	15.00
8 Frank Thomas	60.00
9 Cecil Fielder, Frank Thomas	50.00
10 Ozzie Smith	25.00
11 Derek Jeter	40.00
12 Ozzie Smith, Derek Jeter	40.00

1997 Donruss Elite Passing the Torch Autographs

The first 150 individually numbered sets of the Passing the Torch insert were autographed. This means that cards 3, 6, 9 and 12 are dual-autographed on their double-sided format.

	MT
Complete Set (12):	4500.
Common Autograph:	100.00
1 Cal Ripken Jr.	600.00
2 Alex Rodriguez	500.00
3 Cal Ripken Jr., Alex Rodriguez	1000.
4 Kirby Puckett	400.00
5 Andruw Jones	180.00
6 Kirby Puckett, Andruw Jones	500.00
7 Cecil Fielder	100.00
8 Frank Thomas	450.00
9 Cecil Fielder, Frank Thomas	550.00
10 Ozzie Smith	250.00
11 Derek Jeter	250.00
12 Ozzie Smith, Derek Jeter	450.00

1997 Donruss Elite Stars

Gold, rather than silver, foil differentiates the parallel set of Elite Stars from the regular-issue versions of each of the base cards in the Elite set. The parallels also have a small "Elite Stars" printed at top, flanking the position. Stated odds of finding a Stars insert are about one per five packs.

	MT
Complete Set (150):	600.00
Common Player:	2.00

(Star players in the Elite Star parallel issue valued at 15-30X regular Elites.)

1997 Donruss Elite Turn of the Century

Turn of the Century includes 20 potential year 2000 superstars on an insert set numbered to 3,500. The first 500 of these sets feature an external die-cut design. Cards feature the player over a framed background image on silver foil board, with black strips down each side. Backs have a color photo, a few words about the player and the serial number.

	MT
Complete Set (20):	175.00
Common Player:	4.00
Complete Die-Cut Set (20):	500.00
Die-Cuts: 3x to 4x	
1 Alex Rodriguez	30.00
2 Andruw Jones	20.00
3 Chipper Jones	25.00
4 Todd Walker	8.00
5 Scott Rolen	15.00
6 Trey Beamon	4.00
7 Derek Jeter	25.00
7s Derek Jeter ("SAMPLE" overprint)	15.00
8 Darin Erstad	15.00
9 Tony Clark	8.00
10 Todd Greene	6.00
11 Jason Giambi	4.00
12 Justin Thompson	6.00
13 Ernie Young	4.00
14 Jason Kendall	4.00
15 Alex Ochoa	4.00
15s Alex Ochoa ("SAMPLE" overprint)	4.00
16 Brooks Kieschnick	4.00
17 Bobby Higginson	5.00
17s Bobby Higginson ("SAMPLE" overprint)	6.00
18 Ruben Rivera	4.00
18s Ruben Rivera ("SAMPLE" overprint)	4.00
19 Chan Ho Park	5.00
20 Chad Mottola	4.00

A player's name in *italic* type indicates a rookie card.

1997 Donruss Limited

Each of the 200 base cards in this set features a double-front design showcasing an action photo on each side. The set is divided into four different subsets: Counterparts (100 cards) highlights two different players from the same position; Double Team (40 cards) features some of the majors' top teammate duos; Star Factor (40 cards) consists of two photos of some of the hobby's favorite players; and Unlimited Potential/Talent (20 cards) combines a top veteran with a top rookie prospect. The issue also includes a Limited Exposure parallel set and one multi-tiered insert called Fabric of the Game. Odds of finding any insert card were 1:5 packs. Less than 1,100 base sets were available. Cards were sold in five-card packs for $4.99 each.

	MT
Complete Set (200):	1200.
Common Counterpart:	.50
Common Double Team:	5.00
Common Star Factor:	10.00
Common Unlimited Potential:	10.00
1 Ken Griffey Jr., Rondell White (Counterparts)	5.00
2 Greg Maddux, David Cone (Counterparts)	3.00
3 Gary Sheffield, Moises Alou (Double Team)	6.00
4 Frank Thomas (Star Factor)	50.00
5 Cal Ripken Jr., Kevin Orie (Counterparts)	4.00
6 Vladimir Guerrero, Barry Bonds (Unlimited Potential/Talent)	30.00
7 Eddie Murray, Reggie Jefferson (Counterparts)	.75
8 Manny Ramirez, Marquis Grissom (Double Team)	10.00
9 Mike Piazza (Star Factor)	50.00
10 Barry Larkin, Rey Ordonez (Counterparts)	.75
11 Jeff Bagwell, Eric Karros (Counterparts)	2.00
12 Chuck Knoblauch, Ray Durham (Counterparts)	.75
13 Alex Rodriguez, Edgar Renteria (Counterparts)	4.00
14 Matt Williams, Vinny Castilla (Counterparts)	.75
15 Todd Hollandsworth, Bob Abreu (Counterparts)	.50
16 John Smoltz, Pedro Martinez (Counterparts)	.75
17 Jose Canseco, Chili Davis (Counterparts)	.75

#	Player(s)	Value
18	Jose Cruz, Jr., Ken Griffey Jr. (Unlimited Potential/Talent)	75.00
19	Ken Griffey Jr. (Star Factor)	75.00
20	Paul Molitor, John Olerud (Counterparts)	1.00
21	Roberto Alomar, Luis Castillo (Counterparts)	1.00
22	Derek Jeter, Lou Collier (Counterparts)	3.00
23	Chipper Jones, Robin Ventura (Counterparts)	3.00
24	Gary Sheffield, Ron Gant (Counterparts)	.75
25	Ramon Martinez, Bobby Jones (Counterparts)	.50
26	Mike Piazza, Raul Mondesi (Double Team)	20.00
27	Darin Erstad, Jeff Bagwell (Unlimited Potential/Talent)	30.00
28	Ivan Rodriguez (Star Factor)	20.00
29	J.T. Snow, Kevin Young (Counterparts)	.50
30	Ryne Sandberg, Julio Franco (Counterparts)	1.50
31	Travis Fryman, Chris Snopek (Counterparts)	.50
32	Wade Boggs, Russ Davis (Counterparts)	.75
33	Brooks Kieschnick, Marty Cordova (Counterparts)	.50
34	Andy Pettitte, Denny Neagle (Counterparts)	1.50
35	Paul Molitor, Matt Lawton (Double Team)	8.00
36	Scott Rolen, Cal Ripken Jr. (Unlimited Potential/Talent)	60.00
37	Cal Ripken Jr. (Star Factor)	60.00
38	Jim Thome, Dave Nilsson (Counterparts)	1.00
39	Tony Womack, Carlos Baerga (Counterparts)	.50
40	Nomar Garciaparra, Mark Grudzielanek (Counterparts)	2.50
41	Todd Greene, Chris Widger (Counterparts)	.50
42	Deion Sanders, Bernard Gilkey (Counterparts)	.75
43	Hideo Nomo, Charles Nagy (Counterparts)	1.25
44	Ivan Rodriguez, Rusty Greer (Double Team)	10.00
45	Todd Walker, Chipper Jones (Unlimited Potential/Talent)	50.00
46	Greg Maddux (Star Factor)	50.00
47	Mo Vaughn, Cecil Fielder (Counterparts)	1.50
48	Craig Biggio, Scott Spiezio (Counterparts)	.50
49	Pokey Reese, Jeff Blauser (Counterparts)	.50
50	Ken Caminiti, Joe Randa (Counterparts)	.75
51	Albert Belle, Shawn Green (Counterparts)	1.50
52	Randy Johnson, Jason Dickson (Counterparts)	1.25
53	Hideo Nomo, Chan Ho Park (Double Team)	10.00
54	Scott Spiezio, Chuck Knoblauch (Unlimited Potential/Talent)	15.00
55	Chipper Jones (Star Factor)	50.00
56	Tino Martinez, Ryan McGuire (Counterparts)	.75
57	Eric Young, Wilton Guerrero (Counterparts)	.50
58	Ron Coomer, Dave Hollins (Counterparts)	.50
59	Sammy Sosa, Angel Echevarria (Counterparts)	4.00
60	Dennis Reyes, Jimmy Key (Counterparts)	.50
61	Barry Larkin, Deion Sanders (Double Team)	6.00
62	Wilton Guerrero, Roberto Alomar (Unlimited Potential/Talent)	15.00
63	Albert Belle (Star Factor)	20.00
64	Mark McGwire, Andres Galarraga (Counterparts)	4.00
65	Edgar Martinez, Todd Walker (Counterparts)	.75
66	Steve Finley, Rich Becker (Counterparts)	.50
67	Tom Glavine, Andy Ashby (Counterparts)	.75
68	Sammy Sosa, Ryne Sandberg (Double Team)	30.00
69	Nomar Garciaparra, Alex Rodriguez (Unlimited Potential/Talent)	75.00
70	Jeff Bagwell (Star Factor)	30.00
71	Darin Erstad, Mark Grace (Counterparts)	2.00
72	Scott Rolen, Edgardo Alfonzo (Counterparts)	2.00
73	Kenny Lofton, Lance Johnson (Counterparts)	1.50
74	Joey Hamilton, Brett Tomko (Counterparts)	.50
75	Eddie Murray, Tim Salmon (Double Team)	6.00
76	Dmitri Young, Mo Vaughn (Unlimited Potential/Talent)	20.00
77	Juan Gonzalez (Star Factor)	40.00
78	Frank Thomas, Tony Clark (Counterparts)	4.00
79	Shannon Stewart, Bip Roberts (Counterparts)	.50
80	Shawn Estes, Alex Fernandez (Counterparts)	.50
81	John Smoltz, Javier Lopez (Double Team)	.75
82	Todd Greene, Mike Piazza (Unlimited Potential/Talent)	50.00
83	Derek Jeter (Star Factor)	50.00
84	Dmitri Young, Antone Williamson (Counterparts)	.50
85	Rickey Henderson, Darryl Hamilton (Counterparts)	.50
86	Billy Wagner, Dennis Eckersley (Counterparts)	.50
87	Larry Walker, Eric Young (Double Team)	6.00
88	Mark Kotsay, Juan Gonzalez (Unlimited Potential/Talent)	40.00
89	Barry Bonds (Star Factor)	20.00
90	Will Clark, Jeff Conine (Counterparts)	.75
91	Tony Gwynn, Brett Butler (Counterparts)	2.50
92	John Wetteland, Rod Beck (Counterparts)	.50
93	Bernie Williams, Tino Martinez (Double Team)	8.00
94	Andruw Jones, Kenny Lofton (Unlimited Potential/Talent)	30.00
95	Mo Vaughn (Star Factor)	20.00
96	Joe Carter, Derek Lee (Counterparts)	.50
97	John Mabry, F.P. Santangelo (Counterparts)	.50
98	Esteban Loaiza, Wilson Alvarez (Counterparts)	.50
99	Matt Williams, David Justice (Double Team)	6.00
100	Derek Lee, Frank Thomas (Unlimited Potential/Talent)	60.00
101	Mark McGwire (Star Factor)	80.00
102	Fred McGriff, Paul Sorrento (Counterparts)	.75
103	Jermaine Allensworth, Bernie Williams (Counterparts)	1.25
104	Ismael Valdes, Chris Holt (Counterparts)	.50
105	Fred McGriff, Ryan Klesko (Double Team)	6.00
106	Tony Clark, Mark McGwire (Unlimited Potential/Talent)	100.00
107	Tony Gwynn (Star Factor)	40.00
108	Jeffrey Hammonds, Ellis Burks (Counterparts)	.50
109	Shane Reynolds, Andy Benes (Counterparts)	.50
110	Roger Clemens, Carlos Delgado (Double Team)	12.00
111	Karim Garcia, Albert Belle (Unlimited Potential/Talent)	20.00
112	Paul Molitor (Star Factor)	18.00
113	Trey Beamon, Eric Owens (Counterparts)	.50
114	Curt Schilling, Darryl Kile (Counterparts)	.50
115	Tom Glavine, Michael Tucker (Double Team)	6.00
116	Pokey Reese, Derek Jeter (Unlimited Potential/Talent)	50.00
117	Manny Ramirez (Star Factor)	20.00
118	Juan Gonzalez, Brant Brown (Counterparts)	2.50
119	Juan Guzman, Francisco Cordova (Counterparts)	.50
120	Randy Johnson, Edgar Martinez (Double Team)	8.00
121	Hideki Irabu, Greg Maddux (Unlimited Potential/Talent)	50.00
122	Alex Rodriguez (Star Factor)	60.00
123	Barry Bonds, Quinton McCracken (Counterparts)	1.50
124	Roger Clemens, Alan Benes (Counterparts)	1.50
125	Wade Boggs, Paul O'Neill (Double Team)	6.00
126	Mike Cameron, Larry Walker (Unlimited Potential/Talent)	15.00
127	Gary Sheffield (Star Factor)	10.00
128	Andruw Jones, Raul Mondesi (Counterparts)	2.00
129	Brian Anderson, Terrell Wade (Counterparts)	.50
130	Brady Anderson, Rafael Palmeiro (Double Team)	5.00
131	Neifi Perez, Barry Larkin (Unlimited Potential/Talent)	15.00
132	Ken Caminiti (Star Factor)	10.00
133	Larry Walker, Rusty Greer (Counterparts)	.75
134	Mariano Rivera, Mark Wohlers (Counterparts)	.60
135	Hideki Irabu, Andy Pettitte (Double Team)	10.00
136	Jose Guillen, Tony Gwynn (Unlimited Potential/Talent)	40.00
137	Hideo Nomo (Star Factor)	15.00
138	Vladimir Guerrero, Jim Edmonds (Counterparts)	1.50
139	Justin Thompson, Dwight Gooden (Counterparts)	.50
140	Andres Galarraga, Dante Bichette (Double Team)	6.00
141	Kenny Lofton (Star Factor)	20.00
142	Tim Salmon, Manny Ramirez (Counterparts)	1.50
143	Kevin Brown, Matt Morris (Counterparts)	.50
144	Craig Biggio, Bob Abreu (Double Team)	.50
145	Roberto Alomar (Star Factor)	15.00
146	Jose Guillen, Brian Jordan (Counterparts)	1.50
147	Bartolo Colon, Kevin Appier (Counterparts)	.50
148	Ray Lankford, Brian Jordan (Double Team)	.50
149	Chuck Knoblauch (Star Factor)	15.00
150	Henry Rodriguez, Ray Lankford (Counterparts)	.50
151	Jaret Wright, Ben McDonald (Counterparts)	4.00
152	Bobby Bonilla, Kevin Brown (Double Team)	5.00
153	Barry Larkin (Star Factor)	15.00
154	David Justice, Reggie Sanders (Counterparts)	.75
155	Mike Mussina, Ken Hill (Counterparts)	1.25
156	Mark Grace, Brooks Kieschnick (Double Team)	6.00
157	Jim Thome (Star Factor)	15.00
158	Michael Tucker, Curtis Goodwin (Counterparts)	.50
159	Jeff Suppan, Jeff Fassero (Counterparts)	.50
160	Mike Mussina, Jeffrey Hammonds (Double Team)	10.00
161	John Smoltz (Star Factor)	10.00
162	Moises Alou, Eric Davis (Counterparts)	.50
163	Sandy Alomar Jr., Dan Wilson (Counterparts)	.50
164	Rondell White, Henry Rodriguez (Double Team)	5.00
165	Roger Clemens (Star Factor)	30.00
166	Brady Anderson, Al Martin (Counterparts)	.50

167	Jason Kendall, Charles Johnson (Counterparts)	.50
168	Jason Giambi, Jose Canseco (Double Team)	6.00
169	Larry Walker (Star Factor)	15.00
170	Jay Buhner, Geronimo Berroa (Counterparts)	.75
171	Ivan Rodriguez, Mike Sweeney (Counterparts)	1.25
172	Kevin Appier, Jose Rosado (Double Team)	5.00
173	Bernie Williams (Star Factor)	15.00
174	Todd Dunwoody, Brian Giles (Counterparts)	.75
175	Javier Lopez, Scott Hatteberg (Counterparts)	.60
176	John Jaha, Jeff Cirillo (Double Team)	5.00
177	Andy Pettitte (Star Factor)	15.00
178	Dante Bichette, Butch Huskey (Counterparts)	.75
179	Raul Casanova, Todd Hundley (Counterparts)	.75
180	Jim Edmonds, Garret Anderson (Double Team)	5.00
181	Deion Sanders (Star Factor)	10.00
182	Ryan Klesko, Paul O'Neill (Counterparts)	.75
183	Joe Carter, Pat Hentgen (Double Team)	5.00
184	Brady Anderson (Star Factor)	10.00
185	Carlos Delgado, Wally Joyner (Counterparts)	.50
186	Jermaine Dye, Johnny Damon (Double Team)	5.00
187	Randy Johnson (Star Factor)	15.00
188	Todd Hundley, Carlos Baerga (Double Team)	5.00
189	Tom Glavine (Star Factor)	10.00
190	Damon Mashore, Jason McDonald (Double Team)	5.00
191	Wade Boggs (Star Factor)	10.00
192	Al Martin, Jason Kendall (Double Team)	5.00
193	Matt Williams (Star Factor)	15.00
194	Will Clark, Dean Palmer (Double Team)	6.00
195	Sammy Sosa (Star Factor)	40.00
196	Jose Cruz, Jr., Jay Buhner (Double Team)	25.00
197	Eddie Murray (Star Factor)	10.00
198	Darin Erstad, Jason Dickson (Double Team)	12.00
199	Fred McGriff (Star Factor)	10.00
200	Bubba Trammell, Bobby Higginson (Double Team)	10.00

1997 Donruss Limited Exposure

A complete 200-card parallel set printed on Holographic Poly-Chromium technology on both sides and featuring a special "Limit-ed Exposure" stamp. Less than 40 sets of the Star Factor Limited Exposures are thought to exist.

		MT
Complete Set (200):		12000.
Common Counterpart:		4.00
Common Double Team:		10.00
Common Star Factor:		40.00
Common Unlimited Potential:		25.00
1	Ken Griffey Jr., Rondell White (Counterparts)	75.00
2	Greg Maddux, David Cone (Counterparts)	40.00
3	Gary Sheffield, Moises Alou (Double Team)	12.00
4	Frank Thomas (Star Factor)	400.00
5	Cal Ripken Jr., Kevin Orie (Counterparts)	50.00
6	Vladimir Guerrero, Barry Bonds (Unlimited Potential/Talent)	100.00
7	Eddie Murray, Reggie Jefferson (Counterparts)	8.00
8	Manny Ramirez, Marquis Grissom (Double Team)	20.00
9	Mike Piazza (Star Factor)	400.00
10	Barry Larkin, Rey Ordonez (Counterparts)	6.00
11	Jeff Bagwell, Eric Karros (Counterparts)	25.00
12	Chuck Knoblauch, Ray Durham (Counterparts)	8.00
13	Alex Rodriguez, Edgar Renteria (Counterparts)	50.00
14	Matt Williams, Vinny Castilla (Counterparts)	8.00
15	Todd Hollandsworth, Bob Abreu (Counterparts)	4.00
16	John Smoltz, Pedro Martinez (Counterparts)	6.00
17	Jose Canseco, Chili Davis (Counterparts)	6.00
18	Jose Cruz, Jr., Ken Griffey Jr. (Unlimited Potential/Talent)	500.00
19	Ken Griffey Jr. (Star Factor)	600.00
20	Paul Molitor, John Olerud (Counterparts)	12.00
21	Roberto Alomar, Luis Castillo (Counterparts)	12.00
22	Derek Jeter, Lou Collier (Counterparts)	30.00
23	Chipper Jones, Robin Ventura (Counterparts)	40.00
24	Gary Sheffield, Ron Gant (Counterparts)	8.00
25	Ramon Martinez, Bobby Jones (Counterparts)	4.00
26	Mike Piazza, Raul Mondesi (Double Team)	120.00
27	Darin Erstad, Jeff Bagwell (Unlimited Potential/Talent)	200.00
28	Ivan Rodriguez (Star Factor)	150.00
29	J.T. Snow, Kevin Young (Counterparts)	4.00
30	Ryne Sandberg, Julio Franco (Counterparts)	15.00
31	Travis Fryman, Chris Snopek (Counterparts)	4.00
32	Wade Boggs, Russ Davis (Counterparts)	6.00
33	Brooks Kieschnick, Marty Cordova (Counterparts)	4.00
34	Andy Pettitte, Denny Neagle (Counterparts)	15.00
35	Paul Molitor, Matt Lawton (Double Team)	20.00
36	Scott Rolen, Cal Ripken Jr. (Unlimited Potential/Talent)	400.00
37	Cal Ripken Jr. (Star Factor)	500.00
38	Jim Thome, Dave Nilsson (Counterparts)	8.00
39	Tony Womack, Carlos Baerga (Counterparts)	4.00
40	Nomar Garciaparra, Mark Grudzielanek (Counterparts)	50.00
41	Todd Greene, Chris Widger (Counterparts)	4.00
42	Deion Sanders, Bernard Gilkey (Counterparts)	6.00
43	Hideo Nomo, Charles Nagy (Counterparts)	30.00

44	Ivan Rodriguez, Rusty Greer (Double Team)	50.00
45	Todd Walker, Chipper Jones (Unlimited Potential/Talent)	250.00
46	Greg Maddux (Star Factor)	400.00
47	Mo Vaughn, Cecil Fielder (Counterparts)	15.00
48	Craig Biggio, Scott Spiezio (Counterparts)	4.00
49	Pokey Reese, Jeff Blauser (Counterparts)	4.00
50	Ken Caminiti, Joe Randa (Counterparts)	6.00
51	Albert Belle, Shawn Green (Counterparts)	20.00
52	Randy Johnson, Jason Dickson (Counterparts)	12.00
53	Hideo Nomo, Chan Ho Park (Double Team)	90.00
54	Scott Spiezio, Chuck Knoblauch (Unlimited Potential/Talent)	35.00
55	Chipper Jones (Star Factor)	400.00
56	Tino Martinez, Ryan McGuire (Counterparts)	6.00
57	Eric Young, Wilton Guerrero (Counterparts)	4.00
58	Ron Coomer, Dave Hollins (Counterparts)	4.00
59	Sammy Sosa, Angel Echevarria (Counterparts)	30.00
60	Dennis Reyes, Jimmy Koy (Counterparts)	4.00
61	Barry Larkin, Deion Sanders (Double Team)	15.00
62	Wilton Guerrero, Roberto Alomar (Unlimited Potential/Talent)	35.00
63	Albert Belle (Star Factor)	150.00
64	Mark McGwire, Andres Galarraga (Counterparts)	75.00
65	Edgar Martinez, Todd Walker (Counterparts)	8.00
66	Steve Finley, Rich Becker (Counterparts)	4.00
67	Tom Glavine, Andy Ashby (Counterparts)	6.00
68	Sammy Sosa, Ryne Sandberg (Double Team)	125.00
69	Nomar Garciaparra, Alex Rodriguez (Unlimited Potential/Talent)	400.00
70	Jeff Bagwell (Star Factor)	180.00
71	Darin Erstad, Mark Grace (Counterparts)	18.00
72	Scott Rolen, Edgardo Alfonzo (Counterparts)	25.00
73	Kenny Lofton, Lance Johnson (Counterparts)	15.00
74	Joey Hamilton, Brett Tomko (Counterparts)	4.00
75	Eddie Murray, Tim Salmon (Double Team)	12.00
76	Dmitri Young, Mo Vaughn (Unlimited Potential/Talent)	100.00
77	Juan Gonzalez (Star Factor)	300.00
78	Frank Thomas, Tony Clark (Counterparts)	50.00
79	Shannon Stewart, Bip Roberts (Counterparts)	4.00
80	Shawn Estes, Alex Fernandez (Counterparts)	4.00
81	John Smoltz, Javier Lopez (Double Team)	10.00
82	Todd Greene, Mike Piazza (Unlimited Potential/Talent)	200.00
83	Derek Jeter (Star Factor)	350.00
84	Dmitri Young, Antone Williamson (Counterparts)	4.00
85	Rickey Henderson, Darryl Hamilton (Counterparts)	4.00
86	Billy Wagner, Dennis Eckersley (Counterparts)	4.00
87	Larry Walker, Eric Young (Double Team)	12.00
88	Mark Kotsay, Juan Gonzalez (Unlimited Potential/Talent)	250.00
89	Barry Bonds (Star Factor)	150.00
90	Will Clark, Jeff Conine (Counterparts)	6.00
91	Tony Gwynn, Brett Butler (Counterparts)	10.00
92	John Wetteland, Rod Beck (Counterparts)	4.00

93	Bernie Williams, Tino Martinez (Double Team)	15.00
94	Andruw Jones, Kenny Lofton (Unlimited Potential/Talent)	150.00
95	Mo Vaughn (Star Factor)	150.00
96	Joe Carter, Derrek Lee (Counterparts)	4.00
97	John Mabry, F.P. Santangelo (Counterparts)	4.00
98	Esteban Loaiza, Wilson Alvarez (Counterparts)	4.00
99	Matt Williams, David Justice (Double Team)	10.00
100	Derrek Lee, Frank Thomas (Unlimited Potential/Talent)	400.00
101	Mark McGwire (Star Factor)	600.00
102	Fred McGriff, Paul Sorrento (Counterparts)	5.00
103	Jermaine Allensworth, Bernie Williams (Counterparts)	8.00
104	Ismael Valdes, Chris Holt (Counterparts)	4.00
105	Fred McGriff, Ryan Klesko (Double Team)	12.00
106	Tony Clark, Mark McGwire (Unlimited Potential/Talent)	400.00
107	Tony Gwynn (Star Factor)	300.00
108	Jeffrey Hammonds, Ellis Burks (Counterparts)	4.00
109	Shane Reynolds, Andy Benes (Counterparts)	4.00
110	Roger Clemens, Carlos Delgado (Double Team)	80.00
111	Karim Garcia, Albert Belle (Unlimited Potential/Talent)	100.00
112	Paul Molitor (Star Factor)	75.00
113	Trey Beamon, Eric Owens (Counterparts)	4.00
114	Curt Schilling, Darryl Kile (Counterparts)	4.00
115	Tom Glavine, Michael Tucker (Double Team)	10.00
116	Pokey Reese, Derek Jeter (Unlimited Potential/Talent)	200.00
117	Manny Ramirez (Star Factor)	100.00
118	Juan Gonzalez, Brant Brown (Counterparts)	35.00
119	Juan Guzman, Francisco Cordova (Counterparts)	4.00
120	Randy Johnson, Edgar Martinez (Double Team)	10.00
121	Hideki Irabu, Greg Maddux (Unlimited Potential/Talent)	250.00
122	Alex Rodriguez (Star Factor)	400.00
123	Barry Bonds, Quinton McCracken (Counterparts)	15.00
124	Roger Clemens, Alan Benes (Counterparts)	25.00
125	Wade Boggs, Paul O'Neill (Double Team)	10.00
126	Mike Cameron, Larry Walker (Unlimited Potential/Talent)	25.00
127	Gary Sheffield (Star Factor)	50.00
128	Andruw Jones, Raul Mondesi (Counterparts)	30.00
129	Brian Anderson, Terrell Wade (Counterparts)	4.00
130	Brady Anderson, Rafael Palmeiro (Double Team)	10.00
131	Neifi Perez, Barry Larkin (Unlimited Potential/Talent)	25.00
132	Ken Caminiti (Star Factor)	40.00
133	Larry Walker, Rusty Greer (Counterparts)	5.00
134	Mariano Rivera, Mark Wohlers (Counterparts)	4.00
135	Hideki Irabu, Andy Pettitte (Double Team)	30.00
136	Jose Guillen, Tony Gwynn (Unlimited Potential/Talent)	200.00
137	Hideo Nomo (Star Factor)	200.00
138	Vladimir Guerrero, Jim Edmonds (Counterparts)	20.00
139	Justin Thompson, Dwight Gooden (Counterparts)	4.00
140	Andres Galarraga, Dante Bichette (Double Team)	10.00
141	Kenny Lofton (Star Factor)	125.00
142	Tim Salmon, Manny Ramirez (Counterparts)	12.00
143	Kevin Brown, Matt Morris (Counterparts)	4.00
144	Craig Biggio, Bob Abreu (Double Team)	4.00
145	Roberto Alomar (Star Factor)	100.00
146	Jose Guillen, Brian Jordan (Counterparts)	10.00
147	Bartolo Colon, Kevin Appier (Counterparts)	4.00
148	Ray Lankford, Brian Jordan (Double Team)	10.00
149	Chuck Knoblauch (Star Factor)	60.00
150	Henry Rodriguez, Ray Lankford (Counterparts)	4.00
151	*Jaret Wright*, Ben McDonald (Counterparts)	20.00
152	Bobby Bonilla, Kevin Brown (Double Team)	10.00
153	Barry Larkin (Star Factor)	40.00
154	David Justice, Reggie Sanders (Counterparts)	5.00
155	Mike Mussina, Ken Hill (Counterparts)	8.00
156	Mark Grace, Brooks Kieschnick (Double Team)	10.00
157	Jim Thome (Star Factor)	75.00
158	Michael Tucker, Curtis Goodwin (Counterparts)	4.00
159	Jeff Suppan, Jeff Fassero (Counterparts)	4.00
160	Mike Mussina, Jeffrey Hammonds (Double Team)	15.00
161	John Smoltz (Star Factor)	40.00
162	Moises Alou, Eric Davis (Counterparts)	4.00
163	Sandy Alomar Jr., Dan Wilson (Counterparts)	4.00
164	Rondell White, Henry Rodriguez (Double Team)	10.00
165	Roger Clemens (Star Factor)	200.00
166	Brady Anderson, Al Martin (Counterparts)	4.00
167	Jason Kendall, Charles Johnson (Counterparts)	4.00
168	Jason Giambi, Jose Canseco (Double Team)	12.00
169	Larry Walker (Star Factor)	60.00
170	Jay Buhner, Geronimo Berroa (Counterparts)	4.00
171	Ivan Rodriguez, Mike Sweeney (Counterparts)	12.00
172	Kevin Appier, Jose Rosado (Double Team)	10.00
173	Bernie Williams (Star Factor)	75.00
174	Todd Dunwoody, Brian Giles (Counterparts)	4.00
175	Javier Lopez, Scott Hatteberg (Counterparts)	4.00
176	John Jaha, Jeff Cirillo (Double Team)	10.00
177	Andy Pettitte (Star Factor)	80.00
178	Dante Bichette, Butch Huskey (Counterparts)	6.00
179	Raul Casanova, Todd Hundley (Counterparts)	4.00
180	Jim Edmonds, Garret Anderson (Double Team)	10.00
181	Deion Sanders (Star Factor)	50.00
182	Ryan Klesko, Paul O'Neill (Counterparts)	6.00
183	Joe Carter, Pat Hentgen (Double Team)	10.00
184	Brady Anderson (Star Factor)	40.00
185	Carlos Delgado, Wally Joyner (Counterparts)	4.00
186	Jermaine Dye, Johnny Damon (Double Team)	10.00
187	Randy Johnson (Star Factor)	80.00
188	Todd Hundley, Carlos Baerga (Double Team)	10.00
189	Tom Glavine (Star Factor)	40.00
190	Damon Mashore, Jason McDonald (Double Team)	10.00
191	Wade Boggs (Star Factor)	50.00
192	Al Martin, Jason Kendall (Double Team)	10.00
193	Matt Williams (Star Factor)	50.00
194	Will Clark, Dean Palmer (Double Team)	15.00
195	Sammy Sosa (Star Factor)	250.00
196	Jose Cruz, Jr., Jay Buhner (Double Team)	80.00
197	Eddie Murray (Star Factor)	60.00
198	Darin Erstad, Jason Dickson (Double Team)	60.00
199	Fred McGriff (Star Factor)	50.00
200	Bubba Trammell, Bobby Higginson (Double Team)	15.00

1997 Donruss Limited Fabric of the Game

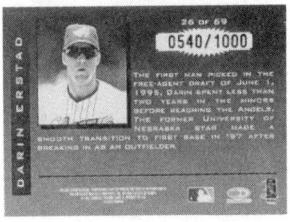

This fractured insert set consists of 69 different cards highlighting three different technologies representing three statistical categories: Canvas (stolen bases), Leather (doubles) and Wood (home runs). Each of the 23 cards in each category are found in varying levels of scarcity: Legendary Material (one card per theme; numbered to 100), Hall of Fame Material (four cards numbered to 250), Superstar Material (five cards numbered to 500), Star Material (six cards numbered to 750), and Major League Material (seven cards numbered to 1,000).

	MT
Complete Set (69):	1800.
Complete Canvas Set (23):	15.00
Rickey Henderson (100)	60.00
Barry Bonds (250)	60.00
Kenny Lofton (250)	60.00
Roberto Alomar (250)	50.00
Ryne Sandberg (250)	60.00
Tony Gwynn (500)	60.00
Barry Larkin (500)	25.00
Brady Anderson (500)	20.00
Chuck Knoblauch (500)	25.00
Craig Biggio (500)	20.00
Sammy Sosa (750)	50.00
Gary Sheffield (750)	25.00
Eric Young (750)	15.00
Larry Walker (750)	30.00
Ken Griffey Jr. (750)	125.00
Deion Sanders (750)	20.00
Raul Mondesi (1,000)	20.00
Rondell White (1,000)	15.00
Derek Jeter (1,000)	50.00
Nomar Garciaparra (1,000)	40.00
Wilton Guerrero (1,000)	10.00
Pokey Reese (1,000)	10.00
Darin Erstad (1,000)	35.00
Complete Leather Set (23):	15.00
Paul Molitor (100)	125.00
Wade Boggs (250)	30.00
Cal Ripken Jr. (250)	160.00

Tony Gwynn (250)	100.00
Joe Carter (250)	25.00
Rafael Palmeiro (500)	25.00
Mark Grace (500)	25.00
Bobby Bonilla (500)	20.00
Andres Galarraga (500)	25.00
Edgar Martinez (500)	20.00
Ken Caminiti (750)	25.00
Ivan Rodriguez (750)	35.00
Frank Thomas (750)	100.00
Jeff Bagwell (750)	50.00
Albert Belle (750)	40.00
Bernie Williams (750)	35.00
Chipper Jones (1,000)	50.00
Rusty Greer (1,000)	10.00
Todd Walker (1,000)	20.00
Scott Rolen (1,000)	40.00
Bob Abreu (1,000)	10.00
Jose Guillen (1,000)	30.00
Jose Cruz, Jr. (1,000)	60.00
Complete Wood Set (23):	15.00
Eddie Murray (100)	100.00
Cal Ripken Jr. (250)	160.00
Barry Bonds (250)	60.00
Mark McGwire (250)	100.00
Fred McGriff (250)	25.00
Ken Griffey Jr. (500)	140.00
Albert Belle (500)	40.00
Frank Thomas (500)	120.00
Juan Gonzalez (500)	60.00
Matt Williams (500)	25.00
Mike Piazza (750)	60.00
Jeff Bagwell (750)	16.00
Mo Vaughn (750)	35.00
Gary Sheffield (750)	25.00
Tim Salmon (750)	20.00
David Justice (750)	20.00
Manny Ramirez (1,000)	25.00
Jim Thome (1,000)	20.00
Tino Martinez (1,000)	20.00
Andruw Jones (1,000)	40.00
Vladimir Guerrero (1,000)	30.00
Tony Clark (1,000)	25.00
Dmitri Young (1,000)	10.00

1997 Donruss Preferred

Each of the 200 base cards is printed on front on an all-foil micro-etched stock. Conventional backs have a color player photo and a few stats. The set is fractured into three different scarcities: 100 Bronze cards, 70 Silver cards, 20 Gold cards and 10 Platinum cards. Instead of traditional packs, cards were sold in five-card collectible tins. A total of 25 different tins were available, and each tin was numbered to 1,200. Four different inserts were included with the product: Staremaster, X-Ponential

Power, Cut To The Chase, and Precious Metals. Odds of finding any insert were 1:4 packs.

	MT
Complete Set (200):	800.00
Common Bronze:	.10
Common Silver:	1.50
Common Gold:	8.00
Cut to the Chase Golds: 2.5x to 3x	
Cut to the Chase Silvers: 3x to 4x	
Cut to the Chase Bronze: 5x to 10x	
Cut to the Chase Platinum: 2x to 3x	
Wax Box:	120.00

1	Frank Thomas P	50.00
2	Ken Griffey Jr. P	80.00
3	Cecil Fielder B	.20
4	Chuck Knoblauch G	8.00
5	Garret Anderson B	.10
6	Greg Maddux P	50.00
7	Matt Williams S	2.00
8	Marquis Grissom S	1.50
9	Jason Isringhausen B	.10
10	Larry Walker S	2.50
11	Charles Nagy B	.10
12	Dan Wilson B	.10
13	Albert Belle G	12.00
14	Javier Lopez B	.20
15	David Cone B	.20
16	Bernard Gilkey B	.10
17	Andres Galarraga S	2.00
18	Bill Pulsipher B	.10
19	Alex Fernandez B	.10
20	Andy Pettitte S	5.00
21	Mark Grudzielanek B	.10
22	Juan Gonzalez P	40.00
23	Reggie Sanders B	.10
24	Kenny Lofton G	10.00
25	Andy Ashby B	.10
26	John Wetteland B	.10
27	Bobby Bonilla B	.10
28	Hideo Nomo G	10.00
29	Joe Carter B	.20
30	Jose Canseco B	.25
31	Ellis Burks B	.10
32	Edgar Martinez S	1.50
33	Chan Ho Park B	.10
34	David Justice B	.40
35	Carlos Delgado B	.10
36	Jeff Cirillo S	1.50
37	Charles Johnson B	.10
38	Manny Ramirez G	10.00
39	Greg Vaughn B	.10
40	Henry Rodriguez B	.10
41	Darryl Strawberry B	.10
42	Jim Thome G	6.00
43	Ryan Klesko S	3.00
44	Jermaine Allensworth B	.10
45	Brian Jordan G	8.00
46	Tony Gwynn P	40.00
47	Rafael Palmeiro G	10.00
48	Dante Bichette S	2.00
49	Ivan Rodriguez G	15.00
50	Mark McGwire G	35.00
51	Tim Salmon S	2.00
52	Roger Clemens B	1.00
53	Matt Lawton B	.10
54	Wade Boggs S	2.00
55	Travis Fryman B	.10
56	Bobby Higginson S	1.50
57	John Jaha S	1.50
58	Rondell White S	1.50
59	Tom Glavine S	2.00
60	Eddie Murray S	4.00
61	Vinny Castilla B	.10
62	Todd Hundley B	.40
63	Jay Buhner S	2.00
64	Paul O'Neill B	.20
65	Steve Finley B	.10
66	Kevin Appier B	.10
67	Ray Durham B	.10
68	Dave Nilsson B	.10
69	Jeff Bagwell G	20.00
70	Al Martin S	1.50
71	Paul Molitor G	10.00
72	Kevin Brown S	1.50
73	Ron Gant B	.10
74	Dwight Gooden B	.10
75	Quinton McCracken B	.10
76	Rusty Greer S	1.50
77	Juan Guzman B	.10
78	Fred McGriff S	1.50
79	Tino Martinez B	.40
80	Ray Lankford B	.10
81	Ken Caminiti G	8.00
82	James Baldwin B	.10

83	Jermaine Dye G	8.00
84	Mark Grace S	2.00
85	Pat Hentgen S	1.50
86	Jason Giambi S	1.50
87	Brian Hunter B	.10
88	Andy Benes B	.10
89	Jose Rosado B	.10
90	Shawn Green B	.10
91	Jason Kendall B	.10
92	Alex Rodriguez P	70.00
93	Chipper Jones P	50.00
94	Barry Bonds G	10.00
95	Brady Anderson G	8.00
96	Ryne Sandberg S	5.00
97	Lance Johnson B	.10
98	Cal Ripken Jr. P	60.00
99	Craig Biggio S	1.50
100	Dean Palmer B	.10
101	Gary Sheffield G	8.00
102	Johnny Damon B	.10
103	Mo Vaughn G	10.00
104	Randy Johnson S	3.00
105	Raul Mondesi S	1.50
106	Roberto Alomar G	10.00
107	Mike Piazza P	50.00
108	Rey Ordonez B	.10
109	Barry Larkin G	8.00
110	Tony Clark S	5.00
111	Bernie Williams S	4.00
112	John Smoltz G	8.00
113	Moises Alou B	.10
114	Will Clark B	.25
115	Sammy Sosa G	20.00
116	Jim Edmonds S	1.50
117	Jeff Conine B	.10
118	Joey Hamilton B	.10
119	Todd Hollandsworth B	.10
120	Troy Percival B	.10
121	Paul Wilson B	.10
122	Ken Hill B	.10
123	Mariano Rivera S	1.50
124	Eric Karros B	.10
125	Derek Jeter G	30.00
126	Eric Young S	1.50
127	John Mabry B	.10
128	Gregg Jefferies B	.10
129	Ismael Valdes S	1.50
130	Marty Cordova B	.10
131	Omar Vizquel B	.10
132	Mike Mussina S	4.00
133	Darin Erstad B	1.00
134	Edgar Renteria S	1.50
135	Billy Wagner B	.10
136	Alex Ochoa B	.10
137	Luis Castillo B	.10
138	Rocky Coppinger B	.10
139	Mike Sweeney B	.10
140	Michael Tucker B	.10
141	Chris Snopek B	.10
142	Dmitri Young S	1.50
143	Andruw Jones P	35.00
144	Mike Cameron S	1.50
145	Brant Brown B	.10
146	Todd Walker G	8.00
147	Nomar Garciaparra G	30.00
148	Glendon Rusch B	.10
149	Karim Garcia S	1.50
150	*Bubba Trammell S*	5.00
151	Todd Greene B	.10
152	Wilton Guerrero G	8.00
153	Scott Spiezio B	.10
154	Brooks Kieschnick B	.10
155	Vladimir Guerrero G	15.00
156	Brian Giles S	1.50
157	Pokey Reese B	.10
158	Jason Dickson G	8.00
159	Kevin Orie S	1.50
160	Scott Rolen G	20.00
161	Bartolo Colon S	1.50
162	Shannon Stewart G	8.00
163	Wendell Magee B	.10
164	Jose Guillen S	4.00
165	Bob Abreu S	1.50
166	*Deivi Cruz B*	1.00
167	Alex Rodriguez B (National Treasures)	2.00
168	Frank Thomas B (National Treasures)	1.50
169	Cal Ripken Jr. B (National Treasures)	1.50
170	Chipper Jones B (National Treasures)	1.00
171	Mike Piazza B (National Treasures)	1.00

172	Tony Gwynn S (National Treasures)	8.00
173	Juan Gonzalez B (National Treasures)	.75
174	Kenny Lofton S (National Treasures)	5.00
175	Ken Griffey Jr. B (National Treasures)	2.00
176	Mark McGwire B (National Treasures)	3.00
177	Jeff Bagwell B (National Treasures)	.75
178	Paul Molitor S (National Treasures)	3.00
179	Andruw Jones B (National Treasures)	1.00
180	Manny Ramirez S (National Treasures)	4.00
181	Ken Caminiti S (National Treasures)	2.00
182	Barry Bonds B (National Treasures)	.50
183	Mo Vaughn B (National Treasures)	.50
184	Derek Jeter B (National Treasures)	1.00
185	Barry Larkin S (National Treasures)	2.00
186	Ivan Rodriguez B (National Treasures)	.30
187	Albert Belle S (National Treasures)	4.00
188	John Smoltz S (National Treasures)	1.50
189	Chuck Knoblauch S (National Treasures)	2.00
190	Brian Jordan S (National Treasures)	1.50
191	Gary Sheffield S (National Treasures)	2.00
192	Jim Thome S (National Treasures)	4.00
193	Brady Anderson S (National Treasures)	1.50
194	Hideo Nomo S (National Treasures)	6.00
195	Sammy Sosa S (National Treasures)	12.00
196	Greg Maddux B (National Treasures)	1.00
197	Checklist(Vladimir Guerrero B)	.75
198	Checklist(Scott Rolen B)	1.00
199	Checklist(Todd Walker B)	.25
200	Checklist(Nomar Garciaparra B)	1.00

1997 Donruss Preferred Cut To The Chase

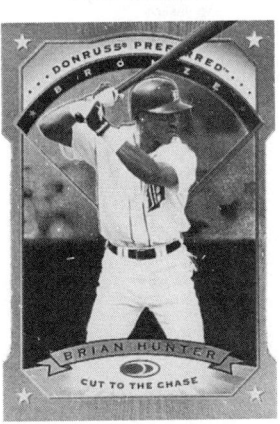

Each of the cards in the Donruss Preferred series can also be found in this parallel set with die-cut borders, in the same bronze, silver, gold and platinum finishes. Multiplier values of the die-cuts are inverse to that usually found, with platinum cards the lowest, followed by gold, silver and bronze. Besides die-cutting, the chase cards feature a "CUT TO THE CHASE" designation at bottom.

	MT
Complete Set (200):	4000.
Common Platinum:	100.00
Common Gold:	12.00
Common Silver:	6.00
Common Bronze:	1.50
(Stars and rookies valued at multiples of regular-issue cards. Platinum: 2.5-3X; Gold: 2.5-3X; Silver: 3-4X; Bronze: 5-10X)	

1997 Donruss Preferred Precious Metals

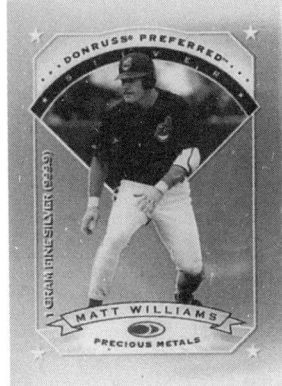

This 25-card partial parallel set features cards printed on actual silver, gold and platinum stock. Only 100 of each card were produced.

		MT
Complete Set (25):		4000.
Common Player:		50.00
1	Frank Thomas	300.00
2	Ken Griffey Jr.	500.00
3	Greg Maddux	300.00
4	Albert Belle	125.00
5	Juan Gonzalez	250.00
6	Kenny Lofton	125.00
7	Tony Gwynn	250.00
8	Ivan Rodriguez	125.00
9	Mark McGwire	500.00
10	Matt Williams	50.00
11	Wade Boggs	50.00
12	Eddie Murray	75.00
13	Jeff Bagwell	150.00
14	Ken Caminiti	75.00
15	Alex Rodriguez	300.00
16	Chipper Jones	250.00
17	Barry Bonds	125.00
18	Cal Ripken Jr.	400.00
19	Mo Vaughn	125.00
20	Mike Piazza	300.00
21	Derek Jeter	300.00
22	Bernie Williams	100.00
23	Andruw Jones	125.00
24	Vladimir Guerrero	150.00
25	Jose Guillen	100.00

A player's name in *italic* type indicates a rookie card.

1997 Donruss Preferred Staremasters

A 20-card insert printed on foil stock and accented with holographic foil stamping, Staremasters is designed to show up-close "game-face" photography. Each card is sequentially numbered to 1,500.

		MT
Complete Set (20):		500.00
Common Player:		12.00
1	Alex Rodriguez	50.00
2	Frank Thomas	60.00
3	Chipper Jones	50.00
4	Cal Ripken Jr.	60.00
5	Mike Piazza	50.00
6	Juan Gonzalez	35.00
7	Derek Jeter	50.00
8	Jeff Bagwell	30.00
8s	Jeff Bagwell (overprinted "SAMPLE")	4.00
9	Ken Griffey Jr.	80.00
10	Tony Gwynn	35.00
11	Barry Bonds	20.00
12	Albert Belle	20.00
13	Greg Maddux	50.00
14	Mark McGwire	80.00
15	Ken Caminiti	12.00
16	Hideo Nomo	20.00
17	Gary Sheffield	12.00
18	Andruw Jones	35.00
19	Mo Vaughn	20.00
20	Ivan Rodriguez	20.00

1997 Donruss Preferred X-Ponential Power

This 20-card die-cut insert contains two top hitters from 10 different teams. Placing the cards of teammates together forms an "X" shape. Cards are printed on thick plastic stock and gold holographic foil stamping and are sequentially numbered to 3,000.

		MT
Complete Set (20):		300.00
Common Player:		5.00
1A	Manny Ramirez	12.00
1B	Jim Thome	10.00
2A	Paul Molitor	8.00
2B	Chuck Knoblauch	5.00
3A	Ivan Rodriguez	10.00
3B	Juan Gonzalez	20.00
4A	Albert Belle	12.00
4B	Frank Thomas	40.00
5A	Roberto Alomar	10.00
5B	Cal Ripken Jr.	40.00
6A	Tim Salmon	5.00
6B	Jim Edmonds	5.00
7A	Ken Griffey Jr.	50.00
7B	Alex Rodriguez	40.00
8A	Chipper Jones	30.00
8B	Andruw Jones	25.00
9A	Mike Piazza	30.00
9B	Raul Mondesi	5.00
10A	Tony Gwynn	20.00
10B	Ken Caminiti	5.00

1997 Donruss Preferred Tins

A total of 25 different players are featured on the lithographed steel tins which were the "packs" of Donruss Preferred baseball. The tins measure 3" x 4-1/2" x 5/8" and are hinged along the left side. Tins were produced in two versions. Predominantly blue tins are the standard package. A premium parallel version is gold-colored and serially numbered within an edition of 1,200. Gold tins were packed one per 24-pack box of Preferred.

		MT
Complete Set, Blue (25):		20.00
Common Tin:		.50
Gold: 5X-10X		
1	Frank Thomas	2.00
2	Ken Griffey Jr.	2.00
3	Andruw Jones	1.25
4	Cal Ripken Jr.	1.50
5	Mike Piazza	1.25
6	Chipper Jones	1.25
7	Alex Rodriguez	1.50
8	Derek Jeter	1.00
9	Juan Gonzalez	.75
10	Albert Belle	.50
11	Tony Gwynn	.75
12	Greg Maddux	.75
13	Jeff Bagwell	.50
14	Roger Clemens	.75
15	Mark McGwire	1.50
16	Gary Sheffield	.50
17	Manny Ramirez	.50
18	Hideo Nomo	.60
19	Kenny Lofton	.50
20	Mo Vaughn	.50
21	Ryne Sandberg	.60
22	Barry Bonds	.75
23	Sammy Sosa	1.00
24	John Smoltz	.50
25	Ivan Rodriguez	.60

1997 Donruss Preferred Tin Boxes

A total of 25 different players are featured on the lithographed steel boxes in which the "packs" of Donruss Preferred baseball were sold. Boxes measure about 5-1/4" x 9-1/4" x 5-3/8". Inside the removable lid is a serial number from within an edition of 1,200 (blue) or 299 (gold). Boxes were produced in two versions. Predominantly blue boxes are the standard package. A premium parallel version is gold-colored.

		MT
Complete Set, Blue (25):		120.00
Common Box:		3.00
Gold: 10X-20X		
1	Frank Thomas	10.00
2	Ken Griffey Jr.	12.00
3	Andruw Jones	5.00
4	Cal Ripken Jr.	9.00
5	Mike Piazza	7.50
6	Chipper Jones	7.50
7	Alex Rodriguez	7.50
8	Derek Jeter	6.00
9	Juan Gonzalez	4.50
10	Albert Belle	2.50
11	Tony Gwynn	4.50
12	Greg Maddux	4.50
13	Jeff Bagwell	3.00
14	Roger Clemens	4.50
15	Mark McGwire	10.00
16	Gary Sheffield	3.00
17	Manny Ramirez	3.00
18	Hideo Nomo	3.50
19	Kenny Lofton	3.00
20	Mo Vaughn	3.00
21	Ryne Sandberg	3.50
22	Barry Bonds	4.50
23	Sammy Sosa	4.00
24	John Smoltz	3.00
25	Ivan Rodriguez	3.50

A player's name in *italic* type indicates a rookie card.

11	Tony Gwynn	.75
12	Greg Maddux	.75
13	Jeff Bagwell	.50
14	Roger Clemens	.75
15	Mark McGwire	1.50
16	Gary Sheffield	.50
17	Manny Ramirez	.50
18	Hideo Nomo	.60
19	Kenny Lofton	.50
20	Mo Vaughn	.50
21	Ryne Sandberg	.60
22	Barry Bonds	.75
23	Sammy Sosa	1.00
24	John Smoltz	.50
25	Ivan Rodriguez	.60

1997 Donruss Signature

Michael Tucker - Braves

		MT
Complete Set (100):		40.00
Common Player:		.20
Platinum Stars: 20x to 40x		
Platinum Yng Stars & RCs: 10x to 20x		
1	Mark McGwire	5.00
2	Kenny Lofton	1.00
3	Tony Gwynn	2.00
4	Tony Clark	.60
5	Tim Salmon	.40
6	Ken Griffey Jr.	4.00
7	Mike Piazza	2.50
8	Greg Maddux	2.50
9	Roberto Alomar	.75
10	Andres Galarraga	.30
11	Roger Clemens	1.50
12	Bernie Williams	.75
13	Rondell White	.30
14	Kevin Appier	.20
15	Ray Lankford	.20
16	Frank Thomas	3.00
17	Will Clark	.35
18	Chipper Jones	2.50
19	Jeff Bagwell	1.75
20	Manny Ramirez	.75
21	Ryne Sandberg	1.00
22	Paul Molitor	.75
23	Gary Sheffield	.40
24	Jim Edmonds	.20
25	Barry Larkin	.30
26	Rafael Palmeiro	.30
27	Alan Benes	.20
28	David Justice	.30
29	Randy Johnson	.60
30	Barry Bonds	1.00
31	Mo Vaughn	1.00
32	Michael Tucker	.20
33	Larry Walker	.40
34	Tino Martinez	.30
35	Jose Guillen	.60
36	Carlos Delgado	.20
37	Jason Dickson	.20
38	Tom Glavine	.30
39	Raul Mondesi	.30
40	*Jose Cruz Jr.*	4.00
41	Johnny Damon	.20
42	Mark Grace	.30
43	Juan Gonzalez	2.00
44	Vladimir Guerrero	1.00
45	Kevin Brown	.20
46	Justin Thompson	.20
47	Eric Young	.20
48	Ron Coomer	.20
49	Mark Kotsay	.40
50	Scott Rolen	2.00
51	Derek Jeter	2.50
52	Jim Thome	.75
53	Fred McGriff	.30
54	Albert Belle	1.00
55	Garret Anderson	.20
56	Wilton Guerrero	.20
57	Jose Canseco	.30
58	Cal Ripken Jr.	3.00
59	Sammy Sosa	1.50

60	Dmitri Young	.20
61	Alex Rodriguez	2.50
62	Javier Lopez	.20
63	Sandy Alomar Jr.	.20
64	Joe Carter	.20
65	Dante Bichette	.30
66	Al Martin	.20
67	Darin Erstad	1.25
68	Pokey Reese	.20
69	Brady Anderson	.30
70	Andruw Jones	2.00
71	Ivan Rodriguez	.75
72	Nomar Garciaparra	2.50
73	Moises Alou	.30
74	Andy Pettitte	.75
75	Jay Buhner	.40
76	Craig Biggio	.40
77	Wade Boggs	.40
78	Shawn Estes	.20
79	Neifi Perez	.20
80	Rusty Greer	.20
81	Pedro J. Martinez	.30
82	Mike Mussina	.75
83	Jason Giambi	.20
84	Hideo Nomo	.75
85	Todd Hundley	.20
86	Deion Sanders	.30
87	Mike Cameron	.20
88	Bobby Bonilla	.30
89	Todd Greene	.20
90	Kevin Orie	.20
91	Ken Caminiti	.30
92	Chuck Knoblauch	.40
93	Matt Morris	.20
94	Matt Williams	.40
95	Pat Hentgen	.20
96	John Smoltz	.30
97	Edgar Martinez	.20
98	Jason Kendall	.20
99	Ken Griffey Jr.	2.00
100	Frank Thomas	1.50

1997 Donruss Signature Autographs

		MT
Complete Set (117):		1700.
Common Player:		5.00

Players signed 3,900 cards unless otherwise noted.

1	Jeff Abbott (3900)	5.00
2	Bob Abreu (3900)	5.00
3	Edgardo Alfonzo (3900)	10.00
4	Roberto Alomar (150)	90.00
5	Sandy Alomar Jr. (1400)	15.00
6	Moises Alou (900)	20.00
7	Garret Anderson (3900)	10.00
8	Andy Ashby (3900)	5.00
9	Trey Beamon (3900)	5.00
10	Alan Benes (3900)	10.00
11	Geronimo Berroa (3900)	5.00
12	Wade Boggs (150)	100.00
13	Kevin L. Brown (3900)	5.00
14	Brett Butler (1400)	15.00
15	Mike Cameron (3900)	15.00
16	Giovanni Carrara (2900)	6.00
17	Luis Castillo (3900)	5.00
18	Tony Clark (3900)	18.00
19	Will Clark (1400)	25.00
20	Lou Collier (3900)	5.00
21	Bartolo Colon (3900)	8.00
22	Ron Coomer (3900)	5.00
23	Marty Cordova (3900)	8.00
24	Jacob Cruz (3900)	12.00
25	Jose Cruz Jr. (900)	75.00
26	Russ Davis (3900)	5.00
27	Jason Dickson (3900)	8.00
28	Todd Dunwoody (3900)	12.00
29	Jermaine Dye (3900)	5.00
30	Jim Edmonds (3900)	15.00
31	Darin Erstad (900)	40.00
32	Bobby Estalella (3900)	8.00
33	Shawn Estes (3900)	10.00
34	Jeff Fassero (3900)	8.00
35	Andres Galarraga (900)	35.00
36	Karim Garcia (3900)	12.00
37	Derrick Gibson (3900)	12.00
38	Brian Giles (3900)	5.00
39	Tom Glavine (150)	60.00
40	Rick Gorecki (900)	5.00
41	Shawn Green (1900)	10.00
42	Todd Greene (3900)	12.00
43	Rusty Greer (3900)	10.00
44	Ben Grieve (3900)	30.00
45	Mark Grudzielanek (3900)	8.00
46	Vladimir Guerrero (1900)	40.00
47	Wilton Guerrero (2150)	8.00
48	Jose Guillen (2900)	20.00
49	Jeffrey Hammonds (2150)	8.00
50	Todd Helton (1400)	25.00
51	Todd Hollandsworth (2900)	10.00
52	Trenidad Hubbard (900)	8.00
53	Todd Hundley (1400)	12.00
54	Bobby Jones (3900)	5.00
55	Brian Jordan (1400)	12.00
56	David Justice (900)	35.00
57	Eric Karros (650)	20.00
58	Jason Kendall (3900)	10.00
59	Jimmy Key (3900)	10.00
60	Brooks Kieschnick (3900)	8.00
61	Ryan Klesko (225)	50.00
62	Paul Konerko (3900)	25.00
63	Mark Kotsay (2400)	30.00
64	Ray Lankford (3900)	10.00
65	Barry Larkin (150)	50.00
66	Derrek Lee (3900)	12.00
67	Esteban Loaiza (3900)	5.00
68	Javier Lopez (1400)	20.00
69	Edgar Martinez (150)	60.00
70	Pedro Martinez (900)	40.00
71	Rafael Medina (3900)	5.00
72	Raul Mondesi (650)	35.00
73	Matt Morris (3900)	10.00
74	Paul O'Neill (900)	25.00
75	Kevin Orie (3900)	8.00
76	David Ortiz (3900)	10.00
77	Rafael Palmeiro (900)	25.00
78	Jay Payton (3900)	10.00
79	Neifi Perez (3900)	8.00
80	Manny Ramirez (900)	35.00
81	Joe Randa (3900)	5.00
82	Calvin Reese (3900)	5.00
83	Edgar Renteria (3900)	10.00
84	Dennis Reyes (3900)	5.00
85	Henry Rodriguez (3900)	8.00
86	Scott Rolen (1900)	50.00
87	Kirk Rueter (2900)	5.00
88	Ryne Sandberg (400)	100.00
89	Dwight Smith (2900)	8.00
90	J.T. Snow (900)	12.00
91	Scott Spiezio (3900)	8.00
92	Shannon Stewart (2900)	10.00
93	Jeff Suppan (1900)	10.00
94	Mike Sweeney (3900)	5.00
95	Miguel Tejada (3900)	30.00
96	Justin Thompson (2400)	10.00
97	Brett Tomko (3900)	10.00
98	Bubba Trammell (3900)	15.00
99	Michael Tucker (3900)	8.00
100	Javier Valentin (3900)	5.00
101	Mo Vaughn (150)	100.00
102	Robin Ventura (1400)	20.00
103	Terrell Wade (3900)	5.00
104	Billy Wagner (3900)	8.00
105	Larry Walker (900)	50.00
106	Todd Walker (2400)	12.00
107	Rondell White (3900)	15.00
108	Kevin Wickander (900)	8.00
109	Chris Widger (3900)	5.00
110	Matt Williams (150)	50.00
111	Antone Williamson (3900)	5.00
112	Dan Wilson (3900)	5.00
113	Tony Womack (3900)	8.00
114	Jaret Wright (3900)	35.00
115	Dmitri Young (3900)	5.00
116	Eric Young (3900)	8.00
117	Kevin Young (3900)	5.00

Modern cards have little collector value in conditions lower than Mint. Figure NM cards at 75% of values shown; EX cards at 40%.

Values shown reflect the market as of January, 1999. On-field performances of current players in the 1999 baseball season are not factored in.

1997 Donruss Signature Millenium Autographs

		MT
Common Player:		15.00
Minor Stars:		30.00
1	Cal Ripken Jr. (400)	375.00
2	Greg Maddux (400)	300.00
3	Alex Rodriguez (400)	300.00
5	Chipper Jones (900)	125.00
7	Barry Bonds (400)	140.00
8	Albert Belle (400)	110.00
9	Juan Gonzalez (900)	140.00
10	Jeff Bagwell (400)	150.00
12	Tony Gwynn (900)	150.00
13	Roger Clemens (400)	220.00
15	Derek Jeter (400)	180.00
17	Gary Sheffield (400)	75.00
18	Larry Walker	50.00
19	Bernie Williams (150)	75.00
21	Eddie Murray (900)	15.00
22	Manny Ramirez	40.00
23	Mo Vaughn	60.00
24	Roberto Alomar	50.00
25	Jim Thome (900)	50.00
26	Ryne Sandberg	80.00
27	David Justice (900)	40.00
29	Barry Larkin	35.00
30	Ivan Rodriguez (400)	75.00
31	Vladimir Guerrero	70.00
33	Rickey Henderson	20.00
34	Edgar Martinez	35.00
35	Ken Caminiti	25.00
37	Chuck Knoblauch (900)	40.00
38	Mike Mussina (900)	50.00
39	Andy Pettitte (900)	50.00
40	Kevin Brown	35.00
41	Craig Biggio	25.00
42	Dante Bichette	25.00
43	Bobby Bonilla (900)	30.00
44	Pat Hentgen	15.00
45	Matt Williams	35.00
46	Rafael Palmeiro	25.00
47	Tom Glavine	15.00
48	Jose Canseco	20.00
49	Wade Boggs	50.00
50	John Smoltz	15.00
51	Brian Jordan	15.00
52	Raul Mondesi (775)	35.00
53	Randy Johnson	25.00
54	Tim Salmon	25.00
55	Ryan Klesko	30.00
56	Mark Grace	25.00
57	Fred McGriff	25.00
58	Jay Buhner (900)	50.00
59	Cecil Fielder	15.00
60	Hideki Irabu	15.00
61	Andruw Jones (900)	90.00
62	Frank Thomas (400)	300.00
63	Andres Galarraga	40.00
64	Rusty Greer	15.00
65	Michael Tucker	15.00
66	Moises Alou	25.00
67	Jim Edmonds	15.00
68	Rondell White	25.00
69	Javier Lopez	25.00

70	Kevin Appler	15.00
71	David Cone	25.00
72	Garret Anderson	15.00
73	Marquis Grissom	20.00
74	Tino Martinez	40.00
75	Eric Young	15.00
76	Sandy Alomar Jr.	25.00
77	Carlos Delgado	25.00
78	Will Clark	25.00
79	Al Martin	15.00
80	Ron Coomer	15.00
81	Jeff Fassero	15.00
82	Alex Fernandez	15.00
83	Dean Palmer	15.00
84	Marty Cordova	15.00
85	Edgar Renteria	25.00
86	Geronimo Berroa	15.00
87	Rick Gorecki	15.00
88	Pedro J. Martinez	50.00
89	John Olerud	25.00
90	Jason Giambi	15.00
91	Mike Sweeney	15.00
92	Jimmy Key	15.00
93	Johnny Damon	15.00
94	Dan Wilson	15.00
95	Ellis Burks	25.00
96	Eric Karros	15.00
97	Henry Rodriguez	15.00
98	Vinny Castilla	25.00
99	Todd Hundley	15.00
100	Ray Lankford	25.00
101	Eric Davis	20.00
102	Mark Grudzielanek	15.00
103	Robin Ventura	25.00
104	John Wetteland	15.00
105	Paul O'Neill	30.00
106	Julio Franco	15.00
107	Reggie Sanders	15.00
108	Lance Johnson	15.00
109	Kevin Wickander	15.00
110	Dwight Smith	15.00
111	Carlos Baerga	15.00
112	Bip Roberts	15.00
113	Jeff Blauser	15.00
114	Jeffrey Hammonds	15.00
115	Darren Daulton	15.00
116	Russ Davis	15.00
117	J.T. Snow	25.00
118	F.P. Santangelo	15.00
119	Brett Butler	15.00
120	Jack McDowell	20.00
121	Curt Schilling	25.00
122	Andy Ashby	15.00
123	Rafael Medina	15.00
124	Steve Finley	15.00
125	Andy Benes	15.00
126	Denny Neagle	25.00
127	Dennis Eckersley	25.00
128	Shawn Estes	20.00
129	Edgardo Alfonzo	25.00
130	Todd Walker	20.00
131	Bobby Jones	15.00
132	Wilton Guerrero	15.00
133	Tony Clark	30.00
134	Dmitri Young	15.00
135	Nomar Garciaparra (650)	175.00
136	Bob Abreu	15.00
137	Scott Rolen	100.00
138	Billy Wagner	15.00
139	Jose Cruz Jr.	75.00
140	Scott Spiezio	15.00
141	Todd Hollandsworth	15.00
142	Kevin Orie	15.00
143	Derrek Lee	15.00
144	Jermaine Allensworth	15.00
145	Jose Rosado	15.00
146	Pokey Reese	15.00
147	Luis Castillo	15.00
148	Brooks Kieschnick	15.00
149	Jose Guillen	25.00
150	Joe Randa	15.00
151	Bubba Trammell	25.00
152	Bartolo Colon	15.00
153	Dennis Reyes	15.00
154	Karim Garcia	20.00
155	Derrick Gibson	15.00
156	Neifi Perez	20.00
157	Kevin Young	15.00
158	Todd Helton	35.00
159	Mike Cameron	15.00
160	Trey Beamon	15.00
161	Brian Giles	15.00
162	Darin Erstad	40.00
163	Lou Collier	15.00
164	Brett Tomko	15.00
165	Tony Womack	20.00
166	Justin Thompson	20.00
167	Chan Ho Park	20.00
168	Alan Benes	15.00
169	Jeff Suppan	15.00
170	Shannon Stewart	15.00
171	Jason Dickson	15.00
172	Matt Morris	20.00
173	Jay Payton	25.00
174	Jeff Abbott	15.00
175	Brant Brown	15.00
176	Javier Valentin	15.00
177	Chris Widger	15.00
178	Antone Williamson	15.00
179	Jason Kendall	15.00
180	Todd Greene	15.00
181	Raul Casanova	15.00
182	Mark Kotsay	35.00
183	Todd Dunwoody	15.00
184	Francisco Cordova	15.00
185	Paul Konerko	50.00
186	Bobby Estalella	25.00
187	Esteban Loaiza	15.00
188	Shawn Green	15.00
189	Ryan McGuire	15.00
190	Jaret Wright	65.00
191	Wally Joyner	15.00
192	Jermaine Dye	15.00
193	Terrell Wade	15.00
194	Giovanni Carrara	15.00
195	Kirk Rueter	15.00
196	Jacob Cruz	15.00
197	Kevin L. Brown	15.00
198	Trenidad Hubbard	15.00
199	Eric Chavez	30.00
200	Jeremi Gonzalez	15.00

1997 Donruss Signature Notable Nicknames

		MT
Complete Set (13):		1600.
Common Player:		50.00
1	Frank Thomas	400.00
2	Mo Vaughn	200.00
3	Fred McGriff	100.00
4	Ivan Rodriguez	150.00
5	Sammy Sosa	250.00
6	Roger Clemens	250.00
7	Billy Wagner	50.00
8	Deion Sanders	60.00
9	Tony Clark	100.00
10	Reggie Jackson	125.00
11	Ernie Banks	200.00
12	Stan Musial	250.00
13	Randy Johnson	150.00

Modern cards have little collector value in conditions lower than Mint. Figure NM cards at 75% of values shown; EX cards at 40%.

1997 Donruss Signature Significant Signatures

		MT
Complete Set (22):		
Common Player:		25.00
1	George Brett	60.00
2	Mike Schmidt	50.00
3	Carl Yastrzemski	50.00
4	Johnny Bench	60.00
5	Don Mattingly	75.00
6	Rod Carew	40.00
7	Steve Carlton	30.00
8	Carlton Fisk	35.00
9	Stan Musial	75.00
10	Jim Palmer	35.00
11	Tom Seaver	60.00
12	Ernie Banks	50.00
13	Larry Doby	45.00
14	Harmon Killebrew	35.00
15	Al Kaline	40.00
16	Brooks Robinson	40.00
17	Frank Robinson	40.00
18	Lou Brock	35.00
19	Yogi Berra	50.00
20	Bob Gibson	40.00
21	Reggie Jackson	50.00
22	Duke Snider	50.00

1997 Donruss Team Sets

A total of 165 cards were part of the Donruss Team Set issue. Packs consisted solely of players from one of 11 different teams. In addition, a full 150-card parallel set called Pennant Edition was available, featuring red and gold foil and a special "Pennant Edition" logo. Cards were sold in five-card packs for $1.99 each.

	MT
Comp. Angels Set (1-15): team issued	2.50
Comp. Braves Set (16-30):	6.00
Comp. Orioles Set (31-45):	3.50

A player's name in *italic* type indicates a rookie card.

Comp. Red Sox Set (46-60):	3.00	
Comp. White Sox Set (61-75):	4.00	
Comp. Indians Set (76-90): team issued 3.00		
Comp. Rockies Set (91-105):	2.50	
Comp. Dodgers Set (106-120):	3.50	
Comp. Yankees Set (121-135):	5.00	
Comp. Mariners Set (136-150):	10.00	
Common Player:	.10	
Pennant Edition Stars: 10x to 15x		
Pennant Edit. Yng Stars & RC: 5x to 10x		
1	Jim Edmonds	.15
2	Tim Salmon	.25
3	Tony Phillips	.10
4	Garret Anderson	.10
5	Troy Percival	.10
6	Mark Langston	.10
7	Chuck Finley	.10
8	Eddie Murray	.40
9	Jim Leyritz	.10
10	Darin Erstad	1.00
11	Jason Dickson	.10
12	Allen Watson	.10
13	Shigetosi Hasegawa	.10
14	Dave Hollins	.10
15	Gary DiSarcina	.10
16	Greg Maddux	2.00
17	Denny Neagle	.15
18	Chipper Jones	2.00
19	Tom Glavine	.20
20	John Smoltz	.20
21	Ryan Klesko	.40
22	Fred McGriff	.30
23	Michael Tucker	.10
24	Kenny Lofton	.75
25	Javier Lopez	.20
26	Mark Wohlers	.10
27	Jeff Blauser	.10
28	Andruw Jones	1.50
29	Tony Graffanino	.10
30	Terrell Wade	.10
31	Brady Anderson	.15
32	Roberto Alomar	.60
33	Rafael Palmeiro	.20
34	Mike Mussina	.60
35	Cal Ripken Jr.	2.50
36	Rocky Coppinger	.10
37	Randy Myers	.10
38	B.J. Surhoff	.10
39	Eric Davis	.10
40	Armando Benitez	.10
41	Jeffrey Hammonds	.10
42	Jimmy Key	.10
43	Chris Hoiles	.10
44	Mike Bordick	.10
45	Pete Incaviglia	.10
46	Mike Stanley	.10
47	Reggie Jefferson	.10
48	Mo Vaughn	.75
49	John Valentin	.10
50	Tim Naehring	.10
51	Jeff Suppan	.10
52	Tim Wakefield	.10
53	Jeff Frye	.10
54	Darren Bragg	.10
55	Steve Avery	.10
56	Shane Mack	.10
57	Aaron Sele	.10
58	Troy O'Leary	.10
59	Rudy Pemberton	.10
60	Nomar Garciaparra	2.00
61	Robin Ventura	.10
62	Wilson Alvarez	.10
63	Roberto Hernandez	.10
64	Frank Thomas	3.00
65	Ray Durham	.10
66	James Baldwin	.10
67	Harold Baines	.10
68	Doug Drabek	.10
69	Mike Cameron	.10
70	Albert Belle	.75
71	Jaime Navarro	.10
72	Chris Snopek	.10
73	Lyle Mouton	.10
74	Dave Martinez	.10
75	Ozzie Guillen	.10
76	Manny Ramirez	.75
77	Jack McDowell	.10
78	Jim Thome	.50
79	Jose Mesa	.10
80	Brian Giles	.10
81	Omar Vizquel	.10
82	Charles Nagy	.10
83	Orel Hershiser	.10
84	Matt Williams	.25
85	Marquis Grissom	.15
86	David Justice	.20
87	Sandy Alomar	.10
88	Kevin Seitzer	.10
89	Julio Franco	.10
90	Bartolo Colon	.10
91	Andres Galarraga	.20
92	Larry Walker	.30
93	Vinny Castilla	.10
94	Dante Bichette	.20
95	Jamey Wright	.10
96	Ellis Burks	.10
97	Eric Young	.10
98	Neifi Perez	.10
99	Quinton McCracken	.10
100	Bruce Ruffin	.10
101	Walt Weiss	.10
102	Roger Bailey	.10
103	Jeff Reed	.10
104	Bill Swift	.10
105	Kirt Manwaring	.10
106	Raul Mondesi	.20
107	Hideo Nomo	.60
108	Roger Cedeno	.10
109	Ismael Valdes	.10
110	Todd Hollandsworth	.10
111	Mike Piazza	2.00
112	Brett Butler	.10
113	Chan Ho Park	.10
114	Ramon Martinez	.10
115	Eric Karros	.10
116	Wilton Guerrero	.10
117	Todd Zeile	.10
118	Karim Garcia	.20
119	Greg Gagne	.10
120	Darren Dreifort	.10
121	Wade Boggs	.25
122	Paul O'Neill	.20
123	Derek Jeter	2.00
124	Tino Martinez	.25
125	David Cone	.20
126	Andy Pettitte	.75
127	Charlie Hayes	.10
128	Mariano Rivera	.20
129	Dwight Gooden	.20
130	Cecil Fielder	.20
131	Not Issued	.10
132	Darryl Strawberry	.15
133	Joe Girardi	.10
134	David Wells	.10
135	Hideki Irabu	1.50
136	Ken Griffey Jr.	3.00
137	Alex Rodriguez	2.50
138	Jay Buhner	.20
139	Randy Johnson	.50
140	Paul Sorrento	.10
141	Edgar Martinez	.10
142	Joey Cora	.10
143	Bob Wells	.10
144	Not Issued	.10
145	Jamie Moyer	.10
146	Jeff Fassero	.10
147	Dan Wilson	.10
148	Jose Cruz, Jr.	2.00
149	Scott Sanders	.10
150	Rich Amaral	.10
151	Brian Jordan	.10
152	Andy Benes	.10
153	Ray Lankford	.10
154	John Mabry	.10
155	Tom Pagnozzi	.10
156	Ron Gant	.10
157	Alan Benes	.10
158	Dennis Eckersley	.10
159	Royce Clayton	.10
160	Todd Stottlemyre	.10
161	Gary Gaetti	.10
162	Willie McGee	.10
163	Delino DeShields	.10
164	Dmitri Young	.10
165	Matt Morris	.10

1997 Donruss Update Cal Ripken

This 10-card set salutes Cal Ripken Jr. and is printed on an all-foil stock with foil stamping. Photos and text are taken from Ripken's autobiography, "The Only Way I Know." The first nine cards of the set were randomly inserted into packs. The 10th card was only available inside the book. Each card found within packs was numbered to 5,000.

		MT
Complete Set (10):		120.00
Common Card:		15.00
1-9	Cal Ripken Jr.	15.00
10	Cal Ripken Jr. (book insert)	24.00

1997 Donruss Team Sets MVP

The top players at each position were available in this 18-card insert set. Each card is sequentially numbered to 1,000.

		MT
Complete Set (18):		500.00
Common Player:		4.00
1	Ivan Rodriguez	15.00
2	Mike Piazza	45.00
3	Frank Thomas	75.00
4	Jeff Bagwell	35.00
5	Chuck Knoblauch	6.00
6	Eric Young	4.00
7	Alex Rodriguez	60.00
8	Barry Larkin	4.00
9	Cal Ripken Jr.	60.00
10	Chipper Jones	45.00
11	Albert Belle	15.00
12	Barry Bonds	15.00
13	Ken Griffey Jr.	75.00
14	Kenny Lofton	15.00
15	Juan Gonzalez	40.00
16	Larry Walker	4.00
17	Roger Clemens	25.00
18	Greg Maddux	45.00

1997 Donruss Update Dominators

This 20-card insert highlights players known for being able to "take over a game." Each card features silver-foil highlights on front and stats on back.

		MT
Complete Set (20):		80.00
Common Player:		2.00
1	Frank Thomas	10.00
2	Ken Griffey Jr.	15.00
3	Greg Maddux	9.00
4	Cal Ripken Jr.	12.00
5	Alex Rodriguez	12.00
6	Albert Belle	4.00
7	Mark McGwire	15.00
8	Juan Gonzalez	7.00
9	Chipper Jones	9.00
10	Hideo Nomo	3.00
11	Roger Clemens	4.00
12	John Smoltz	2.00
13	Mike Piazza	9.00
14	Sammy Sosa	10.00
15	Matt Williams	2.50
16	Kenny Lofton	4.00
17	Barry Larkin	2.00
18	Rafael Palmeiro	2.00
19	Ken Caminiti	2.00
20	Gary Sheffield	2.00

1997 Donruss Update Franchise Features

This hobby-exclusive insert consists of 15 cards designed with a movie poster theme. The double-front design highlights a top veteran player on one side with an up-and-coming rookie on the other. The side featuring the veteran has the designation "Now Playing," while the rookie side carries the banner "Coming Attraction." Each card is printed on an all-foil stock and numbered to 3,000.

		MT
Complete Set (15):		350.00
Common Player:		10.00
1	Ken Griffey Jr., Andruw Jones	50.00
2	Frank Thomas, Darin Erstad	40.00
3	Alex Rodriguez, Nomar Garciaparra	40.00
4	Chuck Knoblauch, Wilton Guerrero	10.00
5	Juan Gonzalez, Jose Cruz Jr.	25.00
6	Chipper Jones, Todd Walker	30.00
7	Barry Bonds, Vladimir Guerrero	15.00
8	Mark McGwire, Dmitri Young	50.00
9	Mike Piazza, Mike Sweeney	30.00
10	Mo Vaughn, Tony Clark	15.00
11	Gary Sheffield, Jose Guillen	5.00
12	Kenny Lofton, Shannon Stewart	15.00

13	Cal Ripken Jr., Scott Rolen	40.00
14	Derek Jeter, Pokey Reese	30.00
15	Tony Gwynn, Bob Abreu	30.00

1997 Donruss Update Power Alley

This 24-card insert is fractured into three different styles: Gold, Blue and Green. Each card is micro-etched and printed on holographic foil board. All cards are sequentially numbered, with the first 250 cards in each level being die-cut. Twelve players' cards feature a green finish and are numbered to 4,000. Eight players are printed on blue cards that are numbered to 2,000. Four players are found on gold cards numbered to 1,000.

		MT
Complete Set (24):		600.00
Common Gold (1-4):		20.00
Common Blue (5-12):		10.00
Common Green (13-24):		5.00
1	Frank Thomas	60.00
2	Ken Griffey Jr.	100.00
3	Cal Ripken Jr.	80.00
4	Jeff Bagwell	30.00
5	Mike Piazza	40.00
6	Andruw Jones	30.00
7	Alex Rodriguez	60.00
8	Albert Belle	10.00
9	Mo Vaughn	10.00
10	Chipper Jones	30.00
11	Juan Gonzalez	30.00
12	Ken Caminiti	10.00
13	Manny Ramirez	10.00
14	Mark McGwire	30.00
15	Kenny Lofton	10.00
16	Barry Bonds	10.00
17	Gary Sheffield	7.50
18	Tony Gwynn	18.00
19	Vladimir Guerrero	15.00
20	Ivan Rodriguez	8.00
21	Paul Molitor	6.00
22	Sammy Sosa	30.00
23	Matt Williams	5.00
24	Derek Jeter	25.00

1997 Donruss Update Press Proofs

This 180-card parallel set is printed on an all-foil stock with foil stamped accents. Each card is numbered "1 of 2,000". Special die-cut gold versions are numbered as "1 of 500".

		MT
Complete Set (180):		650.00
Common Player:		2.00
Stars: 25-35X base card		
Complete Set, Gold (180):		2500.
Common Player, Gold:		7.50
Gold Stars: 4-6X regular press proof		
(See 1997 Donruss Series 2 (#271-450) for checklist, base card values.)		

1997 Donruss Update Rookie Diamond Kings

This popular Donruss insert set features a new twist - all 10 cards feature a promising rookies. Each card is sequentially numbered to 10,000, with the first 500 cards of each player printed on actual canvas.

		MT
Complete Set (10):		75.00
Common Player:		4.00
1	Andruw Jones	15.00
2	Vladimir Guerrero	12.00
3	Scott Rolen	15.00
4	Todd Walker	6.00
5	Bartolo Colon	4.00
6	Jose Guillen	7.00
7	Nomar Garciaparra	20.00
8	Darin Erstad	12.00
9	Dmitri Young	4.00
10	Wilton Guerrero	5.00

1998 Donruss

This 170-card set includes 155 regular player cards, the 10-card Fan Club subset and five checklists. The cards have color photos and the player's name listed at the bottom. The backs have a horizontal layout with stats and a biography on the left and another photo on the right. The base set is paralleled twice. Silver Press Proofs is a silver foil and die-cut parallel numbered "1 of 1,500." Gold Press Proofs is die-cut, has gold foil and is numbered "1 of 500." The inserts are Crusade, Diamond Kings, Longball Leaders, Production Line and Rated Rookies.

		MT
Complete Set (420):		45.00
Complete Series I Set (170):		20.00
Complete Update II Set (250):		25.00
Common Player:		.10
Silver Press Proofs: 6x to 12x		
Production 1,500 sets		
Gold Press Proof Stars: 20x to 40x		
Gold Yng Stars & RC's: 12x to 25x		
Production 500 sets		
Wax Box:		45.00
1	Paul Molitor	.50
2	Juan Gonzalez	1.50
3	Darryl Kile	.10
4	Randy Johnson	.40
5	Tom Glavine	.20
6	Pat Hentgen	.10
7	David Justice	.25
8	Kevin Brown	.10
9	Mike Mussina	.60
10	Ken Caminiti	.20
11	Todd Hundley	.20
12	Frank Thomas	2.50
13	Ray Lankford	.10
14	Justin Thompson	.10
15	Jason Dickson	.10
16	Kenny Lofton	.75
17	Ivan Rodriguez	.60
18	Pedro Martinez	.25
19	Brady Anderson	.20
20	Barry Larkin	.20
21	Chipper Jones	2.00
22	Tony Gwynn	1.50
23	Roger Clemens	1.00
24	Sandy Alomar Jr.	.10
25	Tino Martinez	.20
26	Jeff Bagwell	1.25
27	Shawn Estes	.10
28	Ken Griffey Jr.	3.00
29	Javier Lopez	.20
30	Denny Neagle	.10
31	Mike Piazza	2.00
32	Andres Galarraga	.20
33	Larry Walker	.25
34	Alex Rodriguez	2.50
35	Greg Maddux	2.00
36	Albert Belle	.75
37	Barry Bonds	.75
38	Mo Vaughn	.75
39	Kevin Appier	.10
40	Wade Boggs	.25
41	Garret Anderson	.10
42	Jeffrey Hammonds	.10
43	Marquis Grissom	.10
44	Jim Edmonds	.10
45	Brian Jordan	.10
46	Raul Mondesi	.20
47	John Valentin	.10
48	Brad Radke	.10
49	Ismael Valdes	.10
50	Matt Stairs	.10
51	Matt Williams	.20
52	Reggie Jefferson	.10
53	Alan Benes	.10
54	Charles Johnson	.10
55	Chuck Knoblauch	.25
56	Edgar Martinez	.10
57	Nomar Garciaparra	2.00
58	Craig Biggio	.20
59	Bernie Williams	.50
60	David Cone	.20
61	Cal Ripken Jr.	2.50
62	Mark McGwire	4.00
63	Roberto Alomar	.50
64	Fred McGriff	.20
65	Eric Karros	.10
66	Robin Ventura	.10
67	Darin Erstad	.75
68	Michael Tucker	.10
69	Jim Thome	.40
70	Mark Grace	.25
71	Lou Collier	.10
72	Karim Garcia	.20
73	Alex Fernandez	.10
74	J.T. Snow	.10
75	Reggie Sanders	.10
76	John Smoltz	.25
77	Tim Salmon	.25
78	Paul O'Neill	.20
79	Vinny Castilla	.10
80	Rafael Palmeiro	.20
81	Jaret Wright	1.00
82	Jay Buhner	.20
83	Brett Butler	.10
84	Todd Greene	.10
85	Scott Rolen	1.50
86	Sammy Sosa	1.50
87	Jason Giambi	.10
88	Carlos Delgado	.10
89	Deion Sanders	.25
90	Wilton Guerrero	.10
91	Andy Pettitte	.50
92	Brian Giles	.10
93	Dmitri Young	.10
94	Ron Coomer	.10
95	Mike Cameron	.10
96	Edgardo Alfonzo	.10
97	Jimmy Key	.10
98	Ryan Klesko	.25
99	Andy Benes	.10
100	Derek Jeter	2.00
101	Jeff Fassero	.10
102	Neifi Perez	.10
103	Hideo Nomo	.60
104	Andruw Jones	1.50
105	Todd Helton	.75
106	Livan Hernandez	.20
107	Brett Tomko	.10
108	Shannon Stewart	.10
109	Bartolo Colon	.10
110	Matt Morris	.10
111	Miguel Tejada	.50
112	Pokey Reese	.10
113	Fernando Tatis	.25
114	Todd Dunwoody	.10
115	Jose Cruz Jr.	1.50
116	Chan Ho Park	.10
117	Kevin Young	.10
118	Rickey Henderson	.10
119	Hideki Irabu	.75
120	Francisco Cordova	.10
121	Al Martin	.10
122	Tony Clark	.30
123	Curt Schilling	.10
124	Rusty Greer	.10
125	Jose Canseco	.25
126	Edgar Renteria	.10
127	Todd Walker	.20
128	Wally Joyner	.10
129	Bill Mueller	.10
130	Jose Guillen	.40
131	Manny Ramirez	.50
132	Bobby Higginson	.10
133	Kevin Orie	.10
134	Will Clark	.20
135	Dave Nilsson	.10
136	Jason Kendall	.10
137	Ivan Cruz	.10
138	Gary Sheffield	.25
139	Bubba Trammell	.20
140	Vladimir Guerrero	1.00
141	Dennis Reyes	.25
142	Bobby Bonilla	.20
143	Ruben Rivera	.10
144	Ben Grieve	1.00
145	Moises Alou	.20
146	Tony Womack	.10
147	Eric Young	.10
148	Paul Konerko	1.00
149	Dante Bichette	.20
150	Joe Carter	.15
151	Rondell White	.20
152	Chris Holt	.10
153	Shawn Green	.10
154	Mark Grudzielanek	.10
155	Jermaine Dye	.10
156	Ken Griffey Jr. (Fan Club)	1.50
157	Frank Thomas (Fan Club)	1.25
158	Chipper Jones (Fan Club)	1.00
159	Mike Piazza (Fan Club)	1.00
160	Cal Ripken Jr. (Fan Club)	1.25
161	Greg Maddux (Fan Club)	1.00
162	Juan Gonzalez (Fan Club)	.75
163	Alex Rodriguez (Fan Club)	1.25
164	Mark McGwire (Fan Club)	1.50
165	Derek Jeter (Fan Club)	1.00
166	Larry Walker CL	.20
167	Tony Gwynn CL	.75
168	Tino Martinez CL	.15
169	Scott Rolen CL	.75
170	Nomar Garciaparra CL	1.00
171	Mike Sweeney	.10
172	Dustin Hermanson	.10
173	Darren Dreifort	.10
174	Ron Gant	.20
175	Todd Hollandsworth	.10
176	John Jaha	.10
177	Kerry Wood	4.00
178	Chris Stynes	.10
179	Kevin Elster	.10
180	Derek Bell	.10
181	Darryl Strawberry	.20
182	Damion Easley	.10
183	Jeff Cirillo	.10
184	John Thomson	.10
185	Dan Wilson	.10
186	Jay Bell	.10
187	Bernard Gilkey	.10
188	Marc Valdes	.10
189	Ramon Martinez	.20
190	Charles Nagy	.10
191	Derek Lowe	.10
192	Andy Benes	.10
193	Delino DeShields	.10
194	*Ryan Jackson*	.40
195	Kenny Lofton	.75
196	Chuck Knoblauch	.25
197	Andres Galarraga	.30
198	Jose Canseco	.25
199	John Olerud	.20
200	Lance Johnson	.10
201	Darryl Kile	.10
202	Luis Castillo	.10
203	Joe Carter	.20
204	Dennis Eckersley	.20
205	Steve Finley	.10
206	Esteban Loaiza	.10
207	*Ryan Christenson*	.25
208	Deivi Cruz	.10
209	Mariano Rivera	.10
210	*Mike Judd*	.20
211	Billy Wagner	.10
212	Scott Spiezio	.10
213	Russ Davis	.10
214	Jeff Suppan	.10
215	Doug Glanville	.10
216	Dmitri Young	.10
217	Rey Ordonez	.10
218	Cecil Fielder	.20
219	*Masato Yoshii*	.50
220	Raul Casanova	.10
221	*Rolando Arrojo*	.40
222	Ellis Burks	.10
223	Butch Huskey	.10
224	Brian Hunter	.10
225	Marquis Grissom	.10
226	Kevin Brown	.10
227	Joe Randa	.10

228	Henry Rodriguez	.10
229	Omar Vizquel	.10
230	Fred McGriff	.25
231	Matt Williams	.25
232	Moises Alou	.20
233	Travis Fryman	.20
234	Wade Boggs	.25
235	Pedro Martinez	.40
236	Rickey Henderson	.20
237	Bubba Trammell	.10
238	Mike Caruso	.20
239	Wilson Alvarez	.10
240	Geronimo Berroa	.10
241	Eric Milton	.10
242	Scott Erickson	.10
243	*Todd Erdos*	.20
244	Bobby Hughes	.10
245	Dave Hollins	.10
246	Dean Palmer	.10
247	Carlos Baerga	.10
248	Jose Silva	.10
249	*Jose Cabrera*	.20
250	Tom Evans	.10
251	Marty Cordova	.10
252	*Hanley Frias*	.20
253	Javier Valentin	.10
254	Mario Valdez	.10
255	Joey Cora	.10
256	Mike Lansing	.10
257	Jeff Kent	.10
258	*David Dellucci*	.50
259	*Curtis King*	.10
260	David Segui	.10
261	Royce Clayton	.10
262	Jeff Blauser	.10
263	*Manny Aybar*	.20
264	*Mike Cather*	.20
265	Todd Zeile	.10
266	Richard Hidalgo	.10
267	Dante Powell	.10
268	*Mike DeJean*	.10
269	Ken Cloude	.10
270	Danny Klassen	.20
271	Sean Casey	.25
272	A.J. Hinch	.50
273	*Rich Butler*	.50
274	*Ben Ford*	.10
275	Billy McMillon	.10
276	Wilson Delgado	.10
277	Orlando Cabrera	.10
278	Geoff Jenkins	.10
279	Enrique Wilson	.10
280	Derrek Lee	.10
281	*Marc Pisciotta*	.10
282	Abraham Nunez	.20
283	Aaron Boone	.10
284	Brad Fullmer	.20
285	*Rob Stanifer*	.25
286	Preston Wilson	.10
287	Greg Norton	.10
288	Bobby Smith	.10
289	Josh Booty	.10
290	Russell Branyan	.10
291	Jeremi Gonzalez	.10
292	Michael Coleman	.10
293	Cliff Politte	.10
294	Eric Ludwick	.10
295	Rafael Medina	.10
296	Jason Varitek	.10
297	Ron Wright	.10
298	Mark Kotsay	.25
299	David Ortiz	.25
300	*Frank Catalanotto*	.20
301	Robinson Checo	.10
302	*Kevin Millwood*	1.00
303	Jacob Cruz	.10
304	Javier Vazquez	.10
305	*Magglio Ordonez*	.75
306	Kevin Witt	.10
307	Derrick Gibson	.10
308	Shane Monahan	.10
309	Brian Rose	.10
310	Bobby Estalella	.10
311	Felix Heredia	.10
312	Desi Relaford	.10
313	*Esteban Yan*	.20
314	Ricky Ledee	.10
315	*Steve Woodard*	.25
316	Pat Watkins	.10
317	Damian Moss	.10
318	Bob Abreu	.10
319	Jeff Abbott	.10
320	Miguel Cairo	.10
321	*Rigo Beltran*	.10
322	Tony Saunders	.10
323	Randall Simon	.25

324	Hiram Bocachica	.10
325	Richie Sexson	.10
326	Karim Garcia	.10
327	*Mike Lowell*	.40
328	Pat Cline	.10
329	Matt Clement	.10
330	Scott Elarton	.10
331	*Manuel Barrios*	.10
332	Bruce Chen	.20
333	Juan Encarnacion	.10
334	Travis Lee	2.00
335	Wes Helms	.10
336	*Chad Fox*	.10
337	Donnie Sadler	.10
338	*Carlos Mendoza*	.25
339	Damian Jackson	.10
340	*Julio Ramirez*	.50
341	*John Halama*	.30
342	Edwin Diaz	.10
343	Felix Martinez	.10
344	Eli Marrero	.10
345	Carl Pavano	.10
346	Vladimir Guerrero (Hit List)	.40
347	Barry Bonds (Hit List)	.40
348	Darin Erstad (Hit List)	.40
349	Albert Belle (Hit List)	.40
350	Kenny Lofton (Hit List)	.40
351	Mo Vaughn (Hit List)	.40
352	Jose Cruz Jr. (Hit List)	.30
353	Tony Clark (Hit List)	.25
354	Roberto Alomar (Hit List)	.25
355	Manny Ramirez (Hit List)	.40
356	Paul Molitor (Hit List)	.25
357	Jim Thome (Hit List)	.25
358	Tino Martinez (Hit List)	.20
359	Tim Salmon (Hit List)	.20
360	David Justice (Hit List)	.20
361	Raul Mondesi (Hit List)	.10
362	Mark Grace (Hit List)	.10
363	Craig Biggio (Hit List)	.10
364	Larry Walker (Hit List)	.10
365	Mark McGwire (Hit List)	1.50
366	Juan Gonzalez (Hit List)	.75
367	Derek Jeter (Hit List)	.75
368	Chipper Jones (Hit List)	1.00
369	Frank Thomas (Hit List)	1.00
370	Alex Rodriguez (Hit List)	1.00
371	Mike Piazza (Hit List)	1.00
372	Tony Gwynn (Hit List)	.75
373	Jeff Bagwell (Hit List)	.50
374	Nomar Garciaparra (Hit List)	1.00
375	Ken Griffey Jr. (Hit List)	1.50
376	Livan Hernandez (Untouchables)	.10
377	Chan Ho Park (Untouchables)	.10
378	Mike Mussina (Untouchables)	.25
379	Andy Pettitte (Untouchables)	.25
380	Greg Maddux (Untouchables)	1.00
381	Hideo Nomo (Untouchables)	.25
382	Roger Clemens (Untouchables)	.50
383	Randy Johnson (Untouchables)	.25
384	Pedro Martinez (Untouchables)	.25
385	Jaret Wright (Untouchables)	.40
386	Ken Griffey Jr. (Spirit of the Game)	1.50
387	Todd Helton (Spirit of the Game)	.40
388	Paul Konerko (Spirit of the Game)	.10
389	Cal Ripken Jr. (Spirit of the Game)	1.25
390	Larry Walker (Spirit of the Game)	.10
391	Ken Caminiti (Spirit of the Game)	.10
392	Jose Guillen (Spirit of the Game)	.10
393	Jim Edmonds (Spirit of the Game)	.10
394	Barry Larkin (Spirit of the Game)	.10
395	Bernie Williams (Spirit of the Game)	.25
396	Tony Clark (Spirit of the Game)	.20
397	Jose Cruz Jr. (Spirit of the Game)	.30

398	Ivan Rodriguez (Spirit of the Game)	.40
399	Darin Erstad (Spirit of the Game)	.40
400	Scott Rolen (Spirit of the Game)	.50
401	Mark McGwire (Spirit of the Game)	1.50
402	Andruw Jones (Spirit of the Game)	.40
403	Juan Gonzalez (Spirit of the Game)	.75
404	Derek Jeter (Spirit of the Game)	.75
405	Chipper Jones (Spirit of the Game)	1.00
406	Greg Maddux (Spirit of the Game)	1.00
407	Frank Thomas (Spirit of the Game)	1.00
408	Alex Rodriguez (Spirit of the Game)	1.00
409	Mike Piazza (Spirit of the Game)	1.00
410	Tony Gwynn (Spirit of the Game)	.75
411	Jeff Bagwell (Spirit of the Game)	.50
412	Nomar Garciaparra (Spirit of the Game)	1.00
413	Hideo Nomo (Spirit of the Game)	.25
414	Barry Bonds (Spirit of the Game)	.40
415	Ben Grieve (Spirit of the Game)	.50
416	Checklist(Barry Bonds)	.25
417	Checklist(Mark McGwire)	1.00
418	Checklist(Roger Clemens)	.40
419	Checklist(Livan Hernandez)	.10
420	Checklist(Ken Griffey Jr.)	1.00

1998 Donruss Crusade Green

This 100-card insert was included in 1998 Donruss (40 cards), Leaf (30) and Donruss Update (30). The cards use refractive technology and the background features Crusades era dragons. The cards are sequentially numbered to 250. Crusade Purple (numbered to 100) and Red (25) parallels were also inserted in the three products.

	MT
Complete Set (40):	
Common Player:	10.00
Production 250 sets	
Purples: 1.5x	
Production 100 sets	
Reds: 4x to 6x	
Production 25 sets	
5 Jason Dickson	10.00
6 Todd Greene	20.00

7	Roberto Alomar	30.00
8	Cal Ripken Jr.	150.00
12	Mo Vaughn	50.00
13	Nomar Garciaparra	120.00
16	Mike Cameron	20.00
20	Sandy Alomar Jr.	20.00
21	David Justice	25.00
25	Justin Thompson	10.00
27	Kevin Appier	10.00
33	Tino Martinez	30.00
36	Hideki Irabu	20.00
37	Jose Canseco	25.00
39	Ken Griffey Jr.	200.00
42	Edgar Martinez	20.00
45	Will Clark	25.00
47	Rusty Greer	20.00
50	Shawn Green	10.00
51	Jose Cruz Jr.	50.00
52	Kenny Lofton	40.00
53	Chipper Jones	120.00
62	Kevin Orie	10.00
65	Deion Sanders	20.00
67	Larry Walker	30.00
68	Dante Bichette	20.00
71	Todd Helton	50.00
74	Bobby Bonilla	15.00
75	Kevin Brown	20.00
78	Craig Biggio	20.00
82	Wilton Guerrero	10.00
85	Pedro J. Martinez	40.00
86	Edgardo Alfonzo	15.00
88	Scott Rolen	75.00
89	Francisco Cordova	10.00
90	Jose Guillen	20.00
92	Ray Lankford	20.00
93	Mark McGwire	250.00
94	Matt Morris	15.00
100	Shawn Estes	15.00

1998 Donruss Diamond Kings

Diamond Kings is a 20-card insert featuring a color portrait of the player on the card front. The backs have a ghosted image of the portrait with a player biography and the card's number printed over it. A total of 10,000 sets were produced with the first 500 of each card printed on canvas. A Frank Thomas sample card was also created.

		MT
Complete Set (20):		150.00
Common Player:		4.00
Production 9,500 sets		
Canvas (1st 500 sets): 2x to 4x		
1	Cal Ripken Jr.	20.00
2	Greg Maddux	15.00
3	Ivan Rodriguez	6.00
4	Tony Gwynn	12.00
5	Paul Molitor	4.00
6	Kenny Lofton	6.00
7	Andy Pettitte	5.00
8	Darin Erstad	8.00
9	Randy Johnson	4.00
10	Derek Jeter	15.00
11	Hideo Nomo	5.00
12	David Justice	4.00
13	Bernie Williams	5.00
14	Roger Clemens	8.00
15	Barry Larkin	4.00
16	Andruw Jones	12.00
17	Mike Piazza	15.00
18	Frank Thomas	20.00
19	Alex Rodriguez	20.00
20	Ken Griffey Jr.	25.00

1998 Donruss Longball Leaders

Longball Leaders features 24 top home run hitters. The right border features a home run meter with zero at the bottom, 61 at the top and the player's 1997 home run total marked. Each card is sequentially numbered to 5,000.

		MT
Complete Set (24):		260.00
Common Player:		6.00
Production 5,000 sets		
1	Ken Griffey Jr.	40.00
2	Mark McGwire	50.00
3	Tino Martinez	6.00
4	Barry Bonds	10.00
5	Frank Thomas	30.00
6	Albert Belle	10.00
7	Mike Piazza	25.00
8	Chipper Jones	25.00
9	Vladimir Guerrero	12.00
10	Matt Williams	6.00
11	Sammy Sosa	20.00
12	Tim Salmon	6.00
13	Raul Mondesi	6.00
14	Jeff Bagwell	15.00
15	Mo Vaughn	10.00
16	Manny Ramirez	8.00
17	Jim Thome	8.00
18	Jim Edmonds	6.00
19	Tony Clark	8.00
20	Nomar Garciaparra	25.00
21	Juan Gonzalez	20.00
22	Scott Rolen	20.00
23	Larry Walker	8.00
24	Andres Galarraga	6.00

1998 Donruss Production Line-ob

This 20-card insert was printed on holographic foil board. Inserted in magazine packs, this insert features player's with a high on-base percentage in 1997. Each player's card is sequentially numbered to his on-base percentage from that season. The card back has a player photo and a list of the 20 players with their stat.

		MT
Complete Set (20):		1000.
Common Player:		15.00
1	Frank Thomas (456)	150.00
2	Edgar Martinez (456)	15.00
3	Barry Bonds (446)	40.00
4	Barry Larkin (440)	20.00
5	Mike Piazza (431)	140.00
6	Jeff Bagwell (425)	80.00
7	Gary Sheffield (424)	25.00
8	Mo Vaughn (420)	40.00
9	Craig Biggio (415)	20.00
10	Kenny Lofton (409)	40.00
11	Tony Gwynn (409)	100.00
12	Bernie Williams (408)	30.00
13	Rusty Greer (405)	15.00
14	Brady Anderson (393)	15.00
15	Mark McGwire (393)	200.00
16	Chuck Knoblauch (390)	25.00
17	Roberto Alomar (390)	30.00
18	Ken Griffey Jr. (382)	220.00
19	Chipper Jones (371)	140.00
20	Derek Jeter (370)	125.00

1998 Donruss Production Line-PI

This 20-card insert was printed on holographic board. The set features players with a high power index from 1997. Each card is sequentially numbered to that player's power index from that season.

		MT
Complete Set (20):		600.00
Common Player:		10.00
1	Larry Walker (1,172)	15.00
2	Mike Piazza (1,070)	60.00
3	Frank Thomas (1,067)	80.00
4	Mark McGwire (1,039)	100.00
5	Barry Bonds (1,031)	25.00
6	Ken Griffey Jr. (1,028)	100.00
7	Jeff Bagwell (1,028)	40.00
8	David Justice (1,013)	10.00
9	Jim Thome (1,001)	20.00

10	Mo Vaughn (980)	25.00
11	Tony Gwynn (957)	50.00
12	Manny Ramirez (953)	20.00
13	Bernie Williams (952)	20.00
14	Tino Martinez (948)	10.00
15	Brady Anderson (863)	10.00
16	Chipper Jones (850)	60.00
17	Scott Rolen (846)	50.00
18	Alex Rodriguez (846)	70.00
19	Vladimir Guerrero (833)	25.00
20	Albert Belle (823)	25.00

1998 Donruss Production Line-sg

This 20-card insert was printed on holographic board. It featured players with high slugging percentages in 1997. Each card is sequentially numbered to the player's slugging percentage from that season.

		MT
Complete Set (20):		1000.
Common Player:		15.00
1	Larry Walker (720)	20.00
2	Ken Griffey Jr. (646)	150.00
3	Mark McGwire (646)	150.00
4	Mike Piazza (638)	90.00
5	Frank Thomas (611)	125.00
6	Jeff Bagwell (592)	60.00
7	Juan Gonzalez (589)	70.00
8	Andres Galarraga (585)	15.00
9	Barry Bonds (585)	40.00
10	Jim Thome (579)	25.00
11	Tino Martinez (577)	15.00
12	Mo Vaughn (560)	40.00
13	Raul Mondesi (541)	20.00
14	Manny Ramirez (538)	35.00
15	Nomar Garciaparra (534)	90.00
16	Tim Salmon (517)	20.00
17	Tony Clark (500)	25.00
18	Jose Cruz Jr. (499)	50.00
19	Alex Rodriguez (496)	100.00
20	Cal Ripken Jr. (402)	110.00

1998 Donruss Rated Rookies

This 30-card insert features top young players. The fronts have a color player photo in front of a stars and stripes background, with "Rated Rookies" and the player's name printed on the right. The backs have another photo, basic player information and career highlights.

		MT
Complete Set (30):		70.00
Common Player:		2.00
Medalists (250 sets): 8x to 15x		
1	Mark Kotsay	5.00
2	Neifi Perez	2.00
3	Paul Konerko	4.00
4	Jose Cruz Jr.	10.00
5	Hideki Irabu	3.00
6	Mike Cameron	2.00
7	Jeff Suppan	2.00
8	Kevin Orie	2.00
9	Pokey Reese	2.00
10	Todd Dunwoody	2.00
11	Miguel Tejada	4.00
12	Jose Guillen	3.00
13	Bartolo Colon	2.00
14	Derrek Lee	2.00
15	Antone Williamson	2.00
16	Wilton Guerrero	2.00
17	Jaret Wright	4.00
18	Todd Helton	4.00
19	Shannon Stewart	2.00
20	Nomar Garciaparra	10.00
21	Brett Tomko	2.00
22	Fernando Tatis	4.00
23	Raul Ibanez	2.00

24	Dennis Reyes	2.00
25	Bobby Estalella	2.00
26	Lou Collier	2.00
27	Bubba Trammell	2.00
28	Ben Grieve	5.00
29	Ivan Cruz	2.00
30	Karim Garcia	3.00

Grading Guide

Mint (MT): A perfect card. Well-centered with all corners sharp and square. No creases, stains, edge nicks, surface marks, yellowing or fading.
Near Mint (NM): A nearly perfect card. At first glance, a NM card appears to be perfect. May be slightly off-center. No surface marks, creases or loss of gloss.
Excellent (EX): Corners are still fairly sharp with only moderate wear. Borders may be off-center. No creases or stains on fronts or backs, but may show slight loss of surface luster.
Very Good (VG): Shows obvious handling. May have rounded corners, minor creases, major gum or wax stains. No major creases, tape marks, writing, etc.
Good (G): A well-worn card, but exhibits no intentional damage. May have major or multiple creases. Corners may be rounded well beyond card border.

1998 Donruss Elite

Nomar Garciaparra - SS

Donruss Elite consists of a 150-card base set with two parallels and five inserts. The base cards feature a bordered player photo on the front and another photo on the back with stats and basic player information. The Aspirations parallel is numbered to 750 and the Status parallel is numbered to 100. The base set also includes the 30-card Generations subset and three checklists. The inserts are Back to the Future, Back to the Future Autographs, Craftsmen, Prime Numbers and Prime Numbers Die-Cuts.

		MT
Complete Set (150):		35.00
Common Player:		.15
Wax Box:		65.00
1	Ken Griffey Jr.	4.00
2	Frank Thomas	3.00
3	Alex Rodriguez	2.50
4	Mike Piazza	2.50
5	Greg Maddux	2.50

6	Cal Ripken Jr.	3.00
7	Chipper Jones	2.50
8	Derek Jeter	2.50
9	Tony Gwynn	2.00
10	Andruw Jones	2.00
11	Juan Gonzalez	2.00
12	Jeff Bagwell	1.50
13	Mark McGwire	5.00
14	Roger Clemens	1.50
15	Albert Belle	1.00
16	Barry Bonds	1.00
17	Kenny Lofton	1.00
18	Ivan Rodriguez	.75
19	Manny Ramirez	.75
20	Jim Thome	.50
21	Chuck Knoblauch	.40
22	Paul Molitor	.60
23	Barry Larkin	.30
24	Andy Pettitte	.60
25	John Smoltz	.25
26	Randy Johnson	.50
27	Bernie Williams	.75
28	Larry Walker	.30
29	Mo Vaughn	1.00
30	Bobby Higginson	.15
31	Edgardo Alfonzo	.15
32	Justin Thompson	.15
33	Jeff Suppan	.15
34	Roberto Alomar	.75
35	Hideo Nomo	1.00
36	Rusty Greer	.15
37	Tim Salmon	.30
38	Jim Edmonds	.15
39	Gary Sheffield	.30
40	Ken Caminiti	.25
41	Sammy Sosa	2.00
42	Tony Womack	.15
43	Matt Williams	.30
44	Andres Galarraga	.30
45	Garret Anderson	.15
46	Rafael Palmeiro	.25
47	Mike Mussina	.75
48	Craig Biggio	.25
49	Wade Boggs	.30
50	Tom Glavine	.25
51	Jason Giambi	.15
52	Will Clark	.25
53	David Justice	.25
54	Sandy Alomar Jr.	.15
55	Edgar Martinez	.15
56	Brady Anderson	.25
57	Eric Young	.15
58	Ray Lankford	.15
59	Kevin Brown	.25
60	Raul Mondesi	.30
61	Bobby Bonilla	.20
62	Javier Lopez	.15
63	Fred McGriff	.25
64	Rondell White	.25
65	Todd Hundley	.25
66	Mark Grace	.30
67	Alan Benes	.25
68	Jeff Abbott	.15
69	Bob Abreu	.15
70	Deion Sanders	.30
71	Tino Martinez	.30
72	Shannon Stewart	.15
73	Homer Bush	.15
74	Carlos Delgado	.25
75	Raul Ibanez	.15
76	Hideki Irabu	1.00
77	Jose Cruz Jr.	1.50
78	Tony Clark	.60
79	Wilton Guerrero	.15
80	Vladimir Guerrero	1.25
81	Scott Rolen	2.00
82	Nomar Garciaparra	2.50
83	Darin Erstad	1.00
84	Chan Ho Park	.25
85	Mike Cameron	.15
86	Todd Walker	.25
87	Todd Dunwoody	.15
88	Neifi Perez	.15
89	Brett Tomko	.15
90	Jose Guillen	.40
91	Matt Morris	.15
92	Bartolo Colon	.15
93	Jaret Wright	1.50
94	Shawn Estes	.15
95	Livan Hernandez	.25
96	Bobby Estalella	.15
97	Ben Grieve	1.50
98	Paul Konerko	1.25
99	David Ortiz	.75
100	Todd Helton	1.00
101	Juan Encarnacion	.30

102	Bubba Trammell	.15
103	Miguel Tejada	.75
104	Jacob Cruz	.15
105	Todd Greene	.15
106	Kevin Orie	.15
107	Mark Kotsay	.60
108	Fernando Tatis	.30
109	Jay Payton	.15
110	Pokey Reese	.15
111	Derrek Lee	.25
112	Richard Hidalgo	.15
113	Ricky Ledee	.75
114	Lou Collier	.15
115	Ruben Rivera	.15
116	Shawn Green	.15
117	Moises Alou	.25
118	Ken Griffey Jr. (Generations)	2.00
119	Frank Thomas (Generations)	1.50
120	Alex Rodriguez (Generations)	1.25
121	Mike Piazza (Generations)	1.25
122	Greg Maddux (Generations)	1.25
123	Cal Ripken Jr. (Generations)	1.50
124	Chipper Jones (Generations)	1.25
125	Derek Jeter (Generations)	1.25
126	Tony Gwynn (Generations)	1.00
127	Andruw Jones (Generations)	1.00
128	Juan Gonzalez (Generations)	1.00
129	Jeff Bagwell (Generations)	.75
130	Mark McGwire (Generations)	2.50
131	Roger Clemens (Generations)	.75
132	Albert Belle (Generations)	.50
133	Barry Bonds (Generations)	.50
134	Kenny Lofton (Generations)	.50
135	Ivan Rodriguez (Generations)	.40
136	Manny Ramirez (Generations)	.40
137	Jim Thome (Generations)	.30
138	Chuck Knoblauch (Generations)	.25
139	Paul Molitor (Generations)	.30
140	Barry Larkin (Generations)	.15
141	Mo Vaughn (Generations)	.50
142	Hideki Irabu (Generations)	.50
143	Jose Cruz Jr. (Generations)	1.00
144	Tony Clark (Generations)	.40
145	Vladimir Guerrero (Generations)	.60
146	Scott Rolen (Generations)	1.00
147	Nomar Garciaparra (Generations)	1.25
148	Checklist (Garciaparra) (Hit Streaks)	.75
149	Checklist (Walker) (Long HR-Coors)	.15
150	Checklist (Martinez) (3 HR in game)	.15

1998 Donruss Elite Aspirations

Javier Lopez Aspirations

A parallel edition of 750 of each player are found in this die-cut set. Cards have a scalloped treatment cut into the top and sides and red, rather than silver metallic borders. The word "ASPIRATIONS" in printed on front at bottom-right. Backs have the notation "1 of 750".

	MT
Complete Set (150):	550.00
Common Player:	2.00
(Stars valued 15-25X regular version, rookies at 8-15X.)	

1998 Donruss Elite Status

Mo Vaughn - 1B *Status*

Just 100 serially numbered cards of each player are found in this die-cut parallel set. Cards have a scalloped treatment cut into the top and sides and red, rather than silver metallic borders.

	MT
Common Player:	9.00
(Stars and hot rookie valued at 45-75X regular Elite version.)	

1998 Donruss Elite Back to the Future

These double-front cards feature a veteran or retired star on one side and a young player on the other. The player's name, team and "Back to the Future" are printed in the border. The cards are numbered to 1,500, with the first 100 of each card signed by both players. Exceptions are cards #1 and #6. Ripken and Konerko did not sign the same cards and Frank Thomas did not sign his Back to the Future card. Thomas instead signed 100 copies of his base set card.

		MT
Complete Set (8):		450.00
Common Player:		15.00
Production 1,400 sets		
1	Cal Ripken Jr., Paul Konerko	75.00
2	Jeff Bagwell, Todd Helton	40.00
3	Eddie Mathews, Chipper Jones	50.00
4	Juan Gonzalez, Ben Grieve	60.00
5	Hank Aaron, Jose Cruz Jr.	60.00
6	Frank Thomas, David Ortiz	80.00

7	Nolan Ryan, Greg Maddux	80.00
8	Alex Rodriguez, Nomar Garciaparra	70.00

1998 Donruss Elite Back to the Future Autographs

The first 100 of each card in the Back to the Future insert was autographed by both players. Exceptions are cards #1 and #6. Ripken and Konerko did not sign the same cards and Frank Thomas did not sign his Back to the Future card. Thomas instead signed 100 copies of his base set card.

		MT
Common Autograph:		125.00
F. Thomas Redemption:		450.00
C. Ripken Redemption:		450.00
Production 100 sets		
1	Paul Konerko	125.00
2	Jeff Bagwell, Todd Helton	350.00
3	Eddie Mathews, Chipper Jones	400.00
4	Juan Gonzalez, Ben Grieve	600.00
5	Hank Aaron, Jose Cruz Jr.	500.00
7	Nolan Ryan, Greg Maddux	1000.
8	Alex Rodriguez, Nomar Garciaparra	600.00

1998 Donruss Elite Craftsmen

CRAFTSMEN

MIKE PIAZZA *C* *DODGERS*

This 30-card insert has color player photos on the front and back. The set is sequentially numbered to 3,500. The Master Craftsmen parallel is numbered to 100.

		MT
Complete Set (30):		300.00
Common Player:		4.00
Production 3,500 sets		
Master Craftsman: 6x to 10x		
Production 100 sets		
1	Ken Griffey Jr.	30.00
2	Frank Thomas	20.00
3	Alex Rodriguez	20.00
4	Cal Ripken Jr.	20.00
5	Greg Maddux	20.00
6	Mike Piazza	20.00
7	Chipper Jones	20.00
8	Derek Jeter	15.00
9	Tony Gwynn	15.00
10	Nomar Garciaparra	20.00
11	Scott Rolen	10.00
12	Jose Cruz Jr.	10.00
13	Tony Clark	5.00
14	Vladimir Guerrero	10.00
15	Todd Helton	6.00
16	Ben Grieve	10.00
17	Andruw Jones	10.00
18	Jeff Bagwell	10.00
19	Mark McGwire	30.00
20	Juan Gonzalez	15.00
21	Roger Clemens	12.00
22	Albert Belle	8.00
23	Barry Bonds	8.00
24	Kenny Lofton	8.00
25	Ivan Rodriguez	8.00
26	Paul Molitor	6.00
27	Barry Larkin	4.00
28	Mo Vaughn	8.00
29	Larry Walker	5.00
30	Tino Martinez	4.00

1998 Donruss Elite Prime Numbers

This 36-card insert includes three cards for each of 12 players. Each card has a single number in the background. The three numbers for each player represent a key statistic for the player (ex. Mark McGwire's cards are 3-8-7; his career home run total at the time was 387). Each card in the set is sequentially numbered. The total is dependent upon the player's statistic.

		MT
Common Player:		30.00
1A	Ken Griffey Jr. (94)	350.00
1B	Ken Griffey Jr. (204)	175.00
1C	Ken Griffey Jr. (290)	140.00
2A	Frank Thomas (56)	400.00
2B	Frank Thomas (406)	100.00
2C	Frank Thomas (450)	100.00
3A	Mark McGwire (87)	350.00
3B	Mark McGwire (307)	150.00
3C	Mark McGwire (380)	150.00
4A	Cal Ripken Jr. (17)	1000.
4B	Cal Ripken Jr. (507)	100.00
4C	Cal Ripken Jr. (510)	100.00
5A	Mike Piazza (76)	225.00
5B	Mike Piazza (506)	75.00
5C	Mike Piazza (570)	75.00
6A	Chipper Jones (89)	180.00
6B	Chipper Jones (409)	50.00
6C	Chipper Jones (480)	50.00
7A	Tony Gwynn (72)	200.00
7B	Tony Gwynn (302)	75.00
7C	Tony Gwynn (370)	75.00
8A	Barry Bonds (74)	100.00
8B	Barry Bonds (304)	40.00
8C	Barry Bonds (370)	40.00
9A	Jeff Bagwell (25)	375.00
9B	Jeff Bagwell (405)	50.00
9C	Jeff Bagwell (420)	50.00
10A	Juan Gonzalez (89)	180.00
10B	Juan Gonzalez (509)	60.00
10C	Juan Gonzalez (580)	60.00
11A	Alex Rodriguez (34)	375.00

11B	Alex Rodriguez (504)	75.00
11C	Alex Rodriguez (530)	75.00
12A	Kenny Lofton (54)	120.00
12B	Kenny Lofton (304)	40.00
12C	Kenny Lofton (350)	40.00

1998 Donruss Elite Prime Numbers Die-Cuts

This set is a die-cut parallel of the Prime Numbers insert. Each card is sequentially numbered. The production run for each player is the number featured on his first card times 100, his second card times 10 and his third card is sequentially numbered to the number featured on the card.

		MT
Common Player:		30.00
1A	Ken Griffey Jr. (200)	175.00
1B	Ken Griffey Jr. (90)	400.00
1C	Ken Griffey Jr. (4)	30.00
2A	Frank Thomas (400)	100.00
2B	Frank Thomas (50)	400.00
2C	Frank Thomas (6)	30.00
3A	Mark McGwire (300)	150.00
3B	Mark McGwire (80)	400.00
3C	Mark McGwire (7)	40.00
4A	Cal Ripken Jr. (500)	100.00
4B	Cal Ripken Jr. (10)	30.00
4C	Cal Ripken Jr. (7)	30.00
5A	Mike Piazza (500)	75.00
5B	Mike Piazza (70)	200.00
5C	Mike Piazza (6)	30.00
6A	Chipper Jones (400)	50.00
6B	Chipper Jones (80)	200.00
6C	Chipper Jones (9)	30.00
7A	Tony Gwynn (300)	75.00
7B	Tony Gwynn (70)	180.00
7C	Tony Gwynn (2)	30.00
8A	Barry Bonds (300)	40.00
8B	Barry Bonds (70)	100.00
8C	Barry Bonds (4)	30.00
9A	Jeff Bagwell (400)	50.00
9B	Jeff Bagwell (20)	400.00
9C	Jeff Bagwell (5)	30.00
10A	Juan Gonzalez (500)	60.00
10B	Juan Gonzalez (80)	180.00
10C	Juan Gonzalez (9)	30.00
11A	Alex Rodriguez (500)	75.00
11B	Alex Rodriguez (30)	450.00
11C	Alex Rodriguez (4)	30.00
12A	Kenny Lofton (300)	40.00
12B	Kenny Lofton (50)	120.00
12C	Kenny Lofton (4)	30.00

1998 Donruss Preferred

The Donruss Preferred 200-card base set is broken down into five subsets: 100 Grand Stand cards (5:1), 40 Mezzanine (1:6), 20 Club Level (1:12), 20 Field Box (1:23) and 10 Executive Suite (1:65). The base set is paralleled in the Preferred Seating set. Each subset has a different die-cut in the parallel. Inserts in this product include Great X-Pectations, Precious Metals and Title Waves.

	MT
Complete Set (200):	900.00
Common Grand Stand:	.20
Common Mezzanine:	1.50
Mezz. Inserted 1:6	
Common Club Level:	2.00
C.L. Inserted 1:12	
Common Field Box:	3.00
F.B. Inserted 1:23	
Common Executive Suite:	30.00
E.S. Inserted 1:65	
Wax Box:	100.00
1	Ken Griffey Jr. EX	90.00
2	Frank Thomas EX	75.00
3	Cal Ripken Jr. EX	60.00
4	Alex Rodriguez EX	50.00
5	Greg Maddux EX	50.00
6	Mike Piazza EX	50.00
7	Chipper Jones EX	50.00
8	Tony Gwynn FB	40.00
9	Derek Jeter FB	30.00
10	Jeff Bagwell EX	35.00
11	Juan Gonzalez EX	40.00
12	Nomar Garciaparra EX	50.00
13	Andruw Jones FB	15.00
14	Hideo Nomo FB	15.00
15	Roger Clemens FB	25.00
16	Mark McGwire FB	60.00
17	Scott Rolen FB	20.00
18	Vladimir Guerrero FB	15.00
19	Barry Bonds FB	15.00
20	Darin Erstad FB	15.00
21	Albert Belle FB	15.00
22	Kenny Lofton FB	15.00
23	Mo Vaughn FB	15.00
24	Tony Clark FB	8.00
25	Ivan Rodriguez FB	15.00
26	Larry Walker CL	5.00
27	Eddie Murray CL	4.00
28	Andy Pettitte CL	8.00
29	Roberto Alomar CL	8.00
30	Randy Johnson CL	8.00
31	Manny Ramirez CL	10.00
32	Paul Molitor FB	12.00
33	Mike Mussina CL	8.00
34	Jim Thome FB	10.00
35	Tino Martinez CL	5.00
36	Gary Sheffield CL	5.00
37	Chuck Knoblauch CL	5.00
38	Bernie Williams CL	8.00
39	Tim Salmon CL	6.00
40	Sammy Sosa CL	20.00
41	Wade Boggs MZ	3.00
42	Will Clark GS	.50
43	Andres Galarraga CL	5.00
44	Raul Mondesi CL	5.00
45	Rickey Henderson GS	.20
46	Jose Canseco GS	.50
47	Pedro Martinez GS	.75
48	Jay Buhner GS	.50
49	Ryan Klesko GS	.50
50	Barry Larkin CL	5.00
51	Charles Johnson GS	.20
52	Tom Glavine GS	.50
53	Edgar Martinez CL	2.00
54	Fred McGriff GS	.50
55	Moises Alou MZ	1.50
56	Dante Bichette GS	.50
57	Jim Edmonds CL	2.00
58	Mark Grace MZ	2.50
59	Chan Ho Park MZ	2.50
60	Justin Thompson MZ	1.50
61	John Smoltz MZ	2.50
62	Craig Biggio CL	4.00
63	Ken Caminiti MZ	2.50
64	Deion Sanders MZ	2.50
65	Carlos Delgado GS	.50
66	David Justice CL	4.00
67	J.T. Snow GS	.20
68	Jason Giambi CL	2.00
69	Garret Anderson MZ	.20
70	Rondell White MZ	.50
71	Matt Williams MZ	.60
72	Brady Anderson MZ	.40
73	Eric Karros GS	.50
74	Javier Lopez GS	.40
75	Pat Hentgen GS	.40
76	Todd Hundley GS	.20
77	Ray Lankford GS	.20
78	Denny Neagle GS	.20
79	Henry Rodriguez GS	.20
80	Sandy Alomar Jr. MZ	1.50
81	Rafael Palmeiro MZ	2.50
82	Robin Ventura GS	.40
83	John Olerud GS	.40
84	Omar Vizquel GS	.20
85	Joe Randa GS	.20
86	Lance Johnson GS	.20
87	Kevin Brown GS	.40
88	Curt Schilling GS	.50
89	Ismael Valdes GS	.20
90	Francisco Cordova GS	.20
91	David Cone GS	.40
92	Paul O'Neill GS	.40
93	Jimmy Key GS	.20
94	Brad Radke GS	.20
95	Kevin Appier GS	.20
96	Al Martin GS	.20
97	Rusty Greer MZ	1.50
98	Reggie Jefferson GS	.20
99	Ron Coomer GS	.20
100	Vinny Castilla GS	.40
101	Bobby Bonilla MZ	1.50
102	Eric Young GS	.20
103	Tony Womack GS	.20
104	Jason Kendall GS	.20
105	Jeff Suppan GS	.20
106	Shawn Estes MZ	1.50
107	Shawn Green GS	.20
108	Edgardo Alfonzo MZ	1.50
109	Alan Benes MZ	1.50
110	Bobby Higginson GS	.20
111	Mark Grudzielanek GS	.20
112	Wilton Guerrero GS	.20
113	Todd Greene MZ	1.50
114	Pokey Reese GS	.20
115	Jose Guillen CL	2.00
116	Neifi Perez MZ	1.50
117	Luis Castillo GS	.20
118	Edgar Renteria GS	.20
119	Karim Garcia GS	.20
120	Butch Huskey GS	.20
121	Michael Tucker GS	.20
122	Jason Dickson GS	.20
123	Todd Walker MZ	2.50
124	Brian Jordan GS	.20
125	Joe Carter GS	.20
126	Matt Morris MZ	1.50
127	Brett Tomko MZ	1.50
128	Mike Cameron CL	3.00
129	Russ Davis GS	.20
130	Shannon Stewart MZ	1.50
131	Kevin Orie GS	.20
132	Scott Spiezio GS	.20
133	Brian Giles GS	.20
134	Raul Casanova GS	.20
135	Jose Cruz Jr. CL	10.00
136	Hideki Irabu GS	1.00
137	Bubba Trammell GS	.20
138	Richard Hidalgo CL	2.00
139	Paul Konerko CL	6.00
140	Todd Helton FB	15.00
141	Miguel Tejada CL	8.00
142	Fernando Tatis MZ	1.50
143	Ben Grieve FB	25.00
144	Travis Lee FB	40.00
145	Mark Kotsay CL	8.00
146	Eli Marrero MZ	1.50
147	David Ortiz CL	5.00
148	Juan Encarnacion MZ	1.50
149	Jaret Wright MZ	10.00
150	Livan Hernandez CL	4.00
151	Ruben Rivera GS	.20
152	Brad Fullmer MZ	4.00
153	Dennis Reyes GS	.20
154	Enrique Wilson MZ	1.50
155	Todd Dunwoody MZ	1.50
156	Derrick Gibson MZ	1.50
157	Aaron Boone MZ	1.50
158	Ron Wright MZ	1.50
159	Preston Wilson MZ	1.50
160	Abraham Nunez GS	.20
161	Shane Monahan GS	.20
162	Carl Pavano GS	.50
163	Derrek Lee GS	.50
164	Jeff Abbott GS	.20
165	Wes Helms MZ	.20

166	Brian Rose GS	.50
167	Bobby Estalella GS	.20
168	Ken Griffey Jr. GS	3.00
169	Frank Thomas GS	3.00
170	Cal Ripken Jr. GS	2.50
171	Alex Rodriguez GS	2.00
172	Greg Maddux GS	2.00
173	Mike Piazza GS	2.00
174	Chipper Jones GS	2.00
175	Tony Gwynn GS	1.50
176	Derek Jeter GS	1.50
177	Jeff Bagwell GS	1.00
178	Juan Gonzalez GS	1.50
179	Nomar Garciaparra GS	2.00
180	Andruw Jones GS	.75
181	Hideo Nomo GS	.75
182	Roger Clemens GS	1.25
183	Mark McGwire GS	4.00
184	Scott Rolen GS	1.00
185	Barry Bonds GS	.75
186	Darin Erstad GS	.75
187	Mo Vaughn GS	.75
188	Ivan Rodriguez GS	.75
189	Larry Walker MZ	4.00
190	Andy Pettitte GS	.50
191	Randy Johnson MZ	4.00
192	Paul Molitor GS	.60
193	Jim Thome GS	.50
194	Tino Martinez MZ	4.00
195	Gary Sheffield GS	.40
196	Albert Belle GS	.75
197	Jose Cruz Jr. GS	1.00
198	Todd Helton GS	.75
199	Ben Grieve GS	1.25
200	Paul Konerko GS	.75

1998 Donruss Preferred Great X-pectations

This 26-card insert features a veteran player on one side and a young player on the other. A large "GX" appears in the background on each side. The cards are sequentially numbered to 2,700, with the first 300 of each die-cut around the "GX".

		MT
Complete Set (26):		450.00
Common Player:		6.00
Production 2,700 sets		
Die-Cuts: 3x to 5x		
Production 300 sets		
1	Jeff Bagwell, Travis Lee	25.00
2	Jose Cruz Jr., Ken Griffey Jr.	40.00
3	Larry Walker, Ben Grieve	20.00
4	Frank Thomas, Todd Helton	35.00
5	Jim Thome, Paul Konerko	8.00
6	Alex Rodriguez, Miguel Tejada	30.00
7	Greg Maddux, Livan Hernandez	30.00
8	Roger Clemens, Jaret Wright	20.00
9	Albert Belle, Juan Encarnacion	12.00
10	Mo Vaughn, David Ortiz	12.00
11	Manny Ramirez, Mark Kotsay	10.00
12	Tim Salmon, Brad Fullmer	6.00
13	Cal Ripken Jr., Fernando Tatis	40.00
14	Hideo Nomo, Hideki Irabu	10.00
15	Mike Piazza, Todd Greene	30.00
16	Gary Sheffield, Richard Hidalgo	8.00
17	Paul Molitor, Darin Erstad	12.00
18	Ivan Rodriguez, Eli Marrero	12.00
19	Ken Caminiti, Todd Walker	8.00
20	Tony Gwynn, Jose Guillen	25.00
21	Derek Jeter, Nomar Garciaparra	30.00
22	Chipper Jones, Scott Rolen	30.00
23	Juan Gonzalez, Andruw Jones	25.00
24	Barry Bonds, Vladimir Guerrero	12.00
25	Mark McGwire, Tony Clark	50.00
26	Bernie Williams, Mike Cameron	10.00

1998 Donruss Preferred Precious Metals

Precious Metals is a 30-card partial parallel of the Preferred base set. Each card was printed on stock using real silver, gold or platinum. Fifty complete sets were produced.

		MT
Complete Set (30):		6000.
Common Player:		80.00
Production 50 sets		
1	Ken Griffey Jr.	600.00
2	Frank Thomas	400.00
3	Cal Ripken Jr.	500.00
4	Alex Rodriguez	400.00
5	Greg Maddux	400.00
6	Mike Piazza	400.00
7	Chipper Jones	350.00
8	Tony Gwynn	300.00
9	Derek Jeter	350.00
10	Jeff Bagwell	200.00
11	Juan Gonzalez	300.00
12	Nomar Garciaparra	400.00
13	Andruw Jones	150.00
14	Hideo Nomo	100.00
15	Roger Clemens	250.00
16	Mark McGwire	600.00
17	Scott Rolen	200.00
18	Barry Bonds	150.00
19	Darin Erstad	125.00
20	Kenny Lofton	150.00
21	Mo Vaughn	150.00
22	Ivan Rodriguez	150.00
23	Randy Johnson	100.00
24	Paul Molitor	125.00
25	Jose Cruz Jr.	150.00
26	Paul Konerko	80.00
27	Todd Helton	150.00
28	Ben Grieve	200.00
29	Travis Lee	200.00
30	Mark Kotsay	80.00

1998 Donruss Preferred Seating

Preferred Seating is a die-cut parallel of the base set. Each section of the base set has a different die-cut.

		MT
Complete Set (200):		4000.
Comp. Grand Stand (100):		400.00
Common Grand Stand:		1.50
Comp. Mezzanine (40):		275.00
Common Mezzanine:		5.00
Comp. Club Level (30):		600.00
Common Club Level:		8.00
Comp. Field Box (20):		1000.
Common Field Box:		10.00
Comp. Executive Suite (10):		1800.
Common Executive Suite:		100.00
1	Ken Griffey Jr. EX	300.00
2	Frank Thomas EX	200.00
3	Cal Ripken Jr. EX	220.00
4	Alex Rodriguez EX	200.00
5	Greg Maddux EX	200.00
6	Mike Piazza EX	200.00
7	Chipper Jones EX	200.00
8	Tony Gwynn FB	100.00
9	Derek Jeter FB	100.00
10	Jeff Bagwell EX	125.00
11	Juan Gonzalez EX	150.00
12	Nomar Garciaparra EX	200.00
13	Andruw Jones FB	50.00
14	Hideo Nomo FB	50.00
15	Roger Clemens FB	80.00
16	Mark McGwire FB	200.00
17	Scott Rolen FB	70.00
18	Vladimir Guerrero FB	50.00
19	Barry Bonds FB	50.00
20	Darin Erstad FB	50.00
21	Albert Belle FB	50.00
22	Kenny Lofton FB	50.00
23	Mo Vaughn FB	50.00
24	Tony Clark FB	30.00
25	Ivan Rodriguez FB	50.00
26	Larry Walker CL	30.00
27	Eddie Murray CL	25.00
28	Andy Pettitte CL	30.00
29	Roberto Alomar CL	35.00
30	Randy Johnson CL	30.00
31	Manny Ramirez CL	35.00
32	Paul Molitor FB	40.00
33	Mike Mussina CL	30.00
34	Jim Thome FB	40.00
35	Tino Martinez CL	25.00
36	Gary Sheffield CL	30.00
37	Chuck Knoblauch CL	25.00
38	Bernie Williams CL	30.00
39	Tim Salmon CL	25.00
40	Sammy Sosa CL	75.00
41	Wade Boggs MZ	15.00
42	Will Clark GS	5.00
43	Andres Galarraga CL	25.00
44	Raul Mondesi CL	20.00
45	Rickey Henderson GS	4.00
46	Jose Canseco GS	6.00
47	Pedro Martinez GS	10.00
48	Jay Buhner GS	8.00
49	Ryan Klesko GS	10.00
50	Barry Larkin CL	15.00
51	Charles Johnson GS	2.00
52	Tom Glavine GS	4.00
53	Edgar Martinez CL	15.00
54	Fred McGriff GS	5.00
55	Moises Alou MZ	8.00
56	Dante Bichette GS	6.00
57	Jim Edmonds CL	15.00
58	Mark Grace MZ	15.00
59	Chan Ho Park MZ	15.00
60	Justin Thompson MZ	10.00
61	John Smoltz MZ	15.00
62	Craig Biggio CL	20.00
63	Ken Caminiti MZ	15.00
64	Deion Sanders MZ	15.00
65	Carlos Delgado GS	5.00
66	David Justice CL	25.00
67	J.T. Snow GS	2.00
68	Jason Giambi CL	8.00
69	Garret Anderson MZ	5.00
70	Rondell White MZ	8.00
71	Matt Williams MZ	20.00
72	Brady Anderson MZ	15.00
73	Eric Karros GS	5.00
74	Javier Lopez GS	5.00
75	Pat Hentgen GS	4.00
76	Todd Hundley GS	2.00
77	Ray Lankford GS	2.00
78	Denny Neagle GS	4.00
79	Henry Rodriguez GS	2.00
80	Sandy Alomar Jr. MZ	8.00
81	Rafael Palmeiro MZ	15.00
82	Robin Ventura GS	4.00
83	John Olerud GS	4.00
84	Omar Vizquel GS	2.00
85	Joe Randa GS	2.00
86	Lance Johnson GS	2.00
87	Kevin Brown GS	5.00
88	Curt Schilling GS	5.00
89	Ismael Valdes GS	2.00
90	Francisco Cordova GS	2.00
91	David Cone GS	5.00
92	Paul O'Neill GS	5.00
93	Jimmy Key GS	2.00
94	Brad Radke GS	2.00
95	Kevin Appier GS	2.00
96	Al Martin GS	2.00
97	Rusty Greer MZ	10.00
98	Reggie Jefferson GS	2.00
99	Ron Coomer GS	2.00
100	Vinny Castilla GS	5.00
101	Bobby Bonilla MZ	10.00
102	Eric Young GS	2.00
103	Tony Womack GS	2.00
104	Jason Kendall GS	2.00
105	Jeff Suppan GS	2.00
106	Shawn Estes MZ	5.00
107	Shawn Green GS	2.00
108	Edgardo Alfonzo MZ	5.00
109	Alan Benes MZ	5.00
110	Bobby Higginson GS	2.00
111	Mark Grudzielanek GS	2.00
112	Wilton Guerrero GS	2.00
113	Todd Greene MZ	5.00
114	Pokey Reese GS	2.00
115	Jose Guillen GS	15.00
116	Neifi Perez MZ	5.00
117	Luis Castillo GS	2.00
118	Edgar Renteria GS	2.00
119	Karim Garcia GS	2.00
120	Butch Huskey GS	2.00

121	Michael Tucker GS	2.00
122	Jason Dickson GS	2.00
123	Todd Walker MZ	10.00
124	Brian Jordan GS	2.00
125	Joe Carter GS	4.00
126	Matt Morris MZ	5.00
127	Brett Tomko MZ	5.00
128	Mike Cameron CL	15.00
129	Russ Davis GS	2.00
130	Shannon Stewart MZ	5.00
131	Kevin Orie GS	2.00
132	Scott Spiezio GS	2.00
133	Brian Giles GS	2.00
134	Raul Casanova GS	2.00
135	Jose Cruz Jr. CL	40.00
136	Hideki Irabu GS	10.00
137	Bubba Trammell GS	2.00
138	Richard Hidalgo CL	8.00
139	Paul Konerko CL	12.00
140	Todd Helton FB	20.00
141	Miguel Tejada CL	12.00
142	Fernando Tatis MZ	10.00
143	Ben Grieve FB	25.00
144	Travis Lee FB	100.00
145	Mark Kotsay CL	20.00
146	Eli Marrero MZ	5.00
147	David Ortiz CL	12.00
148	Juan Encarnacion MZ	5.00
149	Jaret Wright MZ	30.00
150	Livan Hernandez CL	8.00
151	Ruben Rivera GS	2.00
152	Brad Fullmer MZ	12.00
153	Dennis Reyes GS	2.00
154	Enrique Wilson MZ	5.00
155	Todd Dunwoody MZ	5.00
156	Derrick Gibson MZ	5.00
157	Aaron Boone MZ	5.00
158	Ron Wright MZ	5.00
159	Preston Wilson MZ	5.00
160	Abraham Nunez GS	2.00
161	Shane Monahan GS	2.00
162	Carl Pavano GS	5.00
163	Derrek Lee GS	5.00
164	Jeff Abbott GS	2.00
165	Wes Helms MZ	5.00
166	Brian Rose GS	5.00
167	Bobby Estalella GS	2.00
168	Ken Griffey Jr. GS	40.00
169	Frank Thomas GS	30.00
170	Cal Ripken Jr. GS	30.00
171	Alex Rodriguez GS	25.00
172	Greg Maddux GS	25.00
173	Mike Piazza GS	25.00
174	Chipper Jones GS	25.00
175	Tony Gwynn GS	20.00
176	Derek Jeter GS	20.00
177	Jeff Bagwell GS	15.00
178	Juan Gonzalez GS	20.00
179	Nomar Garciaparra GS	25.00
180	Andruw Jones GS	12.00
181	Hideo Nomo GS	12.00
182	Roger Clemens GS	15.00
183	Mark McGwire GS	40.00
184	Scott Rolen GS	12.00
185	Barry Bonds GS	10.00
186	Darin Erstad GS	10.00
187	Mo Vaughn GS	10.00
188	Ivan Rodriguez GS	10.00
189	Larry Walker MZ	20.00
190	Andy Pettitte GS	8.00
191	Randy Johnson MZ	15.00
192	Paul Molitor GS	8.00
193	Jim Thome GS	8.00
194	Tino Martinez MZ	15.00
195	Gary Sheffield GS	5.00
196	Albert Belle GS	10.00
197	Jose Cruz Jr. GS	15.00
198	Todd Helton GS	6.00
199	Ben Grieve GS	10.00
200	Paul Konerko GS	8.00

1998 Donruss Preferred Title Waves

This 30-card set features players who won awards or titles between 1993-1997. Printed on plastic stock, each card is sequentially numbered to the year the player won the award. The card fronts feature the Title Waves logo, a color player photo in front of a background of fans and the name of the award the player won.

		MT
Complete Set (30):		700.00
Common Player:		8.00
#'d to year award was won		
1	Nomar Garciaparra	40.00
2	Scott Rolen	25.00
3	Roger Clemens	30.00
4	Gary Sheffield	8.00
5	Jeff Bagwell	30.00
6	Cal Ripken Jr.	50.00
7	Frank Thomas	50.00
8	Ken Griffey Jr.	70.00
9	Larry Walker	10.00
10	Derek Jeter	35.00
11	Juan Gonzalez	35.00
12	Bernie Williams	12.00
13	Andruw Jones	25.00
14	Andy Pettitte	12.00
15	Ivan Rodriguez	15.00
16	Alex Rodriguez	40.00
17	Mark McGwire	80.00
18	Andres Galarraga	10.00
19	Hideo Nomo	15.00
20	Mo Vaughn	15.00
21	Randy Johnson	12.00
22	Chipper Jones	40.00
23	Greg Maddux	40.00
24	Manny Ramirez	15.00
25	Tony Gwynn	35.00
26	Albert Belle	15.00
27	Kenny Lofton	15.00
28	Mike Piazza	40.00
29	Paul Molitor	12.00
30	Barry Bonds	15.00

1998 Donruss Preferred Tins

Donruss Preferred was packaged in collectible tins. Each tin contained five cards and featured one of 24 players on the top. Silver (numbered to 999) and gold (199) parallel tins were also produced and included in hobby-only boxes. The hobby boxes were actually large tins that held 24 tin packs. The 24 tin boxes came in green (numbered to 999) and gold (199) versions. Five-card retail packs came in one of 12 double-wide tins featuring two players on the top.

		MT
Complete Set (26):		20.00
Common Player:		.50
Gold Tins: 10x to 20x		
Production 199 sets		
Silver & Green Tins: 4x to 8x		
Production 999 sets		
1	Todd Helton	.75
2	Ben Grieve	1.00
3	Cal Ripken Jr.	2.00
4	Alex Rodriguez	1.50
5	Greg Maddux	1.50
6	Mike Piazza	1.50
7	Chipper Jones	1.50
8	Travis Lee	1.50
9	Derek Jeter	1.25
10	Jeff Bagwell	1.00
11	Juan Gonzalez	1.25
12	Mark McGwire	2.00
13	Hideo Nomo	.75
14	Roger Clemens	1.00
15	Andruw Jones	.75
16	Paul Molitor	.50
17	Vladimir Guerrero	.75
18	Jose Cruz Jr.	1.50
19	Nomar Garciaparra	1.50
20	Scott Rolen	1.00
21	Ken Griffey Jr.	2.50
22	Larry Walker	.50
25	Frank Thomas	2.00
26	Tony Gwynn	1.25

1998 Donruss Update Crusade Green

This 30-card insert is continued from 1998 Donruss and Leaf baseball sets. Each card features a color player shot in front of a Medieval background. The player's name and background are colored green and each card is numbered to 250. Purple (numbered to 100) and Red (25) parallel versions were also created. Crusade is a 100-card crossbrand insert with 40 cards included in 1998 Donruss and 30 in 1998 Leaf.

		MT
Complete Set (30):		1000.
Common Player:		10.00
Production 250 sets		
Purples (100 sets): 1x to 2x		
Reds (25 sets): 4x to 6x		
1	Tim Salmon	25.00
2	Garret Anderson	10.00
9	Rafael Palmeiro	25.00
10	Brady Anderson	10.00
14	Frank Thomas	125.00
17	Robin Ventura	20.00
22	Matt Williams	25.00
23	Tony Clark	35.00
29	Chuck Knoblauch	25.00
31	Bernie Williams	40.00
32	Derek Jeter	100.00
38	Jason Giambi	10.00
43	Jay Buhner	25.00
44	Juan Gonzalez	100.00
49	Carlos Delgado	20.00
55	Greg Maddux	125.00
57	Tom Glavine	20.00
60	Mark Grace	25.00
61	Sammy Sosa	125.00
63	Barry Larkin	25.00
69	Neifi Perez	10.00
72	Gary Sheffield	25.00
77	Jeff Bagwell	75.00
80	Raul Mondesi	20.00
81	Hideo Nomo	40.00
83	Rondell White	20.00
84	Vladimir Guerrero	50.00
87	Todd Hundley	10.00
96	Brian Jordan	10.00
99	Barry Bonds	50.00

1998 Donruss Update Dominators

This 30-card insert features color player photos and holographic foil.

	MT
Complete Set (30):	200.00
Common Player:	2.50
Approx: 1:12	
1 Roger Clemens	10.00
2 Tony Clark	4.00
3 Darin Erstad	6.00
4 Jeff Bagwell	10.00
5 Ken Griffey Jr.	25.00
6 Andruw Jones	6.00
7 Juan Gonzalez	12.00
8 Ivan Rodriguez	6.00
9 Randy Johnson	4.00
10 Tino Martinez	3.00
11 Mark McGwire	30.00
12 Chuck Knoblauch	3.00
13 Jim Thome	6.00
14 Alex Rodriguez	15.00
15 Hideo Nomo	6.00
16 Jose Cruz Jr.	5.00
17 Chipper Jones	15.00
18 Tony Gwynn	12.00
19 Barry Bonds	6.00
20 Mo Vaughn	6.00
21 Cal Ripken Jr.	20.00
22 Greg Maddux	15.00
23 Manny Ramirez	6.00
24 Andres Galarraga	3.00
25 Vladimir Guerrero	6.00
26 Albert Belle	6.00
27 Nomar Garciaparra	15.00
28 Kenny Lofton	6.00
29 Mike Piazza	15.00
30 Frank Thomas	20.00

1998 Donruss Update Elite

This 20-card insert features color player photos in a diamond-shaped border at the top with the Elite Series logo and player's name at the bottom. The fronts have a cream-colored border. The cards are sequentially numbered to 2,500.

	MT
Complete Set (20):	400.00
Common Player:	5.00
Production 2,500 sets	
1 Jeff Bagwell	20.00
2 Andruw Jones	12.00
3 Ken Griffey Jr.	50.00
4 Derek Jeter	25.00
5 Juan Gonzalez	25.00
6 Mark McGwire	60.00
7 Ivan Rodriguez	15.00
8 Paul Molitor	10.00
9 Hideo Nomo	10.00
10 Mo Vaughn	15.00
11 Chipper Jones	30.00
12 Nomar Garciaparra	30.00
13 Mike Piazza	30.00
14 Frank Thomas	40.00
15 Greg Maddux	30.00
16 Cal Ripken Jr.	40.00
17 Alex Rodriguez	30.00
18 Scott Rolen	18.00
19 Barry Bonds	15.00
20 Tony Gwynn	25.00

1998 Donruss Update FANtasy Team

This 20-card set features the top vote getters from the Donruss online Fan Club ballot box. The top ten make up the 1st Team FANtasy Team and are sequentially numbered to 2,000. The other players are included in the 2nd Team FANtasy Team and are numbered to 4,000. The first 250 cards of each player are die-cut. The front of the cards feature a color photo inside a stars and stripes border.

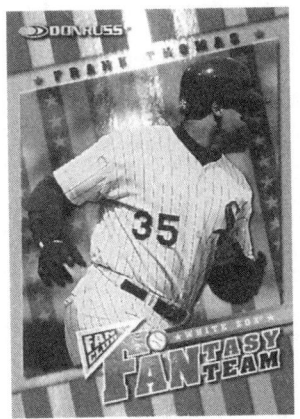

	MT
Complete Set (20):	250.00
Common Player (1-10):	8.00
Common Player (11-20):	4.00
Production 1-10 1,750 sets	
Production 11-20 3,750 sets	
Die-Cuts (1-10): 3x to 4x	
Die-Cuts (11-20): 6x to 8x	
Production 250 sets	
1 Frank Thomas	30.00
2 Ken Griffey Jr.	40.00
3 Cal Ripken Jr.	30.00
4 Jose Cruz Jr.	8.00
5 Travis Lee	25.00
6 Greg Maddux	25.00
7 Alex Rodriguez	25.00
8 Mark McGwire	50.00
9 Chipper Jones	25.00
10 Andruw Jones	10.00
11 Mike Piazza	15.00
12 Tony Gwynn	12.00
13 Larry Walker	4.00
14 Nomar Garciaparra	15.00
15 Jaret Wright	6.00
16 Livan Hernandez	4.00
17 Roger Clemens	10.00
18 Derek Jeter	12.00
19 Scott Rolen	8.00
20 Jeff Bagwell	10.00

1998 Donruss Update Rookie Diamond Kings

The Rookie Diamond Kings insert features color portraits of young players inside a golden border. The player's name, team and Rookie Diamond Kings logo are

listed at the bottom. Each card is sequentially numbered to 10,000 with the first 500 printed on canvas.

	MT
Complete Set (12):	80.00
Common Player:	4.00
Production 9,500 sets	
Die-Cuts: 3x to 5x	
Production 500 sets	
1 Travis Lee	25.00
2 Fernando Tatis	4.00
3 Livan Hernandez	4.00
4 Todd Helton	10.00
5 Derrek Lee	4.00
6 Jaret Wright	10.00
7 Ben Grieve	15.00
8 Paul Konerko	6.00
9 Jose Cruz Jr.	8.00
10 Mark Kotsay	6.00
11 Todd Greene	4.00
12 Brad Fullmer	6.00

1998 Donruss Update Signature Series Preview

This 29-card insert was a surprise addition to Donruss Update. The set features autographs from top rookies and stars. The number of cards produced varies for each player. The card fronts have a color player photo in front of a checkered border with the signature in a white area near the bottom.

	MT
Common Player:	25.00
Sandy Alomar Jr. (96)	50.00
Andy Benes (135)	40.00
Russell Branyan (188)	40.00
Tony Clark (188)	60.00
Juan Encarnacion (193)	30.00
Brad Fullmer (396)	40.00
Juan Gonzalez (108)	250.00
Ben Grieve (100)	150.00
Todd Helton (101)	90.00
Richard Hidalgo (380)	25.00
A.J. Hinch (400)	35.00
Damian Jackson (15)	200.00
Chipper Jones (112)	300.00
Chuck Knoblauch (98)	80.00
Travis Lee (101)	175.00
Mike Lowell (450)	25.00
Greg Maddux (92)	350.00
Kevin Millwood (395)	75.00
Magglio Ordonez (420)	40.00
David Ortiz (393)	25.00
Rafael Palmeiro (107)	75.00
Cal Ripken Jr. (22)	1200.
Alex Rodriguez (23)	1000.
Curt Schilling (100)	75.00
Randall Simon (380)	25.00
Fernando Tatis (400)	25.00
Miguel Tejada (375)	40.00
Robin Ventura (95)	50.00
Kerry Wood (373)	150.00

1998 Donruss Update Sony MLB 99

This 20-card set promotes the MLB '99 game for Sony PlayStation systems. The card front has a color player photo with a red border on two sides. The Donruss, PlayStation and MLB '99 logos appear on the front as well. The backs have a MLB '99 Tip and instructions on entering the PlayStation MLB '99 Sweepstakes.

		MT
Complete Set (20):		10.00
Common Player:		.25
1	Cal Ripken Jr.	2.00
2	Nomar Garciaparra	1.50
3	Barry Bonds	.60
4	Mike Mussina	.50
5	Pedro Martinez	.40
6	Derek Jeter	1.25
7	Andruw Jones	.60
8	Kenny Lofton	.60
9	Gary Sheffield	.25
10	Raul Mondesi	.25
11	Jeff Bagwell	.75
12	Tim Salmon	.25
13	Tom Glavine	.25
14	Ben Grieve	.75
15	Matt Williams	.25
16	Juan Gonzalez	1.25
17	Mark McGwire	2.00
18	Bernie Williams	.40
19	Andres Galarraga	.25
20	Jose Cruz Jr.	.40

F

1993 Finest

This 199-card set uses a process of multi-color metallization; this chromium technology adds depth and dimension to the card.

The set has a 33-card subset of All-Stars; a parallel version of these cards (Refractors) were also recreated with refracting foil using the metallization enhancement process. There is one refracting foil card in every nine packs. Packs have five cards. Each 18-count box contains a 5" x 7" version of one of the 33 All-Star players in the set.

		MT
Complete Set (199):		280.00
Common Player:		1.00
Wax Box:		600.00
1	Dave Justice	2.00
2	Lou Whitaker	1.00
3	Bryan Harvey	1.00
4	Carlos Garcia	1.00
5	Sid Fernandez	1.00
6	Brett Butler	1.00
7	Scott Cooper	1.00
8	B.J. Surhoff	1.00
9	Steve Finley	1.50
10	Curt Schilling	2.00
11	Jeff Bagwell	12.00
12	Alex Cole	1.00
13	John Olerud	1.50
14	John Smiley	1.00
15	Bip Roberts	1.00
16	Albert Belle	6.00
17	Duane Ward	1.00
18	Alan Trammell	1.00
19	Andy Benes	1.50
20	Reggie Sanders	1.00
21	Todd Zeile	1.00
22	Rick Aguilera	1.00
23	Dave Hollins	1.00
24	Jose Rijo	1.00
25	Matt Williams	3.00
26	Sandy Alomar	1.50
27	Alex Fernandez	1.00
28	Ozzie Smith	6.00
29	Ramon Martinez	2.00
30	Bernie Williams	6.00
31	Gary Sheffield	3.00
32	Eric Karros	2.00
33	Frank Viola	1.00
34	Kevin Young	1.00
35	Ken Hill	1.00
36	Tony Fernandez	1.00
37	Tim Wakefield	1.00
38	John Kruk	1.00
39	Chris Sabo	1.00
40	Marquis Grissom	1.50
41	Glenn Davis	1.00
42	Jeff Montgomery	1.00
43	Kenny Lofton	6.00
44	John Burkett	1.00
45	Darryl Hamilton	1.00
46	Jim Abbott	1.00
47	Ivan Rodriguez	6.00
48	Eric Young	1.00
49	Mitch Williams	1.00
50	Harold Reynolds	1.00
51	Brian Harper	1.00
52	Rafael Palmeiro	3.00
53	Bret Saberhagen	1.00
54	Jeff Conine	1.50
55	Ivan Calderon	1.00
56	Juan Guzman	1.00
57	Carlos Baerga	1.00
58	Charles Nagy	1.00
59	Wally Joyner	1.00
60	Charlie Hayes	1.00
61	Shane Mack	1.00
62	Pete Harnisch	1.00
63	George Brett	10.00
64	Lance Johnson	1.00
65	Ben McDonald	1.00
66	Bobby Bonilla	1.50
67	Terry Steinbach	1.00
68	Ron Gant	1.50
69	Doug Jones	1.00
70	Paul Molitor	4.00
71	Brady Anderson	2.00
72	Chuck Finley	1.00
73	Mark Grace	2.00
74	Mike Devereaux	1.00
75	Tony Phillips	1.00
76	Chuck Knoblauch	2.50
77	Tony Gwynn	12.00
78	Kevin Appier	1.00
79	Sammy Sosa	12.00

		MT
80	Mickey Tettleton	1.00
81	Felix Jose	1.00
82	Mark Langston	1.00
83	Gregg Jefferies	1.50
84	Andre Dawson (AS)	1.50
85	Greg Maddux (AS)	15.00
86	Rickey Henderson (AS)	2.00
87	Tom Glavine (AS)	2.50
88	Roberto Alomar (AS)	5.00
89	Darryl Strawberry (AS)	1.50
90	Wade Boggs (AS)	2.00
91	Bo Jackson (AS)	2.00
92	Mark McGwire (AS)	25.00
93	Robin Ventura (AS)	1.50
94	Joe Carter (AS)	1.50
95	Lee Smith (AS)	1.00
96	Cal Ripken, Jr. (AS)	20.00
97	Larry Walker (AS)	3.00
98	Don Mattingly (AS)	10.00
99	Jose Canseco (AS)	2.50
100	Dennis Eckersley (AS)	1.50
101	Terry Pendleton (AS)	1.00
102	Frank Thomas (AS)	20.00
103	Barry Bonds (AS)	6.00
104	Roger Clemens (AS)	12.00
105	Ryne Sandberg (AS)	6.00
106	Fred McGriff (AS)	2.50
107	Nolan Ryan (AS)	25.00
108	Will Clark (AS)	3.00
109	Pat Listach (AS)	1.00
110	Ken Griffey, Jr. (AS)	25.00
111	Cecil Fielder (AS)	1.50
112	Kirby Puckett (AS)	10.00
113	Dwight Gooden (AS)	1.25
114	Barry Larkin (AS)	3.00
115	David Cone (AS)	1.50
116	Juan Gonzalez (AS)	12.00
117	Kent Hrbek	1.00
118	Tim Wallach	1.00
119	Craig Biggio	2.00
120	Bobby Kelly	1.00
121	Greg Olson	1.00
122	Eddie Murray	4.00
123	Wil Cordero	1.00
124	Jay Buhner	3.00
125	Carlton Fisk	1.50
126	Eric Davis	1.00
127	Doug Drabek	1.00
128	Ozzie Guillen	1.00
129	John Wetteland	1.00
130	Andres Galarraga	2.50
131	Ken Caminiti	1.50
132	Tom Candiotti	1.00
133	Pat Borders	1.00
134	Kevin Brown	1.50
135	Travis Fryman	2.00
136	Kevin Mitchell	1.00
137	Greg Swindell	1.00
138	Benny Santiago	1.00
139	Reggie Jefferson	1.00
140	Chris Bosio	1.00
141	Deion Sanders	2.00
142	Scott Erickson	1.00
143	Howard Johnson	1.00
144	Orestes Destrade	1.00
145	Jose Guzman	1.00
146	Chad Curtis	1.00
147	Cal Eldred	1.00
148	Willie Greene	1.00
149	Tommy Greene	1.00
150	Erik Hanson	1.00
151	Bob Welch	1.00
152	John Jaha	1.00
153	Harold Baines	1.00
154	Randy Johnson	5.00
155	Al Martin	1.00
156	*J.T. Snow*	3.00
157	Mike Mussina	6.00
158	Ruben Sierra	1.50
159	Dean Palmer	1.50
160	Steve Avery	1.50
161	Julio Franco	1.00
162	Dave Winfield	2.00
163	Tim Salmon	4.00
164	Tom Henke	1.00
165	Mo Vaughn	6.00
166	John Smoltz	2.00
167	Danny Tartabull	1.00
168	Delino DeShields	1.00
169	Charlie Hough	1.00
170	Paul O'Neill	1.50
171	Darren Daulton	1.50
172	Jack McDowell	1.50
173	Junior Felix	1.00
174	Jimmy Key	1.00
175	George Bell	1.00

176	Mike Stanton	1.00
177	Len Dykstra	1.50
178	Norm Charlton	1.00
179	Eric Anthony	1.00
180	Bob Dibble	1.00
181	Otis Nixon	1.00
182	Randy Myers	1.00
183	Tim Raines	1.00
184	Orel Hershiser	1.00
185	Andy Van Slyke	1.00
186	*Mike Lansing*	2.00
187	Ray Lankford	1.00
188	Mike Morgan	1.00
189	Moises Alou	2.00
190	Edgar Martinez	2.00
191	John Franco	1.00
192	Robin Yount	4.00
193	Bob Tewksbury	1.00
194	Jay Bell	1.00
195	Luis Gonzalez	1.00
196	Dave Fleming	1.00
197	Mike Greenwell	1.00
198	David Nied	1.00
199	Mike Piazza	30.00

1993 Finest
Refractors

This insert set features each of the 199 cards from the regular Topps Finest set recreated with refracting foil using the metallization enhancement process. One refracting foil card was inserted in every nine packs, on average.

		MT
Complete Set (199):		20000.
Common Player:		40.00
1	Dave Justice	200.00
2	Lou Whitaker	40.00
3	Bryan Harvey	100.00
4	Carlos Garcia	40.00
5	Sid Fernandez	40.00
6	Brett Butler	40.00
7	Scott Cooper	40.00
8	B.J. Surhoff	40.00
9	Steve Finley	60.00
10	Curt Schilling	200.00
11	Jeff Bagwell	300.00
12	Alex Cole	125.00
13	John Olerud	75.00
14	John Smiley	40.00
15	Bip Roberts	40.00
16	Albert Belle	200.00
17	Duane Ward	40.00
18	Alan Trammell	60.00
19	Andy Benes	40.00
20	Reggie Sanders	100.00
21	Todd Zeile	40.00
22	Rick Aguilera	40.00
23	Dave Hollins	40.00
24	Jose Rijo	40.00
25	Matt Williams	200.00
26	Sandy Alomar	100.00
27	Alex Fernandez	100.00
28	Ozzie Smith	250.00
29	Ramon Martinez	75.00
30	Bernie Williams	150.00
31	Gary Sheffield	100.00
32	Eric Karros	120.00
33	Frank Viola	40.00
34	Kevin Young	40.00
35	Ken Hill	40.00
36	Tony Fernandez	40.00
37	Tim Wakefield	60.00
38	John Kruk	75.00
39	Chris Sabo	75.00
40	Marquis Grissom	100.00
41	Glenn Davis	75.00
42	Jeff Montgomery	40.00
43	Kenny Lofton	250.00
44	John Burkett	40.00
45	Darryl Hamilton	40.00
46	Jim Abbott	40.00
47	Ivan Rodriguez	400.00
48	Eric Young	40.00
49	Mitch Williams	40.00
50	Harold Reynolds	40.00
51	Brian Harper	40.00
52	Rafael Palmeiro	150.00
53	Bret Saberhagen	40.00
54	Jeff Conine	75.00

55	Ivan Calderon	40.00
56	Juan Guzman	40.00
57	Carlos Baerga	50.00
58	Charles Nagy	50.00
59	Wally Joyner	50.00
60	Charlie Hayes	40.00
61	Shane Mack	40.00
62	Pete Harnisch	40.00
63	George Brett	400.00
64	Lance Johnson	40.00
65	Ben McDonald	40.00
66	Bobby Bonilla	50.00
67	Terry Steinbach	40.00
68	Ron Gant	50.00
69	Doug Jones	40.00
70	Paul Molitor	250.00
71	Brady Anderson	60.00
72	Chuck Finley	40.00
73	Mark Grace	100.00
74	Mike Devereaux	40.00
75	Tony Phillips	60.00
76	Chuck Knoblauch	100.00
77	Tony Gwynn	400.00
78	Kevin Appier	40.00
79	Sammy Sosa	500.00
80	Mickey Tettleton	40.00
81	Felix Jose	40.00
82	Mark Langston	40.00
83	Gregg Jefferies	40.00
84	Andre Dawson (AS)	50.00
85	Greg Maddux (AS)	600.00
86	Rickey Henderson (AS)	75.00
87	Tom Glavine (AS)	80.00
88	Roberto Alomar (AS)	150.00
89	Darryl Strawberry (AS)	75.00
90	Wade Boggs (AS)	80.00
91	Bo Jackson (AS)	60.00
92	Mark McGwire (AS)	800.00
93	Robin Ventura (AS)	60.00
94	Joe Carter (AS)	60.00
95	Lee Smith (AS)	60.00
96	Cal Ripken, Jr. (AS)	1200.
97	Larry Walker (AS)	150.00
98	Don Mattingly (AS)	300.00
99	Jose Canseco (AS)	75.00
100	Dennis Eckersley (AS)	50.00
101	Terry Pendleton (AS)	40.00
102	Frank Thomas (AS)	600.00
103	Barry Bonds (AS)	250.00
104	Roger Clemens (AS)	400.00
105	Ryne Sandberg (AS)	200.00
106	Fred McGriff (AS)	75.00
107	Nolan Ryan (AS)	900.00
108	Will Clark (AS)	75.00
109	Pat Listach (AS)	40.00
110	Ken Griffey, Jr. (AS)	1200.
111	Cecil Fielder (AS)	60.00
112	Kirby Puckett (AS)	300.00
113	Dwight Gooden (AS)	60.00
114	Barry Larkin (AS)	75.00
115	David Cone (AS)	60.00
116	Juan Gonzalez (AS)	800.00
117	Kent Hrbek	40.00
118	Tim Wallach	40.00
119	Craig Biggio	75.00
120	Bobby Kelly	40.00
121	Greg Olson	40.00
122	Eddie Murray	100.00
123	Wil Cordero	40.00
124	Jay Buhner	100.00
125	Carlton Fisk	60.00
126	Eric Davis	40.00
127	Doug Drabek	40.00
128	Ozzie Guillen	40.00
129	John Wetteland	40.00
130	Andres Galarraga	90.00
131	Ken Caminiti	75.00
132	Tom Candiotti	40.00
133	Pat Borders	40.00
134	Kevin Brown	75.00
135	Travis Fryman	75.00
136	Kevin Mitchell	40.00
137	Greg Swindell	40.00
138	Benny Santiago	40.00
139	Reggie Jefferson	40.00
140	Chris Bosio	40.00
141	Deion Sanders	75.00
142	Scott Erickson	40.00
143	Howard Johnson	40.00
144	Orestes Destrade	40.00
145	Jose Guzman	40.00
146	Chad Curtis	40.00
147	Cal Eldred	40.00
148	Willie Greene	40.00
149	Tommy Greene	40.00
150	Erik Hanson	40.00

151	Bob Welch	40.00
152	John Jaha	40.00
153	Harold Baines	40.00
154	Randy Johnson	150.00
155	Al Martin	40.00
156	J.T. Snow	60.00
157	Mike Mussina	200.00
158	Ruben Sierra	40.00
159	Dean Palmer	50.00
160	Steve Avery	40.00
161	Julio Franco	40.00
162	Dave Winfield	50.00
163	Tim Salmon	150.00
164	Tom Henke	40.00
165	Mo Vaughn	250.00
166	John Smoltz	75.00
167	Danny Tartabull	40.00
168	Delino DeShields	40.00
169	Charlie Hough	40.00
170	Paul O'Neill	75.00
171	Darren Daulton	40.00
172	Jack McDowell	40.00
173	Junior Felix	40.00
174	Jimmy Key	40.00
175	George Bell	40.00
176	Mike Stanton	40.00
177	Len Dykstra	50.00
178	Norm Charlton	40.00
179	Eric Anthony	40.00
180	Bob Dibble	40.00
181	Otis Nixon	40.00
182	Randy Myers	40.00
183	Tim Raines	50.00
184	Orel Hershiser	50.00
185	Andy Van Slyke	40.00
186	*Mike Lansing*	60.00
187	Ray Lankford	60.00
188	Mike Morgan	40.00
189	Moises Alou	75.00
190	Edgar Martinez	75.00
191	John Franco	40.00
192	Robin Yount	75.00
193	Bob Tewksbury	60.00
194	Jay Bell	40.00
195	Luis Gonzalez	40.00
196	Dave Fleming	40.00
197	Mike Greenwell	40.00
198	David Nied	40.00
199	Mike Piazza	600.00

1993 Finest
Jumbo All-Stars

These 4-1/2" x 6" cards were produced using the metallization process. Each 18-pack Finest box contains one of the cards, while one of every six cards is enhanced with special refracting foil.

		MT
Complete Set (33):		400.00
Common Player:		4.00
84	Andre Dawson	4.00
85	Greg Maddux	40.00
86	Rickey Henderson	5.00
87	Tom Glavine	8.00
88	Roberto Alomar	12.00
89	Darryl Strawberry	8.00

90	Wade Boggs	8.00
91	Bo Jackson	4.00
92	Mark McGwire	45.00
93	Robin Ventura	5.00
94	Joe Carter	4.00
95	Lee Smith	4.00
96	Cal Ripken, Jr.	50.00
97	Larry Walker	8.00
98	Don Mattingly	20.00
99	Jose Canseco	8.00
100	Dennis Eckersley	4.00
101	Terry Pendleton	4.00
102	Frank Thomas	50.00
103	Barry Bonds	15.00
104	Roger Clemens	20.00
105	Ryne Sandberg	15.00
106	Fred McGriff	6.00
107	Nolan Ryan	50.00
108	Will Clark	8.00
109	Pat Listach	4.00
110	Ken Griffey, Jr.	60.00
111	Cecil Fielder	5.00
112	Kirby Puckett	20.00
113	Dwight Gooden	4.00
114	Barry Larkin	6.00
115	David Cone	5.00
116	Juan Gonzalez	25.00

1994 Finest Promos

Mark McGwire 1B

Forty cards premiering the upcoming 1994 Topps Finest set were issued as a random insert in packs of Topps Series II regular-issue cards. The cards are in the same format as the regular-issue Finest cards and share the same card numbers. On back there is a red "Pre-Production" notice printed diagonally over the statistics.

		MT
Complete Set (40):		140.00
Common Player:		2.50
22	Deion Sanders	6.00
23	Jose Offerman	2.50
26	Alex Fernandez	2.50
31	Steve Finley	2.50
35	Andres Galarraga	3.00
43	Reggie Sanders	3.00
47	Dave Hollins	2.50
52	David Cone	2.50
59	Dante Bichette	3.00
61	Orlando Merced	2.50
62	Brian McRae	2.50
66	Mike Mussina	6.00
76	Mike Stanley	2.50
78	Mark McGwire	8.00
79	Pat Listach	2.50
82	Dwight Gooden	3.00
84	Phil Plantier	2.50
90	Jeff Russell	2.50
92	Gregg Jefferies	2.50
93	Jose Guzman	2.50
100	John Smoltz	3.00
102	Jim Thome	4.00
121	Moises Alou	3.00

125	Devon White	2.50
126	Ivan Rodriguez	3.00
130	Dave Magadan	2.50
136	Ozzie Smith	6.00
141	Chris Hoiles	2.50
149	Jim Abbott	3.00
151	Bill Swift	2.50
154	Edgar Martinez	3.00
157	J.T. Snow	3.00
159	Alan Trammell	3.00
163	Roberto Kelly	2.50
166	Scott Erickson	2.50
168	Scott Cooper	2.50
169	Rod Beck	2.50
177	Dean Palmer	2.50
182	Todd Van Poppel	2.50
185	Paul Sorrento	2.50

1994 Finest

Milt Thompson

The 1994 Baseball's Finest set included two series of 220 cards each. This 440-card set featured two 20-card subsets of 20 superstars and 20 top rookies in each series. Each card has a metallic look to it, using Topps Finest technology. The player' name is across the bottom with Topps Finest logos across the top. Backs picture each player on the top half and statistics on the bottom. Baseball's Finest was limited to 4,000 cases and available to dealers through an allocation process, based on their sales the previous year. Along with the regular-issue set, there was a parallel set, called Refractors, of 440 cards and a 4 x 6-inch version of the 80 subset cards.

		MT
Complete Set (440):		170.00
Common Player:		.50
Series 1 or 2 Wax Box:		50.00
1	Mike Piazza	7.00
2	Kevin Stocker	.50
3	Greg McMichael	.50
4	Jeff Conine	.50
5	Rene Arocha	.50
6	Aaron Sele	.50
7	Brent Gates	.50
8	Chuck Carr	.50
9	Kirk Rueter	.50
10	Mike Lansing	.50
11	Al Martin	.50
12	Jason Bere	.50
13	Troy Neel	.50
14	Armando Reynoso	.50
15	Jeromy Burnitz	.50
16	Rich Amaral	.50
17	David McCarty	.50
18	Tim Salmon	1.50
19	Steve Cooke	.50
20	Wil Cordero	.50
21	Kevin Tapani	.50
22	Deion Sanders	1.50
23	Jose Offerman	.50

24	Mark Langston	.50
25	Ken Hill	.50
26	Alex Fernandez	.60
27	Jeff Blauser	.50
28	Royce Clayton	.50
29	Brad Ausmus	.50
30	Ryan Bowen	.50
31	Steve Finley	.50
32	Charlie Hayes	.50
33	Jeff Kent	.50
34	Mike Henneman	.50
35	Andres Galarraga	1.00
36	Wayne Kirby	.50
37	Joe Oliver	.50
38	Terry Steinbach	.50
39	Ryan Thompson	.50
40	Luis Alicea	.50
41	Randy Velarde	.50
42	Bob Tewksbury	.50
43	Reggie Sanders	.75
44	Brian Williams	.50
45	Joe Orsulak	.50
46	Jose Lind	.50
47	Dave Hollins	.50
48	Graeme Lloyd	.50
49	Jim Gott	.50
50	Andre Dawson	.50
51	Steve Buechele	.50
52	David Cone	.75
53	Ricky Gutierrez	.50
54	Lance Johnson	.50
55	Tino Martinez	.50
56	Phil Hiatt	.50
57	Carlos Garcia	.50
58	Danny Darwin	.50
59	Dante Bichette	1.50
60	Scott Kamieniecki	.50
61	Orlando Merced	.50
62	Brian McRae	.50
63	Pat Kelly	.50
64	Tom Henke	.50
65	Jeff King	.50
66	Mike Mussina	2.00
67	Tim Pugh	.50
68	Robby Thompson	.50
69	Paul O'Neill	.50
70	Hal Morris	.50
71	Ron Karkovice	.50
72	Joe Girardi	.50
73	Eduardo Perez	.50
74	Raul Mondesi	2.00
75	Mike Gallego	.50
76	Mike Stanley	.50
77	Kevin Roberson	.50
78	Mark McGwire	12.00
79	Pat Listach	.50
80	Eric Davis	.50
81	Mike Bordick	.50
82	Dwight Gooden	.60
83	Mike Moore	.50
84	Phil Plantier	.50
85	Darren Lewis	.50
86	Rick Wilkins	.50
87	Darryl Strawberry	.60
88	Rob Dibble	.50
89	Greg Vaughn	.50
90	Jeff Russell	.50
91	Mark Lewis	.50
92	Gregg Jefferies	.50
93	Jose Guzman	.50
94	Kenny Rogers	.50
95	Mark Lemke	.50
96	Mike Morgan	.50
97	Andujar Cedeno	.50
98	Orel Hershiser	.50
99	Greg Swindell	.50
100	John Smoltz	1.00
101	Pedro Martinez	.75
102	Jim Thome	1.50
103	David Segui	.50
104	Charles Nagy	.50
105	Shane Mack	.50
106	John Jaha	.50
107	Tom Candiotti	.50
108	David Wells	.50
109	Bobby Jones	.50
110	Bob Hamelin	.50
111	Bernard Gilkey	.50
112	Chili Davis	.50
113	Todd Stottlemyre	.50
114	Derek Bell	.50
115	Mark McLemore	.50
116	Mark Whiten	.50
117	Mike Devereaux	.50
118	Terry Pendleton	.50
119	Pat Meares	.50

#	Name	Price	#	Name	Price	#	Name	Price
120	Pete Harnisch	.50	216	Larry Walker	1.00	312	Jose Vizcaino	.50
121	Moises Alou	.50	217	Roger Clemens	4.00	313	Rob Butler	.50
122	Jay Buhner	.75	218	Kenny Lofton	3.00	314	Kevin Seitzer	.50
123	Wes Chamberlain	.50	219	Cecil Fielder	1.00	315	Geronimo Pena	.50
124	Mike Perez	.50	220	Darren Daulton	.50	316	Hector Carrasco	.50
125	Devon White	.50	221	John Olerud	.50	317	Eddie Murray	2.00
126	Ivan Rodriguez	2.00	222	Jose Canseco	1.50	318	Roger Salkeld	.50
127	Don Slaught	.50	223	Rickey Henderson	.50	319	Todd Hundley	1.00
128	John Valentin	.50	224	Fred McGriff	1.50	320	Danny Jackson	.50
129	Jaime Navarro	.50	225	Gary Sheffield	1.50	321	Kevin Young	.50
130	Dave Magadan	.50	226	Jack McDowell	.75	322	Mike Greenwell	.50
131	Brady Anderson	.75	227	Rafael Palmeiro	.75	323	Kevin Mitchell	.50
132	Juan Guzman	.50	228	Travis Fryman	.50	324	Chuck Knoblauch	.75
133	John Wetteland	.50	229	Marquis Grissom	.50	325	Danny Tartabull	.50
134	Dave Stewart	.50	230	Barry Bonds	3.00	326	Vince Coleman	.50
135	Scott Servais	.50	231	Carlos Baerga	.50	327	Marvin Freeman	.50
136	Ozzie Smith	2.50	232	Ken Griffey, Jr.	12.00	328	Andy Benes	.50
137	Darrin Fletcher	.50	233	Dave Justice	.75	329	Mike Kelly	.50
138	Jose Mesa	.50	234	Bobby Bonilla	.50	330	Karl Rhodes	.50
139	Wilson Alvarez	.50	235	Cal Ripken	10.00	331	Allen Watson	.50
140	Pete Incaviglia	.50	236	Sammy Sosa	5.00	332	Damion Easley	.50
141	Chris Hoiles	.50	237	Len Dykstra	.50	333	Reggie Jefferson	.50
142	Darryl Hamilton	.50	238	Will Clark	1.00	334	Kevin McReynolds	.50
143	Chuck Finley	.50	239	Paul Molitor	2.00	335	Arthur Rhodes	.50
144	Archi Cianfrocco	.50	240	Barry Larkin	1.00	336	Brian Hunter	.50
145	Bill Wegman	.50	241	Bo Jackson	.75	337	Tom Browning	.50
146	Joey Cora	.50	242	Mitch Williams	.50	338	Pedro Munoz	.50
147	Darrell Whitmore	.50	243	Ron Darling	.50	339	Billy Ripken	.50
148	David Hulse	.50	244	Darryl Kile	.50	340	Gene Harris	.50
149	Jim Abbott	.50	245	Geronimo Berroa	.50	341	Fernando Vina	.50
150	Curt Schilling	.50	246	Gregg Olson	.50	342	Sean Berry	.50
151	Bill Swift	.50	247	Brian Harper	.50	343	Pedro Astacio	.50
152	Tommy Greene	.50	248	Rheal Cormier	.50	344	B.J. Surhoff	.50
153	Roberto Mejia	.50	249	Rey Sanchez	.50	345	Doug Drabek	.50
154	Edgar Martinez	.75	250	Jeff Fassero	.50	346	Jody Reed	.50
155	Roger Pavlik	.50	251	Sandy Alomar	.50	347	Ray Lankford	.50
156	Randy Tomlin	.50	252	Chris Bosio	.50	348	Steve Farr	.50
157	J.T. Snow	.75	253	Andy Stankiewicz	.50	349	Eric Anthony	.50
158	Bob Welch	.50	254	Harold Baines	.50	350	Pete Smith	.50
159	Alan Trammell	.50	255	Andy Ashby	.50	351	Lee Smith	.50
160	Ed Sprague	.50	256	Tyler Green	.50	352	Mariano Duncan	.50
161	Ben McDonald	.60	257	Kevin Brown	.50	353	Doug Strange	.50
162	Derrick May	.50	258	Mo Vaughn	3.00	354	Tim Bogar	.50
163	Roberto Kelly	.50	259	Mike Harkey	.50	355	Dave Weathers	.50
164	Bryan Harvey	.50	260	Dave Henderson	.50	356	Eric Karros	.50
165	Ron Gant	.60	261	Kent Hrbek	.50	357	Randy Myers	.50
166	Scott Erickson	.50	262	Darrin Jackson	.50	358	Chad Curtis	.50
167	Anthony Young	.50	263	Bob Wickman	.50	359	Steve Avery	.50
168	Scott Cooper	.50	264	Spike Owen	.50	360	Brian Jordan	.50
169	Rod Beck	.50	265	Todd Jones	.50	361	Tim Wallach	.50
170	John Franco	.50	266	Pat Borders	.50	362	Pedro Martinez	.75
171	Gary DiSarcina	.50	267	Tom Glavine	1.50	363	Bip Roberts	.50
172	Dave Fleming	.50	268	Dave Nilsson	.50	364	Lou Whitaker	.50
173	Wade Boggs	1.00	269	Rich Batchelor	.50	365	Luis Polonia	.50
174	Kevin Appier	.50	270	Delino DeShields	.50	366	Benny Santiago	.50
175	Jose Bautista	.50	271	Felix Fermin	.50	367	Brett Butler	.50
176	Wally Joyner	.50	272	Orestes Destrade	.50	368	Shawon Dunston	.50
177	Dean Palmer	.50	273	Mickey Morandini	.50	369	Kelly Stinnett	.50
178	Tony Phillips	.50	274	Otis Nixon	.50	370	Chris Turner	.50
179	John Smiley	.50	275	Ellis Burks	.50	371	Ruben Sierra	.50
180	Charlie Hough	.50	276	Greg Gagne	.50	372	Greg Harris	.50
181	Scott Fletcher	.50	277	John Doherty	.50	373	Xavier Hernandez	.50
182	Todd Van Poppel	.50	278	Julio Franco	.50	374	Howard Johnson	.50
183	Mike Blowers	.50	279	Bernie Williams	1.50	375	Duane Ward	.50
184	Willie McGee	.50	280	Rick Aguilera	.50	376	Roberto Hernandez	.50
185	Paul Sorrento	.50	281	Mickey Tettleton	.50	377	Scott Leius	.50
186	Eric Young	.50	282	David Nied	.50	378	Dave Valle	.50
187	Bret Barberie	.50	283	Johnny Ruffin	.50	379	Sid Fernandez	.50
188	Manuel Lee	.50	284	Dan Wilson	.50	380	Doug Jones	.50
189	Jeff Branson	.50	285	Omar Vizquel	.50	381	Zane Smith	.50
190	Jim Deshaies	.50	286	Willie Banks	.50	382	Craig Biggio	.50
191	Ken Caminiti	1.00	287	Erik Pappas	.50	383	Rick White	.50
192	Tim Raines	.50	288	Cal Eldred	.50	384	Tom Pagnozzi	.50
193	Joe Grahe	.50	289	Bobby Witt	.50	385	Chris James	.50
194	Hipolito Pichardo	.50	290	Luis Gonzalez	.50	386	Bret Boone	.50
195	Denny Neagle	.50	291	Greg Pirkl	.50	387	Jeff Montgomery	.50
196	Jeff Gardner	.50	292	Alex Cole	.50	388	Chad Kreuter	.50
197	Mike Benjamin	.50	293	Ricky Bones	.50	389	Greg Hibbard	.50
198	Milt Thompson	.50	294	Denis Boucher	.50	390	Mark Grace	1.00
199	Bruce Ruffin	.50	295	John Burkett	.50	391	Phil Leftwich	.60
200	Chris Hammond	.50	296	Steve Trachsel	.50	392	Don Mattingly	5.00
201	Tony Gwynn	5.00	297	Ricky Jordan	.50	393	Ozzie Guillen	.50
202	Robin Ventura	.75	298	Mark Dewey	.50	394	Gary Gaetti	.50
203	Frank Thomas	8.00	299	Jimmy Key	.50	395	Erik Hanson	.50
204	Kirby Puckett	5.00	300	Mike MacFarlane	.50	396	Scott Brosius	.50
205	Roberto Alomar	3.00	301	Tim Belcher	.50	397	Tom Gordon	.50
206	Dennis Eckersley	.50	302	Carlos Reyes	.50	398	Bill Gullickson	.50
207	Joe Carter	1.00	303	Greg Harris	.50	399	Matt Mieske	.50
208	Albert Belle	4.00	304	*Brian Anderson*	1.00	400	Pat Hentgen	.50
209	Greg Maddux	8.00	305	Terry Mulholland	.50	401	Walt Weiss	.50
210	Ryne Sandberg	3.00	306	Felix Jose	.50	402	Greg Blosser	.50
211	Juan Gonzalez	5.00	307	Darren Holmes	.50	403	Stan Javier	.50
212	Jeff Bagwell	5.00	308	Jose Rijo	.50	404	Doug Henry	.50
213	Randy Johnson	1.50	309	Paul Wagner	.50	405	Ramon Martinez	.50
214	Matt Williams	1.00	310	Bob Scanlan	.50	406	Frank Viola	.50
215	Dave Winfield	.50	311	Mike Jackson	.50	407	Mike Hampton	.50

408	Andy Van Slyke	.50
409	Bobby Ayala	.50
410	Todd Zeile	.50
411	Jay Bell	.50
412	Denny Martinez	.50
413	Mark Portugal	.50
414	Bobby Munoz	.50
415	Kirt Manwaring	.50
416	John Kruk	.50
417	Trevor Hoffman	.50
418	Chris Sabo	.50
419	Bret Saberhagen	.50
420	Chris Nabholz	.50
421	James Mouton	.50
422	Tony Tarasco	.50
423	Carlos Delgado	1.00
424	Rondell White	1.50
425	Javier Lopez	1.00
426	*Chan Ho Park*	1.50
427	Cliff Floyd	.50
428	Dave Staton	.50
429	J.R. Phillips	.50
430	Manny Ramirez	3.00
431	Kurt Abbott	.75
432	Melvin Nieves	.50
433	Alex Gonzalez	.75
434	Rick Helling	.50
435	Danny Bautista	.50
436	Matt Walbeck	.50
437	Ryan Klesko	2.50
438	Steve Karsay	.60
439	Salomon Torres	.50
440	Scott Ruffcorn	.50

1994 Finest Refractors

It takes an experienced eye and good light to detect a Refractor parallel card from a regular-issue Topps Finest. The Refractor utilizes a variation of the Finest metallic printing process to produce rainbow-effect highlights on the card front. The Refractors share the checklist with the regular-issue Finest and were inserted at a rate of about one per 10 packs.

	MT
Complete Set (440):	1750.
Common Player:	1.50
(Star cards valued about 8X-10X corresponding cards in regular Finest)	

1994 Finest Superstar Jumbos

Identical in format to the Superstars subset in the Finest issue, these cards measure about 4" x 5-1/2" and were distributed one per box in Finest foil packs. Backs carry

a card number under the banner with the player's name and position. Since there were 20 rookies and 20 superstars from both Series I and Series II, this is an 80-card set.

		MT
Complete Set (80):		350.00
Common Player:		2.00
1	Mike Piazza	15.00
2	Kevin Stocker	2.00
3	Greg McMichael	2.00
4	Jeff Conine	3.00
5	Rene Arocha	2.00
6	Aaron Sele	2.00
7	Brent Gates	2.00
8	Chuck Carr	2.00
9	Kirk Rueter	2.00
10	Mike Lansing	2.00
11	Al Martin	2.00
12	Jason Bere	2.00
13	Troy Neel	2.00
14	Armando Reynoso	2.00
15	Jeromy Burnitz	2.00
16	Rich Amaral	2.00
17	David McCarty	2.00
18	Tim Salmon	4.00
19	Steve Cooke	2.00
20	Wil Cordero	3.00
201	Tony Gwynn	6.00
202	Robin Ventura	3.00
203	Frank Thomas	30.00
204	Kirby Puckett	15.00
205	Roberto Alomar	9.00
206	Dennis Eckersley	2.00
207	Joe Carter	3.00
208	Albert Belle	12.00
209	Greg Maddux	25.00
210	Ryne Sandberg	7.50
211	Juan Gonzalez	7.50
212	Jeff Bagwell	12.00
213	Randy Johnson	4.50
214	Matt Williams	4.00
215	Dave Winfield	3.50
216	Larry Walker	3.00
217	Roger Clemens	6.00
218	Kenny Lofton	9.00
219	Cecil Fielder	3.00
220	Darren Daulton	2.00
221	John Olerud	2.00
222	Jose Canseco	6.00
223	Rickey Henderson	4.00
224	Fred McGriff	6.00
225	Gary Sheffield	4.00
226	Jack McDowell	2.00
227	Rafael Palmeiro	3.00
228	Travis Fryman	2.00
229	Marquis Grissom	2.00
230	Barry Bonds	12.00
231	Carlos Baerga	3.00
232	Ken Griffey Jr.	35.00
233	Dave Justice	6.00
234	Bobby Bonilla	2.00
235	Cal Ripken	35.00
236	Sammy Sosa	15.00
237	Len Dykstra	2.00
238	Will Clark	4.50
239	Paul Molitor	4.50
240	Barry Larkin	4.50
421	James Mouton	2.00
422	Tony Tarasco	2.00
423	Carlos Delgado	3.00
424	Rondell White	4.00
425	Javier Lopez	3.00
426	Chan Ho Park	3.00
427	Cliff Floyd	3.00
428	Dave Staton	2.00
429	J.R. Phillips	3.00
430	Manny Ramirez	9.00
431	Kurt Abbott	2.00
432	Melvin Nieves	2.00
433	Alex Gonzalez	2.00
434	Rick Helling	2.00
435	Danny Bautista	2.00
436	Matt Walbeck	2.00
437	Ryan Klesko	4.50
438	Steve Karsay	2.00
439	Salomon Torres	2.00
440	Scott Ruffcorn	2.00

> A player's name in *italic* type indicates a rookie card.

1995 Finest

In its third year Topps Finest baseball was produced in a 220-card base set. All cards feature the chrome-printing technology associated with the Finest logo and include a peel-off plastic protector on the card front. Backgrounds are green with gold pinstripes. Behind the action photo at center is a large diamond with each corner intersected by a silver semi-circle. On the Finest Rookies subset which makes up the first 30 cards of the issue, the diamond has a graduated pink to orange center, with flecks of red throughout. Veterans cards have a graduated blue to purple center of the diamond. On the rookies cards there is a teal brand name at top, while the vets show a gold "FINEST". Backs repeat the front background motif in shades of green. There is a player photo at right, with biographical data, 1994 and career stats, and a "Finest Moment" career highlight at left. Finest was sold in seven-card packs with a suggested retail price of $4.99.

		MT
Complete Set (220):		80.00
Common Player:		.25
Series 1 or 2 Wax Box:		100.00
1	Raul Mondesi (Rookie Theme)	.75
2	Kurt Abbott (Rookie Theme)	.30
3	Chris Gomez (Rookie Theme)	.25
4	Manny Ramirez (Rookie Theme)	2.00
5	Rondell White (Rookie Theme)	.50
6	William Van Landingham (Rookie Theme)	.50
7	Jon Lieber (Rookie Theme)	.25
8	Ryan Klesko (Rookie Theme)	1.00
9	John Hudek (Rookie Theme)	.25
10	Joey Hamilton (Rookie Theme)	.75
11	Bob Hamelin (Rookie Theme)	.25
12	Brian Anderson (Rookie Theme)	.25
13	Mike Lieberthal (Rookie Theme)	.25
14	Rico Brogna (Rookie Theme)	.25
15	Rusty Greer (Rookie Theme)	.50
16	Carlos Delgado (Rookie Theme)	.50

17	Jim Edmonds (Rookie Theme)	.75
18	Steve Trachsel (Rookie Theme)	.25
19	Matt Walbeck (Rookie Theme)	.25
20	Armando Benitez (Rookie Theme)	.25
21	Steve Karsay (Rookie Theme)	.25
22	Jose Oliva (Rookie Theme)	.25
23	Cliff Floyd (Rookie Theme)	.25
24	Kevin Foster (Rookie Theme)	.25
25	Javier Lopez (Rookie Theme)	.50
26	Jose Valentin (Rookie Theme)	.25
27	James Mouton (Rookie Theme)	.25
28	Hector Carrasco (Rookie Theme)	.25
29	Orlando Miller (Rookie Theme)	.25
30	Garret Anderson (Rookie Theme)	.25
31	Marvin Freeman	.25
32	Brett Butler	.30
33	Roberto Kelly	.25
34	Rod Beck	.25
35	Jose Rijo	.25
36	Edgar Martinez	.25
37	Jim Thome	1.50
38	Rick Wilkins	.25
39	Wally Joyner	.30
40	Wil Cordero	.25
41	Tommy Greene	.25
42	Travis Fryman	.25
43	Don Slaught	.25
44	Brady Anderson	.50
45	Matt Williams	.75
46	Rene Arocha	.25
47	Rickey Henderson	.40
48	Mike Mussina	1.50
49	Greg McMichael	.25
50	Jody Reed	.25
51	Tino Martinez	.35
52	Dave Clark	.25
53	John Valentin	.25
54	Bret Boone	.25
55	Wait Weiss	.25
56	Kenny Lofton	2.50
57	Scott Leius	.25
58	Eric Karros	.30
59	John Olerud	.30
60	Chris Hoiles	.25
61	Sandy Alomar	.25
62	Tim Wallach	.25
63	Cal Eldred	.25
64	Tom Glavine	.35
65	Mark Grace	.40
66	Rey Sanchez	.25
67	Bobby Ayala	.25
68	Dante Bichette	.75
69	Andres Galarraga	.35
70	Chuck Carr	.25
71	Bobby Witt	.25
72	Steve Avery	.25
73	Bobby Jones	.25
74	Delino DeShields	.25
75	Kevin Tapani	.25
76	Randy Johnson	1.00
77	David Nied	.25
78	Pat Hentgen	.40
79	Tim Salmon	.75
80	Todd Zeile	.25
81	John Wetteland	.25
82	Albert Belle	2.50
83	Ben McDonald	.25
84	Bobby Munoz	.25
85	Bip Roberts	.25
86	Mo Vaughn	2.50
87	Chuck Finley	.25
88	Chuck Knoblauch	.50
89	Frank Thomas	8.00
90	Danny Tartabull	.25
91	Dean Palmer	.25
92	Len Dykstra	.25
93	J.R. Phillips	.25
94	Tom Candiotti	.25
95	Marquis Grissom	.25
96	Barry Larkin	.50
97	Bryan Harvey	.25
98	Dave Justice	.50
99	David Cone	.40
100	Wade Boggs	.50
101	Jason Bere	.25
102	Hal Morris	.25
103	Fred McGriff	.50
104	Bobby Bonilla	.30
105	Jay Buhner	.35
106	Allen Watson	.25
107	Mickey Tettleton	.25
108	Kevin Appier	.25
109	Ivan Rodriguez	2.50
110	Carlos Garcia	.25
111	Andy Benes	.25
112	Eddie Murray	1.00
113	Mike Piazza	6.00
114	Greg Vaughn	.25
115	Paul Molitor	1.50
116	Terry Steinbach	.25
117	Jeff Bagwell	4.00
118	Ken Griffey Jr.	10.00
119	Gary Sheffield	2.00
120	Cal Ripken Jr.	8.00
121	Jeff Kent	.25
122	Jay Bell	.25
123	Will Clark	.75
124	Cecil Fielder	.50
125	Alex Fernandez	.30
126	Don Mattingly	4.00
127	Reggie Sanders	.25
128	Moises Alou	.25
129	Craig Biggio	.25
130	Eddie Williams	.25
131	John Franco	.25
132	John Kruk	.25
133	Jeff King	.25
134	Royce Clayton	.25
135	Doug Drabek	.25
136	Ray Lankford	.25
137	Roberto Alomar	2.50
138	Todd Hundley	.50
139	Alex Cole	.25
140	Shawon Dunston	.25
141	John Roper	.25
142	Mark Langston	.25
143	Tom Pagnozzi	.25
144	Wilson Alvarez	.25
145	Scott Cooper	.25
146	Kevin Mitchell	.25
147	Mark Whiten	.25
148	Jeff Conine	.25
149	Chili Davis	.25
150	Luis Gonzalez	.25
151	Juan Guzman	.25
152	Mike Greenwell	.25
153	Mike Henneman	.25
154	Rick Aguilera	.25
155	Dennis Eckersley	.30
156	Darrin Fletcher	.25
157	Darren Lewis	.25
158	Juan Gonzalez	5.00
159	Dave Hollins	.25
160	Jimmy Key	.25
161	Roberto Hernandez	.25
162	Randy Myers	.25
163	Joe Carter	.35
164	Darren Daulton	.25
165	Mike MacFarlane	.25
166	Bret Saberhagen	.25
167	Kirby Puckett	4.00
168	Lance Johnson	.25
169	Mark McGwire	10.00
170	Jose Canseco	1.00
171	Mike Stanley	.25
172	Lee Smith	.25
173	Robin Ventura	.35
174	Greg Gagne	.25
175	Brian McRae	.25
176	Mike Bordick	.25
177	Rafael Palmeiro	.50
178	Kenny Rogers	.25
179	Chad Curtis	.25
180	Devon White	.25
181	Paul O'Neill	.25
182	Ken Caminiti	.75
183	Dave Nilsson	.25
184	Tim Naehring	.25
185	Roger Clemens	3.00
186	Otis Nixon	.25
187	Tim Raines	.25
188	Dennis Martinez	.25
189	Pedro Martinez	.25
190	Jim Abbott	.25
191	Ryan Thompson	.25
192	Barry Bonds	2.50
193	Joe Girardi	.25
194	Steve Finley	.25
195	John Jaha	.25
196	Tony Gwynn	4.00
197	Sammy Sosa	5.00
198	John Burkett	.25
199	Carlos Baerga	.25
200	Ramon Martinez	.25
201	Aaron Sele	.25
202	Eduardo Perez	.25
203	Alan Trammell	.25
204	Orlando Merced	.25
205	Deion Sanders	.50
206	Robb Nen	.25
207	Jack McDowell	.25
208	Ruben Sierra	.25
209	Bernie Williams	2.00
210	Kevin Seitzer	.25
211	Charles Nagy	.25
212	Tony Phillips	.25
213	Greg Maddux	6.00
214	Jeff Montgomery	.25
215	Larry Walker	.60
216	Andy Van Slyke	.25
217	Ozzie Smith	1.50
218	Geronimo Pena	.25
219	Gregg Jefferies	.25
220	Lou Whitaker	.25

1995 Finest Refractors

A parallel set with a counterpart to each of the 220 cards in the regular Finest emission, the Refractors are printed in a version of the Finest chrome technology that produces a rainbow effect when viewed at the proper angle. The relatively open spaces of the 1995 Finest design make the Refractors easier to spot than the previous years' versions, but just to assist the identification process, Topps placed a small black "REFRACTOR" in the dark green background on the cards' backs, as well. Advertised rate of insertion for the Refractors was about one per 12 packs.

	MT
Complete Set (220):	3000.
Common Player:	8.00

(Star cards valued at 15-25X regular Finest cards; rookies at 10-20X.)

1995 Finest Flame Throwers

The scarcest of the Finest inserts is the nine-card set of baseball hardest throwing pitchers. Flame Throwers cards are found at an average rate of one per 48 packs. Fronts have a central photo of a pitcher bringing his best heat.

Behind the photo is the Flame Throwers typographic logo in tones of red, yellow and orange. Backs have another photo and a bar graph rating the pitcher's skill levels.

		MT
Complete Set (9):		50.00
Common Player:		5.00
1	Jason Bere	5.00
2	Roger Clemens	30.00
3	Juan Guzman	5.00
4	John Hudek	5.00
5	Randy Johnson	12.00
6	Pedro Martinez	8.00
7	Jose Rijo	5.00
8	Bret Saberhagen	6.00
9	John Wetteland	5.00

1995 Finest Power Kings

The emphasis in on youth in this chase set of baseball's top distance threats. Found at a rate of one per 24 packs, on average, the Power Kings inserts have a central photo of the player in batting action. The background, in shades of blue, features lightning strokes. Backs feature another pair of player photos and a bar graph charting the hitter's power skills.

		MT
Complete Set (18):		200.00
Common Player:		4.00
1	Bob Hamelin	4.00
2	Raul Mondesi	6.00
3	Ryan Klesko	8.00
4	Carlos Delgado	4.00
5	Manny Ramirez	10.00
6	Mike Piazza	30.00
7	Jeff Bagwell	20.00
8	Mo Vaughn	15.00
9	Frank Thomas	30.00
10	Ken Griffey Jr.	50.00
11	Albert Belle	12.00
12	Sammy Sosa	25.00
13	Dante Bichette	6.00
14	Gary Sheffield	6.00
15	Matt Williams	8.00
16	Fred McGriff	6.00
17	Barry Bonds	15.00
18	Cecil Fielder	4.00

> Values shown reflect the market as of January, 1999. On-field performances of current players in the 1999 baseball season are not factored in.

1995 Finest Update

Players who changed teams through trades or free agent signings and more of the season's rookie player crop are included in the Finest Update series of 110 cards. The cards are numbered contiguously with the base Finest set and share the same design. Once again, Refractor cards were found on an average of once per 12 packs. Finest Update was sold in seven-card packs with a suggested retail price of $4.99.

		MT
Complete Set (110):		40.00
Common Player:		.25
221	Chipper Jones	6.00
222	Benji Gil	.25
223	Tony Phillips	.25
224	Trevor Wilson	.25
225	Tony Tarasco	.25
226	Roberto Petagine	.25
227	Mike MacFarlane	.25
228	*Hideo Nomo*	12.00
229	Mark McLemore	.25
230	Ron Gant	.60
231	Andujar Cedeno	.25
232	*Mike Mimbs*	.40
233	Jim Abbott	.25
234	Ricky Bones	.25
235	Marty Cordova	2.00
236	Mark Johnson	1.00
237	Marquis Grissom	.25
238	Tom Henke	.25
239	Terry Pendleton	.25
240	John Wetteland	.25
241	Lee Smith	.25
242	Jaime Navarro	.25
243	Luis Alicea	.25
244	Scott Cooper	.25
245	Gary Gaetti	.25
246	Edgardo Alfonzo	.25
247	Brad Clontz	.25
248	Dave Mlicki	.25
249	Dave Winfield	.50
250	*Mark Grudzielanek*	3.00
251	Alex Gonzalez	.25
252	Kevin Brown	.25
253	Esteban Loaiza	.40
254	Vaughn Eshelman	.25
255	Bill Swift	.25
256	Brian McRae	.25
257	*Bobby Higginson*	5.00
258	Jack McDowell	.25
259	Scott Stahoviak	.25
260	Jon Nunnally	.25
261	Charlie Hayes	.25
262	Jacob Brumfield	.25
263	Chad Curtis	.25
264	Heathcliff Slocumb	.25
265	Mark Whiten	.25
266	Mickey Tettleton	.25
267	Jose Mesa	.25
268	Doug Jones	.25

269	Trevor Hoffman	.25
270	Paul Sorrento	.25
271	Shane Andrews	.25
272	Brett Butler	.25
273	Curtis Goodwin	.25
274	Larry Walker	.75
275	Phil Plantier	.25
276	Ken Hill	.25
277	Vinny Castilla	.25
278	Billy Ashley	.25
279	Derek Jeter	6.00
280	Bob Tewksbury	.25
281	Jose Offerman	.25
282	Glenallen Hill	.25
283	Tony Fernandez	.25
284	Mike Devereaux	.25
285	John Burkett	.25
286	Geronimo Berroa	.25
287	Quilvio Veras	.25
288	Jason Bates	.25
289	Lee Tinsley	.25
290	Derek Bell	.25
291	Jeff Fassero	.25
292	Ray Durham	.50
293	Chad Ogea	.25
294	Bill Pulsipher	.50
295	Phil Nevin	.25
296	*Carlos Perez*	1.00
297	Roberto Kelly	.25
298	Tim Wakefield	.25
299	Jeff Manto	.25
300	Brian Hunter	.25
301	C.J. Nitkowski	.25
302	Dustin Hermanson	.25
303	John Mabry	.25
304	Orel Hershiser	.25
305	Ron Villone	.25
306	Sean Bergman	.25
307	Tom Goodwin	.25
308	Al Reyes	.25
309	Todd Stottlemyre	.25
310	Rich Becker	.25
311	Joey Cora	.25
312	Ed Sprague	.25
313	John Smoltz	.75
314	Frank Castillo	.25
315	Chris Hammond	.25
316	Ismael Valdes	.25
317	Pete Harnisch	.25
318	Bernard Gilkey	.25
319	John Kruk	.25
320	Marc Newfield	.25
321	Brian Johnson	.25
322	Mark Portugal	.25
323	David Hulse	.25
324	Luis Ortiz	.25
325	Mike Benjamin	.25
326	Brian Jordan	.25
327	Shawn Green	.45
328	Joe Oliver	.25
329	Felipe Lira	.25
330	Andre Dawson	.35

1995 Finest Update Refractors

The special version of Topps' chromium printing process which creates a rainbow effect was applied to a limited number of each card in the Finest Update set to create a parallel Refractor edition. To assist in identification, a small black "REFRACTOR" is printed on the cards' backs, as well. Refractors are found on average once every 12 packs of Finest Update.

	MT
Complete Set (110):	700.00
Common Player:	6.00
(Star cards valued 15-25X regular Finest Updates; rookies valued 10-20X.)	

A player's name in *italic* type indicates a rookie card.

1996 Finest

Using the same format created for its Finest hockey brand, this 359-card Topps set has 220 commons, 91 uncommons and 47 rares. Cards are randomly chosen for a status. Commons have a bronze trim, while uncommon cards (one in four packs) have a silver trim. Rare cards have gold trim and are found one per every 24 packs. The set has eight themes. Series I themes are Finest Phenoms, Finest Intimidators, Finest Gamers and Finest Sterling, which consists of star players already included within the first three themes. Series II themes are Franchise, Additions, Prodigies and Sterling. Regular-issue cards are not only numbered from 1-359 in the set as a whole, but also numbered within each sub-set. For example, Kirby Puckett's rare card is numbered 18 and S3 (Sterling). Finest Refractor parallel cards were also made. Rare Refractor cards are found one per every 288 packs (less than 150 of these sets were produced), while uncommon Refractors are found one per every 48 packs. Common Refractors are seeded one per every 12 packs.

		MT
Complete Set (359):		1000.
Complete Series I Set (191):		800.00
Complete Series II Set (168):		400.00
Complete Bronze Set (220):		50.00
Complete Series I Bronze Set (110): 25.00		
Complete Series II Bronze Set (110): 25.00		
Common Player:		.25
Complete Gold Set (47):		1000.
Complete Series I Gold Set (25):		700.00
Complete Series II Gold Set (22):		
Common Gold:		10.00
Complete Silver Set (91):		200.00
Complete Series I Silver Set (55):		140.00
Complete Series II Silver Set (36):		75.00
Common Silver:		2.00
Series I Wax Box:		150.00
Series II Wax Box:		90.00
1	Greg Maddux S (Intimidators)	15.00
2	Bernie Williams S (Gamers)	5.00
3	Ivan Rodriguez S (Intimidators)	6.00
4	Marty Cordova G (Phenoms)	10.00
5	Roberto Hernandez S	.25
6	Tony Gwynn G (Gamers)	35.00
7	Barry Larkin S (Sterling)	2.00
8	Terry Pendleton (Gamers)	.25
9	Albert Belle G (Sterling)	25.00
10	Ray Lankford S (Gamers)	2.00
11	Mike Piazza S (Sterling)	15.00
12	Ken Caminiti (Gamers)	.25
13	Larry Walker S (Intimidators)	4.00
14	Matt Williams S (Intimidators)	3.00
15	Dan Miceli (Phenoms)	.25
16	Chipper Jones (Sterling)	3.00
17	John Wetteland (Intimidators)	.25
18	Kirby Puckett G (Sterling)	30.00
19	Tim Naehring (Gamers)	.25
20	Karim Garcia G (Phenoms)	15.00
21	Eddie Murray (Gamers)	.75
22	Tim Salmon S (Intimidators)	3.00
23	Kevin Appier (Intimidators)	.25
24	Ken Griffey Jr. (Sterling)	6.00
25	Cal Ripken Jr. G (Gamers)	60.00
26	Brian McRae (Gamers)	.25
27	Pedro Martinez (Intimidators)	.40
28	Brian Jordan (Gamers)	.25
29	Mike Fetters (Intimidators)	.25
30	Carlos Delgado (Phenoms)	.50
31	Shane Reynolds (Intimidators)	.25
32	Terry Steinbach (Gamers)	.25
33	Hideo Nomo G (Sterling)	25.00
34	Mark Leiter (Gamers)	.25
35	Edgar Martinez S (Intimidators)	2.00
36	David Segui (Gamers)	.25
37	Gregg Jefferies S (Gamers)	2.00
38	Bill Pulsipher S (Phenoms)	2.00
39	Ryne Sandberg G (Gamers)	20.00
40	Fred McGriff (Intimidators)	.75
41	Shawn Green S (Phenoms)	2.00
42	Jeff Bagwell S (Sterling)	35.00
43	Jim Abbott S (Gamers)	2.00
44	Glenallen Hill (Intimidators)	.25
45	Brady Anderson (Gamers)	.25
46	Roger Clemens S (Intimidators)	6.00
47	Jim Thome (Gamers)	.75
48	Frank Thomas (Sterling)	5.00
49	Chuck Knoblauch (Gamers)	.40
50	Lenny Dykstra (Gamers)	.25
51	Jason Isringhausen G (Phenoms)	10.00
52	Rondell White S (Phenoms)	2.00
53	Tom Pagnozzi (Gamers)	.25
54	Dennis Eckersley S (Intimidators)	2.00
55	Ricky Bones (Gamers)	.25
56	David Justice (Intimidators)	.50
57	Steve Avery (Gamers)	.25
58	Robby Thompson (Gamers)	.25
59	Hideo Nomo S (Phenoms)	8.00
60	Gary Sheffield S (Intimidators)	3.00
61	Tony Gwynn (Sterling)	2.50
62	Will Clark S (Gamers)	3.00
63	Denny Neagle (Gamers)	.25
64	Mo Vaughn G (Intimidators)	25.00
65	Bret Boone S (Gamers)	2.00
66	Dante Bichette G (Sterling)	12.00
67	Robin Ventura (Gamers)	.25
68	Rafael Palmeiro S (Intimidators)	2.50
69	Carlos Baerga S (Gamers)	2.00
70	Kevin Seitzer (Gamers)	.25
71	Ramon Martinez (Intimidators)	.25
72	Tom Glavine S (Gamers)	2.00
73	Garret Anderson S (Phenoms)	2.00
74	Mark McGwire G (Intimidators)	80.00
75	Brian Hunter (Phenoms)	.50
76	Alan Benes (Phenoms)	.50
77	Randy Johnson S (Intimidators)	6.00
78	Jeff King S (Gamers)	2.00
79	Kirby Puckett S (Intimidators)	10.00
80	Ozzie Guillen (Gamers)	.25
81	Kenny Lofton G (Intimidators)	25.00
82	Benji Gil (Phenoms)	.25
83	Jim Edmonds G (Gamers)	10.00
84	Cecil Fielder S (Intimidators)	2.00
85	Todd Hundley (Gamers)	.50
86	Reggie Sanders S (Intimidators)	2.00
87	Pat Hentgen (Gamers)	.25
88	Ryan Klesko S (Intimidators)	5.00
89	Chuck Finley (Gamers)	.25
90	Mike Mussina G (Intimidators)	18.00
91	John Valentin S (Intimidators)	2.00
92	Derek Jeter (Phenoms)	4.00
93	Paul O'Neill (Intimidators)	.25
94	Darrin Fletcher (Gamers)	.25
95	Manny Ramirez S (Phenoms)	8.00
96	Delino DeShields (Gamers)	.25
97	Tim Salmon (Sterling)	.75
98	John Olerud (Gamers)	.25
99	Vinny Castilla S (Intimidators)	2.00
100	Jeff Conine G (Gamers)	10.00
101	Tim Wakefield (Gamers)	.25
102	Johnny Damon G (Phenoms)	10.00
103	Dave Stevens (Gamers)	.25
104	Orlando Merced (Gamers)	.25
105	Barry Bonds G (Sterling)	25.00
106	Jay Bell (Gamers)	.25
107	John Burkett (Gamers)	.25
108	Chris Hoiles (Gamers)	.25
109	Carlos Perez S (Phenoms)	2.00
110	Dave Nilsson (Gamers)	.25
111	Rod Beck (Intimidators)	.25
112	Craig Biggio S (Gamers)	2.00
113	Mike Piazza (Intimidators)	4.00
114	Mark Langston (Gamers)	.25
115	Juan Gonzalez S (Intimidators)	12.00
116	Rico Brogna (Gamers)	.25
117	Jose Canseco G (Intimidators)	12.00
118	Tom Goodwin (Gamers)	.25
119	Bryan Rekar (Phenoms)	.25
120	David Cone (Intimidators)	.40
121	Ray Durham S (Phenoms)	2.00
122	Andy Pettitte (Phenoms)	1.50
123	Chili Davis (Intimidators)	.25
124	John Smoltz (Gamers)	.50
125	Heathcliff Slocumb (Intimidators)	.25
126	Dante Bichette (Intimidators)	.50
127	C.J. Nitkowski S (Phenoms)	2.00
128	Alex Gonzalez (Phenoms)	.25
129	Jeff Montgomery (Intimidators)	.25
130	Raul Mondesi S (Intimidators)	2.50
131	Denny Martinez (Gamers)	.25
132	Mel Rojas (Intimidators)	.25
133	Derek Bell (Gamers)	.25
134	Trevor Hoffman (Intimidators)	.25
135	Ken Griffey Jr. G (Intimidators)	90.00
136	Darren Daulton (Gamers)	.25
137	Pete Schourek (Gamers)	.25
138	Phil Nevin (Gamers)	.25
139	Andres Galarraga (Intimidators)	.40
140	Chad Fonville (Phenoms)	.25
141	Chipper Jones G (Phenoms)	50.00
142	Lee Smith S (Intimidators)	2.00
143	Joe Carter S (Gamers)	2.00
144	J.T. Snow (Gamers)	.25
145	Greg Maddux G (Sterling)	50.00
146	Barry Bonds (Intimidators)	1.50
147	Orel Hershiser (Gamers)	.25
148	Quilvio Veras (Phenoms)	.25
149	Will Clark (Sterling)	.50
150	Jose Rijo (Gamers)	.25
151	Mo Vaughn S (Sterling)	8.00
152	Travis Fryman (Gamers)	.25
153	Frank Rodriguez S (Phenoms)	2.00
154	Alex Fernandez (Gamers)	.25
155	Wade Boggs (Gamers)	.50
156	Troy Percival (Phenoms)	.25
157	Moises Alou (Gamers)	.25
158	Javy Lopez (Gamers)	.50
159	Jason Giambi (Phenoms)	.25
160	Steve Finley S (Gamers)	2.00
161	Jeff Bagwell S (Intimidators)	12.00
162	Mark McGwire (Sterling)	5.00
163	Eric Karros (Gamers)	.25
164	Jay Buhner G (Intimidators)	12.00
165	Cal Ripken Jr. S (Sterling)	20.00

166	Mickey Tettleton (Intimidators)	.25
167	Barry Larkin (Intimidators)	.75
168	Lyle Mouton S (Phenoms)	2.00
169	Ruben Sierra (Intimidators)	.25
170	Bill Swift (Gamers)	.25
171	Sammy Sosa S (Intimidators)	12.00
172	Chad Curtis (Gamers)	.25
173	Dean Palmer (Gamers)	.25
174	John Franco S (Gamers)	2.00
175	Bobby Bonilla (Intimidators)	.25
176	Greg Colbrunn (Gamers)	.25
177	Jose Mesa (Intimidators)	.25
178	Mike Greenwell (Gamers)	.25
179	Greg Vaughn S (Intimidators)	2.00
180	Mark Wohlers S (Intimidators)	2.00
181	Doug Drabek (Gamers)	.25
182	Paul O'Neill S (Sterling)	2.00
183	Wilson Alvarez (Gamers)	.25
184	Marty Cordova (Sterling)	.40
185	Hal Morris (Gamers)	.25
186	Frank Thomas G (Intimidators)	70.00
187	Carlos Garcia (Gamers)	.25
188	Albert Belle S (Intimidators)	8.00
189	Mark Grace S (Gamers)	2.00
190	Marquis Grissom (Gamers)	.25
191	Checklist	.25
192	Chipper Jones G	50.00
193	Will Clark	.60
104	Paul Molitor	.75
195	Kenny Rogers	.25
196	Reggie Sanders	.25
197	Roberto Alomar G	20.00
198	Dennis Eckersley G	10.00
199	Raul Mondesi	.75
200	Lance Johnson	.25
201	Alvin Mormon	.25
202	George Arias G	10.00
203	Jack McDowell	.25
204	Randy Myers	.25
205	Harold Baines	.25
206	Marty Cordova	.40
207	Rich Hunter	.25
208	Al Leiter	.25
209	Greg Gagne	.25
210	Ben McDonald	.25
211	Ernie Young S	2.00
212	Terry Adams	.25
213	Paul Sorrento	.25
214	Albert Belle	1.50
215	Mike Blowers	.25
216	Jim Edmonds	.75
217	Felipe Crespo	.25
218	Fred McGriff S	2.50
219	Shawon Dunston	.25
220	Jimmy Haynes	.25
221	Jose Canseco	.75
222	Eric Davis	.25
223	Kimera Bartee S	2.00
224	Tim Raines	.25
225	Tony Phillips	.25
226	Charlie Hayes	.25
227	Eric Owens	.25
228	Roberto Alomar	1.25
229	Rickey Henderson S	2.00
230	Sterling Hitchcock S	2.00
231	Bernard Gilkey S	2.00
232	Hideo Nomo G	20.00
233	Kenny Lofton	1.50
234	Ryne Sandberg S	6.00
235	Greg Maddux S	20.00
236	Mark McGwire	4.00
237	Jay Buhner	.50
238	Craig Biggio	.25
239	Todd Stottlemyre S	2.00
240	Barry Bonds	1.50
241	Jason Kendall S	2.00
242	Paul O'Neill S	2.00
243	Chris Snopek G	10.00
244	Ron Gant	.40
245	Paul Wilson	.40
246	Todd Hollandsworth	.25
247	Todd Zeile	.25
248	David Justice	.50
249	Tim Salmon G	12.00
250	Moises Alou	.25
251	Bob Wolcott	.25
252	David Wells	.25
253	Juan Gonzalez	2.50
254	Andres Galarraga	.50
255	Dave Hollins	.25
256	Devon White S	2.00

257	Sammy Sosa	2.50
258	Ivan Rodriguez	1.00
259	Bip Roberts	.25
260	Tino Martinez	.50
261	Chuck Knoblauch S	2.50
262	Mike Stanley	.25
263	Wally Joyner S	2.00
264	Butch Huskey	.25
265	Jeff Conine	.25
266	Matt Williams G	12.00
267	Mark Grace	.50
268	Jason Schmidt	.25
269	Otis Nixon	.25
270	Randy Johnson G	20.00
271	Kirby Puckett	2.00
272	Andy Fox S	2.00
273	Andy Benes	.25
274	Sean Berry S	.25
275	Mike Piazza	4.00
276	Rey Ordonez	.75
277	Benito Santiago S	2.00
278	Gary Gaetti	.25
279	Paul Molitor G	15.00
280	Robin Ventura	.25
281	Cal Ripken Jr.	5.00
282	Carlos Baerga	.25
283	Roger Cedeno	.25
284	Chad Mottola S	2.00
285	Terrell Wade	.25
286	Kevin Brown	.25
287	Rafael Palmeiro	.50
2R8	Mo Vaughn	1.50
289	Dante Bichette S	2.50
290	Cecil Fielder G	10.00
291	Doc Gooden S	2.00
292	Bob Tewksbury	.25
293	Kevin Mitchell S	2.00
294	Livan Hernandez G	25.00
295	Russ Davis S	2.00
296	Chan Ho Park S	2.00
297	T.J. Mathews	.25
298	Manny Ramirez	1.50
299	Jeff Bagwell	3.00
300	Marty Janzen G	10.00
301	Wade Boggs	.50
302	Larry Walker S	4.00
303	Steve Gibralter	.25
304	B.J. Surhoff	.25
305	Ken Griffey Jr. S	25.00
306	Royce Clayton	.25
307	Sal Fasano	.25
308	Ron Gant G	10.00
309	Gary Sheffield	.75
310	Ken Hill	.25
311	Joe Girardi	.25
312	Matt Lawton	.25
313	Billy Wagner S	2.00
314	Julio Franco	.25
315	Joe Carter	.50
316	Brooks Kieschnick	.25
317	Mike Grace S	3.00
318	Heathcliff Slocumb	.25
319	Barry Larkin	.75
320	Tony Gwynn	2.50
321	Ryan Klesko G	18.00
322	Frank Thomas	5.00
323	Edgar Martinez	.25
324	Jermaine Dye G	10.00
325	Henry Rodriguez	.25
326	Marvin Benard	.25
327	Kenny Lofton S	8.00
328	Derek Bell S	2.00
329	Ugueth Urbina	.25
330	Jason Giambi G	10.00
331	Roger Salkeld	.25
332	Edgar Renteria	.25
333	Ryan Klesko	1.00
334	Ray Lankford	.25
335	Edgar Martinez G	10.00
336	Justin Thompson	.25
337	Gary Sheffield S	4.00
338	Rey Ordonez G	12.00
339	Mark Clark	.25
340	Ruben Rivera	.75
341	Mark Grace S	3.00
342	Matt Williams	.50
343	Francisco Cordova	.40
344	Cecil Fielder	.40
345	Andres Galarraga S	2.50
346	Brady Anderson S	2.50
347	Sammy Sosa G	40.00
348	Mark Grudzielanek	.25
349	Ron Coomer	.25
350	Derek Jeter S	12.00
351	Rich Aurilla	.25
352	Jose Herrera	.25

353	Jay Buhner S	3.00
354	Juan Gonzalez G	40.00
355	Craig Biggio G	10.00
356	Tony Clark	1.00
357	Tino Martinez S	2.50
358	Dan Naulty	.25
359	Checklist	.25

1996 Finest Refractors

Finest Refractor cards were created as a parallel set to Topps' 1996 Finest set. Finest Refractor cards are found one per every 288 packs (less than 150 of these sets were produced), while uncommon Refractors are found one per every 48 packs. Common Refractors are seeded one per every 12 packs.

	MT
Complete Set (359):	7500.
Complete Series I Set (191):	5000.
Complete Series II Set (168):	2500.
Complete Bronze Set (219):	1000.
Complete Series I Bronze Set (110): 400.00	
Complete Series II Bronze Set (109): 600.00	
Common Player:	4.00
Complete Gold Refractor Set (48):	4500.
Complete Series I Gold Set (26):	3000.
Complete Series II Gold Set (22):	1500.
Common Gold:	25.00
Complete Silver Refractor Set (91):	2000.
Complete Series I Silver Set (55):	1500.
Complete Series II Silver Set (36): 600.00	
Common Silver:	10.00

1	Greg Maddux S (Intimidators)	60.00
2	Bernie Williams S (Gamers)	25.00
3	Ivan Rodriguez S (Intimidators)	30.00
4	Marty Cordova G (Phenoms)	25.00
5	Roberto Hernandez (Intimidators)	4.00
6	Tony Gwynn G (Gamers)	150.00
7	Barry Larkin S (Sterling)	15.00
8	Terry Pendleton (Gamers)	4.00
9	Albert Belle G (Sterling)	80.00
10	Ray Lankford S (Gamers)	10.00
11	Mike Piazza S (Sterling)	60.00
12	Ken Caminiti (Gamers)	8.00
13	Larry Walker S (Intimidators)	25.00
14	Matt Williams S (Intimidators)	15.00
15	Dan Miceli (Phenoms)	4.00
16	Chipper Jones (Sterling)	40.00
17	John Wetteland (Intimidators)	4.00
18	Kirby Puckett G (Sterling)	90.00
19	Tim Naehring (Gamers)	4.00
20	Karim Garcia G (Phenoms)	50.00
21	Eddie Murray (Gamers)	12.00
22	Tim Salmon S (Intimidators)	15.00
23	Kevin Appier (Intimidators)	4.00
24	Ken Griffey Jr. (Sterling)	75.00
25	Cal Ripken Jr. G (Gamers)	200.00
26	Brian McRae (Gamers)	4.00
27	Pedro Martinez (Intimidators)	6.00
28	Brian Jordan (Gamers)	4.00
29	Mike Fetters (Intimidators)	4.00
30	Carlos Delgado (Phenoms)	6.00
31	Shane Reynolds (Intimidators)	4.00
32	Terry Steinbach (Gamers)	4.00
33	Hideo Nomo S (Sterling)	75.00
34	Mark Leiter (Gamers)	4.00
35	Edgar Martinez S (Intimidators)	10.00
36	David Segui (Gamers)	4.00
37	Gregg Jefferies S (Gamers)	10.00
38	Bill Pulsipher S (Phenoms)	10.00
39	Ryne Sandberg G (Gamers)	80.00
40	Fred McGriff (Intimidators)	15.00
41	Shawn Green S (Phenoms)	10.00
42	Jeff Bagwell (Sterling)	90.00
43	Jim Abbott S (Gamers)	10.00

#	Player	Price
44	Glenallen Hill (Intimidators)	4.00
45	Brady Anderson (Gamers)	6.00
46	Roger Clemens S (Intimidators)	40.00
47	Jim Thome (Gamers)	12.00
48	Frank Thomas (Sterling)	50.00
49	Chuck Knoblauch (Gamers)	8.00
50	Lenny Dykstra (Gamers)	4.00
51	Jason Isringhausen G (Phenoms)	25.00
52	Rondell White S (Phenoms)	12.00
53	Tom Pagnozzi (Gamers)	4.00
54	Dennis Eckersley S (Intimidators)	10.00
55	Ricky Bones (Gamers)	4.00
56	David Justice (Intimidators)	10.00
57	Steve Avery (Gamers)	4.00
58	Robby Thompson (Gamers)	4.00
59	Hideo Nomo S (Phenoms)	30.00
60	Gary Sheffield S (Intimidators)	15.00
61	Tony Gwynn (Sterling)	30.00
62	Will Clark S (Gamers)	15.00
63	Denny Neagle (Gamers)	4.00
64	Mo Vaughn G (Intimidators)	80.00
65	Bret Boone S (Gamers)	10.00
66	Dante Bichette G (Sterling)	35.00
67	Robin Ventura (Gamers)	4.00
68	Rafael Palmeiro S (Intimidators)	12.00
69	Carlos Baerga S (Gamers)	10.00
70	Kevin Seitzer (Gamers)	4.00
71	Ramon Martinez (Intimidators)	4.00
72	Tom Glavine S (Gamers)	12.00
73	Garret Anderson S (Phenoms)	10.00
74	Mark McGwire G (Intimidators)	250.00
75	Brian Hunter (Phenoms)	4.00
76	Alan Benes (Phenoms)	10.00
77	Randy Johnson S (Intimidators)	30.00
78	Jeff King S (Gamers)	10.00
79	Kirby Puckett S (Intimidators)	50.00
80	Ozzie Guillen (Gamers)	4.00
81	Kenny Lofton G (Intimidators)	80.00
82	Benji Gil (Phenoms)	4.00
83	Jim Edmonds G (Gamers)	30.00
84	Cecil Fielder S (Intimidators)	12.00
85	Todd Hundley (Gamers)	10.00
86	Reggie Sanders S (Intimidators)	10.00
87	Pat Hentgen (Gamers)	4.00
88	Ryan Klesko S (Intimidators)	20.00
89	Chuck Finley (Gamers)	4.00
90	Mike Mussina G (Intimidators)	60.00
91	John Valentin S (Intimidators)	10.00
92	Derek Jeter (Phenoms)	40.00
93	Paul O'Neill (Intimidators)	4.00
94	Darrin Fletcher (Gamers)	4.00
95	Manny Ramirez S (Phenoms)	30.00
96	Delino DeShields (Gamers)	4.00
97	Tim Salmon (Sterling)	10.00
98	John Olerud (Gamers)	4.00
99	Vinny Castilla S (Intimidators)	10.00
100	Jeff Conine G (Gamers)	25.00
101	Tim Wakefield (Gamers)	4.00
102	Johnny Damon G (Phenoms)	25.00
103	Dave Stevens (Gamers)	4.00
104	Orlando Merced (Gamers)	4.00
105	Barry Bonds G (Sterling)	80.00
106	Jay Bell (Gamers)	4.00
107	John Burkett (Gamers)	4.00
108	Chris Hoiles (Gamers)	4.00
109	Carlos Perez S (Phenoms)	10.00
110	Dave Nilsson (Gamers)	4.00
111	Rod Beck (Intimidators)	4.00
112	Craig Biggio S (Gamers)	10.00
113	Mike Piazza (Intimidators)	40.00
114	Mark Langston (Gamers)	4.00
115	Juan Gonzalez S (Intimidators)	50.00
116	Rico Brogna (Gamers)	4.00
117	Jose Canseco (Intimidators)	40.00
118	Tom Goodwin (Gamers)	4.00
119	Bryan Rekar (Phenoms)	4.00
120	David Cone (Intimidators)	7.50
121	Ray Durham S (Phenoms)	10.00
122	Andy Pettitte (Phenoms)	20.00
123	Chili Davis (Intimidators)	4.00
124	John Smoltz (Gamers)	10.00
125	Heathcliff Slocumb (Intimidators)	4.00
126	Dante Bichette (Intimidators)	8.00
127	C.J. Nitkowski S (Phenoms)	10.00
128	Alex Gonzalez (Phenoms)	4.00
129	Jeff Montgomery (Intimidators)	4.00
130	Raul Mondesi S (Intimidators)	15.00
131	Denny Martinez (Gamers)	4.00
132	Mel Rojas (Intimidators)	4.00
133	Derek Bell (Gamers)	4.00
134	Trevor Hoffman (Intimidators)	4.00
135	Ken Griffey Jr. G (Intimidators)	250.00
136	Darren Daulton (Gamers)	4.00
137	Pete Schourek (Gamers)	4.00
138	Phil Nevin (Phenoms)	4.00
139	Andres Galarraga (Intimidators)	6.00
140	Chad Fonville (Phenoms)	4.00
141	Chipper Jones G (Phenoms)	125.00
142	Lee Smith S (Intimidators)	10.00
143	Joe Carter S (Gamers)	12.00
144	J.T. Snow (Gamers)	4.00
145	Greg Maddux G (Sterling)	150.00
146	Barry Bonds (Intimidators)	20.00
147	Orel Hershiser (Gamers)	4.00
148	Quilvio Veras (Phenoms)	4.00
149	Will Clark (Sterling)	8.00
150	Jose Rijo (Gamers)	4.00
151	Mo Vaughn S (Sterling)	30.00
152	Travis Fryman (Gamers)	4.00
153	Frank Rodriguez S (Phenoms)	10.00
154	Alex Fernandez (Gamers)	6.00
155	Wade Boggs (Gamers)	6.00
156	Troy Percival (Phenoms)	4.00
157	Moises Alou (Gamers)	6.00
158	Javy Lopez (Gamers)	6.00
159	Jason Giambi (Phenoms)	4.00
160	Steve Finley S (Gamers)	10.00
161	Jeff Bagwell S (Intimidators)	50.00
162	Mark McGwire (Sterling)	75.00
163	Eric Karros (Gamers)	4.00
164	Jay Buhner G (Intimidators)	35.00
165	Cal Ripken Jr. S (Sterling)	80.00
166	Mickey Tettleton (Intimidators)	4.00
167	Barry Larkin (Intimidators)	10.00
168	Lyle Mouton S (Phenoms)	10.00
169	Ruben Sierra (Intimidators)	4.00
170	Bill Swift (Gamers)	4.00
171	Sammy Sosa S (Intimidators)	40.00
172	Chad Curtis (Gamers)	4.00
173	Dean Palmer (Gamers)	4.00
174	John Franco S (Gamers)	10.00
175	Bobby Bonilla (Intimidators)	6.00
176	Greg Colbrunn (Gamers)	4.00
177	Jose Mesa (Intimidators)	4.00
178	Mike Greenwell (Gamers)	4.00
179	Greg Vaughn S (Intimidators)	10.00
180	Mark Wohlers S (Intimidators)	10.00
181	Doug Drabek (Gamers)	4.00
182	Paul O'Neill S (Sterling)	10.00
183	Wilson Alvarez (Gamers)	4.00
184	Marty Cordova (Sterling)	6.00
185	Hal Morris (Gamers)	4.00
186	Frank Thomas G (Intimidators)	150.00
187	Carlos Garcia (Gamers)	4.00
188	Albert Belle S (Intimidators)	30.00
189	Mark Grace S (Gamers)	15.00
190	Marquis Grissom (Gamers)	6.00
191	Checklist	4.00
192	Chipper Jones G (Gamers)	125.00
193	Will Clark	8.00
194	Paul Molitor	12.00
195	Kenny Rogers	4.00
196	Reggie Sanders	4.00
197	Roberto Alomar G	60.00
198	Dennis Eckersley G	25.00
199	Raul Mondesi	10.00
200	Lance Johnson	4.00
201	Alvin Mormon	4.00
202	George Arias G	25.00
203	Jack McDowell	6.00
204	Randy Myers	4.00
205	Harold Baines	4.00
206	Marty Cordova	4.00
207	Rich Hunter	4.00
208	Al Leiter	4.00
209	Greg Gagne	4.00
210	Ben McDonald	4.00
211	Ernie Young S	10.00
212	Terry Adams	4.00
213	Paul Sorrento	4.00
214	Albert Belle	20.00
215	Mike Blowers	4.00
216	Jim Edmonds	8.00
217	Felipe Crespo	4.00
218	Fred McGriff S	15.00
219	Shawon Dunston	4.00
220	Jimmy Haynes	4.00
221	Jose Canseco	10.00
222	Eric Davis	4.00
223	Kimera Bartee S	10.00
224	Tim Raines	4.00
225	Tony Phillips	4.00
226	Charlie Hayes	4.00
227	Eric Owens	4.00
228	Roberto Alomar	20.00
229	Rickey Henderson S	10.00
230	Sterling Hitchcock S	10.00
231	Bernard Gilkey S	10.00
232	Hideo Nomo G	60.00
233	Kenny Lofton	25.00
234	Ryne Sandberg S	30.00
235	Greg Maddux S	60.00
236	Mark McGwire	75.00
237	Jay Buhner	8.00
238	Craig Biggio	6.00
239	Todd Stottlemyre S	10.00
240	Barry Bonds	20.00
241	Jason Kendall S	10.00
242	Paul O'Neill S	10.00
243	Chris Snopek G	25.00
244	Ron Gant	6.00
245	Paul Wilson	6.00
246	Todd Hollandsworth	4.00
247	Todd Zeile	4.00
248	David Justice	10.00
249	Tim Salmon G	35.00
250	Moises Alou	6.00
251	Bob Wolcott	4.00
252	David Wells	4.00
253	Juan Gonzalez	30.00
254	Andres Galarraga	8.00
255	Dave Hollins	4.00
256	Devon White S	10.00
257	Sammy Sosa	35.00
258	Ivan Rodriguez	15.00
259	Bip Roberts	4.00
260	Tino Martinez	8.00
261	Chuck Knoblauch S	15.00
262	Mike Stanley	4.00
263	Wally Joyner S	10.00
264	Butch Huskey	4.00
265	Jeff Conine	4.00
266	Matt Williams G	35.00
267	Mark Grace	8.00
268	Jason Schmidt	4.00
269	Otis Nixon	4.00
270	Randy Johnson G	40.00
271	Kirby Puckett	20.00
272	Andy Fox S	10.00
273	Andy Benes	4.00
274	Sean Berry S	10.00
275	Mike Piazza	40.00
276	Rey Ordonez	8.00
277	Benito Santiago S	10.00
278	Gary Gaetti	4.00
279	Paul Molitor G	50.00
280	Robin Ventura	4.00
281	Cal Ripken Jr.	50.00
282	Carlos Baerga	4.00
283	Roger Cedeno	4.00
284	Chad Mottola S	10.00
285	Terrell Wade	4.00
286	Kevin Brown	4.00
287	Rafael Palmeiro	8.00
288	Mo Vaughn	25.00
289	Dante Bichette S	15.00
290	Cecil Fielder G	35.00
291	Doc Gooden S	10.00
292	Bob Tewksbury	4.00
293	Kevin Mitchell S	10.00
294	Livan Hernandez G	50.00
295	Russ Davis S	10.00
296	Chan Ho Park S	10.00

297	T.J. Mathews	4.00
298	Manny Ramirez	20.00
299	Jeff Bagwell	30.00
300	Marty Janzen G	25.00
301	Wade Boggs	7.50
302	Larry Walker S	30.00
303	Steve Gibralter	4.00
304	B.J. Surhoff	4.00
305	Ken Griffey Jr. S	100.00
306	Royce Clayton	4.00
307	Sal Fasano	4.00
308	Ron Gant G	30.00
309	Gary Sheffield	12.00
310	Ken Hill	4.00
311	Joe Girardi	4.00
312	Matt Lawton	4.00
313	Billy Wagner S	12.00
314	Julio Franco	4.00
315	Joe Carter	8.00
316	Brooks Kieschnick	4.00
317	Mike Grace S	12.00
318	Heathcliff Slocumb	4.00
319	Barry Larkin	10.00
320	Tony Gwynn	30.00
321	Ryan Klesko G	40.00
322	Frank Thomas	50.00
323	Edgar Martinez	4.00
324	Jermaine Dye G	25.00
325	Henry Rodriguez	4.00
326	Marvin Benard	4.00
327	Kenny Lofton S	30.00
328	Derek Bell S	10.00
329	Ugueth Urbina	4.00
330	Jason Giambi G	30.00
331	Roger Salkeld	4.00
332	Edgar Renteria	8.00
333	Ryan Klesko	12.00
334	Ray Lankford	4.00
335	Edgar Martinez G	30.00
336	Justin Thompson	8.00
337	Gary Sheffield S	15.00
338	Rey Ordonez G	40.00
339	Mark Clark	4.00
340	Ruben Rivera	8.00
341	Mark Grace S	12.00
342	Matt Williams	10.00
343	Francisco Cordova	5.00
344	Cecil Fielder	8.00
345	Andres Galarraga S	12.00
346	Brady Anderson S	12.00
347	Sammy Sosa G	125.00
348	Mark Grudzielanek	4.00
349	Ron Coomer	4.00
350	Derek Jeter S	60.00
351	Rich Aurilia	4.00
352	Jose Herrera	4.00
353	Jay Buhner S	12.00
354	Juan Gonzalez G	125.00
355	Craig Biggio G	35.00
356	Tony Clark	25.00
357	Tino Martinez S	12.00
358	Dan Naulty	4.00
359	Checklist	4.00

1997 Finest

Finest returned for 1997 in its three-tiered format from 1996, but added several new twists. Cards numbered 1-100 were bronze, 101-150 were silver and 151-175 were gold. All cards fit into one of five different subsets, called Warriors, Blue Chips, Power, Hurlers and Masters. The bronze cards were the "common" card, while silvers were found every four packs and golds every 24 packs. Each card had a parallel Refractor version: bronze (1:12), silver (1:48) and gold (1:288). In addition, silver and gold cards had an additional parallel set. Silvers were found in an embossed version (1:16) and embossed Refractor version (1:192), while golds were found in a die-cut/embossed version (1:96) and a die-cut embossed Refractor (1:1152).

		MT
Complete Set (350):		1000.
Complete Series 1 Set (175):		550.00
Complete Series 2 Set (175):		450.00
Complete Bronze Set (200):		35.00
Common Bronze:		.25
Complete Silver Set (100):		250.00
Common Silver:		2.00
Embossed Silvers: 3x		
Complete Gold Set (50):		750.00
Common Gold:		8.00
Embossed Die-Cut Golds: 2x to 3x		
Series 1 Box:		110.00
Series 2 Box:		80.00
1	Barry Bonds B	1.50
2	Ryne Sandberg B	1.50
3	Brian Jordan B	.25
4	Rocky Coppinger B	.25
5	Dante Bichette B	.50
6	Al Martin B	.25
7	Charles Nagy B	.25
8	Otis Nixon B	.25
9	Mark Johnson B	.25
10	Jeff Bagwell B	2.50
11	Ken Hill B	.25
12	Willie Adams B	.25
13	Raul Mondesi B	.50
14	Reggie Sanders B	.25
15	Derek Jeter B	3.00
16	Jermaine Dye B	.50
17	Edgar Renteria B	.50
18	Travis Fryman B	.25
19	Roberto Hernandez B	.25
20	Sammy Sosa B	2.50
21	Garret Anderson B	.25
22	Rey Ordonez B	.50
23	Glenallen Hill B	.25
24	Dave Nilsson B	.25
25	Kevin Brown B	.25
26	Brian McRae B	.25
27	Joey Hamilton B	.25
28	Jamey Wright B	.25
29	Frank Thomas B	4.00
30	Mark McGwire B	5.00
31	Ramon Martinez B	.25
32	Jaime Bluma B	.25
33	Frank Rodriguez B	.25
34	Andy Benes B	.25
35	Jay Buhner B	.50
36	Justin Thompson B	.25
37	Darin Erstad B	2.50
38	Gregg Jefferies B	.25
39	Jeff D'Amico B	.40
40	Pedro Martinez B	.25
41	Nomar Garciaparra B	2.50
42	Jose Valentin B	.25
43	Pat Hentgen B	.25
44	Will Clark B	.50
45	Bernie Williams B	1.00
46	Luis Castillo B	.25
47	B.J. Surhoff B	.25
48	Greg Gagne B	.25
49	Pete Schourek B	.25
50	Mike Piazza B	3.00
51	Dwight Gooden B	.25
52	Javy Lopez B	.40
53	Chuck Finley B	.25
54	James Baldwin B	.25
55	Jack McDowell B	.25
56	Royce Clayton B	.25
57	Carlos Delgado B	.40
58	Neifi Perez B	.25
59	Eddie Taubensee B	.25
60	Rafael Palmeiro B	.50
61	Marty Cordova B	.25
62	Wade Boggs B	.50
63	Rickey Henderson B	.25
64	Mike Hampton B	.25
65	Troy Percival B	.25
66	Barry Larkin B	.75
67	Jermaine Allensworth B	.25
68	Mark Clark B	.25
69	Mike Lansing B	.25
70	Mark Grudzielanek B	.25
71	Todd Stottlemyre B	.25
72	Juan Guzman B	.25
73	John Burkett B	.25
74	Wilson Alvarez B	.25
75	Ellis Burks B	.40
76	Bobby Higginson B	.50
77	Ricky Bottalico B	.25
78	Omar Vizquel B	.25
79	Paul Sorrento B	.25
80	Denny Neagle B	.25
81	Roger Pavlik B	.25
82	Mike Lieberthal B	.25
83	Devon White B	.25
84	John Olerud B	.25
85	Kevin Appier B	.25
86	Joe Girardi B	.25
87	Paul O'Neill B	.40
88	Mike Sweeney B	.25
89	John Smiley B	.25
90	Ivan Rodriguez B	1.00
91	Randy Myers B	.25
92	Bip Roberts B	.25
93	Jose Mesa B	.25
94	Paul Wilson B	.40
95	Mike Mussina B	1.00
96	Ben McDonald B	.25
97	John Mabry B	.25
98	Tom Goodwin B	.25
99	Edgar Martinez B	.40
100	Andruw Jones B	2.50
101	Jose Canseco S	3.00
102	Billy Wagner S	3.00
103	Dante Bichette S	3.00
104	Curt Schilling S	2.00
105	Dean Palmer S	2.00
106	Larry Walker S	5.00
107	Bernie Williams S	6.00
108	Chipper Jones S	15.00
109	Gary Sheffield S	4.00
110	Randy Johnson S	5.00
111	Roberto Alomar S	6.00
112	Todd Walker S	5.00
113	Sandy Alomar S	2.00
114	John Jaha S	2.00
115	Ken Caminiti S	4.00
116	Ryan Klesko S	5.00
117	Mariano Rivera S	3.00
118	Jason Giambi S	2.00
119	Lance Johnson S	2.00
120	Robin Ventura S	2.00
121	Todd Hollandsworth S	2.50
122	Johnny Damon S	2.00
123	William VanLandingham S	2.00
124	Jason Kendall S	2.50
125	Vinny Castilla S	2.50
126	Harold Baines S	2.00
127	Joe Carter S	2.50
128	Craig Biggio S	2.50
129	Tony Clark S	6.00
130	Ron Gant S	2.50
131	David Segui S	2.00
132	Steve Trachsel S	2.00
133	Scott Rolen S	15.00
134	Mike Stanley S	2.00
135	Cal Ripken Jr. S	20.00
136	John Smoltz S	4.00
137	Bobby Jones S	2.00
138	Manny Ramirez S	6.00
139	Ken Griffey Jr. S	25.00
140	Chuck Knoblauch S	3.00
141	Mark Grace S	3.00
142	Chris Snopek S	2.00
143	Hideo Nomo S	6.00
144	Tim Salmon S	4.00
145	David Cone S	3.00
146	Eric Young S	2.50
147	Jeff Brantley S	2.00
148	Jim Thome S	5.00
149	Trevor Hoffman S	2.00
150	Juan Gonzalez S	12.00
151	Mike Piazza S	40.00
152	Ivan Rodriguez G	15.00
153	Mo Vaughn G	15.00
154	Brady Anderson G	10.00
155	Mark McGwire G	75.00

156	Rafael Palmeiro G	10.00
157	Barry Larkin G	10.00
158	Greg Maddux G	40.00
159	Jeff Bagwell G	30.00
160	Frank Thomas G	40.00
161	Ken Caminiti G	10.00
162	Andruw Jones G	20.00
163	Dennis Eckersley G	8.00
164	Jeff Conine G	8.00
165	Jim Edmonds G	8.00
166	Derek Jeter G	40.00
167	Vladimir Guerrero G	30.00
168	Sammy Sosa G	40.00
169	Tony Gwynn G	30.00
170	Andres Galarraga G	10.00
171	Todd Hundley G	10.00
172	Jay Buhner G	10.00
173	Paul Molitor G	12.00
174	Kenny Lofton G	15.00
175	Barry Bonds G	15.00
176	Gary Sheffield B	.50
177	Dmitri Young B	.25
178	Jay Bell B	.25
179	David Wells B	.25
180	Walt Weiss B	.25
181	Paul Molitor B	.75
182	Jose Guillen B	1.50
183	Al Leiter B	.25
184	Mike Fetters B	.25
185	Mark Langston B	.25
186	Fred McGriff B	.40
187	Darrin Fletcher B	.25
188	Brant Brown B	.25
189	Geronimo Berroa B	.25
190	Jim Thome B	1.00
191	Jose Vizcaino B	.25
192	Andy Ashby B	.25
193	Rusty Greer B	.25
194	Brian Hunter B	.25
195	Chris Hoiles B	.25
196	Orlando Merced B	.25
197	Brett Butler B	.25
198	Derek Bell B	.25
199	Bobby Bonilla B	.25
200	Alex Ochoa B	.25
201	Wally Joyner B	.25
202	Mo Vaughn B	1.25
203	Doug Drabek B	.25
204	Tino Martinez B	.50
205	Roberto Alomar B	1.00
206	Brian Giles B	.25
207	Todd Worrell B	.25
208	Alan Benes B	.25
209	Jim Leyritz B	.25
210	Darryl Hamilton B	.25
211	Jimmy Key B	.25
212	Juan Gonzalez B	2.50
213	Vinny Castilla B	.25
214	Chuck Knoblauch B	.40
215	Tony Phillips B	.25
216	Jeff Cirillo B	.25
217	Carlos Garcia B	.25
218	Brooks Kieschnick B	.25
219	Marquis Grissom B	.25
220	Dan Wilson B	.25
221	Greg Vaughn B	.25
222	John Wetteland B	.25
223	Andres Galarraga B	.40
224	Ozzie Guillen B	.25
225	Kevin Elster B	.25
226	Bernard Gilkey B	.25
227	Mike MacFarlane B	.25
228	Heathcliff Slocumb B	.25
229	Wendell Magee Jr. B	.25
230	Carlos Baerga B	.25
231	Kevin Seitzer B	.25
232	Henry Rodriguez B	.25
233	Roger Clemens B	1.50
234	Mark Wohlers B	.25
235	Eddie Murray B	.50
236	Todd Zeile B	.25
237	J.T. Snow B	.25
238	Ken Griffey Jr. B	5.00
239	Sterling Hitchcock B	.25
240	Albert Belle B	1.25
241	Terry Steinbach B	.25
242	Robb Nen B	.25
243	Mark McLemore B	.25
244	Jeff King B	.25
245	Tony Clark B	1.25
246	Tim Salmon B	.40
247	Benito Santiago B	.25
248	Robin Ventura B	.25
249	*Bubba Trammell B*	1.50
250	Chili Davis B	.25
251	John Valentin B	.25

252	Cal Ripken Jr. B	4.00
253	Matt Williams B	.50
254	Jeff Kent B	.25
255	Eric Karros B	.25
256	Ray Lankford B	.25
257	Ed Sprague B	.25
258	Shane Reynolds B	.25
259	Jaime Navarro B	.25
260	Eric Davis B	.25
261	Orel Hershiser B	.25
262	Mark Grace B	.40
263	Rod Beck B	.25
264	Ismael Valdes B	.25
265	Manny Ramirez B	1.25
266	Ken Caminiti B	.40
267	Tim Naehring B	.25
268	Jose Rosado B	.25
269	Greg Colbrunn B	.25
270	Dean Palmer B	.25
271	David Justice B	.50
272	Scott Spiezio B	.25
273	Chipper Jones B	3.00
274	Mel Rojas B	.25
275	Bartolo Colon B	.25
276	Darin Erstad S	12.00
277	Sammy Sosa S	15.00
278	Rafael Palmeiro S	3.00
279	Frank Thomas S	20.00
280	Ruben Rivera S	2.00
281	Hal Morris S	2.00
282	Jay Buhner S	3.00
283	Kenny Lofton S	8.00
284	Jose Canseco S	3.00
285	Alex Fernandez S	2.00
286	Todd Helton S	8.00
287	Andy Pettitte S	6.00
288	John Franco S	2.00
289	Ivan Rodriguez S	6.00
290	Ellis Burks S	2.00
291	Julio Franco S	2.00
292	Mike Piazza S	15.00
293	Brian Jordan S	2.00
294	Greg Maddux S	15.00
295	Bob Abreu S	2.00
296	Rondell White S	2.00
297	Moises Alou S	2.00
298	Tony Gwynn S	12.00
299	Deion Sanders S	3.00
300	Jeff Montgomery S	2.00
301	Ray Durham S	2.00
302	John Wasdin S	2.00
303	Ryne Sandberg S	6.00
304	Delino DeShields S	2.00
305	Mark McGwire S	25.00
306	Andruw Jones S	12.00
307	Kevin Orie S	2.00
308	Matt Williams S	3.00
309	Karim Garcia S	2.00
310	Derek Jeter S	15.00
311	Mo Vaughn S	8.00
312	Brady Anderson S	2.50
313	Barry Bonds S	8.00
314	Steve Finley S	2.00
315	Vladimir Guerrero S	8.00
316	Matt Morris S	2.00
317	Tom Glavine S	3.00
318	Jeff Bagwell S	12.00
319	Albert Belle S	6.00
320	*Hideki Irabu S*	15.00
321	Andres Galarraga S	3.00
322	Cecil Fielder S	2.00
323	Barry Larkin S	3.00
324	Todd Hundley S	3.00
325	Fred McGriff S	3.00
326	Gary Sheffield G	12.00
327	Craig Biggio G	10.00
328	Raul Mondesi G	12.00
329	Edgar Martinez G	8.00
330	Chipper Jones G	40.00
331	Bernie Williams G	12.00
332	Juan Gonzalez G	30.00
333	Ron Gant G	8.00
334	Cal Ripken Jr. G	50.00
335	Larry Walker G	12.00
336	Matt Williams G	10.00
337	Jose Cruz Jr. G	25.00
338	Joe Carter G	8.00
339	Wilton Guerrero G	8.00
340	Cecil Fielder G	8.00
341	Todd Walker G	10.00
342	Ken Griffey Jr. G	60.00
343	Ryan Klesko G	10.00
344	Roger Clemens G	20.00
345	Hideo Nomo G	12.00
346	Dante Bichette G	8.00
347	Albert Belle G	15.00

348	Randy Johnson G	12.00
349	Manny Ramirez G	15.00
350	John Smoltz G	8.00

1997 Finest Refractors

Every card in the '97 Finest set - both regular and parallel - has a Refractor version. The Uncommon parallel set of Refractors feature a mosaic pattern in the background while the Rare embossed die-cut parallel set of Refractors are produced with a hyper-plaid foil design. The number of cards and the insertion ratios for each level of Refractors is as follows: Common (100 cards, 1:12 packs), Uncommon (50, 1:48), Rare (25, 1:288), Embossed Uncommon (50, 1:192), Embossed Die-cut Rare (25, 1:1,152).

	MT
Complete Set (350):	5800.
Complete Series 1 Set (175):	3200.
Complete Series 2 Set (175):	2600.
Complete Bronze Set (200)	800.00
Common Bronze:	4.00
Complete Silver Set (100):	1500.
Common Silver:	10.00
Embossed Silver Refractors: 3x	
Complete Gold Set (50):	3500.
Common Gold:	40.00
Embossed Die-Cut Gold Refractors: 3x	
Wax Box:	95.00
1	Barry Bonds B	20.00
2	Ryne Sandberg B	20.00
3	Brian Jordan B	4.00
4	Rocky Coppinger B	4.00
5	Dante Bichette B	10.00
6	Al Martin B	4.00
7	Charles Nagy B	4.00
8	Otis Nixon B	4.00
9	Mark Johnson B	4.00
10	Jeff Bagwell B	35.00
11	Ken Hill B	4.00
12	Willie Adams B	4.00
13	Raul Mondesi B	10.00
14	Reggie Sanders B	4.00
15	Derek Jeter B	40.00
16	Jermaine Dye B	4.00
17	Edgar Renteria B	4.00
18	Travis Fryman B	4.00
19	Roberto Hernandez B	4.00
20	Sammy Sosa B	25.00
21	Garret Anderson B	4.00
22	Rey Ordonez B	4.00
23	Glenallen Hill B	4.00
24	Dave Nilsson B	4.00
25	Kevin Brown B	4.00
26	Brian McRae B	4.00
27	Joey Hamilton B	4.00
28	Jamey Wright B	4.00
29	Frank Thomas B	40.00
30	Mark McGwire B	75.00
31	Ramon Martinez B	4.00
32	Jaime Bluma B	4.00
33	Frank Rodriguez B	4.00
34	Andy Benes B	4.00
35	Jay Buhner B	8.00
36	Justin Thompson B	4.00
37	Darin Erstad B	25.00
38	Gregg Jefferies B	4.00
39	Jeff D'Amico B	6.00
40	Pedro Martinez B	4.00
41	Nomar Garciaparra B	30.00
42	Jose Valentin B	4.00
43	Pat Hentgen B	4.00
44	Will Clark B	8.00
45	Bernie Williams B	18.00
46	Luis Castillo B	4.00
47	B.J. Surhoff B	4.00
48	Greg Gagne B	4.00
49	Pete Schourek B	4.00
50	Mike Piazza B	40.00
51	Dwight Gooden B	4.00
52	Javy Lopez B	6.00
53	Chuck Finley B	4.00
54	James Baldwin B	4.00

#	Player	Price	#	Player	Price	#	Player	Price
55	Jack McDowell B	4.00	151	Mike Piazza G	200.00	247	Benito Santiago B	4.00
56	Royce Clayton B	4.00	152	Ivan Rodriguez G	75.00	248	Robin Ventura B	4.00
57	Carlos Delgado B	4.00	153	Mo Vaughn G	75.00	249	Bubba Trammell B	8.00
58	Neifi Perez B	4.00	154	Brady Anderson G	40.00	250	Chili Davis B	4.00
59	Eddie Taubensee B	4.00	155	Mark McGwire G	300.00	251	John Valentin B	4.00
60	Rafael Palmeiro B	8.00	156	Rafael Palmeiro G	50.00	252	Cal Ripken Jr. B	50.00
61	Marty Cordova B	4.00	157	Barry Larkin G	50.00	253	Matt Williams B	8.00
62	Wade Boggs B	10.00	158	Greg Maddux G	200.00	254	Jeff Kent B	4.00
63	Rickey Henderson B	4.00	159	Jeff Bagwell G	100.00	255	Eric Karros B	6.00
64	Mike Hampton B	4.00	160	Frank Thomas G	200.00	256	Ray Lankford B	4.00
65	Troy Percival B	4.00	161	Ken Caminiti G	50.00	257	Ed Sprague B	4.00
66	Barry Larkin B	8.00	162	Andruw Jones G	75.00	258	Shane Reynolds B	4.00
67	Jermaine Allensworth B	4.00	163	Dennis Eckersley G	40.00	259	Jaime Navarro B	4.00
68	Mark Clark B	4.00	164	Jeff Conine G	40.00	260	Eric Davis B	4.00
69	Mike Lansing B	4.00	165	Jim Edmonds G	40.00	261	Orel Hershiser B	4.00
70	Mark Grudzielanek B	4.00	166	Derek Jeter G	200.00	262	Mark Grace B	8.00
71	Todd Stottlemyre B	4.00	167	Vladimir Guerrero G	100.00	263	Rod Beck B	4.00
72	Juan Guzman B	4.00	168	Sammy Sosa G	200.00	264	Ismael Valdes B	4.00
73	John Burkett B	4.00	169	Tony Gwynn G	150.00	265	Manny Ramirez B	15.00
74	Wilson Alvarez B	4.00	170	Andres Galarraga G	60.00	266	Ken Caminiti B	6.00
75	Ellis Burks B	6.00	171	Todd Hundley G	40.00	267	Tim Naehring B	4.00
76	Bobby Higginson B	6.00	172	Jay Buhner G	50.00	268	Jose Rosado B	4.00
77	Ricky Bottalico B	4.00	173	Paul Molitor G	65.00	269	Greg Colbrunn B	4.00
78	Omar Vizquel B	4.00	174	Kenny Lofton G	75.00	270	Dean Palmer B	4.00
79	Paul Sorrento B	4.00	175	Barry Bonds G	75.00	271	David Justice B	8.00
80	Denny Neagle B	4.00	176	Gary Sheffield B	8.00	272	Scott Spiezio B	4.00
81	Roger Pavlik B	4.00	177	Dmitri Young B	4.00	273	Chipper Jones B	40.00
82	Mike Lieberthal B	4.00	178	Jay Bell B	4.00	274	Mel Rojas B	4.00
83	Devon White B	4.00	179	David Wells B	4.00	275	Bartolo Colon B	4.00
84	John Olerud B	4.00	180	Walt Weiss B	4.00	276	Darin Erstad S	30.00
85	Kevin Appier B	4.00	181	Paul Molitor B	10.00	277	Sammy Sosa S	70.00
86	Joe Girardi B	4.00	182	Jose Guillen B	15.00	278	Rafael Palmeiro S	12.00
87	Paul O'Neill B	6.00	183	Al Leiter B	4.00	279	Frank Thomas S	75.00
88	Mike Sweeney B	4.00	184	Mike Fetters B	4.00	280	Ruben Rivera S	10.00
89	John Smiley B	4.00	185	Mark Langston B	4.00	281	Hal Morris S	10.00
90	Ivan Rodriguez B	20.00	186	Fred McGriff B	6.00	282	Jay Buhner S	12.00
91	Randy Myers B	4.00	187	Darrin Fletcher B	4.00	283	Kenny Lofton S	30.00
92	Bip Roberts B	4.00	188	Brant Brown B	4.00	284	Jose Canseco S	12.00
93	Jose Mesa B	4.00	189	Geronimo Berroa B	4.00	285	Alex Fernandez S	10.00
94	Paul Wilson B	4.00	190	Jim Thome B	12.00	286	Todd Helton S	20.00
95	Mike Mussina B	15.00	191	Jose Vizcaino B	4.00	287	Andy Pettitte S	25.00
96	Ben McDonald B	4.00	192	Andy Ashby B	4.00	288	John Franco S	10.00
97	John Mabry B	4.00	193	Rusty Greer B	4.00	289	Ivan Rodriguez S	30.00
98	Tom Goodwin B	4.00	194	Brian L. Hunter B	4.00	290	Ellis Burks S	10.00
99	Edgar Martinez B	6.00	195	Chris Hoiles B	4.00	291	Julio Franco S	10.00
100	Andruw Jones B	20.00	196	Orlando Merced B	4.00	292	Mike Piazza S	75.00
101	Jose Canseco S	20.00	197	Brett Butler B	4.00	293	Brian Jordan S	10.00
102	Billy Wagner S	15.00	198	Derek Bell B	4.00	294	Greg Maddux S	75.00
103	Dante Bichette S	20.00	199	Bobby Bonilla B	4.00	295	Bob Abreu S	10.00
104	Curt Schilling S	12.00	200	Alex Ochoa B	4.00	296	Rondell White S	10.00
105	Dean Palmer S	12.00	201	Wally Joyner B	4.00	297	Moises Alou S	10.00
106	Larry Walker S	30.00	202	Mo Vaughn B	15.00	298	Tony Gwynn S	60.00
107	Bernie Williams S	25.00	203	Doug Drabek B	4.00	299	Deion Sanders S	15.00
108	Chipper Jones S	75.00	204	Tino Martinez B	8.00	300	Jeff Montgomery S	10.00
109	Gary Sheffield S	15.00	205	Roberto Alomar B	12.00	301	Ray Durham S	10.00
110	Randy Johnson S	25.00	206	Brian Giles B	4.00	302	John Wasdin S	10.00
111	Roberto Alomar S	25.00	207	Todd Worrell B	4.00	303	Ryne Sandberg S	30.00
112	Todd Walker S	20.00	208	Alan Benes B	4.00	304	Delino DeShields S	10.00
113	Sandy Alomar S	12.00	209	Jim Leyritz B	4.00	305	Mark McGwire S	125.00
114	John Jaha S	10.00	210	Darryl Hamilton B	4.00	306	Andruw Jones S	30.00
115	Ken Caminiti S	15.00	211	Jimmy Key B	4.00	307	Kevin Orie S	10.00
116	Ryan Klesko S	15.00	212	Juan Gonzalez B	30.00	308	Matt Williams S	12.00
117	Mariano Rivera S	12.00	213	Vinny Castilla B	4.00	309	Karim Garcia S	10.00
118	Jason Giambi S	10.00	214	Chuck Knoblauch B	6.00	310	Derek Jeter S	75.00
119	Lance Johnson S	10.00	215	Tony Phillips B	4.00	311	Mo Vaughn S	30.00
120	Robin Ventura S	10.00	216	Jeff Cirillo B	4.00	312	Brady Anderson S	10.00
121	Todd Hollandsworth S	10.00	217	Carlos Garcia B	4.00	313	Barry Bonds S	30.00
122	Johnny Damon S	10.00	218	Brooks Kieschnick B	4.00	314	Steve Finley S	10.00
123	William VanLandingham S	10.00	219	Marquis Grissom B	4.00	315	Vladimir Guerrero S	40.00
124	Jason Kendall S	10.00	220	Dan Wilson B	4.00	316	Matt Morris S	10.00
125	Vinny Castilla S	12.00	221	Greg Vaughn B	6.00	317	Tom Glavine S	10.00
126	Harold Baines S	10.00	222	John Wetteland B	4.00	318	Jeff Bagwell S	40.00
127	Joe Carter S	12.00	223	Andres Galarraga B	8.00	319	Albert Belle S	30.00
128	Craig Biggio S	12.00	224	Ozzie Guillen B	4.00	320	Hideki Irabu S	30.00
129	Tony Clark S	20.00	225	Kevin Elster B	4.00	321	Andres Galarraga S	15.00
130	Ron Gant S	10.00	226	Bernard Gilkey B	4.00	322	Cecil Fielder S	10.00
131	David Segui S	10.00	227	Mike Macfarlane B	4.00	323	Barry Larkin S	12.00
132	Steve Trachsel S	10.00	228	Heathcliff Slocumb B	4.00	324	Todd Hundley S	10.00
133	Scott Rolen S	40.00	229	Wendell Magee Jr. B	4.00	325	Fred McGriff S	12.00
134	Mike Stanley S	10.00	230	Carlos Baerga B	4.00	326	Gary Sheffield G	40.00
135	Cal Ripken Jr. S	100.00	231	Kevin Seitzer B	4.00	327	Craig Biggio G	40.00
136	John Smoltz S	12.00	232	Henry Rodriguez B	4.00	328	Raul Mondesi G	40.00
137	Bobby Jones S	10.00	233	Roger Clemens B	25.00	329	Edgar Martinez G	40.00
138	Manny Ramirez S	30.00	234	Mark Wohlers B	4.00	330	Chipper Jones G	200.00
139	Ken Griffey Jr. S	120.00	235	Eddie Murray B	8.00	331	Bernie Williams G	60.00
140	Chuck Knoblauch S	20.00	236	Todd Zeile B	4.00	332	Juan Gonzalez G	150.00
141	Mark Grace S	20.00	237	J.T. Snow B	4.00	333	Ron Gant G	40.00
142	Chris Snopek S	12.00	238	Ken Griffey Jr. B	60.00	334	Cal Ripken Jr. G	250.00
143	Hideo Nomo S	20.00	239	Sterling Hitchcock B	4.00	335	Larry Walker G	50.00
144	Tim Salmon S	20.00	240	Albert Belle B	15.00	336	Matt Williams G	50.00
145	David Cone S	12.00	241	Terry Steinbach B	4.00	337	Jose Cruz Jr. G	80.00
146	Eric Young S	10.00	242	Robb Nen B	4.00	338	Joe Carter G	40.00
147	Jeff Brantley S	10.00	243	Mark McLemore B	4.00	339	Wilton Guerrero G	40.00
148	Jim Thome S	20.00	244	Jeff King B	4.00	340	Cecil Fielder G	40.00
149	Trevor Hoffman S	12.00	245	Tony Clark B	10.00	341	Todd Walker G	60.00
150	Juan Gonzalez S	60.00	246	Tim Salmon B	8.00	342	Ken Griffey Jr. G	300.00

343	Ryan Klesko G	40.00
344	Roger Clemens G	100.00
345	Hideo Nomo G	60.00
346	Dante Bichette G	50.00
347	Albert Belle G	75.00
348	Randy Johnson G	60.00
349	Manny Ramirez G	75.00
350	John Smoltz G	40.00

1998 Finest

Finest dropped its three-tiered format in 1998 and produced a 275-card set with a thicker 26-point stock, with 150 cards in Series I and 125 in Series II. The catch in 1998 was that each card arrived in Protector, No-Protector, Protector Refractor and No-Protector Refractor versions. Six-card packs sold for a suggested retail price of $5. Finest also included insert sets for the first time since 1995. Included in Series I packs were Centurions, Mystery Finest and Power Zone inserts. Series II had Mystery Finest, Stadium Stars and The Man. Throughout Series I and II, Finest Protector cards are considered base cards, while No-Protector are inserted one per two packs (HTA odds 1:1), No-Protector Refractors are seeded 1:24 packs (HTA odds 1:10) and Finest Refractors are seeded 1:12 packs (HTA odds 1:5).

	MT
Complete Set (275):	90.00
Complete Series I Set (150):	50.00
Complete Series II Set (125):	40.00
Common Player:	.25
No-Protector: 2x to 4x	
Inserted 1:2	
Refractors: 10x to 20x	
Inserted 1:12	
No protector Refract: 15x to 30x	
Inserted 1:24	
Wax Box:	100.00

1	Larry Walker	1.00
2	Andruw Jones	1.75
3	Ramon Martinez	.25
4	Geronimo Berroa	.25
5	David Justice	.60
6	Rusty Greer	.40
7	Chad Ogea	.25
8	Tom Goodwin	.25
9	Tino Martinez	.75
10	Jose Guillen	.50
11	Jeffrey Hammonds	.25
12	Brian McRae	.25
13	Jeremi Gonzalez	.25
14	Craig Counsell	.25
15	Mike Piazza	4.00
16	Greg Maddux	4.00
17	Todd Greene	.25
18	Rondell White	.50
19	Kirk Rueter	.25
20	Tony Clark	1.00
21	Brad Radke	.25
22	Jaret Wright	3.00
23	Carlos Delgado	.25
24	Dustin Hermanson	.50
25	Gary Sheffield	.75
26	Jose Canseco	.50
27	Kevin Young	.25
28	David Wells	.25
29	Mariano Rivera	.50
30	Reggie Sanders	.25
31	Mike Cameron	.50
32	Bobby Witt	.25
33	Kevin Orie	.25
34	Royce Clayton	.25
35	Edgar Martinez	.40
36	Neifi Perez	.25
37	Kevin Appier	.25
38	Darryl Hamilton	.25
39	Michael Tucker	.25
40	Roger Clemens	2.50
41	Carl Everett	.25
42	Mike Sweeney	.25
43	Pat Meares	.25
44	Brian Giles	.25
45	Matt Morris	.25
46	Jason Dickson	.25
47	Rich Loiselle	.25
48	Joe Girardi	.25
49	Steve Trachsel	.25
50	Ben Grieve	3.00
51	Jose Vizcaino	.25
52	Hideki Irabu	1.00
53	J.T. Snow	.25
54	Mike Hampton	.25
55	Dave Nilsson	.25
56	Alex Fernandez	.25
57	Brett Tomko	.25
58	Wally Joyner	.25
59	Kelvim Escobar	.25
60	Roberto Alomar	1.25
61	Todd Jones	.25
62	Paul O'Neill	.50
63	Jamie Moyer	.25
64	Mark Wohlers	.25
65	Jose Cruz Jr.	2.50
66	Troy Percival	.25
67	Rick Reed	.25
68	Will Clark	.50
69	Jamey Wright	.25
70	Mike Mussina	1.25
71	David Cone	.50
72	Ryan Klesko	.75
73	Scott Hatteberg	.25
74	James Baldwin	.25
75	Tony Womack	.25
76	Carlos Perez	.25
77	Charles Nagy	.25
78	Jeromy Burnitz	.25
79	Shane Reynolds	.25
80	Cliff Floyd	.25
81	Jason Kendall	.25
82	Chad Curtis	.25
83	Matt Karchner	.25
84	Ricky Bottalico	.25
85	Sammy Sosa	4.00
86	Javy Lopez	.40
87	Jeff Kent	.25
88	Shawn Green	.25
89	Devon White	.25
90	Tony Gwynn	3.00
91	Bob Tewksbury	.25
92	Derek Jeter	4.00
93	Eric Davis	.25
94	Jeff Fassero	.25
95	Denny Neagle	.50
96	Ismael Valdes	.25
97	Tim Salmon	1.00
98	Mark Grudzielanek	.25
99	Curt Schilling	.75
100	Ken Griffey Jr.	6.00
101	Edgardo Alfonzo	.25
102	Vinny Castilla	.25
103	Jose Rosado	.25
104	Scott Erickson	.25
105	Alan Benes	.50
106	Shannon Stewart	.25
107	Delino DeShields	.25
108	Mark Loretta	.25
109	Todd Hundley	.50
110	Chuck Knoblauch	.75
111	Quinton McCracken	.25
112	F.P. Santangelo	.25
113	Gerald Williams	.25
114	Omar Vizquel	.25
115	John Valentin	.25
116	Damion Easley	.25
117	Matt Lawton	.25
118	Jim Thome	1.00
119	Sandy Alomar	.50
120	Albert Belle	1.50
121	Chris Stynes	.25
122	Butch Huskey	.25
123	Shawn Estes	.25
124	Terry Adams	.25
125	Ivan Rodriguez	1.50
126	Ron Gant	.50
127	John Mabry	.25
128	Jeff Shaw	.25
129	Jeff Montgomery	.25
130	Justin Thompson	.50
131	Livan Hernandez	.50
132	Ugueth Urbina	.25
133	Doug Glanville	.25
134	Troy O'Leary	.25
135	Cal Ripken Jr.	5.00
136	Quilvio Veras	.25
137	Pedro Astacio	.25
138	Willie Greene	.25
139	Lance Johnson	.25
140	Nomar Garciaparra	4.00
141	Jose Offerman	.25
142	Scott Rolen	2.50
143	Derek Bell	.25
144	Johnny Damon	.25
145	Mark McGwire	8.00
146	Chan Ho Park	.50
147	Edgar Renteria	.25
148	Eric Young	.25
149	Craig Biggio	.50
150	Checklist 1-150	.25
151	Frank Thomas	5.00
152	John Wetteland	.25
153	Mike Lansing	.25
154	Pedro Martinez	1.00
155	Rico Brogna	.25
156	Kevin Brown	.40
157	Alex Rodriguez	3.00
158	Wade Boggs	.50
159	Richard Hidalgo	.25
160	Mark Grace	.50
161	Jose Mesa	.25
162	John Olerud	.50
163	Tim Belcher	.25
164	Chuck Finley	.25
165	Brian Hunter	.25
166	Joe Carter	.40
167	Stan Javier	.25
168	Jay Bell	.25
169	Ray Lankford	.25
170	John Smoltz	.40
171	Ed Sprague	.25
172	Jason Giambi	.25
173	Todd Walker	.50
174	Paul Konerko	.75
175	Rey Ordonez	.25
176	Dante Bichette	.50
177	Bernie Williams	1.00
178	Jon Nunnally	.25
179	Rafael Palmeiro	.75
180	Jay Buhner	.50
181	Devon White	.25
182	Jeff D'Amico	.25
183	Walt Weiss	.25
184	Scott Spiezio	.25
185	Moises Alou	.50
186	Carlos Baerga	.25
187	Todd Zeile	.25
188	Gregg Jefferies	.25
189	Mo Vaughn	1.50
190	Terry Steinbach	.25
191	Ray Durham	.25
192	Robin Ventura	.40
193	Jeff Reed	.25
194	Ken Caminiti	.50
195	Eric Karros	.40
196	Wilson Alvarez	.25
197	Gary Gaetti	.25
198	Andres Galarraga	.75
199	Alex Gonzalez	.25
200	Garret Anderson	.25
201	Andy Benes	.25
202	Harold Baines	.25
203	Ron Coomer	.25
204	Dean Palmer	.25
205	Reggie Jefferson	.25
206	John Burkett	.25
207	Jermaine Allensworth	.25
208	Bernard Gilkey	.25
209	Jeff Bagwell	2.00

210	Kenny Lofton	1.50
211	Bobby Jones	.25
212	Bartolo Colon	.50
213	Jim Edmonds	.40
214	Pat Hentgen	.25
215	Matt Williams	.75
216	Bob Abreu	.25
217	Jorge Posada	.25
218	Marty Cordova	.25
219	Ken Hill	.25
220	Steve Finley	.25
221	Jeff King	.25
222	Quinton McCracken	.25
223	Matt Stairs	.25
224	Darin Erstad	1.50
225	Fred McGriff	.50
226	Marquis Grissom	.25
227	Doug Glanville	.25
228	Tom Glavine	.40
229	John Franco	.25
230	Darren Bragg	.25
231	Barry Larkin	.50
232	Trevor Hoffman	.25
233	Brady Anderson	.25
234	Al Martin	.25
235	B.J. Surhoff	.25
236	Ellis Burks	.25
237	Randy Johnson	1.00
238	Mark Clark	.25
239	Tony Saunders	.25
240	Hideo Nomo	.75
241	Brad Fullmer	.50
242	Chipper Jones	4.00
243	Jose Valentin	.25
244	Manny Ramirez	1.50
245	Derrek Lee	.25
246	Jimmy Key	.25
247	Tim Naehring	.25
248	Bobby Higginson	.25
249	Charles Johnson	.25
250	Chili Davis	.25
251	Tom Gordon	.25
252	Mike Lieberthal	.25
253	Billy Wagner	.25
254	Juan Guzman	.25
255	Todd Stottlemyre	.25
256	Brian Jordan	.25
257	Barry Bonds	1.50
258	Dan Wilson	.25
259	Paul Molitor	1.00
260	Juan Gonzalez	3.00
261	Francisco Cordova	.25
262	Cecil Fielder	.50
263	Travis Lee	4.00
264	Kevin Tapani	.25
265	Raul Mondesi	.50
266	Travis Fryman	.25
267	Armando Benitez	.25
268	Pokey Reese	.25
269	Rick Aguilera	.25
270	Andy Pettitte	1.00
271	Jose Vizcaino	.25
272	Kerry Wood	8.00
273	Vladimir Guerrero	1.50
274	John Smiley	.25
275	Checklist 151-275	.25

1998 Finest Centurions

Centurions was a 20-card insert found only Series I hobby (1:153) and Home Team Advantage packs (1:71). The theme of the insert to top players who will lead the game into the next century. Each card is sequentially numbered on the back to 500, while Refractor versions are numbered to 75.

		MT
Complete Set (20):		900.00
Common Player:		25.00
Production 500 sets		
Refractors: 2x to 3x		
Production 75 sets		
C1	Andruw Jones	30.00
C2	Vladimir Guerrero	30.00
C3	Nomar Garciaparra	75.00
C4	Scott Rolen	40.00
C5	Ken Griffey Jr.	120.00
C6	Jose Cruz Jr.	25.00
C7	Barry Bonds	30.00

C8	Mark McGwire	140.00
C9	Juan Gonzalez	60.00
C10	Jeff Bagwell	40.00
C11	Frank Thomas	90.00
C12	Paul Konerko	20.00
C13	Alex Rodriguez	120.00
C14	Mike Piazza	75.00
C15	Travis Lee	90.00
C16	Chipper Jones	75.00
C17	Larry Walker	20.00
C18	Mo Vaughn	30.00
C19	Livan Hernandez	15.00
C20	Jaret Wright	40.00

1998 Finest Mystery Finest

This 50-card insert was seeded one per 36 Series I packs and one per 15 HTA packs. The set included 20 top players, each matched on double sided card with three other players and once with himself. Each side of the card is printed on a chromium finish and arrives with a black opaque protector. Mystery Finest inserts are numbered with a "M" prefix. Refractor versions were seeded one per 64 packs (HTA odds 1:15).

		MT
Complete Set (50):		1000.
Common Player:		8.00
Inserted 1:36		
Refractors: 1.5x to 2.5x		
Inserted 1:144		
M1	Frank Thomas, Ken Griffey Jr.	60.00
M2	Frank Thomas, Mike Piazza	50.00
M3	Frank Thomas, Mark McGwire	50.00
M4	Frank Thomas, Frank Thomas	50.00
M5	Ken Griffey Jr., Mike Piazza	50.00
M6	Ken Griffey Jr., Mark McGwire	60.00
M7	Ken Griffey Jr., Ken Griffey Jr.	65.00
M8	Mike Piazza, Mark McGwire	40.00
M9	Mike Piazza, Mike Piazza	40.00
M10	Mark McGwire, Mark McGwire	60.00
M11	Nomar Garciaparra, Jose Cruz Jr.	25.00
M12	Nomar Garciaparra, Derek Jeter	40.00
M13	Nomar Garciaparra, Andruw Jones	35.00
M14	Nomar Garciaparra, Nomar Garciaparra	40.00
M15	Jose Cruz Jr., Derek Jeter	25.00
M16	Jose Cruz Jr., Andruw Jones	25.00
M17	Jose Cruz Jr., Jose Cruz Jr.	25.00
M18	Derek Jeter, Andruw Jones	35.00
M19	Derek Jeter, Derek Jeter	40.00
M20	Andruw Jones, Andruw Jones	20.00
M21	Cal Ripken Jr., Tony Gwynn	50.00
M22	Cal Ripken Jr., Barry Bonds	45.00
M23	Cal Ripken Jr., Greg Maddux	50.00
M24	Cal Ripken Jr., Cal Ripken Jr.	50.00
M25	Tony Gwynn, Barry Bonds	30.00
M26	Tony Gwynn, Greg Maddux	35.00
M27	Tony Gwynn, Tony Gwynn	30.00
M28	Barry Bonds, Greg Maddux	35.00
M29	Barry Bonds, Barry Bonds	20.00
M30	Greg Maddux, Greg Maddux	40.00
M31	Juan Gonzalez, Larry Walker	30.00
M32	Juan Gonzalez, Andres Galarraga	30.00
M33	Juan Gonzalez, Chipper Jones	35.00
M34	Juan Gonzalez, Juan Gonzalez	30.00
M35	Larry Walker, Andres Galarraga	15.00

M36	Larry Walker, Chipper Jones	20.00
M37	Larry Walker, Larry Walker	15.00
M38	Andres Galarraga, Chipper Jones	20.00
M39	Andres Galarraga, Andres Galarraga	10.00
M40	Chipper Jones, Chipper Jones	40.00
M41	Gary Sheffield, Sammy Sosa	25.00
M42	Gary Sheffield, Jeff Bagwell	20.00
M43	Gary Sheffield, Tino Martinez	15.00
M44	Gary Sheffield, Gary Sheffield	15.00
M45	Sammy Sosa, Jeff Bagwell	25.00
M46	Sammy Sosa, Tino Martinez	15.00
M47	Sammy Sosa, Sammy Sosa	15.00
M48	Jeff Bagwell, Tino Martinez	25.00
M49	Jeff Bagwell, Jeff Bagwell	25.00
M50	Tino Martinez, Tino Martinez	10.00

1998 Finest II Mystery Finest

Fifty more Mystery Finest inserts were seeded in Series II packs at a rate of one per 36 packs (HTA odds 1:15), with Refrators every 1:144 packs (HTA odds 1:64). As with Series I, 20 players are in the insert, with each player featured with three different players on the back or by himself on each side.

		MT
Complete Set (40):		1000.
Common Player:		6.00
Inserted 1:36		
Refractors: 1.5x to 3x		
Inserted 1:144		
M1	Nomar Garciaparra, Frank Thomas	45.00
M2	Nomar Garciaparra, Albert Belle	40.00
M3	Nomar Garciaparra, Scott Rolen	40.00
M4	Frank Thomas, Albert Belle	45.00
M5	Frank Thomas, Scott Rolen	45.00
M6	Albert Belle, Scott Rolen	20.00
M7	Ken Griffey Jr., Jose Cruz	50.00
M8	Ken Griffey Jr., Alex Rodriguez	60.00
M9	Ken Griffey Jr., Roger Clemens	60.00
M10	Jose Cruz, Alex Rodriguez	35.00
M11	Jose Cruz, Roger Clemens	20.00
M12	Alex Rodriguez, Roger Clemens	40.00
M13	Mike Piazza, Barry Bonds	40.00
M14	Mike Piazza, Derek Jeter	40.00
M15	Mike Piazza, Bernie Williams	35.00

M16	Barry Bonds, Derek Jeter	30.00
M17	Barry Bonds, Bernie Williams	15.00
M18	Derek Jeter, Bernie Williams	25.00
M19	Mark McGwire, Jeff Bagwell	50.00
M20	Mark McGwire, Mo Vaughn	45.00
M21	Mark McGwire, Jim Thome	45.00
M22	Jeff Bagwell, Mo Vaughn	20.00
M23	Jeff Bagwell, Jim Thome	20.00
M24	Mo Vaughn, Jim Thome	15.00
M25	Juan Gonzalez, Travis Lee	35.00
M26	Juan Gonzalez, Ben Grieve	30.00
M27	Juan Gonzalez, Fred McGriff	25.00
M28	Travis Lee, Ben Grieve	35.00
M29	Travis Lee, Fred McGriff	30.00
M30	Ben Grieve, Fred McGriff	20.00
M31	Albert Belle, Albert Belle	15.00
M32	Scott Rolen, Scott Rolen	20.00
M33	Alex Rodriguez, Alex Rodriguez	40.00
M34	Roger Clemens, Roger Clemens	20.00
M35	Bernie Williams, Bernie Williams	10.00
M36	Mo Vaughn, Mo Vaughn	15.00
M37	Jim Thome, Jim Thome	10.00
M38	Travis Lee, Travis Lee	30.00
M39	Fred McGriff, Fred McGriff	6.00
M40	Ben Grieve, Ben Grieve	20.00

1998 Finest Oversize

Eight oversized cards were inserted into both Series I and Series II boxes as box toppers. The cards measure 3" x 5" and were inserted one per three boxes, with Refractor versions every six boxes. The oversized cards are similar to the regular-issed cards except for the numbering.

		MT
Complete Set (16):		180.00
Complete Series 1 (8):		120.00
Complete Series 2 (8):		75.00
Common Player:		5.00
Refractors: 1x to 2x		
A1	Mark McGwire	25.00
A2	Cal Ripken Jr.	25.00
A3	Nomar Garciaparra	20.00
A4	Mike Piazza	20.00
A5	Greg Maddux	20.00
A6	Jose Cruz Jr.	8.00
A7	Roger Clemens	10.00
A8	Ken Griffey Jr.	30.00
B1	Frank Thomas	25.00
B2	Bernie Williams	6.00
B3	Randy Johnson	6.00
B4	Chipper Jones	20.00
B5	Manny Ramirez	8.00
B6	Barry Bonds	8.00
B7	Juan Gonzalez	15.00
B8	Jeff Bagwell	10.00

1998 Finest Power Zone

This Series I insert feature Topps' new printing technology which actually changes the color of the card depending on what angle you are viewing it from. This 20-card set was inserted one per 72 packs (HTA odds 1:32).

A player's name in *italic* type indicates a rookie card.

		MT
Complete Set (20):		500.00
Common Player:		10.00
Inserted 1:72 hobby packs		
P1	Ken Griffey Jr.	80.00
P2	Jeff Bagwell	35.00
P3	Jose Cruz Jr.	35.00
P4	Barry Bonds	20.00
P5	Mark McGwire	90.00
P6	Jim Thome	15.00
P7	Mo Vaughn	20.00
P8	Gary Sheffield	12.00
P9	Andres Galarraga	10.00
P10	Nomar Garciaparra	50.00
P11	Rafael Palmeiro	10.00
P12	Sammy Sosa	40.00
P13	Jay Buhner	10.00
P14	Tony Clark	15.00
P15	Mike Piazza	50.00
P16	Larry Walker	12.00
P17	Albert Belle	20.00
P18	Tino Martinez	12.00
P19	Juan Gonzalez	40.00
P20	Frank Thomas	70.00

1998 Finest Stadium Stars

Stadium Stars was a 24-card insert that featured Topps' new lenticular holographic chromium technology. These were exclusive to Series II packs and carried an insertion rate of one per 72 packs (HTA odds 1:32).

		MT
Complete Set (24):		600.00
Common Player:		8.00
Inserted 1:72		
SS1	Ken Griffey Jr.	70.00
SS2	Alex Rodriguez	45.00
SS3	Mo Vaughn	18.00
SS4	Nomar Garciaparra	45.00
SS5	Frank Thomas	50.00
SS6	Albert Belle	18.00
SS7	Derek Jeter	35.00
SS8	Chipper Jones	45.00
SS9	Cal Ripken Jr.	50.00
SS10	Jim Thome	15.00
SS11	Mike Piazza	45.00
SS12	Juan Gonzalez	35.00
SS13	Jeff Bagwell	25.00
SS14	Sammy Sosa	40.00
SS15	Jose Cruz Jr.	15.00
SS16	Gary Sheffield	10.00
SS17	Larry Walker	12.00
SS18	Tony Gwynn	35.00
SS19	Mark McGwire	80.00
SS20	Barry Bonds	18.00
SS21	Tino Martinez	10.00
SS22	Manny Ramirez	18.00
SS23	Ken Caminiti	8.00
SS24	Andres Galarraga	10.00

1998 Finest The Man

This 20-card insert featured the top players in baseball and was exclusive inserted into Series II packs. Regular versions were sequentially numbered to 500 and inserted one per 119 packs, while Refractor versions were numbered to 75 and inserted one per 793 packs.

		MT
Complete Set (20):		1000.
Common Player:		15.00
Production 500 sets		
Refractors: 2x to 3x		
Production 75 sets		
TM1	Ken Griffey Jr.	125.00
TM2	Barry Bonds	30.00
TM3	Frank Thomas	90.00
TM4	Chipper Jones	75.00
TM5	Cal Ripken Jr.	90.00
TM6	Nomar Garciaparra	75.00
TM7	Mark McGwire	125.00
TM8	Mike Piazza	75.00
TM9	Derek Jeter	60.00
TM10	Alex Rodriguez	75.00
TM11	Jose Cruz Jr.	25.00
TM12	Larry Walker	15.00
TM13	Jeff Bagwell	40.00
TM14	Tony Gwynn	60.00
TM15	Travis Lee	40.00
TM16	Juan Gonzalez	60.00
TM17	Scott Rolen	40.00
TM18	Randy Johnson	25.00
TM19	Roger Clemens	40.00
TM20	Greg Maddux	75.00

Grading Guide

Mint (MT): A perfect card. Well-centered with all corners sharp and square. No creases, stains, edge nicks, surface marks, yellowing or fading.

Near Mint (NM): A nearly perfect card. At first glance, a NM card appears to be perfect. May be slightly off-center. No surface marks, creases or loss of gloss.

Excellent (EX): Corners are still fairly sharp with only moderate wear. Borders may be off-center. No creases or stains on fronts or backs, but may show slight loss of surface luster.

Very Good (VG): Shows obvious handling. May have rounded corners, minor creases, major gum or wax stains. No major creases, tape marks, writing, etc.

Good (G): A well-worn card, but exhibits no intentional damage. May have major or multiple creases. Corners may be rounded well beyond card border.

1993 Flair

Designed as Fleer's super-premium card brand, this 300-card set contains extra-thick cards which feature gold stamping and UV coating front and back. Portrait and action photos are combined in a high-tech front picture and there is a muted photo on the back, as well.

		MT
Complete Set (300):		60.00
Common Player:		.25
Wax Box:		60.00
1	Steve Avery	.25
2	Jeff Blauser	.25
3	Ron Gant	.35
4	Tom Glavine	.50
5	Dave Justice	.40
6	Mark Lemke	.25
7	Greg Maddux	5.00
8	Fred McGriff	.75
9	Terry Pendleton	.25
10	Deion Sanders	.50
11	John Smoltz	.50
12	Mike Stanton	.25
13	Steve Buechele	.25
14	Mark Grace	.50
15	Greg Hibbard	.25
16	Derrick May	.25
17	Chuck McElroy	.25
18	Mike Morgan	.25
19	Randy Myers	.25
20	Ryne Sandberg	2.00
21	Dwight Smith	.25
22	Sammy Sosa	6.00
23	Jose Vizcaino	.25
24	Tim Belcher	.25
25	Rob Dibble	.25
26	Roberto Kelly	.25
27	Barry Larkin	.40
28	Kevin Mitchell	.25
29	Hal Morris	.35
30	Joe Oliver	.25
31	Jose Rijo	.25
32	Bip Roberts	.25
33	Chris Sabo	.25
34	Reggie Sanders	.40
35	Dante Bichette	.60
36	Willie Blair	.25
37	Jerald Clark	.25
38	Alex Cole	.25
39	Andres Galarraga	.50
40	Joe Girardi	.25
41	Charlie Hayes	.25
42	Chris Jones	.25
43	David Nied	.25
44	Eric Young	.40
45	Alex Arias	.25
46	Jack Armstrong	.25
47	Bret Barberie	.25
48	Chuck Carr	.25
49	Jeff Conine	.40
50	Orestes Destrade	.25
51	Chris Hammond	.25
52	Bryan Harvey	.25
53	Benito Santiago	.25
54	Gary Sheffield	.75
55	Walt Weiss	.25
56	Eric Anthony	.25
57	Jeff Bagwell	2.50
58	Craig Biggio	.40
59	Ken Caminiti	.50
60	Andujar Cedeno	.25
61	Doug Drabek	.25
62	Steve Finley	.25
63	Luis Gonzalez	.25
64	Pete Harnisch	.25
65	Doug Jones	.25
66	Darryl Kile	.25
67	Greg Swindell	.25
68	Brett Butler	.25
69	Jim Gott	.25
70	Orel Hershiser	.25
71	Eric Karros	.40
72	Pedro Martinez	.60
73	Ramon Martinez	.35
74	Roger McDowell	.25
75	Mike Piazza	5.00
76	Jody Reed	.25
77	Tim Wallach	.25
78	Moises Alou	.50
79	Greg Colbrunn	.25
80	Wil Cordero	.35
81	Delino DeShields	.35
82	Jeff Fassero	.25
83	Marquis Grissom	.50
84	Ken Hill	.25
85	*Mike Lansing*	.60
86	Dennis Martinez	.25
87	Larry Walker	.75
88	John Wetteland	.25
89	Bobby Bonilla	.35
90	Vince Coleman	.25
91	Dwight Gooden	.35
92	Todd Hundley	.50
93	Howard Johnson	.25
94	Eddie Murray	.40
95	Joe Orsulak	.25
96	Bret Saberhagen	.25
97	Darren Daulton	.40
98	Mariano Duncan	.25
99	Len Dykstra	.35
100	Jim Eisenreich	.25
101	Tommy Greene	.25
102	Dave Hollins	.25
103	Pete Incaviglia	.25
104	Danny Jackson	.25
105	John Kruk	.35
106	Terry Mulholland	.25
107	Curt Schilling	.25
108	Mitch Williams	.25
109	Stan Belinda	.25
110	Jay Bell	.25
111	Steve Cooke	.25
112	Carlos Garcia	.25
113	Jeff King	.25
114	Al Martin	.30
115	Orlando Merced	.25
116	Don Slaught	.25
117	Andy Van Slyke	.25
118	Tim Wakefield	.25
119	*Rene Arocha*	.40
120	Bernard Gilkey	.40
121	Gregg Jefferies	.25
122	Ray Lankford	.30
123	Donovan Osborne	.25
124	Tom Pagnozzi	.25
125	Erik Pappas	.25
126	Geronimo Pena	.25
127	Lee Smith	.25
128	Ozzie Smith	1.00
129	Bob Tewksbury	.25
130	Mark Whiten	.30
131	Derek Bell	.25
132	Andy Benes	.25
133	Tony Gwynn	3.00
134	Gene Harris	.25
135	Trevor Hoffman	.25
136	Phil Plantier	.25
137	Rod Beck	.25
138	Barry Bonds	2.00
139	John Burkett	.25
140	Will Clark	.75
141	Royce Clayton	.35
142	Mike Jackson	.25
143	Darren Lewis	.25
144	Kirt Manwaring	.25
145	Willie McGee	.30
146	Bill Swift	.25
147	Robby Thompson	.25
148	Matt Williams	.75
149	Brady Anderson	.40
150	Mike Devereaux	.25
151	Chris Hoiles	.25
152	Ben McDonald	.25
153	Mark McLemore	.25
154	Mike Mussina	1.50
155	Gregg Olson	.25
156	Harold Reynolds	.25
157	Cal Ripken, Jr.	6.00
158	Rick Sutcliffe	.25
159	Fernando Valenzuela	.30
160	Roger Clemens	3.00
161	Scott Cooper	.25
162	Andre Dawson	.35
163	Scott Fletcher	.25
164	Mike Greenwell	.25
165	Greg Harris	.25
166	Billy Hatcher	.25
167	Jeff Russell	.25
168	Mo Vaughn	2.00
169	Frank Viola	.25
170	Chad Curtis	.30
171	Chili Davis	.25
172	Gary DiSarcina	.25
173	Damion Easley	.35
174	Chuck Finley	.25
175	Mark Langston	.25
176	Luis Polonia	.25
177	Tim Salmon	1.50
178	Scott Sanderson	.25
179	*J.T. Snow*	2.00
180	Wilson Alvarez	.35
181	Ellis Burks	.35
182	Joey Cora	.25
183	Alex Fernandez	.35
184	Ozzie Guillen	.25
185	Roberto Hernandez	.25
186	Bo Jackson	.75
187	Lance Johnson	.25
188	Jack McDowell	.35
189	Frank Thomas	6.00
190	Robin Ventura	.50
191	Carlos Baerga	.35
192	Albert Belle	2.00
193	Wayne Kirby	.25
194	Derek Lilliquist	.25
195	Kenny Lofton	2.00
196	Carlos Martinez	.25
197	Jose Mesa	.25
198	Eric Plunk	.25
199	Paul Sorrento	.25
200	John Doherty	.25
201	Cecil Fielder	.50
202	Travis Fryman	.50
203	Kirk Gibson	.25
204	Mike Henneman	.25
205	Chad Kreuter	.25
206	Scott Livingstone	.25
207	Tony Phillips	.30
208	Mickey Tettleton	.25
209	Alan Trammell	.40
210	David Wells	.25
211	Lou Whitaker	.25
212	Kevin Appier	.25
213	George Brett	2.00
214	David Cone	.30
215	Tom Gordon	.25
216	Phil Hiatt	.25
217	Felix Jose	.25
218	Wally Joyner	.30
219	Jose Lind	.25
220	Mike Macfarlane	.25
221	Brian McRae	.25
222	Jeff Montgomery	.25
223	Cal Eldred	.25
224	Darryl Hamilton	.25
225	John Jaha	.30
226	Pat Listach	.30
227	*Graeme Lloyd*	.35
228	Kevin Reimer	.25
229	Bill Spiers	.25
230	B.J. Surhoff	.25
231	Greg Vaughn	.25
232	Robin Yount	1.50
233	Rick Aguilera	.25
234	Jim Deshaies	.25
235	Brian Harper	.25
236	Kent Hrbek	.30
237	Chuck Knoblauch	.50
238	Shane Mack	.25
239	David McCarty	.25
240	Pedro Munoz	.25
241	Mike Pagliarulo	.25
242	Kirby Puckett	3.00
243	Dave Winfield	.40
244	Jim Abbott	.35
245	Wade Boggs	.75
246	Pat Kelly	.25

247 Jimmy Key .25
248 Jim Leyritz .25
249 Don Mattingly 2.50
250 Matt Nokes .25
251 Paul O'Neill .25
252 Mike Stanley .25
253 Danny Tartabull .25
254 Bob Wickman .25
255 Bernie Williams 1.50
256 Mike Bordick .25
257 Dennis Eckersley .30
258 Brent Gates .30
259 Goose Gossage .25
260 Rickey Henderson .40
261 Mark McGwire 10.00
262 Ruben Sierra .40
263 Terry Steinbach .25
264 Bob Welch .25
265 Bobby Witt .25
266 Rich Amaral .25
267 Chris Bosio .25
268 Jay Buhner .50
269 Norm Charlton .25
270 Ken Griffey, Jr. 8.00
271 Erik Hanson .25
272 Randy Johnson 1.00
273 Edgar Martinez .25
274 Tino Martinez .50
275 Dave Valle .25
276 Omar Vizquel .25
277 Kevin Brown .25
278 Jose Canseco .50
279 Julio Franco .25
280 Juan Gonzalez 3.00
281 Tom Henke .25
282 David Hulse .25
283 Rafael Palmeiro .50
284 Dean Palmer .40
285 Ivan Rodriguez 2.00
286 Nolan Ryan 5.00
287 Roberto Alomar 1.50
288 Pat Borders .25
289 Joe Carter .40
290 Juan Guzman .25
291 Pat Hentgen .35
292 Paul Molitor 1.00
293 John Olerud .40
294 Ed Sprague .25
295 Dave Stewart .25
296 Duane Ward .25
297 Devon White .25
298 Checklist .10
299 Checklist .10
300 Checklist .10

1993 Flair
Wave of the Future

Twenty of the game's top prospects were featured in this insert issue randomly packaged in Flair packs. Cards #19-20, Darrell Whitmore and Nigel Wilson, were printed with each other's back; no corrected version was made.

		MT
Complete Set (20):		40.00
Common Player:		1.00
1	Jason Bere	1.00
2	Jeremy Burnitz	2.50
3	Russ Davis	1.00
4	Jim Edmonds	6.00
5	Cliff Floyd	1.50
6	Jeffrey Hammonds	2.00
7	Trevor Hoffman	1.50
8	Domingo Jean	1.00
9	David McCarty	1.00
10	Bobby Munoz	1.00
11	Brad Pennington	1.00
12	Mike Piazza	15.00
13	Manny Ramirez	8.00
14	John Roper	1.00
15	Tim Salmon	5.00
16	Aaron Sele	2.00
17	Allen Watson	1.00
18	Rondell White	5.00
19	Darell Whitmore	1.00
20	Nigel Wilson	1.00

1994 Flair

One of the success stories of 1993 returned with the release of Fleer Flair for 1994. At $4 per pack this is pricey stuff, but collectors apparently liked the look that includes an extremely thick card stock, full-bleed photos and gold-foil stamping on both sides and a protective polyester laminate described by company officials as "far beyond mere UV coating." In addition to the 250 regular-issue cards, there are three 10-card, insert sets; Wave of the Future, Outfield Power and Hot Numbers in Series I, the last with players' images printed on 100% etched foil. Series II inserts included Hot Glove, Infield Power and 10 more Wave of the Future cards.

		MT
Complete Set (450):		75.00
Common Player:		.20
Series 1 or 2 Wax Box:		55.00
1	Harold Baines	.25
2	Jeffrey Hammonds	.30
3	Chris Hoiles	.20
4	Ben McDonald	.20
5	Mark McLemore	.20
6	Jamie Moyer	.20
7	Jim Poole	.20
8	Cal Ripken, Jr.	5.00
9	Chris Sabo	.20
10	Scott Bankhead	.20
11	Scott Cooper	.20
12	Danny Darwin	.20
13	Andre Dawson	.30
14	Billy Hatcher	.20
15	Aaron Sele	.40

15a	Aaron Sele (overprinted "PROMOTIONAL SAMPLE")	6.00
16	John Valentin	.35
17	Dave Valle	.20
18	Mo Vaughn	1.25
19	*Brian Anderson*	.30
20	Gary DiSarcina	.20
21	Jim Edmonds	.60
22	Chuck Finley	.20
23	Bo Jackson	.35
24	Mark Leiter	.20
25	Greg Myers	.20
26	Eduardo Perez	.20
27	Tim Salmon	.75
28	Wilson Alvarez	.20
29	Jason Bere	.30
30	Alex Fernandez	.20
31	Ozzie Guillen	.20
32	Joe Hall	.20
33	Darrin Jackson	.20
34	Kirk McCaskill	.20
35	Tim Raines	.25
36	Frank Thomas	4.00
37	Carlos Baerga	.30
38	Albert Belle	1.25
39	Mark Clark	.30
40	Wayne Kirby	.20
41	Dennis Martinez	.25
42	Charles Nagy	.20
43	Manny Ramirez	1.75
44	Paul Sorrento	.20
45	Jim Thome	.50
46	Eric Davis	.15
47	John Doherty	.20
48	Junior Felix	.20
49	Cecil Fielder	.30
50	Kirk Gibson	.20
51	Mike Moore	.20
52	Tony Phillips	.25
53	Alan Trammell	.30
54	Kevin Appier	.20
55	Stan Belinda	.20
56	Vince Coleman	.20
57	Greg Gagne	.20
58	Bob Hamelin	.20
59	Dave Henderson	.20
60	Wally Joyner	.25
61	Mike Macfarlane	.20
62	Jeff Montgomery	.20
63	Ricky Bones	.20
64	Jeff Bronkey	.20
65	Alex Diaz	.20
66	Cal Eldred	.20
67	Darryl Hamilton	.20
68	John Jaha	.20
69	Mark Kiefer	.20
70	Kevin Seitzer	.20
71	Turner Ward	.20
72	Rich Becker	.20
73	Scott Erickson	.20
74	Keith Garagozzo	.20
75	Kent Hrbek	.25
76	Scott Leius	.20
77	Kirby Puckett	2.00
78	Matt Walkbeck	.20
79	Dave Winfield	.40
80	Mike Gallego	.20
81	Xavier Hernandez	.20
82	Jimmy Key	.20
83	Jim Leyritz	.20
84	Don Mattingly	2.00
85	Matt Nokes	.20
86	Paul O'Neill	.20
87	Melido Perez	.20
88	Danny Tartabull	.20
89	Mike Bordick	.20
90	Ron Darling	.20
91	Dennis Eckersley	.25
92	Stan Javier	.20
93	Steve Karsay	.20
94	Mark McGwire	6.00
95	Troy Neel	.20
96	Terry Steinbach	.20
97	Bill Taylor	.20
98	Eric Anthony	.20
99	Chris Bosio	.20
100	Tim Davis	.20
101	Felix Fermin	.20
102	Dave Fleming	.20
103	Ken Griffey, Jr.	5.00
104	Greg Hibbard	.20
105	Reggie Jefferson	.20
106	Tino Martinez	.30
107	Jack Armstrong	.20
108	Will Clark	.75

#	Name	Price
109	Juan Gonzalez	1.50
110	Rick Helling	.20
111	Tom Henke	.20
112	David Hulse	.20
113	Manuel Lee	.20
114	Doug Strange	.20
115	Roberto Alomar	1.50
116	Joe Carter	.35
117	Carlos Delgado	.35
118	Pat Hentgen	.20
119	Paul Molitor	.60
120	John Olerud	.25
121	Dave Stewart	.25
122	Todd Stottlemyre	.20
123	Mike Timlin	.20
124	Jeff Blauser	.20
125	Tom Glavine	.35
126	Dave Justice	.35
127	Mike Kelly	.25
128	Ryan Klesko	1.00
129	Javier Lopez	.40
130	Greg Maddux	2.50
131	Fred McGriff	.75
132	Kent Mercker	.20
133	Mark Wohlers	.20
134	Willie Banks	.20
135	Steve Buechele	.20
136	Shawon Dunston	.30
137	Jose Guzman	.20
138	Glenallen Hill	.20
139	Randy Myers	.20
140	Karl Rhodes	.20
141	Ryne Sandberg	1.25
142	Steve Trachsel	.35
143	Bret Boone	.20
144	Tom Browning	.20
145	Hector Carrasco	.20
146	Barry Larkin	.30
147	Hal Morris	.20
148	Jose Rijo	.20
149	Reggie Sanders	.30
150	John Smiley	.20
151	Dante Bichette	.50
152	Ellis Burks	.30
153	Joe Girardi	.20
154	Mike Harkey	.20
155	Roberto Mejia	.20
156	Marcus Moore	.20
157	Armando Reynoso	.20
158	Bruce Ruffin	.20
159	Eric Young	.20
160	*Kurt Abbott*	.40
161	Jeff Conine	.35
162	Orestes Destrade	.20
163	Chris Hammond	.20
164	Bryan Harvey	.20
165	Dave Magadan	.20
166	Gary Sheffield	.35
167	David Weathers	.20
168	Andujar Cedeno	.20
169	Tom Edens	.20
170	Luis Gonzalez	.20
171	Pete Harnisch	.20
172	Todd Jones	.20
173	Darryl Kile	.20
174	James Mouton	.30
175	Scott Servais	.20
176	Mitch Williams	.20
177	Pedro Astacio	.20
178	Orel Hershiser	.25
179	Raul Mondesi	1.00
180	Jose Offerman	.20
181	*Chan Ho Park*	.75
182	Mike Piazza	2.50
183	Cory Snyder	.20
184	Tim Wallach	.20
185	Todd Worrell	.20
186	Sean Berry	.20
187	Wil Cordero	.20
188	Darrin Fletcher	.20
189	Cliff Floyd	.30
190	Marquis Grissom	.30
191	Rod Henderson	.20
192	Ken Hill	.20
193	Pedro Martinez	.20
194	Kirk Rueter	.20
195	Jeromy Burnitz	.20
196	John Franco	.20
197	Dwight Gooden	.25
198	Todd Hundley	.25
199	Bobby Jones	.30
200	Jeff Kent	.25
201	Mike Maddux	.20
202	Ryan Thompson	.20
203	Jose Vizcaino	.20
204	Darren Daulton	.20
205	Len Dykstra	.25
206	Jim Eisenreich	.20
207	Dave Hollins	.20
208	Danny Jackson	.20
209	Doug Jones	.20
210	Jeff Juden	.20
211	Ben Rivera	.20
212	Kevin Stocker	.20
213	Milt Thompson	.20
214	Jay Bell	.20
215	Steve Cooke	.20
216	Mark Dewey	.20
217	Al Martin	.20
218	Orlando Merced	.20
219	Don Slaught	.20
220	Zane Smith	.20
221	Rick White	.20
222	Kevin Young	.20
223	Rene Arocha	.20
224	Rheal Cormier	.20
225	Brian Jordan	.25
226	Ray Lankford	.25
227	Mike Perez	.20
228	Ozzie Smith	1.00
229	Mark Whiten	.20
230	Todd Zeile	.25
231	Derek Bell	.25
232	Archi Cianfrocco	.20
233	Ricky Gutierrez	.20
234	Trevor Hoffman	.20
235	Phil Plantier	.20
236	Dave Staton	.20
237	Wally Whitehurst	.20
238	Todd Benzinger	.20
239	Barry Bonds	1.25
240	John Burkett	.20
241	Royce Clayton	.20
242	Bryan Hickerson	.20
243	Mike Jackson	.20
244	Darren Lewis	.20
245	Kirt Manwaring	.20
246	Mark Portugal	.20
247	Salomon Torres	.20
248	Checklist	.20
249	Checklist	.20
250	Checklist	.20
251	Brady Anderson	.40
252	Mike Devereaux	.20
253	Sid Fernandez	.20
254	Leo Gomez	.20
255	Mike Mussina	.75
256	Mike Oquist	.20
257	Rafael Palmeiro	.30
258	Lee Smith	.25
259	Damon Berryhill	.20
260	Wes Chamberlain	.20
261	Roger Clemens	2.00
262	Gar Finnvold	.20
263	Mike Greenwell	.20
264	Tim Naehring	.20
265	Otis Nixon	.20
266	Ken Ryan	.20
267	Chad Curtis	.20
268	Chili Davis	.25
269	Damion Easley	.20
270	Jorge Fabregas	.20
271	Mark Langston	.20
272	Phil Leftwich	.20
273	Harold Reynolds	.20
274	J.T. Snow	.40
275	Joey Cora	.20
276	Julio Franco	.20
277	Roberto Hernandez	.20
278	Lance Johnson	.20
279	Ron Karkovice	.20
280	Jack McDowell	.25
281	Robin Ventura	.40
282	Sandy Alomar Jr.	.25
283	Kenny Lofton	1.50
284	Jose Mesa	.25
285	Jack Morris	.20
286	Eddie Murray	.30
287	Chad Ogea	.20
288	Eric Plunk	.20
289	Paul Shuey	.20
290	Omar Vizquel	.20
291	Danny Bautista	.20
292	Travis Fryman	.30
293	Greg Gohr	.20
294	Chris Gomez	.20
295	Mickey Tettleton	.20
296	Lou Whitaker	.20
297	David Cone	.20
298	Gary Gaetti	.25
299	Tom Gordon	.20
300	Felix Jose	.20
301	Jose Lind	.20
302	Brian McRae	.20
303	Mike Fetters	.20
304	Brian Harper	.20
305	Pat Listach	.20
306	Matt Mieske	.30
307	Dave Nilsson	.20
308	Jody Reed	.20
309	Greg Vaughn	.25
310	Bill Wegman	.20
311	Rick Aguilera	.20
312	Alex Cole	.20
313	Denny Hocking	.20
314	Chuck Knoblauch	.30
315	Shane Mack	.20
316	Pat Meares	.35
317	Kevin Tapani	.20
318	Jim Abbott	.25
319	Wade Boggs	.40
320	Sterling Hitchcock	.20
321	Pat Kelly	.20
322	Terry Mulholland	.20
323	Luis Polonia	.20
324	Mike Stanley	.20
325	Bob Wickman	.20
326	Bernie Williams	1.50
327	Mark Acre	.20
328	Geronimo Berroa	.25
329	Scott Brosius	.20
330	Brent Gates	.20
331	Rickey Henderson	.35
332	Carlos Reyes	.20
333	Ruben Sierra	.25
334	Bobby Witt	.20
335	Bobby Ayala	.20
336	Jay Buhner	.25
337	Randy Johnson	.60
338	Edgar Martinez	.30
339	Bill Risley	.30
340	*Alex Rodriguez*	45.00
341	Roger Salkeld	.25
342	Dan Wilson	.20
343	Kevin Brown	.20
344	Jose Canseco	.65
345	Dean Palmer	.20
346	Ivan Rodriguez	1.00
347	Kenny Rogers	.20
348	Pat Borders	.20
349	Juan Guzman	.20
350	Ed Sprague	.20
351	Devon White	.20
352	Steve Avery	.25
353	Roberto Kelly	.20
354	Mark Lemke	.20
355	Greg McMichael	.20
356	Terry Pendleton	.20
357	John Smoltz	.30
358	Mike Stanton	.20
359	Tony Tarasco	.20
360	Mark Grace	.30
361	Derrick May	.20
362	Rey Sanchez	.20
363	Sammy Sosa	3.00
364	Rick Wilkins	.20
365	Jeff Brantley	.20
366	Tony Fernandez	.20
367	Chuck McElroy	.20
368	Kevin Mitchell	.20
369	John Roper	.20
370	Johnny Ruffin	.20
371	Deion Sanders	1.00
372	Marvin Freeman	.20
373	Andres Galarraga	.40
374	Charlie Hayes	.20
375	Nelson Liriano	.20
376	David Nied	.20
377	Walt Weiss	.20
378	Bret Barberie	.20
379	Jerry Browne	.20
380	Chuck Carr	.20
381	Greg Colbrunn	.20
382	Charlie Hough	.20
383	Kurt Miller	.25
384	Benito Santiago	.25
385	Jeff Bagwell	1.50
386	Craig Biggio	.35
387	Ken Caminiti	.35
388	Doug Drabek	.20
389	Steve Finley	.20
390	John Hudek	.20
391	Orlando Miller	.20
392	Shane Reynolds	.20
393	Brett Butler	.25
394	Tom Candiotti	.20
395	Delino DeShields	.20
396	Kevin Gross	.20

397	Eric Karros	.30
398	Ramon Martinez	.25
399	Henry Rodriguez	.25
400	Moises Alou	.25
401	Jeff Fassero	.20
402	Mike Lansing	.20
403	Mel Rojas	.20
404	Larry Walker	.60
405	John Wetteland	.20
406	Gabe White	.30
407	Bobby Bonilla	.30
408	Josias Manzanillo	.20
409	Bret Saberhagen	.20
410	David Segui	.20
411	Mariano Duncan	.20
412	Tommy Greene	.20
413	Billy Hatcher	.20
414	Ricky Jordan	.20
415	John Kruk	.20
416	Bobby Munoz	.20
417	Curt Schilling	.20
418	Fernando Valenzuela	.25
419	David West	.20
420	Carlos Garcia	.20
421	Brian Hunter	.20
422	Jeff King	.20
423	Jon Lieber	.20
424	Ravelo Manzanillo	.20
425	Denny Neagle	.20
426	Andy Van Slyke	.20
427	Bryan Eversgerd	.20
428	Bernard Gilkey	.25
429	Gregg Jefferies	.25
430	Tom Pagnozzi	.20
431	Bob Tewksbury	.20
432	Allen Watson	.25
433	Andy Ashby	.20
434	Andy Benes	.25
435	Donnie Elliott	.20
436	Tony Gwynn	1.50
437	Joey Hamilton	.75
438	Tim Hyers	.20
439	Luis Lopez	.20
440	Bip Roberts	.20
441	Scott Sanders	.20
442	Rod Beck	.20
443	Dave Burba	.20
444	Darryl Strawberry	.25
445	Bill Swift	.20
446	Robby Thompson	.20
447	*W. VanLandingham*	1.00
448	Matt Williams	1.00
449	Checklist	.20
450	Checklist	.20

1994 Flair
Hot Glove

Hot Glove is a 10-card insert set that was available in packs of 1994 Flair Baseball Series II. It focused on collectible players with outstanding defensive ability. Cards featured a special diecut "glove" design, with the player photo over top of a baseball glove. The fingers of the glove were cut as a border to the card. The

player's name, team and a "Hot Glove" logo was placed in the lower-left hand corner of each card.

		MT
Complete Set (10):		200.00
Common Player:		8.00
1	Barry Bonds	15.00
2	Will Clark	8.00
3	Ken Griffey, Jr.	60.00
4	Kenny Lofton	15.00
5	Greg Maddux	40.00
6	Don Mattingly	15.00
7	Kirby Puckett	20.00
8	Cal Ripken, Jr.	45.00
9	Tim Salmon	10.00
10	Matt Williams	8.00

1994 Flair
Hot Numbers

Hot Numbers is an insert set found in packs of Flair Series I. This was the scarcest insert set in Series I and included the hottest players in baseball in 1994. Each card is printed on 100% etched foil and displays the player in the forefront with a background made up of different numbers floating around. The player's name is printed in gold foil across the bottom-right side and a large foil "Hot Numbers" and that player's uniform number are in a square at the bottom-left corner.

		MT
Complete Set (10):		75.00
Common Player:		1.50
1	Roberto Alomar	4.00
2	Carlos Baerga	1.50
3	Will Clark	2.50
4	Fred McGriff	2.00
5	Paul Molitor	3.00
6	John Olerud	1.50
7	Mike Piazza	20.00
8	Cal Ripken, Jr.	25.00
9	Ryne Sandberg	8.00
10	Frank Thomas	20.00

1994 Flair Infield
Power

Infield Power is a horizontally formatted insert set. Cards show the player batting on one half and in the field on the other half of the card. This is divided by a black, diagonal strip that reads "Infield Power" and the player's name. The set spotlights infielders that often hit the longball. Infield Power was inserted into Series II packs of Flair.

		MT
Complete Set (10):		20.00
Common Player:		.75
1	Jeff Bagwell	2.00
2	Will Clark	1.00
3	Darren Daulton	.75
4	Don Mattingly	2.00
5	Fred McGriff	1.00
6	Rafael Palmeiro	1.00
7	Mike Piazza	5.00
8	Cal Ripken, Jr.	8.00
9	Frank Thomas	6.00
10	Matt Williams	1.00

1994 Flair
Outfield Power

Fleer Flair's Outfield Power was randomly inserted into Series I packs. This vertically formatted card shows the player in the field on top, while the bottom half shows the player at the plate. These two halves are divided by a black strip with "Outfield Power" and the player's name on it.

		MT
Complete Set (10):		25.00
Common Player:		1.00
1	Albert Belle	3.00
2	Barry Bonds	3.00
3	Joe Carter	1.00
4	Len Dykstra	1.00
5	Juan Gonzalez	4.00
6	Ken Griffey, Jr.	12.00
7	Dave Justice	1.50
8	Kirby Puckett	4.00
9	Tim Salmon	1.50
10	Dave Winfield	1.00

1994 Flair
Wave of the Future

Wave of the Future Series I is horizontally formatted and depicts 10 outstanding 1994 rookies who have the potential to become superstars. Each player is featured on a colorful wavelike background. A Wave of the Future gold foil stamp is placed in the bottom-right corner and the player name in gold foil starting in the opposite bottom corner and running across the bottom.

	MT
Complete Set (10):	22.00
Common Player:	1.00
1 Kurt Abbott	1.00
2 Carlos Delgado	2.00
3 Steve Karsay	1.00
4 Ryan Klesko	7.00
5 Javier Lopez	3.00
6 Raul Mondesi	7.00
7 James Mouton	1.50
8 Chan Ho Park	2.00
9 Dave Staton	1.00
10 Rick White	1.00

1994 Flair Wave of the Future 2

Series II of Flair also has a Wave of the Future insert set. Unlike Series I, this 10-card set is vertically formated. The Wave of the Future logo appeared in the left-bottom corner with the player's name stretching across the rest of the bottom. The background has a swirling water effect, on which the player is superimposed.

	MT
Complete Set (10):	70.00
Common Player:	1.00
1 Mark Acre	1.00
2 Chris Gomez	1.00
3 Joey Hamilton	4.00
4 John Hudek	1.00
5 Jon Lieber	1.00
6 Matt Mieske	1.50
7 Orlando Miller	1.50
8 Alex Rodriguez	60.00
9 Tony Tarasco	1.00
10 Bill VanLandingham	1.00

Values shown reflect the market as of January, 1999. On-field performances of current players in the 1999 baseball season are not factored in.

1995 Flair

There's no mistaking that 1995 Flair is Fleer's super-premium brand. Cards are printed on double-thick cardboard with a background of etched metallic foil - gold for National Leaguers, silver for American. A portrait and an action photo are featured on the horizontal front design. Backs are vertically formatted with a borderless action photo, several years worth of stats and foil trim. The basic set was issued in two series of 216 basic cards each, along with several insert sets exclusive to each series. Cards were sold in a hard pack of nine with a suggested retail price of $5.

	MT
Complete Set (432):	60.00
Common Player:	.20
Series 1 or 2 Wax Box:	80.00
1 Brady Anderson	.40
2 Harold Baines	.25
3 Leo Gomez	.20
4 Alan Mills	.20
5 Jamie Moyer	.20
6 Mike Mussina	.75
7 Mike Oquist	.20
8 Arthur Rhodes	.20
9 Cal Ripken Jr.	4.00
10 Roger Clemens	1.50
11 Scott Cooper	.20
12 Mike Greenwell	.20
13 Aaron Sele	.20
14 John Valentin	.25
15 Mo Vaughn	1.25
16 Chad Curtis	.20
17 Gary DiSarcina	.20
18 Chuck Finley	.20
19 Andrew Lorraine	.20
20 Spike Owen	.20
21 Tim Salmon	.40
22 J.T. Snow	.30
23 Wilson Alvarez	.20
24 Jason Bere	.20
25 Ozzie Guillen	.20
26 Mike LaValliere	.20
27 Frank Thomas	4.00
28 Robin Ventura	.30
29 Carlos Baerga	.30
30 Albert Belle	1.25
31 Jason Grimsley	.20
32 Dennis Martinez	.25
33 Eddie Murray	.75
34 Charles Nagy	.20
35 Manny Ramirez	1.00
36 Paul Sorrento	.20
37 John Doherty	.20
38 Cecil Fielder	.30
39 Travis Fryman	.20
40 Chris Gomez	.20
41 Tony Phillips	.25
42 Lou Whitaker	.20
43 David Cone	.20
44 Gary Gaetti	.25
45 Mark Gubicza	.20
46 Bob Hamelin	.20
47 Wally Joyner	.25
48 Rusty Meacham	.20
49 Jeff Montgomery	.20
50 Ricky Bones	.20
51 Cal Eldred	.20
52 Pat Listach	.20
53 Matt Mieske	.20
54 Dave Nilsson	.20

55 Greg Vaughn	.20
56 Bill Wegman	.20
57 Chuck Knoblauch	.35
58 Scott Leius	.20
59 Pat Mahomes	.20
60 Pat Meares	.20
61 Pedro Munoz	.20
62 Kirby Puckett	2.00
63 Wade Boggs	.40
64 Jimmy Key	.20
65 Jim Leyritz	.20
66 Don Mattingly	2.00
67 Paul O'Neill	.20
68 Melido Perez	.20
69 Danny Tartabull	.20
70 John Briscoe	.20
71 Scott Brosius	.20
72 Ron Darling	.20
73 Brent Gates	.20
74 Rickey Henderson	.35
75 Stan Javier	.20
76 Mark McGwire	6.00
77 Todd Van Poppel	.20
78 Bobby Ayala	.20
79 Mike Blowers	.20
80 Jay Buhner	.35
81 Ken Griffey Jr.	5.00
82 Randy Johnson	.75
83 Tino Martinez	.30
84 Jeff Nelson	.20
85 Alex Rodriguez	5.00
86 Will Clark	.50
87 Jeff Frye	.20
88 Juan Gonzalez	2.50
89 Rusty Greer	.25
90 Darren Oliver	.20
91 Dean Palmer	.20
92 Ivan Rodriguez	1.00
93 Matt Whiteside	.20
94 Roberto Alomar	1.00
95 Joe Carter	.30
96 Tony Castillo	.20
97 Juan Guzman	.20
98 Pat Hentgen	.20
99 Mike Huff	.20
100 John Olerud	.25
101 Woody Williams	.20
102 Roberto Kelly	.20
103 Ryan Klesko	.75
104 Javier Lopez	.35
105 Greg Maddux	3.00
106 Fred McGriff	.40
107 Jose Oliva	.20
108 John Smoltz	.35
109 Tony Tarasco	.20
110 Mark Wohlers	.20
111 Jim Bullinger	.20
112 Shawon Dunston	.30
113 Derrick May	.20
114 Randy Myers	.20
115 Karl Rhodes	.20
116 Rey Sanchez	.20
117 Steve Trachsel	.20
118 Eddie Zambrano	.20
119 Bret Boone	.20
120 Brian Dorsett	.20
121 Hal Morris	.20
122 Jose Rijo	.20
123 John Roper	.20
124 Reggie Sanders	.30
125 Pete Schourek	.20
126 John Smiley	.20
127 Ellis Burks	.30
128 Vinny Castilla	.25
129 Marvin Freeman	.20
130 Andres Galarraga	.30
131 Mike Munoz	.20
132 David Nied	.20
133 Bruce Ruffin	.20
134 Walt Weiss	.20
135 Eric Young	.20
136 Greg Colbrunn	.20
137 Jeff Conine	.25
138 Jeremy Hernandez	.20
139 Charles Johnson	.25
140 Robb Nen	.20
141 Gary Sheffield	.60
142 Dave Weathers	.20
143 Jeff Bagwell	1.50
144 Craig Biggio	.30
145 Tony Eusebio	.20
146 Luis Gonzalez	.20
147 John Hudek	.20
148 Darryl Kile	.20
149 Dave Veres	.20
150 Billy Ashley	.20

#	Player	Price
151	Pedro Astacio	.20
152	Rafael Bournigal	.20
153	Delino DeShields	.20
154	Raul Mondesi	.60
155	Mike Piazza	3.00
156	Rudy Seanez	.20
157	Ismael Valdes	.20
158	Tim Wallach	.20
159	Todd Worrell	.20
160	Moises Alou	.25
161	Cliff Floyd	.20
162	Gil Heredia	.20
163	Mike Lansing	.20
164	Pedro Martinez	.20
165	Kirk Rueter	.20
166	Tim Scott	.20
167	Jeff Shaw	.20
168	Rondell White	.30
169	Bobby Bonilla	.25
170	Rico Brogna	.20
171	Todd Hundley	.30
172	Jeff Kent	.20
173	Jim Lindeman	.20
174	Joe Orsulak	.20
175	Bret Saberhagen	.20
176	Toby Borland	.20
177	Darren Daulton	.25
178	Lenny Dykstra	.20
179	Jim Eisenreich	.20
180	Tommy Greene	.20
181	Tony Longmire	.20
182	Bobby Munoz	.20
183	Kevin Stocker	.20
184	Jay Bell	.20
185	Steve Cooke	.20
186	Ravelo Manzanillo	.20
187	Al Martin	.20
188	Denny Neagle	.20
189	Don Slaught	.20
190	Paul Wagner	.20
191	Rene Arocha	.20
192	Bernard Gilkey	.25
193	Jose Oquendo	.20
194	Tom Pagnozzi	.20
195	Ozzie Smith	.75
196	Allen Watson	.20
197	Mark Whiten	.20
198	Andy Ashby	.20
199	Donnie Elliott	.20
200	Bryce Florie	.20
201	Tony Gwynn	2.00
202	Trevor Hoffman	.20
203	Brian Johnson	.20
204	Tim Mauser	.20
205	Bip Roberts	.20
206	Rod Beck	.20
207	Barry Bonds	1.25
208	Royce Clayton	.20
209	Darren Lewis	.20
210	Mark Portugal	.20
211	Kevin Rogers	.20
212	William Van Landingham	.30
213	Matt Williams	.50
214	Checklist	.20
215	Checklist	.20
216	Checklist	.20
217	Bret Barberie	.20
218	Armando Benitez	.20
219	Kevin Brown	.20
220	Sid Fernandez	.20
221	Chris Hoiles	.20
222	Doug Jones	.20
223	Ben McDonald	.20
224	Rafael Palmeiro	.30
225	Andy Van Slyke	.20
226	Jose Canseco	.50
227	Vaughn Eshelman	.20
228	Mike Macfarlane	.20
229	Tim Naehring	.20
230	Frank Rodriguez	.25
231	Lee Tinsley	.20
232	Mark Whiten	.20
233	Garret Anderson	.25
234	Chili Davis	.25
235	Jim Edmonds	.40
236	Mark Langston	.20
237	Troy Percival	.25
238	Tony Phillips	.25
239	Lee Smith	.25
240	Jim Abbott	.25
241	James Baldwin	.20
242	Mike Devereaux	.20
243	Ray Durham	.30
244	Alex Fernandez	.25
245	Roberto Hernandez	.20
246	Lance Johnson	.20
247	Ron Karkovice	.20
248	Tim Raines	.25
249	Sandy Alomar Jr.	.25
250	Orel Hershiser	.25
251	Julian Tavarez	.20
252	Jim Thome	.40
253	Omar Vizquel	.20
254	Dave Winfield	.35
255	Chad Curtis	.20
256	Kirk Gibson	.20
257	Mike Henneman	.20
258	*Bob Higginson*	1.50
259	Felipe Lira	.20
260	Rudy Pemberton	.20
261	Alan Trammell	.25
262	Kevin Appier	.20
263	Pat Borders	.20
264	Tom Gordon	.20
265	Jose Lind	.20
266	Jon Nunnally	.20
267	Dilson Torres	.20
268	Michael Tucker	.30
269	Jeff Cirillo	.20
270	Darryl Hamilton	.20
271	David Hulse	.20
272	Mark Kiefer	.20
273	Graeme Lloyd	.20
274	Joe Oliver	.20
275	Al Reyes	.20
276	Kevin Seitzer	.20
277	Rick Aguilera	.20
278	Marty Cordova	.30
279	Scott Erickson	.20
280	LaTroy Hawkins	.20
281	Brad Radke	.20
282	Kevin Tapani	.20
283	Tony Fernandez	.20
284	Sterling Hitchcock	.20
285	Pat Kelly	.20
286	Jack McDowell	.20
287	Andy Pettitte	2.00
288	Mike Stanley	.20
289	John Wetteland	.25
290	Bernie Williams	1.50
291	Mark Acre	.20
292	Geronimo Berroa	.25
293	Dennis Eckersley	.25
294	Steve Ontiveros	.20
295	Ruben Sierra	.25
296	Terry Steinbach	.25
297	Dave Stewart	.25
298	Todd Stottlemyre	.20
299	Darren Bragg	.20
300	Joey Cora	.20
301	Edgar Martinez	.25
302	Bill Risley	.20
303	Ron Villone	.20
304	Dan Wilson	.20
305	Benji Gil	.20
306	Wilson Heredia	.20
307	Mark McLemore	.20
308	Otis Nixon	.20
309	Kenny Rogers	.20
310	Jeff Russell	.20
311	Mickey Tettleton	.20
312	Bob Tewksbury	.20
313	David Cone	.20
314	Carlos Delgado	.25
315	Alex Gonzalez	.20
316	Shawn Green	.25
317	Paul Molitor	.40
318	Ed Sprague	.20
319	Devon White	.20
320	Steve Avery	.20
321	Jeff Blauser	.20
322	Brad Clontz	.20
323	Tom Glavine	.35
324	Marquis Grissom	.25
325	Chipper Jones	3.00
326	Dave Justice	.40
327	Mark Lemke	.20
328	Kent Mercker	.20
329	Jason Schmidt	.25
330	Steve Buechele	.20
331	Kevin Foster	.20
332	Mark Grace	.35
333	Brian McRae	.20
334	Sammy Sosa	3.00
335	Ozzie Timmons	.20
336	Rick Wilkins	.20
337	Hector Carrasco	.20
338	Ron Gant	.30
339	Barry Larkin	.40
340	Deion Sanders	.40
341	Benito Santiago	.25
342	Roger Bailey	.20
343	Jason Bates	.20
344	Dante Bichette	.50
345	Joe Girardi	.20
346	Bill Swift	.20
347	Mark Thompson	.20
348	Larry Walker	.40
349	Kurt Abbott	.20
350	John Burkett	.20
351	Chuck Carr	.20
352	Andre Dawson	.25
353	Chris Hammond	.20
354	Charles Johnson	.25
355	Terry Pendleton	.20
356	Quilvio Veras	.20
357	Derek Bell	.25
358	Jim Dougherty	.20
359	Doug Drabek	.20
360	Todd Jones	.20
361	Orlando Miller	.20
362	James Mouton	.20
363	Phil Plantier	.20
364	Shane Reynolds	.20
365	Todd Hollandsworth	.40
366	Eric Karros	.25
367	Ramon Martinez	.20
368	*Hideo Nomo*	5.00
369	Jose Offerman	.20
370	Antonio Osuna	.20
371	Todd Williams	.20
372	Shane Andrews	.20
373	Wil Cordero	.20
374	Jeff Fassero	.20
375	Darrin Fletcher	.20
376	*Mark Grudzielanek*	.60
377	*Carlos Perez*	.25
378	Mel Rojas	.20
379	Tony Tarasco	.20
380	Edgardo Alfonzo	.25
381	Brett Butler	.25
382	Carl Everett	.20
383	John Franco	.20
384	Pete Harnisch	.20
385	Bobby Jones	.20
386	Dave Mlicki	.20
387	Jose Vizcaino	.20
388	Ricky Bottalico	.20
389	Tyler Green	.20
390	Charlie Hayes	.20
391	Dave Hollins	.20
392	Gregg Jefferies	.25
393	*Michael Mimbs*	.30
394	Mickey Morandini	.20
395	Curt Schilling	.20
396	Heathcliff Slocumb	.20
397	Jason Christiansen	.20
398	Midre Cummings	.20
399	Carlos Garcia	.20
400	Mark Johnson	.25
401	Jeff King	.20
402	Jon Lieber	.20
403	Esteban Loaiza	.30
404	Orlando Merced	.20
405	*Gary Wilson*	.30
406	Scott Cooper	.20
407	Tom Henke	.20
408	Ken Hill	.20
409	Danny Jackson	.20
410	Brian Jordan	.30
411	Ray Lankford	.25
412	John Mabry	.20
413	Todd Zeile	.25
414	Andy Benes	.25
415	Andres Berumen	.20
416	Ken Caminiti	.30
417	Andujar Cedeno	.20
418	Steve Finley	.20
419	Joey Hamilton	.30
420	Dustin Hermanson	.25
421	Melvin Nieves	.20
422	Roberto Petagine	.20
423	Eddie Williams	.20
424	Glenallen Hill	.20
425	Kirt Manwaring	.20
426	Terry Mulholland	.20
427	J.R. Phillips	.20
428	Joe Rosselli	.20
429	Robby Thompson	.20
430	Checklist	.20
431	Checklist	.20
432	Checklist	.20

A player's name in *italic* type indicates a rookie card.

1995 Flair Cal Ripken, Jr. Enduring Flair

The career of Cal Ripken, Jr., is traced in this insert set found in Series II Flair packs at the average rate of once per dozen packs. Each card has a vintage photo on front, with a large silver-foil "ENDURING" logo toward the bottom. Backs have another color photo, a quote and other information about the milestone. The series was extended by a special mail-in offer for five additional cards which chronicled Ripken's record-breaking 1995 season.

		MT
Complete Set (15):		150.00
Common Ripken:		10.00
1	Rookie Of The Year	10.00
2	1st MVP Season	10.00
3	World Series Highlight	10.00
4	Family Tradition	10.00
5	8,243 Consecutive Innings	10.00
6	95 Consecutive Errorless Games	10.00
7	All-Star MVP	10.00
8	1,000th RBI	10.00
9	287th Home Run	10.00
10	2,000th Consecutive Game	10.00
11	Record-tying Game	12.00
12	Record-breaking Game	12.00
13	Defensive Prowess	12.00
14	Literacy Work	12.00
15	2,153 and Counting	12.00

1995 Flair Hot Gloves

The cream of the crop among Series II Flair inserts is this set featuring fine fielders. Cards have a background of an embossed gold-foil glove, with a color player photo centered in front. Silver foil comprises the card title and player name at bottom and the Flair logo at top. Backs have a white background, a photo of a glove with a career summary overprinted and a player portrait photo in a lower corner. These inserts are found at the average rate of once per 25 packs.

		MT
Complete Set (12):		200.00
Common Player:		8.00
1	Roberto Alomar	15.00
2	Barry Bonds	18.00
3	Ken Griffey Jr.	65.00
4	Marquis Grissom	8.00
5	Barry Larkin	10.00
6	Darren Lewis	8.00
7	Kenny Lofton	18.00
8	Don Mattingly	25.00
9	Cal Ripken Jr.	50.00
10	Ivan Rodriguez	12.00
11	Devon White	8.00
12	Matt Williams	8.00

1995 Flair Hot Numbers

		MT
Complete Set (10):		60.00
Common Player:		3.00
1	Jeff Bagwell	4.50
2	Albert Belle	4.00
3	Barry Bonds	4.00
4	Ken Griffey Jr.	16.00
5	Kenny Lofton	4.00
6	Greg Maddux	10.00
7	Mike Piazza	8.00
8	Cal Ripken Jr.	12.00
9	Frank Thomas	12.00
10	Matt Williams	3.00

1995 Flair Infield Power

Power rays and waves eminating from the player's bat in an action photo are the front design of this Series II chase set. The card title, name and team at bottom, and the Flair logo at top are in silver foil. Backs repeat the wave theme with a player photo on one end and a career summary at the other. These inserts are seeded at the average rate of one per five packs.

		MT
Complete Set (10):		17.50
Common Player:		.75
1	Jeff Bagwell	4.00
2	Darren Daulton	.75
3	Cecil Fielder	1.25
4	Andres Galarraga	1.00
5	Fred McGriff	2.00
6	Rafael Palmeiro	1.25
7	Mike Piazza	5.00
8	Frank Thomas	8.00
9	Mo Vaughn	2.50
10	Matt Williams	1.00

1995 Flair Outfield Power

Laser-like colored rays are the background to the action photo on front and portrait on back of this series. The card title, player name and team, and Flair logo on front are in silver foil. Backs are horizontal, silver-foil enhanced and include a paragraph of career summary. This chase set is seeded at the average rate of one card per six packs of Series I Flair.

		MT
Complete Set (10):		25.00
Common Player:		1.00
1	Albert Belle	2.50
2	Dante Bichette	1.50
3	Barry Bonds	2.50
4	Jose Canseco	2.00
5	Joe Carter	1.50
6	Juan Gonzalez	5.00
7	Ken Griffey Jr.	10.00
8	Kirby Puckett	3.00
9	Gary Sheffield	1.50
10	Ruben Sierra	1.00

1995 Flair Today's Spotlight

The premier insert set in Flair Series I, found once every 30 packs or so, this die-cut issue has the player action photo spotlighted in a 2-3/8" bright spot, with the rest of the photo muted in gray and dark gray. The card title, Flair logo, player name and team are in silver foil. The horizontal backs have a portrait photo in the spotlight and career summary on the side.

		MT
Complete Set (12):		80.00
Common Player:		4.00
1	Jeff Bagwell	20.00
2	Jason Bere	4.00
3	Cliff Floyd	4.00
4	Chuck Knoblauch	8.00
5	Kenny Lofton	10.00
6	Javier Lopez	4.00
7	Raul Mondesi	6.00
8	Mike Mussina	8.00
9	Mike Piazza	30.00
10	Manny Ramirez	8.00
11	Tim Salmon	6.00
12	Frank Thomas	30.00

1995 Flair
Wave Of The Future

The cream of baseball's rookie crop is featured in this Series II insert set, found once per eight packs, on average. Fronts have a graduated color background with a baseball/wave morph, which is repeated at the bottom in silver foil, along with the player name. A color action photo is at center. The player's name, team and "Wave of the Future" are repeated in horizontal rows behind the photo. Horizontal backs repeat the wave logo, have another player photo and a career summary.

		MT
Complete Set (10):		25.00
Common Player:		1.00
1	Jason Bates	1.00
2	Armando Benitez	1.00
3	Marty Cordova	1.75
4	Ray Durham	2.00

5	Vaughn Eshelman	1.00
6	Carl Everett	1.00
7	Shawn Green	2.00
8	Dustin Hermanson	2.00
9	Chipper Jones	12.00
10	Hideo Nomo	8.00

1996 Flair

Fleer's 1996 Flair baseball set has 400 cards, a parallel set and four insert types. Regular card fronts have two photos of the featured players; backs have a photo and career statistics. All cards have a silver-foil version and a gold-foil version, with both versions appearing in equal numbers. The insert sets are Powerline, Diamond Cuts, Wave of the Future and Hot Glove.

		MT
Complete Set (400):		125.00
Common Player:		.25
Wax Box:		55.00
1	Roberto Alomar	2.00
2	Brady Anderson	.40
3	Bobby Bonilla	.35
4	Scott Erickson	.25
5	Jeffrey Hammonds	.25
6	Jimmy Haynes	.25
7	Chris Hoiles	.25
8	Kent Mercker	.25
9	Mike Mussina	1.50
10	Randy Myers	.25
11	Rafael Palmeiro	.40
12	Cal Ripken Jr.	8.00
(12p)	Cal Ripken Jr. (no card #, overprinted "PROMOTIONAL SAMPLE")	5.00
13	B.J. Surhoff	.25
14	David Wells	.25
15	Jose Canseco	.60
16	Roger Clemens	3.00
17	Wil Cordero	.25
18	Tom Gordon	.25
19	Mike Greenwell	.25
20	Dwayne Hosey	.25
21	Jose Malave	.25
22	Tim Naehring	.25
23	Troy O'Leary	.25
24	Aaron Sele	.25
25	Heathcliff Slocumb	.25
26	Mike Stanley	.25
27	Jeff Suppan	.25
28	John Valentin	.25
29	Mo Vaughn	2.00
30	Tim Wakefield	.25
31	Jim Abbott	.25
32	Garret Anderson	.25
33	George Arias	.25
34	Chili Davis	.25
35	Gary DiSarcina	.25
36	Jim Edmonds	.25
37	Chuck Finley	.25
38	Todd Greene	.25
39	Mark Langston	.25
40	Troy Percival	.25

41	Tim Salmon	.50
42	Lee Smith	.25
43	J.T. Snow	.25
44	Randy Velarde	.25
45	Tim Wallach	.25
46	Wilson Alvarez	.25
47	Harold Baines	.25
48	Jason Bere	.25
49	Ray Durham	.25
50	Alex Fernandez	.40
51	Ozzie Guillen	.25
52	Roberto Hernandez	.25
53	Ron Karkovice	.25
54	Darren Lewis	.25
55	Lyle Mouton	.25
56	Tony Phillips	.25
57	Chris Snopek	.25
58	Kevin Tapani	.25
59	Danny Tartabull	.25
30	Frank Thomas	8.00
61	Robin Ventura	.25
62	Sandy Alomar	.25
63	Carlos Baerga	.30
64	Albert Belle	2.50
65	Julio Franco	.25
66	Orel Hershiser	.25
67	Kenny Lofton	2.00
68	Dennis Martinez	.25
69	Jack McDowell	.40
70	Jose Mesa	.25
71	Eddie Murray	.75
72	Charles Nagy	.25
73	Tony Pena	.25
74	Manny Ramirez	2.00
75	Julian Tavarez	.25
76	Jim Thome	1.00
77	Omar Vizquel	.25
78	Chad Curtis	.25
79	Cecil Fielder	.50
80	Travis Fryman	.25
81	Chris Gomez	.25
82	Bob Higginson	.40
83	Mark Lewis	.25
84	Felipe Lira	.25
85	Alan Trammell	.25
86	Kevin Appier	.25
87	Johnny Damon	.40
88	Tom Goodwin	.25
89	Mark Gubicza	.25
90	Bob Hamelin	.25
91	Keith Lockhart	.25
92	Jeff Montgomery	.25
93	Jon Nunnally	.25
94	Bip Roberts	.25
95	Michael Tucker	.25
96	Joe Vitiello	.25
97	Ricky Bones	.25
98	Chuck Carr	.25
99	Jeff Cirillo	.25
100	Mike Fetters	.25
101	John Jaha	.25
102	Mike Matheny	.25
103	Ben McDonald	.25
104	Matt Mieske	.25
105	Dave Nilsson	.25
106	Kevin Seitzer	.25
107	Steve Sparks	.25
108	Jose Valentin	.25
109	Greg Vaughn	.25
110	Rick Aguilera	.25
111	Rich Becker	.25
112	Marty Cordova	.40
113	LaTroy Hawkins	.25
114	Dave Hollins	.25
115	Roberto Kelly	.25
116	Chuck Knoblauch	.50
117	*Matt Lawton*	.25
118	Pat Meares	.25
119	Paul Molitor	1.00
120	Kirby Puckett	4.00
121	Brad Radke	.25
122	Frank Rodriguez	.25
123	Scott Stahoviak	.25
124	Matt Walbeck	.25
125	Wade Boggs	.40
126	David Cone	.35
127	Joe Girardi	.25
128	Dwight Gooden	.35
129	Derek Jeter	5.00
130	Jimmy Key	.25
131	Jim Leyritz	.25
132	Tino Martinez	.25
133	Paul O'Neill	.25
134	Andy Pettitte	2.00
135	Tim Raines	.25
136	Ruben Rivera	1.25

#	Player	Price	#	Player	Price	#	Player	Price
137	Kenny Rogers	.25	233	Mike Kelly	.25	329	Ricky Bottalico	.25
138	Ruben Sierra	.25	234	Barry Larkin	1.00	330	Darren Daulton	.25
139	John Wetteland	.25	235	Hal Morris	.25	331	*David Doster*	.25
140	Bernie Williams	2.00	236	Mark Portugal	.25	332	Lenny Dykstra	.25
141	Tony Batista	.25	237	Jose Rijo	.25	333	Jim Eisenreich	.25
142	Allen Battle	.25	238	Reggie Sanders	.25	334	Sid Fernandez	.25
143	Geronimo Berroa	.40	239	Pete Schourek	.25	335	Gregg Jefferies	.25
144	Mike Bordick	.25	240	John Smiley	.25	336	Mickey Morandini	.25
145	Scott Brosius	.25	241	Eddie Taubensee	.25	337	Benito Santiago	.25
146	Steve Cox	.25	242	Jason Bates	.25	338	Curt Schilling	.25
147	Brent Gates	.25	243	Dante Bichette	1.00	339	Kevin Stocker	.25
148	Jason Giambi	.40	244	Ellis Burks	.25	340	David West	.25
149	Doug Johns	.25	245	Vinny Castilla	.25	341	Mark Whiten	.25
150	Mark McGwire	10.00	246	Andres Galarraga	.50	342	Todd Zeile	.25
151	Pedro Munoz	.25	247	Darren Holmes	.25	343	Jay Bell	.25
152	Ariel Prieto	.25	248	Curt Leskanic	.25	344	John Ericks	.25
153	Terry Steinbach	.25	249	Steve Reed	.25	345	Carlos Garcia	.25
154	Todd Van Poppel	.25	250	Kevin Ritz	.25	346	Charlie Hayes	.25
155	Bobby Ayala	.25	251	Bret Saberhagen	.25	347	Jason Kendall	.25
156	Chris Bosio	.25	252	Bill Swift	.25	348	Jeff King	.25
157	Jay Buhner	.50	253	Larry Walker	.75	349	Mike Kingery	.25
158	Joey Cora	.25	254	Walt Weiss	.25	350	Al Martin	.25
159	Russ Davis	.25	255	Eric Young	.25	351	Orlando Merced	.25
160	Ken Griffey Jr.	10.00	256	Kurt Abbott	.25	352	Dan Miceli	.25
161	Sterling Hitchcock	.25	257	Kevin Brown	.25	353	Denny Neagle	.25
162	Randy Johnson	1.50	258	John Burkett	.25	354	Alan Benes	.40
163	Edgar Martinez	.25	259	Greg Colbrunn	.25	355	Andy Benes	.25
164	Alex Rodriguez	8.00	260	Jeff Conine	.25	356	Royce Clayton	.25
165	Paul Sorrento	.25	261	Andre Dawson	.25	357	Dennis Eckersley	.25
166	Dan Wilson	.25	262	Chris Hammond	.25	358	Gary Gaetti	.25
167	Will Clark	.50	263	Charles Johnson	.25	359	Ron Gant	.40
168	Benji Gil	.25	264	Al Leiter	.25	360	Brian Jordan	.40
169	Juan Gonzalez	4.00	265	Robb Nen	.25	361	Ray Lankford	.25
170	Rusty Greer	.40	266	Terry Pendleton	.25	362	John Mabry	.25
171	Kevin Gross	.25	267	Pat Rapp	.25	363	T.J. Mathews	.25
172	Darryl Hamilton	.25	268	Gary Sheffield	1.50	364	Mike Morgan	.25
173	Mike Henneman	.25	269	Quilvio Veras	.25	365	Donovan Osborne	.25
174	Ken Hill	.25	270	Devon White	.25	366	Tom Pagnozzi	.25
175	Mark McLemore	.25	271	Bob Abreu	.50	367	Ozzie Smith	1.50
176	Dean Palmer	.25	272	Jeff Bagwell	4.00	368	Todd Stottlemyre	.25
177	Roger Pavlik	.25	273	Derek Bell	.25	369	Andy Ashby	.25
178	Ivan Rodriguez	1.50	274	Sean Berry	.25	370	Brad Ausmus	.25
179	Mickey Tettleton	.25	275	Craig Biggio	.25	371	Ken Caminiti	.75
180	Bobby Witt	.25	276	Doug Drabek	.25	372	Andujar Cedeno	.25
181	Joe Carter	.50	277	Tony Eusebio	.25	373	Steve Finley	.25
182	Felipe Crespo	.25	278	Richard Hidalgo	.25	374	Tony Gwynn	4.00
183	Alex Gonzalez	.25	279	Brian Hunter	.25	375	Joey Hamilton	.25
184	Shawn Green	.25	280	Todd Jones	.25	376	Rickey Henderson	.25
185	Juan Guzman	.25	281	Derrick May	.25	377	Trevor Hoffman	.25
186	Erik Hanson	.25	282	Orlando Miller	.25	378	Wally Joyner	.25
187	Pat Hentgen	.25	283	James Mouton	.25	379	Marc Newfield	.25
188	*Sandy Martinez*	.25	284	Shane Reynolds	.25	380	Jody Reed	.25
189	Otis Nixon	.25	285	Greg Swindell	.25	381	Bob Tewksbury	.25
190	John Olerud	.25	286	Mike Blowers	.25	382	Fernando Valenzuela	.25
191	Paul Quantrill	.25	287	Brett Butler	.25	383	Rod Beck	.25
192	Bill Risley	.25	288	Tom Candiotti	.25	384	Barry Bonds	2.00
193	Ed Sprague	.25	289	Roger Cedeno	.25	385	Mark Carreon	.25
194	Steve Avery	.25	290	Delino DeShields	.25	386	Shawon Dunston	.25
195	Jeff Blauser	.25	291	Greg Gagne	.25	387	*Osvaldo Fernandez*	.40
196	Brad Clontz	.25	292	Karim Garcia	1.00	388	Glenallen Hill	.25
197	Jermaine Dye	.60	293	Todd Hollandsworth	.40	389	Stan Javier	.25
198	Tom Glavine	.40	294	Eric Karros	.25	390	Mark Leiter	.25
199	Marquis Grissom	.25	295	Ramon Martinez	.25	391	Kirt Manwaring	.25
200	Chipper Jones	6.00	296	Raul Mondesi	.75	392	Robby Thompson	.25
201	David Justice	.50	297	Hideo Nomo	2.00	393	William VanLandingham	.25
202	Ryan Klesko	1.50	298	Mike Piazza	6.00	394	Allen Watson	.25
203	Mark Lemke	.25	299	Ismael Valdes	.25	395	Matt Williams	.75
204	Javier Lopez	.40	300	Todd Worrell	.25	396	Checklist	.25
205	Greg Maddux	6.00	301	Moises Alou	.25	397	Checklist	.25
206	Fred McGriff	1.00	302	Shane Andrews	.25	398	Checklist	.25
207	Greg McMichael	.25	303	Yamil Benitez	.25	399	Checklist	.25
208	Wonderful Monds	.25	304	Jeff Fassero	.25	400	Checklist	.25
209	Jason Schmidt	.25	305	Darrin Fletcher	.25			
210	John Smoltz	.75	306	Cliff Floyd	.25			
211	Mark Wohlers	.25	307	Mark Grudzielanek	.40			
212	Jim Bullinger	.25	308	Mike Lansing	.25			
213	Frank Castillo	.25	309	Pedro Martinez	.25			
214	Kevin Foster	.25	310	Ryan McGuire	.25			
215	Luis Gonzalez	.25	311	Carlos Perez	.25			
216	Mark Grace	.40	312	Mel Rojas	.25			
217	*Robin Jennings*	.25	313	David Segui	.25			
218	Doug Jones	.25	314	Rondell White	.25			
219	Dave Magadan	.25	315	Edgardo Alfonzo	.25			
220	Brian McRae	.25	316	Rico Brogna	.25			
221	Jaime Navarro	.25	317	Carl Everett	.25			
222	Rey Sanchez	.25	318	John Franco	.25			
223	Ryne Sandberg	2.00	319	Bernard Gilkey	.25			
224	Scott Servais	.25	320	Todd Hundley	.40			
225	Sammy Sosa	6.00	321	Jason Isringhausen	.40			
226	Ozzie Timmons	.25	322	Lance Johnson	.25			
227	Bret Boone	.25	323	Bobby Jones	.25			
228	Jeff Branson	.25	324	Jeff Kent	.25			
229	Jeff Brantley	.25	325	Rey Ordonez	.75			
230	Dave Burba	.25	326	Bill Pulsipher	.25			
231	Vince Coleman	.25	327	Jose Vizcaino	.25			
232	Steve Gibralter	.25	328	Paul Wilson	.40			

1996 Flair Diamond Cuts

Ten of the game's top stars are showcased on these 1996 Fleer Flair insert cards. They are seeded one per every 20 packs.

Modern cards have little collector value in conditions lower than Mint.

Figure NM cards at 75% of values shown; EX cards at 40%.

		MT
Complete Set (12):		125.00
Common Player:		3.00
1	Jeff Bagwell	10.00
2	Albert Belle	6.00
3	Barry Bonds	6.00
4	Juan Gonzalez	12.00
5	Ken Griffey Jr.	25.00
6	Greg Maddux	15.00
7	Eddie Murray	4.00
8	Mike Piazza	15.00
9	Cal Ripken Jr.	20.00
10	Frank Thomas	20.00
11	Mo Vaughn	6.00
12	Matt Williams	4.00

1996 Flair Hot Gloves

Ten top defensive players are highlighted on these die-cut insert cards, a design first made popular in 1994. Hot Gloves can only be found in hobby packs, at a rate of one per every 90 packs.

		MT
Complete Set (10):		450.00
Common Player:		20.00
1	Roberto Alomar	35.00
2	Barry Bonds	45.00
3	Will Clark	20.00
4	Ken Griffey Jr.	120.00
5	Kenny Lofton	40.00
6	Greg Maddux	90.00
7	Mike Piazza	80.00
8	Cal Ripken Jr.	100.00
9	Ivan Rodriguez	40.00
10	Matt Williams	20.00

A player's name in *italic* type indicates a rookie card.

1996 Flair Powerline

Ten of baseball's top power hitters are featured on these 1996 Fleer Flair insert cards. They are the easiest of the Flair inserts to obtain; they are seeded one per every six packs.

		MT
Complete Set (10):		30.00
Common Player:		1.00
1	Albert Belle	2.50
2	Barry Bonds	2.50
3	Juan Gonzalez	3.00
4	Ken Griffey Jr.	10.00
5	Mark McGwire	10.00
6	Mike Piazza	6.00
7	Manny Ramirez	2.50
8	Sammy Sosa	5.00
9	Frank Thomas	8.00
10	Matt Williams	1.50

1996 Flair Wave of the Future

These 1996 Fleer Flair inserts display some of the game's top young talent in baseball. Twenty 1996 rookies and prospects are printed on lenticular cards. They are seeded one per every 72 packs.

		MT
Complete Set (20):		200.00
Common Player:		10.00
1	Bob Abreu	15.00
2	George Arias	10.00
3	Tony Batista	10.00
4	Alan Benes	20.00
5	Yamil Benitez	10.00
6	Steve Cox	10.00
7	David Doster	10.00
8	Jermaine Dye	10.00
9	Osvaldo Fernandez	10.00
10	Karim Garcia	15.00
11	Steve Gibralter	10.00
12	Todd Greene	20.00
13	Richard Hidalgo	10.00
14	Robin Jennings	10.00
15	Jason Kendall	25.00
16	Jose Malave	10.00
17	Wonderful Monds	10.00
18	Rey Ordonez	20.00
19	Ruben Rivera	15.00
20	Paul Wilson	20.00

1997 Flair Showcase

This 540-card set is actually a 180-card set printed in three different versions, all on a super-glossy thick stock. Card fronts feature holographic foil with an action photo of the player silhouetted over a larger portrait image in the background. Each of the 180 base cards has three versions - Style, Grace and Showcase. There are two different parallel sets (Legacy Collection and Legacy Collection Masterpiece) as well as five other inserts: Wave of the Future, Diamond Cuts, Hot Gloves, Emerald, and Million Dollar Moments. Cards were sold exclusively at hobby shops in five-card packs for $4.99.

		MT
Complete Set (180):		2000.
Common Style/Showtime (1-60):		.25
Grace/Showstopper (1-60): 1.5x to 2x		
Showcase/Showpiece (1-60): 10x to 15x		
Common Style/Showpiece (61-120):		.35
Grace/Showtime (61-120): 1x to 2x		
Showcase/Showstopper (61-120): 4x		
Common Style/Showstopper (121-180):		
.25		
Grace/Showpiece (121-180): 2x		
Showcase/Showtime (121-180): 3x		
Wax Box:		170.00
1	Andruw Jones	4.00
2	Derek Jeter	5.00
3	Alex Rodriguez	8.00
4	Paul Molitor	1.50
5	Jeff Bagwell	3.00
6	Scott Rolen	4.00
7	Kenny Lofton	2.00
8	Cal Ripken Jr.	6.00
9	Brady Anderson	.25
10	Chipper Jones	5.00
11	Todd Greene	.25
12	Todd Walker	1.50

#	Player	Price
13	Billy Wagner	.25
14	Craig Biggio	.25
15	Kevin Orie	.25
16	Hideo Nomo	1.50
17	Kevin Appier	.25
18	*Bubba Trammell*	2.00
19	Juan Gonzalez	4.00
20	Randy Johnson	1.50
21	Roger Clemens	3.00
22	Johnny Damon	.25
23	Ryne Sandberg	2.00
24	Ken Griffey Jr.	10.00
25	Barry Bonds	2.00
26	Nomar Garciaparra	5.00
27	Vladimir Guerrero	3.00
28	Ron Gant	.25
29	Joe Carter	.25
30	Tim Salmon	.75
31	Mike Piazza	5.00
32	Barry Larkin	.50
33	Manny Ramirez	2.00
34	Sammy Sosa	6.00
35	Frank Thomas	8.00
36	Melvin Nieves	.25
37	Tony Gwynn	4.00
38	Gary Sheffield	.75
39	Darin Erstad	3.50
40	Ken Caminiti	.50
41	Jermaine Dye	.25
42	Mo Vaughn	2.00
43	Raul Mondesi	.75
44	Greg Maddux	5.00
45	Chuck Knoblauch	.75
46	Andy Pettitte	2.00
47	Deion Sanders	.75
48	Albert Belle	2.50
49	Jamey Wright	.25
50	Rey Ordonez	.25
51	Bernie Williams	1.50
52	Mark McGwire	12.00
53	Mike Mussina	1.50
54	Bob Abreu	.25
55	Reggie Sanders	.25
56	Brian Jordan	.25
57	Ivan Rodriguez	1.50
58	Roberto Alomar	1.50
59	Tim Naehring	.25
60	Edgar Renteria	.25
61	Dean Palmer	.35
62	Benito Santiago	.25
63	David Cone	.50
64	Carlos Delgado	.50
65	Brian Giles	.35
66	Alex Ochoa	.35
67	Rondell White	.35
68	Robin Ventura	.35
69	Eric Karros	.35
70	Jose Valentin	.35
71	Rafael Palmeiro	.50
72	Chris Snopek	.35
73	David Justice	.75
74	Tom Glavine	.50
75	Rudy Pemberton	.35
76	Larry Walker	1.00
77	Jim Thome	1.50
78	Charles Johnson	.35
79	Dante Powell	.35
80	Derrek Lee	.35
81	Jason Kendall	.35
82	Todd Hollandsworth	.35
83	Bernard Gilkey	.35
84	Mel Rojas	.35
85	Dmitri Young	.35
86	Bret Boone	.35
87	Pat Hentgen	.35
88	Bobby Bonilla	.35
89	John Wetteland	.35
90	Todd Hundley	.50
91	Wilton Guerrero	.50
92	Geronimo Berroa	.35
93	Al Martin	.35
94	Danny Tartabull	.35
95	Brian McRae	.35
96	Steve Finley	.35
97	Todd Stottlemyre	.35
98	John Smoltz	.50
99	Matt Williams	1.00
100	Eddie Murray	1.00
101	Henry Rodriguez	.35
102	Marty Cordova	.35
103	Juan Guzman	.35
104	Chili Davis	.35
105	Eric Young	.35
106	Jeff Abbott	.35
107	Shannon Stewart	.35
108	Rocky Coppinger	.35

#	Player	Price
109	Jose Canseco	.75
110	Dante Bichette	.60
111	Dwight Gooden	.35
112	Scott Brosius	.35
113	Steve Avery	.35
114	Andres Galarraga	.60
115	Sandy Alomar Jr.	.35
116	Ray Lankford	.35
117	Jorge Posada	.35
118	Ryan Klesko	1.00
119	Jay Buhner	.60
120	Jose Guillen	1.50
121	Paul O'Neill	.25
122	Jimmy Key	.25
123	Hal Morris	.25
124	Travis Fryman	.25
125	Jim Edmonds	.25
126	Jeff Cirillo	.25
127	Fred McGriff	.60
128	Alan Benes	.50
129	Derek Bell	.25
130	Tony Graffanino	.25
131	Shawn Green	.25
132	Denny Neagle	.25
133	Alex Fernandez	.25
134	Mickey Morandini	.25
135	Royce Clayton	.25
136	Jose Mesa	.25
137	Edgar Martinez	.25
138	Curt Schilling	.25
139	Lance Johnson	.25
140	Andy Benes	.25
141	Charles Nagy	.25
142	Mariano Rivera	.50
143	Mark Wohlers	.25
144	Ken Hill	.25
145	Jay Bell	.25
146	Bob Higginson	.40
147	Mark Grudzielanek	.25
148	Ray Durham	.25
149	John Olerud	.25
150	Joey Hamilton	.25
151	Trevor Hoffman	.25
152	Dan Wilson	.25
153	J.T. Snow	.25
154	Marquis Grissom	.40
155	Yamil Benitez	.25
156	Rusty Greer	.25
157	Darryl Kile	.25
158	Ismael Valdes	.25
159	Jeff Conine	.25
160	Darren Daulton	.25
161	Chan Ho Park	.25
162	Troy Percival	.25
163	Wade Boggs	.50
164	Dave Nilsson	.25
165	Vinny Castilla	.25
166	Kevin Brown	.25
167	Dennis Eckersley	.25
168	Wendell Magee Jr.	.25
169	John Jaha	.25
170	Garret Anderson	.25
171	Jason Giambi	.25
172	Mark Grace	.50
173	Tony Clark	1.50
174	Moises Alou	.40
175	Brett Butler	.25
176	Cecil Fielder	.50
177	Chris Widger	.25
178	Doug Drabek	.25
179	Ellis Burks	.25
180	Shigetosi Hasegawa	.25

1997 Flair Showcase Legacy Collection

This 540-card parallel set is printed on different stock than the regular cards and is sequentially numbered in gold foil. Odds of finding a card is 1:30 packs. Less than 99 complete Legacy Collection sets are available.

A player's name in *italic* type indicates a rookie card.

#	Player	MT
	Common Player:	25.00
	Semistars:	50.00
1	Andruw Jones	125.00
2	Derek Jeter	300.00
3	Alex Rodriguez	300.00
4	Paul Molitor	100.00
5	Jeff Bagwell	200.00
6	Scott Rolen	200.00
7	Kenny Lofton	125.00
8	Cal Ripken Jr.	400.00
9	Brady Anderson	40.00
10	Chipper Jones	300.00
11	Todd Greene	25.00
12	Todd Walker	60.00
13	Billy Wagner	25.00
14	Craig Biggio	40.00
15	Kevin Orie	35.00
16	Hideo Nomo	275.00
17	Kevin Appier	25.00
18	Bubba Trammell	75.00
19	Juan Gonzalez	250.00
20	Randy Johnson	100.00
21	Roger Clemens	200.00
22	Johnny Damon	25.00
23	Ryne Sandberg	140.00
24	Ken Griffey Jr.	500.00
25	Barry Bonds	125.00
26	Nomar Garciaparra	250.00
27	Vladimir Guerrero	150.00
28	Ron Gant	25.00
29	Joe Carter	25.00
30	Tim Salmon	50.00
31	Mike Piazza	300.00
32	Barry Larkin	50.00
33	Manny Ramirez	100.00
34	Sammy Sosa	150.00
35	Frank Thomas	400.00
36	Melvin Nieves	25.00
37	Tony Gwynn	250.00
38	Gary Sheffield	75.00
39	Darin Erstad	150.00
40	Ken Caminiti	50.00
41	Jermaine Dye	25.00
42	Mo Vaughn	125.00
43	Raul Mondesi	60.00
44	Greg Maddux	300.00
45	Chuck Knoblauch	60.00
46	Andy Pettitte	100.00
47	Deion Sanders	60.00
48	Albert Belle	125.00
49	Jamey Wright	25.00
50	Rey Ordonez	25.00
51	Bernie Williams	90.00
52	Mark McGwire	500.00
53	Mike Mussina	100.00
54	Bob Abreu	25.00
55	Reggie Sanders	25.00
56	Brian Jordan	25.00
57	Ivan Rodriguez	100.00
58	Roberto Alomar	100.00
59	Tim Naehring	25.00
60	Edgar Renteria	25.00
61	Dean Palmer	25.00
63	David Cone	40.00
64	Carlos Delgado	40.00
65	Brian Giles	25.00
66	Alex Ochoa	25.00
67	Rondell White	25.00
68	Robin Ventura	25.00
69	Eric Karros	25.00

70	Jose Valentin	25.00
71	Rafael Palmeiro	40.00
72	Chris Snopek	25.00
73	David Justice	50.00
74	Tom Glavine	50.00
75	Rudy Pemberton	25.00
76	Larry Walker	100.00
77	Jim Thome	100.00
78	Charles Johnson	25.00
79	Dante Powell	25.00
80	Derrek Lee	25.00
81	Jason Kendall	25.00
82	Todd Hollandsworth	25.00
83	Bernard Gilkey	25.00
84	Mel Rojas	25.00
85	Dmitri Young	25.00
86	Bret Boone	25.00
87	Pat Hentgen	25.00
88	Bobby Bonilla	40.00
89	John Wetteland	25.00
90	Todd Hundley	50.00
91	Wilton Guerrero	40.00
92	Geronimo Berroa	25.00
93	Al Martin	25.00
94	Danny Tartabull	25.00
95	Brian McRae	25.00
96	Steve Finley	25.00
97	Todd Stottlemyre	25.00
98	John Smoltz	50.00
99	Matt Williams	75.00
100	Eddie Murray	75.00
101	Henry Rodriguez	25.00
102	Marty Cordova	25.00
103	Juan Guzman	25.00
104	Chili Davis	25.00
105	Eric Young	25.00
106	Jeff Abbott	25.00
107	Shannon Stewart	25.00
108	Rocky Coppinger	25.00
109	Jose Canseco	50.00
110	Dante Bichette	50.00
111	Dwight Gooden	25.00
112	Scott Brosius	25.00
113	Steve Avery	25.00
114	Andres Galarraga	50.00
115	Sandy Alomar Jr.	25.00
116	Ray Lankford	25.00
117	Jorge Posada	25.00
118	Ryan Klesko	80.00
119	Jay Buhner	50.00
120	Jose Guillen	75.00
121	Paul O'Neill	40.00
122	Jimmy Key	25.00
123	Hal Morris	25.00
124	Travis Fryman	25.00
125	Jim Edmonds	25.00
126	Jeff Cirillo	25.00
127	Fred McGriff	40.00
128	Alan Benes	50.00
129	Derek Bell	25.00
130	Tony Graffanino	25.00
131	Shawn Green	25.00
132	Denny Neagle	25.00
133	Alex Fernandez	25.00
134	Mickey Morandini	25.00
135	Royce Clayton	25.00
136	Jose Mesa	25.00
137	Edgar Martinez	40.00
138	Curt Schilling	25.00
139	Lance Johnson	25.00
140	Andy Benes	25.00
141	Charles Nagy	25.00
142	Mariano Rivera	50.00
143	Mark Wohlers	25.00
144	Ken Hill	25.00
145	Jay Bell	25.00
146	Bob Higginson	25.00
147	Mark Grudzielanek	25.00
148	Ray Durham	25.00
149	John Olerud	35.00
150	Joey Hamilton	40.00
151	Trevor Hoffman	25.00
152	Dan Wilson	25.00
153	J.T. Snow	35.00
154	Marquis Grissom	40.00
155	Yamil Benitez	25.00
156	Rusty Greer	35.00
157	Darryl Kile	25.00
158	Ismael Valdes	25.00
159	Jeff Conine	25.00
160	Darren Daulton	35.00
161	Chan Ho Park	40.00
162	Troy Percival	25.00
163	Wade Boggs	60.00
164	Dave Nilsson	25.00
165	Vinny Castilla	35.00

166	Kevin Brown	40.00
167	Dennis Eckersley	40.00
168	Wendell Magee Jr.	25.00
169	John Jaha	25.00
170	Garret Anderson	25.00
171	Jason Giambi	25.00
172	Mark Grace	50.00
173	Tony Clark	80.00
174	Moises Alou	40.00
175	Brett Butler	25.00
176	Cecil Fielder	40.00
177	Chris Widger	25.00
178	Doug Drabek	25.00
179	Ellis Burks	25.00
180	Shigetosi Hasegawa	25.00

1997 Flair Showcase Legacy Masterpieces

The insert card chase reached its inevitable zenith with the creation of this series of one-of-a-kind inserts. Each of the 180 players' three cards (Style, Grace, Showpiece) in the '97 Flair Legacy Collection (100 of each) was also produced in an edition of one card and inserted at a rate of about one per 3,000 packs. Instead of the blue metallic foil on front and highlights on back of the regular Legacy cards, the one-of-a-kind cards are highlighted in purple and carry a notation on back that they are "The Only 1 of 1 Masterpiece". Because of the unique nature of each card, values indicated here do not represent actual transactions but are educated estimates based on recently reported sales, advertisements and offers to buy. At present there does not seem to be any premium attached to the "Row 0," "Row 1" or "Row 2" versions, since they are equally scarce.

	MT
Common Player:	600.00

(Recently observed buy/sell asking prices range from $250 for a common player to $10,000 for Ken Griffey, Jr. Also, Bagwell - $2,350.)

1997 Flair Showcase Diamond Cuts

This 20-card insert, found 1:20 packs, features a die-cut design with an action photo of the player appearing above a baseball diamond in the lower background of the cards.

		MT
Complete Set (20):		280.00
Common Player:		5.00
1	Jeff Bagwell	15.00
2	Albert Belle	10.00
3	Ken Caminiti	5.00
4	Juan Gonzalez	18.00
5	Ken Griffey Jr.	35.00
6	Tony Gwynn	18.00
7	Todd Hundley	5.00
8	Andruw Jones	10.00
9	Chipper Jones	25.00
10	Greg Maddux	25.00
11	Mark McGwire	40.00
12	Mike Piazza	25.00
13	Derek Jeter	20.00
14	Manny Ramirez	8.00
15	Cal Ripken Jr.	30.00
16	Alex Rodriguez	25.00
17	Frank Thomas	30.00
18	Mo Vaughn	10.00
19	Bernie Williams	8.00
20	Matt Williams	6.00

1997 Flair Showcase Hot Gloves

Inserted 1:90 packs, Hot Gloves features 15 cards with a die-cut "flame" design saluting some of baseball's best defensive players.

		MT
Complete Set (15):		600.00
Common Player:		10.00
1	Roberto Alomar	20.00
2	Barry Bonds	25.00
3	Juan Gonzalez	50.00
4	Ken Griffey Jr.	100.00
5	Marquis Grissom	10.00
6	Derek Jeter	50.00
7	Chipper Jones	60.00
8	Barry Larkin	10.00
9	Kenny Lofton	25.00
10	Greg Maddux	60.00
11	Mike Piazza	60.00
12	Cal Ripken Jr.	75.00
13	Alex Rodriguez	60.00
14	Ivan Rodriguez	20.00
15	Frank Thomas	75.00

A player's name in *italic* type indicates a rookie card.

1997 Flair Showcase Wave of the Future

This 27-card insert focuses on some of the up-and-coming young stars in the game. Cards were seeded 1:4 packs. A large ocean wave makes up the background of each card front.

		MT
Complete Set (27):		60.00
Common Player:		1.50
1	Todd Greene	1.50
2	Andruw Jones	6.00
3	Randall Simon	1.50
4	Wady Almonte	1.50
5	Pat Cline	1.50
6	Jeff Abbott	1.50
7	Justin Towle	1.50
8	Richie Sexson	1.50
9	Bubba Trammell	3.00
10	Bob Abreu	1.50
11	David Arias (last name actually Ortiz)	2.50
12	Todd Walker	4.00
13	Orlando Cabrera	1.50
14	Vladimir Guerrero	6.00
15	Ricky Ledee	4.00
16	Jorge Posada	2.50
17	Ruben Rivera	1.50
18	Scott Spiezio	1.50
19	Scott Rolen	6.00
20	Emil Brown	1.50
21	Jose Guillen	3.00
22	T.J. Staton	1.50
23	Elieser Marrero	1.50
24	Fernando Tatis	3.00
25	Ryan Jones	1.50
WF1	Hideki Irabu	8.00
WF2	Jose Cruz Jr.	15.00

1998 Flair Showcase Row 0

Row 0 was the most difficult of the four Rows to obtain from packs. Each of these were printed on a horizontal format and featured a prismatic foil background. The first 30 cards were numbered to 250, 30-60 were numbered to 500, 61-90 were numbered to 1,000 and 91-120 were numbered to 2,000.

		MT
Common Player (1-30):		20.00
Production 250 sets		
Common Player (31-60):		6.00
Production 500 sets		
Common Player (61-90):		4.00
Production 1,000 sets		
Common Player (91-120):		2.00
Production 2,000 sets		
1	Ken Griffey Jr.	200.00
2	Travis Lee	80.00
3	Frank Thomas	125.00
4	Ben Grieve	60.00
5	Nomar Garciaparra	125.00
6	Jose Cruz Jr.	50.00
7	Alex Rodriguez	125.00
8	Cal Ripken Jr.	150.00
9	Mark McGwire	250.00
10	Chipper Jones	125.00
11	Paul Konerko	35.00
12	Todd Helton	50.00
13	Greg Maddux	125.00
14	Derek Jeter	125.00
15	Jaret Wright	60.00
16	Livan Hernandez	20.00
17	Mike Piazza	125.00
18	Juan Encarnacion	20.00
19	Tony Gwynn	100.00
20	Scott Rolen	60.00
21	Roger Clemens	85.00
22	Tony Clark	40.00
23	Albert Belle	50.00
24	Mo Vaughn	50.00
25	Andruw Jones	50.00
26	Jason Dickson	20.00
27	Fernando Tatis	25.00
28	Ivan Rodriguez	50.00
29	Ricky Ledee	40.00
30	Darin Erstad	50.00
31	Brian Rose	6.00
32	Magglio Ordonez	30.00
33	Larry Walker	20.00
34	Bobby Higginson	6.00
35	Chili Davis	6.00
36	Barry Bonds	40.00
37	Vladimir Guerrero	40.00
38	Jeff Bagwell	50.00
39	Kenny Lofton	40.00
40	Ryan Klesko	15.00
41	Mike Cameron	6.00
42	Charles Johnson	6.00
43	Andy Pettitte	25.00
44	Juan Gonzalez	75.00
45	Tim Salmon	20.00
46	Hideki Irabu	20.00
47	Paul Molitor	30.00
48	Edgar Renteria	6.00
49	Manny Ramirez	40.00
50	Jim Edmonds	6.00
51	Bernie Williams	30.00
52	Roberto Alomar	30.00
53	David Justice	15.00
54	Rey Ordonez	6.00
55	Ken Caminiti	12.00
56	Jose Guillen	12.00
57	Randy Johnson	25.00
58	Brady Anderson	6.00
59	Hideo Nomo	25.00
60	Tino Martinez	20.00
61	John Smoltz	8.00
62	Joe Carter	8.00
63	Matt Williams	12.00
64	Robin Ventura	6.00
65	Barry Larkin	12.00
66	Dante Bichette	12.00
67	Travis Fryman	4.00
68	Gary Sheffield	15.00
69	Eric Karros	6.00
70	Matt Stairs	4.00
71	Al Martin	4.00
72	Jay Buhner	12.00
73	Ray Lankford	4.00
74	Carlos Delgado	6.00
75	Edgardo Alfonzo	4.00
76	Rondell White	6.00
77	Chuck Knoblauch	12.00
78	Raul Mondesi	8.00
79	Johnny Damon	4.00
80	Matt Morris	4.00
81	Tom Glavine	8.00
82	Kevin Brown	8.00
83	Garret Anderson	4.00
84	Mike Mussina	25.00
85	Pedro Martinez	20.00
86	Craig Biggio	10.00
87	Darryl Kile	4.00
88	Rafael Palmeiro	12.00
89	Jim Thome	20.00
90	Andres Galarraga	15.00
91	Sammy Sosa	40.00
92	Willie Greene	2.00
93	Vinny Castilla	4.00
94	Justin Thompson	2.00
95	Jeff King	2.00
96	Jeff Cirillo	2.00
97	Mark Grudzielanek	2.00
98	Brad Radke	2.00
99	John Olerud	4.00
100	Curt Schilling	4.00
101	Steve Finley	2.00
102	J.T. Snow	2.00
103	Edgar Martinez	2.00
104	Wilson Alvarez	2.00
105	Rusty Greer	2.00
106	Pat Hentgen	2.00
107	David Cone	4.00
108	Fred McGriff	4.00
109	Jason Giambi	2.00
110	Tony Womack	2.00
111	Bernard Gilkey	2.00
112	Alan Benes	4.00
113	Mark Grace	8.00
114	Reggie Sanders	2.00
115	Moises Alou	4.00
116	John Jaha	2.00
117	Henry Rodriguez	2.00
118	Dean Palmer	2.00
119	Mike Lieberthal	2.00
120	Shawn Estes	2.00

1998 Flair Showcase Row 1

Row 1, also referred to as Grace, was the second most difficult type of card to pull from Flair Showcase. All 120 players were featured on this design that contained a foil patterned background. Grace (front)/ Showtime (back) cards were seeded one per six packs, Grace/Showstopper cards were seeded one per 10 packs, Grace/Showdown cards were seeded one per 16 packs and Grace/Showpiece cards were seeded one per 24 packs.

	MT
Commons (1-30):	3.00
Stars (1-30): 2.5x to 5x Row 3	
Commons (31-60):	2.00
Stars (31-60): 3x to 6x Row 3	
Commons (61-90):	1.00
Stars (61-90): 1.5x to 2.5x Row 3	

Commons (91-120):		1.00
Stars (91-120): 2x to 4x Row 3		
1	Ken Griffey Jr.	50.00
2	Travis Lee	30.00
3	Frank Thomas	40.00
4	Ben Grieve	15.00
5	Nomar Garciaparra	30.00
6	Jose Cruz Jr.	8.00
7	Alex Rodriguez	30.00
8	Cal Ripken Jr.	40.00
9	Mark McGwire	60.00
10	Chipper Jones	30.00
11	Paul Konerko	6.00
12	Todd Helton	12.00
13	Greg Maddux	30.00
14	Derek Jeter	25.00
15	Jaret Wright	12.00
16	Livan Hernandez	3.00
17	Mike Piazza	30.00
18	Juan Encarnacion	3.00
19	Tony Gwynn	25.00
20	Scott Rolen	15.00
21	Roger Clemens	15.00
22	Tony Clark	6.00
23	Albert Belle	12.00
24	Mo Vaughn	12.00
25	Andruw Jones	12.00
26	Jason Dickson	3.00
27	Fernando Tatis	4.00
28	Ivan Rodriguez	12.00
29	Ricky Ledee	5.00
30	Darin Erstad	12.00
31	Brian Rose	2.00
32	Magglio Ordonez	12.00
33	Larry Walker	6.00
34	Bobby Higginson	2.00
35	Chili Davis	2.00
36	Barry Bonds	15.00
37	Vladimir Guerrero	15.00
38	Jeff Bagwell	20.00
39	Kenny Lofton	15.00
40	Ryan Klesko	4.00
41	Mike Cameron	2.00
42	Charles Johnson	2.00
43	Andy Pettitte	8.00
44	Juan Gonzalez	30.00
45	Tim Salmon	6.00
46	Hideki Irabu	6.00
47	Paul Molitor	12.00
48	Edgar Renteria	2.00
49	Manny Ramirez	15.00
50	Jim Edmonds	3.00
51	Bernie Williams	12.00
52	Roberto Alomar	12.00
53	David Justice	4.00
54	Rey Ordonez	2.00
55	Ken Caminiti	3.00
56	Jose Guillen	3.00
57	Randy Johnson	8.00
58	Brady Anderson	2.00
59	Hideo Nomo	8.00
60	Tino Martinez	6.00
61	John Smoltz	1.50
62	Joe Carter	1.50
63	Matt Williams	2.00
64	Robin Ventura	1.00
65	Barry Larkin	2.00
66	Dante Bichette	2.00
67	Travis Fryman	1.00
68	Gary Sheffield	2.00
69	Eric Karros	1.00
70	Matt Stairs	1.00
71	Al Martin	1.00
72	Jay Buhner	2.00
73	Ray Lankford	1.00
74	Carlos Delgado	1.50
75	Edgardo Alfonzo	1.00
76	Rondell White	1.50
77	Chuck Knoblauch	2.00
78	Raul Mondesi	1.50
79	Johnny Damon	1.00
80	Matt Morris	1.00
81	Tom Glavine	1.50
82	Kevin Brown	1.50
83	Garret Anderson	1.00
84	Mike Mussina	6.00
85	Pedro Martinez	4.00
86	Craig Biggio	1.50
87	Darryl Kile	1.00
88	Rafael Palmeiro	2.00
89	Jim Thome	4.00
90	Andres Galarraga	3.00
91	Sammy Sosa	25.00
92	Willie Greene	1.00
93	Vinny Castilla	1.50
94	Justin Thompson	1.00
95	Jeff King	1.00
96	Jeff Cirillo	1.00
97	Mark Grudzielanek	1.00
98	Brad Radke	1.00
99	John Olerud	1.50
100	Curt Schilling	1.50
101	Steve Finley	1.00
102	J.T. Snow	1.00
103	Edgar Martinez	1.00
104	Wilson Alvarez	1.00
105	Rusty Greer	1.00
106	Pat Hentgen	1.00
107	David Cone	1.50
108	Fred McGriff	1.50
109	Jason Giambi	1.00
110	Tony Womack	1.00
111	Bernard Gilkey	1.00
112	Alan Benes	1.50
113	Mark Grace	3.00
114	Reggie Sanders	1.00
115	Moises Alou	1.50
116	John Jaha	1.00
117	Henry Rodriguez	1.00
118	Dean Palmer	1.00
119	Mike Lieberthal	1.00
120	Shawn Estes	1.00

1998 Flair Showcase Row 2

Charles Johnson
FLORIDA MARLINS • CATCHER

All 120 players were featured on Row 2, or Style cards in Flair Showcase. These were the second easiest type of card to pull from packs and pictured a still shot of the player on the right side with an action shot on the rest of the card. Style (front)/Showtime (back) cards were inserted one per 2.5 packs. Style/Showstopper cards were inserted one per three packs. Style/Showdown cards were inserted one per 3.5 packs and Style/Showpiece cards were inserted one per four packs.

		MT
Complete Set (120):		140.00
Common Player:		.50
Stars: 1x to 2x Row 3		
1	Ken Griffey Jr.	20.00
2	Travis Lee	12.00
3	Frank Thomas	15.00
4	Ben Grieve	6.00
5	Nomar Garciaparra	12.00
6	Jose Cruz Jr.	4.00
7	Alex Rodriguez	12.00
8	Cal Ripken Jr.	15.00
9	Mark McGwire	25.00
10	Chipper Jones	12.00
11	Paul Konerko	2.50
12	Todd Helton	5.00
13	Greg Maddux	12.00
14	Derek Jeter	10.00
15	Jaret Wright	5.00
16	Livan Hernandez	.50
17	Mike Piazza	12.00
18	Juan Encarnacion	.50
19	Tony Gwynn	10.00
20	Scott Rolen	6.00
21	Roger Clemens	6.00
22	Tony Clark	2.50
23	Albert Belle	5.00
24	Mo Vaughn	5.00
25	Andruw Jones	5.00
26	Jason Dickson	.50
27	Fernando Tatis	1.00
28	Ivan Rodriguez	5.00
29	Ricky Ledee	1.00
30	Darin Erstad	5.00
31	Brian Rose	.50
32	Magglio Ordonez	5.00
33	Larry Walker	2.00
34	Bobby Higginson	.50
35	Chili Davis	.50
36	Barry Bonds	5.00
37	Vladimir Guerrero	5.00
38	Jeff Bagwell	6.00
39	Kenny Lofton	5.00
40	Ryan Klesko	1.50
41	Mike Cameron	.50
42	Charles Johnson	.50
43	Andy Pettitte	3.00
44	Juan Gonzalez	10.00
45	Tim Salmon	1.50
46	Hideki Irabu	2.00
47	Paul Molitor	4.00
48	Edgar Renteria	.50
49	Manny Ramirez	5.00
50	Jim Edmonds	.75
51	Bernie Williams	4.00
52	Roberto Alomar	4.00
53	David Justice	1.50
54	Rey Ordonez	.50
55	Ken Caminiti	.75
56	Jose Guillen	1.00
57	Randy Johnson	3.00
58	Brady Anderson	.50
59	Hideo Nomo	3.00
60	Tino Martinez	2.00
61	John Smoltz	.75
62	Joe Carter	.50
63	Matt Williams	1.50
64	Robin Ventura	.75
65	Barry Larkin	1.50
66	Dante Bichette	1.50
67	Travis Fryman	.50
68	Gary Sheffield	2.00
69	Eric Karros	.50
70	Matt Stairs	.50
71	Al Martin	.50
72	Jay Buhner	1.25
73	Ray Lankford	.50
74	Carlos Delgado	.50
75	Edgardo Alfonzo	.50
76	Rondell White	.75
77	Chuck Knoblauch	1.50
78	Raul Mondesi	.75
79	Johnny Damon	.50
80	Matt Morris	.50
81	Tom Glavine	.75
82	Kevin Brown	.75
83	Garret Anderson	.50
84	Mike Mussina	4.00
85	Pedro Martinez	3.00
86	Craig Biggio	.75
87	Darryl Kile	.50
88	Rafael Palmeiro	1.25
89	Jim Thome	3.00
90	Andres Galarraga	2.00
91	Sammy Sosa	10.00
92	Willie Greene	.50
93	Vinny Castilla	.75
94	Justin Thompson	.50
95	Jeff King	.50
96	Jeff Cirillo	.50
97	Mark Grudzielanek	.50
98	Brad Radke	.50
99	John Olerud	.75
100	Curt Schilling	.75
101	Steve Finley	.50
102	J.T. Snow	.50
103	Edgar Martinez	.50
104	Wilson Alvarez	.50
105	Rusty Greer	.50
106	Pat Hentgen	.50
107	David Cone	.75
108	Fred McGriff	.75
109	Jason Giambi	.50
110	Tony Womack	.50
111	Bernard Gilkey	.50

112	Alan Benes	.75
113	Mark Grace	1.25
114	Reggie Sanders	.50
115	Moises Alou	.75
116	John Jaha	.50
117	Henry Rodriguez	.50
118	Dean Palmer	.50
119	Mike Lieberthal	.50
120	Shawn Estes	.50

1998 Flair Showcase Row 3

Row 3, or Flair, cards were considered the base cards of Flair Showcase. These featured a close-up shot of the player on the right side with an action shot on the right, all over a silver foil background. Flair (front)/Showtime (back) cards were inserted 1:.9 packs, Flair/Showstopper cards were inserted 1:1.1 packs, Flair/Showdown cards were inserted 1:1.5 packs and Flair/Showdown cards were inserted 1:2 packs.

		MT
Complete Set (120):		70.00
Common Player:		.25
Unlisted Stars: 1.00 to 2.00		
1	Ken Griffey Jr.	10.00
2	Travis Lee	4.00
3	Frank Thomas	6.00
4	Ben Grieve	3.00
5	Nomar Garciaparra	6.00
6	Jose Cruz Jr.	2.00
7	Alex Rodriguez	6.00
8	Cal Ripken Jr.	8.00
9	Mark McGwire	12.00
10	Chipper Jones	6.00
11	Paul Konerko	1.50
12	Todd Helton	2.50
13	Greg Maddux	6.00
14	Derek Jeter	5.00
15	Jaret Wright	2.50
16	Livan Hernandez	.25
17	Mike Piazza	6.00
18	Juan Encarnacion	.25
19	Tony Gwynn	5.00
20	Scott Rolen	3.00
21	Roger Clemens	3.00
22	Tony Clark	1.50
23	Albert Belle	2.50
24	Mo Vaughn	2.50
25	Andruw Jones	2.50
26	Jason Dickson	.25
27	Fernando Tatis	.50
28	Ivan Rodriguez	2.50
29	Ricky Ledee	.50
30	Darin Erstad	2.50
31	Brian Rose	.25
32	*Magglio Ordonez*	2.50
33	Larry Walker	1.00
34	Bobby Higginson	.25

35	Chili Davis	.25
36	Barry Bonds	2.50
37	Vladimir Guerrero	2.50
38	Jeff Bagwell	3.00
39	Kenny Lofton	2.50
40	Ryan Klesko	.75
41	Mike Cameron	.25
42	Charles Johnson	.25
43	Andy Pettitte	1.50
44	Juan Gonzalez	5.00
45	Tim Salmon	1.00
46	Hideki Irabu	1.00
47	Paul Molitor	2.00
48	Edgar Renteria	.25
49	Manny Ramirez	2.50
50	Jim Edmonds	.50
51	Bernie Williams	2.00
52	Roberto Alomar	2.00
53	David Justice	.75
54	Rey Ordonez	.25
55	Ken Caminiti	.50
56	Jose Guillen	.50
57	Randy Johnson	1.50
58	Brady Anderson	.25
59	Hideo Nomo	1.50
60	Tino Martinez	1.00
61	John Smoltz	.50
62	Joe Carter	.50
63	Matt Williams	.75
64	Robin Ventura	.50
65	Barry Larkin	.75
66	Dante Bichette	.75
67	Travis Fryman	.25
68	Gary Sheffield	1.00
69	Eric Karros	.40
70	Matt Stairs	.25
71	Al Martin	.25
72	Jay Buhner	.75
73	Ray Lankford	.25
74	Carlos Delgado	.50
75	Edgardo Alfonzo	.25
76	Rondell White	.50
77	Chuck Knoblauch	.75
78	Raul Mondesi	.50
79	Johnny Damon	.25
80	Matt Morris	.25
81	Tom Glavine	.50
82	Kevin Brown	.50
83	Garret Anderson	.25
84	Mike Mussina	2.00
85	Pedro Martinez	1.50
86	Craig Biggio	.50
87	Darryl Kile	.25
88	Rafael Palmeiro	.75
89	Jim Thome	1.50
90	Andres Galarraga	1.00
91	Sammy Sosa	5.00
92	Willie Greene	.25
93	Vinny Castilla	.50
94	Justin Thompson	.25
95	Jeff King	.25
96	Jeff Cirillo	.25
97	Mark Grudzielanek	.25
98	Brad Radke	.25
99	John Olerud	.50
100	Curt Schilling	.50
101	Steve Finley	.25
102	J.T. Snow	.25
103	Edgar Martinez	.25
104	Wilson Alvarez	.25
105	Rusty Greer	.25
106	Pat Hentgen	.25
107	David Cone	.50
108	Fred McGriff	.50
109	Jason Giambi	.25
110	Tony Womack	.25
111	Bernard Gilkey	.25
112	Alan Benes	.50
113	Mark Grace	.75
114	Reggie Sanders	.25
115	Moises Alou	.50
116	John Jaha	.25
117	Henry Rodriguez	.25
118	Dean Palmer	.25
119	Mike Lieberthal	.25
120	Shawn Estes	.25

A player's name in *italic* type indicates a rookie card.

1998 Flair Showcase Legacy

Legacy Collection and Legacy Masterpieces both paralleled all 480 cards in the Flair Showcase set. Each Legacy Collection card displayed the player's name in black plate laminated on the back, with the cards sequential numbering to 100 in gold foil. Each Masterpiece arrived with special foil overstamps on the front and "The Only 1 of 1 Masterpiece" stamped on the back.

		MT
Common Player:		10.00
Semistars:		40.00
Each Player Has Four Different Cards		
Production 100 sets		
1	Ken Griffey Jr.	400.00
2	Travis Lee	150.00
3	Frank Thomas	250.00
4	Ben Grieve	125.00
5	Nomar Garciaparra	250.00
6	Jose Cruz Jr.	100.00
7	Alex Rodriguez	250.00
8	Cal Ripken Jr.	300.00
9	Mark McGwire	500.00
10	Chipper Jones	250.00
11	Paul Konerko	25.00
12	Todd Helton	100.00
13	Greg Maddux	250.00
14	Derek Jeter	225.00
15	Jaret Wright	100.00
16	Livan Hernandez	10.00
17	Mike Piazza	250.00
18	Juan Encarnacion	10.00
19	Tony Gwynn	200.00
20	Scott Rolen	125.00
21	Roger Clemens	150.00
22	Tony Clark	60.00
23	Albert Belle	100.00
24	Mo Vaughn	100.00
25	Andruw Jones	100.00
26	Jason Dickson	10.00
27	Fernando Tatis	15.00
28	Ivan Rodriguez	100.00
29	Ricky Ledee	25.00
30	Darin Erstad	125.00
31	Brian Rose	10.00
32	Magglio Ordonez	50.00
33	Larry Walker	60.00
34	Bobby Higginson	10.00
35	Chili Davis	10.00
36	Barry Bonds	100.00
37	Vladimir Guerrero	125.00
38	Jeff Bagwell	125.00
39	Kenny Lofton	100.00
40	Ryan Klesko	30.00
41	Mike Cameron	15.00
42	Charles Johnson	10.00
43	Andy Pettitte	75.00
44	Juan Gonzalez	200.00
45	Tim Salmon	40.00

46	Hideki Irabu	50.00
47	Paul Molitor	80.00
48	Edgar Renteria	10.00
49	Manny Ramirez	100.00
50	Jim Edmonds	25.00
51	Bernie Williams	80.00
52	Roberto Alomar	80.00
53	David Justice	30.00
54	Rey Ordonez	10.00
55	Ken Caminiti	25.00
56	Jose Guillen	25.00
57	Randy Johnson	75.00
58	Brady Anderson	15.00
59	Hideo Nomo	75.00
60	Tino Martinez	50.00
61	John Smoltz	25.00
62	Joe Carter	20.00
63	Matt Williams	25.00
64	Robin Ventura	20.00
65	Barry Larkin	25.00
66	Dante Bichette	40.00
67	Travis Fryman	20.00
68	Gary Sheffield	25.00
69	Eric Karros	25.00
70	Matt Stairs	10.00
71	Al Martin	10.00
72	Jay Buhner	30.00
73	Ray Lankford	10.00
74	Carlos Delgado	20.00
75	Edgardo Alfonzo	10.00
76	Rondell White	25.00
77	Chuck Knoblauch	30.00
78	Raul Mondesi	25.00
79	Johnny Damon	10.00
80	Matt Morris	10.00
81	Tom Glavine	25.00
82	Kevin Brown	20.00
83	Garret Anderson	10.00
84	Mike Mussina	80.00
85	Pedro Martinez	80.00
86	Craig Biggio	25.00
87	Darryl Kile	10.00
88	Rafael Palmeiro	30.00
89	Jim Thome	60.00
90	Andres Galarraga	60.00
91	Sammy Sosa	300.00
92	Willie Greene	10.00
93	Vinny Castilla	20.00
94	Justin Thompson	10.00
95	Jeff King	10.00
96	Jeff Cirillo	10.00
97	Mark Grudzielanek	10.00
98	Brad Radke	10.00
99	John Olerud	25.00
100	Curt Schilling	20.00
101	Steve Finley	10.00
102	J.T. Snow	10.00
103	Edgar Martinez	20.00
104	Wilson Alvarez	10.00
105	Rusty Greer	15.00
106	Pat Hentgen	10.00
107	David Cone	20.00
108	Fred McGriff	20.00
109	Jason Giambi	10.00
110	Tony Womack	10.00
111	Bernard Gilkey	10.00
112	Alan Benes	20.00
113	Mark Grace	30.00
114	Reggie Sanders	10.00
115	Moises Alou	25.00
116	John Jaha	10.00
117	Henry Rodriguez	10.00
118	Dean Palmer	10.00
119	Mike Lieberthal	10.00
120	Shawn Estes	10.00

1998 Flair Showcase Wave of the Future

Twelve up-and-coming players whose minor league stats and Major League potential are displayed in Wave of the Future. The cards actually contain a plastic card inside a plastic covering that is filled with vegetable oil inside. These were inserted one per 20 packs and are numbered with a "WF" prefix.

		MT
Complete Set (12):		50.00
Common Player:		2.00
Inserted 1:20		
WF1	Travis Lee	20.00
WF2	Todd Helton	6.00
WF3	Ben Grieve	15.00
WF4	Juan Encarnacion	2.00
WF5	Brad Fullmer	4.00
WF6	Ruben Rivera	2.00
WF7	Paul Konerko	4.00
WF8	Derrek Lee	2.00
WF9	Mike Lowell	2.00
WF10	Magglio Ordonez	6.00
WF11	Rich Butler	4.00
WF12	Eli Marrero	2.00

1981 Fleer

STEVE CARLTON
PITCHER OF THE YEAR

For the first time in 18 years, Fleer issued a baseball card set featuring current players. The 660-card effort included numerous errors in the first print run which were subsequently corrected. The 2-1/2" x 3-1/2" cards are numbered by team in order of the previous season's finish. Card fronts feature a full-color photo inside a border which is color-coded by team. Backs are printed in black, grey and yellow on white stock and carry full player statistical information. The player's batting average or earned run average is located in a circle in the upper-right corner of the back. The complete set price in the checklist that follows does not include the higher priced variations.

		MT
Complete Set (660):		50.00
Common Player:		.08
Wax Box:		80.00
1	Pete Rose	2.50
2	Larry Bowa	.10
3	Manny Trillo	.08
4	Bob Boone	.10
5a	Mike Schmidt (portrait)	2.00
5b	Mike Schmidt (batting)	2.00
6a	Steve Carlton ("Lefty" on front)	1.00
6b	Steve Carlton (Pitcher of the Year on front, date 1066 on back)	2.00
6c	Steve Carlton (Pitcher of the Year on front, date 1966 on back)	3.00
7a	Tug McGraw (Game Saver on front)	.50
7b	Tug McGraw (Pitcher on front)	.12
8	Larry Christenson	.08
9	Bake McBride	.08
10	Greg Luzinski	.15
11	Ron Reed	.08
12	Dickie Noles	.08
13	*Keith Moreland*	.08
14	*Bob Walk*	.10
15	Lonnie Smith	.08
16	Dick Ruthven	.08
17	Sparky Lyle	.10
18	Greg Gross	.08
19	Garry Maddox	.10
20	Nino Espinosa	.08
21	George Vukovich	.08
22	John Vukovich	.08
23	Ramon Aviles	.08
24a	Kevin Saucier (Ken Saucier on back)	.15
24b	Kevin Saucier (Kevin Saucier on back)	.50
25	Randy Lerch	.08
26	Del Unser	.08
27	Tim McCarver	.15
28a	George Brett (batting)	4.00
28b	George Brett (portrait)	1.00
29a	Willie Wilson (portrait)	.50
29b	Willie Wilson (batting)	.15
30	Paul Splittorff	.08
31	Dan Quisenberry	.15
32a	Amos Otis (batting)	.50
32b	Amos Otis (portrait)	.10
33	Steve Busby	.08
34	U.L. Washington	.08
35	Dave Chalk	.08
36	Darrell Porter	.08
37	Marty Pattin	.08
38	Larry Gura	.08
39	Renie Martin	.08
40	Rich Gale	.08
41a	Hal McRae (dark blue "Royals" on front)	.40
41b	Hal McRae (light blue "Royals" on front)	.10
42	Dennis Leonard	.08
43	Willie Aikens	.08
44	Frank White	.08
45	Clint Hurdle	.08
46	John Wathan	.08
47	Pete LaCock	.08
48	Rance Mulliniks	.08
49	Jeff Twitty	.08
50	Jamie Quirk	.08
51	Art Howe	.08
52	Ken Forsch	.08
53	Vern Ruhle	.08
54	Joe Niekro	.12
55	Frank LaCorte	.08
56	J.R. Richard	.10
57	Nolan Ryan	8.00
58	Enos Cabell	.08
59	Cesar Cedeno	.12
60	Jose Cruz	.12
61	Bill Virdon	.08
62	Terry Puhl	.08
63	Joaquin Andujar	.08
64	Alan Ashby	.08
65	Joe Sambito	.08
66	Denny Walling	.08
67	Jeff Leonard	.08
68	Luis Pujols	.08
69	Bruce Bochy	.08
70	Rafael Landestoy	.08
71	*Dave Smith*	.08
72	*Danny Heep*	.08

Grading Guide

Mint (MT): A perfect card. Well-centered with all corners sharp and square. No creases, stains, edge nicks, surface marks, yellowing or fading.

Near Mint (NM): A nearly perfect card. At first glance, a NM card appears to be perfect. May be slightly off-center. No surface marks, creases or loss of gloss.

Excellent (EX): Corners are still fairly sharp with only moderate wear. Borders may be off-center. No creases or stains on fronts or backs, but may show slight loss of surface luster.

Very Good (VG): Shows obvious handling. May have rounded corners, minor creases, major gum or wax stains. No major creases, tape marks, writing, etc.

Good (G): A well-worn card, but exhibits no intentional damage. May have major or multiple creases. Corners may be rounded well beyond card border.

No.	Name	Price
73	Julio Gonzalez	.08
74	Craig Reynolds	.08
75	Gary Woods	.08
76	Dave Bergman	.08
77	Randy Niemann	.08
78	Joe Morgan	.75
79a	Reggie Jackson (portrait)	4.00
79b	Reggie Jackson (batting)	2.00
80	Bucky Dent	.08
81	Tommy John	.20
82	Luis Tiant	.12
83	Rick Cerone	.08
84	Dick Howser	.08
85	Lou Piniella	.12
86	Ron Davis	.08
87a	Graig Nettles (Craig on back)	10.00
87b	Graig Nettles (Graig on back)	.15
88	Ron Guidry	.15
89	Rich Gossage	.10
90	Rudy May	.08
91	Gaylord Perry	.75
92	Eric Soderholm	.08
93	Bob Watson	.10
94	Bobby Murcer	.08
95	Bobby Brown	.08
96	Jim Spencer	.08
97	Tom Underwood	.08
98	Oscar Gamble	.08
99	Johnny Oates	.08
100	Fred Stanley	.08
101	Ruppert Jones	.08
102	Dennis Werth	.08
103	Joe Lefebvre	.08
104	Brian Doyle	.08
105	Aurelio Rodriguez	.08
106	Doug Bird	.08
107	Mike Griffin	.08
108	Tim Lollar	.08
109	Willie Randolph	.08
110	Steve Garvey	.40
111	Reggie Smith	.10
112	Don Sutton	.35
113	Burt Hooton	.08
114a	Davy Lopes (Davey) (no finger on back)	.08
114b	Davy Lopes (Davey) (small finger on back)	1.00
115	Dusty Baker	.10
116	Tom Lasorda	.45
117	Bill Russell	.12
118	Jerry Reuss	.08
119	Terry Forster	.08
120a	Bob Welch (Bob on back)	.10
120b	Bob Welch (Robert)	.50
121	Don Stanhouse	.08
122	Rick Monday	.08
123	Derrel Thomas	.08
124	Joe Ferguson	.08
125	Rick Sutcliffe	.10
126a	Ron Cey (no finger on back)	.10
126b	Ron Cey (small finger on back)	1.00
127	Dave Goltz	.08
128	Jay Johnstone	.08
129	Steve Yeager	.08
130	Gary Weiss	.08
131	*Mike Scioscia*	.25
132	Vic Davalillo	.08
133	Doug Rau	.08
134	Pepe Frias	.08
135	Mickey Hatcher	.08
136	*Steve Howe*	.10
137	Robert Castillo	.08
138	Gary Thomasson	.08
139	Rudy Law	.08
140	*Fernando Valenzuela*	1.50
141	Manny Mota	.08
142	Gary Carter	.50
143	Steve Rogers	.08
144	Warren Cromartie	.08
145	Andre Dawson	1.25
146	Larry Parrish	.08
147	Rowland Office	.08
148	Ellis Valentine	.08
149	Dick Williams	.08
150	*Bill Gullickson*	.15
151	Elias Sosa	.08
152	John Tamargo	.08
153	Chris Speier	.08
154	Ron LeFlore	.08
155	Rodney Scott	.08
156	Stan Bahnsen	.08
157	Bill Lee	.08
158	Fred Norman	.08
159	Woodie Fryman	.08
160	Dave Palmer	.08
161	Jerry White	.08
162	Roberto Ramos	.08
163	John D'Acquisto	.08
164	Tommy Hutton	.08
165	*Charlie Lea*	.12
166	Scott Sanderson	.08
167	Ken Macha	.08
168	Tony Bernazard	.08
169	Jim Palmer	1.00
170	Steve Stone	.08
171	Mike Flanagan	.08
172	Al Bumbry	.08
173	Doug DeCinces	.08
174	Scott McGregor	.08
175	Mark Belanger	.08
176	Tim Stoddard	.08
177a	Rick Dempsey (no finger on front)	.08
177b	Rick Dempsey (small finger on front)	1.00
178	Earl Weaver	.40
179	Tippy Martinez	.08
180	Dennis Martinez	.10
181	Sammy Stewart	.08
182	Rich Dauer	.08
183	Lee May	.08
184	Eddie Murray	3.00
185	Benny Ayala	.08
186	John Lowenstein	.08
187	Gary Roenicke	.08
188	Ken Singleton	.10
189	Dan Graham	.08
190	Terry Crowley	.08
191	Kiko Garcia	.08
192	Dave Ford	.08
193	Mark Corey	.08
194	Lenn Sakata	.08
195	Doug DeCinces	.08
196	Johnny Bench	1.50
197	Dave Concepcion	.15
198	Ray Knight	.10
199	Ken Griffey	.12
200	Tom Seaver	1.50
201	Dave Collins	.08
202	George Foster	.12
203	Junior Kennedy	.08
204	Frank Pastore	.08
205	Dan Driessen	.08
206	Hector Cruz	.08
207	Paul Moskau	.08
208	*Charlie Leibrandt*	.25
209	Harry Spilman	.08
210	*Joe Price*	.08
211	Tom Hume	.08
212	Joe Nolan	.08
213	Doug Bair	.08
214	Mario Soto	.08
215a	Bill Bonham (no finger on back)	.08
215b	Bill Bonham (small finger on back)	1.00
216a	George Foster (Slugger on front)	.25
216b	George Foster (Outfield on front)	.20
217	Paul Householder	.08
218	Ron Oester	.08
219	Sam Mejias	.08
220	Sheldon Burnside	.08
221	Carl Yastrzemski	1.50
222	Jim Rice	.12
223	Fred Lynn	.15
224	Carlton Fisk	1.00
225	Rick Burleson	.08
226	Dennis Eckersley	1.00
227	Butch Hobson	.08
228	Tom Burgmeier	.08
229	Garry Hancock	.08
230	Don Zimmer	.08
231	Steve Renko	.08
232	Dwight Evans	.15
233	Mike Torrez	.08
234	Bob Stanley	.08
235	Jim Dwyer	.08
236	Dave Stapleton	.08
237	Glenn Hoffman	.08
238	Jerry Remy	.08
239	Dick Drago	.08
240	Bill Campbell	.08
241	Tony Perez	.20
242	Phil Niekro	.75
243	Dale Murphy	.75
244	Bob Horner	.12
245	Jeff Burroughs	.08
246	Rick Camp	.08
247	Bob Cox	.08
248	Bruce Benedict	.08
249	Gene Garber	.08
250	Jerry Royster	.08
251a	Gary Matthews (no finger on back)	.08
251b	Gary Matthews (small finger on back)	1.00
252	Chris Chambliss	.08
253	Luis Gomez	.08
254	Bill Nahorodny	.08
255	Doyle Alexander	.08
256	Brian Asselstine	.08
257	Biff Pocoroba	.08
258	Mike Lum	.08
259	Charlie Spikes	.08
260	Glenn Hubbard	.08
261	Tommy Boggs	.08
262	Al Hrabosky	.08
263	Rick Matula	.08
264	Preston Hanna	.08
265	Larry Bradford	.08
266	*Rafael Ramirez*	.08
267	Larry McWilliams	.08
268	Rod Carew	1.50
269	Bobby Grich	.10
270	Carney Lansford	.08
271	Don Baylor	.12
272	Joe Rudi	.08
273	Dan Ford	.08
274	Jim Fregosi	.08
275	Dave Frost	.08
276	Frank Tanana	.08
277	Dickie Thon	.08
278	Jason Thompson	.08
279	Rick Miller	.08
280	Bert Campaneris	.08
281	Tom Donohue	.08
282	Brian Downing	.08
283	Fred Patek	.08
284	Bruce Kison	.08
285	Dave LaRoche	.08
286	Don Aase	.08
287	Jim Barr	.08
288	Alfredo Martinez	.08
289	Larry Harlow	.08
290	Andy Hassler	.08
291	Dave Kingman	.12
292	Bill Buckner	.12
293	Rick Reuschel	.08
294	Bruce Sutter	.08
295	Jerry Martin	.08
296	Scot Thompson	.08
297	Ivan DeJesus	.08
298	Steve Dillard	.08
299	Dick Tidrow	.08
300	Randy Martz	.08
301	Lenny Randle	.08
302	Lynn McGlothen	.08
303	Cliff Johnson	.08
304	Tim Blackwell	.08
305	Dennis Lamp	.08
306	Bill Caudill	.08
307	Carlos Lezcano	.08
308	Jim Tracy	.08
309	Doug Capilla	.08
310	Willie Hernandez	.08
311	Mike Vail	.08
312	Mike Krukow	.08
313	Barry Foote	.08
314	Larry Biittner	.08
315	Mike Tyson	.08
316	Lee Mazzilli	.08
317	John Stearns	.08
318	Alex Trevino	.08
319	Craig Swan	.08
320	Frank Taveras	.08
321	Steve Henderson	.08
322	Neil Allen	.08
323	Mark Bomback	.08
324	Mike Jorgensen	.08
325	Joe Torre	.12
326	Elliott Maddox	.08
327	Pete Falcone	.08
328	Ray Burris	.08
329	Claudell Washington	.08
330	Doug Flynn	.08
331	Joel Youngblood	.08
332	Bill Almon	.08
333	Tom Hausman	.08
334	Pat Zachry	.08
335	*Jeff Reardon*	2.50
336	*Wally Backman*	.15
337	Dan Norman	.08
338	Jerry Morales	.08

Number	Name	Price
339	Ed Farmer	.08
340	Bob Molinaro	.08
341	Todd Cruz	.08
342a	Britt Burns (no finger on front)	.10
342b	Britt Burns (small finger on front)	1.00
343	Kevin Bell	.08
344	Tony LaRussa	.12
345	Steve Trout	.08
346	Harold Baines	4.00
347	Richard Wortham	.08
348	Wayne Nordhagen	.08
349	Mike Squires	.08
350	Lamar Johnson	.08
351	Rickey Henderson	6.00
352	Francisco Barrios	.08
353	Thad Bosley	.08
354	Chet Lemon	.08
355	Bruce Kimm	.08
356	Richard Dotson	.08
357	Jim Morrison	.08
358	Mike Proly	.08
359	Greg Pryor	.08
360	Dave Parker	.15
361	Omar Moreno	.08
362a	Kent Tekulve (1071 Waterbury on back)	.15
362b	Kent Tekulve (1971 Waterbury on back)	.50
363	Willie Stargell	.75
364	Phil Garner	.08
365	Ed Ott	.08
366	Don Robinson	.08
367	Chuck Tanner	.08
368	Jim Rooker	.08
369	Dale Berra	.08
370	Jim Bibby	.08
371	Steve Nicosia	.08
372	Mike Easler	.08
373	Bill Robinson	.08
374	Lee Lacy	.08
375	John Candelaria	.08
376	Manny Sanguillen	.08
377	Rick Rhoden	.08
378	Grant Jackson	.08
379	Tim Foli	.08
380	Rod Scurry	.08
381	Bill Madlock	.10
382a	Kurt Bevacqua (photo reversed, backwards "P" on cap)	.15
382b	Kurt Bevacqua (correct photo)	.50
383	Bert Blyleven	.08
384	Eddie Solomon	.08
385	Enrique Romo	.08
386	John Milner	.08
387	Mike Hargrove	.08
388	Jorge Orta	.08
389	Toby Harrah	.08
390	Tom Veryzer	.08
391	Miguel Dilone	.08
392	Dan Spillner	.08
393	Jack Brohamer	.08
394	Wayne Garland	.08
395	Sid Monge	.08
396	Rick Waits	.08
397	Joe Charboneau	.25
398	Gary Alexander	.08
399	Jerry Dybzinski	.08
400	Mike Stanton	.08
401	Mike Paxton	.08
402	Gary Gray	.08
403	Rick Manning	.08
404	Bo Diaz	.08
405	Ron Hassey	.08
406	Ross Grimsley	.08
407	Victor Cruz	.08
408	Len Barker	.08
409	Bob Bailor	.08
410	Otto Velez	.08
411	Ernie Whitt	.08
412	Jim Clancy	.08
413	Barry Bonnell	.08
414	Dave Stieb	.25
415	Damaso Garcia	.10
416	John Mayberry	.08
417	Roy Howell	.08
418	Dan Ainge	5.00
419a	Jesse Jefferson (Pirates on back)	.10
419b	Jesse Jefferson (Blue Jays on back)	.50
420	Joey McLaughlin	.08
421	Lloyd Moseby	.10
422	Al Woods	.08
423	Garth Iorg	.08
424	Doug Ault	.08
425	Ken Schrom	.08
426	Mike Willis	.08
427	Steve Braun	.08
428	Bob Davis	.08
429	Jerry Garvin	.08
430	Alfredo Griffin	.08
431	Bob Mattick	.08
432	Vida Blue	.12
433	Jack Clark	.12
434	Willie McCovey	1.00
435	Mike Ivie	.08
436a	Darrel Evans (Darrel on front)	.15
436b	Darrell Evans (Darrell on front)	.50
437	Terry Whitfield	.08
438	Rennie Stennett	.08
439	John Montefusco	.08
440	Jim Wohlford	.08
441	Bill North	.08
442	Milt May	.08
443	Max Venable	.08
444	Ed Whitson	.08
445	Al Holland	.08
446	Randy Moffitt	.08
447	Bob Knepper	.08
448	Gary Lavelle	.08
449	Greg Minton	.08
450	Johnnie LeMaster	.08
451	Larry Herndon	.08
452	Rich Murray	.08
453	Joe Pettini	.08
454	Allen Ripley	.08
455	Dennis Littlejohn	.08
456	Tom Griffin	.08
457	Alan Hargesheimer	.08
458	Joe Strain	.08
459	Steve Kemp	.08
460	Sparky Anderson	.12
461	Alan Trammell	1.25
462	Mark Fidrych	.12
463	Lou Whitaker	.50
464	Dave Rozema	.08
465	Milt Wilcox	.08
466	Champ Summers	.08
467	Lance Parrish	.20
468	Dan Petry	.08
469	Pat Underwood	.08
470	Rick Peters	.08
471	Al Cowens	.08
472	John Wockenfuss	.08
473	Tom Brookens	.08
474	Richie Hebner	.08
475	Jack Morris	.15
476	Jim Lentine	.08
477	Bruce Robbins	.08
478	Mark Wagner	.08
479	Tim Corcoran	.08
480a	Stan Papi (Pitcher on front)	.15
480b	Stan Papi (Shortstop on front)	.50
481	Kirk Gibson	3.00
482	Dan Schatzeder	.08
483	Amos Otis	.15
484	Dave Winfield	2.50
485	Rollie Fingers	1.00
486	Gene Richards	.08
487	Randy Jones	.08
488	Ozzie Smith	3.00
489	Gene Tenace	.08
490	Bill Fahey	.08
491	John Curtis	.08
492	Dave Cash	.08
493a	Tim Flannery (photo reversed, batting righty)	.15
493b	Tim Flannery (photo correct, batting lefty)	.50
494	Jerry Mumphrey	.08
495	Bob Shirley	.08
496	Steve Mura	.08
497	Eric Rasmussen	.08
498	Broderick Perkins	.08
499	Barry Evans	.08
500	Chuck Baker	.08
501	Luis Salazar	.08
502	Gary Lucas	.08
503	Mike Armstrong	.08
504	Jerry Turner	.08
505	Dennis Kinney	.08
506	Willy Montanez (Willie)	.08
507	Gorman Thomas	.08
508	Ben Oglivie	.08
509	Larry Hisle	.08
510	Sal Bando	.08
511	Robin Yount	3.00
512	Mike Caldwell	.08
513	Sixto Lezcano	.08
514a	Jerry Augustine (Billy Travers photo)	.15
514b	Billy Travers (correct name with photo)	.50
515	Paul Molitor	3.00
516	Moose Haas	.08
517	Bill Castro	.08
518	Jim Slaton	.08
519	Lary Sorensen	.08
520	Bob McClure	.08
521	Charlie Moore	.08
522	Jim Gantner	.08
523	Reggie Cleveland	.08
524	Don Money	.08
525	Billy Travers	.08
526	Buck Martinez	.08
527	Dick Davis	.08
528	Ted Simmons	.08
529	Garry Templeton	.08
530	Ken Reitz	.08
531	Tony Scott	.08
532	Ken Oberkfell	.08
533	Bob Sykes	.08
534	Keith Smith	.08
535	John Littlefield	.08
536	Jim Kaat	.20
537	Bob Forsch	.08
538	Mike Phillips	.08
539	Terry Landrum	.08
540	Leon Durham	.10
541	Terry Kennedy	.08
542	George Hendrick	.08
543	Dane Iorg	.08
544	Mark Littell (photo actually Jeff Little)	.08
545	Keith Hernandez	.12
546	Silvio Martinez	.08
547a	Pete Vuckovich (photo actually Don Hood)	.15
547b	Don Hood (correct name with photo)	.50
548	Bobby Bonds	.10
549	Mike Ramsey	.08
550	Tom Herr	.08
551	Roy Smalley	.08
552	Jerry Koosman	.08
553	Ken Landreaux	.08
554	John Castino	.08
555	Doug Corbett	.08
556	Bombo Rivera	.08
557	Ron Jackson	.08
558	Butch Wynegar	.08
559	Hosken Powell	.08
560	Pete Redfern	.08
561	Roger Erickson	.08
562	Glenn Adams	.08
563	Rick Sofield	.08
564	Geoff Zahn	.08
565	Pete Mackanin	.08
566	Mike Cubbage	.08
567	Darrell Jackson	.08
568	Dave Edwards	.08
569	Rob Wilfong	.08
570	Sal Butera	.08
571	Jose Morales	.08
572	Rick Langford	.08
573	Mike Norris	.08
574	Rickey Henderson	7.00
575	Tony Armas	.08
576	Dave Revering	.08
577	Jeff Newman	.08
578	Bob Lacey	.08
579	Brian Kingman (photo actually Alan Wirth)	.08
580	Mitchell Page	.08
581	Billy Martin	.12
582	Rob Picciolo	.08
583	Mike Heath	.08
584	Mickey Klutts	.08
585	Orlando Gonzalez	.08
586	Mike Davis	.08
587	Wayne Gross	.08
588	Matt Keough	.08
589	Steve McCatty	.08
590	Dwayne Murphy	.08
591	Mario Guerrero	.08
592	Dave McKay	.08
593	Jim Essian	.08
594	Dave Heaverlo	.08
595	Maury Wills	.10
596	Juan Beniquez	.08
597	Rodney Craig	.08

598	Jim Anderson	.08
599	Floyd Bannister	.08
600	Bruce Bochte	.08
601	Julio Cruz	.08
602	Ted Cox	.08
603	Dan Meyer	.08
604	Larry Cox	.08
605	Bill Stein	.08
606	Steve Garvey	.45
607	Dave Roberts	.08
608	Leon Roberts	.08
609	Reggie Walton	.08
610	Dave Edler	.08
611	Larry Milbourne	.08
612	Kim Allen	.08
613	Mario Mendoza	.08
614	Tom Paciorek	.08
615	Glenn Abbott	.08
616	Joe Simpson	.08
617	Mickey Rivers	.08
618	Jim Kern	.08
619	Jim Sundberg	.08
620	Richie Zisk	.08
621	Jon Matlack	.08
622	Fergie Jenkins	.75
623	Pat Corrales	.08
624	Ed Figueroa	.08
625	Buddy Bell	.12
626	Al Oliver	.15
627	Doc Medich	.08
628	Bump Wills	.08
629	Rusty Staub	.10
630	Pat Putnam	.08
631	John Grubb	.08
632	Danny Darwin	.08
633	Ken Clay	.08
634	Jim Norris	.08
635	John Butcher	.08
636	Dave Roberts	.08
637	Billy Sample	.08
638	Carl Yastrzemski	1.25
639	Cecil Cooper	.08
640	Mike Schmidt	2.00
641a	Checklist 1-50 (41 Hal McRae)	.10
641b	Checklist 1-50 (41 Hal McRae Double Threat)	.25
642	Checklist 51-109	.08
643	Checklist 110-168	.08
644a	Checklist 169-220 (202 George Foster)	.10
644b	Checklist 169-220 (202 George Foster "Slugger")	.25
(645a)	Triple Threat(Larry Bowa, Pete Rose, Mike Schmidt) (no number on back)	2.00
645b	Triple Threat(Pete Rose, Larry Bowa, Mike Schmidt) (number on back)	2.00
646	Checklist 221-267	.08
647	Checklist 268-315	.08
648	Checklist 316-359	.08
649	Checklist 360-408	.08
650	Reggie Jackson	2.50
651	Checklist 409-458	.08
652a	Checklist 459-509 (483 Aurelio Lopez)	.10
652b	Checklist 459-506 (no 483)	.25
653	Willie Wilson	.25
654a	Checklist 507-550 (514 Jerry Augustine)	.10
654b	Checklist 507-550 (514 Billy Travers)	.25
655	George Brett	4.00
656	Checklist 551-593	.08
657	Tug McGraw	.15
658	Checklist 594-637	.08
659a	Checklist 640-660 (last number on front is 551)	.10
659b	Checklist 640-660 (last number on front is 483)	.25
660a	Steve Carlton (date 1066 on back)	1.00
660b	Steve Carlton (date 1966 on back)	2.00

Cards before 1981 are priced
Near Mint (NM), Excellent (EX),
and Very Good (VG).

Cards 1981 to present are
priced
Mint (MT), Near Mint (NM), and
Excellent (EX).

1982 Fleer

Fleer's 1982 set did not match the quality of the previous year's effort. Many of the card photos are blurred and have muddied backgrounds. The 2-1/2" x 3-1/2" cards feature color photos bordered by a frame which is color-coded by team. Backs are blue, white, and yellow and contain the player's team logo plus the logos of Major League Baseball and the Major League Baseball Players Association. Due to a lawsuit by Topps, Fleer was forced to issue the set with team logo stickers rather than gum. The complete set price does not include the higher priced variations.

		MT
Complete Set (660):		90.00
Common Player:		.06
Wax Box:		110.00
1	Dusty Baker	.10
2	Robert Castillo	.08
3	Ron Cey	.08
4	Terry Forster	.08
5	Steve Garvey	.20
6	Dave Goltz	.08
7	Pedro Guerrero	.08
8	Burt Hooton	.08
9	Steve Howe	.08
10	Jay Johnstone	.08
11	Ken Landreaux	.08
12	Davey Lopes	.08
13	*Mike Marshall*	.12
14	Bobby Mitchell	.08
15	Rick Monday	.08
16	Tom Niedenfuer	.08
17	*Ted Power*	.08
18	Jerry Reuss	.08
19	Ron Roenicke	.08
20	Bill Russell	.08
21	*Steve Sax*	.45
22	Mike Scioscia	.08
23	Reggie Smith	.08
24	*Dave Stewart*	2.00
25	Rick Sutcliffe	.08
26	Derrel Thomas	.08
27	Fernando Valenzuela	.15
28	Bob Welch	.08
29	Steve Yeager	.08
30	Bobby Brown	.08
31	Rick Cerone	.08
32	Ron Davis	.08
33	Bucky Dent	.10
34	Barry Foote	.08
35	George Frazier	.08
36	Oscar Gamble	.08
37	Rich Gossage	.10
38	Ron Guidry	.15
39	Reggie Jackson	1.50
40	Tommy John	.15
41	Rudy May	.08
42	Larry Milbourne	.08
43	Jerry Mumphrey	.08

44	Bobby Murcer	.10
45	*Gene Nelson*	.08
46	Graig Nettles	.10
47	Johnny Oates	.08
48	Lou Piniella	.12
49	Willie Randolph	.08
50	Rick Reuschel	.08
51	Dave Revering	.08
52	*Dave Righetti*	.45
53	Aurelio Rodriguez	.08
54	Bob Watson	.08
55	Dennis Werth	.08
56	Dave Winfield	2.00
57	Johnny Dench	.90
58	Bruce Berenyi	.08
59	Larry Biittner	.08
60	Scott Brown	.08
61	Dave Collins	.08
62	Geoff Combe	.08
63	Dave Concepcion	.08
64	Dan Driessen	.08
65	Joe Edelen	.08
66	George Foster	.10
67	Ken Griffey	.12
68	Paul Householder	.08
69	Tom Hume	.08
70	Junior Kennedy	.08
71	Ray Knight	.10
72	Mike LaCoss	.08
73	Rafael Landestoy	.08
74	Charlie Leibrandt	.08
75	Sam Mejias	.08
76	Paul Moskau	.08
77	Joe Nolan	.08
78	Mike O'Berry	.08
79	Ron Oester	.08
80	Frank Pastore	.08
81	Joe Price	.08
82	Tom Seaver	.90
83	Mario Soto	.08
84	Mike Vail	.08
85	Tony Armas	.08
86	Shooty Babitt	.08
87	Dave Beard	.08
88	Rick Bosetti	.08
89	Keith Drumright	.08
90	Wayne Gross	.08
91	Mike Heath	.08
92	Rickey Henderson	2.50
93	Cliff Johnson	.08
94	Jeff Jones	.08
95	Matt Keough	.08
96	Brian Kingman	.08
97	Mickey Klutts	.08
98	Rick Langford	.08
99	Steve McCatty	.08
100	Dave McKay	.08
101	Dwayne Murphy	.08
102	Jeff Newman	.08
103	Mike Norris	.08
104	Bob Owchinko	.08
105	Mitchell Page	.08
106	Rob Picciolo	.08
107	Jim Spencer	.08
108	Fred Stanley	.08
109	Tom Underwood	.08
110	Joaquin Andujar	.08
111	Steve Braun	.08
112	Bob Forsch	.08
113	George Hendrick	.08
114	Keith Hernandez	.08
115	Tom Herr	.08
116	Dane Iorg	.08
117	Jim Kaat	.10
118	Tito Landrum	.08
119	Sixto Lezcano	.08
120	Mark Littell	.08
121	John Martin	.08
122	Silvio Martinez	.08
123	Ken Oberkfell	.08
124	Darrell Porter	.08
125	Mike Ramsey	.08
126	Orlando Sanchez	.08
127	Bob Shirley	.08
128	Lary Sorensen	.08
129	Bruce Sutter	.08
130	Bob Sykes	.08
131	Garry Templeton	.08
132	Gene Tenace	.08
133	Jerry Augustine	.08
134	Sal Bando	.08
135	Mark Brouhard	.08
136	Mike Caldwell	.08
137	Reggie Cleveland	.08
138	Cecil Cooper	.08
139	Jamie Easterly	.08

No.	Player	Price	No.	Player	Price	No.	Player	Price
140	Marshall Edwards	.08	235	Dickie Thon	.08	331	Bill Stein	.08
141	Rollie Fingers	.65	236	Denny Walling	.08	332	Jim Sundberg	.08
142	Jim Gantner	.08	237	Gary Woods	.08	333	Mark Wagner	.08
143	Moose Haas	.08	238	*Luis Aguayo*	.08	334	Bump Wills	.08
144	Larry Hisle	.08	239	Ramon Aviles	.08	335	Bill Almon	.08
145	Roy Howell	.08	240	Bob Boone	.10	336	Harold Baines	.25
146	Rickey Keeton	.08	241	Larry Bowa	.08	337	Ross Baumgarten	.08
147	Randy Lerch	.08	242	Warren Brusstar	.08	338	Tony Bernazard	.08
148	Paul Molitor	3.00	243	Steve Carlton	1.00	339	Britt Burns	.08
149	Don Money	.08	244	Larry Christenson	.08	340	Richard Dotson	.08
150	Charlie Moore	.08	245	Dick Davis	.08	341	Jim Essian	.08
151	Ben Oglivie	.08	246	Greg Gross	.08	342	Ed Farmer	.08
152	Ted Simmons	.08	247	Sparky Lyle	.08	343	Carlton Fisk	.90
153	Jim Slaton	.08	248	Garry Maddox	.08	344	Kevin Hickey	.08
154	Gorman Thomas	.08	249	Gary Matthews	.08	345	Lamarr Hoyt (LaMarr)	.08
155	Robin Yount	3.00	250	Bake McBride	.08	346	Lamar Johnson	.08
156	Pete Vukovich	.08	251	Tug McGraw	.10	347	Jerry Koosman	.08
157	Benny Ayala	.08	252	Keith Moreland	.08	348	Rusty Kuntz	.08
158	Mark Belanger	.08	253	Dickie Noles	.08	349	Dennis Lamp	.08
159	Al Bumbry	.08	254	Mike Proly	.08	350	Ron LeFlore	.08
160	Terry Crowley	.08	255	Ron Reed	.08	351	Chet Lemon	.08
161	Rich Dauer	.08	256	Pete Rose	2.00	352	Greg Luzinski	.10
162	Doug DeCinces	.08	257	Dick Ruthven	.08	353	Bob Molinaro	.08
163	Rick Dempsey	.08	258	Mike Schmidt	3.00	354	Jim Morrison	.08
164	Jim Dwyer	.08	259	Lonnie Smith	.08	355	Wayne Nordhagen	.08
165	Mike Flanagan	.08	260	Manny Trillo	.08	356	Greg Pryor	.08
166	Dave Ford	.08	261	Del Unser	.08	357	Mike Squires	.08
167	Dan Graham	.08	262	George Vukovich	.08	358	Steve Trout	.08
168	Wayne Krenchicki	.08	263	Tom Brookens	.08	359	Alan Bannister	.08
169	John Lowenstein	.08	264	George Cappuzzello	.08	360	Len Barker	.08
170	Dennis Martinez	.10	265	Marty Castillo	.08	361	Bert Blyleven	.08
171	Tippy Martinez	.08	266	Al Cowens	.08	362	Joe Charboneau	.10
172	Scott McGregor	.08	267	Kirk Gibson	.12	363	John Denny	.08
173	Jose Morales	.08	268	Richie Hebner	.08	364	Bo Diaz	.08
174	Eddie Murray	3.00	269	Ron Jackson	.08	365	Miguel Dilone	.08
175	Jim Palmer	.75	270	Lynn Jones	.08	366	Jerry Dybzinski	.08
176	*Cal Ripken, Jr.*	50.00	271	Steve Kemp	.08	367	Wayne Garland	.08
177	Gary Roenicke	.08	272	*Rick Leach*	.12	368	Mike Hargrove	.08
178	Lenn Sakata	.08	273	Aurelio Lopez	.08	369	Toby Harrah	.08
179	Ken Singleton	.08	274	Jack Morris	.12	370	Ron Hassey	.08
180	Sammy Stewart	.08	275	Kevin Saucier	.08	371	*Von Hayes*	.25
181	Tim Stoddard	.08	276	Lance Parrish	.10	372	Pat Kelly	.08
182	Steve Stone	.08	277	Rick Peters	.08	373	Duane Kuiper	.08
183	Stan Bahnsen	.08	278	Dan Petry	.08	374	Rick Manning	.08
184	Ray Burris	.08	279	David Rozema	.08	375	Sid Monge	.08
185	Gary Carter	.25	280	Stan Papi	.08	376	Jorge Orta	.08
186	Warren Cromartie	.08	281	Dan Schatzeder	.08	377	Dave Rosello	.08
187	Andre Dawson	.75	282	Champ Summers	.08	378	Dan Spillner	.08
188	*Terry Francona*	.08	283	Alan Trammell	.60	379	Mike Stanton	.08
189	Woodie Fryman	.08	284	Lou Whitaker	.15	380	Andre Thornton	.08
190	Bill Gullickson	.08	285	Milt Wilcox	.08	381	Tom Veryzer	.08
191	Grant Jackson	.08	286	John Wockenfuss	.08	382	Rick Waits	.08
192	Wallace Johnson	.08	287	Gary Allenson	.08	383	Doyle Alexander	.08
193	Charlie Lea	.08	288	Tom Burgmeier	.08	384	Vida Blue	.10
194	Bill Lee	.08	289	Bill Campbell	.08	385	Fred Breining	.08
195	Jerry Manuel	.08	290	Mark Clear	.08	386	Enos Cabell	.08
196	Brad Mills	.08	291	Steve Crawford	.08	387	Jack Clark	.08
197	John Milner	.08	292	Dennis Eckersley	.75	388	Darrell Evans	.10
198	Rowland Office	.08	293	Dwight Evans	.15	389	Tom Griffin	.08
199	David Palmer	.08	294	*Rich Gedman*	.20	390	Larry Herndon	.08
200	Larry Parrish	.08	295	Garry Hancock	.08	391	Al Holland	.08
201	Mike Phillips	.08	296	Glenn Hoffman	.08	392	Gary Lavelle	.08
202	Tim Raines	.75	297	Bruce Hurst	.08	393	Johnnie LeMaster	.08
203	Bobby Ramos	.08	298	Carney Lansford	.08	394	Jerry Martin	.08
204	Jeff Reardon	.12	299	Rick Miller	.08	395	Milt May	.08
205	Steve Rogers	.08	300	Reid Nichols	.08	396	Greg Minton	.08
206	Scott Sanderson	.08	301	*Bob Ojeda*	.25	397	Joe Morgan	.75
207	Rodney Scott (photo actually Tim Raines)	.10	302	Tony Perez	.20	398	Joe Pettini	.08
208	Elias Sosa	.08	303	Chuck Rainey	.08	399	Alan Ripley	.08
209	Chris Speier	.08	304	Jerry Remy	.08	400	Billy Smith	.08
210	*Tim Wallach*	1.00	305	Jim Rice	.15	401	Rennie Stennett	.08
211	Jerry White	.08	306	Joe Rudi	.08	402	Ed Whitson	.08
212	Alan Ashby	.08	307	Bob Stanley	.08	403	Jim Wohlford	.08
213	Cesar Cedeno	.12	308	Dave Stapleton	.08	404	Willie Aikens	.08
214	Jose Cruz	.12	309	Frank Tanana	.08	405	George Brett	4.00
215	Kiko Garcia	.08	310	Mike Torrez	.08	406	Ken Brett	.08
216	Phil Garner	.08	311	John Tudor	.08	407	Dave Chalk	.08
217	Danny Heep	.08	312	Carl Yastrzemski	1.00	408	Rich Gale	.08
218	Art Howe	.08	313	Buddy Bell	.10	409	Cesar Geronimo	.08
219	Bob Knepper	.08	314	Steve Comer	.08	410	Larry Gura	.08
220	Frank LaCorte	.08	315	Danny Darwin	.08	411	Clint Hurdle	.08
221	Joe Niekro	.12	316	John Ellis	.08	412	Mike Jones	.08
222	Joe Pittman	.08	317	John Grubb	.08	413	Dennis Leonard	.08
223	Terry Puhl	.08	318	Rick Honeycutt	.08	414	Renie Martin	.08
224	Luis Pujols	.08	319	Charlie Hough	.08	415	Lee May	.08
225	Craig Reynolds	.08	320	Fergie Jenkins	.65	416	Hal McRae	.12
226	J.R. Richard	.10	321	John Henry Johnson	.08	417	Darryl Motley	.08
227	Dave Roberts	.08	322	Jim Kern	.08	418	Rance Mulliniks	.08
228	Vern Ruhle	.08	323	Jon Matlack	.08	419	Amos Otis	.08
229	Nolan Ryan	9.00	324	Doc Medich	.08	420	*Ken Phelps*	.10
230	Joe Sambito	.08	325	Mario Mendoza	.08	421	Jamie Quirk	.08
231	Tony Scott	.08	326	Al Oliver	.10	422	Dan Quisenberry	.10
232	Dave Smith	.08	327	Pat Putnam	.08	423	Paul Splittorff	.08
233	Harry Spilman	.08	328	Mickey Rivers	.08	424	U.L. Washington	.08
234	Don Sutton	.45	329	Leon Roberts	.08	425	John Wathan	.08
			330	Billy Sample	.08	426	Frank White	.08

#	Player	Price
427	Willie Wilson	.10
428	Brian Asselstine	.08
429	Bruce Benedict	.08
430	Tom Boggs	.08
431	Larry Bradford	.08
432	Rick Camp	.08
433	Chris Chambliss	.08
434	Gene Garber	.08
435	Preston Hanna	.08
436	Bob Horner	.08
437	Glenn Hubbard	.08
438a	Al Hrabosky (All Hrabosky, 5'1" on back)	16.00
438b	Al Hrabosky (Al Hrabosky, 5'1" on back)	1.25
438c	Al Hrabosky (Al Hrabosky, 5'10" on back)	.35
439	Rufino Linares	.08
440	*Rick Mahler*	.12
441	Ed Miller	.08
442	John Montefusco	.08
443	Dale Murphy	.60
444	Phil Niekro	.90
445	Gaylord Perry	.65
446	Biff Pocoroba	.08
447	Rafael Ramirez	.08
448	Jerry Royster	.08
449	Claudell Washington	.08
450	Don Aase	.08
451	Don Baylor	.12
452	Juan Beniquez	.08
453	Rick Burleson	.08
454	Bert Campaneris	.08
455	Rod Carew	1.00
456	Bob Clark	.08
457	Brian Downing	.08
458	Dan Ford	.08
459	Ken Forsch	.08
460	Dave Frost	.08
461	Bobby Grich	.08
462	Larry Harlow	.08
463	John Harris	.08
464	Andy Hassler	.08
465	Butch Hobson	.08
466	Jesse Jefferson	.08
467	Bruce Kison	.08
468	Fred Lynn	.12
469	Angel Moreno	.08
470	Ed Ott	.08
471	Fred Patek	.08
472	Steve Renko	.08
473	*Mike Witt*	.25
474	Geoff Zahn	.08
475	Gary Alexander	.08
476	Dale Berra	.08
477	Kurt Bevacqua	.08
478	Jim Bibby	.08
479	John Candelaria	.08
480	Victor Cruz	.08
481	Mike Easler	.08
482	Tim Foli	.08
483	Lee Lacy	.08
484	Vance Law	.08
485	Bill Madlock	.08
486	Willie Montanez	.08
487	Omar Moreno	.08
488	Steve Nicosia	.08
489	Dave Parker	.20
490	Tony Pena	.10
491	Pascual Perez	.10
492	*Johnny Ray*	.08
493	Rick Rhoden	.08
494	Bill Robinson	.08
495	Don Robinson	.08
496	Enrique Romo	.08
497	Rod Scurry	.08
498	Eddie Solomon	.08
499	Willie Stargell	.75
500	Kent Tekulve	.08
501	Jason Thompson	.08
502	Glenn Abbott	.08
503	Jim Anderson	.08
504	Floyd Bannister	.08
505	Bruce Bochte	.08
506	Jeff Burroughs	.08
507	Bryan Clark	.08
508	Ken Clay	.08
509	Julio Cruz	.08
510	Dick Drago	.08
511	Gary Gray	.08
512	Dan Meyer	.08
513	Jerry Narron	.08
514	Tom Paciorek	.08
515	Casey Parsons	.08
516	Lenny Randle	.08
517	Shane Rawley	.08
518	Joe Simpson	.08
519	Richie Zisk	.08
520	Neil Allen	.08
521	Bob Bailor	.08
522	Hubie Brooks	.10
523	Mike Cubbage	.08
524	Pete Falcone	.08
525	Doug Flynn	.08
526	Tom Hausman	.08
527	Ron Hodges	.08
528	Randy Jones	.08
529	Mike Jorgensen	.08
530	Dave Kingman	.12
531	Ed Lynch	.08
532	Mike Marshall	.08
533	Lee Mazzilli	.08
534	Dyar Miller	.08
535	Mike Scott	.10
536	Rusty Staub	.10
537	John Stearns	.08
538	Craig Swan	.08
539	Frank Taveras	.08
540	Alex Trevino	.08
541	Ellis Valentine	.08
542	Mookie Wilson	.15
543	Joel Youngblood	.08
544	Pat Zachry	.08
545	Glenn Adams	.08
546	Fernando Arroyo	.08
547	John Verhoeven	.08
548	Sal Butera	.08
549	John Castino	.08
550	Don Cooper	.08
551	Doug Corbett	.08
552	Dave Engle	.08
553	Roger Erickson	.08
554	Danny Goodwin	.08
555a	Darrell Jackson (black cap)	1.00
555b	Darrell Jackson (red cap with emblem)	.10
555c	Darrell Jackson (red cap, no emblem)	.25
556	Pete Mackanin	.08
557	Jack O'Connor	.08
558	Hosken Powell	.08
559	Pete Redfern	.08
560	Roy Smalley	.08
561	Chuck Baker	.08
562	Gary Ward	.08
563	Rob Wilfong	.08
564	Al Williams	.08
565	Butch Wynegar	.08
566	Randy Bass	.08
567	Juan Bonilla	.08
568	Danny Boone	.08
569	John Curtis	.08
570	Juan Eichelberger	.08
571	Barry Evans	.08
572	Tim Flannery	.08
573	Ruppert Jones	.08
574	Terry Kennedy	.08
575	Joe Lefebvre	.08
576a	John Littlefield (pitching lefty)	250.00
576b	John Littlefield (pitching righty)	.08
577	Gary Lucas	.08
578	Steve Mura	.08
579	Broderick Perkins	.08
580	Gene Richards	.08
581	Luis Salazar	.08
582	Ozzie Smith	3.00
583	John Urrea	.08
584	Chris Welsh	.08
585	Rick Wise	.08
586	Doug Bird	.08
587	Tim Blackwell	.08
588	Bobby Bonds	.10
589	Bill Buckner	.08
590	Bill Caudill	.08
591	Hector Cruz	.08
592	*Jody Davis*	.10
593	Ivan DeJesus	.08
594	Steve Dillard	.08
595	Leon Durham	.08
596	Rawly Eastwick	.08
597	Steve Henderson	.08
598	Mike Krukow	.08
599	Mike Lum	.08
600	Randy Martz	.08
601	Jerry Morales	.08
602	Ken Reitz	.08
603a	*Lee Smith* (Cubs logo reversed on back)	8.00
603b	*Lee Smith* (corrected)	8.00
604	Dick Tidrow	.08
605	Jim Tracy	.08
606	Mike Tyson	.08
607	Ty Waller	.08
608	Danny Ainge	1.25
609	*Jorge Bell*	1.00
610	Mark Bomback	.08
611	Barry Bonnell	.08
612	Jim Clancy	.08
613	Damaso Garcia	.08
614	Jerry Garvin	.08
615	Alfredo Griffin	.08
616	Garth Iorg	.08
617	Luis Leal	.08
618	Ken Macha	.08
619	John Mayberry	.08
620	Joey McLaughlin	.08
621	Lloyd Moseby	.08
622	Dave Stieb	.08
623	Jackson Todd	.08
624	Willie Upshaw	.08
625	Otto Velez	.08
626	Ernie Whitt	.08
627	Al Woods	.08
628	1981 All-Star Game	.08
629	All-Star Infielders(Bucky Dent, Frank White)	.08
630	Big Red Machine(Dave Concepcion, Dan Driessen, George Foster)	.10
631	Top N.L. Relief Pitcher(Bruce Sutter)	.08
632	Steve & Carlton(Steve Carlton, Gary Fisk)	.25
633	3000th Game, May 25, 1981(Carl Yastrzemski)	.35
634	Dynamic Duo(Johnny Bench, Tom Seaver)	.30
635	West Meets East(Gary Carter, Fernando Valenzuela)	.20
636a	N.L. Strikeout King(Fernando Valenzuela) ("...led the National League...")	1.00
636b	N.L. Strikeout King(Fernando Valenzuela) ("...led the National League)	.35
637	Home Run King(Mike Schmidt)	.50
638	N.L. All-Stars(Gary Carter, Dave Parker)	.20
639	Perfect Game!(Len Barker, Bo Diaz)	.08
640	Pete Rose, Pete Rose, Jr. (Re-Pete)	2.00
641	Phillies' Finest(Steve Carlton, Mike Schmidt, Lonnie Smith)	.50
642	Red Sox Reunion(Dwight Evans, Fred Lynn)	.15
643	Most Hits and Runs(Rickey Henderson)	1.50
644	Most Saves 1981 A.L.(Rollie Fingers)	.15
645	Most 1981 Wins(Tom Seaver)	.25
646a	Yankee Powerhouse(Reggie Jackson, Dave Winfield) (comma after "outfielder" on back)	2.00
646b	Yankee Powerhouse(Reggie Jackson, Dave Winfield) (no comma)	2.00
647	Checklist 1-56	.08
648	Checklist 57-109	.08
649	Checklist 110-156	.08
650	Checklist 157-211	.08
651	Checklist 212-262	.08
652	Checklist 263-312	.08
653	Checklist 313-358	.08
654	Checklist 359-403	.08
655	Checklist 404-449	.08
656	Checklist 450-501	.08
657	Checklist 502-544	.08
658	Checklist 545-585	.08
659	Checklist 586-627	.08
660	Checklist 628-646	.08

A player's name in *italic* type indicates a rookie card.

1983 Fleer

Reggie Smith
FIRST BASE

The 1983 Fleer set features color photos set inside a light brown border. The cards are standard 2-1/2" x 3-1/2". A team logo is located at the card bottom and the word "Fleer" is found at the top. The card backs are designed on a vertical format and include a small black and white photo of the player along with biographical and statistical information. The reverses are done in two shades of brown on white stock. The set was issued with team logo stickers.

		MT
Complete Set (660):		100.00
Common Player:		.06
Wax Box:		180.00
1	Joaquin Andujar	.08
2	Doug Bair	.08
3	Steve Braun	.08
4	Glenn Brummer	.08
5	Bob Forsch	.08
6	David Green	.08
7	George Hendrick	.08
8	Keith Hernandez	.08
9	Tom Herr	.08
10	Dane Iorg	.08
11	Jim Kaat	.12
12	Jeff Lahti	.08
13	Tito Landrum	.08
14	*Dave LaPoint*	.08
15	*Willie McGee*	1.50
16	Steve Mura	.08
17	Ken Oberkfell	.08
18	Darrell Porter	.08
19	Mike Ramsey	.08
20	Gene Roof	.08
21	Lonnie Smith	.08
22	Ozzie Smith	2.50
23	John Stuper	.08
24	Bruce Sutter	.08
25	Gene Tenace	.08
26	Jerry Augustine	.08
27	Dwight Bernard	.08
28	Mark Brouhard	.08
29	Mike Caldwell	.08
30	Cecil Cooper	.08
31	Jamie Easterly	.08
32	Marshall Edwards	.08
33	Rollie Fingers	.60
34	Jim Gantner	.08
35	Moose Haas	.08
36	Roy Howell	.08
37	Peter Ladd	.08
38	Bob McClure	.08
39	Doc Medich	.08
40	Paul Molitor	2.50
41	Don Money	.08
42	Charlie Moore	.08
43	Ben Oglivie	.08
44	Ed Romero	.08
45	Ted Simmons	.08
46	Jim Slaton	.08
47	Don Sutton	.30
48	Gorman Thomas	.08

49	Pete Vuckovich	.08
50	Ned Yost	.08
51	Robin Yount	2.50
52	Benny Ayala	.08
53	Bob Bonner	.08
54	Al Bumbry	.08
55	Terry Crowley	.08
56	*Storm Davis*	.10
57	Rich Dauer	.08
58	Rick Dempsey	.08
59	Jim Dwyer	.08
60	Mike Flanagan	.08
61	Dan Ford	.08
62	Glenn Gulliver	.08
63	John Lowenstein	.08
64	Dennis Martinez	.08
65	Tippy Martinez	.08
66	Scott McGregor	.08
67	Eddie Murray	2.50
68	Joe Nolan	.08
69	Jim Palmer	.90
70	Cal Ripken, Jr.	18.00
71	Gary Roenicke	.08
72	Lenn Sakata	.08
73	Ken Singleton	.08
74	Sammy Stewart	.08
75	Tim Stoddard	.08
76	Don Aase	.08
77	Don Baylor	.08
78	Juan Beniquez	.08
79	Bob Boone	.08
80	Rick Burleson	.08
81	Rod Carew	1.00
82	Bobby Clark	.08
83	Doug Corbett	.08
84	John Curtis	.08
85	Doug DeCinces	.08
86	Brian Downing	.08
87	Joe Ferguson	.08
88	Tim Foli	.08
89	Ken Forsch	.08
90	Dave Goltz	.08
91	Bobby Grich	.08
92	Andy Hassler	.08
93	Reggie Jackson	1.00
94	Ron Jackson	.08
95	Tommy John	.10
96	Bruce Kison	.08
97	Fred Lynn	.10
98	Ed Ott	.08
99	Steve Renko	.08
100	Luis Sanchez	.08
101	Rob Wilfong	.08
102	Mike Witt	.08
103	Geoff Zahn	.08
104	Willie Aikens	.08
105	Mike Armstrong	.08
106	Vida Blue	.08
107	*Bud Black*	.50
108	George Brett	3.50
109	Bill Castro	.08
110	Onix Concepcion	.08
111	Dave Frost	.08
112	Cesar Geronimo	.08
113	Larry Gura	.08
114	Steve Hammond	.08
115	Don Hood	.08
116	Dennis Leonard	.08
117	Jerry Martin	.08
118	Lee May	.08
119	Hal McRae	.08
120	Amos Otis	.08
121	Greg Pryor	.08
122	Dan Quisenberry	.08
123	*Don Slaught*	.20
124	Paul Splittorff	.08
125	U.L. Washington	.08
126	John Wathan	.08
127	Frank White	.08
128	Willie Wilson	.08
129	Steve Bedrosian	.08
130	Bruce Benedict	.08
131	Tommy Boggs	.08
132	Brett Butler	.15
133	Rick Camp	.08
134	Chris Chambliss	.08
135	Ken Dayley	.08
136	Gene Garber	.08
137	Terry Harper	.08
138	Bob Horner	.08
139	Glenn Hubbard	.08
140	Rufino Linares	.08
141	Rick Mahler	.08
142	Dale Murphy	.30
143	Phil Niekro	.60
144	Pascual Perez	.08

145	Biff Pocoroba	.08
146	Rafael Ramirez	.08
147	Jerry Royster	.08
148	Ken Smith	.08
149	Bob Walk	.08
150	Claudell Washington	.08
151	Bob Watson	.08
152	Larry Whisenton	.08
153	Porfirio Altamirano	.08
154	Marty Bystrom	.08
155	Steve Carlton	1.00
156	Larry Christenson	.08
157	Ivan DeJesus	.08
158	John Denny	.08
159	Bob Dernier	.08
160	Bo Diaz	.08
161	Ed Farmer	.08
162	Greg Gross	.08
163	Mike Krukow	.08
164	Garry Maddox	.08
165	Gary Matthews	.08
166	Tug McGraw	.08
167	Bob Molinaro	.08
168	Sid Monge	.08
169	Ron Reed	.08
170	Bill Robinson	.08
171	Pete Rose	3.00
172	Dick Ruthven	.08
173	Mike Schmidt	2.50
174	Manny Trillo	.08
175	Ozzie Virgil	.08
176	George Vukovich	.08
177	Gary Allenson	.08
178	Luis Aponte	.08
179	*Wade Boggs*	12.00
180	Tom Burgmeier	.08
181	Mark Clear	.08
182	Dennis Eckersley	.30
183	Dwight Evans	.08
184	Rich Gedman	.08
185	Glenn Hoffman	.08
186	Bruce Hurst	.08
187	Carney Lansford	.08
188	Rick Miller	.08
189	Reid Nichols	.08
190	Bob Ojeda	.08
191	Tony Perez	.10
192	Chuck Rainey	.08
193	Jerry Remy	.08
194	Jim Rice	.08
195	Bob Stanley	.08
196	Dave Stapleton	.08
197	Mike Torrez	.08
198	John Tudor	.08
199	Julio Valdez	.08
200	Carl Yastrzemski	1.00
201	Dusty Baker	.08
202	Joe Beckwith	.08
203	*Greg Brock*	.08
204	Ron Cey	.08
205	Terry Forster	.08
206	Steve Garvey	.30
207	Pedro Guerrero	.08
208	Burt Hooton	.08
209	Steve Howe	.08
210	Ken Landreaux	.08
211	Mike Marshall	.08
212	*Candy Maldonado*	.15
213	Rick Monday	.08
214	Tom Niedenfuer	.08
215	Jorge Orta	.08
216	Jerry Reuss	.08
217	Ron Roenicke	.08
218	Vicente Romo	.08
219	Bill Russell	.10
220	Steve Sax	.08
221	Mike Scioscia	.08
222	Dave Stewart	.25
223	Derrel Thomas	.08
224	Fernando Valenzuela	.10
225	Bob Welch	.08
226	Ricky Wright	.08
227	Steve Yeager	.08
228	Bill Almon	.08
229	Harold Baines	.15
230	Salome Barojas	.08
231	Tony Bernazard	.08
232	Britt Burns	.08
233	Richard Dotson	.08
234	Ernesto Escarrega	.08
235	Carlton Fisk	.45
236	Jerry Hairston	.08
237	Kevin Hickey	.08
238	LaMarr Hoyt	.08
239	Steve Kemp	.08
240	Jim Kern	.08

#	Player	Price
241	*Ron Kittle*	.08
242	Jerry Koosman	.08
243	Dennis Lamp	.08
244	Rudy Law	.08
245	Vance Law	.08
246	Ron LeFlore	.08
247	Greg Luzinski	.10
248	Tom Paciorek	.08
249	Aurelio Rodriguez	.08
250	Mike Squires	.08
251	Steve Trout	.08
252	Jim Barr	.08
253	Dave Bergman	.08
254	Fred Breining	.08
255	Bob Brenly	.08
256	Jack Clark	.08
257	Chili Davis	.20
258	Darrell Evans	.10
259	Alan Fowlkes	.08
260	Rich Gale	.08
261	Atlee Hammaker	.08
262	Al Holland	.08
263	Duane Kuiper	.08
264	Bill Laskey	.08
265	Gary Lavelle	.08
266	Johnnie LeMaster	.08
267	Renie Martin	.08
268	Milt May	.08
269	Greg Minton	.08
270	Joe Morgan	.60
271	Tom O'Malley	.08
272	Reggie Smith	.08
273	Guy Sularz	.08
274	Champ Summers	.08
275	Max Venable	.08
276	Jim Wohlford	.08
277	Ray Burris	.08
278	Gary Carter	.20
279	Warren Cromartie	.08
280	Andre Dawson	.50
281	Terry Francona	.08
282	Doug Flynn	.08
283	Woody Fryman	.08
284	Bill Gullickson	.08
285	Wallace Johnson	.08
286	Charlie Lea	.08
287	Randy Lerch	.08
288	Brad Mills	.08
289	Dan Norman	.08
290	Al Oliver	.08
291	David Palmer	.08
292	Tim Raines	.25
293	Jeff Reardon	.10
294	Steve Rogers	.08
295	Scott Sanderson	.08
296	Dan Schatzeder	.08
297	Bryn Smith	.08
298	Chris Speier	.08
299	Tim Wallach	.10
300	Jerry White	.08
301	Joel Youngblood	.08
302	Ross Baumgarten	.08
303	Dale Berra	.08
304	John Candelaria	.08
305	Dick Davis	.08
306	Mike Easler	.08
307	Richie Hebner	.08
308	Lee Lacy	.08
309	Bill Madlock	.08
310	Larry McWilliams	.08
311	John Milner	.08
312	Omar Moreno	.08
313	Jim Morrison	.08
314	Steve Nicosia	.08
315	Dave Parker	.12
316	Tony Pena	.08
317	Johnny Ray	.08
318	Rick Rhoden	.08
319	Don Robinson	.08
320	Enrique Romo	.08
321	Manny Sarmiento	.08
322	Rod Scurry	.08
323	Jim Smith	.08
324	Willie Stargell	.60
325	Jason Thompson	.08
326	Kent Tekulve	.08
327a	Tom Brookens (narrow (1/4") brown box at bottom on back)	.45
327b	Tom Brookens (wide (1-1/4") brown box at bottom on back)	.08
328	Enos Cabell	.08
329	Kirk Gibson	.08
330	Larry Herndon	.08
331	Mike Ivie	.08

#	Player	Price
332	*Howard Johnson*	1.00
333	Lynn Jones	.08
334	Rick Leach	.08
335	Chet Lemon	.08
336	Jack Morris	.10
337	Lance Parrish	.10
338	Larry Pashnick	.08
339	Dan Petry	.08
340	Dave Rozema	.08
341	Dave Rucker	.08
342	Elias Sosa	.08
343	Dave Tobik	.08
344	Alan Trammell	.45
345	Jerry Turner	.08
346	Jerry Ujdur	.08
347	Pat Underwood	.08
348	Lou Whitaker	.15
349	Milt Wilcox	.08
350	*Glenn Wilson*	.08
351	John Wockenfuss	.08
352	Kurt Bevacqua	.08
353	Juan Bonilla	.08
354	Floyd Chiffer	.08
355	Luis DeLeon	.08
356	*Dave Dravecky*	.30
357	Dave Edwards	.08
358	Juan Eichelberger	.08
359	Tim Flannery	.08
360	*Tony Gwynn*	26.00
361	Ruppert Jones	.08
362	Terry Kennedy	.08
363	Joe Lefebvre	.08
364	Sixto Lezcano	.08
365	Tim Lollar	.08
366	Gary Lucas	.08
367	John Montefusco	.08
368	Broderick Perkins	.08
369	Joe Pittman	.08
370	Gene Richards	.08
371	Luis Salazar	.08
372	*Eric Show*	.08
373	Garry Templeton	.08
374	Chris Welsh	.08
375	Alan Wiggins	.08
376	Rick Cerone	.08
377	Dave Collins	.08
378	Roger Erickson	.08
379	George Frazier	.08
380	Oscar Gamble	.08
381	Goose Gossage	.08
382	Ken Griffey	.10
383	Ron Guidry	.10
384	Dave LaRoche	.08
385	Rudy May	.08
386	John Mayberry	.08
387	Lee Mazzilli	.08
388	Mike Morgan	.08
389	Jerry Mumphrey	.08
390	Bobby Murcer	.08
391	Graig Nettles	.08
392	Lou Piniella	.08
393	Willie Randolph	.08
394	Shane Rawley	.08
395	Dave Righetti	.08
396	Andre Robertson	.08
397	Roy Smalley	.08
398	Dave Winfield	2.00
399	Butch Wynegar	.08
400	Chris Bando	.08
401	Alan Bannister	.08
402	Len Barker	.08
403	Tom Brennan	.08
404	*Carmelo Castillo*	.08
405	Miguel Dilone	.08
406	Jerry Dybzinski	.08
407	Mike Fischlin	.08
408	Ed Glynn (photo actually Bud Anderson)	.08
409	Mike Hargrove	.08
410	Toby Harrah	.08
411	Ron Hassey	.08
412	Von Hayes	.08
413	Rick Manning	.08
414	Bake McBride	.08
415	Larry Milbourne	.08
416	Bill Nahorodny	.08
417	Jack Perconte	.08
418	Larry Sorensen	.08
419	Dan Spillner	.08
420	Rick Sutcliffe	.08
421	Andre Thornton	.08
422	Rick Waits	.08
423	Eddie Whitson	.08
424	Jesse Barfield	.08
425	Barry Bonnell	.08
426	Jim Clancy	.08

#	Player	Price
427	Damaso Garcia	.08
428	Jerry Garvin	.08
429	Alfredo Griffin	.08
430	Garth Iorg	.08
431	Roy Lee Jackson	.08
432	Luis Leal	.08
433	Buck Martinez	.08
434	Joey McLaughlin	.08
435	Lloyd Moseby	.08
436	Rance Mulliniks	.08
437	Dale Murray	.08
438	Wayne Nordhagen	.08
439	*Gene Petralli*	.08
440	Hosken Powell	.08
441	Dave Stieb	.08
442	Willie Upshaw	.08
443	Ernie Whitt	.08
444	Al Woods	.08
445	Alan Ashby	.08
446	Jose Cruz	.08
447	Kiko Garcia	.08
448	Phil Garner	.08
449	Danny Heep	.08
450	Art Howe	.08
451	Bob Knepper	.08
452	Alan Knicely	.08
453	Ray Knight	.08
454	Frank LaCorte	.08
455	Mike LaCoss	.08
456	Randy Moffitt	.08
457	Joe Niekro	.08
458	Terry Puhl	.08
459	Luis Pujols	.08
460	Craig Reynolds	.08
461	Bert Roberge	.08
462	Vern Ruhle	.08
463	Nolan Ryan	8.00
464	Joe Sambito	.08
465	Tony Scott	.08
466	Dave Smith	.08
467	Harry Spilman	.08
468	Dickie Thon	.08
469	Denny Walling	.08
470	Larry Andersen	.08
471	Floyd Bannister	.08
472	Jim Beattie	.08
473	Bruce Bochte	.08
474	Manny Castillo	.08
475	Bill Caudill	.08
476	Bryan Clark	.08
477	Al Cowens	.08
478	Julio Cruz	.08
479	Todd Cruz	.08
480	Gary Gray	.08
481	Dave Henderson	.10
482	*Mike Moore*	.25
483	Gaylord Perry	.50
484	Dave Revering	.08
485	Joe Simpson	.08
486	Mike Stanton	.08
487	Rick Sweet	.08
488	*Ed Vande Berg*	.08
489	Richie Zisk	.08
490	Doug Bird	.08
491	Larry Bowa	.08
492	Bill Buckner	.08
493	Bill Campbell	.08
494	Jody Davis	.08
495	Leon Durham	.08
496	Steve Henderson	.08
497	Willie Hernandez	.08
498	Fergie Jenkins	.50
499	Jay Johnstone	.08
500	Junior Kennedy	.08
501	Randy Martz	.08
502	Jerry Morales	.08
503	Keith Moreland	.08
504	Dickie Noles	.08
505	Mike Proly	.08
506	Allen Ripley	.08
507	*Ryne Sandberg*	16.00
508	Lee Smith	1.25
509	Pat Tabler	.08
510	Dick Tidrow	.08
511	Bump Wills	.08
512	Gary Woods	.08
513	Tony Armas	.08
514	Dave Beard	.08
515	Jeff Burroughs	.08
516	John D'Acquisto	.08
517	Wayne Gross	.08
518	Mike Heath	.08
519	Rickey Henderson	2.50
520	Cliff Johnson	.08
521	Matt Keough	.08
522	Brian Kingman	.08

523	Rick Langford	.08
524	Davey Lopes	.08
525	Steve McCatty	.08
526	Dave McKay	.08
527	Dan Meyer	.08
528	Dwayne Murphy	.08
529	Jeff Newman	.08
530	Mike Norris	.08
531	Bob Owchinko	.08
532	Joe Rudi	.08
533	Jimmy Sexton	.08
534	Fred Stanley	.08
535	Tom Underwood	.08
536	Neil Allen	.08
537	Wally Backman	.08
538	Bob Bailor	.08
539	Hubie Brooks	.08
540	Carlos Diaz	.08
541	Pete Falcone	.08
542	George Foster	.08
543	Ron Gardenhire	.08
544	Brian Giles	.08
545	Ron Hodges	.08
546	Randy Jones	.08
547	Mike Jorgensen	.08
548	Dave Kingman	.10
549	Ed Lynch	.08
550	Jesse Orosco	.08
551	Rick Ownbey	.08
552	*Charlie Puleo*	.08
553	Gary Rajsich	.08
554	Mike Scott	.08
555	Rusty Staub	.10
556	John Stearns	.08
557	Craig Swan	.08
558	Ellis Valentine	.08
559	Tom Veryzer	.08
560	Mookie Wilson	.08
561	Pat Zachry	.08
562	Buddy Bell	.08
563	John Butcher	.08
564	Steve Comer	.08
565	Danny Darwin	.08
566	Bucky Dent	.08
567	John Grubb	.08
568	Rick Honeycutt	.08
569	Dave Hostetler	.08
570	Charlie Hough	.08
571	Lamar Johnson	.08
572	Jon Matlack	.08
573	Paul Mirabella	.08
574	Larry Parrish	.08
575	Mike Richardt	.08
576	Mickey Rivers	.08
577	Billy Sample	.08
578	*Dave Schmidt*	.08
579	Bill Stein	.08
580	Jim Sundberg	.08
581	Frank Tanana	.08
582	Mark Wagner	.08
583	George Wright	.08
584	Johnny Bench	1.00
585	Bruce Berenyi	.08
586	Larry Biittner	.08
587	Cesar Cedeno	.08
588	Dave Concepcion	.08
589	Dan Driessen	.08
590	Greg Harris	.08
591	Ben Hayes	.08
592	Paul Householder	.08
593	Tom Hume	.08
594	Wayne Krenchicki	.08
595	Rafael Landestoy	.08
596	Charlie Leibrandt	.08
597	*Eddie Milner*	.08
598	Ron Oester	.08
599	Frank Pastore	.08
600	Joe Price	.08
601	Tom Seaver	1.00
602	Bob Shirley	.08
603	Mario Soto	.08
604	Alex Trevino	.08
605	Mike Vail	.08
606	Duane Walker	.08
607	Tom Brunansky	.08
608	Bobby Castillo	.08
609	John Castino	.08
610	Ron Davis	.08
611	Lenny Faedo	.08
612	Terry Felton	.08
613	*Gary Gaetti*	.35
614	Mickey Hatcher	.08
615	Brad Havens	.08
616	Kent Hrbek	.25
617	Randy S. Johnson	.08
618	Tim Laudner	.08

619	Jeff Little	.08
620	Bob Mitchell	.08
621	Jack O'Connor	.08
622	John Pacella	.08
623	Pete Redfern	.08
624	Jesus Vega	.08
625	*Frank Viola*	.90
626	Ron Washington	.08
627	Gary Ward	.08
628	Al Williams	.08
629	Red Sox All-Stars(Mark Clear, Dennis Eckersley, Carl Yastrzemski)	.25
630	300 Career Wins(Terry Bulling, Gaylord Perry)	.15
631	Pride of Venezuela(Dave Concepcion, Manny Trillo)	.10
632	All-Star Infielders(Buddy Bell, Robin Yount)	.20
633	Mr. Vet & Mr. Rookie(Kent Hrbek, Dave Winfield)	.25
634	Fountain of Youth(Pete Rose, Willie Stargell)	.40
635	Big Chiefs(Toby Harrah, Andre Thornton)	.08
636	"Smith Bros."(Lonnie Smith, Ozzie Smith)	.10
637	Base Stealers' Threat(Gary Carter, Bo Diaz)	.10
638	All-Star Catchers(Gary Carter, Carlton Fisk)	.20
639	Rickey Henderson (In Action)	.50
640	Home Run Threats(Reggie Jackson, Ben Oglivie)	.25
641	Two Teams - Same Day(Joel Youngblood)	.08
642	Last Perfect Game(Len Barker, Ron Hassey)	.08
643	Blue(Vida Blue)	.08
644	Black &(Bud Black)	.08
645	Power(Reggie Jackson)	.30
646	Speed &(Rickey Henderson)	.30
647	Checklist 1-51	.08
648	Checklist 52-103	.08
649	Checklist 104-152	.08
650	Checklist 153-200	.08
651	Checklist 201-251	.08
652	Checklist 252-301	.08
653	Checklist 302-351	.08
654	Checklist 352-399	.08
655	Checklist 400-444	.08
656	Checklist 445-489	.08
657	Checklist 490-535	.08
658	Checklist 536-583	.08
659	Checklist 584-628	.08
660	Checklist 629-646	.08

1984 Fleer

Kent Hrbek
FIRST BASE

The 1984 Fleer set contained 660 cards for the fourth consecutive year. The 2-1/2" x 3-1/2" cards feature a color photo surrounded by white borders and horizontal dark blue stripes. The top stripe contains the word "Fleer" with the lower carrying the player's name. Backs have a small black-and-white player photo and are done in blue ink on white stock. The set was issued with team logo stickers.

		MT
Complete Set (660):		100.00
Common Player:		.08
Wax Box:		200.00
1	Mike Boddicker	.08
2	Al Bumbry	.08
3	Todd Cruz	.08
4	Rich Dauer	.08
5	Storm Davis	.08
6	Rick Dempsey	.08
7	Jim Dwyer	.08
8	Mike Flanagan	.08
9	Dan Ford	.08
10	John Lowenstein	.08
11	Dennis Martinez	.12
12	Tippy Martinez	.08
13	Scott McGregor	.08
14	Eddie Murray	4.00
15	Joe Nolan	.08
16	Jim Palmer	1.50
17	Cal Ripken, Jr.	22.00
18	Gary Roenicke	.08
19	Lenn Sakata	.08
20	*John Shelby*	.08
21	Ken Singleton	.08
22	Sammy Stewart	.08
23	Tim Stoddard	.08
24	Marty Bystrom	.08
25	Steve Carlton	3.50
26	Ivan DeJesus	.08
27	John Denny	.08
28	Bob Dernier	.08
29	Bo Diaz	.08
30	Kiko Garcia	.08
31	Greg Gross	.08
32	*Kevin Gross*	.08
33	Von Hayes	.08
34	Willie Hernandez	.08
35	Al Holland	.08
36	*Charles Hudson*	.08
37	Joe Lefebvre	.08
38	Sixto Lezcano	.08
39	Garry Maddox	.08
40	Gary Matthews	.08
41	Len Matuszek	.08
42	Tug McGraw	.08
43	Joe Morgan	.75
44	Tony Perez	.15
45	Ron Reed	.08
46	Pete Rose	7.50
47	*Juan Samuel*	.75
48	Mike Schmidt	8.00
49	Ozzie Virgil	.08
50	*Juan Agosto*	.08
51	Harold Baines	.12
52	Floyd Bannister	.08
53	Salome Barojas	.08
54	Britt Burns	.08
55	Julio Cruz	.08
56	Richard Dotson	.08
57	Jerry Dybzinski	.08
58	Carlton Fisk	2.00
59	Scott Fletcher	.08
60	Jerry Hairston	.08
61	Kevin Hickey	.08
62	Marc Hill	.08
63	LaMarr Hoyt	.08
64	Ron Kittle	.08
65	Jerry Koosman	.08
66	Dennis Lamp	.08
67	Rudy Law	.08
68	Vance Law	.08
69	Greg Luzinski	.12
70	Tom Paciorek	.08
71	Mike Squires	.08
72	Dick Tidrow	.08
73	*Greg Walker*	.08
74	Glenn Abbott	.08
75	Howard Bailey	.08
76	Doug Bair	.08
77	Juan Berenguer	.08
78	Tom Brookens	.08
79	Enos Cabell	.08
80	Kirk Gibson	.08
81	John Grubb	.08
82	Larry Herndon	.08
83	Wayne Krenchicki	.08
84	Rick Leach	.08

No.	Player	Price	No.	Player	Price	No.	Player	Price
85	Chet Lemon	.08	181	Bob Horner	.08	278	Charlie Lea	.08
86	Aurelio Lopez	.08	182	Glenn Hubbard	.08	279	Bryan Little	.08
87	Jack Morris	.08	183	Randy S. Johnson	.08	280	Al Oliver	.10
88	Lance Parrish	.12	184	*Craig McMurtry*	.08	281	Tim Raines	.45
89	Dan Petry	.08	185	Donnie Moore	.08	282	Bobby Ramos	.08
90	Dave Rozema	.08	186	Dale Murphy	.75	283	Jeff Reardon	.08
91	Alan Trammell	.30	187	Phil Niekro	.75	284	Steve Rogers	.08
92	Lou Whitaker	.12	188	Pascual Perez	.08	285	Scott Sanderson	.08
93	Milt Wilcox	.08	189	Biff Pocoroba	.08	286	Dan Schatzeder	.08
94	Glenn Wilson	.08	190	Rafael Ramirez	.08	287	Bryn Smith	.08
95	John Wockenfuss	.08	191	Jerry Royster	.08	288	Chris Speier	.08
96	Dusty Baker	.12	192	Claudell Washington	.08	289	Manny Trillo	08
97	Joe Beckwith	.08	193	Bob Watson	.08	290	Mike Vail	.08
98	Greg Brock	.08	194	Jerry Augustine	.08	291	Tim Wallach	.12
99	Jack Fimple	.08	195	Mark Brouhard	.08	292	Chris Welsh	.08
100	Pedro Guerrero	.08	196	Mike Caldwell	.08	293	Jim Wohlford	.08
101	Rick Honeycutt	.08	197	*Tom Candiotti*	.60	294	Kurt Bevacqua	.08
102	Burt Hooton	.08	198	Cecil Cooper	.08	295	Juan Bonilla	.08
103	Steve Howe	.08	199	Rollie Fingers	.50	296	Bobby Brown	.08
104	Ken Landreaux	.08	200	Jim Gantner	.08	297	Luis DeLeon	.08
105	Mike Marshall	.08	201	Bob L. Gibson	.08	298	Dave Dravecky	.08
106	Rick Monday	.08	202	Moose Haas	.08	299	Tim Flannery	.08
107	Jose Morales	.08	203	Roy Howell	.08	300	Steve Garvey	.45
108	Tom Niedenfuer	.08	204	Pete Ladd	.08	301	Tony Gwynn	12.00
109	*Alejandro Pena*	.08	205	Rick Manning	.08	302	*Andy Hawkins*	.20
110	Jerry Reuss	.08	206	Bob McClure	.08	303	Ruppert Jones	.08
111	Bill Russell	.12	207	Paul Molitor	4.00	304	Terry Kennedy	.08
112	Steve Sax	.08	208	Don Money	.08	305	Tim Lollar	08
113	Mike Scioscia	.08	209	Charlie Moore	.08	306	Gary Lucas	.08
114	Derrel Thomas	.08	210	Ben Oglivie	.08	307	*Kevin McReynolds*	.60
115	Fernando Valenzuela	.12	211	Chuck Porter	.08	308	Sid Monge	.08
116	Bob Welch	.08	212	Ed Romero	.08	309	Mario Ramirez	.08
117	Steve Yeager	.08	213	Ted Simmons	.08	310	Gene Richards	.08
110	Pat Zachry	.08	214	Jim Slaton	.08	311	Luis Salazar	.08
119	Don Baylor	.15	215	Don Sutton	.45	312	Eric Show	.08
120	Bert Campaneris	.08	216	Tom Tellmann	.08	313	Elias Sosa	.08
121	Rick Cerone	.08	217	Pete Vuckovich	.08	314	Garry Templeton	.08
122	*Ray Fontenot*	.08	218	Ned Yost	.08	315	*Mark Thurmond*	.08
123	George Frazier	.08	219	Robin Yount	4.00	316	Ed Whitson	.08
124	Oscar Gamble	.08	220	Alan Ashby	.08	317	Alan Wiggins	.08
125	Goose Gossage	.10	221	Kevin Bass	.08	318	Neil Allen	.08
126	Ken Griffey	.12	222	Jose Cruz	.08	319	Joaquin Andujar	.08
127	Ron Guidry	.10	223	*Bill Dawley*	.08	320	Steve Braun	.08
128	Jay Howell	.08	224	Frank DiPino	.08	321	Glenn Brummer	.08
129	Steve Kemp	.08	225	*Bill Doran*	.08	322	Bob Forsch	.08
130	Matt Keough	.08	226	Phil Garner	.08	323	David Green	.08
131	*Don Mattingly*	30.00	227	Art Howe	.08	324	George Hendrick	.08
132	John Montefusco	.08	228	Bob Knepper	.08	325	Tom Herr	.08
133	Omar Moreno	.08	229	Ray Knight	.08	326	Dane Iorg	.08
134	Dale Murray	.08	230	Frank LaCorte	.08	327	Jeff Lahti	.08
135	Graig Nettles	.10	231	Mike LaCoss	.08	328	Dave LaPoint	.08
136	Lou Piniella	.10	232	Mike Madden	.08	329	Willie McGee	.15
137	Willie Randolph	.08	233	Jerry Mumphrey	.08	330	Ken Oberkfell	.08
138	Shane Rawley	.08	235	Terry Puhl	.08	331	Darrell Porter	.08
139	Dave Righetti	.08	236	Luis Pujols	.08	332	Jamie Quirk	.08
140	Andre Robertson	.08	237	Craig Reynolds	.08	333	Mike Ramsey	.08
141	Bob Shirley	.08	238	Vern Ruhle	.08	334	Floyd Rayford	.08
142	Roy Smalley	.08	239	Nolan Ryan	20.00	335	Lonnie Smith	.08
143	Dave Winfield	3.00	240	Mike Scott	.08	336	Ozzie Smith	4.00
144	Butch Wynegar	.08	241	Tony Scott	.08	337	John Stuper	.08
145	*Jim Acker*	.08	242	Dave Smith	.08	338	Bruce Sutter	.08
146	Doyle Alexander	.08	243	Dickie Thon	.08	339	*Andy Van Slyke*	2.00
147	Jesse Barfield	.08	244	Denny Walling	.08	340	Dave Von Ohlen	.08
148	George Bell	.08	245	Dale Berra	.08	341	Willie Aikens	.08
149	Barry Bonnell	.08	246	Jim Bibby	.08	342	Mike Armstrong	.08
150	Jim Clancy	.08	247	John Candelaria	.08	343	Bud Black	.08
151	Dave Collins	.08	248	*Jose DeLeon*	.08	344	George Brett	7.50
152	*Tony Fernandez*	.50	249	Mike Easler	.08	345	Onix Concepcion	.08
153	Damaso Garcia	.08	250	Cecilio Guante	.08	346	Keith Creel	.08
154	Dave Geisel	.08	251	Richie Hebner	.08	347	Larry Gura	.08
155	Jim Gott	.08	252	Lee Lacy	.08	348	Don Hood	.08
156	Alfredo Griffin	.08	253	Bill Madlock	.08	349	Dennis Leonard	.08
157	Garth Iorg	.08	254	Milt May	.08	350	Hal McRae	.12
158	Roy Lee Jackson	.08	255	Lee Mazzilli	.08	351	Amos Otis	.08
159	Cliff Johnson	.08	256	Larry McWilliams	.08	352	Gaylord Perry	.60
160	Luis Leal	.08	257	Jim Morrison	.08	353	Greg Pryor	.08
161	Buck Martinez	.08	258	Dave Parker	.12	354	Dan Quisenberry	.08
162	Joey McLaughlin	.08	259	Tony Pena	.08	355	Steve Renko	.08
163	Randy Moffitt	.08	260	Johnny Ray	.08	356	Leon Roberts	.08
164	Lloyd Moseby	.08	261	Rick Rhoden	.08	357	*Pat Sheridan*	.08
165	Rance Mulliniks	.08	262	Don Robinson	.08	358	Joe Simpson	.08
166	Jorge Orta	.08	263	Manny Sarmiento	.08	359	Don Slaught	.08
167	Dave Stieb	.10	264	Rod Scurry	.08	360	Paul Splittorff	.08
168	Willie Upshaw	.08	265	Kent Tekulve	.08	361	U.L. Washington	.08
169	Ernie Whitt	.08	266	Gene Tenace	.08	362	John Wathan	.08
170	Len Barker	.08	267	Jason Thompson	.08	363	Frank White	.08
171	Steve Bedrosian	.08	268	*Lee Tunnell*	.08	364	Willie Wilson	.12
172	Bruce Benedict	.08	269	*Marvell Wynne*	.08	365	Jim Barr	.08
173	Brett Butler	.15	270	Ray Burris	.08	366	Dave Bergman	.08
174	Rick Camp	.08	271	Gary Carter	.45	367	Fred Breining	.08
175	Chris Chambliss	.08	272	Warren Cromartie	.08	368	Bob Brenly	.08
176	Ken Dayley	.08	273	Andre Dawson	2.00	369	Jack Clark	.08
177	Pete Falcone	.08	274	Doug Flynn	.08	370	Chili Davis	.12
178	Terry Forster	.08	275	Terry Francona	.08	371	Mark Davis	.08
179	Gene Garber	.08	276	Bill Gullickson	.08	372	Darrell Evans	.08
180	Terry Harper	.08	277	Bob James	.08	373	Atlee Hammaker	.08

#	Player	Price	#	Player	Price	#	Player	Price
374	Mike Krukow	.08	470	Ben Hayes	.08	566	Mickey Hatcher	.08
375	Duane Kuiper	.08	471	Paul Householder	.08	567	Kent Hrbek	.20
376	Bill Laskey	.08	472	Tom Hume	.08	568	Rusty Kuntz	.08
377	Gary Lavelle	.08	473	Alan Knicely	.08	569	Tim Laudner	.08
378	Johnnie LeMaster	.08	474	Eddie Milner	.08	570	Rick Lysander	.08
379	Jeff Leonard	.08	475	Ron Oester	.08	571	Bobby Mitchell	.08
380	Randy Lerch	.08	476	Kelly Paris	.08	572	Ken Schrom	.08
381	Renie Martin	.08	477	Frank Pastore	.08	573	Ray Smith	.08
382	Andy McGaffigan	.08	478	Ted Power	.08	574	*Tim Teufel*	.30
383	Greg Minton	.08	479	Joe Price	.08	575	Frank Viola	.08
384	Tom O'Malley	.08	480	Charlie Puleo	.08	576	Gary Ward	.08
385	Max Venable	.08	481	*Gary Redus*	.25	577	Ron Washington	.08
386	Brad Wellman	.08	482	Bill Scherrer	.08	578	Len Whitehouse	.08
387	Joel Youngblood	.08	483	Mario Soto	.08	579	Al Williams	.08
388	Gary Allenson	.08	484	Alex Trevino	.08	580	Bob Bailor	.08
389	Luis Aponte	.08	485	Duane Walker	.08	581	Mark Bradley	.08
390	Tony Armas	.08	486	Larry Bowa	.08	582	Hubie Brooks	.08
391	Doug Bird	.08	487	Warren Brusstar	.08	583	Carlos Diaz	.08
392	Wade Boggs	4.00	488	Bill Buckner	.08	584	George Foster	.08
393	*Dennis Boyd*	.08	489	Bill Campbell	.08	585	Brian Giles	.08
394	Mike Brown	.08	490	Ron Cey	.08	586	Danny Heep	.08
395	Mark Clear	.08	491	Jody Davis	.08	587	Keith Hernandez	.08
396	Dennis Eckersley	.15	492	Leon Durham	.08	588	Ron Hodges	.08
397	Dwight Evans	.08	493	Mel Hall	.08	589	Scott Holman	.08
398	Rich Gedman	.08	494	Fergie Jenkins	.60	590	Dave Kingman	.15
399	Glenn Hoffman	.08	495	Jay Johnstone	.08	591	Ed Lynch	.08
400	Bruce Hurst	.08	496	*Craig Lefferts*	.20	592	*Jose Oquendo*	.15
401	John Henry Johnson	.08	497	*Carmelo Martinez*	.08	593	Jesse Orosco	.08
402	Ed Jurak	.08	498	Jerry Morales	.08	594	*Junior Ortiz*	.08
403	Rick Miller	.08	499	Keith Moreland	.08	595	Tom Seaver	1.50
404	Jeff Newman	.08	500	Dickie Noles	.08	596	*Doug Sisk*	.08
405	Reid Nichols	.08	501	Mike Proly	.08	597	Rusty Staub	.12
406	Bob Ojeda	.08	502	Chuck Rainey	.08	598	John Stearns	.08
407	Jerry Remy	.08	503	Dick Ruthven	.08	599	Darryl Strawberry	6.00
408	Jim Rice	.08	504	Ryne Sandberg	8.00	600	Craig Swan	.08
409	Bob Stanley	.08	505	Lee Smith	.15	601	*Walt Terrell*	.12
410	Dave Stapleton	.08	506	Steve Trout	.08	602	Mike Torrez	.08
411	John Tudor	.08	507	Gary Woods	.08	603	Mookie Wilson	.08
412	Carl Yastrzemski	.80	508	Juan Beniquez	.08	604	Jamie Allen	.08
413	Buddy Bell	.08	509	Bob Boone	.08	605	Jim Beattie	.08
414	Larry Biittner	.08	510	Rick Burleson	.08	606	Tony Bernazard	.08
415	John Butcher	.08	511	Rod Carew	.90	607	Manny Castillo	.08
416	Danny Darwin	.08	512	Bobby Clark	.08	608	Bill Caudill	.08
417	Bucky Dent	.08	513	John Curtis	.08	609	Bryan Clark	.08
418	Dave Hostetler	.08	514	Doug DeCinces	.08	610	Al Cowens	.08
419	Charlie Hough	.08	515	Brian Downing	.08	611	Dave Henderson	.08
420	Bobby Johnson	.08	516	Tim Foli	.08	612	Steve Henderson	.08
421	Odell Jones	.08	517	Ken Forsch	.08	613	Orlando Mercado	.08
422	Jon Matlack	.08	518	Bobby Grich	.08	614	Mike Moore	.08
423	*Pete O'Brien*	.30	519	Andy Hassler	.08	615	Ricky Nelson	.08
424	Larry Parrish	.08	520	Reggie Jackson	1.50	616	*Spike Owen*	.20
425	Mickey Rivers	.08	521	Ron Jackson	.08	617	Pat Putnam	.08
426	Billy Sample	.08	522	Tommy John	.12	618	Ron Roenicke	.08
427	Dave Schmidt	.08	523	Bruce Kison	.08	619	Mike Stanton	.08
428	*Mike Smithson*	.08	524	Steve Lubratich	.08	620	Bob Stoddard	.08
429	Bill Stein	.08	525	Fred Lynn	.12	621	Rick Sweet	.08
430	Dave Stewart	.15	526	*Gary Pettis*	.08	622	Roy Thomas	.08
431	Jim Sundberg	.08	527	Luis Sanchez	.08	623	Ed Vande Berg	.08
432	Frank Tanana	.08	528	Daryl Sconiers	.08	624	*Matt Young*	.08
433	Dave Tobik	.08	529	Ellis Valentine	.08	625	Richie Zisk	.08
434	Wayne Tolleson	.08	530	Rob Wilfong	.08	626	'83 All-Star Game Record Breaker(Fred Lynn)	.08
435	George Wright	.08	531	Mike Witt	.08			
436	Bill Almon	.08	532	Geoff Zahn	.08	627	'83 All-Star Game Record Breaker(Manny Trillo)	.08
437	*Keith Atherton*	.08	533	Bud Anderson	.08			
438	Dave Beard	.08	534	Chris Bando	.08	628	N.L. Iron Man(Steve Garvey)	.20
439	Tom Burgmeier	.08	535	Alan Bannister	.08			
440	Jeff Burroughs	.08	536	Bert Blyleven	.08	629	A.L. Batting Runner-Up(Rod Carew)	.25
441	*Chris Codiroli*	.08	537	Tom Brennan	.08			
442	*Tim Conroy*	.08	538	Jamie Easterly	.08	630	A.L. Batting Champion(Wade Boggs)	1.00
443	Mike Davis	.08	539	Juan Eichelberger	.08			
444	Wayne Gross	.08	540	Jim Essian	.08	631	Letting Go Of The Raines(Tim Raines)	.20
445	Garry Hancock	.08	541	Mike Fischlin	.08			
446	Mike Heath	.08	542	Julio Franco	.25	632	Double Trouble(Al Oliver)	.08
447	Rickey Henderson	3.00	543	Mike Hargrove	.08	633	All-Star Second Base(Steve Sax)	.08
448	*Don Hill*	.08	544	Toby Harrah	.08			
449	Bob Kearney	.08	545	Ron Hassey	.08	634	All-Star Shortstop(Dickie Thon)	.08
450	Bill Krueger	.08	546	*Neal Heaton*	.08			
451	Rick Langford	.08	547	Bake McBride	.08	635	Ace Firemen(Tippy Martinez, Dan Quisenberry)	.08
452	Carney Lansford	.08	548	Broderick Perkins	.08			
453	Davey Lopes	.08	549	Lary Sorensen	.08	636	Reds Reunited(Joe Morgan, Tony Perez, Pete Rose)	.65
454	Steve McCatty	.08	550	Dan Spillner	.08			
455	Dan Meyer	.08	551	Rick Sutcliffe	.08	637	Backstop Stars(Bob Boone, Lance Parrish)	.12
456	Dwayne Murphy	.08	552	Pat Tabler	.08			
457	Mike Norris	.08	553	Gorman Thomas	.08	638	The Pine Tar Incident, 7/24/83(George Brett, Gaylord Perry)	.30
458	Ricky Peters	.08	554	Andre Thornton	.08			
459	Tony Phillips	2.50	555	George Vukovich	.08	639	1983 No-Hitters(Dave Forsch, Dave Righetti, Mike Warren)	.08
460	Tom Underwood	.08	556	Darrell Brown	.08			
461	Mike Warren	.08	557	Tom Brunansky	.08	640	Retiring Superstars(Johnny Bench, Carl Yastrzemski)	1.00
462	Johnny Bench	.80	558	*Randy Bush*	.08			
463	Bruce Berenyi	.08	559	Bobby Castillo	.08	641	Going Out In Style(Gaylord Perry)	.15
464	Dann Bilardello	.08	560	John Castino	.08			
465	Cesar Cedeno	.08	561	Ron Davis	.08	642	300 Club & Strikeout Record(Steve Carlton)	.20
466	Dave Concepcion	.08	562	Dave Engle	.08			
467	Dan Driessen	.08	563	Lenny Faedo	.08			
468	*Nick Esasky*	.08	564	Pete Filson	.08			
469	Rich Gale	.08	565	Gary Gaetti	.12			

643	The Managers(Joe Altobelli, Paul Owens)	.08
644	The MVP(Rick Dempsey)	.08
645	The Rookie Winner(Mike Boddicker)	.08
646	The Clincher(Scott McGregor)	.08
647	Checklist: Orioles/Royals(Joe Altobelli)	.08
648	Checklist: Phillies/Giants(Paul Owens)	.08
649	Checklist: White Sox/Red Sox(Tony LaRussa)	.08
650	Checklist: Tigers/Rangers(Sparky Anderson)	.08
651	Checklist: Dodgers/A's(Tommy Lasorda)	.10
652	Checklist: Yankees/Reds(Billy Martin)	.08
653	Checklist: Blue Jays/Cubs(Bobby Cox)	.08
654	Checklist: Braves/Angels(Joe Torre)	.08
655	Checklist: Brewers/Indians(Rene Lacheman)	.08
656	Checklist: Astros/Twins(Bob Lillis)	.08
657	Checklist: Pirates/Mets(Chuck Tanner)	.08
658	Checklist: Expos/Mariners(Bill Virdon)	.08
659	Checklist: Padres/Specials(Dick Williams)	.08
660	Checklist: Cardinals/Specials(Whitey Herzog)	.08

1984 Fleer Update

Brett Butler
OUTFIELD

Following the lead of Topps, Fleer issued near the end of the baseball season a 132-card set to update player trades and include rookies not depicted in the regular issue. The cards are identical in design to the regular issue but are numbered U-1 through U-132. Available only as a boxed set through hobby dealers, the set was printed in limited quantities.

		MT
Complete Set (132):		500.00
Common Player:		.25
1	Willie Aikens	.25
2	Luis Aponte	.25
3	Mark Bailey	.25
4	Bob Bailor	.25
5	Dusty Baker	.35
6	Steve Balboni	.25

7	Alan Bannister	.25
8	Marty Barrett	.25
9	Dave Beard	.25
10	Joe Beckwith	.25
11	Dave Bergman	.25
12	Tony Bernazard	.25
13	Bruce Bochte	.25
14	Barry Bonnell	.25
15	Phil Bradley	.25
16	Fred Breining	.25
17	Mike Brown	.25
18	Bill Buckner	.35
19	Ray Burris	.25
20	John Butcher	.25
21	Brett Butler	.50
22	Enos Cabell	.25
23	Bill Campbell	.25
24	Bill Caudill	.25
25	Bobby Clark	.25
26	Bryan Clark	.25
27	*Roger Clemens*	240.00
28	Jaime Cocanower	.25
29	*Ron Darling*	2.50
30	Alvin Davis	.25
31	Bob Dernier	.25
32	Carlos Diaz	.25
33	Mike Easler	.25
34	Dennis Eckersley	10.00
35	Jim Essian	.25
36	Darrell Evans	.35
37	Mike Fitzgerald	.25
38	Tim Foli	.26
39	John Franco	6.00
40	George Frazier	.25
41	Rich Gale	.25
42	Barbaro Garbey	.25
43	*Dwight Gooden*	14.00
44	Goose Gossage	.40
45	Wayne Gross	.25
46	Mark Gubicza	2.00
47	Jackie Gutierrez	.25
48	Toby Harrah	.25
49	Ron Hassey	.25
50	Richie Hebner	.25
51	Willie Hernandez	.25
52	Ed Hodge	.25
53	Ricky Horton	.25
54	Art Howe	.25
55	Dane Iorg	.25
56	Brook Jacoby	.40
57	Dion James	.25
58	Mike Jeffcoat	.25
59	Ruppert Jones	.25
60	Bob Kearney	.25
61	*Jimmy Key*	15.00
62	Dave Kingman	.50
63	Brad Komminsk	.25
64	Jerry Koosman	.25
65	Wayne Krenchicki	.25
66	Rusty Kuntz	.25
67	Frank LaCorte	.25
68	Dennis Lamp	.25
69	Tito Landrum	.25
70	*Mark Langston*	10.00
71	Rick Leach	.25
72	Craig Lefferts	.25
73	Gary Lucas	.25
74	Jerry Martin	.25
75	Carmelo Martinez	.25
76	Mike Mason	.25
77	Gary Matthews	.25
78	Andy McGaffigan	.25
79	Joey McLaughlin	.25
80	Joe Morgan	6.00
81	Darryl Motley	.25
82	Graig Nettles	.50
83	Phil Niekro	4.00
84	Ken Oberkfell	.25
85	Al Oliver	.35
86	Jorge Orta	.25
87	Amos Otis	.25
88	Bob Owchinko	.25
89	Dave Parker	2.00
90	Jack Perconte	.25
91	Tony Perez	4.00
92	Gerald Perry	.35
93	*Kirby Puckett*	200.00
94	Shane Rawley	.25
95	Floyd Rayford	.25
96	Ron Reed	.25
97	R.J. Reynolds	.25
98	Gene Richards	.25
99	*Jose Rijo*	10.00
100	Jeff Robinson	.25
101	Ron Romanick	.25
102	Pete Rose	30.00

103	*Bret Saberhagen*	10.00
104	Scott Sanderson	.25
105	Dick Schofield	.25
106	Tom Seaver	15.00
107	Jim Slaton	.25
108	Mike Smithson	.25
109	Lary Sorensen	.25
110	Tim Stoddard	.25
111	Jeff Stone	.25
112	Champ Summers	.25
113	Jim Sundberg	.25
114	Rick Sutcliffe	.35
115	Craig Swan	.25
116	Derrel Thomas	.25
117	Gorman Thomas	.25
118	Alex Trevino	.25
119	Manny Trillo	.25
120	John Tudor	.25
121	Tom Underwood	.25
122	Mike Vail	.25
123	Tom Waddell	.25
124	Gary Ward	.25
125	Terry Whitfield	.25
126	Curtis Wilkerson	.25
127	Frank Williams	.25
128	Glenn Wilson	.25
129	John Wockenfuss	.25
130	Ned Yost	.25
131	Mike Young	.25
132	Checklist 1-132	.10

1985 Fleer

The 1985 Fleer set consists of 660 cards, each measuring 2-1/2" x 3-1/2". Card fronts feature a color photo plus the player's team logo and the word "Fleer." The photos have a color-coded frame which corresponds to the player's team. A grey border surrounds the frame. Backs are similar in design to previous years, but have two shades of red and black ink on white stock. For the fourth consecutive year, Fleer included special cards and team checklists in the set. Also incorporated in a set for the first time were ten "Major League Prospect" cards, each featuring two rookie hopefuls. The set was issued with team logo stickers.

		MT
Complete Set (660):		130.00
Common Player:		.06
Wax Box:		275.00
1	Doug Bair	.06
2	Juan Berenguer	.06
3	Dave Bergman	.06
4	Tom Brookens	.06
5	Marty Castillo	.06
6	Darrell Evans	.06
7	Barbaro Garbey	.06
8	Kirk Gibson	.06
9	John Grubb	.06
10	Willie Hernandez	.06

#	Player	Price
11	Larry Herndon	.06
12	Howard Johnson	.06
13	Ruppert Jones	.06
14	Rusty Kuntz	.06
15	Chet Lemon	.06
16	Aurelio Lopez	.06
17	Sid Monge	.06
18	Jack Morris	.10
19	Lance Parrish	.10
20	Dan Petry	.06
21	Dave Rozema	.06
22	Bill Scherrer	.06
23	Alan Trammell	.25
24	Lou Whitaker	.15
25	Milt Wilcox	.06
26	Kurt Bevacqua	.06
27	*Greg Booker*	.06
28	Bobby Brown	.06
29	Luis DeLeon	.06
30	Dave Dravecky	.06
31	Tim Flannery	.06
32	Steve Garvey	.35
33	Goose Gossage	.12
34	Tony Gwynn	6.00
35	Greg Harris	.06
36	Andy Hawkins	.06
37	Terry Kennedy	.06
38	Craig Lefferts	.06
39	Tim Lollar	.06
40	Carmelo Martinez	.06
41	Kevin McReynolds	.06
42	Graig Nettles	.10
43	Luis Salazar	.06
44	Eric Show	.06
45	Garry Templeton	.06
46	Mark Thurmond	.06
47	Ed Whitson	.06
48	Alan Wiggins	.06
49	Rich Bordi	.06
50	Larry Bowa	.06
51	Warren Brusstar	.06
52	Ron Cey	.06
53	*Henry Cotto*	.06
54	Jody Davis	.06
55	Bob Dernier	.06
56	Leon Durham	.06
57	Dennis Eckersley	.30
58	George Frazier	.06
59	Richie Hebner	.06
60	Dave Lopes	.06
61	Gary Matthews	.06
62	Keith Moreland	.06
63	Rick Reuschel	.06
64	Dick Ruthven	.06
65	Ryne Sandberg	5.00
66	Scott Sanderson	.06
67	Lee Smith	.10
68	Tim Stoddard	.06
69	Rick Sutcliffe	.06
70	Steve Trout	.06
71	Gary Woods	.06
72	Wally Backman	.06
73	Bruce Berenyi	.06
74	Hubie Brooks	.06
75	Kelvin Chapman	.06
76	Ron Darling	.06
77	Sid Fernandez	.06
78	Mike Fitzgerald	.06
79	George Foster	.06
80	Brent Gaff	.06
81	Ron Gardenhire	.06
82	Dwight Gooden	1.00
83	Tom Gorman	.06
84	Danny Heep	.06
85	Keith Hernandez	.06
86	Ray Knight	.06
87	Ed Lynch	.06
88	Jose Oquendo	.06
89	Jesse Orosco	.06
90	*Rafael Santana*	.06
91	Doug Sisk	.06
92	Rusty Staub	.10
93	Darryl Strawberry	1.00
94	Walt Terrell	.06
95	Mookie Wilson	.06
96	Jim Acker	.06
97	Willie Aikens	.06
98	Doyle Alexander	.06
99	Jesse Barfield	.06
100	George Bell	.06
101	Jim Clancy	.06
102	Dave Collins	.06
103	Tony Fernandez	.06
104	Damaso Garcia	.06
105	Jim Gott	.06
106	Alfredo Griffin	.06
107	Garth Iorg	.06
108	Roy Lee Jackson	.06
109	Cliff Johnson	.06
110	Jimmy Key	2.50
111	Dennis Lamp	.06
112	Rick Leach	.06
113	Luis Leal	.06
114	Buck Martinez	.06
115	Lloyd Moseby	.06
116	Rance Mulliniks	.06
117	Dave Stieb	.06
118	Willie Upshaw	.06
119	Ernie Whitt	.06
120	Mike Armstrong	.06
121	Don Baylor	.12
122	Marty Bystrom	.06
123	Rick Cerone	.06
124	Joe Cowley	.06
125	Brian Dayett	.06
126	Tim Foli	.06
127	Ray Fontenot	.06
128	Ken Griffey	.10
129	Ron Guidry	.10
130	Toby Harrah	.06
131	Jay Howell	.06
132	Steve Kemp	.06
133	Don Mattingly	9.00
134	Bobby Meacham	.06
135	John Montefusco	.06
136	Omar Moreno	.06
137	Dale Murray	.06
138	Phil Niekro	.50
139	*Mike Pagliarulo*	.20
140	Willie Randolph	.06
141	Dennis Rasmussen	.06
142	Dave Righetti	.06
143	Jose Rijo	.40
144	Andre Robertson	.06
145	Bob Shirley	.06
146	Dave Winfield	3.00
147	Butch Wynegar	.06
148	Gary Allenson	.06
149	Tony Armas	.06
150	Marty Barrett	.06
151	Wade Boggs	4.00
152	Dennis Boyd	.06
153	Bill Buckner	.06
154	Mark Clear	.06
155	Roger Clemens	40.00
156	Steve Crawford	.06
157	Mike Easler	.06
158	Dwight Evans	.06
159	Rich Gedman	.06
160	Jackie Gutierrez	.06
161	Bruce Hurst	.06
162	John Henry Johnson	.06
163	Rick Miller	.06
164	Reid Nichols	.06
165	*Al Nipper*	.06
166	Bob Ojeda	.06
167	Jerry Remy	.06
168	Jim Rice	.06
169	Bob Stanley	.06
170	Mike Boddicker	.06
171	Al Bumbry	.06
172	Todd Cruz	.06
173	Rich Dauer	.06
174	Storm Davis	.06
175	Rick Dempsey	.06
176	Jim Dwyer	.06
177	Mike Flanagan	.06
178	Dan Ford	.06
179	Wayne Gross	.06
180	John Lowenstein	.06
181	Dennis Martinez	.10
182	Tippy Martinez	.06
183	Scott McGregor	.06
184	Eddie Murray	2.00
185	Joe Nolan	.06
186	Floyd Rayford	.06
187	Cal Ripken, Jr.	10.00
188	Gary Roenicke	.06
189	Lenn Sakata	.06
190	John Shelby	.06
191	Ken Singleton	.06
192	Sammy Stewart	.06
193	Bill Swaggerty	.06
194	Tom Underwood	.06
195	Mike Young	.06
196	Steve Balboni	.06
197	Joe Beckwith	.06
198	Bud Black	.06
199	George Brett	4.50
200	Onix Concepcion	.06
201	*Mark Gubicza*	.80
202	Larry Gura	.06
203	Mark Huismann	.06
204	Dane Iorg	.06
205	Danny Jackson	.06
206	Charlie Leibrandt	.06
207	Hal McRae	.10
208	Darryl Motley	.06
209	Jorge Orta	.06
210	Greg Pryor	.06
211	Dan Quisenberry	.06
212	Bret Saberhagen	2.00
213	Pat Sheridan	.06
214	Don Slaught	.06
215	U.L. Washington	.06
216	John Wathan	.06
217	Frank White	.06
218	Willie Wilson	.06
219	Neil Allen	.06
220	Joaquin Andujar	.06
221	Steve Braun	.06
222	Danny Cox	.06
223	Bob Forsch	.06
224	David Green	.06
225	George Hendrick	.06
226	Tom Herr	.06
227	*Ricky Horton*	.06
228	Art Howe	.06
229	Mike Jorgensen	.06
230	Kurt Kepshire	.06
231	Jeff Lahti	.06
232	Tito Landrum	.06
233	Dave LaPoint	.06
234	Willie McGee	.15
235	*Tom Nieto*	.06
236	*Terry Pendleton*	2.00
237	Darrell Porter	.06
238	Dave Rucker	.06
239	Lonnie Smith	.06
240	Ozzie Smith	2.50
241	Bruce Sutter	.06
242	Andy Van Slyke	.06
243	Dave Von Ohlen	.06
244	Larry Andersen	.06
245	Bill Campbell	.06
246	Steve Carlton	1.50
247	Tim Corcoran	.06
248	Ivan DeJesus	.06
249	John Denny	.06
250	Bo Diaz	.06
251	Greg Gross	.06
252	Kevin Gross	.06
253	Von Hayes	.06
254	Al Holland	.06
255	Charles Hudson	.06
256	Jerry Koosman	.06
257	Joe Lefebvre	.06
258	Sixto Lezcano	.06
259	Garry Maddox	.06
260	Len Matuszek	.06
261	Tug McGraw	.06
262	Al Oliver	.06
263	Shane Rawley	.06
264	Juan Samuel	.06
265	Mike Schmidt	5.00
266	*Jeff Stone*	.06
267	Ozzie Virgil	.06
268	Glenn Wilson	.06
269	John Wockenfuss	.06
270	Darrell Brown	.06
271	Tom Brunansky	.06
272	Randy Bush	.06
273	John Butcher	.06
274	Bobby Castillo	.06
275	Ron Davis	.06
276	Dave Engle	.06
277	Pete Filson	.06
278	Gary Gaetti	.12
279	Mickey Hatcher	.06
280	Ed Hodge	.06
281	Kent Hrbek	.20
282	Houston Jimenez	.06
283	Tim Laudner	.06
284	Rick Lysander	.06
285	Dave Meier	.06
286	Kirby Puckett	30.00
287	Pat Putnam	.06
288	Ken Schrom	.06
289	Mike Smithson	.06
290	Tim Teufel	.06
291	Frank Viola	.06
292	Ron Washington	.06
293	Don Aase	.06
294	Juan Beniquez	.06
295	Bob Boone	.06
296	Mike Brown	.06
297	Rod Carew	1.50
298	Doug Corbett	.06

No.	Player	Price
299	Doug DeCinces	.06
300	Brian Downing	.06
301	Ken Forsch	.06
302	Bobby Grich	.06
303	Reggie Jackson	2.00
304	Tommy John	.10
305	Curt Kaufman	.06
306	Bruce Kison	.06
307	Fred Lynn	.10
308	Gary Pettis	.06
309	*Ron Romanick*	.06
310	Luis Sanchez	.06
311	Dick Schofield	.06
312	Daryl Sconiers	.06
313	Jim Slaton	.06
314	Derrel Thomas	.06
315	Rob Wilfong	.06
316	Mike Witt	.06
317	Geoff Zahn	.06
318	Len Barker	.06
319	Steve Bedrosian	.06
320	Bruce Benedict	.06
321	Rick Camp	.06
322	Chris Chambliss	.06
323	*Jeff Dedmon*	.06
324	Terry Forster	.06
325	Gene Garber	.06
326	*Albert Hall*	.06
327	Terry Harper	.06
328	Bob Horner	.06
329	Glenn Hubbard	.06
330	Randy S. Johnson	.06
331	Brad Komminsk	.06
332	Rick Mahler	.06
333	Craig McMurtry	.06
334	Donnie Moore	.06
335	Dale Murphy	.50
336	Ken Oberkfell	.06
337	Pascual Perez	.06
338	Gerald Perry	.06
339	Rafael Ramirez	.06
340	Jerry Royster	.06
341	Alex Trevino	.06
342	Claudell Washington	.06
343	Alan Ashby	.06
344	*Mark Bailey*	.06
345	Kevin Bass	.06
346	Enos Cabell	.06
347	Jose Cruz	.06
348	Bill Dawley	.06
349	Frank DiPino	.06
350	Bill Doran	.06
351	Phil Garner	.06
352	Bob Knepper	.06
353	Mike LaCoss	.06
354	Jerry Mumphrey	.06
355	Joe Niekro	.06
356	Terry Puhl	.06
357	Craig Reynolds	.06
358	Vern Ruhle	.06
359	Nolan Ryan	10.00
360	Joe Sambito	.06
361	Mike Scott	.06
362	Dave Smith	.06
363	*Julio Solano*	.06
364	Dickie Thon	.06
365	Denny Walling	.06
366	Dave Anderson	.06
367	Bob Bailor	.06
368	Greg Brock	.06
369	Carlos Diaz	.06
370	Pedro Guerrero	.06
371	*Orel Hershiser*	3.50
372	Rick Honeycutt	.06
373	Burt Hooton	.06
374	*Ken Howell*	.15
375	Ken Landreaux	.06
376	Candy Maldonado	.06
377	Mike Marshall	.06
378	Tom Niedenfuer	.06
379	Alejandro Pena	.06
380	Jerry Reuss	.06
381	*R.J. Reynolds*	.06
382	German Rivera	.06
383	Bill Russell	.06
384	Steve Sax	.06
385	Mike Scioscia	.06
386	*Franklin Stubbs*	.06
387	Fernando Valenzuela	.10
388	Bob Welch	.06
389	Terry Whitfield	.06
390	Steve Yeager	.06
391	Pat Zachry	.06
392	Fred Breining	.06
393	Gary Carter	.40
394	Andre Dawson	.90
395	Miguel Dilone	.06
396	Dan Driessen	.06
397	Doug Flynn	.06
398	Terry Francona	.06
399	Bill Gullickson	.06
400	Bob James	.06
401	Charlie Lea	.06
402	Bryan Little	.06
403	Gary Lucas	.06
404	David Palmer	.06
405	Tim Raines	.30
406	Mike Ramsey	.06
407	Jeff Reardon	.06
408	Steve Rogers	.06
409	Dan Schatzeder	.06
410	Bryn Smith	.06
411	Mike Stenhouse	.06
412	Tim Wallach	.10
413	Jim Wohlford	.06
414	Bill Almon	.06
415	Keith Atherton	.06
416	Bruce Bochte	.06
417	Tom Burgmeier	.06
418	Ray Burris	.06
419	Bill Caudill	.06
420	Chris Codiroli	.06
421	Tim Conroy	.06
422	Mike Davis	.06
423	Jim Essian	.06
424	Mike Heath	.06
425	Rickey Henderson	3.00
426	Donnie Hill	.06
427	Dave Kingman	.12
428	Bill Krueger	.06
429	Carney Lansford	.06
430	Steve McCatty	.06
431	Joe Morgan	.40
432	Dwayne Murphy	.06
433	Tony Phillips	.30
434	Lary Sorensen	.06
435	Mike Warren	.06
436	*Curt Young*	.06
437	Luis Aponte	.06
438	Chris Bando	.06
439	Tony Bernazard	.06
440	Bert Blyleven	.06
441	Brett Butler	.15
442	Ernie Camacho	.06
443	Joe Carter	6.00
444	Carmelo Castillo	.06
445	Jamie Easterly	.06
446	*Steve Farr*	.30
447	Mike Fischlin	.06
448	Julio Franco	.15
449	Mel Hall	.06
450	Mike Hargrove	.06
451	Neal Heaton	.06
452	Brook Jacoby	.06
453	*Mike Jeffcoat*	.06
454	*Don Schulze*	.06
455	Roy Smith	.06
456	Pat Tabler	.06
457	Andre Thornton	.06
458	George Vukovich	.06
459	Tom Waddell	.06
460	Jerry Willard	.06
461	Dale Berra	.06
462	John Candelaria	.06
463	Jose DeLeon	.06
464	Doug Frobel	.06
465	Cecilio Guante	.06
466	Brian Harper	.06
467	Lee Lacy	.06
468	Bill Madlock	.06
469	Lee Mazzilli	.06
470	Larry McWilliams	.06
471	Jim Morrison	.06
472	Tony Pena	.06
473	Johnny Ray	.06
474	Rick Rhoden	.06
475	Don Robinson	.06
476	Rod Scurry	.06
477	Kent Tekulve	.06
478	Jason Thompson	.06
479	John Tudor	.06
480	Lee Tunnell	.06
481	Marvell Wynne	.06
482	Salome Barojas	.06
483	Dave Beard	.06
484	Jim Beattie	.06
485	Barry Bonnell	.06
486	*Phil Bradley*	.06
487	Al Cowens	.06
488	*Alvin Davis*	.06
489	Dave Henderson	.06
490	Steve Henderson	.06
491	Bob Kearney	.06
492	Mark Langston	2.00
493	Larry Milbourne	.06
494	Paul Mirabella	.06
495	Mike Moore	.06
496	Edwin Nunez	.06
497	Spike Owen	.06
498	Jack Perconte	.06
499	Ken Phelps	.06
500	*Jim Presley*	.06
501	Mike Stanton	.06
502	Bob Stoddard	.06
503	Gorman Thomas	.06
504	Ed Vande Berg	.06
505	Matt Young	.06
506	Juan Agosto	.06
507	Harold Baines	.15
508	Floyd Bannister	.06
509	Britt Burns	.06
510	Julio Cruz	.06
511	Richard Dotson	.06
512	Jerry Dybzinski	.06
513	Carlton Fisk	.75
514	Scott Fletcher	.06
515	Jerry Hairston	.06
516	Marc Hill	.06
517	LaMarr Hoyt	.06
518	Ron Kittle	.06
519	Rudy Law	.06
520	Vance Law	.06
521	Greg Luzinski	.10
522	Gene Nelson	.06
523	Tom Paciorek	.06
524	Ron Reed	.06
525	Bert Roberge	.06
526	Tom Seaver	1.25
527	Roy Smalley	.06
528	Dan Spillner	.06
529	Mike Squires	.06
530	Greg Walker	.06
531	Cesar Cedeno	.06
532	Dave Concepcion	.06
533	*Eric Davis*	2.50
534	Nick Esasky	.06
535	Tom Foley	.06
536	*John Franco*	.75
537	Brad Gulden	.06
538	Tom Hume	.06
539	Wayne Krenchicki	.06
540	Andy McGaffigan	.06
541	Eddie Milner	.06
542	Ron Oester	.06
543	Bob Owchinko	.06
544	Dave Parker	.25
545	Frank Pastore	.06
546	Tony Perez	.15
547	Ted Power	.06
548	Joe Price	.06
549	Gary Redus	.06
550	Pete Rose	3.00
551	Jeff Russell	.06
552	Mario Soto	.06
553	*Jay Tibbs*	.06
554	Duane Walker	.06
555	Alan Bannister	.06
556	Buddy Bell	.06
557	Danny Darwin	.06
558	Charlie Hough	.06
559	Bobby Jones	.06
560	Odell Jones	.06
561	*Jeff Kunkel*	.06
562	Mike Mason	.06
563	Pete O'Brien	.06
564	Larry Parrish	.06
565	Mickey Rivers	.06
566	Billy Sample	.06
567	Dave Schmidt	.06
568	Donnie Scott	.06
569	Dave Stewart	.12
570	Frank Tanana	.06
571	Wayne Tolleson	.06
572	Gary Ward	.06
573	Curtis Wilkerson	.06
574	George Wright	.06
575	Ned Yost	.06
576	Mark Brouhard	.06
577	Mike Caldwell	.06
578	Bobby Clark	.06
579	Jaime Cocanower	.06
580	Cecil Cooper	.06
581	Rollie Fingers	.40
582	Jim Gantner	.06
583	Moose Haas	.06
584	Dion James	.06
585	Pete Ladd	.06
586	Rick Manning	.06

587	Bob McClure	.06
588	Paul Molitor	3.00
589	Charlie Moore	.06
590	Ben Oglivie	.06
591	Chuck Porter	.06
592	*Randy Ready*	.06
593	Ed Romero	.06
594	Bill Schroeder	.06
595	Ray Searage	.06
596	Ted Simmons	.06
597	Jim Sundberg	.06
598	Don Sutton	.35
599	Tom Tellmann	.06
600	Rick Waits	.06
601	Robin Yount	3.00
602	Dusty Baker	.10
603	Bob Brenly	.06
604	Jack Clark	.06
605	Chili Davis	.15
606	Mark Davis	.06
607	*Dan Gladden*	.50
608	Atlee Hammaker	.06
609	Mike Krukow	.06
610	Duane Kuiper	.06
611	Bob Lacey	.06
612	Bill Laskey	.06
613	Gary Lavelle	.06
614	Johnnie LeMaster	.06
615	Jeff Leonard	.06
616	Randy Lerch	.06
617	Greg Minton	.06
618	Steve Nicosia	.06
619	Gene Richards	.06
620	*Jeff Robinson*	.06
621	Scot Thompson	.06
622	Manny Trillo	.06
623	Brad Wellman	.06
624	*Frank Williams*	.06
625	Joel Youngblood	.06
626	Cal Ripken, Jr. (In Action)	4.00
627	Mike Schmidt (In Action)	1.50
628	Giving the Signs(Sparky Anderson)	.10
629	A.L. Pitcher's Nightmare(Rickey Henderson, Dave Winfield)	1.00
630	N.L. Pitcher's Nightmare(Ryne Sandberg, Mike Schmidt)	2.00
631	N.L. All-Stars(Gary Carter, Steve Garvey, Ozzie Smith, Darryl Strawberry)	.25
632	All-Star Game Winning Battery(Gary Carter, Charlie Lea)	.12
633	N.L. Pennant Clinchers(Steve Garvey, Goose Gossage)	.20
634	N.L. Rookie Phenoms(Dwight Gooden, Juan Samuel)	.25
635	Toronto's Big Guns(Willie Upshaw)	.06
636	Toronto's Big Guns(Lloyd Moseby)	.06
637	Holland(Al Holland)	.06
638	Tunnell(Lee Tunnell)	.06
639	Reggie Jackson (In Action)	.75
640	Pete Rose (In Action)	.75
641	Father & Son(Cal Ripken, Jr., Cal Ripken, Sr.)	4.00
642	Cubs team	.10
643	1984's Two Perfect Games & One No-Hitter(Jack Morris, David Palmer, Mike Witt)	.06
644	Major League Prospect(Willie Lozado, Vic Mata)	.06
645	Major League Prospect(*Kelly Gruber*), (*Randy O'Neal*)	.15
646	Major League Prospect(*Jose Roman*), (*Joel Skinner*)	.06
647	Major League Prospect(*Steve Kiefer*), (*Danny Tartabull*)	1.50
648	Major League Prospect(*Rob Deer*), (*Alejandro Sanchez*)	.15
649	Major League Prospect(*Shawon Dunston*), (*Bill Hatcher*)	2.00
650	Major League Prospect(*Mike Bielecki*), (*Ron Robinson*)	.10

651	Major League Prospect(*Zane Smith*), (*Paul Zuvella*)	.15
652	Major League Prospect(*Glenn Davis*), (*Joe Hesketh*)	.20
653	Major League Prospect(*Steve Jeltz*), (*John Russell*)	.10
654	Checklist 1-95	.06
655	Checklist 96-195	.06
656	Checklist 196-292	.06
657	Checklist 293-391	.06
658	Checklist 392-481	.06
659	Checklist 482-575	.06
660	Checklist 576-660	.06

1985 Fleer Update

For the second straight year, Fleer issued a 132-card update set. Cards portray traded players on their new teams and also include rookies not depicted in the regular issue. The cards are identical in design to the 1985 Fleer set but are numbered U-1 through U-132. The set was issued with team logo stickers in a specially designed box and was available only through hobby dealers.

		MT
Complete Set (132):		25.00
Common Player:		.10
1	Don Aase	.10
2	Bill Almon	.10
3	Dusty Baker	.15
4	Dale Berra	.10
5	Karl Best	.10
6	Tim Birtsas	.10
7	Vida Blue	.10
8	Rich Bordi	.10
9	Daryl Boston	.15
10	Hubie Brooks	.10
11	Chris Brown	.10
12	Tom Browning	.35
13	Al Bumbry	.10
14	Tim Burke	.10
15	Ray Burris	.10
16	Jeff Burroughs	.10
17	Ivan Calderon	.10
18	Jeff Calhoun	.10
19	Bill Campbell	.10
20	Don Carman	.10
21	Gary Carter	.50
22	Bobby Castillo	.10
23	Bill Caudill	.10
24	Rick Cerone	.10
25	Jack Clark	.10
26	Pat Clements	.10
27	Stewart Cliburn	.10
28	Vince Coleman	.60
29	Dave Collins	.10
30	Fritz Connally	.10
31	Henry Cotto	.10
32	Danny Darwin	.10

33	*Darren Daulton*	6.00
34	Jerry Davis	.10
35	Brian Dayett	.10
36	Ken Dixon	.10
37	Tommy Dunbar	.10
38	Mariano Duncan	.75
39	Bob Fallon	.10
40	Brian Fisher	.10
41	Mike Fitzgerald	.10
42	Ray Fontenot	.10
43	Greg Gagne	.75
44	Oscar Gamble	.10
45	Jim Gott	.10
46	David Green	.10
47	Alfredo Griffin	.10
48	*Ozzie Guillen*	1.50
49	Toby Harrah	.10
50	Ron Hassey	.10
51	Rickey Henderson	2.50
52	Steve Henderson	.10
53	George Hendrick	.10
54	Teddy Higuera	.10
55	Al Holland	.10
56	Burt Hooton	.10
57	Jay Howell	.10
58	LaMarr Hoyt	.10
59	Tim Hulett	.10
60	Bob James	.10
61	Cliff Johnson	.10
62	Howard Johnson	.10
63	Ruppert Jones	.10
64	Steve Kemp	.10
65	Bruce Kison	.10
66	Mike LaCoss	.10
67	Lee Lacy	.10
68	Dave LaPoint	.10
69	Gary Lavelle	.10
70	Vance Law	.10
71	Manny Lee	.10
72	Sixto Lezcano	.10
73	Tim Lollar	.10
74	Urbano Lugo	.10
75	Fred Lynn	.25
76	Steve Lyons	.15
77	Mickey Mahler	.10
78	Ron Mathis	.10
79	Len Matuszek	.10
80	Oddibe McDowell	.10
81	Roger McDowell	.50
82	Donnie Moore	.10
83	Ron Musselman	.10
84	Al Oliver	.15
85	Joe Orsulak	.25
86	Dan Pasqua	.40
87	Chris Pittaro	.10
88	Rick Reuschel	.10
89	Earnie Riles	.10
90	Jerry Royster	.10
91	Dave Rozema	.10
92	Dave Rucker	.10
93	Vern Ruhle	.10
94	Mark Salas	.10
95	Luis Salazar	.10
96	Joe Sambito	.10
97	Billy Sample	.10
98	Alex Sanchez	.10
99	Calvin Schiraldi	.10
100	Rick Schu	.10
101	Larry Sheets	.10
102	Ron Shepherd	.10
103	Nelson Simmons	.10
104	Don Slaught	.10
105	Roy Smalley	.10
106	Lonnie Smith	.10
107	Nate Snell	.10
108	Lary Sorensen	.10
109	Chris Speier	.10
110	Mike Stenhouse	.10
111	Tim Stoddard	.10
112	John Stuper	.10
113	Jim Sundberg	.10
114	Bruce Sutter	.10
115	Don Sutton	.60
116	Bruce Tanner	.10
117	Kent Tekulve	.10
118	Walt Terrell	.10
119	*Mickey Tettleton*	3.00
120	Rich Thompson	.10
121	Louis Thornton	.10
122	Alex Trevino	.10
123	John Tudor	.10
124	Jose Uribe	.10
125	Dave Valle	.20
126	Dave Von Ohlen	.10
127	Curt Wardle	.10
128	U.L. Washington	.10

1986 Fleer

The 1986 Fleer set contains 660 color cards measuring 2-1/2" x 3-1/2". The card fronts feature a player photo enclosed by a dark blue border. The card backs are minus the black-and-white photo that was included in past Fleer efforts. Player biographical and statistical information appear in black and yellow on white stock. As in 1985, Fleer devoted ten cards, entitled "Major League Prospects," to twenty promising rookie players. The 1986 set, as in the previous four years was issued with team logo stickers.

		MT
Complete Set (660):		70.00
Common Player:		.06
Wax Box:		120.00
1	Steve Balboni	.08
2	Joe Beckwith	.08
3	Buddy Biancalana	.08
4	Bud Black	.08
5	George Brett	2.25
6	Onix Concepcion	.08
7	Steve Farr	.08
8	Mark Gubicza	.08
9	Dane Iorg	.08
10	Danny Jackson	.08
11	Lynn Jones	.08
12	Mike Jones	.08
13	Charlie Leibrandt	.08
14	Hal McRae	.10
15	Omar Moreno	.08
16	Darryl Motley	.08
17	Jorge Orta	.08
18	Dan Quisenberry	.08
19	Bret Saberhagen	.15
20	Pat Sheridan	.08
21	Lonnie Smith	.08
22	Jim Sundberg	.08
23	John Wathan	.08
24	Frank White	.08
25	Willie Wilson	.08
26	Joaquin Andujar	.08
27	Steve Braun	.08
28	Bill Campbell	.08
29	Cesar Cedeno	.08
30	Jack Clark	.08
31	Vince Coleman	.30
32	Danny Cox	.08
33	Ken Dayley	.08
34	Ivan DeJesus	.08
35	Bob Forsch	.08
36	Brian Harper	.08
37	Tom Herr	.08
38	Ricky Horton	.08
39	Kurt Kepshire	.08

40	Jeff Lahti	.08
41	Tito Landrum	.08
42	Willie McGee	.10
43	Tom Nieto	.08
44	Terry Pendleton	.10
45	Darrell Porter	.08
46	Ozzie Smith	1.50
47	John Tudor	.08
48	Andy Van Slyke	.08
49	Todd Worrell	.40
50	Jim Acker	.08
51	Doyle Alexander	.08
52	Jesse Barfield	.08
53	George Bell	.08
54	Jeff Burroughs	.08
55	Bill Caudill	.08
56	Jim Clancy	.08
57	Tony Fernandez	.08
58	Tom Filer	.08
59	Damaso Garcia	.08
60	Tom Henke	.08
61	Garth Iorg	.08
62	Cliff Johnson	.08
63	Jimmy Key	.10
64	Dennis Lamp	.08
65	Gary Lavelle	.08
66	Buck Martinez	.08
67	Lloyd Moseby	.08
68	Rance Mulliniks	.08
69	Al Oliver	.08
70	Dave Stieb	.08
71	Louis Thornton	.08
72	Willie Upshaw	.08
73	Ernie Whitt	.08
74	Rick Aguilera	1.00
75	Wally Backman	.08
76	Gary Carter	.35
77	Ron Darling	.08
78	Len Dykstra	2.00
79	Sid Fernandez	.08
80	George Foster	.08
81	Dwight Gooden	.45
82	Tom Gorman	.08
83	Danny Heep	.08
84	Keith Hernandez	.08
85	Howard Johnson	.08
86	Ray Knight	.08
87	Terry Leach	.08
88	Ed Lynch	.08
89	Roger McDowell	.40
90	Jesse Orosco	.08
91	Tom Paciorek	.08
92	Ronn Reynolds	.08
93	Rafael Santana	.08
94	Doug Sisk	.08
95	Rusty Staub	.10
96	Darryl Strawberry	.75
97	Mookie Wilson	.08
98	Neil Allen	.08
99	Don Baylor	.12
100	Dale Berra	.08
101	Rich Bordi	.08
102	Marty Bystrom	.08
103	Joe Cowley	.08
104	Brian Fisher	.08
105	Ken Griffey	.10
106	Ron Guidry	.12
107	Ron Hassey	.08
108	Rickey Henderson	.75
109	Don Mattingly	3.00
110	Bobby Meacham	.08
111	John Montefusco	.08
112	Phil Niekro	.50
113	Mike Pagliarulo	.08
114	Dan Pasqua	.08
115	Willie Randolph	.08
116	Dave Righetti	.08
117	Andre Robertson	.08
118	Billy Sample	.08
119	Bob Shirley	.08
120	Ed Whitson	.08
121	Dave Winfield	1.00
122	Butch Wynegar	.08
123	Dave Anderson	.08
124	Bob Bailor	.08
125	Greg Brock	.08
126	Enos Cabell	.08
127	Bobby Castillo	.08
128	Carlos Diaz	.08
129	Mariano Duncan	.15
130	Pedro Guerrero	.08
131	Orel Hershiser	.15
132	Rick Honeycutt	.08
133	Ken Howell	.08
134	Ken Landreaux	.08
135	Bill Madlock	.08

136	Candy Maldonado	.08
137	Mike Marshall	.08
138	Len Matuszek	.08
139	Tom Niedenfuer	.08
140	Alejandro Pena	.08
141	Jerry Reuss	.08
142	Bill Russell	.08
143	Steve Sax	.08
144	Mike Scioscia	.08
145	Fernando Valenzuela	.10
146	Bob Welch	.08
147	Terry Whitfield	.08
148	Juan Beniquez	.08
149	Bob Boone	.08
150	John Candelaria	.08
151	Rod Carew	.70
152	Stewart Cliburn	.08
153	Doug DeCinces	.08
154	Brian Downing	.08
155	Ken Forsch	.08
156	Craig Gerber	.08
157	Bobby Grich	.08
158	George Hendrick	.08
159	Al Holland	.08
160	Reggie Jackson	1.00
161	Ruppert Jones	.08
162	Urbano Lugo	.08
163	Kirk McCaskill	.25
164	Donnie Moore	.08
165	Gary Pettis	.08
166	Ron Romanick	.08
167	Dick Schofield	.08
168	Daryl Sconiers	.08
169	Jim Slaton	.08
170	Don Sutton	.35
171	Mike Witt	.08
172	Buddy Bell	.08
173	Tom Browning	.08
174	Dave Concepcion	.08
175	Eric Davis	.45
176	Bo Diaz	.08
177	Nick Esasky	.08
178	John Franco	.08
179	Tom Hume	.08
180	Wayne Krenchicki	.08
181	Andy McGaffigan	.08
182	Eddie Milner	.08
183	Ron Oester	.08
184	Dave Parker	.10
185	Frank Pastore	.08
186	Tony Perez	.15
187	Ted Power	.08
188	Joe Price	.08
189	Gary Redus	.08
190	Ron Robinson	.08
191	Pete Rose	.75
192	Mario Soto	.08
193	John Stuper	.08
194	Jay Tibbs	.08
195	Dave Van Gorder	.08
196	Max Venable	.08
197	Juan Agosto	.08
198	Harold Baines	.10
199	Floyd Bannister	.08
200	Britt Burns	.08
201	Julio Cruz	.08
202	Joel Davis	.08
203	Richard Dotson	.08
204	Carlton Fisk	.50
205	Scott Fletcher	.08
206	Ozzie Guillen	.80
207	Jerry Hairston	.08
208	Tim Hulett	.08
209	Bob James	.08
210	Ron Kittle	.08
211	Rudy Law	.08
212	Bryan Little	.08
213	Gene Nelson	.08
214	Reid Nichols	.08
215	Luis Salazar	.08
216	Tom Seaver	1.00
217	Dan Spillner	.08
218	Bruce Tanner	.08
219	Greg Walker	.08
220	Dave Wehrmeister	.08
221	Juan Berenguer	.08
222	Dave Bergman	.08
223	Tom Brookens	.08
224	Darrell Evans	.08
225	Barbaro Garbey	.08
226	Kirk Gibson	.08
227	John Grubb	.08
228	Willie Hernandez	.08
229	Larry Herndon	.08
230	Chet Lemon	.08
231	Aurelio Lopez	.08

129	Ed Whitson	.10
130	Herm Winningham	.10
131	Rich Yett	.10
132	Checklist	.10

No.	Player	Value	No.	Player	Value	No.	Player	Value
232	Jack Morris	.08	328	Craig Lefferts	.08	424	Bill Krueger	.08
233	Randy O'Neal	.08	329	Carmelo Martinez	.08	425	Rick Langford	.08
234	Lance Parrish	.08	330	*Lance McCullers*	.08	426	Carney Lansford	.08
235	Dan Petry	.08	331	Kevin McReynolds	.08	427	Steve McCatty	.08
236	Alex Sanchez	.08	332	Graig Nettles	.08	428	Dwayne Murphy	.08
237	Bill Scherrer	.08	333	Jerry Royster	.08	429	*Steve Ontiveros*	.08
238	Nelson Simmons	.08	334	Eric Show	.08	430	Tony Phillips	.12
239	Frank Tanana	.08	335	Tim Stoddard	.08	431	Jose Rijo	.08
240	Walt Terrell	.08	336	Garry Templeton	.08	432	Mickey Tettleton	.50
241	Alan Trammell	.25	337	Mark Thurmond	.08	433	Luis Aguayo	.08
242	Lou Whitaker	.10	338	Ed Wojna	.08	434	Larry Andersen	.08
243	Milt Wilcox	.08	339	Tony Armas	.08	435	Steve Carlton	.60
244	Hubie Brooks	.08	340	Marty Barrett	.08	436	*Don Carman*	.08
245	*Tim Burke*	.10	341	Wade Boggs	2.00	437	Tim Corcoran	.08
246	Andre Dawson	.30	342	Dennis Boyd	.08	438	*Darren Daulton*	2.50
247	Mike Fitzgerald	.08	343	Bill Buckner	.08	439	John Denny	.08
248	Terry Francona	.08	344	Mark Clear	.08	440	Tom Foley	.08
249	Bill Gullickson	.08	345	Roger Clemens	7.00	441	Greg Gross	.08
250	Joe Hesketh	.08	346	Steve Crawford	.08	442	Kevin Gross	.08
251	Bill Laskey	.08	347	Mike Easler	.08	443	Von Hayes	.08
252	Vance Law	.08	348	Dwight Evans	.08	444	Charles Hudson	.08
253	Charlie Lea	.08	349	Rich Gedman	.08	445	Garry Maddox	.08
254	Gary Lucas	.08	350	Jackie Gutierrez	.08	446	Shane Rawley	.08
255	David Palmer	.08	351	Glenn Hoffman	.08	447	Dave Rucker	.08
256	Tim Raines	.30	352	Bruce Hurst	.08	448	John Russell	.08
257	Jeff Reardon	.08	353	Bruce Kison	.08	449	Juan Samuel	.08
258	Bert Roberge	.08	354	Tim Lollar	.08	450	Mike Schmidt	1.50
259	Dan Schatzeder	.08	355	Steve Lyons	.08	451	Rick Schu	.08
260	Bryn Smith	.08	356	Al Nipper	.08	452	Dave Shipanoff	.08
261	Randy St. Claire	.08	357	Bob Ojeda	.08	453	Dave Stewart	.10
262	Scot Thompson	.08	358	Jim Rice	.08	454	Jeff Stone	.08
263	Tim Wallach	.08	359	Bob Stanley	.08	455	Kent Tekulve	.08
264	U.L. Washington	.08	360	Mike Trujillo	.08	456	Ozzie Virgil	.08
265	*Mitch Webster*	.08	361	Thad Bosley	.08	457	Glenn Wilson	.08
266	*Herm Winningham*	.08	362	Warren Brusstar	.08	458	Jim Beattie	.08
267	*Floyd Youmans*	.08	363	Ron Cey	.08	459	Karl Best	.08
268	Don Aase	.08	364	Jody Davis	.08	460	Barry Bonnell	.08
269	Mike Boddicker	.08	365	Bob Dernier	.08	461	Phil Bradley	.08
270	Rich Dauer	.08	366	Shawon Dunston	.15	462	*Ivan Calderon*	.08
271	Storm Davis	.08	367	Leon Durham	.08	463	Al Cowens	.08
272	Rick Dempsey	.08	368	Dennis Eckersley	.12	464	Alvin Davis	.08
273	Ken Dixon	.08	369	Ray Fontenot	.08	465	Dave Henderson	.08
274	Jim Dwyer	.08	370	George Frazier	.08	466	Bob Kearney	.08
275	Mike Flanagan	.08	371	Bill Hatcher	.08	467	Mark Langston	.08
276	Wayne Gross	.08	372	Dave Lopes	.08	468	Bob Long	.08
277	Lee Lacy	.08	373	Gary Matthews	.08	469	Mike Moore	.08
278	Fred Lynn	.10	374	Ron Meredith	.08	470	Edwin Nunez	.08
279	Tippy Martinez	.08	375	Keith Moreland	.08	471	Spike Owen	.08
280	Dennis Martinez	.08	376	Reggie Patterson	.08	472	Jack Perconte	.08
281	Scott McGregor	.08	377	Dick Ruthven	.08	473	Jim Presley	.08
282	Eddie Murray	1.50	378	Ryne Sandberg	3.00	474	Donnie Scott	.08
283	Floyd Rayford	.08	379	Scott Sanderson	.08	475	Bill Swift	.08
284	Cal Ripken, Jr.	5.00	380	Lee Smith	.12	476	Danny Tartabull	.20
285	Gary Roenicke	.08	381	Lary Sorensen	.08	477	Gorman Thomas	.08
286	Larry Sheets	.08	382	Chris Speier	.08	478	Roy Thomas	.08
287	John Shelby	.08	383	Rick Sutcliffe	.08	479	Ed Vande Berg	.08
288	Nate Snell	.08	384	Steve Trout	.08	480	Frank Wills	.08
289	Sammy Stewart	.08	385	Gary Woods	.08	481	Matt Young	.08
290	Alan Wiggins	.08	386	Bert Blyleven	.08	482	Ray Burris	.08
291	Mike Young	.08	387	Tom Brunansky	.08	483	Jaime Cocanower	.08
292	Alan Ashby	.08	388	Randy Bush	.08	484	Cecil Cooper	.08
293	Mark Bailey	.08	389	John Butcher	.08	485	Danny Darwin	.08
294	Kevin Bass	.08	390	Ron Davis	.08	486	Rollie Fingers	.20
295	Jeff Calhoun	.08	391	Dave Engle	.08	487	Jim Gantner	.08
296	Jose Cruz	.08	392	Frank Eufemia	.08	488	Bob L. Gibson	.08
297	Glenn Davis	.08	393	Pete Filson	.08	489	Moose Haas	.08
298	Bill Dawley	.08	394	Gary Gaetti	.12	490	*Teddy Higuera*	.08
299	Frank DiPino	.08	395	Greg Gagne	.08	491	Paul Householder	.08
300	Bill Doran	.08	396	Mickey Hatcher	.08	492	Pete Ladd	.08
301	Phil Garner	.08	397	Kent Hrbek	.20	493	Rick Manning	.08
302	*Jeff Heathcock*	.08	398	Tim Laudner	.08	494	Bob McClure	.08
303	*Charlie Kerfeld*	.08	399	Rick Lysander	.08	495	Paul Molitor	1.75
304	Bob Knepper	.08	400	Dave Meier	.08	496	Charlie Moore	.08
305	Ron Mathis	.08	401	Kirby Puckett	8.00	497	Ben Oglivie	.08
306	Jerry Mumphrey	.08	402	Mark Salas	.08	498	Randy Ready	.08
307	Jim Pankovits	.08	403	Ken Schrom	.08	499	*Earnie Riles*	.08
308	Terry Puhl	.08	404	Roy Smalley	.08	500	Ed Romero	.08
309	Craig Reynolds	.08	405	Mike Smithson	.08	501	Bill Schroeder	.08
310	Nolan Ryan	7.00	406	Mike Stenhouse	.08	502	Ray Searage	.08
311	Mike Scott	.08	407	Tim Teufel	.08	503	Ted Simmons	.08
312	Dave Smith	.08	408	Frank Viola	.08	504	Pete Vuckovich	.08
313	Dickie Thon	.08	409	Ron Washington	.08	505	Rick Waits	.08
314	Denny Walling	.08	410	Keith Atherton	.08	506	Robin Yount	1.50
315	Kurt Bevacqua	.08	411	Dusty Baker	.10	507	Len Barker	.08
316	Al Bumbry	.08	412	*Tim Birtsas*	.08	508	Steve Bedrosian	.08
317	Jerry Davis	.08	413	Bruce Bochte	.08	509	Bruce Benedict	.08
318	Luis DeLeon	.08	414	Chris Codiroli	.08	510	Rick Camp	.08
319	Dave Dravecky	.08	415	Dave Collins	.08	511	Rick Cerone	.08
320	Tim Flannery	.08	416	Mike Davis	.08	512	Chris Chambliss	.08
321	Steve Garvey	.30	417	Alfredo Griffin	.08	513	Jeff Dedmon	.08
322	Goose Gossage	.08	418	Mike Heath	.08	514	Terry Forster	.08
323	Tony Gwynn	4.00	419	Steve Henderson	.08	515	Gene Garber	.08
324	Andy Hawkins	.08	420	Donnie Hill	.08	516	Terry Harper	.08
325	LaMarr Hoyt	.08	421	Jay Howell	.08	517	Bob Horner	.08
326	Roy Lee Jackson	.08	422	Tommy John	.10	518	Glenn Hubbard	.08
327	Terry Kennedy	.08	423	Dave Kingman	.10	519	*Joe Johnson*	.08

520	Brad Komminsk	.08
521	Rick Mahler	.08
522	Dale Murphy	.30
523	Ken Oberkfell	.08
524	Pascual Perez	.08
525	Gerald Perry	.08
526	Rafael Ramirez	.08
527	*Steve Shields*	.08
528	Zane Smith	.08
529	Bruce Sutter	.08
530	*Milt Thompson*	.10
531	Claudell Washington	.08
532	Paul Zuvella	.08
533	Vida Blue	.08
534	Bob Brenly	.08
535	*Chris Brown*	.08
536	Chili Davis	.10
537	Mark Davis	.08
538	Rob Deer	.08
539	Dan Driessen	.08
540	Scott Garrelts	.08
541	Dan Gladden	.08
542	Jim Gott	.08
543	David Green	.08
544	Atlee Hammaker	.08
545	Mike Jeffcoat	.08
546	Mike Krukow	.08
547	Dave LaPoint	.08
548	Jeff Leonard	.08
549	Greg Minton	.08
550	Alex Trevino	.08
551	Manny Trillo	.08
552	*Jose Uribe*	.08
553	Brad Wellman	.08
554	Frank Williams	.08
555	Joel Youngblood	.08
556	Alan Bannister	.08
557	Glenn Brummer	.08
558	*Steve Buechele*	.10
559	*Jose Guzman*	.08
560	Toby Harrah	.08
561	Greg Harris	.08
562	*Dwayne Henry*	.08
563	Burt Hooton	.08
564	Charlie Hough	.08
565	Mike Mason	.08
566	*Oddibe McDowell*	.08
567	Dickie Noles	.08
568	Pete O'Brien	.08
569	Larry Parrish	.08
570	Dave Rozema	.08
571	Dave Schmidt	.08
572	Don Slaught	.08
573	Wayne Tolleson	.08
574	Duane Walker	.08
575	Gary Ward	.08
576	Chris Welsh	.08
577	Curtis Wilkerson	.08
578	George Wright	.08
579	Chris Bando	.08
580	Tony Bernazard	.08
581	Brett Butler	.12
582	Ernie Camacho	.08
583	Joe Carter	1.00
584	Carmello Castillo (Carmelo)	.08
585	Jamie Easterly	.08
586	Julio Franco	.10
587	Mel Hall	.08
588	Mike Hargrove	.08
589	Neal Heaton	.08
590	Brook Jacoby	.08
591	*Otis Nixon*	.30
592	Jerry Reed	.08
593	Vern Ruhle	.08
594	Pat Tabler	.08
595	Rich Thompson	.08
596	Andre Thornton	.08
597	Dave Von Ohlen	.08
598	George Vukovich	.08
599	Tom Waddell	.08
600	Curt Wardle	.08
601	Jerry Willard	.08
602	Bill Almon	.08
603	Mike Bielecki	.08
604	Sid Bream	.08
605	Mike Brown	.08
606	*Pat Clements*	.08
607	Jose DeLeon	.08
608	Denny Gonzalez	.08
609	Cecilio Guante	.08
610	Steve Kemp	.08
611	Sam Khalifa	.08
612	Lee Mazzilli	.08
613	Larry McWilliams	.08
614	Jim Morrison	.08
615	*Joe Orsulak*	.25

616	Tony Pena	.08
617	Johnny Ray	.08
618	Rick Reuschel	.08
619	R.J. Reynolds	.08
620	Rick Rhoden	.08
621	Don Robinson	.08
622	Jason Thompson	.08
623	Lee Tunnell	.08
624	Jim Winn	.08
625	Marvell Wynne	.08
626	Dwight Gooden (In Action)	.25
627	Don Mattingly (In Action)	1.25
628	Pete Rose (4,192 hits)	.75
629	Rod Carew (3,000 Hits)	.50
630	Phil Niekro, Tom Seaver (300 Wins)	.25
631	Ouch!(Don Baylor)	.10
632	Instant Offense(Tim Raines, Darryl Strawberry)	.25
633	Shortstops Supreme(Cal Ripken, Jr., Alan Trammell)	1.00
634	Boggs & "Hero"(Wade Boggs, George Brett)	1.00
635	Braves Dynamic Duo(Bob Horner, Dale Murphy)	.30
636	Cardinal Ignitors(Vince Coleman, Willie McGee)	.25
637	Terror on the Basepaths(Vince Coleman)	.10
638	Charlie Hustle & Dr. K(Dwight Gooden, Pete Rose)	.50
639	1984 and 1985 A.L. Batting Champs(Wade Boggs, Don Mattingly)	1.00
640	N.L. West Sluggers(Steve Garvey, Dale Murphy, Dave Parker)	.30
641	Staff Aces(Dwight Gooden, Fernando Valenzuela)	.20
642	Blue Jay Stoppers(Jimmy Key, Dave Stieb)	.10
643	A.L. All-Star Backstops(Carlton Fisk, Rich Gedman)	.10
644	Major League Prospect(*Benito Santiago*), (*Gene Walter*)	.90
645	Major League Prospect(*Colin Ward*), (*Mike Woodard*)	.10
646	Major League Prospect(*Kal Daniels*), (*Paul O'Neill*)	3.50
647	Major League Prospect(*Andres Galarraga*), (*Fred Toliver*)	5.00
648	Major League Prospect(*Curt Ford*), (*Bob Kipper*)	.10
649	Major League Prospect(*Jose Canseco*), (*Eric Plunk*)	12.00
650	Major League Prospect(*Mark McLemore*), (*Gus Polidor*)	.40
651	Major League Prospect(*Mickey Brantley*), (*Rob Woodward*)	.10
652	Major League Prospect(*Mark Funderburk*), (*Billy Joe Robidoux*)	.10
653	Major League Prospect(*Cecil Fielder*), (*Cory Snyder*)	6.00
654	Checklist 1-97	.08
655	Checklist 98-196	.08
656	Checklist 197-291	.08
657	Checklist 292-385	.08
658	Checklist 386-482	.08
659	Checklist 483-578	.08
660	Checklist 579-660	.08

Modern cards have little collector value in conditions lower than Mint. Figure NM cards at 75% of values shown; EX cards at 40%.

Values shown reflect the market as of January, 1999. On-field performances of current players in the 1999 baseball season are not factored in.

1986 Fleer All Stars

Fleer's choices for a major league All-Star team make up this 12-card set. The cards were randomly inserted in 35¢ wax packs and 59¢ cello packs. The card fronts have a color photo set against a bright red background for A.L. players or a bright blue background for N.L. players. Backs feature the player's career highlights on a red and blue background.

		MT
Complete Set (12):		19.00
Common Player:		.25
1	Don Mattingly	5.00
2	Tom Herr	.25
3	George Brett	5.00
4	Gary Carter	.75
5	Cal Ripken, Jr.	12.00
6	Dave Parker	.35
7	Rickey Henderson	2.00
8	Pedro Guerrero	.25
9	Dan Quisenberry	.25
10	Dwight Gooden	.50
11	Gorman Thomas	.25
12	John Tudor	.25

1986 Fleer Box Panels

Picking up on a Donruss idea, Fleer issued eight cards in panels of four on the bottoms of the wax and cello pack boxes. The cards are numbered C-1 through C-8 and are 2-1/2" x 3-1/2", with a complete panel measuring 5" x 7-1/8". Included in the eight cards are six players and two team logo/checklist cards.

		MT
Complete Panel Set (2):		3.50
Complete Singles Set (8):		1.75
Common Single Player:		.20
Panel		2.50
1	Royals logo/checklist	.05
2	George Brett	.90
3	Ozzie Guillen	.20
4	Dale Murphy	.40
Panel		1.50
5	Cardinals Logo/Checklist	.05
6	Tom Browning	.20
7	Gary Carter	.35
8	Carlton Fisk	.35

1986 Fleer Future Hall Of Famers

The 1986 Future Hall of Famers set is comprised of six players Fleer felt would gain eventual entrance into the Baseball Hall of Fame. The cards are the standard 2-1/2" x 3-1/2" and were randomly inserted in three-pack rack packs. Card fronts feature a player photo set against a blue background with horizontal light blue stripes. Backs are printed in black on blue and feature career highlights in narrative form.

		MT
Complete Set (6):		15.00
Common Player:		1.75
1	Pete Rose	2.50
2	Steve Carlton	2.00
3	Tom Seaver	2.00
4	Rod Carew	2.00
5	Nolan Ryan	9.00
6	Reggie Jackson	2.00

1986 Fleer Mini

Fleer's 1986 "Classic Miniatures" set contains 120 cards that measure 1-13/16" x 2-9/16". The design of the high-gloss cards is identical to the regular 1986 Fleer set but the player photos are entirely different. The set, which was issued in a specially designed box along with 18 team logo stickers, was available only through hobby dealers.

		MT
Complete Set (120):		6.00
Common Player:		.05
1	George Brett	.80
2	Dan Quisenberry	.05
3	Bret Saberhagen	.08
4	Lonnie Smith	.05
5	Willie Wilson	.05
6	Jack Clark	.05
7	Vince Coleman	.05
8	Tom Herr	.05
9	Willie McGee	.08
10	Ozzie Smith	.20
11	John Tudor	.05
12	Jesse Barfield	.05
13	George Bell	.05
14	Tony Fernandez	.05
15	Damaso Garcia	.05
16	Dave Stieb	.05
17	Gary Carter	.12
18	Ron Darling	.05
19	Dwight Gooden	.15
20	Keith Hernandez	.05
21	Darryl Strawberry	.10
22	Ron Guidry	.10
23	Rickey Henderson	.30
24	Don Mattingly	1.00
25	Dave Righetti	.05
26	Dave Winfield	.45
27	Mariano Duncan	.05
28	Pedro Guerrero	.05
29	Bill Madlock	.05
30	Mike Marshall	.05
31	Fernando Valenzuela	.10
32	Reggie Jackson	.30
33	Gary Pettis	.05
34	Ron Romanick	.05
35	Don Sutton	.15
36	Mike Witt	.05
37	Buddy Bell	.05
38	Tom Browning	.05
39	Dave Parker	.08
40	Pete Rose	.75
41	Mario Soto	.05
42	Harold Baines	.08
43	Carlton Fisk	.12
44	Ozzie Guillen	.05
45	Ron Kittle	.05
46	Tom Seaver	.20
47	Kirk Gibson	.05
48	Jack Morris	.05
49	Lance Parrish	.05
50	Alan Trammell	.15
51	Lou Whitaker	.08
52	Hubie Brooks	.05
53	Andre Dawson	.12
54	Tim Raines	.10
55	Bryn Smith	.05
56	Tim Wallach	.05
57	Mike Boddicker	.05
58	Eddie Murray	.25
59	Cal Ripken, Jr.	2.50
60	John Shelby	.05
61	Mike Young	.05
62	Jose Cruz	.05
63	Glenn Davis	.05
64	Phil Garner	.05
65	Nolan Ryan	2.00
66	Mike Scott	.05
67	Steve Garvey	.12
68	Goose Gossage	.05

69	Tony Gwynn	.30
70	Andy Hawkins	.05
71	Garry Templeton	.05
72	Wade Boggs	.80
73	Roger Clemens	.80
74	Dwight Evans	.05
75	Rich Gedman	.05
76	Jim Rice	.05
77	Shawon Dunston	.15
78	Leon Durham	.05
79	Keith Moreland	.05
80	Ryne Sandberg	.75
81	Rick Sutcliffe	.05
82	Bert Blyleven	.05
83	Tom Brunansky	.05
84	Kent Hrbek	.08
85	Kirby Puckett	.95
86	Bruce Bochte	.05
87	Jose Canseco	1.00
88	Mike Davis	.05
89	Jay Howell	.05
90	Dwayne Murphy	.05
91	Steve Carlton	.20
92	Von Hayes	.05
93	Juan Samuel	.05
94	Mike Schmidt	.50
95	Glenn Wilson	.05
96	Phil Bradley	.05
97	Alvin Davis	.05
98	Jim Presley	.05
99	Danny Tartabull	.05
100	Cecil Cooper	.05
101	Paul Molitor	.15
102	Earnie Riles	.05
103	Robin Yount	.25
104	Bob Horner	.05
105	Dale Murphy	.15
106	Bruce Sutter	.05
107	Claudell Washington	.05
108	Chris Brown	.05
109	Chili Davis	.08
110	Scott Garrelts	.05
111	Oddibe McDowell	.05
112	Pete O'Brien	.05
113	Gary Ward	.05
114	Brett Butler	.12
115	Julio Franco	.08
116	Brook Jacoby	.05
117	Mike Brown	.05
118	Joe Orsulak	.05
119	Tony Pena	.05
120	R.J. Reynolds	.05

1986 Fleer Update

Issued near the end of the baseball season, the 1986 Fleer Update set consists of cards numbered U-1 through U-132. The 2-1/2" x 3-1/2" cards are identical in design to the regular 1986 Fleer set. The purpose of the set is to update player trades and include rookies not depicted in the regular issue. The set was issued with team logo stickers in a specially designed box and was available only through hobby dealers.

		MT
Complete Set (132):		20.00
Common Player:		.08
1	Mike Aldrete	.08
2	Andy Allanson	.08
3	Neil Allen	.08
4	Joaquin Andujar	.08
5	Paul Assenmacher	.08
6	Scott Bailes	.08
7	Jay Baller	.08
8	Scott Bankhead	.08
9	Bill Bathe	.08
10	Don Baylor	.15
11	Billy Beane	.08
12	Steve Bedrosian	.08
13	Juan Beniquez	.08
14	*Barry Bonds*	5.00
15	*Bobby Bonilla*	2.00
16	Rich Bordi	.08
17	Bill Campbell	.08
18	Tom Candiotti	.08
19	John Cangelosi	.08
20	Jose Canseco	4.00
21	Chuck Cary	.08
22	Juan Castillo	.08
23	Rick Cerone	.08
24	John Cerutti	.10
25	*Will Clark*	3.00
26	Mark Clear	.08
27	Darnell Coles	.08
28	Dave Collins	.08
29	Tim Conroy	.08
30	Ed Correa	.08
31	Joe Cowley	.08
32	Bill Dawley	.08
33	Rob Deer	.08
34	John Denny	.08
35	Jim DeShaies	.10
36	*Doug Drabek*	1.00
37	Mike Easler	.08
38	Mark Eichhorn	.12
39	Dave Engle	.08
40	Mike Fischlin	.08
41	Scott Fletcher	.08
42	Terry Forster	.08
43	Terry Francona	.08
44	Andres Galarraga	2.00
45	Lee Guetterman	.08
46	Bill Gullickson	.08
47	Jackie Gutierrez	.08
48	Moose Haas	.08
49	Billy Hatcher	.08
50	Mike Heath	.08
51	Guy Hoffman	.08
52	Tom Hume	.08
53	*Pete Incaviglia*	.40
54	Dane Iorg	.08
55	Chris James	.08
56	Stan Javier	.10
57	Tommy John	.15
58	Tracy Jones	.08
59	*Wally Joyner*	1.00
60	Wayne Krenchicki	.08
61	*John Kruk*	.50
62	Mike LaCoss	.08
63	Pete Ladd	.08
64	Dave LaPoint	.08
65	Mike LaValliere	.20
66	Rudy Law	.08
67	Dennis Leonard	.08
68	Steve Lombardozzi	.08
69	Aurelio Lopez	.08
70	Mickey Mahler	.08
71	Candy Maldonado	.08
72	Roger Mason	.08
73	Greg Mathews	.08
74	Andy McGaffigan	.08
75	Joel McKeon	.08
76	*Kevin Mitchell*	.50
77	Bill Mooneyham	.08
78	Omar Moreno	.08
79	Jerry Mumphrey	.08
80	Al Newman	.08
81	Phil Niekro	.50
82	Randy Niemann	.08
83	Juan Nieves	.08
84	Bob Ojeda	.08
85	Rick Ownbey	.08
86	Tom Paciorek	.08
87	David Palmer	.08
88	Jeff Parrett	.08
89	Pat Perry	.08
90	Dan Plesac	.08
91	Darrell Porter	.08
92	Luis Quinones	.08
93	Rey Quinonez	.08

94	Gary Redus	.08
95	Jeff Reed	.08
96	Bip Roberts	.60
97	Billy Joe Robidoux	.08
98	Gary Roenicke	.08
99	Ron Roenicke	.08
100	Angel Salazar	.08
101	Joe Sambito	.08
102	Billy Sample	.08
103	Dave Schmidt	.08
104	Ken Schrom	.08
105	*Ruben Sierra*	.75
106	Ted Simmons	.08
107	Sammy Stewart	.08
108	Kurt Stillwell	.08
109	Dale Sveum	.08
110	Tim Teufel	.08
111	Bob Tewksbury	.75
112	Andres Thomas	.08
113	Jason Thompson	.08
114	Milt Thompson	.08
115	Rob Thompson	.20
116	Jay Tibbs	.08
117	Fred Toliver	.08
118	Wayne Tolleson	.08
119	Alex Trevino	.08
120	Manny Trillo	.08
121	Ed Vande Berg	.08
122	Ozzie Virgil	.08
123	Tony Walker	.08
124	Gene Walter	.08
125	Duane Ward	.25
126	Jerry Willard	.08
127	Mitch Williams	.30
128	Reggie Williams	.08
129	Bobby Witt	.30
130	Marvell Wynne	.08
131	Steve Yeager	.08
132	Checklist	.05

1987 Fleer

Tim Raines
OUTFIELD

The 1987 Fleer set consists of 660 cards. Fronts feature a graduated blue-to-white border design. The player's name and position appear in the upper-left corner of the card; his team logo is located in the lower-right. Backs are done in blue, red and white and contain an innovative "Pro Scouts Report" feature which rates the player's batting or pitching skills. For the third year in a row, Fleer included its "Major League Prospects" subset. Fleer produced a glossy-finish Collectors Edition set which came housed in a specially-designed tin box. After experiencing a dramatic hike in price during 1987, the glossy set now sells for only a few dollars more than the regular issue.

		MT
Complete Set (660):		70.00
Common Player:		.06
Wax Box:		110.00
1	Rick Aguilera	.06

2	Richard Anderson	.06
3	Wally Backman	.06
4	Gary Carter	.15
5	Ron Darling	.06
6	Len Dykstra	.15
7	*Kevin Elster*	.15
8	Sid Fernandez	.06
9	Dwight Gooden	.35
10	*Ed Hearn*	.06
11	Danny Heep	.06
12	Keith Hernandez	.06
13	Howard Johnson	.06
14	Ray Knight	.06
15	Lee Mazzilli	.06
16	Roger McDowell	.06
17	Kevin Mitchell	.15
18	Randy Niemann	.06
19	Bob Ojeda	.06
20	Jesse Orosco	.06
21	Rafael Santana	.06
22	Doug Sisk	.06
23	Darryl Strawberry	.20
24	Tim Teufel	.06
25	Mookie Wilson	.06
26	Tony Armas	.06
27	Marty Barrett	.06
28	Don Baylor	.12
29	Wade Boggs	.75
30	Oil Can Boyd	.06
31	Bill Buckner	.06
32	Roger Clemens	3.00
33	Steve Crawford	.06
34	Dwight Evans	.06
35	Rich Gedman	.06
36	Dave Henderson	.06
37	Bruce Hurst	.06
38	Tim Lollar	.06
39	Al Nipper	.06
40	Spike Owen	.06
41	Jim Rice	.06
42	Ed Romero	.06
43	Joe Sambito	.06
44	Calvin Schiraldi	.06
45	Tom Seaver	.75
46	*Jeff Sellers*	.06
47	Bob Stanley	.06
48	Sammy Stewart	.06
49	Larry Andersen	.06
50	Alan Ashby	.06
51	Kevin Bass	.06
52	Jeff Calhoun	.06
53	Jose Cruz	.06
54	Danny Darwin	.06
55	Glenn Davis	.06
56	*Jim Deshaies*	.15
57	Bill Doran	.06
58	Phil Garner	.06
59	Billy Hatcher	.06
60	Charlie Kerfeld	.06
61	Bob Knepper	.06
62	Dave Lopes	.06
63	Aurelio Lopez	.06
64	Jim Pankovits	.06
65	Terry Puhl	.06
66	Craig Reynolds	.06
67	Nolan Ryan	4.00
68	Mike Scott	.06
69	Dave Smith	.06
70	Dickie Thon	.06
71	Tony Walker	.06
72	Denny Walling	.06
73	Bob Boone	.06
74	Rick Burleson	.06
75	John Candelaria	.06
76	Doug Corbett	.06
77	Doug DeCinces	.06
78	Brian Downing	.06
79	*Chuck Finley*	1.00
80	Terry Forster	.06
81	Bobby Grich	.06
82	George Hendrick	.06
83	Jack Howell	.06
84	Reggie Jackson	1.00
85	Ruppert Jones	.06
86	Wally Joyner	1.25
87	Gary Lucas	.06
88	Kirk McCaskill	.06
89	Donnie Moore	.06
90	Gary Pettis	.06
91	Vern Ruhle	.06
92	Dick Schofield	.06
93	Don Sutton	.25
94	Rob Wilfong	.06
95	Mike Witt	.06
96	Doug Drabek	.75
97	Mike Easler	.06

#	Player	Price
98	Mike Fischlin	.06
99	Brian Fisher	.06
100	Ron Guidry	.10
101	Rickey Henderson	.35
102	Tommy John	.10
103	Ron Kittle	.06
104	Don Mattingly	2.00
105	Bobby Meacham	.06
106	Joe Niekro	.06
107	Mike Pagliarulo	.06
108	Dan Pasqua	.06
109	Willie Randolph	.06
110	Dennis Rasmussen	.06
111	Dave Righetti	.06
112	Gary Roenicke	.06
113	Rod Scurry	.06
114	Bob Shirley	.06
115	Joel Skinner	.06
116	Tim Stoddard	.06
117	*Bob Tewksbury*	.75
118	Wayne Tolleson	.06
119	Claudell Washington	.06
120	Dave Winfield	.25
121	Steve Buechele	.06
122	*Ed Correa*	.06
123	Scott Fletcher	.06
124	Jose Guzman	.06
125	Toby Harrah	.06
126	Greg Harris	.06
127	Charlie Hough	.06
128	Pete Incaviglia	.08
129	Mike Mason	.06
130	Oddibe McDowell	.06
131	*Dale Mohorcic*	.06
132	Pete O'Brien	.06
133	Tom Paciorek	.06
134	Larry Parrish	.06
135	Geno Petralli	.06
136	Darrell Porter	.06
137	Jeff Russell	.06
138	Ruben Sierra	.75
139	Don Slaught	.06
140	Gary Ward	.06
141	Curtis Wilkerson	.06
142	*Mitch Williams*	.40
143	*Bobby Witt*	.40
144	Dave Bergman	.06
145	Tom Brookens	.06
146	Bill Campbell	.06
147	*Chuck Cary*	.06
148	Darnell Coles	.06
149	Dave Collins	.06
150	Darrell Evans	.06
151	Kirk Gibson	.06
152	John Grubb	.06
153	Willie Hernandez	.06
154	Larry Herndon	.06
155	*Eric King*	.06
156	Chet Lemon	.06
157	Dwight Lowry	.06
158	Jack Morris	.06
159	Randy O'Neal	.10
160	Lance Parrish	.06
161	Dan Petry	.06
162	Pat Sheridan	.06
163	Jim Slaton	.06
164	Frank Tanana	.06
165	Walt Terrell	.06
166	Mark Thurmond	.06
167	Alan Trammell	.25
168	Lou Whitaker	.12
169	Luis Aguayo	.06
170	Steve Bedrosian	.06
171	Don Carman	.06
172	Darren Daulton	.15
173	Greg Gross	.06
174	Kevin Gross	.06
175	Von Hayes	.06
176	Charles Hudson	.06
177	Tom Hume	.06
178	Steve Jeltz	.06
179	*Mike Maddux*	.06
180	Shane Rawley	.06
181	Gary Redus	.06
182	Ron Roenicke	.06
183	*Bruce Ruffin*	.10
184	John Russell	.06
185	Juan Samuel	.06
186	Dan Schatzeder	.06
187	Mike Schmidt	1.00
188	Rick Schu	.06
189	Jeff Stone	.06
190	Kent Tekulve	.06
191	Milt Thompson	.06
192	Glenn Wilson	.06
193	Buddy Bell	.06
194	Tom Browning	.06
195	Sal Butera	.06
196	Dave Concepcion	.06
197	Kal Daniels	.06
198	Eric Davis	.15
199	John Denny	.06
200	Bo Diaz	.06
201	Nick Esasky	.06
202	John Franco	.06
203	Bill Gullickson	.06
204	*Barry Larkin*	5.00
205	Eddie Milner	.06
206	*Rob Murphy*	.06
207	Ron Oester	.06
208	Dave Parker	.12
209	Tony Perez	.15
210	Ted Power	.06
211	Joe Price	.06
212	Ron Robinson	.06
213	Pete Rose	1.00
214	Mario Soto	.06
215	*Kurt Stillwell*	.06
216	Max Venable	.06
217	Chris Welsh	.06
218	*Carl Willis*	.06
219	Jesse Barfield	.06
220	George Bell	.06
221	Bill Caudill	.06
222	*John Cerutti*	.06
223	Jim Clancy	.06
224	*Mark Eichhorn*	.10
225	Tony Fernandez	.06
226	Damaso Garcia	.06
227	Kelly Gruber	.06
228	Tom Henke	.06
229	Garth Iorg	.06
230	Cliff Johnson	.06
231	Joe Johnson	.06
232	Jimmy Key	.15
233	Dennis Lamp	.06
234	Rick Leach	.06
235	Buck Martinez	.06
236	Lloyd Moseby	.06
237	Rance Mulliniks	.06
238	Dave Stieb	.06
239	Willie Upshaw	.06
240	Ernie Whitt	.06
241	*Andy Allanson*	.06
242	*Scott Bailes*	.06
243	Chris Bando	.06
244	Tony Bernazard	.06
245	John Butcher	.06
246	Brett Butler	.15
247	Ernie Camacho	.06
248	Tom Candiotti	.06
249	Joe Carter	.65
250	Carmen Castillo	.06
251	Julio Franco	.08
252	Mel Hall	.06
253	Brook Jacoby	.06
254	Phil Niekro	.25
255	Otis Nixon	.06
256	Dickie Noles	.06
257	Bryan Oelkers	.06
258	Ken Schrom	.06
259	Don Schulze	.06
260	Cory Snyder	.06
261	Pat Tabler	.06
262	Andre Thornton	.06
263	*Rich Yett*	.06
264	*Mike Aldrete*	.06
265	Juan Berenguer	.06
266	Vida Blue	.06
267	Bob Brenly	.06
268	Chris Brown	.06
269	Will Clark	3.50
270	Chili Davis	.08
271	Mark Davis	.06
272	*Kelly Downs*	.06
273	Scott Garrelts	.06
274	Dan Gladden	.06
275	Mike Krukow	.06
276	*Randy Kutcher*	.06
277	Mike LaCoss	.06
278	Jeff Leonard	.06
279	Candy Maldonado	.06
280	Roger Mason	.06
281	Bob Melvin	.06
282	Greg Minton	.06
283	Jeff Robinson	.06
284	Harry Spilman	.06
285	*Rob Thompson*	.40
286	Jose Uribe	.06
287	Frank Williams	.06
288	Joel Youngblood	.06
289	Jack Clark	.06
290	Vince Coleman	.08
291	Tim Conroy	.06
292	Danny Cox	.06
293	Ken Dayley	.06
294	Curt Ford	.06
295	Bob Forsch	.06
296	Tom Herr	.06
297	Ricky Horton	.06
298	Clint Hurdle	.06
299	Jeff Lahti	.06
300	Steve Lake	.06
301	Tito Landrum	.06
302	*Mike LaValliere*	.20
303	*Greg Mathews*	.06
304	Willie McGee	.08
305	Jose Oquendo	.06
306	Terry Pendleton	.08
307	Pat Perry	.06
308	Ozzie Smith	1.00
309	Ray Soff	.06
310	John Tudor	.06
311	Andy Van Slyke	.06
312	Todd Worrell	.06
313	Dann Bilardello	.06
314	Hubie Brooks	.06
315	Tim Burke	.06
316	Andre Dawson	.25
317	Mike Fitzgerald	.06
318	Tom Foley	.06
319	Andres Galarraga	1.00
320	Joe Hesketh	.06
321	Wallace Johnson	.06
322	Wayne Krenchicki	.06
323	Vance Law	.06
324	Dennis Martinez	.10
325	Bob McClure	.06
326	Andy McGaffigan	.06
327	*Al Newman*	.06
328	Tim Raines	.25
329	Jeff Reardon	.06
330	*Luis Rivera*	.06
331	*Bob Sebra*	.06
332	Bryn Smith	.06
333	Jay Tibbs	.06
334	Tim Wallach	.08
335	Mitch Webster	.06
336	Jim Wohlford	.06
337	Floyd Youmans	.06
338	*Chris Bosio*	.25
339	*Glenn Braggs*	.06
340	Rick Cerone	.06
341	Mark Clear	.06
342	*Bryan Clutterbuck*	.06
343	Cecil Cooper	.06
344	Rob Deer	.06
345	Jim Gantner	.06
346	Ted Higuera	.06
347	John Henry Johnson	.06
348	Tim Leary	.06
349	Rick Manning	.06
350	Paul Molitor	1.00
351	Charlie Moore	.06
352	Juan Nieves	.06
353	Ben Oglivie	.06
354	*Dan Plesac*	.12
355	Ernest Riles	.06
356	Billy Joe Robidoux	.06
357	Bill Schroeder	.06
358	*Dale Sveum*	.06
359	Gorman Thomas	.06
360	Bill Wegman	.10
361	Robin Yount	1.00
362	Steve Balboni	.06
363	*Scott Bankhead*	.06
364	Buddy Biancalana	.06
365	Bud Black	.06
366	George Brett	2.00
367	Steve Farr	.06
368	Mark Gubicza	.06
369	Bo Jackson	3.00
370	Danny Jackson	.06
371	*Mike Kingery*	.06
372	Rudy Law	.06
373	Charlie Leibrandt	.06
374	Dennis Leonard	.06
375	Hal McRae	.08
376	Jorge Orta	.06
377	Jamie Quirk	.06
378	Dan Quisenberry	.06
379	Bret Saberhagen	.08
380	Angel Salazar	.06
381	Lonnie Smith	.06
382	Jim Sundberg	.06
383	Frank White	.06
384	Willie Wilson	.06
385	Joaquin Andujar	.06

386	Doug Bair	.06
387	Dusty Baker	.10
388	Bruce Bochte	.06
389	Jose Canseco	2.00
390	Chris Codiroli	.06
391	Mike Davis	.06
392	Alfredo Griffin	.06
393	Moose Haas	.06
394	Donnie Hill	.06
395	Jay Howell	.06
396	Dave Kingman	.10
397	Carney Lansford	.06
398	*David Leiper*	.06
399	*Bill Mooneyham*	.06
400	Dwayne Murphy	.06
401	Steve Ontiveros	.06
402	Tony Phillips	.12
403	Eric Plunk	.06
404	Jose Rijo	.06
405	*Terry Steinbach*	.60
406	Dave Stewart	.10
407	Mickey Tettleton	.08
408	Dave Von Ohlen	.06
409	Jerry Willard	.06
410	Curt Young	.06
411	Bruce Bochy	.06
412	Dave Dravecky	.06
413	Tim Flannery	.06
414	Steve Garvey	.25
415	Goose Gossage	.12
416	Tony Gwynn	2.00
417	Andy Hawkins	.06
418	LaMarr Hoyt	.06
419	Terry Kennedy	.06
420	John Kruk	.40
421	Dave LaPoint	.06
422	Craig Lefferts	.06
423	Carmelo Martinez	.06
424	Lance McCullers	.06
425	Kevin McReynolds	.06
426	Graig Nettles	.06
427	*Bip Roberts*	.75
428	Jerry Royster	.06
429	Benito Santiago	.40
430	Eric Show	.06
431	Bob Stoddard	.06
432	Garry Templeton	.06
433	Gene Walter	.06
434	Ed Whitson	.06
435	Marvell Wynne	.06
436	Dave Anderson	.06
437	Greg Brock	.06
438	Enos Cabell	.06
439	Mariano Duncan	.06
440	Pedro Guerrero	.06
441	Orel Hershiser	.10
442	Rick Honeycutt	.06
443	Ken Howell	.06
444	Ken Landreaux	.06
445	Bill Madlock	.06
446	Mike Marshall	.06
447	Len Matuszek	.06
448	Tom Niedenfuer	.06
449	Alejandro Pena	.06
450	Dennis Powell	.06
451	Jerry Reuss	.06
452	Bill Russell	.08
453	Steve Sax	.06
454	Mike Scioscia	.06
455	Franklin Stubbs	.06
456	Alex Trevino	.06
457	Fernando Valenzuela	.10
458	Ed Vande Berg	.06
459	Bob Welch	.06
460	*Reggie Williams*	.06
461	Don Aase	.06
462	Juan Beniquez	.06
463	Mike Boddicker	.06
464	Juan Bonilla	.06
465	Rich Bordi	.06
466	Storm Davis	.06
467	Rick Dempsey	.06
468	Ken Dixon	.06
469	Jim Dwyer	.06
470	Mike Flanagan	.06
471	Jackie Gutierrez	.06
472	Brad Havens	.06
473	Lee Lacy	.06
474	Fred Lynn	.12
475	Scott McGregor	.06
476	Eddie Murray	1.00
477	Tom O'Malley	.06
478	Cal Ripken, Jr.	4.00
479	Larry Sheets	.06
480	John Shelby	.06
481	Nate Snell	.06

482	Jim Traber	.06
483	Mike Young	.06
484	Neil Allen	.06
485	Harold Baines	.10
486	Floyd Bannister	.06
487	Daryl Boston	.06
488	Ivan Calderon	.06
489	*John Cangelosi*	.06
490	Steve Carlton	.40
491	Joe Cowley	.06
492	Julio Cruz	.06
493	Bill Dawley	.06
494	Jose DeLeon	.06
495	Richard Dotson	.06
496	Carlton Fisk	.60
497	Ozzie Guillen	.06
498	Jerry Hairston	.06
499	Ron Hassey	.06
500	Tim Hulett	.06
501	Bob James	.06
502	Steve Lyons	.06
503	*Joel McKeon*	.06
504	Gene Nelson	.06
505	Dave Schmidt	.06
506	Ray Searage	.06
507	*Bobby Thigpen*	.15
508	Greg Walker	.06
509	Jim Acker	.06
510	Doyle Alexander	.06
511	*Paul Assenmacher*	.06
512	Bruce Benedict	.06
513	Chris Chambliss	.06
514	Jeff Dedmon	.06
515	Gene Garber	.06
516	Ken Griffey	.10
517	Terry Harper	.06
518	Bob Horner	.06
519	Glenn Hubbard	.06
520	Rick Mahler	.06
521	Omar Moreno	.06
522	Dale Murphy	.25
523	Ken Oberkfell	.06
524	Ed Olwine	.06
525	David Palmer	.06
526	Rafael Ramirez	.06
527	Billy Sample	.06
528	Ted Simmons	.06
529	Zane Smith	.06
530	Bruce Sutter	.06
531	*Andres Thomas*	.06
532	Ozzie Virgil	.06
533	*Allan Anderson*	.06
534	Keith Atherton	.06
535	Billy Beane	.06
536	Bert Blyleven	.06
537	Tom Brunansky	.06
538	Randy Bush	.06
539	George Frazier	.06
540	Gary Gaetti	.10
541	Greg Gagne	.06
542	Mickey Hatcher	.06
543	Neal Heaton	.06
544	Kent Hrbek	.15
545	Roy Lee Jackson	.06
546	Tim Laudner	.06
547	Steve Lombardozzi	.06
548	*Mark Portugal*	.50
549	Kirby Puckett	3.00
550	Jeff Reed	.06
551	Mark Salas	.06
552	Roy Smalley	.06
553	Mike Smithson	.06
554	Frank Viola	.06
555	Thad Bosley	.06
556	Ron Cey	.06
557	Jody Davis	.06
558	Ron Davis	.06
559	Bob Dernier	.06
560	Frank DiPino	.06
561	Shawon Dunston	.15
562	Leon Durham	.06
563	Dennis Eckersley	.20
564	Terry Francona	.06
565	Dave Gumpert	.06
566	Guy Hoffman	.06
567	Ed Lynch	.06
568	Gary Matthews	.06
569	Keith Moreland	.06
570	*Jamie Moyer*	.06
571	Jerry Mumphrey	.06
572	Ryne Sandberg	1.00
573	Scott Sanderson	.06
574	Lee Smith	.10
575	Chris Speier	.06
576	Rick Sutcliffe	.06
577	Manny Trillo	.06

578	Steve Trout	.06
579	Karl Best	.06
580	Scott Bradley	.06
581	Phil Bradley	.06
582	Mickey Brantley	.06
583	Mike Brown	.06
584	Alvin Davis	.06
585	*Lee Guetterman*	.06
586	Mark Huismann	.06
587	Bob Kearney	.06
588	Pete Ladd	.06
589	Mark Langston	.06
590	Mike Moore	.06
591	Mike Morgan	.06
592	John Moses	.06
593	Ken Phelps	.06
594	Jim Presley	.06
595	*Rey Quinonez (Quinones)*	.06
596	Harold Reynolds	.06
597	Billy Swift	.06
598	Danny Tartabull	.05
599	Steve Yeager	.06
600	Matt Young	.06
601	Bill Almon	.06
602	*Rafael Belliard*	.06
603	Mike Bielecki	.06
604	Barry Bonds	20.00
605	Bobby Bonilla	2.00
606	Sid Bream	.06
607	Mike Brown	.06
608	Pat Clements	.06
609	*Mike Diaz*	.06
610	Cecilio Guante	.06
611	*Barry Jones*	.06
612	Bob Kipper	.06
613	Larry McWilliams	.06
614	Jim Morrison	.06
615	Joe Orsulak	.06
616	Junior Ortiz	.06
617	Tony Pena	.06
618	Johnny Ray	.06
619	Rick Reuschel	.06
620	R.J. Reynolds	.06
621	Rick Rhoden	.06
622	Don Robinson	.06
623	Bob Walk	.06
624	Jim Winn	.06
625	Youthful Power(Jose Canseco, Pete Incaviglia)	.40
626	300 Game Winners(Phil Niekro, Don Sutton)	.25
627	A.L. Firemen(Don Aase, Dave Righetti)	.06
628	Rookie All-Stars(Jose Canseco, Wally Joyner)	.40
629	Magic Mets(Gary Carter, Dwight Gooden, Keith Hernandez, Darryl Strawberry)	.15
630	N.L. Best Righties(Mike Krukow, Mike Scott)	.06
631	Sensational Southpaws(John Franco, Fernando Valenzuela)	.06
632	Count 'Em(Bob Horner)	.08
633	A.L. Pitcher's Nightmare(Jose Canseco, Kirby Puckett, Jim Rice)	.40
634	All Star Battery(Gary Carter, Roger Clemens)	.25
635	4,000 Strikeouts(Steve Carlton)	.12
636	Big Bats At First Sack(Glenn Davis, Eddie Murray)	.25
637	On Base(Wade Boggs, Keith Hernandez)	.20
638	Sluggers From Left Side(Don Mattingly, Darryl Strawberry)	.40
639	Former MVP's(Dave Parker, Ryne Sandberg)	.12
640	Dr. K. & Super K(Roger Clemens, Dwight Gooden)	.50
641	A.L. West Stoppers(Charlie Hough, Mike Witt)	.06
642	Doubles & Triples(Tim Raines, Juan Samuel)	.06
643	Outfielders With Punch(Harold Baines, Jesse Barfield)	.06
644	Major League Prospects(*Dave Clark*), (*Greg Swindell*)	.30
645	Major League Prospects(*Ron Karkovice*), (*Russ Morman*)	.25

646	Major League Prospects(*Willie Fraser*), (*Devon White*)	1.00
647	Major League Prospects(*Jerry Browne*), (*Mike Stanley*)	.40
648	Major League Prospects(*Phil Lombardi*), (*Dave Magadan*)	.20
649	Major League Prospects(*Ralph Bryant*), (*Jose Gonzalez*)	.10
650	Major League Prospects(*Randy Asadoor*), (*Jimmy Jones*)	.10
651	Major League Prospects(*Marvin Freeman*), (*Tracy Jones*)	.15
652	Major League Prospects(*Kevin Seitzer*, John Stefero*)	.25
653	Major League Prospects(*Steve Fireovid*), (*Rob Nelson*)	.10
654	Checklist 1-95	.06
655	Checklist 96-192	.06
656	Checklist 193-288	.06
657	Checklist 289-384	.06
658	Checklist 385-483	.06
659	Checklist 484-578	.06
660	Checklist 579-660	.06

1987 Fleer '86 World Series

Fleer issued a set of 12 cards highlighting the 1986 World Series between the Boston Red Sox and New York Mets. The sets were available only with Fleer factory sets, both regular and glossy. The cards, 2-1/2" x 3-1/2", have either horizontal or vertical formats. The fronts are bordered in red, white and blue stars and stripes with a thin gold frame around the photo. Backs are printed in red and blue on white stock and include information regarding the photo on the card fronts.

		MT
Complete Set, Regular (12):		2.00
Complete Set, Glossy (12):		3.00
Common Card:		.25
1	Left-Hand Finesse Beats Mets(Bruce Hurst)	.25
2	Wade Boggs, Keith Hernandez	.50
3	Roger Clemens	.75
4	Gary Carter	.35
5	Ron Darling	.25
6	.433 Series Batting Average(Marty Barrett)	.25
7	Dwight Gooden	.35

8	Strategy At Work	.25
9	Dewey!(Dwight Evans)	.25
10	One Strike From Boston Victory(Dave Henderson, Spike Owen)	.25
11	Ray Knight, Darryl Strawberry	.25
12	Series M.V.P.(Ray Knight)	.25

1987 Fleer All Stars

As in 1986, Fleer All Star Team cards were randomly inserted in wax and cello packs. Twelve cards, measuring the standard 2-1/2" x 3-1/2", comprise the set. Fronts feature a full-color player photo set against a gray background for American League players and a black background for National Leaguers. Backs are printed in black, red and white and feature a lengthy player biography. Fleer's choices for a major league All-Star team is once again the theme for the set.

		MT
Complete Set (12):		15.00
Common Player:		.30
1	Don Mattingly	4.00
2	Gary Carter	.50
3	Tony Fernandez	.30
4	Steve Sax	.30
5	Kirby Puckett	5.00
6	Mike Schmidt	3.50
7	Mike Easler	.30
8	Todd Worrell	.30
9	George Bell	.30
10	Fernando Valenzuela	.45
11	Roger Clemens	5.00
12	Tim Raines	.50

1987 Fleer Box Panels

For the second straight year, Fleer produced a special set of cards designed to stimulate sales of their wax and cello pack boxes. In 1987, Fleer issued 16 cards in panels of four on the bottoms of retail boxes. The cards are numbered C-1 through C-16 and are 2-1/2" x 3-1/2" in size. The cards have the

same design as the regular issue set with the player photos and card numbers being different.

		MT
Complete Panel Set (4):		8.00
Complete Singles Set (16):		3.50
Common Panel:		2.25
Common Single Player:		.15
Panel		2.50
1	Mets Logo	.05
6	Keith Hernandez	.15
8	Dale Murphy	.30
14	Ryne Sandberg	.80
Panel		2.25
2	Jesse Barfield	.15
3	George Brett	.80
5	Red Sox Logo	.05
11	Kirby Puckett	.90
Panel		2.75
4	Dwight Gooden	.30
9	Astros Logo	.05
10	Dave Parker	.15
15	Mike Schmidt	.80
Panel		2.50
7	Wally Joyner	.25
12	Dave Righetti	.15
13	Angels Logo	.05
16	Robin Yount	.50

1987 Fleer Glossy Tin

The three-year run of limited edition, glossy collectors' issues by Fleer from 1987-89 has become known to the hobby as "tins" for the colorful lithographed metal boxes in which complete sets were sold. In their debut year a reported 100,000 sets were made, each serial numbered on a sticker attached to the shrink-wrapped tin box. While the glossy version of the 1987 Fleer set once enjoyed a significant premium over regular cards, today that premium has evaporated and, indeed, it can be harder to find a buyer for the glossy version.

	MT
Complete Set (672):	40.00
Common Player:	.06
(Single star cards valued at .75-1X regular-issue 1987 Fleer.)	

Values shown reflect the market as of January, 1999. On-field performances of current players in the 1999 baseball season are not factored in.

1987 Fleer Headliners

KEITH HERNANDEZ
METS • FIRST BASE

A continuation of the 1986 Future Hall of Famers idea, Fleer encountered legal problems with using the Hall of Fame name and abated them by entitling the set "Headliners." The cards were randomly inserted in three-pack rack packs. Fronts feature a player photo set against a beige background with bright red stripes. Backs are printed in black, red and gray and offer a brief biography with an emphasis on the player's performance during the 1986 season.

		MT
Complete Set (6):		6.00
Common Player:		.45
1	Wade Boggs	2.25
2	Jose Canseco	2.00
3	Dwight Gooden	.60
4	Rickey Henderson	1.00
5	Keith Hernandez	.45
6	Jim Rice	.45

1987 Fleer Mini

Cecil Cooper
FIRST BASE

Continuing with an idea originated the previous year, the Fleer "Classic Miniatures" set consists of 120 cards that measure 1-13/16" x 2-9/16". The cards are identical in design to the regular-issue set, but use completely different photos.

The set was issued in a specially prepared collectors box along with 18 team logo stickers. The mini set was available only through hobby dealers.

		MT
Complete Set (120):		4.00
Common Player:		.05
1	Don Aase	.05
2	Joaquin Andujar	.05
3	Harold Baines	.08
4	Jesse Barfield	.05
5	Kevin Bass	.05
6	Don Baylor	.08
7	George Bell	.05
8	Tony Bernazard	.05
9	Bert Blyleven	.05
10	Wade Boggs	.60
11	Phil Bradley	.05
12	Sid Bream	.05
13	George Brett	.60
14	Hubie Brooks	.05
15	Chris Brown	.05
16	Tom Candiotti	.05
17	Jose Canseco	.90
18	Gary Carter	.15
19	Joe Carter	.10
20	Roger Clemens	.40
21	Vince Coleman	.05
22	Cecil Cooper	.05
23	Ron Darling	.05
24	Alvin Davis	.05
25	Chili Davis	.08
26	Eric Davis	.15
27	Glenn Davis	.05
28	Mike Davis	.05
29	Doug DeCinces	.05
30	Rob Deer	.05
31	Jim Deshaies	.05
32	Bo Diaz	.05
33	Richard Dotson	.05
34	Brian Downing	.05
35	Shawon Dunston	.10
36	Mark Eichhorn	.05
37	Dwight Evans	.05
38	Tony Fernandez	.05
39	Julio Franco	.05
40	Gary Gaetti	.08
41	Andres Galarraga	.15
42	Scott Garrelts	.05
43	Steve Garvey	.15
44	Kirk Gibson	.05
45	Dwight Gooden	.10
46	Ken Griffey	.08
47	Mark Gubicza	.05
48	Ozzie Guillen	.05
49	Bill Gullickson	.05
50	Tony Gwynn	.35
51	Von Hayes	.05
52	Rickey Henderson	.40
53	Keith Hernandez	.05
54	Willie Hernandez	.05
55	Ted Higuera	.05
56	Charlie Hough	.05
57	Kent Hrbek	.08
58	Pete Incaviglia	.05
59	Wally Joyner	.08
60	Bob Knepper	.05
61	Mike Krukow	.05
62	Mark Langston	.05
63	Carney Lansford	.05
64	Jim Lindeman	.05
65	Bill Madlock	.05
66	Don Mattingly	1.00
67	Kirk McCaskill	.05
68	Lance McCullers	.05
69	Keith Moreland	.05
70	Jack Morris	.05
71	Jim Morrison	.05
72	Lloyd Moseby	.05
73	Jerry Mumphrey	.05
74	Dale Murphy	.15
75	Eddie Murray	.30
76	Pete O'Brien	.05
77	Bob Ojeda	.05
78	Jesse Orosco	.05
79	Dan Pasqua	.05
80	Dave Parker	.08
81	Larry Parrish	.05
82	Jim Presley	.05
83	Kirby Puckett	.90
84	Dan Quisenberry	.05
85	Tim Raines	.10
86	Dennis Rasmussen	.05
87	Johnny Ray	.05
88	Jeff Reardon	.05
89	Jim Rice	.05
90	Dave Righetti	.05
91	Earnest Riles	.05
92	Cal Ripken, Jr.	2.00
93	Ron Robinson	.05
94	Juan Samuel	.05
95	Ryne Sandberg	.75
96	Steve Sax	.05
97	Mike Schmidt	.45
98	Ken Schrom	.05
99	Mike Scott	.05
100	Ruben Sierra	.08
101	Lee Smith	.08
102	Ozzie Smith	.25
103	Cory Snyder	.05
104	Kent Tekulve	.05
105	Andres Thomas	.05
106	Rob Thompson	.05
107	Alan Trammell	.10
108	John Tudor	.05
109	Fernando Valenzuela	.10
110	Greg Walker	.05
111	Mitch Webster	.05
112	Lou Whitaker	.08
113	Frank White	.05
114	Reggie Williams	.05
115	Glenn Wilson	.05
116	Willie Wilson	.05
117	Dave Winfield	.30
118	Mike Witt	.05
119	Todd Worrell	.05
120	Floyd Youmans	.05

1987 Fleer Update

Steve Carlton
PITCHER

The 1987 update edition brings the regular Fleer set up to date by including traded players and hot rookies. The cards measure 2-1/2" x 3-1/2" and are housed in a specially designed box with 25 team logo stickers. A glossy-coated Fleer Collectors Edition set was also produced.

		MT
Complete Set (132):		30.00
Common Player:		.08
1	Scott Bankhead	.08
2	Eric Bell	.08
3	Juan Beniquez	.08
4	Juan Berenguer	.08
5	Mike Birkbeck	.08
6	Randy Bockus	.08
7	Rod Booker	.08
8	Thad Bosley	.08
9	Greg Brock	.08
10	Bob Brower	.08
11	Chris Brown	.08
12	Jerry Browne	.08
13	Ralph Bryant	.08
14	DeWayne Buice	.08

15	Ellis Burks	.80
16	Casey Candaele	.08
17	Steve Carlton	.40
18	Juan Castillo	.08
19	Chuck Crim	.08
20	Mark Davidson	.08
21	Mark Davis	.08
22	Storm Davis	.08
23	Bill Dawley	.08
24	Andre Dawson	.35
25	Brian Dayett	.08
26	Rick Dempsey	.08
27	Ken Dowell	.08
28	Dave Dravecky	.08
29	Mike Dunne	.08
30	Dennis Eckersley	.25
31	Cecil Fielder	.80
32	Brian Fisher	.08
33	Willie Fraser	.08
34	Ken Gerhart	.08
35	Jim Gott	.08
36	Dan Gladden	.08
37	Mike Greenwell	.15
38	Cecilio Guante	.08
39	Albert Hall	.08
40	Atlee Hammaker	.08
41	Mickey Hatcher	.08
42	Mike Heath	.08
43	Neal Heaton	.08
44	Mike Henneman	.20
45	Guy Hoffman	.08
46	Charles Hudson	.08
47	Chuck Jackson	.08
48	Mike Jackson	.08
49	Reggie Jackson	.60
50	Chris James	.08
51	Dion James	.08
52	Stan Javier	.08
53	Stan Jefferson	.08
54	Jimmy Jones	.08
55	Tracy Jones	.08
56	Terry Kennedy	.08
57	Mike Kingery	.08
58	Ray Knight	.08
59	Gene Larkin	.08
60	Mike LaValliere	.08
61	Jack Lazorko	.08
62	Terry Leach	.08
63	Rick Leach	.08
64	Craig Lefferts	.08
65	Jim Lindeman	.08
66	Bill Long	.08
67	Mike Loynd	.08
68	*Greg Maddux*	10.00
69	Bill Madlock	.08
70	Dave Magadan	.10
71	Joe Magrane	.20
72	Fred Manrique	.08
73	Mike Mason	.08
74	Lloyd McClendon	.08
75	Fred McGriff	3.00
76	Mark McGwire	20.00
77	Mark McLemore	.08
78	Kevin McReynolds	.08
79	Dave Meads	.08
80	Greg Minton	.08
81	John Mitchell	.08
82	Kevin Mitchell	.10
83	John Morris	.08
84	Jeff Musselman	.10
85	Randy Myers	.35
86	Gene Nelson	.08
87	Joe Niekro	.08
88	Tom Nieto	.08
89	Reid Nichols	.08
90	Matt Nokes	.08
91	Dickie Noles	.08
92	Edwin Nunez	.08
93	Jose Nunez	.08
94	Paul O'Neill	.75
95	Jim Paciorek	.08
96	Lance Parrish	.08
97	Bill Pecota	.08
98	Tony Pena	.08
99	Luis Polonia	.15
100	Randy Ready	.08
101	Jeff Reardon	.08
102	Gary Redus	.08
103	Rick Rhoden	.08
104	Wally Ritchie	.08
105	Jeff Robinson	.08
106	Mark Salas	.08
107	Dave Schmidt	.08
108	Kevin Seitzer	.08
109	John Shelby	.08
110	John Smiley	.10

111	Lary Sorenson	.08
112	Chris Speier	.08
113	Randy St. Claire	.08
114	Jim Sundberg	.08
115	B.J. Surhoff	.10
116	Greg Swindell	.15
117	Danny Tartabull	.08
118	Dorn Taylor	.08
119	Lee Tunnell	.08
120	Ed Vande Berg	.08
121	Andy Van Slyke	.08
122	Gary Ward	.08
123	Devon White	.35
124	Alan Wiggins	.08
125	Bill Wilkinson	.08
126	Jim Winn	.08
127	Frank Williams	.08
128	Ken Williams	.08
129	*Matt Williams*	4.00
130	Herm Winningham	.08
131	Matt Young	.08
132	Checklist 1-132	.08

1987 Fleer Update Glossy Tin

The 1987 Fleer glossy tin update set is identical to the regular-issue updates, except for the high-gloss coating on the cards' fronts and the lithographed metal box in which the sets were sold. Production was estimated at 100,000. Because of perceived overproduction, the glossy tin update set and singles currently carry little, if any, premium over the regular-issue updates.

	MT
Complete Set (132):	20.00
Common Player:	.08

(Star cards valued at .75-1X regular version 1987 Fleer updates.)

1988 Fleer

A clean, uncluttered look was the trademark of the 660-card 1988 Fleer set. The cards, which are the standard 2-1/2" x 3-1/2" format, feature blue and red diagonal lines set inside a white border. The player name and position are located on a slant in the upper left corner of the card. The player's team logo appears in the upper right corner. Below the player photo, a blue and red band with the word "Fleer" appears. Card backs include the card number, player personal information and career statistics, plus a

new feature called "At Their Best." This feature graphically shows a player's pitching or hitting statistics for home and road games and how he fared during day games as opposed to night contests. The set includes 19 special cards (#622-640) and 12 "Major League Prospects" cards.

		MT
Complete Set (660):		20.00
Common Player:		.06
Wax Box:		35.00
1	Keith Atherton	.06
2	Don Baylor	.10
3	Juan Berenguer	.06
4	Bert Blyleven	.06
5	Tom Brunansky	.06
6	Randy Bush	.06
7	Steve Carlton	.25
8	*Mark Davidson*	.06
9	George Frazier	.06
10	Gary Gaetti	.08
11	Greg Gagne	.06
12	Dan Gladden	.06
13	Kent Hrbek	.15
14	*Gene Larkin*	.06
15	Tim Laudner	.06
16	Steve Lombardozzi	.06
17	Al Newman	.06
18	Joe Niekro	.06
19	Kirby Puckett	.75
20	Jeff Reardon	.06
21a	Dan Schatzader (incorrect spelling)	.20
21b	Dan Schatzeder (correct spelling)	.06
22	Roy Smalley	.06
23	Mike Smithson	.06
24	*Les Straker*	.06
25	Frank Viola	.06
26	Jack Clark	.06
27	Vince Coleman	.06
28	Danny Cox	.06
29	Bill Dawley	.06
30	Ken Dayley	.06
31	Doug DeCinces	.06
32	Curt Ford	.06
33	Bob Forsch	.06
34	David Green	.06
35	Tom Herr	.06
36	Ricky Horton	.06
37	*Lance Johnson*	.50
38	Steve Lake	.06
39	Jim Lindeman	.06
40	*Joe Magrane*	.10
41	Greg Mathews	.06
42	Willie McGee	.08
43	John Morris	.06
44	Jose Oquendo	.06
45	Tony Pena	.06
46	Terry Pendleton	.06
47	Ozzie Smith	.45
48	John Tudor	.06
49	Lee Tunnell	.06
50	Todd Worrell	.06
51	Doyle Alexander	.06
52	Dave Bergman	.06
53	Tom Brookens	.06
54	Darrell Evans	.06
55	Kirk Gibson	.06
56	Mike Heath	.06
57	*Mike Henneman*	.20
58	Willie Hernandez	.06
59	Larry Herndon	.06
60	Eric King	.06
61	Chet Lemon	.06
62	*Scott Lusader*	.06
63	Bill Madlock	.06
64	Jack Morris	.06
65	Jim Morrison	.06
66	*Matt Nokes*	.15
67	Dan Petry	.06
68a	*Jeff Robinson* (Born 12-13-60 on back)	.25
68b	*Jeff Robinson* (Born 12/14/61 on back)	.10
69	Pat Sheridan	.06
70	Nate Snell	.06
71	Frank Tanana	.06
72	Walt Terrell	.06
73	Mark Thurmond	.06
74	Alan Trammell	.10
75	Lou Whitaker	.08

No.	Player	Price
76	Mike Aldrete	.06
77	Bob Brenly	.06
78	Will Clark	.40
79	Chili Davis	.10
80	Kelly Downs	.06
81	Dave Dravecky	.06
82	Scott Garrelts	.06
83	Atlee Hammaker	.06
84	Dave Henderson	.06
85	Mike Krukow	.06
86	Mike LaCoss	.06
87	Craig Lefferts	.06
88	Jeff Leonard	.06
89	Candy Maldonado	.06
90	Ed Milner	.06
91	Bob Melvin	.06
92	Kevin Mitchell	.08
93	*Jon Perlman*	.06
94	Rick Reuschel	.06
95	Don Robinson	.06
96	Chris Speier	.06
97	Harry Spilman	.06
98	Robbie Thompson	.06
99	Jose Uribe	.06
100	*Mark Wasinger*	.06
101	Matt Williams	2.50
102	Jesse Barfield	.06
103	George Bell	.06
104	Juan Beniquez	.06
105	John Cerutti	.06
106	Jim Clancy	.06
107	*Rob Ducey*	.06
108	Mark Eichhorn	.06
109	Tony Fernandez	.06
110	Cecil Fielder	.25
111	Kelly Gruber	.06
112	Tom Henke	.06
113	Garth Iorq (Iorg)	.06
114	Jimmy Key	.08
115	Rick Leach	.06
116	Manny Lee	.06
117	*Nelson Liriano*	.06
118	Fred McGriff	.50
119	Lloyd Moseby	.06
120	Rance Mulliniks	.06
121	Jeff Musselman	.06
122	*Jose Nunez*	.06
123	Dave Stieb	.06
124	Willie Upshaw	.06
125	Duane Ward	.06
126	Ernie Whitt	.06
127	Rick Aguilera	.06
128	Wally Backman	.06
129	*Mark Carreon*	.12
130	Gary Carter	.10
131	David Cone	.50
132	Ron Darling	.06
133	Len Dykstra	.08
134	Sid Fernandez	.06
135	Dwight Gooden	.10
136	Keith Hernandez	.06
137	*Gregg Jefferies*	.75
138	Howard Johnson	.06
139	Terry Leach	.06
140	*Barry Lyons*	.06
141	Dave Magadan	.06
142	Roger McDowell	.06
143	Kevin McReynolds	.06
144	*Keith Miller*	.06
145	*John Mitchell*	.06
146	Randy Myers	.06
147	Bob Ojeda	.06
148	Jesse Orosco	.06
149	Rafael Santana	.06
150	Doug Sisk	.06
151	Darryl Strawberry	.15
152	Tim Teufel	.06
153	Gene Walter	.06
154	Mookie Wilson	.06
155	*Jay Aldrich*	.06
156	Chris Bosio	.06
157	Glenn Braggs	.06
158	Greg Brock	.06
159	Juan Castillo	.06
160	Mark Clear	.06
161	Cecil Cooper	.06
162	*Chuck Crim*	.06
163	Rob Deer	.06
164	Mike Felder	.06
165	Jim Gantner	.06
166	Ted Higuera	.06
167	Steve Kiefer	.06
168	Rick Manning	.06
169	Paul Molitor	.40
170	Juan Nieves	.06
171	Dan Plesac	.06
172	Earnest Riles	.06
173	Bill Schroeder	.06
174	*Steve Stanicek*	.06
175	B.J. Surhoff	.06
176	Dale Sveum	.06
177	Bill Wegman	.06
178	Robin Yount	.50
179	Hubie Brooks	.06
180	Tim Burke	.06
181	Casey Candaele	.06
182	Mike Fitzgerald	.06
183	Tom Foley	.06
184	Andres Galarraga	.25
185	Neal Heaton	.06
186	Wallace Johnson	.06
187	Vance Law	.06
188	Dennis Martinez	.08
189	Bob McClure	.06
190	Andy McGaffigan	.06
191	Reid Nichols	.06
192	Pascual Perez	.06
193	Tim Raines	.10
194	Jeff Reed	.06
195	Bob Sebra	.06
196	Bryn Smith	.06
197	Randy St. Claire	.06
198	Tim Wallach	.06
199	Mitch Webster	.06
200	Herm Winningham	.06
201	Floyd Youmans	.06
202	*Brad Arnsberg*	.06
203	Rick Cerone	.06
204	Pat Clements	.06
205	Henry Cotto	.06
206	Mike Easler	.06
207	Ron Guidry	.10
208	Bill Gullickson	.06
209	Rickey Henderson	.25
210	Charles Hudson	.06
211	Tommy John	.10
212	*Roberto Kelly*	.40
213	Ron Kittle	.06
214	Don Mattingly	.75
215	Bobby Meacham	.06
216	Mike Pagliarulo	.06
217	Dan Pasqua	.06
218	Willie Randolph	.06
219	Rick Rhoden	.06
220	Dave Righetti	.06
221	Jerry Royster	.06
222	Tim Stoddard	.06
223	Wayne Tolleson	.06
224	Gary Ward	.06
225	Claudell Washington	.06
226	Dave Winfield	.40
227	Buddy Bell	.06
228	Tom Browning	.06
229	Dave Concepcion	.06
230	Kal Daniels	.06
231	Eric Davis	.10
232	Bo Diaz	.06
233	Nick Esasky	.06
234	John Franco	.06
235	Guy Hoffman	.06
236	Tom Hume	.06
237	Tracy Jones	.06
238	*Bill Landrum*	.06
239	Barry Larkin	.20
240	Terry McGriff	.06
241	Rob Murphy	.06
242	Ron Oester	.06
243	Dave Parker	.10
244	Pat Perry	.06
245	Ted Power	.06
246	Dennis Rasmussen	.06
247	Ron Robinson	.06
248	Kurt Stillwell	.06
249	*Jeff Treadway*	.06
250	Frank Williams	.06
251	Steve Balboni	.06
252	Bud Black	.06
253	Thad Bosley	.06
254	George Brett	.75
255	*John Davis*	.06
256	Steve Farr	.06
257	Gene Garber	.06
258	Jerry Gleaton	.06
259	Mark Gubicza	.06
260	Bo Jackson	.25
261	Danny Jackson	.06
262	*Ross Jones*	.06
263	Charlie Leibrandt	.06
264	*Bill Pecota*	.06
265	*Melido Perez*	.15
266	Jamie Quirk	.06
267	Dan Quisenberry	.06
268	Bret Saberhagen	.10
269	Angel Salazar	.06
270	Kevin Seitzer	.06
271	Danny Tartabull	.06
272	*Gary Thurman*	.06
273	Frank White	.06
274	Willie Wilson	.06
275	Tony Bernazard	.06
276	Jose Canseco	.40
277	Mike Davis	.06
278	Storm Davis	.06
279	Dennis Eckersley	.10
280	Alfredo Griffin	.06
281	Rick Honeycutt	.00
282	Jay Howell	.06
283	Reggie Jackson	.30
284	Dennis Lamp	.06
285	Carney Lansford	.06
286	Mark McGwire	4.00
287	Dwayne Murphy	.06
288	Gene Nelson	.06
289	Steve Ontiveros	.06
290	Tony Phillips	.12
291	Eric Plunk	.06
292	*Luis Polonia*	.15
293	*Rick Rodriguez*	.06
294	Terry Steinbach	.06
295	Dave Stewart	.10
296	Curt Young	.06
297	Luis Aguayo	.00
298	Steve Bedrosian	.06
299	Jeff Calhoun	.06
300	Don Carman	.06
301	*Todd Frohwirth*	.06
302	Greg Gross	.06
303	Kevin Gross	.06
304	Von Hayes	.06
305	*Keith Hughes*	.06
306	*Mike Jackson*	.06
307	Chris James	.06
308	Steve Jeltz	.06
309	Mike Maddux	.06
310	Lance Parrish	.08
311	Shane Rawley	.06
312	*Wally Ritchie*	.06
313	Bruce Ruffin	.06
314	Juan Samuel	.06
315	Mike Schmidt	.75
316	Rick Schu	.06
317	Jeff Stone	.06
318	Kent Tekulve	.06
319	Milt Thompson	.06
320	Glenn Wilson	.06
321	Rafael Belliard	.06
322	Barry Bonds	1.00
323	Bobby Bonilla	.20
324	Sid Bream	.06
325	John Cangelosi	.06
326	Mike Diaz	.06
327	Doug Drabek	.06
328	*Mike Dunne*	.06
329	Brian Fisher	.06
330	*Brett Gideon*	.06
331	Terry Harper	.06
332	Bob Kipper	.06
333	Mike LaValliere	.06
334	*Jose Lind*	.15
335	Junior Ortiz	.06
336	*Vicente Palacios*	.06
337	*Bob Patterson*	.12
338	*Al Pedrique*	.06
339	R.J. Reynolds	.06
340	*John Smiley*	.20
341	Andy Van Slyke	.06
342	Bob Walk	.06
343	Marty Barrett	.06
344	*Todd Benzinger*	.06
345	Wade Boggs	.25
346	*Tom Bolton*	.06
347	Oil Can Boyd	.06
348	Ellis Burks	1.00
349	Roger Clemens	.65
350	Steve Crawford	.06
351	Dwight Evans	.06
352	*Wes Gardner*	.06
353	Rich Gedman	.06
354	Mike Greenwell	.15
355	*Sam Horn*	.06
356	Bruce Hurst	.06
357	*John Marzano*	.06
358	Al Nipper	.06
359	Spike Owen	.06
360	*Jody Reed*	.30
361	Jim Rice	.08
362	Ed Romero	.06
363	Kevin Romine	.06

#	Player	Price
364	Joe Sambito	.06
365	Calvin Schiraldi	.06
366	Jeff Sellers	.06
367	Bob Stanley	.06
368	Scott Bankhead	.06
369	Phil Bradley	.06
370	Scott Bradley	.06
371	Mickey Brantley	.06
372	*Mike Campbell*	.06
373	Alvin Davis	.06
374	Lee Guetterman	.06
375	*Dave Hengel*	.06
376	Mike Kingery	.06
377	Mark Langston	.06
378	*Edgar Martinez*	1.50
379	Mike Moore	.06
380	Mike Morgan	.06
381	John Moses	.06
382	*Donnell Nixon*	.06
383	Edwin Nunez	.06
384	Ken Phelps	.06
385	Jim Presley	.06
386	Rey Quinones	.06
387	Jerry Reed	.06
388	Harold Reynolds	.06
389	Dave Valle	.06
390	*Bill Wilkinson*	.08
391	Harold Baines	.06
392	Floyd Bannister	.06
393	Daryl Boston	.06
394	Ivan Calderon	.06
395	Jose DeLeon	.06
396	Richard Dotson	.06
397	Carlton Fisk	.20
398	Ozzie Guillen	.06
399	Ron Hassey	.06
400	Donnie Hill	.06
401	Bob James	.06
402	Dave LaPoint	.06
403	*Bill Lindsey*	.06
404	*Bill Long*	.06
405	Steve Lyons	.06
406	*Fred Manrique*	.06
407	*Jack McDowell*	.75
408	Gary Redus	.06
409	Ray Searage	.06
410	Bobby Thigpen	.06
411	Greg Walker	.06
412	*Kenny Williams*	.06
413	Jim Winn	.06
414	Jody Davis	.06
415	Andre Dawson	.20
416	Brian Dayett	.06
417	Bob Dernier	.06
418	Frank DiPino	.06
419	Shawon Dunston	.12
420	Leon Durham	.06
421	*Les Lancaster*	.10
422	Ed Lynch	.06
423	Greg Maddux	2.00
424	Dave Martinez	.06
425a	Keith Moreland (bunting, photo actually Jody Davis)	3.00
425b	Keith Moreland (standing upright, correct photo)	.06
426	Jamie Moyer	.06
427	Jerry Mumphrey	.06
428	*Paul Noce*	.06
429	Rafael Palmeiro	.75
430	Wade Rowdon	.06
431	Ryne Sandberg	.75
432	Scott Sanderson	.06
433	Lee Smith	.10
434	Jim Sundberg	.06
435	Rick Sutcliffe	.06
436	Manny Trillo	.06
437	Juan Agosto	.06
438	Larry Andersen	.06
439	Alan Ashby	.06
440	Kevin Bass	.06
441	*Ken Caminiti*	2.00
442	*Rocky Childress*	.06
443	Jose Cruz	.06
444	Danny Darwin	.06
445	Glenn Davis	.06
446	Jim Deshaies	.06
447	Bill Doran	.06
448	Ty Gainey	.06
449	Billy Hatcher	.06
450	Jeff Heathcock	.06
451	Bob Knepper	.06
452	*Rob Mallicoat*	.06
453	*Dave Meads*	.06
454	Craig Reynolds	.06
455	Nolan Ryan	1.50
456	Mike Scott	.06
457	Dave Smith	.06
458	Denny Walling	.06
459	*Robbie Wine*	.06
460	*Gerald Young*	.06
461	Bob Brower	.06
462a	Jerry Browne (white player, photo actually Bob Brower)	2.50
462b	Jerry Browne (black player, correct photo)	.06
463	Steve Buechele	.06
464	Edwin Correa	.06
465	*Cecil Espy*	.06
466	Scott Fletcher	.06
467	Jose Guzman	.06
468	Greg Harris	.06
469	Charlie Hough	.06
470	Pete Incaviglia	.06
471	*Paul Kilgus*	.06
472	Mike Loynd	.06
473	Oddibe McDowell	.06
474	Dale Mohorcic	.06
475	Pete O'Brien	.06
476	Larry Parrish	.06
477	Geno Petralli	.06
478	Jeff Russell	.06
479	Ruben Sierra	.08
480	Mike Stanley	.06
481	Curtis Wilkerson	.06
482	Mitch Williams	.06
483	Bobby Witt	.06
484	Tony Armas	.06
485	Bob Boone	.06
486	Bill Buckner	.06
487	*DeWayne Buice*	.06
488	Brian Downing	.06
489	Chuck Finley	.06
490	Willie Fraser	.06
491	Jack Howell	.06
492	Ruppert Jones	.06
493	Wally Joyner	.10
494	Jack Lazorko	.06
495	Gary Lucas	.06
496	Kirk McCaskill	.06
497	Mark McLemore	.06
498	Darrell Miller	.06
499	Greg Minton	.06
500	Donnie Moore	.06
501	Gus Polidor	.06
502	Johnny Ray	.06
503	Mark Ryal	.06
504	Dick Schofield	.06
505	Don Sutton	.20
506	Devon White	.10
507	Mike Witt	.06
508	Dave Anderson	.06
509	Tim Belcher	.06
510	Ralph Bryant	.15
511	*Tim Crews*	.10
512	*Mike Devereaux*	.10
513	Mariano Duncan	.06
514	Pedro Guerrero	.06
515	Jeff Hamilton	.06
516	Mickey Hatcher	.06
517	Brad Havens	.06
518	Orel Hershiser	.10
519	*Shawn Hillegas*	.06
520	Ken Howell	.06
521	Tim Leary	.06
522	Mike Marshall	.06
523	Steve Sax	.06
524	Mike Scioscia	.06
525	Mike Sharperson	.06
526	John Shelby	.06
527	Franklin Stubbs	.06
528	Fernando Valenzuela	.08
529	Bob Welch	.06
530	Matt Young	.06
531	Jim Acker	.06
532	Paul Assenmacher	.06
533	*Jeff Blauser*	.40
534	*Joe Boever*	.06
535	Martin Clary	.06
536	*Kevin Coffman*	.06
537	Jeff Dedmon	.06
538	*Ron Gant*	2.50
539	*Tom Glavine*	2.50
540	Ken Griffey	.08
541	Al Hall	.06
542	Glenn Hubbard	.06
543	Dion James	.06
544	Dale Murphy	.20
545	Ken Oberkfell	.06
546	David Palmer	.06
547	Gerald Perry	.06
548	Charlie Puleo	.06
549	Ted Simmons	.06
550	Zane Smith	.06
551	Andres Thomas	.06
552	Ozzie Virgil	.06
553	Don Aase	.06
554	*Jeff Ballard*	.06
555	Eric Bell	.06
556	Mike Boddicker	.06
557	Ken Dixon	.06
558	Jim Dwyer	.06
559	Ken Gerhart	.06
560	*Rene Gonzales*	.06
561	Mike Griffin	.06
562	John Hayban (Habyan)	.06
563	Terry Kennedy	.06
564	Ray Knight	.06
565	Lee Lacy	.06
566	Fred Lynn	.08
567	Eddie Murray	.25
568	Tom Niedenfuer	.06
569	*Bill Ripken*	.06
570	Cal Ripken, Jr.	1.50
571	Dave Schmidt	.06
572	Larry Sheets	.06
573	*Pete Stanicek*	.06
574	*Mark Williamson*	.06
575	Mike Young	.06
576	Shawn Abner	.06
577	Greg Booker	.06
578	Chris Brown	.06
579	*Keith Comstock*	.06
580	*Joey Cora*	.06
581	Mark Davis	.06
582	Tim Flannery	.06
583	Goose Gossage	.08
584	Mark Grant	.06
585	Tony Gwynn	.65
586	Andy Hawkins	.06
587	Stan Jefferson	.06
588	Jimmy Jones	.06
589	John Kruk	.06
590	*Shane Mack*	.25
591	Carmelo Martinez	.06
592	Lance McCullers	.06
593	*Eric Nolte*	.06
594	Randy Ready	.06
595	Luis Salazar	.06
596	Benito Santiago	.10
597	Eric Show	.06
598	Garry Templeton	.06
599	Ed Whitson	.06
600	Scott Bailes	.06
601	Chris Bando	.06
602	*Jay Bell*	.75
603	Brett Butler	.10
604	Tom Candiotti	.06
605	Joe Carter	.20
606	Carmen Castillo	.06
607	*Brian Dorsett*	.06
608	*John Farrell*	.06
609	Julio Franco	.06
610	Mel Hall	.06
611	*Tommy Hinzo*	.06
612	Brook Jacoby	.06
613	*Doug Jones*	.30
614	Ken Schrom	.06
615	Cory Snyder	.06
616	Sammy Stewart	.06
617	Greg Swindell	.06
618	Pat Tabler	.06
619	Ed Vande Berg	.06
620	*Eddie Williams*	.06
621	Rich Yett	.06
622	Slugging Sophomores (Wally Joyner, Cory Snyder)	.25
623	Dominican Dynamite (George Bell, Pedro Guerrero)	.06
624	Oakland's Power Team (Jose Canseco, Mark McGwire)	2.00
625	Classic Relief (Dan Plesac, Dave Righetti)	.06
626	All Star Righties (Jack Morris, Bret Saberhagen, Mike Witt)	.06
627	Game Closers (Steve Bedrosian, John Franco)	.06
628	Masters of the Double Play (Ryne Sandberg, Ozzie Smith)	.35
629	Rookie Record Setter (Mark McGwire)	2.00
630	Changing the Guard in Boston (Todd Benzinger, Ellis Burks, Mike Greenwell)	.25

631	N.L. Batting Champs(Tony Gwynn, Tim Raines)	.20
632	Pitching Magic(Orel Hershiser, Mike Scott)	.06
633	Big Bats At First(Mark McGwire, Pat Tabler)	1.00
634	Hitting King and the Thief(Tony Gwynn, Vince Coleman)	.12
635	A.L. Slugging Shortstops(Tony Fernandez, Cal Ripken, Jr., Alan Trammell)	.30
636	Tried and True Sluggers(Gary Carter, Mike Schmidt)	.25
637	Crunch Time(Eric Davis)	.10
638	A.L. All Stars(Matt Nokes, Kirby Puckett)	.25
639	N.L. All Stars(Keith Hernandez, Dale Murphy)	.10
640	The "O's" Brothers(Bill Ripken, Cal Ripken, Jr.)	.50
641	Major League Prospects(Mark Grace), (Darrin Jackson)	2.00
642	Major League Prospects(Damon Berryhill), (Jeff Montgomery)	.20
643	Major League Prospects(Felix Fermin), (Jessie Reid)	.10
644	Major League Prospects(Greg Myers), (Greg Tabor)	.10
645	Major League Prospects(Jim Eppard, Joey Meyer)	.06
646	Major League Prospects(Adam Peterson), (Randy Velarde)	.15
647	Major League Prospects(Chris Gwynn), (Peter Smith)	.15
648	Major League Prospects(Greg Jelks), (Tom Newell)	.06
649	Major League Prospects(Mario Diaz), (Clay Parker)	.06
650	Major League Prospects(Jack Savage), (Todd Simmons)	.06
651	Major League Prospects(John Burkett), (Kirt Manwaring)	.25
652	Major League Prospects(Dave Otto), (Walt Weiss)	.40
653	Major League Prospects(Randell Byers (Randall)), (Jeff King)	.50
654a	Checklist 1-101 (21 is Schatzader)	.08
654b	Checklist 1-101 (21 is Schatzeder)	.06
655	Checklist 102-201	.06
656	Checklist 202-296	.06
657	Checklist 297-390	.06
658	Checklist 391-483	.06
659	Checklist 484-575	.06
660	Checklist 576-660	.06

1988 Fleer '87 World Series

Highlights of the 1987 Series are captured in this full-color insert set found only in Fleer's regular 660-card factory sets. This second World Series edition by Fleer features cards framed in red, with a blue and white starred bunting draped over the upper edges of the photo and a brief photo caption printed on a yellow band across the lower border. Numbered card backs are red, white and blue and include a description of the action pictured on the front, with stats for the Series.

MASTERFUL PERFORMANCE
TURNS MOMENTUM IN GAME 5

		MT
Complete Set (12):		2.50
Common Player:		.20
1	"Grand" Hero In Game 1(Dan Gladden)	.20
2	The Cardinals "Bush" Whacked(Randy Bush, Tony Pena)	.20
3	Masterful Performance Turns Momentum(John Tudor)	.20
4	Ozzie Smith	.75
5	Throw Smoke!(Tony Pena, Todd Worrell)	.20
6	Cardinal Attack - Disruptive Speed(Vince Coleman)	.20
7	Herr's Wallop(Dan Driessen, Tom Herr)	.20
8	Kirby Puckett	1.00
9	Kent Hrbek	.30
10	Rich Hacker (coach), Tom Herr, Lee Weyer (umpire)	.20
11	Game 7's Play At The Plate(Don Baylor, Dave Phillips (umpire))	.20
12	Frank Viola	.20

1988 Fleer All Stars

ALAN TRAMMELL

For the third consecutive year, Fleer randomly inserted All Star Team cards in its wax and cello packs. Twelve cards make up the set, with players chosen for the set being Fleer's idea of a major league All-Star team.

		MT
Complete Set (12):		6.00
Common Player:		.25
1	Matt Nokes	.25
2	Tom Henke	.25

3	Ted Higuera	.25
4	Roger Clemens	3.00
5	George Bell	.25
6	Andre Dawson	.45
7	Eric Davis	.35
8	Wade Boggs	1.00
9	Alan Trammell	.35
10	Juan Samuel	.25
11	Jack Clark	.25
12	Paul Molitor	2.00

1988 Fleer Box Panels

Wally Joyner
FIRST BASE

Fleer's third annual box-bottom issue once again included 16 full-color trading cards printed on the bottoms of four different wax and cello pack retail display boxes. Each box contains three player cards and one team logo card. Player cards follow the same design as the basic 1988 Fleer issue. Standard size, the cards are numbered C-1 through C-16.

		MT
Complete Panel Set (4):		8.00
Complete Singles Set (16):		3.00
Common Panel:		2.00
Common Single Player:		.15
Panel		2.00
1	Cardinals Logo	.05
11	Mike Schmidt	.75
14	Dave Stewart	.20
15	Tim Wallach	.15
Panel		2.75
2	Dwight Evans	.15
8	Shane Rawley	.15
10	Ryne Sandberg	.75
13	Tigers Logo	.05
Panel		2.00
3	Andres Galarraga	.30
6	Dale Murphy	.30
9	Giants Logo	.05
12	Kevin Seitzer	.15
Panel		2.75
4	Wally Joyner	.20
5	Twins Logo	.05
7	Kirby Puckett	1.00
16	Todd Worrell	.15

1988 Fleer Glossy Tin

In its second year of production, Fleer radically reduced production numbers on its glossy version of the 1988 baseball card set. With production estimates in the 60,000 set range, values of the '88 tin glossies are about double those of the regular issue cards.

Once again the issue was sold only as complete sets in colorful lithographed metal boxes.

	MT
Complete Set (672):	30.00
Common Player:	.15
(Star cards valued at 2X regular-issue 1988 Fleer version)	

1988 Fleer Headliners

This six-card set was inserted in Fleer three-packs, sold by retail outlets and hobby dealers nationwide. The card fronts feature crisp full-color player cut-outs printed on a grey and white facsimile sports page. "Fleer Headliners 1988" is printed in black and red on a white banner across the top of the card, both front and back. A similar white banner across the card bottom bears the black and white National or American League logo and a red player/team name. Card backs are black on grey with red accents and include the card number and a narrative career summary.

	MT
Complete Set (6):	5.00
Common Player:	.50
1 Don Mattingly	2.00
2 Mark McGwire	3.00
3 Jack Morris	.50
4 Darryl Strawberry	.50
5 Dwight Gooden	.75
6 Tim Raines	.50

1988 Fleer Mini

This third annual issue of miniatures (1-7/8" x 2-5/8") includes 120 high-gloss cards featuring new photos, not copies from the regular issue, although the card designs are identical. Card backs are red, white and blue and include personal data, yearly career stats and a stats breakdown of batting average, slugging percentage and on-base average, listed for day, night, home and road games. Card backs are numbered in alphabetical order by teams which are also listed alphabetically. The set includes 18 team logo stickers with black-and-white aerial stadium photos on the flip sides.

		MT
Complete Set (120):		8.00
Common Player:		.05
1	Eddie Murray	.25
2	Dave Schmidt	.05
3	Larry Sheets	.05
4	Wade Boggs	.65
5	Roger Clemens	.60
6	Dwight Evans	.05
7	Mike Greenwell	.08
8	Sam Horn	.05
9	Lee Smith	.08
10	Brian Downing	.05
11	Wally Joyner	.08
12	Devon White	.08
13	Mike Witt	.05
14	Ivan Calderon	.05
15	Ozzie Guillen	.05
16	Jack McDowell	.08
17	Kenny Williams	.05
18	Joe Carter	.15
19	Julio Franco	.05
20	Pat Tabler	.05
21	Doyle Alexander	.05
22	Jack Morris	.05
23	Matt Nokes	.05
24	Walt Terrell	.05
25	Alan Trammell	.10
26	Bret Saberhagen	.05
27	Kevin Seitzer	.05
28	Danny Tartabull	.05
29	Gary Thurman	.05
30	Ted Higuera	.05
31	Paul Molitor	.35
32	Dan Plesac	.05
33	Robin Yount	.40
34	Gary Gaetti	.05
35	Kent Hrbek	.08
36	Kirby Puckett	.75
37	Jeff Reardon	.05
38	Frank Viola	.05
39	Jack Clark	.05
40	Rickey Henderson	.50
41	Don Mattingly	1.00
42	Willie Randolph	.05
43	Dave Righetti	.05
44	Dave Winfield	.35
45	Jose Canseco	.65
46	Mark McGwire	2.00
47	Dave Parker	.08
48	Dave Stewart	.08
49	Walt Weiss	.05
50	Bob Welch	.05
51	Mickey Brantley	.05
52	Mark Langston	.05
53	Harold Reynolds	.05
54	Scott Fletcher	.05
55	Charlie Hough	.05
56	Pete Incaviglia	.05
57	Larry Parrish	.05
58	Ruben Sierra	.08
59	George Bell	.05
60	Mark Eichhorn	.05
61	Tony Fernandez	.05
62	Tom Henke	.05
63	Jimmy Key	.05
64	Dion James	.05
65	Dale Murphy	.15
66	Zane Smith	.05
67	Andre Dawson	.15
68	Mark Grace	.75
69	Jerry Mumphrey	.05
70	Ryne Sandberg	.65
71	Rick Sutcliffe	.05
72	Kal Daniels	.05
73	Eric Davis	.10
74	John Franco	.05
75	Ron Robinson	.05
76	Jeff Treadway	.05
77	Kevin Bass	.05
78	Glenn Davis	.05
79	Nolan Ryan	1.00
80	Mike Scott	.05
81	Dave Smith	.05
82	Kirk Gibson	.05
83	Pedro Guerrero	.05
84	Orel Hershiser	.10
85	Steve Sax	.05
86	Fernando Valenzuela	.08
87	Tim Burke	.05
88	Andres Galarraga	.15
89	Neal Heaton	.05
90	Tim Raines	.10
91	Tim Wallach	.05
92	Dwight Gooden	.10
93	Keith Hernandez	.05
94	Gregg Jefferies	.25
95	Howard Johnson	.05
96	Roger McDowell	.05
97	Darryl Strawberry	.15
98	Steve Bedrosian	.05
99	Von Hayes	.05
100	Shane Rawley	.05
101	Juan Samuel	.05
102	Mike Schmidt	.60
103	Bobby Bonilla	.10
104	Mike Dunne	.05
105	Andy Van Slyke	.05
106	Vince Coleman	.05
107	Bob Horner	.05
108	Willie McGee	.08
109	Ozzie Smith	.35
110	John Tudor	.05
111	Todd Worrell	.05
112	Tony Gwynn	.45
113	John Kruk	.05
114	Lance McCullers	.05
115	Benito Santiago	.08
116	Will Clark	.40
117	Jeff Leonard	.05
118	Candy Maldonado	.05
119	Kirt Manwaring	.05
120	Don Robinson	.05

1988 Fleer Update

This update set (numbered U-1 through U-132 are 2-1/2" x 3-1/2") features traded veterans and rookies in a mixture of full-color action shots and close-ups, framed by white borders with red and blue stripes. The backs are red, white and blue-grey and include personal info, along with yearly and "At Their Best" (day, night, home, road) stats charts. The set was packaged in white cardboard boxes with red and blue stripes. A glossy-coated edition of the update set was issued in its own box and is valued at two times the regular issue.

		MT
Complete Set (132):		13.00
Common Player:		.06
1	Jose Bautista	.06
2	Joe Orsulak	.06
3	Doug Sisk	.06
4	Craig Worthington	.06
5	Mike Boddicker	.06
6	Rick Cerone	.06
7	Larry Parrish	.06
8	Lee Smith	.10
9	Mike Smithson	.06
10	John Trautwein	.06
11	Sherman Corbett	.06
12	Chili Davis	.10
13	Jim Eppard	.06
14	Bryan Harvey	.25
15	John Davis	.06
16	Dave Gallagher	.06
17	Ricky Horton	.06
18	Dan Pasqua	.06
19	Melido Perez	.06
20	Jose Segura	.06
21	Andy Allanson	.06
22	Jon Perlman	.06
23	Domingo Ramos	.06
24	Rick Rodriguez	.06
25	Willie Upshaw	.06
26	Paul Gibson	.06
27	Don Heinkel	.06
28	Ray Knight	.06
29	Gary Pettis	.06
30	Luis Salazar	.06
31	Mike MacFarlane	.20
32	Jeff Montgomery	.25
33	Ted Power	.06
34	Israel Sanchez	.06
35	Kurt Stillwell	.06
36	Pat Tabler	.06
37	Don August	.06
38	Darryl Hamilton	.30
39	Jeff Leonard	.06
40	Joey Meyer	.06
41	Allan Anderson	.06
42	Brian Harper	.06
43	Tom Herr	.06
44	Charlie Lea	.06
45	John Moses	.06
46	John Candelaria	.06
47	Jack Clark	.06
48	Richard Dotson	.06
49	Al Leiter	.10
50	Rafael Santana	.06
51	Don Slaught	.06
52	Todd Burns	.06
53	Dave Henderson	.06
54	Doug Jennings	.06
55	Dave Parker	.20
56	Walt Weiss	.20
57	Bob Welch	.06
58	Henry Cotto	.06
59	Marion Diaz (Mario)	.06
60	Mike Jackson	.06
61	Bill Swift	.06
62	Jose Cecena	.06
63	Ray Hayward	.06
64	Jim Steels	.06
65	Pat Borders	.20
66	Sil Campusano	.06
67	Mike Flanagan	.06
68	Todd Stottlemyre	.15
69	David Wells	1.50
70	Jose Alvarez	.06
71	Paul Runge	.06
72	Cesar Jimenez (German)	.06
73	Pete Smith	.08
74	*John Smoltz*	3.00
75	Damon Berryhill	.06
76	Goose Gossage	.08
77	Mark Grace	2.00
78	Darrin Jackson	.15
79	Vance Law	.06
80	Jeff Pico	.06
81	Gary Varsho	.06
82	Tim Birtsas	.06
83	Rob Dibble	.20
84	Danny Jackson	.06
85	Paul O'Neill	.25
86	Jose Rijo	.06
87	*Chris Sabo*	.20
88	John Fishel	.06
89	*Craig Biggio*	2.50
90	Terry Puhl	.06
91	Rafael Ramirez	.06
92	Louie Meadows	.06
93	Kirk Gibson	.06
94	Alfredo Griffin	.06
95	Jay Howell	.06
96	Jesse Orosco	.06
97	Alejandro Pena	.06
98	Tracy Woodson	.06
99	John Dopson	.06
100	Brian Holman	.06
101	Rex Hudler	.06
102	Jeff Parrett	.06
103	Nelson Santovenia	.06
104	Kevin Elster	.08
105	Jeff Innis	.06
106	Mackey Sasser	.06
107	Phil Bradley	.06
108	Danny Clay	.06
109	Greg Harris	.06
110	Ricky Jordan	.06
111	David Palmer	.06
112	Jim Gott	.06
113	Tommy Gregg (photo actually Randy Milligan)	.06
114	Barry Jones	.06
115	Randy Milligan	.10
116	Luis Alicea	.10
117	Tom Brunansky	.06
118	John Costello	.06
119	Jose DeLeon	.06
120	Bob Horner	.06
121	Scott Terry	.06
122	*Roberto Alomar*	4.00
123	Dave Leiper	.06
124	Keith Moreland	.06
125	Mark Parent	.06
126	Dennis Rasmussen	.06
127	Randy Bockus	.06
128	Brett Butler	.12
129	Donell Nixon	.06
130	Earnest Riles	.06
131	Roger Samuels	.06
132	Checklist	.06

1988 Fleer Update Glossy Tin

The glossy version of the 1988 Fleer Update set differs from the regular-issue Update set only in the high-gloss finish applied to the cards' fronts and the lithographed metal box in which sets were sold.

	MT
Complete Set (132):	22.00
Common Player:	.15
(Star cards valued about 2X regular-issue 1988 Fleer Updates)	

1989 Fleer

This set includes 660 standard-size cards and was issued with 45 team logo stickers. Individual card fronts feature a grey and white striped background with full-color player photos framed by a bright line of color that slants upward to the right. The set also includes two subsets: 15 Major League Prospects and 12 SuperStar Specials. A special bonus set of 12 All-Star Team cards was randomly inserted in individual wax packs of 15 cards. The last seven cards in the set are checklists, with players listed alphabetically by teams.

		MT
Complete Set (660):		15.00
Common Player:		.05
Wax Box:		18.00
1	Don Baylor	.10
2	*Lance Blankenship*	.10
3	*Todd Burns*	.08
4	Greg Cadaret	.05
5	Jose Canseco	.20
6	Storm Davis	.05
7	Dennis Eckersley	.08
8	Mike Gallego	.05
9	Ron Hassey	.05
10	Dave Henderson	.05
11	Rick Honeycutt	.05
12	Glenn Hubbard	.05
13	Stan Javier	.05
14	*Doug Jennings*	.05
15	*Felix Jose*	.08
16	Carney Lansford	.05
17	Mark McGwire	.75
18	Gene Nelson	.05
19	Dave Parker	.10
20	Eric Plunk	.05
21	Luis Polonia	.05
22	Terry Steinbach	.05
23	Dave Stewart	.08
24	Walt Weiss	.05
25	Bob Welch	.05
26	Curt Young	.05
27	Rick Aguilera	.05
28	Wally Backman	.05
29	Mark Carreon	.05
30	Gary Carter	.15
31	David Cone	.10
32	Ron Darling	.05
33	Len Dykstra	.10
34	Kevin Elster	.05
35	Sid Fernandez	.05
36	Dwight Gooden	.10
37	Keith Hernandez	.05
38	Gregg Jefferies	.20
39	Howard Johnson	.05
40	Terry Leach	.05
41	Dave Magadan	.05
42	Bob McClure	.05
43	Roger McDowell	.05
44	Kevin McReynolds	.05
45	Keith Miller	.05
46	Randy Myers	.05
47	Bob Ojeda	.05
48	Mackey Sasser	.05
49	Darryl Strawberry	.15
50	Tim Teufel	.05
51	*Dave West*	.12
52	Mookie Wilson	.05
53	Dave Anderson	.05
54	Tim Belcher	.05
55	Mike Davis	.05
56	Mike Devereaux	.05
57	Kirk Gibson	.05
58	Alfredo Griffin	.05
59	Chris Gwynn	.05
60	Jeff Hamilton	.05
61a	Danny Heep (Home: San Antonio, TX)	.50
61b	Danny Heep (Home: Lake Hills, TX)	.05
62	Orel Hershiser	.08
63	Brian Holton	.05
64	Jay Howell	.05
65	Tim Leary	.05
66	Mike Marshall	.05
67	*Ramon Martinez*	.40
68	Jesse Orosco	.05
69	Alejandro Pena	.05

No.	Player	Price
70	Steve Sax	.05
71	Mike Scioscia	.05
72	Mike Sharperson	.05
73	John Shelby	.05
74	Franklin Stubbs	.05
75	John Tudor	.05
76	Fernando Valenzuela	.08
77	Tracy Woodson	.05
78	Marty Barrett	.05
79	Todd Benzinger	.05
80	Mike Boddicker	.05
81	Wade Boggs	.25
82	"Oil Can" Boyd	.05
83	Ellis Burks	.08
84	Rick Cerone	.05
85	Roger Clemens	.40
86	*Steve Curry*	.05
87	Dwight Evans	.05
88	Wes Gardner	.05
89	Rich Gedman	.05
90	Mike Greenwell	.08
91	Bruce Hurst	.05
92	Dennis Lamp	.05
93	Spike Owen	.05
94	Larry Parrish	.05
95	*Carlos Quintana*	.08
96	Jody Reed	.05
97	Jim Rice	.05
98a	Kevin Romine (batting follow-thru, photo actually Randy Kutcher)	.40
98b	Kevin Romine (arms crossed on chest, correct photo)	.40
99	Lee Smith	.10
100	Mike Smithson	.05
101	Bob Stanley	.05
102	Allan Anderson	.05
103	Keith Atherton	.05
104	Juan Berenguer	.05
105	Bert Blyleven	.05
106	*Eric Bullock*	.05
107	Randy Bush	.05
108	John Christensen	.05
109	Mark Davidson	.08
110	Gary Gaetti	.05
111	Greg Gagne	.05
112	Dan Gladden	.05
113	*German Gonzalez*	.05
114	Brian Harper	.05
115	Tom Herr	.08
116	Kent Hrbek	.05
117	Gene Larkin	.05
118	Tim Laudner	.05
119	Charlie Lea	.05
120	Steve Lombardozzi	.25
121a	John Moses (Home: Phoenix, AZ)	
121b	John Moses (Home: Tempe, AZ)	.05
122	Al Newman	.05
123	Mark Portugal	.05
124	Kirby Puckett	.40
125	Jeff Reardon	.05
126	Fred Toliver	.05
127	Frank Viola	.05
128	Doyle Alexander	.05
129	Dave Bergman	.05
130a	Tom Brookens (Mike Heath stats on back)	2.00
130b	Tom Brookens (correct stats on back)	.20
131	*Paul Gibson*	.05
132a	Mike Heath (Tom Brookens stats on back)	2.00
132b	Mike Heath (correct stats on back)	.20
133	*Don Heinkel*	.05
134	Mike Henneman	.05
135	Guillermo Hernandez	.05
136	Eric King	.05
137	Chet Lemon	.05
138	Fred Lynn	.08
139	Jack Morris	.05
140	Matt Nokes	.05
141	Gary Pettis	.05
142	Ted Power	.05
143	Jeff Robinson	.05
144	Luis Salazar	.05
145	*Steve Searcy*	.10
146	Pat Sheridan	.05
147	Frank Tanana	.05
148	Alan Trammell	.10
149	Walt Terrell	.05
150	Jim Walewander	.05
151	Lou Whitaker	.08
152	Tim Birtsas	.05
153	Tom Browning	.05
154	*Keith Brown*	.05
155	*Norm Charlton*	.15
156	Dave Concepcion	.05
157	Kal Daniels	.05
158	Eric Davis	.10
159	Bo Diaz	.05
160	*Rob Dibble*	.20
161	Nick Esasky	.05
162	John Franco	.05
163	Danny Jackson	.05
164	Barry Larkin	.15
165	Rob Murphy	.05
166	Paul O'Neill	.15
167	Jeff Reed	.05
168	Jose Rijo	.05
169	Ron Robinson	.05
170	*Chris Sabo*	.15
171	*Candy Sierra*	.05
172	*Van Snider*	.05
173a	Jeff Treadway (blue "target" above head)	8.00
173b	Jeff Treadway (no "target")	.05
174	Frank Williams	.05
175	Herm Winningham	.05
176	Jim Adduci	.05
177	Don August	.05
178	Mike Birkbeck	.05
179	Chris Bosio	.05
180	Glenn Braggs	.05
181	Greg Brock	.05
182	Mark Clear	.05
183	Chuck Crim	.05
184	Rob Deer	.05
185	Tom Filer	.05
186	Jim Gantner	.05
187	*Darryl Hamilton*	.25
188	Ted Higuera	.05
189	Odell Jones	.05
190	Jeffrey Leonard	.05
191	Joey Meyer	.05
192	Paul Mirabella	.05
193	Paul Molitor	.30
194	Charlie O'Brien	.05
195	Dan Plesac	.05
196	*Gary Sheffield*	.75
197	B.J. Surhoff	.05
198	Dale Sveum	.05
199	Bill Wegman	.05
200	Robin Yount	.30
201	Rafael Belliard	.05
202	Barry Bonds	.50
203	Bobby Bonilla	.10
204	Sid Bream	.05
205	Benny Distefano	.05
206	Doug Drabek	.05
207	Mike Dunne	.05
208	Felix Fermin	.05
209	Brian Fisher	.05
210	Jim Gott	.05
211	Bob Kipper	.05
212	Dave LaPoint	.05
213	Mike LaValliere	.05
214	Jose Lind	.05
215	Junior Ortiz	.05
216	Vicente Palacios	.05
217	Tom Prince	.05
218	Gary Redus	.05
219	R.J. Reynolds	.05
220	Jeff Robinson	.05
221	John Smiley	.05
222	Andy Van Slyke	.05
223	Bob Walk	.05
224	Glenn Wilson	.05
225	Jesse Barfield	.05
226	George Bell	.15
227	*Pat Borders*	.15
228	John Cerutti	.05
229	Jim Clancy	.05
230	Mark Eichhorn	.05
231	Tony Fernandez	.05
232	Cecil Fielder	.20
233	Mike Flanagan	.05
234	Kelly Gruber	.05
235	Tom Henke	.05
236	Jimmy Key	.05
237	Rick Leach	.05
238	Manny Lee	.05
239	Nelson Liriano	.05
240	Fred McGriff	.20
241	Lloyd Moseby	.05
242	Rance Mulliniks	.05
243	Jeff Musselman	.05
244	Dave Stieb	.05
245	Todd Stottlemyre	.05
246	Duane Ward	.05
247	David Wells	.05
248	Ernie Whitt	.05
249	Luis Aguayo	.05
250a	Neil Allen (Home: Sarasota, FL)	.25
250b	Neil Allen (Home: Syosset, NY)	.05
251	John Candelaria	.05
252	Jack Clark	.05
253	Richard Dotson	.05
254	Rickey Henderson	.15
255	Tommy John	.10
256	Roberto Kelly	.10
257	Al Leiter	.05
258	Don Mattingly	.50
259	Dale Mohorcic	.05
260	*Hal Morris*	.25
261	Scott Nielsen	.05
262	Mike Pagliarulo	.05
263	*Hipolito Pena*	.05
264	Ken Phelps	.05
265	Willie Randolph	.05
266	Rick Rhoden	.05
267	Dave Righetti	.05
268	Rafael Santana	.05
269	Steve Shields	.05
270	Joel Skinner	.05
271	Don Slaught	.05
272	Claudell Washington	.05
273	Gary Ward	.05
274	Dave Winfield	.15
275	Luis Aquino	.05
276	Floyd Bannister	.05
277	George Brett	.35
278	Bill Buckner	.05
279	*Nick Capra*	.05
280	*Jose DeJesus*	.05
281	Steve Farr	.05
282	Jerry Gleaton	.05
283	Mark Gubicza	.05
284	*Tom Gordon*	.20
285	Bo Jackson	.20
286	Charlie Leibrandt	.05
287	*Mike Macfarlane*	.15
288	Jeff Montgomery	.08
289	Bill Pecota	.05
290	Jamie Quirk	.05
291	Bret Saberhagen	.08
292	Kevin Seitzer	.05
293	Kurt Stillwell	.05
294	Pat Tabler	.05
295	Danny Tartabull	.05
296	Gary Thurman	.05
297	Frank White	.05
298	Willie Wilson	.05
299	Roberto Alomar	.40
300	*Sandy Alomar, Jr.*	.40
301	Chris Brown	.05
302	Mike Brumley	.05
303	Mark Davis	.05
304	Mark Grant	.05
305	Tony Gwynn	.40
306	*Greg Harris*	.05
307	Andy Hawkins	.05
308	Jimmy Jones	.05
309	John Kruk	.05
310	Dave Leiper	.05
311	Carmelo Martinez	.05
312	Lance McCullers	.05
313	Keith Moreland	.05
314	Dennis Rasmussen	.05
315	Randy Ready	.05
316	Benito Santiago	.08
317	Eric Show	.05
318	Todd Simmons	.05
319	Garry Templeton	.05
320	Dickie Thon	.05
321	Ed Whitson	.05
322	Marvell Wynne	.05
323	Mike Aldrete	.05
324	Brett Butler	.10
325	Will Clark	.25
326	Kelly Downs	.05
327	Dave Dravecky	.05
328	Scott Garrelts	.05
329	Atlee Hammaker	.05
330	*Charlie Hayes*	.25
331	Mike Krukow	.05
332	Craig Lefferts	.05
333	Candy Maldonado	.05
334	Kirt Manwaring	.05
335	Bob Melvin	.05
336	Kevin Mitchell	.08
337	Donell Nixon	.05
338	*Tony Perezchica*	.05

No.	Name	Price	No.	Name	Price	No.	Name	Price
339	Joe Price	.05	434	Rafael Palmeiro	.25	528	Oddibe McDowell	.05
340	Rick Reuschel	.05	435	Pat Perry	.05	529	Pete O'Brien	.05
341	Earnest Riles	.05	436	*Jeff Pico*	.05	530	Geno Petralli	.05
342	Don Robinson	.05	437	Ryne Sandberg	.40	531	Jeff Russell	.05
343	Chris Speier	.05	438	Calvin Schiraldi	.05	532	Ruben Sierra	.08
344	Robby Thompson	.05	439	Rick Sutcliffe	.05	533	Mike Stanley	.05
345	Jose Uribe	.05	440a	Manny Trillo ("Throws Rig")	1.50	534	Ed Vande Berg	.05
346	Matt Williams	.25	440b	Manny Trillo ("Throws Right")	.05	535	Curtis Wilkerson	.05
347	*Trevor Wilson*	.15				536	Mitch Williams	.05
348	Juan Agosto	.05	441	*Gary Varsho*	.05	537	Bobby Witt	.05
349	Larry Andersen	.05	442	Mitch Webster	.05	538	Steve Balboni	.05
350a	Alan Ashby ("Throws Rig")	.50	443	*Luis Alicea*	.15	539	Scott Bankhead	.05
350b	Alan Ashby ("Throws Right")	.05	444	Tom Brunansky	.05	540	Scott Bradley	.05
351	Kevin Bass	.05	445	Vince Coleman	.05	541	Mickey Brantley	.05
352	Buddy Bell	.05	446	*John Costello*	.05	542	Jay Buhner	.15
353	Craig Biggio	.30	447	Danny Cox	.05	543	Mike Campbell	.05
354	Danny Darwin	.05	448	Ken Dayley	.05	544	Darnell Coles	.05
355	Glenn Davis	.05	449	Jose DeLeon	.05	545	Henry Cotto	.05
356	Jim Deshaies	.05	450	Curt Ford	.05	546	Alvin Davis	.05
357	Bill Doran	.05	451	Pedro Guerrero	.05	547	Mario Diaz	.05
358	*John Fishel*	.05	452	Bob Horner	.05	548	*Ken Griffey, Jr.*	8.00
359	Billy Hatcher	.05	453	*Tim Jones*	.05	549	*Erik Hanson*	.15
360	Bob Knepper	.05	454	Steve Lake	.05	550	Mike Jackson	.05
361	*Louie Meadows*	.05	455	Joe Magrane	.05	551	Mark Langston	.05
362	Dave Meads	.05	456	Greg Mathews	.05	552	Edgar Martinez	.20
363	Jim Pankovits	.05	457	Willie McGee	.08	553	*Bill McGuire*	.05
364	Terry Puhl	.05	458	Larry McWilliams	.05	554	Mike Moore	.05
365	Rafael Ramirez	.05	459	Jose Oquendo	.05	555	Jim Presley	.05
366	Craig Reynolds	.05	460	Tony Pena	.05	556	Rey Quinones	.05
367	Mike Scott	.05	461	Terry Pendleton	.05	557	Jerry Reed	.05
368	Nolan Ryan	.75	462	*Steve Peters*	.05	558	Harold Reynolds	.05
369	Dave Smith	.05	463	Ozzie Smith	.25	559	*Mike Schooler*	.05
370	Gerald Young	.05	464	Scott Terry	.05	560	Bill Swift	.05
371	Hubie Brooks	.05	465	Denny Walling	.05	561	Dave Valle	.05
372	Tim Burke	.05	466	Todd Worrell	.05	562	Steve Bedrosian	.05
373	*John Dopson*	.10	467	Tony Armas	.05	563	Phil Bradley	.05
374	Mike Fitzgerald	.05	468	*Dante Bichette*	.50	564	Don Carman	.05
375	Tom Foley	.05	469	Bob Boone	.05	565	Bob Dernier	.05
376	Andres Galarraga	.15	470	*Terry Clark*	.05	566	Marvin Freeman	.05
377	Neal Heaton	.05	471	Stew Cliburn	.05	567	Todd Frohwirth	.05
378	Joe Hesketh	.05	472	*Mike Cook*	.05	568	Greg Gross	.05
379	*Brian Holman*	.10	473	*Sherman Corbett*	.05	569	Kevin Gross	.05
380	Rex Hudler	.05	474	Chili Davis	.08	570	Greg Harris	.05
381	*Randy Johnson*	1.00	475	Brian Downing	.05	571	Von Hayes	.05
382	Wallace Johnson	.05	476	Jim Eppard	.05	572	Chris James	.05
383	Tracy Jones	.05	477	Chuck Finley	.05	573	Steve Jeltz	.05
384	Dave Martinez	.05	478	Willie Fraser	.05	574	*Ron Jones*	.05
385	Dennis Martinez	.08	479	*Bryan Harvey*	.25	575	*Ricky Jordan*	.05
386	Andy McGaffigan	.05	480	Jack Howell	.05	576	Mike Maddux	.05
387	Otis Nixon	.05	481	Wally Joyner	.08	577	David Palmer	.05
388	*Johnny Paredes*	.05	482	Jack Lazorko	.05	578	Lance Parrish	.08
389	Jeff Parrett	.05	483	Kirk McCaskill	.05	579	Shane Rawley	.05
390	Pascual Perez	.05	484	Mark McLemore	.05	580	Bruce Ruffin	.05
391	Tim Raines	.08	485	Greg Minton	.05	581	Juan Samuel	.05
392	Luis Rivera	.05	486	Dan Petry	.05	582	Mike Schmidt	.30
393	*Nelson Santovenia*	.05	487	Johnny Ray	.05	583	Kent Tekulve	.05
394	Bryn Smith	.05	488	Dick Schofield	.05	584	Milt Thompson	.05
395	Tim Wallach	.05	489	Devon White	.08	585	*Jose Alvarez*	.05
396	Andy Allanson	.05	490	Mike Witt	.05	586	Paul Assenmacher	.05
397	*Rod Allen*	.05	491	Harold Baines	.08	587	Bruce Benedict	.05
398	Scott Bailes	.05	492	Daryl Boston	.05	588	Jeff Blauser	.05
399	Tom Candiotti	.05	493	Ivan Calderon	.05	589	*Terry Blocker*	.05
400	Joe Carter	.15	494	Mike Diaz	.05	590	Ron Gant	.15
401	Carmen Castillo	.05	495	Carlton Fisk	.15	591	Tom Glavine	.20
402	Dave Clark	.05	496	*Dave Gallagher*	.05	592	Tommy Gregg	.05
403	John Farrell	.05	497	Ozzie Guillen	.05	593	Albert Hall	.05
404	Julio Franco	.08	498	Shawn Hillegas	.05	594	Dion James	.05
405	Don Gordon	.05	499	Lance Johnson	.05	595	Rick Mahler	.05
406	Mel Hall	.05	500	Barry Jones	.05	596	Dale Murphy	.15
407	Brad Havens	.05	501	Bill Long	.05	597	Gerald Perry	.05
408	Brook Jacoby	.05	502	Steve Lyons	.05	598	Charlie Puleo	.05
409	Doug Jones	.05	503	Fred Manrique	.05	599	Ted Simmons	.05
410	*Jeff Kaiser*	.05	504	Jack McDowell	.08	600	Pete Smith	.05
411	*Luis Medina*	.05	505	*Donn Pall*	.12	601	Zane Smith	.05
412	Cory Snyder	.05	506	Kelly Paris	.05	602	John Smoltz	.20
413	Greg Swindell	.05	507	Dan Pasqua	.05	603	Bruce Sutter	.05
414	*Ron Tingley*	.05	508	*Ken Patterson*	.10	604	Andres Thomas	.05
415	Willie Upshaw	.05	509	Melido Perez	.05	605	Ozzie Virgil	.05
416	Ron Washington	.05	510	Jerry Reuss	.05	606	Brady Anderson	.30
417	Rich Yett	.05	511	Mark Salas	.05	607	Jeff Ballard	.05
418	Damon Berryhill	.05	512	Bobby Thigpen	.05	608	*Jose Bautista*	.05
419	Mike Bielecki	.05	513	Mike Woodard	.05	609	Ken Gerhart	.05
420	*Doug Dascenzo*	.05	514	Bob Brower	.05	610	Terry Kennedy	.05
421	Jody Davis	.05	515	Steve Buechele	.05	611	Eddie Murray	.30
422	Andre Dawson	.15	516	*Jose Cecena*	.05	612	Carl Nichols	.05
423	Frank DiPino	.05	517	Cecil Espy	.05	613	Tom Niedenfuer	.05
424	Shawon Dunston	.15	518	Scott Fletcher	.05	614	Joe Orsulak	.05
425	"Goose" Gossage	.08	519	Cecilio Guante	.05	615	*Oswaldo Peraza ((Oswald))*	.05
426	Mark Grace	.30	520	Jose Guzman	.05	616a	Bill Ripken (vulgarity on bat knob)	8.00
427	*Mike Harkey*	.05	521	Ray Hayward	.05	616b	Bill Ripken (scribble over vulgarity)	8.00
428	Darrin Jackson	.05	522	Charlie Hough	.05	616c	Bill Ripken (black box over vulgarity)	.10
429	Les Lancaster	.05	523	Pete Incaviglia	.05	616d	Bill Ripken (vulgarity whited out)	30.00
430	Vance Law	.05	524	Mike Jeffcoat	.05			
431	Greg Maddux	.75	525	Paul Kilgus	.05			
432	Jamie Moyer	.05	526	*Chad Kreuter*	.15			
433	Al Nipper	.05	527	Jeff Kunkel	.05			

617	Cal Ripken, Jr.	.75
618	Dave Schmidt	.05
619	Rick Schu	.05
620	Larry Sheets	.05
621	Doug Sisk	.05
622	Pete Stanicek	.05
623	Mickey Tettleton	.08
624	Jay Tibbs	.05
625	Jim Traber	.05
626	Mark Williamson	.05
627	*Craig Worthington*	.10
628	Speed and Power(Jose Canseco)	.25
629	Pitcher Perfect(Tom Browning)	.05
630	Like Father Like Sons(Roberto Alomar, Sandy Alomar, Jr.)	.25
631	N.L. All-Stars(Will Clark, Rafael Palmeiro)	.20
632	Homeruns Coast to Coast(Will Clark, Darryl Strawberry)	.25
633	Hot Corner's Hot Hitters(Wade Boggs, Carney Lansford)	.10
634	Triple A's(Jose Canseco, Mark McGwire, Terry Steinbach)	.60
635	Dual Heat(Mark Davis, Dwight Gooden)	.10
636	N.L. Pitching Power(David Cone, Danny Jackson)	.05
637	Cannon Arms(Bobby Bonilla, Chris Sabo)	.10
638	Double Trouble(Andres Galarraga, Gerald Perry)	.10
639	Power Center(Eric Davis)	.10
640	Major League Prospects(*Cameron Drew*), (*Steve Wilson*)	.05
641	Major League Prospects(Kevin Brown), (*Kevin Reimer*)	.30
642	Major League Prospects(*Jerald Clark*), (*Brad Pounders*)	.08
643	Major League Prospects(*Mike Capel*), (*Drew Hall*)	.05
644	Major League Prospects(*Joe Girardi*), (*Rolando Roomes*)	.20
645	Major League Prospects(*Marty Brown*), (*Lenny Harris*)	.12
646	Major League Prospects(*Luis de los Santos*), (*Jim Campbell*)	.05
647	Major League Prospects(*Miguel Garcia*), (*Randy Kramer*)	.05
648	Major League Prospects(*Torey Lovullo*), (*Robert Palacios*)	.08
649	Major League Prospects(*Jim Corsi*), (*Bob Milacki*)	.12
650	Major League Prospects(*Grady Hall*), (*Mike Rochford*)	.05
651	Major League Prospects(*Vance Lovelace*), (*Terry Taylor*)	.05
652	Major League Prospects(*Dennis Cook*), (*Ken Hill*)	.25
653	Major League Prospects(*Scott Service*), (*Shane Turner*)	.08
654	Checklist 1-101	.05
655	Checklist 102-200	.05
656	Checklist 201-298	.05
657	Checklist 299-395	.05
658	Checklist 396-490	.05
659	Checklist 491-584	.05
660	Checklist 585-660	.05

Modern cards have little collector value in conditions lower than Mint.
Figure NM cards at 75% of values shown;
EX cards at 40%.

1989 Fleer All-Stars

This special 12-card set represents Fleer's choices for its 1989 Major League All-Star Team. For the fourth consecutive year, Fleer inserted the special cards randomly inside its regular 1989 wax and cello packs. The cards feature two player photos set against a green background with the "1989 Fleer All Star Team" logo bannered across the top, and the player's name, position and team in the lower left corner. The backs contain a narrative player profile.

		MT
Complete Set (12):		8.00
Common Player:		.50
1	Bobby Bonilla	.75
2	Jose Canseco	2.00
3	Will Clark	1.50
4	Dennis Eckersley	.50
5	Julio Franco	.50
6	Mike Greenwell	.50
7	Orel Hershiser	.50
8	Paul Molitor	1.00
9	Mike Scioscia	.50
10	Darryl Strawberry	.60
11	Alan Trammell	.50
12	Frank Viola	.50

1989 Fleer Box Panels

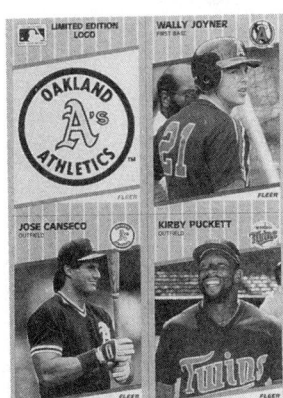

For the fourth consecutive year, Fleer issued a series of cards on the bottom panels of its regular 1989 wax pack boxes. The 28-card set includes 20 players and eight team logo cards, all designed in the identical style of the regular 1989 Fleer set. The box-bottom cards were randomly printed, four cards (three player cards and one team logo) on each bottom panel. The cards are numbered from C-1 to C-28.

		MT
Complete Panel Set (7):		6.00
Complete Singles Set (28):		3.00
Common Single Player:		.15
1	Mets Logo	.05
2	Wade Boggs	.45
3	George Brett	.40
4	Jose Canseco	.50
5	A's Logo	.05
6	Will Clark	.35
7	David Cone	.15
8	Andres Galarraga	.20
9	Dodgers Logo	.05
10	Kirk Gibson	.15
11	Mike Greenwell	.15
12	Tony Gwynn	.45
13	Tigers Logo	.05
14	Orel Hershiser	.15
15	Danny Jackson	.10
16	Wally Joyner	.15
17	Red Sox Logo	.05
18	Yankees Logo	.05
19	Fred McGriff	.25
20	Kirby Puckett	.50
21	Chris Sabo	.15
22	Kevin Seitzer	.10
23	Pirates logo	.05
24	Astros logo	.05
25	Darryl Strawberry	.20
26	Alan Trammell	.20
27	Andy Van Slyke	.10
28	Frank Viola	.10

1989 Fleer For The Record

Fleer's "For the Record" set features six players and their achievements from 1988. Fronts of the standard 2-1/2" x 3-1/2" cards feature a photo of the player set against a red scoreboard background. Card backs are grey and describe individual accomplishments. The cards were distributed randomly in rack packs.

		MT
Complete Set (6):		5.00
Common Player:		.50
1	Wade Boggs	1.00
2	Roger Clemens	1.50

		MT
3	Andres Galarraga	.75
4	Kirk Gibson	.50
5	Greg Maddux	2.00
6	Don Mattingly	1.50

1989 Fleer Glossy Tin

The last of the limited-edition, collector-version glossy tin sets is estimated to have been produced in an edition of about 60,000, creating a significant premium over their counterparts in the regualr Fleer set. The issue was sold only in complete-set form in a lithographed metal box. No glossy version of the '89 Update set was made. Fleer glossy sets were originally wholesaled at $40 each.

	MT
Complete Set (672):	80.00
Common Player:	.25

(Star cards valued at 3X-5X regular 1989 Fleer cards.)

1989 Fleer Update

ROBIN VENTURA
THIRD BASE

FLEER

Fleer produced its sixth consecutive "Update" set in 1989 to supplement the company's regular set. As in the past, the set consisted of 132 cards (numbered U-1 through U-132) that were sold by hobby dealers in special collector's boxes.

		MT
Complete Set (132):		5.00
Common Player:		.06
1	Phil Bradley	.06
2	Mike Devereaux	.06
3	Steve Finley	.30
4	Kevin Hickey	.06
5	Brian Holton	.06
6	Bob Milacki	.06
7	Randy Milligan	.06
8	John Dopson	.06
9	Nick Esasky	.06
10	Rob Murphy	.06
11	Jim Abbott	.20
12	Bert Blyleven	.06
13	Jeff Manto	.06
14	Bob McClure	.06
15	Lance Parrish	.08
16	Lee Stevens	.06
17	Claudell Washington	.06
18	Mark Davis	.06
19	Eric King	.06
20	Ron Kittle	.06
21	Matt Merullo	.06
22	Steve Rosenberg	.06

23	Robin Ventura	.40
24	Keith Atherton	.06
25	Joey (Albert) Belle	2.00
26	Jerry Browne	.06
27	Felix Fermin	.06
28	Brad Komminsk	.06
29	Pete O'Brien	.06
30	Mike Brumley	.06
31	Tracy Jones	.06
32	Mike Schwabe	.06
33	Gary Ward	.06
34	Frank Williams	.06
35	Kevin Appier	.40
36	Bob Boone	.06
37	Luis de los Santos	.06
38	Jim Eisenreich	.06
39	Jaime Navarro	.20
40	Bill Spiers	.06
41	Greg Vaughn	1.50
42	Randy Veres	.06
43	Wally Backman	.06
44	Shane Rawley	.06
45	Steve Balboni	.06
46	Jesse Barfield	.06
47	Alvaro Espinoza	.06
48	Bob Geren	.06
49	Mel Hall	.06
50	Andy Hawkins	.06
51	Hensley Meulens	.06
52	Steve Sax	.06
53	Deion Sanders	.75
54	Rickey Henderson	.15
55	Mike Moore	.06
56	Tony Phillips	.10
57	Greg Briley	.06
58	Gene Harris	.06
59	Randy Johnson	.75
60	Jeffrey Leonard	.06
61	Dennis Powell	.06
62	Omar Vizquel	.30
63	Kevin Brown	.10
64	Julio Franco	.08
65	Jamie Moyer	.06
66	Rafael Palmeiro	.25
67	Nolan Ryan	1.00
68	Francisco Cabrera	.06
69	Junior Felix	.06
70	Al Leiter	.08
71	Alex Sanchez	.06
72	Geronimo Berroa	.20
73	Derek Lilliquist	.06
74	Lonnie Smith	.06
75	Jeff Treadway	.06
76	Paul Kilgus	.06
77	Lloyd McClendon	.06
78	Scott Sanderson	.06
79	Dwight Smith	.06
80	Jerome Walton	.06
81	Mitch Williams	.06
82	Steve Wilson	.06
83	Todd Benzinger	.06
84	Ken Griffey	.08
85	Rick Mahler	.06
86	Rolando Roomes	.06
87	Scott Scudder	.06
88	Jim Clancy	.06
89	Rick Rhoden	.06
90	Dan Schatzeder	.06
91	Mike Morgan	.06
92	Eddie Murray	.20
93	Willie Randolph	.06
94	Ray Searage	.06
95	Mike Aldrete	.06
96	Kevin Gross	.06
97	Mark Langston	.06
98	Spike Owen	.06
99	Zane Smith	.06
100	Don Aase	.06
101	Barry Lyons	.06
102	Juan Samuel	.06
103	Wally Whitehurst	.06
104	Dennis Cook	.06
105	Len Dykstra	.08
106	Charlie Hayes	.15
107	Tommy Herr	.06
108	Ken Howell	.06
109	John Kruk	.06
110	Roger McDowell	.06
111	Terry Mulholland	.10
112	Jeff Parrett	.06
113	Neal Heaton	.06
114	Jeff King	.10
115	Randy Kramer	.06
116	Bill Landrum	.06
117	Cris Carpenter	.06
118	Frank DiPino	.06

119	Ken Hill	.15
120	Dan Quisenberry	.06
121	Milt Thompson	.06
122	Todd Zeile	.25
123	Jack Clark	.06
124	Bruce Hurst	.06
125	Mark Parent	.06
126	Bip Roberts	.06
127	Jeff Brantley	.15
128	Terry Kennedy	.06
129	Mike LaCoss	.06
130	Greg Litton	.06
131	Mike Schmidt	.50
132	Checklist	.06

1989 Fleer World Series

1988
World Series

"BULLDOG"

FLEER

This 12-card set, which depicts highlights of the 1988 World Series, was included as a special sub-set with the regular and glossy factory-collated Fleer set. It was not available as individual cards in wax packs, cello packs or any other form.

		MT
Complete Set, Regular (12):		1.50
Complete Set, Glossy (12):		1.00
Common Card:		.15
1	Dodgers Secret Weapon(Mickey Hatcher)	.15
2	Rookie Starts Series(Tim Belcher)	.15
3	Jose Canseco	.40
4	Dramatic Comeback(Mike Scioscia)	.15
5	Kirk Gibson	.30
6	Orel Hershiser	.30
7	One Swings, Three RBIs(Mike Marshall)	.15
8	Mark McGwire	.75
9	Sax's Speed Wins Game 4(Steve Sax)	.15
10	Series Caps Award Winning Year(Walt Weiss)	.15
11	Orel Hershiser	.25
12	Dodger Blue, World Champs	.25

Modern cards have little collector value in conditions lower than Mint. Figure NM cards at 75% of values shown; EX cards at 40%.

Values shown reflect the market as of January, 1999. On-field performances of current players in the 1999 baseball season are not factored in.

1990 Fleer

FLEER90

George Brett — FIRST BASE

Fleer's 1990 set, its 10th annual baseball card offering, again consisted of 660 cards numbered by team. The front of the cards feature mostly action photos surrounded by one of several different color bands and a white border. The set includes various special cards, including a series of "Major League Prospects," Players of the Decade, team checklist cards and a series of multi-player cards. The backs include complete career stats, player data, and a special "Vital Signs" section showing on-base percentage, slugging percentage, etc. for batters; and strikeout and walk ratios, opposing batting averages, etc. for pitchers.

		MT
Complete Set (660):		10.00
Common Player:		.05
Wax Box:		8.00
1	Lance Blankenship	.05
2	Todd Burns	.05
3	Jose Canseco	.25
4	Jim Corsi	.05
5	Storm Davis	.05
6	Dennis Eckersley	.10
7	Mike Gallego	.05
8	Ron Hassey	.05
9	Dave Henderson	.05
10	Rickey Henderson	.15
11	Rick Honeycutt	.05
12	Stan Javier	.05
13	Felix Jose	.05
14	Carney Lansford	.05
15	Mark McGwire	1.00
16	Mike Moore	.05
17	Gene Nelson	.05
18	Dave Parker	.08
19	Tony Phillips	.08
20	Terry Steinbach	.08
21	Dave Stewart	.08
22	Walt Weiss	.08
23	Bob Welch	.05
24	Curt Young	.05
25	Paul Assenmacher	.05
26	Damon Berryhill	.05
27	Mike Bielecki	.05
28	Kevin Blankenship	.05
29	Andre Dawson	.12
30	Shawon Dunston	.15
31	Joe Girardi	.08
32	Mark Grace	.25
33	Mike Harkey	.05
34	Paul Kilgus	.05
35	Les Lancaster	.05
36	Vance Law	.05
37	Greg Maddux	.60
38	Lloyd McClendon	.05
39	Jeff Pico	.05
40	Ryne Sandberg	.30
41	Scott Sanderson	.05
42	Dwight Smith	.05
43	Rick Sutcliffe	.05
44	*Jerome Walton*	.05
45	Mitch Webster	.05
46	Curt Wilkerson	.05
47	*Dean Wilkins*	.05
48	Mitch Williams	.05
49	Steve Wilson	.05
50	Steve Bedrosian	.05
51	*Mike Benjamin*	.08
52	*Jeff Brantley*	.10
53	Brett Butler	.10
54	Will Clark	.25
55	Kelly Downs	.05
56	Scott Garrelts	.05
57	Atlee Hammaker	.05
58	Terry Kennedy	.05
59	Mike LaCoss	.05
60	Craig Lefferts	.05
61	*Greg Litton*	.05
62	Candy Maldonado	.05
63	Kirt Manwaring	.05
64	*Randy McCament*	.05
65	Kevin Mitchell	.08
66	Donell Nixon	.05
67	Ken Oberkfell	.05
68	Rick Reuschel	.05
69	Ernest Riles	.05
70	Don Robinson	.05
71	Pat Sheridan	.05
72	Chris Speier	.05
73	Robby Thompson	.05
74	Jose Uribe	.05
75	Matt Williams	.25
76	George Bell	.05
77	Pat Borders	.05
78	John Cerutti	.05
79	*Junior Felix*	.05
80	Tony Fernandez	.05
81	Mike Flanagan	.05
82	*Mauro Gozzo*	.05
83	Kelly Gruber	.05
84	Tom Henke	.05
85	Jimmy Key	.05
86	Manny Lee	.05
87	Nelson Liriano	.05
88	Lee Mazzilli	.05
89	Fred McGriff	.20
90	Lloyd Moseby	.05
91	Rance Mulliniks	.05
92	Alex Sanchez	.05
93	Dave Steib	.08
94	Todd Stottlemyre	.05
95	Duane Ward	.05
96	David Wells	.05
97	Ernie Whitt	.05
98	Frank Wills	.05
99	Mookie Wilson	.05
100	*Kevin Appier*	.25
101	Luis Aquino	.05
102	Bob Boone	.05
103	George Brett	.30
104	Jose DeJesus	.05
105	Luis de los Santos	.05
106	Jim Eisenreich	.05
107	Steve Farr	.05
108	Tom Gordon	.20
109	Mark Gubicza	.05
110	Bo Jackson	.20
111	Terry Leach	.05
112	Charlie Leibrandt	.05
113	*Rick Luecken*	.05
114	Mike Macfarlane	.05
115	Jeff Montgomery	.05
116	Bret Saberhagen	.08
117	Kevin Seitzer	.05
118	Kurt Stillwell	.05
119	Pat Tabler	.05
120	Danny Tartabull	.05
121	Gary Thurman	.05
122	Frank White	.05
123	Willie Wilson	.05
124	*Matt Winters*	.05
125	Jim Abbott	.08
126	Tony Armas	.05
127	Dante Bichette	.20
128	Bert Blyleven	.05
129	Chili Davis	.08
130	Brian Downing	.05
131	*Mike Fetters*	.10
132	Chuck Finley	.05
133	Willie Fraser	.05
134	Bryan Harvey	.05
135	Jack Howell	.05
136	Wally Joyner	.10
137	*Jeff Manto*	.10
138	Kirk McCaskill	.05
139	Bob McClure	.05
140	Greg Minton	.05
141	Lance Parrish	.05
142	Dan Petry	.05
143	Johnny Ray	.05
144	Dick Schofield	.05
145	*Lee Stevens*	.10
146	Claudell Washington	.05
147	Devon White	.08
148	Mike Witt	.05
149	Roberto Alomar	.25
150	Sandy Alomar, Jr.	.12
151	Andy Benes	.20
152	Jack Clark	.05
153	Pat Clements	.05
154	Joey Cora	.05
155	Mark Davis	.05
156	Mark Grant	.05
157	Tony Gwynn	.40
158	Greg Harris	.05
159	Bruce Hurst	.05
160	Darrin Jackson	.05
161	Chris James	.05
162	Carmelo Martinez	.05
163	Mike Pagliarulo	.05
164	Mark Parent	.05
165	Dennis Rasmussen	.05
166	Bip Roberts	.05
167	Benito Santiago	.08
168	Calvin Schiraldi	.05
169	Eric Show	.05
170	Garry Templeton	.05
171	Ed Whitson	.05
172	Brady Anderson	.12
173	Jeff Ballard	.05
174	Phil Bradley	.05
175	Mike Devereaux	.05
176	*Steve Finley*	.10
177	Pete Harnisch	.10
178	Kevin Hickey	.05
179	Brian Holton	.05
180	*Ben McDonald*	.25
181	Bob Melvin	.05
182	Bob Milacki	.05
183	Randy Milligan	.05
184	Gregg Olson	.05
185	Joe Orsulak	.05
186	Bill Ripken	.05
187	Cal Ripken, Jr.	.60
188	Dave Schmidt	.05
189	Larry Sheets	.05
190	Mickey Tettleton	.08
191	Mark Thurmond	.05
192	Jay Tibbs	.05
193	Jim Traber	.05
194	Mark Williamson	.05
195	Craig Worthington	.05
196	Don Aase	.05
197	*Blaine Beatty*	.05
198	Mark Carreon	.05
199	Gary Carter	.10
200	David Cone	.05
201	Ron Darling	.05
202	Kevin Elster	.05
203	Sid Fernandez	.05
204	Dwight Gooden	.10
205	Keith Hernandez	.05
206	*Jeff Innis*	.05
207	Gregg Jefferies	.15
208	Howard Johnson	.05
209	Barry Lyons	.05
210	Dave Magadan	.05
211	Kevin McReynolds	.05
212	Jeff Musselman	.05
213	Randy Myers	.05
214	Bob Ojeda	.05
215	Juan Samuel	.05
216	Mackey Sasser	.05
217	Darryl Strawberry	.08
218	Tim Teufel	.05
219	Frank Viola	.05
220	Juan Agosto	.05
221	Larry Anderson	.05
222	*Eric Anthony*	.15
223	Kevin Bass	.05
224	Craig Biggio	.15
225	Ken Caminiti	.15
226	Jim Clancy	.05
227	Danny Darwin	.05
228	Glenn Davis	.05
229	Jim Deshaies	.05
230	Bill Doran	.05
231	Bob Forsch	.05
232	Brian Meyer	.05
233	Terry Puhl	.05

#	Player	Price
234	Rafael Ramirez	.05
235	Rick Rhoden	.05
236	Dan Schatzeder	.05
237	Mike Scott	.05
238	Dave Smith	.05
239	Alex Trevino	.05
240	Glenn Wilson	.05
241	Gerald Young	.05
242	Tom Brunansky	.05
243	Cris Carpenter	.05
244	*Alex Cole*	.05
245	Vince Coleman	.05
246	John Costello	.05
247	Ken Dayley	.05
248	Jose DeLeon	.05
249	Frank DiPino	.05
250	Pedro Guorrero	.05
251	Ken Hill	.08
252	Joe Magrane	.05
253	Willie McGee	.08
254	John Morris	.05
255	Jose Oquendo	.05
256	Tony Pena	.05
257	Terry Pendleton	.05
258	Ted Power	.05
259	Dan Quisenberry	.05
260	Ozzie Smith	.25
261	Scott Terry	.05
262	Milt Thompson	.05
263	Denny Walling	.05
264	Todd Worrell	.05
265	*Todd Zeile*	.15
266	Marty Barrett	.05
267	Mike Boddicker	.05
268	Wade Boggs	.25
269	Ellis Burks	.10
270	Rick Cerone	.05
271	Roger Clemens	.40
272	John Dopson	.05
273	Nick Esasky	.05
274	Dwight Evans	.05
275	Wes Gardner	.05
276	Rich Gedman	.05
277	Mike Greenwell	.08
278	Danny Heep	.05
279	Eric Hetzel	.05
280	Dennis Lamp	.05
281	Rob Murphy	.05
282	Joe Price	.05
283	Carlos Quintana	.05
284	Jody Reed	.05
285	Luis Rivera	.05
286	Kevin Romine	.05
287	Lee Smith	.08
288	Mike Smithson	.05
289	Bob Stanley	.05
290	Harold Baines	.08
291	Kevin Brown	.10
292	Steve Buechele	.05
293	*Scott Coolbaugh*	.05
294	*Jack Daugherty*	.05
295	Cecil Espy	.05
296	Julio Franco	.05
297	*Juan Gonzalez*	2.00
298	Cecilio Guante	.05
299	Drew Hall	.05
300	Charlie Hough	.05
301	Pete Incaviglia	.05
302	Mike Jeffcoat	.05
303	Chad Kreuter	.05
304	Jeff Kunkel	.05
305	Rick Leach	.05
306	Fred Manrique	.05
307	Jamie Moyer	.05
308	Rafael Palmeiro	.15
309	Geno Petralli	.05
310	Kevin Reimer	.05
311	*Kenny Rogers*	.15
312	Jeff Russell	.05
313	Nolan Ryan	.60
314	Ruben Sierra	.08
315	Bobby Witt	.05
316	Chris Bosio	.05
317	Glenn Braggs	.05
318	Greg Brock	.05
319	Chuck Crim	.05
320	Rob Deer	.05
321	Mike Felder	.05
322	Tom Filer	.05
323	*Tony Fossas*	.05
324	Jim Gantner	.05
325	Darryl Hamilton	.05
326	Ted Higuera	.05
327	Mark Knudson	.05
328	Bill Krueger	.05
329	*Tim McIntosh*	.05
330	Paul Molitor	.20
331	*Jaime Navarro*	.15
332	Charlie O'Brien	.05
333	*Jeff Peterek*	.05
334	Dan Plesac	.05
335	Jerry Reuss	.05
336	Gary Sheffield	.25
337	*Bill Spiers*	.05
338	B.J. Surhoff	.05
339	Greg Vaughn	.20
340	Robin Yount	.20
341	Hubie Brooks	.05
342	Tim Burke	.05
343	Mike Fitzgerald	.05
344	Tom Foley	.05
345	Andres Galarraga	.15
346	Damaso Garcia	.05
347	*Marquis Grissom*	.50
348	Kevin Gross	.05
349	Joe Hesketh	.05
350	*Jeff Huson*	.10
351	Wallace Johnson	.05
352	Mark Langston	.05
353	Dave Martinez	.05
354	Dennis Martinez	.08
355	Andy McGaffigan	.05
356	Otis Nixon	.05
357	Spike Owen	.05
358	Pascual Perez	.05
359	Tim Raines	.10
360	Nelson Santovenia	.05
361	Bryn Smith	.05
362	Zane Smith	.05
363	*Larry Walker*	1.25
364	Tim Wallach	.05
365	Rick Aguilera	.05
366	Allan Anderson	.05
367	Wally Backman	.05
368	Doug Baker	.05
369	Juan Berenguer	.05
370	Randy Bush	.05
371	Carmen Castillo	.05
372	*Mike Dyer*	.05
373	Gary Gaetti	.08
374	Greg Gagne	.05
375	Dan Gladden	.05
376	German Gonzalez	.05
377	Brian Harper	.05
378	Kent Hrbek	.08
379	Gene Larkin	.05
380	Tim Laudner	.05
381	John Moses	.05
382	Al Newman	.05
383	Kirby Puckett	.35
384	Shane Rawley	.05
385	Jeff Reardon	.05
386	Roy Smith	.05
387	*Gary Wayne*	.05
388	Dave West	.05
389	Tim Belcher	.05
390	Tim Crews	.05
391	Mike Davis	.05
392	Rick Dempsey	.05
393	Kirk Gibson	.05
394	Jose Gonzalez	.05
395	Alfredo Griffin	.05
396	Jeff Hamilton	.05
397	Lenny Harris	.05
398	Mickey Hatcher	.05
399	Orel Hershiser	.10
400	Jay Howell	.05
401	Mike Marshall	.05
402	Ramon Martinez	.08
403	Mike Morgan	.05
404	Eddie Murray	.20
405	Alejandro Pena	.05
406	Willie Randolph	.05
407	Mike Scioscia	.05
408	Ray Searage	.05
409	Fernando Valenzuela	.08
410	*Jose Vizcaino*	.25
411	*John Wetteland*	.25
412	Jack Armstrong	.05
413	Todd Benzinger	.05
414	Tim Birtsas	.05
415	Tom Browning	.05
416	Norm Charlton	.05
417	Eric Davis	.08
418	Rob Dibble	.05
419	John Franco	.05
420	Ken Griffey, Sr.	.08
421	*Chris Hammond*	.15
422	Danny Jackson	.05
423	Barry Larkin	.15
424	Tim Leary	.05
425	Rick Mahler	.05
426	*Joe Oliver*	.05
427	Paul O'Neill	.15
428	Luis Quinones	.05
429	Jeff Reed	.05
430	Jose Rijo	.05
431	Ron Robinson	.05
432	Rolando Roomes	.05
433	Chris Sabo	.05
434	*Scott Scudder*	.10
435	Herm Winningham	.05
436	Steve Balboni	.05
437	Jesse Barfield	.05
438	*Mike Blowers*	.15
439	Tom Brookens	.05
440	Greg Cadaret	.05
441	Alvaro Espinoza	.05
442	*Bob Geren*	.05
443	Lee Guetterman	.05
444	Mel Hall	.05
445	Andy Hawkins	.05
446	Roberto Kelly	.10
447	Don Mattingly	.40
448	Lance McCullers	.05
449	Hensley Meulens	.05
450	Dale Mohorcic	.05
451	Clay Parker	.05
452	Eric Plunk	.05
453	Dave Righetti	.05
454	Deion Sanders	.25
455	Steve Sax	.05
456	Don Slaught	.05
457	Walt Torrrol	.05
458	Dave Winfield	.15
459	Jay Bell	.05
460	Rafael Belliard	.05
461	Barry Bonds	.40
462	Bobby Bonilla	.10
463	Sid Bream	.05
464	Benny Distefano	.05
465	Doug Drabek	.05
466	Jim Gott	.05
467	Billy Hatcher	.05
468	Neal Heaton	.05
469	Jeff King	.08
470	Bob Kipper	.05
471	Randy Kramer	.05
472	Bill Landrum	.05
473	Mike LaValliere	.05
474	Jose Lind	.05
475	Junior Ortiz	.05
476	Gary Redus	.05
477	*Rick Reed*	.05
478	R.J. Reynolds	.05
479	Jeff Robinson	.05
480	John Smiley	.05
481	Andy Van Slyke	.05
482	Bob Walk	.05
483	Andy Allanson	.05
484	Scott Bailes	.05
485	Albert Belle	.50
486	Bud Black	.05
487	Jerry Browne	.05
488	Tom Candiotti	.05
489	Joe Carter	.10
490	David Clark	.05
491	John Farrell	.05
492	Felix Fermin	.05
493	Brook Jacoby	.05
494	Dion James	.05
495	Doug Jones	.05
496	Brad Komminsk	.05
497	Rod Nichols	.05
498	Pete O'Brien	.05
499	*Steve Olin*	.10
500	Jesse Orosco	.05
501	Joel Skinner	.05
502	Cory Snyder	.05
503	Greg Swindell	.05
504	Rich Yett	.05
505	Scott Bankhead	.05
506	Scott Bradley	.05
507	Greg Briley	.05
508	Jay Buhner	.08
509	Darnell Coles	.05
510	Keith Comstock	.05
511	Henry Cotto	.05
512	Alvin Davis	.05
513	Ken Griffey, Jr.	2.00
514	Erik Hanson	.05
515	Gene Harris	.05
516	Brian Holman	.05
517	Mike Jackson	.05
518	Randy Johnson	.35
519	Jeffrey Leonard	.05
520	Edgar Martinez	.10
521	Dennis Powell	.05

522	Jim Presley	.05
523	Jerry Reed	.05
524	Harold Reynolds	.05
525	Mike Schooler	.05
526	Bill Swift	.05
527	David Valle	.05
528	*Omar Vizquel*	.25
529	Ivan Calderon	.05
530	Carlton Fisk	.10
531	Scott Fletcher	.05
532	Dave Gallagher	.05
533	Ozzie Guillen	.05
534	*Greg Hibbard*	.05
535	Shawn Hillegas	.05
536	Lance Johnson	.05
537	Eric King	.05
538	Ron Kittle	.05
539	Steve Lyons	.05
540	Carlos Martinez	.05
541	*Tom McCarthy*	.05
542	*Matt Merullo*	.05
543	Donn Pall	.05
544	Dan Pasqua	.05
545	Ken Patterson	.05
546	Melido Perez	.05
547	Steve Rosenberg	.05
548	*Sammy Sosa*	5.00
549	Bobby Thigpen	.05
550	Robin Ventura	.15
551	Greg Walker	.05
552	Don Carman	.05
553	*Pat Combs*	.10
554	Dennis Cook	.05
555	Darren Daulton	.08
556	Len Dykstra	.05
557	Curt Ford	.05
558	Charlie Hayes	.05
559	Von Hayes	.05
560	Tom Herr	.05
561	Ken Howell	.05
562	Steve Jeltz	.05
563	Ron Jones	.05
564	Ricky Jordan	.05
565	John Kruk	.05
566	Steve Lake	.05
567	Roger McDowell	.05
568	Terry Mulholland	.05
569	Dwayne Murphy	.05
570	Jeff Parrett	.05
571	Randy Ready	.05
572	Bruce Ruffin	.05
573	Dickie Thon	.05
574	Jose Alvarez	.05
575	Geronimo Berroa	.05
576	Jeff Blauser	.05
577	Joe Boever	.05
578	Marty Clary	.05
579	Jody Davis	.05
580	Mark Eichhorn	.05
581	Darrell Evans	.05
582	Ron Gant	.10
583	Tom Glavine	.10
584	*Tommy Greene*	.15
585	Tommy Gregg	.05
586	*Dave Justice*	.40
587	Mark Lemke	.05
588	Derek Lilliquist	.05
589	Oddibe McDowell	.05
590	Kent Mercker	.20
591	Dale Murphy	.10
592	Gerald Perry	.05
593	Lonnie Smith	.05
594	Pete Smith	.05
595	John Smoltz	.15
596	*Mike Stanton*	.15
597	Andres Thomas	.05
598	Jeff Treadway	.05
599	Doyle Alexander	.05
600	Dave Bergman	.05
601	*Brian Dubois*	.08
602	Paul Gibson	.05
603	Mike Heath	.05
604	Mike Henneman	.05
605	Guillermo Hernandez	.05
606	*Shawn Holman*	.05
607	Tracy Jones	.05
608	Chet Lemon	.05
609	Fred Lynn	.08
610	Jack Morris	.05
611	Matt Nokes	.05
612	Gary Pettis	.05
613	*Kevin Ritz*	.08
614	Jeff Robinson	.05
615	Steve Searcy	.05
616	Frank Tanana	.05
617	Alan Trammell	.10

618	Gary Ward	.05
619	Lou Whitaker	.08
620	Frank Williams	.05
621a	Players of the Decade - 1980(George Brett) (... 10 .390 hitting ...)	2.00
621b	Players of the Decade - 1980(George Brett)	.20
622	Players of the Decade - 1981(Fernando Valenzuela)	.05
623	Players of the Decade - 1982(Dale Murphy)	.05
624a	Players of the Decade - 1983(Cal Ripkin, Jr.) (Ripkin)	3.00
624b	Players of the Decade - 1983(Cal Ripken, Jr.)	.25
625	Players of the Decade - 1984(Ryne Sandberg)	.25
626	Players of the Decade - 1985(Don Mattingly)	.25
627	Players of the Decade - 1986(Roger Clemens)	.25
628	Players of the Decade - 1987(George Bell)	.05
629	Players of the Decade - 1988(Jose Canseco)	.20
630a	Players of the Decade - 1989(Will Clark) (total bases 32)	.85
630b	Players of the Decade - 1989(Will Clark) (total bases 321)	.20
631	Game Savers(Mark Davis, Mitch Williams)	.05
632	Boston Igniters(Wade Boggs, Mike Greenwell)	.10
633	Starter & Stopper(Mark Gubicza, Jeff Russell)	.05
634	League's Best Shortstops(Tony Fernandez, Cal Ripken Jr.)	.15
635	Human Dynamos(Kirby Puckett, Bo Jackson)	.20
636	300 Strikeout Club(Mike Scott, Nolan Ryan)	.10
637	The Dymanic Duo(Will Clark, Kevin Mitchell)	.10
638	A.L. All-Stars(Don Mattingly, Mark McGwire)	.50
639	N.L. East Rivals(Howard Johnson, Ryne Sandberg)	.10
640	Major League Prospects(*Rudy Seanez*), (*Colin Charland*)	.15
641	Major League Prospects(*George Canale*), (*Kevin Maas*)	.15
642	Major League Prospects(*Kelly Mann*), (*Dave Hansen*)	.15
643	Major League Prospects(*Greg Smith*), (*Stu Tate*)	.10
644	Major League Prospects(*Tom Drees*), (*Dan Howitt*)	.08
645	Major League Prospects(*Mike Roesler*), (*Derrick May*)	.15
646	Major League Prospects(*Scott Hemond*), (*Mark Gardner*)	.15
647	Major League Prospects(*John Orton*), (*Scott Leius*)	.15
648	Major League Prospects(*Rich Monteleone*), (*Dana Williams*)	.08
649	Major League Prospects(*Mike Huff*), (*Steve Frey*)	.10
650	Major League Prospects(*Chuck McElroy*), (*Moises Alou*)	.50
651	Major League Prospects(*Bobby Rose*), (*Mike Hartley*)	.10
652	Major League Prospects(*Matt Kinzer*), (*Wayne Edwards*)	.08
653	Major League Prospects(*Delino DeShields*), (*Jason Grimsley*)	.20
654	Athletics, Cubs, Giants & Blue Jays (Checklist)	.05

655	Royals, Angels, Padres & Orioles (Checklist)	.05
656	Mets, Astros, Cardinals & Red Sox (Checklist)	.05
657	Rangers, Brewers, Expos & Twins (Checklist)	.05
658	Dodgers, Reds, Yankees & Pirates (Checklist)	.05
659	Indians, Mariners, White Sox & Phillies (Checklist)	.05
660	Braves, Tigers & Special Cards (Checklist)	.05

1990 Fleer All-Stars

The top players at each position, as selected by Fleer, are featured in this 12-card set inserted in cello packs and some wax packs. The cards measure 2-1/2" x 3-1/2" and feature a unique two-photo format on the card fronts.

		MT
Complete Set (12):		5.00
Common Player:		.20
1	Harold Baines	.25
2	Will Clark	.50
3	Mark Davis	.20
4	Howard Johnson	.20
5	Joe Magrane	.20
6	Kevin Mitchell	.25
7	Kirby Puckett	1.50
8	Cal Ripken	3.00
9	Ryne Sandberg	1.50
10	Mike Scott	.20
11	Ruben Sierra	.25
12	Mickey Tettleton	.20

1990 Fleer Box Panels

For the fifth consecutive year, Fleer issued a series of cards on the bottom panels of its wax pack boxes. This 28-card set features both players and team logo cards. The cards were numbered C-1 to C-28.

		MT
Complete Set, Panels (7):		4.00
Complete Set, Singles (28):		
Common Player:		.05
1	Giants Logo	.05
2	Tim Belcher	.05
3	Roger Clemens	.50
4	Eric Davis	.10
5	Glenn Davis	.05
6	Cubs Logo	.05
7	John Franco	.05
8	Mike Greenwell	.08
9	Athletics logo	.05
10	Ken Griffey, Jr.	2.50
11	Pedro Guerrero	.05
12	Tony Gwynn	.60
13	Blue Jays Logo	.05
14	Orel Hershiser	.10
15	Bo Jackson	.25
16	Howard Johnson	.05
17	Mets Logo	.05
18	Cardinals Logo	.05
19	Don Mattingly	1.00
20	Mark McGwire	1.00
21	Kevin Mitchell	.08
22	Kirby Puckett	.75
23	Royals Logo	.05
24	Orioles Logo	.05
25	Ruben Sierra	.10
26	Dave Stewart	.08
27	Jerome Walton	.05
28	Robin Yount	.25

1990 Fleer League Standouts

Fleer's "League Standouts" are six of baseball's top players distributed randomly in Fleer rack packs. Fronts feature full color photos with a six-dimensional effect. A black and gold frame borders the photo. Backs are yellow and describe the player's accomplishments. The cards measure 2-1/2" x 3-1/2".

		MT
Complete Set (6):		4.00
Common Player:		.50
1	Barry Larkin	.50
2	Don Mattingly	1.00
3	Darryl Strawberry	.50
4	Jose Canseco	.75
5	Wade Boggs	.60
6	Mark Grace	.60

1990 Fleer Soaring Stars

Larry Walker
OF • Montreal Expos

Cards from this 12-card set could be found in 1990 Fleer jumbo cello packs. The cards are styled with a cartoon flavor, featuring astronomical graphics surrounding the player. Backs feature information about the promising young player.

		MT
Complete Set (12):		15.00
Common Player:		.25
1	Todd Zeile	.50
2	Mike Stanton	.25
3	Larry Walker	3.00
4	Robin Ventura	2.00
5	Scott Coolbaugh	.25
6	Ken Griffey, Jr.	12.00
7	Tom Gordon	.35
8	Jerome Walton	.25
9	Junior Felix	.25
10	Jim Abbott	.50
11	Ricky Jordan	.25
12	Dwight Smith	.25

1990 Fleer Update

Fleer produced its seventh consecutive "Update" set in 1990. As in the past, the set consists of 132 cards (numbered U-1 through U-132) that were sold by hobby dealers in special collectors boxes. The cards are designed in the same style as the regular issue. A special Nolan Ryan commemorative card is included in the set.

		MT
Complete Set (132):		5.00
Common Player:		.06
1	Steve Avery	.15
2	Francisco Cabrera	.06
3	Nick Esasky	.06
4	Jim Kremers	.06
5	Greg Olson	.06
6	Jim Presley	.06
7	Shawn Boskie	.06
8	Joe Kraemer	.06
9	Luis Salazar	.06
10	Hector Villanueva	.06
11	Glenn Braggs	.06
12	Mariano Duncan	.06
13	Billy Hatcher	.06
14	Tim Layana	.06
15	Hal Morris	.20
16	Javier Ortiz	.06
17	Dave Rohde	.06
18	Eric Yelding	.10
19	Hubie Brooks	.06
20	Kal Daniels	.06
21	Dave Hansen	.06
22	Mike Hartley	.06
23	Stan Javier	.06
24	Jose Offerman	.15
25	Juan Samuel	.06
26	Dennis Boyd	.06
27	Delino DeShields	.10
28	Steve Frey	.06
29	Mark Gardner	.06
30	Chris Nabholz	.06
31	Bill Sampen	.06
32	Dave Schmidt	.06
33	Daryl Boston	.06
34	Chuck Carr	.20
35	John Franco	.06
36	*Todd Hundley*	.75
37	Julio Machado	.06
38	Alejandro Pena	.06
39	Darren Reed	.06
40	Kelvin Torve	.06
41	Darrel Akerfelds	.06
42	Jose DeJesus	.06
43	Dave Hollins	.20
44	Carmelo Martinez	.06
45	Brad Moore	.06
46	Dale Murphy	.15
47	Wally Backman	.06
48	Stan Belinda	.10
49	Bob Patterson	.06
50	Ted Power	.06
51	Don Slaught	.06
52	Geronimo Pena	.15
53	Lee Smith	.08
54	John Tudor	.06
55	Joe Carter	.15
56	Tom Howard	.06
57	Craig Lefferts	.06
58	Rafael Valdez	.06
59	Dave Anderson	.06
60	Kevin Bass	.06
61	John Burkett	.08
62	Gary Carter	.10
63	Rick Parker	.06
64	Trevor Wilson	.10
65	Chris Hoiles	.20
66	Tim Hulett	.06
67	Dave Johnson	.06
68	Curt Schilling	.30
69	David Segui	.15
70	Tom Brunansky	.06
71	Greg Harris	.06
72	Dana Kiecker	.06
73	Tim Naehring	.15
74	Tony Pena	.06
75	Jeff Reardon	.06
76	Jerry Reed	.06
77	Mark Eichhorn	.06
78	Mark Langston	.06
79	John Orton	.06
80	Luis Polonia	.06
81	Dave Winfield	.15
82	Cliff Young	.06
83	Wayne Edwards	.06
84	Alex Fernandez	.20
85	Craig Grebeck	.06
86	Scott Radinsky	.10
87	Frank Thomas	4.00
88	Beau Allred	.06
89	Sandy Alomar, Jr.	.15
90	*Carlos Baerga*	.25
91	Kevin Bearse	.06
92	Chris James	.06
93	Candy Maldonado	.06

94	Jeff Manto	.06
95	Cecil Fielder	.20
96	*Travis Fryman*	.35
97	Lloyd Moseby	.06
98	Edwin Nunez	.06
99	Tony Phillips	.10
100	Larry Sheets	.06
101	Mark Davis	.06
102	Storm Davis	.06
103	Gerald Perry	.06
104	Terry Shumpert	.06
105	Edgar Diaz	.06
106	Dave Parker	.12
107	Tim Drummond	.06
108	Junior Ortiz	.06
109	Park Pittman	.06
110	Kevin Tapani	.25
111	Oscar Azocar	.06
112	Jim Leyritz	.15
113	Kevin Maas	.06
114	Alan Mills	.12
115	Matt Nokes	.06
116	Pascual Perez	.06
117	Ozzie Canseco	.08
118	Scott Sanderson	.06
119	Tino Martinez	.40
120	Jeff Schaefer	.06
121	Matt Young	.06
122	Brian Bohanon	.10
123	Jeff Huson	.06
124	Ramon Manon	.06
125	Gary Mielke	.06
126	Willie Blair	.06
127	Glenallen Hill	.10
128	*John Olerud*	.35
129	Luis Sojo	.06
130	Mark Whiten	.15
131	Three Decades of No Hitters(Nolan Ryan)	.70
132	Checklist	.06

1990 Fleer World Series

This 12-card set depicts high-lights of the 1989 World Series and was included in the factory-collated Fleer set. Single World Series cards were discovered in cello and rack packs, but this was not intended to happen. Fronts of the 2-1/2" x 3-1/2" cards feature action photos set against a white background with a red and blue " '89 World Series" banner. Backs are pink and white and describe the events of the 1989 Fall Classic.

		MT
Complete Set (12):		1.50
Common Player:		.10
1	The Final Piece To The Puzzle(Mike Moore)	.10
2	Kevin Mitchell	.15
3	Game Two's Crushing Blow	.20

4	Will Clark	.60
5	Jose Canseco	.75
6	Great Leather in the Field	.10
7	Game One And A's Break Out On Top	.10
8	Dave Stewart	.25
9	Parker's Bat Produces Power(Dave Parker)	.25
10	World Series Record Book Game 3	.10
11	Rickey Henderson	.30
12	Oakland A's - Baseball's Best In '89	.25

1991 Fleer

Fleer expanded its 1991 set to include 720 cards. The cards feature yellow borders surrounding full-color action photos. Backs feature a circular portrait photo, biographical information, complete statistics, and career highlights. Once again the cards are numbered alphabetically within team. Because Fleer used more than one printer, many minor variations in photo cropping and typography can be found. The most notable are included in the checklist here.

		MT
Complete Set (720):		10.00
Common Player:		.05
Wax Box:		8.00
1	*Troy Afenir*	.05
2	Harold Baines	.08
3	Lance Blankenship	.05
4	Todd Burns	.05
5	Jose Canseco	.25
6	Dennis Eckersley	.08
7	Mike Gallego	.05
8	Ron Hassey	.05
9	Dave Henderson	.05
10	Rickey Henderson	.15
11	Rick Honeycutt	.05
12	Doug Jennings	.05
13	*Joe Klink*	.05
14	Carney Lansford	.05
15	*Darren Lewis*	.15
16	Willie McGee	.08
17a	Mark McGwire (six-line career summary)	.75
17b	Mark McGwire (seven-line career summary)	.75
18	Mike Moore	.05
19	Gene Nelson	.05
20	Dave Otto	.05
21	Jamie Quirk	.05
22	Willie Randolph	.05
23	Scott Sanderson	.05
24	Terry Steinbach	.05
25	Dave Stewart	.08
26	Walt Weiss	.05
27	Bob Welch	.05
28	Curt Young	.05
29	Wally Backman	.05
30	*Stan Belinda*	.05

31	Jay Bell	.05
32	Rafael Belliard	.05
33	Barry Bonds	.35
34	Bobby Bonilla	.10
35	Sid Bream	.05
36	Doug Drabek	.05
37	*Carlos Garcia*	.15
38	Neal Heaton	.05
39	Jeff King	.05
40	Bob Kipper	.05
41	Bill Landrum	.05
42	Mike LaValliere	.05
43	Jose Lind	.05
44	Carmelo Martinez	.05
45	Bob Patterson	.05
46	Ted Power	.05
47	Gary Redus	.05
48	R.J. Reynolds	.05
49	Don Slaught	.05
50	John Smiley	.05
51	Zane Smith	.05
52	*Randy Tomlin*	.10
53	Andy Van Slyke	.05
54	Bob Walk	.05
55	Jack Armstrong	.05
56	Todd Benzinger	.05
57	Glenn Braggs	.05
58	Keith Brown	.05
59	Tom Browning	.05
60	Norm Charlton	.08
61	Eric Davis	.05
62	Rob Dibble	.05
63	Bill Doran	.05
64	Mariano Duncan	.05
65	Chris Hammond	.05
66	Billy Hatcher	.05
67	Danny Jackson	.05
68	Barry Larkin	.10
69	*Tim Layana*	.05
70	*Terry Lee*	.05
71	Rick Mahler	.05
72	Hal Morris	.08
73	Randy Myers	.05
74	Ron Oester	.05
75	Joe Oliver	.05
76	Paul O'Neill	.10
77	Luis Quinones	.05
78	Jeff Reed	.05
79	Jose Rijo	.05
80	Chris Sabo	.05
81	Scott Scudder	.05
82	Herm Winningham	.05
83	Larry Andersen	.05
84	Marty Barrett	.05
85	Mike Boddicker	.05
86	Wade Boggs	.25
87	Tom Bolton	.05
88	Tom Brunansky	.05
89	Ellis Burks	.12
90	Roger Clemens	.35
91	Scott Cooper	.10
92	John Dopson	.05
93	Dwight Evans	.05
94	Wes Gardner	.05
95	*Jeff Gray*	.05
96	Mike Greenwell	.08
97	Greg Harris	.05
98	*Daryl Irvine*	.05
99	*Dana Kiecker*	.05
100	Randy Kutcher	.05
101	Dennis Lamp	.05
102	Mike Marshall	.05
103	John Marzano	.05
104	Rob Murphy	.05
105a	*Tim Naehring* (seven-line career summary)	.08
105b	*Tim Naehring* (nine-line career summary)	.08
106	Tony Pena	.05
107	*Phil Plantier*	.10
108	Carlos Quintana	.05
109	Jeff Reardon	.05
110	Jerry Reed	.05
111	Jody Reed	.05
112	Luis Rivera	.05
113a	Kevin Romine (one-line career summary)	.05
113b	Kevin Romine (two-line career summary)	.05
114	Phil Bradley	.05
115	Ivan Calderon	.05
116	Wayne Edwards	.05
117	Alex Fernandez	.10
118	Carlton Fisk	.10
119	Scott Fletcher	.05
120	*Craig Grebeck*	.08

No.	Player	Price
121	Ozzie Guillen	.05
122	Greg Hibbard	.05
123	Lance Johnson	.05
124	Barry Jones	.05
125a	Ron Karkovice (two-line career summary)	.05
125b	Ron Karkovice (one-line career summary)	.05
126	Eric King	.05
127	Steve Lyons	.05
128	Carlos Martinez	.05
129	Jack McDowell	.05
130	Donn Pall	.05
131	Dan Pasqua	.05
132	Ken Patterson	.05
133	Melido Perez	.05
134	Adam Peterson	.05
135	*Scott Radinsky*	.08
136	Sammy Sosa	.50
137	Bobby Thigpen	.05
138	Frank Thomas	1.50
139	Robin Ventura	.15
140	Daryl Boston	.05
141	*Chuck Carr*	.15
142	Mark Carreon	.05
143	David Cone	.05
144	Ron Darling	.05
145	Kevin Elster	.05
146	Sid Fernandez	.05
147	John Franco	.05
148	Dwight Gooden	.10
149	Tom Herr	.05
150	Todd Hundley	.10
151	Gregg Jefferies	.10
152	Howard Johnson	.05
153	Dave Magadan	.05
154	Kevin McReynolds	.05
155	Keith Miller	.05
156	Bob Ojeda	.05
157	Tom O'Malley	.05
158	Alejandro Pena	.05
159	*Darren Reed*	.08
160	Mackey Sasser	.05
161	Darryl Strawberry	.10
162	Tim Teufel	.05
163	Kelvin Torve	.05
164	Julio Valera	.05
165	Frank Viola	.05
166	Wally Whitehurst	.05
167	Jim Acker	.05
168	*Derek Bell*	.15
169	George Bell	.05
170	*Willie Blair*	.05
171	Pat Borders	.05
172	John Cerutti	.05
173	Junior Felix	.05
174	Tony Fernandez	.05
175	Kelly Gruber	.05
176	Tom Henke	.05
177	Glenallen Hill	.05
178	Jimmy Key	.08
179	Manny Lee	.05
180	Fred McGriff	.20
181	Rance Mulliniks	.05
182	Greg Myers	.05
183	John Olerud	.15
184	Luis Sojo	.05
185	Dave Steib	.05
186	Todd Stottlemyre	.05
187	Duane Ward	.05
188	David Wells	.05
189	*Mark Whiten*	.15
190	Ken Williams	.05
191	Frank Wills	.05
192	Mookie Wilson	.05
193	Don Aase	.05
194	Tim Belcher	.05
195	Hubie Brooks	.05
196	Dennis Cook	.05
197	Tim Crews	.05
198	Kal Daniels	.05
199	Kirk Gibson	.05
200	Jim Gott	.05
201	Alfredo Griffin	.05
202	Chris Gwynn	.05
203	Dave Hansen	.05
204	Lenny Harris	.05
205	Mike Hartley	.05
206	Mickey Hatcher	.05
207	*Carlos Hernandez*	.10
208	Orel Hershiser	.08
209	Jay Howell	.05
210	Mike Huff	.05
211	Stan Javier	.05
212	Ramon Martinez	.08
213	Mike Morgan	.05
214	Eddie Murray	.15
215	*Jim Neidlinger*	.05
216	Jose Offerman	.05
217	*Jim Poole*	.05
218	Juan Samuel	.05
219	Mike Scioscia	.05
220	Ray Searage	.05
221	Mike Sharperson	.05
222	Fernando Valenzuela	.08
223	Jose Vizcaino	.05
224	Mike Aldrete	.05
225	*Scott Anderson*	.05
226	Dennis Boyd	.05
227	Tim Burke	.05
228	Delino DeShields	.08
229	Mike Fitzgerald	.05
230	Tom Foley	.05
231	Steve Frey	.05
232	Andres Galarraga	.10
233	Mark Gardner	.05
234	Marquis Grissom	.15
235	Kevin Gross	.05
236	Drew Hall	.05
237	Dave Martinez	.05
238	Dennis Martinez	.08
239	Dale Mohorcic	.05
240	*Chris Nabholz*	.05
241	Otis Nixon	.05
242	Junior Noboa	.05
243	Spike Owen	.05
244	Tim Raines	.08
245	*Mel Rojas*	.12
246	*Scott Ruskin*	.05
247	*Bill Sampen*	.05
248	Nelson Santovenia	.05
249	Dave Schmidt	.05
250	Larry Walker	.25
251	Tim Wallach	.05
252	Dave Anderson	.05
253	Kevin Bass	.05
254	Steve Bedrosian	.05
255	Jeff Brantley	.05
256	John Burkett	.08
257	Brett Butler	.10
258	Gary Carter	.08
259	Will Clark	.20
260	*Steve Decker*	.05
261	Kelly Downs	.05
262	Scott Garrelts	.05
263	Terry Kennedy	.05
264	Mike LaCoss (photo on back actually Ken Oberkfell)	.05
265	*Mark Leonard*	.05
266	Greg Litton	.05
267	Kevin Mitchell	.08
268	Randy O'Neal	.05
269	*Rick Parker*	.05
270	Rick Reuschel	.05
271	Ernest Riles	.05
272	Don Robinson	.05
273	Robby Thompson	.05
274	Mark Thurmond	.05
275	Jose Uribe	.05
276	Matt Williams	.20
277	Trevor Wilson	.05
278	*Gerald Alexander*	.05
279	Brad Arnsberg	.05
280	*Kevin Belcher*	.05
281	*Joe Bitker*	.05
282	Kevin Brown	.10
283	Steve Buechele	.05
284	Jack Daugherty	.05
285	Julio Franco	.08
286	Juan Gonzalez	.50
287	*Bill Haselman*	.15
288	Charlie Hough	.05
289	Jeff Huson	.05
290	Pete Incaviglia	.05
291	Mike Jeffcoat	.05
292	Jeff Kunkel	.05
293	Gary Mielke	.05
294	Jamie Moyer	.05
295	Rafael Palmeiro	.10
296	Geno Petralli	.05
297	Gary Pettis	.05
298	Kevin Reimer	.05
299	Kenny Rogers	.05
300	Jeff Russell	.05
301	John Russell	.05
302	Nolan Ryan	.40
303	Ruben Sierra	.08
304	Bobby Witt	.05
305	Jim Abbott	.08
306	Kent Anderson	.05
307	Dante Bichette	.10
308	Bert Blyleven	.05
309	Chili Davis	.08
310	Brian Downing	.05
311	Mark Eichhorn	.05
312	Mike Fetters	.05
313	Chuck Finley	.05
314	Willie Fraser	.05
315	Bryan Harvey	.05
316	Donnie Hill	.05
317	Wally Joyner	.10
318	Mark Langston	.05
319	Kirk McCaskill	.05
320	John Orton	.05
321	Lance Parrish	.08
322	Luis Polonia	.05
323	Johnny Ray	.05
324	Bobby Rose	.05
325	Dick Schofield	.05
326	Rick Schu	.05
327a	Lee Stevens (six-line career summary)	.10
327b	Lee Stevens (seven-line career summary)	.10
328	Devon White	.08
329	Dave Winfield	.12
330	*Cliff Young*	.05
331	Dave Bergman	.05
332	*Phil Clark*	.08
333	Darnell Coles	.05
334	Milt Cuyler	.05
335	Cecil Fielder	.15
336	Travis Fryman	.10
337	Paul Gibson	.05
338	Jerry Don Gleaton	.05
339	Mike Heath	.05
340	Mike Henneman	.05
341	Chet Lemon	.05
342	Lance McCullers	.05
343	Jack Morris	.05
344	Lloyd Moseby	.05
345	Edwin Nunez	.05
346	Clay Parker	.05
347	Dan Petry	.05
348	Tony Phillips	.10
349	Jeff Robinson	.05
350	Mark Salas	.05
351	*Mike Schwabe*	.05
352	Larry Sheets	.05
353	John Shelby	.05
354	Frank Tanana	.05
355	Alan Trammell	.12
356	Gary Ward	.05
357	Lou Whitaker	.08
358	Beau Allred	.05
359	Sandy Alomar,Jr.	.10
360	Carlos Baerga	.10
361	*Kevin Bearse*	.05
362	Tom Brookens	.05
363	Jerry Browne	.05
364	Tom Candiotti	.05
365	Alex Cole	.05
366	John Farrell	.05
367	Felix Fermin	.05
368	Keith Hernandez	.05
369	Brook Jacoby	.05
370	Chris James	.05
371	Dion James	.05
372	Doug Jones	.05
373	Candy Maldonado	.05
374	Steve Olin	.05
375	Jesse Orosco	.05
376	Rudy Seanez	.05
377	Joel Skinner	.05
378	Cory Snyder	.05
379	Greg Swindell	.05
380	Sergio Valdez	.05
381	*Mike Walker*	.05
382	*Colby Ward*	.05
383	*Turner Ward*	.10
384	Mitch Webster	.05
385	Kevin Wickander	.05
386	Darrel Akerfelds	.05
387	Joe Boever	.05
388a	Rod Booker (no 1981 stats)	.05
388b	Rod Booker (1981 stats included)	.10
389	Sil Campusano	.05
390	Don Carman	.05
391	*Wes Chamberlain*	.10
392	Pat Combs	.05
393	Darren Daulton	.05
394	Jose DeJesus	.05
395	Len Dykstra	.08
396	Jason Grimsley	.05
397	Charlie Hayes	.05
398	Von Hayes	.05
399	*Dave Hollins*	.25

400	Ken Howell	.05
401	Ricky Jordan	.05
402	John Kruk	.05
403	Steve Lake	.05
404	*Chuck Malone*	.05
405	Roger McDowell	.05
406	Chuck McElroy	.05
407	*Mickey Morandini*	.10
408	Terry Mulholland	.05
409	Dale Murphy	.10
410	Randy Ready	.05
411	Bruce Ruffin	.05
412	Dickie Thon	.05
413	Paul Assenmacher	.05
414	Damon Berryhill	.05
415	Mike Bielecki	.05
416	*Shawn Boskie*	.08
417	Dave Clark	.05
418	Doug Dascenzo	.05
419a	Andre Dawson (no 1976 stats)	.10
419b	Andre Dawson (1976 stats included)	.10
420	Shawon Dunston	.10
421	Joe Girardi	.05
422	Mark Grace	.20
423	Mike Harkey	.05
424	Les Lancaster	.05
425	Bill Long	.05
426	Greg Maddux	.60
427	Derrick May	.08
428	Jeff Pico	.05
429	Domingo Ramos	.05
430	Luis Salazar	.05
431	Ryne Sandberg	.25
432	Dwight Smith	.05
433	Greg Smith	.05
434	Rick Sutcliffe	.05
435	Gary Varsho	.05
436	*Hector Villanueva*	.05
437	Jerome Walton	.05
438	Curtis Wilkerson	.05
439	Mitch Williams	.05
440	Steve Wilson	.05
441	Marvell Wynne	.05
442	Scott Bankhead	.05
443	Scott Bradley	.05
444	Greg Briley	.05
445	Mike Brumley	.05
446	Jay Buhner	.08
447	*Dave Burba*	.10
448	Henry Cotto	.05
449	Alvin Davis	.05
450	Ken Griffey, Jr.	1.50
451	Erik Hanson	.05
452	Gene Harris	.05
453	Brian Holman	.05
454	Mike Jackson	.05
455	Randy Johnson	.25
456	Jeffrey Leonard	.05
457	Edgar Martinez	.08
458	Tino Martinez	.20
459	Pete O'Brien	.05
460	Harold Reynolds	.05
461	Mike Schooler	.05
462	Bill Swift	.05
463	David Valle	.05
464	Omar Vizquel	.05
465	Matt Young	.05
466	Brady Anderson	.20
467	Jeff Ballard	.05
468	Juan Bell	.05
469a	Mike Devereaux ("six" last word in career summary top line)	.08
469b	Mike Devereaux ("runs" last word in career summary top line)	.08
470	Steve Finley	.05
471	Dave Gallagher	.05
472	*Leo Gomez*	.10
473	Rene Gonzales	.05
474	Pete Harnisch	.05
475	Kevin Hickey	.05
476	*Chris Hoiles*	.10
477	Sam Horn	.05
478	Tim Hulett	.05
479	Dave Johnson	.05
480	Ron Kittle	.05
481	Ben McDonald	.10
482	Bob Melvin	.05
483	Bob Milacki	.05
484	Randy Milligan	.05
485	*John Mitchell*	.05
486	Gregg Olson	.05
487	Joe Orsulak	.05

488	Joe Price	.05
489	Bill Ripken	.05
490	Cal Ripken, Jr.	.75
491	Curt Schilling	.05
492	*David Segui*	.05
493	*Anthony Telford*	.05
494	Mickey Tettleton	.05
495	Mark Williamson	.05
496	Craig Worthington	.05
497	Juan Agosto	.05
498	Eric Anthony	.05
499	Craig Biggio	.10
500	Ken Caminiti	.10
501	Casey Candaele	.05
502	*Andujar Cedeno*	.10
503	Danny Darwin	.05
504	Mark Davidson	.05
505	Glenn Davis	.05
506	Jim Deshaies	.05
507	*Luis Gonzalez*	.25
508	Bill Gullickson	.05
509	Xavier Hernandez	.05
510	Brian Meyer	.05
511	Ken Oberkfell	.05
512	Mark Portugal	.05
513	Rafael Ramirez	.05
514	*Karl Rhodes*	.08
515	Mike Scott	.05
516	*Mike Simms*	.05
517	Dave Smith	.05
518	Franklin Stubbs	.05
519	Glenn Wilson	.05
520	Eric Yelding	.05
521	Gerald Young	.05
522	Shawn Abner	.05
523	Roberto Alomar	.25
524	Andy Benes	.10
525	Joe Carter	.15
526	Jack Clark	.05
527	Joey Cora	.05
528	*Paul Faries*	.05
529	Tony Gwynn	.30
530	Atlee Hammaker	.05
531	Greg Harris	.05
532	*Thomas Howard*	.08
533	Bruce Hurst	.05
534	Craig Lefferts	.05
535	Derek Lilliquist	.05
536	Fred Lynn	.08
537	Mike Pagliarulo	.05
538	Mark Parent	.05
539	Dennis Rasmussen	.05
540	Bip Roberts	.05
541	*Richard Rodriguez*	.05
542	Benito Santiago	.08
543	Calvin Schiraldi	.05
544	Eric Show	.05
545	Phil Stephenson	.05
546	Garry Templeton	.05
547	Ed Whitson	.05
548	Eddie Williams	.05
549	Kevin Appier	.05
550	Luis Aquino	.05
551	Bob Boone	.05
552	George Brett	.25
553	*Jeff Conine*	.30
554	Steve Crawford	.05
555	Mark Davis	.05
556	Storm Davis	.05
557	Jim Eisenreich	.05
558	Steve Farr	.05
559	Tom Gordon	.05
560	Mark Gubicza	.05
561	Bo Jackson	.15
562	Mike Macfarlane	.05
563	*Brian McRae*	.25
564	Jeff Montgomery	.05
565	Bill Pecota	.05
566	Gerald Perry	.05
567	Bret Saberhagen	.08
568	*Jeff Schulz*	.05
569	Kevin Seitzer	.05
570	*Terry Shumpert*	.05
571	Kurt Stillwell	.05
572	Danny Tartabull	.08
573	Gary Thurman	.05
574	Frank White	.05
575	Willie Wilson	.05
576	Chris Bosio	.05
577	Greg Brock	.05
578	George Canale	.05
579	Chuck Crim	.05
580	Rob Deer	.05
581	*Edgar Diaz*	.05
582	*Tom Edens*	.05
583	Mike Felder	.05

584	Jim Gantner	.05
585	Darryl Hamilton	.05
586	Ted Higuera	.05
587	Mark Knudson	.05
588	Bill Krueger	.05
589	Tim McIntosh	.05
590	Paul Mirabella	.05
591	Paul Molitor	.20
592	Jaime Navarro	.08
593	Dave Parker	.12
594	Dan Plesac	.05
595	Ron Robinson	.05
596	Gary Sheffield	.20
597	Bill Spiers	.05
598	B.J. Surhoff	.05
599	Greg Vaughn	.08
600	Randy Veres	.05
601	Robin Yount	.15
602a	Rick Aguilera (five-line career summary)	.08
602b	Rick Aguilera (four-line career summary)	.08
603	Allan Anderson	.05
604	Juan Berenguer	.05
605	Randy Bush	.05
606	Carmen Castillo	.05
607	Tim Drummond	.05
608	*Scott Erickson*	.10
609	Gary Gaetti	.05
610	Greg Gagne	.05
611	Dan Gladden	.05
612	Mark Guthrie	.05
613	Brian Harper	.05
614	Kent Hrbek	.08
615	Gene Larkin	.05
616	Terry Leach	.05
617	Nelson Liriano	.05
618	Shane Mack	.05
619	John Moses	.05
620	*Pedro Munoz*	.10
621	Al Newman	.05
622	Junior Ortiz	.05
623	Kirby Puckett	.30
624	Roy Smith	.05
625	Kevin Tapani	.05
626	Gary Wayne	.05
627	David West	.05
628	Cris Carpenter	.05
629	Vince Coleman	.05
630	Ken Dayley	.05
631	Jose DeLeon	.05
632	Frank DiPino	.05
633	*Bernard Gilkey*	.25
634	Pedro Guerrero	.05
635	Ken Hill	.08
636	Felix Jose	.05
637	*Ray Lankford*	.25
638	Joe Magrane	.05
639	Tom Niedenfuer	.05
640	Jose Oquendo	.05
641	Tom Pagnozzi	.05
642	Terry Pendleton	.05
643	*Mike Perez*	.10
644	Bryn Smith	.05
645	Lee Smith	.08
646	Ozzie Smith	.20
647	Scott Terry	.05
648	Bob Tewksbury	.05
649	Milt Thompson	.05
650	John Tudor	.05
651	Denny Walling	.05
652	*Craig Wilson*	.05
653	Todd Worrell	.05
654	Todd Zeile	.08
655	*Oscar Azocar*	.05
656	Steve Balboni	.05
657	Jesse Barfield	.05
658	Greg Cadaret	.05
659	Chuck Cary	.05
660	Rick Cerone	.05
661	Dave Eiland	.05
662a	Alvaro Espinoza (no 1979-80 stats)	.08
662b	Alvaro Espinoza (1979-80 stats included)	.08
663	Bob Geren	.05
664	Lee Guetterman	.05
665	Mel Hall	.05
666a	Andy Hawkins (no 1978 stats)	.08
666b	Andy Hawkins (1978 stats included)	.08
667	Jimmy Jones	.05
668	Roberto Kelly	.08
669	Dave LaPoint	.05
670	Tim Leary	.05

671	*Jim Leyritz*	.20
672	Kevin Maas	.05
673	Don Mattingly	.40
674	Matt Nokes	.05
675	Pascual Perez	.05
676	Eric Plunk	.05
677	Dave Righetti	.05
678	Jeff Robinson	.05
679	Steve Sax	.05
680	Mike Witt	.05
681	Steve Avery	.08
682	Mike Bell	.05
683	Jeff Blauser	.05
684	Francisco Cabrera	.05
685	Tony Castillo	.05
686	Marty Clary	.05
687	Nick Esasky	.05
688	Ron Gant	.10
689	Tom Glavine	.10
690	Mark Grant	.05
691	Tommy Gregg	.05
692	Dwayne Henry	.05
693	Dave Justice	.25
694	*Jimmy Kremers*	.05
695	Charlie Leibrandt	.05
696	Mark Lemke	.05
697	Oddibe McDowell	.05
698	*Greg Olson*	.05
699	Jeff Parrett	.05
700	Jim Presley	.05
701	*Victor Rosario*	.05
702	Lonnie Smith	.05
703	Pete Smith	.05
704	John Smoltz	.10
705	Mike Stanton	.05
706	Andres Thomas	.05
707	Jeff Treadway	.05
708	*Jim Vatcher*	.05
709	Home Run Kings(Ryne Sandberg, Cecil Fielder)	.15
710	Second Generation Superstars(Barry Bonds, Ken Griffey, Jr.)	.50
711	NLCS Team Leaders(Bobby Bonilla, Barry Larkin)	.15
712	Top Game Savers(Bobby Thigpen, John Franco)	.05
713	Chicago's 100 Club(Andre Dawson, Ryne Sandberg)	.15
714	Checklists(Athletics, Pirates, Reds, Red Sox)	.05
715	Checklists - White Sox, Mets, Blue Jays, Dodgers	.05
716	Checklists(Expos, Giants, Rangers, Angels)	.05
717	Checklists(Tigers, Indians, Phillies, Cubs)	.05
718	Checklists (Mariners, Orioles, Astros, Padres)	.05
719	Checklists(Royals, Brewers, Twins, Cardinals)	.05
720	Checklists(Yankees, Braves, Super Stars)	.05

1991 Fleer All Stars

Three player photos are featured on each card in this special insert set. An action shot and portrait close-up are featured on the front, while a full-figure pose is showcased on the back. The cards were inserted into 1991 Fleer cello packs.

		MT
Complete Set (10):		9.00
Common Player:		.50
1	Ryne Sandberg	1.50
2	Barry Larkin	.60
3	Matt Williams	.60
4	Cecil Fielder	.50
5	Barry Bonds	2.00
6	Rickey Henderson	.50
7	Ken Griffey, Jr.	6.00
8	Jose Canseco	.75
9	Benito Santiago	.50
10	Roger Clemens	1.50

1991 Fleer Box Panels

Unlike past box panel sets, the 1991 Fleer box panels feature a theme; 1990 no-hitters are celebrated on the three different boxes. The cards feature blank backs and are numbered in order of no-hitter on the front. A team logo was included on each box. The card fronts are styled after the 1991 Fleer cards. A special no-hitter logo appears in the lower left corner.

		MT
Complete Set (10):		1.50
Common Player:		.10
1	Mark Langston, Mike Witt	.10
2	Randy Johnson	.50
3	Nolan Ryan	1.00
4	Dave Stewart	.20
5	Fernando Valenzuela	.15
6	Andy Hawkins	.10
7	Melido Perez	.10
8	Terry Mulholland	.10
9	Dave Steib	.10
----	Team Logos	.05

1991 Fleer ProVisions

The illustrations of artist Terry Smith are showcased in this special set. Twelve fantasy portraits were produced for cards inserted into rack packs. Four other ProVision cards were inserted into factory sets. The rack pack cards feature black borders, while the factory cards have white borders. Information on the card backs explains the manner in which Smith painted each player. Factory insert ProVisions are indicated by an "F" suffix in the checklist here.

		MT
Complete Set (12):		3.00
Common Player:		.15
Complete Factory Set (4):		3.00
Common Player:		.40
1	Kirby Puckett	.80
2	Will Clark	.40
3	Ruben Sierra	.15
4	Mark McGwire	1.00
5	Bo Jackson	.25
6	Jose Canseco	.50
7	Dwight Gooden	.15
8	Mike Greenwell	.15
9	Roger Clemens	.50
10	Eric Davis	.20
11	Don Mattingly	1.00
12	Darryl Strawberry	.25
1F	Barry Bonds	1.00
2F	Rickey Henderson	.50
3F	Ryne Sandberg	1.00
4F	Dave Stewart	.40

1991 Fleer Update

Fleer produced its eighth consecutive "Update" set in 1991 to supplement the company's regular set. As in the past, the set consists of 132 cards that were sold by hobby dealers in special collectors boxes. The cards are designed in the same style as the regular Fleer issue.

		MT
Complete Set (132):		4.00
Common Player:		.06
1	Glenn Davis	.06
2	Dwight Evans	.06
3	Jose Mesa	.12

4	Jack Clark	.06
5	Danny Darwin	.06
6	Steve Lyons	.06
7	Mo Vaughn	.65
8	Floyd Bannister	.06
9	Gary Gaetti	.08
10	Dave Parker	.15
11	Joey Cora	.06
12	Charlie Hough	.06
13	Matt Merullo	.06
14	Warren Newson	.10
15	Tim Raines	.10
16	Albert Belle	.30
17	Glenallen Hill	.08
18	Shawn Hillegas	.06
19	Mark Lewis	.10
20	Charles Nagy	.25
21	Mark Whiten	.10
22	John Cerutti	.06
23	Rob Deer	.06
24	Mickey Tettleton	.06
25	Warren Cromartie	.06
26	Kirk Gibson	.06
27	David Howard	.08
28	Brent Mayne	.20
29	Dante Bichette	.10
30	Mark Lee	.06
31	Julio Machado	.06
32	Edwin Nunez	.06
33	Willie Randolph	.06
34	Franklin Stubbs	.06
35	Bill Wegman	.06
36	Chili Davis	.08
37	Chuck Knoblauch	.50
38	Scott Leius	.06
39	Jack Morris	.06
40	Mike Pagliarulo	.06
41	Lenny Webster	.06
42	John Habyan	.06
43	Steve Howe	.06
44	Jeff Johnson	.06
45	Scott Kamieniecki	.10
46	Pat Kelly	.10
47	Hensley Meulens	.06
48	Wade Taylor	.10
49	Bernie Williams	.30
50	Kirk Dressendorfer	.15
51	Ernest Riles	.06
52	Rich DeLucia	.06
53	Tracy Jones	.06
54	Bill Krueger	.06
55	Alonzo Powell	.06
56	Jeff Schaefer	.06
57	Russ Swan	.06
58	John Barfield	.06
59	Rich Gossage	.08
60	Jose Guzman	.06
61	Dean Palmer	.20
62	*Ivan Rodriguez*	1.50
63	Roberto Alomar	.30
64	Tom Candiotti	.06
65	Joe Carter	.20
66	Ed Sprague	.20
67	Pat Tabler	.06
68	Mike Timlin	.15
69	Devon White	.08
70	Rafael Belliard	.06
71	Juan Berenguer	.06
72	Sid Bream	.06
73	Marvin Freeman	.06
74	Kent Mercker	.06
75	Otis Nixon	.06
76	Terry Pendleton	.06
77	George Bell	.06
78	Danny Jackson	.06
79	Chuck McElroy	.06
80	Gary Scott	.06
81	Heathcliff Slocumb	.08
82	Dave Smith	.06
83	Rick Wilkins	.20
84	Freddie Benavides	.08
85	Ted Power	.06
86	Mo Sanford	.15
87	*Jeff Bagwell*	2.50
88	Steve Finley	.06
89	Pete Harnisch	.06
90	Darryl Kile	.10
91	Brett Butler	.12
92	John Candelaria	.06
93	Gary Carter	.12
94	Kevin Gross	.06
95	Bob Ojeda	.06
96	Darryl Strawberry	.15
97	Ivan Calderon	.06
98	Ron Hassey	.06
99	Gilberto Reyes	.06

100	Hubie Brooks	.06
101	Rick Cerone	.06
102	Vince Coleman	.06
103	Jeff Innis	.06
104	Pete Schourek	.15
105	Andy Ashby	.12
106	Wally Backman	.06
107	Darrin Fletcher	.12
108	Tommy Greene	.08
109	John Morris	.06
110	Mitch Williams	.06
111	Lloyd McClendon	.06
112	Orlando Merced	.25
113	Vicente Palacios	.06
114	Gary Varsho	.06
115	John Wehner	.06
116	Rex Hudler	.06
117	Tim Jones	.06
118	Geronimo Pena	.15
119	Gerald Perry	.06
120	Larry Andersen	.06
121	Jerald Clark	.06
122	Scott Coolbaugh	.06
123	Tony Fernandez	.06
124	Darrin Jackson	.06
125	Fred McGriff	.20
126	Jose Mota	.06
127	Tim Teufel	.06
128	Bud Black	.06
129	Mike Felder	.06
130	Willie McGee	.08
131	Dave Righetti	.06
132	Checklist	.06

1991 Fleer World Series

Once again Fleer released a set in honor of the World Series from the previous season. The 1991 issue features only eight cards compared to twelve in 1990. The cards feature white borders surrounding full-color action shots from the 1990 Fall Classic. The card backs feature an overview of the World Series action.

		MT
Complete Set (8):		1.50
Common Player:		.20
1	Eric Davis	.25
2	Billy Hatcher	.20
3	Jose Canseco	.35
4	Rickey Henderson	.25
5	Chris Sabo, Carney Lansford	.20
6	Dave Stewart	.25
7	Jose Rijo	.20
8	Reds Celebrate	.20

A player's name in *italic* type indicates a rookie card.

1992 Fleer

For the second consecutive year, Fleer produced a 720-card set. The standard card fronts feature full-color action photos bordered in green with the player's name, position and team logo on the right border. The backs feature another full-color action photo, biographical information and statistics. A special 12-card Roger Clemens subset is also included in the 1992 Fleer set. Three more Clemens cards were available through a mail-in offer, and 2,000 Roger Clemens autographed cards were inserted in 1992 packs. Once again the cards are numbered according to team. Subsets in the issue included Major League Propects (#652-680), Record Setters (#681-687), League Leaders (#688-697), Superstar Specials (#698-707) and ProVisions (#708-713), which for the first time were part of the regular numbered set rather than limited edition insert cards.

		MT
Complete Set (720):		15.00
Common Player:		.05
Wax Box:		20.00
1	Brady Anderson	.15
2	Jose Bautista	.05
3	Juan Bell	.05
4	Glenn Davis	.05
5	Mike Devereaux	.05
6	Dwight Evans	.05
7	Mike Flanagan	.05
8	Leo Gomez	.05
9	Chris Hoiles	.05
10	Sam Horn	.05
11	Tim Hulett	.05
12	Dave Johnson	.08
13	*Chito Martinez*	.08
14	Ben McDonald	.08
15	Bob Melvin	.05
16	*Luis Mercedes*	.10
17	Jose Mesa	.08
18	Bob Milacki	.05
19	Randy Milligan	.05
20	Mike Mussina	.25
21	Gregg Olson	.05
22	Joe Orsulak	.05
23	Jim Poole	.05
24	*Arthur Rhodes*	.10
25	Billy Ripken	.05
26	Cal Ripken, Jr.	1.00
27	David Segui	.05
28	Roy Smith	.05
29	Anthony Telford	.05
30	Mark Williamson	.05
31	Craig Worthington	.05
32	Wade Boggs	.20
33	Tom Bolton	.05

No.	Player	Value	No.	Player	Value	No.	Player	Value
34	Tom Brunansky	.05	130	Milt Cuyler	.05	226	Bob Geren	.05
35	Ellis Burks	.15	131	*Mike Dalton*	.05	227	Lee Guetterman	.05
36	Jack Clark	.05	132	Rob Deer	.05	228	John Habyan	.05
37	Roger Clemens	.30	133	Cecil Fielder	.10	229	Mel Hall	.05
38	Danny Darwin	.05	134	Travis Fryman	.10	230	Steve Howe	.05
39	Mike Greenwell	.05	135	*Dan Gakeler*	.05	231	*Mike Humphreys*	.08
40	Joe Hesketh	.05	136	Paul Gibson	.05	232	*Scott Kamieniecki*	.10
41	Daryl Irvine	.05	137	Bill Gullickson	.05	233	Pat Kelly	.05
42	Dennis Lamp	.05	138	Mike Henneman	.05	234	Roberto Kelly	.08
43	Tony Pena	.05	139	Pete Incaviglia	.05	235	Tim Leary	.05
44	Phil Plantier	.05	140	*Mark Leiter*	.05	236	Kevin Maas	.05
45	Carlos Quintana	.05	141	*Scott Livingstone*	.15	237	Don Mattingly	.75
46	Jeff Reardon	.05	142	Lloyd Moseby	.05	238	Hensley Meulens	.05
47	Jody Reed	.05	143	Tony Phillips	.10	239	Matt Nokes	.05
48	Luis Rivera	.05	144	Mark Salas	.05	240	Pascual Perez	.05
49	Mo Vaughn	.30	145	Frank Tanana	.05	241	Eric Plunk	.05
50	Jim Abbott	.10	146	Walt Terrell	.05	242	*John Ramos*	.05
51	Kyle Abbott	.05	147	Mickey Tettleton	.05	243	Scott Sanderson	.05
52	*Ruben Amaro, Jr.*	.05	148	Alan Trammell	.10	244	Steve Sax	.05
53	Scott Bailes	.05	149	Lou Whitaker	.08	245	*Wade Taylor*	.15
54	*Chris Beasley*	.05	150	Kevin Appier	.08	246	Randy Velarde	.05
55	Mark Eichhorn	.05	151	Luis Aquino	.05	247	Bernie Williams	.20
56	Mike Fetters	.05	152	Todd Benzinger	.05	248	Troy Afenir	.05
57	Chuck Finley	.05	153	Mike Boddicker	.05	249	Harold Baines	.08
58	Gary Gaetti	.10	154	George Brett	.35	250	Lance Blankenship	.05
59	Dave Gallagher	.05	155	Storm Davis	.05	251	*Mike Bordick*	.10
60	Donnie Hill	.05	156	Jim Eisenreich	.05	252	Jose Canseco	.15
61	Bryan Harvey	.05	157	Kirk Gibson	.05	253	Steve Chitren	.05
62	Wally Joyner	.08	158	Tom Gordon	.05	254	Ron Darling	.05
63	Mark Langston	.05	159	Mark Gubicza	.05	255	Dennis Eckersley	.08
64	Kirk McCaskill	.05	160	*David Howard*	.05	256	Mike Gallego	.05
65	John Orton	.05	161	Mike Macfarlane	.05	257	Dave Henderson	.05
66	Lance Parrish	.05	162	Brent Mayne	.05	258	Rickey Henderson	.20
67	Luis Polonia	.05	163	Brian McRae	.08	259	Rick Honeycutt	.05
68	Bobby Rose	.05	164	Jeff Montgomery	.05	260	Brook Jacoby	.05
69	Dick Schofield	.05	165	Bill Pecota	.05	261	Carney Lansford	.05
70	Luis Sojo	.05	166	*Harvey Pulliam*	.05	262	Mark McGwire	.75
71	Lee Stevens	.05	167	Bret Saberhagen	.08	263	Mike Moore	.05
72	Dave Winfield	.15	168	Kevin Seitzer	.05	264	Gene Nelson	.05
73	Cliff Young	.05	169	Terry Shumpert	.05	265	Jamie Quirk	.05
74	Wilson Alvarez	.08	170	Kurt Stillwell	.05	266	*Joe Slusarski*	.15
75	*Esteban Beltre*	.08	171	Danny Tartabull	.05	267	Terry Steinbach	.05
76	Joey Cora	.05	172	Gary Thurman	.05	268	Dave Stewart	.05
77	*Brian Drahman*	.08	173	Dante Bichette	.12	269	Todd Van Poppel	.08
78	Alex Fernandez	.10	174	Kevin Brown	.05	270	Walt Weiss	.05
79	Carlton Fisk	.12	175	Chuck Crim	.05	271	Bob Welch	.05
80	Scott Fletcher	.05	176	Jim Gantner	.05	272	Curt Young	.05
81	Craig Grebeck	.05	177	Darryl Hamilton	.05	273	Scott Bradley	.05
82	Ozzie Guillen	.05	178	Ted Higuera	.05	274	Greg Briley	.05
83	Greg Hibbard	.05	179	Darren Holmes	.05	275	Jay Buhner	.08
84	Charlie Hough	.05	180	Mark Lee	.05	276	Henry Cotto	.05
85	Mike Huff	.05	181	Julio Machado	.05	277	Alvin Davis	.05
86	Bo Jackson	.15	182	Paul Molitor	.25	278	Rich DeLucia	.05
87	Lance Johnson	.05	183	Jaime Navarro	.05	279	Ken Griffey, Jr.	1.50
88	Ron Karkovice	.05	184	Edwin Nunez	.05	280	Erik Hanson	.05
89	Jack McDowell	.08	185	Dan Plesac	.05	281	Brian Holman	.05
90	Matt Merullo	.05	186	Willie Randolph	.05	282	Mike Jackson	.05
91	*Warren Newson*	.10	187	Ron Robinson	.05	283	Randy Johnson	.20
92	Donn Pall	.05	188	Gary Sheffield	.25	284	Tracy Jones	.05
93	Dan Pasqua	.05	189	Bill Spiers	.05	285	Bill Krueger	.05
94	Ken Patterson	.05	190	B.J. Surhoff	.05	286	Edgar Martinez	.08
95	Melido Perez	.05	191	Dale Sveum	.05	287	Tino Martinez	.12
96	Scott Radinsky	.05	192	Greg Vaughn	.05	288	Rob Murphy	.05
97	Tim Raines	.08	193	Bill Wegman	.05	289	Pete O'Brien	.05
98	Sammy Sosa	.50	194	Robin Yount	.25	290	Alonzo Powell	.05
99	Bobby Thigpen	.05	195	Rick Aguilera	.05	291	Harold Reynolds	.05
100	Frank Thomas	1.50	196	Allan Anderson	.05	292	Mike Schooler	.05
101	Robin Ventura	.15	197	Steve Bedrosian	.05	293	Russ Swan	.05
102	Mike Aldrete	.05	198	Randy Bush	.05	294	Bill Swift	.05
103	Sandy Alomar, Jr.	.08	199	Larry Casian	.05	295	Dave Valle	.05
104	Carlos Baerga	.10	200	Chili Davis	.08	296	Omar Vizquel	.05
105	Albert Belle	.35	201	Scott Erickson	.08	297	Gerald Alexander	.05
106	Willie Blair	.05	202	Greg Gagne	.05	298	Brad Arnsberg	.05
107	Jerry Browne	.05	203	Dan Gladden	.05	299	Kevin Brown	.08
108	Alex Cole	.05	204	Brian Harper	.05	300	Jack Daugherty	.05
109	Felix Fermin	.05	205	Kent Hrbek	.08	301	Mario Diaz	.05
110	Glenallen Hill	.05	206	Chuck Knoblauch	.15	302	Brian Downing	.05
111	Shawn Hillegas	.05	207	Gene Larkin	.05	303	Julio Franco	.05
112	Chris James	.05	208	Terry Leach	.05	304	Juan Gonzalez	.60
113	Reggie Jefferson	.10	209	Scott Leius	.05	305	Rich Gossage	.05
114	Doug Jones	.05	210	Shane Mack	.05	306	Jose Guzman	.05
115	Eric King	.05	211	Jack Morris	.05	307	*Jose Hernandez*	.05
116	Mark Lewis	.05	212	Pedro Munoz	.08	308	Jeff Huson	.05
117	Carlos Martinez	.05	213	*Denny Neagle*	.12	309	Mike Jeffcoat	.05
118	Charles Nagy	.08	214	Al Newman	.05	310	*Terry Mathews*	.05
119	Rod Nichols	.05	215	Junior Ortiz	.05	311	Rafael Palmeiro	.10
120	Steve Olin	.05	216	Mike Pagliarulo	.05	312	Dean Palmer	.08
121	Jesse Orosco	.05	217	Kirby Puckett	.60	313	Geno Petralli	.05
122	Rudy Seanez	.05	218	Paul Sorrento	.05	314	Gary Pettis	.05
123	Joel Skinner	.05	219	Kevin Tapani	.05	315	Kevin Reimer	.05
124	Greg Swindell	.05	220	Lenny Webster	.05	316	Ivan Rodriguez	.20
125	Jim Thome	.40	221	Jesse Barfield	.05	317	Kenny Rogers	.05
126	Mark Whiten	.05	222	Greg Cadaret	.05	318	*Wayne Rosenthal*	.05
127	Scott Aldred	.05	223	Dave Eiland	.05	319	Jeff Russell	.05
128	Andy Allanson	.05	224	Alvaro Espinoza	.05	320	Nolan Ryan	.45
129	John Cerutti	.05	225	Steve Farr	.05	321	Ruben Sierra	.05

No.	Player	Price	No.	Player	Price	No.	Player	Price
322	Jim Acker	.05	418	Jeff Reed	.05	514	Charlie O'Brien	.05
323	Roberto Alomar	.25	419	Jose Rijo	.05	515	Mackey Sasser	.05
324	Derek Bell	.15	420	Chris Sabo	.05	516	*Pete Schourek*	.10
325	Pat Borders	.05	421	Reggie Sanders	.15	517	Julio Valera	.05
326	Tom Candiotti	.05	422	Scott Scudder	.05	518	Frank Viola	.05
327	Joe Carter	.08	423	Glenn Sutko	.05	519	Wally Whitehurst	.05
328	Rob Ducey	.05	424	Eric Anthony	.05	520	*Anthony Young*	.10
329	Kelly Gruber	.05	425	Jeff Bagwell	.60	521	*Andy Ashby*	.10
330	*Juan Guzman*	.25	426	Craig Biggio	.15	522	*Kim Batiste*	.05
331	Tom Henke	.05	427	Ken Caminiti	.15	523	Joe Boever	.05
332	Jimmy Key	.05	428	Casey Candaele	.05	524	Wes Chamberlain	.05
333	Manny Lee	.05	429	Mike Capel	.05	525	Pat Combs	.05
334	Al Leiter	.05	430	Andujar Cedeno	.05	526	Danny Cox	.05
335	*Bob MacDonald*	.05	431	Jim Corsi	.05	527	Darren Daulton	.05
336	Candy Maldonado	.05	432	Mark Davidson	.05	528	Jose DeJesus	.05
337	Rance Mulliniks	.05	433	Steve Finley	.05	529	Len Dykstra	.08
338	Greg Myers	.05	434	Luis Gonzalez	.05	530	Darrin Fletcher	.05
339	John Olerud	.15	435	Pete Harnisch	.05	531	Tommy Greene	.05
340	*Ed Sprague*	.10	436	Dwayne Henry	.05	532	Jason Grimsley	.05
341	Dave Stieb	.05	437	Xavier Hernandez	.05	533	Charlie Hayes	.05
342	Todd Stottlemyre	.05	438	Jimmy Jones	.05	534	Von Hayes	.05
343	*Mike Timlin*	.15	439	*Darryl Kile*	.10	535	Dave Hollins	.08
344	Duane Ward	.05	440	*Rob Mallicoat*	.05	536	Ricky Jordan	.05
345	David Wells	.05	441	*Andy Mota*	.08	537	John Kruk	.05
346	Devon White	.08	442	Al Osuna	.05	538	Jim Lindeman	.05
347	Mookie Wilson	.05	443	Mark Portugal	.05	539	Mickey Morandini	.05
348	Eddie Zosky	.08	444	*Scott Servais*	.10	540	Terry Mulholland	.05
349	Steve Avery	.05	445	Mike Simms	.05	541	Dale Murphy	.12
350	Mike Bell	.05	446	Gerald Young	.05	542	Randy Ready	.05
351	Rafael Belliard	.05	447	Tim Belcher	.05	543	Wally Ritchie	.05
352	Juan Berenguer	.05	448	Brett Butler	.10	544	Bruce Ruffin	.05
353	Jeff Blauser	.05	449	John Candelaria	.05	545	Steve Searcy	.05
354	Sid Bream	.05	450	Gary Carter	.08	546	Dickie Thon	.05
355	Francisco Cabrera	.05	451	Dennis Cook	.05	547	Mitch Williams	.05
356	Marvin Freeman	.05	452	Tim Crews	.05	548	Stan Belinda	.05
357	Ron Gant	.05	453	Kal Daniels	.05	549	Jay Bell	.05
358	Tom Glavine	.10	454	Jim Gott	.05	550	Barry Bonds	.35
359	*Brian Hunter*	.05	455	Alfredo Griffin	.05	551	Bobby Bonilla	.10
360	Dave Justice	.15	456	Kevin Gross	.05	552	Steve Buechele	.05
361	Charlie Leibrandt	.05	457	Chris Gwynn	.05	553	Doug Drabek	.05
362	Mark Lemke	.05	458	Lenny Harris	.05	554	Neal Heaton	.05
363	Kent Mercker	.05	459	Orel Hershiser	.08	555	Jeff King	.05
364	*Keith Mitchell*	.05	460	Jay Howell	.05	556	Bob Kipper	.05
365	Greg Olson	.05	461	Stan Javier	.05	557	Bill Landrum	.05
366	Terry Pendleton	.05	462	Eric Karros	.15	558	Mike LaValliere	.05
367	*Armando Reynoso*	.05	463	Ramon Martinez	.08	559	Jose Lind	.05
368	Deion Sanders	.20	464	Roger McDowell	.05	560	Lloyd McClendon	.05
369	Lonnie Smith	.05	465	Mike Morgan	.05	561	Orlando Merced	.05
370	Pete Smith	.05	466	Eddie Murray	.25	562	Bob Patterson	.05
371	John Smoltz	.10	467	Jose Offerman	.05	563	*Joe Redfield*	.05
372	Mike Stanton	.05	468	Bob Ojeda	.05	564	Gary Redus	.05
373	Jeff Treadway	.05	469	Juan Samuel	.05	565	Rosario Rodriguez	.05
374	*Mark Wohlers*	.15	470	Mike Scioscia	.05	566	Don Slaught	.05
375	Paul Assenmacher	.05	471	Darryl Strawberry	.10	567	John Smiley	.05
376	George Bell	.05	472	*Bret Barberie*	.10	568	Zane Smith	.05
377	Shawn Boskie	.05	473	Brian Barnes	.05	569	Randy Tomlin	.05
378	*Frank Castillo*	.05	474	Eric Bullock	.05	570	Andy Van Slyke	.05
379	Andre Dawson	.12	475	Ivan Calderon	.05	571	Gary Varsho	.05
380	Shawon Dunston	.12	476	Delino DeShields	.08	572	Bob Walk	.05
381	Mark Grace	.20	477	*Jeff Fassero*	.10	573	*John Wehner*	.15
382	Mike Harkey	.05	478	Mike Fitzgerald	.05	574	Juan Agosto	.05
383	Danny Jackson	.05	479	Steve Frey	.05	575	Cris Carpenter	.05
384	Les Lancaster	.05	480	Andres Galarraga	.12	576	Jose DeLeon	.05
385	*Cedric Landrum*	.05	481	Mark Gardner	.05	577	Rich Gedman	.05
386	Greg Maddux	.60	482	Marquis Grissom	.10	578	Bernard Gilkey	.05
387	Derrick May	.05	483	*Chris Haney*	.05	579	Pedro Guerrero	.05
388	Chuck McElroy	.05	484	Barry Jones	.05	580	Ken Hill	.05
389	Ryne Sandberg	.35	485	Dave Martinez	.05	581	Rex Hudler	.05
390	*Heathcliff Slocumb*	.08	486	Dennis Martinez	.08	582	Felix Jose	.05
391	Dave Smith	.05	487	Chris Nabholz	.05	583	Ray Lankford	.05
392	Dwight Smith	.05	488	Spike Owen	.05	584	Omar Olivares	.05
393	Rick Sutcliffe	.05	489	Gilberto Reyes	.05	585	Jose Oquendo	.05
394	Hector Villanueva	.05	490	Mel Rojas	.05	586	Tom Pagnozzi	.05
395	*Chico Walker*	.05	491	Scott Ruskin	.05	587	Geronimo Pena	.05
396	Jerome Walton	.05	492	Bill Sampen	.05	588	Mike Perez	.05
397	*Rick Wilkins*	.15	493	Larry Walker	.20	589	Gerald Perry	.05
398	Jack Armstrong	.05	494	Tim Wallach	.05	590	Bryn Smith	.05
399	*Freddie Benavides*	.10	495	Daryl Boston	.05	591	Lee Smith	.08
400	Glenn Braggs	.05	496	Hubie Brooks	.05	592	Ozzie Smith	.25
401	Tom Browning	.05	497	Tim Burke	.05	593	Scott Terry	.05
402	Norm Charlton	.05	498	Mark Carreon	.05	594	Bob Tewksbury	.05
403	Eric Davis	.08	499	Tony Castillo	.05	595	Milt Thompson	.05
404	Rob Dibble	.05	500	Vince Coleman	.08	596	Todd Zeile	.08
405	Bill Doran	.05	501	David Cone	.12	597	Larry Andersen	.05
406	Mariano Duncan	.05	502	Kevin Elster	.05	598	Oscar Azocar	.05
407	*Kip Gross*	.05	503	Sid Fernandez	.05	599	Andy Benes	.10
408	Chris Hammond	.05	504	John Franco	.05	600	*Ricky Bones*	.08
409	Billy Hatcher	.05	505	Dwight Gooden	.12	601	Jerald Clark	.05
410	*Chris Jones*	.10	506	Todd Hundley	.05	602	Pat Clements	.05
411	Barry Larkin	.10	507	Jeff Innis	.05	603	Paul Faries	.05
412	Hal Morris	.08	508	Gregg Jefferies	.12	604	Tony Fernandez	.05
413	Randy Myers	.05	509	Howard Johnson	.05	605	Tony Gwynn	.35
414	Joe Oliver	.05	510	Dave Magadan	.05	606	Greg Harris	.05
415	Paul O'Neill	.08	511	*Terry McDaniel*	.05	607	Thomas Howard	.05
416	Ted Power	.05	512	Kevin McReynolds	.05	608	Bruce Hurst	.05
417	Luis Quinones	.05	513	Keith Miller	.05	609	Darrin Jackson	.05

610	Tom Lampkin	.05
611	Craig Lefferts	.05
612	*Jim Lewis*	.05
613	Mike Maddux	.05
614	Fred McGriff	.15
615	*Jose Melendez*	.08
616	Jose Mota	.08
617	Dennis Rasmussen	.05
618	Bip Roberts	.05
619	Rich Rodriguez	.05
620	Benito Santiago	.08
621	*Craig Shipley*	.05
622	Tim Teufel	.05
623	*Kevin Ward*	.05
624	Ed Whitson	.05
625	Dave Anderson	.05
626	Kevin Bass	.05
027	*Rod Beck*	.10
628	Bud Black	.05
629	Jeff Brantley	.05
630	John Burkett	.05
631	Will Clark	.20
632	Royce Clayton	.05
633	Steve Decker	.05
634	Kelly Downs	.05
635	Mike Felder	.05
636	Scott Garrelts	.05
637	Eric Gunderson	.05
638	*Bryan Hickerson*	.10
639	Darren Lewis	.08
640	Greg Litton	.05
641	Kirt Manwaring	.05
642	*Paul McClellan*	.05
043	Willie McGee	.08
644	Kevin Mitchell	.05
645	Francisco Olivares	.05
646	*Mike Remlinger*	.08
647	Dave Righetti	.05
648	Robby Thompson	.05
649	Jose Uribe	.05
650	Matt Williams	.15
651	Trevor Wilson	.05
652	Tom Goodwin (Prospects)	.25
653	Terry Bross (Prospects)	.05
654	*Mike Christopher* (Prospects)	.10
655	Kenny Lofton (Prospects)	2.50
656	*Chris Cron* (Prospects)	.10
657	Willie Banks (Prospects)	.10
658	*Pat Rice* (Prospects)	.05
659a	*Rob Mauer* (Prospects)(last name misspelled)	1.00
659b	*Rob Maurer* (Prospects)(corrected)	.12
660	Don Harris (Prospects)	.12
661	Henry Rodriguez (Prospects)	.25
662	*Cliff Brantley* (Prospects)	.08
663	*Mike Linskey* (Prospects)	.05
664	Gary Disarcina (Prospects)	.10
665	*Gil Heredia* (Prospects)	.12
666	*Vinny Castilla* (Prospects)	1.00
667	Paul Abbott (Prospects)	.08
668	Monty Fariss (Prospects)	.08
669	*Jarvis Brown* (Prospects)	.08
670	*Wayne Kirby* (Prospects)	.15
671	*Scott Brosius* (Prospects)	.15
672	Bob Hamelin (Prospects)	.10
673	*Joel Johnston* (Prospects)	.08
674	Tim Spehr (Prospects)	.15
675	*Jeff Gardner* (Prospects)	.10
676	*Rico Rossy* (Prospects)	.10
677	Roberto Hernandez (Prospects)	.20
678	Ted Wood (Prospects)	.08
679	Cal Eldred (Prospects)	.15
680	Sean Berry (Prospects)	.10
681	Rickey Henderson (Stolen Base Record)	.15
682	Nolan Ryan (Record 7th No-hitter)	.25
683	Dennis Martinez (Perfect Game)	.05
684	Wilson Alvarez (Rookie No-hitter)	.05
685	Joe Carter (3 100 RBI Seasons)	.05
686	Dave Winfield (400 Home Runs)	.10
687	David Cone (Ties NL Record Strikeouts)	.05
688	Jose Canseco (League Leaders)	.15
689	Howard Johnson (League Leaders)	.05
690	Julio Franco (League Leaders)	.05

691	Terry Pendleton (League Leaders)	.05
692	Cecil Fielder (League Leaders)	.10
693	Scott Erickson (League Leaders)	.05
694	Tom Glavine (League Leaders)	.05
695	Dennis Martinez (League Leaders)	.05
696	Bryan Harvey (League Leaders)	.05
697	Lee Smith (League Leaders)	.05
698	Super Siblings(Roberto & Sandy Alomar, Roberto & Sandy Alomar)	.15
699	The Indispensables(Bobby Bonilla, Will Clark)	.10
700	Teamwork(Mark Wohlers, Kent Mercker, Alejandro Pena)	.08
701	Tiger Tandems(Chris Jones, Bo Jackson, Gregg Olson, Frank Thomas)	.40
702	The Ignitors(Brett Butler, Paul Molitor)	.20
703	The Indispensables II(Cal Ripken Jr., Joe Carter)	.15
704	Power Packs(Barry Larkin, Kirby Puckett)	.15
705	Today and Tomorrow(Mo Vaughn, Cecil Fielder)	.10
706	Teenage Sensations(Ramon Martinez, Ozzie Guillen)	.08
707	Designated Hitters(Harold Baines, Wade Boggs)	.10
708	Robin Yount (ProVision)	.20
709	Ken Griffey, Jr. (ProVision)	1.00
710	Nolan Ryan (ProVision)	.85
711	Cal Ripken, Jr. (ProVision)	.50
712	Frank Thomas (ProVision)	1.00
713	Dave Justice (ProVision)	.20
714	Checklist 1-101	.05
715	Checklist 102-194	.05
716	Checklist 195-296	.05
717	Checklist 297-397	.05
718	Checklist 398-494	.05
719	Checklist 495-596	.05
720a	Checklist 597-720 (659 Rob Mauer)	.05
720b	Checklist 597-720 (659 Rob Maurer)	.05

1992 Fleer All-Stars

Black borders with gold high-lights are featured on these special wax pack insert cards. The fronts feature glossy action photos with a portrait photo inset. Backs feature career highlights.

		MT
Complete Set (24):		40.00
Common Player:		.40
1	Felix Jose	.40

2	Tony Gwynn	3.00
3	Barry Bonds	2.50
4	Bobby Bonilla	.60
5	Mike LaValliere	.40
6	Tom Glavine	.60
7	Ramon Martinez	.50
8	Lee Smith	.40
9	Mickey Tettleton	.40
10	Scott Erickson	.50
11	Frank Thomas	8.00
12	Danny Tartabull	.40
13	Will Clark	1.00
14	Ryne Sandberg	1.50
15	Terry Pendleton	.40
16	Barry Larkin	.60
17	Rafael Palmeiro	.90
18	Julio Franco	.40
19	Robin Ventura	.75
20	Cal Ripken, Jr.	6.00
21	Joe Carter	.50
22	Kirby Puckett	4.00
23	Ken Griffey, Jr.	9.00
24	Jose Canseco	1.50

1992 Fleer Lumber Co.

Baseball's top power hitters at each position are featured in this nine-card set. Fronts feature full-color action photos bordered in black. Backs feature posed player photos and career highlights. The set was included only in factory sets released to the hobby trade.

		MT
Complete Set (9):		18.00
Common Player:		1.00
1	Cecil Fielder	1.50
2	Mickey Tettleton	1.00
3	Darryl Strawberry	1.50
4	Ryne Sandberg	2.00
5	Jose Canseco	2.00
6	Matt Williams	1.50
7	Cal Ripken, Jr.	5.00
8	Barry Bonds	2.50
9	Ron Gant	1.00

1992 Fleer Roger Clemens

This set chronicles the career highlights of Roger Clemens. The initial 12 cards from the set were in-serted in 1992 Fleer wax packs. A limited number of autographed cards were inserted as well. The additional three cards from the set were available through a mail-in of-fer. The card fronts feature black borders with metallic gold type. The flip side is yellow with black bor-ders.

		MT
Complete Set (15):		14.00
Common Card:		1.00
Autographed Card:		100.00
1	Quiet Storm	1.00
2	Courted by the Mets and Twins	1.00
3	The Show	1.00
4	A Rocket Launched	1.00
5	Time of Trial	1.00
6	Break Through	1.00
7	Play it Again Roger	1.00
8	Business as Usual	1.00
9	Heee's Back	1.00
10	Blood, Sweat and Tears	1.00
11	Prime of Life	1.00
12	Man for Every Season	1.00
13	Cooperstown Bound	2.00
14	The Heat of the Moment	2.00
15	Final Words	2.00

1992 Fleer Rookie Sensations

This 20-card set features the top rookies of 1991 and rookie prospects from 1992. The card fronts feature blue borders with "Rookie Sensations" in gold along the top border. The flip sides feature background information on the player. The cards were randomly inserted in 1992 Fleer cello packs. This issue saw very high prices when initially released then suffered long-term declines as the hobby became inundated with more and more insert sets.

		MT
Complete Set (20):		75.00
Common Player:		1.00
1	Frank Thomas	30.00
2	Todd Van Poppel	1.00
3	Orlando Merced	1.00

4	Jeff Bagwell	12.00
5	Jeff Fassero	1.00
6	Darren Lewis	2.00
7	Milt Cuyler	1.00
8	Mike Timlin	1.00
9	Brian McRae	2.00
10	Chuck Knoblauch	4.50
11	Rich DeLucia	1.00
12	Ivan Rodriguez	9.00
13	Juan Guzman	1.50
14	Steve Chitren	1.00
15	Mark Wohlers	1.50
16	Wes Chamberlain	1.00
17	Ray Lankford	2.00
18	Chito Martinez	1.00
19	Phil Plantier	1.00
20	Scott Leius	1.00

1992 Fleer Smoke 'N Heat

This 12-card set of top pitchers was included in factory sets designated for sale within the general retail trade. Card numbers have an "S" prefix.

		MT
Complete Set (12):		15.00
Common Player:		.50
1	Lee Smith	.50
2	Jack McDowell	.60
3	David Cone	.50
4	Roger Clemens	3.00
5	Nolan Ryan	6.00
6	Scott Erickson	.50
7	Tom Glavine	.75
8	Dwight Gooden	.75
9	Andy Benes	.60
10	Steve Avery	.50
11	Randy Johnson	1.50
12	Jim Abbott	.60

1992 Fleer Team Leaders

White and green borders highlight this insert set from Fleer. The card fronts also feature a special gold-foil "team leaders" logo beneath the full-color player photo. The card backs feature player information. The cards were randomly inserted in 1992 Fleer rack packs.

		MT
Complete Set (20):		110.00
Common Player:		.75
1	Don Mattingly	16.00
2	Howard Johnson	.75
3	Chris Sabo	.75
4	Carlton Fisk	1.50
5	Kirby Puckett	12.00
6	Cecil Fielder	2.00
7	Tony Gwynn	8.00
8	Will Clark	3.00
9	Bobby Bonilla	1.00
10	Len Dykstra	.75
11	Tom Glavine	2.50
12	Rafael Palmeiro	3.00
13	Wade Boggs	3.00
14	Joe Carter	1.00
15	Ken Griffey, Jr.	25.00
16	Darryl Strawberry	1.00
17	Cal Ripken, Jr.	22.00
18	Danny Tartabull	.75
19	Jose Canseco	3.00
20	Andre Dawson	1.00

1992 Fleer Update

This 132-card set was released in boxed set form and features traded players, free agents and top rookies from 1992. The cards are styled after the regular 1992 Fleer and are numbered alphabetically according to team. This set marks the ninth year that Fleer has released an update set. The set includes four black-bordered "Headliner" cards.

		MT
Complete Set (136):		140.00
Common Player:		.20
H1	1992 All-Star Game MVP(Ken Griffey, Jr.)	25.00
H2	3000 Career Hits(Robin Yount)	7.00
H3	Major League Career Saves Record(Jeff Reardon)	.25
H4	Record RBI Performance(Cecil Fielder)	1.50
1	Todd Frohwirth	.20
2	Alan Mills	.20
3	Rick Sutcliffe	.20
4	John Valentin	3.00
5	Frank Viola	.20
6	Bob Zupcic	.20
7	Mike Butcher	.20
8	Chad Curtis	1.50

9	*Damion Easley*	.40
10	Tim Salmon	15.00
11	Julio Valera	.20
12	George Bell	.20
13	Roberto Hernandez	.35
14	Shawn Jeter	.20
15	Thomas Howard	.20
16	Jesse Levis	.40
17	Kenny Lofton	25.00
18	Paul Sorrento	.20
19	Rico Brogna	.35
20	John Doherty	.20
21	Dan Gladden	.20
22	Buddy Groom	.20
23	Shawn Hare	.20
24	John Kiely	.20
25	Kurt Knudsen	.20
26	Gregg Jefferies	.30
27	Wally Joyner	.30
28	Kevin Koslofski	.20
29	Kevin McReynolds	.20
30	Rusty Meacham	.20
31	Keith Miller	.20
32	Hipolito Pichardo	.20
33	James Austin	.20
34	Scott Fletcher	.20
35	*John Jaha*	2.00
36	Pat Listach	.50
37	Dave Nilsson	2.00
38	Kevin Seitzer	.20
39	Tom Edens	.20
40	Pat Mahomes	.65
41	John Smiley	.20
42	Charlie Hayes	.25
43	Sam Militello	.20
44	Andy Stankiewicz	.35
45	Danny Tartabull	.20
46	Bob Wickman	.20
47	Jerry Browne	.20
48	Kevin Campbell	.20
49	Vince Horsman	.20
50	Troy Neel	.50
51	Ruben Sierra	.20
52	Bruce Walton	.20
53	Willie Wilson	.20
54	Bret Boone	3.00
55	Dave Fleming	.65
56	Kevin Mitchell	.20
57	*Jeff Nelson*	.20
58	Shane Turner	.20
59	Jose Canseco	4.00
60	*Jeff Frye*	.30
61	Damilo Leon	.20
62	Roger Pavlik	.30
63	David Cone	.25
64	Pat Hentgen	4.00
65	Randy Knorr	.20
66	Jack Morris	.20
67	Dave Winfield	2.00
68	*David Nied*	.20
69	Otis Nixon	.20
70	Alejandro Pena	.20
71	Jeff Reardon	.20
72	Alex Arias	.25
73	Jim Bullinger	.25
74	Mike Morgan	.20
75	Rey Sanchez	.20
76	Bob Scanlan	.20
77	Sammy Sosa	15.00
78	Scott Bankhead	.20
79	Tim Belcher	.20
80	Steve Foster	.20
81	Willie Greene	.50
82	Bip Roberts	.20
83	Scott Ruskin	.20
84	Greg Swindell	.20
85	Juan Guerrero	.20
86	Butch Henry	.20
87	Doug Jones	.20
88	Brian Williams	.40
89	Tom Candiotti	.20
90	Eric Davis	.25
91	Carlos Hernandez	.20
92	*Mike Piazza*	85.00
93	Mike Sharperson	.20
94	Eric Young	.75
95	Moises Alou	4.00
96	Greg Colbrunn	.20
97	Wil Cordero	3.00
98	Ken Hill	.60
99	John Vander Wal	.40
100	John Wetteland	.20
101	Bobby Bonilla	.35
102	Eric Hilman	.20
103	Pat Howell	.20
104	*Jeff Kent*	4.00

105	Dick Schofield	.20
106	*Ryan Thompson*	.50
107	Chico Walker	.20
108	Juan Bell	.20
109	Mariano Duncan	.20
110	Jeff Grotewold	.25
111	Ben Rivera	.20
112	Curt Schilling	.25
113	Victor Cole	.20
114	Al Martin	2.00
115	Roger Mason	.20
116	Blas Minor	.35
117	Tim Wakefield	.50
118	*Mark Clark*	2.00
119	Rheal Cormier	.35
120	Donovan Osborne	.20
121	Todd Worrell	.20
122	Jeremy Hernandez	.25
123	Randy Myers	.20
124	Frank Seminara	.20
125	Gary Sheffield	3.00
126	Dan Walters	.20
127	Steve Hosey	.40
128	Mike Jackson	.20
129	Jim Pena	.20
130	Cory Snyder	.20
131	Bill Swift	.20
132	Checklist	.05

1993 Fleer

The card fronts feature silver borders with the player's name, team and position in a banner along the left side of the card. The backs feature an action photo of the player with his name in bold behind him. A box featuring biographical information, statistics and player information is located to the right of the action photo. The cards are numbered alphabetically by team. The basic Fleer issue for 1993 was issued in two series of 360 cards each. The 720-card set included a number of subsets and could be found in many different types of packaging with an unprecedented number of inserts sets to spice up each offering.

	MT
Complete Set (720):	35.00
Common Player:	.05
Series 1 or 2 Wax Box:	26.00

1	Steve Avery	.08
2	Sid Bream	.05
3	Ron Gant	.10
4	Tom Glavine	.10
5	Brian Hunter	.05
6	Ryan Klesko	.75
7	Charlie Leibrandt	.05
8	Kent Mercker	.05
9	David Nied	.05
10	Otis Nixon	.05
11	Greg Olson	.05
12	Terry Pendleton	.05

13	Deion Sanders	.25
14	John Smoltz	.12
15	Mike Stanton	.05
16	Mark Wohlers	.05
17	Paul Assenmacher	.05
18	Steve Buechele	.05
19	Shawon Dunston	.12
20	Mark Grace	.15
21	Derrick May	.05
22	Chuck McElroy	.05
23	Mike Morgan	.05
24	Rey Sanchez	.05
25	Ryne Sandberg	.30
26	Bob Scanlan	.05
27	Sammy Sosa	.75
28	Rick Wilkins	.05
29	*Bobby Ayala*	.05
30	Tim Belcher	.05
31	*Jeff Branson*	.12
32	Norm Charlton	.05
33	*Steve Foster*	.05
34	Willie Greene	.08
35	Chris Hammond	.05
36	Milt Hill	.05
37	Hal Morris	.05
38	Joe Oliver	.05
39	Paul O'Neill	.15
40	*Tim Pugh*	.12
41	Jose Rijo	.05
42	Bip Roberts	.05
43	Chris Sabo	.05
44	Reggie Sanders	.10
45	Eric Anthony	.05
46	Jeff Bagwell	.75
47	Craig Biggio	.15
48	Joe Boever	.05
49	Casey Candaele	.05
50	Steve Finley	.05
51	Luis Gonzalez	.05
52	Pete Harnisch	.05
53	Xavier Hernandez	.05
54	Doug Jones	.05
55	Eddie Taubensee	.05
56	Brian Williams	.05
57	*Pedro Astacio*	.12
58	Todd Benzinger	.05
59	Brett Butler	.10
60	Tom Candiotti	.05
61	Lenny Harris	.05
62	Carlos Hernandez	.05
63	Orel Hershiser	.08
64	Eric Karros	.15
65	Ramon Martinez	.08
66	Jose Offerman	.05
67	Mike Scioscia	.05
68	Mike Sharperson	.05
69	*Eric Young*	.08
70	Moises Alou	.10
71	Ivan Calderon	.05
72	*Archi Cianfrocco*	.08
73	Wil Cordero	.08
74	Delino DeShields	.08
75	Mark Gardner	.05
76	Ken Hill	.08
77	*Tim Laker*	.08
78	Chris Nabholz	.05
79	Mel Rojas	.05
80	*John Vander Wal*	.12
81	Larry Walker	.20
82	Tim Wallach	.05
83	John Wetteland	.05
84	Bobby Bonilla	.08
85	Daryl Boston	.05
86	Sid Fernandez	.05
87	*Eric Hillman*	.08
88	Todd Hundley	.12
89	Howard Johnson	.05
90	Jeff Kent	.12
91	Eddie Murray	.20
92	Bill Pecota	.05
93	Bret Saberhagen	.05
94	Dick Schofield	.05
95	Pete Schourek	.05
96	Anthony Young	.05
97	Ruben Amaro Jr.	.05
98	Juan Bell	.05
99	Wes Chamberlain	.05
100	Darren Daulton	.08
101	Mariano Duncan	.05
102	Mike Hartley	.05
103	Ricky Jordan	.05
104	John Kruk	.05
105	Mickey Morandini	.08
106	Terry Mulholland	.05
107	*Ben Rivera*	.05
108	Curt Schilling	.05

No.	Player	Value	No.	Player	Value	No.	Player	Value
109	*Keith Shepherd*	.05	205	Ron Karkovice	.05	301	Bob Welch	.05
110	Stan Belinda	.05	206	Kirk McCaskill	.05	302	Willie Wilson	.05
111	Jay Bell	.05	207	Jack McDowell	.08	303	Bobby Witt	.05
112	Barry Bonds	.40	208	Scott Radinsky	.05	304	Bret Boone	.10
113	Jeff King	.05	209	Tim Raines	.08	305	Jay Buhner	.10
114	Mike LaValliere	.05	210	Frank Thomas	1.50	306	Dave Fleming	.05
115	Jose Lind	.05	211	Robin Ventura	.12	307	Ken Griffey, Jr.	1.50
116	Roger Mason	.05	212	Sandy Alomar Jr.	.08	308	Erik Hanson	.05
117	Orlando Merced	.05	213	Carlos Baerga	.15	309	Edgar Martinez	.08
118	Bob Patterson	.05	214	Dennis Cook	.05	310	Tino Martinez	.15
119	Don Slaught	.05	215	Thomas Howard	.05	311	Jeff Nelson	.05
120	Zane Smith	.05	216	Mark Lewis	.05	312	Dennis Powell	.05
121	Randy Tomlin	.05	217	Derek Lilliquist	.05	313	Mike Schooler	.05
122	Andy Van Slyke	.05	218	Kenny Lofton	.50	314	Russ Swan	.05
123	*Tim Wakefield*	.08	219	Charles Nagy	.05	315	Dave Valle	.05
124	Rheal Cormier	.05	220	Steve Olin	.05	316	Omar Vizquel	.05
125	Bernard Gilkey	.10	221	Paul Sorrento	.05	317	Kevin Brown	.05
126	Felix Jose	.05	222	Jim Thome	.25	318	Todd Burns	.05
127	Ray Lankford	.10	223	Mark Whiten	.05	319	Jose Canseco	.20
128	Bob McClure	.05	224	Milt Cuyler	.05	320	Julio Franco	.05
129	Donovan Osborne	.05	225	Rob Deer	.05	321	Jeff Frye	.12
130	Tom Pagnozzi	.05	226	*John Doherty*	.12	322	Juan Gonzalez	.50
131	Geronimo Pena	.05	227	Cecil Fielder	.12	323	Jose Guzman	.05
132	Mike Perez	.05	228	Travis Fryman	.10	324	Jeff Huson	.05
133	Lee Smith	.08	229	Mike Henneman	.05	325	Dean Palmer	.08
134	Bob Tewksbury	.05	230	*John Kiely*	.05	326	Kevin Reimer	.05
135	Todd Worrell	.05	231	*Kurt Knudsen*	.08	327	Ivan Rodriguez	.40
136	Todd Zeile	.08	232	Scott Livingstone	.05	328	Kenny Rogers	.05
137	Jerald Clark	.05	233	Tony Phillips	.10	329	Dan Smith	.05
138	Tony Gwynn	.30	234	Mickey Tettleton	.08	330	Roberto Alomar	.35
139	Greg Harris	.05	235	Kevin Appier	.08	331	Derek Bell	.12
140	Jeremy Hernandez	.05	236	George Brett	.40	332	Pat Borders	.05
141	Darrin Jackson	.05	237	Tom Gordon	.05	333	Joe Carter	.15
142	Mike Maddux	.05	238	Gregg Jefferies	.10	334	Kelly Gruber	.05
143	Fred McGriff	.20	239	Wally Joyner	.08	335	Tom Henke	.05
144	Jose Melendez	.05	240	*Kevin Koslofski*	.12	336	Jimmy Key	.05
145	Rich Rodriguez	.05	241	Mike Macfarlane	.05	337	Manuel Lee	.05
146	Frank Seminara	.05	242	Brian McRae	.05	338	Candy Maldonado	.05
147	Gary Sheffield	.20	243	Rusty Meacham	.05	339	John Olerud	.15
148	Kurt Stillwell	.05	244	Keith Miller	.05	340	Todd Stottlemyre	.05
149	*Dan Walters*	.10	245	Jeff Montgomery	.05	341	Duane Ward	.05
150	Rod Beck	.05	246	*Hipolito Pichardo*	.05	342	Devon White	.08
151	Bud Black	.05	247	Ricky Bones	.05	343	Dave Winfield	.15
152	Jeff Brantley	.05	248	Cal Eldred	.05	344	Edgar Martinez (League Leaders)	.08
153	John Burkett	.05	249	Mike Fetters	.05			
154	Will Clark	.20	250	Darryl Hamilton	.05	345	Cecil Fielder (League Leaders)	.10
155	Royce Clayton	.05	251	Doug Henry	.05			
156	Mike Jackson	.05	252	John Jaha	.05	346	Kenny Lofton (League Leaders)	.15
157	Darren Lewis	.05	253	Pat Listach	.05			
158	Kirt Manwaring	.05	254	Paul Molitor	.30	347	Jack Morris (League Leaders)	.05
159	Willie McGee	.08	255	Jaime Navarro	.05			
160	Cory Snyder	.05	256	Kevin Seitzer	.05	348	Roger Clemens (League Leaders)	.15
161	Bill Swift	.05	257	B.J. Surhoff	.05			
162	Trevor Wilson	.05	258	Greg Vaughn	.05	349	Fred McGriff (Round Trippers)	.12
163	Brady Anderson	.20	259	Bill Wegman	.05			
164	Glenn Davis	.05	260	Robin Yount	.20	350	Barry Bonds (Round Trippers)	.15
165	Mike Devereaux	.05	261	Rick Aguilera	.05			
166	Todd Frohwirth	.05	262	Chili Davis	.08	351	Gary Sheffield (Round Trippers)	.12
167	Leo Gomez	.05	263	Scott Erickson	.05			
168	Chris Hoiles	.05	264	Greg Gagne	.05	352	Darren Daulton (Round Trippers)	.05
169	Ben McDonald	.05	265	Mark Guthrie	.05			
170	Randy Milligan	.05	266	Brian Harper	.05	353	Dave Hollins (Round Trippers)	.05
171	Alan Mills	.05	267	Kent Hrbek	.08			
172	Mike Mussina	.30	268	Terry Jorgensen	.05	354	Brothers In Blue(Pedro Martinez, Ramon Martinez)	.50
173	Gregg Olson	.05	269	Gene Larkin	.05			
174	Arthur Rhodes	.05	270	Scott Leius	.05	355	Power Packs(Ivan Rodriguez, Kirby Puckett)	.35
175	David Segui	.05	271	Pat Mahomes	.05			
176	Ellis Burks	.12	272	Pedro Munoz	.05	356	Triple Threats(Ryne Sandberg, Gary Sheffield)	.15
177	Roger Clemens	.50	273	Kirby Puckett	.50			
178	Scott Cooper	.05	274	Kevin Tapani	.05	357	Infield Trifecta(Roberto Alomar, Chuck Knoblauch, Carlos Baerga)	.15
179	Danny Darwin	.05	275	Carl Willis	.05			
180	Tony Fossas	.05	276	Steve Farr	.05			
181	*Paul Quantrill*	.08	277	John Habyan	.05	358	Checklist	.05
182	Jody Reed	.05	278	Mel Hall	.05	359	Checklist	.05
183	*John Valentin*	.15	279	Charlie Hayes	.05	360	Checklist	.05
184	Mo Vaughn	.35	280	Pat Kelly	.05	361	Rafael Belliard	.05
185	Frank Viola	.05	281	Don Mattingly	.50	362	Damon Berryhill	.05
186	Bob Zupcic	.05	282	Sam Militello	.05	363	Mike Bielecki	.05
187	Jim Abbott	.08	283	Matt Nokes	.05	364	Jeff Blauser	.05
188	Gary DiSarcina	.05	284	Melido Perez	.05	365	Francisco Cabrera	.05
189	*Damion Easley*	.10	285	Andy Stankiewicz	.05	366	Marvin Freeman	.05
190	Junior Felix	.05	286	Danny Tartabull	.05	367	Dave Justice	.20
191	Chuck Finley	.05	287	Randy Velarde	.05	368	Mark Lemke	.05
192	Joe Grahe	.05	288	Bob Wickman	.05	369	Alejandro Pena	.05
193	Bryan Harvey	.05	289	Bernie Williams	.40	370	Jeff Reardon	.05
194	Mark Langston	.05	290	Lance Blankenship	.05	371	Lonnie Smith	.05
195	John Orton	.05	291	Mike Bordick	.05	372	Pete Smith	.05
196	Luis Polonia	.05	292	Jerry Browne	.05	373	Shawn Boskie	.05
197	Tim Salmon	.40	293	Dennis Eckersley	.10	374	Jim Bullinger	.05
198	Luis Sojo	.05	294	Rickey Henderson	.10	375	Frank Castillo	.05
199	Wilson Alvarez	.05	295	*Vince Horsman*	.12	376	Doug Dascenzo	.05
200	George Bell	.05	296	Mark McGwire	2.50	377	Andre Dawson	.12
201	Alex Fernandez	.08	297	Jeff Parrett	.05	378	Mike Harkey	.05
202	Craig Grebeck	.05	298	Ruben Sierra	.10	379	Greg Hibbard	.05
203	Ozzie Guillen	.05	299	Terry Steinbach	.05	380	Greg Maddux	1.00
204	Lance Johnson	.05	300	Walt Weiss	.05	381	Ken Patterson	.05

No.	Player	Price	No.	Player	Price	No.	Player	Price
382	Jeff Robinson	.05	478	Charlie O'Brien	.05	574	Gary Gaetti	.05
383	Luis Salazar	.05	479	Willie Randolph	.05	575	Scott Lewis	.05
384	Dwight Smith	.05	480	Mackey Sasser	.05	576	Lee Stevens	.05
385	Jose Vizcaino	.05	481	Ryan Thompson	.05	577	Ron Tingley	.05
386	Scott Bankhead	.05	482	Chico Walker	.05	578	Julio Valera	.05
387	Tom Browning	.05	483	Kyle Abbott	.05	579	Shawn Abner	.05
388	Darnell Coles	.05	484	Bob Ayrault	.05	580	Joey Cora	.05
389	Rob Dibble	.05	485	Kim Batiste	.05	581	Chris Cron	.05
390	Bill Doran	.05	486	Cliff Brantley	.05	582	Carlton Fisk	.10
391	Dwayne Henry	.05	487	Jose DeLeon	.05	583	Roberto Hernandez	.05
392	Cesar Hernandez	.05	488	Len Dykstra	.08	584	Charlie Hough	.05
393	Roberto Kelly	.08	489	Tommy Greene	.05	585	Terry Leach	.05
394	Barry Larkin	.10	490	Jeff Grotewold	.05	586	Donn Pall	.05
395	Dave Martinez	.05	491	Dave Hollins	.08	587	Dan Pasqua	.06
396	Kevin Mitchell	.08	492	Danny Jackson	.05	588	Steve Sax	.05
397	Jeff Reed	.05	493	Stan Javier	.05	589	Bobby Thigpen	.05
398	Scott Ruskin	.05	494	Tom Marsh	.05	590	Albert Belle	.40
399	Greg Swindell	.05	495	Greg Matthews	.05	591	Felix Fermin	.05
400	Dan Wilson	.08	496	Dale Murphy	.12	592	Glenallen Hill	.05
401	Andy Ashby	.05	497	*Todd Pratt*	.10	593	Brook Jacoby	.05
402	Freddie Benavides	.05	498	Mitch Williams	.05	594	Reggie Jefferson	.05
403	Dante Bichette	.15	499	Danny Cox	.05	595	Carlos Martinez	.05
404	Willie Blair	.05	500	Doug Drabek	.05	596	Jose Mesa	.08
405	Denis Boucher	.05	501	Carlos Garcia	.05	597	Rod Nichols	.05
406	Vinny Castilla	.10	502	Lloyd McClendon	.05	598	Junior Ortiz	.05
407	Braulio Castillo	.05	503	Denny Neagle	.05	599	Eric Plunk	.05
408	Alex Cole	.05	504	Gary Redus	.05	600	Ted Power	.05
409	Andres Galarraga	.15	505	Bob Walk	.05	601	Scott Scudder	.05
410	Joe Girardi	.05	506	John Wehner	.05	602	Kevin Wickander	.05
411	Butch Henry	.05	507	Luis Alicea	.05	603	Skeeter Barnes	.05
412	Darren Holmes	.05	508	Mark Clark	.05	604	Mark Carreon	.05
413	Calvin Jones	.05	509	Pedro Guerrero	.05	605	Dan Gladden	.05
414	*Steve Reed*	.10	510	Rex Hudler	.05	606	Bill Gullickson	.05
415	Kevin Ritz	.05	511	Brian Jordan	.12	607	Chad Kreuter	.05
416	*Jim Tatum*	.05	512	Omar Olivares	.05	608	Mark Leiter	.05
417	Jack Armstrong	.05	513	Jose Oquendo	.05	609	Mike Munoz	.05
418	Bret Barberie	.05	514	Gerald Perry	.05	610	Rich Rowland	.05
419	Ryan Bowen	.05	515	Bryn Smith	.05	611	Frank Tanana	.05
420	Cris Carpenter	.05	516	Craig Wilson	.05	612	Walt Terrell	.05
421	Chuck Carr	.05	517	Tracy Woodson	.05	613	Alan Trammell	.10
422	Scott Chiamparino	.05	518	Larry Anderson	.05	614	Lou Whitaker	.08
423	Jeff Conine	.12	519	Andy Benes	.05	615	Luis Aquino	.05
424	Jim Corsi	.05	520	Jim Deshaies	.05	616	Mike Boddicker	.05
425	Steve Decker	.05	521	Bruce Hurst	.05	617	Jim Eisenreich	.05
426	Chris Donnels	.05	522	Randy Myers	.05	618	Mark Gubicza	.05
427	Monty Fariss	.05	523	Benito Santiago	.08	619	David Howard	.05
428	*Bob Natal*	.05	524	Tim Scott	.05	620	Mike Magnante	.05
429	*Pat Rapp*	.08	525	Tim Teufel	.05	621	Brent Mayne	.05
430	Dave Weathers	.05	526	Mike Benjamin	.05	622	Kevin McReynolds	.05
431	*Nigel Wilson*	.10	527	Dave Burba	.05	623	*Eddie Pierce*	.05
432	Ken Caminiti	.15	528	Craig Colbert	.05	624	Bill Sampen	.05
433	Andujar Cedeno	.05	529	Mike Felder	.05	625	Steve Shifflett	.05
434	Tom Edens	.05	530	Bryan Hickerson	.05	626	Gary Thurman	.05
435	Juan Guerrero	.05	531	Chris James	.05	627	Curtis Wikerson	.05
436	Pete Incaviglia	.05	532	Mark Leonard	.05	628	Chris Bosio	.05
437	Jimmy Jones	.05	533	Greg Litton	.05	629	Scott Fletcher	.05
438	Darryl Kile	.05	534	Francisco Oliveras	.05	630	Jim Gantner	.05
439	Rob Murphy	.05	535	John Patterson	.05	631	Dave Nilsson	.05
440	Al Osuna	.05	536	Jim Pena	.05	632	Jesse Orosco	.05
441	Mark Portugal	.05	537	Dave Righetti	.05	633	Dan Plesac	.05
442	Scott Servais	.05	538	Robby Thompson	.05	634	Ron Robinson	.05
443	John Candelaria	.05	539	Jose Uribe	.05	635	Bill Spiers	.05
444	Tim Crews	.05	540	Matt Williams	.30	636	Franklin Stubbs	.05
445	Eric Davis	.08	541	Storm Davis	.05	637	Willie Banks	.05
446	Tom Goodwin	.05	542	Sam Horn	.05	638	Randy Bush	.05
447	Jim Gott	.05	543	Tim Hulett	.05	639	Chuck Knoblauch	.20
448	Kevin Gross	.05	544	Craig Lefferts	.05	640	Shane Mack	.05
449	Dave Hansen	.05	545	Chito Martinez	.05	641	Mike Pagliarulo	.05
450	Jay Howell	.05	546	Mark McLemore	.05	642	Jeff Reboulet	.05
451	Roger McDowell	.05	547	Luis Mercedes	.05	643	John Smiley	.05
452	Bob Ojeda	.05	548	Bob Milacki	.05	644	*Mike Trombley*	.08
453	Henry Rodriguez	.08	549	Joe Orsulak	.05	645	Gary Wayne	.05
454	Darryl Strawberry	.10	550	Billy Ripken	.05	646	Lenny Webster	.05
455	Mitch Webster	.05	551	Cal Ripken, Jr.	1.25	647	Tim Burke	.05
456	Steve Wilson	.05	552	Rick Sutcliffe	.05	648	Mike Gallego	.05
457	Brian Barnes	.05	553	Jeff Tackett	.05	649	Dion James	.05
458	Sean Berry	.05	554	Wade Boggs	.25	650	Jeff Johnson	.05
459	Jeff Fassero	.05	555	Tom Brunansky	.05	651	Scott Kamieniecki	.05
460	Darrin Fletcher	.05	556	Jack Clark	.05	652	Kevin Maas	.05
461	Marquis Grissom	.10	557	John Dopson	.05	653	Rich Monteleone	.05
462	Dennis Martinez	.08	558	Mike Gardiner	.05	654	Jerry Nielsen	.05
463	Spike Owen	.05	559	Mike Greenwell	.05	655	Scott Sanderson	.05
464	Matt Stairs	.05	560	Greg Harris	.05	656	Mike Stanley	.05
465	Sergio Valdez	.05	561	Billy Hatcher	.05	657	Gerald Williams	.05
466	Kevin Bass	.05	562	Joe Hesketh	.05	658	Curt Young	.05
467	Vince Coleman	.05	563	Tony Pena	.05	659	Harold Baines	.08
468	Mark Dewey	.05	564	Phil Plantier	.05	660	Kevin Campbell	.05
469	Kevin Elster	.05	565	Luis Rivera	.05	661	Ron Darling	.05
470	Tony Fernandez	.05	566	Herm Winningham	.05	662	Kelly Downs	.05
471	John Franco	.05	567	Matt Young	.05	663	Eric Fox	.05
472	Dave Gallagher	.05	568	Bert Blyleven	.05	664	Dave Henderson	.05
473	Paul Gibson	.05	569	Mike Butcher	.05	665	Rick Honeycutt	.05
474	Dwight Gooden	.12	570	Chuck Crim	.05	666	Mike Moore	.05
475	Lee Guetterman	.05	571	*Chad Curtis*	.10	667	Jamie Quirk	.05
476	Jeff Innis	.05	572	Tim Fortugno	.05	668	Jeff Russell	.05
477	Dave Magadan	.05	573	Steve Frey	.05	669	Dave Stewart	.08

670	Greg Briley	.05
671	Dave Cochrane	.05
672	Henry Cotto	.05
673	Rich DeLucia	.05
674	Brian Fisher	.05
675	Mark Grant	.05
676	Randy Johnson	.35
677	Tim Leary	.05
678	Pete O'Brien	.05
679	Lance Parrish	.08
680	Harold Reynolds	.05
681	Shane Turner	.05
682	Jack Daugherty	.05
683	*David Hulse*	.15
684	Terry Mathews	.05
685	Al Newman	.05
686	Edwin Nunez	.05
687	Rafael Palmeiro	.15
688	Roger Pavlik	.05
689	Geno Petralli	.05
690	Nolan Ryan	.75
691	David Cone	.05
692	Alfredo Griffin	.05
693	Juan Guzman	.08
694	Pat Hentgen	.05
695	Randy Knorr	.05
696	Bob MacDonald	.05
697	Jack Morris	.05
698	Ed Sprague	.05
699	Dave Stieb	.05
700	Pat Tabler	.05
701	Mike Timlin	.05
702	David Wells	.05
703	Eddie Zosky	.05
704	Gary Sheffield (League Leaders)	.10
705	Darren Daulton (League Leaders)	.05
706	Marquis Grissom (League Leaders)	.10
707	Greg Maddux (League Leaders)	.20
708	Bill Swift (League Leaders)	.05
709	Juan Gonzalez (Round Trippers)	.25
710	Mark McGwire (Round Trippers)	1.00
711	Cecil Fielder (Round Trippers)	.10
712	Albert Belle (Round Trippers)	.25
713	Joe Carter (Round Trippers)	.10
714	Power Brokers(Frank Thomas, Cecil Fielder)	.40
715	Unsung Heroes(Larry Walker, Darren Daulton)	.10
716	Hot Corner Hammers(Edgar Martinez, Robin Ventura)	.10
717	Start to Finish(Roger Clemens, Dennis Eckersley)	.15
718	Checklist	.05
719	Checklist	.05
720	Checklist	.05

1993 Fleer All-Stars

Horizontal-format All-Star cards comprised one of the many 1993 Fleer insert issues. Twelve cards of National League All-Stars were included in Series I wax packs, while a dozen American League All-Stars were found in Series II packs. They are among the more popular and valuable of the '93 Fleer inserts.

		MT
		MT
	Complete Set A.L. (12):	30.00
	Complete Set N.L. (12):	15.00
	Common Player:	.75
	AMERICAN LEAGUE	
1	Frank Thomas	8.00
2	Roberto Alomar	2.00
3	Edgar Martinez	.75
4	Pat Listach	.75
5	Cecil Fielder	1.00
6	Juan Gonzalez	4.00
7	Ken Griffey, Jr.	10.00
8	Joe Carter	.75
9	Kirby Puckett	4.00
10	Brian Harper	.75
11	Dave Fleming	.75
12	Jack McDowell	.75
	NATIONAL LEAGUE	
1	Fred McGriff	1.00
2	Delino DeShields	.75
3	Gary Sheffield	1.50
4	Barry Larkin	1.00
5	Felix Jose	.75
6	Larry Walker	1.50
7	Barry Bonds	3.00
8	Andy Van Slyke	.75
9	Darren Daulton	.75
10	Greg Maddux	6.00
11	Tom Glavine	1.00
12	Lee Smith	.75

1993 Fleer Final Edition

This 310-card set was sold as a complete set in its own box. Card numbers have the prefix "F". The set also includes 10 Diamond Tribute cards, which are numbered DT1-DT10.

		MT
	Complete Set (310):	10.00
	Common Player:	.05
1	Steve Bedrosian	.05
2	Jay Howell	.05
3	Greg Maddux	1.50
4	*Greg McMichael*	.05
5	*Tony Tarasco*	.10
6	Jose Bautista	.05
7	Jose Guzman	.05
8	Greg Hibbard	.05
9	Candy Maldonado	.05
10	Randy Myers	.05
11	*Matt Walbeck*	.10
12	Turk Wendell	.05
13	Willie Nelson	.05
14	Greg Cadaret	.05
15	Roberto Kelly	.05
16	Randy Milligan	.05
17	Kevin Mitchell	.05
18	Jeff Reardon	.05
19	John Roper	.05
20	John Smiley	.05
21	Andy Ashby	.05
22	Dante Bichette	.30
23	Willie Blair	.05
24	Pedro Castellano	.05

25	Vinny Castilla	.20
26	Jerald Clark	.05
27	Alex Cole	.05
28	*Scott Fredrickson*	.05
29	*Jay Gainer*	.05
30	Andres Galarraga	.25
31	Joe Girardi	.05
32	Ryan Hawblitzel	.05
33	Charlie Hayes	.05
34	Darren Holmes	.05
35	Chris Jones	.05
36	David Nied	.05
37	*J. Owens*	.10
38	*Lance Painter*	.05
39	Jeff Parrett	.05
40	*Steve Reed*	.05
41	Armando Reynoso	.05
42	Bruce Ruffin	.05
43	*Danny Sheaffer*	.08
44	Keith Shepherd	.05
45	Jim Tatum	.05
46	Gary Wayne	.05
47	Eric Young	.10
48	Luis Aquino	.05
49	Alex Arias	.05
50	Jack Armstrong	.05
51	Bret Barberie	.05
52	Geronimo Berroa	.08
53	Ryan Bowen	.05
54	Greg Briley	.05
55	Chris Carpenter	.05
56	Chuck Carr	.05
57	Jeff Conine	.10
58	Jim Corsi	.05
59	Orestes Destrade	.05
60	Junior Felix	.05
61	Chris Hammond	.05
62	Bryan Harvey	.05
63	Charlie Hough	.05
64	Joe Klink	.05
65	*Richie Lewis*	.10
66	*Mitch Lyden*	.05
67	Bob Natal	.05
68	*Scott Pose*	.05
69	Rich Renteria	.05
70	Benito Santiago	.08
71	Gary Sheffield	.40
72	*Matt Turner*	.10
73	Walt Weiss	.05
74	*Darrell Whitmore*	.10
75	Nigel Wilson	.05
76	Kevin Bass	.05
77	Doug Drabek	.05
78	Tom Edens	.05
79	Chris James	.05
80	Greg Swindell	.05
81	*Omar Daal*	.10
82	Raul Mondesi	1.00
83	Jody Reed	.05
84	Cory Snyder	.05
85	Rick Trlicek	.05
86	Tim Wallach	.05
87	Todd Worrell	.05
88	Tavo Alvarez	.05
89	Frank Bolick	.05
90	Kent Bottenfield	.05
91	Greg Colbrunn	.05
92	Cliff Floyd	.15
93	*Lou Frazier*	.08
94	Mike Gardiner	.05
95	*Mike Lansing*	.30
96	Bill Risley	.05
97	Jeff Shaw	.05
98	Kevin Baez	.05
99	*Tim Bogar*	.10
100	Jeromy Burnitz	.15
101	Mike Draper	.05
102	Darrin Jackson	.05
103	Mike Maddux	.05
104	Joe Orsulak	.05
105	Doug Saunders	.05
106	Frank Tanana	.05
107	Dave Telgheder	.08
108	Larry Anderson	.05
109	Jim Eisenreich	.05
110	Pete Incaviglia	.05
111	Danny Jackson	.05
112	David West	.05
113	Al Martin	.10
114	Blas Minor	.05
115	Dennis Moeller	.05
116	Will Pennyfeather	.05
117	Rich Robertson	.05
118	Ben Shelton	.05
119	Lonnie Smith	.05
120	Freddie Toliver	.05

121	Paul Wagner	.05
122	Kevin Young	.08
123	*Rene Arocha*	.10
124	Gregg Jefferies	.10
125	Paul Kilgus	.05
126	Les Lancaster	.05
127	Joe Magrane	.05
128	Rob Murphy	.05
129	Erik Pappas	.05
130	Stan Royer	.10
131	Ozzie Smith	.40
132	Tom Urbani	.05
133	Mark Whiten	.05
134	Derek Bell	.10
135	Doug Brocall	.05
136	Phil Clark	.05
137	*Mark Ettles*	.05
138	Jeff Gardner	.05
139	*Pat Gomez*	.08
140	Ricky Gutierrez	.05
141	Gene Harris	.05
142	*Kevin Higgins*	.05
143	Trevor Hoffman	.05
144	Phil Plantier	.05
145	*Kerry Taylor*	.05
146	Guillermo Velasquez	.05
147	Wally Whitehurst	.05
148	*Tim Worrell*	.05
149	Todd Benzinger	.05
150	Barry Bonds	.70
151	Greg Brummett	.05
152	Mark Carreon	.05
153	Dave Martinez	.05
154	Jeff Reed	.05
155	Kevin Rogers	.05
156	Harold Baines	.08
157	Damon Buford	.05
158	*Paul Carey*	.05
159	Jeffrey Hammonds	.20
160	Jaime Moyer	.05
161	*Sherman Obando*	.10
162	*John O'Donoghue*	.10
163	Brad Pennington	.05
164	Jim Poole	.05
165	Harold Reynolds	.05
166	Fernando Valenzuela	.08
167	*Jack Voight*	.05
168	Mark Williamson	.05
169	Scott Bankhead	.05
170	Greg Blosser	.05
171	*Jim Byrd*	.05
172	Ivan Calderon	.05
173	Andre Dawson	.12
174	Scott Fletcher	.05
175	Jose Melendez	.05
176	Carlos Quintana	.05
177	Jeff Russell	.05
178	Aaron Sele	.25
179	*Rod Correia*	.05
180	Chili Davis	.08
181	*Jim Edmonds*	1.25
182	Rene Gonzales	.05
183	*Hilly Hathaway*	.05
184	Torey Lovullo	.05
185	Greg Myers	.05
186	Gene Nelson	.05
187	Troy Percival	.05
188	Scott Sanderson	.05
189	*Darryl Scott*	.05
190	*J.T. Snow*	.40
191	Russ Springer	.05
192	Jason Bere	.10
193	Rodney Bolton	.05
194	Ellis Burks	.15
195	Bo Jackson	.12
196	Mike LaValliere	.05
197	Scott Ruffcorn	.20
198	*Jeff Schwartz*	.05
199	Jerry DiPoto	.05
200	Alvaro Espinoza	.05
201	Wayne Kirby	.05
202	*Tom Kramer*	.05
203	Jesse Levis	.05
204	Manny Ramirez	1.00
205	Jeff Treadway	.05
206	*Bill Wertz*	.05
207	Cliff Young	.05
208	Matt Young	.05
209	Kirk Gibson	.05
210	Greg Gohr	.05
211	Bill Krueger	.05
212	Bob MacDonald	.05
213	Mike Moore	.05
214	David Wells	.05
215	*Billy Brewer*	.05
216	David Cone	.15

217	Greg Gagne	.05
218	Mark Gardner	.05
219	Chis Haney	.05
220	Phil Hiatt	.05
221	Jose Lind	.05
222	Juan Bell	.05
223	Tom Brunansky	.05
224	Mike Ignasiak	.05
225	Joe Kmak	.05
226	Tom Lampkin	.05
227	*Graeme Lloyd*	.10
228	Carlos Maldonado	.05
229	Matt Mieske	.08
230	Angel Miranda	.05
231	*Troy O'Leary*	.10
232	Kevin Reimer	.05
233	Larry Casian	.05
234	Jim Deshaies	.05
235	*Eddie Guardado*	.10
236	Chip Hale	.05
237	*Mike Maksudian*	.05
238	David McCarty	.05
239	*Pat Meares*	.10
240	*George Tsamis*	.05
241	Dave Winfield	.15
242	Jim Abbott	.10
243	Wade Boggs	.25
244	*Andy Cook*	.05
245	*Russ Davis*	.15
246	Mike Humphreys	.05
247	Jimmy Key	.05
248	Jim Leyritz	.08
249	Bobby Munoz	.05
250	Paul O'Neill	.08
251	Spike Owen	.05
252	Dave Silvestri	.05
253	*Marcos Armas*	.05
254	Brent Gates	.10
255	Goose Gossage	.05
256	*Scott Lydy*	.05
257	Henry Mercedes	.05
258	*Mike Mohler*	.05
259	Troy Neel	.05
260	Edwin Nunez	.05
261	Craig Paquette	.10
262	Kevin Seitzer	.05
263	Rich Amaral	.05
264	Mike Blowers	.05
265	Chris Bosio	.05
266	Norm Charlton	.05
267	*Jim Converse*	.05
268	*John Cummings*	.10
269	Mike Felder	.05
270	Mike Hampton	.05
271	Bill Haselman	.05
272	Dwayne Henry	.05
273	Greg Litton	.05
274	Mackey Sasser	.05
275	Lee Tinsley	.05
276	David Wainhouse	.05
277	*Jeff Bronkey*	.05
278	Benji Gil	.05
279	Tom Henke	.05
280	Charlie Leibrandt	.05
281	Robb Nen	.10
282	Bill Ripken	.05
283	*Jon Shave*	.05
284	Doug Strange	.05
285	*Matt Whiteside*	.10
286	*Scott Brow*	.05
287	*Willie Canate*	.05
288	Tony Castillo	.05
289	*Domingo Cedeno*	.10
290	Darnell Coles	.05
291	Danny Cox	.05
292	Mark Eichhorn	.05
293	Tony Fernandez	.05
294	Al Leiter	.05
295	Paul Molitor	.40
296	Dave Stewart	.08
297	*Woody Williams*	.05
298	Checklist	.05
299	Checklist	.05
300	Checklist	.05
	DIAMOND TRIBUTE	
1DT	Wade Boggs	.50
2DT	George Brett	1.50
3DT	Andre Dawson	.25
4DT	Carlton Fisk	.25
5DT	Paul Molitor	.90
6DT	Nolan Ryan	4.50
7DT	Lee Smith	.20
8DT	Ozzie Smith	.90
9DT	Dave Winfield	.90
10DT	Robin Yount	.90
1DT	Wade Boggs	.50

2DT	George Brett	1.50
3DT	Andre Dawson	.20
4DT	Carlton Fisk	.20
5DT	Paul Molitor	.60
6DT	Nolan Ryan	4.50
7DT	Lee Smith	.20
8DT	Ozzie Smith	.50
9DT	Dave Winfield	.30
10DT	Robin Yount	1.00

1993 Fleer Golden Moments

Three cards of this insert set were available in both series of wax packs. Fronts feature black borders with gold-foil baseballs in the corners. The player's name appears in a "Golden Moments" banner at the bottom of the photo. Backs have a portrait photo of the player at top-center and a information on the highlight. The cards are unnumbered and are checklisted here alphabetically within series.

		MT
Complete Set (6):		11.00
Common Player:		.75
	SERIES 1	4.00
(1)	George Brett	3.00
(2)	Mickey Morandini	.75
(3)	Dave Winfield	1.25
	SERIES 2	7.00
(1)	Dennis Eckersley	.75
(2)	Bip Roberts	.75
(3)	Frank Thomas, Juan Gonzalez	6.00

1993 Fleer Major League Prospects

Yet another way to package currently hot rookies and future prospects to increase sales of the base product, there were 18 insert cards found in each series' wax packs. Fronts are bordered in black and have gold-foil highlights. Most of the depicted players were a few seasons away from everyday play in the major leagues.

		MT
Complete Set (36):		35.00
Common Player:		.75
	SERIES 1	24.00
1	Melvin Nieves	.75
2	Sterling Hitchcock	1.00
3	Tim Costo	1.00
4	Manny Alexander	1.00
5	Alan Embree	1.00
6	Kevin Young	1.50
7	J.T. Snow	2.00
8	Russ Springer	.75
9	Billy Ashley	.75
10	Kevin Rogers	.75
11	Steve Hosey	.75
12	Eric Wedge	.75
13	Mike Piazza	15.00
14	Jesse Levis	.75
15	Rico Brogna	1.00
16	Alex Arias	.75
17	Rod Brewer	.75
18	Troy Neel	.75
	SERIES 2	12.00
1	Scooter Tucker	.75
2	Kerry Woodson	.75
3	Greg Colbrunn	.75
4	Pedro Martinez	3.00
5	Dave Silvestri	.75
6	Kent Bottenfield	.75
7	Rafael Bournigal	.75
8	J.T. Bruett	.75
9	Dave Mlicki	.75
10	Paul Wagner	.75
11	Mike Williams	.75
12	Henry Mercedes	.75
13	Scott Taylor	.75
14	Dennis Moeller	.75
15	Javier Lopez	5.00
16	Steve Cooke	.75
17	Pete Young	.75
18	Ken Ryan	1.00

1993 Fleer ProVisions

This three-card insert set in Series I wax packs features the base-ball art of Wayne Still. Black-bordered fronts feature a player-fantasy painting at center, with the player's name gold-foil stamped beneath. Backs are also bordered in black and have a white box with a career summary.

		MT
Complete Set (6):		8.00
Common Player:		.75
	SERIES 1	5.00
1	Roberto Alomar	2.00
2	Dennis Eckersley	.75
3	Gary Sheffield	2.00
	SERIES 2	3.00
1	Andy Van Slyke	.75
2	Tom Glavine	1.50
3	Cecil Fielder	1.50

1993 Fleer Rookie Sensations

Ten rookie sensations - some of whom had not been true rookies for several seasons - were featured in this insert issue packaged exclusively in Series 1 and Series 2 cello packs. Card fronts have a player photo set against a silver background and surrounded by a blue border. The player's name and other front printing are in gold foil. Backs are also printed in silver with a blue border. There is a player portrait photo and career summary.

		MT
Complete Set (20):		25.00
Common Player:		1.00
	SERIES 1	20.00
1	Kenny Lofton	15.00
2	Cal Eldred	1.00
3	Pat Listach	1.00
4	Roberto Hernandez	1.00
5	Dave Fleming	1.00
6	Eric Karros	2.50
7	Reggie Sanders	2.00
8	Derrick May	1.00
9	Mike Perez	1.00
10	Donovan Osborne	1.00
	SERIES 2	10.00
1	Moises Alou	3.50
2	Pedro Astacio	1.50
3	Jim Austin	1.00
4	Chad Curtis	1.00
5	Gary DiSarcina	1.00
6	Scott Livingstone	1.00
7	Sam Militello	1.00
8	Arthur Rhodes	1.00
9	Tim Wakefield	1.00
10	Bob Zupcic	1.00

Modern cards have little collector value in conditions lower than Mint.
Figure NM cards at 75% of values shown;
EX cards at 40%.

1993 Fleer Team Leaders

This 20-card insert issue was exclusive to Series 1 and 2 rack packs. Fronts have a portrait photo, with a small action photo superimposed. At the side is a colored bar with the player's name and "Team Leaders" printed vertically. On back is a career summary. Card borders are a light metallic green and both sides of the card are UV coated.

		MT
Complete Set (20):		85.00
Common Player:		1.00
	SERIES 1	70.00
1	Kirby Puckett	10.00
2	Mark McGwire	25.00
3	Pat Listach	1.00
4	Roger Clemens	7.50
5	Frank Thomas	25.00
6	Carlos Baerga	1.00
7	Brady Anderson	1.00
8	Juan Gonzalez	6.00
9	Roberto Alomar	2.50
10	Ken Griffey, Jr.	25.00
	SERIES 2	24.00
1	Will Clark	2.00
2	Terry Pendleton	1.00
3	Ray Lankford	1.00
4	Eric Karros	1.50
5	Gary Sheffield	2.50
6	Ryne Sandberg	5.00
7	Marquis Grissom	1.50
8	John Kruk	1.00
9	Jeff Bagwell	10.00
10	Andy Van Slyke	1.00

1993 Fleer Tom Glavine Career Highlights

This 15-card insert set spotlighted the career highlights of Fleer's 1993 spokesman, Tom Glavine. Twelve cards were available in Series I and Series II packs; cards #13-15 could be obtained only via a special mail offer. A limited number of certified autograph cards were also inserted into packs. Cards #1-4 and 7-10 can each be found with two variations of the writeups on the back. The versions found in Series II packaging are the "correct" backs. Neither version carries a premium value.

		MT
Complete Set (15):		9.00
Common Card:		.75
Autographed Card:		90.00
1	Tom Glavine	.75
2	Tom Glavine	.75
3	Tom Glavine	.75
4	Tom Glavine	.75
5	Tom Glavine	.75
6	Tom Glavine	.75
7	Tom Glavine	.75
8	Tom Glavine	.75
9	Tom Glavine	.75
10	Tom Glavine	.75
11	Tom Glavine	.75
12	Tom Glavine	.75
13	Tom Glavine	.75
14	Tom Glavine	.75
15	Tom Glavine	.75

1994 Fleer

Fleer's 720-card 1994 set, released in one series, includes another 204 insert cards to be pursued by collectors. Every pack includes one of the cards, randomly inserted from among the 12 insert sets. Regular cards have action photos on front, with a team logo in one of the lower corners. The player's name and position is stamped in gold foil around the logo. On back, another color player photo is overprinted with color boxes, data and stats, leaving a clear image of the player's face, 1-1/2" x 1-3/4" in size. Cards are UV coated on both sides.

		MT
Complete Set (720):		45.00
Common Player:		.05
Wax Box:		30.00
1	Brady Anderson	.15
2	Harold Baines	.08
3	Mike Devereaux	.05
4	Todd Frohwirth	.05
5	Jeffrey Hammonds	.25
6	Chris Hoiles	.05
7	Tim Hulett	.05
8	Ben McDonald	.05
9	Mark McLemore	.05
10	Alan Mills	.05
11	Jamie Moyer	.05
12	Mike Mussina	.30
13	Gregg Olson	.05
14	Mike Pagliarulo	.05
15	Brad Pennington	.05
16	Jim Poole	.05
17	Harold Reynolds	.05
18	Arthur Rhodes	.05
19	Cal Ripken, Jr.	3.00
20	David Segui	.05
21	Rick Sutcliffe	.05
22	Fernando Valenzuela	.08
23	Jack Voigt	.05
24	Mark Williamson	.05
25	Scott Bankhead	.05
26	Roger Clemens	1.50
27	Scott Cooper	.05
28	Danny Darwin	.05
29	Andre Dawson	.10
30	Rob Deer	.05
31	John Dopson	.05
32	Scott Fletcher	.05
33	Mike Greenwell	.05
34	Greg Harris	.05
35	Billy Hatcher	.05
36	Bob Melvin	.05
37	Tony Pena	.05
38	Paul Quantrill	.05
39	Carlos Quintana	.05
40	Ernest Riles	.05
41	Jeff Russell	.05
42	Ken Ryan	.05
43	Aaron Sele	.10
44	John Valentin	.15
45	Mo Vaughn	.50
46	Frank Viola	.05
47	Bob Zupcic	.05
48	Mike Butcher	.05
49	Rod Correia	.05
50	Chad Curtis	.10
51	Chili Davis	.08
52	Gary DiSarcina	.05
53	Damion Easley	.10
54	Jim Edmonds	.40
55	Chuck Finley	.05
56	Steve Frey	.05
57	Rene Gonzales	.05
58	Joe Grahe	.05
59	Hilly Hathaway	.05
60	Stan Javier	.05
61	Mark Langston	.05
62	Phil Leftwich	.05
63	Torey Lovullo	.05
64	Joe Magrane	.05
65	Greg Myers	.05
66	Ken Patterson	.05
67	Eduardo Perez	.08
68	Luis Polonia	.05
69	Tim Salmon	.30
69a	Tim Salmon (overprinted PROMOTIONAL SAMPLE)	3.00
70	J.T. Snow	.15
71	Ron Tingley	.05
72	Julio Valera	.05
73	Wilson Alvarez	.05
74	Tim Belcher	.05
75	George Bell	.05
76	Jason Bere	.10
77	Rod Bolton	.05
78	Ellis Burks	.15
79	Joey Cora	.05
80	Alex Fernandez	.08
81	Craig Grebeck	.05
82	Ozzie Guillen	.05
83	Roberto Hernandez	.05
84	Bo Jackson	.15
85	Lance Johnson	.05
86	Ron Karkovice	.05
87	Mike LaValliere	.05
88	Kirk McCaskill	.05
89	Jack McDowell	.05
90	Warren Newson	.05

		MT
91	Dan Pasqua	.05
92	Scott Radinsky	.05
93	Tim Raines	.08
94	Steve Sax	.05
95	Jeff Schwarz	.05
96	Frank Thomas	2.50
97	Robin Ventura	.10
98	Sandy Alomar, Jr.	.08
99	Carlos Baerga	.10
100	Albert Belle	.75
101	Mark Clark	.05
102	Jerry DiPoto	.05
103	Alvaro Espinoza	.05
104	Felix Fermin	.05
105	Jeremy Hernandez	.05
106	Reggie Jefferson	.05
107	Wayne Kirby	.05
108	Tom Kramer	.05
109	Mark Lewis	.05
110	Derek Lilliquist	.05
111	Kenny Lofton	.75
112	Candy Maldonado	.05
113	Jose Mesa	.10
114	Jeff Mutis	.05
115	Charles Nagy	.05
116	Bob Ojeda	.05
117	Junior Ortiz	.05
118	Eric Plunk	.05
119	Manny Ramirez	1.00
120	Paul Sorrento	.05
121	Jim Thome	.35
122	Jeff Treadway	.05
123	Bill Wertz	.05
124	Skeeter Barnes	.05
125	Milt Cuyler	.05
126	Eric Davis	.08
127	John Doherty	.05
128	Cecil Fielder	.15
129	Travis Fryman	.10
130	Kirk Gibson	.05
131	Dan Gladden	.05
132	Greg Gohr	.05
133	Chris Gomez	.05
134	Bill Gullickson	.05
135	Mike Henneman	.05
136	Kurt Knudsen	.05
137	Chad Kreuter	.05
138	Bill Krueger	.05
139	Scott Livingstone	.05
140	Bob MacDonald	.05
141	Mike Moore	.05
142	Tony Phillips	.08
143	Mickey Tettleton	.05
144	Alan Trammell	.08
145	David Wells	.05
146	Lou Whitaker	.05
147	Kevin Appier	.05
148	Stan Belinda	.05
149	George Brett	.50
150	Billy Brewer	.05
151	Hubie Brooks	.05
152	David Cone	.05
153	Gary Gaetti	.08
154	Greg Gagne	.05
155	Tom Gordon	.05
156	Mark Gubicza	.05
157	Chris Gwynn	.05
158	John Habyan	.05
159	Chris Haney	.05
160	Phil Hiatt	.05
161	Felix Jose	.05
162	Wally Joyner	.08
163	Jose Lind	.05
164	Mike Macfarlane	.05
165	Mike Magnante	.05
166	Brent Mayne	.05
167	Brian McRae	.08
168	Kevin McReynolds	.05
169	Keith Miller	.05
170	Jeff Montgomery	.05
171	Hipolito Pichardo	.05
172	Rico Rossy	.05
173	Juan Bell	.05
174	Ricky Bones	.05
175	Cal Eldred	.05
176	Mike Fetters	.05
177	Darryl Hamilton	.05
178	Doug Henry	.05
179	Mike Ignasiak	.05
180	John Jaha	.08
181	Pat Listach	.05
182	Graeme Lloyd	.05
183	Matt Mieske	.05
184	Angel Miranda	.05
185	Jaime Navarro	.05
186	Dave Nilsson	.05

#	Player	Price	#	Player	Price	#	Player	Price
187	Troy O'Leary	.05	283	Norm Charlton	.05	379	Jose Bautista	.05
188	Jesse Orosco	.05	284	Mike Felder	.05	380	Shawn Boskie	.05
189	Kevin Reimer	.05	285	Dave Fleming	.05	381	Steve Buechele	.05
190	Kevin Seitzer	.05	286	Ken Griffey, Jr.	3.00	382	Frank Castillo	.05
191	Bill Spiers	.05	287	Erik Hanson	.05	383	Mark Grace	.15
192	B.J. Surhoff	.05	288	Bill Haselman	.05	384	Jose Guzman	.05
193	Dickie Thon	.05	289	*Brad Holman*	.10	385	Mike Harkey	.05
194	Jose Valentin	.05	290	Randy Johnson	.40	386	Greg Hibbard	.05
195	Greg Vaughn	.08	291	Tim Leary	.05	387	Glenallen Hill	.05
196	Bill Wegman	.05	292	Greg Litton	.05	388	Steve Lake	.05
197	Robin Yount	.20	293	Dave Magadan	.05	389	Derrick May	.05
198	Rick Aguilera	.05	294	Edgar Martinez	.08	390	Chuck McElroy	.05
199	Willie Banks	.05	295	Tino Martinez	.12	391	Mike Morgan	.05
200	Bernardo Brito	.05	296	Jeff Nelson	.05	392	Randy Myers	.05
201	Larry Casian	.05	297	*Erik Plantenberg*	.08	393	Dan Plesac	.05
202	Scott Erickson	.05	298	Mackey Sasser	.05	394	Kevin Roberson	.10
203	Eddie Guardado	.05	299	*Brian Turang*	.08	395	Rey Sanchez	.05
204	Mark Guthrie	.05	300	Dave Valle	.05	396	Ryne Sandberg	.45
205	Chip Hale	.05	301	Omar Vizquel	.05	397	Bob Scanlan	.05
206	Brian Harper	.05	302	Brian Bohanon	.05	398	Dwight Smith	.05
207	Mike Hartley	.05	303	Kevin Brown	.05	399	Sammy Sosa	.75
208	Kent Hrbek	.08	304	Jose Canseco	.35	400	Jose Vizcaino	.05
209	Terry Jorgensen	.05	305	Mario Diaz	.05	401	Rick Wilkins	.05
210	Chuck Knoblauch	.15	306	Julio Franco	.08	402	Willie Wilson	.05
211	Gene Larkin	.05	307	Juan Gonzalez	1.50	403	Eric Yelding	.05
212	Shane Mack	.05	308	Tom Henke	.05	404	Bobby Ayala	.05
213	David McCarty	.10	309	David Hulse	.05	405	Jeff Branson	.05
214	Pat Meares	.05	310	Manuel Lee	.05	406	Tom Browning	.05
215	Pedro Munoz	.05	311	Craig Lefferts	.05	407	Jacob Brumfield	.05
216	Derek Parks	.05	312	Charlie Leibrandt	.05	408	Tim Costo	.08
217	Kirby Puckett	1.25	313	Rafael Palmeiro	.15	409	Rob Dibble	.05
218	Jeff Reboulet	.05	314	Dean Palmer	.05	410	Willie Greene	.05
219	Kevin Tapani	.05	315	Roger Pavlik	.05	411	Thomas Howard	.05
220	Mike Trombley	.05	316	Dan Peltier	.05	412	Roberto Kelly	.05
221	George Tsamis	.05	317	Geno Petralli	.05	413	Bill Landrum	.05
222	Carl Willis	.05	318	Gary Redus	.05	414	Barry Larkin	.15
223	Dave Winfield	.20	319	Ivan Rodriguez	.40	415	*Larry Luebbers*	.05
224	Jim Abbott	.08	320	Kenny Rogers	.05	416	Kevin Mitchell	.08
225	Paul Assenmacher	.05	321	Nolan Ryan	2.50	417	Hal Morris	.08
226	Wade Boggs	.20	322	Doug Strange	.05	418	Joe Oliver	.05
227	Russ Davis	.10	323	Matt Whiteside	.05	419	Tim Pugh	.05
228	Steve Farr	.05	324	Roberto Alomar	.75	420	Jeff Reardon	.05
229	Mike Gallego	.05	325	Pat Borders	.05	421	Jose Rijo	.05
230	Paul Gibson	.05	326	Joe Carter	.20	422	Bip Roberts	.05
231	Steve Howe	.05	327	Tony Castillo	.05	423	John Roper	.05
232	Dion James	.05	328	Darnell Coles	.05	424	Johnny Ruffin	.05
233	Domingo Jean	.05	329	Danny Cox	.05	425	Chris Sabo	.05
234	Scott Kamieniecki	.05	330	Mark Eichhorn	.05	426	Juan Samuel	.05
235	Pat Kelly	.05	331	Tony Fernandez	.05	427	Reggie Sanders	.10
236	Jimmy Key	.05	332	Alfredo Griffin	.05	428	Scott Service	.05
237	Jim Leyritz	.08	333	Juan Guzman	.10	429	John Smiley	.05
238	Kevin Maas	.05	334	Rickey Henderson	.25	430	*Jerry Spradlin*	.05
239	Don Mattingly	1.50	335	Pat Hentgen	.10	431	Kevin Wickander	.05
240	Rich Monteleone	.05	336	Randy Knorr	.05	432	Freddie Benavides	.05
241	Bobby Munoz	.05	337	Al Leiter	.05	433	Dante Bichette	.30
242	Matt Nokes	.05	338	Paul Molitor	.40	434	Willie Blair	.05
243	Paul O'Neill	.05	339	Jack Morris	.05	435	Daryl Boston	.05
244	Spike Owen	.05	340	John Olerud	.15	436	Kent Bottenfield	.05
245	Melido Perez	.05	341	Dick Schofield	.05	437	Vinny Castilla	.15
246	Lee Smith	.08	342	Ed Sprague	.05	438	Jerald Clark	.05
247	Mike Stanley	.05	343	Dave Stewart	.08	439	Alex Cole	.05
248	Danny Tartabull	.05	344	Todd Stottlemyre	.05	440	Andres Galarraga	.15
249	Randy Velarde	.05	345	Mike Timlin	.05	441	Joe Girardi	.05
250	Bob Wickman	.05	346	Duane Ward	.05	442	Greg Harris	.05
251	Bernie Williams	.40	347	Turner Ward	.05	443	Charlie Hayes	.05
252	Mike Aldrete	.05	348	Devon White	.08	444	Darren Holmes	.05
253	Marcos Armas	.05	349	Woody Williams	.05	445	Chris Jones	.05
254	Lance Blankenship	.05	350	Steve Avery	.10	446	Roberto Mejia	.05
255	Mike Bordick	.05	351	Steve Bedrosian	.05	447	David Nied	.05
256	Scott Brosius	.05	352	Rafael Belliard	.05	448	J. Owens	.05
257	Jerry Browne	.05	353	Damon Berryhill	.05	449	Jeff Parrett	.05
258	Ron Darling	.05	354	Jeff Blauser	.05	450	Steve Reed	.05
259	Kelly Downs	.05	355	Sid Bream	.05	451	Armando Reynoso	.05
260	Dennis Eckersley	.08	356	Francisco Cabrera	.05	452	Bruce Ruffin	.05
261	Brent Gates	.10	357	Marvin Freeman	.05	453	Mo Sanford	.05
262	Goose Gossage	.05	358	Ron Gant	.08	454	Danny Sheaffer	.05
263	Scott Hemond	.05	359	Tom Glavine	.15	455	Jim Tatum	.05
264	Dave Henderson	.05	360	Jay Howell	.05	456	Gary Wayne	.05
265	Rick Honeycutt	.05	361	Dave Justice	.15	457	Eric Young	.10
266	Vince Horsman	.05	362	Ryan Klesko	.60	458	Luis Aquino	.05
267	Scott Lydy	.05	363	Mark Lemke	.05	459	Alex Arias	.05
268	Mark McGwire	4.00	364	Javier Lopez	.15	460	Jack Armstrong	.05
269	Mike Mohler	.05	365	Greg Maddux	2.50	461	Bret Barberie	.05
270	Troy Neel	.10	366	Fred McGriff	.20	462	Ryan Bowen	.05
271	Edwin Nunez	.05	367	Greg McMichael	.05	463	Chuck Carr	.05
272	Craig Paquette	.05	368	Kent Mercker	.05	464	Jeff Conine	.12
273	Ruben Sierra	.08	369	Otis Nixon	.05	465	Henry Cotto	.05
274	Terry Steinbach	.05	370	Greg Olson	.05	466	Orestes Destrade	.05
275	Todd Van Poppel	.05	371	Bill Pecota	.05	467	Chris Hammond	.05
276	Bob Welch	.05	372	Terry Pendleton	.05	468	Bryan Harvey	.05
277	Bobby Witt	.05	373	Deion Sanders	.40	469	Charlie Hough	.05
278	Rich Amaral	.05	374	Pete Smith	.05	470	Joe Klink	.05
279	Mike Blowers	.05	375	John Smoltz	.12	471	Richie Lewis	.05
280	Bret Boone	.08	376	Mike Stanton	.05	472	*Bob Natal*	.10
281	Chris Bosio	.05	377	Tony Tarasco	.05	473	*Pat Rapp*	.15
282	Jay Buhner	.08	378	Mark Wohlers	.05	474	*Rich Renteria*	.08

No.	Player	Price
475	Rich Rodriguez	.05
476	Benito Santiago	.08
477	Gary Sheffield	.20
478	Matt Turner	.05
479	David Weathers	.05
480	Walt Weiss	.05
481	Darrell Whitmore	.05
482	Eric Anthony	.05
483	Jeff Bagwell	1.00
484	Kevin Bass	.05
485	Craig Biggio	.15
486	Ken Caminiti	.15
487	Andujar Cedeno	.05
488	Chris Donnels	.05
489	Doug Drabek	.05
490	Steve Finley	.05
491	Luis Gonzalez	.05
492	Pote Harnisch	.05
493	Xavier Hernandez	.05
494	Doug Jones	.05
495	Todd Jones	.05
496	Darryl Kile	.05
497	Al Osuna	.05
498	Mark Portugal	.05
499	Scott Servais	.05
500	Greg Swindell	.05
501	Eddie Taubensee	.05
502	Jose Uribe	.05
503	Brian Williams	.05
504	Billy Ashley	.10
505	Pedro Astacio	.10
506	Brett Butler	.10
507	Tom Candiotti	.05
508	Omar Daal	.05
509	Jim Gott	.05
510	Kevin Gross	.05
511	Dave Hansen	.05
512	Carlos Hernandez	.05
513	Orel Hershiser	.10
514	Eric Karros	.15
515	Pedro Martinez	.25
516	Ramon Martinez	.08
517	Roger McDowell	.05
518	Raul Mondesi	.75
519	Jose Offerman	.05
520	Mike Piazza	2.50
521	Jody Reed	.05
522	Henry Rodriguez	.12
523	Mike Sharperson	.05
524	Cory Snyder	.05
525	Darryl Strawberry	.10
526	Rick Trlicek	.05
527	Tim Wallach	.05
528	Mitch Webster	.05
529	Steve Wilson	.05
530	Todd Worrell	.05
531	Moises Alou	.10
532	Brian Barnes	.05
533	Sean Berry	.05
534	Greg Colbrunn	.05
535	Delino DeShields	.08
536	Jeff Fassero	.05
537	Darrin Fletcher	.05
538	Cliff Floyd	.10
539	Lou Frazier	.05
540	Marquis Grissom	.10
541	Butch Henry	.05
542	Ken Hill	.05
543	Mike Lansing	.10
544	*Brian Looney*	.20
545	Dennis Martinez	.08
546	Chris Nabholz	.05
547	Randy Ready	.05
548	Mel Rojas	.05
549	Kirk Rueter	.05
550	Tim Scott	.05
551	Jeff Shaw	.05
552	Tim Spehr	.05
553	John VanderWal	.05
554	Larry Walker	.30
555	John Wetteland	.05
556	Rondell White	.25
557	Tim Bogar	.08
558	Bobby Bonilla	.08
559	Jeremy Burnitz	.05
560	Sid Fernandez	.05
561	John Franco	.05
562	Dave Gallagher	.05
563	Dwight Gooden	.10
564	Eric Hillman	.05
565	Todd Hundley	.12
566	Jeff Innis	.05
567	Darrin Jackson	.05
568	Howard Johnson	.05
569	Bobby Jones	.05
570	Jeff Kent	.05
571	Mike Maddux	.05
572	Jeff McKnight	.05
573	Eddie Murray	.12
574	Charlie O'Brien	.05
575	Joe Orsulak	.05
576	Bret Saberhagen	.05
577	Pete Schourek	.05
578	Dave Telgheder	.05
579	Ryan Thompson	.05
580	Anthony Young	.05
581	Ruben Amaro	.05
582	Larry Andersen	.05
583	Kim Batiste	.05
584	Wes Chamberlain	.05
585	Darren Daulton	.08
586	Mariano Duncan	.05
587	Len Dykstra	.08
588	Jim Eisenreich	.05
589	Tommy Greene	.05
590	Dave Hollins	.08
591	Pete Incaviglia	.05
592	Danny Jackson	.05
593	Ricky Jordan	.05
594	John Kruk	.05
595	Roger Mason	.05
596	Mickey Morandini	.05
597	Terry Mulholland	.05
598	Todd Pratt	.05
599	Ben Rivera	.05
600	Curt Schilling	.05
601	Kevin Stocker	.05
602	Milt Thompson	.05
603	David West	.05
604	Mitch Williams	.05
605	Jay Bell	.05
606	Dave Clark	.05
607	Steve Cooke	.05
608	Tom Foley	.05
609	Carlos Garcia	.05
610	Joel Johnston	.05
611	Jeff King	.05
612	Al Martin	.08
613	Lloyd McClendon	.05
614	Orlando Merced	.05
615	Blas Minor	.05
616	Denny Neagle	.05
617	*Mark Petkovsek*	.10
618	Tom Prince	.05
619	Don Slaught	.05
620	Zane Smith	.05
621	Randy Tomlin	.05
622	Andy Van Slyke	.05
623	Paul Wagner	.05
624	Tim Wakefield	.05
625	Bob Walk	.05
626	Kevin Young	.10
627	Luis Alicea	.05
628	Rene Arocha	.10
629	Rod Brewer	.05
630	Rheal Cormier	.05
631	Bernard Gilkey	.10
632	Lee Guetterman	.05
633	Gregg Jefferies	.10
634	Brian Jordan	.10
635	Les Lancaster	.05
636	Ray Lankford	.12
637	Rob Murphy	.05
638	Omar Olivares	.05
639	Jose Oquendo	.05
640	Donovan Osborne	.05
641	Tom Pagnozzi	.05
642	Erik Pappas	.05
643	Geronimo Pena	.05
644	Mike Perez	.05
645	Gerald Perry	.05
646	Ozzie Smith	.25
647	Bob Tewksbury	.05
648	Allen Watson	.10
649	Mark Whiten	.05
650	Tracy Woodson	.05
651	Todd Zeile	.08
652	Andy Ashby	.05
653	Brad Ausmus	.05
654	Billy Bean	.05
655	Derek Bell	.12
656	Andy Benes	.08
657	Doug Brocail	.05
658	Jarvis Brown	.05
659	Archi Cianfrocco	.05
660	Phil Clark	.05
661	Mark Davis	.05
662	Jeff Gardner	.05
663	Pat Gomez	.05
664	Ricky Gutierrez	.05
665	Tony Gwynn	1.25
666	Gene Harris	.05
667	Kevin Higgins	.05
668	Trevor Hoffman	.05
669	*Pedro A. Martinez*	.05
670	Tim Mauser	.05
671	Melvin Nieves	.05
672	Phil Plantier	.05
673	Frank Seminara	.05
674	Craig Shipley	.05
675	Kerry Taylor	.05
676	Tim Teufel	.05
677	Guillermo Velasquez	.05
678	Wally Whitehurst	.05
679	Tim Worrell	.05
680	Rod Beck	.05
681	Mike Benjamin	.05
682	Todd Benzinger	.05
683	Bud Black	.05
684	Barry Bonds	.60
685	Jeff Brantley	.05
686	Dave Burba	.05
687	John Burkett	.05
688	Mark Carreon	.05
689	Will Clark	.25
690	Royce Clayton	.08
691	Bryan Hickerson	.05
692	Mike Jackson	.05
693	Darren Lewis	.05
694	Kirt Manwaring	.05
695	Dave Martinez	.05
696	Willie McGee	.08
697	John Patterson	.05
698	Jeff Reed	.05
699	Kevin Rogers	.05
700	Scott Sanderson	.05
701	Steve Scarsone	.05
702	Billy Swift	.05
703	Robby Thompson	.05
704	Matt Williams	.15
705	Trevor Wilson	.05
706	"Brave New World"(Fred McGriff, Ron Gant, Dave Justice)	.10
707	"1-2 Punch"(Paul Molitor, John Olerud)	.10
708	"American Heat"(Mike Mussina, Jack McDowell)	.10
709	"Together Again"(Lou Whitaker, Alan Trammell)	.10
710	"Lone Star Lumber"(Rafael Palmeiro, Juan Gonzalez)	.25
711	"Batmen"(Brett Butler, Tony Gwynn)	.10
712	"Twin Peaks"(Kirby Puckett, Chuck Knoblauch)	.25
713	"Back to Back"(Mike Piazza, Eric Karros)	.50
714	Checklist	.05
715	Checklist	.05
716	Checklist	.05
717	Checklist	.05
718	Checklist	.05
719	Checklist	.05
720	Checklist	.05

1994 Fleer All-Rookie Team

Sharing the format of the basic 1994 Fleer issue, this nine-card set of rookies was available only by redemption of a trade card randomly inserted into foil packs. The exchange card expired Sept. 30, 1994.

		MT
Complete Set (9):		8.00
Common Player:		.50
Exchange Card:		.50
M1	Kurt Abbott	1.00
M2	Rich Becker	1.00
M3	Carlos Delgado	2.00
M4	Jorge Fabregas	1.50
M5	Bob Hamelin	.50
M6	John Hudek	.75
M7	Tim Hyers	.50
M8	Luis Lopez	.50
M9	James Mouton	.75

1994 Fleer All-Stars

Each league's 25 representatives for the 1993 All-Star Game are featured in this insert set. Fronts have a player action photo with a rippling American flag in the top half of the background. The '93 All-Star logo is featured at the bottom, along with a gold-foil impression of the player's name. The flag motif is repeated at top of the card back, along with a player portrait photo set against a red (American League) or blue (National League) background. Odds of finding one of the 50 All-Star inserts are one in every two 15-card foil packs.

		MT
Complete Set (50):		20.00
Common Player:		.25
1	Roberto Alomar	1.00
2	Carlos Baerga	.25
3	Albert Belle	1.00
4	Wade Boggs	.40
5	Joe Carter	.35
6	Scott Cooper	.25
7	Cecil Fielder	.35
8	Travis Fryman	.25
9	Juan Gonzalez	1.50
10	Ken Griffey, Jr.	4.00
11	Pat Hentgen	.25
12	Randy Johnson	.60
13	Jimmy Key	.25
14	Mark Langston	.25
15	Jack McDowell	.25
16	Paul Molitor	.75
17	Jeff Montgomery	.25
18	Mike Mussina	.50
19	John Olerud	.25
20	Kirby Puckett	1.50
21	Cal Ripken, Jr.	4.00
22	Ivan Rodriguez	1.00
23	Frank Thomas	3.00
24	Greg Vaughn	.25
25	Duane Ward	.25
26	Steve Avery	.25
27	Rod Beck	.25
28	Jay Bell	.25
29	Andy Benes	.25
30	Jeff Blauser	.25
31	Barry Bonds	1.00
32	Bobby Bonilla	.25
33	John Burkett	.25
34	Darren Daulton	.25
35	Andres Galarraga	.35
36	Tom Glavine	.35
37	Mark Grace	.40
38	Marquis Grissom	.25
39	Tony Gwynn	1.50
40	Bryan Harvey	.25
41	Dave Hollins	.25
42	Dave Justice	.35
43	Darryl Kile	.25
44	John Kruk	.25
45	Barry Larkin	.35
46	Terry Mulholland	.25
47	Mike Piazza	2.00
48	Ryne Sandberg	1.00
49	Gary Sheffield	.75
50	John Smoltz	.50

1994 Fleer Award Winners

The 1993 MVP, Cy Young and Rookie of the Year award winners from each league are featured in this insert set. Cards are UV coated on both sides. Three different croppings of the same player action photo are featured on the front, with the player's name and other printing in gold foil. Backs have a player portrait and short summary of his previous season's performance. According to the company, odds of finding one of these horizontal-format inserts were one in 37 packs.

		MT
Complete Set (6):		11.00
Common Player:		.75
1	Frank Thomas	4.00
2	Barry Bonds	1.50
3	Jack McDowell	.75
4	Greg Maddux	3.00
5	Tim Salmon	1.00
6	Mike Piazza	3.00

1994 Fleer Golden Moments

Ten highlights from the 1993 Major League baseball season are commemorated in this insert set. Each of the cards has a title which summarizes the historical moment. These inserts were available exclusively in Fleer cards packaged for large retail outlets.

		MT
Complete Set (10):		30.00
Common Player:		.50
1	"Four in One"(Mark Whiten)	.50
2	"Left and Right"(Carlos Baerga)	1.00
3	"3,000 Hit Club"(Dave Winfield)	1.50
4	"Eight Straight"(Ken Griffey, Jr.)	10.00
5	"Triumphant Return"(Bo Jackson)	1.50
6	"Farewell to Baseball"(George Brett)	4.00
7	"Farewell to Baseball"(Nolan Ryan)	8.00
8	"Thirty Times Six"(Fred McGriff)	1.50
9	"Enters 5th Dimension"(Frank Thomas)	8.00
10	"The No-Hit Parade"(Chris Bosio, Jim Abbott, Darryl Kile)	.50

1994 Fleer Golden Moments Super

Super-size (3-1/2" x 5") versions of the Golden Moments insert set were included in hobby cases at the rate of one set, in a specially-printed folder, per 20-box case. Each card carries a serial number designating its position in an edition of 10,000.

		MT
Complete Set (10):		75.00
Common Player:		5.00
1	"Four in One"(Mark Whiten)	5.00
2	"Left and Right"(Carlos Baerga)	6.00
3	"3,000 Hit Club"(Dave Winfield)	7.50
4	"Eight Straight"(Ken Griffey, Jr.)	15.00
5	"Triumphant Return"(Bo Jackson)	7.50
6	"Farewell to Baseball"(George Brett)	10.00
7	"Farewell to Baseball"(Nolan Ryan)	12.50
8	"Thirty Times Six"(Fred McGriff)	7.50
9	"Enters 5th Dimension"(Frank Thomas)	15.00
10	"The No-Hit Parade"(Chris Bosio, Jim Abbott, Darryl Kile)	5.00

A player's name in *italic* type indicates a rookie card.

1994 Fleer League Leaders

Twelve players who led the major leagues in various statistical categories in 1993 are featured in this insert set. Cards are UV coated and have gold-foil stamping on both sides. Within a light metallic green border, card fronts feature a color action photo superimposed over a similar photo in black-and-white. The category in which the player led his league is printed down the right border. Other printing is gold-foil. On back is a color photo and details of the league-leading performance. Stated odds of finding a League Leaders card were one per 17 packs.

		MT
Complete Set (12):		7.00
Common Player:		.25
1	John Olerud	.25
2	Albert Belle	1.00
3	Rafael Palmeiro	.50
4	Kenny Lofton	1.00
5	Jack McDowell	.25
6	Kevin Appier	.25
7	Andres Galarraga	.50
8	Barry Bonds	1.00
9	Len Dykstra	.25
10	Chuck Carr	.25
11	Tom Glavine	.35
12	Greg Maddux	2.50

1994 Fleer Lumber Co.

This insert set features the major leagues' top home run hitters. Inserted only in 21-card jumbo packs, odds of finding one were given as one per five packs. Card fronts feature player action photos against a background resembling the label area of a baseball bat. On back is a background photo of a row of bats on the dirt. A player write-up and close-up photo complete the design.

		MT
Complete Set (10):		15.00
Common Player:		.75
1	Albert Belle	1.50
2	Barry Bonds	1.50
3	Ron Gant	.75
4	Juan Gonzalez	2.50
5	Ken Griffey, Jr.	6.00
6	Dave Justice	.75
7	Fred McGriff	.90
8	Rafael Palmeiro	.75
9	Frank Thomas	5.00
10	Matt Williams	.75

1994 Fleer Major League Prospects

Thirty-five of the game's promising young stars are featured in this insert set. A light green metallic border frames a player photo, with his team logo lightly printed over the background. Most of the printing is gold-foil stamped. Backs have a player photo against a pin-striped background. A light blue box contains career details. Given odds of finding a "Major League Prospects" card are one in six packs.

		MT
Complete Set (35):		15.00
Common Player:		.25
1	Kurt Abbott	.40
2	Brian Anderson	.25
3	Rich Aude	.25
4	Cory Bailey	.25
5	Danny Bautista	.25
6	Marty Cordova	1.00
7	Tripp Cromer	.25
8	Midre Cummings	.25
9	Carlos Delgado	.75
10	Steve Dreyer	.25
11	Steve Dunn	.25
12	Jeff Granger	.25
13	Tyrone Hill	.25
14	Denny Hocking	.40
15	John Hope	.30
16	Butch Huskey	.40
17	Miguel Jimenez	.25
18	Chipper Jones	8.00
19	Steve Karsay	.25
20	Mike Kelly	.25
21	Mike Lieberthal	.25
22	Albie Lopez	.25
23	Jeff McNeely	.35
24	Dan Miceli	.40
25	Nate Minchey	.25
26	Marc Newfield	.35
27	Darren Oliver	.25
28	Luis Ortiz	.25
29	Curtis Pride	.50
30	Roger Salkeld	.35
31	Scott Sanders	.40
32	Dave Staton	.40
33	Salomon Torres	.25
34	Steve Trachsel	.40
35	Chris Turner	.35

1994 Fleer ProVisions

Nine players are featured in this insert set. Cards feature the fantasy artwork of Wayne Still in a format that produces one large image when all nine cards are properly arranged. Besides the art, card fronts feature the player's name in gold-foil. Backs have a background in several shades of red, with the player's name and team at the top in white. A short career summary is printed in black. Odds of finding this particular insert in a pack are one in 12.

		MT
Complete Set (9):		4.00
Common Player:		.25
1	Darren Daulton	.25
2	John Olerud	.25
3	Matt Williams	.50
4	Carlos Baerga	.25
5	Ozzie Smith	.50
6	Juan Gonzalez	1.00
7	Jack McDowell	.20
8	Mike Piazza	2.00
9	Tony Gwynn	1.00

1994 Fleer Rookie Sensations

This insert set features the top rookies from 1993. These inserts were available only in 21-card jumbo packs, with stated odds of one in four packs. Full-bleed fronts have a pair of player photos - one highlighted by a neon outline - superimposed on a graduated background approximating the team colors. Team uniform logo details appear vertically at the right or left side. The player's name is gold-foil stamped in a banner at bottom. The Rookie Sensations and Fleer logos are also gold-imprinted. On back, the team uniform logo is repeated on a white background, along with another player photo and a short write-up.

		MT
Complete Set (20):		20.00
Common Player:		.50
1	Rene Arocha	.50
2	Jason Bere	1.00
3	Jeromy Burnitz	.75
4	Chuck Carr	.50
5	Jeff Conine	1.00
6	Steve Cooke	.50
7	Cliff Floyd	.75
8	Jeffrey Hammonds	1.25
9	Wayne Kirby	.50
10	Mike Lansing	.60
11	Al Martin	.60
12	Greg McMichael	.50
13	Troy Neel	.50
14	Mike Piazza	8.00
15	Armando Reynoso	.50
16	Kirk Rueter	.50
17	Tim Salmon	2.50
18	Aaron Sele	.75
19	J.T. Snow	1.00
20	Kevin Stocker	.50

1994 Fleer Smoke N' Heat

Among the scarcest of the '94 Fleer inserts, available at a stated rate of one per 30 packs, these feature 10 of the top strikeout pitchers in the major leagues. "Metallized" card fronts have a player photo set against an infernal background with large letters, "Smoke 'N Heat". The player's name is in gold foil at bottom. Backs have a similar chaotic hot-red background, a player photo and career summary.

		MT
Complete Set (12):		80.00
Common Player:		1.00
1	Roger Clemens	10.00
2	David Cone	1.50
3	Juan Guzman	1.00
4	Pete Harnisch	1.00
5	Randy Johnson	6.00
6	Mark Langston	1.00
7	Greg Maddux	25.00
8	Mike Mussina	6.00
9	Jose Rijo	1.00
10	Nolan Ryan	35.00
11	Curt Schilling	1.00
12	John Smoltz	5.00

1994 Fleer Team Leaders

A player from each major league team has been chosen for this 28-card insert set. Fronts feature a team logo against a backgound of graduated team colors. Player portrait and action photos are superimposed. At bottom is the player name, team and position, all in gold foil. Backs have a team logo and player photo set against a white background, with a short write-up justifying the player's selection as a "Team Leader." Odds of finding one of these inserts were given as one in eight packs.

		MT
Complete Set (28):		24.00
Common Player:		.25
1	Cal Ripken, Jr.	5.00
2	Mo Vaughn	1.00
3	Tim Salmon	.75
4	Frank Thomas	4.00
5	Carlos Baerga	.40
6	Cecil Fielder	.50
7	Brian McRae	.25
8	Greg Vaughn	.25
9	Kirby Puckett	2.00
10	Don Mattingly	2.00
11	Mark McGwire	6.00
12	Ken Griffey, Jr.	5.00
13	Juan Gonzalez	2.00
14	Paul Molitor	.75
15	Dave Justice	.35
16	Ryne Sandberg	1.00
17	Barry Larkin	.40
18	Andres Galarraga	.40
19	Gary Sheffield	.75
20	Jeff Bagwell	1.50
21	Mike Piazza	2.00
22	Marquis Grissom	.25
23	Bobby Bonilla	.25
24	Len Dykstra	.25
25	Jay Bell	.25
26	Gregg Jefferies	.25
27	Tony Gwynn	1.50
28	Will Clark	.50

1994 Fleer Tim Salmon A.L. Rookie of the Year

The popular Angels Rookie of the Year is featured in a 15-card set produced in what Fleer terms "metallized" format. The first 12 cards in the set were inserted into foil packs at the rate of about one card per box. Three additional cards could be obtained by sending $1.50 and 10 '94 Fleer wrappers to a mail-in offer. On both front and back, the cards have a color player photo set against a metallic-image background.

		MT
Complete Set (15):		30.00
Common Card:		2.00
1	Tim Salmon	2.00
2	Tim Salmon	2.00
3	Tim Salmon	2.00
4	Tim Salmon	2.00
5	Tim Salmon	2.00
6	Tim Salmon	2.00
7	Tim Salmon	2.00
8	Tim Salmon	2.00
9	Tim Salmon	2.00
10	Tim Salmon	2.00
11	Tim Salmon	2.00
12	Tim Salmon	2.00
13	Tim Salmon	4.00
14	Tim Salmon	4.00
15	Tim Salmon	4.00
--	Tim Salmon (autographed edition of 2,000)	75.00

1994 Fleer Update

Rookies, traded players and free agents who changed teams are included in the annual update issue. Cards are in the same format as the regular-issue '94 Fleer set. Cards are numbered alphabetically within team.

		MT
Complete Set (200):		50.00
Common Player:		.10
1	Mark Eichhorn	.10
2	Sid Fernandez	.10
3	Leo Gomez	.10
4	Mike Oquist	.10
5	Rafael Palmeiro	.25
6	Chris Sabo	.10
7	Dwight Smith	.10
8	Lee Smith	.12
9	Damon Berryhill	.10
10	Wes Chamberlain	.10
11	Gar Finnvold	.10
12	Chris Howard	.10
13	Tim Naehring	.10
14	Otis Nixon	.10
15	Brian Anderson	.10
16	Jorge Fabregas	.10
17	Rex Hudler	.10
18	Bo Jackson	.20
19	Mark Leiter	.10
20	Spike Owen	.10
21	Harold Reynolds	.10
22	Chris Turner	.10
23	Dennis Cook	.10
24	Jose DeLeon	.10
25	Julio Franco	.12
26	Joe Hall	.10
27	Darrin Jackson	.10
28	Dane Johnson	.10
29	Norberto Martin	.10
30	Scott Sanderson	.10
31	Jason Grimsley	.10
32	Dennis Martinez	.12
33	Jack Morris	.10
34	Eddie Murray	.20
35	Chad Ogea	.10
36	Tony Pena	.10
37	Paul Shuey	.10
38	Omar Vizquel	.10
39	Danny Bautista	.10
40	Tim Belcher	.10
41	Joe Boever	.10
42	Storm Davis	.10
43	Junior Felix	.10
44	Mike Gardiner	.10
45	Buddy Groom	.10
46	Juan Samuel	.10
47	Vince Coleman	.10
48	Bob Hamelin	.15
49	Dave Henderson	.10
50	Rusty Meacham	.10
51	Terry Shumpert	.10
52	Jeff Bronkey	.10
53	Alex Diaz	.10
54	Brian Harper	.10
55	Jose Mercedes	.10
56	Jody Reed	.10
57	Bob Scanlan	.10
58	Turner Ward	.10
59	Rich Becker	.10
60	Alex Cole	.10
61	Denny Hocking	.10
63	Pat Mahomes	.15
64	Carlos Pulido	.10
65	Dave Stevens	.10
66	Matt Walbeck	.10
67	Xavier Hernandez	.10
68	Sterling Hitchcock	.10
69	Terry Mulholland	.10
70	Luis Polonia	.10
71	Gerald Williams	.10
72	Mark Acre	.10
73	Geronimo Berroa	.10
74	Rickey Henderson	.25
75	Stan Javier	.10
76	Steve Karsay	.10
77	Carlos Reyes	.10
78	Bill Taylor	.10
79	Eric Anthony	.10
80	Bobby Ayala	.10
81	Tim Davis	.10
82	Felix Fermin	.10
83	Reggie Jefferson	.10
84	Keith Mitchell	.10
85	Bill Risley	.15
86	*Alex Rodriguez*	40.00
87	Roger Salkeld	.12
88	Dan Wilson	.12
89	Cris Carpenter	.10
90	Will Clark	.40
91	Jeff Frye	.10
92	Rick Helling	.10
93	Chris James	.10
94	Oddibe McDowell	.10
95	Billy Ripken	.10
96	Carlos Delgado	.30
97	Alex Gonzalez	.25
98	Shawn Green	.20
100	Mike Huff	.10
101	Mike Kelly	.10
102	Roberto Kelly	.10
103	Charlie O'Brien	.10
104	Jose Oliva	.10
105	Gregg Olson	.10
106	Willie Banks	.10
107	Jim Bullinger	.10
108	Chuck Crim	.10
109	Shawon Dunston	.15
110	Karl Rhodes	.10
111	Steve Trachsel	.20
112	Anthony Young	.10
113	Eddie Zambrano	.10
114	Bret Boone	.15
115	Jeff Brantley	.10
116	Hector Carrasco	.15
117	Tony Fernandez	.10
118	Tim Fortugno	.10
119	Erik Hanson	.10
120	Chuck McElroy	.10
121	Deion Sanders	1.00
122	Ellis Burks	.20
123	Marvin Freeman	.10
124	Mike Harkey	.10
125	Howard Johnson	.10
126	Mike Kingery	.10
127	Nelson Liriano	.10
128	Marcus Moore	.10
129	Mike Munoz	.10
130	Kevin Ritz	.10
131	Walt Weiss	.10
132	Kurt Abbott	.15
133	Jerry Browne	.10
134	Greg Colbrunn	.10
135	Jeremy Hernandez	.10
136	Dave Magadan	.10
137	Kurt Miller	.10
138	Robb Nen	.15
139	Jesus Taverez	.10
140	Sid Bream	.10
141	Tom Edens	.10
142	Tony Eusebio	.10
143	John Hudek	.20
144	Brian Hunter	1.00
145	Orlando Miller	.15
146	James Mouton	.20
147	Shane Reynolds	.10
148	Rafael Bournigal	.10
149	Delino DeShields	.10
150	Garey Ingram	.10
151	Chan Ho Park	.20
152	Wil Cordero	.15
153	Pedro Martinez	.25
154	Randy Milligan	.10
155	Lenny Webster	.10
156	Rico Brogna	.10
157	Josias Manzanillo	.10
158	Kevin McReynolds	.10
159	Mike Remlinger	.10
160	David Segui	.10
161	Pete Smith	.10
162	Kelly Stinnett	.15
163	Jose Vizcaino	.10
164	Billy Hatcher	.10
165	Doug Jones	.10
166	Mike Lieberthal	.10
167	Tony Longmire	.10
168	Bobby Munoz	.10
169	Paul Quantrill	.10
170	Heathcliff Slocumb	.10
171	Fernando Valenzuela	.12
172	Mark Dewey	.10
173	Brian Hunter	.10
174	Jon Lieber	.10
175	Ravelo Manzanillo	.10
176	Dan Miceli	.10
177	Rick White	.10
178	Bryan Eversgerd	.10
179	John Habyan	.10
180	Terry McGriff	.10
181	Vicente Palacios	.10
182	Rich Rodriguez	.10
183	Rick Sutcliffe	.10
184	Donnie Elliott	.10
185	Joey Hamilton	.60
186	Tim Hyers	.10
187	Luis Lopez	.10
188	Ray McDavid	.10
189	Bip Roberts	.10
190	Scott Sanders	.10
191	Eddie Williams	.10
192	Steve Frey	.10
193	Pat Gomez	.10
194	Rich Monteleone	.10
195	Mark Portugal	.10
196	Darryl Strawberry	.15
197	Salomon Torres	.10
198	W. Van Landingham	.35
199	Checklist	.10
200	Checklist	.10

1994 Fleer Update Diamond Tribute

These special cards included in the 1994 Fleer Update set feature 10 of baseball's proven superstars. The card front has a color action shot of the player, against a skyline with a baseball pattern among the clouds. The card back is numbered 1 of 8, etc., and includes another photo against a background similar to that used for the card front. A "Diamond Tribute" logo and career summary are also included on the back.

	MT
Complete Set (10):	7.50
Common Player:	.50
1 Barry Bonds	1.00
2 Joe Carter	.50
3 Will Clark	.60
4 Roger Clemens	1.00
5 Tony Gwynn	1.00
6 Don Mattingly	1.00
7 Fred McGriff	.60
8 Eddie Murray	.50
9 Kirby Puckett	1.00
10 Cal Ripken Jr.	3.00

1994 Fleer/ Extra Bases

Extra Bases was a 400-card, oversized set, plus 80 insert cards in four different subsets. The cards, 4-11/16" by 2-1/2", have a full-bleed photo on the front and back, as well as UV coating and color coding by team. As was the case in other Fleer products, Extra Bases contained an insert card in every pack. All 80 insert cards feature gold or silver foil stamping.

	MT
Complete Set (400):	30.00
Common Player:	.10
Wax Box:	30.00
1 Brady Anderson	.20
2 Harold Baines	.12
3 Mike Devereaux	.10
4 Sid Fernandez	.10
5 Jeffrey Hammonds	.25
6 Chris Hoiles	.10
7 Ben McDonald	.10
8 Mark McLemore	.10
9 Mike Mussina	.50
10 Mike Oquist	.10
11 Rafael Palmeiro	.20
12 Cal Ripken, Jr.	3.00
13 Chris Sabo	.10
14 Lee Smith	.12
15 Wes Chamberlain	.10
16 Roger Clemens	.65
17 Scott Cooper	.10
18 Danny Darwin	.10
19 Andre Dawson	.15
20 Mike Greenwell	.10
21 Tim Naehring	.10
22 Otis Nixon	.10
23 Jeff Russell	.10
24 Ken Ryan	.10
25 Aaron Sele	.15
26 John Valentin	.15
27 Mo Vaughn	.50
28 Frank Viola	.10

29 *Brian Anderson*	.15
30 Chad Curtis	.10
31 Chili Davis	.12
32 Gary DiSarcina	.10
33 Damion Easley	.10
34 Jim Edmonds	.30
35 Chuck Finley	.10
36 Bo Jackson	.15
37 Mark Langston	.10
38 Harold Reynolds	.10
39 Tim Salmon	.40
40 Wilson Alvarez	.10
41 James Baldwin	.15
42 Jason Bere	.15
43 Joey Cora	.10
44 *Ray Durham*	.60
45 Alex Fernandez	.15
46 Julio Franco	.10
47 Ozzie Guillen	.10
48 Darrin Jackson	.10
49 Lance Johnson	.10
50 Ron Karkovice	.10
51 Jack McDowell	.12
52 Tim Raines	.10
53 Frank Thomas	2.50
54 Robin Ventura	.15
55 Sandy Alomar Jr.	.12
56 Carlos Baerga	.15
57 Albert Belle	.75
58 Mark Clark	.15
59 Wayne Kirby	.10
60 Kenny Lofton	.75
61 Dennis Martinez	.12
62 Jose Mesa	.12
63 Jack Morris	.10
64 Eddie Murray	.15
65 Charles Nagy	.10
66 Manny Ramirez	.75
67 Paul Shuey	.10
68 Paul Sorrento	.10
69 Jim Thome	.35
70 Omar Vizquel	.10
71 Eric Davis	.12
72 John Doherty	.10
73 Cecil Fielder	.20
74 Travis Fryman	.15
75 Kirk Gibson	.10
76 Gene Harris	.10
77 Mike Henneman	.10
78 Mike Moore	.10
79 Tony Phillips	.15
80 Mickey Tettleton	.10
81 Alan Trammell	.15
82 Lou Whitaker	.10
83 Kevin Appier	.10
84 Vince Coleman	.10
85 David Cone	.10
86 Gary Gaetti	.15
87 Greg Gagne	.10
88 Tom Gordon	.10
89 Jeff Granger	.10
90 Bob Hamelin	.10
91 Dave Henderson	.10
92 Felix Jose	.10
93 Wally Joyner	.12
94 Jose Lind	.10
95 Mike Macfarlane	.10
96 Brian McRae	.10
97 Jeff Montgomery	.10
98 Ricky Bones	.10
99 Jeff Bronkey	.10
100 Alex Diaz	.10
101 Cal Eldred	.10
102 Darryl Hamilton	.10
103 Brian Harper	.10
104 John Jaha	.10
105 Pat Listach	.10
106 Dave Nilsson	.10
107 Jody Reed	.10
108 Kevin Seitzer	.10
109 Greg Vaughn	.15
110 Turner Ward	.10
111 Wes Weger	.12
112 Bill Wegman	.10
113 Rick Aguilera	.10
114 Rich Becker	.10
115 Alex Cole	.10
116 Scott Erickson	.10
117 Kent Hrbek	.12
118 Chuck Knoblauch	.20
119 Scott Leius	.10
120 Shane Mack	.10
121 Pat Mahomes	.10
122 Pat Meares	.10
123 Kirby Puckett	1.00
124 Kevin Tapani	.10

125 Matt Walbeck	.10
126 Dave Winfield	.25
127 Jim Abbott	.15
128 Wade Boggs	.25
129 Mike Gallego	.10
130 Xavier Hernandez	.10
131 Pat Kelly	.10
132 Jimmy Key	.10
133 Don Mattingly	1.00
134 Terry Mulholland	.10
135 Matt Nokes	.10
136 Paul O'Neill	.10
137 Melido Perez	.10
138 Luis Polonia	.10
139 Mike Stanley	.10
140 Danny Tartabull	.10
141 Randy Velarde	.10
142 Bernie Williams	.40
143 Mark Acre	.10
144 Geronimo Berroa	.15
145 Mike Bordick	.10
146 Scott Brosius	.10
147 Ron Darling	.10
148 Dennis Eckersley	.12
149 Brent Gates	.15
150 Rickey Henderson	.20
151 Stan Javier	.10
152 Steve Karsay	.15
153 Mark McGwire	3.00
154 Troy Neel	.10
155 Ruben Sierra	.15
156 Terry Steinbach	.10
157 Bill Taylor	.10
158 Rich Amaral	.10
159 Eric Anthony	.05
160 Bobby Ayala	.10
161 Chris Bosio	.10
162 Jay Buhner	.15
163 Tim Davis	.10
164 Felix Fermin	.10
165 Dave Fleming	.10
166 Ken Griffey, Jr.	3.00
167 Reggie Jefferson	.10
168 Randy Johnson	.40
169 Edgar Martinez	.12
170 Tino Martinez	.15
171 Bill Risley	.10
172 Roger Salkeld	.10
173 *Mac Suzuki*	.20
174 Dan Wilson	.10
175 Kevin Brown	.10
176 Jose Canseco	.40
177 Will Clark	.25
178 Juan Gonzalez	1.50
179 Rick Helling	.10
180 Tom Henke	.10
181 Chris James	.10
182 Manuel Lee	.10
183 Dean Palmer	.10
184 Ivan Rodriguez	.40
185 Kenny Rogers	.10
186 Roberto Alomar	.60
187 Pat Borders	.10
188 Joe Carter	.20
189 Carlos Delgado	.15
190 Juan Guzman	.10
191 Pat Hentgen	.12
192 Paul Molitor	.45
192a Paul Molitor (promotional sample)	6.00
193 John Olerud	.15
194 Ed Sprague	.10
195 Dave Stewart	.12
196 Todd Stottlemyre	.10
197 Duane Ward	.10
198 Devon White	.12
199 Steve Avery	.12
200 Jeff Blauser	.10
201 Tom Glavine	.20
202 Dave Justice	.40
203 Mike Kelly	.10
204 Roberto Kelly	.10
205 Ryan Klesko	.50
206 Mark Lemke	.10
207 Javier Lopez	.25
208 Greg Maddux	2.00
209 Fred McGriff	.35
210 Greg McMichael	.10
211 Kent Mercker	.10
212 Terry Pendleton	.10
213 John Smoltz	.15
214 Tony Tarasco	.10
215 Willie Banks	.10
216 Steve Buechele	.10
217 Shawon Dunston	.15
218 Mark Grace	.15

219	Brooks Kieschnick	.75
220	Derrick May	.10
221	Randy Myers	.10
222	Karl Rhodes	.10
223	Rey Sanchez	.10
224	Sammy Sosa	.75
225	Steve Traschel	.20
226	Rick Wilkins	.10
227	Bret Boone	.10
228	Jeff Brantley	.10
229	Tom Browning	.10
230	Hector Carrasco	.15
231	Rob Dibble	.10
232	Erik Hanson	.10
233	Barry Larkin	.15
234	Kevin Mitchell	.12
235	Hal Morris	12
236	Joe Oliver	.10
237	Jose Rijo	.10
238	Johnny Ruffin	.10
239	Deion Sanders	.40
240	Reggie Sanders	.15
241	John Smiley	.10
242	Dante Bichette	.30
243	Ellis Burks	.15
244	Andres Galarraga	.20
245	Joe Girardi	.10
246	Greg Harris	.10
247	Charlie Hayes	.10
248	Howard Johnson	.10
249	Roberto Mejia	.10
250	Marcus Moore	.10
251	David Nied	.10
252	Armando Reynoso	.10
253	Bruce Ruffin	.10
254	Mark Thompson	.10
255	Walt Weiss	.10
256	Kurt Abbott	.20
257	Bret Barberie	.10
258	Chuck Carr	.10
259	Jeff Conine	.15
260	Chris Hammond	.10
261	Bryan Harvey	.10
262	Jeremy Hernandez	.10
263	Charlie Hough	.10
264	Dave Magadan	.10
265	Benito Santiago	.12
266	Gary Sheffield	.20
267	David Weathers	.10
268	Jeff Bagwell	.75
269	Craig Biggio	.15
270	Ken Caminiti	.15
271	Andujar Cedeno	.10
272	Doug Drabek	.10
273	Steve Finley	.10
274	Luis Gonzalez	.10
275	Pete Harnisch	.10
276	John Hudek	.15
277	Darryl Kile	.10
278	Orlando Miller	.10
279	James Mouton	.15
280	Shane Reynolds	.10
281	Scott Servais	.10
282	Greg Swindell	.10
283	Pedro Astacio	.10
284	Brett Butler	.15
285	Tom Candiotti	.10
286	Delino DeShields	.10
287	Kevin Gross	.10
288	Orel Hershiser	.12
289	Eric Karros	.15
290	Ramon Martinez	.12
291	Raul Mondesi	.50
292	Jose Offerman	.10
293	Chan Ho Park	.25
294	Mike Piazza	2.00
295	Henry Rodriguez	.12
296	Cory Snyder	.10
297	Tim Wallach	.10
298	Todd Worrell	.10
299	Moises Alou	.15
300	Sean Berry	.10
301	Wil Cordero	.15
302	Joey Eischen	.10
303	Jeff Fassero	.10
304	Darrin Fletcher	.10
305	Cliff Floyd	.20
306	Marquis Grissom	.15
307	Ken Hill	.10
308	Mike Lansing	.10
309	Pedro Martinez	.25
310	Mel Rojas	.10
311	Kirk Rueter	.10
312	Larry Walker	.25
313	John Wetteland	.10
314	Rondell White	.30

315	Bobby Bonilla	.15
316	John Franco	.10
317	Dwight Gooden	.15
318	Todd Hundley	.15
319	Bobby Jones	.10
320	Jeff Kent	.15
321	Kevin McReynolds	.10
322	Bill Pulsipher	.20
323	Bret Saberhagen	.10
324	David Segui	.10
325	Pete Smith	.10
326	Kelly Stinnett	.15
327	Ryan Thompson	.10
328	Jose Vizcaino	.10
329	Ricky Bottalico	.10
330	Darren Daulton	.15
331	Mariano Duncan	.10
332	Len Dykstra	.15
333	Tommy Greene	.10
334	Billy Hatcher	.10
335	Dave Hollins	.10
336	Pete Incaviglia	.10
337	Danny Jackson	.10
338	Doug Jones	.10
339	Ricky Jordan	.10
340	John Kruk	.10
341	Curt Schilling	.10
342	Kevin Stocker	.10
343	Jay Bell	.10
344	Steve Cooke	.10
345	Carlos Garcia	.10
346	Brian Hunter	.10
347	Jeff King	.10
348	Al Martin	.10
349	Orlando Merced	.10
350	Denny Neagle	.10
351	Don Slaught	.10
352	Andy Van Slyke	.10
353	Paul Wagner	.10
354	Rick White	.10
355	Luis Alicea	.10
356	Rene Arocha	.10
357	Rheal Cormier	.10
358	Bernard Gilkey	.15
359	Gregg Jefferies	.15
360	Ray Lankford	.15
361	Tom Pagnozzi	.10
362	Mike Perez	.10
363	Ozzie Smith	.45
364	Bob Tewksbury	.10
365	Mark Whiten	.10
366	Todd Zeile	.15
367	Andy Ashby	.10
368	Brad Ausmus	.10
369	Derek Bell	.15
370	Andy Benes	.12
371	Archi Cianfrocco	.10
372	Tony Gwynn	1.00
373	Trevor Hoffman	.10
374	Tim Hyers	.10
375	Pedro Martinez	.15
376	Phil Plantier	.10
377	Bip Roberts	.10
378	Scott Sanders	.10
379	Dave Staton	.10
380	Wally Whitehurst	.10
381	Rod Beck	.10
382	Todd Benzinger	.10
383	Barry Bonds	.65
384	John Burkett	.10
385	Royce Clayton	.10
386	Bryan Hickerson	.10
387	Mike Jackson	.10
388	Darren Lewis	.10
389	Kirt Manwaring	.10
390	Willie McGee	.12
391	Mark Portugal	.10
392	Bill Swift	.10
393	Robby Thompson	.10
394	Salomon Torres	.10
395	Matt Williams	.35
396	Checklist	.10
397	Checklist	.10
398	Checklist	.10
399	Checklist	.10
400	Checklist	.10

1994 Fleer/ Extra Bases Game Breakers

Game Breakers featured 30 big-name stars from both leagues who have exhibited offensive fire-power. This insert set was done in a horizontal format picturing the player in two different shots, one close-up and one slightly further away. The words "Game Breakers" is written across the bottom, with the player name and team in much smaller letters, printed under it.

		MT
Complete Set (30):		20.00
Common Player:		.25
1	Jeff Bagwell	1.50
2	Rod Beck	.25
3	Albert Belle	1.00
4	Barry Bonds	1.50
5	Jose Canseco	.50
6	Joe Carter	.35
7	Roger Clemens	1.00
8	Darren Daulton	.25
9	Len Dykstra	.25
10	Cecil Fielder	.30
11	Tom Glavine	.30
12	Juan Gonzalez	1.50
13	Mark Grace	.35
14	Ken Griffey, Jr.	4.00
15	Dave Justice	.55
16	Greg Maddux	2.50
17	Don Mattingly	1.75
18	Ben McDonald	.25
19	Fred McGriff	.60
20	Paul Molitor	.50
21	John Olerud	.25
22	Mike Piazza	2.50
23	Kirby Puckett	1.50
24	Cal Ripken, Jr.	4.00
25	Tim Salmon	.75
26	Gary Sheffield	.45
27	Frank Thomas	3.00
28	Mo Vaughn	1.00
29	Matt Williams	.75
30	Dave Winfield	.50

Modern cards have little collector value in conditions lower than Mint. Figure NM cards at 75% of values shown; EX cards at 40%.

Values shown reflect the market as of January, 1999. On-field performances of current players in the 1999 baseball season are not factored in.

1994 Fleer/ Extra Bases Major League Hopefuls

Minor league standouts with impressive credentials were showcased in Major League Hopefuls. Each card in this insert set shows the player over a computer enhanced background, with three smaller photos running down the top half, on the left side of the card. The insert set title runs across the bottom and the player's name is just under it on a black strip.

MAJOR LEAGUE HOREFUL
RAY DURHAM

	MT
Complete Set (10):	4.00
Common Player:	.25
1 James Baldwin	.50
2 Ricky Bottalico	.50
3 Ray Durham	1.00
4 Joey Eischen	.35
5 Brooks Kieschnick	1.00
6 Orlando Miller	.35
7 Bill Pulsipher	.25
8 Mac Suzuki	.25
9 Mark Thompson	.25
10 Wes Weger	.35

1994 Fleer/ Extra Bases Pitcher's Duel

Pitcher's Duel was available to collectors who mailed in 10 Extra Bases wrappers. The set features 20 of the top pitchers is baseball. Contained in the set were five American League and five National League cards, with two pitchers from the same league on each card. The front background pictures a wide-angle photo of a major league stadium, viewed from above the diamond, behind home plate. Backs have two more action photos set against a sepia-toned background photo of an Old West street to enhance the shootout theme of the set. Cards are numbered with an "M" prefix.

	MT
Complete Set (10):	12.00
Common Player:	.75
1M Roger Clemens, Jack McDowell	2.00
2M Ben McDonald, Randy Johnson	1.50
3M Jimmy Key, David Cone	1.00
4M Mike Mussina, Aaron Sele	2.00
5M Chuck Finley, Wilson Alvarez	.75

6M Steve Avery, Curt Schilling	.75
7M Greg Maddux, Jose Rijo	5.00
8M Bret Saberhagen, Bob Tewksbury	.75
9M Tom Glavine, Bill Swift	1.00
10M Doug Drabek, Orel Hershiser	.75

1994 Fleer/ Extra Bases Rookie Standouts

Rookie Standouts highlights 20 of the best and brightest first-year players of the 1994 season. Cards picture the player on a baseball background, with a black, jagged-edged "aura" around the player. Names and teams were placed in the bottom-left corner, running up the side. The Rookie Standouts logo, which is a gold glove with a baseball in it and "Rookie Standouts" printed under it, was placed in the bottom-right corner and the Extra Bases logo appears in the upper-left.

	MT
Complete Set (20):	12.00
Common Player:	.25
1 Kurt Abbott	.50
2 Brian Anderson	.35
3 Hector Carrasco	.35
4 Tim Davis	.25
5 Carlos Delgado	.75
6 Cliff Floyd	.60
7 Bob Hamelin	.30
8 Jeffrey Hammonds	.50
9 Rick Helling	.40
10 Steve Karsay	.30
11 Ryan Klesko	2.00
12 Javier Lopez	1.00
13 Raul Mondesi	2.00
14 James Mouton	.35
15 Chan Ho Park	.65
16 Manny Ramirez	2.00
17 Tony Tarasco	.25
18 Steve Trachsel	.25
19 Rick White	.25
20 Rondell White	1.00

Modern cards
have little collector value in
conditions lower than Mint.
Figure NM cards
at 75%
of values shown;
EX cards at 40%.

1994 Fleer/ Extra Bases Second Year Stars

Second-Year Stars contains 1993 rookies who were expected to have an even bigger impact in the 1994 season. Each card features five photos of the player. Four are in a filmstrip down the left side; the remaining two-thirds of the card contain a larger photo. "Second-Year Stars" is printed across the bottom, along with the player name and team. Backs repeat the film-strip motif.

	MT
Complete Set (20):	9.00
Common Player:	.25
1 Bobby Ayala	.25
2 Jason Bere	.50
3 Chuck Carr	.25
4 Jeff Conine	.40
5 Steve Cooke	.25
6 Wil Cordero	.40
7 Carlos Garcia	.25
8 Brent Gates	.30
9 Trevor Hoffman	.30
10 Wayne Kirby	.25
11 Al Martin	.25
12 Pedro Martinez	.50
13 Greg McMichael	.25
14 Troy Neel	.25
15 David Nied	.25
16 Mike Piazza	3.50
17 Kirk Rueter	.25
18 Tim Salmon	1.00
19 Aaron Sele	.75
20 Kevin Stocker	.25

1995 Fleer

Fleer baseball arrived in 1995 with six different designs, one for each division. The basic set contains 600 cards and was sold in 12-card and 18-card packs. National League West cards feature many smaller pictures in the background that are identical to the picture in the forefront, while AL West cards contain an action photo over top of a close-up on the right side and a water colored look on the left side. AL Central cards exhibit numbers pertinent to each player throughout the front design, with the player in the middle. NL East players appear in action on the left half of the card with a colorful, encripted look on the rest. National League Central and American League East feature more standard designs with the player in the forefront, with vital numbers and a color background.

		MT
Complete Set (600):		40.00
Common Player:		.05
Wax Box:		35.00
1	Brady Anderson	.20
2	Harold Baines	.08
3	Damon Buford	.05
4	Mike Devereaux	.05
5	Mark Eichhorn	.05
6	Sid Fernandez	.05
7	Leo Gomez	.05
8	Jeffrey Hammonds	.10
9	Chris Hoiles	.05
10	Rick Krivda	.05
11	Ben McDonald	.05
12	Mark McLemore	.05
13	Alan Mills	.05
14	Jamie Moyer	.05
15	Mike Mussina	.30
16	Mike Oquist	.05
17	Rafael Palmeiro	.10
18	Arthur Rhodes	.05
19	Cal Ripken, Jr.	2.50
20	Chris Sabo	.05
21	Lee Smith	.08
22	Jack Voight	.05
23	Damon Berryhill	.05
24	Tom Brunansky	.05
25	Wes Chamberlain	.05
26	Roger Clemens	.50
27	Scott Cooper	.05
28	Andre Dawson	.15
29	Gar Finnvold	.05
30	Tony Fossas	.05
31	Mike Greenwell	.05
32	Joe Hesketh	.05
33	Chris Howard	.05
34	Chris Nabholz	.05
35	Tim Naehring	.05
36	Otis Nixon	.05
37	Carlos Rodriguez	.05
38	Rich Rowland	.05
39	Ken Ryan	.05
40	Aaron Sele	.10
41	John Valentin	.15
42	Mo Vaughn	.60
43	Frank Viola	.05
44	Danny Bautista	.05
45	Joe Boeven	.05
46	Milt Cuyler	.05
47	Storm Davis	.05
48	John Doherty	.05
49	Junior Felix	.05
50	Cecil Fielder	.15
51	Travis Fryman	.10
52	Mike Gardiner	.05
53	Kirk Gibson	.05
54	Chris Gomez	.05
55	Buddy Groom	.05
56	Mike Henneman	.05

57	Chad Kreuter	.05
58	Mike Moore	.05
59	Tony Phillips	.10
60	Juan Samuel	.05
61	Mickey Tettleton	.05
62	Alan Trammell	.10
63	David Wells	.05
64	Lou Whitaker	.05
65	Jim Abbott	.10
66	Joe Ausanio	.05
67	Wade Boggs	.20
68	Mike Gallego	.05
69	Xavier Hernandez	.05
70	Sterling Hitchcock	.05
71	Steve Howe	.05
72	Scott Kamieniecki	.05
73	Pat Kelly	.05
74	Jimmy Key	.05
75	Jim Leyritz	.05
76	Don Mattingly	1.00
77	Terry Mulholland	.05
78	Paul O'Neill	.05
79	Melido Perez	.05
80	Luis Polonia	.05
81	Mike Stanley	.05
82	Danny Tartabull	.05
83	Randy Velarde	.05
84	Bob Wickman	.05
85	Bernie Williams	.40
86	Gerald Williams	.05
87	Roberto Alomar	.60
88	Pat Borders	.05
89	Joe Carter	.20
90	Tony Castillo	.05
91	Brad Cornett	.05
92	Carlos Delgado	.10
93	Alex Gonzalez	.10
94	Shawn Green	.10
95	Juan Guzman	.05
96	Darren Hall	.05
97	Pat Hentgen	.05
98	Mike Huff	.05
99	Randy Knorr	.05
100	Al Leiter	.05
101	Paul Molitor	.35
102	John Olerud	.10
103	Dick Schofield	.05
104	Ed Sprague	.05
105	Dave Stewart	.08
106	Todd Stottlemyre	.05
107	Devon White	.05
108	Woody Williams	.05
109	Wilson Alvarez	.05
110	Paul Assenmacher	.05
111	Jason Bere	.05
112	Dennis Cook	.05
113	Joey Cora	.05
114	Jose DeLeon	.05
115	Alex Fernandez	.10
116	Julio Franco	.05
117	Craig Graboeck	.05
118	Ozzie Guillen	.05
119	Roberto Hernandez	.05
120	Darrin Jackson	.05
121	Lance Johnson	.05
122	Ron Karkovice	.05
123	Mike LaValliere	.05
124	Norberto Martin	.05
125	Kirk McCaskill	.05
126	Jack McDowell	.05
127	Tim Raines	.10
128	Frank Thomas	2.00
129	Robin Ventura	.10
130	Sandy Alomar Jr.	.08
131	Carlos Baerga	.15
132	Albert Belle	.60
133	Mark Clark	.08
134	Alvaro Espinoza	.05
135	Jason Grimsley	.05
136	Wayne Kirby	.05
137	Kenny Lofton	.75
138	Albie Lopez	.05
139	Dennis Martinez	.08
140	Jose Mesa	.08
141	Eddie Murray	.35
142	Charles Nagy	.05
143	Tony Pena	.05
144	Eric Plunk	.05
145	Manny Ramirez	.60
146	Jeff Russell	.05
147	Paul Shuey	.05
148	Paul Sorrento	.05
149	Jim Thome	.40
150	Omar Vizquel	.05
151	Dave Winfield	.20
152	Kevin Appier	.05

153	Billy Brewer	.05
154	Vince Coleman	.05
155	David Cone	.05
156	Gary Gaetti	.08
157	Greg Gagne	.05
158	Tom Gordon	.05
159	Mark Gubicza	.05
160	Bob Hamelin	.05
161	Dave Henderson	.05
162	Felix Jose	.05
163	Wally Joyner	.10
164	Jose Lind	.05
165	Mike Macfarlane	.05
166	Mike Magnante	.05
167	Brent Mayne	.05
168	Brian McRae	.05
169	Rusty Meacham	.05
170	Jeff Montgomery	.05
171	Hipolito Pichardo	.05
172	Terry Shumpert	.05
173	Michael Tucker	.15
174	Ricky Bones	.05
175	*Jeff Cirillo*	.20
176	Alex Diaz	.05
177	Cal Eldred	.05
178	Mike Fetters	.05
179	Darryl Hamilton	.05
180	Brian Harper	.05
181	John Jaha	.05
182	Pat Listach	.05
183	Graeme Lloyd	.05
184	Jose Mercedes	.05
185	Matt Mieske	.05
186	Dave Nilsson	.05
187	Jody Reed	.05
188	Bob Scanlan	.05
189	Kevin Seitzer	.05
190	Bill Spiers	.05
191	B.J. Surhoff	.05
192	Jose Valentin	.05
193	Greg Vaughn	.10
194	Turner Ward	.05
195	Bill Wegman	.05
196	Rick Aguilera	.05
197	Rich Becker	.05
198	Alex Cole	.05
199	Marty Cordova	.10
200	Steve Dunn	.05
201	Scott Erickson	.05
202	Mark Guthrie	.05
203	Chip Hale	.05
204	LaTroy Hawkins	.15
205	Denny Hocking	.05
206	Chuck Knoblauch	.20
207	Scott Leius	.05
208	Shane Mack	.05
209	Pat Mahomes	.05
210	Pat Meares	.05
211	Pedro Munoz	.05
212	Kirby Puckett	.75
213	Jeff Reboulet	.10
214	Dave Stevens	.05
215	Kevin Tapani	.05
216	Matt Walbeck	.05
217	Carl Willis	.05
218	Brian Anderson	.10
219	Chad Curtis	.05
220	Chili Davis	.08
221	Gary DiSarcina	.05
222	Damion Easley	.05
223	Jim Edmonds	.25
224	Chuck Finley	.05
225	Joe Grahe	.05
226	Rex Hudler	.05
227	Bo Jackson	.10
228	Mark Langston	.05
229	Phil Leftwich	.05
230	Mark Leiter	.05
231	Spike Owen	.05
232	Bob Patterson	.05
233	Troy Percival	.05
234	Eduardo Perez	.05
235	Tim Salmon	.25
236	J.T. Snow	.12
237	Chris Turner	.05
238	Mark Acre	.05
239	Geronimo Berroa	.08
240	Mike Bordick	.05
241	John Briscoe	.05
242	Scott Brosius	.05
243	Ron Darling	.05
244	Dennis Eckersley	.08
245	Brent Gates	.05
246	Rickey Henderson	.20
247	Stan Javier	.05
248	Steve Karsay	.10

#	Name	Price
249	Mark McGwire	4.00
250	Troy Neel	.05
251	Steve Ontiveros	.05
252	Carlos Reyes	.05
253	Ruben Sierra	.08
254	Terry Steinbach	.05
255	Bill Taylor	.05
256	Todd Van Poppel	.05
257	Bobby Witt	.05
258	Rich Amaral	.05
259	Eric Anthony	.05
260	Bobby Ayala	.05
261	Mike Blowers	.05
262	Chris Bosio	.05
263	Jay Buhner	.10
264	John Cummings	.05
265	Tim Davis	.05
266	Felix Fermin	.05
267	Dave Fleming	.05
268	Goose Gossage	.05
269	Ken Griffey, Jr.	2.50
270	Reggie Jefferson	.05
271	Randy Johnson	.40
272	Edgar Martinez	.08
273	Tino Martinez	.15
274	Greg Pirkl	.05
275	Bill Risley	.05
276	Roger Salkeld	.05
277	Luis Sojo	.05
278	Mac Suzuki	.08
279	Dan Wilson	.05
280	Kevin Brown	.05
281	Jose Canseco	.35
282	Cris Carpenter	.05
283	Will Clark	.30
284	Jeff Frye	.05
285	Juan Gonzalez	1.25
286	Rick Helling	.05
287	Tom Henke	.05
288	David Hulse	.05
289	Chris James	.05
290	Manuel Lee	.05
291	Oddibe McDowell	.05
292	Dean Palmer	.05
293	Roger Pavlik	.05
294	Bill Ripken	.05
295	Ivan Rodriguez	.40
296	Kenny Rogers	.05
297	Doug Strange	.05
298	Matt Whiteside	.05
299	Steve Avery	.05
300	Steve Bedrosian	.05
301	Rafael Belliard	.05
302	Jeff Blauser	.05
303	Dave Gallagher	.05
304	Tom Glavine	.15
305	Dave Justice	.20
306	Mike Kelly	.05
307	Roberto Kelly	.05
308	Ryan Klesko	.60
309	Mark Lemke	.05
310	Javier Lopez	.15
311	Greg Maddux	1.50
312	Fred McGriff	.30
313	Greg McMichael	.05
314	Kent Mercker	.05
315	Charlie O'Brien	.05
316	Jose Oliva	.05
317	Terry Pendleton	.05
318	John Smoltz	.20
319	Mike Stanton	.05
320	Tony Tarasco	.05
321	Terrell Wade	.10
322	Mark Wohlers	.05
323	Kurt Abbott	.05
324	Luis Aquino	.05
325	Bret Barberie	.05
326	Ryan Bowen	.05
327	Jerry Browne	.05
328	Chuck Carr	.05
329	Matias Carrillo	.05
330	Greg Colbrunn	.05
331	Jeff Conine	.15
332	Mark Gardner	.05
333	Chris Hammond	.05
334	Bryan Harvey	.05
335	Richie Lewis	.05
336	Dave Magadan	.05
337	Terry Mathews	.05
338	Robb Nen	.05
339	Yorkis Perez	.05
340	Pat Rapp	.05
341	Benito Santiago	.08
342	Gary Sheffield	.35
343	Dave Weathers	.05
344	Moises Alou	.10
345	Sean Berry	.05
346	Wil Cordero	.05
347	Joe Eischen	.05
348	Jeff Fassero	.05
349	Darrin Fletcher	.05
350	Cliff Floyd	.08
351	Marquis Grissom	.10
352	Butch Henry	.05
353	Gil Heredia	.05
354	Ken Hill	.05
355	Mike Lansing	.05
356	Pedro Martinez	.25
357	Mel Rojas	.05
358	Kirk Rueter	.05
359	Tim Scott	.05
360	Jeff Shaw	.05
361	Larry Walker	.25
362	Lenny Webster	.05
363	John Wetteland	.05
364	Rondell White	.15
365	Bobby Bonilla	.10
366	Rico Brogna	.05
367	Jeromy Burnitz	.05
368	John Franco	.05
369	Dwight Gooden	.10
370	Todd Hundley	.15
371	Jason Jacome	.05
372	Bobby Jones	.05
373	Jeff Kent	.05
374	Jim Lindeman	.05
375	Josias Manzanillo	.05
376	Roger Mason	.05
377	Kevin McReynolds	.05
378	Joe Orsulak	.05
379	Bill Pulsipher	.05
380	Bret Saberhagen	.05
381	David Segui	.05
382	Pete Smith	.05
383	Kelly Stinnett	.05
384	Ryan Thompson	.05
385	Jose Vizcaino	.05
386	Toby Borland	.05
387	Ricky Bottalico	.05
388	Darren Daulton	.05
389	Mariano Duncan	.05
390	Len Dykstra	.08
391	Jim Eisenreich	.05
392	Tommy Greene	.05
393	Dave Hollins	.05
394	Pete Incaviglia	.05
395	Danny Jackson	.05
396	Doug Jones	.05
397	Ricky Jordan	.05
398	John Kruk	.05
399	Mike Lieberthal	.05
400	Tony Longmire	.05
401	Mickey Morandini	.05
402	Bobby Munoz	.05
403	Curt Schilling	.05
404	Heathcliff Slocumb	.05
405	Kevin Stocker	.05
406	Fernando Valenzuela	.08
407	David West	.05
408	Willie Banks	.05
409	Jose Bautista	.05
410	Steve Buechele	.05
411	Jim Bullinger	.05
412	Chuck Crim	.05
413	Shawon Dunston	.12
414	Kevin Foster	.05
415	Mark Grace	.20
416	Jose Hernandez	.05
417	Glenallen Hill	.05
418	Brooks Kieschnick	.15
419	Derrick May	.05
420	Randy Myers	.05
421	Dan Plesac	.05
422	Karl Rhodes	.05
423	Rey Sanchez	.05
424	Sammy Sosa	1.00
425	Steve Trachsel	.05
426	Rick Wilkins	.05
427	Anthony Young	.05
428	Eddie Zambrano	.05
429	Bret Boone	.05
430	Jeff Branson	.05
431	Jeff Brantley	.05
432	Hector Carrasco	.05
433	Brian Dorsett	.05
434	Tony Fernandez	.05
435	Tim Fortugno	.05
436	Erik Hanson	.05
437	Thomas Howard	.05
438	Kevin Jarvis	.05
439	Barry Larkin	.20
440	Chuck McElroy	.05
441	Kevin Mitchell	.08
442	Hal Morris	.05
443	Jose Rijo	.05
444	John Roper	.05
445	Johnny Ruffin	.05
446	Deion Sanders	.25
447	Reggie Sanders	.10
448	Pete Schourek	.05
449	John Smiley	.05
450	Eddie Taubensee	.05
451	Jeff Bagwell	.75
452	Kevin Bass	.05
453	Craig Biggio	.12
454	Ken Caminiti	.12
455	Andujar Cedeno	.05
456	Doug Drabek	.05
457	Tony Eusebio	.05
458	Mike Felder	.05
459	Steve Finley	.05
460	Luis Gonzalez	.05
461	Mike Hampton	.05
462	Pete Harnisch	.05
463	John Hudek	.05
464	Todd Jones	.05
465	Darryl Kile	.05
466	James Mouton	.05
467	Shane Reynolds	.05
468	Scott Servais	.05
469	Greg Swindell	.05
470	Dave Veres	.05
471	Brian Williams	.05
472	Jay Bell	.05
473	Jacob Brumfield	.05
474	Dave Clark	.05
475	Steve Cooke	.05
476	Midre Cummings	.05
477	Mark Dewey	.05
478	Tom Foley	.05
479	Carlos Garcia	.05
480	Jeff King	.05
481	Jon Lieber	.05
482	Ravelo Manzanillo	.08
483	Al Martin	.05
484	Orlando Merced	.05
485	Danny Miceli	.05
486	Denny Neagle	.05
487	Lance Parrish	.08
488	Don Slaught	.05
489	Zane Smith	.05
490	Andy Van Slyke	.05
491	Paul Wagner	.05
492	Rick White	.05
493	Luis Alicea	.05
494	Rene Arocha	.05
495	Rheal Cormier	.05
496	Bryan Eversgerd	.05
497	Bernard Gilkey	.10
498	John Habyan	.05
499	Gregg Jefferies	.10
500	Brian Jordan	.15
501	Ray Lankford	.15
502	John Mabry	.08
503	Terry McGriff	.05
504	Tom Pagnozzi	.05
505	Vicente Palacios	.05
506	Geronimo Pena	.05
507	Gerald Perry	.05
508	Rich Rodriguez	.05
509	Ozzie Smith	.35
510	Bob Tewksbury	.05
511	Allen Watson	.10
512	Mark Whiten	.05
513	Todd Zeile	.05
514	Dante Bichette	.30
515	Willie Blair	.05
516	Ellis Burks	.15
517	Marvin Freeman	.05
518	Andres Galarraga	.15
519	Joe Girardi	.05
520	Greg Harris	.05
521	Charlie Hayes	.05
522	Mike Kingery	.05
523	Nelson Liriano	.05
524	Mike Munoz	.05
525	David Nied	.05
526	Steve Reed	.05
527	Kevin Ritz	.05
528	Bruce Ruffin	.05
529	John Vander Wal	.05
530	Walt Weiss	.05
531	Eric Young	.05
532	Billy Ashley	.05
533	Pedro Astacio	.05
534	Rafael Bournigal	.05
535	Brett Butler	.10
536	Tom Candiotti	.05

537	Omar Daal	.05
538	Delino DeShields	.05
539	Darren Dreifort	.05
540	Kevin Gross	.05
541	Orel Hershiser	.08
542	Garey Ingram	.05
543	Eric Karros	.15
544	Ramon Martinez	.08
545	Raul Mondesi	.40
546	Chan Ho Park	.15
547	Mike Piazza	1.25
548	Henry Rodriguez	.10
549	Rudy Seanez	.05
550	Ismael Valdes	.10
551	Tim Wallach	.05
552	Todd Worrell	.05
553	Andy Ashby	.05
554	Brad Ausmus	.05
555	Derek Bell	.10
556	Andy Benes	.08
557	Phil Clark	.05
558	Donnie Elliott	.05
559	Ricky Gutierrez	.05
560	Tony Gwynn	.75
561	Joey Hamilton	.12
562	Trevor Hoffman	.05
563	Luis Lopez	.05
564	Pedro Martinez	.15
565	Tim Mauser	.05
566	Phil Plantier	.05
567	Bip Roberts	.05
568	Scott Sanders	.05
569	Craig Shipley	.05
570	Jeff Tabaka	.05
571	Eddie Williams	.05
572	Rod Beck	.05
573	Mike Benjamin	.05
574	Barry Bonds	.60
575	Dave Burba	.05
576	John Burkett	.05
577	Mark Carreon	.05
578	Royce Clayton	.05
579	Steve Frey	.05
580	Bryan Hickerson	.05
581	Mike Jackson	.05
582	Darren Lewis	.05
583	Kirt Manwaring	.05
584	Rich Monteleone	.05
585	John Patterson	.05
586	J.R. Phillips	.05
587	Mark Portugal	.05
588	Joe Rosselli	.05
589	Darryl Strawberry	.10
590	Bill Swift	.05
591	Robby Thompson	.05
592	William Van Landingham	.05
593	Matt Williams	.20
594	Checklist	.05
595	Checklist	.05
596	Checklist	.05
597	Checklist	.05
598	Checklist	.05
599	Checklist	.05
600	Checklist	.05

1995 Fleer All-Stars

All-Stars are a horizontal, two-sided insert set consisting of 25 cards. A National League All-Star is on one side, while an American League All-Star is on the other, by position. All-Stars are the most common insert in Fleer 1995 baseball, with an insertion ratio of one per three packs.

		MT
Complete Set (25):		16.00
Common Player:		.25
1	Ivan Rodriguez, Mike Piazza	1.50
2	Frank Thomas, Gregg Jefferies	3.00
3	Roberto Alomar, Mariano Duncan	.75
4	Wade Boggs, Matt Williams	.50
5	Cal Ripken, Jr., Ozzie Smith	3.50
6	Joe Carter, Barry Bonds	.50
7	Ken Griffey, Jr., Tony Gwynn	3.50
8	Kirby Puckett, Dave Justice	1.25
9	Jimmy Key, Greg Maddux	2.50
10	Chuck Knoblauch, Wil Cordero	.35
11	Scott Cooper, Ken Caminiti	.25
12	Will Clark, Carlos Garcia	.45
13	Paul Molitor, Jeff Bagwell	.50
14	Travis Fryman, Craig Biggio	.40
15	Mickey Tettleton, Fred McGriff	.25
16	Kenny Lofton, Moises Alou	.40
17	Albert Belle, Marquis Grissom	1.00
18	Paul O'Neill, Dante Bichette	.25
19	David Cone, Ken Hill	.25
20	Mike Mussina, Doug Drabek	.40
21	Randy Johnson, John Hudek	.50
22	Pat Hentgen, Danny Jackson	.25
23	Wilson Alvarez, Rod Beck	.25
24	Lee Smith, Randy Myers	.25
25	Jason Bere, Doug Jones	.30

1995 Fleer Award Winners

Fleer Award Winners contain Fleer's choices of baseball's most outstanding players. This six-card set was only inserted at a rate of one per 24 packs. Each card has an embossed gold foil design, with the gold strip running up the left side and containing the words "Fleer Award Winner" and the player name.

		MT
Complete Set (6):		10.00
Common Player:		.50
1	Frank Thomas	5.00
2	Jeff Bagwell	2.50
3	David Cone	.50
4	Greg Maddux	4.00
5	Bob Hamelin	.50
6	Raul Mondesi	1.00

A player's name in *italic* type indicates a rookie card.

1995 Fleer League Leaders

League Leaders feature players on a horizontal format from 10 statistical categories from both leagues. "League Leader" is placed in a blue strip down the left-side of the card, with their respective league and their name in it. These were inserted at a rate of one per 12 packs.

		MT
Complete Set (10):		10.00
Common Player:		.50
1	Paul O'Neill	.50
2	Ken Griffey, Jr.	5.00
3	Kirby Puckett	1.50
4	Jimmy Key	.50
5	Randy Johnson	1.00
6	Tony Gwynn	1.00
7	Matt Williams	.75
8	Jeff Bagwell	1.50
9	Greg Maddux, Ken Hill	2.50
10	Andy Benes	.50

1995 Fleer Lumber Company

Ten of the top longball hitters were featured in Lumber Company, which were inserted into every 24 12-card retailer packs. They show the power hitter in action, with a wood-grain Lumber Co. logo across the bottom, contain the player's name and team.

		MT
Complete Set (10):		35.00
Common Player:		.75
1	Jeff Bagwell	3.50
2	Albert Belle	3.00
3	Barry Bonds	3.00
4	Jose Canseco	2.00
5	Joe Carter	.75
6	Ken Griffey, Jr.	12.00
7	Fred McGriff	1.50
8	Kevin Mitchell	.75
9	Frank Thomas	10.00
10	Matt Williams	1.00

1995 Fleer Major League Prospects

Major League Prospects showcases 10 of 1995's most promising young players. The set title is repeatedly printed across the background, with the player's name and team in a grey strip across the bottom. These cards were inserted into one every six packs.

		MT
Complete Set (10):		7.00
Common Player:		.25
1	Garret Anderson	1.00
2	James Baldwin	.45
3	Alan Benes	1.00
4	Armando Benitez	.25
5	Ray Durham	1.50
6	Brian Hunter	.50
7a	Derek Jeter (no licensor logos on back)	3.00
7b	Derek Jeter (licensor logos on back)	3.00
8	Charles Johnson	.40
9	Orlando Miller	.25
10	Alex Rodriguez	6.00

1995 Fleer Pro-Visions

Pro-Visions contain six interlocking cards that form one giant picture. These original art cards exhibit the player in a fantasy art background and are inserted into every nine packs.

		MT
Complete Set (6):		4.00
Common Player:		.25
1	Mike Mussina	.50
2	Raul Mondesi	.50
3	Jeff Bagwell	1.25
4	Greg Maddux	1.75
5	Tim Salmon	.50
6	Manny Ramirez	1.00

1995 Fleer Rookie Sensations

A perennial favorite within Fleer products, Rookie Sensations cards were inserted in 18-card packs only, at a rate of one per 16 packs. This 20-card set featured the top rookies from the 1994 season. The player's name and team run up the right side of the card, while the words "Rookie Sensations" appear in the bottom-left corner, separated by a colorful, zig-zagged image of a player.

		MT
Complete Set (20):		40.00
Common Player:		1.00
1	Kurt Abbott	1.25
2	Rico Brogna	1.00
3	Hector Carrasco	1.00
4	Kevin Foster	1.00
5	Chris Gomez	1.00
6	Darren Hall	1.00
7	Bob Hamelin	1.00
8	Joey Hamilton	1.50
9	John Hudek	1.00
10	Ryan Klesko	6.00
11	Javier Lopez	3.00
12	Matt Mieske	1.00
13	Raul Mondesi	6.00
14	Manny Ramirez	12.00
15	Shane Reynolds	1.00
16	Bill Risley	1.00
17	Johnny Ruffin	1.00
18	Steve Trachsel	1.50
19	William Van Landingham	1.50
20	Rondell White	4.00

1995 Fleer Team Leaders

Team Leaders are two-player cards featuring the leading hitter and pitcher from each major league team, one on each side. Inserted at a rate of one per 24 packs, these are only found in 12-card hobby packs. Team Leaders consisted of 28 cards and included a Team Leader logo in the bottom-left corner.

		MT
Complete Set (28):		225.00
Common Player:		2.00
1	Cal Ripken, Jr., Mike Mussina	30.00
2	Mo Vaughn, Roger Clemens	15.00
3	Tim Salmon, Chuck Finley	4.00
4	Frank Thomas, Jack McDowell	25.00
5	Albert Belle, Dennis Martinez	12.00
6	Cecil Fielder, Mike Moore	2.00
7	Bob Hamelin, David Cone	2.00
8	Greg Vaughn, Ricky Bones	2.00
9	Kirby Puckett, Rick Aguilera	15.00
10	Don Mattingly, Jimmy Key	15.00
11	Ruben Sierra, Dennis Eckersley	2.50
12	Ken Griffey, Jr., Randy Johnson	40.00
13	Jose Canseco, Kenny Rogers	4.00
14	Joe Carter, Pat Hentgen	3.00
15	Dave Justice, Greg Maddux	25.00
16	Sammy Sosa, Steve Trachsel	12.00
17	Kevin Mitchell, Jose Rijo	2.00
18	Dante Bichette, Bruce Ruffin	4.00
19	Jeff Conine, Robb Nen	2.50
20	Jeff Bagwell, Doug Drabek	14.00
21	Mike Piazza, Ramon Martinez	20.00
22	Moises Alou, Ken Hill	2.50
23	Bobby Bonilla, Bret Saberhagen	2.00
24	Darren Daulton, Danny Jackson	2.00
25	Jay Bell, Zane Smith	2.00
26	Gregg Jefferies, Bob Tewksbury	2.00
27	Tony Gwynn, Andy Benes	15.00
28	Matt Williams, Rod Beck	3.00

1995 Fleer Update

Fleer carried its "different by design" concept of six formats (one for each division in each league) from the regular set into its 1995 Update issue. The issue consists of 200 cards of 1995's traded, rookie and free agent players, plus five different insert sets. One insert card was found in each regular (12-card, $1.49) and jumbo (18-card, $2.29) pack.

		MT
Complete Set (200):		14.00
Common Player:		.10
Wax Box:		35.00
U1	Manny Alexander	.10
U2	Bret Barberie	.10
U3	Armando Benitez	.10

U4	Kevin Brown	.10
U5	Doug Jones	.10
U6	Sherman Obando	.10
U7	Andy Van Slyke	.10
U8	Stan Belinda	.10
U9	Jose Canseco	.30
U10	Vaughn Eshelman	.10
U11	Mike Macfarlane	.10
U12	Troy O'Leary	.10
U13	Steve Rodriguez	.10
U14	Lee Tinsley	.10
U15	Tim Vanegmond	.10
U16	Mark Whiten	.10
U17	Sean Bergman	.10
U18	Chad Curtis	.10
U19	John Flaherty	.10
U20	*Bob Higginson*	.25
U21	Felipe Lira	.10
U22	Shannon Penn	.10
U23	Todd Steverson	.10
U24	Sean Whiteside	.10
U25	Tony Fernandez	.10
U26	Jack McDowell	.10
U27	Andy Petitte	.10
U28	John Wetteland	.10
U29	David Cone	.10
U30	Mike Timlin	.10
U31	Duane Ward	.10
U32	Jim Abbott	.15
U33	James Baldwin	.10
U34	Mike Devereaux	.10
U35	Ray Durham	.25
U36	Tim Fortugno	.10
U37	Scott Ruffcorn	.10
U38	Chris Sabo	.10
U39	Paul Assenmacher	.10
U40	Bud Black	.10
U41	Orel Hershiser	.12
U42	Julian Tavarez	.10
U43	Dave Winfield	.15
U44	Pat Borders	.10
U45	*Melvin Bunch*	.15
U46	Tom Goodwin	.10
U47	Jon Nunnally	.10
U48	Joe Randa	.10
U49	*Dilson Torres*	.10
U50	Joe Vitiello	.10
U51	David Hulse	.10
U52	Scott Karl	.10
U53	Mark Kiefer	.10
U54	Derrick May	.10
U55	Joe Oliver	.10
U56	Al Reyes	.10
U57	*Steve Sparks*	.15
U58	Jerald Clark	.10
U59	Eddie Guardado	.10
U60	Kevin Maas	.10
U61	David McCarty	.10
U62	*Brad Radke*	.15
U63	Scott Stahoviak	.10
U64	Garret Anderson	.15
U65	Shawn Boskie	.10
U66	Mike James	.10
U67	Tony Phillips	.15
U68	Lee Smith	.12
U69	Mitch Williams	.10
U70	Jim Corsi	.10
U71	Mark Harkey	.10
U72	Dave Stewart	.12
U73	Todd Stottlemyre	.10
U74	Joey Cora	.10
U75	Chad Kreuter	.10
U76	Jeff Nelson	.10
U77	Alex Rodriguez	1.50
U78	Ron Villone	.10
U79	*Bob Wells*	.15
U80	*Jose Alberro*	.15
U81	Terry Burrows	.10
U82	Kevin Gross	.10
U83	Wilson Heredia	.10
U84	Mark McLemore	.10
U85	Otis Nixon	.10
U86	Jeff Russell	.10
U87	Mickey Tettleton	.10
U88	Bob Tewksbury	.10
U89	Pedro Borbon	.10
U90	Marquis Grissom	.12
U91	Chipper Jones	.75
U92	Mike Mordecai	.10
U93	*Jason Schmidt*	.25
U94	John Burkett	.10
U95	Andre Dawson	.15
U96	*Matt Dunbar*	.15
U97	Charles Johnson	.15
U98	Terry Pendleton	.10
U99	Rich Scheid	.10
U100	Quilvio Veras	.10
U101	Bobby Witt	.10
U102	Eddie Zosky	.10
U103	Shane Andrews	.10
U104	Reid Cornelius	.10
U105	*Chad Fonville*	.20
U106	*Mark Grudzielanek*	.30
U107	Roberto Kelly	.10
U108	*Carlos Perez*	.15
U109	Tony Tarasco	.10
U110	Brett Butler	.15
U111	Carl Everett	.10
U112	Pete Harnisch	.10
U113	Doug Henry	.10
U114	Kevin Lomon	.10
U115	Blas Minor	.10
U116	Dave Mlicki	.10
U117	*Ricky Otero*	.15
U118	Norm Charlton	.10
U119	Tyler Green	.10
U120	Gene Harris	.10
U121	Charlie Hayes	.10
U122	Gregg Jefferies	.15
U123	*Michael Mimbs*	.20
U124	Paul Quantrill	.10
U125	Frank Castillo	.10
U126	Brian McRae	.10
U127	Jaime Navarro	.10
U128	Mike Perez	.10
U129	Tanyon Sturtze	.10
U130	Ozzie Timmons	.10
U131	John Courtright	.10
U132	Ron Gant	.15
U133	Xavier Hernandez	.10
U134	Brian Hunter	.10
U135	Benito Santiago	.12
U136	Pete Smith	.10
U137	Scott Sullivan	.10
U138	Derek Bell	.15
U139	Doug Brocail	.10
U140	Ricky Gutierrez	.10
U141	Pedro Martinez	.25
U142	Orlando Miller	.10
U143	Phil Plantier	.10
U144	Craig Shipley	.10
U145	Rich Aude	.10
U146	*Jason Christiansen*	.15
U147	*Freddy Garcia*	.15
U148	Jim Gott	.10
U149	*Mark Johnson*	.20
U150	Esteban Loaiza	.15
U151	Dan Plesac	.10
U152	*Gary Wilson*	.10
U153	Allen Battle	.10
U154	Terry Bradshaw	.10
U155	Scott Cooper	.10
U156	Tripp Cromer	.10
U157	John Frascatore	.10
U158	John Habyan	.10
U159	Tom Henke	.10
U160	Ken Hill	.10
U161	Danny Jackson	.10
U162	Donovan Osborne	.10
U163	Tom Urbani	.10
U164	Roger Bailey	.10
U165	*Jorge Brito*	.15
U166	Vinny Castilla	.15
U167	Darren Holmes	.10
U168	Roberto Mejia	.10
U169	Bill Swift	.10
U170	Mark Thompson	.10
U171	Larry Walker	.40
U172	Greg Hansell	.10
U173	Dave Hansen	.10
U174	Carlos Hernandez	.10
U175	*Hideo Nomo*	3.00
U176	Jose Offerman	.10
U177	Antonio Osuna	.10
U178	Reggie Williams	.10
U179	Todd Williams	.10
U180	Andres Berumen	.10
U181	Ken Caminiti	.15
U182	Andujar Cedeno	.10
U183	Steve Finley	.10
U184	Bryce Florie	.10
U185	Dustin Hermanson	.15
U186	Ray Holbert	.10
U187	Melvin Nieves	.10
U188	Roberto Petagine	.10
U189	Jody Reed	.10
U190	Fernando Valenzuela	.12
U191	Brian Williams	.10
U192	Mark Dewey	.10
U193	Glenallen Hill	.10
U194	*Chris Hook*	.15
U195	Terry Mulholland	.10
U196	Steve Scarsone	.10
U197	Trevor Wilson	.10
U198	Checklist	.10
U199	Checklist	.10
U200	Checklist	.10

1995 Fleer Update Diamond Tribute

Borderless action photos and gold-foil graphics are front features of this chase set honoring perhaps the 10 top names among baseball's veteran players. Backs have another photo and a few sentences describing what makes the player worthy of inclusion in such a set. The Diamond Tribute cards are found on the average of one per five packs.

		MT
Complete Set (10):		7.00
Common Player:		.25
1	Jeff Bagwell	.60
2	Albert Belle	.60
3	Barry Bonds	.60
4	David Cone	.25
5	Dennis Eckersley	.30
6	Ken Griffey Jr.	2.50
7	Rickey Henderson	.40
8	Greg Maddux	2.00
9	Frank Thomas	2.50
10	Matt Williams	.40

1995 Fleer Update Headliners

The most common of the Fleer Update inserts are the Headliners cards found on average of one per three packs. Fronts have an action photo set against a collage of newspaper clippings. The graphics are gold-foil. Backs have another color photo and a "Fleer Times" newspaper background with career summary and/or quotes about the featured player.

		MT
Complete Set (20):		12.00
Common Player:		.25
1	Jeff Bagwell	.75
2	Albert Belle	.75
3	Barry Bonds	.75
4	Jose Canseco	.50
5	Joe Carter	.25
6	Will Clark	.35
7	Roger Clemens	.50
8	Lenny Dykstra	.25
9	Cecil Fielder	.30
10	Juan Gonzalez	1.25
11	Ken Griffey Jr.	3.00
12	Kenny Lofton	1.00
13	Greg Maddux	2.50
14	Fred McGriff	.40
15	Mike Piazza	1.50
16	Kirby Puckett	1.00
17	Tim Salmon	.40
18	Frank Thomas	2.50
19	Mo Vaughn	.60
20	Matt Williams	.50

1995 Fleer Update Rookie Update

Ten of 1995's top rookies are featured in this horizontally formatted insert set. Fronts have an action photo with a large gold-foil "ROOKIE UPDATE" headline at top. Backs have another photo and career summary. Rookie Update chase cards are found on the average of one per four packs.

		MT
Complete Set (10):		17.00
Common Player:		.25
1	Shane Andrews	.40
2	Ray Durham	1.00
3	Shawn Green	1.50
4	Charles Johnson	1.00
5	Chipper Jones	5.00
6	Esteban Loaiza	.40
7	Hideo Nomo	5.00
8	Jon Nunnally	.50
9	Alex Rodriguez	6.00
10	Julian Tavarez	.25

1995 Fleer Update Smooth Leather

These inserts featuring top fielders were found only in pre-priced (magazine) foil packs, at an average rate of one card per 12 packs. Fronts are highlighted with gold-foil graphics. Backs have a glove in the background and explain the player's defensive abilities.

		MT
Complete Set (10):		25.00
Common Player:		.50
1	Roberto Alomar	1.25
2	Barry Bonds	1.50
3	Ken Griffey Jr.	9.00
4	Marquis Grissom	.50
5	Darren Lewis	.50
6	Kenny Lofton	2.00
7	Don Mattingly	2.50
8	Cal Ripken Jr.	10.00
9	Ivan Rodriguez	.75
10	Matt Williams	.90

1995 Fleer Update Soaring Stars

A metallic foil-etched background behind the color player action photo identifies this chase set as the toughest among those in the 1995 Fleer Update issue. The Soaring Star cards are found at the average rate of one per box. Backs are conventionally printed and featured a colorful posterized version of the front background, along with another color photo and a career summary.

		MT
Complete Set (9):		60.00
Common Player:		2.50
1	Moises Alou	2.50
2	Jason Bere	2.50
3	Jeff Conine	2.50
4	Cliff Floyd	2.50
5	Pat Hentgen	2.50
6	Kenny Lofton	14.00
7	Raul Mondesi	8.00
8	Mike Piazza	18.00
9	Tim Salmon	4.00

1996 Fleer

In a radical departure from the UV-coated standard for even base-brand baseball cards, Fleer's 1996 issue is printed on a matte surface. Fronts feature borderless game-action photos with minimal (player ID, Fleer logo) graphic enhancement in gold foil. Backs have a white background, a portrait photo, full pro stats and a few career highlights. The single-series set was sold in basic 11-card packs with one of nearly a dozen insert-set cards in each $1.49 pack. The set is arranged alphabetically by player within team and league.

		MT
Complete Set (600):		60.00
Common Player:		.05
Wax Box:		45.00
1	Manny Alexander	.05
2	Brady Anderson	.20
3	Harold Baines	.08
4	Armando Benitez	.05
5	Bobby Bonilla	.10
6	Kevin Brown	.05
7	Scott Erickson	.05
8	Curtis Goodwin	.05
9	Jeffrey Hammonds	.05
10	Jimmy Haynes	.05
11	Chris Hoiles	.05
12	Doug Jones	.05
13	Rick Krivda	.05
14	Jeff Manto	.05
15	Ben McDonald	.05
16	Jamie Moyer	.05
17	Mike Mussina	.30
18	Jesse Orosco	.05
19	Rafael Palmeiro	.15
20	Cal Ripken Jr.	2.50
20(p)	Cal Ripken Jr. (overprinted "PROMOTIONAL SAMPLE")	8.00
21	Rick Aguilera	.05
22	Luis Alicea	.05
23	Stan Belinda	.05
24	Jose Canseco	.30
25	Roger Clemens	.50
26	Vaughn Eshelman	.05
27	Mike Greenwell	.05
28	Erik Hanson	.05
29	Dwayne Hosey	.05
30	Mike Macfarlane	.05
31	Tim Naehring	.05
32	Troy O'Leary	.05
33	Aaron Sele	.05
34	Zane Smith	.05
35	Jeff Suppan	.05
36	Lee Tinsley	.05
37	John Valentin	.15
38	Mo Vaughn	.75
39	Tim Wakefield	.05
40	Jim Abbott	.10
41	Brian Anderson	.05
42	Garret Anderson	.10
43	Chili Davis	.08

No.	Player	Value
44	Gary DiSarcina	.05
45	Damion Easley	.05
46	Jim Edmonds	.15
47	Chuck Finley	.05
48	Todd Greene	.05
49	Mike Harkey	.05
50	Mike James	.05
51	Mark Langston	.05
52	Greg Myers	.05
53	Orlando Palmeiro	.05
54	Bob Patterson	.05
55	Troy Percival	.05
56	Tony Phillips	.10
57	Tim Salmon	.20
58	Lee Smith	.08
59	J.T. Snow	.10
60	Randy Velarde	.05
61	Wilson Alvarez	.05
62	*Luis Andujar*	.05
63	Jason Bere	.05
64	Ray Durham	.05
65	Alex Fernandez	.05
66	Ozzie Guillen	.05
67	Roberto Hernandez	.05
68	Lance Johnson	.05
69	Matt Karchner	.05
70	Ron Karkovice	.05
71	Norberto Martin	.05
72	Dave Martinez	.05
73	Kirk McCaskill	.05
74	Lyle Mouton	.05
75	Tim Raines	.10
76	Mike Sirotka	.05
77	Frank Thomas	2.50
78	Larry Thomas	.05
79	Robin Ventura	.15
80	Sandy Alomar Jr.	.10
81	Paul Assenmacher	.05
82	Carlos Baerga	.15
83	Albert Belle	.75
84	Mark Clark	.05
85	Alan Embree	.05
86	Alvaro Espinoza	.05
87	Orel Hershiser	.08
88	Ken Hill	.05
89	Kenny Lofton	.75
90	Dennis Martinez	.08
91	Jose Mesa	.08
92	Eddie Murray	.35
93	Charles Nagy	.05
94	Chad Ogea	.05
95	Tony Pena	.05
96	Herb Perry	.05
97	Eric Plunk	.05
98	Jim Poole	.05
99	Manny Ramirez	.75
100	Paul Sorrento	.05
101	Julian Tavarez	.05
102	Jim Thome	.40
103	Omar Vizquel	.05
104	Dave Winfield	.20
105	Danny Bautista	.05
106	Joe Boever	.05
107	Chad Curtis	.05
108	John Doherty	.05
109	Cecil Fielder	.15
110	John Flaherty	.05
111	Travis Fryman	.05
112	Chris Gomez	.05
113	Bob Higginson	.10
114	Mark Lewis	.05
115	Jose Lima	.05
116	Felipe Lira	.05
117	Brian Maxcy	.05
118	C.J. Nitkowski	.05
119	Phil Plantier	.05
120	Clint Sodowsky	.05
121	Alan Trammell	.10
122	Lou Whitaker	.05
123	Kevin Appier	.05
124	Johnny Damon	.20
125	Gary Gaetti	.10
126	Tom Goodwin	.05
127	Tom Gordon	.05
128	Mark Gubicza	.05
129	Bob Hamelin	.05
130	David Howard	.05
131	Jason Jacome	.05
132	Wally Joyner	.10
133	Keith Lockhart	.05
134	Brent Mayne	.05
135	Jeff Montgomery	.05
136	Jon Nunnally	.05
137	Juan Samuel	.05
138	*Mike Sweeney*	.10
139	Michael Tucker	.15
140	Joe Vitiello	.05
141	Ricky Bones	.05
142	Chuck Carr	.05
143	Jeff Cirillo	.05
144	Mike Fetters	.05
145	Darryl Hamilton	.05
146	David Hulse	.05
147	John Jaha	.05
148	Scott Karl	.05
149	Mark Kiefer	.05
150	Pat Listach	.05
151	Mark Loretta	.05
152	Mike Matheny	.05
153	Matt Mieske	.05
154	Dave Nilsson	.05
155	Joe Oliver	.05
156	Al Reyes	.05
157	Kevin Seitzer	.05
158	Steve Sparks	.05
159	B.J. Surhoff	.05
160	Jose Valentin	.05
161	Greg Vaughn	.10
162	Fernando Vina	.05
163	Rich Becker	.05
164	Ron Coomer	.05
165	Marty Cordova	.15
166	Chuck Knoblauch	.20
167	*Matt Lawton*	.10
168	Pat Meares	.05
169	Paul Molitor	.30
170	Pedro Munoz	.05
171	Jose Parra	.05
172	Kirby Puckett	1.00
173	Brad Radke	.05
174	Jeff Reboulet	.05
175	Rich Robertson	.05
176	Frank Rodriguez	.05
177	Scott Stahoviak	.05
178	Dave Stevens	.05
179	Matt Walbeck	.05
180	Wade Boggs	.20
181	David Cone	.05
182	Tony Fernandez	.05
183	Joe Girardi	.05
184	Derek Jeter	1.50
185	Scott Kamieniecki	.05
186	Pat Kelly	.05
187	Jim Leyritz	.05
188	Tino Martinez	.15
189	Don Mattingly	1.00
190	Jack McDowell	.05
191	Jeff Nelson	.05
192	Paul O'Neill	.05
193	Melido Perez	.05
194	Andy Pettitte	1.00
195	Mariano Rivera	.15
196	Ruben Sierra	.08
197	Mike Stanley	.05
198	Darryl Strawberry	.10
199	John Wetteland	.05
200	Bob Wickman	.05
201	Bernie Williams	.40
202	Mark Acre	.05
203	Geronimo Berroa	.05
204	Mike Bordick	.05
205	Scott Brosius	.05
206	Dennis Eckersley	.08
207	Brent Gates	.05
208	Jason Giambi	.10
209	Rickey Henderson	.20
210	Jose Herrera	.05
211	Stan Javier	.05
212	Doug Johns	.05
213	Mark McGwire	4.00
214	Steve Ontiveros	.05
215	Craig Paquette	.05
216	Ariel Prieto	.05
217	Carlos Reyes	.05
218	Terry Steinbach	.05
219	Todd Stottlemyre	.05
220	Danny Tartabull	.05
221	Todd Van Poppel	.05
222	John Wasdin	.05
223	George Williams	.05
224	Steve Wojciechowski	.05
225	Rich Amaral	.05
226	Bobby Ayala	.05
227	Tim Belcher	.05
228	Andy Benes	.08
229	Chris Bosio	.05
230	Darren Bragg	.05
231	Jay Buhner	.15
232	Norm Charlton	.05
233	Vince Coleman	.05
234	Joey Cora	.05
235	Russ Davis	.05
236	Alex Diaz	.05
237	Felix Fermin	.05
238	Ken Griffey Jr.	2.50
239	Sterling Hitchcock	.05
240	Randy Johnson	.25
241	Edgar Martinez	.08
242	Bill Risley	.05
243	Alex Rodriquez	2.50
244	Luis Sojo	.05
245	Dan Wilson	.05
246	Bob Wolcott	.05
247	Will Clark	.30
248	Jeff Frye	.05
249	Benji Gil	.05
250	Juan Gonzalez	1.00
251	Rusty Greer	.05
252	Kevin Gross	.05
253	Roger McDowell	.05
254	Mark McLemore	.05
255	Otis Nixon	.05
256	Luis Ortiz	.05
257	Mike Pagliarulo	.05
258	Dean Palmer	.05
259	Roger Pavlik	.05
260	Ivan Rodriguez	.50
261	Kenny Rogers	.05
262	Jeff Russell	.05
263	Mickey Tettleton	.05
264	Bob Tewksbury	.05
265	Dave Valle	.05
266	Matt Whiteside	.05
267	Roberto Alomar	.75
268	Joe Carter	.15
269	Tony Castillo	.05
270	Domingo Cedeno	.05
271	Timothy Crabtree	.05
272	Carlos Delgado	.10
273	Alex Gonzalez	.05
274	Shawn Green	.05
275	Juan Guzman	.05
276	Pat Hentgen	.05
277	Al Leiter	.05
278	*Sandy Martinez*	.05
279	Paul Menhart	.05
280	John Olerud	.10
281	Paul Quantrill	.05
282	Ken Robinson	.05
283	Ed Sprague	.05
284	Mike Timlin	.05
285	Steve Avery	.05
286	Rafael Belliard	.05
287	Jeff Blauser	.05
288	Pedro Borbon	.05
289	Brad Clontz	.05
290	Mike Devereaux	.05
291	Tom Glavine	.15
292	Marquis Grissom	.10
293	Chipper Jones	1.75
294	David Justice	.20
295	Mike Kelly	.05
296	Ryan Klesko	.50
297	Mark Lemke	.05
298	Javier Lopez	.15
299	Greg Maddux	2.00
300	Fred McGriff	.35
301	Greg McMichael	.05
302	Kent Mercker	.05
303	Mike Mordecai	.05
304	Charlie O'Brien	.05
305	Eduardo Perez	.05
306	Luis Polonia	.05
307	Jason Schmidt	.05
308	John Smoltz	.20
309	Terrell Wade	.05
310	Mark Wohlers	.05
311	Scott Bullett	.05
312	Jim Bullinger	.05
313	Larry Casian	.05
314	Frank Castillo	.05
315	Shawon Dunston	.15
316	Kevin Foster	.05
317	Matt Franco	.05
318	Luis Gonzalez	.05
319	Mark Grace	.20
320	Jose Hernandez	.05
321	Mike Hubbard	.05
322	Brian McRae	.05
323	Randy Myers	.05
324	Jaime Navarro	.05
325	Mark Parent	.05
326	Mike Perez	.05
327	Rey Sanchez	.05
328	Ryne Sandberg	.75
329	Scott Servais	.05
330	Sammy Sosa	1.50
331	Ozzie Timmons	.05

#	Player	Value	#	Player	Value	#	Player	Value
332	Steve Trachsel	.05	428	Tom Candiotti	.05	524	Nelson Liriano	.05
333	Todd Zeile	.10	429	Juan Castro	.05	525	Esteban Loaiza	.10
334	Bret Boone	.05	430	John Cummings	.05	526	Al Martin	.05
335	Jeff Branson	.05	431	Delino DeShields	.05	527	Orlando Merced	.05
336	Jeff Brantley	.05	432	Joey Eischen	.05	528	Dan Miceli	.05
337	Dave Burba	.05	433	Chad Fonville	.15	529	Ramon Morel	.05
338	Hector Carrasco	.05	434	Greg Gagne	.05	530	Denny Neagle	.05
339	Mariano Duncan	.05	435	Dave Hansen	.05	531	Steve Parris	.05
340	Ron Gant	.10	436	Carlos Hernandez	.05	532	Dan Plesac	.05
341	Lenny Harris	.05	437	Todd Hollandsworth	.12	533	Don Slaught	.05
342	Xavier Hernandez	.05	438	Eric Karros	.10	534	Paul Wagner	.05
343	Thomas Howard	.05	439	Roberto Kelly	.05	535	John Wehner	.05
344	Mike Jackson	.05	440	Ramon Martinez	.08	536	Kevin Young	.05
345	Barry Larkin	.15	441	Raul Mondesi	.30	537	Allen Battle	.05
346	Darren Lewis	.05	442	Hideo Nomo	1.00	538	David Bell	.05
347	Hal Morris	.05	443	Antonio Osuna	.05	539	Alan Benes	.15
348	Eric Owens	.05	444	Chan Ho Park	.08	540	Scott Cooper	.05
349	Mark Portugal	.05	445	Mike Piazza	1.75	541	Tripp Cromer	.05
350	Jose Rijo	.05	446	Felix Rodriguez	.05	542	Tony Fossas	.05
351	Reggie Sanders	.10	447	Kevin Tapani	.05	543	Bernard Gilkey	.10
352	Benito Santiago	.08	448	Ismael Valdes	.05	544	Tom Henke	.05
353	Pete Schourek	.05	449	Todd Worrell	.05	545	Brian Jordan	.15
354	John Smiley	.05	450	Moises Alou	.10	546	Ray Lankford	.15
355	Eddie Taubensee	.05	451	Shane Andrews	.05	547	John Mabry	.05
356	Jerome Walton	.05	452	Yamil Benitez	.05	548	T.J. Mathews	.05
357	David Wells	.05	453	Sean Berry	.05	549	Mike Morgan	.05
358	Roger Bailey	.05	454	Wil Cordero	.05	550	Jose Oliva	.05
359	Jason Bates	.05	455	Jeff Fassero	.05	551	Jose Oquendo	.05
360	Dante Bichette	.15	456	Darrin Fletcher	.05	552	Donovan Osborne	.05
361	Ellis Burks	.15	457	Cliff Floyd	.05	553	Tom Pagnozzi	.05
362	Vinny Castilla	.12	458	Mark Grudzielanek	.10	554	Mark Petkovsek	.05
363	Andres Galarraga	.15	459	Gil Heredia	.05	555	Danny Sheaffer	.05
364	Darren Holmes	.05	460	Tim Laker	.05	556	Ozzie Smith	.40
365	Mike Kingery	.05	461	Mike Lansing	.05	557	Mark Sweeney	.05
366	Curt Leskanic	.05	462	Pedro Martinez	.20	558	Allen Watson	.05
367	Quinton McCracken	.05	463	Carlos Perez	.05	559	Andy Ashby	.05
368	Mike Munoz	.05	464	Curtis Pride	.05	560	Brad Ausmus	.05
369	David Nied	.05	465	Mel Rojas	.05	561	Willie Blair	.05
370	Steve Reed	.05	466	Kirk Rueter	.05	562	Ken Caminiti	.15
371	Bryan Rekar	.05	467	*F.P. Santangelo*	.10	563	Andujar Cedeno	.05
372	Kevin Ritz	.05	468	Tim Scott	.05	564	Glenn Dishman	.05
373	Bruce Ruffin	.05	469	David Segui	.05	565	Steve Finley	.05
374	Bret Saberhagen	.05	470	Tony Tarasco	.05	566	Bryce Florie	.05
375	Bill Swift	.05	471	Rondell White	.10	567	Tony Gwynn	.75
376	John Vander Wal	.05	472	Edgardo Alfonzo	.08	568	Joey Hamilton	.10
377	Larry Walker	.30	473	Tim Bogar	.05	569	Dustin Hermanson	.10
378	Walt Weiss	.05	474	Rico Brogna	.05	570	Trevor Hoffman	.05
379	Eric Young	.05	475	Damon Buford	.05	571	Brian Johnson	.05
380	Kurt Abbott	.05	476	Paul Byrd	.05	572	Marc Kroon	.05
381	Alex Arias	.05	477	Carl Everett	.05	573	Scott Livingstone	.05
382	Jerry Browne	.05	478	John Franco	.05	574	Marc Newfield	.05
383	John Burkett	.05	479	Todd Hundley	.15	575	Melvin Nieves	.05
384	Greg Colbrunn	.05	480	Butch Huskey	.10	576	Jody Reed	.05
385	Jeff Conine	.15	481	Jason Isringhausen	.15	577	Bip Roberts	.05
386	Andre Dawson	.20	482	Bobby Jones	.05	578	Scott Sanders	.05
387	Chris Hammond	.05	483	Chris Jones	.05	579	Fernando Valenzuela	.08
388	Charles Johnson	.15	484	Jeff Kent	.05	580	Eddie Williams	.05
389	Terry Mathews	.05	485	Dave Mlicki	.05	581	Rod Beck	.05
390	Robb Nen	.05	486	Robert Person	.05	582	*Marvin Benard*	.05
391	Joe Orsulak	.05	487	Bill Pulsipher	.10	583	Barry Bonds	.75
392	Terry Pendleton	.05	488	Kelly Stinnett	.05	584	Jamie Brewington	.05
393	Pat Rapp	.05	489	Ryan Thompson	.05	585	Mark Carreon	.05
394	Gary Sheffield	.40	490	Jose Vizcaino	.05	586	Royce Clayton	.05
395	Jesus Tavarez	.05	491	Howard Battle	.05	587	Shawn Estes	.05
396	Marc Valdes	.05	492	Toby Borland	.05	588	Glenallen Hill	.05
397	Quilvio Veras	.05	493	Ricky Bottalico	.05	589	Mark Leiter	.05
398	Randy Veres	.05	494	Darren Daulton	.05	590	Kirt Manwaring	.05
399	Devon White	.05	495	Lenny Dykstra	.08	591	David McCarty	.05
400	Jeff Bagwell	1.00	496	Jim Eisenreich	.05	592	Terry Mulholland	.05
401	Derek Bell	.15	497	Sid Fernandez	.05	593	John Patterson	.05
402	Craig Biggio	.10	498	Tyler Green	.05	594	J.R. Phillips	.05
403	John Cangelosi	.05	499	Charlie Hayes	.05	595	Deion Sanders	.20
404	Jim Dougherty	.05	500	Gregg Jefferies	.10	596	Steve Scarsone	.05
405	Doug Drabek	.05	501	Kevin Jordan	.05	597	Robby Thompson	.05
406	Tony Eusebio	.05	502	Tony Longmire	.05	598	Sergio Valdez	.05
407	Ricky Gutierrez	.05	503	Tom Marsh	.05	599	William VanLandingham	.05
408	Mike Hampton	.05	504	Michael Mimbs	.05	600	Matt Williams	.25
409	Dean Hartgraves	.05	505	Mickey Morandini	.05			
410	John Hudek	.05	506	Gene Schall	.05			
411	Brian Hunter	.10	507	Curt Schilling	.05			
412	Todd Jones	.05	508	Heathcliff Slocumb	.05			
413	Darryl Kile	.05	509	Kevin Stocker	.05			
414	Dave Magadan	.05	510	Andy Van Slyke	.05			
415	Derrick May	.05	511	Lenny Webster	.05			
416	Orlando Miller	.05	512	Mark Whiten	.05			
417	James Mouton	.05	513	Mike Williams	.05			
418	Shane Reynolds	.05	514	Jay Bell	.05			
419	Greg Swindell	.05	515	Jacob Brumfield	.05			
420	Jeff Tabaka	.05	516	Jason Christiansen	.05			
421	Dave Veres	.05	517	Dave Clark	.05			
422	Billy Wagner	.10	518	Midre Cummings	.05			
423	*Donne Wall*	.05	519	Angelo Encarnacion	.05			
424	Rick Wilkins	.05	520	John Ericks	.05			
425	Billy Ashley	.10	521	Carlos Garcia	.05			
426	Mike Blowers	.05	522	Mark Johnson	.10			
427	Brett Butler	.10	523	Jeff King	.05			

1996 Fleer
Baseball '96

For a second consecutive year Fleer issued a special version of its Cleveland Indians cards for sale at Revco stores and Jacobs Field. Sold in 10-card packs with a suggested retail price of $1.49, the Revco version Indians team set differs from the regular Fleer cards in the application of UV coating on front and back, the use of silver-rather than gold-foil highlights and the numbering "X of 20". Following up on the Indians team-set issue, Fleer also issued 20-card sets for several other teams, distributed regionally. They were also sold in 10-card packs ($1.99 SRP) and feature UV coating, silver-foil graphics and special numbering. Some cards were updated and feature new photos reflecting trades, free agent signings, etc.

		MT
Complete Set (180):		48.00
Common Player:		.10
	Atlanta Braves team set:	8.00
1	Steve Avery	.10
2	Jeff Blauser	.10
3	Brad Clontz	.10
4	Tom Glavine	.20
5	Marquis Grissom	.15
6	Chipper Jones	2.00
7	David Justice	.50
8	Ryan Klesko	1.00
9	Mark Lemke	.10
10	Javier Lopez	.15
11	Greg Maddux	3.00
12	Fred McGriff	.30
13	Greg McMichael	.10
14	Eddie Perez	.10
15	Jason Schmidt	.10
16	John Smoltz	.25
17	Terrell Wade	.10
18	Mark Wohlers	.10
19	Logo card	.05
20	Checklist	.05
	Baltimore Orioles team set:	8.00
1	Roberto Alomar	1.00
2	Brady Anderson	.15
3	Armando Benitez	.10
4	Bobby Bonilla	.15
5	Scott Erickson	.10
6	Jeffrey Hammonds	.10
7	Jimmy Haynes	.10
8	Chris Hoiles	.10
9	Rick Krivda	.10
10	Kent Mercker	.10
11	Mike Mussina	.20
12	Randy Myers	.10
13	Jesse Orosco	.10
14	Rafael Palmeiro	.40
15	Cal Ripken Jr.	4.00
16	B.J. Surhoff	.10
17	Tony Tarasco	.10
18	David Wells	.10
19	Logo card	.05
20	Checklist	.05
	Boston Red Sox team set:	4.00
1	Stan Belinda	.10
2	Jose Canseco	.75
3	Roger Clemens	1.00
4	Wil Cordero	.10
5	Vaughn Eshelman	.10
6	Tom Gordon	.10
7	Mike Greenwell	.10
8	Dwayne Hosey	.10
9	Kevin Mitchell	.10
10	Tim Naehring	.10

11	Troy O'Leary	.10
12	Aaron Sele	.15
13	Heathcliff Slocumb	.10
14	Mike Stanley	.10
15	Jeff Suppan	.10
16	John Valentin	.15
17	Mo Vaughn	.50
18	Tim Wakefield	.10
19	Logo card	.05
20	Checklist	.05
	Chicago Cubs team set:	4.00
1	Terry Adams	.10
2	Jim Bullinger	.10
3	Frank Castillo	.10
4	Kevin Foster	.10
5	Leo Gomez	.10
6	Luis Gonzalez	.10
7	Mark Grace	.40
8	Jose Hernandez	.10
9	*Robin Jennings*	.10
10	Doug Jones	.10
11	Brooks Kieschnick	.35
12	Brian McRae	.10
13	Jaime Navarro	.10
14	Rey Sanchez	.10
15	Ryne Sandberg	1.50
16	Scott Servais	.10
17	Sammy Sosa	1.00
18	Steve Trachsel	.10
19	Logo card	.05
20	Checklist	.05
	Chicago White Sox team set:	6.00
1	Wilson Alvarez	.10
2	Harold Baines	.10
3	Jason Bere	.10
4	Ray Durham	.15
5	Alex Fernandez	.10
6	Ozzie Guillen	.10
7	Roberto Hernandez	.10
8	Matt Karchner	.10
9	Ron Karkovice	.10
10	Darren Lewis	.10
11	Dave Martinez	.10
12	Lyle Mouton	.10
13	Tony Phillips	.10
14	Chris Snopek	.10
15	Kevin Tapani	.10
16	Danny Tartabull	.10
17	Frank Thomas	3.00
18	Robin Ventura	.20
19	Logo card	.05
20	Checklist	.05
	Cleveland Indians team set:	8.00
1	Sandy Alomar Jr.	.20
2	Paul Assenmacher	.10
3	Carlos Baerga	.15
4	Albert Belle	1.00
5	Orel Hershiser	.15
6	Kenny Lofton	1.00
7	Dennis Martinez	.15
8	Jose Mesa	.10
9	Eddie Murray	.75
10	Charles Nagy	.10
11	Tony Pena	.10
12	Herb Perry	.10
13	Eric Plunk	.10
14	Jim Poole	.10
15	Manny Ramirez	1.50
16	Julian Tavarez	.10
17	Jim Thome	.20
18	Omar Vizquel	.10
19	Logo card	.05
20	Checklist	.05
	Colorado Rockies team set:	4.00
1	Jason Bates	.10
2	Dante Bichette	.75
3	Ellis Burks	.15
4	Vinny Castilla	.25
5	Andres Galarraga	.45
6	Darren Holmes	.10
7	Curt Leskanic	.10
8	Quinton McCracken	.10
9	Mike Munoz	.10
10	Jayhawk Owens	.10
11	Steve Reed	.10
12	Kevin Ritz	.10
13	Bret Saberhagen	.10
14	Bill Swift	.10
15	John Vander Wal	.10
16	Larry Walker	.30
17	Walt Weiss	.10
18	Eric Young	.15
19	Logo card	.05
20	Checklist	.05
	L.A. Dodgers team set:	8.00

1	Mike Blowers	.10
2	Brett Butler	.15
3	Tom Candiotti	.10
4	Roger Cedeno	.10
5	Delino DeShields	.10
6	Chad Fonville	.10
7	Greg Gagne	.10
8	Karim Garcia	.50
9	Todd Hollandsworth	.15
10	Eric Karros	.15
11	Ramon Martinez	.10
12	Raul Mondesi	.50
13	Hideo Nomo	1.50
14	Antonio Osuna	.10
15	Chan Ho Park	.50
16	Mike Piazza	2.50
17	Ismael Valdes	.15
18	Todd Worrell	.10
19	Logo card	.05
20	Checklist	.05
	Texas Rangers team set:	4.00
1	Mark Brandenburg	.10
2	Damon Buford	.15
3	Will Clark	.60
4	Kevin Elster	.10
5	Benji Gil	.10
6	Juan Gonzalez	1.50
7	Rusty Greer	.10
8	Kevin Gross	.10
9	Darryl Hamilton	.10
10	Ken Hill	.10
11	Mark McLemore	.10
12	Dean Palmer	.15
13	Roger Pavlik	.10
14	Ivan Rodriguez	.40
15	Mickey Tettleton	.10
16	Dave Valle	.10
17	Ed Vosberg	.10
18	Matt Whiteside	.10
19	Logo card	.05
20	Checklist	.05

1996 Fleer Checklists

Checklist cards are treated as an insert set in 1996 Fleer, appearing on average once every six packs. Like all other Fleer hobby inserts in the baseball set, the checklists are UV-coated front and back, in contrast to the matte-finish regular issue cards. Checklists have borderless game-action photos on front, with gold-foil typography. Backs have a large Fleer logo and checklist data on a white background.

		MT
Complete Set (10):		5.50
Common Player:		.25
1	Barry Bonds	.40
2	Ken Griffey Jr.	2.00
3	Chipper Jones	1.00
4	Greg Maddux	1.50
5	Mike Piazza	1.25
6	Manny Ramirez	.75

7	Cal Ripken Jr.	1.75
8	Frank Thomas	1.50
9	Mo Vaughn	.50
10	Matt Williams	.25

1996 Fleer Glossy

While Fleer's basic card set for 1996 feature matte-surface cards, a glossy version of each regular card was also issued as a parallel insert set. Other than the UV coating on front and back and the use of silver- rather than gold-foil typography on front, the cards are identical to the regular '96 Fleer player cards. One glossy version card is found in each pack.

	MT
Complete Set (600):	250.00
Common Player:	.25
(Star cards valued at 3X-5X corresponding card in regular 1996 Fleer issue)	

1996 Fleer Golden Memories

Some of the 1995 season's greatest moments are captured in this insert set, a one per 10 pack pick. Fronts have two photos of the player, one in full color in the foreground and one in monochrome as a backdrop. Typography is in prismatic foil vertically down one side. Backs have another color player photo, along with details of the milestone. Two of the cards feature multiple players.

		MT
Complete Set (10):		18.00
Common Player:		.40
1	Albert Belle	1.25
2	Barry Bonds, Sammy Sosa	3.00
3	Greg Maddux	3.00
4	Edgar Martinez	.40
5	Ramon Martinez	.40
6	Mark McGwire	6.00
7	Eddie Murray	.75
8	Cal Ripken Jr.	4.00
9	Frank Thomas	4.00
10	Alan Trammell, Lou Whitaker	.40

1996 Fleer Lumber Company

Once again for 1996, a Fleer "Lumber Company" chase set honors the game's top sluggers. The '96 version has a horizontal format with a rather small player action photo on a background resembling the trademark area of a bat. The "trademark" is actually the player and team name along with the "Lumber Company" ID, printed in textured glossy black ink. Backs repeat the trademark motif and also include a close-up player photo and a few words about his power-hitting numbers. Lumber Company cards are a one per nine pack pick, on average, found only in retail packs.

		MT
Complete Set (12):		18.00
Common Player:		.50
1	Albert Belle	1.25
2	Dante Bichette	.75
3	Barry Bonds	1.25
4	Ken Griffey Jr.	5.00
5	Mark McGwire	6.00
6	Mike Piazza	3.00
7	Manny Ramirez	1.00
8	Tim Salmon	.75
9	Sammy Sosa	3.00
10	Frank Thomas	4.00
11	Mo Vaughn	1.50
12	Matt Williams	.75

1996 Fleer Post-Season Glory

Highlights of the 1995 postseason are featured in this small chase card set. Against a stadium background are multiple photos of the featured player, arranged horizontally. The vertical backs have another player photo down one side, and a description of his play-off performance on the other. Stated odds of picking one of these cards are one per five packs.

		MT
Complete Set (5):		5.00
Common Player:		.25
1	Tom Glavine	.40
2	Ken Griffey Jr.	4.00
3	Orel Hershiser	.25
4	Randy Johnson	.60
5	Jim Thome	.40

1996 Fleer Prospects

Minor leaguers who are expected to make it big in the big time are featured in this insert issue. Fronts feature large portrait photos against pastel backgrounds with player and set ID in prismatic foil. Backs have an action photo and repeat the front background color in a box which details the player's potential and career to date. Average odds of finding a Prospects card are one per six packs.

		MT
Complete Set (10):		5.00
Common Player:		.25
1	Yamil Benitez	.25
2	Roger Cedeno	.50
3	Tony Clark	1.00
4	Micah Franklin	.25
5	Karim Garcia	.75
6	Todd Greene	.25
7	Alex Ochoa	.25
8	Ruben Rivera	1.50
9	Chris Snopek	.25
10	Shannon Stewart	.25

1996 Fleer Road Warriors

A black-and-white country highway photo is the background for the color player action photo on this insert set. Front typography is in silver foil. The players featured are those whose performance on the road is considered outstanding. Backs have a white background, portrait photo and stats bearing out the away-game superiority. These inserts are found at an average pace of one per 13 packs.

		MT
Complete Set (10):		18.00
Common Player:		.75
1	Derek Bell	.75
2	Tony Gwynn	2.50
3	Greg Maddux	4.00
4	Mark McGwire	8.00
5	Mike Piazza	4.00
6	Manny Ramirez	1.50
7	Tim Salmon	1.00
8	Frank Thomas	5.00
9	Mo Vaughn	1.75
10	Matt Williams	.75

1996 Fleer Rookie Sensations

Top rookies of the 1995 season are featured on this chase card set. Horizontally formatted, the cards have an action photo on one side and a large prismatic-foil end strip which displays the player name, team logo and card company identifiers. Backs have a portrait photo on as white background with a few sentences about the player's rookie season. Stated odds of finding one of these inserts is one per 11 packs, on average.

		MT
Complete Set (15):		15.00
Common Player:		.50
1	Garret Anderson	.75
2	Marty Cordova	1.50
3	Johnny Damon	.75
4	Ray Durham	.50
5	Carl Everett	.50
6	Shawn Green	.50
7	Brian Hunter	.75
8	Jason Isringhausen	.75
9	Charles Johnson	.75
10	Chipper Jones	8.00
11	John Mabry	.50
12	Hideo Nomo	3.00
13	Troy Percival	.50
14	Andy Pettitte	4.00
15	Quilvio Veras	.50

1996 Fleer Smoke 'N Heat

Once more using the "Smoke 'N Heat" identifier for a chase set of the game's hardest throwers, Fleer presents these select pitchers in action photos against a black-and-flame background. Front typography is in gold foil. Backs have a large portrait photo, repeat the flame motif as background and have a description of the pitcher's prowess in a black box. The cards are found, on average, once per nine packs.

A player's name in *italic* type indicates a rookie card.

		MT
Complete Set (10):		10.00
Common Player:		.40
1	Kevin Appier	.40
2	Roger Clemens	1.00
3	David Cone	.50
4	Chuck Finley	.40
5	Randy Johnson	1.00
6	Greg Maddux	5.00
7	Pedro Martinez	.50
8	Hideo Nomo	2.50
9	John Smoltz	1.00
10	Todd Stottlemyre	.40

1996 Fleer Team Leaders

One player from each club has been selected for inclusion in the "Team Leaders" chase set. Fronts have action player photos on a background of metallic foil littered with multiple representations of the team logo. Gold-foil lettering identifies the player, team and chase set. Backs have a white background, portrait photo and description of the player's leadership role. Stated rate of insertion for this set is one card per nine packs, on average, found only in hobby packs.

		MT
Complete Set (28):		50.00
Common Player:		.60
1	Cal Ripken Jr.	10.00
2	Mo Vaughn	3.00
3	Jim Edmonds	1.00
4	Frank Thomas	10.00
5	Kenny Lofton	3.00
6	Travis Fryman	.60
7	Gary Gaetti	.60
8	B.J. Surhoff	.60
9	Kirby Puckett	5.00
10	Don Mattingly	5.00
11	Mark McGwire	15.00
12	Ken Griffey Jr.	12.00
13	Juan Gonzalez	6.00
14	Joe Carter	.75
15	Greg Maddux	8.00
16	Sammy Sosa	6.00
17	Barry Larkin	1.00
18	Dante Bichette	1.50
19	Jeff Conine	.75
20	Jeff Bagwell	4.00
21	Mike Piazza	7.00
22	Rondell White	.75
23	Rico Brogna	.60
24	Darren Daulton	.60
25	Jeff King	.60
26	Ray Lankford	.60
27	Tony Gwynn	5.00
28	Barry Bonds	2.50

1996 Fleer Tomorrow's Legends

In this insert set the projected stars of tomorrow are featured in action poses on a busy multi-colored, quartered background of baseball symbols and the globe. Typography is in silver foil. Backs have a portrait photo and large team logo along with an early-career summary. Odds of finding a "Tomorrow's Legends" card are posted at one per 13 packs, on average.

		MT
Complete Set (10):		15.00
Common Player:		.60
1	Garret Anderson	.75
2	Jim Edmonds	.75
3	Brian Hunter	.60
4	Jason Isringhausen	.75
5	Charles Johnson	.60
6	Chipper Jones	5.00
7	Ryan Klesko	2.00
8	Hideo Nomo	3.00
9	Manny Ramirez	3.00
10	Rondell White	.60

1996 Fleer Update

Fleer Update Baseball has 250 cards, including more than 55 rookies, plus traded players and free agents in their new uniforms, 35 Encore subset cards and five checklists. Each card in the regular-issue set also has a parallel "Tiffany Collection" version, which has UV coating and holographic foil stamping in contrast to the matte finish and gold foil of the regular cards. Insert cards include Diamond Tribute, New Horizons, Smooth Leather and Soaring Stars. Each pack also contains a Fleer "Thanks a Million" scratch-off game card, redeemable for prizes.

		MT
Complete Set (250):		15.00
Common Player:		.05
Unlisted Stars: .20 to .30		
U1	Roberto Alomar	.75
U2	Mike Devereaux	.05
U3	*Scott McClain*	.05
U4	Roger McDowell	.05
U5	Kent Mercker	.05
U6	Jimmy Myers	.05
U7	Randy Myers	.05
U8	B.J. Surhoff	.05
U9	Tony Tarasco	.05
U10	David Wells	.05
U11	Wil Cordero	.05
U12	Tom Gordon	.05
U13	Reggie Jefferson	.05
U14	Jose Malave	.05
U15	Kevin Mitchell	.05
U16	Jamie Moyer	.05
U17	Heathcliff Slocumb	.05
U18	Mike Stanley	.05
U19	George Arias	.05
U20	Jorge Fabregas	.05
U21	Don Slaught	.05
U22	Randy Velarde	.05
U23	Harold Baines	.05
U24	*Mike Cameron*	.75
U25	Darren Lewis	.05
U26	Tony Phillips	.05
U27	Bill Simas	.05
U28	Chris Snopek	.05
U29	Kevin Tapani	.05
U30	Danny Tartabull	.05
U31	Julio Franco	.05
U32	Jack McDowell	.10
U33	Kimera Bartee	.05
U34	Mark Lewis	.05
U35	Melvin Nieves	.05
U36	Mark Parent	.05
U37	Eddie Williams	.05
U38	Tim Belcher	.05
U39	Sal Fasano	.05
U40	Chris Haney	.05
U41	Mike Macfarlane	.05
U42	Jose Offerman	.05
U43	Joe Randa	.05
U44	Bip Roberts	.05
U45	Chuck Carr	.05
U46	Bobby Hughes	.05
U47	Graeme Lloyd	.05
U48	Ben McDonald	.05
U49	Kevin Wickander	.05
U50	Rick Aguilera	.05
U51	Mike Durant	.05
U52	Chip Hale	.05
U53	LaTroy Hawkins	.05
U54	Dave Hollins	.05
U55	Roberto Kelly	.05
U56	Paul Molitor	.20
U57	*Dan Naulty*	.10
U58	Mariano Duncan	.05
U59	*Andy Fox*	.05

U60	Joe Girardi	.05
U61	Dwight Gooden	.10
U62	Jimmy Key	.05
U63	*Matt Luke*	.05
U64	Tino Martinez	.05
U65	Jeff Nelson	.05
U66	Tim Raines	.05
U67	Ruben Rivera	.35
U68	Kenny Rogers	.05
U69	Gerald Williams	.05
U70	Tony Batista	.05
U71	Allen Battle	.05
U72	Jim Corsi	.05
U73	Steve Cox	.05
U74	Pedro Munoz	.05
U75	Phil Plantier	.05
U76	Scott Spiezio	.05
U77	Ernie Young	.05
U78	Russ Davis	.05
U79	Sterling Hitchcock	.05
U80	Edwin Hurtado	.05
U81	*Raul Ibanez*	.05
U82	Mike Jackson	.05
U83	Ricky Jordan	.05
U84	Paul Sorrento	.05
U85	Doug Strange	.05
U86	Mark Brandenburg	.05
U87	Damon Buford	.05
U88	Kevin Elster	.05
U89	Darryl Hamilton	.05
U90	Ken Hill	.05
U91	Ed Vosberg	.05
U92	Craig Worthington	.05
U93	Tilson Brito	.05
U94	Giovanni Carrara	.05
U95	Felipe Crespo	.05
U96	Erik Hanson	.05
U97	*Marty Janzen*	.05
U98	Otis Nixon	.05
U99	Charlie O'Brien	.05
U100	Robert Perez	.05
U101	Paul Quantrill	.05
U102	Bill Risley	.05
U103	Juan Samuel	.05
U104	Jermaine Dye	.30
U105	Wonderful Monds	.05
U106	Dwight Smith	.05
U107	Jerome Walton	.05
U108	Terry Adams	.05
U109	Leo Gomez	.05
U110	*Robin Jennings*	.05
U111	Doug Jones	.05
U112	Brooks Kieschnick	.10
U113	Dave Magadan	.05
U114	*Jason Maxwell*	.05
U115	Rodney Myers	.05
U116	Eric Anthony	.05
U117	Vince Coleman	.05
U118	Eric Davis	.05
U119	Steve Gibralter	.05
U120	Curtis Goodwin	.05
U121	Willie Greene	.05
U122	Mike Kelly	.05
U123	Marcus Moore	.05
U124	Chad Mottola	.05
U125	Chris Sabo	.05
U126	Roger Salkeld	.05
U127	Pedro Castellano	.05
U128	Trenidad Hubbard	.05
U129	Jayhawk Owens	.05
U130	Jeff Reed	.05
U131	Kevin Brown	.05
U132	Al Leiter	.05
U133	Matt Mantei	.05
U134	Dave Weathers	.05
U135	Devon White	.05
U136	Bob Abreu	.15
U137	Sean Berry	.05
U138	Doug Brocail	.05
U139	Richard Hidalgo	.05
U140	Alvin Morman	.05
U141	Mike Blowers	.05
U142	Roger Cedeno	.05
U143	Greg Gagne	.05
U144	Karim Garcia	.75
U145	*Wilton Guerrero*	.50
U146	Israel Alcantara	.05
U147	Omar Daal	.05
U148	Ryan McGuire	.05
U149	Sherman Obando	.05
U150	Jose Paniagua	.05
U151	Henry Rodriguez	.05
U152	Andy Stankiewicz	.05
U153	Dave Veres	.05
U154	Juan Acevedo	.05
U155	Mark Clark	.05

U156	Bernard Gilkey	.05
U157	Pete Harnisch	.05
U158	Lance Johnson	.05
U159	Brent Mayne	.05
U160	Rey Ordonez	.25
U161	Kevin Roberson	.05
U162	Paul Wilson	.10
U163	*David Doster*	.05
U164	*Mike Grace*	.40
U165	*Rich Hunter*	.05
U166	Pete Incaviglia	.05
U167	Mike Lieberthal	.05
U168	Terry Mulholland	.05
U169	Ken Ryan	.05
U170	Benito Santiago	.05
U171	*Kevin Sefcik*	.05
U172	Lee Tinsley	.05
U173	Todd Zeile	.05
U174	*Francisco Cordova*	.10
U175	Danny Darwin	.05
U176	Charlie Hayes	.05
U177	Jason Kendall	.05
U178	Mike Kingery	.05
U179	Jon Lieber	.05
U180	Zane Smith	.05
U181	Luis Alicea	.05
U182	Cory Bailey	.05
U183	Andy Benes	.05
U184	Pat Borders	.05
U185	*Mike Busby*	.05
U186	Royce Clayton	.05
U187	Dennis Eckersley	.05
U188	Gary Gaetti	.05
U189	Ron Gant	.10
U190	Aaron Holbert	.05
U191	Willie McGee	.05
U192	*Miguel Mejia*	.05
U193	Jeff Parrett	.05
U194	Todd Stottlemyre	.05
U195	Sean Bergman	.05
U196	Archi Cianfrocco	.05
U197	Rickey Henderson	.05
U198	Wally Joyner	.05
U199	Craig Shipley	.05
U200	Bob Tewksbury	.05
U201	Tim Worrell	.05
U202	*Rich Aurilia*	.05
U203	Doug Creek	.05
U204	Shawon Dunston	.05
U205	*Osvaldo Fernandez*	.10
U206	Mark Gardner	.05
U207	Stan Javier	.05
U208	Marcus Jensen	.05
U209	Chris Singleton	.05
U210	Allen Watson	.05
U211	Jeff Bagwell (Encore)	.60
U212	Derek Bell (Encore)	.05
U213	Albert Belle (Encore)	.40
U214	Wade Boggs (Encore)	.10
U215	Barry Bonds (Encore)	.40
U216	Jose Canseco (Encore)	.15
U217	Marty Cordova (Encore)	.10
U218	Jim Edmonds (Encore)	.10
U219	Cecil Fielder (Encore)	.10
U220	Andres Galarraga (Encore)	.15
U221	Juan Gonzalez (Encore)	.60
U222	Mark Grace (Encore)	.10
U223	Ken Griffey Jr. (Encore)	1.50
U224	Tony Gwynn (Encore)	.60
U225	Jason Isringhausen (Encore)	.10
U226	Derek Jeter (Encore)	.75
U227	Randy Johnson (Encore)	.35
U228	Chipper Jones (Encore)	1.00
U229	Ryan Klesko (Encore)	.40
U230	Barry Larkin (Encore)	.15
U231	Kenny Lofton (Encore)	.50
U232	Greg Maddux (Encore)	1.00
U233	Raul Mondesi (Encore)	.20
U234	Hideo Nomo (Encore)	.40
U235	Mike Piazza (Encore)	1.00
U236	Manny Ramirez (Encore)	.50
U237	Cal Ripken Jr. (Encore)	1.25
U238	Tim Salmon (Encore)	.15
U239	Ryne Sandberg (Encore)	.40
U240	Reggie Sanders (Encore)	.05
U241	Gary Sheffield (Encore)	.20
U242	Sammy Sosa (Encore)	1.00
U243	Frank Thomas (Encore)	1.25
U244	Mo Vaughn (Encore)	.50
U245	Matt Williams (Encore)	.15
U246	Checklist	.05
U247	Checklist	.05
U248	Checklist	.05
U249	Checklist	.05
U250	Checklist	.05

1996 Fleer Update Diamond Tribute

These insert cards are the most difficult to pull from 1996 Fleer Update packs; they are seeded one per every 100 packs. The 10-card set features cards of future Hall of Famers on stock utilizing two different holographic foils and a diamond design, similar to the "Zone" insert cards in Fleer Baseball.

		MT
Complete Set (10):		140.00
Common Player:		4.00
1	Wade Boggs	5.00
2	Barry Bonds	10.00
3	Ken Griffey Jr.	40.00
4	Tony Gwynn	20.00
5	Rickey Henderson	4.00
6	Greg Maddux	25.00
7	Eddie Murray	6.00
8	Cal Ripken Jr.	30.00
9	Ozzie Smith	6.00
10	Frank Thomas	30.00

1996 Fleer Update Headliners

These 20 cards feature newsmakers from 1996. The cards were random inserts in 1996 Fleer Update packs, one per every five retail packs.

		MT
Complete Set (20):		50.00
Common Player:		.50
1	Roberto Alomar	1.50
2	Jeff Bagwell	2.50
3	Albert Belle	2.00
4	Barry Bonds	2.00
5	Cecil Fielder	.50
6	Juan Gonzalez	4.00
7	Ken Griffey Jr.	8.00
8	Tony Gwynn	3.00
9	Randy Johnson	1.00
10	Chipper Jones	5.00
11	Ryan Klesko	1.50

12	Kenny Lofton	2.00
13	Greg Maddux	5.00
14	Hideo Nomo	1.50
15	Mike Piazza	5.00
16	Manny Ramirez	2.00
17	Cal Ripken Jr.	7.00
18	Tim Salmon	.75
19	Frank Thomas	6.00
20	Matt Williams	.75

1996 Fleer Update New Horizons

These 1996 Fleer Update inserts feature 20 promising youngsters with bright futures in the majors. The cards were seeded one per every five hobby packs.

		MT
Complete Set (20):		16.00
Common Player:		.50
1	Bob Abreu	1.50
2	George Arias	.50
3	Tony Batista	.50
4	Steve Cox	.50
5	David Doster	.50
6	Jermaine Dye	2.00
7	Andy Fox	1.00
8	Mike Grace	1.00
9	Todd Greene	1.00
10	Wilton Guerrero	1.50
11	Richard Hidalgo	.75
12	Raul Ibanez	.75
13	Robin Jennings	.50
14	Marcus Jensen	.50
15	Jason Kendall	1.00
16	Brooks Kieschnick	1.00
17	Ryan McGuire	.50
18	Miguel Mejia	.50
19	Rey Ordonez	1.50
20	Paul Wilson	1.00

1996 Fleer Update Smooth Leather

Ten of the game's top fielders are showcased on these 1996 Fleer Update insert cards. The cards were seeded one per every five packs.

		MT
Complete Set (10):		15.00
Common Player:		.50
1	Roberto Alomar	1.25
2	Barry Bonds	1.25
3	Will Clark	.50
4	Ken Griffey Jr.	5.00
5	Kenny Lofton	1.25
6	Greg Maddux	3.00
7	Raul Mondesi	.75
8	Rey Ordonez	1.00
9	Cal Ripken Jr.	5.00
10	Matt Williams	.75

1996 Fleer Update Soaring Stars

Ten of the game's top players are spotlighted on these 1996 Fleer Update inserts. The cards were seeded one per every 11 packs.

		MT
Complete Set (10):		40.00
Common Player:		1.00
1	Jeff Bagwell	3.00
2	Barry Bonds	2.50
3	Juan Gonzalez	5.00
4	Ken Griffey Jr.	10.00
5	Chipper Jones	6.00
6	Greg Maddux	6.00
7	Mike Piazza	6.00
8	Manny Ramirez	2.50
9	Frank Thomas	8.00
10	Matt Williams	1.00

1996 Fleer Zone

The toughest pull (one in 90 packs, average) among the '96 Fleer chase cards is this set evoking the "zone" that the game's great players seek in which their performance is at its peak. The cards have action photos with a background of prismatic foil. Backs are conventionally printed but simulate the foil background and include a player portrait photo plus quotes about the player.

		MT
Complete Set (12):		160.00
Common Player:		6.00
1	Albert Belle	10.00
2	Barry Bonds	10.00
3	Ken Griffey Jr.	40.00
4	Tony Gwynn	20.00
5	Randy Johnson	8.00
6	Kenny Lofton	10.00
7	Greg Maddux	25.00
8	Edgar Martinez	6.00
9	Mike Piazza	25.00
10	Frank Thomas	30.00
11	Mo Vaughn	10.00
12	Matt Williams	8.00

1997 Fleer

Fleer maintained its matte-finish coating for 1997 after it debuted in the 1996 product. The regular-issue set had 500 cards equipped with icons designating All-Stars, League Leaders and World Series cards. There were also 10 checklist cards in the regular-issue set, featuring stars on the front. Fleer arrived in 10-card packs and had a Tiffany Collection parallel set and six different insert sets, including Rookie Sensations, Golden Memories, Team Leaders, Night and Day, Zone and Lumber Company.

		MT
Complete Set (761):		65.00
Complete Series 1 Set (500):		40.00
Complete Series 2 Set (261):		25.00
Common Player:		.05
Complete Tiffany Set (1-761):		3500.
Ser. 1 Tiffany Veteran Stars: 25x to 40x		
Ser. 1 Young Stars & RC's: 15x to 25x		
Ser. 2 Tiffany Veteran Stars: 20x to 30x		
Ser. 2 Yng. Stars & RC's: 10x to 15x		
Wax Box:		50.00
1	Roberto Alomar	.60
2	Brady Anderson	.10
3	Bobby Bonilla	.10
4	Rocky Coppinger	.05
5	Cesar Devarez	.05
6	Scott Erickson	.05
7	Jeffrey Hammonds	.05
8	Chris Hoiles	.05
9	Eddie Murray	.40
10	Mike Mussina	.60
11	Randy Myers	.05
12	Rafael Palmeiro	.15
13	Cal Ripken Jr.	2.50
14	B.J. Surhoff	.05
15	David Wells	.05
16	Todd Zeile	.05
17	Darren Bragg	.05
18	Jose Canseco	.25
19	Roger Clemens	.75
20	Wil Cordero	.05
21	Jeff Frye	.05
22	Nomar Garciaparra	2.00
23	Tom Gordon	.05
24	Mike Greenwell	.05
25	Reggie Jefferson	.05
26	Jose Malave	.05
27	Tim Naehring	.05
28	Troy O'Leary	.05
29	Heathcliff Slocumb	.05
30	Mike Stanley	.05
31	John Valentin	.05
32	Mo Vaughn	1.00
33	Tim Wakefield	.05
34	Garret Anderson	.05
35	George Arias	.05
36	Shawn Boskie	.05
37	Chili Davis	.05
38	Jason Dickson	.25
39	Gary DiSarcina	.05
40	Jim Edmonds	.05
41	Darin Erstad	1.25
42	Jorge Fabregas	.05
43	Chuck Finley	.05
44	Todd Greene	.05
45	*Mike Holtz*	.10
46	Rex Hudler	.05
47	Mike James	.05
48	Mark Langston	.05
49	Troy Percival	.05
50	Tim Salmon	.20
51	Jeff Schmidt	.05
52	J.T. Snow	.05
53	Randy Velarde	.05
54	Wilson Alvarez	.05
55	Harold Baines	.05
56	James Baldwin	.05
57	Jason Bere	.05
58	Mike Cameron	.05
59	Ray Durham	.05
60	Alex Fernandez	.05
61	Ozzie Guillen	.05
62	Roberto Hernandez	.05
63	Ron Karkovice	.05
64	Darren Lewis	.05
65	Dave Martinez	.05
66	Lyle Mouton	.05
67	Greg Norton	.05
68	Tony Phillips	.05
69	Chris Snopek	.05
70	Kevin Tapani	.05
71	Danny Tartabull	.05
72	Frank Thomas	2.50
73	Robin Ventura	.05
74	Sandy Alomar Jr.	.05
75	Albert Belle	.75
76	Mark Carreon	.05
77	Julio Franco	.05
78	Brian Giles	.05
79	Orel Hershiser	.05
80	Kenny Lofton	.75
81	Dennis Martinez	.05
82	Jack McDowell	.05
83	Jose Mesa	.05
84	Charles Nagy	.05
85	Chad Ogea	.05
86	Eric Plunk	.05
87	Manny Ramirez	.75
88	Kevin Seitzer	.05
89	Julian Tavarez	.05
90	Jim Thome	.25
91	Jose Vizcaino	.05
92	Omar Vizquel	.05
93	Brad Ausmus	.05
94	Kimera Bartee	.05
95	Raul Casanova	.05
96	Tony Clark	.60
97	John Cummings	.05
98	Travis Fryman	.05
99	Bob Higginson	.05
100	Mark Lewis	.05
101	Felipe Lira	.05
102	Phil Nevin	.05
103	Melvin Nieves	.05
104	Curtis Pride	.05
105	A.J. Sager	.05
106	Ruben Sierra	.05
107	Justin Thompson	.05
108	Alan Trammell	.05
109	Kevin Appier	.05
110	Tim Belcher	.05
111	Jaime Bluma	.05
112	Johnny Damon	.15
113	Tom Goodwin	.05
114	Chris Haney	.05
115	Keith Lockhart	.05
116	Mike Macfarlane	.05
117	Jeff Montgomery	.05
118	Jose Offerman	.05
119	Craig Paquette	.05
120	Joe Randa	.05
121	Bip Roberts	.05
122	Jose Rosado	.05
123	Mike Sweeney	.05
124	Michael Tucker	.05
125	Jeromy Burnitz	.05
126	Jeff Cirillo	.05
127	Jeff D'Amico	.05
128	Mike Fetters	.05
129	John Jaha	.05
130	Scott Karl	.05
131	Jesse Levis	.05
132	Mark Loretta	.05
133	Mike Matheny	.05
134	Ben McDonald	.05
135	Matt Mieske	.05
136	Marc Newfield	.05
137	Dave Nilsson	.05
138	Jose Valentin	.05
139	Fernando Vina	.05
140	Bob Wickman	.05
141	Gerald Williams	.05
142	Rick Aguilera	.05
143	Rich Becker	.05
144	Ron Coomer	.05
145	Marty Cordova	.10
146	Roberto Kelly	.05
147	Chuck Knoblauch	.10
148	Matt Lawton	.05
149	Pat Meares	.05
150	Travis Miller	.05
151	Paul Molitor	.30
152	Greg Myers	.05
153	Dan Naulty	.05
154	Kirby Puckett	1.00
155	Brad Radke	.05
156	Frank Rodriguez	.05
157	Scott Stahoviak	.05
158	Dave Stevens	.05
159	Matt Walbeck	.05
160	Todd Walker	.50
161	Wade Boggs	.15
162	David Cone	.10
163	Mariano Duncan	.05
164	Cecil Fielder	.15
165	Joe Girardi	.05
166	Dwight Gooden	.05
167	Charlie Hayes	.05
168	Derek Jeter	1.50
169	Jimmy Key	.05
170	Jim Leyritz	.05
171	Tino Martinez	.30
172	*Ramiro Mendoza*	.05
173	Jeff Nelson	.05
174	Paul O'Neill	.75
175	Andy Pettitte	.75
176	Mariano Rivera	.15
177	Ruben Rivera	.35
178	Kenny Rogers	.05
179	Darryl Strawberry	.05
180	John Wetteland	.05
181	Bernie Williams	.40
182	Willie Adams	.05
183	Tony Batista	.05
184	Geronimo Berroa	.05
185	Mike Bordick	.05
186	Scott Brosius	.05
187	Bobby Chouinard	.05
188	Jim Corsi	.05
189	Brent Gates	.05
190	Jason Giambi	.05
191	Jose Herrera	.05
192	*Damon Mashore*	.05
193	Mark McGwire	4.00
194	Mike Mohler	.05
195	Scott Spiezio	.05
196	Terry Steinbach	.05
197	Bill Taylor	.05
198	John Wasdin	.05
199	Steve Wojciechowski	.05
200	Ernie Young	.05
201	Rich Amaral	.05
202	Jay Buhner	.15
203	Norm Charlton	.05

No.	Player	Price	No.	Player	Price	No.	Player	Price
204	Joey Cora	.05	300	Joe Oliver	.05	396	Pete Harnisch	.05
205	Russ Davis	.05	301	Mark Portugal	.05	397	Todd Hundley	.05
206	Ken Griffey Jr.	3.00	302	Roger Salkeld	.05	398	Butch Huskey	.05
207	Sterling Hitchcock	.05	303	Reggie Sanders	.05	399	Jason Isringhausen	.10
208	Brian Hunter	.05	304	Pete Schourek	.05	400	Lance Johnson	.05
209	Raul Ibanez	.05	305	John Smiley	.05	401	Bobby Jones	.05
210	Randy Johnson	.30	306	Eddie Taubensee	.05	402	Alex Ochoa	.05
211	Edgar Martinez	.05	307	Dante Bichette	.20	403	Rey Ordonez	.20
212	Jamie Moyer	.05	308	Ellis Burks	.05	404	Robert Person	.05
213	Alex Rodriguez	3.00	309	Vinny Castilla	.05	405	Paul Wilson	.15
214	Paul Sorrento	.05	310	Andres Galarraga	.15	406	Matt Beech	.05
215	Matt Wagner	.05	311	Curt Leskanic	.05	407	Ron Blazier	.05
216	Bob Wells	.05	312	Quinton McCracken	.05	408	Ricky Bottalico	.05
217	Dan Wilson	.05	313	Neifi Perez	.05	409	Lenny Dykstra	.05
218	Damon Buford	.05	314	Jeff Reed	.05	410	Jim Eisenreich	.05
219	Will Clark	.25	315	Steve Reed	.05	411	Bobby Estalella	.05
220	Kevin Elster	.05	316	Armando Reynoso	.05	412	Mike Grace	.15
221	Juan Gonzalez	1.50	317	Kevin Ritz	.05	413	Gregg Jefferies	.05
222	Rusty Greer	.05	318	Bruce Ruffin	.05	414	Mike Lieberthal	.05
223	Kevin Gross	.05	319	Larry Walker	.30	415	Wendell Magee Jr.	.05
224	Darryl Hamilton	.05	320	Walt Weiss	.05	416	Mickey Morandini	.05
225	Mike Henneman	.05	321	Jamey Wright	.05	417	Ricky Otero	.05
226	Ken Hill	.05	322	Eric Young	.05	418	Scott Rolen	1.50
227	Mark McLemore	.05	323	Kurt Abbott	.05	419	Ken Ryan	.05
228	Darren Oliver	.05	324	Alex Arias	.05	420	Benito Santiago	.05
229	Dean Palmer	.05	325	Kevin Brown	.05	421	Curt Schilling	.05
230	Roger Pavlik	.05	326	Luis Castillo	.15	422	Kevin Sefcik	.05
231	Ivan Rodriguez	.50	327	Greg Colbrunn	.05	423	Jermaine Allensworth	.05
232	Mickey Tettleton	.05	328	Jeff Conine	.05	424	Trey Beamon	.05
233	Bobby Witt	.05	329	Andre Dawson	.05	425	Jay Bell	.05
234	Jacob Brumfield	.05	330	Charles Johnson	.05	426	Francisco Cordova	.10
235	Joe Carter	.20	331	Al Leiter	.05	427	Carlos Garcia	.05
236	Tim Crabtree	.05	332	Ralph Milliard	.05	428	Mark Johnson	.05
237	Carlos Delgado	.05	333	Robb Nen	.05	429	Jason Kendall	.05
238	Huck Flener	.05	334	Pat Rapp	.05	430	Jeff King	.05
239	Alex Gonzalez	.05	335	Edgar Renteria	.25	431	Jon Lieber	.05
240	Shawn Green	.05	336	Gary Sheffield	.25	432	Al Martin	.05
241	Juan Guzman	.05	337	Devon White	.05	433	Orlando Merced	.05
242	Pat Hentgen	.05	338	Bob Abreu	.05	434	Ramon Morel	.05
243	Marty Janzen	.05	339	Jeff Bagwell	1.25	435	Matt Ruebel	.05
244	Sandy Martinez	.05	340	Derek Bell	.05	436	Jason Schmidt	.05
245	Otis Nixon	.05	341	Sean Berry	.05	437	*Marc Wilkins*	.05
246	Charlie O'Brien	.05	342	Craig Biggio	.25	438	Alan Benes	.15
247	John Olerud	.05	343	Doug Drabek	.05	439	Andy Benes	.05
248	Robert Perez	.05	344	Tony Eusebio	.05	440	Royce Clayton	.05
249	Ed Sprague	.05	345	Ricky Gutierrez	.05	441	Dennis Eckersley	.05
250	Mike Timlin	.05	346	Mike Hampton	.05	442	Gary Gaetti	.05
251	Steve Avery	.05	347	Brian Hunter	.05	443	Ron Gant	.10
252	Jeff Blauser	.05	348	Todd Jones	.05	444	Aaron Holbert	.05
253	Brad Clontz	.05	349	Darryl Kile	.05	445	Brian Jordan	.05
254	Jermaine Dye	.20	350	Derrick May	.05	446	Ray Lankford	.05
255	Tom Glavine	.10	351	Orlando Miller	.05	447	John Mabry	.05
256	Marquis Grissom	.05	352	James Mouton	.05	448	T.J. Mathews	.05
257	Andruw Jones	1.50	353	Shane Reynolds	.05	449	Willie McGee	.05
258	Chipper Jones	2.00	354	Billy Wagner	.05	450	Donovan Osborne	.05
259	David Justice	.15	355	Donne Wall	.05	451	Tom Pagnozzi	.05
260	Ryan Klesko	.40	356	Mike Blowers	.05	452	Ozzie Smith	.40
261	Mark Lemke	.05	357	Brett Butler	.05	453	Todd Stottlemyre	.05
262	Javier Lopez	.10	358	Roger Cedeno	.05	454	Mark Sweeney	.05
263	Greg Maddux	2.00	259	Chad Curtis	.05	455	Dmitri Young	.05
264	Fred McGriff	.35	360	Delino DeShields	.05	456	Andy Ashby	.05
265	Greg McMichael	.05	361	Greg Gagne	.05	457	Ken Caminiti	.15
266	Denny Neagle	.05	362	Karim Garcia	.50	458	Archi Cianfrocco	.05
267	Terry Pendleton	.05	363	Wilton Guerrero	.25	459	Steve Finley	.05
268	Eddie Perez	.05	364	Todd Hollandsworth	.15	460	John Flaherty	.05
269	John Smoltz	.15	365	Eric Karros	.05	461	Chris Gomez	.05
270	Terrell Wade	.05	366	Ramon Martinez	.05	462	Tony Gwynn	1.25
271	Mark Wohlers	.05	367	Raul Mondesi	.25	463	Joey Hamilton	.05
272	Terry Adams	.05	368	Hideo Nomo	.60	464	Rickey Henderson	.05
273	Brant Brown	.05	369	Antonio Osuna	.05	465	Trevor Hoffman	.05
274	Leo Gomez	.05	370	Chan Ho Park	.05	466	Brian Johnson	.05
275	Luis Gonzalez	.05	371	Mike Piazza	2.00	467	Wally Joyner	.05
276	Mark Grace	.15	372	Ismael Valdes	.05	468	Jody Reed	.05
277	Tyler Houston	.05	373	Todd Worrell	.05	469	Scott Sanders	.05
278	Robin Jennings	.05	374	Moises Alou	.05	470	Bob Tewksbury	.05
279	Brooks Kieschnick	.05	375	Shane Andrews	.05	471	Fernando Valenzuela	.05
280	Brian McRae	.05	376	Yamil Benitez	.05	472	Greg Vaughn	.05
281	Jaime Navarro	.05	377	Jeff Fassero	.05	473	Tim Worrell	.05
282	Ryne Sandberg	.75	378	Darrin Fletcher	.05	474	Rich Aurilla	.05
283	Scott Servais	.05	379	Cliff Floyd	.05	475	Rod Beck	.05
284	Sammy Sosa	1.50	380	Mark Grudzielanek	.05	476	Marvin Benard	.05
285	*Dave Swartzbaugh*	.05	381	Mike Lansing	.05	477	Barry Bonds	.75
286	Amaury Telemaco	.05	382	Barry Manuel	.05	478	Jay Canizaro	.05
287	Steve Trachsel	.05	383	Pedro J. Martinez	.05	479	Shawon Dunston	.05
288	*Pedro Valdes*	.05	384	Henry Rodriguez	.05	480	Shawn Estes	.05
289	Turk Wendell	.05	385	Mel Rojas	.05	481	Mark Gardner	.05
290	Bret Boone	.05	386	F.P. Santangelo	.05	482	Glenallen Hill	.05
291	Jeff Branson	.05	387	David Segui	.05	483	Stan Javier	.05
292	Jeff Brantley	.05	388	Ugueth Urbina	.05	484	Marcus Jensen	.05
293	Eric Davis	.05	389	Rondell White	.05	485	*Bill Mueller*	.05
294	Willie Greene	.05	390	Edgardo Alfonzo	.05	486	William VanLandingham	.05
295	Thomas Howard	.05	391	Carlos Baerga	.10	487	Allen Watson	.05
296	Barry Larkin	.20	392	Mark Clark	.05	488	Rick Wilkins	.05
297	Kevin Mitchell	.05	393	Alvaro Espinoza	.05	489	Matt Williams	.25
298	Hal Morris	.05	394	John Franco	.05	489p	Matt Williams ("PROMOTIONAL SAMPLE")	3.00
299	Chad Mottola	.05	395	Bernard Gilkey	.05			

No.	Player	Price
490	Desi Wilson	.05
491	Checklist(Albert Belle)	.35
492	Checklist(Ken Griffey Jr.)	1.00
493	Checklist(Andruw Jones)	.50
494	Checklist(Chipper Jones)	.60
495	Checklist(Mark McGwire)	1.00
496	Checklist(Paul Molitor)	.15
497	Checklist(Mike Piazza)	.60
498	Checklist(Cal Ripken Jr.)	.75
499	Checklist(Alex Rodriguez)	1.00
500	Checklist(Frank Thomas)	1.00
501	Kenny Lofton	.75
502	Carlos Perez	.05
503	Tim Raines	.05
504	*Danny Patterson*	.20
505	Derrick May	.05
506	Dave Hollins	.05
507	Felipe Crespo	.05
508	Brian Banks	.05
509	Jeff Kent	.05
510	*Bubba Trammell*	.75
511	Robert Person	.05
512	*David Arias* (last name actually Ortiz)	1.00
513	Ryan Jones	.05
514	David Justice	.15
515	Will Cunnane	.05
516	Russ Johnson	.05
517	John Burkett	.05
518	*Robinson Checo*	.25
519	*Ricardo Rincon*	.15
520	Woody Williams	.05
521	Rick Helling	.05
522	Jorge Posada	.05
523	Kevin Orie	.05
524	*Fernando Tatis*	1.00
525	Jermaine Dye	.05
526	Brian Hunter	.05
527	Greg McMichael	.05
528	Matt Wagner	.05
529	Richie Sexson	.05
530	Scott Ruffcorn	.05
531	Luis Gonzalez	.05
532	Mike Johnson	.05
533	Mark Petkovsek	.05
534	Doug Drabek	.05
535	Jose Canseco	.25
536	Bobby Bonilla	.05
537	J.T. Snow	.05
538	Shawon Dunston	.05
539	John Ericks	.05
540	Terry Steinbach	.05
541	Jay Bell	.05
542	Joe Borowski	.05
543	David Wells	.05
544	*Justin Towle*	.25
545	Mike Blowers	.05
546	Shannon Stewart	.05
547	Rudy Pemberton	.05
548	Bill Swift	.05
549	Osvaldo Fernandez	.05
550	Eddie Murray	.35
551	Don Wengert	.05
552	Brad Ausmus	.05
553	Carlos Garcia	.05
554	Jose Guillen	.60
555	Rheal Cormier	.05
556	Doug Brocail	.05
557	Rex Hudler	.05
558	Armando Benitez	.05
559	Elieser Marrero	.05
560	*Ricky Ledee*	1.50
561	Bartolo Colon	.05
562	Quilvio Veras	.05
563	Alex Fernandez	.05
564	Darren Dreifort	.05
565	Benji Gil	.05
566	Kent Mercker	.05
567	Glendon Rusch	.05
568	*Ramon Tatis*	.05
569	Roger Clemens	1.25
570	Mark Lewis	.05
571	*Emil Brown*	.15
572	Jaime Navarro	.05
573	Sherman Obando	.05
574	John Wasdin	.05
575	Calvin Maduro	.05
576	Todd Jones	.05
577	Orlando Merced	.05
578	Cal Eldred	.05
579	Mark Gubicza	.05
580	Michael Tucker	.05
581	*Tony Saunders*	.50
582	Garvin Alston	.05
583	Joe Roa	.05
584	*Brady Raggio*	.05
585	Jimmy Key	.05
586	*Marc Sagmoen*	.05
587	Jim Bullinger	.05
588	Yorkis Perez	.05
589	*Jose Cruz Jr.*	3.00
590	Mike Stanton	.05
591	*Deivi Cruz*	.50
592	Steve Karsay	.05
593	Mike Trombley	.05
594	Doug Glanville	.05
595	Scott Sanders	.05
596	Thomas Howard	.05
597	T.J. Staton	.05
598	Garrett Stephenson	.05
599	Rico Brogna	.05
600	Albert Belle	.75
601	Jose Vizcaino	.05
602	Chili Davis	.05
603	Shane Mack	.05
604	Jim Eisenreich	.05
605	Todd Zeile	.05
606	Brian Boehringer	.05
607	Paul Shuey	.05
608	Kevin Tapani	.05
609	John Wetteland	.05
610	Jim Leyritz	.05
611	Ray Montgomery	.05
612	Doug Bochtler	.05
613	Wady Almonte	.05
614	Danny Tartabull	.05
615	Orlando Miller	.05
616	Bobby Ayala	.05
617	Tony Graffanino	.05
618	Marc Valdes	.05
619	Ron Villone	.05
620	Derrek Lee	.05
621	Greg Colbrunn	.05
622	*Felix Heredia*	.25
623	Carl Everett	.05
624	Mark Thompson	.05
625	Jeff Granger	.05
626	Damian Jackson	.05
627	Mark Leiter	.05
628	Chris Holt	.05
629	*Dario Veras*	.15
630	Dave Burba	.05
631	Darryl Hamilton	.05
632	Mark Acre	.05
633	Fernando Hernandez	.05
634	Terry Mulholland	.05
635	Dustin Hermanson	.05
636	Delino DeShields	.05
637	Steve Avery	.05
638	*Tony Womack*	.25
639	Mark Whiten	.05
640	Marquis Grissom	.05
641	Xavier Hernandez	.05
642	Eric Davis	.05
643	Bob Tewksbury	.05
644	Dante Powell	.05
645	Carlos Castillo	.05
646	Chris Widger	.05
647	Moises Alou	.05
648	Pat Listach	.05
649	Edgar Ramos	.05
650	Deion Sanders	.20
651	John Olerud	.05
652	Todd Dunwoody	.30
653	*Randall Simon*	1.00
654	Dan Carlson	.05
655	Matt Williams	.25
656	Jeff King	.05
657	Luis Alicea	.05
658	Brian Moehler	.05
659	Ariel Prieto	.05
660	Kevin Elster	.05
661	Mark Hutton	.05
662	Aaron Sele	.05
663	Graeme Lloyd	.05
664	John Burke	.05
665	Mel Rojas	.05
666	Sid Fernandez	.05
667	Pedro Astacio	.05
668	Jeff Abbott	.05
669	Darren Daulton	.05
670	Mike Bordick	.05
671	Sterling Hitchcock	.05
672	Damion Easley	.05
673	Armando Reynoso	.05
674	Pat Cline	.05
675	*Orlando Cabrera*	.30
676	Alan Embree	.05
677	Brian Bevil	.05
678	David Weathers	.05
679	Cliff Floyd	.05
680	Joe Randa	.05
681	Bill Haselman	.05
682	Jeff Fassero	.05
683	Matt Morris	.05
684	Mark Portugal	.05
685	Lee Smith	.05
686	Pokey Reese	.05
687	Benito Santiago	.05
688	Brian Johnson	.05
689	*Brent Brede*	.05
690	Shigetosi Hasegawa	.05
691	Julio Santana	.05
692	Steve Kline	.05
693	Julian Tavarez	.05
694	John Hudek	.05
695	Manny Alexander	.05
696	Roberto Alomar (Encore)	.30
697	Jeff Bagwell (Encore)	.60
698	Barry Bonds (Encore)	.40
699	Ken Caminiti (Encore)	.10
700	Juan Gonzalez (Encore)	.60
701	Ken Griffey Jr. (Encore)	1.50
702	Tony Gwynn (Encore)	.60
703	Derek Jeter (Encore)	1.00
704	Andruw Jones (Encore)	.75
705	Chipper Jones (Encore)	1.00
706	Barry Larkin (Encore)	.25
707	Greg Maddux (Encore)	1.00
708	Mark McGwire (Encore)	2.00
709	Paul Molitor (Encore)	.15
710	Hideo Nomo (Encore)	.30
711	Andy Pettitte (Encore)	.40
712	Mike Piazza (Encore)	1.00
713	Manny Ramirez (Encore)	.40
714	Cal Ripken Jr. (Encore)	1.25
715	Alex Rodriguez (Encore)	1.50
716	Ryne Sandberg (Encore)	.40
717	John Smoltz (Encore)	.05
718	Frank Thomas (Encore)	1.25
719	Mo Vaughn (Encore)	.40
720	Bernie Williams (Encore)	.30
721	Checklist(Tim Salmon)	.05
722	Checklist(Greg Maddux)	.50
723	Checklist(Cal Ripken Jr.)	.75
724	Checklist(Mo Vaughn)	.25
725	Checklist(Ryne Sandberg)	.25
726	Checklist(Frank Thomas)	1.00
727	Checklist(Barry Larkin)	.05
728	Checklist(Manny Ramirez)	.25
729	Checklist(Andres Galarraga)	.05
730	Checklist(Tony Clark)	.25
731	Checklist(Gary Sheffield)	.15
732	Checklist(Jeff Bagwell)	.35
733	Checklist(Kevin Appier)	.05
734	Checklist(Mike Piazza)	.50
735	Checklist(Jeff Cirillo)	.05
736	Checklist(Paul Molitor)	.15
737	Checklist(Henry Rodriguez)	.05
738	Checklist(Todd Hundley)	.10
739	Checklist(Derek Jeter)	.50
740	Checklist(Mark McGwire)	.75
741	Checklist(Curt Schilling)	.05
742	Checklist(Jason Kendall)	.05
743	Checklist(Tony Gwynn)	.40
744	Checklist(Barry Bonds)	.25
745	Checklist(Ken Griffey Jr.)	1.00
746	Checklist(Brian Jordan)	.05
747	Checklist(Juan Gonzalez)	.40
748	Checklist(Joe Carter)	.05
749	Arizona Diamondbacks	.05
750	Tampa Bay Devil Rays	.05
751	*Hideki Irabu*	2.00
752	*Jeremi Gonzalez*	.60
753	*Mario Valdez*	.25
754	Aaron Boone	.05
755	Brett Tomko	.05
756	*Jaret Wright*	4.00
757	Ryan McGuire	.05
758	Jason McDonald	.05
759	*Adrian Brown*	.20
760	*Keith Foulke*	.25
761	Checklist	.05

1997 Fleer Bleacher Blasters

This 10-card insert features some of the game's top power hitters and was found in retail packs only. Cards featured a die-cut "burst" pattern on an etched foil background. Backs have a portrait photo and career highlights. Cards were inserted 1:36 packs.

		MT
Complete Set (10):		60.00
Common Player:		2.00
1	Albert Belle	4.00
2	Barry Bonds	4.00
3	Juan Gonzalez	7.00
4	Ken Griffey Jr.	15.00
5	Mark McGwire	15.00
6	Mike Piazza	9.00
7	Alex Rodriguez	15.00
8	Frank Thomas	10.00
9	Mo Vaughn	4.00
10	Matt Williams	2.00

1997 Fleer Decade of Excellence

A 12-card insert found only 1:36 hobby shop packs. Cards are in a format similar to the 1987 Fleer set and feature vintage photos of players who started their careers no later than the '87 season. Ten percent of the press run received a special foil treatment and designation as "Rare Traditions."

		MT
Complete Set (12):		70.00
Common Player:		3.00
1	Wade Boggs	3.00
2	Barry Bonds	6.00
3	Roger Clemens	8.00
4	Tony Gwynn	10.00
5	Rickey Henderson	3.00
6	Greg Maddux	15.00
7	Mark McGwire	25.00
8	Paul Molitor	4.00
9	Eddie Murray	4.00
10	Cal Ripken Jr.	20.00
11	Ryne Sandberg	6.00
12	Matt Williams	4.00

1997 Fleer Diamond Tribute

Twelve of the game's top stars are highlighted in this set. Fronts feature an embossed rainbow prismatic foil background and gold lettering. Backs have an action photo and a few sentences about the player. They were inserted 1:288 packs.

		MT
Complete Set (12):		500.00
Common Player:		10.00
1	Albert Belle	20.00
2	Barry Bonds	20.00
3	Juan Gonzalez	40.00
4	Ken Griffey Jr.	80.00
5	Tony Gwynn	40.00
6	Greg Maddux	50.00
7	Mark McGwire	100.00
8	Eddie Murray	10.00
9	Mike Piazza	50.00
10	Cal Ripken Jr.	60.00
11	Alex Rodriguez	60.00
12	Frank Thomas	50.00

1997 Fleer Golden Memories

Golden Memories captures 10 different highlights from the 1996 season, and is inserted one per 16 packs. Moments like Dwight Gooden's no hitter, Paul Molitor's 3000th hit and Eddie Murray's 500th home run are highlighted on a horizontal format.

		MT
Complete Set (10):		20.00
Common Player:		.75
1	Barry Bonds	2.00
2	Dwight Gooden	.75
3	Todd Hundley	1.00
4	Mark McGwire	6.00
5	Paul Molitor	1.25
6	Eddie Murray	1.00
7	Hideo Nomo	2.00
8	Mike Piazza	5.00
9	Cal Ripken Jr.	6.00
10	Ozzie Smith	2.00

1997 Fleer Goudey Greats

Using a 2-3/8" x 2-7/8" format reminiscent of 1933 Goudey cards, this 15-card insert offers today's top players in classic old-time design. Cards were inserted 1:8 packs. A limited number (1% of press run) of cards received a special foil treatment and were found only in hobby packs.

		MT
Complete Set (15):		30.00
Common Player:		.50
Foils: 20x to 40x		
1	Barry Bonds	1.00
2	Ken Griffey Jr.	5.00
3	Tony Gwynn	2.00
4	Derek Jeter	3.00
5	Chipper Jones	3.00
6	Kenny Lofton	1.00
7	Greg Maddux	3.00
8	Mark McGwire	5.00
9	Eddie Murray	.50
10	Mike Piazza	3.00
11	Cal Ripken Jr.	4.00
12	Alex Rodriguez	5.00
13	Ryne Sandberg	1.00
14	Frank Thomas	4.00
15	Mo Vaughn	1.00

1997 Fleer Headliners

This 20-card insert highlights the personal achievements of each of the players depicted. Cards were inserted 1:2 packs and feature multi-color foil stamping on the fronts and a newspaper-style account of the player's achievement on the back.

		MT
Complete Set (20):		12.00
Common Player:		.20
1	Jeff Bagwell	.75
2	Albert Belle	.50
3	Barry Bonds	.50
4	Ken Caminiti	.20
5	Juan Gonzalez	.75
6	Ken Griffey Jr.	2.00
7	Tony Gwynn	.75
8	Derek Jeter	1.25
9	Andruw Jones	1.00
10	Chipper Jones	1.25
11	Greg Maddux	1.25
12	Mark McGwire	2.50
13	Paul Molitor	.30
14	Eddie Murray	.30
15	Mike Piazza	1.25
16	Cal Ripken Jr.	1.50
17	Alex Rodriguez	2.00
18	Ryne Sandberg	.50
19	John Smoltz	.20
20	Frank Thomas	1.50

1997 Fleer Lumber Company

Lumber Company inserts were found every 48 retail packs. The cards were printed on a die-cut, spherical wood-like pattern, with the player imposed on the left side. Eighteen of the top power hitters in baseball are highlighted.

		MT
Complete Set (18):		150.00
Common Player:		3.00
1	Brady Anderson	3.00
2	Jeff Bagwell	10.00
3	Albert Belle	8.00
4	Barry Bonds	8.00
5	Jay Buhner	4.00
6	Ellis Burks	3.00
7	Andres Galarraga	4.00
8	Juan Gonzalez	15.00
9	Ken Griffey Jr.	30.00
10	Todd Hundley	3.00
11	Ryan Klesko	4.00
12	Mark McGwire	35.00
13	Mike Piazza	20.00
14	Alex Rodriguez	20.00
15	Gary Sheffield	4.00
16	Sammy Sosa	20.00
17	Frank Thomas	25.00
18	Mo Vaughn	8.00

1997-98 Fleer Million Dollar Moments

By assembling a complete set of 50 baseball "Million Dollar Moments" cards prior to July 31, 1998, a collector could win $50,000 a year through 2018. The catch, of course, is that cards #46-50 were printed in very limited quantities, with only one card #50. (Stated

odds of winning the million were one in nearly 46,000,000.) The Moments cards have player action photos on front vignetted into a black border. The Fleer Million Dollar Moments logo is at top, with the player name and the date and details of his highlight at bottom in orange and white. Backs have the contest rules in fine print. Instant Win versions of some cards were also issued.

		MT
Complete Set (45):		4.00
Common Player:		.05
1	Checklist	.05
2	Derek Jeter	.10
3	Babe Ruth	.25
4	Barry Bonds	.05
5	Brooks Robinson	.05
6	Todd Hundley	.05
7	Johnny Vander Meer	.05
8	Cal Ripken Jr.	.25
9	Bill Mazeroski	.10
10	Chipper Jones	.15
11	Frank Robinson	.05
12	Roger Clemens	.10
13	Bob Feller	.05
14	Mike Piazza	.10
15	Joe Nuxhall	.05
16	Hideo Nomo	.08
17	Jackie Robinson	.25
18	Orel Hershiser	.05
19	Bobby Thomson	.05
20	Joe Carter	.05
21	Al Kaline	.05
22	Bernie Williams	.05
23	Don Larsen	.05
24	Rickey Henderson	.05
25	Maury Wills	.05
26	Andruw Jones	.10
27	Bobby Richardson	.05
28	Alex Rodriguez	.45
29	Jim Bunning	.05
30	Ken Caminiti	.05
31	Bob Gibson	.05
32	Frank Thomas	.40
33	Mickey Lolich	.05
34	John Smoltz	.05
35	Ron Swoboda	.05
36	Albert Belle	.10
37	Chris Chambliss	.05
38	Juan Gonzalez	.10
39	Ron Blomberg	.05
40	John Wetteland	.05
41	Carlton Fisk	.05
42	Mo Vaughn	.08
43	Bucky Dent	.05
44	Greg Maddux	.10
45	Willie Stargell	.05
46	Tony Gwynn	
47	Joel Youngblood	
48	Andy Pettitte ($500 winner)	
49	Mookie Wilson	
50	Jeff Bagwell ($1 million winner)	

1997 Fleer New Horizons

Rookies and prospects expected to make an impact during the 1996 season were featured in this 15-card insert set. Card fronts feature a rainbow foil background with the words "New Horizon" featured prominently on the bottom under the player's name. Cards were inserted 1:4 packs.

		MT
Complete Set (15):		15.00
Common Player:		.25
1	Bob Abreu	.25
2	Jose Cruz Jr.	2.00
3	Darin Erstad	2.00
4	Nomar Garciaparra	2.50
5	Vladimir Guerrero	2.50
6	Wilton Guerrero	.25
7	Jose Guillen	1.00
8	Hideki Irabu	1.50
9	Andruw Jones	2.50
10	Kevin Orie	.25
11	Scott Rolen	2.00
12	Scott Spiezio	.25
13	Bubba Trammell	.75
14	Todd Walker	.50
15	Dmitri Young	.25

1997 Fleer Night & Day

Night and Day spotlighted 10 stars with unusual prowess during night or day games. These lenticular cards carried the toughest insert ratios in Fleer Baseball at one per 288 packs.

		MT
Complete Set (10):		375.00
Common Player:		10.00
1	Barry Bonds	18.00
2	Ellis Burks	10.00
3	Juan Gonzalez	35.00
4	Ken Griffey Jr.	75.00
5	Mark McGwire	80.00
6	Mike Piazza	50.00
7	Manny Ramirez	15.00
8	Alex Rodriguez	60.00
9	John Smoltz	10.00
10	Frank Thomas	60.00

1997 Fleer Rookie Sensations

Rookies Sensations showcased 20 of the top up-and-coming stars in baseball. Appearing every six packs, these inserts have the feaured player in the foreground, with the background look of painted brush strokes.

		MT
Complete Set (20):		18.00
Common Player:		.40
1	Jermaine Allensworth	.40
2	James Baldwin	.40
3	Alan Benes	.60
4	Jermaine Dye	.50
5	Darin Erstad	2.50
6	Todd Hollandsworth	.75
7	Derek Jeter	4.00
8	Jason Kendall	.60
9	Alex Ochoa	.50
10	Rey Ordonez	.75
11	Edgar Renteria	.60
12	Bob Abreu	1.00
13	Nomar Garciaparra	3.00
14	Wilton Guerrero	1.00
15	Andruw Jones	4.00
16	Wendell Magee	1.00
17	Neifi Perez	.40
18	Scott Rolen	3.00
19	Scott Spiezio	.40
20	Todd Walker	1.00

1997 Fleer Soaring Stars

A 12-card insert found 1:12 packs designed to profile players with outstanding statistical performances early in their careers. Fronts have player action photos set against a background of rain-bow holographic stars which appear, disappear and twinkle as the viewing angle is changed. Conventionally printed backs have another player pjoto and a few sentences about his career.

		MT
Complete Set (12):		35.00
Common Player:		.75
1	Albert Belle	1.50
2	Barry Bonds	1.50
3	Juan Gonzalez	3.00
4	Ken Griffey Jr.	6.00
5	Derek Jeter	4.00
6	Andruw Jones	3.00
7	Chipper Jones	4.00
8	Greg Maddux	4.00
9	Mark McGwire	8.00
10	Mike Piazza	4.00
11	Alex Rodriguez	5.00
12	Frank Thomas	5.00

1997 Fleer Sports Illustrated

Fleer teamed up with Sports Illustrated to produce a 180-card World Series Fever set. The regular set is divided into six different subsets: 96 Player Cards, 27 Fresh Faces, 18 Inside Baseball, 18 Slber Vision, 12 covers and 9 Newsmakers. Inserts included the Extra Edition parallel set, Great Shots, Cooperstown Collection and Autographed Mini-Cover Redemption Cards. Cards were sold in six-card packs for $1.99 each.

		MT
Complete Set (180):		40.00
Common Player:		.10
Extra Edition Stars: 15x-25x		
Extra Edition Yng Stars & RC's: 10x-20x		
Wax Box:		50.00
1	Bob Abreu (Fresh Faces)	.10
2	Jaime Bluma (Fresh Faces)	.10
3	Emil Brown (Fresh Faces)	.10
4	Jose Cruz, Jr. (Fresh Faces)	4.00
5	Jason Dickson (Fresh Faces)	.10
6	Nomar Garciaparra (Fresh Faces)	2.50
7	Todd Greene (Fresh Faces)	.20
8	Vladimir Guerrero (Fresh Faces)	1.50
9	Wilton Guerrero (Fresh Faces)	.10
10	Jose Guillen (Fresh Faces)	1.00
11	Hideki Irabu (Fresh Faces)	2.00
12	Russ Johnson (Fresh Faces)	.10
13	Andruw Jones (Fresh Faces)	2.00
14	Damon Mashore (Fresh Faces)	.10
15	Jason McDonald (Fresh Faces)	.10
16	Ryan McGuire (Fresh Faces)	.10
17	Matt Morris (Fresh Faces)	.10
18	Kevin Orie (Fresh Faces)	.10
19	Dante Powell (Fresh Faces)	.10
20	Pokey Reese (Fresh Faces)	.10
21	Joe Roa (Fresh Faces)	.10
22	Scott Rolen (Fresh Faces)	2.00
23	Glendon Rusch (Fresh Faces)	.10
24	Scott Spiezio (Fresh Faces)	.10
25	Bubba Trammell (Fresh Faces)	1.00
26	Todd Walker (Fresh Faces)	.75
27	Jamey Wright (Fresh Faces)	.10
28	Ken Griffey Jr. (Season Highlights)	2.00
29	Tino Martinez (Season Highlights)	.20
30	Roger Clemens (Season Highlights)	.50
31	Hideki Irabu (Season Highlights)	1.00
32	Kevin Brown (Season Highlights)	.10
33	Chipper Jones, Cal Ripken Jr. (Season Highlights)	1.25
34	Sandy Alomar (Season Highlights)	.10
35	Ken Caminiti (Season Highlights)	.20
36	Randy Johnson (Season Highlights)	.40
37	Andy Ashby (Inside Baseball)	.10
38	Jay Buhner (Inside Baseball)	.20
39	Joe Carter (Inside Baseball)	.10
40	Darren Daulton (Inside Baseball)	.10
41	Jeff Fassero (Inside Baseball)	.10
42	Andres Galarraga (Inside Baseball)	.20
43	Rusty Greer (Inside Baseball)	.10
44	Marquis Grissom (Inside Baseball)	.10
45	Joey Hamilton (Inside Baseball)	.10
46	Jimmy Key (Inside Baseball)	.10
47	Ryan Klesko (Inside Baseball)	.50
48	Eddie Murray (Inside Baseball)	.40
49	Charles Nagy (Inside Baseball)	.10
50	Dave Nilsson (Inside Baseball)	.10
51	Ricardo Rincon (Inside Baseball)	.10
52	Billy Wagner (Inside Baseball)	.10
53	Dan Wilson (Inside Baseball)	.10

54	Dmitri Young (Inside Baseball)	.10
55	Roberto Alomar (S.I.BER Vision)	.60
56	Sandy Alomar Jr. (S.I.BER Vision)	.10
57	Scott Brosius (S.I.BER Vision)	.10
58	Tony Clark (S.I.BER Vision)	.50
59	Carlos Delgado (S.I.BER Vision)	.10
60	Jermaine Dye (S.I.BER Vision)	.10
61	Darin Erstad (S.I.BER Vision)	2.00
62	Derek Jeter (S.I.BER Vision)	1.25
63	Jason Kendall (S.I.BER Vision)	.10
64	Hideo Nomo (S.I.BER Vision)	.40
65	Rey Ordonez (S.I.BER Vision)	.10
66	Andy Pettitte (S.I.BER Vision)	.50
67	Manny Ramirez (S.I.BER Vision)	.40
68	Edgar Renteria (S.I.BER Vision)	.10
69	Shane Reynolds (S.I.BER Vision)	.10
70	Alex Rodriguez (S.I.BER Vision)	1.50
71	Ivan Rodriguez (S.I.BER Vision)	.40
72	Jose Rosado (S.I.BER Vision)	.10
73	John Smoltz	.20
74	Tom Glavine	.20
75	Greg Maddux	2.50
76	Chipper Jones	2.50
77	Kenny Lofton	1.00
78	Fred McGriff	.30
79	Kevin Brown	.10
80	Alex Fernandez	.10
81	Al Leiter	.10
82	Bobby Bonilla	.10
83	Gary Sheffield	.30
84	Moises Alou	.20
85	Henry Rodriguez	.10
86	Mark Grudzielanek	.10
87	Pedro Martinez	.25
88	Todd Hundley	.20
89	Bernard Gilkey	.10
90	Bobby Jones	.10
91	Curt Schilling	.10
92	Ricky Bottalico	.10
93	Mike Lieberthal	.10
94	Sammy Sosa	2.00
95	Ryne Sandberg	1.00
96	Mark Grace	.30
97	Deion Sanders	.30
98	Reggie Sanders	.10
99	Barry Larkin	.20
100	Craig Biggio	.20
101	Jeff Bagwell	1.50
102	Derek Bell	.10
103	Brian Jordan	.10
104	Ray Lankford	.10
105	Ron Gant	.10
106	Al Martin	.10
107	Kevin Elster	.10
108	Jermaine Allensworth	.10
109	Vinny Castilla	.10
110	Dante Bichette	.20
111	Larry Walker	.30
112	Mike Piazza	2.50
113	Eric Karros	.10
114	Todd Hollandsworth	.10
115	Raul Mondesi	.25
116	Hideo Nomo	.75
117	Ramon Martinez	.10
118	Ken Caminiti	.25
119	Tony Gwynn	2.00
120	Steve Finley	.10
121	Barry Bonds	1.00
122	J.T. Snow	.10
123	Rod Beck	.10
124	Cal Ripken Jr.	3.00
125	Mike Mussina	.75
126	Brady Anderson	.10
127	Bernie Williams	.75
128	Derek Jeter	2.50
129	Tino Martinez	.30
130	Andy Pettitte	1.00
131	David Cone	.20
132	Mariano Rivera	.20
133	Roger Clemens	1.50
134	Pat Hentgen	.10
135	Juan Guzman	.10
136	Bob Higginson	.10
137	Tony Clark	1.00
138	Travis Fryman	.10
139	Mo Vaughn	1.00
140	Tim Naehring	.10
141	John Valentin	.10
142	Matt Williams	.30
143	David Justice	.30
144	Jim Thome	.60
145	Chuck Knoblauch	.25
146	Paul Molitor	.30
147	Marty Cordova	.10
148	Frank Thomas	3.00
149	Albert Belle	1.00
150	Robin Ventura	.10
151	John Jaha	.10
152	Jeff Cirillo	.10
153	Jose Valentin	.10
154	Jay Bell	.10
155	Jeff King	.10
156	Kevin Appier	.10
157	Ken Griffey Jr.	4.00
158	Alex Rodriguez	3.00
158p	Alex Rodriguez (overprinted "PROMOTIONAL SAMPLE")	3.00
159	Randy Johnson	.60
160	Juan Gonzalez	2.00
161	Will Clark	.25
162	Dean Palmer	.10
163	Tim Salmon	.25
164	Jim Edmonds	.10
165	Jim Leyritz	.10
166	Jose Canseco	.30
167	Jason Giambi	.10
168	Mark McGwire	4.00
169	Barry Bonds	1.00
170	Alex Rodriguez	1.50
171	Roger Clemens	.60
172	Ken Griffey Jr.	2.00
173	Greg Maddux	1.25
174	Mike Piazza	1.25
175	Will Clark, Mark McGwire	2.00
176	Hideo Nomo	.40
177	Cal Ripken Jr.	1.50
178	Ken Griffey Jr., Frank Thomas	1.50
179	Alex Rodriguez, Derek Jeter	1.50
180	John Wetteland	.10

		MT
Complete Set (12):		75.00
Common Player:		5.00
1	Hank Aaron	15.00
2	Yogi Berra	8.00
3	Lou Brock	5.00
4	Rod Carew	5.00
5	Juan Marichal	5.00
6	Al Kaline	5.00
7	Joe Morgan	5.00
8	Brooks Robinson	10.00
9	Willie Stargell	5.00
10	Kirby Puckett	15.00
11	Willie Mays	15.00
12	Frank Robinson	8.00

1997 Fleer Sports Illustrated Extra Edition

Each of the regular cards in the premiere Fleer SI issue is also found in a parallel set designated on front in gold holographic foil as "Extra Edition". Backs of the cards carry a serial number from within a production of 500 of each card.

	MT
Complete Set (180):	850.00
Common Player:	2.50
(Stars and rookies are valued from 25-40X regular-edition cards.)	

1997 Fleer Sports Illustrated Great Shots

A 25-card insert, found one per pack, designed to highlight Sports Illustrated's classic photography. Each card in the set folds out to a 5" x 7" format to showcase a larger photo.

		MT
Complete Set (25):		5.00
Common Player:		.10
(1)	Roberto Alomar	.20
(2)	Andy Ashby	.10
(3)	Albert Belle	.25
(4)	Barry Bonds	.25

A player's name in *italic* type indicates a rookie card.

1997 Fleer Sports Illustrated Auto Mini-Covers

Six different players auto-graphed 250 magazine mini-covers that were available through randomly seeded redemption cards. The players who autographed cards were Hank Aaron, Willie Mays, Frank Robinson, Kirby Puckett, Cal Ripken Jr., and Alex Rodriguez.

	MT
Complete Set (6):	800.00
Common Player:	75.00
Alex Rodriguez	200.00
Cal Ripken Jr.	250.00
Kirby Puckett	125.00
Willie Mays	150.00
Frank Robinson	75.00
Hank Aaron	150.00

1997 Fleer Sports Illustrated Cooperstown Collection

This 12-card insert (found 1:12 packs) lets collectors relive classic SI baseball covers with a description of each issue on the back.

(5)	Jay Buhner	.10
(6)	Vinny Castilla, Andres Galarraga	.10
(7)	Darren Daulton	.10
(8)	Juan Gonzalez	.40
(9)	Ken Griffey Jr.	1.00
(10)	Derek Jeter	.60
(11)	Randy Johnson	.15
(12)	Chipper Jones	.60
(13)	Eric Karros	.10
(14)	Ryan Klesko	.15
(15)	Kenny Lofton	.20
(16)	Greg Maddux	.45
(17)	Mark McGwire	1.00
(18)	Mike Piazza	.50
(19)	Cal Ripken Jr.	.75
(20)	Alex Rodriguez	.60
(21)	Ryne Sandberg	.25
(22)	Deion Sanders	.15
(23)	John Smoltz	.10
(24)	Frank Thomas	1.00
(25)	Mo Vaughn	.45

1997 Fleer Team Leaders

Team Leaders captured the statistical and/or inspirational leaders from all 28 teams. Inserted every 20 packs, these inserts were printed on a horizontal format, with the player's face die-cut in the perimeter of the card.

		MT
Complete Set (28):		120.00
Common Player:		2.00
1	Cal Ripken Jr.	15.00
2	Mo Vaughn	6.00
3	Jim Edmonds	2.00
4	Frank Thomas	15.00
5	Albert Belle	5.00
6	Bob Higginson	2.00
7	Kevin Appier	2.00
8	John Jaha	2.00
9	Paul Molitor	3.00
10	Andy Pettitte	5.00
11	Mark McGwire	25.00
12	Ken Griffey Jr.	20.00
13	Juan Gonzalez	10.00
14	Pat Hentgen	2.00
15	Chipper Jones	12.00
16	Mark Grace	2.50
17	Barry Larkin	2.50
18	Ellis Burks	2.00
19	Gary Sheffield	3.00
20	Jeff Bagwell	10.00
21	Mike Piazza	12.00
22	Henry Rodriguez	2.00
23	Todd Hundley	2.00
24	Curt Schilling	2.00
25	Jeff King	2.00
26	Brian Jordan	2.00
27	Tony Gwynn	12.00
28	Barry Bonds	5.00

1997 Fleer Zone

Twenty of the top hitters in baseball are featured on these holographic cards with the words Zone printed across the front. Zone inserts were found only in hobby packs at a rate of one per 80.

		MT
Complete Set (20):		275.00
Common Player:		5.00
1	Jeff Bagwell	15.00
2	Albert Belle	10.00
3	Barry Bonds	10.00
4	Ken Caminiti	5.00
5	Andres Galarraga	5.00
6	Juan Gonzalez	20.00
7	Ken Griffey Jr.	40.00
8	Tony Gwynn	20.00
9	Chipper Jones	25.00
10	Greg Maddux	25.00
11	Mark McGwire	45.00
12	Dean Palmer	5.00
13	Andy Petitte	10.00
14	Mike Piazza	25.00
15	Alex Rodriguez	30.00
16	Gary Sheffield	8.00
17	John Smoltz	5.00
18	Frank Thomas	25.00
19	Jim Thome	8.00
20	Matt Williams	6.00

1998 Fleer

Fleer was issued in two series in 1998, with 350 cards in Series I and 250 in Series II. Each card featured a borderless color action shot, with backs containing player information. Subsets in Series I included Smoke 'N Heat (301-310), Golden Memories (311-320) and Tale of the Tape (321-340). Golden Memories (1:6 packs) and Tale of the Tape (1:4) were shortprinted. Series II subsets included 25 Unforgetable Moments (571-595). In-

serts in Series I were Vintage '63, Vintage '63 Classic, Decade of Excellence, Decade of Excellence Rare Traditions, Diamond Ink, Diamond Standouts, Lumber Company, Power Game, Rookie Sensations and Zone. Inserts in Series II include: Vintage '63, Vintage '63 Classic, Promising Forecast, In the Clutch, Mickey Mantle: Monumental Moments, Mickey Mantle: Monumental Moments Gold Edition, Diamond Tribute and Diamond Ink. Card No. 7 in the regular set pictures Mickey Mantle.

		MT
Complete Set (600):		75.00
Complete Series I Set (350):		30.00
Complete Series II Set (250):		45.00
Common Player:		.10
Wax Box:		50.00
1	Ken Griffey Jr.	3.00
2	Derek Jeter	2.00
3	Gerald Williams	.10
4	Carlos Delgado	.10
5	Nomar Garciaparra	2.00
6	Gary Sheffield	.30
7	Jeff King	.10
8	Cal Ripken Jr.	2.50
9	Matt Williams	.25
10	Chipper Jones	2.00
11	Chuck Knoblauch	.25
12	Mark Grudzielanek	.10
13	Edgardo Alfonzo	.10
14	Andres Galarraga	.20
15	Tim Salmon	.25
16	Reggie Sanders	.10
17	Tony Clark	.40
18	Jason Kendall	.10
19	Juan Gonzalez	1.50
20	Ben Grieve	1.00
21	Roger Clemens	1.00
22	Raul Mondesi	.20
23	Robin Ventura	.10
24	Derek Lee	.10
25	Mark McGwire	4.00
26	Luis Gonzalez	.10
27	Kevin Brown	.20
28	Kirk Rueter	.10
29	Bobby Estalella	.10
30	Shawn Green	.10
31	Greg Maddux	2.00
32	Jorge Velandia	.10
33	Larry Walker	.25
34	Joey Cora	.10
35	Frank Thomas	2.50
36	*Curtis King*	.10
37	Aaron Boone	.10
38	Curt Schilling	.10
39	Bruce Aven	.10
40	Ben McDonald	.10
41	Andy Ashby	.10
42	Jason McDonald	.10
43	Eric Davis	.10
44	Mark Grace	.25
45	Pedro Martinez	.25
46	Lou Collier	.10
47	Chan Ho Park	.10
48	Shane Halter	.10
49	Brian Hunter	.10
50	Jeff Bagwell	1.25
51	Bernie Williams	.50
52	J.T. Snow	.10
53	Todd Greene	.10
54	Shannon Stewart	.10
55	Darren Bragg	.10
56	Fernando Tatis	.20
57	Darryl Kile	.10
58	Chris Stynes	.10
59	Javier Valentin	.10
60	Brian McRae	.10
61	Tom Evans	.10
62	Randall Simon	.20
63	Darrin Fletcher	.10
64	Jaret Wright	1.50
65	Luis Ordaz	.10
66	Jose Canseco	.20
67	Edgar Renteria	.10
68	Jay Buhner	.20
69	Paul Konerko	1.00
70	Adrian Brown	.10
71	Chris Carpenter	.10
72	Mike Lieberthal	.10

73	Dean Palmer	.10
74	Jorge Fabregas	.10
75	Stan Javier	.10
76	Damion Easley	.10
77	David Cone	.20
78	Aaron Sele	.10
79	Antonio Alfonseca	.10
80	Bobby Jones	.10
81	David Justice	.25
82	Jeffrey Hammonds	.10
83	Doug Glanville	.10
84	Jason Dickson	.10
85	Brad Radke	.10
86	David Segui	.10
87	Greg Vaughn	.10
88	*Mike Cather*	.20
89	Alex Fernandez	.10
90	Billy Taylor	.10
91	Jason Schmidt	.10
92	*Mike DeJean*	.20
93	Domingo Cedeno	.10
94	Jeff Cirillo	.10
95	*Manny Aybar*	.20
96	Jaime Navarro	.10
97	Dennis Reyes	.10
98	Barry Larkin	.20
99	Troy O'Leary	.10
100	Alex Rodriguez	2.50
101	Pat Hentgen	.10
102	Bubba Trammell	.20
103	Glendon Rusch	.10
104	Kenny Lofton	.75
105	Craig Biggio	.20
106	Kelvim Escobar	.10
107	Mark Kotsay	.40
108	Rondell White	.20
109	Darren Oliver	.10
110	Jim Thome	.40
111	Rich Becker	.10
112	Chad Curtis	.10
113	Dave Hollins	.10
114	Bill Mueller	.10
115	Antone Williamson	.10
116	Tony Womack	.10
117	Randy Myers	.10
118	Rico Brogna	.10
119	Pat Watkins	.10
120	Eli Marrero	.10
121	Jay Bell	.10
122	Kevin Tapani	.10
123	*Todd Erdos*	.20
124	Neifi Perez	.10
125	Todd Hundley	.10
126	Jeff Abbott	.10
127	Todd Zeile	.10
128	Travis Fryman	.10
129	Sandy Alomar	.10
130	Fred McGriff	.20
131	Richard Hidalgo	.10
132	Scott Spiezio	.10
133	John Valentin	.10
134	Quilvio Veras	.10
135	Mike Lansing	.10
136	Paul Molitor	.50
137	Randy Johnson	.40
138	Harold Baines	.10
139	Doug Jones	.10
140	Abraham Nunez	.25
141	Alan Benes	.20
142	Matt Perisho	.10
143	Chris Clemons	.10
144	Andy Pettitte	.50
145	Jason Giambi	.10
146	Moises Alou	.20
147	*Chad Fox*	.25
148	Felix Martinez	.10
149	*Carlos Mendoza*	.20
150	Scott Rolen	1.50
151	*Jose Cabrera*	.20
152	Justin Thompson	.10
153	Ellis Burks	.10
154	Pokey Reese	.10
155	Bartolo Colon	.10
156	Ray Durham	.10
157	Ugueth Urbina	.10
158	Tom Goodwin	.10
159	*David Dellucci*	.50
160	Rod Beck	.10
161	Ramon Martinez	.10
162	Joe Carter	.15
163	Kevin Orie	.10
164	Trevor Hoffman	.10
165	Emil Brown	.10
166	Robb Nen	.10
167	Paul O'Neill	.20
168	Ryan Long	.10

169	Ray Lankford	.10
170	Ivan Rodriguez	.60
171	Rick Aguilera	.10
172	Deivi Cruz	.10
173	Ricky Bottalico	.10
174	Garret Anderson	.10
175	Jose Vizcaino	.10
176	Omar Vizquel	.10
177	Jeff Blauser	.10
178	Orlando Cabrera	.10
179	Russ Johnson	.10
180	Matt Stairs	.10
181	Will Cunnane	.10
182	Adam Riggs	.10
183	Matt Morris	.10
184	Mario Valdez	.10
185	Larry Sutton	.10
186	*Marc Pisciotta*	.10
187	Dan Wilson	.10
188	John Franco	.10
189	Darren Daulton	.10
190	Todd Helton	.75
191	Brady Anderson	.20
192	Ricardo Rincon	.10
193	Kevin Stocker	.10
194	Jose Valentin	.10
195	Ed Sprague	.10
196	Ryan McGuire	.10
197	*Scott Eyre*	.25
198	Steve Finley	.10
199	T.J. Mathews	.10
200	Mike Piazza	2.00
201	Mark Wohlers	.10
202	Brian Giles	.10
203	Eduardo Perez	.10
204	Shigetosi Hasegawa	.10
205	Mariano Rivera	.20
206	Jose Rosado	.10
207	Michael Coleman	.10
208	James Baldwin	.10
209	Russ Davis	.10
210	Billy Wagner	.10
211	Sammy Sosa	1.50
212	*Frank Catalanotto*	.25
213	Delino DeShields	.10
214	John Olerud	.10
215	Heath Murray	.10
216	Jose Vidro	.10
217	Jim Edmonds	.20
218	Shawon Dunston	.10
219	Homer Bush	.10
220	Midre Cummings	.10
221	Tony Saunders	.20
222	Jeromy Burnitz	.10
223	Enrique Wilson	.10
224	Chili Davis	.10
225	Jerry DiPoto	.10
226	Dante Powell	.10
227	Javier Lopez	.20
228	*Kevin Polcovich*	.20
229	Deion Sanders	.25
230	Jimmy Key	.10
231	Rusty Greer	.10
232	Reggie Jefferson	.10
233	Ron Coomer	.10
234	Bobby Higginson	.20
235	*Magglio Ordonez*	.75
236	Miguel Tejada	.50
237	Rick Gorecki	.10
238	Charles Johnson	.10
239	Lance Johnson	.10
240	Derek Bell	.10
241	Will Clark	.20
242	Brady Raggio	.10
243	Orel Hershiser	.10
244	Vladimir Guerrero	1.25
245	John LeRoy	.10
246	Shawn Estes	.10
247	Brett Tomko	.10
248	Dave Nilsson	.10
249	Edgar Martinez	.10
250	Tony Gwynn	1.50
251	Mark Bellhorn	.10
252	Jed Hansen	.10
253	Butch Huskey	.10
254	Eric Young	.10
255	Vinny Castilla	.10
256	Hideki Irabu	.75
257	Mike Cameron	.10
258	Juan Encarnacion	.25
259	Brian Rose	.25
260	Brad Ausmus	.10
261	Dan Serafini	.10
262	Willie Greene	.10
263	Troy Percival	.10
264	*Jeff Wallace*	.20

265	Richie Sexson	.10
266	Rafael Palmeiro	.20
267	Brad Fullmer	.10
268	Jeremi Gonzalez	.10
269	*Rob Stanifer*	.25
270	Mickey Morandini	.10
271	Andruw Jones	1.50
272	Royce Clayton	.10
273	Takashi Kashiwada	.40
274	*Steve Woodard*	.25
275	Jose Cruz Jr.	1.50
276	Keith Foulke	.10
277	Brad Rigby	.10
278	Tino Martinez	.20
279	Todd Jones	.10
280	John Wetteland	.10
281	Alex Gonzalez	.10
282	Ken Cloude	.25
283	Jose Guillen	.40
284	Danny Clyburn	.10
285	David Ortiz	.40
286	John Thomson	.10
287	Kevin Appier	.10
288	Ismael Valdes	.10
289	Gary DiSarcina	.10
290	Todd Dunwoody	.10
291	Wally Joyner	.10
292	Charles Nagy	.10
293	Jeff Shaw	.10
294	*Kevin Millwood*	1.00
295	*Rigo Beltran*	.20
296	Jeff Frye	.10
297	Oscar Henriquez	.10
298	Mike Thurman	.10
299	Garrett Stephenson	.10
300	Barry Bonds	.75
301	Roger Clemens (Smoke 'N Heat)	.50
302	David Cone (Smoke 'N Heat)	.15
303	Hideki Irabu (Smoke 'N Heat)	.40
304	Randy Johnson (Smoke 'N Heat)	.20
305	Greg Maddux (Smoke 'N Heat)	1.00
306	Pedro Martinez (Smoke 'N Heat)	.15
307	Mike Mussina (Smoke 'N Heat)	.30
308	Andy Pettitte (Smoke 'N Heat)	.25
309	Curt Schilling (Smoke 'N Heat)	.10
310	John Smoltz (Smoke 'N Heat)	.15
311	Roger Clemens (Golden Memories)	.50
312	Jose Cruz Jr. (Golden Memories)	.75
313	Nomar Garciaparra (Golden Memories)	1.00
314	Ken Griffey Jr. (Golden Memories)	1.50
315	Tony Gwynn (Golden Memories)	.75
316	Hideki Irabu (Golden Memories)	.40
317	Randy Johnson (Golden Memories)	.20
318	Mark McGwire (Golden Memories)	2.00
319	Curt Schilling (Golden Memories)	.10
320	Larry Walker (Golden Memories)	.15
321	Jeff Bagwell (Tale of the Tape)	.60
322	Albert Belle (Tale of the Tape)	.40
323	Barry Bonds (Tale of the Tape)	.40
324	Jay Buhner (Tale of the Tape)	.15
325	Tony Clark (Tale of the Tape)	.20
326	Jose Cruz Jr. (Tale of the Tape)	.75
327	Andres Galarraga (Tale of the Tape)	.15
328	Juan Gonzalez (Tale of the Tape)	.75
329	Ken Griffey Jr. (Tale of the Tape)	1.50
330	Andruw Jones (Tale of the Tape)	.75

No.	Player	Price
331	Tino Martinez (Tale of the Tape)	.15
332	Mark McGwire (Tale of the Tape)	2.00
333	Rafael Palmeiro (Tale of the Tape)	.15
334	Mike Piazza (Tale of the Tape)	1.00
335	Manny Ramirez (Tale of the Tape)	.25
336	Alex Rodriguez (Tale of the Tape)	1.25
337	Frank Thomas (Tale of the Tape)	1.25
338	Jim Thome (Tale of the Tape)	.20
339	Mo Vaughn (Tale of the Tape)	.10
340	Larry Walker (Tale of the Tape)	.15
341	Checklist(Jose Cruz Jr.)	.50
342	Checklist(Ken Griffey Jr.)	1.00
343	Checklist(Derek Jeter)	.60
344	Checklist(Andruw Jones)	.50
345	Checklist(Chipper Jones)	.60
346	Checklist(Greg Maddux)	.60
347	Checklist(Mike Piazza)	.60
348	Checklist(Cal Ripken Jr.)	.75
349	Checklist(Alex Rodriguez)	.75
350	Checklist(Frank Thomas)	1.00
351	Mo Vaughn	.75
352	Andres Galarraga	.25
353	Roberto Alomar	.50
354	Darin Erstad	.75
355	Albert Belle	.75
356	Matt Williams	.25
357	Darryl Kile	.10
358	Kenny Lofton	.75
359	Orel Hershiser	.10
360	Bob Abreu	.10
361	Chris Widger	.10
362	Glenallen Hill	.10
363	Chili Davis	.10
364	Kevin Brown	.15
365	Marquis Grissom	.15
366	Livan Hernandez	.10
367	Moises Alou	.20
368	Matt Lawton	.10
369	Rey Ordonez	.10
370	Kenny Rogers	.10
371	Lee Stevens	.10
372	Wade Boggs	.20
373	Luis Gonzalez	.10
374	Jeff Conine	.10
375	Esteban Loaiza	.10
376	Jose Canseco	.25
377	Henry Rodriguez	.10
378	Dave Burba	.10
379	Todd Hollandsworth	.10
380	Ron Gant	.20
381	Pedro Martinez	.40
382	Ryan Klesko	.30
383	Derrek Lee	.10
384	Doug Glanville	.10
385	David Wells	.10
386	Ken Caminiti	.20
387	Damon Hollins	.10
388	Manny Ramirez	.75
389	Mike Mussina	.60
390	Jay Bell	.10
391	Mike Piazza	.40
392	Mike Lansing	.10
393	Mike Hampton	.10
394	Geoff Jenkins	.10
395	Jimmy Haynes	.10
396	Scott Servais	.10
397	Kent Mercker	.10
398	Jeff Kent	.10
399	Kevin Elster	.10
400	*Masato Yoshii*	.40
401	Jose Vizcaino	.10
402	Javier Martinez	.10
403	David Segui	.10
404	Tony Saunders	.10
405	Karim Garcia	.10
406	Armando Benitez	.10
407	Joe Randa	.10
408	Vic Darensbourg	.10
409	Sean Casey	.20
410	Eric Milton	.20
411	Trey Moore	.10
412	Mike Stanley	.10
413	Tom Gordon	.10
414	Hal Morris	.10
415	Braden Looper	.10
416	Mike Kelly	.10
417	John Smoltz	.10
418	Roger Cedeno	.10
419	Al Leiter	.20
420	Chuck Knoblauch	.30
421	Felix Rodriguez	.10
422	Bip Roberts	.10
423	Ken Hill	.10
424	Jermaine Allensworth	.10
425	Esteban Yan	.10
426	Scott Karl	.10
427	Sean Berry	.10
428	Rafael Medina	.10
429	Javier Vazquez	.10
430	Rickey Henderson	.20
431	*Adam Butler*	.10
432	Todd Stottlemyre	.10
433	Yamil Benitez	.10
434	Sterling Hitchcock	.10
435	Paul Sorrento	.10
436	Bobby Ayala	.10
437	Tim Raines	.10
438	Chris Hoiles	.10
439	Rod Beck	.10
440	Donnie Sadler	.10
441	Charles Johnson	.10
442	Russ Ortiz	.10
443	Pedro Astacio	.10
444	Wilson Alvarez	.10
445	Mike Blowers	.10
446	Todd Zeile	.10
447	Mel Rojas	.10
448	F.P. Santangelo	.10
449	Dmitri Young	.10
450	Brian Anderson	.10
451	Cecil Fielder	.20
452	Roberto Hernandez	.10
453	Todd Walker	.20
454	Tyler Green	.10
455	Jorge Posada	.10
456	Geronimo Berroa	.10
457	Jose Silva	.10
458	Bobby Bonilla	.20
459	Walt Weiss	.10
460	Darren Dreifort	.10
461	B.J. Surhoff	.10
462	Quinton McCracken	.10
463	Derek Lowe	.10
464	Jorge Fabregas	.10
465	Joey Hamilton	.10
466	Brian Jordan	.10
467	Allen Watson	.10
468	John Jaha	.10
469	Heathcliff Slocumb	.10
470	Gregg Jefferies	.10
471	Scott Brosius	.10
472	Chad Ogea	.10
473	A.J. Hinch	.20
474	Bobby Smith	.10
475	Brian Moehler	.10
476	DaRond Stovall	.10
477	Kevin Young	.10
478	Jeff Suppan	.10
479	Marty Cordova	.10
480	*John Halama*	.25
481	Bubba Trammell	.10
482	Mike Caruso	.10
483	Eric Karros	.20
484	Jamey Wright	.10
485	Mike Sweeney	.10
486	Aaron Sele	.10
487	Cliff Floyd	.10
488	Jeff Brantley	.10
489	Jim Leyritz	.10
490	Denny Neagle	.20
491	Travis Fryman	.10
492	Carlos Baerga	.10
493	Eddie Taubensee	.10
494	Darryl Strawberry	.20
495	Brian Johnson	.10
496	Randy Myers	.10
497	Jeff Blauser	.10
498	Jason Wood	.10
499	*Rolando Arrojo*	.40
500	Johnny Damon	.10
501	Jose Mercedes	.10
502	Tony Batista	.10
503	Mike Piazza	2.00
504	Hideo Nomo	.50
505	Chris Gomez	.10
506	*Jesus Sanchez*	.25
507	Al Martin	.10
508	Brian Edmondson	.10
509	Joe Girardi	.10
510	Shayne Bennett	.10
511	Joe Carter	.15
512	Dave Mlicki	.10
513	*Rich Butler*	.50
514	Dennis Eckersley	.10
515	Travis Lee	2.00
516	John Mabry	.10
517	Jose Mesa	.10
518	Phil Nevin	.10
519	Raul Casanova	.10
520	Mike Fetters	.10
521	Gary Sheffield	.25
522	Terry Steinbach	.10
523	Steve Trachsel	.10
524	Josh Booty	.10
525	Darryl Hamilton	.10
526	Mark McLemore	.10
527	Kevin Stocker	.10
528	Bret Boone	.10
529	Shane Andrews	.10
530	Robb Nen	.10
531	Carl Everett	.10
532	LaTroy Hawkins	.10
533	Fernando Vina	.10
534	Michael Tucker	.10
535	Mark Langston	.10
536	Mickey Mantle	5.00
537	Bernard Gilkey	.10
538	Francisco Cordova	.10
539	Mike Bordick	.10
540	Fred McGriff	.20
541	Cliff Politte	.10
542	Jason Varitek	.10
543	Shawon Dunston	.10
544	Brian Meadows	.10
545	Pat Meares	.10
546	Carlos Perez	.10
547	Desi Relaford	.10
548	Antonio Osuna	.10
549	Devon White	.10
550	Sean Runyan	.10
551	Mickey Morandini	.10
552	Dave Martinez	.10
553	Jeff Fassero	.10
554	*Ryan Jackson*	.25
555	Stan Javier	.10
556	Jaime Navarro	.10
557	Jose Offerman	.10
558	*Mike Lowell*	.40
559	Darrin Fletcher	.10
560	Mark Lewis	.10
561	Dante Bichette	.25
562	Chuck Finley	.10
563	Kerry Wood	5.00
564	Andy Benes	.10
565	Freddy Garcia	.10
566	Tom Glavine	.20
567	Jon Nunnally	.10
568	Miguel Cairo	.10
569	Shane Reynolds	.10
570	Roberto Kelly	.10
571	Checklist(Jose Cruz Jr.)	.50
572	Checklist(Ken Griffey Jr.)	1.50
573	Checklist(Mark McGwire)	1.50
574	Checklist(Cal Ripken Jr.)	1.00
575	Checklist(Frank Thomas)	1.00
576	Jeff Bagwell (Unforgettable Moments)	1.50
577	Barry Bonds (Unforgettable Moments)	1.00
578	Tony Clark (Unforgettable Moments)	.75
579	Roger Clemens (Unforgettable Moments)	1.50
580	Jose Cruz Jr. (Unforgettable Moments)	1.00
581	Nomar Garciaparra (Unforgettable Moments)	2.50
582	Juan Gonzalez (Unforgettable Moments)	2.00
583	Ben Grieve (Unforgettable Moments)	1.50
584	Ken Griffey Jr. (Unforgettable Moments)	4.00
585	Tony Gwynn (Unforgettable Moments)	2.00
586	Derek Jeter (Unforgettable Moments)	2.50
587	Randy Johnson (Unforgettable Moments)	.75
588	Chipper Jones (Unforgettable Moments)	2.50
589	Greg Maddux (Unforgettable Moments)	2.50
590	Mark McGwire (Unforgettable Moments)	5.00
591	Andy Pettitte (Unforgettable Moments)	.60

592	Paul Molitor (Unforgettable Moments)	.50
593	Cal Ripken Jr. (Unforgettable Moments)	3.00
594	Alex Rodriguez (Unforgettable Moments)	2.50
595	Scott Rolen (Unforgettable Moments)	1.25
596	Curt Schilling (Unforgettable Moments)	.40
597	Frank Thomas (Unforgettable Moments)	2.50
598	Jim Thome (Unforgettable Moments)	.75
599	Larry Walker (Unforgettable Moments)	.50
600	Bernie Williams (Unforgettable Moments)	.75

1998 Fleer Decade of Excellence

Decade of Excellence inserts were found in one per 72 Series I hobby packs of Fleer Tradition. The 12-card set features 1988 season photos in Fleer's 1988 card design. The set includes only those current players who have been in baseball for ten years or more.

		MT
Complete Set (12):		100.00
Common Player:		4.00
Inserted 1:72		
Rare Traditions: 3x to 5x		
Inserted 1:720		
1	Roberto Alomar	8.00
2	Barry Bonds	10.00
3	Roger Clemens	12.00
4	David Cone	4.00
5	Andres Galarraga	5.00
6	Mark Grace	4.00
7	Tony Gwynn	16.00
8	Randy Johnson	6.00
9	Greg Maddux	24.00
10	Mark McGwire	35.00
11	Paul O'Neill	4.00
12	Cal Ripken Jr.	30.00

1998 Fleer Diamond Standouts

Diamond Standouts were inserted into Series I packs at a rate of one per 12. The 20-card insert set features players over a diamond design silver foil background.

		MT
Complete Set (20):		75.00
Common Player:		1.50
Inserted 1:12		
1	Jeff Bagwell	5.00
2	Barry Bonds	3.00
3	Roger Clemens	5.00
4	Jose Cruz Jr.	5.00
5	Andres Galarraga	1.50
6	Nomar Garciaparra	8.00
7	Juan Gonzalez	6.00
8	Ken Griffey Jr.	12.00
9	Derek Jeter	7.00
10	Randy Johnson	2.00
11	Chipper Jones	8.00
12	Kenny Lofton	3.00
13	Greg Maddux	8.00
14	Pedro Martinez	1.50
15	Mark McGwire	15.00
16	Mike Piazza	8.00
17	Alex Rodriguez	10.00
18	Curt Schilling	1.50
19	Frank Thomas	10.00
20	Larry Walker	2.00

1998 Fleer Diamond Tribute

This 10-card insert was exclusive to Series II packs and seeded one per 300 packs. Cards were printed on a leather- like laminated stock and had silver holofoil stamping.

		MT
Complete Set (10):		400.00
Common Player:		30.00
Inserted 1:300		
DT1	Jeff Bagwell	35.00
DT2	Roger Clemens	35.00
DT3	Nomar Garciaparra	50.00
DT4	Juan Gonzalez	40.00
DT5	Ken Griffey Jr.	80.00
DT6	Mark McGwire	90.00
DT7	Mike Piazza	50.00
DT8	Cal Ripken Jr.	60.00
DT9	Alex Rodriguez	50.00
DT10	Frank Thomas	60.00

A player's name in *italic* type indicates a rookie card.

1998 Fleer In the Clutch

This Series 2 insert features stars who can stand up to pressure of big league ball. Fronts have embossed action photos on a prismatic metallic foil background. Backs have a portrait photo and a few words about the player. Stated insertion rate for the inserts was one per 20 packs on average.

		MT
Complete Set (15):		75.00
Common Player:		1.50
Inserted 1:20		
IC1	Jeff Bagwell	5.00
IC2	Barry Bonds	3.00
IC3	Roger Clemens	5.00
IC4	Jose Cruz Jr.	3.00
IC5	Nomar Garciaparra	8.00
IC6	Juan Gonzalez	6.00
IC7	Ken Griffey Jr.	12.00
IC8	Tony Gwynn	6.00
IC9	Derek Jeter	6.00
IC10	Chipper Jones	8.00
IC11	Greg Maddux	8.00
IC12	Mark McGwire	15.00
IC13	Mike Piazza	8.00
IC14	Frank Thomas	10.00
IC15	Larry Walker	1.50

1998 Fleer Lumber Company

This 15-card set was exclusive to Series I retail packs and inserted one per 36 packs. It included power hitters and featured the insert name in large letters across the top.

Complete Set (15):	MT 200.00
Common Player:	3.00

Inserted 1:36 retail

1	Jeff Bagwell	12.00
2	Barry Bonds	7.00
3	Jose Cruz Jr.	10.00
4	Nomar Garciaparra	20.00
5	Juan Gonzalez	15.00
6	Ken Griffey Jr.	30.00
7	Tony Gwynn	15.00
8	Chipper Jones	20.00
9	Tino Martinez	3.00
10	Mark McGwire	35.00
11	Mike Piazza	20.00
12	Cal Ripken Jr.	25.00
13	Alex Rodriguez	25.00
14	Frank Thomas	25.00
15	Larry Walker	4.00

1998 Fleer Promising Forecast

Potential future stars are showcased in this Series 2 insert. Both front and back have a background of a colorful weather map. Fronts have a glossy player action photo on a matte-finish background. Backs are all-glossy and have a second photo and a few words about the player's potential. Average odds of pulling a Promising Forecast card were stated as one per 12 packs.

Complete Set (20):	MT 30.00
Common Player:	.50

Inserted 1:12

PF1	Rolando Arrojo	1.00
PF2	Sean Casey	1.50
PF3	Brad Fullmer	2.00
PF4	Karim Garcia	.50
PF5	Ben Grieve	4.00
PF6	Todd Helton	3.00
PF7	Richard Hidalgo	.50
PF8	A.J. Hinch	.50
PF9	Paul Konerko	1.50
PF10	Mark Kotsay	1.00
PF11	Derrek Lee	.50
PF12	Travis Lee	5.00
PF13	Eric Milton	.50
PF14	Magglio Ordonez	1.50
PF15	David Ortiz	1.50
PF16	Brian Rose	.50
PF17	Miguel Tejada	1.50
PF18	Jason Varitek	.50
PF19	Enrique Wilson	.50
PF20	Kerry Wood	8.00

A player's name in *italic* type indicates a rookie card.

1998 Fleer Rookie Sensation

Rookie Sensations included 20 gray-bordered cards of the 1997 most promising players who were eligible for the Rookie of the Year award. Each card contained a multi-colored background and was inserted one per 18 packs.

Complete Set (20):	MT 60.00
Common Player:	2.00

Inserted 1:18

1	Mike Cameron	2.00
2	Jose Cruz Jr.	10.00
3	Jason Dickson	2.00
4	Kelvim Escobar	2.00
5	Nomar Garciaparra	12.00
6	Ben Grieve	5.00
7	Vladimir Guerrero	5.00
8	Wilton Guerrero	2.00
9	Jose Guillen	3.00
10	Todd Helton	4.00
11	Livan Hernandez	2.00
12	Hideki Irabu	4.00
13	Andruw Jones	6.00
14	Matt Morris	2.00
15	Magglio Ordonez	2.00
16	Neifi Perez	2.00
17	Scott Rolen	8.00
18	Fernando Tatis	4.00
19	Brett Tomko	2.00
20	Jaret Wright	4.00

1998 Fleer The Power Game

Pitchers and hitters are pictured over a purple metallic background with UV coating in this 20-card insert. Power Game inserts were exclusive to Series I and seeded one per 36 packs.

Complete Set (20):	MT 175.00
Common Player:	3.00

Inserted 1:36

1	Jeff Bagwell	12.00
2	Albert Belle	7.00
3	Barry Bonds	7.00
4	Tony Clark	5.00
5	Roger Clemens	10.00
6	Jose Cruz Jr.	10.00
7	Andres Galarraga	3.00
8	Nomar Garciaparra	20.00
9	Juan Gonzalez	15.00
10	Ken Griffey Jr.	30.00
11	Randy Johnson	5.00
12	Greg Maddux	20.00
13	Pedro Martinez	3.00
14	Tino Martinez	3.00
15	Mark McGwire	35.00
16	Mike Piazza	20.00
17	Curt Schilling	3.00
18	Frank Thomas	25.00
19	Jim Thome	5.00
20	Larry Walker	4.00

1998 Fleer Update

Fleer produced its first Update set since 1994 with this 100-card boxed set. It arrived soon after the conclusion of the 1998 World Series and focused on rookies like J.D. Drew, Rich Croushore, Ryan Bradley, John Rocker, Mike Frank and Benj Sampson, who made their major league debut in September and have not yet had a rookie card yet. The set had 70 rookies, including 15 making their major league debut, 20 traded players and free agents. There was one subset called Season's Highlights that focused on feats like Mark McGwire's 70th home run, Sammy Sosa's single-month home run record and Kerry Wood's 20 strikeout performance.

Complete Set (100):	MT 50.00
Common Player:	.10
U1	Mark McGwire ("Season Highlights" Subset)	3.00
U2	Sammy Sosa ("Season Highlights" Subset)	1.50
U3	Roger Clemens ("Season Highlights" Subset)	.75
U4	Barry Bonds ("Season Highlights" Subset)	.50
U5	Kerry Wood ("Season Highlights" Subset)	2.50
U6	Paul Molitor ("Season Highlights" Subset)	.25
U7	Ken Griffey Jr. ("Season Highlights" Subset)	2.50
U8	Cal Ripken Jr. ("Season Highlights" Subset)	1.50
U9	David Wells ("Season Highlights" Subset)	.10
U10	Alex Rodriguez ("Season Highlights" Subset)	1.00
U11	*Angel Pena*	.30
U12	Bruce Chen	.10
U13	Craig Wilson	.10
U14	*Orlando Hernandez*	6.00
U15	Aramis Ramirez	.25
U16	Aaron Boone	.10
U17	Bob Henley	.10
U18	Juan Guzman	.10
U19	Darryl Hamilton	.10
U20	Jay Payton	.10
U21	*Jeremy Powell*	.25

U22	Ben Davis	.10
U23	Preston Wilson	.10
U24	*Jim Parque*	.20
U25	*Odalis Perez*	.15
U26	Ron Belliard	.10
U27	Royce Clayton	.10
U28	George Lombard	.10
U29	Tony Phillips	.10
U30	*Fernando Seguignol*	.15
U31	*Armando Rios*	.20
U32	Jerry Hairston	.10
U33	*Justin Baughman*	.15
U34	Seth Greisinger	.10
U35	Alex Gonzalez	.10
U36	Michael Barrett	.10
U37	Carlos Beltran	.10
U38	Ellis Burks	.10
U39	Jose Jimenez	.40
U40	Carlos Guillen	.10
U41	Marlon Anderson	.10
U42	Scott Elarton	.10
U43	Glenallen Hill	.10
U44	Shane Monahan	.10
U45	Dennis Martinez	.10
U46	*Carlos Febles*	.20
U47	Carlos Perez	.10
U48	Wilton Guerrero	.10
U49	Randy Johnson	.10
U50	*Brian Simmons*	.25
U51	Carlton Loewer	.10
U52	*Mark DeRosa*	.25
U53	*Tim Young*	.25
U54	Gary Gaetti	.10
U55	Eric Chavez	.75
U56	Carl Pavano	.10
U57	Mike Stanley	.10
U58	Todd Stottlemyre	.10
U59	*Gabe Kapler*	2.00
U60	*Mike Jerzembeck*	.25
U61	*Mitch Meluskey*	.20
U62	Bill Pulsipher	.10
U63	Derrick Gibson	.10
U64	*John Rocker*	.25
U65	Calvin Pickering	.10
U66	Blake Stein	.10
U67	Fernando Tatis	.10
U68	Gabe Alvarez	.10
U69	Jeffrey Hammonds	.10
U70	Adrian Beltre	.50
U71	*Ryan Bradley*	.75
U72	*Edgar Clemente*	.20
U73	*Rick Croushore*	.20
U74	Matt Clement	.10
U75	Dermal Brown	.10
U76	Paul Bako	.10
U77	*Placido Polanco*	.25
U78	Jay Tessmer	.10
U79	Jarrod Washburn	.10
U80	Kevin Witt	.10
U81	Mike Metcalfe	.10
U82	Daryle Ward	.10
U83	*Benj Sampson*	.20
U84	*Mike Kinkade*	.50
U85	Randy Winn	.10
U86	Jeff Shaw	.10
U87	*Troy Glaus*	5.00
U88	Hideo Nomo	.10
U89	Mark Grudzielanek	.10
U90	*Mike Frank*	.25
U91	*Bobby Howry*	.20
U92	*Ryan Minor*	2.00
U93	*Corey Koskie*	.60
U94	*Matt Anderson*	2.00
U95	Joe Carter	.10
U96	Paul Konerko	.10
U97	Sidney Ponson	.10
U98	*Jeremy Giambi*	.75
U99	*Jeff Kubenka*	.20
U100	*J.D. Drew*	30.00

1998 Fleer Vintage '63

Vintage featured 126 different players, with 63 in Series I and 63 in Series II, on the design of 1963 Fleer cards. The insert commemorated the 35th anniversary of Fleer and was seeded one per hobby pack. In addition, Series II featured Mickey Mantle on card No. 67, which completed the original 1963 Fleer set that ended at card No. 66 and wasn't able to include Mantle for licensing reasons. The Mantle card was printed in vintage looking stock and was purposely made to look and feel like the originals. Fleer also printed a Classic parallel version to this insert that contained gold foil on the front and was sequentially numbered to 63 with a "C" prefix on the back.

		MT
Complete Set (126):		35.00
Complete Series I Set (63):		20.00
Complete Series II Set (63):		15.00
Common Player:		.25
Inserted 1:1		
Classics (63 sets): 75x to 120x		
1	Jason Dickson	.25
2	Tim Salmon	.40
3	Andruw Jones	1.00
4	Chipper Jones	1.50
5	Kenny Lofton	.75
6	Greg Maddux	1.50
7	Rafael Palmeiro	.30
8	Cal Ripken Jr.	2.00
9	Nomar Garciaparra	1.50
10	Mark Grace	.40
11	Sammy Sosa	1.50
12	Frank Thomas	2.50
13	Deion Sanders	.30
14	Sandy Alomar	.25
15	David Justice	.40
16	Jim Thome	.50
17	Matt Williams	.30
18	Jaret Wright	1.50
19	Vinny Castilla	.25
20	Andres Galarraga	.40
21	Todd Helton	.75
22	Larry Walker	.40
23	Tony Clark	.40
24	Moises Alou	.25
25	Kevin Brown	.25
26	Charles Johnson	.25
27	Edgar Renteria	.25
28	Gary Sheffield	.40
29	Jeff Bagwell	1.00
30	Craig Biggio	.25
31	Raul Mondesi	.25
32	Mike Piazza	1.50
33	Chuck Knoblauch	.40
34	Paul Molitor	.50
35	Vladimir Guerrero	1.00
36	Pedro J. Martinez	.40
37	Todd Hundley	.25
38	Derek Jeter	1.50
39	Tino Martinez	.40
40	Paul O'Neill	.25
41	Andy Pettitte	.50
42	Mariano Rivera	.50
43	Bernie Williams	.50
44	Ben Grieve	1.50
45	Scott Rolen	1.00
46	Curt Schilling	.25
47	Jason Kendall	.25
48	Tony Womack	.25
49	Ray Lankford	.25
50	Mark McGwire	4.00
51	Matt Morris	.25
52	Tony Gwynn	1.50
53	Barry Bonds	.75
54	Jay Buhner	.25
55	Ken Griffey Jr.	3.00
56	Randy Johnson	.40
57	Edgar Martinez	.25
58	Alex Rodriguez	2.00
59	Juan Gonzalez	1.50
60	Rusty Greer	.25
61	Ivan Rodriguez	.75
62	Roger Clemens	1.25
63	Jose Cruz Jr.	1.50
	Checklist (Vintage '63)	.25
64	Darin Erstad	.75
65	Jay Bell	.25
66	Andy Benes	.25
67	Mickey Mantle	5.00
68	Travis Lee	3.00
69	Matt Williams	.40
70	Andres Galarraga	.40
71	Tom Glavine	.40
72	Ryan Klesko	.40
73	Denny Neagle	.25
74	John Smoltz	.25
75	Roberto Alomar	.50
76	Joe Carter	.25
77	Mike Mussina	.60
78	B.J. Surhoff	.25
79	Dennis Eckersley	.25
80	Pedro Martinez	.40
81	Mo Vaughn	.75
82	Jeff Blauser	.25
83	Henry Rodriguez	.25
84	Albert Belle	.75
85	Sean Casey	.50
86	Travis Fryman	.25
87	Kenny Lofton	.75
88	Darryl Kile	.25
89	Mike Lansing	.25
90	Bobby Bonilla	.25
91	Cliff Floyd	.25
92	Livan Hernandez	.25
93	Derrek Lee	.25
94	Moises Alou	.25
95	Shane Reynolds	.25
96	Jeff Conine	.25
97	Johnny Damon	.25
98	Eric Karros	.25
99	Hideo Nomo	.50
100	Marquis Grissom	.25
101	Matt Lawton	.25
102	Todd Walker	.25
103	Carlos Baerga	.25
104	Bernard Gilkey	.25
105	Rey Ordonez	.25
106	Chili Davis	.25
107	Jason Giambi	.40
108	Chuck Knoblauch	.40
109	Tim Raines	.25
110	Rickey Henderson	.25
111	Bob Abreu	.25
112	Doug Glanville	.25
113	Gregg Jefferies	.25
114	Al Martin	.25
115	Kevin Young	.25
116	Ron Gant	.25
117	Kevin Brown	.25
118	Ken Caminiti	.25
119	Joey Hamilton	.25
120	Jeff Kent	.25
121	Wade Boggs	.50
122	Quinton McCracken	.25
123	Fred McGriff	.40
124	Paul Sorrento	.25
125	Jose Canseco	.40
126	Randy Myers	.25

1998 Fleer Zone

Inserted in one per 288 packs of Series I Fleer Tradition, Zone featured 15 top players printed on rainbow foil and etching.

		MT
Complete Set (15):		800.00
Common Player:		15.00
Inserted 1:288		
1	Jeff Bagwell	50.00
2	Barry Bonds	30.00
3	Roger Clemens	50.00

4	Jose Cruz Jr.	40.00
5	Nomar Garciaparra	75.00
6	Juan Gonzalez	60.00
7	Ken Griffey Jr.	125.00
8	Tony Gwynn	60.00
9	Chipper Jones	75.00
10	Greg Maddux	75.00
11	Mark McGwire	125.00
12	Mike Piazza	75.00
13	Alex Rodriguez	90.00
14	Frank Thomas	90.00
15	Larry Walker	15.00

L

1990 Leaf

FRANK THOMAS 1B

This 528-card set was issued in two 264-card series. The cards were printed on heavy quality stock and both the card fronts and backs have full color player photos. Cards also have an ultra-glossy finish on both the fronts and the backs. A high-tech foil Hall of Fame puzzle features former Yankee great Yogi Berra.

		MT
Complete Set (528):		240.00
Complete Series 1 (264):		100.00
Complete Series 2 (264):		140.00
Common Player:		.25
Series 1 Wax Box:		220.00
Series 2 Wax Box:		300.00
1	Introductory card	.25
2	Mike Henneman	.25
3	Steve Bedrosian	.25
4	Mike Scott	.25
5	Allan Anderson	.25
6	Rick Sutcliffe	.25
7	Gregg Olson	.30
8	Kevin Elster	.25
9	Pete O'Brien	.25
10	Carlton Fisk	.50
11	Joe Magrane	.25
12	Roger Clemens	2.00
13	Tom Glavine	2.00
14	Tom Gordon	.25
15	Todd Benzinger	.25
16	Hubie Brooks	.25
17	Roberto Kelly	.45
18	Barry Larkin	1.00
19	Mike Boddicker	.25
20	Roger McDowell	.25
21	Nolan Ryan	7.00
22	John Farrell	.25
23	Bruce Hurst	.25
24	Wally Joyner	.40
25	Greg Maddux	15.00

26	Chris Bosio	.25
27	John Cerutti	.25
28	Tim Burke	.25
29	Dennis Eckersley	.40
30	Glenn Davis	.25
31	Jim Abbott	.50
32	Mike LaValliere	.25
33	Andres Thomas	.25
34	Lou Whitaker	.35
35	Alvin Davis	.25
36	Melido Perez	.25
37	Craig Biggio	1.25
38	Rick Aguilera	.25
39	Pete Harnisch	.50
40	David Cone	1.00
41	Scott Garrelts	.25
42	Jay Howell	.25
43	Eric King	.25
44	Pedro Guerrero	.25
45	Mike Bielecki	.25
46	Bob Boone	.35
47	Kevin Brown	2.00
48	Jerry Browne	.25
49	Mike Scioscia	.25
50	Chuck Cary	.25
51	Wade Boggs	1.00
52	Von Hayes	.25
53	Tony Fernandez	.25
54	Dennis Martinez	.35
55	Tom Candiotti	.25
56	Andy Benes	1.00
57	Rob Dibble	.25
58	Chuck Crim	.25
59	John Smoltz	3.00
60	Mike Heath	.25
61	Kevin Gross	.25
62	Mark McGwire	10.00
63	Bert Blyleven	.25
64	Bob Walk	.25
65	Mickey Tettleton	.35
66	Sid Fernandez	.25
67	Terry Kennedy	.25
68	Fernando Valenzuela	.40
69	Don Mattingly	3.00
70	Paul O'Neill	.50
71	Robin Yount	1.00
72	Bret Saberhagen	.30
73	Geno Petralli	.25
74	Brook Jacoby	.25
75	Roberto Alomar	2.50
76	Devon White	.35
77	Jose Lind	.25
78	Pat Combs	.25
79	Dave Steib	.25
80	Tim Wallach	.25
81	Dave Stewart	.25
82	*Eric Anthony*	.25
83	Randy Bush	.25
84	Checklist	.25
85	Jaime Navarro	.25
86	Tommy Gregg	.25
87	Frank Tanana	.25
88	Omar Vizquel	1.50
89	Ivan Calderon	.25
90	Vince Coleman	.25
91	Barry Bonds	2.50
92	Randy Milligan	.25
93	Frank Viola	.25
94	Matt Williams	2.00
95	Alfredo Griffin	.25
96	Steve Sax	.25
97	Gary Gaetti	.35
98	Ryne Sandberg	2.00
99	Danny Tartabull	.35
100	Rafael Palmeiro	1.50
101	Jesse Orosco	.25
102	Garry Templeton	.25
103	Frank DiPino	.25
104	Tony Pena	.25
105	Dickie Thon	.25
106	Kelly Gruber	.25
107	*Marquis Grissom*	4.00
108	Jose Canseco	.75
109	Mike Blowers	.25
110	Tom Browning	.25
111	Greg Vaughn	6.00
112	Oddibe McDowell	.25
113	Gary Ward	.25
114	Jay Buhner	1.50
115	Eric Show	.25
116	Bryan Harvey	.45
117	Andy Van Slyke	.25
118	Jeff Ballard	.25
119	Barry Lyons	.25
120	Kevin Mitchell	.40
121	Mike Gallego	.25

122	Dave Smith	.25
123	Kirby Puckett	2.00
124	Jerome Walton	.25
125	Bo Jackson	.75
126	Harold Baines	.35
127	Scott Bankhead	.25
128	Ozzie Guillen	.25
129	Jose Oquendo	.25
130	John Dopson	.25
131	Charlie Hayes	.25
132	Fred McGriff	.75
133	Chet Lemon	.25
134	Gary Carter	.35
135	Rafael Ramirez	.25
136	Shane Mack	.35
137	Mark Grace	1.00
138	Phil Bradley	.25
139	Dwight Gooden	.40
140	Harold Reynolds	.25
141	Scott Fletcher	.25
142	Ozzie Smith	1.50
143	Mike Greenwell	.30
144	Pete Smith	.25
145	Mark Gubicza	.30
146	Chris Sabo	.25
147	Ramon Martinez	.35
148	Tim Leary	.25
149	Randy Myers	.25
150	Jody Reed	.25
151	Bruce Ruffin	.25
152	Jeff Russell	.25
153	Doug Jones	.25
154	Tony Gwynn	3.00
155	Mark Langston	.30
156	Mitch Williams	.25
157	Gary Sheffield	4.00
158	Tom Henke	.25
159	Oil Can Boyd	.25
160	Rickey Henderson	.50
161	Bill Doran	.25
162	Chuck Finley	.25
163	Jeff King	.35
164	Nick Esasky	.25
165	Cecil Fielder	.50
166	Dave Valle	.25
167	Robin Ventura	2.00
168	Jim Deshaies	.25
169	Juan Berenguer	.25
170	Craig Worthington	.25
171	Gregg Jefferies	.50
172	Will Clark	.75
173	Kirk Gibson	.25
174	Checklist	.25
175	Bobby Thigpen	.25
176	John Tudor	.25
177	Andre Dawson	.50
178	George Brett	2.50
179	Steve Buechele	.25
180	Albert Belle	10.00
181	Eddie Murray	1.00
182	Bob Geren	.25
183	Rob Murphy	.25
184	Tom Herr	.25
185	George Bell	.25
186	Spike Owen	.25
187	Cory Snyder	.25
188	Fred Lynn	.30
189	Eric Davis	.40
190	Dave Parker	.35
191	Jeff Blauser	.25
192	Matt Nokes	.25
193	*Delino DeShields*	.50
194	Scott Sanderson	.25
195	Lance Parrish	.25
196	Bobby Bonilla	.40
197	Cal Ripken, Jr.	6.00
198	Kevin McReynolds	.25
199	Robby Thompson	.25
200	Tim Belcher	.25
201	Jesse Barfield	.25
202	Mariano Duncan	.25
203	Bill Spiers	.25
204	Frank White	.25
205	Julio Franco	.35
206	Greg Swindell	.25
207	Benito Santiago	.30
208	Johnny Ray	.25
209	Gary Redus	.25
210	Jeff Parrett	.25
211	Jimmy Key	.35
212	Tim Raines	.35
213	Carney Lansford	.25
214	Gerald Young	.25
215	Gene Larkin	.25
216	Dan Plesac	.25
217	Lonnie Smith	.25

218	Alan Trammell	.40	314	Matt Nokes	.25	410	Tim Layana	.25
219	Jeffrey Leonard	.25	315	Dennis Lamp	.25	411	Chris Gwynn	.25
220	*Sammy Sosa*	100.00	316	Ken Howell	.25	412	Jeff Robinson	.25
221	Todd Zeile	.40	317	Glenallen Hill	.25	413	Scott Scudder	.25
222	Bill Landrum	.25	318	Dave Martinez	.25	414	Kevin Romine	.25
223	Mike Devereaux	.25	319	Chris James	.25	415	Jose DeJesus	.25
224	Mike Marshall	.25	320	Mike Pagliarulo	.25	416	Mike Jeffcoat	.25
225	Jose Uribe	.25	321	Hal Morris	.35	417	Rudy Seanez	.25
226	Juan Samuel	.25	322	Rob Deer	.25	418	Mike Dunne	.25
227	Mel Hall	.25	323	Greg Olson	.25	419	Dick Schofield	.25
228	Kent Hrbek	.40	324	Tony Phillips	.30	420	Steve Wilson	.25
229	Shawon Dunston	.30	325	*Larry Walker*	12.00	421	Bill Krueger	.25
230	Kevin Seitzer	.25	326	Ron Hassey	.25	422	Junior Felix	.25
231	Pete Incaviglia	.25	327	Jack Howell	.25	423	Drew Hall	.25
232	Sandy Alomar	.30	328	John Smiley	.25	424	Curt Young	.25
233	Bip Roberts	.25	329	Steve Finley	.50	425	Franklin Stubbs	.25
234	Scott Terry	.25	330	Dave Magadan	.25	426	Dave Winfield	.40
235	Dwight Evans	.25	331	Greg Litton	.25	427	Rick Reed	.25
236	Ricky Jordan	.25	332	Mickey Hatcher	.25	428	Charlie Leibrandt	.25
237	*John Olerud*	2.00	333	Lee Guetterman	.25	429	Jeff Robinson	.25
238	Zane Smith	.25	334	Norm Charlton	.25	430	Erik Hanson	.40
239	Walt Weiss	.25	335	Edgar Diaz	.25	431	Barry Jones	.25
240	Alvaro Espinoza	.25	336	Willie Wilson	.25	432	Alex Trevino	.25
241	Billy Hatcher	.25	337	Bobby Witt	.25	433	John Moses	.25
242	Paul Molitor	2.00	338	Candy Maldonado	.25	434	Dave Johnson	.25
243	Dale Murphy	.30	339	Craig Lefferts	.25	435	Mackey Sasser	.25
244	Dave Bergman	.25	340	Dante Bichette	3.00	436	Rick Leach	.25
245	Ken Griffey, Jr.	30.00	341	Wally Backman	.25	437	Lenny Harris	.25
246	Ed Whitson	.25	342	Dennis Cook	.25	438	Carlos Martinez	.25
247	Kirk McCaskill	.25	343	Pat Borders	.25	439	Rex Hudler	.25
248	Jay Bell	.25	344	Wallace Johnson	.25	440	Domingo Ramos	.25
249	*Ben McDonald*	1.50	345	Willie Randolph	.25	441	Gerald Perry	.25
250	Darryl Strawberry	.50	346	Danny Darwin	.25	442	John Russell	.25
251	Brett Butler	.30	347	Al Newman	.25	443	*Carlos Baerga*	2.00
252	Terry Steinbach	.25	348	Mark Knudson	.25	444	Checklist	.25
253	Ken Caminiti	2.00	349	Joe Boever	.25	445	Stan Javier	.25
254	Dan Gladden	.25	350	Larry Sheets	.25	446	*Kevin Maas*	.25
255	Dwight Smith	.25	351	Mike Jackson	.25	447	Tom Brunansky	.25
256	Kurt Stillwell	.25	352	Wayne Edwards	.25	448	Carmelo Martinez	.25
257	Ruben Sierra	.30	353	*Bernard Gilkey*	2.50	449	*Willie Blair*	.25
258	Mike Schooler	.25	354	Don Slaught	.25	450	Andres Galarraga	1.50
259	Lance Johnson	.25	355	Joe Orsulak	.25	451	Bud Black	.25
260	Terry Pendleton	.25	356	John Franco	.25	452	Greg Harris	.25
261	Ellis Burks	.40	357	Jeff Brantley	.25	453	Joe Oliver	.40
262	Len Dykstra	.25	358	Mike Morgan	.25	454	Greg Brock	.25
263	Mookie Wilson	.25	359	Deion Sanders	3.00	455	Jeff Treadway	.25
264	Checklist (Nolan Ryan)	.50	360	Terry Leach	.25	456	Lance McCullers	.25
265	Nolan Ryan (No-Hit King)	4.00	361	Les Lancaster	.25	457	Dave Schmidt	.25
266	Brian DuBois	.25	362	Storm Davis	.25	458	Todd Burns	.25
267	Don Robinson	.25	363	Scott Coolbaugh	.25	459	Max Venable	.25
268	Glenn Wilson	.25	364	Checklist	.25	460	Neal Heaton	.25
269	*Kevin Tapani*	.75	365	Cecilio Guante	.25	461	Mark Williamson	.25
270	Marvell Wynne	.25	366	Joey Cora	.25	462	Keith Miller	.25
271	Billy Ripken	.25	367	Willie McGee	.35	463	Mike LaCoss	.25
272	Howard Johnson	.25	368	Jerry Reed	.25	464	*Jose Offerman*	.50
273	Brian Holman	.25	369	Darren Daulton	.40	465	*Jim Leyritz*	.50
274	Dan Pasqua	.25	370	Manny Lee	.25	466	Glenn Braggs	.25
275	Ken Dayley	.25	371	Mark Gardner	.25	467	Ron Robinson	.25
276	Jeff Reardon	.25	372	Rick Honeycutt	.25	468	Mark Davis	.25
277	Jim Presley	.25	373	Steve Balboni	.25	469	Gary Pettis	.25
278	Jim Eisenreich	.25	374	Jack Armstrong	.25	470	Keith Hernandez	.25
279	Danny Jackson	.25	375	Charlie O'Brien	.25	471	Dennis Rasmussen	.25
280	Orel Hershiser	.35	376	Ron Gant	.75	472	Mark Eichhorn	.25
281	Andy Hawkins	.25	377	Lloyd Moseby	.25	473	Ted Power	.25
282	Jose Rijo	.25	378	Gene Harris	.25	474	Terry Mulholland	.30
283	Luis Rivera	.25	379	Joe Carter	.40	475	Todd Stottlemyre	.40
284	John Kruk	.25	380	Scott Bailes	.25	476	Jerry Goff	.25
285	Jeff Huson	.25	381	R.J. Reynolds	.25	477	Gene Nelson	.25
286	Joel Skinner	.25	382	Bob Melvin	.25	478	Rich Gedman	.25
287	Jack Clark	.25	383	Tim Teufel	.25	479	Brian Harper	.25
288	Chili Davis	.35	384	John Burkett	.40	480	Mike Felder	.25
289	Joe Girardi	.30	385	Felix Jose	.25	481	Steve Avery	.50
290	B.J. Surhoff	.25	386	Larry Andersen	.25	482	Jack Morris	.25
291	Luis Sojo	.25	387	David West	.25	483	Randy Johnson	4.00
292	Tom Foley	.25	388	Luis Salazar	.25	484	Scott Radinsky	.25
293	Mike Moore	.25	389	Mike Macfarlane	.25	485	*Stan Belinda*	.25
294	Ken Oberkfell	.25	390	Charlie Hough	.25	486	Jose DeLeon	.25
295	Luis Polonia	.25	391	Greg Briley	.25	487	Brian Holton	.25
296	Doug Drabek	.25	392	Donn Pall	.25	488	Mark Carreon	.40
297	*Dave Justice*	4.00	393	Bryn Smith	.25	489	Trevor Wilson	.25
298	Paul Gibson	.25	394	Carlos Quintana	.25	490	Mike Sharperson	.25
299	Edgar Martinez	1.50	395	Steve Lake	.25	491	*Alan Mills*	.25
300	*Frank Thomas*	60.00	396	*Mark Whiten*	.50	492	John Candelaria	.25
301	Eric Yelding	.25	397	Edwin Nunez	.25	493	Paul Assenmacher	.25
302	Greg Gagne	.25	398	Rick Parker	.25	494	Steve Crawford	.25
303	Brad Komminsk	.25	399	Mark Portugal	.25	495	Brad Arnsberg	.25
304	Ron Darling	.25	400	Roy Smith	.25	496	Sergio Valdez	.25
305	Kevin Bass	.25	401	Hector Villanueva	.25	497	Mark Parent	.25
306	Jeff Hamilton	.25	402	Bob Milacki	.25	498	Tom Pagnozzi	.25
307	Ron Karkovice	.25	403	Alejandro Pena	.25	499	Greg Harris	.25
308	Milt Thompson	.25	404	Scott Bradley	.25	500	Randy Ready	.25
309	Mike Harkey	.25	405	Ron Kittle	.25	501	Duane Ward	.25
310	Mel Stottlemyre	.25	406	Bob Tewksbury	.25	502	Nelson Santovenia	.25
311	Kenny Rogers	.35	407	Wes Gardner	.25	503	Joe Klink	.25
312	Mitch Webster	.25	408	Ernie Whitt	.25	504	Eric Plunk	.25
313	Kal Daniels	.25	409	Terry Shumpert	.25	505	Jeff Reed	.25

506	Ted Higuera	.25
507	Joe Hesketh	.25
508	Dan Petry	.25
509	Matt Young	.25
510	Jerald Clark	.25
511	*John Orton*	.25
512	Scott Ruskin	.25
513	*Chris Hoiles*	.75
514	Daryl Boston	.25
515	Francisco Oliveras	.25
516	Ozzie Canseco	.30
517	*Xavier Hernandez*	.40
518	Fred Manrique	.25
519	Shawn Boskie	.30
520	Jeff Montgomery	.40
521	Jack Daugherty	.25
522	Keith Comstock	.25
523	*Greg Hibbard*	.30
524	Lee Smith	.30
525	Dana Kiecker	.25
526	Darrel Akerfelds	.25
527	Greg Myers	.25
528	Checklist	.25

1991 Leaf

JOHN OLERUD 1B

Silver borders and black insets surround the color action photos on the 1991 Leaf cards. The set was once again released in two series. Series I consists of cards 1-264. Card backs feature an additional player photo, biographical information, statistics and career highlights. The 1991 issue is not considered as scarce as the 1990 release.

		MT
Complete Set (528):		25.00
Common Player:		.05
Series 1 or 2 Wax Box:		28.00
1	The Leaf Card	.05
2	Kurt Stillwell	.05
3	Bobby Witt	.05
4	Tony Phillips	.05
5	Scott Garrelts	.05
6	Greg Swindell	.05
7	Billy Ripken	.05
8	Dave Martinez	.05
9	Kelly Gruber	.05
10	Juan Samuel	.05
11	Brian Holman	.05
12	Craig Biggio	.20
13	Lonnie Smith	.05
14	Ron Robinson	.05
15	Mike LaValliere	.05
16	Mark Davis	.05
17	Jack Daugherty	.05
18	Mike Henneman	.05
19	Mike Greenwell	.05
20	Dave Magadan	.05
21	Mark Williamson	.05
22	Marquis Grissom	.15
23	Pat Borders	.05
24	Mike Scioscia	.05
25	Shawon Dunston	.10
26	Randy Bush	.05

27	John Smoltz	.20
28	Chuck Crim	.05
29	Don Slaught	.05
30	Mike Macfarlane	.05
31	Wally Joyner	.05
32	Pat Combs	.05
33	Tony Pena	.05
34	Howard Johnson	.05
35	Leo Gomez	.05
36	Spike Owen	.05
37	Eric Davis	.10
38	Roberto Kelly	.05
39	Jerome Walton	.05
40	Shane Mack	.05
41	Kent Mercker	.05
42	B.J. Surhoff	.05
43	Jerry Browne	.05
44	Lee Smith	.05
45	Chuck Finley	.05
46	Terry Mulholland	.05
47	Tom Bolton	.05
48	Tom Herr	.05
49	Jim Deshaies	.05
50	Walt Weiss	.05
51	Hal Morris	.10
52	Lee Guetterman	.05
53	Paul Assenmacher	.05
54	Brian Harper	.05
55	Paul Gibson	.05
56	John Burkett	.05
57	Doug Jones	.05
58	Jose Oquendo	.05
59	Dick Schofield	.05
60	Dickie Thon	.05
61	Ramon Martinez	.10
62	Jay Buhner	.20
63	Mark Portugal	.05
64	Bob Welch	.05
65	Chris Sabo	.05
66	Chuck Cary	.05
67	Mark Langston	.10
68	Joe Boever	.05
69	Jody Reed	.05
70	Alejandro Pena	.05
71	Jeff King	.05
72	Tom Pagnozzi	.05
73	Joe Oliver	.05
74	Mike Witt	.05
75	Hector Villanueva	.05
76	Dan Gladden	.05
77	Dave Justice	.25
78	Mike Gallego	.05
79	Tom Candiotti	.05
80	Ozzie Smith	.40
81	Luis Polonia	.05
82	Randy Ready	.05
83	Greg Harris	.05
84	Checklist(Dave Justice)	.15
85	Kevin Mitchell	.10
86	Mark McLemore	.05
87	Terry Steinbach	.05
88	Tom Browning	.05
89	Matt Nokes	.05
90	Mike Harkey	.05
91	Omar Vizquel	.05
92	Dave Bergman	.05
93	Matt Williams	.40
94	Steve Olin	.05
95	Craig Wilson	.05
96	Dave Stieb	.05
97	Ruben Sierra	.10
98	Jay Howell	.05
99	Scott Bradley	.05
100	Eric Yelding	.05
101	Rickey Henderson	.15
102	Jeff Reed	.05
103	Jimmy Key	.10
104	Terry Shumpert	.05
105	Kenny Rogers	.05
106	Cecil Fielder	.30
107	Robby Thompson	.05
108	Alex Cole	.05
109	Randy Milligan	.05
110	Andres Galarraga	.15
111	Bill Spiers	.05
112	Kal Daniels	.05
113	Henry Cotto	.05
114	Casy Candaele	.05
115	Jeff Blauser	.05
116	Robin Yount	.25
117	Ben McDonald	.10
118	Bret Saberhagen	.10
119	Juan Gonzalez	1.25
120	Lou Whitaker	.05
121	Ellis Burks	.15
122	Charlie O'Brien	.05

123	John Smiley	.05
124	Tim Burke	.05
125	John Olerud	.20
126	Eddie Murray	.30
127	Greg Maddux	1.50
128	Kevin Tapani	.05
129	Ron Gant	.15
130	Jay Bell	.05
131	Chris Hoiles	.05
132	Tom Gordon	.05
133	Kevin Seitzer	.05
134	Jeff Huson	.05
135	Jerry Don Gleaton	.05
136	Jeff Brantley	.05
137	Felix Fermin	.05
138	Mike Devereaux	.05
139	Delino DeShields	.05
140	David Wells	.05
141	Tim Crews	.05
142	Erik Hanson	.05
143	Mark Davidson	.05
144	Tommy Gregg	.05
145	Jim Gantner	.05
146	Jose Lind	.05
147	Danny Tartabull	.05
148	Geno Petralli	.05
149	Travis Fryman	.15
150	Tim Naehring	.10
151	Kevin McReynolds	.05
152	Joe Orsulak	.05
153	Steve Frey	.05
154	Duane Ward	.05
155	Stan Javier	.05
156	Damon Berryhill	.05
157	Gene Larkin	.05
158	Greg Olson	.05
159	Mark Knudson	.05
160	Carmelo Martinez	.05
161	Storm Davis	.05
162	Jim Abbott	.10
163	Len Dykstra	.10
164	Tom Brunansky	.05
165	Dwight Gooden	.15
166	Jose Mesa	.05
167	Oil Can Boyd	.05
168	Barry Larkin	.15
169	Scott Sanderson	.05
170	Mark Grace	.15
171	Mark Guthrie	.05
172	Tom Glavine	.40
173	Gary Sheffield	.25
174	Checklist(Roger Clemens)	.15
175	Chris James	.05
176	Milt Thompson	.05
177	Donnie Hill	.05
178	Wes Chamberlain	.05
179	John Marzano	.05
180	Frank Viola	.05
181	Eric Anthony	.05
182	Jose Canseco	.40
183	Scott Scudder	.05
184	Dave Eiland	.05
185	Luis Salazar	.05
186	Pedro Munoz	.05
187	Steve Searcy	.05
188	Don Robinson	.05
189	Sandy Alomar	.10
190	Jose DeLeon	.05
191	John Orton	.05
192	Darren Daulton	.10
193	Mike Morgan	.05
194	Greg Briley	.05
195	Karl Rhodes	.05
196	Harold Baines	.10
197	Bill Doran	.05
198	Alvaro Espinoza	.05
199	Kirk McCaskill	.05
200	Jose DeJesus	.05
201	Jack Clark	.05
202	Daryl Boston	.05
203	Randy Tomlin	.05
204	Pedro Guerrero	.05
205	Billy Hatcher	.05
206	Tim Leary	.05
207	Ryne Sandberg	.60
208	Kirby Puckett	.75
209	Charlie Leibrandt	.05
210	Rick Honeycutt	.05
211	Joel Skinner	.05
212	Rex Hudler	.05
213	Bryan Harvey	.05
214	Charlie Hayes	.05
215	Matt Young	.05
216	Terry Kennedy	.05
217	Carl Nichols	.05
218	Mike Moore	.05

#	Player	Price	#	Player	Price	#	Player	Price
219	Paul O'Neill	.10	316	Beau Allred	.05	412	Dale Murphy	.15
220	Steve Sax	.05	317	Curtis Wilkerson	.05	413	Tim Raines	.15
221	Shawn Boskie	.05	318	Bill Sampen	.05	414	Norm Charlton	.05
222	Rich DeLucia	.05	319	Randy Johnson	.40	415	Greg Cadaret	.05
223	Lloyd Moseby	.05	320	Mike Heath	.05	416	Chris Nabholz	.05
224	Mike Kingery	.05	321	Sammy Sosa	2.00	417	Dave Stewart	.05
225	Carlos Baerga	.10	322	Mickey Tettleton	.15	418	Rich Gedman	.05
226	Bryn Smith	.05	323	Jose Vizcaino	.05	419	Willie Randolph	.05
227	Todd Stottlemyre	.05	324	John Candelaria	.05	420	Mitch Williams	.05
228	Julio Franco	.10	325	David Howard	.12	421	Brook Jacoby	.05
229	Jim Gott	.05	326	Jose Rijo	.05	422	Greg Harris	.05
230	Mike Schooler	.05	327	Todd Zeile	.15	423	Nolan Ryan	2.00
231	Steve Finley	.05	328	Gene Nelson	.05	424	Dave Rohde	.05
232	Dave Henderson	.05	329	Dwayne Henry	.05	425	Don Mattingly	.75
233	Luis Quinones	.05	330	Mike Boddicker	.05	426	Greg Gagne	.05
234	Mark Whiten	.05	331	Ozzie Guillen	.05	427	Vince Coleman	.05
235	Brian McRae	.25	332	Sam Horn	.05	428	Dan Pasqua	.05
236	Rich Gossage	.05	333	Wally Whitehurst	.05	429	Alvin Davis	.05
237	Rob Deer	.05	334	Dave Parker	.10	430	Cal Ripken, Jr.	2.00
238	Will Clark	.25	335	George Brett	.40	431	Jamie Quirk	.05
239	Albert Belle	.50	336	Bobby Thigpen	.05	432	Benito Santiago	.12
240	Bob Melvin	.05	337	Ed Whitson	.05	433	Jose Uribe	.05
241	Larry Walker	.30	338	Ivan Calderon	.05	434	Candy Maldonado	.05
242	Dante Bichette	.40	339	Mike Pagliarulo	.05	435	Junior Felix	.05
243	Orel Hershiser	.15	340	Jack McDowell	.10	436	Deion Sanders	.75
244	Pete O'Brien	.05	341	Dana Kiecker	.05	437	John Franco	.05
245	Pete Harnisch	.10	342	Fred McGriff	.40	438	Greg Hibbard	.05
246	Jeff Treadway	.05	343	Mark Lee	.05	439	Floyd Bannister	.05
247	Julio Machado	.05	344	Alfredo Griffin	.05	440	Steve Howe	.05
248	Dave Johnson	.05	345	Scott Bankhead	.05	441	Steve Decker	.05
249	Kirk Gibson	.05	346	Darrin Jackson	.05	442	Vicente Palacios	.05
250	Kevin Brown	.05	347	Rafael Palmeiro	.25	443	Pat Tabler	.05
251	Milt Cuyler	.05	348	Steve Farr	.05	444	Checklist(Darryl Strawberry)	.10
252	Jeff Reardon	.05	349	Hensley Meulens	.05			
253	David Cone	.10	350	Danny Cox	.05	445	Mike Felder	.05
254	Gary Redus	.05	351	Alan Trammell	.15	446	Al Newman	.05
255	Junior Noboa	.05	352	Edwin Nunez	.05	447	Chris Donnels	.05
256	Greg Myers	.05	353	Joe Carter	.20	448	Rich Rodriguez	.05
257	Dennis Cook	.05	354	Eric Show	.05	449	Turner Ward	.05
258	Joe Girardi	.05	355	Vance Law	.05	450	Bob Walk	.05
259	Allan Anderson	.05	356	Jeff Gray	.05	451	Gilberto Reyes	.05
260	Paul Marak	.05	357	Bobby Bonilla	.15	452	Mike Jackson	.05
261	Barry Bonds	.75	358	Ernest Riles	.05	453	Rafael Belliard	.05
262	Juan Bell	.05	359	Ron Hassey	.05	454	Wayne Edwards	.05
263	Russ Morman	.05	360	Willie McGee	.12	455	Andy Allanson	.05
264	Checklist(George Brett)	.20	361	Mackey Sasser	.05	456	Dave Smith	.05
265	Jerald Clark	.05	362	Glenn Braggs	.05	457	Gary Carter	.15
266	Dwight Evans	.05	363	Mario Diaz	.05	458	Warren Cromartie	.05
267	Roberto Alomar	.50	364	Checklist(Barry Bonds)	.15	459	Jack Armstrong	.05
268	Danny Jackson	.05	365	Kevin Bass	.05	460	Bob Tewksbury	.10
269	Brian Downing	.05	366	Pete Incaviglia	.05	461	Joe Klink	.05
270	John Cerutti	.05	367	Luis Sojo	.05	462	Xavier Hernandez	.05
271	Robin Ventura	.15	368	Lance Parrish	.10	463	Scott Radinsky	.05
272	Wade Boggs	.30	369	Mark Leonard	.05	464	Jeff Robinson	.05
273	Dennis Martinez	.15	370	Heathcliff Slocumb	.05	465	Gregg Jefferies	.40
274	Andy Benes	.15	371	Jimmy Jones	.05	466	Denny Neagle	.15
275	Andy Benes	.15	372	Ken Griffey, Jr.	3.50	467	Carmelo Martinez	.05
276	Tony Fossas	.05	373	Chris Hammond	.10	468	Donn Pall	.05
277	Franklin Stubbs	.05	374	Chili Davis	.10	469	Bruce Hurst	.05
278	John Kruk	.05	375	Joey Cora	.05	470	Eric Bullock	.05
279	Kevin Gross	.05	376	Ken Hill	.15	471	Rick Aguilera	.05
280	Von Hayes	.05	377	Darryl Strawberry	.15	472	Charlie Hough	.05
281	Frank Thomas	3.00	378	Ron Darling	.05	473	Carlos Quintana	.05
282	Rob Dibble	.05	379	Sid Bream	.05	474	Marty Barrett	.05
283	Mel Hall	.05	380	Bill Swift	.05	475	Kevin Brown	.10
284	Rick Mahler	.05	381	Shawn Abner	.05	476	Bobby Ojeda	.05
285	Dennis Eckersley	.15	382	Eric King	.05	477	Edgar Martinez	.20
286	Bernard Gilkey	.25	383	Mickey Morandini	.15	478	Bip Roberts	.05
287	Dan Plesac	.05	384	Carlton Fisk	.15	479	Mike Flanagan	.05
288	Jason Grimsley	.05	385	Steve Lake	.05	480	John Habyan	.05
289	Mark Lewis	.15	386	Mike Jeffcoat	.05	481	Larry Casian	.05
290	Tony Gwynn	.50	387	Darren Holmes	.05	482	Wally Backman	.05
291	Jeff Russell	.05	388	Tim Wallach	.05	483	Doug Dascenzo	.05
292	Curt Schilling	.05	389	George Bell	.05	484	Rick Dempsey	.05
293	Pascual Perez	.05	390	Craig Lefferts	.05	485	Ed Sprague	.10
294	Jack Morris	.05	391	Ernie Whitt	.05	486	Steve Chitren	.05
295	Hubie Brooks	.05	392	Felix Jose	.05	487	Mark McGwire	2.00
296	Alex Fernandez	.40	393	Kevin Maas	.05	488	Roger Clemens	.50
297	Harold Reynolds	.05	394	Devon White	.12	489	Orlando Merced	.05
298	Craig Worthington	.05	395	Otis Nixon	.05	490	Rene Gonzales	.05
299	Willie Wilson	.05	396	Chuck Knoblauch	.50	491	Mike Stanton	.05
300	Mike Maddux	.05	397	Scott Coolbaugh	.05	492	Al Osuna	.05
301	Dave Righetti	.05	398	Glenn Davis	.05	493	Rick Cerone	.05
302	Paul Molitor	.30	399	Manny Lee	.05	494	Mariano Duncan	.05
303	Gary Gaetti	.10	400	Andre Dawson	.15	495	Zane Smith	.05
304	Terry Pendleton	.05	401	Scott Chiamparino	.05	496	John Morris	.05
305	Kevin Elster	.05	402	Bill Gullickson	.05	497	Frank Tanana	.05
306	Scott Fletcher	.05	403	Lance Johnson	.05	498	Junior Ortiz	.05
307	Jeff Robinson	.05	404	Juan Agosto	.05	499	Dave Winfield	.20
308	Jesse Barfield	.05	405	Danny Darwin	.05	500	Gary Varsho	.05
309	Mike LaCoss	.05	406	Barry Jones	.05	501	Chico Walker	.05
310	Andy Van Slyke	.05	407	Larry Andersen	.05	502	Ken Caminiti	.20
311	Glenallen Hill	.05	408	Luis Rivera	.05	503	Ken Griffey, Sr.	.10
312	Bud Black	.05	409	Jaime Navarro	.05	504	Randy Myers	.05
313	Kent Hrbek	.15	410	Roger McDowell	.05	505	Steve Bedrosian	.05
314	Tim Teufel	.05	411	Brett Butler	.15	506	Cory Snyder	.05
315	Tony Fernandez	.05						

507	Cris Carpenter	.05
508	Tim Belcher	.05
509	Jeff Hamilton	.05
510	Steve Avery	.20
511	Dave Valle	.05
512	Tom Lampkin	.05
513	Shawn Hillegas	.05
514	Reggie Jefferson	.15
515	Ron Karkovice	.05
516	Doug Drabek	.05
517	Tom Henke	.05
518	Chris Bosio	.05
519	Gregg Olson	.05
520	Bob Scanlan	.05
521	Alonzo Powell	.05
522	Jeff Ballard	.05
523	Ray Lankford	.25
524	Tommy Greene	.05
525	Mike Timlin	.15
526	Juan Berenguer	.05
527	Scott Erickson	.12
528	Checklist(Sandy Alomar Jr.)	.05

1991 Leaf
Gold Rookies

MO VAUGHN 1B

Special gold rookie and gold bonus cards were randomly inserted in 1991 Leaf packs. Backs have a design similar to the regular-issue cards, but have gold, rather than silver background. Fronts have gold-foil highlights. Card numbers of the issued version have a "BC" prefix, but there is a much rarer second version of the Series 1 cards, which carry card numbers between 265-276.

		MT
Complete Set (26):		30.00
Common Player:		.50
BC1	Scott Leius	.50
BC2	Luis Gonzalez	.50
BC3	Wil Cordero	1.00
BC4	Gary Scott	.50
BC5	Willie Banks	.50
BC6	Arthur Rhodes	.50
BC7	Mo Vaughn	8.00
BC8	Henry Rodriguez	.50
BC9	Todd Van Poppel	.50
BC10	Reggie Sanders	.75
BC11	Rico Brogna	.50
BC12	Mike Mussina	7.50
BC13	Kirk Dressendorfer	.50
BC14	Jeff Bagwell	10.00
BC15	Pete Schourek	.50
BC16	Wade Taylor	.50
BC17	Pat Kelly	.50
BC18	Tim Costo	.50
BC19	Roger Salkeld	.50
BC20	Andujar Cedeno	.50
BC21	Ryan Klesko	7.50
BC22	Mike Huff	.50
BC23	Anthony Young	1.00
BC24	Eddie Zosky	.50
BC25	Nolan Ryan (7th no-hitter)	10.00

BC26	Rickey Henderson (record steal)	2.00
265	Scott Leius	9.00
266	Luis Gonzalez	9.00
267	Wil Cordero	12.00
268	Gary Scott	9.00
269	Willie Banks	9.00
270	Arthur Rhodes	9.00
271	Mo Vaughn	65.00
272	Henry Rodriguez	9.00
273	Todd Van Poppel	9.00
274	Reggie Sanders	12.00
275	Rico Brogna	10.00
276	Mike Mussina	60.00

1992 Leaf

TRAVIS FRYMAN 3B

Two 264-card series comprise this 528-card set. The cards feature action photos on both the front and the back. Silver borders surround the photo on the card front. Each leaf card was also produced in a gold foil version. One gold card was issued per pack and a complete Leaf Gold Edition set can be assembled. Traded players and free agents are shown in uniform with their new teams.

		MT
Complete Set (528):		20.00
Common Player:		.05
Series 1 or 2 Wax Box:		20.00
1	Jim Abbott	.15
2	Cal Eldred	.10
3	Bud Black	.05
4	Dave Howard	.05
5	Luis Sojo	.05
6	Gary Scott	.05
7	Joe Oliver	.10
8	Chris Gardner	.08
9	Sandy Alomar	.10
10	Greg Harris	.05
11	Doug Drabek	.05
12	Darryl Hamilton	.10
13	Mike Mussina	.60
14	Kevin Tapani	.10
15	Ron Gant	.15
16	Mark McGwire	2.00
17	Robin Ventura	.25
18	Pedro Guerrero	.05
19	Roger Clemens	.40
20	Steve Farr	.05
21	Frank Tanana	.05
22	Joe Hesketh	.05
23	Erik Hanson	.05
24	Greg Cadaret	.05
25	Rex Hudler	.05
26	Mark Grace	.15
27	Kelly Gruber	.05
28	Jeff Bagwell	.75
29	Darryl Strawberry	.10
30	Dave Smith	.05
31	Kevin Appier	.10
32	Steve Chitren	.05
33	Kevin Gross	.05
34	Rick Aguilera	.05

35	Juan Guzman	.10
36	Joe Orsulak	.05
37	Tim Raines	.15
38	Harold Reynolds	.05
39	Charlie Hough	.05
40	Tony Phillips	.10
41	Nolan Ryan	1.25
42	Vince Coleman	.05
43	Andy Van Slyke	.05
44	Tim Burke	.05
45	Luis Polonia	.05
46	Tom Browning	.05
47	Willie McGee	.10
48	Gary DiSarcina	.05
49	Mark Lewis	.10
50	Phil Plantier	.05
51	Doug Dascenzo	.05
52	Cal Ripken, Jr.	2.00
53	Pedro Munoz	.05
54	Carlos Hernandez	.05
55	Jerald Clark	.05
56	Jeff Brantley	.05
57	Don Mattingly	.60
58	Roger McDowell	.05
59	Steve Avery	.12
60	John Olerud	.20
61	Bill Gullickson	.05
62	Juan Gonzalez	.60
63	Felix Jose	.05
64	Robin Yount	.25
65	Greg Briley	.05
66	Steve Finley	.05
67	Checklist	.05
68	Tom Gordon	.05
69	Rob Dibble	.05
70	Glenallen Hill	.05
71	Calvin Jones	.05
72	Joe Girardi	.05
73	Barry Larkin	.15
74	Andy Benes	.05
75	Milt Cyler	.05
76	Kevin Bass	.05
77	Pete Harnisch	.05
78	Wilson Alvarez	.05
79	Mike Devereaux	.05
80	Doug Henry	.05
81	Orel Hershiser	.15
82	Shane Mack	.10
83	Mike Macfarlane	.05
84	Thomas Howard	.05
85	Alex Fernandez	.05
86	Reggie Jefferson	.10
87	Leo Gomez	.05
88	Mel Hall	.05
89	Mike Greenwell	.10
90	Jeff Russell	.05
91	Steve Buechele	.05
92	David Cone	.10
93	Kevin Reimer	.05
94	Mark Lemke	.05
95	Bob Tewksbury	.05
96	Zane Smith	.05
97	Mark Eichhorn	.05
98	Kirby Puckett	.75
99	Paul O'Neill	.12
100	Dennis Eckersley	.10
101	Duane Ward	.05
102	Matt Nokes	.05
103	Mo Vaughn	.50
104	Pat Kelly	.05
105	Ron Karkovice	.05
106	Bill Spiers	.05
107	Gary Gaetti	.10
108	Mackey Sasser	.05
109	Robby Thompson	.05
110	Marvin Freeman	.05
111	Jimmy Key	.05
112	Dwight Gooden	.12
113	Charlie Leibrandt	.05
114	Devon White	.10
115	Charles Nagy	.10
116	Rickey Henderson	.25
117	Paul Assenmacher	.05
118	Junior Felix	.05
119	Julio Franco	.10
120	Norm Charlton	.05
121	Scott Servais	.05
122	Gerald Perry	.05
123	Brian McRae	.10
124	Don Slaught	.05
125	Juan Samuel	.05
126	Harold Baines	.12
127	Scott Livingstone	.05
128	Jay Buhner	.10
129	Darrin Jackson	.05
130	Luis Mercedes	.05

#	Name	Price	#	Name	Price	#	Name	Price	#	Name	Price
131	Brian Harper	.05	227	Jose DeLeon	.05	323	Tony Pena	.05
132	Howard Johnson	.05	228	Mike LaValliere	.05	324	Pat Borders	.05
133	Checklist	.05	229	Mark Langston	.08	325	Mike Henneman	.05
134	Dante Bichette	.15	230	Chuck Knoblauch	.20	326	Kevin Brown	.15
135	Dave Righetti	.05	231	Bill Doran	.05	327	Chris Nabholz	.05
136	Jeff Montgomery	.05	232	Dave Henderson	.05	328	Franklin Stubbs	.05
137	Joe Grahe	.05	233	Roberto Alomar	.50	329	Tino Martinez	.15
138	Delino DeShields	.08	234	Scott Fletcher	.05	330	Mickey Morandini	.08
139	Jose Rijo	.08	235	Tim Naehring	.05	331	Checklist	.05
140	Ken Caminiti	.15	236	Mike Gallego	.05	332	Mark Gubicza	.08
141	Steve Olin	.05	237	Lance Johnson	.05	333	Bill Landrum	.05
142	Kurt Stillwell	.05	238	Paul Molitor	.25	334	Mark Whiten	.08
143	Jay Bell	.05	239	Dan Gladden	.05	335	Darren Daulton	.08
144	Jaime Navarro	.05	240	Willie Randolph	.05	336	Rick Wilkins	.08
145	Ben McDonald	.10	241	Will Clark	.30	337	*Brian Jordan*	1.50
146	Greg Gagne	.05	242	Sid Bream	.05	338	Kevin Ward	.05
147	Jeff Blauser	.05	243	Derek Bell	.20	339	Ruben Amaro	.05
148	Carney Lansford	.05	244	Bill Pecota	.05	340	Trevor Wilson	.05
149	Ozzie Guillen	.05	245	Terry Pendleton	.05	341	Andujar Cedeno	.05
150	Milt Thompson	.05	246	Randy Ready	.05	342	Michael Huff	.05
151	Jeff Reardon	.05	247	Jack Armstrong	.05	343	Brady Anderson	.15
152	Scott Sanderson	.05	248	Todd Van Poppel	.10	344	Craig Grebeck	.05
153	Cecil Fielder	.20	249	Shawon Dunston	.15	345	Bobby Ojeda	.05
154	Greg Harris	.05	250	Bobby Rose	.05	346	Mike Pagliarulo	.05
155	Rich DeLucia	.05	251	Jeff Huson	.05	347	Terry Shumpert	.05
156	Roberto Kelly	.05	252	Bip Roberts	.05	348	Dann Bilardello	.05
157	Bryn Smith	.05	253	Doug Jones	.05	349	Frank Thomas	2.50
158	Chuck McElroy	.05	254	Lee Smith	.10	350	Albert Belle	.40
159	Tom Henke	.05	255	George Brett	.40	351	Jose Mesa	.05
160	Luis Gonzalez	.05	256	Randy Tomlin	.05	352	Rich Monteleone	.05
161	Steve Wilson	.05	257	Todd Benzinger	.05	353	Bob Walk	.05
162	Shawn Boskie	.05	258	Dave Stewart	.05	354	Monty Fariss	.05
163	Mark Davis	.05	259	Mark Carreon	.05	355	Luis Rivera	.05
164	Mike Moore	.05	260	Pete O'Brien	.05	356	Anthony Young	.12
165	Mike Scioscia	.05	261	Tim Teufel	.05	357	Geno Petralli	.05
166	Scott Erickson	.10	262	Bob Milacki	.05	358	Otis Nixon	.05
167	Todd Stottlemyre	.10	263	Mark Guthrie	.05	359	Tom Pagnozzi	.05
168	Alvin Davis	.05	264	Darrin Fletcher	.05	360	Reggie Sanders	.15
169	Greg Hibbard	.05	265	Omar Vizquel	.05	361	Lee Stevens	.05
170	David Valle	.05	266	Chris Bosio	.05	362	Kent Hrbek	.15
171	Dave Winfield	.25	267	Jose Canseco	.25	363	Orlando Merced	.05
172	Alan Trammell	.12	268	Mike Boddicker	.05	364	Mike Bordick	.05
173	Kenny Rogers	.05	269	Lance Parrish	.10	365	Dion James	.05
174	John Franco	.05	270	Jose Vizcaino	.05	366	Jack Clark	.05
175	Jose Lind	.05	271	Chris Sabo	.05	367	Mike Stanley	.05
176	Pete Schourek	.10	272	Royce Clayton	.15	368	Randy Velarde	.05
177	Von Hayes	.05	273	Marquis Grissom	.20	369	Dan Pasqua	.05
178	Chris Hammond	.05	274	Fred McGriff	.25	370	Pat Listach	.05
179	John Burkett	.05	275	Barry Bonds	.60	371	Mike Fitzgerald	.05
180	Dickie Thon	.05	276	Greg Vaughn	.15	372	Tom Foley	.05
181	Joel Skinner	.05	277	Gregg Olson	.05	373	Matt Williams	.20
182	Scott Cooper	.05	278	Dave Hollins	.10	374	Brian Hunter	.05
183	Andre Dawson	.15	279	Tom Glavine	.15	375	Joe Carter	.15
184	Billy Ripken	.05	280	Bryan Hickerson	.05	376	Bret Saberhagen	.08
185	Kevin Mitchell	.10	281	Scott Radinsky	.05	377	Mike Stanton	.05
186	Brett Butler	.15	282	Omar Olivares	.05	378	Hubie Brooks	.05
187	Tony Fernandez	.05	283	Ivan Calderon	.05	379	Eric Bell	.05
188	Cory Snyder	.05	284	Kevin Maas	.05	380	Walt Weiss	.05
189	John Habyan	.05	285	Mickey Tettleton	.10	381	Danny Jackson	.05
190	Dennis Martinez	.12	286	Wade Boggs	.25	382	Manuel Lee	.05
191	John Smoltz	.15	287	Stan Belinda	.05	383	Ruben Sierra	.10
192	Greg Myers	.05	288	Bret Barberie	.05	384	Greg Swindell	.05
193	Rob Deer	.05	289	Jose Oquendo	.05	385	Ryan Bowen	.05
194	Ivan Rodriguez	.40	290	Frank Castillo	.05	386	Kevin Ritz	.10
195	Ray Lankford	.25	291	Dave Stieb	.05	387	Curtis Wilkerson	.05
196	Bill Wegman	.05	292	Tommy Greene	.05	388	Gary Varsho	.05
197	Edgar Martinez	.15	293	Eric Karros	.20	389	Dave Hansen	.05
198	Darryl Kile	.10	294	Greg Maddux	2.00	390	Bob Welch	.05
199	Checklist	.05	295	Jim Eisenreich	.05	391	Lou Whitaker	.08
200	Brent Mayne	.05	296	Rafael Palmeiro	.15	392	Ken Griffey, Jr.	3.00
201	Larry Walker	.25	297	Ramon Martinez	.10	393	Mike Maddux	.05
202	Carlos Baerga	.15	298	Tim Wallach	.05	394	Arthur Rhodes	.08
203	Russ Swan	.05	299	Jim Thome	.75	395	Chili Davis	.10
204	Mike Morgan	.05	300	Chito Martinez	.05	396	Eddie Murray	.20
205	Hal Morris	.10	301	Mitch Williams	.05	397	Checklist	.05
206	Tony Gwynn	.75	302	Randy Johnson	.30	398	Dave Cochrane	.05
207	Mark Leiter	.05	303	Carlton Fisk	.10	399	Kevin Seitzer	.05
208	Kirt Manwaring	.05	304	Travis Fryman	.20	400	Ozzie Smith	.25
209	Al Osuna	.05	305	Bobby Witt	.05	401	Paul Sorrento	.05
210	Bobby Thigpen	.05	306	Dave Magadan	.05	402	Les Lancaster	.05
211	Chris Hoiles	.05	307	Alex Cole	.05	403	Junior Noboa	.05
212	B.J. Surhoff	.05	308	Bobby Bonilla	.12	404	Dave Justice	.25
213	Lenny Harris	.05	309	Bryan Harvey	.05	405	Andy Ashby	.08
214	Scott Leius	.05	310	Rafael Belliard	.05	406	Danny Tartabull	.08
215	Gregg Jefferies	.25	311	Mariano Duncan	.05	407	Bill Swift	.05
216	Bruce Hurst	.05	312	Chuck Crim	.05	408	Craig Lefferts	.05
217	Steve Sax	.05	313	John Kruk	.15	409	Tom Candiotti	.05
218	Dave Otto	.05	314	Ellis Burks	.15	410	Lance Blankenship	.05
219	Sam Horn	.05	315	Craig Biggio	.20	411	Jeff Tackett	.05
220	Charlie Hayes	.05	316	Glenn Davis	.05	412	Sammy Sosa	2.00
221	Frank Viola	.05	317	Ryne Sandberg	.35	413	Jody Reed	.05
222	Jose Guzman	.05	318	Mike Sharperson	.05	414	Bruce Ruffin	.05
223	Gary Redus	.05	319	Rich Rodriguez	.05	415	Gene Larkin	.05
224	Dave Gallagher	.05	320	Lee Guetterman	.05	416	John Vanderwal	.05
225	Dean Palmer	.20	321	Benito Santiago	.08	417	Tim Belcher	.05
226	Greg Olson	.05	322	Jose Offerman	.05	418	Steve Frey	.05

419	Dick Schofield	.05
420	Jeff King	.05
421	Kim Batiste	.05
422	Jack McDowell	.12
423	Damon Berryhill	.05
424	Gary Wayne	.05
425	Jack Morris	.08
426	Moises Alou	.15
427	Mark McLemore	.05
428	Juan Guerrero	.05
429	Scott Scudder	.05
430	Eric Davis	.15
431	Joe Slusarski	.05
432	Todd Zeile	.15
433	Dwayne Henry	.05
434	Cliff Brantley	.10
435	Butch Henry	.05
436	Todd Worrell	.05
437	Bob Scanlan	.05
438	Wally Joyner	.12
439	John Flaherty	.05
440	Brian Downing	.05
441	Darren Lewis	.12
442	Gary Carter	.10
443	Wally Ritchie	.05
444	Chris Jones	.05
445	Jeff Kent	.10
446	Gary Sheffield	.25
447	Ron Darling	.05
448	Deion Sanders	.25
449	Andres Galarraga	.20
450	Chuck Finley	.05
451	Derek Lilliquist	.05
452	Carl Willis	.05
453	Wes Chamberlain	.05
454	Roger Mason	.05
455	Spike Owen	.05
456	Thomas Howard	.05
457	Dave Martinez	.05
458	Pete Incaviglia	.05
459	Keith Miller	.05
460	Mike Fetters	.05
461	Paul Gibson	.05
462	George Bell	.05
463	Checklist	.05
464	Terry Mulholland	.10
465	Storm Davis	.05
466	Gary Pettis	.05
467	Randy Bush	.05
468	Ken Hill	.08
469	Rheal Cormier	.05
470	Andy Stankiewicz	.05
471	Dave Burba	.05
472	Henry Cotto	.05
473	Dale Sveum	.05
474	Rich Gossage	.05
475	William Suero	.05
476	Doug Strange	.05
477	Bill Krueger	.05
478	John Wetteland	.15
479	Melido Perez	.05
480	Lonnie Smith	.05
481	Mike Jackson	.05
482	Mike Gardiner	.05
483	David Wells	.05
484	Barry Jones	.05
485	Scott Bankhead	.05
486	Terry Leach	.05
487	Vince Horsman	.05
488	Dave Eiland	.05
489	Alejandro Pena	.05
490	Julio Valera	.05
491	Joe Boever	.05
492	Paul Miller	.05
493	*Arci Cianfrocco*	.10
494	Dave Fleming	.08
495	Kyle Abbott	.08
496	Chad Kreuter	.05
497	Chris James	.05
498	Donnie Hill	.05
499	Jacob Brumfield	.08
500	Ricky Bones	.05
501	Terry Steinbach	.05
502	Bernard Gilkey	.10
503	Dennis Cook	.05
504	Len Dykstra	.10
505	Mike Bielecki	.05
506	Bob Kipper	.05
507	Jose Melendez	.05
508	Rick Sutcliffe	.05
509	Ken Patterson	.05
510	Andy Allanson	.05
511	Al Newman	.05
512	Mark Gardner	.05
513	Jeff Schaefer	.05
514	Jim McNamara	.05

515	Peter Hoy	.05
516	Curt Schilling	.12
517	Kirk McCaskill	.05
518	Chris Gwynn	.05
519	Sid Fernandez	.05
520	Jeff Parrett	.05
521	Scott Ruskin	.05
522	Kevin McReynolds	.05
523	Rick Cerone	.05
524	Jesse Orosco	.05
525	Troy Afenir	.05
526	John Smiley	.05
527	Dale Murphy	.12
528	Leaf Set Card	.05

1992 Leaf Gold Edition

JOSE VIZCAINO IF

This set is a parallel version of Leaf's regular 1992 set. Card fronts do not have silver borders like the regular cards do; black borders and gold foil highlights are seen instead. A Gold Edition card was inserted in each 15-card 1992 Leaf foil pack.

	MT
Complete Set (528):	150.00
Common Player:	.25
(Gold stars 5-7X regular Leaf cards)	

1992 Leaf Gold Rookies

PAT MAHOMES RHP

Two dozen of the major leagues' most promising players are featured in this insert set. Cards 1-12 were randomly included in Se-

ries I foil packs, while cards 13-24 were in Series II packs. Cards, numbered with a BC prefix, are standard size and enhanced with gold foil.

		MT
Complete Set (24):		10.00
Common Player:		.25
1	Chad Curtis	.25
2	Brent Gates	.40
3	Pedro Martinez	1.00
4	Kenny Lofton	4.00
5	Turk Wendell	.25
6	Mark Hutton	.25
7	Todd Hundley	.75
8	Matt Stairs	.25
9	Ed Taubensee	.25
10	David Nied	.25
11	Salomon Torres	.25
12	Bret Boone	.40
13	John Ruffin	.25
14	Ed Martel	.25
15	Rick Trlicek	.25
16	Raul Mondesi	2.00
17	Pat Mahomes	.25
18	Dan Wilson	.25
19	Donovan Osborne	.25
20	Dave Silvestri	.25
21	Gary DiSarcina	.25
22	Denny Neagle	.50
23	Steve Hosey	.25
24	John Doherty	.25

1993 Leaf

JUAN GONZALEZ RANGERS

Leaf issued this set in three series: two 220-card series and a 110-card update set. Card fronts have full-bleed action photos and players' names stamped in gold foil. Color-coded slate corners are used to differentiate teams. Backs have player photos against cityscapes or landmarks from the team's home city, a holographic embossed team logo and 1992 and career statistics. Players from the National League's expansion teams, the Colorado Rockies and Florida Marlins, along with the Cincinnati Reds, California Angels and Seattle Mariners were featured in Series II packs so they could be pictured in their new uniforms. The Update series included a specially numbered "DW" insert card honoring Dave Winfield's 3,000-hit landmark, plus 3,500 special Frank Thomas autographed cards.

A player's name in *italic* type indicates a rookie card.

	MT
Complete Set (550):	50.00
Common Player:	.10
Series 1 or 2 Wax Box:	30.00
Update Wax Box:	45.00

#	Player	MT
1	Ben McDonald	.10
2	Sid Fernandez	.10
3	Juan Guzman	.10
4	Curt Schilling	.15
5	Ivan Rodriguez	.60
6	Don Slaught	.10
7	Terry Steinbach	.10
8	Todd Zeile	.15
9	Andy Stankiewicz	.10
10	Tim Teufel	.10
11	Marvin Freeman	.10
12	Jim Austin	.10
13	Bob Scanlan	.10
14	Rusty Meacham	.10
15	Casey Candaele	.10
16	Travis Fryman	.20
17	Jose Offerman	.10
18	Albert Belle	.75
19	John Vander Wahl (Vander Wal)	.10
20	Dan Pasqua	.10
21	Frank Viola	.10
22	Terry Mulholland	.10
23	Gregg Olson	.10
24	Randy Tomlin	.10
25	Todd Stottlemyre	.10
26	Jose Oquendo	.10
27	Julio Franco	.10
28	Tony Gwynn	1.25
29	Ruben Sierra	.15
30	Bobby Thigpen	.10
31	Jim Bullinger	.10
32	Rick Aguilera	.10
33	Scott Servais	.10
34	Cal Eldred	.10
35	Mike Piazza	2.00
36	Brent Mayne	.10
37	Wil Cordero	.10
38	Milt Cuyler	.10
39	Howard Johnson	.10
40	Kenny Lofton	.75
41	Alex Fernandez	.15
42	Denny Neagle	.10
43	Tony Pena	.10
44	Bob Tewksbury	.10
45	Glenn Davis	.10
46	Fred McGriff	.25
47	John Olerud	.20
48	Steve Hosey	.10
49	Rafael Palmeiro	.20
50	Dave Justice	.20
51	Pete Harnisch	.10
52	Sam Militello	.10
53	Orel Hershiser	.15
54	Pat Mahomes	.10
55	Greg Colbrunn	.10
56	Greg Vaughn	.15
57	Vince Coleman	.10
58	Brian McRae	.15
59	Len Dykstra	.10
60	Dan Gladden	.10
61	Ted Power	.10
62	Donovan Osborne	.10
63	Ron Karkovice	.10
64	Frank Seminara	.10
65	Bob Zupcic	.10
66	Kirt Manwaring	.10
67	Mike Devereaux	.10
68	Mark Lemke	.10
69	Devon White	.10
70	Sammy Sosa	1.50
71	Pedro Astacio	.15
72	Dennis Eckersley	.15
73	Chris Nabholz	.10
74	Melido Perez	.10
75	Todd Hundley	.20
76	Kent Hrbek	.12
77	Mickey Morandini	.10
78	Tim McIntosh	.10
79	Andy Van Slyke	.10
80	Kevin McReynolds	.10
81	Mike Henneman	.10
82	Greg Harris	.10
83	Sandy Alomar Jr.	.12
84	Mike Jackson	.10
85	Ozzie Guillen	.10
86	Jeff Blauser	.10
87	John Valentin	.20
88	Rey Sanchez	.10
89	Rick Sutcliffe	.10
90	Luis Gonzalez	.10
91	Jeff Fassero	.10
92	Kenny Rogers	.10
93	Bret Saberhagen	.10
94	Bob Welch	.10
95	Darren Daulton	.12
96	Mike Gallego	.10
97	Orlando Merced	.10
98	Chuck Knoblauch	.25
99	Bernard Gilkey	.15
100	Billy Ashley	.15
101	Kevin Appier	.10
102	Jeff Brantley	.10
103	Bill Gullickson	.10
104	John Smoltz	.20
105	Paul Sorrento	.10
106	Steve Buechele	.10
107	Steve Sax	.10
108	Andujar Cedeno	.10
109	Billy Hatcher	.10
110	Checklist	.10
111	Alan Mills	.10
112	John Franco	.10
113	Jack Morris	.10
114	Mitch Williams	.10
115	Nolan Ryan	2.00
116	Jay Bell	.10
117	Mike Bordick	.10
118	Geronimo Pena	.10
119	Danny Tartabull	.10
120	Checklist	.10
121	Steve Avery	.15
122	Ricky Bones	.10
123	Mike Morgan	.10
124	Jeff Montgomery	.10
125	Jeff Bagwell	1.00
126	Tony Phillips	.15
127	Lenny Harris	.10
128	Glenallen Hill	.10
129	Marquis Grissom	.15
130	Bernie Williams (name on front is Gerald Williams)	.60
131	Greg Harris	.10
132	Tommy Greene	.10
133	Chris Hoiles	.10
134	Bob Walk	.10
135	Duane Ward	.10
136	Tom Pagnozzi	.10
137	Jeff Huson	.10
138	Kurt Stillwell	.10
139	Dave Henderson	.10
140	Darrin Jackson	.10
141	Frank Castillo	.10
142	Scott Erickson	.10
143	Darryl Kile	.10
144	Bill Wegman	.10
145	Steve Wilson	.10
146	George Brett	.75
147	Moises Alou	.15
148	Lou Whitaker	.10
149	Chico Walker	.10
150	Jerry Browne	.10
151	Kirk McCaskill	.10
152	Zane Smith	.10
153	Matt Young	.12
154	Lee Smith	.10
155	Leo Gomez	.10
156	Dan Walters	.10
157	Pat Borders	.10
158	Matt Williams	.25
159	Dean Palmer	.15
160	John Patterson	.10
161	Doug Jones	.10
162	John Habyan	.10
163	Pedro Martinez	.25
164	Carl Willis	.10
165	Darrin Fletcher	.10
166	B.J. Surhoff	.10
167	Eddie Murray	.25
168	Keith Miller	.10
169	Ricky Jordan	.10
170	Juan Gonzalez	1.25
171	Charles Nagy	.10
172	Mark Clark	.10
173	Bobby Thigpen	.10
174	Tim Scott	.10
175	Scott Cooper	.10
176	Royce Clayton	.10
177	Brady Anderson	.20
178	Sid Bream	.10
179	Derek Bell	.15
180	Otis Nixon	.10
181	Kevin Gross	.10
182	Ron Darling	.10
183	John Wetteland	.10
184	Mike Stanley	.10
185	Jeff Kent	.10
186	Brian Harper	.10
187	Mariano Duncan	.10
188	Robin Yount	.25
189	Al Martin	.10
190	Eddie Zosky	.10
191	Mike Munoz	.10
192	Andy Benes	.10
193	Dennis Cook	.10
194	Bill Swift	.10
195	Frank Thomas	2.50
196	Damon Berryhill	.10
197	Mike Greenwell	.10
198	Mark Grace	.20
199	Darryl Hamilton	.10
200	Derrick May	.10
201	Ken Hill	.10
202	Kevin Brown	.15
203	Dwight Gooden	.15
204	Bobby Witt	.10
205	Juan Bell	.10
206	Kevin Maas	.10
207	Jeff King	.10
208	Scott Leius	.10
209	Rheal Cormier	.10
210	Darryl Strawberry	.15
211	Tom Gordon	.10
212	Bud Black	.10
213	Mickey Tettleton	.10
214	Pete Smith	.10
215	Felix Fermin	.10
216	Rick Wilkins	.10
217	George Bell	.10
218	Eric Anthony	.10
219	Pedro Munoz	.10
220	Checklist	.10
221	Lance Blankenship	.10
222	Deion Sanders	.40
223	Craig Biggio	.20
224	Ryne Sandberg	.60
225	Ron Gant	.15
226	Tom Brunansky	.10
227	Chad Curtis	.10
228	Joe Carter	.15
229	Brian Jordan	.15
230	Brett Butler	.15
231	Frank Bolick	.10
232	Rod Beck	.10
233	Carlos Baerga	.10
234	Eric Karros	.15
235	Jack Armstrong	.10
236	Bobby Bonilla	.15
237	Don Mattingly	1.00
238	Jeff Gardner	.10
239	Dave Hollins	.10
240	Steve Cooke	.10
241	Jose Canseco	.25
242	Ivan Calderon	.10
243	Tim Belcher	.10
244	Freddie Benavides	.10
245	Roberto Alomar	.50
246	Rob Deer	.10
247	Will Clark	.25
248	Mike Felder	.10
249	Harold Baines	.12
250	David Cone	.15
251	Mark Guthrie	.10
252	Ellis Burks	.15
253	Jim Abbott	.15
254	Chili Davis	.10
255	Chris Bosio	.10
256	Bret Barberie	.10
257	Hal Morris	.10
258	Dante Bichette	.25
259	Storm Davis	.10
260	Gary DiSarcina	.10
261	Ken Caminiti	.25
262	Paul Molitor	.40
263	Joe Oliver	.10
264	Pat Listach	.10
265	Gregg Jefferies	.15
266	Jose Guzman	.10
267	Eric Davis	.15
268	Delino DeShields	.12
269	Barry Bonds	.75
270	Mike Bielecki	.10
271	Jay Buhner	.20
272	*Scott Pose*	.15
273	Tony Fernandez	.10
274	Chito Martinez	.10
275	Phil Plantier	.10
276	Pete Incaviglia	.10
277	Carlos Garcia	.10
278	Tom Henke	.10
279	Roger Clemens	1.00
280	Rob Dibble	.10
281	Daryl Boston	.10

No.	Player	Value
282	Greg Gagne	.10
283	Cecil Fielder	.20
284	Carlton Fisk	.15
285	Wade Boggs	.25
286	Damion Easley	.10
287	Norm Charlton	.10
288	Jeff Conine	.15
289	Roberto Kelly	.10
290	Jerald Clark	.10
291	Rickey Henderson	.15
292	Chuck Finley	.10
293	Doug Drabek	.10
294	Dave Stewart	.10
295	Tom Glavine	.20
296	Jaime Navarro	.10
297	Ray Lankford	.15
298	Greg Hibbard	.10
290	Jody Reed	.10
300	Dennis Martinez	.12
301	Dave Martinez	.10
302	Reggie Jefferson	.10
303	*John Cummings*	.25
304	Orestes Destrade	.10
305	Mike Maddux	.10
306	David Segui	.10
307	Gary Sheffield	.30
308	Danny Jackson	.10
309	Criag Lefferts	.10
310	Andre Dawson	.15
311	Barry Larkin	.20
312	Alex Cole	.10
313	Mark Gardner	.10
314	Kirk Gibson	.10
315	Shane Mack	.10
316	Bo Jackson	.15
317	Jimmy Key	.10
318	Greg Myers	.10
319	Ken Griffey, Jr.	3.00
320	Monty Fariss	.10
321	Kevin Mitchell	.10
322	Andres Galarraga	.20
323	Mark McGwire	3.00
324	Mark Langston	.10
325	Steve Finley	.10
326	Greg Maddux	2.00
327	Dave Nilsson	.10
328	Ozzie Smith	.40
329	Candy Maldonado	.10
330	Checklist	.10
331	*Tim Pugh*	.10
332	Joe Girardi	.10
333	Junior Feliz	.10
334	Greg Swindell	.10
335	Ramon Martinez	.15
336	Sean Berry	.10
337	Joe Orsulak	.10
338	Wes Chamberlain	.10
339	Stan Belinda	.10
340	Checklist	.10
341	Bruce Hurst	.10
342	John Burkett	.10
343	Mike Mussina	.60
344	Scott Fletcher	.10
345	Rene Gonzales	.10
346	Roberto Hernandez	.10
347	Carlos Martinez	.10
348	Bill Krueger	.10
349	Felix Jose	.10
350	John Jaha	.15
351	Willie Banks	.10
352	Matt Nokes	.10
353	Kevin Seitzer	.10
354	Erik Hanson	.10
355	*David Hulse*	.10
356	*Domingo Martinez*	.10
357	Greg Olson	.10
358	Randy Myers	.10
359	Tom Browning	.10
360	Charlie Hayes	.10
361	Bryan Harvey	.10
362	Eddie Taubensee	.10
363	Tim Wallach	.10
364	Mel Rojas	.10
365	Frank Tanana	.10
366	John Kruk	.10
367	*Tim Laker*	.10
368	Rich Rodriguez	.10
369	Darren Lewis	.10
370	Harold Reynolds	.10
371	Jose Melendez	.10
372	Joe Grahe	.10
373	Lance Johnson	.10
374	Jose Mesa	.12
375	Scott Livingstone	.10
376	Wally Joyner	.12
377	Kevin Reimer	.10
378	Kirby Puckett	1.00
379	Paul O'Neill	.20
380	Randy Johnson	.35
381	Manuel Lee	.10
382	Dick Schofield	.10
383	Darren Holmes	.10
384	Charlie Hough	.10
385	John Orton	.10
386	Edgar Martinez	.12
387	Terry Pendleton	.10
388	Dan Plesac	.10
389	Jeff Reardon	.10
390	David Nied	.10
391	Dave Magadan	.10
392	Larry Walker	.25
393	Ben Rivera	.10
304	Lonnie Smith	.10
395	Craig Shipley	.10
396	Willie McGee	.12
397	Arthur Rhodes	.10
398	Mike Stanton	.10
399	Luis Polonia	.10
400	Jack McDowell	.12
401	Mike Moore	.10
402	Jose Lind	.10
403	Bill Spiers	.10
404	Kevin Tapani	.10
405	Spike Owen	.10
406	Tino Martinez	.25
407	Charlie Leibrandt	.10
408	Ed Sprague	.10
409	Bryn Smith	.10
410	Benito Santiago	.10
411	Jose Rijo	.10
412	Pete O'Brien	.10
413	Willie Wilson	.10
414	Bip Roberts	.10
415	Eric Young	.15
416	Walt Weiss	.10
417	Milt Thompson	.10
418	Chris Sabo	.10
419	Scott Sanderson	.10
420	Tim Raines	.12
421	Alan Trammell	.15
422	Mike Macfarlane	.10
423	Dave Winfield	.20
424	Bob Wickman	.10
425	David Valle	.10
426	Gary Redus	.10
427	Turner Ward	.10
428	Reggie Sanders	.15
429	Todd Worrell	.10
430	Julio Valera	.10
431	Cal Ripken, Jr.	3.00
432	Mo Vaughn	.75
433	John Smiley	.10
434	Omar Vizquel	.10
435	Billy Ripken	.10
436	Cory Snyder	.10
437	Carlos Quintana	.10
438	Omar Olivares	.10
439	Robin Ventura	.15
440	Checklist	.10
441	Kevin Higgins	.10
442	Carlos Hernandez	.10
443	Dan Peltier	.10
444	Derek Lilliquist	.10
445	Tim Salmon	.50
446	*Sherman Obando*	.10
447	Pat Kelly	.10
448	Todd Van Poppel	.10
449	Mark Whiten	.10
450	Checklist	.10
451	Pat Meares	.10
452	*Tony Tarasco*	.15
453	Chris Gwynn	.10
454	Armando Reynoso	.10
455	Danny Darwin	.10
456	Willie Greene	.10
457	Mike Blowers	.10
458	*Kevin Roberson*	.15
459	*Graeme Lloyd*	.10
460	David West	.10
461	Joey Cora	.10
462	Alex Arias	.10
463	Chad Kreuter	.10
464	Mike Lansing	.15
465	Mike Timlin	.10
466	Paul Wagner	.10
467	Mark Portugal	.10
468	Jim Leyritz	.10
469	Ryan Klesko	.75
470	Mario Diaz	.10
471	Guillermo Velasquez	.10
472	Fernando Valenzuela	.15
473	Raul Mondesi	1.50
474	Mike Pagliarulo	.10
475	Chris Hammond	.10
476	Torey Lovullo	.10
477	Trevor Wilson	.10
478	*Marcos Armas*	.10
479	Dave Gallagher	.10
480	Jeff Treadway	.10
481	Jeff Branson	.10
482	Dickie Thon	.10
483	Eduardo Perez	.15
484	David Wells	.10
485	Brian Williams	.10
486	Domingo Cedeno	.20
487	Tom Candiotti	.10
488	Steve Frey	.10
409	Greg McMichael	.10
490	Marc Newfield	.15
491	Larry Andersen	.10
492	Damon Buford	.15
493	Ricky Gutierrez	.10
494	Jeff Russell	.10
495	Vinny Castilla	.20
496	Wilson Alvarez	.15
497	Scott Bullett	.10
498	Larry Casian	.10
499	Jose Vizcaino	.10
500	*J.T. Snow*	.75
501	Bryan Hickerson	.10
502	Jeremy Hernandez	.20
503	Jeromy Burnitz	.20
504	Steve Farr	.10
505	J. Owens	.15
506	Craig Paquette	.10
507	Jim Eisenreich	.10
508	Matt Whiteside	.10
509	Luis Aquino	.10
510	Mike LaValliere	.10
511	Jim Gott	.10
512	Mark McLemore	.10
513	Randy Milligan	.10
514	Gary Gaetti	.15
515	Lou Frazier	.10
516	Rich Amaral	.10
517	Gene Harris	.10
518	Aaron Sele	.15
519	Mark Wohlers	.10
520	Scott Kamieniecki	.15
521	Kent Mercker	.10
522	Jim Deshaies	.10
523	Kevin Stocker	.20
524	Jason Bere	.10
525	Tim Bogar	.10
526	Brad Pennington	.15
527	*Curt Leskanic*	.15
528	Wayne Kirby	.10
529	Tim Costo	.10
530	Doug Henry	.10
531	Trevor Hoffman	.20
532	Kelly Gruber	.10
533	Mike Harkey	.10
534	John Doherty	.10
535	Erik Pappas	.10
536	Brent Gates	.15
537	Roger McDowell	.10
538	Chris Haney	.10
539	Blas Minor	.10
540	Pat Hentgen	.20
541	Chuck Carr	.10
542	Doug Strange	.10
543	Xavier Hernandez	.10
544	Paul Quantrill	.10
545	Anthony Young	.15
546	Bret Boone	.15
547	Dwight Smith	.10
548	Bobby Munoz	.10
549	Russ Springer	.10
550	Roger Pavlik	.10
----	Dave Winfield (3000 Hits)	4.00
----	Frank Thomas (Autograph)	200.00

Modern cards have little collector value in conditions lower than Mint. Figure NM cards at 75% of values shown; EX cards at 40%.

Values shown reflect the market as of January, 1999. On-field performances of current players in the 1999 baseball season are not factored in.

1993 Leaf Fasttrack

This 20-card insert set was released in two series; cards 1-10 were randomly included in Leaf Series I retail packs, while 11-20 were in Series II packs. Card fronts and backs are similar with a player photo and a diagonal white strip with "on the Fasttrack" printed in black and red. Fronts have the gold embossed Leaf logo, backs have the silver holographic team logo.

		MT
Complete Set (20):		60.00
Common Player:		1.50
1	Frank Thomas	20.00
2	Tim Wakefield	1.50
3	Kenny Lofton	12.00
4	Mike Mussina	6.00
5	Juan Gonzalez	8.00
6	Chuck Knoblauch	3.00
7	Eric Karros	2.00
8	Ray Lankford	2.00
9	Juan Guzman	1.50
10	Pat Listach	1.50
11	Carlos Baerga	1.50
12	Felix Jose	1.50
13	Steve Avery	1.50
14	Robin Ventura	1.50
15	Ivan Rodriguez	5.00
16	Cal Eldred	1.50
17	Jeff Bagwell	12.00
18	Dave Justice	4.00
19	Travis Fryman	2.00
20	Marquis Grissom	2.00

1993 Leaf Frank Thomas

Leaf signed Frank Thomas as its spokesman for 1993, and honored him with a 10-card insert set. Cards 1-5 were randomly included in Series I packs; cards 6-10 were in Series II packs. A custom designed "Frank" logo in a holographic foil stamp is featured on each card front which includes a one-word character trait. On back is a color portrait photo of Thomas superimposed on a Chicago skyline. A paragraph on back describes how the character trait on front applies to Thomas.

		MT
Complete Set:		25.00
Common Card:		3.00
Autographed Card:		200.00
1	Aggressive(Frank Thomas)	3.00
2	Serious(Frank Thomas)	3.00
3	Intense(Frank Thomas)	3.00
4	Confident(Frank Thomas)	3.00
5	Assertive(Frank Thomas)	3.00
6	Power(Frank Thomas)	3.00
7	Control(Frank Thomas)	3.00
8	Strength(Frank Thomas)	3.00
9	Concentration(Frank Thomas)	3.00
10	Preparation(Frank Thomas)	3.00

1993 Leaf Gold All-Stars

Cards 1-10 in this insert set were randomly inserted one per Leaf Series I jumbo packs, while cards 11-20 were in Series II jumbo packs. Cards feature two players per card, one on each side. Only one side is numbered, but both sides have gold foil.

		MT
Complete Set (20):		35.00
Common Player:		.75
1	Ivan Rodriguez, Darren Daulton	1.50
2	Don Mattingly, Fred McGriff	2.50
3	Cecil Fielder, Jeff Bagwell	3.00
4	Carlos Baerga, Ryne Sandberg	2.00
5	Chuck Knoblauch, Delino DeShields	.75
6	Robin Ventura, Terry Pendleton	.75
7	Ken Griffey, Jr., Andy Van Slyke	7.00
8	Joe Carter, Dave Justice	1.00
9	Jose Canseco, Tony Gwynn	2.00
10	Dennis Eckersley, Rob Dibble	.75
11	Mark McGwire, Will Clark	4.00
12	Frank Thomas, Mark Grace	6.00
13	Roberto Alomar, Craig Biggio	2.00
14	Barry Larkin, Cal Ripken, Jr.	6.00
15	Gary Sheffield, Edgar Martinez	1.50
16	Juan Gonzalez, Barry Bonds	3.00
17	Kirby Puckett, Marquis Grissom	2.50
18	Jim Abbott, Tom Glavine	1.00
19	Nolan Ryan, Greg Maddux	8.00
20	Roger Clemens, Doug Drabek	2.00

1993 Leaf Gold Rookies

These cards, numbered 1 of 20 etc., feature 1993 rookies and were randomly inserted into hobby foil packs, 10 players per series. Card fronts feature action photos, while the backs show a player photo against a landmark from his team's city.

		MT
Complete Set (20):		40.00
Common Player:		.50
1	Kevin Young	.50
2	Wil Cordero	1.00
3	Mark Kiefer	.50
4	Gerald Williams	1.00
5	Brandon Wilson	.50
6	Greg Gohr	.50
7	Ryan Thompson	1.50
8	Tim Wakefield	.50
9	Troy Neel	1.00
10	Tim Salmon	8.00
11	Kevin Rogers	.75
12	Rod Bolton	.75
13	Ken Ryan	.50
14	Phil Hiatt	.50
15	Rene Arocha	1.00
16	Nigel Wilson	.50
17	J.T. Snow	3.00
18	Benji Gil	1.00
19	Chipper Jones	18.00
20	Darrell Sherman	.50

1993 Leaf Heading for the Hall

Ten players on the way to the Baseball Hall of Fame are featured in this insert set. Series I Leaf packs had cards 1-5 randomly included; Series II packs had cards 6-10.

		MT
Complete Set (10):		45.00
Common Player:		1.00
1	Nolan Ryan	9.00
2	Tony Gwynn	4.00
3	Robin Yount	2.50
4	Eddie Murray	2.00
5	Cal Ripken, Jr.	12.00
6	Roger Clemens	4.00
7	George Brett	5.00
8	Ryne Sandberg	3.00
9	Kirby Puckett	6.00
10	Ozzie Smith	3.00

1993 Leaf Update Frank Thomas Autograph

This card was a random insert in '93 Leaf Update packs and features a genuine Frank Thomas autograph on front. Unlike the other cards in the set, this has a silver-gray border on front and back. Front has a gold-foil seal in upper-left. Back has a photo of Thomas in his batting follow-through. At bottom on back is a white strip bearing the card's individual serial number from within an edition of 3,500.

		MT
FT	Frank Thomas	200.00

1993 Leaf Update Frank Thomas Super

This 10-card insert set features Leaf's 1993 spokesman, Frank Thomas. Cards, which measure 5" x 7", were included one per every Leaf Update foil box and are identical to the inserts found in Series I and II except in size. Cards are individually numbered. Thomas autographed 3,500 cards.

		MT
Complete Set (10):		90.00
Common Thomas:		10.00
1	Aggressive(Frank Thomas)	10.00
2	Serious(Frank Thomas)	10.00
3	Intense(Frank Thomas)	10.00
4	Confident(Frank Thomas)	10.00
5	Assertive(Frank Thomas)	10.00
6	Power(Frank Thomas)	10.00
7	Control(Frank Thomas)	10.00
8	Strength(Frank Thomas)	10.00
9	Concentration(Frank Thomas)	10.00
10	Preparation(Frank Thomas)	10.00

1993 Leaf Update Gold All-Stars

These 10 cards, featuring 20 all-stars, were randomly inserted in Leaf Update packs. Each card features two players, one on each side. Cards are distinguished from the regular Gold All-Stars by indicating on the front the card is numbered X of 10, with a tiny white "Update" in the red stripe above the card number.

		MT
Complete Set (10):		20.00
Common Player:		.75
1	Mark Langston, Terry Mulholland	.75
2	Ivan Rodriguez, Darren Daulton	1.00
3	John Olerud, John Kruk	.75
4	Roberto Alomar, Ryne Sandberg	2.00
5	Wade Boggs, Gary Sheffield	1.00
6	Cal Ripken, Jr., Barry Larkin	7.00
7	Kirby Puckett, Barry Bonds	4.00
8	Marquis Grissom, Ken Griffey Jr.	6.00
9	Joe Carter, Dave Justice	1.50
10	Mark Grace, Paul Molitor	1.50

1993 Leaf Update Gold Rookies

These five cards were randomly inserted in Leaf Update packs. Cards are similiar in design to the regular Gold Rookies cards, except the logo on the back indicates they are from the Update series.

		MT
Complete Set (5):		25.00
Common Player:		2.00
1	Allen Watson	2.00
2	Jeffrey Hammonds	3.00
3	David McCarty	2.00
4	Mike Piazza	20.00
5	Roberto Meija	2.00

1994 Leaf

Donruss returned its premium-brand Leaf set in 1994 with an announced 25% production cut from the previous season - fewer than 20,000 20-box cases of each 220-card series. Game-action photos dominate the fronts of the cards, borderless at the top and sides. At bottom are team color-coded faux-marble borders with the player's name (last name in gold foil) and team. Backs have a background of the player's home stadium with another action photo superimposed. In a ticket-stub device at upper-left is a portrait photo and a few personal numbers. Previous season and career stats are in white stripes at bottom. The team logo is presented in holographic foil at upper-right. To feature 1994's new stadiums and uniforms, cards of the Indians, Rangers, Brewers and Astros were included only in the second series. Seven different types of insert cards were produced and distributed among the various types of Leaf packaging.

		MT
Complete Set (440):		32.00
Complete Series 1 (220):		15.00
Complete Series 2 (220):		17.00
Common Player:		.10
Series 1 or 2 Wax Box:		40.00
1	Cal Ripken, Jr.	2.50
2	Tony Tarasco	.10
3	Joe Girardi	.10
4	Bernie Williams	.60
5	Chad Kreuter	.10
6	Troy Neel	.15
7	Tom Pagnozzi	.10
8	Kirk Rueter	.10
9	Chris Bosio	.10
10	Dwight Gooden	.12
11	Mariano Duncan	.10
12	Jay Bell	.10
13	Lance Johnson	.10
14	Richie Lewis	.10
15	Dave Martinez	.10

No.	Player	Price
16	Orel Hershiser	.12
17	Rob Butler	.10
18	Glenallen Hill	.10
19	Chad Curtis	.10
20	Mike Stanton	.10
21	Tim Wallach	.10
22	Milt Thompson	.10
23	Kevin Young	.10
24	John Smiley	.10
25	Jeff Montgomery	.10
26	Robin Ventura	.20
27	Scott Lydy	.10
28	Todd Stottlemyre	.10
29	Mark Whiten	.10
30	Robby Thompson	.10
31	Bobby Bonilla	.12
32	Andy Ashby	.10
33	Greg Myers	.10
34	Billy Hatcher	.10
35	Brad Holman	.10
36	Mark McLemore	.10
37	Scott Sanders	.10
38	Jim Abbott	.12
39	David Wells	.10
40	Roberto Kelly	.10
41	Jeff Conine	.10
42	Sean Berry	.10
43	Mark Grace	.15
44	Eric Young	.10
45	Rick Aguilera	.10
46	Chipper Jones	1.50
47	Mel Rojas	.10
48	Ryan Thompson	.10
49	Al Martin	.10
50	Cecil Fielder	.20
51	Pat Kelly	.10
52	Kevin Tapani	.10
53	Tim Costo	.10
54	Dave Hollins	.10
55	Kirt Manwaring	.10
56	Gregg Jefferies	.15
57	Ron Darling	.10
58	Bill Haselman	.10
59	Phil Plantier	.10
60	Frank Viola	.10
61	Todd Zeile	.10
62	Bret Barberie	.10
63	Roberto Mejia	.10
64	Chuck Knoblauch	.15
65	Jose Lind	.10
66	Brady Anderson	.15
67	Ruben Sierra	.12
68	Jose Vizcaino	.10
69	Joe Grahe	.10
70	Kevin Appier	.10
71	Wilson Alvarez	.10
72	Tom Candiotti	.10
73	John Burkett	.10
74	Anthony Young	.10
75	Scott Cooper	.10
76	Nigel Wilson	.10
77	John Valentin	.10
78	Dave McCarty	.10
79	Archi Cianfrocco	.10
80	Lou Whitaker	.10
81	Dante Bichette	.30
82	Mark Dewey	.10
83	Danny Jackson	.10
84	Harold Baines	.12
85	Todd Benzinger	.10
86	Damion Easley	.10
87	Danny Cox	.10
88	Jose Bautista	.10
89	Mike Lansing	.10
90	Phil Hiatt	.10
91	Tim Pugh	.10
92	Tino Martinez	.15
93	Raul Mondesi	.75
94	Greg Maddux	2.00
95	Al Leiter	.10
96	Benito Santiago	.10
97	Len Dykstra	.15
98	Sammy Sosa	1.50
99	Tim Bogar	.10
100	Checklist	.10
101	Deion Sanders	.25
102	Bobby Witt	.10
103	Wil Cordero	.10
104	Rich Amaral	.10
105	Mike Mussina	.40
106	Reggie Sanders	.15
107	Ozzie Guillen	.10
108	Paul O'Neill	.10
109	Tim Salmon	.35
110	Rheal Cormier	.10
111	Billy Ashley	.15
112	Jeff Kent	.10
113	Derek Bell	.12
114	Danny Darwin	.10
115	Chip Hale	.10
116	Tim Raines	.12
117	Ed Sprague	.10
118	Darrin Fletcher	.10
119	Darren Holmes	.10
120	Alan Trammell	.15
121	Don Mattingly	1.00
122	Greg Gagne	.10
123	Jose Offerman	.10
124	Joe Orsulak	.10
125	Jack McDowell	.10
126	Barry Larkin	.15
127	Ben McDonald	.10
128	Mike Bordick	.10
129	Devon White	.12
130	Mike Perez	.10
131	Jay Buhner	.15
132	Phil Leftwich	.10
133	Tommy Greene	.10
134	Charlie Hayes	.10
135	Don Slaught	.10
136	Mike Gallego	.10
137	Dave Winfield	.15
138	Steve Avery	.15
139	Derrick May	.10
140	Bryan Harvey	.10
141	Wally Joyner	.12
142	Andre Dawson	.12
143	Andy Benes	.10
144	John Franco	.10
145	Jeff King	.10
146	Joe Oliver	.10
147	Bill Gullickson	.10
148	Armando Reynoso	.10
149	Dave Fleming	.10
150	Checklist	.10
151	Todd Van Poppel	.10
152	Bernard Gilkey	.12
153	Kevin Gross	.10
154	Mike Devereaux	.10
155	Tim Wakefield	.10
156	Andres Galarraga	.15
157	Pat Meares	.10
158	Jim Leyritz	.10
159	Mike Macfarlane	.10
160	Tony Phillips	.12
161	Brent Gates	.15
162	Mark Langston	.10
163	Allen Watson	.10
164	Randy Johnson	.35
165	Doug Brocail	.10
166	Rob Dibble	.10
167	Roberto Hernandez	.10
168	Felix Jose	.10
169	Steve Cooke	.10
170	Darren Daulton	.12
171	Eric Karros	.12
172	Geronimo Pena	.10
173	Gary DiSarcina	.10
174	Marquis Grissom	.12
175	Joey Cora	.10
176	Jim Eisenreich	.10
177	Brad Pennington	.10
178	Terry Steinbach	.10
179	Pat Borders	.10
180	Steve Buechele	.10
181	Jeff Fassero	.10
182	Mike Greenwell	.10
183	Mike Henneman	.10
184	Ron Karkovice	.10
185	Pat Hentgen	.12
186	Jose Guzman	.10
187	Brett Butler	.15
188	Charlie Hough	.10
189	Terry Pendleton	.10
190	Melido Perez	.10
191	Orestes Destrade	.10
192	Mike Morgan	.10
193	Joe Carter	.20
194	Jeff Blauser	.10
195	Chris Hoiles	.10
196	Ricky Gutierrez	.10
197	Mike Moore	.10
198	Carl Willis	.10
199	Aaron Sele	.12
200	Checklist	.10
201	Tim Naehring	.10
202	Scott Livingstone	.10
203	Luis Alicea	.10
204	*Torey Lovullo*	.10
205	Jim Gott	.10
206	Bob Wickman	.10
207	Greg McMichael	.10
208	Scott Brosius	.10
209	Chris Gwynn	.10
210	Steve Sax	.10
211	Dick Schofield	.10
212	Robb Nen	.15
213	Ben Rivera	.10
214	Vinny Castilla	.15
215	Jamie Moyer	.10
216	Wally Whitehurst	.10
217	Frank Castillo	.10
218	Mike Blowers	.10
219	Tim Scott	.10
220	Paul Wagner	.10
221	Jeff Bagwell	1.00
222	Ricky Bones	.10
223	Sandy Alomar Jr.	.12
224	Rod Beck	.10
225	Roberto Alomar	.75
226	Jack Armstrong	.10
227	Scott Erickson	.10
228	Rene Arocha	.10
229	Eric Anthony	.10
230	Jeromy Burnitz	.15
231	Kevin Brown	.12
232	Tim Belcher	.10
233	Bret Boone	.12
234	Dennis Eckersley	.12
235	Tom Glavine	.20
236	Craig Biggio	.15
237	Pedro Astacio	.12
238	Ryan Bowen	.10
239	Brad Ausmus	.10
240	Vince Coleman	.10
241	Jason Bere	.15
242	Ellis Burks	.15
243	Wes Chamberlain	.10
244	Ken Caminiti	.15
245	Willie Banks	.10
246	Sid Fernandez	.10
247	Carlos Baerga	.15
248	Carlos Garcia	.10
249	Jose Canseco	.30
250	Alex Diaz	.10
251	Albert Belle	.75
252	Moises Alou	.12
253	Bobby Ayala	.10
254	Tony Gwynn	1.00
255	Roger Clemens	1.00
256	Eric Davis	.12
257	Wade Boggs	.30
258	Chili Davis	.10
259	Rickey Henderson	.20
260	Andujar Cedeno	.10
261	Cris Carpenter	.10
262	Juan Guzman	.10
263	Dave Justice	.20
264	Barry Bonds	.75
265	Pete Incaviglia	.10
266	Tony Fernandez	.10
267	Cal Eldred	.10
268	Alex Fernandez	.10
269	Kent Hrbek	.12
270	Steve Farr	.10
271	Doug Drabek	.10
272	Brian Jordan	.15
273	Xavier Hernandez	.10
274	David Cone	.12
275	Brian Hunter	.15
276	Mike Harkey	.10
277	Delino DeShields	.10
278	David Hulse	.10
279	Mickey Tettleton	.10
280	Kevin McReynolds	.10
281	Darryl Hamilton	.10
282	Ken Hill	.10
283	Wayne Kirby	.10
284	Chris Hammond	.10
285	Mo Vaughn	.75
286	Ryan Klesko	.60
287	Rick Wilkins	.10
288	Bill Swift	.10
289	Rafael Palmeiro	.15
290	Brian Harper	.10
291	Chris Turner	.10
292	Luis Gonzalez	.10
293	Kenny Rogers	.10
294	Kirby Puckett	1.00
295	Mike Stanley	.10
296	Carlos Reyes	.10
297	Charles Nagy	.10
298	Reggie Jefferson	.10
299	Bip Roberts	.10
300	Darrin Jackson	.10
301	Mike Jackson	.10
302	Dave Nilsson	.10
303	Ramon Martinez	.12

304	Bobby Jones	.15
305	Johnny Ruffin	.10
306	Brian McRae	.10
307	Bo Jackson	.15
308	Dave Stewart	.10
309	John Smoltz	.12
310	Dennis Martinez	.12
311	Dean Palmer	.15
312	David Nied	.10
313	Eddie Murray	.15
314	Darryl Kile	.10
315	Rick Sutcliffe	.10
316	Shawon Dunston	.15
317	John Jaha	.10
318	Salomon Torres	.10
319	Gary Sheffield	.15
320	Curt Schilling	.10
321	Greg Vaughn	.10
322	Jay Howell	.10
323	Todd Hundley	.15
324	Chris Sabo	.10
325	Stan Javier	.10
326	Willie Greene	.10
327	Hipolito Pichardo	.10
328	Doug Strange	.10
329	Dan Wilson	.10
330	Checklist	.10
331	Omar Vizquel	.10
332	Scott Servais	.10
333	Bob Tewksbury	.10
334	Matt Williams	.30
335	Tom Foley	.10
336	Jeff Russell	.10
337	Scott Leius	.10
338	Ivan Rodriguez	.50
339	Kevin Seitzer	.10
340	Jose Rijo	.10
341	Eduardo Perez	.10
342	Kirk Gibson	.10
343	Randy Milligan	.10
344	Edgar Martinez	.10
345	Fred McGriff	.30
346	Kurt Abbott	.10
347	John Kruk	.10
348	Mike Felder	.10
349	Dave Staton	.10
350	Kenny Lofton	.75
351	Graeme Lloyd	.10
352	David Segui	.10
353	Danny Tartabull	.10
354	Bob Welch	.10
355	Duane Ward	.10
356	Tuffy Rhodes	.10
357	Lee Smith	.12
358	Chris James	.10
359	Walt Weiss	.10
360	Pedro Munoz	.10
361	Paul Sorrento	.10
362	Todd Worrell	.10
363	Bob Hamelin	.10
364	Julio Franco	.10
365	Roberto Petagine	.10
366	Willie McGee	.12
367	Pedro Martinez	.12
368	Ken Griffey, Jr.	3.00
369	B.J. Surhoff	.10
370	Kevin Mitchell	.12
371	John Doherty	.10
372	Manuel Lee	.10
373	Terry Mulholland	.10
374	Zane Smith	.10
375	Otis Nixon	.10
376	Jody Reed	.10
377	Doug Jones	.10
378	John Olerud	.20
379	Greg Swindell	.10
380	Checklist	.10
381	Royce Clayton	.12
382	Jim Thome	.40
383	Steve Finley	.10
384	Ray Lankford	.15
385	Henry Rodriguez	.12
386	Dave Magadan	.10
387	Gary Redus	.10
388	Orlando Merced	.10
389	Tom Gordon	.10
390	Luis Polonia	.10
391	Mark McGwire	3.00
392	Mark Lemke	.10
393	Doug Henry	.10
394	Chuck Finley	.10
395	Paul Molitor	.25
396	Randy Myers	.10
397	Larry Walker	.20
398	Pete Harnisch	.10
399	Darren Lewis	.10
400	Frank Thomas	2.50
401	Jack Morris	.10
402	Greg Hibbard	.10
403	Jeffrey Hammonds	.15
404	Will Clark	.25
405	Travis Fryman	.15
406	Scott Sanderson	.10
407	Gene Harris	.10
408	Chuck Carr	.10
409	Ozzie Smith	.40
410	Kent Mercker	.10
411	Andy Van Slyke	.10
412	Jimmy Key	.10
413	Pat Mahomes	.10
414	John Wetteland	.10
415	Todd Jones	.10
416	Greg Harris	.10
417	Kevin Stocker	.10
418	Juan Gonzalez	1.00
419	Pete Smith	.10
420	Pat Listach	.10
421	Trevor Hoffman	.10
422	Scott Fletcher	.10
423	Mark Lewis	.10
424	Mickey Morandini	.10
425	Ryne Sandberg	.75
426	Erik Hanson	.10
427	Gary Gaetti	.12
428	Harold Reynolds	.10
429	Mark Portugal	.10
430	David Valle	.10
431	Mitch Williams	.10
432	Howard Johnson	.10
433	Hal Morris	.10
434	Tom Henke	.10
435	Shane Mack	.10
436	Mike Piazza	1.50
437	Bret Saberhagen	.10
438	Jose Mesa	.10
439	Jaime Navarro	.10
440	Checklist	.10

1994 Leaf Clean-Up Crew

The number four spot in the line-up is featured on this 12-card insert set (six per series) found only in magazine distributor packaging. Fronts are gold-foil enhanced; backs feature an action photo set against a background of a lineup card on which the player is pencilled into the #4 spot. His 1993 stats when batting clean-up are presented.

		MT
Complete Set (12):		50.00
Complete Series 1 (6):		12.00
Complete Series 2 (6):		40.00
Common Player:		2.00
1	Larry Walker	3.00
2	Andres Galarraga	3.00
3	Dave Hollins	2.00
4	Bobby Bonilla	2.00
5	Cecil Fielder	3.00
6	Danny Tartabull	2.00
7	Juan Gonzalez	12.00
8	Joe Carter	3.00
9	Fred McGriff	4.00
10	Matt Williams	4.00
11	Albert Belle	6.00
12	Harold Baines	2.00

1994 Leaf Frank Thomas Super

An edition of 20,000 super-size versions of Frank Thomas' 1994 Leaf card was produced for inclusion in Series II hobby boxes as a bonus. Except for its 5" x 7" format and a white strip on back bearing a serial number, the card is identical to the normal-size issue.

		MT
400	Frank Thomas	12.00

1994 Leaf Gamers

Leaf jumbo packs are the exclusive venue for the six cards of this insert set which were issued in each series.

		MT
Complete Set (12):		215.00
Complete Series 1 (6):		95.00
Complete Series 2 (6):		120.00
Common Player:		4.00
1	Ken Griffey, Jr.	55.00
2	Len Dykstra	4.00
3	Juan Gonzalez	15.00
4	Don Mattingly	25.00

5	Dave Justice	5.00
6	Mark Grace	5.00
7	Frank Thomas	40.00
8	Barry Bonds	10.00
9	Kirby Puckett	25.00
10	Will Clark	5.00
11	John Kruk	4.00
12	Mike Piazza	20.00

1994 Leaf Gold Rookies

A gold-foil rendered stadium background and huge black "94 Gold Leaf Rookie" serve as a backdrop for a player photo on these insert cards found at the rate of about one per 18 foil packs. The player's name and team are in silver at bottom. Horizontal backs have a ghosted action photo of the player in the background. A portrait photo is in the upper-right corner, above some personal data and stats. Cards are numbered "X of 20".

		MT
Complete Set (20):		16.00
Complete Series 1 (10):		10.00
Complete Series 2 (10):		7.50
Common Player:		.50
1	Javier Lopez	2.00
2	Rondell White	2.50
3	Butch Huskey	.75
4	Midre Cummings	.50
5	Scott Ruffcorn	.50
6	Manny Ramirez	6.00
7	Danny Bautista	.50
8	Russ Davis	.50
9	Steve Karsay	.50
10	Carlos Delgado	1.50
11	Bob Hamelin	.60
12	Marcus Moore	.50
13	Miguel Jimenez	.50
14	Matt Walbeck	.50
15	James Mouton	.75
16	Rich Becker	.50
17	Brian Anderson	.50
18	Cliff Floyd	.75
19	Steve Trachsel	.50
20	Hector Carrasco	.50

1994 Leaf Gold Stars

The "Cadillac" of 1994 Leaf inserts, this 15-card series (#1-8 in Series I; 9-15 in Series II) is found on average only one card per 90 packs. The edition of 10,000 of each player's card is serially numbered. Fronts feature a rather small photo in a diamond-shaped frame

against a green marble-look background. The border, facsimile autograph and several other graphic elements are presented in prismatic foil. The back repeats the basic front design with a few sentences about the player and a serial number strip at bottom.

		MT
Complete Set (15):		300.00
Complete Series 1 (8):		175.00
Complete Series 2 (7):		125.00
Common Player:		10.00
1	Roberto Alomar	20.00
2	Barry Bonds	20.00
3	Dave Justice	12.00
4	Ken Griffey, Jr.	80.00
5	Len Dykstra	10.00
6	Don Mattingly	35.00
7	Andres Galarraga	12.00
8	Greg Maddux	50.00
9	Carlos Baerga	10.00
10	Paul Molitor	15.00
11	Frank Thomas	60.00
12	John Olerud	10.00
13	Juan Gonzalez	30.00
14	Fred McGriff	12.00
15	Jack McDowell	10.00

1994 Leaf MVP Contenders

Found on an average of about once per 36-pack foil box, these inserts were produced in an edition of 10,000 each. Cards found in packs were marked "Silver Collection" on the horizontal fronts, and featured a silver-foil Leaf seal and other enhancements. Persons holding cards of the players selected as N.L. and A.L. MVPs could trade in their Contender card for an individually numbered 5" x 7" card of Leaf spokesman Frank Thomas and be entered in a drawing for one of 5,000 Gold Collection MVP Contender 28-card sets. Winning cards were punch-cancelled and returned to the winner along with his prize.

		MT
Complete Set, Silver:		220.00
Complete Set, Gold:		400.00
Common Player, Silver:		2.50
Common Player, Gold:		5.00
AMERICAN LEAGUE		8.00
1a	Albert Belle (silver)	6.00
1b	Albert Belle (gold)	12.00
2a	Jose Canseco (silver)	3.00
2b	Jose Canseco (gold)	6.00
3a	Joe Carter (silver)	2.50
3b	Joe Carter (gold)	5.00
4a	Will Clark (silver)	3.00
4b	Will Clark (gold)	6.00
5a	Cecil Fielder (silver)	2.50
5b	Cecil Fielder (gold)	5.00
6a	Juan Gonzalez (silver)	8.00
6b	Juan Gonzalez (gold)	15.00
7a	Ken Griffey, Jr. (silver)	35.00
7b	Ken Griffey, Jr. (gold)	60.00
8a	Paul Molitor (silver)	4.00
8b	Paul Molitor (gold)	8.00
9a	Rafael Palmeiro (silver)	2.50
9b	Rafael Palmeiro (gold)	5.00
10a	Kirby Puckett (silver)	10.00
10b	Kirby Puckett (gold)	20.00
11a	Cal Ripken, Jr. (silver)	35.00
11b	Cal Ripken, Jr. (gold)	60.00
12a	Frank Thomas (silver)	30.00
12b	Frank Thomas (gold)	50.00
13a	Mo Vaughn (silver)	3.00
13b	Mo Vaughn (gold)	6.00
14a	Carlos Baerga (silver)	2.50
14b	Carlos Baerga (gold)	5.00
15	AL Bonus Card (silver)	2.50
NATIONAL LEAGUE		2.50
1a	Gary Sheffield (silver)	5.00
1b	Gary Sheffield (gold)	10.00
2a	Jeff Bagwell (silver)	12.00
2b	Jeff Bagwell (gold)	24.00
3a	Dante Bichette (silver)	2.50
3b	Dante Bichette (gold)	5.00
4a	Barry Bonds (silver)	7.00
4b	Barry Bonds (gold)	15.00
5a	Darren Daulton (silver)	2.50
5b	Darren Daulton (gold)	5.00
6a	Andres Galarraga (silver)	2.50
6b	Andres Galarraga (gold)	5.00
7a	Gregg Jefferies (silver)	2.50
7b	Gregg Jefferies (gold)	5.00
8a	Dave Justice (silver)	4.00
8b	Dave Justice (gold)	8.00
9a	Ray Lankford (silver)	2.50
9b	Ray Lankford (gold)	5.00
10a	Fred McGriff (silver)	4.00
10b	Fred McGriff (gold)	8.00
11a	Barry Larkin (silver)	2.50
11b	Barry Larkin (gold)	5.00
12a	Mike Piazza (silver)	12.00
12b	Mike Piazza (gold)	24.00
13a	Deion Sanders (silver)	5.00
13b	Deion Sanders (gold)	10.00
14a	Matt Williams (silver)	4.00
14b	Matt Williams (gold)	8.00
15	NL Bonus Card (silver)	2.50

1994 Leaf Power Brokers

This insert set was unique to Leaf Series II packs and features the game's top sluggers. Horizontal-format fronts have a player photo at left, depicting his power stroke. A fireworks display is featured in the large letters of "POWER" at top. Other gold and silver foil highlights are featured on the black background. Backs have pie charts showing home run facts along with another player photo and a few stats. Stated odds of finding a Power Brokers insert card were one per dozen packs, on average.

		MT
Complete Set (10):		30.00
Common Player:		1.00
1	Frank Thomas	8.00
2	Dave Justice	1.00
3	Barry Bonds	2.00
4	Juan Gonzalez	3.00
5	Ken Griffey, Jr.	10.00
6	Mike Piazza	4.00
7	Cecil Fielder	1.00
8	Fred McGriff	1.00
9	Joe Carter	1.00
10	Albert Belle	2.50

1994 Leaf Slide Show

A new level of high-tech insert card production values was reached with the creation of Leaf's "Slide Show" chase cards. The cards feature a printed acetate center sandwiched between cardboard front and back. The see-through acetate portion of the card is bordered in white to give it the appearance of a slide. The player's name, location and date of the photo are printed on the front of the "slide," with the card number on back. The pseudo-slide is bordered in black (Series I) or white (Series II), with a blue "Slide Show" logo at bottom and a silver-foil Leaf logo. Backs of the Slide Show inserts have a few sentences about the featured player from Frank Thomas, Leaf's official spokesman again in 1994. The first five cards were released in Series I; cards 6-10 in Series II. Stated odds of finding a Slide Show insert are one per 54 packs.

		MT
Complete Set (10):		65.00
Common Player:		1.00
1	Frank Thomas	15.00
2	Mike Piazza	10.00
3	Darren Daulton	1.00
4	Ryne Sandberg	4.00
5	Roberto Alomar	5.00
6	Barry Bonds	5.00
7	Juan Gonzalez	8.00
8	Tim Salmon	2.50
9	Ken Griffey, Jr.	20.00
10	Dave Justice	1.00

1994 Leaf Statistical Standouts

Significant statistical acheivements from the 1993 season are marked in this insert set found in both retail and hobby packs at a rate of about once every 12 packs. Fronts feature player action photos set against a foil background of silver at right and a team color at left. A gold embossed Leaf seal is at upper-left. Backs are bordered in the complementary team color at right, silver at left and have a vertical player photo along with the statistical achievement. Cards are numbered "x-10".

		MT
Complete Set (10):		24.00
Common Player:		1.00
1	Frank Thomas	7.00
2	Barry Bonds	2.00
3	Juan Gonzalez	3.00
4	Mike Piazza	4.00
5	Greg Maddux	5.00
6	Ken Griffey, Jr.	8.00
7	Joe Carter	1.00
8	Dave Winfield	1.00
9	Tony Gwynn	3.00
10	Cal Ripken, Jr.	7.00

1994 Leaf 5th Anniversary

FRANK THOMAS 1B

The card which insured the success of the Leaf brand name when it was re-introduced in 1990, the

Frank Thomas rookie card, was re-issued in a 5th anniversary commemorative form as an insert in the 1994 set. On the chase card, silver foil rays emanate from the White Sox logo at lower-left, while a silver-foil 5th anniversary logo at upper-right replaces the Leaf script on the 1990 version. The card back carries a 1994 copyright. The Thomas anniversary card is found on average of once every 36 Series I hobby packs.

		MT
Complete Set:		5.00
300	Frank Thomas	5.00

1994 Leaf/Limited

Leaf Limited was a 160-card high-end, super premium set printed on the highest quality board stock ever used by Donruss. Production was limited to 3,000 20-box case equivalents, making this the most limited product up to that point in 1994 by Donruss. Card fronts feature silver holographic Spectra Tech foiling and a silhouetted layer action photo over full silver foil. Cards have the team name and logo in silver and player name written in black at the bottom of the card. Leaf Limited appears in silver at the top and the player is bordered in silver on the front. The backs are dull grey or silver with a quote from a baseball personality and a player picture in the top-right corner. Leaf Limited and the card number are printed above the player photo. This card set was highly sought after and very limited. The cards look very unique and truly can't be described in words.

		MT
Complete Set (160):		90.00
Common Player:		.50
Wax Box:		100.00
1	Jeffrey Hammonds	.75
2	Ben McDonald	.50
3	Mike Mussina	2.50
4	Rafael Palmeiro	.75
5	Cal Ripken, Jr.	8.00
6	Lee Smith	.60
7	Roger Clemens	4.00
8	Scott Cooper	.50
9	Andre Dawson	.75
10	Mike Greenwell	.50
11	Aaron Sele	.50

12	Mo Vaughn	3.00
13	*Brian Anderson*	1.50
14	Chad Curtis	.50
15	Chili Davis	.50
16	Gary DiSarcina	.50
17	Mark Langston	.50
18	Tim Salmon	1.00
19	Wilson Alvarez	.50
20	Jason Bere	.50
21	Julio Franco	.50
22	Jack McDowell	.75
23	Tim Raines	.50
24	Frank Thomas	6.00
25	Robin Ventura	1.00
26	Carlos Baerga	.50
27	Albert Belle	3.00
28	Kenny Lofton	3.00
29	Eddie Murray	.75
30	Manny Ramirez	2.50
31	Cecil Fielder	.75
32	Travis Fryman	.50
33	Mickey Tettleton	.50
34	Alan Trammell	.75
35	Lou Whitaker	.50
36	David Cone	.50
37	Gary Gaetti	.50
38	Greg Gagne	.50
39	Bob Hamelin	.50
40	Wally Joyner	.65
41	Brian McRae	.50
42	Ricky Bones	.50
43	Brian Harper	.50
44	John Jaha	.50
45	Pat Listach	.50
46	Dave Nilsson	.50
47	Greg Vaughn	.50
48	Kent Hrbek	.50
49	Chuck Knoblauch	.75
50	Shane Mack	.50
51	Kirby Puckett	2.50
52	Dave Winfield	.75
53	Jim Abbott	.60
54	Wade Boggs	1.00
55	Jimmy Key	.50
56	Don Mattingly	2.50
57	Paul O'Neill	.50
58	Danny Tartabull	.50
59	Dennis Eckersley	.60
60	Rickey Henderson	.75
61	Mark McGwire	15.00
62	Troy Neel	.50
63	Ruben Sierra	.60
64	Eric Anthony	.50
65	Jay Buhner	.75
66	Ken Griffey, Jr.	10.00
67	Randy Johnson	1.50
68	Edgar Martinez	.60
69	Tino Martinez	.75
70	Jose Canseco	1.00
71	Will Clark	1.00
72	Juan Gonzalez	5.00
73	Dean Palmer	.50
74	Ivan Rodriguez	2.00
75	Roberto Alomar	1.50
76	Joe Carter	.75
77	Carlos Delgado	.75
78	Paul Molitor	1.50
79	John Olerud	.50
80	Devon White	.50
81	Steve Avery	.50
82	Tom Glavine	.75
83	Dave Justice	1.00
84	Roberto Kelly	.50
85	Ryan Klesko	1.50
86	Javier Lopez	.75
87	Greg Maddux	6.00
88	Fred McGriff	1.00
89	Shawon Dunston	.50
90	Mark Grace	.75
91	Derrick May	.50
92	Sammy Sosa	8.00
93	Rick Wilkins	.50
94	Bret Boone	.50
95	Barry Larkin	.75
96	Kevin Mitchell	.50
97	Hal Morris	.50
98	Deion Sanders	1.00
99	Reggie Sanders	.50
100	Dante Bichette	1.00
101	Ellis Burks	.50
102	Andres Galarraga	.75
103	Joe Girardi	.50
104	Charlie Hayes	.50
105	Chuck Carr	.50
106	Jeff Conine	.50
107	Bryan Harvey	.50

108	Benito Santiago	.50
109	Gary Sheffield	1.00
110	Jeff Bagwell	3.00
111	Craig Biggio	.75
112	Ken Caminiti	.75
113	Andujar Cedeno	.50
114	Doug Drabek	.50
115	Luis Gonzalez	.50
116	Brett Butler	.50
117	Delino DeShields	.50
118	Eric Karros	.50
119	Raul Mondesi	1.00
120	Mike Piazza	6.00
121	Henry Rodriguez	.50
122	Tim Wallach	.50
123	Moises Alou	.75
124	Cliff Floyd	.50
125	Marquis Grissom	.50
126	Ken Hill	.50
127	Larry Walker	.75
128	John Wetteland	.50
129	Bobby Bonilla	.50
130	John Franco	.50
131	Jeff Kent	.50
132	Bret Saberhagen	.50
133	Ryan Thompson	.50
134	Darren Daulton	.50
135	Mariano Duncan	.50
136	Len Dykstra	.50
137	Danny Jackson	.50
138	John Kruk	.50
139	Jay Bell	.50
140	Jeff King	.50
141	Al Martin	.50
142	Orlando Merced	.50
143	Andy Van Slyke	.50
144	Bernard Gilkey	.50
145	Gregg Jefferies	.60
146	Ray Lankford	.50
147	Ozzie Smith	1.50
148	Mark Whiten	.50
149	Todd Zeile	.50
150	Derek Bell	.50
151	Andy Benes	.50
152	Tony Gwynn	4.00
153	Phil Plantier	.50
154	Bip Roberts	.50
155	Rod Beck	.50
156	Barry Bonds	2.50
157	John Burkett	.50
158	Royce Clayton	.50
159	Bill Swift	.50
160	Matt Williams	1.00

1994 Leaf/ Limited Gold

Leaf Limited Gold was an 18-card insert set randomly packed into Leaf Limited. All cards are individually numbered and feature the starting lineups at each position in both the National League and American League for the 1994 All-Star Game. There were only 10,000 cards of each player produced in this insert set.

		MT
Complete Set (18):		125.00
Common Player:		2.00
1	Frank Thomas	20.00
2	Gregg Jefferies	2.00
3	Roberto Alomar	5.00
4	Mariano Duncan	2.00
5	Wade Boggs	3.00
6	Matt Williams	4.00
7	Cal Ripken, Jr.	25.00
8	Ozzie Smith	6.00
9	Kirby Puckett	8.00
10	Barry Bonds	8.00
11	Ken Griffey, Jr.	30.00
12	Tony Gwynn	15.00
13	Joe Carter	2.50
14	Dave Justice	3.00
15	Ivan Rodriguez	6.00
16	Mike Piazza	20.00
17	Jimmy Key	2.00
18	Greg Maddux	20.00

1994 Leaf/ Limited Rookies

Similar in format to the super-premium Leaf Limited issue, this separate issue features 80 of baseball's brightest young talents.

		MT
Complete Set (80):		35.00
Common Player:		.35
Wax Box:		60.00
1	Charles Johnson	2.00
2	Rico Brogna	.75
3	Melvin Nieves	.35
4	Rich Becker	.50
5	Russ Davis	.50
6	Matt Mieske	.50
7	Paul Shuey	.50
8	Hector Carrasco	.50
9	J.R. Phillips	1.25
10	Scott Ruffcorn	.35
11	Kurt Abbott	.35
12	Danny Bautista	.35
13	Rick White	.35
14	Steve Dunn	.35
15	Joe Ausanio	.35
16	Salomon Torres	.35
17	Rick Bottalico	.50
18	Johnny Ruffin	.35
19	Kevin Foster	.45
20	*W. Van Landingham*	2.00
21	Troy O'Leary	.40
22	Mark Acre	.35
23	Norberto Martin	.35
24	*Jason Jacome*	.50
25	Steve Trachsel	.75
26	Denny Hocking	.45
27	Mike Lieberthal	.35
28	Gerald Williams	.50
29	John Mabry	.50
30	Greg Blosser	.35
31	Carl Everett	.50
32	Steve Karsay	.40
33	Jose Valentin	.35
34	Jon Lieber	.35

35	Chris Gomez	.50
36	Jesus Tavarez	.50
37	Tony Longmire	.50
38	Luis Lopez	.35
39	Matt Walbeck	.35
40	Rikkert Faneyte	.60
41	Shane Reynolds	.35
42	Joey Hamilton	1.50
43	Ismael Valdes	1.50
44	Danny Miceli	.50
45	Darren Bragg	.35
46	Alex Gonzalez	1.00
47	Rick Helling	.35
48	Jose Oliva	.35
49	Jim Edmonds	2.50
50	Miguel Jimenez	.50
51	Tony Eusebio	.45
52	Shawn Green	1.50
53	Billy Ashley	1.00
54	Rondell White	3.00
55	Cory Bailey	.75
56	Tim Davis	.35
57	John Hudek	.75
58	Darren Hall	.50
59	Darren Dreifort	.50
60	Mike Kelly	.40
61	Marcus Moore	.35
62	Garret Anderson	1.00
63	Brian Hunter	2.00
64	Mark Smith	.50
65	Garey Ingram	.50
66	*Rusty Greer*	1.50
67	Marc Newfield	.75
68	Gar Finnvold	.35
69	Paul Spoljaric	.35
70	Ray McDavid	.50
71	Orlando Miller	.75
72	Jorge Fabregas	.45
73	Ray Holbert	.35
74	Armando Benitez	.35
75	Ernie Young	.50
76	James Mouton	.75
77	*Robert Perez*	.75
78	*Chan Ho Park*	1.50
79	Roger Salkeld	.35
80	Tony Tarasco	.45

1994 Leaf/ Limited Rookies Rookie Phenoms

Alex Rodriguez

Similar in format to the other Leaf Limited cards for 1994, these Phenom inserts feature gold-foil background and graphics, rather than silver. Each card is numbered from within an edition of 5,000 of each player.

		MT
Complete Set (10):		175.00
Common Player:		6.00
1	Raul Mondesi	20.00
2	Bob Hamelin	6.00
3	Midre Cummings	6.00
4	Carlos Delgado	12.00
5	Cliff Floyd	8.00

6	Jeffrey Hammonds	6.00
7	Ryan Klesko	20.00
8	Javier Lopez	15.00
9	Manny Ramirez	25.00
10	Alex Rodriguez	70.00

1995 Leaf

Two series of 200 basic cards each, plus numerous insert series, are featured in 1995 Leaf. The basic card design has a borderless action photo on front, with a small portrait photo printed at upper-left on holographic silver foil. The team name is printed in the same foil in large letters down the left side. A script rendition of the player's name is at bottom-right, with the Leaf logo under the portrait photo; both elements are in gold foil. Backs have a couple more player photos. The card number is in white in a silver-foil seal at upper-right. Previous season and career stats are at lower-left. Several of the inserts sets are unique to various package configurations, while others are found in all types of packs.

		MT
Complete Set (400):		40.00
Complete Series 1 (200):		15.00
Complete Series 2 (200):		25.00
Common Player:		.10
Series 1 or 2 Wax Box:		60.00
1	Frank Thomas	2.50
2	Carlos Garcia	.10
3	Todd Hundley	.15
4	Damion Easley	.10
5	Roberto Mejia	.10
6	John Mabry	.10
7	Aaron Sele	.10
8	Kenny Lofton	.75
9	John Doherty	.10
10	Joe Carter	.20
11	Mike Lansing	.10
12	John Valentin	.15
13	Ismael Valdes	.15
14	Dave McCarty	.10
15	Melvin Nieves	.10
16	Bobby Jones	.10
17	Trevor Hoffman	.10
18	John Smoltz	.25
19	Leo Gomez	.10
20	Roger Pavlik	.10
21	Dean Palmer	.10
22	Rickey Henderson	.20
23	Eddie Taubensee	.10
24	Damon Buford	.10
25	Mark Wohlers	.10
26	Jim Edmonds	.20
27	Wilson Alvarez	.10
28	Matt Williams	.35
29	Jeff Montgomery	.10
30	Shawon Dunston	.15
31	Tom Pagnozzi	.10

32	Jose Lind	.10
33	Royce Clayton	.10
34	Cal Eldred	.10
35	Chris Gomez	.10
36	Henry Rodriguez	.10
37	Dave Fleming	.10
38	Jon Lieber	.10
39	Scott Servais	.10
40	Wade Boggs	.25
41	John Olerud	.15
42	Eddie Williams	.10
43	Paul Sorrento	.10
44	Ron Karkovice	.10
45	Kevin Foster	.10
46	Miguel Jimenez	.10
47	Reggie Sanders	.15
48	Rondell White	.15
49	Scott Leius	.10
50	Jose Valentin	.10
51	William Van Landingham	.15
52	Denny Hocking	.10
53	Jeff Fassero	.10
54	Chris Hoiles	.10
55	Walt Weiss	.10
56	Geronimo Berroa	.10
57	Rich Rowland	.10
58	Dave Weathers	.10
59	Sterling Hitchcock	.10
60	Raul Mondesi	.50
61	Rusty Greer	.10
62	Dave Justice	.25
63	Cecil Fielder	.20
64	Brian Jordan	.15
65	Mike Lieberthal	.10
66	Rick Aguilera	.10
67	Chuck Finley	.10
68	Andy Ashby	.10
69	Alex Fernandez	.15
70	Ed Sprague	.10
71	Steve Buechele	.10
72	Willie Greene	.10
73	Dave Nilsson	.10
74	Bret Saberhagen	.10
75	Jimmy Key	.10
76	Darren Lewis	.10
77	Steve Cooke	.10
78	Kirk Gibson	.10
79	Ray Lankford	.15
80	Paul O'Neill	.10
81	Mike Bordick	.10
82	Wes Chamberlain	.10
83	Rico Brogna	.10
84	Kevin Appier	.10
85	Juan Guzman	.10
86	Kevin Seitzer	.10
87	Mickey Morandini	.10
88	Pedro Martinez	.10
89	Matt Mieske	.10
90	Tino Martinez	.15
91	Paul Shuey	.10
92	Bip Roberts	.10
93	Chili Davis	.10
94	Deion Sanders	.35
95	Darrell Whitmore	.10
96	Joe Orsulak	.10
97	Bret Boone	.10
98	Kent Mercker	.10
99	Scott Livingstone	.10
100	Brady Anderson	.15
101	James Mouton	.10
102	Jose Rijo	.10
103	Bobby Munoz	.10
104	Ramon Martinez	.12
105	Bernie Williams	.60
106	Troy Neel	.10
107	Ivan Rodriguez	.50
108	Salomon Torres	.10
109	Johnny Ruffin	.10
110	Darryl Kile	.10
111	Bobby Ayala	.10
112	Ron Darling	.10
113	Jose Lima	.10
114	Joey Hamilton	.15
115	Greg Maddux	2.00
116	Greg Colbrunn	.10
117	Ozzie Guillen	.10
118	Brian Anderson	.10
119	Jeff Bagwell	1.00
120	Pat Listach	.10
121	Sandy Alomar	.10
122	Jose Vizcaino	.10
123	Rick Helling	.10
124	Allen Watson	.10
125	Pedro Munoz	.10
126	Craig Biggio	.15
127	Kevin Stocker	.10

#	Player	Value
128	Wil Cordero	.10
129	Rafael Palmeiro	.20
130	Gar Finnvold	.10
131	Darren Hall	.10
132	Heath Slocumb	.10
133	Darrin Fletcher	.10
134	Cal Ripken Jr.	2.50
135	Dante Bichette	.35
136	Don Slaught	.10
137	Pedro Astacio	.10
138	Ryan Thompson	.10
139	Greg Gohr	.10
140	Javier Lopez	.20
141	Lenny Dykstra	.10
142	Pat Rapp	.10
143	Mark Kiefer	.10
144	Greg Gagne	.10
145	Eduardo Perez	.10
146	Felix Fermin	.10
147	Jeff Frye	.10
148	Terry Steinbach	.10
149	Jim Eisenreich	.10
150	Brad Ausmus	.10
151	Randy Myers	.10
152	Rick White	.10
153	Mark Portugal	.10
154	Delino DeShields	.10
155	Scott Cooper	.10
156	Pat Hentgen	.10
157	Mark Gubicza	.10
158	Carlos Baerga	.15
159	Joe Girardi	.10
160	Rey Sanchez	.10
161	Todd Jones	.10
162	Luis Polonia	.10
163	Steve Trachsel	.10
164	Roberto Hernandez	.10
165	John Patterson	.10
166	Rene Arocha	.10
167	Will Clark	.30
168	Jim Leyritz	.10
169	Todd Van Poppel	.10
170	Robb Nen	.10
171	Midre Cummings	.10
172	Jay Buhner	.20
173	Kevin Tapani	.10
174	Mark Lemke	.10
175	Marcus Moore	.10
176	Wayne Kirby	.10
177	Rich Amaral	.10
178	Lou Whitaker	.10
179	Jay Bell	.10
180	Rick Wilkins	.10
181	Paul Molitor	.35
182	Gary Sheffield	.40
183	Kirby Puckett	1.00
184	Cliff Floyd	.10
185	Darren Oliver	.10
186	Tim Naehring	.10
187	John Hudek	.10
188	Eric Young	.10
189	Roger Salkeld	.10
190	Kirt Manwaring	.10
191	Kurt Abbott	.10
192	David Nied	.10
193	Todd Zeile	.10
194	Wally Joyner	.12
195	Dennis Martinez	.12
196	Billy Ashley	.15
197	Ben McDonald	.10
198	Bob Hamelin	.10
199	Chris Turner	.10
200	Lance Johnson	.10
201	Willie Banks	.10
202	Juan Gonzalez	1.50
203	Scott Sanders	.10
204	Scott Brosius	.10
205	Curt Schilling	.10
206	Alex Gonzalez	.10
207	Travis Fryman	.15
208	Tim Raines	.12
209	Steve Avery	.10
210	Hal Morris	.10
211	Ken Griffey Jr.	3.00
212	Ozzie Smith	.40
213	Chuck Carr	.10
214	Ryan Klesko	.60
215	Robin Ventura	.15
216	Luis Gonzalez	.10
217	Ken Ryan	.10
218	Mike Piazza	1.50
219	Matt Walbeck	.10
220	Jeff Kent	.10
221	Orlando Miller	.10
222	Kenny Rogers	.10
223	J.T. Snow	.15

#	Player	Value
224	Alan Trammell	.12
225	John Franco	.10
226	Gerald Williams	.10
227	Andy Benes	.10
228	Dan Wilson	.10
229	Dave Hollins	.10
230	Vinny Castilla	.10
231	Devon White	.10
232	Fred McGriff	.35
233	Quilvio Veras	.10
234	Tom Candiotti	.10
235	Jason Bere	.10
236	Mark Langston	.10
237	Mel Rojas	.10
238	Chuck Knoblauch	.20
239	Bernard Gilkey	.10
240	Mark McGwire	3.00
241	Kirk Rueter	.10
242	Pat Kelly	.10
243	Ruben Sierra	.10
244	Randy Johnson	.40
245	Shane Reynolds	.10
246	Danny Tartabull	.10
247	Darryl Hamilton	.10
248	Danny Bautista	.10
249	Tom Gordon	.10
250	Tom Glavine	.20
251	Orlando Merced	.10
252	Eric Karros	.15
253	Benji Gil	.10
254	Sean Bergman	.10
255	Roger Clemens	1.00
256	Roberto Alomar	.60
257	Benito Santiago	.10
258	Robby Thompson	.10
259	Marvin Freeman	.10
260	Jose Offerman	.10
261	Greg Vaughn	.10
262	David Segui	.10
263	Geronimo Pena	.10
264	Tim Salmon	.25
265	Eddie Murray	.40
266	Mariano Duncan	.10
267	*Hideo Nomo*	4.00
268	Derek Bell	.10
269	Mo Vaughn	.75
270	Jeff King	.10
271	Edgar Martinez	.15
272	Sammy Sosa	1.50
273	Scott Ruffcorn	.10
274	Darren Daulton	.10
275	John Jaha	.10
276	Andres Galarraga	.20
277	Mark Grace	.20
278	Mike Moore	.10
279	Barry Bonds	.75
280	Manny Ramirez	.75
281	Ellis Burks	.15
282	Greg Swindell	.10
283	Barry Larkin	.25
284	Albert Belle	.75
285	Shawn Green	.10
286	John Roper	.10
287	Scott Erickson	.10
288	Moises Alou	.15
289	Mike Blowers	.10
290	Brent Gates	.10
291	Sean Berry	.10
292	Mike Stanley	.10
293	Jeff Conine	.10
294	Tim Wallach	.10
295	Bobby Bonilla	.15
296	Bruce Ruffin	.10
297	Chad Curtis	.10
298	Mike Greenwell	.10
299	Tony Gwynn	1.00
300	Russ Davis	.10
301	Danny Jackson	.10
302	Pete Harnisch	.10
303	Don Mattingly	1.00
304	Rheal Cormier	.10
305	Larry Walker	.30
306	Hector Carrasco	.10
307	Jason Jacome	.10
308	Phil Plantier	.10
309	Harold Baines	.12
310	Mitch Williams	.10
311	Charles Nagy	.10
312	Ken Caminiti	.20
313	Alex Rodriguez	3.00
314	Chris Sabo	.10
315	Gary Gaetti	.10
316	Andre Dawson	.12
317	Mark Clark	.10
318	Vince Coleman	.10
319	Brad Clontz	.10

#	Player	Value
320	Steve Finley	.10
321	Doug Drabek	.10
322	Mark McLemore	.10
323	Stan Javier	.10
324	Ron Gant	.15
325	Charlie Hayes	.10
326	Carlos Delgado	.10
327	Ricky Bottalico	.10
328	Rod Beck	.10
329	Mark Acre	.10
330	Chris Bosio	.10
331	Tony Phillips	.15
332	Garret Anderson	.15
333	Pat Meares	.10
334	Todd Worrell	.10
335	Marquis Grissom	.10
336	Brent Mayne	.10
337	Lee Tinsley	.10
338	Terry Pendleton	.10
339	David Cone	.10
340	Tony Fernandez	.10
341	Jim Bullinger	.10
342	Armando Benitez	.10
343	John Smiley	.10
344	Dan Miceli	.10
345	Charles Johnson	.15
346	Lee Smith	.12
347	Brian McRae	.10
348	Jim Thome	.40
349	Jose Oliva	.10
350	Terry Mulholland	.10
351	Tom Henke	.10
352	Dennis Eckersley	.12
353	Sid Fernandez	.10
354	Paul Wagner	.10
355	John Dettmer	.10
356	John Wetteland	.10
357	John Burkett	.10
358	Marty Cordova	.20
359	Norm Charlton	.10
360	Mike Devereaux	.10
361	Alex Cole	.10
362	Brett Butler	.15
363	Mickey Tettleton	.10
364	Al Martin	.10
365	Tony Tarasco	.10
366	Pat Mahomes	.10
367	Gary DiSarcina	.10
368	Bill Swift	.10
369	Chipper Jones	1.50
370	Orel Hershiser	.12
371	Kevin Gross	.10
372	Dave Winfield	.25
373	Andujar Cedeno	.10
374	Jim Abbott	.12
375	Glenallen Hill	.10
376	Otis Nixon	.10
377	Roberto Kelly	.10
378	Chris Hammond	.10
379	Mike Macfarlane	.10
380	J.R. Phillips	.10
381	Luis Alicea	.10
382	Bret Barberie	.10
383	Tom Goodwin	.10
384	Mark Whiten	.10
385	Jeffrey Hammonds	.12
386	Omar Vizquel	.10
387	Mike Mussina	.40
388	Rickey Bones	.10
389	Steve Ontiveros	.10
390	Jeff Blauser	.10
391	Jose Canseco	.30
392	Bob Tewksbury	.10
393	Jacob Brumfield	.10
394	Doug Jones	.10
395	Ken Hill	.10
396	Pat Borders	.10
397	Carl Everett	.10
398	Gregg Jefferies	.12
399	Jack McDowell	.12
400	Denny Neagle	.10

1995 Leaf Checklists

Honoring the major 1994 award winners in the American (Series I) and National (Series II) Leagues, checklists for the 1995 Leaf set are not numbered among the regular issue. Horizontal cards have a player action photo at left with his name and team in gold foil at bottom. The award is printed vertically at left with the checklist beginning on the right. Backs continue the checklist on a graduated purple background with the checklist number in a silver-foil seal at top-right.

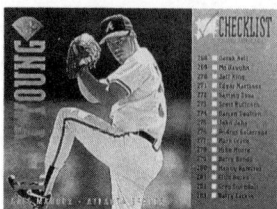

		MT
Complete Set (8):		3.00
Common Player:		.25
1	Checklist 1-67(Bob Hamelin) (Rookie of the Year)	.25
2	Checklist 68-134(David Cone) (Cy Young)	.25
3	Checklist 135-200(Frank Thomas) (MVP)	1.00
4	Series II inserts checklist(Paul O'Neill) (Batting title)	.25
5	Checklist 201-267(Raul Mondesi) (Rookie of the Year)	.50
6	Checklist 268-334(Greg Maddux) (Cy Young)	.60
7	Checklist 335-400(Jeff Bagwell) (MVP)	.40
8	Series 2 inserts checklist(Tony Gwynn) (Batting title)	.50

1995 Leaf Cornerstones

Cornerstones, six of the best first baseman-third baseman combos in baseball, are a six-card insert series found, on average, once every 18 packs in Series I Leaf. Card fronts are horizontally oriented and have a silver prismatic border and player names. Player defensive action photos are set against a background resembling their team logo chiseled into a stone block. Backs have player batting photos at each end with offensive and defensive stats from 1994, and a few words about the duo.

		MT
Complete Set (6):		10.00
Common Player:		1.00
1	Frank Thomas, Robin Ventura	4.00
2	Cecil Fielder, Travis Fryman	1.00
3	Don Mattingly, Wade Boggs	2.00
4	Jeff Bagwell, Ken Caminiti	2.00
5	Will Clark, Dean Palmer	1.50
6	J.R. Phillips, Matt Williams	1.50

1995 Leaf Frank Thomas

The Big Hurt's six seasons in the major leagues are chronicled in this flashy insert set. Silver and gold foil squares are the background for a photo of Thomas on front. Backs repeat the motif with standard print technology and another photo, along with a few words about Thomas' season. The Frank Thomas inserts are found in all types of Series II packs, with odds varying from one in 42 packs to one in 14 packs, depending on card count per pack.

		MT
Complete Set (6):		25.00
Common Thomas:		5.00
1	The Rookie	5.00
2	Sophomore Stardom	5.00
3	Super Star	5.00
4	AL MVP	5.00
5	Back-To-Back	5.00
6	The Big Hurt	5.00

1995 Leaf Gold Stars

Once again the toughest pull among the Leaf inserts are the Gold Leaf Stars found in both series. Found on average of one card per 90-270 packs, depending on pack card count, each of these chase cards is numbered on back within an edition of 10,000. Cards

have fronts printed on metallic foil with the player name at top, the series title at bottom and a vertical stars and stripe device at right all printed in gold foil. A die-cut star appears at bottom-left. Backs are coventionally printed with another player photo and a few sentences about the star. The serial number is in gold foil in a white strip at top.

		MT
Complete Set (14):		200.00
Complete Series 1 (8):		100.00
Complete Series 2 (6):		100.00
Common Player:		6.00
1	Jeff Bagwell	15.00
2	Albert Belle	10.00
3	Tony Gwynn	20.00
4	Ken Griffey Jr.	40.00
5	Barry Bonds	10.00
6	Don Mattingly	15.00
7	Raul Mondesi	8.00
8	Joe Carter	6.00
9	Greg Maddux	25.00
10	Frank Thomas	30.00
11	Mike Piazza	25.00
12	Jose Canseco	8.00
13	Kirby Puckett	30.00
14	Matt Williams	6.00

1995 Leaf Gold Rookies

Every other pack of Series I Leaf Series I is seeded with a Gold Leaf Rookie card. Fronts have a largely white background with a large player photo at left-center and a smaller picture in a rectangle at upper-right. A team-color stripe is at left, while a smaller gray stripe is at top-right. The team name is printed in large gray letters across the center of the card, with the player name in a team color beneath that and above the gold-foil Leaf logo at lower-left. "Gold Leaf Rookies" is printed in gold foil down the right side. Backs repeat the team-color motif with a large action photo of the player in a single color and a smaller color portrait. Full career stats are at bottom.

		MT
Complete Set (16):		8.00
Common Player:		.25
1	Alex Rodriguez	5.00
2	Garret Anderson	.75
3	Shawn Green	.40
4	Armando Benitez	.25
5	Darren Dreifort	.25
6	Orlando Miller	.25
7	Jose Oliva	.25

8	Ricky Bottalico	.25
9	Charles Johnson	.75
10	Brian Hunter	.50
11	Ray McDavid	.25
12	Chan Ho Park	.75
13	Mike Kelly	.25
14	Cory Bailey	.25
15	Alex Gonzalez	.75
16	Andrew Lorraine	.25

1995 Leaf Great Gloves

While the stated emphasis is on fielding prowess in this Series II chase set, players who don't also swing a big stick are ignored. Found as frequently as one per two packs, cards have a detail photo of a glove at left, with an action photo at right. The player name in the Great Gloves logo at bottom-right is in gold foil, as are the Leaf logo at top-left and the team name vertically at right. Backs repeat the glove photo and series logo as background for another player photo and a few words and stats about the player's defense.

		MT
Complete Set (16):		10.00
Common Player:		.25
1	Jeff Bagwell	.60
2	Roberto Alomar	.40
3	Barry Bonds	.40
4	Wade Boggs	.45
5	Andres Galarraga	.25
6	Ken Griffey Jr.	3.00
7	Marquis Grissom	.25
8	Kenny Lofton	.40
9	Barry Larkin	.25
10	Don Mattingly	.75
11	Greg Maddux	2.00
12	Kirby Puckett	.75
13	Ozzie Smith	.50
14	Cal Ripken Jr.	3.00
15	Matt Williams	.35
16	Ivan Rodriguez	.30

1995 Leaf Heading For The Hall

Series II hobby packs were the home of this scarce (one per 75 packs, average) chase set. Eight players deemed to be sure shots for Cooperstown are pictured in a semblance of the famed tombstone-shaped plaque they will someday adorn at the Hall of Fame; in fact the cards are die-cut to that shape. Backs have a sepia-toned photo, career stats and a serial number placing the card within an edition of 5,000.

		MT
Complete Set (8):		200.00
Common Player:		10.00
1	Frank Thomas	30.00
2	Ken Griffey Jr.	50.00
3	Jeff Bagwell	20.00
4	Barry Bonds	15.00
5	Kirby Puckett	20.00
6	Cal Ripken Jr.	40.00
7	Tony Gwynn	25.00
8	Paul Molitor	12.00

1995 Leaf Slideshow

The hold-to-light technology which Leaf debuted with its 1994 Slideshow inserts continued in 1995 with a cross-series concept. The same eight players are featured on these cards in both Series I and II. Each has three clear photos at center, between the spokes of a silver-foil wheel. When both the player's cards are placed side-by-side, the six-picture see-through photo device is complete. Silver-foil and black borders surround the photo wheel on each side of the card. The Slideshow inserts are found on average of just over one per box among all types of pack configurations. Cards were issued with a peelable plastic protector on the front.

	MT
Complete Set (16):	80.00
Complete Series 1 (1a-8a):	40.00
Complete Series 2 (1b-8b):	40.00
Same CL and prices for both series	
Common Player:	4.00
1a Raul Mondesi	5.00

1b	Raul Mondesi	5.00
2a	Frank Thomas	12.00
2b	Frank Thomas	12.00
3a	Fred McGriff	4.00
3b	Fred McGriff	4.00
4a	Cal Ripken Jr.	12.00
4b	Cal Ripken Jr.	12.00
5a	Jeff Bagwell	7.00
5b	Jeff Bagwell	7.00
6a	Will Clark	4.00
6b	Will Clark	4.00
7a	Matt Williams	4.00
7b	Matt Williams	4.00
8a	Ken Griffey Jr.	15.00
8b	Ken Griffey Jr.	15.00

1995 Leaf Statistical Standouts

Embossed red stitches on the large baseball background make the Statistical Standouts chase cards stand out among the inserts in Series I hobby packs (one per 70, average). The leather surface of the ball is also lightly textured, as is the player action photo at center. Printed in gold foil on front are the series name at top, the player's facsimile autograph at lower-center and the Leaf logo and team name at bottom. Backs have a graduated black background with a large team logo at bottom, and a circular player portrait at center. A few words explain why the player's stats stand out among his peers.

		MT
Complete Set (9):		350.00
Common Player:		15.00
1	Joe Carter	15.00
2	Ken Griffey Jr.	125.00
3	Don Mattingly	40.00
4	Fred McGriff	15.00
5	Paul Molitor	25.00
6	Kirby Puckett	40.00
7	Cal Ripken Jr.	100.00
8	Frank Thomas	75.00
9	Matt Williams	20.00

1995 Leaf 300 Club

Issued in both Series I and II Leaf, but only in the retail and magazine packs, at a rate of one per 12-30 packs, depending on pack configuration, 300 Club inserts feature the 18 active players with lifetime .300+ batting averages in a minimum of 1,000 AB. Fronts have color player photos with a large white "300" in the background and "club" in gold foil near the bottom. The player name is in gold foil in an arc above the silver Leaf logo at bottom-center. Large embossed silver triangles in each bottom corner have the team name and player position (left) and career BA (right). Backs have another player photo and highlight his place on the list of .300+ batters.

		MT
Complete Set (18):		100.00
Complete Series 1 (9):		40.00
Complete Series 2 (9):		60.00
Common Player:		1.00
1	Frank Thomas	15.00
2	Paul Molitor	4.00
3	Mike Piazza	15.00
4	Moises Alou	2.00
5	Mike Greenwell	1.00
6	Will Clark	2.50
7	Hal Morris	1.00
8	Edgar Martinez	1.00
9	Carlos Baerga	1.00
10	Ken Griffey Jr.	25.00
11	Wade Boggs	2.50
12	Jeff Bagwell	8.00
13	Tony Gwynn	12.00
14	John Kruk	1.00
15	Don Mattingly	6.00
16	Mark Grace	2.50
17	Kirby Puckett	6.00
18	Kenny Lofton	6.00

1995 Leaf/Limited

Issued in two series of 96 basic cards each, plus inserts, Leaf Limited was a hobby-only product limited to 90,000 numbered 20-pack boxes. Five-card packs had a suggested retail price of $4.99. Fronts of the basic cards have a player action photo on a background of silver holographic foil highlighted with team colors and a gold-foil Leaf Limited logo. Horizontal-format backs have two more player photos, career stats and holographic foil team logos and card numbers.

		MT
Complete Set (192):		60.00
Complete Series 1 (96):		30.00
Complete Series 2 (96):		30.00
Common Player:		.25
Series 1 or 2 Wax Box:		65.00
1	Frank Thomas	5.00
2	Geronimo Berroa	.25
3	Tony Phillips	.25
4	Roberto Alomar	1.00
5	Steve Avery	.25
6	Darryl Hamilton	.25
7	Scott Cooper	.25
8	Mark Grace	.50
9	Billy Ashley	.25
10	Wil Cordero	.25
11	Barry Bonds	1.50
12	Kenny Lofton	1.50
13	Jay Buhner	.50
14	Alex Rodriguez	5.00
15	Bobby Bonilla	.40
16	Brady Anderson	.50
17	Ken Caminiti	.50
18	Charlie Hayes	.25
19	Jay Bell	.25
20	Will Clark	.50
21	Jose Canseco	.50
22	Bret Boone	.25
23	Dante Bichette	.50
24	Kevin Appier	.25
25	Chad Curtis	.25
26	Marty Cordova	.40
27	Jason Bere	.25
28	Jimmy Key	.25
29	Rickey Henderson	.30
30	Tim Salmon	.60
31	Joe Carter	.40
32	Tom Glavine	.40
33	Pat Listach	.25
34	Brian Jordan	.40
35	Brian McRae	.25
36	Eric Karros	.40
37	Pedro Martinez	.50
38	Royce Clayton	.25
39	Eddie Murray	.75
40	Randy Johnson	1.00
41	Jeff Conine	.25
42	Brett Butler	.35
43	Jeffrey Hammonds	.25
44	Andujar Cedeno	.25
45	Dave Hollins	.25
46	Jeff King	.25
47	Benji Gil	.25
48	Roger Clemens	2.00
49	Barry Larkin	.50
50	Joe Girardi	.25
51	Bob Hamelin	.25
52	Travis Fryman	.25
53	Chuck Knoblauch	.50
54	Ray Durham	.40
55	Don Mattingly	2.00
56	Ruben Sierra	.25
57	J.T. Snow	.40
58	Derek Bell	.25
59	David Cone	.40
60	Marquis Grissom	.40
61	Kevin Seitzer	.25
62	Ozzie Smith	1.00
63	Rick Wilkins	.25
64	*Hideo Nomo*	5.00
65	Tony Tarasco	.25
66	Manny Ramirez	1.25
67	Charles Johnson	.50
68	Craig Biggio	.50
69	Bobby Jones	.25
70	Mike Mussina	1.00
71	Alex Gonzalez	.25
72	Gregg Jefferies	.25
73	Rusty Greer	.40
74	Mike Greenwell	.25
75	Hal Morris	.25
76	Paul O'Neill	.40

77	Luis Gonzalez	.25
78	Chipper Jones	4.00
79	Mike Piazza	4.00
80	Rondell White	.50
81	Glenallen Hill	.25
82	Shawn Green	.50
83	Bernie Williams	1.25
84	Jim Thome	1.00
85	Terry Pendleton	.25
86	Rafael Palmeiro	.50
87	Tony Gwynn	3.00
88	Mickey Tettleton	.25
89	John Valentin	.25
90	Deion Sanders	.75
91	Larry Walker	.75
92	Michael Tucker	.25
93	Alan Trammell	.25
94	Tim Raines	.25
95	Dave Justice	.50
96	Tino Martinez	.50
97	Cal Ripken Jr.	5.00
98	Deion Sanders	.75
99	Darren Daulton	.25
100	Paul Molitor	1.00
101	Randy Myers	.25
102	Wally Joyner	.25
103	Carlos Perez	.25
104	Brian Hunter	.25
105	Wade Boggs	.75
106	*Bobby Higginson*	3.00
107	Jeff Kent	.25
108	Jose Offerman	.25
109	Dennis Eckersley	.40
110	Dave Nilsson	.25
111	Chuck Finley	.25
112	Devon White	.25
113	Bip Roberts	.25
114	Ramon Martinez	.25
115	Greg Maddux	4.00
116	Curtis Goodwin	.25
117	John Jaha	.25
118	Ken Griffey Jr.	6.00
119	Geronimo Pena	.25
120	Shawon Dunston	.25
121	Ariel Prieto	.25
122	Kirby Puckett	2.00
123	Carlos Baerga	.25
124	Todd Hundley	.50
125	Tim Naehring	.25
126	Gary Sheffield	.75
127	Dean Palmer	.25
128	Rondell White	.50
129	Greg Gagne	.25
130	Jose Rijo	.25
131	Ivan Rodriguez	1.00
132	Jeff Bagwell	2.00
133	Greg Vaughn	.25
134	Chili Davis	.25
135	Al Martin	.25
136	Kenny Rogers	.25
137	Aaron Sele	.25
138	Raul Mondesi	.50
139	Cecil Fielder	.40
140	Tim Wallach	.25
141	Andres Galarraga	.50
142	Lou Whitaker	.25
143	Jack McDowell	.40
144	Matt Williams	.50
145	Ryan Klesko	.75
146	Carlos Garcia	.25
147	Albert Belle	1.50
148	Ryan Thompson	.25
149	Roberto Kelly	.25
150	Edgar Martinez	.40
151	Robby Thompson	.25
152	Mo Vaughn	1.50
153	Todd Zeile	.25
154	Harold Baines	.25
155	Phil Plantier	.25
156	Mike Stanley	.25
157	Ed Sprague	.25
158	Moises Alou	.40
159	Quilvio Veras	.25
160	Reggie Sanders	.40
161	Delino DeShields	.25
162	Rico Brogna	.25
163	Greg Colbrunn	.25
164	Steve Finley	.25
165	Orlando Merced	.25
166	Mark McGwire	6.00
167	Garret Anderson	.25
168	Paul Sorrento	.25
169	Mark Langston	.25
170	Danny Tartabull	.25
171	Vinny Castilla	.25
172	Javier Lopez	.40

173	Bret Saberhagen	.25
174	Eddie Williams	.25
175	Scott Leius	.25
176	Juan Gonzalez	3.00
177	Gary Gaetti	.25
178	Jim Edmonds	.40
179	John Olerud	.25
180	Lenny Dykstra	.25
181	Ray Lankford	.25
182	Ron Gant	.40
183	Doug Drabek	.25
184	Fred McGriff	.50
185	Andy Benes	.25
186	Kurt Abbott	.25
187	Bernard Gilkey	.25
188	Sammy Sosa	3.00
189	Lee Smith	.25
190	Dennis Martinez	.25
191	Ozzie Guillen	.25
192	Robin Ventura	.25

1995 Leaf/Limited Bat Patrol

Yet another insert of the game's top veteran hitters was featured as chase cards in Series 2 Leaf Limited. The cards have player action photos on front with large silver-foil "BAT / PATROL" lettering at lower-left. Backs are printed on a silver background and include career stats plus another color player photo. The cards were seeded at the rate of one per pack.

		MT
Complete Set (24):		20.00
Common Player:		.50
1	Frank Thomas	4.00
2	Tony Gwynn	2.50
3	Wade Boggs	.50
4	Larry Walker	.50
5	Ken Griffey Jr.	5.00
6	Jeff Bagwell	2.00
7	Manny Ramirez	1.00
8	Mark Grace	.50
9	Kenny Lofton	1.25
10	Mike Piazza	3.00
11	Will Clark	.50
12	Mo Vaughn	1.25
13	Carlos Baerga	.50
14	Rafael Palmeiro	.50
15	Barry Bonds	1.25
16	Kirby Puckett	2.00
17	Roberto Alomar	1.00
18	Barry Larkin	.50
19	Eddie Murray	.75
20	Tim Salmon	.50
21	Don Mattingly	1.50
22	Fred McGriff	.50
23	Albert Belle	1.25
24	Dante Bichette	.50

A player's name in *italic* type indicates a rookie card.

1995 Leaf/Limited Gold

Seeded one per pack in Series I only, this insert set follows the format of the basic Leaf Limited cards, but is distinguished by the presence of gold, rather than silver, holographic foil.

		MT
Complete Set (24):		35.00
Common Player:		.75
1	Frank Thomas	4.00
2	Jeff Bagwell	2.00
3	Raul Mondesi	.75
4	Barry Bonds	1.25
5	Albert Belle	1.25
6	Ken Griffey Jr.	5.00
7	Cal Ripken Jr.	4.00
8	Will Clark	.75
9	Jose Canseco	.75
10	Larry Walker	.75
11	Kirby Puckett	1.50
12	Don Mattingly	1.50
13	Tim Salmon	.75
14	Roberto Alomar	1.00
15	Greg Maddux	3.00
16	Mike Piazza	3.00
17	Matt Williams	.75
18	Kenny Lofton	1.25
19	Alex Rodriquez (Rodriguez)	5.00
20	Tony Gwynn	2.50
21	Mo Vaughn	1.25
22	Chipper Jones	3.00
23	Manny Ramirez	1.00
24	Deion Sanders	.75

1995 Leaf/Limited Lumberjacks

Among the scarcest of 1995 chase cards are the Lumberjacks inserts found in both Series 1 and 2 Leaf Limited at a rate of one per 23 packs on average (less than one per box). Fronts are printed on woodgrain veneer with a large team logo behind a batting action photo of the game's top sluggers. Backs have another photo against a background of tree trunks. A white stripe at bottom carries each card's unique serial number within an edition of 5,000. An even more limited version with black background is limited to 500 numbered cards of each player. Each player can also be found in a promo version.

		MT
Complete Set (16):		275.00
Complete Series 1 Set (8):		175.00
Complete Series 2 Set (8):		100.00
Common Player:		8.00
Black: 3X-5X		
1	Albert Belle	12.00
2	Barry Bonds	12.00
3	Juan Gonzalez	25.00
4	Ken Griffey Jr.	50.00
5	Fred McGriff	8.00
6	Mike Piazza	30.00
7	Kirby Puckett	15.00
8	Mo Vaughn	12.00
9	Frank Thomas	30.00
10	Jeff Bagwell	20.00
11	Matt Williams	8.00
12	Jose Canseco	10.00
13	Raul Mondesi	8.00
14	Manny Ramirez	12.00
15	Cecil Fielder	8.00
16	Cal Ripken Jr.	40.00

1996 Leaf

Reverting to a single-series issue of 220 basic cards, plus numerous insert set bells and whistles, this was the final Leaf set under Donruss' ownership. Regular cards offer large action photos on front and back with a side and bottom border subdued through darkening (front) or lightening (back). Fronts feature silver prismatic-foil graphic highlights while the back includes a circular portrait photo with vital data around. Leaf was sold in both hobby and retail versions, each with some unique inserts. Basic unit was the 12-card foil pack, with suggested retail of $2.49.

	MT
Complete Set (220):	20.00
Common Player:	.10
Unlisted Stars: .20 to .35	
Complete Gold Set (220):	4500.
Common Golds:	8.00
Gold Press Proofs: 75x - 100x	
Complete Silver Set (220):	2200.
Common Silvers:	4.00
Silver Press Proofs: 35x - 50x	
Complete Bronze Set (220):	1000.
Common Bronze:	2.00
Bronze Press Proofs: 15x - 25x	
Wax Box:	50.00

1	John Smoltz	.25
2	Dennis Eckersley	.15
3	Delino DeShields	.10
4	Cliff Floyd	.10
5	Chuck Finley	.10
6	Cecil Fielder	.20
7	Tim Naehring	.10
8	Carlos Perez	.10
9	Brad Ausmus	.10
10	*Matt Lawton*	.10
11	Alan Trammell	.15
12	Steve Finley	.10
13	Paul O'Neill	.10
14	Gary Sheffield	.40
15	Mark McGwire	3.00
16	Bernie Williams	.50
17	Jeff Montgomery	.10
18	Chan Ho Park	.15
19	Greg Vaughn	.10
20	Jeff Kent	.10
21	Cal Ripken Jr.	2.50
22	Charles Johnson	.10
23	Eric Karros	.10
24	Alex Rodriguez	3.00
25	Chris Snopek	.10
26	Jason Isringhausen	.15
27	Chili Davis	.10
28	Chipper Jones	2.00
29	Bret Saberhagen	.10
30	Tony Clark	.60
31	Marty Cordova	.15
32	Dwayne Hosey	.10
33	Fred McGriff	.35
34	Deion Sanders	.25
35	Orlando Merced	.10
36	Brady Anderson	.15
37	Ray Lankford	.15
38	Manny Ramirez	.60
39	Alex Fernandez	.15
40	Greg Colbrunn	.10
41	Ken Griffey Jr.	3.00
42	Mickey Morandini	.10
43	Chuck Knoblauch	.20
44	Quinton McCracken	.10
45	Tim Salmon	.25
46	Jose Mesa	.10
47	Marquis Grissom	.10
48	Checklist	.10
49	Raul Mondesi	.25
50	Mark Grudzielanek	.10
51	Ray Durham	.10
52	Matt Williams	.25
53	Bob Hamelin	.10
54	Lenny Dykstra	.10
55	Jeff King	.10
56	LaTroy Hawkins	.10
57	Terry Pendleton	.10
58	Kevin Stocker	.10
59	Ozzie Timmons	.10
60	David Justice	.20
61	Ricky Bottalico	.10
62	Andy Ashby	.10
63	Larry Walker	.30
64	Jose Canseco	.25
65	Bret Boone	.10
66	Shawn Green	.10
67	Chad Curtis	.10
68	Travis Fryman	.10
69	Roger Clemens	.75
70	David Bell	.10
71	Rusty Greer	.10
72	Bob Higginson	.10
73	Joey Hamilton	.10
74	Kevin Seitzer	.10
75	Julian Tavarez	.10
76	Troy Percival	.10
77	Kirby Puckett	1.00
78	Barry Bonds	.75
79	Michael Tucker	.10
80	Paul Molitor	.30
81	Carlos Garcia	.10
82	Johnny Damon	.15

83	Mike Hampton	.10
84	Ariel Prieto	.10
85	Tony Tarasco	.10
86	Pete Schourek	.10
87	Tom Glavine	.20
88	Rondell White	.15
89	Jim Edmonds	.10
90	Robby Thompson	.10
91	Wade Boggs	.25
92	Pedro Martinez	.10
93	Gregg Jefferies	.15
94	Albert Belle	.75
95	Benji Gil	.10
96	Denny Neagle	.10
97	Mark Langston	.10
98	Sandy Alomar	.10
99	Tony Gwynn	1.25
100	Todd Hundley	.20
101	Dante Bichette	.20
102	Eddie Murray	.40
103	Lyle Mouton	.10
104	John Jaha	.10
105	Checklist	.10
106	Jon Nunnally	.10
107	Juan Gonzalez	1.50
108	Kevin Appier	.10
109	Brian McRae	.10
110	Lee Smith	.10
111	Tim Wakefield	.10
112	Sammy Sosa	1.50
113	Jay Buhner	.15
114	Garret Anderson	.10
115	Edgar Martinez	.10
116	Edgardo Alfonzo	.10
117	Billy Ashley	.10
118	Joe Carter	.20
119	Javy Lopez	.15
120	Bobby Bonilla	.15
121	Ken Caminiti	.25
122	Barry Larkin	.20
123	Shannon Stewart	.10
124	Orel Hershiser	.10
125	Jeff Conine	.10
126	Mark Grace	.20
127	Kenny Lofton	.75
128	Luis Gonzalez	.10
129	Rico Brogna	.10
130	Mo Vaughn	.75
131	Brad Radke	.10
132	Jose Herrera	.10
133	Rick Aguilera	.10
134	Gary DiSarcina	.10
135	Andres Galarraga	.15
136	Carl Everett	.10
137	Steve Avery	.10
138	Vinny Castilla	.10
139	Dennis Martinez	.10
140	John Wetteland	.10
141	Alex Gonzalez	.10
142	Brian Jordan	.15
143	Todd Hollandsworth	.15
144	Terrell Wade	.10
145	Wilson Alvarez	.10
146	Reggie Sanders	.10
147	Will Clark	.25
148	Hideo Nomo	.60
149	J.T. Snow	.10
150	Frank Thomas	2.50
151	Ivan Rodriguez	.60
152	Jay Bell	.10
153	Checklist	.10
154	David Cone	.15
155	Roberto Alomar	.75
156	Carlos Delgado	.15
157	Carlos Baerga	.15
158	Geronimo Berroa	.10
159	Joe Vitiello	.10
160	Terry Steinbach	.10
161	Doug Drabek	.10
162	David Segui	.10
163	Ozzie Smith	.40
164	Kurt Abbott	.10
165	Randy Johnson	.40
166	John Valentin	.10
167	Mickey Tettleton	.10
168	Ruben Sierra	.10
169	Jim Thome	.40
170	Mike Greenwell	.10
171	Quilvio Veras	.10
172	Robin Ventura	.10
173	Bill Pulsipher	.15
174	Rafael Palmeiro	.20
175	Hal Morris	.10
176	Ryan Klesko	.60
177	Eric Young	.10
178	Shane Andrews	.10

179	Brian Hunter	.10
180	Brett Butler	.15
181	John Olerud	.10
182	Moises Alou	.10
183	Glenallen Hill	.10
184	Ismael Valdes	.10
185	Andy Pettitte	1.00
186	Yamil Benitez	.10
187	Jason Bere	.10
188	Dean Palmer	.10
189	Jimmy Haynes	.10
190	Trevor Hoffman	.10
191	Mike Mussina	.40
192	Greg Maddux	2.00
193	Ozzie Guillen	.10
194	Pat Listach	.10
195	Derek Bell	.10
196	Darren Daulton	.10
197	John Mabry	.10
198	Ramon Martinez	.10
199	Jeff Bagwell	1.25
200	Mike Piazza	2.00
201	Al Martin	.10
202	Aaron Sele	.10
203	Ed Sprague	.10
204	Rod Beck	.10
205	Checklist	.10
206	Mike Lansing	.10
207	Craig Biggio	.15
208	Jeffrey Hammonds	.10
209	Dave Nilsson	.10
210	Checklist, Inserts(Dante Bichette, Albert Belle)	.10
211	Derek Jeter	1.50
212	Alan Benes	.20
213	Jason Schmidt	.10
214	Alex Ochoa	.15
215	Ruben Rivera	.40
216	Roger Cedeno	.20
217	Jeff Suppan	.10
218	Billy Wagner	.10
219	Mark Loretta	.10
220	Karim Garcia	.50

1996 Leaf All-Star MVP Contenders

A surprise insert in Leaf boxes was this interactive redemption issue. Twenty leading candidates for MVP honors at the 1996 All-Star Game in Philadelphia were presented in a silver-foil highlighted horizontal format. The player's league logo serves as a background to the color action photo on front; the All-Star logo is in the lower-left corner. Backs have details of the redemption program. Persons who sent in the Mike Piazza card for redemption received a gold version of the set and had their Piazza card punch-cancelled and returned.

	MT
Complete Set (20):	40.00
Common Card:	1.00
Expired: 8-15-96	
Golds: 1x to 1.5x	
1	Frank Thomas	5.00
2	Mike Piazza	5.00
2c	Mike Piazza (redeemed and punch-cancelled)	2.00
3	Sammy Sosa	2.50

4	Cal Ripken Jr.	5.00
5	Jeff Bagwell	2.00
6	Reggie Sanders	.75
7	Mo Vaughn	1.50
8	Tony Gwynn	3.00
9	Dante Bichette	1.00
10	Tim Salmon	1.00
11	Chipper Jones	4.00
12	Kenny Lofton	1.50
13	Manny Ramirez	1.50
14	Barry Bonds	1.50
15	Raul Mondesi	1.00
16	Kirby Puckett	1.50
17	Albert Belle	1.50
18	Ken Griffey Jr.	6.00
19	Greg Maddux	4.00
20	Bonus card	.75

1996 Leaf
All-Star MVP
Contenders Gold

A surprise insert in Leaf boxes was an interactive redemption issue of 20 leading candidates for MVP honors at the 1996 All-Star Game in Philadelphia. The first 5,000 persons who sent in the Mike Piazza card for redemption received a gold version of the set and had their Piazza card punch-cancelled and returned.

		MT
Complete Set (20):		160.00
Common Card:		2.00
1	Frank Thomas	20.00
2	Mike Piazza	12.00
3	Sammy Sosa	5.00
4	Cal Ripken Jr.	20.00
5	Jeff Bagwell	8.00
6	Reggie Sanders	2.00
7	Mo Vaughn	4.00
8	Tony Gwynn	8.00
9	Dante Bichette	2.00
10	Tim Salmon	2.00
11	Chipper Jones	10.00
12	Kenny Lofton	8.00
13	Manny Ramirez	10.00
14	Barry Bonds	3.00
15	Raul Mondesi	4.00
16	Kirby Puckett	4.00
17	Albert Belle	5.00
18	Ken Griffey Jr.	24.00
19	Greg Maddux	18.00

1996 Leaf
Frank Thomas'
Greatest Hits

Die-cut plastic with a background of prismatic foil to simulate a segment of a compact disc is the

format for this insert issue chronicling the career-to-date of Frank Thomas. Backs include a few stats and a portrait photo, plus a gold-foil serial number from within an edition of 5,000. Cards #1-4 are found only in hobby packs; cards #5-7 are exclusive to retail packs (average insertion rate one per 210 packs) and card #8 could be had only through a wrapper redemption.

		MT
Complete Set (8):		180.00
Common Thomas:		25.00
1	1990	40.00
2	1991	40.00
3	1992	40.00
4	1993	40.00
5	1994	40.00
6	1995	40.00
7	Career	40.00
8	MVP	40.00

1996 Leaf
Gold Leaf Stars

A vignetted background of embossed gold metallic cardboard and a Gold Leaf Stars logo in 22-karat gold foil are featured on this limited (2,500 of each) edition insert. Backs include a second color photo of the player and a serial number from within the edition. Gold Leaf Stars were included in both hobby and retail packaging, with an average insertion rate of one per 210 packs.

		MT
Complete Set (15):		350.00
Common Player:		10.00
1	Frank Thomas	50.00
2	Dante Bichette	10.00
3	Sammy Sosa	40.00
4	Ken Griffey Jr.	60.00
5	Mike Piazza	40.00
6	Tim Salmon	10.00
7	Hideo Nomo	12.00
8	Cal Ripken Jr.	50.00
9	Chipper Jones	40.00
10	Albert Belle	15.00
11	Tony Gwynn	30.00
12	Mo Vaughn	15.00
13	Barry Larkin	10.00
14	Manny Ramirez	15.00
15	Greg Maddux	40.00

1996 Leaf
Hats Off

The most technically innovative inserts of 1996 have to be the Hats Off series exclusive to Leaf retail

packs. Front player photos are on a background that is both flocked to simulate the cloth of a baseball cap, plus enhanced with a stiched team logo. The graphics are all in raised textured gold foil. Backs are conventionally printed and include a gold-foil serial number placing each card within an edition of 5,000 per player.

		MT
Complete Set (8):		120.00
Common Player:		5.00
1	Cal Ripken Jr.	30.00
2	Barry Larkin	5.00
3	Frank Thomas	30.00
4	Mo Vaughn	10.00
5	Ken Griffey Jr.	40.00
6	Hideo Nomo	8.00
7	Albert Belle	10.00
8	Greg Maddux	25.00

1996 Leaf
Picture Perfect

Leaf calls the glossy central area of these inserts "pearlized foil," which allows the player action photo to stand out in contrast to the actual wood veneer background. Gold foil graphic highlights complete the design. Backs are conventionally printed and include a gold-foil serial number from within the edition of 5,000 of each player's card. Cards #1-6 are hobby-only inserts, while #7-12 are found in retail packs. Average insertion rate is one per 140 packs.

		MT
Complete Set (12):		220.00
Common Player:		5.00
1	Frank Thomas	30.00
2	Cal Ripken Jr.	30.00
3	Greg Maddux	25.00
4	Manny Ramirez	10.00
5	Chipper Jones	25.00
6	Tony Gwynn	18.00
7	Ken Griffey Jr.	40.00
8	Albert Belle	10.00
9	Jeff Bagwell	18.00
10	Mike Piazza	25.00
11	Mo Vaughn	10.00
12	Barry Bonds	10.00

1996 Leaf Press Proofs

Carrying the parallel edition concept to its inevitable next level, '96 Leaf offered the Press Proof insert cards in three degrees of scarcity, each highlighted with appropriate holographic foil. Like the other '96 Leaf inserts, these are individually serially numbered within its edition limit. At the top of the line are Gold Press Proofs in an edition of only 500 of each card. Silver and Bronze versions were produced in editions of 1,000 and 2,000, respectively. Press Proofs are inserted into both hobby and retail packs at an average rate of one card per 10 packs.

	MT
Complete Set, Gold:	4500.
Complete Set, Silver:	2200.
Complete Set, Bronze:	1000.
Common Player, Gold:	8.00
Common Player, Silver:	4.00
Common Player, Bronze:	2.00
(Press Proof stars valued	
as follows in comparison to	
regular-issue '96 Leaf -	
Gold: 75X-100X Silver: 35X-	
50X Bronze: 15X-20X)	

1996 Leaf Statistical Standouts

The feel of leather complements the game-used baseball background on these hobby-only inserts featuring the game's top names. Backs offer statistical data and a gold-foil serial number placing the card within an edition of 2,500 for each player. Average insertion rate is one per 210 packs.

		MT
Complete Set (8):		350.00
Common Player:		20.00
1	Cal Ripken Jr.	70.00
2	Tony Gwynn	40.00
3	Frank Thomas	70.00
4	Ken Griffey Jr.	90.00
5	Hideo Nomo	20.00
6	Greg Maddux	50.00
7	Albert Belle	25.00
8	Chipper Jones	50.00

1996 Leaf Total Bases

Total-base leaders from 1991-95 are featured in this hobby-only insert set. Card fronts are printed on textured canvas to simulate a base. Fronts are highlighted with gold foil. Backs have stats ranking the player in this category plus a gold-foil serial number from an edition of 5,000 of each player. Total Bases inserts are seeded at an average rate of one per 72 packs.

		MT
Complete Set (12):		125.00
Common Player:		3.00
1	Frank Thomas	25.00
2	Albert Belle	8.00
3	Rafael Palmeiro	4.00
4	Barry Bonds	8.00
5	Kirby Puckett	12.00
6	Joe Carter	3.00
7	Paul Molitor	4.00
8	Fred McGriff	5.00
9	Ken Griffey Jr.	30.00
10	Carlos Baerga	3.00
11	Juan Gonzalez	12.00
12	Cal Ripken Jr.	25.00

1996 Leaf/Limited

Leaf's 1996 Limited set contains 90 of the top rookies and veterans in baseball. There is also a 100-card Limited Gold parallel set which includes the 90 main cards, plus 10 cards from a Limited Rookies insert set. The gold parallel cards are seeded one per every 11 packs. Regular Limited Rookies inserts were seeded one per every seven packs. Two other insert sets were also made - two versions of Lumberjacks and Pennant Craze.

		MT
Complete Set (90):		50.00
Common Player:		.25
Limited Gold Comp. Set (90):		400.00
Limited Golds: 4x to 10x		
Unlisted Stars: .50 to .75		
Wax Box:		75.00
1	Ivan Rodriguez	1.50
2	Roger Clemens	2.50
3	Gary Sheffield	1.00
4	Tino Martinez	.25
5	Sammy Sosa	5.00
6	Reggie Sanders	.25
7	Ray Lankford	.25
8	Manny Ramirez	2.00
9	Jeff Bagwell	3.00
10	Greg Maddux	5.00
11	Ken Griffey Jr.	8.00
12	Rondell White	.25
13	Mike Piazza	5.00
14	Marc Newfield	.25
15	Cal Ripken Jr.	6.00
16	Carlos Delgado	.25
17	Tim Salmon	.50
18	Andres Galarraga	.50
19	Chuck Knoblauch	.50
20	Matt Williams	.50
21	Mark McGwire	8.00
22	Ben McDonald	.25
23	Frank Thomas	6.00
24	Johnny Damon	.25
25	Gregg Jefferies	.25
26	Travis Fryman	.25
27	Chipper Jones	5.00
28	David Cone	.40
29	Kenny Lofton	2.00
30	Mike Mussina	1.00
31	Alex Rodriguez	8.00
32	Carlos Baerga	.25
33	Brian Hunter	.25
34	Juan Gonzalez	4.00
35	Bernie Williams	1.50
36	Wally Joyner	.25
37	Fred McGriff	.75
38	Randy Johnson	1.00
39	Marty Cordova	.25
40	Garret Anderson	.25
41	Albert Belle	2.00
42	Edgar Martinez	.25
43	Barry Larkin	.75
44	Paul O'Neill	.25
45	Cecil Fielder	.50
46	Rusty Greer	.25

47	Mo Vaughn	2.50
48	Dante Bichette	.75
49	Ryan Klesko	1.00
50	Roberto Alomar	2.00
51	Raul Mondesi	.75
52	Robin Ventura	.25
53	Tony Gwynn	3.00
54	Mark Grace	.50
55	Jim Thome	1.00
56	Jason Giambi	.25
57	Tom Glavine	.50
58	Jim Edmonds	.50
59	Pedro Martinez	.25
60	Charles Johnson	.25
61	Wade Boggs	.50
62	Orlando Merced	.25
63	Craig Biggio	.25
64	Brady Anderson	.50
65	Hideo Nomo	1.50
66	Ozzie Smith	1.00
67	Eddie Murray	.75
68	Will Clark	.75
69	Jay Buhner	.50
70	Kirby Puckett	3.00
71	Barry Bonds	2.00
72	Ray Durham	.25
73	Sterling Hitchcock	.25
74	John Smoltz	.75
75	Andre Dawson	.25
76	Joe Carter	.50
77	Ryne Sandberg	1.50
78	Rickey Henderson	.25
79	Brian Jordan	.40
80	Greg Vaughn	.25
81	Andy Pettitte	2.00
82	Dean Palmer	.25
83	Paul Molitor	1.00
84	Rafael Palmeiro	.50
85	Henry Rodriguez	.25
86	Larry Walker	.75
87	Ismael Valdes	.25
88	Derek Bell	.25
89	J.T. Snow	.25
90	Jack McDowell	.25

1996 Leaf/Limited Lumberjacks

Lumberjacks inserts return to Leaf Limited, but the 1996 versions feature an improved maple stock that puts wood grains on both sides of the card. Ten different Lumberjacks are available in two different versions. Regular versions are serial numbered to 5,000, while a special black-bordered Limited Edition version is numbered to 500.

		MT
Complete Set (10):		180.00
Common Player:		6.00
Lumberjack Blacks (500): 3x to 5x		
1	Ken Griffey Jr.	35.00
2	Sammy Sosa	20.00
3	Cal Ripken Jr.	30.00
4	Frank Thomas	30.00
5	Alex Rodriguez	25.00
6	Mo Vaughn	10.00

7	Chipper Jones	25.00
8	Mike Piazza	25.00
9	Jeff Bagwell	15.00
10	Mark McGwire	35.00

1996 Leaf/Limited Pennant Craze

Each card in this insert set is sequentially numbered to 2,500 in silver foil on the back. The top-front of the cards have a die-cut pennant shape and is felt-textured.

		MT
Complete Set (10):		350.00
Common Player:		15.00
1	Juan Gonzalez	40.00
2	Cal Ripken Jr.	60.00
3	Frank Thomas	60.00
4	Ken Griffey Jr.	75.00
5	Albert Belle	20.00
6	Greg Maddux	50.00
7	Paul Molitor	15.00
8	Alex Rodriguez	50.00
9	Barry Bonds	20.00
10	Chipper Jones	50.00

1996 Leaf/Limited Rookies

There are two versions of this 1996 Limited insert set. The cards are reprinted as part of a Limited Gold parallel set, which also includes the regular issue's 90 cards. The gold cards are seeded one per every 11 packs. The top young players are also featured on regular Limited Rookies inserts; these versions are seeded one per every seven packs.

		MT
Complete Set (10):		60.00
Common Player:		3.00
1	Alex Ochoa	3.00
2	Darin Erstad	15.00
3	Ruben Rivera	5.00
4	Derek Jeter	20.00
5	Jermaine Dye	3.00

6	Jason Kendall	3.00
7	Mike Grace	3.00
8	Andruw Jones	15.00
9	Rey Ordonez	4.00
10	George Arias	3.00

1996 Leaf/Preferred

Leaf Preferred consists of 150 cards, a Press Proof parallel set and three insert sets, one of which has its own parallel set, too. While no individual odds are given for insert sets, the overall odds of getting an insert card are one per 10 packs. The Press Proof inserts replace the silver foil name and strip down the left side of the card with gold foil. Press Proof parallels were limited to 250 sets. Another insert set, Silver Leaf Steel, has a card seeded one per pack. This insert set is paralleled by a Gold Leaf Steel set, which appears in much more limited numbers. The two other insert sets are Steel Power and Staremaster.

		MT
Complete Set (150):		40.00
Common Player:		.15
Gold Press Proofs: 25x to 50x		
Unlisted Stars: .25 to .50		
Wax Box:		65.00
1	Ken Griffey Jr.	4.00
2	Rico Brogna	.15
3	Gregg Jefferies	.15
4	Reggie Sanders	.15
5	Manny Ramirez	1.25
6	Shawn Green	.15
7	Tino Martinez	.15
8	Jeff Bagwell	2.00
9	Marc Newfield	.15
10	Ray Lankford	.15
11	Jay Bell	.15
12	Greg Maddux	2.50
13	Frank Thomas	3.00
14	Travis Fryman	.15
15	Mark McGwire	4.00
16	Chuck Knoblauch	.25
17	Sammy Sosa	2.00
18	Matt Williams	.35
19	Roger Clemens	1.00
20	Rondell White	.15
21	Ivan Rodriguez	.75
22	Cal Ripken Jr.	3.00
23	Ben McDonald	.15
24	Kenny Lofton	1.00
25	Mike Piazza	2.50
26	David Cone	.25
27	Gary Sheffield	.75
28	Tim Salmon	.40
29	Andres Galarraga	.30
30	Johnny Damon	.20
31	Ozzie Smith	1.00
32	Carlos Baerga	.20
33	Raul Mondesi	.35

34	Moises Alou	.15
35	Alex Rodriguez	5.00
36	Mike Mussina	1.00
37	Jason Isringhausen	.40
38	Barry Larkin	.40
39	Bernie Williams	.75
40	Chipper Jones	2.50
41	Joey Hamilton	.15
42	Charles Johnson	.15
43	Juan Gonzalez	2.00
44	Greg Vaughn	.15
45	Robin Ventura	.15
46	Albert Belle	1.00
47	Rafael Palmeiro	.25
48	Brian Hunter	.15
49	Mo Vaughn	1.50
50	Paul O'Neill	.15
51	Mark Grace	.25
52	Randy Johnson	.60
53	Pedro Martinez	.15
54	Marty Cordova	.20
55	Garret Anderson	.20
56	Joe Carter	.40
57	Jim Thome	.75
58	Edgardo Alfonzo	.15
59	Dante Bichette	.40
60	Darryl Hamilton	.15
61	Roberto Alomar	1.25
62	Fred McGriff	.60
63	Kirby Puckett	2.00
64	Hideo Nomo	1.00
65	Alex Fernandez	.15
66	Ryan Klesko	1.00
67	Wade Boggs	.25
68	Eddie Murray	.50
69	Eric Karros	.15
70	Jim Edmonds	.25
71	Edgar Martinez	.15
72	Andy Pettitte	1.00
73	Mark Grudzielanek	.15
74	Tom Glavine	.25
75	Ken Caminiti	.50
76	Will Clark	.30
77	Craig Biggio	.15
78	Brady Anderson	.20
79	Tony Gwynn	2.00
80	Larry Walker	.40
81	Brian Jordan	.25
82	Lenny Dykstra	.15
83	Butch Huskey	.15
84	Jack McDowell	.15
85	Cecil Fielder	.25
86	Jose Canseco	.30
87	Jason Giambi	.20
88	Rickey Henderson	.15
89	Kevin Seitzer	.15
90	Carlos Delgado	.15
91	Ryne Sandberg	1.25
92	Dwight Gooden	.15
93	Michael Tucker	.15
94	Barry Bonds	1.25
95	Eric Young	.15
96	Dean Palmer	.15
97	Henry Rodriguez	.15
98	John Mabry	.15
99	J.T. Snow	.15
100	Andre Dawson	.15
101	Ismael Valdes	.15
102	Charles Nagy	.15
103	Jay Buhner	.40
104	Derek Bell	.15
105	Paul Molitor	.75
106	Hal Morris	.15
107	Ray Durham	.15
108	Bernard Gilkey	.15
109	John Valentin	.15
110	Melvin Nieves	.15
111	John Smoltz	.40
112	Terrell Wade	.15
113	Chad Mottola	.15
114	Tony Clark	.75
115	John Wasdin	.15
116	Derek Jeter	2.00
117	Rey Ordonez	.50
118	Jason Thompson	.15
119	*Robin Jennings*	.15
120	*Rocky Coppinger*	.40
121	Billy Wagner	.30
122	Steve Gibralter	.15
123	Jermaine Dye	.40
124	Jason Kendall	.15
125	*Mike Grace*	.50
126	Jason Schmidt	.15
127	Paul Wilson	.25
128	Alan Benes	.25
129	Justin Thompson	.15
130	Brooks Kieschnick	.15
131	George Arias	.15
132	*Osvaldo Fernandez*	.40
133	Todd Hollandsworth	.20
134	Eric Owens	.15
135	Chan Ho Park	.15
136	Mark Loretta	.15
137	Ruben Rivera	.75
138	Jeff Suppan	.15
139	Ugueth Urbina	.15
140	LaTroy Hawkins	.15
141	Chris Snopek	.15
142	Edgar Renteria	.40
143	Raul Casanova	.15
144	Jose Herrera	.15
145	*Matt Lawton*	.15
146	*Ralph Milliard*	.15
147	Checklist	.15
148	Checklist	.15
149	Checklist	.15
150	Checklist	.15

1996 Leaf/Preferred Leaf Steel

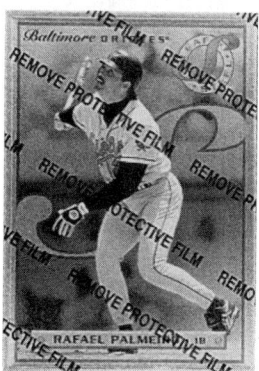

This 77-card insert set has two versions - a silver one and a much more limited gold one. A Silver Leaf Steel card is included in every pack; the parallel versions appear in much more limited numbers.

		MT
Complete Set (77):		100.00
Common Player:		.50
Golds: 6x to 8x		
1	Frank Thomas	8.00
2	Paul Molitor	2.00
3	Kenny Lofton	2.50
4	Travis Fryman	.50
5	Jeff Conine	.50
6	Barry Bonds	2.50
7	Gregg Jefferies	.50
8	Alex Rodriguez	6.00
9	Wade Boggs	.50
10	David Justice	1.00
11	Hideo Nomo	2.00
12	Roberto Alomar	2.00
13	Todd Hollandsworth	.50
14	Mark McGwire	10.00
15	Rafael Palmeiro	1.00
16	Will Clark	1.00
17	Cal Ripken Jr.	8.00
18	Derek Bell	.50
19	Gary Sheffield	1.50
20	Juan Gonzalez	5.00
21	Garret Anderson	.50
22	Mo Vaughn	2.50
23	Robin Ventura	.50
24	Carlos Baerga	.50
25	Tim Salmon	1.00
26	Matt Williams	1.00
27	Fred McGriff	.75
28	Rondell White	.75
29	Ray Lankford	.50
30	Lenny Dykstra	.50
31	J.T. Snow	.50
32	Sammy Sosa	6.00
33	Chipper Jones	6.00
34	Bobby Bonilla	.50
35	Paul Wilson	.50
36	Darren Daulton	.50
37	Larry Walker	1.50
38	Raul Mondesi	1.00
39	Jeff Bagwell	3.00
40	Derek Jeter	5.00
41	Kirby Puckett	2.50
42	Jason Isringhausen	.50
43	Vinny Castilla	.50
44	Jim Edmonds	.75
45	Ron Gant	.50
46	Carlos Delgado	.50
47	Jose Canseco	1.00
48	Tony Gwynn	5.00
49	Mike Mussina	2.00
50	Charles Johnson	.50
51	Mike Piazza	6.00
52	Ken Griffey Jr.	10.00
53	Greg Maddux	6.00
54	Mark Grace	1.00
55	Ryan Klesko	1.00
56	Dennis Eckersley	.50
57	Rickey Henderson	.50
58	Michael Tucker	.50
59	Joe Carter	1.00
60	Randy Johnson	1.50
61	Brian Jordan	.50
62	Shawn Green	.50
63	Roger Clemens	3.00
64	Andres Galarraga	1.50
65	Johnny Damon	.50
66	Ryne Sandberg	2.50
67	Alan Benes	1.00
68	Albert Belle	2.50
69	Barry Larkin	1.00
70	Marty Cordova	.50
71	Dante Bichette	1.00
72	Craig Biggio	.75
73	Reggie Sanders	.50
74	Moises Alou	.75
75	Chuck Knoblauch	1.50
76	Cecil Fielder	.50
77	Manny Ramirez	2.50

1996 Leaf/Preferred Staremaster

These 1996 Leaf Preferred inserts provide a photographic tribute to the stares of 12 top players. Each card is printed on silver holographic card stock and is numbered up to 2,500.

		MT
Complete Set (12):		300.00
Common Player:		10.00
1	Chipper Jones	30.00
2	Alex Rodriguez	30.00
3	Derek Jeter	25.00
4	Tony Gwynn	25.00
5	Frank Thomas	40.00
6	Ken Griffey Jr.	50.00
7	Cal Ripken Jr.	40.00
8	Greg Maddux	40.00
9	Albert Belle	12.00
10	Barry Bonds	12.00
11	Jeff Bagwell	15.00
12	Mike Piazza	40.00

1996 Leaf/Preferred Steel Power

This eight-card Leaf Steel insert set combines micro-etched foil with interior die-cutting to honor the game's top power hitters. Each insert card carries a serial number up to 5,000.

Modern cards have little collector value in conditions lower than Mint.
Figure NM cards at 75% of values shown; EX cards at 40%.

		MT
Complete Set (8):		150.00
Common Player:		8.00
1	Albert Belle	10.00
2	Mo Vaughn	10.00
3	Ken Griffey Jr.	40.00
4	Cal Ripken Jr.	30.00
5	Mike Piazza	25.00
6	Barry Bonds	10.00
7	Jeff Bagwell	18.00
8	Frank Thomas	30.00

1996 Leaf Signature Series

There were 245 Major League Baseball players who autographed cards for Leaf's 1996 Signature Series. At least one authentic signature is guaranteed in every pack. There were 235 players who signed cards in these quantities: Gold (500 autographs), Silver (1,000) and Bronze (3,500). The other 10 players signed fewer autographs - 100 Gold, 200 Silver and 700 Bronze. They are: Kenny Lofton, Mo Vaughn, Frank Thomas, Wade Boggs, Derek Jeter, Manny Ramirez, Paul Molitor, Alex Rodriguez, Raul Mondesi and Roberto Alomar. Each major leaguer signed his cards, including an affidavit that was notarized to guarantee each signature was authentic. In addition, Pinnacle used team clubhouse officials to witness signings. One out of every 48 packs is a super pack containing nothing but autographed cards. In addition, the regular-issue set, which has 100 cards, is paralleled in a Press Proof insert set. These gold version cards are seeded one per every 12 packs.

		MT
Complete Set (150):		75.00
Complete 1st Series Set (100):		50.00
Complete Extended Series Set (50):		25.00
Common Player:		.20
Complete Gold PP Set (150):		1000.
Gold Press Proofs: 8x to 15x		
Complete Platinum Set (150):		3000.
Platinum PP Ser.1 Stars: 30x to 40x		
Platinum PP Ser.2 Stars: 12x to 25x		
Platinum PP Ser. 1 Yng Stars: 20x to 30x		
Platinum PP Ser. 2 Yng Stars: 8x to 20x		
Wax Box:		100.00
1	Mike Piazza	3.00
2	Juan Gonzalez	2.50
3	Greg Maddux	3.00
4	Marc Newfield	.20
5	Wade Boggs	.40
6	Ray Lankford	.20
7	Frank Thomas	4.00
8	Rico Brogna	.20
9	Tim Salmon	.40
10	Ken Griffey Jr.	5.00
11	Manny Ramirez	1.25
12	Cecil Fielder	.40
13	Gregg Jefferies	.20
14	Rondell White	.40
15	Cal Ripken Jr.	4.00
16	Alex Rodriguez	4.00
17	Bernie Williams	1.00
18	Andres Galarraga	.40
19	Mike Mussina	1.00
20	Chuck Knoblauch	.20
21	Joe Carter	.40
22	Jeff Bagwell	2.50
23	Mark McGwire	5.00
24	Sammy Sosa	2.00
25	Reggie Sanders	.20
26	Chipper Jones	3.00
27	Jeff Cirillo	.20
28	Roger Clemens	1.25
29	Craig Biggio	.20
30	Gary Sheffield	.50
31	Paul O'Neill	.20
32	Johnny Damon	.50
33	Jason Isringhausen	.20
34	Jay Bell	.20
35	Henry Rodriguez	.20
36	Matt Williams	.40
37	Randy Johnson	.75
38	Fred McGriff	.50
39	Jason Giambi	.20
40	Ivan Rodriguez	.75
41	Raul Mondesi	.50
42	Barry Larkin	.75
43	Ryan Klesko	1.25
44	Joey Hamilton	.20
45	Todd Hundley	.20
46	Jim Edmonds	.50
47	Dante Bichette	.50
48	Roberto Alomar	1.25
49	Mark Grace	.40
50	Brady Anderson	.40
51	Hideo Nomo	1.25
52	Ozzie Smith	1.00
53	Robin Ventura	.20
54	Andy Pettitte	1.50
55	Kenny Lofton	1.50
56	John Mabry	.20
57	Paul Molitor	.75
58	Rey Ordonez	.75
59	Albert Belle	1.50
60	Charles Johnson	.20
61	Edgar Martinez	.20
62	Derek Bell	.20
63	Carlos Delgado	.20
64	Raul Casanova	.20
65	Ismael Valdes	.20
66	J.T. Snow	.20
67	Derek Jeter	3.00
68	Jason Kendall	.20
69	John Smoltz	.50
70	Chad Mottola	.20
71	Jim Thome	.75
72	Will Clark	.50
73	Mo Vaughn	2.00
74	John Wasdin	.20
75	Rafael Palmeiro	.40
76	Mark Grudzielanek	.20
77	Larry Walker	.30
78	Alan Benes	.40
79	Michael Tucker	.20
80	Billy Wagner	.20
81	Paul Wilson	.50
82	Greg Vaughn	.20
83	Dean Palmer	.20
84	Ryne Sandberg	1.25
85	Eric Young	.20
86	Jay Buhner	.40
87	Tony Clark	.50
88	Jermaine Dye	.40
89	Barry Bonds	1.25
90	Ugueth Urbina	.20
91	Charles Nagy	.20
92	Ruben Rivera	.75
93	Todd Hollandsworth	.20
94	*Darin Erstad*	5.00
95	Brooks Kieschnick	.20
96	Edgar Renteria	.50
97	Lenny Dykstra	.20
98	Tony Gwynn	2.00
99	Kirby Puckett	1.50
100	Checklist	.20
101	Andruw Jones	2.50
102	Alex Ochoa	.20
103	David Cone	.20
104	Rusty Greer	.20
105	Jose Canseco	.40
106	Ken Caminiti	.40
107	Mariano Rivera	.50
108	Ron Gant	.20
109	Darryl Strawberry	.20
110	Vladimir Guerrero	1.50
111	George Arias	.20
112	Jeff Conine	.20
113	Bobby Higginson	.20
114	Eric Karros	.20
115	Brian Hunter	.20
116	Eddie Murray	.50
117	Todd Walker	.75
118	Chan Ho Park	.20
119	John Jaha	.20
120	David Justice	.30
121	Makoto Suzuki	.20
122	Scott Rolen	1.50
123	Tino Martinez	.20
124	Kimera Bartee	.20
125	Garret Anderson	.20
126	Brian Jordan	.20
127	Andre Dawson	.30
128	Javier Lopez	.20
129	Bill Pulsipher	.20
130	Dwight Gooden	.20
131	Al Martin	.20
132	Terrell Wade	.20
133	Steve Gibralter	.20
134	Tom Glavine	.30
135	Kevin Appier	.20
136	Tim Raines	.20
137	Curtis Pride	.20
138	Todd Greene	.20
139	Bobby Bonilla	.20
140	Trey Beamon	.20
141	Marty Cordova	.20
142	Rickey Henderson	.20
143	Ellis Burks	.20
144	Dennis Eckersley	.20
145	Kevin Brown	.20
146	Carlos Baerga	.20
147	Brett Butler	.20
148	Marquis Grissom	.20
149	Karim Garcia	.75
150	Checklist	.20

1996 Leaf Signature Series Autographs

Every pack of 1996 Leaf Signature Series product includes at least one authentically signed card from one of 245 players. There were 235 players who signed three versions in these quantities - 500 Gold, 1,000 Silver and 3,500 Bronze. There are also short-printed autographs for 10 players in quantities of 100 Gold, 200 Silver and 700 Bronze. The short-printed players are designated with an "SP" in the checklist. Cards are numbered alphabetically in the checklist since the autographed cards are unnumbered. Each major leaguer signed a notarized affidavit to guarantee each signature was authentic. Series I style cards of Carlos Delgado, Brian Hunter, Phil Plantier, Jim Thome, Terrell Wade and Ernie Young were signed too late for inclusion in Series 1 packs, and were inserted with Extended. No Bronze cards of Thome were signed.

TERRELL WADE

ATLANTA BRAVES™

	MT
Complete Bronze Set (251):	2000.
Common Bronze Player:	4.00
Silver: 2X	
Gold: 3X-4X	
SP Signatures: 100 Gold, 200 Silver, 700 Bronze	

(1)	Kurt Abbott	4.00
(2)	Juan Acevedo	4.00
(3)	Terry Adams	4.00
(4)	Manny Alexander	4.00
(5)	Roberto Alomar (SP)	100.00
(6)	Moises Alou	12.00
(7)	Wilson Alvarez	4.00
(8)	Garret Anderson	6.00
(9)	Shane Andrews	4.00
(10)	Andy Ashby	4.00
(11)	Pedro Astacio	4.00
(12)	Brad Ausmus	4.00
(13)	Bobby Ayala	4.00
(14)	Carlos Baerga	6.00
(15)	Harold Baines	6.00
(16)	Jason Bates	4.00
(17)	Allen Battle	4.00
(18)	Rich Becker	5.00
(19)	David Bell	4.00
(20)	Rafael Belliard	4.00
(21)	Andy Benes	6.00
(22)	Armando Benitez	4.00
(23)	Jason Bere	4.00
(24)	Geronimo Berroa	4.00
(25)	Willie Blair	4.00
(26)	Mike Blowers	4.00
(27)	Wade Boggs (SP)	140.00
(28)	Ricky Bones	4.00
(29)	Mike Bordick	4.00
(30)	Toby Borland	4.00
(31)	Ricky Bottalico	4.00
(32)	Darren Bragg	4.00
(33)	Jeff Branson	4.00
(34)	Tilson Brito	4.00
(35)	Rico Brogna	4.00
(36)	Scott Brosius	4.00
(37)	Damon Buford	4.00
(38)	Mike Busby	4.00
(39)	Tom Candiotti	4.00
(40)	Frank Castillo	4.00
(41)	Andujar Cedeno	4.00
(42)	Domingo Cedeno	4.00
(43)	Roger Cedeno	4.00

(44)	Norm Charlton	4.00
(45)	Jeff Cirillo	4.00
(46)	Will Clark	20.00
(47)	Jeff Conine	6.00
(48)	Steve Cooke	4.00
(49)	Joey Cora	6.00
(50)	Marty Cordova	4.00
(51)	Rheal Cormier	4.00
(52)	Felipe Crespo	4.00
(53)	Chad Curtis	4.00
(54)	Johnny Damon	12.00
(55)	Russ Davis	4.00
(56)	Andre Dawson	20.00
(57a)	Carlos Delgado (black autograph)	8.00
(57b)	Carlos Delgado (blue autograph)	8.00
(58)	Doug Drabek	4.00
(59)	Darren Dreifort	4.00
(60)	Shawon Dunston	4.00
(61)	Ray Durham	4.00
(62)	Jim Edmonds	5.00
(63)	Joey Eischen	4.00
(64)	Jim Eisenreich	4.00
(65)	Sal Fasano	4.00
(66)	Jeff Fassero	4.00
(67)	Alex Fernandez	7.50
(68)	Darrin Fletcher	4.00
(69)	Chad Fonville	4.00
(70)	Kevin Foster	4.00
(71)	John Franco	4.00
(72)	Julio Franco	5.00
(73)	Marvin Freeman	4.00
(74)	Travis Fryman	6.00
(75)	Gary Gaetti	5.00
(76)	Carlos Garcia	4.00
(77)	Jason Giambi	6.00
(78)	Benji Gil	4.00
(79)	Greg Gohr	4.00
(80)	Chris Gomez	4.00
(81)	Leo Gomez	4.00
(82)	Tom Goodwin	4.00
(83)	Mike Grace	4.00
(84)	Mike Greenwell	4.00
(85)	Rusty Greer	5.00
(86)	Mark Grudzielanek	7.50
(87)	Mark Gubicza	4.00
(88)	Juan Guzman	4.00
(89)	Darryl Hamilton	4.00
(90)	Joey Hamilton	5.00
(91)	Chris Hammond	4.00
(92)	Mike Hampton	4.00
(93)	Chris Haney	4.00
(94)	Todd Haney	4.00
(95)	Erik Hanson	4.00
(96)	Pete Harnisch	4.00
(97)	LaTroy Hawkins	4.00
(98)	Charlie Hayes	4.00
(99)	Jimmy Haynes	4.00
(100)	Roberto Hernandez	4.00
(101)	Bobby Higginson	9.00
(102)	Glenallen Hill	4.00
(103)	Ken Hill	4.00
(104)	Sterling Hitchcock	4.00
(105)	Trevor Hoffman	4.00
(106)	Dave Hollins	4.00
(107)	Dwayne Hosey	4.00
(108)	Thomas Howard	4.00
(109)	Steve Howe	4.00
(110)	John Hudek	4.00
(111)	Rex Hudler	4.00
(112)	Brian Hunter	5.00
(113)	Butch Huskey	5.00
(114)	Mark Hutton	4.00
(115)	Jason Jacome	4.00
(116)	John Jaha	4.00
(117)	Reggie Jefferson	4.00
(118)	Derek Jeter (SP)	175.00
(119)	Bobby Jones	4.00
(120)	Todd Jones	4.00
(121)	Brian Jordan	4.00
(122)	Kevin Jordan	4.00
(123)	Jeff Juden	4.00
(124)	Ron Karkovice	4.00
(125)	Roberto Kelly	4.00
(126)	Mark Kiefer	4.00
(127)	Brooks Kieschnick	5.00
(128)	Jeff King	4.00
(129)	Mike Lansing	4.00
(130)	Matt Lawton	4.00
(131)	Al Leiter	4.00
(132)	Mark Leiter	4.00
(133)	Curtis Leskanic	4.00
(134)	Darren Lewis	4.00
(135)	Mark Lewis	4.00
(136)	Felipe Lira	4.00

(137)	Pat Listach	4.00
(138)	Keith Lockhart	4.00
(139)	Kenny Lofton (SP)	75.00
(140)	John Mabry	4.00
(141)	Mike Macfarlane	4.00
(142)	Kirt Manwaring	4.00
(143)	Al Martin	4.00
(144)	Norberto Martin	4.00
(145)	Dennis Martinez	6.00
(146)	Pedro Martinez	30.00
(147)	Sandy Martinez	4.00
(148)	Mike Matheny	4.00
(149)	T.J. Mathews	4.00
(150)	David McCarty	4.00
(151)	Ben McDonald	4.00
(152)	Pat Meares	4.00
(153)	Orlando Merced	4.00
(154)	Jose Mesa	4.00
(155)	Matt Mieske	4.00
(156)	Orlando Miller	4.00
(157)	Mike Mimbs	4.00
(158)	Paul Molitor (SP)	100.00
(159)	Raul Mondesi (SP)	70.00
(160)	Jeff Montgomery	4.00
(161)	Mickey Morandini	4.00
(162)	Lyle Mouton	4.00
(163)	James Mouton	4.00
(164)	Jamie Moyer	4.00
(165)	Rodney Myers	4.00
(166)	Denny Neagle	5.00
(167)	Robb Nen	4.00
(168)	Marc Newfield	4.00
(169)	Dave Nilsson	4.00
(170)	Jon Nunnally	4.00
(171)	Chad Ogea	4.00
(172)	Troy O'Leary	4.00
(173)	Rey Ordonez	6.00
(174)	Jayhawk Owens	4.00
(175)	Tom Pagnozzi	4.00
(176)	Dean Palmer	4.00
(177)	Roger Pavlik	4.00
(178)	Troy Percival	4.00
(179)	Carlos Perez	4.00
(180)	Robert Perez	4.00
(181)	Andy Pettitte	30.00
(182)	Phil Plantier	4.00
(183)	Mike Potts	4.00
(184)	Curtis Pride	4.00
(185)	Ariel Prieto	6.00
(186)	Bill Pulsipher	4.00
(187)	Brad Radke	4.00
(188)	Manny Ramirez (SP)	60.00
(189)	Joe Randa	4.00
(190)	Pat Rapp	4.00
(191)	Bryan Rekar	4.00
(192)	Shane Reynolds	4.00
(193)	Arthur Rhodes	4.00
(194)	Mariano Rivera	4.00
(195a)	Alex Rodriguez (SP, black autograph)	275.00
(195b)	Alex Rodriguez (SP, blue autograph)	275.00
(196)	Frank Rodriguez	4.00
(197)	Mel Rojas	4.00
(198)	Ken Ryan	4.00
(199)	Bret Saberhagen	6.00
(200)	Tim Salmon	6.00
(201)	Rey Sanchez	4.00
(202)	Scott Sanders	4.00
(203)	Steve Scarsone	4.00
(204)	Curt Schilling	4.00
(205)	Jason Schmidt	4.00
(206)	David Segui	4.00
(207)	Kevin Seitzer	4.00
(208)	Scott Servais	4.00
(209)	Don Slaught	4.00
(210)	Zane Smith	4.00
(211)	Paul Sorrento	4.00
(212)	Scott Stahoviak	4.00
(213)	Mike Stanley	4.00
(214)	Terry Steinbach	4.00
(215)	Kevin Stocker	4.00
(216)	Jeff Suppan	4.00
(217)	Bill Swift	4.00
(218)	Greg Swindell	4.00
(219)	Kevin Tapani	4.00
(220)	Danny Tartabull	4.00
(221)	Julian Tavarez	4.00
(222)	Frank Thomas (SP)	200.00
(223)	Ozzie Timmons	4.00
(224a)	Michael Tucker (black autograph)	4.00
(224b)	Michael Tucker (blue autograph)	4.00
(225)	Ismael Valdez	4.00
(226)	Jose Valentin	4.00

(227)	Todd Van Poppel	4.00
(228)	Mo Vaughn (SP)	80.00
(229)	Quilvio Veras	4.00
(230)	Fernando Vina	4.00
(231)	Joe Vitiello	4.00
(232)	Jose Vizcaino	4.00
(233)	Omar Vizquel	5.00
(234)	Terrell Wade	4.00
(235)	Paul Wagner	4.00
(236)	Matt Walbeck	4.00
(237)	Jerome Walton	4.00
(238)	Turner Ward	4.00
(239)	Allen Watson	4.00
(240)	David Weathers	4.00
(241)	Walt Weiss	4.00
(242)	Turk Wendell	4.00
(243)	Rondell White	5.00
(244)	Brian Williams	4.00
(245)	George Williams	4.00
(246)	Paul Wilson	4.00
(247)	Bobby Witt	4.00
(248)	Bob Wolcott	4.00
(249)	Eric Young	4.00
(250)	Ernie Young	4.00
(251)	Greg Zaun	4.00
---	Frank Thomas (Autographed jumbo)	100.00

1996 Leaf Signature Series Extended Autographs

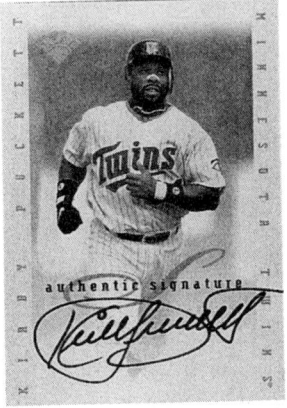

Leaf Signature Series Extended Autograph cards consist of 31 stars and rising prospects, six autographs from Series I that were late inclusions and 186 other major leaguers. The 186 regular players signed 5,000 each, while other signees' totals are listed in parentheses. Signature cards for Alex Rodriguez, Juan Gonzalez and Andruw Jones were only available through redemption cards. Autographed versions are different designs from the regular-issue cards, with two available in each pack. The unnumbered cards are checklisted here in alphabetical order.

		MT
Complete Set (217):		2600.
Common Player:		4.00
Extended Box:		175.00
(1)	Scott Aldred	4.00
(2)	Mike Aldrete	4.00
(3)	Rich Amaral	4.00
(4)	Alex Arias	4.00
(5)	Paul Assenmacher	4.00
(6)	Roger Bailey	4.00
(7)	Erik Bennett	

(8)	Sean Bergman	4.00
(9)	Doug Bochtler	4.00
(10)	Tim Bogar	4.00
(11)	Pat Borders	4.00
(12)	Pedro Borbon	4.00
(13)	Shawn Boskie	4.00
(14)	Rafael Bournigal	4.00
(15)	Mark Brandenburg	4.00
(16)	John Briscoe	4.00
(17)	Jorge Brito	4.00
(18)	Doug Brocail	4.00
(19)	Jay Buhner (SP, 1000)	50.00
(20)	Scott Bullett	4.00
(21)	Dave Burba	4.00
(22)	Ken Caminiti (SP, 1000)	50.00
(23)	John Cangelosi	4.00
(24)	Cris Carpenter	4.00
(25)	Chuck Carr	4.00
(26)	Larry Casian	4.00
(27)	Tony Castillo	4.00
(28)	Jason Christiansen	4.00
(29)	Archi Cianfrocco	4.00
(30)	Mark Clark	4.00
(31)	Terry Clark	4.00
(32)	Roger Clemens (SP, 1000)	150.00
(33)	Jim Converse	4.00
(34)	Dennis Cook	4.00
(35)	Francisco Cordova	5.00
(36)	Jim Corsi	4.00
(37)	Tim Crabtree	4.00
(38)	Doug Creek (SP, 1950)	6.00
(39)	John Cummings	4.00
(40)	Omar Daal	4.00
(41)	Rich DeLucia	4.00
(42)	Mark Dewey	4.00
(43)	Alex Diaz	4.00
(44)	Jermaine Dye (SP, 2500)	16.00
(45)	Ken Edenfield	4.00
(46)	Mark Eichhorn	4.00
(47)	John Ericks	4.00
(48)	Darin Erstad	60.00
(49)	Alvaro Espinoza	4.00
(50)	Jorge Fabregas	4.00
(51)	Mike Fetters	4.00
(52)	John Flaherty	4.00
(53)	Bryce Florie	4.00
(54)	Tony Fossas	4.00
(55)	Lou Frazier	4.00
(56)	Mike Gallego	4.00
(57)	Karim Garcia (SP, 2500)	40.00
(58)	Jason Giambi	4.00
(59)	Ed Giovanola	4.00
(60)	Tom Glavine (SP, 1250)	50.00
(61)	Juan Gonzalez (SP, 1000)	150.00
(62)	Craig Grebeck	4.00
(63)	Buddy Groom	4.00
(64)	Kevin Gross	4.00
(65)	Eddie Guardado	4.00
(66)	Mark Guthrie	4.00
(67)	Tony Gwynn (SP, 1000)	120.00
(68)	Chip Hale	4.00
(69)	Darren Hall	4.00
(70)	Lee Hancock	4.00
(71)	Dave Hansen	4.00
(72)	Bryan Harvey	4.00
(73)	Bill Haselman	4.00
(74)	Mike Henneman	4.00
(75)	Doug Henry	4.00
(76)	Gil Heredia	4.00
(77)	Carlos Hernandez	4.00
(78)	Jose Hernandez	4.00
(79)	Darren Holmes	4.00
(80)	Mark Holzemer	4.00
(81)	Rick Honeycutt	4.00
(82)	Chris Hook	4.00
(83)	Chris Howard	4.00
(84)	Jack Howell	4.00
(85)	David Hulse	4.00
(86)	Edwin Hurtado	4.00
(87)	Jeff Huson	4.00
(88)	Mike James	4.00
(89)	Derek Jeter (SP, 1000)	130.00
(90)	Brian Johnson	4.00
(91)	Randy Johnson (SP, 1000)	60.00
(92)	Mark Johnson	4.00
(93)	Andruw Jones (SP, 2000)	60.00
(94)	Chris Jones	4.00
(95)	Ricky Jordan	4.00
(96)	Matt Karchner	4.00
(97)	Scott Karl	4.00
(98)	Jason Kendall (SP, 2500)	15.00
(99)	Brian Keyser	4.00
(100)	Mike Kingery	4.00
(101)	Wayne Kirby	4.00
(102)	Ryan Klesko (SP, 1000)	40.00

(103)	Chuck Knoblauch (SP, 1000)	60.00
(104)	Chad Kreuter	4.00
(105)	Tom Lampkin	4.00
(106)	Scott Leius	4.00
(107)	Jon Lieber	4.00
(108)	Nelson Liriano	4.00
(109)	Scott Livingstone	4.00
(110)	Graeme Lloyd	4.00
(111)	Kenny Lofton (SP, 1000)	60.00
(112)	Luis Lopez	4.00
(113)	Torey Lovullo	4.00
(114)	Greg Maddux (SP, 500)	300.00
(115)	Mike Maddux	4.00
(116)	Dave Magadan	4.00
(117)	Mike Magnante	4.00
(118)	Joe Magrane	4.00
(119)	Pat Mahomes	4.00
(120)	Matt Mantei	4.00
(121)	John Marzano	4.00
(122)	Terry Matthews	4.00
(123)	Chuck McElroy	4.00
(124)	Fred McGriff (SP, 1000)	30.00
(125)	Mark McLemore	4.00
(126)	Greg McMichael	4.00
(127)	Blas Minor	4.00
(128)	Dave Mlicki	4.00
(129)	Mike Mohler	4.00
(130)	Paul Molitor (SP, 1000)	80.00
(131)	Steve Montgomery	4.00
(132)	Mike Mordecai	4.00
(133)	Mike Morgan	4.00
(134)	Mike Munoz	4.00
(135)	Greg Myers	4.00
(136)	Jimmy Myers	4.00
(137)	Mike Myers	4.00
(138)	Bob Natal	4.00
(139)	Dan Naulty	4.00
(140)	Jeff Nelson	4.00
(141)	Warren Newson	4.00
(142)	Chris Nichting	4.00
(143)	Melvin Nieves	4.00
(144)	Charlie O'Brien	4.00
(145)	Alex Ochoa	4.00
(146)	Omar Olivares	4.00
(147)	Joe Oliver	4.00
(148)	Lance Painter	4.00
(149)	Rafael Palmeiro (SP, 2000)	35.00
(150)	Mark Parent	4.00
(151)	Steve Parris (SP, 1800)	12.00
(152)	Bob Patterson	4.00
(153)	Tony Pena	4.00
(154)	Eddie Perez	4.00
(155)	Yorkis Perez	4.00
(156)	Robert Person	4.00
(157)	Mark Petkovsek	4.00
(158)	Andy Pettitte (SP, 1000)	60.00
(159)	J.R. Phillips	4.00
(160)	Hipolito Pichardo	4.00
(161)	Eric Plunk	4.00
(162)	Jimmy Poole	4.00
(163)	Kirby Puckett (SP, 1000)	150.00
(164)	Paul Quantrill	4.00
(165)	Tom Quinlan	4.00
(166)	Jeff Reboulet	4.00
(167)	Jeff Reed	4.00
(168)	Steve Reed	4.00
(169)	Carlos Reyes	4.00
(170)	Bill Risley	4.00
(171)	Kevin Ritz	4.00
(172)	Kevin Roberson	4.00
(173)	Rich Robertson	4.00
(174)	Alex Rodriguez (SP, 500)	300.00
(175)	Ivan Rodriguez (SP, 1250)	80.00
(176)	Bruce Ruffin	4.00
(177)	Juan Samuel	4.00
(178)	Tim Scott	4.00
(179)	Kevin Sefcik	4.00
(180)	Jeff Shaw	4.00
(181)	Danny Sheaffer	4.00
(182)	Craig Shipley	4.00
(183)	Dave Silvestri	4.00
(184)	Aaron Small	4.00
(185)	John Smoltz (SP, 1000)	50.00
(186)	Luis Sojo	4.00
(187)	Sammy Sosa (SP, 1000)	140.00
(188)	Steve Sparks	4.00
(189)	Tim Spehr	4.00
(190)	Russ Springer	4.00
(191)	Matt Stairs	4.00
(192)	Andy Stankiewicz	4.00
(193)	Mike Stanton	4.00
(194)	Kelly Stinnett	4.00
(195)	Doug Strange	4.00
(196)	Mark Sweeney	4.00
(197)	Jeff Tabaka	4.00

(198)	Jesus Tavarez	4.00
(199)	Frank Thomas (SP, 1000)	200.00
(200)	Larry Thomas	4.00
(201)	Mark Thompson	4.00
(202)	Mike Timlin	4.00
(203)	Steve Trachsel	4.00
(204)	Tom Urbani	4.00
(205)	Julio Valera	4.00
(206)	Dave Valle	4.00
(207)	William VanLandingham	4.00
(208)	Mo Vaughn (SP, 1000)	75.00
(209)	Dave Veres	4.00
(210)	Ed Vosberg	4.00
(211)	Don Wengert	4.00
(212)	Matt Whiteside	4.00
(213)	Bob Wickman	4.00
(214)	Matt Williams (SP, 1250)	45.00
(215)	Mike Williams	4.00
(216)	Woody Williams	4.00
(217)	Craig Worthington	4.00
---	Frank Thomas (Autographed jumbo)	200.00

1996 Leaf/ Signature Extended Autographs - Century Marks

Century Marks consisted of the first 100 autographs by the 31 stars and top prospects, and are designated with a "Century Marks" blue holographic foil logo. Several players' autographed cards were available only by mail-in redemption cards.

		MT
	Common Player:	80.00
(1)	Jay Buhner	125.00
(2)	Ken Caminiti	100.00
(3)	Roger Clemens	350.00
(4)	Jermaine Dye	80.00
(5)	Darin Erstad	200.00
(6)	Karim Garcia	100.00
(7)	Jason Giambi	80.00
(8)	Tom Glavine	100.00
(9)	Juan Gonzalez	300.00
(10)	Tony Gwynn	300.00
(11)	Derek Jeter	275.00
(12)	Randy Johnson	150.00
(13)	Andruw Jones	250.00
(14)	Jason Kendall	80.00
(15)	Ryan Klesko	90.00
(16)	Chuck Knoblauch	140.00
(17)	Kenny Lofton	175.00
(18)	Greg Maddux	600.00
(19)	Fred McGriff	100.00
(20)	Paul Molitor	175.00
(21)	Alex Ochoa	80.00
(22)	Rafael Palmeiro	80.00
(23)	Andy Pettitte	150.00
(24)	Kirby Puckett	300.00
(25)	Alex Rodriguez	400.00
(26)	Ivan Rodriguez	175.00
(27)	John Smoltz	125.00
(28)	Sammy Sosa	350.00
(29)	Frank Thomas	500.00
(30)	Mo Vaughn	175.00
(31)	Matt Williams	100.00

1997 Leaf

Leaf produced a 200-card set for the first series in 1997. The cards featured a grey border, with the featured player in the center. The player's name, team and a Leaf logo were displayed at the bottom center with silver foil, with the team logo in the upper-right hand corner. Cards numbered 188-200 were part of a subset called Legacy Collection. Leaf was the first install- ment of the Fractal Matrix system,

and also included the following in- serts: Banner Season, Dress for Success, Get-A-Grip, Knot-hole Gang and Statistical Standouts.

		MT
Complete Set (400):		50.00
Complete Series I Set (200):		25.00
Complete Series II Set (200):		25.00
Common Player:		.10
Jackie Robinson 1948 Leaf Reprint:		60.00
Wax Box:		45.00
1	Wade Boggs	.20
2	Brian McRae	.10
3	Jeff D'Amico	.10
4	George Arias	.10
5	Billy Wagner	.10
6	Ray Lankford	.10
7	Will Clark	.25
8	Edgar Renteria	.10
9	Alex Ochoa	.10
10	Roberto Hernandez	.10
11	Joe Carter	.20
12	Gregg Jefferies	.10
13	Mark Grace	.20
14	Roberto Alomar	.75
15	Joe Randa	.10
16	Alex Rodriguez	3.00
17	Tony Gwynn	1.25
18	Steve Gibralter	.10
19	Scott Stahoviak	.10
20	Matt Williams	.25
21	Quinton McCracken	.10
22	Ugueth Urbina	.10
23	Jermaine Allensworth	.10
24	Paul Molitor	.40
25	Carlos Delgado	.15
26	Bob Abreu	.10
27	John Jaha	.10
28	Rusty Greer	.10
29	Kimera Bartee	.10
30	Ruben Rivera	.20
31	Jason Kendall	.10
32	Lance Johnson	.10
33	Robin Ventura	.10
34	Kevin Appier	.10
35	John Mabry	.10
36	Ricky Otero	.10
37	Mike Lansing	.10
38	Mark McGwire	4.00
39	Tim Naehring	.10
40	Tom Glavine	.20
41	Rey Ordonez	.15
42	Tony Clark	.50
43	Rafael Palmeiro	.20
44	Pedro Martinez	.20
45	Keith Lockhart	.10
46	Dan Wilson	.10
47	John Wetteland	.10
48	Chan Ho Park	.10
49	Gary Sheffield	.40
50	Shawn Estes	.10
51	Royce Clayton	.10
52	Jaime Navarro	.10
53	Raul Casanova	.10
54	Jeff Bagwell	1.25
55	Barry Larkin	.30
56	Charles Nagy	.10
57	Ken Caminiti	.30

58	Todd Hollandsworth	.10
59	Pat Hentgen	.10
60	Jose Valentin	.10
61	Frank Rodriguez	.10
62	Mickey Tettleton	.10
63	Marty Cordova	.10
64	Cecil Fielder	.20
65	Barry Bonds	.75
66	Scott Servais	.10
67	Ernie Young	.10
68	Wilson Alvarez	.10
69	Mike Grace	.10
70	Shane Reynolds	.10
71	Henry Rodriguez	.10
72	Eric Karros	.10
73	Mark Langston	.10
74	Scott Karl	.10
75	Trevor Hoffman	.10
76	Orel Hershiser	.10
77	John Smoltz	.20
78	Raul Mondesi	.25
79	Jeff Brantley	.10
80	Donne Wall	.10
81	Joey Cora	.10
82	Mel Rojas	.10
83	Chad Mottola	.10
84	Omar Vizquel	.10
85	Greg Maddux	2.00
86	Jamey Wright	.10
87	Chuck Finley	.10
88	Brady Anderson	.10
89	Alex Gonzalez	.10
90	Andy Benes	.10
91	Reggie Jefferson	.10
92	Paul O'Neill	.10
93	Javier Lopez	.20
94	Mark Grudzielanek	.10
95	Marc Newfield	.10
96	Kevin Ritz	.10
97	Fred McGriff	.25
98	Dwight Gooden	.10
99	Hideo Nomo	.75
100	Steve Finley	.10
101	Juan Gonzalez	1.25
102	Jay Buhner	.20
103	Paul Wilson	.10
104	Alan Benes	.10
105	Manny Ramirez	.75
106	Kevin Elster	.10
107	Frank Thomas	2.50
108	Orlando Miller	.10
109	Ramon Martinez	.10
110	Kenny Lofton	.75
111	Bernie Williams	.50
112	Robby Thompson	.10
113	Bernard Gilkey	.10
114	Ray Durham	.10
115	Jeff Cirillo	.10
116	Brian Jordan	.10
117	Rich Becker	.10
118	Al Leiter	.10
119	Mark Johnson	.10
120	Ellis Burks	.10
121	Sammy Sosa	1.50
122	Willie Greene	.10
123	Michael Tucker	.10
124	Eddie Murray	.40
125	Joey Hamilton	.10
126	Antonio Osuna	.10
127	Bobby Higginson	.10
128	Tomas Perez	.10
129	Tim Salmon	.25
130	Mark Wohlers	.10
131	Charles Johnson	.10
132	Randy Johnson	.50
133	Brooks Kieschnick	.10
134	Al Martin	.10
135	Dante Bichette	.20
136	Andy Pettitte	.75
137	Jason Giambi	.10
138	James Baldwin	.10
139	Ben McDonald	.10
140	Shawn Green	.10
141	Geronimo Berroa	.10
142	Jose Offerman	.10
143	Curtis Pride	.10
144	Terrell Wade	.10
145	Ismael Valdes	.10
146	Mike Mussina	.60
147	Mariano Rivera	.20
148	Ken Hill	.10
149	Darin Erstad	1.25
150	Jay Bell	.10
151	Mo Vaughn	.75
152	Ozzie Smith	.50
153	Jose Mesa	.10

154	Osvaldo Fernandez	.10
155	Vinny Castilla	.10
156	Jason Isringhausen	.10
157	B.J. Surhoff	.10
158	Robert Perez	.10
159	Ron Coomer	.10
160	Darren Oliver	.10
161	Mike Mohler	.10
162	Russ Davis	.10
163	Bret Boone	.10
164	Ricky Bottalico	.10
165	Derek Jeter	2.00
166	Orlando Merced	.10
167	John Valentin	.10
168	Andruw Jones	1.50
169	Angel Echevarria	.10
170	Todd Walker	.75
171	Desi Relaford	.10
172	Trey Beamon	.10
173	Brian Giles	.10
174	Scott Rolen	1.25
175	Shannon Stewart	.10
176	Dmitri Young	.10
177	Justin Thompson	.10
178	Trot Nixon	.10
179	Josh Booty	.10
180	Robin Jennings	.10
181	Marvin Benard	.10
182	Luis Castillo	.25
183	Wendell Magee	.10
184	Vladimir Guerrero	1.00
185	Nomar Garciaparra	2.00
186	Ryan Hancock	.10
187	Mike Cameron	.10
188	Cal Ripken Jr. (Legacy)	1.25
189	Chipper Jones (Legacy)	1.00
190	Albert Belle (Legacy)	.50
191	Mike Piazza (Legacy)	1.00
192	Chuck Knoblauch (Legacy)	.10
193	Ken Griffey Jr. (Legacy)	1.50
194	Ivan Rodriguez (Legacy)	.25
195	Jose Canseco (Legacy)	.20
196	Ryne Sandberg (Legacy)	.35
197	Jim Thome (Legacy)	.20
198	Andy Pettitte (Checklist)	.35
199	Andruw Jones (Checklist)	.75
200	Derek Jeter (Checklist)	.60
201	Chipper Jones	2.00
202	Albert Belle	.75
203	Mike Piazza	2.00
204	Ken Griffey Jr.	3.00
205	Ryne Sandberg	.75
206	Jose Canseco	.25
207	Chili Davis	.10
208	Roger Clemens	1.00
209	Deion Sanders	.25
210	Darryl Hamilton	.10
211	Jermaine Dye	.10
212	Matt Williams	.25
213	Kevin Elster	.10
214	John Wetteland	.10
215	Garret Anderson	.10
216	Kevin Brown	.10
217	Matt Lawton	.10
218	Cal Ripken Jr.	2.50
219	Moises Alou	.10
220	Chuck Knoblauch	.20
221	Ivan Rodriguez	.60
222	Travis Fryman	.40
223	Jim Thome	.35
224	Eddie Murray	.10
225	Eric Young	.10
226	Ron Gant	.10
227	Tony Phillips	.10
228	Reggie Sanders	.10
229	Johnny Damon	.10
230	Bill Pulsipher	.10
231	Jim Edmonds	.10
232	Melvin Nieves	.10
233	Ryan Klesko	.40
234	David Cone	.20
235	Derek Bell	.10
236	Julio Franco	.10
237	Juan Guzman	.10
238	Larry Walker	.25
239	Delino DeShields	.10
240	Troy Percival	.10
241	Andres Galarraga	.20
242	Rondell White	.15
243	John Burkett	.10
244	J.T. Snow	.10
245	Alex Fernandez	.10
246	Edgar Martinez	.10
247	Craig Biggio	.15
248	Todd Hundley	.10
249	Jimmy Key	.10
250	Cliff Floyd	.10
251	Jeff Conine	.10
252	Curt Schilling	.10
253	Jeff King	.10
254	Tino Martinez	.20
255	Carlos Baerga	.10
256	Jeff Fassero	.10
257	Dean Palmer	.10
258	Robb Nen	.10
259	Sandy Alomar Jr.	.10
260	Carlos Perez	.10
261	Rickey Henderson	.10
262	Bobby Bonilla	.10
263	Darren Daulton	.10
264	Jim Leyritz	.10
265	Dennis Martinez	.10
266	Butch Huskey	.10
267	Joe Vitiello	.10
268	Steve Trachsel	.10
269	Glenallen Hill	.10
270	Terry Steinbach	.10
271	Mark McLemore	.10
272	Devon White	.10
273	Jeff Kent	.10
274	Tim Raines	.10
275	Carlos Garcia	.10
276	Hal Morris	.10
277	Gary Gaetti	.10
278	John Olerud	.10
279	Wally Joyner	.10
280	Brian Hunter	.10
281	Steve Karsay	.10
282	Denny Neagle	.10
283	Jose Herrera	.10
284	Todd Stottlemyre	.10
285	Bip Roberts	.10
286	Kevin Seitzer	.10
287	Benji Gil	.10
288	Dennis Eckersley	.10
289	Brad Ausmus	.10
290	Otis Nixon	.10
291	Darryl Strawberry	.10
292	Marquis Grissom	.10
293	Darryl Kile	.10
294	Quilvio Veras	.10
295	Tom Goodwin	.10
296	Benito Santiago	.10
297	Mike Bordick	.10
298	Roberto Kelly	.10
299	David Justice	.20
300	Carl Everett	.10
301	Mark Whiten	.10
302	Aaron Sele	.10
303	Darren Dreifort	.10
304	Bobby Jones	.10
305	Fernando Vina	.10
306	Ed Sprague	.10
307	Andy Ashby	.10
308	Tony Fernandez	.10
309	Roger Pavlik	.10
310	Mark Clark	.10
311	Mariano Duncan	.10
312	Tyler Houston	.10
313	Eric Davis	.10
314	Greg Vaughn	.10
315	David Segui	.10
316	Dave Nilsson	.10
317	F.P. Santangelo	.10
318	Wilton Guerrero	1.00
319	Jose Guillen	.10
320	Kevin Orie	.10
321	Derrek Lee	.10
322	*Bubba Trammell*	.75
323	Pokey Reese	.10
324	*Hideki Irabu*	2.00
325	Scott Spiezio	.10
326	Bartolo Colon	.10
327	Damon Mashore	.10
328	Ryan McGuire	.10
329	Chris Carpenter	.10
330	*Jose Cruz Jr.*	4.00
331	Todd Greene	.10
332	Brian Moehler	.10
333	Mike Sweeney	.10
334	Neifi Perez	.10
335	Matt Morris	.10
336	Marvin Benard	.10
337	Karim Garcia	.10
338	Jason Dickson	.10
339	Brant Brown	.10
340	Jeff Suppan	.10
341	*Deivi Cruz*	.50
342	Antone Williamson	.10
343	Curtis Goodwin	.10
344	Brooks Kieschnick	.10
345	*Tony Womack*	.25
346	Rudy Pemberton	.10
347	Todd Dunwoody	.30
348	Frank Thomas (Legacy)	1.25
349	Andruw Jones (Legacy)	.75
350	Alex Rodriguez (Legacy)	1.25
351	Greg Maddux (Legacy)	1.00
352	Jeff Bagwell (Legacy)	.75
353	Juan Gonzalez (Legacy)	.75
354	Barry Bonds (Legacy)	.40
355	Mark McGwire (Legacy)	2.00
356	Tony Gwynn (Legacy)	.75
357	Gary Sheffield (Legacy)	.20
358	Derek Jeter (Legacy)	1.00
359	Manny Ramirez (Legacy)	.40
360	Hideo Nomo (Legacy)	.30
361	Sammy Sosa (Legacy)	.75
362	Paul Molitor (Legacy)	.20
363	Kenny Lofton (Legacy)	.40
364	Eddie Murray (Legacy)	.20
365	Barry Larkin (Legacy)	.10
366	Roger Clemens (Legacy)	.50
367	John Smoltz (Legacy)	.10
368	Alex Rodriguez (Gamers)	1.25
369	Frank Thomas (Gamers)	1.25
370	Cal Ripken Jr. (Gamers)	1.25
371	Ken Griffey Jr. (Gamers)	1.50
372	Greg Maddux (Gamers)	1.00
373	Mike Piazza (Gamers)	1.00
374	Chipper Jones (Gamers)	1.00
375	Albert Belle (Gamers)	.40
376	Chuck Knoblauch (Gamers)	.15
377	Brady Anderson (Gamers)	.10
378	David Justice (Gamers)	.10
379	Randy Johnson (Gamers)	.20
380	Wade Boggs (Gamers)	.15
381	Kevin Brown (Gamers)	.10
382	Tom Glavine (Gamers)	.10
383	Raul Mondesi (Gamers)	.10
384	Ivan Rodriguez (Gamers)	.30
385	Larry Walker (Gamers)	.10
386	Bernie Williams (Gamers)	.30
387	Rusty Greer (Gamers)	.10
388	Rafael Palmeiro (Gamers)	.10
389	Matt Williams (Gamers)	.15
390	Eric Young (Gamers)	.10
391	Fred McGriff (Gamers)	.10
392	Ken Caminiti (Gamers)	.10
393	Roberto Alomar (Gamers)	.30
394	Brian Jordan (Gamers)	.10
395	Mark Grace (Gamers)	.10
396	Jim Edmonds (Gamers)	.10
397	Deion Sanders (Gamers)	.10
398	Checklist(Vladimir Guerrero)	.50
399	Checklist(Darin Erstad)	.60
400	Checklist(Nomar Garciaparra)	.75

1997 Leaf Banner Season

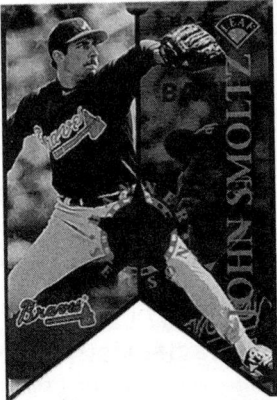

Banner Season was a 15-card insert set that was die-cut and printed on a canvas card stock. Only 2,500 individually numbered sets were produced, with cards only found in pre-priced packs.

		MT
Complete Set (15):		225.00
Common Player:		5.00
1	Jeff Bagwell	20.00
2	Ken Griffey Jr.	50.00
3	Juan Gonzalez	25.00
4	Frank Thomas	25.00
5	Alex Rodriguez	30.00
6	Kenny Lofton	12.00
7	Chuck Knoblauch	6.00
8	Mo Vaughn	12.00
9	Chipper Jones	30.00
10	Ken Caminiti	5.00
11	Craig Biggio	5.00
12	John Smoltz	5.00
13	Pat Hentgen	5.00
14	Derek Jeter	25.00
15	Todd Hollandsworth	5.00

1997 Leaf
Dress for Success

Exclusive to retail packs was an insert called Dress for Success. It included 18 players printed on nylon and flocking card stock. Dress for Success was limited to 3,500 individually numbered sets.

		MT
Complete Set (18):		300.00
Common Player:		5.00
1	Greg Maddux	25.00
2	Cal Ripken Jr.	30.00
3	Albert Belle	10.00
4	Frank Thomas	25.00
5	Dante Bichette	5.00
6	Gary Sheffield	8.00
7	Jeff Bagwell	18.00
8	Mike Piazza	25.00
9	Mark McGwire	50.00
10	Ken Caminiti	8.00
11	Alex Rodriguez	30.00
12	Ken Griffey Jr.	40.00
13	Juan Gonzalez	18.00
14	Brian Jordan	5.00
15	Mo Vaughn	10.00
16	Ivan Rodriguez	8.00
17	Andruw Jones	20.00
18	Chipper Jones	25.00

1997 Leaf
Fractal Matrix

Leaf introduced Fractal Matrix inserts, a 200-card parallel set broken down into three colors and three unique die-cuts. Two fractures break the insert set down by foil background color only (40 Golds, 60 Silvers and 100 Bronze). A second fracture breaks those cards down into color and die-cutting variations. No production numbers or insert ratios were released for either fracture.

		MT
Common Bronze:		2.00
Common Silver:		4.00
Common Gold Z-Axis:		10.00
Common Gold Y-Axis:		20.00
Common Gold X-Axis:		40.00
1	Wade Boggs G/Y	35.00
2	Brian McRae B/Y	2.00
3	Jeff D'Amico B/Y	2.00
4	George Arias B/Y	4.00
5	Billy Wagner S/Y	4.00
6	Ray Lankford B/Z	2.00
7	Will Clark S/Y	10.00
8	Edgar Renteria S/Y	4.00
9	Alex Ochoa S/Y	4.00
10	Roberto Hernandez S/Y	4.00
11	Joe Carter S/Y	6.00
12	Gregg Jefferies B/Y	2.00
13	Mark Grace S/Y	8.00
14	Roberto Alomar G/Y	50.00
15	Joe Randa B/X	2.00
16	Alex Rodriguez G/Z	125.00
17	Tony Gwynn G/Z	75.00
18	Steve Gibralter B/Y	2.00
19	Scott Stahoviak B/X	2.00
20	Matt Williams S/Z	15.00
21	Quinton McCracken B/Y	2.00
22	Ugueth Urbina B/X	2.00
23	Jermaine Allensworth S/X	6.00
24	Paul Molitor G/X	75.00
25	Carlos Delgado S/Y	8.00
26	Bob Abreu S/Y	6.00
27	John Jaha S/Y	6.00
28	Rusty Greer S/Z	4.00
29	Kimera Bartee B/X	2.00
30	Ruben Rivera S/Y	6.00
31	Jason Kendall S/Y	6.00
32	Lance Johnson B/X	2.00
33	Robin Ventura B/Y	2.00
34	Kevin Appier S/X	4.00
35	John Mabry S/Y	4.00
36	Ricky Otero B/X	2.00
37	Mike Lansing B/X	2.00
38	Mark McGwire G/Z	140.00
39	Tim Naehring B/X	2.00
40	Tom Glavine S/Z	6.00
41	Rey Ordonez S/Y	6.00
42	Tony Clark S/Y	20.00
43	Rafael Palmeiro S/Z	10.00
44	Pedro Martinez S/X	4.00
45	Keith Lockhart B/X	2.00
46	Dan Wilson B/Y	2.00
47	John Wetteland B/Y	2.00
48	Chan Ho Park B/X	2.00
49	Gary Sheffield G/Z	25.00
50	Shawn Estes B/X	2.00
51	Royce Clayton B/X	2.00
52	Jaime Navarro B/X	2.00
53	Raul Casanova B/X	2.00
54	Jeff Bagwell G/Z	60.00
55	Barry Larkin G/X	40.00
56	Charles Nagy B/Y	2.00
57	Ken Caminiti G/Y	40.00
58	Todd Hollandsworth S/Z	4.00
59	Pat Hentgen S/X	4.00
60	Jose Valentin B/X	2.00
61	Frank Rodriguez B/X	2.00
62	Mickey Tettleton B/X	2.00
63	Marty Cordova G/X	30.00
64	Cecil Fielder S/X	8.00
65	Barry Bonds G/Z	40.00
66	Scott Servais B/X	2.00
67	Ernie Young B/X	2.00
68	Wilson Alvarez B/X	2.00
69	Mike Grace B/X	2.00
70	Shane Reynolds S/X	6.00
71	Henry Rodriguez S/Y	4.00
72	Eric Karros R/X	2.00
73	Mark Langston B/X	2.00
74	Scott Karl B/X	2.00
75	Trevor Hoffman B/X	2.00
76	Orel Hershiser S/X	4.00
77	John Smoltz G/Y	30.00
78	Raul Mondesi G/Z	25.00
79	Jeff Brantley B/X	2.00
80	Donne Wall B/X	2.00
81	Joey Cora B/X	2.00
82	Mel Rojas B/X	2.00
83	Chad Mottola B/X	2.00
84	Omar Vizquel B/X	2.00
85	Greg Maddux G/Z	120.00
86	Jamey Wright S/Y	6.00
87	Chuck Finley B/X	2.00
88	Brady Anderson G/Y	20.00
89	Alex Gonzalez S/X	6.00
90	Andy Benes B/X	2.00
91	Reggie Jefferson B/X	2.00
92	Paul O'Neill B/Y	4.00
93	Javier Lopez S/X	8.00
94	Mark Grudzielanek S/X	6.00
95	Marc Newfield B/X	2.00
96	Kevin Ritz B/X	2.00
97	Fred McGriff G/Y	25.00
98	Dwight Gooden S/X	6.00
99	Hideo Nomo S/Y	30.00
100	Steve Finley B/X	2.00
101	Juan Gonzalez G/Z	75.00
102	Jay Buhner S/Z	8.00
103	Paul Wilson S/Y	4.00
104	Alan Benes B/Y	4.00
105	Manny Ramirez G/Z	30.00
106	Kevin Elster B/X	2.00
107	Frank Thomas G/Z	140.00
108	Orlando Miller B/X	2.00
109	Ramon Martinez B/X	4.00
110	Kenny Lofton G/Z	45.00
111	Bernie Williams G/Y	50.00
112	Robby Thompson B/X	2.00
113	Bernard Gilkey B/Z	2.00
114	Ray Durham B/X	2.00
115	Jeff Cirillo S/Z	4.00
116	Brian Jordan G/Z	10.00
117	Rich Becker S/Y	4.00
118	Al Leiter B/X	2.00
119	Mark Johnson B/X	2.00
120	Ellis Burks B/Y	4.00
121	Sammy Sosa G/Z	80.00
122	Willie Greene B/X	2.00
123	Michael Tucker B/X	2.00
124	Eddie Murray G/X	40.00
125	Joey Hamilton S/Y	4.00
126	Antonio Osuna B/X	2.00
127	Bobby Higginson S/Y	6.00
128	Tomas Perez B/X	2.00
129	Tim Salmon G/Z	20.00
130	Mark Wohlers B/X	2.00
131	Charles Johnson S/X	4.00
132	Randy Johnson S/Y	20.00
133	Brooks Kieschnick S/X	6.00
134	Al Martin S/Y	4.00
135	Dante Bichette B/X	4.00
136	Andy Pettitte G/Z	45.00
137	Jason Giambi G/Y	20.00
138	James Baldwin S/X	4.00
139	Ben McDonald B/X	2.00
140	Shawn Green S/X	4.00
141	Geronimo Berroa B/Y	2.00
142	Jose Offerman B/X	2.00
143	Curtis Pride B/X	2.00
144	Terrell Wade B/X	2.00
145	Ismael Valdes B/X	4.00
146	Mike Mussina S/Y	25.00
147	Mariano Rivera S/X	10.00
148	Ken Hill B/Y	2.00
149	Darin Erstad G/Z	75.00
150	Jay Bell B/X	2.00
151	Mo Vaughn G/Z	40.00
152	Ozzie Smith G/Z	60.00
153	Jose Mesa B/X	2.00
154	Osvaldo Fernandez B/X	2.00

#	Player	Value
155	Vinny Castilla B/Y	2.00
156	Jason Isringhausen S/Y	4.00
157	B.J. Surhoff B/X	2.00
158	Robert Perez B/X	2.00
159	Ron Coomer B/X	2.00
160	Darren Oliver B/X	2.00
161	Mike Mohler B/X	2.00
162	Russ Davis B/X	2.00
163	Bret Boone B/X	2.00
164	Ricky Bottalico B/X	2.00
165	Derek Jeter G/Z	100.00
166	Orlando Merced B/X	2.00
167	John Valentin B/X	2.00
168	Andruw Jones G/Z	80.00
169	Angel Echevarria B/X	2.00
170	Todd Walker G/Z	30.00
171	Desi Relaford B/Y	2.00
172	Trey Beamon S/X	4.00
173	Brian Giles S/Y	4.00
174	Scott Rolen G/Z	75.00
175	Shannon Stewart S/Z	4.00
176	Dmitri Young G/Z	10.00
177	Justin Thompson B/X	2.00
178	Trot Nixon S/Y	4.00
179	Josh Booty S/Y	4.00
180	Robin Jennings B/X	2.00
181	Marvin Benard B/X	2.00
182	Luis Castillo B/Y	2.00
183	Wendell Magee B/X	2.00
184	Vladimir Guerrero G/X	100.00
185	Nomar Garciaparra G/X	120.00
186	Ryan Hancock B/X	2.00
187	Mike Cameron S/X	12.00
188	Cal Ripken Jr. B/Z (Legacy)	30.00
189	Chipper Jones S/Z (Legacy)	50.00
190	Albert Belle S/X (Legacy)	20.00
191	Mike Piazza B/Z (Legacy)	25.00
192	Chuck Knoblauch S/Y (Legacy)	12.00
193	Ken Griffey Jr. B/Z (Legacy)	40.00
194	Ivan Rodriguez G/Z (Legacy)	30.00
195	Jose Canseco S/X (Legacy)	20.00
196	Ryne Sandberg S/X (Legacy)	40.00
197	Jim Thome G/Y (Legacy)	40.00
198	Checklist(Andy Pettitte B/Y)	12.00
199	Checklist(Andruw Jones B/Y)	20.00
200	Checklist(Derek Jeter S/Y)	60.00
201	Chipper Jones G/X	120.00
202	Albert Belle G/X	50.00
203	Mike Piazza G/Y	100.00
204	Ken Griffey Jr. G/X	350.00
205	Ryne Sandberg G/Z	25.00
206	Jose Canseco S/Y	8.00
207	Chili Davis B/X	2.00
208	Roger Clemens G/Z	30.00
209	Deion Sanders G/Z	15.00
210	Darryl Hamilton B/X	2.00
211	Jermaine Dye S/X	4.00
212	Matt Williams G/Y	25.00
213	Kevin Elster B/X	2.00
214	John Wetteland B/X	4.00
215	Garret Anderson G/Z	10.00
216	Kevin Brown B/X	20.00
217	Matt Lawton S/Y	4.00
218	Cal Ripken Jr. G/X	250.00
219	Moises Alou G/X	20.00
220	Chuck Knoblauch G/Z	15.00
221	Ivan Rodriguez G/Y	40.00
222	Travis Fryman B/Y	2.00
223	Jim Thome G/Z	20.00
224	Eddie Murray S/Z	15.00
225	Eric Young G/Z	10.00
226	Ron Gant S/Y	4.00
227	Tony Phillips B/X	2.00
228	Reggie Sanders B/Y	2.00
229	Johnny Damon S/Z	4.00
230	Bill Pulsipher B/X	2.00
231	Jim Edmonds G/Z	10.00
232	Melvin Nieves B/X	2.00
233	Ryan Klesko G/Z	15.00
234	David Cone S/X	4.00
235	Derek Bell B/Y	2.00
236	Julio Franco S/X	4.00
237	Juan Gonzalez B/X	2.00
238	Larry Walker G/Z	15.00
239	Delino DeShields B/X	2.00
240	Troy Percival B/Y	2.00
241	Andres Galarraga G/Z	12.00
242	Rondell White G/Z	10.00
243	John Burkett B/X	2.00
244	J.T. Snow B/Y	2.00
245	Alex Fernandez S/Y	4.00
246	Edgar Martinez G/Z	10.00
247	Craig Biggio G/Z	10.00
248	Todd Hundley G/Y	20.00
249	Jimmy Key S/X	4.00
250	Cliff Floyd B/Y	2.00
251	Jeff Conine B/X	2.00
252	Curt Schilling B/X	2.00
253	Jeff King B/X	2.00
254	Tino Martinez G/Z	15.00
255	Carlos Baerga S/Y	4.00
256	Jeff Fassero B/X	2.00
257	Dean Palmer S/Y	4.00
258	Robb Nen B/X	2.00
259	Sandy Alomar Jr. S/Y	4.00
260	Carlos Perez B/X	2.00
261	Rickey Henderson S/Y	4.00
262	Bobby Bonilla S/Y	4.00
263	Darren Daulton B/X	2.00
264	Jim Leyritz B/X	2.00
265	Dennis Martinez B/X	2.00
266	Butch Huskey B/X	2.00
267	Joe Vitiello S/Y	4.00
268	Steve Trachsel B/X	2.00
269	Glenallen Hill B/X	2.00
270	Terry Steinbach B/X	2.00
271	Mark McLemore B/X	2.00
272	Devon White B/X	2.00
273	Jeff Kent B/X	2.00
274	Tim Raines B/X	2.00
275	Carlos Garcia B/X	2.00
276	Hal Morris B/X	2.00
277	Gary Gaetti B/X	2.00
278	John Olerud S/Y	4.00
279	Wally Joyner B/X	2.00
280	Brian Hunter S/X	4.00
281	Steve Karsay B/X	2.00
282	Denny Neagle S/X	4.00
283	Jose Herrera B/X	2.00
284	Todd Stottlemyre B/X	2.00
285	Bip Roberts S/X	4.00
286	Kevin Seitzer B/X	2.00
287	Benji Gil B/X	2.00
288	Dennis Eckersley S/X	4.00
289	Brad Ausmus B/X	2.00
290	Otis Nixon B/X	2.00
291	Darryl Strawberry B/X	2.00
292	Marquis Grissom S/Y	4.00
293	Darryl Kile B/X	2.00
294	Quilvio Veras B/X	2.00
295	Tom Goodwin B/X	2.00
296	Benito Santiago B/X	2.00
297	Mike Bordick B/X	2.00
298	Roberto Kelly B/X	2.00
299	David Justice G/Z	15.00
300	Carl Everett B/X	2.00
301	Mark Whiten B/X	2.00
302	Aaron Sele B/X	2.00
303	Darren Dreifort B/X	2.00
304	Bobby Jones B/X	2.00
305	Fernando Vina B/X	2.00
306	Ed Sprague B/X	2.00
307	Andy Ashby S/X	4.00
308	Tony Fernandez B/X	2.00
309	Roger Pavlik B/X	2.00
310	Mark Clark B/X	2.00
311	Mariano Duncan B/X	2.00
312	Tyler Houston B/X	2.00
313	Eric Davis S/Y	4.00
314	Greg Vaughn B/Y	2.00
315	David Segui S/Y	4.00
316	Dave Nilsson S/Y	4.00
317	F.P. Santangelo S/X	4.00
318	Wilton Guerrero G/Z	10.00
319	Jose Guillen G/Z	25.00
320	Kevin Orie S/Y	4.00
321	Derrek Lee G/Z	10.00
322	Bubba Trammell S/Y	15.00
323	Pokey Reese G/Z	10.00
324	Hideki Irabu G/X	100.00
325	Scott Spiezio S/Z	4.00
326	Bartolo Colon G/Z	10.00
327	Damon Mashore S/Y	4.00
328	Ryan McGuire S/Y	4.00
329	Chris Carpenter B/X	2.00
330	Jose Cruz, Jr. G/X	150.00
331	Todd Greene S/Z	6.00
332	Brian Moehler B/X	2.00
333	Mike Sweeney B/Y	2.00
334	Neifi Perez G/Z	10.00
335	Matt Morris S/Y	4.00
336	Marvin Benard B/Y	2.00
337	Karim Garcia S/Z	4.00
338	Jason Dickson S/Y	4.00
339	Brant Brown S/Y	4.00
340	Jeff Suppan S/Z	4.00
341	Deivi Cruz B/X	4.00
342	Antone Williamson G/Z	10.00
343	Curtis Goodwin B/X	2.00
344	Brooks Kieschnick S/Y	4.00
345	Tony Womack B/X	2.00
346	Rudy Pemberton B/X	2.00
347	Todd Dunwoody B/X	2.00
348	Frank Thomas S/Y (Legacy)	50.00
349	Andruw Jones S/X (Legacy)	25.00
350	Alex Rodriguez B/Y (Legacy)	30.00
351	Greg Maddux S/Y (Legacy)	40.00
352	Jeff Bagwell B/Y (Legacy)	20.00
353	Juan Gonzalez S/Z (Legacy)	30.00
354	Barry Bonds B/Y (Legacy)	10.00
355	Mark McGwire B/Y (Legacy)	30.00
356	Tony Gwynn B/Y (Legacy)	20.00
357	Gary Sheffield B/X (Legacy)	4.00
358	Derek Jeter S/X (Legacy)	30.00
359	Manny Ramirez S/Y (Legacy)	15.00
360	Hideo Nomo G/Z (Legacy)	20.00
361	Sammy Sosa B/X (Legacy)	20.00
362	Paul Molitor S/Z (Legacy)	8.00
363	Kenny Lofton B/Y (Legacy)	10.00
364	Eddie Murray B/X (Legacy)	6.00
365	Barry Larkin S/Z (Legacy)	6.00
366	Roger Clemens S/Y (Legacy)	20.00
367	John Smoltz B/Z (Legacy)	2.00
368	Alex Rodriguez S/X (Gamers)	40.00
369	Frank Thomas B/X (Gamers)	30.00
370	Cal Ripken Jr. S/Y (Gamers)	50.00
371	Ken Griffey Jr. S/Y (Gamers)	70.00
372	Greg Maddux B/Y (Gamers)	20.00
373	Mike Piazza S/X (Gamers)	30.00
374	Chipper Jones B/Y (Gamers)	20.00
375	Albert Belle B/X (Gamers)	10.00
376	Chuck Knoblauch B/X (Gamers)	4.00
377	Brady Anderson B/Z (Gamers)	2.00
378	David Justice S/X (Gamers)	8.00
379	Randy Johnson B/Z (Gamers)	8.00
380	Wade Boggs B/X (Gamers)	4.00
381	Kevin Brown B/X (Gamers)	2.00
382	Tom Glavine S/X (Gamers)	20.00
383	Raul Mondesi S/X (Gamers)	6.00
384	Ivan Rodriguez S/X (Gamers)	10.00
385	Larry Walker B/Y (Gamers)	4.00
386	Bernie Williams B/Z (Gamers)	6.00
387	Rusty Greer G/Y (Gamers)	20.00
388	Rafael Palmeiro G/Y (Gamers)	20.00
389	Matt Williams B/X (Gamers)	4.00
390	Eric Young B/X (Gamers)	2.00
391	Fred McGriff B/X (Gamers)	4.00
392	Ken Caminiti B/X (Gamers)	3.00
393	Roberto Alomar B/Z (Gamers)	8.00
394	Brian Jordan B/X (Gamers)	2.00
395	Mark Grace G/Z (Gamers)	15.00
396	Jim Edmonds B/Y (Gamers)	2.00
397	Deion Sanders S/Y (Gamers)	6.00
398	Checklist(Vladimir Guerrero S/Z)	15.00
399	Checklist(Darin Erstad S/Y)	20.00
400	Checklist(Nomar Garciaparra S/Z)	25.00

Modern cards have little collector value in conditions lower than Mint. Figure NM cards at 75% of values shown; EX cards at 40%.

Values shown reflect the market as of January, 1999. On-field performances of current players in the 1999 baseball season are not factored in.

1997 Leaf Fractal Matrix Die-Cut

A second parallel set to the Leaf product, the Fractal Matrix Die-Cuts offer three different die-cut designs with three different styles for each. The Axis-X die-cuts consist of 100 cards (75 bronze, 20 silver and 5 gold), the Axis-Y die-cuts consist of 60 cards (30 silver, 20 bronze, 10 gold), and the Axis-Z die-cuts consist of 40 cards (25 gold, 10 silver, 5 bronze). Odds of finding any of these inserts are 1:6 packs.

		MT
Complete Set (400):		
Common X-Axis:		8.00
Common Y-Axis:		12.00
Y-Axis Unlisted Stars:		20.00
Common Z-Axis:		20.00
Z-Axis Unlisted Stars:		30.00
1	Wade Boggs G/Y	35.00
2	Brian McRae B/Y	12.00
3	Jeff D'Amico B/Y	12.00
4	George Arias S/Y	12.00
5	Billy Wagner S/Y	12.00
6	Ray Lankford B/Z	20.00
7	Will Clark S/Y	20.00
8	Edgar Renteria S/Y	12.00
9	Alex Ochoa S/Y	12.00
11	Joe Carter S/Y	12.00
12	Gregg Jefferies B/Y	12.00
13	Mark Grace S/Y	18.00
14	Roberto Alomar G/Y	50.00
15	Joe Randa B/X	8.00
16	Alex Rodriguez G/Z	250.00
17	Tony Gwynn G/Z	150.00
18	Steve Gibralter B/Y	12.00
19	Scott Stahoviak B/X	8.00
20	Matt Williams S/Z	50.00
21	Quinton McCracken B/Y	12.00
22	Ugueth Urbina B/X	8.00
23	Jermaine Allensworth S/X	8.00
24	Paul Molitor G/X	25.00
25	Carlos Delgado S/Y	12.00
26	Bob Abreu S/Y	12.00
27	John Jaha S/Y	12.00
28	Rusty Greer S/Z	20.00
29	Kimera Bartee B/X	8.00
30	Ruben Rivera S/Y	12.00
31	Jason Kendall S/Y	12.00
32	Lance Johnson B/X	8.00
33	Robin Ventura B/Y	12.00
34	Kevin Appier S/X	8.00
35	John Mabry S/Y	12.00
36	Ricky Otero B/X	8.00
37	Mike Lansing B/X	8.00
38	Mark McGwire G/Z	300.00
39	Tim Naehring B/X	8.00
40	Tom Glavine S/Z	25.00
41	Rey Ordonez S/Y	12.00
42	Tony Clark S/Y	40.00
43	Rafael Palmeiro S/Z	25.00
44	Pedro Martinez B/X	10.00
45	Keith Lockhart B/X	8.00
46	Dan Wilson B/Y	12.00
47	John Wetteland B/Y	12.00
48	Chan Ho Park B/X	8.00
49	Gary Sheffield G/Z	60.00
50	Shawn Estes B/X	8.00
51	Royce Clayton B/X	8.00
52	Jaime Navarro B/X	8.00
53	Raul Casanova B/X	8.00
54	Jeff Bagwell G/Z	150.00
55	Barry Larkin G/Z	12.00
56	Charles Nagy B/Y	12.00
57	Ken Caminiti G/Y	40.00
58	Todd Hullandsworth S/Z	20.00
59	Pat Hentgen S/X	8.00
60	Jose Valentin B/X	8.00
61	Frank Rodriguez B/X	8.00
62	Mickey Tettleton B/X	8.00
63	Marty Cordova G/X	10.00
64	Cecil Fielder S/X	12.00
65	Barry Bonds G/Z	80.00
66	Scott Servais B/X	8.00
67	Ernie Young B/X	8.00
68	Wilson Alvarez B/X	8.00
69	Mike Grace B/X	12.00
70	Shane Reynolds S/X	8.00
71	Henry Rodriguez S/Y	12.00
72	Eric Karros B/X	8.00
73	Mark Langston B/X	8.00
74	Scott Karl B/X	8.00
75	Trevor Hoffman B/X	8.00
76	Orel Hershiser S/X	8.00
77	John Smoltz G/Y	40.00
78	Raul Mondesi G/Z	30.00
79	Jeff Brantley B/X	8.00
80	Donne Wall B/X	8.00
81	Joey Cora B/X	8.00
82	Mel Rojas B/X	8.00
83	Chad Mottola B/X	8.00
84	Omar Vizquel B/X	8.00
85	Greg Maddux G/Z	200.00
86	Jamey Wright S/Y	12.00
87	Chuck Finley B/X	8.00
88	Brady Anderson G/Y	15.00
89	Alex Gonzalez S/X	8.00
90	Andy Benes B/X	8.00
91	Reggie Jefferson B/X	8.00
92	Paul O'Neill B/Y	15.00
93	Javier Lopez S/X	12.00
94	Mark Grudzielanek S/X	8.00
95	Marc Newfield B/X	8.00
96	Kevin Ritz B/X	8.00
97	Fred McGriff G/Y	20.00
98	Dwight Gooden S/X	10.00
99	Hideo Nomo S/Y	60.00
100	Steve Finley B/X	8.00
101	Juan Gonzalez G/Z	150.00
102	Jay Buhner S/Z	25.00
103	Paul Wilson S/Y	12.00
104	Alan Benes B/X	12.00
105	Manny Ramirez G/Z	60.00
106	Kevin Elster B/X	8.00
107	Frank Thomas G/Z	250.00
108	Orlando Miller B/X	8.00
109	Ramon Martinez B/X	8.00
110	Kenny Lofton S/Z	80.00
111	Bernie Williams G/Y	50.00
112	Robby Thompson B/X	8.00
113	Bernard Gilkey B/Z	20.00
114	Ray Durham B/X	8.00
115	Jeff Cirillo S/Z	20.00
116	Brian Jordan G/Z	20.00
117	Rich Becker S/Y	12.00
118	Al Leiter B/X	8.00
119	Mark Johnson B/X	8.00
120	Ellis Burks B/Y	12.00
121	Sammy Sosa G/Z	125.00
122	Willie Greene B/X	8.00
123	Michael Tucker B/X	8.00
124	Eddie Murray G/Y	40.00
125	Joey Hamilton S/Y	12.00
126	Antonio Osuna B/X	8.00
127	Bobby Higginson S/Y	15.00
128	Tomas Perez B/X	8.00
129	Tim Salmon G/Z	30.00
130	Mark Wohlers B/X	8.00
131	Charles Johnson S/X	8.00
132	Randy Johnson G/Y	40.00
133	Brooks Kieschnick S/X	8.00
134	Al Martin S/Y	8.00
135	Dante Bichette B/X	12.00
136	Andy Pettitte G/Z	60.00
137	Jason Giambi G/Y	20.00
138	James Baldwin S/X	8.00
139	Ben McDonald B/X	8.00
140	Shawn Green B/X	8.00
141	Geronimo Berroa B/Y	12.00
142	Jose Offerman B/X	8.00
143	Curtis Pride B/X	8.00
144	Terrell Wade B/X	8.00
145	Ismael Valdes S/X	8.00
146	Mike Mussina S/Y	40.00
147	Mariano Rivera S/X	15.00
148	Ken Hill B/Y	12.00
149	Darin Erstad G/Z	100.00
150	Jay Bell B/X	8.00
151	Mo Vaughn G/Z	80.00
152	Ozzie Smith G/Y	60.00
153	Jose Mesa B/X	8.00
154	Osvaldo Fernandez B/X	8.00
155	Vinny Castilla B/Y	12.00
156	Jason Isringhausen S/Y	12.00
157	B.J. Surhoff B/X	8.00
158	Robert Perez B/X	8.00
159	Ron Coomer B/X	8.00
160	Darren Oliver B/X	8.00
161	Mike Mohler B/X	8.00
162	Russ Davis B/X	8.00
163	Bret Boone B/X	8.00
164	Ricky Bottalico B/X	8.00
165	Derek Jeter G/Z	200.00
166	Orlando Merced B/X	8.00
167	John Valentin B/X	8.00
168	Andruw Jones G/Z	160.00
169	Angel Echevarria B/X	8.00
170	Todd Walker G/Z	50.00
171	Desi Relaford B/Y	12.00
172	Trey Beamon S/X	8.00
173	Brian Giles S/Y	12.00
174	Scott Rolen G/Z	100.00
175	Shannon Stewart S/Z	20.00
176	Dmitri Young S/Z	20.00
177	Justin Thompson B/X	8.00
178	Trot Nixon S/Y	12.00
179	Josh Booty S/Y	12.00
180	Robin Jennings B/X	8.00
181	Marvin Benard B/X	8.00
182	Luis Castillo B/Y	12.00
183	Wendell Magee B/X	8.00
184	Vladimir Guerrero G/X	50.00
185	Nomar Garciaparra G/X	60.00
186	Ryan Hancock B/X	8.00
187	Mike Cameron S/X	15.00
188	Cal Ripken Jr. B/Z (Legacy)	250.00
189	Chipper Jones S/Z (Legacy)	200.00
190	Albert Belle S/Z (Legacy)	80.00
191	Mike Piazza B/Z (Legacy)	200.00
192	Chuck Knoblauch S/Y (Legacy)	20.00
193	Ken Griffey Jr. B/Z (Legacy)	300.00
194	Ivan Rodriguez G/Z (Legacy)	60.00
195	Jose Canseco S/X (Legacy)	20.00
196	Ryne Sandberg S/X (Legacy)	40.00
197	Jim Thome G/Y (Legacy)	50.00
198	Checklist(Andruw Jones B/Y)	40.00
199	Checklist(Andruw Jones B/Y)	100.00
200	Checklist(Derek Jeter S/Y)	120.00
201	Chipper Jones G/X	60.00
202	Albert Belle G/Y	70.00
203	Mike Piazza G/Y	120.00
204	Ken Griffey Jr. G/X	100.00
205	Ryne Sandberg G/Z	75.00
206	Jose Canseco S/X	20.00
207	Chili Davis B/X	8.00
208	Roger Clemens G/X	100.00
209	Deion Sanders G/Z	30.00
210	Darryl Hamilton B/X	8.00
211	Jermaine Dye S/X	8.00
212	Matt Williams G/Y	35.00
213	Kevin Elster B/X	8.00
214	John Wetteland S/X	8.00
215	Garret Anderson G/Z	20.00
216	Kevin Brown G/Z	12.00
217	Matt Lawton B/X	8.00
218	Cal Ripken Jr. G/X	75.00
219	Moises Alou G/Y	15.00
220	Chuck Knoblauch G/Z	40.00
221	Ivan Rodriguez G/Y	50.00
222	Travis Fryman B/Y	12.00
223	Jim Thome G/Z	50.00
224	Eddie Murray S/Z	50.00
225	Eric Young G/Z	20.00
226	Ron Gant S/X	8.00
227	Tony Phillips B/X	8.00
228	Reggie Sanders B/Y	12.00
229	Johnny Damon S/Z	20.00

230	Bill Pulsipher B/X	8.00
231	Jim Edmonds G/Z	25.00
232	Melvin Nieves B/X	8.00
233	Ryan Klesko G/Z	50.00
234	David Cone S/X	8.00
235	Derek Bell B/Y	12.00
236	Julio Franco S/X	8.00
237	Juan Guzman B/X	8.00
238	Larry Walker G/Z	40.00
239	Delino DeShields B/X	8.00
240	Troy Percival B/Y	12.00
241	Andres Galarraga G/Z	30.00
242	Rondell White G/Z	20.00
243	John Burkett B/X	8.00
244	J.T. Snow B/Y	12.00
245	Alex Fernandez S/Y	12.00
246	Edgar Martinez G/Z	20.00
247	Craig Biggio G/Z	20.00
248	Todd Hundley G/Y	15.00
249	Jimmy Key S/X	8.00
250	Cliff Floyd B/Y	12.00
251	Jeff Conine B/Y	12.00
252	Curt Schilling B/X	8.00
253	Jeff King B/X	8.00
254	Tino Martinez G/Z	35.00
255	Carlos Baerga S/Y	12.00
256	Jeff Fassero B/Y	12.00
257	Dean Palmer S/Y	12.00
258	Robb Nen B/X	8.00
259	Sandy Alomar Jr. S/Y	12.00
260	Carlos Perez B/X	8.00
261	Rickey Henderson S/Y	12.00
262	Bobby Bonilla S/Y	12.00
263	Darren Daulton B/X	8.00
264	Jim Leyritz B/X	8.00
265	Dennis Martinez B/X	8.00
266	Butch Huskey B/X	8.00
267	Joe Vitiello B/X	12.00
268	Steve Trachsel B/X	8.00
269	Glenallen Hill B/X	8.00
270	Terry Steinbach B/X	8.00
271	Mark McLemore B/X	8.00
272	Devon White B/X	8.00
273	Jeff Kent B/X	8.00
274	Tim Raines B/X	8.00
275	Carlos Garcia B/X	8.00
276	Hal Morris B/X	8.00
277	Gary Gaetti B/X	8.00
278	John Olerud S/Y	12.00
279	Wally Joyner B/X	8.00
280	Brian Hunter S/X	8.00
281	Steve Karsay B/X	8.00
282	Denny Neagle S/X	8.00
283	Jose Herrera B/X	8.00
284	Todd Stottlemyre B/X	8.00
285	Bip Roberts S/X	8.00
286	Kevin Seitzer B/X	8.00
287	Benji Gil B/X	8.00
288	Dennis Eckersley S/X	8.00
289	Brad Ausmus B/X	8.00
290	Otis Nixon B/X	8.00
291	Darryl Strawberry B/X	8.00
292	Marquis Grissom S/Y	12.00
293	Darryl Kile B/X	8.00
294	Quilvio Veras B/X	8.00
295	Tom Goodwin B/X	8.00
296	Benito Santiago B/X	8.00
297	Mike Bordick B/X	8.00
298	Roberto Kelly B/X	8.00
299	David Justice G/Z	30.00
300	Carl Everett B/X	8.00
301	Mark Whiten B/X	8.00
302	Aaron Sele B/X	8.00
303	Darren Dreifort B/X	8.00
304	Bobby Jones B/X	8.00
305	Fernando Vina B/X	8.00
306	Ed Sprague B/X	8.00
307	Andy Ashby S/X	8.00
308	Tony Fernandez B/X	8.00
309	Roger Pavlik B/X	8.00
310	Mark Clark B/X	8.00
311	Mariano Duncan B/X	8.00
312	Tyler Houston B/X	8.00
313	Eric Davis S/Y	12.00
314	Greg Vaughn B/Y	12.00
315	David Segui S/Y	12.00
316	Dave Nilsson B/X	8.00
317	F.P. Santangelo S/X	8.00
318	Wilton Guerrero G/Z	20.00
319	Jose Guillen G/Z	70.00
320	Kevin Orie S/Y	12.00
321	Derrek Lee G/Z	20.00
322	Bubba Trammell S/Y	50.00
323	Pokey Reese G/Z	20.00
324	Hideki Irabu G/X	50.00
325	Scott Spiezio S/Z	20.00

326	Bartolo Colon G/Z	20.00
327	Damon Mashore S/Y	12.00
328	Ryan McGuire S/Y	12.00
329	Chris Carpenter B/X	8.00
330	Jose Cruz, Jr. G/X	50.00
331	Todd Greene S/Z	30.00
332	Brian Moehler B/X	8.00
333	Mike Sweeney B/Y	12.00
334	Neifi Perez G/Z	20.00
335	Matt Morris S/Y	12.00
336	Marvin Benard B/Y	12.00
337	Karim Garcia S/Z	25.00
338	Jason Dickson S/Y	12.00
339	Brant Brown S/Y	12.00
340	Jeff Suppan S/Z	20.00
341	Deivi Cruz B/X	10.00
342	Antone Williamson G/Z	20.00
343	Curtis Goodwin B/X	8.00
344	Brooks Kieschnick S/Y	12.00
345	Tony Womack B/X	8.00
346	Rudy Pemberton B/X	8.00
347	Todd Dunwoody B/X	8.00
348	Frank Thomas S/Y (Legacy)	125.00
349	Andruw Jones S/X (Legacy)	40.00
350	Alex Rodriguez B/Y (Legacy)	125.00
351	Greg Maddux S/Y (Legacy)	100.00
352	Jeff Bagwell B/Y (Legacy)	75.00
353	Juan Gonzalez S/Y (Legacy)	75.00
354	Barry Bonds B/Y (Legacy)	50.00
355	Mark McGwire B/Y (Legacy)	150.00
356	Tony Gwynn B/Y (Legacy)	75.00
357	Gary Sheffield B/X (Legacy)	12.00
358	Derek Jeter S/X (Legacy)	40.00
359	Manny Ramirez S/Y (Legacy)	35.00
360	Hideo Nomo G/Z (Legacy)	40.00
361	Sammy Sosa B/X (Legacy)	30.00
362	Paul Molitor S/Z (Legacy)	30.00
363	Kenny Lofton B/Y (Legacy)	50.00
364	Eddie Murray B/Y (Legacy)	15.00
365	Barry Larkin S/Z (Legacy)	25.00
366	Roger Clemens S/Y (Legacy)	50.00
367	John Smoltz B/Z (Legacy)	20.00
368	Alex Rodriguez S/X (Gamers)	65.00
369	Frank Thomas B/X (Gamers)	75.00
370	Cal Ripken Jr. S/Y (Gamers)	125.00
371	Ken Griffey Jr. S/Y (Gamers)	175.00
372	Greg Maddux B/X (Gamers)	40.00
373	Mike Piazza S/X (Gamers)	40.00
374	Chipper Jones B/Y (Gamers)	90.00
375	Albert Belle B/X (Gamers)	15.00
376	Chuck Knoblauch B/X (Gamers)	15.00
377	Brady Anderson B/Z (Gamers)	20.00
378	David Justice S/X (Gamers)	12.00
379	Randy Johnson B/Z (Gamers)	40.00
380	Wade Boggs B/X (Gamers)	12.00
381	Kevin Brown B/X (Gamers)	8.00
382	Tom Glavine S/X (Gamers)	12.00
383	Raul Mondesi S/X (Gamers)	12.00
384	Ivan Rodriguez S/X (Gamers)	15.00
385	Larry Walker B/Y (Gamers)	20.00
386	Bernie Williams B/Z (Gamers)	40.00
387	Rusty Greer G/Y (Gamers)	12.00
388	Rafael Palmeiro G/Y (Gamers)	15.00
389	Matt Williams B/X (Gamers)	12.00
390	Eric Young B/X (Gamers)	8.00
391	Fred McGriff B/X (Gamers)	12.00
392	Ken Caminiti B/X (Gamers)	10.00
393	Roberto Alomar B/Z (Gamers)	40.00
394	Brian Jordan B/X (Gamers)	8.00
395	Mark Grace B/X (Gamers)	30.00
396	Jim Edmonds B/Y (Gamers)	12.00
397	Deion Sanders S/Y (Gamers)	18.00
398	Checklist (Vladimir Guerrero S/Z)	50.00
399	Checklist (Darin Erstad S/Y)	50.00
400	Checklist (Nomar Garciaparra S/Z)	75.00

1997 Leaf Get-A-Grip

Get a Grip included 16 double-sided cards, with a star hitter on one side and a star pitcher on the other. The card slated the two stars against each other and explained how the hitter would hit against the pitcher, while featuring the pitcher's top pitch. This insert was printed on silver foilboard with the right side die-cut, and limited to 3,500 numbered sets found only in hobby packs.

		MT
Complete Set (16):		250.00
Common Player:		6.00
1	Ken Griffey Jr., Greg Maddux	40.00
2	John Smoltz, Frank Thomas	30.00
3	Mike Piazza, Andy Pettitte	25.00
4	Randy Johnson, Chipper Jones	25.00
5	Tom Glavine, Alex Rodriguez	35.00
6	Pat Hentgen, Jeff Bagwell	15.00
7	Kevin Brown, Juan Gonzalez	15.00
8	Barry Bonds, Mike Mussina	12.00
9	Hideo Nomo, Albert Belle	12.00
10	Troy Percival, Andruw Jones	15.00
11	Roger Clemens, Brian Jordan	15.00
12	Paul Wilson, Ivan Rodriguez	10.00
13	Andy Benes, Mo Vaughn	12.00
14	Al Leiter, Derek Jeter	25.00
15	Bill Pulsipher, Cal Ripken Jr.	30.00
16	Mariano Rivera, Ken Caminiti	6.00

1997 Leaf Knot-Hole Gang

Knot-Hole Gang pictured 12 hitters against a wood picket fence in the background. Cards were die-cut along the top of the fence and printed on a wood card stock. Set production was limited to 5,000 and these inserts were found in all types of packs.

A player's name in *italic* type indicates a rookie card.

		MT
Complete Set (12):		140.00
Common Player:		4.00
1	Chuck Knoblauch	5.00
2	Ken Griffey Jr.	30.00
3	Frank Thomas	20.00
4	Tony Gwynn	15.00
5	Mike Piazza	20.00
6	Jeff Bagwell	15.00
7	Rusty Greer	4.00
8	Cal Ripken Jr.	25.00
9	Chipper Jones	20.00
10	Ryan Klesko	6.00
11	Barry Larkin	5.00
12	Paul Molitor	6.00

1997 Leaf Leagues of the Nation

A 15-card insert set featuring a double-sided die-cut design. The players on each card represent matchups from the initial rounds of interleague play. Cards were numbered to 2,500 and feature a flocked texture.

		MT
Complete Set (15):		400.00
Common Player:		10.00
1	Juan Gonzalez, Barry Bonds	25.00
2	Cal Ripken Jr., Chipper Jones	40.00
3	Mark McGwire, Ken Caminiti	40.00
4	Derek Jeter, Kenny Lofton	30.00
5	Ivan Rodriguez, Mike Piazza	30.00
6	Ken Griffey Jr., Larry Walker	60.00
7	Frank Thomas, Sammy Sosa	50.00
8	Paul Molitor, Barry Larkin	10.00
9	Albert Belle, Deion Sanders	15.00
10	Matt Williams, Jeff Bagwell	20.00
11	Mo Vaughn, Gary Sheffield	15.00
12	Alex Rodriguez, Tony Gwynn	50.00
13	Tino Martinez, Scott Rolen	30.00

14	Darin Erstad, Wilton Guerrero	25.00
15	Tony Clark, Vladimir Guerrero	20.00

1997 Leaf Statistical Standouts

Statistical Standouts were limited to only 1,000 individually numbered sets. Inserts were printed on leather and die-cut. The set included 15 top stars who excelled beyond their competition in many statistical categories.

		MT
Complete Set (15):		900.00
Common Player:		20.00
1	Albert Belle	30.00
2	Juan Gonzalez	60.00
3	Ken Griffey Jr.	125.00
4	Alex Rodriguez	100.00
5	Frank Thomas	75.00
6	Chipper Jones	75.00
7	Greg Maddux	75.00
8	Mike Piazza	75.00
9	Cal Ripken Jr.	100.00
10	Mark McGwire	150.00
11	Barry Bonds	30.00
12	Derek Jeter	75.00
13	Ken Caminiti	20.00
14	John Smoltz	20.00
15	Paul Molitor	25.00

1997 Leaf Thomas Collection

This six-card insert from Series II features pieces of various game-used Frank Thomas items built into the texture of each card. Jerseys, bats, hats, batting gloves and sweatbands are all featured on the various cards, which are numbered to 100 each.

		MT
Complete Set (6):		2000.
Common Thomas:		350.00
1	Frank Thomas Hat	350.00
2	Frank Thomas Home Jersey	500.00
3	Frank Thomas Batting Glove	350.00
4	Frank Thomas Bat	350.00
5	Frank Thomas Sweatband	350.00
6	Frank Thomas Away Jersey	500.00

1997 Leaf 22kt Gold Stars

A 36-card insert from Series II Leaf, each card features a special 22kt. gold foil embossed stamp on front which is printed on gold foil cardboard. Horizontal backs have a portrait photo on a dark background and are serially numbered to a limit of 2,500 each.

		MT
Complete Set (36):		600.00
Common Player:		5.00
1	Frank Thomas	40.00
2	Alex Rodriguez	40.00
3	Ken Griffey Jr.	60.00
4	Andruw Jones	20.00
5	Chipper Jones	35.00
6	Jeff Bagwell	20.00
7	Derek Jeter	30.00
8	Deion Sanders	5.00
9	Ivan Rodriguez	15.00
10	Juan Gonzalez	30.00
11	Greg Maddux	35.00
12	Andy Pettitte	12.00
13	Roger Clemens	25.00
14	Hideo Nomo	15.00
15	Tony Gwynn	30.00
16	Barry Bonds	15.00
17	Kenny Lofton	15.00
18	Paul Molitor	12.00
19	Jim Thome	7.00
20	Albert Belle	15.00
21	Cal Ripken Jr.	50.00
22	Mark McGwire	60.00
23	Barry Larkin	6.00
24	Mike Piazza	35.00
25	Darin Erstad	20.00
26	Chuck Knoblauch	6.00
27	Vladimir Guerrero	20.00
28	Tony Clark	10.00
29	Scott Rolen	30.00
30	Nomar Garciaparra	40.00
31	Eric Young	5.00
32	Ryne Sandberg	15.00
33	Roberto Alomar	12.00
34	Eddie Murray	6.00
35	Rafael Palmeiro	6.00
36	Jose Guillen	10.00

1997 Leaf Warning Track

A 12-card insert printed on embossed canvas depicting players who are known for making tough catches. Cards were numbered to 3,500.

		MT
Complete Set (18):		100.00
Common Player:		4.00
1	Ken Griffey Jr.	30.00
2	Albert Belle	8.00
3	Barry Bonds	8.00
4	Andruw Jones	8.00
5	Kenny Lofton	8.00
6	Tony Gwynn	15.00
7	Manny Ramirez	8.00
8	Rusty Greer	4.00
9	Bernie Williams	6.00
10	Gary Sheffield	5.00
11	Juan Gonzalez	15.00
12	Raul Mondesi	5.00
13	Brady Anderson	4.00
14	Rondell White	4.00
15	Sammy Sosa	30.00
16	Deion Sanders	4.00
17	David Justice	4.00
18	Jim Edmonds	4.00

1998 Leaf

The 50th Anniversary edition of Leaf Baseball consists of a 200-card base set with three subsets, three parallels and four inserts. The base set has 147 regular cards, a 10-card Curtain Calls subset, Gold Leaf Stars subset (20 cards), Gold Leaf Rookies subset (20 cards) and three checklists. Card #42 does not exist because Leaf retired the number in honor of Jackie Robinson. The base set was paralleled in Fractal Matrix, Fractal Matrix Die-Cuts and Fractal Diamond Axis. Inserts include Crusade, Heading for the Hall, State Representatives and Statistical Standouts.

		MT
Complete Set (200):		200.00
Common Player:		.10
Diamond Axis Stars: 60x-100x		
SP Diamond Axis (148-177): 15x to 25x		
Wax Box:		65.00
1	Rusty Greer	.10
2	Tino Martinez	.25
3	Bobby Bonilla	.15
4	Jason Giambi	.10
5	Matt Morris	.20
6	Craig Counsell	.10
7	Reggie Jefferson	.10
8	Brian Rose	.25
9	Ruben Rivera	.10
10	Shawn Estes	.10
11	Tony Gwynn	1.50
12	Jeff Abbott	.10
13	Jose Cruz Jr.	1.50
14	Francisco Cordova	.10
15	Ryan Klesko	.30
16	Tim Salmon	.30
17	Brett Tomko	.10
18	Matt Williams	.25
19	Joe Carter	.20
20	Harold Baines	.10
21	Gary Sheffield	.25
22	Charles Johnson	.20
23	Aaron Boone	.20
24	Eddie Murray	.20
25	Matt Stairs	.10
26	David Cone	.20
27	Jon Nunnally	.10
28	Chris Stynes	.10
29	Enrique Wilson	.10
30	Randy Johnson	.50
31	Garret Anderson	.10
32	Manny Ramirez	.60
33	Jeff Suppan	.10
34	Rickey Henderson	.10
35	Scott Spiezio	.10
36	Rondell White	.20
37	Todd Greene	.20
38	Delino DeShields	.10
39	Kevin Brown	.20
40	Chili Davis	.10
41	Jimmy Key	.10
42		
43	Mike Mussina	.60
44	Joe Randa	.10
45	Chan Ho Park	.20
46	Brad Radke	.10
47	Geronimo Berroa	.10
48	Wade Boggs	.25
49	Kevin Appier	.10
50	Moises Alou	.20
51	David Justice	.25
52	Ivan Rodriguez	.75
53	J.T. Snow	.20
54	Brian Giles	.10
55	Will Clark	.25
56	Justin Thompson	.10
57	Javier Lopez	.20
58	Hideki Irabu	.30
59	Mark Grudzielanek	.10
60	Abraham Nunez	.10
61	Todd Hollandsworth	.10
62	Jay Bell	.10
63	Nomar Garciaparra	2.00
64	Vinny Castilla	.10
65	Lou Collier	.10
66	Kevin Orie	.10
67	John Valentin	.10
68	Robin Ventura	.20
69	Denny Neagle	.20
70	Tony Womack	.10
71	Dennis Reyes	.10
72	Wally Joyner	.10
73	Kevin Brown	.20
74	Ray Durham	.10
75	Mike Cameron	.20
76	Dante Bichette	.25
77	Jose Guillen	.25
78	Carlos Delgado	.20
79	Paul Molitor	.40
80	Jason Kendall	.10
81	Mark Belhorn	.10
82	Damian Jackson	.10
83	Bill Mueller	.10
84	Kevin Young	.10
85	Curt Schilling	.20
86	Jeffrey Hammonds	.10
87	Sandy Alomar Jr.	.20
88	Bartolo Colon	.10
89	Wilton Guerrero	.10
90	Bernie Williams	.50
91	Deion Sanders	.25
92	Mike Piazza	2.00
93	Butch Huskey	.10
94	Edgardo Alfonzo	.10
95	Alan Benes	.20
96	Craig Biggio	.20
97	Mark Grace	.25
98	Shawn Green	.10
99	Derrek Lee	.25
100	Ken Griffey Jr.	3.00
101	Tim Raines	.10
102	Pokey Reese	.10
103	Lee Stevens	.10
104	Shannon Stewart	.10
105	John Smoltz	.20
106	Frank Thomas	2.50
107	Jeff Fassero	.10
108	Jay Buhner	.20
109	Jose Canseco	.25
110	Omar Vizquel	.10
111	Travis Fryman	.10
112	Dave Nilsson	.10
113	John Olerud	.10
114	Larry Walker	.25
115	Jim Edmonds	.20
116	Bobby Higginson	.20
117	Todd Hundley	.10
118	Paul O'Neill	.20
119	Bip Roberts	.10
120	Ismael Valdes	.10
121	Pedro Martinez	.25
122	Jeff Cirillo	.10
123	Andy Benes	.20
124	Bobby Jones	.10
125	Brian Hunter	.10
126	Darryl Kile	.10
127	Pat Hentgen	.10
128	Marquis Grissom	.10
129	Eric Davis	.10
130	Chipper Jones	2.00
131	Edgar Martinez	.10
132	Andy Pettitte	.50
133	Cal Ripken Jr.	2.50
134	Scott Rolen	1.50
135	Ron Coomer	.10
136	Luis Castillo	.10
137	Fred McGriff	.20
138	Neifi Perez	.10
139	Eric Karros	.20
140	Alex Fernandez	.10
141	Jason Dickson	.10
142	Lance Johnson	.10
143	Ray Lankford	.10
144	Sammy Sosa	2.00
145	Eric Young	.10
146	Bubba Trammell	.20
147	Todd Walker	.20
148	Mo Vaughn (Curtain Calls)	3.00
149	Jeff Bagwell (Curtain Calls)	5.00
150	Kenny Lofton (Curtain Calls)	3.00
151	Raul Mondesi (Curtain Calls)	1.50
152	Mike Piazza (Curtain Calls)	10.00
153	Chipper Jones (Curtain Calls)	8.00
154	Larry Walker (Curtain Calls)	1.50
155	Greg Maddux (Curtain Calls)	10.00
156	Ken Griffey Jr. (Curtain Calls)	15.00
157	Frank Thomas (Curtain Calls)	12.00
158	Darin Erstad (Gold Leaf Stars)	3.00
159	Roberto Alomar (Gold Leaf Stars)	2.00
160	Albert Belle (Gold Leaf Stars)	3.00
161	Jim Thome (Gold Leaf Stars)	1.50
162	Tony Clark (Gold Leaf Stars)	2.00
163	Chuck Knoblauch (Gold Leaf Stars)	1.50
164	Derek Jeter (Gold Leaf Stars)	8.00
165	Alex Rodriguez (Gold Leaf Stars)	8.00
166	Tony Gwynn (Gold Leaf Stars)	6.00
167	Roger Clemens (Gold Leaf Stars)	5.00
168	Barry Larkin (Gold Leaf Stars)	1.00
169	Andres Galarraga (Gold Leaf Stars)	1.00
170	Vladimir Guerrero (Gold Leaf Stars)	3.00
171	Mark McGwire (Gold Leaf Stars)	20.00
172	Barry Bonds (Gold Leaf Stars)	3.00
173	Juan Gonzalez (Gold Leaf Stars)	6.00
174	Andruw Jones (Gold Leaf Stars)	6.00
175	Paul Molitor (Gold Leaf Stars)	2.00
176	Hideo Nomo (Gold Leaf Stars)	3.00
177	Cal Ripken Jr. (Gold Leaf Stars)	12.00
178	Brad Fullmer (Gold Leaf Rookies)	1.50
179	Jaret Wright (Gold Leaf Rookies)	8.00
180	Bobby Estalella (Gold Leaf Rookies)	.75

181	Ben Grieve (Gold Leaf Rookies)	5.00
182	Paul Konerko (Gold Leaf Rookies)	4.00
183	David Ortiz (Gold Leaf Rookies)	1.00
184	Todd Helton (Gold Leaf Rookies)	3.00
185	Juan Encarnacion (Gold Leaf Rookies)	.75
186	Miguel Tejada (Gold Leaf Rookies)	3.00
187	Jacob Cruz (Gold Leaf Rookies)	1.00
188	Mark Kotsay (Gold Leaf Rookies)	1.50
189	Fernando Tatis (Gold Leaf Rookies)	1.00
190	Ricky Ledee (Gold Leaf Rookies)	1.00
191	Richard Hidalgo (Gold Leaf Rookies)	.75
192	Richie Sexson (Gold Leaf Rookies)	.75
193	Luis Ordaz (Gold Leaf Rookies)	.75
194	Eli Marrero (Gold Leaf Rookies)	.75
195	Livan Hernandez (Gold Leaf Rookies)	1.50
196	Homer Bush (Gold Leaf Rookies)	.75
197	Raul Ibanez (Gold Leaf Rookies)	.75
198	Checklist(Nomar Garciaparra)	1.50
199	Checklist(Scott Rolen)	1.00
200	Checklist(Jose Cruz Jr.)	.25

1998 Leaf
Crusade Green

Thirty cards from the cross-brand Crusade insert appear in 1998 Leaf. The cards had Green (250 sets), Purple (100 sets) and Red (25 sets) versions. Forty Crusade cards were in 1998 Donruss and the final 30 were in 1998 Donruss Update.

		MT
Complete Set (30):		1200.
Common Player:		10.00
Purples: 1.5x		
Reds: 4x to 6x		
1	Jim Edmonds	10.00
2	Darin Erstad	50.00
3	Mike Mussina	50.00
4	Albert Belle	60.00
5	Manny Ramirez	50.00
6	Jim Thome	40.00
7	Bubba Trammell	20.00
8	Bobby Higginson	10.00
9	Paul Molitor	40.00
10	Todd Walker	20.00
11	Andy Pettitte	40.00
12	Wade Boggs	30.00
13	Alex Rodriguez	150.00
14	Randy Johnson	50.00
15	Ivan Rodriguez	60.00
16	Roger Clemens	100.00
17	John Smoltz	20.00
18	Andruw Jones	120.00
19	Javier Lopez	10.00
20	Fred McGriff	20.00
21	Pokey Reese	10.00
22	Andres Galarraga	25.00
23	Eric Young	10.00
24	Moises Alou	10.00
25	Ben Grieve	90.00
26	Mike Piazza	160.00
27	Jason Kendall	10.00
28	Alan Benes	20.00
29	Tony Gwynn	120.00
30	Ken Caminiti	25.00

1998 Leaf
Fractal Foundation

Fractal Foundations is a stand-alone product but it parallels the 1998 Leaf set. It contains the Curtain Calls, Gold Leaf Stars and Gold Leaf Rookies subsets and is missing card #42 which Leaf retired in honor of Jackie Robinson. The set was printed on foil board and each card is numbered to 3,999. The set is paralleled in Fractal Materials, Fractal Materials Die-Cuts and Fractal Materials Z2 Axis.

		MT
Complete Set (200):		500.00
Common Player:		1.00
Semistars:		3.00
Unlisted Stars:		5.00
Wax Box:		125.00
1	Rusty Greer	1.00
2	Tino Martinez	3.00
3	Bobby Bonilla	2.00
4	Jason Giambi	1.00
5	Matt Morris	2.00
6	Craig Counsell	1.00
7	Reggie Jefferson	1.00
8	Brian Rose	3.00
9	Ruben Rivera	1.00
10	Shawn Estes	1.00
11	Tony Gwynn	10.00
12	Jeff Abbott	1.00
13	Jose Cruz Jr.	8.00
14	Francisco Cordova	1.00
15	Ryan Klesko	3.00
16	Tim Salmon	3.00
17	Brett Tomko	1.00
18	Matt Williams	3.00
19	Joe Carter	2.00
20	Harold Baines	1.00
21	Gary Sheffield	3.00
22	Charles Johnson	2.00
23	Aaron Boone	1.00
24	Eddie Murray	3.00
25	Matt Stairs	1.00
26	David Cone	2.00
27	Jon Nunnally	1.00
28	Chris Stynes	1.00
29	Enrique Wilson	1.00
30	Randy Johnson	4.00
31	Garret Anderson	1.00
32	Manny Ramirez	5.00
33	Jeff Suppan	1.00
34	Rickey Henderson	1.00
35	Scott Spiezio	1.00
36	Rondell White	2.00
37	Todd Greene	1.00
38	Delino DeShields	1.00
39	Kevin Brown	2.00
40	Chili Davis	1.00
41	Jimmy Key	1.00
42		1.00
43	Mike Mussina	5.00
44	Joe Randa	1.00
45	Chan Ho Park	2.00
46	Brad Radke	1.00
47	Geronimo Berroa	1.00
48	Wade Boggs	3.00
49	Kevin Appier	1.00
50	Moises Alou	2.00

51	David Justice	3.00
52	Ivan Rodriguez	5.00
53	J.T. Snow	1.00
54	Brian Giles	1.00
55	Will Clark	3.00
56	Justin Thompson	1.00
57	Javier Lopez	2.00
58	Hideki Irabu	3.00
59	Mark Grudzielanek	1.00
60	Abraham Nunez	1.00
61	Todd Hollandsworth	1.00
62	Jay Bell	1.00
63	Nomar Garciaparra	12.00
64	Vinny Castilla	2.00
65	Lou Collier	1.00
66	Kevin Orie	1.00
67	John Valentin	1.00
68	Robin Ventura	2.00
69	Denny Neagle	2.00
70	Tony Womack	1.00
71	Dennis Reyes	1.00
72	Wally Joyner	1.00
73	Kevin Brown	2.00
74	Ray Durham	1.00
75	Mike Cameron	2.00
76	Dante Bichette	3.00
77	Jose Guillen	3.00
78	Carlos Delgado	2.00
79	Paul Molitor	4.00
80	Jason Kendall	1.00
81	Mark Belhorn	1.00
82	Damian Jackson	1.00
83	Bill Mueller	1.00
84	Kevin Young	1.00
85	Curt Schilling	2.00
86	Jeffrey Hammonds	1.00
87	Sandy Alomar Jr.	2.00
88	Bartolo Colon	1.00
89	Wilton Guerrero	1.00
90	Bernie Williams	4.00
91	Deion Sanders	3.00
92	Mike Piazza	12.00
93	Butch Huskey	1.00
94	Edgardo Alfonzo	1.00
95	Alan Benes	2.00
96	Craig Biggio	2.00
97	Mark Grace	2.50
98	Shawn Green	1.00
99	Derrek Lee	3.00
100	Ken Griffey Jr.	20.00
101	Tim Raines	1.00
102	Pokey Reese	1.00
103	Lee Stevens	1.00
104	Shannon Stewart	1.00
105	John Smoltz	2.00
106	Frank Thomas	15.00
107	Jeff Fassero	1.00
108	Jay Buhner	3.00
109	Jose Canseco	3.00
110	Omar Vizquel	1.00
111	Travis Fryman	1.00
112	Dave Nilsson	1.00
113	John Olerud	1.00
114	Larry Walker	3.00
115	Jim Edmonds	2.00
116	Bobby Higginson	2.00
117	Todd Hundley	1.00
118	Paul O'Neill	2.00
119	Bip Roberts	1.00
120	Ismael Valdes	1.00
121	Pedro Martinez	4.00
122	Jeff Cirillo	1.00
123	Andy Benes	2.00
124	Bobby Jones	1.00
125	Brian Hunter	1.00
126	Darryl Kile	1.00
127	Pat Hentgen	1.00
128	Marquis Grissom	1.00
129	Eric Davis	1.00
130	Chipper Jones	12.00
131	Edgar Martinez	1.00
132	Andy Pettitte	3.00
133	Cal Ripken Jr.	15.00
134	Scott Rolen	8.00
135	Ron Coomer	1.00
136	Luis Castillo	1.00
137	Fred McGriff	2.00
138	Neifi Perez	1.00
139	Eric Karros	2.00
140	Alex Fernandez	1.00
141	Jason Dickson	1.00
142	Lance Johnson	1.00
143	Ray Lankford	1.00
144	Sammy Sosa	10.00
145	Eric Young	1.00
146	Bubba Trammell	2.00

147	Todd Walker	2.00
148	Mo Vaughn (Curtain Calls)	6.00
149	Jeff Bagwell (Curtain Calls)	8.00
150	Kenny Lofton (Curtain Calls)	5.00
151	Raul Mondesi (Curtain Calls)	2.00
152	Mike Piazza (Curtain Calls)	12.00
153	Chipper Jones (Curtain Calls)	12.00
154	Larry Walker (Curtain Calls)	3.00
155	Greg Maddux (Curtain Calls)	12.00
156	Ken Griffey Jr. (Curtain Calls)	20.00
157	Frank Thomas (Curtain Calls)	15.00
158	Darin Erstad (Gold Leaf Stars)	5.00
159	Roberto Alomar (Gold Leaf Stars)	4.00
160	Albert Belle (Gold Leaf Stars)	5.00
161	Jim Thome (Gold Leaf Stars)	3.00
162	Tony Clark (Gold Leaf Stars)	3.00
163	Chuck Knoblauch (Gold Leaf Stars)	2.50
164	Derek Jeter (Gold Leaf Stars)	10.00
165	Alex Rodriguez (Gold Leaf Stars)	12.00
166	Tony Gwynn (Gold Leaf Stars)	10.00
167	Roger Clemens (Gold Leaf Stars)	8.00
168	Barry Larkin (Gold Leaf Stars)	3.00
169	Andres Galarraga (Gold Leaf Stars)	3.00
170	Vladimir Guerrero (Gold Leaf Stars)	5.00
171	Mark McGwire (Gold Leaf Stars)	25.00
172	Barry Bonds (Gold Leaf Stars)	5.00
173	Juan Gonzalez (Gold Leaf Stars)	10.00
174	Andruw Jones (Gold Leaf Stars)	6.00
175	Paul Molitor (Gold Leaf Stars)	4.00
176	Hideo Nomo (Gold Leaf Stars)	5.00
177	Cal Ripken Jr. (Gold Leaf Stars)	15.00
178	Brad Fullmer (Gold Leaf Rookies)	3.00
179	Jaret Wright (Gold Leaf Rookies)	8.00
180	Bobby Estalella (Gold Leaf Rookies)	1.00
181	Ben Grieve (Gold Leaf Rookies)	8.00
182	Paul Konerko (Gold Leaf Rookies)	4.00
183	David Ortiz (Gold Leaf Rookies)	2.00
184	Todd Helton (Gold Leaf Rookies)	5.00
185	Juan Encarnacion (Gold Leaf Rookies)	1.00
186	Miguel Tejada (Gold Leaf Rookies)	4.00
187	Jacob Cruz (Gold Leaf Rookies)	1.00
188	Mark Kotsay (Gold Leaf Rookies)	2.00
189	Fernando Tatis (Gold Leaf Rookies)	1.00
190	Ricky Ledee (Gold Leaf Rookies)	2.00
191	Richard Hidalgo (Gold Leaf Rookies)	1.00
192	Richie Sexson (Gold Leaf Rookies)	1.00
193	Luis Ordaz (Gold Leaf Rookies)	1.00
194	Eli Marrero (Gold Leaf Rookies)	1.00
195	Livan Hernandez (Gold Leaf Rookies)	2.00
196	Homer Bush (Gold Leaf Rookies)	1.00
197	Raul Ibanez (Gold Leaf Rookies)	1.00

198	Checklist(Nomar Garciaparra)	6.00
199	Checklist(Scott Rolen)	4.00
200	Checklist(Jose Cruz Jr.)	4.00

1998 Leaf Fractal Materials

The Fractal Materials set paralleled 1998 Leaf Fractal Foundations. Every card in the set is sequentially numbered. The 200 card set was printed on four different materials: 100 plastic cards (numbered to 3,250), 50 leather (numbered to 1,000), 30 nylon (500) and 20 wood (250). This set was inserted one per pack.

		MT
Common Plastic (3,250):		1.00
Common Leather (1,000):		4.00
Common Nylon (500):		10.00
Common Wood (250):		25.00
Wax Box:		120.00
1	Rusty Greer N	10.00
2	Tino Martinez W	30.00
3	Bobby Bonilla N	15.00
4	Jason Giambi N	10.00
5	Matt Morris L	8.00
6	Craig Counsell P	1.00
7	Reggie Jefferson P	1.00
8	Brian Rose P	2.00
9	Ruben Rivera L	4.00
10	Shawn Estes L	8.00
11	Tony Gwynn W	100.00
12	Jeff Abbott P	1.00
13	Jose Cruz Jr. W	80.00
14	Francisco Cordova P	1.00
15	Ryan Klesko L	15.00
16	Tim Salmon W	30.00
17	Brett Tomko L	4.00
18	Matt Williams N	20.00
19	Joe Carter P	2.00
20	Harold Baines P	1.00
21	Gary Sheffield N	25.00
22	Charles Johnson L	8.00
23	Aaron Boone P	1.00
24	Eddie Murray N	25.00
25	Matt Stairs P	1.00
26	David Cone P	2.00
27	Jon Nunnally P	1.00
28	Chris Stynes P	1.00
29	Enrique Wilson P	1.00
30	Randy Johnson W	40.00
31	Garret Anderson N	10.00
32	Manny Ramirez W	50.00
33	Jeff Suppan L	4.00
34	Rickey Henderson N	20.00
35	Scott Spiezio P	1.00
36	Rondell White L	8.00
37	Todd Greene N	10.00
38	Delino DeShields P	1.00
39	Kevin Brown L	8.00
40	Chili Davis P	1.00

41	Jimmy Key P	1.00
42		.10
43	Mike Mussina N	30.00
44	Joe Randa P	1.00
45	Chan Ho Park N	15.00
46	Brad Radke P	1.00
47	Geronimo Berroa P	1.00
48	Wade Boggs N	25.00
49	Kevin Appier P	1.00
50	Moises Alou N	15.00
51	David Justice N	20.00
52	Ivan Rodriguez W	50.00
53	J.T. Snow L	6.00
54	Brian Giles P	1.00
55	Will Clark L	15.00
56	Justin Thompson N	10.00
57	Javier Lopez P	2.00
58	Hideki Irabu L	20.00
59	Mark Grudzielanek P	1.00
60	Abraham Nunez P	1.00
61	Todd Hollandsworth P	1.00
62	Jay Bell P	1.00
63	Nomar Garciaparra W	125.00
64	Vinny Castilla P	2.00
65	Lou Collier P	1.00
66	Kevin Orie L	4.00
67	John Valentin P	1.00
68	Robin Ventura P	2.00
69	Denny Neagle P	2.00
70	Tony Womack L	4.00
71	Dennis Reyes L	4.00
72	Wally Joyner P	1.00
73	Kevin Brown P	2.00
74	Ray Durham P	1.00
75	Mike Cameron N	15.00
76	Dante Bichette L	12.00
77	Jose Guillen N	15.00
78	Carlos Delgado L	8.00
79	Paul Molitor W	40.00
80	Jason Kendall P	1.00
81	Mark Belhorn L	4.00
82	Damian Jackson P	1.00
83	Bill Mueller P	1.00
84	Kevin Young P	1.00
85	Curt Schilling P	2.00
86	Jeffrey Hammonds P	1.00
87	Sandy Alomar Jr. L	8.00
88	Bartolo Colon P	2.00
89	Wilton Guerrero L	4.00
90	Bernie Williams N	30.00
91	Deion Sanders N	20.00
92	Mike Piazza W	125.00
93	Butch Huskey L	4.00
94	Edgardo Alfonzo L	4.00
95	Alan Benes L	8.00
96	Craig Biggio N	20.00
97	Mark Grace L	12.00
98	Shawn Green L	4.00
99	Derrek Lee L	10.00
100	Ken Griffey Jr. W	200.00
101	Tim Raines L	1.00
102	Pokey Reese P	1.00
103	Lee Stevens P	1.00
104	Shannon Stewart N	10.00
105	John Smoltz L	10.00
106	Frank Thomas W	160.00
107	Jeff Fassero P	1.00
108	Jay Buhner L	12.00
109	Jose Canseco L	15.00
110	Omar Vizquel P	1.00
111	Travis Fryman P	1.00
112	Dave Nilsson P	1.00
113	John Olerud P	1.00
114	Larry Walker W	30.00
115	Jim Edmonds N	15.00
116	Bobby Higginson L	4.00
117	Todd Hundley L	8.00
118	Paul O'Neill P	2.00
119	Bip Roberts P	1.00
120	Ismael Valdes P	1.00
121	Pedro Martinez N	25.00
122	Jeff Cirillo P	1.00
123	Andy Benes P	1.00
124	Bobby Jones P	1.00
125	Brian Hunter P	1.00
126	Darryl Kile P	1.00
127	Pat Hentgen P	1.00
128	Marquis Grissom P	1.00
129	Eric Davis P	1.00
130	Chipper Jones W	125.00
131	Edgar Martinez N	15.00
132	Andy Pettitte W	40.00
133	Cal Ripken Jr. W	150.00
134	Scott Rolen W	80.00
135	Ron Coomer P	1.00
136	Luis Castillo L	4.00

137	Fred McGriff L	12.00
138	Neifi Perez L	4.00
139	Eric Karros P	2.00
140	Alex Fernandez P	1.00
141	Jason Dickson P	1.00
142	Lance Johnson P	1.00
143	Ray Lankford P	1.00
144	Sammy Sosa N	50.00
145	Eric Young P	1.00
146	Bubba Trammell L	8.00
147	Todd Walker L	8.00
148	Mo Vaughn P (Curtain Calls)	6.00
149	Jeff Bagwell P (Curtain Calls)	8.00
150	Kenny Lofton P (Curtain Calls)	6.00
151	Raul Mondesi P (Curtain Calls)	2.00
152	Mike Piazza P (Curtain Calls)	15.00
153	Chipper Jones P (Curtain Calls)	15.00
154	Larry Walker P (Curtain Calls)	4.00
155	Greg Maddux P (Curtain Calls)	15.00
156	Ken Griffey Jr. P (Curtain Calls)	25.00
157	Frank Thomas P (Curtain Calls)	25.00
158	Darin Erstad L (Gold Leaf Stars)	20.00
159	Roberto Alomar P (Gold Leaf Stars)	5.00
160	Albert Belle L (Gold Leaf Stars)	6.00
161	Jim Thome L (Gold Leaf Stars)	4.00
162	Tony Clark L (Gold Leaf Stars)	5.00
163	Chuck Knoblauch L (Gold Leaf Stars)	4.00
164	Derek Jeter P (Gold Leaf Stars)	12.00
165	Alex Rodriguez P (Gold Leaf Stars)	15.00
166	Tony Gwynn P (Gold Leaf Stars)	12.00
167	Roger Clemens L (Gold Leaf Stars)	35.00
168	Barry Larkin P (Gold Leaf Stars)	3.00
169	Andres Galarraga P (Gold Leaf Stars)	3.00
170	Vladimir Guerrero L (Gold Leaf Stars)	15.00
171	Mark McGwire L (Gold Leaf Stars)	75.00
172	Barry Bonds L (Gold Leaf Stars)	25.00
173	Juan Gonzalez P (Gold Leaf Stars)	12.00
174	Andruw Jones P (Gold Leaf Stars)	8.00
175	Paul Molitor P (Gold Leaf Stars)	5.00
176	Hideo Nomo L (Gold Leaf Stars)	25.00
177	Cal Ripken Jr. P (Gold Leaf Stars)	20.00
178	Brad Fullmer P (Gold Leaf Rookies)	3.00
179	Jaret Wright N (Gold Leaf Rookies)	60.00
180	Bobby Estalella P (Gold Leaf Rookies)	1.00
181	Ben Grieve W (Gold Leaf Rookies)	60.00
182	Paul Konerko W (Gold Leaf Rookies)	25.00
183	David Ortiz N (Gold Leaf Rookies)	12.00
184	Todd Helton W (Gold Leaf Rookies)	40.00
185	Juan Encarnacion N (Gold Leaf Rookies)	10.00
186	Miguel Tejada N (Gold Leaf Rookies)	25.00
187	Jacob Cruz P (Gold Leaf Rookies)	1.00
188	Mark Kotsay N (Gold Leaf Rookies)	25.00
189	Fernando Tatis L (Gold Leaf Rookies)	10.00

190	Ricky Ledee P (Gold Leaf Rookies)	2.00
191	Richard Hidalgo P (Gold Leaf Rookies)	1.00
192	Richie Sexson P (Gold Leaf Rookies)	1.00
193	Luis Ordaz P (Gold Leaf Rookies)	1.00
194	Eli Marrero L (Gold Leaf Rookies)	8.00
195	Livan Hernandez L (Gold Leaf Rookies)	8.00
196	Homer Bush P (Gold Leaf Rookies)	1.00
197	Raul Ibanez P (Gold Leaf Rookies)	1.00
198	Checklist(Nomar Garciaparra P)	10.00
199	Checklist(Scott Rolen P)	5.00
200	Checklist(Jose Cruz Jr. P)	10.00

1998 Leaf Fractal Materials Die-Cut

This parallel set adds a die-cut to the Fractal Materials set. The first 200 of 75 plastic, 15 Leather, five nylon and five wood cards have an x-axis die-cut. The first 100 of 20 plastic, 25 leather, 10 nylon and five wood cards have a y-axis die-cut. The first 50 of five plastic, 10 leather, 15 nylon and 10 wood cards have a z-axis die-cut.

		MT
	Common X (200 of each):	8.00
	Common Y (100):	20.00
	Common Z (50):	40.00
1	Rusty Greer Z	40.00
2	Tino Martinez Y	40.00
3	Bobby Bonilla Y	30.00
4	Jason Giambi Z	40.00
5	Matt Morris Y	30.00
6	Craig Counsell X	8.00
7	Reggie Jefferson X	8.00
8	Brian Rose X	25.00
9	Ruben Rivera Y	20.00
10	Shawn Estes Y	20.00
11	Tony Gwynn X	100.00
12	Jeff Abbott Y	20.00
13	Jose Cruz Jr. Z	200.00
14	Francisco Cordova Y	20.00
15	Ryan Klesko X	25.00
16	Tim Salmon Y	40.00
17	Brett Tomko Y	20.00
18	Matt Williams Y	40.00
19	Joe Carter X	20.00
20	Harold Baines X	8.00
21	Gary Sheffield Z	80.00
22	Charles Johnson Y	30.00
23	Aaron Boone Y	20.00
24	Eddie Murray Y	40.00

25	Matt Stairs X	8.00
26	David Cone X	20.00
27	Jon Nunnally X	8.00
28	Chris Stynes X	8.00
29	Enrique Wilson Y	20.00
30	Randy Johnson Y	40.00
31	Garret Anderson Y	20.00
32	Manny Ramirez Y	75.00
33	Jeff Suppan Y	20.00
34	Rickey Henderson X	15.00
35	Scott Spiezio Y	20.00
36	Rondell White Y	30.00
37	Todd Greene Z	60.00
38	Delino DeShields Y	20.00
39	Kevin Brown X	15.00
40	Chili Davis X	8.00
41	Jimmy Key X	8.00
42		.10
43	Mike Mussina Z	120.00
44	Joe Randa X	8.00
45	Chan Ho Park Y	25.00
46	Brad Radke X	8.00
47	Geronimo Berroa X	8.00
48	Wade Boggs Y	30.00
49	Kevin Appier X	8.00
50	Moises Alou X	15.00
51	David Justice Z	75.00
52	Ivan Rodriguez X	40.00
53	J.T. Snow X	15.00
54	Brian Giles Y	20.00
55	Will Clark X	20.00
56	Justin Thompson Y	25.00
57	Javier Lopez Y	25.00
58	Hideki Irabu X	25.00
59	Mark Grudzielanek X	8.00
60	Abraham Nunez Z	40.00
61	Todd Hollandsworth X	8.00
62	Jay Bell X	8.00
63	Nomar Garciaparra Z	350.00
64	Vinny Castilla Y	25.00
65	Lou Collier Y	20.00
66	Kevin Orie X	8.00
67	John Valentin X	8.00
68	Robin Ventura X	15.00
69	Denny Neagle X	15.00
70	Tony Womack X	8.00
71	Dennis Reyes Y	20.00
72	Wally Joyner X	8.00
73	Kevin Brown X	8.00
74	Ray Durham X	8.00
75	Mike Cameron Y	30.00
76	Dante Bichette X	25.00
77	Jose Guillen Z	60.00
78	Carlos Delgado Y	30.00
79	Paul Molitor X	40.00
80	Jason Kendall X	8.00
81	Mark Belhorn X	8.00
82	Damian Jackson Y	20.00
83	Bill Mueller X	8.00
84	Kevin Young X	8.00
85	Curt Schilling X	20.00
86	Jeffrey Hammonds X	8.00
87	Sandy Alomar Jr. Y	30.00
88	Bartolo Colon Y	20.00
89	Wilton Guerrero Y	20.00
90	Bernie Williams Z	125.00
91	Deion Sanders Y	30.00
92	Mike Piazza Z	400.00
93	Butch Huskey X	8.00
94	Edgardo Alfonzo Y	20.00
95	Alan Benes Z	40.00
96	Craig Biggio X	20.00
97	Mark Grace Y	40.00
98	Shawn Green Y	20.00
99	Derrek Lee Y	30.00
100	Ken Griffey Jr. Z	600.00
101	Tim Raines X	8.00
102	Pokey Reese Y	20.00
103	Lee Stevens X	8.00
104	Shannon Stewart X	8.00
105	John Smoltz Y	30.00
106	Frank Thomas Z	500.00
107	Jeff Fassero X	8.00
108	Jay Buhner Y	40.00
109	Jose Canseco X	25.00
110	Omar Vizquel X	8.00
111	Travis Fryman X	8.00
112	Dave Nilsson X	8.00
113	John Olerud X	15.00
114	Larry Walker X	30.00
115	Jim Edmonds X	40.00
116	Bobby Higginson Y	20.00
117	Todd Hundley Z	40.00
118	Paul O'Neill X	20.00
119	Bip Roberts X	8.00
120	Ismael Valdes X	15.00

121	Pedro Martinez X	25.00
122	Jeff Cirillo X	8.00
123	Andy Benes X	20.00
124	Bobby Jones X	8.00
125	Brian Hunter X	8.00
126	Darryl Kile X	8.00
127	Pat Hentgen X	8.00
128	Marquis Grissom X	8.00
129	Eric Davis X	8.00
130	Chipper Jones Z	400.00
131	Edgar Martinez Z	60.00
132	Andy Pettitte Y	60.00
133	Cal Ripken Jr. Z	450.00
134	Scott Rolen X	80.00
135	Ron Coomer X	8.00
136	Luis Castillo X	8.00
137	Fred McGriff X	25.00
138	Neifi Perez Y	20.00
139	Eric Karros X	20.00
140	Alex Fernandez X	8.00
141	Jason Dickson X	8.00
142	Lance Johnson X	8.00
143	Ray Lankford Y	20.00
144	Sammy Sosa Y	80.00
145	Eric Young Y	20.00
146	Bubba Trammell Z	40.00
147	Todd Walker Z	60.00
148	Mo Vaughn X (Curtain Calls)	40.00
149	Jeff Bagwell X (Curtain Calls)	75.00
150	Kenny Lofton X (Curtain Calls)	40.00
151	Raul Mondesi X (Curtain Calls)	20.00
152	Mike Piazza X (Curtain Calls)	120.00
153	Chipper Jones X (Curtain Calls)	120.00
154	Larry Walker X (Curtain Calls)	30.00
155	Greg Maddux X (Curtain Calls)	120.00
156	Ken Griffey Jr. X (Curtain Calls)	200.00
157	Frank Thomas X (Curtain Calls)	160.00
158	Darin Erstad Y (Gold Leaf Stars)	75.00
159	Roberto Alomar X (Gold Leaf Stars)	40.00
160	Albert Belle X (Gold Leaf Stars)	40.00
161	Jim Thome X (Gold Leaf Stars)	30.00
162	Tony Clark Z (Gold Leaf Stars)	100.00
163	Chuck Knoblauch Z (Gold Leaf Stars)	75.00
164	Derek Jeter X (Gold Leaf Stars)	100.00
165	Alex Rodriguez Y (Gold Leaf Stars)	180.00
166	Tony Gwynn X (Gold Leaf Stars)	100.00
167	Roger Clemens Y (Gold Leaf Stars)	120.00
168	Barry Larkin Y (Gold Leaf Stars)	40.00
169	Andres Galarraga Y (Gold Leaf Stars)	40.00
170	Vladimir Guerrero Y (Gold Leaf Stars)	60.00
171	Mark McGwire Z (Gold Leaf Stars)	400.00
172	Barry Bonds Y (Gold Leaf Stars)	75.00
173	Juan Gonzalez Y (Gold Leaf Stars)	150.00
174	Andruw Jones X (Gold Leaf Stars)	40.00
175	Paul Molitor X (Gold Leaf Stars)	35.00
176	Hideo Nomo Z (Gold Leaf Stars)	125.00
177	Cal Ripken Jr. X (Gold Leaf Stars)	150.00
178	Brad Fullmer Z (Gold Leaf Rookies)	60.00
179	Jaret Wright Z (Gold Leaf Rookies)	240.00
180	Bobby Estalella Y (Gold Leaf Rookies)	20.00
181	Ben Grieve Z (Gold Leaf Rookies)	180.00
182	Paul Konerko Z (Gold Leaf Rookies)	100.00
183	David Ortiz Z (Gold Leaf Rookies)	60.00
184	Todd Helton Z (Gold Leaf Rookies)	125.00
185	Juan Encarnacion Z (Gold Leaf Rookies)	40.00
186	Miguel Tejada Z (Gold Leaf Rookies)	80.00
187	Jacob Cruz X (Gold Leaf Rookies)	8.00
188	Mark Kotsay Z (Gold Leaf Rookies)	80.00
189	Fernando Tatis Y (Gold Leaf Rookies)	40.00
190	Ricky Ledee X (Gold Leaf Rookies)	25.00
191	Richard Hidalgo Z (Gold Leaf Rookies)	40.00
192	Richie Sexson Z (Gold Leaf Rookies)	40.00
193	Luis Ordaz X (Gold Leaf Rookies)	8.00
194	Eli Marrero Z (Gold Leaf Rookies)	40.00
195	Livan Hernandez Z (Gold Leaf Rookies)	75.00
196	Homer Bush X (Gold Leaf Rookies)	8.00
197	Raul Ibanez X (Gold Leaf Rookies)	8.00
198	Checklist(Nomar Garciaparra X)	60.00
199	Checklist(Scott Rolen Z)	125.00
200	Checklist(Jose Cruz Jr. X)	50.00

1998 Leaf Fractal Matrix

Fractal Matrix parallels the 1998 Leaf set. The cards have a metallic-colored finish, with 100 done in bronze, 60 in silver and 40 in gold.

		MT
Complete Set (200):		
Common Bronze:		1.50
Bronze Semistars:		4.00
Common Silver:		5.00
Silver Semistars:		10.00
Common Gold:		10.00
Common G/X Axis:		40.00
Gold Semistars:		20.00
1	Rusty Greer G/Z	10.00
2	Tino Martinez G/Z	20.00
3	Bobby Bonilla S/Y	8.00
4	Jason Giambi S/Y	5.00
5	Matt Morris S/Y	5.00
6	Craig Counsell B/X	1.50
7	Reggie Jefferson B/X	1.50
8	Brian Rose S/Y	15.00
9	Ruben Rivera B/X	3.00
10	Shawn Estes S/Y	5.00
11	Tony Gwynn G/Z	80.00
12	Jeff Abbott B/Y	1.50
13	Jose Cruz Jr. G/Z	80.00
14	Francisco Cordova B/X	1.50
15	Ryan Klesko B/X	8.00
16	Tim Salmon G/Y	30.00
17	Brett Tomko B/X	1.50
18	Matt Williams S/Y	12.00
19	Joe Carter B/X	3.00
20	Harold Baines B/X	1.50
21	Gary Sheffield S/Z	20.00
22	Charles Johnson S/X	5.00
23	Aaron Boone B/X	4.00
24	Eddie Murray G/Y	20.00
25	Matt Stairs B/X	1.50
26	David Cone B/X	4.00
27	Jon Nunnally B/X	1.50
28	Chris Stynes B/X	1.50
29	Enrique Wilson B/Y	1.50
30	Randy Johnson S/Z	30.00
31	Garret Anderson S/Y	5.00
32	Manny Ramirez G/Z	35.00
33	Jeff Suppan S/X	5.00
34	Rickey Henderson B/X	1.50
35	Scott Spiezio B/X	1.50
36	Rondell White S/Y	10.00
37	Todd Greene S/Z	10.00
38	Delino DeShields B/X	1.50
39	Kevin Brown S/Z	8.00
40	Chili Davis B/X	1.50
41	Jimmy Key B/X	1.50
42		1.50
43	Mike Mussina G/Y	40.00
44	Joe Randa B/X	1.50
45	Chan Ho Park S/Z	10.00
46	Brad Radke B/X	1.50
47	Geronimo Berroa B/X	1.50
48	Wade Boggs S/Y	10.00
49	Kevin Appier B/X	1.50
50	Moises Alou S/Y	10.00
51	David Justice G/Y	20.00
52	Ivan Rodriguez G/Z	40.00
53	J.T. Snow B/X	3.00
54	Brian Giles B/X	1.50
55	Will Clark B/X	5.00
56	Justin Thompson S/Y	5.00
57	Javier Lopez S/X	8.00
58	Hideki Irabu B/Z	10.00
59	Mark Grudzielanek B/X	1.50
60	Abraham Nunez S/X	10.00
61	Todd Hollandsworth B/X	1.50
62	Jay Bell B/X	1.50
63	Nomar Garciaparra G/Z	100.00
64	Vinny Castilla B/Y	1.50
65	Lou Collier B/Y	1.50
66	Kevin Orie S/X	5.00
67	John Valentin B/X	1.50
68	Robin Ventura B/X	3.00
69	Denny Neagle B/X	3.00
70	Tony Womack S/Y	5.00
71	Dennis Reyes S/Y	5.00
72	Wally Joyner B/X	1.50
73	Kevin Brown B/Y	3.00
74	Ray Durham B/X	1.50
75	Mike Cameron S/Z	10.00
76	Dante Bichette B/X	4.00
77	Jose Guillen G/Y	20.00
78	Carlos Delgado B/Y	1.50
79	Paul Molitor G/Z	30.00
80	Jason Kendall B/X	1.50
81	Mark Belhorn B/X	1.50
82	Damian Jackson B/X	1.50
83	Bill Mueller B/X	1.50
84	Kevin Young B/X	1.50
85	Curt Schilling B/X	4.00
86	Jeffrey Hammonds B/X	1.50
87	Sandy Alomar Jr. S/Y	10.00
88	Bartolo Colon B/Y	1.50
89	Wilton Guerrero B/Y	1.50
90	Bernie Williams S/Y	40.00
91	Deion Sanders S/Y	12.00
92	Mike Piazza G/X	300.00
93	Butch Huskey B/X	1.50
94	Edgardo Alfonzo S/X	5.00
95	Alan Benes S/Y	10.00
96	Craig Biggio S/Y	10.00
97	Mark Grace S/Y	12.00
98	Shawn Green S/Y	5.00
99	Derrek Lee S/Y	10.00
100	Ken Griffey Jr. G/Z	160.00
101	Tim Raines B/X	1.50
102	Pokey Reese S/X	5.00
103	Lee Stevens B/X	1.50
104	Shannon Stewart S/Y	5.00
105	John Smoltz S/Y	10.00
106	Frank Thomas G/X	350.00
107	Jeff Fassero B/X	1.50

108	Jay Buhner B/Y	4.00
109	Jose Canseco B/X	4.00
110	Omar Vizquel B/X	1.50
111	Travis Fryman B/X	1.50
112	Dave Nilsson B/X	1.50
113	John Olerud B/X	1.50
114	Larry Walker G/Z	25.00
115	Jim Edmonds S/Y	10.00
116	Bobby Higginson S/X	10.00
117	Todd Hundley B/X	8.00
118	Paul O'Neill B/X	3.00
119	Bip Roberts B/X	1.50
120	Ismael Valdes B/X	1.50
121	Pedro Martinez S/Y	15.00
122	Jeff Cirillo B/X	1.50
123	Andy Benes B/X	1.50
124	Bobby Jones B/X	1.50
125	Brian Hunter B/X	1.50
126	Darryl Kile B/X	1.50
127	Pat Hentgen B/X	1.50
128	Marquis Grissom B/X	1.50
129	Eric Davis B/X	1.50
130	Chipper Jones G/Z	100.00
131	Edgar Martinez S/Z	5.00
132	Andy Pettitte G/Z	30.00
133	Cal Ripken Jr. G/X	400.00
134	Scott Rolen G/Z	75.00
135	Ron Coomer B/X	1.50
136	Luis Castillo B/Y	1.50
137	Fred McGriff B/Y	4.00
138	Neifi Perez S/Y	5.00
139	Eric Karros B/X	3.00
140	Alex Fernandez B/X	1.50
141	Jason Dickson B/X	1.50
142	Lance Johnson B/X	1.50
143	Ray Lankford B/Y	1.50
144	Sammy Sosa G/Y	75.00
145	Eric Young B/Y	1.50
146	Bubba Trammell S/Y	10.00
147	Todd Walker S/Y	10.00
148	Mo Vaughn S/X (Curtain Calls)	20.00
149	Jeff Bagwell S/X (Curtain Calls)	30.00
150	Kenny Lofton S/X (Curtain Calls)	20.00
151	Raul Mondesi S/X (Curtain Calls)	10.00
152	Mike Piazza S/X (Curtain Calls)	50.00
153	Chipper Jones S/X (Curtain Calls)	50.00
154	Larry Walker S/X (Curtain Calls)	10.00
155	Greg Maddux S/X (Curtain Calls)	50.00
156	Ken Griffey Jr. S/X (Curtain Calls)	80.00
157	Frank Thomas S/X (Curtain Calls)	60.00
158	Darin Erstad B/Z (Gold Leaf Stars)	8.00
159	Roberto Alomar B/Y (Gold Leaf Stars)	5.00
160	Albert Belle G/Y (Gold Leaf Stars)	25.00
161	Jim Thome G/Y (Gold Leaf Stars)	18.00
162	Tony Clark G/Y (Gold Leaf Stars)	18.00
163	Chuck Knoblauch B/Y (Gold Leaf Stars)	4.00
164	Derek Jeter G/Z (Gold Leaf Stars)	50.00
165	Alex Rodriguez G/Z (Gold Leaf Stars)	50.00
166	Tony Gwynn B/X (Gold Leaf Stars)	25.00
167	Roger Clemens G/Z (Gold Leaf Stars)	30.00
168	Barry Larkin B/Y (Gold Leaf Stars)	4.00
169	Andres Galarraga B/Y (Gold Leaf Stars)	4.00
170	Vladimir Guerrero G/Z (Gold Leaf Stars)	25.00
171	Mark McGwire B/Z (Gold Leaf Stars)	30.00
172	Barry Bonds B/Z (Gold Leaf Stars)	12.00
173	Juan Gonzalez G/Z (Gold Leaf Stars)	40.00
174	Andruw Jones G/Z (Gold Leaf Stars)	40.00
175	Paul Molitor B/X (Gold Leaf Stars)	5.00

176	Hideo Nomo B/Z (Gold Leaf Stars)	15.00
177	Cal Ripken Jr. B/X (Gold Leaf Stars)	20.00
178	Brad Fullmer S/Z (Gold Leaf Rookies)	12.00
179	Jaret Wright G/Z (Gold Leaf Rookies)	50.00
180	Bobby Estalella B/Y (Gold Leaf Rookies)	1.50
181	Ben Grieve G/X (Gold Leaf Rookies)	120.00
182	Paul Konerko G/Z (Gold Leaf Rookies)	30.00
183	David Ortiz G/Z (Gold Leaf Rookies)	15.00
184	Todd Helton G/X (Gold Leaf Rookies)	80.00
185	Juan Encarnacion G/Z (Gold Leaf Rookies)	20.00
186	Miguel Tejada G/Z (Gold Leaf Rookies)	25.00
187	Jacob Cruz B/Y (Gold Leaf Rookies)	3.00
188	Mark Kotsay G/Z (Gold Leaf Rookies)	20.00
189	Fernando Tatis S/Z (Gold Leaf Rookies)	10.00
190	Ricky Ledee S/Y (Gold Leaf Rookies)	12.00
191	Richard Hidalgo S/Y (Gold Leaf Rookies)	5.00
192	Richie Sexson S/Y (Gold Leaf Rookies)	5.00
193	Luis Ordaz B/X (Gold Leaf Rookies)	1.50
194	Eli Marrero S/Z (Gold Leaf Rookies)	8.00
195	Livan Hernandez S/Z (Gold Leaf Rookies)	10.00
196	Homer Bush B/X (Gold Leaf Rookies)	1.50
197	Raul Ibanez B/X (Gold Leaf Rookies)	1.50
198	Checklist(Nomar Garciaparra B/X)	15.00
199	Checklist(Scott Rolen B/X)	10.00
200	Checklist(Jose Cruz Jr. B/X)	15.00

1998 Leaf Fractal Matrix Die-Cut

This parallel set adds a die-cut to the Fractal Matrix set. Three different die-cut versions were created: x-axis, y-axis and z-axis. An x-axis die-cut was added to 75 bronze, 20 silver and five gold cards. A y-axis die-cut was added to 20 bronze, 30 silver and 10 gold cards. Of the 40 z-axis cards, five are bronze, 10 silver and 25 gold.

		MT
	Common X-Axis:	6.00
	Common Y-Axis:	10.00
	Y-Axis Semistars:	20.00
	Common Z-Axis:	20.00
	Z-Axis Semistars:	30.00
1	Rusty Greer G/Z	20.00
2	Tino Martinez G/Z	30.00
3	Bobby Bonilla S/Y	15.00
4	Jason Giambi S/Y	12.00
5	Matt Morris S/Y	15.00
6	Craig Counsell B/X	6.00
7	Reggie Jefferson B/X	6.00
8	Brian Rose S/Y	20.00
9	Ruben Rivera B/X	10.00
10	Shawn Estes S/Y	10.00
11	Tony Gwynn G/Z	150.00
12	Jeff Abbott B/Y	10.00
13	Jose Cruz Jr. G/Z	150.00
14	Francisco Cordova B/X	6.00
15	Ryan Klesko B/X	15.00
16	Tim Salmon G/Y	25.00
17	Brett Tomko B/X	6.00
18	Matt Williams S/Y	20.00
19	Joe Carter B/X	10.00
20	Harold Baines B/X	6.00
21	Gary Sheffield S/Z	40.00
22	Charles Johnson S/X	8.00
23	Aaron Boone B/X	8.00
24	Eddie Murray G/Y	20.00
25	Matt Stairs B/X	6.00
26	David Cone B/X	10.00
27	Jon Nunnally B/X	6.00
28	Chris Stynes B/X	6.00
29	Enrique Wilson B/Y	10.00
30	Randy Johnson S/Z	50.00
31	Garret Anderson S/Y	10.00
32	Manny Ramirez G/Z	60.00
33	Jeff Suppan S/X	6.00
34	Rickey Henderson B/X	6.00
35	Scott Spiezio B/X	6.00
36	Rondell White S/Y	20.00
37	Todd Greene S/Z	30.00
38	Delino DeShields B/X	6.00
39	Kevin Brown S/X	8.00
40	Chili Davis B/X	6.00
41	Jimmy Key B/X	6.00
42		6.00
43	Mike Mussina G/Y	40.00
44	Joe Randa B/X	6.00
45	Chan Ho Park S/Z	30.00
46	Brad Radke B/X	6.00
47	Geronimo Berroa B/X	6.00
48	Wade Boggs S/Y	25.00
49	Kevin Appier B/X	6.00
50	Moises Alou S/Y	15.00
51	David Justice G/Y	25.00
52	Ivan Rodriguez G/Z	75.00
53	J.T. Snow B/X	8.00
54	Brian Giles B/X	6.00
55	Will Clark B/X	20.00
56	Justin Thompson S/Y	10.00
57	Javier Lopez S/X	8.00
58	Hideki Irabu B/Z	50.00
59	Mark Grudzielanek B/X	6.00
60	Abraham Nunez S/X	10.00
61	Todd Hollandsworth B/X	6.00
62	Jay Bell B/X	6.00
63	Nomar Garciaparra G/Z	200.00
64	Vinny Castilla B/Y	10.00
65	Lou Collier B/Y	10.00
66	Kevin Orie S/X	6.00
67	John Valentin B/X	6.00
68	Robin Ventura B/X	8.00
69	Denny Neagle B/X	8.00
70	Tony Womack S/Y	10.00
71	Dennis Reyes S/Y	10.00
72	Wally Joyner B/X	6.00
73	Kevin Brown B/Y	15.00
74	Ray Durham B/X	6.00
75	Mike Cameron S/Z	30.00
76	Dante Bichette B/X	10.00
77	Jose Guillen G/Y	20.00
78	Carlos Delgado B/Y	15.00
79	Paul Molitor G/Z	60.00
80	Jason Kendall B/X	6.00
81	Mark Belhorn B/X	6.00
82	Damian Jackson B/X	6.00
83	Bill Mueller B/X	6.00
84	Kevin Young B/X	6.00
85	Curt Schilling B/X	10.00
86	Jeffrey Hammonds B/X	6.00
87	Sandy Alomar Jr. S/Y	20.00
88	Bartolo Colon B/Y	6.00
89	Wilton Guerrero B/Y	6.00
90	Bernie Williams G/Y	40.00

91	Deion Sanders S/Y	20.00
92	Mike Piazza G/X	75.00
93	Butch Huskey B/X	6.00
94	Edgardo Alfonzo S/X	6.00
95	Alan Benes S/Y	15.00
96	Craig Biggio S/Y	20.00
97	Mark Grace S/Y	25.00
98	Shawn Green S/Y	10.00
99	Derrek Lee S/Y	20.00
100	Ken Griffey Jr. G/Z	300.00
101	Tim Raines B/X	6.00
102	Pokey Reese S/X	6.00
103	Lee Stevens B/X	6.00
104	Shannon Stewart S/Y	10.00
105	John Smoltz S/Y	20.00
106	Frank Thomas G/X	90.00
107	Jeff Fassero B/X	6.00
108	Jay Buhner B/Y	20.00
109	Jose Canseco B/X	10.00
110	Omar Vizquel B/X	6.00
111	Travis Fryman B/X	8.00
112	Dave Nilsson B/X	6.00
113	John Olerud B/X	8.00
114	Larry Walker G/Z	40.00
115	Jim Edmonds S/Y	20.00
116	Bobby Higginson S/X	10.00
117	Todd Hundley S/X	8.00
118	Paul O'Neill B/X	10.00
119	Bip Roberts B/X	6.00
120	Ismael Valdes B/X	6.00
121	Pedro Martinez S/Y	25.00
122	Jeff Cirillo B/X	6.00
123	Andy Benes B/X	6.00
124	Bobby Jones B/X	6.00
125	Brian Hunter B/X	6.00
126	Darryl Kile B/X	6.00
127	Pat Hentgen B/X	6.00
128	Marquis Grissom B/X	6.00
129	Eric Davis B/X	6.00
130	Chipper Jones G/Z	200.00
131	Edgar Martinez S/Z	20.00
132	Andy Pettitte G/Z	60.00
133	Cal Ripken Jr. G/X	100.00
134	Scott Rolen G/Z	150.00
135	Ron Coomer B/X	6.00
136	Luis Castillo B/Y	10.00
137	Fred McGriff B/Y	20.00
138	Neifi Perez B/Y	10.00
139	Eric Karros B/X	8.00
140	Alex Fernandez B/X	6.00
141	Jason Dickson B/X	6.00
142	Lance Johnson B/X	6.00
143	Ray Lankford B/Y	10.00
144	Sammy Sosa G/Y	75.00
145	Eric Young B/Y	10.00
146	Bubba Trammell S/Y	15.00
147	Todd Walker S/Y	20.00
148	Mo Vaughn S/X (Curtain Calls)	15.00
149	Jeff Bagwell S/X (Curtain Calls)	25.00
150	Kenny Lofton S/X (Curtain Calls)	15.00
151	Raul Mondesi S/X (Curtain Calls)	10.00
152	Mike Piazza S/X (Curtain Calls)	40.00
153	Chipper Jones S/X (Curtain Calls)	40.00
154	Larry Walker S/X (Curtain Calls)	10.00
155	Greg Maddux S/X (Curtain Calls)	40.00
156	Ken Griffey Jr. S/X (Curtain Calls)	75.00
157	Frank Thomas S/X (Curtain Calls)	60.00
158	Darin Erstad B/Z (Gold Leaf Stars)	40.00
159	Roberto Alomar B/Y (Gold Leaf Stars)	20.00
160	Albert Belle G/Y (Gold Leaf Stars)	25.00
161	Jim Thome G/Y (Gold Leaf Stars)	18.00
162	Tony Clark G/Y (Gold Leaf Stars)	18.00
163	Chuck Knoblauch B/Y (Gold Leaf Stars)	20.00
164	Derek Jeter G/Z (Gold Leaf Stars)	100.00
165	Alex Rodriguez G/Z (Gold Leaf Stars)	100.00
166	Tony Gwynn B/X (Gold Leaf Stars)	35.00

167	Roger Clemens G/Z (Gold Leaf Stars)	60.00
168	Barry Larkin B/Y (Gold Leaf Stars)	20.00
169	Andres Galarraga B/Y (Gold Leaf Stars)	20.00
170	Vladimir Guerrero G/Z (Gold Leaf Stars)	50.00
171	Mark McGwire B/Z (Gold Leaf Stars)	100.00
172	Barry Bonds B/Z (Gold Leaf Stars)	40.00
173	Juan Gonzalez G/Z (Gold Leaf Stars)	75.00
174	Andruw Jones G/Z (Gold Leaf Stars)	75.00
175	Paul Molitor B/X (Gold Leaf Stars)	15.00
176	Hideo Nomo B/Z (Gold Leaf Stars)	80.00
177	Cal Ripken Jr. B/X (Gold Leaf Stars)	50.00
178	Brad Fullmer S/Z (Gold Leaf Rookies)	35.00
179	Jaret Wright G/Z (Gold Leaf Rookies)	80.00
180	Bobby Estalella B/Y (Gold Leaf Rookies)	10.00
181	Ben Grieve G/X (Gold Leaf Rookies)	30.00
182	Paul Konerko G/Z (Gold Leaf Rookies)	50.00
183	David Ortiz G/Z (Gold Leaf Rookies)	30.00
184	Todd Helton G/X (Gold Leaf Rookies)	15.00
185	Juan Encarnacion G/Z (Gold Leaf Rookies)	30.00
186	Miguel Tejada G/Z (Gold Leaf Rookies)	40.00
187	Jacob Cruz B/Y (Gold Leaf Rookies)	15.00
188	Mark Kotsay G/Z (Gold Leaf Rookies)	35.00
189	Fernando Tatis S/Z (Gold Leaf Rookies)	25.00
190	Ricky Ledee S/Y (Gold Leaf Rookies)	20.00
191	Richard Hidalgo S/Y (Gold Leaf Rookies)	10.00
192	Richie Sexson S/Y (Gold Leaf Rookies)	10.00
193	Luis Ordaz B/X (Gold Leaf Rookies)	6.00
194	Eli Marrero S/Z (Gold Leaf Rookies)	20.00
195	Livan Hernandez S/Z (Gold Leaf Rookies)	30.00
196	Homer Bush B/X (Gold Leaf Rookies)	6.00
197	Raul Ibanez B/X (Gold Leaf Rookies)	6.00
198	Checklist(Nomar Garciaparra B/X)	40.00
199	Checklist(Scott Rolen B/X)	30.00
200	Checklist(Jose Cruz Jr. B/X)	40.00

1998 Leaf Heading for the Hall

This 20-card insert features players destined for the Hall of Fame. The set is sequentially numbered to 3,500.

Modern cards have little collector value in conditions lower than Mint. Figure NM cards at 75% of values shown; EX cards at 40%.

Values shown reflect the market as of January, 1999. On-field performances of current players in the 1999 baseball season are not factored in.

MT

Complete Set (20):		250.00
Common Player:		6.00
1	Roberto Alomar	8.00
2	Jeff Bagwell	15.00
3	Albert Belle	10.00
4	Wade Boggs	6.00
5	Barry Bonds	10.00
6	Roger Clemens	15.00
7	Juan Gonzalez	20.00
8	Ken Griffey Jr.	35.00
9	Tony Gwynn	20.00
10	Barry Larkin	6.00
11	Kenny Lofton	10.00
12	Greg Maddux	25.00
13	Mark McGwire	40.00
14	Paul Molitor	8.00
15	Eddie Murray	6.00
16	Mike Piazza	25.00
17	Cal Ripken Jr.	30.00
18	Ivan Rodriguez	10.00
19	Ryne Sandberg	10.00
20	Frank Thomas	25.00

1998 Leaf State Representatives

This 30-card insert features top players. The background has a picture of the state in which he plays. "State Representatives" is printed at the top with the player's name at the bottom. This set is sequentially numbered to 5,000.

		MT
Complete Set (30):		250.00
Common Player:		4.00
1	Ken Griffey Jr.	25.00
2	Frank Thomas	15.00
3	Alex Rodriguez	15.00

4	Cal Ripken Jr.	20.00
5	Chipper Jones	15.00
6	Andruw Jones	12.00
7	Scott Rolen	12.00
8	Nomar Garciaparra	15.00
9	Tim Salmon	6.00
10	Manny Ramirez	8.00
11	Jose Cruz Jr.	10.00
12	Vladimir Guerrero	10.00
13	Tino Martinez	6.00
14	Larry Walker	6.00
15	Mo Vaughn	8.00
16	Jim Thome	6.00
17	Tony Clark	6.00
18	Derek Jeter	15.00
19	Juan Gonzalez	12.00
20	Jeff Bagwell	10.00
21	Ivan Rodriguez	8.00
22	Mark McGwire	30.00
23	David Justice	4.00
24	Chuck Knoblauch	6.00
25	Andy Pettitte	6.00
26	Raul Mondesi	6.00
27	Randy Johnson	6.00
28	Greg Maddux	15.00
29	Bernie Williams	6.00
30	Rusty Greer	4.00

1998 Leaf Statistical Standouts

This 24-card insert features players with impressive statistics. The cards have a horizontal layout and the feel of leather. The background has a ball and glove with the player's facsimile signature on the ball. Statistical Standouts is numbered to 2,500.

		MT
Complete Set (24):		600.00
Common Player:		10.00
1	Frank Thomas	40.00
2	Ken Griffey Jr.	60.00
3	Alex Rodriguez	40.00
4	Mike Piazza	40.00
5	Greg Maddux	40.00
6	Cal Ripken Jr.	50.00
7	Chipper Jones	40.00
8	Juan Gonzalez	30.00
9	Jeff Bagwell	25.00
10	Mark McGwire	60.00
11	Tony Gwynn	30.00
12	Mo Vaughn	15.00
13	Nomar Garciaparra	40.00
14	Jose Cruz Jr.	25.00
15	Vladimir Guerrero	20.00
16	Scott Rolen	30.00
17	Andy Pettitte	12.00
18	Randy Johnson	12.00
19	Larry Walker	10.00
20	Kenny Lofton	15.00
21	Tony Clark	12.00
22	David Justice	12.00
23	Derek Jeter	35.00
24	Barry Bonds	15.00

Modern cards have little collector value in conditions lower than Mint. Figure NM cards at 75% of values shown; EX cards at 40%.

M

1996 Metal Universe

Certainly one of the most unusual baseball card issues of its era, Fleer's Metal Universe set is distinguished by its colored, textured metallic-foil backgrounds created by comic book illustrators. The effects range from gaudy to grotesque. Glossy player action photos are featured on front, with a steel-colored metallic strip at bottom carrying set and player ID. Conventionally printed backs have a heavy-metal theme with a color player portrait photo at top and a few stats and person data around. The issue was sold in hobby and retail packaging with the basic hobby pack containing eight cards at a suggested retail price of $2.49. Several insert sets were included, along with a platinum parallel edition of the player cards.

		MT
Complete Set (250):		30.00
Common Player:		.10
Wax Box:		40.00
1	Roberto Alomar	1.00
2	Brady Anderson	.20
3	Bobby Bonilla	.15
4	Chris Holles	.10
5	Ben McDonald	.10
6	Mike Mussina	.40
7	Randy Myers	.10
8	Rafael Palmeiro	.20
9	Cal Ripken Jr.	2.50
10	B.J. Surhoff	.10
11	Luis Alicea	.10
12	Jose Canseco	.30
13	Roger Clemens	1.00
14	Wil Cordero	.10
15	Tom Gordon	.10
16	Mike Greenwell	.10
17	Tim Naehring	.10
18	Troy O'Leary	.10
19	Mike Stanley	.10
20	John Valentin	.15
21	Mo Vaughn	.75
22	Tim Wakefield	.10
23	Garret Anderson	.15
24	Chili Davis	.12
25	Gary DiSarcina	.10
26	Jim Edmonds	.20
27	Chuck Finley	.10

28	Todd Greene	.10
29	Mark Langston	.10
30	Troy Percival	.10
31	Tony Phillips	.15
32	Tim Salmon	.30
33	Lee Smith	.12
34	J.T. Snow	.15
35	Ray Durham	.10
36	Alex Fernandez	.15
37	Ozzie Guillen	.10
38	Roberto Hernandez	.10
39	Lyle Mouton	.10
40	Frank Thomas	2.50
41	Robin Ventura	.15
42	Sandy Alomar	.15
43	Carlos Baorga	.15
44	Albert Belle	.75
45	Orel Hershiser	.12
46	Kenny Lofton	.75
47	Dennis Martinez	.12
48	Jack McDowell	.10
49	Jose Mesa	.12
50	Eddie Murray	.40
51	Charles Nagy	.10
52	Manny Ramirez	.75
53	Julian Tavarez	.10
54	Jim Thome	.50
55	Omar Vizquel	.10
56	Chad Curtis	.10
57	Cecil Fielder	.20
58	John Flaherty	.10
59	Travis Fryman	.10
60	Chris Gomez	.10
61	Felipe Lira	.10
62	Kevin Appier	.10
63	Johnny Damon	.15
64	Tom Goodwin	.10
65	Mark Gubicza	.10
66	Jeff Montgomery	.10
67	Jon Nunnally	.10
68	Ricky Bones	.10
69	Jeff Cirillo	.10
70	John Jaha	.10
71	Dave Nilsson	.10
72	Joe Oliver	.10
73	Kevin Seitzer	.10
74	Greg Vaughn	.10
75	Marty Cordova	.20
76	Chuck Knoblauch	.20
77	Pat Meares	.10
78	Paul Molitor	.40
79	Pedro Munoz	.10
80	Kirby Puckett	1.25
81	Brad Radke	.10
82	Scott Stahoviak	.10
83	Matt Walbeck	.10
84	Wade Boggs	.25
85	David Cone	.10
86	Joe Girardi	.10
87	Derek Jeter	1.50
88	Jim Leyritz	.10
89	Tino Martinez	.15
90	Don Mattingly	1.50
91	Paul O'Neill	.10
92	Andy Pettitte	1.25
93	Tim Raines	.15
94	Kenny Rogers	.10
95	Ruben Sierra	.12
96	John Wetteland	.10
97	Bernie Williams	.60
98	Geronimo Berroa	.15
99	Dennis Eckersley	.12
100	Brent Gates	.10
101	Mark McGwire	4.00
102	Steve Ontiveros	.10
103	Terry Steinbach	.10
104	Jay Buhner	.20
105	Vince Coleman	.10
106	Joey Cora	.10
107	Ken Griffey Jr.	3.00
108	Randy Johnson	.40
109	Edgar Martinez	.12
110	Alex Rodriguez	3.00
111	Paul Sorrento	.10
112	Will Clark	.30
113	Juan Gonzalez	1.25
114	Rusty Greer	.10
115	Dean Palmer	.10
116	Ivan Rodriguez	.75
117	Mickey Tettleton	.10
118	Joe Carter	.20
119	Alex Gonzalez	.15
120	Shawn Green	.15
121	Erik Hanson	.10
122	Pat Hentgen	.10
123	*Sandy Martinez*	.10

124	Otis Nixon	.10
125	John Olerud	.15
126	Steve Avery	.10
127	Tom Glavine	.20
128	Marquis Grissom	.15
129	Chipper Jones	2.00
130	David Justice	.20
131	Ryan Klesko	.60
132	Mark Lemke	.10
133	Javier Lopez	.20
134	Greg Maddux	2.00
135	Fred McGriff	.50
136	John Smoltz	.25
137	Mark Wohlers	.10
138	Frank Castillo	.10
139	Shawon Dunston	.15
140	Luis Gonzalez	.10
141	Mark Grace	.20
142	Brian McRae	.10
143	Jaime Navarro	.10
144	Rey Sanchez	.10
145	Ryne Sandberg	.90
146	Sammy Sosa	2.00
147	Bret Boone	.10
148	Curtis Goodwin	.10
149	Barry Larkin	.25
150	Hal Morris	.10
151	Reggie Sanders	.15
152	Pete Schourek	.10
153	John Smiley	.10
154	Dante Bichette	.30
155	Vinny Castilla	.15
156	Andres Galarraga	.20
157	Bret Saberhagen	.10
158	Bill Swift	.10
159	Larry Walker	.40
160	Walt Weiss	.10
161	**Kurt Abbott**	.10
162	John Burkett	.10
163	Greg Colbrunn	.10
164	Jeff Conine	.15
165	Chris Hammond	.10
166	Charles Johnson	.15
167	Al Leiter	.10
168	Pat Rapp	.10
169	Gary Sheffield	.50
170	Quilvio Veras	.10
171	Devon White	.10
172	Jeff Bagwell	1.25
173	Derek Bell	.15
174	Sean Berry	.10
175	Craig Biggio	.15
176	Doug Drabek	.10
177	Tony Eusebio	.10
178	Brian Hunter	.10
179	Orlando Miller	.10
180	Shane Reynolds	.10
181	Mike Blowers	.10
182	Roger Cedeno	.10
183	Eric Karros	.15
184	Ramon Martinez	.12
185	Raul Mondesi	.25
186	Hideo Nomo	.75
187	Mike Piazza	2.00
188	Moises Alou	.15
189	Yamil Benitez	.10
190	Darrin Fletcher	.10
191	Cliff Floyd	.10
192	Pedro J. Martinez	.10
193	Carlos Perez	.10
194	David Segui	.10
195	Tony Tarasco	.10
196	Rondell White	.15
197	Edgardo Alfonzo	.10
198	Rico Brogna	.10
199	Carl Everett	.10
200	Todd Hundley	.20
201	Jason Isringhausen	.20
202	Lance Johnson	.10
203	Bobby Jones	.10
204	Jeff Kent	.10
205	Bill Pulsipher	.15
206	Jose Vizcaino	.10
207	Ricky Bottalico	.10
208	Darren Daulton	.10
209	Lenny Dykstra	.12
210	Jim Eisenreich	.10
211	Gregg Jefferies	.15
212	Mickey Morandini	.10
213	Heathcliff Slocumb	.10
214	Jay Bell	.10
215	Carlos Garcia	.10
216	Jeff King	.10
217	Al Martin	.10
218	Orlando Merced	.10
219	Dan Miceli	.10

220	Denny Neagle	.10
221	Andy Benes	.12
222	Royce Clayton	.10
223	Gary Gaetti	.12
224	Ron Gant	.20
225	Bernard Gilkey	.15
226	Brian Jordan	.20
227	Ray Lankford	.15
228	John Mabry	.10
229	Ozzie Smith	.40
230	Todd Stottlemyre	.10
231	Andy Ashby	.10
232	Brad Ausmus	.10
233	Ken Caminiti	.20
234	Steve Finley	.10
235	Tony Gwynn	1.25
236	Joey Hamilton	.15
237	Rickey Henderson	.20
238	Trevor Hoffman	.10
239	Wally Joyner	.15
240	Rod Beck	.10
241	Barry Bonds	.75
242	Glenallen Hill	.10
243	Stan Javier	.10
244	Mark Leiter	.10
245	Deion Sanders	.25
246	William VanLandingham	.10
247	Matt Williams	.25
248	Checklist	.10
249	Checklist	.10
250	Checklist	.10

1996 Metal Universe Platinum Edition

One of the eight cards in each pack of Fleer Metal baseball is a Platinum Edition parallel insert. Each of the 247 player cards (no checklists) in this special version has the textured foil background rendered only in silver. The second line of the logo/ID strip at bottom also identifies the card as part of the Platinum Edition.

	MT
Complete Set (247):	200.00
Common Player:	.50

(Star cards valued at 2X-3X corresponding cards in regular Fleer Metal issue)

1996 Metal Universe Heavy Metal

Some of the game's biggest hitters are included in this insert set. Action photos of players at bat are set on a silver-foil background on front. Backs have a close-up photo down one side, with praise for the player's power potential down the other. The Heavy Metal inserts can be expected to turn up at an average rate of one per eight packs.

		MT
Complete Set (10):		40.00
Common Player:		2.00
1	Albert Belle	2.50
2	Barry Bonds	2.50
3	Juan Gonzalez	5.00
4	Ken Griffey Jr.	10.00
5	Mark McGwire	12.00
6	Mike Piazza	6.00
7	Sammy Sosa	8.00
8	Frank Thomas	8.00
9	Mo Vaughn	2.50
10	Matt Williams	2.00

1996 Metal Universe Mining for Gold

Available only in retail packs, at an average rate of one per dozen packs, the Mining for Gold insert series focuses on 1995's top rookies. Fronts have player action photos frame and backgrounded with several different gold tones in etched metal foil. Backs are conventionally printed, carrying on the same format with a portrait photo and a few words about the player.

		MT
Complete Set (12):		75.00
Common Player:		2.00
1	Yamil Benitez	2.00
2	Marty Cordova	5.00
3	Shawn Green	2.00
4	Todd Greene	2.00
5	Brian Hunter	2.00
6	Derek Jeter	20.00
7	Charles Johnson	2.00
8	Chipper Jones	20.00
9	Hideo Nomo	10.00
10	Alex Ochoa	3.00
11	Andy Pettitte	9.00
12	Quilvio Veras	2.00

1996 Metal Universe Mother Lode

Medieval designs rendered in textured silver-foil on a plain white background are the setting for the color player photos in this hobby-only insert. Backs also have a silver and white background along with another player photo and some kind of words about his skills. The cards are found at an average rate of one per 12 packs.

		MT
Complete Set (12):		40.00
Common Player:		2.00
1	Barry Bonds	4.00
2	Jim Edmonds	1.50
3	Ken Griffey Jr.	15.00
4	Kenny Lofton	4.00
5	Raul Mondesi	2.00
6	Rafael Palmeiro	2.00
7	Manny Ramirez	4.00
8	Cal Ripken Jr.	12.00
9	Tim Salmon	2.00
10	Ryne Sandberg	4.00
11	Frank Thomas	12.00
12	Matt Williams	2.00

1996 Metal Universe Platinum Portraits

Close-up color photos on a plain metallic-foil background are featured in this insert set. The checklist is heavy in rookie and sophomore players, who are featured in an action photo on back, with a few career details. Platinum Portraits inserts are found in every fourth pack, on average.

		MT
Complete Set (10):		15.00
Common Player:		.50
1	Garret Anderson	.50
2	Marty Cordova	.75
3	Jim Edmonds	.75
4	Jason Isringhausen	.75
5	Chipper Jones	6.00

6	Ryan Klesko	3.00
7	Hideo Nomo	3.00
8	Carlos Perez	.50
9	Manny Ramirez	3.00
10	Rondell White	.75

1996 Metal Universe Titanium

A huge purple-highlighted silver baseball in a star-studded night sky is the background for the action photos of the game's biggest names in this insert series. Backs have a second, more up-close, photo and a few words about the player. Titanium inserts are found in Metal Universe packs at an average rate of one per 24 packs.

		MT
Complete Set (10):		100.00
Common Player:		4.00
1	Albert Belle	6.00
2	Barry Bonds	6.00
3	Ken Griffey Jr.	25.00
4	Tony Gwynn	12.00
5	Greg Maddux	15.00
6	Mike Piazza	15.00
7	Cal Ripken Jr.	20.00
8	Frank Thomas	20.00
9	Mo Vaughn	6.00
10	Matt Williams	4.00

1997 Metal Universe

Metal Universe Baseball arrived in a 250-card set, including three checklists. Each card is printed on 100-percent etched foil with

"comic book" art full-bleed backgrounds, with the player's name, team, position and the Metal Universe logo near the bottom of the card. Backs contain another player photo and key statistics. Metal Universe sold in eight-card packs and contained six different insert sets. They included: Blast Furnace, Magnetic Field, Mining for Gold, Mother Lode, Platinum Portraits and Titanium.

		MT
Complete Set (250):		35.00
Common Player:		.10
Wax Box:		45.00
1	Roberto Alomar	.60
2	Brady Anderson	.15
3	Rocky Coppinger	.10
4	Chris Hoiles	.10
5	Eddie Murray	.40
6	Mike Mussina	.50
7	Rafael Palmeiro	.20
8	Cal Ripken Jr.	2.50
9	B.J. Surhoff	.10
10	Brant Brown	.10
11	Mark Grace	.20
12	Brian McRae	.10
13	Jaime Navarro	.10
14	Ryne Sandberg	.75
15	Sammy Sosa	1.50
16	Amaury Telemaco	.10
17	Steve Trachsel	.10
18	Darren Bragg	.10
19	Jose Canseco	.25
20	Roger Clemens	1.00
21	Nomar Garciaparra	2.00
22	Tom Gordon	.10
23	Tim Naehring	.10
24	Mike Stanley	.10
25	John Valentin	.10
26	Mo Vaughn	.75
27	Jermaine Dye	.20
28	Tom Glavine	.20
29	Marquis Grissom	.10
30	Andruw Jones	1.50
31	Chipper Jones	2.00
32	Ryan Klesko	.50
33	Greg Maddux	2.00
34	Fred McGriff	.30
35	John Smoltz	.25
36	Garret Anderson	.10
37	George Arias	.10
38	Gary DiSarcina	.10
39	Jim Edmonds	.10
40	Darin Erstad	1.00
41	Chuck Finley	.10
42	Troy Percival	.10
43	Tim Salmon	.25
44	Bret Boone	.10
45	Jeff Brantley	.10
46	Eric Davis	.10
47	Barry Larkin	.25
48	Hal Morris	.10
49	Mark Portugal	.10
50	Reggie Sanders	.10
51	John Smiley	.10
52	Wilson Alvarez	.10
53	Harold Baines	.10
54	James Baldwin	.10
55	Albert Belle	.75
56	Mike Cameron	.10
57	Ray Durham	.10
58	Alex Fernandez	.10
59	Roberto Hernandez	.10
60	Tony Phillips	.10
61	Frank Thomas	2.50
62	Robin Ventura	.10
63	Jeff Cirillo	.10
64	Jeff D'Amico	.10
65	John Jaha	.10
66	Scott Karl	.10
67	Ben McDonald	.10
68	Marc Newfield	.10
69	Dave Nilsson	.10
70	Jose Valentin	.10
71	Dante Bichette	.25
72	Ellis Burks	.10
73	Vinny Castilla	.10
74	Andres Galarraga	.20
75	Kevin Ritz	.10
76	Larry Walker	.40
77	Walt Weiss	.10

78	Jamey Wright	.10
79	Eric Young	.10
80	Julio Franco	.10
81	Orel Hershiser	.10
82	Kenny Lofton	.75
83	Jack McDowell	.20
84	Jose Mesa	.10
85	Charles Nagy	.10
86	Manny Ramirez	.75
87	Jim Thome	.40
88	Omar Vizquel	.10
89	Matt Williams	.25
90	Kevin Appier	.10
91	Johnny Damon	.10
92	Chili Davis	.10
93	Tom Goodwin	.10
94	Keith Lockhart	.10
95	Jeff Montgomery	.10
96	Craig Paquette	.10
97	Jose Rosado	.10
98	Michael Tucker	.10
99	Wilton Guerrero	.20
100	Todd Hollandsworth	.10
101	Eric Karros	.10
102	Ramon Martinez	.10
103	Raul Mondesi	.25
104	Hideo Nomo	.75
105	Mike Piazza	2.00
106	Ismael Valdes	.10
107	Todd Worrell	.10
108	Tony Clark	.60
109	Travis Fryman	.10
110	Bob Higginson	.10
111	Mark Lewis	.10
112	Melvin Nieves	.10
113	Justin Thompson	.10
114	Wade Boggs	.20
115	David Cone	.15
116	Cecil Fielder	.20
117	Dwight Gooden	.10
118	Derek Jeter	1.75
119	Tino Martinez	.40
120	Paul O'Neill	.10
121	Andy Pettitte	.75
122	Mariano Rivera	.20
123	Darryl Strawberry	.10
124	John Wetteland	.10
125	Bernie Williams	.40
126	Tony Batista	.10
127	Geronimo Berroa	.10
128	Scott Brosius	.10
129	Jason Giambi	.10
130	Jose Herrera	.10
131	Mark McGwire	4.00
132	John Wasdin	.10
133	Bob Abreu	.10
134	Jeff Bagwell	1.25
135	Derek Bell	.10
136	Craig Biggio	.10
137	Brian Hunter	.10
138	Darryl Kile	.10
139	Orlando Miller	.10
140	Shane Reynolds	.10
141	Billy Wagner	.10
142	Donne Wall	.10
143	Jay Buhner	.20
144	Jeff Fassero	.10
145	Ken Griffey Jr.	3.00
146	Sterling Hitchcock	.10
147	Randy Johnson	.40
148	Edgar Martinez	.10
149	Alex Rodriguez	3.00
149p	Alex Rodriguez (overprinted "PROMOTIONAL SAMPLE")	5.00
150	Paul Sorrento	.10
151	Dan Wilson	.10
152	Moises Alou	.10
153	Darrin Fletcher	.10
154	Cliff Floyd	.10
155	Mark Grudzielanek	.10
156	Vladimir Guerrero	1.00
157	Mike Lansing	.10
158	Pedro Martinez	.10
159	Henry Rodriguez	.10
160	Rondell White	.10
161	Will Clark	.25
162	Juan Gonzalez	1.25
163	Rusty Greer	.10
164	Ken Hill	.10
165	Mark McLemore	.10
166	Dean Palmer	.10
167	Roger Pavlik	.10
168	Ivan Rodriguez	.75
169	Mickey Tettleton	.10
170	Bobby Bonilla	.10

171	Kevin Brown	.10
172	Greg Colbrunn	.10
173	Jeff Conine	.10
174	Jim Eisenreich	.10
175	Charles Johnson	.10
176	Al Leiter	.10
177	Robb Nen	.10
178	Edgar Renteria	.20
179	Gary Sheffield	.40
180	Devon White	.10
181	Joe Carter	.20
182	Carlos Delgado	.10
183	Alex Gonzalez	.10
184	Shawn Green	.10
185	Juan Guzman	.10
186	Pat Hentgen	.10
187	Orlando Merced	.10
188	John Olerud	.10
189	Robert Perez	.10
190	Ed Sprague	.10
191	Mark Clark	.10
192	John Franco	.10
193	Bernard Gilkey	.10
194	Todd Hundley	.10
195	Lance Johnson	.10
196	Bobby Jones	.10
197	Alex Ochoa	.10
198	Rey Ordonez	.20
199	Paul Wilson	.10
200	Ricky Bottalico	.10
201	Gregg Jefferies	.10
202	Wendell Magee Jr.	.10
203	Mickey Morandini	.10
204	Ricky Otero	.10
205	Scott Rolen	1.25
206	Benito Santiago	.10
207	Curt Schilling	.10
208	Rich Becker	.10
209	Marty Cordova	.10
210	Chuck Knoblauch	.10
211	Pat Meares	.10
212	Paul Molitor	.40
213	Frank Rodriguez	.10
214	Terry Steinbach	.10
215	Todd Walker	.60
216	Andy Ashby	.10
217	Ken Caminiti	.25
218	Steve Finley	.10
219	Tony Gwynn	1.00
220	Joey Hamilton	.10
221	Rickey Henderson	.10
222	Trevor Hoffman	.10
223	Wally Joyner	.10
224	Scott Sanders	.10
225	Fernando Valenzuela	.10
226	Greg Vaughn	.10
227	Alan Benes	.10
228	Andy Benes	.10
229	Dennis Eckersley	.10
230	Ron Gant	.10
231	Brian Jordan	.10
232	Ray Lankford	.10
233	John Mabry	.10
234	Tom Pagnozzi	.10
235	Todd Stottlemyre	.10
236	Jermaine Allensworth	.10
237	Francisco Cordova	.15
238	Jason Kendall	.10
239	Jeff King	.10
240	Al Martin	.10
241	Rod Beck	.10
242	Barry Bonds	.75
243	Shawn Estes	.10
244	Mark Gardner	.10
245	Glenallen Hill	.10
246	Bill Mueller	.10
247	J.T. Snow	.10
248	Checklist	.10
249	Checklist	.10
250	Checklist	.10

		MT
Complete Set (12):		150.00
Common Player:		3.00
1	Jeff Bagwell	12.00
2	Albert Belle	8.00
3	Barry Bonds	7.00
4	Andres Galarraga	4.00
5	Juan Gonzalez	15.00
6	Ken Griffey Jr.	30.00
7	Todd Hundley	3.00
8	Mark McGwire	35.00
9	Mike Piazza	20.00
10	Alex Rodriguez	25.00
11	Frank Thomas	25.00
12	Mo Vaughn	8.00

1997 Metal Universe Magnetic Field

Magnetic Field inserts are printed in a horizontal format with prismatic foil backgrounds. This 10-card insert was found every 12 packs of Metal Universe.

		MT
Complete Set (10):		40.00
Common Player:		1.00
1	Roberto Alomar	2.00
2	Jeff Bagwell	4.00
3	Barry Bonds	2.50
4	Ken Griffey Jr.	10.00
5	Derek Jeter	5.00
6	Kenny Lofton	2.50
7	Edgar Renteria	1.00
8	Cal Ripken Jr.	8.00
9	Alex Rodriguez	10.00
10	Matt Williams	1.50

1997 Metal Universe Blast Furnace

Blast Furnace inserts were found only in hobby packs, at a rate of one per 48 packs. The 12-card set was printed on a red-tinted plastic, with the words "Blast Furnace" near the bottom in gold foil with a fire-like border.

1997 Metal Universe Mining for Gold

Mining for Gold was a 10-card insert that featured some of baseball's brightest stars on a die-cut "ingot" design with pearlized gold coating. This insert was found every nine packs.

		MT
Complete Set (10):		20.00
Common Player:		.75
1	Bob Abreu	1.00
2	Kevin Brown	.75
3	Nomar Garciaparra	5.00
4	Vladimir Guerrero	2.50
5	Wilton Guerrero	1.25
6	Andruw Jones	4.00
7	Curt Lyons	.75
8	Neifi Perez	.75
9	Scott Rolen	3.00
10	Todd Walker	2.00

1997 Metal Universe Mother Lode

Mother lode was the most difficult insert out of Metal Universe with a one per 288 pack insertion ratio. Each card in this 10-card inert was printed on etched foil with a plant-type monument in back of the player.

		MT
Complete Set (12):		500.00
Common Player:		15.00
1	Roberto Alomar	20.00
2	Jeff Bagwell	30.00
3	Barry Bonds	25.00
4	Ken Griffey Jr.	100.00
5	Andruw Jones	25.00
6	Chipper Jones	60.00
7	Kenny Lofton	25.00
8	Mike Piazza	60.00
9	Cal Ripken Jr.	75.00
10	Alex Rodriguez	60.00
11	Frank Thomas	60.00
12	Matt Williams	15.00

1997 Metal Universe Platinum Portraits

Each card in the Platinum Portraits insert is printed on a background of platinum-colored etched foil. The 10-card set includes some of the top prospects and rising stars in baseball, and is included every 36 packs.

		MT
Complete Set (10):		60.00
Common Player:		2.50
1	James Baldwin	2.50
2	Jermaine Dye	2.00
3	Todd Hollandsworth	2.50
4	Derek Jeter	15.00
5	Chipper Jones	15.00
6	Jason Kendall	2.50
7	Rey Ordonez	3.00
8	Andy Pettitte	6.00
9	Edgar Renteria	4.00
10	Alex Rodriguez	25.00

1997 Metal Universe Titanium

These retail exclusive inserts include 10 cards and were found every 24 packs. Each card is die-cut on the top-left and bottom-right corner with a silver foil background. Titanium includes some of the most popular players in baseball on cards that are also embossed.

		MT
Complete Set (10):		90.00
Common Player:		2.00
1	Jeff Bagwell	7.00
2	Albert Belle	4.00
3	Ken Griffey Jr.	18.00
4	Chipper Jones	10.00
5	Greg Maddux	10.00
6	Mark McGwire	18.00
7	Mike Piazza	10.00
8	Cal Ripken Jr.	14.00
9	Alex Rodriguez	15.00
10	Frank Thomas	15.00

1997 Metal Universe Emerald Autograph Redemption

Six different young stars were featured in this insert, which was found every 480 hobby packs of Metal Universe. The cards are similar to regular-issue cards, but have green foil highlights. Redemption cards are numbered AU1-AU6. The redemption period expired Jan. 15, 1998.

		MT
Complete Set (6):		200.00
Common Player:		12.50
AU1	Darin Erstad	30.00
AU2	Todd Hollandsworth	15.00
AU3	Alex Ochoa	12.50
AU4	Alex Rodriguez	100.00
AU5	Scott Rolen	35.00
AU6	Todd Walker	20.00

1997 Metal Universe Emerald Autographs

Six different young stars were featured in this insert, which was found every 480 hobby packs of Metal Universe. The cards are similar to regular-issue cards, but have a green foil finish and autograph on the front. Redemption cards are numbered AU1-AU6, the autographed cards have a notation on back, "Certified Emerald Autograph Card".

	MT
Complete Set (6):	400.00
Common Autograph:	25.00
AU1 Darin Erstad	60.00
AU2 Todd Hollandsworth	30.00
AU3 Alex Ochoa	25.00
AU4 Alex Rodriguez	200.00
AU5 Scott Rolen	70.00
AU6 Todd Walker	40.00

1998 Metal Universe

This 220-card single series release captured players over a foil etched, art background that related in some way to them or the city they played in. Metal Universe included a 15-card Hardball Galaxy subset and dealers and media were given an Alex Rodriguez promo card that was identical the base card except for the words "Promotional Sample" written across the back. The set arrived with a parallel called Precious Metal Gems, and included the fol-

lowing insert sets: All-Galactic Team, Diamond Heroes, Platinum Portraits, Titanium and Universal Language.

	MT
Complete Set (220):	30.00
Common Player:	.10
Wax Box:	55.00
1 Jose Cruz Jr.	1.00
2 Jeff Abbott	.10
3 Rafael Palmeiro	.25
4 Ivan Rodriguez	.75
5 Jaret Wright	.75
6 Derek Bell	.10
7 Chuck Finley	.10
8 Travis Fryman	.10
9 Randy Johnson	.50
10 Derrek Lee	.20
11 Bernie Williams	.50
12 Carlos Baerga	.10
13 Ricky Bottalico	.10
14 Ellis Burks	.10
15 Russ Davis	.10
16 Nomar Garciaparra	2.00
17 Joey Hamilton	.10
18 Jason Kendall	.20
19 Darryl Kile	.10
20 Edgardo Alfonzo	.10
21 Moises Alou	.20
22 Bobby Bonilla	.20
23 Jim Edmonds	.20
24 Jose Guillen	.25
25 Chuck Knoblauch	.40
26 Javy Lopez	.20
27 Billy Wagner	.10
28 Kevin Appier	.10
29 Joe Carter	.20
30 Todd Dunwoody	.10
31 Gary Gaetti	.10
32 Juan Gonzalez	1.50
33 Jeffrey Hammonds	.10
34 Roberto Hernandez	.10
35 Dave Nilsson	.10
36 Manny Ramirez	.60
37 Robin Ventura	.20
38 Rondell White	.20
39 Vinny Castilla	.20
40 Will Clark	.25
41 Scott Hatteberg	.10
42 Russ Johnson	.10
43 Ricky Ledee	.50
44 Kenny Lofton	.75
45 Paul Molitor	.50
46 Justin Thompson	.10
47 Craig Biggio	.20
48 Damion Easley	.10
49 Brad Radke	.10
50 Ben Grieve	1.00
51 Mark Bellhorn	.10
52 *Henry Blanco*	.10
53 Mariano Rivera	.20
54 Reggie Sanders	.10
55 Paul Sorrento	.10
56 Terry Steinbach	.10
57 Mo Vaughn	.75
58 Brady Anderson	.20
59 Tom Glavine	.20
60 Sammy Sosa	1.50
61 Larry Walker	.30
62 Rod Beck	.10
63 Jose Canseco	.25
64 Steve Finley	.10
65 Pedro Martinez	.50
66 John Olerud	.20
67 Scott Rolen	1.00
68 Ismael Valdes	.10
69 Andrew Vessel	.10
70 Mark Grudzielanek	.10
71 Eric Karros	.10
72 Jeff Shaw	.10
73 Lou Collier	.10
74 Edgar Martinez	.10
75 Vladimir Guerrero	1.00
76 Paul Konerko	.50
77 Kevin Orie	.10
78 Kevin Polcovich	.10
79 Brett Tomko	.10
80 Jeff Bagwell	1.00
81 Barry Bonds	.75
82 David Justice	.25
83 Hideo Nomo	.60
84 Ryne Sandberg	.75
85 Shannon Stewart	.10
86 Derek Wallace	.10
87 Tony Womack	.10
88 Jason Giambi	.10
89 Mark Grace	.25
90 Pat Hentgen	.10
91 Raul Mondesi	.25
92 Matt Morris	.20
93 Matt Perisho	.10
94 Tim Salmon	.25
95 Jeremi Gonzalez	.10
96 Shawn Green	.10
97 Todd Greene	.10
98 Ruben Rivera	.10
99 Deion Sanders	.20
100 Alex Rodriguez	2.00
101 Will Cunnane	.10
102 Ray Lankford	.10
103 Ryan McGuire	.10
104 Charles Nagy	.10
105 Rey Ordonez	.10
106 Mike Piazza	2.00
107 Tony Saunders	.10
108 Curt Schilling	.20
109 Fernando Tatis	.10
110 Mark McGwire	4.00
111 *David Dellucci*	.50
112 Garret Anderson	.10
113 Shane Bowers	.10
114 David Cone	.20
115 Jeff King	.10
116 Matt Williams	.25
117 Aaron Boone	.10
118 Dennis Eckersley	.20
119 Livan Hernandez	.20
120 Richard Hidalgo	.10
121 Bobby Higginson	.10
122 Tino Martinez	.40
123 Tim Naehring	.10
124 Jose Vidro	.10
125 John Wetteland	.10
126 Jay Bell	.10
127 Albert Belle	.75
128 Marty Cordova	.10
129 Chili Davis	.10
130 Jason Dickson	.10
131 Rusty Greer	.20
132 Hideki Irabu	.40
133 Greg Maddux	2.00
134 Billy Taylor	.10
135 Jim Thome	.50
136 Gerald Williams	.10
137 Jeff Cirillo	.10
138 Delino DeShields	.10
139 Andres Galarraga	.40
140 Willie Greene	.10
141 John Jaha	.10
142 Charles Johnson	.20
143 Ryan Klesko	.40
144 Paul O'Neill	.20
145 Robinson Checo	.10
146 Roberto Alomar	.50
147 Wilson Alvarez	.10
148 Bobby Jones	.10
149 Raul Casanova	.10
150 Andruw Jones	1.00
151 Mike Lansing	.10
152 Mickey Morandini	.10
153 Neifi Perez	.10
154 Pokey Reese	.10
155 Edgar Renteria	.10
156 Eric Young	.10
157 Darin Erstad	1.00
158 Kelvim Escobar	.10
159 Carl Everett	.10
160 Tom Gordon	.10
161 Ken Griffey Jr.	3.00
162 Al Martin	.10
163 Bubba Trammell	.20
164 Carlos Delgado	.10
165 Kevin Brown	.20
166 Ken Caminiti	.20
167 Roger Clemens	1.00
168 Ron Gant	.20
169 Jeff Kent	.10
170 Mike Mussina	.60
171 Dean Palmer	.10
172 Henry Rodriguez	.10
173 Matt Stairs	.10
174 Jay Buhner	.25
175 Frank Thomas	2.50
176 Mike Cameron	.10
177 Johnny Damon	.10
178 Tony Gwynn	1.50
179 John Smoltz	.20
180 B.J. Surhoff	.10
181 Antone Williamson	.10
182 Alan Benes	.20

183	Jeromy Burnitz	.10
184	Tony Clark	.40
185	Shawn Estes	.10
186	Todd Helton	.75
187	Todd Hundley	.10
188	Chipper Jones	2.00
189	Mark Kotsay	.25
190	Barry Larkin	.25
191	Mike Lieberthal	.10
192	Andy Pettitte	.50
193	Gary Sheffield	.30
194	Jeff Suppan	.10
195	Mark Wohlers	.10
196	Dante Bichette	.25
197	Trevor Hoffman	.10
198	J.T. Snow	.20
199	Derek Jeter	2.00
200	Cal Ripken Jr.	2.50
201	*Steve Woodard*	.40
202	Ray Durham	.10
203	Barry Bonds (Hardball Galaxy)	.40
204	Tony Clark (Hardball Galaxy)	.20
205	Roger Clemens (Hardball Galaxy)	.50
206	Ken Griffey Jr. (Hardball Galaxy)	1.50
207	Tony Gwynn (Hardball Galaxy)	.75
208	Derek Jeter (Hardball Galaxy)	1.00
209	Randy Johnson (Hardball Galaxy)	.20
210	Mark McGwire (Hardball Galaxy)	2.00
211	Hideo Nomo (Hardball Galaxy)	.40
212	Mike Piazza (Hardball Galaxy)	1.00
213	Cal Ripken Jr. (Hardball Galaxy)	1.25
214	Alex Rodriguez (Hardball Galaxy)	1.00
215	Frank Thomas (Hardball Galaxy)	1.25
216	Mo Vaughn (Hardball Galaxy)	.40
217	Larry Walker (Hardball Galaxy)	.15
218	Checklist(Ken Griffey Jr.)	1.00
219	Checklist(Alex Rodriguez)	.60
220	Checklist(Frank Thomas)	.75

1998 Metal Universe All-Galactic Team

This 18-card insert captures players over a planet holofoil background. Cards were inserted one per 192 packs.

		MT
Complete Set (18):		750.00
Common Player:		20.00
1	Ken Griffey Jr.	100.00
2	Frank Thomas	75.00

3	Chipper Jones	60.00
4	Albert Belle	25.00
5	Juan Gonzalez	50.00
6	Jeff Bagwell	30.00
7	Andruw Jones	25.00
8	Cal Ripken Jr.	75.00
9	Derek Jeter	50.00
10	Nomar Garciaparra	60.00
11	Darin Erstad	30.00
12	Greg Maddux	60.00
13	Alex Rodriguez	60.00
14	Mike Piazza	60.00
15	Vladimir Guerrero	25.00
16	Jose Cruz Jr.	25.00
17	Mark McGwire	120.00
18	Scott Rolen	30.00

1998 Metal Universe Diamond Heroes

Diamond Heroes displayed six players in a comic book setting. This insert was seeded one per 18 packs and contained a foil etched image of a Marvel comic in the background.

		MT
Complete Set (6):		35.00
Common Player:		1.50
1	Ken Griffey Jr.	10.00
2	Frank Thomas	8.00
3	Andruw Jones	4.00
4	Alex Rodriguez	6.00
5	Jose Cruz Jr.	4.00
6	Cal Ripken Jr.	8.00

1998 Metal Universe Titanium

This die-cut 15-card insert contained color photos printed on embossed, sculpted cards on etched foil. Titanium inserts were seeded one per 96 packs.

		MT
Complete Set (15):		400.00
Common Player:		8.00
1	Ken Griffey Jr.	50.00
2	Frank Thomas	40.00
3	Chipper Jones	30.00
4	Jose Cruz Jr.	20.00
5	Juan Gonzalez	25.00
6	Scott Rolen	20.00
7	Andruw Jones	20.00
8	Cal Ripken Jr.	40.00
9	Derek Jeter	30.00
10	Nomar Garciaparra	30.00
11	Darin Erstad	15.00
12	Greg Maddux	30.00
13	Alex Rodriguez	30.00
14	Mike Piazza	30.00
15	Vladimir Guerrero	15.00

1998 Metal Universe Universal Language

This 20-card insert features illustration and copy done in the player's native language. Cards were die-cut and inserted one per six packs.

		MT
Complete Set (20):		75.00
Common Player:		1.00
1	Ken Griffey Jr.	10.00
2	Frank Thomas	8.00
3	Chipper Jones	6.00
4	Albert Belle	2.50
5	Juan Gonzalez	5.00
6	Jeff Bagwell	4.00
7	Andruw Jones	4.00
8	Cal Ripken Jr.	8.00
9	Derek Jeter	6.00
10	Nomar Garciaparra	6.00
11	Darin Erstad	3.00
12	Greg Maddux	6.00
13	Alex Rodriguez	6.00
14	Mike Piazza	6.00
15	Vladimir Guerrero	3.00
16	Jose Cruz Jr.	4.00
17	Hideo Nomo	2.50
18	Kenny Lofton	2.50
19	Tony Gwynn	5.00
20	Scott Rolen	5.00

1998 Metal Universe Platinum Portraits

This 12-card insert set featured color portraits of top players highlighted with a platinum-colored etched foil frame over it. Platinum Portraits are seeded one per 360 packs of Metal Universe.

		MT
Complete Set (12):		700.00
Common Player:		25.00
1	Ken Griffey Jr.	120.00
2	Frank Thomas	90.00
3	Chipper Jones	75.00
4	Jose Cruz Jr.	25.00
5	Andruw Jones	30.00
6	Cal Ripken Jr.	90.00
7	Derek Jeter	60.00
8	Darin Erstad	30.00
9	Greg Maddux	75.00
10	Alex Rodriguez	90.00
11	Mike Piazza	75.00
12	Vladimir Guerrero	30.00

1998 Metal Universe Precious Metal Gems

Precious Metal Gems included 217 (220 minus three checklist cards) cards from Metal Universe and were serial numbered to 50 sets. Because there were five Ultimate Metal Gems redemption cards (good for a complete set of Metal Gems) available, only serial numberes 1-45 were found in packs (46-50 were held back for the exchage program).

		MT
Common Player:		20.00
Semistars:		60.00
1	Jose Cruz Jr.	100.00
2	Jeff Abbott	20.00
3	Rafael Palmeiro	40.00
4	Ivan Rodriguez	100.00
5	Jaret Wright	100.00
6	Derek Bell	20.00
7	Chuck Finley	20.00
8	Travis Fryman	30.00
9	Randy Johnson	75.00
10	Derrek Lee	20.00
11	Bernie Williams	75.00
12	Carlos Baerga	20.00
13	Ricky Bottalico	20.00
14	Ellis Burks	20.00
15	Russ Davis	20.00
16	Nomar Garciaparra	250.00
17	Joey Hamilton	20.00
18	Jason Kendall	30.00
19	Darryl Kile	20.00
20	Edgardo Alfonzo	20.00
21	Moises Alou	35.00
22	Bobby Bonilla	30.00
23	Jim Edmonds	30.00
24	Jose Guillen	30.00
25	Chuck Knoblauch	40.00
26	Javy Lopez	30.00
27	Billy Wagner	20.00
28	Kevin Appier	20.00
29	Joe Carter	30.00
30	Todd Dunwoody	20.00
31	Gary Gaetti	20.00
32	Juan Gonzalez	200.00
33	Jeffrey Hammonds	20.00
34	Roberto Hernandez	20.00
35	Dave Nilsson	20.00
36	Manny Ramirez	100.00
37	Robin Ventura	30.00
38	Rondell White	30.00
39	Vinny Castilla	30.00
40	Will Clark	40.00
41	Scott Hatteberg	20.00
42	Russ Johnson	20.00
43	Ricky Ledee	35.00
44	Kenny Lofton	100.00
45	Paul Molitor	75.00
46	Justin Thompson	20.00
47	Craig Biggio	40.00
48	Damion Easley	20.00
49	Brad Radke	20.00
50	Ben Grieve	125.00
51	Mark Bellhorn	20.00
52	*Henry Blanco*	20.00
53	Mariano Rivera	30.00
54	Reggie Sanders	20.00
55	Paul Sorrento	20.00
56	Terry Steinbach	20.00
57	Mo Vaughn	100.00
58	Brady Anderson	25.00
59	Tom Glavine	30.00
60	Sammy Sosa	150.00
61	Larry Walker	60.00
62	Rod Beck	20.00
63	Jose Canseco	40.00
64	Steve Finley	20.00
65	Pedro Martinez	75.00
66	John Olerud	40.00
67	Scott Rolen	150.00
68	Ismael Valdes	20.00
69	Andrew Vessel	20.00
70	Mark Grudzielanek	20.00
71	Eric Karros	30.00
72	Jeff Shaw	20.00
73	Lou Collier	20.00
74	Edgar Martinez	30.00
75	Vladimir Guerrero	100.00
76	Paul Konerko	40.00
77	Kevin Orie	20.00
78	Kevin Polcovich	20.00
79	Brett Tomko	20.00
80	Jeff Bagwell	75.00
81	Barry Bonds	100.00
82	David Justice	40.00
83	Hideo Nomo	75.00
84	Ryne Sandberg	100.00
85	Shannon Stewart	20.00
86	Derek Wallace	20.00
87	Tony Womack	20.00
88	Jason Giambi	20.00
89	Mark Grace	40.00
90	Pat Hentgen	20.00
91	Raul Mondesi	40.00
92	Matt Morris	30.00
93	Matt Perisho	20.00
94	Tim Salmon	40.00
95	Jeremi Gonzalez	20.00
96	Shawn Green	20.00
97	Todd Greene	20.00
98	Ruben Rivera	20.00
99	Deion Sanders	30.00
100	Alex Rodriguez	250.00
101	Will Cunnane	20.00
102	Ray Lankford	20.00
103	Ryan McGuire	20.00
104	Charles Nagy	20.00
105	Rey Ordonez	20.00
106	Mike Piazza	250.00
107	Tony Saunders	20.00
108	Curt Schilling	30.00
109	Fernando Tatis	30.00
110	Mark McGwire	400.00
111	*David Dellucci*	30.00
112	Garret Anderson	20.00
113	Shane Bowers	20.00
114	David Cone	30.00
115	Jeff King	20.00
116	Matt Williams	50.00
117	Aaron Boone	20.00
118	Dennis Eckersley	20.00
119	Livan Hernandez	20.00
120	Richard Hidalgo	20.00
121	Bobby Higginson	20.00
122	Tino Martinez	60.00
123	Tim Naehring	20.00
124	Jose Vidro	20.00
125	John Wetteland	20.00
126	Jay Bell	20.00
127	Albert Belle	100.00
128	Marty Cordova	20.00
129	Chili Davis	20.00
130	Jason Dickson	20.00
131	Rusty Greer	20.00
132	Hideki Irabu	50.00
133	Greg Maddux	250.00
134	Billy Taylor	20.00
135	Jim Thome	60.00
136	Gerald Williams	20.00
137	Jeff Cirillo	20.00
138	Delino DeShields	20.00
139	Andres Galarraga	50.00
140	Willie Greene	20.00
141	John Jaha	20.00
142	Charles Johnson	20.00
143	Ryan Klesko	40.00
144	Paul O'Neill	30.00
145	Robinson Checo	20.00
146	Roberto Alomar	75.00
147	Wilson Alvarez	20.00
148	Bobby Jones	20.00
149	Raul Casanova	20.00
150	Andruw Jones	100.00
151	Mike Lansing	20.00
152	Mickey Morandini	20.00
153	Neifi Perez	20.00
154	Pokey Reese	20.00
155	Edgar Renteria	20.00
156	Eric Young	20.00
157	Darin Erstad	100.00
158	Kelvim Escobar	20.00
159	Carl Everett	20.00
160	Tom Gordon	20.00
161	Ken Griffey Jr.	400.00
162	Al Martin	20.00
163	Bubba Trammell	20.00
164	Carlos Delgado	20.00
165	Kevin Brown	30.00
166	Ken Caminiti	30.00
167	Roger Clemens	150.00
168	Ron Gant	20.00
169	Jeff Kent	20.00
170	Mike Mussina	75.00
171	Dean Palmer	20.00
172	Henry Rodriguez	20.00
173	Matt Stairs	20.00
174	Jay Buhner	40.00
175	Frank Thomas	300.00
176	Mike Cameron	20.00
177	Johnny Damon	20.00
178	Tony Gwynn	200.00
179	John Smoltz	30.00
180	B.J. Surhoff	20.00
181	Antone Williamson	20.00
182	Alan Benes	30.00
183	Jeromy Burnitz	20.00
184	Tony Clark	60.00
185	Shawn Estes	20.00
186	Todd Helton	80.00
187	Todd Hundley	20.00
188	Chipper Jones	225.00
189	Mark Kotsay	30.00
190	Barry Larkin	40.00
191	Mike Lieberthal	20.00
192	Andy Pettitte	60.00
193	Gary Sheffield	50.00

Grading Guide

Mint (MT): A perfect card. Well-centered with all corners sharp and square. No creases, stains, edge nicks, surface marks, yellowing or fading.

Near Mint (NM): A nearly perfect card. At first glance, a NM card appears to be perfect. May be slightly off-center. No surface marks, creases or loss of gloss.

Excellent (EX): Corners are still fairly sharp with only moderate wear. Borders may be off-center. No creases or stains on fronts or backs, but may show slight loss of surface luster.

Very Good (VG): Shows obvious handling. May have rounded corners, minor creases, major gum or wax stains. No major creases, tape marks, writing, etc.

194	Jeff Suppan	20.00
195	Mark Wohlers	20.00
196	Dante Bichette	40.00
197	Trevor Hoffman	20.00
198	J.T. Snow	20.00
199	Derek Jeter	200.00
200	Cal Ripken Jr.	300.00
201	Steve Woodard	30.00
202	Ray Durham	20.00
203	Barry Bonds (Hardball Galaxy)	50.00
204	Tony Clark (Hardball Galaxy)	40.00
205	Roger Clemens (Hardball Galaxy)	75.00
206	Ken Griffey Jr. (Hardball Galaxy)	200.00
207	Tony Gwynn (Hardball Galaxy)	100.00
208	Derek Jeter (Hardball Galaxy)	100.00
209	Randy Johnson (Hardball Galaxy)	40.00
210	Mark McGwire (Hardball Galaxy)	200.00
211	Hideo Nomo (Hardball Galaxy)	40.00
212	Mike Piazza (Hardball Galaxy)	125.00
213	Cal Ripken Jr. (Hardball Galaxy)	150.00
214	Alex Rodriguez (Hardball Galaxy)	125.00
215	Frank Thomas (Hardball Galaxy)	150.00
216	Mo Vaughn (Hardball Galaxy)	50.00
217	Larry Walker (Hardball Galaxy)	30.00

P

1993 Pacific

This set marks the first time a major league set was designed entirely for the Spanish-speaking market. Distribution areas included retail markets in the United States, Mexico, South America and the Caribbean. The cards are glossy and are written in Spanish on both sides. Cards are numbered in alphabetical order by team, beginning with Atlanta. Insert sets are titled Prism (20 cards featuring Spanish players and their accomplishments), Beisbol De Estrella (Stars of Baseball), Hot Players and Amigos (a 30-card set which features two players per card).

		MT
Complete Set (660):		20.00
Complete Series 1 (330):		12.00
Complete Series 2 (330):		8.00
Common Player:		.05
1	Rafael Belliard	.05
2	Sid Bream	.05
3	Francisco Cabrera	.05
4	Marvin Freeman	.05
5	Ron Gant	.15
6	Tom Glavine	.15
7	Brian Hunter	.05
8	Dave Justice	.20
9	Ryan Klesko	.50
10	Melvin Nieves	.05
11	Deion Sanders	.30
12	John Smoltz	.15
13	Mark Wohlers	.05
14	Brady Anderson	.15
15	Glenn Davis	.05
16	Mike Devereaux	.05
17	Leo Gomez	.05
18	Chris Hoiles	.05
19	Chito Martinez	.05
20	Ben McDonald	.05
21	Mike Mussina	.15
22	Gregg Olson	.05
23	Joe Orsulak	.05
24	Cal Ripken, Jr.	1.00
25	David Segui	.05
26	Rick Sutcliffe	.05
27	Wade Boggs	.25
28	Tom Brunansky	.05
29	Ellis Burks	.10
30	Roger Clemens	.40
31	John Dopson	.05
32	John Flaherty	.05
33	Mike Greenwell	.05
34	Tony Pena	.05
35	Carlos Quintana	.05
36	Luis Rivera	.05
37	Mo Vaughn	.40
38	Frank Viola	.05
39	Matt Young	.05
40	Scott Bailes	.05
41	Bert Blyleven	.05
42	Chad Curtis	.10
43	Gary DiSarcina	.05
44	Chuck Finley	.05
45	Mike Fitzgerald	.05
46	Gary Gaetti	.08
47	Rene Gonzales	.05
48	Mark Langston	.05
49	Scott Lewis	.05
50	Luis Polonia	.05
51	Tim Salmon	.50
52	Lee Stevens	.05
53	Steve Buechele	.05
54	Frank Castillo	.05
55	Doug Dascenzo	.05
56	Andre Dawson	.15
57	Shawon Dunston	.12
58	Mark Grace	.15
59	Mike Morgan	.05
60	Luis Salazar	.05
61	Rey Sanchez	.05
62	Ryne Sandberg	.50
63	Dwight Smith	.05
64	Jerome Walton	.05
65	Rick Wilkins	.05
66	Wilson Alvarez	.05
67	George Bell	.05
68	Joey Cora	.05
69	Alex Fernandez	.08
70	Carlton Fisk	.10
71	Craig Grebeck	.05
72	Ozzie Guillen	.05
73	Jack McDowell	.10
74	Scott Radinsky	.05
75	Tim Raines	.08
76	Bobby Thigpen	.05
77	Frank Thomas	2.00
78	Robin Ventura	.15
79	Tom Browning	.05
80	Jacob Brumfield	.05
81	Rob Dibble	.05
82	Bill Doran	.05
83	Billy Hatcher	.05
84	Barry Larkin	.20
85	Hal Morris	.05
86	Joe Oliver	.05
87	Jeff Reed	.05
88	Jose Rijo	.05
89	Bip Roberts	.05
90	Chris Sabo	.05
91	Sandy Alomar, Jr.	.08

92	Brad Arnsberg	.05
93	Carlos Baerga	.20
94	Albert Belle	.60
95	Felix Fermin	.05
96	Mark Lewis	.05
97	Kenny Lofton	.50
98	Carlos Martinez	.05
99	Rod Nicholos	.05
100	Dave Rohde	.05
101	Scott Scudder	.05
102	Paul Sorrento	.05
103	Mark Whiten	.05
104	Mark Carreon	.08
105	Milt Cuyler	.05
106	Rob Deer	.05
107	Cecil Fielder	.20
108	Travis Fryman	.10
109	Dan Gladden	.05
110	Bill Gullickson	.05
111	Les Lancaster	.05
112	Mark Leiter	.05
113	Tony Phillips	.08
114	Mickey Tettleton	.05
115	Alan Trammell	.08
116	Lou Whitaker	.05
117	Jeff Bagwell	.50
118	Craig Biggio	.10
119	Joe Boever	.05
120	Casey Candaele	.05
121	Andujar Cedeno	.05
122	Steve Finley	.05
123	Luis Gonzalez	.05
124	Pete Harnisch	.05
125	Jimmy Jones	.05
126	Mark Portugal	.05
127	Rafael Ramirez	.05
128	Mike Simms	.05
129	Eric Yelding	.05
130	Luis Aquino	.05
131	Kevin Appier	.05
132	Mike Boddicker	.05
133	George Brett	.50
134	Tom Gordon	.05
135	Mark Gubicza	.05
136	David Howard	.05
137	Gregg Jefferies	.08
138	Wally Joyner	.08
139	Brian McRae	.05
140	Jeff Montgomery	.05
141	Terry Shumpert	.05
142	Curtis Wilkerson	.05
143	Brett Butler	.10
144	Eric Davis	.08
145	Kevin Gross	.05
146	Dave Hansen	.05
147	Lenny Harris	.05
148	Carlos Hernandez	.05
149	Orel Hershiser	.10
150	Jay Howell	.05
151	Eric Karros	.15
152	Ramon Martinez	.08
153	Jose Offerman	.05
154	Mike Sharperson	.05
155	Darryl Strawberry	.08
156	Jim Gantner	.05
157	Darryl Hamilton	.05
158	Doug Henry	.05
159	John Jaha	.05
160	Pat Listach	.05
161	Jaime Navarro	.05
162	Dave Nilsson	.05
163	Jesse Orosco	.05
164	Kevin Seitzer	.05
165	B.J. Surhoff	.05
166	Greg Vaughn	.08
167	Robin Yount	.30
168	Rick Aguilera	.05
169	Scott Erickson	.05
170	Mark Guthrie	.05
171	Kent Hrbek	.05
172	Chuck Knoblauch	.10
173	Gene Larkin	.05
174	Shane Mack	.05
175	Pedro Munoz	.05
176	Mike Pagliarulo	.05
177	Kirby Puckett	.65
178	Kevin Tapani	.05
179	Gary Wayne	.05
180	Moises Alou	.08
181	Brian Barnes	.05
182	Archie Cianfrocco	.05
183	Delino DeShields	.08
184	Darrin Fletcher	.05
185	Marquis Grissom	.10
186	Ken Hill	.05
187	Dennis Martinez	.08

#	Player	Value	#	Player	Value	#	Player	Value
188	Bill Sampen	.05	284	Rich DeLucia	.05	380	Derrick May	.05
189	John VanderWal	.05	285	Dave Fleming	.05	381	Dan Plesac	.05
190	Larry Walker	.15	286	Ken Griffey, Jr.	2.00	382	Tommy Shields	.05
191	Tim Wallach	.05	287	Erik Hanson	.05	383	Sammy Sosa	1.00
192	Bobby Bonilla	.08	288	Randy Johnson	.20	384	Jose Vizcaino	.05
193	Daryl Boston	.05	289	Tino Martinez	.15	385	Greg Walbeck	.05
194	Vince Coleman	.05	290	Edgar Martinez	.08	386	Ellis Burks	.10
195	Kevin Elster	.05	291	Dave Valle	.05	387	Roberto Hernandez	.05
196	Sid Fernandez	.05	292	Omar Vizquel	.05	388	Mike Huff	.05
197	John Franco	.08	293	Luis Alicea	.05	389	Bo Jackson	.15
198	Dwight Gooden	.08	294	Bernard Gilkey	.10	390	Lance Johnson	.05
199	Howard Johnson	.05	295	Felix Jose	.05	391	Ron Karkovice	.05
200	Willie Randolph	.05	296	Ray Lankford	.12	392	Kirk McCaskill	.05
201	Bret Saberhagen	.05	297	Omar Olivares	.05	393	Donn Pall	.05
202	Dick Schofield	.05	298	Jose Oquendo	.05	394	Dan Pasqua	.05
203	Pete Schourek	.05	299	Tom Pagnozzi	.05	395	Steve Sax	.05
204	Greg Cadaret	.05	300	Geronimo Pena	.05	396	Dave Stieb	.05
205	John Habyan	.05	301	Gerald Perry	.05	397	Bobby Ayala	.05
206	Pat Kelly	.05	302	Ozzie Smith	.40	398	Tim Belcher	.05
207	Kevin Maas	.05	303	Lee Smith	.08	399	Jeff Branson	.05
208	Don Mattingly	.45	304	Bob Tewksbury	.05	400	Cesar Hernandez	.05
209	Matt Nokes	.05	305	Todd Zeile	.10	401	Roberto Kelly	.08
210	Melido Perez	.05	306	Kevin Brown	.08	402	Randy Milligan	.05
211	Scott Sanderson	.05	307	Todd Burns	.05	403	Kevin Mitchell	.08
212	Andy Stankiewicz	.05	308	Jose Canseco	.50	404	Juan Samuel	.05
213	Danny Tartabull	.05	309	Hector Fajardo	.05	405	Reggie Sanders	.15
214	Randy Velarde	.05	310	Julio Franco	.05	406	John Smiley	.05
215	Bernie Williams	.40	311	Juan Gonzalez	.65	407	Dan Wilson	.08
216	Harold Baines	.08	312	Jeff Huson	.05	408	Mike Christopher	.05
217	Mike Bordick	.05	313	Rob Maurer	.05	409	Dennis Cook	.05
218	Scott Brosius	.05	314	Rafael Palmeiro	.15	410	Alvaro Espinoza	.05
219	Jerry Browne	.05	315	Dean Palmer	.10	411	Glenallen Hill	.05
220	Ron Darling	.05	316	Ivan Rodriguez	.40	412	Reggie Jefferson	.08
221	Dennis Eckersley	.08	317	Nolan Ryan	.75	413	Derek Lilliquist	.05
222	Rickey Henderson	.20	318	Dickie Thon	.05	414	Jose Mesa	.08
223	Rick Honeycutt	.05	319	Roberto Alomar	.50	415	Charles Nagy	.05
224	Mark McGwire	1.50	320	Derek Bell	.08	416	Junior Ortiz	.05
225	Ruben Sierra	.08	321	Pat Borders	.05	417	Eric Plunk	.05
226	Terry Steinbach	.05	322	Joe Carter	.20	418	Ted Power	.05
227	Bob Welch	.05	323	Kelly Gruber	.05	419	Scott Aldred	.05
228	Willie Wilson	.05	324	Juan Guzman	.08	420	Andy Ashby	.05
229	Ruben Amaro	.05	325	Manny Lee	.05	421	Freddie Benavides	.05
230	Kim Batiste	.05	326	Jack Morris	.05	422	Dante Bichette	.15
231	Juan Bell	.05	327	John Olerud	.10	423	Willie Blair	.05
232	Wes Chamberlain	.05	328	Ed Sprague	.05	424	Vinny Castilla	.10
233	Darren Daulton	.05	329	Todd Stottlemyre	.05	425	Jerald Clark	.05
234	Mariano Duncan	.05	330	Duane Ward	.05	426	Alex Cole	.05
235	Len Dykstra	.10	331	Steve Avery	.10	427	Andres Galarraga	.10
236	Dave Hollins	.08	332	Damon Berryhill	.05	428	Joe Girardi	.05
237	Stan Javier	.05	333	Jeff Blauser	.05	429	Charlie Hayes	.05
238	John Kruk	.05	334	Mark Lemke	.05	430	Butch Henry	.05
239	Mickey Morandini	.05	335	Greg Maddux	1.00	431	Darren Holmes	.05
240	Terry Mulholland	.05	336	Kent Mercker	.05	432	Dale Murphy	.10
241	Mitch Williams	.05	337	Otis Nixon	.05	433	David Nied	.05
242	Stan Belinda	.05	338	Greg Olson	.05	434	Jeff Parrett	.05
243	Jay Bell	.05	339	Bill Pecota	.05	435	*Steve Reed*	.05
244	Carlos Garcia	.05	340	Terry Pendleton	.08	436	Armando Reynoso	.05
245	Jeff King	.05	341	Mike Stanton	.05	437	Bruce Ruffin	.05
246	Mike LaValliere	.05	342	Todd Frohwirth	.05	438	Bryn Smith	.05
247	Lloyd McClendon	.05	343	Tim Hulett	.05	439	Jim Tatum	.05
248	Orlando Merced	.05	344	Mark McLemore	.05	440	Eric Young	.10
249	Paul Miller	.05	345	Luis Mercedes	.05	441	Skeeter Barnes	.05
250	Gary Redus	.05	346	Alan Mills	.05	442	Tom Bolton	.05
251	Don Slaught	.05	347	Sherman Obando	.05	443	Kirk Gibson	.05
252	Zane Smith	.05	348	Jim Poole	.05	444	Chad Krueter	.05
253	Andy Van Slyke	.05	349	Harold Reynolds	.05	445	Bill Krueger	.05
254	Tim Wakefield	.05	350	Arthur Rhodes	.05	446	Scott Livingstone	.05
255	Andy Benes	.05	351	Jeff Tackett	.05	447	Bob MacDonald	.05
256	Dann Bilardello	.05	352	Fernando Valenzuela	.08	448	Mike Moore	.05
257	Tony Gwynn	.25	353	Scott Bankhead	.05	449	Mike Munoz	.05
258	Greg Harris	.05	354	Ivan Calderon	.05	450	Gary Thurman	.05
259	Darrin Jackson	.05	355	Scott Cooper	.05	451	David Wells	.05
260	Mike Maddux	.05	356	Danny Darwin	.05	452	Alex Arias	.05
261	Fred McGriff	.25	357	Scott Fletcher	.05	453	Jack Armstrong	.05
262	Rich Rodriguez	.05	358	Tony Fossas	.05	454	Bret Barberie	.05
263	Benito Santiago	.05	359	Greg Harris	.05	455	Ryan Bowen	.05
264	Gary Sheffield	.25	360	Joe Hesketh	.05	456	Cris Carpenter	.05
265	Kurt Stillwell	.05	361	Jose Melendez	.05	457	Chuck Carr	.05
266	Tim Teufel	.05	362	Paul Quantrill	.05	458	Jeff Conine	.10
267	Bud Black	.05	363	John Valentin	.10	459	Steve Decker	.05
268	John Burkett	.05	364	Mike Butcher	.05	460	Orestes Destrade	.05
269	Will Clark	.30	365	Chuck Crim	.05	461	Monty Fariss	.05
270	Royce Calyton	.05	366	Chili Davis	.08	462	Junior Felix	.05
271	Bryan Hickerson	.05	367	Damion Easley	.05	463	Bryan Harvey	.05
272	Chris James	.05	368	Steve Frey	.05	464	Trevor Hoffman	.08
273	Darren Lewis	.05	369	Joe Grahe	.05	465	Charlie Hough	.05
274	Willie McGee	.08	370	Greg Myers	.05	466	Dave Magadan	.05
275	Jim McNamara	.05	371	John Orton	.05	467	Bob McClure	.05
276	Francisco Oliveras	.05	372	J.T. Snow	.25	468	Rob Natal	.05
277	Robby Thompson	.05	373	Ron Tingley	.05	469	Scott Pose	.05
278	Matt Williams	.25	374	Julio Valera	.05	470	Rich Renteria	.05
279	Trevor Wilson	.05	375	Paul Assenmacher	.05	471	Benito Santiago	.08
280	Bret Boone	.08	376	Jose Bautista	.05	472	Matt Turner	.05
281	Greg Briley	.05	377	Jose Guzman	.05	473	Walt Weiss	.05
282	Jay Buhner	.08	378	Greg Hibbard	.05	474	Eric Anthony	.05
283	Henry Cotto	.05	379	Candy Maldonado	.05	475	Chris Donnels	.05

476	Doug Drabek	.05	
477	Xavier Hernandez	.05	
478	Doug Jones	.05	
479	Darryl Kile	.05	
480	Scott Servais	.05	
481	Greg Swindell	.05	
482	Eddie Taubensee	.05	
483	Jose Uribe	.05	
484	Brian Williams	.05	
485	Billy Brewer	.05	
486	David Cone	.05	
487	Greg Gagne	.05	
488	Phil Hiatt	.05	
489	Jose Lind	.05	
490	Brent Mayne	.05	
491	Kevin McReynolds	.05	
492	Keith Miller	.05	
403	Hipolito Pichardo	.05	
494	Harvey Pulliam	.05	
495	Rico Rossay	.05	
496	Pedro Astacio	.10	
497	Tom Candiotti	.05	
498	Tom Goodwin	.05	
499	Jim Gott	.05	
500	Pedro Martinez	.08	
501	Roger McDowell	.05	
502	Mike Piazza	1.50	
503	Jody Reed	.05	
504	Rick Trlicek	.05	
505	Mitch Weber	.05	
506	Steve Wilson	.05	
507	James Austin	.05	
508	Ricky Bones	.05	
509	Alex Diaz	.05	
510	Mike Fetters	.05	
511	Teddy Higuera	.05	
512	Graeme Lloyd	.05	
513	Carlos Maldonado	.05	
514	Josias Manzanillo	.05	
515	Kevin Reimer	.05	
516	Bill Spiers	.05	
517	Bill Wegman	.05	
518	Willie Banks	.05	
519	J.T. Bruett	.05	
520	Brian Harper	.05	
521	Terry Jorgensen	.05	
522	Scott Leius	.05	
523	Pat Mahomes	.05	
524	Dave McCarty	.08	
525	Jeff Reboulet	.08	
526	Mike Trombley	.05	
527	Carl Willis	.05	
528	Dave Winfield	.15	
529	Sean Berry	.05	
530	Frank Bolick	.05	
531	Kent Bottenfield	.05	
532	Wil Cordero	.10	
533	Jeff Fassero	.05	
534	Tim Laker	.05	
535	Mike Lansing	.08	
536	Chris Nabholz	.05	
537	Mel Rojas	.08	
538	John Wetteland	.08	
539	Ted Wood (Front photo actually Frank Bolick)	.05	
540	Mike Draper	.05	
541	Tony Fernandez	.05	
542	Todd Hundley	.12	
543	Jeff Innis	.05	
544	Jeff McKnight	.05	
545	Eddie Murray	.25	
546	Charlie O'Brien	.05	
547	Frank Tanana	.05	
548	Ryan Thompson	.08	
549	Chico Walker	.05	
550	Anthony Young	.05	
551	Jim Abbott	.10	
552	Wade Boggs	.25	
553	Steve Farr	.05	
554	Neal Heaton	.05	
555	Steve Howe	.05	
556	Dion James	.05	
557	Scott Kamieniecki	.05	
558	Jimmy Key	.05	
559	Jim Leyritz	.05	
560	Paul O'Neill	.08	
561	Spike Owen	.05	
562	Lance Blankenship	.05	
563	Joe Boever	.05	
564	Storm Davis	.05	
565	Kelly Downs	.05	
566	Eric Fox	.10	
567	Rich Gossage	.05	
568	Dave Henderson	.05	
569	Shawn Hillegas	.05	
570	*Mike Mohler*	.05	

571	Troy Neel	.10
572	Dale Sveum	.05
573	Larry Anderson	.05
574	Bob Ayrault	.05
575	Jose DeLeon	.05
576	Jim Eisenreich	.05
577	Pete Incaviglia	.05
578	Danny Jackson	.05
579	Ricky Jordan	.05
580	Ben Rivera	.05
581	Curt Schilling	.05
582	Milt Thompson	.05
583	David West	.05
584	John Candelaria	.05
585	Steve Cooke	.05
586	Tom Foley	.05
587	Al Martin	.05
588	Blas Minor	.05
589	Dennis Moeller	.05
590	Denny Neagle	.05
591	Tom Prince	.05
592	Randy Tomlin	.05
593	Bob Walk	.05
594	Kevin Young	.10
595	Pat Gomez	.05
596	Ricky Gutierrez	.05
597	Gene Harris	.05
598	Jeremy Hernandez	.05
599	Phil Plantier	.05
600	Tim Scott	.05
601	Frank Seminara	.05
602	Darrell Sherman	.05
603	Craig Shipley	.05
604	Guillermo Velasquez	.05
605	Dan Walters	.05
606	Mike Benjamin	.05
607	Barry Bonds	.35
608	Jeff Brantley	.05
609	Dave Burba	.05
610	Craig Colbert	.05
611	Mike Jackson	.05
612	Kirt Manwaring	.05
613	Dave Martinez	.05
614	Dave Righetti	.05
615	Kevin Rogers	.05
616	Bill Swift	.05
617	Rich Amaral	.05
618	Mike Blowers	.05
619	Chris Bosio	.05
620	Norm Charlton	.05
621	John Cummings	.05
622	Mike Felder	.05
623	Bill Haselman	.05
624	Tim Leary	.05
625	Pete O'Brien	.05
626	Russ Swan	.05
627	Fernando Vina	.05
628	Rene Arocha	.05
629	Rod Brewer	.05
630	Ozzie Canseco	.05
631	Rheal Cormier	.05
632	Brian Jordan	.10
633	Joe Magrane	.05
634	Donovan Osborne	.05
635	Mike Perez	.05
636	Stan Royer	.08
637	Hector Villanueva	.05
638	Tracy Woodson	.05
639	Benji Gil	.05
640	Tom Henke	.05
641	David Hulse	.05
642	Charlie Leibrandt	.05
643	Robb Nen	.05
644	Dan Peltier	.05
645	Billy Ripken	.05
646	Kenny Rogers	.05
647	John Russell	.05
648	Dan Smith	.05
649	Matt Whiteside	.05
650	William Canate	.05
651	Darnell Coles	.05
652	Al Leiter	.05
653	Dominigo Martinez	.05
654	Paul Molitor	.20
655	Luis Sojo	.05
656	Dave Stewart	.05
657	Mike Timlin	.05
658	Turner Ward	.05
659	Devon White	.08
660	Eddie Zosky	.05

1993 Pacific Beisbol Amigos

In groups of two, three or more, and generally from the same team, Latin players are paired in this second series insert set. The cards feature player photos (sometimes posed, sometimes superimposed) on a background of red, white and black baseballs. The players' last names and a card title are printed in Spanish on front and repeated on back. Also on back a few career highlights and stats are printed in red on a marbled background - again all in Spanish.

		MT
Complete Set (30):		24.00
Common Player:		1.00
1	Edgar Martinez	1.50
2	Luis Polonia, Stan Javier	1.00
3	George Bell, Julio Franco	1.00
4	Ozzie Guillen, Ivan Rodriguez	1.50
5	Carlos Baerga, Sandy Alomar Jr.	1.00
6	Sandy Alomar Jr., Alvaro Espinoza, Paul Sorrento, Carlos Baerga, Felix Fermin, Junior Ortiz, Jose Mesa, Carlos Martinez	1.00
7	Sandy Alomar Jr., Roberto Alomar	2.00
8	Jose Lind, Felix Jose	1.00
9	Ricky Bones, Jaime Navarro	1.00
10	Jaime Navarro, Jesse Orosco	1.00
11	Tino Martinez, Edgar Martinez	1.50
12	Juan Gonzalez, Ivan Rodriguez	2.50
13	Juan Gonzalez, Julio Franco	1.50
14	Julio Franco, Jose Canseco, Rafael Palmeiro	1.25
15	Juan Gonzalez, Jose Canseco	2.00
16	Ivan Rodriguez, Benji Gil	1.25
17	Jose Guzman, Frank Castillo	1.00
18	Rey Sanchez, Jose Vizcaino	1.00
19	Derrick May, Sammy Sosa	2.50
20	Sammy Sosa, Candy Maldonado	2.50
21	Jose Rijo, Juan Samuel	1.00
22	Freddie Benavides, Andres Galarraga	1.00
23	Guillermo Velasquez, Benito Santiago	1.00
24	Luis Gonzalez, Andujar Cedeno	1.00
25	Wil Cordero, Dennis Martinez	1.00
26	Moises Alou, Wil Cordero	1.00
27	Ozzie Canseco, Jose Canseco	1.50
28	Jose Oquendo, Luis Alicea	1.00
29	Luis Alicea, Rene Arocha	1.00
30	Geronimo Pena, Luis Alicea	1.00

1993 Pacific Estrellas de Beisbol

Pacific produced a gold-foil "Stars of Baseball" set of 20 that was randomly inserted as part of the company's first series Spanish language Major League set in 1993. Each card features a color action photo on the front surrounded by a gold-foil border. Production was limited to 10,000 of each card.

		MT
Complete Set (20):		75.00
Common Player:		3.00
1	Moises Alou	5.00
2	Bobby Bonilla	7.50
3	Tony Fernandez	3.00
4	Felix Jose	3.00
5	Dennis Martinez	4.00
6	Orlando Merced	3.00
7	Jose Oquendo	3.00
8	Geronimo Pena	3.00
9	Jose Rijo	3.00
10	Benito Santiago	4.00
11	Sandy Alomar Jr.	5.00
12	Carlos Baerga	4.00
13	Jose Canseco	6.00
14	Juan "Igor" Gonzalez	12.00
15	Juan Guzman	3.00
16	Edgar Martinez	4.00
17	Rafael Palmeiro	4.00
18	Ruben Sierra	3.00
19	Danny Tartabull	3.00
20	Omar Vizquel	3.00

1993 Pacific Jugadores Calientes

Three dozen "hot players" with a decidedly Hispanic predominance are featured in this glittery Series II insert set. Player action photos appear in front of a silver prismatic foil background. Names

appear at bottom in boldly styled but hard to read letters in bright colors. Horizontal backs have a pair of player photos and a large team logo, along with a few stats, all printed in Spanish.

		MT
Complete Set (36):		50.00
Common Player:		1.00
1	Rich Amaral	1.00
2	George Brett	4.00
3	Jay Buhner	1.00
4	Roger Clemens	2.00
5	Kirk Gibson	1.00
6	Juan Gonzalez	2.50
7	Ken Griffey Jr.	6.00
8	Bo Jackson	1.00
9	Kenny Lofton	1.50
10	Mark McGwire	4.00
11	Sherman Obando	1.00
12	John Olerud	1.00
13	Carlos Quintana	1.00
14	Ivan Rodriguez	1.25
15	Nolan Ryan	5.00
16	J.T. Snow	1.50
17	Fernando Valenzuela	1.00
18	Dave Winfield	1.50
19	Moises Alou	1.00
20	Jeff Bagwell	2.50
21	Barry Bonds	2.50
22	Bobby Bonilla	1.00
23	Vinny Castilla	1.00
24	Andujar Cedeno	1.00
25	Orestes Destrade	1.00
26	Andres Galarraga	1.50
27	Mark Grace	1.50
28	Tony Gwynn	2.00
29	Roberto Kelly	1.00
30	John Kruk	1.00
31	Dave Magadan	1.00
32	Derrick May	1.00
33	Orlando Merced	1.00
34	Mike Piazza	4.00
35	Armadno Reynoso	1.00
36	Jose Vizcaino	1.00

1993 Pacific Prism Insert

Pacific produced a prism card that was randomly inserted in its Series I Spanish-language set in 1993. Each of the 20 cards has a color photo of a star Latino player on the front superimposed over a prismatic silver-foil background. Card backs contain an action photo and a brief player biography on a marbled background. Production was limited to 10,000 of each card.

		MT
Complete Set (20):		250.00
Common Player:		12.00
1	Francisco Cabrera	12.00
2	Jose Lind	12.00

3	Dennis Martinez	14.00
4	Ramon Martinez	14.00
5	Jose Rijo	12.00
6	Benito Santiago	12.00
7	Roberto Alomar	25.00
8	Sandy Alomar Jr.	14.00
9	Carlos Baerga	12.00
10	George Bell	12.00
11	Jose Canseco	20.00
12	Alex Fernandez	12.00
13	Julio Franco	12.00
14	Igor (Juan) Gonzalez	45.00
15	Ozzie Guillen	12.00
16	Teddy Higuera	12.00
17	Edgar Martinez	12.00
18	Hipolito Pichardo	12.00
19	Luis Polonia	12.00
20	Ivan Rodriguez	15.00

1994 Pacific Crown

Following its 1993 Spanish-language set, Pacific's 1994 "Crown Collection" offering is bi-lingual, featuring both English and Spanish for most of the back printing. Fronts have an action photo which is borderless at the top and sides. A gold-foil line separates the bottom of the photo from a marbled strip that is color-coded by team. The player's name appears in two lines at the left of the strip, a gold-foil crown logo is at left. A Pacific logo appears in one of the upper corners of the photo. Backs have a photo, again borderless at top and sides, with a Pacific logo in one upper corner and the card number and MLB logos in the lower corners. At bottom is a gray marble strip with a few biographical details, 1993 and career stats and a ghost-image color team logo. The 660 cards in the set were issued in a single series.

		MT
Complete Set (660):		35.00
Common Player:		.05
Wax Box:		25.00
1	Steve Avery	.10
2	Steve Bedrosian	.05
3	Damon Beryhill	.05
4	Jeff Blauser	.05
5	Sid Bream	.05
6	Francisco Cabrera	.05
7	Ramon Caraballo	.05
8	Ron Gant	.15
9	Tom Glavine	.15
10	Chipper Jones	1.50
11	Dave Justice	.25
12	Ryan Klesko	.50
13	Mark Lemke	.05
14	Javier Lopez	.20

#	Player	Value	#	Player	Value	#	Player	Value
15	Greg Maddux	2.00	111	Dwight Smith	.05	207	Keith Shepherd	.05
16	Fred McGriff	.25	112	Sammy Sosa	1.00	208	Jim Tatum	.05
17	Greg McMichael	.05	113	Jose Vizcaino	.05	209	Eric Young	.05
18	Kent Mercker	.05	114	Turk Wendell	.08	210	Skeeter Barnes	.05
19	Otis Nixon	.05	115	Rick Wilkins	.05	211	Danny Bautista	.05
20	Terry Pendleton	.05	116	Willie Wilson	.05	212	Tom Bolton	.05
21	Deion Sanders	.30	117	Eddie Zambrano	.05	213	Eric Davis	.08
22	John Smoltz	.15	118	Wilson Alvarez	.05	214	Storm Davis	.05
23	Tony Tarasco	.10	119	Tim Belcher	.05	215	Cecil Fielder	.15
24	Manny Alexander	.10	120	Jason Bere	.08	216	Travis Fryman	.10
25	Brady Anderson	.15	121	Rodney Bolton	.05	217	Kirk Gibson	.05
26	Harold Baines	.08	122	Ellis Burks	.10	218	Dan Gladden	.05
27	Damion Buford (Damon)	.08	123	Joey Cora	.05	219	John Doherty	.05
28	Paul Carey	.05	124	Alex Fernandez	.08	220	Chris Gomez	.05
29	Mike Devereaux	.05	125	Ozzie Guillen	.05	221	David Haas	.05
30	Todd Frohwirth	.05	126	Craig Grebeck	.05	222	Bill Krueger	.05
31	Leo Gomez	.05	127	Roberto Hernandez	.05	223	Chad Kreuter	.05
32	Jeffrey Hammonds	.10	128	Bo Jackson	.15	224	Mark Leiter	.05
33	Chris Hoiles	.05	129	Lance Johnson	.05	225	Bob MacDonald	.05
34	Tim Hulett	.05	130	Ron Karkovice	.05	226	Mike Moore	.05
35	Ben McDonald	.05	131	Mike Lavalliere	.05	227	Tony Phillips	.08
36	Mark McLemore	.05	132	Norberto Martin	.05	228	Rich Rowland	.05
37	Alan Mills	.08	133	Kirk McCaskill	.05	229	Mickey Tettleton	.05
38	Mike Mussina	.20	134	Jack McDowell	.08	230	Alan Trammell	.08
39	Sherman Obando	.05	135	Scott Radinsky	.05	231	David Wells	.05
40	Gregg Olson	.05	136	Tim Raines	.08	232	Lou Whitaker	.05
41	Mike Pagliarulo	.05	137	Steve Sax	.05	233	Luis Aquino	.05
42	Jim Poole	.05	138	Frank Thomas	2.00	234	Alex Arias	.05
43	Harold Reynolds	.05	139	Dan Pasqua	.05	235	Jack Armstrong	.05
44	Cal Ripken, Jr.	2.00	140	Robin Ventura	.15	236	Ryan Bowen	.05
45	David Segui	.05	141	Jeff Branson	.05	237	Chuck Carr	.05
46	Fernando Valenzuela	.08	142	Tom Browning	.05	238	Matias Carrillo	.05
47	Jack Voight	.05	143	Jacob Brumfield	.05	239	Jeff Conine	.10
48	Scott Bankhead	.05	144	Tim Costo	.05	240	Henry Cotto	.05
49	Roger Clemens	.75	145	Rob Dibble	.05	241	Orestes Destrade	.05
50	Scott Cooper	.05	146	Brian Dorsett	.08	242	Chris Hammond	.05
51	Danny Darwin	.05	147	Steve Foster	.05	243	Bryan Harvey	.05
52	Andre Dawson	.10	148	Cesar Hernandez	.05	244	Charlie Hough	.05
53	John Dopson	.05	149	Roberto Kelly	.05	245	Richie Lewis	.05
54	Scott Fletcher	.05	150	Barry Larkin	.15	246	Mitch Lyden	.05
55	Tony Fossas	.05	151	Larry Luebbers	.05	247	Bob Magadan	.05
56	Mike Greenwell	.05	152	Kevin Mitchell	.08	248	Bob Natal	.05
57	Billy Hatcher	.05	153	Joe Oliver	.05	249	Benito Santiago	.08
58	Jeff McNeely	.05	154	Tim Pugh	.05	250	Gary Sheffield	.20
59	Jose Melendez	.05	155	Jeff Reardon	.05	251	Matt Turner	.05
60	Tim Naehring	.05	156	Jose Rijo	.05	252	David Weathers	.05
61	Tony Pena	.05	157	Bip Roberts	.05	253	Walt Weiss	.05
62	Carlos Quintana	.05	158	Chris Sabo	.05	254	Darrell Whitmore	.05
63	Paul Quantrill	.05	159	Juan Samuel	.05	255	Nigel Wilson	.05
64	Luis Rivera	.05	160	Reggie Sanders	.15	256	Eric Anthony	.10
65	Jeff Russell	.05	161	John Smiley	.05	257	Jeff Bagwell	.75
66	Aaron Sele	.10	162	Jerry Spradlin	.05	258	Kevin Bass	.05
67	John Valentin	.10	163	Gary Varsho	.05	259	Craig Biggio	.15
68	Mo Vaughn	.40	164	Sandy Alomar Jr.	.08	260	Ken Caminiti	.15
69	Frank Viola	.05	165	Carlos Baerga	.20	261	Andujar Cedeno	.05
70	Bob Zupcic	.05	166	Albert Belle	.60	262	Chris Donnels	.05
71	Mike Butcher	.05	167	Mark Clark	.05	263	Doug Drabek	.05
72	Ron Correia	.05	168	Alvaro Espinoza	.05	264	Tom Edens	.05
73	Chad Curtis	.08	169	Felix Fermin	.05	265	Steve Finley	.05
74	Chili Davis	.08	170	Reggie Jefferson	.10	266	Luis Gonzalez	.05
75	Gary DiSarcina	.05	171	Wayne Kirby	.05	267	Pete Harnisch	.05
76	Damion Easley	.05	172	Tom Kramer	.05	268	Xavier Hernandez	.05
77	John Farrell	.05	173	Jesse Levis	.05	269	Todd Jones	.05
78	Chuck Finley	.05	174	Kenny Lofton	.60	270	Darryl Kile	.05
79	Joe Grahe	.05	175	Candy Maldonado	.05	271	Al Osuna	.05
80	Stan Javier	.05	176	Carlos Martinez	.05	272	Rick Parker	.05
81	Mark Langston	.05	177	Jose Mesa	.08	273	Mark Portugal	.05
82	Phil Leftwich	.05	178	Jeff Mutis	.05	274	Scott Servais	.05
83	Torey Lovullo	.05	179	Charles Nagy	.05	275	Greg Swindell	.05
84	Joe Magrane	.05	180	Bob Ojeda	.05	276	Eddie Taubensee	.05
85	Greg Myers	.05	181	Junior Ortiz	.05	277	Jose Uribe	.05
86	Eduardo Perez	.05	182	Eric Plunk	.05	278	Brian Williams	.05
87	Luis Polonia	.05	183	Manny Ramirez	.50	279	Kevin Appier	.05
88	Tim Salmon	.25	184	Paul Sorrento	.05	280	Billy Brewer	.05
89	J.T. Snow	.15	185	Jeff Treadway	.05	281	David Cone	.08
90	Kurt Stillwell	.05	186	Bill Wertz	.05	282	Greg Gagne	.05
91	Ron Tingley	.05	187	Freddie Benavides	.05	283	Tom Gordon	.05
92	Chris Turner	.05	188	Dante Bichette	.25	284	Chris Gwynn	.05
93	Julio Valera	.05	189	Willie Blair	.05	285	John Habyan	.05
94	Jose Bautista	.05	190	Daryl Boston	.05	286	Chris Haney	.05
95	Shawn Boskie	.05	191	Pedro Castellano	.05	287	Phil Hiatt	.05
96	Steve Buechele	.05	192	Vinny Castilla	.08	288	David Howard	.05
97	Frank Castillo	.05	193	Jerald Clark	.05	289	Felix Jose	.05
98	Mark Grace	.15	194	Alex Cole	.05	290	Wally Joyner	.08
99	Jose Guzman	.05	195	Andres Galarraga	.10	291	Kevin Koslofski	.05
100	Mike Harkey	.05	196	Joe Girardi	.05	292	Jose Lind	.05
101	Greg Hibbard	.05	197	Charlie Hayes	.05	293	Brent Mayne	.05
102	Doug Jennings	.05	198	Darren Holmes	.05	294	Mike Mcfarlane	.05
103	Derrick May	.05	199	Chris Jones	.05	295	Brian McRae	.05
104	Mike Morgan	.05	200	Curt Leskanic	.05	296	Kevin McReynolds	.05
105	Randy Myers	.05	201	Roberto Mejia	.05	297	Keith Miller	.05
106	Karl Rhodes	.10	202	David Nied	.05	298	Jeff Montgomery	.05
107	Kevin Robinson	.08	203	J. Owens	.12	299	Hipolito Pichardo	.05
108	Rey Sanchez	.05	204	Steve Reed	.05	300	Rico Rossy	.05
109	Ryne Sandberg	.50	205	Armando Reynoso	.05	301	Curtis Wilkerson	.05
110	Tommy Shields	.05	206	Bruce Ruffin	.05	302	Pedro Astacio	.10

303	Rafael Bournigal	.05	399	Sid Fernandez	.05	495	Steve Cooke	.05
304	Brett Butler	.10	400	John Franco	.05	496	Midre Cummings	.15
305	Tom Candiotti	.05	401	Dave Gallagher	.05	497	Mark Dewey	.05
306	Omar Daal	.05	402	Dwight Gooden	.08	498	Carlos Garcia	.05
307	Jim Gott	.05	403	Eric Hillman	.05	499	Jeff King	.05
308	Kevin Gross	.05	404	Todd Hundley	.12	500	Al Martin	.05
309	Dave Hansen	.05	405	Butch Huskey	.10	501	Lloyd McClendon	.05
310	Carlos Hernandez	.05	406	Jeff Innis	.05	502	Orlando Merced	.05
311	Orel Hershiser	.08	407	Howard Johnson	.05	503	Blas Minor	.05
312	Eric Karros	.12	408	Jeff Kent	.05	504	Denny Neagle	.08
313	Pedro Martinez	.08	409	Ced Landrum	.05	505	Tom Prince	.05
314	Ramon Martinez	.10	410	Mike Maddux	.05	506	Don Slaught	.05
315	Roger McDowell	.05	411	Josias Manzanillo	.05	507	Zane Smith	.05
316	Raul Mondesi	.40	412	Jeff McKnight	.05	508	Randy Tomlin	.05
317	Jose Offerman	.05	413	Eddie Murray	.25	509	Andy Van Slyke	.05
318	Mike Piazza	1.25	414	Tito Navarro	.05	510	Paul Wagner	.05
319	Jody Reed	.05	415	Joe Orsulak	.05	511	Tim Wakefield	.05
320	Henry Rodriguez	.08	416	Bret Saberhagen	.05	512	Bob Walk	.05
321	Cory Snyder	.05	417	Dave Telgheder	.05	513	John Wehner	.05
322	Darryl Strawberry	.10	418	Ryan Thompson	.05	514	Kevin Young	.10
323	Tim Wallach	.05	419	Chico Walker	.05	515	Billy Bean	.05
324	Steve Wilson	.05	420	Jim Abbott	.10	516	Andy Benes	.10
325	Juan Bell	.05	421	Wade Boggs	.20	517	Derek Bell	.10
326	Ricky Bones	.05	422	Mike Gallego	.05	518	Doug Brocail	.05
327	Alex Diaz	.05	423	Mark Hutton	.05	519	Jarvis Brown	.05
328	Cal Eldred	.05	424	Dion James	.05	520	Phil Clark	.05
329	Darryl Hamilton	.05	425	Domingo Jean	.05	521	Mark Davis	.05
330	Doug Henry	.05	426	Pat Kelly	.05	522	Jeff Gardner	.05
331	John Jaha	.05	427	Jimmy Key	.05	523	Pat Gomez	.05
332	Pat Listach	.05	428	Jim Leyritz	.05	524	Ricky Gutierrez	.05
333	Graeme Lloyd	.05	429	Kevin Maas	.05	525	Tony Gwynn	.35
334	Carlos Maldonado	.05	430	Don Mattingly	1.00	526	Gene Harris	.05
335	Angel Miranda	.05	431	Bobby Munoz	.05	527	Kevin Higgins	.05
336	Jaime Navarro	.05	432	Matt Nokes	.05	528	Trevor Hoffman	.05
337	Dave Nilsson	.05	433	Paul O'Neill	.08	529	Luis Lopez	.05
338	Rafael Novoa	.05	434	Spike Owen	.05	530	Pedro A. Martinez	.05
339	Troy O'Leary	.05	435	Melido Perez	.05	531	Melvin Nieves	.05
340	Jesse Orosco	.05	436	Lee Smith	.08	532	Phil Plantier	.05
341	Kevin Seitzer	.05	437	Andy Stankiewicz	.05	533	Frank Seminara	.05
342	Bill Spiers	.05	438	Mike Stanley	.05	534	Craig Shipley	.05
343	William Suero	.05	439	Danny Tartabull	.05	535	Tim Tuefel	.05
344	B.J. Surhoff	.05	440	Randy Velarde	.05	536	Guillermo Velasquez	.05
345	Dickie Thon	.05	441	Bernie Williams	.35	537	Wally Whitehurst	.05
346	Jose Valentin	.05	442	Gerald Williams	.08	538	Rod Beck	.05
347	Greg Vaughn	.08	443	Mike Witt	.05	539	Todd Benzinger	.05
348	Robin Yount	.20	444	Marcos Armas	.05	540	Barry Bonds	.50
349	Willie Banks	.05	445	Lance Blankenship	.05	541	Jeff Brantley	.05
350	Bernardo Brito	.05	446	Mike Bordick	.05	542	Dave Burba	.05
351	Scott Erickson	.05	447	Ron Darling	.05	543	John Burkett	.05
352	Mark Guthrie	.05	448	Dennis Eckersley	.10	544	Will Clark	.25
353	Chip Hale	.05	449	Brent Gates	.08	545	Royce Clayton	.08
354	Brian Harper	.05	450	Goose Gossage	.05	546	Brian Hickerson (Bryan)	.05
355	Kent Hrbek	.08	451	Scott Hemond	.08	547	Mike Jackson	.05
356	Terry Jorgenson	.05	452	Dave Henderson	.05	548	Darren Lewis	.08
357	Chuck Knoblauch	.15	453	Shawn Hillegas	.05	549	Kirt Manwaring	.05
358	Gene Larkin	.05	454	Rick Honeycutt	.05	550	Dave Martinez	.05
359	Scott Leius	.05	455	Scott Lydy	.05	551	Willie McGee	.08
360	Shane Mack	.05	456	Mark McGwire	3.00	552	Jeff Reed	.05
361	David McCarty	.08	457	Henry Mercedes	.10	553	Dave Righetti	.05
362	Pat Meares	.05	458	Mike Mohler	.05	554	Kevin Rogers	.05
363	Pedro Munoz	.05	459	Troy Neel	.10	555	Steve Scarsone	.05
364	Derek Parks	.05	460	Edwin Nunez	.05	556	Bill Swift	.05
365	Kirby Puckett	.75	461	Craig Paquette	.05	557	Robby Thompson	.05
366	Jeff Reboulet	.10	462	Ruben Sierra	.08	558	Salomon Torres	.05
367	Kevin Tapani	.05	463	Terry Steinbach	.05	559	Matt Williams	.20
368	Mike Trombley	.05	464	Todd Van Poppel	.05	560	Trevor Wilson	.05
369	George Tsamis	.05	465	Bob Welch	.05	561	Rich Amaral	.05
370	Carl Willis	.05	466	Bobby Witt	.05	562	Mike Blowers	.05
371	Dave Winfield	.15	467	Ruben Amaro	.05	563	Chris Bosio	.05
372	Moises Alou	.10	468	Larry Anderson	.05	564	Jay Buhner	.10
373	Brian Barnes	.05	469	Kim Batiste	.05	565	Norm Charlton	.05
374	Sean Berry	.05	470	Wes Chamberlain	.05	566	Jim Converse	.05
375	Frank Bolick	.05	471	Darren Daulton	.05	567	Rich DeLucia	.05
376	Wil Cordero	.10	472	Mariano Duncan	.05	568	Mike Felder	.05
377	Delino DeShields	.08	473	Len Dykstra	.08	569	Dave Fleming	.05
378	Jeff Fassero	.05	474	Jim Eisenreich	.05	570	Ken Griffey, Jr.	2.50
379	Darren Fletcher	.05	475	Tommy Greene	.05	571	Bill Haselman	.05
380	Cliff Floyd	.12	476	Dave Hollins	.05	572	Dwayne Henry	.05
381	Lou Frazier	.05	477	Pete Incaviglia	.05	573	Brad Holman	.05
382	Marquis Grissom	.15	478	Danny Jackson	.05	574	Randy Johnson	.25
383	Gil Heredia	.05	479	John Kruk	.05	575	Greg Litton	.05
384	Mike Lansing	.08	480	Tony Longmire	.05	576	Edgar Martinez	.10
385	Oreste Marrero	.05	481	Jeff Manto	.05	577	Tino Martinez	.15
386	Dennis Martinez	.08	482	Mike Morandini	.05	578	Jeff Nelson	.05
387	Curtis Pride	.15	483	Terry Mulholland	.05	579	Mark Newfield	.08
388	Mel Rojas	.05	484	Todd Pratt	.05	580	Roger Salkeld	.08
389	Kirk Rueter	.05	485	Ben Rivera	.05	581	Mackey Sasser	.05
390	Joe Siddall	.05	486	Curt Shilling	.05	582	Brian Turang	.05
391	John Vander Wal	.05	487	Kevin Stocker	.05	583	Omar Vizquel	.05
392	Larry Walker	.20	488	Milt Thompson	.05	584	Dave Valle	.05
393	John Wetteland	.05	489	David West	.05	585	Luis Alicea	.05
394	Rondell White	.30	490	Mitch Williams	.05	586	Rene Arocha	.05
395	Tom Bogar	.05	491	Jeff Ballard	.05	587	Rheal Cormier	.05
396	Bobby Bonilla	.10	492	Jay Bell	.05	588	Tripp Cromer	.05
397	Jeromy Burnitz	.05	493	Scott Bullett	.05	589	Bernard Gilkey	.08
398	Mike Draper	.05	494	Dave Clark	.05	590	Lee Guetterman	.05

591	Gregg Jefferies	.10
592	Tim Jones	.05
593	Paul Kilgus	.05
594	Les Lancaster	.05
595	Omar Olivares	.05
596	Jose Oquendo	.05
597	Donovan Osborne	.05
598	Tom Pagnozzi	.05
599	Erik Pappas	.05
600	Geronimo Pena	.05
601	Mike Perez	.05
602	Gerald Perry	.05
603	Stan Royer	.08
604	Ozzie Smith	.25
605	Bob Tewksbury	.05
606	Allen Watson	.05
607	Mark Whiten	.05
608	Todd Zeile	.08
609	Jeff Bronkey	.05
610	Kevin Brown	.08
611	Jose Canseco	.25
612	Doug Dascenzo	.05
613	Butch Davis	.05
614	Mario Diaz	.05
615	Julio Franco	.08
616	Benji Gil	.05
617	Juan Gonzalez	1.00
618	Tom Henke	.05
619	Jeff Huson	.05
620	David Hulse	.05
621	Craig Lefferts	.05
622	Rafael Palmeiro	.10
623	Dean Palmer	.05
624	Bob Patterson	.05
625	Roger Pavlik	.05
626	Gary Redus	.05
627	Ivan Rodriguez	.40
628	Kenny Rogers	.05
629	Jon Shave	.05
630	Doug Strange	.05
631	Matt Whiteside	.05
632	Roberto Alomar	.50
633	Pat Borders	.05
634	Scott Brow	.05
635	Rob Butler	.05
636	Joe Carter	.20
637	Tony Castillo	.05
638	Mark Eichhorn	.05
639	Tony Fernandez	.05
640	Huck Flener	.05
641	Alfredo Griffin	.05
642	Juan Guzman	.08
643	Rickey Henderson	.20
644	Pat Hentgen	.10
645	Randy Knorr	.05
646	Al Leiter	.05
647	Dominigo Martinez	.05
648	Paul Molitor	.30
649	Jack Morris	.05
650	John Olerud	.12
651	Ed Sprague	.05
652	Dave Stewart	.05
653	Devon White	.08
654	Woody Williams	.05
655	Barry Bonds (MVP)	.40
656	Greg Maddux (CY)	.75
657	Jack McDowell (CY)	.10
658	Mike Piazza (ROY)	.75
659	Tim Salmon (ROY)	.25
660	Frank Thomas (MVP)	1.50

1994 Pacific Crown All Latino All-Star Team

Latino All-Stars is the theme of the third insert set found randomly packed in Pacific Spanish for 1994. Cards feature a player action photo on front, with a gold foil pinstripe around the sides and top. The player's name appears in gold script at bottom and there is a baseball logo in the corner. On backs a portrait photo of the player is set against a background of his native flag. Season highlights of 1993 are presented in English and Spanish. Eight thousand sets were produced.

Omar Vizquel

		MT
Complete Set (20):		26.00
Common Player:		1.00
1	Benito Santiago	1.50
2	Dave Magadan	1.00
3	Andres Galarraga	1.50
4	Luis Gonzalez	1.00
5	Jose Offerman	1.00
6	Bobby Bonilla	1.50
7	Dennis Martinez	1.50
8	Mariano Duncan	1.00
9	Orlando Merced	1.00
10	Jose Rijo	1.00
11	Danny Tartabull	1.00
12	Ruben Sierra	1.00
13	Ivan Rodriguez	4.00
14	Juan Gonzalez	8.00
15	Jose Canseco	3.00
16	Rafael Palmeiro	1.50
17	Roberto Alomar	4.00
18	Eduardo Perez	1.00
19	Alex Fernandez	1.00
20	Omar Vizquel	1.00

1994 Pacific Crown Homerun Leaders

TIM SALMON

A gold prismatic background behind a color action player photo is the featured design on this Pacific insert set. Backs have another player photo against a ballfield backdrop. A huge baseball is overprinted with the player's name and number of 1993 homers. A league designation is among the logos featured on back. A total of 8,000 of these inserts sets was the announced production.

		MT
Complete Set (20):		80.00
Common Player:		2.00
1	Juan Gonzalez	9.00
2	Ken Griffey, Jr.	15.00
3	Frank Thomas	12.00
4	Albert Belle	5.00
5	Rafael Palmeiro	2.50
6	Joe Carter	3.00
7	Dean Palmer	2.00
8	Mickey Tettleton	2.00
9	Tim Salmon	3.50
10	Danny Tartabull	2.00
11	Barry Bonds	5.00
12	Dave Justice	3.50
13	Matt Williams	3.00
14	Fred McGriff	3.00
15	Ron Gant	2.00
16	Mike Piazza	9.00
17	Bobby Bonilla	2.00
18	Phil Plantier	2.00
19	Sammy Sosa	10.00
20	Rick Wilkins	2.00

1994 Pacific Crown Jewels of the Crown

BARRY BONDS

One of three inserts into 1994 Pacific Spanish foil packs. The design features a player action photo set against a silver prismatic background. On back is another color player photo against a background of colored silk and a large jewel. Season highlight stats and awards won are presented in both English and Spanish. The announced production run of these inserts was 8,000 sets.

		MT
Complete Set (36):		125.00
Common Player:		2.50
1	Robin Yount	3.00
2	Juan Gonzalez	9.00
3	Rafael Palmeiro	3.00
4	Paul Molitor	4.00
5	Roberto Alomar	5.00
6	John Olerud	2.50
7	Randy Johnson	4.00
8	Ken Griffey, Jr.	15.00
9	Wade Boggs	4.00
10	Don Mattingly	8.00
11	Kirby Puckett	8.00
12	Tim Salmon	4.00
13	Frank Thomas	12.00
14	Fernando Valenzuela (Comeback Player)	2.50
15	Cal Ripken, Jr.	15.00
16	Carlos Baerga	2.50
17	Kenny Lofton	6.00
18	Cecil Fielder	2.50
19	John Burkett	2.50
20	Andres Galarraga (Comeback Player)	2.50
21	Charlie Hayes	2.50
22	Orestes Destrade	2.50

23	Jeff Conine	2.50
24	Jeff Bagwell	6.00
25	Mark Grace	3.00
26	Ryne Sandberg	5.00
27	Gregg Jefferies	2.50
28	Barry Bonds	5.00
29	Mike Piazza	12.00
30	Greg Maddux	12.00
31	Darren Daulton	2.50
32	John Kruk	2.50
33	Len Dykstra, Robby Thompson	2.50
34	Orlando Merced	2.50
35	Tony Gwynn	9.00

1995 Pacific

The base cards in Pacific's Crown Collection baseball issue for 1995 feature borderless color action photos on front, graphically highlighted by the player name at bottom in gold foil and a color team logo in a baseball at lower-left. Backs have a playing field design in the background with a portrait photo at left. At right are 1994 stats, career highlights and a ghosted image of the team logo. Most back printing is in both English and Spanish. The 450 cards in the series are arranged alphabetically within team, with the teams arranged in city-alpha order. Several chase cards series are found in the 12-card foil packs.

		MT
Complete Set (450):		22.00
Common Player:		.05
1	Steve Avery	.05
2	Rafael Belliard	.05
3	Jeff Blauser	.05
4	Tom Glavine	.10
5	Dave Justice	.35
6	Mike Kelly	.05
7	Roberto Kelly	.05
8	Ryan Klesko	.45
9	Mark Lemke	.05
10	Javier Lopez	.15
11	Greg Maddux	1.50
12	Fred McGriff	.25
13	Greg McMichael	.05
14	Jose Oliva	.05
15	John Smoltz	.10
16	Tony Tarasco	.05
17	Brady Anderson	.10
18	Harold Baines	.08
19	Armando Benitez	.05
20	Mike Devereaux	.05
21	Leo Gomez	.05
22	Jeffrey Hammonds	.10
23	Chris Hoiles	.05
24	Ben McDonald	.05
25	Mark McLemore	.05
26	Jamie Moyer	.05

27	Mike Mussina	.25
28	Rafael Palmeiro	.10
29	Jim Poole	.05
30	Cal Ripken Jr.	2.50
31	Lee Smith	.08
32	Mark Smith	.05
33	Jose Canseco	.30
34	Roger Clemens	.60
35	Scott Cooper	.05
36	Andre Dawson	.08
37	Tony Fossas	.05
38	Mike Greenwell	.05
39	Chris Howard	.05
40	Jose Melendez	.05
41	Nate Minchey	.05
42	Tim Naehring	.05
43	Otis Nixon	.05
44	Carlos Rodriguez	.05
45	Aaron Sele	.10
46	Lee Tinsley	.05
47	Sergio Valdez	.05
48	John Valentin	.08
49	Mo Vaughn	.50
50	Brian Anderson	.10
51	Garret Anderson	.20
52	Rod Correia	.05
53	Chad Curtis	.05
54	Mark Dalesandro	.05
55	Chili Davis	.05
56	Gary DiSarcina	.05
57	Damion Easley	.05
58	Jim Edmonds	.20
59	Jorge Fabregas	.05
60	Chuck Finley	.05
61	Bo Jackson	.10
62	Mark Langston	.05
63	Eduardo Perez	.05
64	Tim Salmon	.20
65	J.T. Snow	.10
66	Willie Banks	.05
67	Jose Bautista	.05
68	Shawon Dunston	.10
69	Kevin Foster	.05
70	Mark Grace	.15
71	Jose Guzman	.05
72	Jose Hernandez	.05
73	Blaise Ilsley	.05
74	Derrick May	.05
75	Randy Myers	.05
76	Karl Rhodes	.05
77	Kevin Roberson	.05
78	Rey Sanchez	.05
79	Sammy Sosa	1.00
80	Steve Trachsel	.05
81	Eddie Zambrano	.05
82	Wilson Alvarez	.05
83	Jason Bere	.08
84	Joey Cora	.05
85	Jose DeLeon	.05
86	Alex Fernandez	.08
87	Julio Franco	.05
88	Ozzie Guillen	.05
89	Joe Hall	.05
90	Roberto Hernandez	.05
91	Darrin Jackson	.05
92	Lance Johnson	.05
93	Norberto Martin	.05
94	Jack McDowell	.08
95	Tim Raines	.08
96	Olmedo Saenz	.05
97	Frank Thomas	2.00
98	Robin Ventura	.10
99	Bret Boone	.05
100	Jeff Brantley	.05
101	Jacob Brumfield	.05
102	Hector Carrasco	.05
103	Brian Dorsett	.05
104	Tony Fernandez	.05
105	Willie Greene	.05
106	Erik Hanson	.05
107	Kevin Jarvis	.05
108	Barry Larkin	.15
109	Kevin Mitchell	.05
110	Hal Morris	.05
111	Jose Rijo	.05
112	Johnny Ruffin	.05
113	Deion Sanders	.30
114	Reggie Sanders	.10
115	Sandy Alomar Jr.	.10
116	Ruben Amaro	.05
117	Carlos Baerga	.15
118	Albert Belle	.60
119	Alvaro Espinoza	.05
120	Rene Gonzales	.05
121	Wayne Kirby	.05
122	Kenny Lofton	.45

123	Candy Maldonado	.05
124	Dennis Martinez	.08
125	Eddie Murray	.20
126	Charles Nagy	.05
127	Tony Pena	.05
128	Manny Ramirez	.45
129	Paul Sorrento	.05
130	Jim Thome	.20
131	Omar Vizquel	.05
132	Dante Bichette	.25
133	Ellis Burks	.12
134	Vinny Castilla	.10
135	Marvin Freeman	.05
136	Andres Galarraga	.10
137	Joe Girardi	.05
138	Charlie Hayes	.05
139	Mike Kingery	.05
140	Nelson Liriano	.05
141	Roberto Mejia	.05
142	David Nied	.05
143	Steve Reed	.05
144	Armando Reynoso	.05
145	Bruce Ruffin	.05
146	John Vander Wal	.05
147	Walt Weiss	.05
148	Skeeter Barnes	.05
149	Tim Belcher	.05
150	Junior Felix	.05
151	Cecil Fielder	.15
152	Travis Fryman	.10
153	Kirk Gibson	.05
154	Chris Gomez	.05
155	Buddy Groom	.05
156	Chad Kreuter	.05
157	Mike Moore	.05
158	Tony Phillips	.05
159	Juan Samuel	.05
160	Mickey Tettleton	.05
161	Alan Trammell	.08
162	David Wells	.05
163	Lou Whitaker	.05
164	Kurt Abbott	.05
165	Luis Aquino	.05
166	Alex Arias	.05
167	Bret Barberie	.05
168	Jerry Browne	.05
169	Chuck Carr	.05
170	Matias Carrillo	.05
171	Greg Colbrunn	.05
172	Jeff Conine	.08
173	Carl Everett	.05
174	Robb Nen	.05
175	Yorkis Perez	.05
176	Pat Rapp	.05
177	Benito Santiago	.08
178	Gary Sheffield	.15
179	Darrell Whitmore	.05
180	Jeff Bagwell	.75
181	Kevin Bass	.05
182	Craig Biggio	.10
183	Andujar Cedeno	.05
184	Doug Drabek	.05
185	Tony Eusebio	.05
186	Steve Finley	.05
187	Luis Gonzalez	.05
188	Pete Harnisch	.05
189	John Hudek	.08
190	Orlando Miller	.05
191	James Mouton	.05
192	Roberto Petagine	.05
193	Shane Reynolds	.05
194	Greg Swindell	.05
195	Dave Veres	.05
196	Kevin Appier	.05
197	Stan Belinda	.05
198	Vince Coleman	.05
199	David Cone	.08
200	Gary Gaetti	.08
201	Greg Gagne	.05
202	Mark Gubicza	.05
203	Bob Hamelin	.05
204	Dave Henderson	.05
205	Felix Jose	.05
206	Wally Joyner	.08
207	Jose Lind	.05
208	Mike Macfarlane	.05
209	Brian McRae	.05
210	Jeff Montgomery	.05
211	Hipolito Pichardo	.05
212	Pedro Astacio	.05
213	Brett Butler	.10
214	Omar Daal	.05
215	Delino DeShields	.08
216	Darren Dreifort	.05
217	Carlos Hernandez	.05
218	Orel Hershiser	.08

219	Garey Ingram	.05
220	Eric Karros	.10
221	Ramon Martinez	.08
222	Raul Mondesi	.50
223	Jose Offerman	.05
224	Mike Piazza	1.50
225	Henry Rodriguez	.08
226	Ismael Valdes	.15
227	Tim Wallach	.05
228	Jeff Cirillo	.05
229	Alex Diaz	.05
230	Cal Eldred	.05
231	Mike Fetters	.05
232	Brian Harper	.05
233	Ted Higuera	.05
234	John Jaha	.05
235	Graeme Lloyd	.05
236	Jose Mercedes	.05
237	Jaime Navarro	.05
238	Dave Nilsson	.05
239	Jesse Orosco	.05
240	Jody Reed	.05
241	Jose Valentin	.05
242	Greg Vaughn	.05
243	Turner Ward	.05
244	Rick Aguilera	.05
245	Rich Becker	.05
246	Jim Deshaies	.05
247	Steve Dunn	.05
248	Scott Erickson	.05
249	Kent Hrbek	.08
250	Chuck Knoblauch	.15
251	Scott Leius	.05
252	David McCarty	.05
253	Pat Meares	.05
254	Pedro Munoz	.05
255	Kirby Puckett	.75
256	Carlos Pulido	.05
257	Kevin Tapani	.05
258	Matt Walbeck	.05
259	Dave Winfield	.10
260	Moises Alou	.08
261	Juan Bell	.05
262	Freddie Benavides	.05
263	Sean Berry	.05
264	Wil Cordero	.05
265	Jeff Fassero	.05
266	Darrin Fletcher	.05
267	Cliff Floyd	.12
268	Marquis Grissom	.08
269	Gil Heredia	.05
270	Ken Hill	.05
271	Pedro J. Martinez	.05
272	Mel Rojas	.05
273	Larry Walker	.20
274	John Wetteland	.05
275	Rondell White	.15
276	Tim Bogar	.05
277	Bobby Bonilla	.10
278	Rico Brogna	.05
279	Jeromy Burnitz	.05
280	John Franco	.05
281	Eric Hillman	.05
282	Todd Hundley	.10
283	Jeff Kent	.05
284	Mike Maddux	.05
285	Joe Orsulak	.05
286	Luis Rivera	.05
287	Bret Saberhagen	.05
288	David Segui	.05
289	Ryan Thompson	.05
290	Fernando Vina	.05
291	Jose Vizcaino	.05
292	Jim Abbott	.08
293	Wade Boggs	.20
294	Russ Davis	.05
295	Mike Gallego	.05
296	Xavier Hernandez	.05
297	Steve Howe	.05
298	Jimmy Key	.05
299	Don Mattingly	.75
300	Terry Mulholland	.05
301	Paul O'Neill	.08
302	Luis Polonia	.05
303	Mike Stanley	.05
304	Danny Tartabull	.05
305	Randy Velarde	.05
306	Bob Wickman	.05
307	Bernie Williams	.35
308	Mark Acre	.05
309	Geronimo Berroa	.05
310	Mike Bordick	.05
311	Dennis Eckersley	.08
312	Rickey Henderson	.15
313	Stan Javier	.05
314	Miguel Jimenez	.05

315	Francisco Matos	.05
316	Mark McGwire	3.00
317	Troy Neel	.05
318	Steve Ontiveros	.05
319	Carlos Reyes	.05
320	Ruben Sierra	.08
321	Terry Steinbach	.05
322	Bob Welch	.05
323	Bobby Witt	.05
324	Larry Andersen	.05
325	Kim Batiste	.05
326	Darren Daulton	.05
327	Mariano Duncan	.05
328	Lenny Dykstra	.08
329	Jim Eisenreich	.05
330	Danny Jackson	.05
331	John Kruk	.05
332	Tony Longmire	.05
333	Tom Marsh	.05
334	Mickey Morandini	.05
335	Bobby Munoz	.05
336	Todd Pratt	.05
337	Tom Quinlan	.05
338	Kevin Stocker	.05
339	Fernando Valenzuela	.08
340	Jay Bell	.05
341	Dave Clark	.05
342	Steve Cooke	.05
343	Carlos Garcia	.05
344	Jeff King	.05
345	Jon Lieber	.05
346	Ravelo Manzanillo	.05
347	Al Martin	.05
348	Orlando Merced	.05
349	Denny Neagle	.08
350	Alejandro Pena	.05
351	Don Slaught	.05
352	Zane Smith	.05
353	Andy Van Slyke	.05
354	Rick White	.05
355	Kevin Young	.08
356	Andy Ashby	.05
357	Derek Bell	.10
358	Andy Benes	.08
359	Phil Clark	.05
360	Donnie Elliott	.05
361	Ricky Gutierrez	.05
362	Tony Gwynn	.50
363	Trevor Hoffman	.05
364	Tim Hyers	.05
365	Luis Lopez	.05
366	Jose Martinez	.05
367	Pedro A. Martinez	.05
368	Phil Plantier	.05
369	Bip Roberts	.05
370	A.J. Sager	.05
371	Jeff Tabaka	.05
372	Todd Benzinger	.05
373	Barry Bonds	.50
374	John Burkett	.05
375	Mark Carreon	.08
376	Royce Clayton	.08
377	Pat Gomez	.05
378	Erik Johnson	.05
379	Darren Lewis	.05
380	Kirt Manwaring	.05
381	Dave Martinez	.05
382	John Patterson	.05
383	Mark Portugal	.05
384	Darryl Strawberry	.08
385	Salomon Torres	.05
386	Bill Van Landingham	.05
387	Matt Williams	.20
388	Rich Amaral	.05
389	Bobby Ayala	.05
390	Mike Blowers	.05
391	Chris Bosio	.05
392	Jay Buhner	.08
393	Jim Converse	.05
394	Tim Davis	.05
395	Felix Fermin	.05
396	Dave Fleming	.05
397	Goose Gossage	.05
398	Ken Griffey Jr.	2.50
399	Randy Johnson	.25
400	Edgar Martinez	.08
401	Tino Martinez	.12
402	Alex Rodriguez	2.50
403	Dan Wilson	.05
404	Luis Alicea	.05
405	Rene Arocha	.05
406	Bernard Gilkey	.08
407	Gregg Jefferies	.08
408	Ray Lankford	.10
409	Terry McGriff	.05
410	Omar Olivares	.05

411	Jose Oquendo	.05
412	Vicente Palacios	.05
413	Geronimo Pena	.05
414	Mike Perez	.05
415	Gerald Perry	.05
416	Ozzie Smith	.35
417	Bob Tewksbury	.05
418	Mark Whiten	.05
419	Todd Zeile	.08
420	Esteban Beltre	.05
421	Kevin Brown	.08
422	Cris Carpenter	.05
423	Will Clark	.25
424	Hector Fajardo	.05
425	Jeff Frye	.05
426	Juan Gonzalez	.50
427	Rusty Greer	.05
428	Rick Honeycutt	.05
429	David Hulse	.05
430	Manny Lee	.05
431	Junior Ortiz	.05
432	Dean Palmer	.05
433	Ivan Rodriguez	.45
434	Dan Smith	.05
435	Roberto Alomar	.50
436	Pat Borders	.05
437	Scott Brow	.05
438	Rob Butler	.05
439	Joe Carter	.10
440	Tony Castillo	.05
441	Domingo Cedeno	.05
442	Brad Cornett	.05
443	Carlos Delgado	.10
444	Alex Gonzalez	.10
445	Juan Guzman	.08
446	Darren Hall	.05
447	Paul Molitor	.25
448	John Olerud	.10
449	Robert Perez	.05
450	Devon White	.05

1995 Pacific Gold Crown Die-cut

A die-cut gold holographic foil crown in the background is featured in this chase set. The player's name at bottom is rendered in the same foil. Backs have a dark blue background, a portrait photo and a 1994 season recap.

		MT
Complete Set (20):		250.00
Common Player:		3.00
1	Greg Maddux	25.00
2	Fred McGriff	5.00
3	Rafael Palmeiro	5.00
4	Cal Ripken Jr.	30.00
5	Jose Canseco	4.00
6	Frank Thomas	25.00
7	Albert Belle	10.00
8	Manny Ramirez	8.00
9	Andres Galarraga	3.00
10	Jeff Bagwell	15.00
11	Chan Ho Park	3.00
12	Raul Mondesi	4.00
13	Mike Piazza	25.00

14	Kirby Puckett	15.00
15	Barry Bonds	10.00
16	Ken Griffey Jr.	40.00
17	Alex Rodriguez	32.00
18	Juan Gonzalez	20.00
19	Roberto Alomar	8.00
20	Carlos Delgado	3.00

1995 Pacific Hot Hispanics

Acknowledging its bi-lingual card license and market niche, this insert set of Latinos Destacados (Hot Hispanics) features top Latin players in the majors. The series logo and a gold-foil holographic player name rise from a row of flames at bottom-front. On the reverse is another player photo, on an inferno background, along with 1994 season highlights and a large team logo.

		MT
Complete Set (36):		45.00
Common Player:		1.25
1	Roberto Alomar	5.00
2	Moises Alou	1.50
3	Wilson Alvarez	1.25
4	Carlos Baerga	1.50
5	Geronimo Berroa	1.25
6	Jose Canseco	2.00
7	Hector Carrasco	1.25
8	Wil Cordero	1.25
9	Carlos Delgado	1.25
10	Damion Easley	1.25
11	Tony Eusebio	1.25
12	Hector Fajardo	1.25
13	Andres Galarraga	2.00
14	Carlos Garcia	1.25
15	Chris Gomez	1.25
16	Alex Gonzalez	1.25
17	Juan Gonzalez	8.00
18	Luis Gonzalez	1.25
19	Felix Jose	1.25
20	Javier Lopez	2.00
21	Luis Lopez	1.25
22	Dennis Martinez	1.50
23	Orlando Miller	1.25
24	Raul Mondesi	2.00
25	Jose Oliva	1.25
26	Rafael Palmeiro	2.00
27	Yorkis Perez	1.25
28	Manny Ramirez	6.00
29	Jose Rijo	1.25
30	Alex Rodriguez	16.00
31	Ivan Rodriguez	5.00
32	Carlos Rodriguez	1.25
33	Sammy Sosa	10.00
34	Tony Tarasco	1.25
35	Ismael Valdes	1.50
36	Bernie Williams	4.00

1995 Pacific Marquee Prism

Etched gold holographic foil is the background to the action photos in this insert set. Player names at bottom-front are shadowed in team colors. Backs repeat the front photo in miniature version in a box at one side that offers career stats and a highlight. On the other end is a portrait photo on a background of baseballs.

		MT
Complete Set (36):		125.00
Common Player:		1.50
1	Jose Canseco	2.00
2	Gregg Jefferies	1.50
3	Fred McGriff	2.00
4	Joe Carter	2.00
5	Tim Salmon	2.50
6	Wade Boggs	2.50
7	Dave Winfield	2.00
8	Bob Hamelin	1.50
9	Cal Ripken Jr.	15.00
10	Don Mattingly	8.00
11	Juan Gonzalez	8.00
12	Carlos Delgado	1.50
13	Barry Bonds	7.50
14	Albert Belle	6.00
15	Raul Mondesi	3.00
16	Jeff Bagwell	8.00
17	Mike Piazza	10.00
18	Rafael Palmeiro	2.00
19	Frank Thomas	15.00
20	Matt Williams	2.50
21	Ken Griffey Jr.	20.00
22	Will Clark	3.00
23	Bobby Bonilla	1.50
24	Kenny Lofton	5.00
25	Paul Molitor	4.00
26	Kirby Puckett	8.00
27	Dave Justice	2.00
28	Jeff Conine	1.50
29	Bret Boone	1.50
30	Larry Walker	2.00
31	Cecil Fielder	1.50
32	Manny Ramirez	6.00
33	Javier Lopez	2.00
34	Jimmy Key	1.50
35	Andres Galarraga	2.00
36	Tony Gwynn	8.00

1995 Pacific Prism

The rainbow prismatic foil which is the background ot the action photos on the card fronts provides the visual punch to Pacific's premium brand cards. In a throwback to the 1950s, the cards were sold in single-card packs for $1.75. Production was limited to 2,999 cases of 36-pack boxes. Backs have a large portrait photo on a conventionally printed rainbow background. In keeping with the company's license, the 1994 season summary printed at bottom on back is in both English and Spanish. One checklist, team or Pacific logo was inserted into each pack to protect the Prism card.

		MT
Complete Set (144):		150.00
Common Player:		.50
Wax Box:		48.00
Unlisted Stars:		1.50
1	Dave Justice	1.00
2	Ryan Klesko	1.50
3	Javier Lopez	.75
4	Greg Maddux	10.00
5	Fred McGriff	1.00
6	Tony Tarasco	.50
7	Jeffrey Hammonds	.50
8	Mike Mussina	1.50
9	Rafael Palmeiro	.75
10	Cal Ripken Jr.	12.00
11	Lee Smith	.50
12	Roger Clemens	2.50
13	Scott Cooper	.50
14	Mike Greenwell	.50
15	Carlos Rodriguez	.50
16	Mo Vaughn	4.00
17	Chili Davis	.50
18	Jim Edmonds	.50
19	Jorge Fabregas	.50
20	Bo Jackson	.60
21	Tim Salmon	.75
22	Mark Grace	.75
23	Jose Guzman	.50
24	Randy Myers	.50
25	Rey Sanchez	.50
26	Sammy Sosa	8.00
27	Wilson Alvarez	.50
28	Julio Franco	.50
29	Ozzie Guillen	.50
30	Jack McDowell	.50
31	Frank Thomas	12.00
32	Bret Boone	.50
33	Barry Larkin	1.00
34	Hal Morris	.50
35	Jose Rijo	.50
36	Deion Sanders	1.50
37	Carlos Baerga	.65
38	Albert Belle	4.00
39	Kenny Lofton	3.00
40	Dennis Martinez	.50
41	Manny Ramirez	3.00
42	Omar Vizquel	.50
43	Dante Bichette	1.00
44	Marvin Freeman	.50
45	Andres Galarraga	.75
46	Mike Kingery	.50
47	Danny Bautista	.50
48	Cecil Fielder	.75
49	Travis Fryman	.50
50	Tony Phillips	.50
51	Alan Trammell	.50
52	Lou Whitaker	.50
53	Alex Arias	.50
54	Bret Barberie	.50

55	Jeff Conine	.50
56	Charles Johnson	.70
57	Gary Sheffield	3.00
58	Jeff Bagwell	6.00
59	Craig Biggio	.50
60	Doug Drabek	.50
61	Tony Eusebio	.50
62	Luis Gonzalez	.50
63	David Cone	.50
64	Bob Hamelin	.50
65	Felix Jose	.50
66	Wally Joyner	.50
67	Brian McRae	.50
68	Brett Butler	.50
69	Garey Ingram	.50
70	Ramon Martinez	.50
71	Raul Mondesi	1.00
72	Mike Piazza	10.00
73	Henry Rodriguez	.50
74	Ricky Bones	.50
75	Pat Listach	.50
76	Dave Nilsson	.50
77	Jose Valentin	.50
78	Rick Aguilera	.50
79	Denny Hocking	.50
80	Shane Mack	.50
81	Pedro Munoz	.50
82	Kirby Puckett	6.00
83	Dave Winfield	.75
84	Moises Alou	.50
85	Wil Cordero	.50
86	Cliff Floyd	.50
87	Marquis Grissom	.50
88	Pedro Martinez	.50
89	Larry Walker	.75
90	Bobby Bonilla	.50
91	Jeremy Burnitz	.50
92	John Franco	.50
93	Jeff Kent	.50
94	Jose Vizcaino	.50
95	Wade Boggs	1.00
96	Jimmy Key	.50
97	Don Mattingly	7.00
98	Paul O'Neill	.50
99	Luis Polonia	.50
100	Danny Tartabull	.50
101	Geronimo Berroa	.50
102	Rickey Henderson	.65
103	Ruben Sierra	.50
104	Terry Steinbach	.50
105	Darren Daulton	.50
106	Mariano Duncan	.50
107	Lenny Dykstra	.50
108	Mike Lieberthal	.50
109	Tony Longmire	.50
110	Tom Marsh	.50
111	Jay Bell	.50
112	Carlos Garcia	.50
113	Orlando Merced	.50
114	Andy Van Slyke	.50
115	Derek Bell	.50
116	Tony Gwynn	6.00
117	Luis Lopez	.50
118	Bip Roberts	.50
119	Rod Beck	.50
120	Barry Bonds	5.00
121	Darryl Strawberry	.60
122	Bill Van Landingham	.50
123	Matt Williams	1.00
124	Jay Buhner	.75
125	Felix Fermin	.50
126	Ken Griffey Jr.	15.00
127	Randy Johnson	1.00
128	Edgar Martinez	.50
129	Alex Rodriguez	15.00
130	Rene Arocha	.50
131	Gregg Jefferies	.50
132	Mike Perez	.50
133	Ozzie Smith	3.00
134	Jose Canseco	.75
135	Will Clark	.75
136	Juan Gonzalez	6.00
137	Ivan Rodriguez	3.00
138	Roberto Alomar	3.00
139	Joe Carter	.60
140	Carlos Delgado	.50
141	Alex Gonzalez	.50
142	Juan Guzman	.50
143	Paul Molitor	1.50
144	John Olerud	.50

A player's name in *italic* type indicates a rookie card.

1996 Pacific Crown Collection

Pacific's base set for 1996 features 450 gold-foil enhanced cards. Fronts have borderless game-action photos with the issuer's logo in an upper corner and the player's name at bottom center in gold. Horizontal backs have a portrait photo at right, career highlights in both English and Spanish at left, and 1995 stats at top. Cards were sold in 12-card foil packs which could include one of six types of insert cards.

		MT
Complete Set (450):		30.00
Common Player:		.05
Unlisted Stars: .25 to .35		
Wax Box:		50.00
1	Steve Avery	.05
2	Ryan Klesko	.40
3	Pedro Borbon	.05
4	Chipper Jones	2.00
5	Kent Mercker	.05
6	Greg Maddux	2.00
7	Greg McMichael	.05
8	Mark Wohlers	.05
9	Fred McGriff	.30
10	John Smoltz	.20
11	Rafael Belliard	.05
12	Mark Lemke	.05
13	Tom Glavine	.15
14	Javier Lopez	.15
15	Jeff Blauser	.05
16	Dave Justice	.25
17	Marquis Grissom	.08
18	Greg Maddux (Cy Young (NL))	1.00
19	Randy Myers	.05
20	Scott Servais	.05
21	Sammy Sosa	1.00
22	Kevin Foster	.05
23	Jose Hernandez	.05
24	Jim Bullinger	.05
25	Mike Perez	.05
26	Shawon Dunston	.10
27	Rey Sanchez	.05
28	Frank Castillo	.05
29	Jaime Navarro	.05
30	Brian McRae	.05
31	Mark Grace	.10
32	Roberto Rivera	.05
33	Luis Gonzalez	.05
34	Hector Carrasco	.05
35	Bret Boone	.05
36	Thomas Howard	.05
37	Hal Morris	.05
38	John Smiley	.05
39	Jeff Brantley	.05
40	Barry Larkin	.20
41	Mariano Duncan	.05
42	Xavier Hernandez	.05
43	Pete Schourek	.05
44	Reggie Sanders	.10
45	Dave Burba	.05
46	Jeff Branson	.05

47	Mark Portugal	.05
48	Ron Gant	.10
49	Benito Santiago	.05
50	Barry Larkin (MVP (NL))	.10
51	Steve Reed	.05
52	Kevin Ritz	.05
53	Dante Bichette	.25
54	Darren Holmes	.05
55	Ellis Burks	.08
56	Walt Weiss	.05
57	Armando Reynoso	.05
58	Vinny Castilla	.08
59	Jason Bates	.05
60	Mike Kingery	.05
61	Bryan Rekar	.05
62	Curtis Leskanic	.05
63	Bret Saberhagen	.05
64	Andres Galarraga	.10
65	Larry Walker	.25
66	Joe Girardi	.05
67	Quilvio Veras	.05
68	Robb Nen	.05
69	Mario Diaz	.05
70	Chuck Carr	.05
71	Alex Arias	.05
72	Pat Rapp	.05
73	Rich Garces	.05
74	Kurt Abbott	.05
75	Andre Dawson	.10
76	Greg Colbrunn	.05
77	John Burkett	.05
78	Terry Pendleton	.05
79	Jesus Tavarez	.05
80	Charles Johnson	.15
81	Yorkis Perez	.05
82	Jeff Conine	.08
83	Gary Sheffield	.35
84	Brian Hunter	.05
85	Derrick May	.05
86	Greg Swindell	.05
87	Derek Bell	.08
88	Dave Veres	.05
89	Jeff Bagwell	.75
90	Todd Jones	.05
91	Orlando Miller	.05
92	Pedro A. Martinez	.05
93	Tony Eusebio	.05
94	Craig Biggio	.10
95	Shane Reynolds	.05
96	James Mouton	.05
97	Doug Drabek	.05
98	Dave Magadan	.05
99	Ricky Gutierrez	.05
100	Hideo Nomo	.75
101	Delino DeShields	.05
102	Tom Candiotti	.05
103	Mike Piazza	2.00
104	Ramon Martinez	.08
105	Pedro Astacio	.05
106	Chad Fonville	.05
107	Raul Mondesi	.30
108	Ismael Valdes	.08
109	Jose Offerman	.05
110	Todd Worrell	.05
111	Eric Karros	.10
112	Brett Butler	.10
113	Juan Castro	.05
114	Roberto Kelly	.05
115	Omar Daal	.05
116	Antonio Osuna	.05
117	Hideo Nomo (Rookie of Year (NL))	.40
118	Mike Lansing	.05
119	Mel Rojas	.05
120	Sean Berry	.05
121	David Segui	.05
122	Tavo Alvarez	.05
123	Pedro Martinez	.08
124	*F.P. Santangelo*	.10
125	Rondell White	.10
126	Cliff Floyd	.08
127	Henry Rodriguez	.05
128	Tony Tarasco	.05
129	Yamil Benitez	.05
130	Carlos Perez	.05
131	Wil Cordero	.05
132	Jeff Fassero	.05
133	Moises Alou	.10
134	John Franco	.05
135	Rico Brogna	.05
136	Dave Mlicki	.05
137	Bill Pulsipher	.08
138	Jose Vizcaino	.05
139	Carl Everett	.05
140	Edgardo Alfonzo	.05
141	Bobby Jones	.05

#	Player	Value
142	Alberto Castillo	.05
143	Joe Orsulak	.05
144	Jeff Kent	.05
145	Ryan Thompson	.05
146	Jason Isringhausen	.10
147	Todd Hundley	.15
148	Alex Ochoa	.05
149	Charlie Hayes	.05
150	Michael Mimbs	.05
151	Darren Daulton	.05
152	Toby Borland	.05
153	Andy Van Slyke	.05
154	Mickey Morandini	.05
155	Sid Fernandez	.05
156	Tom Marsh	.05
157	Kevin Stocker	.05
158	Paul Quantrill	.05
159	Gregg Jefferies	.08
160	Ricky Bottalico	.05
161	Lenny Dykstra	.05
162	Mark Whiten	.05
163	Tyler Green	.05
164	Jim Eisenreich	.05
165	Heathcliff Slocumb	.05
166	Esteban Loaiza	.10
167	Rich Aude	.05
168	Jason Christiansen	.05
169	Ramon Morel	.05
170	Orlando Merced	.05
171	Paul Wagner	.05
172	Jeff King	.05
173	Jay Bell	.05
174	Jacob Brumfield	.05
175	Nelson Liriano	.05
176	Dan Miceli	.05
177	Carlos Garcia	.05
178	Denny Neagle	.05
179	Angelo Encarnacion	.05
180	Al Martin	.05
181	Midre Cummings	.05
182	Eddie Williams	.05
183	Roberto Petagine	.05
184	Tony Gwynn	.75
185	Andy Ashby	.05
186	Melvin Nieves	.05
187	Phil Clark	.05
188	Brad Ausmus	.05
189	Bip Roberts	.05
190	Fernando Valenzuela	.08
191	Marc Newfield	.05
192	Steve Finley	.05
193	Trevor Hoffman	.05
194	Andujar Cedeno	.05
195	Jody Reed	.05
196	Ken Caminiti	.25
197	Joey Hamilton	.05
198	Tony Gwynn (Batting Champ. (NL))	.30
199	Shawn Barton	.05
200	Deion Sanders	.35
201	Rikkert Faneyte	.05
202	Barry Bonds	.75
203	Matt Williams	.25
204	Jose Bautista	.05
205	Mark Leiter	.05
206	Mark Carreon	.05
207	Robby Thompson	.05
208	Terry Mulholland	.05
209	Rod Beck	.05
210	Royce Clayton	.05
211	J.R. Phillips	.05
212	Kirt Manwaring	.05
213	Glenallen Hill	.05
214	William Van Landingham	.05
215	Scott Cooper	.05
216	Bernard Gilkey	.08
217	Allen Watson	.05
218	Donovan Osborne	.10
219	Ray Lankford	.05
220	Tony Fossas	.05
221	Tom Pagnozzi	.05
222	John Mabry	.05
223	Tripp Cromer	.05
224	Mark Petkovsek	.05
225	Mike Morgan	.05
226	Ozzie Smith	.40
227	Tom Henke	.05
228	Jose Oquendo	.05
229	Brian Jordan	.10
230	Cal Ripken Jr.	2.00
231	Scott Erickson	.05
232	Harold Baines	.08
233	Jeff Manto	.05
234	Jesse Orosco	.05
235	Jeffrey Hammonds	.05
236	Brady Anderson	.12
237	Manny Alexander	.05
238	Chris Hoiles	.05
239	Rafael Palmeiro	.15
240	Ben McDonald	.05
241	Curtis Goodwin	.05
242	Bobby Bonilla	.08
243	Mike Mussina	.40
244	Kevin Brown	.08
245	Armando Benitez	.05
246	Jose Canseco	.35
247	Erik Hanson	.05
248	Mo Vaughn	.60
249	Tim Naehring	.05
250	Vaughn Eshelman	.05
251	Mike Greenwell	.05
252	Troy O'Leary	.05
253	Tim Wakefield	.05
254	Dwayne Hosey	.05
255	John Valentin	.08
256	Rick Aguilera	.05
257	Mike MacFarlane	.05
258	Roger Clemens	.75
259	Luis Alicea	.05
260	Mo Vaughn (MVP (AL))	.25
261	Mark Langston	.05
262	Jim Edmonds	.15
263	Rod Correia	.05
264	Tim Salmon	.25
265	J.T. Snow	.08
266	Orlando Palmeiro	.05
267	Jorge Fabregas	.05
268	Jim Abbott	.08
269	Eduardo Perez	.05
270	Lee Smith	.08
271	Gary DiSarcina	.05
272	Damion Easley	.05
273	Tony Phillips	.05
274	Garret Anderson	.15
275	Chuck Finley	.05
276	Chili Davis	.05
277	Lance Johnson	.05
278	Alex Fernandez	.08
279	Robin Ventura	.10
280	Chris Snopek	.05
281	Brian Keyser	.05
282	Lyle Mouton	.05
283	*Luis Andujar*	.05
284	Tim Raines	.08
285	Larry Thomas	.05
286	Ozzie Guillen	.05
287	Frank Thomas	2.00
288	Roberto Hernandez	.05
289	Dave Martinez	.05
290	Ray Durham	.05
291	Ron Karkovice	.05
292	Wilson Alvarez	.05
293	Omar Vizquel	.05
294	Eddie Murray	.40
295	Sandy Alomar	.08
296	Orel Hershiser	.08
297	Jose Mesa	.05
298	Julian Tavarez	.05
299	Dennis Martinez	.08
300	Carlos Baerga	.10
301	Manny Ramirez	.75
302	Jim Thome	.35
303	Kenny Lofton	.65
304	Tony Pena	.05
305	Alvaro Espinoza	.05
306	Paul Sorrento	.05
307	Albert Belle	.75
308	Danny Bautista	.05
309	Chris Gomez	.05
310	Jose Lima	.05
311	Phil Nevin	.05
312	Alan Trammell	.10
313	Chad Curtis	.05
314	John Flaherty	.05
315	Travis Fryman	.05
316	Todd Steverson	.05
317	Brian Bohanon	.05
318	Lou Whitaker	.05
319	Bobby Higginson	.15
320	Steve Rodriguez	.05
321	Cecil Fielder	.20
322	Felipe Lira	.05
323	Juan Samuel	.05
324	Bob Hamelin	.05
325	Tom Goodwin	.05
326	Johnny Damon	.15
327	Hipolito Pichardo	.05
328	Dilson Torres	.05
329	Kevin Appier	.05
330	Mark Gubicza	.05
331	Jon Nunnally	.05
332	Gary Gaetti	.08
333	Brent Mayne	.05
334	Brent Cookson	.05
335	Tom Gordon	.05
336	Wally Joyner	.08
337	Greg Gagne	.05
338	Fernando Vina	.05
339	Joe Oliver	.05
340	John Jaha	.05
341	Jeff Cirillo	.05
342	Pat Listach	.05
343	Dave Nilsson	.05
344	Steve Sparks	.05
345	Ricky Bones	.05
346	David Hulse	.05
347	Scott Karl	.05
348	Darryl Hamilton	.05
349	B.J. Surhoff	.05
350	Angel Miranda	.05
351	Sid Roberson	.05
352	Matt Mieske	.05
353	*Jose Valentin*	.05
354	*Matt Lawton*	.05
355	Eddie Guardado	.05
356	Brad Radke	.05
357	Pedro Munoz	.05
358	Scott Stahoviak	.05
359	Erik Schullstrom	.05
360	Pat Meares	.15
361	Marty Cordova	.05
362	Scott Leius	.05
363	Matt Walbeck	.05
364	Rich Becker	.05
365	Kirby Puckett	.75
366	Oscar Munoz	.05
367	Chuck Knoblauch	.20
368	Marty Cordova (Rookie of Year (AL))	.10
369	Bernie Williams	.40
370	Mike Stanley	.05
371	Andy Pettitte	.75
372	Jack McDowell	.08
373	Sterling Hitchcock	.05
374	David Cone	.08
375	Randy Velarde	.05
376	Don Mattingly	1.00
377	Melido Perez	.05
378	Wade Boggs	.25
379	Ruben Sierra	.05
380	Tony Fernandez	.05
381	John Wetteland	.05
382	Mariano Rivera	.15
383	Derek Jeter	1.50
384	Paul O'Neill	.05
385	Mark McGwire	3.00
386	Scott Brosius	.05
387	Don Wengert	.05
388	Terry Steinbach	.05
389	Brent Gates	.05
390	Craig Paquette	.05
391	Mike Bordick	.05
392	Ariel Prieto	.05
393	Dennis Eckersley	.08
394	Carlos Reyes	.05
395	Todd Stottlemyre	.05
396	Rickey Henderson	.20
397	Geronimo Berroa	.05
398	Steve Ontiveros	.05
399	Mike Gallego	.05
400	Stan Javier	.05
401	Randy Johnson	.30
402	Norm Charlton	.05
403	Mike Blowers	.05
404	Tino Martinez	.12
405	Dan Wilson	.05
406	Andy Benes	.05
407	Alex Diaz	.05
408	Edgar Martinez	.08
409	Chris Bosio	.05
410	Ken Griffey Jr.	2.50
411	Luis Sojo	.05
412	Bob Wolcott	.05
413	Vince Coleman	.05
414	Rich Amaral	.05
415	Jay Buhner	.20
416	Alex Rodriguez	2.50
417	Joey Cora	.05
418	Randy Johnson (Cy Young (AL))	.20
419	Edgar Martinez (Batting Champ. (AL))	.05
420	Ivan Rodriguez	.40
421	Mark McLemore	.05
422	Mickey Tettleton	.05
423	Juan Gonzalez	1.25
424	Will Clark	.25
425	Kevin Gross	.05

426	Dean Palmer	.05
427	Kenny Rogers	.05
428	Bob Tewksbury	.05
429	Benji Gil	.05
430	Jeff Russell	.05
431	Rusty Greer	.05
432	Roger Pavlik	.05
433	Esteban Beltre	.05
434	Otis Nixon	.05
435	Paul Molitor	.40
436	Carlos Delgado	.08
437	Ed Sprague	.05
438	Juan Guzman	.05
439	Domingo Cedeno	.05
440	Pat Hentgen	.05
441	Tomas Perez	.05
442	John Olerud	.08
443	Shawn Green	.05
444	Al Leiter	.05
445	Joe Carter	.15
446	Robert Perez	.05
447	Devon White	.05
448	Tony Castillo	.05
449	Alex Gonzalez	.05
450	Roberto Alomar	.60
450p	Roberto Alomar (unmarked promo card, "Games: 128" on back)	15.00

1996 Pacific Crown Cramer's Choice

One of the most unusually shaped baseball cards of all time is the Cramer's Choice insert set from the 1996 Pacific Crown Collection. The set features the 10 best players as chosen by Pacific founder and president Mike Cramer. Cards are in a die-cut pyramidal design 3-1/2" tall and 2-1/2" at the base. The player picture on front is set against a silver-foil background, while the player name and other information is in gold foil on a faux marble base at bottom; the effect is a simulation of a trophy. Backs repeat the marbled background and have a bi-lingual justification from Cramer concerning his choice of the player as one of the 10 best. Average insertion rate is one card per case (720 packs.)

	MT
Complete Set (10):	1000.
Common Player:	40.00
CC1 Roberto Alomar	50.00
CC2 Wade Boggs	40.00
CC3 Cal Ripken Jr.	180.00
CC4 Greg Maddux	125.00
CC5 Frank Thomas	180.00
CC6 Tony Gwynn	110.00
CC7 Mike Piazza	125.00
CC8 Ken Griffey Jr.	225.00
CC9 Manny Ramirez	60.00
CC10 Edgar Martinez	40.00

1996 Pacific Crown Estrellas Latinas

Three dozen of the best contemporary Latino ballplayers are honored in this chase set. Cards feature action photos silhouetted on a black background shot through with gold-foil streaks and stars. The player name, set and insert set logos are in gold at left. Backs have a player portrait photo and English/Spanish career summary. The Latino Stars insert cards are inserted at an average rate of one per nine packs; about four per foil box.

		MT
Complete Set (36):		45.00
Common Player:		1.00
EL1	Roberto Alomar	6.00
EL2	Moises Alou	1.00
EL3	Carlos Baerga	1.50
EL4	Geronimo Berroa	1.00
EL5	Ricky Bones	1.00
EL6	Bobby Bonilla	1.00
EL7	Jose Canseco	2.00
EL8	Vinny Castilla	1.25
EL9	Pedro Martinez	1.25
EL10	John Valentin	1.00
EL11	Andres Galarraga	1.50
EL12	Juan Gonzalez	8.00
EL13	Ozzie Guillen	1.00
EL14	Esteban Loaiza	1.25
EL15	Javier Lopez	2.00
EL16	Dennis Martinez	1.00
EL17	Edgar Martinez	1.50
EL18	Tino Martinez	1.25
EL19	Orlando Merced	1.00
EL20	Jose Mesa	1.00
EL21	Raul Mondesi	2.00
EL22	Jaime Navarro	1.00
EL23	Rafael Palmeiro	2.00
EL24	Carlos Perez	1.50
EL25	Manny Ramirez	5.00
EL26	Alex Rodriguez	15.00
EL27	Ivan Rodriguez	4.00
EL28	David Segui	1.00
EL29	Ruben Sierra	1.00
EL30	Sammy Sosa	8.00
EL31	Julian Tavarez	1.00
EL32	Ismael Valdes	1.00
EL33	Fernando Valenzuela	1.00
EL34	Quilvio Veras	1.00
EL35	Omar Vizquel	1.00
EL36	Bernie Williams	3.00

1996 Pacific Crown Gold Crown Die-Cuts

One of Pacific's most popular inserts of the previous year returns in 1996. The Gold Crown die-cuts have the top of the card cut away to

form a gold-foil crown design with an action photo below. The player's name is also in gold foil. Backs repeat the gold crown design at top, have a portrait photo at lower-right and a few words about the player, in both English and Spanish. Insertion rate was advertised as one per 37 packs, on average.

		MT
Complete Set (36):		325.00
Common Player:		4.00
DC1	Roberto Alomar	8.00
DC2	Will Clark	6.00
DC3	Johnny Damon	4.00
DC4	Don Mattingly	10.00
DC5	Edgar Martinez	4.00
DC6	Manny Ramirez	10.00
DC7	Mike Piazza	25.00
DC8	Quilvio Veras	4.00
DC9	Rickey Henderson	4.00
DC10	Jeff Bagwell	15.00
DC11	Andres Galarraga	6.00
DC12	Tim Salmon	5.00
DC13	Ken Griffey Jr.	40.00
DC14	Sammy Sosa	25.00
DC15	Cal Ripken Jr.	30.00
DC16	Raul Mondesi	6.00
DC17	Jose Canseco	6.00
DC18	Frank Thomas	30.00
DC19	Hideo Nomo	10.00
DC20	Wade Boggs	5.00
DC21	Reggie Sanders	4.00
DC22	Carlos Baerga	4.00
DC23	Mo Vaughn	10.00
DC24	Ivan Rodriguez	10.00
DC25	Kirby Puckett	15.00
DC26	Albert Belle	10.00
DC27	Vinny Castilla	4.00
DC28	Greg Maddux	25.00
DC29	Dante Bichette	5.00
DC30	Deion Sanders	5.00
DC31	Chipper Jones	25.00
DC32	Cecil Fielder	5.00
DC33	Randy Johnson	8.00
DC34	Mark McGwire	40.00
DC35	Tony Gwynn	20.00
DC36	Barry Bonds	10.00

1996 Pacific Crown Hometown of the Players

The hometown roots of 20 top players are examined in this chase set. Fronts have action photos with large areas of the background replaced with textured gold foil, including solid and outline versions of the player's name. Backs have a portrait photo, a representation of the player's native flag and a few words about his hometown. Card numbers have an "HP" prefix and are inserted at an average rate of one per 18 packs; about two per box.

	MT
Complete Set (20):	125.00
Common Player:	3.00
HP1 Mike Piazza	12.00
HP2 Greg Maddux	12.00
HP3 Tony Gwynn	8.00
HP4 Carlos Baerga	3.00
HP5 Don Mattingly	8.00
HP6 Cal Ripken Jr.	12.50
HP7 Chipper Jones	12.00
HP8 Andres Galarraga	3.00
HP9 Manny Ramirez	6.00
HP10 Roberto Alomar	7.00
HP11 Ken Griffey Jr.	18.00
HP12 Jose Canseco	4.00
HP13 Frank Thomas	15.00
HP14 Vinny Castilla	3.00
HP15 Roberto Kelly	3.00
HP16 Dennis Martinez	3.00
HP17 Kirby Puckett	7.00
HP18 Raul Mondesi	4.00
HP19 Hideo Nomo	6.00
HP20 Edgar Martinez	3.00

1996 Pacific Crown Milestones

A textured metallic blue-foil background is featured in this insert set. Behind the player action photo is a spider's web design with flying baseballs, team logo and a number representing the milestone. The player's name is in purple foil, outlined in white, vertically at right. Backs have a portrait photo and bilingual description of the milestone. Average insertion rate for this insert series is one per 37 packs.

	MT
Complete Set (10):	75.00
Common Player:	3.00
M1 Albert Belle	6.00
M2 Don Mattingly	10.00
M3 Tony Gwynn	9.00
M4 Jose Canseco	4.00
M5 Marty Cordova	3.00
M6 Wade Boggs	3.00
M7 Greg Maddux	12.00
M8 Eddie Murray	5.00
M9 Ken Griffey Jr.	20.00
M10 Cal Ripken Jr.	15.00

1996 Pacific Crown October Moments

Post-season baseball has never been better represented on a card than in Pacific's "October Moments" chase set. Color action photos are set again a background of a stadium decked in the traditional Fall Classic bunting, all rendered in metallic copper foil. At bottom is a textured silver strip with the player name in copper and a swirl of fallen leaves. Backs have a repeat of the leaves and bunting themes with a player portrait at center and English/Spanish description of his October heroics. These cards are found at an average rate of once per 37 packs.

	MT
Complete Set (20):	150.00
Common Player:	3.00
OM1 Carlos Baerga	3.00
OM2 Albert Belle	9.00
OM3 Dante Bichette	4.00
OM4 Jose Canseco	4.00
OM5 Tom Glavine	4.00
OM6 Ken Griffey Jr.	30.00
OM7 Randy Johnson	6.00
OM8 Chipper Jones	20.00
OM9 Dave Justice	3.00
OM10 Ryan Klesko	6.00
OM11 Kenny Lofton	9.00
OM12 Javier Lopez	3.00
OM13 Greg Maddux	20.00
OM14 Edgar Martinez	3.00
OM15 Don Mattingly	15.00
OM16 Hideo Nomo	10.00
OM17 Mike Piazza	20.00
OM18 Manny Ramirez	9.00
OM19 Reggie Sanders	3.00
OM20 Jim Thome	6.00

1996 Pacific Prism

Only the best in baseball make the cut for the Prism checklist. Sold in one-card foil packs the cards feature action photos set against an etched silver-foil background highlighted by slashes approximating team colors. Backs are conventionally printed in a horizontal format with a player portrait photo at left center on a purple background. A short 1995 season recap is feature in both English and Spanish. Card numbers are prefixed with a "P".

	MT
Complete Set (144):	150.00
Common Player:	1.00
Golds: 3x to 5x	
Wax Box:	45.00
1 Tom Glavine	1.50
2 Chipper Jones	10.00
3 David Justice	1.50
4 Ryan Klesko	3.00
5 Javier Lopez	1.50
6 Greg Maddux	10.00
7 Fred McGriff	1.50
8 Frank Castillo	1.00
9 Luis Gonzalez	1.00
10 Mark Grace	2.00
11 Brian McRae	1.00
12 Jaime Navarro	1.00
13 Sammy Sosa	8.00
14 Bret Boone	1.00
15 Ron Gant	1.50
16 Barry Larkin	1.50
17 Reggie Sanders	1.00
18 Benito Santiago	1.00
19 Dante Bichette	1.50
20 Vinny Castilla	1.25
21 Andres Galarraga	1.50
22 Bryan Rekar	1.00
23 Roberto Alomar	3.00
23p Roberto Alomar ("Azulejos" rather than "Los Azulajos" on back, unmarked promo card)	15.00
24 Jeff Conine	1.00
25 Andre Dawson	1.00
26 Charles Johnson	1.50
27 Gary Sheffield	2.00
28 Quilvio Veras	1.00
29 Jeff Bagwell	6.00
30 Derek Bell	1.00
31 Craig Biggio	1.00
32 Tony Eusebio	1.00
33 Karim Garcia	2.50
34 Eric Karros	1.00
35 Ramon Martinez	1.00
36 Raul Mondesi	1.50
37 Hideo Nomo	3.00
38 Mike Piazza	10.00
39 Ismael Valdes	1.00
40 Moises Alou	1.00
41 Wil Cordero	1.00
42 Pedro Martinez	1.00
43 Mel Rojas	1.00
44 David Segui	1.00
45 Edgardo Alfonzo	1.00
46 Rico Brogna	1.00
47 John Franco	1.00
48 Jason Isringhausen	1.50
49 Jose Vizcaino	1.00
50 Ricky Bottalico	1.00
51 Darren Daulton	1.00

52	Lenny Dykstra	1.00
53	Tyler Green	1.00
54	Gregg Jefferies	1.00
55	Jay Bell	1.00
56	Jason Christiansen	1.00
57	Carlos Garcia	1.00
58	Esteban Loaiza	1.25
59	Orlando Merced	1.00
60	Andujar Cedeno	1.00
61	Tony Gwynn	6.00
62	Melvin Nieves	1.00
63	Phil Plantier	1.00
64	Fernando Valenzuela	1.00
65	Barry Bonds	5.00
66	J.R. Phillips	1.00
67	Deion Sanders	1.50
68	Matt Williams	2.00
69	Bernard Gilkey	1.00
70	Tom Henke	1.00
71	Brian Jordan	1.00
72	Ozzie Smith	3.00
73	Manny Alexander	1.00
74	Bobby Bonilla	1.00
75	Mike Mussina	2.50
76	Rafael Palmeiro	1.50
77	Cal Ripken Jr.	12.00
78	Jose Canseco	1.50
79	Roger Clemens	5.00
80	John Valentin	1.00
81	Mo Vaughn	4.00
82	Tim Wakefield	1.00
83	Garret Anderson	1.50
84	Damion Easley	1.00
85	Jim Edmonds	1.50
86	Tim Salmon	2.00
87	Wilson Alvarez	1.00
88	Alex Fernandez	1.00
89	Ozzie Guillen	1.00
90	Roberto Hernandez	1.00
91	Frank Thomas	12.00
92	Robin Ventura	1.00
93	Carlos Baerga	1.00
94	Albert Belle	4.00
95	Kenny Lofton	4.00
96	Dennis Martinez	1.00
97	Eddie Murray	2.00
98	Manny Ramirez	3.00
99	Omar Vizquel	1.00
100	Chad Curtis	1.00
101	Cecil Fielder	1.50
102	Felipe Lira	1.00
103	Alan Trammell	1.00
104	Kevin Appier	1.00
105	Johnny Damon	1.00
106	Gary Gaetti	1.00
107	Wally Joyner	1.00
108	Ricky Bones	1.00
109	John Jaha	1.00
110	B.J. Surhoff	1.00
111	Jose Valentin	1.00
112	Fernando Vina	1.00
113	Marty Cordova	1.50
114	Chuck Knoblauch	1.50
115	Scott Leius	1.00
116	Pedro Munoz	1.00
117	Kirby Puckett	6.00
118	Wade Boggs	2.00
119	Don Mattingly	8.00
120	Jack McDowell	1.00
121	Paul O'Neill	1.00
122	Ruben Rivera	1.00
123	Bernie Williams	3.00
124	Geronimo Berroa	1.00
125	Rickey Henderson	2.00
126	Mark McGwire	15.00
127	Terry Steinbach	1.00
128	Danny Tartabull	1.00
129	Jay Buhner	1.00
130	Joey Cora	1.00
131	Ken Griffey Jr.	15.00
132	Randy Johnson	2.00
133	Edgar Martinez	1.00
134	Tino Martinez	1.50
135	Will Clark	2.00
136	Juan Gonzalez	8.00
137	Dean Palmer	1.00
138	Ivan Rodriguez	3.00
139	Mickey Tettleton	1.00
140	Larry Walker	1.50
141	Joe Carter	1.00
142	Carlos Delgado	1.00
143	Alex Gonzalez	1.00
144	Paul Molitor	2.00

1996 Pacific Prism Fence Busters

Home run heroes are featured in this insert set. The player's big swing is photographed in the foreground while a baseball flies out of the etched metallic foil stadium background. The player's name is in blue foil. Backs have another player photo and details of his 1995 season home run output, in both English and Spanish. Cards are numbered with an FB prefix. Stated odds of finding a Fence Busters insert are one per 37 packs, on average.

		MT
Complete Set (19):		175.00
Common Player:		6.00
1	Albert Belle	10.00
2	Dante Bichette	7.00
3	Barry Bonds	10.00
4	Jay Buhner	6.00
5	Jose Canseco	6.00
6	Ken Griffey Jr.	40.00
7	Chipper Jones	25.00
8	David Justice	6.00
9	Eric Karros	6.00
10	Edgar Martinez	6.00
11	Mark McGwire	40.00
12	Eddie Murray	8.00
13	Mike Piazza	25.00
14	Kirby Puckett	15.00
15	Cal Ripken Jr.	35.00
16	Tim Salmon	8.00
17	Sammy Sosa	20.00
18	Frank Thomas	30.00
19	Mo Vaughn	10.00

1996 Pacific Prism Flame Throwers

Burning baseballs are the background for the game's best pitchers in this die-cut insert set. The gold-foil highlighted flames have their tails die-cut at the card's left end. The featured pitcher is shown in action in the foreground. The name at bottom and company logo are in gold foil. Backs are conventionally printed with another action photo and 1995 highlight printed in both English and Spanish. Card numbers carry an FT prefix. Stated odds of finding a Flame Throwers card are one in 73 boxes, about every two boxes.

		MT
Complete Set (10):		160.00
Common Player:		10.00
1	Roger Clemens	25.00
2	David Cone	12.00
3	Tom Glavine	12.00
4	Randy Johnson	20.00
5	Greg Maddux	55.00
6	Ramon Martinez	10.00
7	Jose Mesa	10.00
8	Mike Mussina	20.00
9	Hideo Nomo	30.00
10	Jose Rijo	10.00

1996 Pacific Prism Red Hot Stars

Bright red metallic foil provides the background for these inserts. Color action photos are in the foreground, while player name and multiple team logos are worked into the background. Backs are conventionally printed with another player photo and a few words - in both English and Spanish - about the player's 1995 season. Card numbers have an RH prefix. Stated odds of finding a Red Hot Stars insert are one per 37 packs.

		MT
Complete Set (19):		250.00
Common Player:		4.00
1	Roberto Alomar	8.00
2	Jeff Bagwell	15.00
3	Albert Belle	10.00
4	Wade Boggs	4.00
5	Barry Bonds	10.00
6	Jose Canseco	5.00
7	Ken Griffey Jr.	40.00
8	Tony Gwynn	15.00
9	Randy Johnson	6.00
10	Chipper Jones	20.00
11	Greg Maddux	20.00
12	Edgar Martinez	4.00
13	Don Mattingly	18.00
14	Mike Piazza	20.00
15	Kirby Puckett	15.00
16	Manny Ramirez	8.00
17	Cal Ripken Jr.	30.00
18	Tim Salmon	5.00
19	Frank Thomas	30.00

Modern cards have little collector value in conditions lower than Mint. Figure NM cards at 75% of values shown; EX cards at 40%.

Values shown reflect the market as of January, 1999. On-field performances of current players in the 1999 baseball season are not factored in.

1997 Pacific Crown

The 450-card, regular-sized set was available in 12-card packs. The card fronts feature the player's name in gold foil along the left border with the team logo in the bottom right corner. The card backs feature a head shot of the player in the lower left quadrant with a short highlight in both Spanish and English. Inserted in packs were: Card-Supials, Cramer's Choice, Latinos Of The Major Leagues, Fireworks Die-Cuts, Gold Crown Die-Cuts and Triple Crown Die-Cuts. A parallel silver version (67 sets) was available.

	MT
Complete Set (450):	35.00
Common Player:	.05
Silver Stars: 75x to 120x	
Silver Yng Stars & RCs: 50x to 90x	
Wax Box:	60.00

#	Player	Price
1	Garret Anderson	.05
2	George Arias	.05
3	Chili Davis	.05
4	Gary DiSarcina	.05
5	Jim Edmonds	1.25
6	Darin Erstad	1.25
7	Jorge Fabregas	.05
8	Chuck Finley	.05
9	Rex Hudler	.05
10	Mark Langston	.05
11	Orlando Palmeiro	.05
12	Troy Percival	.05
13	Tim Salmon	.25
14	J.T. Snow	.08
15	Randy Velarde	.05
16	Manny Alexander	.05
17	Roberto Alomar	.60
18	Brady Anderson	.10
19	Armando Benitez	.05
20	Bobby Bonilla	.10
21	Rocky Coppinger	.15
22	Scott Erickson	.05
23	Jeffrey Hammonds	.05
24	Chris Hoiles	.05
25	Eddie Murray	.35
26	Mike Mussina	.60
27	Randy Myers	.05
28	Rafael Palmeiro	.10
29	Cal Ripken Jr.	2.50
30	B.J. Surhoff	.05
31	Tony Tarasco	.05
32	Esteban Beltre	.05
33	Darren Bragg	.05
34	Jose Canseco	.25
35	Roger Clemens	1.00
36	Wil Cordero	.05
37	Alex Delgado	.05
38	Jeff Frye	.05
39	Nomar Garciaparra	1.50
40	Tom Gordon	.05
41	Mike Greenwell	.05
42	Reggie Jefferson	.05
43	Tim Naehring	.05
44	Troy O'Leary	.05
45	Heathcliff Slocumb	.05
46	Lee Tinsley	.05
47	John Valentin	.05
48	Mo Vaughn	1.00
49	Wilson Alvarez	.05
50	Harold Baines	.05
51	Ray Durham	.05
52	Alex Fernandez	.05
53	Ozzie Guillen	.05
54	Roberto Hernandez	.05
55	Ron Karkovice	.05
56	Darren Lewis	.05
57	Norberto Martin	.05
58	Dave Martinez	.05
59	Lyle Mouton	.05
60	Jose Munoz	.05
61	Tony Phillips	.05
62	Rich Sauveur	.05
63	Danny Tartabull	.05
64	Frank Thomas	2.50
65	Robin Ventura	.08
66	Sandy Alomar Jr.	.08
67	Albert Belle	.75
68	Julio Franco	.05
69	Brian Giles	.05
70	Danny Graves	.05
71	Orel Hershiser	.05
72	Jeff Kent	.05
73	Kenny Lofton	.65
74	Dennis Martinez	.05
75	Jack McDowell	.10
76	Jose Mesa	.05
77	Charles Nagy	.05
78	Manny Ramirez	.65
79	Julian Tavarez	.05
80	Jim Thome	.30
81	Jose Vizcaino	.05
82	Omar Vizquel	.05
83	Brad Ausmus	.05
84	Kimera Bartee	.05
85	Raul Casanova	.05
86	Tony Clark	.40
87	Travis Fryman	.05
88	Bobby Higginson	.08
89	Mark Lewis	.05
90	Jose Lima	.05
91	Felipe Lira	.05
92	Phil Nevin	.05
93	Melvin Nieves	.05
94	Curtis Pride	.05
95	Ruben Sierra	.05
96	Alan Trammell	.05
97	Kevin Appier	.05
98	Tim Belcher	.05
99	Johnny Damon	.20
100	Tom Goodwin	.05
101	Bob Hamelin	.05
102	David Howard	.05
103	Jason Jacome	.05
104	Keith Lockhart	.05
105	Mike Macfarlane	.05
106	Jeff Montgomery	.05
107	Jose Offerman	.05
108	Hipolito Pichardo	.05
109	Joe Randa	.05
110	Bip Roberts	.05
111	Chris Stynes	.05
112	Mike Sweeney	.05
113	Joe Vitiello	.05
114	Jeromy Burnitz	.05
115	Chuck Carr	.05
116	Jeff Cirillo	.05
117	Mike Fetters	.05
118	David Hulse	.05
119	John Jaha	.05
120	Scott Karl	.05
121	Jesse Levis	.05
122	Mark Loretta	.05
123	Mike Matheny	.05
124	Ben McDonald	.05
125	Matt Mieske	.05
126	Angel Miranda	.05
127	Dave Nilsson	.05
128	Jose Valentin	.05
129	Fernando Vina	.05
130	Ron Villone	.05
131	Gerald Williams	.05
132	Rick Aguilera	.05
133	Rich Becker	.05
134	Ron Coomer	.05
135	Marty Cordova	.10
136	Eddie Guardado	.05
137	Denny Hocking	.05
138	Roberto Kelly	.05
139	Chuck Knoblauch	.10
140	Matt Lawton	.05
141	Pat Meares	.05
142	Paul Molitor	.25
143	Greg Myers	.05
144	Jeff Reboulet	.05
145	Scott Stahoviak	.05
146	Todd Walker	.50
147	Wade Boggs	.15
148	David Cone	.10
149	Mariano Duncan	.05
150	Cecil Fielder	.15
151	Dwight Gooden	.05
152	Derek Jeter	1.50
153	Jim Leyritz	.05
154	Tino Martinez	.25
155	Paul O'Neill	.05
156	Andy Pettitte	.65
157	Tim Raines	.05
158	Mariano Rivera	.15
159	Ruben Rivera	.20
160	Kenny Rogers	.05
161	Darryl Strawberry	.05
162	John Wetteland	.05
163	Bernie Williams	.50
164	Tony Batista	.05
165	Geronimo Berroa	.05
166	Mike Bordick	.05
167	Scott Brosius	.05
168	Brent Gates	.05
169	Jason Giambi	.05
170	Jose Herrera	.05
171	Brian Lesher	.05
172	*Damon Mashore*	.05
173	Mark McGwire	3.00
174	Ariel Prieto	.05
175	Carlos Reyes	.05
176	Matt Stairs	.05
177	Terry Steinbach	.05
178	John Wasdin	.05
179	Ernie Young	.05
180	Rich Amaral	.05
181	Bobby Ayala	.05
182	Jay Buhner	.15
183	Rafael Carmona	.05
184	Norm Charlton	.05
185	Joey Cora	.05
186	Ken Griffey Jr.	3.00
187	Sterling Hitchcock	.05
188	Dave Hollins	.05
189	Randy Johnson	.35
190	Edgar Martinez	.05
191	Jamie Moyer	.05
192	Alex Rodriguez	3.00
193	Paul Sorrento	.05
194	Salomon Torres	.05
195	Bob Wells	.05
196	Dan Wilson	.05
197	Will Clark	.25
198	Kevin Elster	.05
199	Rene Gonzales	.05
200	Juan Gonzalez	1.50
201	Rusty Greer	.05
202	Darryl Hamilton	.05
203	Mike Henneman	.05
204	Ken Hill	.05
205	Mark McLemore	.05
206	Darren Oliver	.05
207	Dean Palmer	.05
208	Roger Pavlik	.05
209	Ivan Rodriguez	.65
210	Kurt Stillwell	.05
211	Mickey Tettleton	.05
212	Bobby Witt	.05
213	Tilson Brito	.05
214	Jacob Brumfield	.05
215	Miguel Cairo	.10
216	Joe Carter	.20
217	Felipe Crespo	.05
218	Carlos Delgado	.05
219	Alex Gonzalez	.05
220	Shawn Green	.05
221	Juan Guzman	.05
222	Pat Hentgen	.05
223	Charlie O'Brien	.05
224	John Olerud	.05
225	Robert Perez	.05
226	Tomas Perez	.05
227	Juan Samuel	.05
228	Ed Sprague	.05
229	Mike Timlin	.05
230	Rafael Belliard	.05
231	Jermaine Dye	.20
232	Tom Glavine	.10
233	Marquis Grissom	.05

234	Andruw Jones	1.50
235	Chipper Jones	2.00
236	David Justice	.20
237	Ryan Klesko	.50
238	Mark Lemke	.05
239	Javier Lopez	.15
240	Greg Maddux	2.00
241	Fred McGriff	.35
242	Denny Neagle	.05
243	Eddie Perez	.05
244	John Smoltz	.15
245	Mark Wohlers	.05
246	Brant Brown	.05
247	Scott Bullett	.05
248	Leo Gomez	.05
249	Luis Gonzalez	.05
250	Mark Grace	.15
251	Jose Hernandez	.05
252	Brooks Kieschnick	.05
253	Brian McRae	.05
254	Jaime Navarro	.05
255	Mike Perez	.05
256	Rey Sanchez	.05
257	Ryne Sandberg	.75
258	Scott Servais	.05
259	Sammy Sosa	1.50
260	*Pedro Valdes*	.05
261	Turk Wendell	.05
262	Bret Boone	.05
263	Jeff Branson	.05
264	Jeff Brantley	.05
265	Dave Burba	.05
266	Hector Carrasco	.05
267	Eric Davis	.05
268	Willie Greene	.05
269	Lenny Harris	.05
270	Thomas Howard	.05
271	Barry Larkin	.20
272	Hal Morris	.05
273	Joe Oliver	.05
274	Eric Owens	.05
275	Jose Rijo	.05
276	Reggie Sanders	.05
277	Eddie Taubensee	.05
278	Jason Bates	.05
279	Dante Bichette	.20
280	Ellis Burks	.05
281	Vinny Castilla	.05
282	Andres Galarraga	.15
283	Quinton McCracken	.05
284	Jayhawk Owens	.05
285	Jeff Reed	.05
286	Bryan Rekar	.05
287	Armando Reynoso	.05
288	Kevin Ritz	.05
289	Bruce Ruffin	.05
290	John Vander Wal	.05
291	Larry Walker	.25
292	Walt Weiss	.05
293	Eric Young	.05
294	Kurt Abbott	.05
295	Alex Arias	.05
296	Miguel Batista	.05
297	Kevin Brown	.05
298	Luis Castillo	.10
299	Greg Colbrunn	.05
300	Jeff Conine	.05
301	Charles Johnson	.05
302	Al Leiter	.05
303	Robb Nen	.05
304	Joe Orsulak	.05
305	Yorkis Perez	.05
306	Edgar Renteria	.25
307	Gary Sheffield	.25
308	Jesus Tavarez	.05
309	Quilvio Veras	.05
310	Devon White	.05
311	Jeff Bagwell	1.25
312	Derek Bell	.05
313	Sean Berry	.05
314	Craig Biggio	.05
315	Doug Drabek	.05
316	Tony Eusebio	.05
317	Ricky Gutierrez	.05
318	Xavier Hernandez	.05
319	Brian L. Hunter	.05
320	Darryl Kile	.05
321	Derrick May	.05
322	Orlando Miller	.05
323	James Mouton	.05
324	Bill Spiers	.05
325	Pedro Astacio	.05
326	Brett Butler	.05
327	Juan Castro	.05
328	Roger Cedeno	.05
329	Delino DeShields	.05

330	Karim Garcia	.50
331	Todd Hollandsworth	.10
332	Eric Karros	.05
333	Oreste Marrero	.05
334	Ramon Martinez	.05
335	Raul Mondesi	.25
336	Hideo Nomo	.65
337	Antonio Osuna	.05
338	Chan Ho Park	.05
339	Mike Piazza	2.00
340	Ismael Valdes	.05
341	Moises Alou	.05
342	Omar Daal	.05
343	Jeff Fassero	.05
344	Cliff Floyd	.05
345	Mark Grudzielanek	.05
346	Mike Lansing	.05
347	Pedro Martinez	.05
348	Sherman Obando	.05
349	Jose Paniagua	.05
350	Henry Rodriguez	.05
351	Mel Rojas	.05
352	F.P. Santangelo	.05
353	Dave Segui	.05
354	Dave Silvestri	.05
355	Ugueth Urbina	.05
356	Rondell White	.05
357	Edgardo Alfonzo	.05
358	Carlos Baerga	.10
359	Tim Bogar	.05
360	Rico Brogna	.05
361	Alvaro Espinoza	.05
362	Carl Everett	.05
363	John Franco	.05
364	Bernard Gilkey	.05
365	Todd Hundley	.05
366	Butch Huskey	.05
367	Jason Isringhausen	.10
368	Bobby Jones	.05
369	Lance Johnson	.05
370	Brent Mayne	.05
371	Alex Ochoa	.05
372	Rey Ordonez	.20
373	Ron Blazier	.05
374	Ricky Bottalico	.05
375	David Doster	.05
376	Lenny Dykstra	.05
377	Jim Eisenreich	.05
378	Bobby Estalella	.05
379	Gregg Jefferies	.05
380	Kevin Jordan	.05
381	Ricardo Jordan	.05
382	Mickey Morandini	.05
383	Ricky Otero	.05
384	Benito Santiago	.05
385	Gene Schall	.05
386	Curt Schilling	.05
387	Kevin Sefcik	.05
388	Kevin Stocker	.05
389	Jermaine Allensworth	.05
390	Jay Bell	.05
391	Jason Christiansen	.05
392	Francisco Cordova	.10
393	Mark Johnson	.05
394	Jason Kendall	.05
395	Jeff King	.05
396	Jon Lieber	.05
397	Nelson Liriano	.05
398	Esteban Loaiza	.10
399	Al Martin	.05
400	Orlando Merced	.05
401	Ramon Morel	.05
402	Luis Alicea	.05
403	Alan Benes	.15
404	Andy Benes	.05
405	Terry Bradshaw	.05
406	Royce Clayton	.05
407	Dennis Eckersley	.05
408	Gary Gaetti	.05
409	Mike Gallego	.05
410	Ron Gant	.10
411	Brian Jordan	.05
412	Ray Lankford	.05
413	John Mabry	.05
414	Willie McGee	.05
415	Tom Pagnozzi	.05
416	Ozzie Smith	.40
417	Todd Stottlemyre	.05
418	Mark Sweeney	.05
419	Andy Ashby	.05
420	Ken Caminiti	.10
421	Archi Cianfrocco	.05
422	Steve Finley	.05
423	Chris Gomez	.05
424	Tony Gwynn	1.25
425	Joey Hamilton	.05

426	Rickey Henderson	.05
427	Trevor Hoffman	.05
428	Brian Johnson	.05
429	Wally Joyner	.05
430	Scott Livingstone	.05
431	Jody Reed	.05
432	Craig Shipley	.05
433	Fernando Valenzuela	.05
434	Greg Vaughn	.05
435	Rich Aurilia	.05
436	Kim Batiste	.05
437	Jose Bautista	.05
438	Rod Beck	.05
439	Marvin Benard	.05
440	Barry Bonds	.75
441	Shawon Dunston	.05
442	Shawn Estes	.05
443	Osvaldo Fernandez	.05
444	Stan Javier	.05
445	David McCarty	.05
446	*Bill Mueller*	.05
447	Steve Scarsone	.05
448	Robby Thompson	.05
449	Rick Wilkins	.05
450	Matt Williams	.25

1997 Pacific Crown Card-Supials

The 36-card, regular-sized set was inserted every 37 packs of 1997 Pacific Crown baseball. The card fronts feature a gold-foil spiral with the player's name printed along a curve on the bottom edge. The team logo appears in the lower right corner. The card backs feature an action shot and are numbered "x of 36." The cards come with a mini (1-1/4" x 1-3/4") card that slides into a pocket on the back. The mini cards are of a different player, but depict the same action shot as the larger card backs.

		MT
Complete Set (72):		550.00
Complete Large Set (36):		350.00
Complete Small Set (36):		200.00
Common Large:		4.00
Small Cards: 50%		
1	Roberto Alomar	6.00
2	Brady Anderson	4.00
3	Eddie Murray	6.00
4	Cal Ripken Jr.	25.00
5	Jose Canseco	5.00
6	Mo Vaughn	8.00
7	Frank Thomas	25.00
8	Albert Belle	8.00
9	Omar Vizquel	4.00
10	Chuck Knoblauch	4.00
11	Paul Molitor	6.00
12	Wade Boggs	4.00
13	Derek Jeter	20.00
14	Andy Pettitte	7.50
15	Mark McGwire	30.00
16	Jay Buhner	4.00
17	Ken Griffey Jr.	30.00
18	Alex Rodriguez	25.00
19	Juan Gonzalez	15.00
20	Ivan Rodriguez	6.00
21	Andruw Jones	15.00
22	Chipper Jones	20.00
23	Ryan Klesko	5.00
24	Greg Maddux	20.00
25	Ryne Sandberg	8.00
26	Andres Galarraga	4.00
27	Gary Sheffield	5.00
28	Jeff Bagwell	15.00
29	Todd Hollandsworth	4.00
30	Hideo Nomo	6.00
31	Mike Piazza	20.00
32	Todd Hundley	4.00
33	Dennis Eckersley	4.00
34	Ken Caminiti	4.00
35	Tony Gwynn	15.00
36	Barry Bonds	8.00

3	Albert Belle	50.00
4	Andy Pettitte	40.00
5	Ken Griffey Jr.	200.00
6	Alex Rodriguez	125.00
7	Chipper Jones	125.00
8	John Smoltz	40.00
9	Mike Piazza	125.00
10	Tony Gwynn	100.00

1997 Pacific Crown Fireworks Die-Cuts

The 20-card, regular-sized, die-cut set was inserted every 73 packs of 1997 Crown. The card fronts feature a color action shot with generic fireworks over a stadium on the upper half. The horizontal card backs contain close-up shots with highlights in Spanish and English. The cards are numbered with the "FW" prefix.

		MT
Complete Set (20):		400.00
Common Player:		6.00
1	Roberto Alomar	12.00
2	Brady Anderson	6.00
3	Eddie Murray	8.00
4	Cal Ripken Jr.	40.00
5	Frank Thomas	40.00
6	Albert Belle	12.00
7	Derek Jeter	30.00
8	Andy Pettitte	12.00
9	Bernie Williams	10.00
10	Mark McGwire	40.00
11	Ken Griffey Jr.	50.00
12	Alex Rodriguez	40.00
13	Juan Gonzalez	20.00
14	Andruw Jones	25.00
15	Chipper Jones	30.00
16	Hideo Nomo	10.00
17	Mike Piazza	30.00
18	Henry Rodriguez	6.00
19	Tony Gwynn	25.00
20	Barry Bonds	12.00

1997 Pacific Crown Cramer's Choice Awards

The 10-card, regular-sized set was inserted every 721 packs and features a die-cut pyramid design. A color player photo is imaged over silver foil with the player's name and position in gold foil over a green marble background along the bottom. The card backs feature a headshot with a brief career highlight in both Spanish and English. The cards are numbered with a "CC" prefix.

		MT
Complete Set (10):		900.00
Common Player:		40.00
1	Roberto Alomar	40.00
2	Frank Thomas	150.00

1997 Pacific Crown Gold Crown Die-Cuts

The 36-card, regular-sized, die-cut set was inserted every 37 packs. The card fronts feature a die-cut, gold-foil crown on the top border and the player's name appears in gold along the bottom edge. The card backs contain a headshot and a Spanish/English highlight and are numbered with the "GC" prefix.

		MT
Complete Set (36):		400.00
Common Player:		4.00
1	Roberto Alomar	10.00
2	Brady Anderson	4.00
3	Mike Mussina	8.00
4	Eddie Murray	8.00
5	Cal Ripken Jr.	30.00
6	Jose Canseco	5.00
7	Frank Thomas	30.00
8	Albert Belle	9.00
9	Omar Vizquel	4.00
10	Wade Boggs	4.00
11	Derek Jeter	20.00
12	Andy Pettitte	9.00
13	Mariano Rivera	4.00
14	Bernie Williams	8.00
15	Mark McGwire	40.00
16	Ken Griffey Jr.	40.00
17	Edgar Martinez	4.00
18	Alex Rodriguez	30.00
19	Juan Gonzalez	20.00
20	Ivan Rodriguez	12.00
21	Andruw Jones	20.00
22	Chipper Jones	25.00
23	Ryan Klesko	6.00
24	John Smoltz	5.00
25	Ryne Sandberg	10.00
26	Andres Galarraga	4.00
27	Edgar Renteria	6.00
28	Jeff Bagwell	18.00
29	Todd Hollandsworth	4.00
30	Hideo Nomo	8.00
31	Mike Piazza	25.00
32	Todd Hundley	4.00
33	Brian Jordan	4.00
34	Ken Caminiti	5.00
35	Tony Gwynn	15.00
36	Barry Bonds	10.00

1997 Pacific Crown Latinos of the Major Leagues

The 36-card, regular-sized set was inserted twice every 37 packs. The card fronts feature a color action shot over the player's name in gold foil. The card backs have another action shot and a Spanish/English highlight.

		MT
Complete Set (36):		60.00
Common Player:		1.50
1	George Arias	1.50
2	Roberto Alomar	4.00
3	Rafael Palmeiro	2.00
4	Bobby Bonilla	2.00
5	Jose Canseco	2.00
6	Wilson Alvarez	1.50
7	Dave Martinez	1.50
8	Julio Franco	1.50
9	Manny Ramirez	4.00
10	Omar Vizquel	1.50
11	Marty Cordova	1.50
12	Roberto Kelly	1.50
13	Tino Martinez	2.00
14	Mariano Rivera	2.00
15	Ruben Rivera	1.50
16	Bernie Williams	4.00
17	Geronimo Berroa	1.50
18	Joey Cora	1.50
19	Edgar Martinez	1.50
20	Alex Rodriguez	12.00
21	Juan Gonzalez	10.00
22	Ivan Rodriguez	5.00
23	Andruw Jones	10.00
24	Javier Lopez	2.00
25	Sammy Sosa	8.00
26	Vinny Castilla	2.00
27	Andres Galarraga	2.00
28	Ramon Martinez	2.00
29	Raul Mondesi	2.50
30	Ismael Valdes	1.50
31	Pedro Martinez	2.00
32	Henry Rodriguez	1.50
33	Carlos Baerga	1.50
34	Rey Ordonez	1.50
35	Fernando Valenzuela	1.50
36	Osvaldo Fernandez	1.50

1997 Pacific Crown Triple Crown Die-Cuts

The 20-card, regular-sized, die-cut set was inserted every 145 packs of Crown baseball. The horizontal card fronts feature the same gold-foil, die-cut crown as on the Gold Crown Die-Cut inserts. The card backs feature a headshot, Spanish/English text and are numbered with the "TC" prefix.

		MT
Complete Set (20):		450.00
Common Player:		10.00
1	Brady Anderson	8.00
2	Rafael Palmeiro	10.00
3	Mo Vaughn	20.00
4	Frank Thomas	60.00
5	Albert Belle	20.00
6	Jim Thome	15.00
7	Cecil Fielder	8.00
8	Mark McGwire	75.00
9	Ken Griffey Jr.	75.00
10	Alex Rodriguez	50.00
11	Juan Gonzalez	40.00

12	Andruw Jones	25.00
13	Chipper Jones	50.00
14	Dante Bichette	8.00
15	Ellis Burks	8.00
16	Andres Galarraga	10.00
17	Jeff Bagwell	25.00
18	Mike Piazza	50.00
19	Ken Caminiti	10.00
20	Barry Bonds	20.00

1997 Pacific Invincible

The 1997 Pacific Invincible 150-card set was sold in three-card packs. The card fronts feature gold foil parallel lines with a color action shot. The bottom right quadrant contains a transparent cel headshot. The card backs have Spanish/English text and another color action shot. The reverse cel has the player's hat team logo air-brushed off to prevent reverse print. Insert sets are: Sluggers & Hurlers, Sizzling Lumber, Gate Attractions, Gems of the Diamond (2:1), and Light Blue (retail only) and Platinum (hobby) parallel sets of the 150 baseb cards.

		MT
Complete Set (150):		150.00
Common Player:		1.00
Light Blues: 3X to 6X		
Platinums: 3X to 5X		
Wax Box:		70.00
1	Chili Davis	1.00
2	Jim Edmonds	1.50
3	Darin Erstad	5.00
4	Orlando Palmeiro	1.00
5	Tim Salmon	2.00
6	J.T. Snow	1.00
7	Roberto Alomar	2.50
8	Brady Anderson	1.50
9	Eddie Murray	2.00
10	Mike Mussina	2.50
11	Rafael Palmeiro	1.50
12	Cal Ripken Jr.	12.00
13	Jose Canseco	1.50
14	Roger Clemens	5.00
15	Nomar Garciaparra	7.00
16	Reggie Jefferson	1.00
17	Mo Vaughn	4.00
18	Wilson Alvarez	1.00
19	Harold Baines	1.00
20	Alex Fernandez	1.00
21	Danny Tartabull	1.00
22	Frank Thomas	12.00
23	Robin Ventura	1.00
24	Sandy Alomar Jr.	1.00
25	Albert Belle	4.00
26	Kenny Lofton	4.00
27	Jim Thome	2.50

28	Omar Vizquel	1.00
29	Raul Casanova	1.00
30	Tony Clark	3.00
31	Travis Fryman	1.00
32	Bobby Higginson	1.00
33	Melvin Nieves	1.00
34	Justin Thompson	1.00
35	Johnny Damon	1.00
36	Tom Goodwin	1.00
37	Jeff Montgomery	1.00
38	Jose Offerman	1.00
39	John Jaha	1.00
40	Jeff Cirillo	1.00
41	Dave Nilsson	1.00
42	Jose Valentin	1.00
43	Fernando Vina	1.00
44	Marty Cordova	1.00
45	Roberto Kelly	1.00
46	Chuck Knoblauch	1.50
47	Paul Molitor	2.50
48	Todd Walker	4.00
49	Wade Boggs	1.50
50	Cecil Fielder	2.00
51	Derek Jeter	8.00
52	Tino Martinez	1.50
53	Andy Pettitte	3.00
54	Mariano Rivera	1.50
55	Bernie Williams	2.50
56	Tony Batista	1.00
57	Geronimo Berroa	1.00
58	Jason Giambi	1.00
59	Mark McGwire	15.00
60	Terry Steinbach	1.00
61	Jay Buhner	1.50
62	Joey Cora	1.00
63	Ken Griffey Jr.	15.00
64	Edgar Martinez	1.00
65	Alex Rodriguez	12.00
66	Paul Sorrento	1.00
67	Will Clark	1.50
68	Juan Gonzalez	7.00
69	Rusty Greer	1.00
70	Dean Palmer	1.00
71	Ivan Rodriguez	3.00
72	Joe Carter	1.50
73	Carlos Delgado	1.50
74	Juan Guzman	1.00
75	Pat Hentgen	1.00
76	Ed Sprague	1.00
77	Jermaine Dye	1.50
78	Andruw Jones	7.00
79	Chipper Jones	10.00
80	Ryan Klesko	2.00
81	Javier Lopez	1.50
82	Greg Maddux	10.00
83	John Smoltz	2.00
84	Mark Grace	1.50
85	Luis Gonzalez	1.00
86	Brooks Kieschnick	1.00
87	Jaime Navarro	1.00
88	Ryne Sandberg	4.00
89	Sammy Sosa	8.00
90	Bret Boone	1.00
91	Jeff Brantley	1.00
92	Eric Davis	1.00
93	Barry Larkin	2.00
94	Reggie Sanders	1.00
95	Ellis Burks	1.00
96	Dante Bichette	2.00
97	Vinny Castilla	1.00
98	Andres Galarraga	1.50
99	Eric Young	1.00
100	Kevin Brown	1.00
101	Jeff Conine	1.00
102	Charles Johnson	1.00
103	Edgar Renteria	1.50
104	Gary Sheffield	2.00
105	Jeff Bagwell	7.00
106	Derek Bell	1.00
107	Sean Berry	1.00
108	Craig Biggio	1.00
109	Shane Reynolds	1.00
110	Karim Garcia	2.00
111	Todd Hollandsworth	1.50
112	Ramon Martinez	1.00
113	Raul Mondesi	2.00
114	Hideo Nomo	3.00
115	Mike Piazza	10.00
116	Ismael Valdes	1.00
117	Moises Alou	1.00
118	Mark Grudzielanek	1.00
119	Pedro Martinez	1.00
120	Henry Rodriguez	1.00
121	F.P. Santangelo	1.00
122	Carlos Baerga	1.00
123	Bernard Gilkey	1.00

		MT
124	Todd Hundley	1.50
125	Lance Johnson	1.00
126	Alex Ochoa	1.00
127	Rey Ordonez	1.50
128	Lenny Dykstra	1.00
129	Gregg Jefferies	1.00
130	Ricky Otero	1.00
131	Benito Santiago	1.00
132	Jermaine Allensworth	1.00
133	Francisco Cordova	1.25
134	Carlos Garcia	1.00
135	Jason Kendall	1.00
136	Al Martin	1.00
137	Dennis Eckersley	1.50
138	Ron Gant	2.00
139	Brian Jordan	1.00
140	John Mabry	1.00
141	Ozzie Smith	3.00
142	Ken Caminiti	2.00
143	Steve Finley	1.00
144	Tony Gwynn	6.00
145	Wally Joyner	1.00
146	Fernando Valenzuela	1.00
147	Barry Bonds	5.00
148	Jacob Cruz	2.00
149	Osvaldo Fernandez	1.00
150	Matt Williams	2.00

1997 Pacific Invincible Gate Attractions

The 32-card, regular-sized set was inserted every 73 packs of Pacific Invincible baseball. The card fronts feature a generic baseball glove background with the player's name and position in a gold-foil circle. The center of the card is a cel action shot within a common baseball image. The player's team logo appears in the upper right corner. The card backs contain a headshot in the upper left corner with highlights in Spanish and English. The player's image in the cel is etched in gray in reverse. The cards are numbered with the "GA" prefix.

		MT
Complete Set (32):		600.00
Common Player:		8.00
1	Roberto Alomar	12.00
2	Brady Anderson	8.00
3	Cal Ripken Jr.	50.00
4	Frank Thomas	50.00
5	Kenny Lofton	12.00
6	Omar Vizquel	8.00
7	Paul Molitor	12.00
8	Wade Boggs	10.00
9	Derek Jeter	40.00
10	Andy Pettitte	12.00
11	Bernie Williams	12.00
12	Geronimo Berroa	8.00
13	Mark McGwire	60.00

14	Ken Griffey Jr.	60.00
15	Alex Rodriguez	50.00
16	Juan Gonzalez	30.00
17	Andruw Jones	30.00
18	Chipper Jones	40.00
19	Greg Maddux	40.00
20	Ryne Sandberg	15.00
21	Sammy Sosa	25.00
22	Andres Galarraga	8.00
23	Jeff Bagwell	25.00
24	Todd Hollandsworth	8.00
25	Hideo Nomo	10.00
26	Mike Piazza	40.00
27	Todd Hundley	8.00
28	Lance Johnson	8.00
29	Ozzie Smith	15.00
30	Ken Caminiti	10.00
31	Tony Gwynn	30.00
32	Barry Bonds	15.00

1997 Pacific Invincible Gems of the Diamond

Essentially the base set for 1997 Pacific Prism Invincible, these cards are found two per three-card pack. Fronts of the 2-1/2" x 3-1/2" cards have action photos with earth-tone borders and a color team logo at bottom. Backs have a large player portrait photos in a diamond at right-center and are numbered with a "GD-" prefix.

		MT
Complete Set (220):		50.00
Common Player:		.15
1	Jim Abbott	.15
2	Shawn Boskie	.15
3	Gary DiSarcina	.15
4	Jim Edmonds	.25
5	Todd Greene	.15
6	Jack Howell	.15
7	Jeff Schmidt	.15
8	Shad Williams	.15
9	Roberto Alomar	.50
10	Cesar Devarez	.15
11	Alan Mills	.15
12	Eddie Murray	.30
13	Jesse Orosco	.15
14	Arthur Rhodes	.15
15	Bill Ripken	.15
16	Cal Ripken Jr.	3.00
17	Mark Smith	.15
18	Roger Clemens	1.50
19	Vaughn Eshelman	.15
20	Rich Garces	.15
21	Bill Haselman	.15
22	Dwayne Hosey	.15
23	Mike Maddux	.15
24	Jose Malave	.15
25	Aaron Sele	.15
26	James Baldwin	.15
27	Pat Borders	.15

28	Mike Cameron	.15
29	Tony Castillo	.15
30	Domingo Cedeno	.15
31	Greg Norton	.15
32	Frank Thomas	3.00
33	Albert Belle	.75
34	Einar Diaz	.15
35	Alan Embree	.15
36	Albie Lopez	.15
37	Chad Ogea	.15
38	Tony Pena	.15
39	Joe Roa	.15
40	Fausto Cruz	.15
41	Joey Eischen	.15
42	Travis Fryman	.15
43	Mike Myers	.15
44	A.J. Sager	.15
45	Duane Singleton	.15
46	Justin Thompson	.15
47	Jeff Granger	.15
48	Les Norman	.15
49	Jon Nunnally	.15
50	Craig Paquette	.15
51	Michael Tucker	.15
52	Julio Valera	.15
53	Kevin Young	.15
54	Cal Eldred	.15
55	Ramon Garcia	.15
56	Marc Newfield	.15
57	Al Reyes	.15
58	Tim Unroe	.15
59	Tim Vanegmond	.15
60	Turner Ward	.15
61	Bob Wickman	.15
62	Chuck Knoblauch	.25
63	Paul Molitor	.50
64	Kirby Puckett	.75
65	Tom Quinlan	.15
66	Rich Robertson	.15
67	Dave Stevens	.15
68	Matt Walbeck	.15
69	Wade Boggs	.50
70	Tony Fernandez	.15
71	Andy Fox	.15
72	Joe Girardi	.15
73	Charlie Hayes	.15
74	Pat Kelly	.15
75	Jeff Nelson	.15
76	Melido Perez	.15
77	Mark Acre	.15
78	Allen Battle	.15
79	Rafael Bournigal	.15
80	Mark McGwire	5.00
81	Pedro Munoz	.15
82	Scott Spiezio	.15
83	Don Wengert	.15
84	Steve Wojciechowski	.15
85	Alex Diaz	.15
86	Ken Griffey Jr.	5.00
87	Raul Ibanez	.25
88	Mike Jackson	.15
89	John Marzano	.15
90	Greg McCarthy	.15
91	Alex Rodriguez	3.00
92	Andy Sheets	.15
93	Makoto Suzuki	.15
94	Benji Gil	.15
95	Juan Gonzalez	2.00
96	Kevin Gross	.15
97	Gil Heredia	.15
98	Luis Ortiz	.15
99	Jeff Russell	.15
100	Dave Valle	.15
101	Marty Janzen	.15
102	Sandy Martinez	.15
103	Julio Mosquera	.15
104	Otis Nixon	.15
105	Paul Spoljaric	.15
106	Shannon Stewart	.15
107	Woody Williams	.15
108	Steve Avery	.15
109	Mike Bielecki	.15
110	Pedro Borbon	.15
111	Ed Giovanola	.15
112	Chipper Jones	2.50
113	Greg Maddux	2.50
114	Mike Mordecai	.15
115	Terrell Wade	.15
116	Terry Adams	.15
117	Brian Dorsett	.15
118	Doug Glanville	.15
119	Tyler Houston	.15
120	Robin Jennings	.15
121	Ryne Sandberg	.75
122	Terry Shumpert	.15
123	Amaury Telemaco	.15

124	Steve Trachsel	.15
125	Curtis Goodwin	.15
126	Mike Kelly	.15
127	Chad Mottola	.15
128	Mark Portugal	.15
129	Roger Salkeld	.15
130	John Smiley	.15
131	Lee Smith	.20
132	Roger Bailey	.15
133	Andres Galarraga	.25
134	Darren Holmes	.15
135	Curtis Leskanic	.15
136	Mike Munoz	.15
137	Jeff Reed	.15
138	Mark Thompson	.15
139	Jamey Wright	.15
140	Andre Dawson	.20
141	Craig Grebeck	.15
142	Matt Mantei	.15
143	Billy McMillon	.15
144	Kurt Miller	.15
145	Ralph Milliard	.15
146	Bob Natal	.15
147	Joe Siddall	.15
148	Bob Abreu	.20
149	Doug Brocail	.15
150	Danny Darwin	.15
151	Mike Hampton	.15
152	Todd Jones	.15
153	Kirt Manwaring	.15
154	Alvin Morman	.15
155	Billy Ashley	.15
156	Tom Candiotti	.15
157	Darren Dreifort	.15
158	Greg Gagne	.15
159	Wilton Guerrero	.15
160	Hideo Nomo	.50
161	Mike Piazza	2.50
162	Tom Prince	.15
163	Todd Worrell	.15
164	Moises Alou	.20
165	Shane Andrews	.15
166	Derek Aucoin	.15
167	Raul Chavez	.15
168	Darrin Fletcher	.15
169	Mark Leiter	.15
170	Henry Rodriguez	.15
171	Dave Veres	.15
172	Paul Byrd	.15
173	Alberto Castillo	.15
174	Mark Clark	.15
175	Rey Ordonez	.20
176	Roberto Petagine	.15
177	Andy Tomberlin	.15
178	Derek Wallace	.15
179	Paul Wilson	.20
180	Ruben Amaro, Jr.	.15
181	Toby Borland	.15
182	Rich Hunter	.15
183	Tony Longmire	.15
184	Wendell Magee Jr.	.15
185	Bobby Munoz	.15
186	Scott Rolen	.75
187	Mike Williams	.15
188	Trey Beamon	.15
189	Jason Christiansen	.15
190	Elmer Dessens	.15
191	Angelo Encarnacion	.25
192	Carlos Garcia	.15
193	Mike Kingery	.15
194	Chris Peters	.15
195	Tony Womack	.25
196	Brian Barber	.15
197	David Bell	.15
198	Tony Fossas	.15
199	Rick Honeycutt	.15
200	T.J. Mathews	.15
201	Miguel Mejia	.15
202	Donovan Osborne	.15
203	Ozzie Smith	.50
204	Andres Berumen	.15
205	Ken Caminiti	.25
206	Chris Gwynn	.15
207	Tony Gwynn	2.00
208	Rickey Henderson	.20
209	Scott Sanders	.15
210	Jason Thompson	.15
211	Fernando Valenzuela	.15
212	Tim Worrell	.15
213	Barry Bonds	.75
214	Jay Canizaro	.15
215	Doug Creek	.15
216	Jacob Cruz	.15
217	Glenallen Hill	.15
218	Tom Lampkin	.15
219	Jim Poole	.15
220	Desi Wilson	.15

1997 Pacific Invincible Sizzling Lumber

The 36-card, regular-sized, die-cut set was inserted every 37 packs of Ivincible. The cards have die-cut flames along the right border with a bat running parallel. The player's name appears in gold foil along the top border with his position in English and Spanish in gold foil along the bottom. The card backs feature a headshot in the upper half and contain Spanish and English text. The cards are numbered with the "SL" prefix.

		MT
Complete Set (36):		350.00
Common Player:		4.00
1A	Cal Ripken Jr.	30.00
1B	Rafael Palmeiro	5.00
1C	Roberto Alomar	8.00
2A	Frank Thomas	30.00
2B	Robin Ventura	4.00
2C	Harold Baines	4.00
3A	Albert Belle	10.00
3B	Manny Ramirez	8.00
3C	Kenny Lofton	10.00
4A	Derek Jeter	25.00
4B	Bernie Williams	8.00
4C	Wade Boggs	5.00
5A	Mark McGwire	40.00
5B	Jason Giambi	4.00
5C	Geronimo Berroa	4.00
6A	Ken Griffey Jr.	40.00
6B	Alex Rodriguez	25.00
6C	Jay Buhner	5.00
7A	Juan Gonzalez	20.00
7B	Dean Palmer	4.00
7C	Ivan Rodriguez	10.00
8A	Ryan Klesko	5.00
8B	Chipper Jones	25.00
8C	Andruw Jones	20.00
9A	Dante Bichette	5.00
9B	Andres Galarraga	5.00
9C	Vinny Castilla	4.00
10A	Jeff Bagwell	20.00
10B	Craig Biggio	4.00
10C	Derek Bell	4.00
11A	Mike Piazza	25.00
11B	Raul Mondesi	6.00
11C	Karim Garcia	6.00
12A	Tony Gwynn	20.00
12B	Ken Caminiti	6.00
12C	Greg Vaughn	4.00

A player's name in *italic* type indicates a rookie card.

1997 Pacific Invincible Sluggers & Hurlers

The 24-card, regular-sized set was inserted every 145 packs of Pacific Invincible baseball. The cards are numbered with an "SH-xA" or "SH-xaB." Each "A" card is the left half of a two-card set with the two players from the same team having their logo in the fit-together center. Each card has the player's name printed in gold foil along the bottom border with gold-foil swirls around the team logo. The card backs have a circular headshot with text in English and Spanish.

	MT
Complete Set (24):	1000.
Common Player:	15.00
SH-1a Cal Ripken Jr.	80.00
SH-1b Mike Mussina	20.00
SH-2a Jose Canseco	20.00
SH-2b Roger Clemens	30.00
SH-3a Frank Thomas	80.00
SH-3b Wilson Alvarez	15.00
SH-4a Kenny Lofton	20.00
SH-4b Orel Hershiser	15.00
SH-5a Derek Jeter	60.00
SH-5b Andy Pettitte	20.00
SH-6a Ken Griffey Jr.	100.00
SH-6b Randy Johnson	20.00
SH-7a Alex Rodriguez	80.00
SH-7b Jamie Moyer	15.00
SH-8a Andruw Jones	50.00
SH-8b Greg Maddux	60.00
SH-9a Chipper Jones	60.00
SH-9b John Smoltz	18.00
SH-10a Jeff Bagwell	40.00
SH-10b Shane Reynolds	15.00
SH-11a Mike Piazza	60.00
SH-11b Hideo Nomo	22.00
SH-12a Tony Gwynn	40.00
SH-12b Fernando Valenzuela	15.00

1998 Pacific

1998 Pacific Baseball is a 450-card, bilingual set. The base set features full-bleed photos with the Pacific Crown Collection logo in the upper left and the player's name, position and team at the bottom. Inserts include Cramer's Choice Awards, In The Cage Laser-Cuts, Home Run Hitters, Team Checklist Laser-Cuts, Gold Crown Die-Cuts and Latinos of the Major Leagues.

		MT
Complete Set (450):		35.00
Common Player:		.10
Silvers: 2x to 4x		
Inserted 1:1 H		
Reds: 2x to 4x		
Inserted 1:1 R		
Platinum Blues: 40x to 80x		
Inserted 1:73		
1	Luis Alicea	.10
2	Garret Anderson	.10
3	Jason Dickson	.10
4	Gary DiSarcina	.10
5	Jim Edmonds	.20
6	Darin Erstad	.75
7	Chuck Finley	.10
8	Shigetosi Hasegawa	.10
9	Rickey Henderson	.10
10	Dave Hollins	.10
11	Mark Langston	.10
12	Orlando Palmeiro	.10
13	Troy Percival	.10
14	Tony Phillips	.10
15	Tim Salmon	.30
16	Allen Watson	.10
17	Roberto Alomar	.60
18	Brady Anderson	.20
19	Harold Baines	.10
20	Armando Benitez	.10
21	Geronimo Berroa	.10
22	Mike Bordick	.10
23	Eric Davis	.10
24	Scott Erickson	.10
25	Chris Hoiles	.10
26	Jimmy Key	.10
27	Aaron Ledesma	.10
28	Mike Mussina	.60
29	Randy Myers	.10
30	Jesse Orosco	.10
31	Rafael Palmeiro	.25
32	Jeff Reboulet	.10
33	Cal Ripken Jr.	2.50
34	B.J. Surhoff	.10
35	Steve Avery	.10
36	Darren Bragg	.10
37	Wil Cordero	.10
38	Jeff Frye	.10
39	Nomar Garciaparra	2.00
40	Tom Gordon	.10
41	Bill Haselman	.10
42	Scott Hatteberg	.10
43	Butch Henry	.10
44	Reggie Jefferson	.10
45	Tim Naehring	.10
46	Troy O'Leary	.10
47	Jeff Suppan	.10
48	John Valentin	.10
49	Mo Vaughn	.75
50	Tim Wakefield	.10
51	James Baldwin	.10
52	Albert Belle	.75
53	Tony Castillo	.10
54	Doug Drabek	.10
55	Ray Durham	.10
56	Jorge Fabregas	.10
57	Ozzie Guillen	.10
58	Matt Karchner	.10
59	Norberto Martin	.10
60	Dave Martinez	.10
61	Lyle Mouton	.10
62	Jaime Navarro	.10
63	Frank Thomas	2.50
64	Mario Valdez	.10
65	Robin Ventura	.20
66	Sandy Alomar Jr.	.20
67	Paul Assenmacher	.10
68	Tony Fernandez	.10
69	Brian Giles	.20
70	Marquis Grissom	.10
71	Orel Hershiser	.10
72	Mike Jackson	.10
73	David Justice	.30
74	Albie Lopez	.10
75	Jose Mesa	.10
76	Charles Nagy	.10
77	Chad Ogea	.10
78	Manny Ramirez	.60
79	Jim Thome	.40
80	Omar Vizquel	.10
81	Matt Williams	.25
82	Jaret Wright	1.00
83	Willie Blair	.10
84	Raul Casanova	.10
85	Tony Clark	.40
86	Deivi Cruz	.10
87	Damion Easley	.10
88	Travis Fryman	.20
89	Bobby Higginson	.20
90	Brian Hunter	.10
91	Todd Jones	.10
92	Dan Miceli	.10
93	Brian Moehler	.10
94	Melvin Nieves	.10
95	Jody Reed	.10
96	Justin Thompson	.10
97	Bubba Trammell	.20
98	Kevin Appier	.10
99	Jay Bell	.10
100	Yamil Benitez	.10
101	Johnny Damon	.10
102	Chili Davis	.10
103	Jermaine Dye	.10
104	Jed Hansen	.10
105	Jeff King	.10
106	Mike Macfarlane	.10
107	Felix Martinez	.10
108	Jeff Montgomery	.10
109	Jose Offerman	.10
110	Dean Palmer	.20
111	Hipolito Pichardo	.10
112	Jose Rosado	.10
113	Jeromy Burnitz	.10
114	Jeff Cirillo	.10
115	Cal Eldred	.10
116	John Jaha	.10
117	Doug Jones	.10
118	Scott Karl	.10
119	Jesse Levis	.10
120	Mark Loretta	.10
121	Ben McDonald	.10
122	Jose Mercedes	.10
123	Matt Mieske	.10
124	Dave Nilsson	.10
125	Jose Valentin	.10
126	Fernando Vina	.10
127	Gerald Williams	.10
128	Rick Aguilera	.10
129	Rich Becker	.10
130	Ron Coomer	.10
131	Marty Cordova	.10
132	Eddie Guardado	.10
133	LaTroy Hawkins	.10
134	Denny Hocking	.10
135	Chuck Knoblauch	.30
136	Matt Lawton	.10
137	Pat Meares	.10
138	Paul Molitor	.50
139	David Ortiz	.40
140	Brad Radke	.10
141	Terry Steinbach	.10
142	Bob Tewksbury	.10
143	Javier Valentin	.10
144	Wade Boggs	.25
145	David Cone	.20
146	Chad Curtis	.10
147	Cecil Fielder	.20
148	Joe Girardi	.10
149	Dwight Gooden	.20
150	Hideki Irabu	.75
151	Derek Jeter	2.00
152	Tino Martinez	.25
153	Ramiro Mendoza	.10
154	Paul O'Neill	.20
155	Andy Pettitte	.60
156	Jorge Posada	.10
157	Mariano Rivera	.20
158	Rey Sanchez	.10
159	Luis Sojo	.10
160	David Wells	.10
161	Bernie Williams	.50
162	Rafael Bournigal	.10
163	Scott Brosius	.10
164	Jose Canseco	.20
165	Jason Giambi	.10
166	Ben Grieve	1.00
167	Dave Magadan	.10
168	Brent Mayne	.10
169	Jason McDonald	.10
170	Izzy Molina	.10
171	Ariel Prieto	.10
172	Carlos Reyes	.10
173	Scott Spiezio	.10
174	Matt Stairs	.10
175	Bill Taylor	.10
176	Dave Telgheder	.10
177	Steve Wojciechowski	.10
178	Rich Amaral	.10
179	Bobby Ayala	.10
180	Jay Buhner	.25
181	Rafael Carmona	.10
182	Ken Cloude	.10
183	Joey Cora	.10
184	Russ Davis	.10
185	Jeff Fassero	.10
186	Ken Griffey Jr.	3.00
187	Raul Ibanez	.10
188	Randy Johnson	.50
189	Roberto Kelly	.10
190	Edgar Martinez	.20
191	Jamie Moyer	.10
192	Omar Olivares	.10
193	Alex Rodriguez	2.00
194	Heathcliff Slocumb	.10
195	Paul Sorrento	.10
196	Dan Wilson	.10
197	Scott Bailes	.10
198	John Burkett	.10
199	Domingo Cedeno	.10
200	Will Clark	.25
201	*Hanley Frias*	.10
202	Juan Gonzalez	1.50
203	Tom Goodwin	.10
204	Rusty Greer	.20
205	Wilson Heredia	.10
206	Darren Oliver	.10
207	Billy Ripken	.10
208	Ivan Rodriguez	.60
209	Lee Stevens	.10
210	Fernando Tatis	.25
211	John Wetteland	.10
212	Bobby Witt	.10
213	Jacob Brumfield	.10
214	Joe Carter	.20
215	Roger Clemens	1.00
216	Felipe Crespo	.10
217	Jose Cruz Jr.	1.00
218	Carlos Delgado	.20
219	Mariano Duncan	.10
220	Carlos Garcia	.10
221	Alex Gonzalez	.10
222	Juan Guzman	.10
223	Pat Hentgen	.10
224	Orlando Merced	.10
225	Tomas Perez	.10
226	Paul Quantrill	.10
227	Benito Santiago	.10
228	Woody Williams	.10
229	Rafael Belliard	.10
230	Jeff Blauser	.10
231	Pedro Borbon	.10
232	Tom Glavine	.20
233	Tony Graffanino	.10
234	Andruw Jones	1.50
235	Chipper Jones	2.00
236	Ryan Klesko	.30

237 Mark Lemke	.10	
238 Kenny Lofton	.75	
239 Javier Lopez	.20	
240 Fred McGriff	.25	
241 Greg Maddux	2.00	
242 Denny Neagle	.10	
243 John Smoltz	.20	
244 Michael Tucker	.10	
245 Mark Wohlers	.10	
246 Manny Alexander	.10	
247 Miguel Batista	.10	
248 Mark Clark	.10	
249 Doug Glanville	.10	
250 Jeremi Gonzalez	.10	
251 Mark Grace	.25	
252 Jose Hernandez	.10	
253 Lance Johnson	.10	
254 Brooks Kieschnick	.10	
255 Kevin Orie	.10	
256 Ryne Sandberg	.75	
257 Scott Servais	.10	
258 Sammy Sosa	1.50	
259 Kevin Tapani	.10	
260 Ramon Tatis	.10	
261 Bret Boone	.10	
262 Dave Burba	.10	
263 Brook Fordyce	.10	
264 Willie Greene	.10	
265 Barry Larkin	.25	
266 Pedro A. Martinez	.10	
267 Hal Morris	.10	
268 Joe Oliver	.10	
269 Eduardo Perez	.10	
270 Pokey Reese	.10	
271 Felix Rodriguez	.10	
272 Deion Sanders	.25	
273 Reggie Sanders	.10	
274 Jeff Shaw	.10	
275 Scott Sullivan	.10	
276 Brett Tomko	.10	
277 Roger Bailey	.10	
278 Dante Bichette	.25	
279 Ellis Burks	.10	
280 Vinny Castilla	.20	
281 Frank Castillo	.10	
282 *Mike DeJean*	.10	
283 Andres Galarraga	.25	
284 Darren Holmes	.10	
285 Kirt Manwaring	.10	
286 Quinton McCracken	.10	
287 Neifi Perez	.10	
288 Steve Reed	.10	
289 John Thomson	.10	
290 Larry Walker	.30	
291 Walt Weiss	.10	
292 Kurt Abbott	.10	
293 Antonio Alfonseca	.10	
294 Moises Alou	.20	
295 Alex Arias	.10	
296 Bobby Bonilla	.20	
297 Kevin Brown	.20	
298 Craig Counsell	.10	
299 Darren Daulton	.10	
300 Jim Eisenreich	.10	
301 Alex Fernandez	.10	
302 Felix Heredia	.10	
303 Livan Hernandez	.20	
304 Charles Johnson	.20	
305 Al Leiter	.10	
306 Robb Nen	.10	
307 Edgar Renteria	.10	
308 Gary Sheffield	.30	
309 Devon White	.10	
310 Bob Abreu	.10	
311 Brad Ausmus	.10	
312 Jeff Bagwell	1.25	
313 Derek Bell	.10	
314 Sean Berry	.10	
315 Craig Biggio	.20	
316 Ramon Garcia	.10	
317 Luis Gonzalez	.10	
318 Ricky Gutierrez	.10	
319 Mike Hampton	.10	
320 Richard Hidalgo	.10	
321 Thomas Howard	.10	
322 Darryl Kile	.10	
323 Jose Lima	.10	
324 Shane Reynolds	.10	
325 Bill Spiers	.10	
326 Tom Candiotti	.10	
327 Roger Cedeno	.10	
328 Greg Gagne	.10	
329 Karim Garcia	.10	
330 Wilton Guerrero	.10	
331 Todd Hollandsworth	.10	
332 Eric Karros	.20	
333 Ramon Martinez	.10	
334 Raul Mondesi	.25	
335 Otis Nixon	.10	
336 Hideo Nomo	.75	
337 Antonio Osuna	.10	
338 Chan Ho Park	.20	
339 Mike Piazza	2.00	
340 Dennis Reyes	.10	
341 Ismael Valdes	.10	
342 Todd Worrell	.10	
343 Todd Zeile	.10	
344 Darrin Fletcher	.10	
345 Mark Grudzielanek	.10	
346 Vladimir Guerrero	1.00	
347 Dustin Hermanson	.10	
348 Mike Lansing	.10	
349 Pedro J. Martinez	.25	
350 Ryan McGuire	.10	
351 Jose Paniagua	.10	
352 Carlos Perez	.10	
353 Henry Rodriguez	.10	
354 F.P. Santangelo	.10	
355 David Segui	.10	
356 Ugueth Urbina	.10	
357 Marc Valdes	.10	
358 Jose Vidro	.10	
359 Rondell White	.20	
360 Juan Acevedo	.10	
361 Edgardo Alfonzo	.10	
362 Carlos Baerga	.10	
363 Carl Everett	.10	
364 John Franco	.10	
365 Bernard Gilkey	.10	
366 Todd Hundley	.20	
367 Butch Huskey	.10	
368 Bobby Jones	.10	
369 Takashi Kashiwada	.40	
370 Greg McMichael	.10	
371 Brian McRae	.10	
372 Alex Ochoa	.10	
373 John Olerud	.10	
374 Rey Ordonez	.10	
375 Turk Wendell	.10	
376 Ricky Bottalico	.10	
377 Rico Brogna	.10	
378 Lenny Dykstra	.10	
379 Bobby Estalella	.10	
380 Wayne Gomes	.10	
381 Tyler Green	.10	
382 Gregg Jefferies	.10	
383 Mark Leiter	.10	
384 Mike Lieberthal	.10	
385 Mickey Morandini	.10	
386 Scott Rolen	1.50	
387 Curt Schilling	.20	
388 Kevin Stocker	.10	
389 Danny Tartabull	.10	
390 Jermaine Allensworth	.10	
391 Adrian Brown	.10	
392 Jason Christiansen	.10	
393 Steve Cooke	.10	
394 Francisco Cordova	.10	
395 Jose Guillen	.40	
396 Jason Kendall	.10	
397 Jon Lieber	.10	
398 Esteban Loaiza	.10	
399 Al Martin	.10	
400 *Kevin Polcovich*	.20	
401 Joe Randa	.10	
402 Ricardo Rincon	.10	
403 Tony Womack	.10	
404 Kevin Young	.10	
405 Andy Benes	.10	
406 Royce Clayton	.10	
407 Delino DeShields	.10	
408 Mike Difelice	.10	
409 Dennis Eckersley	.20	
410 John Frascatore	.10	
411 Gary Gaetti	.10	
412 Ron Gant	.20	
413 Brian Jordan	.10	
414 Ray Lankford	.10	
415 Willie McGee	.10	
416 Mark McGwire	4.00	
417 Matt Morris	.10	
418 Luis Ordaz	.10	
419 Todd Stottlemyre	.10	
420 Andy Ashby	.10	
421 Jim Bruske	.10	
422 Ken Caminiti	.25	
423 Will Cunnane	.10	
424 Steve Finley	.10	
425 John Flaherty	.10	
426 Chris Gomez	.10	
427 Tony Gwynn	1.50	
428 Joey Hamilton	.20	
429 Carlos Hernandez		.10
430 Sterling Hitchcock		.10
431 Trevor Hoffman		.10
432 Wally Joyner		.10
433 Greg Vaughn		.10
434 Quilvio Veras		.10
435 Wilson Alvarez		.10
436 Rod Beck		.10
437 Barry Bonds		.75
438 Jacob Cruz		.10
439 Shawn Estes		.10
440 Darryl Hamilton		.10
441 Roberto Hernandez		.10
442 Glenallen Hill		.10
443 Stan Javier		.10
444 Brian Johnson		.10
445 Jeff Kont		.10
446 Bill Mueller		.10
447 Kirk Rueter		.10
448 J.T. Snow		.10
449 Julian Tavarez		.10
450 Jose Vizcaino		.10

1998 Pacific Cramer's Choice

Cramer's Choice Awards is a 10-card die-cut insert. The cards feature the top player at each position as selected by Pacific CEO Mike Cramer. Each card is shaped like a trophy. Cramer's Choice Awards were inserted one per 721 packs of 1998 Pacific Baseball.

		MT
Complete Set (10):		900.00
Common Player:		40.00
Inserted 1:721		
1	Greg Maddux	120.00
2	Roberto Alomar	40.00
3	Cal Ripken Jr.	150.00
4	Nomar Garciaparra	120.00
5	Larry Walker	40.00
6	Mike Piazza	120.00
7	Mark McGwire	200.00
8	Tony Gwynn	100.00
9	Ken Griffey Jr.	200.00
10	Roger Clemens	75.00

1998 Pacific Gold Crown Die-Cuts

Gold Crown Die-Cuts is a 36-card insert seeded one per 37 packs. Each card has a holographic silver foil background and gold etching. The cards are die-cut around a crown design at the top.

	MT
Complete Set (36):	400.00
Common Player:	4.00
1 Chipper Jones	25.00
2 Greg Maddux	25.00
3 Denny Neagle	4.00
4 Roberto Alomar	8.00
5 Rafael Palmeiro	6.00
6 Cal Ripken Jr.	30.00
7 Nomar Garciaparra	25.00
8 Mo Vaughn	10.00
9 Frank Thomas	40.00
10 Sandy Alomar Jr.	4.00
11 David Justice	5.00
12 Manny Ramirez	8.00
13 Andres Galarraga	5.00
14 Larry Walker	6.00
15 Moises Alou	4.00
16 Livan Hernandez	4.00
17 Gary Sheffield	6.00
18 Jeff Bagwell	15.00
19 Raul Mondesi	6.00
20 Hideo Nomo	10.00
21 Mike Piazza	25.00
22 Derek Jeter	25.00
23 Tino Martinez	5.00
24 Bernie Williams	8.00
25 Ben Grieve	12.00
26 Mark McGwire	45.00
27 Tony Gwynn	20.00
28 Barry Bonds	10.00
29 Ken Griffey Jr.	40.00
30 Randy Johnson	8.00
31 Edgar Martinez	4.00
32 Alex Rodriguez	25.00
33 Juan Gonzalez	20.00
34 Ivan Rodriguez	8.00
35 Roger Clemens	15.00
36 Jose Cruz Jr.	12.00

1998 Pacific Home Run Hitters

This 20-card set was inserted one per 73 packs. The full-foil cards feature a color player photo with their home run total from 1997 embossed in the background.

	MT
Complete Set (20):	220.00
Common Player:	6.00
1 Rafael Palmeiro	6.00
2 Mo Vaughn	10.00
3 Sammy Sosa	25.00
4 Albert Belle	10.00
5 Frank Thomas	40.00
6 David Justice	6.00
7 Jim Thome	8.00
8 Matt Williams	6.00
9 Vinny Castilla	6.00
10 Andres Galarraga	6.00
11 Larry Walker	8.00
12 Jeff Bagwell	15.00
13 Mike Piazza	25.00
14 Tino Martinez	6.00
15 Mark McGwire	45.00
16 Barry Bonds	10.00
17 Jay Buhner	6.00
18 Ken Griffey Jr.	40.00
19 Alex Rodriguez	25.00
20 Juan Gonzalez	20.00

A player's name in *italic* type indicates a rookie card.

1998 Pacific In the Cage

This 20-card insert features top players in a die-cut batting cage. The netting on the cage is laser-cut. In The Cage Laser-Cuts were inserted one per 145 packs.

	MT
Complete Set (20):	550.00
Common Player:	10.00
1 Chipper Jones	50.00
2 Roberto Alomar	15.00
3 Cal Ripken Jr.	60.00
4 Nomar Garciaparra	50.00
5 Frank Thomas	70.00
6 Sandy Alomar Jr.	10.00
7 David Justice	10.00
8 Larry Walker	12.00
9 Bobby Bonilla	10.00
10 Mike Piazza	50.00
11 Tino Martinez	10.00
12 Bernie Williams	15.00
13 Mark McGwire	80.00
14 Tony Gwynn	40.00
15 Barry Bonds	20.00
16 Ken Griffey Jr.	80.00
17 Edgar Martinez	10.00
18 Alex Rodriguez	50.00
19 Juan Gonzalez	40.00
20 Ivan Rodriguez	15.00

1998 Pacific Latinos of the Major Leagues

This 36-card set (2:37) features Major League players of Hispanic descent. The background has a world map on the left, the player's team logo in the center and an American flag on the right.

	MT
Complete Set (36):	75.00
Common Player:	1.50
Inserted 2:37	
1 Andruw Jones	8.00
2 Javier Lopez	1.50
3 Roberto Alomar	4.00
4 Geronimo Berroa	1.50
5 Rafael Palmeiro	2.00
6 Nomar Garciaparra	10.00
7 Sammy Sosa	10.00
8 Ozzie Guillen	1.50
9 Sandy Alomar Jr.	1.50
10 Manny Ramirez	4.00
11 Omar Vizquel	1.50
12 Vinny Castilla	1.50
13 Andres Galarraga	2.50
14 Moises Alou	1.50
15 Bobby Bonilla	1.50
16 Livan Hernandez	1.50
17 Edgar Renteria	1.50
18 Wilton Guerrero	1.50
19 Raul Mondesi	2.50
20 Ismael Valdes	1.50
21 Fernando Vina	1.50
22 Pedro Martinez	2.00
23 Edgardo Alfonzo	1.50
24 Carlos Baerga	1.50
25 Rey Ordonez	1.50
26 Tino Martinez	2.00
27 Mariano Rivera	1.50
28 Bernie Williams	4.00
29 Jose Canseco	2.50
30 Joey Cora	1.50
31 Roberto Kelly	1.50
32 Edgar Martinez	1.50
33 Alex Rodriguez	10.00
34 Juan Gonzalez	8.00
35 Ivan Rodriguez	5.00
36 Jose Cruz Jr.	6.00

1998 Pacific Team Checklists

Team Checklists is a 30-card insert in the bilingual Pacific Baseball set. One card was created for each team. A player photo is featured on the right with the team logo laser-cut into a bat barrel design on the left.

	MT
Complete Set (30):	240.00
Common Player:	3.00
1 Tim Salmon, Jim Edmonds	4.00
2 Cal Ripken Jr., Roberto Alomar	25.00
3 Nomar Garciaparra, Mo Vaughn	20.00
4 Frank Thomas, Albert Belle	30.00
5 Sandy Alomar Jr., Manny Ramirez	5.00
6 Justin Thompson, Tony Clark	5.00
7 Johnny Damon, Jermaine Dye	3.00
8 Dave Nilsson, Jeff Cirillo	3.00
9 Paul Molitor, Chuck Knoblauch	5.00
10 Tino Martinez, Derek Jeter	8.00
11 Ben Grieve, Jose Canseco	10.00
12 Ken Griffey Jr., Alex Rodriguez	30.00
13 Juan Gonzalez, Ivan Rodriguez	15.00
14 Jose Cruz Jr., Roger Clemens	10.00
15 Greg Maddux, Chipper Jones	20.00
16 Sammy Sosa, Mark Grace	10.00
17 Barry Larkin, Deion Sanders	4.00
18 Larry Walker, Andres Galarraga	4.00

19	Moises Alou, Bobby Bonilla	3.00
20	Jeff Bagwell, Craig Biggio	12.00
21	Mike Piazza, Hideo Nomo	20.00
22	Pedro Martinez, Henry Rodriguez	4.00
23	Rey Ordonez, Carlos Baerga	3.00
24	Curt Schilling, Scott Rolen	8.00
25	Al Martin, Tony Womack	3.00
26	Mark McGwire, Dennis Eckersley	30.00
27	Tony Gwynn, Wally Joyner	15.00
28	Barry Bonds, J.T. Snow	8.00
29	Matt Williams, Jay Bell	5.00
30	Fred McGriff, Roberto Hernandez	4.00

1998 Pacific Aurora

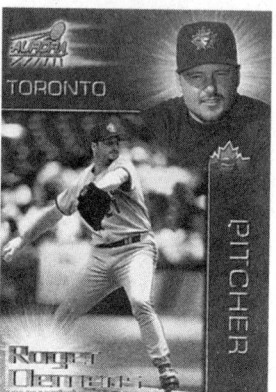

The Aurora base set consists of 200 cards printed on 24-point board. The cards have a color photo bordered on two sides by a thick green border. A headshot of the player appears in the corner of the border. Inserts include Pennant Fever (with three parallels), Hardball Cel-Fusions, Kings of the Major Leagues, On Deck Laser-Cuts and Pacific Cubes.

		MT
Complete Set (200):		40.00
Common Player:		.15
Wax Box:		90.00
1	Garret Anderson	.15
2	Jim Edmonds	.25
3	Darin Erstad	.75
4	Cecil Fielder	.25
5	Chuck Finley	.15
6	Todd Greene	.15
7	Ken Hill	.15
8	Tim Salmon	.40
9	Roberto Alomar	.60
10	Brady Anderson	.15
11	Joe Carter	.25
12	Mike Mussina	.60
13	Rafael Palmeiro	.25
14	Cal Ripken Jr.	2.50
15	B.J. Surhoff	.15
16	Steve Avery	.15
17	Nomar Garciaparra	2.00
18	Pedro Martinez	.50
19	John Valentin	.15
20	Jason Varitek	.15
21	Mo Vaughn	.75
22	Albert Belle	.75
23	Ray Durham	.15
24	*Magglio Ordonez*	.75
25	Frank Thomas	2.50
26	Robin Ventura	.25
27	Sandy Alomar Jr.	.25
28	Travis Fryman	.15
29	Dwight Gooden	.25
30	David Justice	.50
31	Kenny Lofton	.75
32	Manny Ramirez	.75
33	Jim Thome	.50
34	Omar Vizquel	.15
35	Enrique Wilson	.15
36	Jaret Wright	1.00
37	Tony Clark	.50
38	Bobby Higginson	.15
39	Brian Hunter	.15
40	Bip Roberts	.15
41	Justin Thompson	.15
42	Jeff Conine	.15
43	Johnny Damon	.15
44	Jermaine Dye	.15
45	Jeff King	.15
46	Jeff Montgomery	.15
47	Hal Morris	.15
48	Dean Palmer	.15
49	Terry Pendleton	.15
50	Rick Aguilera	.15
51	Marty Cordova	.15
52	Paul Molitor	.50
53	Otis Nixon	.15
54	Brad Radke	.15
55	Terry Steinbach	.15
56	Todd Walker	.40
57	Chili Davis	.15
58	Derek Jeter	1.50
59	Chuck Knoblauch	.40
60	Tino Martinez	.40
61	Paul O'Neill	.40
62	Andy Pettitte	.60
63	Mariano Rivera	.25
64	Bernie Williams	.60
65	Jason Giambi	.15
66	Ben Grieve	1.00
67	Rickey Henderson	.25
68	A.J. Hinch	.40
69	Kenny Rogers	.15
70	Jay Buhner	.40
71	Joey Cora	.15
72	Ken Griffey Jr.	3.00
73	Randy Johnson	.60
74	Edgar Martinez	.25
75	Jamie Moyer	.15
76	Alex Rodriguez	2.00
77	David Segui	.15
78	*Rolando Arrojo*	.50
79	Wade Boggs	.40
80	Roberto Hernandez	.15
81	Dave Martinez	.15
82	Fred McGriff	.40
83	Paul Sorrento	.15
84	Kevin Stocker	.15
85	Will Clark	.40
86	Juan Gonzalez	1.50
87	Tom Goodwin	.15
88	Rusty Greer	.25
89	Ivan Rodriguez	.75
90	John Wetteland	.15
91	Jose Canseco	.40
92	Roger Clemens	1.00
93	Jose Cruz Jr.	.75
94	Carlos Delgado	.25
95	Pat Hentgen	.15
96	Jay Bell	.15
97	Andy Benes	.25
98	Karim Garcia	.15
99	Travis Lee	2.00
100	Devon White	.15
101	Matt Williams	.40
102	Andres Galarraga	.40
103	Tom Glavine	.25
104	Andruw Jones	.75
105	Chipper Jones	2.00
106	Ryan Klesko	.40
107	Javy Lopez	.25
108	Greg Maddux	2.00
109	Walt Weiss	.15
110	Rod Beck	.15
111	Jeff Blauser	.15
112	Mark Grace	.40
113	Lance Johnson	.15
114	Mickey Morandini	.15
115	Henry Rodriguez	.15
116	Sammy Sosa	1.50
117	Kerry Wood	4.00
118	Lenny Harris	.15
119	Damian Jackson	.15
120	Barry Larkin	.40
121	Reggie Sanders	.15
122	Brett Tomko	.15
123	Dante Bichette	.40
124	Ellis Burks	.15
125	Vinny Castilla	.25
126	Todd Helton	.75
127	Darryl Kile	.15
128	Larry Walker	.40
129	Bobby Bonilla	.25
130	Livan Hernandez	.25
131	Charles Johnson	.15
132	Derrek Lee	.15
133	Edgar Renteria	.15
134	Gary Sheffield	.50
135	Moises Alou	.25
136	Jeff Bagwell	1.00
137	Derek Bell	.15
138	Craig Biggio	.40
139	*John Halama*	.40
140	Mike Hampton	.15
141	Richard Hidalgo	.15
142	Wilton Guerrero	.15
143	Todd Hollandsworth	.15
144	Eric Karros	.25
145	Paul Konerko	.40
146	Raul Mondesi	.40
147	Hideo Nomo	.60
148	Chan Ho Park	.40
149	Mike Piazza	2.00
150	Jeromy Burnitz	.15
151	Todd Dunn	.15
152	Marquis Grissom	.15
153	John Jaha	.15
154	Dave Nilsson	.15
155	Fernando Vina	.15
156	Mark Grudzielanek	.15
157	Vladimir Guerrero	.75
158	F.P. Santangelo	.15
159	Jose Vidro	.15
160	Rondell White	.25
161	Edgardo Alfonzo	.15
162	Carlos Baerga	.15
163	John Franco	.15
164	Todd Hundley	.15
165	Brian McRae	.15
166	John Olerud	.25
167	Rey Ordonez	.15
168	*Masato Yoshii*	.50
169	Ricky Bottalico	.15
170	Doug Glanville	.15
171	Gregg Jefferies	.15
172	Desi Relaford	.15
173	Scott Rolen	1.00
174	Curt Schilling	.25
175	Jose Guillen	.25
176	Jason Kendall	.15
177	Al Martin	.15
178	Abraham Nunez	.15
179	Kevin Young	.15
180	Royce Clayton	.15
181	Delino DeShields	.15
182	Gary Gaetti	.15
183	Ron Gant	.25
184	Brian Jordan	.15
185	Ray Lankford	.15
186	Willie McGee	.15
187	Mark McGwire	4.00
188	Kevin Brown	.15
189	Ken Caminiti	.25
190	Steve Finley	.15
191	Tony Gwynn	1.50
192	Wally Joyner	.15
193	Ruben Rivera	.15
194	Quilvio Veras	.15
195	Barry Bonds	.75
196	Shawn Estes	.15
197	Orel Hershiser	.15
198	Jeff Kent	.15
199	Robb Nen	.15
200	J.T. Snow	.15

1998 Pacific Aurora Cubes

A cardboard cube presenting player photos on top and three sides, plus a side of stats was created as a hobby-only insert for Pacific Aurora. The assembled, shrink-wrapped cubes were packed one per box.

Modern cards have little collector value in conditions lower than Mint. Figure NM cards at 75% of values shown; EX cards at 40%.

		MT
Complete Set (20):		140.00
Common Player:		3.00
Inserted 1:box		
1	Travis Lee	6.00
2	Chipper Jones	12.00
3	Greg Maddux	12.00
4	Cal Ripken Jr.	15.00
5	Nomar Garciaparra	12.00
6	Frank Thomas	15.00
7	Manny Ramirez	5.00
8	Larry Walker	2.50
9	Hideo Nomo	4.00
10	Mike Piazza	12.00
11	Derek Jeter	10.00
12	Ben Grieve	6.00
13	Mark McGwire	20.00
14	Tony Gwynn	10.00
15	Barry Bonds	5.00
16	Ken Griffey Jr.	20.00
17	Alex Rodriguez	12.00
18	Wade Boggs	2.50
19	Juan Gonzalez	10.00
20	Jose Cruz Jr.	5.00

1998 Pacific Aurora Hardball

Hardball Cel-Fusions is a 20-card insert seeded one per 73 packs. The cards feature a die-cut cel baseball fused to a foiled and etched card.

		MT
Complete Set (20):		500.00
Common Player:		10.00
Inserted 1:73		
1	Travis Lee	40.00
2	Chipper Jones	40.00
3	Greg Maddux	40.00

4	Cal Ripken Jr.	50.00
5	Nomar Garciaparra	40.00
6	Frank Thomas	50.00
7	David Justice	10.00
8	Jeff Bagwell	20.00
9	Hideo Nomo	15.00
10	Mike Piazza	40.00
11	Derek Jeter	40.00
12	Ben Grieve	20.00
13	Scott Rolen	20.00
14	Mark McGwire	60.00
15	Tony Gwynn	30.00
16	Ken Griffey Jr.	60.00
17	Alex Rodriguez	40.00
18	Ivan Rodriguez	15.00
19	Roger Clemens	20.00
20	Jose Cruz Jr.	15.00

1998 Pacific Aurora Kings of the Major Leagues

This 10-card insert features star players on fully-foiled cards. Kings of the Major Leagues was seeded one per 361 packs.

		MT
Complete Set (10):		850.00
Common Player:		20.00
Inserted 1:361		
1	Chipper Jones	90.00
2	Greg Maddux	90.00
3	Cal Ripken Jr.	110.00
4	Nomar Garciaparra	90.00
5	Frank Thomas	110.00
6	Mike Piazza	90.00
7	Mark McGwire	150.00
8	Tony Gwynn	75.00
9	Ken Griffey Jr.	150.00
10	Alex Rodriguez	90.00

1998 Pacific Aurora On Deck Laser-Cut

On Deck Laser-Cuts is a 20-card insert seeded four per 37 packs of 1998 Pacific Aurora Baseball.

		MT
Complete Set (20):		70.00
Common Player:		1.00
Inserted 1:9		
1	Travis Lee	3.00
2	Chipper Jones	6.00
3	Greg Maddux	6.00
4	Cal Ripken Jr.	8.00
5	Nomar Garciaparra	6.00

6	Frank Thomas	8.00
7	Manny Ramirez	2.50
8	Larry Walker	1.00
9	Hideo Nomo	2.00
10	Mike Piazza	6.00
11	Derek Jeter	6.00
12	Ben Grieve	4.00
13	Mark McGwire	12.00
14	Tony Gwynn	5.00
15	Barry Bonds	2.50
16	Ken Griffey Jr.	10.00
17	Alex Rodriguez	8.00
18	Wade Boggs	1.00
19	Juan Gonzalez	5.00
20	Jose Cruz Jr.	2.50

1998 Pacific Aurora Pennant Fever

Pennant Fever is a 50-card insert seeded one per pack. Each card is fully foiled and etched. The color player image is duplicated in the upper left corner with an image stamped in gold foil. Pennant Fever has three parallels. The Silver retail parallel is numbered to 250, Platinum Blue is numbered to 100 and the Copper hobby parallel is numbered to 20. Tony Gwynn signed his card serially numbered one in each insert.

		MT
Complete Set (50):		20.00
Common Player:		.25
Inserted 1:1		
Silvers: 40x to 75x		
Production 250 sets		
Platinum Blues: 60x to 100x		
Production 100 sets		
1	Tony Gwynn	1.00
2	Derek Jeter	1.25
3	Alex Rodriguez	1.25
4	Paul Molitor	.40
5	Nomar Garciaparra	1.25
6	Jeff Bagwell	.75
7	Ivan Rodriguez	.50
8	Cal Ripken Jr.	1.50
9	Matt Williams	.25
10	Chipper Jones	1.25
11	Edgar Martinez	.25
12	Wade Boggs	.25
13	Paul Konerko	.25
14	Ben Grieve	.75
15	Sandy Alomar Jr.	.25
16	Travis Lee	.75
17	Scott Rolen	.75
18	Ryan Klesko	.25
19	Juan Gonzalez	1.00
20	Albert Belle	.50
21	Roger Clemens	.75
22	Javy Lopez	.25
23	Jose Cruz Jr.	.50
24	Ken Griffey Jr.	2.00
25	Mark McGwire	2.50
26	Brady Anderson	.25
27	Jaret Wright	1.00
28	Roberto Alomar	.40
29	Joe Carter	.25
30	Hideo Nomo	.40
31	Mike Piazza	1.25
32	Andres Galarraga	.25
33	Larry Walker	.25
34	Tim Salmon	.25
35	Frank Thomas	1.50
36	Moises Alou	.25
37	David Justice	.40
38	Manny Ramirez	.50
39	Jim Edmonds	.25
40	Barry Bonds	.50
41	Jim Thome	.40
42	Mo Vaughn	.50
43	Rafael Palmeiro	.25
44	Darin Erstad	.50
45	Pedro Martinez	.40
46	Greg Maddux	1.25
47	Jose Canseco	.25
48	Vladimir Guerrero	.50
49	Bernie Williams	.40
50	Randy Johnson	.40

1998 Pacific Crown Royale

The Crown Royale base set consists of 144 die-cut cards. The cards have a horizontal layout and are die-cut around a crown design at the top. The cards are double-foiled and etched. Inserts include Diamond Knights, Pillars of the Game, Race to the Record, All-Star Die-Cuts, Firestone on Baseball and Cramer's Choice Awards.

		MT
Complete Set (144):		125.00
Common Player:		.50
1	Garret Anderson	.50
2	Jim Edmonds	.75
3	Darin Erstad	2.50
4	Tim Salmon	1.00
5	Jarrod Washburn	.50
6	David Dellucci	.50
7	Travis Lee	6.00
8	Devon White	.50
9	Matt Williams	1.00
10	Andres Galarraga	1.00
11	Tom Glavine	.75
12	Andruw Jones	2.50
13	Chipper Jones	6.00
14	Ryan Klesko	1.00
15	Javy Lopez	.75
16	Greg Maddux	6.00
17	Walt Weiss	.50
18	Roberto Alomar	1.50
19	Harold Baines	.50
20	Eric Davis	.50
21	Mike Mussina	2.00
22	Rafael Palmeiro	1.00
23	Cal Ripken Jr.	8.00
24	Nomar Garciaparra	6.00
25	Pedro Martinez	2.50
26	Troy O'Leary	.50
27	Mo Vaughn	2.50
28	Tim Wakefield	.50
29	Mark Grace	1.00
30	Mickey Morandini	.50
31	Sammy Sosa	8.00
32	Kerry Wood	10.00
33	Albert Belle	2.50
34	Mike Caruso	.50
35	Ray Durham	.50
36	Frank Thomas	8.00
37	Robin Ventura	.75
38	Bret Boone	.50
39	Sean Casey	.50
40	Barry Larkin	.75
41	Reggie Sanders	.50
42	Sandy Alomar Jr.	.50
43	David Justice	1.00
44	Kenny Lofton	2.50
45	Manny Ramirez	2.50
46	Jim Thome	1.50
47	Omar Vizquel	.50
48	Jaret Wright	2.50
49	Dante Bichette	.75
50	Ellis Burks	.50
51	Vinny Castilla	.75
52	Todd Helton	2.00
53	Larry Walker	1.00
54	Tony Clark	1.50
55	Damion Easley	.50
56	Bobby Higginson	.50
57	Cliff Floyd	.50
58	Livan Hernandez	.50
59	Derrek Lee	.50
60	Edgar Renteria	.50
61	Moises Alou	.75
62	Jeff Bagwell	3.00
63	Derek Bell	.50
64	Craig Biggio	.75
65	Johnny Damon	.50
66	Jeff King	.50
67	Hal Morris	.50
68	Dean Palmer	.50
69	Bobby Bonilla	.50
70	Eric Karros	.75
71	Raul Mondesi	.75
72	Gary Sheffield	.75
73	Jeromy Burnitz	.50
74	Jeff Cirillo	.50
75	Marquis Grissom	.50
76	Fernando Vina	.50
77	Marty Cordova	.50
78	Pat Meares	.50
79	Paul Molitor	1.60
80	Terry Steinbach	.50
81	Todd Walker	.75
82	Brad Fullmer	1.00
83	Vladimir Guerrero	2.50
84	Carl Pavano	.50
85	Rondell White	.75
86	Carlos Baerga	.50
87	Hideo Nomo	1.50
88	John Olerud	.75
89	Rey Ordonez	.50
90	Mike Piazza	6.00
91	*Masato Yoshii*	1.50
92	*Orlando Hernandez*	10.00
93	Hideki Irabu	1.50
94	Derek Jeter	5.00
95	Chuck Knoblauch	1.00
96	Ricky Ledee	.75
97	Tino Martinez	1.00
98	Paul O'Neill	.75
99	Bernie Williams	2.00
100	Jason Giambi	.50
101	Ben Grieve	3.00
102	Rickey Henderson	.50
103	Matt Stairs	.50
104	Bob Abreu	.50
105	Doug Glanville	.50
106	Scott Rolen	3.00
107	Curt Schilling	.50
108	Jose Guillen	.50
109	Jason Kendall	.75
110	Jason Schmidt	.50
111	Kevin Young	.50
112	Delino DeShields	.50
113	Brian Jordan	.50
114	Ray Lankford	.75
115	Mark McGwire	12.00
116	Tony Gwynn	5.00
117	Wally Joyner	.50
118	Ruben Rivera	.50
119	Greg Vaughn	.75
120	Rich Aurilia	.50
121	Barry Bonds	2.50
122	Bill Mueller	.50
123	Robb Nen	.50
124	Jay Buhner	1.00
125	Ken Griffey Jr.	10.00
126	Edgar Martinez	.75
127	Shane Monahan	.50
128	Alex Rodriguez	8.00
129	David Segui	.50
130	*Rolando Arrojo*	2.00
131	Wade Boggs	.75
132	Quinton McCracken	.50
133	Fred McGriff	.75
134	Bobby Smith	.50
135	Will Clark	1.00
136	Juan Gonzalez	5.00
137	Rusty Greer	.75
138	Ivan Rodriguez	2.50
139	Aaron Sele	.50
140	John Wetteland	.50
141	Jose Canseco	1.00
142	Roger Clemens	4.00
143	Carlos Delgado	.50
144	Shawn Green	.50

1998 Pacific Crown Royale All-Star

This 20-card insert was seeded one per 25 packs. The featured players all participated in the 1998 All-Star Game. The background features the sun rising over a mountain with a die-cut at the top of the card.

		MT
Complete Set (20):		350.00
Common Player:		5.00
1	Roberto Alomar	10.00
2	Cal Ripken Jr.	40.00
3	Kenny Lofton	15.00
4	Jim Thome	8.00
5	Derek Jeter	25.00
6	David Wells	5.00
7	Ken Griffey Jr.	50.00
8	Alex Rodriguez	40.00
9	Juan Gonzalez	25.00
10	Ivan Rodriguez	15.00
11	Gary Sheffield	5.00
12	Chipper Jones	30.00
13	Greg Maddux	30.00
14	Walt Weiss	5.00
15	Larry Walker	8.00
16	Craig Biggio	5.00
17	Mike Piazza	30.00
18	Mark McGwire	50.00
19	Tony Gwynn	25.00
20	Barry Bonds	15.00

1998 Pacific Crown Royale Cramer's Choice Awards

Premium-sized Cramer's Choice Awards were inserted one per box. The ten players in the set are featured on a die-cut card designed to resemble a trophy. Pacific CEO Mike Cramer signed and hand-numbered ten sets of Cramer's Choice Awards.

		MT
Complete Set (10):		100.00
Common Player:		5.00
1	Cal Ripken Jr.	15.00
2	Ken Griffey Jr.	20.00
3	Alex Rodriguez	15.00
4	Juan Gonzalez	10.00
5	Travis Lee	12.00
6	Chipper Jones	12.00
7	Greg Maddux	12.00
8	Kerry Wood	20.00
9	Mark McGwire	20.00
10	Tony Gwynn	10.00

1998 Pacific Crown Royale Diamond Knights

Diamond Knights is a 25-card, one per pack insert. Each card features a color action photo and the player's name, team and position listed in a Medieval-type border at the bottom.

		MT
Complete Set (25):		40.00
Common Player:		.75
Inserted 1:1		
1	Andres Galarraga	1.00
2	Chipper Jones	3.00
3	Greg Maddux	3.00
4	Cal Ripken Jr.	4.00
5	Nomar Garciaparra	3.00
6	Mo Vaughn	1.25
7	Kerry Wood	5.00
8	Frank Thomas	4.00
9	Vinny Castilla	.75
10	Jeff Bagwell	1.50
11	Craig Biggio	.75
12	Paul Molitor	1.00
13	Mike Piazza	3.00
14	Orlando Hernandez	4.00
15	Derek Jeter	2.50
16	Ricky Ledee	.75
17	Mark McGwire	6.00
18	Tony Gwynn	2.50
19	Barry Bonds	1.25
20	Ken Griffey Jr.	5.00
21	Alex Rodriguez	4.00
22	Wade Boggs	.75
23	Juan Gonzalez	2.50
24	Ivan Rodriguez	1.25
25	Jose Canseco	1.00

1998 Pacific Crown Royale Firestone on Baseball

This 26-card insert features star players with commentary by sports personality Roy Firestone. The fronts feature a color photo of the player and a portrait of Firestone in the lower right corner. The card backs have text by Firestone on what makes the featured player great. Firestone signed a total of 300 cards in this insert.

Values shown reflect the market as of January, 1999. On-field performances of current players in the 1999 baseball season are not factored in.

		MT
Complete Set (26):		400.00
Common Player:		4.00
Inserted 1:12		
1	Travis Lee	25.00
2	Chipper Jones	25.00
3	Greg Maddux	25.00
4	Cal Ripken Jr.	30.00
5	Nomar Garciaparra	25.00
6	Mo Vaughn	10.00
7	Kerry Wood	40.00
8	Frank Thomas	30.00
9	Manny Ramirez	10.00
10	Larry Walker	6.00
11	Gary Sheffield	4.00
12	Paul Molitor	8.00
13	Hideo Nomo	6.00
14	Mike Piazza	25.00
15	Ben Grieve	15.00
16	Mark McGwire	40.00
17	Tony Gwynn	20.00
18	Barry Bonds	10.00
19	Ken Griffey Jr.	40.00
20	Randy Johnson	8.00
21	Alex Rodriquez	30.00
22	Wade Boggs	4.00
23	Juan Gonzalez	20.00
24	Ivan Rodriguez	10.00
25	Roger Clemens	18.00
26	Roy Firestone	4.00

1998 Pacific Crown Royale HomeRun Fever

Home Run Fever (10 cards, 1:73) features players who had a shot at breaking Roger Maris' home run record in 1998. The card fronts have a player photo on the left and a blackboard with numbers from 1 to 60 on the right. Ten circles featuring disappearing ink contained numbers 61 through 70. Collectors could rub the circles to reveal the player's potential record home run total.

		MT
Complete Set (10):		450.00
Common Player:		15.00
1	Andres Galarraga	20.00
2	Sammy Sosa	75.00
3	Albert Belle	30.00
4	Jim Thome	20.00
5	Mark McGwire	120.00
6	Greg Vaughn	15.00
7	Ken Griffey Jr.	120.00
8	Alex Rodriguez	100.00
9	Juan Gonzalez	60.00
10	Jose Canseco	20.00

1998 Pacific Crown Royale Pillars of the Game

This 25-card insert was seeded one per pack. Each card features a star player with a background of holographic silver foil.

		MT
Complete Set (25):		40.00
Common Player:		.75
Inserted 1:1		
1	Jim Edmonds	.75
2	Travis Lee	3.00
3	Chipper Jones	3.00
4	Tom Glavine, John Smoltz, Greg Maddux	2.00
5	Cal Ripken Jr.	4.00
6	Nomar Garciaparra	3.00
7	Mo Vaughn	1.25
8	Sammy Sosa	4.00
9	Kerry Wood	5.00
10	Frank Thomas	4.00
11	Jim Thome	1.00
12	Larry Walker	1.00
13	Moises Alou	.75
14	Raul Mondesi	1.00
15	Mike Piazza	3.00
16	Hideki Irabu	1.00
17	Bernie Williams	1.00
18	Ben Grieve	1.50
19	Scott Rolen	1.50
20	Mark McGwire	6.00
21	Tony Gwynn	2.50
22	Ken Griffey Jr.	5.00
23	Alex Rodriguez	4.00
24	Juan Gonzalez	2.50
25	Roger Clemens	2.00

1998 Pacific Invincible

Invincible Baseball consists of a 150-card base set. The base cards have a horizontal layout and feature a player photo on the left and a headshot in a cel window on the right. The regular cards were inserted one per five-card pack. Silver (2:37) and Platinum Blue (1:73) parallels were also created. Inserts include Moments in Time, Team Checklists, Photoengravings, Interleague Players, Gems of the Diamond and Cramer's Choice Awards.

		MT
Complete Set (150):		175.00
Common Player:		1.00
Silvers: 2x to 4x		
Inserted 2:37		
Ice Blues: 8x to 15x		
Inserted 1:73		
Wax Box:		90.00
1	Garret Anderson	1.00
2	Jim Edmonds	1.50
3	Darin Erstad	4.00
4	Chuck Finley	1.00
5	Tim Salmon	2.00
6	Roberto Alomar	3.00
7	Brady Anderson	1.50
8	Geronimo Berroa	1.00
9	Eric Davis	1.00
10	Mike Mussina	3.00
11	Rafael Palmeiro	2.00
12	Cal Ripken Jr.	12.00
13	Steve Avery	1.00
14	Nomar Garciaparra	9.00
15	John Valentin	1.00
16	Mo Vaughn	4.00
17	Albert Belle	4.00
18	Ozzie Guillen	1.00
19	Norberto Martin	1.00
20	Frank Thomas	12.00
21	Robin Ventura	1.00
22	Sandy Alomar Jr.	1.00
23	David Justice	1.50
24	Kenny Lofton	4.00
25	Manny Ramirez	3.00
26	Jim Thome	2.50
27	Omar Vizquel	1.00
28	Matt Williams	2.00
29	Jaret Wright	8.00
30	Raul Casanova	1.00
31	Tony Clark	2.50
32	Deivi Cruz	1.00
33	Bobby Higginson	1.00
34	Justin Thompson	1.00
35	Yamil Benitez	1.00
36	Johnny Damon	1.00
37	Jermaine Dye	1.00
38	Jed Hansen	1.00
39	Larry Sutton	1.00
40	Jeromy Burnitz	1.00
41	Jeff Cirillo	1.00
42	Dave Nilsson	1.00
43	Jose Valentin	1.00
44	Fernando Vina	1.00
45	Marty Cordova	1.00
46	Chuck Knoblauch	2.00
47	Paul Molitor	3.00
48	Brad Radke	1.00
49	Terry Steinbach	1.00
50	Wade Boggs	1.50
51	Hideki Irabu	2.00
52	Derek Jeter	9.00
53	Tino Martinez	2.00
54	Andy Pettitte	3.00
55	Mariano Rivera	1.50
56	Bernie Williams	3.00
57	Jose Canseco	1.50
58	Jason Giambi	1.00
59	Ben Grieve	6.00
60	Aaron Small	1.00
61	Jay Buhner	2.00
62	Ken Cloude	1.00
63	Joey Cora	1.00
64	Ken Griffey Jr.	15.00
65	Randy Johnson	3.00
66	Edgar Martinez	1.50
67	Alex Rodriguez	9.00
68	Will Clark	1.50
69	Juan Gonzalez	8.00
70	Rusty Greer	1.00
71	Ivan Rodriguez	4.00
72	Joe Carter	1.50
73	Roger Clemens	5.00
74	Jose Cruz Jr.	5.00
75	Carlos Delgado	1.00
76	Andruw Jones	7.00
77	Chipper Jones	9.00
78	Ryan Klesko	2.00
79	Javier Lopez	1.50
80	Greg Maddux	9.00
81	Miguel Batista	1.00
82	Jeremi Gonzalez	1.00
83	Mark Grace	2.00
84	Kevin Orie	1.00
85	Sammy Sosa	8.00
86	Barry Larkin	1.50
87	Deion Sanders	1.50
88	Reggie Sanders	1.00
89	Chris Stynes	1.00
90	Dante Bichette	1.50
91	Vinny Castilla	1.00
92	Andres Galarraga	2.00
93	Neifi Perez	1.00
94	Larry Walker	2.00
95	Moises Alou	1.00
96	Bobby Bonilla	1.00
97	Kevin Brown	1.00
98	Craig Counsell	1.00
99	Livan Hernandez	2.00
100	Edgar Renteria	1.00
101	Gary Sheffield	2.00
102	Jeff Bagwell	7.00
103	Craig Biggio	1.50
104	Luis Gonzalez	1.00
105	Darryl Kile	1.00
106	Wilton Guerrero	1.00
107	Eric Karros	1.50
108	Ramon Martinez	1.50
109	Raul Mondesi	2.00
110	Hideo Nomo	4.00
111	Chan Ho Park	1.50
112	Mike Piazza	9.00
113	Mark Grudzielanek	1.00
114	Vladimir Guerrero	4.00
115	Pedro Martinez	2.00
116	Henry Rodriguez	1.00
117	David Segui	1.00
118	Edgardo Alfonzo	1.00
119	Carlos Baerga	1.00
120	John Franco	1.00
121	John Olerud	1.00
122	Rey Ordonez	1.00
123	Ricky Bottalico	1.00
124	Gregg Jefferies	1.00
125	Mickey Morandini	1.00
126	Scott Rolen	6.00
127	Curt Schilling	1.50
128	Jose Guillen	2.00
129	Esteban Loaiza	1.00
130	Al Martin	1.00
131	Tony Womack	1.00
132	Dennis Eckersley	1.00
133	Gary Gaetti	1.00
134	Curtis King	1.00
135	Ray Lankford	1.00
136	Mark McGwire	15.00
137	Ken Caminiti	1.50
138	Steve Finley	1.00
139	Tony Gwynn	7.00
140	Carlos Hernandez	1.00
141	Wally Joyner	1.00
142	Barry Bonds	4.00
143	Jacob Cruz	1.00
144	Shawn Estes	1.00
145	Stan Javier	1.00
146	J.T. Snow	1.50
147	Nomar Garciaparra	6.00
148	Scott Rolen	4.00
149	Ken Griffey Jr.	10.00
150	Larry Walker	1.50

1998 Pacific Invincible Cramer's Choice

The 10-card Cramer's Choice Awards insert features top players on cards with a die-cut trophy design. This set has six different foil variations, each with a different production number. Green (99 hand-numbered sets), Dark Blue (80), Light Blue (50), Red (25), Gold (15) and Purple (10) versions were included in Invincible.

		MT
Complete Green Set (10):		1100.
Common Green (99 sets):		50.00
Dark Blues (80 sets): .8x to 1.25x		
Light Blues (50 sets): 1x to 1.5x		
Reds (25 sets): 1.5x to 3x		
Golds (15 sets): 2.5x to 5x		
Purples (10 sets): 3x to 6x		
1	Greg Maddux	150.00
2	Roberto Alomar	50.00
3	Cal Ripken Jr.	200.00
4	Nomar Garciaparra	150.00
5	Larry Walker	50.00
6	Mike Piazza	150.00
7	Mark McGwire	250.00
8	Tony Gwynn	125.00
9	Ken Griffey Jr.	250.00
10	Roger Clemens	100.00

1998 Pacific Invincible Gems of the Diamond

Gems of the Diamond is a 220-card insert seeded four per pack. The cards feature a color photo inside a white border.

		MT
Complete Set (220):		30.00
Common Player:		.10
1	Jim Edmonds	.20
2	Todd Greene	.20
3	Ken Hill	.10
4	Mike Holtz	.10
5	Mike James	.10
6	Chad Kreuter	.10
7	Tim Salmon	.30
8	Roberto Alomar	.60
9	Brady Anderson	.20
10	David Dellucci	.10
11	Jeffrey Hammonds	.10
12	Mike Mussina	.60
13	Rafael Palmeiro	.25
14	Arthur Rhodes	.10
15	Cal Ripken Jr.	2.50
16	Nerio Rodriguez	.10
17	Tony Tarasco	.10
18	Lenny Webster	.10
19	Mike Benjamin	.10
20	Rich Garces	.10
21	Nomar Garciaparra	2.00
22	Shane Mack	.10
23	Jose Malave	.10
24	Jesus Tavarez	.10
25	Mo Vaughn	.75
26	John Wasdin	.10
27	Jeff Abbott	.10
28	Albert Belle	.75
29	Mike Cameron	.25
30	Al Levine	.10
31	Robert Machado	.10
32	Greg Norton	.10
33	Magglio Ordonez	.75
34	Mike Sirotka	.10
35	Frank Thomas	2.50
36	Mario Valdez	.10

37	Sandy Alomar Jr.	.20
38	David Justice	.25
39	Jack McDowell	.10
40	Eric Plunk	.10
41	Manny Ramirez	.60
42	Kevin Seitzer	.10
43	Paul Shuey	.10
44	Omar Vizquel	.10
45	Kimera Bartee	.10
46	Glenn Dishman	.10
47	Orlando Miller	.10
48	Mike Myers	.10
49	Phil Nevin	.10
50	A.J. Sager	.10
51	Ricky Bones	.10
52	Scott Cooper	.10
53	Shane Halter	.10
54	David Howard	.10
55	Glendon Rusch	.10
56	Joe Vitiello	.10
57	Jeff D'Amico	.10
58	Mike Fetters	.10
59	Mike Matheny	.10
60	Jose Mercedes	.10
61	Ron Villone	.10
62	Jack Voigt	.10
63	Brent Brede	.10
64	Chuck Knoblauch	.25
65	Paul Molitor	.50
66	Todd Ritchie	.10
67	Frankie Rodriguez	.10
68	Scott Stahoviak	.10
69	Greg Swindell	.10
70	Todd Walker	.20
71	Wade Boggs	.20
72	Hideki Irabu	.30
73	Derek Jeter	1.75
74	Pat Kelly	.10
75	Graeme Lloyd	.10
76	Tino Martinez	.25
77	Jeff Nelson	.10
78	Scott Pose	.10
79	Mike Stanton	.10
80	Darryl Strawberry	.10
81	Bernie Williams	.60
82	Tony Batista	.10
83	Mark Bellhorn	.10
84	Ben Grieve	1.25
85	Pat Lennon	.10
86	Brian Lesher	.10
87	Miguel Tejada	.75
88	George Williams	.10
89	Joey Cora	.10
90	Rob Ducey	.10
91	Ken Griffey Jr.	3.00
92	Randy Johnson	.50
93	Edgar Martinez	.10
94	John Marzano	.10
95	Greg McCarthy	.10
96	Alex Rodriguez	2.00
97	Andy Sheets	.10
98	Mike Timlin	.10
99	Lee Tinsley	.10
100	Damon Buford	.10
101	Alex Diaz	.10
102	Benji Gil	.10
103	Juan Gonzalez	1.50
104	Eric Gunderson	.10
105	Danny Patterson	.10
106	Ivan Rodriguez	.75
107	Mike Simms	.10
108	Luis Andujar	.10
109	Joe Carter	.20
110	Roger Clemens	1.00
111	Jose Cruz Jr.	1.50
112	Shawn Green	.10
113	Robert Perez	.10
114	Juan Samuel	.10
115	Ed Sprague	.10
116	Shannon Stewart	.10
117	Danny Bautista	.10
118	Chipper Jones	2.00
119	Ryan Klesko	.30
120	Keith Lockhart	.10
121	Javier Lopez	.10
122	Greg Maddux	2.00
123	Kevin Millwood	.75
124	Mike Mordecai	.10
125	Eddie Perez	.10
126	Randall Simon	.25
127	Miguel Cairo	.10
128	Dave Clark	.10
129	Kevin Foster	.10
130	Mark Grace	.25
131	Tyler Houston	.10
132	Mike Hubbard	.10
133	Kevin Orie	.10
134	Ryne Sandberg	.75
135	Sammy Sosa	1.00
136	Lenny Harris	.10
137	Kent Mercker	.10
138	Mike Morgan	.10
139	Deion Sanders	.20
140	Chris Stynes	.10
141	Gabe White	.10
142	Jason Bates	.10
143	Vinny Castilla	.10
144	Andres Galarraga	.25
145	Curtis Leskanic	.10
146	Jeff McCurry	.10
147	Mike Munoz	.10
148	Larry Walker	.30
149	Jamey Wright	.10
150	Moises Alou	.20
151	Bobby Bonilla	.10
152	Kevin Brown	.10
153	John Cangelosi	.10
154	Jeff Conine	.10
155	Cliff Floyd	.10
156	Jay Powell	.10
157	Edgar Renteria	.10
158	Tony Saunders	.10
159	Gary Sheffield	.25
160	Jeff Bagwell	1.25
161	Tim Bogar	.10
162	Tony Eusebio	.10
163	Chris Holt	.10
164	Ray Montgomery	.10
165	Luis Rivera	.10
166	Eric Anthony	.10
167	Brett Butler	.10
168	Juan Castro	.10
169	Tripp Cromer	.10
170	Raul Mondesi	.25
171	Hideo Nomo	.75
172	Mike Piazza	2.00
173	Tom Prince	.10
174	Adam Riggs	.10
175	Shane Andrews	.10
176	Shayne Bennett	.10
177	Raul Chavez	.10
178	Pedro Martinez	.30
179	Sherman Obando	.10
180	Andy Stankiewicz	.10
181	Alberto Castillo	.10
182	Shawn Gilbert	.10
183	Luis Lopez	.10
184	Roberto Petagine	.10
185	Armando Reynoso	.10
186	Midre Cummings	.10
187	Kevin Jordan	.10
188	Desi Relaford	.10
189	Scott Rolen	1.25
190	Ken Ryan	.10
191	Kevin Sefcik	.10
192	Emil Brown	.10
193	Lou Collier	.10
194	Francisco Cordova	.10
195	Kevin Elster	.10
196	Mark Smith	.10
197	Marc Wilkins	.10
198	Manny Aybar	.10
199	Jose Bautista	.10
200	David Bell	.10
201	Rigo Beltran	.10
202	Delino DeShields	.10
203	Dennis Eckersley	.10
204	John Mabry	.10
205	Eli Marrero	.10
206	Willie McGee	.10
207	Mark McGwire	4.00
208	Ken Caminiti	.20
209	Tony Gwynn	1.50
210	Chris Jones	.10
211	Craig Shipley	.10
212	Pete Smith	.10
213	Jorge Velandia	.10
214	Dario Veras	.10
215	Rich Aurilia	.10
216	Damon Berryhill	.10
217	Barry Bonds	.75
218	Osvaldo Fernandez	.10
219	Dante Powell	.10
220	Rich Rodriguez	.10

1998 Pacific Invincible Interleague Players

Interleague Players is a 30-card insert featuring 15 sets of players - one National League and one American League player. The dark blue backgrounds have red lightning bolts and the white borders are made of a leather-like material. When a set of players is placed next to each other, they form the MLB Interleague logo in the center. Interleague Players cards were inserted one per 73 packs.

		MT
Complete Set (30):		950.00
Common Player:		8.00
Inserted 1:73		
1A	Roberto Alomar	20.00
1N	Craig Biggio	10.00
2A	Cal Ripken Jr.	80.00
2N	Chipper Jones	60.00
3A	Nomar Garciaparra	60.00
3N	Scott Rolen	40.00
4A	Mo Vaughn	25.00
4N	Andres Galarraga	12.00
5A	Frank Thomas	80.00
5N	Tony Gwynn	50.00
6A	Albert Belle	25.00
6N	Barry Bonds	25.00
7A	Hideki Irabu	15.00
7N	Hideo Nomo	25.00
8A	Derek Jeter	60.00
8N	Rey Ordonez	8.00
9A	Tino Martinez	15.00
9N	Mark McGwire	100.00
10A	Alex Rodriguez	60.00
10N	Edgar Renteria	8.00
11A	Ken Griffey Jr.	100.00
11N	Larry Walker	15.00
12A	Randy Johnson	20.00
12N	Greg Maddux	60.00
13A	Ivan Rodriguez	25.00
13N	Mike Piazza	60.00
14A	Roger Clemens	40.00
14N	Pedro Martinez	15.00
15A	Jose Cruz Jr.	30.00
15N	Wilton Guerrero	8.00

1998 Pacific Invincible Moments in Time

Moments in Time (20 cards, 1:145) is designed as a baseball scoreboard. The cards have a horizontal layout with the date of an important game in the player's career at the top. The player's stats from the game are featured and a picture is located on the scoreboard screen.

		MT
Complete Set (20):		900.00
Common Player:		15.00
Inserted 1:145		
1	Chipper Jones	70.00
2	Cal Ripken Jr.	100.00
3	Frank Thomas	80.00
4	David Justice	15.00
5	Andres Galarraga	20.00
6	Larry Walker	25.00
7	Livan Hernandez	20.00
8	Wilton Guerrero	15.00
9	Hideo Nomo	35.00
10	Mike Piazza	70.00
11	Pedro Martinez	25.00
12	Bernie Williams	25.00
13	Ben Grieve	50.00
14	Scott Rolen	45.00
15	Mark McGwire	120.00
16	Tony Gwynn	60.00
17	Ken Griffey Jr.	120.00
18	Alex Rodriguez	70.00
19	Juan Gonzalez	60.00
20	Jose Cruz Jr.	50.00

1998 Pacific Invincible Photoengravings

Photoengravings is an 18-card insert seeded one per 37 packs. Each card has a unique "old-style" design with a player photo in a frame in the center.

		MT
Complete Set (18):		300.00
Common Player:		4.00
Inserted 1:37		
1	Greg Maddux	25.00
2	Cal Ripken Jr.	30.00
3	Nomar Garciaparra	25.00
4	Frank Thomas	30.00
5	Larry Walker	8.00
6	Mike Piazza	25.00
7	Hideo Nomo	10.00
8	Pedro Martinez	6.00
9	Derek Jeter	25.00
10	Tino Martinez	6.00
11	Mark McGwire	40.00
12	Tony Gwynn	20.00
13	Barry Bonds	10.00

14	Ken Griffey Jr.	40.00
15	Alex Rodriguez	25.00
16	Ivan Rodriguez	10.00
17	Roger Clemens	15.00
18	Jose Cruz Jr.	15.00

1998 Pacific Invincible Team Checklists

Team Checklists is a 30-card insert seeded 2:37. The fronts feature a player collage with the team logo in the background. The back has a complete checklist for that team in Invincible.

		MT
Complete Set (30):		200.00
Common Player:		3.00
Inserted 2:37		
1	Anaheim Angels	6.00
2	Atlanta Braves	15.00
3	Baltimore Orioles	20.00
4	Boston Red Sox	15.00
5	Chicago Cubs	4.00
6	Chicago White Sox	20.00
7	Cincinnati Reds	3.00
8	Cleveland Indians	5.00
9	Colorado Rockies	4.00
10	Detroit Tigers	5.00
11	Florida Marlins	4.00
12	Houston Astros	10.00
13	Kansas City Royals	3.00
14	Los Angeles Dodgers	15.00
15	Milwaukee Brewers	3.00
16	Minnesota Twins	5.00
17	Montreal Expos	6.00
18	New York Mets	3.00
19	New York Yankees	15.00
20	Oakland Athletics	10.00
21	Philadelphia Phillies	10.00
22	Pittsburgh Pirates	3.00
23	St. Louis Cardinals	10.00
24	San Diego Padres	12.00
25	San Francisco Giants	6.00
26	Seattle Mariners	25.00
27	Texas Rangers	12.00
28	Toronto Blue Jays	15.00
29	Arizona Diamondbacks	5.00
30	Tampa Bay Devil Rays	5.00

1998 Pacific Omega

The Omega base set consists of 250 three-image cards. The horizontal cards feature a color player photo in the center with the image duplicated in foil on the right. Another color photo is on the left. The photos are divided by a baseball

seam design. Inserts in the set include Prisms, Face to Face, EO Portraits, Online and Rising Stars.

		MT
Complete Set (250):		35.00
Common Player:		.10
Wax Box:		60.00
1	Garret Anderson	.10
2	Gary DiSarcina	.10
3	Jim Edmonds	.20
4	Darin Erstad	.75
5	Cecil Fielder	.20
6	Chuck Finley	.10
7	Shigetosi Hasegawa	.10
8	Tim Salmon	.25
9	Brian Anderson	.10
10	Jay Bell	.10
11	Andy Benes	.10
12	Yamil Benitez	.10
13	Jorge Fabregas	.10
14	Travis Lee	2.00
15	Devon White	.10
16	Matt Williams	.30
17	Andres Galarraga	.25
18	Tom Glavine	.20
19	Andruw Jones	.75
20	Chipper Jones	2.00
21	Ryan Klesko	.25
22	Javy Lopez	.10
23	Greg Maddux	2.00
24	*Kevin Millwood*	1.00
25	Denny Neagle	.10
26	John Smoltz	.20
27	Roberto Alomar	.60
28	Brady Anderson	.10
29	Joe Carter	.20
30	Eric Davis	.10
31	Jimmy Key	.10
32	Mike Mussina	.60
33	Rafael Palmeiro	.25
34	Cal Ripken Jr.	2.50
35	B.J. Surhoff	.10
36	Dennis Eckersley	.10
37	Nomar Garciaparra	2.00
38	Reggie Jefferson	.10
39	Derek Lowe	.10
40	Pedro Martinez	.50
41	Brian Rose	.10
42	John Valentin	.10
43	Jason Varitek	.10
44	Mo Vaughn	.75
45	Jeff Blauser	.10
46	Jeremi Gonzalez	.10
47	Mark Grace	.25
48	Lance Johnson	.10
49	Kevin Orie	.10
50	Henry Rodriguez	.10
51	Sammy Sosa	1.50
52	Kerry Wood	4.00
53	Albert Belle	.75
54	Mike Cameron	.10
55	Mike Caruso	.10
56	Ray Durham	.10
57	Jaime Navarro	.10
58	Greg Norton	.10
59	*Magglio Ordonez*	.75
60	Frank Thomas	2.50
61	Robin Ventura	.20
62	Bret Boone	.10
63	Willie Greene	.10
64	Barry Larkin	.25
65	Jon Nunnally	.10
66	Eduardo Perez	.10
67	Reggie Sanders	.10
68	Brett Tomko	.10
69	Sandy Alomar Jr.	.20
70	Travis Fryman	.10
71	David Justice	.25
72	Kenny Lofton	.75
73	Charles Nagy	.10
74	Manny Ramirez	.75
75	Jim Thome	.40
76	Omar Vizquel	.10
77	Enrique Wilson	.10
78	Jaret Wright	.75
79	Dante Bichette	.25
80	Ellis Burks	.10
81	Vinny Castilla	.20
82	Todd Helton	.75
83	Darryl Kile	.10
84	Mike Lansing	.10
85	Neifi Perez	.10
86	Larry Walker	.40
87	Raul Casanova	.10
88	Tony Clark	.50

89	Luis Gonzalez	.10
90	Bobby Higginson	.10
91	Brian Hunter	.10
92	Bip Roberts	.10
93	Justin Thompson	.10
94	Josh Booty	.10
95	Craig Counsell	.10
96	Livan Hernandez	.10
97	*Ryan Jackson*	.50
98	Mark Kotsay	.25
99	Derrek Lee	.10
100	Mike Piazza	2.00
101	Edgar Renteria	.10
102	Cliff Floyd	.10
103	Moises Alou	.20
104	Jeff Bagwell	1.00
105	Derrick Bell	.10
106	Sean Berry	.10
107	Craig Biggio	.20
108	*John Halama*	.25
109	Richard Hidalgo	.10
110	Shane Reynolds	.10
111	Tim Belcher	.10
112	Brian Bevil	.10
113	Jeff Conine	.10
114	Johnny Damon	.10
115	Jeff King	.10
116	Jeff Montgomery	.10
117	Dean Palmer	.10
118	Terry Pendleton	.10
119	Bobby Bonilla	.20
120	Wilton Guerrero	.10
121	Todd Hollandsworth	.10
122	Charles Johnson	.10
123	Eric Karros	.20
124	Paul Konerko	.25
125	Ramon Martinez	.10
126	Raul Mondesi	.25
127	Hideo Nomo	.50
128	Gary Sheffield	.30
129	Ismael Valdes	.10
130	Jeromy Burnitz	.10
131	Jeff Cirillo	.10
132	Todd Dunn	.10
133	Marquis Grissom	.10
134	John Jaha	.10
135	Scott Karl	.10
136	Dave Nilsson	.10
137	Jose Valentin	.10
138	Fernando Vina	.10
139	Rick Aguilera	.10
140	Marty Cordova	.10
141	Pat Meares	.10
142	Paul Molitor	.50
143	David Ortiz	.20
144	Brad Radke	.10
145	Terry Steinbach	.10
146	Todd Walker	.20
147	Shane Andrews	.10
148	Brad Fullmer	.25
149	Mark Grudzielanek	.10
150	Vladimir Guerrero	.75
151	F.P. Santangelo	.10
152	Jose Vidro	.10
153	Rondell White	.20
154	Carlos Baerga	.10
155	Bernard Gilkey	.10
156	Todd Hundley	.10
157	Butch Huskey	.10
158	Bobby Jones	.10
159	Brian McRae	.10
160	John Olerud	.20
161	Rey Ordonez	.10
162	*Masato Yoshii*	.50
163	David Cone	.20
164	Hideki Irabu	.50
165	Derek Jeter	1.50
166	Chuck Knoblauch	.30
167	Tino Martinez	.30
168	Paul O'Neill	.20
169	Andy Pettitte	.50
170	Mariano Rivera	.20
171	Darryl Strawberry	.20
172	David Wells	.10
173	Bernie Williams	.50
174	*Ryan Christenson*	.20
175	Jason Giambi	.10
176	Ben Grieve	1.00
177	Rickey Henderson	.10
178	A.J. Hinch	.30
179	Kenny Rogers	.10
180	Ricky Bottalico	.10
181	Rico Brogna	.10
182	Doug Glanville	.10
183	Gregg Jefferies	.10
184	Mike Lieberthal	.10

185	Scott Rolen	1.00
186	Curt Shilling	.20
187	Jermaine Allensworth	.10
188	Lou Collier	.10
189	Jose Guillen	.25
190	Jason Kendall	.10
191	Al Martin	.10
192	Tony Womack	.10
193	Kevin Young	.10
194	Royce Clayton	.10
195	Delino DeShields	.10
196	Gary Gaetti	.10
197	Ron Gant	.20
198	Brian Jordan	.10
199	Ray Lankford	.10
200	Mark McGwire	4.00
201	Todd Stottlemyre	.10
202	Kevin Brown	.20
203	Ken Caminiti	.20
204	Steve Finley	.10
205	Tony Gwynn	1.50
206	Carlos Hernandez	.10
207	Wally Joyner	.10
208	Greg Vaughn	.25
209	Barry Bonds	.75
210	Shawn Estes	.10
211	Orel Hershiser	.10
212	Stan Javier	.10
213	Jeff Kent	.10
214	Bill Mueller	.10
215	Robb Nen	.10
216	J.T. Snow	.10
217	Jay Buhner	.25
218	Ken Cloude	.25
219	Joey Cora	.10
220	Ken Griffey Jr.	3.00
221	Glenallen Hill	.10
222	Randy Johnson	.50
223	Edgar Martinez	.10
224	Jamie Moyer	.10
225	Alex Rodriguez	2.00
226	David Segui	.10
227	Dan Wilson	.10
228	*Rolando Arrojo*	.40
229	Wade Boggs	.25
230	Miguel Cairo	.10
231	Roberto Hernandez	.10
232	Quinton McCracken	.10
233	Fred McGriff	.20
234	Paul Sorrento	.10
235	Kevin Stocker	.10
236	Will Clark	.20
237	Juan Gonzalez	1.50
238	Rusty Greer	.10
239	Rick Helling	.10
240	Roberto Kelly	.10
241	Ivan Rodriguez	.75
242	Aaron Sele	.10
243	John Wetteland	.10
244	Jose Canseco	.25
245	Roger Clemens	1.00
246	Jose Cruz Jr.	.50
247	Carlos Delgado	.10
248	Alex Gonzalez	.10
249	Ed Sprague	.10
250	Shannon Stewart	.10

EO Portraits is a 20-card insert seeded 1:73. Each card has a color player photo with a player portrait laser-cut into the card. A "1-of-1" parallel features a laser-cut number on the card as well.

		MT
Complete Set (20):		350.00
Common Player:		5.00
Inserted 1:73		
1	Cal Ripken Jr.	30.00
2	Nomar Garciaparra	25.00
3	Mo Vaughn	10.00
4	Frank Thomas	30.00
5	Manny Ramirez	10.00
6	Ben Grieve	15.00
7	Ken Griffey Jr.	40.00
8	Alex Rodriguez	25.00
9	Juan Gonzalez	20.00
10	Ivan Rodriguez	10.00
11	Travis Lee	20.00
12	Greg Maddux	25.00
13	Chipper Jones	25.00
14	Kerry Wood	35.00
15	Larry Walker	5.00
16	Jeff Bagwell	15.00
17	Mike Piazza	25.00
18	Mark McGwire	40.00
19	Tony Gwynn	20.00
20	Barry Bonds	10.00

1998 Pacific Omega Face to Face

Face to Face features two star players on each card. It is a 10-card insert seeded one per 145 packs.

		MT
Complete Set (10):		200.00
Common Player:		8.00
Inserted 1:145		
1	Alex Rodriguez, Nomar Garciaparra	25.00
2	Mark McGwire, Ken Griffey Jr.	60.00
3	Mike Piazza, Sandy Alomar Jr.	25.00
4	Kerry Wood, Roger Clemens	35.00
5	Cal Ripken Jr., Paul Molitor	30.00
6	Tony Gwynn, Wade Boggs	20.00
7	Frank Thomas, Chipper Jones	30.00
8	Travis Lee, Ben Grieve	20.00
9	Hideo Nomo, Hideki Irabu	8.00
10	Juan Gonzalez, Manny Ramirez	20.00

Values quoted in this guide reflect the
retail price of a card — the price a collector
can expect to pay when buying a card
from a dealer.

The wholesale price — that which a collector can expect to receive from a dealer when selling cards — will be significantly lower, depending on desirability and condition.

1998 Pacific Omega EO Portraits

MARK McGWIRE   St. Louis

1998 Pacific Omega Online

Online is a 36-card insert seeded four per 37 packs. The foiled and etched cards feature a color player photo in front of a hi-tech designed background. The card fronts also include the internet address for the player's web site on bigleaguers.com.

		MT
Complete Set (36):		140.00
Common Player:		1.00
Inserted 1:9		
1	Cal Ripken Jr.	10.00
2	Nomar Garciaparra	8.00
3	Pedro Martinez	2.00
4	Mo Vaughn	3.00
5	Frank Thomas	10.00
6	Sandy Alomar Jr.	1.00
7	Manny Ramirez	3.00
8	Jaret Wright	3.00
9	Paul Molitor	2.50
10	Derek Jeter	6.00
11	Bernie Williams	2.00
12	Ben Grieve	4.00
13	Ken Griffey Jr.	12.00
14	Edgar Martinez	1.00
15	Alex Rodriguez	8.00
16	Wade Boggs	1.50
17	Juan Gonzalez	6.00
18	Ivan Rodriguez	3.00
19	Roger Clemens	4.00
20	Travis Lee	6.00
21	Matt Williams	1.50
22	Andres Galarraga	1.50
23	Chipper Jones	8.00
24	Greg Maddux	8.00
25	Sammy Sosa	6.00
26	Kerry Wood	15.00
27	Barry Larkin	1.50
28	Larry Walker	2.00
29	Derrek Lee	1.00
30	Jeff Bagwell	4.00
31	Hideo Nomo	2.00
32	Mike Piazza	8.00
33	Scott Rolen	4.00
34	Mark McGwire	15.00
35	Tony Gwynn	6.00
36	Barry Bonds	3.00

1998 Pacific Omega Prism

This 20-card insert was seeded one per 37 packs. The card fronts feature prismatic foil technology.

A player's name in *italic* type indicates a rookie card.

		MT
Complete Set (20):		220.00
Common Player:		3.00
Inserted 1:37		
1	Cal Ripken Jr.	20.00
2	Nomar Garciaparra	15.00
3	Pedro Martinez	4.00
4	Frank Thomas	20.00
5	Manny Ramirez	6.00
6	Brian Giles	3.00
7	Derek Jeter	12.00
8	Ben Grieve	8.00
9	Ken Griffey Jr.	25.00
10	Alex Rodriguez	15.00
11	Juan Gonzalez	12.00
12	Travis Lee	12.00
13	Chipper Jones	15.00
14	Greg Maddux	15.00
15	Kerry Wood	25.00
16	Larry Walker	4.00
17	Hideo Nomo	5.00
18	Mike Piazza	15.00
19	Mark McGwire	25.00
20	Tony Gwynn	12.00

1998 Pacific Omega Rising Stars

Rising Stars is a four-tiered hobby-only insert. The 20 cards were seeded four per 37 packs. Each card featured three rookies and each tier has a different foil color. A parallel of the insert is sequentially numbered. Tier One cards are numbered to 100, Tier Two to 50, Tier Three to 25 and Tier 4 to one.

		MT
Complete Set (30):		55.00
Common Player:		1.00
Inserted 1:9		
1	Nerio Rodriguez, Sidney Ponson	1.00
2	Frank Catalanotto, Roberto Duran, Sean Runyan	1.00
3	Kevin L. Brown, Carlos Almanzar	1.00
4	Aaron Boone, Pat Watkins, Scott Winchester	1.00
5	Brian Meadows, Andy Larkin, Antonio Alfonseca	1.00
6	DaRond Stovall, Trey Moore, Shayne Bennett	1.00
7	Felix Martinez, Larry Sutton, Brian Bevil	1.00
8	Homer Bush, Mike Buddie	1.00
9	Rich Butler, Esteban Yan	2.50
10	Damon Hollins, Brian Edmondson	1.00

11	Lou Collier, Jose Silva, Javier Martinez	1.00
12	Steve Sinclair, Mark Dalesandro	1.00
13	Jason Varitek, Brian Rose, Brian Shouse	2.00
14	Mike Caruso, Jeff Abbott, Tom Fordham	2.00
15	Jason Johnson, Bobby Smith	1.00
16	Dave Berg, Mark Kotsay, Jesus Sanchez	3.00
17	Richard Hidalgo, John Halama, Trever Miller	2.00
18	Geoff Jenkins, Bobby Hughes, Steve Woodard	2.00
19	Eli Marrero, Cliff Politte, Mike Busby	1.00
20	Desi Relaford, Darrin Winston	1.00
21	Todd Helton, Bobby Jones	4.00
22	Rolando Arrojo, Miguel Cairo, Dan Carlson	3.00
23	David Ortiz, Javier Valentin, Eric Milton	2.00
24	Magglio Ordonez, Greg Norton	3.00
25	Brad Fullmer, Javier Vazquez, Rick DeHart	2.00
26	Paul Konerko, Matt Luke	3.00
27	Derrek Lee, Ryan Jackson, John Roskos	2.00
28	Ben Grieve, A.J. Hinch, Ryan Christenson	5.00
29	Travis Lee, Karim Garcia, David Dellucci	8.00
30	Kerry Wood, Marc Pisciotta	12.00

1998 Pacific Online

Online Baseball consists of an 800-card base set with one parallel. The base set features 750 players on cards that list the internet address of the player's home page on the bigleaguers.com web site. Twenty players have two cards and each of the 30 teams has a checklist that lists the team's web site. The Web Cards set parallels the 750 player cards. It has a serial number that can be entered at the bigleaguers.com web site to determine if a prize has been won. MT

Values shown reflect the market as of January, 1999.
On-field performances of current players in the 1999 baseball season are not factored in.

Complete Set (780):	100.00		
Common Player:	.15		
Web Star Cards: 2x to 3x			
Yng Stars & RCs: 1.5x to 2x			
Inserted 1:1			

#	Player	Price	#	Player	Price	#	Player	Price
1	Garret Anderson	.15	92	Jimmy Key	.15	188	Brook Fordyce	.15
2	*Rich DeLucia*	.40	93	Terry Mathews	.15	189	Willie Greene	.15
3	Jason Dickson	.15	94	Alan Mills	.15	190	Pete Harnisch	.15
4	Gary DiSarcina	.15	95	Mike Mussina	.75	191	Lenny Harris	.15
5	Jim Edmonds	.15	96	Jesse Orosco	.15	192	Mark Hutton	.15
6	Darin Erstad	1.50	97	Rafael Palmeiro	.25	193	Damian Jackson	.15
7	Cecil Fielder	.25	98	Sidney Ponson	.15	194	Ricardo Jordan	.15
8	Chuck Finley	.15	99	Jeff Reboulet	.15	195	Barry Larkin	.30
9	Carlos Carcia	.15	100	Arthur Rhodes	.15	196	Eduardo Perez	.15
10	Shigetosi Hasegawa	.15	101	Cal Ripken Jr.	2.50	197	Pokey Reese	.15
11	Ken Hill	.15	102	Nerio Rodriguez	.15	198	Mike Remlinger	.15
12	Dave Hollins	.15	103	B.J. Surhoff	.15	199	Reggie Sanders	.15
13	Mike Holtz	.15	104	Lenny Webster	.15	200	Jeff Shaw	.15
14	Mike James	.15	105	Cal Ripken Jr.	3.00	201	Chris Stynes	.15
15	Norberto Martin	.15	106	Steve Avery	.15	202	Scott Sullivan	.15
16	Damon Mashore	.15	107	Mike Benjamin	.15	203	Eddie Taubensee	.15
17	Jack McDowell	.15	108	Darren Bragg	.15	204	Brett Tomko	.15
18	Phil Nevin	.15	109	Damon Buford	.15	205	Pat Watkins	.15
19	Omar Olivares	.15	110	Jim Corsi	.15	206	David Weathers	.15
20	Troy Percival	.15	111	Dennis Eckersley	.15	207	Gabe White	.15
21	Rich Robertson	.15	112	Rich Garces	.15	208	Scott Winchester	.15
22	Tim Salmon	.30	113	Nomar Garciaparra	2.50	209	Barry Larkin	.25
23	Craig Shipley	.15	114	Tom Gordon	.15	210	Sandy Alomar Jr.	.15
24	Matt Walbeck	.15	115	Scott Hatteberg	.15	211	Paul Assenmacher	.15
25	Allen Watson	.15	116	Butch Henry	.15	212	Geronimo Berroa	.15
26	Jim Edmonds	.15	117	Reggie Jefferson	.15	213	Pat Borders	.15
27	Brian Anderson	.15	118	Mark Lemke	.15	214	Jeff Branson	.15
28	Tony Batista	.15	119	Darren Lewis	.15	215	Dave Burba	.15
29	Jay Bell	.15	120	Jim Leyritz	.15	216	Bartolo Colon	.30
30	Andy Benes	.15	121	Derek Lowe	.15	217	Shawon Dunston	.15
31	Yamil Benitez	.15	122	Pedro Martinez	.75	218	Travis Fryman	.15
32	Willie Blair	.15	123	Troy O'Leary	.15	219	Brian Giles	.15
33	Brent Brede	.15	124	Brian Rose	.15	220	Dwight Gooden	.15
34	Scott Brow	.15	125	Bret Saberhagen	.15	221	Mike Jackson	.15
35	Omar Daal	.15	126	Donnie Sadler	.15	222	David Justice	.40
36	David Dellucci	.15	127	Brian Shouse	.15	223	Kenny Lofton	1.00
37	Edwin Diaz	.15	128	John Valentin	.15	224	Jose Mesa	.15
38	Jorge Fabregas	.15	129	Jason Varitek	.15	225	Alvin Morman	.15
39	Andy Fox	.15	130	Mo Vaughn	1.00	226	Charles Nagy	.15
40	Karim Garcia	.15	131	Tim Wakefield	.15	227	Chad Ogea	.15
41	Travis Lee	2.00	132	John Wasdin	.15	228	Eric Plunk	.15
42	Barry Manuel	.15	133	Nomar Garciaparra	2.50	229	Manny Ramirez	1.00
43	Gregg Olson	.15	134	Terry Adams	.15	230	Paul Shuey	.15
44	Felix Rodriguez	.15	135	Manny Alexander	.15	231	Jim Thome	.60
45	Clint Sodowsky	.15	136	Rod Beck	.15	232	Ron Villone	.15
46	Russ Springer	.15	137	Jeff Blauser	.15	233	Omar Vizquel	.15
47	Andy Stankiewicz	.15	138	Brant Brown	.15	234	Enrique Wilson	.15
48	Kelly Stinnett	.15	139	Mark Clark	.15	235	Jaret Wright	1.00
49	Jeff Suppan	.15	140	Jeremi Gonzalez	.15	236	Manny Ramirez	1.00
50	Devon White	.15	141	Mark Grace	.25	237	Pedro Astacio	.15
51	Matt Williams	.15	142	Jose Hernandez	.15	238	Jason Bates	.15
52	Travis Lee	1.00	143	Tyler Houston	.15	239	Dante Bichette	.30
53	Danny Bautista	.15	144	Lance Johnson	.15	240	Ellis Burks	.15
54	Rafael Belliard	.15	145	Sandy Martinez	.15	241	Vinny Castilla	.25
55	*Adam Butler*	.30	146	Matt Mieske	.15	242	Greg Colbrunn	.15
56	Mike Cather	.15	147	Mickey Morandini	.15	243	Mike DeJean	.15
57	Brian Edmondson	.15	148	Terry Mulholland	.15	244	Jerry Dipoto	.15
58	Alan Embree	.15	149	Kevin Orie	.15	245	Curtis Goodwin	.15
59	Andres Galarraga	.40	150	Bob Patterson	.15	246	Todd Helton	.75
60	Tom Glavine	.30	151	Marc Pisciotta	.15	247	Bobby Jones	.15
61	Tony Graffanino	.15	152	Henry Rodriguez	.15	248	Darryl Kile	.15
62	Andruw Jones	1.00	153	Scott Servais	.15	249	Mike Lansing	.15
63	Chipper Jones	2.00	154	Sammy Sosa	2.50	250	Curtis Leskanic	.15
64	Ryan Klesko	.30	155	Kevin Tapani	.15	251	Nelson Liriano	.15
65	Keith Lockhart	.15	156	Steve Trachsel	.15	252	Kirt Manwaring	.15
66	Javy Lopez	.15	157	Kerry Wood	4.00	253	Chuck McElroy	.15
67	Greg Maddux	2.50	158	Kerry Wood	4.00	254	Mike Munoz	.15
68	Dennis Martinez	.15	159	Jeff Abbott	.15	255	Neifi Perez	.15
69	*Kevin Millwood*	2.00	160	James Baldwin	.15	256	Jeff Reed	.15
70	Denny Neagle	.15	161	Albert Belle	1.00	257	Mark Thompson	.15
71	Eddie Perez	.15	162	Jason Bere	.15	258	John Vander Wal	.15
72	Curtis Pride	.15	163	Mike Cameron	.15	259	Dave Veres	.15
73	John Smoltz	.25	164	Mike Caruso	.15	260	Larry Walker	.40
74	Michael Tucker	.15	165	Carlos Castillo	.15	261	Jamey Wright	.15
75	Walt Weiss	.15	166	Tony Castillo	.15	262	Larry Walker	.25
76	Gerald Williams	.15	167	Ray Durham	.15	263	Kimera Bartee	.15
77	Mark Wohlers	.15	168	Scott Eyre	.15	264	Doug Brocail	.15
78	Chipper Jones	1.00	169	Tom Fordham	.15	265	Raul Casanova	.15
79	Roberto Alomar	.40	170	Keith Foulke	.15	266	Frank Castillo	.15
80	Brady Anderson	.15	171	Lou Frazier	.15	267	Frank Catalanotto	.15
81	Harold Baines	.15	172	Matt Karchner	.15	268	Tony Clark	.75
82	Armando Benitez	.15	173	Chad Kreuter	.15	269	Deivi Cruz	.15
83	Mike Bordick	.15	174	Jaime Navarro	.15	270	Roberto Duran	.15
84	Joe Carter	.15	175	Greg Norton	.15	271	Damion Easley	.15
85	Norm Charlton	.15	176	Charlie O'Brien	.15	272	Bryce Florie	.15
86	Eric Davis	.15	177	Magglio Ordonez	.75	273	Luis Gonzalez	.15
87	Doug Drabek	.15	178	Ruben Sierra	.15	274	Bob Higginson	.15
88	Scott Erickson	.15	179	Bill Simas	.15	275	Brian Hunter	.15
89	Jeffrey Hammonds	.15	180	Mike Sirotka	.15	276	Todd Jones	.15
90	Chris Hoiles	.15	181	Chris Snopek	.15	277	Greg Keagle	.15
91	Scott Kamieniecki	.15	182	Frank Thomas	2.50	278	Jeff Manto	.15
			183	Robin Ventura	.15	279	Brian Moehler	.15
			184	Frank Thomas	1.50	280	Joe Oliver	.15
			185	Stan Belinda	.15	281	Joe Randa	.15
			186	Aaron Boone	.15	282	Billy Ripken	.15
			187	Bret Boone	.15	283	Bip Roberts	.15

#	Player	Price
284	Sean Runyan	.15
285	A.J. Sager	.15
286	Justin Thompson	.15
287	Tony Clark	.50
288	Antonio Alfonseca	.15
289	Dave Berg	.15
290	Josh Booty	.15
291	John Cangelosi	.15
292	Craig Counsell	.15
293	Vic Darensbourg	.15
294	Cliff Floyd	.15
295	Oscar Henriquez	.15
296	Felix Heredia	.15
297	*Ryan Jackson*	.15
298	Mark Kotsay	.40
299	Andy Larkin	.15
300	Derrek Lee	.15
301	Brian Meadows	.15
302	Rafael Medina	.15
303	Jay Powell	.15
304	Edgar Renteria	.15
305	*Jesus Sanchez*	.30
306	Rob Stanifer	.15
307	Greg Zaun	.15
308	Derrek Lee	.15
309	Moises Alou	.25
310	Brad Ausmus	.15
311	Jeff Bagwell	1.50
312	Derek Bell	.15
313	Sean Bergman	.15
314	Sean Berry	.15
315	Craig Biggio	.25
316	Tim Bogar	.15
317	Jose Cabrera	.15
318	Dave Clark	.15
319	Tony Eusebio	.15
320	Carl Everett	.15
321	Ricky Gutierrez	.15
322	John Halama	.15
323	Mike Hampton	.15
324	Doug Henry	.15
325	Richard Hidalgo	.15
326	Jack Howell	.15
327	Jose Lima	.15
328	Mike Magnante	.15
329	Trever Miller	.15
330	C.J. Nitkowski	.15
331	Shane Reynolds	.15
332	Bill Spiers	.15
333	Billy Wagner	.15
334	Jeff Bagwell	.75
335	Tim Belcher	.15
336	Brian Bevil	.15
337	Johnny Damon	.15
338	Jermaine Dye	.15
339	Sal Fasano	.15
340	Shane Halter	.15
341	Chris Haney	.15
342	Jed Hansen	.15
343	Jeff King	.15
344	Jeff Montgomery	.15
345	Hal Morris	.15
346	Jose Offerman	.15
347	Dean Palmer	.15
348	Terry Pendleton	.15
349	Hipolito Pichardo	.15
350	Jim Pittsley	.15
351	Pat Rapp	.15
352	Jose Rosado	.15
353	Glendon Rusch	.15
354	Scott Service	.15
355	Larry Sutton	.15
356	Mike Sweeney	.15
357	Joe Vitiello	.15
358	Matt Whisenant	.15
359	Ernie Young	.15
360	Jeff King	.15
361	Bobby Bonilla	.15
362	Jim Bruske	.15
363	Juan Castro	.15
364	Roger Cedeno	.15
365	Mike Devereaux	.15
366	Darren Dreifort	.15
367	Jim Eisenreich	.15
368	Wilton Guerrero	.15
369	Mark Guthrie	.15
370	Darren Hall	.15
371	Todd Hollandsworth	.15
372	Thomas Howard	.15
373	Trenidad Hubbard	.15
374	Charles Johnson	.15
375	Eric Karros	.15
376	Paul Konerko	.40
377	Matt Luke	.15
378	Ramon Martinez	.15
379	Raul Mondesi	.30
380	Hideo Nomo	.75
381	Antonio Osuna	.15
382	Chan Ho Park	.30
383	Tom Prince	.15
384	Scott Radinsky	.15
385	Gary Sheffield	.40
386	Ismael Valdes	.15
387	Jose Vizcaino	.15
388	Eric Young	.15
389	Gary Sheffield	.40
390	Jeromy Burnitz	.15
391	Jeff Cirillo	.15
392	Cal Eldred	.15
393	Chad Fox	.15
394	Marquis Grissom	.15
395	Bob Hamelin	.15
396	Bobby Hughes	.15
397	Darrin Jackson	.15
398	John Jaha	.15
399	Geoff Jenkins	.15
400	Doug Jones	.15
401	Jeff Juden	.15
402	Scott Karl	.15
403	Jesse Levis	.15
404	Mark Loretta	.15
405	Mike Matheny	.15
406	Jose Mercedes	.15
407	Mike Myers	.15
408	Marc Newfield	.15
409	Dave Nilsson	.15
410	Al Reyes	.15
411	Jose Valentin	.15
412	Fernando Vina	.15
413	Paul Wagner	.15
414	Bob Wickman	.15
415	Steve Woodard	.15
416	Marquis Grissom	.15
417	Rick Aguilera	.15
418	Ron Coomer	.15
419	Marty Cordova	.15
420	Brent Gates	.15
421	Eddie Guardado	.15
422	Denny Hocking	.15
423	Matt Lawton	.15
424	Pat Meares	.15
425	Orlando Merced	.15
426	Eric Milton	.15
427	Paul Molitor	.75
428	Mike Morgan	.15
429	Dan Naulty	.15
430	Otis Nixon	.15
431	Alex Ochoa	.15
432	David Ortiz	.15
433	Brad Radke	.15
434	Todd Ritchie	.15
435	Frank Rodriguez	.15
436	Terry Steinbach	.15
437	Greg Swindell	.15
438	Bob Tewksbury	.15
439	Mike Trombley	.15
440	Javier Valentin	.15
441	Todd Walker	.40
442	Paul Molitor	.40
443	Shane Andrews	.15
444	Miguel Batista	.15
445	Shayne Bennett	.15
446	Rick DeHart	.15
447	Brad Fullmer	.40
448	Mark Grudzielanek	.15
449	Vladimir Guerrero	1.25
450	Dustin Hermanson	.15
451	Steve Kline	.15
452	Scott Livingstone	.15
453	Mike Maddux	.15
454	Derrick May	.15
455	Ryan McGuire	.15
456	Trey Moore	.15
457	Mike Mordecai	.15
458	Carl Pavano	.15
459	Carlos Perez	.15
460	F.P. Santangelo	.15
461	DaRond Stovall	.15
462	Anthony Telford	.15
463	Ugueth Urbina	.15
464	Marc Valdes	.15
465	Jose Vidro	.15
466	Rondell White	.25
467	Chris Widger	.15
468	Vladimir Guerrero	.60
469	Edgardo Alfonzo	.15
470	Carlos Baerga	.15
471	Rich Becker	.15
472	Brian Bohanon	.15
473	Alberto Castillo	.15
474	Dennis Cook	.15
475	John Franco	.15
476	Matt Franco	.15
477	Bernard Gilkey	.15
478	John Hudek	.15
479	Butch Huskey	.15
480	Bobby Jones	.15
481	Al Leiter	.25
482	Luis Lopez	.15
483	Brian McRae	.15
484	Dave Mlicki	.15
485	John Olerud	.25
486	Rey Ordonez	.15
487	Craig Paquette	.15
488	Mike Piazza	2.50
489	Todd Pratt	.15
490	Mel Rojas	.15
491	Tim Spehr	.15
492	Turk Wendell	.15
493	*Masato Yoshii*	.40
494	Mike Piazza	1.25
495	Willie Banks	.15
496	Scott Brosius	.15
497	Mike Buddie	.15
498	Homer Bush	.15
499	David Cone	.15
500	Chad Curtis	.15
501	Chili Davis	.15
502	Joe Girardi	.15
503	Darren Holmes	.15
504	Hideki Irabu	.40
505	Derek Jeter	2.50
506	Chuck Knoblauch	.50
507	Graeme Lloyd	.15
508	Tino Martinez	.40
509	Ramiro Mendoza	.15
510	Jeff Nelson	.15
511	Paul O'Neill	.40
512	Andy Pettitte	.60
513	Jorge Posada	.25
514	Tim Raines	.15
515	Mariano Rivera	.25
516	Luis Sojo	.15
517	Mike Stanton	.15
518	Darryl Strawberry	.25
519	Dale Sveum	.15
520	David Wells	.15
521	Bernie Williams	.75
522	Bernie Williams	.40
523	Kurt Abbott	.15
524	Mike Blowers	.15
525	Rafael Bournigal	.15
526	Tom Candiotti	.15
527	Ryan Christenson	.15
528	Mike Fetters	.15
529	Jason Giambi	.15
530	Ben Grieve	1.25
531	Buddy Groom	.15
532	Jimmy Haynes	.15
533	Rickey Henderson	.15
534	A.J. Hinch	.15
535	Mike Macfarlane	.15
536	Dave Magadan	.15
537	T.J. Mathews	.15
538	Jason McDonald	.15
539	Kevin Mitchell	.15
540	Mike Mohler	.15
541	Mike Oquist	.15
542	Ariel Prieto	.15
543	Kenny Rogers	.15
544	Aaron Small	.15
545	Scott Spiezio	.15
546	Matt Stairs	.15
547	Bill Taylor	.15
548	Dave Telgheder	.15
549	Jack Voigt	.15
550	Ben Grieve	.60
551	Bob Abreu	.15
552	Ruben Amaro	.15
553	Alex Arias	.15
554	Matt Beech	.15
555	Ricky Bottalico	.15
556	Billy Brewer	.15
557	Rico Brogna	.15
558	Doug Glanville	.15
559	Wayne Gomes	.15
560	Mike Grace	.15
561	Tyler Green	.15
562	Rex Hudler	.15
563	Gregg Jefferies	.15
564	Kevin Jordan	.15
565	Mark Leiter	.15
566	Mark Lewis	.15
567	Mike Lieberthal	.15
568	Mark Parent	.15
569	Yorkis Perez	.15
570	Desi Relaford	.15
571	Scott Rolen	1.25

572	Curt Schilling	.25
573	Kevin Sefcik	.15
574	Jerry Spradlin	.15
575	Garrett Stephenson	.15
576	Darrin Winston	.15
577	Scott Rolen	.60
578	Jermaine Allensworth	.15
579	Jason Christiansen	.15
580	Lou Collier	.15
581	Francisco Cordova	.15
582	Elmer Dessens	.15
583	Freddy Garcia	.15
584	Jose Guillen	.25
585	Jason Kendall	.15
586	Jon Lieber	.15
587	Esteban Loaiza	.15
588	Al Martin	.15
589	Javier Martinez	.15
590	Chris Peters	.15
591	Kevin Polcovich	.15
592	Ricardo Rincon	.15
593	Jason Schmidt	.15
594	Jose Silva	.15
595	Mark Smith	.15
596	Doug Strange	.15
597	Turner Ward	.15
598	Marc Wilkins	.15
599	Mike Williams	.15
600	Tony Womack	.15
601	Kevin Young	.15
602	Tony Womack	.15
603	Manny Aybar	.15
604	Kent Bottenfield	.15
605	Jeff Brantley	.15
606	Mike Busby	.15
607	Royce Clayton	.15
608	Delino DeShields	.15
609	John Frascatore	.15
610	Gary Gaetti	.15
611	Ron Gant	.15
612	David Howard	.15
613	Brian Hunter	.15
614	Brian Jordan	.15
615	Tom Lampkin	.15
616	Ray Lankford	.15
617	Braden Looper	.15
618	John Mabry	.15
619	Eli Marrero	.15
620	Willie McGee	.15
621	Mark McGwire	5.00
622	Kent Mercker	.15
623	Matt Morris	.15
624	Donovan Osborne	.15
625	Tom Pagnozzi	.15
626	Lance Painter	.15
627	Mark Petkovsek	.15
628	Todd Stottlemyre	.15
629	Mark McGwire	2.50
630	Andy Ashby	.15
631	Brian Boehringer	.15
632	Kevin Brown	.25
633	Ken Caminiti	.25
634	Steve Finley	.15
635	Ed Giovanola	.15
636	Chris Gomez	.15
637	Tony Gwynn	2.00
638	Joey Hamilton	.15
639	Carlos Hernandez	.15
640	Sterling Hitchcock	.15
641	Trevor Hoffman	.15
642	Wally Joyner	.15
643	Dan Miceli	.15
644	James Mouton	.15
645	Greg Myers	.15
646	Carlos Reyes	.15
647	Andy Sheets	.15
648	Pete Smith	.15
649	Mark Sweeney	.15
650	Greg Vaughn	.15
651	Quilvio Veras	.15
652	Tony Gwynn	1.00
653	Rich Aurilia	.15
654	Marvin Benard	.15
655	Barry Bonds	1.00
656	Danny Darwin	.15
657	Shawn Estes	.15
658	Mark Gardner	.15
659	Darryl Hamilton	.15
660	Charlie Hayes	.15
661	Orel Hershiser	.15
662	Stan Javier	.15
663	Brian Johnson	.15
664	John Johnstone	.15
665	Jeff Kent	.15
666	Brent Mayne	.15
667	Bill Mueller	.15
668	Robb Nen	.15
669	Jim Poole	.15
670	Steve Reed	.15
671	Rich Rodriguez	.15
672	Kirk Rueter	.15
673	Rey Sanchez	.15
674	J.T. Snow	.15
675	Julian Tavarez	.15
676	Barry Bonds	.50
677	Rich Amaral	.15
678	Bobby Ayala	.15
679	Jay Buhner	.30
680	Ken Cloude	.15
681	Joey Cora	.15
682	Russ Davis	.15
683	Rob Ducey	.15
684	Jeff Fassero	.15
685	Tony Fossas	.15
686	Ken Griffey Jr.	4.00
687	Glenallen Hill	.15
688	Jeff Huson	.15
689	Randy Johnson	.75
690	Edgar Martinez	.15
691	John Marzano	.15
692	Jamie Moyer	.15
693	Alex Rodriguez	2.50
694	David Segui	.15
695	Heathcliff Slocumb	.15
696	Paul Spoljaric	.15
697	Bill Swift	.15
698	Mike Timlin	.15
699	Bob Wells	.15
700	Dan Wilson	.15
701	Ken Griffey Jr.	2.00
702	Wilson Alvarez	.15
703	*Rolando Arrojo*	.75
704	Wade Boggs	.30
705	Rich Butler	.25
706	Miguel Cairo	.15
707	Mike Difelice	.15
708	John Flaherty	.15
709	Roberto Hernandez	.15
710	Mike Kelly	.15
711	Aaron Ledesma	.15
712	Albie Lopez	.15
713	Dave Martinez	.15
714	Quinton McCracken	.15
715	Fred McGriff	.25
716	Jim Mecir	.15
717	Tony Saunders	.15
718	Bobby Smith	.15
719	Paul Sorrento	.15
720	Dennis Springer	.15
721	Kevin Stocker	.15
722	Ramon Tatis	.15
723	Bubba Trammell	.15
724	Esteban Yan	.15
725	Wade Boggs	.30
726	Luis Alicea	.15
727	Scott Bailes	.15
728	John Burkett	.15
729	Domingo Cedeno	.15
730	Will Clark	.40
731	Kevin Elster	.15
732	Juan Gonzalez	2.00
733	Tom Goodwin	.15
734	Rusty Greer	.15
735	Eric Gunderson	.15
736	Bill Haselman	.15
737	Rick Helling	.15
738	Roberto Kelly	.15
739	Mark McLemore	.15
740	Darren Oliver	.15
741	Danny Patterson	.15
742	Roger Pavlik	.15
743	Ivan Rodriguez	1.00
744	Aaron Sele	.15
745	Mike Simms	.15
746	Lee Stevens	.15
747	Fernando Tatis	.15
748	John Wetteland	.15
749	Bobby Witt	.15
750	Juan Gonzalez	1.00
751	Carlos Almanzar	.15
752	Kevin Brown	.25
753	Jose Canseco	.40
754	Chris Carpenter	.15
755	Roger Clemens	1.50
756	Felipe Crespo	.15
757	Jose Cruz Jr.	1.00
758	Mark Dalesandro	.15
759	Carlos Delgado	.15
760	Kelvim Escobar	.15
761	Tony Fernandez	.15
762	Darrin Fletcher	.15
763	Alex Gonzalez	.15
764	Craig Grebeck	.15
765	Shawn Green	.15
766	Juan Guzman	.15
767	Erik Hanson	.15
768	Pat Hentgen	.15
769	Randy Myers	.15
770	Robert Person	.15
771	Dan Plesac	.15
772	Paul Quantrill	.15
773	Bill Risley	.15
774	Juan Samuel	.15
775	Steve Sinclair	.15
776	Ed Sprague	.15
777	Mike Stanley	.15
778	Shannon Stewart	.15
779	Woody Williams	.15
780	Roger Clemens	.75

1998 Pacific Paramount

Paramount was Pacific's first fully-licensed baseball card product. The 250 base cards feature full-bleed photos with the player's name and team listed at the bottom. The base set is paralleled three times. Gold retail (1:1), Copper hobby (1:1) and Platinum Blue (1:73) versions were included. Inserts in the product are Special Delivery Die-Cuts, Team Checklist Die-Cuts, Cooperstown Bound, Fielder's Choice Laser-Cuts and Inaugural Issue.

	MT
Complete Set (250):	20.00
Common Player:	.10
Unlisted Stars: .30 to .60	
Golds: 1.5x to 3x	
Coppers: 1.5x to 3x	
Golds & Coppers 1:1	
Reds: 2x to 3x	
Inserted 1:ANCO pack	
Platinum Blue: 40x to 80x	
Inserted 1:73	
Holographic Silvers: 40x to 100x	
Production 99 sets	
Wax Box:	48.00
1	Garret Anderson	.10
2	Gary DiSarcina	.10
3	Jim Edmonds	.20
4	Darin Erstad	.50
5	Cecil Fielder	.20
6	Chuck Finley	.10
7	Todd Greene	.10
8	Shigetoshi Hasegawa	.10
9	Tim Salmon	.30
10	Roberto Alomar	.50
11	Brady Anderson	.20
12	Joe Carter	.20
13	Eric Davis	.10
14	Ozzie Guillen	.10
15	Mike Mussina	.50

16	Rafael Palmeiro	.25
17	Cal Ripken Jr.	2.00
18	B.J. Surhoff	.10
19	Steve Avery	.10
20	Nomar Garciaparra	1.50
21	Reggie Jefferson	.10
22	Pedro Martinez	.25
23	Tim Naehring	.10
24	John Valentin	.10
25	Mo Vaughn	.60
26	James Baldwin	.10
27	Albert Belle	.60
28	Ray Durham	.10
29	Benji Gil	.10
30	Jaime Navarro	.10
31	*Magglio Ordonez*	.75
32	Frank Thomas	2.00
33	Robin Ventura	.20
34	Sandy Alomar Jr.	.20
35	Geronimo Berroa	.10
36	Travis Fryman	.10
37	David Justice	.25
38	Kenny Lofton	.60
39	Charles Nagy	.10
40	Manny Ramirez	.60
41	Jim Thome	.40
42	Omar Vizquel	.10
43	Jaret Wright	1.25
44	Raul Casanova	.10
45	*Frank Catalanotto*	.20
46	Tony Clark	.40
47	Bobby Higginson	.10
48	Brian Hunter	.10
49	Todd Jones	.10
50	Bip Roberts	.10
51	Justin Thompson	.10
52	Kevin Appier	.10
53	Johnny Damon	.10
54	Jermaine Dye	.10
55	Jeff King	.10
56	Jeff Montgomery	.10
57	Dean Palmer	.10
58	Jose Rosado	.10
59	Larry Sutton	.10
60	Rick Aguilera	.10
61	Marty Cordova	.10
62	Pat Meares	.10
63	Paul Molitor	.40
64	Otis Nixon	.10
65	Brad Radke	.10
66	Terry Steinbach	.10
67	Todd Walker	.25
68	Hideki Irabu	.50
69	Derek Jeter	1.25
70	Chuck Knoblauch	.30
71	Tino Martinez	.40
72	Paul O'Neill	.20
73	Andy Pettitte	.40
74	Mariano Rivera	.25
75	Bernie Williams	.50
76	Mark Bellhorn	.10
77	Tom Candiotti	.10
78	Jason Giambi	.10
79	Ben Grieve	1.00
80	Rickey Henderson	.10
81	Jason McDonald	.10
82	Aaron Small	.10
83	Miguel Tejada	.10
84	Jay Buhner	.25
85	Joey Cora	.10
86	Jeff Fassero	.10
87	Ken Griffey Jr.	2.50
88	Randy Johnson	.40
89	Edgar Martinez	.20
90	Alex Rodriguez	1.50
91	David Segui	.10
92	Dan Wilson	.10
93	Wilson Alvarez	.10
94	Wade Boggs	.25
95	Miguel Cairo	.10
96	John Flaherty	.10
97	Dave Martinez	.10
98	Quinton McCracken	.10
99	Fred McGriff	.25
100	Paul Sorrento	.10
101	Kevin Stocker	.10
102	John Burkett	.10
103	Will Clark	.25
104	Juan Gonzalez	1.25
105	Rusty Greer	.20
106	Roberto Kelly	.10
107	Ivan Rodriguez	.60
108	Fernando Tatis	.10
109	John Wetteland	.10
110	Jose Canseco	.25
111	Roger Clemens	1.00
112	Jose Cruz Jr.	.50
113	Carlos Delgado	.20
114	Alex Gonzalez	.10
115	Pat Hentgen	.10
116	Ed Sprague	.10
117	Shannon Stewart	.10
118	Brian Anderson	.10
119	Jay Bell	.10
120	Andy Benes	.20
121	Yamil Benitez	.10
122	Jorge Fabregas	.10
123	Travis Lee	2.00
124	Devon White	.10
125	Matt Williams	.25
126	Bob Wolcott	.10
127	Andres Galarraga	.25
128	Tom Glavine	.20
129	Andruw Jones	.60
130	Chipper Jones	1.50
131	Ryan Klesko	.30
132	Javy Lopez	.10
133	Greg Maddux	1.50
134	Denny Neagle	.20
135	John Smoltz	.20
136	Rod Beck	.10
137	Jeff Blauser	.10
138	Mark Grace	.25
139	Lance Johnson	.10
140	Mickey Morandini	.10
141	Kevin Orie	.10
142	Sammy Sosa	1.50
143	Aaron Boone	.10
144	Bret Boone	.10
145	Dave Burba	.10
146	Lenny Harris	.10
147	Barry Larkin	.25
148	Reggie Sanders	.10
149	Brett Tomko	.10
150	Pedro Astacio	.10
151	Dante Bichette	.20
152	Ellis Burks	.10
153	Vinny Castilla	.20
154	Todd Helton	.50
155	Darryl Kile	.10
156	Jeff Reed	.10
157	Larry Walker	.30
158	Bobby Bonilla	.20
159	Todd Dunwoody	.10
160	Livan Hernandez	.20
161	Charles Johnson	.20
162	Mark Kotsay	.50
163	Derrek Lee	.10
164	Edgar Renteria	.10
165	Gary Sheffield	.30
166	Moises Alou	.20
167	Jeff Bagwell	1.00
168	Derek Bell	.10
169	Craig Biggio	.20
170	Mike Hampton	.10
171	Richard Hidalgo	.10
172	Chris Holt	.10
173	Shane Reynolds	.10
174	Wilton Guerrero	.10
175	Eric Karros	.20
176	Paul Konerko	.25
177	Ramon Martinez	.20
178	Raul Mondesi	.25
179	Hideo Nomo	.50
180	Chan Ho Park	.20
181	Mike Piazza	1.50
182	Ismael Valdes	.10
183	Jeromy Burnitz	.10
184	Jeff Cirillo	.10
185	Todd Dunn	.10
186	Marquis Grissom	.10
187	John Jaha	.10
188	Doug Jones	.10
189	Dave Nilsson	.10
190	Jose Valentin	.10
191	Fernando Vina	.10
192	Orlando Cabrera	.10
193	Steve Falteisek	.10
194	Mark Grudzielanek	.10
195	Vladimir Guerrero	.50
196	Carlos Perez	.10
197	F.P. Santangelo	.10
198	Jose Vidro	.10
199	Rondell White	.20
200	Edgardo Alfonzo	.10
201	Carlos Baerga	.10
202	John Franco	.10
203	Bernard Gilkey	.10
204	Todd Hundley	.20
205	Butch Huskey	.10
206	Bobby Jones	.10
207	Brian McRae	.10
208	John Olerud	.20
209	Rey Ordonez	.10
210	Ricky Bottalico	.10
211	Bobby Estalella	.10
212	Doug Glanville	.10
213	Gregg Jefferies	.10
214	Mike Lieberthal	.10
215	Desi Relaford	.10
216	Scott Rolen	.75
217	Curt Schilling	.25
218	Adrian Brown	.10
219	Emil Brown	.10
220	Francisco Cordova	.10
221	Jose Guillen	.40
222	Al Martin	.10
223	Abraham Nunez	.10
224	Tony Womack	.10
225	Kevin Young	.10
226	Alan Benes	.20
227	Royce Clayton	.10
228	Gary Gaetti	.10
229	Ron Gant	.20
230	Brian Jordan	.20
231	Ray Lankford	.10
232	Mark McGwire	3.00
233	Todd Stottlemyre	.10
234	Kevin Brown	.20
235	Ken Caminiti	.20
236	Steve Finley	.10
237	Tony Gwynn	1.25
238	Wally Joyner	.10
239	Ruben Rivera	.10
240	Greg Vaughn	.10
241	Quilvio Veras	.10
242	Barry Bonds	.60
243	Jacob Cruz	.10
244	Shawn Estes	.20
245	Orel Hershiser	.10
246	Stan Javier	.10
247	Brian Johnson	.10
248	Jeff Kent	.10
249	Robb Nen	.10
250	J.T. Snow	.10

1998 Pacific Paramount Cooperstown Bound

Cooperstown Bound is a 10-card insert seeded one per 361 packs. Each card features a color player photo with a silver foil column on the left. The cards are fully foiled and etched.

		MT
Complete Set (10):		450.00
Common Player:		15.00
Inserted 1:361		
Pacific Proofs: 5x to 8x		
Production 20 sets		
1	Greg Maddux	60.00
2	Cal Ripken Jr.	80.00
3	Frank Thomas	80.00
4	Mike Piazza	60.00

5	Paul Molitor	20.00
6	Mark McGwire	100.00
7	Tony Gwynn	50.00
8	Barry Bonds	25.00
9	Ken Griffey Jr.	100.00
10	Wade Boggs	15.00

1998 Pacific Paramount Fielder's Choice

Fielder's Choice Laser-Cuts is a 20-card insert seeded one per 73 packs. Each card is die-cut around a baseball glove that appears in the background. The webbing of the glove is laser-cut.

		MT
Complete Set (20):		400.00
Common Player:		5.00
Inserted 1:73		
1	Chipper Jones	30.00
2	Greg Maddux	30.00
3	Cal Ripken Jr.	40.00
4	Nomar Garciaparra	30.00
5	Frank Thomas	40.00
6	David Justice	5.00
7	Larry Walker	8.00
8	Jeff Bagwell	20.00
9	Hideo Nomo	10.00
10	Mike Piazza	30.00
11	Derek Jeter	25.00
12	Ben Grieve	20.00
13	Mark McGwire	50.00
14	Tony Gwynn	25.00
15	Barry Bonds	15.00
16	Ken Griffey Jr.	50.00
17	Alex Rodriguez	30.00
18	Wade Boggs	5.00
19	Ivan Rodriguez	15.00
20	Jose Cruz Jr.	12.00

1998 Pacific Paramount Inaugural Issue

A special edition of Pacific's premiere Paramount issue was created to mark the new brand's introduction on May 27 at the debut SportsFest '98 show in Philadelphia. Each of the cards from the Paramount issue was printed with a gold-foil "INAUGURAL ISSUE May 27, 1998" logo, was embossed with Pacific and SportsFest logos at center and hand-numbered at bottom from within an edition of just 20 cards each.

		MT
Common Player:		6.00

(Stars and rookies valued at 50-75X regular Paramount version.)

1998 Pacific Paramount Special Delivery

Special Delivery cards are die-cut to resemble a postage stamp. Each card front is foiled and etched and features three photos of the player. Special Delivery is a 20-card insert seeded one per 37 packs.

		MT
Complete Set (20):		240.00
Common Player:		3.00
Inserted 1:37		
1	Chipper Jones	20.00
2	Greg Maddux	20.00
3	Cal Ripken Jr.	25.00
4	Nomar Garciaparra	20.00
5	Pedro Martinez	6.00
6	Frank Thomas	25.00
7	David Justice	4.00
8	Larry Walker	5.00
9	Jeff Bagwell	12.00
10	Hideo Nomo	6.00
11	Mike Piazza	20.00
12	Vladimir Guerrero	8.00
13	Derek Jeter	15.00
14	Ben Grieve	10.00
15	Mark McGwire	30.00
16	Tony Gwynn	15.00
17	Barry Bonds	8.00
18	Ken Griffey Jr.	30.00
19	Alex Rodriguez	20.00
20	Jose Cruz Jr.	6.00

1998 Pacific Paramount Team Checklist

Team Checklists (30 cards, 2:37) feature a player photo surrounded by two bats. The card is die-cut around the photo and the bats at the top. The bottom has the player's name, position and team.

		MT
Complete Set (30):		150.00
Common Player:		1.50
Inserted 1:18		
1	Tim Salmon	3.00
2	Cal Ripken Jr.	15.00
3	Nomar Garciaparra	12.00
4	Frank Thomas	15.00
5	Manny Ramirez	5.00
6	Tony Clark	4.00
7	Dean Palmer	1.50
8	Paul Molitor	4.00
9	Derek Jeter	12.00
10	Ben Grieve	8.00
11	Ken Griffey Jr.	20.00
12	Wade Boggs	2.00
13	Ivan Rodriguez	5.00
14	Roger Clemens	8.00
15	Matt Williams	2.50
16	Chipper Jones	12.00
17	Sammy Sosa	10.00
18	Barry Larkin	2.00
19	Larry Walker	3.00
20	Livan Hernandez	1.50
21	Jeff Bagwell	8.00
22	Mike Piazza	12.00
23	John Jaha	1.50
24	Vladimir Guerrero	5.00
25	Todd Hundley	1.50
26	Scott Rolen	8.00
27	Kevin Young	1.50
28	Mark McGwire	25.00
29	Tony Gwynn	10.00
30	Barry Bonds	5.00

1998 Pacific Revolution

Pacific Revolution Baseball consists of a 150-card base set. The base cards are dual-foiled, etched and embossed. Inserts include Showstoppers, Prime Time Performers Laser-Cuts, Foul Pole Laser-Cuts, Major League Icons and Shadow Series.

		MT
Complete Set (150):		90.00
Common Player:		.40
Wax Box:		80.00
1	Garret Anderson	.40
2	Jim Edmonds	.40
3	Darin Erstad	2.50
4	Chuck Finley	.40
5	Tim Salmon	1.00
6	Jay Bell	.40
7	Travis Lee	6.00
8	Devon White	.40
9	Matt Williams	1.00
10	Andres Galarraga	1.00
11	Tom Glavine	.60
12	Andruw Jones	2.50
13	Chipper Jones	6.00
14	Ryan Klesko	1.00
15	Javy Lopez	.60
16	Greg Maddux	6.00
17	Walt Weiss	.40
18	Roberto Alomar	2.00
19	Joe Carter	.60
20	Mike Mussina	2.00
21	Rafael Palmeiro	1.00
22	Cal Ripken Jr.	8.00
23	B.J. Surhoff	.40
24	Nomar Garciaparra	6.00
25	Reggie Jefferson	.40
26	Pedro Martinez	2.00
27	Troy O'Leary	.40
28	Mo Vaughn	2.50
29	Mark Grace	1.00
30	Mickey Morandini	.40
31	Henry Rodriguez	.40
32	Sammy Sosa	5.00
33	Kerry Wood	12.00
34	Albert Belle	2.50
35	Ray Durham	.40
36	*Magglio Ordonez*	2.50
37	Frank Thomas	8.00
38	Robin Ventura	.40
39	Bret Boone	.40
40	Barry Larkin	.75
41	Reggie Sanders	.40
42	Brett Tomko	.40
43	Sandy Alomar	.60
44	David Justice	.75
45	Kenny Lofton	2.50
46	Manny Ramirez	2.50
47	Jim Thome	1.50
48	Omar Vizquel	.40
49	Jaret Wright	2.50
50	Dante Bichette	.75
51	Ellis Burks	.40
52	Vinny Castilla	.40
53	Todd Helton	2.50
54	Larry Walker	1.50
55	Tony Clark	1.50
56	Deivi Cruz	.40
57	Damion Easley	.40
58	Bobby Higginson	.40
59	Brian Hunter	.40
60	Cliff Floyd	.40
61	Livan Hernandez	.40
62	Derrek Lee	.40
63	Edgar Renteria	.40
64	Moises Alou	.75
65	Jeff Bagwell	3.00
66	Derek Bell	.40
67	Craig Biggio	.75
68	Richard Hidalgo	.40
69	Johnny Damon	.40
70	Jeff King	.40
71	Hal Morris	.40
72	Dean Palmer	.40
73	Bobby Bonilla	.60
74	Charles Johnson	.40
75	Paul Konerko	.75
76	Raul Mondesi	.75
77	Gary Sheffield	1.00
78	Jeromy Burnitz	.40
79	Marquis Grissom	.40
80	Dave Nilsson	.40
81	Fernando Vina	.40
82	Marty Cordova	.40
83	Pat Meares	.40
84	Paul Molitor	2.00
85	Brad Radke	.40
86	Terry Steinbach	.40
87	Todd Walker	.75
88	Brad Fullmer	.75
89	Vladimir Guerrero	2.50
90	Carl Pavano	.40
91	Rondell White	.75
92	Bernard Gilkey	.40
93	Hideo Nomo	2.00
94	John Olerud	.75
95	Rey Ordonez	.40
96	Mike Piazza	6.00
97	*Masato Yoshii*	1.50
98	Hideki Irabu	1.50
99	Derek Jeter	5.00
100	Chuck Knoblauch	1.00
101	Tino Martinez	1.00
102	Paul O'Neill	.75
103	Darryl Strawberry	.60
104	Bernie Williams	2.00
105	Jason Giambi	.40
106	Ben Grieve	3.00
107	Rickey Henderson	.40
108	Matt Stairs	.40
109	Doug Glanville	.40
110	Desi Relaford	.40
111	Scott Rolen	3.00
112	Curt Schilling	.75
113	Jason Kendall	.75
114	Al Martin	.40
115	Jason Schmidt	.40
116	Kevin Young	.40
117	Delino DeShields	.40
118	Gary Gaetti	.40
119	Brian Jordan	.40
120	Ray Lankford	.40
121	Mark McGwire	12.00
122	Kevin Brown	.60
123	Steve Finley	.40
124	Tony Gwynn	5.00
125	Wally Joyner	.40
126	Greg Vaughn	.40
127	Barry Bonds	2.50
128	Orel Hershiser	.40
129	Jeff Kent	.40
130	Bill Mueller	.40
131	Jay Buhner	1.00
132	Ken Griffey Jr.	10.00
133	Randy Johnson	2.00
134	Edgar Martinez	.40
135	Alex Rodriguez	6.00
136	David Segui	.40
137	*Rolando Arrojo*	4.00
138	Wade Boggs	.75
139	Quinton McCracken	.40
140	Fred McGriff	.60
141	Will Clark	.75
142	Juan Gonzalez	5.00
143	Tom Goodwin	.40
144	Ivan Rodriguez	2.50
145	Aaron Sele	.40
146	John Wetteland	.40
147	Jose Canseco	1.00
148	Roger Clemens	3.00
149	Jose Cruz Jr.	2.50
150	Carlos Delgado	.40

1998 Pacific Revolution Foul Pole

Foul Pole Laser-Cuts is a 20-card insert seeded one per 49 packs. Each card features a color player photo on the left and a foul pole on the right. The foul pole design includes netting that is laser cut.

Values shown reflect the market as of January, 1999. On-field performances of current players in the 1999 baseball season are not factored in.

		MT
Complete Set (20):		350.00
Common Player:		6.00
Inserted 1:49		
1	Cal Ripken Jr.	35.00
2	Nomar Garciaparra	30.00
3	Mo Vaughn	12.00
4	Frank Thomas	35.00
5	Manny Ramirez	12.00
6	Bernie Williams	10.00
7	Ben Grieve	15.00
8	Ken Griffey Jr.	50.00
9	Alex Rodriguez	30.00
10	Juan Gonzalez	25.00
11	Ivan Rodriguez	12.00
12	Travis Lee	25.00
13	Chipper Jones	30.00
14	Sammy Sosa	25.00
15	Vinny Castilla	6.00
16	Moises Alou	6.00
17	Gary Sheffield	6.00
18	Mike Piazza	30.00
19	Mark McGwire	60.00
20	Barry Bonds	12.00

1998 Pacific Revolution Major League Icons

Major League Icons is a 10-card insert seeded one per 121 packs. Each card features a player photo on a die-cut shield, with the shield on a flaming stand.

		MT
Complete Set (10):		500.00
Common Player:		30.00
Inserted 1:121		
1	Cal Ripken Jr.	60.00

2	Nomar Garciaparra	50.00
3	Frank Thomas	60.00
4	Ken Griffey Jr.	80.00
5	Alex Rodriguez	50.00
6	Chipper Jones	50.00
7	Kerry Wood	50.00
8	Mike Piazza	50.00
9	Mark McGwire	90.00
10	Tony Gwynn	40.00

1998 Pacific Revolution Prime Time Performers

Prime Time Performers is a 20-card insert seeded one per 25 packs. The cards are designed like a TV program guide with the team logo laser-cut on the TV screen. The color player photo is located on the left.

		MT
Complete Set (20):		350.00
Common Player:		6.00
Inserted 1:25		
1	Cal Ripken Jr.	30.00
2	Nomar Garciaparra	25.00
3	Frank Thomas	30.00
4	Jim Thome	6.00
5	Hideki Irabu	8.00
6	Derek Jeter	20.00
7	Ben Grieve	15.00
8	Ken Griffey Jr.	35.00
9	Alex Rodriguez	25.00
10	Juan Gonzalez	20.00
11	Ivan Rodriguez	10.00
12	Travis Lee	20.00
13	Chipper Jones	25.00
14	Greg Maddux	25.00
15	Kerry Wood	30.00
16	Larry Walker	6.00
17	Jeff Bagwell	15.00
18	Mike Piazza	25.00
19	Mark McGwire	40.00
20	Tony Gwynn	20.00

1998 Pacific Revolution Rookies and Hardball Heroes

		MT
Complete Set (30):		100.00
Common Player:		.50
Inserted 1:6		
Gold (1-20): 8x to 15x		
Gold (1-20) Production 50 sets		
1	Justin Baughman	.50
2	Jarrod Washburn	.50
3	Travis Lee	5.00
4	Kerry Wood	10.00
5	Magglio Ordonez	2.00
6	Todd Helton	2.50
7	Derek Lee	1.50
8	Richard Hidalgo	1.00
9	Mike Caruso	1.00
10	David Ortiz	2.00
11	Brad Fullmer	2.00
12	Masato Yoshii	1.00
13	Orlando Hernandez	8.00
14	Ricky Ledee	1.00
15	Ben Grieve	5.00

16	Carlton Loewer	1.00
17	Desi Relaford	.50
18	Ruben Rivera	.50
19	Rolando Arrojo	3.00
20	Matt Perisho	.50
21	Chipper Jones	8.00
22	Greg Maddux	8.00
23	Cal Ripken Jr.	10.00
24	Nomar Garciaparra	8.00
25	Frank Thomas	8.00
26	Mark McGwire	15.00
27	Tony Gwynn	6.00
28	Ken Griffey Jr.	12.00
29	Alex Rodriguez	8.00
30	Juan Gonzalez	6.00

1998 Pacific Revolution Shadows

Shadows is a full parallel of the Revolution base set. Limited to 99 sequentially numbered sets, each card is embossed with a special "Shadow Series" stamp.

		MT
Complete Set (150):		
Common Player:		15.00
Production 99 sets		
1	Garret Anderson	15.00
2	Jim Edmonds	15.00
3	Darin Erstad	60.00
4	Chuck Finley	15.00
5	Tim Salmon	30.00
6	Jay Bell	15.00
7	Travis Lee	125.00
8	Devon White	15.00
9	Matt Williams	30.00
10	Andres Galarraga	30.00
11	Tom Glavine	25.00
12	Andruw Jones	60.00
13	Chipper Jones	150.00
14	Ryan Klesko	30.00
15	Javy Lopez	20.00
16	Greg Maddux	150.00
17	Walt Weiss	15.00
18	Roberto Alomar	50.00
19	Joe Carter	20.00
20	Mike Mussina	50.00
21	Rafael Palmeiro	30.00
22	Cal Ripken Jr.	200.00
23	B.J. Surhoff	15.00
24	Nomar Garciaparra	150.00
25	Reggie Jefferson	15.00
26	Pedro Martinez	50.00
27	Troy O'Leary	15.00
28	Mo Vaughn	60.00
29	Mark Grace	30.00
30	Mickey Morandini	15.00
31	Henry Rodriguez	15.00
32	Sammy Sosa	125.00
33	Kerry Wood	150.00
34	Albert Belle	60.00
35	Ray Durham	15.00
36	*Magglio Ordonez*	40.00
37	Frank Thomas	200.00
38	Robin Ventura	15.00
39	Bret Boone	15.00
40	Barry Larkin	25.00
41	Reggie Sanders	15.00
42	Brett Tomko	15.00
43	Sandy Alomar	20.00
44	David Justice	25.00
45	Kenny Lofton	60.00
46	Manny Ramirez	60.00
47	Jim Thome	40.00
48	Omar Vizquel	15.00
49	Jaret Wright	60.00
50	Dante Bichette	30.00
51	Ellis Burks	15.00
52	Vinny Castilla	15.00
53	Todd Helton	60.00
54	Larry Walker	40.00
55	Tony Clark	40.00
56	Deivi Cruz	15.00
57	Damion Easley	15.00
58	Bobby Higginson	15.00
59	Brian Hunter	15.00
60	Cliff Floyd	15.00
61	Livan Hernandez	15.00
62	Derek Lee	15.00
63	Edgar Renteria	15.00
64	Moises Alou	25.00

65	Jeff Bagwell	80.00
66	Derek Bell	15.00
67	Craig Biggio	25.00
68	Richard Hidalgo	15.00
69	Johnny Damon	15.00
70	Jeff King	15.00
71	Hal Morris	15.00
72	Dean Palmer	15.00
73	Bobby Bonilla	20.00
74	Charles Johnson	15.00
75	Paul Konerko	25.00
76	Raul Mondesi	25.00
77	Gary Sheffield	40.00
78	Jeromy Burnitz	15.00
79	Marquis Grissom	15.00
80	Dave Nilsson	15.00
81	Fernando Vina	15.00
82	Marty Cordova	15.00
83	Pat Meares	15.00
84	Paul Molitor	50.00
85	Brad Radke	15.00
86	Terry Steinbach	15.00
87	Todd Walker	25.00
88	Brad Fullmer	25.00
89	Vladimir Guerrero	60.00
90	Carl Pavano	15.00
91	Rondell White	20.00
92	Bernard Gilkey	15.00
93	Hideo Nomo	50.00
94	John Olerud	25.00
95	Rey Ordonez	15.00
96	Mike Piazza	150.00
97	*Masato Yoshii*	30.00
98	Hideki Irabu	30.00
99	Derek Jeter	125.00
100	Chuck Knoblauch	30.00
101	Tino Martinez	40.00
102	Paul O'Neill	25.00
103	Darryl Strawberry	25.00
104	Bernie Williams	50.00
105	Jason Giambi	15.00
106	Ben Grieve	80.00
107	Rickey Henderson	15.00
108	Matt Stairs	15.00
109	Doug Glanville	15.00
110	Desi Relaford	15.00
111	Scott Rolen	80.00
112	Curt Schilling	25.00
113	Jason Kendall	25.00
114	Al Martin	15.00
115	Jason Schmidt	15.00
116	Kevin Young	15.00
117	Delino DeShields	15.00
118	Gary Gaetti	15.00
119	Brian Jordan	15.00
120	Ray Lankford	15.00
121	Mark McGwire	250.00
122	Kevin Brown	25.00
123	Steve Finley	15.00
124	Tony Gwynn	125.00
125	Wally Joyner	15.00
126	Greg Vaughn	60.00
127	Barry Bonds	60.00
128	Orel Hershiser	15.00
129	Jeff Kent	15.00
130	Bill Mueller	15.00
131	Jay Buhner	30.00
132	Ken Griffey Jr.	250.00
133	Randy Johnson	50.00
134	Edgar Martinez	20.00
135	Alex Rodriguez	150.00
136	David Segui	15.00
137	*Rolando Arrojo*	30.00
138	Wade Boggs	25.00
139	Quinton McCracken	15.00
140	Fred McGriff	25.00
141	Will Clark	25.00
142	Juan Gonzalez	125.00
143	Tom Goodwin	15.00
144	Ivan Rodriguez	60.00
145	Aaron Sele	15.00
146	John Wetteland	15.00
147	Jose Canseco	30.00
148	Roger Clemens	90.00
149	Jose Cruz Jr.	60.00
150	Carlos Delgado	15.00

Modern cards have little collector value in conditions lower than Mint.
Figure NM cards at 75% of values shown;
EX cards at 40%.

1998 Pacific Revolution Showstoppers

This 36-card insert was seeded two per 25 packs. The cards feature holographic foil. The color photo is centered above the team logo and the Showstoppers logo.

		MT
Complete Set (36):		275.00
Common Player:		2.00
Inserted 1:12		
1	Cal Ripken Jr.	20.00
2	Nomar Garciaparra	15.00
3	Pedro Martinez	5.00
4	Mo Vaughn	6.00
5	Frank Thomas	20.00
6	Manny Ramirez	6.00
7	Jim Thome	5.00
8	Jaret Wright	6.00
9	Paul Molitor	6.00
10	Orlando Hernandez	12.00
11	Derek Jeter	12.00
12	Bernie Williams	6.00
13	Ben Grieve	8.00
14	Ken Griffey Jr.	25.00
15	Alex Rodriguez	15.00
16	Wade Boggs	3.00
17	Juan Gonzalez	12.00
18	Ivan Rodriguez	6.00
19	Jose Canseco	4.00
20	Roger Clemens	10.00
21	Travis Lee	15.00
22	Andres Galarraga	4.00
23	Chipper Jones	15.00
24	Greg Maddux	15.00
25	Sammy Sosa	12.00
26	Kerry Wood	20.00
27	Vinny Castilla	2.00
28	Larry Walker	4.00
29	Moises Alou	2.00
30	Raul Mondesi	3.00
31	Gary Sheffield	4.00
32	Hideo Nomo	5.00
33	Mike Piazza	15.00
34	Mark McGwire	25.00
35	Tony Gwynn	12.00
36	Barry Bonds	6.00

1992 Pinnacle

Score entered the high-end card market with the release of this 620-card set. The cards feature black borders surrounding a white frame with a full-color action photo inside. The player extends beyond the natural background. The backs are horizontal and feature a close-up photo, statistics, team logo, biographical information and player information. Several subsets can

be found within the set including "Idols, Sidelines, Grips, Shades" and "Technicians".

		MT
Complete Set (620):		45.00
Common Player:		.10
1	Frank Thomas	3.00
2	Benito Santiago	.10
3	Carlos Baerga	.15
4	Cecil Fielder	.30
5	Barry Larkin	.15
6	Ozzie Smith	.30
7	Willie McGee	.10
8	Paul Molitor	.30
9	Andy Van Slyke	.10
10	Ryne Sandberg	.50
11	Kevin Seitzer	.10
12	Len Dykstra	.25
13	Edgar Martinez	.15
14	Ruben Sierra	.15
15	Howard Johnson	.10
16	Dave Henderson	.10
17	Devon White	.10
18	Terry Pendleton	.10
19	Steve Finley	.10
20	Kirby Puckett	.75
21	Orel Hershiser	.10
22	Hal Morris	.15
23	Don Mattingly	.75
24	Delino DeShields	.15
25	Dennis Eckersley	.15
26	Ellis Burks	.10
27	Jay Buhner	.10
28	Matt Williams	.25
29	Lou Whitaker	.10
30	Alex Fernandez	.12
31	Albert Belle	.75
32	Todd Zeile	.12
33	Tony Pena	.10
34	Jay Bell	.10
35	Rafael Palmeiro	.25
36	Wes Chamberlain	.10
37	George Bell	.10
38	Robin Yount	.40
39	Vince Coleman	.10
40	Bruce Hurst	.10
41	Harold Baines	.10
42	Chuck Finley	.10
43	Ken Caminiti	.10
44	Ben McDonald	.25
45	Roberto Alomar	.75
46	Chili Davis	.10
47	Bill Doran	.10
48	Jerald Clark	.10
49	Jose Lind	.10
50	Nolan Ryan	2.00
51	Phil Plantier	.25
52	Gary DiSarcina	.10
53	Kevin Bass	.10
54	Pat Kelly	.10
55	Mark Wohlers	.10
56	Walt Weiss	.10
57	Lenny Harris	.10
58	Ivan Calderon	.10
59	Harold Reynolds	.10
60	George Brett	.75
61	Gregg Olson	.10
62	Orlando Merced	.10
63	Steve Decker	.10
64	John Franco	.10
65	Greg Maddux	2.00
66	Alex Cole	.10
67	Dave Hollins	.15
68	Kent Hrbek	.10
69	Tom Pagnozzi	.10
70	Jeff Bagwell	1.00
71	Jim Gantner	.10
72	Matt Nokes	.10
73	Brian Harper	.10
74	Andy Benes	.15
75	Tom Glavine	.25
76	Terry Steinbach	.10
77	Dennis Martinez	.10
78	John Olerud	.20
79	Ozzie Guillen	.10
80	Darryl Strawberry	.10
81	Gary Gaetti	.10
82	Dave Righetti	.10
83	Chris Hoiles	.15
84	Andujar Cedeno	.20
85	Jack Clark	.10
86	David Howard	.10
87	Bill Gullickson	.10
88	Bernard Gilkey	.15
89	Kevin Elster	.10

90	Kevin Maas	.10
91	Mark Lewis	.10
92	Greg Vaughn	.10
93	Bret Barberie	.10
94	Dave Smith	.10
95	Roger Clemens	.50
96	Doug Drabek	.10
97	Omar Vizquel	.10
98	Jose Guzman	.10
99	Juan Samuel	.10
100	Dave Justice	.20
101	Tom Browning	.10
102	Mark Gubicza	.10
103	Mickey Morandini	.10
104	Ed Whitson	.10
105	Lance Parrish	.10
106	Scott Erickson	.10
107	Jack McDowell	.30
108	Dave Stieb	.10
109	Mike Moore	.10
110	Travis Fryman	.10
111	Dwight Gooden	.10
112	Fred McGriff	.35
113	Alan Trammell	.12
114	Roberto Kelly	.15
115	Andre Dawson	.15
116	Bill Landrum	.10
117	Brian McRae	.10
119	Chuck Knoblauch	.15
120	Steve Olin	.10
121	Robin Ventura	.30
122	Will Clark	.25
123	Tino Martinez	.15
124	Dale Murphy	.15
125	Pete O'Brien	.10
126	Ray Lankford	.15
127	Juan Gonzalez	.75
128	Ron Gant	.15
129	Marquis Grissom	.20
130	Jose Canseco	.40
131	Mike Greenwell	.15
132	Mark Langston	.10
133	Brett Butler	.10
134	Kelly Gruber	.10
135	Chris Sabo	.10
136	Mark Grace	.20
137	Tony Fernandez	.10
138	Glenn Davis	.10
139	Pedro Munoz	.15
140	Craig Biggio	.12
141	Pete Schourek	.10
142	Mike Boddicker	.10
143	Robby Thompson	.10
144	Mel Hall	.10
145	Bryan Harvey	.10
146	Mike LaValliere	.10
147	John Kruk	.12
148	Joe Carter	.25
149	Greg Olson	.10
150	Julio Franco	.10
151	Darryl Hamilton	.10
152	Felix Fermin	.10
153	Jose Offerman	.12
154	Paul O'Neill	.12
155	Tommy Greene	.10
156	Ivan Rodriguez	.60
157	Dave Stewart	.12
158	Jeff Reardon	.10
159	Felix Jose	.10
160	Doug Dascenzo	.10
161	Tim Wallach	.10
162	Dan Plesac	.10
163	Luis Gonzalez	.10
164	Mike Henneman	.10
165	Mike Devereaux	.10
166	Luis Polonia	.10
167	Mike Sharperson	.10
168	Chris Donnels	.10
169	Greg Harris	.10
170	Deion Sanders	.50
171	Mike Schooler	.10
172	Jose DeJesus	.10
173	Jeff Montgomery	.10
174	Milt Cuyler	.10
175	Wade Boggs	.20
176	Kevin Tapani	.10
177	Bill Spiers	.10
178	Tim Raines	.15
179	Randy Milligan	.10
180	Rob Dibble	.10
181	Kirt Manwaring	.10
182	Pascual Perez	.10
183	Juan Guzman	.25
184	John Smiley	.10
185	David Segui	.10
186	Omar Olivares	.10

#	Player	Price
187	Joe Slusarski	.10
188	Erik Hanson	.10
189	Mark Portugal	.10
190	Walt Terrell	.10
191	John Smoltz	.15
192	Wilson Alvarez	.15
193	Jimmy Key	.10
194	Larry Walker	.25
195	Lee Smith	.12
196	Pete Harnisch	.12
197	Mike Harkey	.10
198	Frank Tanana	.10
199	Terry Mulholland	.10
200	Cal Ripken, Jr.	2.50
201	Dave Magadan	.10
202	Bud Black	.10
203	Terry Shumpert	.10
204	Mike Mussina	.75
205	Mo Vaughn	.75
206	Steve Farr	.10
207	Darrin Jackson	.10
208	Jerry Browne	.10
209	Jeff Russell	.10
210	Mike Scioscia	.10
211	Rick Aguilera	.10
212	Jaime Navarro	.10
213	Randy Tomlin	.10
214	Bobby Thigpen	.10
215	Mark Gardner	.10
216	Norm Charlton	.10
217	Mark McGwire	3.00
219	Bob Tewksbury	.10
220	Junior Felix	.10
221	Sam Horn	.10
222	Jody Reed	.10
223	Luis Sojo	.10
224	Jerome Walton	.10
225	Darryl Kile	.10
226	Mickey Tettleton	.15
227	Dan Pasqua	.10
228	Jim Gott	.10
229	Bernie Williams	.40
230	Shane Mack	.10
231	Steve Avery	.25
232	Dave Valle	.10
233	Mark Leonard	.10
234	Spike Owen	.10
235	Gary Sheffield	.25
236	Steve Chitren	.10
237	Zane Smith	.10
238	Tom Gordon	.10
239	Jose Oquendo	.10
240	Todd Stottlemyre	.10
241	Darren Daulton	.15
242	Tim Naehring	.12
243	Tony Phillips	.10
244	Shawon Dunston	.12
245	Manuel Lee	.10
246	Mike Pagliarulo	.10
247	Jim Thome (Rookie Prospect)	.30
248	Luis Mercedes (Rookie Prospect)	.15
249	Cal Eldred (Rookie Prospect)	.25
250	Derek Bell (Rookie Prospect)	.20
251	Arthur Rhodes (Rookie Prospect)	.15
252	Scott Cooper (Rookie Prospect)	.20
253	Roberto Hernandez (Rookie Prospect)	.15
254	Mo Sanford (Rookie Prospect)	.15
255	Scott Servais (Rookie Prospect)	.10
256	Eric Karros (Rookie Prospect)	.20
259	Joel Johnston (Rookie Prospect)	.12
260	John Wehner (Rookie Prospect)	.12
261	Gino Minutelli (Rookie Prospect)	.12
262	Greg Gagne	.10
263	Stan Royer (Rookie Prospect)	.15
264	Carlos Garcia (Rookie Prospect)	.20
265	Andy Ashby (Rookie Prospect)	.12
266	Kim Batiste (Rookie Prospect)	.10
267	Julio Valera (Rookie Prospect)	.12
268	Royce Clayton (Rookie Prospect)	.15
269	Gary Scott (Rookie Prospect)	.10
270	Kirk Dressendorfer (Rookie Prospect)	.10
271	Sean Berry (Rookie Prospect)	.12
272	Lance Dickson (Rookie Prospect)	.12
273	Rob Maurer (Rookie Prospect)	.10
274	Scott Brosius (Rookie Prospect)	.20
275	Dave Fleming (Rookie Prospect)	.20
276	Lenny Webster (Rookie Prospect)	.12
278	Freddie Benavides (Rookie Prospect)	.12
279	Harvey Pulliam (Rookie Prospect)	.12
280	Jeff Carter (Rookie Prospect)	.12
281	Jim Abbott, Nolan Ryan (Idols)	.15
282	Wade Boggs, George Brett (Idols)	.15
283	Ken Griffey Jr., Rickey Henderson (Idols)	.75
284	Dale Murphy, Wally Joyner (Idols)	.15
285	Chuck Knoblauch, Ozzie Smith (Idols)	.15
286	Robin Ventura, Lou Gehrig (Idols)	.25
287	Robin Yount (Sidelines - Motocross)	.35
288	Bob Tewksbury (Sidelines - Cartoonist)	.12
289	Kirby Puckett (Sidelines - Pool Player)	.40
290	Kenny Lofton (Sidelines - Basketball Player)	.75
291	Jack McDowell (Sidelines - Guitarist)	.15
292	John Burkett (Sidelines - Bowler)	.12
293	Dwight Smith (Sidelines - Singer)	.12
294	Nolan Ryan (Sidelines - Cattle Rancher)	1.00
295	*Manny Ramirez* (1st Round Draft Pick)	4.00
296	*Cliff Floyd* (1st Round Draft Pick)	.50
297	*Al Shirley* (1st Round Draft Pick)	.20
298	*Brian Barber* (1st Round Draft Pick)	.30
299	*Jon Farrell* (1st Round Draft Pick)	.30
300	*Scott Ruffcorn* (1st Round Draft Pick)	.40
301	*Tyrone Hill* (1st Round Draft Pick)	.20
302	*Benji Gil* (1st Round Draft Pick)	.50
303	*Tyler Green* (1st Round Draft Pick)	.30
304	Allen Watson (Shades)	.15
305	Jay Buhner (Shades)	.12
306	Roberto Alomar (Shades)	.35
307	Chuck Knoblauch (Shades)	.10
308	Darryl Strawberry (Shades)	.10
309	Danny Tartabull (Shades)	.12
310	Bobby Bonilla (Shades)	.10
311	Mike Felder	.10
312	Storm Davis	.10
313	Tim Teufel	.10
314	Tom Brunansky	.10
315	Rex Hudler	.10
316	Dave Otto	.10
317	Jeff King	.10
318	Dan Gladden	.10
319	Bill Pecota	.10
320	Franklin Stubbs	.10
321	Gary Carter	.15
322	Melido Perez	.10
323	Eric Davis	.15
324	Greg Myers	.10
325	Pete Incaviglia	.10
326	Von Hayes	.10
327	Greg Swindell	.10
328	Steve Sax	.10
329	Chuck McElroy	.10
330	Gregg Jefferies	.20
331	Joe Oliver	.10
332	Paul Faries	.10
333	David West	.10
334	Craig Grebeck	.10
335	Chris Hammond	.10
336	Billy Ripken	.10
337	Scott Sanderson	.10
338	Dick Schofield	.10
339	Bob Milacki	.10
340	Kevin Reimer	.10
341	Jose DeLeon	.10
342	Henry Cotto	.10
343	Daryl Boston	.10
344	Kevin Gross	.10
345	Milt Thompson	.10
346	Luis Rivera	.10
347	Al Osuna	.10
348	Rob Deer	.10
349	Tim Leary	.10
350	Mike Stanton	.10
351	Dean Palmer	.15
352	Trevor Wilson	.10
353	Mark Eichhorn	.10
354	Scott Aldred	.10
355	Mark Whiten	.15
356	Leo Gomez	.10
357	Rafael Belliard	.10
358	Carlos Quintana	.10
359	Mark Davis	.10
360	Chris Nabholz	.10
361	Carlton Fisk	.15
362	Joe Orsulak	.10
363	Eric Anthony	.05
364	Greg Hibbard	.10
365	Scott Leius	.10
366	Hensley Meulens	.10
367	Chris Bosio	.10
368	Brian Downing	.10
369	Sammy Sosa	2.00
370	Stan Belinda	.10
371	Joe Grahe	.10
372	Luis Salazar	.10
373	Lance Johnson	.10
374	Kal Daniels	.10
375	Dave Winfield	.35
376	Brook Jacoby	.10
377	Mariano Duncan	.10
378	Ron Darling	.10
379	Randy Johnson	.40
380	Chito Martinez	.10
381	Andres Galarraga	.12
382	Willie Randolph	.10
383	Charles Nagy	.10
384	Tim Belcher	.10
385	Duane Ward	.10
386	Vicente Palacios	.10
387	Mike Gallego	.10
388	Rich DeLucia	.10
389	Scott Radinsky	.10
390	Damon Berryhill	.10
391	Kirk McCaskill	.10
392	Pedro Guerrero	.10
393	Kevin Mitchell	.10
394	Dickie Thon	.10
395	Bobby Bonilla	.12
396	Bill Wegman	.10
397	Dave Martinez	.10
398	Rick Sutcliffe	.10
399	Larry Andersen	.10
400	Tony Gwynn	.75
401	Rickey Henderson	.30
402	Greg Cadaret	.10
403	Keith Miller	.10
404	Bip Roberts	.10
405	Kevin Brown	.12
406	Mitch Williams	.10
407	Frank Viola	.10
408	Darren Lewis	.10
409	Bob Walk	.10
410	Bob Walk	.10
411	Todd Frohwirth	.10
412	Brian Hunter	.10
413	Ron Karkovice	.10
414	Mike Morgan	.10
415	Joe Hesketh	.10
416	Don Slaught	.10
417	Tom Henke	.10
418	Kurt Stillwell	.10
419	Hector Villanueva	.10
420	Glenallen Hill	.10
421	Pat Borders	.10
422	Charlie Hough	.10
423	Charlie Leibrandt	.10
424	Eddie Murray	.20
425	Jesse Barfield	.10

426	Mark Lemke	.10
427	Kevin McReynolds	.10
428	Gilberto Reyes	.10
429	Ramon Martinez	.10
430	Steve Buechele	.10
431	David Wells	.10
432	Kyle Abbott (Rookie Prospect)	.15
433	John Habyan	.10
434	Kevin Appier	.15
435	Gene Larkin	.10
436	Sandy Alomar, Jr.	.10
437	Mike Jackson	.10
438	Todd Benzinger	.10
439	Teddy Higuera	.10
440	Reggie Sanders (Rookie Prospect)	.20
441	Mark Carreon	.10
442	Bret Saberhagen	.10
443	Gene Nelson	.10
444	Jay Howell	.10
445	Roger McDowell	.10
446	Sid Bream	.10
447	Mackey Sasser	.10
448	Bill Swift	.10
449	Hubie Brooks	.10
450	David Cone	.10
451	Bobby Witt	.10
452	Brady Anderson	.10
453	Lee Stevens	.10
454	Luis Aquino	.10
455	Carney Lansford	.10
456	Carlos Hernandez (Rookie Prospect)	.15
457	Danny Jackson	.10
458	Gerald Young	.10
459	Tom Candiotti	.10
460	Billy Hatcher	.10
461	John Wetteland	.15
462	Mike Bordick	.10
463	Don Robinson	.10
464	Jeff Johnson	.10
465	Lonnie Smith	.10
466	Paul Assenmacher	.10
467	Alvin Davis	.10
468	Jim Eisenreich	.10
469	Brent Mayne	.10
470	Jeff Brantley	.10
471	Tim Burke	.10
472	Pat Mahomes (Rookie Prospect)	.25
473	Ryan Bowen	.20
474	Bryn Smith	.10
475	Mike Flanagan	.10
476	Reggie Jefferson (Rookie Prospect)	.15
477	Jeff Blauser	.10
478	Craig Lefferts	.10
479	Todd Worrell	.10
480	Scott Scudder	.10
481	Kirk Gibson	.10
482	Kenny Rogers	.10
483	Jack Morris	.12
484	Russ Swan	.10
485	Mike Huff	.10
486	Ken Hill	.15
487	Geronimo Pena	.10
488	Charlie O'Brien	.10
489	Mike Maddux	.10
490	Scott Livingstone (Rookie Prospect)	.12
491	Carl Willis	.10
492	Kelly Downs	.10
493	Dennis Cook	.10
494	Joe Magrane	.10
495	Bob Kipper	.10
496	Jose Mesa	.10
497	Charlie Hayes	.10
498	Joe Girardi	.10
499	Doug Jones	.10
500	Barry Bonds	.75
501	Bill Krueger	.10
502	Glenn Braggs	.10
503	Eric King	.10
504	Frank Castillo	.10
505	Mike Gardiner	.10
506	Cory Snyder	.10
507	Steve Howe	.10
508	Jose Rijo	.10
509	Sid Fernandez	.10
510	Archi Cianfrocco (Rookie Prospect)	.20
511	Mark Guthrie	.10
512	Bob Ojeda	.10
513	John Doherty (Rookie Prospect)	.15

514	Dante Bichette	.10
515	Juan Berenguer	.10
516	Jeff Robinson	.10
517	Mike MacFarlane	.10
518	Matt Young	.10
519	Otis Nixon	.10
520	Brian Holman	.10
521	Chris Haney	.20
522	Jeff Kent (Rookie Prospect)	.40
523	Chad Curtis (Rookie Prospect)	.50
524	Vince Horsman	.10
525	Rod Nichols	.10
526	Peter Hoy (Rookie Prospect)	.15
527	Shawn Boskie	.12
528	Alejandro Pena	.10
529	Dave Durba (Rookie Prospect)	.10
530	Ricky Jordan	.10
531	David Silvestri (Rookie Prospect)	.20
532	John Patterson (Rookie Prospect)	.20
533	Jeff Branson (Rookie Prospect)	.12
534	Derrick May (Rookie Prospect)	.15
535	Esteban Beltre (Rookie Prospect)	.20
536	Jose Melendez	.15
537	Wally Joyner	.12
538	Eddie Taubensee (Rookie Prospect)	.12
539	Jim Abbott	.20
540	Brian Williams (Rookie Prospect)	.15
541	Donovan Osborne (Rookie Prospect)	.15
542	Patrick Lennon (Rookie Prospect)	.20
543	Mike Groppuso (Rookie Prospect)	.10
544	Jarvis Brown (Rookie Prospect)	.10
545	Shawn Livesy (1st Round Draft Pick)	.20
546	Jeff Ware (1st Round Draft Pick)	.15
547	Danny Tartabull	.10
548	Bobby Jones (1st Round Draft Pick)	.75
549	Ken Griffey, Jr.	4.00
550	Rey Sanchez (Rookie Prospect)	.25
551	Pedro Astacio (Rookie Prospect)	.25
552	Juan Guerrero (Rookie Prospect)	.12
553	Jacob Brumfield (Rookie Prospect)	.12
554	Ben Rivera (Rookie Prospect)	.12
555	Brian Jordan (Rookie Prospect)	1.00
556	Denny Neagle (Rookie Prospect)	.12
557	Cliff Brantley (Rookie Prospect)	.12
558	Anthony Young (Rookie Prospect)	.10
559	John VanderWal (Rookie Prospect)	.15
560	Monty Fariss (Rookie Prospect)	.15
561	Russ Springer (Rookie Prospect)	.20
562	Pat Listach (Rookie Prospect)	.15
563	Pat Hentgen (Rookie Prospect)	.20
564	Andy Stankiewicz (Rookie Prospect)	.10
565	Mike Perez (Rookie Prospect)	.15
566	Mike Bielecki	.10
567	Butch Henry (Rookie Prospect)	.12
568	Dave Nilsson (Rookie Prospect)	.30
569	Scott Hatteberg (Rookie Prospect)	.20
570	Ruben Amaro, Jr. (Rookie Prospect)	.10
571	Todd Hundley (Rookie Prospect)	.15

572	Moises Alou (Rookie Prospect)	.20
573	Hector Fajardo (Rookie Prospect)	.15
574	Todd Van Poppel (Rookie Prospect)	.25
575	Willie Banks (Rookie Prospect)	.15
576	Bob Zupcic (Rookie Prospect)	.10
577	J.J. Johnson (1st Round Draft Pick)	.15
578	John Burkett	.10
579	Trever Miller (1st Round Draft Pick)	.15
580	Scott Bankhead	10
581	Rich Amaral (Rookie Prospect)	.10
582	Kenny Lofton (Rookie Prospect)	1.00
583	Matt Stairs (Rookie Prospect)	.20
584	Don Mattingly, Rod Carew (Idols)	.20
585	Jack Morris, Steve Avery (Idols)	.20
586	Roberto Alomar, Sandy Alomar (Idols)	.25
587	Scott Sanderson, Catfish Hunter (Idols)	.10
588	Dave Justice, Willie Stargell (Idols)	.30
589	Rex Hudler, Roger Staubach (Idols)	.10
590	David Cone, Jackie Gleason (Idols)	.12
591	Willie Davis, Tony Gwynn (Idols)	.15
592	Orel Hershiser (Sidelines - Golfer)	.15
593	John Wetteland (Sidelines - Musician)	.15
594	Tom Glavine (Sidelines - Hockey Player)	.15
595	Randy Johnson (Sidelines - Photographer)	.20
596	Jim Gott (Sidelines - Black Belt)	.10
597	Donald Harris	.10
598	Shawn Hare	.15
599	Chris Gardner	.10
600	Rusty Meacham	.10
601	Benito Santiago (Shades)	.15
602	Eric Davis (Shades)	.15
603	Jose Lind (Shades)	.10
604	Dave Justice (Shades)	.30
605	Tim Raines (Shades)	.15
606	Randy Tomlin (Grips - Vulcan Change)	.15
607	Jack McDowell (Grips - Split-finger)	.20
608	Greg Maddux (Grips - Circle change)	.30
609	Charles Nagy (Grips - Slider)	.10
610	Tom Candiotti (Grips - Knuckleball)	.10
611	David Cone (Grips - Curveball)	.10
612	Steve Avery (Grips - Fastball)	.25
613	Rod Beck	.30
614	Rickey Henderson (Technician - Base Stealing)	.25
615	Benito Santiago (Technician - Catching)	.10
616	Ruben Sierra (Technician - Outfield)	.15
617	Ryne Sandberg (Technician - Infield)	.40
618	Nolan Ryan (Technician - Pitching)	.75
619	Brett Butler (Technician - Bunting)	.10
620	Dave Justice (Technician - Hitting)	.30

1992 Pinnacle Rookie Idols

Carrying on with the Idols sub-set theme in the regular issue, these Series II foil-pack inserts feature 18 of the year's rookie prospects sharing cards with their baseball heroes. Both front and back are horizontal in format and include photos of both the rookie and his idol.

		MT
Complete Set (18):		95.00
Common Player:		3.00
1	Reggie Sanders, Eric Davis	3.00
2	Hector Fajardo, Jim Abbott	3.00
3	Gary Cooper, George Brett	10.00
4	Mark Wohlers, Roger Clemens	8.00
5	Luis Mercedes, Julio Franco	3.00
6	Willie Banks, Dwight Gooden	3.00
7	Kenny Lofton, Rickey Henderson	15.00
8	Keith Mitchell, Dave Henderson	3.00
9	Kim Batiste, Barry Larkin	3.00
10	Thurman Munson, Todd Hundley	7.50
11	Eddie Zosky, Cal Ripken Jr.	20.00
12	Todd Van Poppel, Nolan Ryan	20.00
13	Ryne Sandberg, Jim Thome	15.00
14	Dave Fleming, Bobby Murcer	3.00
15	Royce Clayton, Ozzie Smith	7.50
16	Don Harris, Darryl Strawberry	3.00
17	Alan Trammell, Chad Curtis	3.00
18	Derek Bell, Dave Winfield	4.00

1992 Pinnacle Rookies

Styled after the regular 1992 Score Pinnacle cards, this 30-card boxed set features the top rookies of 1992. The cards have a player action photo which is borderless on the top and sides. Beneath the photo a team color-coded strip carries the player's name in gold foil, with a round gold-bordered team logo at left. A black strip at bottom has the notation "1992 Rookie".

Horizontal-format backs follow a similar design and include a bit of player information, Pinnacle's anti-counterfeiting strip and some gold-foil enhancements.

		MT
Complete Set (30):		6.00
Common Player:		.20
1	Luis Mercedes	.25
2	Scott Cooper	.20
3	Kenny Lofton	2.00
4	John Doherty	.25
5	Pat Listach	.25
6	Andy Stankiewicz	.20
7	Derek Bell	.35
8	Gary DiSarcina	.20
9	Roberto Hernandez	.25
10	Joel Johnston	.25
11	Pat Mahomes	.25
12	Todd Van Poppel	.20
13	Dave Fleming	.20
14	Monty Fariss	.20
15	Gary Scott	.20
16	Moises Alou	.40
17	Todd Hundley	.25
18	Kim Batiste	.20
19	Denny Neagle	.25
20	Donovan Osborne	.20
21	Mark Wohlers	.20
22	Reggie Sanders	.40
23	Brian Williams	.20
24	Eric Karros	.75
25	Frank Seminara	.20
26	Royce Clayton	.20
27	Dave Nilsson	.30
28	Matt Stairs	.20
29	Chad Curtis	.35
30	Carlos Hernandez	.20

1992 Pinnacle Slugfest

Each specially marked Slugfest jumbo pack of '92 Pinnacle contained one of these horizontal-format cards of the game's top hitters. The player's name is printed in gold foil at the bottom of the card, along with a red and white Slugfest logo. Backs, which are vertical in orientation, have a color player photo, a career summary and a few lifetime stats. er photo, a career summary and a few lifetime stats.

		MT
Complete Set (15):		35.00
Common Player:		1.00
1	Cecil Fielder	1.50
2	Mark McGwire	12.00
3	Jose Canseco	1.50
4	Barry Bonds	3.00
5	Dave Justice	1.00
6	Bobby Bonilla	1.00
7	Ken Griffey, Jr.	12.00
8	Ron Gant	1.00
9	Ryne Sandberg	3.00
10	Ruben Sierra	1.00
11	Frank Thomas	10.00
12	Will Clark	2.00
13	Kirby Puckett	4.00
14	Cal Ripken, Jr.	9.00
15	Jeff Bagwell	4.00

1992 Pinnacle Team Pinnacle

The most sought-after and valuable of the 1992 Pinnacle insert cards is this 12-piece set of "two-headed" cards. An American and a National League superstar at each position are featured on each card, with two cards each for starting and relief pitchers. The ultra-realistic artwork of Chris Greco is featured on the cards, which were inserted into Series I foil packs.

		MT
Complete Set (12):		100.00
Common Player:		4.00
1	Roger Clemens, Ramon Martinez	10.00
2	Jim Abbott, Steve Avery	5.00
3	Benito Santiago, Ivan Rodriguez	5.00
4	Frank Thomas, Will Clark	25.00
5	Roberto Alomar, Ryne Sandberg	15.00
6	Robin Ventura, Matt Williams	8.00
7	Cal Ripken, Jr., Barry Larkin	25.00
8	Danny Tartabull, Barry Bonds	10.00
9	Brett Butler, Ken Griffey Jr.	25.00
10	Ruben Sierra, Dave Justice	10.00
11	Dennis Eckersley, Rob Dibble	4.00
12	Scott Radinsky, John Franco	4.00

1992 Pinnacle Team 2000

Young stars who were projected to be the game's superstars in the year 2000 were chosen for this 80-card insert set found three at a time in jumbo packs. Cards #1-40 were included in Series I packaging, while cards #41-80 were inserted with Series II Pinnacle. Cards feature gold foil highlights on both front and back.

		MT
Complete Set (80):		30.00
Common Player:		.10
1	Mike Mussina	1.25
2	Phil Plantier	.10
3	Frank Thomas	4.00
4	Travis Fryman	.20
5	Kevin Appier	.10
6	Chuck Knoblauch	.40
7	Pat Kelly	.10
8	Ivan Rodriguez	1.00
9	Dave Justice	.25
10	Jeff Bagwell	2.00
11	Marquis Grissom	.20
12	Andy Benes	.10
13	Gregg Olson	.10
14	Kevin Morton	.10
15	Tim Naehring	.10
16	Dave Hollins	.10
17	Sandy Alomar Jr.	.10
18	Albert Belle	1.25
19	Charles Nagy	.10
20	Brian McRae	.10
21	Larry Walker	.40
22	Delino DeShields	.10
23	Jeff Johnson	.10
24	Bernie Williams	1.00
25	Jose Offerman	.10
26	Juan Gonzalez	2.00
27	Juan Guzman	.10
28	Eric Anthony	.10
29	Brian Hunter	.10
30	John Smoltz	.30
31	Deion Sanders	.30
32	Greg Maddux	2.50
33	Andujar Cedeno	.10
34	Royce Clayton	.10
35	Kenny Lofton	1.50
36	Cal Eldred	.10
37	Jim Thome	.60
38	Gary DiSarcina	.10
39	Brian Jordan	.75
40	Chad Curtis	.10
41	Ben McDonald	.10
42	Jim Abbott	.15
43	Robin Ventura	.25
44	Milt Cuyler	.10
45	Gregg Jefferies	.15
46	Scott Radinsky	.10
47	Ken Griffey, Jr.	5.00
48	Roberto Alomar	1.50
49	Ramon Martinez	.10
50	Bret Barberie	.10
51	Ray Lankford	.20
52	Leo Gomez	.10
53	Tommy Greene	.20
54	Mo Vaughn	1.50
55	Sammy Sosa	3.00
56	Carlos Baerga	.10
57	Mark Lewis	.10
58	Carlos Baerga	.20
59	Gary Sheffield	.65
60	Scott Erickson	.10
61	Pedro Munoz	.10
62	Tino Martinez	.15
63	Darren Lewis	.10
64	Dean Palmer	.10
65	John Olerud	.15
66	Steve Avery	.10
67	Pete Harnisch	.10
68	Luis Gonzalez	.10
69	Kim Batiste	.10
70	Reggie Sanders	.15
71	Luis Mercedes	.10
72	Todd Van Poppel	.10
73	Gary Scott	.10
74	Monty Fariss	.10
75	Kyle Abbott	.10
76	Eric Karros	.25
77	Mo Sanford	.10
78	Todd Hundley	.50
79	Reggie Jefferson	.10
80	Pat Mahomes	.15

1993 Pinnacle

Ruben Sierra   PINNACLE

This 620-card set offers many of the same features which made the first Pinnacle set so popular in 1992. Subsets are titled Rookies, Now & Then (which shows the player as he looks now and as a rookie), Idols (active players and their heroes on the same card), Hometown Heroes (players who are playing with their hometown team), Draft Picks and Rookies. More than 100 rookies and 10 draft picks are featured. All regular cards have an action photo, a black border and the Pinnacle name stamped in gold. Series I cards feature portraits of players on the two new expansion teams; Series II cards feature action shots of them. Team Pinnacle insert cards return, while Rookie Team Pinnacle cards make their debut. Other insert sets are titled Team 2001, Slugfest and Tribute, which features five cards each of Nolan Ryan and George Brett.

		MT
Complete Set (620):		50.00
Complete Series 1 (310):		25.00
Complete Series 2 (310):		25.00
Common Player:		.05
Series 1 or 2 Wax Box:		45.00
1	Gary Sheffield	.30
2	Cal Eldred	.15
3	Larry Walker	.25
4	Deion Sanders	.25
5	Dave Fleming	.10
6	Carlos Baerga	.10
7	Bernie Williams	.40
8	John Kruk	.08
9	Jimmy Key	.05
10	Jeff Bagwell	1.00
11	Jim Abbott	.05
12	Terry Steinbach	.05
13	Bob Tewksbury	.05
14	Eric Karros	.15
15	Ryne Sandberg	.60
16	Will Clark	.30
17	Edgar Martinez	.15
18	Eddie Murray	.20
19	Andy Van Slyke	.05
20	Cal Ripken, Jr.	2.50
21	Ivan Rodriguez	.50
22	Barry Larkin	.20
23	Don Mattingly	1.00
24	Gregg Jefferies	.05
25	Roger Clemens	1.00
26	Cecil Fielder	.20
27	Kent Hrbek	.05
28	Robin Ventura	.08
29	Rickey Henderson	.15
30	Roberto Alomar	.60
31	Luis Polonia	.05
32	Andujar Cedeno	.05

33	Pat Listach	.08
34	Mark Grace	.20
35	Otis Nixon	.05
36	Felix Jose	.05
37	Mike Sharperson	.05
38	Dennis Martinez	.05
39	Willie McGee	.05
40	Kenny Lofton	.75
41	Randy Johnson	.40
42	Andy Benes	.05
43	Bobby Bonilla	.10
44	Mike Mussina	.60
45	Len Dykstra	.15
46	Ellis Burks	.05
47	Chris Sabo	.05
48	Jay Bell	.05
49	Jose Canseco	.25
50	Craig Biggio	.20
51	Wally Joyner	.05
52	Mickey Tettleton	.05
53	Tim Raines	.05
54	Brian Harper	.05
55	Rene Gonzales	.05
56	Mark Langston	.05
57	Jack Morris	.05
58	Mark McGwire	3.00
59	Ken Caminiti	.15
60	Terry Pendleton	.05
61	Dave Nilsson	.05
62	Tom Pagnozzi	.05
63	Mike Morgan	.05
64	Darryl Strawberry	.10
65	Charles Nagy	.05
66	Ken Hill	.05
67	Matt Williams	.25
68	Jay Buhner	.15
69	Vince Coleman	.05
70	Brady Anderson	.05
71	Fred McGriff	.30
72	Ben McDonald	.05
73	Terry Mulholland	.05
74	Randy Tomlin	.05
75	Nolan Ryan	2.50
76	Frank Viola	.05
77	Jose Rijo	.05
78	Shane Mack	.05
79	Travis Fryman	.15
80	Jack McDowell	.10
81	Mark Gubicza	.05
82	Matt Nokes	.05
83	Bert Blyleven	.05
84	Eric Anthony	.05
85	Mike Bordick	.15
86	John Olerud	.15
87	B.J. Surhoff	.05
88	Bernard Gilkey	.05
89	Shawon Dunston	.05
90	Tom Glavine	.15
91	Brett Butler	.05
92	Moises Alou	.15
93	Albert Belle	.75
94	Darren Lewis	.05
95	Omar Vizquel	.05
96	Dwight Gooden	.10
97	Gregg Olson	.05
98	Tony Gwynn	1.00
99	Darren Daulton	.05
100	Dennis Eckersley	.05
101	Rob Dibble	.05
102	Mike Greenwell	.05
103	Jose Lind	.05
104	Julio Franco	.05
105	Tom Gordon	.05
106	Scott Livingstone	.05
107	Chuck Knoblauch	.20
108	Frank Thomas	3.00
109	Melido Perez	.05
110	Ken Griffey, Jr.	3.00
111	Harold Baines	.05
112	Gary Gaetti	.05
113	Pete Harnisch	.05
114	David Wells	.05
115	Charlie Leibrandt	.05
116	Ray Lankford	.20
117	Kevin Seitzer	.05
118	Robin Yount	.30
119	Lenny Harris	.05
120	Chris James	.05
121	Delino DeShields	.05
122	Kirt Manwaring	.05
123	Glenallen Hill	.05
124	Hensley Meulens	.05
125	Darrin Jackson	.05
126	Todd Hundley	.15
127	Dave Hollins	.15
128	Sam Horn	.05

129	Roberto Hernandez	.05
130	Vicente Palacios	.05
131	George Brett	.75
132	Dave Martinez	.05
133	Kevin Appier	.05
134	Pat Kelly	.05
135	Pedro Munoz	.05
136	Mark Carreon	.05
137	Lance Johnson	.05
138	Devon White	.05
139	Julio Valera	.05
140	Eddie Taubensee	.05
141	Willie Wilson	.05
142	Stan Belinda	.05
143	John Smoltz	.15
144	Darryl Hamilton	.05
145	Sammy Sosa	1.50
146	Carlos Hernandez	.05
147	Tom Candiotti	.05
148	Mike Felder	.05
149	Rusty Meacham	.05
150	Ivan Calderon	.05
151	Pete O'Brien	.05
152	Erik Hanson	.05
153	Billy Ripken	.05
154	Kurt Stillwell	.05
155	Jeff Kent	.05
156	Mickey Morandini	.05
157	Randy Milligan	.05
158	Reggie Sanders	.15
159	Luis Rivera	.05
160	Orlando Merced	.05
161	Dean Palmer	.05
162	Mike Perez	.05
163	Scott Erikson	.05
164	Kevin McReynolds	.05
165	Kevin Maas	.05
166	Ozzie Guillen	.05
167	Rob Deer	.05
168	Danny Tartabull	.05
169	Lee Stevens	.05
170	Dave Henderson	.05
171	Derek Bell	.05
172	Steve Finley	.05
173	Greg Olson	.05
174	Geronimo Pena	.05
175	Paul Quantrill	.05
176	Steve Buechele	.05
177	Kevin Gross	.05
178	Tim Wallach	.05
179	Dave Valle	.05
180	Dave Silvestri	.05
181	Bud Black	.05
182	Henry Rodriguez	.05
183	Tim Teufel	.05
184	Mark McLemore	.05
185	Bret Saberhagen	.05
186	Chris Hoiles	.05
187	Ricky Jordan	.05
188	Don Slaught	.05
189	Mo Vaughn	.75
190	Joe Oliver	.05
191	Juan Gonzalez	1.00
192	Scott Leius	.05
193	Milt Cuyler	.05
194	Chris Haney	.05
195	Ron Karkovice	.05
196	Steve Farr	.05
197	John Orton	.05
198	Kelly Gruber	.05
199	Ron Darling	.05
200	Ruben Sierra	.10
201	Chuck Finley	.05
202	Mike Moore	.05
203	Pat Borders	.05
204	Sid Bream	.05
205	Todd Zeile	.05
206	Rick Wilkins	.05
207	Jim Gantner	.05
208	Frank Castillo	.05
209	Dave Hansen	.05
210	Trevor Wilson	.05
211	Sandy Alomar, Jr.	.15
212	Sean Berry	.05
213	Tino Martinez	.25
214	Chito Martinez	.05
215	Dan Walters	.05
216	John Franco	.05
217	Glenn Davis	.05
218	Mariano Duncan	.05
219	Mike LaValliere	.05
220	Rafael Palmeiro	.20
221	Jack Clark	.05
222	Hal Morris	.05
223	Ed Sprague	.05
224	John Valentin	.10
225	Sam Militello	.05
226	Bob Wickman	.05
227	Damion Easley	.15
228	John Jaha	.10
229	Bob Ayrault	.05
230	Mo Sanford (Expansion Draft)	.05
231	Walt Weiss (Expansion Draft)	.05
232	Dante Bichette (Expansion Draft)	.35
233	Steve Decker (Expansion Draft)	.05
234	Jerald Clark (Expansion Draft)	.05
235	Bryan Harvey (Expansion Draft)	.05
236	Joe Girardi (Expansion Draft)	.05
237	Dave Magadan (Expansion Draft)	.05
238	David Nied (Rookie Prospect)	.10
239	*Eric Wedge* (Rookie Prospect)	.15
240	Rico Brogna (Rookie Prospect)	.05
241	J.T. Bruett (Rookie Prospect)	.05
242	Jonathan Hurst (Rookie Prospect)	.05
243	Bret Boone (Rookie Prospect)	.25
244	Manny Alexander (Rookie Prospect)	.15
245	Scooter Tucker (Rookie Prospect)	.05
246	Troy Neel (Rookie Prospect)	.10
247	Eddie Zosky (Rookie Prospect)	.05
248	Melvin Nieves (Rookie Prospect)	.15
249	Ryan Thompson (Rookie Prospect)	.12
250	Shawn Barton (Rookie Prospect)	.15
251	Ryan Klesko (Rookie Prospect)	.75
252	Mike Piazza (Rookie Prospect)	2.50
253	Steve Hosey (Rookie Prospect)	.15
254	Shane Reynolds (Rookie Prospect)	.05
255	Dan Wilson (Rookie Prospect)	.15
256	Tom Marsh (Rookie Prospect)	.05
257	Barry Manuel (Rookie Prospect)	.05
258	Paul Miller (Rookie Prospect)	.05
259	Pedro Martinez (Rookie Prospect)	.25
260	Steve Cooke (Rookie Prospect)	.15
261	Johnny Guzman (Rookie Prospect)	.05
262	Mike Butcher (Rookie Prospect)	.08
263	Bien Figueroa (Rookie Prospect)	.08
264	Rich Rowland (Rookie Prospect)	.08
265	Shawn Jeter (Rookie Prospect)	.10
266	Gerald Williams (Rookie Prospect)	.08
267	Derek Parks (Rookie Prospect)	.05
268	Henry Mercedes (Rookie Prospect)	.08
269	*David Hulse* (Rookie Prospect)	.10
270	*Tim Pugh* (Rookie Prospect)	.10
271	William Suero (Rookie Prospect)	.05
272	Ozzie Canseco (Rookie Prospect)	.05
273	Fernando Ramsey (Rookie Prospect)	.12
274	Bernardo Brito (Rookie Prospect)	.05
275	Dave Mlicki (Rookie Prospect)	.08
276	Tim Salmon (Rookie Prospect)	.60
277	Mike Raczka (Rookie Prospect)	.05
278	*Ken Ryan* (Rookie Prospect)	.25
279	Rafael Bournigal (Rookie Prospect)	.10
280	Wil Cordero (Rookie Prospect)	.15
281	Billy Ashley (Rookie Prospect)	.15
282	Paul Wagner (Rookie Prospect)	.10
283	Blas Minor (Rookie Prospect)	.10
284	Rick Trlicek (Rookie Prospect)	.05
285	Willie Greene (Rookie Prospect)	.15
286	Ted Wood (Rookie Prospect)	.05
287	Phil Clark (Rookie Prospect)	.05
288	Jesse Levis (Rookie Prospect)	.08
289	Tony Gwynn (Now & Then)	.40
290	Nolan Ryan (Now & Then)	1.00
291	Dennis Martinez (Now & Then)	.05
292	Eddie Murray (Now & Then)	.15
293	Robin Yount (Now & Then)	.30
294	George Brett (Now & Then)	.40
295	Dave Winfield (Now & Then)	.15
296	Bert Blyleven (Now & Then)	.05
297	Jeff Bagwell (Idols - Carl Yastrzemski)	.40
298	John Smoltz (Idols - Jack Morris)	.10
299	Larry Walker (Idols - Mike Bossy)	.20
300	Gary Sheffield (Idols - Barry Larkin)	.15
301	Ivan Rodriguez (Idols - Carlton Fisk)	.25
302	Delino DeShields (Idols - Malcolm X)	.05
303	Tim Salmon (Idols - Dwight Evans)	.25
304	Bernard Gilkey (Hometown Heroes)	.05
305	Cal Ripken, Jr. (Hometown Heroes)	1.00
306	Barry Larkin (Hometown Heroes)	.10
307	Kent Hrbek (Hometown Heroes)	.05
308	Rickey Henderson (Hometown Heroes)	.05
309	Darryl Strawberry (Hometown Heroes)	.05
310	John Franco (Hometown Heroes)	.05
311	Todd Stottlemyre	.05
312	Luis Gonzalez	.05
313	Tommy Greene	.05
314	Randy Velarde	.05
315	Steve Avery	.10
316	Jose Oquendo	.05
317	Rey Sanchez	.05
318	Greg Vaughn	.08
319	Orel Hershiser	.05
320	Paul Sorrento	.05
321	Royce Clayton	.05
322	John Vander Wal	.05
323	Henry Cotto	.05
324	Pete Schourek	.05
325	David Segui	.05
326	Arthur Rhodes	.05
327	Bruce Hurst	.05
328	Wes Chamberlain	.05
329	Ozzie Smith	.35
330	Scott Cooper	.10
331	Felix Fermin	.05
332	Mike Macfarlane	.05
333	Dan Gladden	.05
334	Kevin Tapani	.05
335	Steve Sax	.05
336	Jeff Montgomery	.05
337	Gary DiSarcina	.05
338	Lance Blankenship	.05
339	Brian Williams	.05
340	Duane Ward	.05
341	Chuck McElroy	.05
342	Joe Magrane	.05
343	Jaime Navarro	.05
344	Dave Justice	.25
345	Jose Offerman	.05

#	Player	Value
346	Marquis Grissom	.15
347	Bill Swift	.05
348	Jim Thome	.50
349	Archi Cianfrocco	.05
350	Anthony Young	.05
351	Leo Gomez	.05
352	Bill Gullickson	.05
353	Alan Trammell	.05
354	Dan Pasqua	.05
355	Jeff King	.05
356	Kevin Brown	.05
357	Tim Belcher	.05
358	Bip Roberts	.05
359	Brent Mayne	.05
360	Rheal Cormier	.05
361	Mark Guthrie	.05
362	Craig Grebeck	.05
363	Andy Stankiewicz	.05
364	Juan Guzman	.08
365	Bobby Witt	.05
366	Mark Portugal	.05
367	Brian McRae	.05
368	Mark Lemke	.05
369	Bill Wegman	.05
370	Donovan Osborne	.05
371	Derrick May	.08
372	Carl Willis	.05
373	Chris Nabholz	.05
374	Mark Lewis	.05
375	John Burkett	.05
376	Luis Mercedes	.05
377	Ramon Martinez	.20
378	Kyle Abbott	.05
379	Mark Wohlers	.05
380	Bob Walk	.05
381	Kenny Rogers	.05
382	Tim Naehring	.05
383	Alex Fernandez	.05
384	Keith Miller	.05
385	Mike Henneman	.05
386	Rick Aguilera	.05
387	George Bell	.05
388	Mike Gallego	.05
389	Howard Johnson	.05
390	Kim Batiste	.05
391	Jerry Browne	.05
392	Damon Berryhill	.05
393	Ricky Bones	.05
394	Omar Olivares	.05
395	Mike Harkey	.05
396	Pedro Astacio	.15
397	John Wetteland	.05
398	Rod Beck	.05
399	Thomas Howard	.05
400	Mike Devereaux	.05
401	Tim Wakefield	.10
402	Curt Schilling	.05
403	Zane Smith	.05
404	Bob Zupcic	.05
405	Tom Browning	.05
406	Tony Phillips	.05
407	John Doherty	.05
408	Pat Mahomes	.05
409	John Habyan	.05
410	Steve Olin	.05
411	Chad Curtis	.15
412	Joe Grahe	.05
413	John Patterson	.05
414	Brian Hunter	.05
415	Doug Henry	.05
416	Lee Smith	.05
417	Bob Scanlan	.05
418	Kent Mercker	.05
419	Mel Rojas	.05
420	Mark Whiten	.05
421	Carlton Fisk	.12
422	Candy Maldonado	.05
423	Doug Drabek	.05
424	Wade Boggs	.20
425	Mark Davis	.05
426	Kirby Puckett	1.00
427	Joe Carter	.20
428	Paul Molitor	.40
429	Eric Davis	.08
430	Darryl Kile	.05
431	Jeff Parrett (Expansion Draft)	.05
432	Jeff Blauser	.05
433	Dan Plesac	.05
434	Andres Galarraga (Expansion Draft)	.15
435	Jim Gott	.05
436	Jose Mesa	.05
437	Ben Rivera	.05
438	Dave Winfield	.15
439	Norm Charlton	.05
440	Chris Bosio	.05
441	Wilson Alvarez	.05
442	Dave Stewart	.05
443	Doug Jones	.05
444	Jeff Russell	.05
445	Ron Gant	.12
446	Paul O'Neill	.15
447	Charlie Hayes (Expansion Draft)	.05
448	Joe Hesketh	.05
449	Chris Hammond	.05
450	Hipolito Pichardo	.05
451	Scott Radinsky	.05
452	Bobby Thigpen	.05
453	Xavier Hernandez	.08
454	Lonnie Smith	.05
455	*Jamie Arnold* (1st Draft Pick)	.25
456	B.J. Wallace (1st Draft Pick)	.15
457	*Derek Jeter* (Rookie Prospect)	6.00
458	*Jason Kendall* (Rookie Prospect)	1.50
459	Rick Helling (Rookie Prospect)	.15
460	*Derek Wallace* (Rookie Prospect)	.25
461	*Sean Lowe* (Rookie Prospect)	.25
462	*Shannon Stewart* (Rookie Prospect)	.50
463	*Benji Grigsby* (Rookie Prospect)	.25
464	*Todd Steverson* (Rookie Prospect)	.25
465	*Dan Serafini* (Rookie Prospect)	.25
466	Michael Tucker (Rookie Prospect)	.15
467	Chris Roberts (Rookie Prospect)	.25
468	*Pete Janicki* (1st Draft Pick)	.15
469	*Jeff Schmidt* (1st Draft Pick)	.15
470	Don Mattingly (Now & Then)	.40
471	Cal Ripken, Jr. (Now & Then)	1.00
472	Jack Morris (Now & Then)	.05
473	Terry Pendleton (Now & Then)	.05
474	Dennis Eckersley (Now & Then)	.10
475	Carlton Fisk (Now & Then)	.12
476	Wade Boggs (Now & Then)	.20
477	Len Dykstra (Idols - Ken Stabler)	.12
478	Danny Tartabull (Idols - Jose Tartabull)	.15
479	Jeff Conine (Idols - Dale Murphy)	.10
480	Gregg Jefferies (Idols - Ron Cey)	.15
481	Paul Molitor (Idols - Harmon Killebrew)	.20
482	John Valentin (Idols - Dave Concepcion)	.10
483	Alex Arias (Idols - Dave Winfield)	.10
484	Barry Bonds (Hometown Heroes)	.50
485	Doug Drabek (Hometown Heroes)	.08
486	Dave Winfield (Hometown Heroes)	.12
487	Brett Butler (Hometown Heroes)	.10
488	Harold Baines (Hometown Heroes)	.10
489	David Cone (Hometown Heroes)	.15
490	Willie McGee (Hometown Heroes)	.10
491	Robby Thompson	.05
492	Pete Incaviglia	.05
493	Manuel Lee	.05
494	Rafael Belliard	.05
495	Scott Fletcher	.05
496	Jeff Frye	.05
497	Andre Dawson	.15
498	Mike Scioscia	.05
499	Spike Owen	.05
500	Sid Fernandez	.05
501	Joe Orsulak	.05
502	Benito Santiago (Expansion Draft)	.05
503	Dale Murphy	.05
504	Barry Bonds	.75
505	Jose Guzman	.05
506	Tony Pena	.05
507	Greg Swindell	.05
508	Mike Pagliarulo	.05
509	Lou Whitaker	.05
510	Greg Gagne	.05
511	Butch Henry (Expansion Draft)	.05
512	Jeff Brantley	.05
513	Jack Armstrong (Expansion Draft)	.05
514	Danny Jackson	.05
515	Junior Felix (Expansion Draft)	.05
516	Milt Thompson	.05
517	Greg Maddux	2.00
518	Eric Young (Expansion Draft)	.05
519	Jody Reed	.05
520	Roberto Kelly	.05
521	Darren Holmes (Expansion Draft)	.05
522	Craig Lefferts	.05
523	Charlie Hough (Expansion Draft)	.05
524	Bo Jackson	.15
525	Bill Spiers	.05
526	Orestes Destrade (Expansion Draft)	.05
527	Greg Hibbard	.05
528	Roger McDowell	.05
529	Cory Snyder	.05
530	Harold Reynolds	.05
531	Kevin Reimer	.05
532	Rick Sutcliffe	.05
533	Tony Fernandez	.05
534	Tom Brunansky	.05
535	Jeff Reardon	.05
536	Chili Davis	.05
537	Bob Ojeda	.05
538	Greg Colbrunn	.05
539	Phil Plantier	.08
540	Brian Jordan	.12
541	Pete Smith	.05
542	Frank Tanana	.05
543	John Smiley	.05
544	David Cone	.05
545	Daryl Boston (Expansion Draft)	.05
546	Tom Henke	.05
547	Bill Krueger	.05
548	Freddie Benavides (Expansion Draft)	.05
549	Randy Myers	.05
550	Reggie Jefferson	.05
551	Kevin Mitchell	.05
552	Dave Stieb	.05
553	Bret Barberie (Expansion Draft)	.05
554	Tim Crews	.05
555	Doug Dascenzo	.05
556	Alex Cole (Expansion Draft)	.05
557	Jeff Innis	.05
558	Carlos Garcia	.15
559	Steve Howe	.05
560	Kirk McCaskill	.05
561	Frank Seminara	.05
562	Cris Carpenter (Expansion Draft)	.05
563	Mike Stanley	.05
564	Carlos Quintana	.05
565	Mitch Williams	.05
566	Juan Bell	.05
567	Eric Fox	.05
568	Al Leiter	.05
569	Mike Stanton	.05
570	Scott Kamieniecki	.05
571	Ryan Bowen (Expansion Draft)	.05
572	Andy Ashby (Expansion Draft)	.05
573	Bob Welch	.05
574	Scott Sanderson	.05
575	Joe Kmak (Rookie Prospect)	.05
576	Scott Pose (Rookie Prospect/ Expansion Draft)	.15
577	Ricky Gutierrez (Rookie Prospect)	.15
578	Mike Trombley (Rookie Prospect)	.12
579	*Sterling Hitchcock* (Rookie Prospect)	.25
580	Rodney Bolton (Rookie Prospect)	.12
581	Tyler Green (Rookie Prospect)	.15

582	Tim Costo (Rookie Prospect)	.12
583	*Tim Laker* (Rookie Prospect)	.15
584	*Steve Reed* (Rookie Prospect/ Expansion Draft)	.12
585	Tom Kramer (Rookie Prospect)	.15
586	Robb Nen (Rookie Prospect)	.10
587	*Jim Tatum* (Rookie Prospect)	.08
588	Frank Bolick (Rookie Prospect)	.15
589	Kevin Young (Rookie Prospect)	.15
590	*Matt Whiteside* (Rookie Prospect)	.15
591	Cesar Hernandez (Rookie Prospect)	.15
592	*Mike Mohler* (Rookie Prospect)	.15
593	Alan Embree (Rookie Prospect)	.15
594	Terry Jorgensen (Rookie Prospect)	.08
595	*John Cummings* (Rookie Prospect)	.25
596	Domingo Martinez (Rookie Prospect)	.12
597	Benji Gil (Rookie Prospect)	.15
598	*Todd Pratt* (Rookie Prospect)	.15
599	*Rene Arocha* (Rookie Prospect)	.25
600	Dennis Moeller (Rookie Prospect)	.20
601	Jeff Conine (Rookie Prospect/ Expansion Draft)	.25
602	Trevor Hoffman (Rookie Prospect/ Expansion Draft)	.15
603	Daniel Smith (Rookie Prospect)	.12
604	Lee Tinsley (Rookie Prospect)	.12
605	Dan Peltier (Rookie Prospect)	.12
606	Billy Brewer (Rookie Prospect)	.15
607	Matt Walbeck (Rookie Prospect)	.20
608	Richie Lewis (Rookie Prospect/ Expansion Draft)	.12
609	*J.T. Snow* (Rookie Prospect)	.75
610	Pat Gomez (Rookie Prospect)	.12
611	Phil Hiatt (Rookie Prospect)	.10
612	Alex Arias (Rookie Prospect/ Expansion Draft)	.12
613	Kevin Rogers (Rookie Prospect)	.15
614	Al Martin (Rookie Prospect)	.15
615	Greg Gohr (Rookie Prospect)	.12
616	*Grame Lloyd* (Rookie Prospect)	.15
617	Kent Bottenfield (Rookie Prospect)	.15
618	Chuck Carr (Rookie Prospect/ Expansion Draft)	.15
619	*Darrell Sherman* (Rookie Prospect)	.10
620	*Mike Lansing* (Rookie Prospect)	.25

1993 Pinnacle Expansion Opening Day

This nine-card set features 18 players for the two N.L. expansion teams: the Florida Marlins and Colorado Rockies. Each card side shows a projected Opening Day starter for each team. Cards were available one per every Series II hobby box. Complete sets were available through a special mail-in offer.

A player's name in *italic* type indicates a rookie card.

		MT
Complete Set (9):		5.00
Common Player:		.35
1	Charlie Hough, David Nied	.75
2	Benito Santiago, Joe Girardi	.45
3	Orestes Destrade, Andres Galarraga	1.50
4	Bret Barberie, Eric Young	.40
5	Dave Magadan, Charlie Hayes	.75
6	Walt Weiss, Freddie Benevides	.40
7	Jeff Conine, Jerald Clark	.50
8	Scott Pose, Alex Cole	.40
9	Junior Felix, Dante Bichette	.75

1993 Pinnacle Rookie Team Pinnacle

These 10 cards were randomly inserted into Score Pinnacle Series II packs. Rookie Team Pinnacle is written in gold foil on both sides of the card. Cards are numbered 1 of 10, etc., and use the special Dufex process. Each card shows two players painted by artist Christopher Greco. Stated odds of finding a Rookie Team Pinnacle insert were given as one in 90 packs.

		MT
Complete Set (10):		90.00
Common Player:		5.00
1	Pedro Martinez, Mike Trombley	10.00
2	Kevin Rogers, Sterling Hitchcock	5.00
3	Mike Piazza, Jesse Levis	50.00
4	Ryan Klesko, J.T. Snow	12.00
5	John Patterson, Bret Boone	5.00

6	Domingo Martinez, Kevin Young	5.00
7	Wil Cordero, Manny Alexander	8.00
8	Steve Hosey, Tim Salmon	15.00
9	Ryan Thompson, Gerald Williams	5.00
10	Melvin Nieves, David Hulse	5.00

1993 Pinnacle Slugfest

Baseball's top sluggers are featured in this 30-card insert set. Cards were available one per Series II jumbo packs. Slugfest is written in gold foil on the card front.

		MT
Complete Set (30):		45.00
Common Player:		.50
1	Juan Gonzalez	2.50
2	Mark McGwire	15.00
3	Cecil Fielder	1.25
4	Joe Carter	1.00
5	Fred McGriff	1.50
6	Barry Bonds	3.50
7	Gary Sheffield	.75
8	Dave Hollins	.50
9	Frank Thomas	12.00
10	Danny Tartabull	.50
11	Albert Belle	3.00
12	Ruben Sierra	.50
13	Larry Walker	1.00
14	Jeff Bagwell	3.50
15	Dave Justice	.75
16	Kirby Puckett	5.00
17	John Kruk	.50
18	Howard Johnson	.50
19	Darryl Strawberry	.50
20	Will Clark	1.50
21	Kevin Mitchell	.50
22	Mickey Tettleton	.50
23	Don Mattingly	5.00
24	Jose Canseco	1.50
25	Sam Millitello	.50
26	Andre Dawson	.75
27	Ryne Sandberg	3.00
28	Ken Griffey, Jr.	15.00
29	Carlos Baerga	.75
30	Travis Fryman	1.00

1993 Pinnacle Team Pinnacle

These cards were randomly inserted in Pinnacle Series I packs; cards were included one in about every 24 packs. Each card features two players painted by artist Christopher Greco. An eleventh card, featuring relief pitchers, was available only via a mail-in offer.

		MT
Complete Set (11):		90.00
Common Player:		6.00
1	Greg Maddux, Mike Mussina	25.00
2	Tom Glavine, John Smiley	4.00
3	Darren Daulton, Ivan Rodriguez	8.00
4	Fred McGriff, Frank Thomas	30.00
5	Delino DeShields, Carlos Baerga	3.00
6	Gary Sheffield, Edgar Martinez	6.00
7	Ozzie Smith, Pat Listach	6.00
8	Barry Bonds, Juan Gonzalez	15.00
9	Kirby Puckett, Andy Van Slyke	10.00
10	Larry Walker, Joe Carter	5.00
11	Rick Aguilera, Rob Dibble	3.00

1993 Pinnacle Team 2001

This insert set features 30 players who are expected to be stars in the year 2001. Cards were randomly inserted into 27-card jumbo packs from Series I.

		MT
Complete Set (30):		25.00
Common Player:		.40
1	Wil Cordero	.40
2	Cal Eldred	.40
3	Mike Mussina	2.00
4	Chuck Knoblauch	1.00
5	Melvin Nieves	.40
6	Tim Wakefield	.40
7	Carlos Baerga	.40
8	Bret Boone	.40
9	Jeff Bagwell	4.00
10	Travis Fryman	.75
11	Royce Clayton	.40

12	Delino DeShields	.40
13	Juan Gonzalez	2.50
14	Pedro Martinez	1.00
15	Bernie Williams	2.00
16	Billy Ashley	.75
17	Marquis Grissom	.75
18	Kenny Lofton	2.50
19	Ray Lankford	.40
20	Tim Salmon	1.50
21	Steve Hosey	.40
22	Charles Nagy	.40
23	Dave Fleming	.40
24	Reggie Sanders	.40
25	Sam Militello	.40
26	Eric Karros	.75
27	Ryan Klesko	1.50
28	Dean Palmer	.40
29	Ivan Rodriguez	3.00
30	Sterling Hitchcock	.40

1993 Pinnacle Tribute

These two future Hall of Famers each have five-card sets devoted to their career achievements. Each card commemorates a milestone reached by George Brett or Nolan Ryan. Cards were random inserts in 1993 Score Pinnacle Series II packs, about one per every 24 packs. Fronts have a gold-foil stamped "Tribute" vertically at right.

		MT
Complete Set (10):		60.00
George Brett Card (1-5):		5.00
Nolan Ryan Card (6-10):		10.00
1	Kansas City Royalty(George Brett)	6.00
2	The Chase for .400(George Brett)	6.00
3	Pine Tar Pandemonium - "The Bat"	6.00
4	MVP and a World Series, Too(George Brett)	6.00
5	3,000 or Bust(George Brett)	6.00
6	The Rookie(Nolan Ryan)	10.00
7	Angel of No Mercy(Nolan Ryan)	10.00
8	Astronomical Success(Nolan Ryan)	10.00
9	5,000 Ks(Nolan Ryan)	10.00
10	No-Hitter No. 7(Nolan Ryan)	10.00

1994 Pinnacle

Typical of each card company's 1994 mid-priced brand, Pinnacle features full bleed photos, gold-foil stamping and UV coating. On front, player and team names appear in a shield-and-bar motif in the lower-left corner. On horizontal backs, the front photo is reproduced as a subdued background photo, over which are printed recent stats and a few biographical details. A different player photo is featured at left. Pinnacle's trademarks appear at lower-right, while the brand's optical-variable anti-counterfeiting device is at bottom center. Subsets include major award winners, Rookie Prospects and Draft Picks which are appropriately noted with gold-foil lettering on front. The issue was produced in two series of 270 cards each.

		MT
Complete Set (540):		35.00
Complete Series 1 (270):		20.00
Complete Series 2 (270):		15.00
Common Player:		.10
Series 1 & 2 Wax Box:		38.00
1	Frank Thomas	2.50
2	Carlos Baerga	.15
3	Sammy Sosa	1.50
4	Tony Gwynn	1.00
5	John Olerud	.15
6	Ryne Sandberg	.75
7	Moises Alou	.15
8	Steve Avery	.15
9	Tim Salmon	.40
10	Cecil Fielder	.25
11	Greg Maddux	2.00
12	Barry Larkin	.20
13	Mike Devereaux	.10
14	Charlie Hayes	.10
15	Albert Belle	.75
16	Andy Van Slyke	.10
17	Mo Vaughn	.50
18	Brian McRae	.10
19	Cal Eldred	.10
20	Craig Biggio	.10
21	Kirby Puckett	1.00
22	Derek Bell	.10
23	Don Mattingly	1.00
24	John Burkett	.10
25	Roger Clemens	1.00
26	Barry Bonds	.75
27	Paul Molitor	.40
28	Mike Piazza	1.00
29	Robin Ventura	.15
30	Jeff Conine	.15
31	Wade Boggs	.20
32	Dennis Eckersley	.10
33	Bobby Bonilla	.10
34	Len Dykstra	.15
35	Manny Alexander	.10
36	Ray Lankford	.10
37	Greg Vaughn	.10
38	Chuck Finley	.10
39	Todd Benzinger	.10
40	Dave Justice	.40
41	Rob Dibble	.10
42	Tom Henke	.10
43	David Nied	.10
44	Sandy Alomar Jr.	.10
45	Pete Harnisch	.10
46	Jeff Russell	.10
47	Terry Mulholland	.10

#	Name	Price	#	Name	Price	#	Name	Price
48	Kevin Appier	.10	144	Danny Jackson	.10	240	Nigel Wilson	.20
49	Randy Tomlin	.10	145	Allen Watson	.10	241	*Drew Denson*	.20
50	Cal Ripken, Jr.	3.00	146	Scott Fletcher	.10	242	Raul Mondesi	.50
51	Andy Benes	.15	147	Delino DeShields	.10	243	Luis Ortiz	.10
52	Jimmy Key	.10	148	Shane Mack	.10	244	Manny Ramirez	.75
53	Kirt Manwaring	.10	149	Jim Eisenreich	.15	245	Greg Blosser	.10
54	Kevin Tapani	.10	150	Troy Neel	.10	246	Rondell White	.20
55	Jose Guzman	.10	151	Jay Bell	.10	247	Steve Karsay	.10
56	Todd Stottlemyre	.10	152	B.J. Surhoff	.10	248	Scott Stahoviak	.10
57	Jack McDowell	.10	153	Mark Whiten	.10	249	Jose Valentin	.10
58	Orel Hershiser	.10	154	Mike Henneman	.10	250	Marc Newfield	.15
59	Chris Hammond	.10	155	Todd Hundley	.10	251	Keith Kessinger	.10
60	Chris Nabholz	.10	156	Greg Myers	.10	252	Carl Everett	.10
61	Ruben Sierra	.15	157	Ryan Klesko	.75	253	John O'Donoghue	.10
62	Dwight Gooden	.10	158	Dave Fleming	.10	254	Turk Wendell	.10
63	John Kruk	.10	159	Mickey Morandini	.10	255	Scott Ruffcorn	.15
64	Omar Vizquel	.10	160	Blas Minor	.10	256	Tony Tarasco	.15
65	Tim Naehring	.10	161	Reggie Jefferson	.10	257	Andy Cook	.10
66	Dwight Smith	.10	162	David Hulse	.10	258	Matt Mieske	.10
67	Mickey Tettleton	.10	163	Greg Swindell	.10	259	Luis Lopez	.10
68	J.T. Snow	.20	164	Roberto Hernandez	.10	260	Ramon Caraballo	.10
69	Greg McMichael	.10	165	Brady Anderson	.10	261	Salomon Torres	.10
70	Kevin Mitchell	.10	166	Jack Armstrong	.10	262	*Brooks Kieschnick*	1.25
71	Kevin Brown	.10	167	Phil Clark	.10	263	*Daron Kirkreit*	.25
72	Scott Cooper	.30	168	Melido Perez	.10	264	*Bill Wagner*	.20
73	Jim Thome	.10	169	Darren Lewis	.10	265	*Matt Drews*	.10
74	Joe Girardi	.10	170	Sam Horn	.10	266	Scott Christman	.10
75	Eric Anthony	.10	171	Mike Harkey	.10	267	*Torii Hunter*	.40
76	Orlando Merced	.10	172	Juan Guzman	.10	268	*Jamey Wright*	.40
77	Felix Jose	.10	173	Bob Natal	.10	269	Jeff Granger	.10
78	Tommy Greene	.10	174	Deion Sanders	.35	270	*Trot Nixon*	.50
79	Bernard Gilkey	.15	175	Carlos Quintana	.10	271	Randy Myers	.10
80	Phil Plantier	.10	176	Mel Rojas	.10	272	Trevor Hoffman	.10
81	Danny Tartabull	.10	177	Willie Banks	.10	273	Bob Wickman	.10
82	Trevor Wilson	.10	178	Ben Rivera	.10	274	Willie McGee	.10
83	Chuck Knoblauch	.10	179	Kenny Lofton	.60	275	Hipolito Pichardo	.10
84	Rick Wilkins	.10	180	Leo Gomez	.10	276	Bobby Witt	.10
85	Devon White	.10	181	Roberto Mejia	.10	277	Gregg Olson	.10
86	Lance Johnson	.15	182	Mike Perez	.10	278	Randy Johnson	.25
87	Eric Karros	.15	183	Travis Fryman	.15	279	Robb Nen	.10
88	Gary Sheffield	.15	184	Ben McDonald	.10	280	Paul O'Neill	.10
89	Wil Cordero	.10	185	Steve Frey	.10	281	Lou Whitaker	.10
90	Ron Darling	.10	186	Kevin Young	.10	282	Chad Curtis	.10
91	Darren Daulton	.10	187	Dave Magadan	.10	283	Doug Henry	.10
92	Joe Orsulak	.10	188	Bobby Munoz	.10	284	Tom Glavine	.15
93	Steve Cooke	.10	189	Pat Rapp	.10	285	Mike Greenwell	.10
94	Darryl Hamilton	.15	190	Jose Offerman	.10	286	Roberto Kelly	.10
95	Aaron Sele	.10	191	Vinny Castilla	.10	287	Roberto Alomar	.60
96	John Doherty	.10	192	Ivan Calderon	.10	288	Charlie Hough	.10
97	Gary DiSarcina	.10	193	Ken Caminiti	.10	289	Alex Fernandez	.15
98	Jeff Blauser	.10	194	Benji Gil	.10	290	Jeff Bagwell	1.00
99	John Smiley	.10	195	Chuck Carr	.10	291	Wally Joyner	.10
100	Ken Griffey, Jr.	3.00	196	Derrick May	.10	292	Andujar Cedeno	.10
101	Dean Palmer	.10	197	Pat Kelly	.10	293	Rick Aguilera	.10
102	Felix Fermin	.10	198	Jeff Brantley	.10	294	Darryl Strawberry	.10
103	Jerald Clark	.10	199	Jose Lind	.10	295	Mike Mussina	.40
104	Doug Drabek	.10	200	Steve Buechele	.10	296	Jeff Gardner	.10
105	Curt Schilling	.10	201	Wes Chamberlain	.10	297	Chris Gwynn	.10
106	Jeff Montgomery	.10	202	Eduardo Perez	.10	298	Matt Williams	.30
107	Rene Arocha	.10	203	Bret Saberhagen	.10	299	Brent Gates	.15
108	Carlos Garcia	.10	204	Gregg Jefferies	.15	300	Mark McGwire	3.00
109	Wally Whitehurst	.15	205	Darrin Fletcher	.10	301	Jim Deshaies	.10
110	Jim Abbott	.10	206	Kent Hrbek	.10	302	Edgar Martinez	.10
111	Royce Clayton	.10	207	Kim Batiste	.10	303	Danny Darwin	.10
112	Chris Hoiles	.10	208	Jeff King	.10	304	Pat Meares	.10
113	Mike Morgan	.10	209	Donovan Osborne	.10	305	Benito Santiago	.10
114	Joe Magrane	.10	210	Dave Nilsson	.10	306	Jose Canseco	.30
115	Tom Candiotti	.10	211	Al Martin	.10	307	Jim Gott	.10
116	Ron Karkovice	.10	212	Mike Moore	.10	308	Paul Sorrento	.10
117	Ryan Bowen	.10	213	Sterling Hitchcock	.15	309	Scott Kamieniecki	.10
118	Rod Beck	.10	214	Geronimo Pena	.10	310	Larry Walker	.25
119	John Wetteland	.10	215	Kevin Higgins	.10	311	Mark Langston	.10
120	Terry Steinbach	.10	216	Norm Charlton	.10	312	John Jaha	.10
121	Dave Hollins	.10	217	Don Slaught	.10	313	Stan Javier	.10
122	Jeff Kent	.10	218	Mitch Williams	.10	314	Hal Morris	.10
123	Ricky Bones	.10	219	Derek Lilliquist	.10	315	Robby Thompson	.10
124	Brian Jordan	.10	220	Armando Reynoso	.10	316	Pat Hentgen	.10
125	Chad Kreuter	.10	221	Kenny Rogers	.10	317	Tom Gordon	.10
126	John Valentin	.10	222	Doug Jones	.10	318	Joey Cora	.10
127	Billy Hathaway	.10	223	Luis Aquino	.10	319	Luis Alicea	.10
128	Wilson Alvarez	.10	224	Mike Oquist	.10	320	Andre Dawson	.15
129	Tino Martinez	.10	225	Darryl Scott	.10	321	Darryl Kile	.10
130	Rodney Bolton	.10	226	Kurt Abbott	.10	322	Jose Rijo	.10
131	David Segui	.10	227	Andy Tomberlin	.10	323	Luis Gonzalez	.10
132	Wayne Kirby	.10	228	Norberto Martin	.10	324	Billy Ashley	.15
133	Eric Young	.10	229	Pedro Castellano	.10	325	David Cone	.10
134	Scott Servais	.10	230	*Curtis Pride*	.25	326	Bill Swift	.10
135	Scott Radinsky	.10	231	Jeff McNeely	.15	327	Phil Hiatt	.10
136	Bret Barberie	.10	232	Scott Lydy	.10	328	Craig Paquette	.10
137	John Roper	.10	233	Darren Oliver	.10	329	Bob Welch	.10
138	Ricky Gutierrez	.10	234	Danny Bautista	.10	330	Tony Phillips	.10
139	Bernie Williams	.50	235	Butch Huskey	.10	331	Archi Cianfrocco	.10
140	Bud Black	.10	236	Chipper Jones	1.00	332	Dave Winfield	.15
141	Jose Vizcaino	.10	237	Eddie Zambrano	.10	333	David McCarty	.15
142	Gerald Williams	.10	238	Jean Domingo	.10	334	Al Leiter	.10
143	Duane Ward	.10	239	Javier Lopez	.30	335	Tom Browning	.10

336	Mark Grace	.10
337	Jose Mesa	.10
338	Mike Stanley	.10
339	Roger McDowell	.10
340	Damion Easley	.10
341	Angel Miranda	.10
342	John Smoltz	.10
343	Jay Buhner	.10
344	Bryan Harvey	.10
345	Joe Carter	.20
346	Dante Bichette	.30
347	Jason Bere	.20
348	Frank Viola	.10
349	Ivan Rodriguez	.50
350	Juan Gonzalez	1.00
351	Steve Finley	.10
352	Mike Felder	.10
353	Ramon Martinez	.10
354	Greg Gagne	.10
355	Ken Hill	.10
356	Pedro Munoz	.10
357	Todd Van Poppel	.15
358	Marquis Grissom	.12
359	Milt Cuyler	.10
360	Reggie Sanders	.12
361	Scott Erickson	.10
362	Billy Hatcher	.10
363	Gene Harris	.10
364	Rene Gonzales	.10
365	Kevin Rogers	.10
366	Eric Plunk	.10
367	Todd Zeile	.10
368	John Franco	.10
369	Brett Butler	.10
370	Bill Spiers	.10
371	Terry Pendleton	.10
372	Chris Bosio	.10
373	Orestes Destrade	.10
374	Dave Stewart	.10
375	Darren Holmes	.10
376	Doug Strange	.10
377	Brian Turang	.15
378	Carl Willis	.10
379	Mark McLemore	.10
380	Bobby Jones	.35
381	Scott Sanders	.12
382	Kirk Rueter	.15
383	Randy Velarde	.10
384	Fred McGriff	.35
385	Charles Nagy	.10
386	Rich Amaral	.10
387	Geronimo Berroa	.10
388	Eric Davis	.10
389	Ozzie Smith	.25
390	Alex Arias	.10
391	Brad Ausmus	.10
392	Cliff Floyd	.20
393	Roger Salkeld	.10
394	Jim Edmonds	.40
395	Jeromy Burnitz	.15
396	Dave Staton	.10
397	Rob Butler	.10
398	Marcos Armas	.10
399	Darrell Whitmore	.15
400	Ryan Thompson	.15
401	*Ross Powell*	.25
402	Joe Oliver	.10
403	Paul Carey	.12
404	Bob Hamelin	.12
405	Chris Turner	.12
406	Nate Minchey	.15
407	*Lonnie Maclin*	.20
408	Harold Baines	.10
409	Brian Williams	.20
410	Johnny Ruffin	.10
411	*Julian Tavarez*	.50
412	Mark Hutton	.20
413	Carlos Delgado	.40
414	Chris Gomez	.20
415	Mike Hampton	.25
416	Alex Diaz	.10
417	Jeffrey Hammonds	.20
418	Jayhawk Owens	.15
419	J.R. Phillips	.15
420	*Cory Bailey*	.25
421	Denny Hocking	.15
422	Jon Shave	.25
423	Damon Buford	.25
424	Troy O'Leary	.15
425	Tripp Cromer	.15
426	Albie Lopez	.15
427	Tony Fernandez	.10
428	Ozzie Guillen	.10
429	Alan Trammell	.10
430	*John Wasdin*	.50
431	Marc Valdes	.15
432	*Brian Anderson*	.25
433	*Matt Brunson*	.25
434	*Wayne Gomes*	.50
435	*Jay Powell*	.25
436	*Kirk Presley*	1.00
437	*Jon Ratliff*	.40
438	*Derrek Lee*	2.00
439	Tom Pagnozzi	.10
440	Kent Mercker	.10
441	*Phil Leftwich*	.20
442	Jamie Moyer	.10
443	John Flaherty	.10
444	Mark Wohlers	.10
445	Jose Bautista	.10
446	Andres Galarraga	.15
447	Mark Lemke	.10
448	Tim Wakefield	.10
449	Pat Listach	.10
450	Rickey Henderson	.15
451	Mike Gallego	.10
452	Bob Tewksbury	.10
453	Kirk Gibson	.10
454	Pedro Astacio	.10
455	Mike Lansing	.10
456	Sean Berry	.10
457	Bob Walk	.10
458	Chili Davis	.10
459	Ed Sprague	.10
460	Kevin Stocker	.10
461	Mike Stanton	.10
462	Tim Raines	.10
463	Mike Bordick	.10
464	David Wells	.10
465	Tim Laker	.10
466	Cory Snyder	.10
467	Alex Cole	.10
468	Pete Incaviglia	.10
469	Roger Pavlik	.10
470	Greg W. Harris	.10
471	Xavier Hernandez	.10
472	Erik Hanson	.10
473	Jesse Orosco	.10
474	Greg Colbrunn	.10
475	Harold Reynolds	.10
476	Greg Harris	.10
477	Pat Borders	.10
478	Melvin Nieves	.15
479	Mariano Duncan	.10
480	Greg Hibbard	.10
481	Tim Pugh	.10
482	Bobby Ayala	.10
483	Sid Fernandez	.10
484	Tim Wallach	.10
485	Randy Milligan	.10
486	Walt Weiss	.10
487	Matt Walbeck	.20
488	Mike Macfarlane	.10
489	Jerry Browne	.10
490	Chris Sabo	.10
491	Tim Belcher	.10
492	Spike Owen	.10
493	Rafael Palmeiro	.15
494	Brian Harper	.10
495	Eddie Murray	.15
496	Ellis Burks	.10
497	Karl Rhodes	.10
498	Otis Nixon	.10
499	Lee Smith	.10
500	Bip Roberts	.10
501	Pedro Martinez	.10
502	Brian L. Hunter	.15
503	Tyler Green	.12
504	Bruce Hurst	.10
505	Alex Gonzalez	.30
506	Mark Portugal	.10
507	Bob Ojeda	.10
508	Dave Henderson	.10
509	Bo Jackson	.20
510	Bret Boone	.12
511	Mark Eichhorn	.10
512	Luis Polonia	.10
513	Will Clark	.35
514	Dave Valle	.10
515	Dan Wilson	.10
516	Dennis Martinez	.10
517	Jim Leyritz	.10
518	Howard Johnson	.10
519	Jody Reed	.10
520	Julio Franco	.10
521	Jeff Reardon	.10
522	Willie Greene	.15
523	Shawon Dunston	.10
524	Keith Mitchell	.10
525	Rick Helling	.15
526	Mark Kiefer	.10
527	*Chan Ho Park*	.50
528	Tony Longmire	.12
529	Rich Becker	.15
530	Tim Hyers	.10
531	Darrin Jackson	.10
532	Jack Morris	.10
533	Rick White	.10
534	Mike Kelly	.15
535	James Mouton	.25
536	Steve Trachsel	.30
537	Tony Eusebio	.15
538	Kelly Stinnett	.10
539	Paul Spoljaric	.15
540	Darren Dreifort	.25

1994 Pinnacle Artist's Proof

A specially designated version of the regular Pinnacle set, described as the first day's production of the first 1,000 of each card, was issued as a random pack insert. Cards feature a small gold-foil "Artist's Proof" rectangle embossed above the player/team name shield on front. In all other respects the cards are identical to the regular-issue versions.

	MT
Complete Set (540):	3800.
Complete Series 1 (270):	2600.
Complete Series 2 (270):	1200.
Common Player:	3.00
(Star cards valued at 35-50X regular Pinnacle version)	

1994 Pinnacle Museum Collection

Each card in the 1994 Pinnacle set was produced in a parallel "Museum Collection" version. The inserts were produced utilizing the company's Dufex foil-printing technology on front, with rays emanating from the Pinnacle logo. Backs are virtually identical to the regular-issue version except for the substitution of a "1994 Museum Collection" logo for the optical-variable anti-counterfeiting bar at bottom-center. Museums were random package inserts, appearing at the rate of about once per four packs.

	MT
Complete Set (540):	1400.
Complete Series 1 (270):	850.00
Complete Series 2 (270):	550.00
Common Player:	1.00
(Star cards valued at 15-20X regular Pinnacle version)	

1994 Pinnacle Rookie Team Pinnacle

The very popular Rookie Team Pinnacle insert card tradition continued in 1994 with a series of nine "two-headed" cards featuring the top prospect from each league at each position. The cards again feature the ultra-realistic artwork of Chris Greco. Each side is enhanced with gold-foil presentations of the player's name, the Pinnacle logo and the Rookie Team Pinnacle logo. The inserts were packaged, on average, one per 90 packs of hobby foil only.

		MT
Complete Set (9):		100.00
Common Player:		5.00
1	Carlos Delgado, Javier Lopez	15.00
2	Bob Hamelin, J.R. Phillips	8.00
3	Jon Shave, Keith Kessinger	5.00
4	Butch Huskey, Luis Ortiz	5.00
5	Chipper Jones, Kurt Abbott	35.00
6	Rondell White, Manny Ramirez	35.00
7	Cliff Floyd, Jeffrey Hammonds	10.00
8	Marc Newfield, Nigel Wilson	6.00
9	Salomon Torres, Mark Hutton	5.00

1994 Pinnacle Run Creators

This insert set, exclusive to Pinnacle jumbo packaging, features the top 44 performers of the previous season in the arcane statistic of "runs created." Fronts have an action player photo on which the stadium background has been muted in soft-focus red or blue. The player's last name appears at right in gold foil; the logo, "The Run Creators" is in one of the lower corners. Backs are printed in teal with a color team logo at center, beneath the stats that earned the player's inclusion in the series. The player's runs created are in gold foil above the write-up. Cards are numbered with an "RC" prefix.

		MT
Complete Set (44):		150.00
Common Player:		1.50
1	John Olerud	1.50
2	Frank Thomas	15.00
3	Ken Griffey, Jr.	20.00
4	Paul Molitor	2.00
5	Rafael Palmeiro	2.00
6	Roberto Alomar	5.00
7	Juan Gonzalez	8.00
8	Albert Belle	5.00
9	Travis Fryman	1.50
10	Rickey Henderson	1.50
11	Tony Phillips	1.50
12	Mo Vaughn	4.00
13	Tim Salmon	2.00
14	Kenny Lofton	6.00
15	Carlos Baerga	3.50
16	Greg Vaughn	1.50
17	Jay Buhner	1.50
18	Chris Hoiles	1.50
19	Mickey Tettleton	1.50
20	Kirby Puckett	8.00
21	Danny Tartabull	1.50
22	Devon White	1.50
23	Barry Bonds	5.00
24	Lenny Dykstra	1.50
25	John Kruk	1.50
26	Fred McGriff	2.50
27	Gregg Jefferies	1.50
28	Mike Piazza	8.00
29	Jeff Blauser	1.50
30	Andres Galarraga	1.50
31	Darren Daulton	1.50
32	Dave Justice	3.00
33	Craig Biggio	1.50
34	Mark Grace	2.00
35	Tony Gwynn	8.00
36	Jeff Bagwell	6.00
37	Jay Bell	1.50
38	Marquis Grissom	2.00
39	Matt Williams	2.00
40	Charlie Hayes	1.50
41	Dante Bichette	2.00
42	Bernard Gilkey	1.50
43	Brett Butler	1.50
44	Rick Wilkins	1.50

1994 Pinnacle Team Pinnacle

The double-sided Team Pinnacle insert set features 18 of the top players in the game. Team Pinnacle shows two card fronts, one on each side. They were inserted into 1994 Pinnacle Baseball Series II at a rate of one every 90 packs.

		MT
Complete Set (9):		200.00
Common Player:		10.00
1	Jeff Bagwell, Frank Thomas	50.00
2	Carlos Baerga, Robby Thompson	10.00
3	Matt Williams, Dean Palmer	10.00
4	Cal Ripken, Jr., Jay Bell	50.00
5	Ivan Rodriguez, Mike Piazza	30.00
6	Len Dykstra, Ken Griffey, Jr.	55.00
7	Juan Gonzalez, Barry Bonds	25.00
8	Tim Salmon, Dave Justice	12.00
9	Greg Maddux, Jack McDowell	35.00

1994 Pinnacle Tribute

A hobby-only insert set, found approximately one per 18 foil packs, this nine-card series honors players who reached significant season or career milestones or otherwise had special achievements in

1993. Fronts feature full-bleed action photos. At left is a black strip with "TRIBUTE" in gold foil. A colored strip at bottom has the player name in gold foil and a short description of why he is being feted beneath. The Pinnacle logo is in gold foil at top. The same gold-foil enhancements are found on back, along with a portrait photo. In a black box at bottom are details of the tribute. The Pinnacle optical-variable anti-counterfeiting device is at bottom center. Card numbers are prefixed with "TR".

		MT
Complete Set (18):		60.00
Common Player:		1.50
1	Paul Molitor	3.00
2	Jim Abbott	1.50
3	Dave Winfield	1.50
4	Bo Jackson	1.50
5	Dave Justice	2.00
6	Len Dykstra	1.50
7	Mike Piazza	8.00
8	Barry Bonds	4.00
9	Randy Johnson	2.00
10	Ozzie Smith	3.00
11	Mark Whiten	1.50
12	Greg Maddux	8.00
13	Cal Ripken, Jr.	15.00
14	Frank Thomas	12.00
15	Juan Gonzalez	7.00
16	Roberto Alomar	3.00
17	Ken Griffey, Jr.	15.00
18	Lee Smith	1.50

1995 Pinnacle

THOME

The 1995 Pinnacle set was produced in two series of 225 base cards each, plus inserts. Fronts have borderless photos with a large embossed gold foil "wave" at bottom containing the player's last name and team logo. Backs are horizontally formatted and have a portrait photo at left, an action photo at right and a few sentences about the player at center. Stats at the bottom offer previous year, career and career-best numbers. Subsets with the base cards include rookie specials in Series I and II which have a design featuring a green stripe at one side or bottom with the player's name in gold and a special round gold-foil logo. A similar design, with red stripes, is used for Series I cards only featuring Draft Picks. In Series II, a 30-card Swing Men subset has

a blue vortex background design and special gold-foil identifier. Basic pack configurations offered 12-card ($2.49) and 15-card ($2.99) counts in both retail and hobby versions, each with some unique inserts.

		MT
Complete Set (450):		30.00
Complete Series 1 (225):		15.00
Complete Series 2 (225):		15.00
Common Player:		.10
Set 1 or 2 Hobby Box:		45.00
Set 1 or 2 Retail Box:		60.00
1	Jeff Bagwell	1.00
2	Roger Clemens	.75
3	Mark Whiten	.10
4	Shawon Dunston	.10
5	Bobby Bonilla	.15
6	Kevin Tapani	.10
7	Eric Karros	.15
8	Cliff Floyd	.10
9	Pat Kelly	.10
10	Jeffrey Hammonds	.10
11	Jeff Conine	.10
12	Fred McGriff	.25
13	Chris Bosio	.10
14	Mike Mussina	.40
15	Danny Bautista	.10
16	Mickey Morandini	.10
17	Chuck Finley	.10
18	Jim Thome	.40
19	Luis Ortiz	.10
20	Walt Weiss	.10
21	Don Mattingly	1.00
22	Bob Hamelin	.10
23	Melido Perez	.10
24	Kevin Mitchell	.10
25	John Smoltz	.25
26	Hector Carrasco	.10
27	Pat Hentgen	.10
28	Derrick May	.10
29	Mike Kingery	.10
30	Chuck Carr	.10
31	Billy Ashley	.10
32	Todd Hundley	.15
33	Luis Gonzalez	.10
34	Marquis Grissom	.10
35	Jeff King	.10
36	Eddie Williams	.10
37	Tom Pagnozzi	.10
38	Chris Hoiles	.10
39	Sandy Alomar	.10
40	Mike Greenwell	.10
41	Lance Johnson	.10
42	Junior Felix	.10
43	Felix Jose	.10
44	Scott Leius	.10
45	Ruben Sierra	.10
46	Kevin Seitzer	.10
47	Wade Boggs	.20
48	Reggie Jefferson	.10
49	Jose Canseco	.30
50	Dave Justice	.20
51	John Smiley	.10
52	Joe Carter	.25
53	Rick Wilkins	.10
54	Ellis Burks	.10
55	Dave Weathers	.10
56	Pedro Astacio	.10
57	Ryan Thompson	.10
58	James Mouton	.10
59	Mel Rojas	.10
60	Orlando Merced	.10
61	Matt Williams	.30
62	Bernard Gilkey	.10
63	J.R. Phillips	.10
64	Lee Smith	.10
65	Jim Edmonds	.25
66	Darrin Jackson	.10
67	Scott Cooper	.10
68	Ron Karkovice	.10
69	Chris Gomez	.10
70	Kevin Appier	.10
71	Bobby Jones	.15
72	Doug Drabek	.10
73	Matt Mieske	.10
74	Sterling Hitchcock	.10
75	John Valentin	.10
76	Reggie Sanders	.15
77	Wally Joyner	.10
78	Turk Wendell	.10
79	Wendell Hayes	.10
80	Bret Barberie	.10
81	Troy Neel	.10
82	Ken Caminiti	.25
83	Milt Thompson	.10
84	Paul Sorrento	.10
85	Trevor Hoffman	.10
86	Jay Bell	.10
87	Mark Portugal	.10
88	Sid Fernandez	.10
89	Charles Nagy	.10
90	Jeff Montgomery	.10
91	Chuck Knoblauch	.20
92	Jeff Frye	.10
93	Tony Gwynn	1.00
94	John Olerud	.10
95	David Nied	.10
96	Chris Hammond	.10
97	Edgar Martinez	.15
98	Kevin Stocker	.10
99	Jeff Fassero	.10
100	Curt Schilling	.10
101	Dave Clark	.10
102	Delino DeShields	.10
103	Leo Gomez	.10
104	Dave Hollins	.10
105	Tim Naehring	.10
106	Otis Nixon	.10
107	Ozzie Guillen	.10
108	Jose Lind	.10
109	Stan Javier	.10
110	Greg Vaughn	.10
111	Chipper Jones	2.00
112	Ed Sprague	.10
113	Mike Macfarlane	.10
114	Steve Finley	.10
115	Ken Hill	.10
116	Carlos Garcia	.10
117	Lou Whitaker	.10
118	Todd Zeile	.10
119	Gary Sheffield	.40
120	Ben McDonald	.10
121	Pete Harnisch	.10
122	Ivan Rodriguez	.50
123	Wilson Alvarez	.10
124	Travis Fryman	.15
125	Pedro Munoz	.10
126	Mark Lemke	.10
127	Jose Valentin	.10
128	Ken Griffey Jr.	3.00
129	Omar Vizquel	.10
130	Milt Cuyler	.10
131	Steve Traschel	.25
132	Alex Rodriguez	3.00
133	Garret Anderson	.20
134	Armando Benitez	.10
135	Shawn Green	.20
136	Jorge Fabregas	.10
137	Orlando Miller	.10
138	Rikkert Faneyte	.10
139	Ismael Valdes	.10
140	Jose Oliva	.10
141	Aaron Small	.10
142	Tim Davis	.10
143	Ricky Bottalico	.10
144	Mike Matheny	.10
145	Roberto Petagine	.10
146	Fausto Cruz	.10
147	Bryce Florie	.10
148	Jose Lima	.10
149	John Hudek	.10
150	Duane Singleton	.10
151	John Mabry	.10
152	Robert Eenhoorn	.10
153	Jon Lieber	.10
154	Garey Ingram	.10
155	Paul Shuey	.10
156	Mike Lieberthal	.10
157	Steve Dunn	.10
158	Charles Johnson	.15
159	Ernie Young	.10
160	Jose Martinez	.10
161	Kurt Miller	.10
162	Joey Eischen	.10
163	Dave Stevens	.10
164	Brian Hunter	.15
165	Jeff Cirillo	.15
166	Mark Smith	.10
167	*McKay Christensen*	.20
168	C.J. Nitkowski	.10
169	*Antone Williamson*	.50
170	Paul Konerko	2.50
171	*Scott Elarton*	.50
172	Jacob Shumate	.10
173	Terrence Long	.20
174	*Mark Johnson*	.25
175	Ben Grieve	3.00
176	*Jayson Peterson*	.20

#	Player	Price
177	Checklist	.10
178	Checklist	.10
179	Checklist	.10
180	Checklist	.10
181	Brian Anderson	.15
182	Steve Buechele	.10
183	Mark Clark	.10
184	Cecil Fielder	.20
185	Steve Avery	.10
186	Devon White	.10
187	Craig Shipley	.10
188	Brady Anderson	.15
189	Kenny Lofton	.75
190	Alex Cole	.10
191	Brent Gates	.10
192	Dean Palmer	.10
193	Alex Gonzalez	.15
194	Steve Cooke	.10
195	Ray Lankford	.10
196	Mark McGwire	3.00
197	Marc Newfield	.10
198	Pat Rapp	.10
199	Darren Lewis	.10
200	Carlos Baerga	.15
201	Rickey Henderson	.15
202	Kurt Abbott	.10
203	Kirt Manwaring	.10
204	Cal Ripken Jr.	3.00
205	Darren Daulton	.10
206	Greg Colbrunn	.10
207	Darryl Hamilton	.10
208	Bo Jackson	.15
209	Tony Phillips	.10
210	Geronimo Berroa	.10
211	Rich Becker	.10
212	Tony Tarasco	.10
213	Karl Rhodes	.10
214	Phil Plantier	.10
215	J.T. Snow	.20
216	Mo Vaughn	.50
217	Greg Gagne	.10
218	Rickey Bones	.10
219	Mike Bordick	.10
220	Chad Curtis	.10
221	Royce Clayton	.10
222	Roberto Alomar	.60
223	Jose Rijo	.10
224	Ryan Klesko	.50
225	Mark Langston	.10
226	Frank Thomas	2.50
227	Juan Gonzalez	1.50
228	Ron Gant	.15
229	Javier Lopez	.20
230	Sammy Sosa	2.00
231	Kevin Brown	.10
232	Gary DiSarcina	.10
233	Albert Belle	.75
234	Jay Buhner	.20
235	Pedro Martinez	.10
236	Bob Tewksbury	.10
237	Mike Piazza	2.00
238	Darryl Kile	.10
239	Bryan Harvey	.10
240	Andres Galarraga	.20
241	Jeff Blauser	.10
242	Jeff Kent	.10
243	Bobby Munoz	.10
244	Greg Maddux	2.00
245	Paul O'Neill	.10
246	Lenny Dykstra	.10
247	Todd Van Poppel	.10
248	Bernie Williams	.40
249	Glenallen Hill	.10
250	Duane Ward	.10
251	Dennis Eckersley	.10
252	Pat Mahomes	.10
253	Rusty Greer (photo actually Jeff Frye)	.10
254	Roberto Kelly	.10
255	Randy Myers	.10
256	Scott Ruffcorn	.10
257	Robin Ventura	.10
258	Eduardo Perez	.10
259	Aaron Sele	.10
260	Paul Molitor	.35
261	Juan Guzman	.10
262	Darren Oliver	.10
263	Mike Stanley	.10
264	Tom Glavine	.20
265	Rico Brogna	.10
266	Craig Biggio	.15
267	Darrell Whitmore	.10
268	Jimmy Key	.10
269	Will Clark	.30
270	David Cone	.15
271	Brian Jordan	.15
272	Barry Bonds	.75
273	Danny Tartabull	.10
274	Ramon Martinez	.10
275	Al Martin	.10
276	Fred McGriff (Swing Men)	.25
277	Carlos Delgado (Swing Men)	.15
278	Juan Gonzalez (Swing Men)	.50
279	Shawn Green (Swing Men)	.10
280	Carlos Baerga (Swing Men)	.15
281	Cliff Floyd (Swing Men)	.10
282	Ozzie Smith (Swing Men)	.25
283	Alex Rodriguez (Swing Men)	1.50
284	Kenny Lofton (Swing Men)	.40
285	Dave Justice (Swing Men)	.20
286	Tim Salmon (Swing Men)	.15
287	Manny Ramirez (Swing Men)	.75
288	Will Clark (Swing Men)	.20
289	Garret Anderson (Swing Men)	.15
290	Billy Ashley (Swing Men)	.10
291	Tony Gwynn (Swing Men)	.50
292	Raul Mondesi (Swing Men)	.25
293	Rafael Palmeiro (Swing Men)	.15
294	Matt Williams (Swing Men)	.15
295	Don Mattingly (Swing Men)	.50
296	Kirby Puckett (Swing Men)	.50
297	Paul Molitor (Swing Men)	.20
298	Albert Belle (Swing Men)	.40
299	Barry Bonds (Swing Men)	.40
300	Mike Piazza (Swing Men)	.75
301	Jeff Bagwell (Swing Men)	.50
302	Frank Thomas (Swing Men)	1.25
303	Chipper Jones (Swing Men)	.75
304	Ken Griffey Jr. (Swing Men)	1.50
305	Cal Ripken Jr. (Swing Men)	1.50
306	Eric Anthony	.10
307	Todd Benzinger	.10
308	Jacob Brumfield	.10
309	Wes Chamberlain	.10
310	Tino Martinez	.10
311	Roberto Mejia	.10
312	Jose Offerman	.10
313	David Segui	.10
314	Eric Young	.10
315	Rey Sanchez	.10
316	Raul Mondesi	.50
317	Bret Boone	.10
318	Andre Dawson	.10
319	Brian McRae	.10
320	Dave Nilsson	.10
321	Moises Alou	.10
322	Don Slaught	.10
323	Dave McCarty	.10
324	Mike Huff	.10
325	Rick Aguilera	.10
326	Rod Beck	.10
327	Kenny Rogers	.10
328	Andy Benes	.10
329	Allen Watson	.10
330	Randy Johnson	.35
331	Willie Greene	.10
332	Hal Morris	.10
333	Ozzie Smith	.35
334	Jason Bere	.10
335	Scott Erickson	.10
336	Dante Bichette	.35
337	Willie Banks	.10
338	Eric Davis	.10
339	Rondell White	.10
340	Kirby Puckett	1.00
341	Deion Sanders	.30
342	Eddie Murray	.40
343	Mike Harkey	.10
344	Joey Hamilton	.15
345	Roger Salkeld	.10
346	Wil Cordero	.10
347	John Wetteland	.10
348	Geronimo Pena	.10
349	Kirk Gibson	.10
350	Manny Ramirez	.75
351	William Van Landingham	.10
352	B.J. Surhoff	.10
353	Ken Ryan	.10
354	Terry Steinbach	.10
355	Bret Saberhagen	.10
356	John Jaha	.10
357	Joe Girardi	.10
358	Steve Karsay	.10
359	Alex Fernandez	.15
360	Salomon Torres	.10
361	John Burkett	.10
362	Derek Bell	.10
363	Tom Henke	.10
364	Gregg Jefferies	.10
365	Jack McDowell	.15
366	Andujar Cedeno	.10
367	Dave Winfield	.10
368	Carl Everett	.10
369	Danny Jackson	.10
370	Jeromy Burnitz	.10
371	Mark Grace	.20
372	Larry Walker	.25
373	Bill Swift	.10
374	Dennis Martinez	.10
375	Mickey Tettleton	.10
376	Mel Nieves	.10
377	Cal Eldred	.10
378	Orel Hershiser	.10
379	David Wells	.10
380	Gary Gaetti	.10
381	Tim Raines	.10
382	Barry Larkin	.25
383	Jason Jacome	.10
384	Tim Wallach	.10
385	Robby Thompson	.10
386	Frank Viola	.10
387	Dave Stewart	.10
388	Ron Darling	.10
389	Ron Darling	.10
390	Carlos Delgado	.15
391	Tim Salmon	.20
392	Alan Trammell	.10
393	Kevin Foster	.10
394	Jim Abbott	.10
395	John Kruk	.10
396	Andy Van Slyke	.10
397	Dave Magadan	.10
398	Rafael Palmeiro	.20
399	Mike Devereaux	.10
400	Benito Santiago	.10
401	Brett Butler	.10
402	John Franco	.10
403	Matt Walbeck	.10
404	Terry Pendleton	.10
405	Chris Sabo	.10
406	Andrew Lorraine	.10
407	Dan Wilson	.10
408	Mike Lansing	.10
409	Ray McDavid	.10
410	Shane Andrews	.10
411	Tom Gordon	.10
412	Chad Ogea	.10
413	James Baldwin	.10
414	Russ Davis	.10
415	Ray Holbert	.10
416	Ray Durham	.15
417	Matt Nokes	.10
418	Rodney Henderson	.10
419	Gabe White	.10
420	Todd Hollandsworth	.15
421	Midre Cummings	.10
422	Harold Baines	.10
423	Troy Percival	.10
424	Joe Vitiello	.10
425	Andy Ashby	.10
426	Michael Tucker	.10
427	Mark Gubicza	.10
428	Jim Bullinger	.10
429	Jose Malave	.10
430	Pete Schourek	.10
431	Bobby Ayala	.10
432	Marvin Freeman	.10
433	Pat Listach	.10
434	Eddie Taubensee	.10
435	Steve Howe	.10
436	Kent Mercker	.10
437	Hector Fajardo	.10
438	Scott Kamienecki	.10
439	Robb Nen	.10
440	Mike Kelly	.10
441	Tom Candiotti	.10
442	Albie Lopez	.10
443	Jeff Granger	.10
444	Rich Aude	.10
445	Luis Polonia	.10
446	A.L. Checklist (Frank Thomas)	1.00
447	A.L. Checklist (Ken Griffey Jr.)	1.00
448	N.L. Checklist (Mike Piazza)	.50
449	N.L. Checklist (Jeff Bagwell)	.40
450	Insert Checklist (Frank Thomas, Ken Griffey Jr., Mike Piazza, Jeff Bagwell)	1.50

A player's name in *italic* type indicates a rookie card.

1995 Pinnacle Artist's Proof

Said to represent the first 1,000 of each card printed, the Artist's Proof chase set is a parallel issue with a counterpart for each of the regular-issue cards. The proofs differ in the use of silver, rather than gold foil for front graphic highlights, and the inclusion of a rectangular silver-foil "ARTIST'S PROOF" logo on front. The AP inserts were reported seeded at an average rate of one per 26 packs.

	MT
Complete Set (450):	1800.
Complete Series 1 (225):	900.00
Complete Series 2 (225):	900.00
Common Player:	3.00
Stars: 15x to 25x	
Yng Stars & RCs: 8x to 15x	
(Star cards valued at 35-40X regular Pinnacle version)	

1995 Pinnacle Museum Collection

Pinnacle's Dufex foil-printing technology on the card fronts differentiates the cards in this parallel insert set from the corresponding cards in the regular issue. Backs have a rectangular "1995 Museum Collection" logo at the lower-left. Museum inserts are found at an average rate of one per four packs. Because of production difficulties, trade cards had to be issued in place of seven of the rookie cards in Series 2. Those redemption cards were valid only through Dec. 31, 1995. MT

> A player's name in *italic* type indicates a rookie card.

Complete Set (450):	400.00
Complete Series 1 (225):	200.00
Complete Series 2 (225):	200.00
Common Player:	.75
Stars: 4x to 8x	
Yng Stars & RCs: 3x to 6x	
(Star cards valued at 20-25X regular Pinnacle version)	

1995 Pinnacle E.T.A. '95

This hobby-only chase card set identifies six players who were picked to arrive in the major leagues for a 1995 debut. Both front and back have borderless action photos on which the background has been subdued and posterized. Gold-foil headlines on each side of the card give the player's credentials. These inserts are found on average of once per 24 packs.

		MT
Complete Set (6):		24.00
Common Player:		1.00
1	Ben Grieve	20.00
2	Alex Ochoa	2.00
3	Joe Vitiello	1.00
4	Johnny Damon	6.00
5	Trey Beamon	3.00
6	Brooks Kieschnick	4.00

1995 Pinnacle Gate Attraction

Series II jumbo packs are the exclusive source for this chase set. Printed on metallic foil, the cards have a color photo at top and a second photo at bottom that is shown in gold tones only. A "Gate Attraction" seal is in the lower-left corner. Backs have a large portrait photo on a color-streaked background, plus a few words about the player.

		MT
Complete Set (18):		100.00
Common Player:		1.50
1	Ken Griffey Jr.	20.00
2	Frank Thomas	15.00
3	Cal Ripken Jr.	15.00
4	Jeff Bagwell	8.00
5	Mike Piazza	12.00
6	Barry Bonds	5.00
7	Kirby Puckett	6.00
8	Albert Belle	5.00
9	Tony Gwynn	10.00
10	Raul Mondesi	2.00
11	Will Clark	2.00
12	Don Mattingly	6.00
13	Roger Clemens	7.00
14	Paul Molitor	4.00
15	Matt Williams	2.00
16	Greg Maddux	12.00
17	Kenny Lofton	4.00
18	Cliff Floyd	1.50

1995 Pinnacle New Blood

Both hobby and retail packs of Series II Pinnacle hide this insert set of young stars, at an average rate of one card per 90 packs. A player photo appears in the red and silver foil-printed background, and there is a color action photo in the foreground. Conventionally printed backs feature the same photos, but with their prominence reversed. A few words of text describe the player's star potential.

		MT
Complete Set (9):		55.00
Common Player:		2.00
1	Alex Rodriguez	25.00
2	Shawn Green	4.00
3	Brian Hunter	3.00
4	Garret Anderson	4.00
5	Charles Johnson	7.50
6	Chipper Jones	20.00
7	Carlos Delgado	4.00
8	Billy Ashley	2.00
9	J.R. Phillips	2.00

1995 Pinnacle Performers

Series I jumbos were the only place to find this chase set. Fronts have a deep red background with a golden pyramid at center and a silver apex, all in foil printing. A color player action photo is in the center foreground. The reverse repeats the front photo in the background, in one color, and has a second color photo, along with a few words about the player.

		MT
Complete Set (18):		90.00
Common Player:		2.00
1	Frank Thomas	20.00
2	Albert Belle	6.00
3	Barry Bonds	7.50
4	Juan Gonzalez	8.00
5	Andres Galarraga	2.50
6	Raul Mondesi	3.00
7	Paul Molitor	4.00
8	Tim Salmon	3.00
9	Mike Piazza	12.00
10	Gregg Jefferies	2.00
11	Will Clark	3.00
12	Greg Maddux	15.00
13	Manny Ramirez	7.50
14	Kirby Puckett	10.00
15	Shawn Green	3.00
16	Rafael Palmeiro	3.00
17	Paul O'Neill	2.00
18	Jason Bere	2.00

1995 Pinnacle Red Hot

These Series II inserts are found at an average rate of one per 16 packs and feature top veterans stars. Fronts have a large action photo on right, over a background of foil-printed red and yellow flames. A vertical strip at left of graduated red tones has a player portrait photo and the "RED HOT" flame logo, again printed on foil. Backs are conventionally printed and have a black background with large flaming "RED HOT" letters and a color player photo.

		MT
Complete Set (25):		80.00
Common Player:		1.50
1	Cal Ripken Jr.	12.00
2	Ken Griffey Jr.	15.00
3	Frank Thomas	12.00
4	Jeff Bagwell	6.00
5	Mike Piazza	10.00
6	Barry Bonds	4.00
7	Albert Belle	4.00
8	Tony Gwynn	6.00
9	Kirby Puckett	6.00
10	Don Mattingly	6.00
11	Matt Williams	1.50
12	Greg Maddux	10.00
13	Raul Mondesi	2.00
14	Paul Molitor	3.00
15	Manny Ramirez	4.00
16	Joe Carter	1.50
17	Will Clark	2.00
18	Roger Clemens	5.00
19	Tim Salmon	1.50
20	Dave Justice	1.50
21	Kenny Lofton	4.00
22	Deion Sanders	1.50
23	Roberto Alomar	3.00
24	Cliff Floyd	1.50
25	Carlos Baerga	1.50

1995 Pinnacle Team Pinnacle Pin Trade Cards

In one of the hobby's first major attempts to cross-promote pin- and card-collecting, Series 2 Pinnacle packs offered a special insert set of cards which could be redeemed for a collector's pin of the same player. Seeded at the rate of one per 48 regular packs and one per 36 jumbo packs, the pin redemption cards were valid until Nov. 15, 1995. Payment of $2 handling fee was required for redemption.

		MT
Complete Set (18):		75.00
Common Player:		2.00
1	Greg Maddux	6.00
2	Mike Mussina	2.00
3	Mike Piazza	6.00
4	Carlos Delgado	2.00
5	Jeff Bagwell	4.00
6	Frank Thomas	6.00
7	Craig Biggio	2.00
8	Roberto Alomar	4.00
9	Ozzie Smith	3.00
10	Cal Ripken Jr.	8.00
11	Matt Williams	3.00
12	Travis Fryman	2.00
13	Barry Bonds	5.00
14	Ken Griffey Jr.	8.00
15	Dave Justice	2.00
16	Albert Belle	4.00
17	Tony Gwynn	5.00
18	Kirby Puckett	5.00

1995 Pinnacle Team Pinnacle Collector Pins

Redemption cards in Series 2 packs could be traded in (until Nov. 15, 1995) for an enameled pin of the player pictured on the trade card. Pins are about 1-3/8" x 1-1/4". A raised relief portrait of the player is at center with his name in pennants above and his team logo at bottom, along with the Pinnacle logo. Backs are gold-tone with a post-and-button style of pinback. The unnumbered pins are listed here in the same sequence as the redemption cards.

		MT
Complete Set (18):		150.00
Common Player:		4.00
(1)	Greg Maddux	12.00
(2)	Mike Mussina	4.00
(3)	Mike Piazza	12.00
(4)	Carlos Delgado	4.00
(5)	Jeff Bagwell	8.00
(6)	Frank Thomas	15.00
(7)	Craig Biggio	4.00
(8)	Roberto Alomar	8.00
(9)	Ozzie Smith	6.00
(10)	Cal Ripken Jr.	16.00
(11)	Matt Williams	6.00
(12)	Travis Fryman	4.00
(13)	Barry Bonds	10.00
(14)	Ken Griffey Jr.	16.00
(15)	Dave Justice	4.00
(16)	Albert Belle	8.00
(17)	Tony Gwynn	10.00
(18)	Kirby Puckett	10.00

1995 Pinnacle Upstarts

Thirty of the most dominant young players in the game were featured in this insert series. Cards are printed with most of the photo's background covered by the legs of a large blue and gold star device, which includes the team logo at its red center. A blue circular "'95 UP-STARTS" logo at bottom-left has the player name in gold. These cards are exclusive to Series I, found at an average rate of one per eight packs.

		MT
Complete Set (30):		35.00
Common Player:		.50
1	Frank Thomas	12.00
2	Roberto Alomar	2.50
3	Mike Piazza	7.00
4	Javier Lopez	.60
5	Albert Belle	4.50
6	Carlos Delgado	.55
7	Rusty Greer	.55
8	Tim Salmon	.75
9	Raul Mondesi	.65
10	Juan Gonzalez	6.00
11	Manny Ramirez	3.50
12	Sammy Sosa	10.00
13	Jeff Kent	.50
14	Melvin Nieves	.50
15	Rondell White	.50
16	Shawn Green	.50
17	Bernie Williams	1.25
18	Aaron Sele	.55
19	Jason Bere	.50
20	Joey Hamilton	.50
21	Mike Kelly	.50
22	Wil Cordero	.50
23	Moises Alou	.60
24	Roberto Kelly	.50
25	Deion Sanders	1.25
26	Steve Karsay	.50
27	Bret Boone	.50
28	Willie Greene	.50
29	Billy Ashley	.50
30	Brian Anderson	.50

1995 Pinnacle White Hot

Similar in format to the Red Hot inserts, and featuring the same players, the hobby-only White Hot cards are a chase set of a chase set. Seeded once per 36 packs on average (more than twice as scarce as the Red Hots), the White Hot cards have fronts totally printed in the Dufex process, with predominantly blue and white background colors, while the backs are highlighted by blue foil printing in the "WHITE HOT" background lettering on black background.

		MT
Complete Set (25):		200.00
Common Player:		4.00
1	Cal Ripken Jr.	25.00
2	Ken Griffey Jr.	30.00
3	Frank Thomas	25.00
4	Jeff Bagwell	12.00
5	Mike Piazza	20.00
6	Barry Bonds	8.00
7	Albert Belle	8.00
8	Tony Gwynn	15.00
9	Kirby Puckett	10.00
10	Don Mattingly	10.00
11	Matt Williams	4.00
12	Greg Maddux	20.00
13	Raul Mondesi	4.00
14	Paul Molitor	4.00
15	Manny Ramirez	7.00
16	Joe Carter	4.00
17	Will Clark	4.00
18	Roger Clemens	8.00
19	Tim Salmon	4.00
20	Dave Justice	4.00
21	Kenny Lofton	8.00
22	Deion Sanders	6.00
23	Roberto Alomar	6.00
24	Cliff Floyd	4.00
25	Carlos Baerga	4.00

1996 Pinnacle

RUBEN RIVERA

Pinnacle issued a 399-card regular-issue set with borderless front photos highlighted by prismatic gold-foil graphics in the shape of a triangle at bottom. The player's name is in black in the triangle. Backs have another player photo along with stats and data. Parallel Starburst and Starburst Artist's Proof sets contain only 200 of the cards in the base issue. Series I inserts include a Cal Ripken Jr. "Tribute" card, numbered "1 of 1" (seeded one per every 150 packs). The other five Series I inserts are Team Pinnacle, Pinnacle Power, Team Tomorrow, Essence of the Game and First Rate. Series II inserts the Christie Brinkley Collection, Project Stardom, Skylines, Slugfest and Team Spirit. Pinnacle was sold in 10-card hobby and retail foil packs, and 18-card jumbo packs.

		MT
Complete Set (399):		35.00
Complete Series 1 (200):		18.00
Complete Series 2 (200):		18.00
Common Player:		.10
Unlisted Stars: .20 to .35		
Wax Box:		35.00
1	Greg Maddux	2.00
2	Bill Pulsipher	.15
3	Dante Bichette	.25
4	Mike Piazza	2.00
5	Garret Anderson	.10
6	Steve Finley	.10
7	Andy Benes	.10
8	Chuck Knoblauch	.10
9	Tom Gordon	.10
10	Jeff Bagwell	1.25
11	Wil Cordero	.10
12	John Mabry	.10
13	Jeff Frye	.10
14	Travis Fryman	.15
15	John Wetteland	.10
16	Jason Bates	.10
17	Danny Tartabull	.10
18	Charles Nagy	.10
19	Robin Ventura	.10
20	Reggie Sanders	.10
21	Dave Clark	.10
22	Jaime Navarro	.10
23	Joey Hamilton	.10
24	Al Leiter	.10
25	Deion Sanders	.25
26	Tim Salmon	.20
27	Tino Martinez	.15
28	Mike Greenwell	.10
29	Phil Plantier	.10
30	Bobby Bonilla	.10
31	Kenny Rogers	.10
32	Chili Davis	.10
33	Joe Carter	.15
34	Mike Mussina	.40
35	Matt Mieske	.10
36	Jose Canseco	.30
37	Brad Radke	.10
38	Juan Gonzalez	1.50
39	David Segui	.10
40	Alex Fernandez	.10
41	Jeff Kent	.10
42	Todd Zeile	.10
43	Darryl Strawberry	.10
44	Jose Rijo	.10
45	Ramon Martinez	.10
46	Manny Ramirez	.75
47	Gregg Jefferies	.10
48	Bryan Rekar	.10
49	Jeff King	.10
50	John Olerud	.10
51	Marc Newfield	.10
52	Charles Johnson	.15
53	Robby Thompson	.10
54	Brian Hunter	.10
55	Mike Blowers	.10
56	Keith Lockhart	.10
57	Ray Lankford	.10
58	Tim Wallach	.10
59	Ivan Rodriguez	.50
60	Ed Sprague	.10
61	Paul Molitor	.20
62	Eric Karros	.10
63	Glenallen Hill	.10
64	Jay Bell	.10
65	Tom Pagnozzi	.10
66	Greg Colbrunn	.10
67	Edgar Martinez	.10
68	Paul Sorrento	.10
69	Kirt Manwaring	.10
70	Pete Schourek	.10
71	Orlando Merced	.10
72	Shawon Dunston	.10
73	Ricky Bottalico	.10
74	Brady Anderson	.15
75	Steve Ontiveros	.10
76	Jim Abbott	.10
77	Carl Everett	.10
78	Mo Vaughn	.75
79	Pedro Martinez	.10
80	Harold Baines	.10
81	Marty Cordova	.10
82	Ken Griffey Jr.	3.00
83	Gary Sheffield	.40
84	Charlie Hayes	.10
85	Bernie Williams	.50
86	Jason Giambi	.15
87	Mark Langston	.10
88	Mark Whiten	.10
89	Greg Vaughn	.10

No.	Player	Price
90	Barry Larkin	.20
91	Cliff Floyd	.15
92	Sammy Sosa	1.50
93	Andres Galarraga	.15
94	Dave Nilsson	.10
95	James Mouton	.10
96	Marquis Grissom	.10
97	Matt Williams	.25
98	John Jaha	.10
99	Don Mattingly	1.00
100	Tim Naehring	.10
101	Kevin Appier	.10
102	Bobby Higginson	.10
103	Andy Pettitte	.90
104	Ozzie Smith	.40
105	Kenny Lofton	.75
106	Ken Caminiti	.15
107	Walt Weiss	.10
108	Jack McDowell	.10
109	Brian McRae	.10
110	Gary Gaetti	.10
111	Curtis Goodwin	.10
112	Dennis Martinez	.10
113	Omar Vizquel	.10
114	Chipper Jones	2.00
115	Mark Gubicza	.10
116	Ruben Sierra	.10
117	Eddie Murray	.40
118	Chad Curtis	.10
119	Hal Morris	.10
120	Ben McDonald	.10
121	Alan Trammell	.10
122	Steve Avery	.10
123	Jeff Cirillo	.10
124	John Valentin	.10
125	Bernie Williams	.25
126	Andre Dawson	.10
127	Dave Winfield	.10
128	B.J. Surhoff	.10
129	Jeff Blauser	.10
130	Mark McGwire	3.00
131	Hideo Nomo	.60
132	Tony Tarasco	.10
133	Jason Bere	.10
134	Ken Griffey Jr. (The Naturals)	1.50
135	Frank Thomas (The Naturals)	1.50
136	Cal Ripken Jr. (The Naturals)	1.25
137	Albert Belle (The Naturals)	.40
138	Mike Piazza (The Naturals)	1.00
139	Dante Bichette (The Naturals)	.15
140	Sammy Sosa (The Naturals)	.75
141	Mo Vaughn (The Naturals)	.30
142	Tim Salmon (The Naturals)	.15
143	Reggie Sanders (The Naturals)	.10
144	Cecil Fielder (The Naturals)	.15
145	Jim Edmonds (The Naturals)	.10
146	Rafael Palmeiro (The Naturals)	.10
147	Edgar Martinez (The Naturals)	.10
148	Barry Bonds (The Naturals)	.30
149	Manny Ramirez (The Naturals)	.40
150	Larry Walker (The Naturals)	.15
151	Jeff Bagwell (The Naturals)	.50
152	Ron Gant (The Naturals)	.10
153	Andres Galarraga (The Naturals)	.10
154	Eddie Murray (The Naturals)	.20
155	Kirby Puckett (The Naturals)	.50
156	Will Clark (The Naturals)	.15
157	Don Mattingly (The Naturals)	.60
158	Mark McGwire (The Naturals)	1.50
159	Dean Palmer (The Naturals)	.10
160	Matt Williams (The Naturals)	.15
161	Fred McGriff (The Naturals)	.20
162	Joe Carter (The Naturals)	.10
163	Juan Gonzalez (The Naturals)	.60
164	Karim Garcia	.20
165	Ruben Rivera	.25
166	Tony Clark	.50
167	Brian Barber	.10
168	Billy Wagner	.10
169	Terrell Wade	.10
170	Johnny Damon	.20
171	Derek Jeter	1.50
172	Phil Nevin	.10
173	Steve Gibralter	.10
174	C.J. Nitkowski	.10
175	Joe Vitiello	.10
176	Roger Cedeno	.10
177	Ron Coomer	.10
178	Arquimedez Pozo	.10
179	Jimmy Haynes	.10
180	Jorge Posada	.10
181	Dwayne Hosey	.10
182	Makoto Suzuki	.10
183	Jim Pittsley	.10
184	Tim Unroe	.10
185	LaTroy Hawkins	.10
186	Nigel Wilson	.10
187	Shannon Stewart	.20
188	Chris Snopek	.10
189	Mariano Rivera	.20
190	Jose Herrera	.10
191	Chris Stynes	.10
192	Larry Thomas	.10
193	David Bell	.10
194	Checklist	.10
195	Checklist	.10
196	Checklist	.10
197	Checklist	.10
198	Checklist	.10
199	Checklist	.10
200	Checklist	.10
201	Frank Thomas	2.50
202	Michael Tucker	.10
203	Kirby Puckett	1.00
204	Alex Gonzalez	.10
205	Tony Gwynn	1.00
206	Moises Alou	.10
207	Albert Belle	.75
208	Barry Bonds	.75
209	Fred McGriff	.40
210	Dennis Eckersley	.10
211	Craig Biggio	.10
212	David Cone	.10
213	Will Clark	.25
214	Cal Ripken Jr.	2.50
215	Wade Boggs	.20
216	Pete Schourek	.10
217	Darren Daulton	.10
218	Carlos Baerga	.20
219	Larry Walker	.30
220	Denny Neagle	.10
221	Jim Edmonds	.15
222	Lee Smith	.10
223	Jason Isringhausen	.20
224	Jay Buhner	.20
225	John Olerud	.10
226	Jeff Conine	.10
227	Dean Palmer	.10
228	Jim Abbott	.10
229	Raul Mondesi	.30
230	Tom Glavine	.15
231	Kevin Seitzer	.10
232	Lenny Dykstra	.10
233	Brian Jordan	.10
234	Rondell White	.10
235	Bret Boone	.10
236	Randy Johnson	.35
237	Paul O'Neill	.10
238	Jim Thome	.40
239	Edgardo Alfonzo	.10
240	Terry Pendleton	.10
241	Harold Baines	.10
242	Roberto Alomar	.60
243	Mark Grace	.15
244	Derek Bell	.10
245	Vinny Castilla	.10
246	Cecil Fielder	.15
247	Roger Clemens	.75
248	Orel Hershiser	.10
249	J.T. Snow	.10
250	Rafael Palmeiro	.20
251	Bret Saberhagen	.10
252	Todd Hollandsworth	.20
253	Ryan Klesko	.50
254	Greg Maddux (Hardball Heroes)	1.00
255	Ken Griffey Jr. (Hardball Heroes)	1.50
256	Hideo Nomo (Hardball Heroes)	.40
257	Frank Thomas (Hardball Heroes)	1.50
258	Cal Ripken Jr. (Hardball Heroes)	1.25
259	Jeff Bagwell (Hardball Heroes)	.50
260	Barry Bonds (Hardball Heroes)	.40
261	Mo Vaughn (Hardball Heroes)	.25
262	Albert Belle (Hardball Heroes)	.40
263	Sammy Sosa (Hardball Heroes)	.50
264	Reggie Sanders (Hardball Heroes)	.10
265	Mike Piazza (Hardball Heroes)	1.00
266	Chipper Jones (Hardball Heroes)	1.00
267	Tony Gwynn (Hardball Heroes)	.60
268	Kirby Puckett (Hardball Heroes)	.40
269	Wade Boggs (Hardball Heroes)	.15
270	Will Clark (Hardball Heroes)	.15
271	Gary Sheffield (Hardball Heroes)	.15
272	Dante Bichette (Hardball Heroes)	.15
273	Randy Johnson (Hardball Heroes)	.20
274	Matt Williams (Hardball Heroes)	.15
275	Alex Rodriguez (Hardball Heroes)	2.00
276	Tim Salmon (Hardball Heroes)	.20
277	Johnny Damon (Hardball Heroes)	.20
278	Manny Ramirez (Hardball Heroes)	.50
279	Derek Jeter (Hardball Heroes)	1.00
280	Eddie Murray (Hardball Heroes)	.20
281	Ozzie Smith (Hardball Heroes)	.20
282	Garret Anderson (Hardball Heroes)	.10
283	Raul Mondesi (Hardball Heroes)	.20
284	Terry Steinbach	.10
285	Carlos Garcia	.10
286	Dave Justice	.20
287	Eric Anthony	.10
288	Benji Gil	.10
289	Bob Hamelin	.10
290	Dwayne Hosey	.10
291	Andy Pettitte	.75
292	Rod Beck	.10
293	Shane Andrews	.10
294	Julian Tavarez	.10
295	Willie Greene	.10
296	Ismael Valdes	.10
297	Glenallen Hill	.10
298	Troy Percival	.10
299	Ray Durham	.10
300	Jeff Conine (.300 Series)	.10
301.8	Ken Griffey Jr. (.300 Series)	1.50
302	Will Clark (.300 Series)	.20
303	Mike Greenwell (.300 Series)	.10
304.9	Carlos Baerga (.300 Series)	.15
305.3	Paul Molitor (.300 Series)	.20
305.6	Jeff Bagwell (.300 Series)	.50
306	Mark Grace (.300 Series)	.15
307	Don Mattingly (.300 Series)	.60
308	Hal Morris (.300 Series)	.10
309	Butch Huskey	.10
310	Ozzie Guillen	.10
311	Erik Hanson	.10
312	Kenny Lofton (.300 Series)	.40
313	Edgar Martinez (.300 Series)	.10
314	Kurt Abbott	.10
315	John Smoltz	.20
316	Ariel Prieto	.10
317	Mark Carreon	.10
318	Kirby Puckett (.300 Series)	.40
319	Carlos Perez	.10
320	Gary DiSarcina	.10
321	Trevor Hoffman	.10
322	Mike Piazza (.300 Series)	1.00
323	Frank Thomas (.300 Series)	1.50
324	Juan Acevedo	.10
325	Bip Roberts	.10
326	Javier Lopez	.15
327	Benito Santiago	.10
328	Mark Lewis	.10
329	Royce Clayton	.10

330	Tom Gordon	.10
331	Ben McDonald	.10
332	Dan Wilson	.10
333	Ron Gant	.15
334	Wade Boggs (.300 Series)	.10
335	Paul Molitor	.25
336	Tony Gwynn (.300 Series)	.60
337	Sean Berry	.10
338	Rickey Henderson	.10
339	Wil Cordero	.10
340	Kent Mercker	.10
341	Kenny Rogers	.10
342	Ryne Sandberg	.75
343	Charlie Hayes	.10
344	Andy Benes	.10
345	Sterling Hitchcock	.10
346	Bernard Gilkey	.10
347	Julio Franco	.10
348	Ken Hill	.10
349	Russ Davis	.10
350	Mike Blowers	.10
351	B.J. Surhoff	.10
352	Lance Johnson	.10
353	Darryl Hamilton	.10
354	Shawon Dunston	.10
355	Rick Aguilera	.10
356	Danny Tartabull	.10
357	Todd Stottlemyre	.10
358	Mike Bordick	.10
359	Jack McDowell	.10
360	Todd Zeile	.10
361	Tino Martinez	.10
362	Greg Gagne	.10
363	Mike Kelly	.10
364	Tim Raines	.10
365	Ernie Young	.10
366	Mike Stanley	.10
367	Wally Joyner	.10
368	Karim Garcia	.40
369	Paul Wilson	.25
370	Sal Fasano	.10
371	Jason Schmidt	.10
372	*Livan Hernandez*	1.00
373	George Arias	.10
374	Steve Gibralter	.10
375	Jermaine Dye	.25
376	Jason Kendall	.10
377	Brooks Kieschnick	.10
378	Jeff Ware	.10
379	Alan Benes	.25
380	Rey Ordonez	.50
381	Jay Powell	.10
382	*Osvaldo Fernandez*	.15
383	*Wilton Guerrero*	.75
384	Eric Owens	.10
385	George Williams	.10
386	Chan Ho Park	.10
387	Jeff Suppan	.10
388	*F.P. Santangelo*	.10
389	Terry Adams	.10
390	Bob Abreu	.10
391	*Matt Luke*	.10
392	*Mike Busby*	.10
393	Checklist(Cal Ripken Jr.)	1.00
394	Checklist(Ken Griffey Jr.)	1.25
395	Checklist(Frank Thomas)	1.25
396	Checklist(Chipper Jones)	.60
397	Checklist(Greg Maddux)	.75
398	Checklist(Mike Piazza)	.60
399	Checklist(Ken Griffey Jr., Frank Thomas, Cal Ripken Jr., Greg Maddux, Chipper Jones, Mike Piazza)	.75

1996 Pinnacle Christie Brinkley Collection

Supermodel Christie Brinkley exclusively took photos for these 1996 Pinnacle Series II inserts. The 16 cards capture players from the 1995 World Series participants during a spring training photo session. Cards were seeded one per every 23 hobby packs or 32 retail packs.

A player's name in *italic* type indicates a rookie card.

		MT
Complete Set (16):		30.00
Common Player:		1.50
1	Greg Maddux	8.00
2	Ryan Klesko	3.25
3	Dave Justice	1.75
4	Tom Glavine	1.50
5	Chipper Jones	8.00
6	Fred McGriff	2.25
7	Javier Lopez	1.75
8	Marquis Grissom	1.50
9	Jason Schmidt	1.50
10	Albert Belle	4.50
11	Manny Ramirez	4.00
12	Carlos Baerga	1.50
13	Sandy Alomar	1.50
14	Jim Thome	2.25
15	Julio Franco	1.50
16	Kenny Lofton	4.00

1996 Pinnacle Essence of the Game

Essence of the Game is an 18-card insert set found only in hobby packs at a one per 23 packs rate in Series 1. Cards are printed on clear plastic with the front photo also appearing in an inverted fashion on back. Micro-etched Dufex printing technology is utilized on the front of the cards.

		MT
Complete Set (18):		90.00
Common Player:		1.25
1	Cal Ripken Jr.	12.00
2	Greg Maddux	9.00
3	Frank Thomas	9.00
4	Matt Williams	2.50
5	Chipper Jones	9.00
6	Reggie Sanders	1.25
7	Ken Griffey Jr.	15.00
8	Kirby Puckett	6.00
9	Hideo Nomo	3.50

10	Mike Piazza	9.00
11	Jeff Bagwell	6.00
12	Mo Vaughn	4.00
13	Albert Belle	3.50
14	Tim Salmon	2.50
15	Don Mattingly	6.00
16	Will Clark	2.50
17	Eddie Murray	3.00
18	Barry Bonds	4.50

1996 Pinnacle First Rate

Retail-exclusive First Rate showcases 18 former first round draft picks now in the majors. Printed in Dufex foil throughout, a red swirl pattern covers the left 2/3 of the card front. Backs show the player again, within a large numeral "1". These inserts are found at an average rate of one per 23 packs in Series 1.

		MT
Complete Set (18):		120.00
Common Player:		2.50
1	Ken Griffey Jr.	30.00
2	Frank Thomas	20.00
3	Mo Vaughn	8.00
4	Chipper Jones	20.00
5	Alex Rodriguez	25.00
6	Kirby Puckett	10.00
7	Gary Sheffield	4.00
8	Matt Williams	3.00
9	Barry Bonds	8.00
10	Craig Biggio	2.50
11	Robin Ventura	2.50
12	Michael Tucker	2.50
13	Derek Jeter	15.00
14	Manny Ramirez	7.00
15	Barry Larkin	3.00
16	Shawn Green	2.50
17	Will Clark	4.00
18	Mark McGwire	30.00

1996 Pinnacle Pinnacle Power

Pinnacle Powers inserts are seeded at the rate of one per 47 packs in both hobby and retail Series 1. Twenty different sluggers are featured on a two-layered front. The bottom layer is silver Dufex foil with solid black on top; a color action photo of the player is at center, giving the card a die-cut appearance.

		MT
Complete Set (20):		100.00
Common Player:		2.00
1	Frank Thomas	15.00
2	Mo Vaughn	6.00
2p	Mo Vaughn (promo)	3.00
3	Ken Griffey Jr.	25.00
4	Matt Williams	3.00
5	Barry Bonds	6.00
6	Reggie Sanders	2.00
7	Mike Piazza	15.00
8	Jim Edmonds	2.00
9	Dante Bichette	2.00
10	Sammy Sosa	12.00
11	Jeff Bagwell	10.00
12	Fred McGriff	4.00
13	Albert Belle	6.00
14	Tim Salmon	3.00
15	Joe Carter	2.00
16	Manny Ramirez	5.00
17	Eddie Murray	4.00
18	Cecil Fielder	2.00
19	Larry Walker	4.00
20	Juan Gonzalez	12.00

1996 Pinnacle Project Stardom

These 1996 Pinnacle inserts cards feature young players on their way to stardom. The cards, which use Dufex technology, are seeded one per every 35 packs of Series II hobby packs.

		MT
Complete Set (18):		120.00
Common Player:		2.50
1	Paul Wilson	2.50
2	Derek Jeter	25.00
3	Karim Garcia	8.00
4	Johnny Damon	2.50
5	Alex Rodriguez	40.00
6	Chipper Jones	25.00
7	Todd Walker	5.00
8	Bob Abreu	2.50
9	Alan Benes	4.00
10	Richard Hidalgo	2.50
11	Brooks Kieschnick	4.00
12	Garret Anderson	4.00
13	Livan Hernandez	6.00
14	Manny Ramirez	8.00
15	Jermaine Dye	2.50
16	Todd Hollandsworth	4.00
17	Raul Mondesi	6.00
18	Ryan Klesko	8.00

1996 Pinnacle Skylines

These 1996 Pinnacle inserts feature cards printed on a clear plastic stock. The cards were seeded one per every 29 Series II magazine packs, and one per 50 retail packs.

		MT
Complete Set (18):		200.00
Common Player:		4.00
1	Ken Griffey Jr.	40.00
2	Frank Thomas	25.00
3	Greg Maddux	25.00
4	Cal Ripken Jr.	25.00
5	Albert Belle	8.00
6	Mo Vaughn	8.00
7	Mike Piazza	20.00
8	Wade Boggs	4.00
9	Will Clark	4.00
10	Barry Bonds	8.00
11	Gary Sheffield	4.00
12	Hideo Nomo	5.00
13	Tony Gwynn	15.00
14	Kirby Puckett	8.00
15	Chipper Jones	20.00
16	Jeff Bagwell	10.00
17	Manny Ramirez	6.00
18	Raul Mondesi	4.00

1996 Pinnacle Slugfest

These 1996 Pinnacle Series II inserts feature 18 of the game's heaviest hitters on all-foil Dufex cards. The cards were seeded one per every 35 retail packs.

		MT
Complete Set (18):		150.00
Common Player:		3.00
1	Frank Thomas	25.00
2	Ken Griffey Jr.	35.00
3	Jeff Bagwell	15.00
4	Barry Bonds	10.00
5	Mo Vaughn	8.00
6	Albert Belle	8.00
7	Mike Piazza	22.00
8	Matt Williams	5.00
9	Dante Bichette	4.00

10	Sammy Sosa	15.00
11	Gary Sheffield	6.00
12	Reggie Sanders	3.00
13	Manny Ramirez	8.00
14	Eddie Murray	5.00
15	Juan Gonzalez	16.00
16	Dean Palmer	3.00
17	Rafael Palmeiro	4.00
18	Cecil Fielder	3.00

1996 Pinnacle Starburst

For 1996 Pinnacle abbreviated its parallel insert set to just half of the cards from the base issue. Only 200 select players are included in the Starburst Dufex-printed parallel set found on average of once per seven hobby packs and once per 10 retail packs. An Artist's Proof version of the Starbursts, a parallel set within a parallel set, are inserted once per 47 (hobby) or 67 (retail) packs. On these super-premium inserts the Artist's Proof logo is repeated throughout the Dufex background.

		MT
Complete Set (200):		600.00
Complete Series 1 (100):		300.00
Complete Series 2 (100):		300.00
Common Player:		1.00
Complete Artist's Proof Set (200):		1800.
Artist's Proofs: 3X to 4X		
1	Greg Maddux	20.00
2	Bill Pulsipher	2.00
3	Dante Bichette	2.50
4	Mike Piazza	20.00
5	Garret Anderson	1.50
6	Chuck Knoblauch	1.00
7	Jeff Bagwell	15.00
8	Wil Cordero	1.00
9	Travis Fryman	1.00
10	Reggie Sanders	1.00
11	Deion Sanders	4.00
12	Tim Salmon	4.00
13	Tino Martinez	1.50
14	Bobby Bonilla	1.00
15	Joe Carter	1.50
16	Mike Mussina	4.00
17	Jose Canseco	3.00
18	Manny Ramirez	10.00
19	Gregg Jefferies	1.00
20	Charles Johnson	1.00
21	Brian Hunter	1.00
22	Ray Lankford	1.00
23	Ivan Rodriguez	3.00
24	Paul Molitor	2.00
25	Eric Karros	1.00
26	Edgar Martinez	1.00
27	Shawon Dunston	1.00
28	Mo Vaughn	10.00
29	Pedro Martinez	1.00
30	Marty Cordova	1.50
31	Ken Caminiti	1.50

32	Gary Sheffield	2.00
33	Shawn Green	1.00
34	Cliff Floyd	1.00
35	Andres Galarraga	1.50
36	Matt Williams	2.00
37	Don Mattingly	15.00
38	Kevin Appier	1.00
39	Ozzie Smith	4.00
40	Kenny Lofton	10.00
41	Ken Griffey Jr.	40.00
42	Jack McDowell	1.50
43	Gary Gaetti	1.00
44	Dennis Martinez	1.00
45	Chipper Jones	20.00
46	Eddie Murray	3.00
47	Bernie Williams	2.50
48	Andre Dawson	1.00
49	Dave Winfield	1.00
50	B.J. Surhoff	1.00
51	Barry Larkin	1.50
52	Alan Trammell	1.00
53	Sammy Sosa	8.00
54	Hideo Nomo	7.50
55	Mark McGwire	30.00
56	Jay Bell	1.00
57	Juan Gonzalez	15.00
58	Chili Davis	1.00
59	Robin Ventura	1.00
60	John Mabry	1.00
61	Ken Griffey Jr. (Naturals)	20.00
62	Frank Thomas (Naturals)	15.00
63	Cal Ripken Jr. (Naturals)	18.00
64	Albert Belle (Naturals)	5.00
65	Mike Piazza (Naturals)	12.00
66	Dante Bichette (Naturals)	1.50
67	Sammy Sosa (Naturals)	5.00
68	Mo Vaughn (Naturals)	4.00
69	Tim Salmon (Naturals)	2.50
70	Reggie Sanders (Naturals)	1.00
71	Cecil Fielder (Naturals)	1.50
72	Jim Edmonds (Naturals)	1.00
73	Rafael Palmeiro (Naturals)	1.50
74	Edgar Martinez (Naturals)	1.00
75	Barry Bonds (Naturals)	6.00
76	Manny Ramirez (Naturals)	7.00
77	Larry Walker (Naturals)	1.00
78	Jeff Bagwell (Naturals)	10.00
79	Ron Gant (Naturals)	1.00
80	Andres Galarraga (Naturals)	1.00
81	Eddie Murray (Naturals)	1.50
82	Kirby Puckett (Naturals)	9.00
83	Will Clark (Naturals)	2.00
84	Don Mattingly (Naturals)	10.00
85	Mark McGwire (Naturals)	15.00
86	Dean Palmer (Naturals)	1.00
87	Matt Williams (Naturals)	2.00
88	Fred McGriff (Naturals)	2.50
89	Joe Carter (Naturals)	1.00
90	Juan Gonzalez (Naturals)	10.00
91	Alex Ochoa	1.00
92	Ruben Rivera	2.00
93	Tony Clark	6.00
94	Pete Schourek	1.00
95	Terrell Wade	1.00
96	Johnny Damon	2.00
97	Derek Jeter	8.00
98	Phil Nevin	1.00
99	Robert Perez	1.00
100	Dustin Hermanson	1.00
101	Frank Thomas	25.00
102	Michael Tucker	1.00
103	Kirby Puckett	12.00
104	Alex Gonzalez	1.00
105	Tony Gwynn	15.00
106	Moises Alou	1.00
107	Albert Belle	10.00
108	Barry Bonds	10.00
109	Fred McGriff	5.00
110	Dennis Eckersley	1.00
111	Craig Biggio	1.00
112	David Cone	1.00
113	Will Clark	2.00
114	Cal Ripken Jr.	30.00
115	Wade Boggs	2.00
116	Pete Schourek	1.00
117	Darren Daulton	1.00
118	Carlos Baerga	1.50
119	Larry Walker	2.00
120	Denny Neagle	1.00
121	Jim Edmonds	1.00
122	Lee Smith	1.00
123	Jason Isringhausen	2.00
124	Jay Buhner	1.50
125	John Olerud	1.00
126	Jeff Conine	1.00

127	Dean Palmer	1.00
128	Jim Abbott	1.00
129	Raul Mondesi	2.00
130	Tom Glavine	1.00
131	Kevin Seitzer	1.00
132	Lenny Dykstra	1.00
133	Brian Jordan	1.00
134	Rondell White	1.00
135	Bret Boone	1.00
136	Randy Johnson	4.00
137	Paul O'Neill	1.00
138	Jim Thome	3.00
139	Edgardo Alfonzo	1.00
140	Terry Pendleton	1.00
141	Harold Baines	1.00
142	Roberto Alomar	8.00
143	Mark Grace	1.50
144	Derek Bell	1.00
145	Vinny Castilla	1.00
146	Cecil Fielder	1.50
147	Roger Clemens	4.00
148	Orel Hershiser	1.00
149	J.T. Snow	1.00
150	Rafael Palmeiro	1.50
151	Bret Saberhagen	1.00
152	Todd Hollandsworth	1.50
153	Ryan Klesko	8.00
154	Greg Maddux (Hardball Heroes)	12.00
155	Ken Griffey Jr. (Hardball Heroes)	20.00
156	Hideo Nomo (Hardball Heroes)	5.00
157	Frank Thomas (Hardball Heroes)	15.00
158	Cal Ripken Jr. (Hardball Heroes)	18.00
159	Jeff Bagwell (Hardball Heroes)	9.00
160	Barry Bonds (Hardball Heroes)	6.00
161	Mo Vaughn (Hardball Heroes)	7.50
162	Albert Belle (Hardball Heroes)	6.00
163	Sammy Sosa (Hardball Heroes)	5.00
164	Reggie Sanders (Hardball Heroes)	1.00
165	Mike Piazza (Hardball Heroes)	12.00
166	Chipper Jones (Hardball Heroes)	12.00
167	Tony Gwynn (Hardball Heroes)	8.00
168	Kirby Puckett (Hardball Heroes)	6.00
169	Wade Boggs (Hardball Heroes)	1.50
170	Will Clark (Hardball Heroes)	1.50
171	Gary Sheffield (Hardball Heroes)	1.50
172	Dante Bichette (Hardball Heroes)	1.50
173	Randy Johnson (Hardball Heroes)	2.00
174	Matt Williams (Hardball Heroes)	2.00
175	Alex Rodriguez (Hardball Heroes)	20.00
176	Tim Salmon (Hardball Heroes)	1.50
177	Johnny Damon (Hardball Heroes)	1.50
178	Manny Ramirez (Hardball Heroes)	6.00
179	Derek Jeter (Hardball Heroes)	10.00
180	Eddie Murray (Hardball Heroes)	2.50
181	Ozzie Smith (Hardball Heroes)	2.50
182	Garret Anderson (Hardball Heroes)	1.00
183	Raul Mondesi (Hardball Heroes)	1.50
184	Jeff Conine (.300 Series)	1.00
185	Ken Griffey Jr. (.300 Series)	20.00
186	Will Clark (.300 Series)	1.50
187	Mike Greenwell (.300 Series)	1.00
188	Carlos Baerga (.300 Series)	1.00
189	Paul Molitor (.300 Series)	1.50
190	Jeff Bagwell (.300 Series)	9.00
191	Mark Grace (.300 Series)	1.00
192	Don Mattingly (.300 Series)	9.00

193	Hal Morris (.300 Series)	1.00
194	Kenny Lofton (.300 Series)	5.00
195	Edgar Martinez (.300 Series)	1.00
196	Kirby Puckett (.300 Series)	7.00
197	Mike Piazza (.300 Series)	12.00
198	Frank Thomas (.300 Series)	12.00
199	Wade Boggs (.300 Series)	1.50
200	Tony Gwynn (.300 Series)	8.00

1996 Pinnacle Team Pinnacle

Team Pinnacle inserts offer 18 players in a double-sided nine-card set. Each card can be found with Dufex printing on one side and regular gold-foil printing on the other. Inserted one per 72 packs of Series 1, Team Pinnacle pairs up an American League player and a National Leaguer at the same position on each card.

		MT
Complete Set (9):		100.00
Common Player:		4.00
1	Frank Thomas, Jeff Bagwell	20.00
2	Chuck Knoblauch, Craig Biggio	5.00
3	Jim Thome, Matt Williams	6.00
4	Barry Larkin, Cal Ripken Jr.	20.00
5	Barry Bonds, Tim Salmon	8.00
6	Ken Griffey Jr., Reggie Sanders	25.00
7	Albert Belle, Sammy Sosa	15.00
8	Ivan Rodriguez, Mike Piazza	15.00
9	Greg Maddux, Randy Johnson	15.00

1996 Pinnacle Team Spirit

One in every 72 1996 Pinnacle Series II hobby packs or every 103 retail packs has one of these die-cut insert cards. Each card has a holographic baseball design behind an embossed glossy action photo of the player on a flat black background. Backs are conventionally printed.

		MT
Complete Set (12):		200.00
Common Player:		7.50
1	Greg Maddux	25.00
2	Ken Griffey Jr.	40.00
3	Derek Jeter	20.00
4	Mike Piazza	25.00
5	Cal Ripken Jr.	30.00
6	Frank Thomas	25.00
7	Jeff Bagwell	16.00
8	Mo Vaughn	10.00
9	Albert Belle	10.00
10	Chipper Jones	25.00
11	Johnny Damon	7.50
12	Barry Bonds	10.00

1996 Pinnacle Team Tomorrow

Team Tomorrow showcases 10 young superstars on a horizontal Dufex design. While the player appears twice on the card front, the left side is merely a close-up of the same shot appearing on the right. These inserts are exclusive to Series 1 jumbo packs, found on average at the rate of one per 19 packs.

		MT
Complete Set (10):		100.00
Common Player:		3.00
1	Ruben Rivera	5.00
2	Johnny Damon	3.00
3	Raul Mondesi	5.00
4	Manny Ramirez	10.00
5	Hideo Nomo	10.00
6	Chipper Jones	25.00
7	Garret Anderson	3.00
8	Alex Rodriguez	40.00
9	Derek Jeter	25.00
10	Karim Garcia	8.00

1996 Pinnacle/ Aficionado

Pinnacle's 1996 Aficionado set gives every card its own character; each card is printed as an all-wood card with a maple wood grain. The 200 regular issue cards include 160 cards in sepia-tone, giving each an antique-looking finish. The horizontal card front also has a rainbow holographic foil image of the player featured. His name is in foil in a panel at the bottom. The back has positional comparison statistics that show how each player compares with the league average at that position and the league average at that position in different eras. There are also 60 four-color cards, which include 25 four-color rookie cards, and a 10-card Global Reach subset. This subset, which honors baseball's international flavor, features Aficionado's new heliogram printing process. Artist's Proof parallel cards, seeded one per every 35 packs, were also created. These cards mirror the regular issue and use a unique gold foil stamp on them. There were also three insert sets created: Slick Picks, Rivals and Magic Numbers.

		MT
Complete Set (200):		60.00
Common Player:		.20
Unlisted Stars: .40 to .60		
Veteran Star Artist's Proofs: 20x to 30x		
Young Star Artist's Proofs: 10x to 20x		
Wax Box:		50.00
1	Jack McDowell	.25
2	Jay Bell	.20
3	Rafael Palmeiro	.30
4	Wally Joyner	.20
5	Ozzie Smith	.75
6	Mark McGwire	5.00
7	Kevin Seitzer	.20
8	Fred McGriff	.50
9	Roger Clemens	1.50
9s	Roger Clemens (marked "SAMPLE")	5.00
10	Randy Johnson	.75
11	Cecil Fielder	.25
12	David Cone	.30
13	Chili Davis	.20
14	Andres Galarraga	.40
15	Joe Carter	.35
16	Ryne Sandberg	1.25
17	Paul O'Neill	.40
18	Cal Ripken Jr.	4.00
19	Wade Boggs	.40
20	Greg Gagne	.20
21	Edgar Martinez	.20
22	Greg Maddux	3.00
23	Ken Caminiti	.50
24	Kirby Puckett	2.00
25	Craig Biggio	.40
26	Will Clark	.40
27	Ron Gant	.25
28	Eddie Murray	.50
29	Lance Johnson	.20
30	Tony Gwynn	2.50
31	Dante Bichette	.50
32	Darren Daulton	.20
33	Danny Tartabull	.20
34	Jeff King	.20
35	Tom Glavine	.35
36	Rickey Henderson	.20
37	Jose Canseco	.35
38	Barry Larkin	.45
39	Dennis Martinez	.20
40	Ruben Sierra	.20
41	Bobby Bonilla	.30
42	Jeff Conine	.20
43	Lee Smith	.20
44	Charlie Hayes	.20
45	Walt Weiss	.20
46	Jay Buhner	.30
47	Kenny Rogers	.20
48	Paul Molitor	.50
49	Hal Morris	.20
50	Todd Stottlemyre	.20
51	Mike Stanley	.20
52	Mark Grace	.40
53	Lenny Dykstra	.20
54	Andre Dawson	.20
55	Dennis Eckersley	.20

56	Ben McDonald	.20
57	Ray Lankford	.20
58	Mo Vaughn	1.25
59	Frank Thomas	4.00
60	Julio Franco	.20
61	Jim Abbott	.20
62	Greg Vaughn	.20
63	Marquis Grissom	.30
64	Tino Martinez	.50
65	Kevin Appier	.20
66	Matt Williams	.40
67	Sammy Sosa	2.50
68	Larry Walker	.60
69	Ivan Rodriguez	.75
70	Eric Karros	.20
71	Bernie Williams	.75
72	Carlos Baerga	.20
73	Jeff Bagwell	1.50
74	Pete Schourek	.20
75	Ken Griffey Jr.	5.00
76	Bernard Gilkey	.20
77	Albert Belle	1.25
78	Chuck Knoblauch	.40
79	John Smoltz	.40
80	Barry Bonds	1.25
81	Vinny Castilla	.20
82	John Olerud	.20
83	Mike Mussina	1.00
84	Alex Fernandez	.20
85	Shawon Dunston	.20
86	Travis Fryman	.20
87	Moises Alou	.35
88	Dean Palmer	.20
89	Gregg Jefferies	.20
90	Jim Thome	.75
91	Dave Justice	.40
92	B.J. Surhoff	.20
93	Ramon Martinez	.20
94	Gary Sheffield	.60
95	Andy Benes	.20
96	Reggie Sanders	.20
97	Roberto Alomar	1.00
98	Omar Vizquel	.20
99	Juan Gonzalez	2.50
100	Robin Ventura	.20
101	Jason Isringhausen	.20
102	Greg Colbrunn	.20
103	Brian Jordan	.20
104	Shawn Green	.20
105	Brian Hunter	.20
106	Rondell White	.30
107	Ryan Klesko	.75
107s	Ryan Klesko (marked "SAMPLE")	4.00
108	Sterling Hitchcock	.20
109	Manny Ramirez	1.00
110	Bret Boone	.20
111	Michael Tucker	.20
112	Julian Tavarez	.20
113	Benji Gil	.20
114	Kenny Lofton	1.00
115	Mike Kelly	.20
116	Ray Durham	.20
117	Trevor Hoffman	.20
118	Butch Huskey	.20
119	Phil Nevin	.20
120	Pedro Martinez	.40
121	Wil Cordero	.20
122	Tim Salmon	.50
123	Jim Edmonds	.40
124	Mike Piazza	3.00
125	Rico Brogna	.20
126	John Mabry	.20
127	Chipper Jones	3.00
128	Johnny Damon	.20
129	Raul Mondesi	.40
130	Denny Neagle	.20
131	Marc Newfield	.20
132	Hideo Nomo	1.25
133	Joe Vitiello	.20
134	Garret Anderson	.20
135	Dave Nilsson	.20
136	Alex Rodriguez	5.00
137	Russ Davis	.20
138	Frank Rodriguez	.20
139	Royce Clayton	.20
140	John Valentin	.20
141	Marty Cordova	.20
142	Alex Gonzalez	.20
143	Carlos Delgado	.20
144	Willie Greene	.20
145	Cliff Floyd	.20
146	Bobby Higginson	.40
147	J.T. Snow	.20
148	Derek Bell	.20
149	Edgardo Alfonzo	.20

150	Charles Johnson	.20
151	Hideo Nomo (Global Reach)	.45
152	Larry Walker (Global Reach)	.30
153	Bob Abreu (Global Reach)	.20
154	Karim Garcia (Global Reach)	.40
155	Dave Nilsson (Global Reach)	.20
156	Chan Ho Park (Global Reach)	.20
157	Dennis Martinez (Global Reach)	.20
158	Sammy Sosa (Global Reach)	1.00
159	Rey Ordonez (Global Reach)	.40
160	Roberto Alomar (Global Reach)	.50
161	George Arias	.20
162	Jason Schmidt	.20
163	Derek Jeter	3.00
164	Chris Snopek	.20
165	Todd Hollandsworth	.25
166	Sal Fasano	.20
167	Jay Powell	.20
168	Paul Wilson	.40
169	Jim Pittsley	.20
170	LaTroy Hawkins	.20
171	Bob Abreu	.30
172	*Mike Grace*	.35
173	Karim Garcia	.75
174	Richard Hidalgo	.20
175	Felipe Crespo	.20
176	Terrell Wade	.20
177	Steve Gibralter	.20
178	Jermaine Dye	.20
179	Alan Benes	.40
180	*Wilton Guerrero*	.90
181	Brooks Kieschnick	.20
182	Roger Cedeno	.20
183	*Osvaldo Fernandez*	.20
184	*Matt Lawton*	.20
185	George Williams	.20
186	Jimmy Haynes	.20
187	*Mike Busby*	.20
188	Chan Ho Park	.40
189	Marc Barcelo	.20
190	Jason Kendall	.20
191	Rey Ordonez	.50
192	Tyler Houston	.20
193	John Wasdin	.20
194	Jeff Suppan	.20
195	Jeff Ware	.20
196	Checklist	.20
197	Checklist	.20
198	Checklist	.20
199	Checklist	.20
200	Checklist	.20

1996 Pinnacle/ Aficionado First Pitch Previews

This parallel set differs from the regularly issued version in that there is a "FIRST PITCH / PREVIEW" label printed on the front on the end opposite the heliogram player portrait. Also, whereas on the regular cards, the player portrait is in silver metallic composition, the First Pitch Preview cards have the portrait in gold. These cards were most often obtained by visiting Pinnacle's site on the Internet and answering a trivia question.

	MT
Complete Set (200):	750.00
Common Player:	2.50
(Star cards valued at 8X-10X regular Aficionado edition.)	

1996 Pinnacle/ Aficionado Magic Numbers

This 1996 Pinnacle Aficionado insert set focuses on 10 of the game's best players by printing them directly on to a wooden card, each of which carries the distinct grain and color of natural wood. The cards, seeded one per every 72 packs, take current players and compare them with other players who have worn the same uniform number. These cards have the most exclusive ratio of the inserts.

		MT
Complete Set (10):		200.00
Common Player:		6.00
1	Ken Griffey Jr.	50.00
2	Greg Maddux	30.00
3	Frank Thomas	40.00
4	Mo Vaughn	12.00
5	Jeff Bagwell	20.00
6	Chipper Jones	30.00
7	Albert Belle	12.00
8	Cal Ripken Jr.	40.00
9	Matt Williams	7.50
10	Sammy Sosa	25.00

1996 Pinnacle/ Aficionado Rivals

	MT
Complete Set (200):	750.00
Common Player:	2.50

These 1996 Pinnacle Aficionado inserts concentrate on the many matchups and rivalries that make baseball fun. Each card uses spot embossing on it. The cards are seeded one per every 24 packs.

		MT
Complete Set (24):		175.00
Common Player:		6.00
1	Ken Griffey Jr., Frank Thomas	20.00
2	Frank Thomas, Cal Ripken Jr.	20.00
3	Cal Ripken Jr., Mo Vaughn	10.00
4	Mo Vaughn, Ken Griffey Jr.	15.00
5	Ken Griffey Jr., Cal Ripken Jr.	20.00
6	Frank Thomas, Mo Vaughn	15.00
7	Cal Ripken Jr., Ken Griffey Jr.	20.00
8	Mo Vaughn, Frank Thomas	15.00
9	Ken Griffey Jr., Mo Vaughn	15.00
10	Frank Thomas, Ken Griffey Jr.	20.00
11	Cal Ripken Jr., Frank Thomas	20.00
12	Mo Vaughn, Cal Ripken Jr.	10.00
13	Mike Piazza, Jeff Bagwell	8.00
14	Jeff Bagwell, Barry Bonds	7.50
15	Jeff Bagwell, Mike Piazza	10.00
16	Tony Gwynn, Mike Piazza	8.00
17	Mike Piazza, Barry Bonds	8.00
18	Jeff Bagwell, Tony Gwynn	7.50
19	Barry Bonds, Mike Piazza	8.00
20	Tony Gwynn, Jeff Bagwell	7.50
21	Mike Piazza, Tony Gwynn	8.00
22	Barry Bonds, Jeff Bagwell	7.50
23	Tony Gwynn, Barry Bonds	7.50
24	Barry Bonds, Tony Gwynn	7.50

1996 Pinnacle/ Aficionado Slick Picks

This 1996 Pinnacle Aficionado insert set pictures 32 of the best players in baseball on cards which use Spectroetch printing. Each card also notes where that player was selected in the annual draft, emphasizing that there are numerous bargains available throughout the amateur draft. The cards were seeded one per every 10 packs, making them the easiest to obtain of the set's insert cards.

		MT
Complete Set (32):		175.00
Common Player:		2.00
1	Mike Piazza	12.00
2	Cal Ripken Jr.	15.00
3	Ken Griffey Jr.	20.00
4	Paul Wilson	2.00
5	Frank Thomas	15.00
6	Mo Vaughn	5.00
7	Barry Bonds	5.00
8	Albert Belle	5.00
9	Jeff Bagwell	8.00
10	Dante Bichette	3.00
11	Hideo Nomo	6.00
12	Raul Mondesi	3.00
13	Manny Ramirez	4.00
14	Greg Maddux	12.00
15	Tony Gwynn	10.00
16	Ryne Sandberg	5.00

17	Reggie Sanders	2.00
18	Derek Jeter	12.00
19	Johnny Damon	2.00
20	Alex Rodriguez	15.00
21	Ryan Klesko	3.00
22	Jim Thome	4.00
23	Kenny Lofton	4.00
24	Tino Martinez	4.00
25	Randy Johnson	4.00
26	Wade Boggs	3.00
27	Juan Gonzalez	10.00
28	Kirby Puckett	8.00
29	Tim Salmon	3.00
30	Chipper Jones	12.00
31	Garret Anderson	2.00
32	Eddie Murray	4.00

1997 Pinnacle

MARIANO RIVERA

The '97 Pinnacle baseball set consists of 200 base cards. The card fronts consist of the player's name stamped within a foil baseball diamond-shape at the bottom of each card. Card backs contain summaries of the players' 1996 and lifetime statistics. Included within the base set is a 30-card Rookies subset, a 12-card Clout subset and three checklists. Inserts include two parallel sets (Artist's Proof and Museum Collection), Passport to the Majors, Shades, Team Pinnacle, Cardfrontations, and Home/Away. Cards were sold in 10-card packs for $2.49 each.

		MT
Complete Set (200):		20.00
Common Player:		.10
Wax Box:		45.00
1	Cecil Fielder	.15
2	Garret Anderson	.10
3	Charles Nagy	.10
4	Darryl Hamilton	.10
5	Greg Myers	.10
6	Eric Davis	.10
7	Jeff Frye	.10
8	Marquis Grissom	.10
9	Curt Schilling	.10
10	Jeff Fassero	.10
11	Alan Benes	.20
12	Orlando Miller	.10
13	Alex Fernandez	.10
14	Andy Pettitte	.75
15	Andre Dawson	.10
16	Mark Grudzielanek	.10
17	Joe Vitiello	.10
18	Juan Gonzalez	1.25
19	Mark Whiten	.10
20	Lance Johnson	.10
21	Trevor Hoffman	.10
22	Marc Newfield	.10
23	Jim Eisenreich	.10
24	Joe Carter	.20
25	Jose Canseco	.25

26	Bill Swift	.10
27	Ellis Burks	.10
28	Ben McDonald	.10
29	Edgar Martinez	.10
30	Jamie Moyer	.10
31	Chan Ho Park	.10
32	Carlos Delgado	.10
33	Kevin Mitchell	.10
34	Carlos Garcia	.10
35	Darryl Strawberry	.10
36	Jim Thome	.30
37	Jose Offerman	.10
38	Ryan Klesko	.40
39	Ruben Sierra	.10
40	Devon White	.10
41	Brian Jordan	.10
42	Tony Gwynn	1.25
43	Rafael Palmeiro	.15
44	Dante Bichette	.20
45	Scott Stahoviak	.10
46	Roger Cedeno	.10
47	Ivan Rodriguez	.50
48	Bob Abreu	.10
49	Darryl Kile	.10
50	Darren Dreifort	.10
51	Shawon Dunston	.10
52	Mark McGwire	4.00
53	Tim Salmon	.25
54	Gene Schall	.10
55	Roger Clemens	1.00
56	Rondell White	.20
57	Ed Sprague	.10
58	Craig Paquette	.10
59	David Segui	.10
60	Jaime Navarro	.10
61	Tom Glavine	.15
62	Jeff Brantley	.10
63	Kimera Bartee	.10
64	Fernando Vina	.10
65	Eddie Murray	.40
66	Lenny Dykstra	.10
67	Kevin Elster	.10
68	Vinny Castilla	.10
69	Todd Greene	.10
70	Brett Butler	.10
71	Robby Thompson	.10
72	Reggie Jefferson	.10
73	Todd Hundley	.10
74	Jeff King	.10
75	Ernie Young	.10
76	Jeff Bagwell	1.25
77	Dan Wilson	.10
78	Paul Molitor	.25
79	Kevin Seitzer	.10
80	Kevin Brown	.10
81	Ron Gant	.15
82	Dwight Gooden	.10
83	Todd Stottlemyre	.10
84	Ken Caminiti	.15
85	James Baldwin	.10
86	Jermaine Dye	.15
87	Harold Baines	.10
88	Pat Hentgen	.10
89	Frank Rodriguez	.10
90	Mark Johnson	.10
91	Jason Kendall	.10
92	Alex Rodriguez	3.00
93	Alan Trammell	.10
94	Scott Brosius	.10
95	Delino DeShields	.10
96	Chipper Jones	2.00
97	Barry Bonds	.75
98	Brady Anderson	.15
99	Ryne Sandberg	.75
100	Albert Belle	.75
101	Jeff Cirillo	.10
102	Frank Thomas	2.50
103	Mike Piazza	2.00
104	Rickey Henderson	.10
105	Rey Ordonez	.20
106	Mark Grace	.20
107	Terry Steinbach	.10
108	Ray Durham	.10
109	Barry Larkin	.25
110	Tony Clark	.50
111	Bernie Williams	.50
112	John Smoltz	.15
113	Moises Alou	.10
114	Alex Gonzalez	.10
115	Rico Brogna	.10
116	Eric Karros	.10
117	Jeff Conine	.10
118	Todd Hollandsworth	.15
119	Troy Percival	.10
120	Paul Wilson	.15
121	Orel Hershiser	.10

122	Ozzie Smith	.40
123	Dave Hollins	.10
124	Ken Hill	.10
125	Rick Wilkins	.10
126	Scott Servais	.10
127	Fernando Valenzuela	.10
128	Mariano Rivera	.15
129	Mark Loretta	.10
130	Shane Reynolds	.10
131	Darren Oliver	.10
132	Steve Trachsel	.10
133	Darren Bragg	.10
134	Jason Dickson	.35
135	Darren Fletcher	.10
136	Gary Gaetti	.10
137	Joey Cora	.10
138	Terry Pendleton	.10
139	Derek Jeter	1.50
140	Danny Tartabull	.10
141	John Flaherty	.10
142	B.J. Surhoff	.10
143	Mark Sweeney	.10
144	Chad Mottola	.10
145	Andujar Cedeno	.10
146	Tim Belcher	.10
147	Mark Thompson	.10
148	Rafael Bournigal	.10
149	Marty Cordova	.10
150	Osvaldo Fernandez	.10
151	Mike Stanley	.10
152	Ricky Bottalico	.10
153	Donnie Wall	.10
154	Omar Vizquel	.10
155	Mike Mussina	.60
156	Brant Brown	.10
157	F.P. Santangelo	.10
158	Ryan Hancock	.10
159	Jeff D'Amico	.10
160	Luis Castillo	.20
161	Darin Erstad	1.25
162	Ugueth Urbina	.10
163	Andruw Jones	1.50
164	Steve Gibralter	.10
165	Robin Jennings	.10
166	Mike Cameron	.10
167	George Arias	.10
168	Chris Stynes	.10
169	Justin Thompson	.10
170	Jamey Wright	.10
171	Todd Walker	.50
172	Nomar Garciaparra	2.00
173	Jose Paniagua	.10
174	Marvin Benard	.10
175	Rocky Coppinger	.10
176	Quinton McCracken	.10
177	Amaury Telemaco	.10
178	Neifi Perez	.10
179	Todd Greene	.10
180	Jason Thompson	.10
181	Wilton Guerrero	.20
182	Edgar Renteria	.20
183	Billy Wagner	.10
184	Alex Ochoa	.10
185	Billy McMillon	.10
186	Kenny Lofton	.75
187	Andres Galarraga (Clout)	.15
188	Chuck Knoblauch (Clout)	.15
189	Greg Maddux (Clout)	2.00
190	Mo Vaughn (Clout)	1.00
191	Cal Ripken Jr. (Clout)	2.50
192	Hideo Nomo (Clout)	.60
193	Ken Griffey Jr. (Clout)	3.00
194	Sammy Sosa (Clout)	1.50
195	Jay Buhner (Clout)	.15
196	Manny Ramirez (Clout)	.65
197	Matt Williams (Clout)	.25
198	Andruw Jones CL	.75
199	Darin Erstad CL	.50
200	Trey Beamon CL	.10

1997 Pinnacle Artist's Proofs

The 200-card, regular-sized parallel set was randomly inserted in packs of 1997 Pinnacle baseball. Of the 200 cards, 125 were done in bronze foil (common), 50 in silver (uncommon) and 25 gold (rare). The card fronts feature a color action shot over a foil background. "Artist's Proof" is stamped along the lower edge. The card backs contain a large headshot with stats and a brief highlight text.

		MT
Complete Set (200):		3000.
Common Bronze (125):		6.00
Common Silver (50):		10.00
Common Gold (25):		15.00
1	Cecil Fielder B	8.00
2	Garret Anderson B	5.00
3	Charles Nagy B	5.00
4	Darryl Hamilton B	5.00
5	Greg Myers B	5.00
6	Eric Davis B	5.00
7	Jeff Frye B	5.00
8	Marquis Grissom S	10.00
9	Curt Schilling B	5.00
10	Jeff Fassero B	5.00
11	Alan Benes S	15.00
12	Orlando Miller B	5.00
13	Alex Fernandez B	8.00
14	Andy Pettitte G	50.00
15	Andre Dawson B	5.00
16	Mark Grudzielanek B	5.00
17	Joe Vitiello B	5.00
18	Juan Gonzalez G	125.00
19	Mark Whiten B	5.00
20	Lance Johnson B	5.00
21	Trevor Hoffman B	5.00
22	Marc Newfield B	5.00
23	Jim Eisenreich B	5.00
24	Joe Carter S	12.00
25	Jose Canseco S	15.00
26	Bill Swift B	5.00
27	Ellis Burks B	5.00
28	Ben McDonald B	5.00
29	Edgar Martinez S	10.00
30	Jamie Moyer B	5.00
31	Chan Ho Park S	10.00
32	Carlos Delgado S	10.00
33	Kevin Mitchell B	5.00
34	Carlos Garcia B	5.00
35	Darryl Strawberry G	15.00
36	Jim Thome G	40.00
37	Jose Offerman B	5.00
38	Ryan Klesko S	30.00
39	Ruben Sierra B	5.00
40	Devon White B	5.00
41	Brian Jordan G	15.00
42	Tony Gwynn G	100.00
43	Rafael Palmeiro S	12.00
44	Dante Bichette B	8.00
45	Scott Stahoviak B	5.00
46	Roger Cedeno B	5.00
47	Ivan Rodriguez G	40.00
48	Bob Abreu S	10.00
49	Darryl Kile B	5.00
50	Darren Dreifort B	5.00
51	Shawon Dunston B	5.00
52	Mark McGwire S	175.00
53	Tim Salmon S	15.00
54	Gene Schall B	5.00
55	Roger Clemens B	50.00
56	Rondell White S	10.00
57	Ed Sprague B	5.00
58	Craig Paquette B	5.00
59	David Segui B	5.00
60	Jaime Navarro B	5.00
61	Tom Glavine S	12.00
62	Jeff Brantley B	5.00
63	Kimera Bartee B	5.00
64	Fernando Vina B	5.00
65	Eddie Murray S	20.00
66	Lenny Dykstra B	5.00
67	Kevin Elster B	5.00
68	Vinny Castilla B	5.00
69	Todd Greene S	10.00
70	Brett Butler B	5.00
71	Robby Thompson B	5.00
72	Reggie Jefferson B	5.00
73	Todd Hundley S	10.00
74	Jeff King B	5.00
75	Ernie Young S	5.00
76	Jeff Bagwell G	125.00
77	Dan Wilson B	5.00
78	Paul Molitor G	50.00
79	Kevin Seitzer B	5.00
80	Kevin Brown S	10.00
81	Ron Gant S	10.00
82	Dwight Gooden S	10.00
83	Todd Stottlemyre B	5.00
84	Ken Caminiti G	30.00
85	James Baldwin B	5.00
86	Jermaine Dye S	15.00
87	Harold Baines B	5.00
88	Pat Hentgen B	5.00
89	Frank Rodriguez B	5.00
90	Mark Johnson B	5.00
91	Jason Kendall S	10.00
92	Alex Rodriguez G	200.00
93	Alan Trammell B	5.00
94	Scott Brosius B	5.00
95	Delino DeShields B	5.00
96	Chipper Jones S	120.00
97	Barry Bonds S	50.00
98	Brady Anderson S	12.00
99	Ryne Sandberg S	50.00
100	Albert Belle G	60.00
101	Jeff Cirillo B	5.00
102	Frank Thomas G	160.00
103	Mike Piazza S	120.00
104	Rickey Henderson B	6.00
105	Rey Ordonez S	15.00
106	Mark Grace S	12.00
107	Terry Steinbach B	5.00
108	Ray Durham B	5.00
109	Barry Larkin S	15.00
110	Tony Clark S	40.00
111	Bernie Williams G	35.00
112	John Smoltz G	30.00
113	Moises Alou B	5.00
114	Alex Gonzalez B	5.00
115	Rico Brogna B	5.00
116	Eric Karros B	5.00
117	Jeff Conine S	10.00
118	Todd Hollandsworth G	20.00
119	Troy Percival S	10.00
120	Paul Wilson S	15.00
121	Orel Hershiser B	5.00
122	Ozzie Smith S	25.00
123	Dave Hollins B	5.00
124	Ken Hill B	5.00
125	Rick Wilkins B	5.00
126	Scott Servais B	5.00
127	Fernando Valenzuela B	5.00
128	Mariano Rivera G	25.00
129	Mark Loretta B	5.00
130	Shane Reynolds S	10.00
131	Darren Oliver B	5.00
132	Steve Trachsel B	5.00
133	Darren Bragg B	5.00
134	Jason Dickson B	10.00
135	Darren Fletcher B	5.00
136	Gary Gaetti B	5.00
137	Joey Cora B	5.00
138	Terry Pendleton B	5.00
139	Derek Jeter G	150.00
140	Danny Tartabull B	5.00
141	John Flaherty B	5.00
142	B.J. Surhoff B	5.00
143	Mark Sweeney B	5.00
144	Chad Mottola B	5.00
145	Andujar Cedeno B	5.00
146	Tim Belcher B	5.00
147	Mark Thompson B	5.00
148	Rafael Bournigal B	5.00
149	Marty Cordova S	10.00
150	Osvaldo Fernandez B	5.00
151	Mike Stanley B	5.00
152	Ricky Bottalico B	5.00
153	Donnie Wall B	5.00
154	Omar Vizquel B	5.00
155	Mike Mussina S	30.00
156	Brant Brown B	5.00
157	F.P. Santangelo S	10.00
158	Ryan Hancock B	5.00
159	Jeff D'Amico B	5.00
160	Luis Castillo B	10.00
161	Darin Erstad G	75.00
162	Ugueth Urbina B	5.00
163	Andruw Jones G	100.00
164	Steve Gibralter B	5.00
165	Robin Jennings S	10.00
166	Mike Cameron B	5.00
167	George Arias S	10.00
168	Chris Stynes B	5.00
169	Justin Thompson B	5.00
170	Jamey Wright B	5.00
171	Todd Walker G	30.00
172	Nomar Garciaparra B	75.00
173	Jose Paniagua B	5.00
174	Marvin Benard B	5.00
175	Rocky Coppinger B	5.00
176	Quinton McCracken B	5.00
177	Amaury Telemaco B	5.00
178	Neifi Perez B	5.00
179	Todd Greene B	5.00
180	Jason Thompson B	5.00
181	Wilton Guerrero B	10.00
182	Edgar Renteria S	15.00
183	Billy Wagner B	10.00
184	Alex Ochoa G	15.00
185	Billy McMillon B	5.00
186	Kenny Lofton B (Clout)	15.00
187	Andres Galarraga B (Clout)	8.00
188	Chuck Knoblauch G (Clout)	15.00
189	Greg Maddux S (Clout)	80.00
190	Mo Vaughn S (Clout)	40.00
191	Cal Ripken Jr. G (Clout)	125.00
192	Hideo Nomo S (Clout)	30.00
193	Ken Griffey Jr. G (Clout)	250.00
194	Sammy Sosa S (Clout)	50.00
195	Jay Buhner S (Clout)	10.00
196	Manny Ramirez G (Clout)	40.00
197	Matt Williams B (Clout)	8.00
198	Andruw Jones CL B	30.00
199	Darin Erstad CL B	25.00
200	Trey Beamon CL B	5.00

1997 Pinnacle Museum Collection

Each of the 200 cards in 1997 Pinnacle Series I was also issued in a graphically enhanced Museum Collection parallel set. The Museum cards utilize basically the same design as the regular-issue Pinnacle cards, but the front is printed in the company's Dufex gold-foil technology. On back, a small rectangular logo verifies the card's special status.

	MT
Complete Set (200):	600.00
Common Player:	1.00
Veteran Stars: 10-15X	
Young Stars/Rookies: 4-8X	
(See 1997 Pinnacle for checklist and regular-issue card values.)	

1997 Pinnacle Cardfrontations

The 20-card, regular-sized, hobby-only set was inserted every 23 packs of 1997 Pinnacle baseball. The card fronts depict a player headshot imaged over a foil rainbow background. The same player is then pictured in action shots with the "Cardfrontation" logo in gold foil in the lower right half. The player's name appears in gold foil below the gold-foil team logo. The card backs depict another player's headshot with a short text describing interaction between the two players. The cards are numbered as "x of 20."

		MT
Complete Set (20):		225.00
Common Player:		4.00
1	Greg Maddux, Mike Piazza	20.00
2	Tom Glavine, Ken Caminiti	4.00
3	Randy Johnson, Cal Ripken Jr.	25.00
4	Kevin Appier, Mark McGwire	25.00
5	Andy Pettitte, Juan Gonzalez	15.00
6	Pat Hentgen, Albert Belle	12.00
7	Hideo Nomo, Chipper Jones	20.00
8	Ismael Valdes, Sammy Sosa	12.00
9	Mike Mussina, Manny Ramirez	8.00
10	David Cone, Jay Buhner	4.00
11	Mark Wohlers, Gary Sheffield	5.00
12	Alan Benes, Barry Bonds	10.00
13	Roger Clemens, Ivan Rodriguez	8.00
14	Mariano Rivera, Ken Griffey Jr.	35.00
15	Dwight Gooden, Frank Thomas	30.00
16	John Wetteland, Darin Erstad	15.00
17	John Smoltz, Brian Jordan	4.00
18	Kevin Brown, Jeff Bagwell	15.00
19	Jack McDowell, Alex Rodriguez	35.00
20	Charles Nagy, Bernie Williams	4.00

1997 Pinnacle Home/Away

The 24-card, regular-sized, die-cut set was inserted every 33 retail packs. The background on front and back is a facsimile of the player's home or road jersey. A color action photo is on front with gold-foil graphics. Backs have a few words about the player.

		MT
Complete Set (12):		175.00
Common Player:		5.00
1	Chipper Jones	20.00

2	Ken Griffey Jr.	30.00
3	Mike Piazza	20.00
4	Frank Thomas	20.00
5	Jeff Bagwell	12.00
6	Alex Rodriguez	25.00
7	Barry Bonds	8.00
8	Mo Vaughn	8.00
9	Derek Jeter	20.00
10	Mark McGwire	30.00
11	Cal Ripken Jr.	25.00
12	Albert Belle	8.00

1997 Pinnacle Passport to the Majors

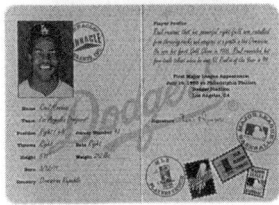

The 25-card, regular-sized set was inserted every 36 packs of 1997 Pinnacle baseball. The cards fold out and resemble a mini passport.

		MT
Complete Set (25):		160.00
Common Player:		3.00
1	Greg Maddux	15.00
1s	Greg Maddux ("SAMPLE" overprint)	10.00
2	Ken Griffey Jr.	25.00
3	Frank Thomas	15.00
4	Cal Ripken Jr.	20.00
5	Mike Piazza	15.00
6	Alex Rodriguez	25.00
7	Mo Vaughn	8.00
8	Chipper Jones	15.00
9	Roberto Alomar	6.00
10	Edgar Martinez	3.00
11	Javier Lopez	3.00
12	Ivan Rodriguez	5.00
13	Juan Gonzalez	12.00
14	Carlos Baerga	3.00
15	Sammy Sosa	12.00
16	Manny Ramirez	7.00
17	Raul Mondesi	4.00
18	Henry Rodriguez	3.00
19	Rafael Palmeiro	3.00
20	Rey Ordonez	4.00
21	Hideo Nomo	6.00
22	Makoto Suzuki	3.00
23	Chan Ho Park	3.00
24	Larry Walker	4.00
25	Ruben Rivera	5.00

A player's name in *italic* type indicates a rookie card.

1997 Pinnacle Shades

The 10-card, regular-sized set was inserted every 23 retail packs of Pinnacle baseball. The horizontal cards are die-cut at the top of a pair of sunglasses whose lenses contain color portrait and action pictures of the player. The player face beneath the shades is printed on silver foil stock. Backs have a mirror-image of the front photos in the lenses and a baseball diamond in the background.

		MT
Complete Set (10):		75.00
Common Player:		3.00
1	Ken Griffey Jr.	20.00
2	Juan Gonzalez	10.00
3	John Smoltz	3.00
4	Gary Sheffield	4.00
5	Cal Ripken Jr.	15.00
6	Mo Vaughn	5.00
7	Brian Jordan	3.00
8	Mike Piazza	12.00
9	Frank Thomas	12.00
10	Alex Rodriguez	12.00

1997 Pinnacle Team Pinnacle

The 10-card, regular-sized set features top National League players from a position on one side with the best American League players on the other. One side of the card is in Dufex printing and there is actually two versions of each card, as either side can feature the Dufex foil. Team Pinnacle is inserted every 90 packs.

		MT
Complete Set (10):		250.00
Common Player:		10.00
1	Frank Thomas, Jeff Bagwell	40.00
2	Chuck Knoblauch, Eric Young	10.00
3	Ken Caminiti, Jim Thome	12.00
4	Alex Rodriguez, Chipper Jones	40.00
5	Mike Piazza, Ivan Rodriguez	30.00
6	Albert Belle, Barry Bonds	15.00
7	Ken Griffey Jr., Ellis Burks	50.00
8	Juan Gonzalez, Gary Sheffield	25.00
9	John Smoltz, Andy Pettitte	15.00
10	All Players	40.00

1997 New Pinnacle

In lieu of a second series of Pinnacle Baseball, the company offered collectors New Pinnacle, a 200-card set sold in 10-card packs for $2.99 each. Two parallel versions of the 200-card set exist in Museum Collection and Artist's Proof. Other inserts include Press Plates, Spellbound, Keeping the Pace and Interleague Encounter. Collectors who obtained four Press Plates of the same player's card back or front were eligible to win cash prizes.

	MT
Complete Set (200):	25.00
Common Player:	.10
Museum Collection Complete Set (200):	500.00
Common Museum:	1.50
Museum Veteran Stars: 10x to 15x	
Museum Yng Stars & RCs: 5x to 10x	
Wax Box:	45.00
1 Ken Griffey Jr.	3.00
2 Sammy Sosa	1.50
3 Greg Maddux	2.00
4 Matt Williams	.35
5 Jason Isringhausen	.10
6 Gregg Jefferies	.10
7 Chili Davis	.10
8 Paul O'Neill	.10
9 Larry Walker	.35
10 Ellis Burks	.10
11 Cliff Floyd	.10
12 Albert Belle	.75
13 Javier Lopez	.20
14 David Cone	.20
15 Jose Canseco	.30
16 Todd Zeile	.10
17 Bernard Gilkey	.10
18 Andres Galarraga	.20
19 Chris Snopek	.10
20 Tim Salmon	.25
21 Roger Clemens	1.00
22 Reggie Sanders	.10
23 John Jaha	.10
24 Andy Pettitte	.75
25 Kenny Lofton	.75
26 Robb Nen	.10
27 John Wetteland	.10
28 Bobby Bonilla	.10
29 Hideo Nomo	.60
30 Cecil Fielder	.20
31 Garret Anderson	.10
32 Pat Hentgen	.10
33 David Justice	.20
34 Billy Wagner	.10
35 Al Leiter	.10
36 Mark Wohlers	.10
37 Rondell White	.10
38 Charles Johnson	.10
39 Mark Grace	.20
40 Pedro Martinez	.20

41 Tom Goodwin	.10
42 Manny Ramirez	.75
43 Greg Vaughn	.10
44 Brian Jordan	.10
45 Mike Piazza	2.00
46 Roberto Hernandez	.10
47 Wade Boggs	.20
48 Scott Sanders	.10
49 Alex Gonzalez	.10
50 Kevin Brown	.10
51 Bob Higginson	.10
52 Ken Caminiti	.25
53 Derek Jeter	2.00
54 Carlos Baerga	.10
55 Jay Buhner	.20
56 Tim Naehring	.10
57 Jeff Bagwell	1.25
58 Steve Finley	.10
59 Kevin Appier	.10
60 Jay Bell	.10
61 Ivan Rodriguez	.60
62 Terrell Wade	.10
63 Rusty Greer	.10
64 Juan Guzman	.10
65 Fred McGriff	.30
66 Tino Martinez	.25
67 Ray Lankford	.10
68 Juan Gonzalez	1.25
69 Ron Gant	.10
70 Jack McDowell	.10
71 Tony Gwynn	1.25
72 Joe Carter	.10
73 Wilson Alvarez	.10
74 Jason Giambi	.10
75 Brian Hunter	.10
76 Michael Tucker	.10
77 Andy Benes	.10
78 Brady Anderson	.20
79 Ramon Martinez	.10
80 Troy Percival	.10
81 Alex Rodriguez	3.00
82 Jim Thome	.50
83 Denny Neagle	.10
84 Rafael Palmeiro	.20
85 Jose Valentin	.10
86 Marc Newfield	.10
87 Mariano Rivera	.20
88 Alan Benes	.20
89 Jimmy Key	.10
90 Joe Randa	.10
91 Cal Ripken Jr.	2.50
92 Craig Biggio	.20
93 Dean Palmer	.10
94 Gary Sheffield	.35
95 Ismael Valdez	.10
96 John Valentin	.10
97 Johnny Damon	.10
98 Mo Vaughn	.75
99 Paul Sorrento	.10
100 Randy Johnson	.60
101 Raul Mondesi	.20
102 Roberto Alomar	.60
103 Royce Clayton	.10
104 Mark Grudzielanek	.10
105 Wally Joyner	.10
106 Wil Cordero	.10
107 Will Clark	.25
108 Chuck Knoblauch	.25
109 Derek Bell	.10
110 Henry Rodriguez	.10
111 Edgar Renteria	.10
112 Travis Fryman	.10
113 Eric Young	.10
114 Sandy Alomar Jr.	.10
115 Darin Erstad	1.25
116 Barry Larkin	.10
117 Barry Bonds	.75
118 Frank Thomas	2.50
119 Carlos Delgado	.10
120 Jason Kendall	.10
121 Todd Hollandsworth	.10
122 Jim Edmonds	.10
123 Chipper Jones	2.00
124 Jeff Fassero	.10
125 Deion Sanders	.30
126 Matt Lawton	.10
127 Ryan Klesko	.50
128 Mike Mussina	.75
129 Paul Molitor	.50
130 Dante Bichette	.20
131 Bill Pulsipher	.10
132 Todd Hundley	.20
133 J.T. Snow	.10
134 Chuck Finley	.10
135 Shawn Green	.10
136 Charles Nagy	.10

137 Willie Greene	.10
138 Marty Cordova	.10
139 Eddie Murray	.40
140 Ryne Sandberg	.75
141 Alex Fernandez	.10
142 Mark McGwire	4.00
143 Eric Davis	.10
144 Jermaine Dye	.10
145 Ruben Sierra	.10
146 Damon Buford	.10
147 John Smoltz	.20
148 Alex Ochoa	.10
149 Moises Alou	.10
150 Rico Brogna	.10
151 Terry Steinbach	.10
152 Jeff King	.10
153 Carlos Garcia	.10
154 Tom Glavine	.20
155 Edgar Martinez	.10
156 Kevin Elster	.10
157 Darryl Hamilton	.10
158 Jason Dickson	.20
159 Kevin Orie	.10
160 *Bubba Trammell*	1.00
161 Jose Guillen	1.00
162 Brant Brown	.10
163 Wendell Magee	.10
164 Scott Spiezio	.10
165 Todd Walker	.50
166 *Rod Myers*	.10
167 Damon Mashore	.10
168 Wilton Guerrero	.20
169 Vladimir Guerrero	1.00
170 Nomar Garciaparra	2.00
171 Shannon Stewart	.10
172 Scott Rolen	1.50
173 Bob Abreu	.10
174 *Danny Patterson*	.20
175 Andruw Jones	1.50
176 Brian Giles	.10
177 Dmitri Young	.10
178 Cal Ripken Jr. (East Meets West)	1.25
179 Chuck Knoblauch (East Meets West)	.20
180 Alex Rodriguez (East Meets West)	1.50
181 Andres Galarraga (East Meets West)	.15
182 Pedro Martinez (East Meets West)	.15
183 Brady Anderson (East Meets West)	.10
184 Barry Bonds (East Meets West)	.40
185 Ivan Rodriguez (East Meets West)	.30
186 Gary Sheffield (East Meets West)	.20
187 Denny Neagle (East Meets West)	.10
188 Mark McGwire (Aura)	2.00
189 Ellis Burks (Aura)	.10
190 Alex Rodriguez (Aura)	1.50
191 Mike Piazza (Aura)	1.00
192 Barry Bonds (Aura)	.40
193 Albert Belle (Aura)	.40
194 Chipper Jones (Aura)	1.00
195 Juan Gonzalez (Aura)	.60
196 Brady Anderson (Aura)	.10
197 Frank Thomas (Aura)	1.25
198 Checklist(Vladimir Guerrero)	.50
199 Checklist(Todd Walker)	.25
200 Checklist(Scott Rolen)	.60

1997 New Pinnacle Artist's Proof

This 200-card parallel set features a special AP seal and foil treatment and is fractured into three levels of scarcity - Red (125 cards), Blue (50 cards) and Green (25 cards). Cards were inserted at a rate of 1:39 packs.

A player's name in *italic* type indicates a rookie card.

	MT
Common Red Artist's Proof:	5.00
Red Artist's Proofs: 15x to 20x	
Common Blue Artist's Proof:	15.00
Blue Artist's Proofs: 35x to 50x	
Common Green Artist's Proof:	30.00
Green Artist's Proofs: 50x to 75x	

(See 1997 New Pinnacle for checklist and base values.)

1997 New Pinnacle Interleague Encounter

Inserted 1:240 packs, this 10-card set showcases 20 American League and National League rivals with the date of their first interleague match-up on double-sided mirror mylar cards.

		MT
	Complete Set (10):	700.00
	Common Player:	20.00
1	Albert Belle, Brian Jordan	30.00
2	Andruw Jones, Brady Anderson	60.00
3	Ken Griffey Jr., Tony Gwynn	125.00
4	Cal Ripken Jr., Chipper Jones	80.00
5	Mike Piazza, Ivan Rodriguez	60.00
6	Derek Jeter, Vladimir Guerrero	60.00
7	Greg Maddux, Mo Vaughn	60.00
8	Alex Rodriguez, Hideo Nomo	100.00
9	Juan Gonzalez, Barry Bonds	50.00
10	Frank Thomas, Jeff Bagwell	100.00

1997 New Pinnacle Keeping the Pace

The top sluggers who are considered candidates to break Roger Maris' single-season record of 61 home runs are featured in this 18-card insert set. Cards feature Dot Matrix holographic borders and backgrounds on front. Backs present career stats of an all-time great and project future numbers for the current player. The cards were inserted 1:89 packs.

A player's name in *italic* type indicates a rookie card.

		MT
	Complete Set (18):	500.00
	Common Player:	6.00
1	Juan Gonzalez	35.00
2	Greg Maddux	50.00
3	Ivan Rodriguez	20.00
4	Ken Griffey Jr.	75.00
5	Alex Rodriguez	50.00
6	Barry Bonds	20.00
7	Frank Thomas	60.00
8	Chuck Knoblauch	10.00
9	Derek Jeter	35.00
10	Roger Clemens	25.00
11	Kenny Lofton	20.00
12	Tony Gwynn	35.00
13	Troy Percival	6.00
14	Cal Ripken Jr.	60.00
15	Andy Pettitte	15.00
16	Hideo Nomo	15.00
17	Randy Johnson	15.00
18	Mike Piazza	50.00

1997 New Pinnacle Press Plates

Just when collectors thought they had seen every type of pack insert chase card imaginable, New Pinnacle proved them wrong by cutting up and inserting into packs (about one per 1,250) the metal plates used to print the regular cards in the set. There are black, blue, red and yellow plates for the front and back of each card. Rather than touting the collector value of the plates, Pinnacle created a treasure hunt by offering $20,000-35,000 to anybody assembling a complete set of four plates for either the front or back of any card. The $35,000, which would have been awarded for completion prior to Aug. 22, was unclaimed. The amount decreased to $20,000 for any set redeemed by the end of 1997.

(Because of the unique nature of each press plate, no current market value can be quoted.)

1997 New Pinnacle Spellbound

Each of the 50 cards in this insert features a letter of the alphabet as the basic card design. The letters can be used to spell out the names of nine players featured in the set. Cards featured micro-etched foil and are inserted 1:19 packs. Cards of Griffey, Ripken and the Jones were inserted only in hobby packs; retail packs have cards of Belle, Thomas, Piazza and the Rodriguezes. Values shown are per card; multiply by number of cards to determine a player's set value.

	MT
Complete Set (50):	600.00
1-5AB Albert Belle	5.00
1-6AJ Andruw Jones	8.00
1-4AR Alex Rodriguez	15.00
1-7CJ Chipper Jones	15.00
1-6CR Cal Ripken Jr.	20.00
1-5FT Frank Thomas	20.00
1-5IR Ivan Rodriguez	6.00
1-6KG Ken Griffey Jr.	25.00
1-6MP Mike Piazza	15.00

1997 Pinnacle Certified

This 150-card base features a mirror-like mylar finish and a peel-off protector on each card front. Backs feature the player's 1996 statistics against each opponent. There are four different parallel sets, each with varying degrees of scarcity - Certified Red (1:5), Mirror Red (1:99), Mirror Blue (1:199) and Mirror Gold (1:299). Other inserts include Lasting Impressions, Certified Team, and Certified Gold Team. Cards were sold in six-card packs for a suggested price of $4.99.

		MT
Complete Set (150):		40.00
Common Player:		.15

Certified Red Stars: 4x to 8x
Certified Red Yng Star & RCs: 3x to 6x
Common Mirror Red:
Mirror Red Minor Stars: 25.00
Mirror Red Stars: 40x to 80x
Mirror Red Yng Stars & RCs: 30x to 50x
Common Mirror Blue: 30.00
Mirror Blue Minor Stars: 50.00
Mirror Blue Stars: 100x to 150x
Mirr. Blue Yng Stars & RCs: 75x to 125x
Common Mirror Gold: 75.00
Mirror Gold Minor Stars: 150.00
Mirror Gold Stars: 300x to 450x
Mirr. Gold Yng Stars & RCs: 200x to 350x
Jose Cruz Jr. Redemption: 25.00
Wax Box: 115.00

1	Barry Bonds	1.25
2	Mo Vaughn	1.25
3	Matt Williams	.50
4	Ryne Sandberg	1.25
5	Jeff Bagwell	2.00
6	Alan Benes	.15
7	John Wetteland	.15
8	Fred McGriff	.40
9	Craig Biggio	.25
10	Bernie Williams	1.00
11	Brian L. Hunter	.15
12	Sandy Alomar Jr.	.15
13	Ray Lankford	.15
14	Ryan Klesko	.50
15	Jermaine Dye	.15
16	Andy Benes	.15
17	Albert Belle	1.25
18	Tony Clark	1.00
19	Dean Palmer	.15
20	Bernard Gilkey	.15
21	Ken Caminiti	.30
22	Alex Rodriguez	4.00
23	Tim Salmon	.40
24	Larry Walker	.50
25	Barry Larkin	.30
26	Mike Piazza	3.00
27	Brady Anderson	.15
28	Cal Ripken Jr.	4.00
29	Charles Nagy	.15
30	Paul Molitor	.75
31	Darin Erstad	1.50
32	Rey Ordonez	.15
33	Wally Joyner	.15
34	David Cone	.25
35	Sammy Sosa	2.50
36	Dante Bichette	.30
37	Eric Karros	.15
38	Omar Vizquel	.15
39	Roger Clemens	1.50
40	Joe Carter	.15
41	Frank Thomas	4.00
42	Javier Lopez	.15
43	Mike Mussina	1.00
44	Gary Sheffield	.50
45	Tony Gwynn	2.00
46	Jason Kendall	.15
47	Jim Thome	.75
48	Andres Galarraga	.30
49	Mark McGwire	5.00
50	Troy Percival	.15
51	Derek Jeter	3.00
52	Todd Hollandsworth	.15
53	Ken Griffey Jr.	5.00
54	Randy Johnson	.75
55	Pat Hentgen	.15
56	Rusty Greer	.15
57	John Jaha	.15
58	Kenny Lofton	1.25
59	Chipper Jones	3.00
60	Robb Nen	.15
61	Rafael Palmeiro	.30
62	Mariano Rivera	.25
63	Hideo Nomo	1.00
64	Greg Vaughn	.15
65	Ron Gant	.15
66	Eddie Murray	.40
67	John Smoltz	.30
68	Manny Ramirez	1.25
69	Juan Gonzalez	2.00
70	F.P. Santangelo	.15
71	Moises Alou	.15
72	Alex Ochoa	.15
73	Chuck Knoblauch	.30
74	Raul Mondesi	.30
75	J.T. Snow	.15
76	Rickey Henderson	.15
77	Bobby Bonilla	.15
78	Wade Boggs	.30
79	Ivan Rodriguez	1.00
80	Brian Jordan	.15
81	Al Leiter	.15
82	Jay Buhner	.30
83	Greg Maddux	3.00
84	Edgar Martinez	.15
85	Kevin Brown	.15
86	Eric Young	.15
87	Todd Hundley	.30
88	Ellis Burks	.15
89	Marquis Grissom	.15
90	Jose Canseco	.40
91	Henry Rodriguez	.15
92	Andy Pettitte	1.25
93	Mark Grudzielanek	.15
94	Dwight Gooden	.15
95	Roberto Alomar	1.00
96	Paul Wilson	.15
97	Will Clark	.30
98	Rondell White	.15
99	Charles Johnson	.15
100	Jim Edmonds	.15
101	Jason Giambi	.15
102	Billy Wagner	.15
103	Edgar Renteria	.15
104	Johnny Damon	.15
105	Jason Isringhausen	.15
106	Andruw Jones	2.50
107	Jose Guillen	1.25
108	Kevin Orie	.15
109	Brian Giles	.15
110	Danny Patterson	.15
111	Vladimir Guerrero	1.50
112	Scott Rolen	2.00
113	Damon Mashore	.15
114	Nomar Garciaparra	2.50
115	Todd Walker	.75
116	Wilton Guerrero	.15
117	Bob Abreu	.15
118	Brooks Kieschnick	.15
119	Pokey Reese	.15
120	Todd Greene	.15
121	Dmitri Young	.15
122	Raul Casanova	.15
123	Glendon Rusch	.15
124	Jason Dickson	.15
125	Jorge Posada	.15
126	*Rod Myers*	.15
127	*Bubba Trammell*	1.50
128	Scott Spiezio	.15
129	*Hideki Irabu*	5.00
130	Wendell Magee	.15
131	Bartolo Colon	.15
132	Chris Holt	.15
133	Calvin Maduro	.15
134	Ray Montgomery	.15
135	Shannon Stewart	.15
136	Ken Griffey Jr. (Certified Stars)	2.50
137	Vladimir Guerrero (Certified Stars)	.75
138	Roger Clemens (Certified Stars)	.75
139	Mark McGwire (Certified Stars)	2.50
140	Albert Belle (Certified Stars)	.60
141	Derek Jeter (Certified Stars)	1.50
142	Juan Gonzalez (Certified Stars)	1.00
143	Greg Maddux (Certified Stars)	1.50
144	Alex Rodriguez (Certified Stars)	2.00
145	Jeff Bagwell (Certified Stars)	1.00
146	Cal Ripken Jr. (Certified Stars)	2.00
147	Tony Gwynn (Certified Stars)	1.00
148	Frank Thomas (Certified Stars)	2.00
149	Hideo Nomo (Certified Stars)	.50
150	Andruw Jones (Certified Stars)	1.25

1997 Pinnacle Certified Lasting Impression

This 20-card insert features a die-cut design and a mirror mylar finish and pictures some of baseball's top veteran stars. Backs are conventionally printed and include a color portrait photo and a few words about the player. Cards were inserted 1:19 packs.

		MT
Complete Set (20):		220.00
Common Player:		4.00
1	Cal Ripken Jr.	30.00
2	Ken Griffey Jr.	40.00
3	Mo Vaughn	10.00
4	Brian Jordan	4.00
5	Mark McGwire	40.00
6	Chuck Knoblauch	6.00
7	Sammy Sosa	20.00
8	Brady Anderson	4.00
9	Frank Thomas	25.00
10	Tony Gwynn	18.00
11	Roger Clemens	10.00
12	Alex Rodriguez	30.00
13	Paul Molitor	8.00
14	Kenny Lofton	10.00
15	John Smoltz	4.00
16	Roberto Alomar	8.00
17	Randy Johnson	8.00
18	Ryne Sandberg	10.00
19	Manny Ramirez	10.00
20	Mike Mussina	8.00

A player's name in *italic* type indicates a rookie card.

1997 Pinnacle Certified Red

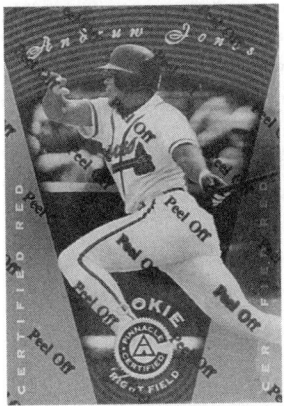

This parallel set features a red tint to the triangular mylar background left and right of the photo on the front. "CERTIFIED RED" is printed vertically on both edges. Backs are identical to regular Certified cards. A peel-off protection coating is on the front of the card. Cards were inserted 1:5 packs.

	MT
Common Certified Red:	2.00
Certified Red Semistars:	4.00
Stars: 4x to 8x	
Yng Stars & RC's: 3x to 6x	
(See 1997 Pinnacle Certified for checklist and base values.)	

1997 Pinnacle Certified Mirror Red

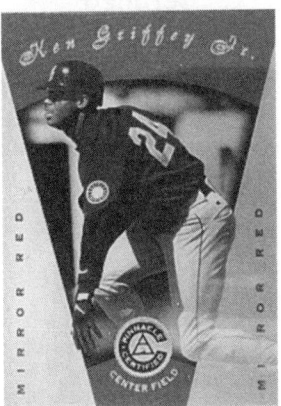

This parallel set features a red design element on the front of each card. Cards were inserted 1:99 packs.

	MT
Common Mirror Red:	15.00
Mirror Red Semistars:	25.00
Stars: 40x to 75x	
Young Stars & RCs: 30x to 50x	
(See 1997 Pinnacle Certified for checklist and base values.)	

1997 Pinnacle Certified Mirror Blue

This parallel set features a blue design element on the front of each card. Cards were inserted 1:199 packs.

	MT
Common Mirror Blue:	30.00
Mirror Blue Semistars:	50.00
Mirror Blue Stars: 100x to 150x	
Mirror Blue Yng Stars & RCs: 75x to 125x	
(See 1997 Pinnacle Certified for checklist and base values.)	

1997 Pinnacle Certified Mirror Gold

This parallel set features a holographic gold design on the front of each card. Cards were inserted 1:299 packs.

	MT
Common Mirror Gold:	75.00
Mirror Gold Semistars:	150.00
Mirror Gold Stars: 300x to 450x	
Yng Stars & RCs: 200x to 350x	
(See 1997 Pinnacle Certified for checklist and base values.)	

1997 Totally Certified Platinum Red

Totally Certified doesn't have a true base set. Instead, the product consists of three different 150-card parallel sets. Packs consisted of three cards for $6.99 each. The first of three parallels is the Platinum Red set, inserted two per pack, and featuring micro-etched holographic mylar stock with red accents and foil stamping. Each card in the Red set is sequentially-numbered to 3,999.

	MT
Complete Set (150):	500.00
Common Player:	1.50
Minor Stars:	3.00
Wax Box:	185.00
1 Barry Bonds	8.00
2 Mo Vaughn	8.00
3 Matt Williams	3.00
4 Ryne Sandberg	8.00
5 Jeff Bagwell	12.00
6 Alan Benes	1.50
7 John Wetteland	1.50
8 Fred McGriff	2.50
9 Craig Biggio	2.50
10 Bernie Williams	6.00
11 Brian Hunter	1.50
12 Sandy Alomar Jr.	1.50
13 Ray Lankford	1.50
14 Ryan Klesko	4.00
15 Jermaine Dye	1.50
16 Andy Benes	1.50
17 Albert Belle	10.00
18 Tony Clark	8.00
19 Dean Palmer	1.50
20 Bernard Gilkey	1.50
21 Ken Caminiti	4.00
22 Alex Rodriguez	25.00
23 Tim Salmon	4.00
24 Larry Walker	5.00
25 Barry Larkin	4.00
26 Mike Piazza	18.00
27 Brady Anderson	1.50
28 Cal Ripken Jr.	25.00
29 Charles Nagy	1.50
30 Paul Molitor	6.00
31 Darin Erstad	10.00
32 Rey Ordonez	1.50
33 Wally Joyner	1.50
34 David Cone	1.50
35 Sammy Sosa	15.00
36 Dante Bichette	3.00
37 Eric Karros	1.50
38 Omar Vizquel	1.50
39 Roger Clemens	12.00
40 Joe Carter	1.50
41 Frank Thomas	25.00
42 Javier Lopez	1.50
43 Mike Mussina	6.00
44 Gary Sheffield	4.00
45 Tony Gwynn	15.00
46 Jason Kendall	1.50
47 Jim Thome	6.00
48 Andres Galarraga	4.00
49 Mark McGwire	30.00
50 Troy Percival	1.50
51 Derek Jeter	18.00
52 Todd Hollandsworth	1.50
53 Ken Griffey Jr.	30.00
54 Randy Johnson	6.00
55 Pat Hentgen	1.50
56 Rusty Greer	1.50
57 John Jaha	1.50
58 Kenny Lofton	8.00
59 Chipper Jones	18.00
60 Robb Nen	1.50
61 Rafael Palmeiro	3.00
62 Mariano Rivera	2.50
63 Hideo Nomo	6.00
64 Greg Vaughn	1.50
65 Ron Gant	1.50
66 Eddie Murray	4.00
67 John Smoltz	3.00
68 Manny Ramirez	8.00
69 Juan Gonzalez	15.00
70 F.P. Santangelo	1.50
71 Moises Alou	2.50
72 Alex Ochoa	1.50
73 Chuck Knoblauch	3.00
74 Raul Mondesi	3.00
75 J.T. Snow	1.50
76 Rickey Henderson	1.50
77 Bobby Bonilla	2.50
78 Wade Boggs	3.00
79 Ivan Rodriguez	6.00
80 Brian Jordan	1.50
81 Al Leiter	1.50
82 Jay Buhner	3.00
83 Greg Maddux	18.00
84 Edgar Martinez	1.50
85 Kevin Brown	1.50
86 Eric Young	1.50
87 Todd Hundley	2.50
88 Ellis Burks	1.50
89 Marquis Grissom	1.50
90 Jose Canseco	3.00
91 Henry Rodriguez	1.50
92 Andy Pettitte	8.00
93 Mark Grudzielanek	1.50
94 Dwight Gooden	1.50
95 Roberto Alomar	6.00
96 Paul Wilson	1.50
97 Will Clark	3.00
98 Rondell White	2.50
99 Charles Johnson	1.50
100 Jim Edmonds	2.50
101 Jason Giambi	1.50

102	Billy Wagner	1.50
103	Edgar Renteria	1.50
104	Johnny Damon	1.50
105	Jason Isringhausen	1.50
106	Andruw Jones	15.00
107	Jose Guillen	8.00
108	Kevin Orie	1.50
109	Brian Giles	1.50
110	Danny Patterson	1.50
111	Vladimir Guerrero	10.00
112	Scott Rolen	15.00
113	Damon Mashore	1.50
114	Nomar Garciaparra	18.00
115	Todd Walker	5.00
116	Wilton Guerrero	1.50
117	Bob Abreu	1.50
118	Brooks Kieschnick	1.50
119	Pokey Reese	1.50
120	Todd Greene	1.50
121	Dmitri Young	1.50
122	Raul Casanova	1.50
123	Glendon Rusch	1.50
124	Jason Dickson	1.50
125	Jorge Posada	1.50
126	Rod Myers	1.50
127	Bubba Trammell	6.00
128	Scott Spiezio	1.50
129	Hideki Irabu	10.00
130	Wendell Magee	1.50
131	Bartolo Colon	1.50
132	Chris Holt	1.50
133	Calvin Maduro	1.50
134	Ray Montgomery	1.50
135	Shannon Stewart	1.50
136	Ken Griffey Jr. (Certified Stars)	15.00
137	Vladimir Guerrero (Certified Stars)	5.00
138	Roger Clemens (Certified Stars)	6.00
139	Mark McGwire (Certified Stars)	15.00
140	Albert Belle (Certified Stars)	5.00
141	Derek Jeter (Certified Stars)	9.00
142	Juan Gonzalez (Certified Stars)	8.00
143	Greg Maddux (Certified Stars)	9.00
144	Alex Rodriguez (Certified Stars)	12.00
145	Jeff Bagwell (Certified Stars)	6.00
146	Cal Ripken Jr. (Certified Stars)	12.00
147	Tony Gwynn (Certified Stars)	8.00
148	Frank Thomas (Certified Stars)	12.00
149	Hideo Nomo (Certified Stars)	3.00
150	Andruw Jones (Certified Stars)	8.00

1997 Totally Certified Platinum Blue

Featuring blue accents and foil stamping, the Platinum Blue cards are sequentially numbered to 1,999 and inserted one per pack.

		MT
Complete Set (150):		1000.
Common Player:		3.00
Minor Stars:		6.00
1	Barry Bonds	15.00
2	Mo Vaughn	15.00
3	Matt Williams	6.00
4	Ryne Sandberg	15.00
5	Jeff Bagwell	25.00
6	Alan Benes	3.00
7	John Wetteland	3.00
8	Fred McGriff	5.00
9	Craig Biggio	5.00
10	Bernie Williams	12.00
11	Brian Hunter	3.00
12	Sandy Alomar Jr.	3.00
13	Ray Lankford	3.00
14	Ryan Klesko	8.00
15	Jermaine Dye	3.00
16	Andy Benes	3.00

17	Albert Belle	20.00
18	Tony Clark	15.00
19	Dean Palmer	3.00
20	Bernard Gilkey	3.00
21	Ken Caminiti	8.00
22	Alex Rodriguez	50.00
23	Tim Salmon	8.00
24	Larry Walker	10.00
25	Barry Larkin	8.00
26	Mike Piazza	35.00
27	Brady Anderson	3.00
28	Cal Ripken Jr.	50.00
29	Charles Nagy	3.00
30	Paul Molitor	12.00
31	Darin Erstad	20.00
32	Rey Ordonez	3.00
33	Wally Joyner	3.00
34	David Cone	3.00
35	Sammy Sosa	30.00
36	Dante Bichette	6.00
37	Eric Karros	3.00
38	Omar Vizquel	3.00
39	Roger Clemens	25.00
40	Joe Carter	3.00
41	Frank Thomas	50.00
42	Javier Lopez	3.00
43	Mike Mussina	12.00
44	Gary Sheffield	8.00
45	Tony Gwynn	30.00
46	Jason Kendall	3.00
47	Jim Thome	12.00
48	Andres Galarraga	8.00
49	Mark McGwire	75.00
50	Troy Percival	3.00
51	Derek Jeter	35.00
52	Todd Hollandsworth	3.00
53	Ken Griffey Jr.	60.00
54	Randy Johnson	12.00
55	Pat Hentgen	3.00
56	Rusty Greer	3.00
57	John Jaha	3.00
58	Kenny Lofton	15.00
59	Chipper Jones	35.00
60	Robb Nen	3.00
61	Rafael Palmeiro	6.00
62	Mariano Rivera	5.00
63	Hideo Nomo	12.00
64	Greg Vaughn	3.00
65	Ron Gant	3.00
66	Eddie Murray	8.00
67	John Smoltz	6.00
68	Manny Ramirez	15.00
69	Juan Gonzalez	30.00
70	F.P. Santangelo	3.00
71	Moises Alou	5.00
72	Alex Ochoa	3.00
73	Chuck Knoblauch	6.00
74	Raul Mondesi	6.00
75	J.T. Snow	3.00
76	Rickey Henderson	5.00
77	Bobby Bonilla	5.00
78	Wade Boggs	6.00
79	Ivan Rodriguez	12.00
80	Brian Jordan	3.00
81	Al Leiter	3.00
82	Jay Buhner	6.00
83	Greg Maddux	35.00
84	Edgar Martinez	3.00
85	Kevin Brown	3.00
86	Eric Young	3.00
87	Todd Hundley	5.00
88	Ellis Burks	3.00
89	Marquis Grissom	3.00
90	Jose Canseco	6.00
91	Henry Rodriguez	3.00
92	Andy Pettitte	15.00
93	Mark Grudzielanek	3.00
94	Dwight Gooden	3.00
95	Roberto Alomar	12.00
96	Paul Wilson	3.00
97	Will Clark	6.00
98	Rondell White	5.00
99	Charles Johnson	3.00
100	Jim Edmonds	5.00
101	Jason Giambi	3.00
102	Billy Wagner	3.00
103	Edgar Renteria	3.00
104	Johnny Damon	3.00
105	Jason Isringhausen	3.00
106	Andruw Jones	30.00
107	Jose Guillen	15.00
108	Kevin Orie	3.00
109	Brian Giles	3.00
110	Danny Patterson	3.00
111	Vladimir Guerrero	20.00
112	Scott Rolen	30.00

113	Damon Mashore	3.00
114	Nomar Garciaparra	35.00
115	Todd Walker	10.00
116	Wilton Guerrero	3.00
117	Bob Abreu	3.00
118	Brooks Kieschnick	3.00
119	Pokey Reese	3.00
120	Todd Greene	3.00
121	Dmitri Young	3.00
122	Raul Casanova	3.00
123	Glendon Rusch	3.00
124	Jason Dickson	3.00
125	Jorge Posada	3.00
126	Rod Myers	3.00
127	Bubba Trammell	12.00
128	Scott Spiezio	3.00
129	Hideki Irabu	20.00
130	Wendell Magee	3.00
131	Bartolo Colon	3.00
132	Chris Holt	3.00
133	Calvin Maduro	3.00
134	Ray Montgomery	3.00
135	Shannon Stewart	3.00
136	Ken Griffey Jr. (Certified Stars)	30.00
137	Vladimir Guerrero (Certified Stars)	10.00
138	Roger Clemens (Certified Stars)	12.00
139	Mark McGwire (Certified Stars)	40.00
140	Albert Belle (Certified Stars)	10.00
141	Derek Jeter (Certified Stars)	18.00
142	Juan Gonzalez (Certified Stars)	15.00
143	Greg Maddux (Certified Stars)	18.00
144	Alex Rodriguez (Certified Stars)	25.00
145	Jeff Bagwell (Certified Stars)	12.00
146	Cal Ripken Jr. (Certified Stars)	25.00
147	Tony Gwynn (Certified Stars)	15.00
148	Frank Thomas (Certified Stars)	25.00
149	Hideo Nomo (Certified Stars)	6.00
150	Andruw Jones (Certified Stars)	15.00

1997 Totally Certified Platinum Gold

The most difficult to find of the Totally Certified cards, the Platinum Gold versions are sequentially-numbered to 30 per card and inserted 1:79 packs.

		MT
Common Player:		60.00
Minor Stars:		6.00
1	Barry Bonds	400.00
2	Mo Vaughn	400.00

3	Matt Williams	150.00
4	Ryne Sandberg	400.00
5	Jeff Bagwell	600.00
6	Alan Benes	60.00
7	John Wetteland	60.00
8	Fred McGriff	125.00
9	Craig Biggio	100.00
10	Bernie Williams	300.00
11	Brian Hunter	60.00
12	Sandy Alomar Jr.	60.00
13	Ray Lankford	60.00
14	Ryan Klesko	150.00
15	Jermaine Dye	60.00
16	Andy Benes	60.00
17	Albert Belle	500.00
18	Tony Clark	300.00
19	Dean Palmer	60.00
20	Bernard Gilkey	60.00
21	Ken Caminiti	150.00
22	Alex Rodriguez	900.00
23	Tim Salmon	150.00
24	Larry Walker	200.00
25	Barry Larkin	150.00
26	Mike Piazza	700.00
27	Brady Anderson	75.00
28	Cal Ripken Jr.	900.00
29	Charles Nagy	60.00
30	Paul Molitor	300.00
31	Darin Erstad	450.00
32	Rey Ordonez	60.00
33	Wally Joyner	60.00
34	David Cone	75.00
35	Sammy Sosa	500.00
36	Dante Bichette	125.00
37	Eric Karros	60.00
38	Omar Vizquel	60.00
39	Roger Clemens	600.00
40	Joe Carter	60.00
41	Frank Thomas	900.00
42	Javier Lopez	75.00
43	Mike Mussina	300.00
44	Gary Sheffield	200.00
45	Tony Gwynn	700.00
46	Jason Kendall	60.00
47	Jim Thome	300.00
48	Andres Galarraga	150.00
49	Mark McGwire	1000.
50	Troy Percival	60.00
51	Derek Jeter	750.00
52	Todd Hollandsworth	60.00
53	Ken Griffey Jr.	1400.
54	Randy Johnson	300.00
55	Pat Hentgen	60.00
56	Rusty Greer	60.00
57	John Jaha	60.00
58	Kenny Lofton	400.00
59	Chipper Jones	750.00
60	Robb Nen	60.00
61	Rafael Palmeiro	125.00
62	Mariano Rivera	75.00
63	Hideo Nomo	700.00
64	Greg Vaughn	60.00
65	Ron Gant	60.00
66	Eddie Murray	300.00
67	John Smoltz	100.00
68	Manny Ramirez	350.00
69	Juan Gonzalez	700.00
70	F.P. Santangelo	60.00
71	Moises Alou	75.00
72	Alex Ochoa	60.00
73	Chuck Knoblauch	150.00
74	Raul Mondesi	125.00
75	J.T. Snow	60.00
76	Rickey Henderson	60.00
77	Bobby Bonilla	75.00
78	Wade Boggs	150.00
79	Ivan Rodriguez	350.00
80	Brian Jordan	60.00
81	Al Leiter	60.00
82	Jay Buhner	125.00
83	Greg Maddux	750.00
84	Edgar Martinez	75.00
85	Kevin Brown	60.00
86	Eric Young	60.00
87	Todd Hundley	100.00
88	Ellis Burks	60.00
89	Marquis Grissom	75.00
90	Jose Canseco	125.00
91	Henry Rodriguez	60.00
92	Andy Pettitte	300.00
93	Mark Grudzielanek	60.00
94	Dwight Gooden	75.00
95	Roberto Alomar	300.00
96	Paul Wilson	60.00
97	Will Clark	150.00
98	Rondell White	100.00

99	Charles Johnson	60.00
100	Jim Edmonds	75.00
101	Jason Giambi	60.00
102	Billy Wagner	60.00
103	Edgar Renteria	60.00
104	Johnny Damon	60.00
105	Jason Isringhausen	60.00
106	Andruw Jones	500.00
107	Jose Guillen	250.00
108	Kevin Orie	60.00
109	Brian Giles	60.00
110	Danny Patterson	60.00
111	Vladimir Guerrero	400.00
112	Scott Rolen	500.00
113	Damon Mashore	60.00
114	Nomar Garciaparra	600.00
115	Todd Walker	150.00
116	Wilton Guerrero	60.00
117	Bob Abreu	60.00
118	Brooks Kieschnick	60.00
119	Pokey Reese	60.00
120	Todd Greene	60.00
121	Dmitri Young	60.00
122	Raul Casanova	60.00
123	Glendon Rusch	60.00
124	Jason Dickson	60.00
125	Jorge Posada	60.00
126	Rod Myers	60.00
127	Bubba Trammell	250.00
128	Scott Spiezio	60.00
129	Hideki Irabu	350.00
130	Wendell Magee	60.00
131	Bartolo Colon	60.00
132	Chris Holt	60.00
133	Calvin Maduro	60.00
134	Ray Montgomery	60.00
135	Shannon Stewart	60.00
136	Ken Griffey Jr. (Certified Stars)	700.00
137	Vladimir Guerrero (Certified Stars)	200.00
138	Roger Clemens (Certified Stars)	300.00
139	Mark McGwire (Certified Stars)	500.00
140	Albert Belle (Certified Stars)	250.00
141	Derek Jeter (Certified Stars)	400.00
142	Juan Gonzalez (Certified Stars)	350.00
143	Greg Maddux (Certified Stars)	400.00
144	Alex Rodriguez (Certified Stars)	450.00
145	Jeff Bagwell (Certified Stars)	300.00
146	Cal Ripken Jr. (Certified Stars)	450.00
147	Tony Gwynn (Certified Stars)	350.00
148	Frank Thomas (Certified Stars)	450.00
149	Hideo Nomo (Certified Stars)	350.00
150	Andruw Jones (Certified Stars)	250.00

1997 Pinnacle Certified Team

The top 20 players in the game are honored on cards with frosted silver mylar printing. Cards were inserted 1:19 packs. A parallel version of this set, Certified Gold Team, has a gold mylar design with each card numbered to 500.

		MT
Complete Set (20):		300.00
Common Player:		4.00
Gold Teams: 4x		
1	Frank Thomas	25.00
2	Jeff Bagwell	18.00
3	Derek Jeter	25.00
4	Chipper Jones	25.00
5	Alex Rodriguez	30.00
6	Ken Caminiti	4.00
7	Cal Ripken Jr.	30.00
8	Mo Vaughn	10.00
9	Ivan Rodriguez	10.00
10	Mike Piazza	25.00
11	Juan Gonzalez	20.00
12	Barry Bonds	10.00
13	Ken Griffey Jr.	40.00
14	Andruw Jones	15.00
15	Albert Belle	10.00
16	Gary Sheffield	6.00
17	Andy Pettitte	8.00
18	Hideo Nomo	8.00
19	Greg Maddux	25.00
20	John Smoltz	4.00

1997 Pinnacle Inside

The first baseball card set to be sold within a sealed tin can, Inside Baseball consisted of a 150-card base set featuring both a color and black-and-white photo of the player on the front of the card. Included in the base set were 20 Rookies cards and three checklists. Inserts include the Club Edition and Diamond Edition parallel sets, Dueling Dugouts and Fortysomething. In addition, 24 different cans, each featuring a different player, were available. Cans containing one pack of 10 cards were sold for $2.99 each.

	MT
Complete Set (150):	35.00
Common Player:	.10
Club Edition Complete Set (150):	500.00
Common Club Edition:	.75
Club Edition Stars: 5x to 10x	
Club Edition Yng Stars & RC's: 3x to 6x	
Common Diamond Edition:	15.00
Diamond Edition Stars: 40x to 70x	
Diamond Edition Yng Stars: 30x to 50x	
1 David Cone	.10

2	Sammy Sosa	2.00
3	Joe Carter	.10
4	Juan Gonzalez	2.00
5	Hideo Nomo	.75
6	Moises Alou	.10
7	Marc Newfield	.10
8	Alex Rodriguez	3.00
9	Kimera Bartee	.10
10	Chuck Knoblauch	.25
11	Jason Isringhausen	.10
12	Jermaine Allensworth	.10
13	Frank Thomas	3.00
14	Paul Molitor	.75
15	John Mabry	.10
16	Greg Maddux	2.50
17	Rafael Palmeiro	.20
18	Brian Jordan	.10
19	Ken Griffey Jr.	4.00
20	Brady Anderson	.10
21	Ruben Sierra	.10
22	Travis Fryman	.10
23	Cal Ripken Jr.	3.00
24	Will Clark	.25
25	Todd Hollandsworth	.10
26	Kevin Brown	.10
27	Mike Piazza	2.50
28	Craig Biggio	.20
29	Paul Wilson	.10
30	Andres Galarraga	.20
31	Chipper Jones	2.50
32	Jason Giambi	.10
33	Ernie Young	.10
34	Marty Cordova	.10
35	Albert Belle	1.00
36	Roger Clemens	1.50
37	Ryne Sandberg	1.00
38	Henry Rodriguez	.10
39	Jay Buhner	.20
40	Raul Mondesi	.20
41	Jeff Fassero	.10
42	Edgar Martinez	.10
43	Trey Beamon	.10
44	Mo Vaughn	1.00
45	Gary Sheffield	.35
46	Ray Durham	.10
47	Brett Butler	.10
48	Ivan Rodriguez	.75
49	Fred McGriff	.25
50	Dean Palmer	.10
51	Rickey Henderson	.10
52	Andy Pettitte	1.00
53	Bobby Bonilla	.10
54	Shawn Green	.10
55	Tino Martinez	.40
56	Tony Gwynn	2.00
57	Tom Glavine	.20
58	Eric Young	.10
59	Kevin Appier	.10
60	Barry Bonds	1.00
61	Wade Boggs	.20
62	Jason Kendall	.10
63	Jeff Bagwell	2.00
64	Jeff Conine	.10
65	Greg Vaughn	.10
66	Eric Karros	.10
67	Manny Ramirez	1.00
68	John Smoltz	.20
69	Terrell Wade	.10
70	John Wetteland	.10
71	Kenny Lofton	1.00
72	Jim Thome	.75
73	Bill Pulsipher	.10
74	Darryl Strawberry	.10
75	Roberto Alomar	.75
76	Bobby Higginson	.10
77	James Baldwin	.10
78	Mark McGwire	5.00
79	Jose Canseco	.25
80	Mark Grudzielanek	.10
81	Ryan Klesko	.50
82	Javier Lopez	.10
83	Ken Caminiti	.20
84	Dave Nilsson	.10
85	Tim Salmon	.20
86	Cecil Fielder	.20
87	Derek Jeter	2.50
88	Garret Anderson	.10
89	Dwight Gooden	.10
90	Carlos Delgado	.10
91	Ugueth Urbina	.10
92	Chan Ho Park	.10
93	Eddie Murray	.40
94	Alex Ochoa	.10
95	Rusty Greer	.10
96	Mark Grace	.20
97	Pat Hentgen	.10

98	John Jaha	.10
99	Charles Johnson	.10
100	Jermaine Dye	.10
101	Quinton McCracken	.10
102	Troy Percival	.10
103	Shane Reynolds	.10
104	Rondell White	.10
105	Charles Nagy	.10
106	Alan Benes	.10
107	Tom Goodwin	.10
108	Ron Gant	.10
109	Dan Wilson	.10
110	Darin Erstad	1.50
111	Matt Williams	.25
112	Barry Larkin	.20
113	Mariano Rivera	.15
114	Larry Walker	.40
115	Jim Edmonds	.10
116	Michael Tucker	.10
117	Todd Hundley	.20
118	Alex Fernandez	.10
119	J.T. Snow	.10
120	Ellis Burks	.10
121	Steve Finley	.10
122	Mike Mussina	.75
123	Curtis Pride	.10
124	Derek Bell	.10
125	Dante Bichette	.20
126	Terry Steinbach	.10
127	Randy Johnson	.75
128	Andruw Jones	2.00
129	Vladimir Guerrero	1.50
130	Ruben Rivera	.10
131	Billy Wagner	.10
132	Scott Rolen	2.00
133	Rey Ordonez	.10
134	Karim Garcia	.10
135	George Arias	.10
136	Todd Greene	.10
137	Robin Jennings	.10
138	Raul Casanova	.10
139	Josh Booty	.10
140	Edgar Renteria	.10
141	Chad Mottola	.10
142	Dmitri Young	.10
143	Tony Clark	.75
144	Todd Walker	.75
145	Kevin Brown	.10
146	Nomar Garciaparra	2.50
147	Neifi Perez	.10
148	Derek Jeter, Todd Hollandsworth	.40
149	Pat Hentgen, John Smoltz	.10
150	Juan Gonzalez, Ken Caminiti	.30

1997 Pinnacle Inside Cans

In addition to the cards, collectors had the option of collecting the 24 different player cans which are "the packs" in which the cards were sold. About the size of a can of peas (3" diameter, 4-1/2" tall, the cans feature several color and black-and-white reproductions of the player's Inside card. The package had to be opened with a can opener to access the cards. Values shown are for empty cans which have been opened from the bottom; top-opened cans have little collectible value.

		MT
Complete Set (24):		20.00
Common Can:		.50
Sealed Cans: 2x to 3x		
1	Ken Griffey Jr.	2.50
2	Juan Gonzalez	1.25
3	Frank Thomas	2.00
4	Cal Ripken Jr.	2.00
5	Derek Jeter	1.50
6	Andruw Jones	1.50
7	Alex Rodriguez	2.50
8	Mike Piazza	1.50
9	Mo Vaughn	.75
10	Jeff Bagwell	1.00
11	Ken Caminiti	.50
12	Andy Pettitte	.75
13	Barry Bonds	.75
14	Mark McGwire	3.00
15	Ryan Klesko	.50
16	Manny Ramirez	.60
17	Ivan Rodriguez	.50
18	Chipper Jones	1.50
19	Albert Belle	.75
20	Tony Gwynn	1.25
21	Kenny Lofton	.65
22	Greg Maddux	1.25
23	Hideo Nomo	.60
24	John Smoltz	.50

1997 Pinnacle Inside Club Edition

A 150-card parallel set featuring a special silver foil design and "CLUB EDITION" notation on back, these cards were inserted 1:7 can of Inside.

	MT
Complete Club Edition Set (150):	500.00
Common Club Edition:	.75
Stars: 5x to 10x	
Yng Stars & RCs: 3x to 6x	

(See 1997 Pinnacle Inside for checklist and base values.)

1997 Pinnacle Inside Diamond Edition

A second parallel set, this time featuring a special die-cut design and gold holographic stamping. Cards were inserted 1:63 packs.

	MT
Common Diamond Edition:	15.00
Stars: 40x to 70x	
Yng Stars & RCs: 30x to 50x	
(See 1997 Pinnacle Inside for checklist and base values.)	

1997 Pinnacle Inside Dueling Dugouts

98m1232f

This 20-card insert set features a veteran player on one side, a rising star on the other, and a spinning wheel that reveals their respective achievements in various statistical categories. Cards were inserted 1:23 packs.

		MT
Complete Set (20):		325.00
Common Player:		8.00
1	Alex Rodriguez, Cal Ripken Jr.	50.00
2	Jeff Bagwell, Ken Caminiti	20.00
3	Barry Bonds, Albert Belle	15.00
4	Mike Piazza, Ivan Rodriguez	25.00
5	Chuck Knoblauch, Roberto Alomar	15.00
6	Ken Griffey Jr., Andruw Jones	50.00
7	Chipper Jones, Jim Thome	25.00
8	Frank Thomas, Mo Vaughn	40.00
9	Fred McGriff, Mark McGwire	50.00
10	Brian Jordan, Tony Gwynn	20.00
11	Barry Larkin, Derek Jeter	20.00
12	Kenny Lofton, Bernie Williams	15.00
13	Juan Gonzalez, Manny Ramirez	20.00
14	Will Clark, Rafael Palmeiro	10.00
15	Greg Maddux, Roger Clemens	20.00
16	John Smoltz, Andy Pettitte	15.00
17	Mariano Rivera, John Wetteland	8.00
18	Hideo Nomo, Mike Mussina	15.00
19	Todd Hollandsworth, Darin Erstad	15.00
20	Vladimir Guerrero, Karim Garcia	15.00

1997 Pinnacle Inside Fortysomething

The top home run hitters in the game are pictured in this 16-card set. Cards were inserted 1:47 packs.

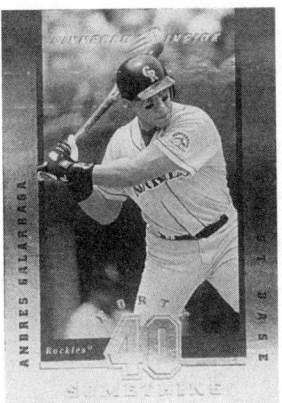

		MT
Complete Set (16):		300.00
Common Player:		8.00
1	Juan Gonzalez	40.00
2	Barry Bonds	20.00
3	Ken Caminiti	10.00
4	Mark McGwire	80.00
5	Todd Hundley	8.00
6	Albert Belle	20.00
7	Ellis Burks	8.00
8	Jay Buhner	8.00
9	Brady Anderson	8.00
10	Vinny Castilla	8.00
11	Mo Vaughn	20.00
12	Ken Griffey Jr.	80.00
13	Sammy Sosa	40.00
14	Andres Galarraga	10.00
15	Gary Sheffield	15.00
16	Frank Thomas	60.00

1997 Pinnacle Mint Collection

The 30-card Mint Collection set came in three-card packs that also contained two coins. The cards came in two versions: die-cut and foil. Three foil versions appear with Bronze Act as the common with Silver (1:15) and Gold (1:48) appearing. The coins that come with each pack arrive in brass, silver and gold and can be matched up with the corresponding player die-cut card. The card fronts feature a player action shot on the left side with a shadowed headshot on the right. On the die-cut versions, the coin-size hole is in the lower right

quadrant while the foil team stamp for the common cards is in the same location. The card backs are numbered as "x of 30" and deliver a short text.

		MT
Complete Set (30):		20.00
Common Player:		.25
Bronze Cards: 2x		40.00
Silver Cards: 4x to 8x		
Gold Cards: 10x to 20x		
Wax Box:		50.00
1	Ken Griffey Jr.	2.50
2	Frank Thomas	2.00
3	Alex Rodriguez	2.50
4	Cal Ripken Jr.	2.00
5	Mo Vaughn	.75
6	Juan Gonzalez	1.25
7	Mike Piazza	1.75
8	Albert Belle	.75
9	Chipper Jones	1.75
10	Andruw Jones	1.50
11	Greg Maddux	1.75
12	Hideo Nomo	.40
13	Jeff Bagwell	1.25
14	Manny Ramirez	.75
15	Mark McGwire	4.00
16	Derek Jeter	1.75
17	Sammy Sosa	1.50
18	Barry Bonds	.75
19	Chuck Knoblauch	.25
20	Dante Bichette	.25
21	Tony Gwynn	1.25
22	Ken Caminiti	.40
23	Gary Sheffield	.40
24	Tim Salmon	.25
25	Ivan Rodriguez	.50
26	Henry Rodriguez	.25
27	Barry Larkin	.25
28	Ryan Klesko	.50
29	Brian Jordan	.25
30	Jay Buhner	.25

1997 Pinnacle Mint Collection Coins

Two coins from the 30-coin set were included in each three-card pack of 1997 Pinnacle Mint Collection. Brass coins are common while nickel-silver coins were inserted every 20 packs and gold-plated coins were inserted every 48 packs. Redemption cards for solid silver coins were found every 2,300 packs and a redemption card for a solid gold coin was inserted in 47,200 packs. The front of the coins feature the player's headshot while the backs have a baseball diamond with "Limited Edition, Pinnacle Mint Collection 1997" printed.

A player's name in *italic* type indicates a rookie card.

		MT
Complete Set (30):		65.00
Common Brass Coin:		1.00
Minor Brass Stars:		1.50
Nickel Coins: 2x to 4x		
Gold Plated Coins: 6x to 10x		
1	Ken Griffey Jr.	10.00
2	Frank Thomas	8.00
3	Alex Rodriguez	10.00
4	Cal Ripken Jr.	8.00
5	Mo Vaughn	2.50
6	Juan Gonzalez	4.00
7	Mike Piazza	6.00
8	Albert Belle	2.50
9	Chipper Jones	6.00
10	Andruw Jones	5.00
11	Greg Maddux	6.00
12	Hideo Nomo	2.00
13	Jeff Bagwell	4.00
14	Manny Ramirez	2.50
15	Mark McGwire	10.00
16	Derek Jeter	4.00
17	Sammy Sosa	5.00
18	Barry Bonds	2.50
19	Chuck Knoblauch	1.00
20	Dante Bichette	1.50
21	Tony Gwynn	4.00
22	Ken Caminiti	1.50
23	Gary Sheffield	1.50
24	Tim Salmon	1.00
25	Ivan Rodriguez	2.00
26	Henry Rodriguez	1.00
27	Barry Larkin	1.00
28	Ryan Klesko	1.50
29	Brian Jordan	1.00
30	Jay Buhner	1.00

1997 Pinnacle X-Press

The 150-card set features 115 base cards, a 22-card Rookies subset, 10 Peak Performers and three checklist cards. Each of the regular cards features a horizontal design with two photos of each player on the front of the card and his name across the bottom. There are a number of inserts in this product, including Swing for the Fences (regular player cards as well as base and booster cards that can be used to accumulate points for a sweepstakes), Men of Summer, Far & Away, Melting Pot, Metal Works silver and Metal Works

Gold. Cards were sold in eight-card packs for $1.99 each. X-Press Metal Works boxes were also available for $14.99 and contained a regular pack, one metal card and a master deck used to play the Swing for the Fences game.

		MT
Complete Set (150):		20.00
Common Player:		.05
Men of Summer: 3x to 5x		
1	Larry Walker	.20
2	Andy Pettitte	.60
3	Matt Williams	.20
4	Juan Gonzalez	1.25
5	Frank Thomas	2.00
6	Kenny Lofton	.60
7	Ken Griffey Jr.	2.50
8	Andres Galarraga	.15
9	Greg Maddux	1.50
10	Hideo Nomo	.40
11	Cecil Fielder	.15
12	Jose Canseco	.15
13	Tony Gwynn	1.25
14	Eddie Murray	.20
15	Alex Rodriguez	2.00
16	Mike Piazza	1.50
17	Ken Hill	.05
18	Chuck Knoblauch	.15
19	Ellis Burks	.05
20	Rafael Palmeiro	.15
21	Vinny Castilla	.05
22	Rusty Greer	.05
23	Chipper Jones	1.50
24	Rey Ordonez	.05
25	Mariano Rivera	.15
26	Garret Anderson	.05
27	Edgar Martinez	.10
28	Dante Bichette	.15
29	Todd Hundley	.15
30	Barry Bonds	.60
31	Barry Larkin	.15
32	Derek Jeter	1.50
33	Marquis Grissom	.10
34	David Justice	.20
35	Ivan Rodriguez	.50
36	Jay Buhner	.15
37	Fred McGriff	.20
38	Brady Anderson	.15
39	Tony Clark	.60
40	Eric Young	.05
41	Charles Nagy	.05
42	Mark McGwire	3.00
43	Paul O'Neill	.15
44	Tino Martinez	.15
45	Ryne Sandberg	.60
46	Bernie Williams	.40
47	Albert Belle	.60
48	Jeff Cirillo	.05
49	Tim Salmon	.15
50	Steve Finley	.05
51	Lance Johnson	.05
52	John Smoltz	.15
53	Javier Lopez	.10
54	Roger Clemens	.60
55	Kevin Appier	.05
56	Ken Caminiti	.20
57	Cal Ripken Jr.	2.00
58	Moises Alou	.15
59	Marty Cordova	.05
60	David Cone	.15
61	Manny Ramirez	.50
62	Ray Durham	.05
63	Jermaine Dye	.05
64	Craig Biggio	.15
65	Will Clark	.20
66	Omar Vizquel	.05
67	Bernard Gilkey	.05
68	Greg Vaughn	.05
69	Wade Boggs	.15
70	Dave Nilsson	.05
71	Mark Grace	.15
72	Dean Palmer	.05
73	Sammy Sosa	1.50
74	Mike Mussina	.50
75	Alex Fernandez	.05
76	Henry Rodriguez	.05
77	Travis Fryman	.05
78	Jeff Bagwell	1.00
79	Pat Hentgen	.05
80	Gary Sheffield	.20
81	Jim Edmonds	.15
82	Darin Erstad	1.00
83	Mark Grudzielanek	.05

84	Jim Thome	.40
85	Bobby Higginson	.15
86	Al Martin	.05
87	Jason Giambi	.05
88	Mo Vaughn	.60
89	Jeff Conine	.05
90	Edgar Renteria	.05
91	Andy Ashby	.05
92	Ryan Klesko	.30
93	John Jaha	.05
94	Paul Molitor	.40
95	Brian Hunter	.05
96	Randy Johnson	.40
97	Joey Hamilton	.05
98	Billy Wagner	.05
99	John Wetteland	.05
100	Jeff Fassero	.05
101	Rondell White	.15
102	Kevin Brown	.15
103	Andy Benes	.15
104	Raul Mondesi	.15
105	Todd Hollandsworth	.05
106	Alex Ochoa	.05
107	Bobby Bonilla	.15
108	Brian Jordan	.05
109	Tom Glavine	.15
110	Ron Gant	.15
111	Jason Kendall	.05
112	Roberto Alomar	.40
113	Troy Percival	.05
114	Michael Tucker	.05
115	Joe Carter	.15
116	Andruw Jones	1.25
117	Nomar Garciaparra	1.25
118	Todd Walker	.20
119	Jose Guillen	.50
120	*Bubba Trammell*	.50
121	Wilton Guerrero	.10
122	Bob Abreu	.05
123	Vladimir Guerrero	.75
124	Dmitri Young	.05
125	Kevin Orie	.05
126	Glendon Rusch	.05
127	Brooks Kieschnick	.05
128	Scott Spiezio	.05
129	Brian Giles	.05
130	Jason Dickson	.15
131	Damon Mashore	.05
132	Wendell Magee	.05
133	Matt Morris	.05
134	Scott Rolen	1.25
135	Shannon Stewart	.05
136	*Deivi Cruz*	.25
137	*Hideki Irabu*	1.50
138	Larry Walker (Peak Performers)	.15
139	Ken Griffey Jr. (Peak Performers)	1.00
140	Frank Thomas (Peak Performers)	1.00
141	Ivan Rodriguez (Peak Performers)	.20
142	Randy Johnson (Peak Performers)	.20
143	Mark McGwire (Peak Performers)	1.00
144	Tino Martinez (Peak Performers)	.10
145	Tony Clark (Peak Performers)	.25
146	Mike Piazza (Peak Performers)	.60
147	Alex Rodriguez (Peak Performers)	.75
148	Checklist(Roger Clemens)	.25
149	Checklist(Greg Maddux)	.50
150	Checklist(Hideo Nomo)	.20

1997 Pinnacle X-Press Far & Away

This 18-card insert highlights the top home run hitters in baseball and is printed with Dufex technology. Cards were inserted 1:19 packs.

A player's name in *italic* type indicates a rookie card.

		MT
Complete Set (18):		100.00
Common Player:		1.50
Men of Summer: 2x to 4x		
1	Albert Belle	5.00
2	Mark McGwire	25.00
3	Frank Thomas	15.00
4	Mo Vaughn	5.00
5	Jeff Bagwell	8.00
6	Juan Gonzalez	10.00
7	Mike Piazza	12.00
8	Andruw Jones	10.00
9	Chipper Jones	12.00
10	Gary Sheffield	2.50
11	Sammy Sosa	10.00
12	Darin Erstad	7.00
13	Jay Buhner	1.50
14	Ken Griffey Jr.	20.00
15	Ken Caminiti	1.50
16	Brady Anderson	1.50
17	Manny Ramirez	4.00
18	Alex Rodriguez	15.00

1997 Pinnacle X-Press Melting Pot

This 20-card insert showcases the talents of major leaguers from various countries. Each card in the set is numbered to 500 and utilizes heliogram print technology.

		MT
Complete Set (20):		650.00
Common Player:		10.00
1	Jose Guillen	20.00
2	Vladimir Guerrero	35.00
3	Andruw Jones	50.00
4	Larry Walker	15.00
5	Manny Ramirez	20.00
6	Ken Griffey Jr.	100.00
7	Alex Rodriguez	75.00
7p	Alex Rodriguez (overprinted "SAMPLE")	6.00
8	Frank Thomas	75.00
9	Juan Gonzalez	50.00
10	Ivan Rodriguez	20.00
11	Hideo Nomo	20.00
12	Rafael Palmeiro	10.00
13	Dave Nilsson	10.00
14	Nomar Garciaparra	50.00
15	Wilton Guerrero	10.00
16	Sammy Sosa	60.00
17	Edgar Renteria	10.00
18	Cal Ripken Jr.	75.00
19	Derek Jeter	60.00
20	Rey Ordonez	10.00

A player's name in *italic* type indicates a rookie card.

1997 Pinnacle X-Press Metal Works

These randomly inserted redemption cards provide collectors with the opportunity to receive a metal card of one of 20 different players. Redemption cards for Silver Metal Works cards were inserted 1:470 packs, while redemptions cards for Gold Metal Works cards were inserted 1:950 packs.

		MT
Complete Set (20):		100.00
Common Player:		2.50
Gold Redemption Card:		50.00
Silver Redemption Card:		25.00
1	Ken Griffey Jr.	12.50
2	Frank Thomas	12.50
3	Andruw Jones	6.00
4	Alex Rodriguez	10.00
5	Derek Jeter	7.50
6	Cal Ripken Jr.	10.00
7	Mike Piazza	7.50
8	Chipper Jones	7.50
9	Juan Gonzalez	7.50
10	Greg Maddux	7.50
11	Tony Gwynn	6.00
12	Jeff Bagwell	5.00
13	Albert Belle	3.00
14	Mark McGwire	15.00
15	Nomar Garciaparra	6.00
16	Mo Vaughn	3.00
17	Andy Pettitte	3.00
18	Manny Ramirez	2.50
19	Kenny Lofton	3.00
20	Roger Clemens	4.00

1997 Pinnacle X-Press Men of Summer

This parallel set of the 150 cards in the base X-Press issue differs in that the fronts are printed on foil backgrounds and the backs have a notation "MEN OF SUMMER" printed in gold vertically at top.

	MT
Complete Set (150):	80.00
Common Player:	.25
(Star cards valued at 3X-5X regular X-Press version)	

1997 Pinnacle X-Press Swing for the Fences

These inserts allow collectors to play an interactive game based on the number of home runs hit by the home run champions of each league. Player Cards feature 60 different players and were inserted 1:2 packs. Base Cards feature a number between 20-42 printed on them and are found one in every master deck. Booster Cards feature a plus-or-minus point total (i.e. +7, -2) that can be used to add or subtract points to get to the winning home run total. Booster Cards are found 1:2 packs, while Base Cards are found one per master deck. Collectors who accumulated the winning home run totals were eligible to win prizes ranging from autographs to a trip to the 1998 All-Star Game.

		MT
Complete Set (60):		5.00
Common Player:		.05
1	Ken Griffey Jr.	1.00
2	Tony Clark	.25
3	Tino Martinez	.10
4	Sandy Alomar Jr.	.05
5	Mark McGwire	.75
6	Jay Bell	.05
7	Geronimo Berroa	.05
8	Tim Naehring	.05
9	Juan Gonzalez	.50
10	Frank Thomas	1.00
11	Jose Canseco	.15
12	Jim Thome	.15
13	Dean Palmer	.05
14	Albert Belle	.30
15	Matt Williams	.10
16	Brady Anderson	.05
17	Mo Vaughn	.25
18	Cal Ripken Jr.	.75
19	Cecil Fielder	.10
20	Jay Buhner	.10
21	Rafael Palmeiro	.05
22	Tim Salmon	.10
23	Edgar Martinez	.05
24	John Jaha	.05
25	Carlos Delgado	.05
26	Terry Steinbach	.05
27	David Justice	.10
28	Dave Nilsson	.05
29	Joe Carter	.05
30	Jim Edmonds	.05
31	Larry Walker	.10
32	Mike Lieberthal	.05
33	Raul Mondesi	.10
34	Vinny Castilla	.05

35	Moises Alou	.05
36	Ellis Burks	.05
37	Jeff Kent	.05
38	Henry Rodriguez	.05
39	Mike Piazza	.60
40	Barry Bonds	.25
41	Dante Bichette	.10
42	Jeff Bagwell	.40
43	Ken Caminiti	.05
44	Chipper Jones	.60
45	Ron Gant	.05
46	Barry Larkin	.05
47	Fred McGriff	.10
48	Andres Galarraga	.10
49	Gary Sheffield	.10
50	Todd Hundley	.10
51	Sammy Sosa	.25
52	Bernard Gilkey	.05
53	Vladimir Guerrero	.30
54	Bobby Bonilla	.05
55	Derek Bell	.05
56	Javier Lopez	.05
57	Rondell White	.10
58	Ryan Klesko	.15
59	Todd Zeile	.05
60	Brian Jordan	.05

1997 Pinnacle X-Press Swing/Fences Gold

Collectors who correctly matched Swing for the Fences insert game cards of the final 1997 season American and National home run champions with proper point cards equal to the number of home runs each hit could exchange them for a randopm assortment of 10 upgraded cards featuring gold-foil highlights and a premium card stock. The first 1,000 redemptions received an autographed Andruw Jones gold card. The redemption period ended March 1, 1998.

	MT
Complete Set (60):	200.00
Common Player:	2.00
Andruw Jones Autograph:	150.00

(Star player and hot rookie cards valued at 3-6X regular Swing/Fences version.)

1998 Pinnacle

Pinnacle Baseball consists of a 200-card base set. The regular cards feature full-bleed photos on the front. Three different backs were produced for each card: home stats, away stats and seasonal stats. The set includes 157 regular cards, 24 Rookies, six Field of Vision, 10 Goin' Jake cards and three checklists. Parallel sets include Artist's Proofs, Press Plates and Museum Collection. Inserts include Epix, Hit it Here, Spellbound and Uncut.

		MT
Complete Set (200):		20.00
Common Player:		.10
1	Tony Gwynn (All-Star)	1.50
2	Pedro Martinez (All-Star)	.25
3	Kenny Lofton (All-Star)	.75
4	Curt Schilling (All-Star)	.10
5	Shawn Estes (All-Star)	.10
6	Tom Glavine (All-Star)	.20
7	Mike Piazza (All-Star)	2.00
8	Ray Lankford (All-Star)	.10
9	Barry Larkin (All-Star)	.20
10	Tony Womack (All-Star)	.10
11	Jeff Blauser (All-Star)	.10
12	Rod Beck (All-Star)	.10
13	Larry Walker (All-Star)	.30
14	Greg Maddux (All-Star)	2.00
15	Mark Grace (All-Star)	.20
16	Ken Caminiti (All-Star)	.20
17	Bobby Jones (All-Star)	.10
18	Chipper Jones (All-Star)	2.00
19	Javier Lopez (All-Star)	.10
20	Moises Alou (All-Star)	.20
21	Royce Clayton (All-Star)	.10
22	Darryl Kile (All-Star)	.10
23	Barry Bonds (All-Star)	.75
24	Steve Finley (All-Star)	.10
25	Andres Galarraga (All-Star)	.25
26	Denny Neagle (All-Star)	.10
27	Todd Hundley (All-Star)	.15
28	Jeff Bagwell	.75
29	Andy Pettitte	.35
30	Darin Erstad	.75
31	Carlos Delgado	.15
32	Matt Williams	.25
33	Will Clark	.20
34	Vinny Castilla	.15
35	Brad Radke	.10
36	John Olerud	.20
37	Andruw Jones	1.50
38	Jason Giambi	.10
39	Scott Rolen	1.50
40	Gary Sheffield	.30
41	Jimmy Key	.10
42	Kevin Appier	.10
43	Wade Boggs	.25
44	Hideo Nomo	.60
45	Manny Ramirez	.60
46	Wilton Guerrero	.10
47	Travis Fryman	.15
48	Chili Davis	.10
49	Jeromy Burnitz	.10
50	Craig Biggio	.20
51	Tim Salmon	.25
52	Jose Cruz Jr.	1.50
53	Sammy Sosa	1.50
54	Hideki Irabu	1.00
55	Chan Ho Park	.20
56	Robin Ventura	.10

57	Jose Guillen	.30
58	Deion Sanders	.25
59	Jose Canseco	.20
60	Jay Buhner	.20
61	Rafael Palmeiro	.20
62	Vladimir Guerrero	1.00
63	Mark McGwire	4.00
64	Derek Jeter	2.00
65	Bobby Bonilla	.20
66	Raul Mondesi	.20
67	Paul Molitor	.40
68	Joe Carter	.15
69	Marquis Grissom	.10
70	Juan Gonzalez	1.50
71	Kevin Orie	.10
72	Rusty Greer	.10
73	Henry Rodriguez	.10
74	Fernando Tatis	.25
75	John Valentin	.10
76	Matt Morris	.10
77	Ray Durham	.10
78	Geronimo Berroa	.10
79	Scott Brosius	.10
80	Willie Greene	.10
81	Rondell White	.20
82	Doug Drabek	.10
83	Derek Bell	.10
84	Butch Huskey	.10
85	Doug Jones	.10
86	Jeff Kent	.10
87	Jim Edmonds	.10
88	Mark McLemore	.10
89	Todd Zeile	.10
90	Edgardo Alfonzo	.10
91	Carlos Baerga	.10
92	Jorge Fabregas	.10
93	Alan Benes	.20
94	Troy Percival	.10
95	Edgar Renteria	.10
96	Jeff Fassero	.10
97	Reggie Sanders	.10
98	Dean Palmer	.10
99	J.T. Snow	.20
100	Dave Nilsson	.10
101	Dan Wilson	.10
102	Robb Nen	.10
103	Damion Easley	.10
104	Kevin Foster	.10
105	Jose Offerman	.10
106	Steve Cooke	.10
107	Matt Stairs	.10
108	Darryl Hamilton	.10
109	Steve Karsay	.10
110	Gary DiSarcina	.10
111	Dante Bichette	.25
112	Billy Wagner	.10
113	David Segui	.10
114	Bobby Higginson	.10
115	Jeffrey Hammonds	.10
116	Kevin Brown	.20
117	Paul Sorrento	.10
118	Mark Leiter	.10
119	Charles Nagy	.10
120	Danny Patterson	.10
121	Brian McRae	.10
122	Jay Bell	.10
123	Jamie Moyer	.10
124	Carl Everett	.10
125	Greg Colbrunn	.10
126	Jason Kendall	.10
127	Luis Sojo	.10
128	Mike Lieberthal	.10
129	Reggie Jefferson	.10
130	Cal Eldred	.10
131	Orel Hershiser	.10
132	Doug Glanville	.10
133	Willie Blair	.10
134	Neifi Perez	.10
135	Sean Berry	.10
136	Chuck Finley	.10
137	Alex Gonzalez	.10
138	Dennis Eckersley	.20
139	Kenny Rogers	.10
140	Troy O'Leary	.10
141	Roger Bailey	.10
142	Yamil Benitez	.10
143	Wally Joyner	.10
144	Bobby Witt	.10
145	Pete Schourek	.10
146	Terry Steinbach	.10
147	B.J. Surhoff	.10
148	Esteban Loaiza	.10
149	Heathcliff Slocumb	.10
150	Ed Sprague	.10
151	Gregg Jefferies	.10
152	Scott Erickson	.10

153	Jaime Navarro	.10
154	David Wells	.10
155	Alex Fernandez	.10
156	Tim Belcher	.10
157	Mark Grudzielanek	.10
158	Scott Hatteberg	.10
159	Paul Konerko	1.00
160	Ben Grieve	1.00
161	Abraham Nunez	.25
162	Shannon Stewart	.10
163	Jaret Wright	1.00
164	Derrek Lee	.10
165	Todd Dunwoody	.10
166	*Steve Woodard*	.25
167	Ryan McGuire	.10
168	Jeremi Gonzalez	.10
169	Mark Kotsay	.50
170	Brett Tomko	.10
171	Bobby Estalella	.10
172	Livan Hernandez	.20
173	Todd Helton	.75
174	Garrett Stephenson	.10
175	Pokey Reese	.10
176	Tony Saunders	.20
177	Antone Williamson	.10
178	Bartolo Colon	.10
179	Karim Garcia	.10
180	Juan Encarnacion	.25
181	Jacob Cruz	.10
182	Alex Rodriguez (Field of Vision)	1.00
183	Cal Ripken Jr., Roberto Alomar (Field of Vision)	1.00
184	Roger Clemens (Field of Vision)	.50
185	Derek Jeter (Field of Vision)	1.00
186	Frank Thomas (Field of Vision)	1.50
187	Ken Griffey Jr. (Field of Vision)	1.50
188	Mark McGwire (Goin' Jake)	2.00
189	Tino Martinez (Goin' Jake)	.10
190	Larry Walker (Goin' Jake)	.15
191	Brady Anderson (Goin' Jake)	.10
192	Jeff Bagwell (Goin' Jake)	.50
193	Ken Griffey Jr. (Goin' Jake)	1.50
194	Chipper Jones (Goin' Jake)	1.00
195	Ray Lankford (Goin' Jake)	.10
196	Jim Thome (Goin' Jake)	.20
197	Nomar Garciaparra (Goin' Jake)	1.00
198	Checklist (1997 HR Contest)	.10
199	Checklist (1997 HR Contest Winner)	.10
200	Checklist (Overall View of the Park)	.10

1998 Pinnacle Artist's Proofs

Artist's Proof is a 100-card partial parallel of the Pinnacle base set. The gold-foil Dufex cards were renumbered and inserted one per 39 packs.

		MT
Complete Set (100):		800.00
Common Player:		3.00
Inserted 1:39		
Museums: .25x to .35x		
Inserted 1:9		
1	Tony Gwynn (All-Star)	30.00
2	Pedro J. Martinez (All-Star)	8.00
3	Kenny Lofton (All-Star)	15.00
4	Curt Schilling (All-Star)	3.00
5	Shawn Estes (All-Star)	3.00
6	Tom Glavine (All-Star)	6.00
7	Mike Piazza (All-Star)	40.00
8	Ray Lankford (All-Star)	3.00
9	Barry Larkin (All-Star)	6.00
10	Tony Womack (All-Star)	3.00
11	Jeff Blauser (All-Star)	3.00
12	Rod Beck (All-Star)	3.00
13	Larry Walker (All-Star)	8.00
14	Greg Maddux (All-Star)	40.00
15	Mark Grace (All-Star)	6.00
16	Ken Caminiti (All-Star)	6.00
17	Bobby Jones (All-Star)	3.00
18	Chipper Jones (All-Star)	40.00
19	Javier Lopez (All-Star)	4.00
20	Moises Alou (All-Star)	4.00
21	Royce Clayton (All-Star)	3.00
22	Darryl Kile (All-Star)	3.00
23	Barry Bonds (All-Star)	15.00
24	Steve Finley (All-Star)	3.00
25	Andres Galarraga (All-Star)	8.00
26	Denny Neagle (All-Star)	4.00
27	Todd Hundley (All-Star)	4.00
28	Jeff Bagwell	25.00
29	Andy Pettitte	12.00
30	Darin Erstad	12.00
31	Carlos Delgado	3.00
32	Matt Williams	5.00
33	Will Clark	5.00
34	Brad Radke	3.00
35	John Olerud	4.00
36	Andruw Jones	30.00
37	Scott Rolen	30.00
38	Gary Sheffield	8.00
39	Jimmy Key	3.00
40	Wade Boggs	5.00
41	Hideo Nomo	15.00
42	Manny Ramirez	12.00
43	Wilton Guerrero	3.00
44	Travis Fryman	3.00
45	Craig Biggio	5.00
46	Tim Salmon	6.00
47	Jose Cruz Jr.	30.00
48	Sammy Sosa	40.00
49	Hideki Irabu	12.00
50	Jose Guillen	6.00
51	Deion Sanders	5.00
52	Jose Canseco	5.00
53	Jay Buhner	5.00
54	Rafael Palmeiro	5.00
55	Vladimir Guerrero	20.00
56	Mark McGwire	75.00
57	Derek Jeter	40.00
58	Bobby Bonilla	4.00
59	Raul Mondesi	5.00
60	Paul Molitor	10.00
61	Joe Carter	4.00
62	Marquis Grissom	4.00
63	Juan Gonzalez	30.00
64	Dante Bichette	5.00
65	Shannon Stewart (Rookie)	3.00
66	Jaret Wright (Rookie)	25.00
67	Derrek Lee (Rookie)	3.00
68	Todd Dunwoody (Rookie)	3.00
69	Steve Woodard (Rookie)	3.00
70	Ryan McGuire (Rookie)	3.00
71	Jeremi Gonzalez (Rookie)	5.00
72	Mark Kotsay (Rookie)	10.00
73	Brett Tomko (Rookie)	3.00
74	Bobby Estalella (Rookie)	5.00
75	Livan Hernandez (Rookie)	5.00
76	Todd Helton (Rookie)	15.00
77	Garrett Stephenson (Rookie)	3.00
78	Pokey Reese (Rookie)	3.00
79	Tony Saunders (Rookie)	5.00
80	Antone Williamson (Rookie)	3.00
81	Bartolo Colon (Rookie)	3.00
82	Karim Garcia (Rookie)	5.00
83	Juan Encarnacion (Rookie)	8.00
84	Jacob Cruz (Rookie)	6.00
85	Alex Rodriguez (Field of Vision)	25.00
86	Cal Ripken Jr., Roberto Alomar (Field of Vision)	25.00

87	Roger Clemens (Field of Vision)	12.00
88	Derek Jeter (Field of Vision)	20.00
89	Frank Thomas (Field of Vision)	30.00
90	Ken Griffey Jr. (Field of Vision)	35.00
91	Mark McGwire (Goin' Jake)	40.00
92	Tino Martinez (Goin' Jake)	4.00
93	Larry Walker (Goin' Jake)	5.00
94	Brady Anderson (Goin' Jake)	3.00
95	Jeff Bagwell (Goin' Jake)	12.00
96	Ken Griffey Jr. (Goin' Jake)	35.00
97	Chipper Jones (Goin' Jake)	20.00
98	Ray Lankford (Goin' Jake)	3.00
99	Jim Thome (Goin' Jake)	6.00
100	Nomar Garciaparra (Goin' Jake)	20.00

1998 Pinnacle Epix

This cross-brand insert was included in Pinnacle, Score, Pinnacle Certified and Zenith. Twenty-four cards were seeded in Pinnacle packs (1:21). The four-tiered set highlights a memorable Game, Season, Moment and Play in a player's career. The dot matrix hologram cards came in three colors: orange, purple and emerald.

		MT
Common Game & Play:		6.00
Common Season (7-12):		15.00
Common Moment (13-18):		30.00
Purples: 1.5x		
Emeralds: 2x to 3x		
1	Ken Griffey Jr. G	40.00
2	Juan Gonzalez G	20.00
3	Jeff Bagwell G	15.00
4	Ivan Rodriguez G	8.00
5	Nomar Garciaparra G	25.00
6	Ryne Sandberg G	10.00
7	Frank Thomas S	100.00
8	Derek Jeter S	60.00
9	Tony Gwynn S	50.00
10	Albert Belle S	25.00
11	Scott Rolen S	50.00
12	Barry Larkin S	15.00
13	Alex Rodriguez M	120.00
14	Cal Ripken Jr. M	150.00
15	Chipper Jones M	120.00
16	Roger Clemens M	75.00
17	Mo Vaughn M	50.00
18	Mark McGwire M	175.00
19	Mike Piazza P	25.00
20	Andruw Jones P	20.00
21	Greg Maddux P	25.00
22	Barry Bonds P	12.00
23	Paul Molitor P	8.00
24	Eddie Murray P	6.00

1998 Pinnacle Hit it Here

Hit it Here is a 10-card insert seeded one per 17 packs. The micro-etched silver foil cards feature a color player photo with a red "Hit it Here" target on the left. Each card has a serial number. If the pictured player hit for the cycle on Opening Day 1998, the collector with the correct serially numbered card would win $1 million.

		MT
Complete Set (10):		75.00
Common Player:		3.00
Inserted 1:17		
1	Larry Walker	3.00
2	Ken Griffey Jr.	20.00
3	Mike Piazza	12.00
4	Frank Thomas	15.00
5	Barry Bonds	5.00
6	Albert Belle	5.00
7	Tino Martinez	3.00
8	Mark McGwire	25.00
9	Juan Gonzalez	10.00
10	Jeff Bagwell	8.00

1998 Pinnacle Inside

Pinnacle Inside Baseball featured cards in a can. The 150 base cards featured full-bleed photos on the front with stats on the right and the player's name and position at the bottom. The Club Edition parallel (1:7) is printed on silver foil board and the Diamond Edition parallel (1:67) is printed on prismatic foil board. Each pack of cards was packaged inside a collectible can. Inserts include Behind the Numbers and Stand Up Guys.

		MT
Complete Set (150):		40.00
Common Player:		.15
Club Editions: 6x to 12x		
Inserted 1:7		
Diamond Editions: 40x to 70x		
Inserted 1:67		
1	Darin Erstad	1.00
2	Derek Jeter	2.50
3	Alex Rodriguez	2.50
4	Bobby Higginson	.15
5	Nomar Garciaparra	2.50
6	Kenny Lofton	1.00
7	Ivan Rodriguez	1.00
8	Cal Ripken Jr.	3.00
9	Todd Hundley	.15
10	Chipper Jones	2.50
11	Barry Larkin	.40
12	Roberto Alomar	.75
13	Mo Vaughn	1.00
14	Sammy Sosa	2.00
15	Sandy Alomar Jr.	.25
16	Albert Belle	1.00
17	Scott Rolen	1.50
18	Pokey Reese	.15
19	Ryan Klesko	.30
20	Andres Galarraga	.40
21	Justin Thompson	.25
22	Gary Sheffield	.40
23	David Justice	.40
24	Ken Griffey Jr.	4.00
25	Andruw Jones	2.00
26	Jeff Bagwell	1.50
27	Vladimir Guerrero	1.25
28	Mike Piazza	2.50
29	Chuck Knoblauch	.40
30	Rondell White	.25
31	Greg Maddux	2.50
32	Andy Pettitte	.75
33	Larry Walker	.40
34	Bobby Estalella	.15
35	Frank Thomas	3.00
36	Tony Womack	.15
37	Tony Gwynn	2.00
38	Barry Bonds	1.00
39	Randy Johnson	.75
40	Mark McGwire	5.00
41	Juan Gonzalez	2.00
42	Tim Salmon	.40
43	John Smoltz	.25
44	Rafael Palmeiro	.40
45	Mark Grace	.40
46	Mike Cameron	.25
47	Jim Thome	.50
48	Neifi Perez	.15
49	Kevin Brown	.40
50	Craig Biggio	.40
51	Bernie Williams	.75
52	Hideo Nomo	.75
53	Bob Abreu	.15
54	Edgardo Alfonzo	.15
55	Wade Boggs	.40
56	Jose Guillen	.40
57	Ken Caminiti	.40
58	Paul Molitor	.75
59	Shawn Estes	.15
60	Edgar Martinez	.15
61	Livan Hernandez	.40
62	Ray Lankford	.15
63	Rusty Greer	.25
64	Jim Edmonds	.25
65	Tom Glavine	.25
66	Alan Benes	.15
67	Will Clark	.25
68	Garret Anderson	.15
69	Javier Lopez	.25
70	Mike Mussina	.75
71	Kevin Orie	.15
72	Matt Williams	.40
73	Bobby Bonilla	.25
74	Ruben Rivera	.25
75	Jason Giambi	.15
76	Todd Walker	.40
77	Tino Martinez	.40
78	Matt Morris	.15
79	Fernando Tatis	.25
80	Todd Greene	.15
81	Fred McGriff	.25
82	Brady Anderson	.25
83	Mark Kotsay	.40
84	Raul Mondesi	.40
85	Moises Alou	.25
86	Roger Clemens	1.50
87	Wilton Guerrero	.15
88	Shannon Stewart	.15
89	Chan Ho Park	.25
90	Carlos Delgado	.15
91	Jose Cruz Jr.	1.50
92	Shawn Green	.15
93	Robin Ventura	.25
94	Reggie Sanders	.15
95	Orel Hershiser	.15
96	Dante Bichette	.25
97	Charles Johnson	.15
98	Pedro Martinez	.40
99	Mariano Rivera	.40
100	Joe Randa	.15
101	Jeff Kent	.15
102	Jay Buhner	.30
103	Brian Jordan	.15
104	Jason Kendall	.15
105	Scott Spiezio	.15
106	Desi Relaford	.15
107	Bernard Gilkey	.15
108	Manny Ramirez	.75
109	Tony Clark	.75
110	Eric Young	.15
111	Johnny Damon	.15
112	Glendon Rusch	.15
113	Ben Grieve	2.00
114	Homer Bush	.15
115	Miguel Tejada	1.00
116	Lou Collier	.15
117	Derrek Lee	.15
118	Jacob Cruz	.15
119	Raul Ibanez	.15
120	Ryan McGuire	.15
121	Antone Williamson	.15
122	Abraham Nunez	.15
123	Jeff Abbott	.15
124	Brett Tomko	.15
125	Richie Sexson	.15
126	Todd Helton	1.00
127	Juan Encarnacion	.15
128	Richard Hidalgo	.15
129	Paul Konerko	1.00
130	Brad Fullmer	1.00
131	Jeremi Gonzalez	.15
132	Jaret Wright	2.50
133	Derek Jeter (Inside Tips)	1.00
134	Frank Thomas (Inside Tips)	1.50
135	Nomar Garciaparra (Inside Tips)	1.00
136	Kenny Lofton (Inside Tips)	.50
137	Jeff Bagwell (Inside Tips)	.75
138	Todd Hundley (Inside Tips)	.15
139	Alex Rodriguez (Inside Tips)	1.00
140	Ken Griffey Jr. (Inside Tips)	2.00
141	Sammy Sosa (Inside Tips)	1.00
142	Greg Maddux (Inside Tips)	1.00
143	Albert Belle (Inside Tips)	.50
144	Cal Ripken Jr. (Inside Tips)	1.50
145	Mark McGwire (Inside Tips)	2.50
146	Chipper Jones (Inside Tips)	1.00
147	Charles Johnson (Inside Tips)	.15
148	Checklist(Ken Griffey Jr.)	1.50
149	Checklist(Jose Cruz Jr.)	.75
150	Checklist(Larry Walker)	.20

1998 Pinnacle Inside Behind the Numbers

Behind the Numbers is a 20-card insert seeded one per 23 cans. The card front features the player's number in the background and the card is die-cut around it. The back has text explaining why the player wears that number.

A player's name in *italic* type indicates a rookie card.

		MT
Complete Set (20):		500.00
Common Player:		8.00
Inserted 1:23		
1	Ken Griffey Jr.	60.00
2	Cal Ripken Jr.	50.00
3	Alex Rodriguez	40.00
4	Jose Cruz Jr.	25.00
5	Mike Piazza	40.00
6	Nomar Garciaparra	40.00
7	Scott Rolen	25.00
8	Andruw Jones	25.00
9	Frank Thomas	50.00
10	Mark McGwire	70.00
11	Ivan Rodriguez	15.00
12	Greg Maddux	40.00
13	Roger Clemens	25.00
14	Derek Jeter	30.00
15	Tony Gwynn	30.00
16	Ben Grieve	25.00
17	Jeff Bagwell	25.00
18	Chipper Jones	40.00
19	Hideo Nomo	15.00
20	Sandy Alomar Jr.	8.00

1998 Pinnacle Inside Cans

Ten-card packs of Pinnacle Inside were packaged in collectible cans. The 24 cans featured a player photo or team logo. Cans were created to honor the Florida Marlins' world championship and the expansion Arizona and Tampa Bay teams. Gold parallel versions of the cans were found one every 47 cans.

		MT
Complete Set (23):		25.00
Common Can:		.40
Sealed Cans: 2x to 3x		
Gold Cans: 10x		
1	Ken Griffey Jr.	2.50
2	Frank Thomas	2.50
3	Alex Rodriguez	1.50
4	Andruw Jones	1.25
5	Mike Piazza	1.50
6	Ben Grieve	1.00
7	Hideo Nomo	.50
8	Vladimir Guerrero	.60
9	Roger Clemens	1.00
10	Tony Gwynn	1.25
11	Mark McGwire	3.00
12	Cal Ripken Jr.	2.00
13	Jose Cruz Jr.	1.00
14	Greg Maddux	1.50
15	Chipper Jones	1.50
16	Derek Jeter	1.50
17	Juan Gonzalez	1.25
18	Nomar Garciaparra (AL ROY)	1.50
19	Scott Rolen (NL ROY)	1.00
20	World Series Winner	.50
21	Larry Walker (NL MVP)	.50
22	Tampa Bay Devil Rays	.40
23	Arizona Diamondbacks	.40

1998 Pinnacle Inside Club Edition

This parallel set is virtually identical to the regular Inside cards, except for the addition of a "CLUB EDITION" notice to the right of the player's first name, and the use of gold foil highlights instead of silver on front.

		MT
Complete Set (xx):		400.00
Common Player:		1.00
Club Editions: 5x to 10x		
Inserted 1:7		
(Stars and rookies valued 6-10X regular version.)		

1998 Pinnacle Inside Stand Up Guys

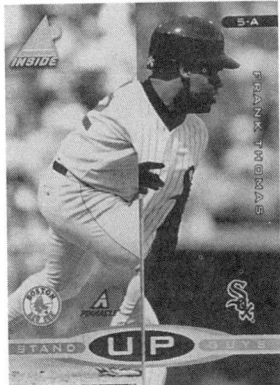

This 50-card insert was seeded one per can. Each card has a match. The two cards join together in the center to form a stand up collectible featuring four Major League players.

		MT
Complete Set (100):		40.00
Common Player:		.25
Inserted 1:1		
1a	Ken Griffey Jr.	2.00
1b	Cal Ripken Jr.	1.50
1c	Tony Gwynn	1.00
1d	Mike Piazza	1.25

2a	Andruw Jones	.75
2b	Alex Rodriguez	1.25
2c	Scott Rolen	.75
2d	Nomar Garciaparra	1.25
3a	Andruw Jones	.75
3b	Greg Maddux	1.25
3c	Javier Lopez	.25
3d	Chipper Jones	1.25
4a	Jay Buhner	.25
4b	Randy Johnson	.40
4c	Ken Griffey Jr.	2.00
4d	Alex Rodriguez	1.25
5a	Frank Thomas	2.00
5b	Jeff Bagwell	.75
5c	Mark McGwire	2.00
5d	Mo Vaughn	.50
6a	Nomar Garciaparra	1.25
6b	Derek Jeter	1.00
6c	Alex Rodriguez	1.25
6d	Barry Larkin	.25
7a	Mike Piazza	1.25
7b	Ivan Rodriguez	.50
7c	Charles Johnson	.25
7d	Javier Lopez	.25
8a	Cal Ripken Jr.	1.50
8b	Chipper Jones	1.25
8c	Ken Caminiti	.25
8d	Scott Rolen	.75
9a	Jose Cruz Jr.	.75
9b	Vladimir Guerrero	.50
9c	Andruw Jones	.75
9d	Jose Guillen	.25
10a	Larry Walker	.40
10b	Dante Bichette	.25
10c	Ellis Burks	.25
10d	Neifi Perez	.25
11a	Juan Gonzalez	1.00
11b	Sammy Sosa	1.50
11c	Vladimir Guerrero	.50
11d	Manny Ramirez	.40
12a	Greg Maddux	1.25
12b	Roger Clemens	.75
12c	Hideo Nomo	.50
12d	Randy Johnson	.50
13a	Ben Grieve	.60
13b	Paul Konerko	.50
13c	Jose Cruz Jr.	.75
13d	Fernando Tatis	.25
14a	Ryne Sandberg	.50
14b	Chuck Knoblauch	.40
14c	Roberto Alomar	.40
14d	Craig Biggio	.25
15a	Cal Ripken Jr.	1.50
15b	Brady Anderson	.25
15c	Rafael Palmeiro	.25
15d	Roberto Alomar	.40
16a	Darin Erstad	.50
16b	Jim Edmonds	.25
16c	Tim Salmon	.40
16d	Garret Anderson	.25
17a	Mike Piazza	1.25
17b	Hideo Nomo	.40
17c	Raul Mondesi	.25
17d	Eric Karros	.25
18a	Ivan Rodriguez	.50
18b	Juan Gonzalez	1.00
18c	Will Clark	.40
18d	Rusty Greer	.25
19a	Derek Jeter	1.00
19b	Bernie Williams	.40
19c	Tino Martinez	.40
19d	Andy Pettitte	.40
20a	Kenny Lofton	.50
20b	Ken Griffey Jr.	2.00
20c	Brady Anderson	.25
20d	Bernie Williams	.40
21a	Paul Molitor	.40
21b	Eddie Murray	.25
21c	Ryne Sandberg	.50
21d	Rickey Henderson	.25
22a	Tony Clark	.40
22b	Frank Thomas	2.00
22c	Jeff Bagwell	.75
22d	Mark McGwire	2.00
23a	Manny Ramirez	.40
23b	Jim Thome	.40
23c	David Justice	.25
23d	Sandy Alomar Jr.	.25
24a	Barry Bonds	.50
24b	Albert Belle	.50
24c	Jeff Bagwell	.75
24d	Dante Bichette	.25
25a	Ken Griffey Jr.	2.00
25b	Frank Thomas	2.00
25c	Alex Rodriguez	1.25
25d	Andruw Jones	.75

1998 Pinnacle Mint Collection

Mint Collection consists of 30 cards and 30 matching coins with numerous parallels of each. The horizontal cards come in four different versions. The base card features a player photo on the left with a circular bronze foil team logo on the right. The base cards were inserted one per hobby pack and two per retail pack. Die-cut versions removed the team logo and were inserted two per hobby and one per retail packs. Silver Mint Team (1:15 hobby, 1:23 retail) and Gold Mint Team (1:47 hobby, 1:71 retail) parallels were printed on silver foil and gold foil board, respectively.

	MT
Complete Set (30):	20.00
Common Die-Cut:	.25
Bronze: 1.5x to 2x	
Inserted 1:1 H	
Silver: 4x to 8x	
Inserted 1:15 H	
Gold: 8x to 15x	
Inserted 1:47 H	
Wax Box:	80.00
1 Jeff Bagwell	1.00
2 Albert Belle	.75
3 Barry Bonds	.75
4 Tony Clark	.50
5 Roger Clemens	1.00
6 Juan Gonzalez	1.25
7 Ken Griffey Jr.	2.50
8 Tony Gwynn	1.25
9 Derek Jeter	1.50
10 Randy Johnson	.40
11 Chipper Jones	1.50
12 Greg Maddux	1.50
13 Tino Martinez	.40
14 Mark McGwire	3.00
15 Hideo Nomo	.75
16 Andy Pettitte	.50
17 Mike Piazza	1.50
18 Cal Ripken Jr.	2.00
19 Alex Rodriguez	1.50
20 Ivan Rodriguez	.75
21 Sammy Sosa	1.50
22 Frank Thomas	2.00
23 Mo Vaughn	.75
24 Larry Walker	.40
25 Jose Cruz Jr.	1.00
26 Nomar Garciaparra	1.50
27 Vladimir Guerrero	.75
28 Livan Hernandez	.25
29 Andruw Jones	1.25
30 Scott Rolen	1.00

1998 Pinnacle Mint Collection Coins

Two base coins were included in each pack of Mint Collection. The coins feature the player's image, name and number on the front along with his team's name and logo. The back has the Mint Collection logo. Seven parallels were included: Nickel-Silver (1:41), Bronze Proof (numbered to 500), Silver Proof (numbered to 250), Gold Proof (numbered to 100), Gold-Plated (1:199), Solid Silver (1:288 hobby, 1:960 retail) and Solid Gold by redemption (1-of-1).

MT

	MT
Complete Set (30):	60.00
Common Brass Coin:	.75
Nickel: 3x to 6x	
Inserted 1:41	
Silver: 12x to 25x	
Inserted 1:288 H, 1:960 R	
Gold: 10x to 25x	
Inserted 1:199	
1 Jeff Bagwell	2.50
2 Albert Belle	1.50
3 Barry Bonds	1.50
4 Tony Clark	1.00
5 Roger Clemens	2.50
6 Juan Gonzalez	3.00
7 Ken Griffey Jr.	6.00
8 Tony Gwynn	3.00
9 Derek Jeter	4.00
10 Randy Johnson	1.00
11 Chipper Jones	4.00
12 Greg Maddux	4.00
13 Tino Martinez	1.00
14 Mark McGwire	6.00
15 Hideo Nomo	1.50
16 Andy Pettitte	1.00
17 Mike Piazza	4.00
18 Cal Ripken Jr.	5.00
19 Alex Rodriguez	4.00
20 Ivan Rodriguez	1.50
21 Sammy Sosa	3.00
22 Frank Thomas	5.00
23 Mo Vaughn	1.50
24 Larry Walker	1.00
25 Jose Cruz Jr.	2.50
26 Nomar Garciaparra	4.00
27 Vladimir Guerrero	1.50
28 Livan Hernandez	.75
29 Andruw Jones	3.00
30 Scott Rolen	2.50

1998 Pinnacle Mint Collection Mint Gems

Mint Gems is a six-card insert printed on silver foil board. The cards were inserted 1:31 hobby packs and 1:47 retail. The oversized Mint Gems coins are twice the size of the regular coins. The six coins were inserted 1:31 hobby packs.

	MT
Complete Set (6)	50.00
Common Player:	4.00
Coins: .5x to 1x	
1 Ken Griffey Jr.	20.00
2 Larry Walker	4.00
3 Roger Clemens	8.00
4 Pedro Martinez	4.00
5 Nomar Garciaparra	12.00
6 Scott Rolen	10.00

1998 Pinnacle Performers

Pinnacle Performers consists of a 150-card base set. The Peak Performers parallel adds silver foil to the base cards and was inserted 1:7. Inserts in the home run-themed product include Big Bang, Launching Pad, Player's Card and Power Trip.

	MT
Complete Set (150):	20.00
Common Player:	.10
Peak Performers: 3x to 6x	
Inserted 1:7	
1 Ken Griffey Jr.	2.50
2 Frank Thomas	2.00
3 Cal Ripken Jr.	2.00
4 Alex Rodriguez	1.50
5 Greg Maddux	1.50
6 Mike Piazza	1.50
7 Chipper Jones	1.50
8 Tony Gwynn	1.25
9 Derek Jeter	1.25
10 Jeff Bagwell	.75
11 Juan Gonzalez	1.25
12 Nomar Garciaparra	1.50
13 Andruw Jones	.60
14 Hideo Nomo	.40
15 Roger Clemens	.75
16 Mark McGwire	3.00
17 Scott Rolen	.75
18 Vladimir Guerrero	.60
19 Barry Bonds	.60
20 Darin Erstad	.60
21 Albert Belle	.60
22 Kenny Lofton	.60
23 Bernie Williams	.60
24 Tony Clark	.40
25 Ivan Rodriguez	.60
26 Jose Cruz Jr.	.50
27 Larry Walker	.30
28 Jaret Wright	.60
29 Andy Pettitte	.50
30 Roberto Alomar	.50
31 Randy Johnson	.40
32 Manny Ramirez	.60
33 Paul Molitor	.40
34 Mike Mussina	.50
35 Jim Thome	.40
36 Tino Martinez	.25
37 Gary Sheffield	.25
38 Chuck Knoblauch	.25
39 Bernie Williams	.50
40 Tim Salmon	.20
41 Sammy Sosa	1.00
42 Wade Boggs	.20
43 Will Clark	.20
44 Andres Galarraga	.25
45 Raul Mondesi	.20
46 Rickey Henderson	.10

47	Jose Canseco	.25
48	Pedro Martinez	.50
49	Jay Buhner	.20
50	Ryan Klesko	.25
51	Barry Larkin	.25
52	Charles Johnson	.10
53	Tom Glavine	.20
54	Edgar Martinez	.10
55	Fred McGriff	.20
56	Moises Alou	.20
57	Dante Bichette	.20
58	Jim Edmonds	.20
59	Mark Grace	.25
60	Chan Ho Park	.20
61	Justin Thompson	.10
62	John Smoltz	.20
63	Craig Biggio	.20
64	Ken Caminiti	.20
65	Richard Hidalgo	.10
66	Carlos Delgado	.10
67	David Justice	.25
68	J.T. Snow	.10
69	Jason Giambi	.10
70	Garret Anderson	.10
71	Rondell White	.20
72	Matt Williams	.25
73	Brady Anderson	.10
74	Eric Karros	.20
75	Javier Lopez	.10
76	Pat Hentgen	.10
77	Todd Hundley	.10
78	Ray Lankford	.10
79	Denny Neagle	.10
80	Sandy Alomar Jr.	.20
81	Jason Kendall	.10
82	Omar Vizquel	.10
83	Kevin Brown	.20
84	Kevin Appier	.10
85	Al Martin	.10
86	Rusty Greer	.10
87	Bobby Bonilla	.20
88	Shawn Estes	.10
89	Rafael Palmeiro	.25
90	Edgar Renteria	.10
91	Alan Benes	.20
92	Bobby Higginson	.10
93	Mark Grudzielanek	.10
94	Jose Guillen	.20
95	Neifi Perez	.10
96	Jeff Abbott	.10
97	Todd Walker	.25
98	Eric Young	.10
99	Brett Tomko	.10
100	Mike Cameron	.10
101	Karim Garcia	.10
102	Brian Jordan	.10
103	Jeff Suppan	.10
104	Robin Ventura	.20
105	Henry Rodriguez	.10
106	Shannon Stewart	.10
107	Kevin Orie	.10
108	Bartolo Colon	.20
109	Bob Abreu	.10
110	Vinny Castilla	.20
111	Livan Hernandez	.10
112	Derrek Lee	.10
113	Mark Kotsay	.25
114	Todd Greene	.10
115	Edgardo Alfonzo	.10
116	A.J. Hinch	.40
117	Paul Konerko	.30
118	Todd Helton	.60
119	Miguel Tejada	.30
120	Fernando Tatis	.20
121	Ben Grieve	.75
122	Travis Lee	1.50
123	Kerry Wood	3.00
124	Eli Marrero	.10
125	David Ortiz	.10
126	Juan Encarnacion	.10
127	Brad Fullmer	.25
128	Richie Sexson	.10
129	Aaron Boone	.10
130	Enrique Wilson	.10
131	Javier Valentin	.10
132	Abraham Nunez	.10
133	Ricky Ledee	.25
134	Carl Pavano	.10
135	Bobby Estalella	.10
136	Homer Bush	.10
137	Brian Rose	.10
138	Ken Griffey Jr. (Far and Away)	1.25
139	Frank Thomas (Far and Away)	1.00

140	Cal Ripken Jr. (Far and Away)	1.00
141	Alex Rodriguez (Far and Away)	.75
142	Greg Maddux (Far and Away)	.75
143	Chipper Jones (Far and Away)	.75
144	Mike Piazza (Far and Away)	.75
145	Tony Gwynn (Far and Away)	.60
146	Derek Jeter (Far and Away)	.60
147	Jeff Bagwell (Far and Away)	.40
148	Checklist(Hideo Nomo)	.20
149	Checklist(Roger Clemens)	.40
150	Checklist(Greg Maddux)	.60

1998 Pinnacle Performers Big Bang

This 20-card insert features top power hitters. The micro-etched cards are sequentially numbered to 2,500. Each player has a Seasonal Outburst parallel, with a red overlay and numbered to that player's best seasonal home run total.

		MT
Complete Set (20):		175.00
Common Player:		4.00
Production 5,000 sets		
1	Ken Griffey Jr.	25.00
2	Frank Thomas	18.00
3	Mike Piazza	15.00
4	Chipper Jones	15.00
5	Alex Rodriguez	15.00
6	Nomar Garciaparra	15.00
7	Jeff Bagwell	8.00
8	Cal Ripken Jr.	18.00
9	Albert Belle	6.00
10	Mark McGwire	30.00
11	Juan Gonzalez	12.00
12	Larry Walker	4.00
13	Tino Martinez	4.00
14	Jim Thome	5.00
15	Manny Ramirez	6.00
16	Barry Bonds	6.00
17	Mo Vaughn	6.00
18	Jose Cruz Jr.	5.00
19	Tony Clark	5.00
20	Andruw Jones	6.00

1998 Pinnacle Performers Big Bang Season Outburst

Season Outburst parallels the Big Bang insert. The cards have a red overlay and are sequentially numbered to each player's season-high home run total.

	MT
Common Player:	40.00
#'d to players home run total from 1997	
1 Ken Griffey Jr. (56)	250.00
2 Frank Thomas (35)	220.00
3 Mike Piazza (40)	175.00
4 Chipper Jones (21)	220.00
5 Alex Rodriguez (23)	250.00
6 Nomar Garciaparra (30)	200.00
7 Jeff Bagwell (43)	140.00
8 Cal Ripken Jr. (17)	350.00
9 Albert Belle (30)	80.00
10 Mark McGwire (58)	275.00
11 Juan Gonzalez (42)	150.00
12 Larry Walker (49)	40.00
13 Tino Martinez (44)	40.00
14 Jim Thome (40)	40.00
15 Manny Ramirez (26)	80.00
16 Barry Bonds (40)	70.00
17 Mo Vaughn (35)	75.00
18 Jose Cruz Jr. (26)	100.00
19 Tony Clark (32)	50.00
20 Andruw Jones (18)	125.00

1998 Pinnacle Performers Launching Pad

Launching Pad is a 20-card insert seeded one per nine packs. It features top sluggers on foil-on-foil cards with an outer space background.

		MT
Complete Set (20):		75.00
Common Player:		1.50
Inserted 1:9		
1	Ben Grieve	3.00
2	Ken Griffey Jr.	10.00
3	Derek Jeter	5.00
4	Frank Thomas	8.00
5	Travis Lee	6.00
6	Vladimir Guerrero	2.50
7	Tony Gwynn	5.00
8	Jose Cruz Jr.	2.00
9	Cal Ripken Jr.	8.00
10	Chipper Jones	6.00
11	Scott Rolen	3.00
12	Andruw Jones	2.50
13	Ivan Rodriguez	2.50
14	Todd Helton	2.50
15	Nomar Garciaparra	6.00
16	Mark McGwire	12.00
17	Gary Sheffield	1.50
18	Bernie Williams	2.00
19	Alex Rodriguez	6.00
20	Mike Piazza	6.00

1998 Pinnacle Performers Power Trip

This 10-card insert was seeded 1:21. Printed on silver foil, each card is sequentially-numbered to 10,000.

	MT
Complete Set (10):	80.00
Common Player:	2.50
Production 10,000 sets	
1 Frank Thomas	12.00
2 Alex Rodriguez	10.00
3 Nomar Garciaparra	10.00
4 Jeff Bagwell	5.00
5 Cal Ripken Jr.	12.00
6 Mike Piazza	10.00
7 Chipper Jones	10.00
8 Ken Griffey Jr.	15.00
9 Mark McGwire	18.00
10 Juan Gonzalez	8.00

1998 Pinnacle Performers Swing for the Fences

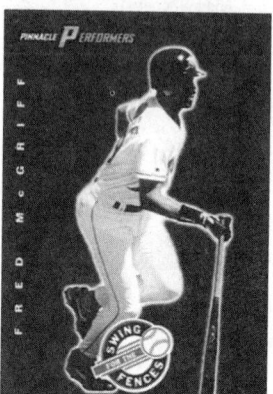

Pinnacle Performers included the "Swing for the Fences" sweepstakes. Fifty players were featured on cards with numbers on an all-red background. Fifty Home Run Points cards were also inserted, with each card featuring a point total on the front. Collectors who found the player cards of the AL and NL home run leaders, as well as enough point cards to match each of their season totals, were eligible to win prizes. A player or point card was inserted in each pack.

	MT
Complete Set (50):	20.00
Common Player:	.20
Inserted 1:1	
1 Brady Anderson	.20
2 Albert Belle	.60
3 Jay Buhner	.30
4 Jose Canseco	.30
5 Tony Clark	.50
6 Jose Cruz Jr.	.50
7 Jim Edmonds	.20
8 Cecil Fielder	.20
9 Travis Fryman	.20
10 Nomar Garciaparra	1.50
11 Juan Gonzalez	1.25
12 Ken Griffey Jr.	2.50
13 David Justice	.30
14 Travis Lee	1.50
15 Edgar Martinez	.20
16 Tino Martinez	.30
17 Rafael Palmeiro	.30
18 Manny Ramirez	.60
19 Cal Ripken Jr.	2.00
20 Alex Rodriguez	1.50
21 Tim Salmon	.30
22 Frank Thomas	2.00
23 Jim Thome	.40
24 Mo Vaughn	.60
25 Bernie Williams	.50
26 Fred McGriff	.25

27 Jeff Bagwell	.75
28 Dante Bichette	.30
29 Barry Bonds	.60
30 Ellis Burks	.20
31 Ken Caminiti	.20
32 Vinny Castilla	.20
33 Andres Galarraga	.30
34 Vladimir Guerrero	.60
35 Todd Helton	.60
36 Todd Hundley	.20
37 Andruw Jones	.60
38 Chipper Jones	1.50
39 Eric Karros	.20
40 Ryan Klesko	.30
41 Ray Lankford	.20
42 Mark McGwire	2.50
43 Raul Mondesi	.25
44 Mike Piazza	1.50
45 Scott Rolen	.75
46 Gary Sheffield	.30
47 Sammy Sosa	1.00
48 Larry Walker	.40
49 Matt Williams	.30
50 WILDCARD	.20

1998 Pinnacle Plus

Pinnacle Plus consists of a 200-card base set. Five subsets are included: Field of Vision, Naturals, All-Stars, Devil Rays and Diamondbacks. Artist's Proof is a 60-card partial parallel of the base set, inserted 1:35 packs. Gold Artist's Proof cards are numbered to 100 and Mirror Artist's Proofs are 1-of-1 inserts. Inserts include Lasting Memories, Yardwork, A Piece of the Game, All-Star Epix, Team Pinnacle, Gold Team Pinnacle, Pinnabilia and Certified Souvenir.

	MT
Complete Set (200):	25.00
Common Player:	.10
Nolan Ryan Auto. Baseball (1,000)	85.00
1 Roberto Alomar (All-star)	.50
2 Sandy Alomar Jr. (All-star)	.15
3 Brady Anderson (All-star)	.10
4 Albert Belle (All-star)	.75
5 Jeff Cirillo (All-star)	.10
6 Roger Clemens (All-star)	1.00
7 David Cone (All-star)	.20
8 Nomar Garciaparra (All-star)	2.00
9 Ken Griffey Jr. (All-star)	3.00
10 Jason Dickson (All-star)	.10
11 Edgar Martinez (All-star)	.10
12 Tino Martinez (All-star)	.25
13 Randy Johnson (All-star)	.50
14 Mark McGwire (All-star)	3.00
15 David Justice (All-star)	.25
16 Mike Mussina (All-star)	.50
17 Chuck Knoblauch (All-star)	.30
18 Joey Cora (All-star)	.10
19 Pat Hentgen (All-star)	.10
20 Randy Myers (All-star)	.10
21 Cal Ripken Jr. (All-star)	2.50
22 Mariano Rivera (All-star)	.20
23 Jose Rosado (All-star)	.10
24 Frank Thomas (All-star)	2.00
25 Alex Rodriguez (All-star)	2.00
26 Justin Thompson (All-star)	.10
27 Ivan Rodriguez (All-star)	.75
28 Bernie Williams (All-star)	.50
29 Pedro Martinez	.50
30 Tony Clark	.40
31 Garret Anderson	.10
32 Travis Fryman	.10
33 Mike Piazza	2.00
34 Carl Pavano	.10
35 *Kevin Millwood*	1.25
36 Miguel Tejada	.20
37 Willie Blair	.10
38 Devon White	.10
39 Andres Galarraga	.30
40 Barry Larkin	.20
41 Al Leiter	.20
42 Moises Alou	.20
43 Eric Young	.10
44 John Jaha	.10
45 Bernard Gilkey	.10

46 Freddy Garcia	.10
47 Ruben Rivera	.10
48 Robb Nen	.10
49 Ray Lankford	.10
50 Kenny Lofton	.75
51 Joe Carter	.10
52 Jason McDonald	.10
53 Quinton McCracken	.10
54 Kerry Wood	3.00
55 Mike Lansing	.10
56 Chipper Jones	1.50
57 Barry Bonds	.75
58 Brad Fullmer	.25
59 Jeff Bagwell	1.00
60 Rondell White	.20
61 Geronimo Berroa	.10
62 *Magglio Ordonez*	.50
63 Dwight Gooden	.10
64 Brian Hunter	.10
65 Todd Walker	.20
66 *Frank Catalanotto*	.20
67 Tony Saunders	.10
68 Travis Lee	1.00
69 Michael Tucker	.10
70 Reggie Sanders	.10
71 Derrek Lee	.10
72 Larry Walker	.25
73 Marquis Grissom	.10
74 Craig Biggio	.10
75 Kevin Brown	.20
76 J.T. Snow	.10
77 Eric Davis	.10
78 Jeff Abbott	.10
79 Jermaine Dye	.10
80 Otis Nixon	.10
81 Curt Schilling	.20
82 Enrique Wilson	.10
83 Tony Gwynn	1.50
84 Orlando Cabrera	.10
85 Ramon Martinez	.10
86 Greg Vaughn	.20
87 Alan Benes	.10
88 Dennis Eckersley	.10
89 Jim Thome	.40
90 Juan Encarnacion	.25
91 Jeff King	.10
92 Shannon Stewart	.10
93 Roberto Hernandez	.10
94 Raul Ibanez	.10
95 Darryl Kile	.10
96 Charles Johnson	.10
97 Rich Becker	.10
98 Hal Morris	.10
99 Ismael Valdes	.10
100 Orel Hershiser	.10
101 Mo Vaughn	.75
102 Aaron Boone	.10
103 Jeff Conine	.10
104 Paul O'Neill	.25
105 Tom Candiotti	.10
106 Wilson Alvarez	.10
107 Mike Stanley	.10
108 Carlos Delgado	.10
109 Tony Batista	.10
110 Dante Bichette	.25
111 Henry Rodriguez	.10
112 Karim Garcia	.10
113 Shane Reynolds	.10
114 Ken Caminiti	.20
115 Jose Silva	.10
116 Juan Gonzalez	1.50
117 Brian Jordan	.10
118 Jim Leyritz	.10
119 Manny Ramirez	.75
120 Fred McGriff	.20
121 Brooks Kieschnick	.10
122 Sean Casey	.25
123 John Smoltz	.20
124 Rusty Greer	.10
125 Cecil Fielder	.10
126 Mike Cameron	.20
127 Reggie Jefferson	.10
128 Bobby Higginson	.10
129 Kevin Appier	.10
130 Robin Ventura	.10
131 Ben Grieve	1.00
132 Wade Boggs	.25
133 Jose Cruz Jr.	.75
134 Jeff Suppan	.10
135 Vinny Castilla	.20
136 Sammy Sosa	2.00
137 Mark Wohlers	.10
138 Jay Bell	.10
139 Brett Tomko	.10
140 Gary Sheffield	.25
141 Tim Salmon	.25

142	Jaret Wright	.75
143	Kenny Rogers	.10
144	Brian Anderson	.10
145	Darrin Fletcher	.10
146	John Flaherty	.10
147	Dmitri Young	.10
148	Andruw Jones	.75
149	Matt Williams	.25
150	Bobby Bonilla	.20
151	Mike Hampton	.10
152	Al Martin	.10
153	Mark Grudzielanek	.10
154	Dave Nilsson	.10
155	Roger Cedeno	.10
156	Greg Maddux	2.00
157	Mark Kotsay	.40
158	Steve Finley	.10
159	Wilson Delgado	.10
160	Ron Gant	.10
161	Jim Edmonds	.10
162	Jeff Blauser	.10
163	Dave Burba	.10
164	Pedro Astacio	.10
165	Livan Hernandez	.10
166	Neifi Perez	.10
167	Ryan Klesko	.20
168	Fernando Tatis	.10
169	Richard Hidalgo	.10
170	Carlos Perez	.10
171	Bob Abreu	.10
172	Francisco Cordova	.10
173	Todd Helton	.40
174	Doug Glanville	.10
175	Brian Rose	.10
176	Yamil Benitez	.10
177	Darin Erstad	.75
178	Scott Rolen	.75
179	John Wetteland	.10
180	Paul Sorrento	.10
181	Walt Weiss	.10
182	Vladimir Guerrero	.75
183	Ken Griffey Jr. (The Naturals)	1.50
184	Alex Rodriguez (The Naturals)	1.00
185	Cal Ripken Jr. (The Naturals)	1.00
186	Frank Thomas (The Naturals)	1.00
187	Chipper Jones (The Naturals)	.75
188	Hideo Nomo (The Naturals)	.30
189	Nomar Garciaparra (The Naturals)	1.00
190	Mike Piazza (The Naturals)	1.00
191	Greg Maddux (The Naturals)	1.00
192	Tony Gwynn (The Naturals)	.75
193	Mark McGwire (The Naturals)	1.50
194	Roger Clemens (The Naturals)	.50
195	Mike Piazza (Field of Vision)	1.00
196	Mark McGwire (Field of Vision)	1.50
197	Chipper Jones (Field of Vision)	.75
198	Larry Walker (Field of Vision)	.20
199	Hideo Nomo (Field of Vision)	.30
200	Barry Bonds (Field of Vision)	.40

1998 Pinnacle Plus Artist's Proofs

Artist's Proofs is a 60-card partial parallel of the Pinnacle Plus base set. The dot matrix hologram cards were inserted 1:35. Gold Artist's Proofs added a gold finish and are sequentially numbered to 100. Mirror Artist's Proofs are a "1-of-1" insert.

A player's name in *italic* type indicates a rookie card.

		MT
Complete Set (60):		500.00
Common Player:		2.50
Inserted 1:35		
Golds: 3x to 5x		
Production 100 sets		
1	Roberto Alomar (All-Star)	12.00
2	Albert Belle (All-Star)	15.00
3	Roger Clemens (All-Star)	25.00
4	Nomar Garciaparra (All-Star)	40.00
5	Ken Griffey Jr. (All-Star)	60.00
6	Tino Martinez (All-Star)	6.00
7	Randy Johnson (All-Star)	10.00
8	Mark McGwire (All-Star)	75.00
9	David Justice (All-Star)	4.00
10	Chuck Knoblauch (All-Star)	5.00
11	Cal Ripken Jr. (All-Star)	50.00
12	Frank Thomas (All-Star)	40.00
13	Alex Rodriguez (All-Star)	40.00
14	Ivan Rodriguez (All-Star)	15.00
15	Bernie Williams (All-Star)	12.00
16	Pedro Martinez	10.00
17	Tony Clark	10.00
18	Mike Piazza	40.00
19	Miguel Tejada	4.00
20	Andres Galarraga	5.00
21	Barry Larkin	4.00
22	Kenny Lofton	15.00
23	Chipper Jones	30.00
24	Barry Bonds	15.00
25	Brad Fullmer	4.00
26	Jeff Bagwell	20.00
27	Todd Walker	4.00
28	Travis Lee	20.00
29	Larry Walker	5.00
30	Craig Biggio	2.50
31	Tony Gwynn	30.00
32	Jim Thome	5.00
33	Juan Encarnacion	4.00
34	Mo Vaughn	15.00
35	Karim Garcia	4.00
36	Ken Caminiti	4.00
37	Juan Gonzalez	30.00
38	Manny Ramirez	15.00
39	Fred McGriff	4.00
40	Rusty Greer	2.50
41	Bobby Higginson	2.50
42	Ben Grieve	15.00
43	Wade Boggs	4.00
44	Jose Cruz Jr.	12.00
45	Sammy Sosa	40.00
46	Gary Sheffield	4.00
47	Tim Salmon	4.00
48	Jaret Wright	12.00
49	Andruw Jones	15.00
50	Matt Williams	4.00
51	Greg Maddux	40.00
52	Jim Edmonds	2.50
53	Livan Hernandez	2.50
54	Neifi Perez	2.50
55	Fernando Tatis	2.50
56	Richard Hidalgo	2.50
57	Todd Helton	12.00
58	Darin Erstad	15.00
59	Scott Rolen	15.00
60	Vladimir Guerrero	18.00

1998 Pinnacle Plus All-Star Epix

The All-Star Epix insert is part of the cross-brand Epix set. This 12-card set honors the All-Star Game achievements of baseball's stars on cards with dot matrix holograms. All-Star Epix was seeded 1:21.

		MT
Complete Set (12):		160.00
Common Player:		5.00
Purples: .75x to 1.5x		
Emeralds: 2x to 3x		
Overall Odds 1:21		
13	Alex Rodriguez	30.00
14	Cal Ripken Jr.	30.00
15	Chipper Jones	15.00
16	Roger Clemens	15.00
17	Mo Vaughn	10.00
18	Mark McGwire	40.00
19	Mike Piazza	20.00
20	Andruw Jones	8.00

21	Greg Maddux	20.00
22	Barry Bonds	10.00
23	Paul Molitor	8.00
24	Hideo Nomo	5.00

1998 Pinnacle Plus A Piece of the Game

Inserted 1:17 hoby packs (1:19 retail), this 10-card insert features baseball's top players on micro-etched foil cards.

		MT
Complete Set (10):		75.00
Common Player:		3.00
Inserted 1:19		
1	Ken Griffey Jr.	15.00
2	Frank Thomas	10.00
3	Alex Rodriguez	10.00
4	Chipper Jones	8.00
5	Cal Ripken Jr.	10.00
6	Mike Piazza	10.00
7	Greg Maddux	10.00
8	Juan Gonzalez	8.00
9	Nomar Garciaparra	10.00
10	Larry Walker	3.00

1998 Pinnacle Plus Lasting Memories

Lasting Memories is a 30-card insert seeded 1:5. Printed on foil board, the cards feature a player photo with a sky background.

		MT
Complete Set (30):		40.00
Common Player:		.50
Inserted 1:5		
1	Nomar Garciaparra	3.00
2	Ken Griffey Jr.	5.00
3	Livan Hernandez	.50
4	Hideo Nomo	.75
5	Ben Grieve	1.50
6	Scott Rolen	1.50
7	Roger Clemens	2.00
8	Cal Ripken Jr.	4.00
9	Mo Vaughn	1.25
10	Frank Thomas	3.00
11	Mark McGwire	6.00
12	Barry Larkin	.50
13	Matt Williams	.50
14	Jose Cruz Jr.	1.00
15	Andruw Jones	1.25
16	Mike Piazza	3.00
17	Jeff Bagwell	1.50
18	Chipper Jones	3.00
19	Juan Gonzalez	2.50
20	Kenny Lofton	1.25
21	Greg Maddux	3.00
22	Ivan Rodriguez	1.25
23	Alex Rodriguez	4.00
24	Derek Jeter	3.00
25	Albert Belle	1.25
26	Barry Bonds	1.25
27	Larry Walker	.75
28	Sammy Sosa	4.00
29	Tony Gwynn	2.50
30	Randy Johnson	1.00

1998 Pinnacle Plus Team Pinnacle

Team Pinnacle is a 15-card, double-sided insert. Printed on mirror-mylar, the cards were inserted 1:71. The hobby-only Gold Team Pinnacle parallel was inserted 1:199 packs.

		MT
Complete Set (15):		300.00
Common Player:		10.00
Inserted 1:71		
Golds: 1.5x to 2x		
Inserted 1:199		
1	Mike Piazza, Ivan Rodriguez	30.00

2	Mark McGwire, Mo Vaughn	60.00
3	Roberto Alomar, Craig Biggio	10.00
4	Alex Rodriguez, Barry Larkin	30.00
5	Cal Ripken Jr., Chipper Jones	40.00
6	Ken Griffey Jr., Larry Walker	50.00
7	Juan Gonzalez, Tony Gwynn	25.00
8	Albert Belle, Barry Bonds	12.00
9	Kenny Lofton, Andruw Jones	12.00
10	Tino Martinez, Jeff Bagwell	15.00
11	Frank Thomas, Andres Galarraga	30.00
12	Roger Clemens, Greg Maddux	30.00
13	Pedro Martinez, Hideo Nomo	10.00
14	Nomar Garciaparra, Scott Rolen	30.00
15	Ben Grieve, Paul Konerko	15.00

1998 Pinnacle Plus Yardwork

Yardwork is a 15-card insert seeded one per 19 packs. It features the top home run hitters in Major League Baseball.

		MT
Complete Set (15):		30.00
Common Player:		.75
Inserted 1:9		
1	Mo Vaughn	1.50
2	Frank Thomas	4.00
3	Albert Belle	1.50
4	Nomar Garciaparra	4.00
5	Tony Clark	1.00
6	Tino Martinez	.75
7	Ken Griffey Jr.	6.00
8	Juan Gonzalez	3.00
9	Sammy Sosa	4.00
10	Jose Cruz Jr.	1.25
11	Jeff Bagwell	2.00
12	Mike Piazza	4.00
13	Larry Walker	.75
14	Mark McGwire	8.00
15	Barry Bonds	1.50

1988 Score

MARK McGWIRE

A fifth member joined the group of nationally distributed baseball cards in 1988. Titled "Score," the cards are characterized by extremely sharp color photography and printing. Card backs are full-color also and carry a player portrait along with a brief biography, player data and statistics. The 660 cards in the set are standard 2-1/2" x 3-1/2" format. The fronts come with one of six different border colors which are equally divided at 110 cards per color. The Score set was produced by Major League Marketing, the same company that marketed the "triple-action" Sportflics card sets.

		MT
Complete Set (660):		15.00
Common Player:		.05
Wax Box:		10.00
1	Don Mattingly	.50
2	Wade Boggs	.20
3	Tim Raines	.08
4	Andre Dawson	.15
5	Mark McGwire	1.50
6	Kevin Seitzer	.05
7	Wally Joyner	.08
8	Jesse Barfield	.05
9	Pedro Guerrero	.05
10	Eric Davis	.08
11	George Brett	.35
12	Ozzie Smith	.25
13	Rickey Henderson	.15
14	Jim Rice	.05
15	*Matt Nokes*	.05
16	Mike Schmidt	.40
17	Dave Parker	.08
18	Eddie Murray	.20
19	Andres Galarraga	.10
20	Tony Fernandez	.05
21	Kevin McReynolds	.05
22	B.J. Surhoff	.05
23	Pat Tabler	.05
24	Kirby Puckett	.45
25	Benny Santiago	.08
26	Ryne Sandberg	.40
27	Kelly Downs	.05
28	Jose Cruz	.05
29	Pete O'Brien	.05
30	Mark Langston	.05
31	Lee Smith	.08
32	Juan Samuel	.05
33	Kevin Bass	.05
34	R.J. Reynolds	.05
35	Steve Sax	.05
36	John Kruk	.08
37	Alan Trammell	.08
38	Chris Bosio	.05
39	Brook Jacoby	.05
40	Willie McGee	.08
41	Dave Magadan	.05
42	Fred Lynn	.05
43	Kent Hrbek	.12
44	Brian Downing	.05
45	Jose Canseco	.25
46	Jim Presley	.05
47	Mike Stanley	.05
48	Tony Pena	.05
49	David Cone	.10
50	Rick Sutcliffe	.05
51	Doug Drabek	.05
52	Bill Doran	.05
53	Mike Scioscia	.05
54	Candy Maldonado	.05
55	Dave Winfield	.15
56	Lou Whitaker	.08
57	Tom Henke	.05
58	Ken Gerhart	.05
59	Glenn Braggs	.05
60	Julio Franco	.05
61	Charlie Leibrandt	.05
62	Gary Gaetti	.08
63	Bob Boone	.05
64	*Luis Polonia*	.10
65	Dwight Evans	.05
66	Phil Bradley	.05
67	Mike Boddicker	.05
68	Vince Coleman	.08
69	Howard Johnson	.05
70	Tim Wallach	.08
71	Keith Moreland	.05
72	Barry Larkin	.20
73	Alan Ashby	.05
74	Rick Rhoden	.05
75	Darrell Evans	.05
76	Dave Stieb	.05
77	Dan Plesac	.05
78	Will Clark	.25
79	Frank White	.05
80	Joe Carter	.15
81	Mike Witt	.05
82	Terry Steinbach	.05
83	Alvin Davis	.05
84	Tom Herr	.05
85	Vance Law	.05
86	Kal Daniels	.05
87	Rick Honeycutt	.05
88	Alfredo Griffin	.05
89	Bret Saberhagen	.08
90	Bert Blyleven	.05
91	Joff Reardon	.05
92	Cory Snyder	.05
93	Greg Walker	.05
94	*Joe Magrane*	.10
95	Rob Deer	.05
96	Ray Knight	.05
97	Casey Candaele	.05
98	John Cerutti	.05
99	Buddy Bell	.05
100	Jack Clark	.05
101	Eric Bell	.05
102	Willie Wilson	.08
103	Dave Schmidt	.05
104	Dennis Eckersley	.10
105	Don Sutton	.12
106	Danny Tartabull	.08
107	Fred McGriff	.25
108	*Les Straker*	.05
109	Lloyd Moseby	.05
110	Roger Clemens	.35
111	Glenn Hubbard	.05
112	*Ken Williams*	.05
113	Ruben Sierra	.10
114	Stan Jefferson	.05
115	Milt Thompson	.05
116	Bobby Bonilla	.08
117	Wayne Tolleson	.05
118	Matt Williams	.20
119	Chet Lemon	.05
120	Dale Sveum	.05
121	Dennis Boyd	.05
122	Brett Butler	.10
123	Terry Kennedy	.05
124	Jack Howell	.05
125	Curt Young	.05
126a	Dale Valle (first name incorrect)	.25
126b	Dave Valle (correct spelling)	.05
127	Curt Wilkerson	.05
128	Tim Teufel	.05
129	Ozzie Virgil	.05
130	Brian Fisher	.05
131	Lance Parrish	.08
132	Tom Browning	.05
133a	Larry Anderson (incorrect spelling)	.25
133b	Larry Andersen (correct spelling)	.05
134a	Bob Brenley (incorrect spelling)	.25
134b	Bob Brenly (correct spelling)	.05
135	Mike Marshall	.05
136	Gerald Perry	.05
137	Bobby Meacham	.05
138	Larry Herndon	.05
139	*Fred Manrique*	.05
140	Charlie Hough	.05
141	Ron Darling	.05
142	Herm Winningham	.05
143	Mike Diaz	.05
144	*Mike Jackson*	.05
145	Denny Walling	.05
146	Rob Thompson	.05
147	Franklin Stubbs	.05
148	Albert Hall	.05
149	Bobby Witt	.05
150	Lance McCullers	.05
151	Scott Bradley	.05
152	Mark McLemore	.05
153	Tim Laudner	.05
154	Greg Swindell	.05
155	Marty Barrett	.05
156	Mike Heath	.05
157	Gary Ward	.05
158a	Lee Mazilli (incorrect spelling)	.25
158b	Lee Mazzilli (correct spelling)	.05
159	Tom Foley	.05
160	Robin Yount	.25

#	Player	Price
161	Steve Bedrosian	.05
162	Bob Walk	.05
163	Nick Esasky	.05
164	*Ken Caminiti*	.75
165	Jose Uribe	.05
166	Dave Anderson	.05
167	Ed Whitson	.05
168	Ernie Whitt	.05
169	Cecil Cooper	.05
170	Mike Pagliarulo	.05
171	Pat Sheridan	.05
172	Chris Bando	.05
173	Lee Lacy	.05
174	Steve Lombardozzi	.05
175	Mike Greenwell	.08
176	Greg Minton	.05
177	Moose Haas	.05
178	Mike Kingery	.05
179	Greg Harris	.05
180	Bo Jackson	.20
181	Carmelo Martinez	.05
182	Alex Trevino	.05
183	Ron Oester	.05
184	Danny Darwin	.05
185	Mike Krukow	.05
186	Rafael Palmeiro	.20
187	Tim Burke	.05
188	Roger McDowell	.05
189	Garry Templeton	.05
190	Terry Pendleton	.08
191	Larry Parrish	.05
192	Rey Quinones	.05
193	Joaquin Andujar	.05
194	Tom Brunansky	.05
195	Donnie Moore	.05
196	Dan Pasqua	.05
197	Jim Gantner	.05
198	Mark Eichhorn	.05
199	John Grubb	.05
200	*Bill Ripken*	.05
201	*Sam Horn*	.05
202	Todd Worrell	.05
203	Terry Leach	.05
204	Garth Iorg	.05
205	Brian Dayett	.05
206	Bo Diaz	.05
207	Craig Reynolds	.05
208	Brian Holton	.05
209	Marvelle Wynne (Marvell)	.05
210	Dave Concepcion	.05
211	Mike Davis	.05
212	Devon White	.08
213	Mickey Brantley	.05
214	Greg Gagne	.05
215	Oddibe McDowell	.05
216	Jimmy Key	.05
217	Dave Bergman	.05
218	Calvin Schiraldi	.05
219	Larry Sheets	.05
220	Mike Easler	.05
221	Kurt Stillwell	.05
222	*Chuck Jackson*	.05
223	Dave Martinez	.05
224	Tim Leary	.05
225	Steve Garvey	.12
226	Greg Mathews	.05
227	Doug Sisk	.05
228	Dave Henderson	.05
229	Jimmy Dwyer	.05
230	Larry Owen	.05
231	Andre Thornton	.05
232	Mark Salas	.05
233	Tom Brookens	.05
234	Greg Brock	.05
235	Rance Mulliniks	.05
236	Bob Brower	.05
237	Joe Niekro	.05
238	Scott Bankhead	.05
239	Doug DeCinces	.05
240	Tommy John	.10
241	Rich Gedman	.05
242	Ted Power	.05
243	*Dave Meads*	.05
244	Jim Sundberg	.05
245	Ken Oberkfell	.05
246	Jimmy Jones	.05
247	Ken Landreaux	.05
248	Jose Oquendo	.05
249	*John Mitchell*	.05
250	Don Baylor	.08
251	Scott Fletcher	.05
252	Al Newman	.05
253	Carney Lansford	.05
254	Johnny Ray	.05
255	Gary Pettis	.05
256	Ken Phelps	.05
257	Rick Leach	.05
258	Tim Stoddard	.05
259	Ed Romero	.05
260	Sid Bream	.05
261a	Tom Neidenfuer (incorrect spelling)	.25
261b	Tom Niedenfuer (correct spelling)	.05
262	Rick Dempsey	.05
263	Lonnie Smith	.05
264	Bob Forsch	.05
265	Barry Bonds	.50
266	Willie Randolph	.05
267	Mike Ramsey	.05
268	Don Slaught	.05
269	Mickey Tettleton	.08
270	Jerry Reuss	.05
271	Marc Sullivan	.05
272	Jim Morrison	.05
273	Steve Balboni	.05
274	Dick Schofield	.05
275	John Tudor	.05
276	*Gene Larkin*	.05
277	Harold Reynolds	.05
278	Jerry Browne	.05
279	Willie Upshaw	.05
280	Ted Higuera	.05
281	Terry McGriff	.05
282	Terry Puhl	.05
283	*Mark Wasinger*	.05
284	Luis Salazar	.05
285	Ted Simmons	.05
286	John Shelby	.05
287	*John Smiley*	.15
288	Curt Ford	.05
289	Steve Crawford	.05
290	Dan Quisenberry	.05
291	Alan Wiggins	.05
292	Randy Bush	.05
293	John Candelaria	.05
294	Tony Phillips	.08
295	Mike Morgan	.05
296	Bill Wegman	.05
297a	Terry Franconia (incorrect spelling)	.25
297b	Terry Francona (correct spelling)	.05
298	Mickey Hatcher	.05
299	Andres Thomas	.05
300	Bob Stanley	.05
301	*Alfredo Pedrique*	.05
302	Jim Lindeman	.05
303	Wally Backman	.05
304	Paul O'Neill	.15
305	Hubie Brooks	.05
306	Steve Buechele	.05
307	Bobby Thigpen	.05
308	George Hendrick	.05
309	John Moses	.05
310	Ron Guidry	.08
311	Bill Schroeder	.05
312	*Jose Nunez*	.05
313	Bud Black	.05
314	Joe Sambito	.05
315	Scott McGregor	.05
316	Rafael Santana	.05
317	Frank Williams	.05
318	Mike Fitzgerald	.05
319	Rick Mahler	.05
320	Jim Gott	.05
321	Mariano Duncan	.05
322	Jose Guzman	.05
323	Lee Guetterman	.05
324	Dan Gladden	.05
325	Gary Carter	.10
326	Tracy Jones	.05
327	Floyd Youmans	.05
328	Bill Dawley	.05
329	*Paul Noce*	.05
330	Angel Salazar	.05
331	Goose Gossage	.08
332	George Frazier	.05
333	Ruppert Jones	.05
334	Billy Jo Robidoux	.05
335	Mike Scott	.05
336	Randy Myers	.05
337	Bob Sebra	.05
338	Eric Show	.05
339	Mitch Williams	.05
340	Paul Molitor	.30
341	Gus Polidor	.05
342	Steve Trout	.05
343	Jerry Don Gleaton	.05
344	Bob Knepper	.05
345	Mitch Webster	.05
346	John Morris	.05
347	Andy Hawkins	.05
348	Dave Leiper	.05
349	Ernest Riles	.05
350	Dwight Gooden	.12
351	Dave Righetti	.05
352	Pat Dodson	.05
353	John Habyan	.05
354	Jim Deshaies	.05
355	Butch Wynegar	.05
356	Bryn Smith	.05
357	Matt Young	.05
358	*Tom Pagnozzi*	.05
359	Floyd Rayford	.05
360	Darryl Strawberry	.10
361	Sal Butera	.05
362	Domingo Ramos	.05
363	Chris Brown	.05
364	Jose Gonzalez	.05
365	Dave Smith	.05
366	Andy McGaffigan	.05
367	Stan Javier	.05
368	Henry Cotto	.05
369	Mike Birkbeck	.05
370	Len Dykstra	.08
371	Dave Collins	.05
372	Spike Owen	.05
373	Geno Petralli	.05
374	Ron Karkovice	.05
375	Shane Rawley	.05
376	*DeWayne Buice*	.05
377	*Bill Pecota*	.05
378	Leon Durham	.05
379	Ed Olwine	.05
380	Bruce Hurst	.05
381	Bob McClure	.05
382	Mark Thurmond	.05
383	Buddy Biancalana	.05
384	Tim Conroy	.05
385	Tony Gwynn	.30
386	Greg Gross	.05
387	*Barry Lyons*	.05
388	Mike Felder	.05
389	Pat Clements	.05
390	Ken Griffey	.08
391	Mark Davis	.05
392	Jose Rijo	.05
393	Mike Young	.05
394	Willie Fraser	.05
395	Dion James	.05
396	*Steve Shields*	.05
397	Randy St. Claire	.05
398	Danny Jackson	.05
399	Cecil Fielder	.20
400	Keith Hernandez	.05
401	Don Carman	.05
402	*Chuck Crim*	.05
403	Rob Woodward	.05
404	Junior Ortiz	.05
405	Glenn Wilson	.05
406	Ken Howell	.05
407	Jeff Kunkel	.05
408	Jeff Reed	.05
409	Chris James	.05
410	Zane Smith	.05
411	Ken Dixon	.05
412	Ricky Horton	.05
413	Frank DiPino	.05
414	*Shane Mack*	.15
415	Danny Cox	.05
416	Andy Van Slyke	.05
417	Danny Heep	.05
418	John Cangelosi	.05
419a	John Christiansen (incorrect spelling)	.25
419b	John Christensen (correct spelling)	.05
420	*Joey Cora*	.08
421	Mike LaValliere	.05
422	Kelly Gruber	.05
423	Bruce Benedict	.05
424	Len Matuszek	.05
425	Kent Tekulve	.05
426	Rafael Ramirez	.05
427	Mike Flanagan	.05
428	Mike Gallego	.05
429	Juan Castillo	.05
430	Neal Heaton	.05
431	Phil Garner	.05
432	*Mike Dunne*	.05
433	Wallace Johnson	.05
434	Jack O'Connor	.05
435	Steve Jeltz	.05
436	*Donnell Nixon*	.05
437	Jack Lazorko	.05
438	*Keith Comstock*	.05
439	Jeff Robinson	.05

440	Graig Nettles	.08
441	Mel Hall	.05
442	*Gerald Young*	.05
443	Gary Redus	.05
444	Charlie Moore	.05
445	Bill Madlock	.05
446	Mark Clear	.05
447	Greg Booker	.05
448	Rick Schu	.05
449	Ron Kittle	.05
450	Dale Murphy	.10
451	Bob Dernier	.05
452	Dale Mohorcic	.05
453	Rafael Belliard	.05
454	Charlie Puleo	.05
455	Dwayne Murphy	.05
456	Jim Eisenreich	.05
457	David Palmer	.05
458	Dave Stewart	.08
459	Pascual Perez	.05
460	Glenn Davis	.05
461	Dan Petry	.05
462	Jim Winn	.05
463	Darrell Miller	.05
464	Mike Moore	.05
465	Mike LaCoss	.05
466	Steve Farr	.05
467	Jerry Mumphrey	.05
468	Kevin Gross	.05
469	Bruce Bochy	.05
470	Orel Hershiser	.08
471	Eric King	.05
472	*Ellis Burks*	.30
473	Darren Daulton	.08
474	Mookie Wilson	.05
475	Frank Viola	.05
476	Ron Robinson	.05
477	Bob Melvin	.05
478	Jeff Musselman	.05
479	Charlie Kerfeld	.05
480	Richard Dotson	.05
481	Kevin Mitchell	.10
482	Gary Roenicke	.05
483	Tim Flannery	.05
484	Rich Yett	.05
485	Pete Incaviglia	.08
486	Rick Cerone	.05
487	Tony Armas	.05
488	Jerry Reed	.05
489	Davey Lopes	.05
490	Frank Tanana	.05
491	Mike Loynd	.05
492	Bruce Ruffin	.05
493	Chris Speier	.05
494	Tom Hume	.05
495	Jesse Orosco	.05
496	*Robby Wine, Jr.*	.05
497	*Jeff Montgomery*	.20
498	Jeff Dedmon	.05
499	Luis Aguayo	.05
500	Reggie Jackson (1968-75)	.20
501	Reggie Jackson (1976)	.20
502	Reggie Jackson (1977-81)	.20
503	Reggie Jackson (1982-86)	.20
504	Reggie Jackson (1987)	.20
505	Billy Hatcher	.05
506	Ed Lynch	.05
507	Willie Hernandez	.05
508	Jose DeLeon	.05
509	Joel Youngblood	.05
510	Bob Welch	.05
511	Steve Ontiveros	.05
512	Randy Ready	.05
513	Juan Nieves	.05
514	Jeff Russell	.05
515	Von Hayes	.05
516	Mark Gubicza	.05
517	Ken Dayley	.05
518	Don Aase	.05
519	Rick Reuschel	.05
520	*Mike Henneman*	.15
521	Rick Aguilera	.05
522	Jay Howell	.05
523	Ed Correa	.05
524	Manny Trillo	.05
525	Kirk Gibson	.08
526	*Wally Ritchie*	.05
527	Al Nipper	.05
528	Atlee Hammaker	.05
529	Shawon Dunston	.12
530	Jim Clancy	.05
531	Tom Paciorek	.05
532	Joel Skinner	.05
533	Scott Garrelts	.05
534	Tom O'Malley	.05
535	John Franco	.05

536	*Paul Kilgus*	.05
537	Darrell Porter	.05
538	Walt Terrell	.05
539	*Bill Long*	.05
540	George Bell	.05
541	Jeff Sellers	.05
542	*Joe Boever*	.05
543	Steve Howe	.05
544	Scott Sanderson	.05
545	Jack Morris	.08
546	*Todd Benzinger*	.08
547	Steve Henderson	.05
548	Eddie Milner	.05
549	*Jeff Robinson*	.05
550	Cal Ripken, Jr.	.60
551	Jody Davis	.05
552	Kirk McCaskill	.05
553	Craig Lefferts	.05
554	Darnell Coles	.05
555	Phil Niekro	.25
556	Mike Aldrete	.05
557	Pat Perry	.05
558	Juan Agosto	.05
559	Rob Murphy	.05
560	Dennis Rasmussen	.05
561	Manny Lee	.05
562	*Jeff Blauser*	.10
563	Bob Ojeda	.05
564	Dave Dravecky	.05
565	Gene Garber	.05
566	Ron Roenicke	.05
567	*Tommy Hinzo*	.05
568	*Eric Nolte*	.05
569	Ed Hearn	.05
570	*Mark Davidson*	.05
571	*Jim Walewander*	.05
572	Donnie Hill	.05
573	Jamie Moyer	.05
574	Ken Schrom	.05
575	Nolan Ryan	.60
576	Jim Acker	.05
577	Jamie Quirk	.05
578	*Jay Aldrich*	.05
579	Claudell Washington	.05
580	Jeff Leonard	.05
581	Carmen Castillo	.05
582	Daryl Boston	.05
583	*Jeff DeWillis*	.05
584	*John Marzano*	.05
585	Bill Gullickson	.05
586	Andy Allanson	.05
587	Lee Tunnell	.05
588	Gene Nelson	.05
589	Dave LaPoint	.05
590	Harold Baines	.08
591	Bill Buckner	.05
592	Carlton Fisk	.15
593	Rick Manning	.05
594	*Doug Jones*	.08
595	Tom Candiotti	.05
596	Steve Lake	.05
597	*Jose Lind*	.10
598	*Ross Jones*	.05
599	Gary Matthews	.05
600	Fernando Valenzuela	.08
601	Dennis Martinez	.08
602	*Les Lancaster*	.08
603	Ozzie Guillen	.05
604	Tony Bernazard	.05
605	Chili Davis	.08
606	Roy Smalley	.05
607	Ivan Calderon	.05
608	Jay Tibbs	.05
609	Guy Hoffman	.05
610	Doyle Alexander	.05
611	Mike Bielecki	.05
612	*Shawn Hillegas*	.05
613	Keith Atherton	.05
614	Eric Plunk	.05
615	Sid Fernandez	.05
616	Dennis Lamp	.05
617	Dave Engle	.05
618	Harry Spilman	.05
619	Don Robinson	.05
620	*John Farrell*	.05
621	*Nelson Liriano*	.05
622	Floyd Bannister	.05
623	*Randy Milligan*	.10
624	*Kevin Elster*	.05
625	*Jody Reed*	.15
626	*Shawn Abner*	.05
627	*Kirt Manwaring*	.15
628	*Pete Stanicek*	.05
629	*Rob Ducey*	.05
630	Steve Kiefer	.05
631	*Gary Thurman*	.05

632	*Darrel Akerfelds*	.05
633	Dave Clark	.05
634	*Roberto Kelly*	.25
635	Keith Hughes	.05
636	John Davis	.05
637	Mike Devereaux	.10
638	*Tom Glavine*	.75
639	Keith Miller	.05
640	Chris Gwynn	.05
641	Tim Crews	.05
642	*Mackey Sasser*	.05
643	*Vicente Palacios*	.05
644	Kevin Romine	.05
645	*Gregg Jefferies*	.25
646	*Jeff Treadway*	.05
647	*Ron Gant*	.25
648	Rookie Sluggors(Mark McGwire, Matt Nokes)	.75
649	Speed and Power(Tim Raines, Eric Davis)	.10
650	Game Breakers(Jack Clark, Don Mattingly)	.20
651	Super Shortstops(Tony Fernandez, Cal Ripken, Jr., Alan Trammell)	.25
652	Vince Coleman (Highlight)	.05
653	Kirby Puckett (Highlight)	.30
654	Benito Santiago (Highlight)	.05
655	Juan Nieves (Highlight)	.05
656	Steve Bedrosian (Highlight)	.05
657	Mike Schmidt (Highlight)	.20
658	Don Mattingly (Highlight)	.30
659	Mark McGwire (Highlight)	.75
660	Paul Molitor (Highlight)	.15

1988 Score Glossy

With production of a reported 5,000 sets, there is a significant premium attached to the glossy version of Score's debut baseball card issue. The specially packaged collector's edition features cards with a high-gloss front finish and was sold only as a complete set.

	MT
Complete Set (660):	200.00
Common Player:	.50
(Star cards valued at 20-25X regular Score version)	

1988 Score Traded/Rookie

This 110-card set featuring rookies and traded veterans is similar in design to the 1988 Score set, except for a change in border color. Individual standard-size player cards (2-1/2" x 3-1/2") feature a bright orange border framing action photos highlighted by a thin white outline. The player name (in white) is centered in the bottom margin, flanked by three yellow stars lower left and a yellow Score logo lower right. The backs carry full-color player portraits on a cream-colored background, plus team name and logo, personal information and a purple stats chart that lists year-by-year and major league totals. A brief player profile follows the stats chart and, on some cards, information is included about the player's trade or acquisition. The boxed update set also includes 10 Magic Motion 3-D trivia cards.

		MT
Complete Set (110):		50.00
Common Player:		.20
1T	Jack Clark	.20
2T	Danny Jackson	.20
3T	Brett Butler	.20
4T	Kurt Stillwell	.20
5T	Tom Brunansky	.20
6T	Dennis Lamp	.20
7T	Jose DeLeon	.20
8T	Tom Herr	.20
9T	Keith Moreland	.20
10T	Kirk Gibson	.30
11T	Bud Black	.20
12T	Rafael Ramirez	.20
13T	Luis Salazar	.20
14T	Goose Gossage	.25
15T	Bob Welch	.20
16T	Vance Law	.20
17T	Ray Knight	.20
18T	Dan Quisenberry	.20
19T	Don Slaught	.20
20T	Lee Smith	.25
21T	Rick Cerone	.20
22T	Pat Tabler	.20
23T	Larry McWilliams	.20
24T	Rick Horton	.20
25T	Graig Nettles	.20
26T	Dan Petry	.20
27T	Jose Rijo	.25
28T	Chili Davis	.30
29T	Dickie Thon	.20
30T	Mackey Sasser	.20
31T	Mickey Tettleton	.20
32T	Rick Dempsey	.20
33T	Ron Hassey	.20
34T	Phil Bradley	.20
35T	Jay Howell	.20
36T	Bill Buckner	.20
37T	Alfredo Griffin	.20
38T	Gary Pettis	.20
39T	Calvin Schiraldi	.20
40T	John Candelaria	.20
41T	Joe Orsulak	.20
42T	Willie Upshaw	.20
43T	Herm Winningham	.20
44T	Ron Kittle	.20
45T	Bob Dernier	.20
46T	Steve Balboni	.20
47T	Steve Shields	.20
48T	Henry Cotto	.20
49T	Dave Henderson	.20
50T	Dave Parker	.25
51T	Mike Young	.20
52T	Mark Salas	.20
53T	Mike Davis	.20
54T	Rafael Santana	.20
55T	Don Baylor	.35
56T	Dan Pasqua	.20
57T	Ernest Riles	.20
58T	Glenn Hubbard	.20
59T	Mike Smithson	.20
60T	Richard Dotson	.20
61T	Jerry Reuss	.20
62T	Mike Jackson	.20
63T	Floyd Bannister	.20
64T	Jesse Orosco	.20
65T	Larry Parrish	.20
66T	Jeff Bittiger	.20
67T	Ray Hayward	.20
68T	Ricky Jordan	.20
69T	Tommy Gregg	.20
70T	*Brady Anderson*	5.00
71T	Jeff Montgomery	.25
72T	Darryl Hamilton	.75
73T	Cecil Espy	.20
74T	Greg Briley	.20
75T	Joey Meyer	.20
76T	Mike Macfarlane	.25
77T	Oswald Peraza	.20
78T	Jack Armstrong	.20
79T	Don Heinkel	.20
80T	*Mark Grace*	12.00
81T	Steve Curry	.20
82T	Damon Berryhill	.20
83T	Steve Ellsworth	.20
84T	Pete Smith	.20
85T	*Jack McDowell*	2.50
86T	Rob Dibble	.25
87T	Bryan Harvey	.35
88T	John Dopson	.25
89T	Dave Gallagher	.20
90T	Todd Stottlemyre	2.00
91T	Mike Schooler	.20
92T	Don Gordon	.20
93T	Sil Campusano	.20
94T	Jeff Pico	.20
95T	*Jay Buhner*	8.00
96T	Nelson Santovenia	.20
97T	Al Leiter	2.50
98T	Luis Alicea	.25
99T	Pat Borders	1.00
100T	Chris Sabo	.30
101T	Tim Belcher	.25
102T	Walt Weiss	.40
103T	*Craig Biggio*	12.00
104T	Don August	.20
105T	*Roberto Alomar*	20.00
106T	Todd Burns	.20
107T	John Costello	.20
108T	Melido Perez	.25
109T	Darrin Jackson	.50
110T	Orestes Destrade	.20

1988 Score Traded/Rookie Glossy

Among the scarcest of the major card companies' high-gloss collector's editions of the late 1980s is the 1988 Score Rookie/Traded issue. Production of the regular-finish set was limited in itself and the glossy version is moreso, adding a significant premium value.

	MT
Complete Set (110):	565.00
Common Player:	1.50
(Star cards valued at 5-7X regular version Traded/Rookie cards)	

1989 Score

This set of 660 cards plus 56 Magic Motion trivia cards is the second annual basic issue from Score. Full-color player photos highlight

651 individual players and 9 season highlights, including the first Wrigley Field night game. Action photos are framed by thin brightly colored borders (green, cyan blue, purple, orange, red, royal blue) with a baseball diamond logo/player name beneath the photo. Full-color player close-ups (1-5/16" x 1-5/8") are printed on the pastel-colored backs, along with personal information, stats and career highlights. The cards measure 2-1/2" x 3-1/2".

		MT
Complete Set (660):		10.00
Common Player:		.05
Wax Box:		9.00
1	Jose Canseco	.20
2	Andre Dawson	.10
3	Mark McGwire	1.50
4	Benny Santiago	.08
5	Rick Reuschel	.05
6	Fred McGriff	.20
7	Kal Daniels	.05
8	Gary Gaetti	.05
9	Ellis Burks	.08
10	Darryl Strawberry	.15
11	Julio Franco	.05
12	Lloyd Moseby	.05
13	*Jeff Pico*	.05
14	Johnny Ray	.05
15	Cal Ripken, Jr.	.60
16	Dick Schofield	.05
17	Mel Hall	.05
18	Bill Ripken	.05
19	Brook Jacoby	.05
20	Kirby Puckett	.35
21	Bill Doran	.05
22	Pete O'Brien	.05
23	Matt Nokes	.05
24	Brian Fisher	.05
25	Jack Clark	.05
26	Gary Pettis	.05
27	Dave Valle	.05
28	Willie Wilson	.08
29	Curt Young	.05
30	Dale Murphy	.10
31	Barry Larkin	.15
32	Dave Stewart	.08
33	Mike LaValliere	.05
34	Glenn Hubbard	.05
35	Ryne Sandberg	.25
36	Tony Pena	.05
37	Greg Walker	.05
38	Von Hayes	.05
39	Kevin Mitchell	.08
40	Tim Raines	.08
41	Keith Hernandez	.05
42	Keith Moreland	.05
43	Ruben Sierra	.10
44	Chet Lemon	.05
45	Willie Randolph	.05
46	Andy Allanson	.05
47	Candy Maldonado	.05
48	Sid Bream	.05
49	Denny Walling	.05
50	Dave Winfield	.10
51	Alvin Davis	.05
52	Cory Snyder	.05
53	Hubie Brooks	.05
54	Chili Davis	.08
55	Kevin Seitzer	.05
56	Jose Uribe	.05
57	Tony Fernandez	.05
58	Tim Teufel	.05
59	Oddibe McDowell	.05
60	Les Lancaster	.05
61	Billy Hatcher	.05
62	Dan Gladden	.05
63	Marty Barrett	.05
64	Nick Esasky	.05
65	Wally Joyner	.08
66	Mike Greenwell	.08
67	Ken Williams	.05
68	Bob Horner	.08
69	Steve Sax	.05
70	Rickey Henderson	.15
71	Mitch Webster	.05
72	Rob Deer	.05
73	Jim Presley	.05
74	Albert Hall	.05
75a	George Brett ("At age 33 ...")	1.00
75b	George Brett ("At age 35 ...")	.30

No.	Player	Price
76	Brian Downing	.05
77	Dave Martinez	.05
78	Scott Fletcher	.05
79	Phil Bradley	.05
80	Ozzie Smith	.25
81	Larry Sheets	.05
82	Mike Aldrete	.05
83	Darnell Coles	.05
84	Len Dykstra	.10
85	Jim Rice	.05
86	Jeff Treadway	.05
87	Jose Lind	.05
88	Willie McGee	.08
89	Mickey Brantley	.05
90	Tony Gwynn	.40
91	R.J. Reynolds	.05
92	Milt Thompson	.05
93	Kevin MoReynolds	.05
94	Eddie Murray	.20
95	Lance Parrish	.08
96	Ron Kittle	.05
97	Gerald Young	.05
98	Ernie Whitt	.05
99	Jeff Reed	.05
100	Don Mattingly	.40
101	Gerald Perry	.05
102	Vance Law	.05
103	John Shelby	.05
104	*Chris Sabo*	.15
105	Danny Tartabull	.08
106	Glenn Wilson	.05
107	Mark Davidson	.05
108	Dave Parker	.10
109	Eric Davis	.08
110	Alan Trammell	.10
111	Ozzie Virgil	.05
112	Frank Tanana	.05
113	Rafael Ramirez	.05
114	Dennis Martinez	.08
115	Jose DeLeon	.05
116	Bob Ojeda	.05
117	Doug Drabek	.05
118	Andy Hawkins	.05
119	Greg Maddux	.50
120	Cecil Fielder (reversed negative)	.20
121	Mike Scioscia	.05
122	Dan Petry	.05
123	Terry Kennedy	.05
124	Kelly Downs	.05
125	Greg Gross	.05
126	Fred Lynn	.10
127	Barry Bonds	.50
128	Harold Baines	.08
129	Doyle Alexander	.05
130	Kevin Elster	.05
131	Mike Heath	.05
132	Teddy Higuera	.05
133	Charlie Leibrandt	.05
134	Tim Laudner	.05
135a	Ray Knight (photo reversed)	.40
135b	Ray Knight (correct photo)	.05
136	Howard Johnson	.05
137	Terry Pendleton	.08
138	Andy McGaffigan	.05
139	Ken Oberkfell	.05
140	Butch Wynegar	.05
141	Rob Murphy	.05
142	*Rich Renteria*	.05
143	Jose Guzman	.05
144	Andres Galarraga	.15
145	Rick Horton	.05
146	Frank DiPino	.05
147	Glenn Braggs	.05
148	John Kruk	.10
149	Mike Schmidt	.30
150	Lee Smith	.08
151	Robin Yount	.20
152	Mark Eichhorn	.05
153	DeWayne Buice	.05
154	B.J. Surhoff	.05
155	Vince Coleman	.08
156	Tony Phillips	.05
157	Willie Fraser	.05
158	Lance McCullers	.05
159	Greg Gagne	.05
160	Jesse Barfield	.05
161	Mark Langston	.05
162	Kurt Stillwell	.05
163	Dion James	.05
164	Glenn Davis	.05
165	Walt Weiss	.08
166	Dave Concepcion	.05
167	Alfredo Griffin	.05
168	*Don Heinkel*	.05
169	Luis Rivera	.05
170	Shane Rawley	.05
171	Darrell Evans	.05
172	Robby Thompson	.05
173	Jody Davis	.05
174	Andy Van Slyke	.08
175	Wade Boggs	.20
176	Garry Templeton	.05
177	Gary Redus	.05
178	Craig Lefferts	.05
179	Carney Lansford	.05
180	Ron Darling	.05
181	Kirk McCaskill	.05
182	Tony Armas	.05
183	Steve Farr	.05
184	Tom Brunansky	.05
185	*Bryan Harvey*	.10
186	Mike Marshall	.05
187	Bo Diaz	.05
188	Willie Upshaw	.05
189	Mike Pagliarulo	.05
190	Mike Krukow	.05
191	Tommy Herr	.05
192	Jim Pankovits	.05
193	Dwight Evans	.05
194	Kelly Gruber	.05
195	Bobby Bonilla	.10
196	Wallace Johnson	.05
197	Dave Stieb	.05
198	*Pat Borders*	.25
199	Rafael Palmeiro	.20
200	Dwight Gooden	.10
201	Pete Incaviglia	.08
202	Chris James	.05
203	Marvell Wynne	.05
204	Pat Sheridan	.05
205	Don Baylor	.08
206	Paul O'Neill	.15
207	Pete Smith	.05
208	Mark McLemore	.05
209	Henry Cotto	.05
210	Kirk Gibson	.05
211	Claudell Washington	.05
212	Randy Bush	.05
213	Joe Carter	.15
214	Bill Buckner	.05
215	Bert Blyleven	.05
216	Brett Butler	.05
217	Lee Mazzilli	.05
218	Spike Owen	.05
219	Bill Swift	.05
220	Tim Wallach	.08
221	David Cone	.15
222	Don Carman	.05
223	Rich Gossage	.10
224	Bob Walk	.05
225	Dave Righetti	.05
226	Kevin Bass	.05
227	Kevin Gross	.05
228	Tim Burke	.05
229	Rick Mahler	.05
230	Lou Whitaker	.08
231	*Luis Alicea*	.10
232	Roberto Alomar	.30
233	Bob Boone	.05
234	Dickie Thon	.05
235	Shawon Dunston	.08
236	Pete Stanicek	.05
237	Craig Biggio	.15
238	Dennis Boyd	.05
239	Tom Candiotti	.05
240	Gary Carter	.10
241	Mike Stanley	.05
242	Ken Phelps	.05
243	Chris Bosio	.05
244	Les Straker	.05
245	Dave Smith	.05
246	John Candelaria	.05
247	Joe Orsulak	.05
248	Storm Davis	.05
249	Floyd Bannister	.05
250	Jack Morris	.08
251	Bret Saberhagen	.08
252	Tom Niedenfuer	.05
253	Neal Heaton	.05
254	Eric Show	.05
255	Juan Samuel	.05
256	Dale Sveum	.05
257	Jim Gott	.05
258	Scott Garrelts	.05
259	Larry McWilliams	.05
260	Steve Bedrosian	.05
261	Jack Howell	.05
262	Jay Tibbs	.05
263	Jamie Moyer	.05
264	Doug Sisk	.05
265	Todd Worrell	.05
266	John Farrell	.05
267	Dave Collins	.05
268	Sid Fernandez	.05
269	Tom Brookens	.05
270	Shane Mack	.05
271	Paul Kilgus	.05
272	Chuck Crim	.05
273	Bob Knepper	.05
274	Mike Moore	.05
275	Guillermo Hernandez	.05
276	Dennis Eckersley	.10
277	Graig Nettles	.05
278	Rich Dotson	.05
279	Larry Herndon	.05
280	Gene Larkin	.05
281	Roger McDowell	.05
282	Greg Swindell	.08
283	Juan Agosto	.05
284	Jeff Robinson	.05
285	Mike Dunne	.05
286	Greg Mathews	.05
287	Kent Tekulve	.05
288	Jerry Mumphrey	.05
289	Jack McDowell	.15
290	Frank Viola	.05
291	Mark Gubicza	.05
292	Dave Schmidt	.05
293	Mike Henneman	.08
294	Jimmy Jones	.05
295	Charlie Hough	.05
296	Rafael Santana	.05
297	Chris Speier	.05
298	Mike Witt	.05
299	Pascual Perez	.05
300	Nolan Ryan	.60
301	Mitch Williams	.05
302	Mookie Wilson	.05
303	Mackey Sasser	.05
304	John Cerutti	.05
305	Jeff Reardon	.05
306	Randy Myers	.05
307	Greg Brock	.05
308	Bob Welch	.05
309	Jeff Robinson	.05
310	Harold Reynolds	.05
311	Jim Walewander	.05
312	Dave Magadan	.05
313	Jim Gantner	.05
314	Walt Terrell	.05
315	Wally Backman	.05
316	Luis Salazar	.05
317	Rick Rhoden	.05
318	Tom Henke	.05
319	*Mike Macfarlane*	.15
320	Dan Plesac	.05
321	Calvin Schiraldi	.05
322	Stan Javier	.05
323	Devon White	.08
324	Scott Bradley	.05
325	Bruce Hurst	.05
326	Manny Lee	.05
327	Rick Aguilera	.05
328	Bruce Ruffin	.05
329	Ed Whitson	.05
330	Bo Jackson	.15
331	Ivan Calderon	.05
332	Mickey Hatcher	.05
333	Barry Jones	.05
334	Ron Hassey	.05
335	Bill Wegman	.05
336	Damon Berryhill	.05
337	Steve Ontiveros	.05
338	Dan Pasqua	.05
339	Bill Pecota	.05
340	Greg Cadaret	.05
341	Scott Bankhead	.05
342	Ron Guidry	.08
343	Danny Heep	.05
344	Bob Brower	.05
345	Rich Gedman	.05
346	*Nelson Santovenia*	.05
347	George Bell	.08
348	Ted Power	.05
349	Mark Grant	.05
350a	Roger Clemens (778 wins)	2.00
350b	Roger Clemens (78 wins)	.30
351	Bill Long	.05
352	Jay Bell	.05
353	Steve Balboni	.05
354	Bob Kipper	.05
355	Steve Jeltz	.05
356	Jesse Orosco	.05
357	Bob Dernier	.05
358	Mickey Tettleton	.05
359	Duane Ward	.05
360	Darrin Jackson	.05

#	Player	Price
361	Rey Quinones	.05
362	Mark Grace	.15
363	Steve Lake	.05
364	Pat Perry	.05
365	Terry Steinbach	.05
366	Alan Ashby	.05
367	Jeff Montgomery	.05
368	Steve Buechele	.05
369	Chris Brown	.05
370	Orel Hershiser	.08
371	Todd Benzinger	.05
372	Ron Gant	.15
373	Paul Assenmacher	.05
374	Joey Meyer	.05
375	Neil Allen	.05
376	Mike Davis	.05
377	Jeff Parrett	.05
378	Jay Howell	.05
379	Rafael Belliard	.05
380	Luis Polonia	.05
381	Keith Atherton	.05
382	Kent Hrbek	.10
383	Bob Stanley	.05
384	Dave LaPoint	.05
385	Rance Mulliniks	.05
386	Melido Perez	.05
387	Doug Jones	.05
388	Steve Lyons	.05
389	Alejandro Pena	.05
390	Frank White	.05
391	Pat Tabler	.05
392	Eric Plunk	.05
393	Mike Maddux	.05
394	Allan Anderson	.05
395	Bob Brenly	.05
396	Rick Cerone	.05
397	Scott Terry	.05
398	Mike Jackson	.05
399	Bobby Thigpen	.05
400	Don Sutton	.08
401	Cecil Espy	.05
402	Junior Ortiz	.05
403	Mike Smithson	.05
404	Bud Black	.05
405	Tom Foley	.05
406	Andres Thomas	.05
407	Rick Sutcliffe	.05
408	Brian Harper	.05
409	John Smiley	.05
410	Juan Nieves	.05
411	Shawn Abner	.05
412	Wes Gardner	.05
413	Darren Daulton	.10
414	Juan Berenguer	.05
415	Charles Hudson	.05
416	Rick Honeycutt	.05
417	Greg Booker	.05
418	Tim Belcher	.05
419	Don August	.05
420	Dale Mohorcic	.05
421	Steve Lombardozzi	.05
422	Atlee Hammaker	.05
423	Jerry Don Gleaton	.05
424	Scott Bailes	.05
425	Bruce Sutter	.05
426	Randy Ready	.05
427	Jerry Reed	.05
428	Bryn Smith	.05
429	Tim Leary	.05
430	Mark Clear	.05
431	Terry Leach	.05
432	John Moses	.05
433	Ozzie Guillen	.05
434	Gene Nelson	.05
435	Gary Ward	.05
436	Luis Aguayo	.05
437	Fernando Valenzuela	.10
438	Jeff Russell	.05
439	Cecilio Guante	.05
440	Don Robinson	.05
441	Rick Anderson	.05
442	Tom Glavine	.25
443	Daryl Boston	.05
444	Joe Price	.05
445	Stewart Cliburn	.05
446	Manny Trillo	.05
447	Joel Skinner	.05
448	Charlie Puleo	.05
449	Carlton Fisk	.10
450	Will Clark	.25
451	Otis Nixon	.05
452	Rick Schu	.05
453	Todd Stottlemyre	.10
454	Tim Birtsas	.05
455	*Dave Gallagher*	.05
456	Barry Lyons	.05
457	Fred Manrique	.05
458	Ernest Riles	.05
459	*Doug Jennings*	.05
460	Joe Magrane	.05
461	Jamie Quirk	.05
462	*Jack Armstrong*	.05
463	Bobby Witt	.05
464	Keith Miller	.05
465	*Todd Burns*	.05
466	*John Dopson*	.05
467	Rich Yett	.05
468	Craig Reynolds	.05
469	Dave Bergman	.05
470	Rex Hudler	.05
471	Eric King	.05
472	Joaquin Andujar	.05
473	*Sil Campusano*	.05
474	Terry Mulholland	.05
475	Mike Flanagan	.05
476	Greg Harris	.05
477	Tommy John	.10
478	Dave Anderson	.05
479	Fred Toliver	.05
480	Jimmy Key	.05
481	Donell Nixon	.05
482	Mark Portugal	.05
483	Tom Pagnozzi	.05
484	Jeff Kunkel	.05
485	Frank Williams	.05
486	Jody Reed	.05
487	Roberto Kelly	.10
488	Shawn Hillegas	.05
489	Jerry Reuss	.05
490	Mark Davis	.05
491	Jeff Sellers	.05
492	Zane Smith	.05
493	Al Newman	.05
494	Mike Young	.05
495	Larry Parrish	.05
496	Herm Winningham	.05
497	Carmen Castillo	.05
498	Joe Hesketh	.05
499	Darrell Miller	.05
500	Mike LaCoss	.05
501	Charlie Lea	.05
502	Bruce Benedict	.05
503	Chuck Finley	.05
504	Brad Wellman	.05
505	Tim Crews	.05
506	Ken Gerhart	.05
507a	Brian Holton (Born: 1/25/65, Denver)	.15
507b	Brian Holton (Born: 11/29/59, McKeesport)	.05
508	Dennis Lamp	.05
509	Bobby Meacham	.05
510	Tracy Jones	.05
511	Mike Fitzgerald	.05
512	*Jeff Bittiger*	.05
513	Tim Flannery	.05
514	Ray Hayward	.05
515	Dave Leiper	.05
516	Rod Scurry	.05
517	Carmelo Martinez	.05
518	Curtis Wilkerson	.05
519	Stan Jefferson	.05
520	Dan Quisenberry	.05
521	Lloyd McClendon	.05
522	Steve Trout	.05
523	Larry Andersen	.05
524	Don Aase	.05
525	Bob Forsch	.05
526	Geno Petralli	.05
527	Angel Salazar	.05
528	*Mike Schooler*	.05
529	Jose Oquendo	.05
530	Jay Buhner	.15
531	Tom Bolton	.05
532	Al Nipper	.05
533	Dave Henderson	.05
534	*John Costello*	.05
535	Donnie Moore	.05
536	Mike Laga	.05
537	Mike Gallego	.05
538	Jim Clancy	.05
539	Joel Youngblood	.05
540	Rick Leach	.05
541	Kevin Romine	.05
542	Mark Salas	.05
543	Greg Minton	.05
544	Dave Palmer	.05
545	Dwayne Murphy	.05
546	Jim Deshaies	.05
547	Don Gordon	.05
548	*Ricky Jordan*	.10
549	Mike Boddicker	.05
550	Mike Scott	.05
551	Jeff Ballard	.05
552a	Jose Rijo (uniform number #24 on card back)	.15
552b	Jose Rijo (uniform number #27 on card back)	.08
553	Danny Darwin	.05
554	Tom Browning	.05
555	Danny Jackson	.05
556	Rick Dempsey	.05
557	Jeffrey Leonard	.05
558	Jeff Musselman	.05
559	Ron Robinson	.05
560	John Tudor	.05
561	Don Slaught	.05
562	Dennis Rasmussen	.05
563	Brady Anderson	.25
564	Pedro Guerrero	.05
565	Paul Molitor	.20
566	*Terry Clark*	.05
567	Terry Puhl	.05
568	Mike Campbell	.05
569	Paul Mirabella	.05
570	Jeff Hamilton	.05
571	*Oswald Peraza*	.05
572	Bob McClure	.05
573	*Jose Bautista*	.10
574	Alex Trevino	.05
575	John Franco	.05
576	*Mark Parent*	.05
577	Nelson Liriano	.05
578	Steve Shields	.05
579	Odell Jones	.05
580	Al Leiter	.05
581	Dave Stapleton	.05
582	1988 World Series(Jose Canseco, Kirk Gibson, Orel Hershiser, Dave Stewart)	.10
583	Donnie Hill	.05
584	Chuck Jackson	.05
585	Rene Gonzales	.05
586	Tracy Woodson	.05
587	Jim Adduci	.05
588	Mario Soto	.05
589	Jeff Blauser	.05
590	Jim Traber	.05
591	Jon Perlman	.05
592	Mark Williamson	.05
593	Dave Meads	.05
594	Jim Eisenreich	.05
595	*Paul Gibson*	.05
596	Mike Birkbeck	.05
597	Terry Francona	.05
598	Paul Zuvella	.05
599	Franklin Stubbs	.05
600	Gregg Jefferies	.10
601	John Cangelosi	.05
602	Mike Sharperson	.05
603	Mike Diaz	.05
604	*Gary Varsho*	.05
605	*Terry Blocker*	.05
606	Charlie O'Brien	.05
607	Jim Eppard	.05
608	John Davis	.05
609	Ken Griffey, Sr.	.08
610	Buddy Bell	.05
611	Ted Simmons	.05
612	Matt Williams	.25
613	Danny Cox	.05
614	Al Pedrique	.05
615	Ron Oester	.05
616	John Smoltz	.20
617	Bob Melvin	.05
618	*Rob Dibble*	.15
619	Kirt Manwaring	.05
620	Felix Fermin	.05
621	*Doug Dascenzo*	.05
622	*Bill Brennan*	.05
623	*Carlos Quintana*	.10
624	*Mike Harkey*	.10
625	*Gary Sheffield*	.75
626	*Tom Prince*	.05
627	*Steve Searcy*	.05
628	*Charlie Hayes*	.25
629	*Felix Jose*	.10
630	*Sandy Alomar*	.25
631	*Derek Lilliquist*	.10
632	Geronimo Berroa	.08
633	*Luis Medina*	.05
634	*Tom Gordon*	.10
635	*Ramon Martinez*	.50
636	*Craig Worthington*	.05
637	Edgar Martinez	.15
638	*Chad Krueter*	.05
639	*Ron Jones*	.05
640	*Van Snider*	.05

641	*Lance Blankenship*	.10
642	*Dwight Smith*	.05
643	*Cameron Drew*	.05
644	*Jerald Clark*	.10
645	*Randy Johnson*	.75
646	*Norm Charlton*	.10
647	Todd Frohwirth	.05
648	*Luis de los Santos*	.05
649	*Tim Jones*	.05
650	*Dave West*	.10
651	*Bob Milacki*	.10
652	1988 Highlight (Wrigley Field)	.05
653	1988 Highlight(Orel Hershiser)	.10
654a	1988 Highlight(Wade Boggs) ("...sixth consecutive seaason..." on back)	2.00
654b	1988 Highlight(Wade Boggs) ("season" corrected)	.10
655	1988 Highlight(Jose Canseco)	.15
656	1988 Highlight(Doug Jones)	.05
657	1988 Highlight(Rickey Henderson)	.12
658	1988 Highlight(Tom Browning)	.05
659	1988 Highlight(Mike Greenwell)	.08
660	1988 Highlight(Joe Morgan) (A.L. Win Streak)	.05

1989 Score Traded

Score issued its second consecutive traded set in 1989 to supplement and update its regular set. The 110-card traded set features the same basic card design as the regular 1989 Score set. The set consists of rookies and traded players pictured with correct teams. The set was sold by hobby dealers in a special box that included an assortment of "Magic Motion" trivia cards.

		MT
Complete Set (110):		10.00
Common Player:		.06
1T	Rafael Palmeiro	.35
2T	Nolan Ryan	1.50
3T	Jack Clark	.06
4T	Dave LaPoint	.06
5T	Mike Moore	.06
6T	Pete O'Brien	.06
7T	Jeffrey Leonard	.06
8T	Rob Murphy	.06
9T	Tom Herr	.06
10T	Claudell Washington	.06
11T	Mike Pagliarulo	.06
12T	Steve Lake	.06
13T	Spike Owen	.06
14T	Andy Hawkins	.06

15T	Todd Benzinger	.06
16T	Mookie Wilson	.06
17T	Bert Blyleven	.06
18T	Jeff Treadway	.06
19T	Bruce Hurst	.06
20T	Steve Sax	.06
21T	Juan Samuel	.06
22T	Jesse Barfield	.06
23T	Carmelo Castillo	.06
24T	Terry Leach	.06
25T	Mark Langston	.06
26T	Eric King	.06
27T	Steve Balboni	.06
28T	Len Dykstra	.10
29T	Keith Moreland	.06
30T	Terry Kennedy	.06
31T	Eddie Murray	.20
32T	Mitch Williams	.06
33T	Jeff Parrett	.06
34T	Wally Backman	.06
35T	Julio Franco	.10
36T	Lance Parrish	.06
37T	Nick Esasky	.06
38T	Luis Polonia	.06
39T	Kevin Gross	.06
40T	John Dopson	.06
41T	Willie Randolph	.06
42T	Jim Clancy	.06
43T	Tracy Jones	.06
44T	Phil Bradley	.06
45T	Milt Thompson	.06
46T	Chris James	.06
47T	Scott Fletcher	.06
48T	Kal Daniels	.06
49T	Steve Bedrosian	.06
50T	Rickey Henderson	.15
51T	Dion James	.06
52T	Tim Leary	.06
53T	Roger McDowell	.06
54T	Mel Hall	.06
55T	Dickie Thon	.06
56T	Zane Smith	.06
57T	Danny Heep	.06
58T	Bob McClure	.06
59T	Brian Holton	.06
60T	Randy Ready	.06
61T	Bob Melvin	.06
62T	Harold Baines	.08
63T	Lance McCullers	.06
64T	Jody Davis	.06
65T	Darrell Evans	.06
66T	Joel Youngblood	.06
67T	Frank Viola	.06
68T	Mike Aldrete	.06
69T	Greg Cadaret	.06
70T	John Kruk	.12
71T	Pat Sheridan	.06
72T	Oddibe McDowell	.06
73T	Tom Brookens	.06
74T	Bob Boone	.06
75T	Walt Terrell	.06
76T	Joel Skinner	.06
77T	Randy Johnson	.75
78T	Felix Fermin	.06
79T	Rick Mahler	.06
80T	Rich Dotson	.06
81T	Cris Carpenter	.06
82T	Bill Spiers	.06
83T	Junior Felix	.10
84T	Joe Girardi	.15
85T	Jerome Walton	.06
86T	Greg Litton	.06
87T	Greg Harris	.06
88T	Jim Abbott	.15
89T	Kevin Brown	.25
90T	John Wetteland	.40
91T	Gary Wayne	.06
92T	Rich Monteleone	.06
93T	Bob Geren	.06
94T	Clay Parker	.06
95T	Steve Finley	.25
96T	Gregg Olson	.06
97T	Ken Patterson	.06
98T	*Ken Hill*	.25
99T	Scott Scudder	.06
100T	*Ken Griffey, Jr.*	8.00
101T	Jeff Brantley	.06
102T	Donn Pall	.06
103T	Carlos Martinez	.06
104T	Joe Oliver	.06
105T	Omar Vizquel	.15
106T	*Albert Belle*	1.50
107T	Kenny Rogers	.06
108T	Mark Carreon	.10
109T	Rolando Roomes	.06
110T	Pete Harnisch	.25

1990 Score

The regular Score set increased to 704 cards in 1990. Included were a series of cards picturing first-round draft picks, an expanded subset of rookie cards, four World Series specials, five Highlight cards, and a 13-card "Dream Team" series featuring the game's top players pictured on old tobacco-style cards. For the first time in a Score set, team logos are displayed on the card fronts Card backs include a full-color portrait photo with player data. A one-paragraph write-up of each player was again provided by former Sports Illustrated editor Les Woodcock. The Score set was again distributed with "Magic Motion" trivia cards, this year using "Baseball's Most Valuable Players" as its theme.

		MT
Complete Set (704):		15.00
Common Player:		.05
Wax Box:		15.00
1	Don Mattingly	.25
2	Cal Ripken, Jr.	.60
3	Dwight Evans	.05
4	Barry Bonds	.40
5	Kevin McReynolds	.05
6	Ozzie Guillen	.05
7	Terry Kennedy	.05
8	Bryan Harvey	.05
9	Alan Trammell	.10
10	Cory Snyder	.05
11	Jody Reed	.05
12	Roberto Alomar	.30
13	Pedro Guerrero	.05
14	Gary Redus	.05
15	Marty Barrett	.05
16	Ricky Jordan	.05
17	Joe Magrane	.05
18	Sid Fernandez	.05
19	Rich Dotson	.05
20	Jack Clark	.05
21	Bob Walk	.05
22	Ron Karkovice	.05
23	Lenny Harris	.05
24	Phil Bradley	.05
25	Andres Galarraga	.15
26	Brian Downing	.05
27	Dave Martinez	.05
28	Eric King	.05
29	Barry Lyons	.05
30	Dave Schmidt	.05
31	Mike Boddicker	.05
32	Tom Foley	.05
33	Brady Anderson	.08
34	Jim Presley	.05
35	Lance Parrish	.08
36	Von Hayes	.05
37	Lee Smith	.08
38	Herm Winningham	.05
39	Alejandro Pena	.05

#	Player	Price
40	Mike Scott	.05
41	Joe Orsulak	.05
42	Rafael Ramirez	.05
43	Gerald Young	.05
44	Dick Schofield	.05
45	Dave Smith	.05
46	Dave Magadan	.05
47	Dennis Martinez	.08
48	Greg Minton	.05
49	Milt Thompson	.05
50	Orel Hershiser	.10
51	Bip Roberts	.05
52	Jerry Browne	.05
53	Bob Ojeda	.05
54	Fernando Valenzuela	.08
55	Matt Nokes	.05
56	Brook Jacoby	.05
57	Frank Tanana	.05
58	Scott Fletcher	.05
59	Ron Oester	.05
60	Bob Boone	.05
61	Dan Gladden	.05
62	Darnell Coles	.05
63	Gregg Olson	.05
64	Todd Burns	.05
65	Todd Benzinger	.05
66	Dale Murphy	.10
67	Mike Flanagan	.05
68	Jose Oquendo	.05
69	Cecil Espy	.05
70	Chris Sabo	.05
71	Shane Rawley	.05
72	Tom Brunansky	.05
73	Vance Law	.05
74	B.J. Surhoff	.05
75	Lou Whitaker	.08
76	Ken Caminiti	.08
77	Nelson Liriano	.05
78	Tommy Gregg	.05
79	Don Slaught	.05
80	Eddie Murray	.20
81	Joe Boever	.05
82	Charlie Leibrandt	.05
83	Jose Lind	.05
84	Tony Phillips	.05
85	Mitch Webster	.05
86	Dan Plesac	.05
87	Rick Mahler	.05
88	Steve Lyons	.05
89	Tony Fernandez	.05
90	Ryne Sandberg	.30
91	Nick Esasky	.05
92	Luis Salazar	.05
93	Pete Incaviglia	.05
94	Ivan Calderon	.05
95	Jeff Treadway	.05
96	Kurt Stillwell	.05
97	Gary Sheffield	.25
98	Jeffrey Leonard	.05
99	Andres Thomas	.05
100	Roberto Kelly	.15
101	Alvaro Espinoza	.05
102	Greg Gagne	.05
103	John Farrell	.05
104	Willie Wilson	.05
105	Glenn Braggs	.05
106	Chet Lemon	.05
107	Jamie Moyer	.05
108	Chuck Crim	.05
109	Dave Valle	.05
110	Walt Weiss	.05
111	Larry Sheets	.05
112	Don Robinson	.05
113	Danny Heep	.05
114	Carmelo Martinez	.05
115	Dave Gallagher	.05
116	Mike LaValliere	.05
117	Bob McClure	.05
118	Rene Gonzales	.05
119	Mark Parent	.05
120	Wally Joyner	.08
121	Mark Gubicza	.05
122	Tony Pena	.05
123	Carmen Castillo	.05
124	Howard Johnson	.05
125	Steve Sax	.05
126	Tim Belcher	.05
127	Tim Burke	.05
128	Al Newman	.05
129	Dennis Rasmussen	.05
130	Doug Jones	.05
131	Fred Lynn	.08
132	Jeff Hamilton	.05
133	German Gonzalez	.05
134	John Morris	.05
135	Dave Parker	.10
136	Gary Pettis	.05
137	Dennis Boyd	.05
138	Candy Maldonado	.05
139	Rick Cerone	.05
140	George Brett	.30
141	Dave Clark	.05
142	Dickie Thon	.05
143	Junior Ortiz	.05
144	Don August	.05
145	Gary Gaetti	.05
146	Kirt Manwaring	.05
147	Jeff Reed	.05
148	Jose Alvarez	.05
149	Mike Schooler	.05
150	Mark Grace	.20
151	Geronimo Berroa	.05
152	Barry Jones	.05
153	Geno Petralli	.05
154	Jim Deshaies	.05
155	Barry Larkin	.12
156	Alfredo Griffin	.05
157	Tom Henke	.05
158	Mike Jeffcoat	.05
159	Bob Welch	.05
160	Julio Franco	.05
161	Henry Cotto	.05
162	Terry Steinbach	.05
163	Damon Berryhill	.05
164	Tim Crews	.05
165	Tom Browning	.05
166	Frd Manrique	.05
167	Harold Reynolds	.05
168a	Ron Hassey (uniform #27 on back)	.05
168b	Ron Hassey (uniform #24 on back)	.50
169	Shawon Dunston	.08
170	Bobby Bonilla	.10
171	Tom Herr	.05
172	Mike Heath	.05
173	Rich Gedman	.05
174	Bill Ripken	.05
175	Pete O'Brien	.05
176a	Lloyd McClendon (uniform number 1 on back)	1.00
176b	Lloyd McClendon (uniform number 10 on back)	.05
177	Brian Holton	.05
178	Jeff Blauser	.05
179	Jim Eisenreich	.05
180	Bert Blyleven	.05
181	Rob Murphy	.05
182	Bill Doran	.05
183	Curt Ford	.05
184	Mike Henneman	.05
185	Eric Davis	.08
186	Lance McCullers	.05
187	*Steve Davis*	.05
188	Bill Wegman	.05
189	Brian Harper	.05
190	Mike Moore	.05
191	Dale Mohorcic	.05
192	Tim Wallach	.05
193	Keith Hernandez	.05
194	Dave Righetti	.05
195a	Bret Saberhagen ("joke" on card back)	.25
195b	Bret Saberhagen ("joker" on card back)	.30
196	Paul Kilgus	.05
197	Bud Black	.05
198	Juan Samuel	.05
199	Kevin Seitzer	.05
200	Darryl Strawberry	.12
201	Dave Steib	.05
202	Charlie Hough	.05
203	Jack Morris	.05
204	Rance Mulliniks	.05
205	Alvin Davis	.05
206	Jack Howell	.05
207	Ken Patterson	.05
208	Terry Pendleton	.08
209	Craig Lefferts	.05
210	Kevin Brown	.10
211	Dan Petry	.05
212	Dave Leiper	.05
213	Daryl Boston	.05
214	Kevin Hickey	.05
215	Mike Krukow	.05
216	Terry Francona	.05
217	Kirk McCaskill	.05
218	Scott Bailes	.05
219	Bob Forsch	.05
220	Mike Aldrete	.05
221	Steve Buechele	.05
222	Jesse Barfield	.05
223	Juan Berenguer	.05
224	Andy McGaffigan	.05
225	Pete Smith	.05
226	Mike Witt	.05
227	Jay Howell	.05
228	Scott Bradley	.05
229	*Jerome Walton*	.08
230	Greg Swindell	.05
231	Atlee Hammaker	.05
232	Mike Devereaux	.05
233	Ken Hill	.25
234	Craig Worthington	.05
235	Scott Terry	.05
236	Brett Butler	.05
237	Doyle Alexander	.05
238	Dave Anderson	.05
239	Bob Milacki	.05
240	Dwight Smith	.05
241	Otis Nixon	.05
242	Pat Tabler	.05
243	Derek Lilliquist	.05
244	Danny Tartabull	.08
245	Wade Boggs	.25
246	Scott Garrelts	.05
247	Spike Owen	.05
248	Norm Charlton	.05
249	Gerald Perry	.05
250	Nolan Ryan	.60
251	Kevin Gross	.05
252	Randy Milligan	.05
253	Mike LaCoss	.05
254	Dave Bergman	.05
255	Tony Gwynn	.25
256	Felix Fermin	.05
257	Greg Harris	.05
258	*Junior Felix*	.10
259	Mark Davis	.05
260	Vince Coleman	.08
261	Paul Gibson	.05
262	Mitch Williams	.05
263	Jeff Russell	.05
264	*Omar Vizquel*	.10
265	Andre Dawson	.10
266	Storm Davis	.05
267	Guillermo Hernandez	.05
268	Mike Felder	.05
269	Tom Candiotti	.05
270	Bruce Hurst	.05
271	Fred McGriff	.25
272	Glenn Davis	.05
273	John Franco	.05
274	Rich Yett	.05
275	Craig Biggio	.10
276	Gene Larkin	.05
277	Rob Dibble	.05
278	Randy Bush	.05
279	Kevin Bass	.05
280a	Bo Jackson ("Watham" on back)	.15
280b	Bo Jackson ("Wathan" on back)	1.00
281	Wally Backman	.05
282	Larry Andersen	.05
283	Chris Bosio	.05
284	Juan Agosto	.05
285	Ozzie Smith	.25
286	George Bell	.08
287	Rex Hudler	.05
288	Pat Borders	.05
289	Danny Jackson	.05
290	Carlton Fisk	.10
291	Tracy Jones	.05
292	Allan Anderson	.05
293	Johnny Ray	.05
294	Lee Guetterman	.05
295	Paul O'Neill	.08
296	Carney Lansford	.05
297	Tom Brookens	.05
298	Claudell Washington	.05
299	Hubie Brooks	.05
300	Will Clark	.25
301	*Kenny Rogers*	.20
302	Darrell Evans	.05
303	Greg Briley	.05
304	Donn Pall	.05
305	Teddy Higuera	.05
306	Dan Pasqua	.05
307	Dave Winfield	.20
308	Dennis Powell	.05
309	Jose DeLeon	.05
310	Roger Clemens	.25
311	Melido Perez	.05
312	Devon White	.08
313	Dwight Gooden	.08
314	*Carlos Martinez*	.08
315	Dennis Eckersley	.08

No.	Player	Price
316	Clay Parker	.05
317	Rick Honeycutt	.05
318	Tim Laudner	.05
319	Joe Carter	.20
320	Robin Yount	.25
321	Felix Jose	.05
322	Mickey Tettleton	.08
323	Mike Gallego	.05
324	Edgar Martinez	.05
325	Dave Henderson	.05
326	Chili Davis	.08
327	Steve Balboni	.05
328	Jody Davis	.05
329	Shawn Hillegas	.05
330	Jim Abbott	.20
331	John Dopson	.05
332	Mark Williamson	.05
333	Jeff Robinson	.05
334	John Smiley	.05
335	Bobby Thigpen	.05
336	Garry Templeton	.05
337	Marvell Wynne	.05
338a	Ken Griffey, Sr. (uniform #25 on card back)	.25
338b	Ken Griffey, Sr. (uniform #30 on card back)	3.00
339	*Steve Finley*	.25
340	Ellis Burks	.08
341	Frank Williams	.05
342	Mike Morgan	.05
343	Kevin Mitchell	.08
344	Joel Youngblood	.05
345	Mike Greenwell	.10
346	Glenn Wilson	.05
347	John Costello	.05
348	Wes Gardner	.05
349	Jeff Ballard	.05
350	Mark Thurmond	.05
351	Randy Myers	.05
352	Shawn Abner	.05
353	Jesse Orosco	.05
354	Greg Walker	.05
355	Pete Harnisch	.08
356	Steve Farr	.05
357	Dave LaPoint	.05
358	Willie Fraser	.05
359	Mickey Hatcher	.05
360	Rickey Henderson	.15
361	Mike Fitzgerald	.05
362	Bill Schroeder	.05
363	Mark Carreon	.05
364	Ron Jones	.05
365	Jeff Montgomery	.05
366	Bill Krueger	.05
367	John Cangelosi	.05
368	Jose Gonzalez	.05
369	*Greg Hibbard*	.10
370	John Smoltz	.15
371	*Jeff Brantley*	.08
372	Frank White	.05
373	Ed Whitson	.05
374	Willie McGee	.05
375	Jose Canseco	.25
376	Randy Ready	.05
377	Don Aase	.05
378	Tony Armas	.05
379	Steve Bedrosian	.05
380	Chuck Finley	.05
381	Kent Hrbek	.10
382	Jim Gantner	.05
383	Mel Hall	.05
384	Mike Marshall	.05
385	Mark McGwire	1.50
386	Wayne Tolleson	.05
387	Brian Holton	.05
388	*John Wetteland*	.20
389	Darren Daulton	.05
390	Rob Deer	.05
391	John Moses	.05
392	Todd Worrell	.05
393	Chuck Cary	.05
394	Stan Javier	.05
395	Willie Randolph	.05
396	Bill Buckner	.05
397	Robby Thompson	.05
398	Mike Scioscia	.05
399	Lonnie Smith	.05
400	Kirby Puckett	.30
401	Mark Langston	.05
402	Danny Darwin	.05
403	Greg Maddux	.60
404	Lloyd Moseby	.05
405	Rafael Palmeiro	.15
406	Chad Kreuter	.05
407	Jimmy Key	.05
408	Tim Birtsas	.05
409	Tim Raines	.10
410	Dave Stewart	.08
411	*Eric Yelding*	.15
412	*Kent Anderson*	.05
413	Les Lancaster	.05
414	Rick Dempsey	.05
415	Randy Johnson	.35
416	Gary Carter	.10
417	Rolando Roomes	.05
418	Dan Schatzeder	.05
419	Bryn Smith	.05
420	Ruben Sierra	.15
421	Steve Jeltz	.05
422	Ken Oberkfell	.05
423	Sid Bream	.05
424	Jim Clancy	.05
425	Kelly Gruber	.05
426	Rick Leach	.05
427	Len Dykstra	.10
428	Jeff Pico	.05
429	John Cerutti	.05
430	David Cone	.08
431	Jeff Kunkel	.05
432	Luis Aquino	.05
433	Ernie Whitt	.05
434	Bo Diaz	.05
435	Steve Lake	.05
436	Pat Perry	.05
437	Mike Davis	.05
438	Cecilio Guante	.05
439	Duane Ward	.05
440	Andy Van Slyke	.08
441	Gene Nelson	.05
442	Luis Polonia	.05
443	Kevin Elster	.05
444	Keith Moreland	.05
445	Roger McDowell	.05
446	Ron Darling	.05
447	Ernest Riles	.05
448	Mookie Wilson	.05
449a	*Bill Spiers* (66 missing for year of birth)	1.25
449b	*Bill Spiers* (1966 for birth year)	.15
450	Rick Sutcliffe	.05
451	Nelson Santovenia	.05
452	Andy Allanson	.05
453	Bob Melvin	.05
454	Benny Santiago	.08
455	Jose Uribe	.05
456	Bill Landrum	.05
457	Bobby Witt	.05
458	Kevin Romine	.05
459	Lee Mazzilli	.05
460	Paul Molitor	.20
461	Ramon Martinez	.15
462	Frank DiPino	.05
463	Walt Terrell	.05
464	*Bob Geren*	.05
465	Rick Reuchel	.05
466	Mark Grant	.05
467	John Kruk	.08
468	Gregg Jefferies	.20
469	R.J. Reynolds	.05
470	Harold Baines	.05
471	Dennis Lamp	.05
472	Tom Gordon	.05
473	Terry Puhl	.05
474	Curtis Wilkerson	.05
475	Dan Quisenberry	.05
476	Oddibe McDowell	.05
477a	Zane Smith (Career ERA 3.93)	1.50
477b	Zane Smith	.05
478	Franklin Stubbs	.05
479	Wallace Johnson	.05
480	Jay Tibbs	.05
481	Tom Glavine	.15
482	Manny Lee	.05
483	Joe Hesketh	.05
484	Mike Bielecki	.05
485	Greg Brock	.05
486	Pascual Perez	.05
487	Kirk Gibson	.08
488	Scott Sanderson	.05
489	Domingo Ramos	.05
490	Kal Daniels	.05
491a	David Wells (reversed negative on back photo)	3.00
491b	David Wells (corrected)	.05
492	Jerry Reed	.05
493	Eric Show	.05
494	Mike Pagliarulo	.05
495	Ron Robinson	.05
496	Brad Komminsk	.05
497	*Greg Litton*	.05
498	Chris James	.05
499	Luis Quinones	.05
500	Frank Viola	.05
501	Tim Teufel	.05
502	Terry Leach	.05
503	Matt Williams	.25
504	Tim Leary	.05
505	Doug Drabek	.05
506	Mariano Duncan	.05
507	Charlie Hayes	.05
508	Albert Belle	.50
509	Pat Sheridan	.05
510	Mackey Sasser	.05
511	Jose Rijo	.05
512	Mike Smithson	.05
513	Gary Ward	.05
514	Dion James	.05
515	Jim Gott	.05
516	Drew Hall	.05
517	Doug Bair	.05
518	*Scott Scudder*	.10
519	Rick Aguilera	.05
520	Rafael Belliard	.05
521	Jay Buhner	.10
522	Jeff Reardon	.05
523	Steve Rosenberg	.05
524	Randy Velarde	.10
525	Jeff Musselman	.05
526	Bill Long	.05
527	*Gary Wayne*	.05
528	*Dave Johnson*	.05
529	Ron Kittle	.05
530	Erik Hanson	.10
531	Steve Wilson	.10
532	Joey Meyer	.05
533	Curt Young	.05
534	Kelly Downs	.05
535	Joe Girardi	.05
536	Lance Blankenship	.05
537	Greg Mathews	.05
538	Donell Nixon	.05
539	Mark Knudson	.05
540	*Jeff Wetherby*	.05
541	Darrin Jackson	.05
542	Terry Mulholland	.05
543	Eric Hetzel	.05
544	*Rick Reed*	.05
545	Dennis Cook	.05
546	Mike Jackson	.05
547	Brian Fisher	.05
548	*Gene Harris*	.05
549	Jeff King	.10
550	Dave Dravecky (Salute)	.10
551	Randy Kutcher	.05
552	Mark Portugal	.05
553	*Jim Corsi*	.05
554	Todd Stottlemyre	.05
555	Scott Bankhead	.05
556	Ken Dayley	.05
557	*Rick Wrona*	.15
558	*Sammy Sosa*	5.00
559	Keith Miller	.05
560	Ken Griffey, Jr.	2.00
561a	Ryne Sandberg (Highlight, 3B on front)	10.00
561b	Ryne Sandberg (Highlight, no position)	.25
562	Billy Hatcher	.05
563	Jay Bell	.05
564	*Jack Daugherty*	.05
565	*Rich Monteleone*	.05
566	Bo Jackson (All-Star MVP)	.25
567	*Tony Fossas*	.05
568	Roy Smith	.05
569	*Jaime Navarro*	.15
570	Lance Johnson	.05
571	*Mike Dyer*	.05
572	*Kevin Ritz*	.10
573	Dave West	.05
574	*Gary Mielke*	.05
575	Scott Lusader	.05
576	*Joe Oliver*	.10
577	Sandy Alomar, Jr.	.08
578	Andy Benes	.25
579	Tim Jones	.05
580	*Randy McCament*	.05
581	Curt Schilling	.10
582	*John Orton*	.05
583a	*Milt Cuyler* (998 games)	2.00
583b	*Milt Cuyler* (98 games)	.15
584	*Eric Anthony*	.25
585	*Greg Vaughn*	.30
586	Deion Sanders	.30
587	Jose DeJesus	.05
588	*Chip Hale*	.15
589	*John Olerud*	.25

590	Steve Olin	.08
591	Marquis Grissom	.60
592	Moises Alou	.20
593	Mark Lemke	.05
594	Dean Palmer	.30
595	Robin Ventura	.35
596	Tino Martinez	.10
597	Mike Huff	.08
598	Scott Hemond	.08
599	Wally Whitehurst	.10
600	Todd Zeile	.15
601	Glenallen Hill	.10
602	Hal Morris	.15
603	Juan Bell	.05
604	Bobby Rose	.05
605	Matt Merullo	.10
606	Kevin Maas	.05
607	Randy Nosek	.05
608a	Billy Bates ("12 triples" mentioned in second-last line ine)	.05
608b	Billy Bates (triples not mentioned)	.50
609	Mike Stanton	.10
610	Goose Gozzo	.10
611	Charles Nagy	.25
612	Scott Coolbaugh	.05
613	Jose Vizcaino	.25
614	Greg Smith	.05
615	Jeff Huson	.10
616	Mickey Weston	.08
617	John Pawlowski	.08
618a	Joe Skalski (uniform #27 on card back)	.15
618b	Joe Skalski (uniform #67 on card back)	2.00
619	Bernie Williams	1.00
620	Shawn Holman	.05
621	Gary Eave	.05
622	Darrin Fletcher	.15
623	Pat Combs	.10
624	Mike Blowers	.08
625	Kevin Appier	.15
626	Pat Austin	.05
627	Kelly Mann	.05
628	Matt Kinzer	.05
629	Chris Hammond	.15
630	Dean Wilkins	.08
631	Larry Walker	1.00
632	Blaine Beatty	.10
633a	Tom Barrett (uniform #29 on card back)	.15
633b	Tom Barrett (uniform #14 on card back)	2.00
634	Stan Belinda	.10
635	Tex Smith	.05
636	Hensley Meulens	.08
637	Juan Gonzalez	2.00
638	Lenny Webster	.10
639	Mark Gardner	.10
640	Tommy Greene	.25
641	Mike Hartley	.08
642	Phil Stephenson	.05
643	Kevin Mmahat	.15
644	Ed Whited	.05
645	Delino DeShields	.25
646	Kevin Blankenship	.10
647	Paul Sorrento	.20
648	Mike Roesler	.15
649	Jason Grimsley	.10
650	Dave Justice	.50
651	Scott Cooper	.15
652	Dave Eiland	.08
653	Mike Munoz	.05
654	Jeff Fischer	.05
655	Terry Jorgenson	.05
656	George Canale	.05
657	Brian DuBois	.08
658	Carlos Quintana	.05
659	Luis de los Santos	.05
660	Jerald Clark	.05
661	Donald Harris (1st Round Pick)	.12
662	Paul Coleman (1st Round Pick)	.20
663	Frank Thomas (1st Round Pick)	3.00
664	Brent Mayne (1st Round Pick)	.10
665	Eddie Zosky (1st Round Pick)	.10
666	Steve Hosey (1st Round Pick)	.25
667	Scott Bryant (1st Round Pick)	.10
668	Tom Goodwin (1st Round Pick)	.10
669	Cal Eldred (1st Round Pick)	.25
670	Earl Cunningham (1st Round Pick)	.10
671	Alan Zinter (1st Round Pick)	.15
672	Chuck Knoblauch (1st Round Pick)	.50
672(a)	Chuck Knoblauch (3,000 autographed cards with a special hologram on back were inserted into 1992 rack packs)	75.00
673	Kyle Abbott (1st Round Pick)	.10
674	Roger Salkeld (1st Round Pick)	.15
675	Mo Vaughn (1st Round Pick)	1.00
676	Kiki Jones (1st Round Pick)	.10
677	Tyler Houston (1st Round Pick)	.12
678	Jeff Jackson (1st Round Pick)	.12
679	Greg Gohr (1st Round Pick)	.10
680	Ben McDonald (1st Round Pick)	.25
681	Greg Blosser (1st Round Pick)	.15
682	Willie Green ((Greene) 1st Round Pick)	.15
683	Wade Boggs (Dream Team)	.10
684	Will Clark (Dream Team)	.20
685	Tony Gwynn (Dream Team)	.20
686	Rickey Henderson (Dream Team)	.10
687	Bo Jackson (Dream Team)	.15
688	Mark Langston (Dream Team)	.10
689	Barry Larkin (Dream Team)	.15
690	Kirby Puckett (Dream Team)	.25
691	Ryne Sandberg (Dream Team)	.25
692	Mike Scott (Dream Team)	.10
693	Terry Steinbach (Dream Team)	.10
694	Bobby Thigpen (Dream Team)	.05
695	Mitch Williams (Dream Team)	.10
696	Nolan Ryan (Highlight)	.60
697	Bo Jackson (FB/BB)	1.00
698	Rickey Henderson (ALCS MVP)	.10
699	Will Clark (NLCS MVP)	.15
700	World Series Games 1-2	.10
701	Lights Out: Candlestick	.12
702	World Series Game 3	.12
703	World Series Wrap-up	.30
704	Wade Boggs (Highlight)	.10

1990 Score Rookie Dream Team

MARK LEMKE   BRAVES-2B

This 10-card "Rookie Dream Team" set, in the same format as those found in the regular-issue 1990 Score, was available only in factory sets for the hobby trade. Factory sets for general retail outlets did not include these cards, nor were they available in Score packs. Cards carry a "B" prefix to their numbers.

		MT
Complete Set:		4.00
Common Player:		.25
1	A. Bartlett Giamatti	.25
2	Pat Combs	.25
3	Todd Zeile	.40
4	Luis de los Santos	.25
5	Mark Lemke	.25
6	Robin Ventura	1.00
7	Jeff Huson	.25
8	Greg Vaughn	.30
9	Marquis Grissom	2.00
10	Eric Anthony	.25

1990 Score Traded

This 110-card set features players with new teams as well as 1990 Major League rookies. The cards feature full-color action photos framed in yellow with an orange border. The player's ID appears in green below the photo. The team logo is displayed next to the player's name. The card backs feature posed player photos and follow the style of the regular 1990 Score issue. The cards are numbered 1T-110T. Young hockey phenom Eric Lindros is featured trying out for the Toronto Blue Jays.

		MT
Complete Set (110):		9.00
Common Player:		.06
1T	Dave Winfield	.20
2T	Kevin Bass	.06
3T	Nick Esasky	.06
4T	Mitch Webster	.06
5T	Pascual Perez	.06
6T	Gary Pettis	.06
7T	Tony Pena	.06
8T	Candy Maldonado	.06
9T	Cecil Fielder	.25
10T	Carmelo Martinez	.06
11T	Mark Langston	.06
12T	Dave Parker	.15
13T	Don Slaught	.06
14T	Tony Phillips	.08
15T	John Franco	.06
16T	Randy Myers	.06
17T	Jeff Reardon	.06
18T	Sandy Alomar, Jr.	.15
19T	Joe Carter	.15
20T	Fred Lynn	.06
21T	Storm Davis	.06
22T	Craig Lefferts	.06
23T	Pete O'Brien	.06
24T	Dennis Boyd	.06
25T	Lloyd Moseby	.06
26T	Mark Davis	.06

27T	Tim Leary	.06
28T	Gerald Perry	.06
29T	Don Aase	.06
30T	Ernie Whitt	.06
31T	Dale Murphy	.10
32T	Alejandro Pena	.06
33T	Juan Samuel	.06
34T	Hubie Brooks	.06
35T	Gary Carter	.10
36T	Jim Presley	.06
37T	Wally Backman	.06
38T	Matt Nokes	.06
39T	Dan Petry	.06
40T	Franklin Stubbs	.06
41T	Jeff Huson	.06
42T	Billy Hatcher	.06
43T	Terry Leach	.06
44T	Phil Bradley	.06
45T	Claudell Washington	.06
46T	Luis Polonia	.06
47T	Daryl Boston	.06
48T	Lee Smith	.08
49T	Tom Brunansky	.06
50T	Mike Witt	.06
51T	Willie Randolph	.06
52T	Stan Javier	.06
53T	Brad Komminsk	.06
54T	John Candelaria	.06
55T	Bryn Smith	.06
56T	Glenn Braggs	.06
57T	Keith Hernandez	.06
58T	Ken Oberkfell	.06
59T	Steve Jeltz	.06
60T	Chris James	.06
61T	Scott Sanderson	.06
62T	Bill Long	.06
63T	Rick Cerone	.06
64T	Scott Bailes	.06
65T	Larry Sheets	.06
66T	Junior Ortiz	.06
67T	Francisco Cabrera	.06
68T	Gary DiSarcina	.10
69T	Greg Olson	.06
70T	Beau Allred	.06
71T	Oscar Azocar	.06
72T	Kent Mercker	.08
73T	John Burkett	.15
74T	*Carlos Baerga*	.50
75T	Dave Hollins	.45
76T	*Todd Hundley*	.75
77T	Rick Parker	.08
78T	Steve Cummings	.08
79T	Bill Sampen	.08
80T	Jerry Kutzler	.08
81T	Derek Bell	.40
82T	Kevin Tapani	.30
83T	Jim Leyritz	.25
84T	*Ray Lankford*	.75
85T	Wayne Edwards	.08
86T	Frank Thomas	5.00
87T	Tim Naehring	.10
88T	Willie Blair	.10
89T	Alan Mills	.10
90T	Scott Radinsky	.08
91T	Howard Farmer	.06
92T	Julio Machado	.06
93T	Rafael Valdez	.06
94T	Shawn Boskie	.10
95T	David Segui	.20
96T	Chris Hoiles	.10
97T	D.J. Dozier	.08
98T	Hector Villanueva	.06
99T	Eric Gunderson	.06
100T	*Eric Lindros*	2.00
101T	Dave Otto	.06
102T	Dana Kiecker	.06
103T	Tim Drummond	.06
104T	Mickey Pina	.06
105T	Craig Grebeck	.06
106T	*Bernard Gilkey*	.40
107T	Tim Layana	.06
108T	Scott Chiamparino	.06
109T	Steve Avery	.15
110T	Terry Shumpert	.06

1991 Score

Score introduced a two series format in 1991. The first series includes cards 1-441. Score cards once again feature multiple border colors within the set, several subsets (Master Blaster, K-Man, High-lights and Riflemen), full-color action photos on the front and portraits on the flip side. Score eliminated display of the player's uniform number on the 1991 cards. Black-and-white Dream Team cards, plus Prospects and #1 Draft Picks highlight the 1991 set. The second series was released in February of 1991.

		MT
Complete Set (893):		15.00
Common Player:		.05
Wax Box:		10.00
1	Jose Canseco	.30
2	Ken Griffey, Jr.	1.25
3	Ryne Sandberg	.25
4	Nolan Ryan	.50
5	Bo Jackson	.15
6	Bret Saberhagen	.05
7	Will Clark	.20
8	Ellis Burks	.10
9	Joe Carter	.20
10	Rickey Henderson	.25
11	Ozzie Guillen	.05
12	Wade Boggs	.20
13	Jerome Walton	.05
14	John Franco	.05
15	Ricky Jordan	.05
16	Wally Backman	.05
17	Rob Dibble	.05
18	Glenn Braggs	.05
19	Cory Snyder	.05
20	Kal Daniels	.05
21	Mark Langston	.05
22	Kevin Gross	.05
23	Don Mattingly	.30
24	Dave Righetti	.05
25	Roberto Alomar	.30
26	Robby Thompson	.05
27	Jack McDowell	.05
28	Bip Roberts	.05
29	Jay Howell	.05
30	Dave Steib	.05
31	Johnny Ray	.05
32	Steve Sax	.05
33	Terry Mulholland	.05
34	Lee Guetterman	.05
35	Tim Raines	.12
36	Scott Fletcher	.05
37	Lance Parrish	.08
38	Tony Phillips	.05
39	Todd Stottlemyre	.08
40	Alan Trammell	.08
41	Todd Burns	.05
42	Mookie Wilson	.05
43	Chris Bosio	.05
44	Jeffrey Leonard	.05
45	Doug Jones	.05
46	Mike Scott	.05
47	Andy Hawkins	.05
48	Harold Reynolds	.05
49	Paul Molitor	.15
50	John Farrell	.05
51	Danny Darwin	.05
52	Jeff Blauser	.05
53	John Tudor	.05
54	Milt Thompson	.05
55	Dave Justice	.30

56	*Greg Olson*	.05
57	*Willie Blair*	.12
58	*Rick Parker*	.10
59	*Shawn Boskie*	.15
60	Kevin Tapani	.10
61	Dave Hollins	.10
62	*Scott Radinsky*	.12
63	Francisco Cabrera	.05
64	*Tim Layana*	.12
65	*Jim Leyritz*	.12
66	Wayne Edwards	.08
67	Lee Stevens	.15
68	*Bill Sampen*	.15
69	*Craig Grebeck*	.10
70	John Burkett	.15
71	*Hector Villanueva*	.05
72	*Oscar Azocar*	.05
73	*Alan Mills*	.15
74	Carlos Baerga	.45
75	Charles Nagy	.05
76	Tim Drummond	.05
77	*Dana Kiecker*	.05
78	*Tom Edens*	.05
79	Kent Mercker	.05
80	Steve Avery	.20
81	Lee Smith	.08
82	Dave Martinez	.05
83	Dave Winfield	.12
84	Bill Spiers	.05
85	Dan Pasqua	.05
86	Randy Milligan	.05
87	Tracy Jones	.05
88	Greg Myers	.05
89	Keith Hernandez	.05
90	Todd Benzinger	.05
91	Mike Jackson	.05
92	Mike Stanley	.05
93	Candy Maldonado	.05
94	John Kruk	.05
95	Cal Ripken, Jr.	.75
96	Willie Fraser	.05
97	Mike Felder	.05
98	Bill Landrum	.05
99	Chuck Crim	.05
100	Chuck Finley	.05
101	Kirt Manwaring	.05
102	Jaime Navarro	.05
103	Dickie Thon	.05
104	Brian Downing	.05
105	Jim Abbott	.12
106	Tom Brookens	.05
107	Darryl Hamilton	.05
108	Bryan Harvey	.05
109	Greg Harris	.05
110	Greg Swindell	.05
111	Juan Berenguer	.05
112	Mike Heath	.05
113	Scott Bradley	.05
114	Jack Morris	.05
115	Barry Jones	.05
116	Kevin Romine	.05
117	Garry Templeton	.05
118	Scott Sanderson	.05
119	Roberto Kelly	.08
120	George Brett	.30
121	Oddibe McDowell	.05
122	Jim Acker	.05
123	Bill Swift	.05
124	Eric King	.05
125	Jay Buhner	.10
126	Matt Young	.05
127	Alvaro Espinoza	.05
128	Greg Hibbard	.05
129	Jeff Robinson	.05
130	Mike Greenwell	.08
131	Dion James	.05
132	Donn Pall	.05
133	Lloyd Moseby	.05
134	Randy Velarde	.05
135	Allan Anderson	.05
136	Mark Davis	.05
137	Eric Davis	.08
138	Phil Stephenson	.05
139	Felix Fermin	.05
140	Pedro Guerrero	.05
141	Charlie Hough	.05
142	Mike Henneman	.05
143	Jeff Montgomery	.05
144	Lenny Harris	.05
145	Bruce Hurst	.05
146	Eric Anthony	.08
147	Paul Assenmacher	.05
148	Jesse Barfield	.05
149	Carlos Quintana	.05
150	Dave Stewart	.12
151	Roy Smith	.05

#	Player	Price
152	Paul Gibson	.05
153	Mickey Hatcher	.05
154	Jim Eisenreich	.05
155	Kenny Rogers	.05
156	Dave Schmidt	.05
157	Lance Johnson	.05
158	Dave West	.05
159	Steve Balboni	.05
160	Jeff Brantley	.05
161	Craig Biggio	.08
162	Brook Jacoby	.05
163	Dan Gladden	.05
164	Jeff Reardon	.05
165	Mark Carreon	.05
166	Mel Hall	.05
167	Gary Mielke	.05
168	Cecil Fielder	.20
169	Darrin Jackson	.05
170	Rick Aguilera	.05
171	Walt Weiss	.05
172	Steve Farr	.05
173	Jody Reed	.05
174	Mike Jeffcoat	.05
175	Mark Grace	.10
176	Larry Sheets	.05
177	Bill Gullickson	.05
178	Chris Gwynn	.05
179	Melido Perez	.05
180	Sid Fernandez	.05
181	Tim Burke	.05
182	Gary Pettis	.05
183	Rob Murphy	.05
184	Craig Lefferts	.05
185	Howard Johnson	.05
186	Ken Caminiti	.05
187	Tim Belcher	.05
188	Greg Cadaret	.05
189	Matt Williams	.20
190	Dave Magadan	.05
191	Geno Petralli	.05
192	Jeff Robinson	.05
193	Jim Deshaies	.05
194	Willie Randolph	.05
195	George Bell	.08
196	Hubie Brooks	.05
197	Tom Gordon	.05
198	Mike Fitzgerald	.05
199	Mike Pagliarulo	.05
200	Kirby Puckett	.25
201	Shawon Dunston	.08
202	Dennis Boyd	.05
203	Junior Felix	.05
204	Alejandro Pena	.05
205	Pete Smith	.05
206	Tom Glavine	.10
207	Luis Salazar	.05
208	John Smoltz	.08
209	Doug Dascenzo	.05
210	Tim Wallach	.08
211	Greg Gagne	.05
212	Mark Gubicza	.05
213	Mark Parent	.05
214	Ken Oberkfell	.05
215	Gary Carter	.08
216	Rafael Palmeiro	.10
217	Tom Niedenfuer	.05
218	Dave LaPoint	.05
219	Jeff Treadway	.05
220	Mitch Williams	.05
221	Jose DeLeon	.05
222	Mike LaValliere	.05
223	Darrel Akerfelds	.05
224	Kent Anderson	.05
225	Dwight Evans	.05
226	Gary Redus	.05
227	Paul O'Neill	.08
228	Marty Barrett	.05
229	Tom Browning	.05
230	Terry Pendleton	.08
231	Jack Armstrong	.05
232	Mike Boddicker	.05
233	Neal Heaton	.05
234	Marquis Grissom	.10
235	Bert Blyleven	.05
236	Curt Young	.05
237	Don Carman	.05
238	Charlie Hayes	.05
239	Mark Knudson	.05
240	Todd Zeile	.08
241	Larry Walker	.20
242	Jerald Clark	.05
243	Jeff Ballard	.05
244	Jeff King	.05
245	Tom Brunansky	.05
246	Darren Daulton	.08
247	Scott Terry	.05
248	Rob Deer	.05
249	Brady Anderson	.05
250	Len Dykstra	.15
251	Greg Harris	.05
252	Mike Hartley	.05
253	Joey Cora	.05
254	Ivan Calderon	.05
255	Ted Power	.05
256	Sammy Sosa	.75
257	Steve Buechele	.05
258	Mike Devereaux	.05
259	Brad Komminsk	.05
260	Teddy Higuera	.05
261	Shawn Abner	.05
262	Dave Valle	.05
263	Jeff Huson	.05
264	Edgar Martinez	.10
265	Carlton Fisk	.10
266	Steve Finley	.05
267	John Wetteland	.08
268	Kevin Appier	.08
269	Steve Lyons	.05
270	Mickey Tettleton	.05
271	Luis Rivera	.05
272	Steve Jeltz	.05
273	R.J. Reynolds	.05
274	Carlos Martinez	.05
275	Dan Plesac	.05
276	Mike Morgan	.05
277	Jeff Russell	.05
278	Pete Incaviglia	.05
279	Kevin Seitzer	.05
280	Bobby Thigpen	.05
281	Stan Javier	.05
282	Henry Cotto	.05
283	Gary Wayne	.05
284	Shane Mack	.05
285	Brian Holman	.05
286	Gerald Perry	.05
287	Steve Crawford	.05
288	Nelson Liriano	.05
289	Don Aase	.05
290	Randy Johnson	.20
291	Harold Baines	.05
292	Kent Hrbek	.08
293	Les Lancaster	.05
294	Jeff Musselman	.05
295	Kurt Stillwell	.05
296	Stan Belinda	.05
297	Lou Whitaker	.05
298	Glenn Wilson	.05
299	Omar Vizquel	.05
300	Ramon Martinez	.10
301	Dwight Smith	.05
302	Tim Crews	.05
303	Lance Blankenship	.05
304	Sid Bream	.05
305	Rafael Ramirez	.05
306	Steve Wilson	.05
307	Mackey Sasser	.05
308	Franklin Stubbs	.05
309	Jack Daugherty	.05
310	Eddie Murray	.15
311	Bob Welch	.05
312	Brian Harper	.05
313	Lance McCullers	.05
314	Dave Smith	.05
315	Bobby Bonilla	.10
316	Jerry Don Gleaton	.05
317	Greg Maddux	.75
318	Keith Miller	.05
319	Mark Portugal	.05
320	Robin Ventura	.12
321	Bob Ojeda	.05
322	Mike Harkey	.05
323	Jay Bell	.05
324	Mark McGwire	1.50
325	Gary Gaetti	.05
326	Jeff Pico	.05
327	Kevin McReynolds	.05
328	Frank Tanana	.05
329	Eric Yelding	.05
330	Barry Bonds	.40
331	*Brian McRae*	.20
332	*Pedro Munoz*	.08
333	*Daryl Irvine*	.08
334	Chris Hoiles	.15
335	*Thomas Howard*	.08
336	*Jeff Schulz*	.08
337	Jeff Manto	.08
338	Beau Allred	.05
339	*Mike Bordick*	.15
340	Todd Hundley	.10
341	*Jim Vatcher*	.05
342	Luis Sojo	.05
343	*Jose Offerman*	.15
344	*Pete Coachman*	.15
345	Mike Benjamin	.10
346	*Ozzie Canseco*	.05
347	Tim McIntosh	.05
348	*Phil Plantier*	.15
349	Terry Shumpert	.05
350	Darren Lewis	.15
351	*David Walsh*	.05
352	Scott Chiamparino	.05
353	*Julio Valera*	.08
354	*Anthony Telford*	.08
355	Kevin Wickander	.10
356	Tim Naehring	.12
357	*Jim Poole*	.05
358	Mark Whiten	.10
359	Terry Wells	.05
360	Rafael Valdez	.05
361	Mel Stottlemyre	.08
362	*David Segui*	.10
363	Paul Abbott	.08
364	Steve Howard	.15
365	Karl Rhodes	.15
366	Rafael Novoa	.10
367	*Joe Grahe*	.15
368	*Darren Reed*	.15
369	Jeff McKnight	.10
370	Scott Leius	.10
371	*Mark Dewey*	.10
372	*Mark Lee*	.10
373	Rosario Rodriguez	.15
374	Chuck McElroy	.05
375	*Mike Bell*	.05
376	Mickey Morandini	.05
377	*Bill Haselman*	.12
378	*Dave Pavlas*	.10
379	Derrick May	.10
380	*Jeromy Burnitz* (1st Draft Pick)	.25
381	*Donald Peters* (1st Draft Pick)	.10
382	*Alex Fernandez* (1st Draft Pick)	.15
383	*Mike Mussina* (1st Draft Pick)	1.25
384	*Daniel Smith* (1st Draft Pick)	.12
385	*Lance Dickson* (1st Draft Pick)	.10
386	*Carl Everett* (1st Draft Pick)	.05
387	*Thomas Nevers* (1st Draft Pick)	.15
388	*Adam Hyzdu* (1st Draft Pick)	.15
389	*Todd Van Poppel* (1st Draft Pick)	.10
390	*Rondell White* (1st Draft Pick)	.50
391	*Marc Newfield* (1st Draft Pick)	.15
392	Julio Franco (AS)	.05
393	Wade Boggs (AS)	.12
394	Ozzie Guillen (AS)	.05
395	Cecil Fielder (AS)	.15
396	Ken Griffey, Jr. (AS)	.40
397	Rickey Henderson (AS)	.15
398	Jose Canseco (AS)	.10
399	Roger Clemens (AS)	.15
400	Sandy Alomar, Jr. (AS)	.05
401	Bobby Thigpen (AS)	.05
402	Bobby Bonilla (Master Blaster)	.10
403	Eric Davis (Master Blaster)	.10
404	Fred McGriff (Master Blaster)	.25
405	Glenn Davis (Master Blaster)	.05
406	Kevin Mitchell (Master Blaster)	.10
407	Rob Dibble (K-Man)	.10
408	Ramon Martinez (K-Man)	.15
409	David Cone (K-Man)	.10
410	Bobby Witt (K-Man)	.05
411	Mark Langston (K-Man)	.10
412	Bo Jackson (Rifleman)	.15
413	Shawon Dunston (Rifleman)	.10
414	Jesse Barfield (Rifleman)	.08
415	Ken Caminiti (Rifleman)	.08
416	Benito Santiago (Rifleman)	.08
417	Nolan Ryan (Highlight)	.35
418	Bobby Thigpen (HL)	.05
419	Ramon Martinez (HL)	.10
420	Bo Jackson (HL)	.15
421	Carlton Fisk (HL)	.10
422	Jimmy Key	.05
423	Junior Noboa	.05
424	Al Newman	.05
425	Pat Borders	.05
426	Von Hayes	.05
427	Tim Teufel	.05

No.	Player	Price
428	Eric Plunk	.05
429	John Moses	.05
430	Mike Witt	.05
431	Otis Nixon	.05
432	Tony Fernandez	.05
433	Rance Mulliniks	.05
434	Dan Petry	.05
435	Bob Geren	.05
436	Steve Frey	.05
437	Jamie Moyer	.05
438	Junior Ortiz	.05
439	Tom O'Malley	.05
440	Pat Combs	.05
441	Jose Canseco (Dream Team)	.60
442	Alfredo Griffin	.05
443	Andres Galarraga	.08
444	Bryn Smith	.05
445	Andre Dawson	.10
446	Juan Samuel	.05
447	Mike Aldrete	.05
448	Ron Gant	.10
449	Fernando Valenzuela	.08
450	Vince Coleman	.08
451	Kevin Mitchell	.08
452	Spike Owen	.05
453	Mike Bielecki	.05
454	Dennis Martinez	.08
455	Brett Butler	.05
456	Ron Darling	.05
457	Dennis Rasmussen	.05
458	Ken Howell	.05
459	Steve Bedrosian	.05
460	Frank Viola	.05
461	Jose Lind	.05
462	Chris Sabo	.05
463	Dante Bichette	.10
464	Rick Mahler	.05
465	John Smiley	.05
466	Devon White	.05
467	John Orton	.05
468	Mike Stanton	.05
469	Billy Hatcher	.05
470	Wally Joyner	.12
471	Gene Larkin	.05
472	Doug Drabek	.08
473	Gary Sheffield	.10
474	David Wells	.05
475	Andy Van Slyke	.05
476	Mike Gallego	.05
477	B.J. Surhoff	.05
478	Gene Nelson	.05
479	Mariano Duncan	.05
480	Fred McGriff	.20
481	Jerry Browne	.05
482	Alvin Davis	.05
483	Bill Wegman	.05
484	Dave Parker	.08
485	Dennis Eckersley	.12
486	Erik Hanson	.12
487	Bill Ripken	.05
488	Tom Candiotti	.05
489	Mike Schooler	.05
490	Gregg Olson	.05
491	Chris James	.05
492	Pete Harnisch	.05
493	Julio Franco	.05
494	Greg Briley	.05
495	Ruben Sierra	.12
496	Steve Olin	.05
497	Mike Fetters	.05
498	Mark Williamson	.05
499	Bob Tewksbury	.05
500	Tony Gwynn	.25
501	Randy Myers	.05
502	Keith Comstock	.05
503	Craig Worthington	.05
504	Mark Eichhorn	.05
505	Barry Larkin	.12
506	Dave Johnson	.05
507	Bobby Witt	.05
508	Joe Orsulak	.05
509	Pete O'Brien	.05
510	Brad Arnsberg	.05
511	Storm Davis	.05
512	Bob Milacki	.05
513	Bill Pecota	.05
514	Glenallen Hill	.08
515	Danny Tartabull	.10
516	Mike Moore	.05
517	Ron Robinson	.05
518	Mark Gardner	.05
519	Rick Wrona	.05
520	Mike Scioscia	.05
521	Frank Wills	.05
522	Greg Brock	.05
523	Jack Clark	.05
524	Bruce Ruffin	.05
525	Robin Yount	.15
526	Tom Foley	.05
527	Pat Perry	.05
528	Greg Vaughn	.05
529	Wally Whitehurst	.05
530	Norm Charlton	.05
531	Marvell Wynne	.05
532	Jim Gantner	.05
533	Greg Litton	.05
534	Manny Lee	.05
535	Scott Bailes	.05
536	Charlie Leibrandt	.05
537	Roger McDowell	.05
538	Andy Benes	.10
539	Rick Honeycutt	.05
540	Dwight Gooden	.08
541	Scott Garrelts	.05
542	Dave Clark	.05
543	Lonnie Smith	.05
544	Rick Rueschel	.05
545	Delino DeShields	.12
546	Mike Sharperson	.05
547	Mike Kingery	.05
548	Terry Kennedy	.05
549	David Cone	.08
550	Orel Hershiser	.12
551	Matt Nokes	.05
552	Eddie Williams	.05
553	Frank DiPino	.05
554	Fred Lynn	.05
555	Alex Cole	.05
556	Terry Leach	.05
557	Chet Lemon	.05
558	Paul Mirabella	.05
559	Bill Long	.05
560	Phil Bradley	.05
561	Duane Ward	.05
562	Dave Bergman	.05
563	Eric Show	.05
564	Xavier Hernandez	.08
565	Jeff Parrett	.05
566	Chuck Cary	.05
567	Ken Hill	.08
568	Bob Welch	.05
569	John Mitchell	.05
570	Travis Fryman	.25
571	Derek Lilliquist	.05
572	Steve Lake	.05
573	*John Barfield*	.05
574	Randy Bush	.05
575	Joe Magrane	.05
576	Edgar Diaz	.05
577	Casy Candaele	.05
578	Jesse Orosco	.05
579	Tom Henke	.05
580	Rick Cerone	.05
581	Drew Hall	.05
582	Tony Castillo	.05
583	Jimmy Jones	.05
584	Rick Reed	.05
585	Joe Girardi	.05
586	*Jeff Gray*	.05
587	Luis Polonia	.05
588	Joe Klink	.05
589	Rex Hudler	.05
590	Kirk McCaskill	.05
591	Juan Agosto	.05
592	Wes Gardner	.05
593	*Rich Rodriguez*	.05
594	Mitch Webster	.05
595	Kelly Gruber	.05
596	Dale Mohorcic	.05
597	Willie McGee	.05
598	Bill Krueger	.05
599	Bob Walk	.05
600	Kevin Maas	.05
601	Danny Jackson	.05
602	Craig McMurtry	.05
603	Curtis Wilkerson	.05
604	Adam Peterson	.05
605	Sam Horn	.05
606	Tommy Gregg	.05
607	Ken Dayley	.05
608	Carmelo Castillo	.05
609	John Shelby	.05
610	Don Slaught	.05
611	Calvin Schiraldi	.05
612	Dennis Lamp	.05
613	Andres Thomas	.05
614	Jose Gonzales	.05
615	Randy Ready	.05
616	Kevin Bass	.05
617	Mike Marshall	.05
618	Daryl Boston	.05
619	Andy McGaffigan	.05
620	Joe Oliver	.05
621	Jim Gott	.05
622	Jose Oquendo	.05
623	Jose DeJesus	.05
624	Mike Brumley	.05
625	John Olerud	.25
626	Ernest Riles	.05
627	Gene Harris	.05
628	Jose Uribe	.05
629	Darnell Coles	.05
630	Carney Lansford	.05
631	Tim Leary	.05
632	Tim Hulett	.05
633	Kevin Elster	.05
634	Tony Fossas	.05
035	Francisco Oliveras	.05
636	Bob Patterson	.05
637	Gary Ward	.05
638	Rene Gonzales	.05
639	Don Robinson	.05
640	Darryl Strawberry	.12
641	Dave Anderson	.05
642	Scott Scudder	.05
643	*Reggie Harris*	.10
644	Dave Henderson	.05
645	Ben McDonald	.10
646	Bob Kipper	.05
647	Hal Morris	.15
648	Tim Birtsas	.05
649	Steve Searcy	.05
650	Dale Murphy	.12
651	Ron Oester	.05
652	Mike LaCoss	.05
653	Ron Jones	.05
654	Kelly Downs	.05
655	Roger Clemens	.20
656	Herm Winningham	.05
657	Trevor Wilson	.08
658	Jose Rijo	.08
659	Dann Bilardello	.05
660	Gregg Jefferies	.15
661	Doug Drabek (All-Star)	.05
662	Randy Myers (AS)	.05
663	Benito Santiago (AS)	.05
664	Will Clark (AS)	.15
665	Ryne Sandberg (AS)	.15
666	Barry Larkin (AS)	.08
667	Matt Williams (AS)	.12
668	Barry Bonds (AS)	.20
669	Eric Davis (AS)	.08
670	Bobby Bonilla (AS)	.05
671	*Chipper Jones* (1st Draft Pick)	3.00
672	*Eric Christopherson* (1st Draft Pick)	.15
673	*Robbie Beckett* (1st Draft Pick)	.15
674	*Shane Andrews* (1st Draft Pick)	.20
675	*Steve Karsay* (1st Draft Pick)	.25
676	*Aaron Holbert* (1st Draft Pick)	.10
677	*Donovan Osborne* (1st Draft Pick)	.10
678	*Todd Ritchie* (1st Draft Pick)	.15
679	*Ron Walden* (1st Draft Pick)	.10
680	*Tim Costo* (1st Draft Pick)	.20
681	*Dan Rijo* (1st Draft Pick)	.15
682	*Kurt Miller* (1st Draft Pick)	.15
683	*Mike Lieberthal* (1st Draft Pick)	.25
684	Roger Clemens (K-Man)	.15
685	Dwight Gooden (K-Man)	.08
686	Nolan Ryan (K-Man)	.30
687	Frank Viola (K-Man)	.08
688	Erik Hanson (K-Man)	.08
689	Matt Williams (Master Blaster)	.10
690	Jose Canseco (Master Blaster)	.12
691	Darryl Strawberry (Master Blaster)	.10
692	Bo Jackson (Master Blaster)	.12
693	Cecil Fielder (Master Blaster)	.12
694	Sandy Alomar, Jr. (Rifleman)	.08
695	Cory Snyder (Rifleman)	.05
696	Eric Davis (Rifleman)	.08
697	Ken Griffey, Jr. (Rifleman)	.50
698	Andy Van Slyke (Rifleman)	.05
699	Mark Langston, Mike Witt (No-hitter)	.08
700	Randy Johnson (No-hitter)	.10
701	Nolan Ryan (No-hitter)	.30
702	Dave Stewart (No-hitter)	.08

703	Fernando Valenzuela (No-hitter)	.08
704	Andy Hawkins (No-hitter)	.05
705	Melido Perez (No-hitter)	.05
706	Terry Mulholland (No-hitter)	.05
707	Dave Stieb (No-hitter)	.05
708	*Brian Barnes*	.05
709	*Bernard Gilkey*	.20
710	*Steve Decker*	.10
711	*Paul Faries*	.12
712	*Paul Marak*	.10
713	*Wes Chamberlain*	.10
714	*Kevin Belcher*	.10
715	Dan Boone	.05
716	*Steve Adkins*	.10
717	*Geronimo Pena*	.10
718	*Howard Farmer*	.08
719	*Mark Leonard*	.10
720	Tom Lampkin	.05
721	*Mike Gardiner*	.10
722	*Jeff Conine*	.40
723	*Efrain Valdez*	.05
724	Chuck Malone	.08
725	*Leo Gomez*	.12
726	*Paul McClellan*	.15
727	*Mark Leiter*	.10
728	*Rich DeLucia*	.15
729	Mel Rojas	.25
730	*Hector Wagner*	.10
731	*Ray Lankford*	.25
732	*Turner Ward*	.15
733	*Gerald Alexander*	.10
734	*Scott Anderson*	.10
735	Tony Perezchica	.05
736	Jimmy Kremers	.05
737	American Flag	.25
738	*Mike York*	.10
739	Mike Rochford	.06
740	Scott Aldred	.05
741	*Rico Brogna*	.15
742	*Dave Burba*	.10
743	*Ray Stephens*	.10
744	*Eric Gunderson*	.08
745	*Troy Afenir*	.08
746	*Jeff Shaw*	.08
747	*Orlando Merced*	.15
748	*Omar Oliveras*	.05
749	Jerry Kutzler	.05
750	Mo Vaughn	.50
751	*Matt Stark*	.05
752	*Randy Hennis*	.05
753	*Andujar Cedeno*	.08
754	Kelvin Torve	.08
755	Joe Kraemer	.08
756	Phil Clark	.08
757	*Ed Vosberg*	.08
758	*Mike Perez*	.10
759	*Scott Lewis*	.10
760	*Steve Chitren*	.10
761	*Ray Young*	.10
762	*Andres Santana*	.15
763	*Rodney McCray*	.05
764	*Sean Berry*	.10
765	Brent Mayne	.05
766	*Mike Simms*	.15
767	*Glenn Sutko*	.05
768	Gary Disarcina	.05
769	George Brett (HL)	.20
770	Cecil Fielder (HL)	.08
771	Jim Presley	.05
772	John Dopson	.05
773	Bo Jackson (Breaker)	.25
774	Brent Knackert	.08
775	Bill Doran	.05
776	Dick Schofield	.05
777	Nelson Santovenia	.05
778	Mark Guthrie	.05
779	Mark Lemke	.05
780	Terry Steinbach	.05
781	Tom Bolton	.05
782	*Randy Tomlin*	.10
783	Jeff Kunkel	.05
784	Felix Jose	.05
785	Rick Sutcliffe	.05
786	John Cerutti	.05
787	Jose Vizcaino	.05
788	Curt Schilling	.05
789	Ed Whitson	.05
790	Tony Pena	.05
791	John Candelaria	.05
792	Carmelo Martinez	.05
793	Sandy Alomar, Jr.	.08
794	*Jim Neidlinger*	.05
795	Red's October(Barry Larkin, Chris Sabo)	.08
796	Paul Sorrento	.05

797	Tom Pagnozzi	.05
798	Tino Martinez	.10
799	Scott Ruskin	.08
800	Kirk Gibson	.08
801	Walt Terrell	.05
802	John Russell	.05
803	Chili Davis	.08
804	Chris Nabholz	.08
805	Juan Gonzalez	.60
806	Ron Hassey	.05
807	Todd Worrell	.05
808	Tommy Greene	.05
809	Joel Skinner	.05
810	Benito Santiago	.08
811	Pat Tabler	.05
812	*Scott Erickson*	.10
813	Moises Alou	.30
814	Dale Sveum	.05
815	Ryne Sandberg (Man of the Year)	.20
816	Rick Dempsey	.05
817	Scott Bankhead	.05
818	Jason Grimsley	.05
819	Doug Jennings	.05
820	Tom Herr	.05
821	Rob Ducey	.05
822	Luis Quinones	.05
823	Greg Minton	.05
824	Mark Grant	.05
825	Ozzie Smith	.10
826	Dave Eiland	.05
827	Danny Heep	.05
828	Hensley Meulens	.05
829	Charlie O'Brien	.05
830	Glenn Davis	.05
831	John Marzano	.05
832	Steve Ontiveros	.05
833	Ron Karkovice	.05
834	Jerry Goff	.05
835	Ken Griffey, Sr.	.08
836	Kevin Reimer	.05
837	Randy Kutcher	.05
838	Mike Blowers	.05
839	Mike Macfarlane	.05
840	Frank Thomas	1.25
841	Ken Griffey Sr., Ken Griffey Jr.	.50
842	Jack Howell	.05
843	Mauro Gozzo	.05
844	Gerald Young	.05
845	Zane Smith	.05
846	Kevin Brown	.05
847	Sil Campusano	.05
848	Larry Andersen	.05
849	Cal Ripken, Jr. (Franchise)	.12
850	Roger Clemens (Franchise)	.15
851	Sandy Alomar, Jr. (Franchise)	.05
852	Alan Trammell (Franchise)	.05
853	George Brett (Franchise)	.15
854	Robin Yount (Franchise)	.10
855	Kirby Puckett (Franchise)	.12
856	Don Mattingly (Franchise)	.12
857	Rickey Henderson (Franchise)	.12
858	Ken Griffey, Jr. (Franchise)	.50
859	Ruben Sierra (Franchise)	.10
860	John Olerud (Franchise)	.20
861	Dave Justice (Franchise)	.15
862	Ryne Sandberg (Franchise)	.15
863	Eric Davis (Franchise)	.05
864	Darryl Strawberry (Franchise)	.08
865	Tim Wallach (Franchise)	.05
866	Dwight Gooden (Franchise)	.08
867	Len Dykstra (Franchise)	.10
868	Barry Bonds (Franchise)	.25
869	Todd Zeile (Franchise)	.05
870	Benito Santiago (Franchise)	.05
871	Will Clark (Franchise)	.12
872	Craig Biggio (Franchise)	.05
873	Wally Joyner (Franchise)	.05
874	Frank Thomas (Franchise)	.75
875	Rickey Henderson (MVP)	.10
876	Barry Bonds (MVP)	.25
877	Bob Welch (Cy Young)	.05
878	Doug Drabek (Cy Young)	.05
879	Sandy Alomar, Jr. (ROY)	.08
880	Dave Justice (ROY)	.25
881	Damon Berryhill	.05
882	Frank Viola (Dream Team)	.05
883	Dave Stewart (Dream Team)	.08
884	Doug Jones (Dream Team)	.05
885	Randy Myers (Dream Team)	.05

886	Will Clark (Dream Team)	.30
887	Roberto Alomar (Dream Team)	.25
888	Barry Larkin (Dream Team)	.12
889	Wade Boggs (Dream Team)	.20
890	Rickey Henderson (Dream Team)	.15
891	Kirby Puckett (Dream Team)	.40
892	Ken Griffey, Jr. (Dream Team)	1.50
893	Benito Santiago (Dream Team)	.08

1991 Score Cooperstown

This seven-card set was included as an insert in every factory set. The card fronts are white, with an oval-vignetted player portrait. The backs have green borders surrounding a yellow background which contains a summary of the player's career. Cards are numbered B1-B7.

		MT
Complete Set (7):		7.50
Common Player:		.50
1	Wade Boggs	1.00
2	Barry Larkin	.50
3	Ken Griffey, Jr.	5.00
4	Rickey Henderson	.50
5	George Brett	2.00
6	Will Clark	.50
7	Nolan Ryan	4.00

1991 Score Hot Rookies

These standard-size cards were inserted one per every 100-card 1991 Score blister pack. Action photos with white borders are featured on the front, and "Hot Rookie" is written in yellow at the top. The background is shaded from yellow to orange. The backs are numbered and each has a color mug shot and a career summary.

		MT
Complete Set (10):		18.00
Common Player:		.50
1	Dave Justice	2.00
2	Kevin Maas	.50
3	Hal Morris	.75
4	Frank Thomas	7.00
5	Jeff Conine	1.50
6	Sandy Alomar Jr.	.75
7	Ray Lankford	.75
8	Steve Decker	.50
9	Juan Gonzalez	4.00
10	Jose Offerman	.50

1991 Score
Mickey Mantle

The Rookie

This special set recalls Mickey Mantle's career as a Yankee. Card fronts are glossy and have red and white borders. The card's caption appears at the bottom in a blue stripe. The backs have a photo and a summary of the caption, plus the card number and serial number. Dealers and media members who were on Score's mailing list received the seven-card sets, which were limited to 5,000 sets produced.

		MT
Complete Set (7):		300.00
Common Player:		50.00
Autographed Card:		500.00
1	The Rookie	50.00
2	Triple Crown	50.00
3	World Series	50.00
4	Going, Going, Gone	50.00
5	Speed and Grace	50.00
6	A True Yankee	50.00
7	Twilight	50.00

1991 Score
Rookies

This 40-card boxed set did not receive much attention in the hobby world, but features some of the top young players of 1991. The card fronts feature full-color action photos with a "Rookies" banner along the side border. The backs feature statistics and a player profile. This set was available through hobby dealers and is Score's first release of its kind.

		MT
Complete Set (40):		5.00
Common Player:		.10
1	Mel Rojas	.10
2	Ray Lankford	.15
3	Scott Aldred	.25
4	Turner Ward	.10
5	Omar Olivares	.10
6	Mo Vaughn	.50
7	Phil Clark	.10
8	Brent Mayne	.10
9	Scott Lewis	.10
10	Brian Barnes	.10
11	Bernard Gilkey	.25
12	Steve Decker	.10
13	Paul Marak	.10
14	Wes Chamberlain	.10
15	Kevin Belcher	.10
16	Steve Adkins	.10
17	Geronimo Pena	.10
18	Mark Leonard	.10
19	Jeff Conine	.25
20	Leo Gomez	.10
21	Chuck Malone	.10
22	Beau Allred	.10
23	Todd Hundley	.25
24	Lance Dickson	.10
25	Mike Benjamin	.10
26	Jose Offerman	.15
27	Terry Shumpert	.10
28	Darren Lewis	.25
29	Scott Chiamparino	.10
30	Tim Naehring	.10
31	David Segui	.10
32	Karl Rhodes	.10
33	Mickey Morandini	.15
34	Chuck McElroy	.10
35	Tim McIntosh	.10
36	Derrick May	.10
37	Rich DeLucia	.10
38	Tino Martinez	.35
39	Hensley Meulens	.10
40	Andujar Cedeno	.10

1991 Score
Traded

This 110-card set features players with new teams as well as 1991 Major League rookies. The cards are designed in the same style as the regular 1991 Score issue. The cards once again feature a "T" designation along with the card number. The complete set was sold at hobby shops in a special box.

		MT
Complete Set (110):		4.00
Common Player:		.06
1	Bo Jackson	.20
2	Mike Flanagan	.06
3	Pete Incaviglia	.06
4	Jack Clark	.06
5	Hubie Brooks	.06
6	Ivan Calderon	.06
7	Glenn Davis	.06
8	Wally Backman	.06
9	Dave Smith	.06
10	Tim Raines	.15
11	Joe Carter	.10
12	Sid Bream	.06
13	George Bell	.06
14	Steve Bedrosian	.06
15	Willie Wilson	.06
16	Darryl Strawberry	.12
17	Danny Jackson	.06
18	Kirk Gibson	.06
19	Willie McGee	.10
20	Junior Felix	.06
21	Steve Farr	.06
22	Pat Tabler	.06
23	Brett Butler	.10
24	Danny Darwin	.06
25	Mickey Tettleton	.06
26	Gary Carter	.10
27	Mitch Williams	.06
28	Candy Maldonado	.06
29	Otis Nixon	.06
30	Brian Downing	.06
31	Tom Candiotti	.06
32	John Candelaria	.06
33	Rob Murphy	.06
34	Deion Sanders	.35
35	Willie Randolph	.06
36	Pete Harnisch	.06
37	Dante Bichette	.12
38	Garry Templeton	.06
39	Gary Gaetti	.08
40	John Cerutti	.06
41	Rick Cerone	.06
42	Mike Pagliarulo	.06
43	Ron Hassey	.06
44	Roberto Alomar	.30
45	Mike Boddicker	.06
46	Bud Black	.06
47	Rob Deer	.06
48	Devon White	.06
49	Luis Sojo	.06
50	Terry Pendleton	.06
51	Kevin Gross	.06
52	Mike Huff	.06
53	Dave Righetti	.06
54	Matt Young	.06
55	Ernest Riles	.06
56	Bill Gullickson	.06
57	Vince Coleman	.06
58	Fred McGriff	.15
59	Franklin Stubbs	.06
60	Eric King	.06
61	Cory Snyder	.06
62	Dwight Evans	.06
63	Gerald Perry	.06
64	Eric Show	.06
65	Shawn Hillegas	.06
66	Tony Fernandez	.06
67	Tim Teufel	.06
68	Mitch Webster	.06
69	Mike Heath	.06

70	Chili Davis	.08
71	Larry Andersen	.06
72	Gary Varsho	.06
73	Juan Berenguer	.06
74	Jack Morris	.06
75	Barry Jones	.06
76	Rafael Belliard	.06
77	Steve Buechele	.06
78	Scott Sanderson	.06
79	Bob Ojeda	.06
80	Curt Schilling	.06
81	Brian Drahman	.06
82	*Ivan Rodriguez*	2.00
83	David Howard	.10
84	Heath Slocumb	.06
85	Mike Timlin	.06
86	Darryl Kile	.25
87	Pete Schourek	.10
88	Bruce Walton	.06
89	Al Osuna	.06
90	Gary Scott	.06
91	Doug Simons	.06
92	Chris Jones	.06
93	Chuck Knoblauch	.45
94	Dana Allison	.06
95	Erik Pappas	.06
96	*Jeff Bagwell*	2.50
97	Kirk Dressendorfer	.06
98	Freddie Benavides	.06
99	*Luis Gonzalez*	.15
100	Wade Taylor	.06
101	Ed Sprague	.10
102	Bob Scanlan	.06
103	Rick Wilkins	.10
104	Chris Donnels	.06
105	Joe Slusarski	.06
106	Mark Lewis	.10
107	Pat Kelly	.12
108	John Briscoe	.06
109	Luis Lopez	.06
110	Jeff Johnson	.06

1992 Score

Score used a two series format for the second consecutive year in 1992. Cards 1-442 are featured in the first series. Fronts feature full-color game action photos. Backs feature color head shots of the players, team logo and career stats on a vertical layout. Several sub-sets are included in 1992, including a five-card Joe DiMaggio set. DiMaggio autographed cards were also inserted into random packs. Cards 736-772 can be found with or without a "Rookie Prospects" banner on the card front.

		MT
Complete Set (893):		15.00
Common Player:		.05
Series 1 or 2 Wax Box:		10.00
1	Ken Griffey, Jr.	1.50
2	Nolan Ryan	.90
3	Will Clark	.25

4	Dave Justice	.20
5	Dave Henderson	.05
6	Bret Saberhagen	.08
7	Fred McGriff	.15
8	Erik Hanson	.05
9	Darryl Strawberry	.10
10	Dwight Gooden	.12
11	Juan Gonzalez	.60
12	Mark Langston	.05
13	Lonnie Smith	.05
14	Jeff Montgomery	.05
15	Roberto Alomar	.25
16	Delino DeShields	.08
17	Steve Bedrosian	.05
18	Terry Pendleton	.05
19	Mark Carreon	.05
20	Mark McGwire	2.00
21	Roger Clemens	.25
22	Chuck Crim	.05
23	Don Mattingly	.50
24	Dickie Thon	.05
25	Ron Gant	.08
26	Milt Cuyler	.05
27	Mike Macfarlane	.05
28	Dan Gladden	.05
29	Melido Perez	.05
30	Willie Randolph	.05
31	Albert Belle	.30
32	Dave Winfield	.15
33	Jimmy Jones	.05
34	Kevin Gross	.05
35	Andres Galarraga	.10
36	Mike Devereaux	.05
37	Chris Bosio	.05
38	Mike LaValliere	.05
39	Gary Gaetti	.05
40	Felix Jose	.05
41	Alvaro Espinoza	.05
42	Rick Aguilera	.05
43	Mike Gallego	.05
44	Eric Davis	.08
45	George Bell	.05
46	Tom Brunansky	.05
47	Steve Farr	.05
48	Duane Ward	.05
49	David Wells	.05
50	Cecil Fielder	.12
51	Walt Weiss	.05
52	Todd Zeile	.10
53	Doug Jones	.05
54	Bob Walk	.05
55	Rafael Palmeiro	.10
56	Rob Deer	.05
57	Paul O'Neill	.08
58	Jeff Reardon	.05
59	Randy Ready	.05
60	Scott Erickson	.05
61	Paul Molitor	.25
62	Jack McDowell	.05
63	Jim Acker	.05
64	Jay Buhner	.08
65	Travis Fryman	.08
66	Marquis Grissom	.10
67	Mike Harkey	.05
68	Luis Polonia	.05
69	Ken Caminiti	.08
70	Chris Sabo	.05
71	Gregg Olson	.05
72	Carlton Fisk	.10
73	Juan Samuel	.05
74	Todd Stottlemyre	.05
75	Andre Dawson	.12
76	Alvin Davis	.05
77	Bill Doran	.05
78	B.J. Surhoff	.05
79	Kirk McCaskill	.05
80	Dale Murphy	.08
81	Jose DeLeon	.05
82	Alex Fernandez	.20
83	Ivan Calderon	.05
84	Brent Mayne	.05
85	Jody Reed	.05
86	Randy Tomlin	.05
87	Randy Milligan	.05
88	Pascual Perez	.05
89	Hensley Meulens	.05
90	Joe Carter	.10
91	Mike Moore	.05
92	Ozzie Guillen	.05
93	Shawn Hillegas	.05
94	Chili Davis	.08
95	Vince Coleman	.05
96	Jimmy Key	.05
97	Billy Ripken	.05
98	Dave Smith	.05
99	Tom Bolton	.05

100	Barry Larkin	.10
101	Kenny Rogers	.05
102	Mike Boddicker	.05
103	Kevin Elster	.05
104	Ken Hill	.05
105	Charlie Leibrandt	.05
106	Pat Combs	.05
107	Hubie Brooks	.05
108	Julio Franco	.05
109	Vicente Palacios	.05
110	Kal Daniels	.05
111	Bruce Hurst	.05
112	Willie McGee	.05
113	Ted Power	.05
114	Milt Thompson	.05
115	Doug Drabek	.05
116	Rafael Belliard	.05
117	Scott Garrelts	.05
118	Terry Mulholland	.05
119	Jay Howell	.05
120	Danny Jackson	.05
121	Scott Ruskin	.05
122	Robin Ventura	.15
123	Bip Roberts	.05
124	Jeff Russell	.05
125	Hal Morris	.05
126	Teddy Higuera	.05
127	Luis Sojo	.05
128	Carlos Baerga	.20
129	Jeff Ballard	.05
130	Tom Gordon	.05
131	Sid Bream	.05
132	Rance Mulliniks	.05
133	Andy Benes	.10
134	Mickey Tettleton	.05
135	Rich DeLucia	.05
136	Tom Pagnozzi	.05
137	Harold Baines	.05
138	Danny Darwin	.05
139	Kevin Bass	.05
140	Chris Nabholz	.05
141	Pete O'Brien	.05
142	Jeff Treadway	.05
143	Mickey Morandini	.05
144	Eric King	.05
145	Danny Tartabull	.05
146	Lance Johnson	.05
147	Casey Candaele	.05
148	Felix Fermin	.05
149	Rich Rodriguez	.05
150	Dwight Evans	.05
151	Joe Klink	.05
152	Kevin Reimer	.05
153	Orlando Merced	.05
154	Mel Hall	.05
155	Randy Myers	.05
156	Greg Harris	.05
157	Jeff Brantley	.05
158	Jim Eisenreich	.05
159	Luis Rivera	.05
160	Cris Carpenter	.05
161	Bruce Ruffin	.05
162	Omar Vizquel	.05
163	Gerald Alexander	.05
164	Mark Guthrie	.05
165	Scott Lewis	.05
166	Bill Sampen	.05
167	Dave Anderson	.05
168	Kevin McReynolds	.05
169	Jose Vizcaino	.05
170	Bob Geren	.05
171	Mike Morgan	.05
172	Jim Gott	.05
173	Mike Pagliarulo	.05
174	Mike Jeffcoat	.05
175	Craig Lefferts	.05
176	Steve Finley	.05
177	Wally Backman	.05
178	Kent Mercker	.05
179	John Cerutti	.05
180	Jay Bell	.05
181	Dale Sveum	.05
182	Greg Gagne	.05
183	Donnie Hill	.05
184	Rex Hudler	.05
185	Pat Kelly	.05
186	Jeff Robinson	.05
187	Jeff Gray	.05
188	Jerry Willard	.05
189	Carlos Quintana	.05
190	Dennis Eckersley	.08
191	Kelly Downs	.05
192	Gregg Jefferies	.10
193	Darrin Fletcher	.05
194	Mike Jackson	.05
195	Eddie Murray	.12

196	Billy Landrum	.05
197	Eric Yelding	.05
198	Devon White	.05
199	Larry Walker	.15
200	Ryne Sandberg	.25
201	Dave Magadan	.05
202	Steve Chitren	.05
203	Scott Fletcher	.05
204	Dwayne Henry	.05
205	Scott Coolbaugh	.05
206	Tracy Jones	.05
207	Von Hayes	.05
208	Bob Melvin	.05
209	Scott Scudder	.05
210	Luis Gonzalez	.05
211	Scott Sanderson	.05
212	Chris Donnels	.05
213	Heath Slocumb	.05
214	Mike Timlin	.05
215	Brian Harper	.05
216	Juan Berenguer	.05
217	Mike Henneman	.05
218	Bill Spiers	.05
219	Scott Terry	.05
220	Frank Viola	.05
221	Mark Eichhorn	.05
222	Ernest Riles	.05
223	Ray Lankford	.10
224	Pete Harnisch	.05
225	Bobby Bonilla	.10
226	Mike Scioscia	.05
227	Joel Skinner	.05
228	Brian Holman	.05
229	Gilberto Reyes	.05
230	Matt Williams	.20
231	Jaime Navarro	.05
232	Jose Rijo	.05
233	Atlee Hammaker	.05
234	Tim Teufel	.05
235	John Kruk	.05
236	Kurt Stillwell	.05
237	Dan Pasqua	.05
238	Tim Crews	.05
239	Dave Gallagher	.05
240	Leo Gomez	.05
241	Steve Avery	.20
242	Bill Gullickson	.05
243	Mark Portugal	.05
244	Lee Guetterman	.05
245	Benny Santiago	.08
246	Jim Gantner	.05
247	Robby Thompson	.05
248	Terry Shumpert	.05
249	Mike Bell	.05
250	Harold Reynolds	.05
251	Mike Felder	.05
252	Bill Pecota	.05
253	Bill Krueger	.05
254	Alfredo Griffin	.05
255	Lou Whitaker	.05
256	Roy Smith	.05
257	Jerald Clark	.05
258	Sammy Sosa	.75
259	Tim Naehring	.05
260	Dave Righetti	.05
261	Paul Gibson	.05
262	Chris James	.05
263	Larry Andersen	.05
264	Storm Davis	.05
265	Jose Lind	.05
266	Greg Hibbard	.05
267	Norm Charlton	.05
268	Paul Kilgus	.05
269	Greg Maddux	.75
270	Ellis Burks	.08
271	Frank Tanana	.05
272	Gene Larkin	.05
273	Ron Hassey	.05
274	Jeff Robinson	.05
275	Steve Howe	.05
276	Daryl Boston	.05
277	Mark Lee	.05
278	Jose Segura	.05
279	Lance Blankenship	.05
280	Don Slaught	.05
281	Russ Swan	.05
282	Bob Tewksbury	.05
283	Geno Petralli	.05
284	Shane Mack	.05
285	Bob Scanlan	.05
286	Tim Leary	.05
287	John Smoltz	.10
288	Pat Borders	.05
289	Mark Davidson	.05
290	Sam Horn	.05
291	Lenny Harris	.05

292	Franklin Stubbs	.05
293	Thomas Howard	.05
294	Steve Lyons	.05
295	Francisco Oliveras	.05
296	Terry Leach	.05
297	Barry Jones	.05
298	Lance Parrish	.05
299	Wally Whitehurst	.05
300	Bob Welch	.05
301	Charlie Hayes	.05
302	Charlie Hough	.05
303	Gary Redus	.05
304	Scott Bradley	.05
305	Jose Oquendo	.05
306	Pete Incaviglia	.05
307	Marvin Freeman	.05
308	Gary Pettis	.05
309	Joe Slusarski	.05
310	Kevin Seitzer	.05
311	Jeff Reed	.05
312	Pat Tabler	.05
313	Mike Maddux	.05
314	Bob Milacki	.05
315	Eric Anthony	.05
316	Dante Bichette	.05
317	Steve Decker	.05
318	Jack Clark	.05
319	Doug Dascenzo	.05
320	Scott Leius	.08
321	Jim Lindeman	.05
322	Bryan Harvey	.05
323	Spike Owen	.05
324	Roberto Kelly	.05
325	Stan Belinda	.05
326	Joey Cora	.05
327	Jeff Innis	.05
328	Willie Wilson	.05
329	Juan Agosto	.05
330	Charles Nagy	.05
331	Scott Bailes	.05
332	Pete Schourek	.08
333	Mike Flanagan	.05
334	Omar Olivares	.05
335	Dennis Lamp	.05
336	Tommy Greene	.05
337	Randy Velarde	.05
338	Tom Lampkin	.05
339	John Russell	.05
340	Bob Kipper	.05
341	Todd Burns	.05
342	Ron Jones	.05
343	Dave Valle	.05
344	Mike Heath	.05
345	John Olerud	.25
346	Gerald Young	.05
347	Ken Patterson	.05
348	Les Lancaster	.05
349	Steve Crawford	.05
350	John Candelaria	.05
351	Mike Aldrete	.05
352	Mariano Duncan	.05
353	Julio Machado	.05
354	Ken Williams	.05
355	Walt Terrell	.05
356	Mitch Williams	.05
357	Al Newman	.05
358	Bud Black	.05
359	Joe Hesketh	.05
360	Paul Assenmacher	.05
361	Bo Jackson	.12
362	Jeff Blauser	.05
363	Mike Brumley	.05
364	Jim Deshaies	.05
365	Brady Anderson	.05
366	Chuck McElroy	.05
367	Matt Merullo	.05
368	Tim Belcher	.05
369	Luis Aquino	.05
370	Joe Oliver	.05
371	Greg Swindell	.05
372	Lee Stevens	.05
373	Mark Knudson	.05
374	Bill Wegman	.05
375	Jerry Don Gleaton	.05
376	Pedro Guerrero	.05
377	Randy Bush	.05
378	Greg Harris	.05
379	Eric Plunk	.05
380	Jose DeJesus	.05
381	Bobby Witt	.05
382	Curtis Wilkerson	.05
383	Gene Nelson	.05
384	Wes Chamberlain	.05
385	Tom Henke	.05
386	Mark Lemke	.05
387	Greg Briley	.05

388	Rafael Ramirez	.05
389	Tony Fossas	.05
390	Henry Cotto	.05
391	Tim Hulett	.05
392	Dean Palmer	.05
393	Glenn Braggs	.05
394	Mark Salas	.05
395	Rusty Meacham	.08
396	Andy Ashby	.10
397	Jose Melendez	.05
398	Warren Newson	.08
399	Frank Castillo	.05
400	Chito Martinez	.05
401	Bernie Williams	.25
402	Derek Bell	.12
403	Javier Ortiz	.05
404	Tim Sherrill	.08
405	Rob MacDonald	.05
406	Phil Plantier	.05
407	Troy Afenir	.05
408	Gino Minutelli	.05
409	Reggie Jefferson	.10
410	Mike Remlinger	.08
411	Carlos Rodriguez	.10
412	Joe Redfield	.05
413	Alonzo Powell	.05
414	Scott Livingstone	.08
415	Scott Kamieniecki	.08
416	Tim Spehr	.10
417	Brian Hunter	.05
418	Ced Landrum	.05
419	Bret Barberie	.05
420	Kevin Morton	.08
421	Doug Henry	.10
422	Doug Piatt	.08
423	Pat Rice	.08
424	Juan Guzman	.08
425	Nolan Ryan (No-Hit)	.30
426	Tommy Greene (No-Hit)	.10
427	Bob Milacki, Mike Flanagan, Mark Williamson, Gregg Olson (No-Hit)	.10
428	Wilson Alvarez (No-Hit)	.08
429	Otis Nixon (Highlight)	.05
430	Rickey Henderson (Highlight)	.10
431	Cecil Fielder (All-Star)	.10
432	Julio Franco (AS)	.05
433	Cal Ripken, Jr. (AS)	.20
434	Wade Boggs (AS)	.10
435	Joe Carter (AS)	.05
436	Ken Griffey, Jr. (AS)	.60
437	Ruben Sierra (AS)	.05
438	Scott Erickson (AS)	.05
439	Tom Henke (AS)	.05
440	Terry Steinbach (AS)	.05
441	Rickey Henderson (Dream Team)	.15
442	Ryne Sandberg (Dream Team)	.25
443	Otis Nixon	.05
444	Scott Radinsky	.05
445	Mark Grace	.15
446	Tony Pena	.05
447	Billy Hatcher	.05
448	Glenallen Hill	.05
449	Chris Gwynn	.05
450	Tom Glavine	.08
451	John Habyan	.05
452	Al Osuna	.05
453	Tony Phillips	.05
454	Greg Cadaret	.05
455	Rob Dibble	.05
456	Rick Honeycutt	.05
457	Jerome Walton	.05
458	Mookie Wilson	.05
459	Mark Gubicza	.05
460	Craig Biggio	.08
461	Dave Cochrane	.05
462	Keith Miller	.05
463	Alex Cole	.05
464	Pete Smith	.05
465	Brett Butler	.05
466	Jeff Huson	.05
467	Steve Lake	.05
468	Lloyd Moseby	.05
469	Tim McIntosh	.05
470	Dennis Martinez	.08
471	Greg Myers	.05
472	Mackey Sasser	.05
473	Junior Ortiz	.05
474	Greg Olson	.05
475	Steve Sax	.05
476	Ricky Jordan	.05
477	Max Venable	.05
478	Brian McRae	.10

No.	Player	Value	No.	Player	Value	No.	Player	Value
479	Doug Simons	.05	575	Tom Candiotti	.05	671	Curt Schilling	.05
480	Rickey Henderson	.15	576	Jeff Bagwell	.50	672	Brian Bohanon	.05
481	Gary Varsho	.05	577	Brook Jacoby	.05	673	Cecil Espy	.05
482	Carl Willis	.05	578	Chico Walker	.05	674	Joe Grahe	.05
483	*Rick Wilkins*	.10	579	Brian Downing	.05	675	Sid Fernandez	.05
484	Donn Pall	.05	580	Dave Stewart	.08	676	Edwin Nunez	.05
485	Edgar Martinez	.08	581	Francisco Cabrera	.05	677	Hector Villanueva	.05
486	Tom Foley	.05	582	Rene Gonzales	.05	678	Sean Berry	.05
487	Mark Williamson	.05	583	Stan Javier	.05	679	Dave Eiland	.05
488	Jack Armstrong	.05	584	Randy Johnson	.25	680	David Cone	.05
489	Gary Carter	.08	585	Chuck Finley	.05	681	Mike Bordick	.05
490	Ruben Sierra	.05	586	Mark Gardner	.05	682	Tony Castillo	.05
491	Gerald Perry	.05	587	Mark Whiten	.05	683	John Barfield	.05
492	Rob Murphy	.05	588	Garry Templeton	.05	684	Jeff Hamilton	.05
493	Zane Smith	.05	589	Gary Sheffield	.15	685	Ken Dayley	.05
494	*Darryl Kile*	.10	590	Ozzie Smith	.20	686	Carmelo Martinez	.05
495	Kelly Gruber	.05	591	Candy Maldonado	.05	687	Mike Capel	.05
496	Jerry Browne	.05	592	Mike Sharperson	.05	688	Scott Chiamparino	.05
497	Darryl Hamilton	.05	593	Carlos Martinez	.05	689	Rich Gedman	.05
498	Mike Stanton	.05	594	Scott Bankhead	.05	690	Rich Monteleone	.05
499	Mark Leonard	.05	595	Tim Wallach	.05	691	Alejandro Pena	.05
500	Jose Canseco	.15	596	Tino Martinez	.05	692	Oscar Azocar	.05
501	Dave Martinez	.05	597	Roger McDowell	.05	693	Jim Poole	.05
502	Jose Guzman	.05	598	Cory Snyder	.05	694	Mike Gardiner	.05
503	Terry Kennedy	.05	599	Andujar Cedeno	.05	695	Steve Buechele	.05
504	*Ed Sprague*	.08	600	Kirby Puckett	.30	696	Rudy Seanez	.05
505	Frank Thomas	1.50	601	Rick Parker	.05	697	Paul Abbott	.05
506	Darren Daulton	.05	602	Todd Hundley	.05	698	Steve Searcy	.05
507	Kevin Tapani	.05	603	Greg Litton	.05	699	Jose Offerman	.05
508	Luis Salazar	.05	604	Dave Johnson	.05	700	Ivan Rodriguez	.30
509	Paul Faries	.05	605	John Franco	.05	701	Joe Girardi	.05
510	Sandy Alomar, Jr.	.08	606	Mike Fetters	.05	702	Tony Perezchica	.05
511	Jeff King	.05	607	Luis Alicea	.05	703	Paul McClellan	.05
512	Gary Thurman	.05	608	Trevor Wilson	.05	704	*David Howard*	.08
513	Chris Hammond	.05	609	Rob Ducey	.05	705	Dan Petry	.05
514	*Pedro Munoz*	.10	610	Ramon Martinez	.08	706	Jack Howell	.05
515	Alan Trammell	.08	611	Dave Burba	.05	707	Jose Mesa	.05
516	Geronimo Pena	.05	612	Dwight Smith	.05	708	Randy St. Claire	.05
517	Rodney McCray	.05	613	Kevin Maas	.05	709	Kevin Brown	.05
518	Manny Lee	.05	614	John Costello	.05	710	Ron Darling	.05
519	Junior Felix	.05	615	Glenn Davis	.05	711	Jason Grimsley	.05
520	Kirk Gibson	.05	616	Shawn Abner	.05	712	John Orton	.05
521	Darrin Jackson	.05	617	Scott Hemond	.05	713	Shawn Boskie	.05
522	John Burkett	.05	618	Tom Prince	.05	714	Pat Clements	.05
523	Jeff Johnson	.05	619	Wally Ritchie	.05	715	Brian Barnes	.05
524	Jim Corsi	.05	620	Jim Abbott	.08	716	*Luis Lopez*	.05
525	Robin Yount	.15	621	Charlie O'Brien	.05	717	Bob McClure	.05
526	Jamie Quirk	.05	622	Jack Daugherty	.05	718	Mark Davis	.05
527	Bob Ojeda	.05	623	Tommy Gregg	.05	719	Dann Billardello	.05
528	Mark Lewis	.05	624	Jeff Shaw	.05	720	Tom Edens	.05
529	Bryn Smith	.08	625	Tony Gwynn	.35	721	Willie Fraser	.05
530	Kent Hrbek	.08	626	Mark Leiter	.05	722	Curt Young	.05
531	Dennis Boyd	.05	627	Jim Clancy	.05	723	Neal Heaton	.05
532	Ron Karkovice	.05	628	Tim Layana	.05	724	Craig Worthington	.05
533	Don August	.05	629	Jeff Schaefer	.05	725	Mel Rojas	.05
534	Todd Frohwirth	.05	630	Lee Smith	.08	726	Daryl Irvine	.05
535	Wally Joyner	.08	631	Wade Taylor	.05	727	Roger Mason	.05
536	Dennis Rasmussen	.05	632	Mike Simms	.05	728	Kirk Dressendorfer	.05
537	Andy Allanson	.05	633	Terry Steinbach	.05	729	Scott Aldred	.05
538	Rich Gossage	.05	634	Shawon Dunston	.08	730	Willie Blair	.05
539	John Marzano	.05	635	Tim Raines	.08	731	Allan Anderson	.05
540	Cal Ripken, Jr.	1.00	636	Kirt Manwaring	.05	732	Dana Kiecker	.05
541	Bill Swift	.05	637	Warren Cromartie	.05	733	Jose Gonzalez	.05
542	Kevin Appier	.05	638	Luis Quinones	.05	734	Brian Drahman	.05
543	Dave Bergman	.05	639	Greg Vaughn	.05	735	Brad Komminsk	.05
544	Bernard Gilkey	.10	640	Kevin Mitchell	.05	736	*Arthur Rhodes*	.10
545	Mike Greenwell	.05	641	Chris Hoiles	.05	737	*Terry Mathews*	.05
546	Jose Uribe	.05	642	Tom Browning	.05	738	*Jeff Fassero*	.05
547	Jesse Orosco	.05	643	Mitch Webster	.05	739	*Mike Magnante*	.05
548	Bob Patterson	.05	644	Steve Olin	.05	740	*Kip Gross*	.05
549	Mike Stanley	.05	645	Tony Fernandez	.05	741	*Jim Hunter*	.05
550	Howard Johnson	.05	646	Juan Bell	.05	742	*Jose Mota*	.05
551	Joe Orsulak	.05	647	Joe Boever	.05	743	Joe Bitker	.05
552	Dick Schofield	.05	648	Carney Lansford	.05	744	*Tim Mauser*	.05
553	Dave Hollins	.05	649	Mike Benjamin	.05	745	*Ramon Garcia*	.05
554	David Segui	.05	650	George Brett	.25	746	*Rod Beck*	.25
555	Barry Bonds	.40	651	Tim Burke	.05	747	*Jim Austin*	.05
556	Mo Vaughn	.35	652	Jack Morris	.05	748	*Keith Mitchell*	.05
557	Craig Wilson	.05	653	Orel Hershiser	.08	749	*Wayne Rosenthal*	.05
558	Bobby Rose	.05	654	Mike Schooler	.05	750	*Bryan Hickerson*	.05
559	Rod Nichols	.05	655	Andy Van Slyke	.05	751	*Bruce Egloff*	.05
560	Len Dykstra	.05	656	Dave Stieb	.05	752	*John Wehner*	.05
561	Craig Grebeck	.05	657	Dave Clark	.05	753	Darren Holmes	.05
562	Darren Lewis	.10	658	Ben McDonald	.08	754	Dave Hansen	.05
563	Todd Benzinger	.05	659	John Smiley	.05	755	Mike Mussina	.25
564	Ed Whitson	.05	660	Wade Boggs	.12	756	*Anthony Young*	.05
565	Jesse Barfield	.05	661	Eric Bullock	.05	757	Ron Tingley	.05
566	Lloyd McClendon	.05	662	Eric Show	.05	758	*Ricky Bones*	.08
567	Dan Plesac	.05	663	Lenny Webster	.05	759	*Mark Wohlers*	.10
568	Danny Cox	.05	664	Mike Huff	.05	760	Wilson Alvarez	.10
569	Skeeter Barnes	.05	665	Rick Sutcliffe	.05	761	*Harvey Pulliam*	.05
570	Bobby Thigpen	.05	666	Jeff Manto	.05	762	Ryan Bowen	.10
571	Deion Sanders	.10	667	Mike Fitzgerald	.05	763	Terry Bross	.05
572	Chuck Knoblauch	.05	668	Matt Young	.05	764	*Joel Johnston*	.05
573	Matt Nokes	.05	669	Dave West	.05	765	*Terry McDaniel*	.05
574	Herm Winningham	.05	670	Mike Hartley	.05	766	*Esteban Beltre*	.05

767	*Rob Maurer*	.05
768	Ted Wood	.05
769	*Mo Sanford*	.10
770	Jeff Carter	.05
771	Gil Heredia	.08
772	Monty Fariss	.05
773	Will Clark (AS)	.10
774	Ryne Sandberg (AS)	.15
775	Barry Larkin (AS)	.08
776	Howard Johnson (AS)	.05
777	Barry Bonds (AS)	.25
778	Brett Butler (AS)	.05
779	Tony Gwynn (AS)	.15
780	Ramon Martinez (AS)	.05
781	Lee Smith (AS)	.05
782	Mike Scioscia (AS)	.05
783	Dennis Martinez (Highlight)	.05
784	Donnie Martinez (No-Hit)	.05
785	Mark Gardner (No-Hit)	.05
786	Bret Saberhagen (No-Hit)	.05
787	Kent Mercker, Mark Wohlers, Alejandro Pena (No-Hit)	.05
788	Cal Ripken (MVP)	.20
789	Terry Pendleton (MVP)	.05
790	Roger Clemens (CY)	.15
791	Tom Glavine (CY)	.05
792	Chuck Knoblauch (ROY)	.10
793	Jeff Bagwell (ROY)	.25
794	Cal Ripken, Jr. (Man of the Year)	.15
795	David Cone (Highlight)	.05
796	Kirby Puckett (Highlight)	.15
797	Steve Avery (Highlight)	.05
798	Jack Morris (Highlight)	.05
799	*Allen Watson*	.25
800	*Manny Ramirez*	1.50
801	*Cliff Floyd*	.40
802	*Al Shirley*	.05
803	*Brian Barber*	.05
804	*Jon Farrell*	.05
805	*Brent Gates*	.25
806	*Scott Ruffcorn*	.20
807	*Tyrone Hill*	.20
808	*Benji Gil*	.20
809	*Aaron Sele*	.30
810	*Tyler Green*	.25
811	Chris Jones	.05
812	Steve Wilson	.05
813	*Cliff Young*	.08
814	*Don Wakamatsu*	.05
815	*Mike Humphreys*	.05
816	*Scott Servais*	.05
817	*Rico Rossy*	.05
818	*John Ramos*	.05
819	Rob Mallicoat	.05
820	*Milt Hill*	.08
821	Carlos Garcia	.05
822	Stan Royer	.08
823	*Jeff Plympton*	.10
824	*Braulio Castillo*	.12
825	*David Haas*	.05
826	*Luis Mercedes*	.10
827	Eric Karros	.20
828	*Shawn Hare*	.10
829	Reggie Sanders	.20
830	Tom Goodwin	.10
831	*Dan Gakeler*	.05
832	*Stacy Jones*	.05
833	*Kim Batiste*	.05
834	Cal Eldred	.05
835	*Chris George*	.05
836	*Wayne Housie*	.05
837	Mike Ignasiak	.05
838	*Josias Manzanillo*	.05
839	Jim Olander	.05
840	*Gary Cooper*	.05
841	Royce Clayton	.05
842	Hector Fajardo	.05
843	Blaine Beatty	.05
844	*Jorge Pedre*	.05
845	Kenny Lofton	.30
846	Scott Brosius	.15
847	*Chris Cron*	.05
848	Denis Boucher	.05
849	Kyle Abbott	.10
850	Bob Zupcic	.05
851	*Rheal Cormier*	.15
852	*Jim Lewis*	.05
853	Anthony Telford	.05
854	*Cliff Brantley*	.05
855	*Kevin Campbell*	.05
856	*Craig Shipley*	.05
857	Chuck Carr	.05
858	*Tony Eusebio*	.05
859	Jim Thome	.25

860	*Vinny Castilla*	1.00
861	Dann Howitt	.05
862	Kevin Ward	.05
863	*Steve Wapnick*	.05
864	Rod Brewer	.05
865	Todd Van Poppel	.08
866	*Jose Hernandez*	.05
867	*Amalio Carreno*	.05
868	*Calvin Jones*	.05
869	*Jeff Gardner*	.05
870	*Jarvis Brown*	.05
871	*Eddie Taubensee*	.05
872	*Andy Mota*	.05
873	Chris Haney (Front photo actually Scott Ruskin)	.05
874	Roberto Hernandez	.10
875	*Laddie Renfroe*	.05
876	Scott Cooper	.05
877	*Armando Reynoso*	.05
878	Ty Cobb (Memorabilia)	.30
879	Babe Ruth (Memorabilia)	.40
880	Honus Wagner (Memorabilia)	.20
881	Lou Gehrig (Memorabilia)	.30
882	Satchel Paige (Memorabilia)	.20
883	Will Clark (Dream Team)	.20
884	Cal Ripken, Jr. (Dream Team)	.35
885	Wade Boggs (Dream Team)	.20
886	Kirby Puckett (Dream Team)	.30
887	Tony Gwynn (Dream Team)	.30
889	Scott Erickson (Dream Team)	.05
890	Tom Glavine (Dream Team)	.15
891	Rob Dibble (Dream Team)	.05
892	Mitch Williams (Dream Team)	.05
893	Frank Thomas (Dream Team)	1.00

1992 Score Factory Inserts

Game 6

Available exclusively in factory sets these 17 cards are divided into four subsets commemorating the 1991 World Series, potential Hall of Famers, the career of Joe DiMaggio and Carl Yastrzemski's 1967 Triple Crown season. Cards carry a "B" prefix to the card number.

		MT
Complete Set (17):		10.00
Common World Series (1-7):		.20
Common Cooperstown (8-11):		1.00
Common DiMaggio (12-14):		.50
Common Yastrzemski (15-17):		.25
1	World Series Game 1(Greg Gagne)	.20
2	World Series Game 2(Scott Leius)	.20
3	World Series Game 3(David Justice, Brian Harper)	.20
4	World Series Game 4(Lonnie Smith, Brian Harper)	.20
5	World Series Game 5(David Justice)	.40
6	World Series Game 6(Kirby Puckett)	.75
7	World Series Game 7(Gene Larkin)	.20
8	Carlton Fisk (Cooperstown)	.60
9	Ozzie Smith (Cooperstown)	1.00
10	Dave Winfield (Cooperstown)	1.00
11	Robin Yount (Cooperstown)	1.00
12	Joe DiMaggio (The Hard Hitter)	1.00
13	Joe DiMaggio (The Stylish Fielder)	1.00
14	Joe DiMaggio (The Champion Player)	1.00
15	Carl Yastrzemski (The Impossible Dream)	.25
16	Carl Yastrzemski (The Triple Crown)	.25
17	Carl Yastrzemski (The World Series)	.25

1992 Score Hot Rookies

This 10-card rookie issue was produced as an insert in special blister packs of 1992 Score cards sold at retail outlets. Action photos on front and portraits on back are set against white backgrounds with orange highlights. Cards are standard 2-1/2" x 3-1/2".

		MT
Complete Set (10):		60.00
Common Player:		2.00
1	Cal Eldred	2.00
2	Royce Clayton	4.00
3	Kenny Lofton	35.00
4	Todd Van Poppel	2.00
5	Scott Cooper	3.00
6	Todd Hundley	5.00
7	Tino Martinez	5.00
8	Anthony Telford	2.00
9	Derek Bell	9.00
10	Reggie Jefferson	2.00

1992 Score Impact Players

Scott Cooper - 3B

Jumbo packs of 1992 Score Series I and II cards contained five of these special inserts labeled "90's Impact Players". Front action photos contrast with portrait photos on the backs, which are color-coded by team. Cards #1-45 were packaged with Series I, cards #46-90 were included in Series II packs.

		MT
Complete Set (90):		20.00
Common Player:		.10
1	Chuck Knoblauch	.25
2	Jeff Bagwell	1.00
3	Juan Guzman	.10
4	Milt Cuyler	.10
5	Ivan Rodriguez	.50
6	Rich DeLucia	.10
7	Orlando Merced	.10
8	Ray Lankford	.20
9	Brian Hunter	.10
10	Roberto Alomar	.60
11	Wes Chamberlain	.10
12	Steve Avery	.15
13	Scott Erickson	.10
14	Jim Abbott	.15
15	Mark Whiten	.10
16	Leo Gomez	.10
17	Doug Henry	.10
18	Brent Mayne	.10
19	Charles Nagy	.10
20	Phil Plantier	.10
21	Mo Vaughn	.60
22	Craig Biggio	.20
23	Derek Bell	.20
24	Royce Clayton	.15
25	Gary Cooper	.10
26	Scott Cooper	.10
27	Juan Gonzalez	1.00
28	Ken Griffey, Jr.	3.00
29	Larry Walker	.35
30	John Smoltz	.20
31	Todd Hundley	.15
32	Kenny Lofton	.75
33	Andy Mota	.10
34	Todd Zeile	.10
35	Arthur Rhodes	.10
36	Jim Thome	.25
37	Todd Van Poppel	.10
38	Mark Wohlers	.10
39	Anthony Young	.10
40	Sandy Alomar Jr.	.15
41	John Olerud	.25
42	Robin Ventura	.25
43	Frank Thomas	2.50
44	Dave Justice	.50
45	Hal Morris	.10
46	Ruben Sierra	.10
47	Travis Fryman	.10
48	Mike Mussina	.20
49	Tom Glavine	.15
50	Barry Larkin	.20
51	Will Clark	.30
52	Jose Canseco	.45
53	Bo Jackson	.25
54	Dwight Gooden	.15
55	Barry Bonds	1.00
56	Fred McGriff	.40
57	Roger Clemens	.75
58	Benito Santiago	.10
59	Darryl Strawberry	.15
60	Cecil Fielder	.20
61	John Franco	.10
62	Matt Williams	.25
63	Marquis Grissom	.15
64	Danny Tartabull	.10
65	Ron Gant	.20
66	Paul O'Neill	.15
67	Devon White	.10
68	Rafael Palmeiro	.25
69	Tom Gordon	.12
70	Shawon Dunston	.15
71	Rob Dibble	.10
72	Eddie Zosky	.10
73	Jack McDowell	.10
74	Len Dykstra	.10
75	Ramon Martinez	.12
76	Reggie Sanders	.20
77	Greg Maddux	1.50
78	Ellis Burks	.20
79	John Smiley	.10
80	Roberto Kelly	.10
81	Ben McDonald	.10
82	Mark Lewis	.10
83	Jose Rijo	.10
84	Ozzie Guillen	.10
85	Lance Dickson	.10
86	Kim Batiste	.10
87	Gregg Olson	.10
88	Andy Benes	.15
89	Cal Eldred	.10
90	David Cone	.15

1992 Score Joe DiMaggio

Colorized vintage photos are featured on the front and back of each of five Joe DiMaggio tribute cards which were issued as random inserts in 1992 Score Series I packs. A limited number (1,800) of each card were autographed. Curiously, the cards carry a 1993 copyright date.

		MT
Complete Set (5):		100.00
Common Player:		25.00
Autographed Card:		450.00
1	Joe DiMaggio (The Minors)	25.00
2	Joe DiMaggio (The Rookie)	25.00
3	Joe DiMaggio (The MVP)	25.00
4	Joe DiMaggio (The Streak)	25.00
5	Joe DiMaggio (The Legend)	25.00

1992 Score Rookie & Traded

This 110-card set features traded players, free agents and top rookies from 1992. The cards are styled after the regular 1992 Score cards. Cards 80-110 feature the rookies. The set was released as a boxed set and was available only through hobby dealers.

		MT
Complete Set (110):		20.00
Common Player:		.05
1	Gary Sheffield	.30
2	Kevin Seitzer	.05
3	Danny Tartabull	.08
4	Steve Sax	.05
5	Bobby Bonilla	.08
6	Frank Viola	.05
7	Dave Winfield	.45
8	Rick Sutcliffe	.05
9	Jose Canseco	.65
10	Greg Swindell	.05
11	Eddie Murray	.40
12	Randy Myers	.05
13	Wally Joyner	.08
14	Kenny Lofton	8.00
15	Jack Morris	.05
16	Charlie Hayes	.05
17	Pete Incaviglia	.05
18	Kevin Mitchell	.08
19	Kurt Stillwell	.05
20	Bret Saberhagen	.05
21	Steve Buechele	.05
22	John Smiley	.05
23	Sammy Sosa	4.00
24	George Bell	.05
25	Curt Schilling	.05
26	Dick Schofield	.05
27	David Cone	.05

28	Dan Gladden	.05
29	Kirk McCaskill	.05
30	Mike Gallego	.05
31	Kevin McReynolds	.05
32	Bill Swift	.05
33	Dave Martinez	.05
34	Storm Davis	.05
35	Willie Randolph	.05
36	Melido Perez	.05
37	Mark Carreon	.05
38	Doug Jones	.05
39	Gregg Jefferies	.20
40	Mike Jackson	.05
41	Dickie Thon	.05
42	Eric King	.05
43	Herm Winningham	.05
44	Derek Lilliquist	.05
45	Dave Anderson	.05
46	Jeff Reardon	.05
47	Scott Bankhead	.05
48	Cory Snyder	.05
49	Al Newman	.05
50	Keith Miller	.05
51	Dave Burba	.05
52	Bill Pecota	.05
53	Chuck Crim	.05
54	Mariano Duncan	.05
55	Dave Gallagher	.05
56	Chris Gwynn	.05
57	Scott Ruskin	.05
58	Jack Armstrong	.05
59	Gary Carter	.10
60	Andres Galarraga	.30
61	Ken Hill	.15
62	Eric Davis	.08
63	Ruben Sierra	.08
64	Darrin Fletcher	.05
65	Tim Belcher	.05
66	Mike Morgan	.05
67	Scott Scudder	.05
68	Tom Candiotti	.05
69	Hubie Brooks	.05
70	Kal Daniels	.05
71	Bruce Ruffin	.05
72	Billy Hatcher	.05
73	Bob Melvin	.05
74	Lee Guetterman	.05
75	Rene Gonzales	.05
76	Kevin Bass	.05
77	Tom Bolton	.05
78	John Wetteland	.20
79	Bip Roberts	.05
80	Pat Listach	.10
81	John Doherty	.08
82	Sam Militello	.05
83	*Brian Jordan*	1.50
84	Jeff Kent	.60
85	Dave Fleming	.15
86	Jeff Tackett	.05
87	*Chad Curtis*	.50
88	Eric Fox	.05
89	Denny Neagle	.25
90	Donovan Osborne	.10
91	Carlos Hernandez	.05
92	Tim Wakefield	.10
93	Tim Salmon	5.00
94	Dave Nilsson	.25
95	Mike Perez	.12
96	Pat Hentgen	.30
97	Frank Seminara	.05
98	Ruben Amaro, Jr.	.05
99	Archi Cianfrocco	.05
100	Andy Stankiewicz	.05
101	Jim Bullinger	.08
102	Pat Mahomes	.15
103	Hipolito Pichardo	.05
104	Bret Boone	.50
105	John Vander Wal	.15
106	Vince Horsman	.05
107	James Austin	.05
108	Brian Williams	.05
109	Dan Walters	.05
110	Wil Cordero	1.00

1992 Score Rookies

A selection of 40 1992 rookie players is featured in this boxed set. Fronts have green borders with a red and white "1992 ROOKIE" notation printed vertically to the left of a color action photo. Backs repeat the notation on a graduated blue background with a player color portrait photo at top, biographical details and a career summary at center and appropriate logos at bottom.

		MT
Complete Set (40):		6.00
Common Player:		.10
1	Todd Van Poppel	.10
2	Kyle Abbott	.15
3	Derek Bell	.25
4	Jim Thome	.25
5	Mark Wohlers	.10
6	Todd Hundley	.25
7	Arthur Rhodes	.10
8	John Ramos	.10
9	Chris George	.10
10	Kenny Lofton	2.00
11	Ted Wood	.10
12	Royce Clayton	.35
13	Scott Cooper	.10
14	Anthony Young	.10
15	Joel Johnston	.10
16	Andy Mota	.10
17	Lenny Webster	.10
18	Andy Ashby	.10
19	Jose Mota	.10
20	Tim McIntosh	.10
21	Terry Bross	.10
22	Harvey Pulliam	.10
23	Hector Fajardo	.10
24	Esteban Beltre	.10
25	Gary DiSarcina	.15
26	Mike Humphreys	.10
27	Jarvis Brown	.10
28	Gary Cooper	.10
29	Chris Donnels	.10
30	Monty Fariss	.10
31	Eric Karros	.65
32	Braulio Castillo	.10
33	Cal Eldred	.15
34	Tom Goodwin	.10
35	Reggie Sanders	.75
36	Scott Servais	.15
37	Kim Batiste	.10
38	Eric Wedge	.10
39	Willie Banks	.10
40	Mo Sanford	.10

1992 Score The Franchise

CARL YASTRZEMSKI

This four-card set, in both autographed and unautographed form, was a random insert in various premium packaging of Score's 1992 Series II cards. Each of the four cards was produced in an edition of 150,000, with 2,000 of each player's card being autographed and 500 of the triple-player card carrying the autographs of all three superstars.

		MT
Complete Set (4):		30.00
Common Player:		8.00
Musial Autograph:		200.00
Mantle Autograph:		400.00
Yastrzemski Autograph:		150.00
Triple Autograph:		1000.
1	Stan Musial	8.00
2	Mickey Mantle	12.00
3	Carl Yastrzemski	8.00
4	Stan Musial, Mickey Mantle, Carl Yastrzemski	9.00

1993 Score

CHUCK KNOBLAUCH

Score's 1993 cards have white borders surrounding color action photographs. The player's name is at the bottom of the card, while his team's name and position appears on the left side in a color band. Backs have color portraits, statistics and text. Subsets feature rookies, award winners, draft picks, highlights, World Series highlights, all-star caricatures, dream team players, and the Man of the Year (Kirby Puckett). Insert sets include: Boys of Summer, the Franchise and Stat Leaders, which feature Select's card design.

		MT
Complete Set (660):		30.00
Common Player:		.05
Wax Box:		18.00
1	Ken Griffey, Jr.	1.50
2	Gary Sheffield	.20
3	Frank Thomas	1.50
4	Ryne Sandberg	.40
5	Larry Walker	.20
6	Cal Ripken, Jr.	1.25
7	Roger Clemens	.75
8	Bobby Bonilla	.10
9	Carlos Baerga	.10
10	Darren Daulton	.08
11	Travis Fryman	.08
12	Andy Van Slyke	.05
13	Jose Canseco	.20
14	Roberto Alomar	.35
15	Tom Glavine	.10
16	Barry Larkin	.15
17	Gregg Jefferies	.08
18	Craig Biggio	.10
19	Shane Mack	.05
20	Brett Butler	.08
21	Dennis Eckersley	.10
22	Will Clark	.20
23	Don Mattingly	.50
24	Tony Gwynn	.75
25	Ivan Rodriguez	.30
26	Shawon Dunston	.08
27	Mike Mussina	.30
28	Marquis Grissom	.08
29	Charles Nagy	.05
30	Len Dykstra	.08
31	Cecil Fielder	.10
32	Jay Bell	.05
33	B.J. Surhoff	.05
34	Bob Tewksbury	.05
35	Danny Tartabull	.05
36	Terry Pendleton	.05
37	Jack Morris	.05
38	Hal Morris	.05
39	Luis Polonia	.05
40	Ken Caminiti	.15
41	Robin Ventura	.10
42	Darryl Strawberry	.08
43	Wally Joyner	.08
44	Fred McGriff	.15
45	Kevin Tapani	.05
46	Matt Williams	.15
47	Robin Yount	.20
48	Ken Hill	.05
49	Edgar Martinez	.08
50	Mark Grace	.15
51	Juan Gonzalez	.75
52	Curt Schilling	.05
53	Dwight Gooden	.10
54	Chris Hoiles	.05
55	Frank Viola	.05
56	Ray Lankford	.10
57	George Brett	.40
58	Kenny Lofton	.50
59	Nolan Ryan	1.00
60	Mickey Tettleton	.05
61	John Smoltz	.10
62	Howard Johnson	.05
63	Eric Karros	.08
64	Rick Aguilera	.05
65	Steve Finley	.05
66	Mark Langston	.05
67	Bill Swift	.05
68	John Olerud	.15
69	Kevin McReynolds	.05
70	Jack McDowell	.05
71	Rickey Henderson	.10
72	Brian Harper	.05
73	Mike Morgan	.05
74	Rafael Palmeiro	.15
75	Dennis Martinez	.08
76	Tino Martinez	.15
77	Eddie Murray	.20
78	Ellis Burks	.10
79	John Kruk	.05
80	Gregg Olson	.05
81	Bernard Gilkey	.10
82	Milt Cuyler	.05
83	Mike LaValliere	.05
84	Albert Belle	.40
85	Bip Roberts	.05
86	Melido Perez	.05
87	Otis Nixon	.05
88	Bill Spiers	.05
89	Jeff Bagwell	.75
90	Orel Hershiser	.08
91	Andy Benes	.10
92	Devon White	.05
93	Willie McGee	.05
94	Ozzie Guillen	.05
95	Ivan Calderon	.05
96	Keith Miller	.05
97	Steve Buechele	.05
98	Kent Hrbek	.08
99	Dave Hollins	.05
100	Mike Bordick	.05
101	Randy Tomlin	.05
102	Omar Vizquel	.05
103	Lee Smith	.08
104	Leo Gomez	.05
105	Jose Rijo	.05
106	Mark Whiten	.05
107	Dave Justice	.15
108	Eddie Taubensee	.05
109	Lance Johnson	.05
110	Felix Jose	.05
111	Mike Harkey	.05
112	Randy Milligan	.05
113	Anthony Young	.05
114	Rico Brogna	.05
115	Bret Saberhagen	.05
116	Sandy Alomar, Jr.	.10
117	Terry Mulholland	.05
118	Darryl Hamilton	.05
119	Todd Zeile	.10
120	Bernie Williams	.35
121	Zane Smith	.05
122	Derek Bell	.10
123	Deion Sanders	.20
124	Luis Sojo	.05
125	Joe Oliver	.05
126	Craig Grebeck	.05
127	Andujar Cedeno	.05

#	Player	Price	#	Player	Price	#	Player	Price
128	Brian McRae	.05	224	*Brad Brink*	.05	320	*Mark Clark*	.08
129	Jose Offerman	.05	225	*Barry Manual*	.05	321	Pedro Martinez	.20
130	Pedro Munoz	.05	226	*Kevin Koslofski*	.05	322	*Al Martin*	.10
131	Bud Black	.05	227	*Ryan Thompson*	.10	323	Mike Macfarlane	.05
132	Mo Vaughn	.40	228	*Mike Munoz*	.05	324	*Rey Sanchez*	.08
133	Bruce Hurst	.05	229	*Dan Wilson*	.10	325	*Roger Pavlik*	.05
134	Dave Henderson	.05	230	*Peter Hoy*	.08	326	Troy Neel	.10
135	Tom Pagnozzi	.05	231	*Pedro Astacio*	.20	327	*Kerry Woodson*	.05
136	Erik Hanson	.05	232	Matt Stairs	.05	328	*Wayne Kirby*	.08
137	Orlando Merced	.05	233	*Jeff Reboulet*	.05	329	*Ken Ryan*	.15
138	Dean Palmer	.08	234	*Manny Alexander*	.08	330	*Jesse Levis*	.05
139	John Franco	.05	235	Willie Banks	.05	331	James Austin	.05
140	Brady Anderson	.15	236	*John Jaha*	.10	332	Dan Walters	.05
141	Ricky Jordan	.05	237	*Scooter Tucker*	.08	333	Brian Williams	.05
142	Jeff Blauser	.05	238	*Russ Springer*	.05	334	Wil Cordero	.10
143	Sammy Sosa	.75	239	*Paul Miller*	.05	335	Bret Boone	.10
144	Bob Walk	.05	240	*Dan Peltier*	.05	336	Hipolito Pichardo	.05
145	Delino DeShields	.08	241	*Ozzie Canseco*	.05	337	Pat Mahomes	.05
146	Kevin Brown	.08	242	*Ben Rivera*	.05	338	Andy Stankiewicz	.05
147	Mark Lemke	.05	243	*John Valentin*	.20	339	Jim Bullinger	.05
148	Chuck Knoblauch	.20	244	Henry Rodriguez	.08	340	Archi Cianfrocco	.05
149	Chris Sabo	.05	245	*Derek Parks*	.05	341	Ruben Amaro, Jr.	.05
150	Bobby Witt	.05	246	Carlos Garcia	.10	342	Frank Seminara	.05
151	Luis Gonzalez	.05	247	*Tim Pugh*	.10	343	Pat Hentgen	.05
152	Ron Karkovice	.05	248	*Melvin Nieves*	.10	344	Dave Nilsson	.05
153	Jeff Brantley	.05	249	*Rich Amaral*	.05	345	Mike Perez	.05
154	Kevin Appier	.05	250	*Willie Greene*	.15	346	Tim Salmon	.40
155	Darrin Jackson	.05	251	*Tim Scott*	.05	347	*Tim Wakefield*	.15
156	Kelly Gruber	.05	252	*Dave Silvestri*	.08	348	Carlos Hernandez	.05
157	Royce Clayton	.08	253	*Rob Mallicoat*	.05	349	Donovan Osborne	.05
158	Chuck Finley	.05	254	*Donald Harris*	.08	350	Denny Naegle	.10
159	Jeff King	.05	255	*Craig Colbert*	.05	351	Sam Militello	.05
160	Greg Vaughn	.05	256	Jose Guzman	.05	352	Eric Fox	.05
161	Geronimo Pena	.05	257	*Domingo Martinez*	.05	353	John Doherty	.05
162	Steve Farr	.05	258	*William Suero*	.05	354	Chad Curtis	.05
163	Jose Oquendo	.05	259	*Juan Guerrero*	.05	355	Jeff Tackett	.05
164	Mark Lewis	.05	260	*J.T. Snow*	.50	356	Dave Fleming	.05
165	John Wetteland	.05	261	Tony Pena	.05	357	Pat Listach	.05
166	Mike Henneman	.05	262	*Tim Fortugno*	.05	358	Kevin Wickander	.05
167	Todd Hundley	.10	263	*Tom Marsh*	.05	359	John VanderWal	.05
168	Wes Chamberlain	.05	264	*Kurt Knudsen*	.05	360	Arthur Rhodes	.05
169	Steve Avery	.05	265	*Tim Costo*	.05	361	Bob Scanlan	.05
170	Mike Devereaux	.05	266	*Steve Shifflett*	.05	362	Bob Zupcic	.05
171	Reggie Sanders	.10	267	*Billy Ashley*	.20	363	Mel Rojas	.05
172	Jay Buhner	.15	268	Jerry Nielsen	.05	364	Jim Thome	.30
173	Eric Anthony	.05	269	*Pete Young*	.05	365	Bill Pecota	.05
174	John Burkett	.05	270	*Johnny Guzman*	.05	366	Mark Carreon	.05
175	Tom Candiotti	.05	271	Greg Colbrunn	.10	367	Mitch Williams	.05
176	Phil Plantier	.05	272	Jeff Nelson	.05	368	Cal Eldred	.05
177	Doug Henry	.05	273	*Kevin Young*	.08	369	Stan Belinda	.05
178	Scott Leius	.05	274	Jeff Frye	.08	370	Pat Kelly	.05
179	Kirt Manwaring	.05	275	*J.T. Bruett*	.05	371	Pheal Cormier	.05
180	Jeff Parrett	.05	276	*Todd Pratt*	.05	372	Juan Guzman	.05
181	Don Slaught	.05	277	*Mike Butcher*	.05	373	Damon Berryhill	.05
182	Scott Radinsky	.05	278	*John Flaherty*	.10	374	Gary DiSarcina	.05
183	Luis Alicea	.05	279	*John Patterson*	.08	375	Norm Charlton	.05
184	Tom Gordon	.05	280	*Eric Hillman*	.05	376	Roberto Hernandez	.05
185	Rick Wilkins	.05	281	*Bien Figueros*	.05	377	Scott Kamieniecki	.05
186	Todd Stottlemyre	.05	282	*Shane Reynolds*	.10	378	Rusty Meacham	.05
187	Moises Alou	.15	283	*Rich Rowland*	.05	379	Kurt Stillwell	.05
188	Joe Grahe	.05	284	*Steve Foster*	.05	380	Lloyd McClendon	.05
189	Jeff Kent	.05	285	*Dave Mlicki*	.05	381	Mark Leonard	.05
190	Bill Wegman	.05	286	Mike Piazza	1.50	382	Jerry Browne	.05
191	Kim Batiste	.05	287	*Mike Trombley*	.08	383	Glenn Davis	.05
192	Matt Nokes	.05	288	*Jim Pena*	.05	384	Randy Johnson	.25
193	Mark Wohlers	.05	289	*Bob Ayrault*	.08	385	Mike Greenwell	.05
194	Paul Sorrento	.05	290	*Henry Mercedes*	.08	386	Scott Chiamparino	.05
195	Chris Hammond	.05	291	Bob Wickman	.05	387	George Bell	.05
196	Scott Livingstone	.05	292	*Jacob Brumfield*	.05	388	Steve Olin	.05
197	Doug Jones	.05	293	*David Hulse*	.10	389	Chuck McElroy	.05
198	Scott Cooper	.05	294	Ryan Klesko	.40	390	Mark Gardner	.05
199	Ramon Martinez	.08	295	Doug Linton	.05	391	Rod Beck	.05
200	Dave Valle	.05	296	Steve Cooke	.05	392	Dennis Rasmussen	.05
201	Mariano Duncan	.05	297	Eddie Zosky	.05	393	Charlie Leibrandt	.05
202	Ben McDonald	.05	298	Gerald Williams	.08	394	Julio Franco	.05
203	Darren Lewis	.05	299	*Jonathan Hurst*	.08	395	Pete Harnisch	.05
204	Kenny Rogers	.05	300	*Larry Carter*	.05	396	Sid Bream	.05
205	Manuel Lee	.05	301	*William Pennyfeather*	.05	397	Milt Thompson	.05
206	Scott Erickson	.05	302	*Cesar Hernandez*	.05	398	Glenallen Hill	.05
207	Dan Gladden	.05	303	*Steve Hosey*	.08	399	Chico Walker	.05
208	Bob Welch	.05	304	*Blas Minor*	.08	400	Alex Cole	.05
209	Greg Olson	.05	305	*Jeff Grotewold*	.05	401	Trevor Wilson	.05
210	Dan Pasqua	.05	306	*Bernardo Brito*	.05	402	Jeff Conine	.05
211	Tim Wallach	.05	307	*Rafael Bournigal*	.08	403	Kyle Abbott	.05
212	Jeff Montgomery	.05	308	*Jeff Branson*	.08	404	Tom Browning	.05
213	Derrick May	.05	309	*Tom Quinlan*	.05	405	Jerald Clark	.05
214	Ed Sprague	.05	310	*Pat Gomez*	.08	406	Vince Horsman	.05
215	David Haas	.05	311	*Sterling Hitchcock*	.10	407	Kevin Mitchell	.05
216	Darrin Fletcher	.05	312	*Kent Bottenfield*	.08	408	Pete Smith	.05
217	Brian Jordan	.10	313	Alan Trammell	.08	409	Jeff Innis	.05
218	Jaime Navarro	.05	314	Cris Colon	.05	410	Mike Timlin	.05
219	Randy Velarde	.05	315	*Paul Wagner*	.05	411	Charlie Hayes	.05
220	Ron Gant	.10	316	*Matt Maysey*	.05	412	Alex Fernandez	.05
221	Paul Quantrill	.05	317	Mike Stanton	.05	413	Jeff Russell	.05
222	Damion Easley	.05	318	*Rick Trlicek*	.05	414	Jody Reed	.05
223	Charlie Hough	.05	319	*Kevin Rogers*	.08	415	Mickey Morandini	.05

416	Darnell Coles	.05
417	Xavier Hernandez	.05
418	Steve Sax	.05
419	Joe Girardi	.05
420	Mike Fetters	.05
421	Danny Jackson	.05
422	Jim Gott	.05
423	Tim Belcher	.05
424	Jose Mesa	.05
425	Junior Felix	.05
426	Thomas Howard	.05
427	Julio Valera	.05
428	Dante Bichette	.25
429	Mike Sharperson	.05
430	Darryl Kile	.05
431	Lonnie Smith	.05
432	Monty Fariss	.05
433	Reggie Jefferson	.05
434	Bob McClure	.05
435	Craig Lefferts	.05
436	Duane Ward	.05
437	Shawn Abner	.05
438	Roberto Kelly	.05
439	Paul O'Neill	.08
440	Alan Mills	.05
441	Roger Mason	.05
442	Gary Pettis	.05
443	Steve Lake	.05
444	Gene Larkin	.05
445	Larry Anderson	.05
446	Doug Dascenzo	.05
447	Daryl Boston	.05
448	John Candelaria	.05
449	Storm Davis	.05
450	Tom Edens	.05
451	Mike Maddux	.05
452	Tim Naehring	.05
453	John Orton	.05
454	Joey Cora	.05
455	Chuck Crim	.05
456	Dan Plesac	.05
457	Mike Bielecki	.05
458	*Terry Jorgensen*	.05
459	John Habyan	.05
460	Pete O'Brien	.05
461	Jeff Treadway	.05
462	Frank Castillo	.05
463	Jimmy Jones	.05
464	Tommy Greene	.05
465	Tracy Woddson	.06
466	Rich Rodriguez	.05
467	Joe Hesketh	.05
468	Greg Myers	.05
469	Kirk McCaskill	.05
470	Ricky Bones	.05
471	Lenny Webster	.05
472	Francisco Cabrera	.05
473	Turner Ward	.05
474	Dwayne Henry	.05
475	Al Osuna	.05
476	Craig Wilson	.05
477	Chris Nabholz	.05
478	Rafael Belliard	.05
479	Terry Leach	.05
480	Tim Teufel	.05
481	Dennis Eckersley (Award Winner)	.08
482	Barry Bonds (Award Winner)	.20
483	Dennis Eckersley (Award Winner)	.08
484	Greg Maddux (Award Winner)	.50
485	Pat Listach (ROY)	.08
486	Eric Karros (ROY)	.15
487	*Jamie Arnold*	.10
488	B.J. Wallace	.10
489	*Derek Jeter*	4.00
490	*Jason Kendall*	.75
491	Rick Helling	.08
492	*Derek Wallace*	.15
493	Sean Lowe	.10
494	*Shannon Stewart*	.15
495	*Benji Grigsby*	.15
496	*Todd Steverson*	.15
497	*Dan Serafini*	.15
498	Michael Tucker	.10
499	Chris Roberts (Draft Pick)	.08
500	Pete Janicki (Draft Pick)	.08
501	*Jeff Schmidt*	.10
502	Edgar Martinez (All-Star)	.05
503	Omar Vizquel (AS)	.05
504	Ken Griffey, Jr. (AS)	.75
505	Kirby Puckett (AS)	.25
506	Joe Carter (AS)	.10
507	Ivan Rodriguez (AS)	.15

508	Jack Morris (AS)	.05
509	Dennis Eckersley (AS)	.05
510	Frank Thomas (AS)	.75
511	Roberto Alomar (AS)	.15
512	Mickey Morandini (Highlight)	.05
513	Dennis Eckersley (Highlight)	.08
514	Jeff Reardon (Highlight)	.05
515	Danny Tartabull (Highlight)	.05
516	Bip Roberts (Highlight)	.05
517	George Brett (Highlight)	.30
518	Robin Yount (Highlight)	.15
519	Kevin Gross (Highlight)	.05
520	Ed Sprague (World Series Highlight)	.05
521	Dave Winfield (World Series Highlight)	.10
522	Ozzie Smith (AS)	.15
523	Barry Bonds (AS)	.15
524	Andy Van Slyke (AS)	.05
525	Tony Gwynn (AS)	.30
526	Darren Daulton (AS)	.05
527	Greg Maddux (AS)	.50
528	Fred McGriff (AS)	.08
529	Lee Smith (AS)	.05
530	Ryne Sandberg (AS)	.25
531	Gary Sheffield (AS)	.15
532	Ozzie Smith (Dream Team)	.15
533	Kirby Puckett (Dream Team)	.25
534	Gary Sheffield (Dream Team)	.15
535	Andy Van Slyke (Dream Team)	.05
536	Ken Griffey, Jr. (Dream Team)	.75
537	Ivan Rodriguez (Dream Team)	.10
538	Charles Nagy (Dream Team)	.05
539	Tom Glavine (Dream Team)	.10
540	Dennis Eckersley (Dream Team)	.08
541	Frank Thomas (Dream Team)	.75
542	Roberto Alomar (Dream Team)	.15
543	Sean Barry	.05
544	Mike Schooler	.05
545	Chuck Carr	.05
546	Lenny Harris	.05
547	Gary Scott	.05
548	Derek Lilliquist	.05
549	Brian Hunter	.05
550	Kirby Puckett (MOY)	.25
551	Jim Eisenreich	.05
552	Andre Dawson	.10
553	David Nied	.05
554	Spike Owen	.05
555	Greg Gagne	.05
556	Sid Fernandez	.05
557	Mark McGwire	2.00
558	Bryan Harvey	.05
559	Harold Reynolds	.05
560	Barry Bonds	.40
561	*Eric Wedge*	.10
562	Ozzie Smith	.35
563	Rick Sutcliffe	.05
564	Jeff Reardon	.05
565	*Alex Arias*	.05
566	Greg Swindell	.05
567	Brook Jacoby	.05
568	Pete Incaviglia	.05
569	*Butch Henry*	.08
570	Eric Davis	.08
571	Kevin Seitzer	.05
572	Tony Fernandez	.05
573	*Steve Reed*	.08
574	Cory Snyder	.05
575	Joe Carter	.15
576	Greg Maddux	1.00
577	Bert Blyleven	.05
578	Kevin Bass	.05
579	Carlton Fisk	.10
580	Doug Drabek	.05
581	Mark Gubicza	.05
582	Bobby Thigpen	.05
583	Chili Davis	.08
584	Scott Bankhead	.05
585	Harold Baines	.08
586	*Eric Young*	.08
587	Lance Parrish	.08
588	Juan Bell	.05
589	Bob Ojeda	.05
590	Joe Orsulak	.05

591	Benito Santiago	.08
592	Wade Boggs	.20
593	Robby Thompson	.05
594	Erik Plunk	.05
595	Hensley Meulens	.05
596	Lou Whitaker	.05
597	Dale Murphy	.10
598	Paul Molitor	.30
599	Greg W. Harris	.05
600	Darren Holmes	.05
601	Dave Martinez	.05
602	Tom Henke	.05
603	Mike Benjamin	.05
604	Rene Gonzales	.05
605	Roger McDowell	.05
606	Kirby Puckett	.75
607	Randy Myers	.05
608	Ruben Sierra	.08
609	Wilson Alvarez	.05
610	Dave Segui	.05
611	Juan Samuel	.05
612	Tom Brunansky	.05
613	Willie Randolph	.05
614	Tony Phillips	.08
615	Candy Maldonado	.05
616	Chris Bosio	.05
617	Bret Barberie	.05
618	Scott Sanderson	.05
619	Ron Darling	.05
620	Dave Winfield	.10
621	Mike Felder	.05
622	Greg Hibbard	.05
623	Mike Scioscia	.05
624	John Smiley	.05
625	Alejandro Pena	.05
626	Terry Steinbach	.05
627	Freddie Benavides	.05
628	Kevin Reimer	.05
629	Braulio Castillo	.05
630	Dave Stieb	.05
631	Dave Magadan	.05
632	Scott Fletcher	.05
633	Cris Carpenter	.05
634	Kevin Maas	.05
635	Todd Worrell	.05
636	Rob Deer	.05
637	Dwight Smith	.05
638	Chito Martinez	.05
639	Jimmy Key	.05
640	Greg Harris	.05
641	Mike Moore	.05
642	Pat Borders	.05
643	Bill Gullickson	.05
644	Gary Gaetti	.08
645	David Howard	.05
646	Jim Abbott	.10
647	Willie Wilson	.05
648	David Wells	.05
649	Andres Galarraga	.08
650	Vince Coleman	.05
651	Rob Dibble	.05
652	Frank Tanana	.05
653	Steve Decker	.05
654	David Cone	.08
655	Jack Armstrong	.05
656	Dave Stewart	.05
657	Billy Hatcher	.05
658	Tim Raines	.08
659	Walt Weiss	.05
660	Jose Lind	.05

1993 Score Boys of Summer

These cards were available as inserts only in Score 35-card Super Packs, about one in every four packs. Borderless fronts have a color action photo of the player superimposed over the sun. The player's name is in black script in a green strip at bottom, along with a subset logo. On back is a player portrait, again with the sun as a background. Subset, company, team and major league logos are in color on the right, and there is a short career summary on the green background at bottom.

		MT
Complete Set (30):		50.00
Common Player:		.75
1	Billy Ashley	1.00
2	Tim Salmon	10.00
3	Pedro Martinez	6.00
4	Luis Mercedes	.75
5	Mike Piazza	30.00
6	Troy Neel	1.00
7	Melvin Nieves	.75
8	Ryan Klesko	8.00
9	Ryan Thompson	1.00
10	Kevin Young	1.00
11	Gerald Williams	1.00
12	Willie Greene	1.00
13	John Patterson	.75
14	Carlos Garcia	1.00
15	Eddie Zosky	.75
16	Sean Berry	1.00
17	Rico Brogna	1.00
18	Larry Carter	.75
19	Bobby Ayala	.75
20	Alan Embree	.75
21	Donald Harris	.75
22	Sterling Hitchcock	1.00
23	David Nied	.75
24	Henry Mercedes	.75
25	Ozzie Canseco	.75
26	David Hulse	.75
27	Al Martin	1.00
28	Dan Wilson	1.00
29	Paul Miller	.75
30	Rich Rowland	.75

1993 Score Gold Dream Team

This 11-player insert set consists of the same players in the regular set's Dream Team subset, except the cards are gold-foil

stamped. There is an unnumbered header card in the set, which was available only via a mail-in offer.

		MT
Complete Set (12):		12.00
Common Player:		.50
1	Ozzie Smith	1.50
2	Kirby Puckett	2.50
3	Gary Sheffield	1.00
4	Andy Van Slyke	.50
5	Ken Griffey, Jr.	5.00
6	Ivan Rodriguez	1.00
7	Charles Nagy	.50
8	Tom Glavine	.75
9	Dennis Eckersley	.75
10	Frank Thomas	4.00
11	Roberto Alomar	1.00
---	Header card	.05

1993 Score The Franchise

These glossy inserts have full-bleed color action photos against a darkened background so that the player stands out. Cards could be found in 16-card packs only; odds of finding one are 1 in every 24 packs. The fronts have gold-foil highlights.

		MT
Complete Set (28):		100.00
Common Player:		1.00
1	Cal Ripken, Jr.	25.00
2	Roger Clemens	10.00
3	Mark Langston	1.00
4	Frank Thomas	25.00
5	Carlos Baerga	1.00
6	Cecil Fielder	2.00
7	Gregg Jefferies	1.00
8	Robin Yount	4.00
9	Kirby Puckett	12.00
10	Don Mattingly	12.00
11	Dennis Eckersley	1.00
12	Ken Griffey, Jr.	30.00
13	Juan Gonzalez	10.00
14	Roberto Alomar	5.00
15	Terry Pendleton	1.00
16	Ryne Sandberg	7.00
17	Barry Larkin	3.00
18	Jeff Bagwell	12.00
19	Brett Butler	1.00
20	Larry Walker	3.00
21	Bobby Bonilla	1.50
22	Darren Daulton	1.00
23	Andy Van Slyke	1.00
24	Ray Lankford	1.00
25	Gary Sheffield	4.00
26	Will Clark	2.00
27	Bryan Harvey	1.00
28	David Nied	1.00

A player's name in *italic* type indicates a rookie card.

1994 Score

Score's 1994 set, with a new design and UV coating, was issued in two series of 330 cards each. The cards, which use more action photos than before, have dark blue borders with the player's name in a team color-coded strip at the bottom. A special Gold Rush card, done for each card in the set, is included in every pack. Series I includes American League checklists, which are printed on the backs of cards depicting panoramic views of each team's ballpark. Series II has the National League team checklists. Insert sets include Dream Team players, and National (Series I packs) and American League Gold Stars (Series II packs), which use the Gold Rush process and appear once every 18 packs.

		MT
Complete Set (660):		30.00
Common Player:		.05
Series 1 or 2 Wax Box:		36.00
1	Barry Bonds	.40
2	John Olerud	.10
3	Ken Griffey, Jr.	1.50
4	Jeff Bagwell	.60
5	John Burkett	.05
6	Jack McDowell	.05
7	Albert Belle	.30
8	Andres Galarraga	.10
9	Mike Mussina	.25
10	Will Clark	.25
11	Travis Fryman	.10
12	Tony Gwynn	.40
13	Robin Yount	.25
14	Dave Magadan	.05
15	Paul O'Neill	.05
16	Ray Lankford	.10
17	Damion Easley	.05
18	Andy Van Slyke	.05
19	Brian McRae	.05
20	Ryne Sandberg	.35
21	Kirby Puckett	.50
22	Dwight Gooden	.10
23	Don Mattingly	1.00
24	Kevin Mitchell	.05
25	Roger Clemens	.50
26	Eric Karros	.10
27	Juan Gonzalez	.50
28	John Kruk	.05
29	Gregg Jefferies	.08
30	Tom Glavine	.10
31	Ivan Rodriguez	.30
32	Jay Bell	.05
33	Randy Johnson	.15
34	Darren Daulton	.05
35	Rickey Henderson	.15
36	Eddie Murray	.20
37	Brian Harper	.05
38	Delino DeShields	.05
39	Jose Lind	.05

40	Benito Santiago	.05
41	Frank Thomas	1.50
42	Mark Grace	.15
43	Roberto Alomar	.40
44	Andy Benes	.05
45	Luis Polonia	.05
46	Brett Butler	.08
47	Terry Steinbach	.05
48	Craig Biggio	.05
49	Greg Vaughn	.05
50	Charlie Hayes	.05
51	Mickey Tettleton	.05
52	Jose Rijo	.05
53	Carlos Baerga	.20
54	Jeff Blauser	.05
55	Leo Gomez	.05
56	Bob Tewksbury	.05
57	Mo Vaughn	.30
58	Orlando Merced	.05
59	Tino Martinez	.15
60	Len Dykstra	.05
61	Jose Canseco	.25
62	Tony Fernandez	.05
63	Donovan Osborne	.05
64	Ken Hill	.05
65	Kent Hrbek	.08
66	Bryan Harvey	.05
67	Wally Joyner	.08
68	Derrick May	.05
69	Lance Johnson	.05
70	Willie McGee	.08
71	Mark Langston	.05
72	Terry Pendleton	.05
73	Joe Carter	.15
74	Barry Larkin	.15
75	Jimmy Key	.05
76	Joe Girardi	.05
77	B.J. Surhoff	.05
78	Pete Harnisch	.05
79	Lou Whitaker	.05
80	Cory Snyder	.05
81	Kenny Lofton	.50
82	Fred McGriff	.25
83	Mike Greenwell	.05
84	Mike Perez	.05
85	Cal Ripken, Jr.	1.50
86	Don Slaught	.05
87	Omar Vizquel	.05
88	Curt Schilling	.05
89	Chuck Knoblauch	.10
90	Moises Alou	.08
91	Greg Gagne	.05
92	Bret Saberhagen	.05
93	Ozzie Guillen	.05
94	Matt Williams	.15
95	Chad Curtis	.05
96	Mike Harkey	.05
97	Devon White	.05
98	Walt Weiss	.05
99	Kevin Brown	.05
100	Gary Sheffield	.15
101	Wade Boggs	.25
102	Orel Hershiser	.08
103	Tony Phillips	.08
104	Andujar Cedeno	.05
105	Bill Spiers	.05
106	Otis Nixon	.05
107	Felix Fermin	.05
108	Bip Roberts	.05
109	Dennis Eckersley	.08
110	Dante Bichette	.25
111	Ben McDonald	.05
112	Jim Poole	.05
113	John Dopson	.05
114	Rob Dibble	.05
115	Jeff Treadway	.05
116	Ricky Jordan	.05
117	Mike Henneman	.05
118	Willie Blair	.05
119	Doug Henry	.05
120	Gerald Perry	.05
121	Greg Myers	.05
122	John Franco	.05
123	Roger Mason	.05
124	Chris Hammond	.05
125	Hubie Brooks	.05
126	Kent Mercker	.05
127	Jim Abbott	.08
128	Kevin Bass	.05
129	Rick Aguilera	.05
130	Mitch Webster	.05
131	Eric Plunk	.05
132	Mark Carreon	.05
133	Dave Stewart	.05
134	Willie Wilson	.05
135	Dave Fleming	.05
136	Jeff Tackett	.05
137	Geno Petralli	.05
138	Gene Harris	.05
139	Scott Bankhead	.05
140	Trevor Wilson	.05
141	Alvaro Espinoza	.05
142	Ryan Bowen	.05
143	Mike Moore	.05
144	Bill Pecota	.05
145	Jaime Navarro	.05
146	Jack Daugherty	.05
147	Bob Wickman	.05
148	Chris Jones	.05
149	Todd Stottlemyre	.05
150	Brian Williams	.05
151	Chuck Finley	.05
152	Lenny Harris	.05
153	Alex Fernandez	.08
154	Candy Maldonado	.05
155	Jeff Montgomery	.05
156	David West	.05
157	Mark Williamson	.05
158	Milt Thompson	.05
159	Ron Darling	.05
160	Stan Belinda	.05
161	Henry Cotto	.05
162	Mel Rojas	.05
163	Doug Strange	.05
164	Rene Arocha (1993 Rookie)	.10
165	Tim Hulett	.05
166	Steve Avery	.08
167	Jim Thome	.15
168	Tom Browning	.05
169	Mario Diaz	.05
170	Steve Reed (1993 Rookie)	.05
171	Scott Livingstone	.05
172	Chris Donnels	.05
173	John Jaha	.05
174	Carlos Hernandez	.05
175	Dion James	.05
176	Bud Black	.05
177	Tony Castillo	.05
178	Jose Guzman	.05
179	Torey Lovullo	.05
180	John Vander Wal	.05
181	Mike LaValliere	.05
182	Sid Fernandez	.05
183	Brent Mayne	.05
184	Terry Mulholland	.05
185	Willie Banks	.05
186	Steve Cooke (1993 Rookie)	.05
187	Brent Gates (1993 Rookie)	.10
188	Erik Pappas (1993 Rookie)	.10
189	Bill Haselman (1993 Rookie)	.05
190	Fernando Valenzuela	.08
191	Gary Redus	.05
192	Danny Darwin	.05
193	Mark Portugal	.05
194	Derek Lilliquist	.05
195	Charlie O'Brien	.05
196	Matt Nokes	.05
197	Danny Sheaffer	.05
198	Bill Gullickson	.05
199	Alex Arias (1993 Rookie)	.10
200	Mike Fetters	.05
201	Brian Jordan	.12
202	Joe Grahe	.05
203	Tom Candiotti	.05
204	Jeremy Stanton	.05
205	Mike Stanton	.05
206	David Howard	.05
207	Darren Holmes	.05
208	Rick Honeycutt	.05
209	Danny Jackson	.05
210	Rich Amaral (1993 Rookie)	.05
211	Blas Minor (1993 Rookie)	.10
212	Kenny Rogers	.05
213	Jim Leyritz	.05
214	Mike Morgan	.05
215	Dan Gladden	.05
216	Randy Velarde	.05
217	Mitch Williams	.05
218	Hipolito Pichardo	.05
219	Dave Burba	.05
220	Wilson Alvarez	.05
221	Bob Zupcic	.05
222	Francisco Cabrera	.05
223	Julio Valera	.05
224	Paul Assenmacher	.05
225	Jeff Branson	.05
226	Todd Frohwirth	.05
227	Armando Reynoso	.05
228	Rich Rowland (1993 Rookie)	.05
229	Freddie Benavides	.05
230	Wayne Kirby (1993 Rookie)	.05
231	Darryl Kile	.05
232	Skeeter Barnes	.05
233	Ramon Martinez	.08
234	Tom Gordon	.05
235	Dave Gallagher	.05
236	Ricky Bones	.05
237	Larry Andersen	.05
238	Pat Meares (1993 Rookie)	.08
239	Zane Smith	.05
240	Tim Leary	.05
241	Phil Clark	.05
242	Danny Cox	.05
243	Mike Jackson	.05
244	Mike Gallego	.05
245	Lee Smith	.08
246	Todd Jones (1993 Rookie)	.05
247	Steve Bedrosian	.05
248	Troy Neel	.10
249	Jose Bautista	.05
250	Steve Frey	.05
251	Jeff Reardon	.05
252	Stan Javier	.05
253	Mo Sanford (1993 Rookie)	.05
254	Steve Sax	.05
255	Luis Aquino	.05
256	Domingo Jean (1993 Rookie)	.05
257	Scott Servais	.05
258	Brad Pennington (1993 Rookie)	.08
259	Dave Hansen	.05
260	Goose Gossage	.05
261	Jeff Fassero	.05
262	Junior Ortiz	.05
263	Anthony Young	.05
264	Chris Bosio	.05
265	Ruben Amaro, Jr.	.05
266	Mark Eichhorn	.05
267	Dave Clark	.05
268	Gary Thurman	.05
269	Les Lancaster	.05
270	Jamie Moyer	.05
271	Ricky Gutierrez (1993 Rookie)	.10
272	Greg Harris	.05
273	Mike Benjamin	.05
274	Gene Nelson	.05
275	Damon Berryhill	.05
276	Scott Radinsky	.05
277	Mike Aldrete	.05
278	Jerry DiPoto (1993 Rookie)	.05
279	Chris Haney	.05
280	Richie Lewis (1993 Rookie)	.05
281	Jarvis Brown	.05
282	Juan Bell	.05
283	Joe Klink	.05
284	Graeme Lloyd (1993 Rookie)	.05
285	Casey Candaele	.05
286	Bob MacDonald	.05
287	Mike Sharperson	.05
288	Gene Larkin	.05
289	Brian Barnes	.05
290	David McCarty (1993 Rookie)	.10
291	Jeff Innis	.05
292	Bob Patterson	.05
293	Ben Rivera	.05
294	John Habyan	.05
295	Rich Rodriguez	.05
296	Edwin Nunez	.05
297	Rod Brewer	.05
298	Mike Timlin	.05
299	Jesse Orosco	.05
300	Gary Gaetti	.08
301	Todd Benzinger	.05
302	Jeff Nelson	.05
303	Rafael Belliard	.05
304	Matt Whiteside	.05
305	Vinny Castilla	.08
306	Matt Turner	.05
307	Eduardo Perez	.05
308	Joel Johnston	.05
309	Chris Gomez	.10
310	Pat Rapp	.05
311	Jim Tatum	.05
312	Kirk Rueter	.05
313	John Flaherty	.05
314	Tom Kramer	.05
315	Mark Whiten (Highlights)	.05
316	Chris Bosio (Highlights)	.05
317	Orioles Checklist	.05
318	Red Sox Checklist	.05
319	Angels Checklist	.05
320	White Sox Checklist	.05

#	Name	Price	#	Name	Price	#	Name	Price
321	Indians Checklist	.05	417	John Valentin	.08	513	Bo Jackson	.15
322	Tigers Checklist	.05	418	Tim Wakefield	.05	514	Dennis Martinez	.08
323	Royals Checklist	.05	419	Jose Mesa	.05	515	Phil Hiatt	.05
324	Brewers Checklist	.05	420	Bernard Gilkey	.10	516	Jeff Kent	.10
325	Twins Checklist	.05	421	Kirk Gibson	.05	517	*Brooks Kieschnick*	.50
326	Yankees Checklist	.05	422	Dave Justice	.15	518	*Kirk Presley*	.35
327	Athletics Checklist	.05	423	Tom Brunansky	.05	519	Kevin Seitzer	.05
328	Mariners Checklist	.05	424	John Smiley	.05	520	Carlos Garcia	.05
329	Rangers Checklist	.05	425	Kevin Maas	.05	521	Mike Blowers	.05
330	Blue Jays Checklist	.05	426	Doug Drabek	.05	522	Luis Alicea	.05
331	Frank Viola	.05	427	Paul Molitor	.20	523	David Hulse	.05
332	Ron Gant	.10	428	Darryl Strawberry	.10	524	Greg Maddux	1.25
333	Charles Nagy	.05	429	Tim Naehring	.05	525	Gregg Olson	.05
334	Roberto Kelly	.05	430	Bill Swift	.05	526	Hal Morris	.05
335	Brady Anderson	.12	431	Ellis Burks	.12	527	Daron Kirkreit	.10
336	Alex Cole	.05	432	Greg Hibbard	.05	528	David Nied	.05
337	Alan Trammell	.10	433	Felix Jose	.05	529	Jeff Russell	.05
338	Derek Bell	.10	434	Bret Barberie	.05	530	Kevin Gross	.05
339	Bernie Williams	.40	435	Pedro Munoz	.05	531	John Doherty	.05
340	Jose Offerman	.05	436	Darrin Fletcher	.05	532	*Matt Brunson*	.10
341	Bill Wegman	.05	437	Bobby Witt	.05	533	Dave Nilsson	.05
342	Ken Caminiti	.10	438	Wes Chamberlain	.05	534	Randy Myers	.05
343	Pat Borders	.05	439	Mackey Sasser	.05	535	Steve Farr	.05
344	Kirt Manwaring	.05	440	Mark Whiten	.05	536	*Billy Wagner*	.30
345	Chili Davis	.05	441	Harold Reynolds	.05	537	Darnell Coles	.05
346	Steve Buechele	.05	442	Greg Olson	.05	538	Frank Tanana	.05
347	Robin Ventura	.10	443	Billy Hatcher	.05	539	Tim Salmon	.25
348	Teddy Higuera	.05	444	Joe Oliver	.05	540	Kim Batiste	.05
349	Jerry Browne	.05	445	Sandy Alomar Jr.	.08	541	George Bell	.05
350	Scott Kamieniecki	.05	446	Tim Wallach	.05	542	Tom Henke	.05
351	Kevin Tapani	.05	447	Karl Rhodes	.05	543	Sam Horn	.05
352	Marquis Grissom	.08	448	Royce Clayton	.10	544	Doug Jones	.05
353	Jay Buhner	.08	449	Cal Eldred	.05	545	Scott Leius	.05
354	Dave Hollins	.05	450	Rick Wilkins	.05	546	Al Martin	.05
355	Dan Wilson	.05	451	Mike Stanley	.05	547	Bob Welch	.05
356	Bob Walk	.05	452	Charlie Hough	.05	548	*Scott Christman*	.10
357	Chris Hoiles	.08	453	Jack Morris	.05	549	Norm Charlton	.05
358	Todd Zeile	.05	454	*Jon Ratliff*	.05	550	Mark McGwire	2.00
359	Kevin Appier	.05	455	Rene Gonzales	.05	551	Greg McMichael	.05
360	Chris Sabo	.05	456	Eddie Taubensee	.05	552	Tim Costo	.05
361	David Segui	.05	457	Roberto Hernandez	.05	553	Rodney Bolton	.05
362	Jerald Clark	.05	458	Todd Hundley	.12	554	Pedro Martinez	.05
363	Tony Pena	.05	459	Mike MacFarlane	.05	555	Marc Valdes	.05
364	Steve Finley	.05	460	Mickey Morandini	.05	556	Darrell Whitmore	.05
365	Roger Pavlik	.05	461	Scott Erickson	.05	557	Tim Bogar	.05
366	John Smoltz	.10	462	Lonnie Smith	.05	558	Steve Karsay	.10
367	Scott Fletcher	.05	463	Dave Henderson	.05	559	Danny Bautista	.05
368	Jody Reed	.05	464	Ryan Klesko	.40	560	Jeffrey Hammonds	.15
369	David Wells	.05	465	Edgar Martinez	.10	561	Aaron Sele	.10
370	Jose Vizcaino	.05	466	Tom Pagnozzi	.05	562	Russ Springer	.05
371	Pat Listach	.05	467	Charlie Leibrandt	.05	563	Jason Bere	.10
372	Orestes Destrade	.05	468	*Brian Anderson*	.10	564	Billy Brewer	.05
373	Danny Tartabull	.05	469	Harold Baines	.08	565	Sterling Hitchcock	.05
374	Greg W. Harris	.05	470	Tim Belcher	.05	566	Bobby Munoz	.05
375	Juan Guzman	.15	471	Andre Dawson	.10	567	Craig Paquette	.05
376	Larry Walker	.15	472	Eric Young	.05	568	Bret Boone	.08
377	Gary DiSarcina	.05	473	Paul Sorrento	.05	569	Dan Peltier	.05
378	Bobby Bonilla	.10	474	Luis Gonzalez	.05	570	Jeromy Burnitz	.05
379	Tim Raines	.08	475	Rob Deer	.05	571	*John Wasdin*	.15
380	Tommy Greene	.05	476	Mike Piazza	1.00	572	Chipper Jones	1.00
381	Chris Gwynn	.05	477	Kevin Reimer	.05	573	*Jamey Wright*	.10
382	Jeff King	.05	478	Jeff Gardner	.05	574	*Jeff Granger*	.10
383	Shane Mack	.05	479	Melido Perez	.05	575	*Jay Powell*	.10
384	Ozzie Smith	.25	480	Darren Lewis	.05	576	Ryan Thompson	.05
385	*Eddie Zambrano*	.10	481	Duane Ward	.05	577	Lou Frazier	.05
386	Mike Devereaux	.05	482	Rey Sanchez	.05	578	Paul Wagner	.05
387	Erik Hanson	.05	483	Mark Lewis	.05	579	Brad Ausmus	.05
388	Scott Cooper	.05	484	Jeff Conine	.08	580	Jack Voigt	.05
389	Dean Palmer	.05	485	Joey Cora	.05	581	Kevin Rogers	.05
390	John Wetteland	.05	486	*Trot Nixon*	.35	582	Damon Buford	.05
391	Reggie Jefferson	.05	487	Kevin McReynolds	.05	583	Paul Quantrill	.05
392	Mark Lemke	.05	488	Mike Lansing	.05	584	Marc Newfield	.10
393	Cecil Fielder	.12	489	Mike Pagliarulo	.05	585	*Derrek Lee*	.50
394	Reggie Sanders	.10	490	Mariano Duncan	.05	586	Shane Reynolds	.05
395	Darryl Hamilton	.05	491	Mike Bordick	.05	587	Cliff Floyd	.15
396	Daryl Boston	.05	492	Kevin Young	.05	588	Jeff Schwarz	.05
397	Pat Kelly	.05	493	Dave Valle	.05	589	*Ross Powell*	.10
398	Joe Orsulak	.05	494	*Wayne Gomes*	.10	590	Gerald Williams	.05
399	Ed Sprague	.05	495	Rafael Palmeiro	.10	591	Mike Trombley	.05
400	Eric Anthony	.05	496	Deion Sanders	.25	592	Ken Ryan	.05
401	Scott Sanderson	.05	497	Rick Sutcliffe	.05	593	John O'Donoghue	.05
402	Jim Gott	.05	498	Randy Milligan	.05	594	Rod Correia	.05
403	Ron Karkovice	.05	499	Carlos Quintana	.05	595	Darrell Sherman	.05
404	Phil Plantier	.05	500	Chris Turner	.05	596	Steve Scarsone	.05
405	David Cone	.05	501	Thomas Howard	.05	597	Sherman Obando	.05
406	Robby Thompson	.05	502	Greg Swindell	.05	598	Kurt Abbott	.05
407	Dave Winfield	.15	503	Chad Kreuter	.05	599	Dave Telgheder	.05
408	Dwight Smith	.05	504	Eric Davis	.08	600	Rick Trlicek	.05
409	Ruben Sierra	.08	505	Dickie Thon	.05	601	Carl Everett	.10
410	Jack Armstrong	.05	506	*Matt Drews*	.10	602	Luis Ortiz	.05
411	Mike Felder	.05	507	Spike Owen	.05	603	*Larry Luebbers*	.10
412	Wil Cordero	.05	508	Rod Beck	.05	604	Kevin Roberson	.10
413	Julio Franco	.05	509	Pat Hentgen	.05	605	Butch Huskey	.10
414	Howard Johnson	.05	510	Sammy Sosa	.75	606	Benji Gil	.05
415	Mark McLemore	.05	511	J.T. Snow	.08	607	Todd Van Poppel	.05
416	Pete Incaviglia	.05	512	Chuck Carr	.05	608	Mark Hutton	.05

609	Chip Hale	.05
610	Matt Maysey	.05
611	Scott Ruffcorn	.05
612	Hilly Hathaway	.05
613	Allen Watson	.10
614	Carlos Delgado	.25
615	Roberto Mejia	.05
616	Turk Wendell	.05
617	Tony Tarasco	.10
618	Raul Mondesi	.40
619	Kevin Stocker	.10
620	Javier Lopez	.25
621	*Keith Kessinger*	.15
622	Bob Hamelin	.05
623	John Roper	.05
624	Len Dykstra (World Series)	.08
625	Joe Carter (World Series)	.10
626	Jim Abbott (Highlight)	.08
627	Lee Smith (Highlight)	.08
628	Ken Griffey, Jr. (HL)	1.00
629	Dave Winfield (Highlight)	.08
630	Darryl Kile (Highlight)	.05
631	Frank Thomas (MVP)	1.00
632	Barry Bonds (MVP)	.25
633	Jack McDowell (Cy Young)	.05
634	Greg Maddux (Cy Young)	.75
635	Tim Salmon (ROY)	.15
636	Mike Piazza (ROY)	.40
637	*Brian Turang*	.15
638	Rondell White	.25
639	Nigel Wilson	.05
640	*Torii Hunter*	.10
641	Salomon Torres	.05
642	Kevin Higgins	.05
643	Eric Wedge	.05
644	Roger Salkeld	.05
645	Manny Ramirez	.50
646	Jeff McNeely	.05
647	Braves Checklist	.05
648	Cubs Checklist	.05
649	Reds Checklist	.05
650	Rockies Checklist	.05
651	Marlins Checklist	.05
652	Astros Checklist	.05
653	Dodgers Checklist	.05
654	Expos Checklist	.05
655	Mets Checklist	.05
656	Phillies Checklist	.05
657	Pirates Checklist	.05
658	Cardinals Checklist	.05
659	Padres Checklist	.05
660	Giants Checklist	.05

1994 Score Gold Rush

Opting to include one insert card in each pack of its 1994 product, Score created a "Gold Rush" version of each card in its regular set. Gold Rush cards are basically the same as their counterparts with a few enhancements. Card fronts are printed on foil with a gold border and a Score Gold Rush logo in one of the upper corners. The back-

ground of the photo has been metalized, allowing the color player portion to stand out in sharp contrast. Backs are identical to the regular cards except for the appearance of a large Gold Rush logo under the typography.

	MT
Complete Set (660):	200.00
Common Player:	.25
Stars 3X-7X:	

(Gold Rush cards are valued at 3-7X the same card in 1994 Score regular-issue.)

1994 Score Boys of Summer

A heavy emphasis on rookies and recent rookies is noted in this 1994 Score insert set. Released in two series, cards #1-30 with Score's Series I and #31-60 packaged with Series II, card fronts feature a color action photo on which the background has been rendered in a blurred watercolor effect. A hotcolor aura separates the player from the background. The player's name appears vertically in gold foil. Backs have backgrounds in reds and orange with a portrait-style player photo on one side and a large "Boys of Summer" logo on the other. A short description of the player's talents appears at center.

		MT
Complete Set (60):		130.00
Complete Series 1 (30):		65.00
Complete Series 2 (30):		65.00
Common Player:		1.00
1	Jeff Conine	2.00
2	Aaron Sele	2.00
3	Kevin Stocker	1.00
4	Pat Meares	1.00
5	Jeromy Burnitz	1.50
6	Mike Piazza	20.00
7	Allen Watson	1.00
8	Jeffrey Hammonds	2.00
9	Kevin Roberson	1.00
10	Hilly Hathaway	1.00
11	Kirk Reuter	1.00
12	Eduardo Perez	1.00
13	Ricky Gutierrez	1.00
14	Domingo Jean	1.00
15	David Nied	1.00
16	Wayne Kirby	1.00
17	Mike Lansing	2.00
18	Jason Bere	2.00
19	Brent Gates	2.00
20	Javier Lopez	6.00
21	Greg McMichael	1.00

22	David Hulse	1.00
23	Roberto Mejia	1.00
24	Tim Salmon	5.00
25	Rene Arocha	1.00
26	Bret Boone	2.00
27	David McCarty	1.00
28	Todd Van Poppel	1.00
29	Lance Painter	1.00
30	Erik Pappas	1.00
31	Chuck Carr	1.00
32	Mark Hutton	1.00
33	Jeff McNeely	1.00
34	Willie Greene	1.00
35	Nigel Wilson	1.00
36	Rondell White	5.00
37	Brian Turang	1.00
38	Manny Ramirez	15.00
39	Salomon Torres	1.00
40	Melvin Nieves	1.00
41	Ryan Klesko	9.00
42	Keith Kessinger	1.00
43	Eric Wedge	1.00
44	Bob Hamelin	1.00
45	Carlos Delgado	3.00
46	Marc Newfield	2.00
47	Raul Mondesi	10.00
48	Tim Costo	1.00
49	Pedro Martinez	3.00
50	Steve Karsay	1.50
51	Danny Bautista	1.00
52	Butch Huskey	1.50
53	Kurt Abbott	1.50
54	Darrell Sherman	1.00
55	Damon Buford	1.00
56	Ross Powell	1.00
57	Darrell Whitmore	1.00
58	Chipper Jones	20.00
59	Jeff Granger	1.00
60	Cliff Floyd	2.00

1994 Score Dream Team

Score's 1994 "Dream Team," one top player at each position, was featured in a 10-card insert set. The stars were decked out in vintage uniforms and equipment for the photos. Green and black bars at top and bottom frame the photo, and all printing on the front is in gold foil. Backs have a white background with green highlights. A color player portrait photo is featured, along with a brief justification for the player's selection to the squad. Cards are UV coated on both sides. Stated odds of finding a Dream Team insert were given as one per 72 packs.

		MT
Complete Set (10):		85.00
Common Player:		4.00
1	Mike Mussina	8.00
2	Tom Glavine	6.00

3	Don Mattingly	25.00
4	Carlos Baerga	6.00
5	Barry Larkin	7.50
6	Matt Williams	7.50
7	Juan Gonzalez	25.00
8	Andy Van Slyke	4.00
9	Larry Walker	6.00
10	Mike Stanley	4.00

1994 Score Gold Stars

Limited to inclusion in hobby packs, Score's 60-card "Gold Stars" insert set features 30 National League players, found in Series I packs, and 30 American Leaguers inserted with Series II. Stated odds of finding a Gold Stars card were listed on the wrapper as one in 18 packs. A notation on the cards' back indicates that no more than 6,500 sets of Gold Stars were produced. The high-tech cards feature a color player action photo, the full-bleed background of which has been converted to metallic tones. Backs have a graduated gold background with a portrait-style color player photo.

		MT
Complete Set (60):		140.00
Common Player:		1.00
1	Barry Bonds	8.00
2	Orlando Merced	1.00
3	Mark Grace	2.50
4	Darren Daulton	1.00
5	Jeff Blauser	1.00
6	Deion Sanders	4.00
7	John Kruk	1.00
8	Jeff Bagwell	10.00
9	Gregg Jefferies	1.00
10	Matt Williams	3.00
11	Andres Galarraga	3.00
12	Jay Bell	1.00
13	Mike Piazza	20.00
14	Ron Gant	1.00
15	Barry Larkin	2.50
16	Tom Glavine	2.00
17	Len Dykstra	1.00
18	Fred McGriff	2.00
19	Andy Van Slyke	1.00
20	Gary Sheffield	2.50
21	John Burkett	1.00
22	Dante Bichette	4.00
23	Tony Gwynn	15.00
24	Dave Justice	2.00
25	Marquis Grissom	1.50
26	Bobby Bonilla	1.00
27	Larry Walker	3.00
28	Brett Butler	1.00
29	Robby Thompson	1.00
30	Jeff Conine	1.00
31	Joe Carter	1.00
32	Ken Griffey, Jr.	30.00

33	Juan Gonzalez	15.00
34	Rickey Henderson	1.00
35	Bo Jackson	1.00
36	Cal Ripken, Jr.	25.00
37	John Olerud	1.50
38	Carlos Baerga	1.00
39	Jack McDowell	1.00
40	Cecil Fielder	1.50
41	Kenny Lofton	8.00
42	Roberto Alomar	6.00
43	Randy Johnson	4.00
44	Tim Salmon	4.00
45	Frank Thomas	20.00
46	Albert Belle	8.00
47	Greg Vaughn	1.50
48	Travis Fryman	1.00
49	Don Mattingly	8.00
50	Wade Boggs	2.00
51	Mo Vaughn	8.00
52	Kirby Puckett	8.00
53	Devon White	1.00
54	Tony Phillips	1.00
55	Brian Harper	1.00
56	Chad Curtis	1.00
57	Paul Molitor	5.00
58	Ivan Rodriguez	8.00
59	Rafael Palmeiro	2.00
60	Brian McRae	1.00

1994 Score The Cycle

Leaders in the previous season's production of singles, doubles, triples and home runs are featured in this insert set which was packaged with Series II Score. Player action photos pop out of a circle at center and are surrounded by dark blue borders. "The Cycle" in printed in green at top. The player's name is in gold foil at bottom, printed over an infield diagram in a green strip. The stat which earned the player inclusion in the set is in gold foil at bottom right. On back are the rankings for the statistical category. Cards are numbered with a "TC" prefix.

		MT
Complete Set (20):		275.00
Common Player:		5.00
1	Brett Butler	6.00
2	Kenny Lofton	25.00
3	Paul Molitor	12.00
4	Carlos Baerga	6.00
5	Gregg Jefferies, Tony Phillips	5.00
6	John Olerud	6.00
7	Charlie Hayes	5.00
8	Len Dykstra	5.00
9	Dante Bichette	8.00
10	Devon White	5.00
11	Lance Johnson	5.00
12	Joey Cora, Steve Finley	5.00

13	Tony Fernandez	5.00
14	David Hulse, Brett Butler	5.00
15	Jay Bell, Brian McRae, Mickey Morandini	5.00
16	Juan Gonzalez, Barry Bonds	20.00
17	Ken Griffey, Jr.	65.00
18	Frank Thomas	50.00
19	Dave Justice	12.00
20	Matt Williams, Albert Belle	12.00

1994 Score Rookie/Traded

Score Rookie & Traded completed the 1994 Score baseball issue with a 165-card update set. These were available in both retail and hobby packs. Score issued Super Rookies and Changing Places insert sets, as well as a Traded Redemption card and a parallel Gold Rush set. Basic cards features red front borders. Team logos are in a bottom corner in a gold polygon. One of the upper corners contains a green polygon with a gold Score logo. Most cards #71-163 feature a square multi-colored "Rookie '94" logo in a lower corner. Backs of all cards have a purple background. Traded players' card backs are vertical and contain two additional photos. Backs of the rookie cards are horizontal and feature a portrait photo at left. The "Rookie '94" logo is repeated in the upper-right corner. This is in reverse of the card fronts, on which traded players have a single photo and rookie cards have both portrait and action photos.

		MT
Complete Set (165):		8.00
Common Player:		.05
Wax Box:		25.00
1	Will Clark	.25
2	Lee Smith	.08
3	Bo Jackson	.15
4	Ellis Burks	.10
5	Eddie Murray	.15
6	Delino DeShields	.05
7	Erik Hanson	.05
8	Rafael Palmeiro	.20
9	Luis Polonia	.05
10	Omar Vizquel	.05
11	Kurt Abbott	.05
12	Vince Coleman	.05
13	Rickey Henderson	.25
14	Terry Mulholland	.05
15	Greg Hibbard	.05
16	Walt Weiss	.05
17	Chris Sabo	.05

18	Dave Henderson	.05
19	Rick Sutcliffe	.05
20	Harold Reynolds	.05
21	Jack Morris	.05
22	Dan Wilson	.05
23	Dave Magadan	.05
24	Dennis Martinez	.08
25	Wes Chamberlain	.05
26	Otis Nixon	.05
27	Eric Anthony	.05
28	Randy Milligan	.05
29	Julio Franco	.05
30	Kevin McReynolds	.05
31	Anthony Young	.05
32	Brian Harper	.05
33	Lenny Harris	.05
34	Eddie Taubensee	.05
35	David Segui	.05
36	Stan Javier	.05
37	Felix Fermin	.05
38	Darrin Jackson	.05
39	Tony Fernandez	.05
40	Jose Vizcaino	.05
41	Willie Banks	.05
42	Brian Hunter	.05
43	Reggie Jefferson	.05
44	Junior Felix	.05
45	Jack Armstrong	.05
46	Bip Roberts	.05
47	Jerry Browne	.05
48	Marvin Freeman	.05
49	Jody Reed	.05
50	Alex Cole	.05
51	Sid Fernandez	.05
52	Pete Smith	.05
53	Xavier Hernandez	.05
54	Scott Sanderson	.05
55	Turner Ward	.05
56	Rex Hudler	.05
57	Deion Sanders	.35
58	Sid Bream	.05
59	Tony Pena	.05
60	Bret Boone	.05
61	Bobby Ayala	.05
62	Pedro Martinez	.05
63	Howard Johnson	.05
64	Mark Portugal	.05
65	Roberto Kelly	.05
66	Spike Owen	.05
67	Jeff Treadway	.05
68	Mike Harkey	.05
69	Doug Jones	.05
70	Steve Farr	.05
71	Billy Taylor	.05
72	Manny Ramirez	1.00
73	Bob Hamelin	.05
74	Steve Karsay	.05
75	Ryan Klesko	.50
76	Cliff Floyd	.10
77	Jeffrey Hammonds	.20
78	Javier Lopez	.20
79	Roger Salkeld	.05
80	Hector Carrasco	.05
81	Gerald Williams	.05
82	Raul Mondesi	.75
83	Sterling Hitchcock	.05
84	Danny Bautista	.05
85	Chris Turner	.05
86	Shane Reynolds	.05
87	Rondell White	.20
88	Salomon Torres	.05
89	Turk Wendell	.05
90	Tony Tarasco	.05
91	Shawn Green	.05
92	Greg Colbrunn	.05
93	Eddie Zambrano	.05
94	Rich Becker	.05
95	Chris Gomez	.08
96	John Patterson	.05
97	Derek Parks	.05
98	Rich Rowland	.05
99	James Mouton	.10
100	Tim Hyers	.15
101	Jose Valentin	.05
102	Carlos Delgado	.15
103	Robert Esenhoorn	.05
104	John Hudek	.10
105	Domingo Cedeno	.05
106	Denny Hocking	.10
107	Greg Pirkl	.05
108	Mark Smith	.05
109	Paul Shuey	.05
110	Jorge Fabregas	.05
111	Rikkert Faneyte	.05
112	Rob Butler	.05
113	Darren Oliver	.05

114	Troy O'Leary	.05
115	Scott Brow	.05
116	Tony Eusebio	.05
117	Carlos Reyes	.05
118	J.R. Phillips	.10
119	Alex Diaz	.05
120	Charles Johnson	.15
121	Nate Minchey	.05
122	Scott Sanders	.05
123	Daryl Boston	.05
124	Joey Hamilton	.30
125	Brian Anderson	.25
126	Dan Miceli	.05
127	Tom Brunansky	.05
128	Dave Staton	.05
129	Mike Oquist	.05
130	John Mabry	.15
131	Norberto Martin	.05
132	Hector Fajardo	.05
133	Mark Hutton	.05
134	Fernando Vina	.05
135	Lee Tinsley	.05
136	*Chan Ho Park*	.25
137	Paul Spoljaric	.05
138	Matias Carrillo	.05
139	Mark Kiefer	.05
140	Stan Royer	.05
141	Bryan Eversgerd	.10
143	Joe Hall	.10
144	Johnny Ruffin	.05
145	Alex Gonzalez	.25
146	Keith Lockhart	.10
147	Tom Marsh	.05
148	Tony Longmire	.05
149	Keith Mitchell	.05
150	Melvin Nieves	.05
151	Kelly Stinnett	.15
152	Miguel Jimenez	.05
153	Jeff Juden	.05
154	Matt Walbeck	.05
155	Marc Newfield	.05
156	Matt Mieske	.05
157	Marcus Moore	.05
158	Jose Lima	.10
159	Mike Kelly	.05
160	Jim Edmonds	.30
161	Steve Trachsel	.25
162	Greg Blosser	.05
163	Mark Acre	.10
164	AL Checklist	.05
165	NL Checklist	.05

1994 Score Rookie/Traded Gold Rush

Each pack of Score Rookie and Traded cards included one Gold Rush parallel version of one of the set's cards. The insert cards feature fronts that are printed directly on gold foil and include a Gold Rush logo in an upper corner.

	MT
Complete Set (165):	45.00
Common Player:	.25
(Single-player Gold Rush cards valued at 3-5X regular Rookie/Traded version.)	

1994 Score Rookie/Traded Changing Places

Changing Places documented the relocation of 10 veteran superstars. Cards were inserted into one of every 36 retail or hobby packs. Fronts have a color photo of the player in his new uniform and are enhanced with red foil. Backs have a montage of color and black-and-white photos and a few words about the trade.

		MT
Complete Set (10):		20.00
Common Player:		1.00
1	Will Clark	4.00
2	Rafael Palmeiro	3.00
3	Roberto Kelly	1.00
4	Bo Jackson	2.00
5	Otis Nixon	1.00
6	Rickey Henderson	2.50
7	Ellis Burks	1.50
8	Lee Smith	1.00
9	Delino DeShields	1.00
10	Deion Sanders	6.00

1994 Score Rookie/Traded Redemption Card

The Score Rookie and Traded Redemption card was inserted at a rate of one every 240 packs. It gave collectors a chance to mail in for the best rookie in the annual September call-up: Alex Rodriguez

		MT
---	September Call-Up redemption card (expired)	24.00 2.00
---	Alex Rodriguez	60.00

1994 Score Rookie/Traded Super Rookies

Super Rookies is an 18-card set honoring baseball's brightest young stars. Super Rookies appear only in hobby packs at a rate of one

every 36 packs. Fronts are printed on foil, with a multi-colored border. Backs feature another photo, most of which is rendered in single-color blocks, along with a few words about the player and a large Super Rookie logo. Cards are numbered with an SU prefix.

		MT
Complete Set (18):		60.00
Common Player:		1.50
1	Carlos Delgado	3.00
2	Manny Ramirez	12.00
3	Ryan Klesko	9.00
4	Raul Mondesi	8.00
5	Bob Hamelin	1.50
6	Steve Karsay	1.50
7	Jeffrey Hammonds	2.00
8	Cliff Floyd	2.00
9	Kurt Abbott	2.00
10	Marc Newfield	1.50
11	Javier Lopez	5.00
12	Rich Becker	1.50
13	Greg Pirkl	1.50
14	Rondell White	4.00
15	James Mouton	1.50
16	Tony Tarasco	1.50
17	Brian Anderson	2.00
18	Jim Edmonds	6.00

1995 Score

CAL RIPKEN JR.

Score 1995 Baseball is composed of 605 cards, issued in two series; the first comprising 330 cards, the second, 275. Basic cards have photos placed on a dirt-like background with a green strip running up each side. The player's name, position, and team logo is given in white letters on a blue strip across the bottom. Backs resemble the fronts, except with a smaller, portrait photo of the player, which leaves room for statistics and biographical information. Score had a parallel set of Gold Rush cards, along with several other series of inserts. Eleven players in Series II can be found in two team variations as the result of a redemption program for updated cards.

		MT
Complete Set (605):		24.00
Complete Series 1 (330):		12.00
Complete Series 2 (275):		12.00
Common Player:		.05
Series 1 or 2 Wax Box:		27.00
1	Frank Thomas	2.00
2	Roberto Alomar	.40
3	Cal Ripken, Jr.	2.00
4	Jose Canseco	.25

5	Matt Williams	.25
6	Esteban Beltre	.05
7	Domingo Cedeno	.05
8	John Valentin	.05
9	Glenallen Hill	.05
10	Rafael Belliard	.05
11	Randy Myers	.05
12	Mo Vaughn	.40
13	Hector Carrasco	.05
14	Chili Davis	.05
15	Dante Bichette	.25
16	Darren Jackson	.05
17	Mike Piazza	1.00
18	Junior Felix	.05
19	Moises Alou	.08
20	Mark Gubicza	.05
21	Bret Saberhagen	.08
22	Len Dykstra	.05
23	Steve Howe	.05
24	Mark Dewey	.05
25	Brian Harper	.05
26	Ozzie Smith	.30
27	Scott Erickson	.05
28	Tony Gwynn	.75
29	Bob Welch	.05
30	Barry Bonds	.40
31	Leo Gomez	.05
32	Greg Maddux	1.25
33	Mike Greenwell	.05
34	Sammy Sosa	1.00
35	Darnell Coles	.05
36	Tommy Greene	.05
37	Will Clark	.20
38	Steve Ontiveros	.05
39	Stan Javier	.05
40	Bip Roberts	.05
41	Paul O'Neill	.05
42	Bill Haselman	.05
43	Shane Mack	.05
44	Orlando Merced	.05
45	Kevin Seitzer	.05
46	Trevor Hoffman	.05
47	Greg Gagne	.05
48	Jeff Kent	.05
49	Tony Phillips	.08
50	Ken Hill	.05
51	Carlos Baerga	.10
52	Henry Rodriguez	.05
53	Scott Sanderson	.05
54	Jeff Conine	.08
55	Chris Turner	.05
56	Ken Caminiti	.15
57	Harold Baines	.08
58	Charlie Hayes	.05
59	Roberto Kelly	.05
60	John Olerud	.10
61	Tim Davis	.05
62	Rich Rowland	.05
63	Rey Sanchez	.05
64	Junior Ortiz	.05
65	Ricky Gutierrez	.05
66	Rex Hudler	.05
67	Johnny Ruffin	.05
68	Jay Buhner	.10
69	Tom Pagnozzi	.05
70	Julio Franco	.05
71	Eric Young	.05
72	Mike Bordick	.05
73	Don Slaught	.05
74	Goose Gossage	.05
75	Lonnie Smith	.05
76	Jimmy Key	.05
77	Dave Hollins	.05
78	Mickey Tettleton	.05
79	Luis Gonzalez	.05
80	Dave Winfield	.10
81	Ryan Thompson	.05
82	Felix Jose	.05
83	Rusty Meacham	.05
84	Darryl Hamilton	.05
85	John Wetteland	.05
86	Tom Brunansky	.05
87	Mark Lemke	.05
88	Spike Owen	.05
89	Shawon Dunston	.08
90	Wilson Alvarez	.05
91	Lee Smith	.08
92	Scott Kamieniecki	.05
93	Jacob Brumfield	.05
94	Kirk Gibson	.05
95	Joe Girardi	.05
96	Mike Macfarlane	.05
97	Greg Colbrunn	.05
98	Ricky Bones	.05
99	Delino DeShields	.05
100	Pat Meares	.05

101	Jeff Fassero	.05
102	Jim Leyritz	.05
103	Gary Redus	.05
104	Terry Steinbach	.05
105	Kevin McReynolds	.05
106	Felix Fermin	.05
107	Danny Jackson	.05
108	Chris James	.05
109	Jeff King	.05
110	Pat Hentgen	.05
111	Gerald Perry	.05
112	Tim Raines	.08
113	Eddie Williams	.05
114	Jamie Moyer	.05
115	Bud Black	.05
116	Chris Gomez	.05
117	Luis Lopez	.05
118	Roger Clemens	.50
119	Javier Lopez	.20
120	Dave Nilsson	.05
121	Karl Rhodes	.05
122	Rick Aguilera	.05
123	Tony Fernandez	.05
124	Bernie Williams	.40
125	James Mouton	.05
126	Mark Langston	.05
127	Mike Lansing	.05
128	Tino Martinez	.12
129	Joe Orsulak	.05
130	David Hulse	.05
131	Pete Incaviglia	.05
132	Mark Clark	.05
133	Tony Eusebio	.05
134	Chuck Finley	.05
135	Lou Frazier	.05
136	Craig Grebeck	.05
137	Kelly Stinnett	.05
138	Paul Shuey	.08
139	David Nied	.05
140	Billy Brewer	.05
141	Dave Weathers	.05
142	Scott Leius	.05
143	Brian Jordan	.10
144	Melido Perez	.05
145	Tony Tarasco	.05
146	Dan Wilson	.05
147	Rondell White	.20
148	Mike Henneman	.05
149	Brian Johnson	.10
150	Tom Henke	.05
151	John Patterson	.05
152	Bobby Witt	.05
153	Eddie Taubensee	.05
154	Pat Borders	.05
155	Ramon Martinez	.08
156	Mike Kingery	.05
157	Zane Smith	.05
158	Benito Santiago	.05
159	Matias Carrillo	.05
160	Scott Brosius	.05
161	Dave Clark	.05
162	Mark McLemore	.05
163	Curt Schilling	.05
164	J.T. Snow	.10
165	Rod Beck	.05
166	Scott Fletcher	.05
167	Bob Tewksbury	.05
168	Mike LaValliere	.05
169	Dave Hansen	.05
170	Pedro Martinez	.05
171	Kirk Rueter	.05
172	Jose Lind	.05
173	Luis Alicea	.05
174	Mike Moore	.05
175	Andy Ashby	.05
176	Jody Reed	.05
177	Darryl Kile	.05
178	Carl Willis	.05
179	Jeromy Burnitz	.05
180	Mike Gallego	.05
181	*W. Van Landingham*	.15
182	Sid Fernandez	.05
183	Kim Batiste	.05
184	Greg Myers	.05
185	Steve Avery	.10
186	Steve Farr	.05
187	Robb Nen	.08
188	Dan Pasqua	.05
189	Bruce Ruffin	.05
190	Jose Valentin	.05
191	Willie Banks	.05
192	Mike Aldrete	.05
193	Randy Milligan	.05
194	Steve Karsay	.08
195	Mike Stanley	.05
196	Jose Mesa	.05

197	Tom Browning	.05
198	John Vander Wal	.05
199	Kevin Brown	.05
200	Mike Oquist	.05
201	Greg Swindell	.05
202	Eddie Zambrano	.05
203	Joe Boever	.05
204	Gary Varsho	.05
205	Chris Gwynn	.05
206	David Howard	.05
207	Jerome Walton	.05
208	Danny Darwin	.05
209	Darryl Strawberry	.08
210	Todd Van Poppel	.05
211	Scott Livingstone	.05
212	Dave Fleming	.05
213	Todd Worrell	.05
214	Carlos Delgado	.15
215	Bill Pecota	.05
216	Jim Lindeman	.05
217	Rick White	.05
218	Jose Oquendo	.05
219	Tony Castillo	.05
220	Fernando Vina	.05
221	Jeff Bagwell	.60
222	Randy Johnson	.25
223	Albert Belle	.40
224	Chuck Carr	.05
225	Mark Leiter	.05
226	Hal Morris	.05
227	Robin Ventura	.10
228	Mike Munoz	.05
229	Jim Thome	.25
230	Mario Diaz	.05
231	John Doherty	.05
232	Bobby Jones	.05
233	Raul Mondesi	.35
234	Ricky Jordan	.05
235	John Jaha	.05
236	Carlos Garcia	.05
237	Kirby Puckett	.75
238	Orel Hershiser	.08
239	Don Mattingly	.75
240	Sid Bream	.05
241	Brent Gates	.05
242	Tony Longmire	.05
243	Robby Thompson	.05
244	Rick Sutcliffe	.05
245	Dean Palmer	.05
246	Marquis Grissom	.05
247	Paul Molitor	.25
248	Mark Carreon	.05
249	Jack Voight	.05
250	Greg McMichael	.05
251	Damon Berryhill	.05
252	Brian Dorsett	.08
253	Jim Edmonds	.20
254	Barry Larkin	.15
255	Jack McDowell	.08
256	Wally Joyner	.08
257	Eddie Murray	.25
258	Lenny Webster	.05
259	Milt Cuyler	.05
260	Todd Benzinger	.05
261	Vince Coleman	.05
262	Todd Stottlemyre	.05
263	Turner Ward	.05
264	Ray Lankford	.10
265	Matt Walbeck	.05
266	Deion Sanders	.20
267	Gerald Williams	.05
268	Jim Gott	.05
269	Jeff Frye	.05
270	Jose Rijo	.05
271	Dave Justice	.15
272	Ismael Valdes	.08
273	Ben McDonald	.05
274	Darren Lewis	.05
275	Graeme Lloyd	.05
276	Luis Ortiz	.05
277	Julian Tavarez	.05
278	Mark Dalesandro	.08
279	Brett Merriman	.05
280	Ricky Bottalico	.05
281	Robert Eenhoorn	.05
282	Rikkert Faneyte	.05
283	Mike Kelly	.05
284	Mark Smith	.05
285	Turk Wendell	.05
286	Greg Blosser	.05
287	Garey Ingram	.10
288	Jorge Fabregas	.05
289	Blaise Ilsley	.10
290	Joe Hall	.05
291	Orlando Miller	.05
292	Jose Lima	.05
293	Greg O'Halloran	.05
294	Mark Kiefer	.05
295	Jose Oliva	.05
296	Rich Becker	.05
297	Brian Hunter	.10
298	Dave Silvestri	.05
299	*Armando Benitez*	.15
300	Darren Dreifort	.05
301	John Mabry	.05
302	Greg Pirkl	.05
303	J.R. Phillips	.05
304	Shawn Green	.15
305	Roberto Petagine	.05
306	Keith Lockhart	.05
307	Jonathon Hurst	.05
308	Paul Spoljaric	.05
309	Mike Lieberthal	.05
310	Garret Anderson	.10
311	John Johnston	.05
312	Alex Rodriguez	2.00
313	Kent Mercker	.05
314	John Valentin	.05
315	Kenny Rogers	.05
316	Fred McGriff	.20
317	Atlanta Braves, Baltimore Orioles	.05
318	Chicago Cubs, Boston Red Sox	.05
319	Cincinnati Reds, California Angels	.05
320	Colorado Rockies, Chicago White Sox	.05
321	Cleveland Indians, Florida Marlins	.05
322	Houston Astros, Detroit Tigers	.05
323	Los Angels Dodgers, Kansas City Royals	.05
324	Montreal Expos, Milwaukee Brewers	.05
325	New York Mets, Minnesota Twins	.05
326	Philadelphia Phillies, New York Yankees	.05
327	Pittsburgh Pirates, Oakland Athletics	.05
328	San Diego Padres, Seattle Mariners	.05
329	San Francisco Giants, Texas Rangers	.05
330	St. Louis Cardinals, Toronto Blue Jays	.05
331	Pedro Munoz	.05
332	Ryan Klesko	.40
333a	Andre Dawson (Red Sox)	.05
333b	Andre Dawson (Marlins)	.40
334	Derrick May	.05
335	Aaron Sele	.05
336	Kevin Mitchell	.05
337	Steve Traschel	.10
338	Andres Galarraga	.10
339a	Terry Pendleton (Braves)	.05
339b	Terry Pendleton (Marlins)	.15
340	Gary Sheffield	.30
341	Travis Fryman	.05
342	Bo Jackson	.10
343	Gary Gaetti	.05
344a	Brett Butler (Dodgers)	.08
344b	Brett Butler (Mets)	.25
345	B. J. Surhoff	.05
346a	Larry Walker (Expos)	.15
346b	Larry Walker (Rockies)	.50
347	Kevin Tapani	.05
348	Rick Wilkins	.05
349	Wade Boggs	.15
350	Mariano Duncan	.05
351	Ruben Sierra	.05
352a	Andy Van Slyke (Pirates)	.05
352b	Andy Van Slyke (Orioles)	.25
353	Reggie Jefferson	.05
354	Gregg Jefferies	.10
355	Tim Naehring	.05
356	John Roper	.05
357	Joe Carter	.15
358	Kurt Abbott	.05
359	Lenny Harris	.05
360	Lance Johnson	.05
361	Brian Anderson	.10
362	Jim Eisenreich	.05
363	Jerry Browne	.05
364	Mark Grace	.15
365	Devon White	.05
366	Reggie Sanders	.10
367	Ivan Rodriguez	.35
368	Kirt Manwaring	.05
369	Pat Kelly	.05
370	Ellis Burks	.12
371	Charles Nagy	.05
372	Kevin Bass	.05
373	Lou Whitaker	.05
374	Rene Arocha	.05
375	Derrick Parks	.05
376	Mark Whiten	.05
377	Mark McGwire	2.50
378	Doug Drabek	.05
379	Greg Vaughn	.05
380	Al Martin	.05
381	Ron Darling	.05
382	Tim Wallach	.05
383	Alan Trammell	.08
384	Randy Velarde	.05
385	Chris Sabo	.05
386	Wil Cordero	.05
307	Darrin Fletcher	.05
388	David Segui	.05
389	Steve Buechele	.05
390	Otis Nixon	.05
391	Jeff Brantley	.05
392a	Chad Curtis (Angels)	.05
392b	Chad Curtis (Tigers)	.25
393	Cal Eldred	.05
394	Jason Bere	.05
395	Bret Barberie	.05
396	Paul Sorrento	.05
397	Steve Finley	.05
398	Cecil Fielder	.15
399	Eric Karros	.08
400	Jeff Montgomery	.05
401	Cliff Floyd	.10
402	Matt Mieske	.05
403	Brian Hunter	.05
404	Alex Cole	.05
405	Kevin Stocker	.05
406	Eric Davis	.08
407	Marvin Freeman	.05
408	Dennis Eckersley	.08
409	Todd Zeile	.10
410	Keith Mitchell	.05
411	Andy Benes	.05
412	Juan Bell	.05
413	Royce Clayton	.05
414	Ed Sprague	.05
415	Mike Mussina	.25
416	Todd Hundley	.15
417	Pat Listach	.05
418	Joe Oliver	.05
419	Rafael Palmeiro	.15
420	Tim Salmon	.15
421	Brady Anderson	.10
422	Kenny Lofton	.40
423	Craig Biggio	.08
424	Bobby Bonilla	.10
425	Kenny Rogers	.05
426	Derek Bell	.05
427a	Scott Cooper (Red Sox)	.05
427b	Scott Cooper (Cardinals)	.25
428	Ozzie Guillen	.05
429	Omar Vizquel	.05
430	Phil Plantier	.05
431	Chuck Knoblauch	.10
432	Darren Daulton	.05
433	Bob Hamelin	.05
434	Tom Glavine	.15
435	Walt Weiss	.05
436	Jose Vizcaino	.05
437	Ken Griffey Jr.	2.00
438	Jay Bell	.05
439	Juan Gonzalez	1.00
440	Jeff Blauser	.05
441	Rickey Henderson	.15
442	Bobby Ayala	.05
443a	David Cone (Royals)	.05
443b	David Cone (Blue Jays)	.50
444	Pedro J. Martinez	.05
445	Manny Ramirez	.50
446	Mark Portugal	.05
447	Damion Easley	.05
448	Gary DiSarcina	.05
449	Roberto Hernandez	.05
450	Jeffrey Hammonds	.10
451	Jeff Treadway	.05
452a	Jim Abbott (Yankees)	.08
452b	Jim Abbott (White Sox)	.25
453	Carlos Rodriguez	.05
454	Joey Cora	.05
455	Bret Boone	.05
456	Danny Tartabull	.05
457	John Franco	.05
458	Roger Salkeld	.05
459	Fred McGriff	.30
460	Pedro Astacio	.05
461	Jon Lieber	.05

462	Luis Polonia	.05
463	Geronimo Pena	.05
464	Tom Gordon	.05
465	Brad Ausmus	.05
466	Willie McGee	.08
467	Doug Jones	.15
468	John Smoltz	.05
469	Troy Neel	.05
470	Luis Sojo	.05
471	John Smiley	.05
472	Rafael Bournigal	.05
473	Billy Taylor	.05
474	Juan Guzman	.05
475	Dave Magadan	.05
476	Mike Devereaux	.05
477	Andujar Cedeno	.05
478	Edgar Martinez	.08
479	Troy Neel	.05
480	Allen Watson	.05
481	Ron Karkovice	.05
482	Joey Hamilton	.05
483	Vinny Castilla	.08
484	Kevin Gross	.05
485	Bernard Gilkey	.08
486	John Burkett	.05
487	Matt Nokes	.05
488	Mel Rojas	.05
489	Craig Shipley	.05
490	Chip Hale	.05
491	Bill Swift	.05
492	Pat Rapp	.05
493a	Brian McRae (Royals)	.05
493b	Brian McRae (Cubs)	.35
494	Mickey Morandini	.05
495	Tony Pena	.05
496	Danny Bautista	.05
497	Armando Reynoso	.05
498	Ken Ryan	.05
499	Billy Ripken	.05
500	Pat Mahomes	.05
501	Mark Acre	.05
502	Geronimo Berroa	.05
503	Norberto Martin	.05
504	Chad Kreuter	.05
505	Howard Johnson	.05
506	Eric Anthony	.05
507	Mark Wohlers	.05
508	Scott Sanders	.05
509	Pete Harnisch	.05
510	Wes Chamberlain	.05
511	Tom Candiotti	.05
512	Albie Lopez	.05
513	Denny Neagle	.05
514	Sean Berry	.05
515	Billy Hatcher	.05
516	Todd Jones	.05
517	Wayne Kirby	.05
518	Butch Henry	.05
519	Sandy Alomar Jr.	.08
520	Kevin Appier	.05
521	Robert Mejia	.05
522	Steve Cooke	.05
523	Terry Shumpert	.05
524	Mike Jackson	.05
525	Kent Mercker	.05
526	David Wells	.05
527	Juan Samuel	.05
528	Salomon Torres	.05
529	Duane Ward	.05
530a	Rob Dibble (Reds)	.05
530b	Rob Dibble (White Sox)	.25
531	Mike Blowers	.05
532	Mark Eichhorn	.05
533	Alex Diaz	.05
534	Dan Miceli	.05
535	Jeff Branson	.05
536	Dave Stevens	.05
537	Charlie O'Brien	.05
538	Shane Reynolds	.05
539	Rich Amaral	.05
540	Rusty Greer	.05
541	Alex Arias	.05
542	Eric Plunk	.05
543	John Hudek	.05
544	Kirk McCaskill	.05
545	Jeff Reboulet	.05
546	Sterling Hitchcock	.05
547	Warren Newson	.05
548	Bryan Harvey	.05
549	Mike Huff	.05
550	Lance Parrish	.05
551	Ken Griffey Jr. (Hitters Inc.)	1.00
552	Matt Williams (Hitters Inc.)	.15
553	Roberto Alomar (Hitters Inc.)	.20
554	Jeff Bagwell (Hitters Inc.)	.35

555	Dave Justice (Hitters Inc.)	.10
556	Cal Ripken Jr. (Hitters Inc.)	1.00
557	Albert Belle (Hitters Inc.)	.20
558	Mike Piazza (Hitters Inc.)	.50
559	Kirby Puckett (Hitters Inc.)	.40
560	Wade Boggs (Hitters Inc.)	.15
561	Tony Gwynn (Hitters Inc.)	.40
562	Barry Bonds (Hitters Inc.)	.25
563	Mo Vaughn (Hitters Inc.)	.20
564	Don Mattingly (Hitters Inc.)	.50
565	Carlos Baerga (Hitters Inc.)	.10
566	Paul Molitor (Hitters Inc.)	.20
567	Raul Mondesi (Hitters Inc.)	.15
568	Manny Ramirez (Hitters Inc.)	.25
569	Alex Rodriguez (Hitters Inc.)	1.00
570	Will Clark (Hitters Inc.)	.15
571	Frank Thomas (Hitters Inc.)	1.00
572	Moises Alou (Hitters Inc.)	.05
573	Jeff Conine (Hitters Inc.)	.05
574	Joe Ausanio	.05
575	Charles Johnson	.10
576	Ernie Young	.05
577	Jeff Granger	.05
578	Robert Perez	.05
579	Melvin Nieves	.05
580	Gar Finnvold	.05
581	Duane Singleton	.05
582	Chan Ho Park	.15
583	Fausto Cruz	.05
584	Dave Staton	.05
585	Denny Hocking	.05
586	Nate Minchey	.05
587	Marc Newfield	.08
588	Jayhawk Owens	.05
589	Darren Bragg	.05
590	Kevin King	.05
591	Kurt Miller	.05
592	Aaron Small	.05
593	Troy O'Leary	.05
594	Phil Stidham	.05
595	Steve Dunn	.05
596	Cory Bailey	.10
597	Alex Gonzalez	.10
598	Jim Bowie	.05
599	Jeff Cirillo	.10
600	Mark Hutton	.05
601	Russ Davis	.05
602	Team Checklist	.05
603	Team Checklist	.05
604	Team Checklist	.05
605	Team Checklist	.05
----	"You Trade 'em" redemption card (Expired Dec. 31, 1995)	.50

1995 Score Ad Prize Cards

In a series of ads in hobby and public media, Score offered a pair of special cards as prizes in a mail-in offer. Cards feature the same basic design as 1995 Score, but are printed on platinum foil on front. Backs are conventionally printed with a portrait photo and a few words about the player.

		MT
Complete Set (2):		50.00
Common Player:		15.00
AD1	Alex Rodriguez	35.00
AD2	Ivan Rodriguez	15.00

1995 Score Airmail

Young ballplayers with a propensity for hitting the long ball are featured in this insert set found only in Series II jumbo packs. Cards have a player batting action photo set in sky-and-clouds background. A gold-foil stamp in the upper-left corner identifies the series. Backs have a background photo of sunset and dark clouds, with a player portrait photo in the foreground. A few stats and sentences describe the player's power hitting potential. Cards have an AM prefix to the number. Stated odds for insertion rate are an average of one Airmail chase card per 24 packs.

		MT
Complete Set (18):		70.00
Common Player:		2.00
1	Bob Hamelin	2.00
2	John Mabry	2.00
3	Marc Newfield	2.00
4	Jose Oliva	2.00
5	Charles Johnson	5.00
6	Russ Davis	2.00
7	Ernie Young	2.00
8	Billy Ashley	2.00
9	Ryan Klesko	6.00
10	J.R. Phillips	2.00
11	Cliff Floyd	3.00
12	Carlos Delgado	3.00
13	Melvin Nieves	2.00
14	Raul Mondesi	5.00
15	Manny Ramirez	6.00
16	Mike Kelly	2.00
17	Alex Rodriguez	28.00
18	Rusty Greer	4.00

Modern cards have little collector value in conditions lower than Mint. Figure NM cards at 75% of values shown; EX cards at 40%.

Values shown reflect the market as of January, 1999. On-field performances of current players in the 1999 baseball season are not factored in.

1995 Score Draft Picks

Antone Williamson

These cards were randomly included in 1995 Score hobby packs at a rate of one per every 36 packs. The cards showcase 18 of baseball's potential superstars and document their professional beginnings. The card front has the player's team logo and name in the lower-right corner. " '94 Draft Pick" appears in the upper-right corner. The front also has a mug shot and an action shot of the player. The card back has a portrait and career summary and is numbered with a DP prefix.

		MT
Complete Set (18):		30.00
Common Player:		1.00
1	McKay Christensen	1.00
2	Brett Wagner	1.00
3	Paul Wilson	2.00
4	C.J. Nitkowski	1.00
5	Josh Booty	4.00
6	Antone Williamson	1.50
7	Paul Konerko	10.00
8	Scott Elarton	4.00
9	Jacob Shumate	1.00
10	Terrence Long	1.00
11	Mark Johnson	1.00
12	Ben Grieve	15.00
13	Doug Million	1.00
14	Jayson Peterson	1.00
15	Dustin Hermanson	3.00
16	Matt Smith	1.50
17	Kevin Witt	1.00
18	Brian Buchanon	1.00

1995 Score Dream Team Gold

The Major Leagues' top players at each position are featured in this Series I insert set. Fronts are printed entirely on rainbow holographic foil and feature a large and a small player action photo. Backs have a

single-color version of one of the front photos as well as a color portrait photo in a circle at center, all in conventional printing technology. Card numbers have a DG prefix.

		MT
Complete Set (12):		120.00
Common Player:		2.00
1	Frank Thomas	25.00
2	Roberto Alomar	6.00
3	Cal Ripken Jr.	25.00
4	Matt Williams	4.00
5	Mike Piazza	20.00
6	Albert Belle	8.00
7	Ken Griffey Jr.	30.00
8	Tony Gwynn	15.00
9	Paul Molitor	6.00
10	Jimmy Key	2.00
11	Greg Maddux	20.00
12	Lee Smith	2.00

1995 Score Double Gold Champions

ROGER CLEMENS

A dozen veteran players, who have won at least two of the game's top awards are designated as "Double Gold Champs," in this Series II hobby insert set. Fronts have horizontal action photos at top, with a speckled red border at bottom. Vertical backs have a portrait photo and a list of the major awards won by the player. Cards have a GC prefix to the number. These chase cards were reportedly inserted at an average rate of one per 36.

		MT
Complete Set (11):		85.00
Common Player:		3.00
1	Frank Thomas	15.00
2	Ken Griffey Jr.	20.00
3	Barry Bonds	5.00
4	Tony Gwynn	8.00
5	Don Mattingly	8.00
6	Greg Maddux	12.00
7	Roger Clemens	5.00
8	Kenny Lofton	6.00
9	Jeff Bagwell	7.00
10	Matt Williams	3.00
11	Kirby Puckett	8.00

1995 Score Gold Rush

Besides being collectible in their own right, the gold-foil printed parallel versions of the Score regular-issue cards could be collected into team sets and exchanged with a trade card for platinum versions. The deadline for redemption of Series I was July 1, 1995; Oct. 1, 1995, for Series II. Gold Rush cards were found either one or two per pack, depending on pack card count. Gold Rush versions exist for each card in the Score set and have fronts that are identical to the regu-

lar cards except they are printed on foil and have gold borders. Backs of the Gold Rush cards have a small rectangular "GOLD RUSH" logo overprinted.

TOM HENKE RP

	MT
Complete Set (605):	175.00
Complete Series 1:	100.00
Complete Series 2:	75.00
Common Player:	.25
(Star Gold Rush cards are valued about 7X the regular-issue Score versions.)	

1995 Score Hall of Gold

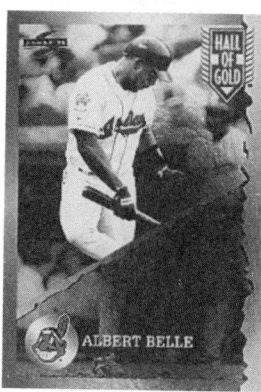

ALBERT BELLE

Hall of Gold inserts picture 110 of the top players on gold foil cards. Each card front has the Hall of Gold logo in an upper corner, plus a color action photo of the player, and his name and team logo at the bottom. The card back is numbered using an "HG" prefix and includes another color photo of the player, his team's name, his position, and a career summary. Cards were inserted one per every six regular 1995 Score packs and one per every two jumbo packs. Updated versions of five traded players were issued in Series II, available only via mail-in offer with a trade card found randomly inserted in packs.

A player's name in *italic* type indicates a rookie card.

		MT
Complete Set (110):		100.00
Complete Series 1 (55):		60.00
Complete Series 2 (55):		40.00
Common Player:		.25
1	Ken Griffey Jr.	10.00
2	Matt Williams	.50
3	Roberto Alomar	1.50
4	Jeff Bagwell	3.00
5	Dave Justice	.50
6	Cal Ripken Jr.	8.00
7	Randy Johnson	.50
8	Barry Larkin	.50
9	Albert Belle	3.00
10	Mike Piazza	6.00
11	Kirby Puckett	3.00
12	Moises Alou	.30
13	Jose Canseco	.75
14	Tony Gwynn	3.00
15	Roger Clemens	3.00
16	Barry Bonds	3.00
17	Mo Vaughn	2.00
18	Greg Maddux	6.00
19	Dante Bichette	.75
20	Will Clark	.75
21	Len Dykstra	.25
22	Don Mattingly	3.00
23	Carlos Baerga	.30
24	Ozzie Smith	.75
25	Paul Molitor	.75
26	Paul O'Neill	.25
27	Deion Sanders	1.00
28	Jeff Conine	.25
29	John Olerud	.25
30	Jose Rijo	.25
31	Sammy Sosa	4.00
32	Robin Ventura	.25
33	Raul Mondesi	1.00
34	Eddie Murray	.75
35	Marquis Grissom	.25
36	Darryl Strawberry	.25
37	Dave Nilsson	.25
38	Manny Ramirez	2.00
39	Delino DeShields	.25
40	Lee Smith	.25
41	Alex Rodriguez	10.00
42	Julio Franco	.25
43	Bret Saberhagen	.25
44	Ken Hill	.25
45	Roberto Kelly	.25
46	Hal Morris	.25
47	Jimmy Key	.25
48	Terry Steinbach	.25
49	Mickey Tettleton	.25
50	Tony Phillips	.25
51	Carlos Garcia	.25
52	Jim Edmonds	.50
53	Rod Beck	.25
54	Shane Mack	.25
55	Ken Caminiti	.25
56	Frank Thomas	8.00
57	Kenny Lofton	2.50
58	Jack McDowell	.25
59	Jason Bere	.25
60	Joe Carter	.25
61	Gary Sheffield	.50
62	Andres Galarraga	.25
63	Gregg Jefferies	.25
64	Bobby Bonilla	.25
65	Tom Glavine	.25
66	John Smoltz	.40
67	Fred McGriff	.60
68	Craig Biggio	.25
69	Reggie Sanders	.25
70	Kevin Mitchell	.25
71a	Larry Walker (Expos)	.50
71b	Larry Walker (Rockies)	1.50
72	Carlos Delgado	.25
73	Andujar Cedeno	.25
74	Ivan Rodriguez	.75
75	Ryan Klesko	1.50
76a	John Kruk (Phillies)	.25
76b	John Kruk (White Sox)	.75
77a	Brian McRae (Royals)	.25
77b	Brian McRae (Cubs)	.75
78	Tim Salmon	.50
79	Travis Fryman	.25
80	Chuck Knoblauch	.25
81	Jay Bell	.25
82	Cecil Fielder	.40
83	Cliff Floyd	.25
84	Ruben Sierra	.25
85	Mike Mussina	1.50
86	Mark Grace	.55
87	Dennis Eckersley	.25
88	Dennis Martinez	.25

89	Rafael Palmeiro	.25
90	Ben McDonald	.25
91	Dave Hollins	.25
92	Steve Avery	.25
93a	David Cone (Royals)	.25
93b	David Cone (Blue Jays)	.75
94	Darren Daulton	.25
95	Bret Boone	.25
96	Wade Boggs	.50
97	Doug Drabek	.25
98	Derek Bell	.25
99	Jim Thome	.75
100	Chili Davis	.25
101	Jeffrey Hammonds	.25
102	Rickey Henderson	.25
103	Brett Butler	.25
104	Tim Wallach	.25
105	Wil Cordero	.25
106	Mark Whiten	.25
107	Bob Hamelin	.25
108	Rondell White	.25
109	Devon White	.25
110a	Tony Tarasco (Braves)	.25
110b	Tony Tarasco (Expos)	.75
----	Redemption trade card	.50
	(Expired Dec. 31, 1995)	

1995 Score Rookie Dream Team

These Series II inserts feature a dozen of 1995's best rookie prospects. Fronts are printed on a silver-foil background. The words "ROOKIE DREAM TEAM" are formed of sky-and-cloud images within the letters. Horizontal backs repeat the motif and include another player photo in a vignette at center. Card numbers have an RDT prefix.

		MT
Complete Set (12):		55.00
Common Player:		2.00
1	J.R. Phillips	2.00
2	Alex Gonzalez	4.00
3	Alex Rodriguez	28.00
4	Jose Oliva	2.00
5	Charles Johnson	5.00
6	Shawn Green	4.00
7	Brian Hunter	4.00
8	Garret Anderson	3.00
9	Julian Tavarez	2.00
10	Jose Lima	2.00
11	Armando Benitez	2.00
12	Ricky Bottalico	2.50

1995 Score Rookie Greatness

This single-card insert set is the toughest pull among the 1995 Score chase cards. Honoring slugging Braves star Ryan Klesko, the card is inserted at the rate of one per 720 retail packs. An even scarcer autographed version of the card in an edition of just over 6,000 was also created for insertion into hobby packs.

		MT
Complete Set (2):		100.00
RG1	Ryan Klesko	25.00
SG1	Ryan Klesko (autographed)	75.00

1995 Score Score Rules

Series I jumbo packs were the only sources for "Score Rules" insert set of rookie and veteran stars. A color player photo at left has a team logo toward the bottom, beneath which is a gold-foil "tie tack" device with the league initials and position. At top-right is a baseball which appears to be dripping orange and green goop down the card. The player's last name is presented vertically with a sepia photo of the player within the letters. Backs repeat the green baseball and ooze motif, with three progressive color proof versions of the sepia front photo and a few sentences about the star. Cards are numbered with an "SR" prefix.

	MT
Complete Set (30):	100.00
Common Player:	1.50
1 Ken Griffey, Jr.	20.00
2 Frank Thomas	15.00
3 Mike Piazza	12.00
4 Jeff Bagwell	10.00
5 Alex Rodriguez	20.00
6 Albert Belle	5.00
7 Matt Williams	2.00
8 Roberto Alomar	3.00
9 Barry Bonds	6.00
10 Raul Mondesi	3.00
11 Jose Canseco	2.50
12 Kirby Puckett	8.00
13 Fred McGriff	2.50
14 Kenny Lofton	6.00
15 Greg Maddux	12.00
16 Juan Gonzalez	10.00
17 Cliff Floyd	1.50
18 Cal Ripken, Jr.	15.00
19 Will Clark	2.50
20 Tim Salmon	2.50
21 Paul O'Neill	1.50
22 Jason Bere	1.50
23 Tony Gwynn	9.00
24 Manny Ramirez	4.00
25 Don Mattingly	9.00
26 Dave Justice	2.00
27 Javier Lopez	1.50
28 Ryan Klesko	2.00
29 Carlos Delgado	1.50
30 Mike Mussina	3.00

1996 Score

Large, irregularly shaped action photos are featured on the fronts of the basic cards in the 1996 Score issue. Backs feature a portrait photo (in most cases) at left and a full slate of major and minor league stats at right, along with a few words about the player. Slightly different design details and a "ROOK-IE" headline identify that subset within the regular issue. A wide variety of insert cards was produced, most of them exclusive to one type of packaging.

	MT
Complete Set (510):	32.00
Complete Series 1 (275):	18.00
Complete Series 2 (235):	15.00
Common Player:	.05
Series 1 or 2 Wax Box:	28.00
1 Will Clark	.25
2 Rich Becker	.05
3 Ryan Klesko	.40
4 Jim Edmonds	.10
5 Barry Larkin	.20
6 Jim Thome	.25
7 Raul Mondesi	.25
8 Don Mattingly	.75
9 Jeff Conine	.08
10 Rickey Henderson	.20
11 Chad Curtis	.05
12 Darren Daulton	.05
13 Larry Walker	.25
14 Carlos Garcia	.05
15 Carlos Baerga	.10
16 Tony Gwynn	.75
17 Jon Nunally	.05
18 Deion Sanders	.25
19 Mark Grace	.20
20 Alex Rodriguez	2.50
21 Frank Thomas	2.00
22 Brian Jordan	.15
23 J.T. Snow	.08
24 Shawn Green	.10
25 Tim Wakefield	.05
26 Curtis Goodwin	.05
27 John Smoltz	.15
28 Devon White	.05
29 Brian Hunter	.10
30 Rusty Greer	.05
31 Rafael Palmeiro	.10
32 Bernard Gilkey	.10
33 John Valentin	.05
34 Randy Johnson	.20
35 Garret Anderson	.10
36 Rikkert Faneyte	.05
37 Ray Durham	.05
38 Bip Roberts	.05
39 Jaime Navarro	.05
40 Mark Johnson	.05
41 Darren Lewis	.05
42 Tyler Green	.05
43 Bill Pulsipher	.10
44 Jason Giambi	.15
45 Kevin Ritz	.05
46 Jack McDowell	.05
47 Felipe Lira	.05
48 Rico Brogna	.05
49 Terry Pendleton	.05
50 Rondell White	.10
51 Andre Dawson	.10
52 Kirby Puckett	.75
53 Wally Joyner	.08
54 B.J. Surhoff	.05
55 Chan Ho Park	.08
56 Greg Vaughn	.05
57 Roberto Alomar	.40
58 Dave Justice	.15
59 Kevin Seitzer	.05
60 Cal Ripken Jr.	2.00
61 Ozzie Smith	.25
62 Mo Vaughn	.60
63 Ricky Bones	.05
64 Gary DiSarcina	.05
65 Matt Williams	.25
66 Wilson Alvarez	.05
67 Lenny Dykstra	.08
68 Brian McRae	.05
69 Todd Stottlemyre	.05
70 Bret Boone	.05
71 Sterling Hitchcock	.05
72 Albert Belle	.50
73 Todd Hundley	.15
74 Vinny Castilla	.10
75 Moises Alou	.05
76 Cecil Fielder	.15
77 Brad Radke	.05
78 Quilvio Veras	.05
79 Eddie Murray	.35
80 James Mouton	.05
81 Pat Listach	.05
82 Mark Gubicza	.05
83 Dave Winfield	.20
84 Fred McGriff	.30
85 Darryl Hamilton	.05
86 Jeffrey Hammonds	.05
87 Pedro Munoz	.05
88 Craig Biggio	.10
89 Cliff Floyd	.05
90 Tim Naehring	.05
91 Brett Butler	.08
92 Kevin Foster	.05
93 Patrick Kelly	.05
94 John Smiley	.05
95 Terry Steinbach	.05
96 Orel Hershiser	.08
97 Darrin Fletcher	.05
98 Walt Weiss	.05
99 John Wetteland	.05
100 Alan Trammell	.08
101 Steve Avery	.05
102 Tony Eusebio	.05
103 Sandy Alomar	.08
104 Joe Girardi	.05
105 Rick Aguilera	.05
106 Tony Tarasco	.05
107 Chris Hammond	.05
108 Mike McFarlane	.05
109 Doug Drabek	.05
110 Derek Bell	.08
111 Ed Sprague	.05
112 Todd Hollandsworth	.15
113 Otis Nixon	.05
114 Keith Lockhart	.05
115 Donovan Osborne	.05
116 Dave Magadan	.05
117 Edgar Martinez	.10
118 Chuck Carr	.05
119 J.R. Phillips	.05
120 Sean Bergman	.05
121 Andujar Cedeno	.05
122 Eric Young	.05
123 Al Martin	.05
124 Ken Hill	.05
125 Jim Eisenreich	.05
126 Benito Santiago	.05
127 Ariel Prieto	.05
128 Jim Bullinger	.05
129 Russ Davis	.05
130 Jim Abbott	.08
131 Jason Isringhausen	.10
132 Carlos Perez	.05
133 David Segui	.05
134 Troy O'Leary	.05
135 Pat Meares	.05
136 Chris Hoiles	.05
137 Ismael Valdes	.10
138 Jose Oliva	.05
139 Carlos Delgado	.10
140 Tom Goodwin	.05
141 Bob Tewksbury	.05
142 Chris Gomez	.05
143 Jose Oquendo	.05
144 Mark Lewis	.05
145 Salomon Torres	.05
146 Luis Gonzalez	.05
147 Mark Carreon	.05
148 Lance Johnson	.05
149 Melvin Nieves	.05
150 Lee Smith	.08
151 Jacob Brumfield	.05
152 Armando Benitez	.05
153 Curt Shilling	.05
154 Javier Lopez	.15
155 Frank Rodriguez	.05
156 Alex Gonzalez	.10
157 Todd Worrell	.05
158 Benji Gil	.05
159 Greg Gagne	.05
160 Tom Henke	.05
161 Randy Myers	.05
162 Joey Cora	.05
163 Scott Ruffcorn	.05
164 William VanLandingham	.05
165 Tony Phillips	.08
166 Eddie Williams	.05
167 Bobby Bonilla	.10
168 Denny Neagle	.05
169 Troy Percival	.05
170 Billy Ashley	.05
171 Andy Van Slyke	.05
172 Jose Offerman	.05
173 Mark Parent	.05
174 Edgardo Alfonzo	.05
175 Trevor Hoffman	.05
176 David Cone	.10
177 Dan Wilson	.05
178 Steve Ontiveros	.05
179 Dean Palmer	.05
180 Mike Kelly	.05
181 Jim Leyritz	.05
182 Ron Karkovice	.05
183 Kevin Brown	.05
184 *Jose Valentin*	.05
185 Jorge Fabregas	.05
186 Jose Mesa	.05
187 Brent Mayne	.05
188 Carl Everett	.05
189 Paul Sorrento	.05
190 Pete Shourek	.05
191 Scott Kamieniecki	.05
192 Roberto Hernandez	.05
193 Randy Johnson (Radar Rating)	.10
194 Greg Maddux (Radar Rating)	.75
195 Hideo Nomo (Radar Rating)	.25
196 David Cone (Radar Rating)	.05
197 Mike Mussina (Radar Rating)	.15
198 Andy Benes (Radar Rating)	.05
199 Kevin Appier (Radar Rating)	.05
200 John Smoltz (Radar Rating)	.10

#	Player	Value	#	Player	Value	#	Player	Value
201	John Wetteland (Radar Rating)	.05	295	Mike Blowers	.05	391	Midre Cummings	.05
202	Mark Wohlers (Radar Rating)	.05	296	Paul O'Neill	.05	392	Scott Leius	.05
			297	Dave Nilsson	.05	393	Manny Alexander	.05
203	Stan Belinda	.05	298	Dante Bichette	.15	394	Brent Gates	.05
204	Brian Anderson	.05	299	Marty Cordova	.15	395	Rey Sanchez	.05
205	Mike Devereaux	.05	300	Jay Bell	.05	396	Andy Pettitte	.60
206	Mark Wohlers	.05	301	Mike Mussina	.30	397	Jeff Cirillo	.05
207	Omar Vizquel	.05	302	Ivan Rodriguez	.40	398	Kurt Abbott	.05
208	Jose Rijo	.05	303	Jose Canseco	.25	399	Lee Tinsley	.05
209	Willie Blair	.05	304	Jeff Bagwell	.75	400	Paul Assenmacher	.05
210	Jamie Moyer	.05	305	Manny Ramirez	.45	401	Scott Erickson	.05
211	Craig Shipley	.05	306	Dennis Martinez	.08	402	Todd Zeile	.08
212	Shane Reynolds	.05	307	Charlie Hayes	.05	403	Tom Pagnozzi	.05
213	Chad Fonville	.05	308	Joe Carter	.15	404	Ozzie Guillen	.05
214	Jose Vizcaino	.05	309	Travis Fryman	.05	405	Jeff Frye	.05
215	Sid Fernandez	.05	310	Mark McGwire	3.00	406	Kirt Manwaring	.05
216	Andy Ashby	.05	311	Reggie Sanders	.10	407	Chad Ogea	.05
217	Frank Castillo	.05	312	Julian Tavarez	.05	408	Harold Baines	.08
218	Kevin Tapani	.05	313	Jeff Montgomery	.05	409	Jason Bere	.05
219	Kent Mercker	.05	314	Andy Benes	.05	410	Chuck Finley	.05
220	Karim Garcia	.30	315	John Jaha	.05	411	Jeff Fassero	.05
221	Chris Snopek	.05	316	Jeff Kent	.05	412	Joey Hamilton	.05
222	Tim Unroe	.10	317	Mike Piazza	1.50	413	John Olerud	.12
223	Johnny Damon	.10	318	Erik Hanson	.05	414	Kevin Stocker	.05
224	LaTroy Hawkins	.10	319	Kenny Rogers	.05	415	Eric Anthony	.05
225	Mariano Rivera	.20	320	Hideo Nomo	.50	416	Aaron Sele	.05
226	Jose Alberro	.05	321	Gregg Jefferies	.10	417	Chris Bosio	.05
227	Angel Martinez	.05	322	Chipper Jones	1.50	418	Michael Mimbs	.05
228	Jason Schmidt	.05	323	Jay Buhner	.15	419	Orlando Miller	.05
229	Tony Clark	.40	324	Dennis Eckersley	.08	420	Stan Javier	.05
230	Kevin Jordan	.05	325	Kenny Lofton	.50	421	Matt Mieske	.05
231	Mark Thompson	.05	326	Robin Ventura	.10	422	Jason Bates	.05
232	Jim Dougherty	.05	327	Tom Glavine	.15	423	Orlando Merced	.05
333	Roger Cedeno	.10	328	Tim Salmon	.15	424	John Flaherty	.05
234	Ugueth Urbina	.10	329	Andres Galarraga	.10	425	Reggie Jefferson	.05
235	Ricky Otero	.05	330	Hal Morris	.05	426	Scott Stahoviak	.05
236	Mark Smith	.05	331	Brady Anderson	.10	427	John Burkett	.05
237	Brian Barber	.05	332	Chili Davis	.05	428	Rod Beck	.05
238	Marc Kroon	.05	333	Roger Clemens	.60	429	Bill Swift	.05
239	Joe Rosselli	.05	334	Marquis Grissom	.10	430	Scott Cooper	.05
240	Derek Jeter	1.00	335	Mike Greenwell	.05	431	Mel Rojas	.05
241	Michael Tucker	.05	336	Sammy Sosa	1.50	432	Todd Van Poppel	.05
242	*Joe Borowski*	.05	337	Ron Gant	.10	433	Bobby Jones	.05
243	Joe Vitiello	.05	338	Ken Caminiti	.10	434	Mike Harkey	.05
244	Orlando Palmeiro	.05	339	Danny Tartabull	.05	435	Sean Berry	.05
245	James Baldwin	.05	340	Barry Bonds	.50	436	Glenallen Hill	.05
246	Alan Embree	.05	341	Ben McDonald	.05	437	Ryan Thompson	.05
247	Shannon Penn	.05	342	Ruben Sierra	.05	438	Luis Alicea	.05
248	Chris Stynes	.05	343	Bernie Williams	.40	439	Esteban Loaiza	.10
249	Oscar Munoz	.05	344	Wil Cordero	.05	440	Jeff Reboulet	.05
250	Jose Herrera	.05	345	Wade Boggs	.20	441	Vince Coleman	.05
251	Scott Sullivan	.05	346	Gary Gaetti	.08	442	Ellis Burks	.10
252	Reggie Williams	.05	347	Greg Colbrunn	.05	443	Allen Battle	.05
253	Mark Grudzielanek	.10	348	Juan Gonzalez	1.00	444	Jimmy Key	.05
254	Kevin Jordan	.05	349	Marc Newfield	.05	445	Ricky Bottalico	.05
255	Terry Bradshaw	.05	350	Charles Nagy	.05	446	Delino DeShields	.05
256	*F.P. Santangelo*	.05	351	Robby Thompson	.05	447	Albie Lopez	.05
257	Doug Johns	.05	352	Roberto Petagine	.05	448	Mark Petkovsek	.05
258	George Williams	.05	353	Darryl Strawberry	.10	449	Tim Raines	.08
259	Larry Thomas	.05	354	Tino Martinez	.12	450	Bryan Harvey	.05
260	Rudy Pemberton	.05	355	Eric Karros	.10	451	Pat Hentgen	.05
261	Jim Pittsley	.10	356	Cal Ripken Jr.	1.00	452	Tim Laker	.05
262	Les Norman	.05	357	Cecil Fielder	.15	453	Tom Gordon	.05
263	Ruben Rivera	.20	358	Kirby Puckett	.30	454	Phil Plantier	.05
264	*Cesar Devarez*	.05	359	Jim Edmonds	.10	455	Ernie Young	.05
265	Greg Zaun	.08	360	Matt Williams	.15	456	Pete Harnisch	.05
266	Eric Owens	.05	361	Alex Rodriguez	1.00	457	Roberto Kelly	.05
267	John Frascatore	.10	362	Barry Larkin	.15	458	Mark Portugal	.05
268	Shannon Stewart	.05	363	Rafael Palmeiro	.10	459	Mark Leiter	.05
269	Checklist	.05	364	David Cone	.10	460	Tony Pena	.05
270	Checklist	.05	365	Roberto Alomar	.25	461	Roger Pavlik	.05
271	Checklist	.05	366	Eddie Murray	.15	462	Jeff King	.05
272	Checklist	.05	367	Randy Johnson	.15	463	Bryan Rekar	.05
273	Checklist	.05	368	Ryan Klesko	.20	464	Al Leiter	.05
274	Checklist	.05	369	Raul Mondesi	.20	465	Phil Nevin	.05
275	Checklist	.05	370	Mo Vaughn	.35	466	Jose Lima	.05
276	Greg Maddux	1.50	371	Will Clark	.15	467	Mike Stanley	.05
277	Pedro Martinez	.05	372	Carlos Baerga	.15	468	David McCarty	.05
278	Bobby Higginson	.05	373	Frank Thomas	1.00	469	Herb Perry	.05
279	Ray Lankford	.12	374	Larry Walker	.15	470	Geronimo Berroa	.05
280	Shawon Dunston	.05	375	Garret Anderson	.10	471	David Wells	.05
281	Gary Sheffield	.25	376	Edgar Martinez	.05	472	Vaughn Eshelman	.05
282	Ken Griffey Jr.	2.50	377	Don Mattingly	.40	473	Greg Swindell	.05
283	Paul Molitor	.25	378	Tony Gwynn	.40	474	Steve Sparks	.05
284	Kevin Appier	.05	379	Albert Belle	.25	475	Luis Sojo	.05
285	Chuck Knoblauch	.12	380	Jason Isringhausen	.20	476	Derrick May	.05
286	Alex Fernandez	.05	381	Ruben Rivera	.20	477	Joe Oliver	.05
287	Steve Finley	.05	382	Johnny Damon	.10	478	Alex Arias	.05
288	Jeff Blauser	.05	383	Karim Garcia	.20	479	Brad Ausmus	.05
289	Charles Johnson	.12	384	Derek Jeter	.50	480	Gabe White	.05
290	John Franco	.05	385	David Justice	.15	481	Pat Rapp	.05
291	Mark Langston	.05	386	Royce Clayton	.05	482	Damon Buford	.05
292	Bret Saberhagen	.05	387	Mark Whiten	.05	483	Turk Wendell	.05
293	John Mabry	.05	388	Mickey Tettleton	.05	484	Jeff Brantley	.05
294	Ramon Martinez	.08	389	Steve Trachsel	.05	485	Curtis Leskanic	.05
			390	Danny Bautista	.05	486	Robb Nen	.05

487	Lou Whitaker	.05
488	Melido Perez	.05
489	Luis Polonia	.05
490	Scott Brosius	.05
491	Robert Perez	.05
492	*Mike Sweeney*	.05
493	Mark Loretta	.05
494	Alex Ochoa	.05
495	*Matt Lawton*	.05
496	Shawn Estes	.05
497	John Wasdin	.05
498	Marc Kroon	.05
499	Chris Snopek	.05
500	Jeff Suppan	.05
501	Terrell Wade	.05
502	*Marvin Benard*	.05
503	Chris Widger	.05
504	Quinton McCracken	.05
505	Bob Wolcott	.05
506	C.J. Nitkowski	.05
507	Aaron Ledesma	.05
508	Scott Hatteberg	.05
509	Jimmy Haynes	.05
510	Howard Battle	.05

1996 Score All-Stars

An exclusive insert found only in 20-card Series 2 jumbo packs at an average rate of one per nine packs, these inserts feature the game's top stars printed in a rainbow holographic-foil technology.

		MT
Complete Set (20):		80.00
Common Player:		1.00
1	Frank Thomas	12.00
2	Albert Belle	4.00
3	Ken Griffey Jr.	16.00
4	Cal Ripken Jr.	12.00
5	Mo Vaughn	4.00
6	Matt Williams	2.00
7	Barry Bonds	4.00
8	Dante Bichette	1.00
9	Tony Gwynn	6.50
10	Greg Maddux	10.00
11	Randy Johnson	2.50
12	Hideo Nomo	2.50
13	Tim Salmon	2.00
14	Jeff Bagwell	5.00
15	Edgar Martinez	1.00
16	Reggie Sanders	1.00
17	Larry Walker	2.00
18	Chipper Jones	10.00
19	Manny Ramirez	3.00
20	Eddie Murray	2.00

1996 Score Big Bats

Gold-foil printing highlights cards of 20 of the game's top hitters found in this retail-packaging exclu-

sive insert set. Stated odds of picking a Big Bats card are one in 31 packs.

		MT
Complete Set (20):		150.00
Common Player:		2.50
1	Cal Ripken Jr.	20.00
2	Ken Griffey Jr.	25.00
3	Frank Thomas	20.00
4	Jeff Bagwell	10.00
5	Mike Piazza	15.00
6	Barry Bonds	7.00
7	Matt Williams	3.00
8	Raul Mondesi	3.00
9	Tony Gwynn	10.00
10	Albert Belle	6.00
11	Manny Ramirez	7.00
12	Carlos Baerga	2.50
13	Mo Vaughn	7.00
14	Derek Bell	2.50
15	Larry Walker	3.00
16	Kenny Lofton	6.00
17	Edgar Martinez	2.50
18	Reggie Sanders	2.50
19	Eddie Murray	3.50
20	Chipper Jones	15.00

1996 Score Cal Ripken Tribute

The toughest pick among the 1996 Score inserts is this special card marking Cal Ripken's 2,131st consecutive game. The insertion rate is one per 300 packs hobby and retail, one per 150 jumbo packs.

		MT
2131	Cal Ripken Jr. (Tribute)	16.00

1996 Score Diamond Aces

Thirty of the top veterans and young stars are included in this jumbo-only insert set, seeded at a rate of one per eight packs.

		MT
Complete Set (30):		125.00
Common Player:		2.50
1	Hideo Nomo	6.00
2	Brian Hunter	2.50
3	Ray Durham	2.50
4	Frank Thomas	25.00
5	Cal Ripken Jr.	25.00
6	Barry Bonds	8.00
7	Greg Maddux	20.00
8	Chipper Jones	18.00
9	Raul Mondesi	3.00
10	Mike Piazza	18.00
11	Derek Jeter	15.00
12	Bill Pulsipher	2.50
13	Larry Walker	3.00
14	Ken Griffey Jr.	30.00
15	Alex Rodriguez	30.00
16	Manny Ramirez	8.00
17	Mo Vaughn	8.00
18	Reggie Sanders	2.50
19	Derek Bell	2.50
20	Jim Edmonds	3.00
21	Albert Belle	8.00
22	Eddie Murray	4.00
23	Tony Gwynn	10.00
24	Jeff Bagwell	10.00
25	Carlos Baerga	2.50
26	Matt Williams	3.00
27	Garret Anderson	2.50
28	Todd Hollandsworth	3.00
29	Johnny Damon	3.00
30	Tim Salmon	3.00

1996 Score Dream Team

The hottest player at each position is honored in the Dream Team insert set. Once again featured on holographic foil printing technology, the cards are found in all types of Score packaging at a rate of once per 72 packs.

	MT
Complete Set (9):	100.00
Common Player:	4.00
1 Cal Ripken Jr.	20.00
2 Frank Thomas	20.00
3 Carlos Baerga	4.00
4 Matt Williams	5.00
5 Mike Piazza	15.00
6 Barry Bonds	7.00
7 Ken Griffey Jr.	25.00
8 Manny Ramirez	6.00
9 Greg Maddux	15.00

1996 Score Dugout Collection

The concept of a partial parallel set, including the stars and rookies but not the journeymen and bench warmers, was initiated with Score's "Dugout Collection," with fewer than half of the cards from the regular series chosen for inclusion. The white borders of the regular cards are replaced with copper-foil and background printing is also done on foil in this special version. On back is a special "Dugout Collection '96" logo. Advertised insertion rate of the copper-version cards is one per three packs.

	MT
Complete Set (110):	45.00
Common Player:	.25
1 Greg Maddux	2.50
2 Pedro Martinez	.25
3 Bobby Higginson	.25
4 Ray Lankford	.25
5 Shawon Dunston	.25
6 Gary Sheffield	.40
7 Ken Griffey Jr.	6.00
8 Paul Molitor	1.25
9 Kevin Appier	.25
10 Chuck Knoblauch	.50
11 Alex Fernandez	.25
12 Steve Finley	.25
13 Jeff Blauser	.25
14 Charles Johnson	.25
15 John Franco	.25
16 Mark Langston	.25
17 Bret Saberhagen	.25
18 John Mabry	.25
19 Ramon Martinez	.25
20 Mike Blowers	.25
21 Paul O'Neill	.25
22 Dave Nilsson	.25
23 Dante Bichette	.40
24 Marty Cordova	.25
25 Jay Bell	.25
26 Mike Mussina	.35
27 Ivan Rodriguez	.40
28 Jose Canseco	.40
29 Jeff Bagwell	.60

30 Manny Ramirez	.45
31 Dennis Martinez	.25
32 Charlie Hayes	.25
33 Joe Carter	.25
34 Travis Fryman	.25
35 Mark McGwire	2.00
36 Reggie Sanders	.35
37 Julian Tavarez	.25
38 Jeff Montgomery	.25
39 Andy Benes	.25
40 John Jaha	.25
41 Jeff Kent	.25
42 Mike Piazza	2.00
43 Erik Hanson	.25
44 Kenny Rogers	.25
45 Hideo Nomo	1.25
46 Gregg Jefferies	.25
47 Chipper Jones	2.50
48 Jay Buhner	.35
49 Dennis Eckersley	.25
50 Kenny Lofton	.35
51 Robin Ventura	.25
52 Tom Glavine	.25
53 Tim Salmon	.35
54 Andres Galarraga	.35
55 Hal Morris	.25
56 Brady Anderson	.40
57 Chili Davis	.25
58 Roger Clemens	.50
59 Marquis Grissom	.25
60 Mike Greenwell	.25
61 Sammy Sosa	1.50
62 Ron Gant	.25
63 Ken Caminiti	.25
64 Danny Tartabull	.25
65 Barry Bonds	1.50
66 Ben McDonald	.25
67 Ruben Sierra	.25
68 Bernie Williams	.50
69 Wil Cordero	.25
70 Wade Boggs	.40
71 Gary Gaetti	.25
72 Greg Colbrunn	.25
73 Juan Gonzalez	.60
74 Marc Newfield	.25
75 Charles Nagy	.25
76 Robby Thompson	.25
77 Roberto Petagine	.25
78 Darryl Strawberry	.35
79 Tino Martinez	.25
80 Eric Karros	.25
81 Cal Ripken Jr. (Star Struck)	5.00
82 Cecil Fielder (Star Struck)	.40
83 Kirby Puckett (Star Struck)	1.50
84 Jim Edmonds (Star Struck)	.25
85 Matt Williams (Star Struck)	.25
86 Alex Rodriguez (Star Struck)	6.00
87 Barry Larkin (Star Struck)	.40
88 Rafael Palmeiro (Star Struck)	.35
89 David Cone (Star Struck)	.25
90 Roberto Alomar (Star Struck)	.50
91 Eddie Murray (Star Struck)	.40
92 Randy Johnson (Star Struck)	.35
93 Ryan Klesko (Star Struck)	.45
94 Raul Mondesi (Star Struck)	.40
95 Mo Vaughn (Star Struck)	.60
96 Will Clark (Star Struck)	.40
97 Carlos Baerga (Star Struck)	.25
98 Frank Thomas (Star Struck)	5.00
99 Larry Walker (Star Struck)	.40
100 Garret Anderson (Star Struck)	.25
101 Edgar Martinez (Star Struck)	.25
102 Don Mattingly (Star Struck)	.60
103 Tony Gwynn (Star Struck)	.50
104 Albert Belle (Star Struck)	1.50
105 Jason Isringhausen (Star Struck)	.25
106 Ruben Rivera (Star Struck)	.35
107 Johnny Damon (Star Struck)	.35
108 Karim Garcia (Star Struck)	.35
109 Derek Jeter (Star Struck)	.45
110 David Justice (Star Struck)	.35

A player's name in *italic* type indicates a rookie card.

1996 Score Dugout Collection Artist's Proofs

A parallel set within a parallel set, the Artist's Proof logo added to the copper-foil design of the Dugout Collection cards raises the odds of finding one to just once in 36 packs.

	MT
Complete Set (110):	250.00

(Artist's Proofs stars valued at 6X-8X of regular Dugout Collection versions)

1996 Score Future Franchise

Future Franchise is the most difficult insert to pull from packs of Series 2, at the rate of once per 72 packs, on average. Sixteen young stars are showcased on holographic gold-foil printing in the set.

	MT
Complete Set (16):	150.00
Common Player:	5.00
1 Jason Isringhausen	5.00
2 Chipper Jones	35.00
3 Derek Jeter	25.00
4 Alex Rodriguez	55.00
5 Alex Ochoa	5.00
6 Manny Ramirez	15.00
7 Johnny Damon	6.00
8 Ruben Rivera	8.00
9 Karim Garcia	10.00
10 Garret Anderson	5.00
11 Marty Cordova	5.00
12 Bill Pulsipher	5.00
13 Hideo Nomo	12.00
14 Marc Newfield	5.00
15 Charles Johnson	5.00
16 Raul Mondesi	7.00

1996 Score Gold Stars

Appearing once in every 15 packs of Series 2, Gold Stars are labeled with a stamp in the upper-left corner. The set contains 30 top current stars printed on gold-foil and seeded at the average rate of one per 15 packs.

		MT
Complete Set (30):		60.00
Common Player:		.75
1	Ken Griffey Jr.	8.00
2	Frank Thomas	8.00
3	Reggie Sanders	.75
4	Tim Salmon	1.00
5	Mike Piazza	6.00
6	Tony Gwynn	4.00
7	Gary Sheffield	1.00
8	Matt Williams	1.00
9	Bernie Williams	1.50
10	Jason Isringhausen	.75
11	Albert Belle	2.50
12	Chipper Jones	6.00
13	Edgar Martinez	.75
14	Barry Larkin	1.25
15	Barry Bonds	2.50
16	Jeff Bagwell	4.00
17	Greg Maddux	6.00
18	Mo Vaughn	3.00
19	Ryan Klesko	1.50
20	Sammy Sosa	6.00
21	Darren Daulton	.75
22	Ivan Rodriguez	1.50
23	Dante Bichette	1.00
24	Hideo Nomo	1.50
25	Cal Ripken Jr.	8.00
26	Rafael Palmeiro	1.00
27	Larry Walker	1.00
28	Carlos Baerga	.75
29	Randy Johnson	1.50
30	Manny Ramirez	2.50

1996 Score Numbers Game

Some of the 1995 season's most impressive statistical accomplishments are featured in this chase set. Cards are enhanced with gold foil and found in all types of Score packs at an average rate of one per 15 packs.

		MT
Complete Set (30):		60.00
Common Player:		.75
1	Cal Ripken Jr.	8.00
2	Frank Thomas	8.00
3	Ken Griffey Jr.	10.00
4	Mike Piazza	6.00
5	Barry Bonds	2.50
6	Greg Maddux	6.00
7	Jeff Bagwell	4.00
8	Derek Bell	.75
9	Tony Gwynn	4.00
10	Hideo Nomo	1.50
11	Raul Mondesi	1.25
12	Manny Ramirez	2.50
13	Albert Belle	2.50
14	Matt Williams	1.00
15	Jim Edmonds	.75
16	Edgar Martinez	.75
17	Mo Vaughn	3.00
18	Reggie Sanders	.75
19	Chipper Jones	6.00
20	Larry Walker	1.00
21	Juan Gonzalez	5.00
22	Kenny Lofton	2.50
23	Don Mattingly	4.00
24	Ivan Rodriguez	1.25
25	Randy Johnson	1.50
26	Derek Jeter	5.00
27	J.T. Snow	.75
28	Will Clark	1.00
29	Rafael Palmeiro	1.00
30	Alex Rodriguez	8.00

1996 Score Power Pace

Power Pace is exclusive to retail packs in Series 2, where they are found on average every 31 packs. Eighteen top power hitters are featured in this issue in a gold-foil design.

		MT
Complete Set (18):		90.00
Common Player:		2.50
1	Mark McGwire	30.00
2	Albert Belle	6.00
3	Jay Buhner	3.00
4	Frank Thomas	20.00
5	Matt Williams	3.00
6	Gary Sheffield	3.00
7	Mike Piazza	15.00
8	Larry Walker	3.00
9	Mo Vaughn	7.00
10	Rafael Palmeiro	3.00
11	Dante Bichette	3.00
12	Ken Griffey Jr.	25.00
13	Barry Bonds	6.00
14	Manny Ramirez	6.00
15	Sammy Sosa	15.00
16	Tim Salmon	3.00
17	Dave Justice	2.50
18	Eric Karros	2.50

1996 Score Reflexions

Appearing only in hobby packs this insert set pairs 20 veteran stars with 20 up-and-coming players in a foil-printed format. Odds of finding a Reflexions insert are stated as one per 31 packs.

		MT
Complete Set (20):		150.00
Common Player:		2.00
1	Cal Ripken Jr., Chipper Jones	30.00
2	Ken Griffey Jr., Alex Rodriguez	40.00
3	Frank Thomas, Mo Vaughn	30.00
4	Kenny Lofton, Brian Hunter	5.00
5	Don Mattingly, J.T. Snow	6.00
6	Manny Ramirez, Raul Mondesi	6.00
7	Tony Gwynn, Garret Anderson	8.00
8	Rafael Alomar, Carlos Baerga	5.00
9	Andre Dawson, Larry Walker	3.00
10	Barry Larkin, Derek Jeter	15.00
11	Barry Bonds, Reggie Sanders	6.00
12	Mike Piazza, Albert Belle	15.00
13	Wade Boggs, Edgar Martinez	2.00
14	David Cone, John Smoltz	2.00
15	Will Clark, Jeff Bagwell	7.50
16	Mark McGwire, Cecil Fielder	35.00
17	Greg Maddux, Mike Mussina	15.00
18	Randy Johnson, Hideo Nomo	4.00
19	Jim Thome, Dean Palmer	3.00
20	Chuck Knoblauch, Craig Biggio	2.00

1996 Score Titantic Taters

One of the more creative names in the 1996 insert lineup, Titanic Taters are found one in every 31 packs of Series 2 hobby. Gold-foil fronts feature 18 of the game's heaviest hitters.

		MT
Complete Set (18):		100.00
Common Player:		2.50
1	Albert Belle	6.00
2	Frank Thomas	20.00
3	Mo Vaughn	7.00
4	Ken Griffey Jr.	25.00
5	Matt Williams	3.00
6	Mark McGwire	30.00
7	Dante Bichette	3.00

8	Tim Salmon	3.00
9	Jeff Bagwell	8.00
10	Rafael Palmeiro	3.00
11	Mike Piazza	14.00
12	Cecil Fielder	3.00
13	Larry Walker	3.00
14	Sammy Sosa	15.00
15	Manny Ramirez	6.00
16	Gary Sheffield	3.00
17	Barry Bonds	6.00
18	Jay Buhner	3.00

1997 Score

A total of 551 cards make up the base set, with 330 cards sold in Series I and 221 making up Series II. The basic card design features a color action photo surrounded by a white border. The player's name is above the photo, with the team name underneath. Backs feature text and statistics against a white background with the image of the team logo ghosted into the background. Two parallel insert sets - Artist's Proof and Showcase Series - were part of each series. Other inserts in Series I were Pitcher Perfect, The Franchise, The Glowing Franchise, Titanic Taters (retail exclusive), Stellar Season (magazine packs only), and The Highlight Zone (hobby exclusive). Series II inserts were Blastmasters, Heart of the Order and Stand and Deliver. Cards were sold in 10-card packs for 99 cents each.

		MT
Complete Set (551):		35.00
Complete Series 1 Set (330):		20.00
Complete Series 2 Set (221):		15.00
Common Player:		.05
Wax Box:		30.00
1	Jeff Bagwell	.75
2	Mickey Tettleton	.05
3	Johnny Damon	.15
4	Jeff Conine	.05
5	Bernie Williams	.40
6	Will Clark	.20
7	Ryan Klesko	.30
8	Cecil Fielder	.10
9	Paul Wilson	.05
10	Gregg Jefferies	.05
11	Chili Davis	.05
12	Albert Belle	.50
13	Ken Hill	.05
14	Cliff Floyd	.05
15	Jaime Navarro	.05
16	Ismael Valdes	.05
17	Jeff King	.05
18	Chris Bosio	.05
19	Reggie Sanders	.05

20	Darren Daulton	.05
21	Ken Caminiti	.05
22	Mike Piazza	1.25
23	Chad Mottola	.05
24	Darin Erstad	.75
25	Dante Bichette	.15
26	Frank Thomas	1.50
27	Ben McDonald	.05
28	Raul Casanova	.05
29	Kevin Ritz	.05
30	Garret Anderson	.05
31	Jason Kendall	.05
32	Billy Wagner	.05
33	David Justice	.05
34	Marty Cordova	.05
35	Derek Jeter	.75
36	Trevor Hoffman	.05
37	Geronimo Berroa	.05
38	Walt Weiss	.05
39	Kirt Manwaring	.05
40	Alex Gonzalez	.05
41	Sean Berry	.05
42	Kevin Appier	.05
43	Rusty Greer	.05
44	Pete Incaviglia	.05
45	Rafael Palmeiro	.10
46	Eddie Murray	.25
47	Moises Alou	.05
48	Mark Lewis	.05
49	Hal Morris	.05
50	Edgar Renteria	.25
51	Rickey Henderson	.05
52	Pat Listach	.05
53	John Wasdin	.05
54	James Baldwin	.05
55	Brian Jordan	.05
56	Edgar Martinez	.05
57	Wil Cordero	.05
58	Danny Tartabull	.05
59	Keith Lockhart	.05
60	Rico Brogna	.05
61	Ricky Bottalico	.05
62	Terry Pendleton	.05
63	Bret Boone	.05
64	Charlie Hayes	.05
65	Marc Newfield	.05
66	Sterling Hitchcock	.05
67	Roberto Alomar	.50
68	John Jaha	.05
69	Greg Colbrunn	.05
70	Sal Fasano	.05
71	Brooks Kieschnick	.05
72	Pedro Martinez	.05
73	Kevin Elster	.05
74	Ellis Burks	.05
75	Chuck Finley	.05
76	John Olerud	.05
77	Jay Bell	.05
78	Allen Watson	.05
79	Darryl Strawberry	.05
80	Orlando Miller	.05
81	Jose Herrera	.05
82	Andy Pettitte	.40
83	Juan Guzman	.05
84	Alan Benes	.05
85	Jack McDowell	.10
86	Ugueth Urbina	.05
87	Rocky Coppinger	.05
88	Jeff Cirillo	.05
89	Tom Glavine	.15
90	Robby Thompson	.05
91	Barry Bonds	.50
92	Carlos Delgado	.05
93	Mo Vaughn	.50
94	Ryne Sandberg	.40
95	Alex Rodriguez	2.00
96	Brady Anderson	.10
97	Scott Brosius	.05
98	Dennis Eckersley	.05
99	Brian McRae	.05
100	Rey Ordonez	.25
101	John Valentin	.05
102	Brett Butler	.05
103	Eric Karros	.05
104	Harold Baines	.05
105	Javier Lopez	.15
106	Alan Trammell	.05
107	Jim Thome	.25
108	Frank Rodriguez	.05
109	Bernard Gilkey	.05
110	Reggie Jefferson	.05
111	Scott Stahoviak	.05
112	Steve Gibralter	.05
113	Todd Hollandsworth	.05
114	Ruben Rivera	.30
115	Dennis Martinez	.05

116	Mariano Rivera	.25
117	John Smoltz	.20
118	John Mabry	.05
119	Tom Gordon	.05
120	Alex Ochoa	.05
121	Jamey Wright	.05
122	Dave Nilsson	.05
123	Bobby Bonilla	.05
124	Al Leiter	.05
125	Rick Aguilera	.05
126	Jeff Brantley	.05
127	Kevin Brown	.05
128	George Arias	.05
129	Darren Oliver	.05
130	Bill Pulsipher	.05
131	Roberto Hernandez	.05
132	Delino DeShields	.05
133	Mark Grudzielanek	.05
134	John Wetteland	.05
135	Carlos Baerga	.10
136	Paul Sorrento	.05
137	Leo Gomez	.05
138	Andy Ashby	.05
139	Julio Franco	.05
140	Brian Hunter	.05
141	Jermaine Dye	.20
142	Tony Clark	.40
143	Ruben Sierra	.05
144	Donovan Osborne	.05
145	Mark McLemore	.05
146	Terry Steinbach	.05
147	Bob Wells	.05
148	Chan Ho Park	.05
149	Tim Salmon	.20
150	Paul O'Neill	.05
151	Cal Ripken Jr.	1.50
152	Wally Joyner	.05
153	Omar Vizquel	.05
154	Mike Mussina	.40
155	Andres Galarraga	.15
156	Ken Griffey Jr.	2.00
157	Kenny Lofton	.50
158	Ray Durham	.05
159	Hideo Nomo	.40
160	Ozzie Guillen	.05
161	Roger Pavlik	.05
162	Manny Ramirez	.50
163	Mark Lemke	.05
164	Mike Stanley	.05
165	Chuck Knoblauch	.05
166	Kimera Bartee	.05
167	Wade Boggs	.15
168	Jay Buhner	.15
169	Eric Young	.05
170	Jose Canseco	.20
171	Dwight Gooden	.05
172	Fred McGriff	.20
173	Sandy Alomar Jr.	.05
174	Andy Benes	.05
175	Dean Palmer	.05
176	Larry Walker	.25
177	Charles Nagy	.05
178	David Cone	.05
179	Mark Grace	.10
180	Robin Ventura	.05
181	Roger Clemens	.60
182	Bobby Witt	.05
183	Vinny Castilla	.05
184	Gary Sheffield	.15
185	Dan Wilson	.05
186	Roger Cedeno	.05
187	Mark McGwire	3.00
188	Darren Bragg	.05
189	Quinton McCracken	.05
190	Randy Myers	.05
191	Jeromy Burnitz	.05
192	Randy Johnson	.25
193	Chipper Jones	1.25
194	Greg Vaughn	.05
195	Travis Fryman	.05
196	Tim Naehring	.05
197	B.J. Surhoff	.05
198	Juan Gonzalez	.75
199	Terrell Wade	.05
200	Jeff Frye	.05
201	Joey Cora	.05
202	Raul Mondesi	.15
203	Ivan Rodriguez	.50
204	Armando Reynoso	.05
205	Jeffrey Hammonds	.05
206	Darren Dreifort	.05
207	Kevin Seitzer	.05
208	Tino Martinez	.25
209	Jim Bruske	.05
210	Jeff Suppan	.05
211	Mark Carreon	.05

#	Player	Price
212	Wilson Alvarez	.05
213	John Burkett	.05
214	Tony Phillips	.05
215	Greg Maddux	1.25
216	Mark Whiten	.05
217	Curtis Pride	.05
218	Lyle Mouton	.05
219	Todd Hundley	.05
220	Greg Gagne	.05
221	Rich Amaral	.05
222	Tom Goodwin	.05
223	Chris Hoiles	.05
224	Jayhawk Owens	.05
225	Kenny Rogers	.05
226	Mike Greenwell	.05
227	Mark Wohlers	.05
228	Henry Rodriguez	.05
229	Robert Perez	.05
230	Jeff Kent	.05
231	Darryl Hamilton	.05
232	Alex Fernandez	.05
233	Ron Karkovice	.05
234	Jimmy Haynes	.05
235	Craig Biggio	.05
236	Ray Lankford	.05
237	Lance Johnson	.05
238	Matt Williams	.20
239	Chad Curtis	.05
240	Mark Thompson	.05
241	Jason Giambi	.05
242	Barry Larkin	.20
243	Paul Molitor	.20
244	Sammy Sosa	1.00
245	Kevin Tapani	.05
246	Marquis Grissom	.05
247	Joe Carter	.15
248	Ramon Martinez	.05
249	Tony Gwynn	.75
250	Andy Fox	.05
251	Troy O'Leary	.05
252	Warren Newson	.05
253	Troy Percival	.05
254	Jamie Moyer	.05
255	Danny Graves	.05
256	David Wells	.05
257	Todd Zeile	.05
258	Raul Ibanez	.05
259	Tyler Houston	.05
260	LaTroy Hawkins	.05
261	Joey Hamilton	.05
262	Mike Sweeney	.05
263	Brant Brown	.05
264	Pat Hentgen	.05
265	Mark Johnson	.05
266	Robb Nen	.05
267	Justin Thompson	.05
268	Ron Gant	.05
269	Jeff D'Amico	.05
270	Shawn Estes	.05
271	Derek Bell	.05
272	Fernando Valenzuela	.05
273	Luis Castillo	.10
274	Ray Montgomery	.05
275	Ed Sprague	.05
276	F.P. Santangelo	.05
277	Todd Greene	.05
278	Butch Huskey	.05
279	Steve Finley	.05
280	Eric Davis	.05
281	Shawn Green	.05
282	Al Martin	.05
283	Michael Tucker	.05
284	Shane Reynolds	.05
285	Matt Mieske	.05
286	Jose Rosado	.05
287	Mark Langston	.05
288	Ralph Milliard	.05
289	Mike Lansing	.05
290	Scott Servais	.05
291	Royce Clayton	.05
292	Mike Grace	.15
293	James Mouton	.05
294	Charles Johnson	.05
295	Gary Gaetti	.05
296	Kevin Mitchell	.05
297	Carlos Garcia	.05
298	Desi Relaford	.05
299	Jason Thompson	.05
300	Osvaldo Fernandez	.05
301	Fernando Vina	.05
302	Jose Offerman	.05
303	Yamil Benitez	.05
304	J.T. Snow	.05
305	Rafael Bournigal	.05
306	Jason Isringhausen	.05
307	Bob Higginson	.05
308	*Nerio Rodriguez*	.25
309	Brian Giles	.05
310	Andruw Jones	1.00
311	Billy McMillon	.05
312	Arquimedez Pozo	.05
313	Jermaine Allensworth	.05
314	Luis Andujar	.05
315	Angel Echevarria	.05
316	Karim Garcia	.30
317	Trey Beamon	.05
318	Makoto Suzuki	.05
319	Robin Jennings	.05
320	Dmitri Young	.05
321	*Damon Mashore*	.05
322	Wendell Magee	.05
323	*Dax Jones*	.05
324	Todd Walker	.40
325	Marvin Benard	.05
326	*Brian Raabe*	.05
327	Marcus Jensen	.05
328	Checklist	.05
329	Checklist	.05
330	Checklist	.05
331	Norm Charlton	.05
332	Bruce Ruffin	.05
333	John Wetteland	.05
334	Marquis Grissom	.05
335	Sterling Hitchcock	.05
336	John Olerud	.05
337	David Wells	.05
338	Chili Davis	.05
339	Mark Lewis	.05
340	Kenny Lofton	.50
341	Alex Fernandez	.05
342	Ruben Sierra	.05
343	Delino DeShields	.05
344	John Wasdin	.05
345	Dennis Martinez	.05
346	Kevin Elster	.05
347	Bobby Bonilla	.10
348	Jaime Navarro	.05
349	Chad Curtis	.05
350	Terry Steinbach	.05
351	Ariel Prieto	.05
352	Jeff Kent	.05
353	Carlos Garcia	.05
354	Mark Whiten	.05
355	Todd Zeile	.05
356	Eric Davis	.05
357	Greg Colbrunn	.05
358	Moises Alou	.05
359	Allen Watson	.05
360	Jose Canseco	.20
361	Matt Williams	.25
362	Jeff King	.05
363	Darryl Hamilton	.05
364	Mark Clark	.05
365	J.T. Snow	.05
366	Kevin Mitchell	.05
367	Orlando Miller	.05
368	Rico Brogna	.05
369	Mike James	.05
370	Brad Ausmus	.05
371	Darryl Kile	.05
372	Edgardo Alfonzo	.05
373	Julian Tavarez	.05
374	Darren Lewis	.05
375	Steve Karsay	.05
376	Lee Stevens	.05
377	Albie Lopez	.05
378	Orel Hershiser	.05
379	Lee Smith	.05
380	Rick Helling	.05
381	Carlos Perez	.05
382	Tony Tarasco	.05
383	Melvin Nieves	.05
384	Benji Gil	.05
385	Devon White	.05
386	Armando Benitez	.05
387	Bill Swift	.05
388	John Smiley	.05
389	Midre Cummings	.05
390	Tim Belcher	.05
391	Tim Raines	.05
392	Todd Worrell	.05
393	Quilvio Veras	.05
394	Matt Lawton	.05
395	Aaron Sele	.05
396	Bip Roberts	.05
397	Denny Neagle	.05
398	Tyler Green	.05
399	Hipolito Pichardo	.05
400	Scott Erickson	.05
401	Bobby Jones	.05
402	Jim Edmonds	.05
403	Chad Ogea	.05
404	Cal Eldred	.05
405	Pat Listach	.05
406	Todd Stottlemyre	.05
407	Phil Nevin	.05
408	Otis Nixon	.05
409	Billy Ashley	.05
410	Jimmy Key	.05
411	Mike Timlin	.05
412	Joe Vitiello	.05
413	Rondell White	.05
414	Jeff Fassero	.05
415	Rex Hudler	.05
416	Curt Schilling	.05
417	Rich Becker	.05
418	William VanLandingham	.05
419	Chris Snopek	.05
420	David Segui	.05
421	Eddie Murray	.25
422	Shane Andrews	.05
423	Gary DiSarcina	.05
424	Brian Hunter	.05
425	Willie Greene	.05
426	Felipe Crespo	.05
427	Jason Bates	.05
428	Albert Belle	.50
429	Rey Sanchez	.05
430	Roger Clemens	.75
431	Deion Sanders	.20
432	Ernie Young	.05
433	Jay Bell	.05
434	Jeff Blauser	.05
435	Lenny Dykstra	.05
436	Chuck Carr	.05
437	Russ Davis	.05
438	Carl Everett	.05
439	Damion Easley	.05
440	Pat Kelly	.05
441	Pat Rapp	.05
442	David Justice	.15
443	Graeme Lloyd	.05
444	Damon Buford	.05
445	Jose Valentin	.05
446	Jason Schmidt	.05
447	Dave Martinez	.05
448	Danny Tartabull	.05
449	Jose Vizcaino	.05
450	Steve Avery	.05
451	Mike Devereaux	.05
452	Jim Eisenreich	.05
453	Mark Leiter	.05
454	Roberto Kelly	.05
455	Benito Santiago	.05
456	Steve Trachsel	.05
457	Gerald Williams	.05
458	Pete Schourek	.05
459	Esteban Loaiza	.05
460	Mel Rojas	.05
461	Tim Wakefield	.05
462	Tony Fernandez	.05
463	Doug Drabek	.05
464	Joe Girardi	.05
465	Mike Bordick	.05
466	Jim Leyritz	.05
467	Erik Hanson	.05
468	Michael Tucker	.05
469	*Tony Womack*	.25
470	Doug Glanville	.05
471	Rudy Pemberton	.05
472	Keith Lockhart	.05
473	Nomar Garciaparra	1.25
474	Scott Rolen	.75
475	Jason Dickson	.15
476	Glendon Rusch	.05
477	Todd Walker	.40
478	Dmitri Young	.05
479	*Rod Myers*	.05
480	Wilton Guerrero	.15
481	Jorge Posada	.05
482	Brant Brown	.05
483	*Bubba Trammell*	.60
484	Jose Guillen	.50
485	Scott Spiezio	.05
486	Bob Abreu	.05
487	Chris Holt	.05
488	*Deivi Cruz*	.25
489	Vladimir Guerrero	.60
490	Julio Santana	.05
491	Ray Montgomery	.05
492	Kevin Orie	.05
493	Todd Hundley (Goin' Yard)	.10
494	Tim Salmon (Goin' Yard)	.15
495	Albert Belle (Goin' Yard)	.25
496	Manny Ramirez (Goin' Yard)	.25
497	Rafael Palmeiro (Goin' Yard)	.10

498	Juan Gonzalez (Goin' Yard)	.40
499	Ken Griffey Jr. (Goin' Yard)	1.00
500	Andruw Jones (Goin' Yard)	.50
501	Mike Piazza (Goin' Yard)	.60
502	Jeff Bagwell (Goin' Yard)	.40
503	Bernie Williams (Goin' Yard)	.20
504	Barry Bonds (Goin' Yard)	.25
505	Ken Caminiti (Goin' Yard)	.10
506	Darin Erstad (Goin' Yard)	.50
507	Alex Rodriguez (Goin' Yard)	1.00
508	Frank Thomas (Goin' Yard)	1.00
509	Chipper Jones (Goin' Yard)	.60
510	Mo Vaughn (Goin' Yard)	.25
511	Mark McGwire (Goin' Yard)	1.50
512	Fred McGriff (Goin' Yard)	.15
513	Jay Buhner (Goin' Yard)	.10
514	Jim Thome (Goin' Yard)	.15
515	Gary Sheffield (Goin' Yard)	.15
516	Dean Palmer (Goin' Yard)	.05
517	Henry Rodriguez (Goin' Yard)	.05
518	Andy Pettitte (Rock & Fire)	.25
519	Mike Mussina (Rock & Fire)	.20
520	Greg Maddux (Rock & Fire)	.60
521	John Smoltz (Rock & Fire)	.10
522	Hideo Nomo (Rock & Fire)	.20
523	Troy Percival (Rock & Fire)	.05
524	John Wetteland (Rock & Fire)	.05
525	Roger Clemens (Rock & Fire)	.25
526	Charles Nagy (Rock & Fire)	.05
527	Mariano Rivera (Rock & Fire)	.10
528	Tom Glavine (Rock & Fire)	.10
529	Randy Johnson (Rock & Fire)	.20
530	Jason Isringhausen (Rock & Fire)	.05
531	Alex Fernandez (Rock & Fire)	.05
532	Kevin Brown (Rock & Fire)	.05
533	Chuck Knoblauch (True Grit)	.10
534	Rusty Greer (True Grit)	.05
535	Tony Gwynn (True Grit)	.40
536	Ryan Klesko (True Grit)	.20
537	Ryne Sandberg (True Grit)	.25
538	Barry Larkin (True Grit)	.10
539	Will Clark (True Grit)	.10
540	Kenny Lofton (True Grit)	.25
541	Paul Molitor (True Grit)	.15
542	Roberto Alomar (True Grit)	.20
543	Rey Ordonez (True Grit)	.05
544	Jason Giambi (True Grit)	.05
545	Derek Jeter (True Grit)	.60
546	Cal Ripken Jr. (True Grit)	.75
547	Ivan Rodriguez (True Grit)	.20
548	Checklist(Ken Griffey Jr.)	.75
549	Checklist(Frank Thomas)	.75
550	Checklist(Mike Piazza)	.50
551	*Hideki Irabu*	1.50

1997 Score Blast Masters

This 18-card set was inserted into every 35 Series II retail packs and every 23 hobby packs. The set displays the top power hitters in the game over a prismatic gold foil background. The word "Blast" is printed across the top, while "Master" is printed across the bottom, both in red. Backs are predominantly black with a color player photo at center.

		MT
Complete Set (18):		125.00
Common Player:		2.00
1	Mo Vaughn	6.00
2	Mark McGwire	30.00
3	Juan Gonzalez	10.00
4	Albert Belle	6.00
5	Barry Bonds	6.00
6	Ken Griffey Jr.	25.00
7	Andruw Jones	10.00
8	Chipper Jones	15.00
9	Mike Piazza	15.00
10	Jeff Bagwell	10.00
11	Dante Bichette	2.00
12	Alex Rodriguez	25.00
13	Gary Sheffield	3.00
14	Ken Caminiti	2.00
15	Sammy Sosa	15.00
16	Vladimir Guerrero	8.00
17	Brian Jordan	2.00
18	Tim Salmon	3.00

1997 Score Heart of the Order

This 36-card set was distributed in Series II retail and hobby packs, with cards 1-18 in retail (one per 23 packs) and cards 19-36 in hobby (one per 15). The cards are printed in a horizontal format, with some of the top hitters in the game included in the insert. Fronts are highlighted in red metallic foil. Backs have a color portrait photo and a few words about the player.

		MT
Complete Set (36):		170.00
Complete Retail Set (1-18):		100.00
Complete Hobby Set (19-36):		70.00
Common Player:		1.50
1	Ivan Rodriguez	4.00
2	Will Clark	2.00
3	Juan Gonzalez	10.00
4	Frank Thomas	15.00
5	Albert Belle	5.00
6	Robin Ventura	1.50
7	Alex Rodriguez	15.00
8	Ken Griffey Jr.	20.00
9	Jay Buhner	1.50
10	Roberto Alomar	4.00
11	Rafael Palmeiro	2.00
12	Cal Ripken Jr.	15.00
13	Manny Ramirez	5.00
14	Matt Williams	2.50
15	Jim Thome	3.00
16	Wade Boggs	2.00
17	Derek Jeter	10.00
18	Bernie Williams	4.00
19	Chipper Jones	12.00
20	Andruw Jones	8.00
21	Ryan Klesko	4.00
22	Wilton Guerrero	1.50
23	Mike Piazza	12.00

24	Raul Mondesi	2.50
25	Tony Gwynn	10.00
26	Ken Caminiti	2.00
27	Greg Vaughn	1.50
28	Brian Jordan	1.50
29	Ron Gant	1.50
30	Dmitri Young	1.50
31	Darin Erstad	7.00
32	Jim Edmonds	1.50
33	Tim Salmon	2.00
34	Chuck Knoblauch	2.00
35	Paul Molitor	3.00
36	Todd Walker	5.00

1997 Score Pitcher Perfect

Seattle Mariners' star pitcher and accomplished photographer Randy Johnson makes his picks for the top talent in this 1997 Score Series I insert set. Fronts have player photos with a gold-foil filmstrip graphic at bottom featuring player names and a portrait of The Big Unit. Backs have additional color photos in a filmstrip design and a few words about the player.

		MT
Complete Set (15):		70.00
Common Player:		1.50
1	Cal Ripken Jr.	12.00
2	Alex Rodriguez	12.00
3	Cal Ripken Jr., Alex Rodriguez	12.00
4	Edgar Martinez	1.50
5	Ivan Rodriguez	2.00
6	Mark McGwire	15.00
7	Tim Salmon	2.00
8	Chili Davis	1.50
9	Joe Carter	2.00
10	Frank Thomas	12.00
11	Will Clark	2.00
12	Mo Vaughn	5.00
13	Wade Boggs	3.00
14	Ken Griffey Jr.	15.00
15	Randy Johnson	2.00

1997 Score Premium Stock

This is an upscale version of Score's regular 1997 issue, designated for hobby sales only. The cards are basically the same as the regular issue, except for the use of gray borders on front and an embossed gold-foil "Premium Stock" logo.

		MT
Complete Set (551):		70.00
Common Player:		.10
	(Star cards and rookies valued at 1.5-2X same cards in regular issue)	

1997 Score Showcase

A silver metallic-foil background distinguishes the cards in this parallel set, inserted at a rate of about one per seven packs of both hobby and retail.

	MT
Complete Set (551):	450.00
Common Player:	.50
(Stars and rookies valued about 4-8X same cards in regular issue)	

1997 Score Showcase Artist's Proofs

This is a parallel of the Show-case parallel set covering all 330 cards of the base '97 Score set. The Artist's Proofs cards carry over the textured silver foil background of the Showcase cards on front, and are marked with a round red "ARTIST'S PROOF" logo.

	MT
Complete Set (330):	750.00
Common Player:	1.50
(Star cards valued at 20X-40X regular Score cards.)	

1997 Score Stand & Deliver

This 24-card insert was printed on a silver foil background, with the series name and team logo in gold foil across the bottom. Cards were found in Series II packs one per 71 retail, one per 41 hobby. Card numbers 21-24 (Florida Marlins) were designated as the winning group, meaning the first 225 collectors that mailed in the complete four card set received a gold upgrade version of the set framed in glass.

		MT
Complete Set (24):		325.00
Common Player:		4.00
1	Andruw Jones	20.00
2	Greg Maddux	30.00
3	Chipper Jones	30.00
4	John Smoltz	4.00
5	Ken Griffey Jr.	50.00
6	Alex Rodriguez	40.00
7	Jay Buhner	4.00
8	Randy Johnson	10.00
9	Derek Jeter	25.00
10	Andy Pettitte	12.00
11	Bernie Williams	12.00
12	Mariano Rivera	4.00
13	Mike Piazza	30.00
14	Hideo Nomo	10.00
15	Raul Mondesi	4.00
16	Todd Hollandsworth	4.00

17	Manny Ramirez	15.00
18	Jim Thome	10.00
19	David Justice	6.00
20	Matt Williams	8.00
21	Juan Gonzalez	25.00
22	Jeff Bagwell	20.00
23	Cal Ripken Jr.	40.00
24	Frank Thomas	40.00

1997 Score Stellar Season

These 1997 Score Series I inserts were seeded one per every 17 magazine packs.

		MT
Complete Set (18):		90.00
Common Player:		2.00
1	Juan Gonzalez	9.00
2	Chuck Knoblauch	4.00
3	Jeff Bagwell	7.50
4	John Smoltz	3.00
5	Mark McGwire	25.00
6	Ken Griffey Jr.	20.00
7	Frank Thomas	15.00
8	Alex Rodriguez	15.00
9	Mike Piazza	12.00
10	Albert Belle	5.00
11	Roberto Alomar	4.00
12	Sammy Sosa	12.00
13	Mo Vaughn	5.00
14	Brady Anderson	2.00
15	Henry Rodriguez	2.00
16	Eric Young	2.00
17	Gary Sheffield	2.00
18	Ryan Klesko	3.00

1997 Score Team Collection

Team sets consisting of 15 players each were produced for 10 different teams. Each card is similar in design to the regular 1997 Score set except for a special foil stamping at the bottom of the card that corresponds with team colors. In a parallel "Platinum" version, seeded one per six packs, the background and team foil on front are replaced with silver prismatic foil. A top of the line parallel set, "Premier" utilizes gold foil highlights on fronts and is found one per 31 packs. Team Collection was sold in five-card, single-team packs with a suggested retail price of about $1.29. It was reported that 100 cases of each team were issued.

		MT
Complete Set (150):		60.00
Common Player:		.25
Platinums: 4x to 6x		
Premiers: 15x to 20x		
Braves Wax Box:		80.00
Orioles Wax Box:		70.00
Red Sox Wax Box:		60.00
White Sox Wax Box:		70.00
Indians Wax Box:		70.00
Rockies Wax Box:		55.00
Dodgers Wax Box:		70.00
Yankees Wax Box:		75.00
Mariners Wax Box:		120.00
Rangers Wax Box:		60.00
	Atlanta Braves	8.00
1	Ryan Klesko	.60
2	David Justice	.35
3	Terry Pendleton	.25
4	Tom Glavine	.35
5	Javier Lopez	.35
6	John Smoltz	.35
7	Jermaine Dye	.40
8	Mark Lemke	.25
9	Fred McGriff	.40
10	Chipper Jones	2.50
11	Terrell Wade	.25
12	Greg Maddux	2.50
13	Mark Wohlers	.25
14	Marquis Grissom	.25
15	Andruw Jones	2.50
	Baltimore Orioles	5.00
1	Rafael Palmeiro	.35
2	Eddie Murray	.50
3	Roberto Alomar	1.00
4	Rocky Coppinger	.25
5	Brady Anderson	.35
6	Bobby Bonilla	.35
7	Cal Ripken Jr.	3.00
8	Mike Mussina	.50
9	Nerio Rodriguez	.25
10	Randy Myers	.25
11	B.J. Surhoff	.25
12	Jeffrey Hammonds	.25
13	Chris Hoiles	.25
14	Jimmy Haynes	.25
15	David Wells	.25
	Boston Red Sox	4.00
1	Wil Cordero	.25
2	Mo Vaughn	1.50
3	John Valentin	.25
4	Reggie Jefferson	.25
5	Tom Gordon	.25
6	Mike Stanley	.25
7	Jose Canseco	.40
8	Roger Clemens	.75
9	Darren Bragg	.25
10	Jeff Frye	.25
11	Jeff Suppan	.25
12	Mike Greenwell	.25
13	Arquimedez Pozo	.25
14	Tim Naehring	.25
15	Troy O'Leary	.25
	Chicago White Sox	6.00
1	Frank Thomas	4.00
2	James Baldwin	.25
3	Danny Tartabull	.25
4	Jeff Darwin	.25
5	Harold Baines	.25
6	Roberto Hernandez	.25

7	Ray Durham	.25
8	Robin Ventura	.25
9	Wilson Alvarez	.25
10	Lyle Mouton	.25
11	Alex Fernandez	.30
12	Ron Karkovice	.25
13	Kevin Tapani	.25
14	Tony Phillips	.25
15	Mike Cameron	.25
	Cleveland Indians	6.00
1	Albert Belle	1.50
2	Jack McDowell	.30
3	Jim Thome	.60
4	Dennis Martinez	.25
5	Julio Franco	.25
6	Omar Vizquel	.25
7	Kenny Lofton	1.25
8	Manny Ramirez	1.25
9	Sandy Alomar Jr.	.25
10	Charles Nagy	.25
11	Kevin Seitzer	.25
12	Mark Carreon	.25
13	Jeff Kent	.25
14	Danny Graves	.25
15	Brian Giles	.25
	Colorado Rockies	4.00
1	Dante Bichette	.40
2	Kevin Ritz	.25
3	Walt Weiss	.25
4	Ellis Burks	.25
5	Jamey Wright	.25
6	Andres Galarraga	.35
7	Eric Young	.25
8	Larry Walker	.50
9	Vinny Castilla	.25
10	Quinton McCracken	.25
11	Armando Reynoso	.25
12	Jayhawk Owens	.25
13	Mark Thompson	.25
14	John Burke	.25
15	Bruce Ruffin	.25
	Los Angeles Dodgers	6.00
1	Ismael Valdez	.25
2	Mike Piazza	2.50
3	Todd Hollandsworth	.40
4	Delino DeShields	.25
5	Chan Ho Park	.25
6	Roger Cedeno	.25
7	Raul Mondesi	.40
8	Darren Dreifort	.25
9	Jim Bruske	.25
10	Greg Gagne	.25
11	Chad Curtis	.25
12	Ramon Martinez	.25
13	Brett Butler	.25
14	Eric Karros	.25
15	Hideo Nomo	.75
	New York Yankees	6.00
1	Bernie Williams	.75
2	Cecil Fielder	.40
3	Derek Jeter	2.50
4	Darryl Strawberry	.25
5	Andy Pettitte	1.00
6	Ruben Rivera	.50
7	Mariano Rivera	.40
8	John Wetteland	.25
9	Paul O'Neill	.25
10	Wade Boggs	.40
11	Dwight Gooden	.25
12	David Cone	.35
13	Tino Martinez	.25
14	Kenny Rogers	.25
15	Andy Fox	.25
	Seattle Mariners	12.00
1	Chris Bosio	.25
2	Edgar Martinez	.25
3	Alex Rodriguez	4.00
4	Paul Sorrento	.25
5	Bob Wells	.25
6	Ken Griffey Jr.	4.00
7	Jay Buhner	.40
8	Dan Wilson	.25
9	Randy Johnson	.40
10	Joey Cora	.25
11	Mark Whiten	.25
12	Rich Amaral	.25
13	Raul Ibanez	.25
14	Jamie Moyer	.25
15	Makoto Suzuki	.25
	Texas Rangers	5.00
1	Mickey Tettleton	.25
2	Will Clark	.40
3	Ken Hill	.25
4	Rusty Greer	.25
5	Kevin Elster	.25
6	Darren Oliver	.25

7	Mark McLemore	.25
8	Roger Pavlik	.25
9	Dean Palmer	.25
10	Bobby Witt	.25
11	Juan Gonzalez	2.00
12	Ivan Rodriguez	.50
13	Darryl Hamilton	.25
14	John Burkett	.25
15	Warren Newson	.25

1997 Score
Team Collection
Platinum Team

Team sets consisting of 15 players each were produced for 10 different teams. Each card is similar in design to the regular 1997 Score set except for a special foil stamping at the bottom of the card that corresponds with team colors. In a parallel "Platinum" version, seeded one per six packs, the background and team foil on front are replaced with silver prismatic foil. Backs are overprinted in gold script, "Platinum Team." Team Collection was sold in five-card, single-team packs with a suggested retail price of about $1.29. It was reported that 100 cases of each team were issued.

		MT
Complete Set (150):		250.00
Common Player:		2.00
	(Star cards valued at 4X-6X same cards in regular Team Collection.)	

1997 Score
Team Collection
Premier Club

Team sets consisting of 15 players each were produced for 10 different teams. Each card is similar in design to the regular 1997 Score set except for a special foil stamping at the bottom of the card that corresponds with team colors. In a top of the line parallel "Premier Club" version, seeded one per 31 packs, the background and team foil on front are replaced with gold prismatic foil, and backs are overprinted "Premier Club" in gold script. Team Collection was sold in five-card, single-team packs with a suggested retail price of about $1.29. It was reported that 100 cases of each team were issued.

		MT
Complete Set (150):		900.00
Common Player:		6.00
	(Star cards valued at 15X to 20X regular Team Collection version.)	

1997 Score
The Franchise

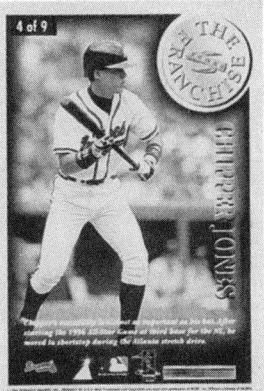

There were two versions made for these 1997 Score Series I inserts - regular and The Glowing Franchise, which has glow-in-the-dark highlights. The regular version is seeded one per 72 packs; glow-in-the-dark cards are seeded one per 240 packs, and generally valued about 2-3x regular.

		MT
Complete Set (9):		120.00
Common Player:		4.00
1	Ken Griffey Jr.	30.00
2	John Smoltz	4.00
3	Cal Ripken Jr.	25.00
4	Chipper Jones	20.00
5	Mike Piazza	20.00
6	Albert Belle	10.00
7	Frank Thomas	25.00
8	Sammy Sosa	15.00
9	Roberto Alomar	10.00

1997 Score
The Highlight Zone

Exclusive to 1997 Score Series I hobby packs are these Highlight Zone inserts, seeded one per every 35 packs. Within the 18-card set, card numbers 1-9 are in regular hobby packs, while numbers 10-18 are found only in premium stock packs.

		MT
Complete Set (18):		120.00
Common Player:		2.00
1	Frank Thomas	15.00
2	Ken Griffey Jr.	20.00
3	Mo Vaughn	7.00
4	Albert Belle	5.00
5	Mike Piazza	12.00
6	Barry Bonds	5.00
7	Greg Maddux	12.00
8	Sammy Sosa	12.00
9	Jeff Bagwell	8.00
10	Alex Rodriguez	15.00
11	Chipper Jones	12.00
12	Brady Anderson	2.00
13	Ozzie Smith	4.00
14	Edgar Martinez	2.00
15	Cal Ripken Jr.	15.00
16	Ryan Klesko	4.00
17	Randy Johnson	4.00
18	Eddie Murray	3.50

1997 Score Titanic Taters

Some of the game's most powerful hitters are featured on these 1997 Score Series I inserts. The cards were seeded one per every 35 retail packs.

		MT
Complete Set (18):		120.00
Common Player:		3.00
1	Mark McGwire	30.00
2	Mike Piazza	15.00
3	Ken Griffey Jr.	25.00
4	Juan Gonzalez	12.00
5	Frank Thomas	20.00
6	Albert Belle	6.00
7	Sammy Sosa	15.00
8	Jeff Bagwell	10.00
9	Todd Hundley	3.00
10	Ryan Klesko	4.00
11	Brady Anderson	3.00
12	Mo Vaughn	8.00
13	Jay Buhner	3.00
14	Greg Vaughn	3.00
15	Barry Bonds	6.00
16	Gary Sheffield	4.00
17	Alex Rodriguez	20.00
18	Cecil Fielder	3.00

1998 Score

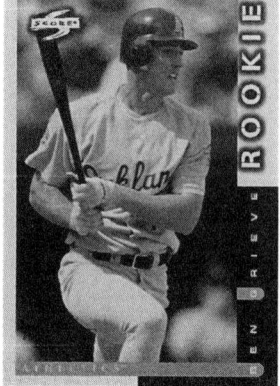

The cards in the 270-card base set feature a color photo inside a black and white border. The player's name is printed in the left border. The entire base set is paralleled in the silver-foil Showcase Series (1:5). The Artist's Proof partial parallel gives a prismatic foil treatment to 165 base cards and was seeded 1:23. Inserts included All-Stars, Complete Players and Epix.

		MT
Complete Set (270):		15.00
Common Player:		.05
Showcases: 3x to 6x		
Inserted 1:7		
Artist's Proofs: 10x to 20x		
Inserted 1:35		
Wax Box:		32.00
1	Andruw Jones	1.00
2	Dan Wilson	.05
3	Hideo Nomo	.40
4	Chuck Carr	.05
5	Barry Bonds	.50
6	Jack McDowell	.05
7	Albert Belle	.50
8	Francisco Cordova	.05
9	Greg Maddux	1.25
10	Alex Rodriguez	1.50
11	Steve Avery	.05
12	Chuck McElroy	.05
13	Larry Walker	.20
14	Hideki Irabu	.75
15	Roberto Alomar	.40
16	Neifi Perez	.05
17	Jim Thome	.30
18	Rickey Henderson	.05
19	Andres Galarraga	.20
20	Jeff Fassero	.05
21	Kevin Young	.05
22	Derek Jeter	1.25
23	Andy Benes	.05
24	Mike Piazza	1.25
25	Todd Stottlemyre	.05
26	Michael Tucker	.05
27	Denny Neagle	.05
28	Javier Lopez	.10
29	Aaron Sele	.05
30	Ryan Klesko	.25
31	Dennis Eckersley	.10
32	Quinton McCracken	.05
33	Brian Anderson	.05
34	Ken Griffey Jr.	2.00
35	Shawn Estes	.05
36	Tim Wakefield	.05
37	Jimmy Key	.05
38	Jeff Bagwell	.75
39	Edgardo Alfonzo	.05
40	Mike Cameron	.05
41	Mark McGwire	2.50
42	Tino Martinez	.15
43	Cal Ripken Jr.	1.50
44	Curtis Goodwin	.05
45	Bobby Ayala	.05
46	Sandy Alomar Jr.	.10
47	Bobby Jones	.05
48	Omar Vizquel	.05
49	Roger Clemens	.75
50	Tony Gwynn	1.00
51	Chipper Jones	1.25
52	Ron Coomer	.05
53	Dmitri Young	.05
54	Brian Giles	.05
55	Steve Finley	.05
56	David Cone	.10
57	Andy Pettitte	.50
58	Wilton Guerrero	.05
59	Deion Sanders	.15
60	Carlos Delgado	.05
61	Jason Giambi	.05
62	Ozzie Guillen	.05
63	Jay Bell	.05
64	Barry Larkin	.15
65	Sammy Sosa	1.00
66	Bernie Williams	.40
67	Terry Steinbach	.05
68	Scott Rolen	1.00
69	Melvin Nieves	.05
70	Craig Biggio	.10
71	Todd Greene	.05
72	Greg Gagne	.05
73	Shigetosi Hasegawa	.05
74	Mark McLemore	.05
75	Darren Bragg	.05
76	Brett Butler	.05
77	Ron Gant	.10
78	Mike Difelice	.05
79	Charles Nagy	.05
80	Scott Hatteberg	.05
81	Brady Anderson	.15
82	Jay Buhner	.15
83	Todd Hollandsworth	.05
84	Geronimo Berroa	.05
85	Jeff Suppan	.05
86	Pedro Martinez	.20
87	Roger Cedeno	.05
88	Ivan Rodriguez	.40
89	Jaime Navarro	.05
90	Chris Hoiles	.05
91	Nomar Garciaparra	1.25
92	Rafael Palmeiro	.15
93	Darin Erstad	.75
94	Kenny Lofton	.50
95	Mike Timlin	.05
96	Chris Clemons	.05
97	Vinny Castilla	.10
98	Charlie Hayes	.05
99	Lyle Mouton	.05
100	Jason Dickson	.05
101	Justin Thompson	.05
102	Pat Kelly	.05
103	Chan Ho Park	.05
104	Ray Lankford	.05
105	Frank Thomas	1.50
106	Jermaine Allensworth	.05
107	Doug Drabek	.05
108	Todd Hundley	.15
109	Carl Everett	.05
110	Edgar Martinez	.05
111	Robin Ventura	.05
112	John Wetteland	.05
113	Mariano Rivera	.15
114	Jose Rosado	.05
115	Ken Caminiti	.15
116	Paul O'Neill	.15
117	Tim Salmon	.20
118	Eduardo Perez	.05
119	Mike Jackson	.05
120	John Smoltz	.10
121	Brant Brown	.05
122	John Mabry	.05
123	Chuck Knoblauch	.20
124	Reggie Sanders	.05
125	Ken Hill	.05
126	Mike Mussina	.40
127	Chad Curtis	.05
128	Todd Worrell	.05
129	Chris Widger	.05
130	Damon Mashore	.05
131	Kevin Brown	.10
132	Bip Roberts	.05
133	Tim Naehring	.05
134	Dave Martinez	.05
135	Jeff Blauser	.05
136	David Justice	.20
137	Dave Hollins	.05
138	Pat Hentgen	.05
139	Darren Daulton	.05
140	Ramon Martinez	.05
141	Raul Casanova	.05
142	Tom Glavine	.15
143	J.T. Snow	.05
144	Tony Graffanino	.05
145	Randy Johnson	.35
146	Orlando Merced	.05
147	Jeff Juden	.05
148	Darryl Kile	.05
149	Ray Durham	.05
150	Alex Fernandez	.05
151	Joey Cora	.05
152	Royce Clayton	.05
153	Randy Myers	.05
154	Charles Johnson	.05
155	Alan Benes	.05
156	Mike Bordick	.05
157	Heathcliff Slocumb	.05
158	Roger Bailey	.05
159	Reggie Jefferson	.05
160	Ricky Bottalico	.05
161	Scott Erickson	.05
162	Matt Williams	.20
163	Robb Nen	.05
164	Matt Stairs	.05
165	Ismael Valdes	.05
166	Lee Stevens	.05
167	Gary DiSarcina	.05
168	Brad Radke	.05
169	Mike Lansing	.05

170	Armando Benitez	.05
171	Mike James	.05
172	Russ Davis	.05
173	Lance Johnson	.05
174	Joey Hamilton	.05
175	John Valentin	.05
176	David Segui	.05
177	David Wells	.05
178	Delino DeShields	.05
179	Eric Karros	.10
180	Jim Leyritz	.05
181	Raul Mondesi	.15
182	Travis Fryman	.05
183	Todd Zeile	.05
184	Brian Jordan	.05
185	Rey Ordonez	.05
186	Jim Edmonds	.05
187	Terrell Wade	.05
188	Marquis Grissom	.10
189	Chris Snopek	.05
190	Shane Reynolds	.05
191	Jeff Frye	.05
192	Paul Sorrento	.05
193	James Baldwin	.05
194	Brian McRae	.05
195	Fred McGriff	.15
196	Troy Percival	.05
197	Rich Amaral	.05
198	Juan Guzman	.05
199	Cecil Fielder	.10
200	Willie Blair	.05
201	Chili Davis	.05
202	Gary Gaetti	.05
203	B.J. Surhoff	.05
204	Steve Cooke	.05
205	Chuck Finley	.05
206	Jeff Kent	.05
207	Ben McDonald	.05
208	Jeffrey Hammonds	.05
209	Tom Goodwin	.05
210	Billy Ashley	.05
211	Wil Cordero	.05
212	Shawon Dunston	.05
213	Tony Phillips	.05
214	Jamie Moyer	.05
215	John Jaha	.05
216	Troy O'Leary	.05
217	Brad Ausmus	.05
218	Garret Anderson	.05
219	Wilson Alvarez	.05
220	Kent Mercker	.05
221	Wade Boggs	.15
222	Mark Wohlers	.05
223	Kevin Appier	.05
224	Tony Fernandez	.05
225	Ugueth Urbina	.05
226	Gregg Jefferies	.05
227	Mo Vaughn	.50
228	Arthur Rhodes	.05
229	Jorge Fabregas	.05
230	Mark Gardner	.05
231	Shane Mack	.05
232	Jorge Posada	.05
233	Jose Cruz Jr.	.75
234	Paul Konerko	.60
235	Derrek Lee	.05
236	*Steve Woodard*	.15
237	Todd Dunwoody	.05
238	Fernando Tatis	.20
239	Jacob Cruz	.05
240	*Pokey Reese*	.05
241	Mark Kotsay	.30
242	Matt Morris	.05
243	*Antone Williamson*	.05
244	Ben Grieve	.60
245	Ryan McGuire	.05
246	*Lou Collier*	.05
247	*Shannon Stewart*	.05
248	*Brett Tomko*	.05
249	Bobby Estalella	.05
250	*Livan Hernandez*	.05
251	Todd Helton	.40
252	Jaret Wright	.75
253	Darryl Hamilton (Interleague Moments)	.05
254	Stan Javier (Interleague Moments)	.05
255	Glenallen Hill (Interleague Moments)	.05
256	Mark Gardner (Interleague Moments)	.05
257	Cal Ripken Jr. (Interleague Moments)	.75
258	Mike Mussina (Interleague Moments)	.20
259	Mike Piazza (Interleague Moments)	.60
260	Sammy Sosa (Interleague Moments)	.50
261	Todd Hundley (Interleague Moments)	.05
262	Eric Karros (Interleague Moments)	.05
263	Denny Neagle (Interleague Moments)	.05
264	Jeromy Burnitz (Interleague Moments)	.05
265	Greg Maddux (Interleague Moments)	.60
266	Tony Clark (Interleague Moments)	.20
267	Vladimir Guerrero (Interleague Moments)	.40
268	Checklist	.05
269	Checklist	.05
270	Checklist	.05

1998 Score All-Stars

All-Stars is a 20-card insert featuring the top players in baseball. The cards were inserted one per 35 packs.

		MT
Complete Set (20):		125.00
Common Player:		2.00
Inserted 1:35		
1	Mike Piazza	15.00
2	Ivan Rodriguez	6.00
3	Frank Thomas	20.00
4	Mark McGwire	30.00
5	Ryne Sandberg	6.00
6	Roberto Alomar	4.00
7	Cal Ripken Jr.	20.00
8	Barry Larkin	2.00
9	Paul Molitor	3.00
10	Travis Fryman	2.00
11	Kirby Puckett	6.00
12	Tony Gwynn	12.00
13	Ken Griffey Jr.	25.00
14	Juan Gonzalez	12.00
15	Barry Bonds	6.00
16	Andruw Jones	10.00
17	Roger Clemens	10.00
18	Randy Johnson	4.00
19	Greg Maddux	15.00
20	Dennis Eckersley	2.00

1998 Score Complete Players

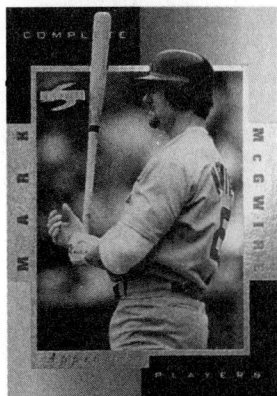

Complete Players is a 30-card insert featuring 10 players who can do it all. Each player had three cards displaying their variety of skills. The cards feature holographic foil stamping and were inserted 1:5.

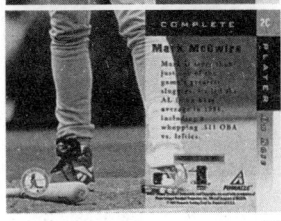

		MT
Complete Set (10):		60.00
Common Player:		1.50
Inserted 1:23		
1	Ken Griffey Jr.	12.00
2	Mark McGwire	15.00
3	Derek Jeter	8.00
4	Cal Ripken Jr.	10.00
5	Mike Piazza	8.00
6	Darin Erstad	4.00
7	Frank Thomas	10.00
8	Andruw Jones	6.00
9	Nomar Garciaparra	8.00
10	Manny Ramirez	3.00

1998 Score Epix

Epix is a cross-brand insert, with 24 cards appearing in Score. The cards are printed on 20-point stock with dot matrix hologram technology. The cards honor the top Play, Game, Season and Moment in a players career and come in Orange, Purple and Emerald versions. Game cards were inserted 1:141, Plays 1:171, Seasons 1:437 and Moments 1:757.

		MT
Complete Set (24):		800.00
Common Game and Play (1-12):		6.00
Common Season (13-18):		15.00
Common Moment (19-24):		25.00
Purple: 1.5x		
Emeralds: 2x to 3x		
1	Ken Griffey Jr. P	40.00
2	Juan Gonzalez P	20.00
3	Jeff Bagwell P	15.00
4	Ivan Rodriguez P	10.00
5	Nomar Garciaparra P	25.00
6	Ryne Sandberg P	10.00
7	Frank Thomas G	35.00
8	Derek Jeter G	20.00
9	Tony Gwynn G	18.00
10	Albert Belle G	8.00
11	Scott Rolen G	15.00
12	Barry Larkin G	6.00
13	Alex Rodriguez S	80.00
14	Cal Ripken Jr. S	80.00
15	Chipper Jones S	60.00
16	Roger Clemens S	40.00
17	Mo Vaughn S	25.00

18	Mark McGwire S	90.00
19	Mike Piazza M	90.00
20	Andruw Jones M	75.00
21	Greg Maddux M	90.00
22	Barry Bonds M	35.00
23	Paul Molitor M	25.00
24	Eddie Murray M	20.00

1998 Score First Pitch

		MT
Complete Set (20):		60.00
Common Player:		1.50
Inserted 1:11 All-Star Edition		
1	Ken Griffey Jr.	8.00
2	Frank Thomas	5.00
3	Alex Rodriguez	5.00
4	Cal Ripken Jr.	6.00
5	Chipper Jones	5.00
6	Juan Gonzalez	4.00
7	Derek Jeter	4.00
8	Mike Piazza	5.00
9	Andruw Jones	2.00
10	Nomar Garciaparra	5.00
11	Barry Bonds	2.00
12	Jeff Bagwell	3.00
13	Scott Rolen	3.00
14	Hideo Nomo	1.50
15	Roger Clemens	3.00
16	Mark McGwire	10.00
17	Greg Maddux	5.00
18	Albert Belle	2.00
19	Ivan Rodriguez	2.00
20	Mo Vaughn	2.00

1998 Score Loaded Lineup

		MT
Complete Set (10):		60.00
Common Player:		2.50
Inserted 1:45 All-Star Edition		
LL1	Chuck Knoblauch	2.50
LL2	Tony Gwynn	8.00
LL3	Frank Thomas	10.00
LL4	Ken Griffey Jr.	15.00
LL5	Mike Piazza	10.00
LL6	Barry Bonds	4.00
LL7	Cal Ripken Jr.	12.00
LL8	Paul Molitor	3.00
LL9	Nomar Garciaparra	10.00
LL10	Greg Maddux	10.00

Modern cards have little collector value in conditions lower than Mint. Figure NM cards at 75% of values shown; EX cards at 40%.

1998 Score New Season

		MT
Complete Set (15):		60.00
Common Player:		2.00
Inserted 1:23 All-Star Edition		
NS1	Kenny Lofton	3.00
NS2	Nomar Garciaparra	8.00
NS3	Todd Helton	2.50
NS4	Miguel Tejada	2.00
NS5	Jaret Wright	4.00
NS6	Alex Rodriguez	8.00
NS7	Vladimir Guerrero	3.00
NS8	Ken Griffey Jr.	12.00
NS9	Ben Grieve	4.00
NS10	Travis Lee	6.00
NS11	Jose Cruz Jr.	3.00
NS12	Paul Konerko	2.00
NS13	Frank Thomas	8.00
NS14	Chipper Jones	8.00
NS15	Cal Ripken Jr.	10.00

1998 Score Rookie & Traded

Score Rookie/Traded consists of a 270-card base set. The base cards have a white and gray border with the player's name on the left. The Showcase Series parallels 110 base cards and was inserted 1:7. Artist's Proofs is a 50-card partial parallel done on prismatic foil and inserted 1:35. Inserts included All-Star Epix, Complete Players and Star Gazing.

		MT
Complete Set (270):		25.00
Common SP (1-50):		.25
Common Player (51-270):		.10
Artist's Proofs (1-50): 5x to 10x		
Artist's Proofs (51-270): 10x to 20x		
Inserted 1:35		
Show (1-50): 1.5x to 3x		
Show (51-270): 2.5x to 4x		
Inserted 1:7		
Paul Konerko Auto. (500):		50.00
Wax Box:		28.00
1	Tony Clark	.50
2	Juan Gonzalez	1.50
3	Frank Thomas	2.50
4	Greg Maddux	2.00
5	Barry Larkin	.40
6	Derek Jeter	1.50
7	Randy Johnson	.50
8	Roger Clemens	1.00
9	Tony Gwynn	1.50
10	Barry Bonds	.75
11	Jim Edmonds	.25
12	Bernie Williams	.50
13	Ken Griffey Jr.	3.00
14	Tim Salmon	.40

15	Mo Vaughn	.75
16	David Justice	.40
17	Jose Cruz Jr.	.50
18	Andruw Jones	.75
19	Sammy Sosa	1.25
20	Jeff Bagwell	1.00
21	Scott Rolen	1.00
22	Darin Erstad	.75
23	Andy Pettitte	.50
24	Mike Mussina	.50
25	Mark McGwire	3.00
26	Hideo Nomo	.50
27	Chipper Jones	2.00
28	Cal Ripken Jr.	2.50
29	Chuck Knoblauch	.40
30	Alex Rodriguez	2.00
31	Jim Thome	.50
32	Mike Piazza	2.00
33	Ivan Rodriguez	.75
34	Roberto Alomar	.50
35	Nomar Garciaparra	2.00
36	Albert Belle	.75
37	Vladimir Guerrero	.75
38	Raul Mondesi	.25
39	Larry Walker	.40
40	Manny Ramirez	.75
41	Tino Martinez	.40
42	Craig Biggio	.25
43	Jay Buhner	.40
44	Kenny Lofton	.75
45	Pedro Martinez	.60
46	Edgar Martinez	.25
47	Gary Sheffield	.30
48	Jose Guillen	.25
49	Ken Caminiti	.25
50	Bobby Higginson	.25
51	Alan Benes	.20
52	Shawn Green	.10
53	Ron Coomer	.10
54	Charles Nagy	.10
55	Steve Karsay	.10
56	Matt Morris	.10
57	Bobby Jones	.10
58	Jason Kendall	.10
59	Jeff Conine	.10
60	Joe Girardi	.10
61	Mark Kotsay	.30
62	Eric Karros	.20
63	Bartolo Colon	.10
64	Mariano Rivera	.20
65	Alex Gonzalez	.10
66	Scott Spiezio	.10
67	Luis Castillo	.10
68	Joey Cora	.10
69	Mark McLemore	.10
70	Reggie Jefferson	.10
71	Lance Johnson	.10
72	Damian Jackson	.10
73	Jeff D'Amico	.10
74	David Ortiz	.10
75	J.T. Snow	.10
76	Todd Hundley	.10
77	Billy Wagner	.10
78	Vinny Castilla	.20
79	Ismael Valdes	.10
80	Neifi Perez	.10
81	Derek Bell	.10
82	Ryan Klesko	.30
83	Rey Ordonez	.10
84	Carlos Garcia	.10
85	Curt Schilling	.20
86	Robin Ventura	.20
87	Pat Hentgen	.10
88	Glendon Rusch	.10
89	Hideki Irabu	.40
90	Antone Williamson	.10
91	Denny Neagle	.10
92	Kevin Orie	.10
93	Reggie Sanders	.10
94	Brady Anderson	.10
95	Andy Benes	.10
96	John Valentin	.10
97	Bobby Bonilla	.20
98	Walt Weiss	.10
99	Robin Jennings	.10
100	Marty Cordova	.10
101	Brad Ausmus	.10
102	Brian Rose	.10
103	Calvin Maduro	.10
104	Raul Casanova	.10
105	Jeff King	.10
106	Sandy Alomar	.20
107	Tim Naehring	.10
108	Mike Cameron	.10
109	Omar Vizquel	.10
110	Brad Radke	.10

111	Jeff Fassero	.10
112	Deivi Cruz	.10
113	Dave Hollins	.10
114	Dean Palmer	.10
115	Esteban Loaiza	.10
116	Brian Giles	.10
117	Steve Finley	.10
118	Jose Canseco	.25
119	Al Martin	.10
120	Eric Young	.10
121	Curtis Goodwin	.10
122	Ellis Burks	.10
123	Mike Hampton	.10
124	Lou Collier	.10
125	John Olerud	.20
126	Ramon Martinez	.10
127	Todd Dunwoody	.10
128	Jermaine Allensworth	.10
129	Eduardo Perez	.10
130	Dante Bichette	.25
131	Edgar Renteria	.10
132	Bob Abreu	.10
133	Rondell White	.20
134	Michael Coleman	.10
135	Jason Giambi	.10
136	Brant Brown	.10
137	Michael Tucker	.10
138	Dave Nilsson	.10
139	Benito Santiago	.10
140	Ray Durham	.10
141	Jeff Kent	.10
142	Matt Stairs	.10
143	Kevin Young	.10
144	Eric Davis	.10
145	John Wetteland	.10
146	Esteban Yan	.10
147	Wilton Guerrero	.10
148	Moises Alou	.20
149	Edgardo Alfonzo	.10
150	Andy Ashby	.10
151	Todd Walker	.20
152	Jermaine Dye	.10
153	Brian Hunter	.10
154	Shawn Estes	.10
155	Bernard Gilkey	.10
156	Tony Womack	.10
157	John Smoltz	.20
158	Delino DeShields	.10
159	Jacob Cruz	.10
160	Javier Valentin	.10
161	Chris Hoiles	.10
162	Garret Anderson	.10
163	Dan Wilson	.10
164	Paul O'Neill	.20
165	Matt Williams	.25
166	Travis Fryman	.10
167	Javier Lopez	.10
168	Ray Lankford	.10
169	Bobby Estalella	.10
170	Henry Rodriguez	.10
171	Quinton McCracken	.10
172	Jaret Wright	.50
173	Darryl Kile	.10
174	Wade Boggs	.25
175	Orel Hershiser	.10
176	B.J. Surhoff	.10
177	Fernando Tatis	.20
178	Carlos Delgado	.10
179	Jorge Fabregas	.10
180	Tony Saunders	.10
181	Devon White	.10
182	Dmitri Young	.10
183	Ryan McGuire	.10
184	Mark Bellhorn	.10
185	Joe Carter	.20
186	Kevin Stocker	.10
187	Mike Lansing	.10
188	Jason Dickson	.10
189	Charles Johnson	.10
190	Will Clark	.25
191	Shannon Stewart	.10
192	Johnny Damon	.10
193	Todd Greene	.10
194	Carlos Baerga	.10
195	David Cone	.20
196	Pokey Reese	.10
197	Livan Hernandez	.10
198	Tom Glavine	.20
199	Geronimo Berroa	.10
200	Darryl Hamilton	.10
201	Terry Steinbach	.10
202	Robb Nen	.10
203	Ron Gant	.10
204	Rafael Palmeiro	.25
205	Rickey Henderson	.10
206	Justin Thompson	.10

207	Jeff Suppan	.10
208	Kevin Brown	.20
209	Jimmy Key	.10
210	Brian Jordan	.10
211	Aaron Sele	.10
212	Fred McGriff	.20
213	Jay Bell	.10
214	Andres Galarraga	.25
215	Mark Grace	.25
216	Brett Tomko	.10
217	Francisco Cordova	.10
218	Rusty Greer	.10
219	Bubba Trammell	.10
220	Derrek Lee	.10
221	Brian Anderson	.10
222	Mark Grudzielanek	.10
223	Marquis Grissom	.10
224	Gary DiSarcina	.10
225	Jim Leyritz	.10
226	Jeffrey Hammonds	.10
227	Karim Garcia	.10
228	Chan Ho Park	.30
229	Brooks Kieschnick	.10
230	Trey Beamon	.10
231	Kevin Appier	.10
232	Wally Joyner	.10
233	Richie Sexson	.10
234	*Frank Catalanotto*	.20
235	Rafael Medina	.10
236	Travis Lee	1.50
237	Eli Marrero	.10
238	Carl Pavano	.25
239	Enrique Wilson	.10
240	Richard Hidalgo	.10
241	Todd Helton	.50
242	Ben Grieve	.75
243	Mario Valdez	.10
244	*Magglio Ordonez*	.50
245	Juan Encarnacion	.10
246	Russell Branyan	.10
247	Sean Casey	.20
248	Abraham Nunez	.10
249	Brad Fullmer	.25
250	Paul Konerko	.25
251	Miguel Tejada	.30
252	*Mike Lowell*	.30
253	Ken Griffey Jr. (Spring Training)	1.00
254	Frank Thomas (Spring Training)	.75
255	Alex Rodriguez (Spring Training)	.60
256	Jose Cruz Jr. (Spring Training)	.25
257	Jeff Bagwell (Spring Training)	.30
258	Chipper Jones (Spring Training)	.60
259	Mo Vaughn (Spring Training)	.25
260	Nomar Garciaparra (Spring Training)	.60
261	Jim Thome (Spring Training)	.20
262	Derek Jeter (Spring Training)	.50
263	Mike Piazza (Spring Training)	.60
264	Tony Gwynn (Spring Training)	.50
265	Scott Rolen (Spring Training)	.30
266	Andruw Jones (Spring Training)	.25
267	Cal Ripken Jr. (Spring Training)	.75
268	Checklist(Ken Griffey Jr.)	.75
269	Checklist(Cal Ripken Jr.)	.50
270	Checklist(Jose Cruz Jr.)	.20

1998 Score
Rookie & Traded
All-Star Epix

All-Star Epix is a 12-card insert seeded 1:61. The cards honor the top All-Star Game moments of 12 star players. The dot matrix hologram cards were printed in orange, purple and emerald versions.

		MT
Complete Set (12):		475.00
Common Player:		15.00
Purples: 1x to 2x		
Emeralds: 2x to 4x		
1	Ken Griffey Jr.	100.00
2	Juan Gonzalez	50.00
3	Jeff Bagwell	30.00
4	Ivan Rodriguez	25.00
5	Nomar Garciaparra	60.00
6	Ryne Sandberg	25.00
7	Frank Thomas	75.00
8	Derek Jeter	50.00
9	Tony Gwynn	50.00
10	Albert Belle	25.00
11	Scott Rolen	30.00
12	Barry Larkin	15.00

1998 Score
Rookie & Traded
Complete Players

Complete Players is a 30-card insert seeded one per 11 packs. The set highlights 10 players who can do it all on the field. Each player has three cards showcasing one of their talents. The cards feature holographic foil stamping.

		MT
Complete Set (30):		90.00
Common Player:		1.50
3 cards per player		
Inserted 1:11		
1	Ken Griffey Jr.	8.00
2	Larry Walker	1.50
3	Alex Rodriguez	5.00
4	Jose Cruz	1.50
5	Jeff Bagwell	3.00
6	Greg Maddux	5.00
7	Ivan Rodriguez	2.50
8	Roger Clemens	3.00
9	Chipper Jones	5.00
10	Hideo Nomo	1.50

1998 Score
Rookie & Traded
Star Gazing

Printed on micro-etched foil board, Star Gazing features 20 top players and was seeded 1:35.

		MT
Complete Set (20):		150.00
Common Player:		3.00
Inserted 1:35		
1	Ken Griffey Jr.	20.00
2	Frank Thomas	15.00
3	Chipper Jones	12.00
4	Mark McGwire	25.00
5	Cal Ripken Jr.	15.00
6	Mike Piazza	12.00
7	Nomar Garciaparra	12.00
8	Derek Jeter	10.00
9	Juan Gonzalez	10.00
10	Vladimir Guerrero	5.00
11	Alex Rodriguez	12.00
12	Tony Gwynn	10.00
13	Andruw Jones	5.00
14	Scott Rolen	7.00
15	Jose Cruz	4.00
16	Mo Vaughn	5.00
17	Bernie Williams	4.00
18	Greg Maddux	12.00
19	Tony Clark	3.00
20	Ben Grieve	6.00

Values shown reflect the market as of January, 1999. On-field performances of current players in the 1999 baseball season are not factored in.

1993 Select

This 400-card set from Score is designed for the mid-priced card market. The card fronts feature green borders on two sides of the card with the photo filling the remaining portion of the card front. The backs feature an additional photo, player information and statistics. Cards numbered 271-360 are devoted to rookies and draft picks.

		MT
Complete Set (405):		30.00
Common Player:		.05
Wax Box:		30.00
1	Barry Bonds	.75
2	Ken Griffey, Jr.	3.00
3	Will Clark	.25
4	Kirby Puckett	1.00
5	Tony Gwynn	1.00
6	Frank Thomas	2.50
7	Tom Glavine	.15
8	Roberto Alomar	.50
9	Andre Dawson	.15
10	Ron Darling	.05
11	Bobby Bonilla	.15
12	Danny Tartabull	.05
13	Darren Daulton	.10
14	Roger Clemens	1.00
15	Ozzie Smith	.30
16	Mark McGwire	4.00
17	Terry Pendleton	.05
18	Cal Ripken, Jr.	2.50
19	Fred McGriff	.20
20	Cecil Fielder	.15
21	Darryl Strawberry	.15
22	Robin Yount	.25
23	Barry Larkin	.20
24	Don Mattingly	.75
25	Craig Biggio	.15
26	Sandy Alomar Jr.	.15
27	Larry Walker	.30
28	Junior Felix	.05
29	Eddie Murray	.15
30	Robin Ventura	.15
31	Greg Maddux	2.00
32	Dave Winfield	.10
33	John Kruk	.05
34	Wally Joyner	.05
35	Andy Van Slyke	.05
36	Chuck Knoblauch	.20
37	Tom Pagnozzi	.05
38	Dennis Eckersley	.10
39	Dave Justice	.20
40	Juan Gonzalez	1.50
41	Gary Sheffield	.35
42	Paul Molitor	.40
43	Delino DeShields	.05
44	Travis Fryman	.10
45	Hal Morris	.10
46	Gregg Olson	.05
47	Ken Caminiti	.20
48	Wade Boggs	.20
49	Orel Hershiser	.10
50	Albert Belle	.75
51	Bill Swift	.05

52	Mark Langston	.05
53	Joe Girardi	.05
54	Keith Miller	.05
55	Gary Carter	.10
56	Brady Anderson	.15
57	Dwight Gooden	.10
58	Julio Franco	.05
59	Len Dykstra	.10
60	Mickey Tettleton	.05
61	Randy Tomlin	.05
62	B.J. Surhoff	.05
63	Todd Zeile	.05
64	Roberto Kelly	.05
65	Rob Dibble	.05
66	Leo Gomez	.05
67	Doug Jones	.05
68	Ellis Burks	.10
69	Miko Scioscia	.05
70	Charles Nagy	.05
71	Cory Snyder	.05
72	Devon White	.05
73	Mark Grace	.20
74	Luis Polonia	.05
75	John Smiley	.05
76	Carlton Fisk	.15
77	Luis Sojo	.05
78	George Brett	.75
79	Mitch Williams	.05
80	Kent Hrbek	.05
81	Jay Bell	.05
82	Edgar Martinez	.10
83	Lee Smith	.05
84	Deion Sanders	.25
85	Bill Gullickson	.05
86	Paul O'Neill	.15
87	Kevin Seitzer	.05
88	Steve Finley	.15
89	Mel Hall	.05
90	Nolan Ryan	1.50
91	Eric Davis	.10
92	Mike Mussina	.50
93	Tony Fernandez	.05
94	Frank Viola	.05
95	Matt Williams	.25
96	Joe Carter	.15
97	Ryne Sandberg	.60
98	Jim Abbott	.10
99	Marquis Grissom	.15
100	George Bell	.05
101	Howard Johnson	.05
102	Kevin Appier	.10
103	Dale Murphy	.10
104	Shane Mack	.05
105	Jose Lind	.05
106	Rickey Henderson	.15
107	Bob Tewksbury	.05
108	Kevin Mitchell	.05
109	Steve Avery	.05
110	Candy Maldonado	.05
111	Bip Roberts	.05
112	Lou Whitaker	.05
113	Jeff Bagwell	1.00
114	Dante Bichette	.25
115	Brett Butler	.10
116	Melido Perez	.05
117	Andy Benes	.10
118	Randy Johnson	.35
119	Willie McGee	.05
120	Jody Reed	.05
121	Shawon Dunston	.10
122	Carlos Baerga	.10
123	Bret Saberhagen	.05
124	John Olerud	.20
125	Ivan Calderon	.05
126	Bryan Harvey	.05
127	Terry Mulholland	.05
128	Ozzie Guillen	.05
129	Steve Buechele	.05
130	Kevin Tapani	.05
131	Felix Jose	.05
132	Terry Steinbach	.05
133	Ron Gant	.15
134	Harold Reynolds	.05
135	Chris Sabo	.05
136	Ivan Rodriguez	.50
137	Eric Anthony	.05
138	Mike Henneman	.05
139	Robby Thompson	.05
140	Scott Fletcher	.05
141	Bruce Hurst	.05
142	Kevin Maas	.05
143	Tom Candiotti	.05
144	Chris Hoiles	.05
145	Mike Morgan	.05
146	Mark Whiten	.05
147	Dennis Martinez	.10

148	Tony Pena	.05
149	Dave Magadan	.05
150	Mark Lewis	.05
151	Mariano Duncan	.05
152	Gregg Jefferies	.05
153	Doug Drabek	.05
154	Brian Harper	.05
155	Ray Lankford	.15
156	Carney Lansford	.05
157	Mike Sharperson	.05
158	Jack Morris	.05
159	Otis Nixon	.05
160	Steve Sax	.05
161	Mark Lemke	.05
162	Rafael Palmeiro	.20
163	Jose Rijo	.05
164	Omar Vizquel	.05
165	Sammy Sosa	1.50
166	Milt Cuyler	.05
167	John Franco	.05
168	Darryl Hamilton	.05
169	Ken Hill	.05
170	Mike Devereaux	.05
171	Don Slaught	.05
172	Steve Farr	.05
173	Bernard Gilkey	.10
174	Mike Fetters	.05
175	Vince Coleman	.05
176	Kevin McReynolds	.05
177	John Smoltz	.15
178	Greg Gagne	.05
179	Greg Swindell	.05
180	Juan Guzman	.05
181	Kal Daniels	.05
182	Rick Sutcliffe	.05
183	Orlando Merced	.05
184	Bill Wegman	.05
185	Mark Gardner	.05
186	Rob Deer	.05
187	Dave Hollins	.05
188	Jack Clark	.05
189	Brian Hunter	.05
190	Tim Wallach	.05
191	Tim Belcher	.05
192	Walt Weiss	.05
193	Kurt Stillwell	.05
194	Charlie Hayes	.05
195	Willie Randolph	.05
196	Jack McDowell	.05
197	Jose Offerman	.05
198	Chuck Finley	.05
199	Darrin Jackson	.05
200	Kelly Gruber	.05
201	John Wetteland	.10
202	Jay Buhner	.20
203	Mike LaValliere	.05
204	Kevin Brown	.05
205	Luis Gonzalez	.05
206	Rick Aguilera	.05
207	Norm Charlton	.05
208	Mike Bordick	.05
209	Charlie Leibrandt	.05
210	Tom Brunansky	.05
211	Tom Henke	.05
212	Randy Milligan	.05
213	Ramon Martinez	.10
214	Mo Vaughn	.75
215	Randy Myers	.05
216	Greg Hibbard	.05
217	Wes Chamberlain	.05
218	Tony Phillips	.05
219	Pete Harnisch	.05
220	Mike Gallego	.05
221	Bud Black	.05
222	Greg Vaughn	.05
223	Milt Thompson	.05
224	Ben McDonald	.05
225	Billy Hatcher	.05
226	Paul Sorrento	.05
227	Mark Gubicza	.05
228	Mike Greenwell	.05
229	Curt Schilling	.05
230	Alan Trammell	.10
231	Zane Smith	.05
232	Bobby Thigpen	.05
233	Greg Olson	.05
234	Joe Orsulak	.05
235	Joe Oliver	.05
236	Tim Raines	.10
237	Juan Samuel	.05
238	Chili Davis	.10
239	Spike Owen	.05
240	Dave Stewart	.05
241	Jim Eisenreich	.05
242	Phil Plantier	.05
243	Sid Fernandez	.05

244	Dan Gladden	.05
245	Mickey Morandini	.05
246	Tino Martinez	.20
247	Kirt Manwaring	.05
248	Dean Palmer	.10
249	Tom Browning	.05
250	Brian McRae	.05
251	Scott Leius	.05
252	Bert Blyleven	.05
253	Scott Erickson	.05
254	Bob Welch	.05
255	Pat Kelly	.05
256	Felix Fermin	.05
257	Harold Baines	.10
258	Duane Ward	.05
259	Bill Spiers	.05
260	Jaime Navarro	.05
261	Scott Sanderson	.05
262	Gary Gaetti	.05
263	Bob Ojeda	.05
264	Jeff Montgomery	.05
265	Scott Bankhead	.05
266	Lance Johnson	.05
267	Rafael Belliard	.05
268	Kevin Reimer	.05
269	Benito Santiago	.05
270	Mike Moore	.05
271	Dave Fleming	.05
272	Moises Alou	.15
273	Pat Listach	.05
274	Reggie Sanders	.10
275	Kenny Lofton	.65
276	Donovan Osborne	.05
277	Rusty Meacham	.05
278	Eric Karros	.15
279	Andy Stankiewicz	.05
280	Brian Jordan	.10
281	Gary DiSarcina	.05
282	Mark Wohlers	.05
283	Dave Nilsson	.05
284	Anthony Young	.05
285	Jim Bullinger	.05
286	Derek Bell	.10
287	Brian Williams	.10
288	Julio Valera	.05
289	Dan Walters	.05
290	Chad Curtis	.05
291	Michael Tucker	.05
292	Bob Zupcic	.05
293	Todd Hundley	.20
294	Jeff Tackett	.05
295	Greg Colbrunn	.05
296	Cal Eldred	.05
297	Chris Roberts	.05
298	John Doherty	.05
299	Denny Neagle	.10
300	Arthur Rhodes	.05
301	Mark Clark	.05
302	Scott Cooper	.05
303	*Jamie Arnold*	.25
304	Jim Thome	.25
305	Frank Seminara	.05
306	Kurt Knudsen	.05
307	Tim Wakefield	.05
308	John Jaha	.05
309	Pat Hentgen	.10
310	B.J. Wallace	.05
311	Roberto Hernandez	.05
312	Hipolito Pichardo	.05
313	Eric Fox	.05
314	Willie Banks	.05
315	Sam Militello	.05
316	Vince Horsman	.05
317	Carlos Hernandez	.15
318	Jeff Kent	.05
319	Mike Perez	.05
320	Scott Livingstone	.05
321	Jeff Conine	.15
322	James Austin	.05
323	John Vander Wal	.05
324	Pat Mahomes	.05
325	Pedro Astacio	.12
326	Bret Boone	.10
327	Matt Stairs	.10
328	Damion Easley	.10
329	Ben Rivera	.05
330	Reggie Jefferson	.10
331	Luis Mercedes	.05
332	Kyle Abbott	.10
333	Eddie Taubensee	.05
334	Tim McIntosh	.05
335	Phil Clark	.05
336	Wil Cordero	.10
337	Russ Springer	.12
338	Craig Colbert	.10
339	Tim Salmon	.50

340	Braulio Castillo	.05
341	Donald Harris	.05
342	Eric Young	.15
343	Bob Wickman	.05
344	John Valentin	.15
345	Dan Wilson	.15
346	Steve Hosey	.12
347	Mike Piazza	2.50
348	Willie Greene	.12
349	Tom Goodwin	.05
350	Eric Hillman	.05
351	*Steve Reed*	.12
352	*Dan Serafini*	.15
353	*Todd Steverson*	.15
354	Benji Grigsby	.05
355	*Shannon Stewart*	.25
356	Sean Lowe	.15
357	Derek Wallace	.15
358	Rick Helling	.05
359	*Jason Kendall*	1.50
360	*Derek Jeter*	6.00
361	David Cone	.15
362	Jeff Reardon	.05
363	Bobby Witt	.05
364	Jose Canseco	.25
365	Jeff Russell	.05
366	Ruben Sierra	.10
367	Alan Mills	.05
368	Matt Nokes	.05
369	Pat Borders	.05
370	Pedro Munoz	.05
371	Danny Jackson	.05
372	Geronimo Pena	.05
373	Craig Lefferts	.05
374	Joe Grahe	.05
375	Roger McDowell	.05
376	Jimmy Key	.05
377	Steve Olin	.05
378	Glenn Davis	.05
379	Rene Gonzales	.05
380	Manuel Lee	.05
381	Ron Karkovice	.05
382	Sid Bream	.05
383	Gerald Williams	.05
384	Lenny Harris	.05
385	*J.T. Snow*	.75
386	Dave Stieb	.05
387	Kirk McCaskill	.05
388	Lance Parrish	.05
389	Craig Greback	.05
390	Rick Wilkins	.05
391	Manny Alexander	.05
392	Mike Schooler	.05
393	Bernie Williams	.50
394	Kevin Koslofski	.05
395	Willie Wilson	.05
396	Jeff Parrett	.05
397	Mike Harkey	.05
398	Frank Tanana	.05
399	Doug Henry	.05
400	Royce Clayton	.05
401	Eric Wedge	.05
402	Derrick May	.05
403	Carlos Garcia	.05
404	Henry Rodriguez	.10
405	Ryan Klesko	.45

1993 Select Aces

Cards from this set feature 24 of the top pitchers from 1992 and were included one per every 27-card Super Pack. The fronts have a picture of the player in action against an Ace card background. Backs have text and a portrait in the middle of a card suit for an Ace.

		MT
Complete Set (24):		75.00
Common Player:		2.00
1	Roger Clemens	20.00
2	Tom Glavine	5.00
3	Jack McDowell	2.00
4	Greg Maddux	25.00
5	Jack Morris	2.00
6	Dennis Martinez	2.50
7	Kevin Brown	3.00
8	Dwight Gooden	3.00
9	Kevin Appier	2.00
10	Mike Morgan	2.00
11	Juan Guzman	2.00
12	Charles Nagy	2.00
13	John Smiley	2.00
14	Ken Hill	2.00
15	Bob Tewksbury	2.00
16	Doug Drabek	2.00
17	John Smoltz	4.00
18	Greg Swindell	2.00
19	Bruce Hurst	2.00
20	Mike Mussina	12.00
21	Cal Eldred	2.00
22	Melido Perez	2.00
23	Dave Fleming	2.00
24	Kevin Tapani	2.00

1993 Select Rookies

Top newcomers in 1992 are featured in this 21-card insert set. Cards were randomly inserted in 15-card hobby packs. The fronts, printed on metallic foil, have a Score Select Rookies logo on the front. The backs have text and a player portrait.

		MT
Complete Set (21):		90.00
Common Player:		2.00
1	Pat Listach	2.00
2	Moises Alou	5.00
3	Reggie Sanders	4.00
4	Kenny Lofton	40.00
5	Eric Karros	4.00
6	Brian Williams	2.00
7	Donovan Osborne	2.00
8	Sam Militello	2.00
9	Chad Curtis	2.00
10	Bob Zupcic	2.00
11	Tim Salmon	25.00
12	Jeff Conine	5.00
13	Pedro Astacio	3.00
14	Arthur Rhodes	2.00
15	Cal Eldred	2.00

16	Tim Wakefield	2.00
17	Andy Stankiewicz	2.00
18	Wil Cordero	3.00
19	Todd Hundley	8.00
20	Dave Fleming	2.00
21	Bret Boone	3.00

1993 Select Stars

The top 24 players from 1992 are featured in this insert set. Cards were randomly inserted in 15-card retail packs. Fronts are printed on metallic foil.

		MT
Complete Set (24):		150.00
Common Player:		2.00
1	Fred McGriff	3.00
2	Ryne Sandberg	9.00
3	Ozzie Smith	9.00
4	Gary Sheffield	4.00
5	Darren Daulton	3.00
6	Andy Van Slyke	2.00
7	Barry Bonds	10.00
8	Tony Gwynn	20.00
9	Greg Maddux	25.00
10	Tom Glavine	3.00
11	John Franco	2.00
12	Lee Smith	2.00
13	Cecil Fielder	3.00
14	Roberto Alomar	7.50
15	Cal Ripken, Jr.	30.00
16	Edgar Martinez	2.00
17	Ivan Rodriguez	8.00
18	Kirby Puckett	18.00
19	Ken Griffey, Jr.	40.00
20	Joe Carter	2.00
21	Roger Clemens	18.00
22	Dave Fleming	2.00
23	Paul Molitor	9.00
24	Dennis Eckersley	3.00

1993 Select Stat Leaders

This 90-card set features 1992 American League and National League leaders in various statistical categories. Each card front indicates the league and the category in which the player finished at or near the top. The backs have a list of the leaders; the pictured player's name is in larger type size. Cards were inserted one per foil pack.

A player's name in *italic* type indicates a rookie card.

		MT
Complete Set (90):		10.00
Common Player:		.10
1	Edgar Martinez	.10
2	Kirby Puckett	.50
3	Frank Thomas	1.00
4	Gary Sheffield	.15
5	Andy Van Slyke	.10
6	John Kruk	.10
7	Kirby Puckett	.50
8	Carlos Baerga	.10
9	Paul Molitor	.25
10	Andy Van Slyke, Terry Pendleton	.10
11	Ryne Sandberg	.40
12	Mark Grace	.20
13	Frank Thomas	1.00
14	Don Mattingly	.50
15	Ken Griffey, Jr.	1.00
16	Andy Van Slyke	.10
17	Mariano Duncan, Jerald Clark, Ray Lankford	.10
18	Marquis Grissom, Terry Pendleton	.10
19	Lance Johnson	.10
20	Mike Devereaux	.10
21	Brady Anderson	.15
22	Deion Sanders	.20
23	Steve Finley	.10
24	Andy Van Slyke	.10
25	Juan Gonzalez	.40
26	Mark McGwire	.75
27	Cecil Fielder	.15
28	Fred McGriff	.20
29	Barry Bonds	.40
30	Gary Sheffield	.20
31	Cecil Fielder	.15
32	Joe Carter	.15
33	Frank Thomas	1.00
34	Darren Daulton	.10
35	Terry Pendleton	.10
36	Fred McGriff	.20
37	Tony Phillips	.10
38	Frank Thomas	1.00
39	Roberto Alomar	.25
40	Barry Bonds	.40
41	Dave Hollins	.10
42	Andy Van Slyke	.10
43	Mark McGwire	.75
44	Edgar Martinez	.15
45	Frank Thomas	1.00
46	Barry Bonds	.40
47	Gary Sheffield	.20
48	Fred McGriff	.20
49	Frank Thomas	1.00
50	Danny Tartabull	.10
51	Roberto Alomar	.25
52	Barry Bonds	.40
53	John Kruk	.10
54	Brett Butler	.10
55	Kenny Lofton	.40
56	Pat Listach	.10
57	Brady Anderson	.15
58	Marquis Grissom	.15
59	Delino DeShields	.10
60	Steve Finley, Bip Roberts	.10
61	Jack McDowell	.10
62	Kevin Brown	.10
63	Melido Perez	.10
64	Terry Mulholland	.10
65	Curt Schilling	.10

66	John Smoltz, Doug Drabek, Greg Maddux	.50
67	Dennis Eckersley	.10
68	Rick Aguilera	.10
69	Jeff Montgomery	.10
70	Lee Smith	.10
71	Randy Myers	.10
72	John Wetteland	.10
73	Randy Johnson	.20
74	Melido Perez	.10
75	Roger Clemens	.40
76	John Smoltz	.15
77	David Cone	.15
78	Greg Maddux	.60
79	Roger Clemens	.40
80	Kevin Appier	.10
81	Mike Mussina	.30
82	Bill Swift	.10
83	Bob Tewksbury	.10
84	Greg Maddux	.60
85	Kevin Brown	.10
86	Jack McDowell	.10
87	Roger Clemens	.40
88	Tom Glavine	.10
89	Ken Hill, Bob Tewksbury	.10
90	Dennis Martinez, Mike Morgan	.10

1993 Select Triple Crown

This three-card set commemorates the Triple Crown seasons of Hall of Famers Mickey Mantle, Frank Robinson and Carl Yastrzemski. Cards were randomly inserted in 15-card hobby packs. Card fronts have a green metallic-look textured border, with the player's name at top in gold, and "Triple Crown" in gold at bottom. There are other silver and green highlights around the photo, which feature the player set against a metallized background. Dark green backs have a player photo and information on his Triple Crown season.

		MT
Complete Set (3):		125.00
Common Player:		25.00
1	Mickey Mantle	90.00
2	Frank Robinson	25.00
3	Carl Yastrzemski	25.00

1993 Select Rookie/Traded

Production of this 150-card set was limited to 1,950 numbered cases. Several future Hall of Famers and six dozen top rookies are featured in the set. Cards were available in packs rather than collated sets and include randomly inserted FX cards, which feature Nolan Ryan (two per 24-box case), Tim Salmon and Mike Piazza (one per 576 packs) and All-Star Rookie Team members (one per 58 packs).

		MT
Complete Set (150):		30.00
Common Player:		.15
Wax Box:		55.00
1	Rickey Henderson	.25
2	Rob Deer	.15
3	Tim Belcher	.15
4	Gary Sheffield	.40
5	Fred McGriff	.35
6	Mark Whiten	.15
7	Jeff Russell	.15
8	Harold Baines	.15
9	Dave Winfield	.25
10	Ellis Burks	.15
11	Andre Dawson	.15
12	Gregg Jefferies	.15
13	Jimmy Key	.15
14	Harold Reynolds	.15
15	Tom Henke	.15
16	Paul Molitor	.65
17	Wade Boggs	.35
18	David Cone	.30
19	Tony Fernandez	.15
20	Roberto Kelly	.15
21	Paul O'Neill	.30
22	Jose Lind	.15
23	Barry Bonds	3.00
24	Dave Stewart	.15
25	Randy Myers	.15
26	Benito Santiago	.15
27	Tim Wallach	.15
28	Greg Gagne	.15
29	Kevin Mitchell	.15
30	Jim Abbott	.15
31	Lee Smith	.15
32	Bobby Munoz	.20
33	Mo Sanford	.25
34	John Roper	.15
35	David Hulse	.20
36	Pedro Martinez	1.50
37	Chuck Carr	.15
38	Armando Reynoso	.25
39	Ryan Thompson	.25
40	Carlos Garcia	.20
41	Matt Whiteside	.15
42	Benji Gil	.15
43	Rodney Bolton	.15
44	J.T. Snow	1.00
45	David McCarty	.15
46	Paul Quantrill	.15
47	Al Martin	.15
48	Lance Painter	.15
49	Lou Frazier	.15
50	Eduardo Perez	.15
51	Kevin Young	.20
52	Mike Trombley	.15
53	Sterling Hitchcock	.35
54	Tim Bogar	.25
55	Hilly Hathaway	.25
56	Wayne Kirby	.15
57	Craig Paquette	.15
58	Bret Boone	.25
59	Greg McMichael	.20
60	Mike Lansing	.35
61	Brent Gates	.25
62	Rene Arocha	.25
63	Ricky Gutierrez	.25
64	Kevin Rogers	.20
65	Ken Ryan	.40
66	Phil Hiatt	.15
67	Pat Meares	.25
68	Troy Neel	.20
69	Steve Cooke	.15
70	Sherman Obando	.15
71	Blas Minor	.15
72	Angel Miranda	.15
73	Tom Kramer	.20
74	Chip Hale	.20
75	Brad Pennington	.25
76	Graeme Lloyd	.15
77	Darrell Whitmore	.20
78	David Nied	.15
79	Todd Van Poppel	.15
80	Chris Gomez	.25
81	Jason Bere	.15
82	Jeffrey Hammonds	.25
83	Brad Ausmus	.20
84	Kevin Stocker	.15
85	Jeromy Burnitz	.20
86	Aaron Sele	.25
87	Roberto Mejia	.15
88	Kirk Rueter	.25
89	Kevin Roberson	.25
90	Allen Watson	.35
91	Charlie Leibrandt	.15
92	Eric Davis	.15
93	Jody Reed	.15
94	Danny Jackson	.15
95	Gary Gaetti	.15
96	Norm Charlton	.15
97	Doug Drabek	.15
98	Scott Fletcher	.15
99	Greg Swindell	.15
100	John Smiley	.15
101	Kevin Reimer	.15
102	Andres Galarraga	.15
103	Greg Hibbard	.15
104	Chris Hammond	.15
105	Darnell Coles	.15
106	Mike Felder	.15
107	Jose Guzman	.15
108	Chris Bosio	.15
109	Spike Owen	.15
110	Felix Jose	.15
111	Cory Snyder	.15
112	Craig Lefferts	.15
113	David Wells	.15
114	Pete Incaviglia	.15
115	Mike Pagliarulo	.15
116	Dave Magadan	.15
117	Charlie Hough	.15
118	Ivan Calderon	.15
119	Manuel Lee	.15
120	Bob Patterson	.15
121	Bob Ojeda	.15
122	Scott Bankhead	.15
123	Greg Maddux	4.00
124	Chili Davis	.15
125	Milt Thompson	.15
126	Dave Martinez	.15
127	Frank Tanana	.15
128	Phil Plantier	.15
129	Juan Samuel	.15
130	Eric Young	.20
131	Joe Orsulak	.15
132	Derek Bell	.15
133	Darrin Jackson	.15
134	Tom Brunansky	.15
135	Jeff Reardon	.15
136	Kevin Higgins	.15
137	Joel Johnston	.15
138	Rick Trlicek	.15
139	Richie Lewis	.25
140	Jeff Gardner	.20
141	Jack Voigt	.15
142	Rod Correia	.15
143	Billy Brewer	.15
144	Terry Jorgensen	.15
145	Rich Amaral	.15
146	Sean Berry	.20
147	Dan Peltier	.20
148	Paul Wagner	.35
149	Damon Buford	.20
150	Wil Cordero	.15

1993 Select Rookie/Traded All-Star Rookies

KEVIN STOCKER

'93 ALL-STAR ROOKIE TEAM

These cards were randomly inserted into the Score Select Rookie/Traded packs, making them among the scarcest of the year's many "chase" cards. Card fronts feature metallic foil printing. Backs have a few words about the player. Stated odds of finding an All-Star Rookie Team insert card are one per 58 packs.

		MT
Complete Set (10):		100.00
Common Player:		3.00
1	Jeff Conine	5.00
2	Brent Gates	3.00
3	Mike Lansing	4.00
4	Kevin Stocker	5.00
5	Mike Piazza	75.00
6	Jeffrey Hammonds	5.00
7	David Hulse	3.00
8	Tim Salmon	25.00
9	Rene Arocha	3.00
10	Greg McMichael	3.00

1993 Select Rookie/Traded Inserts

Three cards honoring the 1993 Rookies of the Year and retiring superstar Nolan Ryan were issued as random inserts in the Select Rookie/Traded packs. Cards are printed with metallic foil front backgrounds.

Stated odds of finding a Piazza or Salmon card are about one per 24-box case; Ryan cards are found on average two per case.

	MT
Complete Set (3):	150.00
Common Player:	25.00
1NR Nolan Ryan	60.00
1ROY Tim Salmon	25.00
2ROY Mike Piazza	75.00

1994 Select

Both series of this premium brand from the Score/Pinnacle line-up offered 210 regular cards for a combined 420 cards, and seven insert sets. The announced press runs for Series I and II was 4,950 20-box cases. Cards have a horizontal format with a color action photo at right and a second action photo at left done in a single team color-coded hue. The player's last name is dropped out of a vertical gold-foil strip between the two photos, with his first name in white at top-center. Backs are vertically oriented with yet another color action photo at center. In a vertical bar at right, matching the color-coding on front and printed over the photo are 1993 and career stats, a "Select Stat," and a few sentences about the player. The appropriate logos and Pinnacle's optical-variable counterfeiting device are at bottom-center. Thirty of the final 33 cards in the first series are a "1994 Rookie Prospect" subset, so noted in a special gold-foil logo on front.

	MT
Complete Set (420):	40.00
Complete Series 1 (210):	25.00
Complete Series 2 (210):	15.00
Common Player:	.10
Series 1 Wax Box:	30.00
Series 2 Wax Box:	20.00
1 Ken Griffey, Jr.	3.50
2 Greg Maddux	2.00
3 Paul Molitor	.40
4 Mike Piazza	2.00
5 Jay Bell	.10
6 Frank Thomas	2.50
7 Barry Larkin	.20
8 Paul O'Neill	.10
9 Darren Daulton	.10
10 Mike Greenwell	.10
11 Chuck Carr	.10
12 Joe Carter	.15
13 Lance Johnson	.10
14 Jeff Blauser	.10
15 Chris Hoiles	.10
16 Rick Wilkins	.10
17 Kirby Puckett	1.00
18 Larry Walker	.25
19 Randy Johnson	.40
20 Bernard Gilkey	.10
21 Devon White	.10
22 Randy Myers	.10
23 Don Mattingly	1.00
24 John Kruk	.10
25 Ozzie Guillen	.10
26 Jeff Conine	.10
27 Mike Macfarlane	.10
28 Dave Hollins	.10
29 Chuck Knoblauch	.15
30 Ozzie Smith	.50
31 Harold Baines	.10
32 Ryne Sandberg	.60
33 Ron Karkovice	.10
34 Terry Pendleton	.10
35 Wally Joyner	.10
36 Mike Mussina	.40
37 Felix Jose	.10
38 Derrick May	.10
39 Scott Cooper	.10
40 Jose Rijo	.10
41 Robin Ventura	.15
42 Charlie Hayes	.10
43 Jimmy Key	.10
44 Eric Karros	.10
45 Ruben Sierra	.10
46 Ryan Thompson	.10
47 Brian McRae	.10
48 Pat Hentgen	.10
49 John Valentin	.10
50 Al Martin	.10
51 Jose Lind	.10
52 Kevin Stocker	.10
53 Mike Gallego	.10
54 Dwight Gooden	.12
55 Brady Anderson	.15
56 Jeff King	.10
57 Mark McGwire	3.00
58 Sammy Sosa	1.50
59 Ryan Bowen	.10
60 Mark Lemke	.10
61 Roger Clemens	1.00
62 Brian Jordan	.12
63 Andres Galarraga	.15
64 Kevin Appier	.10
65 Don Slaught	.10
66 Mike Blowers	.10
67 Wes Chamberlain	.10
68 Troy Neel	.10
69 John Wetteland	.10
70 Joe Girardi	.10
71 Reggie Sanders	.10
72 Edgar Martinez	.15
73 Todd Hundley	.15
74 Pat Borders	.10
75 Roberto Mejia	.10
76 David Cone	.10
77 Tony Gwynn	.75
78 Jim Abbott	.12
79 Jay Buhner	.15
80 Mark McLemore	.10
81 Wil Cordero	.10
82 Pedro Astacio	.10
83 Bob Tewksbury	.10
84 Dave Winfield	.15
85 Jeff Kent	.10
86 Todd Van Poppel	.10
87 Steve Avery	.10
88 Mike Lansing	.10
89 Len Dykstra	.10
90 Jose Guzman	.10
91 Brian Hunter	.10
92 Tim Raines	.12
93 Andre Dawson	.15
94 Joe Orsulak	.10
95 Ricky Jordan	.10
96 Billy Hatcher	.10
97 Jack McDowell	.10
98 Tom Pagnozzi	.10
99 Darryl Strawberry	.12
100 Mike Stanley	.10
101 Bret Saberhagen	.10
102 Willie Greene	.10
103 Bryan Harvey	.10
104 Tim Bogar	.10
105 Jack Voight	.10
106 Brad Ausmus	.10
107 Ramon Martinez	.10
108 Mike Perez	.10
109 Jeff Montgomery	.10
110 Danny Darwin	.10
111 Wilson Alvarez	.10
112 Kevin Mitchell	.10
113 David Nied	.10
114 Rich Amaral	.10
115 Stan Javier	.10
116 Mo Vaughn	.50
117 Ben McDonald	.10
118 Tom Gordon	.10
119 Carlos Garcia	.10
120 Phil Plantier	.10
121 Mike Morgan	.10
122 Pat Meares	.10
123 Kevin Young	.10
124 Jeff Fassero	.10
125 Gene Harris	.10
126 Bob Welch	.10
127 Walt Weiss	.10
128 Bobby Witt	.10
129 Andy Van Slyke	.10
130 Steve Cooke	.10
131 Mike Devereaux	.10
132 Joey Cora	.10
133 Bret Barberie	.10
134 Orel Hershiser	.10
135 Ed Sprague	.10
136 Shawon Dunston	.10
137 Alex Arias	.10
138 Archi Cianfrocco	.10
139 Tim Wallach	.10
140 Bernie Williams	.50
141 Karl Rhodes	.10
142 Pat Kelly	.10
143 Dave Magadan	.10
144 Kevin Tapani	.10
145 Eric Young	.10
146 Derek Bell	.10
147 Dante Bichette	.35
148 Geronimo Pena	.10
149 Joe Oliver	.10
150 Orestes Destrade	.10
151 Tim Naehring	.10
152 Ray Lankford	.10
153 Phil Clark	.10
154 David McCarty	.10
155 Tommy Greene	.10
156 Wade Boggs	.30
157 Kevin Gross	.10
158 Hal Morris	.10
159 Moises Alou	.10
160 Rick Aguilera	.10
161 Curt Schilling	.10
162 Chip Hale	.10
163 Tino Martinez	.15
164 Mark Whiten	.10
165 Dave Stewart	.10
166 Steve Buechele	.10
167 Bobby Jones	.25
168 Darrin Fletcher	.10
169 John Smiley	.10
170 Cory Snyder	.10
171 Scott Erickson	.10
172 Kirk Rueter	.10
173 Dave Fleming	.10
174 John Smoltz	.20
175 Ricky Gutierrez	.10
176 Mike Bordick	.10
177 Chan Ho Park	.35
178 Alex Gonzalez	.25
179 Steve Karsay	.15
180 Jeffrey Hammonds	.15
181 Manny Ramirez	.70
182 Salomon Torres	.10
183 Raul Mondesi	.30
184 James Mouton	.10
185 Cliff Floyd	.12
186 Danny Bautista	.10
187 Kurt Abbott	.35
188 Javier Lopez	.15
189 John Patterson	.10
190 Greg Blosser	.10
191 Bob Hamelin	.10
192 Tony Eusebio	.10
193 Carlos Delgado	.15
194 Chris Gomez	.10
195 Kelly Stinnett	.10
196 Shane Reynolds	.10
197 Ryan Klesko	.60
198 Jim Edmonds	.30
199 James Hurst	.10
200 Dave Staton	.20
201 Rondell White	.30
202 Keith Mitchell	.10
203 Darren Oliver	.10
204 Mike Matheny	.10
205 Chris Turner	.10

206	Matt Mieske	.10
207	N.L. team checklist	.10
208	N.L. team checklist	.10
209	A.L. team checklist	.10
210	A.L. team checklist	.10
211	Barry Bonds	.75
212	Juan Gonzalez	1.00
213	Jim Eisenreich	.10
214	Ivan Rodriguez	.50
215	Tony Phillips	.10
216	John Jaha	.10
217	Lee Smith	.10
218	Bip Roberts	.10
219	Dave Hansen	.10
220	Pat Listach	.10
221	Willie McGee	.10
222	Damion Easley	.10
223	Dean Palmer	.10
224	Mike Moore	.10
225	Brian Harper	.10
226	Gary DiSarcina	.10
227	Delino DeShields	.10
228	Otis Nixon	.10
229	Roberto Alomar	.65
230	Mark Grace	.25
231	Kenny Lofton	.65
232	Gregg Jefferies	.10
233	Cecil Fielder	.15
234	Jeff Bagwell	1.00
235	Albert Belle	.65
236	Dave Justice	.35
237	Tom Henke	.10
238	Bobby Bonilla	.10
239	John Olerud	.15
240	Robby Thompson	.10
241	Dave Valle	.10
242	Marquis Grissom	.15
243	Greg Swindell	.10
244	Todd Zeile	.10
245	Dennis Eckersley	.10
246	Jose Offerman	.10
247	Greg McMichael	.10
248	Tim Belcher	.10
249	Cal Ripken, Jr.	2.50
250	Tom Glavine	.15
251	Luis Polonia	.10
252	Bill Swift	.10
253	Juan Guzman	.10
254	Rickey Henderson	.15
255	Terry Mulholland	.10
256	Gary Sheffield	.15
257	Terry Steinbach	.10
258	Brett Butler	.10
259	Jason Bere	.10
260	Doug Strange	.10
261	Kent Hrbek	.10
262	Graeme Lloyd	.10
263	Lou Frazier	.10
264	Charles Nagy	.10
265	Bret Boone	.10
266	Kirk Gibson	.10
267	Kevin Brown	.10
269	Matt Williams	.35
270	Greg Gagne	.10
271	Mariano Duncan	.10
272	Jeff Russell	.10
273	Eric Davis	.10
274	Shane Mack	.10
275	Jose Vizcaino	.10
276	Jose Canseco	.30
277	Roberto Hernandez	.10
278	Royce Clayton	.10
279	Carlos Baerga	.15
280	Pete Incaviglia	.10
281	Brent Gates	.10
282	Jeromy Burnitz	.10
283	Chili Davis	.10
284	Pete Harnisch	.10
285	Alan Trammell	.10
286	Eric Anthony	.10
287	Ellis Burks	.15
288	Julio Franco	.10
289	Jack Morris	.10
290	Erik Hanson	.10
291	Chuck Finley	.10
292	Reggie Jefferson	.10
293	Kevin McReynolds	.10
294	Greg Hibbard	.10
295	Travis Fryman	.10
296	Craig Biggio	.10
297	Kenny Rogers	.10
298	Dave Henderson	.10
299	Jim Thome	.30
300	Rene Arocha	.10
301	Pedro Munoz	.10
302	David Hulse	.10

303	Greg Vaughn	.10
304	Darren Lewis	.10
305	Deion Sanders	.35
306	Danny Tartabull	.10
307	Darryl Hamilton	.10
308	Andujar Cedeno	.10
309	Tim Salmon	.30
310	Tony Fernandez	.10
311	Alex Fernandez	.10
312	Roberto Kelly	.10
313	Harold Reynolds	.10
314	Chris Sabo	.10
315	Howard Johnson	.10
316	Mark Portugal	.10
317	Rafael Palmeiro	.20
318	Pete Smith	.10
319	Will Clark	.30
320	Henry Rodriguez	.10
321	Omar Vizquel	.10
322	David Segui	.10
323	Lou Whitaker	.10
324	Felix Fermin	.10
325	Spike Owen	.10
326	Darryl Kile	.10
327	Chad Kreuter	.10
328	Rod Beck	.10
329	Eddie Murray	.25
330	B.J. Surhoff	.10
331	Mickey Tettleton	.10
332	Pedro Martinez	.10
333	Roger Pavlik	.10
334	Eddie Taubensee	.10
335	John Doherty	.10
336	Jody Reed	.10
337	Aaron Sele	.15
338	Leo Gomez	.10
339	Dave Nilsson	.10
340	Rob Dibble	.10
341	John Burkett	.10
342	Wayne Kirby	.10
343	Dan Wilson	.10
344	Armando Reynoso	.10
345	Chad Curtis	.10
346	Dennis Martinez	.10
347	Cal Eldred	.10
348	Luis Gonzalez	.10
349	Doug Drabek	.10
350	Jim Leyritz	.10
351	Mark Langston	.10
352	Darrin Jackson	.10
353	Sid Fernandez	.10
354	Benito Santiago	.10
355	Kevin Seitzer	.10
356	Bo Jackson	.20
357	David Wells	.10
358	Paul Sorrento	.10
359	Ken Caminiti	.10
360	Eduardo Perez	.10
361	Orlando Merced	.10
362	Steve Finley	.10
363	Andy Benes	.10
364	Manuel Lee	.10
365	Todd Benzinger	.10
366	Sandy Alomar Jr.	.10
367	Rex Hudler	.10
368	Mike Henneman	.10
369	Vince Coleman	.10
370	Kirt Manwaring	.10
371	Ken Hill	.10
372	Glenallen Hill	.10
373	Sean Berry	.10
374	Geronimo Berroa	.10
375	Duane Ward	.10
376	Allen Watson	.10
377	Marc Newfield	.15
378	Dan Miceli	.10
379	Denny Hocking	.10
380	Mark Kiefer	.10
381	Tony Tarasco	.10
382	Tony Longmire	.10
383	*Brian Anderson*	.25
384	Fernando Vina	.10
385	Hector Carrasco	.15
386	Mike Kelly	.10
387	Greg Colbrunn	.10
388	Roger Salkeld	.10
389	Steve Trachsel	.15
390	Rich Becker	.15
391	*Billy Taylor*	.10
392	Rich Rowland	.10
393	Carl Everett	.10
394	Johnny Ruffin	.10
395	*Keith Lockhart*	.15
396	J.R. Phillips	.10
397	Sterling Hitchcock	.10
398	Jorge Fabregas	.10

399	Jeff Granger	.10
400	*Eddie Zambrano*	.15
401	*Rikkert Faneyte*	.10
402	Gerald Williams	.10
403	Joey Hamilton	.10
404	*Joe Hall*	.10
405	*John Hudek*	.15
406	Roberto Petagine	.10
407	Charles Johnson	.20
408	Mark Smith	.10
409	Jeff Juden	.10
410	*Carlos Pulido*	.12
411	Paul Shuey	.10
412	Rob Butler	.10
413	Mark Acre	.10
414	Greg Pirkl	.10
415	Melvin Nieves	.10
416	*Tim Hyers*	.10
417	N.L. checklist	.10
418	N.L. checklist	.10
419	A.L. checklist	.10
420	A.L. checklist	.10

1994 Select Crown Contenders

Candidates for the major baseball annual awards are featured in this subset. Horizontal-format cards have a color player photo printed on a holographic foil background. Backs are vertically oriented with a player portrait photo and justification for the player's inclusion in the set. Cards are numbered with a "CC" prefix and feature a special optical-variable anti-counterfeiting device at bottom-center. According to stated odds of one card on average in every 24 packs it has been estimated that fewer than 12,000 of each Crown Contenders card was produced.

		MT
Complete Set (10):		100.00
Common Player:		2.00
1	Len Dykstra	2.00
2	Greg Maddux	18.00
3	Roger Clemens	7.00
4	Randy Johnson	5.00
5	Frank Thomas	25.00
6	Barry Bonds	7.00
7	Juan Gonzalez	12.00
8	John Olerud	4.00
9	Mike Piazza	18.00
10	Ken Griffey, Jr.	30.00

1994 Select MVP

Paul Molitor was the 1994 Select MVP and is featured in this one card set. Molitor is pictured in front of three distinct foil designs across the rest of the card.

Modern cards have little collector value in conditions lower than Mint.
Figure NM cards at 75% of values shown;
EX cards at 40%.

MVP1 Paul Molitor   MT 15.00

1994 Select Rookie of the Year

Carlos Delgado was the 1994 Select Rookie of the Year. Delgado is pictured on top of a glowing foil background with his initials in large capital letters in the background and Rookie of the Year printed across the bottom.

		MT
		10.00
RY1	Carlos Delgado	10.00

1994 Select Rookie Surge

Each series of 1994 Score Select offered a chase card set of nine top rookies. Fronts feature action photos set against a rainbow-colored metallic foil background. Backs have a portrait photo and a few words about the player. Cards are numbered with an "RS" prefix and were inserted at an average rate of one per 48 packs.

		MT
Complete Set (18):		150.00
Complete Series 1 (9):		60.00
Complete Series 2 (9):		90.00
Common Player:		3.00
1	Cliff Floyd	4.00
2	Bob Hamelin	3.00
3	Ryan Klesko	15.00
4	Carlos Delgado	4.50
5	Jeffrey Hammonds	3.00
6	Rondell White	10.00
7	Salomon Torres	3.00
8	Steve Karsay	3.00
9	Javier Lopez	12.00
10	Manny Ramirez	30.00
11	Tony Tarasco	3.00
12	Kurt Abbott	3.00
13	Chan Ho Park	5.00
14	Rich Becker	3.00
15	James Mouton	3.00
16	Alex Gonzalez	6.00
17	Raul Mondesi	20.00
18	Steve Trachsel	3.00

1994 Select Salute

With odds of finding one of these cards stated at one per 360 packs, it is estimated that only about 4,000 of each of this two-card chase set were produced.

		MT
Complete Set (2):		175.00
1	Cal Ripken, Jr.	150.00
2	Dave Winfield	25.00

1994 Select Skills

Select Skills is a 10-card insert that was randomly inserted into every 24 packs. Ten specific skills were designated and matched with the player whom, in the opinion of Select officials, demonstrated that particular skill the best in baseball. Each card is printed on a foil background with the player name running along the lower right side of the card and the skill that they are being featured for along the bottom.

		MT
Complete Set (10):		50.00
Common Player:		3.00
1	Randy Johnson	5.00
2	Barry Larkin	4.00
3	Len Dykstra	3.00
4	Kenny Lofton	8.00
5	Juan Gonzalez	12.00
6	Barry Bonds	9.00
7	Marquis Grissom	3.00
8	Ivan Rodriguez	7.00
9	Larry Walker	4.00
10	Travis Fryman	3.00

1995 Select

The 250 regular-issue cards in Pinnacle's mid-price brand baseball set feature three basic formats. Veteran players' cards are presented in a horizontal design which features an action photo at left. At right is a portrait in a trapezoidal gold-foil frame set against a team color-coordinated marbled background. The team logo beneath the portrait and the player's name below that are printed in gold foil. Backs feature a black-and-white photo with a few career highlights, 1994 and Major League cumulative stats, and a "Select Stat" printed in red. The colored marble effect is carried over from the front. The Select Rookie cards which are grouped toward the end of the set are vertical in format and feature a borderless player photo with a gold-foil band at bottom which includes the player name and team logo, along with waves of gold emanating from the logo. Backs have a small, narrow color photo at left, with a large sepia version of the same photo ghosted at center and overprinted with a career summary. At bottom are 1994 and career stats. Ending the set are a series of "Show Time" cards of top prospects. Cards feature large gold-foil "Show Time" and team logos at bottom, with a facsimile autograph printed above. The player photo is shown as if at a curtain raising, with spotlight effects behind. Backs repeat the curtain and spotlight motif and feature another player photo, with autograph above. Production of this hobby-only product was stated as 4,950 cases, which translates to about 110,000 of each regular-issue card. A special card (#251) of Hideo Nomo was added to the set later. It was not issued in foil packs, but distributed to dealers who had purchased Select cases.

		MT
	Complete Set (251):	20.00
	Common Player:	.10
	Wax Box:	40.00
1	Cal Ripken Jr.	2.50
2	Robin Ventura	.10
3	Al Martin	.10
4	Jeff Frye	.10
5	Darryl Strawberry	.15
6	Chan Ho Park	.15
7	Steve Avery	.10
8	Bret Boone	.10
9	Danny Tartabull	.10
10	Dante Bichette	.25
11	Rondell White	.20
12	Dave McCarty	.10
13	Bernard Gilkey	.10
14	Mark McGwire	3.00
15	Ruben Sierra	.10
16	Wade Boggs	.20
17	Mike Piazza	2.00
18	Jeffrey Hammonds	.10
19	Mike Mussina	.35
20	Darryl Kile	.10
21	Greg Maddux	2.00
22	Frank Thomas	2.50
23	Kevin Appier	.10
24	Jay Bell	.10
25	Kirk Gibson	.10
26	Pat Hentgen	.10
27	Joey Hamilton	.10
28	Bernie Williams	.40
29	Aaron Sele	.12
30	Delino DeShields	.10
31	Danny Bautista	.10
32	Jim Thome	.35
33	Rikkert Faneyte	.10
34	Roberto Alomar	.60
35	Paul Molitor	.35
36	Allen Watson	.10
37	Jeff Bagwell	1.00
38	Jay Buhner	.15
39	Marquis Grissom	.12
40	Jim Edmonds	.25
41	Ryan Klesko	.50
42	Fred McGriff	.30
43	Tony Tarasco	.10
44	Darren Daulton	.10
45	Marc Newfield	.10
46	Barry Bonds	.75
47	Bobby Bonilla	.10
48	Greg Pirkl	.10
49	Steve Karsay	.10
50	Bob Hamelin	.10
51	Javier Lopez	.15
52	Barry Larkin	.25
53	Kevin Young	.10
54	Sterling Hitchcock	.10
55	Tom Glavine	.15
56	Carlos Delgado	.10
57	Darren Oliver	.10
58	Cliff Floyd	.12
59	Tim Salmon	.20
60	Albert Belle	.65
61	Salomon Torres	.10
62	Gary Sheffield	.40
63	Ivan Rodriguez	.50
64	Charles Nagy	.10
65	Eduardo Perez	.10
66	Terry Steinbach	.10
67	Dave Justice	.20
68	Jason Bere	.10
69	Dave Nilsson	.10
70	Brian Anderson	.10
71	Billy Ashley	.10
72	Roger Clemens	.75
73	Jimmy Key	.10
74	Wally Joyner	.10
75	Andy Benes	.10
76	Ray Lankford	.10
77	Jeff Kent	.10
78	Moises Alou	.10
79	Kirby Puckett	1.00
80	Joe Carter	.20
81	Manny Ramirez	.55
82	J.R. Phillips	.10
83	Matt Mieske	.10
84	John Olerud	.12
85	Andres Galarraga	.10
86	Juan Gonzalez	1.00
87	Pedro Martinez	.10
88	Dean Palmer	.10
89	Ken Griffey Jr.	3.00
90	Brian Jordan	.15
91	Hal Morris	.10
92	Lenny Dykstra	.10
93	Wil Cordero	.10
94	Tony Gwynn	1.00
95	Alex Gonzalez	.10
96	Cecil Fielder	.12
97	Mo Vaughn	.75
98	John Valentin	.10
99	Will Clark	.25
100	Geronimo Pena	.10
101	Don Mattingly	1.00
102	Charles Johnson	.15
103	Raul Mondesi	.35
104	Reggie Sanders	.10
105	Royce Clayton	.10
106	Reggie Jefferson	.10
107	Craig Biggio	.10
108	Jack McDowell	.10
109	James Mouton	.10
110	Mike Greenwell	.10
111	David Cone	.10
112	Matt Williams	.25
113	Garret Anderson	.10
114	Carlos Garcia	.10
115	Alex Fernandez	.10
116	Deion Sanders	.30
117	Chili Davis	.10
118	Mike Kelly	.10
119	Jeff Conine	.10
120	Kenny Lofton	.55
121	Rafael Palmeiro	.20
122	Chuck Knoblauch	.15
123	Ozzie Smith	.40
124	Carlos Baerga	.10
125	Brett Butler	.10
126	Sammy Sosa	1.50
127	Ellis Burks	.10
128	Bret Saberhagen	.10
129	Doug Drabek	.10
130	Dennis Martinez	.10
131	Paul O'Neill	.10
132	Travis Fryman	.10
133	Brent Gates	.10
134	Rickey Henderson	.25
135	Randy Johnson	.35
136	Mark Langston	.10
137	Greg Colbrunn	.10
138	Jose Rijo	.10
139	Bryan Harvey	.10
140	Dennis Eckersley	.10
141	Ron Gant	.10
142	Carl Everett	.10
143	Jeff Granger	.10
144	Ben McDonald	.10
145	Kurt Abbott	.10
146	Jim Abbott	.10
147	Jason Jacome	.10
148	Rico Brogna	.10
149	Cal Eldred	.10
150	Rich Becker	.10
151	Pete Harnisch	.10
152	Roberto Petagine	.10
153	Jacob Brumfield	.10
154	Todd Hundley	.10
155	Roger Cedeno	.10
156	Harold Baines	.10
157	Steve Dunn	.10
158	Tim Belk	.10
159	Marty Cordova	.10
160	Russ Davis	.10
161	Jose Malave	.10
162	Brian Hunter	.10
163	Andy Pettitte	.60
164	Brooks Kieschnick	.15
165	Midre Cummings	.10
166	Frank Rodriguez	.10
167	Chad Mottola	.10
168	Brian Barber	.10
169	Tim Unroe	.10
170	Shane Andrews	.10
171	Kevin Flora	.10
172	Ray Durham	.20
173	Chipper Jones	2.00
174	Butch Huskey	.10
175	Ray McDavid	.10
176	Jeff Cirillo	.10
177	Terry Pendleton	.10
178	Scott Ruffcorn	.10
179	Ray Holbert	.10
180	Joe Randa	.10
181	Jose Oliva	.10
182	Andy Van Slyke	.10
183	Albie Lopez	.10
184	Chad Curtis	.10
185	Ozzie Guillen	.10
186	Chad Ogea	.10
187	Dan Wilson	.10
188	Tony Fernandez	.10
189	John Smoltz	.25
190	Willie Greene	.10
191	Darren Lewis	.10
192	Orlando Miller	.10
193	Kurt Miller	.10
194	Andrew Lorraine	.10
195	Ernie Young	.10
196	Jimmy Haynes	.10
197	*Raul Casanova*	.20
198	Joe Vitiello	.10
199	Brad Woodall	.10
200	Juan Acevedo	.10
201	Michael Tucker	.10
202	Shawn Green	.10
203	Alex Rodriguez	3.00
204	Julian Tavarez	.10
205	Jose Lima	.10
206	Wilson Alvarez	.10
207	Rich Aude	.10
208	Armando Benitez	.10
209	Dwayne Hosey	.10
210	Gabe White	.10
211	Joey Eischen	.10
212	Bill Pulsipher	.15
213	Robby Thompson	.10
214	Toby Borland	.10
215	Rusty Greer	.10
216	Fausto Cruz	.10
217	Luis Ortiz	.10
218	Duane Singleton	.10
219	Troy Percival	.10
220	Gregg Jefferies	.10
221	Mark Grace	.25
222	Mickey Tettleton	.10
223	Phil Plantier	.10
224	Larry Walker	.25
225	Ken Caminiti	.20
226	Dave Winfield	.25
227	Brady Anderson	.15
228	Kevin Brown	.10
229	Andujar Cedeno	.10
230	Roberto Kelly	.10
231	Jose Canseco	.30
231	(Scott Ruffcorn) (Showtime)	.10
232	Billy Ashley (Showtime)	.10
234	J.R. Phillips (Showtime)	.10
235	Chipper Jones (Showtime)	.75
236	Charles Johnson (Showtime)	.15
237	Midre Cummings (Showtime)	.10
238	Brian Hunter (Showtime)	.10
239	Garret Anderson (Showtime)	.10
240	Shawn Green (Showtime)	.15
241	Alex Rodriguez (Showtime)	1.50
242	Checklist #1(Frank Thomas)	1.25
243	Checklist #2(Ken Griffey Jr.)	1.25
244	Checklist #3(Albert Belle)	.30
245	Checklist #4(Cal Ripken Jr.)	1.00
246	Checklist #5(Barry Bonds)	.35
247	Checklist #6(Raul Mondesi)	.20
248	Checklist #7(Mike Piazza)	.60
249	Checklist #8(Jeff Bagwell)	.50
250	Checklist #9(Jeff Bagwell, Frank Thomas, Ken Griffey Jr., Mike Piazza)	.50
251	Hideo Nomo	6.00

A player's name in *italic* type indicates a rookie card.

1995 Select Artist's Proofs

Among the scarcest and most valuable of 1995's baseball card inserts are the Select Artist's Proof parallel set. While an AP card is found on average once per 24 packs, the limited print run of the basic Select set means that only about 475 of each of the 250 regular-issue cards in the Select set were made in this edition. The AP inserts have a gold-foil "ARTIST'S PROOF" line at bottom, and other gold-foil highlights are embossed, rather than merely stamped on, as on regular Select cards.

	MT
Complete Set (250):	3000.
Common Player:	5.00
(Star Select Artist's Proof cards valued about 100-125X regular-issue versions.)	

1995 Select Big Sticks

With fronts printed in what Pinnacle describes as "holographic Gold Rush technology," the Big Sticks chase card issue offers a dozen of the game's big hitters in action photos superimposed over their team logo. Conventionally printed backs have another player photo, along with a summary of career highlights and description of the player's power potential. Stated odds of pulling a Big Sticks chase card are one per 48 packs, on average.

		MT
Complete Set (12):		100.00
Common Player:		4.00
BS1	Frank Thomas	20.00
BS2	Ken Griffey Jr.	25.00
BS3	Cal Ripken Jr.	20.00
BS4	Mike Piazza	15.00
BS5	Don Mattingly	10.00
BS6	Will Clark	4.00
BS7	Tony Gwynn	12.00
BS8	Jeff Bagwell	10.00
BS9	Barry Bonds	6.00
BS10	Paul Molitor	5.00
BS11	Matt Williams	4.00
BS12	Albert Belle	5.00

1995 Select Can't Miss

A mix of rookies and sophomore standouts, along with a few players of slightly longer service are presented in this chase set. Cards feature color player action photos printed on a metallic red background, with their last name in gold foil at lower-left. An umpire on the "Can't Miss" logo is at upper-left. Backs repeat the logo, have a tall, narrow player photo, a few biographical details and a paragraph of career summary.

		MT
Complete Set (12):		70.00
Common Player:		2.00
CM1	Cliff Floyd	3.00
CM2	Ryan Klesko	5.00
CM3	Charles Johnson	5.00
CM4	Raul Mondesi	4.00
CM5	Manny Ramirez	6.00
CM6	Billy Ashley	2.00
CM7	Alex Gonzalez	2.50
CM8	Carlos Delgado	3.00
CM9	Garret Anderson	3.00
CM10	Alex Rodriguez	30.00
CM11	Chipper Jones	20.00
CM12	Shawn Green	2.00

1995 Select Sure Shots

Ten of Select's picks for future stardom are featured in this chase set, the toughest find of any of the 1995 Select inserts, at an average rate of one per 90 packs. Card fronts feature player action photos set against a gold "Dufex" foil printed background with a Sure Shots logo vertically at left. Backs have a blue background with a few words about the player and a portrait photo at left.

		MT
Complete Set (10):		60.00
Common Player:		2.00
SS1	Ben Grieve	30.00
SS2	Kevin Witt	2.00
SS3	Mark Farris	2.00
SS4	Paul Konerko	20.00
SS5	Dustin Hermanson	12.00
SS6	Ramon Castro	2.00
SS7	McKay Christensen	2.00
SS8	Brian Buchanan	4.00
SS9	Paul Wilson	4.00
SS10	Terrence Long	2.00

1996 Select

Select's 1996 baseball set has 200 cards in it, including 35 rookies, five checklists and 10 Lineup Leaders subset cards. All 200 cards are also reprinted as part of an Artist's Proof parallel set, using a holographic Artist's Proof logo. Cards were seeded one per every 35 packs; there were approximately 435 sets produced. Three insert sets were also created: Claim to Fame, En Fuego and Team Nucleus.

		MT
Complete Set (200):		20.00
Common Player:		.10
Unlisted Stars: .20 to .35		
Wax Box:		40.00
1	Wade Boggs	.20
2	Shawn Green	.10
3	Andres Galarraga	.15
4	Bill Pulsipher	.15
5	Chuck Knoblauch	.10
6	Ken Griffey Jr.	2.50
7	Greg Maddux	1.50
8	Manny Ramirez	.75
9	Ivan Rodriguez	.50
10	Tim Salmon	.25
11	Frank Thomas	2.00
12	Jeff Bagwell	1.00
13	Travis Fryman	.15
14	Kenny Lofton	.75
15	Matt Williams	.25
16	Jay Bell	.10
17	Ken Caminiti	.10
18	Ray Lankford	.10
19	Cal Ripken Jr.	2.00
20	Roger Clemens	.60
21	Carlos Baerga	.15
22	Mike Piazza	1.50
23	Gregg Jefferies	.10
24	Reggie Sanders	.10
25	Rondell White	.10
26	Sammy Sosa	1.50
27	Kevin Appier	.10
28	Kevin Seitzer	.10
29	Gary Sheffield	.10
30	Mike Mussina	.40
31	Mark McGwire	3.00
32	Barry Larkin	.20

33	Marc Newfield	.10
34	Ismael Valdes	.10
35	Marty Cordova	.20
36	Albert Belle	.75
37	Johnny Damon	.25
38	Garret Anderson	.10
39	Cecil Fielder	.15
40	John Mabry	.10
41	Chipper Jones	1.50
42	Omar Vizquel	.10
43	Jose Rijo	.10
44	Charles Johnson	.10
45	Alex Rodriquez	2.50
46	Rico Brogna	.10
47	Joe Carter	.20
48	Mo Vaughn	.75
49	Moises Alou	.10
50	Raul Mondesi	.30
51	Robin Ventura	.10
52	Jim Thome	.40
53	Dave Justice	.20
54	Jeff King	.10
55	Brian Hunter	.15
56	Juan Gonzalez	1.00
57	John Olerud	.10
58	Rafael Palmeiro	.20
59	Tony Gwynn	1.00
60	Eddie Murray	.35
61	Jason Isringhausen	.25
62	Dante Bichette	.20
63	Randy Johnson	.35
64	Kirby Puckett	1.00
65	Jim Edmonds	.15
66	David Cone	.15
67	Ozzie Smith	.25
68	Fred McGriff	.35
69	Darren Daulton	.10
70	Edgar Martinez	.10
71	J.T. Snow	.10
72	Butch Huskey	.10
73	Hideo Nomo	.50
74	Pedro Martinez	.10
75	Bobby Bonilla	.15
76	Jeff Conine	.10
77	Ryan Klesko	.50
78	Bernie Williams	.40
79	Andre Dawson	.10
80	Trevor Hoffman	.10
81	Mark Grace	.15
82	Benji Gil	.10
83	Eric Karros	.10
84	Pete Schourek	.10
85	Edgardo Alfonzo	.10
86	Jay Buhner	.20
87	Vinny Castilla	.10
88	Bret Boone	.10
89	Ray Durham	.10
90	Brian Jordan	.10
91	Jose Canseco	.25
92	Paul O'Neill	.10
93	Chili Davis	.10
94	Tom Glavine	.15
95	Julian Tavarez	.10
96	Derek Bell	.10
97	Will Clark	.25
98	Larry Walker	.25
99	Denny Neagle	.10
100	Alex Fernandez	.10
101	Barry Bonds	.60
102	Ben McDonald	.10
103	Andy Pettitte	1.25
104	Tino Martinez	.10
105	Sterling Hitchcock	.10
106	Royce Clayton	.10
107	Jim Abbott	.10
108	Rickey Henderson	.10
109	Ramon Martinez	.10
110	Paul Molitor	.25
111	Dennis Eckersley	.10
112	Alex Gonzalez	.10
113	Marquis Grissom	.10
114	Greg Vaughn	.10
115	Lance Johnson	.10
116	Todd Stottlemyre	.10
117	Jack McDowell	.15
118	Ruben Sierra	.10
119	Brady Anderson	.15
120	Julio Franco	.10
121	Brooks Kieshnick	.15
122	Roberto Alomar	.50
123	Greg Gagne	.10
124	Wally Joyner	.10
125	John Smoltz	.20
126	John Valentin	.10
127	Russ Davis	.10
128	Joe Vitiello	.10

129	Shawon Dunston	.10
130	Frank Rodriguez	.10
131	Charlie Hayes	.10
132	Andy Benes	.10
133	B.J. Surhoff	.10
134	Dave Nilsson	.10
135	Carlos Delgado	.15
136	Walt Weiss	.10
137	Mike Stanley	.10
138	Greg Colbrunn	.10
139	Mike Kelly	.10
140	Ryne Sandberg	.50
141	Lee Smith	.10
142	Dennis Martinez	.10
143	Bernard Gilkey	.10
144	Lenny Dykstra	.10
145	Danny Tartabull	.10
146	Dean Palmer	.10
147	Craig Biggio	.10
148	Juan Acevedo	.10
149	Michael Tucker	.10
150	Bobby Higginson	.10
151	Ken Griffey Jr. (Line Up Leaders)	1.25
152	Frank Thomas (Line Up Leaders)	1.00
153	Cal Ripken Jr. (Line Up Leaders)	1.00
154	Albert Belle (Line Up Leaders)	.40
155	Mike Piazza (Line Up Leaders)	.60
156	Barry Bonds (Line Up Leaders)	.25
157	Sammy Sosa (Line Up Leaders)	.75
158	Mo Vaughn (Line Up Leaders)	.25
159	Greg Maddux (Line Up Leaders)	.75
160	Jeff Bagwell (Line Up Leaders)	.50
161	Derek Jeter	1.25
162	Paul Wilson	.25
163	Chris Snopek	.10
164	Jason Schmidt	.20
165	Jimmy Haynes	.10
166	George Arias	.10
167	Steve Gibralter	.10
168	Bob Wolcott	.10
169	Jason Kendall	.10
170	Greg Zaun	.10
171	Quinton McCracken	.10
172	Alan Benes	.25
173	Rey Ordonez	.40
174	Ugueth Urbina	.10
175	*Osvaldo Fernandez*	.20
176	Yamil Benitez	.10
177	Sal Fasano	.10
178	*Mike Grace*	.20
179	Chan Ho Park	.10
180	Robert Perez	.10
181	Todd Hollandsworth	.20
182	*Wilton Guerrero*	.75
183	John Wasdin	.10
184	Jim Pittsley	.10
185	LaTroy Hawkins	.10
186	Jay Powell	.10
187	Felipe Crespo	.10
188	Jermaine Dye	.25
189	Bob Abreu	.10
190	*Matt Luke*	.15
191	Richard Hidalgo	.10
192	Karim Garcia	.35
193	Tavo Alvarez	.10
194	*Andy Fox*	.10
195	Terrell Wade	.10
196	Frank Thomas CL	.75
197	Ken Griffey Jr.	1.00
198	Greg Maddux CL	.60
199	Mike Piazza CL	.50
200	Cal Ripken Jr. CL	.75

1996 Select Artist's Proofs

Approximately once per 35 packs, a card from this parallel chase set is encountered among 1996 Select. Reported production was 435 sets. The Artist's Proof cards are distinguished by a holographic logo testifying to their status on the front of the card.

	MT
Complete Set (200):	2500.
Common Player:	2.50

(Star cards valued at 60X-80X regular Select edition)

1996 Select Claim to Fame

Twenty different stars are featured on these 1996 Select insert cards. Each card is numbered "1 of 2100" and uses an external die-cut design. The cards were seeded one per every 72 packs.

		MT
Complete Set (20):		300.00
Common Player:		4.00
1	Cal Ripken Jr.	40.00
2	Greg Maddux	30.00
3	Ken Griffey Jr.	50.00
4	Frank Thomas	40.00
5	Mo Vaughn	15.00
6	Albert Belle	12.00
7	Jeff Bagwell	20.00
8	Sammy Sosa	25.00
8s	Sammy Sosa (overprinted "SAMPLE")	10.00
9	Reggie Sanders	4.00
10	Hideo Nomo	10.00
11	Chipper Jones	30.00
12	Mike Piazza	30.00
13	Matt Williams	6.00
14	Tony Gwynn	20.00
15	Johnny Damon	4.00
16	Dante Bichette	4.00
17	Kirby Puckett	15.00
18	Barry Bonds	12.00
19	Randy Johnson	8.00
20	Eddie Murray	6.00

1996 Select En Fuego

ESPN announcer Dan Patrick is featured on his own card in this set, inspired by his Sportscenter catch phrase "en fuego," which means "on fire." Patrick's teammate, Keith Olberman, wrote the card backs. The 25 cards, printed on all-foil Dufex stock, are seeded one peer every 48 packs of 1996 Select baseball.

A player's name in *italic* type indicates a rookie card.

		MT
Complete Set (25):		200.00
Common Player:		3.00
1	Ken Griffey Jr.	30.00
2	Frank Thomas	25.00
3	Cal Ripken Jr.	25.00
4	Greg Maddux	20.00
5	Jeff Bagwell	12.00
6	Barry Bonds	8.00
7	Mo Vaughn	8.00
8	Albert Belle	8.00
9	Sammy Sosa	15.00
10	Reggie Sanders	3.00
11	Mike Piazza	20.00
12	Chipper Jones	20.00
13	Tony Gwynn	15.00
14	Kirby Puckett	10.00
15	Wade Boggs	4.00
16	Dan Patrick	3.00
17	Gary Sheffield	5.00
18	Dante Bichette	4.00
19	Randy Johnson	5.00
20	Matt Williams	3.00
21	Alex Rodriguez	25.00
22	Tim Salmon	4.00
23	Johnny Damon	3.00
24	Manny Ramirez	6.00
25	Hideo Nomo	8.00

1996 Select
Team Nucleus

This 1996 Select insert set pays tribute to the three top players from each Major League Baseball team; each card features the three teammates on it. The cards are printed on a clear plastic, utilizing a holographic micro-etched design. They are seeded one per every 18 packs.

		MT
Complete Set (28):		120.00
Common Player:		2.00
1	Albert Belle, Manny Ramirez, Carlos Baerga	5.00
2	Ray Lankford, Brian Jordan, Ozzie Smith	4.00
3	Jay Bell, Jeff King, Denny Neagle	2.00
4	Dante Bichette, Andres Galarraga, Larry Walker	4.00
5	Mark McGwire, Mike Bordick, Terry Steinbach	12.00

6	Bernie Williams, Wade Boggs, David Cone	5.00
7	Joe Carter, Alex Gonzalez, Shawn Green	2.50
8	Roger Clemens, Mo Vaughn, Jose Canseco	5.00
9	Ken Griffey Jr., Edgar Martinez, Randy Johnson	15.00
10	Gregg Jefferies, Darren Daulton, Lenny Dykstra	2.00
11	Mike Piazza, Raul Mondesi, Hideo Nomo	12.00
12	Greg Maddux, Chipper Jones, Ryan Klesko	15.00
13	Cecil Fielder, Travis Fryman, Phil Nevin	2.50
14	Ivan Rodriguez, Will Clark, Juan Gonzalez	5.00
15	Ryne Sandberg, Sammy Sosa, Mark Grace	12.00
16	Gary Sheffield, Charles Johnson, Andre Dawson	3.00
17	Johnny Damon, Michael Tucker, Kevin Appier	4.00
18	Barry Bonds, Matt Williams, Rod Beck	4.00
19	Kirby Puckett, Chuck Knoblauch, Marty Cordova	5.00
20	Cal Ripken Jr., Bobby Bonilla, Mike Mussina	12.00
21	Jason Isringhausen, Bill Pulsipher, Rico Brogna	3.00
22	Tony Gwynn, Ken Caminiti, Marc Newfield	5.00
23	Tim Salmon, Garret Anderson, Jim Edmonds	3.00
24	Moises Alou, Rondell White, Cliff Floyd	2.00
25	Barry Larkin, Reggie Sanders, Bret Boone	3.00
26	Jeff Bagwell, Craig Biggio, Derek Bell	7.50
27	Frank Thomas, Robin Ventura, Alex Fernandez	12.00
28	John Jaha, Greg Vaughn, Kevin Seitzer	2.00

1997 Select

The base set is made up of 150 cards printed on a thick, 16-point stock. Each card in the regular set features a distinctive silver-foil treatment and either a red (100 cards) or blue (50 cards) foil accent. Subsets include 40 Rookies, eight Super Stars and two checklists. Inserts include two parallel sets, (Artist's Proof and Registered Gold), Tools of the Trade, Mirror Blue Tools of the Trade, and Rookie Revolution. The cards were sold only at hobby shops in six-card packs for $2.99 each.

		MT
Complete Set (150):		45.00
Common Player:		.10
Prices listed for Red Cards:		
Blues 2x listed prices		
Registered Gold Reds: 5x to 10x		
Registered Gold Blues: 20x to 35x		
Artist's Proofs Reds: 25x to 50x		
Artist's Proofs Blues: 80x to 100x		
Wax Box:		50.00
1	Juan Gonzalez	1.25
2	Mo Vaughn	.75
3	Tony Gwynn	1.25
4	Manny Ramirez	.75
5	Jose Canseco	.25
6	David Cone	.15
7	Chan Ho Park	.10
8	Frank Thomas	2.50
9	Todd Hollandsworth	.10
10	Marty Cordova	.10
11	Gary Sheffield	.30
12	John Smoltz	.20
13	Mark Grudzielanek	.10
14	Sammy Sosa	1.50
15	Paul Molitor	.40
16	Kevin Brown	.10
17	Albert Belle	.75
18	Eric Young	.10
19	John Wetteland	.10
20	Ryan Klesko	.40
21	Joe Carter	.15
22	Alex Ochoa	.10
23	Greg Maddux	2.00
24	Roger Clemens	1.00
25	Ivan Rodriguez	.50
26	Barry Bonds	.75
27	Kenny Lofton	.75
28	Javy Lopez	.15
29	Hideo Nomo	.60
30	Rusty Greer	.10
31	Rafael Palmeiro	.15
32	Mike Piazza	2.00
33	Ryne Sandberg	.75
34	Wade Boggs	.20
35	Jim Thome	.40
36	Ken Caminiti	.20
37	Mark Grace	.15
38	Brian Jordan	.10
39	Craig Biggio	.15
40	Henry Rodriguez	.10
41	Dean Palmer	.10
42	Jason Kendall	.10
43	Bill Pulsipher	.10
44	Tim Salmon	.20
45	Marc Newfield	.10
46	Pat Hentgen	.10
47	Ken Griffey Jr.	3.00
48	Paul Wilson	.10
49	Jay Buhner	.20
50	Rickey Henderson	.10
51	Jeff Bagwell	1.25
52	Cecil Fielder	.15
53	Alex Rodriguez	3.00
54	John Jaha	.10
55	Brady Anderson	.10
56	Andres Galarraga	.20
57	Raul Mondesi	.25
58	Andy Pettitte	.75
59	Roberto Alomar	.50
60	Derek Jeter	2.00
61	Charles Johnson	.10
62	Travis Fryman	.10
63	Chipper Jones	2.00
64	Edgar Martinez	.10
65	Bobby Bonilla	.10
66	Greg Vaughn	.10
67	Bobby Higginson	.10
68	Garret Anderson	.10
69	Chuck Knoblauch	.15
70	Jermaine Dye	.10
71	Cal Ripken Jr.	2.50
72	Jason Giambi	.10
73	Trey Beamon	.10
74	Shawn Green	.10
75	Mark McGwire	4.00
76	Carlos Delgado	.10
77	Jason Isringhausen	.10
78	Randy Johnson	.60
79	Troy Percival	.10
80	Ron Gant	.15
81	Ellis Burks	.10
82	Mike Mussina	.50
83	Todd Hundley	.20
84	Jim Edmonds	.10
85	Charles Nagy	.10
86	Dante Bichette	.20

87	Mariano Rivera	.15
88	Matt Williams	.30
89	Rondell White	.10
90	Steve Finley	.10
91	Alex Fernandez	.15
92	Barry Larkin	.20
93	Tom Goodwin	.10
94	Will Clark	.30
95	Michael Tucker	.10
96	Derek Bell	.10
97	Larry Walker	.40
98	Alan Benes	.20
99	Tom Glavine	.20
100	Darin Erstad	1.25
101	Andruw Jones	1.50
102	Scott Rolen	1.50
103	Todd Walker	.50
104	Dmitri Young	.10
105	Vladimir Guerrero	1.00
106	Nomar Garciaparra	2.00
107	*Danny Patterson*	.20
108	Karim Garcia	.15
109	Todd Greene	.10
110	Ruben Rivera	.15
111	Raul Casanova	.10
112	Mike Cameron	.10
113	Bartolo Colon	.10
114	*Rod Myers*	.10
115	Todd Dunn	.10
116	Torii Hunter	.10
117	Jason Dickson	.20
118	*Gene Kingsale*	.20
119	Rafael Medina	.10
120	Raul Ibanez	.10
121	*Bobby Henley*	.20
122	Scott Spiezio	.10
123	*Bobby Smith*	.20
124	J.J. Johnson	.10
125	*Bubba Trammell*	1.00
126	Jeff Abbott	.10
127	Neifi Perez	.10
128	Derrek Lee	.10
129	*Kevin Brown*	.10
130	Mendy Lopez	.10
131	Kevin Orie	.10
132	Ryan Jones	.10
133	Juan Encarnacion	.50
134	Jose Guillen	.75
135	Greg Norton	.10
136	Richie Sexson	.10
137	Jay Payton	.10
138	Bob Abreu	.10
139	*Ronnie Belliard*	.50
140	Wilton Guerrero	.10
141	Alex Rodriguez (Select Stars)	1.50
142	Juan Gonzalez (Select Stars)	.60
143	Ken Caminiti (Select Stars)	.15
144	Frank Thomas (Select Stars)	1.25
145	Ken Griffey Jr. (Select Stars)	1.50
146	John Smoltz (Select Stars)	.15
147	Mike Piazza (Select Stars)	1.00
148	Derek Jeter (Select Stars)	1.00
149	Frank Thomas CL	.75
150	Ken Griffey Jr. CL	.75

1997 Select Autographs

Four top candidates for the 1997 Rookie of the Year Award - Wilton Guerrero, Jose Guillen, Andruw Jones and Todd Walker - each signed a limited number of their Select Rookie cards. Jones signed 2,500 cards while each of the other players signed 3,000 each.

Modern cards have little collector value in conditions lower than Mint. Figure NM cards at 75% of values shown; EX cards at 40%.

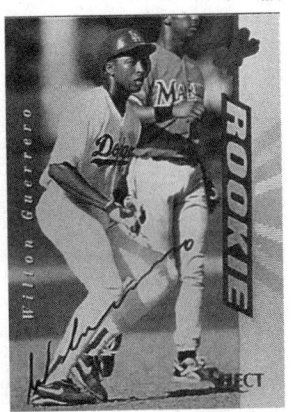

MT

Complete Set (4):		125.00
Common Autograph:		35.00
AU1	Wilton Guerrero	35.00
AU2	Jose Guillen	30.00
AU3	Andruw Jones	50.00
AU4	Todd Walker	40.00

1997 Select Registered Gold

This parallel insert set, like the regular issue, can be found with 100 red-foil and 50 blue-foil enhanced cards. They differ from the regular issue in the use of gold foil instead of silver on the right side of the front. Also, the inserts have "Registered Gold" printed vertically on the right side of the photo. Backs are identical to the regular issue. Red-foil Registered Gold cards are found on average of once every 11 packs; blue-foiled cards are a 1 in 47 pick.

	MT
Complete Set (15):	1200.
Common Red Gold:	2.00
Common Blue Gold:	4.00
(Stars and rookies valued at 5X-10X cards in regular issue)	

1997 Select Rookie Revolution

MT

This 20-card insert highlights some of the top young stars in the game. Cards feature a silver micro-etched mylar design on front. Backs are sequentially numbered and contain a few words about the player. Odds of finding a card are 1:56 packs.

		MT
Complete Set (20):		200.00
Common Player:		6.00
1	Andruw Jones	20.00
2	Derek Jeter	30.00
3	Todd Hollandsworth	6.00
4	Edgar Renteria	6.00
5	Jason Kendall	6.00
6	Rey Ordonez	6.00
7	F.P. Santangelo	6.00
8	Jermaine Dye	6.00
9	Alex Ochoa	6.00
10	Vladimir Guerrero	20.00
11	Dmitri Young	6.00
12	Todd Walker	12.00
13	Scott Rolen	25.00
14	Nomar Garciaparra	30.00
15	Ruben Rivera	8.00
16	Darin Erstad	20.00
17	Todd Greene	6.00
18	Mariano Rivera	6.00
19	Trey Beamon	6.00
20	Karim Garcia	8.00

1997 Select Tools of the Trade

A 25-card insert featuring a double-front design salutes a top veteran player on one side and a promising youngster on the other. Cards feature a silver-foil card stock with gold-foil stamping. Cards were inserted 1:9 packs. A parallel to this set - Blue Mirror Tools of the Trade - features blue-foil stock with an insert ratio of 1:240 packs.

		MT
Complete Set (25):		200.00
Common Player:		3.00
Mirror Blues: 8x to 12x		
1	Ken Griffey Jr., Andruw Jones	20.00
2	Greg Maddux, Andy Pettitte	15.00
3	Cal Ripken Jr., Chipper Jones	20.00
4	Mike Piazza, Jason Kendall	12.00
5	Albert Belle, Karim Garcia	8.00
6	Mo Vaughn, Dmitri Young	8.00
7	Juan Gonzalez, Vladimir Guerrero	12.00
8	Tony Gwynn, Jermaine Dye	12.00
9	Barry Bonds, Alex Ochoa	8.00
10	Jeff Bagwell, Jason Giambi	12.00
11	Kenny Lofton, Darin Erstad	12.00

12	Gary Sheffield, Manny Ramirez	8.00
13	Tim Salmon, Todd Hollandsworth	3.00
14	Sammy Sosa, Ruben Rivera	12.00
15	Paul Molitor, George Arias	6.00
16	Jim Thome, Todd Walker	6.00
17	Wade Boggs, Scott Rolen	8.00
18	Ryne Sandberg, Chuck Knoblauch	8.00
19	Mark McGwire, Frank Thomas	20.00
20	Ivan Rodriguez, Charles Johnson	7.00
21	Brian Jordan, Trey Beamon	3.00
22	Roger Clemens, Troy Percival	10.00
23	John Smoltz, Mike Mussina	6.00
24	Alex Rodriguez, Rey Ordonez	20.00
25	Derek Jeter, Nomar Garciaparra	15.00

1995 SkyBox E-Motion

This is a super-premium debut issue from the newly merged Fleer/SkyBox company. Printed on double-thick cardboard, card fronts have borderless photos marred by the presence of four gold-foil "viewfinder" corner marks. The player's last name and team are printed in gold foil near the bottom. On each card there is a large silver-foil word printed in block letters; either a nickname or an emotion or attribute associated with the player. Backs have two more player photos, 1994 and career stats and a few biographical bits. Eight-cards packs were issued with a suggested retail price of $4.99.

		MT
Complete Set (200):		40.00
Common Player:		.15
Wax Box:		80.00
1	Brady Anderson	.25
2	Kevin Brown	.15
3	Curtis Goodwin	.15
4	Jeffrey Hammonds	.15
5	Ben McDonald	.15
6	Mike Mussina	.75
7	Rafael Palmeiro	.25
8	Cal Ripken Jr.	3.00
9	Jose Canseco	.40
10	Roger Clemens	1.00
11	Vaughn Eshelman	.15
12	Mike Greenwell	.15
13	Erik Hanson	.15
14	Tim Naehring	.15

15	Aaron Sele	.15
16	John Valentin	.15
17	Mo Vaughn	1.00
18	Chili Davis	.15
19	Gary DiSarcina	.15
20	Chuck Finley	.15
21	Tim Salmon	.40
22	Lee Smith	.15
23	J.T. Snow	.15
24	Jim Abbott	.15
25	Jason Bere	.15
26	Ray Durham	.15
27	Ozzie Guillen	.15
28	Tim Raines	.15
29	Frank Thomas	3.00
30	Robin Ventura	.20
31	Carlos Baerga	.15
32	Albert Belle	1.00
33	Orel Hershiser	.15
34	Kenny Lofton	.75
35	Dennis Martinez	.15
36	Eddie Murray	.60
37	Manny Ramirez	.75
38	Julian Tavarez	.15
39	Jim Thome	.50
40	Dave Winfield	.25
41	Chad Curtis	.15
42	Cecil Fielder	.20
43	Travis Fryman	.15
44	Kirk Gibson	.15
45	*Bob Higginson*	1.50
46	Alan Trammell	.15
47	Lou Whitaker	.15
48	Kevin Appier	.15
49	Gary Gaetti	.15
50	Jeff Montgomery	.15
51	Jon Nunnally	.15
52	Ricky Bones	.15
53	Cal Eldred	.15
54	Joe Oliver	.15
55	Kevin Seitzer	.15
56	Marty Cordova	.15
57	Chuck Knoblauch	.25
58	Kirby Puckett	1.50
59	Wade Boggs	.40
60	Derek Jeter	1.75
61	Jimmy Key	.15
62	Don Mattingly	1.50
63	Jack McDowell	.15
64	Paul O'Neill	.15
65	Andy Pettitte	1.00
66	Ruben Rivera	.75
67	Mike Stanley	.15
68	John Wetteland	.15
69	Geronimo Berroa	.15
70	Dennis Eckersley	.20
71	Rickey Henderson	.25
72	Mark McGwire	4.00
73	Steve Ontiveros	.15
74	Ruben Sierra	.15
75	Terry Steinbach	.15
76	Jay Buhner	.25
77	Ken Griffey Jr.	4.00
78	Randy Johnson	.60
79	Edgar Martinez	.25
80	Tino Martinez	.25
81	Marc Newfield	.15
82	Alex Rodriguez	4.00
83	Will Clark	.40
84	Benji Gil	.15
85	Juan Gonzalez	1.50
86	Rusty Greer	.15
87	Dean Palmer	.15
88	Ivan Rodriguez	.75
89	Kenny Rogers	.15
90	Roberto Alomar	1.00
91	Joe Carter	.15
92	David Cone	.25
93	Alex Gonzalez	.15
94	Shawn Green	.20
95	Pat Hentgen	.15
96	Paul Molitor	.35
97	John Olerud	.15
98	Devon White	.15
99	Steve Avery	.15
100	Tom Glavine	.25
101	Marquis Grissom	.15
102	Chipper Jones	2.00
103	Dave Justice	.25
104	Ryan Klesko	.60
105	Javier Lopez	.25
106	Greg Maddux	2.50
107	Fred McGriff	.40
108	John Smoltz	.30
109	Shawon Dunston	.15
110	Mark Grace	.25

111	Brian McRae	.15
112	Randy Myers	.15
113	Sammy Sosa	2.00
114	Steve Trachsel	.15
115	Bret Boone	.15
116	Ron Gant	.25
117	Barry Larkin	.25
118	Deion Sanders	.40
119	Reggie Sanders	.15
120	Pete Schourek	.15
121	John Smiley	.15
122	Jason Bates	.15
123	Dante Bichette	.50
124	Vinny Castilla	.15
125	Andres Galarraga	.25
126	Larry Walker	.40
127	Greg Colbrunn	.15
128	Jeff Conine	.15
129	Andre Dawson	.20
130	Chris Hammond	.15
131	Charles Johnson	.15
132	Gary Sheffield	.60
133	Quilvio Veras	.15
134	Jeff Bagwell	1.25
135	Derek Bell	.15
136	Craig Biggio	.15
137	Jim Dougherty	.15
138	John Hudek	.15
139	Orlando Miller	.15
140	Phil Plantier	.15
141	Eric Karros	.20
142	Ramon Martinez	.15
143	Raul Mondesi	.50
144	*Hideo Nomo*	4.00
145	Mike Piazza	2.00
146	Ismael Valdes	.15
147	Todd Worrell	.15
148	Moises Alou	.15
149	*Yamil Benitez*	.15
150	Wil Cordero	.15
151	Jeff Fassero	.15
152	Cliff Floyd	.15
153	Pedro Martinez	.40
154	*Carlos Perez*	.25
155	Tony Tarasco	.15
156	Rondell White	.15
157	Edgardo Alfonzo	.15
158	Bobby Bonilla	.15
159	Rico Brogna	.15
160	Bobby Jones	.15
161	Bill Pulsipher	.20
162	Bret Saberhagen	.15
163	Ricky Bottalico	.15
164	Darren Daulton	.15
165	Lenny Dykstra	.15
166	Charlie Hayes	.15
167	Dave Hollins	.15
168	Gregg Jefferies	.15
169	*Michael Mimbs*	.40
170	Curt Schilling	.15
171	Heathcliff Slocumb	.15
172	Jay Bell	.15
173	*Micah Franklin*	.20
174	*Mark Johnson*	.40
175	Jeff King	.15
176	Al Martin	.15
177	Dan Miceli	.15
178	Denny Neagle	.15
179	Bernard Gilkey	.15
180	Ken Hill	.15
181	Brian Jordan	.20
182	Ray Lankford	.15
183	Ozzie Smith	.75
184	Andy Benes	.15
185	Ken Caminiti	.25
186	Steve Finley	.15
187	Tony Gwynn	1.50
188	Joey Hamilton	.20
189	Melvin Nieves	.15
190	Scott Sanders	.15
191	Rod Beck	.15
192	Barry Bonds	.75
193	Royce Clayton	.15
194	Glenallen Hill	.15
195	Darren Lewis	.15
196	Mark Portugal	.15
197	Matt Williams	.40
198	Checklist	.15
199	Checklist	.15
200	Checklist	.15

A player's name in *italic* type indicates a rookie card.

1995 SkyBox E-Motion Cal Ripken Jr. Timeless

A white background with a clockface and gold-foil "TIMELESS" logo are the standard elements of this insert tribute to Cal Ripken, Jr. Each card front features a large color photo and a smaller sepia photo contemporary to some phase of his career. The first 10 cards in the set chronicle Ripken's career through 1994. A special mail-in offer provided five more cards featuring highlights of his 1995 season.

		MT
Complete Set (15):		60.00
Common Player:		5.00
1	High School Pitcher	5.00
2	Role Model	5.00
3	Rookie of the Year	5.00
4	1st MVP Season	5.00
5	95 Consecutive Errorless Games	5.00
6	All-Star MVP	5.00
7	Conditioning	5.00
8	Shortstop HR Record	5.00
9	Literacy Work	5.00
10	2000th Consecutive Game	5.00
11	All-Star Selection	5.00
12	Record-tying Game	5.00
13	Record-breaking Game	5.00
14	2,153 and Counting	5.00
15	Birthday	5.00

1995 SkyBox E-Motion N-Tense

A colored wave-pattern printed on metallic foil is the background for the action photo of one of baseball's top sluggers in this chase card set. A huge rainbow prismatic foil "N" appears in an upper corner. The player's name and team are at lower-right in gold foil. Backs are conventionally printed and repeat the front's patterned background, with another color player photo and a shaded box with a few career highlights.

A player's name in *italic* type indicates a rookie card.

		MT
Complete Set (12):		150.00
Common Player:		4.00
1	Jeff Bagwell	12.00
2	Albert Belle	10.00
3	Barry Bonds	10.00
4	Cecil Fielder	4.00
5	Ron Gant	4.00
6	Ken Griffey Jr.	40.00
7	Mark McGwire	35.00
8	Mike Piazza	25.00
9	Manny Ramirez	10.00
10	Frank Thomas	30.00
11	Mo Vaughn	10.00
12	Matt Williams	6.00

1995 SkyBox E-Motion Masters

Ten of the game's top veterans are featured in this chase card set. A large close-up photo in a single team-related color in the background, with a color action photo in the foreground. Backs have a borderless color photo and a top to bottom color bar with some good words about the player. The Masters inserts are found at an average rate of one per eight packs.

		MT
Complete Set (10):		70.00
Common Player:		2.50
1	Barry Bonds	4.00
2	Juan Gonzalez	6.00
3	Ken Griffey Jr.	15.00
4	Tony Gwynn	6.00
5	Kenny Lofton	4.00
6	Greg Maddux	10.00
7	Raul Mondesi	3.00
8	Cal Ripken Jr.	12.00
9	Frank Thomas	12.00
10	Matt Williams	3.00

1995 SkyBox E-Motion Rookies

A bold colored background with outline white letters repeating the word "ROOKIE" is the frame for the central action photo in this insert series. The top of the photo is vignetted with a white circle that has the player's name in gold at left, and his team in white at right. Backs repeat the front background and include a player portrait photo and a few sentences about his potential. Rookie inserts are found at an average rate of one per five packs.

		MT
Complete Set (10):		24.00
Common Player:		1.00
1	Edgardo Alfonzo	1.50
2	Jason Bates	1.00
3	Marty Cordova	2.00
4	Ray Durham	2.00
5	Alex Gonzalez	1.75
6	Shawn Green	2.00
7	Charles Johnson	2.50
8	Chipper Jones	8.00
9	Hideo Nomo	6.00
10	Alex Rodriguez	8.00

1996 SkyBox E-Motion XL

Each card in SkyBox's 1996 E-Motion XL Baseball arrives on two layers of stock - a die-cut matte frame over a UV-coated card. The frames come in three colors - blue, green and maroon (but each player has only one color version). The

300-card set also includes four insert sets: Legion of Boom, D-Fense, N-Tense and Rare Breed.

		MT
	Complete Set (300):	70.00
	Common Player:	.20
	Wax Box:	65.00
1	Roberto Alomar	1.50
2	Brady Anderson	.40
3	Bobby Bonilla	.20
4	Jeffrey Hammonds	.20
5	Chris Hoiles	.20
6	Mike Mussina	1.00
7	Randy Myers	.20
8	Rafael Palmeiro	.40
9	Cal Ripken Jr.	5.00
10	B.J. Surhoff	.20
11	Jose Canseco	.50
12	Roger Clemens	2.00
13	Wil Cordero	.20
14	Mike Greenwell	.20
15	Dwayne Hosey	.20
16	Tim Naehring	.20
17	Troy O'Leary	.20
18	Mike Stanley	.20
19	John Valentin	.20
20	Mo Vaughn	2.00
21	Jim Abbott	.20
22	Garret Anderson	.20
23	George Arias	.20
24	Chili Davis	.30
25	Jim Edmonds	.30
26	Chuck Finley	.20
27	Todd Greene	.20
28	Mark Langston	.20
29	Troy Percival	.20
30	Tim Salmon	.40
31	Lee Smith	.20
32	J.T. Snow	.20
33	Harold Baines	.20
34	Jason Bere	.20
35	Ray Durham	.20
36	Alex Fernandez	.20
37	Ozzie Guillen	.20
38	Darren Lewis	.20
39	Lyle Mouton	.20
40	Tony Phillips	.20
41	Danny Tartabull	.20
42	Frank Thomas	4.00
43	Robin Ventura	.20
44	Sandy Alomar	.20
45	Carlos Baerga	.35
46	Albert Belle	1.50
47	Julio Franco	.20
48	Orel Hershiser	.20
49	Kenny Lofton	1.50
50	Dennis Martinez	.20
51	Jack McDowell	.40
52	Jose Mesa	.20
53	Eddie Murray	.75
54	Charles Nagy	.20
55	Manny Ramirez	1.50
55p	Manny Ramirez (overprinted "PROMOTIONAL SAMPLE")	3.00
56	Jim Thome	1.00
57	Omar Vizquel	.20
58	Chad Curtis	.20
59	Cecil Fielder	.40
60	Travis Fryman	.20
61	Chris Gomez	.20
62	Felipe Lira	.20
63	Alan Trammell	.20
64	Kevin Appier	.20
65	Johnny Damon	.50
66	Tom Goodwin	.20
67	Mark Gubicza	.20
68	Jeff Montgomery	.20
69	Jon Nunnally	.20
70	Bip Roberts	.20
71	Ricky Bones	.20
72	Chuck Carr	.20
73	John Jaha	.20
74	Ben McDonald	.20
75	Matt Mieske	.20
76	Dave Nilsson	.20
77	Kevin Seitzer	.20
78	Greg Vaughn	.20
79	Rick Aguilera	.20
80	Marty Cordova	.25
81	Roberto Kelly	.20
82	Chuck Knoblauch	.20
83	Pat Meares	.20
84	Paul Molitor	.75
85	Kirby Puckett	2.00
86	Brad Radke	.20
87	Wade Boggs	.40
88	David Cone	.35
89	Dwight Gooden	.20
90	Derek Jeter	3.50
91	Tino Martinez	.40
92	Paul O'Neill	.20
93	Andy Pettitte	1.50
94	Tim Raines	.20
95	Ruben Rivera	.75
96	Kenny Rogers	.20
97	Ruben Sierra	.20
98	John Wetteland	.20
99	Bernie Williams	1.50
100	Allen Battle	.20
101	Geronimo Berroa	.20
102	Brent Gates	.20
103	Doug Johns	.20
104	Mark McGwire	6.00
105	Pedro Munoz	.20
106	Ariel Prieto	.20
107	Terry Steinbach	.20
108	Todd Van Poppel	.20
109	Chris Bosio	.20
110	Jay Buhner	.50
111	Joey Cora	.20
112	Russ Davis	.20
113	Ken Griffey Jr.	7.00
114	Sterling Hitchcock	.20
115	Randy Johnson	1.25
116	Edgar Martinez	.20
117	Alex Rodriguez	7.00
118	Paul Sorrento	.20
119	Dan Wilson	.20
120	Will Clark	.20
121	Juan Gonzalez	3.00
122	Rusty Greer	.20
123	Kevin Gross	.20
124	Ken Hill	.20
125	Dean Palmer	.20
126	Roger Pavlik	.20
127	Ivan Rodriguez	1.50
128	Mickey Tettleton	.20
129	Joe Carter	.40
130	Carlos Delgado	.20
131	Alex Gonzalez	.20
132	Shawn Green	.20
133	Erik Hanson	.20
134	Pat Hentgen	.20
135	Otis Nixon	.20
136	John Olerud	.20
137	Ed Sprague	.20
138	Steve Avery	.20
139	Jermaine Dye	.50
140	Tom Glavine	.40
141	Marquis Grissom	.20
142	Chipper Jones	3.50
143	David Justice	.40
144	Ryan Klesko	1.25
145	Javier Lopez	.40
146	Greg Maddux	3.50
147	Fred McGriff	.75
148	Jason Schmidt	.20
149	John Smoltz	.75
150	Mark Wohlers	.20
151	Jim Bullinger	.20
152	Frank Castillo	.20
153	Kevin Foster	.20
154	Luis Gonzalez	.20
155	Mark Grace	.40
156	Brian McRae	.20
157	Jaime Navarro	.20
158	Rey Sanchez	.20
159	Ryne Sandberg	2.00
160	Sammy Sosa	3.00
161	Bret Boone	.20
162	Jeff Brantley	.20
163	Vince Coleman	.20
164	Steve Gibralter	.20
165	Curtis Goodwin	.20
166	Barry Larkin	.50
167	Hal Morris	.20
168	Mark Portugal	.20
169	Reggie Sanders	.20
170	Pete Schourek	.20
171	John Smiley	.20
172	Jason Bates	.20
173	Dante Bichette	.40
174	Ellis Burks	.20
175	Vinny Castilla	.20
176	Andres Galarraga	.40
177	Kevin Ritz	.20
178	Bill Swift	.20
179	Larry Walker	.40
180	Walt Weiss	.20
181	Eric Young	.20
182	Kurt Abbott	.20
183	Kevin Brown	.20
184	John Burkett	.20
185	Greg Colbrunn	.20
186	Jeff Conine	.20
187	Chris Hammond	.20
188	Charles Johnson	.20
189	Terry Pendleton	.20
190	Pat Rapp	.20
191	Gary Sheffield	1.00
192	Quilvio Veras	.20
193	Devon White	.20
194	Jeff Bagwell	2.50
195	Derek Bell	.20
196	Sean Berry	.20
197	Craig Biggio	.20
198	Doug Drabek	.20
199	Tony Eusebio	.20
200	Mike Hampton	.20
201	Brian Hunter	.40
202	Derrick May	.20
203	Orlando Miller	.20
204	Shane Reynolds	.20
205	Mike Blowers	.20
206	Tom Candiotti	.20
207	Delino DeShields	.20
208	Greg Gagne	.20
209	Karim Garcia	.75
210	Todd Hollandsworth	.30
211	Eric Karros	.20
212	Ramon Martinez	.20
213	Raul Mondesi	.40
214	Hideo Nomo	1.50
215	Mike Piazza	3.50
216	Ismael Valdes	.20
217	Todd Worrell	.20
218	Moises Alou	.20
219	Yamil Benitez	.20
220	Jeff Fassero	.20
221	Darrin Fletcher	.20
222	Cliff Floyd	.20
223	Pedro Martinez	.40
224	Carlos Perez	.20
225	Mel Rojas	.20
226	David Segui	.20
227	Rondell White	.20
228	Rico Brogna	.20
229	Carl Everett	.20
230	John Franco	.20
231	Bernard Gilkey	.20
232	Todd Hundley	.20
233	Jason Isringhausen	.40
234	Lance Johnson	.20
235	Bobby Jones	.20
236	Jeff Kent	.20
237	Rey Ordonez	.75
238	Bill Pulsipher	.20
239	Jose Vizcaino	.20
240	Paul Wilson	.50
241	Ricky Bottalico	.20
242	Darren Daulton	.20
243	Lenny Dykstra	.20
244	Jim Eisenreich	.20
245	Sid Fernandez	.20
246	Gregg Jefferies	.20
247	Mickey Morandini	.20
248	Benito Santiago	.20
249	Curt Schilling	.20
250	Mark Whiten	.20
251	Todd Zeile	.20
252	Jay Bell	.20
253	Carlos Garcia	.20
254	Charlie Hayes	.20
255	Jason Kendall	.20
256	Jeff King	.20
257	Al Martin	.20
258	Orlando Merced	.20
259	Dan Miceli	.20
260	Denny Neagle	.20
261	Alan Benes	.40
262	Andy Benes	.20
263	Royce Clayton	.20
264	Dennis Eckersley	.20
265	Gary Gaetti	.20
266	Ron Gant	.40
267	Brian Jordan	.20
268	Ray Lankford	.20
269	John Mabry	.20
270	Tom Pagnozzi	.20
271	Ozzie Smith	1.00
272	Todd Stottlemyre	.20
273	Andy Ashby	.20
274	Brad Ausmus	.20
275	Ken Caminiti	.40
276	Steve Finley	.20

277	Tony Gwynn	2.00
278	Joey Hamilton	.20
279	Rickey Henderson	.20
280	Trevor Hoffman	.20
281	Wally Joyner	.20
282	Jody Reed	.20
283	Bob Tewksbury	.20
284	Fernando Valenzuela	.20
285	Rod Beck	.20
286	Barry Bonds	1.50
287	Mark Carreon	.20
288	Shawon Dunston	.20
289	*Osvaldo Fernandez*	.30
290	Glenallen Hill	.20
291	Stan Javier	.20
292	Mark Leiter	.20
293	Kirt Manwaring	.20
294	Robby Thompson	.20
295	William VanLandingham	.20
296	Allen Watson	.20
297	Matt Williams	.50
298	Checklist	.20
299	Checklist	.20
300	Checklist	.20

1996 SkyBox E-Motion XL D-Fense

Ten top defensive players are featured on these 1996 SkyBox E-Motion XL insert cards. The cards were seeded at a rate of one per every four packs.

		MT
Complete Set (10):		40.00
Common Player:		1.00
1	Roberto Alomar	4.00
2	Barry Bonds	4.00
3	Mark Grace	1.00
4	Ken Griffey Jr.	15.00
5	Kenny Lofton	4.00
6	Greg Maddux	8.00
7	Raul Mondesi	1.50
8	Cal Ripken Jr.	10.00
9	Ivan Rodriguez	2.50
10	Matt Williams	1.50

1996 SkyBox E-Motion XL Legion of Boom

The top power hitters in baseball are featured on these 1996 SkyBox E-Motion XL insert cards. The cards, exclusive to hobby packs at a ratio of one per every 36 packs, have translucent card backs.

		MT
Complete Set (12):		200.00
Common Player:		6.00
1	Albert Belle	15.00
2	Barry Bonds	15.00
3	Juan Gonzalez	25.00
4	Ken Griffey Jr.	60.00
5	Mark McGwire	60.00
6	Mike Piazza	30.00
7	Manny Ramirez	15.00
8	Tim Salmon	10.00
9	Sammy Sosa	30.00
10	Frank Thomas	30.00
11	Mo Vaughn	15.00
12	Matt Williams	10.00

1996 SkyBox E-Motion XL N-Tense

Ten top clutch performers are featured on these 1996 SkyBox E-Motion XL insert cards. The cards, which use an N-shaped die-cut design, were included one per every 12 packs.

		MT
Complete Set (10):		100.00
Common Player:		3.00
1	Albert Belle	6.00
2	Barry Bonds	7.00
3	Jose Canseco	4.00
4	Ken Griffey Jr.	25.00
5	Tony Gwynn	10.00
6	Randy Johnson	6.00
7	Greg Maddux	15.00
8	Cal Ripken Jr.	20.00
9	Frank Thomas	15.00
10	Matt Williams	3.00

1996 SkyBox E-Motion XL Rare Breed

These 1996 E-Motion XL inserts are the most difficult to find; they are seeded one per every 100 packs. The cards showcase top young stars on 3-D lenticular design, similar to the Hot Numbers in Fleer Flair basketball.

		MT
Complete Set (10):		240.00
Common Player:		10.00
1	Garret Anderson	12.00
2	Marty Cordova	15.00
3	Brian Hunter	12.00
4	Jason Isringhausen	15.00
5	Charles Johnson	15.00
6	Chipper Jones	70.00
7	Raul Mondesi	15.00
8	Hideo Nomo	25.00
9	Manny Ramirez	35.00
10	Rondell White	12.00

1997 SkyBox E-X2000

The premiere issue of E-X2000 consists of 100 base cards designed with "SkyView" technology, utilizing a die-cut holofoil border and the player silhouetted in front of a transparent "window" featuring a variety of sky patterns. Inserts include two sequentially-numbered parallel sets - Credentials (1:50 packs) and Essential Credentials

(1:200 packs) - as well as Emerald Autograph Exchange Cards, A Cut Above, Hall of Nothing, and Star Date. Cards were sold in two-card packs for $3.99 each.

		MT
Complete Set (100):		100.00
Common Player:		1.00
Credentials Stars: 12x to 20x		
Credentials RC's & Yng Stars: 8x to 12x		
Essential Credentials: 25x to 50x		
Unlisted Stars: 1.50 to 2		
Wax Box:		85.00
1	Jim Edmonds	1.00
2	Darin Erstad	4.00
3	Eddie Murray	2.00
4	Roberto Alomar	2.00
5	Brady Anderson	1.00
6	Mike Mussina	2.00
7	Rafael Palmeiro	1.50
8	Cal Ripken Jr.	8.00
9	Steve Avery	1.00
10	Nomar Garciaparra	6.00
11	Mo Vaughn	2.50
12	Albert Belle	2.50
13	Mike Cameron	1.00
14	Ray Durham	1.00
15	Frank Thomas	8.00
16	Robin Ventura	1.00
17	Manny Ramirez	2.50
18	Jim Thome	2.00
19	Matt Williams	1.50
20	Tony Clark	2.00
21	Travis Fryman	1.00
22	Bob Higginson	1.00
23	Kevin Appier	1.00
24	Johnny Damon	1.00
25	Jermaine Dye	1.00
26	Jeff Cirillo	1.00
27	Ben McDonald	1.00
28	Chuck Knoblauch	1.50
29	Paul Molitor	2.50
30	Todd Walker	2.00
31	Wade Boggs	1.50
32	Cecil Fielder	1.25
33	Derek Jeter	6.00
34	Andy Pettitte	2.50
35	Ruben Rivera	1.00
36	Bernie Williams	2.00
37	Jose Canseco	1.50
38	Mark McGwire	12.00
39	Jay Buhner	1.50
40	Ken Griffey Jr.	10.00
41	Randy Johnson	2.00
42	Edgar Martinez	1.00
43	Alex Rodriguez	8.00
44	Dan Wilson	1.00
45	Will Clark	1.50
46	Juan Gonzalez	5.00
47	Ivan Rodriguez	2.50
48	Joe Carter	1.00
49	Roger Clemens	3.00
50	Juan Guzman	1.00
51	Pat Hentgen	1.00
52	Tom Glavine	1.50
53	Andruw Jones	5.00
54	Chipper Jones	6.00
55	Ryan Klesko	1.50
56	Kenny Lofton	2.50
57	Greg Maddux	6.00
58	Fred McGriff	1.50
59	John Smoltz	1.25
60	Mark Wohlers	1.00
61	Mark Grace	1.50
62	Ryne Sandberg	2.50
63	Sammy Sosa	6.00
64	Barry Larkin	1.50
65	Deion Sanders	1.50
66	Reggie Sanders	1.00
67	Dante Bichette	1.50
68	Ellis Burks	1.00
69	Andres Galarraga	1.50
70	Moises Alou	1.00
71	Kevin Brown	1.00
72	Cliff Floyd	1.00
73	Edgar Renteria	1.00
74	Gary Sheffield	1.50
75	Bob Abreu	1.00
76	Jeff Bagwell	4.00
77	Craig Biggio	1.50
78	Todd Hollandsworth	1.00
79	Eric Karros	1.00
80	Raul Mondesi	1.50
81	Hideo Nomo	2.50
82	Mike Piazza	6.00
83	Vladimir Guerrero	3.00
84	Henry Rodriguez	1.00
85	Todd Hundley	1.50
86	Rey Ordonez	1.00
87	Alex Ochoa	1.00
88	Gregg Jefferies	1.00
89	Scott Rolen	5.00
90	Jermaine Allensworth	1.00
91	Jason Kendall	1.00
92	Ken Caminiti	1.50
93	Tony Gwynn	5.00
94	Rickey Henderson	1.00
95	Barry Bonds	2.50
96	J.T. Snow	1.00
97	Dennis Eckersley	1.00
98	Ron Gant	1.00
99	Brian Jordan	1.00
100	Ray Lankford	1.00

1997 SkyBox E-X2000 A Cut Above

Some of the game's elite players are featured in this 1:288 pack insert that features a die-cut design resembling a saw blade. Printed on silver-foil stock, the player's name and Cut Above logo are embossed on front. On back is another color photo and a few words about the player.

		MT
Complete Set (10):		500.00
Common Player:		20.00
1	Frank Thomas	100.00
2	Ken Griffey Jr.	120.00
3	Alex Rodriguez	100.00
4	Albert Belle	30.00
5	Juan Gonzalez	60.00
6	Mark McGwire	120.00
7	Mo Vaughn	30.00
8	Manny Ramirez	30.00
9	Barry Bonds	30.00
10	Fred McGriff	20.00

1997 SkyBox E-X2000 Credentials

This parallel set features different colored foils from the base cards, as well as different images on the "window." Cards are sequentially numbered on back within an issue of 299. Cards were inserted 1:50 packs.

	MT
Common Player:	12.00
Minor Stars:	20.00
Credentials Stars: 12x to 20x	
Yng Stars & RC's: 8x to 12x	
(See E-X2000 for checklist, base card values)	

1997 SkyBox E-X2000 Emerald Autograph Redemptions

Inserted 1:480 packs, these cards can be exchanged for autographed cards or memorabilia from one to six different major leaguers.

		MT
Complete Set (6):		450.00
Common Player:		25.00
AU1	Darin Erstad	80.00
AU2	Todd Hollandsworth	25.00
AU3	Alex Ochoa	25.00
AU4	Alex Rodriguez	200.00
AU5	Scott Rolen	90.00
AU6	Todd Walker	40.00

1997 SkyBox E-X2000 Essential Credentials

A sequentially-numbered parallel set, found one per 200 packs, and limited to 99 total sets.

		MT
Common Player:		25.00
1	Jim Edmonds	25.00
2	Darin Erstad	150.00
3	Eddie Murray	50.00
4	Roberto Alomar	100.00
5	Brady Anderson	35.00
6	Mike Mussina	100.00
7	Rafael Palmeiro	50.00
8	Cal Ripken Jr.	350.00
9	Steve Avery	25.00
10	Nomar Garciaparra	250.00
11	Mo Vaughn	125.00
12	Albert Belle	125.00
13	Mike Cameron	25.00
14	Ray Durham	25.00
15	Frank Thomas	350.00
16	Robin Ventura	25.00
17	Manny Ramirez	100.00
18	Jim Thome	100.00
19	Matt Williams	50.00
20	Tony Clark	100.00
21	Travis Fryman	25.00
22	Bob Higginson	25.00
23	Kevin Appier	25.00
24	Johnny Damon	25.00
25	Jermaine Dye	25.00
26	Jeff Cirillo	25.00
27	Ben McDonald	25.00
28	Chuck Knoblauch	50.00
29	Paul Molitor	100.00
30	Todd Walker	50.00
31	Wade Boggs	50.00
32	Cecil Fielder	40.00
33	Derek Jeter	250.00
34	Andy Pettitte	125.00
35	Ruben Rivera	25.00
36	Bernie Williams	100.00
37	Jose Canseco	50.00
38	Mark McGwire	500.00
39	Jay Buhner	50.00
40	Ken Griffey Jr.	500.00
41	Randy Johnson	100.00
42	Edgar Martinez	25.00
43	Alex Rodriguez	350.00
44	Dan Wilson	25.00
45	Will Clark	50.00
46	Juan Gonzalez	220.00
47	Ivan Rodriguez	125.00
48	Joe Carter	40.00
49	Roger Clemens	175.00
50	Juan Guzman	25.00

51	Pat Hentgen	25.00
52	Tom Glavine	40.00
53	Andruw Jones	125.00
54	Chipper Jones	275.00
55	Ryan Klesko	40.00
56	Kenny Lofton	125.00
57	Greg Maddux	275.00
58	Fred McGriff	40.00
59	John Smoltz	40.00
60	Mark Wohlers	25.00
61	Mark Grace	50.00
62	Ryne Sandberg	125.00
63	Sammy Sosa	200.00
64	Barry Larkin	40.00
65	Deion Sanders	40.00
66	Reggie Sanders	25.00
67	Dante Bichette	40.00
68	Ellis Burks	25.00
69	Andres Galarraga	40.00
70	Moises Alou	40.00
71	Kevin Brown	25.00
72	Cliff Floyd	25.00
73	Edgar Renteria	25.00
74	Gary Sheffield	50.00
75	Bob Abreu	25.00
76	Jeff Bagwell	180.00
77	Craig Biggio	50.00
78	Todd Hollandsworth	25.00
79	Eric Karros	25.00
80	Raul Mondesi	40.00
81	Hideo Nomo	150.00
82	Mike Piazza	275.00
83	Vladimir Guerrero	125.00
84	Henry Rodriguez	25.00
85	Todd Hundley	30.00
86	Rey Ordonez	25.00
87	Alex Ochoa	25.00
88	Gregg Jefferies	25.00
89	Scott Rolen	180.00
90	Jermaine Allensworth	25.00
91	Jason Kendall	25.00
92	Ken Caminiti	40.00
93	Tony Gwynn	200.00
94	Rickey Henderson	25.00
95	Barry Bonds	125.00
96	J.T. Snow	25.00
97	Dennis Eckersley	25.00
98	Ron Gant	35.00
99	Brian Jordan	25.00
100	Ray Lankford	25.00

1997 SkyBox
E-X2000
Hall or Nothing

This 20-card insert, featuring players who are candidates for the Hall of Fame, utilizes a die-cut design on plastic stock. Stately architectural details and brush bronze highlights frame the player picture on front. The player silhouette on back contains career information. Cards were inserted 1:20 packs.

		MT
Complete Set (20):		300.00
Common Player:		3.00
1	Frank Thomas	25.00
2	Ken Griffey Jr.	40.00
3	Eddie Murray	6.00
4	Cal Ripken Jr.	30.00
5	Ryne Sandberg	10.00
6	Wade Boggs	3.00
7	Roger Clemens	10.00
8	Tony Gwynn	20.00
9	Alex Rodriguez	30.00
10	Mark McGwire	50.00
11	Barry Bonds	10.00
12	Greg Maddux	25.00
13	Juan Gonzalez	20.00
14	Albert Belle	10.00
15	Mike Piazza	25.00
16	Jeff Bagwell	20.00
17	Dennis Eckersley	3.00
18	Mo Vaughn	10.00
19	Roberto Alomar	8.00
20	Kenny Lofton	10.00

1997 SkyBox
E-X2000
Star Date 2000

A 15-card set highlighting young stars that are likely to be the game's top players in the year 2000. Cards were inserted 1:9 packs.

		MT
Complete Set (15):		60.00
Common Player:		2.00
1	Alex Rodriguez	10.00
2	Andruw Jones	6.00
3	Andy Pettitte	4.00
4	Brooks Kieschnick	2.00
5	Chipper Jones	8.00
6	Darin Erstad	8.00
7	Derek Jeter	8.00
8	Jason Kendall	3.00
9	Jermaine Dye	2.00
10	Neifi Perez	2.00
11	Scott Rolen	8.00
12	Todd Hollandsworth	2.00
13	Todd Walker	4.00
14	Tony Clark	4.00
15	Vladimir Guerrero	8.00

1998 SkyBox
Dugout Axcess

Dugout Axcess was a 150-card set that attempted to provide collectors with an inside look at baseball. The cards were printed on "playing card" quality stock and used unique information and photography. The

product arrived in 12-card packs with an Inside Axcess parallel set that was individually numbered to 50 sets. Six different inserts sets were available, including Double Header, Frequent Flyers, Dishwashers, Superheroes, Gronks and Autograph Redemptions.

		MT
Complete Set (150):		20.00
Common Player:		.10
Unlisted Stars: .30 to .60		
Inside Axcess Stars: 100x to 150x		
Inside Axcess Yng Stars & RCs: 50x-100x		
Production 50 sets		
Wax Box:		45.00
1	Travis Lee	1.00
2	Matt Williams	.25
3	Andy Benes	.15
4	Chipper Jones	1.50
5	Ryan Klesko	.25
6	Greg Maddux	1.50
7	Sammy Sosa	2.00
8	Henry Rodriguez	.10
9	Mark Grace	.25
10	Barry Larkin	.20
11	Bret Boone	.10
12	Reggie Sanders	.10
13	Vinny Castilla	.10
14	Larry Walker	.30
15	Darryl Kile	.10
16	Charles Johnson	.10
17	Edgar Renteria	.10
18	Gary Sheffield	.30
19	Jeff Bagwell	.75
20	Craig Biggio	.20
21	Moises Alou	.20
22	Mike Piazza	1.50
23	Hideo Nomo	.40
24	Raul Mondesi	.20
25	John Jaha	.10
26	Jeff Cirillo	.10
27	Jeromy Burnitz	.10
28	Mark Grudzielanek	.10
29	Vladimir Guerrero	.60
30	Rondell White	.20
31	Edgardo Alfonzo	.10
32	Rey Ordonez	.10
33	Bernard Gilkey	.10
34	Scott Rolen	.75
35	Curt Schilling	.20
36	Ricky Bottalico	.10
37	Tony Womack	.10
38	Al Martin	.10
39	Jason Kendall	.10
40	Ron Gant	.20
41	Mark McGwire	3.00
42	Ray Lankford	.10
43	Tony Gwynn	1.25
44	Ken Caminiti	.20
45	Kevin Brown	.10
46	Barry Bonds	.60
47	J.T. Snow	.10
48	Shawn Estes	.10
49	Jim Edmonds	.10
50	Tim Salmon	.30

51	Jason Dickson	.10
52	Cal Ripken Jr.	2.00
53	Mike Mussina	.50
54	Roberto Alomar	.50
55	Mo Vaughn	.60
56	Pedro Martinez	.50
57	Nomar Garciaparra	1.50
58	Albert Belle	.60
59	Frank Thomas	1.50
60	Robin Ventura	.20
61	Jim Thome	.40
62	Sandy Alomar Jr.	.20
63	Jaret Wright	.75
64	Bobby Higginson	.10
65	Tony Clark	.30
66	Justin Thompson	.10
67	Dean Palmer	.10
68	Kevin Appier	.10
69	Johnny Damon	.10
70	Paul Molitor	.40
71	Marty Cordova	.10
72	Brad Radke	.10
73	Derek Jeter	1.50
74	Bernie Williams	.40
75	Andy Pettitte	.40
76	Matt Stairs	.10
77	Ben Grieve	.75
78	Jason Giambi	.10
79	Randy Johnson	.40
80	Ken Griffey Jr.	2.50
81	Alex Rodriguez	1.50
82	Fred McGriff	.20
83	Wade Boggs	.20
84	Wilson Alvarez	.10
85	Juan Gonzalez	1.25
86	Ivan Rodriguez	.60
87	Fernando Tatis	.20
88	Roger Clemens	.75
89	Jose Cruz Jr.	.50
90	Shawn Green	.10
91	Jeff Suppan (Little Dawgs)	.10
92	Eli Marrero (Little Dawgs)	.10
93	*Mike Lowell* (Little Dawgs)	.30
94	Ben Grieve (Little Dawgs)	.75
95	Cliff Politte (Little Dawgs)	.10
96	*Rolando Arrojo* (Little Dawgs)	.40
97	Mike Caruso (Little Dawgs)	.10
98	Miguel Tejada (Little Dawgs)	.20
99	Rod Myers (Little Dawgs)	.10
100	Juan Encarnacion (Little Dawgs)	.10
101	Enrique Wilson (Little Dawgs)	.10
102	Brian Giles (Little Dawgs)	.10
103	*Magglio Ordonez* (Little Dawgs)	.50
104	Brian Rose (Little Dawgs)	.10
105	*Ryan Jackson* (Little Dawgs)	.25
106	Mark Kotsay (Little Dawgs)	.30
107	Desi Relaford (Little Dawgs)	.10
108	A.J. Hinch (Little Dawgs)	.10
109	Eric Milton (Little Dawgs)	.10
110	Ricky Ledee (Little Dawgs)	.25
111	Karim Garcia (Little Dawgs)	.10
112	Derrek Lee (Little Dawgs)	.10
113	Brad Fullmer (Little Dawgs)	.10
114	Travis Lee (Little Dawgs)	1.00
115	Greg Norton (Little Dawgs)	.10
116	Rich Butler (Little Dawgs)	.10
117	*Masato Yoshii* (Little Dawgs)	.40
118	Paul Konerko (Little Dawgs)	.25
119	Richard Hidalgo (Little Dawgs)	.10
120	Todd Helton (Little Dawgs)	.40
121	Nomar Garciaparra (7th Inning Sketch)	.75
122	Scott Rolen (7th Inning Sketch)	.40
123	Cal Ripken Jr. (7th Inning Sketch)	1.00
124	Derek Jeter (7th Inning Sketch)	.60
125	Mike Piazza (7th Inning Sketch)	.75
126	Tony Gwynn (7th Inning Sketch)	.60
127	Mark McGwire (7th Inning Sketch)	1.50
128	Kenny Lofton (7th Inning Sketch)	.30
129	Greg Maddux (7th Inning Sketch)	.75
130	Jeff Bagwell (7th Inning Sketch)	.40
131	Randy Johnson (7th Inning Sketch)	.25
132	Alex Rodriguez (7th Inning Sketch)	.75
133	Mo Vaughn (Name Plates)	.30
134	Chipper Jones (Name Plates)	.75
135	Juan Gonzalez (Name Plates)	.60
136	Tony Clark (Name Plates)	.20
137	Fred McGriff (Name Plates)	.10
138	Roger Clemens (Name Plates)	.40
139	Ken Griffey Jr. (Name Plates)	1.25
140	Ivan Rodriguez (Name Plates)	.30
141	Vinny Castilla (Trivia Card)	.10
142	Livan Hernandez (Trivia Card)	.10
143	Jose Cruz Jr. (Trivia Card)	.25
144	Andruw Jones (Trivia Card)	.30
145	Rafael Palmeiro (Trivia Card)	.20
146	Chuck Knoblauch (Trivia Card)	.10
147	Jay Buhner (Trivia Card)	.10
148	Andres Galarraga (Trivia Card)	.10
149	Frank Thomas (Trivia Card)	1.00
150	Todd Hundley (Trivia Card)	.10

1998 SkyBox Dugout Axcess Autograph Redemptions

This 150-card parallel set was sequentially numbered to 50 sets, with each card containing a stamped logo on the front and serial numbering on the back.

		MT
Common Ball:		15.00
Common Glove:		50.00
Inserted 1:96		
1	Jay Buhner (Ball)	25.00
2	Roger Clemens (Ball)	120.00
3	Jose Cruz Jr. (Ball)	40.00
4	Darin Erstad (Glove)	220.00
5	Nomar Garciaparra (Ball)	100.00
6	Tony Gwynn (Ball)	100.00
7	Roberto Hernandez (Ball)	15.00
8	Todd Hollandsworth (Glove)	50.00
9	Greg Maddux (Ball)	180.00
10	Alex Ochoa (Glove)	50.00
11	Alex Rodriguez (Ball)	160.00
12	Scott Rolen (Glove)	250.00
13	Scott Rolen (Ball)	80.00
14	Todd Walker (Glove)	75.00
15	Tony Womack (Ball)	15.00

1998 SkyBox Dugout Axcess Dishwashers

This 10-card set was a tribute to the game's best pitchers who "clean the home plate of opposing batters." Cards were inserted one per eight packs.

Modern cards have little collector value in conditions lower than Mint. Figure NM cards at 75% of values shown; EX cards at 40%.

Values shown reflect the market as of January, 1999. On-field performances of current players in the 1999 baseball season are not factored in.

		MT
Complete Set (10):		6.00
Common Player:		.10
Inserted 1:8		
D1	Greg Maddux	3.00
D2	Kevin Brown	.10
D3	Pedro Martinez	1.00
D4	Randy Johnson	.75
D5	Curt Schilling	.40
D6	John Smoltz	.10
D7	Darryl Kile	.10
D8	Roger Clemens	2.00
D9	Andy Pettitte	.75
D10	Mike Mussina	1.00

1998 SkyBox Dugout Axcess Double Header

Double Header featured 20 players on cards that doubled as game pieces. The game instructions were on the card and required two dice to play. These were inserted at a rate of two per pack.

		MT
Complete Set (20):		5.00
Common Player:		.10
Inserted 2:1		
DH1	Jeff Bagwell	.30
DH2	Albert Belle	.25
DH3	Barry Bonds	.25
DH4	Derek Jeter	.50
DH5	Tony Clark	.20
DH6	Nomar Garciaparra	.60
DH7	Juan Gonzalez	.50
DH8	Ken Griffey Jr.	1.00
DH9	Chipper Jones	.60
DH10	Kenny Lofton	.25
DH11	Mark McGwire	1.00

DH12	Mo Vaughn	.25
DH13	Mike Piazza	.60
DH14	Cal Ripken Jr.	.75
DH15	Ivan Rodriguez	.25
DH16	Scott Rolen	.30
DH17	Frank Thomas	.75
DH18	Tony Gwynn	.50
DH19	Travis Lee	.50
DH20	Jose Cruz Jr.	.20

1998 SkyBox Dugout Axcess Frequent Flyers

The game's top 10 base stealers were included in Frequent Flyers. This insert was designed to look like airline frequent flyer cards and was inserted one per four packs.

		MT
Complete Set (10):		3.00
Common Player:		.25
Inserted 1:4		
FF1	Brian Hunter	.25
FF2	Kenny Lofton	.75
FF3	Chuck Knoblauch	.40
FF4	Tony Womack	.25
FF5	Marquis Grissom	.25
FF6	Craig Biggio	.25
FF7	Barry Bonds	.75
FF8	Tom Goodwin	.25
FF9	Delino DeShields	.25
FF10	Eric Young	.25

1998 SkyBox Dugout Axcess Gronks

Gronks featured 10 of the top home run hitters and was a hobby exclusive insert. The name of the insert originated from shortstop Greg Gagne, and the cards were inserted in one per 72 packs.

		MT
Complete Set (10):		150.00
Common Player:		6.00
Inserted 1:72		
G1	Jeff Bagwell	15.00
G2	Albert Belle	10.00
G3	Juan Gonzalez	20.00
G4	Ken Griffey Jr.	40.00
G5	Mark McGwire	40.00
G6	Mike Piazza	25.00
G7	Frank Thomas	30.00
G8	Mo Vaughn	10.00
G9	Ken Caminiti	6.00
G10	Tony Clark	6.00

1998 SkyBox Dugout Axcess SuperHeroes

SuperHeroes combined 10 top superstars with the Marvel Comics superhero with whom they share a common trait in this 10-card insert set. Cards were inserted at a rate of one per 20 packs.

		MT
Complete Set (10):		60.00
Common Player:		2.00
Inserted 1:20		
SH1	Barry Bonds	4.00
SH2	Andres Galarraga	2.00
SH3	Ken Griffey Jr.	15.00
SH4	Chipper Jones	10.00
SH5	Andruw Jones	4.00
SH6	Hideo Nomo	2.50
SH7	Cal Ripken Jr.	12.00
SH8	Alex Rodriguez	10.00
SH9	Frank Thomas	12.00
SH10	Mo Vaughn	4.00

1998 SkyBox E-X2001

This super-premium set featured 100 players on a layered, diecut design utilizing mirror-image silhouetted photography and etched holofoil treatment over a clear, 20-point plastic card.

Values shown reflect the market as of January, 1999. On-field performances of current players in the 1999 baseball season are not factored in.

		MT
Complete Set (100):		90.00
Common Player:		.75
Unlisted Stars: 1.50 to 2.00		
Kerry Wood Exchange:		15.00
Wax Box:		100.00
1	Alex Rodriguez	6.00
2	Barry Bonds	2.50
3	Greg Maddux	6.00
4	Roger Clemens	4.00
5	Juan Gonzalez	5.00
6	Chipper Jones	6.00
7	Derek Jeter	5.00
8	Frank Thomas	8.00
9	Cal Ripken Jr.	8.00
10	Ken Griffey Jr.	10.00
11	Mark McGwire	12.00
12	Hideo Nomo	2.00
13	Tony Gwynn	5.00
14	Ivan Rodriguez	2.50
15	Mike Piazza	6.00
16	Roberto Alomar	2.00
17	Jeff Bagwell	4.00
18	Andruw Jones	2.50
19	Albert Belle	2.50
20	Mo Vaughn	2.50
21	Kenny Lofton	2.50
22	Gary Sheffield	.75
23	Tony Clark	1.50
24	Mike Mussina	2.00
25	Barry Larkin	.75
26	Moises Alou	.75
27	Brady Anderson	.75
28	Andy Pettitte	1.50
29	Sammy Sosa	8.00
30	Raul Mondesi	.75
31	Andres Galarraga	1.00
32	Chuck Knoblauch	1.00
33	Jim Thome	1.50
34	Craig Biggio	.75
35	Jay Buhner	.75
36	Rafael Palmeiro	.75
37	Curt Schilling	.75
38	Tino Martinez	1.00
39	Pedro Martinez	1.50
40	Jose Canseco	1.00
41	Jeff Cirillo	.75
42	Dean Palmer	.75
43	Tim Salmon	1.50
44	Jason Giambi	.75
45	Bobby Higginson	.75
46	Jim Edmonds	.75
47	David Justice	1.00
48	John Olerud	.75
49	Ray Lankford	.75
50	Al Martin	.75
51	Mike Lieberthal	.75
52	Henry Rodriguez	.75
53	Edgar Renteria	.75
54	Eric Karros	.75
55	Marquis Grissom	.75
56	Wilson Alvarez	.75
57	Darryl Kile	.75
58	Jeff King	.75
59	Shawn Estes	.75
60	Tony Womack	.75
61	Willie Greene	.75
62	Ken Caminiti	1.00
63	Vinny Castilla	.75
64	Mark Grace	1.00

65	Ryan Klesko	1.00
66	Robin Ventura	.75
67	Todd Hundley	.75
68	Travis Fryman	.75
69	Edgar Martinez	.75
70	Matt Williams	1.00
71	Paul Molitor	1.50
72	Kevin Brown	.75
73	Randy Johnson	1.50
74	Bernie Williams	1.50
75	Manny Ramirez	2.50
76	Fred McGriff	.75
77	Tom Glavine	.75
78	Carlos Delgado	.75
79	Larry Walker	1.00
80	Hideki Irabu	1.50
81	Ryan McGuire	.75
82	Justin Thompson	.75
83	Kevin Orie	.75
84	Jon Nunnally	.75
85	Mark Kotsay	2.00
86	Todd Walker	.75
87	Jason Dickson	.75
88	Fernando Tatis	.75
89	Karim Garcia	.75
90	Ricky Ledee	1.50
91	Paul Konerko	1.50
92	Jaret Wright	3.00
93	Darin Erstad	2.50
94	Livan Hernandez	1.00
95	Nomar Garciaparra	6.00
96	Jose Cruz Jr.	2.00
97	Scott Rolen	4.00
98	Ben Grieve	3.00
99	Vladimir Guerrero	3.00
100	Travis Lee	4.00

1998 SkyBox E-X2001 Cheap Seat Treats

This 20-card die-cut insert arrived in the shape of a stadium seat. Inserted at one per 24 packs, Cheap Seat Treats included some of the top home run hitters and were numbered with a "CS" prefix.

		MT
Complete Set (20):		325.00
Common Player:		4.00
Inserted 1:24		
CS1	Frank Thomas	50.00
CS2	Ken Griffey Jr.	60.00
CS3	Mark McGwire	70.00
CS4	Tino Martinez	8.00
CS5	Larry Walker	10.00
CS6	Juan Gonzalez	30.00
CS7	Mike Piazza	40.00
CS8	Jeff Bagwell	25.00
CS9	Tony Clark	10.00
CS10	Albert Belle	15.00
CS11	Andres Galarraga	8.00
CS12	Jim Thome	10.00
CS13	Mo Vaughn	15.00
CS14	Barry Bonds	15.00
CS15	Vladimir Guerrero	15.00
CS16	Scott Rolen	20.00
CS17	Travis Lee	40.00
CS18	David Justice	4.00
CS19	Jose Cruz Jr.	15.00
CS20	Andruw Jones	15.00

1998 SkyBox E-X2001 Essential Credentials "Future"

Essential Credentials Future, along with Essential Credentials Now, paralleled all 100 cards in the base set. Production varied depending on the card number, with the exact production number of each player determined by subtracting his card number from 101. Since Essential Credentials Now was numbered to that player's card number, the two equalled production of 101.

		MT
Complete Set (100):		
Common Player:		20.00
1	Alex Rodriguez (100)	250.00
2	Barry Bonds (99)	100.00
3	Greg Maddux (98)	250.00
4	Roger Clemens (97)	150.00
5	Juan Gonzalez (96)	200.00
6	Chipper Jones (95)	200.00
7	Derek Jeter (94)	200.00
8	Frank Thomas (93)	300.00
9	Cal Ripken Jr. (92)	300.00
10	Ken Griffey Jr. (91)	400.00
11	Mark McGwire (90)	450.00
12	Hideo Nomo (89)	125.00
13	Tony Gwynn (88)	200.00
14	Ivan Rodriguez (87)	100.00
15	Mike Piazza (86)	250.00
16	Roberto Alomar (85)	75.00
17	Jeff Bagwell (84)	150.00
18	Andruw Jones (83)	100.00
19	Albert Belle (82)	90.00
20	Mo Vaughn (81)	100.00
21	Kenny Lofton (80)	90.00
22	Gary Sheffield (79)	50.00
23	Tony Clark (78)	50.00
24	Mike Mussina (77)	75.00
25	Barry Larkin (76)	50.00
26	Moises Alou (75)	30.00
27	Brady Anderson (74)	25.00
28	Andy Pettitte (73)	60.00
29	Sammy Sosa (72)	75.00
30	Raul Mondesi (71)	40.00
31	Andres Galarraga (70)	75.00
32	Chuck Knoblauch (69)	60.00
33	Jim Thome (68)	100.00
34	Craig Biggio (67)	50.00
35	Jay Buhner (66)	50.00
36	Rafael Palmeiro (65)	50.00
37	Curt Schilling (64)	40.00
38	Tino Martinez (63)	75.00
39	Pedro Martinez (62)	125.00
40	Jose Canseco (61)	75.00
41	Jeff Cirillo (60)	20.00
42	Dean Palmer (59)	20.00
43	Tim Salmon (58)	75.00
44	Jason Giambi (57)	30.00
45	Bobby Higginson (56)	40.00
46	Jim Edmonds (55)	40.00
47	David Justice (54)	75.00
48	John Olerud (53)	30.00
49	Ray Lankford (52)	35.00
50	Al Martin (51)	20.00
51	Mike Lieberthal (50)	20.00
52	Henry Rodriguez (49)	30.00
53	Edgar Renteria (48)	30.00
54	Eric Karros (47)	40.00
55	Marquis Grissom (46)	30.00
56	Wilson Alvarez (45)	20.00
57	Darryl Kile (44)	25.00
58	Jeff King (43)	20.00
59	Shawn Estes (42)	25.00
60	Tony Womack (41)	20.00
61	Willie Greene (40)	25.00
62	Ken Caminiti (39)	75.00
63	Vinny Castilla (38)	50.00

64	Mark Grace (37)	75.00
65	Ryan Klesko (36)	60.00
66	Robin Ventura (35)	50.00
67	Todd Hundley (34)	40.00
68	Travis Fryman (33)	40.00
69	Edgar Martinez (32)	80.00
70	Matt Williams (31)	90.00
71	Paul Molitor (30)	180.00
72	Kevin Brown (29)	60.00
73	Randy Johnson (28)	180.00
74	Bernie Williams (27)	150.00
75	Manny Ramirez (26)	200.00
76	Fred McGriff (25)	120.00
77	Tom Glavine (24)	100.00
78	Carlos Delgado (23)	75.00
79	Larry Walker (22)	250.00
80	Hideki Irabu (21)	125.00
81	Ryan McGuire (20)	50.00
82	Justin Thompson (19)	80.00
83	Kevin Orie (18)	75.00
84	Jon Nunnally (17)	50.00
85	Mark Kotsay (16)	180.00
86	Todd Walker (15)	150.00
87	Jason Dickson (14)	80.00
88	Fernando Tatis (13)	120.00
89	Karim Garcia (12)	100.00
90	Ricky Ledee (11)	120.00
91	Paul Konerko (10)	150.00
92	Jaret Wright (9)	300.00
93	Darin Erstad (8)	20.00
94	Livan Hernandez (7)	20.00
95	Nomar Garciaparra (6)	20.00
96	Jose Cruz (5)	20.00
97	Scott Rolen (4)	20.00
98	Ben Grieve (3)	20.00
99	Vladimir Guerrero (2)	20.00
100	Travis Lee (1)	20.00

1998 SkyBox E-X2001 Essential Credentials "Now"

Essential Credentials Now, along with Essential Credentials Future, paralleled all 100 cards in the base set. Production for each card was limited to that player's card number so that together with Essential Credentials Furture, production equalled 101.

		MT
Complete Set (100):		
Common Player:		20.00
1	Alex Rodriguez (1)	20.00
2	Barry Bonds (2)	20.00
3	Greg Maddux (3)	20.00
4	Roger Clemens (4)	20.00
5	Juan Gonzalez (5)	20.00
6	Chipper Jones (6)	20.00
7	Derek Jeter (7)	20.00
8	Frank Thomas (8)	20.00
9	Cal Ripken Jr. (9)	20.00
10	Ken Griffey Jr. (10)	20.00
11	Mark McGwire (11)	20.00

12	Hideo Nomo (12)	350.00
13	Tony Gwynn (13)	550.00
14	Ivan Rodriguez (14)	350.00
15	Mike Piazza (15)	600.00
16	Roberto Alomar (16)	250.00
17	Jeff Bagwell (17)	450.00
18	Andruw Jones (18)	300.00
19	Albert Belle (19)	250.00
20	Mo Vaughn (20)	275.00
21	Kenny Lofton (21)	275.00
22	Gary Sheffield (22)	175.00
23	Tony Clark (23)	150.00
24	Mike Mussina (24)	220.00
25	Barry Larkin (25)	150.00
26	Moises Alou (26)	75.00
27	Brady Anderson (27)	60.00
28	Andy Pettitte (28)	150.00
29	Sammy Sosa (29)	250.00
30	Raul Mondesi (30)	100.00
31	Andres Galarraga (31)	120.00
32	Chuck Knoblauch (32)	120.00
33	Jim Thome (33)	150.00
34	Craig Biggio (34)	80.00
35	Jay Buhner (35)	100.00
36	Rafael Palmeiro (36)	75.00
37	Curt Schilling (37)	50.00
38	Tino Martinez (38)	100.00
39	Pedro Martinez (39)	150.00
40	Jose Canseco (40)	100.00
41	Jeff Cirillo (41)	25.00
42	Dean Palmer (42)	25.00
43	Tim Salmon (43)	75.00
44	Jason Giambi (44)	40.00
45	Bobby Higginson (45)	40.00
46	Jim Edmonds (46)	50.00
47	David Justice (47)	75.00
48	John Olerud (48)	35.00
49	Ray Lankford (49)	35.00
50	Al Martin (50)	25.00
51	Mike Lieberthal (51)	20.00
52	Henry Rodriguez (52)	25.00
53	Edgar Renteria (53)	30.00
54	Eric Karros (54)	40.00
55	Marquis Grissom (55)	30.00
56	Wilson Alvarez (56)	20.00
57	Darryl Kile (57)	25.00
58	Jeff King (58)	25.00
59	Shawn Estes (59)	25.00
60	Tony Womack (60)	25.00
61	Willie Greene (61)	25.00
62	Ken Caminiti (62)	50.00
63	Vinny Castilla (63)	40.00
64	Mark Grace (64)	50.00
65	Ryan Klesko (65)	50.00
66	Robin Ventura (66)	40.00
67	Todd Hundley (67)	30.00
68	Travis Fryman (68)	35.00
69	Edgar Martinez (69)	40.00
70	Matt Williams (70)	60.00
71	Paul Molitor (71)	75.00
72	Kevin Brown (72)	25.00
73	Randy Johnson (73)	75.00
74	Bernie Williams (74)	60.00
75	Manny Ramirez (75)	75.00
76	Fred McGriff (76)	40.00
77	Tom Glavine (77)	40.00
78	Carlos Delgado (78)	25.00
79	Larry Walker (79)	75.00
80	Hideki Irabu (80)	50.00
81	Ryan McGuire (81)	20.00
82	Justin Thompson (82)	30.00
83	Kevin Orie (83)	25.00
84	Jon Nunnally (84)	20.00
85	Mark Kotsay (85)	50.00
86	Todd Walker (86)	40.00
87	Jason Dickson (87)	30.00
88	Fernando Tatis (88)	30.00
89	Karim Garcia (89)	30.00
90	Ricky Ledee (90)	40.00
91	Paul Konerko (91)	75.00
92	Jaret Wright (92)	120.00
93	Darin Erstad (93)	75.00
94	Livan Hernandez (94)	30.00
95	Nomar Garciaparra (95)	180.00
96	Jose Cruz Jr.(96)	100.00
97	Scott Rolen (97)	140.00
98	Ben Grieve (98)	120.00
99	Vladimir Guerrero (99)	100.00
100	Travis Lee (100)	200.00

A player's name in *italic* type indicates a rookie card.

1998 SkyBox E-X2001 Destination: Cooperstown

Destination: Cooperstown captured a mixture of rising young stars and top veterans on die-cut cards that were inserted one per 720 packs. This insert included 15 players and was numbered with a "DC" prefix.

		MT
Complete Set (15):		2500.
Common Player:		60.00
Inserted 1:720		
DC1	Alex Rodriguez	250.00
DC2	Frank Thomas	300.00
DC3	Cal Ripken Jr.	300.00
DC4	Roger Clemens	160.00
DC5	Greg Maddux	250.00
DC6	Chipper Jones	250.00
DC7	Ken Griffey Jr.	400.00
DC8	Mark McGwire	450.00
DC9	Tony Gwynn	200.00
DC10	Mike Piazza	250.00
DC11	Jeff Bagwell	160.00
DC12	Jose Cruz Jr.	100.00
DC13	Derek Jeter	200.00
DC14	Hideo Nomo	90.00
DC15	Ivan Rodriguez	100.00

1998 SkyBox E-X2001 Signature 2001

Seventeen top young and future stars signed cards for Signature 2001 inserts in E-X2001. The cards featured the player over a blue and white, sky-like background, with an embossed SkyBox seal of authenticity. Backs were horizontal and also included a Certificate of Authenticity. These cards were unnumbered and inserted one per 60 packs.

		MT
Complete Set (17):		400.00
Common Player:		15.00
Inserted 1:60		
1	Ricky Ledee	15.00
2	Derrick Gibson	15.00
3	Mark Kotsay	25.00
4	Kevin Millwood	40.00
5	Brad Fullmer	25.00
6	Todd Walker	20.00
7	Ben Grieve	50.00
8	Tony Clark	20.00
9	Jaret Wright	25.00

10	Randall Simon	15.00
11	Paul Konerko	20.00
12	Todd Helton	25.00
13	David Ortiz	15.00
14	Alex Gonzalez	15.00
15	Bobby Estalella	15.00
16	Alex Rodriguez	120.00
17	Mike Lowell	20.00

1998 SkyBox E-X2001 Star Date 2001

Star Date 2001 displayed 15 of the top rising stars on a space/planet background. This insert was seeded one per 12 packs and was numbered with a "SD" prefix.

		MT
Complete Set (15):		60.00
Common Player:		2.00
Inserted 1:12		
SD1	Travis Lee	20.00
SD2	Jose Cruz Jr.	6.00
SD3	Paul Konerko	4.00
SD4	Bobby Estalella	2.00
SD5	Magglio Ordonez	5.00
SD6	Juan Encarnacion	2.00
SD7	Richard Hidalgo	2.00
SD8	Abraham Nunez	2.00
SD9	Sean Casey	4.00
SD10	Todd Helton	5.00
SD11	Brad Fullmer	4.00
SD12	Ben Grieve	15.00
SD13	Livan Hernandez	2.00
SD14	Jaret Wright	10.00
SD15	Todd Dunwoody	2.00

1993 SP

Upper Deck's first super-premium baseball card issue features 290 cards in the single-series set; 252 are individual player cards, while the remainder includes a Premier Prospects subset featuring top prospects (20 cards), 18 All-Stars and a Platinum Power insert set of 20 top home run hitters. Cards, which were available in 12-card foil packs, feature borderless color photos and UV coating on the front, plus a special logo using lenticular printing. Foil is also used intricately in the design. Backs have a large color photo and statistics. Cards are numbered and color-coded by team.

		MT
Complete Set (290):		110.00
Common Player:		.15
Wax Box:		150.00
1	Roberto Alomar	1.50
2	Wade Boggs	.40
3	Joe Carter	.50
4	Ken Griffey, Jr.	10.00
5	Mark Langston	.15
6	John Olerud	.50
7	Kirby Puckett	4.00
8	Cal Ripken, Jr.	8.00
9	Ivan Rodriguez	2.50
10	Barry Bonds	2.50
11	Darren Daulton	.20
12	Marquis Grissom	.20
13	Dave Justice	.40
14	John Kruk	.15
15	Barry Larkin	.75
16	Terry Mulholland	.15
17	Ryne Sandberg	2.50
18	Gary Sheffield	.40
19	Chad Curtis	.20
20	Chili Davis	.15
21	Gary DiSarcina	.15
22	Damion Easley	.15
23	Chuck Finley	.15
24	Luis Polonia	.15
25	Tim Salmon	2.00
26	J.T. Snow	1.00
27	Russ Springer	.15
28	Jeff Bagwell	5.00
29	Craig Biggio	.25
30	Ken Caminiti	.40
31	Andujar Cedeno	.15
32	Doug Drabek	.15
33	Steve Finley	.15
34	Luis Gonzalez	.15
35	Pete Harnisch	.15
36	Darryl Kile	.15
37	Mike Bordick	.15
38	Dennis Eckersley	.20
39	Brent Gates	.15
40	Rickey Henderson	.20
41	Mark McGwire	10.00
42	Craig Paquette	.15
43	Ruben Sierra	.15
44	Terry Steinbach	.15
45	Todd Van Poppel	.15
46	Pat Borders	.15
47	Tony Fernandez	.15
48	Juan Guzman	.15
49	Pat Hentgen	.20
50	Paul Molitor	1.50
51	Jack Morris	.15
52	Ed Sprague	.15
53	Duane Ward	.15
54	Devon White	.15
55	Steve Avery	.15
56	Jeff Blauser	.15
57	Ron Gant	.25
58	Tom Glavine	.40
59	Greg Maddux	7.00
60	Fred McGriff	.40
61	Terry Pendleton	.15
62	Deion Sanders	1.50
63	John Smoltz	.40
64	Cal Eldred	.15
65	Darryl Hamilton	.15
66	John Jaha	.15
67	Pat Listach	.15
68	Jaime Navarro	.15
69	Kevin Reimer	.15
70	B.J. Surhoff	.15
71	Greg Vaughn	.15
72	Robin Yount	.75
73	Rene Arocha	.25
74	Bernard Gilkey	.15
75	Gregg Jefferies	.15
76	Ray Lankford	.15
77	Tom Pagnozzi	.15
78	Lee Smith	.15
79	Ozzie Smith	1.50
80	Bob Tewksbury	.15
81	Mark Whiten	.15
82	Steve Buechele	.15
83	Mark Grace	.30
84	Jose Guzman	.15
85	Derrick May	.15
86	Mike Morgan	.15
87	Randy Myers	.15
88	Kevin Roberson	.40
89	Sammy Sosa	5.00
90	Rick Wilkins	.15
91	Brett Butler	.15
92	Eric Davis	.15
93	Orel Hershiser	.20
94	Eric Karros	.20
95	Ramon Martinez	.20
96	Raul Mondesi	1.25
97	Jose Offerman	.15
98	Mike Piazza	7.50
99	Darryl Strawberry	.25
100	Moises Alou	.25
101	Wil Cordero	.15
102	Delino DeShields	.15
103	Darrin Fletcher	.15
104	Ken Hill	.15
105	Mike Lansing	.40
106	Dennis Martinez	.15
107	Larry Walker	.75
108	John Wetteland	.15
109	Rod Beck	.15
110	John Burkett	.15
111	Will Clark	.75
112	Royce Clayton	.15
113	Darren Lewis	.15
114	Willie McGee	.15
115	Bill Swift	.15
116	Robby Thompson	.15
117	Matt Williams	.75
118	Sandy Alomar Jr.	.15
119	Carlos Baerga	.20
120	Albert Belle	2.50
121	Reggie Jefferson	.15
122	Kenny Lofton	2.50
123	Wayne Kirby	.15
124	Carlos Martinez	.15
125	Charles Nagy	.15
126	Paul Sorrento	.15
127	Rich Amaral	.15
128	Jay Buhner	.40
129	Norm Charlton	.15
130	Dave Fleming	.15
131	Erik Hanson	.15
132	Randy Johnson	1.50
133	Edgar Martinez	.30
134	Tino Martinez	.50
135	Omar Vizquel	.15
136	Bret Barberie	.15
137	Chuck Carr	.15
138	Jeff Conine	.15
139	Orestes Destrade	.15
140	Chris Hammond	.15
141	Bryan Harvey	.15
142	Benito Santiago	.15
143	Walt Weiss	.15
144	Darrell Whitmore	.30
145	Tim Bolger	.15
146	Bobby Bonilla	.20
147	Jeromy Burnitz	.30
148	Vince Coleman	.15
149	Dwight Gooden	.20
150	Todd Hundley	.50
151	Howard Johnson	.15
152	Eddie Murray	.50
153	Bret Saberhagen	.15
154	Brady Anderson	.25
155	Mike Devereaux	.15
156	Jeffrey Hammonds	.50
157	Chris Hoiles	.15
158	Ben McDonald	.20
159	Mark McLemore	.15
160	Mike Mussina	1.50
161	Gregg Olson	.15
162	David Segui	.15
163	Derek Bell	.15
164	Andy Benes	.25
165	Archi Cianfrocco	.15
166	Ricky Gutierrez	.15
167	Tony Gwynn	3.00
168	Gene Harris	.15
169	Trevor Hoffman	.15
170	Ray McDavid	.40
171	Phil Plantier	.15
172	Mariano Duncan	.15
173	Len Dykstra	.15
174	Tommy Greene	.15
175	Dave Hollins	.15
176	Pete Incaviglia	.15
177	Mickey Morandini	.15
178	Curt Schilling	.25
179	Kevin Stocker	.20
180	Mitch Williams	.15
181	Stan Belinda	.15
182	Jay Bell	.15
183	Steve Cooke	.15
184	Carlos Garcia	.15
185	Jeff King	.15
186	Orlando Merced	.15
187	Don Slaught	.15
188	Andy Van Slyke	.15
189	Kevin Young	.20
190	Kevin Brown	.25
191	Jose Canseco	.75
192	Julio Franco	.15
193	Benji Gil	.15
194	Juan Gonzalez	2.50
195	Tom Henke	.15
196	Rafael Palmeiro	.50
197	Dean Palmer	.15
198	Nolan Ryan	8.00
199	Roger Clemens	3.00
200	Scott Cooper	.15
201	Andre Dawson	.20
202	Mike Greenwell	.15
203	Carlos Quintana	.15
204	Jeff Russell	.15
205	Aaron Sele	.40
206	Mo Vaughn	2.00
207	Frank Viola	.15
208	Rob Dibble	.15
209	Roberto Kelly	.15
210	Kevin Mitchell	.15
211	Hal Morris	.15
212	Joe Oliver	.15
213	Jose Rijo	.15
214	Bip Roberts	.15
215	Chris Sabo	.15
216	Reggie Sanders	.15
217	Dante Bichette	.50
218	Jerald Clark	.15
219	Alex Cole	.15
220	Andres Galarraga	.40
221	Joe Girardi	.15
222	Charlie Hayes	.15
223	Robert Mejia	.20
224	Armando Reynoso	.15
225	Eric Young	.15
226	Kevin Appier	.20
227	George Brett	3.50
228	David Cone	.30
229	Phil Hiatt	.15
230	Felix Jose	.15
231	Wally Joyner	.15
232	Mike Macfarlane	.15
233	Brian McRae	.15
234	Jeff Montgomery	.15
235	Rob Deer	.15
236	Cecil Fielder	.60
237	Travis Fryman	.15
238	Mike Henneman	.15
239	Tony Phillips	.15
240	Mickey Tettleton	.15
241	Alan Trammell	.15
242	David Wells	.15
243	Lou Whitaker	.15
244	Rick Aguilera	.15
245	Scott Erickson	.15
246	Brian Harper	.15
247	Kent Hrbek	.15
248	Chuck Knoblauch	.40
249	Shane Mack	.15
250	David McCarty	.15
251	Pedro Munoz	.15
252	Dave Winfield	.20
253	Alex Fernandez	.30
254	Ozzie Guillen	.15
255	Bo Jackson	.30
256	Lance Johnson	.15
257	Ron Karkovice	.15
258	Jack McDowell	.25
259	Tim Raines	.15
260	Frank Thomas	8.00
261	Robin Ventura	.25
262	Jim Abbott	.15

263	Steve Farr	.15
264	Jimmy Key	.25
265	Don Mattingly	4.00
266	Paul O'Neill	.25
267	Mike Stanley	.15
268	Danny Tartabull	.15
269	Bob Wickman	.15
270	Bernie Williams	1.25
271	Jason Bere	.15
272	*Roger Cedeno*	.75
273	*Johnny Damon*	2.00
274	*Russ Davis*	.50
275	Carlos Delgado	1.00
276	Carl Everett	.25
277	Cliff Floyd	.50
278	Alex Gonzalez	1.50
279	*Derek Jeter*	35.00
280	Chipper Jones	8.00
281	Javier Lopez	1.00
282	*Chad Mottola*	.40
283	Marc Newfield	.25
284	Eduardo Perez	.25
285	Manny Ramirez	4.00
286	*Todd Steverson*	.40
287	Michael Tucker	.50
288	Allen Watson	.25
289	Rondell White	1.50
290	Dmitri Young	.50

1993 SP
Platinum Power

This 20-card insert set features 20 of the game's top home run hitters. The top of each insert card features a special die cut treatment. Backs are numbered with a PP prefix.

		MT
Complete Set (20):		200.00
Common Player:		4.00
1	Albert Belle	12.50
2	Barry Bonds	12.50
3	Joe Carter	6.00
4	Will Clark	9.00
5	Darren Daulton	4.00
6	Cecil Fielder	6.00
7	Ron Gant	5.00
8	Juan Gonzalez	20.00
9	Ken Griffey, Jr.	50.00
10	Dave Hollins	4.00
11	Dave Justice	6.00
12	Fred McGriff	6.00
13	Mark McGwire	40.00
14	Dean Palmer	4.00
15	Mike Piazza	30.00
16	Tim Salmon	7.50
17	Ryne Sandberg	12.50
18	Gary Sheffield	7.50
19	Frank Thomas	40.00
20	Matt Williams	7.50

1994 SP

The second edition of Upper Deck's top-shelf SP brand features each card with a front background printed on metallic foil; the first 20 cards in the set, a series of "Prospects," have front backgrounds of textured metallic foil. Backs are printed with standard processes and include a color player photo a few stats and typical copyright notice and logos. Each foil pack contains one card featuring a special die-cut treatment at top.

		MT
Complete Set (200):		75.00
Common Player:		.15
Wax Box:		150.00
1	*Mike Bell*	1.00
2	*D.J. Boston*	.15
3	Johnny Damon	.40
4	*Brad Fullmer*	5.00
5	Joey Hamilton	.50
6	Todd Hollandsworth	1.00
7	Brian Hunter	1.00
8	*LaTroy Hawkins*	1.00
9	*Brooks Kieschnick*	2.00
10	*Derrek Lee*	4.00
11	*Trot Nixon*	.50
12	Alex Ochoa	.20
13	*Chan Ho Park*	2.00
14	*Kirk Presley*	1.00
15	*Alex Rodriguez*	55.00
16	*Jose Silva*	.30
17	*Terrell Wade*	.50
18	*Billy Wagner*	1.00
19	*Glenn Williams*	1.00
20	Preston Wilson	.25
21	Brian Anderson	.20
22	Chad Curtis	.15
23	Chili Davis	.15
24	Bo Jackson	.25
25	Mark Langston	.15
26	Tim Salmon	.40
27	Jeff Bagwell	1.50
28	Craig Biggio	.20
29	Ken Caminiti	.40
30	Doug Drabek	.15
31	John Hudek	.15
32	Greg Swindell	.15
33	Brent Gates	.15
34	Rickey Henderson	.20
35	Steve Karsay	.15
36	Mark McGwire	5.00
37	Ruben Sierra	.15
38	Terry Steinbach	.15
39	Roberto Alomar	1.00
40	Joe Carter	.15
41	Carlos Delgado	.25
42	Alex Gonzalez	.25
43	Juan Guzman	.15
44	Paul Molitor	.65
45	John Olerud	.20
46	Devon White	.15
47	Steve Avery	.15
48	Jeff Blauser	.15
49	Tom Glavine	.30
50	Dave Justice	.25
51	Roberto Kelly	.15
52	Ryan Klesko	.75
53	Javier Lopez	.30
54	Greg Maddux	3.00

55	Fred McGriff	.35
56	Ricky Bones	.15
57	Cal Eldred	.15
58	Brian Harper	.15
59	Pat Listach	.15
60	B.J. Surhoff	.15
61	Greg Vaughn	.15
62	Bernard Gilkey	.15
63	Gregg Jefferies	.15
64	Ray Lankford	.15
65	Ozzie Smith	.65
66	Bob Tewksbury	.15
67	Mark Whiten	.15
68	Todd Zeile	.15
69	Mark Grace	.25
70	Randy Myers	.15
71	Ryne Sandberg	1.00
72	Sammy Sosa	2.50
73	Steve Trachsel	.20
74	Rick Wilkins	.15
75	Brett Butler	.15
76	Delino DeShields	.15
77	Orel Hershiser	.15
78	Eric Karros	.20
79	Raul Mondesi	.60
80	Mike Piazza	2.50
81	Tim Wallach	.15
82	Moises Alou	.15
83	Cliff Floyd	.15
84	Marquis Grissom	.15
85	Pedro J. Martinez	.50
86	Larry Walker	.40
87	John Wetteland	.15
88	Rondell White	.35
89	Rod Beck	.15
90	Barry Bonds	1.25
91	John Burkett	.15
92	Royce Clayton	.15
93	Billy Swift	.15
94	Robby Thompson	.15
95	Matt Williams	.40
96	Carlos Baerga	.20
97	Albert Belle	1.50
98	Kenny Lofton	1.00
99	Dennis Martinez	.15
100	Eddie Murray	.50
101	Manny Ramirez	1.00
102	Eric Anthony	.15
103	Chris Bosio	.15
104	Jay Buhner	.20
105	Ken Griffey, Jr.	5.00
106	Randy Johnson	.50
107	Edgar Martinez	.20
108	Chuck Carr	.15
109	Jeff Conine	.15
110	Carl Everett	.15
111	Chris Hammond	.15
112	Bryan Harvey	.15
113	Charles Johnson	.25
114	Gary Sheffield	.50
115	Bobby Bonilla	.25
116	Dwight Gooden	.20
117	Todd Hundley	.25
118	Bobby Jones	.25
119	Jeff Kent	.15
120	Bret Saberhagen	.15
121	Jeffrey Hammonds	.15
122	Chris Hoiles	.15
123	Ben McDonald	.15
124	Mike Mussina	1.00
125	Rafael Palmeiro	.35
126	Cal Ripken, Jr.	4.00
127	Lee Smith	.15
128	Derek Bell	.15
129	Andy Benes	.20
130	Tony Gwynn	1.50
131	Trevor Hoffman	.15
132	Phil Plantier	.15
133	Bip Roberts	.15
134	Darren Daulton	.15
135	Len Dykstra	.15
136	Dave Hollins	.15
137	Danny Jackson	.15
138	John Kruk	.15
139	Kevin Stocker	.15
140	Jay Bell	.15
141	Carlos Garcia	.15
142	Jeff King	.15
143	Orlando Merced	.15
144	Andy Van Slyke	.15
145	Paul Wagner	.15
146	Jose Canseco	.40
147	Will Clark	.40
148	Juan Gonzalez	2.50
149	Rick Helling	.15
150	Dean Palmer	.15

151	Ivan Rodriguez	1.00
152	Roger Clemens	1.50
153	Scott Cooper	.15
154	Andre Dawson	.20
155	Mike Greenwell	.15
156	Aaron Sele	.25
157	Mo Vaughn	1.00
158	Bret Boone	.15
159	Barry Larkin	.20
160	Kevin Mitchell	.15
161	Jose Rijo	.15
162	Deion Sanders	.40
163	Reggie Sanders	.20
164	Dante Bichette	.40
165	Ellis Burks	.20
166	Andres Galarraga	.30
167	Charlie Hayes	.15
168	David Nied	.15
169	Walt Weiss	.15
170	Kevin Appier	.15
171	David Cone	.20
172	Jeff Granger	.20
173	Felix Jose	.15
174	Wally Joyner	.15
175	Brian McRae	.15
176	Cecil Fielder	.20
177	Travis Fryman	.15
178	Mike Henneman	.15
179	Tony Phillips	.15
180	Mickey Tettleton	.15
181	Alan Trammell	.15
182	Rick Aguilera	.15
183	Rich Becker	.15
184	Scott Erickson	.15
185	Chuck Knoblauch	.25
186	Kirby Puckett	1.50
187	Dave Winfield	.20
188	Wilson Alvarez	.15
189	Jason Bere	.15
190	Alex Fernandez	.20
191	Julio Franco	.15
192	Jack McDowell	.20
193	Frank Thomas	4.00
194	Robin Ventura	.20
195	Jim Abbott	.15
196	Wade Boggs	.25
197	Jimmy Key	.15
198	Don Mattingly	2.00
199	Paul O'Neill	.20
200	Danny Tartabull	.15

1994 SP Die-Cut

Upper Deck SP Die-cuts are a 200-card parallel set inserted at the rate of one per foil pack. Each card has a die-cut top instead of the flat-top found on regular SP cards. Die-cuts also have a silver-foil Upper Deck hologram logo on back, in contrast to the gold-tone hologram found on regular SP cards. This is an effort to prevent fraudulent replication by any crook with a pair of scissors.

		MT
Complete Set (200):		150.00
Common Player:		.25
	(Star cards valued at 1.5-3X corresponding cards in regular SP issue)	

1994 SP Holoview Blue

Holoview F/X Blue is a 38-card set utilizing Holoview printing technology, which features 200 frames of video to produce a true, three-dimensional image on the bottom third of each card. The hologram is bordered in blue and there is a blue stripe running down the right side of the card. Backs are done with a blue background and feature a player photo over top of bold letters reading "HoloView FX". This insert could be found in one per five packs of SP baseball.

		MT
Complete Set (38):		175.00
Common Player:		2.00
1	Roberto Alomar	7.50
2	Kevin Appier	2.00
3	Jeff Bagwell	10.00
4	Jose Canseco	4.00
5	Roger Clemens	10.00
6	Carlos Delgado	2.00
7	Cecil Fielder	3.00
8	Cliff Floyd	2.00
9	Travis Fryman	2.00
10	Andres Galarraga	3.00
11	Juan Gonzalez	12.00
12	Ken Griffey, Jr.	30.00
13	Tony Gwynn	10.00
14	Jeffrey Hammonds	2.00
15	Bo Jackson	2.50
16	Michael Jordan	30.00
17	Dave Justice	4.00
18	Steve Karsay	2.00
19	Jeff Kent	2.00
20	Brooks Kieschnick	3.00
21	Ryan Klesko	7.50
22	John Kruk	2.00
23	Barry Larkin	3.00
24	Pat Listach	2.00
25	Don Mattingly	12.00
26	Mark McGwire	30.00
27	Raul Mondesi	4.00
28	Trot Nixon	2.00
29	Mike Piazza	14.00
30	Kirby Puckett	9.00
31	Manny Ramirez	7.50
32	Cal Ripken, Jr.	20.00
33	Alex Rodriguez	45.00
34	Tim Salmon	4.00
35	Gary Sheffield	4.00
36	Ozzie Smith	6.00
37	Sammy Sosa	20.00
38	Andy Van Slyke	2.00

1994 SP Holoview Red

HoloView F/X Red is a parallel set to the Blue insert. Once again, this 38-card set utilizes Holoview printing technology. However, these cards have a red border surrounding the hologram and along the right side, as well as a red background on the back and a large "SPECIAL FX" under the player photo. Holoview red cards also have die-cut tops. Red cards are much scarcer than blue; the red being inserted once per 75 packs of SP baseball.

		MT
Complete Set (38):		2000.
Common Player:		7.50
1	Roberto Alomar	25.00
2	Kevin Appier	7.50
3	Jeff Bagwell	50.00
4	Jose Canseco	20.00
5	Roger Clemens	60.00
6	Carlos Delgado	10.00
7	Cecil Fielder	12.00
8	Cliff Floyd	8.00
9	Travis Fryman	7.50
10	Andres Galarraga	12.00
11	Juan Gonzalez	70.00
12	Ken Griffey, Jr.	200.00
13	Tony Gwynn	75.00
14	Jeffrey Hammonds	7.50
15	Bo Jackson	10.00
16	Michael Jordan	250.00
17	Dave Justice	15.00
18	Steve Karsay	7.50
19	Jeff Kent	7.50
20	Brooks Kieschnick	10.00
21	Ryan Klesko	20.00
22	John Kruk	7.50
23	Barry Larkin	12.00
24	Pat Listach	7.50
25	Don Mattingly	40.00
26	Mark McGwire	175.00
27	Raul Mondesi	25.00
28	Trot Nixon	10.00
29	Mike Piazza	100.00
30	Kirby Puckett	40.00
31	Manny Ramirez	40.00
32	Cal Ripken, Jr.	125.00
33	Alex Rodriguez	200.00
34	Tim Salmon	20.00
35	Gary Sheffield	25.00
36	Ozzie Smith	40.00
37	Sammy Sosa	80.00
38	Andy Van Slyke	7.50

1995 SP

Foil highlights and die-cut specialty cards are once again featured in Upper Deck's premium-brand SP baseball card issue. The 207-card set opens with four die-cut tribute cards, followed by 20 Premier Prospect die-cuts printed on metallic foil backgrounds with copper-foil highlights. The three checklists follow, also die-cut. The regular player cards in the set are arranged in team-alphabetical order within league. Card fronts feature photos which are borderless at top, bottom and right. On the left is a gold-highlighted metallic foil border of blue for N.L., red for A.L. Backs have a large photo at top, with a few stats and career highlights at bottom, along with a gold infield-shaped hologram. The SP insert program consists of a "SuperbaFoil" parallel set, in which each card's normal foil highlights are replaced with silver foil; a 48-card Special F/X set utilizing holographic portraits, and, a 20-card Platinum Power set. The hobby-only SP was issued in eight-card foil packs with a $3.99 suggested retail price.

Bret Saberhagen

	MT
Complete Set (207):	40.00
Common Player:	.15
Wax Box:	55.00
1 Cal Ripken Jr. (Salute)	3.00
2 Nolan Ryan (Salute)	2.00
3 George Brett (Salute)	1.00
4 Mike Schmidt (Salute)	.75
5 Dustin Hermanson (Premier Prospects)	.25
6 Antonio Osuna (Premier Prospects)	.30
7 *Mark Grudzielanek* (Premier Prospects)	.75
8 Ray Durham (Premier Prospects)	.30
9 Ugueth Urbina (Premier Prospects)	.20
10 Ruben Rivera (Premier Prospects)	1.50
11 Curtis Goodwin (Premier Prospects)	.15
12 Jimmy Hurst (Premier Prospects)	.15
13 Jose Malave (Premier Prospects)	.15
14 *Hideo Nomo* (Premier Prospects)	3.00
15 Juan Acevedo (Premier Prospects)	.15
16 Tony Clark (Premier Prospects)	1.50
17 Jim Pittsley (Premier Prospects)	.15
18 *Freddy Garcia* (Premier Prospects)	.30
19 *Carlos Perez* (Premier Prospects)	.25
20 *Raul Casanova* (Premier Prospects)	.50
21 Quilvio Veras (Premier Prospects)	.25
22 Edgardo Alfonzo (Premier Prospects)	.15
23 Marty Cordova (Premier Prospects)	.25
24 C.J. Nitkowski (Premier Prospects)	.25
25 Checklist 1-69(Wade Boggs)	.25
26 Checklist 70-138(Dave Winfield)	.25
27 Checklist 139-207(Eddie Murray)	.50
28 Dave Justice	.30
29 Marquis Grissom	.15
30 Fred McGriff	.50
31 Greg Maddux	2.50
32 Tom Glavine	.30
33 Steve Avery	.15
34 Chipper Jones	2.00
35 Sammy Sosa	2.50
36 Jaime Navarro	.15
37 Randy Myers	.15
38 Mark Grace	.25
39 Todd Zeile	.15
40 Brian McRae	.15
41 Reggie Sanders	.15
42 Ron Gant	.25
43 Deion Sanders	.40
44 Barry Larkin	.40
45 Bret Boone	.15
46 Jose Rijo	.15
47 Jason Bates	.15
48 Andres Galarraga	.40
49 Bill Swift	.15
50 Larry Walker	.40
51 Vinny Castilla	.15
52 Dante Bichette	.40
53 Jeff Conine	.15
54 John Burkett	.15
55 Gary Sheffield	.40
56 Andre Dawson	.25
57 Terry Pendleton	.15
58 Charles Johnson	.30
59 Brian L. Hunter	.25
60 Jeff Bagwell	1.25
61 Craig Biggio	.25
62 Phil Nevin	.15
63 Doug Drabek	.15
64 Derek Bell	.15
65 Raul Mondesi	.50
66 Eric Karros	.15
67 Roger Cedeno	.15
68 Delino DeShields	.15
69 Ramon Martinez	.15
70 Mike Piazza	2.00
71 Billy Ashley	.15
72 Jeff Fassero	.15
73 Shane Andrews	.15
74 Wil Cordero	.15
75 Tony Tarasco	.15
76 Rondell White	.25
77 Pedro J. Martinez	.25
78 Moises Alou	.15
79 Rico Brogna	.15
80 Bobby Bonilla	.25
81 Jeff Kent	.15
82 Brett Butler	.15
83 Bobby Jones	.15
84 Bill Pulsipher	.15
85 Bret Saberhagen	.15
86 Gregg Jefferies	.15
87 Lenny Dykstra	.15
88 Dave Hollins	.15
89 Charlie Hayes	.15
90 Darren Daulton	.15
91 Curt Schilling	.15
92 Heathcliff Slocumb	.15
93 Carlos Garcia	.15
94 Denny Neagle	.15
95 Jay Bell	.15
96 Orlando Merced	.15
97 Dave Clark	.15
98 Bernard Gilkey	.15
99 Scott Cooper	.15
100 Ozzie Smith	.50
100(P)Ken Griffey Jr. ("For Promotional Use Only" overprinted on back)	6.00
101 Tom Henke	.15
102 Ken Hill	.15
103 Brian Jordan	.15
104 Ray Lankford	.15
105 Tony Gwynn	1.25
106 Andy Benes	.15
107 Ken Caminiti	.30
108 Steve Finley	.15
109 Joey Hamilton	.25
110 Bip Roberts	.15
111 Eddie Williams	.15
112 Rod Beck	.15
113 Matt Williams	.50
114 Glenallen Hill	.15
115 Barry Bonds	1.00
116 Robby Thompson	.15
117 Mark Portugal	.15
118 Brady Anderson	.30
119 Mike Mussina	.60
120 Rafael Palmeiro	.30
121 Chris Hoiles	.15
122 Harold Baines	.15
123 Jeffrey Hammonds	.15
124 Tim Naehring	.15
125 Mo Vaughn	.75
126 Mike Macfarlane	.15
127 Roger Clemens	1.00
128 John Valentin	.15
129 Aaron Sele	.15
130 Jose Canseco	.40
131 J.T. Snow	.25
132 Mark Langston	.15
133 Chili Davis	.15
134 Chuck Finley	.15
135 Tim Salmon	.35
136 Tony Phillips	.15
137 Jason Bere	.15
138 Robin Ventura	.15
139 Tim Raines	.15
140a Frank Thomas (5-yr. BA .326)	3.00
140b Frank Thomas (5-yr. BA .303)	8.00
141 Alex Fernandez	.15
142 Jim Abbott	.15
143 Wilson Alvarez	.15
144 Carlos Baerga	.15
145 Albert Belle	1.00
146 Jim Thome	.50
147 Dennis Martinez	.15
148 Eddie Murray	.50
149 Dave Winfield	.25
150 Kenny Lofton	1.00
151 Manny Ramirez	.75
152 Chad Curtis	.15
153 Lou Whitaker	.15
154 Alan Trammell	.15
155 Cecil Fielder	.35
156 Kirk Gibson	.15
157 Michael Tucker	.25
158 Jon Nunnally	.15
159 Wally Joyner	.15
160 Kevin Appier	.15
161 Jeff Montgomery	.15
162 Greg Gagne	.15
163 Ricky Bones	.15
164 Cal Eldred	.15
165 Greg Vaughn	.15
166 Kevin Seitzer	.15
167 Jose Valentin	.15
168 Joe Oliver	.15
169 Rick Aguilera	.15
170 Kirby Puckett	1.50
171 Scott Stahoviak	.15
172 Kevin Tapani	.15
173 Chuck Knoblauch	.25
174 Rich Becker	.15
175 Don Mattingly	1.50
176 Jack McDowell	.30
177 Jimmy Key	.15
178 Paul O'Neill	.15
179 John Wetteland	.15
180 Wade Boggs	.35
181 Derek Jeter	2.50
182 Rickey Henderson	.25
183 Terry Steinbach	.15
184 Ruben Sierra	.15
185 Mark McGwire	4.00
186 Todd Stottlemyre	.15
187 Dennis Eckersley	.15
188 Alex Rodriguez	4.00
189 Randy Johnson	.50
190 Ken Griffey Jr.	4.00
190a	60.00
191 Tino Martinez	.30
192 Jay Buhner	.40
193 Edgar Martinez	.25
194 Mickey Tettleton	.15
195 Juan Gonzalez	1.75
196 Benji Gil	.15

197	Dean Palmer	.15
198	Ivan Rodriguez	.75
199	Kenny Rogers	.15
200	Will Clark	.40
201	Roberto Alomar	.75
202	David Cone	.25
203	Paul Molitor	.50
204	Shawn Green	.25
205	Joe Carter	.25
206	Alex Gonzalez	.15
207	Pat Hentgen	.15

1995 SP Platinum Power

This die-cut insert set features the game's top power hitters in color action photos set against a background of two-toned gold rays emanating from the SP logo at lower-right. Player name, team and position are printed in white in a black band at bottom. Backs repeat the golden ray effect in the background and have a color photo at center. Career and 1994 stats are presented. An infield-shaped gold foil hologram is at lower-right. Cards have a PP prefix. Stated odds of finding one of the 20 Platinum Power inserts are one per five packs.

		MT
Complete Set (20):		20.00
Common Player:		.50
PP1	Jeff Bagwell	2.00
PP2	Barry Bonds	1.50
PP3	Ron Gant	.50
PP4	Fred McGriff	.75
PP5	Raul Mondesi	.75
PP6	Mike Piazza	3.00
PP7	Larry Walker	.75
PP8	Matt Williams	.75
PP9	Albert Belle	1.50
PP10	Cecil Fielder	.50
PP11	Juan Gonzalez	2.00
PP12	Ken Griffey Jr.	5.00
PP13	Mark McGwire	5.00
PP14	Eddie Murray	1.00
PP15	Manny Ramirez	1.50
PP16	Cal Ripken Jr.	4.00
PP17	Tim Salmon	.75
PP18	Frank Thomas	4.00
PP19	Jim Thome	.75
PP20	Mo Vaughn	1.50

1995 SP Special F/X

By far the preferred pick of the '95 SP insert program is the Special F/X set of 48. The cards have a color

action photo on front, printed on a metallic foil background. A 3/4" square holographic portrait is printed on the front. Backs are printed in standard technology and include another photo and a few stats and career highlights. Stated odds of finding a Special F/X card are 1 per 75 packs, or about one per two boxes.

		MT
Complete Set (48):		700.00
Common Player:		5.00
1	Jose Canseco	8.00
2	Roger Clemens	30.00
3	Mo Vaughn	20.00
4	Tim Salmon	8.00
5	Chuck Finley	5.00
6	Robin Ventura	5.00
7	Jason Bere	5.00
8	Carlos Baerga	5.00
9	Albert Belle	20.00
10	Kenny Lofton	20.00
11	Manny Ramirez	20.00
12	Jeff Montgomery	5.00
13	Kirby Puckett	20.00
14	Wade Boggs	8.00
15	Don Mattingly	20.00
16	Cal Ripken Jr.	60.00
17	Ruben Sierra	5.00
18	Ken Griffey Jr.	75.00
19	Randy Johnson	15.00
20	Alex Rodriguez	75.00
21	Will Clark	8.00
22	Juan Gonzalez	35.00
23	Roberto Alomar	12.00
24	Joe Carter	8.00
25	Alex Gonzalez	5.00
26	Paul Molitor	12.00
27	Ryan Klesko	10.00
28	Fred McGriff	8.00
29	Greg Maddux	50.00
30	Sammy Sosa	50.00
31	Bret Boone	5.00
32	Barry Larkin	8.00
33	Reggie Sanders	5.00
34	Dante Bichette	8.00
35	Andres Galarraga	10.00
36	Charles Johnson	5.00
37	Gary Sheffield	10.00
38	Jeff Bagwell	25.00
39	Craig Biggio	5.00
40	Eric Karros	5.00
41	Billy Ashley	5.00
42	Raul Mondesi	8.00
43	Mike Piazza	50.00
44	Rondell White	5.00
45	Bret Saberhagen	5.00
46	Tony Gwynn	40.00
47	Melvin Nieves	5.00
48	Matt Williams	8.00

1995 SP SuperbaFoil

This chase set parallels the 207 regular cards in the SP issue. Cards were found at the rate of one

per eight-card foil pack. SuperbaFoil cards feature a silver-rainbow metallic foil in place of the gold, copper, red or blue foil highlights on regular-issue SP cards. On back, the SuperbaFoil inserts have a silver hologram instead of the gold version found on standard cards.

	MT
Complete Set (207):	80.00
Common Player:	.25
Veteran Stars: 2X to 3X	
Young Stars and Rookies: 1X to 2X	
(See 1995 SP for checklist and base values.)	

1995 SP/Championship

Championship was a version of Upper Deck's popular SP line designed for sale in retail outlets. The first 20 cards in the set are a "Diamond in the Rough" subset featuring hot rookies printed on textured metallic foil background. Regular player cards are arranged by team within league, alphabetically by city name. Each team set is led off with a "Pro Files" card of a star player; those card backs feature team season and post-season results. Each of the regular player cards has a borderless action photo on front, highlighted with a gold-foil SP Championship logo. The team name is in a blue-foil oval on National Leaguers' cards; red on American Leaguers. Backs have a portrait photo, a few stats and career highlights. Situated between the N.L. and A.L. cards in the checklist are a subset of 15 October Legends. A parallel set of cards with die-cut tops was inserted into the six-card foil packs at the rate of one per pack. A special card honoring Cal Ripken's consecutive-game record was issued as a super-scarce insert.

		MT
Complete Set (200):		40.00
Common Player:		.15
Die-Cuts: 1.5x to 2x:		
Wax Box:		90.00
1	*Hideo Nomo* (Diamonds in the Rough)	3.00
2	Roger Cedeno (Diamonds in the Rough)	.15

3	Curtis Goodwin (Diamonds in the Rough)	.15
4	Jon Nunnally (Diamonds in the Rough)	.15
5	Bill Pulsipher (Diamonds in the Rough)	.35
6	C.J. Nitkowski (Diamonds in the Rough)	.15
7	Dustin Hermanson (Diamonds in the Rough)	.15
8	Marty Cordova (Diamonds in the Rough)	.25
9	Ruben Rivera (Diamonds in the Rough)	.75
10	*Ariel Prieto* (Diamonds in the Rough)	.25
11	Edgardo Alfonzo (Diamonds in the Rough)	.15
12	Ray Durham (Diamonds in the Rough)	.25
13	Quilvio Veras (Diamonds in the Rough)	.15
14	Ugueth Urbina (Diamonds in the Rough)	.25
15	*Carlos Perez* (Diamonds in the Rough)	.20
16	*Glenn Dishman* (Diamonds in the Rough)	.25
17	Jeff Suppan (Diamonds in the Rough)	.15
18	Jason Bates (Diamonds in the Rough)	.15
19	Jason Isringhausen (Diamonds in the Rough)	1.00
20	Derek Jeter (Diamonds in the Rough)	1.50
21	Fred McGriff (Major League ProFiles)	.40
22	Marquis Grissom	.15
23	Fred McGriff	.50
24	Tom Glavine	.25
25	Greg Maddux	2.00
26	Chipper Jones	1.50
27	Sammy Sosa (Major League ProFiles)	1.50
28	Randy Myers	.15
29	Mark Grace	.25
30	Sammy Sosa	.75
31	Todd Zeile	.15
32	Brian McRae	.15
33	Ron Gant (Major League ProFiles)	.15
34	Reggie Sanders	.15
35	Ron Gant	.20
36	Barry Larkin	.30
37	Bret Boone	.15
38	John Smiley	.15
39	Larry Walker (Major League ProFiles)	.25
40	Andres Galarraga	.25
41	Bill Swift	.15
42	Larry Walker	.35
43	Vinny Castilla	.15
44	Dante Bichette	.50
45	Jeff Conine (Major League ProFiles)	.15
46	Charles Johnson	.15
47	Gary Sheffield	.30
48	Andre Dawson	.15
49	Jeff Conine	.15
50	Jeff Bagwell (Major League ProFiles)	.40
51	Phil Nevin	.15
52	Craig Biggio	.15
53	Brian L. Hunter	.20
54	Doug Drabek	.15
55	Jeff Bagwell	1.00
56	Derek Bell	.15
57	Mike Piazza (Major League ProFiles)	.60
58	Raul Mondesi	.40
59	Eric Karros	.20
60	Mike Piazza	1.50
61	Ramon Martinez	.20
62	Billy Ashley	.15
63	Rondell White (Major League ProFiles)	.20
64	Jeff Fassero	.15
65	Moises Alou	.15
66	Tony Tarasco	.15
67	Rondell White	.20
68	Pedro J. Martinez	.25
69	Bobby Jones (Major League ProFiles)	.15
70	Bobby Bonilla	.20
71	Bobby Jones	.15
72	Bret Saberhagen	.15
73	Darren Daulton (Major League ProFiles)	.15
74	Darren Daulton	.15
75	Gregg Jefferies	.15
76	Tyler Green	.15
77	Heathcliff Slocumb	.15
78	Lenny Dykstra	.15
79	Jay Bell (Major League ProFiles)	.15
80	Denny Neagle	.15
81	Orlando Merced	.15
82	Jay Bell	.15
83	Ozzie Smith (Major League ProFiles)	.30
84	Ken Hill	.15
85	Ozzie Smith	.50
86	Bernard Gilkey	.15
87	Ray Lankford	.15
88	Tony Gwynn (Major League ProFiles)	.50
89	Ken Caminiti	.25
90	Tony Gwynn	1.00
91	Joey Hamilton	.15
92	Bip Roberts	.15
93	Deion Sanders (Major League ProFiles)	.25
94	Glenallen Hill	.15
95	Matt Williams	.30
96	Barry Bonds	.75
97	Rod Beck	.15
98	Eddie Murray (Checklist)	.25
99	Cal Ripken Jr. (Checklist)	1.50
100	Roberto Alomar (October Legends)	.40
101	George Brett (October Legends)	.75
102	Joe Carter (Ocober Legends)	.20
103	Will Clark (October Legends)	.25
104	Dennis Eckersley (October Legends)	.15
105	Whitey Ford (October Legends)	.40
106	Steve Garvey (October Legends)	.15
107	Kirk Gibson (October Legends)	.15
108	Orel Hershiser (October Legends)	.15
109	Reggie Jackson (October Legends)	.50
110	Paul Molitor (October Legends)	.25
111	Kirby Puckett (October Legends)	.75
112	Mike Schmidt (October Legends)	.50
113	Dave Stewart (October Legends)	.15
114	Alan Trammell (October Legends)	.15
115	Cal Ripken Jr. (Major League ProFiles)	1.75
116	Brady Anderson	.20
117	Mike Mussina	.50
118	Rafael Palmeiro	.25
119	Chris Hoiles	.15
120	Cal Ripken Jr.	3.00
121	Mo Vaughn (Major League ProFiles)	.35
122	Roger Clemens	.75
123	Tim Naehring	.15
124	John Valentin	.15
125	Mo Vaughn	.75
126	Tim Wakefield	.15
127	Jose Canseco	.35
128	Rick Aguilera	.15
129	Chili Davis (Major League ProFiles)	.15
130	Lee Smith	.15
131	Jim Edmonds	.30
132	Chuck Finley	.15
133	Chili Davis	.15
134	J.T. Snow	.15
135	Tim Salmon	.30
136	Frank Thomas (Major League ProFiles)	1.25
137	Jason Bere	.15
138	Robin Ventura	.15
139	Tim Raines	.15
140	Frank Thomas	2.50
141	Alex Fernandez	.15
142	Eddie Murray (Major League ProFiles)	.25
143	Carlos Baerga	.15
144	Eddie Murray	.40
145	Albert Belle	.75
146	Jim Thome	.40
147	Dennis Martinez	.15
148	Dave Winfield	.15
149	Kenny Lofton	.75
150	Manny Ramirez	.75
151	Cecil Fielder (Major League ProFiles)	.20
152	Lou Whitaker	.15
153	Alan Trammell	.15
154	Kirk Gibson	.15
155	Cecil Fielder	.25
156	*Bobby Higginson*	1.50
157	Kevin Appier (Major League ProFiles)	.15
158	Wally Joyner	.15
159	Jeff Montgomery	.15
160	Kevin Appier	.15
161	Gary Gaetti	.15
162	Greg Gagne	.15
163	Ricky Bones (Major League ProFiles)	.15
164	Greg Vaughn	.15
165	Kevin Seitzer	.15
166	Ricky Bones	.15
167	Kirby Puckett (Major League ProFiles)	.40
168	Pedro Munoz	.15
169	Chuck Knoblauch	.25
170	Kirby Puckett	1.00
171	Don Mattingly (Major League ProFiles)	.50
172	Wade Boggs	.25
173	Paul O'Neill	.15
174	John Wetteland	.15
175	Don Mattingly	1.00
176	Jack McDowell	.20
177	Mark McGwire (Major League ProFiles)	2.00
178	Rickey Henderson	.15
179	Terry Steinbach	.15
180	Ruben Sierra	.15
181	Mark McGwire	3.00
182	Dennis Eckersley	.15
183	Ken Griffey Jr. (Major League ProFiles)	1.75
184	Alex Rodriguez	3.00
185	Ken Griffey Jr.	3.00
186	Randy Johnson	.60
187	Jay Buhner	.25
188	Edgar Martinez	.20
189	Will Clark (Major League ProFiles)	.25
190	Juan Gonzalez	1.25
191	Benji Gil	.15
192	Ivan Rodriguez	.60
193	Kenny Rogers	.15
194	Will Clark	.30
195	Paul Molitor (Major League ProFiles)	.25
196	Roberto Alomar	.60
197	David Cone	.20
198	Paul Molitor	.35
199	Shawn Green	.25
200	Joe Carter	.25
CR1	Cal Ripken Jr. (2,131 games tribute)	40.00
CR1	Cal Ripken Jr. 2,131 games tribute DC	100.00

1995 SP/Championship Classic Performances

Vintage action photos are featured in this chase set marking great post-season performances of modern times. The cards have a wide red strip at top with "CLASSIC PERFORMANCES" in gold-foil; the player's name, team and the SP Championship embossed logo at bottom are also in gold. Backs have a portrait photo and description of the highlight along with stats from that series. Regular Classic Performances cards are found at a stated rate of one per 15 foil packs, with die-cut versions in every 75 packs, on average. The die-cuts have silver UD holograms on back as opposed to the gold hologram found on regular versions of the chase cards.

		MT
Complete Set (10):		40.00
Common Player:		2.50
Complete Die-Cut Set (10):		200.00
Common Die-Cuts:		10.00
CP1	Reggie Jackson (Game 6 of '77 WS)	3.00
CP1	Reggie Jackson (die-cut)	15.00
CP2	Nolan Ryan (Game 3 of '69 WS)	20.00
CP2	Nolan Ryan (die-cut)	100.00
CP3	Kirk Gibson (Game 1 of '88 WS)	2.50
CP3	Kirk Gibson (die-cut)	10.00
CP4	Joe Carter (Game 6 of '93 WS)	3.00
CP4	Joe Carter (die-cut)	15.00
CP5	George Brett (Game 3 of '80 ALCS)	8.00
CP5	George Brett (die-cut)	40.00
CP6	Roberto Alomar (Game 4 of '92 ALCS)	6.00
CP6	Roberto Alomar (die-cut)	30.00
CP7	Ozzie Smith (Game 5 of '85 NLCS)	4.00
CP7	Ozzie Smith (die-cut)	20.00
CP8	Kirby Puckett (Game 6 of '91 WS)	8.00
CP8	Kirby Puckett (die-cut)	40.00
CP9	Bret Saberhagen (Game 7 of '85 WS)	2.50
CP9	Bret Saberhagen (die-cut)	10.00
CP10	Steve Garvey (Game 4 of '84 NLCS)	2.50
CP10	Steve Garvey (die-cut)	10.00

1995 SP/Championship Destination: Fall Classic

Colored foil background printing and copper-foil graphic highlights are featured on this insert set picturing players who, for the most part, had yet to make a post-season appearance prior to 1995's expanded playoffs. Found at a stated average rate of one per 40 foil packs, the cards have short career summaries and another photo on back. A die-cut version of the cards was also issued, with a silver UD hologram on back rather than the

gold found on the standard chase cards. The die-cut Fall Classic cards were inserted at a rate of one per 75 packs.

		MT
Complete Set (9):		100.00
Common Player:		4.00
Complete Die-Cut Set (9):		160.00
Common Die-Cut:		8.00
1	Ken Griffey Jr.	25.00
1	Ken Griffey Jr. (die-cut)	40.00
2	Frank Thomas	20.00
2	Frank Thomas (die-cut)	40.00
3	Albert Belle	6.00
3	Albert Belle (die-cut)	10.00
4	Mike Piazza	15.00
4	Mike Piazza (die-cut)	25.00
5	Don Mattingly	10.00
5	Don Mattingly (die-cut)	20.00
6	Hideo Nomo	8.00
6	Hideo Nomo (die-cut)	12.00
7	Greg Maddux	15.00
7	Greg Maddux (die-cut)	25.00
8	Fred McGriff	4.00
8	Fred McGriff (die-cut)	8.00
9	Barry Bonds	8.00
9	Barry Bonds (die-cut)	12.00

1995 SP/Championship Die-Cuts

Each of the 200 cards in the regular SP championship issue, plus the 20 insert cards, can also be found in a parallel chase card set with die-cut tops. One die-cut card was found in each six-card foil pack, making them five times

scarcer than the regular cards. To prevent regular cards from being fraudulently cut, factory-issue die-cuts have the Upper Deck hologram on back in silver tone, rather than the gold holograms found on regular cards.

	MT
Complete Set (200):	90.00
Common Player:	.25
Veteran Stars: 2X to 3X	
Young Stars and Rookies: 1X to 2X	
(See 1995 SP/Championship for checklist and base values.)	

1996 SP

This 188-card set, distributed through hobby-only channels, features tremendous photography, including two photos on the front, and six insert sets. The inserts sets are Heroes, Marquee Matchups Blue and Die-Cut Marquee Matchups Red, Holoview Special F/X Blue and Die-Cut Holoview Special F/X Red, and the continuation of the Cal Ripken Collection.

		MT
Complete Set (188):		40.00
Common Player:		.15
Unlisted Stars: .30 to .50		
Wax Box:		60.00
1	Rey Ordonez (Premier Prospects)	.40
2	George Arias (Premier Prospects)	.15
3	*Osvaldo Fernandez* (Premier Prospects)	.30
4	*Darin Erstad* (Premier Prospects)	10.00
5	Paul Wilson (Premier Prospects)	.30
6	Richard Hidalgo (Premier Prospects)	.15
7	Bob Wolcott (Premier Prospects)	.15
8	Jimmy Haynes (Premier Prospects)	.15
9	Edgar Renteria (Premier Prospects)	.35
10	Alan Benes (Premier Prospects)	.30
11	Chris Snopek (Premier Prospects)	.15
12	Billy Wagner (Premier Prospects)	.30
13	*Mike Grace* (Premier Prospects)	.40
14	Todd Greene (Premier Prospects)	.15
15	Karim Garcia (Premier Prospects)	.75
16	John Wasdin (Premier Prospects)	.15

17	Jason Kendall (Premier Prospects)	.15
18	Bob Abreu (Premier Prospects)	.40
19	Jermaine Dye (Premier Prospects)	.25
20	Jason Schmidt (Premier Prospects)	.15
21	Javy Lopez	.25
22	Ryan Klesko	.75
23	Tom Glavine	.25
24	John Smoltz	.35
25	Greg Maddux	2.50
26	Chipper Jones	2.50
27	Fred McGriff	.40
28	David Justice	.20
29	Roberto Alomar	.75
30	Cal Ripken Jr.	3.00
31	Jeffrey Hammonds	.15
32	Bobby Bonilla	.15
33	Mike Mussina	.75
34	Randy Myers	.15
35	Rafael Palmeiro	.25
36	Brady Anderson	.25
37	Tim Naehring	.15
38	Jose Canseco	.40
39	Roger Clemens	1.00
40	Mo Vaughn	1.00
41	*Jose Valentin*	.30
42	Kevin Mitchell	.15
43	Chili Davis	.15
44	Garret Anderson	.15
45	Tim Salmon	.40
46	Chuck Finley	.15
47	Mark Langston	.15
48	Jim Abbott	.15
49	J.T. Snow	.15
50	Jim Edmonds	.25
51	Sammy Sosa	2.50
52	Brian McRae	.15
53	Ryne Sandberg	1.25
54	Mark Grace	.25
55	Jaime Navarro	.15
56	Harold Baines	.15
57	Robin Ventura	.15
58	Tony Phillips	.15
59	Alex Fernandez	.25
60	Frank Thomas	2.50
61	Ray Durham	.15
62	Bret Boone	.15
63	Barry Larkin	.40
64	Pete Schourek	.15
65	Reggie Sanders	.15
66	John Smiley	.15
67	Carlos Baerga	.15
68	Jim Thome	.60
69	Eddie Murray	.60
70	Albert Belle	1.00
71	Dennis Martinez	.15
72	Jack McDowell	.25
73	Kenny Lofton	1.00
74	Manny Ramirez	1.00
75	Dante Bichette	.35
76	Vinny Castilla	.15
77	Andres Galarraga	.35
78	Walt Weiss	.15
79	Ellis Burks	.15
80	Larry Walker	.40
81	Cecil Fielder	.25
82	Melvin Nieves	.15
83	Travis Fryman	.15
84	Chad Curtis	.15
85	Alan Trammell	.15
86	Gary Sheffield	.50
87	Charles Johnson	.15
88	Andre Dawson	.15
89	Jeff Conine	.15
90	Greg Colbrunn	.15
91	Derek Bell	.15
92	Brian Hunter	.15
93	Doug Drabek	.15
94	Craig Biggio	.25
95	Jeff Bagwell	1.50
96	Kevin Appier	.15
97	Jeff Montgomery	.15
98	Michael Tucker	.15
99	Bip Roberts	.15
100	Johnny Damon	.15
101	Eric Karros	.15
102	Raul Mondesi	.40
103	Ramon Martinez	.15
104	Ismael Valdes	.15
105	Mike Piazza	2.50
106	Hideo Nomo	.75
107	Chan Ho Park	.15
108	Ben McDonald	.15

109	Kevin Seitzer	.15
110	Greg Vaughn	.15
111	Jose Valentin	.15
112	Rick Aguilera	.15
113	Marty Cordova	.15
114	Brad Radke	.15
115	Kirby Puckett	1.50
116	Chuck Knoblauch	.25
117	Paul Molitor	.50
118	Pedro Martinez	.25
119	Mike Lansing	.15
120	Rondell White	.15
121	Moises Alou	.15
122	Mark Grudzielanek	.15
123	Jeff Fassero	.15
124	Rico Brogna	.15
125	Jason Isringhausen	.15
126	Jeff Kent	.15
127	Bernard Gilkey	.15
128	Todd Hundley	.25
129	David Cone	.25
130	Andy Pettitte	1.25
131	Wade Boggs	.25
132	Paul O'Neill	.25
133	Ruben Sierra	.15
134	John Wetteland	.15
135	Derek Jeter	2.00
136	Geronimo Pena	.15
137	Terry Steinbach	.15
138	Ariel Prieto	.15
139	Scott Brosius	.15
140	Mark McGwire	4.00
141	Lenny Dykstra	.15
142	Todd Zeile	.15
143	Benito Santiago	.15
144	Mickey Morandini	.15
145	Gregg Jefferies	.15
146	Denny Neagle	.15
147	Orlando Merced	.15
148	Charlie Hayes	.15
149	Carlos Garcia	.15
150	Jay Bell	.15
151	Ray Lankford	.15
152	Alan Benes	.25
153	Dennis Eckersley	.15
154	Gary Gaetti	.15
155	Ozzie Smith	.75
156	Ron Gant	.25
157	Brian Jordan	.15
158	Ken Caminiti	.40
159	Rickey Henderson	.15
160	Tony Gwynn	1.50
161	Wally Joyner	.15
162	Andy Ashby	.15
163	Steve Finley	.15
164	Glenallen Hill	.15
165	Matt Williams	.40
166	Barry Bonds	1.00
167	William VanLandingham	.15
168	Rod Beck	.15
169	Randy Johnson	.50
170	Ken Griffey Jr.	4.00
170p	Ken Griffey Jr. (unmarked promo; bio on back says, ". . . against Cleveland" as opposed to ". . . against the Indians")	20.00
171	Alex Rodriguez	5.00
172	Edgar Martinez	.15
173	Jay Buhner	.25
174	Russ Davis	.15
175	Juan Gonzalez	1.75
176	Mickey Tettleton	.15
177	Will Clark	.40
178	Ken Hill	.15
179	Dean Palmer	.15
180	Ivan Rodriguez	.60
181	Carlos Delgado	.15
182	Alex Gonzalez	.15
183	Shawn Green	.15
184	Erik Hanson	.15
185	Joe Carter	.25
186	Checklist(Hideo Nomo)	.40
187	Checklist(Cal Ripken Jr.)	1.50
188	Checklist(Ken Griffey Jr.)	2.00

1996 SP Baseball Heroes

This 1996 insert set is a continuation of the series which began in 1990. These cards, numbered 81-90, feature nine of today's top stars, plus a Ken Griffey Jr. header card (#81). The cards were seeded one per every 96 packs. MT

Complete Set (10):		275.00
Common Player:		10.00
81	Ken Griffey Jr. Header	40.00
82	Frank Thomas	40.00
83	Albert Belle	15.00
84	Barry Bonds	15.00
85	Chipper Jones	40.00
86	Hideo Nomo	10.00
87	Mike Piazza	40.00
88	Manny Ramirez	15.00
89	Greg Maddux	40.00
90	Ken Griffey Jr.	60.00

1996 SP Marquee Matchups Blue

This 20-card Upper Deck SP insert set contains cards that allow collectors to match up the game's top players against each other, such as Greg Maddux against Cal Ripken Jr. The design and stadiums in the background match together when the two cards are next to each other. Blue versions are seeded one per every five packs. Red versions, with die-cut tops but otherwise identical to the blue, are found on average of once in 61 packs.

A player's name in *italic* type indicates a rookie card.

		MT
Complete Set (20):		50.00
Common Player:		1.00
Complete Die-Cut Set:		200.00
Die-Cuts: 3x to 5x		
MM1	Ken Griffey Jr.	8.00
MM2	Hideo Nomo	1.50
MM3	Derek Jeter	5.00
MM4	Rey Ordonez	1.00
MM5	Tim Salmon	1.00
MM6	Mike Piazza	5.00
MM7	Mark McGwire	8.00
MM8	Barry Bonds	2.00
MM9	Cal Ripken Jr.	6.00
MM10	Greg Maddux	5.00
MM11	Albert Belle	2.00
MM12	Barry Larkin	1.50
MM13	Jeff Bagwell	4.00
MM14	Juan Gonzalez	4.00
MM15	Frank Thomas	5.00
MM16	Sammy Sosa	5.00
MM17	Mike Mussina	1.50
MM18	Chipper Jones	5.00
MM19	Roger Clemens	2.00
MM20	Fred McGriff	1.50

1996 SP
Ripken Collection

The last five cards of the Cal Ripken Jr. Collection, which began in Collector's Choice Series I, are featured in this Upper Deck SP product. These five cards, numbered 18-22, cover Ripken's early days, including his 1982 Rookie of the Year Award, his Major League debut, and photos of him playing third base. Ripken Collection inserts are found one per every 45 packs.

		MT
Complete Set (5):		50.00
Common Ripken:		10.00
18	Cal Ripken Jr.	10.00
19	Cal Ripken Jr.	10.00
20	Cal Ripken Jr.	10.00
21	Cal Ripken Jr.	10.00
22	Cal Ripken Jr.	10.00

1996 SP
SpecialFX

These 48 cards capture Upper Deck Holoview technology. Blue versions were seeded one per every five packs of 1996 Upper Deck SP baseball.

		MT
Complete Set (48):		200.00
Common Player:		2.00
1	Greg Maddux	12.00
2	Eric Karros	2.00
3	Mike Piazza	12.00
4	Raul Mondesi	3.00
5	Hideo Nomo	4.00
6	Jim Edmonds	2.00
7	Jason Isringhausen	2.00
8	Jay Buhner	2.00
9	Barry Larkin	3.00
10	Ken Griffey Jr.	20.00
11	Gary Sheffield	3.00
12	Craig Biggio	2.00
13	Paul Wilson	3.00
14	Rondell White	2.00
15	Chipper Jones	12.00
16	Kirby Puckett	6.00
17	Ron Gant	2.00
18	Wade Boggs	3.00
19	Fred McGriff	2.50
20	Cal Ripken Jr.	15.00
21	Jason Kendall	2.00
22	Johnny Damon	2.00
23	Kenny Lofton	5.00
24	Roberto Alomar	4.00
25	Barry Bonds	5.00
26	Dante Bichette	3.00
27	Mark McGwire	20.00
28	Rafael Palmeiro	3.00
29	Juan Gonzalez	8.00
30	Albert Belle	5.00
31	Randy Johnson	4.00
32	Jose Canseco	3.00
33	Sammy Sosa	10.00
34	Eddie Murray	3.00
35	Frank Thomas	12.00
36	Tom Glavine	2.00
37	Matt Williams	3.00
38	Roger Clemens	5.00
39	Paul Molitor	4.00
40	Tony Gwynn	10.00
41	Mo Vaughn	5.00
42	Tim Salmon	3.00
43	Manny Ramirez	5.00
44	Jeff Bagwell	8.00
45	Edgar Martinez	2.00
46	Rey Ordonez	2.00
47	Osvaldo Fernandez	2.00
48	Livan Hernandez	2.00

1996 SP
SpecialFX Red

These 1996 Upper Deck SP red die-cut cards use Upper Deck's Holoview technology. They are scarcer than the blue versions; these being seeded one per every 75 packs.

Modern cards have little collector value in conditions lower than Mint.
Figure NM cards at 75% of values shown;
EX cards at 40%.

		MT
Complete Set (48):		800.00
Common Player:		8.00
1	Greg Maddux	60.00
2	Eric Karros	8.00
3	Mike Piazza	60.00
4	Raul Mondesi	12.00
5	Hideo Nomo	20.00
6	Jim Edmonds	8.00
7	Jason Isringhausen	8.00
8	Jay Buhner	12.00
9	Barry Larkin	12.00
10	Ken Griffey Jr.	100.00
11	Gary Sheffield	15.00
12	Craig Biggio	8.00
13	Paul Wilson	12.00
14	Rondell White	8.00
15	Chipper Jones	60.00
16	Kirby Puckett	40.00
17	Ron Gant	8.00
18	Wade Boggs	10.00
19	Fred McGriff	12.00
20	Cal Ripken Jr.	80.00
21	Jason Kendall	8.00
22	Johnny Damon	8.00
23	Kenny Lofton	25.00
24	Roberto Alomar	20.00
25	Barry Bonds	25.00
26	Dante Bichette	15.00
27	Mark McGwire	100.00
28	Rafael Palmeiro	15.00
29	Juan Gonzalez	45.00
30	Albert Belle	25.00
31	Randy Johnson	20.00
32	Jose Canseco	15.00
33	Sammy Sosa	60.00
34	Eddie Murray	15.00
35	Frank Thomas	60.00
36	Tom Glavine	8.00
37	Matt Williams	15.00
38	Roger Clemens	25.00
39	Paul Molitor	20.00
40	Tony Gwynn	40.00
41	Mo Vaughn	25.00
42	Tim Salmon	12.00
43	Manny Ramirez	25.00
44	Jeff Bagwell	40.00
45	Edgar Martinez	8.00
46	Rey Ordonez	8.00
47	Osvaldo Fernandez	8.00
48	Livan Hernandez	8.00

1996 SPx

Upper Deck's 1996 SPX set has 60 players in it, which are each paralleled as a Gold version (one per every seven packs). Base cards feature a new look with a different perimeter die-cut design from those used in the past for basketball and football sets. A 10-card insert set, Bound for Glory, was also produced. Tribute cards were also made for Ken Griffey Jr. and Mike Piazza, with scarcer autographed versions also produced for each player.

		MT
Complete Set (60):		100.00
Common Player:		1.00
Complete Gold Set (60):		300.00
Golds: 1.5x to 3x		
Wax Box:		65.00
1	Greg Maddux	6.00
2	Chipper Jones	6.00
3	Fred McGriff	1.50
4	Tom Glavine	1.00
5	Cal Ripken Jr.	8.00
6	Roberto Alomar	2.00
7	Rafael Palmeiro	1.00
8	Jose Canseco	1.50
9	Roger Clemens	3.00
10	Mo Vaughn	2.50
11	Jim Edmonds	1.00
12	Tim Salmon	1.50
13	Sammy Sosa	5.00
14	Ryne Sandberg	2.50
15	Mark Grace	1.00
16	Frank Thomas	8.00
17	Barry Larkin	1.50
18	Kenny Lofton	2.50
19	Albert Belle	2.50
20	Eddie Murray	1.50
21	Manny Ramirez	2.50
22	Dante Bichette	1.50
23	Larry Walker	1.50
24	Vinny Castilla	1.00
25	Andres Galarraga	1.50
26	Cecil Fielder	1.00
27	Gary Sheffield	1.50
28	Craig Biggio	1.00
29	Jeff Bagwell	3.00
30	Derek Bell	1.00
31	Johnny Damon	1.00
32	Eric Karros	1.00
33	Mike Piazza	6.00
34	Raul Mondesi	1.50
35	Hideo Nomo	2.00
36	Kirby Puckett	3.00
37	Paul Molitor	2.00
38	Marty Cordova	1.00
39	Rondell White	1.00
40	Jason Isringhausen	1.00
41	Paul Wilson	1.00
42	Rey Ordonez	1.00
43	Derek Jeter	6.00
44	Wade Boggs	1.50
45	Mark McGwire	12.00
46	Jason Kendall	1.00
47	Ron Gant	1.00
48	Ozzie Smith	2.00
49	Tony Gwynn	5.00
50	Ken Caminiti	1.50
51	Barry Bonds	2.50
52	Matt Williams	1.50
53	Osvaldo Fernandez	1.00
54	Jay Buhner	1.00
55	Ken Griffey Jr.	12.00
55p	Ken Griffey Jr. (overprinted "For Promotional Use Only")	15.00
56	Randy Johnson	2.00
57	Alex Rodriguez	8.00
58	Juan Gonzalez	5.00
59	Joe Carter	1.00
60	Carlos Delgado	1.00

1996 SPx Bound for Glory

Some of baseball's best players are highlighted on these 1996 Upper Deck SPX insert cards. The cards were seeded one per every 24 packs. Fronts of the die-cut cards feature a color photograph on a background of silver-foil holographic portrait and action photos. Backs have another portrait photo, stats, career highlights and logos.

		MT
Complete Set (10):		150.00
Common Player:		8.00
1	Ken Griffey Jr.	30.00
2	Frank Thomas	25.00
3	Barry Bonds	8.00
4	Cal Ripken Jr.	25.00
5	Greg Maddux	20.00
6	Chipper Jones	20.00
7	Roberto Alomar	7.00
8	Manny Ramirez	8.00
9	Tony Gwynn	15.00
10	Mike Piazza	20.00

1996 SPx Ken Griffey Jr. Commemorative

Seattle Mariners' star Ken Griffey Jr. has this tribute card in Upper Deck's 1996 SPX set. The card was seeded one per every 75 packs. Autographed versions were also produced; these cards were seeded one per every 2,000 packs.

		MT
Ken Griffey Jr. (KG1)		20.00
KG1	Ken Griffey Jr.	20.00
KG1	Ken Griffey Jr. (autographed)	350.00

1996 SPx Mike Piazza Tribute

Los Angeles Dodgers' star catcher Mike Piazza is featured on this 1996 Upper Deck SPX insert card.

Normal versions of the card are found one per every 95 packs, making it scarcer than the Ken Griffey Jr. inserts. Autographed Piazza cards are seeded one per every 2,000 packs.

		MT
Mike Piazza (MP1)		10.00
MP1	Mike Piazza	10.00
MP1	Mike Piazza (autographed)	200.00

1997 SP

The fifth anniversary edition of SP Baseball features 184 regular cards sold in eight-card packs for $4.39. Card fronts feature the player's name in gold foil-stamping at bottom. Team name and position are vertically at one edge. Backs have two more photos along with "Best Year" and career stats. Inserts include Marquee Matchups, Special FX, Inside Info, Baseball Heroes, Game Film, SPx Force, and Autographed Vintage SP Cards.

		MT
Complete Set (184):		40.00
Common Player:		.15
Wax Box:		100.00
1	Andruw Jones (Great Futures)	2.00
2	Kevin Orie (Great Futures)	.15
3	Nomar Garciaparra (Great Futures)	1.50
4	Jose Guillen (Great Futures)	1.50
5	Todd Walker (Great Futures)	1.00
6	Derrick Gibson (Great Futures)	.25
7	Aaron Boone (Great Futures)	.25
8	Bartolo Colon (Great Futures)	.15
9	Derrek Lee (Great Futures)	.25
10	Vladimir Guerrero (Great Futures)	1.50
11	Wilton Guerrero (Great Futures)	.15
12	Luis Castillo (Great Futures)	.15
13	Jason Dickson (Great Futures)	.15
14	Bubba Trammell (Great Futures)	1.50
15	Jose Cruz Jr. (Great Futures)	4.00
16	Eddie Murray	.50
17	Darin Erstad	1.50
18	Garret Anderson	.15
19	Jim Edmonds	.15
20	Tim Salmon	.40
21	Chuck Finley	.15

22	John Smoltz	.30
23	Greg Maddux	2.50
24	Kenny Lofton	1.00
25	Chipper Jones	2.50
26	Ryan Klesko	.60
27	Javier Lopez	.15
28	Fred McGriff	.40
29	Roberto Alomar	.75
30	Rafael Palmeiro	.30
31	Mike Mussina	.75
32	Brady Anderson	.15
33	Rocky Coppinger	.15
34	Cal Ripken Jr.	3.00
35	Mo Vaughn	1.00
36	Steve Avery	.15
37	Tom Gordon	.15
38	Tim Naehring	.15
39	Troy O'Leary	.15
40	Sammy Sosa	2.50
41	Brian McRae	.15
42	Mel Rojas	.15
43	Ryne Sandberg	1.00
44	Mark Grace	.30
45	Albert Belle	1.00
46	Robin Ventura	.15
47	Roberto Hernandez	.15
48	Ray Durham	.15
49	Harold Baines	.15
50	Frank Thomas	3.00
51	Bret Boone	.15
52	Reggie Sanders	.15
53	Deion Sanders	.40
54	Hal Morris	.15
55	Barry Larkin	.30
56	Jim Thome	.75
57	Marquis Grissom	.15
58	David Justice	.50
59	Charles Nagy	.15
60	Manny Ramirez	1.00
61	Matt Williams	.40
62	Jack McDowell	.15
63	Vinny Castilla	.15
64	Dante Bichette	.25
65	Andres Galarraga	.25
66	Ellis Burks	.15
67	Larry Walker	.50
68	Eric Young	.15
69	Brian L. Hunter	.15
70	Travis Fryman	.15
71	Tony Clark	1.00
72	Bobby Higginson	.15
73	Melvin Nieves	.15
74	Jeff Conine	.15
75	Gary Sheffield	.50
76	Moises Alou	.15
77	Edgar Renteria	.15
78	Alex Fernandez	.15
79	Charles Johnson	.15
80	Bobby Bonilla	.15
81	Darryl Kile	.15
82	Derek Bell	.15
83	Shane Reynolds	.15
84	Craig Biggio	.25
85	Jeff Bagwell	2.00
86	Billy Wagner	.15
87	Chili Davis	.15
88	Kevin Appier	.15
89	Jay Bell	.15
90	Johnny Damon	.15
91	Jeff King	.15
92	Hideo Nomo	.75
93	Todd Hollandsworth	.15
94	Eric Karros	.15
95	Mike Piazza	2.50
96	Ramon Martinez	.15
97	Todd Worrell	.15
98	Raul Mondesi	.40
99	Dave Nilsson	.15
100	John Jaha	.15
101	Jose Valentin	.15
102	Jeff Cirillo	.15
103	Jeff D'Amico	.15
104	Ben McDonald	.15
105	Paul Molitor	.50
106	Rich Becker	.15
107	Frank Rodriguez	.15
108	Marty Cordova	.15
109	Terry Steinbach	.15
110	Chuck Knoblauch	.30
111	Mark Grudzielanek	.15
112	Mike Lansing	.15
113	Pedro J. Martinez	.30
114	Henry Rodriguez	.15
115	Rondell White	.15
116	Rey Ordonez	.15
117	Carlos Baerga	.15
118	Lance Johnson	.15
119	Bernard Gilkey	.15
120	Todd Hundley	.30
121	John Franco	.15
122	Bernie Williams	.75
123	David Cone	.30
124	Cecil Fielder	.25
125	Derek Jeter	2.50
126	Tino Martinez	.40
127	Mariano Rivera	.25
128	Andy Pettitte	1.00
129	Wade Boggs	.40
130	Mark McGwire	5.00
131	Jose Canseco	.40
132	Geronimo Berroa	.15
133	Jason Giambi	.15
134	Ernie Young	.15
135	Scott Rolen	1.50
136	Ricky Bottalico	.15
137	Curt Schilling	.15
138	Gregg Jefferies	.15
139	Mickey Morandini	.15
140	Jason Kendall	.15
141	Kevin Elster	.15
142	Al Martin	.15
143	Joe Randa	.15
144	Jason Schmidt	.15
145	Ray Lankford	.15
146	Brian Jordan	.15
147	Andy Benes	.15
148	Alan Benes	.25
149	Gary Gaetti	.15
150	Ron Gant	.15
151	Dennis Eckersley	.15
152	Rickey Henderson	.15
153	Joey Hamilton	.15
154	Ken Caminiti	.40
155	Tony Gwynn	2.00
156	Steve Finley	.15
157	Trevor Hoffman	.15
158	Greg Vaughn	.15
159	J.T. Snow	.15
160	Barry Bonds	1.00
161	Glenallen Hill	.15
162	William VanLandingham	.15
163	Jeff Kent	.15
164	Jay Buhner	.30
165	Ken Griffey Jr.	4.00
166	Alex Rodriguez	4.00
167	Randy Johnson	.75
168	Edgar Martinez	.15
169	Dan Wilson	.15
170	Ivan Rodriguez	.75
171	Roger Pavlik	.15
172	Will Clark	.30
173	Dean Palmer	.15
174	Rusty Greer	.15
175	Juan Gonzalez	2.00
176	John Wetteland	.15
177	Joe Carter	.15
178	Ed Sprague	.15
179	Carlos Delgado	.15
180	Roger Clemens	1.00
181	Juan Guzman	.15
182	Pat Hentgen	.15
183	Ken Griffey Jr.	4.00
184	*Hideki Irabu*	4.00

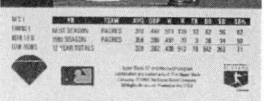

To celebrate the fifth anniversary of its premium SP brand, Upper Deck went into the hobby market to buy nearly 3,000 previous years' cards for a special insert program in 1997 SP packs. Various SP cards from 1993-96 issues and inserts were autographed by star players and a numbered holographic seal added on back. The number of each particular card signed ranged widely from fewer than 10 to more than 100. Numbers in parentheses in the checklist are the quantity reported signed for that card. All cards were inserted into foil packs except those of Mo Vaughn, which were a mail-in redemption.

		MT
Common Autograph:		25.00
	1993 SP	
4	Ken Griffey Jr. (16)	2000.
28	Jeff Bagwell (7)	25.00
167	Tony Gwynn (17)	700.00
280	Chipper Jones (34)	400.00
	1993 SP Platinum Power	
PP9	Ken Griffey Jr. (5)	25.00
	1994 SP	
6	Todd Hollandsworth (167)	25.00
15	Alex Rodriguez (94)	350.00
105	Ken Griffey Jr. (103)	800.00
114	Gary Sheffield (130)	75.00
130	Tony Gwynn (367)	175.00
	1994 SP Holoview Blue	
13	Tony Gwynn (31)	400.00
	1994 SP Holoview Red	
35	Gary Sheffield (4)	25.00
	1995 SP	
34	Chipper Jones (60)	350.00
60	Jeff Bagwell (173)	140.00
75	Gary Sheffield (221)	40.00
105	Tony Gwynn (64)	215.00
188	Alex Rodriguez (63)	400.00
190	Ken Griffey Jr. (38)	1100.00
195	Jay Buhner (57)	75.00
	1996 SP	
1	Rey Ordonez (111)	25.00
18	Gary Sheffield (58)	75.00
26	Chipper Jones (102)	250.00
40	Mo Vaughn (250)	80.00
95	Jeff Bagwell (292)	100.00
160	Tony Gwynn (20)	450.00
170	Ken Griffey Jr. (312)	400.00
171	Alex Rodriguez (73)	400.00
173	Jay Buhner (79)	80.00
	1996 SP Marquee Matchups	
MM13	Jeff Bagwell (23)	400.00
MM4	Rey Ordonez (40)	40.00
	1996 SP Special F/X	
8	Jay Buhner (27)	95.00

1997 SP
Autographed Inserts

A player's name in *italic* type indicates a rookie card.

1997 SP
Baseball Heroes

First started in 1990, this single-player insert continues with a salute to Ken Griffey Jr. Each card in the set is numbered to 2,000.

		MT
Complete Set (10):		300.00
Common Griffey Jr.:		35.00
91	Ken Griffey Jr.	40.00
92	Ken Griffey Jr.	40.00
93	Ken Griffey Jr.	40.00
94	Ken Griffey Jr.	40.00
95	Ken Griffey Jr.	40.00
96	Ken Griffey Jr.	40.00
97	Ken Griffey Jr.	40.00
98	Ken Griffey Jr.	40.00
99	Ken Griffey Jr.	40.00
100	Ken Griffey Jr.	40.00

1997 SP
Game Film

A 10-card insert utilizing pieces of actual game footage to highlight the top stars in the game. Only 500 of each card were available.

		MT
Complete Set (10):		750.00
Common Player:		25.00
GF1	Alex Rodriguez	100.00
GF2	Frank Thomas	100.00
GF3	Andruw Jones	40.00
GF4	Cal Ripken Jr.	120.00
GF5	Mike Piazza	100.00
GF6	Derek Jeter	75.00
GF7	Mark McGwire	150.00
GF8	Chipper Jones	80.00
GF9	Barry Bonds	40.00
GF10	Ken Griffey Jr.	150.00

1997 SP
Inside Info

Each of the 25 cards in this insert feature a pull-out panel describing the player's major accomplishments. Both front and back are printed on metallic-foil stock. Cards were inserted one per box.

		MT
Complete Set (25):		250.00
Common Player:		4.00
1	Ken Griffey Jr.	30.00
2	Mark McGwire	35.00
3	Kenny Lofton	7.00

4	Paul Molitor	8.00
5	Frank Thomas	20.00
6	Greg Maddux	20.00
7	Mo Vaughn	7.00
8	Cal Ripken Jr.	25.00
9	Jeff Bagwell	12.00
10	Alex Rodriguez	25.00
11	John Smoltz	4.00
12	Manny Ramirez	7.00
13	Sammy Sosa	20.00
14	Vladimir Guerrero	10.00
15	Albert Belle	8.00
16	Mike Piazza	20.00
17	Derek Jeter	20.00
18	Scott Rolen	12.00
19	Tony Gwynn	12.00
20	Barry Bonds	7.00
21	Ken Caminiti	4.00
22	Chipper Jones	20.00
23	Juan Gonzalez	15.00
24	Roger Clemens	8.00
25	Andruw Jones	15.00

1997 SP
Marquee Matchups

A 20-card die-cut set designed to highlight top interleague matchups. When the matching cards are put together, a third player is highlighted in the background. Cards were inserted 1:5 packs.

		MT
Complete Set (30):		50.00
Common Player:		1.00
MM1	Ken Griffey Jr.	8.00
MM2	Andres Galarraga	1.50
MM2	Juan Gonzalez	5.00
MM3	Barry Bonds	2.50
MM4	Mark McGwire	10.00
MM4	Jose Canseco	1.50
MM5	Mike Piazza	5.00
MM6	Tim Salmon	1.50
MM6	Hideo Nomo	2.00
MM7	Tony Gwynn	4.00
MM8	Alex Rodriguez	6.00
MM8	Ken Caminiti	1.00
MM9	Chipper Jones	5.00
MM10	Derek Jeter	5.00
MM10	Andruw Jones	2.50
MM11	Manny Ramirez	2.50
MM12	Jeff Bagwell	3.00
MM12	Matt Williams	1.50
MM13	Greg Maddux	5.00
MM14	Cal Ripken Jr.	6.00
MM14	Brady Anderson	1.00
MM15	Mo Vaughn	2.50
MM16	Gary Sheffield	1.50
MM16	Vladimir Guerrero	3.00
MM17	Jim Thome	2.00
MM18	Barry Larkin	1.50
MM18	Deion Sanders	1.00
MM19	Frank Thomas	5.00
MM20	Sammy Sosa	6.00
MM20	Albert Belle	2.50

1997 SP
Special FX

Color 3-D motion portraits are front and center on these cards that also feature a die-cut design. The rest of the front includes color action photos printed on silver-foil stock.that also feature a die-cut design. Backs have another color photo. The Alex Rodriguez card features the 1996 die-cut design since it was not available in the '96 set and is numbered 49 of 49. Cards were inserted 1:9 packs.

		MT
Complete Set (48):		250.00
Common Player:		3.00
1	Ken Griffey Jr.	25.00
2	Frank Thomas	20.00
3	Barry Bonds	6.00
4	Albert Belle	6.00
5	Mike Piazza	15.00
6	Greg Maddux	15.00
7	Chipper Jones	15.00
8	Cal Ripken Jr.	20.00
9	Jeff Bagwell	10.00
10	Alex Rodriguez	20.00
11	Mark McGwire	30.00
12	Kenny Lofton	6.00
13	Juan Gonzalez	12.00
14	Mo Vaughn	6.00
15	John Smoltz	3.00
16	Derek Jeter	12.00
17	Tony Gwynn	12.00
18	Ivan Rodriguez	6.00
19	Barry Larkin	3.00
20	Sammy Sosa	15.00
21	Mike Mussina	5.00
22	Gary Sheffield	4.00
23	Brady Anderson	3.00
24	Roger Clemens	8.00
25	Ken Caminiti	3.00
26	Roberto Alomar	5.00
27	Hideo Nomo	5.00
28	Bernie Williams	5.00
29	Todd Hundley	3.00
30	Manny Ramirez	6.00
31	Eric Karros	3.00
32	Tim Salmon	4.00
33	Jay Buhner	4.00
34	Andy Pettitte	5.00
35	Jim Thome	5.00
36	Ryne Sandberg	6.00
37	Matt Williams	4.00
38	Ryan Klesko	4.00
39	Jose Canseco	4.00
40	Paul Molitor	4.00
41	Eddie Murray	4.00
42	Darin Erstad	8.00
43	Todd Walker	5.00
44	Wade Boggs	3.00
45	Andruw Jones	10.00
46	Scott Rolen	12.00

47	Vladimir Guerrero	8.00
48	not issued	
49	Alex Rodriguez	20.00

1997 SP SPx Force

Each of the 10 cards in this set feature four different players. Cards are individually numbered to 500. In addition, a number of players signed 100 versions of their SPx Force cards that are also randomly inserted into packs.

		MT
Complete Set (10):		1000.
Common Player:		50.00
1	Ken Griffey Jr., Jay Buhner, Andres Galarraga, Dante Bichette	200.00
2	Albert Belle, Brady Anderson, Mark McGwire, Cecil Fielder	80.00
3	Mo Vaughn, Ken Caminiti, Frank Thomas, Jeff Bagwell	150.00
4	Gary Sheffield, Sammy Sosa, Barry Bonds, Jose Canseco	75.00
5	Greg Maddux, Roger Clemens, John Smoltz, Randy Johnson	125.00
6	Alex Rodriguez, Derek Jeter, Chipper Jones, Rey Ordonez	200.00
7	Todd Hollandsworth, Mike Piazza, Raul Mondesi, Hideo Nomo	100.00
8	Juan Gonzalez, Manny Ramirez, Roberto Alomar, Ivan Rodriguez	100.00
9	Tony Gwynn, Wade Boggs, Eddie Murray, Paul Molitor	90.00
10	Andruw Jones, Vladimir Guerrero, Todd Walker, Scott Rolen	125.00

1997 SP SPx Force Autographs

Ten players signed cards for this insert, which was serially numbered to 100. The cards were randomly seeded in packs except the Mo Vaughn card which was available by redemption.

		MT
Complete Set (10):		3000.
Common Player:		125.00
1	Ken Griffey Jr.	900.00
3	Mo Vaughn	150.00
4	Gary Sheffield	150.00
5	Greg Maddux	400.00
6	Alex Rodriguez	500.00
7	Todd Hollandsworth	125.00
8	Roberto Alomar	200.00
9	Tony Gwynn	350.00
10	Andruw Jones	250.00

1997 SPx

Fifty cards, each featuring a perimeter die-cut design and a 3-D holoview photo, make up the SPx base set. Five different parallel sets

- Steel (1:1 pack), Bronze (1:1), Silver (1:1), Gold (1:17) and Grand Finale (50 per card) - are found as inserts, as are Cornerstones of the Game, Bound for Glory and Bound for Glory Signature cards. Packs contain three cards and carried a suggested retail price of $5.99.

	MT
Complete Set (50):	60.00
Common Player:	.75
Silvers: 1.5x	
Bronzes: 2x	
Steels: 2x to 3x	
Golds: 8x to 12x	
Wax box:	100.00

1	Eddie Murray	1.00
2	Darin Erstad	4.00
3	Tim Salmon	1.00
4	Andruw Jones	3.00
5	Chipper Jones	4.00
6	John Smoltz	.75
7	Greg Maddux	4.00
8	Kenny Lofton	1.50
9	Roberto Alomar	1.25
10	Rafael Palmeiro	.75
11	Brady Anderson	.75
12	Cal Ripken Jr.	5.00
13	Nomar Garciaparra	2.50
14	Mo Vaughn	1.50
15	Ryne Sandberg	1.50
16	Sammy Sosa	4.00
17	Frank Thomas	5.00
18	Albert Belle	1.50
19	Barry Larkin	.75
20	Deion Sanders	.75
21	Manny Ramirez	1.50
22	Jim Thome	1.25
23	Dante Bichette	.75
24	Andres Galarraga	.75
25	Larry Walker	1.00
26	Gary Sheffield	1.00
27	Jeff Bagwell	2.50
28	Raul Mondesi	.75
29	Hideo Nomo	1.50
30	Mike Piazza	4.00
31	Paul Molitor	1.00
32	Todd Walker	1.00
33	Vladimir Guerrero	2.00
34	Todd Hundley	.75
35	Andy Pettitte	1.50
36	Derek Jeter	4.00
37	Jose Canseco	.75
38	Mark McGwire	8.00
39	Scott Rolen	2.50
40	Ron Gant	.75
41	Ken Caminiti	.75
42	Tony Gwynn	3.00
43	Barry Bonds	1.50
44	Jay Buhner	.75
45	Ken Griffey Jr.	6.00
46	Alex Rodriguez	6.00
47	*Jose Cruz Jr.*	5.00
48	Juan Gonzalez	3.00
49	Ivan Rodriguez	1.25
50	Roger Clemens	1.50

1997 SPx Bound for Glory

A 20-card insert utilizing Holoview technology and sequentially numbered to 1,500 per card. Five players (Andruw Jones, Gary Sheffield, Alex Rodriguez, Ken Griffey Jr. and Jeff Bagwell) signed versions of their cards as part of the Bound For Glory Supreme Signatures set.

		MT
Complete Set (20):		550.00
Common Player:		15.00
1	Andruw Jones	20.00
2	Chipper Jones	40.00
3	Greg Maddux	40.00
4	Kenny Lofton	20.00
5	Cal Ripken Jr.	50.00
6	Mo Vaughn	20.00
7	Frank Thomas	50.00
8	Albert Belle	15.00
9	Manny Ramirez	15.00
10	Gary Sheffield	10.00
11	Jeff Bagwell	25.00
12	Mike Piazza	40.00
13	Derek Jeter	40.00
14	Mark McGwire	75.00
15	Tony Gwynn	30.00
16	Ken Caminiti	10.00
17	Barry Bonds	20.00
18	Alex Rodriguez	50.00
19	Ken Griffey Jr.	70.00
20	Juan Gonzalez	30.00

1997 SPx Bound for Glory Supreme Signatures

This five-card set featured autographs from the players and was sequentially numbered to 250.

		MT
Complete Set (5):		1000.
Common Player:		75.00
1	Jeff Bagwell	200.00
2	Ken Griffey Jr.	450.00
3	Andruw Jones	100.00
4	Alex Rodriguez	275.00
5	Gary Sheffield	75.00

1997 SPx Cornerstones of the Game

A 20-card insert utilizing a double-front design highlighting 40 of the top players in the game. Each card is sequentially numbered to 500.

		MT
Complete Set (10):		750.00
Common Player:		25.00
1	Ken Griffey Jr., Barry Bonds	120.00
2	Frank Thomas, Albert Belle	80.00
3	Chipper Jones, Greg Maddux	75.00
4	Tony Gwynn, Paul Molitor	60.00
5	Andruw Jones, Vladimir Guerrero	60.00
6	Jeff Bagwell, Ryne Sandberg	50.00
7	Mike Piazza, Ivan Rodriguez	75.00
8	Cal Ripken Jr., Eddie Murray	80.00
9	Mo Vaughn, Mark McGwire	80.00
10	Alex Rodriguez, Derek Jeter	80.00

1998 SP Authentic

The SP Authentic base set consists of 198 cards, including the 30-card Future Watch subset and one checklist card. The base cards have a color photo inside a thick white border. Inserts include Chirography, Sheer Dominance and SP Authentics.

ROGER CLEMENS
to Toronto Blue Jays™

		MT
Complete Set (198):		50.00
Common Player:		.25
Wax Box:		110.00
1	Travis Lee (Future Watch)	3.00
2	Mike Caruso (Future Watch)	.40
3	Kerry Wood (Future Watch)	6.00
4	Mark Kotsay (Future Watch)	.50
5	Magglio Ordonez (Future Watch)	1.50
6	Scott Elarton (Future Watch)	.25
7	Carl Pavano (Future Watch)	.25
8	A.J. Hinch (Future Watch)	.25
9	Rolando Arrojo (Future Watch)	.75
10	Ben Grieve (Future Watch)	1.50
11	Gabe Alvarez (Future Watch)	.25
12	Mike Kinkade (Future Watch)	1.50
13	Bruce Chen (Future Watch)	.25
14	Juan Encarnacion (Future Watch)	.25
15	Todd Helton (Future Watch)	1.25
16	Aaron Boone (Future Watch)	.25
17	Sean Casey (Future Watch)	.50
18	Ramon Hernandez (Future Watch)	.25
19	Daryle Ward (Future Watch)	.25
20	Paul Konerko (Future Watch)	.50
21	David Ortiz (Future Watch)	.25
22	Derrek Lee (Future Watch)	.25
23	Brad Fullmer (Future Watch)	.40
24	Javier Vazquez (Future Watch)	.25
25	Miguel Tejada (Future Watch)	.75
26	David Dellucci (Future Watch)	.25
27	Alex Gonzalez (Future Watch)	.25
28	Matt Clement (Future Watch)	.25
29	Eric Milton (Future Watch)	.25
30	Russell Branyan (Future Watch)	.25
31	Chuck Finley	.25
32	Jim Edmonds	.25
33	Darren Erstad	1.25
34	Jason Dickson	.25
35	Tim Salmon	.50
36	Cecil Fielder	.40
37	Todd Greene	.25
38	Andy Benes	.25
39	Jay Bell	.25
40	Matt Williams	.50
41	Brian Anderson	.25
42	Karim Garcia	.25
43	Javy Lopez	.25
44	Tom Glavine	.50
45	Greg Maddux	3.00
46	Andruw Jones	1.25
47	Chipper Jones	3.00
48	Ryan Klesko	.50
49	John Smoltz	.40
50	Andres Galarraga	.50
51	Rafael Palmeiro	.50

52	Mike Mussina	1.00
53	Roberto Alomar	1.00
54	Joe Carter	.25
55	Cal Ripken Jr.	4.00
56	Brady Anderson	.25
57	Mo Vaughn	1.25
58	John Valentin	.25
59	Dennis Eckersley	.25
60	Nomar Garciaparra	3.00
61	Pedro J. Martinez	1.00
62	Jeff Blauser	.25
63	Kevin Orie	.25
64	Henry Rodriguez	.25
65	Mark Grace	.50
66	Albert Belle	1.25
67	Mike Cameron	.25
68	Robin Ventura	.25
69	Frank Thomas	4.00
70	Barry Larkin	.50
71	Brett Tomko	.25
72	Willie Greene	.25
73	Reggie Sanders	.25
74	Sandy Alomar Jr.	.40
75	Kenny Lofton	1.25
76	Jaret Wright	1.25
77	David Justice	.25
78	Omar Vizquel	.25
79	Manny Ramirez	1.25
80	Jim Thome	.75
81	Travis Fryman	.25
82	Neifi Perez	.25
83	Mike Lansing	.25
84	Vinny Castilla	.25
85	Larry Walker	.75
86	Dante Bichette	.50
87	Darryl Kile	.25
88	Justin Thompson	.25
89	Damion Easley	.25
90	Tony Clark	.75
91	Bobby Higginson	.25
92	Brian L. Hunter	.25
93	Edgar Renteria	.25
94	Craig Counsell	.25
95	Mike Piazza	3.00
96	Livan Hernandez	.25
97	Todd Zeile	.25
98	Richard Hidalgo	.25
99	Moises Alou	.50
100	Jeff Bagwell	1.50
101	Mike Hampton	.25
102	Craig Biggio	.50
103	Dean Palmer	.25
104	Tim Belcher	.25
105	Jeff King	.25
106	Jeff Conine	.25
107	Johnny Damon	.25
108	Hideo Nomo	1.00
109	Raul Mondesi	.50
110	Gary Sheffield	.75
111	Ramon Martinez	.40
112	Chan Ho Park	.50
113	Eric Young	.25
114	Charles Johnson	.25
115	Eric Karros	.40
116	Bobby Bonilla	.40
117	Jeromy Burnitz	.25
118	Carl Eldred	.25
119	Jeff D'Amico	.25
120	Marquis Grissom	.25
121	Dave Nilsson	.25
122	Brad Radke	.25
123	Marty Cordova	.25
124	Ron Coomer	.25
125	Paul Molitor	1.00
126	Todd Walker	.50
127	Rondell White	.40
128	Mark Grudzielanek	.25
129	Carlos Perez	.25
130	Vladimir Guerrero	1.25
131	Dustin Hermanson	.25
132	Butch Huskey	.25
133	John Franco	.25
134	Rey Ordonez	.25
135	Todd Hundley	.25
136	Edgardo Alfonzo	.25
137	Bobby Jones	.25
138	John Olerud	.40
139	Chili Davis	.25
140	Tino Martinez	.75
141	Andy Pettitte	.75
142	Chuck Knoblauch	.50
143	Bernie Williams	1.00
144	David Cone	.40
145	Derek Jeter	2.50
146	Paul O'Neill	.50
147	Rickey Henderson	.40

148	Jason Giambi	.25
149	Kenny Rogers	.25
150	Scott Rolen	1.50
151	Curt Schilling	.40
152	Ricky Bottalico	.25
153	Mike Lieberthal	.25
154	Francisco Cordova	.25
155	Jose Guillen	.50
156	Jason Schmidt	.25
157	Jason Kendall	.25
158	Kevin Young	.25
159	Delino DeShields	.25
160	Mark McGwire	5.00
161	Ray Lankford	.25
162	Brian Jordan	.25
163	Ron Gant	.25
164	Todd Stottlemyre	.25
165	Ken Caminiti	.50
166	Kevin Brown	.40
167	Trevor Hoffman	.25
168	Steve Finley	.25
169	Wally Joyner	.25
170	Tony Gwynn	2.50
171	Shawn Estes	.25
172	J.T. Snow	.25
173	Jeff Kent	.25
174	Robb Nen	.25
175	Barry Bonds	1.25
176	Randy Johnson	1.00
177	Edgar Martinez	.40
178	Jay Buhner	.75
179	Alex Rodriguez	3.00
180	Ken Griffey Jr.	5.00
181	Ken Cloude	.25
182	Wade Boggs	.50
183	Tony Saunders	.25
184	Wilson Alvarez	.25
185	Fred McGriff	.40
186	Roberto Hernandez	.25
187	Kevin Stocker	.25
188	Fernando Tatis	.40
189	Will Clark	.50
190	Juan Gonzalez	2.50
191	Rusty Greer	.25
192	Ivan Rodriguez	1.25
193	Jose Canseco	.50
194	Carlos Delgado	.25
195	Roger Clemens	1.75
196	Pat Hentgen	.25
197	Randy Myers	.25
198	Checklist(Ken Griffey Jr.)	2.00

1998 SP Authentic Chirography

Chirography is a 30-card insert seeded one per 25 packs. The featured player signed his cards in the white border at the bottom.

		MT
Complete Set (30):		
Common autograph:		15.00
Inserted 1:25		
RA	Roberto Alomar	75.00

RB	Russell Branyan	15.00
SC	Sean Casey	25.00
TC	Tony Clark	30.00
RC	Roger Clemens	175.00
JC	Jose Cruz Jr.	60.00
DE	Darin Erstad	60.00
NG	Nomar Garciaparra	150.00
BG	Ben Grieve	75.00
KG	Ken Griffey Jr.	300.00
VG	Vladimir Guerrero	75.00
TG	Tony Gwynn	160.00
TH	Todd Helton	50.00
LH	Livan Hernandez	25.00
CJ	Charles Johnson	25.00
AJ	Andruw Jones	60.00
CHIP	Chipper Jones	160.00
PK	Paul Konerko	40.00
MK	Mark Kotsay	40.00
RL	Ray Lankford	25.00
TL	Travis Lee	110.00
PM	Paul Molitor	75.00
MM	Mike Mussina	70.00
AR	Alex Rodriguez	180.00
IR	Ivan Rodriguez	80.00
SR	Scott Rolen	75.00
DL	Gary Sheffield	35.00
MT	Miguel Tejada	40.00
JW	Jaret Wright	75.00
MV	Mo Vaughn	80.00

1998 SP Authentic Sheer Dominance

Sheer Dominance is a 42-card insert. The base set is inserted one per three packs. The Sheer Dominance Gold parallel is sequentially numbered to 2,000 and the Titanium parallel is numbered to 100. The cards feature a player photo inside a white border. The background color corresponds to the level of the insert.

	MT
Complete Set (42):	120.00
Common Player:	1.00
Inserted 1:3	
Golds: 3x	
Production 2,000 sets	
SD1 Ken Griffey Jr.	12.00
SD2 Rickey Henderson	1.00
SD3 Jaret Wright	3.00
SD4 Craig Biggio	1.50
SD5 Travis Lee	8.00
SD6 Kenny Lofton	3.00
SD7 Raul Mondesi	1.50
SD8 Cal Ripken Jr.	10.00
SD9 Matt Williams	2.00
SD10 Mark McGwire	12.00
SD11 Alex Rodriguez	8.00
SD12 Fred McGriff	1.00
SD13 Scott Rolen	4.00
SD14 Paul Molitor	2.50

SD15	Nomar Garciaparra	8.00
SD16	Vladimir Guerrero	3.00
SD17	Andruw Jones	3.00
SD18	Manny Ramirez	3.00
SD19	Tony Gwynn	6.00
SD20	Barry Bonds	3.00
SD21	Ben Grieve	4.00
SD22	Ivan Rodriguez	3.00
SD23	Jose Cruz Jr.	3.00
SD24	Pedro J. Martinez	2.50
SD25	Chipper Jones	8.00
SD26	Albert Belle	3.00
SD27	Todd Helton	3.00
SD28	Paul Konerko	1.50
SD29	Sammy Sosa	6.00
SD30	Frank Thomas	10.00
SD31	Greg Maddux	8.00
SD32	Randy Johnson	2.50
SD33	Larry Walker	2.00
SD34	Roberto Alomar	2.50
SD35	Roger Clemens	4.00
SD36	Mo Vaughn	3.00
SD37	Jim Thome	2.00
SD38	Jeff Bagwell	4.00
SD39	Tino Martinez	2.00
SD40	Mike Piazza	8.00
SD41	Derek Jeter	6.00
SD42	Juan Gonzalez	6.00

1998 SP Authentic Sheer Dominance Titanium

Sheer Dominance Titanium is a parallel of the 42-card Sheer Dominance insert. The cards are numbered to 100 and have a gray background with "Titanium" printed across it.

	MT
Common Player:	20.00
Production 100 sets	
SD1 Ken Griffey Jr.	300.00
SD2 Rickey Henderson	20.00
SD3 Jaret Wright	75.00
SD4 Craig Biggio	40.00
SD5 Travis Lee	180.00
SD6 Kenny Lofton	75.00
SD7 Raul Mondesi	40.00
SD8 Cal Ripken Jr.	225.00
SD9 Matt Williams	40.00
SD10 Mark McGwire	250.00
SD11 Alex Rodriguez	200.00
SD12 Fred McGriff	25.00
SD13 Scott Rolen	100.00
SD14 Paul Molitor	60.00
SD15 Nomar Garciaparra	180.00
SD16 Vladimir Guerrero	75.00
SD17 Andruw Jones	75.00
SD18 Manny Ramirez	75.00
SD19 Tony Gwynn	150.00
SD20 Barry Bonds	75.00
SD21 Ben Grieve	100.00
SD22 Ivan Rodriguez	75.00

SD23	Jose Cruz Jr.	75.00
SD24	Pedro J. Martinez	60.00
SD25	Chipper Jones	200.00
SD26	Albert Belle	75.00
SD27	Todd Helton	75.00
SD28	Paul Konerko	30.00
SD29	Sammy Sosa	150.00
SD30	Frank Thomas	225.00
SD31	Greg Maddux	200.00
SD32	Randy Johnson	60.00
SD33	Larry Walker	50.00
SD34	Roberto Alomar	60.00
SD35	Roger Clemens	100.00
SD36	Mo Vaughn	75.00
SD37	Jim Thome	50.00
SD38	Jeff Bagwell	100.00
SD39	Tino Martinez	50.00
SD40	Mike Piazza	200.00
SD41	Derek Jeter	150.00
SD42	Juan Gonzalez	150.00

1998 SP Authentic SP Authentics

The 15 SP Authentics cards can be redeemed for autographed memorabilia. Each card was good for a different signed item from a Major League player. The cards were inserted one per 320 packs.

		MT
Complete Set (15):		
Common Player:		
TC1	Ken Griffey Jr.	
TC2	Ken Griffey Jr.	
TC3	Robin Ventura	
TC4	Raul Mondesi	
TC5	Albert Belle	
TC6	Brian Jordan	
TC7	Roberto Alomar	
TC8	Ken Griffey Jr.	
TC9	Ken Griffey Jr.	
TC10	Tony Gwynn	
TC11	Greg Maddux	
TC12	Alex Rodriguez	
TC13	Gary Sheffield	
TC14	Jay Buhner	
TC15	Ken Griffey Jr.	

1998 SPx Finite

SPx Finite is an all-sequentially numbered set that was released in two 180-card series. The base set for the first series consisted of five subsets: 90 regular cards (numbered to 9,000), 30 Star Focus (7,000), 30 Youth Movement (5,000), 20 Power Explosion (4,000) and 10 Heroes of the Game (2,000). The set is paralleled in the Radiance and Spectrum sets. Radiance regular cards are numbered to 4,500, Star Focus to 3,500, Youth Movement to 2,500, Power Explosion to 1,000 and Heroes of the Game to 100. Spectrum regular cards are numbered to 2,250, Star Focus to 1,750, Youth Movement to 1,250, Power Explosion to 50 and Heroes of the Game to 1. The Series Two base set had 90 regular cards (numbered to 9,000), 30 Power Passion (7,000), 30 Youth Movement (5,000), 20 Tradewinds (4,000) and 10 Cornerstones of the Game (2,000). Series Two also had the Radiance and Spectrum parallel. Radiance regular cards are numbered to 4,500, Power Passion to 3,500, Youth Movement to 2,500, Tradewinds to 1,000 and Cornerstones of the Game to 100. Spectrum regular cards are numbered to 2,250, Power Passion to 1,750, Youth Movement to 1,250, Tradewinds to 50 and Cornerstones of the Game to 1. The only insert is Home Run Hysteria.

		MT
Complete Set (360):		2000.
Common Youth Movement (1-30, 181-210):		1.00
Radiance Youth Movement (2,500): 2x		
Spectrum Youth Movement (1,250): 4x		
Common Power Explosion (31-50):		3.00
Radiance Power Explosion (1,000): 4x		
Common Reg. Card (51-140, 241-330):		1.00
Radiance Regular Card (4,500): 2x		
Spectrum Regular Card (2,250): 4x		
Common Star Focus (141-170):		1.50
Radiance Star Focus (3,500): 2x		
Spectrum Star Focus (1,750): 4x		
Common Heroes of the Game (171-180):		12.00
Common Power Passion (211-240):		1.50
Radiance Power Passion (3,500) 2x		
Spectrum Power Passion (1,750) 4x		
Common Tradewinds (331-350):		2.50
Radiance Tradewinds (1,000) 4x		
Common Cornerstones (351-360):		12.00
Wax Box:		95.00

1	Nomar Garciaparra (Youth Movement)	15.00
2	Miguel Tejada (Youth Movement)	2.50
3	Mike Cameron (Youth Movement)	1.00
4	Ken Cloude (Youth Movement)	2.00
5	Jaret Wright (Youth Movement)	10.00
6	Mark Kotsay (Youth Movement)	2.50
7	Craig Counsell (Youth Movement)	1.00
8	Jose Guillen (Youth Movement)	2.00
9	Neifi Perez (Youth Movement)	1.00
10	Jose Cruz Jr. (Youth Movement)	6.00
11	Brett Tomko (Youth Movement)	1.00
12	Matt Morris (Youth Movement)	1.50
13	Justin Thompson (Youth Movement)	1.00
14	Jeremi Gonzalez (Youth Movement)	1.00
15	Scott Rolen (Youth Movement)	10.00
16	Vladimir Guerrero (Youth Movement)	6.00
17	Brad Fullmer (Youth Movement)	2.50
18	Brian Giles (Youth Movement)	1.00
19	Todd Dunwoody (Youth Movement)	1.00
20	Ben Grieve (Youth Movement)	8.00
21	Juan Encarnacion (Youth Movement)	1.00
22	Aaron Boone (Youth Movement)	1.00
23	Richie Sexson (Youth Movement)	1.00
24	Richard Hidalgo (Youth Movement)	1.00
25	Andruw Jones (Youth Movement)	6.00
26	Todd Helton (Youth Movement)	6.00
27	Paul Konerko (Youth Movement)	3.00
28	Dante Powell (Youth Movement)	1.00
29	Elieser Marrero (Youth Movement)	1.00
30	Derek Jeter (Youth Movement)	15.00
31	Mike Piazza (Power Explosion)	15.00
32	Tony Clark (Power Explosion)	4.00
33	Larry Walker (Power Explosion)	3.00
34	Jim Thome (Power Explosion)	4.00
35	Juan Gonzalez (Power Explosion)	12.00
36	Jeff Bagwell (Power Explosion)	10.00
37	Jay Buhner (Power Explosion)	3.00
38	Tim Salmon (Power Explosion)	3.00
39	Albert Belle (Power Explosion)	6.00
40	Mark McGwire (Power Explosion)	12.00
41	Sammy Sosa (Power Explosion)	8.00
42	Mo Vaughn (Power Explosion)	6.00
43	Manny Ramirez (Power Explosion)	6.00
44	Tino Martinez (Power Explosion)	3.00
45	Frank Thomas (Power Explosion)	20.00
46	Nomar Garciaparra (Power Explosion)	15.00
47	Alex Rodriguez (Power Explosion)	15.00
48	Chipper Jones (Power Explosion)	15.00
49	Barry Bonds (Power Explosion)	6.00
50	Ken Griffey Jr. (Power Explosion)	25.00
51	Jason Dickson	1.00
52	Jim Edmonds	1.50
53	Darin Erstad	4.00
54	Tim Salmon	2.00
55	Chipper Jones	10.00
56	Ryan Klesko	2.00
57	Tom Glavine	1.50
58	Denny Neagle	1.00
59	John Smoltz	1.00
60	Javy Lopez	1.00
61	Roberto Alomar	3.00
62	Rafael Palmeiro	1.50
63	Mike Mussina	4.00
64	Cal Ripken Jr.	12.00
65	Mo Vaughn	4.00
66	Tim Naehring	1.00
67	John Valentin	1.00
68	Mark Grace	2.00
69	Kevin Orie	1.00
70	Sammy Sosa	6.00
71	Albert Belle	4.00
72	Frank Thomas	12.00
73	Robin Ventura	1.50
74	David Justice	2.00
75	Kenny Lofton	4.00
76	Omar Vizquel	1.00
77	Manny Ramirez	4.00
78	Jim Thome	2.50
79	Dante Bichette	2.00
80	Larry Walker	2.00
81	Vinny Castilla	1.50
82	Ellis Burks	1.00
83	Bobby Higginson	1.00
84	Brian L. Hunter	1.00
85	Tony Clark	2.50
86	Mike Hampton	1.00
87	Jeff Bagwell	6.00
88	Craig Biggio	2.00
89	Derek Bell	1.00
90	Mike Piazza	10.00
91	Ramon Martinez	1.00
92	Raul Mondesi	2.00
93	Hideo Nomo	3.00
94	Eric Karros	1.50
95	Paul Molitor	3.00
96	Marty Cordova	1.00
97	Brad Radke	1.00
98	Mark Grudzielanek	1.00
99	Carlos Perez	1.00
100	Rondell White	1.50
101	Todd Hundley	1.00
102	Edgardo Alfonzo	1.00
103	John Franco	1.00
104	John Olerud	1.50
105	Tino Martinez	2.00
106	David Cone	1.50
107	Paul O'Neill	1.50
108	Andy Pettitte	2.50
109	Bernie Williams	3.00
110	Rickey Henderson	1.50
111	Jason Giambi	1.00
112	Matt Stairs	1.00
113	Gregg Jefferies	1.00
114	Rico Brogna	1.00
115	Curt Schilling	1.50
116	Jason Schmidt	1.00
117	Jose Guillen	2.00
118	Kevin Young	1.00
119	Ray Lankford	1.00
120	Mark McGwire	8.00
121	Delino DeShields	1.00
122	Ken Caminiti	2.00
123	Tony Gwynn	8.00
124	Trevor Hoffman	1.00
125	Barry Bonds	4.00
126	Jeff Kent	1.00
127	Shawn Estes	1.00
128	J.T. Snow	1.00
129	Jay Buhner	2.00
130	Ken Griffey Jr.	15.00
131	Dan Wilson	1.00
132	Edgar Martinez	1.00
133	Alex Rodriguez	10.00
134	Rusty Greer	1.00
135	Juan Gonzalez	8.00
136	Fernando Tatis	1.00
137	Ivan Rodriguez	4.00
138	Carlos Delgado	1.50
139	Pat Hentgen	1.00
140	Roger Clemens	6.00
141	Chipper Jones (Star Focus)	12.00
142	Greg Maddux (Star Focus)	12.00
143	Rafael Palmeiro (Star Focus)	2.00
144	Mike Mussina (Star Focus)	4.00
145	Cal Ripken Jr. (Star Focus)	14.00
146	Nomar Garciaparra (Star Focus)	12.00
147	Mo Vaughn (Star Focus)	5.00
148	Sammy Sosa (Star Focus)	6.00
149	Albert Belle (Star Focus)	5.00
150	Frank Thomas (Star Focus)	14.00
151	Jim Thome (Star Focus)	4.00
152	Kenny Lofton (Star Focus)	5.00
153	Manny Ramirez (Star Focus)	5.00
154	Larry Walker (Star Focus)	2.50
155	Jeff Bagwell (Star Focus)	8.00
156	Craig Biggio (Star Focus)	1.50
157	Mike Piazza (Star Focus)	12.00
158	Paul Molitor (Star Focus)	4.00
159	Derek Jeter (Star Focus)	10.00
160	Tino Martinez (Star Focus)	2.50
161	Curt Schilling (Star Focus)	1.50
162	Mark McGwire (Star Focus)	10.00
163	Tony Gwynn (Star Focus)	8.00
164	Barry Bonds (Star Focus)	5.00
165	Ken Griffey Jr. (Star Focus)	18.00
166	Randy Johnson (Star Focus)	3.00
167	Alex Rodriguez (Star Focus)	12.00
168	Juan Gonzalez (Star Focus)	10.00
169	Ivan Rodriguez (Star Focus)	5.00
170	Roger Clemens (Star Focus)	8.00
171	Greg Maddux (Heroes of the Game)	30.00
172	Cal Ripken Jr. (Heroes of the Game)	40.00
173	Frank Thomas (Heroes of the Game)	40.00
174	Jeff Bagwell (Heroes of the Game)	20.00
175	Mike Piazza (Heroes of the Game)	30.00
176	Mark McGwire (Heroes of the Game)	25.00
177	Barry Bonds (Heroes of the Game)	12.00
178	Ken Griffey Jr. (Heroes of the Game)	50.00

179	Alex Rodriguez (Heroes of the Game)	30.00
180	Roger Clemens (Heroes of the Game)	20.00
181	Mike Caruso	1.00
182	David Ortiz	2.00
183	Gabe Alvarez	1.00
184	Gary Matthews Jr.	1.00
185	Kerry Wood	20.00
186	Carl Pavano	1.00
187	Alex Gonzalez	1.00
188	Masato Yoshii	2.00
189	Larry Sutton	1.00
190	Russell Branyan	1.00
191	Bruce Chen	1.00
192	Rolando Arrojo	2.50
193	Ryan Christenson	1.00
194	Cliff Politte	1.00
195	A.J. Hinch	1.00
196	Kevin Witt	1.00
197	Daryle Ward	1.00
198	Corey Koskie	1.00
199	Mike Lowell	1.00
200	Travis Lee	10.00
201	Kevin Millwood	1.00
202	Robert Smith	1.00
203	Magglio Ordonez	1.00
204	Eric Milton	1.00
205	Geoff Jenkins	1.00
206	Rich Butler	1.00
207	*Mike Kinkade*	1.00
208	Braden Looper	1.00
209	Matt Clement	1.00
210	Derrek Lee	1.00
211	Randy Johnson	3.00
212	John Smoltz	1.50
213	Roger Clemens	5.00
214	Curt Schilling	2.00
215	Pedro J. Martinez	4.00
216	Vinny Castilla	1.00
217	Jose Cruz Jr.	4.00
218	Jim Thome	2.50
219	Alex Rodriguez	10.00
220	Frank Thomas	10.00
221	Tim Salmon	2.00
222	Larry Walker	2.50
223	Albert Belle	4.00
224	Manny Ramirez	4.00
225	Mark McGwire	18.00
226	Mo Vaughn	4.00
227	Andres Galarraga	2.00
228	Scott Rolen	4.00
229	Travis Lee	8.00
230	Mike Piazza	10.00
231	Nomar Garciaparra	10.00
232	Andruw Jones	4.00
233	Barry Bonds	4.00
234	Jeff Bagwell	5.00
235	Juan Gonzalez	8.00
236	Tino Martinez	2.00
237	Vladimir Guerrero	4.00
238	Rafael Palmeiro	2.00
239	Russell Branyan	1.00
240	Ken Griffey Jr.	15.00
241	Cecil Fielder	1.00
242	Chuck Finley	1.00
243	Jay Bell	1.00
244	Andy Benes	1.00
245	Matt Williams	1.50
246	Brian Anderson	1.00
247	David Dellucci	1.00
248	Andres Galarraga	2.00
249	Andruw Jones	2.50
250	Greg Maddux	6.00
251	Brady Anderson	1.00
252	Joe Carter	1.00
253	Eric Davis	1.00
254	Pedro J. Martinez	2.50
255	Nomar Garciaparra	6.00
256	Dennis Eckersley	1.00
257	Henry Rodriguez	1.00
258	Jeff Blauser	1.00
259	Jaime Navarro	1.00
260	Ray Durham	1.00
261	Chris Stynes	1.00
262	Willie Greene	1.00
263	Reggie Sanders	1.00
264	Bret Boone	1.00
265	Barry Larkin	1.50
266	Travis Fryman	1.00
267	Charles Nagy	1.00
268	Sandy Alomar Jr.	1.00
269	Darryl Kile	1.00
270	Mike Lansing	1.00
271	Pedro Astacio	1.00
272	Damion Easley	1.00
273	Joe Randa	1.00
274	Luis Gonzalez	1.00
275	Mike Piazza	6.00
276	Todd Zeile	1.00
277	Edgar Renteria	1.00
278	Livan Hernandez	1.00
279	Cliff Floyd	1.00
280	Moises Alou	1.50
281	Billy Wagner	1.00
282	Jeff King	1.00
283	Hal Morris	1.00
284	Johnny Damon	1.00
285	Dean Palmer	1.00
286	Tim Belcher	1.00
287	Eric Young	1.00
288	Bobby Bonilla	1.00
289	Gary Sheffield	1.50
290	Chan Ho Park	1.50
291	Charles Johnson	1.00
292	Jeff Cirillo	1.00
293	Jeromy Burnitz	1.00
294	Jose Valentin	1.00
295	Marquis Grissom	1.00
296	Todd Walker	1.00
297	Terry Steinbach	1.00
298	Rick Aguilera	1.00
299	Vladimir Guerrero	2.50
300	Rey Ordonez	1.00
301	Butch Huskey	1.00
302	Bernard Gilkey	1.00
303	Mariano Rivera	1.50
304	Chuck Knoblauch	1.50
305	Derek Jeter	5.00
306	Ricky Bottalico	1.00
307	Bob Abreu	1.00
308	Scott Rolen	3.00
309	Al Martin	1.00
310	Jason Kendall	1.00
311	Brian Jordan	1.00
312	Ron Gant	1.00
313	Todd Stottlemyre	1.00
314	Greg Vaughn	1.00
315	J. Kevin Brown	1.00
316	Wally Joyner	1.00
317	Robb Nen	1.00
318	Orel Hershiser	1.00
319	Russ Davis	1.00
320	Randy Johnson	2.00
321	Quinton McCracken	1.00
322	Tony Saunders	1.00
323	Wilson Alvarez	1.00
324	Wade Boggs	1.50
325	Fred McGriff	1.50
326	Lee Stevens	1.00
327	John Wetteland	1.00
328	Jose Canseco	1.50
329	Randy Myers	1.00
330	Jose Cruz Jr.	2.50
331	Matt Williams	3.00
332	Andres Galarraga	4.00
333	Walt Weiss	2.50
334	Joe Carter	2.50
335	Pedro J. Martinez	5.00
336	Henry Rodriguez	2.50
337	Travis Fryman	2.50
338	Darryl Kile	2.50
339	Mike Lansing	2.50
340	Mike Piazza	12.00
341	Moises Alou	3.00
342	Charles Johnson	2.50
343	Chuck Knoblauch	4.00
344	Rickey Henderson	2.50
345	J. Kevin Brown	3.00
346	Orel Hershiser	2.50
347	Wade Boggs	3.00
348	Fred McGriff	3.00
349	Jose Canseco	3.00
350	Gary Sheffield	3.00
351	Travis Lee	20.00
352	Nomar Garciaparra	25.00
353	Frank Thomas	30.00
354	Cal Ripken Jr.	30.00
355	Mark McGwire	50.00
356	Mike Piazza	30.00
357	Alex Rodriguez	30.00
358	Barry Bonds	10.00
359	Tony Gwynn	20.00
360	Ken Griffey Jr.	40.00

A player's name in *italic* type indicates a rookie card.

1998 SPx Finite Home Run Hysteria

Home Run Hysteria is a 10-card insert in SPx Finite Series Two. The cards were sequentially numbered to 62.

	MT
Common Player:	75.00
Production 62 sets	
HR1 Ken Griffey Jr.	350.00
HR2 Mark McGwire	450.00
HR3 Sammy Sosa	300.00
HR4 Albert Belle	120.00
HR5 Alex Rodriguez	250.00
HR6 Greg Vaughn	75.00
HR7 Andres Galarraga	90.00
HR8 Vinny Castilla	75.00
HR9 Juan Gonzalez	200.00
HR10 Chipper Jones	250.00

1998 SPx Finite Radiance Cornerstones

Radiance Cornerstones of the Game is a parallel of the 10-card subset. The cards have two images of the player on the front and are numbered to 100.

	MT
Common Player (100 sets):	40.00
351 Travis Lee	100.00
352 Nomar Garciaparra	200.00
353 Frank Thomas	175.00
354 Cal Ripken Jr.	225.00
355 Mark McGwire	350.00
356 Mike Piazza	200.00
357 Alex Rodriguez	200.00
358 Barry Bonds	75.00
359 Tony Gwynn	150.00
360 Ken Griffey Jr.	300.00

1998 SPx Finite Radiance Heroes of the Game

Radiance Heroes of the Game is a parallel of the 10-card subset. The cards have a horizontal layout and are numbered to 100.

	MT
Common Player:	50.00
Production 100 sets	
171 Greg Maddux	150.00
172 Cal Ripken Jr.	200.00
173 Frank Thomas	150.00
174 Jeff Bagwell	60.00
175 Mike Piazza	150.00
176 Mark McGwire	300.00
177 Barry Bonds	50.00
178 Ken Griffey Jr.	250.00
179 Alex Rodriguez	150.00
180 Roger Clemens	90.00

1998 SPx Finite Spectrum Power Explosion

Spectrum Power Explosion is a parallel of the 20-card subset in Series One. The horizontal cards have two images of the player and are numbered to 50.

	MT
Common Player:	40.00
Semistars:	100.00
Production 50 sets	
31 Mike Piazza	250.00
32 Tony Clark	75.00
33 Larry Walker	75.00
34 Jim Thome	75.00
35 Juan Gonzalez	200.00
36 Jeff Bagwell	125.00
37 Jay Buhner	60.00
38 Tim Salmon	40.00
39 Albert Belle	100.00
40 Mark McGwire	500.00
41 Sammy Sosa	250.00
42 Mo Vaughn	100.00
43 Manny Ramirez	100.00
44 Tino Martinez	60.00
45 Frank Thomas	250.00
46 Nomar Garciaparra	250.00
47 Alex Rodriguez	250.00
48 Chipper Jones	250.00
49 Barry Bonds	100.00
50 Ken Griffey Jr.	400.00

1998 SPx Finite Spectrum Tradewinds

Spectrum Tradewinds is a parallel of the 20-card subset in Series Two. The horizontal cards have two images of the player and are numbered to 50.

	MT
Common Player (50 sets):	40.00
331 Matt Williams	60.00
332 Andres Galarraga	80.00
333 Walt Weiss	40.00
334 Joe Carter	60.00
335 Pedro J. Martinez	150.00
336 Henry Rodriguez	40.00
337 Travis Fryman	50.00
338 Darryl Kile	40.00
339 Mike Lansing	40.00
340 Mike Piazza	300.00
341 Moises Alou	60.00
342 Charles Johnson	40.00
343 Chuck Knoblauch	80.00
344 Rickey Henderson	50.00
345 Kevin Brown	60.00
346 Orel Hershiser	40.00
347 Wade Boggs	60.00
348 Fred McGriff	60.00
349 Jose Canseco	80.00
350 Gary Sheffield	80.00

1998 Sports Illustrated

The second of three Sports Illustrated releases of 1998 from Fleer contained 200 cards and fea-tured exclusive Sports Illustrated photography and commentary. Cards arrived in six-card packs and carried a Sports Illustrated logo in a top corner. The set included a Travis Lee One to Watch cards (#201) that was inserted just before going to press. Subsets included: Baseball's Best (129-148), One to Watch (149-176), and '97 in Review (177-200). Inserts sets include: Extra Edition and First Edition parallels, Autographs, Covers, Editor's Choice and Opening Day Mini Posters.

	MT
Complete Set (201):	25.00
Common Player:	.10
Wax Box:	42.00
1 Edgardo Alfonzo	.10
2 Roberto Alomar	.50
3 Sandy Alomar	.10
4 Moises Alou	.20
5 Brady Anderson	.20
6 Garret Anderson	.10
7 Kevin Appier	.10
8 Jeff Bagwell	1.00
9 Jay Bell	.10
10 Albert Belle	.75
11 Dante Bichette	.25
12 Craig Biggio	.20
13 Barry Bonds	.75
14 Bobby Bonilla	.20
15 Kevin Brown	.20
16 Jay Buhner	.25
17 Ellis Burks	.20
18 Mike Cameron	.20
19 Ken Caminiti	.20
20 Jose Canseco	.25
21 Joe Carter	.20
22 Vinny Castilla	.10
23 Jeff Cirillo	.10
24 Tony Clark	.50
25 Will Clark	.25
26 Roger Clemens	1.00
27 David Cone	.20
28 Jose Cruz Jr.	1.00
29 Carlos Delgado	.10
30 Jason Dickson	.10
31 Dennis Eckersley	.10
32 Jim Edmonds	.20
33 Scott Erickson	.10
34 Darin Erstad	.75
35 Shawn Estes	.10
36 Jeff Fassero	.10
37 Alex Fernandez	.10
38 Chuck Finley	.10
39 Steve Finley	.10
40 Travis Fryman	.10
41 Andres Galarraga	.25
42 Ron Gant	.20
43 Nomar Garciaparra	1.50
44 Jason Giambi	.10
45 Tom Glavine	.20
46 Juan Gonzalez	1.50
47 Mark Grace	.25
48 Willie Green	.10
49 Rusty Greer	.20
50 Ben Grieve	1.25
51 Ken Griffey Jr.	3.00
52 Mark Grudzielanek	.10
53 Vladimir Guerrero	1.00
54 Juan Guzman	.10
55 Tony Gwynn	1.50
56 Joey Hamilton	.10
57 Rickey Henderson	.10
58 Pat Hentgen	.20
59 Livan Hernandez	.20
60 Bobby Higginson	.10
61 Todd Hundley	.20
62 Hideki Irabu	.35
63 John Jaha	.10
64 Derek Jeter	1.50
65 Charles Johnson	.10
66 Randy Johnson	.50
67 Andruw Jones	.75
68 Bobby Jones	.10
69 Chipper Jones	2.00
70 Brian Jordan	.10
71 David Justice	.25
72 Eric Karros	.10
73 Jeff Kent	.10
74 Jimmy Key	.10
75 Darryl Kile	.10
76 Jeff King	.10
77 Ryan Klesko	.30
78 Chuck Knoblauch	.25
79 Ray Lankford	.10
80 Barry Larkin	.20
81 Kenny Lofton	.75
82 Greg Maddux	2.00
83 Al Martin	.10
84 Edgar Martinez	.20
85 Pedro Martinez	.25
86 Tino Martinez	.25
87 Mark McGwire	4.00
88 Paul Molitor	.40
89 Raul Mondesi	.25
90 Jamie Moyer	.10
91 Mike Mussina	.60
92 Tim Naehring	.10
93 Charles Nagy	.10
94 Denny Neagle	.20
95 Dave Nilsson	.10
96 Hideo Nomo	.60
97 Rey Ordonez	.10
98 Dean Palmer	.10
99 Rafael Palmeiro	.20
100 Andy Pettitte	.50
101 Mike Piazza	2.00
102 Brad Radke	.10
103 Manny Ramirez	.60
104 Edgar Renteria	.10
105 Cal Ripken Jr.	2.50
106 Alex Rodriguez	2.00
107 Henry Rodriguez	.10
108 Ivan Rodriguez	.75
109 Scott Rolen	1.00
110 Tim Salmon	.30
111 Curt Schilling	.25
112 Gary Sheffield	.25
113 John Smoltz	.20
114 J.T. Snow	.10
115 Sammy Sosa	2.00
116 Matt Stairs	.10
117 Shannon Stewart	.10
118 Frank Thomas	2.00
119 Jim Thome	.40
120 Justin Thompson	.20
121 Mo Vaughn	.75
122 Robin Ventura	.20
123 Larry Walker	.40
124 Rondell White	.20
125 Bernie Williams	.60
126 Matt Williams	.25
127 Tony Womack	.10
128 Jaret Wright	1.75
129 Edgar Renteria (Baseball's Best)	.10
130 Kenny Lofton (Baseball's Best)	.40
131 Tony Gwynn (Baseball's Best)	.75
132 Mark McGwire (Baseball's Best)	2.00
133 Craig Biggio (Baseball's Best)	.10
134 Charles Johnson (Baseball's Best)	.10
135 J.T. Snow (Baseball's Best)	.10
136 Ken Caminiti (Baseball's Best)	.10

137	Vladimir Guerrero (Baseball's Best)	.40
138	Jim Edmonds (Baseball's Best)	.10
139	Randy Johnson (Baseball's Best)	.25
140	Darryl Kile (Baseball's Best)	.10
141	John Smoltz (Baseball's Best)	.10
142	Greg Maddux (Baseball's Best)	1.00
143	Andy Pettitte (Baseball's Best)	.25
144	Ken Griffey Jr. (Baseball's Best)	1.50
145	Mike Piazza (Baseball's Best)	1.00
146	Todd Greene (Baseball's Best)	.10
147	Vinny Castilla (Baseball's Best)	.10
148	Derek Jeter (Baseball's Best)	.75
149	Travis Lee (One to Watch)	5.00
150	Mike Gulan (One to Watch)	.10
151	Randall Simon (One to Watch)	.20
152	Michael Coleman (One to Watch)	.10
153	Brian Rose (One to Watch)	.25
154	*Scott Eyre* (One to Watch)	.25
155	*Magglio Ordonez* (One to Watch)	.75
156	Todd Helton (One to Watch)	.75
157	Juan Encarnacion (One to Watch)	.10
158	Mark Kotsay (One to Watch)	.50
159	Josh Booty (One to Watch)	.10
160	*Melvin Rosario* (One to Watch)	.25
161	Shane Halter (One to Watch)	.10
162	Paul Konerko (One to Watch)	1.00
163	*Henry Blanco* (One to Watch)	.20
164	Antone Williamson (One to Watch)	.10
165	Brad Fullmer (One to Watch)	.20
166	Ricky Ledee (One to Watch)	.50
167	Ben Grieve (One to Watch)	.60
168	*Frank Catalanotto* (One to Watch)	.20
169	Bobby Estalella (One to Watch)	.10
170	Dennis Reyes (One to Watch)	.10
171	Kevin Polcovich (One to Watch)	.10
172	Jacob Cruz (One to Watch)	.10
173	Ken Cloude (One to Watch)	.10
174	Eli Marrero (One to Watch)	.10
175	Fernando Tatis (One to Watch)	.10
176	Tom Evans (One to Watch)	.10
177	Everett, Garciaparra (97 in Review)	.75
178	Eric Davis (97 in Review)	.10
179	Roger Clemens (97 in Review)	.50
180	Butler, Murray (97 in Review)	.10
181	Frank Thomas (97 in Review)	1.25
182	Curt Schilling (97 in Review)	.10
183	Jeff Bagwell (97 in Review)	.50
184	McGwire, Griffey (97 in Review)	1.50
185	Kevin Brown (97 in Review)	.10
186	Cordova, Rincon (97 in Review)	.10
187	Charles Johnson (97 in Review)	.10
188	Hideki Irabu (97 in Review)	.20
189	Tony Gwynn (97 in Review)	.75
190	Sandy Alomar (97 in Review)	.10
191	Ken Griffey Jr. (97 in Review)	1.50
192	Larry Walker (97 in Review)	.20
193	Roger Clemens (97 in Review)	.50
194	Pedro Martinez (97 in Review)	.20
195	Nomar Garciaparra (97 in Review)	.75

196	Scott Rolen (97 in Review)	.50
197	Brian Anderson (97 in Review)	.10
198	Tony Saunders (97 in Review)	.10
199	Fla. Celebration (97 in Review)	.10
200	Livan Hernandez (97 in Review)	.10
201	Travis Lee	4.00

1998 Sports Illustrated Autographs

This six-card insert featured autographs of players with the following production: Brock 500, Cruz Jr. 250, Fingers 500, Grieve 250, Konerko 250 and Robinson 500. The Konerko and Greive cards were availble through redemptions.

	MT
Complete Set (6):	400.00
Common Player:	30.00
Jose Cruz Jr. (250)	100.00
Ben Grieve (250)	90.00
Paul Konerko (250)	60.00
Lou Brock (500)	75.00
Rollie Fingers (500)	30.00
Brooks Robinson (250)	75.00

1998 Sports Illustrated Covers

This 10-card insert set pictures actual Sports Illustrated covers on trading cards. The cards are numbered with a "C" prefix and inserted one per nine packs.

		MT
Complete Set (10):		45.00
Common Player:		2.50
Inserted 1:9		
C1	Griffey, Piazza	10.00
C2	Derek Jeter	6.00
C3	Ken Griffey Jr.	12.00
C4	Cal Ripken Jr.	10.00
C5	Manny Ramirez	4.00
C6	Jay Buhner	2.50
C7	Matt Williams	3.00
C8	Randy Johnson	4.00
C9	Deion Sanders	2.50
C10	Jose Canseco	2.50

A player's name in *italic* type indicates a rookie card.

1998 Sports Illustrated Editor's Choice

Ken GRIFFEY, Jr.

Editor's Choice includes 10 top players in 1998 as profiled by the editors of Sports Illustrated. Cards are numbered with an "EC" prefix and seeded one per 24 packs.

		MT
Complete Set (10):		100.00
Common Player:		4.00
Inserted 1:24		
EP1	Ken Griffey Jr.	20.00
EP2	Alex Rodriguez	12.00
EP3	Frank Thomas	15.00
EP4	Mark McGwire	25.00
EP5	Greg Maddux	12.00
EP6	Derek Jeter	12.00
EP7	Cal Ripken Jr.	15.00
EP8	Nomar Garciaparra	12.00
EP9	Jeff Bagwell	8.00
EP10	Jose Cruz Jr.	8.00

1998 Sports Illustrated Extra Edition

Extra Edition was a 201-card parallel set that included a holofoil stamp on the front and sequential numbering to 250 on the back. There was also a First Edition version of these that was identical on the front, but contained the text "The Only 1 of 1 First Edition" written in purple lettering on the card back.

		MT
Common Player:		8.00
Semistars:		20.00
Production 250 sets		
1	Edgardo Alfonzo	8.00
2	Roberto Alomar	40.00
3	Sandy Alomar	8.00
4	Moises Alou	12.00
5	Brady Anderson	12.00
6	Garret Anderson	8.00
7	Kevin Appier	8.00
8	Jeff Bagwell	80.00
9	Jay Bell	8.00
10	Albert Belle	50.00
11	Dante Bichette	15.00
12	Craig Biggio	15.00
13	Barry Bonds	50.00
14	Bobby Bonilla	12.00
15	Kevin Brown	15.00
16	Jay Buhner	15.00
17	Ellis Burks	.20
18	Mike Cameron	15.00

19	Ken Caminiti	15.00
20	Jose Canseco	15.00
21	Joe Carter	12.00
22	Vinny Castilla	8.00
23	Jeff Cirillo	8.00
24	Tony Clark	35.00
25	Will Clark	20.00
26	Roger Clemens	80.00
27	David Cone	12.00
28	Jose Cruz Jr.	50.00
29	Carlos Delgado	8.00
30	Jason Dickson	8.00
31	Dennis Eckersley	8.00
32	Jim Edmonds	12.00
33	Scott Erickson	8.00
34	Darin Erstad	50.00
35	Shawn Estes	8.00
36	Jeff Fassero	8.00
37	Alex Fernandez	8.00
38	Chuck Finley	8.00
39	Steve Finley	8.00
40	Travis Fryman	12.00
41	Andres Galarraga	20.00
42	Ron Gant	12.00
43	Nomar Garciaparra	100.00
44	Jason Giambi	8.00
45	Tom Glavine	15.00
46	Juan Gonzalez	100.00
47	Mark Grace	15.00
48	Willie Green	8.00
49	Rusty Greer	12.00
50	Ben Grieve	75.00
51	Ken Griffey Jr.	200.00
52	Mark Grudzielanek	8.00
53	Vladimir Guerrero	50.00
54	Juan Guzman	8.00
55	Tony Gwynn	100.00
56	Joey Hamilton	8.00
57	Rickey Henderson	8.00
58	Pat Hentgen	12.00
59	Livan Hernandez	12.00
60	Bobby Higginson	8.00
61	Todd Hundley	12.00
62	Hideki Irabu	20.00
63	John Jaha	8.00
64	Derek Jeter	100.00
65	Charles Johnson	8.00
66	Randy Johnson	40.00
67	Andruw Jones	50.00
68	Bobby Jones	8.00
69	Chipper Jones	120.00
70	Brian Jordan	8.00
71	David Justice	20.00
72	Eric Karros	8.00
73	Jeff Kent	8.00
74	Jimmy Key	8.00
75	Darryl Kile	8.00
76	Jeff King	8.00
77	Ryan Klesko	25.00
78	Chuck Knoblauch	20.00
79	Ray Lankford	8.00
80	Barry Larkin	15.00
81	Kenny Lofton	50.00
82	Greg Maddux	120.00
83	Al Martin	8.00
84	Edgar Martinez	12.00
85	Pedro Martinez	25.00
86	Tino Martinez	20.00
87	Mark McGwire	250.00
88	Paul Molitor	35.00
89	Raul Mondesi	20.00
90	Jamie Moyer	8.00
91	Mike Mussina	40.00
92	Tim Naehring	8.00
93	Charles Nagy	8.00
94	Denny Neagle	12.00
95	Dave Nilsson	8.00
96	Hideo Nomo	40.00
97	Rey Ordonez	8.00
98	Dean Palmer	8.00
99	Rafael Palmeiro	15.00
100	Andy Pettitte	35.00
101	Mike Piazza	120.00
102	Brad Radke	8.00
103	Manny Ramirez	40.00
104	Edgar Renteria	8.00
105	Cal Ripken Jr.	150.00
106	Alex Rodriguez	120.00
107	Henry Rodriguez	8.00
108	Ivan Rodriguez	50.00
109	Scott Rolen	60.00
110	Tim Salmon	25.00
111	Curt Schilling	15.00
112	Gary Sheffield	20.00
113	John Smoltz	12.00
114	J.T. Snow	8.00
115	Sammy Sosa	120.00
116	Matt Stairs	8.00
117	Shannon Stewart	8.00
118	Frank Thomas	125.00
119	Jim Thome	30.00
120	Justin Thompson	15.00
121	Mo Vaughn	50.00
122	Robin Ventura	15.00
123	Larry Walker	25.00
124	Rondell White	15.00
125	Bernie Williams	40.00
126	Matt Williams	20.00
127	Tony Womack	8.00
128	Jaret Wright	100.00
129	Edgar Renteria (Baseball's Best)	8.00
130	Kenny Lofton (Baseball's Best)	25.00
131	Tony Gwynn (Baseball's Best)	50.00
132	Mark McGwire (Baseball's Best)	100.00
133	Craig Biggio (Baseball's Best)	12.00
134	Charles Johnson (Baseball's Best)	8.00
135	J.T. Snow (Baseball's Best)	8.00
136	Ken Caminiti (Baseball's Best)	12.00
137	Vladimir Guerrero (Baseball's Best)	25.00
138	Jim Edmonds (Baseball's Best)	12.00
139	Randy Johnson (Baseball's Best)	20.00
140	Darryl Kile (Baseball's Best)	8.00
141	John Smoltz (Baseball's Best)	12.00
142	Greg Maddux (Baseball's Best)	60.00
143	Andy Pettitte (Baseball's Best)	20.00
144	Ken Griffey Jr. (Baseball's Best)	100.00
145	Mike Piazza (Baseball's Best)	60.00
146	Todd Greene (Baseball's Best)	8.00
147	Vinny Castilla (Baseball's Best)	8.00
148	Derek Jeter (Baseball's Best)	25.00
149	Travis Lee (One to Watch)	100.00
150	Mike Gulan (One to Watch)	8.00
151	Randall Simon (One to Watch)	12.00
152	Michael Coleman (One to Watch)	8.00
153	Brian Rose (One to Watch)	15.00
154	*Scott Eyre* (One to Watch)	12.00
155	Magglio Ordonez (One to Watch)	25.00
156	Todd Helton (One to Watch)	35.00
157	Juan Encarnacion (One to Watch)	8.00
158	Mark Kotsay (One to Watch)	20.00
159	Josh Booty (One to Watch)	8.00
160	*Melvin Rosario* (One to Watch)	12.00
161	Shane Halter (One to Watch)	8.00
162	Paul Konerko (One to Watch)	35.00
163	*Henry Blanco* (One to Watch)	8.00
164	Antone Williamson (One to Watch)	8.00
165	Brad Fullmer (One to Watch)	15.00
166	Ricky Ledee (One to Watch)	20.00
167	Ben Grieve (One to Watch)	35.00
168	Frank Catalanotto (One to Watch)	8.00
169	Bobby Estalella (One to Watch)	8.00
170	Dennis Reyes (One to Watch)	8.00
171	Kevin Polcovich (One to Watch)	8.00
172	Jacob Cruz (One to Watch)	8.00
173	Ken Cloude (One to Watch)	8.00
174	Eli Marrero (One to Watch)	8.00
175	Fernando Tatis (One to Watch)	8.00
176	Tom Evans (One to Watch)	8.00
177	Everett, Garciaparra (97 in Review)	25.00
178	Eric Davis (97 in Review)	8.00
179	Roger Clemens (97 in Review)	40.00
180	Butler, Murray (97 in Review)	8.00
181	Frank Thomas (97 in Review)	75.00
182	Curt Schilling (97 in Review)	8.00
183	Jeff Bagwell (97 in Review)	40.00
184	McGwire, Griffey (97 in Review)	80.00
185	Kevin Brown (97 in Review)	8.00
186	Cordova, Rincon (97 in Review)	8.00
187	Charles Johnson (97 in Review)	8.00
188	Hideki Irabu (97 in Review)	12.00
189	Tony Gwynn (97 in Review)	40.00
190	Sandy Alomar (97 in Review)	8.00
191	Ken Griffey Jr. (97 in Review)	100.00
192	Larry Walker (97 in Review)	15.00
193	Roger Clemens (97 in Review)	40.00
194	Pedro Martinez (97 in Review)	20.00
195	Nomar Garciaparra (97 in Review)	40.00
196	Scott Rolen (97 in Review)	30.00
197	Brian Anderson (97 in Review)	8.00
198	Tony Saunders (97 in Review)	8.00
199	Fla. Celebration (97 in Review)	15.00
200	Livan Hernandez (97 in Review)	12.00

1998 Sports Illustrated Mini-Posters

Thirty 5" x 7" mini-posters were available at a rate of one per pack. The posters took the top player or two from each team and added their 1998 schedule. Backs were blank so the cards are numbered on the front with a "OD" prefix.

	MT
Complete Set (30):	8.00
Common Player:	.15
Inserted 1:1	
OD1 Tim Salmon	.25
OD2 Travis Lee	1.50
OD3 Smoltz, Maddux	.75
OD4 Cal Ripken Jr.	1.00
OD5 Nomar Garciaparra	.75
OD6 Sammy Sosa	.50
OD7 Frank Thomas	1.25
OD8 Barry Larkin	.15
OD9 David Justice	.15
OD10 Larry Walker	.25

OD11	Tony Clark	.40
OD12	Livan Hernandez	.15
OD13	Jeff Bagwell	.60
OD14	Kevin Appier	.15
OD15	Mike Piazza	1.00
OD16	Fernando Vina	.15
OD17	Chuck Knoblauch	.25
OD18	Vladimir Guerrero	.40
OD19	Rey Ordonez	.15
OD20	Bernie Williams	.40
OD21	Matt Stairs	.15
OD22	Curt Schilling	.15
OD23	Tony Womack	.15
OD24	Mark McGwire	2.00
OD25	Tony Gwynn	.75
OD26	Barry Bonds	.50
OD27	Ken Griffey Jr.	1.50
OD28	Fred McGriff	.25
OD29	Gonzalez, Rodriguez	.75
OD30	Roger Clemens	.75

1998 Sports Illustrated Then & Now

Manny Ramirez

Then and Now was the first of three Sports Illustrated Baseball releases in 1998. It contained 150 cards and sold in six-card packs, with five cards and a mini- poster. Fronts carried photos of active and retired players, as well as rookies. There was only one subset - A Place in History (37-53) - and it compared statistics between current players and retired greats. The product arrived with an Extra Edition parallel set, Art of the Game, Autograph Redemptions, Covers and Great Shots inserts. There was also an Alex Rodriguez checklist/mini-poster seeded every 12th pack.

		MT
Complete Set (150):		25.00
Common Player:		.10
Extra Edition Stars: 25x to 40x		
Yng Stars & RC's: 15x to 25x		
Production 500 sets		
Wax Box:		45.00
1	Luis Aparicio (Legends of the Game)	.10
2	Richie Ashburn (Legends of the Game)	.10
3	Ernie Banks (Legends of the Game)	.75
4	Yogi Berra (Legends of the Game)	.75
5	Lou Boudreau (Legends of the Game)	.10
6	Lou Brock (Legends of the Game)	.25

7	Jim Bunning (Legends of the Game)	.10
8	Rod Carew (Legends of the Game)	.25
9	Bob Feller (Legends of the Game)	.25
10	Rollie Fingers (Legends of the Game)	.10
11	Bob Gibson (Legends of the Game)	.50
12	Fergie Jenkins (Legends of the Game)	.10
13	Al Kaline (Legends of the Game)	.25
14	George Kell (Legends of the Game)	.10
15	Harmon Killebrew (Legends of the Game)	.50
16	Ralph Kiner (Legends of the Game)	.10
17	Tommy Lasorda (Legends of the Game)	.10
18	Juan Marichal (Legends of the Game)	.10
19	Eddie Mathews (Legends of the Game)	.40
20	Willie Mays (Legends of the Game)	1.50
21	Willie McCovey (Legends of the Game)	.10
22	Joe Morgan (Legends of the Game)	.10
23	Gaylord Perry (Legends of the Game)	.10
24	Kirby Puckett (Legends of the Game)	1.00
25	Pee Wee Reese (Legends of the Game)	.10
26	Phil Rizzuto (Legends of the Game)	.25
27	Robin Roberts (Legends of the Game)	.10
28	Brooks Robinson (Legends of the Game)	.75
29	Frank Robinson (Legends of the Game)	.50
30	Red Schoendienst (Legends of the Game)	.10
31	Enos Slaughter (Legends of the Game)	.10
32	Warren Spahn (Legends of the Game)	.50
33	Willie Stargell (Legends of the Game)	.20
34	Earl Weaver (Legends of the Game)	.10
35	Billy Williams (Legends of the Game)	.20
36	Early Wynn (Legends of the Game)	.10
37	Rickey Henderson (A Place in History)	.10
38	Greg Maddux (A Place in History)	1.50
39	Mike Mussina (A Place in History)	.50
40	Cal Ripken Jr. (A Place in History)	2.00
41	Albert Belle (A Place in History)	.60
42	Frank Thomas (A Place in History)	2.00
43	Jeff Bagwell (A Place in History)	.75
44	Paul Molitor (A Place in History)	.40
45	Chuck Knoblauch (A Place in History)	.25
46	Todd Hundley (A Place in History)	.10
47	Bernie Williams (A Place in History)	.40
48	Tony Gwynn (A Place in History)	1.00
49	Barry Bonds (A Place in History)	.60
50	Ken Griffey Jr. (A Place in History)	2.50
51	Randy Johnson (A Place in History)	.50
52	Mark McGwire (A Place in History)	3.00
53	Roger Clemens (A Place in History)	.75
54	Jose Cruz Jr. (A Place in History)	1.00

55	Roberto Alomar (Legends of Today)	.50
56	Sandy Alomar (Legends of Today)	.10
57	Brady Anderson (Legends of Today)	.10
58	Kevin Appier (Legends of Today)	.10
59	Jeff Bagwell (Legends of Today)	.75
60	Albert Belle (Legends of Today)	.60
61	Dante Bichette (Legends of Today)	.20
62	Craig Biggio (Legends of Today)	.20
63	Barry Bonds (Legends of Today)	.60
64	Kevin Brown (Legends of Today)	.10
65	Jay Buhner (Legends of Today)	.20
66	Ellis Burks (Legends of Today)	.10
67	Ken Caminiti (Legends of Today)	.25
68	Jose Canseco (Legends of Today)	.25
69	Joe Carter (Legends of Today)	.10
70	Vinny Castilla (Legends of Today)	.10
71	Tony Clark (Legends of Today)	.40
72	Roger Clemens (Legends of Today)	.75
73	David Cone (Legends of Today)	.20
74	Jose Cruz Jr. (Legends of Today)	1.00
75	Jason Dickson (Legends of Today)	.10
76	Jim Edmonds (Legends of Today)	.10
77	Scott Erickson (Legends of Today)	.10
78	Darin Erstad (Legends of Today)	.60
79	Alex Fernandez (Legends of Today)	.10
80	Steve Finley (Legends of Today)	.10
81	Travis Fryman (Legends of Today)	.10
82	Andres Galarraga (Legends of Today)	.25
83	Nomar Garciaparra (Legends of Today)	2.00
84	Tom Glavine (Legends of Today)	.20
85	Juan Gonzalez (Legends of Today)	1.50
86	Mark Grace (Legends of Today)	.25
87	Willie Greene (Legends of Today)	.10
88	Ken Griffey Jr. (Legends of Today)	2.50
89	Vladimir Guerrero (Legends of Today)	1.00
90	Tony Gwynn (Legends of Today)	1.00
91	Livan Hernandez (Legends of Today)	.10
92	Bobby Higginson (Legends of Today)	.10
93	Derek Jeter (Legends of Today)	1.50
94	Charles Johnson (Legends of Today)	.10
95	Randy Johnson (Legends of Today)	.40
96	Andruw Jones (Legends of Today)	1.00
97	Chipper Jones (Legends of Today)	1.50
98	David Justice (Legends of Today)	.25
99	Eric Karros (Legends of Today)	.10
100	Jason Kendall (Legends of Today)	.10
101	Jimmy Key (Legends of Today)	.10
102	Darryl Kile (Legends of Today)	.10

103	Chuck Knoblauch (Legends of Today)	.25
104	Ray Lankford (Legends of Today)	.10
105	Barry Larkin (Legends of Today)	.20
106	Kenny Lofton (Legends of Today)	.60
107	Greg Maddux (Legends of Today)	1.50
108	Al Martin (Legends of Today)	.10
109	Edgar Martinez (Legends of Today)	.10
110	Pedro Martinez (Legends of Today)	.25
111	Ramon Martinez (Legends of Today)	.10
112	Tino Martinez (Legends of Today)	.25
113	Mark McGwire (Legends of Today)	3.00
114	Raul Mondesi (Legends of Today)	.25
115	Matt Morris (Legends of Today)	.10
116	Charles Nagy (Legends of Today)	.10
117	Denny Neagle (Legends of Today)	.10
118	Hideo Nomo (Legends of Today)	.75
119	Dean Palmer (Legends of Today)	.10
120	Andy Pettitte (Legends of Today)	.50
121	Mike Piazza (Legends of Today)	1.50
122	Manny Ramirez (Legends of Today)	.50
123	Edgar Renteria (Legends of Today)	.10
124	Cal Ripken Jr. (Legends of Today)	2.00
125	Alex Rodriguez (Legends of Today)	1.50
126	Henry Rodriguez (Legends of Today)	.10
127	Ivan Rodriguez (Legends of Today)	.60
128	Scott Rolen (Legends of Today)	1.00
129	Tim Salmon (Legends of Today)	.25
130	Curt Schilling (Legends of Today)	.10
131	Gary Sheffield (Legends of Today)	.25
132	John Smoltz (Legends of Today)	.20
133	Sammy Sosa (Legends of Today)	2.00
134	Frank Thomas (Legends of Today)	2.50
135	Jim Thome (Legends of Today)	.50
136	Mo Vaughn (Legends of Today)	.60
137	Robin Ventura (Legends of Today)	.10
138	Larry Walker (Legends of Today)	.25
139	Bernie Williams (Legends of Today)	.40
140	Matt Williams (Legends of Today)	.25
141	Jaret Wright (Legends of Today)	1.00
142	Michael Coleman (Legends of the Future)	.10
143	Juan Encarnacion (Legends of the Future)	.20
144	Brad Fullmer (Legends of the Future)	.25
145	Ben Grieve (Legends of the Future)	1.00
146	Todd Helton (Legends of the Future)	.75
147	Paul Konerko (Legends of the Future)	.75
148	Derrek Lee (Legends of the Future)	.20
149	*Magglio Ordonez* (Legends of the Future)	.75
150	Enrique Wilson (Legends of the Future)	.10

1998 Sports Illustrated Then & Now Art of the Game

"Brooks"

Art of the Game was an eight-card insert featuring reproductions of original artwork of current and retired baseball stars done by eight popular sports artists, including world renowned T.S. O'Connell. They are numbered with a "AG" prefix and inserted one per nine packs.

		MT
Complete Set (8):		45.00
Common Player:		3.00
Inserted 1:9		
AG1	It's Gone	10.00
AG2	Alex Rodriguez	8.00
AG3	Mike Piazza	8.00
AG4	Brooks Robinson	5.00
AG5	David Justice (All-Star)	4.00
AG6	Cal Ripken Jr.	10.00
AG7	The Prospect and the Prospector	3.00
AG8	Barry Bonds	5.00

1998 Sports Illustrated Then & Now Autographs

Six autograph redemption cards were randomly inserted into packs of Then & Now and could be exchanged prior to the Nov. 1, 1999. The signed cards were produced in the following quantities: Clemens 250, Gibson 500, Gwynn 250, Killebrew 500, Mays 250 and Rolen 250. Four of the six cards, excluing Gibson and Rolen, used the same fronts as the Covers insert. Gibson and Rolen cards both featured unique card fronts.

	MT
Complete Set (6):	600.00
Common Autograph:	70.00
Bob Gibson (500)	70.00
Tony Gwynn (250)	200.00
Roger Clemens (250)	200.00
Scott Rolen (250)	125.00
Willie Mays (250)	175.00
Harmon Killebrew (500)	70.00

1998 Sports Illustrated Then & Now Covers

This 12-card insert features color shots of six actual Sports Illustrated covers, including six current players and six retired players. The cards are numbered with a "C" prefix and were seeded one per 18 packs.

		MT
Complete Set (12):		75.00
Common Player:		4.00
Inserted 1:18		
C1	Lou Brock (10/16/67)	4.00
C2	Kirby Puckett (4/6/92)	8.00
C3	Harmon Killebrew (4/8/63 - inside)	4.00
C4	Eddie Mathews (8/16/54)	10.00
C5	Willie Mays (5/22/72)	10.00
C6	Frank Robinson (10/6/69)	8.00
C7	Cal Ripken Jr. (9/11/95)	12.00
C8	Roger Clemens (5/12/86)	8.00
C9	Ken Griffey Jr. (10/16/95)	15.00
C10	Mark McGwire (6/1/92)	20.00
C11	Tony Gwynn (7/28/97)	8.00
C12	Ivan Rodriguez (8/11/97)	5.00

1998 Sports Illustrated Then & Now Great Shots!

This 25-card set featured 5" x 7" fold-out mini-posters using Sports Illustrated photos. Great Shots were inserted one per pack and contained a mix of retired and current players.

		MT
Complete Set (25):		5.00
Common Player:		.10
Inserted 1:1		
1	Ken Griffey Jr.	1.00
2	Frank Thomas	1.00
3	Alex Rodriguez	.60
4	Andruw Jones	.40
5	Chipper Jones	.60
6	Cal Ripken Jr.	.75
7	Mark McGwire	2.00
8	Derek Jeter	.60
9	Greg Maddux	.60
10	Jeff Bagwell	.40
11	Mike Piazza	.60
12	Scott Rolen	.40
13	Nomar Garciaparra	.60
14	Jose Cruz Jr.	.50
15	Charles Johnson	.10
16	Fergie Jenkins	.10
17	Lou Brock	.10
18	Bob Gibson	.10
19	Harmon Killebrew	.10
20	Juan Marichal	.10
21	Brooks Robinson	.25
22	Rod Carew	.20
23	Yogi Berra	.25
24	Willie Mays	.50
25	Kirby Puckett	.50

1998 Sports Illustrated Then & Now Road to Cooperstown

Road to Cooperstown features 10 current players who are having Hall of Fame careers. The insert name is printed across the back in bold, gold letters. Cards are numbered with a "RC" prefix and were inserted one per 24 packs.

		MT
Complete Set (10):		80.00
Common Player:		2.00
Inserted 1:24		
RC1	Barry Bonds	5.00
RC2	Roger Clemens	8.00
RC3	Ken Griffey Jr.	20.00
RC4	Tony Gwynn	10.00
RC5	Rickey Henderson	2.00
RC6	Greg Maddux	12.00
RC7	Paul Molitor	4.00
RC8	Mike Piazza	12.00
RC9	Cal Ripken Jr.	15.00
RC10	Frank Thomas	20.00

1998 Sports Illustrated World Series Fever

The third and final Sports Illustrated release of 1998 contained 150 cards and focused on the World Series while recapping memorable moments from the season. The set also included many stars of tomorrow, like Kerry Wood, Orlando Hernandez, Ben Grieve and Travis Lee. Once again, all the photos were taken from Sports Illustrated archives. The set has two subsets - 10 Magnificent Moments and 20 Cover Collection. The set is paralleled twice in Extra and First Edition parallel sets, and has three insert sets - MVP Collection, Reggie Jackson's Picks and Autumn Excellence.

		MT
Complete Set (150):		25.00
Common Player:		.10
Wax Box:		42.00
1	Mickey Mantle (Covers)	3.00
2	1957 World Series Preview (Covers)	.20
3	1958 World Series Preview (Covers)	.20
4	1959 World Series Preview (Covers)	.20
5	1962 World Series (Covers)	.20
6	Lou Brock (Covers)	.40
7	Brooks Robinson (Covers)	.75
8	Frank Robinson (Covers)	.50
9	1974 World Series (Covers)	.20
10	Reggie Jackson (Covers)	.50
11	1985 World Series (Covers)	.20
12	1987 World Series (Covers)	.20
13	Orel Hershiser (Covers)	.10
14	Rickey Henderson (Covers)	.10
15	1991 World Series (Covers)	.20
16	1992 World Series (Covers)	.10
17	Joe Carter (Covers)	.10
18	1995 World Series (Covers)	.20
19	1996 World Series (Covers)	.40
20	Edgar Renteria (Covers)	.10
21	Bill Mazeroski (Magnificent Moments)	.10
22	Joe Carter (Magnificent Moments)	.10
23	Carlton Fisk (Magnificent Moments)	.10
24	Bucky Dent (Magnificent Moments)	.10
25	Mookie Wilson (Magnificent Moments)	.10
26	Enos Slaughter (Magnificent Moments)	.10
27	Mickey Lolich (Magnificent Moments)	.10
28	Bobby Richardson (Magnificent Moments)	.10
29	Kirk Gibson (Magnificent Moments)	.10
30	Edgar Renteria (Magnificent Moments)	.10
31	Albert Belle	.75
32	Kevin Brown	.10
33	Brian Rose	.10
34	Ron Gant	.20
35	Jeromy Burnitz	.10
36	Andres Galarraga	.40
37	Jim Edmonds	.10
38	Jose Cruz Jr.	.75
39	Mark Grudzielanek	.10
40	Shawn Estes	.10
41	Mark Grace	.25
42	Nomar Garciaparra	2.00
43	Juan Gonzalez	1.50
44	Tom Glavine	.20
45	Brady Anderson	.10
46	Tony Clark	.50
47	Jeff Cirillo	.10
48	Dante Bichette	.25
49	Ben Grieve	1.00
50	Ken Griffey Jr.	3.00
51	Edgardo Alfonzo	.10
52	Roger Clemens	1.00
53	Pat Hentgen	.10
54	Todd Helton	.75
55	Andy Benes	.10
56	Tony Gwynn	1.50
57	Andruw Jones	.75
58	Bobby Higginson	.10
59	Bobby Jones	.10
60	Darryl Kile	.10
61	Chan Ho Park	.25
62	Charles Johnson	.10
63	Rusty Greer	.10
64	Travis Fryman	.10
65	Derek Jeter	1.50
66	Jay Buhner	.25
67	Chuck Knoblauch	.40
68	David Justice	.40
69	Brian Hunter	.10
70	Eric Karros	.20
71	Edgar Martinez	.10
72	Chipper Jones	2.00
73	Barry Larkin	.25
74	Mike Lansing	.10
75	Craig Biggio	.25
76	Al Martin	.10
77	Barry Bonds	.75
78	Randy Johnson	.50
79	Ryan Klesko	.25
80	Mark McGwire	4.00
81	Fred McGriff	.25
82	Javy Lopez	.10
83	Kenny Lofton	.75
84	Sandy Alomar Jr.	.10
85	Matt Morris	.10
86	Paul Konerko	.25
87	Ray Lankford	.10
88	Kerry Wood	4.00
89	Roberto Alomar	.50
90	Greg Maddux	2.00
91	Travis Lee	2.00
92	Moises Alou	.25
93	Dean Palmer	.10
94	Hideo Nomo	.50
95	Ken Caminiti	.20
96	Pedro Martinez	.75
97	Raul Mondesi	.25
98	Denny Neagle	.20
99	Tino Martinez	.30
100	Mike Mussina	.60
101	Kevin Appier	.10
102	Vinny Castilla	.20
103	Jeff Bagwell	1.00
104	Paul O'Neill	.20
105	Rey Ordonez	.10
106	Vladimir Guerrero	1.00
107	Rafael Palmeiro	.25
108	Alex Rodriguez	2.00
109	Andy Pettitte	.50
110	Carl Pavano	.20
111	Henry Rodriguez	.10
112	Gary Sheffield	.25
113	Curt Schilling	.20
114	John Smoltz	.20
115	Reggie Sanders	.10
116	Scott Rolen	1.00
117	Mike Piazza	2.00
118	Manny Ramirez	.75
119	Cal Ripken Jr.	2.50
120	Brad Radke	.10

121	Tim Salmon	.30
122	Brett Tomko	.10
123	Robin Ventura	.10
124	Mo Vaughn	.75
125	A.J. Hinch	.10
126	Derrek Lee	.10
127	*Orlando Hernandez*	3.00
128	Aramis Ramirez	.75
129	Frank Thomas	2.50
130	J.T. Snow	.10
131	*Magglio Ordonez*	.75
132	Bobby Bonilla	.20
133	Marquis Grissom	.10
134	Jim Thome	.50
135	Justin Thompson	.10
136	Matt Williams	.30
137	Matt Stairs	.10
138	Wade Boggs	.25
139	Chuck Finley	.10
140	Jaret Wright	.75
141	Ivan Rodriguez	.75
142	Brad Fullmer	.25
143	Bernie Williams	.50
144	Jason Giambi	.10
145	Larry Walker	.40
146	Tony Womack	.10
147	Sammy Sosa	2.00
148	Rondell White	.20
149	Todd Stottlemyre	.10
150	Shane Reynolds	.10

1998 Sports Illustrated WS Fever Autumn Excellence

Autumn Excellence honors players with the most select World Series records. The 10-card set was seeded one per 24 packs, while rarer Gold versions were seeded one per 240 packs.

		MT
Complete Set (10):		60.00
Common Player:		2.00
Inserted 1:24		
Golds: 3x to 5x		
Inserted 1:240		
AE1	Willie Mays	6.00
AE2	Kirby Puckett	8.00
AE3	Babe Ruth	25.00
AE4	Reggie Jackson	4.00
AE5	Whitey Ford	2.00
AE6	Lou Brock	4.00
AE7	Mickey Mantle	15.00
AE8	Yogi Berra	5.00
AE9	Bob Gibson	4.00
AE10	Don Larsen	2.00

A player's name in *italic* type indicates a rookie card.

1998 Sports Illustrated WS Fever Extra Edition

Extra Edition paralleled the entire 150-card base set and were identified by a gold foil stamp on the card front and sequential numbering to 98 sets on the back. World Series Fever also included one-of-one paralell versions called First Edition. These had the same fronts, but were numbered 1 of 1 on the back.

		MT
Common Player:		15.00
Semistars:		40.00
Extra Edition Stars: 50x to 80x		
Extra Edition Yng Stars & RCs:30x to 50x		
Production 98 sets		
1	Mickey Mantle (Covers)	75.00
2	1957 World Series Preview (Covers)	25.00
3	1958 World Series Preview (Covers)	25.00
4	1959 World Series Preview (Covers)	25.00
5	1962 World Series (Covers)	20.00
6	Lou Brock (Covers)	30.00
7	Brooks Robinson (Covers)	40.00
8	Frank Robinson (Covers)	40.00
9	1974 World Series (Covers)	25.00
10	Reggie Jackson (Covers)	50.00
11	1985 World Series (Covers)	20.00
12	1987 World Series (Covers)	25.00
13	Orel Hershiser (Covers)	15.00
14	Rickey Henderson (Covers)	15.00
15	1991 World Series (Covers)	25.00
16	1992 World Series (Covers)	15.00
17	Joe Carter (Covers)	15.00
18	1995 World Series (Covers)	25.00
19	1996 World Series (Covers)	40.00
20	Edgar Renteria (Covers)	15.00
21	Bill Mazeroski (Magnificent Moments)	15.00
22	Joe Carter (Magnificent Moments)	15.00
23	Carlton Fisk (Magnificent Moments)	15.00
24	Bucky Dent (Magnificent Moments)	15.00
25	Mookie Wilson (Magnificent Moments)	15.00
26	Enos Slaughter (Magnificent Moments)	15.00
27	Mickey Lolich (Magnificent Moments)	15.00
28	Bobby Richardson (Magnificent Moments)	15.00
29	Kirk Gibson (Magnificent Moments)	15.00
30	Edgar Renteria (Magnificent Moments)	15.00
31	Albert Belle	60.00
32	Kevin Brown	15.00
33	Brian Rose	15.00
34	Ron Gant	20.00
35	Jeromy Burnitz	15.00
36	Andres Galarraga	30.00
37	Jim Edmonds	15.00
38	Jose Cruz Jr.	60.00
39	Mark Grudzielanek	15.00
40	Shawn Estes	15.00
41	Mark Grace	25.00
42	Nomar Garciaparra	150.00
43	Juan Gonzalez	125.00
44	Tom Glavine	20.00
45	Brady Anderson	15.00
46	Tony Clark	40.00
47	Jeff Cirillo	15.00
48	Dante Bichette	25.00
49	Ben Grieve	80.00
50	Ken Griffey Jr.	250.00
51	Edgardo Alfonzo	15.00
52	Roger Clemens	90.00
53	Pat Hentgen	15.00
54	Todd Helton	50.00
55	Andy Benes	15.00
56	Tony Gwynn	125.00

57	Andruw Jones	60.00
58	Bobby Higginson	15.00
59	Bobby Jones	15.00
60	Darryl Kile	15.00
61	Chan Ho Park	30.00
62	Charles Johnson	15.00
63	Rusty Greer	15.00
64	Travis Fryman	15.00
65	Derek Jeter	120.00
66	Jay Buhner	30.00
67	Chuck Knoblauch	35.00
68	David Justice	30.00
69	Brian Hunter	15.00
70	Eric Karros	20.00
71	Edgar Martinez	15.00
72	Chipper Jones	150.00
73	Barry Larkin	25.00
74	Mike Lansing	15.00
75	Craig Biggio	25.00
76	Al Martin	15.00
77	Barry Bonds	60.00
78	Randy Johnson	40.00
79	Ryan Klesko	25.00
80	Mark McGwire	275.00
81	Fred McGriff	25.00
82	Javy Lopez	15.00
83	Kenny Lofton	60.00
84	Sandy Alomar Jr.	15.00
85	Matt Morris	15.00
86	Paul Konerko	25.00
87	Ray Lankford	15.00
88	Kerry Wood	180.00
89	Roberto Alomar	40.00
90	Greg Maddux	150.00
91	Travis Lee	150.00
92	Moises Alou	25.00
93	Dean Palmer	15.00
94	Hideo Nomo	40.00
95	Ken Caminiti	20.00
96	Pedro Martinez	60.00
97	Raul Mondesi	25.00
98	Denny Neagle	20.00
99	Tino Martinez	30.00
100	Mike Mussina	50.00
101	Kevin Appier	15.00
102	Vinny Castilla	20.00
103	Jeff Bagwell	75.00
104	Paul O'Neill	20.00
105	Rey Ordonez	15.00
106	Vladimir Guerrero	60.00
107	Rafael Palmeiro	25.00
108	Alex Rodriguez	150.00
109	Andy Pettitte	40.00
110	Carl Pavano	20.00
111	Henry Rodriguez	15.00
112	Gary Sheffield	25.00
113	Curt Schilling	20.00
114	John Smoltz	20.00
115	Reggie Sanders	15.00
116	Scott Rolen	75.00
117	Mike Piazza	150.00
118	Manny Ramirez	60.00
119	Cal Ripken Jr.	200.00
120	Brad Radke	15.00
121	Tim Salmon	25.00
122	Brett Tomko	15.00
123	Robin Ventura	15.00
124	Mo Vaughn	60.00
125	A.J. Hinch	15.00
126	Derrek Lee	15.00
127	Orlando Hernandez	100.00
128	Aramis Ramirez	30.00
129	Frank Thomas	200.00
130	J.T. Snow	15.00
131	Magglio Ordonez	35.00
132	Bobby Bonilla	20.00
133	Marquis Grissom	15.00
134	Jim Thome	40.00
135	Justin Thompson	15.00
136	Matt Williams	30.00
137	Matt Stairs	15.00
138	Wade Boggs	25.00
139	Chuck Finley	15.00
140	Jaret Wright	50.00
141	Ivan Rodriguez	60.00
142	Brad Fullmer	25.00
143	Bernie Williams	40.00
144	Jason Giambi	15.00
145	Larry Walker	40.00
146	Tony Womack	15.00
147	Sammy Sosa	125.00
148	Rondell White	20.00
149	Todd Stottlemyre	15.00
150	Shane Reynolds	15.00

1998 Sports Illustrated WS Fever MVP Collection

This 10-card insert set features select MVPs from the World Series. Card fronts contain a shot of the player over a white border with the year in black letters and the insert and player's name in blue foil. MVP Collection inserts were seeded one per four packs and numbered with a "MC" prefix.

		MT
Complete Set (10):		15.00
Common Player:		1.50
Inserted 1:4		
MC1	Frank Robinson	3.00
MC2	Brooks Robinson	4.00
MC3	Willie Stargell	1.50
MC4	Bret Saberhagen	1.50
MC5	Rollie Fingers	1.50
MC6	Orel Hershiser	1.50
MC7	Paul Molitor	4.00
MC8	Tom Glavine	1.50
MC9	John Wetteland	1.50
MC10	Livan Hernandez	1.50

1998 Sports Illustrated WS Fever Reggie Jackson Picks

Reggie Jackson's Picks contains top players that Jackson believes have what it takes to perform on center stage in the World Series. Fronts have a shot of the player with his name in the background, and a head shot of Reggie Jackson in the bottom right corner. These were numbered with a "RP" prefix and inserted one per 12 packs.

		MT
Complete Set (15):		140.00
Common Player:		3.00
Inserted 1:12		
R1	Paul O'Neill	3.00
R2	Barry Bonds	6.00
R3	Ken Griffey Jr.	25.00
R4	Juan Gonzalez	12.00
R5	Greg Maddux	15.00
R6	Mike Piazza	15.00
R7	Larry Walker	4.00
R8	Mo Vaughn	6.00
R9	Roger Clemens	8.00
R10	John Smoltz	3.00
R11	Alex Rodriguez	15.00
R12	Frank Thomas	20.00
R13	Mark McGwire	30.00
R14	Jeff Bagwell	8.00
R15	Randy Johnson	5.00

1991 Stadium Club

One of the most popular sets of 1991, this 600-card issue was released in two 300-card series. The cards were available in foil packs only. No factory sets were available. The cards feature borderless high gloss photos on the front and a player evaluation and card photo on the back. Stadium Club cards were considered scarce in many areas, this driving up the price per pack. A special Stadium Club membership package was made available for $29.95 with 10 proof of purchase seals from wrappers.

		MT
Complete Set (600):		150.00
Complete Series 1 (300):		90.00
Complete Series 2 (300):		60.00
Common Player:		.20
Series 1 Wax Box:		110.00
Series 2 Wax Box:		60.00
1	Dave Stewart	.25
2	Wally Joyner	.30
3	Shawon Dunston	.35
4	Darren Daulton	.30
5	Will Clark	.75
6	Sammy Sosa	6.00
7	Dan Plesac	.20
8	Marquis Grissom	.60
9	Erik Hanson	.20
10	Geno Petralli	.20
11	Jose Rijo	.20
12	Carlos Quintana	.20
13	Junior Ortiz	.20
14	Bob Walk	.20
15	Mike Macfarlane	.20
16	Eric Yelding	.20
17	Bryn Smith	.20
18	Bip Roberts	.20
19	Mike Scioscia	.20
20	Mark Williamson	.20
21	Don Mattingly	2.00
22	John Franco	.20
23	Chet Lemon	.20
24	Tom Henke	.20
25	Jerry Browne	.20
26	Dave Justice	1.00
27	Mark Langston	.20
28	Damon Berryhill	.20
29	Kevin Bass	.20
30	Scott Fletcher	.20
31	Moises Alou	.40
32	Dave Valle	.20
33	Jody Reed	.20
34	Dave West	.20
35	Kevin McReynolds	.20
36	Pat Combs	.20
37	Eric Davis	.25
38	Bret Saberhagen	.20
39	Stan Javier	.20
40	Chuck Cary	.20
41	Tony Phillips	.25
42	Lee Smith	.25
43	Tim Teufel	.20
44	Lance Dickson	.20
45	Greg Litton	.20
46	Teddy Higuera	.20
47	Edgar Martinez	.35
48	Steve Avery	.25
49	Walt Weiss	.20
50	David Segui	.20
51	Andy Benes	.35
52	Karl Rhodes	.20
53	Neal Heaton	.20
54	Dan Gladden	.20
55	Luis Rivera	.20
56	Kevin Brown	.20
57	Frank Thomas	10.00
58	Terry Mulholland	.20
59	Dick Schofield	.20
60	Ron Darling	.20
61	Sandy Alomar, Jr.	.30
62	Dave Stieb	.20
63	Alan Trammell	.30
64	Matt Nokes	.20
65	Lenny Harris	.20
66	Milt Thompson	.20
67	Storm Davis	.20
68	Joe Oliver	.20
69	Andres Galarraga	.45
70	Ozzie Guillen	.20
71	Ken Howell	.20
72	Garry Templeton	.20
73	Derrick May	.20
74	Xavier Hernandez	.20
75	Dave Parker	.25
76	Rick Aguilera	.20
77	Robby Thompson	.20
78	Pete Incaviglia	.20
79	Bob Welch	.20
80	Randy Milligan	.20
81	Chuck Finley	.20
82	Alvin Davis	.20
83	Tim Naehring	.20
84	Jay Bell	.20
85	Joe Magrane	.20
86	Howard Johnson	.20
87	Jack McDowell	.25
88	Kevin Seitzer	.20
89	Bruce Ruffin	.20
90	Fernando Valenzuela	.25
91	Terry Kennedy	.20
92	Barry Larkin	.60
93	Larry Walker	.75
94	Luis Salazar	.20
95	Gary Sheffield	.75
96	Bobby Witt	.20
97	Lonnie Smith	.20
98	Bryan Harvey	.20
99	Mookie Wilson	.20
100	Dwight Gooden	.25
101	Lou Whitaker	.20
102	Ron Karkovice	.20
103	Jesse Barfield	.20
104	Jose DeJesus	.20
105	Benito Santiago	.25
106	Brian Holman	.20

No.	Player	Price
107	Rafael Ramirez	.20
108	Ellis Burks	.30
109	Mike Bielecki	.20
110	Kirby Puckett	4.00
111	Terry Shumpert	.20
112	Chuck Crim	.20
113	Todd Benzinger	.20
114	Brian Barnes	.20
115	Carlos Baerga	.60
116	Kal Daniels	.20
117	Dave Johnson	.20
118	Andy Van Slyke	.20
119	John Burkett	.30
120	Rickey Henderson	.40
121	Tim Jones	.20
122	Daryl Irvine	.20
123	Ruben Sierra	.30
124	Jim Abbott	.50
125	Daryl Boston	.20
126	Greg Maddux	4.00
127	Von Hayes	.20
128	Mike Fitzgerald	.20
129	Wayne Edwards	.20
130	Greg Briley	.20
131	Rob Dibble	.20
132	Gene Larkin	.20
133	David Wells	.20
134	Steve Balboni	.20
135	Greg Vaughn	.20
136	Mark Davis	.20
137	Dave Rohde	.20
138	Eric Show	.20
139	Bobby Bonilla	.30
140	Dana Kiecker	.20
141	Gary Pettis	.20
142	Dennis Boyd	.20
143	Mike Benjamin	.20
144	Luis Polonia	.20
145	Doug Jones	.20
146	Al Newman	.20
147	Alex Fernandez	.40
148	Bill Doran	.20
149	Kevin Elster	.20
150	Len Dykstra	.40
151	Mike Gallego	.20
152	Tim Belcher	.20
153	Jay Buhner	.40
154	Ozzie Smith	.75
155	Jose Canseco	.60
156	Gregg Olson	.20
157	Charlie O'Brien	.20
158	Frank Tanana	.20
159	George Brett	2.50
160	Jeff Huson	.20
161	Kevin Tapani	.20
162	Jerome Walton	.20
163	Charlie Hayes	.20
164	Chris Bosio	.20
165	Chris Sabo	.20
166	Lance Parrish	.25
167	Don Robinson	.20
168	Manuel Lee	.20
169	Dennis Rasmussen	.20
170	Wade Boggs	.90
171	Bob Geren	.20
172	Mackey Sasser	.20
173	Julio Franco	.20
174	Otis Nixon	.20
175	Bert Blyleven	.20
176	Craig Biggio	.60
177	Eddie Murray	.50
178	Randy Tomlin	.20
179	Tino Martinez	.50
180	Carlton Fisk	.80
181	Dwight Smith	.20
182	Scott Garrelts	.20
183	Jim Gantner	.20
184	Dickie Thon	.20
185	John Farrell	.20
186	Cecil Fielder	.40
187	Glenn Braggs	.20
188	Allan Anderson	.20
189	Kurt Stillwell	.20
190	Jose Oquendo	.20
191	Joe Orsulak	.20
192	Ricky Jordan	.20
193	Kelly Downs	.20
194	Delino DeShields	.25
195	Omar Vizquel	.20
196	Mark Carreon	.20
197	Mike Harkey	.20
198	Jack Howell	.20
199	Lance Johnson	.20
200	Nolan Ryan	8.00
201	John Marzano	.20
202	Doug Drabek	.20
203	Mark Lemke	.20
204	Steve Sax	.20
205	Greg Harris	.20
206	B.J. Surhoff	.20
207	Todd Burns	.20
208	Jose Gonzalez	.20
209	Mike Scott	.20
210	Dave Magadan	.75
211	Dante Bichette	.20
212	Trevor Wilson	.20
213	Hector Villanueva	.20
214	Dan Pasqua	.20
215	Greg Colbrunn	.20
216	Mike Jeffcoat	.20
217	Harold Reynolds	.35
218	Paul O'Neill	.20
219	Mark Guthrie	.20
220	Barry Bonds	1.25
221	Jimmy Key	.20
222	Billy Ripken	.20
223	Tom Pagnozzi	.20
224	Bo Jackson	.50
225	Sid Fernandez	.20
226	Mike Marshall	.20
227	John Kruk	.20
228	Mike Fetters	.20
229	Eric Anthony	.20
230	Ryne Sandberg	1.50
231	Carney Lansford	.20
232	Melido Perez	.20
233	Jose Lind	.20
234	Darryl Hamilton	.20
235	Tom Browning	.20
236	Spike Owen	.20
237	Juan Gonzalez	6.00
238	Felix Fermin	.20
239	Keith Miller	.20
240	Mark Gubicza	.20
241	Kent Anderson	.20
242	Alvaro Espinoza	.20
243	Dale Murphy	.40
244	Orel Hershiser	.30
245	Paul Molitor	1.00
246	Eddie Whitson	.20
247	Joe Girardi	.20
248	Kent Hrbek	.25
249	Bill Sampen	.20
250	Kevin Mitchell	.25
251	Mariano Duncan	.20
252	Scott Bradley	.20
253	Mike Greenwell	.20
254	Tom Gordon	.20
255	Todd Zeile	.25
256	Bobby Thigpen	.20
257	Gregg Jefferies	.40
258	Kenny Rogers	.20
259	Shane Mack	.30
260	Zane Smith	.20
261	Mitch Williams	.20
262	Jim DeShaies	.20
263	Dave Winfield	.50
264	Ben McDonald	.25
265	Randy Ready	.20
266	Pat Borders	.20
267	Jose Uribe	.20
268	Derek Lilliquist	.20
269	Greg Brock	.20
270	Ken Griffey, Jr.	15.00
271	Jeff Gray	.20
272	Danny Tartabull	.25
273	Dennis Martinez	.35
274	Robin Ventura	.35
275	Randy Myers	.20
276	Jack Daugherty	.20
277	Greg Gagne	.20
278	Jay Howell	.20
279	Mike LaValliere	.20
280	Rex Hudler	.20
281	Mike Simms	.20
282	Kevin Maas	.20
283	Jeff Ballard	.20
284	Dave Henderson	.20
285	Pete O'Brien	.20
286	Brook Jacoby	.20
287	Mike Henneman	.20
288	Greg Olson	.20
289	Greg Myers	.20
290	Mark Grace	.40
291	Shawn Abner	.20
292	Frank Viola	.20
293	Lee Stevens	.20
294	Jason Grimsley	.20
295	Matt Williams	.75
296	Ron Robinson	.20
297	Tom Brunansky	.20
298	Checklist	.20
299	Checklist	.20
300	Checklist	.20
301	Darryl Strawberry	.40
302	Bud Black	.20
303	Harold Baines	.25
304	Roberto Alomar	1.50
305	Norm Charlton	.20
306	Gary Thurman	.20
307	Mike Felder	.20
308	Tony Gwynn	2.50
309	Roger Clemens	2.00
310	Andre Dawson	.50
311	Scott Radinsky	.20
312	Bob Melvin	.20
313	Kirk McCaskill	.20
314	Pedro Guerrero	.20
315	Walt Terrell	.20
316	Sam Horn	.20
317	*Wes Chamberlain*	.30
318	*Pedro Munoz*	.30
319	Roberto Kelly	.20
320	Mark Portugal	.20
321	Tim McIntosh	.20
322	Jesse Orosco	.20
323	Gary Green	.20
324	Greg Harris	.20
325	Hubie Brooks	.20
326	Chris Nabholz	.20
327	Terry Pendleton	.35
328	Eric King	.20
329	Chili Davis	.20
330	Anthony Telford	.20
331	Kelly Gruber	.20
332	Dennis Eckersley	.30
333	Mel Hall	.20
334	Bob Kipper	.20
335	Willie McGee	.25
336	Steve Olin	.20
337	Steve Buechele	.20
338	Scott Leius	.20
339	Hal Morris	.30
340	Jose Offerman	.25
341	Kent Mercker	.20
342	Ken Griffey	.20
343	Pete Harnisch	.20
344	Kirk Gibson	.20
345	Dave Smith	.20
346	Dave Martinez	.20
347	Atlee Hammaker	.20
348	Brian Downing	.20
349	Todd Hundley	.35
350	Candy Maldonado	.20
351	Dwight Evans	.20
352	Steve Searcy	.20
353	Gary Gaetti	.25
354	Jeff Reardon	.20
355	Travis Fryman	.30
356	Dave Righetti	.20
357	Fred McGriff	.75
358	Don Slaught	.20
359	Gene Nelson	.20
360	Billy Spiers	.20
361	Lee Guetterman	.20
362	Darren Lewis	.25
363	Duane Ward	.20
364	Lloyd Moseby	.20
365	John Smoltz	.75
366	Felix Jose	.25
367	David Cone	.30
368	Wally Backman	.20
369	Jeff Montgomery	.20
370	Rich Garces	.20
371	Billy Hatcher	.20
372	Bill Swift	.20
373	Jim Eisenreich	.20
374	Rob Ducey	.20
375	Tim Crews	.20
376	Steve Finley	.20
377	Jeff Blauser	.20
378	Willie Wilson	.20
379	Gerald Perry	.20
380	Jose Mesa	.20
381	Pat Kelly	.25
382	Matt Merullo	.20
383	Ivan Calderon	.20
384	Scott Chiamparino	.20
385	Lloyd McClendon	.20
386	Dave Bergman	.20
387	Ed Sprague	.40
388	*Jeff Bagwell*	10.00
389	Brett Butler	.30
390	Larry Andersen	.20
391	Glenn Davis	.20
392	Alex Cole (photo of Otis Nixon)	.20
393	Mike Heath	.20

394	Danny Darwin	.20
395	Steve Lake	.20
396	Tim Layana	.20
397	Terry Leach	.20
398	Bill Wegman	.20
399	Mark McGwire	8.00
400	Mike Boddicker	.20
401	Steve Howe	.20
402	Bernard Gilkey	.45
403	Thomas Howard	.20
404	Rafael Belliard	.20
405	Tom Candiotti	.20
406	Rene Gonzalez	.20
407	Chuck McElroy	.20
408	Paul Sorrento	.25
409	Randy Johnson	1.50
410	Brady Anderson	.50
411	Dennis Cook	.20
412	Mickey Tettleton	.25
413	Mike Stanton	.20
414	Ken Oberkfell	.20
415	Rick Honeycutt	.20
416	Nelson Santovenia	.20
417	Bob Tewksbury	.20
418	Brent Mayne	.20
419	Steve Farr	.20
420	Phil Stephenson	.20
421	Jeff Russell	.20
422	Chris James	.20
423	Tim Leary	.20
424	Gary Carter	.30
425	Glenallen Hill	.20
426	Matt Young	.20
427	Sid Bream	.20
428	Greg Swindell	.20
429	Scott Aldred	.20
430	Cal Ripken, Jr.	5.00
431	Bill Landrum	.20
432	Ernie Riles	.20
433	Danny Jackson	.20
434	Casey Candaele	.20
435	Ken Hill	.40
436	Jaime Navarro	.20
437	Lance Blankenship	.20
438	Randy Velarde	.20
439	Frank DiPino	.20
440	Carl Nichols	.20
441	Jeff Robinson	.20
442	Deion Sanders	.75
443	Vincente Palacios	.20
444	Devon White	.20
445	John Cerutti	.20
446	Tracy Jones	.20
447	Jack Morris	.20
448	Mitch Webster	.20
449	Bob Ojeda	.20
450	Oscar Azocar	.20
451	Luis Aquino	.20
452	Mark Whiten	.30
453	Stan Belinda	.20
454	Ron Gant	.45
455	Jose DeLeon	.20
456	Mark Salas	.20
457	Junior Felix	.20
458	Wally Whitehurst	.20
459	*Phil Plantier*	.35
460	Juan Berenguer	.20
461	Franklin Stubbs	.20
462	Joe Boever	.20
463	Tim Wallach	.20
464	Mike Moore	.20
465	Albert Belle	2.50
466	Mike Witt	.20
467	Craig Worthington	.20
468	Jerald Clark	.20
469	Scott Terry	.20
470	Milt Cuyler	.20
471	John Smiley	.20
472	Charles Nagy	.20
473	Alan Mills	.20
474	John Russell	.20
475	Bruce Hurst	.20
476	Andujar Cedeno	.20
477	Dave Eiland	.20
478	*Brian McRae*	.75
479	Mike LaCoss	.20
480	Chris Gwynn	.20
481	Jamie Moyer	.20
482	John Olerud	.30
483	Efrain Valdez	.20
484	Sil Campusano	.20
485	Pascual Perez	.20
486	Gary Redus	.20
487	Andy Hawkins	.20
488	Cory Snyder	.20
489	Chris Hoiles	.30

490	Ron Hassey	.20
491	Gary Wayne	.20
492	Mark Lewis	.35
493	Scott Coolbaugh	.20
494	Gerald Young	.20
495	Juan Samuel	.20
496	Willie Fraser	.20
497	Jeff Treadway	.20
498	Vince Coleman	.20
499	Cris Carpenter	.20
500	Jack Clark	.20
501	Kevin Appier	.30
502	Rafael Palmeiro	.50
503	Hensley Meulens	.20
504	George Bell	.20
505	Tony Pena	.20
506	Roger McDowell	.20
507	Luis Sojo	.20
508	Mike Schooler	.20
509	Robin Yount	.75
510	Jack Armstrong	.20
511	Rick Cerone	.20
512	Curt Wilkerson	.20
513	Joe Carter	.30
514	Tim Burke	.20
515	Tony Fernandez	.20
516	Ramon Martinez	.25
517	Tim Hulett	.20
518	Terry Steinbach	.20
519	Pete Smith	.20
520	Ken Caminiti	.30
521	Shawn Boskie	.20
522	Mike Pagliarulo	.20
523	Tim Raines	.30
524	Alfredo Griffin	.20
525	Henry Cotto	.20
526	Mike Stanley	.20
527	Charlie Leibrandt	.20
528	Jeff King	.20
529	Eric Plunk	.20
530	Tom Lampkin	.20
531	Steve Bedrosian	.20
532	Tom Herr	.20
533	Craig Lefferts	.20
534	Jeff Reed	.20
535	Mickey Morandini	.20
536	Greg Cadaret	.20
537	Ray Lankford	.50
538	John Candelaria	.20
539	Rob Deer	.20
540	Brad Arnsberg	.20
541	Mike Sharperson	.20
542	Jeff Robinson	.20
543	Mo Vaughn	6.00
544	Jeff Parrett	.20
545	Willie Randolph	.20
546	Herm Winningham	.20
547	Jeff Innis	.20
548	Chuck Knoblauch	2.00
549	Tommy Greene	.35
550	Jeff Hamilton	.20
551	Barry Jones	.20
552	Ken Dayley	.20
553	Rick Dempsey	.20
554	Greg Smith	.20
555	Mike Devereaux	.20
556	Keith Comstock	.20
557	Paul Faries	.20
558	Tom Glavine	.60
559	Craig Grebeck	.20
560	Scott Erickson	.30
561	Joel Skinner	.20
562	Mike Morgan	.20
563	Dave Gallagher	.20
564	Todd Stottlemyre	.20
565	Rich Rodriguez	.25
566	*Craig Wilson*	.25
567	Jeff Brantley	.20
568	Scott Kamieniecki	.20
569	Steve Decker	.20
570	Juan Agosto	.20
571	Tommy Gregg	.20
572	Kevin Wickander	.20
573	Jamie Quirk	.20
574	Jerry Don Gleaton	.20
575	Chris Hammond	.20
576	*Luis Gonzalez*	.50
577	Russ Swan	.20
578	*Jeff Conine*	2.00
579	Charlie Hough	.20
580	Jeff Kunkel	.20
581	Darrel Akerfelds	.20
582	Jeff Manto	.20
583	Alejandro Pena	.20
584	Mark Davidson	.20
585	Bob MacDonald	.20

586	Paul Assenmacher	.20
587	Dan Wilson	.30
588	Tom Bolton	.20
589	Brian Harper	.20
590	John Habyan	.20
591	John Orton	.20
592	Mark Gardner	.20
593	Turner Ward	.20
594	Bob Patterson	.20
595	Edwin Nunez	.20
596	Gary Scott	.20
597	Scott Bankhead	.20
598	Checklist	.20
599	Checklist	.20
600	Checklist	.20

1992 Stadium Club

This 900-card set was released in three 100-card series. Like the 1991 issue, the cards feature borderless high-gloss photos on the front. The flip sides feature the player's first Topps card and a player evaluation. Topps released updated cards in the third series for traded player and free agents. Several players appear on two cards. Special Members Choice cards are included in the set. Series III features special inserts of the last three number one draft picks: Phil Nevin, Brien Taylor and Chipper Jones.

	MT
Complete Set (900):	70.00
Common Player:	.10
Series 1,2,3 Wax Box:	28.00

1	Cal Ripken, Jr.	4.00
2	Eric Yelding	.10
3	Geno Petralli	.10
4	Wally Backman	.10
5	Milt Cuyler	.10
6	Kevin Bass	.10
7	Dante Bichette	.30
8	Ray Lankford	.20
9	Mel Hall	.10
10	Joe Carter	.20
11	Juan Samuel	.10
12	Jeff Montgomery	.10
13	Glenn Braggs	.10
14	Henry Cotto	.10
15	Deion Sanders	.60
16	Dick Schofield	.10
17	David Cone	.10
18	Chili Davis	.10
19	Tom Foley	.10
20	Ozzie Guillen	.10
21	Luis Salazar	.10
22	Terry Steinbach	.10
23	Chris James	.10
24	Jeff King	.10
25	Carlos Quintana	.10
26	Mike Maddux	.10
27	Tommy Greene	.10
28	Jeff Russell	.10
29	Steve Finley	.10

#	Name	Price	#	Name	Price	#	Name	Price
30	Mike Flanagan	.10	126	Mark Portugal	.10	222	Jeff Gray	.10
31	Darren Lewis	.10	127	Calvin Jones	.10	223	Paul Gibson	.10
32	Mark Lee	.10	128	Mike Heath	.10	224	Bobby Thigpen	.10
33	Willie Fraser	.10	129	Todd Van Poppel	.10	225	Mike Mussina	.75
34	Mike Henneman	.10	130	Benny Santiago	.12	226	Darrin Jackson	.10
35	Kevin Maas	.10	131	Gary Thurman	.10	227	Luis Gonzalez	.10
36	Dave Hansen	.10	132	Joe Girardi	.10	228	Greg Briley	.10
37	Erik Hanson	.10	133	Dave Eiland	.10	229	Brent Mayne	.10
38	Bill Doran	.10	134	Orlando Merced	.10	230	Paul Molitor	.35
39	Mike Boddicker	.10	135	Joe Orsulak	.10	231	Al Leiter	.10
40	Vince Coleman	.10	136	John Burkett	.10	232	Andy Van Slyke	.10
41	Devon White	.10	137	Ken Dayley	.10	233	Ron Tingley	.10
42	Mark Gardner	.10	138	Ken Hill	.10	234	Bernard Gilkey	.15
43	Scott Lewis	.10	139	Walt Terrell	.10	235	Kent Hrbek	.12
44	Juan Berenguer	.10	140	Mike Scioscia	.10	236	Eric Karros	.15
45	Carney Lansford	.10	141	Junior Felix	.10	237	Randy Velarde	.10
46	Curt Wilkerson	.10	142	Ken Caminiti	.20	238	Andy Allanson	.10
47	Shane Mack	.10	143	Carlos Baerga	.15	239	Willie McGee	.12
48	Bip Roberts	.10	144	Tony Fossas	.10	240	Juan Gonzalez	1.00
49	Greg Harris	.10	145	Craig Grebeck	.10	241	Karl Rhodes	.10
50	Ryne Sandberg	.50	146	Scott Bradley	.10	242	Luis Mercedes	.10
51	Mark Whiten	.10	147	Kent Mercker	.10	243	Billy Swift	.10
52	Jack McDowell	.10	148	Derrick May	.10	244	Tommy Gregg	.10
53	Jimmy Jones	.10	149	Jerald Clark	.10	245	David Howard	.10
54	Steve Lake	.10	150	George Brett	.75	246	Dave Hollins	.10
55	Bud Black	.10	151	Luis Quinones	.10	247	Kip Gross	.10
56	Dave Valle	.10	152	Mike Pagliarulo	.10	248	Walt Weiss	.10
57	Kevin Reimer	.10	153	Jose Guzman	.10	249	Mackey Sasser	.10
58	Rich Gedman	.10	154	Charlie O'Brien	.10	250	Cecil Fielder	.20
59	Travis Fryman	.10	155	Darren Holmes	.10	251	Jerry Browne	.10
60	Steve Avery	.10	156	Joe Boever	.10	252	Doug Dascenzo	.10
61	Francisco de la Rosa	.10	157	Rich Monteleone	.10	253	Darryl Hamilton	.10
62	Scott Hemond	.10	158	Reggie Harris	.10	254	Dann Bilardello	.10
63	Hal Morris	.10	159	Roberto Alomar	.75	255	Luis Rivera	.10
64	Hensley Meulens	.10	160	Robby Thompson	.10	256	Larry Walker	.40
65	Frank Castillo	.10	161	Chris Hoiles	.10	257	Ron Karkovice	.10
66	Gene Larkin	.10	162	Tom Pagnozzi	.10	258	Bob Tewksbury	.10
67	Jose DeLeon	.10	163	Omar Vizquel	.10	259	Jimmy Key	.10
68	Al Osuna	.10	164	John Candelaria	.10	260	Bernie Williams	.60
69	Dave Cochrane	.10	165	Terry Shumpert	.10	261	Gary Wayne	.10
70	Robin Ventura	.25	166	Andy Mota	.10	262	Mike Simms	.10
71	John Cerutti	.10	167	Scott Bailes	.10	263	John Orton	.10
72	Kevin Gross	.10	168	Jeff Blauser	.10	264	Marvin Freeman	.10
73	Ivan Calderon	.10	169	Steve Olin	.10	265	Mike Jeffcoat	.10
74	Mike Macfarlane	.10	170	Doug Drabek	.10	266	Roger Mason	.10
75	Stan Belinda	.10	171	Dave Bergman	.10	267	Edgar Martinez	.15
76	Shawn Hillegas	.10	172	Eddie Whitson	.10	268	Henry Rodriguez	.10
77	Pat Borders	.10	173	Gilberto Reyes	.10	269	Sam Horn	.10
78	Jim Vatcher	.10	174	Mark Grace	.20	270	Brian McRae	.10
79	Bobby Rose	.10	175	Paul O'Neill	.15	271	Kirt Manwaring	.10
80	Roger Clemens	.75	176	Greg Cadaret	.10	272	Mike Bordick	.10
81	Craig Worthington	.10	177	Mark Williamson	.10	273	Chris Sabo	.10
82	Jeff Treadway	.10	178	Casey Candaele	.10	274	Jim Olander	.10
83	Jamie Quirk	.10	179	Candy Maldonado	.10	275	Greg Harris	.10
84	Randy Bush	.10	180	Lee Smith	.12	276	Dan Gakeler	.10
85	Anthony Young	.10	181	Harold Reynolds	.10	277	Bill Sampen	.10
86	Trevor Wilson	.10	182	Dave Justice	.20	278	Joel Skinner	.10
87	Jaime Navarro	.10	183	Lenny Webster	.10	279	Curt Schilling	.10
88	Les Lancaster	.10	184	Donn Pall	.10	280	Dale Murphy	.25
89	Pat Kelly	.10	185	Gerald Alexander	.10	281	Lee Stevens	.10
90	Alvin Davis	.10	186	Jack Clark	.10	282	Lonnie Smith	.10
91	Larry Andersen	.10	187	Stan Javier	.10	283	Manuel Lee	.10
92	Rob Deer	.10	188	Ricky Jordan	.10	284	Shawn Boskie	.10
93	Mike Sharperson	.10	189	Franklin Stubbs	.10	285	Kevin Seitzer	.10
94	Lance Parrish	.10	190	Dennis Eckersley	.12	286	Stan Royer	.15
95	Cecil Espy	.10	191	Danny Tartabull	.10	287	John Dopson	.10
96	Tim Spehr	.10	192	Pete O'Brien	.10	288	Scott Bullett	.15
97	Dave Stieb	.10	193	Mark Lewis	.10	289	Ken Patterson	.10
98	Terry Mulholland	.10	194	Mike Felder	.10	290	Todd Hundley	.15
99	Dennis Boyd	.10	195	Mickey Tettleton	.10	291	Tim Leary	.10
100	Barry Larkin	.15	196	Dwight Smith	.10	292	Brett Butler	.12
101	Ryan Bowen	.10	197	Shawn Abner	.10	293	Gregg Olson	.10
102	Felix Fermin	.10	198	Jim Leyritz	.10	294	Jeff Brantley	.10
103	Luis Alicea	.10	199	Mike Devereaux	.10	295	Brian Holman	.10
104	Tim Hulett	.10	200	Craig Biggio	.15	296	Brian Harper	.10
105	Rafael Belliard	.10	201	Kevin Elster	.10	297	Brian Bohanon	.10
106	Mike Gallego	.10	202	Rance Mulliniks	.10	298	Checklist 1-100	.10
107	Dave Righetti	.10	203	Tony Fernandez	.10	299	Checklist 101-200	.10
108	Jeff Schaefer	.10	204	Allan Anderson	.10	300	Checklist 201-300	.10
109	Ricky Bones	.10	205	Herm Winningham	.10	301	Frank Thomas	3.00
110	Scott Erickson	.10	206	Tim Jones	.10	302	Lloyd McClendon	.10
111	Matt Nokes	.10	207	Ramon Martinez	.12	303	Brady Anderson	.20
112	Bob Scanlan	.10	208	Teddy Higuera	.10	304	Julio Valera	.10
113	Tom Candiotti	.10	209	John Kruk	.15	305	Mike Aldrete	.10
114	Sean Berry	.10	210	Jim Abbott	.15	306	Joe Oliver	.10
115	Kevin Morton	.10	211	Dean Palmer	.15	307	Todd Stottlemyre	.10
116	Scott Fletcher	.10	212	Mark Davis	.10	308	Rey Sanchez	.10
117	B.J. Surhoff	.10	213	Jay Buhner	.12	309	Gary Sheffield	.25
118	Dave Magadan	.10	214	Jesse Barfield	.10	310	Andujar Cedeno	.10
119	Bill Gullickson	.10	215	Kevin Mitchell	.12	311	Kenny Rogers	.10
120	Marquis Grissom	.20	216	Mike LaValliere	.10	312	Bruce Hurst	.10
121	Lenny Harris	.10	217	Mark Wohlers	.10	313	Mike Schooler	.10
122	Wally Joyner	.15	218	Dave Henderson	.10	314	Mike Benjamin	.10
123	Kevin Brown	.10	219	Dave Smith	.10	315	Chuck Finley	.10
124	Braulio Castillo	.10	220	Albert Belle	.75	316	Mark Lemke	.10
125	Eric King	.10	221	Spike Owen	.10	317	Scott Livingstone	.10

#	Player	Value
318	Chris Nabholz	.10
319	Mike Humphreys	.10
320	Pedro Guerrero	.10
321	Willie Banks	.10
322	Tom Goodwin	.10
323	Hector Wagner	.10
324	Wally Ritchie	.10
325	Mo Vaughn	.60
326	Joe Klink	.10
327	Cal Eldred	.10
328	Daryl Boston	.10
329	Mike Huff	.10
330	Jeff Bagwell	1.25
331	Bob Milacki	.10
332	Tom Prince	.10
333	Pat Tabler	.10
334	Ced Landrum	.10
335	Reggie Jefferson	.10
336	Mo Sanford	.10
337	Kevin Ritz	.10
338	Gerald Perry	.10
339	Jeff Hamilton	.10
340	Tim Wallach	.10
341	Jeff Huson	.10
342	Jose Melendez	.10
343	Willie Wilson	.10
344	Mike Stanton	.10
345	Joel Johnston	.10
346	Lee Guetterman	.10
347	Francisco Olivares	.10
348	Dave Burba	.10
349	Tim Crews	.10
350	Scott Leius	.10
351	Danny Cox	.10
352	Wayne Housie	.10
353	Chris Donnels	.10
354	Chris George	.10
355	Gerald Young	.10
356	Roberto Hernandez	.10
357	Neal Heaton	.10
358	Todd Frohwirth	.10
359	Jose Vizcaino	.10
360	Jim Thome	.60
361	Craig Wilson	.10
362	Dave Haas	.10
363	Billy Hatcher	.10
364	John Barfield	.10
365	Luis Aquino	.10
366	Charlie Leibrandt	.10
367	Howard Farmer	.10
368	Bryn Smith	.10
369	Mickey Morandini	.10
370	Jose Canseco (Members Choice, should have been #597)	.50
371	Jose Uribe	.10
372	Bob MacDonald	.10
373	Luis Sojo	.10
374	Craig Shipley	.10
375	Scott Bankhead	.10
376	Greg Gagne	.10
377	Scott Cooper	.10
378	Jose Offerman	.10
379	Billy Spiers	.10
380	John Smiley	.10
381	Jeff Carter	.10
382	Heathcliff Slocumb	.10
383	Jeff Tackett	.10
384	John Kiely	.10
385	John Vander Wal	.10
386	Omar Olivares	.10
387	Ruben Sierra	.12
388	Tom Gordon	.10
389	Charles Nagy	.10
390	Dave Stewart	.10
391	Pete Harnisch	.10
392	Tim Burke	.10
393	Roberto Kelly	.10
394	Freddie Benavides	.10
395	Tom Glavine	.20
396	Wes Chamberlain	.10
397	Eric Gunderson	.10
398	Dave West	.10
399	Ellis Burks	.15
400	Ken Griffey, Jr.	6.00
401	Thomas Howard	.10
402	Juan Guzman	.10
403	Mitch Webster	.10
404	Matt Merullo	.10
405	Steve Buechele	.10
406	Danny Jackson	.10
407	Felix Jose	.10
408	Doug Piatt	.10
409	Jim Eisenreich	.10
410	Bryan Harvey	.10
411	Jim Austin	.10

#	Player	Value
412	Jim Poole	.10
413	Glenallen Hill	.10
414	Gene Nelson	.10
415	Ivan Rodriguez	.75
416	Frank Tanana	.10
417	Steve Decker	.10
418	Jason Grimsley	.10
419	Tim Layana	.10
420	Don Mattingly	1.25
421	Jerome Walton	.10
422	Rob Ducey	.10
423	Andy Benes	.15
424	John Marzano	.10
425	Gene Harris	.10
426	Tim Raines	.15
427	Bret Barberie	.10
428	Harvey Pulliam	.10
429	Cris Carpenter	.10
430	Howard Johnson	.10
431	Orel Hershiser	.12
432	Brian Hunter	.10
433	Kevin Tapani	.10
434	Rick Reed	.10
435	Ron Witmeyer	.10
436	Gary Gaetti	.15
437	Alex Cole	.10
438	Chito Martinez	.10
439	Greg Litton	.10
440	Julio Franco	.10
441	Mike Munoz	.10
442	Erik Pappas	.10
443	Pat Combs	.10
444	Lance Johnson	.10
445	Ed Sprague	.10
446	Mike Greenwell	.10
447	Milt Thompson	.10
448	Mike Magnante	.10
449	Chris Haney	.10
450	Robin Yount	.75
451	Rafael Ramirez	.10
452	Gino Minutelli	.10
453	Tom Lampkin	.10
454	Tony Perezchica	.10
455	Dwight Gooden	.15
456	Mark Guthrie	.10
457	Jay Howell	.10
458	Gary DiSarcina	.10
459	John Smoltz	.15
460	Will Clark	.50
461	Dave Otto	.10
462	Rob Maurer	.10
463	Dwight Evans	.10
464	Tom Brunansky	.10
465	*Shawn Hare*	.10
466	Geronimo Pena	.10
467	Alex Fernandez	.15
468	Greg Myers	.10
469	Jeff Fassero	.10
470	Len Dykstra	.15
471	Jeff Johnson	.10
472	Russ Swan	.10
473	Archie Corbin	.10
474	Chuck McElroy	.10
475	Mark McGwire	4.00
476	Wally Whitehurst	.10
477	Tim McIntosh	.10
478	Sid Bream	.10
479	Jeff Juden	.10
480	Carlton Fisk	.15
481	Jeff Plympton	.10
482	Carlos Martinez	.10
483	Jim Gott	.10
484	Bob McClure	.10
485	Tim Teufel	.10
486	Vicente Palacios	.10
487	Jeff Reed	.10
488	Tony Phillips	.12
489	Mel Rojas	.10
490	Ben McDonald	.10
491	Andres Santana	.10
492	Chris Beasley	.10
493	Mike Timlin	.10
494	Brian Downing	.10
495	Kirk Gibson	.10
496	Scott Sanderson	.10
497	Nick Esasky	.10
498	*Johnny Guzman*	.10
499	Mitch Williams	.10
500	Kirby Puckett	1.00
501	Mike Harkey	.10
502	Jim Gantner	.10
503	Bruce Egloff	.10
504	Josias Manzanillo	.15
505	Delino DeShields	.10
506	Rheal Cormier	.10
507	Jay Bell	.10

#	Player	Value
508	Rich Rowland	.10
509	Scott Servais	.10
510	Terry Pendleton	.10
511	Rich DeLucia	.10
512	Warren Newson	.10
513	Paul Faries	.10
514	Kal Daniels	.10
515	Jarvis Brown	.10
516	Rafael Palmeiro	.25
517	Kelly Downs	.10
518	Steve Chitren	.10
519	Moises Alou	.20
520	Wade Boggs	.25
521	Pete Schourek	.10
522	Scott Terry	.10
523	Kevin Appier	.10
524	Gary Redus	.10
525	George Bell	.10
526	Jeff Kaiser	.10
527	Alvaro Espinoza	.10
528	Luis Polonia	.10
529	Darren Daulton	.12
530	Norm Charlton	.10
531	John Olerud	.20
532	Dan Plesac	.10
533	Billy Ripken	.10
534	Rod Nichols	.10
535	Joey Cora	.10
536	Harold Baines	.12
537	Bob Ojeda	.10
538	Mark Leonard	.10
539	Danny Darwin	.10
540	Shawon Dunston	.15
541	Pedro Munoz	.10
542	Mark Gubicza	.10
543	Kevin Baez	.10
544	Todd Zeile	.15
545	Don Slaught	.10
546	Tony Eusebio	.10
547	Alonzo Powell	.10
548	Gary Pettis	.10
549	Brian Barnes	.10
550	Lou Whitaker	.10
551	Keith Mitchell	.10
552	Oscar Azocar	.10
553	Stu Cole	.10
554	Steve Wapnick	.10
555	Derek Bell	.15
556	Luis Lopez	.10
557	Anthony Telford	.10
558	Tim Mauser	.10
559	Glenn Sutko	.10
560	Darryl Strawberry	.15
561	Tom Bolton	.10
562	Cliff Young	.10
563	Bruce Walton	.10
564	Chico Walker	.10
565	John Franco	.10
566	Paul McClellan	.10
567	Paul Abbott	.10
568	Gary Varsho	.10
569	Carlos Maldonado	.10
570	Kelly Gruber	.10
571	Jose Oquendo	.10
572	Steve Frey	.10
573	Tino Martinez	.20
574	Bill Haselman	.10
575	Eric Anthony	.15
576	John Habyan	.10
577	Jeffrey McNeely	.10
578	Chris Bosio	.10
579	Joe Grahe	.10
580	Fred McGriff	.40
581	Rick Honeycutt	.10
582	Matt Williams	.60
583	Cliff Brantley	.10
584	Rob Dibble	.10
585	Skeeter Barnes	.10
586	Greg Hibbard	.10
587	Randy Milligan	.10
588	Checklist 301-400	.10
589	Checklist 401-500	.10
590	Checklist 501-600	.10
591	Frank Thomas (Members Choice)	2.50
592	Dave Justice (Members Choice)	.20
593	Roger Clemens (Members Choice)	.40
594	Steve Avery (Members Choice)	.15
595	Cal Ripken, Jr. (Members Choice)	2.00
596	Barry Larkin (Members Choice)	.15
597	Not issued (See #370)	

#	Player	Value
598	Will Clark (Members Choice)	.35
599	Cecil Fielder (Members Choice)	.15
600	Ryne Sandberg (Members Choice)	.40
601	Chuck Knoblauch (Members Choice)	.20
602	Dwight Gooden (Members Choice)	.15
603	Ken Griffey, Jr. (Members Choice)	2.75
604	Barry Bonds (Members Choice)	.75
605	Nolan Ryan (Members Choice)	1.50
606	Jeff Bagwell (Members Choice)	1.00
607	Robin Yount (Members Choice)	.25
608	Bobby Bonilla (Members Choice)	.15
609	George Brett (Members Choice)	.50
610	Howard Johnson (Members Choice)	.10
611	Esteban Beltre	.10
612	Mike Christopher	.10
613	Troy Afenir	.10
614	Mariano Duncan	.10
615	Doug Henry	.10
616	Doug Jones	.10
617	Alvin Davis	.10
618	Craig Lefferts	.10
619	Kevin McReynolds	.10
620	Barry Bonds	.75
621	Turner Ward	.15
622	Joe Magrane	.10
623	Mark Parent	.10
624	Tom Browning	.10
625	John Smiley	.10
626	Steve Wilson	.10
627	Mike Gallego	.10
628	Sammy Sosa	1.50
629	Rico Rossy	.10
630	Royce Clayton	.15
631	Clay Parker	.10
632	Pete Smith	.10
633	Jeff McKnight	.10
634	Jack Daugherty	.10
635	Steve Sax	.10
636	Joe Hesketh	.10
637	Vince Horsman	.10
638	Eric King	.10
639	Joe Boever	.10
640	Jack Morris	.10
641	Arthur Rhodes	.10
642	Bob Melvin	.10
643	Rick Wilkins	.10
644	Scott Scudder	.10
645	Bip Roberts	.10
646	Julio Valera	.10
647	Kevin Campbell	.10
648	Steve Searcy	.10
649	Scott Kamieniecki	.10
650	Kurt Stillwell	.10
651	Bob Welch	.10
652	Andres Galarraga	.15
653	Mike Jackson	.10
654	Bo Jackson	.15
655	Sid Fernandez	.10
656	Mike Bielecki	.10
657	Jeff Reardon	.10
658	Wayne Rosenthal	.10
659	Eric Bullock	.10
660	Eric Davis	.15
661	Randy Tomlin	.10
662	Tom Edens	.10
663	Rob Murphy	.10
664	Leo Gomez	.10
665	Greg Maddux	2.00
666	Greg Vaughn	.15
667	Wade Taylor	.10
668	Brad Arnsberg	.10
669	Mike Moore	.10
670	Mark Langston	.10
671	Barry Jones	.10
672	Bill Landrum	.10
673	Greg Swindell	.10
674	Wayne Edwards	.10
675	Greg Olson	.10
676	*Bill Pulsipher*	.90
677	Bobby Witt	.10
678	Mark Carreon	.10
679	Patrick Lennon	.10
680	Ozzie Smith	.40
681	John Briscoe	.10
682	Matt Young	.10
683	Jeff Conine	.15
684	Phil Stephenson	.10
685	Ron Darling	.10
686	Bryan Hickerson	.10
687	Dale Sveum	.10
688	Kirk McCaskill	.10
689	Rich Amaral	.10
690	Danny Tartabull	.10
691	Donald Harris	.10
692	Doug Davis	.10
693	John Farrell	.10
694	Paul Gibson	.10
695	Kenny Lofton	2.00
696	Mike Fetters	.10
697	Rosario Rodriguez	.10
698	Chris Jones	.10
699	Jeff Manto	.10
700	Rick Sutcliffe	.10
701	Scott Bankhead	.10
702	Donnie Hill	.10
703	Todd Worrell	.10
704	Rene Gonzales	.10
705	Rick Cerone	.10
706	Tony Pena	.10
707	Paul Sorrento	.10
708	Gary Scott	.10
709	Junior Noboa	.10
710	Wally Joyner	.15
711	Charlie Hayes	.10
712	Rich Rodriguez	.10
713	Rudy Seanez	.10
714	Jim Bullinger	.10
715	Jeff Robinson	.10
716	Jeff Branson	.10
717	Andy Ashby	.10
718	Dave Burba	.10
719	Rich Gossage	.10
720	Randy Johnson	.50
721	David Wells	.10
722	Paul Kilgus	.10
723	Dave Martinez	.10
724	Denny Neagle	.10
725	Andy Stankiewicz	.10
726	Rick Aguilera	.10
727	Junior Ortiz	.10
728	Storm Davis	.10
729	Don Robinson	.10
730	Ron Gant	.15
731	Paul Assenmacher	.10
732	Mark Gardiner	.10
733	Milt Hill	.10
734	Jeremy Hernandez	.10
735	Ken Hill	.10
736	Xavier Hernandez	.10
737	Gregg Jefferies	.15
738	Dick Schofield	.10
739	Ron Robinson	.10
740	Sandy Alomar	.12
741	Mike Stanley	.10
742	Butch Henry	.10
743	Floyd Bannister	.10
744	Brian Drahman	.10
745	Dave Winfield	.50
746	Bob Walk	.10
747	Chris James	.10
748	Don Prybylinski	.10
749	Dennis Rasmussen	.10
750	Rickey Henderson	.25
751	Chris Hammond	.10
752	Bob Kipper	.10
753	Dave Rohde	.10
754	Hubie Brooks	.10
755	Bret Saberhagen	.10
756	Jeff Robinson	.10
757	*Pat Listach*	.15
758	Bill Wegman	.10
759	John Wetteland	.10
760	Phil Plantier	.10
761	Wilson Alvarez	.10
762	Scott Aldred	.10
763	*Armando Reynoso*	.15
764	Todd Benzinger	.10
765	Kevin Mitchell	.12
766	Gary Sheffield	.25
767	Allan Anderson	.10
768	Rusty Meacham	.10
769	Rick Parker	.10
770	Nolan Ryan	3.00
771	Jeff Ballard	.10
772	Cory Snyder	.10
773	Denis Boucher	.10
774	Jose Gonzales	.10
775	Juan Guerrero	.10
776	Ed Nunez	.10
777	Scott Ruskin	.10
778	Terry Leach	.10
779	Carl Willis	.10
780	Bobby Bonilla	.15
781	Duane Ward	.10
782	Joe Slusarski	.10
783	David Segui	.10
784	Kirk Gibson	.10
785	Frank Viola	.10
786	Keith Miller	.10
787	Mike Morgan	.10
788	Kim Batiste	.10
789	Sergio Valdez	.10
790	Eddie Taubensee	.10
791	Jack Armstrong	.10
792	Scott Fletcher	.10
793	Steve Farr	.10
794	Dan Pasqua	.10
795	Eddie Murray	.25
796	John Morris	.10
797	Francisco Cabrera	.10
798	Mike Perez	.10
799	Ted Wood	.10
800	Jose Rijo	.10
801	Danny Gladden	.10
802	Arci Cianfrocco	.10
803	Monty Fariss	.10
804	Roger McDowell	.10
805	Randy Myers	.10
806	Kirk Dressendorfer	.10
807	Zane Smith	.10
808	Glenn Davis	.10
809	Torey Lovullo	.10
810	Andre Dawson	.15
811	Bill Pecota	.10
812	Ted Power	.10
813	Willie Blair	.10
814	Dave Fleming	.10
815	Chris Gwynn	.10
816	Jody Reed	.10
817	Mark Dewey	.10
818	Kyle Abbott	.10
819	Tom Henke	.10
820	Kevin Seitzer	.10
821	Al Newman	.10
822	Tim Sherrill	.10
823	Chuck Crim	.10
824	Darren Reed	.10
825	Tony Gwynn	.60
826	Steve Foster	.10
827	Steve Howe	.10
828	Brook Jacoby	.10
829	Rodney McCray	.10
830	Chuck Knoblauch	.15
831	John Wehner	.10
832	Scott Garrelts	.10
833	Alejandro Pena	.10
834	Jeff Parrett	.10
835	Juan Bell	.10
836	Lance Dickson	.10
837	Darryl Kile	.10
838	Efrain Valdez	.10
839	*Bob Zupcic*	.10
840	George Bell	.10
841	Dave Gallagher	.10
842	Tim Belcher	.10
843	Jeff Shaw	.10
844	Mike Fitzgerald	.10
845	Gary Carter	.15
846	John Russell	.10
847	*Eric Hillman*	.15
848	Mike Witt	.10
849	Curt Wilkerson	.10
850	Alan Trammell	.15
851	Rex Hudler	.10
852	*Michael Walkden*	.10
853	Kevin Ward	.10
854	Tim Naehring	.10
855	Bill Swift	.10
856	Damon Berryhill	.10
857	Mark Eichhorn	.10
858	Hector Villanueva	.10
859	Jose Lind	.10
860	Denny Martinez	.12
861	Bill Krueger	.10
862	Mike Kingery	.10
863	Jeff Innis	.10
864	Derek Lilliquist	.10
865	Reggie Sanders	.15
866	Ramon Garcia	.10
867	Bruce Ruffin	.10
868	Dickie Thon	.10
869	Melido Perez	.10
870	Ruben Amaro	.10
871	Alan Mills	.10
872	Matt Sinatro	.10

873	Eddie Zosky	.15
874	Pete Incaviglia	.10
875	Tom Candiotti	.10
876	Bob Patterson	.10
877	Neal Heaton	.10
878	*Terrel Hansen*	.15
879	Dave Eiland	.10
880	Von Hayes	.10
881	Tim Scott	.10
882	Otis Nixon	.10
883	Herm Winningham	.10
884	Dion James	.10
885	Dave Wainhouse	.10
886	Frank DiPino	.10
887	Dennis Cook	.10
888	Jose Mesa	.10
889	Mark Leiter	.10
890	Willie Randolph	.10
891	Craig Colbert	.10
892	Dwayne Henry	.10
893	Jim Lindeman	.10
894	Charlie Hough	.10
895	Gil Heredia	.10
896	Scott Chiamparino	.10
897	Lance Blankenship	.10
898	Checklist 601-700	.10
899	Checklist 701-800	.10
900	Checklist 801-900	.10

1992 Stadium Club First Draft Picks

Issued as inserts with Stadium Club Series III, this three-card set features the No. 1 draft picks of 1990-92. Fronts have a full-bleed photo with S.C. logo and player name in the lower-right corner. At bottom-lerft is a red strip is a gold-foil stamping, "#1 Draft Pick of the '90's". An orage circle at upper-right has the year the player was the No. 1 choice. The basic red-and-black back has a color photo, a few biographical and draft details and a gold facsimile autograph among other gold-foil highlights.

		MT
Complete Set (3):		9.00
Common Player:		2.00
1	Chipper Jones	8.00
2	Brien Taylor	1.00
3	Phil Nevin	1.00

1992 Stadium Club Master Photos

Uncropped versions of the photos which appear on regular Stadium Club cards are featured on these large-format (5" x 7") cards. The photos are set against a white background and trimmed with holo-graphic foil. Backs are blank and the cards are unnumbered. Members of Topps' Stadium Club received a Master Photo in their members' packs for 1992. The cards were also available as inserts in special boxes of Stadium Club cards sold at Wal-Mart stores.

		MT
Complete Set (15):		45.00
Common Player:		2.00
(1)	Wade Boggs	2.50
(2)	Barry Bonds	4.00
(3)	Jose Canseco	3.00
(4)	Will Clark	2.50
(5)	Cecil Fielder	2.50
(6)	Dwight Gooden	2.00
(7)	Ken Griffey, Jr.	8.00
(8)	Rickey Henderson	2.50
(9)	Lance Johnson	2.00
(10)	Cal Ripken, Jr.	7.50
(11)	Nolan Ryan	7.50
(12)	Deion Sanders	3.00
(13)	Darryl Strawberry	2.00
(14)	Danny Tartabull	2.00
(15)	Frank Thomas	6.00

1992 Stadium Club Special Edition (SkyDome)

This 200-card special Stadium Club set from Topps was uniquely packaged in a plastic replica of the Toronto SkyDome, the home of the 1991 All-Star Game. Featured in the set are members of Team USA, All-Stars, draft picks, top prospects and hight cards from the World Series between the Twins and Braves. The cards are styled much like the regular Stadium Club cards. Some cards have been found with incorrect gold-foil identifiers as well as the correct version.

		MT
Complete Set (200):		20.00
Common Player:		.10
1	*Terry Adams*	.10
2	Tommy Adams	.10
3	Rick Aguilera	.10
4	Ron Allen	.10
5	Roberto Alomar (All-Star)	.50
6	Sandy Alomar	.15
7	Greg Anthony	.10
8	James Austin	.10
9	Steve Avery	.12
10	Harold Baines	.12
11	*Brian Barber*	.15
12	Jon Barnes	.10
13	George Bell	.10
14	Doug Bennett	.10
15	Sean Bergman	.10
16	Bill Bliss	.10
17	Craig Biggio	.20
18	Wade Boggs (AS)	.30
19	Bobby Bonilla (AS)	.10
20	Russell Brock	.10
21	Tarrik Brock	.10
22	Tom Browning	.10
23	Brett Butler	.12
24	Ivan Calderon	.10
25	Joe Carter	.15
26	Joe Caruso	.10
27	Dan Cholowsky	.10
28	Will Clark (AS)	.20
29	Roger Clemens (AS)	.40
30	Shawn Curran	.10
31	Chris Curtis	.10
32	Chili Davis	.10
33	Andre Dawson	.15
34	Joe DeBerry	.10
35	John Dettmer	.10
36	Rob Dibble	.10
37	*John Donati*	.10
38	Dave Doorneweerd	.10
39	Darren Dreifort	.15
40	Mike Durant	.10
41	Chris Durkin	.10
42	Dennis Eckersley	.12
43	*Brian Edmondson*	.10
44	*Vaughn Eshelman*	.25
45	*Shawn Estes*	1.00
46	*Jorge Fabregas*	.15
47	Jon Farrell	.10
48	Cecil Fielder (AS)	.15
49	Carlton Fisk	.15
50	Tim Flannelly	.10
51	*Cliff Floyd*	.50
52	Julio Franco	.10
53	Greg Gagne	.10
54	*Chris Gambs*	.10
55	Ron Gant	.15
56	Brent Gates	.25
57	Dwayne Gerald	.10
58	Jason Giambi	.60
59	*Benji Gil*	.30
60	Mark Gipner	.10
61	Danny Gladden	.10
62	Tom Glavine	.20
63	Jimmy Gonzalez	.10
64	Jeff Granger	.10
65	Dan Grapenthien	.10
66	Dennis Gray	.10
67	*Shawn Green*	1.00
68	Tyler Green	.15
69	Todd Greene	1.00
70	Ken Griffey, Jr. (AS)	2.50
71	Kelly Gruber	.10
72	Ozzie Guillen	.10
73	Tony Gwynn (AS)	.50
74	Shane Halter	.10
75	Jeffrey Hammonds	.25
76	Larry Hanlon	.10
77	Pete Harnisch	.10
78	Mike Harrison	.10
79	Bryan Harvey	.10
80	Scott Hatteberg	.15
81	Rick Helling	.10
82	Dave Henderson	.10
83	Rickey Henderson (AS)	.20
84	Tyrone Hill	.10
85	*Todd Hollandsworth*	1.50
86	Brian Holliday	.10
87	Terry Horn	.10

88	Jeff Hostetler	.10
89	Kent Hrbek	.12
90	Mark Hubbard	.10
91	Charles Johnson	1.50
92	Howard Johnson	.10
93	Todd Johnson	.10
94	*Bobby Jones*	.75
95	Dan Jones	.10
96	Felix Jose	.10
97	Dave Justice	.30
98	Jimmy Key	.10
99	*Marc Kroom*	.10
100	John Kruk	.10
101	Mark Langston	.10
102	Barry Larkin	.25
103	Mike LaValliere	.10
104a	Scott Leius (1991 N.L. All-Star - error)	.10
104b	Scott Leius (1991 World Series - correct)	.10
105	Mark Lemke	.10
106	Donnie Leshnock	.10
107	Jimmy Lewis	.10
108	Shawn Livesy	.10
109	Ryan Long	.10
110	Trevor Mallory	.10
111	Denny Martinez	.12
112	Justin Mashore	.10
113	Jason McDonald	.10
114	Jack McDowell	.10
115	Tom McKinnon	.10
116	Billy McKinnon	.10
117	*Buck McNabb*	.20
118	Jim Mecir	.10
119	Dan Melendez	.10
120	*Shawn Miller*	.20
121	Trever Miller	.15
122	Paul Molitor	.35
123	Vincent Moore	.10
124	Mike Morgan	.10
125	Jack Morris (World Series)	.10
126	Jack Morris (All-Star)	.10
127	Sean Mulligan	.10
128	Eddie Murray	.30
129	Mike Neill	.10
130	Phil Nevin	.10
131	Mark O'Brien	.10
132	*Alex Ochoa*	.25
133	*Chad Ogea*	.20
134	Greg Olson	.10
135	Paul O'Neill	.12
136	Jared Osentowski	.10
137	Mike Pagliarulo	.10
138	Rafael Palmeiro	.20
139	Rodney Pedraza	.10
140	Tony Phillips	.10
141	*Scott Pisciotta*	.10
142	Chris Pritchett	.10
143	Jason Pruitt	.10
144a	Kirby Puckett (1991 N.L. All-Star - error)	.75
144b	Kirby Puckett (1991 World Series - correct)	.75
145	Kirby Puckett (AS)	.75
146	*Manny Ramirez*	6.00
147	Eddie Ramos	.10
148	Mark Ratekin	.10
149	Jeff Reardon	.10
150	Sean Rees	.10
151	*Calvin Reese*	.25
152	*Desmond Relaford*	.20
153	Eric Richardson	.10
154	Cal Ripken, Jr. (AS)	2.50
155	Chris Roberts	.15
156	Mike Robertson	.10
157	Steve Rodriguez	.10
158	Mike Rossiter	.10
159	Scott Ruffcorn	.10
160a	Chris Sabo (1991 World Series - error)	.10
160b	Chris Sabo (1991 N.L. All-Star - correct)	.10
161	Juan Samuel	.10
162	Ryne Sandberg (AS)	.50
163	Scott Sanderson	.10
164	Benito Santiago	.10
165	*Gene Schall*	.10
166	Chad Schoenvogel	.10
167	*Chris Seelbach*	.10
168	*Aaron Sele*	.50
169	Basil Shabazz	.10
170	*Al Shirley*	.10
171	Paul Shuey	.10
172	Ruben Sierra	.10
173	John Smiley	.10
174	Lee Smith	.12

175	Ozzie Smith	.30
176	Tim Smith	.10
177	Zane Smith	.10
178	John Smoltz	.12
179	Scott Stahoviak	.10
180	Kennie Steenstra	.10
181	Kevin Stocker	.10
182	*Chris Stynes*	.10
183	Danny Tartabull	.10
184	Brien Taylor	.15
185	Todd Taylor	.10
186	Larry Thomas	.10
187a	*Ozzie Timmons*	.15
187b	David Tuttle (should be #188)	.10
188	Not issued	
189	Andy Van Slyke	.10
190a	Frank Viola (1991 World Series - error)	.10
190b	Frank Viola (1991 N.L. All-Star - correct)	.10
191	Michael Walkden	.10
192	Jeff Ware	.10
193	*Allen Watson*	.15
194	Steve Whitaker	.10
195a	Jerry Willard (1991 Draft Pick - error)	.10
195b	Jerry Willard (1991 World Series - correct)	.10
196	Craig Wilson	.10
197	Chris Wimmer	.15
198	*Steve Wojciechowski*	.10
199	Joel Wolfe	.10
200	Ivan Zweig	.10

1993 Stadium Club

Topps' premium set for 1993 was issued in three series, two 300-card series and a final series of 150. Boxes contained 24 packs this year, compared to 36 in the past. Packs had 14 cards and an insert card. Each box had a 5" x 7" Master Photo card.

		MT
Complete Set (750):		60.00
Complete Series 1 (300):		20.00
Complete Series 2 (300):		30.00
Complete Series 3 (150):		10.00
Common Player:		.10
Series 1,2,3 Wax Box:		28.00
1	Pat Borders	.10
2	Greg Maddux	2.50
3	Daryl Boston	.10
4	Bob Ayrault	.10
5	Tony Phillips	.10
6	Damion Easley	.10
7	Kip Gross	.10
8	Jim Thome	.40
9	Tim Belcher	.10
10	Gary Wayne	.10
11	Sam Militello	.10
12	Mike Magnante	.10
13	Tim Wakefield	.12

14	Tim Hulett	.10
15	Rheal Cormier	.10
16	Juan Guerrero	.10
17	Rich Gossage	.10
18	Tim Laker	.10
19	Darrin Jackson	.10
20	Jack Clark	.10
21	Roberto Hernandez	.10
22	Dean Palmer	.15
23	Harold Reynolds	.10
24	Dan Plesac	.10
25	Brent Mayne	.10
26	Pat Hentgen	.15
27	Luis Sojo	.10
28	Ron Gant	.15
29	Paul Gibson	.10
30	Bip Roberts	.10
31	Mickey Tettleton	.10
32	Randy Velarde	.10
33	Brian McRae	.10
34	Wes Chamberlain	.10
35	Wayne Kirby	.10
36	Rey Sanchez	.10
37	Jesse Orosco	.10
38	Mike Stanton	.10
39	Royce Clayton	.15
40	Cal Ripken, Jr.	2.50
41	John Dopson	.10
42	Gene Larkin	.10
43	Tim Raines	.12
44	Randy Myers	.10
45	Clay Parker	.10
46	Mike Scioscia	.10
47	Pete Incaviglia	.10
48	Todd Van Poppel	.15
49	Ray Lankford	.15
50	Eddie Murray	.25
51	Barry Bonds	.75
52	Gary Thurman	.10
53	Bob Wickman	.10
54	Joey Cora	.10
55	Kenny Rogers	.10
56	Mike Devereaux	.10
57	Kevin Seitzer	.10
58	Rafael Belliard	.10
59	David Wells	.10
60	Mark Clark	.10
61	Carlos Baerga	.15
62	Scott Brosius	.10
63	Jeff Grotewold	.10
64	Rick Wrona	.10
65	Kurt Knudsen	.10
66	Lloyd McClendon	.10
67	Omar Vizquel	.10
68	Jose Vizcaino	.10
69	Rob Ducey	.10
70	Casey Candaele	.10
71	Ramon Martinez	.15
72	Todd Hundley	.20
73	John Marzano	.10
74	Derek Parks	.10
75	Jack McDowell	.15
76	Tim Scott	.10
77	Mike Mussina	.40
78	Delino DeShields	.10
79	Chris Bosio	.10
80	Mike Bordick	.10
81	Rod Beck	.10
82	Ted Power	.10
83	John Kruk	.12
84	Steve Shifflett	.10
85	Danny Tartabull	.10
86	Mike Greenwell	.10
87	Jose Melendez	.10
88	Craig Wilson	.10
89	Melvin Nieves	.15
90	Ed Sprague	.10
91	Willie McGee	.10
92	Joe Orsulak	.10
93	Jeff King	.10
94	Dan Pasqua	.10
95	Brian Harper	.10
96	Joe Oliver	.10
97	Shane Turner	.10
98	Lenny Harris	.10
99	Jeff Parrett	.10
100	Luis Polonia	.10
101	Kent Bottenfield	.10
102	Albert Belle	.75
103	Mike Maddux	.10
104	Randy Tomlin	.10
105	Andy Stankiewicz	.10
106	Rico Rossy	.10
107	Joe Hesketh	.10
108	Dennis Powell	.10
109	Derrick May	.10

#	Player	Price
110	Pete Harnisch	.10
111	Kent Mercker	.10
112	Scott Fletcher	.10
113	Rex Hudler	.10
114	Chico Walker	.10
115	Rafael Palmeiro	.20
116	Mark Leiter	.10
117	Pedro Munoz	.15
118	Jim Bullinger	.10
119	Ivan Calderon	.10
120	Mike Timlin	.10
121	Rene Gonzales	.10
122	Greg Vaughn	.10
123	Mike Flanagan	.10
124	Mike Hartley	.10
125	Jeff Montgomery	.10
126	Mike Gallego	.10
127	Don Slaught	.10
128	Charlie O'Brien	.10
129	Jose Offerman	.10
130	Mark Wohlers	.10
131	Eric Fox	.10
132	Doug Strange	.10
133	Jeff Frye	.10
134	Wade Boggs	.20
135	Lou Whitaker	.10
136	Craig Grebeck	.10
137	Rich Rodriguez	.10
138	Jay Bell	.10
139	Felix Fermin	.10
140	Denny Martinez	.10
141	Eric Anthony	.10
142	Roberto Alomar	.50
143	Darren Lewis	.10
144	Mike Blowers	.10
145	Scott Bankhead	.10
146	Jeff Reboulet	.10
147	Frank Viola	.10
148	Bill Pecota	.10
149	Carlos Hernandez	.10
150	Bobby Witt	.10
151	Sid Bream	.10
152	Todd Zeile	.15
153	Dennis Cook	.10
154	Brian Bohanon	.10
155	Pat Kelly	.10
156	Milt Cuyler	.10
157	Juan Bell	.10
158	Randy Milligan	.10
159	Mark Gardner	.10
160	Pat Tabler	.10
161	Jeff Reardon	.10
162	Ken Patterson	.10
163	Bobby Bonilla	.15
164	Tony Pena	.10
165	Greg Swindell	.10
166	Kirk McCaskill	.10
167	Doug Drabek	.10
168	Franklin Stubbs	.10
169	Ron Tingley	.10
170	Willie Banks	.10
171	Sergio Valdez	.10
172	Mark Lemke	.10
173	Robin Yount	.40
174	Storm Davis	.10
175	Dan Walters	.10
176	Steve Farr	.10
177	Curt Wilkerson	.10
178	Luis Alicea	.10
179	Russ Swan	.10
180	Mitch Williams	.10
181	Wilson Alvarez	.10
182	Carl Willis	.10
183	Craig Biggio	.20
184	Sean Berry	.10
185	Trevor Wilson	.10
186	Jeff Tackett	.10
187	Ellis Burks	.10
188	Jeff Branson	.10
189	Matt Nokes	.10
190	John Smiley	.10
191	Danny Gladden	.10
192	Mike Boddicker	.10
193	Roger Pavlik	.10
194	Paul Sorrento	.10
195	Vince Coleman	.10
196	Gary DiSarcina	.10
197	Rafael Bournigal	.10
198	Mike Schooler	.10
199	Scott Ruskin	.10
200	Frank Thomas	2.50
201	Kyle Abbott	.10
202	Mike Perez	.10
203	Andre Dawson	.15
204	Bill Swift	.10
205	Alejandro Pena	.10
206	Dave Winfield	.20
207	Andujar Cedeno	.10
208	Terry Steinbach	.10
209	Chris Hammond	.10
210	Todd Burns	.10
211	Hipolito Pichardo	.10
212	John Kiely	.10
213	Tim Teufel	.10
214	Lee Guetterman	.10
215	Geronimo Pena	.10
216	Brett Butler	.10
217	Bryan Hickerson	.10
218	Rick Trlicek	.10
219	Lee Stevens	.10
220	Roger Clemens	1.00
221	Carlton Fisk	.15
222	Chili Davis	.10
223	Walt Terrell	.10
224	Jim Eisenreich	.10
225	Ricky Bones	.10
226	Henry Rodriguez	.10
227	Ken Hill	.15
228	Rick Wilkins	.10
229	Ricky Jordan	.10
230	Bernard Gilkey	.10
231	Tim Fortugno	.10
232	Geno Petralli	.10
233	Jose Rijo	.10
234	Jim Leyritz	.10
235	Kevin Campbell	.10
236	Al Osuna	.10
237	Pete Smith	.10
238	Pete Schourek	.10
239	Moises Alou	.20
240	Donn Pall	.10
241	Denny Neagle	.10
242	Dan Peltier	.10
243	Scott Scudder	.10
244	Juan Guzman	.10
245	Dave Burba	.10
246	Rick Sutcliffe	.10
247	Tony Fossas	.10
248	Mike Munoz	.10
249	Tim Salmon	.50
250	Rob Murphy	.10
251	Roger McDowell	.10
252	Lance Parrish	.10
253	Cliff Brantley	.10
254	Scott Leius	.10
255	Carlos Martinez	.10
256	Vince Horsman	.10
257	Oscar Azocar	.10
258	Craig Shipley	.10
259	Ben McDonald	.15
260	Jeff Brantley	.10
261	Damon Berryhill	.10
262	Joe Grahe	.10
263	Dave Hansen	.10
264	Rich Amaral	.10
265	*Tim Pugh*	.20
266	Dion James	.10
267	Frank Tanana	.10
268	Stan Belinda	.10
269	Jeff Kent	.10
270	Bruce Ruffin	.10
271	Xavier Hernandez	.10
272	Darrin Fletcher	.10
273	Tino Martinez	.10
274	Benny Santiago	.15
275	Scott Radinsky	.10
276	Mariano Duncan	.10
277	Kenny Lofton	.75
278	Dwight Smith	.10
279	Joe Carter	.20
280	Tim Jones	.10
281	Jeff Huson	.10
282	Phil Plantier	.10
283	Kirby Puckett	1.00
284	Johnny Guzman	.10
285	Mike Morgan	.10
286	Chris Sabo	.10
287	Matt Williams	.30
288	Checklist 1-100	.10
289	Checklist 101-200	.10
290	Checklist 201-300	.10
291	Dennis Eckersley (Members Choice)	.15
292	Eric Karros (Members Choice)	.15
293	Pat Listach (Members Choice)	.10
294	Andy Van Slyke (Members Choice)	.10
295	Robin Ventura (Members Choice)	.15
296	Tom Glavine (Members Choice)	.15
297	Juan Gonzalez (Members Choice)	.50
298	Travis Fryman (Members Choice)	.15
299	Larry Walker (Members Choice)	.20
300	Gary Sheffield (Members Choice)	.20
301	Chuck Finley	.10
302	Luis Gonzalez	.10
303	Darryl Hamilton	.10
304	Bien Figueroa	.10
305	Ron Darling	.10
306	Jonathan Hurst	.10
307	Mike Sharperson	.10
308	Mike Christopher	.10
309	Marvin Freeman	.10
310	Jay Buhner	.25
311	Butch Henry	.10
312	Greg Harris	.10
313	Darren Daulton	.10
314	Chuck Knoblauch	.25
315	Greg Harris	.10
316	John Franco	.10
317	John Wehner	.10
318	Donald Harris	.10
319	Benny Santiago	.10
320	Larry Walker	.30
321	Randy Knorr	.10
322	*Ramon D. Martinez*	.15
323	Mike Stanley	.10
324	Bill Wegman	.10
325	Tom Candiotti	.10
326	Glenn Davis	.10
327	Chuck Crim	.10
328	Scott Livingstone	.10
329	Eddie Taubensee	.10
330	George Bell	.10
331	Edgar Martinez	.15
332	Paul Assenmacher	.10
333	Steve Hosey	.10
334	Mo Vaughn	.75
335	Bret Saberhagen	.10
336	Mike Trombley	.10
337	Mark Lewis	.10
338	Terry Pendleton	.10
339	Dave Hollins	.10
340	Jeff Conine	.12
341	Bob Tewksbury	.10
342	Billy Ashley	.30
343	Zane Smith	.10
344	John Wetteland	.10
345	Chris Hoiles	.10
346	Frank Castillo	.10
347	Bruce Hurst	.10
348	Kevin McReynolds	.10
349	Dave Henderson	.10
350	Ryan Bowen	.10
351	Sid Fernandez	.10
352	Mark Whiten	.10
353	Nolan Ryan	2.00
354	Rick Aguilera	.10
355	Mark Langston	.10
356	Jack Morris	.10
357	Rob Deer	.10
358	Dave Fleming	.10
359	Lance Johnson	.10
360	Joe Millette	.10
361	Wil Cordero	.15
362	Chito Martinez	.10
363	Scott Servais	.10
364	Bernie Williams	.60
365	Pedro Martinez	.10
366	Ryne Sandberg	.60
367	Brad Ausmus	.10
368	Scott Cooper	.10
369	Rob Dibble	.10
370	Walt Weiss	.10
371	Mark Davis	.10
372	Orlando Merced	.10
373	Mike Jackson	.10
374	Kevin Appier	.10
375	Esteban Beltre	.10
376	Joe Slusarski	.10
377	William Suero	.10
378	Pete O'Brien	.10
379	Alan Embree	.15
380	Lenny Webster	.10
381	Eric Davis	.10
382	Duane Ward	.10
383	John Habyan	.10
384	Jeff Bagwell	1.00
385	Ruben Amaro	.10
386	Julio Valera	.10

387	Robin Ventura	.25
388	Archi Cianfrocco	.10
389	Skeeter Barnes	.10
390	Tim Costo	.10
391	Luis Mercedes	.10
392	Jeremy Hernandez	.10
393	Shawon Dunston	.10
394	Andy Van Slyke	.10
395	Kevin Maas	.10
396	Kevin Brown	.10
397	J.T. Bruett	.10
398	Darryl Strawberry	.10
399	Tom Pagnozzi	.10
400	Sandy Alomar	.10
401	Keith Miller	.10
402	Rich DeLucia	.10
403	Shawn Abner	.10
404	Howard Johnson	.10
405	Mike Benjamin	.10
406	*Roberto Mejia*	.15
407	Mike Butcher	.10
408	Deion Sanders	.25
409	Todd Stottlemyre	.10
410	Scott Kamieniecki	.10
411	Doug Jones	.10
412	John Burkett	.10
413	Lance Blankenship	.10
414	Jeff Parrett	.10
415	Barry Larkin	.20
416	Alan Trammell	.10
417	Mark Kiefer	.10
418	Gregg Olson	.10
419	Mark Grace	.25
420	Shane Mack	.10
421	Bob Walk	.10
422	Curt Schilling	.10
423	Erik Hanson	.10
424	George Brett	.60
425	Reggie Jefferson	.10
426	Mark Portugal	.10
427	Ron Karkovice	.10
428	Matt Young	.10
429	Troy Neel	.15
430	Hector Fajardo	.10
431	Dave Righetti	.10
432	Pat Listach	.15
433	Jeff Innis	.10
434	Bob MacDonald	.10
435	Brian Jordan	.10
436	Jeff Blauser	.10
437	*Mike Myers*	.12
438	Frank Seminara	.10
439	Rusty Meacham	.10
440	Greg Briley	.10
441	Derek Lilliquist	.10
442	John Vander Wal	.10
443	Scott Erickson	.10
444	Bob Scanlan	.10
445	Todd Frohwirth	.10
446	Tom Goodwin	.10
447	William Pennyfeather	.10
448	Travis Fryman	.15
449	Mickey Morandini	.10
450	Greg Olson	.10
451	Trevor Hoffman	.10
452	Dave Magadan	.10
453	Shawn Jeter	.15
454	Andres Galarraga	.25
455	Ted Wood	.10
456	Freddie Benavides	.10
457	Junior Felix	.10
458	Alex Cole	.10
459	John Orton	.10
460	Eddie Zosky	.10
461	Dennis Eckersley	.15
462	Lee Smith	.12
463	John Smoltz	.20
464	Ken Caminiti	.10
465	Melido Perez	.10
466	Tom Marsh	.10
467	Jeff Nelson	.10
468	Jesse Levis	.10
469	Chris Nabholz	.10
470	Mike Mcfarlane	.10
471	Reggie Sanders	.15
472	Chuck McElroy	.10
473	Kevin Gross	.10
474	*Matt Whiteside*	.15
475	Cal Eldred	.10
476	Dave Gallagher	.10
477	Len Dykstra	.15
478	Mark McGwire	4.00
479	David Segui	.10
480	Mike Henneman	.10
481	Bret Barberie	.10
482	Steve Sax	.10
483	Dave Valle	.10
484	Danny Darwin	.10
485	Devon White	.10
486	Eric Plunk	.10
487	Jim Gott	.10
488	Scooter Tucker	.10
489	Omar Oliveres	.10
490	Greg Myers	.10
491	Brian Hunter	.10
492	Kevin Tapani	.10
493	Rich Monteleone	.10
494	Steve Buechele	.10
495	Bo Jackson	.25
496	Mike LaValliere	.10
497	Mark Leonard	.10
498	Daryl Boston	.10
499	Jose Canseco	.25
500	Brian Barnes	.10
501	Randy Johnson	.50
502	Tim McIntosh	.10
503	Cecil Fielder	.25
504	Derek Bell	.15
505	Kevin Koslofski	.10
506	Darren Holmes	.10
507	Brady Anderson	.10
508	John Valentin	.15
509	Jerry Browne	.10
510	Fred McGriff	.25
511	Pedro Astacio	.15
512	Gary Gaetti	.10
513	*John Burke*	.25
514	Dwight Gooden	.15
515	Thomas Howard	.10
516	*Darrell Whitmore*	.20
517	Ozzie Guillen	.10
518	Darryl Kile	.10
519	Rich Rowland	.10
520	Carlos Delgado	.50
521	Doug Henry	.10
522	Greg Colbrunn	.10
523	Tom Gordon	.10
524	Ivan Rodriguez	.75
525	Kent Hrbek	.12
526	Eric Young	.12
527	Rod Brewer	.10
528	Eric Karros	.15
529	Marquis Grissom	.15
530	Rico Brogna	.10
531	Sammy Sosa	1.50
532	Bret Boone	.15
533	Luis Rivera	.10
534	Hal Morris	.10
535	Monty Fariss	.10
536	Leo Gomez	.10
537	Wally Joyner	.12
538	Tony Gwynn	1.00
539	Mike Williams	.10
540	Juan Gonzalez	1.00
541	Ryan Klesko	1.00
542	Ryan Thompson	.15
543	Chad Curtis	.15
544	Orel Hershiser	.12
545	Carlos Garcia	.10
546	Bob Welch	.10
547	Vinny Castilla	.15
548	Ozzie Smith	.40
549	Luis Salazar	.10
550	Mark Guthrie	.10
551	Charles Nagy	.15
552	Alex Fernandez	.10
553	Mel Rojas	.10
554	Orestes Destrade	.10
555	Mark Gubicza	.10
556	Steve Finley	.10
557	Don Mattingly	1.00
558	Rickey Henderson	.20
559	Tommy Greene	.10
560	Arthur Rhodes	.10
561	Alfredo Griffin	.10
562	Will Clark	.25
563	Bob Zupcic	.10
564	Chuck Carr	.10
565	Henry Cotto	.10
566	Billy Spiers	.10
567	Jack Armstrong	.10
568	Kurt Stillwell	.10
569	David McCarty	.15
570	Joe Vitiello	.25
571	Gerald Williams	.10
572	Dale Murphy	.15
573	Scott Aldred	.10
574	Bill Gullickson	.10
575	Bobby Thigpen	.10
576	Glenallen Hill	.10
577	Dwayne Henry	.10
578	Calvin Jones	.10
579	Al Martin	.15
580	Ruben Sierra	.20
581	Andy Benes	.10
582	Anthony Young	.10
583	Shawn Boskie	.10
584	*Scott Pose*	.15
585	Mike Piazza	3.00
586	Donovan Osborne	.10
587	James Austin	.10
588	Checklist 301-400	.10
589	Checklist 401-500	.10
590	Checklist 501-600	.10
591	Ken Griffey, Jr. (Members Choice)	2.00
592	Ivan Rodriguez (Members Choice)	.40
593	Carlos Baerga (Members Choice)	.10
594	Fred McGriff (Members Choice)	.20
595	Mark McGwire (Members Choice)	2.00
596	Roberto Alomar (Members Choice)	.40
597	Kirby Puckett (Members Choice)	.40
598	Marquis Grissom (Members Choice)	.15
599	John Smoltz (Members Choice)	.10
600	Ryne Sandberg (Members Choice)	.40
601	Wade Boggs	.20
602	Jeff Reardon	.10
603	Billy Ripken	.10
604	Bryan Harvey	.10
605	Carlos Quintana	.10
606	Greg Hibbard	.10
607	Ellis Burks	.10
608	Greg Swindell	.10
609	Dave Winfield	.20
610	Charlie Hough	.10
611	Chili Davis	.10
612	Jody Reed	.10
613	Mark Williamson	.10
614	Phil Plantier	.15
615	Jim Abbott	.15
616	Dante Bichette	.35
617	Mark Eichhorn	.10
618	Gary Sheffield	.25
619	*Richie Lewis*	.20
620	Joe Girardi	.10
621	Jaime Navarro	.10
622	Willie Wilson	.10
623	Scott Fletcher	.10
624	Bud Black	.10
625	Tom Brunansky	.10
626	Steve Avery	.15
627	Paul Molitor	.40
628	Gregg Jefferies	.15
629	Dave Stewart	.12
630	Javier Lopez	.35
631	Greg Gagne	.10
632	Bobby Kelly	.10
633	Mike Fetters	.10
634	Ozzie Canseco	.10
635	Jeff Russell	.10
636	Pete Incaviglia	.10
637	Tom Henke	.10
638	Chipper Jones	1.50
639	Jimmy Key	.10
640	Dave Martinez	.10
641	Dave Stieb	.10
642	Milt Thompson	.10
643	Alan Mills	.10
644	Tony Fernandez	.10
645	Randy Bush	.10
646	Joe Magrane	.10
647	Ivan Calderon	.10
648	Jose Guzman	.10
649	John Olerud	.25
650	Tom Glavine	.20
651	Julio Franco	.10
652	Armando Reynoso	.10
653	Felix Jose	.10
654	Ben Rivera	.10
655	Andre Dawson	.15
656	Mike Harkey	.10
657	Kevin Seitzer	.10
658	Lonnie Smith	.10
659	Norm Charlton	.10
660	Dave Justice	.40
661	Fernando Valenzuela	.10
662	Dan Wilson	.15
663	Mark Gardner	.10
664	Doug Dascenzo	.10

665	Greg Maddux	2.50
666	Harold Baines	.10
667	Randy Myers	.10
668	Harold Reynolds	.10
669	Candy Maldonado	.10
670	Al Leiter	.10
671	Jerald Clark	.10
672	Doug Drabek	.10
673	Kirk Gibson	.10
674	*Steve Reed*	.10
675	Mike Felder	.10
676	Ricky Gutierrez	.10
677	Spike Owen	.10
678	Otis Nixon	.10
679	Scott Sanderson	.10
680	Mark Carreon	.10
681	Troy Percival	.10
682	Kevin Stocker	.10
683	*Jim Converse*	.15
684	Barry Bonds	.75
685	Greg Gohr	.10
686	Tim Wallach	.10
687	Matt Mieske	.10
688	Robby Thompson	.10
689	Brien Taylor	.15
690	Kirt Manwaring	.10
691	*Mike Lansing*	.25
692	Steve Decker	.10
693	Mike Moore	.10
694	Kevin Mitchell	.12
695	Phil Hiatt	.10
696	*Tony Tarasco*	.15
697	Benji Gil	.25
698	Jeff Juden	.10
699	Kevin Reimer	.10
700	Andy Ashby	.10
701	John Jaha	.15
702	*Tim Bogar*	.20
703	David Cone	.10
704	Willie Greene	.15
705	*David Hulse*	.15
706	Cris Carpenter	.10
707	Ken Griffey, Jr.	3.00
708	Steve Bedrosian	.10
709	Dave Nilsson	.10
710	Paul Wagner	.10
711	B.J. Surhoff	.10
712	*Rene Arocha*	.20
713	Manny Lee	.10
714	Brian Williams	.10
715	*Sherman Obando*	.15
716	Terry Mulholland	.10
717	Paul O'Neill	.20
718	David Nied	.15
719	*J.T. Snow*	.75
720	Nigel Wilson	.20
721	Mike Bielecki	.10
722	Kevin Young	.10
723	Charlie Leibrandt	.10
724	Frank Bolick	.10
725	*Jon Shave*	.15
726	Steve Cooke	.15
727	*Domingo Martinez*	.15
728	Todd Worrell	.10
729	Jose Lind	.10
730	*Jim Tatum*	.10
731	Mike Hampton	.10
732	Mike Draper	.10
733	Henry Mercedes	.15
734	*John Johnstone*	.15
735	Mitch Webster	.10
736	Russ Springer	.10
737	Rob Natal	.10
738	Steve Howe	.10
739	*Darrell Sherman*	.15
740	Pat Mahomes	.10
741	Alex Arias	.10
742	Damon Buford	.10
743	Charlie Hayes	.10
744	Guillermo Velasquez	.15
745	Checklist 601-750	.10
746	Frank Thomas (Members Choice)	2.50
747	Barry Bonds (Members Choice)	.35
748	Roger Clemens (Members Choice)	.50
749	Joe Carter (Members Choice)	.15
750	Greg Maddux (Members Choice)	1.50

A player's name in *italic* type indicates a rookie card.

1993 Stadium Club 1st Day Production

Inserted at the rate of about one per wax box, with an estimated production of 2,000 apiece, First Day Production cards are regular-issue Stadium Club cards on which an embossed silver holographic foil logo has been added. Because values for FDP cards are up to 50 times greater than for regular cards, collectors should be aware that fake FDP cards have been created by cutting the logo off a common-player card and gluing it to a star card.

	MT
Complete Set (750):	4000.
Complete Series 1 (1-300)	1400.
Complete Series 2 (301-600)	1800.
Complete Series 3 (601-750)	800.00
Common Player:	2.00
(Star cards valued at 35X-50X same cards in regular Stadium Club issue.)	

1993 Stadium Club Master Photos

Each box of 1993 Stadium Club packs included one Master Photo premium insert. Prize cards good for three Master Photos in a mail-in offer were also included in each of the three series. The 5" x 7" Master Photos feature wide white borders and a large Stadium Club logo at top, highlighted by prismatic foil. The same foil is used as a border for a larger-format version of the player's regular S.C. card at the center of the Master Photo. A "Members Only" version of each of the 1993 Master Photos was available as a premium with the purchase of a Members Only Stadium Club set. the Members Only Master Photos have a gold-foil seal in the upper-right corner.

	MT
Complete Set (30):	25.00
Common Player:	.50

Series I

(1)	Carlos Baerga	.50
(2)	Delino DeShields	.50
(3)	Brian McRae	.50
(4)	Sam Militello	.50
(5)	Joe Oliver	.50
(6)	Kirby Puckett	2.00

Series II

(13)	George Brett	2.00
(14)	Jose Canseco	.75
(15)	Will Clark	.75
(16)	Travis Fryman	.50
(17)	Dwight Gooden	.75
(18)	Mark Grace	.75

Series III

(25)	Barry Bonds	2.00
(26)	Ken Griffey, Jr.	5.00
(27)	Greg Maddux	4.00
(28)	David Nied	.50
(29)	J.T. Snow	1.00
(30)	Brien Taylor	.50

1993 Stadium Club Special (Murphy)

Though the packaging and the cards themselves identify this 200-card set as a 1992 issue, it was not released until 1993 and is thought of by the hobby at large as a 1993 set. The set is sold in a plastic replica of Jack Murphy Stadium in San Diego, venue for the 1993 All-Star Game. Fifty-six of the cards feature players from that contest and are so identified by a line of gold-foil on the card front and an All-Star logo on back. Twenty-five members of the 1992 Team U.S.A. Olympic baseball squad are also included in the set, with appropriate logos and notations front and back. There are 19 cards depicting action and stars of the the 1992 League Championships and World Series. The other 100 cards in the set are 1992 draft picks. All cards have the same basic format as the regular-issue 1992 Topps Stadium Club cards, full-bleed photos on front and back, UV coating on both sides and gold-foil highlights on front. Besides the 200 standard-size cards, the Special Edition set included a dozen "Master Photos," 5" x 7" white-bordered premium cards.

	MT
Complete Set (200):	24.00
Common Player:	.10

1	Dave Winfield	.15
2	Juan Guzman	.10
3	Tony Gwynn	1.00
4	Chris Roberts	.20
5	Benny Santiago	.10
6	Sherard Clinkscales	.10
7	*Jonathan Nunnally*	.35
8	Chuck Knoblauch	.30
9	*Bob Wolcott*	.10

10	Steve Rodriguez	.10	
11	*Mark Williams*	.10	
12	*Danny Clyburn*	.15	
13	Darren Dreifort	.15	
14	Andy Van Slyke	.10	
15	Wade Boggs	.25	
16	Scott Patton	.10	
17	Gary Sheffield	.25	
18	Ron Villone	.10	
19	Roberto Alomar	.50	
20	Marc Valdes	.10	
21	Daron Kirkreit	.10	
22	Jeff Granger	.15	
23	Levon Largusa	.10	
24	Jimmy Key	.10	
25	Kevin Pearson	.10	
26	Michael Moore	.10	
27	*Preston Wilson*	.20	
28	Kirby Puckett	1.00	
29	*Tim Crabtree*	.15	
30	Bip Roberts	.10	
31	Kelly Gruber	.10	
32	Tony Fernandez	.10	
33	Jason Angel	.10	
34	Calvin Murray	.10	
35	Chad McConnell	.15	
36	Jason Moler	.10	
37	Mark Lemke	.10	
38	Tom Knauss	.10	
39	Larry Mitchell	.10	
40	Doug Mirabelli	.10	
41	Everett Stull II	.10	
42	Chris Wimmer	.10	
43	*Dan Serafini*	.10	
44	Ryne Sandberg	.50	
45	Steve Lyons	.10	
46	Ryan Freeburg	.10	
47	Ruben Sierra	.10	
48	David Mysel	.10	
49	Joe Hamilton	.15	
50	Steve Rodriguez	.10	
51	Tim Wakefield	.10	
52	Scott Gentile	.10	
53	Doug Jones	.10	
54	Willie Brown	.10	
55	*Chad Mottola*	.20	
56	Ken Griffey, Jr.	3.00	
57	Jon Lieber	.10	
58	Denny Martinez	.15	
59	Joe Petcka	.10	
60	Benji Simonton	.10	
61	Brett Backlund	.10	
62	Damon Berryhill	.10	
63	Juan Guzman	.10	
64	Doug Hecker	.10	
65	Jamie Arnold	.10	
66	Bob Tewksbury	.10	
67	Tim Leger	.10	
68	Todd Etler	.10	
69	Lloyd McClendon	.10	
70	Kurt Ehmann	.10	
71	Rick Magdaleno	.10	
72	Tom Pagnozzi	.10	
73	Jeffrey Hammonds	.15	
74	Joe Carter	.15	
75	Chris Holt	.10	
76	Charles Johnson	1.00	
77	Bob Walk	.10	
78	Fred McGriff	.20	
79	Tom Evans	.10	
80	Scott Klingenbeck	.10	
81	Chad McConnell	.15	
82	Chris Eddy	.10	
83	Phil Nevin	.15	
84	John Kruk	.10	
85	Tony Sheffield	.10	
86	John Smoltz	.20	
87	Trevor Humphry	.10	
88	Charles Nagy	.10	
89	Sean Runyan	.10	
90	Mike Gulan	.10	
91	Darren Daulton	.10	
92	Otis Nixon	.10	
93	Nomar Garciaparra	12.00	
94	Larry Walker	.35	
95	Hut Smith	.10	
96	Rick Helling	.15	
97	Roger Clemens	1.00	
98	Ron Gant	.15	
99	Kenny Felder	.10	
100	Steve Murphy	.10	
101	Mike Smith	.10	
102	Terry Pendleton	.10	
103	Tim Davis	.10	
104	Jeff Patzke	.10	
105	Craig Wilson	.10	
106	Tom Glavine	.20	
107	Mark Langston	.10	
108	Mark Thompson	.10	
109	*Eric Owens*	.10	
110	Keith Johnson	.10	
111	Robin Ventura	.20	
112	Ed Sprague	.10	
113	*Jeff Schmidt*	.10	
114	Don Wengert	.10	
115	Craig Biggio	.20	
116	Kenny Carlyle	.10	
117	*Derek Jeter*	8.00	
118	Manuel Lee	.10	
119	Jeff Haas	.10	
120	Roger Bailey	.10	
121	Sean Lowe	.10	
122	Rick Aguilera	.10	
123	Sandy Alomar	.15	
124	Derek Wallace	.15	
125	B.J. Wallace	.15	
126	Greg Maddux	2.00	
127	Tim Moore	.10	
128	Lee Smith	.10	
129	Todd Steverson	.15	
130	Chris Widger	.15	
131	Paul Molitor	.40	
132	Chris Smith	.10	
133	*Chris Gomez*	.20	
134	Jimmy Baron	.10	
135	John Smoltz	.10	
136	Pat Borders	.10	
137	Donnie Leshnock	.10	
138	Gus Gandarillos	.10	
139	Will Clark	.25	
140	*Ryan Luzinski*	.10	
141	Cal Ripken, Jr.	3.00	
142	B.J. Wallace	.15	
143	*Trey Beamon*	.40	
144	Norm Charlton	.10	
145	Mike Mussina	.35	
146	Billy Owens	.10	
147	Ozzie Smith	.40	
148	*Jason Kendall*	3.00	
149	*Mike Matthews*	.10	
150	David Spykstra	.10	
151	Benji Grigsby	.10	
152	Sean Smith	.10	
153	Mark McGwire	4.00	
154	David Cone	.20	
155	*Shon Walker*	.25	
156	Jason McDowell	.10	
157	Jack McDowell	.10	
158	Paxton Briley	.10	
159	Edgar Martinez	.10	
160	Brian Sackinsky	.10	
161	Barry Bonds	.60	
162	Roberto Kelly	.10	
163	Jeff Alkire	.10	
164	Mike Sharperson	.10	
165	Jamie Taylor	.10	
166	John Saffer	.10	
167	Jerry Browne	.10	
168	Travis Fryman	.10	
169	Brady Anderson	.15	
170	Chris Roberts	.20	
171	Lloyd Peever	.10	
172	Francisco Cabrera	.10	
173	Ramiro Martinez	.10	
174	Jeff Alkire	.10	
175	Ivan Rodriguez	.50	
176	Kevin Brown	.10	
177	Chad Roper	.10	
178	Rod Henderson	.10	
179	Dennis Eckersley	.20	
180	*Shannon Stewart*	.20	
181	DeShawn Warren	.10	
182	Lonnie Smith	.10	
183	Willie Adams	.10	
184	Jeff Montgomery	.10	
185	Damon Hollins	.10	
186	Byron Matthews	.10	
187	Harold Baines	.10	
188	Rick Greene	.15	
189	Carlos Baerga	.15	
190	Brandon Cromer	.10	
191	Roberto Alomar	.50	
192	Rich Ireland	.10	
193	Steve Montgomery	.10	
194	Brant Brown	1.50	
195	Ritchie Moody	.10	
196	Michael Tucker	.20	
197	*Jason Varitek*	.50	
198	David Manning	.15	
199	Marquis Riley	.10	
200	Jason Giambi	.25	

1993 Stadium Club I Inserts

Four bonus cards were produced as special inserts in Series I Stadium Club packs. Two of the full-bleed, gold-foil enhanced cards honor Robin Yount and George Brett for achieving the 3,000-hit mark, while the other two commemorate the first picks in the 1993 expansion draft by the Colorado Rockies (David Nied) and Marlins (Nigel Wilson).

		MT
Complete Set (4):		7.50
Common Player:		.75
1	Robin Yount (3,000 hits)	2.50
2	George Brett (3,000 hits)	4.00
3	David Nied (#1 pick)	.75
4	Nigel Wilson (#1 pick)	.75

1993 Stadium Club II Inserts

Cross-town and regional rivals were featured in this four-card insert set found, on average, one per 24 packs of Series II Stadium Club. Each of the two-faced cards is typical S.C. quality with gold-foil stamping and UV coating front and back.

		MT
Complete Set (4):		12.00
Common Card:		2.00
1	Pacific Terrific(Will Clark, Mark McGwire)	4.00

2	Broadway Stars(Dwight Gooden, Don Mattingly)	2.00
3	Second City Sluggers(Ryne Sandberg, Frank Thomas)	4.00
4	Pacific Terrific(Ken Griffey, Jr., Darryl Strawberry)	4.00

1993 Stadium Club III Inserts

Team "firsts" - first game, first pitch, first batter, etc. - for the 1993 expansion Florida Marlins and Colorado Rockies are featured on this pair of inserts found in Series III Stadium Club packs. Fronts featured game-action photos with the player's name in gold foil. On back is a stadium scene with the team first overprinted in black. At top the team name and Stadium Club logo are in gold foil.

		MT
Complete Set:		1.50
Common Player:		.50
1	David Nied	.50
2	Charlie Hough	.50

1994 Stadium Club

Issued in three series to a total of 720 cards, Topps' mid-price brand features a hip look and a wide range of insert specials. The regular cards feature a borderless photo with the player's name presented in a unique typewriter/label maker style at bottom. The player's last name and Topps Stadium Club logo at top are in red foil. Backs feature another player photo, some personal data and a headlined career summary. Various stats and skills rankings complete the data. Subsets within the issue include cards annotated with Major League debut dates, 1993 awards won, home run club cards, cards featuring two or three players, and Final Tribute cards for George Brett and Nolan Ryan.

		MT
Complete Set (720):		40.00
Common Player:		.10
Series 1,2,3 Wax Box:		20.00
1	Robin Yount	.40

2	Rick Wilkins	.10
3	Steve Scarsone	.10
4	Gary Sheffield	.40
5	George Brett	.75
6	Al Martin	.10
7	Joe Oliver	.10
8	Stan Belinda	.10
9	Denny Hocking	.10
10	Roberto Alomar	.75
11	Luis Polonia	.10
12	Scott Hemond	.10
13	Joey Reed	.10
14	Mel Rojas	.10
15	Junior Ortiz	.10
16	Harold Baines	.12
17	Brad Pennington	.10
18	Jay Bell	.10
19	Tom Henke	.10
20	Jeff Branson	.10
21	Roberto Mejia	.10
22	Pedro Munoz	.10
23	Matt Nokes	.10
24	Jack McDowell	.10
25	Cecil Fielder	.20
26	Tony Fossas	.10
27	Jim Eisenreich	.10
28	Anthony Young	.10
29	Chuck Carr	.10
30	Jeff Treadway	.10
31	Chris Nabholz	.10
32	Tom Candiotti	.10
33	Mike Maddux	.10
34	Nolan Ryan	2.00
35	Luis Gonzalez	.10
36	Tim Salmon	.50
37	Mark Whiten	.10
38	Roger McDowell	.10
39	Royce Clayton	.12
40	Troy Neel	.10
41	Mike Harkey	.10
42	Darrin Fletcher	.10
43	Wayne Kirby	.10
44	Rich Amaral	.10
45	Robb Nen	.10
46	Tim Teufel	.10
47	Steve Cooke	.10
48	Jeff McNeely	.10
49	Jeff Montgomery	.10
50	Skeeter Barnes	.10
51	Scott Stahoviak	.10
52	Pat Kelly	.10
53	Brady Anderson	.20
54	Mariano Duncan	.10
55	Brian Bohanon	.10
56	Jerry Spradlin	.10
57	Ron Karkovice	.10
58	Jeff Gardner	.10
59	Bobby Bonilla	.15
60	Tino Martinez	.15
61	Todd Benzinger	.10
62	*Steve Trachsel*	.35
63	Brian Jordan	.15
64	Steve Bedrosian	.10
65	Brent Gates	.10
66	Shawn Green	.20
67	Sean Berry	.10
68	Joe Klink	.10
69	Fernando Valenzuela	.12
70	Andy Tomberlin	.10
71	Tony Pena	.10
72	Eric Young	.10
73	Chris Gomez	.10
74	Paul O'Neill	.12
75	Ricky Gutierrez	.10
76	Brad Holman	.10
77	Lance Painter	.10
78	Mike Butcher	.10
79	Sid Bream	.10
80	Sammy Sosa	1.50
81	Felix Fermin	.10
82	Todd Hundley	.20
83	Kevin Higgins	.10
84	Todd Pratt	.10
85	Ken Griffey, Jr.	3.00
86	John O'Donoghue	.10
87	Rick Renteria	.10
88	John Burkett	.10
89	Jose Vizcaino	.10
90	Kevin Seitzer	.10
91	Bobby Witt	.10
92	Chris Turner	.10
93	Omar Vizquel	.10
94	Dave Justice	.25
95	David Segui	.10
96	Dave Hollins	.10
97	Doug Strange	.10

98	Jerald Clark	.10
99	Mike Moore	.10
100	Joey Cora	.10
101	Scott Kamieniecki	.10
102	Andy Benes	.15
103	Chris Bosio	.10
104	Rey Sanchez	.10
105	John Jaha	.10
106	Otis Nixon	.10
107	Rickey Henderson	.25
108	Jeff Bagwell	1.00
109	Gregg Jefferies	.12
110	Topps Trios(Roberto Alomar, Paul Molitor, John Olerud)	.25
111	Topps Trios(Ron Gant, David Justice, Fred McGriff)	.25
112	Topps Trios(Juan Gonzalez, Rafael Palmeiro, Dean Palmer)	.20
113	Greg Swindell	.10
114	Bill Hasleman	.10
115	Phil Plantier	.15
116	Ivan Rodriguez	.75
117	Kevin Tapani	.10
118	Mike LaValliere	.10
119	Tim Costo	.10
120	Mickey Morandini	.10
121	Brett Butler	.12
122	Tom Pagnozzi	.10
123	Ron Gant	.15
124	Damion Easley	.10
125	Dennis Eckersley	.12
126	Matt Mieske	.10
127	Cliff Floyd	.10
128	*Julian Tavarez*	.20
129	Arthur Rhodes	.10
130	Dave West	.10
131	Tim Naehring	.10
132	Freddie Benavides	.10
133	Paul Assenmacher	.10
134	David McCarty	.10
135	Jose Lind	.10
136	Reggie Sanders	.15
137	Don Slaught	.10
138	Andujar Cedeno	.10
139	Rob Deer	.10
140	Mike Piazza	1.50
141	Moises Alou	.15
142	Tom Foley	.10
143	Benny Santiago	.10
144	Sandy Alomar	.12
145	Carlos Hernandez	.10
146	Luis Alicea	.10
147	Tom Lampkin	.10
148	Ryan Klesko	1.00
149	Juan Guzman	.10
150	Scott Servais	.10
151	Tony Gwynn	1.00
152	Tim Wakefield	.10
153	David Nied	.10
154	Chris Haney	.10
155	Danny Bautista	.10
156	Randy Velarde	.10
157	Darrin Jackson	.10
158	*J.R. Phillips*	.20
159	Greg Gagne	.10
160	Luis Aquino	.10
161	John Vander Wal	.10
162	Randy Myers	.10
163	Ted Power	.10
164	Scott Brosius	.10
165	Len Dykstra	.12
166	Jacob Brumfield	.10
167	Bo Jackson	.20
168	Eddie Taubensee	.10
169	Carlos Baerga	.15
170	Tim Bogar	.10
171	Jose Canseco	.35
172	Greg Blosser	.10
173	Chili Davis	.10
174	Randy Knorr	.10
175	Mike Perez	.10
176	Henry Rodriguez	.12
177	*Brian Turang*	.15
178	Roger Pavlik	.10
179	Aaron Sele	.15
180	Tale of 2 Players(Fred McGriff, Gary Sheffield)	.20
181	Tale of 2 Players(J.T. Snow, Tim Salmon)	.20
182	Roberto Hernandez	.10
183	Jeff Reboulet	.10
184	John Doherty	.10
185	Danny Sheaffer	.10
186	Bip Roberts	.10

#	Player	Price	#	Player	Price	#	Player	Price
187	Denny Martinez	.12	275	Rick Aguilera	.10	371	Andre Dawson	.15
188	Darryl Hamilton	.10	276	Ramon Martinez	.12	372	Bobby Kelly	.10
189	Eduardo Perez	.10	277	Orlando Merced	.10	373	Cal Ripken, Jr.	2.50
190	Pete Harnisch	.10	278	Guillermo Velasquez	.10	374	Craig Biggio	.15
191	Rick Gossage	.10	279	Mark Hutton	.10	375	Dan Pasqua	.10
192	Mickey Tettleton	.10	280	Larry Walker	.25	376	Dave Nilsson	.10
193	Lenny Webster	.10	281	Kevin Gross	.10	377	Duane Ward	.10
194	Lance Johnson	.10	282	Jose Offerman	.10	378	Greg Vaughn	.10
195	Don Mattingly	1.00	283	Jim Leyritz	.10	379	Jeff Fassero	.10
196	Gregg Olson	.10	284	Jamie Moyer	.10	380	Jerry Dipoto	.10
197	Mark Gubicza	.10	285	Frank Thomas	2.50	381	John Patterson	.10
198	Scott Fletcher	.10	286	Derek Bell	.12	382	Kevin Brown	.10
199	Jon Shave	.10	287	Derrick May	.10	383	Kevin Roberson	.10
200	Tim Mauser	.10	288	Dave Winfield	.20	384	Joe Orsulak	.10
201	Jeromy Burnitz	.10	289	Curt Schilling	.10	385	Hilly Hathaway	.10
202	Rob Dibble	.10	290	Carlos Quintana	.10	386	Mike Greenwell	.10
203	Will Clark	.40	291	Bob Natal	.10	387	Orestes Destrade	.10
204	Steve Buechele	.10	292	David Cone	.15	388	Mike Gallego	.10
205	Brian Williams	.10	293	Al Osuna	.10	389	Ozzie Guillen	.10
206	Carlos Garcia	.10	294	Bob Hamelin	.10	390	Raul Mondesi	.75
207	Mark Clark	.10	295	Chad Curtis	.10	391	Scott Lydy	.10
208	Rafael Palmeiro	.15	296	Danny Jackson	.10	392	Tom Urbani	.10
209	Eric Davis	.12	297	Bob Welch	.10	393	Wil Cordero	.10
210	Pat Meares	.10	298	Felix Jose	.10	394	Tony Longmire	.10
211	Chuck Finley	.10	299	Jay Buhner	.15	395	Todd Zeile	.12
212	Jason Bere	.10	300	Joe Carter	.15	396	Scott Cooper	.10
213	Gary DiSarcina	.10	301	Kenny Lofton	.75	397	Ryne Sandberg	.60
214	Tony Fernandez	.10	302	*Kirk Rueter*	.15	398	Ricky Bones	.10
215	B.J. Surhoff	.10	303	Kim Batiste	.10	399	Phil Clark	.10
216	Lee Guetterman	.10	304	Mike Morgan	.10	400	Orel Hershiser	.12
217	Tim Wallach	.10	305	Pat Borders	.10	401	Mike Henneman	.10
218	Kirt Manwaring	.10	306	Rene Arocha	.10	402	Mark Lemke	.10
219	Albert Belle	.75	307	Ruben Sierra	.12	403	Mark Grace	.20
220	Dwight Gooden	.15	308	Steve Finley	.10	404	Ken Ryan	.10
221	Archi Cianfrocco	.10	309	Travis Fryman	.10	405	John Smoltz	.20
222	Terry Mulholland	.10	310	Zane Smith	.10	406	Jeff Conine	.10
223	Hipolito Pichardo	.10	311	Willie Wilson	.10	407	Greg Harris	.10
224	Kent Hrbek	.15	312	Trevor Hoffman	.10	408	Doug Drabek	.10
225	Criag Grebeck	.10	313	Terry Pendleton	.10	409	Dave Fleming	.10
226	Todd Jones	.10	314	Salomon Torres	.10	410	Danny Tartabull	.10
227	Mike Bordick	.10	315	Robin Ventura	.15	411	Chad Kreuter	.10
228	John Olerud	.15	316	Randy Tomlin	.10	412	Brad Ausmus	.10
229	Jeff Blauser	.10	317	Dave Stewart	.10	413	Ben McDonald	.10
230	Alex Arias	.10	318	Mike Benjamin	.10	414	Barry Larkin	.25
231	Bernard Gilkey	.15	319	Matt Turner	.10	415	Bret Barberie	.10
232	Denny Neagle	.10	320	Manny Ramirez	.75	416	Chuck Knoblauch	.20
233	*Pedro Borbon*	.15	321	Kevin Young	.10	417	Ozzie Smith	.35
234	Dick Schofield	.10	322	Ken Caminiti	.25	418	Ed Sprague	.10
235	Matias Carrillo	.10	323	Joe Girardi	.10	419	Matt Williams	.30
236	Juan Bell	.10	324	Jeff McKnight	.10	420	Jeremy Hernandez	.10
237	Mike Hampton	.10	325	Gene Harris	.10	421	Jose Bautista	.10
238	Barry Bonds	.75	326	Devon White	.10	422	Kevin Mitchell	.10
239	Cris Carpenter	.10	327	Darryl Kile	.10	423	Manuel Lee	.10
240	Eric Karros	.15	328	Craig Paquette	.10	424	Mike Devereaux	.10
241	Greg McMichael	.10	329	Cal Eldred	.10	425	Omar Olivares	.10
242	Pat Hentgen	.10	330	Bill Swift	.10	426	Rafael Belliard	.10
243	Tim Pugh	.10	331	Alan Trammell	.15	427	Richie Lewis	.10
244	Vinny Castilla	.10	332	Armando Reynoso	.10	428	Ron Darling	.10
245	Charlie Hough	.10	333	Brent Mayne	.10	429	Shane Mack	.10
246	Bobby Munoz	.10	334	Chris Donnels	.10	430	Tim Hulett	.10
247	Kevin Baez	.10	335	Darryl Strawberry	.15	431	Wally Joyner	.12
248	Todd Frohwirth	.10	336	Dean Palmer	.10	432	Wes Chamberlain	.10
249	Charlie Hayes	.10	337	Frank Castillo	.10	433	Tom Browning	.10
250	Mike Macfarlane	.10	338	Jeff King	.10	434	Scott Radinsky	.10
251	Danny Darwin	.10	339	John Franco	.10	435	Rondell White	.25
252	Ben Rivera	.10	340	Kevin Appier	.10	436	Rod Beck	.10
253	Dave Henderson	.10	341	Lance Blankenship	.10	437	Rheal Cormier	.10
254	Steve Avery	.15	342	Mark McLemore	.10	438	Randy Johnson	.40
255	Tim Belcher	.10	343	Pedro Astacio	.10	439	Pete Schourek	.10
256	Dan Plesac	.10	344	Rich Batchelor	.10	440	Mo Vaughn	.60
257	Jim Thome	.40	345	Ryan Bowen	.10	441	Mike Timlin	.10
258	Albert Belle (35+ HR Hitter)	.30	346	Terry Steinbach	.10	442	Mark Langston	.10
259	Barry Bonds (35+ HR Hitter)	.35	347	Troy O'Leary	.10	443	Lou Whitaker	.10
260	Ron Gant (35+ HR Hitter)	.15	348	Willie Blair	.10	444	Kevin Stocker	.10
261	Juan Gonzalez (35+ HR Hitter)	.50	349	Wade Boggs	.25	445	Ken Hill	.10
262	Ken Griffey, Jr. (35+ HR Hitter)	1.50	350	Tim Raines	.12	446	John Wetteland	.10
263	Dave Justice (35+ HR Hitter)	.20	351	Scott Livingstone	.10	447	J.T. Snow	.15
264	Fred McGriff (35+ HR Hitter)	.20	352	Rod Carreia	.10	448	Erik Pappas	.10
265	Rafael Palmeiro (35+ HR Hitter)	.10	353	Ray Lankford	.15	449	David Hulse	.10
266	Mike Piazza (35+ HR Hitter)	.75	354	Pat Listach	.10	450	Darren Daulton	.10
267	Frank Thomas (35+ HR Hitter)	1.50	355	Milt Thompson	.10	451	Chris Hoiles	.10
268	Matt Williams (35+ HR Hitter)	.15	356	Miguel Jimenez	.10	452	Bryan Harvey	.10
269a	Checklist 1-135	.10	357	Marc Newfield	.15	453	Darren Lewis	.10
269b	Checklist 271-408	.10	358	Mark McGwire	4.00	454	Andres Galarraga	.20
270a	Checklist 136-270	.10	359	Kirby Puckett	.75	455	Joe Hesketh	.10
270b	Checklist 409-540	.10	360	Kent Mercker	.10	456	Jose Valentin	.10
271	Mike Stanley	.10	361	John Kruk	.10	457	Dan Peltier	.10
272	Tony Tarasco	.10	362	Jeff Kent	.10	458	Joe Boever	.10
273	Teddy Higuera	.10	363	Hal Morris	.10	459	Kevin Rogers	.10
274	Ryan Thompson	.10	364	Edgar Martinez	.15	460	Craig Shipley	.10
			365	Dave Magadan	.10	461	Alvaro Espinoza	.10
			366	Dante Bichette	.25	462	Wilson Alvarez	.10
			367	Chris Hammond	.10	463	Cory Snyder	.10
			368	Bret Saberhagen	.10	464	Candy Maldonado	.10
			369	Billy Ripken	.10	465	Blas Minor	.10
			370	Bill Gullickson	.10	466	Rod Bolton	.10

467	Kenny Rogers	.10
468	Greg Myers	.10
469	Jimmy Key	.10
470	Tony Castillo	.10
471	Mike Stanton	.10
472	Deion Sanders	.25
473	Tito Navarro	.10
474	Mike Gardiner	.10
475	Steve Reed	.10
476	John Roper	.10
477	Mike Trombley	.10
478	Charles Nagy	.10
479	Larry Casian	.10
480	Eric Hillman	.10
481	Bill Wertz	.10
482	Jeff Schwarz	.10
483	John Valentin	.12
484	Carl Willis	.10
485	Gary Gaetti	.12
486	Bill Pecota	.10
487	John Smiley	.10
488	Mike Mussina	.40
489	*Mike Ignasiak*	.15
490	Billy Brewer	.10
491	Jack Voigt	.10
492	Mike Munoz	.10
493	Lee Tinsley	.10
494	Bob Wickman	.10
495	Roger Salkeld	.10
496	Thomas Howard	.10
497	Mark Davis	.10
498	Dave Clark	.10
499	Turk Wendell	.10
500	Rafael Bournigal	.10
501	Chip Hale	.10
502	Matt Whiteside	.10
503	Brian Koelling	.10
504	Jeff Reed	.10
505	Paul Wagner	.10
506	Torey Lovullo	.10
507	Curtis Leskanic	.10
508	Derek Lilliquist	.10
509	Joe Magrane	.10
510	Mackey Sasser	.10
511	Lloyd McClendon	.10
512	*Jayhawk Owens*	.15
513	*Woody Williams*	.15
514	Gary Redus	.10
515	Tim Spehr	.10
516	Jim Abbott	.12
517	Lou Frazier	.10
518	Erik Plantenberg	.10
519	Tim Worrell	.10
520	Brian McRae	.10
521	*Chan Ho Park*	2.00
522	Mark Wohlers	.10
523	Geronimo Pena	.10
524	Andy Ashby	.10
525	Tale of 2 Players(Tim Raines, Andre Dawson)	.10
526	Tale of 2 Players(Paul Molitor, Dave Winfield)	.35
527	Joe Carter (RBI Leader)	.20
528	Frank Thomas (HR Leader)	1.50
529	Ken Griffey, Jr. (TB Leader)	1.50
530	Dave Justice (HR Leader)	.20
531	Gregg Jefferies (AVG Leader)	.10
532	Barry Bonds (HR Leader)	.35
533	John Kruk (Quick Start)	.10
534	Roger Clemens (Quick Start)	.20
535	Cecil Fielder (Quick Start)	.20
536	Ruben Sierra (Quick Start)	.10
537	Tony Gwynn (Quick Start)	.40
538	Tom Glavine (Quick Start)	.15
539	Not issued, see #269	
540	Not issued, see #270	
541	Ozzie Smith (Career Leader)	.25
542	Eddie Murray (Career Leader)	.25
543a	Lee Smith (Career Leader)	.10
543b	Lonnie Smith (should be #643)	.10
544	Greg Maddux	2.00
545	Denis Boucher	.10
546	Mark Gardner	.10
547	Bo Jackson	.15
548	Eric Anthony	.10
549	Delino DeShields	.10
550	Turner Ward	.10
551	Scott Sanderson	.10
552	Hector Carrasco	.10
553	Tony Phillips	.12
554	Melido Perez	.10

555	Mike Felder	.10
556	Jack Morris	.10
557	Rafael Palmeiro	.20
558	Shane Reynolds	.10
559	Pete Incaviglia	.10
560	Greg Harris	.10
561	Matt Walbeck	.10
562	Todd Van Poppel	.10
563	Todd Stottlemyre	.10
564	Ricky Bones	.10
565	Mike Jackson	.10
566	Kevin McReynolds	.10
567	Melvin Nieves	.10
568	Juan Gonzalez	1.00
569	Frank Viola	.10
570	Vince Coleman	.10
571	*Brian Anderson*	.20
572	Omar Vizquel	.10
573	Bernie Williams	.50
574	Tom Glavine	.20
575	Mitch Williams	.10
576	Shawon Dunston	.12
577	Mike Lansing	.10
578	Greg Pirkl	.10
579	Sid Fernandez	.10
580	Doug Jones	.10
581	Walt Weiss	.10
582	Tim Belcher	.10
583	Alex Fernandez	.10
584	Alex Cole	.10
585	Greg Cadaret	.10
586	Bob Tewksbury	.10
587	Dave Hansen	.10
588	*Kurt Abbott*	.25
589	*Rick White*	.15
590	Kevin Bass	.10
591	Geronimo Berroa	.10
592	Jaime Navarro	.10
593	Steve Farr	.10
594	Jack Armstrong	.10
595	Steve Howe	.10
596	Jose Rijo	.10
597	Otis Nixon	.10
598	Robby Thompson	.10
599	Kelly Stinnett	.10
600	Carlos Delgado	.20
601	*Brian Johnson*	.15
602	Gregg Olson	.10
603	Jim Edmonds	.30
604	Mike Blowers	.10
605	Lee Smith	.12
606	Pat Rapp	.10
607	Mike Magnante	.10
608	Karl Rhodes	.10
609	Jeff Juden	.10
610	Rusty Meacham	.10
611	Pedro Martinez	.10
612	Todd Worrell	.10
613	Stan Javier	.10
614	Mike Hampton	.10
615	Jose Guzman	.10
616	Xavier Hernandez	.10
617	David Wells	.10
618	John Habyan	.10
619	Chris Nabholz	.10
620	Bobby Jones	.15
621	Chris James	.10
622	Ellis Burks	.15
623	Erik Hanson	.10
624	Pat Meares	.10
625	Harold Reynolds	.10
626	Bob Hamelin (Rookie Rocker)	.10
627	Manny Ramirez (Rookie Rocker)	.40
628	Ryan Klesko (Rookie Rocker)	.40
629	Carlos Delgado (Rookie Rocker)	.25
630	Javier Lopez (Rookie Rocker)	.20
631	Steve Karsay (Rookie Rocket)	.15
632	Rick Helling (Rookie Rocket)	.10
633	Steve Trachsel (Rookie Rocket)	.15
634	Hector Carrasco (Rookie Rocket)	.10
635	Andy Stankiewicz	.10
636	Paul Sorrento	.10
637	Scott Erickson	.10
638	Chipper Jones	1.50
639	Luis Polonia	.10
640	Howard Johnson	.10
641	John Dopson	.10

642	Jody Reed	.10
643	Not issued, see #543	
644	Mark Portugal	.10
645	Paul Molitor	.40
646	Paul Assenmacher	.10
647	Hubie Brooks	.10
648	Gary Wayne	.10
649	Sean Berry	.10
650	Roger Clemens	.50
651	Brian Hunter	.10
652	Wally Whitehurst	.10
653	Allen Watson	.10
654	Rickey Henderson	.25
655	Sid Bream	.10
656	Dan Wilson	.10
657	Ricky Jordan	.10
658	Sterling Hitchcock	.10
659	Darrin Jackson	.10
660	Junior Felix	.10
661	Tom Brunansky	.10
662	Jose Vizcaino	.10
663	Mark Leiter	.10
664	Gil Heredia	.10
665	Fred McGriff	.30
666	Will Clark	.30
667	Al Leiter	.10
668	James Mouton	.10
669	Billy Bean	.10
670	Scott Leius	.10
671	Bret Boone	.10
672	Darren Holmes	.10
673	Dave Weathers	.10
674	Eddie Murray	.50
675	Felix Fermin	.10
676	Chris Sabo	.10
677	Billy Spiers	.10
678	Aaron Sele	.10
679	Juan Samuel	.10
680	Julio Franco	.10
681	Heathcliff Slocumb	.10
682	Denny Martinez	.12
683	Jerry Browne	.10
684	*Pedro A. Martinez*	.15
685	Rex Hudler	.10
686	Willie McGee	.12
687	Andy Van Slyke	.10
688	Pat Mahomes	.10
689	Dave Henderson	.10
690	Tony Eusebio	.10
691	Rick Sutcliffe	.10
692	Willie Banks	.10
693	Alan Mills	.10
694	Jeff Treadway	.10
695	Alex Gonzalez	.25
696	David Segui	.10
697	Rick Helling	.10
698	Bip Roberts	.10
699	*Jeff Cirillo*	.15
700	Terry Mulholland	.10
701	Marvin Freeman	.10
702	Jason Bere	.15
703	Javier Lopez	.35
704	Greg Hibbard	.10
705	Tommy Greene	.10
706	Marquis Grissom	.10
707	Brian Harper	.10
708	Steve Karsay	.10
709	Jeff Brantley	.10
710	Jeff Russell	.10
711	Bryan Hickerson	.10
712	*Jim Pittsley*	.20
713	Bobby Ayala	.10
714	John Smoltz (Fantastic Finisher)	.20
715	Jose Rijo (Fantastic Finisher)	.10
716	Greg Maddux (Fantastic Finisher)	1.00
717	Matt Williams (Fantastic Finisher)	.25
718	Frank Thomas (Fantastic Finisher)	1.25
719	Ryne Sandberg (Fantastic Finisher)	.40
720	Checklist	.10

Modern cards have little collector value in conditions lower than Mint.
Figure NM cards at 75% of values shown;
EX cards at 40%.

1994 Stadium Club Dugout Dirt

Cartoons of some of baseball's top stars are featured on the backs of this 12-card insert set. Fronts are virtually identical in format to regular S.C. cards, except the logo and box with the player's last name are in gold-foil, rather than red. Stated odds of finding a Dugout Dirt insert card were one per six packs, on average. Cards can also be found with a gold "Members Only" seal on front.

		MT
Complete Set (12):		12.00
Common Player:		.25
1	Mike Piazza (Catch of the Day)	1.75
2	Dave Winfield (The Road to 3,000)	.50
3	John Kruk (From Coal Mine to Gold Mine)	.25
4	Cal Ripken, Jr. (On Track)	4.00
5	Jack McDowell (Chin Music)	.25
6	Barry Bonds (The Bonds Market)	1.00
7	Ken Griffey, Jr. (Gold Gloves/All-Star)	4.00
8	Tim Salmon (The Salmon Run)	.50
9	Frank Thomas (Big Hurt)	3.00
10	Jeff Kent (Super Kent)	.25
11	Randy Johnson (High Heat)	.50
12	Darren Daulton (Daulton's Gym)	.25

1994 Stadium Club Finest

This insert set was included only in Series III packs of Topps Stadium Club, at the rate of one card per six packs, on average. Cards utilize Topps Finest technology and feature a player action photo on front, set against a red-and-gold sunburst background. Backs have a player portrait photo, a few stats and appropriate logos. Cards can also be found with a "Members Only" logo on front.

		MT
Complete Set (10):		35.00
Common Player:		1.00
1	Jeff Bagwell	2.50
2	Albert Belle	2.00
3	Barry Bonds	2.50
4	Juan Gonzalez	4.00
5	Ken Griffey, Jr.	10.00
6	Marquis Grissom	1.00
7	David Justice	1.00
8	Mike Piazza	5.00
9	Tim Salmon	1.50
10	Frank Thomas	8.00

1994 Stadium Club 1st Day Production

A special silver-foil emboss-ment designating "1st Day Issue" was placed on fewer than 2,000 of each of the 720 regular cards in the '94 Stadium Club set. Inserted at the rate of one per 24 foil packs and one per 15 jumbo packs, the cards are otherwise identical to the regular S.C. cards.

	MT
Complete Set (720):	2900.
Common Player:	2.50
(Star cards valued at 30X-50X corresponding cards in regular SC issue)	

1994 Stadium Club Golden Rainbow

Found at the rate of one per pack, Stadium Club "Golden Rainbow" cards were issued for each of the 720 cards in the regular set. These inserts are distinguished by the use of gold prismatic foil high-lights for the S.C. logo and box with the player's last name, instead of the red foil found on regular S.C. cards.

	MT
Complete Set (720):	150.00
Common Player:	.50
Veteran Stars: 2X to 4X	
Young Stars and Rookies: 1.5X to 2.5X	
(Star players valued at 2X-4X same card in the regular Stadium Club set.)	

1994 Stadium Club Draft Picks

Produced well after the end of the strike-truncated 1994 baseball season, this set was largely ignored by the hobby at the time of issue. The full-bleed card fronts feature up-close and personal poses of 1994's top draft picks in major league uniforms, giving the hobby a good first look at tomorrow's stars. A home plate design in an upper corner has "Draft '94 Pick" in gold-foil. The player's name is printed in gold foil down one of the sides. Backs are horizontally arranged and have a parti-colored back-ground that includes standard scouting report phrases. There is another color portrait of the player at one end with his name and posi-tion printed above. At the opposite end are the team by which the play-er was drafted, a few biographical details, some amateur and pro ca-reer highlights and a box detailing how the team's other recent draft picks at that round have fared.

		MT
Complete Set (90):		22.00
Common Player:		.25
1	Jacob Shumate	.35
2	C.J. Nitkowski	.40
3	Doug Million	.25
4	Matt Smith	.35
5	Kevin Lovinger	.25
6	Alberto Castillo	.25
7	Mike Russell	.25
8	Dan Lock	.25
9	Tom Szimanski	.25
10	Aaron Boone	.45
11	Jayson Peterson	.40
12	Mark Johnson	.40
13	Cade Gaspar	.25
14	George Lombard	.50
15	Russ Johnson	.40
16	Travis Miller	.35
17	Jay Payton	.75
18	Brian Buchanan	.35
19	Jacob Cruz	1.50
20	Gary Rath	.30
21	Ramon Castro	.35
22	Tommy Davis	.25
23	Tony Terry	.25
24	Jerry Whittaker	.25
25	Mike Darr	.25
26	Doug Webb	.25
27	Jason Camilli	.25
28	Brad Rigby	.25
29	Ryan Nye	.25
30	Carl Dale	.25
31	Andy Taulbee	.25
32	Trey Moore	.25
33	John Crowther	.25
34	Joe Giuliano	.25
35	Brian Rose	.25
36	Paul Failla	.25
37	Brian Meadows	.25
38	Oscar Robles	.25
39	Mike Metcalff	.25
40	Larry Barnes	.25
41	Paul Ottavinia	.25
42	Chris McBride	.25
43	Ricky Stone	.25
44	Billy Blythe	.25
45	Eddie Priest	.35
46	Scott Forster	.25
47	Eric Pickett	.25
48	Matt Beaumont	.25
49	Darrell Nicolas	.25

50	Mike Hampton	.25
51	Paul O'Malley	.25
52	Steve Shoemaker	.35
53	Jason Sikes	.30
54	Bryan Farson	.25
55	Yates Hall	.25
56	Troy Brohawn	.25
57	Dan Hower	.25
58	Clay Caruthers	.25
59	Pepe McNeal	.25
60	Ray Ricken	.25
61	Scott Shores	.25
62	Eddie Brooks	.25
63	Dave Kauflin	.25
64	David Meyer	.25
65	Geoff Blum	.25
66	Roy Marsh	.25
67	Ryan Beeney	.25
68	Derek Dukart	.25
69	Nomar Garciaparra	6.00
70	Jason Kelley	.25
71	Jesse Ibarra	.40
72	Bucky Buckles	.25
73	Mark Little	.25
74	Heath Murray	.25
75	Greg Morris	.25
76	Mike Halperin	.25
77	Wes Helms	.65
78	Ray Brown	.25
79	Kevin Brown	.65
80	Paul Konerko	1.50
81	Mike Thurman	.25
82	Paul Wilson	.65
83	Terrence Long	.25
84	Ben Grieve	2.00
85	Mark Farris	.25
86	Bret Wagner	.25
87	Dustin Hermanson	.60
88	Kevin Witt	.25
89	Corey Pointer	.30
90	Tim Grieve	.40

1994 Stadium Club Draft Picks First Day Issue

Identical to the regular-issue S.C. Draft Picks cards except for a silver-foil First Day Issue logo on front, this parallel set was found on the average of one card per six packs of S.C. Draft Picks.

	MT
Complete Set (90):	250.00
Common Player:	2.00
(Star cards valued at 6X-10X same cards in regular SC Draft Picks issue)	

1995 Stadium Club

SHANE REYNOLDS

Topps' upscale brand was issued for 1995 in three series of, respectively, 270, 225 and 135 cards.

Fronts have borderless color photos with a gold-foil device at bottom holding the team logo. Also in gold are the player's name at bottom and the Stadium Club logo at top. Backs have another player photo at left with a pair of computer-enhanced close-ups above it. At right are bar graphs detailing the player's '94 stats and his skills rankings. A number of specially designed subsets - "Best Seat in the House, Cover Story, MLB Debut," etc., are spread throughout the issue, which also includes a full slate of chase cards depending on the series and packaging.

	MT
Complete Set (630):	55.00
Complete Series 1 (270):	20.00
Complete Series 2 (225):	20.00
Complete High Series (135):	15.00
Common Player:	.10
First Day Production (1-270) Comp. Set: 225.00	
Common First Day Production:	.50
Veteran Stars: 6X to 10X	
Young Stars: 4X to 6X	
Random Inserts in Topps Ser. 2 Packs and	
10 per Factory Set.	
Series 1 or 2 Wax Box:	40.00
Series 3 Wax Box:	45.00

1	Cal Ripken Jr.	2.50
2	Bo Jackson	.15
3	Bryan Harvey	.10
4	Curt Schilling	.10
5	Bruce Ruffin	.10
6	Travis Fryman	.10
7	Jim Abbott	.12
8	David McCarty	.10
9	Gary Gaetti	.12
10	Roger Clemens	.75
11	Carlos Garcia	.10
12	Lee Smith	.12
13	Bobby Ayala	.10
14	Charles Nagy	.10
15	Lou Frazier	.10
16	Rene Arocha	.10
17	Carlos Delgado	.15
18	Steve Finley	.10
19	Ryan Klesko	.60
20	Cal Eldred	.10
21	Rey Sanchez	.10
22	Ken Hill	.10
23	Benny Santiago	.10
24	Julian Tavarez	.10
25	Jose Vizcaino	.10
26	Andy Benes	.10
27	Mariano Duncan	.10
28	Checklist A	.10
29	Shawon Dunston	.12
30	Rafael Palmeiro	.15
31	Dean Palmer	.10
32	Andres Galarraga	.15
33	Joey Cora	.10
34	Mickey Tettleton	.10
35	Barry Larkin	.15
36	Carlos Baerga	.20
37	Orel Hershiser	.12
38	Jody Reed	.10
39	Paul Molitor	.25
40	Jim Edmonds	.15
41	Bob Tewksbury	.10
42	John Patterson	.10
43	Ray McDavid	.10
44	Zane Smith	.10
45	Bret Saberhagen	.10
46	Greg Maddux	1.00
47	Frank Thomas	1.25
48	Carlos Baerga	.25
49	Billy Spiers	.10
50	Stan Javier	.10
51	Rex Hudler	.10
52	Denny Hocking	.10
53	Todd Worrell	.10
54	Mark Clark	.10
55	Hipilito Pichardo	.10
56	Bob Wickman	.10
57	Raul Mondesi	.50
58	Steve Cooke	.10
59	Rod Beck	.10

60	Tim Davis	.10
61	Jeff Kent	.10
62	John Valentin	.10
63	Alex Arias	.10
64	Steve Reed	.10
65	Ozzie Smith	.25
66	Terry Pendleton	.10
67	Kenny Rogers	.10
68	Vince Coleman	.10
69	Tom Pagnozzi	.10
70	Roberto Alomar	.75
71	Darrin Jackson	.10
72	Dennis Eckersley	.12
73	Jay Buhner	.12
74	Darren Lewis	.10
75	Dave Weathers	.10
76	Matt Walbeck	.10
77	Brad Ausmus	.10
78	Danny Bautista	.10
79	Bob Hamelin	.10
80	Steve Traschel	.20
81	Ken Ryan	.10
82	Chris Turner	.10
83	David Segui	.10
84	Ben McDonald	.10
85	Wade Boggs	.25
86	John Vander Wal	.10
87	Sandy Alomar	.12
88	Ron Karkovice	.10
89	Doug Jones	.10
90	Gary Sheffield	.25
91	Ken Caminiti	.15
92	Chris Bosio	.10
93	Kevin Tapani	.10
94	Walt Weiss	.10
95	Erik Hanson	.10
96	Ruben Sierra	.10
97	Nomar Garciaparra	2.50
98	Terrence Long	.10
99	Jacob Shumate	.10
100	Paul Wilson	.30
101	Kevin Witt	.10
102	Paul Konerko	2.50
103	Ben Grieve	3.00
104	Mark Johnson	.25
105	Cade Gaspar	.20
106	Mark Farris	.10
107	Dustin Hermanson	.15
108	Scott Elarton	.50
109	Doug Million	.10
110	Matt Smith	.10
111	Brian Buchanan	.20
112	Jayson Peterson	.20
113	Bret Wagner	.10
114	C.J. Nitkowski	.15
115	Ramon Castro	.25
116	Rafael Bournigal	.10
117	Jeff Fassero	.10
118	Bobby Bonilla	.12
119	Ricky Gutierrez	.10
120	Roger Pavlik	.10
121	Mike Greenwell	.10
122	Deion Sanders	.25
123	Charlie Hayes	.10
124	Paul O'Neill	.12
125	Jay Bell	.10
126	Royce Clayton	.12
127	Willie Banks	.10
128	Mark Wohlers	.10
129	Todd Jones	.10
130	Todd Stottlemyre	.10
131	Will Clark	.30
132	Wilson Alvarez	.10
133	Chili Davis	.10
134	Dave Burba	.10
135	Chris Hoiles	.10
136	Jeff Blauser	.10
137	Jeff Reboulet	.10
138	Bret Saberhagen	.10
139	Kirk Rueter	.10
140	Dave Nilsson	.10
141	Pat Borders	.10
142	Ron Darling	.10
143	Derek Bell	.12
144	Dave Hollins	.10
145	Juan Gonzalez	1.25
146	Andre Dawson	.15
147	Jim Thome	.12
148	Larry Walker	.20
149	Mike Piazza	1.25
150	Mike Perez	.10
151	Steve Avery	.12
152	Dan Wilson	.10
153	Andy Van Slyke	.10
154	Junior Felix	.10
155	Jack McDowell	.10

#	Player	Price	#	Player	Price	#	Player	Price
156	Danny Tartabull	.10	252	Bret Boone	.10	338	Gary DiSarcina	.10
157	Willie Blair	.10	253	Al Martin	.10	339	Joey Hamilton	.15
158	William Van Landingham	.10	254	Armando Benitez	.10	340	Randy Johnson	.40
159	Robb Nen	.10	255	Wil Cordero	.10	341	Jim Leyritz	.10
160	Lee Tinsley	.10	256	Al Leiter	.10	342	Bobby Jones	.10
161	Ismael Valdes	.10	257	Luis Gonzalez	.10	343	Jaime Navarro	.10
162	Juan Guzman	.10	258	Charlie O'Brien	.10	344	Bip Roberts	.10
163	Scott Servais	.10	259	Tim Wallach	.10	345	Steve Karsay	.10
164	Cliff Floyd	.15	260	Scott Sanders	.10	346	Kevin Stocker	.10
165	Allen Watson	.10	261	Tom Henke	.10	347	Jose Canseco	.30
166	Eddie Taubensee	.10	262	Otis Nixon	.10	348	Bill Wegman	.10
167	Scott Hemond	.10	263	Darren Daulton	.10	349	Rondell White	.20
168	Jeff Tackett	.10	264	Manny Ramirez	.75	350	Mo Vaughn	.60
169	Chad Curtis	.10	265	Bret Barberie	.10	351	Joe Orsulak	.10
170	Rico Brogna	.10	266	Mel Rojas	.10	352	Pat Meares	.10
171	Luis Polonia	.10	267	John Burkett	.10	353	Albie Lopez	.10
172	Checklist B	.10	268	Brady Anderson	.20	354	Edgar Martinez	.10
173	Lance Johnson	.10	269	John Roper	.10	355	Brian Jordan	.10
174	Sammy Sosa	1.50	270	Shane Reynolds	.10	356	Tommy Greene	.10
175	Mike MacFarlane	.10	271	Barry Bonds	.75	357	Chuck Carr	.10
176	Darryl Hamilton	.10	272	Alex Fernandez	.10	358	Pedro Astacio	.10
177	Rick Aguilera	.10	273	Brian McRae	.10	359	Russ Davis	.10
178	Dave West	.10	274	Todd Zeile	.10	360	Chris Hammond	.10
179	Mike Gallego	.10	275	Greg Swindell	.10	361	Gregg Jefferies	.10
180	Marc Newfield	.10	276	Johnny Ruffin	.10	362	Shane Mack	.10
181	Steve Buechele	.10	277	Troy Neel	.10	363	Fred McGriff	.30
182	David Wells	.10	278	Eric Karros	.15	364	Pat Rapp	.10
183	Tom Glavine	.15	279	John Hudek	.10	365	Bill Swift	.10
184	Joe Girardi	.10	280	Thomas Howard	.10	366	Checklist	.10
185	Craig Biggio	.12	281	Joe Carter	.20	367	Robin Ventura	.15
186	Eddie Murray	.20	282	Mike Devereaux	.10	368	Bobby Witt	.10
187	Kevin Gross	.10	283	Butch Henry	.10	369	Karl Rhodes	.10
188	Sid Fernandez	.10	284	Reggie Jefferson	.10	370	Eddie Williams	.10
189	John Franco	.10	285	Mark Lemke	.10	371	John Jaha	.10
190	Bernard Gilkey	.15	286	Jeff Montgomery	.10	372	Steve Howe	.10
191	Matt Williams	.35	287	Ryan Thompson	.10	373	Leo Gomez	.10
192	Darrin Fletcher	.10	288	Paul Shuey	.10	374	Hector Fajardo	.10
193	Jeff Conine	.10	289	Mark McGwire	4.00	375	Jeff Bagwell	.60
194	Ed Sprague	.10	290	Bernie Williams	.50	376	Mark Acre	.10
195	Eduardo Perez	.10	291	Mickey Morandini	.10	377	Wayne Kirby	.10
196	Scott Livingstone	.10	292	Scott Leius	.10	378	Mark Portugal	.10
197	Ivan Rodriguez	.75	293	David Hulse	.10	379	Jesus Tavarez	.10
198	Orlando Merced	.10	294	Greg Gagne	.10	380	Jim Lindeman	.10
199	Ricky Bones	.10	295	Moises Alou	.10	381	Don Mattingly	1.00
200	Javier Lopez	.20	296	Geronimo Berroa	.10	382	Trevor Hoffman	.10
201	Miguel Jimenez	.10	297	Eddie Zambrano	.10	383	Chris Gomez	.10
202	Terry McGriff	.10	298	Alan Trammell	.12	384	Garret Anderson	.20
203	Mike Lieberthal	.10	299	Don Slaught	.10	385	Bobby Munoz	.10
204	David Cone	.10	300	Jose Rijo	.10	386	Jon Lieber	.10
205	Todd Hundley	.15	301	Joe Ausanio	.10	387	Rick Helling	.10
206	Ozzie Guillen	.10	302	Tim Raines	.10	388	Marvin Freeman	.10
207	Alex Cole	.10	303	Melido Perez	.10	389	Juan Castillo	.10
208	Tony Phillips	.12	304	Kent Mercker	.10	390	Jeff Cirillo	.15
209	Jim Eisenreich	.10	305	James Mouton	.15	391	Sean Berry	.10
210	Greg Vaughn	.10	306	Luis Lopez	.10	392	Hector Carrasco	.10
211	Barry Larkin	.15	307	Mike Kingery	.10	393	Mark Grace	.20
212	Don Mattingly	.50	308	Willie Greene	.10	394	Pat Kelly	.10
213	Mark Grace	.15	309	Cecil Fielder	.15	395	Tim Naehring	.10
214	Jose Canseco	.35	310	Scott Kamieniecki	.10	396	Greg Pirkl	.10
215	Joe Carter	.15	311	Mike Greenwell (Best Seat in the House)	.10	397	John Smoltz	.15
216	David Cone	.12	312	Bobby Bonilla (Best Seat in the House)	.10	398	Robby Thompson	.10
217	Sandy Alomar	.12	313	Andres Galarraga (Best Seat in the House)	.10	399	Rick White	.10
218	Al Martin	.10	314	Cal Ripken Jr. (Best Seat in the House)	1.25	400	Frank Thomas	2.50
219	Roberto Kelly	.10	315	Matt Williams (Best Seat in the House)	.25	401	Jeff Conine (Cover Story)	.10
220	Paul Sorrento	.10	316	Tom Pagnozzi (Best Seat in the House)	.10	402	Jose Valentin (Cover Story)	.10
221	Tony Fernandez	.10	317	Len Dykstra (Best Seat in the House)	.10	403	Carlos Baerga (Cover Story)	.10
222	Stan Belinda	.10	318	Frank Thomas (Best Seat in the House)	1.25	404	Rick Aguilera (Cover Story)	.10
223	Mike Stanley	.10	319	Kirby Puckett (Best Seat in the House)	.75	405	Wilson Alvarez (Cover Story)	.10
224	Doug Drabek	.10	320	Mike Piazza (Best Seat in the House)	.75	406	Juan Gonzalez (Cover Story)	.50
225	Todd Van Poppel	.10	321	Jason Jacome	.10	407	Barry Larkin (Cover Story)	.10
226	Matt Mieske	.10	322	Brian Hunter	.10	408	Ken Hill (Cover Story)	.10
227	Tino Martinez	.15	323	Brent Gates	.10	409	Chuck Carr (Cover Story)	.10
228	Andy Ashby	.10	324	Jim Converse	.10	410	Tim Raines (Cover Story)	.10
229	Midre Cummings	.10	325	Damion Easley	.10	411	Bryan Eversgerd	.10
230	Jeff Frye	.10	326	Dante Bichette	.15	412	Phil Plantier	.10
231	Hal Morris	.10	327	Kurt Abbott	.10	413	Josias Manzanillo	.10
232	Jose Lind	.10	328	Scott Cooper	.10	414	Roberto Kelly	.10
233	Shawn Green	.10	329	Mike Henneman	.10	415	Rickey Henderson	.20
234	Rafael Belliard	.10	330	Orlando Miller	.10	416	John Smiley	.10
235	Randy Myers	.10	331	John Kruk	.10	417	Kevin Brown	.10
236	Frank Thomas	2.50	332	Jose Oliva	.10	418	Jimmy Key	.10
237	Darren Daulton	.10	333	Reggie Sanders	.10	419	Wally Joyner	.12
238	Sammy Sosa	.75	334	Omar Vizquel	.10	420	Roberto Hernandez	.10
239	Cal Ripken Jr.	1.25	335	Devon White	.10	421	Felix Fermin	.10
240	Jeff Bagwell	.60	336	Mike Morgan	.10	422	Checklist	.10
241	Ken Griffey Jr.	3.00	337	J.R. Phillips	.10	423	Greg Vaughn	.10
242	Brett Butler	.15				424	Ray Lankford	.15
243	Derrick May	.10				425	Greg Maddux	2.00
244	Pat Listach	.10				426	Mike Mussina	.40
245	Mike Bordick	.10				427	Geronimo Pena	.10
246	Mark Langston	.10				428	David Nied	.10
247	Randy Velarde	.10				429	Scott Erickson	.10
248	Julio Franco	.10				430	Kevin Mitchell	.10
249	Chuck Knoblauch	.15						
250	Bill Gullickson	.10						
251	Dave Henderson	.10						

431	Mike Lansing	.10
432	Brian Anderson	.15
433	Jeff King	.10
434	Ramon Martinez	.12
435	Kevin Seitzer	.10
436	Salomon Torres	.10
437	Brian Hunter	.10
438	Melvin Nieves	.10
439	Mike Kelly	.10
440	Marquis Grissom	.12
441	Chuck Finley	.10
442	Len Dykstra	.10
443	Ellis Burks	.15
444	Harold Baines	.12
445	Kevin Appier	.10
446	Dave Justice	.20
447	Darryl Kile	.10
448	John Olerud	.15
449	Greg McMichael	.10
450	Kirby Puckett	1.00
451	Jose Valentin	.10
452	Rick Wilkins	.10
453	Arthur Rhodes	.10
454	Pat Hentgen	.10
455	Tom Gordon	.10
456	Tom Candiotti	.10
457	Jason Bere	.15
458	Wes Chamberlain	.10
459	Greg Colbrunn	.10
460	John Doherty	.10
461	Kevin Foster	.10
462	Mark Whiten	.10
463	Terry Steinbach	.10
464	Aaron Sele	.15
465	Kirt Manwaring	.10
466	Darren Hall	.10
467	Delino DeShields	.10
468	Andujar Cedeno	.10
469	Billy Ashley	.10
470	Kenny Lofton	.75
471	Pedro Munoz	.10
472	John Wetteland	.10
473	Tim Salmon	.20
474	Denny Neagle	.10
475	Tony Gwynn	1.00
476	Vinny Castilla	.10
477	Steve Dreyer	.10
478	Jeff Shaw	.10
479	Chad Ogea	.10
480	Scott Ruffcorn	.10
481	Lou Whitaker	.10
482	J.T. Snow	.10
483	Rich Rowland	.10
484	Dennis Martinez	.12
485	Pedro Martinez	.10
486	Rusty Greer	.10
487	Dave Fleming	.10
488	John Dettmer	.10
489	Albert Belle	.75
490	Ravelo Manzanillo	.10
491	Henry Rodriguez	.10
492	Andrew Lorraine	.25
493	Dwayne Hosey	.10
494	Mike Blowers	.10
495	Turner Ward	.10
496	Fred McGriff (Extreme Corps)	.20
497	Sammy Sosa (Extreme Corps)	.75
498	Barry Larkin (Extreme Corps)	.15
499	Andres Galarraga (Extreme Corps)	.10
500	Gary Sheffield (Extreme Corps)	.20
501	Jeff Bagwell (Extreme Corps)	.40
502	Mike Piazza (Extreme Corps)	.60
503	Moises Alou (Extreme Corps)	.10
504	Bobby Bonilla (Extreme Corps)	.10
505	Darren Daulton (Extreme Corps)	.10
506	Jeff King (Extreme Corps)	.10
507	Ray Lankford (Extreme Corps)	.10
508	Tony Gwynn (Extreme Corps)	.50
509	Barry Bonds (Extreme Corps)	.35
510	Cal Ripken Jr. (Extreme Corps)	1.25
511	Mo Vaughn (Extreme Corps)	.30

512	Tim Salmon (Extreme Corps)	.20
513	Frank Thomas (Extreme Corps)	1.25
514	Albert Belle (Extreme Corps)	.40
515	Cecil Fielder (Extreme Corps)	.10
516	Kevin Appier (Extreme Corps)	.10
517	Greg Vaughn (Extreme Corps)	.10
518	Kirby Puckett (Extreme Corps)	.50
519	Paul O'Neill (Extreme Corps)	.10
520	Ruben Sierra (Extreme Corps)	.10
521	Ken Griffey Jr. (Extreme Corps)	1.25
522	Will Clark (Extreme Corps)	.25
523	Joe Carter (Extreme Corps)	.10
524	Antonio Osuna	.10
525	Glenallen Hill	.10
526	Alex Gonzalez	.10
527	Dave Stewart	.10
528	Ron Gant	.15
529	Jason Bates	.10
530	Mike Macfarlane	.10
531	Esteban Loaiza	.15
532	Joe Randa	.10
533	Dave Winfield	.20
534	Danny Darwin	.10
535	Pete Harnisch	.10
536	Joey Cora	.10
537	Jaime Navarro	.10
538	Marty Cordova	.15
539	Andujar Cedeno	.10
540	Mickey Tettleton	.10
541	Andy Van Slyke	.10
542	*Carlos Perez*	.20
543	Chipper Jones	1.50
544	Tony Fernandez	.10
545	Tom Henke	.10
546	Pat Borders	.10
547	Chad Curtis	.10
548	Ray Durham	.15
549	Joe Oliver	.10
550	Jose Mesa	.10
551	Steve Finley	.10
552	Otis Nixon	.10
553	Jacob Brumfield	.10
554	Bill Swift	.10
555	Quilvio Veras	.10
556	*Hideo Nomo*	5.00
557	Joe Vitiello	.10
558	Mike Perez	.10
559	Charlie Hayes	.10
560	*Brad Radke*	.20
561	Darren Bragg	.10
562	Orel Hershiser	.12
563	Edgardo Alfonzo	.10
564	Doug Jones	.10
565	Andy Pettitte	.75
566	Benito Santiago	.10
567	John Burkett	.10
568	Brad Clontz	.10
569	Jim Abbott	.12
570	Joe Rosselli	.10
571	*Mark Grudzielanek*	.75
572	Dustin Hermanson	.10
573	Benji Gil	.10
574	Mark Whiten	.10
575	Mike Ignasiak	.10
576	Kevin Ritz	.10
577	Paul Quantrill	.10
578	Andre Dawson	.12
579	Jerald Clark	.10
580	Frank Rodriguez	.10
581	Mark Kiefer	.10
582	Trevor Wilson	.10
583	*Gary Wilson*	.20
584	Andy Stankiewicz	.10
585	Felipe Lira	.10
586	*Mike Mimbs*	.20
587	Jon Nunnally	.10
588	*Tomas Perez*	.15
589	Checklist	.10
590	Todd Hollandsworth	.15
591	Roberto Petagine	.10
592	Mariano Rivera	.10
593	Mark McLemore	.10
594	Bobby Witt	.10
595	Jose Offerman	.10
596	Jason Christiansen	.10
597	Jeff Manto	.10

598	Jim Dougherty	.10
599	Juan Acevedo	.10
600	Troy O'Leary	.10
601	Ron Villone	.10
602	Tripp Cromer	.10
603	Steve Scarsone	.10
604	Lance Parrish	.12
605	Ozzie Timmons	.10
606	Ray Holbert	.10
607	Tony Phillips	.12
608	Phil Plantier	.10
609	Shane Andrews	.10
610	Heathcliff Slocumb	.10
611	*Bobby Higginson*	1.50
612	Bob Tewksbury	.10
613	Terry Pendleton	.10
614	Scott Cooper (Trans-Action)	.10
615	John Wetteland (Trans-Action)	.10
616	Ken Hill (Trans-Action)	.10
617	Marquis Grissom (Trans-Action)	.10
618	Larry Walker (Trans-Action)	.25
619	Derek Bell (Trans-Action)	.10
620	David Cone (Trans-Action)	.10
621	Ken Caminiti (Trans-Action)	.10
622	Jack McDowell (Trans-Action)	.10
623	Vaughn Eshelman (Trans-Action)	.10
624	Brian McRae (Trans-Action)	.10
625	Gregg Jefferies (Trans-Action)	.10
626	Kevin Brown (Trans-Action)	.10
627	Lee Smith (Trans-Action)	.10
628	Tony Tarasco (Trans-Action)	.10
629	Brett Butler (Trans-Action)	.10
630	Jose Canseco (Trans-Action)	.35

1995 Stadium Club Clear Cut

Among the most technically advanced of 1995's insert cards is the Clear Cut chase set found in Series I and II packs. Cards feature a color player action photo printed on see-through plastic. There is a rainbow-hued trapezoid behind the player with an overall background tinted in blue, green and gold. The player's name is in white in a vertical blue bar at right. Backs have a few stats and data in a blue bar vertically at left. Each of the cards can also be found in a version with the round Members Only seal embossed into the plastic at lower-left.

	MT
Complete Set (28):	100.00
Complete Series 1 (14):	45.00
Complete Series 2 (14):	55.00
Common Player:	1.00
1 Mike Piazza	10.00

2	Ruben Sierra	1.00
3	Tony Gwynn	8.00
4	Frank Thomas	20.00
5	Fred McGriff	3.00
6	Rafael Palmeiro	1.00
7	Bobby Bonilla	1.00
8	Chili Davis	1.00
9	Hal Morris	1.00
10	Jose Canseco	2.00
11	Jay Bell	1.00
12	Kirby Puckett	8.00
13	Gary Sheffield	4.00
14	Bob Hamelin	1.00
15	Jeff Bagwell	7.00
16	Albert Belle	6.00
17	Sammy Sosa	15.00
18	Ken Griffey Jr.	24.00
19	Todd Zeile	1.00
20	Mo Vaughn	6.00
21	Moises Alou	1.00
22	Paul O'Neill	1.00
23	Andres Galarraga	1.00
24	Greg Vaughn	1.00
25	Len Dykstra	1.00
26	Joe Carter	1.00
27	Barry Bonds	6.00
28	Cecil Fielder	1.00

1995 Stadium Club
Crunch Time

Series I rack packs were the exclusive provenance of these cards featuring baseball's top run creators. Fronts are printed on rainbow prismatic foil. The central color action photo is repeated as an enlarged background photo, along with a team logo. At bottom in gold foil are the player name and Crunch Time logo. Backs have a positive and a negative image of the same photo as background to a pie chart and stats relative to the player's runs-created stats.

		MT
Complete Set (20):		30.00
Common Player:		1.00
1	Jeff Bagwell	2.50
2	Kirby Puckett	3.00
3	Frank Thomas	6.00
4	Albert Belle	2.00
5	Julio Franco	1.00
6	Jose Canseco	1.50
7	Paul Molitor	2.00
8	Joe Carter	1.00
9	Ken Griffey Jr.	8.00
10	Larry Walker	1.50
11	Dante Bichette	1.50
12	Carlos Baerga	1.00
13	Fred McGriff	1.50
14	Ruben Sierra	1.00
15	Will Clark	1.50
16	Moises Alou	1.00
17	Rafael Palmeiro	1.00
18	Travis Fryman	1.00
19	Barry Bonds	2.50
20	Cal Ripken Jr.	6.00

1995 Stadium Club
Crystal Ball

Multi-colored swirls around a clear central circle with the player's photo, all printed on foil, are the front design for this Series III insert. Backs have a portrait photo in a floating crystal ball image at one side. At the other end are year-by-year minor league stats and a few words about each of the player's seasons. This insert was also produced in an edition of 4,000 bearing a gold-foil "Members Only" seal, sold in complete Stadium Club Members Only factory sets.

		MT
Complete Set (15):		70.00
Common Player:		2.50
1	Chipper Jones	20.00
2	Dustin Hermanson	2.50
3	Ray Durham	4.00
4	Phil Nevin	2.50
5	Billy Ashley	3.00
6	Shawn Green	4.00
7	Jason Bates	2.50
8	Benji Gil	2.50
9	Marty Cordova	5.00
10	Quilvio Veras	2.50
11	Mark Grudzielanek	5.00
12	Ruben Rivera	8.00
13	Bill Pulsipher	3.00
14	Derek Jeter	20.00
15	LaTroy Hawkins	2.50

1995 Stadium Club
1st Day Issue

Series II hobby packs of Topps baseball featured a chase set of Stadium Club 1st Day Issue cards, #1-270. The FDI cards have a small gold embossed seal on front. Cards were seeded on an average of one per six packs.

		MT
Complete Set (270):		225.00
Common Player:		.50
	(Stars, rookies and special interest cards valued at 5X-10X regular TSC)	

1995 Stadium Club
Power Zone

The performance in several parks around the league is chronicled on the back of these Series III

inserts. Fronts are printed on foil and feature a player swinging into an exploding asteroid. His name is printed vertically down one side in prismatic glitter foil. Backs also have a portrait photo and a baseball with a weird red and green vapor trail. A special edition of 4,000 each of these inserts was included with the purchase of Stadium Club Members Only factory sets; those cards have an embossed gold-foil seal on front.

		MT
Complete Set (12):		55.00
Common Player:		1.50
1	Jeff Bagwell	6.00
2	Albert Belle	5.00
3	Barry Bonds	5.00
4	Joe Carter	1.50
5	Cecil Fielder	1.50
6	Andres Galarraga	1.50
7	Ken Griffey Jr.	15.00
8	Paul Molitor	2.00
9	Fred McGriff	2.00
10	Rafael Palmeiro	1.50
11	Frank Thomas	12.00
12	Matt Williams	2.00

1995 Stadium Club
Ring Leaders

With a background that looks like an explosion at a jewelry factory, these cards feature players who have won championship, All-Star or other award rings. Fronts are foil-printed with a player action photo on a background of flying rings and stars, and, - for some reason - an attacking eagle. Backs repeat the background motif, have a player portrait in an oval frame at top-left, photos of some of his rings and a list of rings won. Cards were random inserts in both Series I and II; complete sets could also be won in Stadium Clug's phone card insert contest. A version with the Members Only gold seal was also issued for each.

		MT
Complete Set (40):		275.00
Complete Series 1 (20):		125.00
Complete Series 2 (20):		150.00
Common Player:		2.00
1	Jeff Bagwell	14.00
2	Mark McGwire	40.00

3	Ozzie Smith	7.00
4	Paul Molitor	4.00
5	Darryl Strawberry	2.00
6	Eddie Murray	4.00
7	Tony Gwynn	12.00
8	Jose Canseco	4.00
9	Howard Johnson	2.00
10	Andre Dawson	2.00
11	Matt Williams	4.00
12	Tim Raines	2.00
13	Fred McGriff	4.00
14	Ken Griffey Jr.	35.00
15	Gary Sheffield	6.00
16	Dennis Eckersley	2.00
17	Kevin Mitchell	2.00
18	Will Clark	3.00
19	Darren Daulton	2.00
20	Paul O'Neill	2.00
21	Julio Franco	2.00
22	Albert Belle	10.00
23	Juan Gonzalez	18.00
24	Kirby Puckett	15.00
25	Joe Carter	2.00
26	Frank Thomas	30.00
27	Cal Ripken Jr.	30.00
28	John Olerud	3.00
29	Ruben Sierra	2.00
30	Barry Bonds	8.00
31	Cecil Fielder	2.00
32	Roger Clemens	8.00
33	Don Mattingly	18.00
34	Terry Pendleton	2.00
35	Rickey Henderson	3.00
36	Dave Winfield	3.00
37	Edgar Martinez	2.00
38	Wade Boggs	4.00
39	Willie McGee	2.00
40	Andres Galarraga	2.00

13	Paul O'Neill	1.50
14	Kenny Lofton	6.00
15	Larry Walker	2.50
16	Scott Cooper	1.50
17	Barry Larkin	2.00
18	Matt Williams	3.00
19	John Wetteland	1.50
20	Randy Johnson	2.50

1995 Stadium Club
Virtual Reality

A partial parallel set found one per foil pack, two per rack pack, these cards share the basic front and back with the corresponding Gonzalez card in the regular S.C. issue. On front, however, is a "Virtual Reality" seal around the team logo at bottom (gold foil in Series I, silver-foil in Series II). Backs differ in that instead of actual 1994 season stats, they present a bar graph of computer projected stats representing full 162-game season instead of the strike-shortened reality. Each of these inserts can also be found in a version bearing the round gold- (Series I) or silver-foil (Series II) Members Only seal on the front.

		MT
Complete Set (270):		80.00
Complete Series I (135):		40.00
Complete Series II (135):		40.00
Common Player:		.25
1	Cal Ripken Jr.	7.50
2	Travis Fryman	.25
3	Jim Abbott	.30
4	Gary Gaetti	.30
5	Roger Clemens	2.00
6	Carlos Garcia	.25
7	Lee Smith	.30
8	Bobby Ayala	.25
9	Charles Nagy	.25
10	Rene Arocha	.25
11	Carlos Delgado	.35
12	Steve Finley	.25
13	Ryan Klesko	.75
14	Cal Eldred	.25
15	Rey Sanchez	.25
16	Ken Hill	.25
17	Jose Vizcaino	.25
18	Andy Benes	.25
19	Shawon Dunston	.30
20	Rafael Palmeiro	.40
21	Dean Palmer	.25
22	Joey Cora	.25
23	Mickey Tettleton	.25
24	Barry Larkin	.50
25	Carlos Baerga	.25
26	Orel Hershiser	.25
27	Jody Reed	.25
28	Paul Molitor	1.00
29	Jim Edmonds	.25
30	Bob Tewksbury	.25

1995 Stadium Club
Super Skills

These random hobby pack inserts in both Series I and II are printed on rainbow prismatic foil which features as a background an enlarged version of the front photo. The S.C. and Super Skills logos are printed in gold foil in opposite corners, while the player's name is in blue at bottom-right. Backs repeat the enlarged background image of a close-up foreground photo, while a few choice words about the player's particular specialties are in white at left. Each card can also be found in a version featuring the Members Only gold-foil seal on front.

		MT
Complete Set (20):		55.00
Complete Series 1 (9):		25.00
Complete Series 2 (11):		30.00
Common Player:		1.50
1	Roberto Alomar	5.00
2	Barry Bonds	6.00
3	Jay Buhner	2.00
4	Chuck Carr	1.50
5	Don Mattingly	10.00
6	Raul Mondesi	3.00
7	Tim Salmon	2.50
8	Deion Sanders	2.50
9	Devon White	1.50
10	Mark Whiten	1.50
11	Ken Griffey Jr.	25.00
12	Marquis Grissom	2.00

31	Ray McDavid	.25
32	Stan Javier	.25
33	Todd Worrell	.25
34	Bob Wickman	.25
35	Raul Mondesi	1.00
36	Rod Beck	.25
37	Jeff Kent	.25
38	John Valentin	.25
39	Ozzie Smith	1.00
40	Terry Pendleton	.25
41	Kenny Rogers	.25
42	Vince Coleman	.25
43	Roberto Alomar	1.50
44	Darrin Jackson	.25
45	Dennis Eckersley	.30
46	Jay Buhner	.40
47	Dave Weathers	.25
48	Danny Bautista	.25
49	Bob Hamelin	.25
50	Steve Trachsel	.25
51	Ben McDonald	.25
52	Wade Boggs	.50
53	Sandy Alomar	.25
54	Ron Karkovice	.25
55	Doug Jones	.25
56	Gary Sheffield	1.50
57	Ken Caminiti	.75
58	Kevin Tapani	.25
59	Ruben Sierra	.25
60	Bobby Bonilla	.30
61	Deion Sanders	1.50
62	Charlie Hayes	.25
63	Paul O'Neill	.25
64	Jay Bell	.25
65	Todd Jones	.25
66	Todd Stottlemyre	.25
67	Will Clark	1.00
68	Wilson Alvarez	.25
69	Chili Davis	.25
70	Chris Hoiles	.25
71	Bret Saberhagen	.25
72	Dave Nilsson	.25
73	Derek Bell	.25
74	Juan Gonzalez	2.50
75	Andre Dawson	.35
76	Jim Thome	.60
77	Larry Walker	.60
78	Mike Piazza	5.00
79	Dan Wilson	.25
80	Junior Felix	.25
81	Jack McDowell	.25
82	Danny Tartabull	.25
83	William Van Landingham	.25
84	Robb Nen	.25
85	Ismael Valdes	.25
86	Juan Guzman	.25
87	Cliff Floyd	.25
88	Rico Brogna	.25
89	Luis Polonia	.25
90	Lance Johnson	.25
91	Sammy Sosa	5.00
92	Dave West	.25
93	Tom Glavine	.35
94	Joe Girardi	.25
95	Craig Biggio	.25
96	Eddie Murray	.75
97	Kevin Gross	.25
98	John Franco	.25
99	Matt Williams	.75
100	Darrin Fletcher	.25
101	Jeff Conine	.25
102	Ed Sprague	.25
103	Ivan Rodriguez	1.50
104	Orlando Merced	.25
105	Ricky Bones	.25
106	David Cone	.40
107	Todd Hundley	.40
108	Alex Cole	.25
109	Tony Phillips	.25
110	Jim Eisenreich	.25
111	Paul Sorrento	.25
112	Mike Stanley	.25
113	Doug Drabek	.25
114	Matt Mieske	.25
115	Tino Martinez	.35
116	Midre Cummings	.25
117	Hal Morris	.25
118	Shawn Green	.25
119	Randy Myers	.25
120	Ken Griffey Jr.	7.50
121	Brett Butler	.30
122	Julio Franco	.25
123	Chuck Knoblauch	.50
124	Bret Boone	.25
125	Wil Cordero	.25
126	Luis Gonzalez	.25

127	Tim Wallach	.25
128	Scott Sanders	.25
129	Tom Henke	.25
130	Otis Nixon	.25
131	Darren Daulton	.25
132	Manny Ramirez	1.50
133	Bret Barberie	.25
134	Brady Anderson	.40
135	Shane Reynolds	.25
136	Barry Bonds	1.50
137	Alex Fernandez	.25
138	Brian McRae	.25
139	Todd Zeile	.25
140	Greg Swindell	.25
141	Troy Neel	.25
142	Eric Karros	.25
143	John Hudek	.25
144	Joe Carter	.35
145	Mike Devereaux	.25
146	Butch Henry	.25
147	Mark Lemke	.25
148	Jeff Montgomery	.25
149	Ryan Thompson	.25
150	Bernie Williams	.75
151	Scott Leius	.25
152	Greg Gagne	.25
153	Moises Alou	.25
154	Geronimo Berroa	.25
155	Alan Trammell	.25
156	Don Slaught	.25
157	Jose Rijo	.25
158	Tim Raines	.25
159	Melido Perez	.25
160	Kent Mercker	.25
161	James Mouton	.25
162	Luis Lopez	.25
163	Mike Kingery	.25
164	Cecil Fielder	.35
165	Scott Kamieniecki	.25
166	Brent Gates	.25
167	Jason Jacome	.25
168	Dante Bichette	.75
169	Kurt Abbott	.25
170	Mike Henneman	.25
171	John Kruk	.25
172	Jose Oliva	.25
173	Reggie Sanders	.40
174	Omar Vizquel	.25
175	Devon White	.25
176	Mark McGwire	10.00
177	Gary DiSarcina	.25
178	Joey Hamilton	.25
179	Randy Johnson	1.00
180	Jim Leyritz	.25
181	Bobby Jones	.25
182	Bip Roberts	.25
183	Jose Canseco	.75
184	Mo Vaughn	1.00
185	Edgar Martinez	.25
186	Tommy Greene	.25
187	Chuck Carr	.25
188	Pedro Astacio	.25
189	Shane Mack	.25
190	Fred McGriff	.75
191	Pat Rapp	.25
192	Bill Swift	.25
193	Robin Ventura	.35
194	Bobby Witt	.25
195	Steve Howe	.25
196	Leo Gomez	.25
197	Hector Fajardo	.25
198	Jeff Bagwell	2.50
199	Rondell White	.40
200	Don Mattingly	2.50
201	Trevor Hoffman	.25
202	Chris Gomez	.25
203	Bobby Munoz	.25
204	Marvin Freeman	.25
205	Sean Berry	.25
206	Mark Grace	.40
207	Pat Kelly	.25
208	Eddie Williams	.25
209	Frank Thomas	6.00
210	Bryan Eversgerd	.25
211	Phil Plantier	.25
212	Roberto Kelly	.25
213	Rickey Henderson	.40
214	John Smiley	.25
215	Kevin Brown	.25
216	Jimmy Key	.25
217	Wally Joyner	.25
218	Roberto Hernandez	.25
219	Felix Fermin	.25
220	Greg Vaughn	.25
221	Ray Lankford	.35
222	Greg Maddux	5.00

223	Mike Mussina	1.00
224	David Nied	.25
225	Scott Erickson	.25
226	Kevin Mitchell	.25
227	Brian Anderson	.25
228	Jeff King	.25
229	Ramon Martinez	.25
230	Kevin Seitzer	.25
231	Marquis Grissom	.25
232	Chuck Finley	.25
233	Len Dykstra	.25
234	Ellis Burks	.30
235	Harold Baines	.25
236	Kevin Appier	.25
237	Dave Justice	.40
238	Darryl Kile	.25
239	John Olerud	.35
240	Greg McMichael	.25
241	Kirby Puckett	2.50
242	Jose Valentin	.25
243	Rick Wilkins	.25
244	Pat Hentgen	.25
245	Tom Gordon	.25
246	Tom Candiotti	.25
247	Jason Bere	.25
248	Wes Chamberlain	.25
249	Jeff Cirillo	.25
250	Kevin Foster	.25
251	Mark Whiten	.25
252	Terry Steinbach	.25
253	Aaron Sele	.25
254	Kirt Manwaring	.25
255	Delino DeShields	.25
256	Andujar Cedeno	.25
257	Kenny Lofton	1.50
258	John Wetteland	.25
259	Tim Salmon	.50
260	Denny Neagle	.25
261	Tony Gwynn	2.50
262	Lou Whitaker	.25
263	J.T. Snow	.25
264	Dennis Martinez	.25
265	Pedro Martinez	.25
266	Rusty Greer	.25
267	Dave Fleming	.25
268	John Dettmer	.25
269	Albert Belle	2.00
270	Henry Rodriguez	.25

1995 Stadium Club VR Extremist

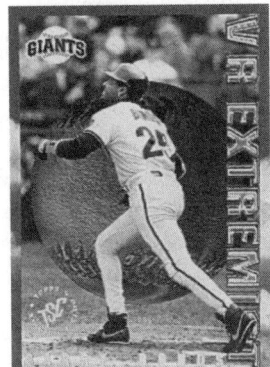

A huge silver-blue metallic baseball separates the player from the background of the photo in this Series II insert found only in rack packs. A blue sky and clouds provides the front border. The player rises out of the clouds in a back photo in the foreground of which are some pie-in-the-sky stats. The metallic baseball is also repeated on the back, with the player's name in orange script on the sweet spot. Each card was also issued in the Members Only boxed set in a version with a round silver-foil Members Only seal on front.

	MT
Complete Set (10):	80.00
Common Player:	2.00
VRE1 Barry Bonds	7.00
VRE2 Ken Griffey Jr.	30.00
VRE3 Jeff Bagwell	8.00
VRE4 Albert Belle	8.00
VRE5 Frank Thomas	25.00
VRE6 Tony Gwynn	10.00
VRE7 Kenny Lofton	7.00
VRE8 Deion Sanders	4.00
VRE9 Ken Hill	2.00
VRE10 Jimmy Key	2.00

1996 Stadium Club

Consisting of 450 cards in a pair of 225-card series, Stadium Club continued Topps' 1996 tribute to Mickey Mantle with 19 Retrospective inserts. Cards feature full-bleed photos with gold-foil graphic highlights. Backs offer a TSC Skills Matrix along with another player photo, some biographical data and stats. Team TSC is the only subset with 45 cards each in Series I and II. Stadium Club was issued in retail and hobby packs, with inserts found at differing ratios in each type of packaging.

		MT
Complete Set (450):		40.00
Complete Series 1 Set (225):		20.00
Complete Series 2 Set (225):		20.00
Common Player:		.10
Unlisted Stars: .20 to .40		
Series 1 or 2 Wax Box:		40.00
1	(Hideo Nomo (Extreme Player))	.75
2	Paul Molitor	.40
3	Garret Anderson (Extreme Player)	.15
4	Jose Mesa (Extreme Player)	.10
5	Vinny Castilla (Extreme Player)	.12
6	Mike Mussina (Extreme Player)	.40
7	Ray Durham (Extreme Player)	.10
8	Jack McDowell (Extreme Player)	.10
9	Juan Gonzalez (Extreme Player)	1.50
10	Chipper Jones (Extreme Player)	2.00
11	Deion Sanders (Extreme Player)	.25
12	Rondell White (Extreme Player)	.15
13	Tom Henke (Extreme Player)	.10
14	Derek Bell (Extreme Player)	.12
15	Randy Myers (Extreme Player)	.10
16	Randy Johnson (Extreme Player)	.40

17	Len Dykstra (Extreme Player)	.10
18	Bill Pulsipher (Extreme Player)	.10
19	Greg Colbrunn	.10
20	David Wells	.10
21	Chad Curtis (Extreme Player)	.10
22	Roberto Hernandez (Extreme Player)	.10
23	Kirby Puckett (Extreme Player)	1.00
24	Joe Vitiello	.10
25	Roger Clemens (Extreme Player)	1.00
26	Al Martin	.10
27	Chad Ogea	.10
28	David Segui	.10
29	Joey Hamilton	.10
30	Dan Wilson	.10
31	Chad Fonville (Extreme Player)	.15
32	Bernard Gilkey (Extreme Player)	.15
33	Kevin Seitzer	.10
34	Shawn Green (Extreme Player)	.15
35	Rick Aguilera (Extreme Player)	.10
36	Gary DiSarcina	.10
37	Jaime Navarro	.10
38	Doug Jones	.10
39	Brent Gates	.10
40	Dean Palmer (Extreme Player)	.12
41	Pat Rapp	.10
42	Tony Clark	.50
43	Bill Swift	.10
44	Randy Velarde	.10
45	Matt Williams (Extreme Player)	.30
46	John Mabry	.10
47	Mike Fetters	.10
48	Orlando Miller	.10
49	Tom Glavine (Extreme Player)	.15
50	Delino DeShields (Extreme Player)	.10
51	Scott Erickson	.10
52	Andy Van Slyke	.10
53	Jim Bullinger	.10
54	Lyle Mouton	.10
55	Bret Saberhagen	.10
56	Benito Santiago (Extreme Player)	.10
57	Dan Miceli	.10
58	Carl Everett	.10
59	Rod Beck (Extreme Player)	.10
60	Phil Nevin	.10
61	Jason Giambi	.20
62	Paul Menhart	.10
63	Eric Karros (Extreme Player)	.15
64	Allen Watson	.10
65	Jeff Cirillo	.10
66	Lee Smith (Extreme Player)	.12
67	Sean Berry	.10
68	Luis Sojo	.10
69	Jeff Montgomery (Extreme Player)	.10
70	Todd Hundley (Extreme Player)	.20
71	John Burkett	.10
72	Mark Gubicza	.10
73	Don Mattingly (Extreme Player)	1.00
74	Jeff Brantley	.10
75	Matt Walbeck	.10
76	Steve Parris	.10
77	Ken Caminiti (Extreme Player)	.40
78	Kirt Manwaring	.10
79	Greg Vaughn	.10
80	Pedro Martinez (Extreme Player)	.10
81	Benji Gil	.10
82	Heathcliff Slocumb (Extreme Player)	.10
83	Joe Girardi (Extreme Player)	.10
84	Sean Bergman	.10
85	Matt Karchner	.10
86	Butch Huskey	.10
87	Mike Morgan	.10
88	Todd Worrell (Extreme Player)	.10

89	Mike Bordick	.10
90	Bip Roberts (Extreme Player)	.10
91	Mike Hampton	.10
92	Troy O'Leary	.10
93	Wally Joyner	.12
94	Dave Stevens	.10
95	Cecil Fielder (Extreme Player)	.15
96	Wade Boggs (Extreme Player)	.20
97	Hal Morris	.10
98	Mickey Tettleton (Extreme Player)	.10
99	Jeff Kent (Extreme Player)	.10
100	Denny Martinez	.12
101	Luis Gonzalez (Extreme Player)	.10
102	John Jaha	.10
103	Javy Lopez (Extreme Player)	.20
104	Mark McGwire (Extreme Player)	4.00
105	Ken Griffey Jr. (Extreme Player)	3.00
106	Darren Daulton (Extreme Player)	.10
107	Bryan Rekar	.10
108	Mike Macfarlane (Extreme Player)	.10
109	Gary Gaetti (Extreme Player)	.12
110	Shane Reynolds (Extreme Player)	.10
111	Pat Meares	.10
112	Jason Schmidt	.10
113	Otis Nixon	.10
114	John Franco (Extreme Player)	.10
115	Marc Newfield	.10
116	Andy Benes (Extreme Player)	.10
117	Ozzie Guillen	.10
118	Brian Jordan (Extreme Player)	.15
119	Terry Pendleton (Extreme Player)	.10
120	Chuck Finley (Extreme Player)	.10
121	Scott Stahoviak	.10
122	Sid Fernandez	.10
123	Derek Jeter (Extreme Player)	1.50
124	John Smiley (Extreme Player)	.10
125	David Bell	.10
126	Brett Butler (Extreme Player)	.12
127	Doug Drabek (Extreme Player)	.10
128	J.T. Snow (Extreme Player)	.10
129	Joe Carter (Extreme Player)	.15
130	Dennis Eckersley (Extreme Player)	.12
131	Marty Cordova (Extreme Player)	.20
132	Greg Maddux (Extreme Player)	2.50
133	Tom Goodwin	.10
134	Andy Ashby	.10
135	Paul Sorrento (Extreme Player)	.10
136	Ricky Bones	.10
137	Shawon Dunston (Extreme Player)	.15
138	Moises Alou (Extreme Player)	.12
139	Mickey Morandini	.10
140	Ramon Martinez (Extreme Player)	.12
141	Royce Clayton (Extreme Player)	.10
142	Brad Ausmus	.10
143	Kenny Rogers (Extreme Player)	.10
144	Tim Naehring (Extreme Player)	.10
145	Chris Gomez (Extreme Player)	.10
146	Bobby Bonilla (Extreme Player)	.12
147	Wilson Alvarez	.10
148	Johnny Damon (Extreme Player)	.20
149	Pat Hentgen	.10

150	Andres Galarraga (Extreme Player)	.20
151	David Cone (Extreme Player)	.15
152	Lance Johnson (Extreme Player)	.10
153	Carlos Garcia	.10
154	Doug Johns	.10
155	Midre Cummings	.10
156	Steve Sparks	.10
157	*Sandy Martinez*	.10
158	William Van Landingham	.10
159	Dave Justice (Extreme Player)	.20
160	Mark Grace (Extreme Player)	.15
161	Robb Nen (Extreme Player)	.10
162	Mike Greenwell (Extreme Player)	.10
163	Brad Radke	.10
164	Edgardo Alfonzo	.10
165	Mark Leiter	.10
166	Walt Weiss	.10
167	Mel Rojas (Extreme Player)	.10
168	Bret Boone (Extreme Player)	.10
169	Ricky Bottalico	.10
170	Bobby Higginson	.10
171	Trevor Hoffman	.10
172	Jay Bell (Extreme Player)	.10
173	Gabe White	.10
174	Curtis Goodwin	.10
175	Tyler Green	.10
176	Roberto Alomar (Extreme Player)	.75
177	Sterling Hitchcock	.10
178	Ryan Klesko (Extreme Player)	.60
179	*Donne Wall*	.10
180	Brian McRae	.10
181	Will Clark (Team TSC)	.20
182	Frank Thomas (Team TSC)	2.50
183	Jeff Bagwell (Team TSC)	1.50
184	Mo Vaughn (Team TSC)	1.00
185	Tino Martinez (Team TSC)	.15
186	Craig Biggio (Team TSC)	.10
187	Chuck Knoblauch (Team TSC)	.25
188	Carlos Baerga (Team TSC)	.15
189	Quilvio Veras (Team TSC)	.10
190	Luis Alicea (Team TSC)	.10
191	Jim Thome (Team TSC)	.30
192	Mike Blowers (Team TSC)	.10
193	Robin Ventura (Team TSC)	.10
194	Jeff King (Team TSC)	.10
195	Tony Phillips (Team TSC)	.10
196	John Valentin (Team TSC)	.10
197	Barry Larkin (Team TSC)	.20
198	Cal Ripken Jr. (Team TSC)	3.00
199	Omar Vizquel (Team TSC)	.10
200	Kurt Abbott (Team TSC)	.10
201	Albert Belle (Team TSC)	1.50
202	Barry Bonds (Team TSC)	.75
203	Ron Gant (Team TSC)	.10
204	Dante Bichette (Team TSC)	.25
205	Jeff Conine (Team TSC)	.10
206	Jim Edmonds (Team TSC)	.15
207	Stan Javier (Team TSC)	.10
208	Kenny Lofton (Team TSC)	1.00
209	Ray Lankford (Team TSC)	.15
210	Bernie Williams (Team TSC)	.60
211	Jay Buhner (Team TSC)	.15
212	Paul O'Neill (Team TSC)	.10
213	Tim Salmon (Team TSC)	.25
214	Reggie Sanders (Team TSC)	.10
215	Manny Ramirez (Team TSC)	.60
216	Mike Piazza (Team TSC)	2.50
217	Mike Stanley (Team TSC)	.10
218	Tony Eusebio (Team TSC)	.10
219	Chris Hoiles (Team TSC)	.10
220	Ron Karkovice (Team TSC)	.10
221	Edgar Martinez (Team TSC)	.10
222	Chili Davis (Team TSC)	.10
223	Jose Canseco (Team TSC)	.35
224	Eddie Murray (Team TSC)	.40
225	Geronimo Berroa (Team TSC)	.10
226	Chipper Jones (Team TSC)	2.50
227	Garret Anderson (Team TSC)	.20
228	Marty Cordova (Team TSC)	.20
229	Jon Nunnally (Team TSC)	.10
230	Brian Hunter (Team TSC)	.10

231	Shawn Green (Team TSC)	.10	
232	Ray Durham (Team TSC)	.10	
233	Alex Gonzalez (Team TSC)	.10	
234	Bobby Higginson (Team TSC)	.15	
235	Randy Johnson (Team TSC)	.40	
236	Al Leiter (Team TSC)	.10	
237	Tom Glavine (Team TSC)	.15	
238	Kenny Rogers (Team TSC)	.10	
239	Mike Hampton (Team TSC)	.10	
240	David Wells (Team TSC)	.10	
241	Jim Abbott (Team TSC)	.12	
242	Denny Neagle (Team TSC)	.10	
243	Wilson Alvarez (Team TSC)	.10	
244	John Smiley (Team TSC)	.10	
245	Greg Maddux (Team TSC)	2.50	
246	Andy Ashby (Team TSC)	.10	
247	Hideo Nomo (Team TSC)	.60	
248	Pat Rapp (Team TSC)	.10	
249	Tim Wakefield (Team TSC)	.10	
250	John Smoltz (Team TSC)	.25	
251	Joey Hamilton (Team TSC)	.10	
252	Frank Castillo (Team TSC)	.10	
253	Denny Martinez (Team TSC)	.10	
254	Jaime Navarro (Team TSC)	.10	
255	Karim Garcia (Team TSC)	.40	
256	Bob Abreu (Team TSC)	.30	
257	Butch Huskey (Team TSC)	.15	
258	Ruben Rivera (Team TSC)	.50	
259	Johnny Damon (Team TSC)	.15	
260	Derek Jeter (Team TSC)	2.00	
261	Dennis Eckersley (Team TSC)	.10	
262	Jose Mesa (Team TSC)	.10	
263	Tom Henke (Team TSC)	.10	
264	Rick Aguilera (Team TSC)	.10	
265	Randy Myers (Team TSC)	.10	
266	John Franco (Team TSC)	.10	
267	Jeff Brantley (Team TSC)	.10	
268	John Wetteland (Team TSC)	.10	
269	Mark Wohlers (Team TSC)	.10	
270	Rod Beck (Team TSC)	.10	
271	Barry Larkin	.20	
272	Paul O'Neill	.10	
273	Bobby Jones	.10	
274	Will Clark	.25	
275	Steve Avery	.10	
276	Jim Edmonds	.20	
277	John Olerud	.15	
278	Carlos Perez	.10	
279	Chris Hoiles	.10	
280	Jeff Conine	.10	
281	Jim Eisenreich	.10	
282	Jason Jacome	.10	
283	Ray Lankford	.15	
284	John Wasdin	.10	
285	Frank Thomas	2.50	
286	Jason Isringhausen	.15	
287	Glenallen Hill	.10	
288	Esteban Loaiza	.15	
289	Bernie Williams	.60	
290	Curtis Leskanic	.10	
291	Scott Cooper	.10	
292	Curt Schilling	.10	
293	Eddie Murray	.50	
294	Rick Krivda	.10	
295	Domingo Cedeno	.10	
296	Jeff Fassero	.10	
297	Albert Belle	.75	
298	Craig Biggio	.15	
299	Fernando Vina	.10	
300	Edgar Martinez	.15	
301	Tony Gwynn	1.00	
302	Felipe Lira	.10	
303	Mo Vaughn	.75	
304	Alex Fernandez	.15	
305	Keith Lockhart	.10	
306	Roger Pavlik	.10	
307	Lee Tinsley	.10	
308	Omar Vizquel	.10	
309	Scott Servais	.10	
310	Danny Tartabull	.10	
311	Chili Davis	.10	
312	Cal Eldred	.10	
313	Roger Cedeno	.15	
314	Chris Hammond	.10	
315	Rusty Greer	.15	
316	Brady Anderson	.20	
317	Ron Villone	.10	
318	Mark Carreon	.10	
319	Larry Walker	.30	
320	Pete Harnisch	.10	
321	Robin Ventura	.15	

322	Tim Belcher	.10
323	Tony Tarasco	.10
324	Juan Guzman	.10
325	Kenny Lofton	.75
326	Kevin Foster	.10
327	Wil Cordero	.10
328	Troy Percival	.10
329	Turk Wendell	.10
330	Thomas Howard	.10
331	Carlos Baerga	.15
332	B.J. Surhoff	.10
333	Jay Buhner	.15
334	Andujar Cedeno	.10
335	Jeff King	.10
336	Dante Bichette	.25
337	Alan Trammell	.15
338	Scott Leius	.10
339	Chris Snopek	.10
340	Roger Bailey	.10
341	Jacob Brumfield	.10
342	Jose Canseco	.35
343	Rafael Palmeiro	.25
344	Quilvio Veras	.10
345	Darrin Fletcher	.10
346	Carlos Delgado	.10
347	Tony Eusebio	.10
348	Ismael Valdes	.10
349	Terry Steinbach	.10
350	Orel Hershiser	.12
351	Kurt Abbott	.10
352	Jody Reed	.10
353	David Howard	.10
354	Ruben Sierra	.10
355	John Ericks	.10
356	Buck Showalter	.10
357	Jim Thome	.40
358	Geronimo Berroa	.10
359	Robby Thompson	.10
360	Jose Vizcaino	.10
361	Jeff Frye	.10
362	Kevin Appier	.10
363	Pat Kelly	.10
364	Ron Gant	.15
365	Luis Alicea	.10
366	Armando Benitez	.10
367	Rico Brogna	.10
368	Manny Ramirez	.75
369	Mike Lansing	.10
370	Sammy Sosa	2.00
371	Don Wengert	.10
372	Dave Nilsson	.10
373	Sandy Alomar	.12
374	Joey Cora	.10
375	Larry Thomas	.10
376	John Valentin	.10
377	Kevin Ritz	.10
378	Steve Finley	.10
379	Frank Rodriguez	.10
380	Ivan Rodriguez	.60
381	Alex Ochoa	.10
382	Mark Lemke	.10
383	Scott Brosius	.10
384	James Mouton	.10
385	Mark Langston	.10
386	Ed Sprague	.10
387	Joe Oliver	.10
388	Steve Ontiveros	.10
389	Rey Sanchez	.10
390	Mike Henneman	.10
391	*Jose Valentin*	.10
392	Tom Candiotti	.10
393	Damon Buford	.10
394	Erik Hanson	.10
395	Mark Smith	.10
396	Pete Schourek	.10
397	John Flaherty	.10
398	Dave Martinez	.10
399	Tommy Greene	.10
400	Gary Sheffield	.40
401	Glenn Dishman	.10
402	Barry Bonds	.60
403	Tom Pagnozzi	.10
404	Todd Stottlemyre	.10
405	Tim Salmon	.25
406	John Hudek	.10
407	Fred McGriff	.30
408	Orlando Merced	.10
409	Brian Barber	.10
410	Ryan Thompson	.10
411	Mariano Rivera	.25
412	Eric Young	.10
413	Chris Bosio	.10
414	Chuck Knoblauch	.20
415	Jamie Moyer	.10
416	Chan Ho Park	.15
417	Mark Portugal	.10

418	Tim Raines	.10
419	Antonio Osuna	.10
420	Todd Zeile	.10
421	Steve Wojciechowski	.10
422	Marquis Grissom	.15
423	Norm Charlton	.10
424	Cal Ripken Jr.	3.00
425	Gregg Jefferies	.12
426	Mike Stanton	.10
427	Tony Fernandez	.10
428	Jose Rijo	.10
429	Jeff Bagwell	1.00
430	Raul Mondesi	.30
431	Travis Fryman	.10
432	Ron Karkovice	.10
433	Alan Benes	.15
434	Tony Phillips	.12
435	Reggie Sanders	.15
436	Andy Pettitte	1.00
437	*Matt Lawton*	.10
438	Jeff Blauser	.10
439	Michael Tucker	.10
440	Mark Loretta	.10
441	Charlie Hayes	.10
442	Mike Piazza	2.00
443	Shane Andrews	.10
444	Jeff Suppan	.10
445	Steve Rodriguez	.10
446	Mike Matheny	.10
447	Trenidad Hubbard	.10
448	Denny Hocking	.10
449	Mark Grudzielanek	.12
450	Joe Randa	.10

1996 Stadium Club Bash & Burn

Inserted in one per 24 retail packs and one per 48 hobby packs of Series II, Bash & Burn includes 10 players on double-fronted cards. Both sides are foil-etched with the Bash side highlighting home runs and runs batted in for 1995 and career, and the Burn side featured stolen base and runs scored leaders for 1995 and career.

	MT
Complete Set (10):	30.00
Common Player:	2.50
B&B1 Sammy Sosa	20.00
B&B2 Barry Bonds	10.00
B&B3 Reggie Sanders	3.00
B&B4 Craig Biggio	2.50
B&B5 Raul Mondesi	5.00
B&B6 Ron Gant	3.00
B&B7 Ray Lankford	2.50
B&B8 Glenallen Hill	2.50
B&B9 Chad Curtis	2.50
B&B10 John Valentin	2.50

A player's name in *italic* type indicates a rookie card.

1996 Stadium Club Extreme Player - Bronze

A special interactive version of 179 players' cards in 1996 Stadium Club was issued as an insert set across Series I and II. Specially stamped with an "Extreme Player" logo in bronze (1 per 12 packs average), silver (1:24) or gold (1:48), the cards have backs which detail a contest by which the player's on-field performance was used to rank each by position. At season's end, cards of the winning players at each position could be redeemed for special prizes. Bronze winners' cards could be redeemed for a set of 10 bronze foil-stamped cards featuring the Extreme Player winners at each position.

	MT
Complete Bronze Set (179):	200.00
Complete Series 1 Bronze (90):	100.00
Complete Series 2 Bronze (89):	100.00
Common Bronze:	1.00
Silvers 2x Bronze:	
Golds 4x Bronze:	

1	(Hideo Nomo)	7.00
3	Garret Anderson	1.50
4	Jose Mesa	1.00
5	Vinny Castilla	1.00
6	Mike Mussina	4.00
7	Ray Durham	1.00
8	Jack McDowell	1.00
9	Juan Gonzalez	7.50
10	Chipper Jones	12.50
11	Deion Sanders	2.00
12	Rondell White	1.00
13	Tom Henke	1.00
14	Derek Bell	1.00
15	Randy Myers	1.00
16	Randy Johnson	4.00
17	Len Dykstra	1.00
18	Bill Pulsipher	1.00
21	Chad Curtis	1.00
22	Roberto Hernandez	1.00
23	Kirby Puckett	7.00
25	Roger Clemens	3.00
31	Chad Fonville	1.00
32	Bernard Gilkey	1.50
34	Shawn Green	1.00
35	Rick Aguilera	1.00
40	Dean Palmer	1.00
45	Matt Williams	5.00
49	Tom Glavine	2.00
50	Delino DeShields	1.00
56	Benito Santiago	1.00
59	Rod Beck	1.00
63	Eric Karros	1.00
66	Lee Smith	1.00
69	Jeff Montgomery	1.00
70	Todd Hundley	2.00
73	Don Mattingly	8.00
77	Ken Caminiti	1.50
80	Pedro Martinez	1.50

82	Heathcliff Slocumb	1.00
83	Joe Girardi	1.00
88	Todd Worrell	1.00
90	Bip Roberts	1.00
95	Cecil Fielder	1.00
96	Wade Boggs	2.50
98	Mickey Tettleton	1.00
99	Jeff Kent	1.00
101	Luis Gonzalez	1.00
103	Javier Lopez	2.00
104	Mark McGwire	10.00
105	Ken Griffey Jr.	25.00
106	Darren Daulton	1.00
108	Mike Macfarlane	1.00
109	Gary Gaetti	1.00
110	Shane Reynolds	1.00
114	John Franco	1.00
116	Andy Benes	1.00
118	Brian Jordan	1.00
119	Terry Pendleton	1.00
120	Chuck Finley	1.00
123	Derek Jeter	3.00
124	John Smiley	1.00
126	Brett Butler	1.00
127	Doug Drabek	1.00
128	J.T. Snow	1.00
129	Joe Carter	1.00
130	Dennis Eckersley	1.00
131	Marty Cordova	1.00
132	Greg Maddux	15.00
135	Paul Sorrento	1.00
137	Shawon Dunston	1.00
138	Moises Alou	1.00
140	Ramon Martinez	1.00
141	Royce Clayton	1.00
143	Kenny Rogers	1.00
144	Tim Naehring	1.00
145	Chris Gomez	1.00
146	Bobby Bonilla	1.00
148	Johnny Damon	1.50
150	Andres Galarraga	1.00
151	David Cone	1.50
152	Lance Johnson	1.00
159	Dave Justice	2.00
160	Mark Grace	2.00
161	Robb Nen	1.00
162	Mike Greenwell	1.00
167	Mel Rojas	1.00
168	Bret Boone	1.00
172	Jay Bell	1.00
176	Roberto Alomar	6.00
178	Ryan Klesko	5.00
271	Barry Larkin	2.00
272	Paul O'Neill	1.00
274	Will Clark	2.50
275	Steve Avery	1.00
276	Jim Edmonds	1.50
277	John Olerud	2.00
279	Chris Hoiles	1.00
280	Jeff Conine	1.00
283	Ray Lankford	1.00
285	Frank Thomas	20.00
286	Jason Isringhausen	2.00
287	Glenallen Hill	1.00
289	Bernie Williams	3.00
290	Eddie Murray	1.50
296	Jeff Fassero	1.00
297	Albert Belle	8.00
298	Craig Biggio	1.00
300	Edgar Martinez	1.00
301	Tony Gwynn	10.00
303	Mo Vaughn	5.00
304	Alex Fernandez	1.00
308	Omar Vizquel	1.00
310	Danny Tartabull	1.00
316	Brady Anderson	2.00
319	Larry Walker	1.50
321	Robin Ventura	1.00
325	Kenny Lofton	5.00
327	Wil Cordero	1.00
328	Troy Percival	2.00
331	Carlos Baerga	2.00
333	Jay Buhner	1.00
335	Jeff King	1.00
336	Dante Bichette	2.00
337	Alan Trammell	1.00
342	Jose Canseco	2.00
343	Rafael Palmeiro	1.00
344	Quilvio Veras	1.00
345	Darrin Fletcher	1.00
347	Tony Eusebio	1.00
348	Ismael Valdes	1.00
349	Terry Steinbach	1.00
350	Orel Hershiser	1.00
351	Kurt Abbott	1.00
354	Ruben Sierra	1.00

357	Jim Thome	2.00
358	Geronimo Berroa	1.00
359	Robby Thompson	1.00
360	Jose Vizcaino	1.00
362	Kevin Appier	1.00
364	Ron Gant	1.00
367	Rico Brogna	1.00
368	Manny Ramirez	5.00
370	Sammy Sosa	15.00
373	Sandy Alomar	1.00
378	Steve Finley	1.00
380	Ivan Rodriguez	1.00
382	Mark Lemke	1.00
385	Mark Langston	1.00
386	Ed Sprague	1.00
388	Steve Ontiveros	1.00
392	Tom Candiotti	1.00
394	Erik Hanson	1.00
396	Pete Schourek	1.00
400	Gary Sheffield	2.50
402	Barry Bonds	8.00
403	Tom Pagnozzi	1.00
404	Todd Stottlemyre	1.00
405	Tim Salmon	4.00
407	Fred McGriff	2.00
408	Orlando Merced	1.00
412	Eric Young	1.00
414	Chuck Knoblauch	2.00
417	Mark Portugal	1.00
418	Tim Raines	1.00
420	Todd Zeile	1.00
422	Marquis Grissom	1.00
423	Norm Charlton	1.00
424	Cal Ripken Jr.	20.00
425	Gregg Jefferies	1.00
428	Jose Rijo	1.00
429	Jeff Bagwell	8.00
430	Raul Mondesi	2.00
431	Travis Fryman	1.00
434	Tony Phillips	1.00
435	Reggie Sanders	1.00
436	Andy Pettitte	3.00
438	Jeff Blauser	1.00
441	Charlie Hayes	1.00
442	Mike Piazza	18.00

1996 Stadium Club Extreme Player - Silver

A special interactive version of 179 player's cards in 1996 Stadium Club was issued as an insert set across Series I and II. Specially stamped with an "Extreme Player" logo in bronze (1 per 12 packs average), silver (1 per 24 packs) or gold (1 per 48 packs), the cards have backs which detail a contest by which the player's on-field performance was used to rank each by position. At season's end, cards of the winning players at each position could be redeemed for special prizes. Silver winners' cards could be redeemed for a set of 10 Finest Refractor cards featuring the Extreme Player winners at each position.

	MT
Complete Silver Set (179):	600.00
Complete Series 1 Silver (90):	180.00
Complete Series 2 Silver (89):	180.00
Common Silver:	2.00

1	(Hideo Nomo)	14.00
3	Garret Anderson	3.00
4	Jose Mesa	3.00
5	Vinny Castilla	2.00
6	Mike Mussina	8.00
7	Ray Durham	2.00
8	Jack McDowell	2.00
9	Juan Gonzalez	15.00
10	Chipper Jones	24.00
11	Deion Sanders	5.00
12	Rondell White	2.00
13	Tom Henke	2.00
14	Derek Bell	2.00
15	Randy Myers	2.00
16	Randy Johnson	10.00
17	Len Dykstra	2.00

18	Bill Pulsipher	2.00
21	Chad Curtis	2.00
22	Roberto Hernandez	2.00
23	Kirby Puckett	12.00
25	Roger Clemens	6.00
31	Chad Fonville	2.00
32	Bernard Gilkey	2.00
34	Shawn Green	2.00
35	Rick Aguilera	2.00
40	Dean Palmer	2.00
45	Matt Williams	8.00
49	Tom Glavine	2.00
50	Delino DeShields	2.00
56	Benito Santiago	2.00
59	Rod Beck	2.00
63	Eric Karros	2.00
66	Lee Smith	2.00
69	Jeff Montgomery	2.00
70	Todd Hundley	4.00
73	Don Mattingly	15.00
77	Ken Caminiti	2.00
80	Pedro Martinez	2.00
82	Heathcliff Slocumb	2.00
83	Joe Girardi	2.00
88	Todd Worrell	2.00
90	Bip Roberts	2.00
95	Cecil Fielder	2.00
96	Wade Boggs	5.00
98	Mickey Tettleton	2.00
99	Jeff Kent	2.00
101	Luis Gonzalez	2.00
103	Javier Lopez	4.00
104	Mark McGwire	8.00
105	Ken Griffey Jr.	50.00
106	Darren Daulton	2.00
108	Mike Macfarlane	2.00
109	Gary Gaetti	2.00
110	Shane Reynolds	2.00
114	John Franco	2.00
116	Andy Benes	2.00
118	Brian Jordan	2.00
119	Terry Pendleton	2.00
120	Chuck Finley	2.00
123	Derek Jeter	6.00
124	John Smiley	2.00
126	Brett Butler	2.00
127	Doug Drabek	2.00
128	J.T. Snow	2.00
129	Joe Carter	2.00
130	Dennis Eckersley	2.00
131	Marty Cordova	3.00
132	Greg Maddux	40.00
135	Paul Sorrento	2.00
137	Shawon Dunston	2.00
138	Moises Alou	2.00
140	Ramon Martinez	2.00
141	Royce Clayton	2.00
143	Kenny Rogers	2.00
144	Tim Naehring	2.00
145	Chris Gomez	2.00
146	Bobby Bonilla	2.00
148	Johnny Damon	3.00
150	Andres Galarraga	2.00
151	David Cone	3.00
152	Lance Johnson	2.00
159	Dave Justice	4.00
160	Mark Grace	3.00
161	Robb Nen	2.00
162	Mike Greenwell	2.00
167	Mel Rojas	2.00
168	Bret Boone	2.00
172	Jay Bell	2.00
176	Roberto Alomar	15.00
178	Ryan Klesko	10.00
271	Barry Larkin	6.00
272	Paul O'Neill	2.00
274	Will Clark	6.00
275	Steve Avery	2.00
276	Jim Edmonds	3.00
277	John Olerud	2.00
279	Chris Hoiles	2.00
280	Jeff Conine	2.00
283	Ray Lankford	2.00
285	Frank Thomas	40.00
286	Jason Isringhausen	4.00
287	Glenallen Hill	2.00
289	Bernie Williams	4.00
290	Eddie Murray	3.00
296	Jeff Fassero	2.00
297	Albert Belle	12.00
298	Craig Biggio	2.00
300	Edgar Martinez	2.00
301	Tony Gwynn	18.00
303	Mo Vaughn	10.00
304	Alex Fernandez	2.00
308	Omar Vizquel	2.00
310	Danny Tartabull	2.00
316	Brady Anderson	4.00
319	Larry Walker	3.00
321	Robin Ventura	2.00
325	Kenny Lofton	10.00
327	Wil Cordero	2.00
328	Troy Percival	3.00
331	Carlos Baerga	3.00
333	Jay Buhner	2.00
335	Jeff King	2.00
336	Dante Bichette	5.00
337	Alan Trammell	2.00
342	Jose Canseco	4.00
343	Rafael Palmeiro	3.00
344	Quilvio Veras	2.00
345	Darrin Fletcher	2.00
347	Tony Eusebio	2.00
348	Ismael Valdes	2.00
349	Terry Steinbach	2.00
350	Orel Hershiser	2.00
351	Kurt Abbott	2.00
354	Ruben Sierra	2.00
357	Jim Thome	4.00
358	Geronimo Berroa	2.00
359	Robby Thompson	2.00
360	Jose Vizcaino	2.00
362	Kevin Appier	2.00
364	Ron Gant	2.00
367	Rico Brogna	2.00
368	Manny Ramirez	10.00
370	Sammy Sosa	20.00
373	Sandy Alomar	2.00
378	Steve Finley	2.00
380	Ivan Rodriguez	8.00
382	Mark Lemke	2.00
385	Mark Langston	2.00
386	Ed Sprague	2.00
388	Steve Ontiveros	2.00
392	Tom Candiotti	2.00
394	Erik Hanson	2.00
396	Pete Schourek	2.00
400	Gary Sheffield	5.00
402	Barry Bonds	18.00
403	Tom Pagnozzi	2.00
404	Todd Stottlemyre	2.00
405	Tim Salmon	8.00
407	Fred McGriff	8.00
408	Orlando Merced	2.00
412	Eric Young	2.00
414	Chuck Knoblauch	5.00
417	Mark Portugal	2.00
418	Tim Raines	2.00
420	Todd Zeile	2.00
422	Marquis Grissom	2.00
423	Norm Charlton	2.00
424	Cal Ripken Jr.	40.00
425	Gregg Jefferies	2.00
428	Jose Rijo	2.00
429	Jeff Bagwell	16.00
430	Raul Mondesi	4.00
431	Travis Fryman	2.00
434	Tony Phillips	2.00
435	Reggie Sanders	2.00
436	Andy Pettitte	8.00
438	Jeff Blauser	2.00
441	Charlie Hayes	2.00
442	Mike Piazza	36.00

1996 Stadium Club Extreme Player - Gold

A special interactive version of 179 players' cards in 1996 Stadium Club was issued as an insert set across Series 1 and 2. Specially stamped with an "Extreme Player" logo in bronze (1 per 12 packs average), silver (1:24) or gold (1:48 packs), the cards have backs which detail a contest by which the player's on-field performance was used to rank each by position. At season's end, cards of the winning players at each position could be redeemed for special prizes. Gold winners' cards could be redeemed for a Finest Refractor card mounted on bronze featuring that Extreme Player.

		MT
Complete Gold Set (179):		1200.
Complete Series 1 Gold (90):		360.00
Complete Series 2 Gold (89):		360.00
Common Gold:		4.00
1	(Hideo Nomo)	28.00
3	Garret Anderson	6.00
4	Jose Mesa	6.00
5	Vinny Castilla	4.00
6	Mike Mussina	16.00
7	Ray Durham	4.00
8	Jack McDowell	4.00
9	Juan Gonzalez	25.00
10	Chipper Jones	48.00
11	Deion Sanders	10.00
12	Rondell White	4.00
13	Tom Henke	4.00
14	Derek Bell	4.00
15	Randy Myers	4.00
16	Randy Johnson	20.00
17	Len Dykstra	4.00
18	Bill Pulsipher	4.00
21	Chad Curtis	4.00
22	Roberto Hernandez	4.00
23	Kirby Puckett	24.00
25	Roger Clemens	12.00
31	Chad Fonville	4.00
32	Bernard Gilkey	4.00
34	Shawn Green	4.00
35	Rick Aguilera	4.00
40	Dean Palmer	4.00
45	Matt Williams	24.00
49	Tom Glavine	8.00
50	Delino DeShields	4.00
56	Benito Santiago	4.00
59	Rod Beck	4.00
63	Eric Karros	4.00
66	Lee Smith	4.00
69	Jeff Montgomery	4.00
70	Todd Hundley	8.00
73	Don Mattingly	30.00
77	Ken Caminiti	4.00
80	Pedro Martinez	4.00
82	Heathcliff Slocumb	4.00
83	Joe Girardi	4.00
88	Todd Worrell	4.00
90	Bip Roberts	4.00
95	Cecil Fielder	4.00
96	Wade Boggs	6.00
98	Mickey Tettleton	4.00
99	Jeff Kent	4.00
101	Luis Gonzalez	4.00
103	Javier Lopez	8.00
104	Mark McGwire	20.00
105	Ken Griffey Jr.	100.00
106	Darren Daulton	4.00
108	Mike Macfarlane	4.00
109	Gary Gaetti	4.00
110	Shane Reynolds	4.00
114	John Franco	4.00
116	Andy Benes	4.00
118	Brian Jordan	4.00
119	Terry Pendleton	4.00
120	Chuck Finley	4.00
123	Derek Jeter	12.00
124	John Smiley	4.00
126	Brett Butler	4.00
127	Doug Drabek	4.00
128	J.T. Snow	4.00
129	Joe Carter	4.00
130	Dennis Eckersley	4.00
131	Marty Cordova	10.00
132	Greg Maddux	80.00
135	Paul Sorrento	4.00
137	Shawon Dunston	4.00
138	Moises Alou	4.00
140	Ramon Martinez	4.00
141	Royce Clayton	4.00
143	Kenny Rogers	4.00
144	Tim Naehring	4.00
145	Chris Gomez	4.00
146	Bobby Bonilla	4.00
148	Johnny Damon	8.00
150	Andres Galarraga	4.00
151	David Cone	4.00
152	Lance Johnson	4.00
159	Dave Justice	7.50
160	Mark Grace	6.00
161	Robb Nen	4.00
162	Mike Greenwell	4.00
167	Mel Rojas	4.00
168	Bret Boone	4.00
172	Jay Bell	4.00
176	Roberto Alomar	24.00
178	Ryan Klesko	24.00
271	Barry Larkin	12.00

272	Paul O'Neill	4.00
274	Will Clark	12.00
275	Steve Avery	4.00
276	Jim Edmonds	6.00
277	John Olerud	4.00
279	Chris Hoiles	4.00
280	Jeff Conine	4.00
283	Ray Lankford	4.00
285	Frank Thomas	80.00
286	Jason Isringhausen	8.00
287	Glenallen Hill	4.00
289	Bernie Williams	8.00
290	Eddie Murray	6.00
296	Jeff Fassero	4.00
297	Albert Belle	35.00
298	Craig Biggio	4.00
300	Edgar Martinez	4.00
301	Tony Gwynn	40.00
303	Mo Vaughn	20.00
304	Alex Fernandez	4.00
308	Omar Vizquel	4.00
310	Danny Tartabull	4.00
316	Brady Anderson	8.00
319	Larry Walker	4.00
321	Robin Ventura	4.00
325	Kenny Lofton	20.00
327	Wil Cordero	4.00
328	Troy Percival	4.00
331	Carlos Baerga	4.00
333	Jay Buhner	6.00
335	Jeff King	4.00
336	Dante Bichette	10.00
337	Alan Trammell	4.00
342	Jose Canseco	6.00
343	Rafael Palmeiro	4.00
344	Quilvio Veras	4.00
345	Darrin Fletcher	4.00
347	Tony Eusebio	4.00
348	Ismael Valdes	4.00
349	Terry Steinbach	4.00
350	Orel Hershiser	4.00
351	Kurt Abbott	4.00
354	Ruben Sierra	4.00
357	Jim Thome	8.00
358	Geronimo Berroa	4.00
359	Robby Thompson	4.00
360	Jose Vizcaino	4.00
362	Kevin Appier	4.00
364	Ron Gant	4.00
367	Rico Brogna	4.00
368	Manny Ramirez	20.00
370	Sammy Sosa	40.00
373	Sandy Alomar	4.00
378	Steve Finley	4.00
380	Ivan Rodriguez	4.00
382	Mark Lemke	4.00
385	Mark Langston	4.00
386	Ed Sprague	4.00
388	Steve Ontiveros	4.00
392	Tom Candiotti	4.00
394	Erik Hanson	4.00
396	Pete Schourek	4.00
400	Gary Sheffield	10.00
402	Barry Bonds	35.00
403	Tom Pagnozzi	4.00
404	Todd Stottlemyre	4.00
405	Tim Salmon	10.00
407	Fred McGriff	10.00
408	Orlando Merced	4.00
412	Eric Young	4.00
414	Chuck Knoblauch	9.00
417	Mark Portugal	4.00
418	Tim Raines	4.00
420	Todd Zeile	4.00
422	Marquis Grissom	4.00
423	Norm Charlton	4.00
424	Cal Ripken Jr.	80.00
425	Gregg Jefferies	4.00
428	Jose Rijo	4.00
429	Jeff Bagwell	32.00
430	Raul Mondesi	10.00
431	Travis Fryman	4.00
434	Tony Phillips	4.00
435	Reggie Sanders	4.00
436	Andy Pettitte	15.00
438	Jeff Blauser	4.00
441	Charlie Hayes	4.00
442	Mike Piazza	72.00

A player's name in *italic* type indicates a rookie card.

1996 Stadium Club Mega Heroes

ANDRES GALARRAGA

Ten herois players are matched with a comic book-style illustration depicting their nickname in the Mega Heroes insert set. Printed on foil-board in a defraction technology, the cards are found, on average, once per 48 Series I hobby packs and twice as often in retail packs.

		MT
Complete Set (10):		80.00
Common Player:		4.00
1	Frank Thomas	25.00
2	Ken Griffey Jr.	30.00
3	Hideo Nomo	8.00
4	Ozzie Smith	8.00
5	Will Clark	5.00
6	Jack McDowell	4.00
7	Andres Galarraga	4.00
8	Roger Clemens	8.00
9	Deion Sanders	6.00
10	Mo Vaughn	12.00

1996 Stadium Club Metalists

FRANK THOMAS

Eight players who have won two or more major awards in their careers are featured in this Series II insert. Cards are printed on foil-board and feature intricate laser-cut designs that depict the player's

face. Metalist inserts are found one per 96 retail and one per 48 hobby packs, on average.

		MT
Complete Set (8):		75.00
Common Player:		2.50
M1	Jeff Bagwell	10.00
M2	Barry Bonds	10.00
M3	Jose Canseco	4.00
M4	Roger Clemens	7.50
M5	Dennis Eckersley	2.50
M6	Greg Maddux	20.00
M7	Cal Ripken Jr.	25.00
M8	Frank Thomas	20.00

1996 Stadium Club Mickey Mantle Retrospective

MICKEY MANTLE

Following the success of the Mantle reprints in Topps baseball, Stadium Club produced a series of 19 Mickey Mantle Retrospective inserts; nine black-and-white cards in Series I and 10 color cards in Series II. The cards chronicle Mantle's career and provide insights from baseball contemporaries. Throughout both series, the Mantle cards are found on an average of once per 24 retail packs and once per 12 hobby packs.

	MT
Complete Set (19):	200.00
Complete Series I (9):	120.00
Complete Series II (10):	100.00
Common Player:	12.00
MM1 Mickey Mantle (1950, minor league)	15.00
MM2 Mickey Mantle (1951)	15.00
MM3 Mickey Mantle (1951)	15.00
MM4 Mickey Mantle (1953)	15.00
MM5 Mickey Mantle (1954)(w/ Yogi Berra)	15.00
MM6 Mickey Mantle (1956)	15.00
MM7 Mickey Mantle (1957)	15.00
MM8 Mickey Mantle (1958)(w/ Casey Stengel)	15.00
MM9 Mickey Mantle (1959)	15.00
MM10 Mickey Mantle (1960)(w/ Elston Howard)	12.00
MM11 Mickey Mantle (1961)	12.00
MM12 Mickey Mantle (1961)(w/ Roger Maris)	18.00
MM13 Mickey Mantle (1962)	12.00
MM14 Mickey Mantle (1963)	12.00
MM15 Mickey Mantle (1964)	12.00
MM16 Mickey Mantle	12.00
MM17 Mickey Mantle (1968)	12.00
MM18 Mickey Mantle (1969)	12.00
MM19 Mickey Mantle (In Memoriam)	12.00

1996 Stadium Club Midsummer Matchups

These inserts salute 1995 National League and American League All-Stars on back-to-back etched-foil cards. Players are matched by position in the 10-card set. Average insertion rate is one per 48 hobby packs and one per 24 retail packs in Series I.

		MT
Complete Set (10):		100.00
Common Player:		4.00
M1	Hideo Nomo, Randy Johnson	8.00
M2	Mike Piazza, Ivan Rodriguez	20.00
M3	Fred McGriff, Frank Thomas	25.00
M4	Craig Biggio, Carlos Baerga	4.00
M5	Vinny Castilla, Wade Boggs	5.00
M6	Barry Larkin, Cal Ripken Jr.	25.00
M7	Barry Bonds, Albert Belle	10.00
M8	Len Dykstra, Kenny Lofton	10.00
M9	Tony Gwynn, Kirby Puckett	12.00
M10	Ron Gant, Edgar Martinez	4.00

1996 Stadium Club Power Packed

Topps' Power Matrix technology is used to showcase 15 of the biggest, strongest players in this Series II insert set. Card backs feature a diagram of the player's home park with baseball graphics measuring this home runs during the 1995 season. The inserts are a one in 48 packs pick, on average, both hobby and retail.

		MT
Complete Set (15):		110.00
Common Player:		3.00
PP1	Albert Belle	8.00
PP2	Mark McGwire	30.00
PP3	Jose Canseco	5.00
PP4	Mike Piazza	20.00
PP5	Ron Gant	4.00
PP6	Ken Griffey Jr.	30.00
PP7	Mo Vaughn	10.00
PP8	Cecil Fielder	4.00
PP9	Tim Salmon	5.00
PP10	Frank Thomas	20.00
PP11	Juan Gonzalez	15.00
PP12	Andres Galarraga	4.00
PP13	Fred McGriff	6.00
PP14	Jay Buhner	4.00
PP15	Dante Bichette	5.00

1996 Stadium Club Power Streak

The best power hitters in baseball are featured in Power Matrix technology on these Series I inserts. Average insertion rate is one per 24 hobby and 48 retail packs.

		MT
Complete Set (15):		80.00
Common Player:		3.00
PS1	Randy Johnson	6.00
PS2	Hideo Nomo	6.00
PS3	Albert Belle	8.00
PS4	Dante Bichette	4.00
PS5	Jay Buhner	4.00
PS6	Frank Thomas	15.00
PS7	Mark McGwire	30.00
PS8	Rafael Palmeiro	4.00
PS9	Mo Vaughn	9.00
PS10	Sammy Sosa	15.00
PS11	Larry Walker	4.00
PS12	Gary Gaetti	3.00
PS13	Tim Salmon	4.00
PS14	Barry Bonds	8.00
PS15	Jim Edmonds	4.00

1996 Stadium Club Prime Cuts

The purest swings in baseball are the focus on these laser-cut, defraction-foil inserts found in Series I packs at an average rate of one per 36 hobby and 72 retail packs.

		MT
Complete Set (8):		60.00
Common Player:		3.00
PC1	Albert Belle	6.00
PC2	Barry Bonds	6.00
PC3	Ken Griffey Jr.	25.00
PC4	Tony Gwynn	10.00
PC5	Edgar Martinez	3.00
PC6	Rafael Palmeiro	4.00
PC7	Mike Piazza	15.00
PC8	Frank Thomas	15.00

1996 Stadium Club TSC Awards

TSC Awards insert cards allowed Topps' experts to honor best performances, newcomer, comeback, etc. The cards are found in Series II packs at an average rate of one per 24 retail and 48 hobby packs.

		MT
Complete Set (10):		50.00
Common Player:		2.00
1	Cal Ripken Jr.	15.00
2	Albert Belle	6.00
3	Tom Glavine	2.00
4	Jeff Conine	2.00
5	Ken Griffey Jr.	18.00
6	Hideo Nomo	4.00
7	Greg Maddux	10.00
8	Chipper Jones	10.00
9	Randy Johnson	4.00
10	Jose Mesa	2.00

1997 Stadium Club

Stadium Club totalled 390 cards in 1997, and was issued in two Series of 195 cards each. In Series I, card numbers 182-195 are a rookie subset called TSC 2000. In

Series II, card numbers 376-390 form a subset called Stadium Slugger. Stadium Club, which arrived in nine-card hobby packs and six-card retail packs, is printed on an improved 20-point stock with Topps' Super Color process. Series I included five co-Signers, 11 Instavision, 20 Millennium, 10 Pure Gold, 60 TSC Matrix and 12 Firebrand inserts. Series II continued these inserts, except instead of Firebrand, Series II had Patent Leather.

	MT
Complete Set (390):	80.00
Complete Series I Set (195):	40.00
Complete Series II Set (195):	40.00
Common Player:	.10
Wax Box:	50.00

#	Player	Price
1	Chipper Jones	2.00
2	Gary Sheffield	.40
3	Kenny Lofton	.60
4	Brian Jordan	.10
5	Mark McGwire	4.00
6	Charles Nagy	.10
7	Tim Salmon	.25
8	Cal Ripken Jr.	2.50
9	Jeff Conine	.10
10	Paul Molitor	.30
11	Mariano Rivera	.20
12	Pedro Martinez	.10
13	Jeff Bagwell	1.25
14	Bobby Bonilla	.10
15	Barry Bonds	.75
16	Ryan Klesko	.50
17	Barry Larkin	.20
18	Jim Thome	.30
19	Jay Buhner	.15
20	Juan Gonzalez	1.50
21	Mike Mussina	.30
22	Kevin Appier	.10
23	Eric Karros	.10
24	Steve Finley	.10
25	Ed Sprague	.10
26	Bernard Gilkey	.10
27	Tony Phillips	.10
28	Henry Rodriguez	.10
29	John Smoltz	.20
30	Dante Bichette	.20
31	Mike Piazza	2.00
32	Paul O'Neill	.10
33	Billy Wagner	.10
34	Reggie Sanders	.10
35	John Jaha	.10
36	Eddie Murray	.40
37	Eric Young	.10
38	Roberto Hernandez	.10
39	Pat Hentgen	.10
40	Sammy Sosa	1.50
41	Todd Hundley	.10
42	Mo Vaughn	1.00
43	Robin Ventura	.10
44	Mark Grudzielanek	.10
45	Shane Reynolds	.10
46	Andy Pettitte	.75
47	Fred McGriff	.25
48	Rey Ordonez	.20
49	Will Clark	.25
50	Ken Griffey Jr.	3.00
51	Todd Worrell	.10
52	Rusty Greer	.10
53	Mark Grace	.20
54	Tom Glavine	.20
55	Derek Jeter	1.50
56	Rafael Palmeiro	.15
57	Bernie Williams	.60
58	Marty Cordova	.10
59	Andres Galarraga	.15
60	Ken Caminiti	.35
61	Garret Anderson	.10
62	Denny Martinez	.10
63	Mike Greenwell	.10
64	David Segui	.10
65	Julio Franco	.10
66	Rickey Henderson	.20
67	Ozzie Guillen	.10
68	Pete Harnisch	.10
69	Chan Ho Park	.10
70	Harold Baines	.10
71	Mark Clark	.10
72	Steve Avery	.10
73	Brian Hunter	.10
74	Pedro Astacio	.10
75	Jack McDowell	.10
76	Gregg Jefferies	.10
77	Jason Kendall	.10
78	Todd Walker	.75
79	B.J. Surhoff	.10
80	Moises Alou	.20
81	Fernando Vina	.10
82	Darryl Strawberry	.10
83	Jose Rosado	.10
84	Chris Gomez	.10
85	Chili Davis	.10
86	Alan Benes	.10
87	Todd Hollandsworth	.10
88	Jose Vizcaino	.10
89	Edgardo Alfonzo	.10
90	Ruben Rivera	.30
91	Donovan Osborne	.10
92	Doug Glanville	.10
93	Gary DiSarcina	.10
94	Brooks Kieschnick	.10
95	Bobby Jones	.10
96	Raul Casanova	.10
97	Jermaine Allensworth	.10
98	Kenny Rogers	.10
99	Mark McLemore	.10
100	Jeff Fassero	.10
101	Sandy Alomar	.10
102	Chuck Finley	.10
103	Eric Owens	.10
104	Billy McMillon	.10
105	Dwight Gooden	.10
106	Sterling Hitchcock	.10
107	Doug Drabek	.10
108	Paul Wilson	.15
109	Chris Snopek	.10
110	Al Leiter	.10
111	Bob Tewksbury	.10
112	Todd Greene	.10
113	Jose Valentin	.10
114	Delino DeShields	.10
115	Mike Bordick	.10
116	Pat Meares	.10
117	Mariano Duncan	.10
118	Steve Trachsel	.10
119	Luis Castillo	.25
120	Andy Benes	.10
121	Donne Wall	.10
122	Alex Gonzalez	.10
123	Dan Wilson	.10
124	Omar Vizquel	.10
125	Devon White	.10
126	Darryl Hamilton	.10
127	Orlando Merced	.10
128	Royce Clayton	.10
129	William VanLandingham	.10
130	Terry Steinbach	.10
131	Jeff Blauser	.10
132	Jeff Cirillo	.10
133	Roger Pavlik	.10
134	Danny Tartabull	.10
135	Jeff Montgomery	.10
136	Bobby Higginson	.10
137	Mike Grace	.10
138	Kevin Elster	.10
139	Brian Giles	.10
140	Rod Beck	.10
141	Ismael Valdes	.10
142	Scott Brosius	.10
143	Mike Fetters	.10
144	Gary Gaetti	.10
145	Mike Lansing	.10
146	Glenallen Hill	.10
147	Shawn Green	.10
148	Mel Rojas	.10
149	Joey Cora	.10
150	John Smiley	.10
151	Marvin Benard	.10
152	Curt Schilling	.10
153	Dave Nilsson	.10
154	Edgar Renteria	.20
155	Joey Hamilton	.10
156	Carlos Garcia	.10
157	Nomar Garciaparra	2.00
158	Kevin Ritz	.10
159	Keith Lockhart	.10
160	Justin Thompson	.10
161	Terry Adams	.10
162	Jamey Wright	.10
163	Otis Nixon	.10
164	Michael Tucker	.10
165	Mike Stanley	.10
166	Ben McDonald	.10
167	John Mabry	.10
168	Troy O'Leary	.10
169	Mel Nieves	.10
170	Bret Boone	.10
171	Mike Timlin	.10
172	Scott Rolen	1.50
173	Reggie Jefferson	.10
174	Neifi Perez	.10
175	Brian McRae	.10
176	Tom Goodwin	.10
177	Aaron Sele	.10
178	Benny Santiago	.10
179	Frank Rodriguez	.10
180	Eric Davis	.10
181	Andruw Jones (TSC 2000)	4.00
182	Todd Walker (TSC 2000)	1.50
183	Wes Helms (TSC 2000)	1.00
184	*Nelson Figueroa* (TSC 2000)	.75
185	Vladimir Guerrero (TSC 2000)	4.00
186	Billy McMillon (TSC 2000)	.40
187	Todd Helton (TSC 2000)	2.00
188	Nomar Garciaparra (TSC 2000)	4.00
189	Katsuhiro Maeda (TSC 2000)	1.00
190	Russell Branyan (TSC 2000)	.75
191	Glendon Rusch (TSC 2000)	.25
192	Bartolo Colon (TSC 2000)	.25
193	Scott Rolen (TSC 2000)	3.00
194	Angel Echevarria (TSC 2000)	.10
195	Bob Abreu (TSC 2000)	.25
196	Greg Maddux	2.00
197	Joe Carter	.20
198	Alex Ochoa	.20
199	Ellis Burks	.20
200	Ivan Rodriguez	.60
201	Marquis Grissom	.10
202	Trevor Hoffman	.10
203	Matt Williams	.30
204	Carlos Delgado	.15
205	Ramon Martinez	.10
206	Chuck Knoblauch	.20
207	Juan Guzman	.10
208	Derek Bell	.10
209	Roger Clemens	1.00
210	Vladimir Guerrero	1.00
211	Cecil Fielder	.20
212	Hideo Nomo	.60
213	Frank Thomas	2.50
214	Greg Vaughn	.10
215	Javy Lopez	.20
216	Raul Mondesi	.25
217	Wade Boggs	.20
218	Carlos Baerga	.10
219	Tony Gwynn	1.25
220	Tino Martinez	.25
221	Vinny Castilla	.20
222	Lance Johnson	.10
223	David Justice	.25
224	Rondell White	.20
225	Dean Palmer	.10
226	Jim Edmonds	.10
227	Albert Belle	.75
228	Alex Fernandez	.20
229	Ryne Sandberg	.75
230	Jose Mesa	.10
231	David Cone	.20
232	Troy Percival	.10
233	Edgar Martinez	.10
234	Jose Canseco	.25
235	Kevin Brown	.10
236	Ray Lankford	.10
237	Karim Garcia	.20
238	J.T. Snow	.10
239	Dennis Eckersley	.10
240	Roberto Alomar	.60
241	John Valentin	.10
242	Ron Gant	.20
243	Geronimo Berroa	.10
244	Manny Ramirez	.75
245	Travis Fryman	.10
246	Denny Neagle	.10
247	Randy Johnson	.60
248	Darin Erstad	1.25
249	Mark Wohlers	.10
250	Ken Hill	.10
251	Larry Walker	.35
252	Craig Biggio	.10
253	Brady Anderson	.10
254	John Wetteland	.10
255	Andruw Jones	2.50
256	Turk Wendell	.10
257	Jason Isringhausen	.10
258	Jaime Navarro	.10
259	Sean Berry	.10
260	Albie Lopez	.10
261	Jay Bell	.10

262	Bobby Witt	.10
263	Tony Clark	.50
264	Tim Wakefield	.10
265	Brad Radke	.10
266	Tim Belcher	.10
267	Mark Lewis	.10
268	Roger Cedeno	.10
269	Tim Naehring	.10
270	Kevin Tapani	.10
271	Joe Randa	.10
272	Randy Myers	.10
273	Dave Burba	.10
274	Mike Sweeney	.10
275	Danny Graves	.10
276	Chad Mottola	.10
277	Ruben Sierra	.10
278	Norm Charlton	.10
279	Scott Servais	.10
280	Jacob Cruz	.10
281	Mike Macfarlane	.10
282	Rich Becker	.10
283	Shannon Stewart	.10
284	Gerald Williams	.10
285	Jody Reed	.10
286	Jeff D'Amico	.10
287	Walt Weiss	.10
288	Jim Leyritz	.10
289	Francisco Cordova	.15
290	F.P. Santangelo	.10
291	Scott Erickson	.10
292	Hal Morris	.10
293	Ray Durham	.10
294	Andy Ashby	.10
295	Darryl Kile	.10
296	Jose Paniagua	.10
297	Mickey Tettleton	.10
298	Joe Girardi	.10
299	Rocky Coppinger	.10
300	Bob Abreu	.20
301	John Olerud	.10
302	Paul Shuey	.10
303	Jeff Brantley	.10
304	Bob Wells	.10
305	Kevin Seitzer	.10
306	Shawon Dunston	.10
307	Jose Herrera	.10
308	Butch Huskey	.10
309	Jose Offerman	.10
310	Rick Aguilera	.10
311	Greg Gagne	.10
312	John Burkett	.10
313	Mark Thompson	.10
314	Alvaro Espinoza	.10
315	Todd Stottlemyre	.10
316	Al Martin	.10
317	James Baldwin	.10
318	Cal Eldred	.10
319	Sid Fernandez	.10
320	Mickey Morandini	.10
321	Robb Nen	.10
322	Mark Lemke	.10
323	Pete Schourek	.10
324	Marcus Jensen	.10
325	Rich Aurilia	.10
326	Jeff King	.10
327	Scott Stahoviak	.10
328	Ricky Otero	.10
329	Antonio Osuna	.10
330	Chris Hoiles	.10
331	Luis Gonzalez	.10
332	Wil Cordero	.10
333	Johnny Damon	.10
334	Mark Langston	.10
335	Orlando Miller	.10
336	Jason Giambi	.10
337	Damian Jackson	.10
338	David Wells	.10
339	Bip Roberts	.10
340	Matt Ruebel	.10
341	Tom Candiotti	.10
342	Wally Joyner	.10
343	Jimmy Key	.10
344	Tony Batista	.10
345	Paul Sorrento	.10
346	Ron Karkovice	.10
347	Wilson Alvarez	.10
348	John Flaherty	.10
349	Rey Sanchez	.10
350	John Vander Wal	.10
351	Jermaine Dye	.15
352	Mike Hampton	.10
353	Greg Colbrunn	.10
354	Heathcliff Slocumb	.10
355	Ricky Bottalico	.10
356	Marty Janzen	.10
357	Orel Hershiser	.10

358	Rex Hudler	.10
359	Amaury Telemaco	.10
360	Darrin Fletcher	.10
361	Robert Person	.10
362	Russ Davis	.10
363	Allen Watson	.10
364	Mike Lieberthal	.10
365	Dave Stevens	.10
366	Jay Powell	.10
367	Tony Fossas	.10
368	Bob Wolcott	.10
369	Mark Loretta	.10
370	Shawn Estes	.10
371	Sandy Martinez	.10
372	Wendell Magee Jr.	.10
373	John Franco	.10
374	Tom Pagnozzi	.10
375	Willie Adams	.10
376	Chipper Jones (Stadium Sluggers)	4.00
377	Mo Vaughn (Stadium Sluggers)	2.00
378	Frank Thomas (Stadium Sluggers)	3.00
379	Albert Belle (Stadium Sluggers)	1.50
380	Andres Galarraga (Stadium Sluggers)	.25
381	Gary Sheffield (Stadium Sluggers)	.25
382	Jeff Bagwell (Stadium Sluggers)	2.50
383	Mike Piazza (Stadium Sluggers)	4.00
384	Mark McGwire (Stadium Sluggers)	8.00
385	Ken Griffey Jr. (Stadium Sluggers)	6.00
386	Barry Bonds (Stadium Sluggers)	1.50
387	Juan Gonzalez (Stadium Sluggers)	3.00
388	Brady Anderson (Stadium Sluggers)	.10
389	Ken Caminiti (Stadium Sluggers)	.25
390	Jay Buhner (Stadium Sluggers)	.15

1997 Stadium Club Co-Signers

Each Series of Stadium Club included five different Co-Signers, with an insertion ratio of one per 168 hobby packs. These double-sided cards featured authentic autographs from each star, one per side.

		MT
Complete Set (10):		650.00
Complete Series 1 Set (5):		325.00
Complete Series 2 Set (5):		350.00
Common Autograph:		50.00
CO1	Andy Pettitte, Derek Jeter	125.00
CO2	Paul Wilson, Todd Hundley	50.00
CO3	Jermaine Dye, Mark Wohlers	50.00
CO4	Scott Rolen, Gregg Jefferies	100.00
CO5	Todd Hollandsworth, Jason Kendall	50.00
CO6	Alan Benes, Robin Ventura	50.00
CO7	Eric Karros, Raul Mondesi	50.00
CO8	Rey Ordonez, Nomar Garciaparra	125.00
CO9	Rondell White, Marty Cordova	50.00
CO10	Tony Gwynn, Karim Garcia	125.00

1997 Stadium Club Firebrand

This 12-card insert was found only in packs sold at retail chains. Cards were inserted 1:36 packs. The hortizonal format cards are printed on thin wood stock, die-cut at top. Fronts are trimmed in gold foil.

		MT
Complete Set (12):		125.00
Common Player:		4.00
F1	Jeff Bagwell	12.00
F2	Albert Belle	8.00
F3	Barry Bonds	8.00
F4	Andres Galarraga	4.00
F5	Ken Griffey Jr.	30.00
F6	Brady Anderson	4.00
F7	Mark McGwire	35.00
F8	Chipper Jones	20.00
F9	Frank Thomas	25.00
F10	Mike Piazza	20.00
F11	Mo Vaughn	8.00
F12	Juan Gonzalez	15.00

1997 Stadium Club Firebrand Redemption

Because of production problems with its "Laser-Etched Wood" technology, Stadium Club was unable to package the Firebrand insert cards with the rest of the issue. Instead, a redemption card was substituted. The redemption card pictures the Firebrand card on its horizontal front; the back has details for exchanging the redemption card for the actual wood-printed, die-cut version. The exchange offer ended Sept. 30, 1997.

		MT
Complete Set (12):		85.00
Common Player:		3.00
F1	Jeff Bagwell	8.00
F2	Albert Belle	5.00
F3	Barry Bonds	5.00

		MT
F4	Andres Galarraga	3.00
F5	Ken Griffey Jr.	20.00
F6	Brady Anderson	3.00
F7	Mark McGwire	15.00
F8	Chipper Jones	13.50
F9	Frank Thomas	20.00
F10	Mike Piazza	13.50
F11	Mo Vaughn	5.00
F12	Juan Gonzalez	10.00

1997 Stadium Club Instavision

Instavision features holographic cards with exciting moments from the 1996 playoffs and World Series. Inserted one per 24 hobby packs and one per 36 retail packs, these cards are printed on a horizontal, plastic card. Cards carry an "I" prefix, with the first 10 found in Series I and the final 12 in Series II.

		MT
Complete Set (22):		100.00
Complete Series I Set (10):		40.00
Complete Series II Set (12):		60.00
Common Player:		3.00
I1	Eddie Murray	4.00
I2	Paul Molitor	6.00
I3	Todd Hundley	4.00
I4	Roger Clemens	8.00
I5	Barry Bonds	6.00
I6	Mark McGwire	25.00
I7	Brady Anderson	3.00
I8	Barry Larkin	5.00
I9	Ken Caminiti	5.00
I10	Hideo Nomo	8.00
I11	Bernie Williams	6.00
I12	Juan Gonzalez	12.00
I13	Andy Pettitte	8.00
I14	Albert Belle	8.00
I15	John Smoltz	4.00
I16	Brian Jordan	3.00
I17	Derek Jeter	15.00
I18	Ken Caminiti	5.00
I19	John Wetteland	3.00
I20	Brady Anderson	3.00
I21	Andruw Jones	10.00
I22	Jim Leyritz	3.00

1997 Stadium Club Millenium

Millennium was a 40-card insert that was released with 20 cards in Series I and Series II. The set featured 40 top prospects and rookies on a silver foil, holographic front, with a Future Forecast section on the back. Cards carried an "M" prefix and were numbered consecutively M1-M40. Millennium inserts were found every 24 hobby packs and every 36 retail packs.

		MT
Complete Set (40):		190.00
Complete Series I Set (20):		90.00
Complete Series II Set (20):		100.00
Common Player:		3.00
M1	Derek Jeter	25.00
M2	Mark Grudzielanek	3.00
M3	Jacob Cruz	3.00
M4	Ray Durham	3.00
M5	Tony Clark	8.00
M6	Chipper Jones	25.00
M7	Luis Castillo	3.00
M8	Carlos Delgado	4.00
M9	Brant Brown	3.00
M10	Jason Kendall	3.00
M11	Alan Benes	4.00
M12	Rey Ordonez	4.00
M13	Justin Thompson	4.00
M14	Jermaine Allensworth	3.00
M15	Brian Hunter	3.00
M16	Marty Cordova	4.00
M17	Edgar Renteria	4.00
M18	Karim Garcia	5.00
M19	Todd Greene	3.00
M20	Paul Wilson	4.00
M21	Andruw Jones	20.00
M22	Todd Walker	8.00
M23	Alex Ochoa	4.00
M24	Bartolo Colon	4.00
M25	Wendell Magee Jr.	4.00
M26	Jose Rosado	4.00
M27	Katsuhiro Maeda	3.00
M28	Bob Abreu	5.00
M29	Brooks Kieschnick	3.00
M30	Derrick Gibson	3.00
M31	Mike Sweeney	3.00
M32	Jeff D'Amico	4.00
M33	Chad Mottola	3.00
M34	Chris Snopek	3.00
M35	Jaime Bluma	3.00
M36	Vladimir Guerrero	12.00
M37	Nomar Garciaparra	20.00
M38	Scott Rolen	15.00
M39	Dmitri Young	3.00
M40	Neifi Perez	3.00

1997 Stadium Club Patent Leather

Patent Leather featured 13 of the top gloves in baseball on a leather, die-cut card. The cards carry a "PL" prefix and are inerted one per 36 retail packs.

		MT
Complete Set (13):		100.00
Common Player:		5.00
PL1	Ivan Rodriguez	8.00
PL2	Ken Caminiti	6.00
PL3	Barry Bonds	10.00
PL4	Ken Griffey Jr.	35.00
PL5	Greg Maddux	20.00
PL6	Craig Biggio	5.00
PL7	Andres Galarraga	5.00
PL8	Kenny Lofton	10.00
PL9	Barry Larkin	5.00
PL10	Mark Grace	5.00
PL11	Rey Ordonez	5.00
PL12	Roberto Alomar	8.00
PL13	Derek Jeter	20.00

1997 Stadium Club Pure Gold

Pure Gold featured 20 of the top players in baseball on gold, embossed foil cards. Cards carry a "PG" prefix and were inserted every 72 hobby packs and every 108 retail packs. The first 10 cards were in Series I packs, while the final 10 cards are exclusive to Series II.

		MT
Complete Set (20):		450.00
Complete Series I Set (10):		200.00
Complete Series II Set (10):		250.00
Common Player:		
PG1	Brady Anderson	8.00
PG2	Albert Belle	15.00
PG3	Dante Bichette	8.00
PG4	Barry Bonds	15.00
PG5	Jay Buhner	8.00
PG6	Tony Gwynn	30.00
PG7	Chipper Jones	40.00
PG8	Mark McGwire	70.00
PG9	Gary Sheffield	12.00
PG10	Frank Thomas	40.00
PG11	Juan Gonzalez	30.00
PG12	Ken Caminiti	10.00
PG13	Kenny Lofton	15.00
PG14	Jeff Bagwell	30.00
PG15	Ken Griffey Jr.	60.00
PG16	Cal Ripken Jr.	50.00
PG17	Mo Vaughn	15.00
PG18	Mike Piazza	40.00
PG19	Derek Jeter	40.00
PG20	Andres Galarraga	8.00

1997 Stadium Club TSC Matrix

TSC Matrix consists of 120 cards from Series I and II reprinted with Power Matrix technology. In each Series, 60 of the 190 cards were selected for inclusion in TSC Matrix and inserted every 12 hobby packs and every 18 retail packs. Each insert carries the TSC Matrix logo in a top corner of the card.

		MT
Complete Set (120):		400.00
Complete Series I Set (60):		200.00
Complete Series II Set (60):		200.00
Common Player:		1.00
Unlisted Stars: 10x		
1	Chipper Jones	25.00
2	Gary Sheffield	5.00
3	Kenny Lofton	10.00
4	Brian Jordan	1.00
5	Mark McGwire	40.00
6	Charles Nagy	1.00
7	Tim Salmon	2.00
8	Cal Ripken Jr.	30.00
9	Jeff Conine	1.00
10	Paul Molitor	4.00
11	Mariano Rivera	2.00
12	Pedro Martinez	1.00
13	Jeff Bagwell	15.00
14	Bobby Bonilla	1.00
15	Barry Bonds	8.00
16	Ryan Klesko	5.00
17	Barry Larkin	2.00
18	Jim Thome	4.00
19	Jay Buhner	2.00
20	Juan Gonzalez	15.00
21	Mike Mussina	4.00
22	Kevin Appier	1.00
23	Eric Karros	1.00
24	Steve Finley	1.00
25	Ed Sprague	1.00
26	Bernard Gilkey	1.00
27	Tony Phillips	1.00
28	Henry Rodriguez	1.00
29	John Smoltz	2.00
30	Dante Bichette	2.00
31	Mike Piazza	25.00
32	Paul O'Neill	1.50
33	Billy Wagner	1.50
34	Reggie Sanders	1.00
35	John Jaha	1.00
36	Eddie Murray	4.00
37	Eric Young	1.00
38	Roberto Hernandez	1.00
39	Pat Hentgen	1.00
40	Sammy Sosa	20.00
41	Todd Hundley	1.00
42	Mo Vaughn	10.00
43	Robin Ventura	1.00
44	Mark Grudzielanek	1.00
45	Shane Reynolds	1.00
46	Andy Pettitte	10.00
47	Fred McGriff	2.50
48	Rey Ordonez	2.00
49	Will Clark	2.50
50	Ken Griffey Jr.	40.00
51	Todd Worrell	1.00
52	Rusty Greer	1.00
53	Mark Grace	2.00
54	Tom Glavine	1.50
55	Derek Jeter	20.00
56	Rafael Palmeiro	1.50
57	Bernie Williams	8.00
58	Marty Cordova	1.00
59	Andres Galarraga	2.00
60	Ken Caminiti	3.00

196	Greg Maddux	25.00
197	Joe Carter	2.00
198	Alex Ochoa	1.00
199	Ellis Burks	1.00
200	Ivan Rodriguez	8.00
201	Marquis Grissom	1.00
202	Trevor Hoffman	1.00
203	Matt Williams	4.00
204	Carlos Delgado	1.00
205	Ramon Martinez	1.00
206	Chuck Knoblauch	2.00
207	Juan Guzman	1.00
208	Derek Bell	1.00
209	Roger Clemens	8.00
210	Vladimir Guerrero	12.00
211	Cecil Fielder	2.00
212	Hideo Nomo	8.00
213	Frank Thomas	35.00
214	Greg Vaughn	1.00
215	Javy Lopez	2.00
216	Raul Mondesi	2.00
217	Wade Boggs	2.00
218	Carlos Baerga	1.00
219	Tony Gwynn	20.00
220	Tino Martinez	2.00
221	Vinny Castilla	1.00
222	Lance Johnson	1.00
223	David Justice	2.00
224	Rondell White	1.00
225	Dean Palmer	1.00
226	Jim Edmonds	1.00
227	Albert Belle	10.00
228	Alex Fernandez	2.00
229	Ryne Sandberg	12.00
230	Jose Mesa	1.00
231	David Cone	2.00
232	Troy Percival	1.00
233	Edgar Martinez	1.00
234	Jose Canseco	3.00
235	Kevin Brown	1.00
236	Ray Lankford	1.00
237	Karim Garcia	4.00
238	J.T. Snow	1.00
239	Dennis Eckersley	1.00
240	Roberto Alomar	8.00
241	John Valentin	1.00
242	Ron Gant	2.00
243	Geronimo Berroa	1.00
244	Manny Ramirez	10.00
245	Travis Fryman	1.00
246	Denny Neagle	1.00
247	Randy Johnson	6.00
248	Darin Erstad	15.00
249	Mark Wohlers	1.00
250	Ken Hill	1.00
251	Larry Walker	2.00
252	Craig Biggio	1.00
253	Brady Anderson	1.50
254	John Wetteland	1.00
255	Andruw Jones	20.00

1998 Stadium Club

Stadium Club was issued in two separate series for 1998, with 200 odd-numbered cards in Series I and 200 even- numbered cards in Series II. Retail packs contained six cards and an SRP of $2, hobby packs contained nine cards and an SRP of $3 and HTA packs contained 15 cards and an SRP of $5. Three subets were included in the set, with Future Stars (361-379) and Draft Picks (381-399) both being odd-numbered and Traded (356-400) being even- numbered. Inserts in Series I include: First Day Issue parallels (retail), One of a Kind parallels (hobby), Printing Plates parallels (HTA), Bowman Previews, Co-Signers (hobby), In the Wings, Never Comprimise, and Triumvirates (retail). Inserts in Series II include: First Day Issue parallels (retail), One of a Kind parallels (hobby), Printing Plates parallels (HTA), Bowman Prospect Previews, Co-Signers (hobby), Playing with Passion, Royal Court and Triumvirates (retail).

		MT
Complete Set (400):		75.00
Complete Series I (200):		40.00
Complete Series II (200):		35.00
Common Player:		.10
Cal Ripken Screen Play Sound Chip: 20.00		
Wax Box:		65.00
1	Chipper Jones	2.00
2	Frank Thomas	2.00
3	Vladimir Guerrero	1.00
4	Ellis Burks	.10
5	John Franco	.10
6	Paul Molitor	.50
7	Rusty Greer	.10
8	Todd Hundley	.10
9	Brett Tomko	.10
10	Eric Karros	.20
11	Mike Cameron	.10
12	Jim Edmonds	.10
13	Bernie Williams	.50
14	Denny Neagle	.20
15	Jason Dickson	.10
16	Sammy Sosa	2.00
17	Brian Jordan	.10
18	Jose Vidro	.10
19	Scott Spiezio	.10
20	Jay Buhner	.25
21	Jim Thome	.40
22	Sandy Alomar	.20
23	Devon White	.10
24	Roberto Alomar	.60
25	John Flaherty	.10
26	John Wetteland	.10
27	Willie Greene	.10
28	Gregg Jefferies	.10
29	Johnny Damon	.10
30	Barry Larkin	.25
31	Chuck Knoblauch	.25
32	Mo Vaughn	.75
33	Tony Clark	.40
34	Marty Cordova	.10
35	Vinny Castilla	.10
36	Jeff King	.10
37	Reggie Jefferson	.10
38	Mariano Rivera	.20
39	Jermaine Allensworth	.10
40	Livan Hernandez	.10
41	Heathcliff Slocumb	.10
42	Jacob Cruz	.10
43	Barry Bonds	.75
44	Dave Magadan	.10
45	Chan Ho Park	.10
46	Jeremi Gonzalez	.10
47	Jeff Cirillo	.10
48	Delino DeShields	.10
49	Craig Biggio	.20
50	Benito Santiago	.10
51	Mark Clark	.10
52	Fernando Vina	.10
53	F.P. Santangelo	.10
54	*Pep Harris*	.25
55	Edgar Renteria	.10
56	Jeff Bagwell	1.25
57	Jimmy Key	.10
58	Bartolo Colon	.10
59	Curt Schilling	.20

#	Player	Price
60	Steve Finley	.10
61	Andy Ashby	.10
62	John Burkett	.10
63	Orel Hershiser	.10
64	Pokey Reese	.10
65	Scott Servais	.10
66	Todd Jones	.10
67	Javy Lopez	.20
68	Robin Ventura	.20
69	Miguel Tejada	.50
70	Raul Casanova	.10
71	Reggie Sanders	.10
72	Edgardo Alfonzo	.10
73	Dean Palmer	.10
74	Todd Stottlemyre	.10
75	David Wells	.10
76	Troy Percival	.10
77	Albert Belle	.75
78	Pat Hentgen	.20
79	Brian Hunter	.10
80	Richard Hidalgo	.10
81	Darren Oliver	.10
82	Mark Wohlers	.10
83	Cal Ripken Jr.	2.50
84	Hideo Nomo	.60
85	Derrek Lee	.20
86	Stan Javier	.10
87	Rey Ordonez	.10
88	Randy Johnson	.60
89	Jeff Kent	.10
90	Brian McRae	.10
91	Manny Ramirez	.60
92	Trevor Hoffman	.10
93	Doug Glanville	.10
94	Todd Walker	.20
95	Andy Benes	.10
96	Jason Schmidt	.10
97	Mike Matheny	.10
98	Tim Naehring	.10
99	Jeff Blauser	.10
100	Jose Rosado	.10
101	Roger Clemens	1.00
102	Pedro Astacio	.10
103	Mark Bellhorn	.10
104	Paul O'Neill	.20
105	Darin Erstad	.75
106	Mike Lieberthal	.10
107	Wilson Alvarez	.10
108	Mike Mussina	.60
109	George Williams	.10
110	Cliff Floyd	.10
111	Shawn Estes	.10
112	Mark Grudzielanek	.10
113	Tony Gwynn	1.50
114	Alan Benes	.20
115	Terry Steinbach	.10
116	Greg Maddux	2.00
117	Andy Pettitte	.50
118	Dave Nilsson	.10
119	Deivi Cruz	.10
120	Carlos Delgado	.10
121	Scott Hatteberg	.10
122	John Olerud	.20
123	Moises Alou	.20
124	Garret Anderson	.10
125	Royce Clayton	.10
126	Dante Powell	.10
127	Tom Glavine	.20
128	Gary DiSarcina	.10
129	Terry Adams	.10
130	Raul Mondesi	.30
131	Dan Wilson	.10
132	Al Martin	.10
133	Mickey Morandini	.10
134	Rafael Palmeiro	.25
135	Juan Encarnacion	.25
136	Jim Pittsley	.10
137	*Magglio Ordonez*	.75
138	Will Clark	.30
139	Todd Helton	1.00
140	Kelvim Escobar	.10
141	Esteban Loaiza	.10
142	John Jaha	.10
143	Jeff Fassero	.10
144	Harold Baines	.10
145	Butch Huskey	.10
146	Pat Meares	.10
147	Brian Giles	.10
148	Ramiro Mendoza	.10
149	John Smoltz	.20
150	Felix Martinez	.10
151	Jose Valentin	.10
152	Brad Rigby	.10
153	Ed Sprague	.10
154	Mike Hampton	.10
155	Mike Lansing	.10
156	Ray Lankford	.10
157	Bobby Bonilla	.20
158	Bill Mueller	.10
159	Jeffrey Hammonds	.10
160	Charles Nagy	.10
161	Rich Loiselle	.10
162	Al Leiter	.10
163	Larry Walker	.25
164	Chris Hoiles	.10
165	Jeff Montgomery	.10
166	Francisco Cordova	.10
167	James Baldwin	.10
168	Mark McLemore	.10
169	Kevin Appier	.10
170	Jamey Wright	.10
171	Nomar Garciaparra	2.00
172	Matt Franco	.10
173	Armando Benitez	.10
174	Jeromy Burnitz	.10
175	Ismael Valdes	.10
176	Lance Johnson	.10
177	Paul Sorrento	.10
178	Rondell White	.20
179	Kevin Elster	.10
180	Jason Giambi	.10
181	Carlos Baerga	.10
182	Russ Davis	.10
183	Ryan McGuire	.10
184	Eric Young	.10
185	Ron Gant	.10
186	Manny Alexander	.10
187	Scott Karl	.10
188	Brady Anderson	.10
189	Randall Simon	.10
190	Tim Belcher	.10
191	Jaret Wright	1.00
192	Dante Bichette	.25
193	John Valentin	.10
194	Darren Bragg	.10
195	Mike Sweeney	.10
196	Craig Counsell	.10
197	Jaime Navarro	.10
198	Todd Dunn	.10
199	Ken Griffey Jr.	3.00
200	Juan Gonzalez	1.50
201	Billy Wagner	.10
202	Jeff D'Amico	.10
203	Mark McGwire	4.00
204	Jeff D'Amico	.10
205	Rico Brogna	.10
206	Todd Hollandsworth	.10
207	Chad Curtis	.10
208	Tom Goodwin	.10
209	Neifi Perez	.10
210	Derek Bell	.10
211	Quilvio Veras	.10
212	Greg Vaughn	.10
213	Roberto Hernandez	.10
214	Arthur Rhodes	.10
215	Cal Eldred	.10
216	Bill Taylor	.10
217	Todd Greene	.10
218	Mario Valdez	.10
219	Ricky Bottalico	.10
220	Frank Rodriguez	.10
221	Rich Becker	.10
222	Roberto Duran	.10
223	Ivan Rodriguez	.75
224	Mike Jackson	.10
225	Deion Sanders	.25
226	Tony Womack	.10
227	Mark Kotsay	.50
228	Steve Trachsel	.10
229	Ryan Klesko	.35
230	Ken Cloude	.25
231	Luis Gonzalez	.10
232	Gary Gaetti	.10
233	Michael Tucker	.10
234	Shawn Green	.10
235	Ariel Prieto	.10
236	Kirt Manwaring	.10
237	Omar Vizquel	.10
238	Matt Beech	.10
239	Justin Thompson	.20
240	Bret Boone	.10
241	Derek Jeter	2.00
242	Ken Caminiti	.25
243	Jay Bell	.10
244	Kevin Tapani	.10
245	Jason Kendall	.10
246	Jose Guillen	.20
247	Mike Bordick	.10
248	Dustin Hermanson	.10
249	Darrin Fletcher	.10
250	Dave Hollins	.10
251	Ramon Martinez	.20
252	Hideki Irabu	.50
253	Mark Grace	.25
254	Jason Isringhausen	.10
255	Jose Cruz Jr.	1.50
256	Brian Johnson	.10
257	Brad Ausmus	.10
258	Andruw Jones	.75
259	Doug Jones	.10
260	Jeff Shaw	.10
261	Chuck Finley	.10
262	Gary Sheffield	.30
263	David Segui	.10
264	John Smiley	.10
265	Tim Salmon	.25
266	J.T. Snow Jr.	.10
267	Alex Fernandez	.10
268	Matt Stairs	.10
269	B.J. Surhoff	.10
270	Keith Foulke	.10
271	Edgar Martinez	.10
272	Shannon Stewart	.10
273	Eduardo Perez	.10
274	Wally Joyner	.10
275	Kevin Young	.10
276	Eli Marrero	.10
277	Brad Radke	.10
278	Jamie Moyer	.10
279	Joe Girardi	.10
280	Troy O'Leary	.10
281	Aaron Sele	.10
282	Jose Offerman	.10
283	Scott Erickson	.10
284	Sean Berry	.10
285	Shigetosi Hasegawa	.10
286	Felix Heredia	.10
287	Willie McGee	.10
288	Alex Rodriguez	3.00
289	Ugueth Urbina	.10
290	Jon Lieber	.10
291	Fernando Tatis	.10
292	Chris Stynes	.10
293	Bernard Gilkey	.10
294	Joey Hamilton	.10
295	Matt Karchner	.10
296	Paul Wilson	.10
297	Mel Nieves	.10
298	*Kevin Millwood*	1.50
299	Quinton McCracken	.10
300	Jerry DiPoto	.10
301	Jermaine Dye	.10
302	Travis Lee	2.50
303	Ron Coomer	.10
304	Matt Williams	.25
305	Bobby Higginson	.10
306	Jorge Fabregas	.10
307	Hal Morris	.10
308	Jay Bell	.10
309	Joe Randa	.10
310	Andy Benes	.10
311	Sterling Hitchcock	.10
312	Jeff Suppan	.10
313	Shane Reynolds	.10
314	Willie Blair	.10
315	Scott Rolen	1.50
316	Wilson Alvarez	.10
317	David Justice	.25
318	Fred McGriff	.25
319	Bobby Jones	.10
320	Wade Boggs	.30
321	Tim Wakefield	.10
322	Tony Saunders	.10
323	David Cone	.20
324	Roberto Hernandez	.10
325	Jose Canseco	.25
326	Kevin Stocker	.10
327	Gerald Williams	.10
328	Quinton McCracken	.10
329	Mark Gardner	.10
330	Ben Grieve (Prime Rookie)	1.50
331	Kevin Brown	.20
332	*Mike Lowell* (Prime Rookie)	.40
333	Jed Hansen	
334	Abraham Nunez (Prime Rookie)	.25
335	John Thomson	.10
336	Derrek Lee (Prime Rookie)	.10
337	Mike Piazza	2.00
338	Brad Fullmer (Prime Rookie)	.10
339	Ray Durham	.10
340	Kerry Wood (Prime Rookie)	5.00
341	*Kevin Polcovich*	.10
342	Russ Johnson (Prime Rookie)	.10
343	Darryl Hamilton	.10
344	David Ortiz (Prime Rookie)	.40

345	Kevin Orie	.10
346	Sean Casey (Prime Rookie)	.50
347	Juan Guzman	.10
348	Ruben Rivera (Prime Rookie)	.10
349	Rick Aguilera	.10
350	Bobby Estalella (Prime Rookie)	.10
351	Bobby Witt	.10
352	Paul Konerko (Prime Rookie)	.50
353	Matt Morris	.10
354	Carl Pavano (Prime Rookie)	.20
355	Todd Zeile	.10
356	Kevin Brown (Transaction)	.10
357	Alex Gonzalez	.10
358	Chuck Knoblauch (Transaction)	.40
359	Joey Cora	.10
360	Mike Lansing (Transaction)	.10
361	Adrian Beltre (Future Stars)	3.00
362	Dennis Eckersley (Transaction)	.10
363	A.J. Hinch (Future Stars)	1.50
364	Kenny Lofton (Transaction)	.75
365	Alex Gonzalez (Future Stars)	.10
366	Henry Rodriguez (Transaction)	.10
367	*Mike Stoner* (Future Stars)	2.00
368	Darryl Kile (Transaction)	.10
369	Carl Pavano (Future Stars)	.50
370	Walt Weiss (Transaction)	.10
371	Kris Benson (Future Stars)	.75
372	Cecil Fielder (Transaction)	.10
373	Dermal Brown (Future Stars)	1.50
374	Rod Beck (Transaction)	.10
375	Eric Milton (Future Stars)	1.00
376	Travis Fryman (Transaction)	.10
377	Preston Wilson (Future Stars)	.10
378	Chili Davis (Transaction)	.10
379	Travis Lee (Future Stars)	5.00
380	Jim Leyritz (Transaction)	.10
381	Vernon Wells (Draft Picks)	1.50
382	Joe Carter (Transaction)	.10
383	J.J. Davis (Draft Picks)	1.00
384	Marquis Grissom (Transaction)	.10
385	*Mike Cuddyer* (Draft Picks)	1.50
386	Rickey Henderson (Transaction)	.10
387	*Chris Enochs* (Draft Picks)	1.00
388	Andres Galarraga (Transaction)	.40
389	Jason Dellaero (Draft Picks)	.20
390	Robb Nen (Transaction)	.10
391	Mark Mangum (Draft Picks)	.10
392	Jeff Blauser (Transaction)	.10
393	Adam Kennedy (Draft Picks)	.20
394	Bob Abreu (Transaction)	.10
395	*Jack Cust* (Draft Picks)	1.00
396	Jose Vizcaino (Transaction)	.10
397	Jon Garland (Draft Picks)	.50
398	Pedro Martinez (Transaction)	.40
399	Aaron Akin (Draft Picks)	.10
400	Jeff Conine (Transaction)	.10

1998 Stadium Club Bowman Prospect Preview

Bowman Prospect Previews were inserted into Series II retail and hobby packs at a rate of one per 12 and HTA packs at one per four. The 10-card insert previews the upcoming 1998 Bowman set and includes top prospects that are expected to make an impact in 1998.

A player's name in *italic* type indicates a rookie card.

		MT
Complete Set (10):		20.00
Common Player:		1.00
Inserted 1:12		
BP1	Ben Grieve	8.00
BP2	Brad Fullmer	2.50
BP3	Ryan Anderson	6.00
BP4	Mark Kotsay	2.00
BP5	Bobby Estalella	1.00
BP6	Juan Encarnacion	2.00
BP7	Todd Helton	3.00
BP8	Mike Lowell	1.00
BP9	A.J. Hinch	2.00
BP10	Richard Hidalgo	1.00

1998 Stadium Club 98 Bowman Preview

This Series I insert gave collectors a sneak peak at Bowman's 50th anniversary set, with 10 top veterans displayed on the 1998 Bowman design. The cards were inserted one per 12 packs and numbered with a "BP" prefix.

		MT
Complete Set (10):		50.00
Common Player:		1.00
Inserted 1:12		
BP1	Nomar Garciaparra	8.00
BP2	Scott Rolen	6.00
BP3	Ken Griffey Jr.	12.00
BP4	Frank Thomas	10.00
BP5	Larry Walker	1.50
BP6	Mike Piazza	8.00
BP7	Chipper Jones	8.00
BP8	Tino Martinez	1.00
BP9	Mark McGwire	15.00
BP10	Barry Bonds	3.00

1998 Stadium Club Co-Signers

Co-Signers were inserted into both Series I and II hobby and HTA packs. The complete set is 36 cards and contains two top players one side along with both autographs. The were available in three levels of scarcity - Groups A, B and C. Seeding is as follows: Series I Group A 1:4,372 hobby and 1:2,623 HTA, Series I Group B 1:1,457 hobby and HTA 1:874, Series I Group C 1:121 hobby and 1:73 HTA, Series II Group A 1:4,702 hobby and 1:2,821 HTA, Series II Group B 1:1,567 hobby and 1:940 HTA, Series II Group C 1:1:131 hobby and 1:78 HTA.

		MT
Common Player:		50.00
Group A 1:4,372		
Group B 1:1,457		
Group C 1:121		
CS1	Nomar Garciaparra, Scott Rolen	50.00
CS2	Nomar Garciaparra, Derek Jeter	250.00
CS3	Nomar Garciaparra, Eric Karros	120.00
CS4	Scott Rolen, Derek Jeter	150.00
CS5	Scott Rolen, Eric Karros	150.00
CS6	Derek Jeter, Eric Karros	50.00
CS7	Travis Lee, Jose Cruz Jr.	250.00
CS8	Travis Lee, Mark Kotsay	125.00
CS9	Travis Lee, Paul Konerko	50.00
CS10	Jose Cruz Jr., Mark Kotsay	50.00
CS11	Jose Cruz Jr., Paul Konerko	150.00
CS12	Mark Kotsay, Paul Konerko	125.00
CS13	Tony Gwynn, Larry Walker	50.00
CS14	Tony Gwynn, Mark Grudzielanek	125.00
CS15	Tony Gwynn, Andres Galarraga	200.00
CS16	Larry Walker, Mark Grudzielanek	100.00
CS17	Larry Walker, Andres Galarraga	50.00
CS18	Mark Grudzielanek, Andres Galarraga	50.00
CS19	Sandy Alomar, Roberto Alomar	50.00
CS20	Sandy Alomar, Andy Pettitte	50.00
CS21	Sandy Alomar, Tino Martinez	80.00
CS22	Roberto Alomar, Andy Pettitte	125.00
CS23	Roberto Alomar, Tino Martinez	75.00
CS24	Andy Pettitte, Tino Martinez	50.00
CS25	Tony Clark, Todd Hundley	50.00
CS26	Tony Clark, Tim Salmon	100.00
CS27	Tony Clark, Robin Ventura	50.00
CS28	Todd Hundley, Tim Salmon	50.00
CS29	Todd Hundley, Robin Ventura	50.00
CS30	Tim Salmon, Robin Ventura	50.00
CS31	Roger Clemens, Randy Johnson	200.00
CS32	Roger Clemens, Jaret Wright	50.00
CS33	Roger Clemens, Matt Morris	100.00
CS34	Randy Johnson, Jaret Wright	100.00
CS35	Randy Johnson, Matt Morris	50.00
CS36	Jaret Wright, Matt Morris	125.00

1998 Stadium Club First Day Issue

This retail-only parallel set was individually numbered to 200 and inserted through both series. First Day Issue cards were inserted in one per 44 Series I packs and one per 47 Series II packs.

		MT
Common Player:		8.00
Semistars:		15.00
Production 200 sets		
1	Chipper Jones	75.00
2	Frank Thomas	90.00
3	Vladimir Guerrero	30.00
4	Ellis Burks	8.00
5	John Franco	8.00
6	Paul Molitor	25.00
7	Rusty Greer	15.00
8	Todd Hundley	15.00
9	Brett Tomko	8.00
10	Eric Karros	15.00
11	Mike Cameron	15.00
12	Jim Edmonds	8.00
13	Bernie Williams	25.00
14	Denny Neagle	15.00
15	Jason Dickson	8.00
16	Sammy Sosa	80.00
17	Brian Jordan	8.00
18	Jose Vidro	8.00
19	Scott Spiezio	8.00
20	Jay Buhner	20.00
21	Jim Thome	25.00
22	Sandy Alomar	15.00
23	Devon White	8.00
24	Roberto Alomar	30.00
25	John Flaherty	8.00
26	John Wetteland	8.00
27	Willie Greene	8.00
28	Gregg Jefferies	8.00
29	Johnny Damon	8.00
30	Barry Larkin	15.00
31	Chuck Knoblauch	20.00
32	Mo Vaughn	40.00
33	Tony Clark	25.00
34	Marty Cordova	8.00
35	Vinny Castilla	12.00
36	Jeff King	8.00
37	Reggie Jefferson	8.00
38	Mariano Rivera	15.00
39	Jermaine Allensworth	8.00
40	Livan Hernandez	15.00
41	Heathcliff Slocumb	8.00
42	Jacob Cruz	8.00
43	Barry Bonds	40.00
44	Dave Magadan	8.00
45	Chan Ho Park	20.00
46	Jeremi Gonzalez	8.00
47	Jeff Cirillo	8.00
48	Delino DeShields	8.00
49	Craig Biggio	15.00
50	Benito Santiago	8.00
51	Mark Clark	8.00
52	Fernando Vina	8.00
53	F.P. Santangelo	8.00
54	*Pep Harris*	8.00
55	Edgar Renteria	8.00
56	Jeff Bagwell	60.00
57	Jimmy Key	8.00
58	Bartolo Colon	8.00
59	Curt Schilling	15.00
60	Steve Finley	8.00
61	Andy Ashby	8.00
62	John Burkett	8.00
63	Orel Hershiser	8.00
64	Pokey Reese	8.00
65	Scott Servais	8.00
66	Todd Jones	8.00
67	Javy Lopez	15.00
68	Robin Ventura	15.00
69	Miguel Tejada	20.00
70	Raul Casanova	8.00
71	Reggie Sanders	8.00
72	Edgardo Alfonzo	8.00
73	Dean Palmer	8.00
74	Todd Stottlemyre	12.00
75	David Wells	8.00
76	Troy Percival	8.00
77	Albert Belle	40.00
78	Pat Hentgen	8.00
79	Brian Hunter	8.00
80	Richard Hidalgo	8.00
81	Darren Oliver	8.00
82	Mark Wohlers	8.00
83	Cal Ripken Jr.	100.00
84	Hideo Nomo	40.00
85	Derrek Lee	15.00
86	Stan Javier	8.00
87	Rey Ordonez	8.00
88	Randy Johnson	30.00
89	Jeff Kent	8.00
90	Brian McRae	8.00
91	Manny Ramirez	35.00
92	Trevor Hoffman	8.00
93	Doug Glanville	8.00
94	Todd Walker	15.00
95	Andy Benes	8.00
96	Jason Schmidt	8.00
97	Mike Matheny	8.00
98	Tim Naehring	8.00
99	Jeff Blauser	8.00
100	Jose Rosado	8.00
101	Roger Clemens	70.00
102	Pedro Astacio	8.00
103	Mark Bellhorn	8.00
104	Paul O'Neill	15.00
105	Darin Erstad	25.00
106	Mike Lieberthal	8.00
107	Wilson Alvarez	8.00
108	Mike Mussina	30.00
109	George Williams	8.00
110	Cliff Floyd	8.00
111	Shawn Estes	8.00
112	Mark Grudzielanek	8.00
113	Tony Gwynn	70.00
114	Alan Benes	15.00
115	Terry Steinbach	8.00
116	Greg Maddux	80.00
117	Andy Pettitte	25.00
118	Dave Nilsson	8.00
119	Deivi Cruz	8.00
120	Carlos Delgado	15.00
121	Scott Hatteberg	8.00
122	John Olerud	15.00
123	Moises Alou	15.00
124	Garret Anderson	8.00
125	Royce Clayton	8.00
126	Dante Powell	8.00
127	Tom Glavine	15.00
128	Gary DiSarcina	8.00
129	Terry Adams	8.00
130	Raul Mondesi	20.00
131	Dan Wilson	8.00
132	Al Martin	8.00
133	Mickey Morandini	8.00
134	Rafael Palmeiro	15.00
135	Juan Encarnacion	12.00
136	Jim Pittsley	8.00
137	Magglio Ordonez	20.00
138	Will Clark	20.00
139	Todd Helton	30.00
140	Kelvim Escobar	8.00
141	Esteban Loaiza	8.00
142	John Jaha	8.00
143	Jeff Fassero	8.00
144	Harold Baines	8.00
145	Butch Huskey	8.00
146	Pat Meares	8.00
147	Brian Giles	8.00
148	Ramiro Mendoza	8.00
149	John Smoltz	15.00
150	Felix Martinez	8.00
151	Jose Valentin	8.00
152	Brad Rigby	8.00
153	Ed Sprague	8.00
154	Mike Hampton	8.00
155	Mike Lansing	8.00
156	Ray Lankford	8.00
157	Bobby Bonilla	15.00
158	Bill Mueller	8.00
159	Jeffrey Hammonds	8.00
160	Charles Nagy	8.00
161	Rich Loiselle	8.00
162	Al Leiter	8.00
163	Larry Walker	20.00
164	Chris Hoiles	8.00
165	Jeff Montgomery	8.00
166	Francisco Cordova	8.00
167	James Baldwin	8.00
168	Mark McLemore	8.00
169	Kevin Appier	8.00
170	Jamey Wright	8.00
171	Nomar Garciaparra	80.00
172	Matt Franco	8.00
173	Armando Benitez	8.00
174	Jeromy Burnitz	8.00
175	Ismael Valdes	8.00
176	Lance Johnson	8.00
177	Paul Sorrento	8.00
178	Rondell White	15.00
179	Kevin Elster	8.00
180	Jason Giambi	8.00
181	Carlos Baerga	8.00
182	Russ Davis	8.00
183	Ryan McGuire	8.00
184	Eric Young	8.00
185	Ron Gant	15.00
186	Manny Alexander	8.00
187	Scott Karl	8.00
188	Brady Anderson	12.00
189	Randall Simon	15.00
190	Tim Belcher	8.00
191	Jaret Wright	40.00
192	Dante Bichette	15.00
193	John Valentin	8.00
194	Darren Bragg	8.00
195	Mike Sweeney	8.00
196	Craig Counsell	8.00
197	Jaime Navarro	8.00
198	Todd Dunn	8.00
199	Ken Griffey Jr.	150.00
200	Juan Gonzalez	70.00
201	Billy Wagner	8.00
202	Jeff D'Amico	8.00
203	Mark McGwire	160.00
204	Jeff D'Amico	8.00
205	Rico Brogna	8.00
206	Todd Hollandsworth	8.00
207	Chad Curtis	8.00
208	Tom Goodwin	8.00
209	Neifi Perez	8.00
210	Derek Bell	8.00
211	Quilvio Veras	8.00
212	Greg Vaughn	8.00
213	Roberto Hernandez	8.00
214	Arthur Rhodes	8.00
215	Cal Eldred	8.00
216	Bill Taylor	8.00
217	Todd Greene	8.00
218	Mario Valdez	8.00
219	Ricky Bottalico	8.00
220	Frank Rodriguez	8.00
221	Rich Becker	8.00
222	Roberto Duran	8.00
223	Ivan Rodriguez	40.00
224	Mike Jackson	8.00
225	Deion Sanders	15.00
226	Tony Womack	8.00
227	Mark Kotsay	15.00
228	Steve Trachsel	8.00
229	Ryan Klesko	20.00
230	Ken Cloude	12.00
231	Luis Gonzalez	8.00
232	Gary Gaetti	8.00
233	Michael Tucker	8.00
234	Shawn Green	8.00
235	Ariel Prieto	8.00
236	Kirt Manwaring	8.00
237	Omar Vizquel	8.00
238	Matt Beech	8.00
239	Justin Thompson	8.00
240	Bret Boone	8.00
241	Derek Jeter	75.00
242	Ken Caminiti	15.00
243	Jay Bell	8.00
244	Kevin Tapani	8.00
245	Jason Kendall	8.00
246	Jose Guillen	15.00
247	Mike Bordick	8.00
248	Dustin Hermanson	8.00
249	Darrin Fletcher	8.00
250	Dave Hollins	8.00
251	Ramon Martinez	15.00
252	Hideki Irabu	25.00
253	Mark Grace	20.00
254	Jason Isringhausen	8.00
255	Jose Cruz Jr.	60.00
256	Brian Johnson	8.00
257	Brad Ausmus	8.00
258	Andruw Jones	35.00
259	Doug Jones	8.00
260	Jeff Shaw	8.00
261	Chuck Finley	8.00
262	Gary Sheffield	20.00
263	David Segui	8.00
264	John Smiley	8.00
265	Tim Salmon	20.00
266	J.T. Snow Jr.	8.00
267	Alex Fernandez	8.00
268	Matt Stairs	8.00
269	B.J. Surhoff	8.00
270	Keith Foulke	8.00
271	Edgar Martinez	12.00
272	Shannon Stewart	8.00
273	Eduardo Perez	8.00
274	Wally Joyner	8.00
275	Kevin Young	8.00
276	Eli Marrero	8.00
277	Brad Radke	8.00
278	Jamie Moyer	8.00
279	Joe Girardi	8.00
280	Troy O'Leary	8.00
281	Aaron Sele	12.00
282	Jose Offerman	8.00
283	Scott Erickson	8.00
284	Sean Berry	8.00

285	Shigetosi Hasegawa	8.00
286	Felix Heredia	8.00
287	Willie McGee	8.00
288	Alex Rodriguez	100.00
289	Ugueth Urbina	8.00
290	Jon Lieber	8.00
291	Fernando Tatis	8.00
292	Chris Stynes	8.00
293	Bernard Gilkey	8.00
294	Joey Hamilton	8.00
295	Matt Karchner	8.00
296	Paul Wilson	8.00
297	Mel Nieves	8.00
298	Kevin Millwood	30.00
299	Quinton McCracken	8.00
300	Jerry DiPoto	8.00
301	Jermaine Dye	8.00
302	Travis Lee	60.00
303	Ron Coomer	8.00
304	Matt Williams	20.00
305	Bobby Higginson	8.00
306	Jorge Fabregas	8.00
307	Hal Morris	8.00
308	Jay Bell	8.00
309	Joe Randa	8.00
310	Andy Benes	8.00
311	Sterling Hitchcock	8.00
312	Jeff Suppan	8.00
313	Shane Reynolds	8.00
314	Willie Blair	8.00
315	Scott Rolen	50.00
316	Wilson Alvarez	8.00
317	David Justice	20.00
318	Fred McGriff	15.00
319	Bobby Jones	8.00
320	Wade Boggs	15.00
321	Tim Wakefield	8.00
322	Tony Saunders	8.00
323	David Cone	15.00
324	Roberto Hernandez	8.00
325	Jose Canseco	20.00
326	Kevin Stocker	8.00
327	Gerald Williams	8.00
328	Quinton McCracken	8.00
329	Mark Gardner	8.00
330	Ben Grieve (Prime Rookie)	65.00
331	Kevin Brown	8.00
332	Mike Lowell (Prime Rookie)	8.00
333	Jed Hansen	8.00
334	Abraham Nunez (Prime Rookie)	8.00
335	John Thomson	8.00
336	Derrek Lee (Prime Rookie)	15.00
337	Mike Piazza	90.00
338	Brad Fullmer (Prime Rookie)	20.00
339	Ray Durham	8.00
340	Kerry Wood (Prime Rookie)	100.00
341	*Kevin Polcovich*	8.00
342	Russ Johnson (Prime Rookie)	8.00
343	Darryl Hamilton	8.00
344	David Ortiz (Prime Rookie)	10.00
345	Kevin Orie	8.00
346	Sean Casey (Prime Rookie)	25.00
347	Juan Guzman	8.00
348	Ruben Rivera (Prime Rookie)	8.00
349	Rick Aguilera	8.00
350	Bobby Estalella (Prime Rookie)	8.00
351	Bobby Witt	8.00
352	Paul Konerko (Prime Rookie)	25.00
353	Matt Morris	8.00
354	Carl Pavano (Prime Rookie)	15.00
355	Todd Zeile	8.00
356	Kevin Brown (Transaction)	8.00
357	Alex Gonzalez	8.00
358	Chuck Knoblauch (Transaction)	20.00
359	Joey Cora	8.00
360	Mike Lansing (Transaction)	8.00
361	Adrian Beltre (Future Stars)	40.00
362	Dennis Eckersley (Transaction)	8.00
363	A.J. Hinch (Future Stars)	8.00
364	Kenny Lofton (Transaction)	20.00
365	Alex Gonzalez (Future Stars)	8.00
366	Henry Rodriguez (Transaction)	8.00
367	*Mike Stoner* (Future Stars)	35.00
368	Darryl Kile (Transaction)	8.00
369	Carl Pavano (Future Stars)	8.00
370	Walt Weiss (Transaction)	8.00

371	Kris Benson (Future Stars)	25.00
372	Cecil Fielder (Transaction)	12.00
373	Dermal Brown (Future Stars)	35.00
374	Rod Beck (Transaction)	8.00
375	Eric Milton (Future Stars)	25.00
376	Travis Fryman (Transaction)	8.00
377	Preston Wilson (Future Stars)	8.00
378	Chili Davis (Transaction)	8.00
379	Travis Lee (Future Stars)	60.00
380	Jim Leyritz (Transaction)	8.00
381	Vernon Wells (Draft Picks)	20.00
382	Joe Carter (Transaction)	8.00
383	J.J. Davis (Draft Picks)	15.00
384	Marquis Grissom (Transaction)	8.00
385	*Mike Cuddyer* (Draft Picks)	25.00
386	Rickey Henderson (Transaction)	8.00
387	*Chris Enochs* (Draft Picks)	15.00
388	Andres Galarraga (Transaction)	20.00
389	Jason Dellaero (Draft Picks)	8.00
390	Robb Nen (Transaction)	8.00
391	Mark Mangum (Draft Picks)	8.00
392	Jeff Blauser (Transaction)	8.00
393	Adam Kennedy (Draft Picks)	8.00
394	Bob Abreu (Transaction)	8.00
395	*Jack Cust* (Draft Picks)	15.00
396	Jose Vizcaino (Transaction)	8.00
397	Jon Garland (Draft Picks)	12.00
398	Pedro Martinez (Transaction)	25.00
399	Aaron Akin (Draft Picks)	8.00
400	Jeff Conine (Transaction)	8.00

1998 Stadium Club
In the Wings

ELI MARRERO

In the Wings was a Series I insert found every 36 packs. It included 15 future stars on uniluster technology.

		MT
Complete Set (15):		90.00
Common Player:		3.00
Inserted 1:36		
W1	Juan Encarnacion	5.00
W2	Brad Fullmer	6.00
W3	Ben Grieve	20.00
W4	Todd Helton	15.00
W5	Richard Hidalgo	3.00
W6	Russ Johnson	3.00
W7	Paul Konerko	15.00
W8	Mark Kotsay	8.00
W9	Derrek Lee	6.00
W10	Travis Lee	25.00
W11	Eli Marrero	3.00
W12	David Ortiz	3.00
W13	Randall Simon	5.00
W14	Shannon Stewart	3.00
W15	Fernando Tatis	5.00

1998 Stadium Club
Never Compromise

Never Compromise was a 20-card insert found in packs of Series I. Cards were inserted one per 12 packs and numbered with a "NC" prefix.

		MT
Complete Set (20):		120.00
Common Player:		1.00
Inserted 1:12		
NC1	Cal Ripken Jr.	15.00
NC2	Ivan Rodriguez	5.00
NC3	Ken Griffey Jr.	20.00
NC4	Frank Thomas	15.00
NC5	Tony Gwynn	10.00
NC6	Mike Piazza	12.00
NC7	Randy Johnson	3.00
NC8	Greg Maddux	12.00
NC9	Roger Clemens	8.00
NC10	Derek Jeter	12.00
NC11	Chipper Jones	12.00
NC12	Barry Bonds	5.00
NC13	Larry Walker	2.00
NC14	Jeff Bagwell	8.00
NC15	Barry Larkin	1.00
NC16	Ken Caminiti	1.00
NC17	Mark McGwire	25.00
NC18	Manny Ramirez	4.00
NC19	Tim Salmon	2.00
NC20	Paul Molitor	3.00

1998 Stadium Club
One of a Kind

This hobby-only parallel set included all 400 cards from Series I and II printed on a silver mirror-board stock. Cards were sequentially numbered to 150 and inserted one per 21 Series I packs and one per 24 Series II packs.

		MT
Common Player:		8.00
Semistars:		15.00
Production 150 sets		
1	Chipper Jones	90.00
2	Frank Thomas	90.00
3	Vladimir Guerrero	40.00
4	Ellis Burks	8.00
5	John Franco	8.00
6	Paul Molitor	30.00
7	Rusty Greer	15.00
8	Todd Hundley	15.00
9	Brett Tomko	8.00
10	Eric Karros	15.00
11	Mike Cameron	15.00
12	Jim Edmonds	8.00
13	Bernie Williams	30.00
14	Denny Neagle	15.00
15	Jason Dickson	8.00

#	Player	Price
16	Sammy Sosa	100.00
17	Brian Jordan	8.00
18	Jose Vidro	8.00
19	Scott Spiezio	8.00
20	Jay Buhner	20.00
21	Jim Thome	25.00
22	Sandy Alomar	15.00
23	Devon White	8.00
24	Roberto Alomar	30.00
25	John Flaherty	8.00
26	John Wetteland	8.00
27	Willie Greene	8.00
28	Gregg Jefferies	8.00
29	Johnny Damon	8.00
30	Barry Larkin	20.00
31	Chuck Knoblauch	20.00
32	Mo Vaughn	40.00
33	Tony Clark	25.00
34	Marty Cordova	8.00
35	Vinny Castilla	12.00
36	Jeff King	8.00
37	Reggie Jefferson	8.00
38	Mariano Rivera	15.00
39	Jermaine Allensworth	8.00
40	Livan Hernandez	15.00
41	Heathcliff Slocumb	8.00
42	Jacob Cruz	8.00
43	Barry Bonds	40.00
44	Dave Magadan	8.00
45	Chan Ho Park	20.00
46	Jeremi Gonzalez	8.00
47	Jeff Cirillo	8.00
48	Delino DeShields	8.00
49	Craig Biggio	15.00
50	Benito Santiago	8.00
51	Mark Clark	8.00
52	Fernando Vina	8.00
53	F.P. Santangelo	8.00
54	*Pep Harris*	8.00
55	Edgar Renteria	8.00
56	Jeff Bagwell	60.00
57	Jimmy Key	8.00
58	Bartolo Colon	8.00
59	Curt Schilling	15.00
60	Steve Finley	8.00
61	Andy Ashby	8.00
62	John Burkett	8.00
63	Orel Hershiser	8.00
64	Pokey Reese	8.00
65	Scott Servais	8.00
66	Todd Jones	8.00
67	Javy Lopez	15.00
68	Robin Ventura	15.00
69	Miguel Tejada	20.00
70	Raul Casanova	8.00
71	Reggie Sanders	8.00
72	Edgardo Alfonzo	8.00
73	Dean Palmer	8.00
74	Todd Stottlemyre	12.00
75	David Wells	8.00
76	Troy Percival	8.00
77	Albert Belle	40.00
78	Pat Hentgen	8.00
79	Brian Hunter	8.00
80	Richard Hidalgo	8.00
81	Darren Oliver	8.00
82	Mark Wohlers	8.00
83	Cal Ripken Jr.	125.00
84	Hideo Nomo	40.00
85	Derrek Lee	15.00
86	Stan Javier	8.00
87	Rey Ordonez	8.00
88	Randy Johnson	30.00
89	Jeff Kent	8.00
90	Brian McRae	8.00
91	Manny Ramirez	40.00
92	Trevor Hoffman	8.00
93	Doug Glanville	8.00
94	Todd Walker	15.00
95	Andy Benes	8.00
96	Jason Schmidt	8.00
97	Mike Matheny	8.00
98	Tim Naehring	8.00
99	Jeff Blauser	8.00
100	Jose Rosado	8.00
101	Roger Clemens	70.00
102	Pedro Astacio	8.00
103	Mark Bellhorn	8.00
104	Paul O'Neill	15.00
105	Darin Erstad	25.00
106	Mike Lieberthal	8.00
107	Wilson Alvarez	8.00
108	Mike Mussina	30.00
109	George Williams	8.00
110	Cliff Floyd	8.00
111	Shawn Estes	8.00
112	Mark Grudzielanek	8.00
113	Tony Gwynn	80.00
114	Alan Benes	15.00
115	Terry Steinbach	8.00
116	Greg Maddux	90.00
117	Andy Pettitte	30.00
118	Dave Nilsson	8.00
119	Deivi Cruz	8.00
120	Carlos Delgado	15.00
121	Scott Hatteberg	8.00
122	John Olerud	15.00
123	Moises Alou	15.00
124	Garret Anderson	8.00
125	Royce Clayton	8.00
126	Dante Powell	8.00
127	Tom Glavine	15.00
128	Gary DiSarcina	8.00
129	Terry Adams	8.00
130	Raul Mondesi	20.00
131	Dan Wilson	8.00
132	Al Martin	8.00
133	Mickey Morandini	8.00
134	Rafael Palmeiro	15.00
135	Juan Encarnacion	15.00
136	Jim Pittsley	8.00
137	Magglio Ordonez	20.00
138	Will Clark	20.00
139	Todd Helton	40.00
140	Kelvim Escobar	8.00
141	Esteban Loaiza	8.00
142	John Jaha	8.00
143	Jeff Fassero	8.00
144	Harold Baines	8.00
145	Butch Huskey	8.00
146	Pat Meares	8.00
147	Brian Giles	8.00
148	Ramiro Mendoza	8.00
149	John Smoltz	15.00
150	Felix Martinez	8.00
151	Jose Valentin	8.00
152	Brad Rigby	8.00
153	Ed Sprague	8.00
154	Mike Hampton	8.00
155	Mike Lansing	8.00
156	Ray Lankford	8.00
157	Bobby Bonilla	15.00
158	Bill Mueller	8.00
159	Jeffrey Hammonds	8.00
160	Charles Nagy	8.00
161	Rich Loiselle	8.00
162	Al Leiter	8.00
163	Larry Walker	25.00
164	Chris Hoiles	8.00
165	Jeff Montgomery	8.00
166	Francisco Cordova	8.00
167	James Baldwin	8.00
168	Mark McLemore	8.00
169	Kevin Appier	8.00
170	Jamey Wright	8.00
171	Nomar Garciaparra	90.00
172	Matt Franco	8.00
173	Armando Benitez	8.00
174	Jeromy Burnitz	8.00
175	Ismael Valdes	8.00
176	Lance Johnson	8.00
177	Paul Sorrento	8.00
178	Rondell White	15.00
179	Kevin Elster	8.00
180	Jason Giambi	8.00
181	Carlos Baerga	8.00
182	Russ Davis	8.00
183	Ryan McGuire	8.00
184	Eric Young	8.00
185	Ron Gant	15.00
186	Manny Alexander	8.00
187	Scott Karl	8.00
188	Brady Anderson	12.00
189	Randall Simon	15.00
190	Tim Belcher	8.00
191	Jaret Wright	40.00
192	Dante Bichette	20.00
193	John Valentin	8.00
194	Darren Bragg	8.00
195	Mike Sweeney	8.00
196	Craig Counsell	8.00
197	Jaime Navarro	8.00
198	Todd Dunn	8.00
199	Ken Griffey Jr.	180.00
200	Juan Gonzalez	80.00
201	Billy Wagner	8.00
202	Jeff D'Amico	8.00
203	Mark McGwire	200.00
204	Jeff D'Amico	8.00
205	Rico Brogna	8.00
206	Todd Hollandsworth	8.00
207	Chad Curtis	8.00
208	Tom Goodwin	8.00
209	Neifi Perez	8.00
210	Derek Bell	8.00
211	Quilvio Veras	8.00
212	Greg Vaughn	8.00
213	Roberto Hernandez	8.00
214	Arthur Rhodes	8.00
215	Cal Eldred	8.00
216	Bill Taylor	8.00
217	Todd Greene	8.00
218	Mario Valdez	8.00
219	Ricky Bottalico	8.00
220	Frank Rodriguez	8.00
221	Rich Becker	8.00
222	Roberto Duran	8.00
223	Ivan Rodriguez	40.00
224	Mike Jackson	8.00
225	Deion Sanders	15.00
226	Tony Womack	8.00
227	Mark Kotsay	15.00
228	Steve Trachsel	8.00
229	Ryan Klesko	25.00
230	Ken Cloude	15.00
231	Luis Gonzalez	8.00
232	Gary Gaetti	8.00
233	Michael Tucker	8.00
234	Shawn Green	8.00
235	Ariel Prieto	8.00
236	Kirt Manwaring	8.00
237	Omar Vizquel	8.00
238	Matt Beech	8.00
239	Justin Thompson	8.00
240	Bret Boone	8.00
241	Derek Jeter	90.00
242	Ken Caminiti	20.00
243	Jay Bell	8.00
244	Kevin Tapani	8.00
245	Jason Kendall	8.00
246	Jose Guillen	15.00
247	Mike Bordick	8.00
248	Dustin Hermanson	8.00
249	Darrin Fletcher	8.00
250	Dave Hollins	8.00
251	Ramon Martinez	15.00
252	Hideki Irabu	25.00
253	Mark Grace	20.00
254	Jason Isringhausen	8.00
255	Jose Cruz Jr.	75.00
256	Brian Johnson	8.00
257	Brad Ausmus	8.00
258	Andruw Jones	40.00
259	Doug Jones	8.00
260	Jeff Shaw	8.00
261	Chuck Finley	8.00
262	Gary Sheffield	20.00
263	David Segui	8.00
264	John Smiley	8.00
265	Tim Salmon	20.00
266	J.T. Snow Jr.	8.00
267	Alex Fernandez	8.00
268	Matt Stairs	8.00
269	B.J. Surhoff	8.00
270	Keith Foulke	8.00
271	Edgar Martinez	12.00
272	Shannon Stewart	8.00
273	Eduardo Perez	8.00
274	Wally Joyner	8.00
275	Kevin Young	8.00
276	Eli Marrero	8.00
277	Brad Radke	8.00
278	Jamie Moyer	8.00
279	Joe Girardi	8.00
280	Troy O'Leary	8.00
281	Aaron Sele	15.00
282	Jose Offerman	8.00
283	Scott Erickson	8.00
284	Sean Berry	8.00
285	Shigetosi Hasegawa	8.00
286	Felix Heredia	8.00
287	Willie McGee	8.00
288	Alex Rodriguez	150.00
289	Ugueth Urbina	8.00
290	Jon Lieber	8.00
291	Fernando Tatis	8.00
292	Chris Stynes	8.00
293	Bernard Gilkey	8.00
294	Joey Hamilton	8.00
295	Matt Karchner	8.00
296	Paul Wilson	8.00
297	Mel Nieves	8.00
298	Kevin Millwood	40.00
299	Quinton McCracken	8.00
300	Jerry DiPoto	8.00
301	Jermaine Dye	8.00
302	Travis Lee	70.00
303	Ron Coomer	8.00

304	Matt Williams	20.00
305	Bobby Higginson	8.00
306	Jorge Fabregas	8.00
307	Hal Morris	8.00
308	Jay Bell	8.00
309	Joe Randa	8.00
310	Andy Benes	8.00
311	Sterling Hitchcock	8.00
312	Jeff Suppan	8.00
313	Shane Reynolds	8.00
314	Willie Blair	8.00
315	Scott Rolen	70.00
316	Wilson Alvarez	8.00
317	David Justice	25.00
318	Fred McGriff	20.00
319	Bobby Jones	8.00
320	Wade Boggs	15.00
321	Tim Wakefield	8.00
322	Tony Saunders	8.00
323	David Cone	15.00
324	Roberto Hernandez	8.00
325	Jose Canseco	20.00
326	Kevin Stocker	8.00
327	Gerald Williams	8.00
328	Quinton McCracken	8.00
329	Mark Gardner	8.00
330	Ben Grieve (Prime Rookie)	75.00
331	Kevin Brown	8.00
332	Mike Lowell (Prime Rookie)	8.00
333	Jed Hansen	8.00
334	Abraham Nunez (Prime Rookie)	8.00
335	John Thomson	8.00
336	Derrek Lee (Prime Rookie)	15.00
337	Mike Piazza	90.00
338	Brad Fullmer (Prime Rookie)	20.00
339	Ray Durham	8.00
340	Kerry Wood (Prime Rookie)	125.00
341	*Kevin Polcovich*	8.00
342	Russ Johnson (Prime Rookie)	8.00
343	Darryl Hamilton	8.00
344	David Ortiz (Prime Rookie)	10.00
345	Kevin Orie	8.00
346	Sean Casey (Prime Rookie)	30.00
347	Juan Guzman	8.00
348	Ruben Rivera (Prime Rookie)	8.00
349	Rick Aguilera	8.00
350	Bobby Estalella (Prime Rookie)	8.00
351	Bobby Witt	8.00
352	Paul Konerko (Prime Rookie)	30.00
353	Matt Morris	8.00
354	Carl Pavano (Prime Rookie)	15.00
355	Todd Zeile	8.00
356	Kevin Brown (Transaction)	8.00
357	Alex Gonzalez	8.00
358	Chuck Knoblauch (Transaction)	25.00
359	Joey Cora	8.00
360	Mike Lansing (Transaction)	8.00
361	Adrian Beltre (Future Stars)	50.00
362	Dennis Eckersley (Transaction)	8.00
363	A.J. Hinch (Future Stars)	8.00
364	Kenny Lofton (Transaction)	20.00
365	Alex Gonzalez (Future Stars)	8.00
366	Henry Rodriguez (Transaction)	8.00
367	*Mike Stoner* (Future Stars)	40.00
368	Darryl Kile (Transaction)	8.00
369	Carl Pavano (Future Stars)	8.00
370	Walt Weiss (Transaction)	8.00
371	Kris Benson (Future Stars)	25.00
372	Cecil Fielder (Transaction)	15.00
373	Dermal Brown (Future Stars)	40.00
374	Rod Beck (Transaction)	8.00
375	Eric Milton (Future Stars)	30.00
376	Travis Fryman (Transaction)	8.00
377	Preston Wilson (Future Stars)	8.00
378	Chili Davis (Transaction)	8.00
379	Travis Lee (Future Stars)	75.00
380	Jim Leyritz (Transaction)	8.00
381	Vernon Wells (Draft Picks)	25.00
382	Joe Carter (Transaction)	8.00
383	J.J. Davis (Draft Picks)	20.00
384	Marquis Grissom (Transaction)	8.00
385	*Mike Cuddyer* (Draft Picks)	30.00

386	Rickey Henderson (Transaction)	8.00
387	*Chris Enochs* (Draft Picks)	20.00
388	Andres Galarraga (Transaction)	20.00
389	Jason Dellaero (Draft Picks)	8.00
390	Robb Nen (Transaction)	8.00
391	Mark Mangum (Draft Picks)	8.00
392	Jeff Blauser (Transaction)	8.00
393	Adam Kennedy (Draft Picks)	8.00
394	Bob Abreu (Transaction)	8.00
395	*Jack Cust* (Draft Picks)	20.00
396	Jose Vizcaino (Transaction)	8.00
397	Jon Garland (Draft Picks)	15.00
398	Pedro Martinez (Transaction)	30.00
399	Aaron Akin (Draft Picks)	8.00
400	Jeff Conine (Transaction)	8.00

1998 Stadium Club
Playing with Passion

This Series II insert displayed 10 players with a strong desire to win. The cards were inserted one per 12 packs and numbered with a "P" prefix.

		MT
Complete Set (10):		40.00
Common Player:		1.50
Inserted 1:12		
P1	Bernie Williams	2.00
P2	Jim Edmonds	1.50
P3	Chipper Jones	6.00
P4	Cal Ripken Jr.	8.00
P5	Craig Biggio	1.50
P6	Juan Gonzalez	5.00
P7	Alex Rodriguez	6.00
P8	Tino Martinez	2.00
P9	Mike Piazza	6.00
P10	Ken Griffey Jr.	10.00

1998 Stadium Club
Royal Court

Fifteen players were showcased on uniluster technology for this Series II insert. The set is broken up into 10 Kings (veterans) and five Princes (rookies) and inserted one per 36 packs.

Modern cards have little collector value in conditions lower than Mint.
Figure NM cards at 75% of values shown;
EX cards at 40%.

		MT
Complete Set (15):		180.00
Common Player:		3.00
Inserted 1:36		
RC1	Ken Griffey Jr.	30.00
RC2	Frank Thomas	20.00
RC3	Mike Piazza	20.00
RC4	Chipper Jones	20.00
RC5	Mark McGwire	40.00
RC6	Cal Ripken Jr.	25.00
RC7	Jeff Bagwell	10.00
RC8	Barry Bonds	8.00
RC9	Juan Gonzalez	15.00
RC10	Alex Rodriguez	20.00
RC11	Travis Lee	15.00
RC12	Paul Konerko	5.00
RC13	Todd Helton	5.00
RC14	Ben Grieve	10.00
RC15	Mark Kotsay	3.00

1998 Stadium Club
Triumvirate

Triumvirates were included in both series of Stadium Club and were available only in retail packs. Series I had 24 players, with three players from eight different teams, while Series II had 30 players, with three players from 10 different positions. The cards were all die-cut and fit together to form one three-card panel. Three different versions of each card were available - Luminous (regular) versions were seeded one per 48 packs, Luminescent versions were seeded one per 192 packs and Illuminator versions were seeded one per 384 packs.

		MT
Complete Set (54):		700.00
Complete Series I (24):		300.00
Complete Series II (30):		400.00
Common Player:		4.00
Luminous 1:48		
Luminescents 1:192: 1.5x to 3x		
Illuminators 1:384: 3x to 5x		
T1a	Chipper Jones	30.00
T1b	Andruw Jones	20.00
T1c	Kenny Lofton	12.00
T2a	Derek Jeter	30.00
T2b	Bernie Williams	10.00
T2c	Tino Martinez	4.00
T3a	Jay Buhner	6.00
T3b	Edgar Martinez	4.00
T3c	Ken Griffey Jr.	50.00
T4a	Albert Belle	12.00
T4b	Robin Ventura	4.00
T4c	Frank Thomas	40.00
T5a	Brady Anderson	4.00
T5b	Cal Ripken Jr.	40.00
T5c	Rafael Palmeiro	6.00
T6a	Mike Piazza	30.00
T6b	Raul Mondesi	6.00
T6c	Eric Karros	4.00
T7a	Vinny Castilla	4.00
T7b	Andres Galarraga	6.00
T7c	Larry Walker	6.00
T8a	Jim Thome	8.00
T8b	Manny Ramirez	10.00
T8c	David Justice	6.00
T9a	Mike Mussina	10.00
T9b	Greg Maddux	30.00
T9c	Randy Johnson	10.00
T10a	Mike Piazza	30.00
T10b	Sandy Alomar	4.00
T10c	Ivan Rodriguez	12.00
T11a	Mark McGwire	40.00
T11b	Tino Martinez	6.00
T11c	Frank Thomas	40.00
T12a	Roberto Alomar	10.00
T12b	Chuck Knoblauch	8.00
T12c	Craig Biggio	4.00
T13a	Cal Ripken Jr.	40.00
T13b	Chipper Jones	30.00
T13c	Ken Caminiti	4.00
T14a	Derek Jeter	30.00
T14b	Nomar Garciaparra	30.00
T14c	Alex Rodriguez	30.00
T15a	Barry Bonds	12.00
T15b	David Justice	6.00
T15c	Albert Belle	12.00
T16a	Bernie Williams	8.00
T16b	Ken Griffey Jr.	50.00
T16c	Ray Lankford	4.00
T17a	Tim Salmon	6.00
T17b	Larry Walker	6.00
T17c	Tony Gwynn	25.00
T18a	Paul Molitor	10.00
T18b	Edgar Martinez	4.00
T18c	Juan Gonzalez	25.00

1991 Studio

Donruss introduced this 264-card set in 1991. The cards feature maroon borders surrounding black and white posed player photos. The card backs are printed in black and white and feature personal data, career highlights, hobbies and interests and the player's hero. The

cards were released in foil packs only and feature a special Rod Carew puzzle.

IVAN CALDERON, LF

		MT
Complete Set (264):		18.00
Common Player:		.12
Wax Box:		27.00
1	Glenn Davis	.12
2	Dwight Evans	.12
3	Leo Gomez	.12
4	Chris Hoiles	.12
5	Sam Horn	.12
6	Ben McDonald	.12
7	Randy Milligan	.12
8	Gregg Olson	.12
9	Cal Ripken, Jr.	2.00
10	David Segui	.15
11	Wade Boggs	.35
12	Ellis Burks	.20
13	Jack Clark	.12
14	Roger Clemens	.75
15	Mike Greenwell	.12
16	Tim Naehring	.12
17	Tony Pena	.12
18	*Phil Plantier*	.12
19	Jeff Reardon	.12
20	Mo Vaughn	1.00
21	Jimmy Reese	.15
22	Jim Abbott	.15
23	Bert Blyleven	.12
24	Chuck Finley	.12
25	Gary Gaetti	.15
26	Wally Joyner	.15
27	Mark Langston	.15
28	Kirk McCaskill	.12
29	Lance Parrish	.15
30	Dave Winfield	.25
31	Alex Fernandez	.12
32	Carlton Fisk	.20
33	Scott Fletcher	.12
34	Greg Hibbard	.12
35	Charlie Hough	.12
36	Jack McDowell	.15
37	Tim Raines	.15
38	Sammy Sosa	2.00
39	Bobby Thigpen	.12
40	Frank Thomas	4.00
41	Sandy Alomar	.15
42	John Farrell	.12
43	Glenallen Hill	.12
44	Brook Jacoby	.12
45	Chris James	.12
46	Doug Jones	.12
47	Eric King	.12
48	Mark Lewis	.12
49	Greg Swindell	.12
50	Mark Whiten	.12
51	Milt Cuyler	.12
52	Rob Deer	.12
53	Cecil Fielder	.25
54	Travis Fryman	.15
55	Bill Gullickson	.12
56	Lloyd Moseby	.12
57	Frank Tanana	.12
58	Mickey Tettleton	.15
59	Alan Trammell	.20
60	Lou Whitaker	.12
61	Mike Boddicker	.12
62	George Brett	.50
63	Jeff Conine	.25
64	Warren Cromartie	.12
65	Storm Davis	.12
66	Kirk Gibson	.12
67	Mark Gubicza	.15
68	*Brian McRae*	.40
69	Bret Saberhagen	.15
70	Kurt Stillwell	.12
71	Tim McIntosh	.12
72	Candy Maldonado	.12
73	Paul Molitor	.50
74	Willie Randolph	.12
75	Ron Robinson	.12
76	Gary Sheffield	.25
77	Franklin Stubbs	.12
78	B.J. Surhoff	.12
79	Greg Vaughn	.15
80	Robin Yount	.45
81	Rick Aguilera	.12
82	Steve Bedrosian	.12
83	Scott Erickson	.15
84	Greg Gagne	.12
85	Dan Gladden	.12
86	Brian Harper	.12
87	Kent Hrbek	.15
88	Shane Mack	.12
89	Jack Morris	.12
90	Kirby Puckett	.60
91	Jesse Barfield	.12
92	Steve Farr	.12
93	Steve Howe	.12
94	Roberto Kelly	.12
95	Tim Leary	.12
96	Kevin Maas	.12
97	Don Mattingly	.75
98	Hensley Meulens	.12
99	Scott Sanderson	.12
100	Steve Sax	.12
101	Jose Canseco	.30
102	Dennis Eckersley	.15
103	Dave Henderson	.12
104	Rickey Henderson	.25
105	Rick Honeycutt	.12
106	Mark McGwire	4.00
107	Dave Stewart	.12
108	Eric Show	.12
109	*Todd Van Poppel*	.12
110	Bob Welch	.12
111	Alvin Davis	.12
112	Ken Griffey, Jr.	4.00
113	Ken Griffey, Sr.	.12
114	Erik Hanson	.12
115	Brian Holman	.12
116	Randy Johnson	.40
117	Edgar Martinez	.15
118	Tino Martinez	.20
119	Harold Reynolds	.12
120	David Valle	.12
121	Kevin Belcher	.12
122	Scott Chiamparino	.12
123	Julio Franco	.15
124	Juan Gonzalez	1.50
125	Rich Gossage	.12
126	Jeff Kunkel	.12
127	Rafael Palmeiro	.25
128	Nolan Ryan	2.00
129	Ruben Sierra	.15
130	Bobby Witt	.12
131	Roberto Alomar	.50
132	Tom Candiotti	.12
133	Joe Carter	.15
134	Ken Dayley	.12
135	Kelly Gruber	.12
136	John Olerud	.20
137	Dave Stieb	.12
138	Turner Ward	.12
139	Devon White	.15
140	Mookie Wilson	.12
141	Steve Avery	.12
142	Sid Bream	.12
143	Nick Esasky	.12
144	Ron Gant	.20
145	Tom Glavine	.25
146	Dave Justice	.25
147	Kelly Mann	.12
148	Terry Pendleton	.12
149	John Smoltz	.20
150	Jeff Treadway	.12
151	George Bell	.12
152	Shawn Boskie	.12
153	Andre Dawson	.15
154	Lance Dickson	.12
155	Shawon Dunston	.15
156	Joe Girardi	.12
157	Mark Grace	.25
158	Ryne Sandberg	.50
159	Gary Scott	.12
160	Dave Smith	.12

161	Tom Browning	.12
162	Eric Davis	.15
163	Rob Dibble	.12
164	Mariano Duncan	.12
165	Chris Hammond	.12
166	Billy Hatcher	.12
167	Barry Larkin	.25
168	Hal Morris	.12
169	Paul O'Neill	.15
170	Chris Sabo	.12
171	Eric Anthony	.12
172	*Jeff Bagwell*	3.00
173	Craig Biggio	.20
174	Ken Caminitti	.20
175	Jim Deshaies	.12
176	Steve Finley	.12
177	Pete Harnisch	.12
178	Darryl Kile	.12
179	Curt Schilling	.12
180	Mike Scott	.12
181	Brett Butler	.15
182	Gary Carter	.15
183	Orel Hershiser	.15
184	Ramon Martinez	.15
185	Eddie Murray	.25
186	Jose Offerman	.12
187	Bob Ojeda	.12
188	Juan Samuel	.12
189	Mike Scioscia	.12
190	Darryl Strawberry	.15
191	Moises Alou	.15
192	Brian Barnes	.12
193	Oil Can Boyd	.12
194	Ivan Calderon	.12
195	Delino DeShields	.12
196	Mike Fitzgerald	.12
197	Andres Galarraga	.20
198	Marquis Grissom	.20
199	Bill Sampen	.12
200	Tim Wallach	.12
201	Daryl Boston	.12
202	Vince Coleman	.12
203	John Franco	.12
204	Dwight Gooden	.15
205	Tom Herr	.12
206	Gregg Jefferies	.15
207	Howard Johnson	.12
208	Dave Magadan	.12
209	Kevin McReynolds	.12
210	Frank Viola	.12
211	Wes Chamberlain	.12
212	Darren Daulton	.12
213	Len Dykstra	.15
214	Charlie Hayes	.12
215	Ricky Jordan	.12
216	Steve Lake	.12
217	Roger McDowell	.12
218	Mickey Morandini	.12
219	Terry Mulholland	.12
220	Dale Murphy	.20
221	Jay Bell	.12
222	Barry Bonds	.75
223	Bobby Bonilla	.15
224	Doug Drabek	.12
225	Bill Landrum	.12
226	Mike LaValliere	.12
227	Jose Lind	.12
228	Don Slaught	.12
229	John Smiley	.12
230	Andy Van Slyke	.12
231	Bernard Gilkey	.15
232	Pedro Guerrero	.12
233	Rex Hudler	.12
234	Ray Lankford	.20
235	Joe Magrane	.12
236	Jose Oquendo	.12
237	Lee Smith	.15
238	Ozzie Smith	.45
239	Milt Thompson	.12
240	Todd Zeile	.12
241	Larry Andersen	.12
242	Andy Benes	.15
243	Paul Faries	.12
244	Tony Fernandez	.12
245	Tony Gwynn	.60
246	Atlee Hammaker	.12
247	Fred McGriff	.30
248	Bip Roberts	.12
249	Benito Santiago	.15
250	Ed Whitson	.12
251	Dave Anderson	.12
252	Mike Benjamin	.12
253	John Burkett	.12
254	Will Clark	.35
255	Scott Garrelts	.12
256	Willie McGee	.15

257	Kevin Mitchell	.12
258	Dave Righetti	.12
259	Matt Williams	.35
260	Black & Decker(Bud Black,	.20
	Steve Decker)	
261	Checklist	.05
262	Checklist	.05
263	Checklist	.05
264	Checklist	.05

1992 Studio

PETE HARNISCH   RHP
Houston Astros

Donruss introduced the Studio line in 1991 and released another 264-card set entitled Leaf Studio for 1992. The cards feature a color player closeup with a large, rough-textured black-and-white photo of the player in the background. Tan borders surround the photos. The cards were only released in foil packs. Special Heritage insert cards featuring top players in vintage uniforms could be found in foil and jumbo packs.

		MT
Complete Set (264):		15.00
Common Player:		.10
Wax Box:		22.00
1	Steve Avery	.10
2	Sid Bream	.10
3	Ron Gant	.15
4	Tom Glavine	.15
5	Dave Justice	.25
6	Mark Lemke	.10
7	Greg Olson	.10
8	Terry Pendleton	.10
9	Deion Sanders	.40
10	John Smoltz	.15
11	Doug Dascenzo	.10
12	Andre Dawson	.15
13	Joe Girardi	.10
14	Mark Grace	.25
15	Greg Maddux	1.50
16	Chuck McElroy	.10
17	Mike Morgan	.10
18	Ryne Sandberg	.50
19	Gary Scott	.10
20	Sammy Sosa	1.50
21	Norm Charlton	.10
22	Rob Dibble	.10
23	Barry Larkin	.25
24	Hal Morris	.10
25	Paul O'Neill	.15
26	Jose Rijo	.10
27	Bip Roberts	.10
28	Chris Sabo	.10
29	Reggie Sanders	.20
30	Greg Swindell	.10
31	Jeff Bagwell	.75
32	Craig Biggio	.15
33	Ken Caminiti	.20
34	Andujar Cedeno	.10
35	Steve Finley	.10
36	Pete Harnisch	.10
37	Butch Henry	.10
38	Doug Jones	.10

39	Darryl Kile	.10
40	Eddie Taubensee	.10
41	Brett Butler	.15
42	Tom Candiotti	.10
43	Eric Davis	.15
44	Orel Hershiser	.15
45	Eric Karros	.20
46	Ramon Martinez	.15
47	Jose Offerman	.10
48	Mike Scioscia	.10
49	Mike Sharperson	.10
50	Darryl Strawberry	.15
51	Bret Barbarie	.10
52	Ivan Calderon	.10
53	Gary Carter	.15
54	Delino DeShields	.10
55	Marquis Grissom	.15
56	Ken Hill	.10
57	Dennis Martinez	.15
58	Spike Owen	.10
59	Larry Walker	.25
60	Tim Wallach	.10
61	Bobby Bonilla	.12
62	Tim Burke	.10
63	Vince Coleman	.10
64	John Franco	.10
65	Dwight Gooden	.15
66	Todd Hundley	.15
67	Howard Johnson	.10
68	Eddie Murray	.25
69	Bret Saberhagen	.15
70	Anthony Young	.10
71	Kim Batiste	.10
72	Wes Chamberlain	.10
73	Darren Daulton	.12
74	Mariano Duncan	.10
75	Len Dykstra	.15
76	John Kruk	.10
77	Mickey Morandini	.10
78	Terry Mulholland	.10
79	Dale Murphy	.20
80	Mitch Williams	.10
81	Jay Bell	.10
82	Barry Bonds	.60
83	Steve Buechele	.10
84	Doug Drabek	.10
85	Mike LaValliere	.10
86	Jose Lind	.10
87	Denny Neagle	.12
88	Randy Tomlin	.10
89	Andy Van Slyke	.10
90	Gary Varsho	.10
91	Pedro Guerrero	.10
92	Rex Hudler	.10
93	Brian Jordan	.15
94	Felix Jose	.10
95	Donovan Osborne	.10
96	Tom Pagnozzi	.10
97	Lee Smith	.15
98	Ozzie Smith	.35
99	Todd Worrell	.10
100	Todd Zeile	.15
101	Andy Benes	.15
102	Jerald Clark	.10
103	Tony Fernandez	.10
104	Tony Gwynn	.35
105	Greg Harris	.10
106	Fred McGriff	.30
107	Benito Santiago	.15
108	Gary Sheffield	.25
109	Kurt Stillwell	.10
110	Tim Teufel	.10
111	Kevin Bass	.10
112	Jeff Brantley	.10
113	John Burkett	.10
114	Will Clark	.25
115	Royce Clayton	.10
116	Mike Jackson	.10
117	Darren Lewis	.10
118	Bill Swift	.10
119	Robby Thompson	.10
120	Matt Williams	.25
121	Brady Anderson	.20
122	Glenn Davis	.10
123	Mike Devereaux	.10
124	Chris Hoiles	.10
125	Sam Horn	.10
126	Ben McDonald	.10
127	Mike Mussina	.30
128	Gregg Olson	.10
129	Cal Ripken, Jr.	1.50
130	Rick Sutcliffe	.10
131	Wade Boggs	.30
132	Roger Clemens	.65
133	Greg Harris	.10
134	Tim Naehring	.10

135	Tony Pena	.10
136	Phil Plantier	.10
137	Jeff Reardon	.10
138	Jody Reed	.10
139	Mo Vaughn	.50
140	Frank Viola	.10
141	Jim Abbott	.15
142	Hubie Brooks	.10
143	*Chad Curtis*	.20
144	Gary DiSarcina	.10
145	Chuck Finley	.10
146	Bryan Harvey	.10
147	Von Hayes	.10
148	Mark Langston	.12
149	Lance Parrish	.10
150	Lee Stevens	.10
151	George Bell	.10
152	Alex Fernandez	.10
153	Greg Hibbard	.10
154	Lance Johnson	.10
155	Kirk McCaskill	.10
156	Tim Raines	.15
157	Steve Sax	.10
158	Bobby Thigpen	.10
159	Frank Thomas	2.50
160	Robin Ventura	.25
161	Sandy Alomar, Jr.	.15
162	Jack Armstrong	.10
163	Carlos Baerga	.15
164	Albert Belle	.60
165	Alex Cole	.10
166	Glenallen Hill	.10
167	Mark Lewis	.10
168	Kenny Lofton	.50
169	Paul Sorrento	.10
170	Mark Whiten	.10
171	Milt Cuyler (color photo actually Lou Whitaker)	.10
172	Rob Deer	.10
173	Cecil Fielder	.20
174	Travis Fryman	.20
175	Mike Henneman	.10
176	Tony Phillips	.12
177	Frank Tanana	.10
178	Mickey Tettleton	.10
179	Alan Trammell	.15
180	Lou Whitaker	.10
181	George Brett	.65
182	Tom Gordon	.10
183	Mark Gubicza	.10
184	Gregg Jefferies	.15
185	Wally Joyner	.12
186	Brent Mayne	.10
187	Brian McRae	.12
188	Kevin McReynolds	.10
189	Keith Miller	.10
190	Jeff Montgomery	.10
191	Dante Bichette	.20
192	Ricky Bones	.10
193	Scott Fletcher	.10
194	Paul Molitor	.35
195	Jaime Navarro	.10
196	Franklin Stubbs	.10
197	B.J. Surhoff	.10
198	Greg Vaughn	.10
199	Bill Wegman	.10
200	Robin Yount	.35
201	Rick Aguilera	.10
202	Scott Erickson	.10
203	Greg Gagne	.10
204	Brian Harper	.10
205	Kent Hrbek	.15
206	Scott Leius	.10
207	Shane Mack	.12
208	Pat Mahomes	.10
209	Kirby Puckett	.65
210	John Smiley	.10
211	Mike Gallego	.10
212	Charlie Hayes	.10
213	Pat Kelly	.10
214	Roberto Kelly	.10
215	Kevin Maas	.10
216	Don Mattingly	.75
217	Matt Nokes	.10
218	Melido Perez	.10
219	Scott Sanderson	.10
220	Danny Tartabull	.10
221	Harold Baines	.12
222	Jose Canseco	.35
223	Dennis Eckersley	.12
224	Dave Henderson	.10
225	Carney Lansford	.10
226	Mark McGwire	4.00
227	Mike Moore	.10
228	Randy Ready	.10
229	Terry Steinbach	.10

230	Dave Stewart	.10
231	Jay Buhner	.10
232	Ken Griffey, Jr.	3.00
233	Erik Hanson	.10
234	Randy Johnson	.25
235	Edgar Martinez	.12
236	Tino Martinez	.15
237	Kevin Mitchell	.10
238	Pete O'Brien	.10
239	Harold Reynolds	.10
240	David Valle	.10
241	Julio Franco	.12
242	Juan Gonzalez	.60
243	Jose Guzman	.10
244	Rafael Palmeiro	.25
245	Dean Palmer	.10
246	Ivan Rodriguez	.50
247	Jeff Russell	.10
248	Nolan Ryan	1.50
249	Ruben Sierra	.10
250	Dickie Thon	.10
251	Roberto Alomar	.40
252	Derek Bell	.15
253	Pat Borders	.10
254	Joe Carter	.20
255	Kelly Gruber	.10
256	Juan Guzman	.10
257	Jack Morris	.10
258	John Olerud	.20
259	Devon White	.15
260	Dave Winfield	.30
261	Checklist	.05
262	Checklist	.05
263	Checklist	.05
264	History card	.05

1992 Studio Heritage

Superstars of 1992 were photographed in vintage-style uniforms in this 14-card insert set found in packages of Studio's 1992 issue. Cards #1-8 could be found in standard foil packs while #9-14 were inserted in Studio jumbos. Cards featured a sepia-tone photo bordered in turquoise and highlighted with copper foil. Cards carry a "BC" prefix to the card number on back.

		MT
Complete Set (14):		22.00
Common Player:		1.00
1	Ryne Sandberg	1.50
2	Carlton Fisk	1.00
3	Wade Boggs	1.50
4	Jose Canseco	1.50
5	Don Mattingly	3.00
6	Darryl Strawberry	1.00
7	Cal Ripken, Jr.	5.00
8	Will Clark	1.00
9	Andre Dawson	1.00
10	Andy Van Slyke	1.00
11	Paul Molitor	1.50
12	Jeff Bagwell	2.00
13	Darren Daulton	1.00
14	Kirby Puckett	3.00

1993 Studio

This 220-card set features full-bleed photos. The player's portrait appears against one of several backgrounds featuring his team's uniform. His signature and the Studio logo are printed in gold foil. Backs have an extreme closeup partial portrait of the player and insights into his personality.

		MT
Complete Set (220):		20.00
Common Player:		.08
Wax Box:		28.00
1	Dennis Eckersley	.10
2	Chad Curtis	.12
3	Eric Anthony	.08
4	Roberto Alomar	.50
5	Steve Avery	.08
6	Cal Eldred	.08
7	Bernard Gilkey	.12
8	Steve Buechele	.08
9	Brett Butler	.12
10	Terry Mulholland	.08
11	Moises Alou	.15
12	Barry Bonds	.75
13	Sandy Alomar Jr.	.12
14	Chris Bosio	.08
15	Scott Sanderson	.08
16	Bobby Bonilla	.12
17	Brady Anderson	.15
18	Derek Bell	.15
19	Wes Chamberlain	.08
20	Jay Bell	.08
21	Kevin Brown	.10
22	Roger Clemens	1.00
23	Roberto Kelly	.08
24	Dante Bichette	.20
25	George Brett	.75
26	Rob Deer	.08
27	Brian Harper	.08
28	George Bell	.08
29	Jim Abbott	.12
30	Dave Henderson	.08
31	Wade Boggs	.20
32	Chili Davis	.08
33	Ellis Burks	.12
34	Jeff Bagwell	1.00
35	Kent Hrbek	.10
36	Pat Borders	.08
37	Cecil Fielder	.15
38	Sid Bream	.08
39	Greg Gagne	.08
40	Darryl Hamilton	.08
41	Jerald Clark	.08
42	Mark Grace	.20
43	Barry Larkin	.15
44	John Burkett	.08
45	Scott Cooper	.08
46	*Mike Lansing*	.25
47	Jose Canseco	.25
48	Will Clark	.25
49	Carlos Garcia	.08

50	Carlos Baerga	.15
51	Darren Daulton	.10
52	Jay Buhner	.08
53	Andy Benes	.12
54	Jeff Conine	.12
55	Mike Devereaux	.08
56	Vince Coleman	.08
57	Terry Steinbach	.08
58	*J.T. Snow*	.75
59	Greg Swindell	.08
60	Devon White	.08
61	John Smoltz	.12
62	Todd Zeile	.12
63	Rick Wilkins	.08
64	Tim Wallach	.08
65	John Wetteland	.08
66	Matt Williams	.30
67	Paul Sorrento	.08
68	David Valle	.08
69	Walt Weiss	.08
70	John Franco	.08
71	Nolan Ryan	2.50
72	Frank Viola	.08
73	Chris Sabo	.08
74	David Nied	.08
75	Kevin McReynolds	.08
76	Lou Whitaker	.08
77	Dave Winfield	.20
78	Robin Ventura	.15
79	Spike Owen	.08
80	Cal Ripken, Jr.	2.50
81	Dan Walter	.08
82	Mitch Williams	.08
83	Tim Wakefield	.08
84	Rickey Henderson	.20
85	Gary DiSarcina	.08
86	Craig Biggio	.10
87	Joe Carter	.15
88	Ron Gant	.15
89	John Jaha	.10
90	Gregg Jefferies	.08
91	Jose Guzman	.08
92	Eric Karros	.15
93	Wil Cordero	.15
94	Royce Clayton	.08
95	Albert Belle	.75
96	Ken Griffey, Jr.	3.00
97	Orestes Destrade	.08
98	Tony Fernandez	.08
99	Leo Gomez	.08
100	Tony Gwynn	1.00
101	Len Dykstra	.12
102	Jeff King	.08
103	Julio Franco	.08
104	Andre Dawson	.12
105	Randy Milligan	.08
106	Alex Cole	.08
107	Phil Hiatt	.08
108	Travis Fryman	.15
109	Chuck Knoblauch	.12
110	Bo Jackson	.15
111	Pat Kelly	.08
112	Bret Saberhagen	.10
113	Ruben Sierra	.08
114	Tim Salmon	.40
115	Doug Jones	.08
116	Ed Sprague	.08
117	Terry Pendleton	.08
118	Robin Yount	.40
119	Mark Whiten	.08
120	Checklist	.08
121	Sammy Sosa	1.50
122	Darryl Strawberry	.12
123	Larry Walker	.25
124	Robby Thompson	.08
125	Carlos Martinez	.08
126	Edgar Martinez	.10
127	Benito Santiago	.10
128	Howard Johnson	.08
129	Harold Reynolds	.08
130	Craig Shipley	.08
131	Curt Schilling	.08
132	Andy Van Slyke	.08
133	Ivan Rodriguez	.50
134	Mo Vaughn	.75
135	Bip Roberts	.08
136	Charlie Hayes	.08
137	Brian McRae	.08
138	Mickey Tettleton	.08
139	Frank Thomas	2.50
140	Paul O'Neill	.12
141	Mark McGwire	4.00
142	Damion Easley	.10
143	Ken Caminiti	.20
144	Juan Guzman	.10
145	Tom Glavine	.15

146	Pat Listach	.08
147	Lee Smith	.10
148	Derrick May	.08
149	Ramon Martinez	.10
150	Delino DeShields	.10
151	Kirt Manwaring	.08
152	Reggie Jefferson	.08
153	Randy Johnson	.40
154	Dave Magadan	.08
155	Dwight Gooden	.12
156	Chris Hoiles	.08
157	Fred McGriff	.20
158	Dave Hollins	.10
159	Al Martin	.10
160	Juan Gonzalez	1.00
161	Mike Greenwell	.08
162	Kevin Mitchell	.10
163	Andres Galarraga	.20
164	Wally Joyner	.12
165	Kirk Gibson	.08
166	Pedro Munoz	.08
167	Ozzie Guillen	.08
168	Jimmy Key	.08
169	Kevin Seitzer	.08
170	Luis Polonia	.08
171	Luis Gonzalez	.08
172	Paul Molitor	.40
173	Dave Justice	.20
174	B.J. Surhoff	.08
175	Ray Lankford	.15
176	Ryne Sandberg	.50
177	Jody Reed	.08
178	Marquis Grissom	.15
179	Willie McGee	.10
180	Kenny Lofton	.75
181	Junior Felix	.08
182	Jose Offerman	.08
183	John Kruk	.08
184	Orlando Merced	.08
185	Rafael Palmeiro	.25
186	Billy Hatcher	.08
187	Joe Oliver	.08
188	Joe Girardi	.08
189	Jose Lind	.08
190	Harold Baines	.10
191	Mike Pagliarulo	.08
192	Lance Johnson	.08
193	Don Mattingly	1.00
194	Doug Drabek	.08
195	John Olerud	.20
196	Greg Maddux	2.00
197	Greg Vaughn	.12
198	Tom Pagnozzi	.08
199	Willie Wilson	.08
200	Jack McDowell	.10
201	Mike Piazza	2.00
202	Mike Mussina	.50
203	Charles Nagy	.08
204	Tino Martinez	.20
205	Charlie Hough	.08
206	Todd Hundley	.20
207	Gary Sheffield	.25
208	Mickey Morandini	.08
209	Don Slaught	.08
210	Dean Palmer	.15
211	Jose Rijo	.08
212	Vinny Castilla	.10
213	Tony Phillips	.10
214	Kirby Puckett	1.00
215	Tim Raines	.12
216	Otis Nixon	.08
217	Ozzie Smith	.40
218	Jose Vizcaino	.08
220	Checklist	.08

FRANK THOMAS
COLLECTION

		MT
Complete Set (5):		20.00
Common Player:		4.00
1	Childhood	4.00
2	Baseball Memories	4.00
3	Importance of Family	4.00
4	Performance	4.00
5	On Being a Role Model	4.00

1993 Studio Heritage

HERITAGE

OZZIE SMITH

All types of 1993 Leaf Studio packs were candidates for having one of 12 Heritage cards inserted in them. The fronts feature the player posing in an old-time uniform, framed in turquiose with copper highlights. The backs have a mug shot surrounded by an ornate frame and describe the uniform on the front. Team trivia is also included.

		MT
Complete Set (12):		20.00
Common Player:		1.00
1	George Brett	4.00
2	Juan Gonzalez	4.00
3	Roger Clemens	2.50
4	Mark McGwire	12.00
5	Mark Grace	1.50
6	Ozzie Smith	2.00
7	Barry Larkin	1.00
8	Frank Thomas	8.00
9	Carlos Baerga	1.00
10	Eric Karros	1.00
11	J.T. Snow	1.00
12	John Kruk	1.00

1993 Studio Frank Thomas

This five-card set is devoted to Frank Thomas. Cards were randomly included in all types of 1993 Leaf Studio packs. Topics covered on the cards include Thomas' childhood, his baseball memories, his family, his performance and being a role model.

A player's name in *italic* type indicates a rookie card.

1993 Studio Silhouettes

These insert cards were randomly included in jumbo packs only. The card fronts feature a ghosted image of the player against an action silhouette on a gray background. The player's name is in bronze foil at bottom. Backs have a player action photo and description of career highlights.

		MT
Complete Set (10):		25.00
Common Player:		1.00
1	Frank Thomas	8.00
2	Barry Bonds	2.50
3	Jeff Bagwell	4.00
4	Juan Gonzalez	3.00
5	Travis Fryman	1.00
6	J.T. Snow	1.50
7	John Kruk	1.00
8	Jeff Blauser	1.00
9	Mike Piazza	6.00
10	Nolan Ryan	7.50

1993 Studio Superstars on Canvas

Ten players are featured on these insert cards, which were available in hobby and retail packs. The cards show player portraits which mix photography and artwork.

		MT
Complete Set (10):		25.00
Common Player:		1.00
1	Ken Griffey, Jr.	12.00
2	Jose Canseco	1.50
3	Mark McGwire	15.00
4	Mike Mussina	2.00
5	Joe Carter	1.00
6	Frank Thomas	10.00
7	Darren Daulton	1.00
8	Mark Grace	1.50
9	Andres Galarraga	1.00
10	Barry Bonds	3.00

1994 Studio

Studio baseball from Donruss returned in mid-August, 1994, with a three-time MVP spokesman, several jazzy and short-printed inserts subsets and a reduced overall production figure that represents a sharp drop from 1993. Barry Bonds is the MVP whose mug adorns Studio counter boxes and advertisements. According to Donruss officials, production was limited to 8,000 cases of 20 boxes each, which represents a 35 percent decrease from 1993 and works out to about 315,000 of each card. Only 2,000 cases were earmarked for retail distribution and no jumbo packs were produced. Studio 1994 features 220 cards issued in one series, once again with close-up personal portraits of the top stars in the game. Each card is foil-stamped with a borderless design and UV coating front and back. The front of the card features the player in the foreground with his locker in the background. As in the previous three Studio offerings, the backs of the cards contain personal information about the players.

		MT
Complete Set (220):		20.00
Common Player:		.10
Wax Box:		25.00
1	Dennis Eckersley	.10
2	Brent Gates	.10
3	Rickey Henderson	.25
4	Mark McGwire	4.00
5	Troy Neel	.10
6	Ruben Sierra	.10
7	Terry Steinbach	.10
8	Chad Curtis	.10
9	Chili Davis	.10
10	Gary DiSarcina	.10
11	Damion Easley	.10
12	Bo Jackson	.25
13	Mark Langston	.10
14	Eduardo Perez	.10
15	Tim Salmon	.25
16	Jeff Bagwell	1.00
17	Craig Biggio	.20
18	Ken Caminiti	.20
19	Andujar Cedeno	.10
20	Doug Drabek	.10
21	Steve Finley	.10
22	Luis Gonzalez	.10
23	Darryl Kile	.10
24	Roberto Alomar	.75
25	Pat Borders	.10
26	Joe Carter	.15
27	Carlos Delgado	.12
28	Pat Hentgen	.10
29	Paul Molitor	.30
30	John Olerud	.15
31	Ed Sprague	.10
32	Devon White	.10
33	Steve Avery	.10
34	Tom Glavine	.15
35	David Justice	.20
36	Roberto Kelly	.10
37	Ryan Klesko	.40
38	Javier Lopez	.15
39	Greg Maddux	2.00
40	Fred McGriff	.25
41	Terry Pendleton	.10
42	Ricky Bones	.10
43	Darryl Hamilton	.10
44	Brian Harper	.10
45	John Jaha	.10
46	Dave Nilsson	.10
47	Kevin Seitzer	.10
48	Greg Vaughn	.12
49	Turner Ward	.10
50	Bernard Gilkey	.10
51	Gregg Jefferies	.10
52	Ray Lankford	.15
53	Tom Pagnozzi	.10
54	Ozzie Smith	.30
55	Bob Tewksbury	.10
56	Mark Whiten	.10
57	Todd Zeile	.10
58	Steve Buechele	.10
59	Shawon Dunston	.10
60	Mark Grace	.25
61	Derrick May	.10
62	Tuffy Rhodes	.10
63	Ryne Sandberg	.60
64	Sammy Sosa	1.50
65	Rick Wilkins	.10
66	Brett Butler	.15
67	Delino DeShields	.10
68	Orel Hershiser	.10
69	Eric Karros	.15
70	Raul Mondesi	.35
71	Jose Offerman	.10
72	Mike Piazza	1.50
73	Tim Wallach	.10
74	Moises Alou	.10
75	Sean Berry	.10
76	Wil Cordero	.10
77	Cliff Floyd	.10
78	Marquis Grissom	.15
79	Ken Hill	.10
80	Larry Walker	.25
81	John Wetteland	.10
82	Rod Beck	.10
83	Barry Bonds	.75
84	Royce Clayton	.10
85	Darren Lewis	.10
86	Willie McGee	.10
87	Bill Swift	.10
88	Robby Thompson	.10
89	Matt Williams	.25
90	Sandy Alomar Jr.	.10
91	Carlos Baerga	.10
92	Albert Belle	.75
93	Kenny Lofton	.75
94	Eddie Murray	.30
95	Manny Ramirez	.40
96	Paul Sorrento	.10
97	Jim Thome	.25
98	Rich Amaral	.10
99	Eric Anthony	.10
100	Jay Buhner	.20
101	Ken Griffey, Jr.	3.00
102	Randy Johnson	.25
103	Edgar Martinez	.10
104	Tino Martinez	.25
105	*Kurt Abbott*	.15
106	Bret Barberie	.10
107	Chuck Carr	.10
108	Jeff Conine	.10

109	Chris Hammond	.10
110	Bryan Harvey	.10
111	Benito Santiago	.10
112	Gary Sheffield	.35
113	Bobby Bonilla	.10
114	Dwight Gooden	.15
115	Todd Hundley	.10
116	Bobby Jones	.10
117	Jeff Kent	.10
118	Kevin McReynolds	.10
119	Bret Saberhagen	.10
120	Ryan Thompson	.10
121	Harold Baines	.10
122	Mike Devereaux	.10
123	Jeffrey Hammonds	.10
124	Ben McDonald	.10
125	Mike Mussina	.25
126	Rafael Palmeiro	.20
127	Cal Ripken, Jr.	2.50
128	Lee Smith	.10
129	Brad Ausmus	.10
130	Derek Bell	.10
131	Andy Benes	.10
132	Tony Gwynn	.75
133	Trevor Hoffman	.10
134	Scott Livingstone	.10
135	Phil Plantier	.10
136	Darren Daulton	.10
137	Mariano Duncan	.10
138	Len Dykstra	.10
139	Dave Hollins	.10
140	Pete Incaviglia	.10
141	Danny Jackson	.10
142	John Kruk	.10
143	Kevin Stocker	.10
144	Jay Bell	.10
145	Carlos Garcia	.10
146	Jeff King	.10
147	Al Martin	.10
148	Orlando Merced	.10
149	Don Slaught	.10
150	Andy Van Slyke	.10
151	Kevin Brown	.10
152	Jose Canseco	.30
153	Will Clark	.25
154	Juan Gonzalez	1.00
155	David Hulse	.10
156	Dean Palmer	.10
157	Ivan Rodriguez	.50
158	Kenny Rogers	.10
159	Roger Clemens	1.00
160	Scott Cooper	.10
161	Andre Dawson	.10
162	Mike Greenwell	.10
163	Otis Nixon	.10
164	Aaron Sele	.10
165	John Valentin	.10
166	Mo Vaughn	.45
167	Bret Boone	.10
168	Barry Larkin	.20
169	Kevin Mitchell	.10
170	Hal Morris	.10
171	Jose Rijo	.10
172	Deion Sanders	.25
173	Reggie Sanders	.10
174	John Smiley	.10
175	Dante Bichette	.30
176	Ellis Burks	.10
177	Andres Galarraga	.15
178	Joe Girardi	.10
179	Charlie Hayes	.10
180	Roberto Mejia	.10
181	Walt Weiss	.10
182	David Cone	.10
183	Gary Gaetti	.10
184	Greg Gagne	.10
185	Felix Jose	.10
186	Wally Joyner	.10
187	Mike Macfarlane	.10
188	Brian McRae	.10
189	Eric Davis	.10
190	Cecil Fielder	.15
191	Travis Fryman	.10
192	Tony Phillips	.10
193	Mickey Tettleton	.10
194	Alan Trammell	.10
195	Lou Whitaker	.10
196	Kent Hrbek	.10
197	Chuck Knoblauch	.15
198	Shane Mack	.10
199	Pat Meares	.10
200	Kirby Puckett	.75
201	Matt Walbeck	.10
202	Dave Winfield	.15
203	Wilson Alvarez	.10
204	Alex Fernandez	.10

205	Julio Franco	.10
206	Ozzie Guillen	.10
207	Jack McDowell	.10
208	Tim Raines	.10
209	Frank Thomas	2.50
210	Robin Ventura	.10
211	Jim Abbott	.10
212	Wade Boggs	.25
213	Pat Kelly	.10
214	Jimmy Key	.10
215	Don Mattingly	1.00
216	Paul O'Neill	.10
217	Mike Stanley	.10
218	Danny Tartabull	.10
219	Checklist	.10
220	Checklist	.10

1994 Studio Editor's Choice

Printed in similitude to a strip of color slide film, each of the cards in this insert set feature a complete player photo at center, with partial "frames" at top and bottom. Printed on acetate, the back of the card shows a reversed image of the front. Stated odds of finding an Editor's Choice insert card are about one per box of 36 packs.

		MT
Complete Set (8):		45.00
Common Player:		1.00
1	Barry Bonds	5.00
2	Frank Thomas	12.00
3	Ken Griffey, Jr.	15.00
4	Andres Galarraga	1.00
5	Juan Gonzalez	5.00
6	Tim Salmon	2.00
7	Paul O'Neill	1.00
8	Mike Piazza	8.00

1994 Studio Gold Stars

The scarcest of the 1994 Studio chase cards, only 5,000 cards of each of the 10 players were produced. Printed on acetate, fronts feature an action photo set against a clear plastic background. At bottom is a large gold-foil seal. Backs have another player photo, within the silhouette of the front photo, and a black-and-white version of the seal, including the card's unique serial number. According to the series wrapper, odds of finding a Gold Series Star card are one in 120 packs.

		MT
Complete Set (10):		300.00
Common Player:		10.00
1	Tony Gwynn	25.00
2	Barry Bonds	20.00
3	Frank Thomas	50.00
4	Ken Griffey, Jr.	70.00
5	Joe Carter	10.00
6	Mike Piazza	40.00
7	Cal Ripken, Jr.	60.00
8	Greg Maddux	40.00
9	Juan Gonzalez	25.00
10	Don Mattingly	25.00

1994 Studio Heritage

Besides picturing today's players in vintage uniforms, the 1994 Studio Heritage inserts have the player portraits set against sepia-toned photos of old ballparks. Fronts are enhanced by copper-foil logos and by a round device at upper-left containing the player's name, team and year represented. Backs have a second color player photo and a short write-up about the team represented. Unlike the other cards in the set, the Heritage cards are printed on a porous cardboard stock to enhance the image of antiquity. Stated odds of finding a Heritage Collection insert card are one in nine packs.

		MT
Complete Set (8):		15.00
Common Player:		1.00
1	Barry Bonds	2.00
2	Frank Thomas	6.00

3	Joe Carter	1.00
4	Don Mattingly	3.00
5	Ryne Sandberg	2.50
6	Javier Lopez	1.50
7	Gregg Jefferies	1.00
8	Mike Mussina	1.50

1994 Studio Silver Stars

Each of the 10 players in this insert set was produced in an edition of 10,000 cards. Printed on acetate, fronts feature action photos set against a clear plastic background with a silver-foil seal at bottom. Within the player silhouette on back, a second photo is printed. The back also features a black-and-white version of the seal, including the card's unique serial number. Stated odds of picking a Silver Series Star are one per 60 packs, on average.

		MT
Complete Set (10):		80.00
Common Player:		4.00
1	Tony Gwynn	8.00
2	Barry Bonds	5.00
3	Frank Thomas	15.00
4	Ken Griffey, Jr.	20.00
5	Joe Carter	4.00
6	Mike Piazza	15.00
7	Cal Ripken, Jr.	15.00
8	Greg Maddux	12.00
9	Juan Gonzalez	8.00
10	Don Mattingly	8.00

1995 Studio

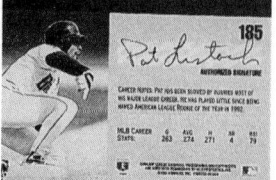

Known since its inception as a brand name for its innovative design, Studio did not disappoint in 1995, unveiling a baseball card with a credit card look. In horizontal format the cards feature embossed stats and data on front, plus a team logo hologram. Backs have a color player photo, facsimile autograph and simulated magnetic data strip to carry through the credit card impression.

		MT
Complete Set (200):		40.00
Common Player:		.10
Wax Box:		48.00
1	Frank Thomas	2.50
2	Jeff Bagwell	1.00
3	Don Mattingly	1.50
4	Mike Piazza	2.00
5	Ken Griffey Jr.	3.00
6	Greg Maddux	2.00
7	Barry Bonds	.75
8	Cal Ripken Jr.	2.50
9	Jose Canseco	.30
10	Paul Molitor	.40
11	Kenny Lofton	.75
12	Will Clark	.30
13	Tim Salmon	.30
14	Joe Carter	.25
15	Albert Belle	.75
16	Roger Clemens	.75
17	Roberto Alomar	.60
18	Alex Rodriguez	3.00
19	Raul Mondesi	.40
20	Deion Sanders	.30
21	Juan Gonzalez	1.50
22	Kirby Puckett	1.00
23	Fred McGriff	.30
24	Matt Williams	.30
25	Tony Gwynn	.75
26	Cliff Floyd	.10
27	Travis Fryman	.10
28	Shawn Green	.15
29	Mike Mussina	.35
30	Bob Hamelin	.10
31	Dave Justice	.20
32	Manny Ramirez	.75
33	David Cone	.10
34	Marquis Grissom	.12
35	Moises Alou	.12
36	Carlos Baerga	.15
37	Barry Larkin	.25
38	Robin Ventura	.15
39	Mo Vaughn	.75
40	Jeffrey Hammonds	.15
41	Ozzie Smith	.35
42	Andres Galarraga	.15
43	Carlos Delgado	.15
44	Lenny Dykstra	.12
45	Cecil Fielder	.15
46	Wade Boggs	.35
47	Gregg Jefferies	.12
48	Randy Johnson	.30
49	Rafael Palmeiro	.20
50	Craig Biggio	.10
51	Steve Avery	.10
52	Ricky Bottalico	.10
53	Chris Gomez	.10
54	Carlos Garcia	.10
55	Brian Anderson	.10
56	Wilson Alvarez	.10
57	Roberto Kelly	.10
58	Larry Walker	.25
59	Dean Palmer	.10
60	Rick Aguilera	.10
61	Javy Lopez	.20
62	Shawon Dunston	.15
63	William Van Landingham	.10
64	Jeff Kent	.10
65	David McCarty	.10
66	Armando Benitez	.10
67	Brett Butler	.12
68	Bernard Gilkey	.15
69	Joey Hamilton	.15
70	Chad Curtis	.10
71	Dante Bichette	.25
72	Chuck Carr	.10
73	Pedro Martinez	.10
74	Ramon Martinez	.12
75	Rondell White	.20
76	Alex Fernandez	.10
77	Dennis Martinez	.12

78	Sammy Sosa	1.50
79	Bernie Williams	.40
80	Lou Whitaker	.10
81	Kurt Abbott	.10
82	Tino Martinez	.15
83	Willie Greene	.10
84	Garret Anderson	.15
85	Jose Rijo	.10
86	Jeff Montgomery	.10
87	Mark Langston	.10
88	Reggie Sanders	.15
89	Rusty Greer	.10
90	Delino DeShields	.10
91	Jason Bere	.10
92	Lee Smith	.12
93	Devon White	.10
94	John Wetteland	.10
95	Luis Gonzalez	.10
96	Greg Vaughn	.10
97	Lance Johnson	.10
98	Alan Trammell	.12
99	Bret Saberhagen	.10
100	Jack McDowell	.12
101	Trevor Hoffman	.10
102	Dave Nilsson	.10
103	Bryan Harvey	.10
104	Chuck Knoblauch	.20
105	Bobby Bonilla	.15
106	Hal Morris	.10
107	Mark Whiten	.10
108	Phil Plantier	.10
109	Ryan Klesko	.60
110	Greg Gagne	.10
111	Ruben Sierra	.10
112	J.R. Phillips	.10
113	Terry Steinbach	.10
114	Jay Buhner	.15
115	Ken Caminiti	.25
116	Gary DiSarcina	.10
117	Ivan Rodriguez	.50
118	Bip Roberts	.10
119	Jay Bell	.10
120	Ken Hill	.10
121	Mike Greenwell	.10
122	Rick Wilkins	.10
123	Rickey Henderson	.20
124	Dave Hollins	.10
125	Terry Pendleton	.10
126	Rich Becker	.10
127	Billy Ashley	.10
128	Derek Bell	.12
129	Dennis Eckersley	.12
130	Andujar Cedeno	.10
131	John Jaha	.10
132	Chuck Finley	.10
133	Steve Finley	.10
134	Danny Tartabull	.10
135	Jeff Conine	.10
136	Jon Lieber	.10
137	Jim Abbott	.12
138	Steve Traschel	.10
139	Bret Boone	.10
140	Charles Johnson	.15
141	Mark McGwire	4.00
142	Eddie Murray	.40
143	Doug Drabek	.10
144	Steve Cooke	.10
145	Kevin Seitzer	.10
146	Rod Beck	.10
147	Eric Karros	.15
148	Tim Raines	.12
149	Joe Girardi	.10
150	Aaron Sele	.10
151	Robby Thompson	.10
152	Chan Ho Park	.15
153	Ellis Burks	.15
154	Brian McRae	.10
155	Jimmy Key	.10
156	Rico Brogna	.10
157	Ozzie Guillen	.10
158	Chili Davis	.10
159	Darren Daulton	.10
160	Chipper Jones	2.00
161	Walt Weiss	.10
162	Paul O'Neill	.12
163	Al Martin	.10
164	John Valentin	.10
165	Tim Wallach	.10
166	Scott Erickson	.10
167	Ryan Thompson	.10
168	Todd Zeile	.10
169	Scott Cooper	.10
170	Matt Mieske	.10
171	Allen Watson	.10
172	Brian Hunter	.10
173	Kevin Stocker	.10

174	Cal Eldred	.10
175	Tony Phillips	.10
176	Ben McDonald	.10
177	Mark Grace	.20
178	Midre Cummings	.10
179	Orlando Merced	.10
180	Jeff King	.10
181	Gary Sheffield	.40
182	Tom Glavine	.20
183	Edgar Martinez	.15
184	Steve Karsay	.10
185	Pat Listach	.10
186	Wil Cordero	.10
187	Brady Anderson	.15
188	Bobby Jones	.10
189	Andy Benes	.10
190	Ray Lankford	.15
191	John Doherty	.10
192	Wally Joyner	.12
193	Jim Thome	.40
194	Royce Clayton	.10
195	John Olerud	.15
196	Steve Buechele	.10
197	Harold Baines	.10
198	Geronimo Berroa	.10
199	Checklist	.10
200	Checklist	.10

1995 Studio Gold

The chase cards in 1995 Studio are plastic versions of some of the regular cards. The round-cornered plastic format of the inserts gives them an even greater similitude to credit cards. The first 50 numbers in the regular set are reproduced in a parallel Studio Gold plastic version, found one per pack, except for those packs which have a platinum card.

		MT
Complete Set (50):		30.00
Common Player:		.25
1	Frank Thomas	3.00
2	Jeff Bagwell	1.50
3	Don Mattingly	1.50
4	Mike Piazza	2.00
5	Ken Griffey Jr.	4.00
6	Greg Maddux	3.00
7	Barry Bonds	1.00
8	Cal Ripken Jr.	3.00
9	Jose Canseco	.50
10	Paul Molitor	.75
11	Kenny Lofton	1.00
12	Will Clark	.50
13	Tim Salmon	.40
14	Joe Carter	.25
15	Albert Belle	.75
16	Roger Clemens	1.50
17	Roberto Alomar	.75
18	Alex Rodriguez	4.00
19	Raul Mondesi	.50
20	Deion Sanders	.50
21	Juan Gonzalez	2.00
22	Kirby Puckett	1.50
23	Fred McGriff	.40
24	Matt Williams	.40
25	Tony Gwynn	1.50
26	Cliff Floyd	.25
27	Travis Fryman	.25
28	Shawn Green	.25
29	Mike Mussina	.75
30	Bob Hamelin	.25
31	Dave Justice	.50
32	Manny Ramirez	.60

33	David Cone	.25
34	Marquis Grissom	.25
35	Moises Alou	.25
36	Carlos Baerga	.25
37	Barry Larkin	.35
38	Robin Ventura	.25
39	Mo Vaughn	1.00
40	Jeffrey Hammonds	.25
41	Ozzie Smith	.75
42	Andres Galarraga	.40
43	Carlos Delgado	.25
44	Lenny Dykstra	.25
45	Cecil Fielder	.25
46	Wade Boggs	.50
47	Gregg Jefferies	.25
48	Randy Johnson	.50
49	Rafael Palmeiro	.40
50	Craig Biggio	.25

1995 Studio Platinum

Found at the rate of one per 10 packs, Studio Platinum cards are silver-toned plastic versions of the first 25 cards from the regular set.

		MT
Complete Set (25):		100.00
Common Player:		1.50
1	Frank Thomas	12.00
2	Jeff Bagwell	6.00
3	Don Mattingly	5.00
4	Mike Piazza	8.00
5	Ken Griffey Jr.	15.00
6	Greg Maddux	8.00
7	Barry Bonds	4.00
8	Cal Ripken Jr.	12.00
9	Jose Canseco	2.00
10	Paul Molitor	2.50
11	Kenny Lofton	4.00
12	Will Clark	1.50
13	Tim Salmon	1.50
14	Joe Carter	1.50
15	Albert Belle	4.00
16	Roger Clemens	5.00
17	Roberto Alomar	2.00
18	Alex Rodriguez	15.00
19	Raul Mondesi	1.50
20	Deion Sanders	1.50
21	Juan Gonzalez	8.00
22	Kirby Puckett	6.00
23	Fred McGriff	1.50
24	Matt Williams	1.50
25	Tony Gwynn	8.00

1996 Studio

The 1996 Studio set is the first Donruss product to be released under the Pinnacle Brands flagship. The 150-card set has three parallel sets - Bronze Press Proofs (2,000 sets), Silver Press Proofs (found only in magazine packs, 100 sets), and Gold Press Proofs (500 sets). Three insert sets were also made - Hit Parade, Masterstrokes and Stained Glass Stars.

A player's name in *italic* type indicates a rookie card.

		MT
Complete Set (150):		20.00
Common Player:		.10
Wax Box:		45.00
1	Cal Ripken Jr.	2.50
2	Alex Gonzalez	.10
3	Roger Cedeno	.15
4	Todd Hollandsworth	.15
5	Gregg Jefferies	.10
6	Ryne Sandberg	.75
7	Eric Karros	.10
8	Jeff Conine	.10
9	Rafael Palmeiro	.20
10	Bip Roberts	.10
11	Roger Clemens	1.00
12	Tom Glavine	.20
13	Jason Giambi	.15
14	Rey Ordonez	.40
15	Chan Ho Park	.10
16	Vinny Castilla	.10
17	Butch Huskey	.10
18	Greg Maddux	2.00
19	Bernard Gilkey	.10
20	Marquis Grissom	.10
21	Chuck Knoblauch	.20
22	Ozzie Smith	.50
23	Garret Anderson	.10
24	J.T. Snow	.10
25	John Valentin	.10
26	Barry Larkin	.25
27	Bobby Bonilla	.15
28	Todd Zeile	.10
29	Roberto Alomar	.65
30	Ramon Martinez	.10
31	Jeff King	.10
32	Dennis Eckersley	.10
33	Derek Jeter	1.50
34	Edgar Martinez	.10
35	Geronimo Berroa	.10
36	Hal Morris	.10
37	Troy Percival	.10
38	Jason Isringhausen	.20
39	Greg Vaughn	.10
40	Robin Ventura	.10
41	Craig Biggio	.10
42	Will Clark	.30
43	Sammy Sosa	1.50
44	Bernie Williams	.50
45	Kenny Lofton	.65
46	Wade Boggs	.20
47	Javy Lopez	.15
48	Reggie Sanders	.10
49	Jeff Bagwell	1.25
50	Fred McGriff	.35
51	Charles Johnson	.10
52	Darren Daulton	.10
53	Jose Canseco	.30
54	Cecil Fielder	.20
55	Raul Mondesi	.30
56	Tim Salmon	.25
57	Carlos Delgado	.10
58	David Cone	.15
59	Tim Raines	.10
60	Lyle Mouton	.10
61	Wally Joyner	.10
62	Bret Boone	.10
63	Hideo Nomo	.60
64	Gary Sheffield	.40
65	Alex Rodriguez	3.00
66	Russ Davis	.10
67	Checklist	.10
68	Marty Cordova	.10

69	Ruben Sierra	.10
70	Jose Mesa	.10
71	Matt Williams	.30
72	Chipper Jones	2.00
73	Randy Johnson	.40
74	Kirby Puckett	1.00
75	Jim Edmonds	.10
76	Barry Bonds	.75
77	David Segui	.10
78	Larry Walker	.30
79	Jason Kendall	.10
80	Mike Piazza	2.00
81	Brian Hunter	.10
82	Julio Franco	.10
83	Jay Bell	.10
84	Kevin Seitzer	.10
85	John Smoltz	.20
86	Joe Carter	.20
87	Ray Durham	.10
88	Carlos Baerga	.15
89	Ron Gant	.15
90	Orlando Merced	.10
91	Lee Smith	.10
92	Pedro Martinez	.10
93	Frank Thomas	2.50
94	Al Martin	.10
95	Chad Curtis	.10
96	Eddie Murray	.40
97	Rusty Greer	.10
98	Jay Buhner	.20
99	Rico Brogna	.10
100	Todd Hundley	.20
101	Moises Alou	.10
102	Chili Davis	.10
103	Ismael Valdes	.10
104	Mo Vaughn	.60
105	Juan Gonzalez	1.25
106	Mark Grudzielanek	.10
107	Derek Bell	.10
108	Shawn Green	.10
109	David Justice	.20
110	Paul O'Neill	.10
111	Kevin Appier	.10
112	Ray Lankford	.10
113	Travis Fryman	.10
114	Manny Ramirez	.65
115	Brooks Kieschnick	.10
116	Ken Griffey Jr.	3.00
117	Jeffrey Hammonds	.10
118	Mark McGwire	4.00
119	Denny Neagle	.10
120	Quilvio Veras	.10
121	Alan Benes	.20
122	Rondell White	.10
123	*Osvaldo Fernandez*	.20
124	Andres Galarraga	.20
125	Johnny Damon	.20
126	Lenny Dykstra	.10
127	Jason Schmidt	.10
128	Mike Mussina	.50
129	Ken Caminiti	.25
130	Michael Tucker	.10
131	LaTroy Hawkins	.10
132	Checklist	.10
133	Delino DeShields	.10
134	Dave Nilsson	.10
135	Jack McDowell	.15
136	Joey Hamilton	.10
137	Dante Bichette	.20
138	Paul Molitor	.20
139	Ivan Rodriguez	.50
140	Mark Grace	.20
141	Paul Wilson	.25
142	Orel Hershiser	.10
143	Albert Belle	.65
144	Tino Martinez	.10
145	Tony Gwynn	1.00
146	George Arias	.10
147	Brian Jordan	.15
148	Brian McRae	.10
149	Rickey Henderson	.10
150	Ryan Klesko	.50

1996 Studio Hit Parade

These die-cut inserts resemble an album with half of the record pulled out of the sleeve. Hit Parade cards, which feature top long ball hitters, were seeded one per every 36 packs. The cards were individu-ally numbered up to 7,500. Each card can also be found in a sample version which has a "XXXX/5000" serial number on back.

		MT
Complete Set (10):		100.00
Common Player:		4.00
1	Tony Gwynn	10.00
2	Ken Griffey Jr.	25.00
3	Frank Thomas	15.00
4	Jeff Bagwell	8.00
5	Kirby Puckett	6.00
6	Mike Piazza	18.00
7	Barry Bonds	6.00
8	Albert Belle	6.00
9	Tim Salmon	4.00
10	Mo Vaughn	6.00

1996 Studio Masterstrokes

Only 5,000 each of these 1996 Studio insert cards were made. The cards simulate oil painting detail on an embossed canvas-feel front. Backs are glossy and individually serial numbered. They are found on average of once per 70 packs. Sample versions of each card over-printed as such on the back and numbered "PROMO/5000" are also known.

		MT
Complete Set (8):		100.00
Common Player:		5.00
1	Tony Gwynn	9.00
2	Mike Piazza	12.50
3	Jeff Bagwell	8.00
4	Manny Ramirez	6.00
5	Cal Ripken Jr.	20.00
6	Frank Thomas	15.00
7	Ken Griffey Jr.	25.00
8	Greg Maddux	12.50

1996 Studio Press Proofs

The basic 150-card 1996 Stu-dio set was also produced in three parallel press proof versions. Each is basically identical to the regular-issue cards except for appropriately colored foil highlights on front and a notation of edition size in the circle around the portrait photo on back. Bronze press proofs were issued in an edition of 2,000 each and were inserted at an average rate of one per six packs. Gold press proofs were an edition of 500 with an aver-age insertion rate of one per 24 packs. The silver press proofs were inserted only into magazine packs and limited to just 150 cards of each.

	MT
Complete Set, Bronze (150):	400.00
Common Player, Bronze:	.50
Bronze Rookies, Stars: 4X-10X	
Complete Set, Gold (150):	2000.00
Common Player, Gold:	3.00
Gold Rookies, Stars: 15X-50X	
Common Player, Silver:	10.00
Silver Rookies, Stars: 40X-80X	
(See 1996 Studio for checklist, base card values)	

Modern cards have little collector value in conditions lower than Mint. Figure NM cards at 75% of values shown; EX cards at 40%.

Values shown reflect the market as of January, 1999. On-field performances of current players in the 1999 baseball season are not factored in.

1996 Studio Stained Glass Stars

Twelve superstars are featured on these clear, die-cut plastic cards which resemble stained glass windows. These 1996 Studio inserts were seeded one per every 30 packs.

		MT
Complete Set (12):		90.00
Common Player:		4.00
1	Cal Ripken Jr.	12.50
2	Ken Griffey Jr.	15.00
3	Frank Thomas	12.00
4	Greg Maddux	10.00
5	Chipper Jones	10.00
6	Mike Piazza	10.00
7	Albert Belle	4.00
8	Jeff Bagwell	9.00
9	Hideo Nomo	4.00
10	Barry Bonds	4.00
11	Manny Ramirez	6.00
12	Kenny Lofton	4.00

1997 Studio

Innovations in both product and packaging marked the seventh annual issue of Donruss' Studio brand. As in the past, the 165 cards in the base set rely on high-quality front photos to bring out the players' personalities. For '97, the photos are set against a background of variously shaded gray horizontal stripes. Backs have a second player photo, often an action shot, along with a short career summary.

The "pack" for '97 Studio is something totally new to the hobby. An 8-1/2" x 12" cardboard envelope, complete with a zip strip opener in the style of an express-mail envelope, contains a cello pack of five standard-size cards plus either an 8" x 10" Studio Portrait card or an 8" x 10" version of the Master Strokes insert. Suggested retail price at issue was $2.49 per pack. Regular-size Master Strokes cards are one of several insert series which includes silver and gold press proofs and die-cut plastic Hard Hats.

		MT
Complete Set (165):		30.00
Common Player:		.10
Silver Press Proof Stars: 8x to 15x		
Silver Yng Stars & RCs: 5x to 10x		
Gold Press Proof Stars: 25x to 40x		
Gold Yng Stars & RCs: 15x to 30x		
Wax Box:		45.00
1	Frank Thomas	2.50
2	Gary Sheffield	.30
3	Jason Isringhausen	.10
4	Ron Gant	.10
5	Andy Pettitte	.75
6	Todd Hollandsworth	.10
7	Troy Percival	.10
8	Mark McGwire	4.00
9	Barry Larkin	.20
10	Ken Caminiti	.20
11	Paul Molitor	.40
12	Travis Fryman	.10
13	Kevin Brown	.10
14	Robin Ventura	.10
15	Andres Galarraga	.20
16	Ken Griffey Jr.	3.00
17	Roger Clemens	1.00
18	Alan Benes	.20
19	David Justice	.25
20	Damon Buford	.10
21	Mike Piazza	2.00
22	Ray Durham	.10
23	Billy Wagner	.10
24	Dean Palmer	.10
25	David Cone	.20
26	Ruben Sierra	.10
27	Henry Rodriguez	.10
28	Ray Lankford	.10
29	Jamey Wright	.10
30	Brady Anderson	.15
31	Tino Martinez	.20
32	Manny Ramirez	.75
33	Jeff Conine	.10
34	Dante Bichette	.20
35	Jose Canseco	.25
36	Mo Vaughn	.75
37	Sammy Sosa	1.50
38	Mark Grudzielanek	.10
39	Mike Mussina	.60
40	Bill Pulsipher	.10
41	Ryne Sandberg	.75
42	Rickey Henderson	.10
43	Alex Rodriguez	3.00
44	Eddie Murray	.40
45	Ernie Young	.10
46	Joey Hamilton	.10
47	Wade Boggs	.20
48	Rusty Greer	.10
49	Carlos Delgado	.10
50	Ellis Burks	.10
51	Cal Ripken Jr.	2.50
52	Alex Fernandez	.10
53	Wally Joyner	.10
54	James Baldwin	.10
55	Juan Gonzalez	1.25
56	John Smoltz	.20
57	Omar Vizquel	.10
58	Shane Reynolds	.10
59	Barry Bonds	.75
60	Jason Kendall	.10
61	Marty Cordova	.10
62	Charles Johnson	.10
63	John Jaha	.10
64	Chan Ho Park	.10
65	Jermaine Allensworth	.10
66	Mark Grace	.20
67	Tim Salmon	.20
68	Edgar Martinez	.10
69	Marquis Grissom	.10
70	Craig Biggio	.20
71	Bobby Higginson	.10
72	Kevin Seitzer	.10
73	Hideo Nomo	.60
74	Dennis Eckersley	.10
75	Bobby Bonilla	.10
76	Dwight Gooden	.10
77	Jeff Cirillo	.10
78	Brian McRae	.10
79	Chipper Jones	2.00
80	Jeff Fassero	.10
81	Fred McGriff	.25
82	Garret Anderson	.10
83	Eric Karros	.10
84	Derek Bell	.10
85	Kenny Lofton	.75
86	John Mabry	.10
87	Pat Hentgen	.10
88	Greg Maddux	2.00
89	Jason Giambi	.10
90	Al Martin	.10
91	Derek Jeter	2.00
92	Rey Ordonez	.10
93	Will Clark	.25
94	Kevin Appier	.10
95	Roberto Alomar	.50
96	Joe Carter	.15
97	Bernie Williams	.50
98	Albert Belle	.75
99	Greg Vaughn	.10
100	Tony Clark	.50
101	Matt Williams	.30
102	Jeff Bagwell	1.25
103	Reggie Sanders	.10
104	Mariano Rivera	.20
105	Larry Walker	.35
106	Shawn Green	.10
107	Alex Ochoa	.10
108	Ivan Rodriguez	.60
109	Eric Young	.10
110	Javier Lopez	.20
111	Brian Hunter	.10
112	Raul Mondesi	.25
113	Randy Johnson	.60
114	Tony Phillips	.10
115	Carlos Garcia	.10
116	Moises Alou	.10
117	Paul O'Neill	.10
118	Jim Thome	.40
119	Jermaine Dye	.10
120	Wilson Alvarez	.10
121	Rondell White	.10
122	Michael Tucker	.10
123	Mike Lansing	.10
124	Tony Gwynn	1.25
125	Ryan Klesko	.50
126	Jim Edmonds	.10
127	Chuck Knoblauch	.20
128	Rafael Palmeiro	.20
129	Jay Buhner	.20
130	Tom Glavine	.20
131	Julio Franco	.10
132	Cecil Fielder	.20
133	Paul Wilson	.10
134	Deion Sanders	.25
135	Alex Gonzalez	.10
136	Charles Nagy	.10
137	Andy Ashby	.10
138	Edgar Renteria	.10
139	Pedro Martinez	.20
140	Brian Jordan	.10
141	Todd Hundley	.20
142	Marc Newfield	.10
143	Darryl Strawberry	.10
144	Dan Wilson	.10
145	Brian Giles	.10
146	Bartolo Colon	.10
147	Shannon Stewart	.10
148	Scott Spiezio	.10
149	Andruw Jones	1.50
150	Karim Garcia	.10
151	Vladimir Guerrero	1.00
152	George Arias	.10
153	Brooks Kieschnick	.10
154	Todd Walker	.50
155	Scott Rolen	1.50
156	Todd Greene	.10
157	Dmitri Young	.10
158	Ruben Rivera	.10
159	Trey Beamon	.10
160	Nomar Garciaparra	2.00
161	Bob Abreu	.15
162	Darin Erstad	1.25
163	Ken Griffey Jr. CL	1.00
164	Frank Thomas CL	1.00
165	Alex Rodriguez CL	1.00

1997 Studio Hard Hats

Die-cut plastic is used to represent a player's batting helmet in this set of '97 Studio inserts. A player action photo appears in the foreground with his name and other graphic elements in silver foil. Backs feature a small portrait photo, short career summary and a serial number from within the edition of 5,000 of each card.

		MT
Complete Set (24):		160.00
Common Player:		2.00
1	Ivan Rodriguez	6.00
2	Albert Belle	6.00
3	Ken Griffey Jr.	25.00
4	Chuck Knoblauch	4.00
5	Frank Thomas	15.00
6	Cal Ripken Jr.	20.00
7	Todd Walker	4.00
8	Alex Rodriguez	15.00
9	Jim Thome	4.00
10	Mike Piazza	15.00
11	Barry Larkin	4.00
12	Chipper Jones	15.00
13	Derek Jeter	15.00
14	Jermaine Dye	2.00
15	Jason Giambi	2.00
16	Tim Salmon	4.00
17	Brady Anderson	2.00
18	Rondell White	2.00
19	Bernie Williams	4.00
20	Juan Gonzalez	12.00
21	Karim Garcia	2.00
22	Scott Rolen	8.00
23	Darin Erstad	6.00
24	Brian Jordan	2.00

1997 Studio Master Strokes

The look and feel of a painting on canvas is the effect presented by '97 Studio's Master Strokes inserts. Card fronts feature unique player action art and are highlight-ed by gold-foil graphics. Each card has a facsimile autograph on front. UV-coated backs are team-color coordinated and have a few sentences about the player. Gold-foil serial numbering identifies the card from an edition of 2,000 of each player.

		MT
Complete Set (24):		600.00
Common Player:		10.00
1	Derek Jeter	30.00
2	Jeff Bagwell	20.00
3	Ken Griffey Jr.	60.00
4	Barry Bonds	15.00
5	Frank Thomas	50.00
6	Andy Pettitte	12.00
7	Mo Vaughn	15.00
8	Alex Rodriguez	40.00
9	Andruw Jones	15.00
10	Kenny Lofton	15.00
11	Cal Ripken Jr.	50.00
12	Greg Maddux	40.00
13	Manny Ramirez	15.00
14	Mike Piazza	40.00
14p	Mike Piazza (promo)	10.00
15	Vladimir Guerrero	15.00
16	Albert Belle	15.00
17	Chipper Jones	40.00
18	Hideo Nomo	12.00
19	Sammy Sosa	40.00
20	Tony Gwynn	25.00
21	Gary Sheffield	10.00
22	Mark McGwire	70.00
23	Juan Gonzalez	30.00
24	Paul Molitor	12.00

1997 Studio Master Strokes 8x10

The look and feel of a painting on canvas is the effect presented by the 8" x 10" version of '97 Studio's Master Strokes inserts. Card fronts feature unique player action art and are highlighted by gold-foil graphics. Each card has a facsimile autograph on front. UV-coated backs are team-color coordinated and have a few sentences about the player. Gold-foil serial numbering identifies the card from an edition of 5,000 of each player - making the super-size version more than twice as common as the 2-1/2" x 3-1/2" version.

		MT
Complete Set (24):		220.00
Common Player:		4.00
1	Derek Jeter	15.00
2	Jeff Bagwell	10.00
3	Ken Griffey Jr.	25.00
4	Barry Bonds	6.00
5	Frank Thomas	20.00
6	Andy Pettitte	6.00
7	Mo Vaughn	6.00
8	Alex Rodriguez	20.00
9	Andruw Jones	12.00
10	Kenny Lofton	6.00
11	Cal Ripken Jr.	20.00
12	Greg Maddux	15.00
13	Manny Ramirez	6.00
14	Mike Piazza	15.00
15	Vladimir Guerrero	8.00
16	Albert Belle	6.00
17	Chipper Jones	15.00
18	Hideo Nomo	6.00
19	Sammy Sosa	15.00
20	Tony Gwynn	10.00
21	Gary Sheffield	4.00
22	Mark McGwire	25.00
23	Juan Gonzalez	10.00
24	Paul Molitor	6.00

A player's name in *italic* type indicates a rookie card.

1997 Studio Portraits

Perhaps the most innovative feature of '97 Studio is the 8" x 10" Portrait cards which come one per pack (except when a pack contains a Master Strokes 8x10). Virtually identical to the player's regular-size Studio card, the jumbo version has the word "PORTRAIT" in black beneath the team name on front. Backs have different card numbers than the same player's card in the regular set. The Portrait cards are produced with a special UV coating on front to facilitate autographing. Pre-autographed cards of three youngsters in the series were included as random pack inserts.

		MT
Complete Set (24):		40.00
Common Player:		.50
1	Ken Griffey Jr.	5.00
1s	Frank Thomas (overprinted "SAMPLE")	.50
2	Frank Thomas	4.00
3	Alex Rodriguez	4.00
4	Andruw Jones	2.50
5	Cal Ripken Jr.	4.00
6	Greg Maddux	3.00
7	Mike Piazza	3.00
8	Chipper Jones	3.00
9	Albert Belle	1.25
10	Derek Jeter	3.00
11	Juan Gonzalez	2.00
12	Todd Walker	1.00
12a	Todd Walker (autographed edition of 1,250)	40.00
13	Mark McGwire	6.00
14	Barry Bonds	1.00
15	Jeff Bagwell	2.00
16	Manny Ramirez	1.00
17	Kenny Lofton	1.00
18	Mo Vaughn	1.00
19	Hideo Nomo	.75
20	Tony Gwynn	2.00
21	Vladimir Guerrero	1.50
21a	Vladimir Guerrero (autographed edition of 500)	100.00
22	Gary Sheffield	.50
23	Ryne Sandberg	1.00
24	Scott Rolen	1.50
24a	Scott Rolen (autographed edition of 1,000)	75.00

1997 Studio Press Proofs

Each of the 165 cards in the base set of '97 Studio was also produced in a pair of Press Proof versions as random pack inserts. Fronts of the Press Proofs have either silver or gold holographic foil replacing the silver foil graphics found on regular cards, as well as foil strips down each side. Backs are identical to the regular issue. The silver Press Proofs were issued in an edition of 1,500 of each player; the golds are limited to 500 of each.

	MT
Complete Set, Silver (165):	350.00
Complete Set, Gold (165):	850.00
Common Player, Silver:	1.50
Common Player, Gold:	4.00
(Silver stars valued at 8-15X regular cards; gold at 15-40X.)	

1998 Studio

The Donruss Studio base set consists of 220 regular-sized cards and 36 8-x-10 portraits. The base cards feature a posed photo with an action shot in the background, surrounded by a white border. Silver Studio Proofs (numbered to 1,000) and Gold Studio Proofs (300) parallel the regular-size base set. Inserts included Freeze Frame, Hit Parade and Masterstrokes.

		MT
Complete Set (220):		35.00
Common Player:		.15
Unlisted Stars: .30 to .60		
Silver Proof Stars: 8x to 12x		
Silver Yng Stars & RCs: 5x to 10x		
Production 1,000 sets		
Wax Box:		50.00
1	Tony Clark	.40
2	Jose Cruz Jr.	.75
3	Ivan Rodriguez	.75
4	Mo Vaughn	.75
5	Kenny Lofton	.75
6	Will Clark	.25
7	Barry Larkin	.25
8	Jay Bell	.15
9	Kevin Young	.15
10	Francisco Cordova	.15
11	Justin Thompson	.15
12	Paul Molitor	.50
13	Jeff Bagwell	1.25
14	Jose Canseco	.30
15	Scott Rolen	1.00
16	Wilton Guerrero	.15
17	Shannon Stewart	.15
18	Hideki Irabu	.50
19	Michael Tucker	.15
20	Joe Carter	.15
21	Gabe Alvarez	.15
22	Ricky Ledee	.40
23	Karim Garcia	.15
24	Eli Marrero	.15
25	Scott Elarton	.15
26	Mario Valdez	.15
27	Ben Grieve	1.00
28	Paul Konerko	.40
29	*Esteban Yan*	.25
30	Esteban Loaiza	.15
31	Delino DeShields	.15
32	Bernie Williams	.50
33	Joe Randa	.15
34	Randy Johnson	.50
35	Brett Tomko	.15
36	*Todd Erdos*	.25
37	Bobby Higginson	.15
38	Jason Kendall	.15
39	Ray Lankford	.15
40	Mark Grace	.30
41	Andy Pettitte	.50
42	Alex Rodriguez	2.00
43	Hideo Nomo	.50
44	Sammy Sosa	2.00
45	J.T. Snow	.15
46	Jason Varitek	.25
47	Vinny Castilla	.15
48	Neifi Perez	.15
49	Todd Walker	.15
50	Mike Cameron	.15
51	Jeffrey Hammonds	.15
52	Deivi Cruz	.15
53	Brian Hunter	.15
54	Al Martin	.15
55	Ron Coomer	.15
56	Chan Ho Park	.15
57	Pedro Martinez	.40
58	Darin Erstad	.75
59	Albert Belle	.75
60	Nomar Garciaparra	2.00
61	Tony Gwynn	1.50
62	Mike Piazza	2.00
63	Todd Helton	.75
64	David Ortiz	.40
65	Todd Dunwoody	.15
66	Orlando Cabrera	.15
67	Ken Cloude	.15
68	Andy Benes	.25
69	Mariano Rivera	.25
70	Cecil Fielder	.25
71	Brian Jordan	.15
72	Darryl Kile	.15
73	Reggie Jefferson	.15
74	Shawn Estes	.15
75	Bobby Bonilla	.15
76	Denny Neagle	.25
77	Robin Ventura	.25
78	Omar Vizquel	.15
79	Craig Biggio	.30
80	Moises Alou	.25
81	Garret Anderson	.15
82	Eric Karros	.25
83	Dante Bichette	.30
84	Charles Johnson	.15
85	Rusty Greer	.15
86	Travis Fryman	.25
87	Fernando Tatis	.25
88	Wilson Alvarez	.15
89	Carl Pavano	.15
90	Brian Rose	.15
91	Geoff Jenkins	.15
92	*Magglio Ordonez*	.75
93	David Segui	.15
94	David Cone	.25
95	John Smoltz	.15
96	Jim Thome	.50
97	Gary Sheffield	.40
98	Barry Bonds	.75
99	Andres Galarraga	.40
100	Brad Fullmer	.40
101	Bobby Estalella	.15
102	Enrique Wilson	.15
103	*Frank Catalanotto*	.20
104	*Mike Lowell*	.40
105	Kevin Orie	.15
106	Matt Morris	.15
107	Pokey Reese	.15
108	Shawn Green	.15
109	Tony Womack	.15
110	Ken Caminiti	.25
111	Roberto Alomar	.50
112	Ken Griffey Jr.	3.00
113	Cal Ripken Jr.	2.50
114	Lou Collier	.15
115	Larry Walker	.40
116	Fred McGriff	.30
117	Jim Edmonds	.25
118	Edgar Martinez	.15
119	Matt Williams	.40
120	Ismael Valdes	.15
121	Bartolo Colon	.15
122	Jeff Cirillo	.15
123	*Steve Woodard*	.25
124	*Kevin Millwood*	1.00
125	Derrick Gibson	.15
126	Jacob Cruz	.15
127	Russell Branyan	.15
128	Sean Casey	.40
129	Derrek Lee	.15
130	Paul O'Neill	.25
131	Brad Radke	.15
132	Kevin Appier	.15
133	John Olerud	.25
134	Alan Benes	.25
135	Todd Greene	.15
136	*Carlos Mendoza*	.25
137	Wade Boggs	.30
138	Jose Guillen	.25
139	Tino Martinez	.30
140	Aaron Boone	.15
141	Abraham Nunez	.15
142	Preston Wilson	.15
143	Randall Simon	.20
144	Dennis Reyes	.15
145	Mark Kotsay	.30
146	Richard Hidalgo	.15
147	Travis Lee	2.00
148	*Hanley Frias*	.15
149	Ruben Rivera	.15
150	Rafael Medina	.15
151	Dave Nilsson	.15
152	Curt Schilling	.25
153	Brady Anderson	.15
154	Carlos Delgado	.15
155	Jason Giambi	.15
156	Pat Hentgen	.15
157	Tom Glavine	.25
158	Ryan Klesko	.30
159	Chipper Jones	2.00
160	Juan Gonzalez	1.50
161	Mark McGwire	4.00
162	Vladimir Guerrero	1.00
163	Derek Jeter	1.50
164	Manny Ramirez	.75
165	Mike Mussina	.60
166	Rafael Palmeiro	.30
167	Henry Rodriguez	.15
168	Jeff Suppan	.15
169	Eric Milton	.15
170	Scott Spiezio	.15
171	Wilson Delgado	.15
172	Bubba Trammell	.15
173	Ellis Burks	.15
174	Jason Dickson	.15
175	Butch Huskey	.15
176	Edgardo Alfonzo	.15
177	Eric Young	.15
178	Marquis Grissom	.15
179	Lance Johnson	.15
180	Kevin Brown	.25
181	Sandy Alomar Jr.	.25
182	Todd Hundley	.15
183	Rondell White	.25
184	Javier Lopez	.25
185	Damian Jackson	.15
186	Raul Mondesi	.40
187	Rickey Henderson	.25
188	David Justice	.40
189	Jay Buhner	.30
190	Jaret Wright	1.00
191	Miguel Tejada	.40
192	Ron Wright	.15
193	Livan Hernandez	.15
194	A.J. Hinch	.50
195	Richie Sexson	.15
196	Bob Abreu	.15
197	Luis Castillo	.15
198	Michael Coleman	.15
199	Greg Maddux	2.00
200	Frank Thomas	2.50
201	Andruw Jones	.75
202	Roger Clemens	1.25
203	Tim Salmon	.40
204	Chuck Knoblauch	.40
205	Wes Helms	.15
206	Juan Encarnacion	.15
207	Russ Davis	.15
208	John Valentin	.15
209	Tony Saunders	.15
210	Mike Sweeney	.15
211	Steve Finley	.15
212	*David Dellucci*	.50
213	Edgar Renteria	.15
214	Jeremi Gonzalez	.15
215	Checklist(Jeff Bagwell)	.60
216	Checklist(Mike Piazza)	1.00
217	Checklist(Greg Maddux)	1.00
218	Checklist(Cal Ripken Jr.)	1.25
219	Checklist(Frank Thomas)	1.25
220	Checklist(Ken Griffey Jr.)	1.50

1998 Studio
Freeze Frame

Freeze Frame is a 30-card insert sequentially numbered to 5,000. The cards are designed to look like a piece of film with a color action photo. The first 500 of each card are die-cut.

Values shown reflect the market as of January, 1999. On-field performances of current players in the 1999 baseball season are not factored in.

Gold Proofs is a parallel of the 220-card base set. The cards feature gold holo-foil treatments and are sequentially numbered to 300.

		MT
Common Player:		5.00
Semistars:		25.00
Production 300 sets		
1	Tony Clark	30.00
2	Jose Cruz Jr.	40.00
3	Ivan Rodriguez	50.00
4	Mo Vaughn	50.00
5	Kenny Lofton	50.00
6	Will Clark	25.00
7	Barry Larkin	25.00
8	Jay Bell	5.00
9	Kevin Young	5.00
10	Francisco Cordova	5.00
11	Justin Thompson	5.00
12	Paul Molitor	40.00
13	Jeff Bagwell	75.00
14	Jose Canseco	25.00
15	Scott Rolen	60.00
16	Wilton Guerrero	5.00
17	Shannon Stewart	5.00
18	Hideki Irabu	25.00
19	Michael Tucker	5.00
20	Joe Carter	10.00
21	Gabe Alvarez	5.00
22	Ricky Ledee	15.00
23	Karim Garcia	5.00
24	Eli Marrero	5.00
25	Scott Elarton	5.00
26	Mario Valdez	5.00
27	Ben Grieve	60.00
28	Paul Konerko	15.00
29	*Esteban Yan*	5.00
30	Esteban Loaiza	5.00
31	Delino DeShields	5.00
32	Bernie Williams	40.00
33	Joe Randa	5.00
34	Randy Johnson	35.00
35	Brett Tomko	5.00
36	Todd Erdos	5.00
37	Bobby Higginson	5.00
38	Jason Kendall	5.00
39	Ray Lankford	5.00
40	Mark Grace	25.00
41	Andy Pettitte	35.00
42	Alex Rodriguez	120.00
43	Hideo Nomo	40.00
44	Sammy Sosa	75.00
45	J.T. Snow	5.00
46	Jason Varitek	5.00
47	Vinny Castilla	15.00
48	Neifi Perez	5.00
49	Todd Walker	5.00
50	Mike Cameron	5.00
51	Jeffrey Hammonds	5.00
52	Deivi Cruz	5.00
53	Brian Hunter	5.00
54	Al Martin	5.00
55	Ron Coomer	5.00
56	Chan Ho Park	15.00
57	Pedro Martinez	40.00
58	Darin Erstad	50.00
59	Albert Belle	50.00
60	Nomar Garciaparra	120.00
61	Tony Gwynn	100.00
62	Mike Piazza	120.00
63	Todd Helton	30.00
64	David Ortiz	15.00
65	Todd Dunwoody	5.00
66	Orlando Cabrera	5.00
67	Ken Cloude	5.00
68	Andy Benes	15.00
69	Mariano Rivera	15.00
70	Cecil Fielder	15.00
71	Brian Jordan	15.00
72	Darryl Kile	5.00
73	Reggie Jefferson	5.00
74	Shawn Estes	5.00
75	Bobby Bonilla	15.00
76	Denny Neagle	15.00
77	Robin Ventura	15.00
78	Omar Vizquel	5.00
79	Craig Biggio	20.00
80	Moises Alou	15.00
81	Garret Anderson	5.00
82	Eric Karros	15.00
83	Dante Bichette	25.00
84	Charles Johnson	15.00
85	Rusty Greer	5.00
86	Travis Fryman	5.00

		MT
Complete Set (30):		325.00
Common Player:		4.00
Production 4,500 sets		
Die-Cuts: 2x to 4x		
Production 500 sets		
1	Ken Griffey Jr.	30.00
2	Derek Jeter	15.00
3	Ben Grieve	10.00
4	Cal Ripken Jr.	25.00
5	Alex Rodriguez	20.00
6	Greg Maddux	20.00
7	David Justice	6.00
8	Mike Piazza	20.00
9	Chipper Jones	20.00
10	Randy Johnson	6.00
11	Jeff Bagwell	12.00
12	Nomar Garciaparra	20.00
13	Andruw Jones	8.00
14	Frank Thomas	25.00
15	Scott Rolen	10.00
16	Barry Bonds	8.00
17	Kenny Lofton	8.00
18	Ivan Rodriguez	8.00
19	Chuck Knoblauch	6.00
20	Jose Cruz Jr.	8.00
21	Bernie Williams	6.00
22	Tony Gwynn	15.00
23	Juan Gonzalez	15.00
24	Gary Sheffield	4.00
25	Roger Clemens	12.00
26	Travis Lee	25.00
27	Brad Fullmer	8.00
28	Tim Salmon	6.00
29	Raul Mondesi	4.00
30	Roberto Alomar	6.00

1998 Studio
Gold Proofs

87	Fernando Tatis	15.00
88	Wilson Alvarez	5.00
89	Carl Pavano	5.00
90	Brian Rose	5.00
91	Geoff Jenkins	5.00
92	Magglio Ordonez	25.00
93	David Segui	5.00
94	David Cone	15.00
95	John Smoltz	15.00
96	Jim Thome	40.00
97	Gary Sheffield	25.00
98	Barry Bonds	50.00
99	Andres Galarraga	25.00
100	Brad Fullmer	25.00
101	Bobby Estalella	5.00
102	Enrique Wilson	5.00
103	Frank Catalanotto	5.00
104	Mike Lowell	5.00
105	Kevin Orie	5.00
106	Matt Morris	5.00
107	Pokey Reese	5.00
108	Shawn Green	5.00
109	Tony Womack	5.00
110	Ken Caminiti	15.00
111	Roberto Alomar	40.00
112	Ken Griffey Jr.	200.00
113	Cal Ripken Jr.	150.00
114	Lou Collier	5.00
115	Larry Walker	30.00
116	Fred McGriff	20.00
117	Jim Edmonds	15.00
118	Edgar Martinez	5.00
119	Matt Williams	25.00
120	Ismael Valdes	5.00
121	Bartolo Colon	5.00
122	Jeff Cirillo	5.00
123	Steve Woodard	5.00
124	*Kevin Millwood*	40.00
125	Derrick Gibson	5.00
126	Jacob Cruz	5.00
127	Russell Branyan	5.00
128	Sean Casey	15.00
129	Derrek Lee	5.00
130	Paul O'Neill	15.00
131	Brad Radke	5.00
132	Kevin Appier	5.00
133	John Olerud	15.00
134	Alan Benes	15.00
135	Todd Greene	5.00
136	Carlos Mendoza	5.00
137	Wade Boggs	25.00
138	Jose Guillen	15.00
139	Tino Martinez	25.00
140	Aaron Boone	5.00
141	Abraham Nunez	5.00
142	Preston Wilson	5.00
143	Randall Simon	5.00
144	Dennis Reyes	5.00
145	Mark Kotsay	15.00
146	Richard Hidalgo	5.00
147	Travis Lee	120.00
148	Hanley Frias	5.00
149	Ruben Rivera	5.00
150	Rafael Medina	5.00
151	Dave Nilsson	5.00
152	Curt Schilling	15.00
153	Brady Anderson	5.00
154	Carlos Delgado	15.00
155	Jason Giambi	5.00
156	Pat Hentgen	5.00
157	Tom Glavine	15.00
158	Ryan Klesko	25.00
159	Chipper Jones	120.00
160	Juan Gonzalez	100.00
161	Mark McGwire	220.00
162	Vladimir Guerrero	50.00
163	Derek Jeter	100.00
164	Manny Ramirez	50.00
165	Mike Mussina	40.00
166	Rafael Palmeiro	25.00
167	Henry Rodriguez	5.00
168	Jeff Suppan	5.00
169	Eric Milton	5.00
170	Scott Spiezio	5.00
171	Wilson Delgado	5.00
172	Bubba Trammell	5.00
173	Ellis Burks	5.00
174	Jason Dickson	5.00
175	Butch Huskey	5.00
176	Edgardo Alfonzo	5.00
177	Eric Young	5.00
178	Marquis Grissom	5.00
179	Lance Johnson	5.00
180	Kevin Brown	15.00
181	Sandy Alomar Jr.	15.00
182	Todd Hundley	5.00

183	Rondell White	15.00
184	Javier Lopez	15.00
185	Damian Jackson	5.00
186	Raul Mondesi	20.00
187	Rickey Henderson	15.00
188	David Justice	25.00
189	Jay Buhner	20.00
190	Jaret Wright	50.00
191	Miguel Tejada	15.00
192	Ron Wright	5.00
193	Livan Hernandez	5.00
194	A.J. Hinch	5.00
195	Richie Sexson	5.00
196	Bob Abreu	5.00
197	Luis Castillo	5.00
198	Michael Coleman	5.00
199	Greg Maddux	120.00
200	Frank Thomas	150.00
201	Andruw Jones	50.00
202	Roger Clemens	75.00
203	Tim Salmon	25.00
204	Chuck Knoblauch	25.00
205	Wes Helms	5.00
206	Juan Encarnacion	5.00
207	Russ Davis	5.00
208	John Valentin	5.00
209	Tony Saunders	5.00
210	Mike Sweeney	5.00
211	Steve Finley	5.00
212	David Dellucci	5.00
213	Edgar Renteria	5.00
214	Jeremi Gonzalez	5.00
215	Checklist(Jeff Bagwell)	40.00
216	Checklist(Mike Piazza)	60.00
217	Checklist(Greg Maddux)	60.00
218	Checklist(Cal Ripken Jr.)	75.00
219	Checklist(Frank Thomas)	75.00
220	Checklist(Ken Griffey Jr.)	100.00

1998 Studio
Hit Parade

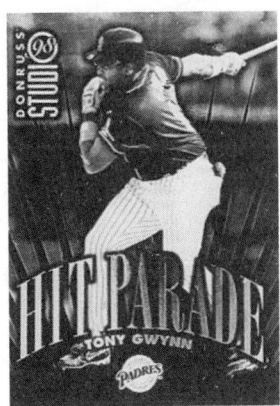

These 20 cards are printed on micro-etched foil board. This set honors baseball's top hitters and is sequentially numbered to 5,000.

		MT
Complete Set (20):		140.00
Common Player:		4.00
Production 5,000 sets		
1	Tony Gwynn	12.00
2	Larry Walker	4.00
3	Mike Piazza	15.00
4	Frank Thomas	20.00
5	Manny Ramirez	6.00
6	Ken Griffey Jr.	25.00
7	Todd Helton	6.00
8	Vladimir Guerrero	6.00
9	Albert Belle	6.00
10	Jeff Bagwell	10.00
11	Juan Gonzalez	12.00
12	Jim Thome	4.00
13	Scott Rolen	8.00
14	Tino Martinez	4.00
15	Mark McGwire	30.00
16	Barry Bonds	6.00
17	Tony Clark	4.00

18	Mo Vaughn	6.00
19	Darin Erstad	6.00
20	Paul Konerko	4.00

1998 Studio
Masterstrokes

Printed on a canvas-like material, these 20 cards are numbered to 1,000.

		MT
Complete Set (20):		700.00
Common Player:		15.00
Production 1,000 sets		
1	Travis Lee	35.00
2	Kenny Lofton	20.00
3	Mo Vaughn	20.00
4	Ivan Rodriguez	20.00
5	Roger Clemens	30.00
6	Mark McGwire	100.00
7	Hideo Nomo	15.00
8	Andruw Jones	20.00
9	Nomar Garciaparra	50.00
10	Juan Gonzalez	40.00
11	Jeff Bagwell	25.00
12	Derek Jeter	50.00
13	Tony Gwynn	50.00
14	Chipper Jones	50.00
15	Mike Piazza	50.00
16	Greg Maddux	50.00
17	Alex Rodriguez	60.00
18	Cal Ripken Jr.	60.00
19	Frank Thomas	50.00
20	Ken Griffey Jr.	80.00

1998 Studio
Sony MLB 99

Twenty Sony MLB '99 sweepstakes cards were inserted one per two Studio packs. The fronts feature a color action shot and the backs have sweepstakes rules and a MLB '99 tip.

		MT
Complete Set (20):		10.00
Common Player:		.25
1	Cal Ripken Jr.	2.00
2	Nomar Garciaparra	1.50
3	Barry Bonds	.60
4	Mike Mussina	.50
5	Pedro Martinez	.40
6	Derek Jeter	1.25
7	Andruw Jones	.60
8	Kenny Lofton	.60
9	Gary Sheffield	.25
10	Raul Mondesi	.25
11	Jeff Bagwell	.75
12	Tim Salmon	.25
13	Tom Glavine	.25
14	Ben Grieve	.75
15	Matt Williams	.25
16	Juan Gonzalez	1.25
17	Mark McGwire	3.00
18	Bernie Williams	.40
19	Andres Galarraga	.25
20	Jose Cruz Jr.	.40

1998 Studio
8x10 Portraits

One Studio 8-x-10 was included in each pack. The cards were blown-up versions of the regular-size base cards, which were inserted seven per pack. The large portraits are paralleled in the Gold Proofs set, which adds gold holofoil to the cards. Gold Proofs are numbered to 300.

		MT
Complete Set (36):		50.00
Common Player:		.50
Inserted 1:1		
1	Travis Lee	4.00
2	Todd Helton	1.25
3	Ben Grieve	1.50
4	Paul Konerko	.50
5	Jeff Bagwell	2.00
6	Derek Jeter	2.50
7	Ivan Rodriguez	1.50
8	Cal Ripken Jr.	4.00
9	Mike Piazza	3.00
10	Chipper Jones	3.00
11	Frank Thomas	4.00
12	Tony Gwynn	2.50
13	Nomar Garciaparra	3.00
14	Juan Gonzalez	2.50
15	Greg Maddux	3.00
16	Hideo Nomo	1.00
17	Scott Rolen	1.50
18	Barry Bonds	1.50
19	Ken Griffey Jr.	5.00
20	Alex Rodriguez	3.00
21	Roger Clemens	2.00
22	Mark McGwire	6.00
23	Jose Cruz Jr.	1.50
24	Andruw Jones	1.50
25	Tino Martinez	.50
26	Mo Vaughn	1.50
27	Vladimir Guerrero	1.50
28	Tony Clark	1.00
29	Andy Pettitte	1.00
30	Jaret Wright	1.50
31	Paul Molitor	1.00
32	Darin Erstad	1.50
33	Larry Walker	.50
34	Chuck Knoblauch	.50
35	Barry Larkin	.50
36	Kenny Lofton	1.50

Modern cards have little collector value in conditions lower than Mint. Figure NM cards at 75% of values shown; EX cards at 40%.

1998 Studio 8x10 Portraits Gold Proofs

This parallel of the 8-x-10 base set adds gold holo-foil treatments to the 36 cards, which are sequentially numbered to 300.

		MT
Common Player:		25.00
Unlisted Stars:		40.00
Production 300 sets		
1	Travis Lee	75.00
2	Todd Helton	40.00
3	Ben Grieve	50.00
4	Paul Konerko	25.00
5	Jeff Bagwell	60.00
6	Derek Jeter	75.00
7	Ivan Rodriguez	40.00
8	Cal Ripken Jr.	120.00
9	Mike Piazza	100.00
10	Chipper Jones	100.00
11	Frank Thomas	100.00
12	Tony Gwynn	75.00
13	Nomar Garciaparra	100.00
14	Juan Gonzalez	75.00
15	Greg Maddux	100.00
16	Hideo Nomo	30.00
17	Scott Rolen	50.00
18	Barry Bonds	40.00
19	Ken Griffey Jr.	150.00
20	Alex Rodriguez	100.00
21	Roger Clemens	60.00
22	Mark McGwire	175.00
23	Jose Cruz Jr.	40.00
24	Andruw Jones	40.00
25	Tino Martinez	25.00
26	Mo Vaughn	40.00
27	Vladimir Guerrero	40.00
28	Tony Clark	25.00
29	Andy Pettitte	25.00
30	Jaret Wright	40.00
31	Paul Molitor	40.00
32	Darin Erstad	40.00
33	Larry Walker	25.00
34	Chuck Knoblauch	25.00
35	Barry Larkin	25.00
36	Kenny Lofton	40.00

1995 Summit

A late-season release, Summit introduced the Score label to a premium brand card. Printed on extra heavy cardboard stock and UV coated on both sides the veteran player cards (#1-111) feature horizontal or vertical action photos with the player's name and team logo printed in gold-foil on front. Backs have a player portrait photo along with his 1994 stats in monthly charted form. The rookie cards subset (#112-173) have a large black "ROOKIE" on top-front while the back has a short career summary instead of stats. Other subsets include "BAT SPEED" (#174-188), honoring top hitters, and "SPECIAL DELIVERY" (#189-193), featuring top pitchers. Each are designated on front with special gold-foil logos. Seven checklists close out the regular 200-card set. The Summit issued featured a four-tiered chase card program, including a parallel "Nth Degree" set. Summit was a hobby-only issue sold in 7-card foil packs.

		MT
Complete Set (200):		25.00
Common Player:		.10
Wax Box:		40.00
1	Ken Griffey Jr.	3.00
2	Alex Fernandez	.15
3	Fred McGriff	.35
4	Ben McDonald	.10
5	Rafael Palmeiro	.15
6	Tony Gwynn	1.00
7	Jim Thome	.40
8	Ken Hill	.10
9	Barry Bonds	.75
10	Barry Larkin	.25
11	Albert Belle	.75
12	Billy Ashley	.10
13	Matt Williams	.25
14	Andy Benes	.10
15	Midre Cummings	.10
16	J.R. Phillips	.10
17	Edgar Martinez	.15
18	Manny Ramirez	.60
19	Jose Canseco	.35
20	Chili Davis	.10
21	Don Mattingly	1.00
22	Bernie Williams	.40
23	Tom Glavine	.20
24	Robin Ventura	.15
25	Jeff Conine	.10
26	Mark Grace	.20
27	Mark McGwire	4.00
28	Carlos Delgado	.20
29	Greg Colbrunn	.10
30	Greg Maddux	2.00
31	Craig Biggio	.20
32	Kirby Puckett	1.00
33	Derek Bell	.12
34	Lenny Dykstra	.10
35	Tim Salmon	.25
36	Deion Sanders	.25
37	Moises Alou	.10
38	Ray Lankford	.10
39	Willie Greene	.10
40	Ozzie Smith	.35
41	Roger Clemens	.75
42	Andres Galarraga	.20
43	Gary Sheffield	.40
44	Sammy Sosa	1.50
45	Larry Walker	.35
46	Kevin Appier	.10
47	Raul Mondesi	.40
48	Kenny Lofton	.75
49	Darryl Hamilton	.10
50	Roberto Alomar	.60
51	Hal Morris	.10
52	Cliff Floyd	.10
53	Brent Gates	.10
54	Rickey Henderson	.20
55	John Olerud	.15
56	Gregg Jefferies	.10
57	Cecil Fielder	.20
58	Paul Molitor	.35
59	Bret Boone	.10
60	Greg Vaughn	.10
61	Wally Joyner	.12
62	Jeffrey Hammonds	.10
63	James Mouton	.10
64	Omar Vizquel	.10
65	Wade Boggs	.20
66	Terry Steinbach	.10
67	Wil Cordero	.10
68	Joey Hamilton	.10
69	Rico Brogna	.10
70	Darren Daulton	.10
71	Chuck Knoblauch	.20
72	Bob Hamelin	.10
73	Carl Everett	.10
74	Joe Carter	.15
75	Dave Winfield	.20
76	Bobby Bonilla	.12
77	Paul O'Neill	.15
78	Javier Lopez	.20
79	Cal Ripken Jr.	2.50
80	David Cone	.15
81	Bernard Gilkey	.10
82	Ivan Rodriguez	.50
83	Dean Palmer	.10
84	Jason Bere	.10
85	Will Clark	.25
86	Scott Cooper	.10
87	Royce Clayton	.10
88	Mike Piazza	1.75
89	Ryan Klesko	.50
90	Juan Gonzalez	1.50
91	Travis Fryman	.10
92	Frank Thomas	2.50
93	Eduardo Perez	.10
94	Mo Vaughn	.75
95	Jay Bell	.10
96	Jeff Bagwell	1.00
97	Randy Johnson	.30
98	Jimmy Key	.10
99	Dennis Eckersley	.10
100	Carlos Baerga	.15
101	Eddie Murray	.35
102	Mike Mussina	.40
103	Brian Anderson	.10
104	Jeff Cirillo	.10
105	Dante Bichette	.25
106	Bret Saberhagen	.12
107	Jeff Kent	.12
108	Ruben Sierra	.10
109	Kirk Gibson	.10
110	Reggie Sanders	.15
111	Dave Justice	.20
112	Benji Gil	.10
113	Vaughn Eshelman	.10
114	*Carlos Perez*	.20
115	Chipper Jones	1.75
116	Shane Andrews	.10
117	Orlando Miller	.10
118	Scott Ruffcorn	.10
119	Jose Oliva	.10
120	Joe Vitiello	.10
121	Jon Nunnally	.10
122	Garret Anderson	.15
123	Curtis Goodwin	.10
124	*Mark Grudzielanek*	.35
125	Alex Gonzalez	.15
126	David Bell	.10
127	Dustin Hermanson	.10
128	Dave Nilsson	.10
129	Wilson Heredia	.10
130	Charles Johnson	.20
131	Frank Rodriguez	.10
132	Alex Ochoa	.10
133	Alex Rodriguez	3.00
134	*Bobby Higginson*	1.50
135	Edgardo Alfonzo	.12
136	Armando Benitez	.10
137	Rich Aude	.10
138	Tim Naehring	.10
139	Joe Randa	.10
140	Quilvio Veras	.10
141	*Hideo Nomo*	3.00
142	Ray Holbert	.10
143	Michael Tucker	.10
144	Chad Mottola	.10
145	John Valentin	.10
146	James Baldwin	.10
147	Esteban Loaiza	.10
148	Marty Cordova	.15
149	*Juan Acevedo*	.10
150	*Tim Unroe*	.10
151	Brad Clontz	.10
152	Steve Rodriguez	.10
153	Rudy Pemberton	.10
154	Ozzie Timmons	.10
155	Ricky Otero	.10
156	Allen Battle	.10
157	Joe Roselli	.10
158	Roberto Petagine	.10
159	Todd Hollandsworth	.15
160	Shannon Penn	.10
161	Antonio Osuna	.10
162	Russ Davis	.10
163	Jason Giambi	.10
164	Terry Bradshaw	.10
165	Ray Durham	.10
166	Todd Steverson	.10
167	Tim Belk	.10
168	Andy Pettitte	.75

169	Roger Cedeno	.10
170	Jose Parra	.10
171	Scott Sullivan	.10
172	LaTroy Hawkins	.10
173	Jeff McCurry	.10
174	Ken Griffey Jr. (Bat Speed)	1.50
175	Frank Thomas (Bat Speed)	1.25
176	Cal Ripken Jr. (Bat Speed)	1.25
177	Jeff Bagwell (Bat Speed)	.50
178	Mike Piazza (Bat Speed)	.60
179	Barry Bonds (Bat Speed)	.35
180	Matt Williams (Bat Speed)	.20
181	Don Mattingly (Bat Speed)	.50
182	Will Clark (Bat Speed)	.20
183	Tony Gwynn (Bat Speed)	.40
184	Kirby Puckett (Bat Speed)	.50
185	Jose Canseco (Bat Speed)	.20
186	Paul Molitor (Bat Speed)	.20
187	Albert Belle (Bat Speed)	.40
188	Joe Carter (Bat Speed)	.15
189	Greg Maddux (Special Delivery)	1.00
190	Roger Clemens (Special Delivery)	.40
191	David Cone (Special Delivery)	.10
192	Mike Mussina (Special Delivery)	.20
193	Randy Johnson (Special Delivery)	.15
194	Checklist(Frank Thomas)	.75
195	Checklist(Ken Griffey Jr.)	.75
196	Checklist(Cal Ripken Jr.)	.60
197	Checklist(Jeff Bagwell)	.30
198	Checklist(Mike Piazza)	.40
199	Checklist(Barry Bonds)	.25
200	Checklist(Mo Vaughn, Matt Williams)	.20

1995 Summit Big Bang

The game's top sluggers are featured in this insert set. The front is printed on prismatic metallic foil, a process which Score calls "Spectroetch," with large and small action photos. Backs are conventionally printed and have a large photo with a career highlight printed beneath. The toughest of the Summit chase cards, these are found on the average of once every two boxes (72 packs).

		MT
Complete Set (20):		250.00
Common Player:		3.00
BB1	Ken Griffey Jr.	50.00
BB2	Frank Thomas	30.00
BB3	Cal Ripken Jr.	40.00
BB4	Jeff Bagwell	20.00
BB5	Mike Piazza	30.00
BB6	Barry Bonds	12.00
BB7	Matt Williams	4.00
BB8	Don Mattingly	15.00
BB9	Will Clark	4.00
BB10	Tony Gwynn	25.00
BB11	Kirby Puckett	20.00
BB12	Jose Canseco	5.00
BB13	Paul Molitor	10.00
BB14	Albert Belle	12.00
BB15	Joe Carter	3.00
BB16	Rafael Palmeiro	4.00
BB17	Fred McGriff	4.00
BB18	Dave Justice	3.00
BB19	Tim Salmon	5.00
BB20	Mo Vaughn	12.00

1995 Summit New Age

Printed on metallic foil in a horizontal format, the New Age inserts were seeded at a rate of about one per 18 packs. Red and silver colors predominate on front, while the backs are printed in standard technology and feature a second photo and a short career summary of the players who were generally in their second or third Major League season in 1995.

		MT
Complete Set (15):		50.00
Common Player:		1.00
1	Cliff Floyd	1.00
2	Manny Ramirez	8.00
3	Raul Mondesi	5.00
4	Alex Rodriguez	30.00
5	Billy Ashley	1.00
6	Alex Gonzalez	1.00
7	Michael Tucker	1.00
8	Charles Johnson	3.00
9	Carlos Delgado	3.00
10	Benji Gil	1.00
11	Chipper Jones	25.00
12	Todd Hollandsworth	2.50
13	Frank Rodriguez	1.00
14	Shawn Green	2.00
15	Ray Durham	2.00

1995 Summit Nth Degree

	MT
Complete Set (200):	400.00
Common Player:	1.00
Stars: 6x to 10x	
Yng Stars & RCs: 3x to 6x	

(Star Nth Degree cards are valued about 12-15X the regular Summit versions.)

1995 Summit 21 Club

Metallic foil printing on front and back distinguishes this set of chase cards. A large red-foil "21 / CLUB" logo on each side identifies the theme of this set, professed to be that age during the 1995 baseball season. The players are pictured in action pose on front and a portrait on back. On average the 21 Club cards are seeded one per box (36 packs).

		MT
Complete Set (9):		30.00
Common Player:		3.00
TC1	Bob Abreu	5.00
TC2	Pokey Reese	3.00
TC3	Edgardo Alfonzo	3.00
TC4	Jim Pittsley	3.00
TC5	Ruben Rivera	8.00
TC6	Chan Ho Park	5.00
TC7	Julian Tavarez	3.00
TC8	Ismael Valdes	4.00
TC9	Dmitri Young	3.00

1996 Summit

Pinnacle's 1996 Summit baseball has 200 cards, including 35 rookies, four checklists and 10 Deja Vu subset cards. Each card is also reprinted in three parallel versions - Above and Beyond (one per seven packs), Artist's Proofs (one in 36) and a retail-only silver foil-bordered version. Above and Beyond cards use an all-prismatic foil design; Artist's Proof cards have holographic foil stamping. Five insert sets were produced: Big Bang; Mirage (a parallel set to Big Bang); Hitters, Inc.; Ballparks; and Positions (found one per every 50 magazine packs).

		MT
Complete Set (200):		20.00
Common Player:		.10
Unlisted Stars: .20 to .35		
Wax Box:		40.00
1	Mike Piazza	2.00
2	Matt Williams	.30
3	Tino Martinez	.20
4	Reggie Sanders	.10
5	Ray Durham	.10
6	Brad Radke	.10

7	Jeff Bagwell	1.25
8	Ron Gant	.15
9	Lance Johnson	.10
10	Kevin Seitzer	.10
11	Dante Bichette	.25
12	Ivan Rodriguez	.50
13	Jim Abbott	.10
14	Greg Colbrunn	.10
15	Rondell White	.10
16	Shawn Green	.10
17	Gregg Jefferies	.10
18	Omar Vizquel	.10
19	Cal Ripken Jr.	2.50
20	Mark McGwire	4.00
21	Wally Joyner	.10
22	Chili Davis	.10
23	Jose Canseco	.30
24	Royce Clayton	.10
25	Jay Bell	.10
26	Travis Fryman	.10
27	Jeff King	.10
28	Todd Hundley	.20
29	Joe Vitiello	.10
30	Russ Davis	.10
31	Mo Vaughn	.75
32	Raul Mondesi	.30
33	Ray Lankford	.10
34	Mike Stanley	.10
35	B.J. Surhoff	.10
36	Greg Vaughn	.10
37	Todd Stottlemyre	.10
38	Carlos Delgado	.15
39	Kenny Lofton	.75
40	Hideo Nomo	.60
41	Sterling Hitchcock	.10
42	Pete Schourek	.10
43	Edgardo Alfonzo	.10
44	Ken Hill	.10
45	Ken Caminiti	.25
46	Bobby Higginson	.10
47	Michael Tucker	.10
48	David Cone	.20
49	Cecil Fielder	.20
50	Brian Hunter	.10
51	Charles Johnson	.10
52	Bobby Bonilla	.15
53	Eddie Murray	.40
54	Kenny Rogers	.10
55	Jim Edmonds	.20
56	Trevor Hoffman	.10
57	Kevin Mitchell	.10
58	Ruben Sierra	.10
59	Benji Gil	.10
60	Juan Gonzalez	1.50
61	Larry Walker	.40
62	Jack McDowell	.15
63	Shawon Dunston	.10
64	Andy Benes	.10
65	Jay Buhner	.20
66	Rickey Henderson	.10
67	Alex Gonzalez	.10
68	Mike Kelly	.10
69	Fred McGriff	.35
70	Ryne Sandberg	.75
71	Ernie Young	.10
72	Kevin Appier	.10
73	Moises Alou	.10
74	John Jaha	.10
75	J.T. Snow	.10
76	Jim Thome	.40
77	Kirby Puckett	.75
78	Hal Morris	.10
79	Robin Ventura	.10
80	Ben McDonald	.10
81	Tim Salmon	.20
82	Albert Belle	.75
83	Marquis Grissom	.10
84	Alex Rodriguez	3.00
85	Manny Ramirez	.75
86	Ken Griffey Jr.	3.00
87	Sammy Sosa	1.50
88	Frank Thomas	2.00
89	Lee Smith	.10
90	Marty Cordova	.15
91	Greg Maddux	2.00
92	Lenny Dykstra	.10
93	Butch Huskey	.10
94	Garret Anderson	.10
95	Mike Bordick	.10
96	Dave Justice	.20
97	Chad Curtis	.10
98	Carlos Baerga	.15
99	Jason Isringhausen	.20
100	Gary Sheffield	.40
101	Roger Clemens	1.25
102	Ozzie Smith	.40

103	Ramon Martinez	.10
104	Paul O'Neill	.10
105	Will Clark	.25
106	Tom Glavine	.15
107	Barry Bonds	.75
108	Barry Larkin	.25
109	Derek Bell	.10
110	Randy Johnson	.40
111	Jeff Conine	.10
112	John Mabry	.10
113	Julian Tavarez	.10
114	Gary DiSarcina	.10
115	Andres Galarraga	.20
116	Marc Newfield	.10
117	Frank Rodriguez	.10
118	Brady Anderson	.15
119	Mike Mussina	.40
120	Orlando Merced	.10
121	Melvin Nieves	.10
122	Brian Jordan	.15
123	Rafael Palmeiro	.20
124	Johnny Damon	.15
125	Wil Cordero	.10
126	Chipper Jones	2.00
127	Eric Karros	.10
128	Darren Daulton	.10
129	Vinny Castilla	.10
130	Joe Carter	.20
131	Bernie Williams	.50
132	Bernard Gilkey	.10
133	Bret Boone	.10
134	Tony Gwynn	1.25
135	Dave Nilsson	.10
136	Ryan Klesko	.60
137	Paul Molitor	.25
138	John Olerud	.10
139	Craig Biggio	.10
140	John Valentin	.10
141	Chuck Knoblauch	.20
142	Edgar Martinez	.10
143	Rico Brogna	.10
144	Dean Palmer	.10
145	Mark Grace	.20
146	Roberto Alomar	.75
147	Alex Fernandez	.15
148	Andre Dawson	.10
149	Wade Boggs	.25
150	Mark Lewis	.10
151	Gary Gaetti	.10
152	Paul Wilson, Roger Clemens (Deja Vu)	.30
153	Rey Ordonez, Ozzie Smith (Deja Vu)	.35
154	Derek Jeter, Cal Ripken Jr. (Deja Vu)	1.00
155	Alan Benes, Andy Benes (Deja Vu)	.10
156	Jason Kendall, Mike Piazza (Deja Vu)	.60
157	Ryan Klesko, Frank Thomas (Deja Vu)	1.00
158	Johnny Damon, Ken Griffey Jr. (Deja Vu)	1.00
159	Karim Garcia, Sammy Sosa (Deja Vu)	1.00
160	Raul Mondesi, Tim Salmon (Deja Vu)	.20
161	Chipper Jones, Matt Williams (Deja Vu)	.60
162	Rey Ordonez	.40
163	Bob Wolcott	.10
164	Brooks Kieschnick	.15
165	Steve Gibralter	.10
166	Bob Abreu	.20
167	Greg Zaun	.10
168	Tavo Alvarez	.10
169	Sal Fasano	.10
170	George Arias	.10
171	Derek Jeter	1.50
172	*Livan Hernandez*	2.00
173	Alan Benes	.20
174	George Williams	.10
175	John Wasdin	.10
176	Chan Ho Park	.10
177	Paul Wilson	.25
178	Jeff Suppan	.20
179	Quinton McCracken	.10
180	*Wilton Guerrero*	.90
181	Eric Owens	.10
182	Felipe Crespo	.10
183	LaTroy Hawkins	.10
184	Jason Schmidt	.20
185	Terrell Wade	.10
186	*Mike Grace*	.30
187	Chris Snopek	.10
188	Jason Kendall	.20

189	Todd Hollandsworth	.20
190	Jim Pittsley	.10
191	Jermaine Dye	.20
192	*Mike Busby*	.10
193	Richard Hidalgo	.10
194	Tyler Houston	.10
195	Jimmy Haynes	.10
196	Karim Garcia	.40
197	Ken Griffey Jr. (Checklist)	1.50
198	Frank Thomas (Checklist)	1.25
199	Greg Maddux (Checklist)	1.00
200	Cal Ripken Jr. (Checklist)	1.50

1996 Summit Above & Beyond

These 200 insert cards parallel Pinnacle's 1996 Summit set, using all-prismatic foil for each card. The cards were seeded one per every four packs.

	MT
Complete Set (200):	400.00
Common Player:	1.00

Stars: 5x to 10x
Yng Stars & RCs: 3x to 6x
(Star cards valued at 10X-12X regular Summit version.)

1996 Summit Artist's Proof

Holographic-foil highlights and an "ARTIST'S PROOF" notation on the front photo distinguish the cards in this parallel edition. The AP cards are found once per 36 packs.

	MT
Complete Set (200):	1500.
Common Player:	2.00

Stars: 15x to 30x
Yng Stars & RCs: 10x to 20x
(Artist's Proof star cards valued at 25-40X regular-edition Summit version.)

1996 Summit Ballparks

These 18 cards feature images of players superimposed over their respective teams' ballparks. The cards were seeded one per every 18 packs of 1996 Pinnacle Summit baseball.

		MT
Complete Set (18):		220.00
Common Player:		4.00
1	Cal Ripken Jr.	25.00
2	Albert Belle	8.00
3	Dante Bichette	4.00
4	Mo Vaughn	10.00
5	Ken Griffey Jr.	35.00
6	Derek Jeter	15.00
7	Juan Gonzalez	15.00
8	Greg Maddux	20.00
9	Frank Thomas	25.00
10	Ryne Sandberg	8.00
11	Mike Piazza	20.00
12	Johnny Damon	6.00
13	Barry Bonds	8.00
14	Jeff Bagwell	12.00
15	Paul Wilson	4.00
16	Tim Salmon	4.00
17	Kirby Puckett	12.00
18	Tony Gwynn	12.00

1996 Summit Big Bang

Sixteen of the biggest hitters are featured on these 1996 Pinnacle Summit insert cards. The cards, seeded one per every 72 packs, use Spectroetched backgrounds with foil highlights.

		MT
Complete Set (16):		500.00
Common Player:		10.00
Mirages: 1x		
1	Frank Thomas	75.00
2	Ken Griffey Jr.	120.00
3	Albert Belle	30.00
4	Mo Vaughn	30.00
5	Barry Bonds	30.00
6	Cal Ripken Jr.	90.00
7	Jeff Bagwell	35.00
8	Mike Piazza	75.00
9	Ryan Klesko	20.00
10	Manny Ramirez	30.00
11	Tim Salmon	15.00
12	Dante Bichette	10.00
13	Sammy Sosa	60.00
14	Raul Mondesi	10.00
15	Chipper Jones	60.00
16	Garret Anderson	10.00

1996 Summit Big Bang Mirage

These 18 cards form a parallel version to Pinnacle's Big Bang inserts. The cards, found one per every 72 packs, use an all-new

technology that creates a floating background behind the player's image. By holding the card in direct sunlight or an incandescent bulb, a collector can see three dimensions and a floating baseball that seems to levitate in the background.

		MT
Complete Set (16):		800.00
Common Player:		10.00
1	Frank Thomas	120.00
2	Ken Griffey Jr.	150.00
3	Albert Belle	40.00
4	Mo Vaughn	40.00
5	Barry Bonds	40.00
6	Cal Ripken Jr.	120.00
7	Jeff Bagwell	60.00
8	Mike Piazza	90.00
9	Ryan Klesko	20.00
10	Manny Ramirez	30.00
11	Tim Salmon	15.00
12	Dante Bichette	10.00
13	Sammy Sosa	50.00
14	Raul Mondesi	10.00
15	Chipper Jones	90.00
16	Garret Anderson	10.00

1996 Summit Foil

This parallel issue was an exclusive in Summit retail packaging. The black borders of the regular Summit versions have been replaced on these cards by silver foil.

	MT
Complete Set (200):	50.00
Common Player:	.25
(Star foils valued at 2-3X regular Summit version.)	

1996 Summit Hitters, Inc.

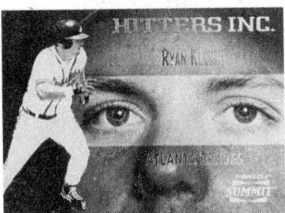

This 1996 Pinnacle Summit set honors 16 top hitters. The cards, seeded one per every 36 packs, puts an embossed highlight on an enlarged photo of the player's eyes.

		MT
Complete Set (16):		200.00
Common Player:		5.00
1	Tony Gwynn	15.00
2	Mo Vaughn	12.00
3	Tim Salmon	5.00
4	Ken Griffey Jr.	40.00
5	Sammy Sosa	25.00
6	Frank Thomas	25.00
7	Wade Boggs	5.00
8	Albert Belle	10.00
9	Cal Ripken Jr.	30.00
10	Manny Ramirez	10.00
11	Ryan Klesko	10.00
11p	Ryan Klesko (overprinted "SAMPLE")	4.50
12	Dante Bichette	5.00
13	Mike Piazza	25.00
14	Chipper Jones	25.00
15	Ryne Sandberg	10.00
16	Matt Williams	5.00

1996 Summit Positions

This insert issue features top players at each position. It is an exclusive magazine pack find, seeded about one per 50 packs. Fronts have action photos of three top players at the position on a baseball infield background at top. Close-ups of those photo appear at bottom, separated by a gold-foil strip. Backs have narrow action photos of each player, a few stats and a serial number from within an edition of 1,500 each.

		MT
Complete Set (9):		200.00
Common Card:		12.00
1	Jeff Bagwell, Mo Vaughn, Frank Thomas (First Base)	30.00
2	Roberto Alomar, Craig Biggio, Chuck Knoblauch (Second Base)	12.00
3	Matt Williams, Jim Thome, Chipper Jones (Third Base)	16.00
4	Barry Larkin, Cal Ripken Jr., Alex Rodriguez (Short Stop)	35.00
5	Mike Piazza, Ivan Rodriguez, Charles Johnson (Catcher)	24.00
6	Hideo Nomo, Greg Maddux, Randy Johnson (Pitcher)	18.00
7	Barry Bonds, Albert Belle, Ryan Klesko (Left Field)	10.00
8	Johnny Damon, Jim Edmonds, Ken Griffey Jr. (Center Field)	35.00
9	Manny Ramirez, Gary Sheffield, Sammy Sosa	25.00

T

1981 Topps

This is another 726-card set of 2-1/2" x 3-1/2" cards from Topps. The cards have the usual color photo with all cards from the same team sharing the same color borders. Player names appear under the photo with team and position on a baseball cap at lower-left. The Topps logo returned in a small baseball in the lower-right. Card backs include the usual stats along with a headline and a cartoon if there was room. Specialty cards include previous season recordbreakers, highlights of the playoffs and World Series, along with the final appearance of team cards. Eleven cards on each of the six press sheets were double-printed.

		MT
Complete Set (726):		60.00
Common Player:		.08
Wax Box:		110.00
1	Batting Leaders(George Brett, Bill Buckner)	.75
2	Home Run Leaders(Reggie Jackson, Ben Oglivie, Mike Schmidt)	.80
3	RBI Leaders(Cecil Cooper, Mike Schmidt)	.30
4	Stolen Base Leaders(Rickey Henderson, Ron LeFlore)	.50
5	Victory Leaders(Steve Carlton, Steve Stone)	.15
6	Strikeout Leaders(Len Barker, Steve Carlton)	.15
7	ERA Leaders(Rudy May, Don Sutton)	.10
8	Leading Firemen(Rollie Fingers, Tom Hume, Dan Quisenberry)	.10
9	Pete LaCock (DP)	.08
10	Mike Flanagan	.08
11	Jim Wohlford (DP)	.08
12	Mark Clear	.08
13	Joe Charboneau	.20
14	John Tudor	.20
15	Larry Parrish	.08
16	Ron Davis	.08
17	Cliff Johnson	.08
18	Glenn Adams	.08
19	Jim Clancy	.08
20	Jeff Burroughs	.08
21	Ron Oester	.08
22	Danny Darwin	.08
23	Alex Trevino	.08
24	Don Stanhouse	.08
25	Sixto Lezcano	.08
26	U.L. Washington	.08
27	Champ Summers (DP)	.08
28	Enrique Romo	.08
29	Gene Tenace	.08
30	Jack Clark	.08
31	Checklist 1-121 (DP)	.08
32	Ken Oberkfell	.08
33	Rick Honeycutt	.08
34	Aurelio Rodriguez	.08
35	Mitchell Page	.08
36	Ed Farmer	.08
37	Gary Roenicke	.08
38	Win Remmerswaal	.08
39	Tom Veryzer	.08
40	Tug McGraw	.10
41	Rangers Future Stars(Bob Babcock, John Butcher, Jerry Don Gleaton)	.08
42	Jerry White (DP)	.08
43	Jose Morales	.08
44	Larry McWilliams	.08
45	Enos Cabell	.08
46	Rick Bosetti	.08
47	Ken Brett	.08
48	Dave Skaggs	.08
49	Bob Shirley	.08
50	Dave Lopes	.10
51	Bill Robinson (DP)	.08
52	Hector Cruz	.08
53	Kevin Saucier	.08
54	Ivan DeJesus	.08
55	Mike Norris	.08
56	Buck Martinez	.08
57	Dave Roberts	.08
58	Joel Youngblood	.08
59	Dan Petry	.08
60	Willie Randolph	.08
61	Butch Wynegar	.08
62	Joe Pettini	.08
63	Steve Renko (DP)	.08
64	Brian Asselstine	.08
65	Scott McGregor	.08
66	Royals Future Stars(Manny Castillo, Tim Ireland, Mike Jones)	.08
67	Ken Kravec	.08
68	Matt Alexander (DP)	.08
69	Ed Halicki	.08
70	Al Oliver (DP)	.10
71	Hal Dues	.08
72	Barry Evans (DP)	.08
73	Doug Bair	.08
74	Mike Hargrove	.08
75	Reggie Smith	.10
76	Mario Mendoza	.08
77	Mike Barlow	.08
78	Steve Dillard	.08
79	Bruce Robbins	.08
80	Rusty Staub	.12
81	Dave Stapleton	.08
82	Astros Future Stars(Danny Heep, Alan Knicely, Bobby Sprowl) (DP)	.08
83	Mike Proly	.08
84	Johnnie LeMaster	.08
85	Mike Caldwell	.08
86	Wayne Gross	.08
87	Rick Camp	.08
88	Joe Lefebvre	.08
89	Darrell Jackson	.08
90	Bake McBride	.08
91	Tim Stoddard (DP)	.08
92	Mike Easler	.08
93	Ed Glynn (DP)	.08
94	Harry Spilman (DP)	.08
95	Jim Sundberg	.08
96	A's Future Stars(Dave Beard), (Ernie Camacho, Pat Dempsey)	.08
97	Chris Speier	.08
98	Clint Hurdle	.08
99	Eric Wilkins	.08
100	Rod Carew	2.00
101	Benny Ayala	.08
102	Dave Tobik	.08
103	Jerry Martin	.08
104	Terry Forster	.08
105	Jose Cruz	.12
106	Don Money	.08
107	Rich Wortham	.08
108	Bruce Benedict	.08
109	Mike Scott	.08
110	Carl Yastrzemski	2.00
111	Greg Minton	.08
112	White Sox Future Stars(Rusty Kuntz, Fran Mullins, Leo Sutherland)	.08
113	Mike Phillips	.08
114	Tom Underwood	.08
115	Roy Smalley	.08
116	Joe Simpson	.08
117	Pete Falcone	.08
118	Kurt Bevacqua	.08
119	Tippy Martinez	.08
120	Larry Bowa	.12
121	Larry Harlow	.08
122	John Denny	.08
123	Al Cowens	.08
124	Jerry Garvin	.08
125	Andre Dawson	.90
126	Charlie Leibrandt	.40
127	Rudy Law	.08
128	Gary Allenson (DP)	.08
129	Art Howe	.08
130	Larry Gura	.08
131	Keith Moreland	.20
132	Tommy Boggs	.08
133	Jeff Cox	.08
134	Steve Mura	.08
135	Gorman Thomas	.08
136	Doug Capilla	.08
137	Hosken Powell	.08
138	Rich Dotson (DP)	.20
139	Oscar Gamble	.08
140	Bob Forsch	.08
141	Miguel Dilone	.08
142	Jackson Todd	.08
143	Dan Meyer	.08
144	Allen Ripley	.08
145	Mickey Rivers	.08
146	Bobby Castillo	.08
147	Dale Berra	.08
148	Randy Niemann	.08
149	Joe Nolan	.08
150	Mark Fidrych	.12
151	Claudell Washington (DP)	.08
152	John Urrea	.08
153	Tom Poquette	.08
154	Rick Langford	.08
155	Chris Chambliss	.08
156	Bob McClure	.08
157	John Wathan	.08
158	Fergie Jenkins	.90
159	Brian Doyle	.08
160	Garry Maddox	.08
161	Dan Graham	.08
162	Doug Corbett	.08
163	Billy Almon	.08
164	Lamarr Hoyt (LaMarr)	.12
165	Tony Scott	.08
166	Floyd Bannister	.08
167	Terry Whitfield	.08
168	Don Robinson (DP)	.08
169	John Mayberry	.08
170	Ross Grimsley	.08
171	Gene Richards	.08
172	Gary Woods	.08
173	Bump Wills	.08
174	Doug Rau	.08
175	Dave Collins	.08
176	Mike Krukow	.08
177	Rick Peters	.08
178	Jim Essian (DP)	.08
179	Rudy May	.08
180	Pete Rose	3.00
181	Elias Sosa	.08
182	Bob Grich	.10
183	Dick Davis (DP)	.08
184	Jim Dwyer	.08
185	Dennis Leonard	.08
186	Wayne Nordhagen	.08
187	Mike Parrott	.08
188	Doug DeCinces	.08
189	Craig Swan	.08
190	Cesar Cedeno	.08
191	Rick Sutcliffe	.08
192	Braves Future Stars(Terry Harper, Ed Miller), (Rafael Ramirez)	.10
193	Pete Vuckovich	.08
194	Rod Scurry	.08
195	Rich Murray	.08
196	Duffy Dyer	.08
197	Jim Kern	.08
198	Jerry Dybzinski	.08
199	Chuck Rainey	.08
200	George Foster	.12
201	Johnny Bench (Record Breaker)	.45
202	Steve Carlton (Record Breaker)	.45
203	Bill Gullickson (Record Breaker)	.08
204	Ron LeFlore, Rodney Scott (Record Breaker)	.08
205	Pete Rose (Record Breaker)	1.50
206	Mike Schmidt (Record Breaker)	1.50
207	Ozzie Smith (Record Breaker)	1.50
208	Willie Wilson (Record Breaker)	.08
209	Dickie Thon (DP)	.08
210	Jim Palmer	1.50
211	Derrel Thomas	.08
212	Steve Nicosia	.08
213	Al Holland	.08
214	Angels Future Stars(Ralph Botting, Jim Dorsey, John Harris)	.08
215	Larry Hisle	.08
216	John Henry Johnson	.08

No.	Player	Value
217	Rich Hebner	.08
218	Paul Splittorff	.08
219	Ken Landreaux	.08
220	Tom Seaver	2.50
221	Bob Davis	.08
222	Jorge Orta	.08
223	Roy Lee Jackson	.08
224	Pat Zachry	.08
225	Ruppert Jones	.08
226	Manny Sanguillen (DP)	.08
227	Fred Martinez	.08
228	Tom Paciorek	.08
229	Rollie Fingers	.90
230	George Hendrick	.08
231	Joe Beckwith	.08
232	Mickey Klutts	.08
233	Skip Lockwood	.08
234	Lou Whitaker	.25
235	Scott Sanderson	.08
236	Mike Ivie	.08
237	Charlie Moore	.08
238	Willie Hernandez	.08
239	Rick Miller (DP)	.08
240	Nolan Ryan	12.00
241	Checklist 122-242 (DP)	.08
242	Chet Lemon	.08
243	Sal Butera	.08
244	Cardinals Future Stars(Tito Landrum, Al Olmsted, Andy Rincon)	.08
245	Ed Figueroa	.08
246	Ed Ott (DP)	.08
247	Glenn Hubbard (DP)	.08
248	Joey McLaughlin	.08
249	Larry Cox	.08
250	Ron Guidry	.20
251	Tom Brookens	.08
252	Victor Cruz	.08
253	Dave Bergman	.08
254	Ozzie Smith	7.50
255	Mark Littell	.08
256	Bombo Rivera	.08
257	Rennie Stennett	.08
258	Joe Price	.08
259	Mets Future Stars(Juan Berenguer), (Hubie Brooks), (Mookie Wilson)	.75
260	Ron Cey	.15
261	Rickey Henderson	7.00
262	Sammy Stewart	.08
263	Brian Downing	.08
264	Jim Norris	.08
265	John Candelaria	.08
266	Tom Herr	.08
267	Stan Bahnsen	.08
268	Jerry Royster	.08
269	Ken Forsch	.08
270	Greg Luzinski	.10
271	Bill Castro	.08
272	Bruce Kimm	.08
273	Stan Papi	.08
274	Craig Chamberlain	.08
275	Dwight Evans	.10
276	Dan Spillner	.08
277	Alfredo Griffin	.08
278	Rick Sofield	.08
279	Bob Knepper	.08
280	Ken Griffey	.08
281	Fred Stanley	.08
282	Mariners Future Stars(Rick Anderson, Greg Biercevicz, Rodney Craig)	.08
283	Billy Sample	.08
284	Brian Kingman	.08
285	Jerry Turner	.08
286	Dave Frost	.08
287	Lenn Sakata	.08
288	Bob Clark	.08
289	Mickey Hatcher	.08
290	Bob Boone (DP)	.08
291	Aurelio Lopez	.08
292	Mike Squires	.08
293	Charlie Lea	.15
294	Mike Tyson (DP)	.08
295	Hal McRae	.12
296	Bill Nahorodny (DP)	.08
297	Bob Bailor	.08
298	Buddy Solomon	.08
299	Elliott Maddox	.08
300	Paul Molitor	5.00
301	Matt Keough	.08
302	Dodgers Future Stars(Jack Perconte), (Mike Scioscia), (Fernando Valenzuela)	2.50
303	Johnny Oates	.08
304	John Castino	.08
305	Ken Clay	.08
306	Juan Beniquez (DP)	.08
307	Gene Garber	.08
308	Rick Manning	.08
309	Luis Salazar	.08
310	Vida Blue (DP)	.08
311	Freddie Patek	.08
312	Rick Rhoden	.08
313	Luis Pujols	.08
314	Rich Dauer	.08
315	Kirk Gibson	3.00
316	Craig Minetto	.08
317	Lonnie Smith	.08
318	Steve Yeager	.08
319	Rowland Office	.08
320	Tom Burgmeier	.08
321	Leon Durham	.15
322	Neil Allen	.08
323	Jim Morrison (DP)	.08
324	Mike Willis	.08
325	Ray Knight	.08
326	Biff Pocoroba	.08
327	Moose Haas	.08
328	Twins Future Stars(Dave Engle, Greg Johnston, Gary Ward)	.12
329	Joaquin Andujar	.08
330	Frank White	.08
331	Dennis Lamp	.08
332	Lee Lacy (DP)	.08
333	Sid Monge	.08
334	Dane Iorg	.08
335	Rick Cerone	.08
336	Eddie Whitson	.08
337	Lynn Jones	.08
338	Checklist 243-363	.08
339	John Ellis	.08
340	Bruce Kison	.08
341	Dwayne Murphy	.08
342	Eric Rasmussen (DP)	.08
343	Frank Taveras	.08
344	Byron McLaughlin	.08
345	Warren Cromartie	.08
346	Larry Christenson (DP)	.08
347	Harold Baines	6.00
348	Bob Sykes	.08
349	Glenn Hoffman	.08
350	J.R. Richard	.12
351	Otto Velez	.08
352	Dick Tidrow (DP)	.08
353	Terry Kennedy	.08
354	Mario Soto	.08
355	Bob Horner	.10
356	Padres Future Stars(George Stablein, Craig Stimac, Tom Tellmann)	.08
357	Jim Slaton	.08
358	Mark Wagner	.08
359	Tom Hausman	.08
360	Willie Wilson	.10
361	Joe Strain	.08
362	Bo Diaz	.08
363	Geoff Zahn	.08
364	Mike Davis	.08
365	Graig Nettles (DP)	.12
366	Mike Ramsey	.08
367	Denny Martinez	.10
368	Leon Roberts	.08
369	Frank Tanana	.08
370	Dave Winfield	4.00
371	Charlie Hough	.08
372	Jay Johnstone	.08
373	Pat Underwood	.08
374	Tom Hutton	.08
375	Dave Concepcion	.10
376	Ron Reed	.08
377	Jerry Morales	.08
378	Dave Rader	.08
379	Lary Sorensen	.08
380	Willie Stargell	1.00
381	Cubs Future Stars(Carlos Lezcano, Steve Macko, Randy Martz)	.08
382	Paul Mirabella	.08
383	Eric Soderholm (DP)	.08
384	Mike Sadek	.08
385	Joe Sambito	.08
386	Dave Edwards	.08
387	Phil Niekro	.90
388	Andre Thornton	.08
389	Marty Pattin	.08
390	Cesar Geronimo	.08
391	Dave Lemanczyk (DP)	.08
392	Lance Parrish	.10
393	Broderick Perkins	.08
394	Woodie Fryman	.08
395	Scot Thompson	.08
396	Bill Campbell	.08
397	Julio Cruz	.08
398	Ross Baumgarten	.08
399	Orioles Future Stars(Mike Boddicker, Mark Corey), (Floyd Rayford)	.20
400	Reggie Jackson	2.50
401	A.L. Championships (Royals Sweep Yankees)	.75
402	N.L. Championships (Phillies Squeak Past Astros)	.35
403	World Series (Phillies Beat Royals In 6)	.25
404	World Series Summary (Phillies Win First World Series)	.25
405	Nino Espinosa	.08
406	Dickie Noles	.08
407	Ernie Whitt	.08
408	Fernando Arroyo	.08
409	Larry Herndon	.08
410	Bert Campaneris	.08
411	Terry Puhl	.08
412	Britt Burns	.08
413	Tony Bernazard	.08
414	John Pacella (DP)	.08
415	Ben Oglivie	.08
416	Gary Alexander	.08
417	Dan Schatzeder	.08
418	Bobby Brown	.08
419	Tom Hume	.08
420	Keith Hernandez	.10
421	Bob Stanley	.08
422	Dan Ford	.08
423	Shane Rawley	.08
424	Yankees Future Stars(Tim Lollar, Bruce Robinson, Dennis Werth)	.08
425	Al Bumbry	.08
426	Warren Brusstar	.08
427	John D'Acquisto	.08
428	John Stearns	.08
429	Mick Kelleher	.08
430	Jim Bibby	.08
431	Dave Roberts	.08
432	Len Barker	.08
433	Rance Mulliniks	.08
434	Roger Erickson	.08
435	Jim Spencer	.08
436	Gary Lucas	.08
437	Mike Heath (DP)	.08
438	John Montefusco	.08
439	Denny Walling	.08
440	Jerry Reuss	.08
441	Ken Reitz	.08
442	Ron Pruitt	.08
443	Jim Beattie (DP)	.08
444	Garth Iorg	.08
445	Ellis Valentine	.08
446	Checklist 364-484	.08
447	Junior Kennedy (DP)	.08
448	Tim Corcoran	.08
449	Paul Mitchell	.08
450	Dave Kingman (DP)	.10
451	Indians Future Stars(Chris Bando, Tom Brennan, Sandy Wihtol)	.08
452	Renie Martin	.08
453	Rob Wilfong (DP)	.08
454	Andy Hassler	.08
455	Rick Burleson	.08
456	Jeff Reardon	1.75
457	Mike Lum	.08
458	Randy Jones	.08
459	Greg Gross	.08
460	Rich Gossage	.10
461	Dave McKay	.08
462	Jack Brohamer	.08
463	Milt May	.08
464	Adrian Devine	.08
465	Bill Russell	.08
466	Bob Molinaro	.08
467	Dave Stieb	.12
468	Johnny Wockenfuss	.08
469	Jeff Leonard	.08
470	Manny Trillo	.08
471	Mike Vail	.08
472	Dyar Miller (DP)	.08
473	Jose Cardenal	.08
474	Mike LaCoss	.08
475	Buddy Bell	.08
476	Jerry Koosman	.08
477	Luis Gomez	.08

No.	Player	Price
478	Juan Eichelberger	.08
479	Expos Future Stars(*Bobby Pate*), (*Tim Raines*), (*Roberto Ramos*)	4.00
480	Carlton Fisk	.90
481	Bob Lacey (DP)	.08
482	Jim Gantner	.08
483	Mike Griffin	.08
484	Max Venable (DP)	.08
485	Garry Templeton	.08
486	Marc Hill	.08
487	Dewey Robinson	.08
488	*Damaso Garcia*	.08
489	John Littlefield (photo actually Mark Riggins)	.08
490	Eddie Murray	5.00
491	Gordy Pladson	.08
492	Barry Foote	.08
493	Dan Quisenberry	.15
494	*Bob Walk*	.20
495	Dusty Baker	.12
496	Paul Dade	.08
497	Fred Norman	.08
498	Pat Putnam	.08
499	Frank Pastore	.08
500	Jim Rice	.15
501	Tim Foli (DP)	.08
502	Giants Future Stars(Chris Bourjos, Al Hargesheimer, Mike Rowland)	.08
503	Steve McCatty	.08
504	Dale Murphy	.90
505	Jason Thompson	.08
506	Phil Huffman	.08
507	Jamie Quirk	.08
508	Rob Dressler	.08
509	Pete Mackanin	.08
510	Lee Mazzilli	.08
511	Wayne Garland	.08
512	Gary Thomasson	.08
513	Frank LaCorte	.08
514	George Riley	.08
515	Robin Yount	4.00
516	Doug Bird	.08
517	Richie Zisk	.08
518	Grant Jackson	.08
519	John Tamargo (DP)	.08
520	Steve Stone	.08
521	Sam Mejias	.08
522	Mike Colbern	.08
523	John Fulgham	.08
524	Willie Aikens	.08
525	Mike Torrez	.08
526	Phillies Future Stars(Marty Bystrom, Jay Loviglio, Jim Wright)	.08
527	Danny Goodwin	.08
528	Gary Matthews	.08
529	Dave LaRoche	.08
530	Steve Garvey	.75
531	John Curtis	.08
532	Bill Stein	.08
533	Jesus Figueroa	.08
534	*Dave Smith*	.15
535	Omar Moreno	.08
536	Bob Owchinko (DP)	.08
537	Ron Hodges	.08
538	Tom Griffin	.08
539	Rodney Scott	.08
540	Mike Schmidt (DP)	4.00
541	Steve Swisher	.08
542	Larry Bradford (DP)	.08
543	Terry Crowley	.08
544	Rich Gale	.08
545	Johnny Grubb	.08
546	Paul Moskau	.08
547	Mario Guerrero	.08
548	Dave Goltz	.08
549	Jerry Remy	.08
550	Tommy John	.25
551	Pirates Future Stars(*Vance Law*), (*Tony Pena*), (*Pascual Perez*)	.75
552	Steve Trout	.08
553	Tim Blackwell	.08
554	Bert Blyleven	.12
555	Cecil Cooper	.08
556	Jerry Mumphrey	.08
557	Chris Knapp	.08
558	Barry Bonnell	.08
559	Willie Montanez	.08
560	Joe Morgan	.90
561	Dennis Littlejohn	.08
562	Checklist 485-605	.08
563	Jim Kaat	.25
564	Ron Hassey (DP)	.08
565	Burt Hooton	.08
566	Del Unser	.08
567	Mark Bomback	.08
568	Dave Revering	.08
569	Al Williams (DP)	.08
570	Ken Singleton	.08
571	Todd Cruz	.08
572	Jack Morris	.35
573	Phil Garner	.08
574	Bill Caudill	.08
575	Tony Perez	.25
576	Reggie Cleveland	.08
577	Blue Jays Future Stars(Luis Leal, Brian Milner), (*Ken Schrom*)	.10
578	*Bill Gullickson*	.20
579	Tim Flannery	.08
580	Don Baylor	.15
581	Roy Howell	.08
582	Gaylord Perry	.90
583	Larry Milbourne	.08
584	Randy Lerch	.08
585	Amos Otis	.08
586	Silvio Martinez	.08
587	Jeff Newman	.08
588	Gary Lavelle	.08
589	Lamar Johnson	.08
590	Bruce Sutter	.08
591	John Lowenstein	.08
592	Steve Comer	.08
593	Steve Kemp	.08
594	Preston Hanna (DP)	.08
595	Butch Hobson	.08
596	Jerry Augustine	.08
597	Rafael Landestoy	.08
598	George Vukovich (DP)	.08
599	Dennis Kinney	.08
600	Johnny Bench	3.00
601	Don Aase	.08
602	Bobby Murcer	.08
603	John Verhoeven	.08
604	Rob Picciolo	.08
605	Don Sutton	.80
606	Reds Future Stars(Bruce Berenyi, Geoff Combe, Paul Householder) (DP)	.08
607	Dave Palmer	.08
608	Greg Pryor	.08
609	Lynn McGlothen	.08
610	Darrell Porter	.08
611	Rick Matula (DP)	.08
612	Duane Kuiper	.08
613	Jim Anderson	.08
614	Dave Rozema	.08
615	Rick Dempsey	.08
616	Rick Wise	.08
617	Craig Reynolds	.08
618	John Milner	.08
619	Steve Henderson	.08
620	Dennis Eckersley	.75
621	Tom Donohue	.08
622	Randy Moffitt	.08
623	Sal Bando	.08
624	Bob Welch	.08
625	Bill Buckner	.10
626	Tigers Future Stars(Dave Steffen, Jerry Ujdur, Roger Weaver)	.08
627	Luis Tiant	.10
628	Vic Correll	.08
629	Tony Armas	.08
630	Steve Carlton	2.50
631	Ron Jackson	.08
632	Alan Bannister	.08
633	Bill Lee	.08
634	Doug Flynn	.08
635	Bobby Bonds	.10
636	Al Hrabosky	.08
637	Jerry Narron	.08
638	Checklist 606	.08
639	Carney Lansford	.08
640	Dave Parker	.50
641	Mark Belanger	.08
642	Vern Ruhle	.08
643	*Lloyd Moseby*	.20
644	Ramon Aviles (DP)	.08
645	Rick Reuschel	.08
646	Marvis Foley	.08
647	Dick Drago	.08
648	Darrell Evans	.12
649	Manny Sarmiento	.08
650	Bucky Dent	.08
651	Pedro Guerrero	.08
652	John Montague	.08
653	Bill Fahey	.08
654	Ray Burris	.08
655	Dan Driessen	.08
656	Jon Matlack	.08
657	Mike Cubbage (DP)	.08
658	Milt Wilcox	.08
659	Brewers Future Stars(John Flinn, Ed Romero, Ned Yost)	.08
660	Gary Carter	.80
661	Orioles Team(Earl Weaver)	.25
662	Red Sox Team(Ralph Houk)	.10
663	Angels Team(Jim Fregosi)	.10
664	White Sox Team(Tony LaRussa)	.25
665	Indians Team(Dave Garcia)	.10
666	Tigers Team(Sparky Anderson)	.30
667	Royals Team(Jim Frey)	.10
668	Brewers Team(Bob Rodgers)	.10
669	Twins Team(John Goryl)	.10
670	Yankees Team(Gene Michael)	.25
671	A's Team(Billy Martin)	.25
672	Mariners Team(Maury Wills)	.15
673	Rangers Team(Don Zimmer)	.15
674	Blue Jays Team(Bobby Mattick)	.10
675	Braves Team(Bobby Cox)	.15
676	Cubs Team(Joe Amalfitano)	.15
677	Reds Team(John McNamara)	.10
678	Astros Team(Bill Virdon)	.10
679	Dodgers Team(Tom Lasorda)	.40
680	Expos Team(Dick Williams)	.15
681	Mets Team(Joe Torre)	.25
682	Phillies Team(Dallas Green)	.25
683	Pirates Team(Chuck Tanner)	.15
684	Cardinals Team(Whitey Herzog)	.25
685	Padres Team(Frank Howard)	.15
686	Giants Team(Dave Bristol)	.10
687	Jeff Jones	.08
688	Kiko Garcia	.08
689	Red Sox Future Stars(*Bruce Hurst*, Keith MacWhorter), (*Reid Nichols*)	.60
690	Bob Watson	.08
691	Dick Ruthven	.08
692	Lenny Randle	.08
693	*Steve Howe*	.20
694	Bud Harrelson (DP)	.08
695	Kent Tekulve	.08
696	Alan Ashby	.08
697	Rick Waits	.08
698	Mike Jorgensen	.08
699	Glenn Abbott	.08
700	George Brett	6.00
701	Joe Rudi	.08
702	George Medich	.08
703	Alvis Woods	.08
704	Bill Travers (DP)	.08
705	Ted Simmons	.08
706	Dave Ford	.08
707	Dave Cash	.08
708	Doyle Alexander	.08
709	Alan Trammell (DP)	.95
710	Ron LeFlore (DP)	.08
711	Joe Ferguson	.08
712	Bill Bonham	.08
713	Bill North	.08
714	Pete Redfern	.08
715	Bill Madlock	.10
716	Glenn Borgmann	.08
717	Jim Barr (DP)	.08
718	Larry Biittner	.08
719	Sparky Lyle	.08
720	Fred Lynn	.12
721	Toby Harrah	.08
722	Joe Niekro	.08
723	Bruce Bochte	.08
724	Lou Piniella	.10
725	Steve Rogers	.08
726	Rick Monday	.08

A player's name in *italic* type indicates a rookie card.

1981 Topps Traded

The 132 cards in this extension set are numbered from 727 to 858, technically making them a high-numbered series of the regular Topps set. The set was not packaged in gum packs, but rather placed in a specially designed red box and sold through baseball card dealers only. While many complained about the method, the fact remains, even at higher prices, the set has done well for its owners as it features not only mid-season trades, but also single-player rookie cards of some of the hottest prospects. The cards measure 2-1/2" x 3-1/2".

		MT
Complete Set (132):		35.00
Common Player:		.20
727	Danny Ainge	8.00
728	Doyle Alexander	.20
729	Gary Alexander	.20
730	Billy Almon	.20
731	Joaquin Andujar	.20
732	Bob Bailor	.20
733	Juan Beniquez	.20
734	Dave Bergman	.20
735	Tony Bernazard	.20
736	Larry Biittner	.20
737	Doug Bird	.20
738	Bert Blyleven	.30
739	Mark Bomback	.20
740	Bobby Bonds	.25
741	Rick Bosetti	.20
742	Hubie Brooks	.35
743	Rick Burleson	.20
744	Ray Burris	.20
745	Jeff Burroughs	.20
746	Enos Cabell	.20
747	Ken Clay	.20
748	Mark Clear	.20
749	Larry Cox	.20
750	Hector Cruz	.20
751	Victor Cruz	.20
752	Mike Cubbage	.20
753	Dick Davis	.20
754	Brian Doyle	.20
755	Dick Drago	.20
756	Leon Durham	.20
757	Jim Dwyer	.20
758	Dave Edwards	.20
759	Jim Essian	.20
760	Bill Fahey	.20
761	Rollie Fingers	2.50
762	Carlton Fisk	5.00
763	Barry Foote	.20
764	Ken Forsch	.20
765	Kiko Garcia	.20
766	Cesar Geronimo	.20
767	Gary Gray	.20
768	Mickey Hatcher	.20
769	Steve Henderson	.20
770	Marc Hill	.20
771	Butch Hobson	.20

772	Rick Honeycutt	.20
773	Roy Howell	.20
774	Mike Ivie	.20
775	Roy Lee Jackson	.20
776	Cliff Johnson	.20
777	Randy Jones	.20
778	Ruppert Jones	.20
779	Mick Kelleher	.20
780	Terry Kennedy	.20
781	Dave Kingman	.20
782	Bob Knepper	.20
783	Ken Kravec	.20
784	Bob Lacey	.20
785	Dennis Lamp	.20
786	Rafael Landestoy	.20
787	Ken Landreaux	.20
788	Carney Lansford	.20
789	Dave LaRoche	.20
790	Joe Lefebvre	.20
791	Ron LeFlore	.20
792	Randy Lerch	.20
793	Sixto Lezcano	.20
794	John Littlefield	.20
795	Mike Lum	.20
796	Greg Luzinski	.50
797	Fred Lynn	.20
798	Jerry Martin	.20
799	Buck Martinez	.20
800	Gary Matthews	.20
801	Mario Mendoza	.20
802	Larry Milbourne	.20
803	Rick Miller	.20
804	John Montefusco	.20
805	Jerry Morales	.20
806	Jose Morales	.20
807	Joe Morgan	3.00
808	Jerry Mumphrey	.20
809	Gene Nelson	.20
810	Ed Ott	.20
811	Bob Owchinko	.20
812	Gaylord Perry	2.50
813	Mike Phillips	.20
814	Darrell Porter	.20
815	Mike Proly	.20
816	Tim Raines	12.00
817	Lenny Randle	.20
818	Doug Rau	.20
819	Jeff Reardon	1.50
820	Ken Reitz	.20
821	Steve Renko	.20
822	Rick Reuschel	.20
823	Dave Revering	.20
824	Dave Roberts	.20
825	Leon Roberts	.20
826	Joe Rudi	.20
827	Kevin Saucier	.20
828	Tony Scott	.20
829	Bob Shirley	.20
830	Ted Simmons	.20
831	Lary Sorensen	.20
832	Jim Spencer	.20
833	Harry Spilman	.20
834	Fred Stanley	.20
835	Rusty Staub	.45
836	Bill Stein	.20
837	Joe Strain	.20
838	Bruce Sutter	.20
839	Don Sutton	2.50
840	Steve Swisher	.20
841	Frank Tanana	.20
842	Gene Tenace	.20
843	Jason Thompson	.20
844	Dickie Thon	.20
845	Bill Travers	.20
846	Tom Underwood	.20
847	John Urrea	.20
848	Mike Vail	.20
849	Ellis Valentine	.20
850	Fernando Valenzuela	2.00
851	Pete Vuckovich	.20
852	Mark Wagner	.20
853	Bob Walk	.20
854	Claudell Washington	.20
855	Dave Winfield	12.00
856	Geoff Zahn	.20
857	Richie Zisk	.20
858	Checklist 727-858	.10

1982 Topps

At 792 cards, this was the largest issue produced up to that time, eliminating the need for double-printed cards. The 2-1/2" x 3-1/2" cards feature a front color photo with a pair of stripes down the left side. Under the player's photo are found his name, team and position. A facsimile autograph runs across the front of the picture. Specialty cards include great performances of the previous season, All-Stars, statistical leaders and "In Action" cards (indicated by "IA" in listings below). Managers and hitting/pitching leaders have cards, while rookies are shown as "Future Stars" on group cards.

		MT
Complete Set (792):		125.00
Common Player:		.08
Wax Box:		250.00
1	Steve Carlton (1981 Highlight)	.25
2	Ron Davis (1981 Highlight)	.08
3	Tim Raines (1981 Highlight)	.15
4	Pete Rose (1981 Highlight)	.60
5	Nolan Ryan (1981 Highlight)	3.00
6	Fernando Valenzuela (1981 Highlight)	.10
7	Scott Sanderson	.08
8	Rich Dauer	.08
9	Ron Guidry	.15
10	Ron Guidry (In Action)	.15
11	Gary Alexander	.08
12	Moose Haas	.08
13	Lamar Johnson	.08
14	Steve Howe	.10
15	Ellis Valentine	.08
16	Steve Comer	.08
17	Darrell Evans	.15
18	Fernando Arroyo	.08
19	Ernie Whitt	.08
20	Garry Maddox	.08
21	Orioles Future Stars(Bob Bonner), (Cal Ripken, Jr.), (Jeff Schneider)	80.00
22	Jim Beattie	.08
23	Willie Hernandez	.08
24	Dave Frost	.08
25	Jerry Remy	.08
26	Jorge Orta	.08
27	Tom Herr	.08
28	John Urrea	.08
29	Dwayne Murphy	.08
30	Tom Seaver	2.00
31	Tom Seaver (In Action)	1.00
32	Gene Garber	.08
33	Jerry Morales	.08
34	Joe Sambito	.08
35	Willie Aikens	.08
36	Rangers Batting/Pitching Leaders(George Medich, Al Oliver)	.08
37	Dan Graham	.08
38	Charlie Lea	.08
39	Lou Whitaker	.30
40	Dave Parker	.35
41	Dave Parker (In Action)	.15
42	Rick Sofield	.08
43	Mike Cubbage	.08
44	Britt Burns	.08

45	Rick Cerone	.08
46	Jerry Augustine	.08
47	Jeff Leonard	.08
48	Bobby Castillo	.08
49	Alvis Woods	.08
50	Buddy Bell	.08
51	Chicago Cubs Future Stars(*Jay Howell*), (*Carlos Lezcano*), (*Ty Waller*)	.40
52	Larry Andersen	.08
53	Greg Gross	.08
54	Ron Hassey	.08
55	Rick Burleson	.08
56	Mark Littell	.08
57	Craig Reynolds	.08
58	John D'Acquisto	.08
59	*Rich Gedman*	.08
60	Tony Armas	.10
61	Tommy Boggs	.08
62	Mike Tyson	.08
63	Mario Soto	.08
64	Lynn Jones	.08
65	Terry Kennedy	.08
66	Astros Batting/Pitching Leaders(Art Howe, Nolan Ryan)	.50
67	Rich Gale	.08
68	Roy Howell	.08
69	Al Williams	.08
70	Tim Raines	1.00
71	Roy Lee Jackson	.08
72	Rick Auerbach	.08
73	Buddy Solomon	.08
74	Bob Clark	.08
75	Tommy John	.30
76	Greg Pryor	.08
77	Miguel Dilone	.08
78	George Medich	.08
79	Bob Bailor	.08
80	Jim Palmer	1.00
81	Jim Palmer (In Action)	.30
82	Bob Welch	.15
83	Yankees Future Stars(*Steve Balboni*), (*Andy McGaffigan*), (*Andre Robertson*)	.15
84	Rennie Stennett	.08
85	Lynn McGlothen	.08
86	Dane Iorg	.08
87	Matt Keough	.08
88	Biff Pocoroba	.08
89	Steve Henderson	.08
90	Nolan Ryan	12.00
91	Carney Lansford	.08
92	Brad Havens	.08
93	Larry Hisle	.08
94	Andy Hassler	.08
95	Ozzie Smith	3.00
96	Royals Batting/Pitching Leaders(George Brett, Larry Gura)	.35
97	Paul Moskau	.08
98	Terry Bulling	.08
99	Barry Bonnell	.08
100	Mike Schmidt	3.00
101	Mike Schmidt (In Action)	1.25
102	Dan Briggs	.08
103	Bob Lacey	.08
104	Rance Mulliniks	.08
105	Kirk Gibson	.40
106	Enrique Romo	.08
107	Wayne Krenchicki	.08
108	Bob Sykes	.08
109	Dave Revering	.08
110	Carlton Fisk	1.00
111	Carlton Fisk (In Action)	.60
112	Billy Sample	.08
113	Steve McCatty	.08
114	Ken Landreaux	.08
115	Gaylord Perry	.55
116	Jim Wohlford	.08
117	Rawly Eastwick	.08
118	Expos Future Stars(*Terry Francona*), (*Brad Mills*), (*Bryn Smith*)	.08
119	Joe Pittman	.08
120	Gary Lucas	.08
121	Ed Lynch	.08
122	Jamie Easterly	.08
123	Danny Goodwin	.08
124	Reid Nichols	.08
125	Danny Ainge	2.00
126	Braves Batting/Pitching Leaders(Rick Mahler, Claudell Washington)	.08
127	Lonnie Smith	.08
128	Frank Pastore	.08
129	Checklist 1-132	.08
130	Julio Cruz	.08
131	Stan Bahnsen	.08
132	Lee May	.08
133	Pat Underwood	.08
134	Dan Ford	.08
135	Andy Rincon	.08
136	Lenn Sakata	.08
137	George Cappuzzello	.08
138	Tony Pena	.10
139	Jeff Jones	.08
140	Ron LeFlore	.08
141	Indians Future Stars(Chris Bando, Tom Brennan), (*Von Hayes*)	.20
142	Dave LaRoche	.08
143	Mookie Wilson	.12
144	Fred Breining	.08
145	Bob Horner	.10
146	Mike Griffin	.08
147	Denny Walling	.08
148	Mickey Klutts	.08
149	Pat Putnam	.08
150	Ted Simmons	.08
151	Dave Edwards	.08
152	Ramon Aviles	.08
153	Roger Erickson	.08
154	Dennis Werth	.08
155	Otto Velez	.08
156	A's Batting/Pitching Leaders(Rickey Henderson, Steve McCatty)	.15
157	Steve Crawford	.08
158	Brian Downing	.08
159	Larry Biittner	.08
160	Luis Tiant	.10
161	Batting Leaders(Carney Lansford, Bill Madlock)	.08
162	Home Run Leaders(Tony Armas, Dwight Evans, Bobby Grich, Eddie Murray, Mike Schmidt)	.25
163	RBI Leaders(Eddie Murray, Mike Schmidt)	.50
164	Stolen Base Leaders(Rickey Henderson, Tim Raines)	.50
165	Victory Leaders(Denny Martinez, Steve McCatty, Jack Morris, Tom Seaver, Pete Vuckovich)	.20
166	Strikeout Leaders(Len Barker, Fernando Valenzuela)	.08
167	ERA Leaders(Steve McCatty, Nolan Ryan)	1.50
168	Leading Relievers(Rollie Fingers, Bruce Sutter)	.20
169	Charlie Leibrandt	.08
170	Jim Bibby	.08
171	Giants Future Stars(*Bob Brenly*), (*Chili Davis*), (*Bob Tufts*)	3.00
172	Bill Gullickson	.08
173	Jamie Quirk	.08
174	Dave Ford	.08
175	Jerry Mumphrey	.08
176	Dewey Robinson	.08
177	John Ellis	.08
178	Dyar Miller	.08
179	Steve Garvey	.60
180	Steve Garvey (In Action)	.30
181	Silvio Martinez	.08
182	Larry Herndon	.08
183	Mike Proly	.08
184	Mick Kelleher	.08
185	Phil Niekro	1.00
186	Cardinals Batting/Pitching Leaders(Bob Forsch, Keith Hernandez)	.08
187	Jeff Newman	.08
188	Randy Martz	.08
189	Glenn Hoffman	.08
190	J.R. Richard	.12
191	*Tim Wallach*	2.50
192	Broderick Perkins	.08
193	Darrell Jackson	.08
194	Mike Vail	.08
195	Paul Molitor	4.00
196	Willie Upshaw	.08
197	Shane Rawley	.08
198	Chris Speier	.08
199	Don Aase	.08
200	George Brett	5.00
201	George Brett (In Action)	2.50
202	Rick Manning	.08
203	Blue Jays Future Stars(*Jesse Barfield*, Brian Milner, Boomer Wells)	.50
204	Gary Roenicke	.08
205	Neil Allen	.08
206	Tony Bernazard	.08
207	Rod Scurry	.08
208	Bobby Murcer	.08
209	Gary Lavelle	.08
210	Keith Hernandez	.12
211	Dan Petry	.08
212	Mario Mendoza	.08
213	*Dave Stewart*	4.00
214	Brian Asselstine	.08
215	Mike Krukow	.08
216	White Sox Batting/Pitching Leaders(Dennis Lamp, Chet Lemon)	.08
217	Bo McLaughlin	.08
218	Dave Roberts	.08
219	John Curtis	.08
220	Manny Trillo	.08
221	Jim Slaton	.08
222	Butch Wynegar	.08
223	Lloyd Moseby	.08
224	Bruce Bochte	.08
225	Mike Torrez	.08
226	Checklist 133-264	.08
227	Ray Burris	.08
228	Sam Mejias	.08
229	Geoff Zahn	.08
230	Willie Wilson	.10
231	Phillies Future Stars(*Mark Davis*), (*Bob Dernier*), (*Ozzie Virgil*)	.20
232	Terry Crowley	.08
233	Duane Kuiper	.08
234	Ron Hodges	.08
235	Mike Easler	.08
236	John Martin	.08
237	Rusty Kuntz	.08
238	Kevin Saucier	.08
239	Jon Matlack	.08
240	Bucky Dent	.12
241	Bucky Dent (In Action)	.08
242	Milt May	.08
243	Bob Owchinko	.08
244	Rufino Linares	.08
245	Ken Reitz	.08
246	Mets Batting/Pitching Leaders(Hubie Brooks, Mike Scott)	.08
247	Pedro Guerrero	.10
248	Frank LaCorte	.08
249	Tim Flannery	.08
250	Tug McGraw	.12
251	Fred Lynn	.20
252	Fred Lynn (In Action)	.10
253	Chuck Baker	.08
254	*George Bell*	1.00
255	Tony Perez	.25
256	Tony Perez (In Action)	.10
257	Larry Harlow	.08
258	Bo Diaz	.08
259	Rodney Scott	.08
260	Bruce Sutter	.10
261	Tigers Future Stars(Howard Bailey, Marty Castillo, Dave Rucker)	.08
262	Doug Bair	.08
263	Victor Cruz	.08
264	Dan Quisenberry	.10
265	Al Bumbry	.08
266	Rick Leach	.08
267	Kurt Bevacqua	.08
268	Rickey Keeton	.08
269	Jim Essian	.08
270	Rusty Staub	.15
271	Larry Bradford	.08
272	Bump Wills	.08
273	Doug Bird	.08
274	*Bob Ojeda*	.60
275	Bob Watson	.08
276	Angels Batting/Pitching Leaders(Rod Carew, Ken Forsch)	.25
277	Terry Puhl	.08
278	John Littlefield	.08
279	Bill Russell	.08
280	Ben Oglivie	.08
281	John Verhoeven	.08
282	Ken Macha	.08
283	Brian Allard	.08
284	Bob Grich	.10
285	Sparky Lyle	.08
286	Bill Fahey	.08

287	Alan Bannister	.08
288	Garry Templeton	.08
289	Bob Stanley	.08
290	Ken Singleton	.08
291	Pirates Future Stars(Vance Law, Bob Long), (Johnny Ray)	.15
292	Dave Palmer	.08
293	Rob Picciolo	.08
294	Mike LaCoss	.08
295	Jason Thompson	.08
296	Bob Walk	.08
297	Clint Hurdle	.08
298	Danny Darwin	.08
299	Steve Trout	.08
300	Reggie Jackson	3.00
301	Reggie Jackson (In Action)	1.50
302	Doug Flynn	.08
303	Bill Caudill	.08
304	Johnnie LeMaster	.08
305	Don Sutton	.65
306	Don Sutton (In Action)	.20
307	Randy Bass	.08
308	Charlie Moore	.08
309	Pete Redfern	.08
310	Mike Hargrove	.08
311	Dodgers Batting/Pitching Leaders(Dusty Baker, Burt Hooton)	.08
312	Lenny Randle	.08
313	John Harris	.08
314	Buck Martinez	.08
315	Burt Hooton	.08
316	Steve Braun	.08
317	Dick Ruthven	.08
318	Mike Heath	.08
319	Dave Rozema	.08
320	Chris Chambliss	.08
321	Chris Chambliss (In Action)	.08
322	Garry Hancock	.08
323	Bill Lee	.08
324	Steve Dillard	.08
325	Jose Cruz	.08
326	Pete Falcone	.08
327	Joe Nolan	.08
328	Ed Farmer	.08
329	U.L. Washington	.08
330	Rick Wise	.08
331	Benny Ayala	.08
332	Don Robinson	.08
333	Brewers Future Stars(Frank DiPino, Marshall Edwards, Chuck Porter)	.08
334	Aurelio Rodriguez	.08
335	Jim Sundberg	.08
336	Mariners Batting/Pitching Leaders(Glenn Abbott, Tom Paciorek)	.08
337	Pete Rose (All-Star)	1.00
338	Dave Lopes (All-Star)	.08
339	Mike Schmidt (All-Star)	1.00
340	Dave Concepcion (All-Star)	.08
341	Andre Dawson (All-Star)	.40
342a	George Foster (All-Star no autograph)	2.25
342b	George Foster (All-Star autograph on front)	.20
343	Dave Parker (All-Star)	.20
344	Gary Carter (All-Star)	.20
345	Fernando Valenzuela (All-Star)	.10
346	Tom Seaver (All-Star)	.75
347	Bruce Sutter (All-Star)	.08
348	Derrel Thomas	.08
349	George Frazier	.08
350	Thad Bosley	.08
351	Reds Future Stars(Scott Brown, Geoff Combe, Paul Householder)	.08
352	Dick Davis	.08
353	Jack O'Connor	.08
354	Roberto Ramos	.08
355	Dwight Evans	.10
356	Denny Lewallyn	.08
357	Butch Hobson	.08
358	Mike Parrott	.08
359	Jim Dwyer	.08
360	Len Barker	.08
361	Rafael Landestoy	.08
362	Jim Wright	.08
363	Bob Molinaro	.08
364	Doyle Alexander	.08
365	Bill Madlock	.10
366	Padres Batting/Pitching Leaders(Juan Eichelberger, Luis Salazar)	.08

367	Jim Kaat	.20
368	Alex Trevino	.08
369	Champ Summers	.08
370	Mike Norris	.08
371	Jerry Don Gleaton	.08
372	Luis Gomez	.08
373	Gene Nelson	.08
374	Tim Blackwell	.08
375	Dusty Baker	.08
376	Chris Welsh	.08
377	Kiko Garcia	.08
378	Mike Caldwell	.08
379	Rob Wilfong	.08
380	Dave Stieb	.25
381	Red Sox Future Stars(Bruce Hurst, Dave Schmidt, Julio Valdez)	.25
382	Joe Simpson	.08
383a	Pascual Perez (no position on front)	8.00
383b	Pascual Perez ("Pitcher" on front)	.10
384	Keith Moreland	.08
385	Ken Forsch	.08
386	Jerry White	.08
387	Tom Veryzer	.08
388	Joe Rudi	.08
389	George Vukovich	.08
390	Eddie Murray	4.00
391	Dave Tobik	.08
392	Rick Bosetti	.08
393	Al Hrabosky	.08
394	Checklist 265-396	.08
395	Omar Moreno	.08
396	Twins Batting/Pitching Leaders(Fernando Arroyo, John Castino)	.08
397	Ken Brett	.08
398	Mike Squires	.08
399	Pat Zachry	.08
400	Johnny Bench	1.50
401	Johnny Bench (In Action)	.40
402	Bill Stein	.08
403	Jim Tracy	.08
404	Dickie Thon	.08
405	Rick Reuschel	.08
406	Al Holland	.08
407	Danny Boone	.08
408	Ed Romero	.08
409	Don Cooper	.08
410	Ron Cey	.10
411	Ron Cey (In Action)	.08
412	Luis Leal	.08
413	Dan Meyer	.08
414	Elias Sosa	.08
415	Don Baylor	.12
416	Marty Bystrom	.08
417	Pat Kelly	.08
418	Rangers Future Stars(John Butcher, Bobby Johnson), (Dave Schmidt)	.08
419	Steve Stone	.12
420	George Hendrick	.08
421	Mark Clear	.08
422	Cliff Johnson	.08
423	Stan Papi	.08
424	Bruce Benedict	.08
425	John Candelaria	.10
426	Orioles Batting/Pitching Leaders(Eddie Murray, Sammy Stewart)	.25
427	Ron Oester	.08
428	Lamarr Hoyt (LaMarr)	.08
429	John Wathan	.08
430	Vida Blue	.10
431	Vida Blue (In Action)	.10
432	Mike Scott	.08
433	Alan Ashby	.08
434	Joe Lefebvre	.08
435	Robin Yount	3.50
436	Joe Strain	.08
437	Juan Berenguer	.08
438	Pete Mackanin	.08
439	Dave Righetti	.90
440	Jeff Burroughs	.08
441	Astros Future Stars(Danny Heep, Billy Smith, Bobby Sprowl)	.08
442	Bruce Kison	.08
443	Mark Wagner	.08
444	Terry Forster	.08
445	Larry Parrish	.08
446	Wayne Garland	.08
447	Darrell Porter	.08
448	Darrell Porter (In Action)	.08
449	Luis Aguayo	.08

450	Jack Morris	.35
451	Ed Miller	.08
452	Lee Smith	8.00
453	Art Howe	.08
454	Rick Langford	.08
455	Tom Burgmeier	.08
456	Cubs Batting & Pitching Ldrs.(Bill Buckner, Randy Martz)	.08
457	Tim Stoddard	.08
458	Willie Montanez	.08
459	Bruce Berenyi	.08
460	Jack Clark	.08
461	Rich Dotson	.08
462	Dave Chalk	.08
463	Jim Kern	.08
464	Juan Bonilla	.08
465	Lee Mazzilli	.08
466	Randy Lerch	.08
467	Mickey Hatcher	.08
468	Floyd Bannister	.08
469	Ed Ott	.08
470	John Mayberry	.08
471	Royals Future Stars(Atlee Hammaker, Mike Jones, Darryl Motley)	.15
472	Oscar Gamble	.08
473	Mike Stanton	.08
474	Ken Oberkfell	.08
475	Alan Trammell	.45
476	Brian Kingman	.08
477	Steve Yeager	.08
478	Ray Searage	.08
479	Rowland Office	.08
480	Steve Carlton	1.00
481	Steve Carlton (In Action)	.40
482	Glenn Hubbard	.08
483	Gary Woods	.08
484	Ivan DeJesus	.08
485	Kent Tekulve	.08
486	Yankees Batting & Pitching Ldrs.(Tommy John, Jerry Mumphrey)	.10
487	Bob McClure	.08
488	Ron Jackson	.08
489	Rick Dempsey	.08
490	Dennis Eckersley	.20
491	Checklist 397-528	.08
492	Joe Price	.08
493	Chet Lemon	.08
494	Hubie Brooks	.08
495	Dennis Leonard	.08
496	Johnny Grubb	.08
497	Jim Anderson	.08
498	Dave Bergman	.08
499	Paul Mirabella	.08
500	Rod Carew	1.00
501	Rod Carew (In Action)	.40
502	Braves Future Stars(Steve Bedrosian), (Brett Butler, Larry Owen)	2.00
503	Julio Gonzalez	.08
504	Rick Peters	.08
505	Graig Nettles	.10
506	Graig Nettles (In Action)	.08
507	Terry Harper	.08
508	Jody Davis	.15
509	Harry Spilman	.08
510	Fernando Valenzuela	.25
511	Ruppert Jones	.08
512	Jerry Dybzinski	.08
513	Rick Rhoden	.08
514	Joe Ferguson	.08
515	Larry Bowa	.10
516	Larry Bowa (In Action)	.08
517	Mark Brouhard	.08
518	Garth Iorg	.08
519	Glenn Adams	.08
520	Mike Flanagan	.08
521	Billy Almon	.08
522	Chuck Rainey	.08
523	Gary Gray	.08
524	Tom Hausman	.08
525	Ray Knight	.08
526	Expos Batting & Pitching Ldrs.(Warren Cromartie, Bill Gullickson)	.08
527	John Henry Johnson	.08
528	Matt Alexander	.08
529	Allen Ripley	.08
530	Dickie Noles	.08
531	A's Future Stars(Rich Bordi, Mark Budaska, Kelvin Moore)	.08
532	Toby Harrah	.08
533	Joaquin Andujar	.08

534	Dave McKay	.08
535	Lance Parrish	.12
536	Rafael Ramirez	.08
537	Doug Capilla	.08
538	Lou Piniella	.12
539	Vern Ruhle	.08
540	Andre Dawson	.80
541	Barry Evans	.08
542	Ned Yost	.08
543	Bill Robinson	.08
544	Larry Christenson	.08
545	Reggie Smith	.12
546	Reggie Smith (In Action)	.08
547	Rod Carew (All-Star)	.25
548	Willie Randolph (All-Star)	.08
549	George Brett (All-Star)	1.50
550	Bucky Dent (All-Star)	.10
551	Reggie Jackson (All-Star)	.80
552	Ken Singleton (All-Star)	.08
553	Dave Winfield (All-Star)	.60
554	Carlton Fisk (All-Star)	.20
555	Scott McGregor (All-Star)	.08
556	Jack Morris (All-Star)	.10
557	Rich Gossage (All-Star)	.10
558	John Tudor	.08
559	Indians Batting & Pitching Ldrs.(Bert Blyleven, Mike Hargrove)	.08
560	Doug Corbett	.08
561	Cardinals Future Stars(Glenn Brummer, Luis DeLeon, Gene Roof)	.08
562	Mike O'Berry	.08
563	Ross Baumgarten	.08
564	Doug DeCinces	.08
565	Jackson Todd	.08
566	Mike Jorgensen	.08
567	Bob Babcock	.08
568	Joe Pettini	.08
569	Willie Randolph	.08
570	Willie Randolph (In Action)	.08
571	Glenn Abbott	.08
572	Juan Beniquez	.08
573	Rick Waits	.08
574	Mike Ramsey	.08
575	Al Cowens	.08
576	Giants Batting & Pitching Ldrs.(Vida Blue, Milt May)	.08
577	Rick Monday	.08
578	Shooty Babitt	.08
579	*Rick Mahler*	.08
580	Bobby Bonds	.10
581	Ron Reed	.08
582	Luis Pujols	.08
583	Tippy Martinez	.08
584	Hosken Powell	.08
585	Rollie Fingers	.35
586	Rollie Fingers (In Action)	.15
587	Tim Lollar	.08
588	Dale Berra	.08
589	Dave Stapleton	.08
590	Al Oliver	.12
591	Al Oliver (In Action)	.08
592	Craig Swan	.08
593	Billy Smith	.08
594	Renie Martin	.08
595	Dave Collins	.08
596	Damaso Garcia	.08
597	Wayne Nordhagen	.08
598	Bob Galasso	.08
599	White Sox Future Stars(Jay Loviglio, Reggie Patterson, Leo Sutherland)	.08
600	Dave Winfield	2.50
601	Sid Monge	.08
602	Freddie Patek	.08
603	Rich Hebner	.08
604	Orlando Sanchez	.08
605	Steve Rogers	.08
606	Blue Jays Batting & Pitching Ldrs.(John Mayberry, Dave Stieb)	.08
607	Leon Durham	.08
608	Jerry Royster	.08
609	Rick Sutcliffe	.12
610	Rickey Henderson	3.50
611	Joe Niekro	.08
612	Gary Ward	.08
613	Jim Foli	.08
614	Juan Eichelberger	.08
615	Bob Boone	.12
616	Bob Boone (In Action)	.10
617	Scott McGregor	.08
618	Tim Foli	.08
619	Bill Campbell	.08
620	Ken Griffey	.08

621	Ken Griffey (In Action)	.08
622	Dennis Lamp	.08
623	Mets Future Stars(Ron Gardenhire), *(Terry Leach)*, *(Tim Leary)*	.20
624	Fergie Jenkins	.65
625	Hal McRae	.12
626	Randy Jones	.08
627	Enos Cabell	.08
628	Bill Travers	.08
629	Johnny Wockenfuss	.08
630	Joe Charboneau	.10
631	Gene Tenace	.08
632	Bryan Clark	.08
633	Mitchell Page	.08
634	Checklist 529-660	.08
635	Ron Davis	.08
636	Phillies Batting & Pitching Ldrs.(Steve Carlton, Pete Rose)	.40
637	Rick Camp	.08
638	John Milner	.08
639	Ken Kravec	.08
640	Cesar Cedeno	.08
641	Steve Mura	.08
642	Mike Scioscia	.08
643	Pete Vuckovich	.08
644	John Castino	.08
645	Frank White	.08
646	Frank White (In Action)	.08
647	Warren Brusstar	.08
648	Jose Morales	.08
649	Ken Clay	.08
650	Carl Yastrzemski	1.50
651	Carl Yastrzemski (In Action)	.60
652	Steve Nicosia	.08
653	Angels Future Stars(Tom Brunansky), (Luis Sanchez), *(Daryl Sconiers)*	.40
654	Jim Morrison	.08
655	Joel Youngblood	.08
656	Eddie Whitson	.08
657	Tom Poquette	.08
658	Tito Landrum	.08
659	Fred Martinez	.08
660	Dave Concepcion	.12
661	Dave Concepcion (In Action)	.10
662	Luis Salazar	.08
663	Hector Cruz	.08
664	Dan Spillner	.08
665	Jim Clancy	.08
666	Tigers Batting & Pitching Ldrs.(Steve Kemp, Dan Petry)	.08
667	Jeff Reardon	.55
668	Dale Murphy	1.25
669	Larry Milbourne	.08
670	Steve Kemp	.08
671	Mike Davis	.08
672	Bob Knepper	.08
673	Keith Drumright	.08
674	Dave Goltz	.08
675	Cecil Cooper	.08
676	Sal Butera	.08
677	Alfredo Griffin	.08
678	Tom Paciorek	.08
679	Sammy Stewart	.08
680	Gary Matthews	.08
681	Dodgers Future Stars(Mike Marshall), (Ron Roenicke), *(Steve Sax)*	.75
682	Jesse Jefferson	.08
683	Phil Garner	.08
684	Harold Baines	.30
685	Bert Blyleven	.12
686	Gary Allenson	.08
687	Greg Minton	.08
688	Leon Roberts	.08
689	Lary Sorensen	.08
690	Dave Kingman	.10
691	Dan Schatzeder	.08
692	Wayne Gross	.08
693	Cesar Geronimo	.08
694	Dave Wehrmeister	.08
695	Warren Cromartie	.08
696	Pirates Batting & Pitching Ldrs.(Bill Madlock, Buddy Solomon)	.08
697	John Montefusco	.08
698	Tony Scott	.08
699	Dick Tidrow	.08
700	George Foster	.12
701	George Foster (In Action)	.08
702	Steve Renko	.08

703	Brewers Batting & Pitching Ldrs.(Cecil Cooper, Pete Vuckovich)	.08
704	Mickey Rivers	.08
705	Mickey Rivers (In Action)	.08
706	Barry Foote	.08
707	Mark Bomback	.08
708	Gene Richards	.08
709	Don Money	.08
710	Jerry Reuss	.08
711	Mariners Future Stars(Dave Edler), (Dave Henderson), *(Reggie Walton)*	.60
712	Denny Martinez	.10
713	Del Unser	.08
714	Jerry Koosman	.10
715	Willie Stargell	.80
716	Willie Stargell (In Action)	.30
717	Rick Miller	.08
718	Charlie Hough	.08
719	Jerry Narron	.08
720	Greg Luzinski	.15
721	Greg Luzinski (In Action)	.08
722	Jerry Martin	.08
723	Junior Kennedy	.08
724	Dave Rosello	.08
725	Amos Otis	.08
726	Amos Otis (In Action)	.08
727	Sixto Lezcano	.08
728	Aurelio Lopez	.08
729	Jim Spencer	.08
730	Gary Carter	.80
731	Padres Future Stars(Mike Armstrong, Doug Gwosdz, Fred Kuhaulua)	.08
732	Mike Lum	.08
733	Larry McWilliams	.08
734	Mike Ivie	.08
735	Rudy May	.08
736	Jerry Turner	.08
737	Reggie Cleveland	.08
738	Dave Engle	.08
739	Joey McLaughlin	.08
740	Dave Lopes	.08
741	Dave Lopes (In Action)	.08
742	Dick Drago	.08
743	John Stearns	.08
744	*Mike Witt*	.50
745	Bake McBride	.08
746	Andre Thornton	.08
747	John Lowenstein	.08
748	Marc Hill	.08
749	Bob Shirley	.08
750	Jim Rice	.15
751	Rick Honeycutt	.08
752	Lee Lacy	.08
753	Tom Brookens	.08
754	Joe Morgan	.70
755	Joe Morgan (In Action)	.20
756	Reds Batting & Pitching Ldrs.(Ken Griffey, Tom Seaver)	.30
757	Tom Underwood	.08
758	Claudell Washington	.08
759	Paul Splittorff	.08
760	Bill Buckner	.12
761	Dave Smith	.08
762	Mike Phillips	.08
763	Tom Hume	.08
764	Steve Swisher	.08
765	Gorman Thomas	.08
766	Twins Future Stars(Lenny Faedo), (Kent Hrbek), *(Tim Laudner)*	2.00
767	Roy Smalley	.08
768	Jerry Garvin	.08
769	Richie Zisk	.08
770	Rich Gossage	.15
771	Rich Gossage (In Action)	.08
772	Bert Campaneris	.08
773	John Denny	.08
774	Jay Johnstone	.08
775	Bob Forsch	.08
776	Mark Belanger	.08
777	Tom Griffin	.08
778	Kevin Hickey	.08
779	Grant Jackson	.08
780	Pete Rose	2.50
781	Pete Rose (In Action)	1.00
782	Frank Taveras	.08
783	*Greg Harris*	.15
784	Milt Wilcox	.08
785	Dan Driessen	.08
786	Red Sox Batting & Pitching Ldrs.(Carney Lansford, Mike Torrez)	.08

787	Fred Stanley	.08
788	Woodie Fryman	.08
789	Checklist 661-792	.08
790	Larry Gura	.08
791	Bobby Brown	.08
792	Frank Tanana	.08

1982 Topps Traded

Topps released its second straight 132-card Traded set in September of 1982. Again, the 2-1/2" x 3-1/2" cards feature not only players who had been traded during the season, but also promising rookies who were given their first individual cards. The cards follow the basic design of the regular issues, but have their backs printed in red rather than the regular-issue green. As in 1981, the cards were not available in normal retail outlets and could only be purchased through regular baseball card dealers. Unlike the previous year, the cards are numbered 1-132 with the letter "T" following the number.

		MT
Complete Set (132):		250.00
Common Player:		.20
1T	Doyle Alexander	.20
2T	Jesse Barfield	.20
3T	Ross Baumgarten	.20
4T	Steve Bedrosian	.20
5T	Mark Belanger	.20
6T	Kurt Bevacqua	.20
7T	Tim Blackwell	.20
8T	Vida Blue	.25
9T	Bob Boone	.30
10T	Larry Bowa	.25
11T	Dan Briggs	.20
12T	Bobby Brown	.20
13T	Tom Brunansky	.40
14T	Jeff Burroughs	.20
15T	Enos Cabell	.20
16T	Bill Campbell	.20
17T	Bobby Castillo	.20
18T	Bill Caudill	.20
19T	Cesar Cedeno	.20
20T	Dave Collins	.20
21T	Doug Corbett	.20
22T	Al Cowens	.20
23T	Chili Davis	2.00
24T	Dick Davis	.20
25T	Ron Davis	.20
26T	Doug DeCinces	.20
27T	Ivan DeJesus	.20
28T	Bob Dernier	.20
29T	Bo Diaz	.20
30T	Roger Erickson	.20
31T	Jim Essian	.20
32T	Ed Farmer	.20
33T	Doug Flynn	.20
34T	Tim Foli	.20
35T	Dan Ford	.20
36T	George Foster	.40

37T	Dave Frost	.20
38T	Rich Gale	.20
39T	Ron Gardenhire	.20
40T	Ken Griffey	.25
41T	Greg Harris	.20
42T	Von Hayes	.20
43T	Larry Herndon	.20
44T	Kent Hrbek	4.00
45T	Mike Ivie	.20
46T	Grant Jackson	.20
47T	Reggie Jackson	12.00
48T	Ron Jackson	.20
49T	Fergie Jenkins	2.50
50T	Lamar Johnson	.20
51T	Randy Johnson	.20
52T	Jay Johnstone	.20
53T	Mick Kelleher	.20
54T	Steve Kemp	.20
55T	Junior Kennedy	.20
56T	Jim Kern	.20
57T	Ray Knight	.20
58T	Wayne Krenchicki	.20
59T	Mike Krukow	.20
60T	Duane Kuiper	.20
61T	Mike LaCoss	.20
62T	Chet Lemon	.20
63T	Sixto Lezcano	.20
64T	Dave Lopes	.20
65T	Jerry Martin	.20
66T	Renie Martin	.20
67T	John Mayberry	.20
68T	Lee Mazzilli	.20
69T	Bake McBride	.20
70T	Dan Meyer	.20
71T	Larry Milbourne	.20
72T	Eddie Milner	.20
73T	Sid Monge	.20
74T	John Montefusco	.20
75T	Jose Morales	.20
76T	Keith Moreland	.20
77T	Jim Morrison	.20
78T	Rance Mulliniks	.20
79T	Steve Mura	.20
80T	Gene Nelson	.20
81T	Joe Nolan	.20
82T	Dickie Noles	.20
83T	Al Oliver	.30
84T	Jorge Orta	.20
85T	Tom Paciorek	.20
86T	Larry Parrish	.20
87T	Jack Perconte	.20
88T	Gaylord Perry	2.50
89T	Rob Picciolo	.20
90T	Joe Pittman	.20
91T	Hosken Powell	.20
92T	Mike Proly	.20
93T	Greg Pryor	.20
94T	Charlie Puleo	.20
95T	Shane Rawley	.20
96T	Johnny Ray	.20
97T	Dave Revering	.20
98T	Cal Ripken, Jr.	220.00
99T	Allen Ripley	.20
100T	Bill Robinson	.20
101T	Aurelio Rodriguez	.20
102T	Joe Rudi	.20
103T	Steve Sax	1.00
104T	Dan Schatzeder	.20
105T	Bob Shirley	.20
106T	Eric Show	.20
107T	Roy Smalley	.20
108T	Lonnie Smith	.20
109T	Ozzie Smith	25.00
110T	Reggie Smith	.20
111T	Lary Sorensen	.20
112T	Elias Sosa	.20
113T	Mike Stanton	.20
114T	Steve Stroughter	.20
115T	Champ Summers	.20
116T	Rick Sutcliffe	.40
117T	Frank Tanana	.20
118T	Frank Taveras	.20
119T	Garry Templeton	.20
120T	Alex Trevino	.20
121T	Jerry Turner	.20
122T	Ed Vande Berg	.20
123T	Tom Veryzer	.20
124T	Ron Washington	.20
125T	Bob Watson	.20
126T	Dennis Werth	.20
127T	Eddie Whitson	.20
128T	Rob Wilfong	.20
129T	Bump Wills	.20
130T	Gary Woods	.20
131T	Butch Wynegar	.20
132T	Checklist 1-132	.20

1983 Topps

The 1983 Topps set totals 792 cards. Missing among the regular 2-1/2" x 3-1/2" cards are some form of future stars cards, as Topps was saving them for the now-established late season "Traded" set. The 1983 cards carry a large color photo as well as a smaller color photo on the front, quite similar in design to the 1963 set. Team colors frame the card, which, at the bottom, have the player's name, position and team. At the upper right-hand corner is a Topps Logo. The backs are horizontal and include statistics, personal information and 1982 highlights. Specialty cards include record-breaking performances, league leaders, All-Stars, numbered check-lists "Team Leaders" and "Super Veteran" cards which are horizontal with a current and first-season picture of the honored player.

		MT
Complete Set (792):		140.00
Common Player:		.08
Wax Box:		230.00
1	Tony Armas (Record Breaker)	.10
2	Rickey Henderson (Record Breaker)	.75
3	Greg Minton (Record Breaker)	.08
4	Lance Parrish (Record Breaker)	.08
5	Manny Trillo (Record Breaker)	.08
6	John Wathan (Record Breaker)	.08
7	Gene Richards	.08
8	Steve Balboni	.08
9	Joey McLaughlin	.08
10	Gorman Thomas	.08
11	Billy Gardner	.08
12	Paul Mirabella	.08
13	Larry Herndon	.08
14	Frank LaCorte	.08
15	Ron Cey	.10
16	George Vukovich	.08
17	Kent Tekulve	.08
18	Kent Tekulve (Super Veteran)	.08
19	Oscar Gamble	.08
20	Carlton Fisk	.70
21	Orioles Batting & Pitching Ldrs.(Eddie Murray, Jim Palmer)	.25
22	Randy Martz	.08
23	Mike Heath	.08
24	Steve Mura	.08
25	Hal McRae	.08
26	Jerry Royster	.08

27	Doug Corbett	.08
28	Bruce Bochte	.08
29	Randy Jones	.08
30	Jim Rice	.12
31	Bill Gullickson	.08
32	Dave Bergman	.08
33	Jack O'Connor	.08
34	Paul Householder	.08
35	Rollie Fingers	.55
36	Rollie Fingers (Super Veteran)	.15
37	Darrell Johnson	.08
38	Tim Flannery	.08
39	Terry Puhl	.08
40	Fernando Valenzuela	.20
41	Jerry Turner	.08
42	Dale Murray	.08
43	Bob Dernier	.08
44	Don Robinson	.08
45	John Mayberry	.08
46	Richard Dotson	.08
47	Dave McKay	.08
48	Lary Sorensen	.08
49	*Willie McGee*	1.50
50	Bob Horner	.10
51	Cubs Batting & Pitching Ldrs.(Leon Durham, Fergie Jenkins)	.10
52	*Onix Concepcion*	.08
53	Mike Witt	.08
54	Jim Maler	.08
55	Mookie Wilson	.08
56	Chuck Rainey	.08
57	Tim Blackwell	.08
58	Al Holland	.08
59	Benny Ayala	.08
60	Johnny Bench	1.50
61	Johnny Bench (Super Veteran)	.60
62	Bob McClure	.08
63	Rick Monday	.08
64	Bill Stein	.08
65	Jack Morris	.20
66	Bob Lillis	.08
67	Sal Butera	.08
68	*Eric Show*	.15
69	Lee Lacy	.08
70	Steve Carlton	1.00
71	Steve Carlton (Super Veteran)	.30
72	Tom Paciorek	.08
73	Allen Ripley	.08
74	Julio Gonzalez	.08
75	Amos Otis	.08
76	Rick Mahler	.08
77	Hosken Powell	.08
78	Bill Caudill	.08
79	Mick Kelleher	.08
80	George Foster	.10
81	Yankees Batting & Pitching Ldrs.(Jerry Mumphrey, Dave Righetti)	.08
82	Bruce Hurst	.08
83	*Ryne Sandberg*	27.50
84	Milt May	.08
85	Ken Singleton	.08
86	Tom Hume	.08
87	Joe Rudi	.08
88	Jim Gantner	.08
89	Leon Roberts	.08
90	Jerry Reuss	.08
91	Larry Milbourne	.08
92	Mike LaCoss	.08
93	John Castino	.08
94	Dave Edwards	.08
95	Alan Trammell	.75
96	Dick Howser	.08
97	Ross Baumgarten	.08
98	Vance Law	.08
99	Dickie Noles	.08
100	Pete Rose	2.00
101	Pete Rose (Super Veteran)	1.00
102	Dave Beard	.08
103	Darrell Porter	.08
104	Bob Walk	.08
105	Don Baylor	.12
106	Gene Nelson	.08
107	Mike Jorgensen	.08
108	Glenn Hoffman	.08
109	Luis Leal	.08
110	Ken Griffey	.08
111	Expos Batting & Pitching Ldrs.(Al Oliver, Steve Rogers)	.08
112	Bob Shirley	.08
113	Ron Roenicke	.08

114	Jim Slaton	.08
115	Chili Davis	.50
116	Dave Schmidt	.08
117	Alan Knicely	.08
118	Chris Welsh	.08
119	Tom Brookens	.08
120	Len Barker	.08
121	Mickey Hatcher	.08
122	Jimmy Smith	.08
123	George Frazier	.08
124	Marc Hill	.08
125	Leon Durham	.08
126	Joe Torre	.10
127	Preston Hanna	.08
128	Mike Ramsey	.08
129	Checklist 1-132	.08
130	Dave Stieb	.15
131	Ed Ott	.08
132	Todd Cruz	.08
133	Jim Barr	.08
134	Hubie Brooks	.08
135	Dwight Evans	.10
136	Willie Aikens	.08
137	Woodie Fryman	.08
138	Rick Dempsey	.08
139	Bruce Berenyi	.08
140	Willie Randolph	.08
141	Indians Batting & Pitching Ldrs.(Toby Harrah, Rick Sutcliffe)	.08
142	Mike Caldwell	.08
143	Joe Pettini	.08
144	Mark Wagner	.08
145	Don Sutton	.50
146	Don Sutton (Super Veteran)	.20
147	Rick Leach	.08
148	Dave Roberts	.08
149	Johnny Ray	.08
150	Bruce Sutter	.10
151	Bruce Sutter (Super Veteran)	.08
152	Jay Johnstone	.08
153	Jerry Koosman	.10
154	Johnnie LeMaster	.08
155	Dan Quisenberry	.12
156	Billy Martin	.12
157	Steve Bedrosian	.08
158	Rob Wilfong	.08
159	Mike Stanton	.08
160	Dave Kingman	.12
161	Dave Kingman (Super Veteran)	.10
162	Mark Clear	.08
163	Cal Ripken, Jr.	24.00
164	Dave Palmer	.08
165	Dan Driessen	.08
166	John Pacella	.08
167	Mark Brouhard	.08
168	Juan Eichelberger	.08
169	Doug Flynn	.08
170	Steve Howe	.08
171	Giants Batting & Pitching Ldrs.(Bill Laskey, Joe Morgan)	.08
172	Vern Ruhle	.08
173	Jim Morrison	.08
174	Jerry Ujdur	.08
175	Bo Diaz	.08
176	Dave Righetti	.08
177	Harold Baines	.75
178	Luis Tiant	.12
179	Luis Tiant (Super Veteran)	.08
180	Rickey Henderson	3.00
181	Terry Felton	.08
182	Mike Fischlin	.08
183	*Ed Vande Berg*	.08
184	Bob Clark	.08
185	Tim Lollar	.08
186	Whitey Herzog	.10
187	Terry Leach	.08
188	Rick Miller	.08
189	Dan Schatzeder	.08
190	Cecil Cooper	.08
191	Joe Price	.08
192	Floyd Rayford	.08
193	Harry Spilman	.08
194	Cesar Geronimo	.08
195	Bob Stoddard	.08
196	Bill Fahey	.08
197	*Jim Eisenreich*	.50
198	Kiko Garcia	.08
199	Marty Bystrom	.08
200	Rod Carew	.90
201	Rod Carew (Super Veteran)	.35

202	Blue Jays Batting & Pitching Ldrs.(Damaso Garcia, Dave Stieb)	.08
203	Mike Morgan	.08
204	Junior Kennedy	.08
205	Dave Parker	.40
206	Ken Oberkfell	.08
207	Rick Camp	.08
208	Dan Meyer	.08
209	*Mike Moore*	.60
210	Jack Clark	.08
211	John Denny	.08
212	John Stearns	.08
213	Tom Burgmeier	.08
214	Jerry White	.08
215	Mario Soto	.08
216	Tony LaRussa	.10
217	Tim Stoddard	.08
218	Roy Howell	.08
219	Mike Armstrong	.08
220	Dusty Baker	.08
221	Joe Niekro	.12
222	Damaso Garcia	.08
223	John Montefusco	.08
224	Mickey Rivers	.08
225	Enos Cabell	.08
226	Enrique Romo	.08
227	Chris Bando	.08
228	Joaquin Andujar	.08
229	Phillies Batting/Pitching Leaders(Steve Carlton, Bo Diaz)	.15
230	Fergie Jenkins	.60
231	Fergie Jenkins (Super Veteran)	.20
232	Tom Brunansky	.08
233	Wayne Gross	.08
234	Larry Andersen	.08
235	Claudell Washington	.08
236	Steve Renko	.08
237	Dan Norman	.08
238	*Bud Black*	.55
239	Dave Stapleton	.08
240	Rich Gossage	.12
241	Rich Gossage (Super Veteran)	.08
242	Joe Nolan	.08
243	Duane Walker	.08
244	Dwight Bernard	.08
245	Steve Sax	.08
246	George Bamberger	.08
247	Dave Smith	.08
248	Bake McBride	.08
249	Checklist 133-264	.08
250	Bill Buckner	.12
251	*Alan Wiggins*	.08
252	Luis Aguayo	.08
253	Larry McWilliams	.08
254	Rick Cerone	.08
255	Gene Garber	.08
256	Gene Garber (Super Veteran)	.08
257	Jesse Barfield	.08
258	Manny Castillo	.08
259	Jeff Jones	.08
260	Steve Kemp	.08
261	Tigers Batting & Pitching Ldrs.(Larry Herndon, Dan Petry)	.08
262	Ron Jackson	.08
263	Renie Martin	.08
264	Jamie Quirk	.08
265	Joel Youngblood	.08
266	Paul Boris	.08
267	Terry Francona	.08
268	*Storm Davis*	.08
269	Ron Oester	.08
270	Dennis Eckersley	.90
271	Ed Romero	.08
272	Frank Tanana	.08
273	Mark Belanger	.08
274	Terry Kennedy	.08
275	Ray Knight	.08
276	Gene Mauch	.08
277	Rance Mulliniks	.08
278	Kevin Hickey	.08
279	Greg Gross	.08
280	Bert Blyleven	.15
281	Andre Robertson	.08
282	Reggie Smith	.08
283	Reggie Smith (Super Veteran)	.08
284	Jeff Lahti	.08
285	Lance Parrish	.12
286	Rick Langford	.08
287	Bobby Brown	.08

No.	Player	Value
288	*Joe Cowley*	.08
289	Jerry Dybzinski	.08
290	Jeff Reardon	.20
291	Pirates Batting & Pitching Ldrs.(John Candelaria, Bill Madlock)	.08
292	Craig Swan	.08
293	Glenn Gulliver	.08
294	Dave Engle	.08
295	Jerry Remy	.08
296	Greg Harris	.08
297	Ned Yost	.08
298	Floyd Chiffer	.08
299	George Wright	.08
300	Mike Schmidt	3.50
301	Mike Schmidt (Super Veteran)	1.00
302	Ernie Whitt	.08
303	Miguel Dilone	.08
304	Dave Rucker	.08
305	Larry Bowa	.10
306	Tom Lasorda	.25
307	Lou Piniella	.10
308	Jesus Vega	.08
309	Jeff Leonard	.08
310	Greg Luzinski	.12
311	Glenn Brummer	.08
312	Brian Kingman	.08
313	Gary Gray	.08
314	Ken Dayley	.08
315	Rick Burleson	.08
316	Paul Splittorff	.08
317	Gary Rajsich	.08
318	John Tudor	.08
319	Lenn Sakata	.08
320	Steve Rogers	.08
321	Brewers Batting & Pitching Ldrs.(Pete Vuckovich, Robin Yount)	.20
322	Dave Van Gorder	.08
323	Luis DeLeon	.08
324	Mike Marshall	.08
325	Von Hayes	.08
326	Garth Iorg	.08
327	Bobby Castillo	.08
328	Craig Reynolds	.08
329	Randy Niemann	.08
330	Buddy Bell	.10
331	Mike Krukow	.08
332	*Glenn Wilson*	.08
333	Dave LaRoche	.08
334	Dave LaRoche (Super Veteran)	.08
335	Steve Henderson	.08
336	Rene Lachemann	.08
337	Tito Landrum	.08
338	Bob Owchinko	.08
339	Terry Harper	.08
340	Larry Gura	.08
341	Doug DeCinces	.08
342	Atlee Hammaker	.08
343	Bob Bailor	.08
344	Roger LaFrancois	.08
345	Jim Clancy	.08
346	Joe Pittman	.08
347	Sammy Stewart	.08
348	Alan Bannister	.08
349	Checklist 265-396	.08
350	Robin Yount	3.00
351	Reds Batting & Pitching Ldrs.(Cesar Cedeno, Mario Soto)	.08
352	Mike Scioscia	.08
353	Steve Comer	.08
354	Randy S. Johnson	.08
355	Jim Bibby	.08
356	Gary Woods	.08
357	*Len Matuszek*	.08
358	Jerry Garvin	.08
359	Dave Collins	.08
360	Nolan Ryan	12.00
361	Nolan Ryan (Super Veteran)	5.00
362	Bill Almon	.08
363	*John Stuper*	.08
364	Brett Butler	.60
365	Dave Lopes	.10
366	Dick Williams	.08
367	Bud Anderson	.08
368	Richie Zisk	.08
369	Jesse Orosco	.08
370	Gary Carter	.25
371	Mike Richardt	.08
372	Terry Crowley	.08
373	Kevin Saucier	.08
374	Wayne Krenchicki	.08
375	Pete Vuckovich	.08
376	Ken Landreaux	.08
377	Lee May	.08
378	Lee May (Super Veteran)	.08
379	Guy Sularz	.08
380	Ron Davis	.08
381	Red Sox Batting & Pitching Ldrs.(Jim Rice, Bob Stanley)	.08
382	Bob Knepper	.08
383	Ozzie Virgil	.08
384	*Dave Dravecky*	.50
385	Mike Easler	.08
386	Rod Carew (All-Star)	.40
387	Bob Grich (All-Star)	.08
388	George Brett (All-Star)	1.25
389	Robin Yount (All-Star)	.60
390	Reggie Jackson (All-Star)	.75
391	Rickey Henderson (All-Star)	.40
392	Fred Lynn (All-Star)	.08
393	Carlton Fisk (All-Star)	.15
394	Pete Vuckovich (All-Star)	.08
395	Larry Gura (All-Star)	.08
396	Dan Quisenberry (All-Star)	.08
397	Pete Rose (All-Star)	.75
398	Manny Trillo (All-Star)	.08
399	Mike Schmidt (All-Star)	1.00
400	Dave Concepcion (All-Star)	.08
401	Dale Murphy (All-Star)	.20
402	Andre Dawson (All-Star)	.40
403	Tim Raines (All-Star)	.25
404	Gary Carter (All-Star)	.20
405	Steve Rogers (All-Star)	.08
406	Steve Carlton (All-Star)	.50
407	Bruce Sutter (All-Star)	.08
408	Rudy May	.08
409	Marvis Foley	.08
410	Phil Niekro	.75
411	Phil Niekro (Super Veteran)	.25
412	Rangers Batting & Pitching Ldrs.(Buddy Bell, Charlie Hough)	.08
413	Matt Keough	.08
414	Julio Cruz	.08
415	Bob Forsch	.08
416	Joe Ferguson	.08
417	Tom Hausman	.08
418	Greg Pryor	.08
419	Steve Crawford	.08
420	Al Oliver	.10
421	Al Oliver (Super Veteran)	.08
422	George Cappuzzello	.08
423	*Tom Lawless*	.08
424	Jerry Augustine	.08
425	Pedro Guerrero	.08
426	Earl Weaver	.20
427	Roy Lee Jackson	.08
428	Champ Summers	.08
429	Eddie Whitson	.08
430	Kirk Gibson	.35
431	*Gary Gaetti*	.75
432	Porfirio Altamirano	.08
433	Dale Berra	.08
434	Dennis Lamp	.08
435	Tony Armas	.08
436	Bill Campbell	.08
437	Rick Sweet	.08
438	*Dave LaPoint*	.08
439	Rafael Ramirez	.08
440	Ron Guidry	.20
441	Astros Batting & Pitching Ldrs.(Ray Knight, Joe Niekro)	.08
442	Brian Downing	.08
443	Don Hood	.08
444	Wally Backman	.08
445	Mike Flanagan	.08
446	Reid Nichols	.08
447	Bryn Smith	.08
448	Darrell Evans	.15
449	*Eddie Milner*	.08
450	Ted Simmons	.08
451	Ted Simmons (Super Veteran)	.08
452	Lloyd Moseby	.08
453	Lamar Johnson	.08
454	Bob Welch	.08
455	Sixto Lezcano	.08
456	Lee Elia	.08
457	Milt Wilcox	.08
458	Ron Washington	.08
459	Ed Farmer	.08
460	Roy Smalley	.08
461	Steve Trout	.08
462	Steve Nicosia	.08
463	Gaylord Perry	.50
464	Gaylord Perry (Super Veteran)	.20
465	Lonnie Smith	.08
466	Tom Underwood	.08
467	Rufino Linares	.08
468	Dave Goltz	.08
469	Ron Gardenhire	.08
470	Greg Minton	.08
471	Royals Batting & Pitching Ldrs.(Vida Blue, Willie Wilson)	.08
472	Gary Allenson	.08
473	John Lowenstein	.08
474	Ray Burris	.08
475	Cesar Cedeno	.08
476	Rob Picciolo	.08
477	Tom Niedenfuer	.08
478	Phil Garner	.08
479	Charlie Hough	.08
480	Toby Harrah	.08
481	Scot Thompson	.08
482	*Tony Gwynn*	60.00
483	Lynn Jones	.08
484	Dick Ruthven	.08
485	Omar Moreno	.08
486	Clyde King	.08
487	Jerry Hairston	.08
488	Alfredo Griffin	.08
489	Tom Herr	.08
490	Jim Palmer	.90
491	Jim Palmer (Super Veteran)	.20
492	Paul Serna	.08
493	Steve McCatty	.08
494	Bob Brenly	.08
495	Warren Cromartie	.08
496	Tom Veryzer	.08
497	Rick Sutcliffe	.08
498	*Wade Boggs*	20.00
499	Jeff Little	.08
500	Reggie Jackson	2.00
501	Reggie Jackson (Super Veteran)	.75
502	Braves Batting & Pitching Ldrs.(Dale Murphy, Phil Niekro)	.30
503	Moose Haas	.08
504	Don Werner	.08
505	Garry Templeton	.08
506	*Jim Gott*	.25
507	Tony Scott	.08
508	Tom Filer	.08
509	Lou Whitaker	.15
510	Tug McGraw	.10
511	Tug McGraw (Super Veteran)	.08
512	Doyle Alexander	.08
513	Fred Stanley	.08
514	Rudy Law	.08
515	Gene Tenace	.08
516	Bill Virdon	.08
517	Gary Ward	.08
518	Bill Laskey	.08
519	Terry Bulling	.08
520	Fred Lynn	.12
521	Bruce Benedict	.08
522	Pat Zachry	.08
523	Carney Lansford	.08
524	Tom Brennan	.08
525	Frank White	.08
526	Checklist 397-528	.08
527	Larry Biittner	.08
528	Jamie Easterly	.08
529	Tim Laudner	.08
530	Eddie Murray	3.00
531	Athletics Batting & Pitching Ldrs.(Rickey Henderson, Rick Langford)	.15
532	Dave Stewart	.75
533	Luis Salazar	.08
534	John Butcher	.08
535	Manny Trillo	.08
536	Johnny Wockenfuss	.08
537	Rod Scurry	.08
538	Danny Heep	.08
539	Roger Erickson	.08
540	Ozzie Smith	3.00
541	Britt Burns	.08
542	Jody Davis	.08
543	Alan Fowlkes	.08
544	Larry Whisenton	.08
545	Floyd Bannister	.08
546	Dave Garcia	.08
547	Geoff Zahn	.08
548	Brian Giles	.08
549	*Charlie Puleo*	.08
550	Carl Yastrzemski	1.00

551	Carl Yastrzemski (Super Veteran)	.40
552	Tim Wallach	.25
553	Denny Martinez	.10
554	Mike Vail	.08
555	Steve Yeager	.08
556	Willie Upshaw	.08
557	Rick Honeycutt	.08
558	Dickie Thon	.08
559	Pete Redfern	.08
560	Ron LeFlore	.08
561	Cardinals Batting & Pitching Ldrs.(Joaquin Andujar, Lonnie Smith)	.08
562	Dave Rozema	.08
563	Juan Bonilla	.08
564	Sid Monge	.08
565	Bucky Dent	.08
566	Manny Sarmiento	.08
567	Joe Simpson	.08
568	Willie Hernandez	.08
569	Jack Perconte	.08
570	Vida Blue	.08
571	Mickey Klutts	.08
572	Bob Watson	.08
573	Andy Hassler	.08
574	Glenn Adams	.08
575	Neil Allen	.08
576	Frank Robinson	.12
577	Luis Aponte	.08
578	David Green	.08
579	Rich Dauer	.08
580	Tom Seaver	2.00
581	Tom Seaver (Super Veteran)	.50
582	Marshall Edwards	.08
583	Terry Forster	.08
584	Dave Hostetler	.08
585	Jose Cruz	.08
586	*Frank Viola*	1.50
587	Ivan DeJesus	.08
588	Pat Underwood	.08
589	Alvis Woods	.08
590	Tony Pena	.08
591	White Sox Batting & Pitching Ldrs.(LaMarr Hoyt, Greg Luzinski)	.08
592	Shane Rawley	.08
593	Broderick Perkins	.08
594	Eric Rasmussen	.08
595	Tim Raines	.60
596	Randy S. Johnson	.08
597	Mike Proly	.08
598	Dwayne Murphy	.08
599	Don Aase	.08
600	George Brett	4.00
601	Ed Lynch	.08
602	Rich Gedman	.08
603	Joe Morgan	.60
604	Joe Morgan (Super Veteran)	.15
605	Gary Roenicke	.08
606	Bobby Cox	.08
607	Charlie Leibrandt	.08
608	Don Money	.08
609	Danny Darwin	.08
610	Steve Garvey	.50
611	Bert Roberge	.08
612	Steve Swisher	.08
613	Mike Ivie	.08
614	Ed Glynn	.08
615	Garry Maddox	.08
616	Bill Nahorodny	.08
617	Butch Wynegar	.08
618	LaMarr Hoyt	.08
619	Keith Moreland	.08
620	Mike Norris	.08
621	Mets Batting & Pitching Ldrs.(Craig Swan, Mookie Wilson)	.08
622	Dave Edler	.08
623	Luis Sanchez	.08
624	Glenn Hubbard	.08
625	Ken Forsch	.08
626	Jerry Martin	.08
627	Doug Bair	.08
628	Julio Valdez	.08
629	Charlie Lea	.08
630	Paul Molitor	3.00
631	Tippy Martinez	.08
632	Alex Trevino	.08
633	Vicente Romo	.08
634	Max Venable	.08
635	Graig Nettles	.10
636	Graig Nettles (Super Veteran)	

637	Pat Corrales	.08
638	Dan Petry	.08
639	Art Howe	.08
640	Andre Thornton	.08
641	Billy Sample	.08
642	Checklist 529-660	.08
643	Bump Wills	.08
644	Joe Lefebvre	.08
645	Bill Madlock	.10
646	Jim Essian	.08
647	Bobby Mitchell	.08
648	Jeff Burroughs	.08
649	Tommy Boggs	.08
650	George Hendrick	.08
651	Angels Batting & Pitching Ldrs.(Rod Carew, Mike Witt)	.12
652	Butch Hobson	.08
653	Ellis Valentine	.08
654	Bob Ojeda	.10
655	Al Bumbry	.08
656	Dave Frost	.08
657	Mike Gates	.08
658	Frank Pastore	.08
659	Charlie Moore	.08
660	Mike Hargrove	.08
661	Bill Russell	.08
662	Joe Sambito	.08
663	Tom O'Malley	.08
664	Bob Molinaro	.08
665	Jim Sundberg	.08
666	Sparky Anderson	.12
667	Dick Davis	.08
668	Larry Christenson	.08
669	Mike Squires	.08
670	Jerry Mumphrey	.08
671	Lenny Faedo	.08
672	Jim Kaat	.20
673	Jim Kaat (Super Veteran)	.10
674	Kurt Bevacqua	.08
675	Jim Beattie	.08
676	Biff Pocoroba	.08
677	Dave Revering	.08
678	Juan Beniquez	.08
679	Mike Scott	.08
680	Andre Dawson	1.50
681	Dodgers Batting & Pitching Ldrs.(Pedro Guerrero, Fernando Valenzuela)	.10
682	Bob Stanley	.08
683	Dan Ford	.08
684	Rafael Landestoy	.08
685	Lee Mazzilli	.08
686	Randy Lerch	.08
687	U.L. Washington	.08
688	Jim Wohlford	.08
689	Ron Hassey	.08
690	Kent Hrbek	.70
691	Dave Tobik	.08
692	Denny Walling	.08
693	Sparky Lyle	.08
694	Sparky Lyle (Super Veteran)	.08
695	Ruppert Jones	.08
696	Chuck Tanner	.08
697	Barry Foote	.08
698	Tony Bernazard	.08
699	Lee Smith	2.50
700	Keith Hernandez	.12
701	Batting Leaders(Al Oliver, Willie Wilson)	.08
702	Home Run Leaders(Reggie Jackson, Dave Kingman, Gorman Thomas)	.15
703	Runs Batted In Leaders(Hal McRae, Dale Murphy, Al Oliver)	.10
704	Stolen Base Leaders(Rickey Henderson, Tim Raines)	.20
705	Victory Leaders(Steve Carlton, LaMarr Hoyt)	.10
706	Strikeout Leaders(Floyd Bannister, Steve Carlton)	.10
707	Earned Run Average Leaders(Steve Rogers, Rick Sutcliffe)	.08
708	Leading Firemen(Dan Quisenberry, Bruce Sutter)	.08
709	Jimmy Sexton	.08
710	Willie Wilson	.08
711	Mariners Batting & Pitching Ldrs.(Jim Beattie, Bruce Bochte)	.08
712	Bruce Kison	.08
713	Ron Hodges	.08
714	Wayne Nordhagen	.08

715	Tony Perez	.15
716	Tony Perez (Super Veteran)	.08
717	Scott Sanderson	.08
718	Jim Dwyer	.08
719	Rich Gale	.08
720	Dave Concepcion	.10
721	John Martin	.08
722	Jorge Orta	.08
723	Randy Moffitt	.08
724	Johnny Grubb	.08
725	Dan Spillner	.08
726	Harvey Kuenn	.08
727	Chet Lemon	.08
728	Ron Reed	.08
729	Jerry Morales	.08
730	Jason Thompson	.08
731	Al Williams	.08
732	Dave Henderson	.08
733	Buck Martinez	.08
734	Steve Braun	.08
735	Tommy John	.25
736	Tommy John (Super Veteran)	.10
737	Mitchell Page	.08
738	Tim Foli	.08
739	Rick Ownbey	.08
740	Rusty Staub	.15
741	Rusty Staub (Super Veteran)	.10
742	Padres Batting & Pitching Ldrs.(Terry Kennedy, Tim Lollar)	.08
743	Mike Torrez	.08
744	Brad Mills	.08
745	Scott McGregor	.08
746	John Wathan	.08
747	Fred Breining	.08
748	Derrel Thomas	.08
749	Jon Matlack	.08
750	Ben Oglivie	.08
751	Brad Havens	.08
752	Luis Pujols	.08
753	Elias Sosa	.08
754	Bill Robinson	.08
755	John Candelaria	.08
756	Russ Nixon	.08
757	Rick Manning	.08
758	Aurelio Rodriguez	.08
759	Doug Bird	.08
760	Dale Murphy	.75
761	Gary Lucas	.08
762	Cliff Johnson	.08
763	Al Cowens	.08
764	Pete Falcone	.08
765	Bob Boone	.12
766	Barry Bonnell	.08
767	Duane Kuiper	.08
768	Chris Speier	.08
769	Checklist 661-792	.08
770	Dave Winfield	2.50
771	Twins Batting & Pitching Ldrs.(Bobby Castillo, Kent Hrbek)	.08
772	Jim Kern	.08
773	Larry Hisle	.08
774	Alan Ashby	.08
775	Burt Hooton	.08
776	Larry Parrish	.08
777	John Curtis	.08
778	Rich Hebner	.08
779	Rick Waits	.08
780	Gary Matthews	.08
781	Rick Rhoden	.08
782	Bobby Murcer	.08
783	Bobby Murcer (Super Veteran)	.08
784	Jeff Newman	.08
785	Dennis Leonard	.08
786	Ralph Houk	.08
787	Dick Tidrow	.08
788	Dane Iorg	.08
789	Bryan Clark	.08
790	Bob Grich	.08
791	Gary Lavelle	.08
792	Chris Chambliss	.08

1983 Topps Traded

These 2-1/2" x 3-1/2" cards mark a continuation of the traded set introduced in 1981. The 132 cards retain the basic design of the year's regular issue, with their numbering being 1-132 with the "T" suffix. Cards in the set include traded players, new managers and promising rookies. Sold only through dealers, the set was in heavy demand as it contained the first cards of Darryl Strawberry, Ron Kittle, Julio Franco and Mel Hall. While some of those cards were very hot in 1983, it seems likely that some of the rookies may not live up to their initial promise.

		MT
Complete Set (132):		50.00
Common Player:		.10
1T	Neil Allen	.10
2T	Bill Almon	.10
3T	Joe Altobelli	.10
4T	Tony Armas	.10
5T	Doug Bair	.10
6T	Steve Baker	.10
7T	Floyd Bannister	.10
8T	Don Baylor	.50
9T	Tony Bernazard	.10
10T	Larry Biittner	.10
11T	Dann Bilardello	.10
12T	Doug Bird	.10
13T	Steve Boros	.10
14T	Greg Brock	.10
15T	Mike Brown	.10
16T	Tom Burgmeier	.10
17T	Randy Bush	.10
18T	Bert Campaneris	.10
19T	Ron Cey	.10
20T	Chris Codiroli	.10
21T	Dave Collins	.10
22T	Terry Crowley	.10
23T	Julio Cruz	.10
24T	Mike Davis	.10
25T	Frank DiPino	.10
26T	Bill Doran	.25
27T	Jerry Dybzinski	.10
28T	Jamie Easterly	.10
29T	Juan Eichelberger	.10
30T	Jim Essian	.10
31T	Pete Falcone	.10
32T	Mike Ferraro	.10
33T	Terry Forster	.10
34T	*Julio Franco*	4.00
35T	Rich Gale	.10
36T	Kiko Garcia	.10
37T	Steve Garvey	2.00
38T	Johnny Grubb	.10
39T	Mel Hall	.25
40T	Von Hayes	.25
41T	Danny Heep	.10
42T	Steve Henderson	.10
43T	Keith Hernandez	.10
44T	Leo Hernandez	.10
45T	Willie Hernandez	.10
46T	Al Holland	.10
47T	Frank Howard	.15
48T	Bobby Johnson	.10
49T	Cliff Johnson	.10
50T	Odell Jones	.10
51T	Mike Jorgensen	.10
52T	Bob Kearney	.10
53T	Steve Kemp	.10

54T	Matt Keough	.10
55T	Ron Kittle	.10
56T	Mickey Klutts	.10
57T	Alan Knicely	.10
58T	Mike Krukow	.10
59T	Rafael Landestoy	.10
60T	Carney Lansford	.10
61T	Joe Lefebvre	.10
62T	Bryan Little	.10
63T	Aurelio Lopez	.10
64T	Mike Madden	.10
65T	Rick Manning	.10
66T	Billy Martin	.35
67T	Lee Mazzilli	.10
68T	Andy McGaffigan	.10
69T	Craig McMurtry	.10
70T	John McNamara	.10
71T	Orlando Mercado	.10
72T	Larry Milbourne	.10
73T	Randy Moffitt	.10
74T	Sid Monge	.10
75T	Jose Morales	.10
76T	Omar Moreno	.10
77T	Joe Morgan	4.00
78T	Mike Morgan	.10
79T	Dale Murray	.10
80T	Jeff Newman	.10
81T	Pete O'Brien	.50
82T	Jorge Orta	.10
83T	Alejandro Pena	.10
84T	Pascual Perez	.20
85T	Tony Perez	1.50
86T	Broderick Perkins	.10
87T	*Tony Phillips*	4.00
88T	Charlie Puleo	.10
89T	Pat Putnam	.10
90T	Jamie Quirk	.10
91T	Doug Rader	.10
92T	Chuck Rainey	.10
93T	Bobby Ramos	.10
94T	Gary Redus	.10
95T	Steve Renko	.10
96T	Leon Roberts	.10
97T	Aurelio Rodriguez	.10
98T	Dick Ruthven	.10
99T	Daryl Sconiers	.10
100T	Mike Scott	.10
101T	Tom Seaver	7.50
102T	John Shelby	.10
103T	Bob Shirley	.10
104T	Joe Simpson	.10
105T	Doug Sisk	.10
106T	Mike Smithson	.10
107T	Elias Sosa	.10
108T	*Darryl Strawberry*	12.00
109T	Tom Tellmann	.10
110T	Gene Tenace	.10
111T	Gorman Thomas	.10
112T	Dick Tidrow	.10
113T	Dave Tobik	.10
114T	Wayne Tolleson	.10
115T	Mike Torrez	.10
116T	Manny Trillo	.10
117T	Steve Trout	.10
118T	Lee Tunnell	.10
119T	Mike Vail	.10
120T	Ellis Valentine	.10
121T	Tom Veryzer	.10
122T	George Vukovich	.10
123T	Rick Waits	.10
124T	Greg Walker	.10
125T	Chris Welsh	.10
126T	Len Whitehouse	.10
127T	Eddie Whitson	.10
128T	Jim Wohlford	.10
129T	Matt Young	.10
130T	Joel Youngblood	.10
131T	Pat Zachry	.10
132T	Checklist 1-132	.10

1984 Topps

Another 792-card regular set from Topps. For the second straight year, the 2-1/2" x 3-1/2" cards featured a color action photo on the front along with a small portrait photo in the lower left. The team name runs in big letters down the left side, while the player's name and position runs under the large action photo. In the upper right-

hand corner is the Topps logo. Backs have a team logo in the upper right corner, along with statistics, personal information and a few highlights. The backs have an unusual and hard-to-read red and purple coloring. Specialty cards include past season highlights, team leaders, major league statistical leaders, All-Stars, active career leaders and numbered checklists. Again, promising rookies were saved for the traded set. Late in 1984, Topps introduced a specially boxed "Tiffany" edition of the 1984 set, with the cards printed on white cardboard with a glossy finish. A total of 10,000 sets were produced. Prices for Tiffany edition superstars can run from six to eight times the value of the "regular" edition, while common cards sell in the 40¢ range.

		MT
Complete Set (792):		60.00
Common Player:		.08
Wax Box:		90.00
1	Steve Carlton (1983 Highlight)	.25
2	Rickey Henderson (1983 Highlight)	.40
3	Dan Quisenberry (1983 Highlight)	.08
4	Steve Carlton, Gaylord Perry, Nolan Ryan (1983 Highlight)	.75
5	Bob Forsch, Dave Righetti, Mike Warren (1983 Highlight)	.08
6	Johnny Bench, Gaylord Perry, Carl Yastrzemski (1983 Highlight)	.30
7	Gary Lucas	.08
8	*Don Mattingly*	16.00
9	Jim Gott	.08
10	Robin Yount	2.00
11	Twins Batting & Pitching Leaders(Kent Hrbek, Ken Schrom)	.08
12	Billy Sample	.08
13	Scott Holman	.08
14	Tom Brookens	.08
15	Burt Hooton	.08
16	Omar Moreno	.08
17	John Denny	.08
18	Dale Berra	.08
19	*Ray Fontenot*	.08
20	Greg Luzinski	.12
21	Joe Altobelli	.08
22	Bryan Clark	.08
23	Keith Moreland	.08
24	John Martin	.08
25	Glenn Hubbard	.08
26	Bud Black	.08
27	Daryl Sconiers	.08
28	Frank Viola	.20
29	Danny Heep	.08

30	Wade Boggs	4.00
31	*Andy McGaffigan*	.08
32	Bobby Ramos	.08
33	Tom Burgmeier	.08
34	Eddie Milner	.08
35	Don Sutton	.20
36	Denny Walling	.08
37	Rangers Batting & Pitching Leaders(Buddy Bell, Rick Honeycutt)	.08
38	Luis DeLeon	.08
39	Garth Iorg	.08
40	Dusty Baker	.08
41	Tony Bernazard	.08
42	Johnny Grubb	.08
43	Ron Reed	.08
44	Jim Morrison	.08
45	Jerry Mumphrey	.08
46	Ray Smith	.08
47	Rudy Law	.08
48	Julio Franco	.60
49	John Stuper	.08
50	Chris Chambliss	.08
51	Jim Frey	.08
52	Paul Splittorff	.08
53	Juan Beniquez	.08
54	Jesse Orosco	.08
55	Dave Concepcion	.12
56	Gary Allenson	.08
57	Dan Schatzeder	.08
58	Max Venable	.08
59	Sammy Stewart	.08
60	Paul Molitor	2.00
61	*Chris Codiroli*	.08
62	Dave Hostetler	.08
63	Ed Vande Berg	.08
64	Mike Scioscia	.08
65	Kirk Gibson	.30
66	Astros Batting & Pitching Leaders(Jose Cruz, Nolan Ryan)	.25
67	Gary Ward	.08
68	Luis Salazar	.08
69	Rod Scurry	.08
70	Gary Matthews	.08
71	Leo Hernandez	.08
72	Mike Squires	.08
73	Jody Davis	.08
74	Jerry Martin	.08
75	Bob Forsch	.08
76	Alfredo Griffin	.08
77	Brett Butler	.10
78	Mike Torrez	.08
79	Rob Wilfong	.08
80	Steve Rogers	.08
81	Billy Martin	.10
82	Doug Bird	.08
83	Richie Zisk	.08
84	Lenny Faedo	.08
85	Atlee Hammaker	.08
86	*John Shelby*	.08
87	Frank Pastore	.08
88	Rob Picciolo	.08
89	*Mike Smithson*	.08
90	Pedro Guerrero	.08
91	Dan Spillner	.08
92	Lloyd Moseby	.08
93	Bob Knepper	.08
94	Mario Ramirez	.08
95	Aurelio Lopez	.08
96	Royals Batting & Pitching Leaders(Larry Gura, Hal McRae)	.08
97	LaMarr Hoyt	.08
98	Steve Nicosia	.08
99	*Craig Lefferts*	.25
100	Reggie Jackson	1.50
101	Porfirio Altamirano	.08
102	Ken Oberkfell	.08
103	Dwayne Murphy	.08
104	Ken Dayley	.08
105	Tony Armas	.08
106	Tim Stoddard	.08
107	Ned Yost	.08
108	Randy Moffitt	.08
109	Brad Wellman	.08
110	Ron Guidry	.10
111	Bill Virdon	.08
112	Tom Niedenfuer	.08
113	Kelly Paris	.08
114	Checklist 1-132	.08
115	Andre Thornton	.08
116	George Bjorkman	.08
117	Tom Veryzer	.08
118	Charlie Hough	.08
119	Johnny Wockenfuss	.08

120	Keith Hernandez	.10
121	*Pat Sheridan*	.08
122	Cecilio Guante	.08
123	Butch Wynegar	.08
124	Damaso Garcia	.08
125	Britt Burns	.08
126	Braves Batting & Pitching Leaders(Craig McMurtry, Dale Murphy)	.10
127	Mike Madden	.08
128	Rick Manning	.08
129	Bill Laskey	.08
130	Ozzie Smith	1.50
131	Batting Leaders(Wade Boggs, Bill Madlock)	.25
132	Home Run Leaders(Jim Rice, Mike Schmidt)	.30
133	RBI Leaders(Cecil Cooper, Dale Murphy, Jim Rice)	.25
134	Stolen Base Leaders(Rickey Henderson, Tim Raines)	.25
135	Victory Leaders(John Denny, LaMarr Hoyt)	.08
136	Strikeout Leaders(Steve Carlton, Jack Morris)	.12
137	Earned Run Average Leaders(Atlee Hammaker, Rick Honeycutt)	.08
138	Leading Firemen(Al Holland, Dan Quisenberry)	.08
139	Bert Campaneris	.08
140	Storm Davis	.08
141	Pat Corrales	.08
142	Rich Gale	.08
143	Jose Morales	.08
144	*Brian Harper*	.35
145	Gary Lavelle	.08
146	Ed Romero	.08
147	Dan Petry	.08
148	Joe Lefebvre	.08
149	Jon Matlack	.08
150	Dale Murphy	.40
151	Steve Trout	.08
152	Glenn Brummer	.08
153	Dick Tidrow	.08
154	Dave Henderson	.08
155	Frank White	.08
156	Athletics Batting & Pitching Leaders(Tim Conroy, Rickey Henderson)	.15
157	Gary Gaetti	.25
158	John Curtis	.08
159	Darryl Cias	.08
160	Mario Soto	.08
161	*Junior Ortiz*	.10
162	Bob Ojeda	.08
163	Lorenzo Gray	.08
164	Scott Sanderson	.08
165	Ken Singleton	.08
166	Jamie Nelson	.08
167	Marshall Edwards	.08
168	Juan Bonilla	.08
169	Larry Parrish	.08
170	Jerry Reuss	.08
171	Frank Robinson	.12
172	Frank DiPino	.08
173	*Marvell Wynne*	.08
174	Juan Berenguer	.08
175	Graig Nettles	.15
176	Lee Smith	.15
177	Jerry Hairston	.08
178	Bill Krueger	.08
179	Buck Martinez	.08
180	Manny Trillo	.08
181	Roy Thomas	.08
182	Darryl Strawberry	2.50
183	Al Williams	.08
184	Mike O'Berry	.08
185	Sixto Lezcano	.08
186	Cardinals Batting & Pitching Leaders(Lonnie Smith, John Stuper)	.08
187	Luis Aponte	.08
188	Bryan Little	.08
189	*Tim Conroy*	.08
190	Ben Oglivie	.08
191	Mike Boddicker	.08
192	*Nick Esasky*	.08
193	Darrell Brown	.08
194	Domingo Ramos	.08
195	Jack Morris	.25
196	Don Slaught	.12
197	Garry Hancock	.08
198	*Bill Doran*	.15
199	Willie Hernandez	.08

200	Andre Dawson	.75
201	Bruce Kison	.08
202	Bobby Cox	.08
203	Matt Keough	.08
204	*Bobby Meacham*	.08
205	Greg Minton	.08
206	*Andy Van Slyke*	.75
207	Donnie Moore	.08
208	*Jose Oquendo*	.15
209	Manny Sarmiento	.08
210	Joe Morgan	.30
211	Rick Sweet	.08
212	Broderick Perkins	.08
213	Bruce Hurst	.08
214	Paul Householder	.08
215	Tippy Martinez	.08
216	White Sox Batting & Pitching Leaders(Richard Dotson, Carlton Fisk)	.15
217	Alan Ashby	.08
218	Rick Waits	.08
219	Joe Simpson	.08
220	Fernando Valenzuela	.15
221	Cliff Johnson	.08
222	Rick Honeycutt	.08
223	Wayne Krenchicki	.08
224	Sid Monge	.08
225	Lee Mazzilli	.08
226	Juan Eichelberger	.08
227	Steve Braun	.08
228	John Rabb	.08
229	Paul Owens	.08
230	Rickey Henderson	1.75
231	Gary Woods	.08
232	Tim Wallach	.12
233	Checklist 133-264	.08
234	Rafael Ramirez	.08
235	*Matt Young*	.08
236	Ellis Valentine	.08
237	John Castino	.08
238	Reid Nichols	.08
239	Jay Howell	.10
240	Eddie Murray	1.50
241	Billy Almon	.08
242	Alex Trevino	.08
243	Pete Ladd	.08
244	Candy Maldonado	.08
245	Rick Sutcliffe	.10
246	Mets Batting & Pitching Leaders(Tom Seaver, Mookie Wilson)	.25
247	Onix Concepcion	.08
248	*Bill Dawley*	.08
249	Jay Johnstone	.08
250	Bill Madlock	.10
251	Tony Gwynn	4.00
252	Larry Christenson	.08
253	Jim Wohlford	.08
254	Shane Rawley	.08
255	Bruce Benedict	.08
256	Dave Geisel	.08
257	Julio Cruz	.08
258	Luis Sanchez	.08
259	Sparky Anderson	.12
260	Scott McGregor	.08
261	Bobby Brown	.08
262	*Tom Candiotti*	.25
263	Jack Fimple	.08
264	Doug Frobel	.08
265	*Donnie Hill*	.08
266	Steve Lubratich	.08
267	*Carmelo Martinez*	.08
268	Jack O'Connor	.08
269	Aurelio Rodriguez	.08
270	*Jeff Russell*	.20
271	Moose Haas	.08
272	Rick Dempsey	.08
273	Charlie Puleo	.08
274	Rick Monday	.08
275	Len Matuszek	.08
276	Angels Batting & Pitching Leaders(Rod Carew, Geoff Zahn)	.20
277	Eddie Whitson	.08
278	Jorge Bell	.20
279	Ivan DeJesus	.08
280	Floyd Bannister	.08
281	Larry Milbourne	.08
282	Jim Barr	.08
283	Larry Biittner	.08
284	Howard Bailey	.08
285	Darrell Porter	.08
286	Lary Sorensen	.08
287	Warren Cromartie	.08
288	Jim Beattie	.08
289	Randy S. Johnson	.08

290	Dave Dravecky	.10
291	Chuck Tanner	.08
292	Tony Scott	.08
293	Ed Lynch	.08
294	U.L. Washington	.08
295	Mike Flanagan	.08
296	Jeff Newman	.08
297	Bruce Berenyi	.08
298	Jim Gantner	.08
299	John Butcher	.08
300	Pete Rose	2.00
301	Frank LaCorte	.08
302	Barry Bonnell	.08
303	Marty Castillo	.08
304	Warren Brusstar	.08
305	Roy Smalley	.08
306	Dodgers Batting & Pitching Leaders(Pedro Guerrero, Bob Welch)	
307	Bobby Mitchell	.08
308	Ron Hassey	.08
309	*Tony Phillips*	1.00
310	Willie McGee	.15
311	Jerry Koosman	.08
312	Jorge Orta	.08
313	Mike Jorgensen	.08
314	Orlando Mercado	.08
315	Bob Grich	.08
316	Mark Bradley	.08
317	Greg Pryor	.08
318	Bill Gullickson	.08
319	Al Bumbry	.08
320	Bob Stanley	.08
321	Harvey Kuenn	.08
322	Ken Schrom	.08
323	Alan Knicely	.08
324	*Alejandro Pena*	.15
325	Darrell Evans	.12
326	Bob Kearney	.08
327	Ruppert Jones	.08
328	Vern Ruhle	.08
329	Pat Tabler	.08
330	John Candelaria	.08
331	Bucky Dent	.12
332	*Kevin Gross*	.15
333	Larry Herndon	.08
334	Chuck Rainey	.08
335	Don Baylor	.12
336	Mariners Batting & Pitching Leaders(Pat Putnam, Matt Young)	.08
337	Kevin Hagen	.08
338	Mike Warren	.08
339	Roy Lee Jackson	.08
340	Hal McRae	.08
341	Dave Tobik	.08
342	Tim Foli	.08
343	Mark Davis	.08
344	Rick Miller	.08
345	Kent Hrbek	.40
346	Kurt Bevacqua	.08
347	Allan Ramirez	.08
348	Toby Harrah	.08
349	Bob L. Gibson	.08
350	George Foster	.08
351	Russ Nixon	.08
352	Dave Stewart	.30
353	Jim Anderson	.08
354	Jeff Burroughs	.08
355	Jason Thompson	.08
356	Glenn Abbott	.08
357	Ron Cey	.08
358	Bob Dernier	.08
359	*Jim Acker*	.08
360	Willie Randolph	.08
361	Dave Smith	.08
362	David Green	.08
363	Tim Laudner	.08
364	Scott Fletcher	.15
365	Steve Bedrosian	.08
366	Padres Batting & Pitching Leaders(Dave Dravecky, Terry Kennedy)	.08
367	Jamie Easterly	.08
368	Hubie Brooks	.08
369	Steve McCatty	.08
370	Tim Raines	.50
371	Dave Gumpert	.08
372	Gary Roenicke	.08
373	Bill Scherrer	.08
374	Don Money	.08
375	Dennis Leonard	.08
376	*Dave Anderson*	.08
377	Danny Darwin	.08
378	Bob Brenly	.08
379	Checklist 265-396	.08

380	Steve Garvey	.35
381	Ralph Houk	.08
382	Chris Nyman	.08
383	Terry Puhl	.08
384	*Lee Tunnell*	.08
385	Tony Perez	.15
386	George Hendrick (All-Star)	.08
387	Johnny Ray (All-Star)	.08
388	Mike Schmidt (All-Star)	.50
389	Ozzie Smith (All-Star)	.40
390	Tim Raines (All-Star)	.25
391	Dale Murphy (All-Star)	.20
392	Andre Dawson (All-Star)	.25
393	Gary Carter (All-Star)	.15
394	Steve Rogers (All-Star)	.08
395	Steve Carlton (All-Star)	.25
396	Jesse Orosco (All-Star)	.08
397	Eddie Murray (All-Star)	.40
398	Lou Whitaker (All-Star)	.15
399	George Brett (All-Star)	.75
400	Cal Ripken, Jr. (All-Star)	3.00
401	Jim Rice (All-Star)	.15
402	Dave Winfield (All-Star)	.30
403	Lloyd Moseby (All-Star)	.08
404	Ted Simmons (All-Star)	.08
405	LaMarr Hoyt (All-Star)	.08
406	Ron Guidry (All-Star)	.10
407	Dan Quisenberry (All-Star)	.08
408	Lou Piniella	.12
409	*Juan Agosto*	.08
410	Claudell Washington	.08
411	Houston Jimenez	.08
412	Doug Rader	.08
413	*Spike Owen*	.20
414	Mitchell Page	.08
415	Tommy John	.25
416	Dane Iorg	.08
417	Mike Armstrong	.08
418	Ron Hodges	.08
419	John Henry Johnson	.08
420	Cecil Cooper	.10
421	Charlie Lea	.08
422	Jose Cruz	.08
423	Mike Morgan	.08
424	Dann Bilardello	.08
425	Steve Howe	.10
426	Orioles Batting & Pitching Leaders(Mike Boddicker, Cal Ripken, Jr.)	1.00
427	Rick Leach	.08
428	Fred Breining	.08
429	*Randy Bush*	.08
430	Rusty Staub	.12
431	Chris Bando	.08
432	*Charlie Hudson*	.08
433	Rich Hebner	.08
434	Harold Baines	.15
435	Neil Allen	.08
436	Rick Peters	.08
437	Mike Proly	.08
438	Biff Pocoroba	.08
439	Bob Stoddard	.08
440	Steve Kemp	.08
441	Bob Lillis	.08
442	Byron McLaughlin	.08
443	Benny Ayala	.08
444	Steve Renko	.08
445	Jerry Remy	.08
446	Luis Pujols	.08
447	Tom Brunansky	.08
448	Ben Hayes	.08
449	Joe Pettini	.08
450	Gary Carter	.30
451	Bob Jones	.08
452	Chuck Porter	.08
453	Willie Upshaw	.08
454	Joe Beckwith	.08
455	Terry Kennedy	.08
456	Cubs Batting & Pitching Leaders(Fergie Jenkins, Keith Moreland)	.10
457	Dave Rozema	.08
458	Kiko Garcia	.08
459	Kevin Hickey	.08
460	Dave Winfield	1.50
461	Jim Maler	.08
462	Lee Lacy	.08
463	Dave Engle	.08
464	Jeff Jones	.08
465	Mookie Wilson	.08
466	Gene Garber	.08
467	Mike Ramsey	.08
468	Geoff Zahn	.08
469	Tom O'Malley	.08
470	Nolan Ryan	7.00
471	Dick Howser	.08

472	Mike Brown	.08
473	Jim Dwyer	.08
474	Greg Bargar	.08
475	*Gary Redus*	.15
476	Tom Tellmann	.08
477	Rafael Landestoy	.08
478	Alan Bannister	.08
479	Frank Tanana	.08
480	Ron Kittle	.08
481	*Mark Thurmond*	.08
482	Enos Cabell	.08
483	Fergie Jenkins	.20
484	Ozzie Virgil	.08
485	Rick Rhoden	.08
486	Yankees Batting & Pitching Leaders(Don Baylor, Ron Guidry)	.12
487	Ricky Adams	.08
488	Jesse Barfield	.08
489	Dave Von Ohlen	.08
490	Cal Ripken, Jr.	6.00
491	Bobby Castillo	.08
492	Tucker Ashford	.08
493	Mike Norris	.08
494	Chili Davis	.12
495	Rollie Fingers	.20
496	Terry Francona	.08
497	Bud Anderson	.08
498	Rich Gedman	.08
499	Mike Witt	.08
500	George Brett	3.00
501	Steve Henderson	.08
502	Joe Torre	.08
503	Elias Sosa	.08
504	Mickey Rivers	.08
505	Pete Vuckovich	.08
506	Ernie Whitt	.08
507	Mike LaCoss	.08
508	Mel Hall	.08
509	Brad Havens	.08
510	Alan Trammell	.30
511	Marty Bystrom	.08
512	Oscar Gamble	.08
513	Dave Beard	.08
514	Floyd Rayford	.08
515	Gorman Thomas	.08
516	Expos Batting & Pitching Leaders(Charlie Lea, Al Oliver)	.08
517	John Moses	.08
518	*Greg Walker*	.08
519	Ron Davis	.08
520	Bob Boone	.10
521	Pete Falcone	.08
522	Dave Bergman	.08
523	Glenn Hoffman	.08
524	Carlos Diaz	.08
525	Willie Wilson	.08
526	Ron Oester	.08
527	Checklist 397-528	.08
528	Mark Brouhard	.08
529	*Keith Atherton*	.08
530	Dan Ford	.08
531	Steve Boros	.08
532	Eric Show	.08
533	Ken Landreaux	.08
534	*Pete O'Brien*	.25
535	Bo Diaz	.08
536	Doug Bair	.08
537	Johnny Ray	.08
538	Kevin Bass	.08
539	George Frazier	.08
540	George Hendrick	.08
541	Dennis Lamp	.08
542	Duane Kuiper	.08
543	*Craig McMurtry*	.08
544	Cesar Geronimo	.08
545	Bill Buckner	.10
546	Indians Batting & Pitching Leaders(Mike Hargrove, Lary Sorensen)	.08
547	Mike Moore	.08
548	Ron Jackson	.08
549	*Walt Terrell*	.20
550	Jim Rice	.12
551	Scott Ullger	.08
552	Ray Burris	.08
553	Joe Nolan	.08
554	Ted Power	.08
555	Greg Brock	.08
556	Joey McLaughlin	.08
557	Wayne Tolleson	.08
558	Mike Davis	.08
559	Mike Scott	.08
560	Carlton Fisk	.60
561	Whitey Herzog	.10

562	Manny Castillo	.08
563	Glenn Wilson	.08
564	Al Holland	.08
565	Leon Durham	.08
566	Jim Bibby	.08
567	Mike Heath	.08
568	Pete Filson	.08
569	Bake McBride	.08
570	Dan Quisenberry	.12
571	Bruce Bochy	.08
572	Jerry Royster	.08
573	Dave Kingman	.15
574	Brian Downing	.08
575	Jim Clancy	.08
576	Giants Batting & Pitching Leaders(Atlee Hammaker, Jeff Leonard)	.08
577	Mark Clear	.08
578	Lenn Sakata	.08
579	Bob James	.08
580	Lonnie Smith	.08
581	*Jose DeLeon*	.08
582	Bob McClure	.08
583	Derrel Thomas	.08
584	Dave Schmidt	.08
585	Dan Driessen	.08
586	Joe Niekro	.12
587	Von Hayes	.08
588	Milt Wilcox	.08
589	Mike Easler	.08
590	Dave Stieb	.12
591	Tony LaRussa	.10
592	Andre Robertson	.08
593	Jeff Lahti	.08
594	Gene Richards	.08
595	Jeff Reardon	.30
596	Ryne Sandberg	5.00
597	Rick Camp	.08
598	Rusty Kuntz	.08
599	*Doug Sisk*	.08
600	Rod Carew	.75
601	John Tudor	.08
602	John Wathan	.08
603	Renie Martin	.08
604	John Lowenstein	.08
605	Mike Caldwell	.08
606	Blue Jays Batting & Pitching Leaders(Lloyd Moseby, Dave Stieb)	.08
607	Tom Hume	.08
608	Bobby Johnson	.08
609	Dan Meyer	.08
610	Steve Sax	.08
611	Chet Lemon	.08
612	Harry Spilman	.08
613	Greg Gross	.08
614	Len Barker	.08
615	Garry Templeton	.08
616	Don Robinson	.08
617	Rick Cerone	.08
618	Dickie Noles	.08
619	Jerry Dybzinski	.08
620	Al Oliver	.15
621	Frank Howard	.10
622	Al Cowens	.08
623	Ron Washington	.08
624	Terry Harper	.08
625	Larry Gura	.08
626	Bob Clark	.08
627	Dave LaPoint	.08
628	Ed Jurak	.08
629	Rick Langford	.08
630	Ted Simmons	.08
631	Denny Martinez	.10
632	Tom Foley	.08
633	Mike Krukow	.08
634	Mike Marshall	.08
635	Dave Righetti	.08
636	Pat Putnam	.08
637	Phillies Batting & Pitching Leaders(John Denny, Gary Matthews)	.08
638	George Vukovich	.08
639	Rick Lysander	.08
640	Lance Parrish	.10
641	Mike Richardt	.08
642	Tom Underwood	.08
643	Mike Brown	.08
644	Tim Lollar	.08
645	Tony Pena	.10
646	Checklist 529-660	.08
647	Ron Roenicke	.08
648	Len Whitehouse	.08
649	Tom Herr	.08
650	Phil Niekro	.50
651	John McNamara	.08

652	Rudy May	.08
653	Dave Stapleton	.08
654	Bob Bailor	.08
655	Amos Otis	.08
656	Bryn Smith	.08
657	Thad Bosley	.08
658	Jerry Augustine	.08
659	Duane Walker	.08
660	Ray Knight	.08
661	Steve Yeager	.08
662	Tom Brennan	.08
663	Johnnie LeMaster	.08
664	Dave Stegman	.08
665	Buddy Bell	.08
666	Tigers Batting & Pitching Leaders(Jack Morris, Lou Whitaker)	.12
667	Vance Law	.08
668	Larry McWilliams	.08
669	Dave Lopes	.10
670	Rich Gossage	.10
671	Jamie Quirk	.08
672	Ricky Nelson	.08
673	Mike Walters	.08
674	Tim Flannery	.08
675	Pascual Perez	.08
676	Brian Giles	.08
677	Doyle Alexander	.08
678	Chris Speier	.08
679	Art Howe	.08
680	Fred Lynn	.25
681	Tom Lasorda	.25
682	Dan Morogiello	.08
683	*Marty Barrett*	.08
684	Bob Shirley	.08
685	Willie Aikens	.08
686	Joe Price	.08
687	Roy Howell	.08
688	George Wright	.08
689	Mike Fischlin	.08
690	Jack Clark	.08
691	*Steve Lake*	.08
692	Dickie Thon	.08
693	Alan Wiggins	.08
694	Mike Stanton	.08
695	Lou Whitaker	.25
696	Pirates Batting & Pitching Leaders(Bill Madlock, Rick Rhoden)	.10
697	Dale Murray	.08
698	Marc Hill	.08
699	Dave Rucker	.08
700	Mike Schmidt	2.50
701	NL Active Career Batting Leaders(Bill Madlock, Dave Parker, Pete Rose)	.25
702	NL Active Career Hit Leaders(Tony Perez, Pete Rose, Rusty Staub)	.25
703	NL Active Career Home Run Leaders(Dave Kingman, Tony Perez, Mike Schmidt)	.25
704	NL Active Career RBI Leaders(Al Oliver, Tony Perez, Rusty Staub)	.15
705	NL Active Career Stolen Bases Leaders(Larry Bowa, Cesar Cedeno, Joe Morgan)	.10
706	NL Active Career Victory Leaders(Steve Carlton, Fergie Jenkins, Tom Seaver)	.25
707	NL Active Career Strikeout Leaders(Steve Carlton, Nolan Ryan, Tom Seaver)	.35
708	NL Active Career ERA Leaders(Steve Carlton, Steve Rogers, Tom Seaver)	.25
709	NL Active Career Save Leaders(Gene Garber, Tug McGraw, Bruce Sutter)	.12
710	AL Active Career Batting Leaders(George Brett, Rod Carew, Cecil Cooper)	.30
711	AL Active Career Hit Leaders(Bert Campaneris, Rod Carew, Reggie Jackson)	.25
712	AL Active Career Home Run Leaders(Reggie Jackson, Greg Luzinski, Graig Nettles)	.20

713	AL Active Career RBI Leaders(Reggie Jackson, Graig Nettles, Ted Simmons)	.15
714	AL Active Career Stolen Bases Leaders(Bert Campaneris, Dave Lopes, Omar Moreno)	.08
715	AL Active Career Victory Leaders(Tommy John, Jim Palmer, Don Sutton)	.25
716	AL Active Strikeout Leaders(Bert Blyleven, Jerry Koosman, Don Sutton)	.15
717	AL Active Career ERA Leaders(Rollie Fingers, Ron Guidry, Jim Palmer)	.15
718	AL Active Career Save Leaders(Rollie Fingers, Rich Gossage, Dan Quisenberry)	.15
719	Andy Hassler	.08
720	Dwight Evans	.10
721	Del Crandall	.08
722	Bob Welch	.08
723	Rich Dauer	.08
724	Eric Rasmussen	.08
725	Cesar Cedeno	.08
726	Brewers Batting & Pitching Leaders(Moose Haas, Ted Simmons)	.08
727	Joel Youngblood	.08
728	Tug McGraw	.12
729	Gene Tenace	.08
730	Bruce Sutter	.15
731	Lynn Jones	.08
732	Terry Crowley	.08
733	Dave Collins	.08
734	Odell Jones	.08
735	Rick Burleson	.08
736	Dick Ruthven	.08
737	Jim Essian	.08
738	*Bill Schroeder*	.08
739	Bob Watson	.08
740	Tom Seaver	1.50
741	Wayne Gross	.08
742	Dick Williams	.08
743	Don Hood	.08
744	Jamie Allen	.08
745	Dennis Eckersley	.15
746	Mickey Hatcher	.08
747	Pat Zachry	.08
748	Jeff Leonard	.08
749	Doug Flynn	.08
750	Jim Palmer	1.00
751	Charlie Moore	.08
752	Phil Garner	.08
753	Doug Gwosdz	.08
754	Kent Tekulve	.08
755	Garry Maddox	.08
756	Reds Batting & Pitching Leaders(Ron Oester, Mario Soto)	.08
757	Larry Bowa	.10
758	Bill Stein	.08
759	Richard Dotson	.08
760	Bob Horner	.08
761	John Montefusco	.08
762	Rance Mulliniks	.08
763	Craig Swan	.08
764	Mike Hargrove	.08
765	Ken Forsch	.08
766	Mike Vail	.08
767	Carney Lansford	.08
768	Champ Summers	.08
769	Bill Caudill	.08
770	Ken Griffey	.08
771	Billy Gardner	.08
772	Jim Slaton	.08
773	Todd Cruz	.08
774	Tom Gorman	.08
775	Dave Parker	.30
776	Craig Reynolds	.08
777	Tom Paciorek	.08
778	*Andy Hawkins*	.15
779	Jim Sundberg	.08
780	Steve Carlton	.90
781	Checklist 661-792	.08
782	Steve Balboni	.08
783	Luis Leal	.08
784	Leon Roberts	.08
785	Joaquin Andujar	.08
786	Red Sox Batting & Pitching Leaders(Wade Boggs, Bob Ojeda)	.30

787	Bill Campbell	.08
788	Milt May	.08
789	Bert Blyleven	.15
790	Doug DeCinces	.08
791	Terry Forster	.08
792	Bill Russell	.08

1984 Topps Tiffany

In 1984 Topps introduced a specially boxed, limited edition version of its baseball card set. Sold only through hobby dealers, the cards differed from regular-issue 1984 Topps cards in their use of white cardboard stock and the application of a high-gloss finish to the front of the card. Production was limited to a reported 10,000 sets. The nickname "Tiffany" was coined by collectors to identify the glossy collectors edition.

	MT
Complete Set (792):	200.00
Common Player:	.15

(Star cards valued at 6X-8X corresponding cards in regular-issue 1984 Topps)

1984 Topps Traded

The popular Topps Traded set returned for its fourth year in 1984 with another 132-card set. The 2-1/2" x 3-1/2" cards have an identical design to the regular Topps cards except that the back cardboard is white and the card numbers carry a "T" suffix. As before, the set was sold only through hobby dealers. Also as before, players who changed teams, new managers and promising rookies are included in the set. The presence of several promising young rookies in especially high demand from investors and speculators had made this one of the most expensive Topps issues of recent years. A glossy-finish "Tiffany" version of the set was also issued, valued at four to five times the price of the normal Traded cards.

	MT
Complete Set (132):	45.00
Common Player:	.25
1T	Willie Aikens	.25
2T	Luis Aponte	.25
3T	Mike Armstrong	.25

4T	Bob Bailor	.25
5T	Dusty Baker	.50
6T	Steve Balboni	.25
7T	Alan Bannister	.25
8T	Dave Beard	.25
9T	Joe Beckwith	.25
10T	Bruce Berenyi	.25
11T	Dave Bergman	.25
12T	Tony Bernazard	.25
13T	Yogi Berra	.60
14T	Barry Bonnell	.25
15T	Phil Bradley	.25
16T	Fred Breining	.25
17T	Bill Buckner	.25
18T	Ray Burris	.25
19T	John Butcher	.25
20T	Brett Butler	.25
21T	Enos Cabell	.25
22T	Bill Campbell	.25
23T	Bill Caudill	.25
24T	Bob Clark	.25
25T	Bryan Clark	.25
26T	Jaime Cocanower	.25
27T	*Ron Darling*	1.00
28T	Alvin Davis	.25
29T	Ken Dayley	.25
30T	Jeff Dedmon	.25
31T	Bob Dernier	.25
32T	Carlos Diaz	.25
33T	Mike Easler	.25
34T	Dennis Eckersley	4.00
35T	Jim Essian	.25
36T	Darrell Evans	.25
37T	Mike Fitzgerald	.25
38T	Tim Foli	.25
39T	George Frazier	.25
40T	Rich Gale	.25
41T	Barbaro Garbey	.25
42T	*Dwight Gooden*	3.00
43T	Rich Gossage	.40
44T	Wayne Gross	.25
45T	Mark Gubicza	.90
46T	Jackie Gutierrez	.25
47T	Mel Hall	.25
48T	Toby Harrah	.25
49T	Ron Hassey	.25
50T	Rich Hebner	.25
51T	Willie Hernandez	.25
52T	Ricky Horton	.25
53T	Art Howe	.25
54T	Dane Iorg	.25
55T	Brook Jacoby	.25
56T	Mike Jeffcoat	.25
57T	Dave Johnson	.25
58T	Lynn Jones	.25
59T	Ruppert Jones	.25
60T	Mike Jorgensen	.25
61T	Bob Kearney	.25
62T	*Jimmy Key*	3.00
63T	Dave Kingman	.25
64T	Jerry Koosman	.25
65T	Wayne Krenchicki	.25
66T	Rusty Kuntz	.25
67T	Rene Lachemann	.25
68T	Frank LaCorte	.25
69T	Dennis Lamp	.25
70T	*Mark Langston*	3.00
71T	Rick Leach	.25
72T	Craig Lefferts	.25
73T	Gary Lucas	.25
74T	Jerry Martin	.25
75T	Carmelo Martinez	.25
76T	Mike Mason	.25
77T	Gary Matthews	.25
78T	Andy McGaffigan	.25
79T	Larry Milbourne	.25
80T	Sid Monge	.25
81T	Jackie Moore	.25
82T	Joe Morgan	3.00
83T	Graig Nettles	.25
84T	Phil Niekro	3.00
85T	Ken Oberkfell	.25
86T	Mike O'Berry	.25
87T	Al Oliver	.25
88T	Jorge Orta	.25
89T	Amos Otis	.25
90T	Dave Parker	1.50
91T	Tony Perez	1.00
92T	Gerald Perry	.75
93T	Gary Pettis	.25
94T	Rob Picciolo	.25
95T	Vern Rapp	.25
96T	Floyd Rayford	.25
97T	Randy Ready	.25
98T	Ron Reed	.25
99T	Gene Richards	.25

100T	*Jose Rijo*	2.00
101T	Jeff Robinson	.25
102T	Ron Romanick	.25
103T	Pete Rose	8.00
104T	*Bret Saberhagen*	4.00
105T	Juan Samuel	.50
106T	Scott Sanderson	.25
107T	Dick Schofield	.25
108T	Tom Seaver	6.00
109T	Jim Slaton	.25
110T	Mike Smithson	.25
111T	Lary Sorensen	.25
112T	Tim Stoddard	.25
113T	Champ Summers	.25
114T	Jim Sundberg	.25
115T	Rick Sutcliffe	.25
116T	Craig Swan	.25
117T	Tim Teufel	.50
118T	Derrel Thomas	.25
119T	Gorman Thomas	.25
120T	Alex Trevino	.25
121T	Manny Trillo	.25
122T	John Tudor	.25
123T	Tom Underwood	.25
124T	Mike Vail	.25
125T	Tom Waddell	.25
126T	Gary Ward	.25
127T	Curt Wilkerson	.25
128T	Frank Williams	.25
129T	Glenn Wilson	.25
130T	Johnny Wockenfuss	.25
131T	Ned Yost	.25
132T	Checklist 1-132	.25

1984 Topps Traded Tiffany

Following up on its inaugural Tiffany collectors edition, Topps produced a special glossy version of its Traded set for 1984, as well. Cards in this special boxed set differ from regular Traded cards only in the use of white cardboard stock with a high-gloss finish coat on front.

	MT
Complete Set (132):	100.00
Common Player:	.15

(Star cards valued at 3X-4X regular Topps Traded)

1984 Topps All-Star Glossy Set of 22

These 2-1/2" x 3-1/2" cards were a result of the success of Topps' efforts the previous year with glossy cards on a mail-in basis. A 22-card set, the cards are divided evenly between the two leagues. Each All-Star Game starter for both leagues, the managers and the honorary team captains have an All-Star Glossy card. The cards feature a large color photo on the front with an All-Star banner across the top and the league emblem in the lower left. The player's name and position appear below the photo. Backs have a name, team, position and card number along with the phrase "1983 All-Star Game Commemorative Set". The '84 Glossy All-Stars were distributed one card per pack in Topps rack packs that year.

		MT
Complete Set (22):		4.00
Common Player:		.20
1	Harvey Kuenn	.20
2	Rod Carew	.50
3	Manny Trillo	.20
4	George Brett	.80
5	Robin Yount	.60
6	Jim Rice	.20
7	Fred Lynn	.20
8	Dave Winfield	.50
9	Ted Simmons	.20
10	Dave Stieb	.20
11	Carl Yastrzemski	.50
12	Whitey Herzog	.20
13	Al Oliver	.20
14	Steve Sax	.20
15	Mike Schmidt	.80
16	Ozzie Smith	.50
17	Tim Raines	.35
18	Andre Dawson	.35
19	Dale Murphy	.35
20	Gary Carter	.35
21	Mario Soto	.20
22	Johnny Bench	.60

1985 Topps

Holding the line at 792 cards, Topps did initiate some major design changes in its 2-1/2" x 3-1/2" cards in 1985. The use of two photos on the front was discontinued in favor of one large color photo. The Topps logo appears in the upper left-hand corner. At the bottom runs a diagonal rectangular box with the team name. It joins a team logo, and below that point runs the player's position and name. The backs feature statistics, biographical information and a trivia question. Some interesting specialty sets were introduced in 1985, including the revival of the father/son theme from 1976, a subset of the 1984 U.S. Olympic Baseball Team mem-

bers and a set featuring #1 draft choices since the inception of the baseball draft in 1965. Again in 1985, a glossy-finish "Tiffany" edition of the regular set was produced, though the number was cut back to 5,000 sets. Values range from four times regular value for common cards to five-six times for high-demand stars and rookie cards.

		MT
Complete Set (792):		240.00
Common Player:		.06
Wax Box:		400.00
1	Carlton Fisk (Record Breaker)	.25
2	Steve Garvey (Record Breaker)	.10
3	Dwight Gooden (Record Breaker)	.25
4	Cliff Johnson (Record Breaker)	.06
5	Joe Morgan (Record Breaker)	.10
6	Pete Rose (Record Breaker)	.45
7	Nolan Ryan (Record Breaker)	1.50
8	Juan Samuel (Record Breaker)	.06
9	Bruce Sutter (Record Breaker)	.06
10	Don Sutton (Record Breaker)	.10
11	Ralph Houk	.06
12	Dave Lopes	.06
13	Tim Lollar	.06
14	Chris Bando	.06
15	Jerry Koosman	.06
16	Bobby Meacham	.06
17	Mike Scott	.06
18	Mickey Hatcher	.06
19	George Frazier	.06
20	Chet Lemon	.06
21	Lee Tunnell	.06
22	Duane Kuiper	.06
23	Bret Saberhagen	1.25
24	Jesse Barfield	.06
25	Steve Bedrosian	.06
26	Roy Smalley	.06
27	Bruce Berenyi	.06
28	Dann Bilardello	.06
29	Odell Jones	.06
30	Cal Ripken, Jr.	4.00
31	Terry Whitfield	.06
32	Chuck Porter	.06
33	Tito Landrum	.06
34	Ed Nunez	.06
35	Graig Nettles	.10
36	Fred Breining	.06
37	Reid Nichols	.06
38	Jackie Moore	.06
39	Johnny Wockenfuss	.06
40	Phil Niekro	.50
41	Mike Fischlin	.06
42	Luis Sanchez	.06
43	Andre David	.06
44	Dickie Thon	.06
45	Greg Minton	.06
46	Gary Woods	.06
47	Dave Rozema	.06
48	Tony Fernandez	.15
49	Butch Davis	.06
50	John Candelaria	.06
51	Bob Watson	.06
52	Jerry Dybzinski	.06
53	Tom Gorman	.06
54	Cesar Cedeno	.06
55	Frank Tanana	.06
56	Jim Dwyer	.06
57	Pat Zachry	.06
58	Orlando Mercado	.06
59	Rick Waits	.06
60	George Hendrick	.06
61	Curt Kaufman	.06
62	Mike Ramsey	.06
63	Steve McCatty	.06
64	*Mark Bailey*	.06
65	Bill Buckner	.06
66	Dick Williams	.06
67	*Rafael Santana*	.06
68	Von Hayes	.06
69	*Jim Winn*	.06
70	Don Baylor	.08
71	Tim Laudner	.06
72	Rick Sutcliffe	.08
73	Rusty Kuntz	.06
74	Mike Krukow	.06
75	Willie Upshaw	.06
76	Alan Bannister	.06
77	Joe Beckwith	.06
78	Scott Fletcher	.08
79	Rick Mahler	.06
80	Keith Hernandez	.06
81	Lenn Sakata	.06
82	Joe Price	.06
83	Charlie Moore	.06
84	Spike Owen	.06
85	Mike Marshall	.06
86	Don Aase	.06
87	David Green	.06
88	Bryn Smith	.06
89	Jackie Gutierrez	.06
90	Rich Gossage	.10
91	Jeff Burroughs	.06
92	Paul Owens	.06
93	*Don Schulze*	.06
94	Toby Harrah	.06
95	Jose Cruz	.06
96	Johnny Ray	.06
97	Pete Filson	.06
98	Steve Lake	.06
99	Milt Wilcox	.06
100	George Brett	2.00
101	Jim Acker	.06
102	Tommy Dunbar	.06
103	Randy Lerch	.06
104	Mike Fitzgerald	.06
105	Ron Kittle	.06
106	Pascual Perez	.06
107	Tom Foley	.06
108	Darnell Coles	.06
109	Gary Roenicke	.06
110	Alejandro Pena	.06
111	Doug DeCinces	.06
112	Tom Tellmann	.06
113	Tom Herr	.06
114	Bob James	.06
115	Rickey Henderson	1.00
116	Dennis Boyd	.08
117	Greg Gross	.06
118	Eric Show	.06
119	Pat Corrales	.06
120	Steve Kemp	.06
121	Checklist 1-132	.06
122	Tom Brunansky	.06
123	Dave Smith	.06
124	Rich Hebner	.06
125	Kent Tekulve	.06
126	Ruppert Jones	.06
127	*Mark Gubicza*	.25
128	Ernie Whitt	.06
129	Gene Garber	.06
130	Al Oliver	.10
131	Father - Son(Buddy Bell, Gus Bell)	.10
132	Father - Son(Dale Berra, Yogi Berra)	.20
133	Father - Son(Bob Boone, Ray Boone)	.12
134	Father - Son(Terry Francona, Tito Francona)	.06
135	Father - Son(Bob Kennedy, Terry Kennedy)	.06
136	Father - Son(Bill Kunkel, Jeff Kunkel)	.06
137	Father - Son(Vance Law, Vern Law)	.10
138	Father - Son(Dick Schofield, Dick Schofield, Jr.)	.06
139	Father - Son(Bob Skinner, Joel Skinner)	.06
140	Father - Son(Roy Smalley, Jr., Roy Smalley III)	.06
141	Father - Son(Dave Stenhouse, Mike Stenhouse)	.06
142	Father - Son(Dizzy Trout, Steve Trout)	.06
143	Father - Son(Ozzie Virgil, Ozzie Virgil)	.06
144	Ron Gardenhire	.06
145	*Alvin Davis*	.06
146	Gary Redus	.06
147	Bill Swaggerty	.06
148	Steve Yeager	.06
149	Dickie Noles	.06
150	Jim Rice	.08

#	Player	Price	#	Player	Price	#	Player	Price
151	Moose Haas	.06	247	Wayne Tolleson	.06	338	Britt Burns	.06
152	Steve Braun	.06	248	Terry Forster	.06	339	Danny Heep	.06
153	Frank LaCorte	.06	249	Harold Baines	.06	340	Robin Yount	.60
154	Argenis Salazar	.06	250	Jesse Orosco	.06	341	Floyd Rayford	.06
155	Yogi Berra	.10	251	Brad Gulden	.06	342	Ted Power	.06
156	Craig Reynolds	.06	252	Dan Ford	.06	343	Bill Russell	.06
157	Tug McGraw	.10	253	*Sid Bream*	.10	344	Dave Henderson	.06
158	Pat Tabler	.06	254	Pete Vuckovich	.06	345	Charlie Lea	.06
159	Carlos Diaz	.06	255	Lonnie Smith	.06	346	*Terry Pendleton*	.75
160	Lance Parrish	.15	256	Mike Stanton	.06	347	Rick Langford	.06
161	Ken Schrom	.06	257	Brian Little (Bryan)	.06	348	Bob Boone	.06
162	*Benny Distefano*	.06	258	Mike Brown	.06	349	Domingo Ramos	.06
163	Dennis Eckersley	.25	259	Gary Allenson	.06	350	Wade Boggs	1.00
164	Jorge Orta	.06	260	Dave Righetti	.06	351	Juan Agosto	.06
165	Dusty Baker	.06	261	Checklist 133-264	.06	352	Joe Morgan	.30
166	Keith Atherton	.06	262	*Greg Booker*	.06	353	Julio Solano	.06
167	Rufino Linares	.06	263	Mel Hall	.06	354	Andre Robertson	.06
168	Garth Iorg	.06	264	Joe Sambito	.06	355	Bert Blyleven	.10
169	Dan Spillner	.06	265	Juan Samuel	.12	356	Dave Meier	.06
170	George Foster	.08	266	Frank Viola	.10	357	Rich Bordi	.06
171	Bill Stein	.06	267	*Henry Cotto*	.06	358	Tony Pena	.06
172	Jack Perconte	.06	268	Chuck Tanner	.06	359	Pat Sheridan	.06
173	Mike Young	.06	269	*Doug Baker*	.06	360	Steve Carlton	.45
174	Rick Honeycutt	.06	270	Dan Quisenberry	.10	361	Alfredo Griffin	.06
175	Dave Parker	.25	271	Tim Foli (#1 Draft Pick)	.06	362	Craig McMurtry	.06
176	Bill Schroeder	.06	272	Jeff Burroughs (#1 Draft Pick)		363	Ron Hodges	.06
177	Dave Von Ohlen	.06				364	Richard Dotson	.06
178	Miguel Dilone	.06	273	Bill Almon (#1 Draft Pick)	.06	365	Danny Ozark	.06
179	Tommy John	.20	274	Floyd Bannister (#1 Draft Pick)	.06	366	Todd Cruz	.06
180	Dave Winfield	1.00				367	Keefe Cato	.06
181	Roger Clemens	15.00	275	Harold Baines (#1 Draft Pick)	.10	368	Dave Bergman	.06
182	Tim Flannery	.06				369	*R.J. Reynolds*	.10
183	Larry McWilliams	.06	276	Bob Horner (#1 Draft Pick)	.10	370	Bruce Sutter	.10
184	Carmen Castillo	.06	277	Al Chambers (#1 Draft Pick)	.06	371	Mickey Rivers	.06
185	Al Holland	.06	278	Darryl Strawberry (#1 Draft Pick)	.30	372	Roy Howell	.06
186	Bob Lillis	.06				373	Mike Moore	.06
187	Mike Walters	.06	279	Mike Moore (#1 Draft Pick)	.10	374	Brian Downing	.06
188	Greg Pryor	.06	280	*Shawon Dunston (#1 Draft Pick)*	.40	375	Jeff Reardon	.08
189	Warren Brusstar	.06				376	Jeff Newman	.06
190	Rusty Staub	.12	281	*Tim Belcher (#1 Draft Pick)*	.30	377	Checklist 265-396	.06
191	Steve Nicosia	.06	282	*Shawn Abner (#1 Draft Pick)*	.06	378	Alan Wiggins	.06
192	Howard Johnson	.08	283	Fran Mullins	.06	379	Charles Hudson	.06
193	Jimmy Key	1.00	284	Marty Bystrom	.06	380	Ken Griffey	.06
194	Dave Stegman	.06	285	Dan Driessen	.06	381	Roy Smith	.06
195	Glenn Hubbard	.06	286	Rudy Law	.06	382	Denny Walling	.06
196	Pete O'Brien	.06	287	Walt Terrell	.06	383	Rick Lysander	.06
197	Mike Warren	.06	288	*Jeff Kunkel*	.06	384	Jody Davis	.06
198	Eddie Milner	.06	289	Tom Underwood	.06	385	Jose DeLeon	.06
199	Denny Martinez	.08	290	Cecil Cooper	.06	386	*Dan Gladden*	.30
200	Reggie Jackson	.75	291	Bob Welch	.06	387	*Buddy Biancalana*	.06
201	Burt Hooton	.06	292	Brad Komminsk	.06	388	Bert Roberge	.06
202	Gorman Thomas	.06	293	*Curt Young*	.06	389	Rod Dedeaux (Team USA)	.06
203	Bob McClure	.06	294	*Tom Nieto*	.06	390	Sid Akins (Team USA)	.06
204	Art Howe	.06	295	Joe Niekro	.08	391	Flavio Alfaro (Team USA)	.06
205	Steve Rogers	.06	296	Ricky Nelson	.06	392	Don August (Team USA)	.08
206	Phil Garner	.06	297	Gary Lucas	.06	393	*Scott Bankhead* (Team USA)	.10
207	Mark Clear	.06	298	Marty Barrett	.06	394	Bob Caffrey (Team USA)	.06
208	Champ Summers	.06	299	Andy Hawkins	.06	395	Mike Dunne (Team USA)	.12
209	Bill Campbell	.06	300	Rod Carew	.35	396	Gary Green (Team USA)	.08
210	Gary Matthews	.06	301	John Montefusco	.06	397	John Hoover (Team USA)	.06
211	Clay Christiansen	.06	302	Tim Corcoran	.06	398	*Shane Mack* (Team USA)	.25
212	George Vukovich	.06	303	*Mike Jeffcoat*	.06	399	John Marzano (Team USA)	.10
213	Billy Gardner	.06	304	Gary Gaetti	.12	400	Oddibe McDowell (Team USA)	.10
214	John Tudor	.06	305	Dale Berra	.06			
215	Bob Brenly	.06	306	Rick Reuschel	.06	401	*Mark McGwire* (Team USA)	200.00
216	Jerry Don Gleaton	.06	307	Sparky Anderson	.08	402	Pat Pacillo (Team USA)	.06
217	Leon Roberts	.06	308	John Wathan	.06	403	*Cory Snyder* (Team USA)	.30
218	Doyle Alexander	.06	309	Mike Witt	.06	404	*Billy Swift* (Team USA)	.40
219	Gerald Perry	.06	310	Manny Trillo	.06	405	Tom Veryzer	.06
220	Fred Lynn	.15	311	Jim Gott	.06	406	Len Whitehouse	.06
221	Ron Reed	.06	312	Marc Hill	.06	407	Bobby Ramos	.06
222	Hubie Brooks	.06	313	Dave Schmidt	.06	408	Sid Monge	.06
223	Tom Hume	.06	314	Ron Oester	.06	409	Brad Wellman	.06
224	Al Cowens	.06	315	Doug Sisk	.06	410	Bob Horner	.06
225	Mike Boddicker	.06	316	John Lowenstein	.06	411	Bobby Cox	.06
226	Juan Beniquez	.06	317	*Jack Lazorko*	.06	412	Bud Black	.06
227	Danny Darwin	.06	318	Ted Simmons	.06	413	Vance Law	.06
228	Dion James	.06	319	Jeff Jones	.06	414	Gary Ward	.06
229	Dave LaPoint	.06	320	Dale Murphy	.20	415	Ron Darling	.08
230	Gary Carter	.25	321	*Ricky Horton*	.06	416	Wayne Gross	.06
231	Dwayne Murphy	.06	322	Dave Stapleton	.06	417	*John Franco*	.30
232	Dave Beard	.06	323	Andy McGaffigan	.06	418	Ken Landreaux	.06
233	Ed Jurak	.06	324	Bruce Bochy	.06	419	Mike Caldwell	.06
234	Jerry Narron	.06	325	John Denny	.06	420	Andre Dawson	.60
235	Garry Maddox	.06	326	Kevin Bass	.06	421	Dave Rucker	.06
236	Mark Thurmond	.06	327	Brook Jacoby	.06	422	Carney Lansford	.06
237	Julio Franco	.35	328	Bob Shirley	.06	423	Barry Bonnell	.06
238	Jose Rijo	.40	329	Ron Washington	.06	424	*Al Nipper*	.06
239	Tim Teufel	.06	330	Leon Durham	.06	425	Mike Hargrove	.06
240	Dave Stieb	.06	331	Bill Laskey	.06	426	Verne Ruhle	.06
241	Jim Frey	.06	332	Brian Harper	.06	427	Mario Ramirez	.06
242	Greg Harris	.06	333	Willie Hernandez	.06	428	Larry Andersen	.06
243	Barbaro Garbey	.06	334	Dick Howser	.06	429	Rick Cerone	.06
244	Mike Jones	.06	335	Bruce Benedict	.06	430	Ron Davis	.06
245	Chili Davis	.10	336	Rance Mulliniks	.06	431	U.L. Washington	.06
246	Mike Norris	.06	337	Billy Sample	.06	432	Thad Bosley	.06

433	Jim Morrison	.06
434	Gene Richards	.06
435	Dan Petry	.06
436	Willie Aikens	.06
437	Al Jones	.06
438	Joe Torre	.08
439	Junior Ortiz	.06
440	Fernando Valenzuela	.08
441	Duane Walker	.06
442	Ken Forsch	.06
443	George Wright	.06
444	Tony Phillips	.15
445	Tippy Martinez	.06
446	Jim Sundberg	.06
447	Jeff Lahti	.06
448	Derrel Thomas	.06
449	*Phil Bradley*	.10
450	Steve Garvey	.25
451	Bruce Hurst	.06
452	John Castino	.06
453	Tom Waddell	.06
454	Glenn Wilson	.06
455	Bob Knepper	.06
456	Tim Foli	.06
457	Cecilio Guante	.06
458	Randy S. Johnson	.06
459	Charlie Leibrandt	.06
460	Ryne Sandberg	2.50
461	Marty Castillo	.06
462	Gary Lavelle	.06
463	Dave Collins	.06
464	*Mike Mason*	.06
465	Bob Grich	.06
466	Tony LaRussa	.08
467	Ed Lynch	.06
468	Wayne Krenchicki	.06
469	Sammy Stewart	.06
470	Steve Sax	.06
471	Pete Ladd	.06
472	Jim Essian	.06
473	Tim Wallach	.08
474	Kurt Kepshire	.06
475	Andre Thornton	.06
476	*Jeff Stone*	.06
477	Bob Ojeda	.06
478	Kurt Bevacqua	.06
479	Mike Madden	.06
480	Lou Whitaker	.12
481	Dale Murray	.06
482	Harry Spilman	.06
483	Mike Smithson	.06
484	Larry Bowa	.06
485	Matt Young	.06
486	Steve Balboni	.06
487	*Frank Williams*	.06
488	Joel Skinner	.06
489	Bryan Clark	.06
490	Jason Thompson	.06
491	Rick Camp	.06
492	Dave Johnson	.06
493	*Orel Hershiser*	1.50
494	Rich Dauer	.06
495	Mario Soto	.06
496	Donnie Scott	.06
497	Gary Pettis	.06
498	Ed Romero	.06
499	Danny Cox	.06
500	Mike Schmidt	1.50
501	Dan Schatzeder	.06
502	Rick Miller	.06
503	Tim Conroy	.06
504	Jerry Willard	.06
505	Jim Beattie	.06
506	*Franklin Stubbs*	.06
507	Ray Fontenot	.06
508	John Shelby	.06
509	Milt May	.06
510	Kent Hrbek	.15
511	Lee Smith	.10
512	Tom Brookens	.06
513	Lynn Jones	.06
514	Jeff Cornell	.06
515	Dave Concepcion	.06
516	Roy Lee Jackson	.06
517	Jerry Martin	.06
518	Chris Chambliss	.06
519	Doug Rader	.06
520	LaMarr Hoyt	.06
521	Rick Dempsey	.06
522	Paul Molitor	.75
523	Candy Maldonado	.06
524	Rob Wilfong	.06
525	Darrell Porter	.06
526	Dave Palmer	.06
527	Checklist 397-528	.06
528	Bill Krueger	.06
529	Rich Gedman	.06
530	Dave Dravecky	.06
531	Joe Lefebvre	.06
532	Frank DiPino	.06
533	Tony Bernazard	.06
534	Brian Dayett	.06
535	Pat Putnam	.06
536	Kirby Puckett	7.00
537	Don Robinson	.06
538	Keith Moreland	.06
539	Aurelio Lopez	.06
540	Claudell Washington	.06
541	Mark Davis	.06
542	Don Slaught	.06
543	Mike Squires	.06
544	Bruce Kison	.06
545	Lloyd Moseby	.06
546	Brent Gaff	.06
547	Pete Rose	.60
548	Larry Parrish	.06
549	Mike Scioscia	.06
550	Scott McGregor	.06
551	Andy Van Slyke	.15
552	Chris Codiroli	.06
553	Bob Clark	.06
554	Doug Flynn	.06
555	Bob Stanley	.06
556	Sixto Lezcano	.06
557	Len Barker	.06
558	Carmelo Martinez	.06
559	Jay Howell	.08
560	Bill Madlock	.12
561	Darryl Motley	.06
562	Houston Jimenez	.06
563	Dick Ruthven	.06
564	Alan Ashby	.06
565	Kirk Gibson	.15
566	Ed Vande Berg	.06
567	Joel Youngblood	.06
568	Cliff Johnson	.06
569	Ken Oberkfell	.06
570	Darryl Strawberry	.40
571	Charlie Hough	.06
572	Tom Paciorek	.06
573	*Jay Tibbs*	.06
574	Joe Altobelli	.06
575	Pedro Guerrero	.06
576	Jaime Cocanower	.06
577	Chris Speier	.06
578	Terry Francona	.06
579	*Ron Romanick*	.06
580	Dwight Evans	.06
581	Mark Wagner	.06
582	Ken Phelps	.06
583	Bobby Brown	.06
584	Kevin Gross	.06
585	Butch Wynegar	.06
586	Bill Scherrer	.06
587	Doug Frobel	.06
588	Bobby Castillo	.06
589	Bob Dernier	.06
590	Ray Knight	.06
591	Larry Herndon	.06
592	*Jeff Robinson*	.06
593	Rick Leach	.06
594	Curt Wilkerson	.06
595	Larry Gura	.06
596	Jerry Hairston	.06
597	Brad Lesley	.06
598	Jose Oquendo	.06
599	Storm Davis	.06
600	Pete Rose	.60
601	Tom Lasorda	.20
602	*Jeff Dedmon*	.06
603	Rick Manning	.06
604	Daryl Sconiers	.06
605	Ozzie Smith	.75
606	Rich Gale	.06
607	Bill Almon	.06
608	Craig Lefferts	.06
609	Broderick Perkins	.06
610	Jack Morris	.10
611	Ozzie Virgil	.06
612	Mike Armstrong	.06
613	Terry Puhl	.06
614	Al Williams	.06
615	Marvell Wynne	.06
616	Scott Sanderson	.06
617	Willie Wilson	.06
618	Pete Falcone	.06
619	Jeff Leonard	.06
620	Dwight Gooden	1.00
621	Marvis Foley	.06
622	Luis Leal	.06
623	Greg Walker	.06
624	Benny Ayala	.06
625	Mark Langston	1.00
626	German Rivera	.06
627	*Eric Davis*	.45
628	Rene Lachemann	.06
629	Dick Schofield	.06
630	Tim Raines	.15
631	Bob Forsch	.06
632	Bruce Bochte	.06
633	Glenn Hoffman	.06
634	Bill Dawley	.06
635	Terry Kennedy	.06
636	Shane Rawley	.06
637	Brett Butler	.06
638	*Mike Pagliarulo*	.12
639	Ed Hodge	.06
640	Steve Henderson	.06
641	Rod Scurry	.06
642	Dave Owen	.06
643	Johnny Grubb	.06
644	Mark Huismann	.06
645	Damaso Garcia	.06
646	Scot Thompson	.06
647	Rafael Ramirez	.06
648	Bob Jones	.06
649	Sid Fernandez	.10
650	Greg Luzinski	.08
651	Jeff Russell	.08
652	Joe Nolan	.06
653	Mark Brouhard	.06
654	Dave Anderson	.06
655	Joaquin Andujar	.06
656	Chuck Cottier	.06
657	Jim Slaton	.06
658	Mike Stenhouse	.06
659	Checklist 529-660	.06
660	Tony Gwynn	2.50
661	Steve Crawford	.06
662	Mike Heath	.06
663	Luis Aguayo	.06
664	*Steve Farr*	.30
665	Don Mattingly	3.00
666	Mike LaCoss	.06
667	Dave Engle	.06
668	Steve Trout	.06
669	Lee Lacy	.06
670	Tom Seaver	.40
671	Dane Iorg	.06
672	Juan Berenguer	.06
673	Buck Martinez	.06
674	Atlee Hammaker	.06
675	Tony Perez	.10
676	*Albert Hall*	.06
677	Wally Backman	.06
678	Joey McLaughlin	.06
679	Bob Kearney	.06
680	Jerry Reuss	.06
681	Ben Oglivie	.06
682	Doug Corbett	.06
683	Whitey Herzog	.06
684	Bill Doran	.06
685	Bill Caudill	.06
686	Mike Easler	.06
687	Bill Gullickson	.06
688	Len Matuszek	.06
689	Luis DeLeon	.06
690	Alan Trammell	.20
691	Dennis Rasmussen	.06
692	Randy Bush	.06
693	Tim Stoddard	.06
694	Joe Carter	3.00
695	Rick Rhoden	.06
696	John Rabb	.06
697	Onix Concepcion	.06
698	Jorge Bell	.12
699	Donnie Moore	.06
700	Eddie Murray	1.25
701	Eddie Murray (All-Star)	.40
702	Damaso Garcia (All-Star)	.06
703	George Brett (All-Star)	.50
704	Cal Ripken, Jr. (All-Star)	2.00
705	Dave Winfield (All-Star)	.50
706	Rickey Henderson (All-Star)	.25
707	Tony Armas (All-Star)	.06
708	Lance Parrish (All-Star)	.08
709	Mike Boddicker (All-Star)	.06
710	Frank Viola (All-Star)	.06
711	Dan Quisenberry (All-Star)	.06
712	Keith Hernandez (All-Star)	.06
713	Ryne Sandberg (All-Star)	.60
714	Mike Schmidt (All-Star)	.45
715	Ozzie Smith (All-Star)	.25
716	Dale Murphy (All-Star)	.15
717	Tony Gwynn (All-Star)	.50
718	Jeff Leonard (All-Star)	.06
719	Gary Carter (All-Star)	.12
720	Rick Sutcliffe (All-Star)	.06

721	Bob Knepper (All-Star)	.06
722	Bruce Sutter (All-Star)	.06
723	Dave Stewart	.12
724	Oscar Gamble	.06
725	Floyd Bannister	.06
726	Al Bumbry	.06
727	Frank Pastore	.06
728	Bob Bailor	.06
729	Don Sutton	.20
730	Dave Kingman	.12
731	Neil Allen	.06
732	John McNamara	.06
733	Tony Scott	.06
734	John Henry Johnson	.06
735	Garry Templeton	.06
736	Jerry Mumphrey	.06
737	Bo Diaz	.06
738	Omar Moreno	.06
739	Ernie Camacho	.06
740	Jack Clark	.06
741	John Butcher	.06
742	Ron Hassey	.06
743	Frank White	.06
744	Doug Bair	.06
745	Buddy Bell	.06
746	Jim Clancy	.06
747	Alex Trevino	.06
748	Lee Mazzilli	.06
749	Julio Cruz	.06
750	Rollie Fingers	.20
751	Kelvin Chapman	.06
752	Bob Owchinko	.06
753	Greg Brock	.06
754	Larry Milbourne	.06
755	Ken Singleton	.06
756	Rob Picciolo	.06
757	Willie McGee	.12
758	Ray Burris	.06
759	Jim Fanning	.06
760	Nolan Ryan	5.00
761	Jerry Remy	.06
762	Eddie Whitson	.06
763	Kiko Garcia	.06
764	Jamie Easterly	.06
765	Willie Randolph	.06
766	Paul Mirabella	.06
767	Darrell Brown	.06
768	Ron Cey	.06
769	Joe Cowley	.06
770	Carlton Fisk	.30
771	Geoff Zahn	.06
772	Johnnie LeMaster	.06
773	Hal McRae	.06
774	Dennis Lamp	.06
775	Mookie Wilson	.06
776	Jerry Royster	.06
777	Ned Yost	.06
778	Mike Davis	.06
779	Nick Esasky	.06
780	Mike Flanagan	.06
781	Jim Gantner	.06
782	Tom Niedenfuer	.06
783	Mike Jorgensen	.06
784	Checklist 661-792	.06
785	Tony Armas	.06
786	Enos Cabell	.06
787	Jim Wohlford	.06
788	Steve Comer	.06
789	Luis Salazar	.06
790	Ron Guidry	.10
791	Ivan DeJesus	.06
792	Darrell Evans	.08

1985 Topps Tiffany

In its second year of producing a high-gloss collectors edition of its regular baseball card set, Topps cut production to a reported 5,000 sets. Other than the use of white cardboard stock and the glossy front coating, the cards in this specially boxed set are identical to regular 1985 Topps cards.

	MT
Complete Set (792):	650.00
Common Player:	.25
(Star cards valued at 3X-5X corresponding cards in regular 1985 Topps issue)	

1985 Topps Traded

By 1985, the Topps Traded set had become a yearly feature, and Topps continued the tradition with another 132-card set. The 2-1/2" x 3-1/2" cards followed the pattern of being virtually identical in design to the regular cards issued by Topps. Sold only through established hobby dealers, the set features traded veterans and promising rookies. A glossy-finish "Tiffany" edition of the set is valued at four times normal Traded card value for commons, up to five or six times normal value for superstars and hot rookies.

		MT
Complete Set (132):		11.00
Common Player:		.10
1T	Don Aase	.10
2T	Bill Almon	.10
3T	Benny Ayala	.10
4T	Dusty Baker	.15
5T	George Bamberger	.10
6T	Dale Berra	.10
7T	Rich Bordi	.10
8T	Daryl Boston	.20
9T	Hubie Brooks	.10
10T	Chris Brown	.10
11T	Tom Browning	.50
12T	Al Bumbry	.10
13T	Ray Burris	.10
14T	Jeff Burroughs	.10
15T	Bill Campbell	.10
16T	Don Carman	.10
17T	Gary Carter	.45
18T	Bobby Castillo	.10
19T	Bill Caudill	.10
20T	Rick Cerone	.10
21T	Bryan Clark	.10
22T	Jack Clark	.10
23T	Pat Clements	.10
24T	*Vince Coleman*	.60
25T	Dave Collins	.10
26T	Danny Darwin	.10
27T	Jim Davenport	.10
28T	Jerry Davis	.10
29T	Brian Dayett	.10
30T	Ivan DeJesus	.10
31T	Ken Dixon	.10
32T	Mariano Duncan	.50
33T	John Felske	.10
34T	Mike Fitzgerald	.10
35T	Ray Fontenot	.10
36T	Greg Gagne	.35
37T	Oscar Gamble	.10
38T	Scott Garrelts	.15
39T	Bob L. Gibson	.10
40T	Jim Gott	.10
41T	David Green	.10
42T	Alfredo Griffin	.10
43T	*Ozzie Guillen*	1.25
44T	Eddie Haas	.10
45T	Terry Harper	.10
46T	Toby Harrah	.10
47T	Greg Harris	.10
48T	Ron Hassey	.10
49T	Rickey Henderson	3.00
50T	Steve Henderson	.10
51T	George Hendrick	.10
52T	Joe Hesketh	.10
53T	Teddy Higuera	.10
54T	Donnie Hill	.10
55T	Al Holland	.10
56T	Burt Hooton	.10
57T	Jay Howell	.10
58T	Ken Howell	.15
59T	LaMarr Hoyt	.10
60T	Tim Hulett	.10
61T	Bob James	.10
62T	Steve Jeltz	.10
63T	Cliff Johnson	.10
64T	Howard Johnson	.25
65T	Ruppert Jones	.10
66T	Steve Kemp	.10
67T	Bruce Kison	.10
68T	Alan Knicely	.10
69T	Mike LaCoss	.10
70T	Lee Lacy	.10
71T	Dave LaPoint	.10

72T	Gary Lavelle	.10
73T	Vance Law	.10
74T	Johnnie LeMaster	.10
75T	Sixto Lezcano	.10
76T	Tim Lollar	.10
77T	Fred Lynn	.20
78T	Billy Martin	.20
79T	Ron Mathis	.10
80T	Len Matuszek	.10
81T	Gene Mauch	.10
82T	Oddibe McDowell	.10
83T	Roger McDowell	.50
84T	John McNamara	.10
85T	Donnie Moore	.10
86T	Gene Nelson	.10
87T	Steve Nicosia	.10
88T	Al Oliver	.10
89T	Joe Orsulak	.20
90T	Rob Picciolo	.10
91T	Chris Pittaro	.10
92T	Jim Presley	.10
93T	Rick Reuschel	.10
94T	Bert Roberge	.10
95T	Bob Rodgers	.10
96T	Jerry Royster	.10
97T	Dave Rozema	.10
98T	Dave Rucker	.10
99T	Vern Ruhle	.10
100T	Paul Runge	.10
101T	Mark Salas	.10
102T	Luis Salazar	.10
103T	Joe Sambito	.10
104T	Rick Schu	.10
105T	Donnie Scott	.10
106T	Larry Sheets	.10
107T	Don Slaught	.10
108T	Roy Smalley	.10
109T	Lonnie Smith	.10
110T	Nate Snell	.10
111T	Chris Speier	.10
112T	Mike Stenhouse	.10
113T	Tim Stoddard	.10
114T	Jim Sundberg	.10
115T	Bruce Sutter	.10
116T	Don Sutton	1.00
117T	Kent Tekulve	.10
118T	Tom Tellmann	.10
119T	Walt Terrell	.10
120T	*Mickey Tettleton*	2.00
121T	Derrel Thomas	.10
122T	Rich Thompson	.10
123T	Alex Trevino	.10
124T	John Tudor	.10
125T	Jose Uribe	.10
126T	Bobby Valentine	.10
127T	Dave Von Ohlen	.10
128T	U.L. Washington	.10
129T	Earl Weaver	.20
130T	Eddie Whitson	.10
131T	Herm Winningham	.10
132T	Checklist 1-132	.10

1985 Topps Traded Tiffany

This specially boxed collectors version of the Topps Traded sets features cards that differ only in the use of a high-gloss finish coat on the fronts.

	MT
Complete Set (132):	50.00
Common Player:	.25
(Star cards valued at 3X-4X corresponding cards in regular Topps Traded issue)	

Modern cards have little collector value in conditions lower than Mint. Figure NM cards at 75% of values shown; EX cards at 40%.

Values shown reflect the market as of January, 1999. On-field performances of current players in the 1999 baseball season are not factored in.

1985 Topps All-Star Glossy Set of 22

This was the second straight year for this set of 22 cards featuring the starting players, honorary captains and managers in the All-Star Game. The set is virtually identical to that of the previous year in design with a color photo, All-Star banner, league emblem, and player ID on the front. Fronts have a high-gloss finish. The cards were available as inserts in Topps rack packs.

	MT
Complete Set (22):	4.00
Common Player:	.20
1 Paul Owens	.20
2 Steve Garvey	.30
3 Ryne Sandberg	.60
4 Mike Schmidt	.75
5 Ozzie Smith	.30
6 Tony Gwynn	.60
7 Dale Murphy	.30
8 Darryl Strawberry	.30
9 Gary Carter	.30
10 Charlie Lea	.20
11 Willie McCovey	.40
12 Joe Altobelli	.20
13 Rod Carew	.40
14 Lou Whitaker	.20
15 George Brett	.80
16 Cal Ripken, Jr.	1.00
17 Dave Winfield	.35
18 Chet Lemon	.20
19 Reggie Jackson	.45
20 Lance Parrish	.20
21 Dave Stieb	.20
22 Hank Greenberg	.25

1986 Topps

The 1986 Topps set consists of 792 cards. Fronts of the 2-1/2" x 3-1/2" cards feature color photos with the Topps logo in the upper right-hand corner while the player's position is in the lower left-hand corner. Above the picture is the team name, while below it is the player's name. The borders are a departure from previous practice, as the top 7/8" is black, while the remainder was white. There are no card numbers 51 and 171 in the set; the card that should have been #51, Bobby Wine, shares #57 with Bill Doran, while #171, Bob Rodgers, shares #141 with Chuck Cottier. Once again, a 5,000-set glossy-finish "Tiffany" edition was produced. Values are four to six times higher than the same card in the regular issue.

	MT
Complete Set (792):	30.00
Common Player:	.05
Wax Box:	30.00
1 Pete Rose	.90
2 Pete Rose (Special 1963-66)	.45
3 Pete Rose (Special 1967-70)	.30
4 Pete Rose (Special 1971-74)	.30
5 Pete Rose (Special 1975-78)	.30
6 Pete Rose (Special 1972-82)	.30
7 Pete Rose (Special 1983-85)	.30
8 Dwayne Murphy	.05
9 Roy Smith	.05
10 Tony Gwynn	1.00
11 Bob Ojeda	.05
12 *Jose Uribe*	.05
13 Bob Kearney	.05
14 Julio Cruz	.05
15 Eddie Whitson	.05
16 Rick Schu	.05
17 Mike Stenhouse	.05
18 Brent Gaff	.05
19 Rich Hebner	.05
20 Lou Whitaker	.08
21 George Bamberger	.05
22 Duane Walker	.05
23 *Manny Lee*	.05
24 Len Barker	.05
25 Willie Wilson	.05
26 Frank DiPino	.05
27 Ray Knight	.05
28 Eric Davis	.15
29 Tony Phillips	.05
30 Eddie Murray	.60
31 Jamie Easterly	.05
32 Steve Yeager	.05
33 Jeff Lahti	.05
34 Ken Phelps	.05
35 Jeff Reardon	.05
36 Tigers Leaders(Lance Parrish)	.05
37 Mark Thurmond	.05
38 Glenn Hoffman	.05
39 Dave Rucker	.05
40 Ken Griffey	.05
41 Brad Wellman	.05
42 Geoff Zahn	.05
43 Dave Engle	.05
44 *Lance McCullers*	.05
45 Damaso Garcia	.05
46 Billy Hatcher	.05
47 Juan Berenguer	.05
48 Bill Almon	.05
49 Rick Manning	.05
50 Dan Quisenberry	.08
51 Not issued, see #57	
52 Chris Welsh	.05
53 *Len Dykstra*	1.00
54 John Franco	.10
55 Fred Lynn	.12
56 Tom Niedenfuer	.05
57a Bill Doran	.05
57b Bobby Wine (supposed to be #51)	.05
58 Bill Krueger	.05

59 Andre Thornton	.05
60 Dwight Evans	.05
61 Karl Best	.05
62 Bob Boone	.05
63 Ron Roenicke	.05
64 Floyd Bannister	.05
65 Dan Driessen	.05
66 Cardinals Leaders(Bob Forsch)	.05
67 Carmelo Martinez	.05
68 Ed Lynch	.05
69 Luis Aguayo	.05
70 Dave Winfield	.50
71 Ken Schrom	.05
72 Shawon Dunston	.15
73 Randy O'Neal	.05
74 Rance Mulliniks	.05
75 Jose DeLeon	.05
76 Dion James	.05
77 Charlie Leibrandt	.05
78 Bruce Benedict	.05
79 Dave Schmidt	.05
80 Darryl Strawberry	.25
81 Gene Mauch	.05
82 Tippy Martinez	.05
83 Phil Garner	.05
84 Curt Young	.05
85 Tony Perez	.12
86 Tom Waddell	.05
87 Candy Maldonado	.05
88 Tom Nieto	.05
89 Randy St. Claire	.05
90 Garry Templeton	.05
91 Steve Crawford	.05
92 Al Cowens	.05
93 Scot Thompson	.05
94 Rich Bordi	.05
95 Ozzie Virgil	.05
96 Blue Jay Leaders(Jim Clancy)	.05
97 Gary Gaetti	.12
98 Dick Ruthven	.05
99 Buddy Biancalana	.05
100 Nolan Ryan	3.00
101 Dave Bergman	.05
102 *Joe Orsulak*	.15
103 Luis Salazar	.05
104 Sid Fernandez	.05
105 Gary Ward	.05
106 Ray Burris	.05
107 Rafael Ramirez	.05
108 Ted Power	.05
109 Len Matuszek	.05
110 Scott McGregor	.05
111 Roger Craig	.05
112 Bill Campbell	.05
113 U.L. Washington	.05
114 Mike Brown	.05
115 Jay Howell	.05
116 Brook Jacoby	.05
117 Bruce Kison	.05
118 Jerry Royster	.05
119 Barry Bonnell	.05
120 Steve Carlton	.30
121 Nelson Simmons	.05
122 Pete Filson	.05
123 Greg Walker	.05
124 Luis Sanchez	.05
125 Luis Sanchez	.05
126 Mets Leaders(Mookie Wilson)	.05
127 *Jack Howell*	.05
128 John Wathan	.05
129 Jeff Dedmon	.05
130 Alan Trammell	.15
131 Checklist 1-132	.05
132 Razor Shines	.05
133 Andy McGaffigan	.05
134 Carney Lansford	.05
135 Joe Niekro	.05
136 Mike Hargrove	.05
137 Charlie Moore	.05
138 Mark Davis	.05
139 Daryl Boston	.05
140 John Candelaria	.05
141a Chuck Cottier	.05
141b Bob Rodgers (supposed to be #171)	.05
142 Bob Jones	.05
143 Dave Van Gorder	.05
144 Doug Sisk	.05
145 Pedro Guerrero	.05
146 Jack Perconte	.05
147 Larry Sheets	.05
148 Mike Heath	.05
149 Brett Butler	.05

#	Player	Price
150	Joaquin Andujar	.05
151	Dave Stapleton	.05
152	Mike Morgan	.05
153	Ricky Adams	.05
154	Bert Roberge	.05
155	Bob Grich	.05
156	White Sox Leaders(Richard Dotson)	.05
157	Ron Hassey	.05
158	Derrel Thomas	.05
159	Orel Hershiser	.15
160	Chet Lemon	.05
161	Lee Tunnell	.05
162	Greg Gagne	.05
163	Pete Ladd	.05
164	Steve Balboni	.05
165	Mike Davis	.05
166	Dickie Thon	.05
167	Zane Smith	.05
168	Jeff Burroughs	.05
169	George Wright	.05
170	Gary Carter	.20
171	Not issued, see #141	
172	Jerry Reed	.05
173	Wayne Gross	.05
174	Brian Snyder	.05
175	Steve Sax	.05
176	Jay Tibbs	.05
177	Joel Youngblood	.05
178	Ivan DeJesus	.05
179	*Stu Cliburn*	.05
180	Don Mattingly	1.00
181	Al Nipper	.05
182	Bobby Brown	.05
183	Larry Andersen	.05
184	Tim Laudner	.05
185	Rollie Fingers	.20
186	Astros Leaders(Jose Cruz)	.05
187	Scott Fletcher	.05
188	Bob Dernier	.05
189	Mike Mason	.05
190	George Hendrick	.05
191	Wally Backman	.05
192	Milt Wilcox	.05
193	Daryl Sconiers	.05
194	Craig McMurtry	.05
195	Dave Concepcion	.05
196	Doyle Alexander	.05
197	Enos Cabell	.05
198	Ken Dixon	.05
199	Dick Howser	.05
200	Mike Schmidt	1.00
201	Vince Coleman (Record Breaker)	.10
202	Dwight Gooden (Record Breaker)	.15
203	Keith Hernandez (Record Breaker)	.05
204	Phil Niekro (Record Breaker)	.15
205	Tony Perez (Record Breaker)	.08
206	Pete Rose (Record Breaker)	.50
207	Fernando Valenzuela (Record Breaker)	.08
208	Ramon Romero	.05
209	Randy Ready	.05
210	Calvin Schiraldi	.05
211	Ed Wojna	.05
212	Chris Speier	.05
213	Bob Shirley	.05
214	Randy Bush	.05
215	Frank White	.05
216	A's Leaders(Dwayne Murphy)	.05
217	Bill Scherrer	.05
218	Randy Hunt	.05
219	Dennis Lamp	.05
220	Bob Horner	.05
221	Dave Henderson	.05
222	Craig Gerber	.05
223	Atlee Hammaker	.05
224	Cesar Cedeno	.05
225	Ron Darling	.05
226	Lee Lacy	.05
227	Al Jones	.05
228	Tom Lawless	.05
229	Bill Gullickson	.05
230	Terry Kennedy	.05
231	Jim Frey	.05
232	Rick Rhoden	.05
233	Steve Lyons	.05
234	Doug Corbett	.05
235	Butch Wynegar	.05
236	Frank Eufemia	.05
237	Ted Simmons	.05
238	Larry Parrish	.05
239	Joel Skinner	.05
240	Tommy John	.10
241	Tony Fernandez	.05
242	Rich Thompson	.05
243	Johnny Grubb	.05
244	Craig Lefferts	.05
245	Jim Sundberg	.05
246	Phillies Leaders(Steve Carlton)	.10
247	Terry Harper	.05
248	Spike Owen	.05
249	Rob Deer	.05
250	Dwight Gooden	.25
251	Rich Dauer	.05
252	Bobby Castillo	.05
253	Dann Bilardello	.05
254	*Ozzie Guillen*	.30
255	Tony Armas	.05
256	Kurt Kepshire	.05
257	Doug DeCinces	.05
258	*Tim Burke*	.05
259	Dan Pasqua	.08
260	Tony Pena	.05
261	Bobby Valentine	.05
262	Mario Ramirez	.05
263	Checklist 133-264	.05
264	Darren Daulton	1.00
265	Ron Davis	.05
266	Keith Moreland	.05
267	Paul Molitor	.75
268	Mike Scott	.05
269	Dane Iorg	.05
270	Jack Morris	.08
271	Dave Collins	.05
272	Tim Tolman	.05
273	Jerry Willard	.05
274	Ron Gardenhire	.05
275	Charlie Hough	.05
276	Yankees Leaders(Willie Randolph)	.05
277	Jaime Cocanower	.05
278	Sixto Lezcano	.05
279	Al Pardo	.05
280	Tim Raines	.12
281	Steve Mura	.05
282	Jerry Mumphrey	.05
283	Mike Fischlin	.05
284	Brian Dayett	.05
285	Buddy Bell	.05
286	Luis DeLeon	.05
287	*John Christensen*	.05
288	Don Aase	.05
289	Johnnie LeMaster	.05
290	Carlton Fisk	.30
291	Tom Lasorda	.20
292	Chuck Porter	.05
293	Chris Chambliss	.05
294	Danny Cox	.05
295	Kirk Gibson	.10
296	Geno Petralli	.05
297	Tim Lollar	.05
298	Craig Reynolds	.05
299	Bryn Smith	.05
300	George Brett	1.00
301	Dennis Rasmussen	.05
302	Greg Gross	.05
303	Curt Wardle	.05
304	*Mike Gallego*	.12
305	Phil Bradley	.05
306	Padres Leaders(Terry Kennedy)	.05
307	Dave Sax	.05
308	Ray Fontenot	.05
309	John Shelby	.05
310	Greg Minton	.05
311	Dick Schofield	.05
312	Tom Filer	.05
313	Joe DeSa	.05
314	Frank Pastore	.05
315	Mookie Wilson	.05
316	Sammy Khalifa	.05
317	Ed Romero	.05
318	Terry Whitfield	.05
319	Rick Camp	.05
320	Jim Rice	.05
321	Earl Weaver	.20
322	Bob Forsch	.05
323	Jerry Davis	.05
324	Dan Schatzeder	.05
325	Juan Beniquez	.05
326	Kent Tekulve	.05
327	Mike Pagliarulo	.08
328	Pete O'Brien	.05
329	Kirby Puckett	4.00
330	Rick Sutcliffe	.05
331	Alan Ashby	.05
332	Darryl Motley	.05
333	Tom Henke	.10
334	Ken Oberkfell	.05
335	Don Sutton	.25
336	Indians Leaders(Andre Thornton)	.05
337	Darnell Coles	.05
338	Jorge Bell	.12
339	Bruce Berenyi	.05
340	Cal Ripken, Jr.	4.50
341	Frank Williams	.05
342	Gary Redus	.05
343	Carlos Diaz	.05
344	Jim Wohlford	.05
345	Donnie Moore	.05
346	Bryan Little	.05
347	*Teddy Higuera*	.08
348	Cliff Johnson	.05
349	Mark Clear	.05
350	Jack Clark	.05
351	Chuck Tanner	.05
352	Harry Spilman	.05
353	Keith Atherton	.05
354	Tony Bernazard	.05
355	Lee Smith	.10
356	Mickey Hatcher	.05
357	Ed Vande Berg	.05
358	Rick Dempsey	.05
359	Mike LaCoss	.05
360	Lloyd Moseby	.05
361	Shane Rawley	.05
362	Tom Paciorek	.05
363	Terry Forster	.05
364	Reid Nichols	.05
365	Mike Flanagan	.05
366	Reds Leaders(Dave Concepcion)	.05
367	Aurelio Lopez	.05
368	Greg Brock	.05
369	Al Holland	.05
370	*Vince Coleman*	.35
371	Bill Stein	.05
372	Ben Oglivie	.05
373	*Urbano Lugo*	.05
374	Terry Francona	.05
375	Rich Gedman	.05
376	Bill Dawley	.05
377	Joe Carter	1.25
378	Bruce Bochte	.05
379	Bobby Meacham	.05
380	LaMarr Hoyt	.05
381	Ray Miller	.05
382	*Ivan Calderon*	.05
383	Chris Brown	.05
384	Steve Trout	.05
385	Cecil Cooper	.05
386	*Cecil Fielder*	2.50
387	Steve Kemp	.05
388	Dickie Noles	.05
389	Glenn Davis	.10
390	Tom Seaver	.35
391	Julio Franco	.10
392	John Russell	.05
393	Chris Pittaro	.05
394	Checklist 265-396	.05
395	Scott Garrelts	.05
396	Red Sox Leaders(Dwight Evans)	.05
397	*Steve Buechele*	.20
398	*Earnie Riles*	.05
399	Bill Swift	.10
400	Rod Carew	.30
401	Fernando Valenzuela (Turn Back the Clock)	.10
402	Tom Seaver (Turn Back the Clock)	.15
403	Willie Mays (Turn Back the Clock)	.20
404	Frank Robinson (Turn Back the Clock)	.15
405	Roger Maris (Turn Back the Clock)	.25
406	Scott Sanderson	.05
407	Sal Butera	.05
408	Dave Smith	.05
409	*Paul Runge*	.05
410	Dave Kingman	.10
411	Sparky Anderson	.08
412	Jim Clancy	.05
413	Tim Flannery	.05
414	Tom Gorman	.05
415	Hal McRae	.05
416	Denny Martinez	.08
417	R.J. Reynolds	.05

No.	Player	Price	No.	Player	Price	No.	Player	Price
418	Alan Knicely	.05	512	Thad Bosley	.05	605	Dennis Boyd	.05
419	Frank Wills	.05	513	Ron Washington	.05	606	Royals Leaders(Hal McRae)	.05
420	Von Hayes	.05	514	Mike Jones	.05	607	Ken Dayley	.05
421	Dave Palmer	.05	515	Darrell Evans	.05	608	Bruce Bochy	.05
422	Mike Jorgensen	.05	516	Giants Leaders(Greg Minton)	.05	609	Barbaro Garbey	.05
423	Dan Spillner	.05	517	*Milt Thompson*	.05	610	Ron Guidry	.08
424	Rick Miller	.05	518	Buck Martinez	.05	611	Gary Woods	.05
425	Larry McWilliams	.05	519	Danny Darwin	.05	612	Richard Dotson	.05
426	Brewers Leaders(Charlie Moore)	.05	520	Keith Hernandez	.05	613	Roy Smalley	.05
427	Joe Cowley	.05	521	Nate Snell	.05	614	Rick Waits	.05
428	Max Venable	.05	522	Bob Bailor	.05	615	Johnny Ray	.05
429	Greg Booker	.05	523	Joe Price	.05	616	Glenn Brummer	.05
430	Kent Hrbek	.10	524	Darrell Miller	.05	617	Lonnie Smith	.05
431	George Frazier	.05	525	Marvell Wynne	.05	618	Jim Pankovits	.05
432	Mark Bailey	.05	526	Charlie Lea	.05	619	Danny Heep	.05
433	Chris Codiroli	.05	527	Checklist 397-528	.05	620	Bruce Sutter	.05
434	Curt Wilkerson	.05	528	Terry Pendleton	.15	621	John Felske	.05
435	Bill Caudill	.05	529	Marc Sullivan	.05	622	Gary Lavelle	.05
436	Doug Flynn	.05	530	Rich Gossage	.10	623	Floyd Rayford	.05
437	Rick Mahler	.05	531	Tony LaRussa	.05	624	Steve McCatty	.05
438	Clint Hurdle	.05	532	*Don Carman*	.05	625	Bob Brenly	.05
439	Rick Honeycutt	.05	533	Billy Sample	.05	626	Roy Thomas	.05
440	Alvin Davis	.05	534	Jeff Calhoun	.05	627	Ron Oester	.05
441	Whitey Herzog	.05	535	Toby Harrah	.05	628	*Kirk McCaskill*	.15
442	Ron Robinson	.05	536	Jose Rijo	.10	629	*Mitch Webster*	.05
443	Bill Buckner	.05	537	Mark Salas	.05	630	Fernando Valenzuela	.08
444	Alex Trevino	.05	538	Dennis Eckersley	.10	631	Steve Braun	.05
445	Bert Blyleven	.10	539	Glenn Hubbard	.05	632	Dave Von Ohlen	.05
446	Lenn Sakata	.05	540	Dan Petry	.05	633	Jackie Gutierrez	.05
447	Jerry Don Gleaton	.05	541	Jorge Orta	.05	634	Roy Lee Jackson	.05
448	*Herm Winningham*	.05	542	Don Schulze	.05	635	Jason Thompson	.05
449	Rod Scurry	.05	543	Jerry Narron	.05	636	Cubs Leaders(Lee Smith)	.08
450	Graig Nettles	.08	544	Eddie Milner	.05	637	Rudy Law	.05
451	Mark Brown	.05	545	Jimmy Key	.15	638	John Butcher	.05
452	Bob Clark	.05	546	Mariners Leaders(Dave Henderson)	.05	639	Bo Diaz	.05
453	Steve Jeltz	.05	547	*Roger McDowell*	.12	640	Jose Cruz	.05
454	Burt Hooton	.05	548	Mike Young	.05	641	Wayne Tolleson	.05
455	Willie Randolph	.05	549	Bob Welch	.05	642	Ray Searage	.05
456	Braves Leaders(Dale Murphy)	.10	550	Tom Herr	.05	643	Tom Brookens	.05
457	Mickey Tettleton	.75	551	Dave LaPoint	.05	644	Mark Gubicza	.12
458	Kevin Bass	.05	552	Marc Hill	.05	645	Dusty Baker	.05
459	Luis Leal	.05	553	Jim Morrison	.05	646	Mike Moore	.05
460	Leon Durham	.05	554	Paul Householder	.05	647	Mel Hall	.05
461	Walt Terrell	.05	555	Hubie Brooks	.05	648	Steve Bedrosian	.05
462	Domingo Ramos	.05	556	John Denny	.05	649	Ronn Reynolds	.05
463	Jim Gott	.05	557	Gerald Perry	.05	650	Dave Stieb	.05
464	Ruppert Jones	.05	558	Tim Stoddard	.05	651	Billy Martin	.08
465	Jesse Orosco	.05	559	Tommy Dunbar	.05	652	Tom Browning	.05
466	Tom Foley	.05	560	Dave Righetti	.05	653	Jim Dwyer	.05
467	Bob James	.05	561	Bob Lillis	.05	654	Ken Howell	.05
468	Mike Scioscia	.05	562	Joe Beckwith	.05	655	Manny Trillo	.05
469	Storm Davis	.05	563	Alejandro Sanchez	.05	656	Brian Harper	.05
470	Bill Madlock	.08	564	Warren Brusstar	.05	657	Juan Agosto	.05
471	Bobby Cox	.05	565	Tom Brunansky	.05	658	Rob Wilfong	.05
472	Joe Hesketh	.05	566	Alfredo Griffin	.05	659	Checklist 529-660	.05
473	Mark Brouhard	.05	567	Jeff Barkley	.05	660	Steve Garvey	.15
474	John Tudor	.05	568	Donnie Scott	.05	661	Roger Clemens	3.50
475	Juan Samuel	.05	569	Jim Acker	.05	662	Bill Schroeder	.05
476	Ron Mathis	.05	570	Rusty Staub	.10	663	Neil Allen	.05
477	Mike Easler	.05	571	Mike Jeffcoat	.05	664	Tim Corcoran	.05
478	Andy Hawkins	.05	572	Paul Zuvella	.05	665	Alejandro Pena	.05
479	*Bob Melvin*	.05	573	Tom Hume	.05	666	Rangers Leaders(Charlie Hough)	.05
480	*Oddibe McDowell*		574	Ron Kittle	.05	667	Tim Teufel	.05
481	Scott Bradley	.05	575	Mike Boddicker	.05	668	Cecilio Guante	.05
482	Rick Lysander	.05	576	Expos Leaders(Andre Dawson)	.10	669	Ron Cey	.05
483	George Vukovich	.05	577	Jerry Reuss	.05	670	Willie Hernandez	.05
484	Donnie Hill	.05	578	Lee Mazzilli	.05	671	Lynn Jones	.05
485	Gary Matthews	.05	579	Jim Slaton	.05	672	Rob Picciolo	.05
486	Angels Leaders(Bob Grich)	.05	580	Willie McGee	.08	673	Ernie Whitt	.05
487	Bret Saberhagen	.25	581	Bruce Hurst	.05	674	Pat Tabler	.05
488	Lou Thornton	.05	582	Jim Gantner	.05	675	Claudell Washington	.05
489	Jim Winn	.05	583	Al Bumbry	.05	676	Matt Young	.05
490	Jeff Leonard	.05	584	*Brian Fisher*	.05	677	Nick Esasky	.05
491	Pascual Perez	.05	585	Garry Maddox	.05	678	Dan Gladden	.05
492	Kelvin Chapman	.05	586	Greg Harris	.05	679	Britt Burns	.05
493	Gene Nelson	.05	587	Rafael Santana	.05	680	George Foster	.08
494	Gary Roenicke	.05	588	Steve Lake	.05	681	Dick Williams	.05
495	Mark Langston	.20	589	Sid Bream	.05	682	Junior Ortiz	.05
496	Jay Johnstone	.05	590	Bob Knepper	.05	683	Andy Van Slyke	.05
497	John Stuper	.05	591	Jackie Moore	.05	684	Bob McClure	.05
498	Tito Landrum	.05	592	Frank Tanana	.05	685	Tim Wallach	.05
499	Bob L. Gibson	.05	593	Jesse Barfield	.05	686	Jeff Stone	.05
500	Rickey Henderson	.50	594	Chris Bando	.05	687	Mike Trujillo	.05
501	Dave Johnson	.05	595	Dave Parker	.15	688	Larry Herndon	.05
502	Glen Cook	.05	596	Onix Concepcion	.05	689	Dave Stewart	.12
503	Mike Fitzgerald	.05	597	Sammy Stewart	.05	690	Ryne Sandberg	1.50
504	Denny Walling	.05	598	Jim Presley	.05	691	Mike Madden	.05
505	Jerry Koosman	.05	599	*Rick Aguilera*	.50	692	Dale Berra	.05
506	Bill Russell	.05	600	Dale Murphy	.12	693	Tom Tellmann	.05
507	*Steve Ontiveros*	.12	601	Gary Lucas	.05	694	Garth Iorg	.05
508	Alan Wiggins	.05	602	*Mariano Duncan*	.25	695	Mike Smithson	.05
509	Ernie Camacho	.05	603	Bill Laskey	.05	696	Dodgers Leaders(Bill Russell)	.05
510	Wade Boggs	.90	604	Gary Pettis	.05	697	Bud Black	.05
511	Ed Nunez	.05						

698	Brad Komminsk	.05
699	Pat Corrales	.05
700	Reggie Jackson	.25
701	Keith Hernandez (All-Star)	.05
702	Tom Herr (All-Star)	.05
703	Tim Wallach (All-Star)	.05
704	Ozzie Smith (All-Star)	.15
705	Dale Murphy (All-Star)	.10
706	Pedro Guerrero (All-Star)	.05
707	Willie McGee (All-Star)	.05
708	Gary Carter (All-Star)	.10
709	Dwight Gooden (All-Star)	.10
710	John Tudor (All-Star)	.05
711	Jeff Reardon (All-Star)	.05
712	Don Mattingly (All-Star)	.40
713	Damasco Garcia (All-Star)	.05
714	George Brett (All-Star)	.50
715	Cal Ripken, Jr. (All-Star)	1.00
716	Rickey Henderson (All-Star)	.25
717	Dave Winfield (All-Star)	.20
718	George Bell (All-Star)	.05
719	Carlton Fisk (All-Star)	.12
720	Bret Saberhagen (All-Star)	.15
721	Ron Guidry (All-Star)	.10
722	Dan Quisenberry (All-Star)	.05
723	Marty Bystrom	.05
724	Tim Hulett	.05
725	Mario Soto	.05
726	Orioles Leaders(Rick Dempsey)	.05
727	David Green	.05
728	Mike Marshall	.05
729	Jim Beattie	.05
730	Ozzie Smith	.30
731	Don Robinson	.05
732	*Floyd Youmans*	.05
733	Ron Romanick	.05
734	Marty Barrett	.05
735	Dave Dravecky	.08
736	Glenn Wilson	.05
737	Pete Vuckovich	.05
738	Andre Robertson	.05
739	Dave Rozema	.05
740	Lance Parrish	.08
741	Pete Rose	.40
742	Frank Viola	.08
743	Pat Sheridan	.05
744	Lary Sorensen	.05
745	Willie Upshaw	.05
746	Denny Gonzalez	.05
747	Rick Cerone	.05
748	Steve Henderson	.05
749	Ed Jurak	.05
750	Gorman Thomas	.05
751	Howard Johnson	.08
752	Mike Krukow	.05
753	Dan Ford	.05
754	*Pat Clements*	.05
755	Harold Baines	.10
756	Pirates Leaders(Rick Rhoden)	.05
757	Darrell Porter	.05
758	Dave Anderson	.05
759	Moose Haas	.05
760	Andre Dawson	.30
761	Don Slaught	.05
762	Eric Show	.05
763	Terry Puhl	.05
764	Kevin Gross	.05
765	Don Baylor	.08
766	Rick Langford	.05
767	Jody Davis	.05
768	Vern Ruhle	.05
769	*Harold Reynolds*	.25
770	Vida Blue	.05
771	John McNamara	.05
772	Brian Downing	.05
773	Greg Pryor	.05
774	Terry Leach	.05
775	Al Oliver	.10
776	Gene Garber	.05
777	Wayne Krenchicki	.05
778	Jerry Hairston	.05
779	Rick Reuschel	.05
780	Robin Yount	.50
781	Joe Nolan	.05
782	Ken Landreaux	.05
783	Ricky Horton	.05
784	Alan Bannister	.05
785	Bob Stanley	.05
786	Twins Leaders(Mickey Hatcher)	.05
787	Vance Law	.05
788	Marty Castillo	.05
789	Kurt Bevacqua	.05
790	Phil Niekro	.30
791	Checklist 661-792	.05
792	Charles Hudson	.05

1986 Topps Tiffany

A total of only 5,000 of these specially boxed collectors edition sets was reported produced. Sold only through hobby dealers the cards differ from the regular-issue 1986 Topps cards only in the use of white cardboard stock and the application of a high-gloss finish on the cards' fronts.

	MT
Complete Set (792):	100.00
Common Player:	.25
(Star cards valued at 4X-6X corresponding cards in regular 1986 Topps issue)	

1986 Topps Box Panels

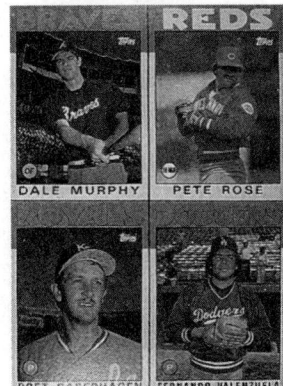

Following the lead of Donruss, which introduced the concept in 1985, Topps produced special cards on the bottom panels of wax boxes. Individual cards measure 2-1/2" x 3-1/2", the same as regular cards. Design of the cards is virtually identical with regular '86 Topps, though the top border is in red, rather than black. The cards are lettered "A" through "P", rather than numbered on the back.

		MT
Complete Panel Set:		10.00
Complete Singles Set:		5.00
Common Panel:		1.50
Common Single Player:		.15
Panel		3.25
A	Jorge Bell	.20
B	Wade Boggs	.40
C	George Brett	.60
D	Vince Coleman	.25
Panel		1.50
E	Carlton Fisk	.25
F	Dwight Gooden	.20
G	Pedro Guerrero	.15
H	Ron Guidry	.15
Panel		3.00
I	Reggie Jackson	.50
J	Don Mattingly	1.00
K	Oddibe McDowell	.15
L	Willie McGee	.15
Panel		2.50
M	Dale Murphy	.35
N	Pete Rose	1.00
O	Bret Saberhagen	.15
P	Fernando Valenzuela	.20

1986 Topps Traded

This 132-card set of 2-1/2" x 3-1/2" cards was, at issue, one of the most popular sets of recent times. As always, the set features traded veterans, including such players as Phil Niekro and Tom Seaver. They were not, however, the reason for the excitement. The demand stemmed from a better than usual crop of rookies appearing in the set. Among those are Jose Canseco, Wally Joyner, Will Clark, Barry Bonds and the first card of Bo Jackson. As in the previous two years, a glossy-finish "Tiffany" edition of 5,000 Traded sets was produced. The "Tiffany" cards are worth three to five times the value of the regular Traded cards.

		MT
Complete Set (132):		12.00
Common Player:		.10
1T	Andy Allanson	.10
2T	Neil Allen	.10
3T	Joaquin Andujar	.10
4T	Paul Assenmacher	.10
5T	Scott Bailes	.10
6T	Don Baylor	.15
7T	Steve Bedrosian	.10
8T	Juan Beniquez	.10
9T	Juan Berenguer	.10
10T	Mike Bielecki	.10
11T	*Barry Bonds*	4.00
12T	*Bobby Bonilla*	1.50
13T	Juan Bonilla	.10
14T	Rich Bordi	.10
15T	Steve Boros	.10
16T	Rick Burleson	.10
17T	Bill Campbell	.10
18T	Tom Candiotti	.10
19T	John Cangelosi	.10
20T	Jose Canseco	4.00
21T	Carmen Castillo	.10
22T	Rick Cerone	.10
23T	John Cerutti	.10
24T	*Will Clark*	3.00
25T	Mark Clear	.10
26T	Darnell Coles	.10
27T	Dave Collins	.10
28T	Tim Conroy	.10
29T	Joe Cowley	.10
30T	Joel Davis	.10
31T	Rob Deer	.10
32T	John Denny	.10
33T	Mike Easler	.10
34T	Mark Eichhorn	.15
35T	Steve Farr	.10
36T	Scott Fletcher	.10
37T	Terry Forster	.10
38T	Terry Francona	.10
39T	Jim Fregosi	.10
40T	Andres Galarraga	1.50
41T	Ken Griffey	.12
42T	Bill Gullickson	.10
43T	Jose Guzman	.10
44T	Moose Haas	.10
45T	Billy Hatcher	.10
46T	Mike Heath	.10
47T	Tom Hume	.10
48T	*Pete Incaviglia*	.20
49T	Dane Iorg	.10
50T	*Bo Jackson*	1.50
51T	*Wally Joyner*	.75
52T	Charlie Kerfeld	.10
53T	Eric King	.10
54T	Bob Kipper	.10
55T	Wayne Krenchicki	.10
56T	*John Kruk*	.35
57T	Mike LaCoss	.10
58T	Pete Ladd	.10
59T	Mike Laga	.10
60T	Hal Lanier	.10
61T	Dave LaPoint	.10
62T	Rudy Law	.10
63T	Rick Leach	.10
64T	Tim Leary	.10
65T	Dennis Leonard	.10
66T	Jim Leyland	.20
67T	Steve Lyons	.10
68T	Mickey Mahler	.10

69T	Candy Maldonado	.10
70T	Roger Mason	.10
71T	Bob McClure	.10
72T	Andy McGaffigan	.10
73T	Gene Michael	.10
74T	*Kevin Mitchell*	.30
75T	Omar Moreno	.10
76T	Jerry Mumphrey	.10
77T	Phil Niekro	.75
78T	Randy Niemann	.10
79T	Juan Nieves	.10
80T	Otis Nixon	.25
81T	Bob Ojeda	.10
82T	Jose Oquendo	.10
83T	Tom Paciorek	.10
84T	Dave Palmer	.10
85T	Frank Pastore	.10
86T	Lou Piniella	.10
87T	Dan Plesac	.12
88T	Darrell Porter	.10
89T	Rey Quinones	.10
90T	Gary Redus	.10
91T	Bip Roberts	.25
92T	Billy Jo Robidoux	.10
93T	Jeff Robinson	.10
94T	Gary Roenicke	.10
95T	Ed Romero	.10
96T	Argenis Salazar	.10
97T	Joe Sambito	.10
98T	Billy Sample	.10
99T	Dave Schmidt	.10
100T	Ken Schrom	.10
101T	Tom Seaver	.60
102T	Ted Simmons	.10
103T	Sammy Stewart	.10
104T	Kurt Stillwell	.10
105T	Franklin Stubbs	.10
106T	Dale Sveum	.10
107T	Chuck Tanner	.10
108T	Danny Tartabull	.30
109T	Tim Teufel	.10
110T	Bob Tewksbury	.50
111T	Andres Thomas	.10
112T	Milt Thompson	.10
113T	Robby Thompson	.35
114T	Jay Tibbs	.10
115T	Wayne Tolleson	.10
116T	Alex Trevino	.10
117T	Manny Trillo	.10
118T	Ed Vande Berg	.10
119T	Ozzie Virgil	.10
120T	Bob Walk	.10
121T	Gene Walter	.10
122T	Claudell Washington	.10
123T	Bill Wegman	.20
124T	Dick Williams	.10
125T	Mitch Williams	.15
126T	Bobby Witt	.20
127T	Todd Worrell	.15
128T	George Wright	.10
129T	Ricky Wright	.10
130T	Steve Yeager	.10
131T	Paul Zuvella	.10
132T	Checklist	.10

1986 Topps Traded Tiffany

This collectors edition differs from the regular 1986 Topps Traded set only in the use of a high-gloss front finish. The set was sold only through hobby channels in a specially design box.

	MT
Complete Set (132):	75.00
Common Player:	.25
(Star cards valued at 3X-4X corresponding cards in regular Topps Traded)	

1986 Topps All-Star Glossy Set of 22

As in previous years, Topps continued to make the popular glossy-surfaced cards as an insert in rack packs. The All-Star Glossy set of 2-1/2" x 3-1/2" cards shows little design change from previous years. Cards feature a front color photo and All-Star banner at the top. The bottom has the player's name and position. The set includes the All-Star starting teams as well as the managers and honorary captains.

		MT
Complete Set (22):		4.00
Common Player:		.20
1	Sparky Anderson	.20
2	Eddie Murray	.60
3	Lou Whitaker	.20
4	George Brett	.80
5	Cal Ripken, Jr.	1.00
6	Jim Rice	.20
7	Rickey Henderson	.50
8	Dave Winfield	.50
9	Carlton Fisk	.30
10	Jack Morris	.20
11	A.L. All-Star Team	.20
12	Dick Williams	.20
13	Steve Garvey	.30
14	Tom Herr	.20
15	Graig Nettles	.20
16	Ozzie Smith	.40
17	Tony Gwynn	.75
18	Dale Murphy	.40
19	Darryl Strawberry	.35
20	Terry Kennedy	.20
21	LaMarr Hoyt	.20
22	N.L. All-Star Team	.20

1986 Topps Mini League Leaders

MIKE SCHMIDT

Topps had long experimented with bigger cards, but in 1986, they also decided to try smaller ones. These 2-1/8" x 2-15/16" cards feature top players in a number of categories. Sold in plastic packs as a regular Topps issue, the 66-card set is attractive as well as innovative. The cards feature color photos and a minimum of added information on the fronts where only the player's name and Topps logo appear. Backs limited information as well, but do feature enough to justify the player's inclusion in a set of league leaders.

		MT
Complete Set (66):		6.00
Common Player:		.10
1	Eddie Murray	.45
2	Cal Ripken, Jr.	1.00
3	Wade Boggs	.50
4	Dennis Boyd	.10
5	Dwight Evans	.10
6	Bruce Hurst	.10
7	Gary Pettis	.10
8	Harold Baines	.15
9	Floyd Bannister	.10
10	Britt Burns	.10
11	Carlton Fisk	.15
12	Brett Butler	.15
13	Darrell Evans	.10
14	Jack Morris	.10
15	Lance Parrish	.10
16	Walt Terrell	.10
17	Steve Balboni	.10
18	George Brett	.80
19	Charlie Leibrandt	.10
20	Bret Saberhagen	.15
21	Lonnie Smith	.10
22	Willie Wilson	.10
23	Bert Blyleven	.10
24	Mike Smithson	.10
25	Frank Viola	.10
26	Ron Guidry	.10
27	Rickey Henderson	.40
28	Don Mattingly	.90
29	Dave Winfield	.30
30	Mike Moore	.10
31	Gorman Thomas	.10
32	Toby Harrah	.10
33	Charlie Hough	.10
34	Doyle Alexander	.10
35	Jimmy Key	.10
36	Dave Stieb	.10
37	Dale Murphy	.30
38	Keith Moreland	.10
39	Ryne Sandberg	.50
40	Tom Browning	.10
41	Dave Parker	.15
42	Mario Soto	.10
43	Nolan Ryan	1.00
44	Pedro Guerrero	.10
45	Orel Hershiser	.15
46	Mike Scioscia	.10
47	Fernando Valenzuela	.15
48	Bob Welch	.10
49	Tim Raines	.15
50	Gary Carter	.15
51	Sid Fernandez	.10
52	Dwight Gooden	.25
53	Keith Hernandez	.10
54	Juan Samuel	.10
55	Mike Schmidt	.80
56	Glenn Wilson	.10
57	Rick Reuschel	.10
58	Joaquin Andujar	.10
59	Jack Clark	.10
60	Vince Coleman	.15
61	Danny Cox	.10
62	Tom Herr	.10
63	Willie McGee	.10
64	John Tudor	.10
65	Tony Gwynn	.60
66	Checklist	.10

1987 Topps

Many collectors feel that Topps' 1987 set of 792 card is a future classic. The 2-1/2" x 3-1/2" design is closely akin to the 1962 set in that the player photo is set against a woodgrain border. Instead of a rolling corner, as in 1962, the player photos in '87 feature a couple of clipped corners at top left and bottom right, where the team logo and player name appear. The player's position is not given on the front of the card. For the first time in several years, the trophy which designates members of Topps All-Star Rookie Team returned to the card design. As in the previous three years, Topps issued a glossy-finish "Tiffany" edition of their 792-card set. However, it was speculated that as many as 50,000 sets were produced as opposed to the 5,000 sets printed in 1985 and 1986. Because of the large print run, the values for the Tiffany cards are only 3-4 times higher than the same card in the regular issue.

		MT
Complete Set (792):		12.00
Common Player:		.05
Wax Box:		15.00
1	Roger Clemens (Record Breaker)	.30
2	Jim Deshaies (Record Breaker)	.05
3	Dwight Evans (Record Breaker)	.05
4	Dave Lopes (Record Breaker)	.05
5	Dave Righetti (Record Breaker)	.05
6	Ruben Sierra (Record Breaker)	.05
7	Todd Worrell (Record Breaker)	.05
8	Terry Pendleton	.05
9	Jay Tibbs	.05
10	Cecil Cooper	.05
11	Indians Leaders(Jack Aker, Chris Bando, Phil Niekro)	.10
12	Jeff Sellers	.05
13	Nick Esasky	.05
14	Dave Stewart	.08
15	Claudell Washington	.05
16	Pat Clements	.05
17	Pete O'Brien	.05
18	Dick Howser	.05
19	Matt Young	.05
20	Gary Carter	.10
21	Mark Davis	.05
22	Doug DeCinces	.05
23	Lee Smith	.08
24	Tony Walker	.05
25	Bert Blyleven	.08
26	Greg Brock	.05
27	Joe Cowley	.05
28	Rick Dempsey	.05
29	Jimmy Key	.08
30	Tim Raines	.12

31	Braves Leaders(Glenn Hubbard, Rafael Ramirez)	.05
32	Tim Leary	.05
33	Andy Van Slyke	.05
34	Jose Rijo	.05
35	Sid Bream	.05
36	Eric King	.05
37	Marvell Wynne	.05
38	Dennis Leonard	.05
39	Marty Barrett	.05
40	Dave Righetti	.05
41	Bo Diaz	.05
42	Gary Redus	.05
43	Gene Michael	.05
44	Greg Harris	.05
45	Jim Presley	.05
46	Danny Gladden	.05
47	Dennis Powell	.05
48	Wally Backman	.05
49	Terry Harper	.05
50	Dave Smith	.05
51	Mel Hall	.05
52	Keith Atherton	.05
53	Ruppert Jones	.05
54	Bill Dawley	.05
55	Tim Wallach	.05
56	Brewers Leaders(Jamie Cocanower, Paul Molitor, Charlie Moore, Herm Starrette)	.10
57	Scott Nielsen	.05
58	Thad Bosley	.05
59	Ken Dayley	.05
60	Tony Pena	.05
61	Bobby Thigpen	.05
62	Bobby Meacham	.05
63	Fred Toliver	.05
64	Harry Spilman	.05
65	Tom Browning	.05
66	Marc Sullivan	.05
67	Bill Swift	.05
68	Tony LaRussa	.05
69	Lonnie Smith	.05
70	Charlie Hough	.05
71	Mike Aldrete	.05
72	Walt Terrell	.05
73	Dave Anderson	.05
74	Dan Pasqua	.05
75	Ron Darling	.05
76	Rafael Ramirez	.05
77	Bryan Oelkers	.05
78	Tom Foley	.05
79	Juan Nieves	.05
80	Wally Joyner	.35
81	Padres Leaders(Andy Hawkins, Terry Kennedy)	.05
82	Rob Murphy	.05
83	Mike Davis	.05
84	Steve Lake	.05
85	Kevin Bass	.05
86	Nate Snell	.05
87	Mark Salas	.05
88	Ed Wojna	.05
89	Ozzie Guillen	.05
90	Dave Stieb	.05
91	Harold Reynolds	.05
92a	Urbano Lugo (no trademark on front)	.10
92b	Urbano Lugo (trademark on front)	.05
93	Jim Leyland	.05
94	Calvin Schiraldi	.05
95	Oddibe McDowell	.05
96	Frank Williams	.05
97	Glenn Wilson	.05
98	Bill Scherrer	.05
99	Darryl Motley	.05
100	Steve Garvey	.12
101	Carl Willis	.05
102	Paul Zuvella	.05
103	Rick Aguilera	.05
104	Billy Sample	.05
105	Floyd Youmans	.05
106	Blue Jays Leaders(George Bell, Willie Upshaw)	.05
107	John Butcher	.05
108	Jim Gantner (photo reversed)	.05
109	R.J. Reynolds	.05
110	John Tudor	.05
111	Alfredo Griffin	.05
112	Alan Ashby	.05
113	Neil Allen	.05
114	Billy Beane	.05
115	Donnie Moore	.05
116	Mike Stanley	.05

117	Jim Beattie	.05
118	Bobby Valentine	.05
119	Ron Robinson	.05
120	Eddie Murray	.40
121	Kevin Romine	.05
122	Jim Clancy	.05
123	John Kruk	.20
124	Ray Fontenot	.05
125	Bob Brenly	.05
126	Mike Loynd	.05
127	Vance Law	.05
128	Checklist 1-132	.05
129	Rick Cerone	.05
130	Dwight Gooden	.10
131	Pirates Leaders(Sid Bream, Tony Pena)	.05
132	Paul Assenmacher	.05
133	Jose Oquendo	.05
134	Rich Yett	.05
135	Mike Easler	.05
136	Ron Romanick	.05
137	Jerry Willard	.05
138	Roy Lee Jackson	.05
139	Devon White	.45
140	Bret Saberhagen	.10
141	Herm Winningham	.05
142	Rick Sutcliffe	.05
143	Steve Boros	.05
144	Mike Scioscia	.05
145	Charlie Kerfeld	.05
146	Tracy Jones	.05
147	Randy Niemann	.05
148	Dave Collins	.05
149	Ray Searage	.05
150	Wade Boggs	.40
151	Mike LaCoss	.05
152	Toby Harrah	.05
153	Duane Ward	.25
154	Tom O'Malley	.05
155	Eddie Whitson	.05
156	Mariners Leaders(Bob Kearney, Phil Regan, Matt Young)	.05
157	Danny Darwin	.05
158	Tim Teufel	.05
159	Ed Olwine	.05
160	Julio Franco	.10
161	Steve Ontiveros	.05
162	Mike LaValliere	.10
163	Kevin Gross	.05
164	Sammy Khalifa	.05
165	Jeff Reardon	.05
166	Bob Boone	.05
167	Jim Deshaies	.08
168	Lou Piniella	.05
169	Ron Washington	.05
170	Bo Jackson (Future Stars)	.75
171	Chuck Cary	.05
172	Ron Oester	.05
173	Alex Trevino	.05
174	Henry Cotto	.05
175	Bob Stanley	.05
176	Steve Buechele	.05
177	Keith Moreland	.05
178	Cecil Fielder	.40
179	Bill Wegman	.05
180	Chris Brown	.05
181	Cardinals Leaders(Mike LaValliere, Ozzie Smith, Ray Soff)	.10
182	Lee Lacy	.05
183	Andy Hawkins	.05
184	Bobby Bonilla	.75
185	Roger McDowell	.05
186	Bruce Benedict	.05
187	Mark Huismann	.05
188	Tony Phillips	.05
189	Joe Hesketh	.05
190	Jim Sundberg	.05
191	Charles Hudson	.05
192	Cory Snyder	.05
193	Roger Craig	.05
194	Kirk McCaskill	.05
195	Mike Pagliarulo	.05
196	Randy O'Neal	.05
197	Mark Bailey	.05
198	Lee Mazzilli	.05
199	Mariano Duncan	.05
200	Pete Rose	.45
201	John Cangelosi	.05
202	Ricky Wright	.05
203	Mike Kingery	.05
204	Sammy Stewart	.05
205	Graig Nettles	.05
206	Twins Leaders(Tim Laudner, Frank Viola)	.05

No.	Name	Price
207	George Frazier	.05
208	John Shelby	.05
209	Rick Schu	.05
210	Lloyd Moseby	.05
211	John Morris	.05
212	Mike Fitzgerald	.05
213	*Randy Myers*	.30
214	Omar Moreno	.05
215	Mark Langston	.08
216	B.J. Surhoff (Future Stars)	.15
217	Chris Codiroli	.05
218	Sparky Anderson	.08
219	Cecilio Guante	.05
220	Joe Carter	.20
221	Vern Ruhle	.05
222	Denny Walling	.05
223	Charlie Leibrandt	.05
224	Wayne Tolleson	.05
225	Mike Smithson	.05
226	Max Venable	.05
227	*Jamie Moyer*	.05
228	Curt Wilkerson	.05
229	*Mike Birkbeck*	.05
230	Don Baylor	.08
231	Giants Leaders(Bob Brenly, Mike Krukow)	.05
232	*Reggie Williams*	.05
233	*Russ Morman*	.05
234	Pat Sheridan	.05
235	Alvin Davis	.05
236	Tommy John	.10
237	Jim Morrison	.05
238	Bill Krueger	.05
239	Juan Espino	.05
240	Steve Balboni	.05
241	Danny Heep	.05
242	Rick Mahler	.05
243	Whitey Herzog	.05
244	Dickie Noles	.05
245	Willie Upshaw	.05
246	Jim Dwyer	.05
247	Jeff Reed	.05
248	Gene Walter	.05
249	Jim Pankovits	.05
250	Teddy Higuera	.05
251	Rob Wilfong	.05
252	Denny Martinez	.05
253	Eddie Milner	.05
254	*Bob Tewksbury*	.20
255	Juan Samuel	.05
256	Royals Leaders(George Brett, Frank White)	.15
257	Bob Forsch	.05
258	Steve Yeager	.05
259	*Mike Greenwell*	.25
260	Vida Blue	.05
261	Ruben Sierra	.30
262	Jim Winn	.05
263	Stan Javier	.05
264	Checklist 133-264	.05
265	Darrell Evans	.05
266	*Jeff Hamilton*	.05
267	Howard Johnson	.05
268	Pat Corrales	.05
269	Cliff Speck	.05
270	Jody Davis	.05
271	Mike Brown	.05
272	Andres Galarraga	.40
273	Gene Nelson	.05
274	*Jeff Hearron*	.05
275	LaMarr Hoyt	.05
276	Jackie Gutierrez	.05
277	Juan Agosto	.05
278	Gary Pettis	.05
279	*Dan Plesac*	.05
280	Jeffrey Leonard	.05
281	Reds Leaders(Bo Diaz, Bill Gullickson, Pete Rose)	.10
282	Jeff Calhoun	.05
283	*Doug Drabek*	.40
284	John Moses	.05
285	Dennis Boyd	.05
286	Mike Woodard	.05
287	Dave Von Ohlen	.05
288	Tito Landrum	.05
289	Bob Kipper	.05
290	Leon Durham	.05
291	*Mitch Williams*	.25
292	Franklin Stubbs	.05
293	Bob Rodgers	.05
294	Steve Jeltz	.05
295	Len Dykstra	.10
296	*Andres Thomas*	.05
297	Don Schulze	.05
298	Larry Herndon	.05
299	Joel Davis	.05
300	Reggie Jackson	.25
301	*Luis Aquino*	.05
302	Bill Schroeder	.05
303	Juan Berenguer	.05
304	Phil Garner	.05
305	John Franco	.05
306	Red Sox Leaders(Rich Gedman, John McNamara, Tom Seaver)	.10
307	*Lee Guetterman*	.05
308	Don Slaught	.05
309	Mike Young	.05
310	Frank Viola	.05
311	Rickey Henderson (Turn Back the Clock)	.12
312	Reggie Jackson (Turn Back the Clock)	.10
313	Roberto Clemente (Turn Back the Clock)	.25
314	Carl Yastrzemski (Turn Back the Clock)	.10
315	Maury Wills (Turn Back the Clock)	.08
316	Brian Fisher	.05
317	Clint Hurdle	.05
318	Jim Fregosi	.05
319	*Greg Swindell*	.10
320	Barry Bonds	1.25
321	Mike Laga	.05
322	Chris Bando	.05
323	*Al Newman*	.05
324	Dave Palmer	.05
325	Garry Templeton	.05
326	Mark Gubicza	.08
327	*Dale Sveum*	.05
328	Bob Welch	.05
329	Ron Roenicke	.05
330	Mike Scott	.05
331	Mets Leaders(Gary Carter, Keith Hernandez, Dave Johnson, Darryl Strawberry)	.10
332	Joe Price	.05
333	Ken Phelps	.05
334	*Ed Correa*	.05
335	Candy Maldonado	.05
336	*Allan Anderson*	.05
337	Darrell Miller	.05
338	Tim Conroy	.05
339	Donnie Hill	.05
340	Roger Clemens	.75
341	Mike Brown	.05
342	Bob James	.05
343	Hal Lanier	.05
344a	Joe Niekro (copyright outside yellow on back)	.30
344b	Joe Niekro (copyright inside yellow on back)	.05
345	Andre Dawson	.15
346	Shawon Dunston	.08
347	Mickey Brantley	.05
348	Carmelo Martinez	.05
349	Storm Davis	.05
350	Keith Hernandez	.05
351	Gene Garber	.05
352	Mike Felder	.05
353	Ernie Camacho	.05
354	Jamie Quirk	.05
355	Don Carman	.05
356	White Sox Leaders(Ed Brinkman, Julio Cruz)	.05
357	*Steve Fireovid*	.05
358	Sal Butera	.05
359	Doug Corbett	.05
360	Pedro Guerrero	.05
361	Mark Thurmond	.05
362	*Luis Quinones*	.05
363	Jose Guzman	.05
364	Randy Bush	.05
365	Rick Rhoden	.05
366	Mark McGwire	4.00
367	Jeff Lahti	.05
368	John McNamara	.05
369	Brian Dayett	.05
370	Fred Lynn	.08
371	*Mark Eichhorn*	.05
372	Jerry Mumphrey	.05
373	Jeff Dedmon	.05
374	Glenn Hoffman	.05
375	Ron Guidry	.10
376	Scott Bradley	.05
377	John Henry Johnson	.05
378	Rafael Santana	.05
379	John Russell	.05
380	Rich Gossage	.08
381	Expos Leaders(Mike Fitzgerald, Bob Rodgers)	.05
382	Rudy Law	.05
383	Ron Davis	.05
384	Johnny Grubb	.05
385	Orel Hershiser	.10
386	Dickie Thon	.05
387	*T.R. Bryden*	.05
388	Geno Petralli	.05
389	Jeff Robinson	.05
390	Gary Matthews	.05
391	Jay Howell	.05
392	Checklist 265-396	.05
393	Pete Rose	.35
394	Mike Bielecki	.05
395	Damaso Garcia	.05
396	Tim Lollar	.05
397	Greg Walker	.05
398	Brad Havens	.05
399	Curt Ford	.05
400	George Brett	.50
401	Billy Jo Robidoux	.05
402	Mike Trujillo	.05
403	Jerry Royster	.05
404	Doug Sisk	.05
405	Brook Jacoby	.05
406	Yankees Leaders(Rickey Henderson, Don Mattingly)	.25
407	Jim Acker	.05
408	John Mizerock	.05
409	Milt Thompson	.05
410	Fernando Valenzuela	.08
411	Darnell Coles	.05
412	Eric Davis	.08
413	Moose Haas	.05
414	Joe Orsulak	.05
415	*Bobby Witt*	.08
416	Tom Nieto	.05
417	Pat Perry	.05
418	Dick Williams	.05
419	*Mark Portugal*	.10
420	Will Clark	1.25
421	Jose DeLeon	.05
422	Jack Howell	.05
423	Jaime Cocanower	.05
424	Chris Speier	.05
425	Tom Seaver	.30
426	Floyd Rayford	.05
427	Ed Nunez	.05
428	Bruce Bochy	.05
429	Tim Pyznarski (Future Stars)	.05
430	Mike Schmidt	.40
431	Dodgers Leaders(Tom Niedenfuer, Ron Perranoski, Alex Trevino)	.05
432	Jim Slaton	.05
433	*Ed Hearn*	.05
434	Mike Fischlin	.05
435	Bruce Sutter	.08
436	*Andy Allanson*	.05
437	Ted Power	.05
438	*Kelly Downs*	.05
439	Karl Best	.05
440	Willie McGee	.05
441	*Dave Leiper*	.05
442	Mitch Webster	.05
443	John Felske	.05
444	Jeff Russell	.05
445	Dave Lopes	.05
446	*Chuck Finley*	.25
447	Bill Almon	.05
448	*Chris Bosio*	.10
449	Pat Dodson (Future Stars)	.05
450	Kirby Puckett	1.00
451	Joe Sambito	.05
452	Dave Henderson	.05
453	*Scott Terry*	.05
454	Luis Salazar	.05
455	Mike Boddicker	.05
456	A's Leaders(Carney Lansford, Tony LaRussa, Mickey Tettleton, Dave Von Ohlen)	.05
457	Len Matuszek	.05
458	Kelly Gruber	.05
459	Dennis Eckersley	.10
460	Darryl Strawberry	.10
461	Craig McMurtry	.05
462	Scott Fletcher	.05
463	Tom Candiotti	.05
464	Butch Wynegar	.05
465	Todd Worrell	.05
466	Kal Daniels	.05
467	Randy St. Claire	.05
468	George Bamberger	.05
469	*Mike Diaz*	.05
470	Dave Dravecky	.05
471	Ronn Reynolds	.05

No.	Player	Price
472	Bill Doran	.05
473	Steve Farr	.05
474	Jerry Narron	.05
475	Scott Garrelts	.05
476	Danny Tartabull	.05
477	Ken Howell	.05
478	Tim Laudner	.05
479	*Bob Sebra*	.05
480	Jim Rice	.05
481	Phillies Leaders(Von Hayes, Juan Samuel, Glenn Wilson)	.05
482	Daryl Boston	.05
483	Dwight Lowry	.05
484	Jim Traber	.05
485	Tony Fernandez	.05
486	Otis Nixon	.05
487	Dave Gumpert	.05
488	Ray Knight	.05
489	Bill Gullickson	.05
490	Dale Murphy	.12
491	*Ron Karkovice*	.10
492	Mike Heath	.05
493	Tom Lasorda	.10
494	*Barry Jones*	.05
495	Gorman Thomas	.05
496	Bruce Bochte	.05
497	*Dale Mohorcic*	.05
498	Bob Kearney	.05
499	*Bruce Ruffin*	.08
500	Don Mattingly	.50
501	Craig Lefferts	.05
502	Dick Schofield	.05
503	Larry Andersen	.05
504	Mickey Hatcher	.05
505	Bryn Smith	.05
506	Orioles Leaders(Rich Bordi, Rick Dempsey, Earl Weaver)	.10
507	Dave Stapleton	.05
508	*Scott Bankhead*	.05
509	Enos Cabell	.05
510	Tom Henke	.05
511	Steve Lyons	.05
512	*Dave Magadan* (Future Stars)	.20
513	Carmen Castillo	.05
514	Orlando Mercado	.05
515	Willie Hernandez	.05
516	Ted Simmons	.05
517	Mario Soto	.05
518	Gene Mauch	.05
519	Curt Young	.05
520	Jack Clark	.05
521	Rick Reuschel	.05
522	Checklist 397-528	.05
523	Earnie Riles	.05
524	Bob Shirley	.05
525	Phil Bradley	.05
526	Roger Mason	.05
527	Jim Wohlford	.05
528	Ken Dixon	.05
529	*Alvaro Espinoza*	.45
530	Tony Gwynn	.05
531	Astros Leaders(Yogi Berra, Hal Lanier, Denis Menke, Gene Tenace)	
532	Jeff Stone	.05
533	Argenis Salazar	.05
534	Scott Sanderson	.05
535	Tony Armas	.05
536	*Terry Mulholland*	.35
537	Rance Mulliniks	.05
538	Tom Niedenfuer	.05
539	Reid Nichols	.05
540	Terry Kennedy	.05
541	*Rafael Belliard*	.05
542	Ricky Horton	.05
543	Dave Johnson	.05
544	Zane Smith	.05
545	Buddy Bell	.05
546	Mike Morgan	.05
547	Rob Deer	.05
548	*Bill Mooneyham*	.05
549	Bob Melvin	.05
550	*Pete Incaviglia*	.25
551	Frank Wills	.05
552	Larry Sheets	.05
553	*Mike Maddux*	.05
554	Buddy Biancalana	.05
555	Dennis Rasmussen	.05
556	Angels Leaders(Bob Boone, Marcel Lachemann, Mike Witt)	.05
557	*John Cerutti*	.05
558	Greg Gagne	.05
559	Lance McCullers	.05
560	Glenn Davis	.05
561	*Rey Quinones*	.05
562	*Bryan Clutterbuck*	.05
563	John Stefero	.05
564	Larry McWilliams	.05
565	Dusty Baker	.05
566	Tim Hulett	.05
567	*Greg Mathews*	.05
568	Earl Weaver	.10
569	Wade Rowdon	.05
570	Sid Fernandez	.05
571	Ozzie Virgil	.05
572	Pete Ladd	.05
573	Hal McRae	.05
574	Manny Lee	.05
575	Pat Tabler	.05
576	Frank Pastore	.05
577	Dann Bilardello	.05
578	Billy Hatcher	.05
579	Rick Burleson	.05
580	Mike Krukow	.05
581	Cubs Leaders(Ron Cey, Steve Trout)	.05
582	Bruce Berenyi	.05
583	Junior Ortiz	.05
584	Ron Kittle	.05
585	*Scott Bailes*	.05
586	Ben Oglivie	.05
587	Eric Plunk	.05
588	Wallace Johnson	.05
589	Steve Crawford	.05
590	Vince Coleman	.05
591	Spike Owen	.05
592	Chris Welsh	.05
593	Chuck Tanner	.05
594	Rick Anderson	.05
595	Keith Hernandez (All-Star)	.05
596	Steve Sax (All-Star)	.05
597	Mike Schmidt (All-Star)	.20
598	Ozzie Smith (All-Star)	.10
599	Tony Gwynn (All-Star)	.20
600	Dave Parker (All-Star)	.08
601	Darryl Strawberry (All-Star)	.10
602	Gary Carter (All-Star)	.10
603a	Dwight Gooden (All-Star, no trademark on front)	.25
603b	Dwight Gooden (All-Star, trademark on front)	.10
604	Fernando Valenzuela (All-Star)	.08
605	Todd Worrell (All-Star)	.05
606a	Don Mattingly (All-Star, no trademark on front)	1.25
606b	Don Mattingly (All-Star, trademark on front)	.25
607	Tony Bernazard (All-Star)	.05
608	Wade Boggs (All-Star)	.20
609	Cal Ripken, Jr. (All-Star)	.60
610	Jim Rice (All-Star)	.05
611	Kirby Puckett (All-Star)	.40
612	George Bell (All-Star)	.05
613	Lance Parrish (All-Star)	.05
614	Roger Clemens (All-Star)	.20
615	Teddy Higuera (All-Star)	.05
616	Dave Righetti (All-Star)	.05
617	Al Nipper	.05
618	Tom Kelly	.05
619	Jerry Reed	.05
620	Jose Canseco	.75
621	Danny Cox	.05
622	*Glenn Braggs*	.10
623	*Kurt Stillwell*	.05
624	Tim Burke	.05
625	Mookie Wilson	.05
626	Joel Skinner	.05
627	Ken Oberkfell	.05
628	Bob Walk	.05
629	Larry Parrish	.05
630	John Candelaria	.05
631	Tigers Leaders(Sparky Anderson, Mike Heath, Willie Hernandez)	.05
632	Rob Woodward	.05
633	Jose Uribe	.05
634	*Rafael Palmeiro*	1.00
635	Ken Schrom	.05
636	Darren Daulton	.10
637	*Bip Roberts*	.15
638	Rich Bordi	.05
639	Gerald Perry	.05
640	Mark Clear	.05
641	Domingo Ramos	.05
642	Al Pulido	.05
643	Ron Shepherd	.05
644	John Denny	.05
645	Dwight Evans	.05
646	Mike Mason	.05
647	Tom Lawless	.05
648	*Barry Larkin*	.75
649	Mickey Tettleton	.10
650	Hubie Brooks	.05
651	Benny Distefano	.05
652	Terry Forster	.05
653	Kevin Mitchell	.10
654	Checklist 529-660	.05
655	Jesse Barfield	.05
656	Rangers Leaders(Bobby Valentine, Rickey Wright)	
657	Tom Waddell	.05
658	*Robby Thompson*	.15
659	Aurelio Lopez	.05
660	Bob Horner	.05
661	Lou Whitaker	.08
662	Frank DiPino	.05
663	Cliff Johnson	.05
664	Mike Marshall	.05
665	Rod Scurry	.05
666	Von Hayes	.05
667	Ron Hassey	.05
668	Juan Bonilla	.05
669	Bud Black	.05
670	Jose Cruz	.05
671a	Ray Soff (no "D*" before copyright line)	.20
671b	Ray Soff ("D*" before copyright line)	.05
672	Chili Davis	.08
673	Don Sutton	.20
674	Bill Campbell	.05
675	Ed Romero	.05
676	Charlie Moore	.05
677	Bob Grich	.05
678	Carney Lansford	.05
679	Kent Hrbek	.08
680	Ryne Sandberg	.50
681	George Bell	.08
682	Jerry Reuss	.05
683	Gary Roenicke	.05
684	Kent Tekulve	.05
685	Jerry Hairston	.05
686	Doyle Alexander	.05
687	Alan Trammell	.12
688	Juan Beniquez	.05
689	Darrell Porter	.05
690	Dane Iorg	.05
691	Dave Parker	.10
692	Frank White	.05
693	Terry Puhl	.05
694	Phil Niekro	.25
695	Chico Walker	.05
696	Gary Lucas	.05
697	Ed Lynch	.05
698	Ernie Whitt	.05
699	Ken Landreaux	.05
700	Dave Bergman	.05
701	Willie Randolph	.05
702	Greg Gross	.05
703	Dave Schmidt	.05
704	Jesse Orosco	.05
705	Bruce Hurst	.05
706	Rick Manning	.05
707	Bob McClure	.05
708	Scott McGregor	.05
709	Dave Kingman	.08
710	Gary Gaetti	.10
711	Ken Griffey	.05
712	Don Robinson	.05
713	Tom Brookens	.05
714	Dan Quisenberry	.05
715	Bob Dernier	.05
716	Rick Leach	.05
717	Ed Vande Berg	.05
718	Steve Carlton	.20
719	Tom Hume	.05
720	Richard Dotson	.05
721	Tom Herr	.05
722	Bob Knepper	.05
723	Brett Butler	.05
724	Greg Minton	.05
725	George Hendrick	.05
726	Frank Tanana	.05
727	Mike Moore	.05
728	Tippy Martinez	.05
729	Tom Paciorek	.05
730	Eric Show	.05
731	Dave Concepcion	.05
732	Manny Trillo	.05
733	Bill Caudill	.05
734	Bill Madlock	.05
735	Rickey Henderson	.25
736	Steve Bedrosian	.05

737	Floyd Bannister	.05
738	Jorge Orta	.05
739	Chet Lemon	.05
740	Rich Gedman	.05
741	Paul Molitor	.25
742	Andy McGaffigan	.05
743	Dwayne Murphy	.05
744	Roy Smalley	.05
745	Glenn Hubbard	.05
746	Bob Ojeda	.05
747	Johnny Ray	.05
748	Mike Flanagan	.05
749	Ozzie Smith	.25
750	Steve Trout	.05
751	Garth Iorg	.05
752	Dan Petry	.05
753	Rick Honeycutt	.05
754	Dave LaPoint	.05
755	Luis Aguayo	.05
756	Carlton Fisk	.20
757	Nolan Ryan	1.25
758	Tony Bernazard	.05
759	Joel Youngblood	.05
760	Mike Witt	.05
761	Greg Pryor	.05
762	Gary Ward	.05
763	Tim Flannery	.05
764	Bill Buckner	.05
765	Kirk Gibson	.05
766	Don Aase	.05
767	Ron Cey	.05
768	Dennis Lamp	.05
769	Steve Sax	.05
770	Dave Winfield	.35
771	Shane Rawley	.05
772	Harold Baines	.05
773	Robin Yount	.30
774	Wayne Krenchicki	.05
775	Joaquin Andujar	.05
776	Tom Brunansky	.05
777	Chris Chambliss	.05
778	Jack Morris	.08
779	Craig Reynolds	.05
780	Andre Thornton	.05
781	Atlee Hammaker	.05
782	Brian Downing	.05
783	Willie Wilson	.05
784	Cal Ripken, Jr.	1.00
785	Terry Francona	.05
786	Jimy Williams	.05
787	Alejandro Pena	.05
788	Tim Stoddard	.05
789	Dan Schatzeder	.05
790	Julio Cruz	.05
791	Lance Parrish	.08
792	Checklist 661-792	.05

1987 Topps Tiffany

Produced in much greater quantity than the previous years' sets, this specially boxed collectors edition differs from the regular 1987 Topps cards only in its use of white cardboard stock and a high-gloss finish on the cards' fronts.

	MT
Complete Set (792):	60.00
Common Player:	.15

(Star cards valued at 3X-5X corresponding cards in regular 1987 Topps)

1987 Topps Box Panels

Offering baseball cards on retail boxes for a second straight year, Topps reduced the size of the cards to 2-1/8" x 3". Four different wax pack boxes were available, each featuring two cards that were placed on the sides of the boxes. The card fronts are identical in design to the regular issue cards. The backs are printed in blue and yellow and carry a commentary imitating a newspaper format. The cards are numbered A through H.

		MT
Complete Singles Set (8):		1.00
Complete Panel Set (4):		4.00
Common Panel:		.75
Common Single Player:		.15
Panel		1.00
A	Don Baylor	.15
B	Steve Carlton	.30
Panel		.75
C	Ron Cey	.15
D	Cecil Cooper	.15
Panel		1.00
E	Rickey Henderson	.35
F	Jim Rice	.15
Panel		1.25
G	Don Sutton	.25
H	Dave Winfield	.35

1987 Topps Traded

The Topps Traded set consists of 132 cards as have all Traded sets issued by Topps since 1981. The cards measure the standard 2-1/2" x 3-1/2" and are identical in design to the regular edition set. The purpose of the set is to update player trades and feature rookies not included in the regular issue. As they had done the previous three years, Topps produced a glossy-coated "Tiffany" edition of the Traded set. The Tiffany edition cards are valued at two to three times greater than the regular Traded cards.

		MT
Complete Set (132):		9.00
Common Player:		.08
1T	Bill Almon	.08
2T	Scott Bankhead	.08
3T	Eric Bell	.08
4T	Juan Beniquez	.08
5T	Juan Berenguer	.08
6T	Greg Booker	.08
7T	Thad Bosley	.08
8T	Larry Bowa	.08
9T	Greg Brock	.08
10T	Bob Brower	.08
11T	Jerry Browne	.10
12T	Ralph Bryant	.08
13T	DeWayne Buice	.08
14T	Ellis Burks	.75
15T	Ivan Calderon	.08
16T	Jeff Calhoun	.08
17T	Casey Candaele	.08
18T	John Cangelosi	.08
19T	Steve Carlton	.30
20T	Juan Castillo	.08
21T	Rick Cerone	.08
22T	Ron Cey	.08
23T	John Christensen	.08
24T	Dave Cone	.75
25T	Chuck Crim	.08
26T	Storm Davis	.08
27T	Andre Dawson	.25
28T	Rick Dempsey	.08
29T	Doug Drabek	.15
30T	Mike Dunne	.08
31T	Dennis Eckersley	.30
32T	Lee Elia	.08
33T	Brian Fisher	.08
34T	Terry Francona	.08
35T	Willie Fraser	.08
36T	Billy Gardner	.08
37T	Ken Gerhart	.08
38T	Danny Gladden	.08
39T	Jim Gott	.08
40T	Cecilio Guante	.08
41T	Albert Hall	.08
42T	Terry Harper	.08
43T	Mickey Hatcher	.08
44T	Brad Havens	.08
45T	Neal Heaton	.08
46T	Mike Henneman	.25
47T	Donnie Hill	.08
48T	Guy Hoffman	.08
49T	Brian Holton	.08
50T	Charles Hudson	.08
51T	Danny Jackson	.08
52T	Reggie Jackson	.50
53T	Chris James	.08
54T	Dion James	.08
55T	Stan Jefferson	.08
56T	Joe Johnson	.08
57T	Terry Kennedy	.08
58T	Mike Kingery	.08
59T	Ray Knight	.08
60T	Gene Larkin	.10
61T	Mike LaValliere	.08
62T	Jack Lazorko	.08
63T	Terry Leach	.08
64T	Tim Leary	.08
65T	Jim Lindeman	.08
66T	Steve Lombardozzi	.08
67T	Bill Long	.08
68T	Barry Lyons	.08
69T	Shane Mack	.20
70T	*Greg Maddux*	8.00
71T	Bill Madlock	.08
72T	Joe Magrane	.12
73T	Dave Martinez	.08
74T	Fred McGriff	1.50
75T	Mark McLemore	.15
76T	Kevin McReynolds	.10
77T	Dave Meads	.08
78T	Eddie Milner	.08
79T	Greg Minton	.08
80T	John Mitchell	.08
81T	Kevin Mitchell	.12
82T	Charlie Moore	.08
83T	Jeff Musselman	.08
84T	Gene Nelson	.08
85T	Graig Nettles	.08
86T	Al Newman	.08
87T	Reid Nichols	.08
88T	Tom Niedenfuer	.08
89T	Joe Niekro	.08
90T	Tom Nieto	.08
91T	Matt Nokes	.10
92T	Dickie Noles	.08
93T	Pat Pacillo	.08
94T	Lance Parrish	.10
95T	Tony Pena	.08
96T	Luis Polonia	.20
97T	Randy Ready	.08
98T	Jeff Reardon	.08
99T	Gary Redus	.08
100T	Jeff Reed	.08
101T	Rick Rhoden	.08
102T	Cal Ripken, Sr.	.08
103T	Wally Ritchie	.08
104T	Jeff Robinson	.08
105T	Gary Roenicke	.08
106T	Jerry Royster	.08
107T	Mark Salas	.08
108T	Luis Salazar	.08
109T	Benny Santiago	.35
110T	Dave Schmidt	.08
111T	Kevin Seitzer	.12
112T	John Shelby	.08
113T	Steve Shields	.08
114T	John Smiley	.25
115T	Chris Speier	.08
116T	Mike Stanley	.12
117T	Terry Steinbach	.25
118T	Les Straker	.08
119T	Jim Sundberg	.08
120T	Danny Tartabull	.15
121T	Tom Trebelhorn	.08
122T	Dave Valle	.08
123T	Ed Vande Berg	.08
124T	Andy Van Slyke	.08
125T	Gary Ward	.08
126T	Alan Wiggins	.08
127T	Bill Wilkinson	.08
128T	Frank Williams	.08
129T	*Matt Williams*	4.00
130T	Jim Winn	.08
131T	Matt Young	.08
132T	Checklist 1T-132T	.08

1987 Topps Traded Tiffany

The cards in this specially boxed limited edition version of the Traded set differ from the regular-issue cards only in the application of a high-gloss finish to the cards' fronts.

	MT
Complete Set (132):	25.00
Common Player:	.25
(Star cards valued at 2X-3X corresponding cards in regular Topps Traded)	

1987 Topps All-Star Glossy Set of 22

For the fourth consecutive year, Topps produced an All-Star Game commemorative set of 22 cards. The glossy cards, 2-1/2" x 3-1/2", were included in rack packs. Using the same basic design as in previous efforts with a few minor changes, the 1987 edition features American and National League logos on the card fronts. Cards #1-12 feature representatives from the American League, while #13-22 are National Leaguers.

		MT
Complete Set (22):		4.00
Common Player:		.15
1	Whitey Herzog	.15
2	Keith Hernandez	.15
3	Ryne Sandberg	.50
4	Mike Schmidt	.70
5	Ozzie Smith	.50
6	Tony Gwynn	.50
7	Dale Murphy	.25
8	Darryl Strawberry	.20
9	Gary Carter	.25
10	Dwight Gooden	.20
11	Fernando Valenzuela	.15
12	Dick Howser	.15
13	Wally Joyner	.15
14	Lou Whitaker	.15
15	Wade Boggs	.40
16	Cal Ripken, Jr.	1.00
17	Dave Winfield	.40
18	Rickey Henderson	.40
19	Kirby Puckett	.50
20	Lance Parrish	.15
21	Roger Clemens	.50
22	Teddy Higuera	.15

A player's name in *italic* type indicates a rookie card.

1987 Topps Glossy Rookies

The 1987 Topps Glossy Rookies set of 22 cards was introduced with Topps' new 100-card "Jumbo Packs". Intended for sale in supermarkets, the jumbo packs contained one glossy card. Measuring the standard 2-1/2" x 3-1/2" size, the special insert cards feature the top rookies from the previous season.

		MT
Complete Set (22):		4.00
Common Player:		.10
1	Andy Allanson	.10
2	John Cangelosi	.10
3	Jose Canseco	1.50
4	Will Clark	1.50
5	Mark Eichhorn	.10
6	Pete Incaviglia	.20
7	Wally Joyner	.30
8	Eric King	.10
9	Dave Magadan	.10
10	John Morris	.10
11	Juan Nieves	.10
12	Rafael Palmeiro	.60
13	Billy Jo Robidoux	.10
14	Bruce Ruffin	.10
15	Ruben Sierra	.20
16	Cory Snyder	.10
17	Kurt Stillwell	.10
18	Dale Sveum	.10
19	Danny Tartabull	.10
20	Andres Thomas	.10
21	Robby Thompson	.10
22	Todd Worrell	.10

1987 Topps Mini League Leaders

DENNIS RASMUSSEN

Returning for 1987, the Topps "Major League Leaders" set was increased in size from 66 to 76 cards. The 2-1/8" x 3" cards feature woodgrain borders that encompass a white-bordered color photo. Backs are printed in yellow, orange and brown and list the player's official ranking based on his 1986 American or National League statistics. The players featured are those who finished the top five in their leagues' various batting and pitching categories. The cards were sold in plastic-wrapped packs, seven cards plus a game card per pack.

		MT
Complete Set (77):		4.00
Common Player:		.05
1	Bob Horner	.05
2	Dale Murphy	.15
3	Lee Smith	.10
4	Eric Davis	.10
5	John Franco	.05
6	Dave Parker	.08
7	Kevin Bass	.05
8	Glenn Davis	.05
9	Bill Doran	.05
10	Bob Knepper	.05
11	Mike Scott	.05
12	Dave Smith	.05
13	Mariano Duncan	.05
14	Orel Hershiser	.10
15	Steve Sax	.05
16	Fernando Valenzuela	.08
17	Tim Raines	.08
18	Jeff Reardon	.05
19	Floyd Youmans	.05
20	Gary Carter	.08
21	Ron Darling	.05
22	Sid Fernandez	.05
23	Dwight Gooden	.08
24	Keith Hernandez	.05
25	Bob Ojeda	.05
26	Darryl Strawberry	.10
27	Steve Bedrosian	.05
28	Von Hayes	.05
29	Juan Samuel	.05
30	Mike Schmidt	.30
31	Rick Rhoden	.05
32	Vince Coleman	.05
33	Danny Cox	.05
34	Todd Worrell	.05
35	Tony Gwynn	.30
36	Mike Krukow	.05
37	Candy Maldonado	.05
38	Don Aase	.05
39	Eddie Murray	.20
40	Cal Ripken, Jr.	1.00
41	Wade Boggs	.30
42	Roger Clemens	.35
43	Bruce Hurst	.05
44	Jim Rice	.05
45	Wally Joyner	.10
46	Donnie Moore	.05
47	Gary Pettis	.05
48	Mike Witt	.05
49	John Cangelosi	.05
50	Tom Candiotti	.05
51	Joe Carter	.10
52	Pat Tabler	.05
53	Kirk Gibson	.05
54	Willie Hernandez	.05
55	Jack Morris	.05
56	Alan Trammell	.10
57	George Brett	.40
58	Willie Wilson	.05
59	Rob Deer	.05
60	Teddy Higuera	.05
61	Bert Blyleven	.05
62	Gary Gaetti	.05
63	Kirby Puckett	.35
64	Rickey Henderson	.20
65	Don Mattingly	.45
66	Dennis Rasmussen	.05
67	Dave Righetti	.05
68	Jose Canseco	.30
69	Dave Kingman	.05
70	Phil Bradley	.05
71	Mark Langston	.05
72	Pete O'Brien	.05

73	Jesse Barfield	.05
74	George Bell	.05
75	Tony Fernandez	.05
76	Tom Henke	.05
77	Checklist	.05

1988 Topps

The 1988 Topps set features a clean, attractive design. The full-color player photo is surrounded by a thin color frame which is encompassed by a white border. The player's name appears in the lower-right corner in a diagonal colored strip. The team nickname is in large letters at the top of the card. Backs feature black print on orange and gray stock and include the usual player personal and career statistics. Many of the cards contain a new feature titled "This Way To The Clubhouse", which explains how the player joined his current team. The 792-card set includes a number of special subsets including "Future Stars", "Turn Back The Clock", All-Star teams, All-Star rookie selections, and Record Breakers. All cards measure 2-1/2" x 3-1/2".

		MT
Complete Set (792):		15.00
Common Player:		.05
Wax Box:		8.00
1	Vince Coleman (Record Breakers)	.05
2	Don Mattingly (Record Breakers)	.15
3a	Mark McGwire (Record Breakers, white triangle by left foot)	1.50
3b	Mark McGwire (Record Breakers, no white triangle)	.50
4a	Eddie Murray (Record Breakers, no mention of record on front)	.30
4b	Eddie Murray (Record Breakers, record in box on front)	.20
5	Joe Niekro, Phil Niekro (Record Breakers)	.15
6	Nolan Ryan (Record Breakers)	.40
7	Benito Santiago (Record Breakers)	.10
8	Kevin Elster (Future Stars)	.05
9	Andy Hawkins	.05
10	Ryne Sandberg	.40
11	Mike Young	.05
12	Bill Schroeder	.05
13	Andres Thomas	.05
14	Sparky Anderson	.05
15	Chili Davis	.08
16	Kirk McCaskill	.05

17	Ron Oester	.05
18a	*Al Leiter* (Future Stars, no "NY" on shirt, photo actually Steve George)	.25
18b	*Al Leiter* (Future Stars, "NY" on shirt, correct photo)	.10
19	*Mark Davidson*	.05
20	Kevin Gross	.05
21	Red Sox Leaders(Wade Boggs, Spike Owen)	.10
22	Greg Swindell	.05
23	Ken Landreaux	.05
24	Jim Deshaies	.05
25	Andres Galarraga	.20
26	Mitch Williams	.05
27	R.J. Reynolds	.05
28	*Jose Nunez*	.05
29	Argenis Salazar	.05
30	Sid Fernandez	.05
31	Bruce Bochy	.05
32	Mike Morgan	.05
33	Rob Deer	.05
34	Ricky Horton	.05
35	Harold Baines	.08
36	Jamie Moyer	.05
37	Ed Romero	.05
38	Jeff Calhoun	.05
39	Gerald Perry	.05
40	Orel Hershiser	.08
41	Bob Melvin	.05
42	*Bill Landrum*	.05
43	Dick Schofield	.05
44	Lou Piniella	.05
45	Kent Hrbek	.08
46	Darnell Coles	.05
47	Joaquin Andujar	.05
48	Alan Ashby	.05
49	Dave Clark	.05
50	Hubie Brooks	.05
51	Orioles Leaders(Eddie Murray, Cal Ripken, Jr.)	.25
52	Don Robinson	.05
53	Curt Wilkerson	.05
54	Jim Clancy	.05
55	Phil Bradley	.05
56	Ed Hearn	.05
57	*Tim Crews*	.05
58	Dave Magadan	.05
59	Danny Cox	.05
60	Rickey Henderson	.15
61	*Mark Knudson*	.05
62	Jeff Hamilton	.05
63	Jimmy Jones	.05
64	*Ken Caminiti*	.75
65	Leon Durham	.05
66	Shane Rawley	.05
67	Ken Oberkfell	.05
68	Dave Dravecky	.05
69	*Mike Hart*	.05
70	Roger Clemens	.50
71	Gary Pettis	.05
72	Dennis Eckersley	.08
73	Randy Bush	.05
74	Tom Lasorda	.10
75	Joe Carter	.15
76	Denny Martinez	.08
77	Tom O'Malley	.05
78	Dan Petry	.05
79	Ernie Whitt	.05
80	Mark Langston	.05
81	Reds Leaders(John Franco, Ron Robinson)	.05
82	*Darrel Akerfelds*	.05
83	Jose Oquendo	.05
84	Cecilio Guante	.05
85	Howard Johnson	.05
86	Ron Karkovice	.05
87	Mike Mason	.05
88	Earnie Riles	.05
89	*Gary Thurman*	.05
90	Dale Murphy	.10
91	*Joey Cora*	.20
92	Len Matuszek	.05
93	Bob Sebra	.05
94	*Chuck Jackson*	.05
95	Lance Parrish	.08
96	*Todd Benzinger*	.10
97	Scott Garrelts	.05
98	*Rene Gonzales*	.05
99	Chuck Finley	.05
100	Jack Clark	.05
101	Allan Anderson	.05
102	Barry Larkin	.15
103	Curt Young	.05
104	Dick Williams	.05
105	Jesse Orosco	.05

106	*Jim Walewander*	.05
107	Scott Bailes	.05
108	Steve Lyons	.05
109	Joel Skinner	.05
110	Teddy Higuera	.05
111	Expos Leaders(Hubie Brooks, Vance Law)	.05
112	*Les Lancaster*	.05
113	Kelly Gruber	.05
114	Jeff Russell	.05
115	Johnny Ray	.05
116	Jerry Don Gleaton	.05
117	*James Steels*	.05
118	Bob Welch	.05
119	*Robbie Wine*	.05
120	Kirby Puckett	.40
121	Checklist 1-132	.05
122	Tony Bernazard	.05
123	Tom Candiotti	.05
124	Ray Knight	.05
125	Bruce Hurst	.05
126	Steve Jeltz	.05
127	Jim Gott	.05
128	Johnny Grubb	.05
129	Greg Minton	.05
130	Buddy Bell	.05
131	Don Schulze	.05
132	Donnie Hill	.05
133	Greg Mathews	.05
134	Chuck Tanner	.05
135	Dennis Rasmussen	.05
136	Brian Dayett	.05
137	Chris Bosio	.05
138	Mitch Webster	.05
139	Jerry Browne	.05
140	Jesse Barfield	.05
141	Royals Leaders(George Brett, Bret Saberhagen)	.20
142	Andy Van Slyke	.05
143	Mickey Tettleton	.08
144	*Don Gordon*	.05
145	Bill Madlock	.05
146	*Donell Nixon*	.05
147	Bill Buckner	.05
148	Carmelo Martinez	.05
149	Ken Howell	.05
150	Eric Davis	.08
151	Bob Knepper	.05
152	*Jody Reed*	.15
153	John Habyan	.05
154	Jeff Stone	.05
155	Bruce Sutter	.05
156	Gary Matthews	.05
157	Atlee Hammaker	.05
158	Tim Hulett	.05
159	*Brad Arnsberg*	.05
160	Willie McGee	.08
161	Bryn Smith	.05
162	Mark McLemore	.05
163	Dale Mohorcic	.05
164	Dave Johnson	.05
165	Robin Yount	.25
166	*Rick Rodriguez*	.05
167	Rance Mulliniks	.05
168	Barry Jones	.05
169	*Ross Jones*	.05
170	Rich Gossage	.08
171	Cubs Leaders(Shawon Dunston, Manny Trillo)	.05
172	*Lloyd McClendon*	.05
173	Eric Plunk	.05
174	Phil Garner	.05
175	Kevin Bass	.05
176	Jeff Reed	.05
177	Frank Tanana	.05
178	Dwayne Henry	.05
179	Charlie Puleo	.05
180	Terry Kennedy	.05
181	Dave Cone	.20
182	Ken Phelps	.05
183	Tom Lawless	.05
184	Ivan Calderon	.05
185	Rick Rhoden	.05
186	Rafael Palmeiro	.25
187	Steve Kiefer	.05
188	John Russell	.05
189	*Wes Gardner*	.05
190	Candy Maldonado	.05
191	John Cerutti	.05
192	Devon White	.05
193	Brian Fisher	.05
194	Tom Kelly	.05
195	Dan Quisenberry	.05
196	Dave Engle	.05
197	Lance McCullers	.05
198	Franklin Stubbs	.05

474	Tom Brookens	.05
475	Pete Rose	.20
476	Dave Stewart	.05
477	Jamie Quirk	.05
478	Sid Bream	.05
479	Brett Butler	.08
480	Dwight Gooden	.10
481	Mariano Duncan	.05
482	Mark Davis	.05
483	*Rod Booker*	.05
484	Pat Clements	.05
485	Harold Reynolds	.05
486	*Pat Keedy*	.05
487	Jim Pankovits	.05
488	Andy McGaffigan	.05
489	Dodgers Leaders(Pedro Guerrero, Fernando Valenzuela)	.08
490	Larry Parrish	.05
491	B.J. Surhoff	.05
492	Doyle Alexander	.05
493	Mike Greenwell	.08
494	*Wally Ritchie*	.05
495	Eddie Murray	.20
496	Guy Hoffman	.05
497	Kevin Mitchell	.08
498	Bob Boone	.05
499	Eric King	.05
500	Andre Dawson	.10
501	Tim Birtsas	.05
502	Danny Gladden	.05
503	*Junior Noboa*	.05
504	Bob Rodgers	.05
505	Willie Upshaw	.05
506	John Cangelosi	.05
507	Mark Gubicza	.08
508	Tim Teufel	.05
509	Bill Dawley	.05
510	Dave Winfield	.15
511	Joel Davis	.05
512	Alex Trevino	.05
513	Tim Flannery	.05
514	Pat Sheridan	.05
515	Juan Nieves	.05
516	Jim Sundberg	.05
517	Ron Robinson	.05
518	Greg Gross	.05
519	Mariners Leaders(Phil Bradley, Harold Reynolds)	.05
520	Dave Smith	.05
521	Jim Dwyer	.05
522	*Bob Patterson*	.05
523	Gary Roenicke	.05
524	Gary Lucas	.05
525	Marty Barrett	.05
526	Juan Berenguer	.05
527	Steve Henderson	.05
528a	Checklist 397-528 (#455 is Steve Carlton)	.05
528b	Checklist 397-528 (#455 is Shawn Hillegas)	.05
529	Tim Burke	.05
530	Gary Carter	.10
531	Rich Yett	.05
532	Mike Kingery	.05
533	*John Farrell*	.05
534	John Wathan	.05
535	Ron Guidry	.10
536	John Morris	.05
537	Steve Buechele	.05
538	Bill Wegman	.05
539	Mike LaValliere	.05
540	Bret Saberhagen	.08
541	Juan Beniquez	.05
542	*Paul Noce*	.05
543	Kent Tekulve	.05
544	Jim Traber	.05
545	Don Baylor	.08
546	John Candelaria	.05
547	*Felix Fermin*	.05
548	*Shane Mack*	.10
549	Braves Leaders(Ken Griffey, Dion James, Dale Murphy, Gerald Perry)	.08
550	Pedro Guerrero	.05
551	Terry Steinbach	.05
552	Mark Thurmond	.05
553	Tracy Jones	.05
554	Mike Smithson	.05
555	Brook Jacoby	.05
556	*Stan Clarke*	.05
557	Craig Reynolds	.05
558	Bob Ojeda	.05
559	*Ken Williams*	.05
560	Tim Wallach	.05
561	Rick Cerone	.05

562	Jim Lindeman	.05
563	Jose Guzman	.05
564	Frank Lucchesi	.05
565	Lloyd Moseby	.05
566	*Charlie O'Brien*	.05
567	Mike Diaz	.05
568	Chris Brown	.05
569	Charlie Leibrandt	.05
570	Jeffrey Leonard	.05
571	*Mark Williamson*	.05
572	Chris James	.05
573	Bob Stanley	.05
574	Graig Nettles	.05
575	Don Sutton	.10
576	*Tommy Hinzo*	.05
577	Tom Browning	.05
578	Gary Gaetti	.08
579	Mets Leaders(Gary Carter, Kevin McReynolds)	.08
580	Mark McGwire	.75
581	Tito Landrum	.05
582	*Mike Henneman*	.15
583	Dave Valle	.05
584	Steve Trout	.05
585	Ozzie Guillen	.05
586	Bob Forsch	.05
587	Terry Puhl	.05
588	*Jeff Parrett*	.05
589	Geno Petralli	.05
590	George Bell	.05
591	Doug Drabek	.05
592	Dale Sveum	.05
593	Bob Tewksbury	.05
594	Bobby Valentine	.05
595	Frank White	.05
596	John Kruk	.05
597	Gene Garber	.05
598	Lee Lacy	.05
599	Calvin Schiraldi	.05
600	Mike Schmidt	.25
601	Jack Lazorko	.05
602	Mike Aldrete	.05
603	Rob Murphy	.05
604	Chris Bando	.05
605	Kirk Gibson	.05
606	Moose Haas	.05
607	Mickey Hatcher	.05
608	Charlie Kerfeld	.05
609	Twins Leaders(Gary Gaetti, Kent Hrbek)	.08
610	Keith Hernandez	.05
611	Tommy John	.08
612	Curt Ford	.05
613	Bobby Thigpen	.05
614	Herm Winningham	.05
615	Jody Davis	.05
616	*Jay Aldrich*	.05
617	Oddibe McDowell	.05
618	Cecil Fielder	.15
619	*Mike Dunne*	.05
620	Cory Snyder	.05
621	Gene Nelson	.05
622	Kal Daniels	.05
623	Mike Flanagan	.05
624	Jim Leyland	.05
625	Frank Viola	.05
626	Glenn Wilson	.05
627	*Joe Boever*	.05
628	Dave Henderson	.05
629	Kelly Downs	.05
630	Darrell Evans	.05
631	Jack Howell	.05
632	*Steve Shields*	.05
633	*Barry Lyons*	.05
634	Jose DeLeon	.05
635	Terry Pendleton	.08
636	Charles Hudson	.05
637	*Jay Bell*	.25
638	Steve Balboni	.05
639	Brewers Leaders(Glenn Braggs, Tony Muser)	.05
640	Garry Templeton	.05
641	Rick Honeycutt	.05
642	Bob Dernier	.05
643	*Rocky Childress*	.05
644	Terry McGriff	.05
645	*Matt Nokes*	.08
646	Checklist 529-660	.05
647	Pascual Perez	.05
648	Al Newman	.05
649	*DeWayne Buice*	.05
650	Cal Ripken, Jr.	.60
651	*Mike Jackson*	.08
652	Bruce Benedict	.05
653	Jeff Sellers	.05
654	Roger Craig	.05

655	Len Dykstra	.12
656	Lee Guetterman	.05
657	Gary Redus	.05
658	Tim Conroy	.05
659	Bobby Meacham	.05
660	Rick Reuschel	.05
661	Nolan Ryan (Turn Back the Clock)	.35
662	Jim Rice (Turn Back the Clock)	.05
663	Ron Blomberg (Turn Back the Clock)	.05
664	Bob Gibson (Turn Back the Clock)	.10
665	Stan Musial (Turn Back the Clock)	.15
666	Mario Soto	.05
667	Luis Quinones	.05
668	Walt Terrell	.05
669	Phillies Leaders(Lance Parrish, Mike Ryan)	.05
670	Dan Plesac	.05
671	Tim Laudner	.05
672	*John Davis*	.05
673	Tony Phillips	.05
674	Mike Fitzgerald	.05
675	Jim Rice	.05
676	Ken Dixon	.05
677	Eddie Milner	.05
678	Jim Acker	.05
679	Darrell Miller	.05
680	Charlie Hough	.05
681	Bobby Bonilla	.15
682	Jimmy Key	.08
683	Julio Franco	.08
684	Hal Lanier	.05
685	Ron Darling	.05
686	Terry Francona	.05
687	Mickey Brantley	.05
688	Jim Winn	.05
689	*Tom Pagnozzi*	.05
690	Jay Howell	.05
691	Dan Pasqua	.05
692	Mike Birkbeck	.05
693	Benny Santiago	.10
694	*Eric Nolte*	.05
695	Shawon Dunston	.15
696	Duane Ward	.05
697	Steve Lombardozzi	.05
698	Brad Havens	.05
699	Padres Leaders(Tony Gwynn, Benny Santiago)	.15
700	George Brett	.30
701	Sammy Stewart	.05
702	Mike Gallego	.05
703	Bob Brenly	.05
704	Dennis Boyd	.05
705	Juan Samuel	.05
706	Rick Mahler	.05
707	Fred Lynn	.08
708	Gus Polidor	.05
709	George Frazier	.05
710	Darryl Strawberry	.10
711	Bill Gullickson	.05
712	John Moses	.05
713	Willie Hernandez	.05
714	Jim Fregosi	.05
715	Todd Worrell	.05
716	Lenn Sakata	.05
717	Jay Baller	.05
718	Mike Felder	.05
719	Denny Walling	.05
720	Tim Raines	.10
721	Pete O'Brien	.05
722	Manny Lee	.05
723	Bob Kipper	.05
724	Danny Tartabull	.05
725	Mike Boddicker	.05
726	Alfredo Griffin	.05
727	Greg Booker	.05
728	Andy Allanson	.05
729	Blue Jays Leaders(George Bell, Fred McGriff)	.10
730	John Franco	.05
731	Rick Schu	.05
732	Dave Palmer	.05
733	Spike Owen	.05
734	Craig Lefferts	.05
735	Kevin McReynolds	.05
736	Matt Young	.05
737	Butch Wynegar	.05
738	Scott Bankhead	.05
739	Daryl Boston	.05
740	Rick Sutcliffe	.05
741	Mike Easler	.05
742	Mark Clear	.05

743	Larry Herndon	.05
744	Whitey Herzog	.05
745	Bill Doran	.05
746	*Gene Larkin*	.10
747	Bobby Witt	.05
748	Reid Nichols	.05
749	Mark Eichhorn	.05
750	Bo Jackson	.20
751	Jim Morrison	.05
752	Mark Grant	.05
753	Danny Heep	.05
754	Mike LaCoss	.05
755	Ozzie Virgil	.05
756	Mike Maddux	.05
757	*John Marzano*	.05
758	*Eddie Williams*	.08
759	A's Leaders(Jose Canseco, Mark McGwire)	.50
760	Mike Scott	.05
761	Tony Armas	.05
762	Scott Bradley	.05
763	Doug Sisk	.05
764	Greg Walker	.05
765	Neal Heaton	.05
766	Henry Cotto	.05
767	*Jose Lind* (Future Stars)	.15
768	Dickie Noles	.05
769	Cecil Cooper	.05
770	Lou Whitaker	.05
771	Ruben Sierra	.08
772	Sal Butera	.05
773	Frank Williams	.05
774	Gene Mauch	.05
775	Dave Stieb	.05
776	Checklist 661-792	.05
777	Lonnie Smith	.05
778a	*Keith Comstock* (white team letters)	.60
778b	*Keith Comstock* (blue team letters)	.15
779	*Tom Glavine*	.50
780	Fernando Valenzuela	.10
781	*Keith Hughes*	.05
782	*Jeff Ballard*	.05
783	Ron Roenicke	.05
784	Joe Sambito	.05
785	Alvin Davis	.05
786	Joe Price	.05
787	Bill Almon	.05
788	Ray Searage	.05
789	Indians Leaders(Joe Carter, Cory Snyder)	.10
790	Dave Righetti	.05
791	Ted Simmons	.05
792	John Tudor	.05

1988 Topps Tiffany

Sharing a checklist with the regular issue 1988 Topps baseball set, this specially boxed, limited-edition (30,000 sets) features cards printed on white cardboard stock with high-gloss front finish. Topps offered the sets directly to the public in ads in USA Today and Sporing News at a price of $99.

	MT
Complete Set (792):	75.00
Common Player:	.15

(Star cards valued at 3X-5X corresponding cards in regular 1988 Topps issue)

1988 Topps Box Panels

After a one-year hiatus during which they appeared on the sides of Topps wax pack display boxes, Topps retail box cards returned to box bottoms in 1988. The series includes 16 standard-size baseball cards, four cards per each of four different display boxes. Card fronts follow the same design as the 1988

Topps basic issue; full-color player photos, framed in yellow, surrounded by a white border; diagonal player name lower-right; team name in large letters at the top. Card backs are "numbered" A through P and are printed in black and orange.

		MT
Complete Panel Set (4):		3.00
Complete Singles Set (16):		1.50
Common Panel:		.50
Common Single Player:		.05
	Panel	.50
A	Don Baylor	.08
B	Steve Bedrosian	.05
C	Juan Beniquez	.05
D	Bob Boone	.05
	Panel	.70
E	Darrell Evans	.05
F	Tony Gwynn	.40
G	John Kruk	.05
H	Marvell Wynne	.05
	Panel	.60
I	Joe Carter	.10
J	Eric Davis	.08
K	Howard Johnson	.05
L	Darryl Strawberry	.08
	Panel	2.00
M	Rickey Henderson	.20
N	Nolan Ryan	.50
O	Mike Schmidt	.30
P	Kent Tekulve	.05
	Panel	.50
A	Don Baylor	.08
B	Steve Bedrosian	.06
C	Juan Beniquez	.04
D	Bob Boone	.06
	Panel	.70
E	Darrell Evans	.06
F	Tony Gwynn	.15
G	John Kruk	.13
H	Marvell Wynne	.04
	Panel	.60
I	Joe Carter	.13
J	Eric Davis	.13
K	Howard Johnson	.06
L	Darryl Strawberry	.10
	Panel	2.00
M	Rickey Henderson	.25
N	Nolan Ryan	.40
O	Mike Schmidt	.20
P	Kent Tekulve	.04

1988 Topps Traded

In addition to new players and traded veterans, 21 members of the U.S.A. Olympic Baseball team are showcased in this 132-card set, numbered 1T-132T. The 2-1/2" x 3-1/2" cards follow the same design as the basic Topps issue - white borders, large full-color photos, team name (or U.S.A.) in large bold letters at the top of the card face, player name on a diagonal stripe across the lower-right corner. Topps had issued its traded series each year since 1981 in boxed complete sets available only through hobby dealers.

		MT
Complete Set (132):		14.00
Common Player:		.06
1T	*Jim Abbott* (USA)	.25
2T	Juan Agosto	.06
3T	Luis Alicea	.15
4T	*Roberto Alomar*	3.00
5T	*Brady Anderson*	1.00
6T	Jack Armstrong	.25
7T	Don August	.06
8T	Floyd Bannister	.06
9T	Bret Barberie (USA)	.25
10T	Jose Bautista	.15
11T	Don Baylor	.15
12T	Tim Belcher	.06
13T	Buddy Bell	.06
14T	*Andy Benes* (USA)	1.00

15T	Damon Berryhill	.06
16T	Bud Black	.06
17T	Pat Borders	.15
18T	Phil Bradley	.06
19T	Jeff Branson (USA)	.06
20T	Tom Brunansky	.06
21T	*Jay Buhner*	1.50
22T	Brett Butler	.15
23T	Jim Campanis (USA)	.15
24T	Sil Campusano	.06
25T	John Candelaria	.06
26T	Jose Cecena	.06
27T	Rick Cerone	.06
28T	Jack Clark	.06
29T	Kevin Coffman	.06
30T	Pat Combs (USA)	.10
31T	Henry Cotto	.06
32T	Chili Davis	.10
33T	Mike Davis	.06
34T	Jose DeLeon	.06
35T	Richard Dotson	.06
36T	Cecil Espy	.06
37T	Tom Filer	.06
38T	Mike Fiore (USA)	.10
39T	*Ron Gant*	.50
40T	Kirk Gibson	.06
41T	Rich Gossage	.10
42T	*Mark Grace*	2.00
43T	Alfredo Griffin	.06
44T	Ty Griffin (USA)	.10
45T	Bryan Harvey	.15
46T	Ron Hassey	.06
47T	Ray Hayward	.06
48T	Dave Henderson	.06
49T	Tom Herr	.06
50T	Bob Horner	.06
51T	Ricky Horton	.06
52T	Jay Howell	.06
53T	Glenn Hubbard	.06
54T	Jeff Innis	.10
55T	Danny Jackson	.06
56T	Darrin Jackson	.15
57T	Roberto Kelly	.15
58T	Ron Kittle	.06
59T	Ray Knight	.06
60T	Vance Law	.06
61T	Jeffrey Leonard	.06
62T	Mike Macfarlane	.15
63T	Scotti Madison	.06
64T	Kirt Manwaring	.15
65T	Mark Marquess (USA)	.06
66T	*Tino Martinez* (USA)	5.00
67T	Billy Masse (USA)	.06
68T	*Jack McDowell*	.40
69T	Jack McKeon	.06
70T	Larry McWilliams	.06
71T	Mickey Morandini (USA)	.25
72T	Keith Moreland	.06
73T	Mike Morgan	.06
74T	Charles Nagy (USA)	1.00
75T	Al Nipper	.06
76T	Russ Nixon	.06
77T	Jesse Orosco	.06
78T	Joe Orsulak	.06
79T	Dave Palmer	.06
80T	Mark Parent	.10
81T	Dave Parker	.10
82T	Dan Pasqua	.10
83T	Melido Perez	.10
84T	Steve Peters	.06
85T	Dan Petry	.06
86T	Gary Pettis	.06
87T	Jeff Pico	.06
88T	Jim Poole (USA)	.10
89T	Ted Power	.06
90T	Rafael Ramirez	.06
91T	Dennis Rasmussen	.06
92T	Jose Rijo	.10
93T	Earnie Riles	.06
94T	Luis Rivera	.06
95T	Doug Robbins (USA)	.10
96T	Frank Robinson	.15
97T	Cookie Rojas	.06
98T	Chris Sabo	.15
99T	Mark Salas	.06
100T	Luis Salazar	.06
101T	Rafael Santana	.06
102T	Nelson Santovenia	.10
103T	Mackey Sasser	.06
104T	Calvin Schiraldi	.06
105T	Mike Schooler	.06
106T	Scott Servais (USA)	.15
107T	Dave Silvestri (USA)	.10
108T	Don Slaught	.06
109T	Joe Slusarski (USA)	.10
110T	Lee Smith	.10

111T	Pete Smith	.15
112T	Jim Snyder	.06
113T	Ed Sprague (USA)	.50
114T	Pete Stanicek	.10
115T	Kurt Stillwell	.06
116T	Todd Stottlemyre	.15
117T	Bill Swift	.06
118T	Pat Tabler	.06
119T	Scott Terry	.06
120T	Mickey Tettleton	.10
121T	Dickie Thon	.06
122T	Jeff Treadway	.06
123T	Willie Upshaw	.06
124T	*Robin Ventura*	1.50
125T	Ron Washington	.06
126T	Walt Weiss	.30
127T	Bob Welch	.06
128T	David Wells	1.00
129T	Glenn Wilson	.06
130T	Ted Wood (USA)	.10
131T	Don Zimmer	.06
132T	Checklist 1T-132T	.06

1988 Topps Traded Tiffany

The high-gloss front surface is all that distinguishes this limited-edition, hobby-only collectors version from the regular Topps Traded boxed set.

	MT
Complete Set (132):	55.00
Common Player:	.15
(Star cards valued at 3X-4X corresponding cards in regular Topps Traded issue)	

1988 Topps All-Star Glossy Set of 22

The fifth edition of Topps' special All-Star inserts was included in the company's 1988 rack packs. The 1987 American and National League All-Star lineup, plus honorary captains Jim Hunter and Billy Williams, are featured on the 2-1/2" x 3-1/2" cards. The glossy full-color fronts contain player photos centered between a red and yellow "1987 All-Star" logo at top and the player name (also red and yellow) which is printed in the bottom margin. A league logo is in the lower-left corner. Card backs are printed in red and blue on a white background, with the title and All-Star logo emblem printed above the player name and card number.

		MT
		MT
Complete Set (22):		3.00
Common Player:		.15
1	John McNamara	.15
2	Don Mattingly	1.00
3	Willie Randolph	.15
4	Wade Boggs	.65
5	Cal Ripken, Jr.	1.50
6	George Bell	.15
7	Rickey Henderson	.50
8	Dave Winfield	.40
9	Terry Kennedy	.15
10	Bret Saberhagen	.15
11	Catfish Hunter	.15
12	Davey Johnson	.15
13	Jack Clark	.15
14	Ryne Sandberg	.65
15	Mike Schmidt	.75
16	Ozzie Smith	.50
17	Eric Davis	.20
18	Andre Dawson	.20
19	Darryl Strawberry	.20
20	Gary Carter	.20
21	Mike Scott	.15
22	Billy Williams	.20

1988 Topps American Baseball

DWIGHT EVANS OF/1B

This 88-card set, unlike Topps' United Kingdom football cards, was made available for distribution by U.S. hobby dealers. Cards were packaged in checklist-backed boxes with an American flag on the top flap. The 2-1/4" x 3" cards feature full-color player photos printed on white stock. The team name, printed in team colors, intersects the red frame at the top of the card. A bright yellow name banner appears below the photo. Backs have bright blue borders and cartoon-style horizontal layouts. The card number appears within a circle of red stars upper left, beside the player's name and team logo. A red banner containing the player career stats runs the length of the card back. The lower half of the flip side features a caricature of the player and a one-line caption. Below the cartoon, a short "Talkin' Baseball" paragraph provides elementary baseball information, obviously designed to acquaint soccer-playing European collectors with American baseball rules and terminology. A glossy edition of the set was issued and is valued at 2-3 times greater than the regular issue.

		MT
		MT
Complete Set (88):		8.00
Common Player:		.10
1	Harold Baines	.15
2	Steve Bedrosian	.10
3	George Bell	.10
4	Wade Boggs	.65
5	Barry Bonds	.75
6	Bob Boone	.10
7	George Brett	.80
8	Hubie Brooks	.10
9	Ivan Calderon	.10
10	Jose Canseco	.60
11	Gary Carter	.20
12	Joe Carter	.20
13	Jack Clark	.10
14	Will Clark	.45
15	Roger Clemens	.75
16	Vince Coleman	.10
17	Alvin Davis	.10
18	Eric Davis	.12
19	Glenn Davis	.10
20	Andre Dawson	.15
21	Mike Dunne	.10
22	Dwight Evans	.10
23	Tony Fernandez	.10
24	John Franco	.10
25	Gary Gaetti	.12
26	Kirk Gibson	.10
27	Dwight Gooden	.15
28	Pedro Guerrero	.10
29	Tony Gwynn	.40
30	Billy Hatcher	.10
31	Rickey Henderson	.35
32	Tom Henke	.10
33	Keith Hernandez	.10
34	Orel Hershiser	.15
35	Teddy Higuera	.10
36	Charlie Hough	.10
37	Kent Hrbek	.12
38	Brook Jacoby	.10
39	Dion James	.10
40	Wally Joyner	.15
41	John Kruk	.10
42	Mark Langston	.10
43	Jeffrey Leonard	.10
44	Candy Maldonado	.10
45	Don Mattingly	1.00
46	Willie McGee	.15
47	Mark McGwire	1.50
48	Kevin Mitchell	.12
49	Paul Molitor	.40
50	Jack Morris	.10
51	Lloyd Moseby	.10
52	Dale Murphy	.20
53	Eddie Murray	.40
54	Matt Nokes	.10
55	Dave Parker	.12
56	Larry Parrish	.10
57	Kirby Puckett	.75
58	Tim Raines	.15
59	Willie Randolph	.10
60	Harold Reynolds	.10
61	Cal Ripken, Jr.	1.50
62	Nolan Ryan	1.00
63	Bret Saberhagen	.10
64	Juan Samuel	.10
65	Ryne Sandberg	.65
66	Benny Santiago	.12
67	Mike Schmidt	.75
68	Mike Scott	.10
69	Kevin Seitzer	.10
70	Larry Sheets	.10
71	Ruben Sierra	.15
72	Ozzie Smith	.40
73	Zane Smith	.10
74	Cory Snyder	.10
75	Dave Stewart	.10
76	Darryl Strawberry	.15
77	Rick Sutcliffe	.10
78	Danny Tartabull	.12
79	Alan Trammell	.15
80	Fernando Valenzuela	.12
81	Andy Van Slyke	.10
82	Frank Viola	.10
83	Greg Walker	.10
84	Tim Wallach	.10
85	Dave Winfield	.30
86	Mike Witt	.10
87	Robin Yount	.35
88	Checklist	.10

A player's name in *italic* type indicates a rookie card.

1988 Topps Big Baseball

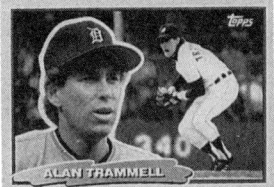

Topps Big Baseball cards (2-5/8" x 3-3/4") were issued in three series, 88 cards per series (a total set of 264 cards) sold in seven-card packs. The glossy cards are similar in format, both front and back, to the 1956 Topps set. Each card features a portrait and a game-action photo on the front, framed by a wide white border. A white outline highlights the portrait. The player's name appears at bottom on a splash of color that fades from yellow to orange to red to pink. On the card back, the player's name is printed in large red letters across the top, followed by his team name and position in black. Personal info is printed in a red rectangle beside a Topps baseball logo bearing the card number. A triple cartoon strip, in full-color, illustrates career highlights, performance, personal background, etc. A red, white and blue statistics box (pitching, batting, fielding) is printed across the bottom.

		MT
Complete Set (264):		21.00
Common Player:		.05
1	Paul Molitor	.45
2	Milt Thompson	.05
3	Billy Hatcher	.05
4	Mike Witt	.05
5	Vince Coleman	.05
6	Dwight Evans	.05
7	Tim Wallach	.05
8	Alan Trammell	.10
9	Will Clark	.60
10	Jeff Reardon	.05
11	Dwight Gooden	.15
12	Benny Santiago	.10
13	Jose Canseco	.60
14	Dale Murphy	.15
15	George Bell	.05
16	Ryne Sandberg	.60
17	Brook Jacoby	.05
18	Fernando Valenzuela	.10
19	Scott Fletcher	.05
20	Eric Davis	.10
21	Willie Wilson	.05
22	B.J. Surhoff	.05
23	Steve Bedrosian	.05
24	Dave Winfield	.45
25	Bobby Bonilla	.10
26	Larry Sheets	.05
27	Ozzie Guillen	.05
28	Checklist 1-88	.05
29	Nolan Ryan	1.50
30	Bob Boone	.05
31	Tom Herr	.05
32	Wade Boggs	.60
33	Neal Heaton	.05
34	Doyle Alexander	.05
35	Candy Maldonado	.05
36	Kirby Puckett	.85
37	Gary Carter	.10
38	Lance McCullers	.08
39a	Terry Steinbach (black Topps logo on front)	.12
39b	Terry Steinbach (white Topps logo on front)	.12
40	Gerald Perry	.05
41	Tom Henke	.05
42	Leon Durham	.05
43	Cory Snyder	.05
44	Dale Sveum	.05
45	Lance Parrish	.08
46	Steve Sax	.05
47	Charlie Hough	.05
48	Kal Daniels	.05
49	Bo Jackson	.25
50	Ron Guidry	.05
51	Bill Doran	.05
52	Wally Joyner	.10
53	Terry Pendleton	.05
54	Marty Barrett	.05
55	Andres Galarraga	.15
56	Larry Herndon	.05
57	Kevin Mitchell	.08
58	Greg Gagne	.05
59	Keith Hernandez	.05
60	John Kruk	.05
61	Mike LaValliere	.05
62	Cal Ripken, Jr.	2.00
63	Ivan Calderon	.05
64	Alvin Davis	.05
65	Luis Polonia	.05
66	Robin Yount	.25
67	Juan Samuel	.05
68	Andres Thomas	.05
69	Jeff Musselman	.05
70	Jerry Mumphrey	.05
71	Joe Carter	.15
72	Mike Scioscia	.05
73	Pete Incaviglia	.25
74	Barry Larkin	.25
75	Frank White	.05
76	Willie Randolph	.05
77	Kevin Bass	.05
78	Brian Downing	.05
79	Willie McGee	.10
80	Ellis Burks	.20
81	Hubie Brooks	.05
82	Darrell Evans	.05
83	Robby Thompson	.05
84	Kent Hrbek	.10
85	Ron Darling	.05
86	Stan Jefferson	.05
87	Teddy Higuera	.05
88	Mike Schmidt	.85
89	Barry Bonds	.75
90	Jim Presley	.05
91	Orel Hershiser	.08
92	Jesse Barfield	.05
93	Tom Candiotti	.05
94	Bret Saberhagen	.05
95	Jose Uribe	.05
96	Tom Browning	.05
97	Johnny Ray	.05
98	Mike Morgan	.05
100	Jim Sundberg	.05
101	Roger McDowell	.05
102	Randy Ready	.05
103	Mike Gallego	.05
104	Steve Buechele	.05
105	Greg Walker	.05
106	Jose Lind	.05
107	Steve Trout	.05
108	Rick Rhoden	.05
109	Jim Pankovits	.05
110	Ken Griffey	.05
111	Danny Cox	.05
112	Franklin Stubbs	.05
113	Lloyd Moseby	.05
114	Mel Hall	.05
115	Kevin Seitzer	.15
116	Tim Raines	.15
117	Juan Castillo	.05
118	Roger Clemens	.75
119	Mike Aldrete	.05
120	Mario Soto	.05
121	Jack Howell	.05
122	Rick Schu	.05
123	Jeff Robinson	.05
124	Doug Drabek	.05
125	Henry Cotto	.05
126	Checklist 89-176	.05
127	Gary Gaetti	.08
128	Rick Sutcliffe	.05
129	Howard Johnson	.05
130	Chris Brown	.05
131	Dave Henderson	.05
132	Curt Wilkerson	.05
133	Mike Marshall	.05
134	Kelly Gruber	.05
135	Julio Franco	.08
136	Kurt Stillwell	.05
137	Donnie Hill	.05
138	Mike Pagliarulo	.05
139	Von Hayes	.05
140	Mike Scott	.05
141	Bob Kipper	.05
142	Harold Reynolds	.05
143	Bob Brenly	.05
144	Dave Concepcion	.05
145	Devon White	.10
146	Jeff Stone	.05
147	Chet Lemon	.05
148	Ozzie Virgil	.05
149	Todd Worrell	.05
150	Mitch Webster	.05
151	Rob Deer	.05
152	Rich Gedman	.05
153	Andre Dawson	.15
154	Mike Davis	.05
155	Nelson Liriano	.05
156	Greg Swindell	.05
157	George Brett	.50
158	Kevin McReynolds	.05
159	Brian Fisher	.05
160	Mike Kingery	.05
161	Tony Gwynn	.65
162	Don Baylor	.08
163	Jerry Browne	.05
164	Dan Pasqua	.05
165	Rickey Henderson	.25
166	Brett Butler	.10
167	Nick Esasky	.05
168	Kirk McCaskill	.05
169	Fred Lynn	.08
170	Jack Morris	.05
171	Pedro Guerrero	.05
172	Dave Stieb	.05
173	Pat Tabler	.05
174	Floyd Bannister	.05
175	Rafael Belliard	.05
176	Mark Langston	.05
177	Greg Mathews	.05
178	Claudell Washington	.05
179	Mark McGwire	1.50
180	Bert Blyleven	.05
181	Jim Rice	.05
182	Mookie Wilson	.05
183	Willie Fraser	.05
184	Andy Van Slyke	.05
185	Matt Nokes	.05
186	Eddie Whitson	.05
187	Tony Fernandez	.05
188	Rick Reuschel	.05
189	Ken Phelps	.05
190	Juan Nieves	.05
191	Kirk Gibson	.05
192	Glenn Davis	.05
193	Zane Smith	.05
194	Jose DeLeon	.05
195	Gary Ward	.05
196	Pascual Perez	.05
197	Carlton Fisk	.12
198	Oddibe McDowell	.05
199	Mark Gubicza	.05
200	Glenn Hubbard	.05
201	Frank Viola	.05
202	Jody Reed	.05
203	Len Dykstra	.10
204	Dick Schofield	.05
205	Sid Bream	.05
206	Guillermo Hernandez	.05
207	Keith Moreland	.05
208	Mark Eichhorn	.05
209	Rene Gonzales	.05
210	Dave Valle	.05
211	Tom Brunansky	.05
212	Charles Hudson	.05
213	John Farrell	.05
214	Jeff Treadway	.05
215	Eddie Murray	.35
216	Checklist 177-264	.05
217	Greg Brock	.05
218	John Shelby	.05
219	Craig Reynolds	.05
220	Dion James	.05

221	Carney Lansford	.05
222	Juan Berenguer	.05
223	Luis Rivera	.05
224	Harold Baines	.10
225	Shawon Dunston	.12
226	Luis Aguayo	.05
227	Pete O'Brien	.05
228	Ozzie Smith	.45
229	Don Mattingly	.90
230	Danny Tartabull	.10
231	Andy Allanson	.05
232	John Franco	.05
233	Mike Greenwell	.08
234	Bob Ojeda	.05
235	Chili Davis	.08
236	Mike Dunne	.05
237	Jim Morrison	.05
238	Carmelo Martinez	.05
239	Ernie Whitt	.05
240	Scott Garrelts	.05
241	Mike Moore	.05
242	Dave Parker	.12
243	Tim Laudner	.05
244	Bill Wegman	.05
245	Bob Horner	.05
246	Rafael Santana	.05
247	Alfredo Griffin	.05
248	Mark Bailey	.05
249	Ron Gant	.20
250	Bryn Smith	.05
251	Lance Johnson	.05
252	Sam Horn	.05
253	Darryl Strawberry	.15
254	Chuck Finley	.05
255	Darnell Coles	.05
256	Mike Henneman	.05
257	Andy Hawkins	.05
258	Jim Clancy	.05
259	Atlee Hammaker	.05
260	Glenn Wilson	.05
261	Larry McWilliams	.05
262	Jack Clark	.05
263	Walt Weiss	.10
264	Gene Larkin	.05

1988 Topps Glossy Rookies

MATT NOKES

The Topps 1988 Rookies special insert cards follow the same basic design as the All-Star inserts. The set consists of 22 standard-size cards found one per pack in 100-card jumbo cellos. Large, glossy color player photos are printed on a white background below a red, yellow and blue "1987 Rookies" banner. A red and yellow player name appears beneath the photo. Red, white and blue card backs bear the title of the special insert set, the Rookies logo emblem, player name and card number.

		MT
Complete Set (22):		5.00
Common Player:		.20
1	Billy Ripken	.20

2	Ellis Burks	.50
3	Mike Greenwell	.25
4	DeWayne Buice	.20
5	Devon White	.25
6	Fred Manrique	.20
7	Mike Henneman	.20
8	Matt Nokes	.20
9	Kevin Seitzer	.20
10	B.J. Surhoff	.25
11	Casey Candaele	.20
12	Randy Myers	.30
13	Mark McGwire	4.00
14	Luis Polonia	.20
15	Terry Steinbach	.25
16	Mike Dunne	.20
17	Al Pedrique	.20
18	Benny Santiago	.30
19	Kelly Downs	.20
20	Joe Magrane	.20
21	Jerry Browne	.20
22	Jeff Musselman	.20

1988 Topps Mini League Leaders

WADE BOGGS

The third consecutive issue of Topps mini-cards (2-1/8" x 3") includes 77 cards spotlighting the top five ranked pitchers and batters. This set is unique in that it was the first time Topps included full-color player photos on both the front and back. Glossy action shots on the card fronts fade into a white border with a Topps logo in an upper corner. The player's name is printed in bold black letters beneath the photo. Horizontal reverses feature circular player photos on a blue and white background with the card number, player name, personal information, 1987 ranking and lifetime/1987 stats printed in red, black and yellow lettering.

		MT
Complete Set (77):		4.00
Common Player:		.09
1	Wade Boggs	.65
2	Roger Clemens	.75
3	Dwight Evans	.09
4	DeWayne Buice	.09
5	Brian Downing	.09
6	Wally Joyner	.15
7	Ivan Calderon	.09
8	Carlton Fisk	.15
9	Gary Redus	.09
10	Darrell Evans	.09
11	Jack Morris	.09
12	Alan Trammell	.15
13	Lou Whitaker	.12
14	Bret Saberhagen	.09
15	Kevin Seitzer	.09
16	Danny Tartabull	.12

17	Willie Wilson	.09
18	Teddy Higuera	.09
19	Paul Molitor	.50
20	Dan Plesac	.09
21	Robin Yount	.50
22	Kent Hrbek	.12
23	Kirby Puckett	.75
24	Jeff Reardon	.09
25	Frank Viola	.09
26	Rickey Henderson	.45
27	Don Mattingly	.90
28	Willie Randolph	.09
29	Dave Righetti	.09
30	Jose Canseco	.65
31	Mark McGwire	1.00
32	Dave Stewart	.09
33	Phil Bradley	.09
34	Mark Langston	.09
35	Harold Reynolds	.09
36	Charlie Hough	.09
37	George Bell	.09
38	Tom Henke	.09
39	Jimmy Key	.09
40	Dion James	.09
41	Dale Murphy	.15
42	Zane Smith	.09
43	Andre Dawson	.12
44	Lee Smith	.12
45	Rick Sutcliffe	.09
46	Eric Davis	.12
47	John Franco	.09
48	Dave Parker	.12
49	Billy Hatcher	.09
50	Nolan Ryan	1.50
51	Mike Scott	.09
52	Pedro Guerrero	.09
53	Orel Hershiser	.12
54	Fernando Valenzuela	.12
55	Bob Welch	.09
56	Andres Galarraga	.15
57	Tim Raines	.15
58	Tim Wallach	.09
59	Len Dykstra	.12
60	Dwight Gooden	.12
61	Howard Johnson	.09
62	Roger McDowell	.09
63	Darryl Strawberry	.15
64	Steve Bedrosian	.09
65	Shane Rawley	.09
66	Juan Samuel	.09
67	Mike Schmidt	.60
68	Mike Dunne	.09
69	Jack Clark	.09
70	Vince Coleman	.09
71	Willie McGee	.15
72	Ozzie Smith	.50
73	Todd Worrell	.09
74	Tony Gwynn	.70
75	John Kruk	.09
76	Rick Rueschel	.09
77	Checklist	.09

1989 Topps

RUBEN SIERRA

Ten top young players from the June, 1988, draft are featured on "#1 Draft Pick" cards in this full-color basic set of 792 standard-size baseball cards. An additional five cards salute 1989 Future Stars, 22 cards highlight All-Stars, seven contain Record Breakers, five are designated Turn Back The Clock, and six contain checklists. This set features the familiar white borders, but upper-left and lower-right photo corners have been rounded off. A curved name banner in bright red or blue is beneath the team name in large script in the lower-right corner. The card backs are printed in black on a red background and include personal information and complete minor and major league stats. Another new addition in this set is the special Monthly Scoreboard chart that lists monthly stats (April through September) in two of several categories (hits, run, home runs, stolen bases, RBIs, wins, strikeouts, games or saves).

		MT
Complete Set (792):		10.00
Common Player:		.05
Wax Box:		9.00
1	George Bell (Record Breaker)	.05
2	Wade Boggs (Record Breaker)	.12
3	Gary Carter (Record Breaker)	.05
4	Andre Dawson (Record Breaker)	.05
5	Orel Hershiser (Record Breaker)	.05
6	Doug Jones (Record Breaker)	.05
7	Kevin McReynolds (Record Breaker)	.05
8	Dave Eiland	.05
9	Tim Teufel	.05
10	Andre Dawson	.10
11	Bruce Sutter	.05
12	Dale Sveum	.05
13	Doug Sisk	.05
14	Tom Kelly	.05
15	Robby Thompson	.05
16	Ron Robinson	.05
17	Brian Downing	.05
18	Rick Rhoden	.05
19	Greg Gagne	.05
20	Steve Bedrosian	.05
21	White Sox Leaders(Greg Walker)	.05
22	Tim Crews	.05
23	Mike Fitzgerald	.05
24	Larry Andersen	.05
25	Frank White	.05
26	Dale Mohorcic	.05
27	Orestes Destrade	.05
28	Mike Moore	.05
29	Kelly Gruber	.05
30	Dwight Gooden	.08
31	Terry Francona	.05
32	Dennis Rasmussen	.05
33	B.J. Surhoff	.05
34	Ken Williams	.05
35	John Tudor	.05
36	Mitch Webster	.05
37	Bob Stanley	.05
38	Paul Runge	.05
39	Mike Maddux	.05
40	Steve Sax	.05
41	Terry Mulholland	.08
42	Jim Eppard	.05
43	Guillermo Hernandez	.05
44	Jim Snyder	.05
45	Kal Daniels	.05
46	Mark Portugal	.05
47	Carney Lansford	.05
48	Tim Burke	.05
49	Craig Biggio	.40
50	George Bell	.05
51	Angels Leaders(Mark McLemore)	.05
52	Bob Brenly	.05
53	Ruben Sierra	.10
54	Steve Trout	.05

55	Julio Franco	.05
56	Pat Tabler	.05
57	Alejandro Pena	.05
58	Lee Mazzilli	.05
59	Mark Davis	.05
60	Tom Brunansky	.05
61	Neil Allen	.05
62	Alfredo Griffin	.05
63	Mark Clear	.05
64	Alex Trevino	.05
65	Rick Reuschel	.05
66	Manny Trillo	.05
67	Dave Palmer	.05
68	Darrell Miller	.05
69	Jeff Ballard	.05
70	Mark McGwire	1.50
71	Mike Boddicker	.05
72	John Moses	.05
73	Pascual Perez	.05
74	Nick Leyva	.05
75	Tom Henke	.05
76	Terry Blocker	.05
77	Doyle Alexander	.05
78	Jim Sundberg	.05
79	Scott Bankhead	.05
80	Cory Snyder	.05
81	Expos Leaders(Tim Raines)	.08
82	Dave Leiper	.05
83	Jeff Blauser	.10
84	Bill Bene (#1 Draft Pick)	.05
85	Kevin McReynolds	.05
86	Al Nipper	.05
87	Larry Owen	.05
88	Darryl Hamilton	.10
89	Dave LaPoint	.05
90	Vince Coleman	.05
91	Floyd Youmans	.05
92	Jeff Kunkel	.05
93	Ken Howell	.05
94	Chris Speier	.05
95	Gerald Young	.05
96	Rick Cerone	.05
97	Greg Mathews	.05
98	Larry Sheets	.05
99	Sherman Corbett	.05
100	Mike Schmidt	.25
101	Les Straker	.05
102	Mike Gallego	.05
103	Tim Birtsas	.05
104	Dallas Green	.05
105	Ron Darling	.05
106	Willie Upshaw	.05
107	Jose DeLeon	.05
108	Fred Manrique	.05
109	Hipolito Pena	.05
110	Paul Molitor	.25
111	Reds Leaders(Eric Davis)	.05
112	Jim Presley	.05
113	Lloyd Moseby	.05
114	Bob Kipper	.05
115	Jody Davis	.05
116	Jeff Montgomery	.05
117	Dave Anderson	.05
118	Checklist 1-132	.05
119	Terry Puhl	.05
120	Frank Viola	.05
121	Garry Templeton	.05
122	Lance Johnson	.05
123	Spike Owen	.05
124	Jim Traber	.05
125	Mike Krukow	.05
126	Sid Bream	.05
127	Walt Terrell	.05
128	Milt Thompson	.05
129	Terry Clark	.05
130	Gerald Perry	.05
131	Dave Otto	.05
132	Curt Ford	.05
133	Bill Long	.05
134	Don Zimmer	.05
135	Jose Rijo	.05
136	Joey Meyer	.05
137	Geno Petralli	.05
138	Wallace Johnson	.05
139	Mike Flanagan	.05
140	Shawon Dunston	.12
141	Indians Leaders(Brook Jacoby)	.05
142	Mike Diaz	.05
143	Mike Campbell	.05
144	Jay Bell	.05
145	Dave Stewart	.05
146	Gary Pettis	.05
147	DeWayne Buice	.05
148	Bill Pecota	.05
149	Doug Dascenzo	.05

150	Fernando Valenzuela	.08
151	Terry McGriff	.05
152	Mark Thurmond	.05
153	Jim Pankovits	.05
154	Don Carman	.05
155	Marty Barrett	.05
156	Dave Gallagher	.05
157	Tom Glavine	.20
158	Mike Aldrete	.05
159	Pat Clements	.05
160	Jeffrey Leonard	.05
161	Gregg Olson (#1 Draft Pick)	.10
162	John Davis	.05
163	Bob Forsch	.05
164	Hal Lanier	.05
165	Mike Dunne	.05
166	Doug Jennings	.05
167	Steve Searcy (Future Star)	.05
168	Willie Wilson	.05
169	Mike Jackson	.05
170	Tony Fernandez	.05
171	Braves Leaders(Andres Thomas)	.05
172	Frank Williams	.05
173	Mel Hall	.05
174	Todd Burns	.08
175	John Shelby	.05
176	Jeff Parrett	.05
177	Monty Fariss (#1 Draft Pick)	.08
178	Mark Grant	.05
179	Ozzie Virgil	.05
180	Mike Scott	.05
181	Craig Worthington	.05
182	Bob McClure	.05
183	Oddibe McDowell	.05
184	John Costello	.05
185	Claudell Washington	.05
186	Pat Perry	.05
187	Darren Daulton	.10
188	Dennis Lamp	.05
189	Kevin Mitchell	.08
190	Mike Witt	.05
191	Sil Campusano	.05
192	Paul Mirabella	.05
193	Sparky Anderson	.05
194	Greg Harris	.10
195	Ozzie Guillen	.05
196	Denny Walling	.05
197	Neal Heaton	.05
198	Danny Heep	.05
199	Mike Schooler	.05
200	George Brett	.30
201	Blue Jays Leaders(Kelly Gruber)	.05
202	Brad Moore	.05
203	Rob Ducey	.05
204	Brad Havens	.05
205	Dwight Evans	.05
206	Roberto Alomar	.50
207	Terry Leach	.05
208	Tom Pagnozzi	.05
209	Jeff Bittiger	.05
210	Dale Murphy	.10
211	Mike Pagliarulo	.05
212	Scott Sanderson	.05
213	Rene Gonzales	.05
214	Charlie O'Brien	.05
215	Kevin Gross	.05
216	Jack Howell	.05
217	Joe Price	.05
218	Mike LaValliere	.05
219	Jim Clancy	.05
220	Gary Gaetti	.08
221	Cecil Espy	.05
222	Mark Lewis (#1 Draft Pick)	.08
223	Jay Buhner	.15
224	Tony LaRussa	.05
225	Ramon Martinez	.50
226	Bill Doran	.05
227	John Farrell	.05
228	Nelson Santovenia	.05
229	Jimmy Key	.05
230	Ozzie Smith	.25
231	Padres Leaders(Roberto Alomar)	.15
232	Ricky Horton	.05
233	Gregg Jefferies (Future Star)	.25
234	Tom Browning	.05
235	John Kruk	.05
236	Charles Hudson	.05
237	Glenn Hubbard	.05
238	Eric King	.05
239	Tim Laudner	.05
240	Greg Maddux	.50
241	Brett Butler	.08

#	Player	Price
242	Ed Vande Berg	.05
243	Bob Boone	.05
244	Jim Acker	.05
245	Jim Rice	.05
246	Rey Quinones	.05
247	Shawn Hillegas	.05
248	Tony Phillips	.05
249	Tim Leary	.05
250	Cal Ripken, Jr.	.60
251	*John Dopson*	.05
252	Billy Hatcher	.05
253	*Jose Alvarez*	.05
254	Tom LaSorda	.15
255	Ron Guidry	.08
256	Benny Santiago	.08
257	Rick Aguilera	.05
258	Checklist 133-264	.05
259	Larry McWilliams	.05
260	Dave Winfield	.15
261	Cardinals Leaders(Tom Brunansky)	.05
262	*Jeff Pico*	.05
263	Mike Felder	.05
264	*Rob Dibble*	.10
265	Kent Hrbek	.10
266	Luis Aquino	.05
267	Jeff Robinson	.05
268	Keith Miller	.05
269	Tom Bolton	.05
270	Wally Joyner	.08
271	Jay Tibbs	.05
272	Ron Hassey	.05
273	Jose Lind	.05
274	Mark Eichhorn	.05
275	Danny Tartabull	.05
276	Paul Kilgus	.05
277	Mike Davis	.05
278	Andy McGaffigan	.05
279	Scott Bradley	.05
280	Bob Knepper	.05
281	Gary Redus	.05
282	*Cris Carpenter*	.08
283	Andy Allanson	.05
284	Jim Leyland	.05
285	John Candelaria	.05
286	Darrin Jackson	.05
287	Juan Nieves	.05
288	Pat Sheridan	.05
289	Ernie Whitt	.05
290	John Franco	.05
291	Mets Leaders(Darryl Strawberry)	.12
292	*Jim Corsi*	.05
293	Glenn Wilson	.05
294	Juan Berenguer	.05
295	Scott Fletcher	.05
296	Ron Gant	.12
297	*Oswald Peraza*	.05
298	Chris James	.05
299	*Steve Ellsworth*	.05
300	Darryl Strawberry	.12
301	Charlie Leibrandt	.05
302	Gary Ward	.05
303	Felix Fermin	.05
304	Joel Youngblood	.05
305	Dave Smith	.05
306	Tracy Woodson	.05
307	Lance McCullers	.05
308	Ron Karkovice	.05
309	Mario Diaz	.05
310	Rafael Palmeiro	.15
311	Chris Bosio	.05
312	Tom Lawless	.05
313	Denny Martinez	.08
314	Bobby Valentine	.05
315	Greg Swindell	.05
316	Walt Weiss	.05
317	*Jack Armstrong*	.05
318	Gene Larkin	.05
319	Greg Booker	.05
320	Lou Whitaker	.05
321	Red Sox Leaders(Jody Reed)	.05
322	John Smiley	.05
323	Gary Thurman	.05
324	*Bob Milacki*	.05
325	Jesse Barfield	.05
326	Dennis Boyd	.05
327	*Mark Lemke*	.05
328	Rick Honeycutt	.05
329	Bob Melvin	.05
330	Eric Davis	.08
331	Curt Wilkerson	.05
332	Tony Armas	.05
333	Bob Ojeda	.05
334	Steve Lyons	.05
335	Dave Righetti	.05
336	Steve Balboni	.05
337	Calvin Schiraldi	.05
338	Jim Adduci	.05
339	Scott Bailes	.05
340	Kirk Gibson	.05
341	Jim Deshaies	.05
342	Tom Brookens	.05
343	*Gary Sheffield* (Future Star)	.75
344	Tom Trebelhorn	.05
345	Charlie Hough	.05
346	Rex Hudler	.05
347	John Cerutti	.05
348	Ed Hearn	.05
349	*Ron Jones*	.05
350	Andy Van Slyke	.05
351	Giants Leaders(Bob Melvin)	.05
352	Rick Schu	.05
353	Marvell Wynne	.05
354	Larry Parrish	.05
355	Mark Langston	.05
356	Kevin Elster	.05
357	Jerry Reuss	.05
358	*Ricky Jordan*	.05
359	Tommy John	.08
360	Ryne Sandberg	.30
361	Kelly Downs	.05
362	Jack Lazorko	.05
363	Rich Yett	.05
364	Rob Deer	.05
365	Mike Henneman	.05
366	Herm Winningham	.05
367	*Johnny Paredes*	.05
368	Brian Holton	.05
369	Ken Caminiti	.05
370	Dennis Eckersley	.08
371	Manny Lee	.05
372	Craig Lefferts	.05
373	Tracy Jones	.05
374	John Wathan	.05
375	Terry Pendleton	.05
376	Steve Lombardozzi	.05
377	Mike Smithson	.05
378	Checklist 265-396	.05
379	Tim Flannery	.05
380	Rickey Henderson	.10
381	Orioles Leaders(Larry Sheets)	.05
382	John Smoltz	.40
383	Howard Johnson	.05
384	Mark Salas	.05
385	Von Hayes	.05
386	Andres Galarraga (All-Star)	.15
387	Ryne Sandberg (All-Star)	.15
388	Bobby Bonilla (All-Star)	.05
389	Ozzie Smith (All-Star)	.15
390	Darryl Strawberry (All-Star)	.10
391	Andre Dawson (All-Star)	.08
392	Andy Van Slyke (All-Star)	.05
393	Gary Carter (All-Star)	.08
394	Orel Hershiser (All-Star)	.08
395	Danny Jackson (All-Star)	.05
396	Kirk Gibson (All-Star)	.05
397	Don Mattingly (All-Star)	.20
398	Julio Franco (All-Star)	.05
399	Wade Boggs (All-Star)	.15
400	Alan Trammell (All-Star)	.05
401	Jose Canseco (All-Star)	.15
402	Mike Greenwell (All-Star)	.05
403	Kirby Puckett (All-Star)	.20
404	Bob Boone (All-Star)	.05
405	Roger Clemens (All-Star)	.20
406	Frank Viola (All-Star)	.05
407	Dave Winfield (All-Star)	.10
408	Greg Walker	.05
409	Ken Dayley	.05
410	Jack Clark	.05
411	Mitch Williams	.05
412	Barry Lyons	.05
413	Mike Kingery	.05
414	Jim Fregosi	.05
415	Rich Gossage	.08
416	Fred Lynn	.08
417	Mike LaCoss	.05
418	Bob Dernier	.05
419	Tom Filer	.05
420	Joe Carter	.10
421	Kirk McCaskill	.05
422	Bo Diaz	.05
423	Brian Fisher	.05
424	Luis Polonia	.05
425	Jay Howell	.05
426	Danny Gladden	.05
427	Eric Show	.05
428	Craig Reynolds	.05
429	Twins Leaders(Greg Gagne)	.05
430	Mark Gubicza	.05
431	Luis Rivera	.05
432	*Chad Kreuter*	.08
433	Albert Hall	.05
434	*Ken Patterson*	.08
435	Len Dykstra	.10
436	Bobby Meacham	.05
437	Andy Benes (#1 Draft Pick)	.40
438	Greg Gross	.05
439	Frank DiPino	.05
440	Bobby Bonilla	.10
441	Jerry Reed	.05
442	Jose Oquendo	.05
443	*Rod Nichols*	.05
444	Moose Stubing	.05
445	Matt Nokes	.05
446	Rob Murphy	.05
447	Donell Nixon	.05
448	Eric Plunk	.05
449	Carmelo Martinez	.05
450	Roger Clemens	.40
451	Mark Davidson	.05
452	*Israel Sanchez*	.05
453	Tom Prince	.05
454	Paul Assenmacher	.05
455	Johnny Ray	.05
456	Tim Belcher	.05
457	Mackey Sasser	.05
458	*Donn Pall*	.05
459	Mariners Leaders(Dave Valle)	.05
460	Dave Stieb	.05
461	Buddy Bell	.05
462	Jose Guzman	.05
463	Steve Lake	.05
464	Bryn Smith	.05
465	Mark Grace	.20
466	Chuck Crim	.05
467	Jim Walewander	.05
468	Henry Cotto	.05
469	*Jose Bautista*	.05
470	Lance Parrish	.08
471	*Steve Curry*	.05
472	Brian Harper	.05
473	Don Robinson	.05
474	Bob Rodgers	.05
475	Dave Parker	.10
476	Jon Perlman	.05
477	Dick Schofield	.05
478	Doug Drabek	.05
479	*Mike Macfarlane*	.10
480	Keith Hernandez	.05
481	Chris Brown	.05
482	*Steve Peters*	.05
483	Mickey Hatcher	.05
484	Steve Shields	.05
485	Hubie Brooks	.05
486	Jack McDowell	.10
487	Scott Lusader	.05
488	Kevin Coffman	.05
489	Phillies Leaders(Mike Schmidt)	.15
490	*Chris Sabo*	.15
491	Mike Birkbeck	.05
492	Alan Ashby	.05
493	Todd Benzinger	.05
494	Shane Rawley	.05
495	Candy Maldonado	.05
496	Dwayne Henry	.05
497	Pete Stanicek	.05
498	Dave Valle	.05
499	*Don Heinkel*	.05
500	Jose Canseco	.20
501	Vance Law	.05
502	Duane Ward	.05
503	Al Newman	.05
504	Bob Walk	.05
505	Pete Rose	.20
506	Kirt Manwaring	.05
507	Steve Farr	.05
508	Wally Backman	.05
509	Bud Black	.05
510	Bob Horner	.05
511	Richard Dotson	.05
512	Donnie Hill	.05
513	Jesse Orosco	.05
514	Chet Lemon	.05
515	Barry Larkin	.15
516	Eddie Whitson	.05
517	Greg Brock	.05
518	Bruce Ruffin	.05
519	Yankees Leaders(Willie Randolph)	.05
520	Rick Sutcliffe	.05

No.	Player	Value
521	Mickey Tettleton	.05
522	*Randy Kramer*	.05
523	Andres Thomas	.05
524	Checklist 397-528	.08
525	Chili Davis	.05
526	Wes Gardner	.05
527	Dave Henderson	.05
528	*Luis Medina*	.05
529	Tom Foley	.05
530	Nolan Ryan	.50
531	Dave Hengel	.05
532	Jerry Browne	.05
533	Andy Hawkins	.05
534	Doc Edwards	.05
535	Todd Worrell	.05
536	Joel Skinner	.05
537	Pete Smith	.05
538	Juan Castillo	.05
539	Barry Jones	.05
540	Bo Jackson	.20
541	Cecil Fielder	.15
542	Todd Frohwirth	.05
543	Damon Berryhill	.05
544	Jeff Sellers	.05
545	Mookie Wilson	.05
546	Mark Williamson	.05
547	Mark McLemore	.05
548	Bobby Witt	.05
549	Cubs Leaders(Jamie Moyer)	.05
550	Orel Hershiser	.08
551	Randy Ready	.05
552	Greg Cadaret	.05
553	Luis Salazar	.05
554	Nick Esasky	.05
555	Bert Blyleven	.05
556	Bruce Fields	.05
557	*Keith Miller*	.05
558	Dan Pasqua	.05
559	Juan Agosto	.05
560	Tim Raines	.08
561	Luis Aguayo	.05
562	Danny Cox	.05
563	Bill Schroeder	.05
564	Russ Nixon	.05
565	Jeff Russell	.05
566	Al Pedrique	.05
567	David Wells	.05
568	Mickey Brantley	.05
569	*German Jimenez*	.05
570	Tony Gwynn	.40
571	Billy Ripken	.05
572	Atlee Hammaker	.05
573	Jim Abbott (#1 Draft Pick)	.15
574	Dave Clark	.05
575	Juan Samuel	.05
576	Greg Minton	.05
577	Randy Bush	.05
578	John Morris	.05
579	Astros Leaders(Glenn Davis)	.05
580	Harold Reynolds	.05
581	Gene Nelson	.05
582	Mike Marshall	.05
583	*Paul Gibson*	.05
584	Randy Velarde	.10
585	Harold Baines	.05
586	Joe Boever	.05
587	Mike Stanley	.05
588	*Luis Alicea*	.10
589	Dave Meads	.05
590	Andres Galarraga	.15
591	Jeff Musselman	.05
592	John Cangelosi	.05
593	Drew Hall	.05
594	Jimy Williams	.05
595	Teddy Higuera	.05
596	Kurt Stillwell	.05
597	*Terry Taylor*	.05
598	Ken Gerhart	.05
599	Tom Candiotti	.05
600	Wade Boggs	.25
601	Dave Dravecky	.05
602	Devon White	.05
603	Frank Tanana	.05
604	Paul O'Neill	.15
605a	Bob Welch (missing Complete Major League Pitching Record line)	2.00
605b	Bob Welch (contains Complete Major League Pitching Record line)	.08
606	Rick Dempsey	.05
607	*Willie Ansley* (#1 Draft Pick)	.05
608	Phil Bradley	.05
609	Tigers Leaders(Frank Tanana)	.05
610	Randy Myers	.08
611	Don Slaught	.05
612	Dan Quisenberry	.05
613	*Gary Varsho*	.05
614	Joe Hesketh	.05
615	Robin Yount	.25
616	*Steve Rosenberg*	.05
617	*Mark Parent*	.05
618	Rance Mulliniks	.05
619	Checklist 529-660	.05
620	Barry Bonds	.35
621	Rick Mahler	.05
622	Stan Javier	.05
623	Fred Toliver	.05
624	Jack McKeon	.05
625	Eddie Murray	.15
626	Jeff Reed	.05
627	Greg Harris	.05
628	Matt Williams	.25
629	Pete O'Brien	.05
630	Mike Greenwell	.08
631	Dave Bergman	.05
632	*Bryan Harvey*	.10
633	Daryl Boston	.05
634	Marvin Freeman	.05
635	Willie Randolph	.05
636	Bill Wilkinson	.05
637	Carmen Castillo	.05
638	Floyd Bannister	.05
639	Athletics Leaders(Walt Weiss)	.05
640	Willie McGee	.05
641	Curt Young	.05
642	Argenis Salazar	.05
643	*Louie Meadows*	.05
644	Lloyd McClendon	.05
645	Jack Morris	.05
646	Kevin Bass	.05
647	*Randy Johnson*	.75
648	*Sandy Alomar* (Future Star)	.30
649	Stewart Cliburn	.05
650	Kirby Puckett	.35
651	Tom Niedenfuer	.05
652	Rich Gedman	.05
653	*Tommy Barrett*	.05
654	Whitey Herzog	.05
655	Dave Magadan	.05
656	Ivan Calderon	.05
657	Joe Magrane	.05
658	R.J. Reynolds	.05
659	Al Leiter	.05
660	Will Clark	.20
661	Dwight Gooden (Turn Back the Clock)	.10
662	Lou Brock (Turn Back the Clock)	.08
663	Hank Aaron (Turn Back the Clock)	.15
664	Gil Hodges (Turn Back the Clock)	.08
665	Tony Oliva (Turn Back the Clock)	.08
666	Randy St. Claire	.05
667	Dwayne Murphy	.05
668	Mike Bielecki	.05
669	Dodgers Leaders(Orel Hershiser)	.08
670	Kevin Seitzer	.05
671	Jim Gantner	.05
672	Allan Anderson	.05
673	Don Baylor	.08
674	Otis Nixon	.05
675	Bruce Hurst	.05
676	Ernie Riles	.05
677	Dave Schmidt	.05
678	Dion James	.05
679	Willie Fraser	.05
680	Gary Carter	.10
681	Jeff Robinson	.05
682	Rick Leach	.05
683	*Jose Cecena*	.05
684	Dave Johnson	.05
685	Jeff Treadway	.05
686	Scott Terry	.05
687	Alvin Davis	.05
688	Zane Smith	.05
689	Stan Jefferson	.05
690	Doug Jones	.05
691	Roberto Kelly	.10
692	Steve Ontiveros	.05
693	*Pat Borders*	.20
694	Les Lancaster	.05
695	Carlton Fisk	.10
696	Don August	.05
697	Franklin Stubbs	.05
698	Keith Atherton	.05
699	Pirates Leaders(Al Pedrique)	.05
700	Don Mattingly	.35
701	Storm Davis	.05
702	Jamie Quirk	.05
703	Scott Garrelts	.05
704	*Carlos Quintana*	.05
705	Terry Kennedy	.05
706	Pete Incaviglia	.05
707	Steve Jeltz	.05
708	Chuck Finley	.05
709	Tom Herr	.05
710	Dave Cone	.15
711	*Candy Sierra*	.05
712	Bill Swift	.05
713	Ty Griffin (#1 Draft Pick)	.05
714	Joe M. Morgan	.05
715	Tony Pena	.05
716	Wayne Tolleson	.05
717	Jamie Moyer	.05
718	Glenn Braggs	.05
719	Danny Darwin	.05
720	Tim Wallach	.05
721	*Ron Tingley*	.05
722	Todd Stottlemyre	.05
723	Rafael Belliard	.05
724	Jerry Don Gleaton	.05
725	Terry Steinbach	.05
726	Dickie Thon	.05
727	Joe Orsulak	.05
728	Charlie Puleo	.05
729	Rangers Leaders(Steve Buechele)	.05
730	Danny Jackson	.05
731	Mike Young	.05
732	Steve Buechele	.05
733	*Randy Bockus*	.05
734	Jody Reed	.05
735	Roger McDowell	.05
736	Jeff Hamilton	.05
737	*Norm Charlton*	.15
738	Darnell Coles	.05
739	Brook Jacoby	.05
740	Dan Plesac	.05
741	Ken Phelps	.05
742	*Mike Harkey* (Future Star)	.08
743	Mike Heath	.05
744	Roger Craig	.05
745	Fred McGriff	.15
746	*German Gonzalez*	.05
747	Wil Tejada	.05
748	Jimmy Jones	.05
749	Rafael Ramirez	.05
750	Bret Saberhagen	.05
751	Ken Oberkfell	.05
752	Jim Gott	.05
753	Jose Uribe	.05
754	Bob Brower	.05
755	Mike Scioscia	.05
756	*Scott Medvin*	.05
757	Brady Anderson	.25
758	Gene Walter	.05
759	Brewers Leaders(Rob Deer)	.05
760	Lee Smith	.05
761	*Dante Bichette*	1.00
762	Bobby Thigpen	.05
763	Dave Martinez	.05
764	Robin Ventura (#1 Draft Pick)	.40
765	Glenn Davis	.05
766	Cecilio Guante	.05
767	*Mike Capel*	.05
768	Bill Wegman	.05
769	Junior Ortiz	.05
770	Alan Trammell	.10
771	Ron Kittle	.05
772	Ron Oester	.05
773	Keith Moreland	.05
774	Frank Robinson	.10
775	Jeff Reardon	.05
776	Nelson Liriano	.05
777	Ted Power	.05
778	Bruce Benedict	.05
779	Craig McMurtry	.05
780	Pedro Guerrero	.05
781	*Greg Briley*	.05
782	Checklist 661-792	.05
783	*Trevor Wilson*	.10
784	*Steve Avery* (#1 Draft Pick)	.20
785	Ellis Burks	.12
786	Melido Perez	.05
787	*Dave West*	.10
788	Mike Morgan	.05

789	Royals Leaders(Bo Jackson)	.12
790	Sid Fernandez	.05
791	Jim Lindeman	.05
792	Rafael Santana	.05

1989 Topps Tiffany

This special hobby-only edition shares the checklist with the regular 1989 Topps set. Cards are identical except for the use of white cardboard stock and the high-gloss front coating.

	MT
Complete Set (792):	75.00
Common Player:	.10
(Star cards valued at 3x-4X corresponding cards in regular 1989 Topps issue)	

1989 Topps Box Panels

Continuing its practice of printing baseball cards on the bottom panels of its wax pack boxes, Topps in 1989 issued a special 16-card set, printing four cards on each of four different box-bottom panels. The cards are identical in design to the regular 1989 Topps cards. They are designated by letter (from A through P) rather than by number.

		MT
Complete Panel Set (4):		10.00
Complete Singles Set: (16):		7.50
Common Panel:		1.50
Common Single Player:		.10
	Panel	1.50
A	George Brett	1.00
B	Bill Buckner	.10
C	Darrell Evans	.10
D	Rich Gossage	.10
	Panel	2.50
E	Greg Gross	.10
F	Rickey Henderson	.50
G	Keith Hernandez	.10
H	Tom Lasorda	.25
	Panel	7.50
I	Jim Rice	.10
J	Cal Ripken, Jr.	2.00
K	Nolan Ryan	1.50
L	Mike Schmidt	1.00
	Panel	1.50
M	Bruce Sutter	.10
N	Don Sutton	.25
O	Kent Tekulve	.10
P	Dave Winfield	.50

1989 Topps Traded

For the ninth straight year, Topps issued its annual 132-card "Traded" set at the end of the 1989 baseball season. The set, which was packaged in a special box and sold by hobby dealers, includes traded players and rookies who were not in the regular 1989 Topps set.

		MT
Complete Set (132):		7.00
Common Player:		.05
1T	Don Aase	.05
2T	Jim Abbott	.15
3T	Kent Anderson	.05
4T	Keith Atherton	.05
5T	Wally Backman	.05
6T	Steve Balboni	.05
7T	Jesse Barfield	.05
8T	Steve Bedrosian	.05
9T	Todd Benzinger	.05
10T	Geronimo Berroa	.10
11T	Bert Blyleven	.05
12T	Bob Boone	.05
13T	Phil Bradley	.05
14T	Jeff Brantley	.05
15T	Kevin Brown	.15
16T	Jerry Browne	.05
17T	Chuck Cary	.05
18T	Carmen Castillo	.05
19T	Jim Clancy	.05
20T	Jack Clark	.05
21T	Bryan Clutterbuck	.05
22T	Jody Davis	.05
23T	Mike Devereaux	.05
24T	Frank DiPino	.05
25T	Benny Distefano	.05
26T	John Dopson	.05
27T	Len Dykstra	.10
28T	Jim Eisenreich	.05
29T	Nick Esasky	.05
30T	Alvaro Espinoza	.05
31T	Darrell Evans	.05
32T	Junior Felix	.05
33T	Felix Fermin	.05
34T	Julio Franco	.08
35T	Terry Francona	.05
36T	Cito Gaston	.05
37T	Bob Geren (photo actually Mike Fennell)	.05
38T	*Tom Gordon*	.10
39T	Tommy Gregg	.05
40T	Ken Griffey	.10
41T	Ken Griffey, Jr.	8.00
42T	Kevin Gross	.05
43T	Lee Guetterman	.05
44T	Mel Hall	.05
45T	Erik Hanson	.20
46T	Gene Harris	.05
47T	Andy Hawkins	.05
48T	Rickey Henderson	.15
49T	Tom Herr	.05
50T	*Ken Hill*	.40
51T	Brian Holman	.05

52T	Brian Holton	.05
53T	Art Howe	.05
54T	Ken Howell	.05
55T	Bruce Hurst	.05
56T	Chris James	.05
57T	Randy Johnson	.75
58T	Jimmy Jones	.05
59T	Terry Kennedy	.05
60T	Paul Kilgus	.05
61T	Eric King	.05
62T	Ron Kittle	.05
63T	John Kruk	.05
64T	Randy Kutcher	.05
65T	Steve Lake	.05
66T	Mark Langston	.10
67T	Dave LaPoint	.05
68T	Rick Leach	.05
69T	Terry Leach	.05
70T	Jim Levebvre	.05
71T	Al Leiter	.05
72T	Jeffrey Leonard	.05
73T	Derek Lilliquist	.05
74T	Rick Mahler	.05
75T	Tom McCarthy	.05
76T	Lloyd McClendon	.05
77T	Lance McCullers	.05
78T	Oddibe McDowell	.05
79T	Roger McDowell	.05
80T	Larry McWilliams	.05
81T	Randy Milligan	.05
82T	Mike Moore	.05
83T	Keith Moreland	.05
84T	Mike Morgan	.05
85T	Jamie Moyer	.05
86T	Rob Murphy	.05
87T	Eddie Murray	.20
88T	Pete O'Brien	.05
89T	Gregg Olson	.05
90T	Steve Ontiveros	.05
91T	Jesse Orosco	.05
92T	Spike Owen	.05
93T	Rafael Palmeiro	.30
94T	Clay Parker	.05
95T	Jeff Parrett	.05
96T	Lance Parrish	.08
97T	Dennis Powell	.05
98T	Rey Quinones	.05
99T	Doug Rader	.05
100T	Willie Randolph	.05
101T	Shane Rawley	.05
102T	Randy Ready	.05
103T	Bip Roberts	.05
104T	Kenny Rogers	.25
105T	Ed Romero	.05
106T	Nolan Ryan	1.50
107T	Luis Salazar	.05
108T	Juan Samuel	.05
109T	Alex Sanchez	.05
110T	*Deion Sanders*	.75
111T	Steve Sax	.05
112T	Rick Schu	.05
113T	Dwight Smith	.05
114T	Lonnie Smith	.05
115T	Billy Spiers	.10
116T	Kent Tekulve	.05
117T	Walt Terrell	.05
118T	Milt Thompson	.05
119T	Dickie Thon	.05
120T	Jeff Torborg	.05
121T	Jeff Treadway	.05
122T	*Omar Vizquel*	.30
123T	Jerome Walton	.05
124T	Gary Ward	.05
125T	Claudell Washington	.05
126T	Curt Wilkerson	.05
127T	Eddie Williams	.05
128T	Frank Williams	.05
129T	Ken Williams	.05
130T	Mitch Williams	.10
131T	Steve Wilson	.10
---	Topps Magazine subscription offer card	.05

1989 Topps Traded Tiffany

The Topps Traded set was issued in a specially boxed, hobby-only editions. Cards are identical to the regular-issue Topps Traded cards except for the application of a high-gloss to the fronts.

	MT
Complete Set (132):	40.00
Common Player:	.15
(Star cards valued at 3X-4X corresponding cards in regular Topps Traded issue)	

1989 Topps All-Star Glossy Set of 22

The glossy All-Stars were included in the Topps 1989 rack packs. Format was very similar to the sets produced since 1984. Besides the starting lineups of the 1988 All-Star Game, the set included the managers and honorary team captains, Bobby Doerr and Willie Stargell.

		MT
Complete Set (22):		2.50
Common Player:		.05
1	Tom Kelly	.05
2	Mark McGwire	1.50
3	Paul Molitor	.15
4	Wade Boggs	.30
5	Cal Ripken, Jr.	.90
6	Jose Canseco	.30
7	Rickey Henderson	.15
8	Dave Winfield	.15
9	Terry Steinbach	.05
10	Frank Viola	.05
11	Bobby Doerr	.05
12	Whitey Herzog	.05
13	Will Clark	.15
14	Ryne Sandberg	.40
15	Bobby Bonilla	.10
16	Ozzie Smith	.20
17	Vince Coleman	.05
18	Andre Dawson	.10
19	Darryl Strawberry	.10
20	Gary Carter	.10
21	Dwight Gooden	.10
22	Willie Stargell	.10

1989 Topps American Baseball

For the second consecutive year Topps released an 88-card set of baseball cards available in both the United States and the United Kingdom. The mini-sized cards (2-1/4" x 3") are printed on white stock with a low-gloss finish. The game-action color player photo is outlined in red, white, and blue and framed in white. Backs are horizontal and include a characterization cartoon along with biographical information and statistics. The cards were sold in packs of five with a stick of bubble gum.

BRADY ANDERSON

		MT
Complete Set (88):		9.00
Common Player:		.10
1	Brady Anderson	.20
2	Harold Baines	.12
3	George Bell	.10
4	Wade Boggs	.60
5	Barry Bonds	.90
6	Bobby Bonilla	.15
7	George Brett	.80
8	Hubie Brooks	.10
9	Tom Brunansky	.10
10	Jay Buhner	.15
11	Brett Butler	.12
12	Jose Canseco	.60
13	Joe Carter	.15
14	Jack Clark	.10
15	Will Clark	.45
16	Roger Clemens	.60
17	Dave Cone	.12
18	Alvin Davis	.10
19	Eric Davis	.12
20	Glenn Davis	.10
21	Andre Dawson	.12
22	Bill Doran	.10
23	Dennis Eckersley	.12
24	Dwight Evans	.10
25	Tony Fernandez	.10
26	Carlton Fisk	.12
27	John Franco	.10
28	Andres Galarraga	.15
29	Ron Gant	.15
30	Kirk Gibson	.10
31	Dwight Gooden	.15
32	Mike Greenwell	.10
33	Mark Gubicza	.10
34	Pedro Gurrero	.10
35	Ozzie Guillen	.10
36	Tony Gwynn	.50
37	Rickey Henderson	.25
38	Orel Hershiser	.15
39	Teddy Higuera	.10
40	Charlie Hough	.10
41	Kent Hrbek	.12
42	Bruce Hurst	.10
43	Bo Jackson	.20
44	Gregg Jefferies	.15
45	Ricky Jordan	.10
46	Wally Joyner	.12
47	Mark Langston	.10
48	Mike Marshall	.10
49	Don Mattingly	1.00
50	Fred McGriff	.25
51	Mark McGwire	1.50
52	Kevin McReynolds	.10
53	Paul Molitor	.35
54	Jack Morris	.10
55	Dale Murphy	.15
56	Eddie Murray	.30
57	Pete O'Brien	.10
58	Rafael Palmeiro	.15
59	Gerald Perry	.10
60	Kirby Puckett	.75
61	Tim Raines	.15
62	Johnny Ray	.10
63	Rick Reuschel	.10
64	Cal Ripken	2.00
65	Chris Sabo	.10
66	Juan Samuel	.10
67	Ryne Sandberg	.60
68	Benny Santiago	.12
69	Steve Sax	.10
70	Mike Schmidt	.90
71	Ruben Sierra	.12
72	Ozzie Smith	.25
73	Cory Snyder	.10
74	Dave Stewart	.10
75	Darryl Strawberry	.15
76	Greg Swindell	.10
77	Alan Trammell	.12
78	Fernando Valenzuela	.12
79	Andy Van Slyke	.10
80	Frank Viola	.10
81	Claudell Washington	.10
82	Walt Weiss	.10
83	Lou Whitaker	.10
84	Dave Winfield	.25
85	Mike Witt	.10
86	Gerald Young	.10
87	Robin Yount	.25
88	Checklist	.10

1989 Topps Batting Leaders

WADE BOGGS

The active career batting leaders are showcased in this 22-card set. The 2-1/2" x 3-1/2" cards are printed on super glossy stock with full-color photos and bright red borders. A "Top Active Career Batting Leaders" cup is displayed in a lower corner. The player's name appears above the photo. This set is specially numbered in accordance to career batting average. Wade Boggs is featured on card #1 as the top active career batting leader. The flip sides present batting statistics. One batting leader card was included in each K-Mart blister pack, which also includes 100 cards from the 1989 regular Topps set.

		MT
Complete Set (22):		19.00
Common Player:		.50
1	Wade Boggs	1.50
2	Tony Gwynn	2.00
3	Don Mattingly	2.50
4	Kirby Puckett	2.50
5	George Brett	2.00
6	Pedro Guerrero	.60
7	Tim Raines	.50
8	Keith Hernandez	.50
9	Jim Rice	.50
10	Paul Molitor	1.50
11	Eddie Murray	1.50

12	Willie McGee	.50
13	Dave Parker	.50
14	Julio Franco	.50
15	Rickey Henderson	.90
16	Kent Hrbek	.75
17	Willie Wilson	.50
18	Johnny Ray	.50
19	Pat Tabler	.50
20	Carney Lansford	.50
21	Robin Yount	1.00
22	Alan Trammell	.50

1989 Topps Big Baseball

Known by collectors as Topps "Big Baseball," the cards in this 330-card set measure 2-5/8" x 3-3/4" and are patterned after the 1956 Topps cards. The glossy card fronts are horizontally-designed and include two photos of each player, a portrait alongside an action photo. The backs include 1988 and career stats, but are dominated by a color cartoon featuring the player. Members of the 1988 Team U.S.A. Olympic baseball team are included in the set, which was issued in three series of 110 cards each.

		MT
Complete Set (330):		22.00
Common Player:		.05
1	Orel Hershiser	.15
2	Harold Reynolds	.05
3	Jody Davis	.05
4	Greg Walker	.05
5	Barry Bonds	.60
6	Bret Saberhagen	.05
7	Johnny Ray	.05
8	Mike Fiore	.05
9	Juan Castillo	.05
10	Todd Burns	.05
11	Carmelo Martinez	.05
12	Geno Petralli	.05
13	Mel Hall	.05
14	Tom Browning	.05
15	Fred McGriff	.15
16	Kevin Elster	.05
17	Tim Leary	.05
18	Jim Rice	.05
19	Bret Barberie	.10
20	Jay Buhner	.05
21	Atlee Hammaker	.05
22	Lou Whitaker	.05
23	Paul Runge	.05
24	Carlton Fisk	.08
25	Jose Lind	.05
26	Mark Gubicza	.08
27	Billy Ripken	.05
28	Mike Pagliarulo	.05
29	Jim Deshaies	.05

30	Mark McLemore	.05
31	Scott Terry	.05
32	Franklin Stubbs	.05
33	Don August	.05
34	Mark McGwire	1.50
35	Eric Show	.05
36	Cecil Espy	.05
37	Ron Tingley	.05
38	Mickey Brantley	.05
39	Paul O'Neill	.08
40	Ed Sprague	.25
41	Len Dykstra	.10
42	Roger Clemens	.60
43	Ron Gant	.15
44	Dan Pasqua	.05
45	Jeff Robinson	.05
46	George Brett	.70
47	Bryn Smith	.05
48	Mike Marshall	.05
49	Doug Robbins	.05
50	Don Mattingly	.90
51	Mike Scott	.05
52	Steve Jeltz	.05
53	Dick Schofield	.05
54	Tom Brunansky	.05
55	Gary Sheffield	.75
56	Dave Valle	.05
57	Carney Lansford	.05
58	Tony Gwynn	.50
59	Checklist	.05
60	Damon Berryhill	.05
61	Jack Morris	.05
62	Brett Butler	.10
63	Mickey Hatcher	.05
64	Bruce Sutter	.05
65	Robin Ventura	.50
66	Junior Oritiz	.05
67	Pat Tabler	.05
68	Greg Swindell	.05
69	Jeff Branson	.10
70	Manny Lee	.05
71	Dave Magadan	.05
72	Rich Gedman	.05
73	Tim Raines	.08
74	Mike Maddux	.05
75	Jim Presley	.05
76	Chuck Finley	.05
77	Jose Oquendo	.05
78	Rob Deer	.05
79	Jay Howell	.05
80	Terry Steinbach	.05
81	Eddie Whitson	.05
82	Ruben Sierra	.08
83	Bruce Benedict	.05
84	Fred Manrique	.05
85	John Smiley	.05
86	Mike Macfarlane	.05
87	Rene Gonzales	.05
88	Charles Hudson	.05
90	Les Straker	.05
91	Carmen Castillo	.05
92	Tracy Woodson	.05
93	Tino Martinez	.65
94	Herm Winningham	.05
95	Kelly Gruber	.05
96	Terry Leach	.05
97	Jody Reed	.05
98	Nelson Santovenia	.05
99	Tony Armas	.05
100	Greg Brock	.05
101	Dave Stewart	.05
102	Roberto Alomar	.25
103	Jim Sundberg	.05
104	Albert Hall	.05
105	Steve Lyons	.05
106	Sid Bream	.05
107	Danny Tartabull	.05
108	Rick Dempsey	.05
109	Rich Renteria	.05
110	Ozzie Smith	.20
111	Steve Sax	.05
112	Kelly Downs	.05
113	Larry Sheets	.05
114	Andy Benes	.50
115	Pete O'Brien	.05
116	Kevin McReynolds	.05
117	Juan Berenguer	.05
118	Billy Hatcher	.05
119	Rick Cerone	.05
120	Andre Dawson	.08
121	Storm Davis	.05
122	Devon White	.05
123	Alan Trammell	.08
124	Vince Coleman	.05
125	Al Leiter	.05
126	Dale Sveum	.05

127	Pete Incaviglia	.05
128	Dave Stieb	.05
129	Kevin Mitchell	.08
130	Dave Schmidt	.05
131	Gary Redus	.05
132	Ron Robinson	.05
133	Darnell Coles	.05
134	Benny Santiago	.08
135	John Farrell	.05
136	Willie Wilson	.05
137	Steve Bedrosian	.05
138	Don Slaught	.05
139	Darryl Strawberry	.15
140	Frank Viola	.05
141	Dave Silvestri	.10
142	Carlos Quintana	.05
143	Vance Law	.05
144	Dave Parker	.05
145	Tim Belcher	.05
146	Will Clark	.35
147	Mark Williamson	.05
148	Ozzie Guillen	.05
149	Kirk McCaskill	.05
150	Pat Sheridan	.05
151	Terry Pendleton	.05
152	Roberto Kelly	.08
153	Joey Meyer	.05
154	Mark Grant	.05
155	Joe Carter	.10
156	Steve Buechele	.05
157	Tony Fernandez	.05
158	Jeff Reed	.05
159	Bobby Bonilla	.12
160	Henry Cotto	.05
161	Kurt Stillwell	.05
162	Mickey Morandini	.25
163	Robby Thompson	.05
164	Rick Schu	.05
165	Stan Jefferson	.05
166	Ron Darling	.05
167	Kirby Puckett	.50
168	Bill Doran	.05
169	Dennis Lamp	.05
170	Ty Griffin	.10
171	Ron Hassey	.05
172	Dale Murphy	.08
173	Andres Galarraga	.12
174	Tim Flannery	.05
175	Cory Snyder	.05
176	Checklist	.05
177	Tommy Barrett	.05
178	Dan Petry	.05
179	Billy Masse	.05
180	Terry Kennedy	.05
181	Joe Orsulak	.05
182	Doyle Alexander	.05
183	Willie McGee	.05
184	Jim Gantner	.05
185	Keith Hernandez	.05
186	Greg Gagne	.05
187	Kevin Bass	.05
188	Mark Eichhorn	.05
189	Mark Grace	.25
190	Jose Canseco	.60
191	Bobby Witt	.05
192	Rafael Santana	.05
193	Dwight Evans	.05
194	Greg Booker	.05
195	Brook Jacoby	.05
196	Rafael Belliard	.05
197	Candy Maldonado	.05
198	Mickey Tettleton	.08
199	Barry Larkin	.12
200	Frank White	.05
201	Wally Joyner	.10
202	Chet Lemon	.05
203	Joe Magrane	.05
204	Glenn Braggs	.05
205	Scott Fletcher	.05
206	Gary Ward	.05
207	Nelson Liriano	.05
208	Howard Johnson	.05
209	Kent Hrbek	.08
210	Ken Caminiti	.12
211	Mike Greenwell	.08
212	Ryne Sandberg	.50
213	Joe Slusarski	.10
214	Donnell Nixon	.05
215	Tim Wallach	.05
216	John Kruk	.05
217	Charles Nagy	.25
218	Alvin Davis	.05
219	Oswald Peraza	.05
220	Mike Schmidt	.50
221	Spike Owen	.05
222	Mike Smithson	.05

223	Dion James	.05
224	Ernie Whitt	.05
225	Mike Davis	.05
226	Gene Larkin	.05
227	Pat Combs	.25
228	Jack Howell	.05
229	Ron Oester	.05
230	Paul Gibson	.05
231	Mookie Wilson	.05
232	Glenn Hubbard	.05
233	Shawon Dunston	.05
234	Otis Nixon	.05
235	Melido Perez	.05
236	Jerry Browne	.05
237	Rick Rhoden	.05
238	Bo Jackson	.25
239	Randy Velarde	.05
240	Jack Clark	.05
241	Wade Boggs	.60
242	Lonnie Smith	.05
243	Mike Flanagan	.05
244	Willie Randolph	.05
245	Oddibe McDowell	.05
246	Ricky Jordan	.05
247	Greg Briley	.05
248	Rex Hudler	.05
249	Robin Yount	.25
250	Lance Parrish	.05
251	Chris Sabo	.05
252	Mike Henneman	.05
253	Gregg Jefferies	.15
254	Curt Young	.05
255	Andy Van Slyke	.05
256	Rod Booker	.05
257	Rafael Palmeiro	.12
258	Jose Uribe	.05
259	Ellis Burks	.15
260	John Smoltz	.10
261	Tom Foley	.05
262	Lloyd Moseby	.05
263	Jim Poole	.10
264	Gary Gaetti	.08
265	Bob Dernier	.05
266	Harold Baines	.08
267	Tom Candiotti	.05
268	Rafael Ramirez	.05
269	Bob Boone	.05
270	Buddy Bell	.05
271	Rickey Henderson	.20
272	Willie Fraser	.05
273	Eric Davis	.08
274	Jeff Robinson	.05
275	Damaso Garcia	.05
276	Sid Fernandez	.05
277	Stan Javier	.05
278	Marty Barrett	.05
279	Gerald Perry	.05
280	Rob Ducey	.05
281	Mike Scioscia	.05
282	Randy Bush	.05
283	Tom Herr	.05
284	Glenn Wilson	.05
285	Pedro Guerrero	.05
286	Cal Ripken, Jr.	.95
287	Randy Johnson	.20
288	Julio Franco	.05
289	Ivan Calderon	.05
290	Rich Yett	.05
291	Scott Servais	.10
292	Bill Pecota	.05
293	Ken Phelps	.05
294	Chili Davis	.05
295	Manny Trillo	.05
296	Mike Boddicker	.05
297	Geronimo Berroa	.05
298	Todd Stottlemyre	.05
299	Kirk Gibson	.05
300	Wally Backman	.05
301	Hubie Brooks	.05
302	Von Hayes	.05
303	Matt Nokes	.05
304	Dwight Gooden	.10
305	Walt Weiss	.05
306	Mike LaValliere	.05
307	Cris Carpenter	.10
308	Ted Wood	.05
309	Jeff Russell	.05
310	Dave Gallagher	.05
311	Andy Allanson	.05
312	Craig Reynolds	.05
313	Kevin Seitzer	.05
314	Dave Winfield	.20
315	Andy McGaffigan	.05
316	Nick Esasky	.05
317	Jeff Blauser	.05
318	George Bell	.05

319	Eddie Murray	.25
320	Mark Davidson	.05
321	Juan Samuel	.05
322	Jim Abbott	.25
323	Kal Daniels	.05
324	Mike Brumley	.05
325	Gary Carter	.10
326	Dave Henderson	.05
327	Checklist	.05
328	Garry Templeton	.05
329	Pat Perry	.05
330	Paul Molitor	.20

1989 Topps Double Headers All-Stars

This scarce test issue was produced in two versions, an All-Stars set and a set of exclusively Mets and Yankees players. The "cards" are two-sided miniature (1-5/8" x 2-1/4") reproductions of the player's 1989 Topps card and his Topps rookie card, encased in a clear plastic stand.

		MT
Complete Set (24):		45.00
Common Player:		1.00
(1)	Alan Ashby	1.00
(2)	Wade Boggs	3.00
(3)	Bobby Bonilla	2.00
(4)	Jose Canseco	3.00
(5)	Will Clark	3.00
(6)	Roger Clemens	4.00
(7)	Andre Dawson	1.50
(8)	Dennis Eckersley	1.50
(9)	Carlton Fisk	1.50
(10)	John Franco	1.00
(11)	Julio Franco	1.00
(12)	Kirk Gibson	1.00
(13)	Mike Greenwell	1.00
(14)	Orel Hershiser	1.50
(15)	Danny Jackson	1.00
(16)	Don Mattingly	6.00
(17)	Mark McGwire	6.00
(18)	Kirby Puckett	5.00
(19)	Ryne Sandberg	3.00
(20)	Ozzie Smith	3.00
(21)	Darryl Strawberry	1.50
(22)	Alan Trammell	1.00
(23)	Andy Van Slyke	1.00
(24)	Frank Viola	1.00

1989 Topps Glossy Rookies Set of 22

Bearing the same design and style of the past two years, Topps featured the top first-year players from the 1988 season in this glossy set. The full-color player photo appears beneath the "1988 Rookies" banner. The player's name is displayed beneath the photo. The flip side features the "1988 Rookies Commemorative Set" logo followed by the player ID and card number. Glossy rookies were found only in 100-card jumbo cello packs.

		MT
Complete Set (22):		7.00
Common Player:		.30
1	Roberto Alomar	1.00
2	Brady Anderson	.60
3	Tim Belcher	.30
4	Damon Berryhill	.30
5	Jay Buhner	.50
6	Kevin Elster	.30
7	Cecil Espy	.30
8	Dave Gallagher	.30
9	Ron Gant	.50
10	Paul Gibson	.30
11	Mark Grace	.80
12	Darrin Jackson	.30
13	Gregg Jefferies	.60
14	Ricky Jordan	.30
15	Al Leiter	.40
16	Melido Perez	.30
17	Chris Sabo	.30
18	Nelson Santovenia	.30
19	Mackey Sasser	.30
20	Gary Sheffield	.80
21	Walt Weiss	.40
22	David Wells	.40

1989 Topps Mini League Leaders

This 77-card set features baseball's statistical leaders from the 1988 season. It is referred to as a "mini" set because of the cards' small (2-1/8" x 3") size. The glossy cards feature action photos that have a soft focus on all edges. The player's team and name appear along the bottom of the card. The back features a head-shot of the player along with his 1988 season ranking and stats.

		MT
Complete Set (77):		4.00
Common Player:		.09
1	Dale Murphy	.15
2	Gerald Perry	.09
3	Andre Dawson	.15
4	Greg Maddux	.90
5	Rafael Palmeiro	.15
6	Tom Browning	.09
7	Kal Daniels	.09
8	Eric Davis	.12
9	John Franco	.09
10	Danny Jackson	.09
11	Barry Larkin	.25
12	Jose Rijo	.09
13	Chris Sabo	.09
14	Nolan Ryan	.90
15	Mike Scott	.09
16	Gerald Young	.09
17	Kirk Gibson	.09
18	Orel Hershiser	.15
19	Steve Sax	.09
20	John Tudor	.09
21	Hubie Brooks	.09
22	Andres Galarraga	.15
23	Otis Nixon	.09
24	Dave Cone	.12
25	Sid Fernandez	.09
26	Dwight Gooden	.12
27	Kevin McReynolds	.09
28	Darryl Strawberry	.12
29	Juan Samuel	.09
30	Bobby Bonilla	.12
31	Sid Bream	.09
32	Jim Gott	.09
33	Andy Van Slyke	.09
34	Vince Coleman	.09
35	Jose DeLeon	.09
36	Joe Magrane	.09
37	Ozzie Smith	.25
38	Todd Worrell	.09
39	Tony Gwynn	.60
40	Brett Butler	.09
41	Will Clark	.40
42	Rick Reuschel	.09
43	Checklist	.09
44	Eddie Murray	.30
45	Wade Boggs	.60
46	Roger Clemens	.45
47	Dwight Evans	.09
48	Mike Greenwell	.12
49	Bruce Hurst	.09
50	Johnny Ray	.09
51	Doug Jones	.09
52	Greg Swindell	.09
53	Gary Pettis	.09
54	George Brett	.65
55	Mark Gubicza	.09
56	Willie Wilson	.09
57	Teddy Higuera	.09
58	Paul Molitor	.25
59	Robin Yount	.30
60	Allan Anderson	.09
61	Gary Gaetti	.12
62	Kirby Puckett	.65
63	Jeff Reardon	.09
64	Frank Viola	.09
65	Jack Clark	.09
66	Rickey Henderson	.25
67	Dave Winfield	.25
68	Jose Canseco	.60
69	Dennis Eckersley	.12
70	Mark McGwire	1.50
71	Dave Stewart	.09
72	Alvin Davis	.09
73	Mark Langston	.09
74	Harold Reynolds	.09
75	George Bell	.09
76	Tony Fernandez	.09
77	Fred McGriff	.20

1990 Topps

JOEY BELLE

The 1990 Topps set again included 792 cards, and sported a newly-designed front that featured six different color schemes. The set led off with a special four-card salute to Nolan Ryan, and features other specials including All-Stars, Number 1 Draft Picks, Record Breakers, managers, rookies, and "Turn Back the Clock" cards. The set also includes a special card commemorating A. Bartlett Giamatti, the late baseball commissioner. Backs are printed in black on a chartreuse background. The set features 725 different individual player cards, the most ever, including 138 players' first appearance in a regular Topps set.

		MT
Complete Set (792):		15.00
Common Player:		.05
Wax Box:		10.00
1	Nolan Ryan	.50
2	Nolan Ryan (Mets)	.20
3	Nolan Ryan (Angels)	.20
4	Nolan Ryan (Astros)	.20
5	Nolan Ryan (Rangers)	.20
6	Vince Coleman (Record Breaker)	.05
7	Rickey Henderson (Record Breaker)	.10
8	Cal Ripken, Jr. (Record Breaker)	.40
9	Eric Plunk	.05
10	Barry Larkin	.10
11	Paul Gibson	.05
12	Joe Girardi	.05
13	Mark Williamson	.05
14	*Mike Fetters*	.10
15	Teddy Higuera	.05
16	*Kent Anderson*	.05
17	Kelly Downs	.05
18	Carlos Quintana	.05
19	Al Newman	.05
20	Mark Gubicza	.08
21	Jeff Torborg	.05
22	Bruce Ruffin	.05
23	Randy Velarde	.05
24	Joe Hesketh	.05
25	Willie Randolph	.05
26	Don Slaught	.05
27	Rick Leach	.05
28	Duane Ward	.05
29	John Cangelosi	.05
30	David Cone	.08
31	Henry Cotto	.05
32	John Farrell	.05
33	Greg Walker	.05
34	*Tony Fossas*	.05
35	Benito Santiago	.08
36	John Costello	.05
37	Domingo Ramos	.05
38	Wes Gardner	.05
39	Curt Ford	.05
40	Jay Howell	.05
41	Matt Williams	.20
42	Jeff Robinson	.05
43	Dante Bichette	.15
44	*Roger Salkeld* (#1 Draft Pick)	.25
45	Dave Parker	.08
46	Rob Dibble	.05
47	Brian Harper	.05
48	Zane Smith	.05
49	Tom Lawless	.05
50	Glenn Davis	.05
51	Doug Rader	.05
52	*Jack Daugherty*	.10
53	Mike LaCoss	.05
54	Joel Skinner	.05
55	Darrell Evans	.05
56	Franklin Stubbs	.05
57	Greg Vaughn	.05
58	Keith Miller	.05
59	Ted Power	.05
60	George Brett	.25
61	Deion Sanders	.60
62	Ramon Martinez	.10
63	Mike Pagliarulo	.05
64	Danny Darwin	.05
65	Devon White	.05
66	*Greg Litton*	.05
67	Scott Sanderson	.05
68	Dave Henderson	.05
69	Todd Frohwirth	.05
70	Mike Greenwell	.08
71	Allan Anderson	.05
72	*Jeff Huson*	.10
73	Bob Milacki	.05
74	*Jeff Jackson* (#1 Draft Pick)	.10
75	Doug Jones	.05
76	Dave Valle	.05
77	Dave Bergman	.05
78	Mike Flanagan	.05
79	Ron Kittle	.05
80	Jeff Russell	.05
81	Bob Rodgers	.05
82	Scott Terry	.05
83	Hensley Meulens	.05
84	Ray Searage	.05
85	Juan Samuel	.05
86	Paul Kilgus	.05
87	*Rick Luecken*	.10
88	Glenn Braggs	.05
89	*Clint Zavaras*	.10
90	Jack Clark	.05
91	*Steve Frey*	.10
92	Mike Stanley	.05
93	Shawn Hillegas	.05
94	Herm Winningham	.05
95	Todd Worrell	.05
96	Jody Reed	.05
97	Curt Schilling	.10
98	Jose Gonzalez	.05
99	*Rich Monteleone*	.10
100	Will Clark	.30
101	Shane Rawley	.05
102	Stan Javier	.05
103	Marvin Freeman	.05
104	Bob Knepper	.05
105	Randy Myers	.05
106	Charlie O'Brien	.05
107	Fred Lynn	.08
108	Rod Nichols	.05
109	Roberto Kelly	.08
110	Tommy Helms	.05
111	Ed Whited	.05
112	Glenn Wilson	.05
113	Manny Lee	.05
114	Mike Bielecki	.05
115	Tony Pena	.05
116	Floyd Bannister	.05
117	Mike Sharperson	.05
118	Erik Hanson	.05
119	Billy Hatcher	.05
120	John Franco	.05
121	Robin Ventura	.15
122	Shawn Abner	.05
123	Rich Gedman	.05
124	Dave Dravecky	.05
125	Kent Hrbek	.08
126	Randy Kramer	.05
127	Mike Devereaux	.05
128	Checklist 1-132	.05
129	Ron Jones	.05
130	Bert Blyleven	.05
131	Matt Nokes	.05
132	Lance Blankenship	.05
133	Ricky Horton	.05

#	Player	Price
134	*Earl Cunningham (#1 Draft Pick)*	.05
135	Dave Magadan	.05
136	Kevin Brown	.08
137	*Marty Pevey*	.08
138	Al Leiter	.05
139	Greg Brock	.05
140	Andre Dawson	.12
141	John Hart	.05
142	*Jeff Wetherby*	.05
143	Rafael Belliard	.05
144	Bud Black	.05
145	Terry Steinbach	.05
146	*Rob Richie*	.08
147	Chuck Finley	.05
148	Edgar Martinez	.10
149	Steve Farr	.05
150	Kirk Gibson	.05
151	Rick Mahler	.05
152	Lonnie Smith	.05
153	Randy Milligan	.05
154	Mike Maddux	.05
155	Ellis Burks	.12
156	Ken Patterson	.05
157	Craig Biggio	.10
158	Craig Lefferts	.05
159	Mike Felder	.05
160	Dave Righetti	.05
161	Harold Reynolds	.05
162	*Todd Zeile*	.20
163	Phil Bradley	.05
164	*Jeff Juden (#1 Draft Pick)*	.35
165	Walt Weiss	.05
166	Bobby Witt	.05
167	Kevin Appier	.12
168	Jose Lind	.05
169	Richard Dotson	.05
170	George Bell	.05
171	Russ Nixon	.05
172	Tom Lampkin	.05
173	Tim Belcher	.05
174	Jeff Kunkel	.05
175	Mike Moore	.05
176	Luis Quinones	.05
177	Mike Henneman	.05
178	Chris James	.05
179	Brian Holton	.05
180	Rock Raines	.10
181	Juan Agosto	.05
182	Mookie Wilson	.05
183	Steve Lake	.05
184	Danny Cox	.05
185	Ruben Sierra	.08
186	Dave LaPoint	.05
187	*Rick Wrona*	.05
188	Mike Smithson	.05
189	Dick Schofield	.05
190	Rick Reuschel	.05
191	Pat Borders	.05
192	Don August	.05
193	Andy Benes	.15
194	Glenallen Hill	.10
195	Tim Burke	.05
196	Gerald Young	.05
197	Doug Drabek	.05
198	Mike Marshall	.05
199	*Sergio Valdez*	.05
200	Don Mattingly	.25
201	Cito Gaston	.05
202	Mike Macfarlane	.05
203	*Mike Roesler*	.05
204	Bob Dernier	.05
205	Mark Davis	.05
206	Nick Esasky	.05
207	Bob Ojeda	.05
208	Brook Jacoby	.05
209	Greg Mathews	.05
210	Ryne Sandberg	.30
211	John Cerutti	.05
212	Joe Orsulak	.05
213	Scott Bankhead	.05
214	Terry Francona	.05
215	Kirk McCaskill	.05
216	Ricky Jordan	.05
217	Don Robinson	.05
218	Wally Backman	.05
219	Donn Pall	.05
220	Barry Bonds	.40
221	*Gary Mielke*	.10
222	Kurt Stillwell	.05
223	Tommy Gregg	.05
224	*Delino DeShields*	.25
225	Jim Deshaies	.05
226	Mickey Hatcher	.05
227	*Kevin Tapani*	.30
228	Dave Martinez	.05
229	David Wells	.05
230	Keith Hernandez	.05
231	Jack McKeon	.05
232	Darnell Coles	.05
233	Ken Hill	.25
234	Mariano Duncan	.05
235	Jeff Reardon	.05
236	Hal Morris	.15
237	Kevin Ritz	.10
238	Felix Jose	.05
239	Eric Show	.05
240	Mark Grace	.15
241	Mike Krukow	.05
242	Fred Manrique	.05
243	Barry Jones	.05
244	Bill Schroeder	.05
245	Roger Clemens	.25
246	Jim Eisenreich	.05
247	Jerry Reed	.05
248	Dave Anderson	.05
249	*Mike Smith*	.05
250	Jose Canseco	.30
251	Jeff Blauser	.05
252	Otis Nixon	.05
253	Mark Portugal	.05
254	Francisco Cabrera	.05
255	Bobby Thigpen	.05
256	Marvell Wynne	.05
257	Jose DeLeon	.05
258	Barry Lyons	.05
259	Lance McCullers	.05
260	Eric Davis	.08
261	Whitey Herzog	.05
262	Checklist 133-264	.05
263	*Mel Stottlemyre, Jr.*	.10
264	Bryan Clutterbuck	.05
265	Pete O'Brien	.05
266	German Gonzalez	.05
267	Mark Davidson	.05
268	Rob Murphy	.05
269	Dickie Thon	.05
270	Dave Stewart	.05
271	Chet Lemon	.05
272	Bryan Harvey	.05
273	Bobby Bonilla	.08
274	*Goose Gozzo*	.10
275	Mickey Tettleton	.08
276	Gary Thurman	.05
277	Lenny Harris	.05
278	Pascual Perez	.05
279	Steve Buechele	.05
280	Lou Whitaker	.05
281	Kevin Bass	.05
282	Derek Lilliquist	.05
283	Albert Belle	.50
284	*Mark Gardner*	.10
285	Willie McGee	.08
286	Lee Guetterman	.05
287	Vance Law	.05
288	Greg Briley	.05
289	Norm Charlton	.05
290	Robin Yount	.25
291	Dave Johnson	.05
292	Jim Gott	.05
293	Mike Gallego	.05
294	Craig McMurtry	.05
295	Fred McGriff	.25
296	Jeff Ballard	.05
297	Tom Herr	.05
298	Danny Gladden	.05
299	Adam Peterson	.05
300	Bo Jackson	.20
301	Don Aase	.05
302	*Marcus Lawton*	.05
303	Rick Cerone	.05
304	Marty Clary	.05
305	Eddie Murray	.20
306	Tom Niedenfuer	.05
307	Bip Roberts	.05
308	Jose Guzman	.05
309	*Eric Yelding*	.10
310	Steve Bedrosian	.05
311	Dwight Smith	.05
312	Dan Quisenberry	.05
313	Gus Polidor	.05
314	*Donald Harris (#1 Draft Pick)*	.10
315	Bruce Hurst	.05
316	Carney Lansford	.05
317	*Mark Guthrie*	.05
318	Wallace Johnson	.05
319	Dion James	.05
320	Dave Steib	.05
321	Joe M. Morgan	.05
322	Junior Ortiz	.05
323	Willie Wilson	.05
324	Pete Harnisch	.05
325	Robby Thompson	.05
326	*Tom McCarthy*	.05
327	Ken Williams	.05
328	Curt Young	.05
329	Oddibe McDowell	.05
330	Ron Darling	.05
331	*Juan Gonzalez*	2.00
332	Paul O'Neill	.08
333	Bill Wegman	.05
334	Johnny Ray	.05
335	Andy Hawkins	.05
336	Ken Griffey, Jr.	2.00
337	Lloyd McClendon	.05
338	Dennis Lamp	.05
339	Dave Clark	.05
340	Fernando Valenzuela	.08
341	Tom Foley	.05
342	Alex Trevino	.05
343	Frank Tanana	.05
344	*George Canale*	.05
345	Harold Baines	.08
346	Jim Presley	.05
347	*Junior Felix*	.05
348	*Gary Wayne*	.08
349	*Steve Finley*	.15
350	Bret Saberhagen	.08
351	Roger Craig	.05
352	Bryn Smith	.05
353	Sandy Alomar	.08
354	*Stan Belinda*	.10
355	Marty Barrett	.05
356	Randy Ready	.05
357	Dave West	.05
358	Andres Thomas	.05
359	Jimmy Jones	.05
360	Paul Molitor	.20
361	*Randy McCament*	.05
362	Damon Berryhill	.05
363	Dan Petry	.05
364	Rolando Roomes	.05
365	Ozzie Guillen	.05
366	Mike Heath	.05
367	Mike Morgan	.05
368	Bill Doran	.05
369	Todd Burns	.05
370	Tim Wallach	.05
371	Jimmy Key	.08
372	Terry Kennedy	.05
373	Alvin Davis	.05
374	*Steve Cummings*	.05
375	Dwight Evans	.05
376	Checklist 265-396	.05
377	*Mickey Weston*	.05
378	Luis Salazar	.05
379	Steve Rosenberg	.05
380	Dave Winfield	.20
381	Frank Robinson	.10
382	Jeff Musselman	.05
383	John Morris	.05
384	*Pat Combs*	.05
385	Fred McGriff (All-Star)	.15
386	Julio Franco (All-Star)	.10
387	Wade Boggs (All-Star)	.15
388	Cal Ripken, Jr. (All-Star)	.40
389	Robin Yount (All-Star)	.15
390	Ruben Sierra (All-Star)	.10
391	Kirby Puckett (All-Star)	.20
392	Carlton Fisk (All-Star)	.10
393	Bret Saberhagen (All-Star)	.10
394	Jeff Ballard (All-Star)	.05
395	Jeff Russell (All-Star)	.05
396	A. Bartlett Giamatti	.30
397	Will Clark (All-Star)	.15
398	Ryne Sandberg (All-Star)	.20
399	Howard Johnson (All-Star)	.10
400	Ozzie Smith (All-Star)	.15
401	Kevin Mitchell (All-Star)	.10
402	Eric Davis (All-Star)	.10
403	Tony Gwynn (All-Star)	.20
404	Craig Biggio (All-Star)	.10
405	Mike Scott (All-Star)	.05
406	Joe Magrane (All-Star)	.05
407	Mark Davis (All-Star)	.05
408	Trevor Wilson	.08
409	Tom Brunansky	.05
410	Joe Boever	.05
411	Ken Phelps	.05
412	Jamie Moyer	.05
413	*Brian DuBois*	.10
414a	*Frank Thomas No Name (#1 Draft Pick, no name on front)*	1600.
414b	*Frank Thomas (#1 Draft Pick, name on front)*	4.00
415	Shawon Dunston	.12
416	*Dave Johnson*	.05

No.	Player	Price
417	Jim Gantner	.05
418	Tom Browning	.05
419	*Beau Allred*	.05
420	Carlton Fisk	.08
421	Greg Minton	.05
422	Pat Sheridan	.05
423	Fred Toliver	.05
424	Jerry Reuss	.05
425	Bill Landrum	.05
426	Jeff Hamilton	.05
427	Carmem Castillo	.05
428	*Steve Davis*	.12
429	Tom Kelly	.05
430	Pete Incaviglia	.05
431	Randy Johnson	.30
432	Damaso Garcia	.05
433	*Steve Olin*	.12
434	Mark Carreon	.10
435	Kevin Seitzer	.05
436	Mel Hall	.05
437	Les Lancaster	.05
438	Greg Myers	.05
439	Jeff Parrett	.05
440	Alan Trammell	.10
441	Bob Kipper	.05
442	Jerry Browne	.05
443	Cris Carpenter	.05
444	*Kyle Abbott* (FDP)	.10
445	Danny Jackson	.05
446	Dan Pasqua	.05
447	Atlee Hammaker	.05
448	Greg Gagne	.05
449	Dennis Rasmussen	.05
450	Rickey Henderson	.20
451	Mark Lemke	.05
452	Luis de los Santos	.05
453	Jody Davis	.05
454	Jeff King	.10
455	Jeffrey Leonard	.05
456	Chris Gwynn	.05
457	Gregg Jefferies	.15
458	Bob McClure	.05
459	Jim Lefebvre	.05
460	Mike Scott	.05
461	*Carlos Martinez*	.05
462	Denny Walling	.05
463	Drew Hall	.05
464	*Jerome Walton*	.08
465	Kevin Gross	.05
466	Rance Mulliniks	.05
467	Juan Nieves	.05
468	Billy Ripken	.05
469	John Kruk	.05
470	Frank Viola	.05
471	Mike Brumley	.05
472	Jose Uribe	.05
473	Joe Price	.05
474	Rich Thompson	.05
475	Bob Welch	.05
476	Brad Komminsk	.05
477	Willie Fraser	.05
478	Mike LaValliere	.05
479	Frank White	.05
480	Sid Fernandez	.05
481	Garry Templeton	.05
482	*Steve Carter*	.05
483	Alejandro Pena	.05
484	Mike Fitzgerald	.05
485	John Candelaria	.05
486	Jeff Treadway	.05
487	Steve Searcy	.05
488	Ken Oberkfell	.05
489	Nick Leyva	.05
490	Dan Plesac	.05
491	*Dave Cochrane*	.05
492	Ron Oester	.05
493	*Jason Grimsley*	.10
494	Terry Puhl	.05
495	Lee Smith	.08
496	Cecil Espy	.05
497	Dave Schmidt	.05
498	Rick Schu	.05
499	Bill Long	.05
500	Kevin Mitchell	.08
501	Matt Young	.05
502	Mitch Webster	.05
503	Randy St. Claire	.05
504	Tom O'Malley	.05
505	Kelly Gruber	.05
506	Tom Glavine	.15
507	Gary Redus	.05
508	Terry Leach	.05
509	Tom Pagnozzi	.05
510	Dwight Gooden	.10
511	Clay Parker	.05
512	Gary Pettis	.05
513	Mark Eichhorn	.05
514	Andy Allanson	.05
515	Len Dykstra	.10
516	Tim Leary	.05
517	Roberto Alomar	.30
518	Bill Krueger	.05
519	Bucky Dent	.05
520	Mitch Williams	.05
521	Craig Worthington	.05
522	Mike Dunne	.05
523	Jay Bell	.05
524	Daryl Boston	.05
525	Wally Joyner	.10
526	Checklist 397-528	.05
527	Ron Hassey	.05
528	*Kevin Wickander*	.10
529	Greg Harris	.05
530	Mark Langston	.05
531	Ken Caminiti	.12
532	Cecilio Guante	.05
533	Tim Jones	.05
534	Louie Meadows	.05
535	John Smoltz	.15
536	*Bob Geren*	.05
537	Mark Grant	.05
538	*Billy Spiers*	.05
539	Neal Heaton	.05
540	Danny Tartabull	.08
541	Pat Perry	.05
542	Darren Daulton	.08
543	Nelson Liriano	.05
544	Dennis Boyd	.05
545	Kevin McReynolds	.05
546	Kevin Hickey	.05
547	Jack Howell	.05
548	Pat Clements	.05
549	Don Zimmer	.05
550	Julio Franco	.08
551	Tim Crews	.05
552	*Mike Smith*	.05
553	*Scott Scudder*	.05
554	Jay Buhner	.08
555	Jack Morris	.05
556	Gene Larkin	.05
557	*Jeff Innis*	.05
558	Rafael Ramirez	.05
559	Andy McGaffigan	.05
560	Steve Sax	.05
561	Ken Dayley	.05
562	Chad Kreuter	.05
563	Alex Sanchez	.05
564	*Tyler Houston* (#1 Draft Pick)	.10
565	Scott Fletcher	.05
566	Mark Knudson	.05
567	Ron Gant	.15
568	John Smiley	.05
569	Ivan Calderon	.05
570	Cal Ripken, Jr.	.50
571	Brett Butler	.10
572	Greg Harris	.05
573	Danny Heep	.05
574	Bill Swift	.05
575	Lance Parrish	.08
576	*Mike Dyer*	.05
577	Charlie Hayes	.10
578	Joe Magrane	.05
579	Art Howe	.05
580	Joe Carter	.15
581	Ken Griffey	.05
582	Rick Honeycutt	.05
583	Bruce Benedict	.05
584	*Phil Stephenson*	.05
585	Kal Daniels	.05
586	Ed Nunez	.05
587	Lance Johnson	.05
588	Rick Rhoden	.05
589	Mike Aldrete	.05
590	Ozzie Smith	.20
591	Todd Stottlemyre	.05
592	R.J. Reynolds	.05
593	Scott Bradley	.05
594	*Luis Sojo*	.05
595	Greg Swindell	.05
596	Jose DeJesus	.05
597	Chris Bosio	.05
598	Brady Anderson	.20
599	Frank Williams	.05
600	Darryl Strawberry	.12
601	Luis Rivera	.05
602	Scott Garrelts	.05
603	Tony Armas	.05
604	Ron Robinson	.05
605	Mike Scioscia	.05
606	Storm Davis	.05
607	Steve Jeltz	.05
608	*Eric Anthony*	.25
609	Sparky Anderson	.05
610	Pedro Guerrero	.05
611	Walt Terrell	.05
612	Dave Gallagher	.05
613	Jeff Pico	.05
614	Nelson Santovenia	.05
615	Rob Deer	.05
616	Brian Holman	.05
617	Geronimo Berroa	.05
618	Eddie Whitson	.05
619	Rob Ducey	.05
620	*Tony Castillo*	.05
621	Melido Perez	.05
622	Sid Bream	.05
623	Jim Corsi	.05
624	Darrin Jackson	.05
625	Roger McDowell	.05
626	Bob Melvin	.05
627	Jose Rijo	.05
628	Candy Maldonado	.05
629	Eric Hetzel	.05
630	Gary Gaetti	.08
631	*John Wetteland*	.25
632	Scott Lusader	.05
633	Dennis Cook	.05
634	Luis Polonia	.05
635	Brian Downing	.05
636	Jesse Orosco	.05
637	Craig Reynolds	.05
638	Jeff Montgomery	.05
639	Tony LaRussa	.05
640	Rick Sutcliffe	.05
641	*Doug Strange*	.05
642	Jack Armstrong	.05
643	Alfredo Griffin	.05
644	Paul Assenmacher	.05
645	Jose Oquendo	.05
646	Checklist 529-660	.05
647	Rex Hudler	.05
648	Jim Clancy	.05
649	*Dan Murphy*	.05
650	Mike Witt	.05
651	Rafael Santana	.05
652	Mike Boddicker	.05
653	John Moses	.05
654	*Paul Coleman* (#1 Draft Pick)	.10
655	Gregg Olson	.05
656	Mackey Sasser	.05
657	Terry Mulholland	.05
658	Donell Nixon	.05
659	Greg Cadaret	.05
660	Vince Coleman	.05
661	Dick Howser (Turn Back the Clock)	.05
662	Mike Schmidt (Turn Back the Clock)	.08
663	Fred Lynn (Turn Back the Clock)	.05
664	Johnny Bench (Turn Back the Clock)	.08
665	Sandy Koufax (Turn Back the Clock)	.08
666	Brian Fisher	.05
667	Curt Wilkerson	.05
668	*Joe Oliver*	.10
669	Tom Lasorda	.15
670	Dennis Eckersley	.08
671	Bob Boone	.05
672	Roy Smith	.05
673	Joey Meyer	.05
674	Spike Owen	.05
675	Jim Abbott	.10
676	Randy Kutcher	.05
677	Jay Tibbs	.05
678	Kirt Manwaring	.05
679	Gary Ward	.05
680	Howard Johnson	.05
681	Mike Schooler	.05
682	Dann Bilardello	.05
683	*Kenny Rogers*	.10
684	*Julio Machado*	.05
685	Tony Fernandez	.05
686	Carmelo Martinez	.05
687	Tim Birtsas	.05
688	Milt Thompson	.05
689	Rich Yett	.05
690	Mark McGwire	1.50
691	Chuck Cary	.05
692	*Sammy Sosa*	5.00
693	Calvin Schiraldi	.05
694	*Mike Stanton*	.05
695	Tom Henke	.05
696	B.J. Surhoff	.05
697	Mike Davis	.05
698	*Omar Vizquel*	.10
699	Jim Leyland	.05

700	Kirby Puckett	.25
701	*Bernie Williams*	1.00
702	Tony Phillips	.08
703	*Jeff Brantley*	.12
704	*Chip Hale*	.10
705	Claudell Washington	.05
706	Geno Petralli	.05
707	Luis Aquino	.05
708	Larry Sheets	.05
709	Juan Berenguer	.05
710	Von Hayes	.05
711	Rick Aguilera	.05
712	Todd Benzinger	.05
713	*Tim Drummond*	.10
714	*Marquis Grissom*	.50
715	Greg Maddux	.60
716	Steve Balboni	.05
717	Ron Kakovice	.05
718	Gary Sheffield	.20
719	*Wally Whitehurst*	.05
720	Andres Galarraga	.15
721	Lee Mazzilli	.05
722	Felix Fermin	.05
723	Jeff Robinson	.05
724	Juan Bell	.10
725	Terry Pendleton	.05
726	Gene Nelson	.05
727	Pat Tabler	.05
728	Jim Acker	.05
729	Bobby Valentine	.05
730	Tony Gwynn	.25
731	Don Carman	.05
732	Ernie Riles	.05
733	John Dopson	.05
734	Kevin Elster	.05
735	Charlie Hough	.05
736	Rick Dempsey	.05
737	Chris Sabo	.05
738	*Gene Harris*	.05
739	Dale Sveum	.05
740	Jesse Barfield	.05
741	Steve Wilson	.05
742	Ernie Whitt	.05
743	Tom Candiotti	.05
744	*Kelly Mann*	.05
745	Hubie Brooks	.05
746	Dave Smith	.05
747	Randy Bush	.05
748	Doyle Alexander	.05
749	Mark Parent	.05
750	Dale Murphy	.10
751	Steve Lyons	.05
752	Tom Gordon	.05
753	Chris Speier	.05
754	Bob Walk	.05
755	Rafael Palmeiro	.10
756	Ken Howell	.05
757	*Larry Walker*	1.00
758	Mark Thurmond	.05
759	Tom Trebelhorn	.05
760	Wade Boggs	.25
761	Mike Jackson	.05
762	Doug Dascenzo	.05
763	Denny Martinez	.08
764	Tim Teufel	.05
765	Chili Davis	.08
766	Brian Meyer	.05
767	Tracy Jones	.05
768	Chuck Crim	.05
769	*Greg Hibbard*	.08
770	Cory Snyder	.05
771	Pete Smith	.05
772	Jeff Reed	.05
773	Dave Leiper	.05
774	*Ben McDonald*	.25
775	Andy Van Slyke	.05
776	Charlie Leibrandt	.05
777	Tim Laudner	.05
778	Mike Jeffcoat	.05
779	Lloyd Moseby	.05
780	Orel Hershiser	.08
781	Mario Diaz	.05
782	Jose Alvarez	.05
783	Checklist 661-792	.05
784	Scott Bailes	.05
785	Jim Rice	.05
786	Eric King	.05
787	Rene Gonzales	.05
788	Frank DiPino	.05
789	John Wathan	.05
790	Gary Carter	.10
791	Alvaro Espinoza	.05
792	Gerald Perry	.05

1990 Topps Tiffany

This specially boxed version of Topps' 1990 baseball card set was sold through hobby channels only. The checklist is identical to the regular-issue Topps set and the cards are nearly so. The Tiffany version features white cardboard stock and a high-gloss finish on the fronts.

	MT
Complete Set (792):	95.00
Common Player:	.10
(Star cards valued at 3X-4X corresponding cards in regular Topps issue)	

1990 Topps Box Panels

This special 16-card set features four cards on four different box-bottom panels. The cards are identical in design to the regular 1990 Topps cards. The cards are designated by letter.

		MT
Complete Panel Set (4):		7.00
Complete Singles Set (16):		5.00
Common Panel:		1.25
Common Single Player:		.10
Panel		2.00
A	Wade Boggs	.30
B	George Brett	.50
C	Andre Dawson	.15
D	Darrell Evans	.10
Panel		1.25
E	Dwight Gooden	.15
F	Rickey Henderson	.25
G	Tom Lasorda	.15
H	Fred Lynn	.10
Panel		1.25
I	Mark McGwire	1.00
J	Dave Parker	.10
K	Jeff Reardon	.10
L	Rick Reuschel	.10
Panel		6.00
M	Jim Rice	.10
N	Cal Ripken, Jr.	1.50
O	Nolan Ryan	1.00
P	Ryne Sandberg	.50

1990 Topps Traded

For the first time, Topps "Traded" series cards were made available nationwide in retail wax packs. The 132-card set was also sold in complete boxed form as it has been in recent years. The wax pack traded cards feature gray backs, while the boxed set cards feature white backs. The cards are numbered 1T-132T and showcase rookies, players who changed teams and new managers.

		MT
Complete Set (132):		4.00
Common Player:		.05
1T	Darrel Akerfelds	.05
2T	Sandy Alomar, Jr.	.10
3T	Brad Arnsberg	.05
4T	Steve Avery	.15
5T	Wally Backman	.05
6T	*Carlos Baerga*	.50
7T	Kevin Bass	.05
8T	Willie Blair	.05
9T	Mike Blowers	.05
10T	Shawn Boskie	.10
11T	Daryl Boston	.05
12T	Dennis Boyd	.05
13T	Glenn Braggs	.05
14T	Hubie Brooks	.05
15T	Tom Brunansky	.05
16T	John Burkett	.20
17T	Casey Candaele	.05
18T	John Candelaria	.05
19T	Gary Carter	.10
20T	Joe Carter	.15
21T	Rick Cerone	.05
22T	Scott Coolbaugh	.05
23T	Bobby Cox	.05
24T	Mark Davis	.05
25T	Storm Davis	.05
26T	Edgar Diaz	.05
27T	Wayne Edwards	.10
28T	Mark Eichhorn	.05
29T	Scott Erickson	.20
30T	Nick Esasky	.05
31T	Cecil Fielder	.15
32T	John Franco	.05
33T	*Travis Fryman*	.35
34T	Bill Gullickson	.05
35T	Darryl Hamilton	.05
36T	Mike Harkey	.05
37T	Bud Harrelson	.05
38T	Billy Hatcher	.05
39T	Keith Hernandez	.05
40T	Joe Hesketh	.05
41T	Dave Hollins	.25
42T	Sam Horn	.05
43T	Steve Howard	.05
44T	*Todd Hundley*	.50
45T	Jeff Huson	.05
46T	Chris James	.05
47T	Stan Javier	.05
48T	*Dave Justice*	.50
49T	Jeff Kaiser	.05
50T	Dana Kiecker	.05
51T	Joe Klink	.05
52T	Brent Knackert	.05
53T	Brad Komminsk	.05
54T	Mark Langston	.05
55T	Tim Layana	.10
56T	Rick Leach	.05
57T	Terry Leach	.05
58T	Tim Leary	.05
59T	Craig Lefferts	.05
60T	Charlie Leibrandt	.05
61T	Jim Leyritz	.20
62T	Fred Lynn	.08
63T	Kevin Maas	.05
64T	Shane Mack	.08
65T	Candy Maldonado	.05
66T	Fred Manrique	.05
67T	Mike Marshall	.05
68T	Carmelo Martinez	.05
69T	John Marzano	.05
70T	Ben McDonald	.15
71T	Jack McDowell	.08
72T	John McNamara	.05
73T	Orlando Mercado	.05
74T	Stump Merrill	.05
75T	Alan Mills	.05
76T	Hal Morris	.15
77T	Lloyd Moseby	.05
78T	Randy Myers	.08
79T	Tim Naehring	.15
80T	Junior Noboa	.05
81T	Matt Nokes	.05
82T	Pete O'Brien	.05
83T	*John Olerud*	.35
84T	Greg Olson	.05
85T	Junior Ortiz	.05
86T	Dave Parker	.10

87T	Rick Parker	.15
88T	Bob Patterson	.05
89T	Alejandro Pena	.05
90T	Tony Pena	.05
91T	Pascual Perez	.05
92T	Gerald Perry	.05
93T	Dan Petry	.05
94T	Gary Pettis	.05
95T	Tony Phillips	.08
96T	Lou Pinella	.05
97T	Luis Polonia	.05
98T	Jim Presley	.05
99T	Scott Radinsky	.15
100T	Willie Randolph	.05
101T	Jeff Reardon	.05
102T	Greg Riddoch	.05
103T	Jeff Robinson	.05
104T	Ron Robinson	.05
105T	Kevin Romine	.05
106T	Scott Ruskin	.05
107T	John Russell	.05
108T	Bill Sampen	.05
109T	Juan Samuel	.05
110T	Scott Sanderson	.05
111T	Jack Savage	.05
112T	Dave Schmidt	.05
113T	Red Schoendienst	.08
114T	Terry Shumpert	.05
115T	Matt Sinatro	.05
116T	Don Slaught	.05
117T	Bryn Smith	.05
118T	Lee Smith	.08
119T	Paul Sorrento	.20
120T	Franklin Stubbs	.05
121T	Russ Swan	.05
122T	Bob Tewksbury	.10
123T	Wayne Tolleson	.05
124T	John Tudor	.05
125T	Randy Veres	.10
126T	Hector Villanueva	.05
127T	Mitch Webster	.05
128T	Ernie Whitt	.05
129T	Frank Wills	.05
130T	Dave Winfield	.20
131T	Matt Young	.05
132T	Checklist	.05

1990 Topps
Traded Tiffany

Identical to the regular Topps Traded issue except for the glossy front surface, this special hobby-only boxed set shares the same checklist.

	MT
Complete Set (132):	22.00
Common Player:	.15
(Star cards valued at 4X-6X corresponding cards in regular Topps Traded issue)	

1990 Topps
All-Star Glossy
Set of 22

One glossy All-Star card was included in each 1990 Topps rack pack. The cards measure 2-1/2" x 3-1/2" and feature a similar style to past glossy All-Star cards. Special cards of All-Star team captains Carl Yastrzemski and Don Drysdale are included in the set.

		MT
Complete Set (22):		4.00
Common Player:		.12
1	Tom Lasorda	.15
2	Will Clark	.25
3	Ryne Sandberg	.40
4	Howard Johnson	.12
5	Ozzie Smith	.40
6	Kevin Mitchell	.15
7	Eric Davis	.15
8	Tony Gwynn	.50
9	Benny Santiago	.15
10	Rick Rueschel	.12
11	Don Drysdale	.20
12	Tony LaRussa	.12
13	Mark McGwire	1.50
14	Julio Franco	.15
15	Wade Boggs	.30
16	Cal Ripken, Jr.	.90
17	Bo Jackson	.25
18	Kirby Puckett	.50
19	Ruben Sierra	.12
20	Terry Steinbach	.12
21	Dave Stewart	.12
22	Carl Yastrzemski	.20

1990 Topps
Batting Leaders

Once again produced as an exclusive insert in jumbo blister packs for K-Mart stores, the 1990 career batting leaders cards are similar in concept and design to the previous year's issue; in fact, some of the same player photos were used. The 22 cards in the set are arranged roughly in order of the players' standings in lifetime batting average. Cards fronts are bordered in bright green; backs are printed in red, white and dark green.

		MT
Complete Set (22):		18.00
Common Player:		.50
1	Wade Boggs	1.50
2	Tony Gwynn	2.00
3	Kirby Puckett	2.50
4	Don Mattingly	2.50
5	George Brett	2.00
6	Pedro Guerrero	.50
7	Tim Raines	.60
8	Paul Molitor	1.50
9	Jim Rice	.50
10	Keith Hernandez	.50
11	Julio Franco	.50
12	Carney Lansford	.50
13	Dave Parker	.50
14	Willie McGee	.50
15	Robin Yount	1.00
16	Tony Fernandez	.50
17	Eddie Murray	1.00
18	Johnny Ray	.50
19	Lonnie Smith	.50
20	Phil Bradley	.50
21	Rickey Henderson	.90
22	Kent Hrbek	.75

1990 Topps
Big Baseball

For the third consecutive year, Topps issued a 330-card set of oversized cards (2-5/8" x 3-3/4") in three 110-card series. The cards are reminiscent of Topps cards from the mid-1950s in that they feature players in portrait and action shots. The 1990 set has action photos in freeze frames. As in previous years, the cards are printed on white card stock with a glossy finish on the front. The card backs include 1989 and career hitting, fielding and pitching stats and a player cartoon.

		MT
Complete Set (330):		18.00
Common Player:		.05
1	Dwight Evans	.05
2	Kirby Puckett	.65
3	Kevin Gross	.05
4	Ron Hassey	.05
5	Lloyd McClendon	.05
6	Bo Jackson	.25
7	Lonnie Smith	.05
8	Alvaro Espinoza	.05
9	Roberto Alomar	.25
10	Glenn Braggs	.05
11	David Cone	.10
12	Claudell Washington	.05
13	Pedro Guerrero	.05
14	Todd Benzinger	.05
15	Jeff Russell	.05
16	Terry Kennedy	.05
17	Kelly Gruber	.05
18	Alfredo Griffin	.05
19	Mark Grace	.15
20	Dave Winfield	.20
21	Bret Saberhagen	.05
22	Roger Clemens	.30
23	Bob Walk	.05
24	Dave Magadan	.05
25	Spike Owen	.05
26	Jody Davis	.05
27	Kent Hrbek	.08
28	Mark McGwire	1.50

#	Name	Price	#	Name	Price	#	Name	Price	#	Name	Price
29	Eddie Murray	.30	125	Benito Santiago	.08	221	Cory Snyder	.05
30	Paul O'Neill	.08	126	Milt Thompson	.05	222	Billy Hatcher	.05
31	Jose DeLeon	.05	127	Rafael Palmeiro	.12	223	Bud Black	.05
32	Steve Lyons	.05	128	Barry Bonds	.75	224	Will Clark	.25
33	Dan Plesac	.05	129	Mike Bielecki	.05	225	Kevin Tapani	.10
34	Jack Howell	.05	130	Lou Whitaker	.05	226	Mike Pagliarulo	.05
35	Greg Briley	.05	131	Bob Ojeda	.05	227	Dave Parker	.08
36	Andy Hawkins	.05	132	Dion James	.05	228	Ben McDonald	.12
37	Cecil Espy	.05	133	Denny Martinez	.08	229	Carlos Baerga	.25
38	Rick Sutcliffe	.05	134	Fred McGriff	.25	230	Roger McDowell	.05
39	Jack Clark	.05	135	Terry Pendleton	.05	231	Delino DeShields	.10
40	Dale Murphy	.12	136	Pat Combs	.05	232	Mark Langston	.05
41	Mike Henneman	.05	137	Kevin Mitchell	.08	233	Wally Backman	.05
42	Rick Honeycutt	.05	138	Marquis Grissom	.15	234	Jim Eisenreich	.05
43	Willie Randolph	.05	139	Chris Bosio	.05	235	Mike Schooler	.05
44	Marty Barrett	.05	140	Omar Vizquel	.05	236	Kevin Bass	.05
45	Willie Wilson	.05	141	Steve Sax	.05	237	John Farrell	.05
46	Wallace Johnson	.05	142	Nelson Liriano	.05	238	Kal Daniels	.05
47	Greg Brock	.05	143	Kevin Elster	.05	239	Tony Phillips	.08
48	Tom Browning	.05	144	Dan Pasqua	.05	240	Todd Stottlemyre	.05
49	Gerald Young	.05	145	Dave Smith	.05	241	Greg Olson	.05
50	Dennis Eckersley	.08	146	Craig Worthington	.05	242	Charlie Hough	.05
51	Scott Garrelts	.05	147	Dan Gladden	.05	243	Mariano Duncan	.05
52	Gary Redus	.05	148	Oddibe McDowell	.05	244	Billy Ripken	.05
53	Al Newman	.05	149	Bip Roberts	.05	245	Joe Carter	.12
54	Darryl Boston	.05	150	Randy Ready	.05	246	Tim Belcher	.05
55	Ron Oester	.05	151	Dwight Smith	.05	247	Roberto Kelly	.05
56	Danny Tartabull	.08	152	Ed Whitson	.05	248	Candy Maldonado	.05
57	Gregg Jefferies	.12	153	George Bell	.05	249	Mike Scott	.05
58	Tom Foley	.05	154	Tim Raines	.10	250	Ken Griffey, Jr.	2.00
59	Robin Yount	.20	155	Sid Fernandez	.05	251	Nick Esasky	.05
60	Pat Borders	.05	156	Henry Cotto	.05	252	Tom Gordon	.05
61	Mike Greenwell	.08	157	Harold Baines	.08	253	John Tudor	.05
62	Shawon Dunston	.10	158	Willie McGee	.08	254	Gary Gaetti	.08
63	Steve Buechele	.05	159	Bill Doran	.05	255	Neal Heaton	.05
64	Dave Stewart	.05	160	Steve Balboni	.05	256	Jerry Browne	.05
65	Jose Oquendo	.05	161	Pete Smith	.05	257	Jose Rijo	.05
66	Ron Gant	.15	162	Frank Viola	.05	258	Mike Boddicker	.05
67	Mike Scioscia	.05	163	Gary Sheffield	.25	259	Brett Butler	.08
68	Randy Velarde	.05	164	Bill Landrum	.05	260	Andy Benes	.10
69	Charlie Hayes	.05	165	Tony Fernandez	.05	261	Kevin Brown	.08
70	Tim Wallach	.05	166	Mike Heath	.05	262	Hubie Brooks	.05
71	Eric Show	.05	167	Jody Reed	.05	263	Randy Milligan	.05
72	Eric Davis	.08	168	Wally Joyner	.08	264	John Franco	.05
73	Mike Gallego	.05	169	Robby Thompson	.05	265	Sandy Alomar	.10
74	Rob Deer	.05	170	Ken Caminiti	.10	266	Dave Valle	.05
75	Ryne Sandberg	.50	171	Nolan Ryan	1.50	267	Jerome Walton	.05
76	Kevin Seitzer	.05	172	Ricky Jordan	.05	268	Bob Boone	.05
77	Wade Boggs	.45	173	Lance Blankenship	.05	269	Ken Howell	.05
78	Greg Gagne	.05	174	Dwight Gooden	.10	270	Jose Canseco	.35
79	John Smiley	.05	175	Ruben Sierra	.08	271	Joe Magrane	.05
80	Ivan Calderon	.05	176	Carlton Fisk	.12	272	Brian DuBois	.05
81	Pete Incaviglia	.05	177	Garry Templeton	.05	273	Carlos Quintana	.05
82	Orel Hershiser	.08	178	Mike Devereaux	.05	274	Lance Johnson	.05
83	Carney Lansford	.05	179	Mookie Wilson	.05	275	Steve Bedrosian	.05
84	Mike Fitzgerald	.05	180	Jeff Blauser	.05	276	Brook Jacoby	.05
85	Don Mattingly	.75	181	Scott Bradley	.05	277	Fred Lynn	.08
86	Chet Lemon	.05	182	Luis Salazar	.05	278	Jeff Ballard	.05
87	Rolando Roomes	.05	183	Rafael Ramirez	.05	279	Otis Nixon	.05
88	Bill Spiers	.05	184	Vince Coleman	.05	280	Chili Davis	.08
89	Pat Tabler	.05	185	Doug Drabek	.05	281	Joe Oliver	.05
90	Danny Heep	.05	186	Darryl Strawberry	.10	282	Brian Holman	.05
91	Andre Dawson	.15	187	Tim Burke	.05	283	Juan Samuel	.05
92	Randy Bush	.05	188	Jesse Barfield	.05	284	Rick Aguilera	.05
93	Tony Gwynn	.30	189	Barry Larkin	.20	285	Jeff Reardon	.05
94	Tom Brunansky	.05	190	Alan Trammell	.10	286	Sammy Sosa	1.00
95	Johnny Ray	.05	191	Steve Lake	.05	287	Carmelo Martinez	.05
96	Matt Williams	.30	192	Derek Lilliquist	.05	288	Greg Swindell	.05
97	Barry Lyons	.05	193	Don Robinson	.05	289	Erik Hanson	.05
98	Jeff Hamilton	.05	194	Kevin McReynolds	.05	290	Tony Pena	.05
99	Tom Glavine	.10	195	Melido Perez	.05	291	Pascual Perez	.05
100	Ken Griffey, Sr.	.05	196	Jose Lind	.05	292	Rickey Henderson	.25
101	Tom Henke	.05	197	Eric Anthony	.05	293	Kurt Stillwell	.05
102	Dave Righetti	.05	198	B.J. Surhoff	.05	294	Todd Zeile	.15
103	Paul Molitor	.20	199	John Olerud	.25	295	Bobby Thigpen	.05
104	Mike LaValliere	.05	200	Mike Moore	.05	296	Larry Walker	.15
105	Frank White	.05	201	Mark Gubicza	.05	297	Rob Murphy	.05
106	Bob Welch	.05	202	Phil Bradley	.05	298	Mitch Webster	.05
107	Ellis Burks	.10	203	Ozzie Smith	.25	299	Devon White	.08
108	Andres Galarraga	.12	204	Greg Maddux	.90	300	Len Dykstra	.10
109	Mitch Williams	.05	205	Julio Franco	.05	301	Keith Hernandez	.05
110	Checklist	.05	206	Tom Herr	.05	302	Gene Larkin	.05
111	Craig Biggio	.08	207	Scott Fletcher	.05	303	Jeffrey Leonard	.05
112	Dave Steib	.05	208	Bobby Bonilla	.10	304	Jim Presley	.05
113	Ron Darling	.05	209	Bob Geren	.05	305	Lloyd Moseby	.05
114	Bert Blyleven	.05	210	Junior Felix	.05	306	John Smoltz	.10
115	Dickie Thon	.05	211	Dick Schofield	.05	307	Sam Horn	.05
116	Carlos Martinez	.05	212	Jim Deshaies	.05	308	Greg Litton	.05
117	Jeff King	.05	213	Jose Uribe	.05	309	Dave Henderson	.05
118	Terry Steinbach	.05	214	John Kruk	.05	310	Mark McLemore	.05
119	Frank Tanana	.05	215	Ozzie Guillen	.05	311	Gary Pettis	.05
120	Mark Lemke	.05	216	Howard Johnson	.05	312	Mark Davis	.05
121	Chris Sabo	.05	217	Andy Van Slyke	.05	313	Cecil Fielder	.15
122	Glenn Davis	.05	218	Tim Laudner	.05	314	Jack Armstrong	.05
123	Mel Hall	.05	219	Manny Lee	.05	315	Alvin Davis	.05
124	Jim Gantner	.05	220	Checklist	.05	316	Doug Jones	.05

317	Eric Yelding	.05
318	Joe Orsulak	.05
319	Chuck Finley	.05
320	Glenn Wilson	.05
321	Harold Reynolds	.05
322	Teddy Higuera	.05
323	Lance Parrish	.08
324	Bruce Hurst	.05
325	Dave West	.05
326	Kirk Gibson	.05
327	Cal Ripken, Jr.	1.75
328	Rick Reuschel	.05
329	Jim Abbott	.10
330	Checklist	.05

1990 Topps Double Headers

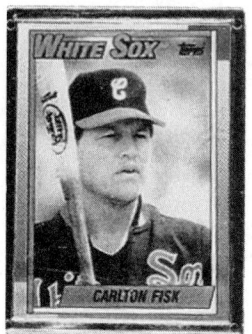

For a second (and final) year, Topps produced an issue of mini cards encased in plastic stands and marketed as Double Headers. Each piece features a 1-5/8" x 2-1/4" reproduction of the player's Topps rookie card, backed by a reproduction of his card from the regular 1990 Topps set. The size of the DH set was increased from 24 in 1989 to 72 for 1990. The novelties were sold for 50 cents apiece. The unnumbered cards are checklisted here alphabetically.

		MT
Complete Set (72):		40.00
Common Player:		.25
(1)	Jim Abbott	.35
(2)	Jeff Ballard	.25
(3)	George Bell	.25
(4)	Wade Boggs	1.00
(5)	Barry Bonds	2.00
(6)	Bobby Bonilla	.35
(7)	Ellis Burks	.35
(8)	Jose Canseco	1.50
(9)	Joe Carter	.35
(10)	Will Clark	.75
(11)	Roger Clemens	.75
(12)	Vince Coleman	.25
(13)	Alvin Davis	.25
(14)	Eric Davis	.30
(15)	Glenn Davis	.25
(16)	Mark Davis	.25
(17)	Andre Dawson	.40
(18)	Shawon Dunston	.40
(19)	Dennis Eckersley	.30
(20)	Sid Fernandez	.25
(21)	Tony Fernandez	.25
(22)	Chuck Finley	.25
(23)	Carlton Fisk	.35
(24)	Julio Franco	.30
(25)	Gary Gaetti	.25
(26)	Dwight Gooden	.30
(27)	Mark Grace	.35
(28)	Mike Greenwell	.25
(29)	Ken Griffey, Jr.	4.00
(30)	Pedro Guerrero	.25
(31)	Tony Gwynn	1.00
(32)	Von Hayes	.25
(33)	Rickey Henderson	.50
(34)	Orel Hershiser	.30

(35)	Bo Jackson	.40
(36)	Gregg Jefferies	.35
(37)	Howard Johnson	.25
(38)	Ricky Jordan	.25
(39)	Carney Lansford	.25
(40)	Barry Larkin	.35
(41)	Greg Maddux	2.50
(42)	Joe Magrane	.25
(43)	Don Mattingly	2.00
(44)	Fred McGriff	.60
(45)	Mark McGwire	3.00
(46)	Kevin McReynolds	.25
(47)	Kevin Mitchell	.30
(48)	Gregg Olson	.25
(49)	Kirby Puckett	1.50
(50)	Tim Raines	.30
(51)	Harold Reynolds	.25
(52)	Cal Ripken, Jr.	4.00
(53)	Nolan Ryan	4.00
(54)	Bret Saberhagen	.30
(55)	Ryne Sandberg	2.00
(56)	Benito Santiago	.30
(57)	Steve Sax	.25
(58)	Mike Scioscia	.25
(59)	Mike Scott	.25
(60)	Ruben Sierra	.30
(61)	Lonnie Smith	.25
(62)	Ozzie Smith	.50
(63)	Dave Stewart	.25
(64)	Darryl Strawberry	.35
(65)	Greg Swindell	.25
(66)	Alan Trammell	.30
(67)	Frank Viola	.25
(68)	Tim Wallach	.25
(69)	Jerome Walton	.25
(70)	Lou Whitaker	.25
(71)	Mitch Williams	.25
(72)	Robin Yount	.60

1990 Topps Glossy Rookies

KEN GRIFFEY, JR.

While the size of the annual glossy rookies set increased to 33 cards from previous years' issues of 22, the format remained identical in 1990. Above the player photo is a colored banner with "1989 Rookies." The player's name appears in red in a yellow bar beneath the photo. Backs are printed in red and blue and contain a shield design with the notation, "1989 Rookies Commemorative Set". The player's name, position and team are listed below, along with a card number. Cards are numbered alphabetically in the set. The glossy rookies were found one per pack in jumbo (100-card) cello packs.

		MT
Complete Set (33):		12.00
Common Player:		.25
1	Jim Abbott	.35
2	Joey Belle	1.00

3	Andy Benes	.35
4	Greg Briley	.25
5	Kevin Brown	.25
6	Mark Carreon	.35
7	Mike Devereaux	.25
8	Junior Felix	.25
9	Bob Geren	.25
10	Tom Gordon	.30
11	Ken Griffey, Jr.	3.00
12	Pete Harnisch	.30
13	Greg W. Harris	.25
14	Greg Hibbard	.25
15	Ken Hill	.40
16	Gregg Jefferies	.45
17	Jeff King	.35
18	Derek Lilliquist	.25
19	Carlos Martinez	.25
20	Ramon Martinez	.35
21	Bob Milacki	.25
22	Gregg Olson	.25
23	Donn Pall	.25
24	Kenny Rogers	.25
25	Gary Sheffield	.50
26	Dwight Smith	.25
27	Billy Spiers	.25
28	Omar Vizquel	.30
29	Jerome Walton	.25
30	Dave West	.25
31	John Wetteland	.35
32	Steve Wilson	.25
33	Craig Worthington	.25

1990 Topps Mini League Leaders

NOLAN RYAN

The last in a five-year string of mini cards, the 1990 league leaders' set offers players who were in the top five in major batting and pitching stats during the 1989 season. Fronts of the 2-1/8" x 3" cards mimic the regular Topps' design for 1990; featuring an action photo with multi-colored borders. Backs offer a round player portrait photo and information about the statistical achievement, all printed in full color. Cards are numbered alphabetically within teams. The 1990 minis are considerably scarcer than the previous years' offerings.

		MT
Complete Set (88):		15.00
Common Player:		.10
1	Jeff Ballard	.10
2	Phil Bradley	.10
3	Wade Boggs	.50
4	Roger Clemens	.75
5	Nick Esasky	.10
6	Jody Reed	.10
7	Bert Blyleven	.10
8	Chuck Finley	.10
9	Kirk McCaskill	.10

10	Devon White	.10
11	Ivan Calderon	.10
12	Bobby Thigpen	.10
13	Joe Carter	.15
14	Gary Pettis	.10
15	Tom Gordon	.10
16	Bo Jackson	.25
17	Bret Saberhagen	.12
18	Kevin Seitzer	.10
19	Chris Bosio	.10
20	Paul Molitor	.50
21	Dan Plesac	.10
22	Robin Yount	.50
23	Kirby Puckett	1.00
24	Don Mattingly	1.00
25	Steve Sax	.10
26	Storm Davis	.10
27	Dennis Eckersley	.12
28	Rickey Henderson	.25
29	Carney Lansford	.10
30	Mark McGwire	1.50
31	Mike Moore	.10
32	Dave Stewart	.10
33	Alvin Davis	.10
34	Harold Reynolds	.10
35	Mike Schooler	.10
36	Cecil Espy	.10
37	Julio Franco	.12
38	Jeff Russell	.10
39	Nolan Ryan	2.00
40	Ruben Sierra	.12
41	George Bell	.10
42	Tony Fernandez	.10
43	Fred McGriff	.25
44	Dave Steib	.10
45	Checklist	.05
46	Lonnie Smith	.10
47	John Smoltz	.15
48	Mike Bielecki	.10
49	Mark Grace	.25
50	Greg Maddux	1.50
51	Ryne Sandberg	.75
52	Mitch Williams	.10
53	Eric Davis	.15
54	John Franco	.10
55	Glenn Davis	.10
56	Mike Scott	.10
57	Tim Belcher	.10
58	Orel Hershiser	.15
59	Jay Howell	.10
60	Eddie Murray	.30
61	Tim Burke	.10
62	Mark Langston	.10
63	Tim Raines	.12
64	Tim Wallach	.10
65	David Cone	.12
66	Sid Fernandez	.10
67	Howard Johnson	.10
68	Juan Samuel	.10
69	Von Hayes	.10
70	Barry Bonds	1.00
71	Bobby Bonilla	.12
72	Andy Van Slyke	.10
73	Vince Coleman	.10
74	Jose DeLeon	.10
75	Pedro Guerrero	.10
76	Joe Magrane	.10
77	Roberto Alomar	.25
78	Jack Clark	.10
79	Mark Davis	.10
80	Tony Gwynn	.65
81	Bruce Hurst	.10
82	Eddie Whitson	.10
83	Brett Butler	.15
84	Will Clark	.25
85	Scott Garrelts	.10
86	Kevin Mitchell	.12
87	Rick Reuschel	.10
88	Robby Thompson	.10

1990 Topps 1989 Major League Debut

This 150-card set chronicles the debut date of all 1989 Major League rookies. Two checklist cards are also included in this boxed set, listing the players in order of debut date, though the cards are numbered alphabetically. The card fronts resemble the 1990 Topps cards in style. A debut banner appears in an upper corner. The flip sides are horizontal and are printed in black on yellow stock, providing an overview of the player's first game. The set is packaged in a special collectors box and was only available through hobby dealers.

SEPTEMBER 1, 1989
MAJOR LEAGUE DEBUT

MIKE BLOWERS

		MT
Complete Set (150):		18.00
Common Player:		.10
1	Jim Abbott	.30
2	Beau Allred	.10
3	Wilson Alvarez	.25
4	Kent Anderson	.10
5	Eric Anthony	.12
6	Kevin Appier	.20
7	Larry Arndt	.10
8	John Barfield	.10
9	Billy Bates	.10
10	Kevin Batiste	.10
11	Blaine Beatty	.10
12	Stan Belinda	.10
13	Juan Bell	.10
14	Joey Belle	2.00
15	Andy Benes	.30
16	Mike Benjamin	.10
17	Geronimo Berroa	.10
18	Mike Blowers	.10
19	Brian Brady	.10
20	Francisco Cabrera	.10
21	George Canale	.10
22	Jose Cano	.10
23	Steve Carter	.10
24	Pat Combs	.10
25	Scott Coolbaugh	.10
26	Steve Cummings	.10
27	Pete Dalena	.10
28	Jeff Datz	.10
29	Bobby Davidson	.10
30	Drew Denson	.10
31	Gary DiSarcina	.15
32	Brian DuBois	.10
33	Mike Dyer	.10
34	Wayne Edwards	.10
35	Junior Felix	.10
36	Mike Fetters	.10
37	Steve Finley	.25
38	Darren Fletcher	.25
39	LaVel Freeman	.10
40	Steve Frey	.10
41	Mark Gardner	.10
42	Joe Girardi	.20
43	Juan Gonzalez	3.00
44	Goose Gozzo	.10
45	Tommy Greene	.15
46	Ken Griffey, Jr.	5.00
47	Jason Grimsley	.10
48	Marquis Grissom	.75
49	Mark Guthrie	.10
50	Chip Hale	.10
51	John Hardy	.10
52	Gene Harris	.10
53	Mike Hartley	.10
54	Scott Hemond	.10
55	Xavier Hernandez	.10
56	Eric Hetzel	.10

57	Greg Hibbard	.10
58	Mark Higgins	.10
59	Glenallen Hill	.15
60	Chris Hoiles	.15
61	Shawn Holman	.10
62	Dann Howitt	.10
63	Mike Huff	.10
64	Terry Jorgenson	.10
65	Dave Justice	2.00
66	Jeff King	.20
67	Matt Kinzer	.10
68	Joe Kraemer	.10
69	Marcus Lawton	.10
70	Derek Lilliquist	.10
71	Scott Little	.10
72	Greg Litton	.10
73	Rick Lueken	.10
74	Julio Machado	.10
75	Tom Magrann	.10
76	Kelly Mann	.10
77	Randy McCament	.10
78	Ben McDonald	.25
79	Chuck McElroy	.10
80	Jeff McKnight	.10
81	Kent Mercker	.10
82	Matt Merullo	.10
83	Hensley Meulens	.10
84	Kevin Mmahat	.10
85	Mike Munoz	.10
86	Dan Murphy	.10
87	Jaime Navarro	.15
88	Randy Nosek	.10
89	John Olerud	.50
90	Steve Olin	.10
91	Joe Oliver	.12
92	Francisco Oliveras	.10
93	Greg Olson	.10
94	John Orton	.10
95	Dean Palmer	.20
96	Ramon Pena	.10
97	Jeff Peterek	.10
98	Marty Pevey	.10
99	Rusty Richards	.10
100	Jeff Richardson	.10
101	Rob Richie	.10
102	Kevin Ritz	.10
103	Rosario Rodriguez	.10
104	Mike Roesler	.10
105	Kenny Rogers	.15
106	Bobby Rose	.10
107	Alex Sanchez	.10
108	Deion Sanders	.60
109	Jeff Schaefer	.10
110	Jeff Schulz	.10
111	Mike Schwabe	.10
112	Dick Scott	.10
113	Scott Scudder	.10
114	Rudy Seanez	.10
115	Joe Skalski	.10
116	Dwight Smith	.10
117	Greg Smith	.10
118	Mike Smith	.10
119	Paul Sorrento	.15
120	Sammy Sosa	20.00
121	Billy Spiers	.10
122	Mike Stanton	.10
123	Phil Stephenson	.10
124	Doug Strange	.10
125	Russ Swan	.10
126	Kevin Tapani	.25
127	Stu Tate	.10
128	Greg Vaughn	.30
129	Robin Ventura	.40
130	Randy Veres	.10
131	Jose Vizcaino	.15
132	Omar Vizquel	.15
133	Larry Walker	1.00
134	Jerome Walton	.10
135	Gary Wayne	.10
136	Lenny Webster	.10
137	Mickey Weston	.10
138	Jeff Wetherby	.10
139	John Wetteland	.20
140	Ed Whited	.10
141	Wally Whitehurst	.10
142	Kevin Wickander	.10
143	Dean Wilkins	.10
144	Dana Williams	.10
145	Paul Wilmet	.10
146	Craig Wilson	.10
147	Matt Winters	.10
148	Eric Yelding	.10
149	Clint Zavaras	.10
150	Todd Zeile	.25
----	Checklist (1 of 2)	.05
----	Checklist (2 of 2)	.05

1991 Topps

Topps celebrated its 40th anniversary in 1991 with the biggest promotional campaign in baseball card history. More than 300,000 vintage Topps cards (or certificates redeemable for valuable older cards) produced from 1952 to 1990 were randomly inserted in packs. Also a grand prize winner received a complete set from each year, and others received a single set from 1952-1990. The 1991 Topps card fronts feature the "Topps 40 Years of Baseball" logo in the upper-left corner. Colored borders frame the player photos. All players of the same team have cards with the same frame/border colors. Both action and posed shots appear in full-color on the card fronts. The flip sides are printed horizontally and feature complete statistics. Record Breakers and other special cards were once again included in the set. The cards measure 2-1/2" x 3-1/2".

		MT
Complete Set (792):		15.00
Common Player:		.05
Wax Box:		9.00
1	Nolan Ryan	.40
2	George Brett (Record Breaker)	.15
3	Carlton Fisk (Record Breaker)	.05
4	Kevin Maas (Record Breaker)	.05
5	Cal Ripken, Jr. (Record Breaker)	.50
6	Nolan Ryan (Record Breaker)	.25
7	Ryne Sandberg (Record Breaker)	.10
8	Bobby Thigpen (Record Breaker)	.05
9	Darrin Fletcher	.10
10	Gregg Olson	.05
11	Roberto Kelly	.05
12	Paul Assenmacher	.05
13	Mariano Duncan	.05
14	Dennis Lamp	.05
15	Von Hayes	.05
16	Mike Heath	.05
17	Jeff Brantley	.05
18	Nelson Liriano	.05
19	Jeff Robinson	.05
20	Pedro Guerrero	.05
21	Joe M. Morgan	.05
22	Storm Davis	.05
23	Jim Gantner	.05
24	Dave Martinez	.05
25	Tim Belcher	.05
26	Luis Sojo	.05
27	Bobby Witt	.05
28	Alvaro Espinoza	.05
29	Bob Walk	.05
30	Gregg Jefferies	.15
31	Colby Ward	.05
32	Mike Simms	.05
33	Barry Jones	.05
34	Atlee Hammaker	.05
35	Greg Maddux	.75
36	Donnie Hill	.05
37	Tom Bolton	.05
38	Scott Bradley	.05
39	Jim Neidlinger	.10
40	Kevin Mitchell	.08
41	Ken Dayley	.05
42a	Chris Hoiles (white inner photo frame)	.20
42b	Chris Hoiles (gray inner photo frame)	.20
43	Roger McDowell	.05
44	Mike Felder	.05
45	Chris Sabo	.05
46	Tim Drummond	.05
47	Brook Jacoby	.05
48	Dennis Boyd	.05
49a	Pat Borders (40 stolen bases in Kinston 1986)	.20
49b	Pat Borders (0 stolen bases in Kinston 1986)	.10
50	Bob Welch	.05
51	Art Howe	.05
52	Francisco Oliveras	.05
53	Mike Sharperson	.05
54	Gary Mielke	.05
55	Jeffrey Leonard	.05
56	Jeff Parrett	.05
57	Jack Howell	.05
58	Mel Stottlemyre	.05
59	Eric Yelding	.05
60	Frank Viola	.05
61	Stan Javier	.05
62	Lee Guetterman	.05
63	Milt Thompson	.05
64	Tom Herr	.05
65	Bruce Hurst	.05
66	Terry Kennedy	.05
67	Rick Honeycutt	.05
68	Gary Sheffield	.20
69	Steve Wilson	.05
70	Ellis Burks	.12
71	Jim Acker	.05
72	Junior Ortiz	.05
73	Craig Worthington	.05
74	Shane Andrews (#1 Draft Pick)	.20
75	Jack Morris	.05
76	Jerry Browne	.05
77	Drew Hall	.05
78	Geno Petralli	.05
79	Frank Thomas	1.50
80a	Fernando Valenzuela (no diamond after 104 ER in 1990)	.25
80b	Fernando Valenzuela (diamond after 104 ER in 1990)	.10
81	Cito Gaston	.05
82	Tom Glavine	.12
83	Daryl Boston	.05
84	Bob McClure	.05
85	Jesse Barfield	.05
86	Les Lancaster	.05
87	Tracy Jones	.05
88	Bob Tewksbury	.05
89	Darren Daulton	.08
90	Danny Tartabull	.05
91	Greg Colbrunn (Future Star)	.10
92	Danny Jackson	.05
93	Ivan Calderon	.05
94	John Dopson	.05
95	Paul Molitor	.15
96	Trevor Wilson	.05
97a	Brady Anderson (3H, 2RBI in Sept. scoreboard)	.25
97b	Brady Anderson (14H, 3 RBI in Sept. scoreboard)	.15
98	Sergio Valdez	.05
99	Chris Gwynn	.05
100a	Don Mattingly (10 hits 1990)	.60
100b	Don Mattingly (101 hits in 1990)	.45
101	Rob Ducey	.05
102	Gene Larkin	.05
103	Tim Costo (#1 Draft Pick)	.10
104	Don Robinson	.05
105	Kevin McReynolds	.05
106	Ed Nunez	.05
107	Luis Polonia	.05
108	Matt Young	.05
109	Greg Riddoch	.05
110	Tom Henke	.05
111	Andres Thomas	.05
112	Frank DiPino	.05
113	Carl Everett (#1 Draft Pick)	.20
114	Lance Dickson (Future Star)	.10
115	Hubie Brooks	.05
116	Mark Davis	.05
117	Dion James	.05
118	Tom Edens	.05
119	Carl Nichols	.05
120	Joe Carter	.10
121	Eric King	.05
122	Paul O'Neill	.08
123	Greg Harris	.05
124	Randy Bush	.05
125	Steve Bedrosian	.05
126	Bernard Gilkey	.20
127	Joe Price	.05
128	Travis Fryman	.10
129	Mark Eichhorn	.05
130	Ozzie Smith	.20
131a	Checklist 1 (Phil Bradley #727)	.05
131b	Checklist 1 (Phil Bradley #717)	.05
132	Jamie Quirk	.05
133	Greg Briley	.05
134	Kevin Elster	.05
135	Jerome Walton	.05
136	Dave Schmidt	.05
137	Randy Ready	.05
138	Jamie Moyer	.05
139	Jeff Treadway	.05
140	Fred McGriff	.15
141	Nick Leyva	.05
142	Curtis Wilkerson	.05
143	John Smiley	.05
144	Dave Henderson	.05
145	Lou Whitaker	.05
146	Dan Plesac	.05
147	Carlos Baerga	.15
148	Rey Palacios	.05
149	Al Osuna	.05
150	Cal Ripken, Jr.	.75
151	Tom Browning	.05
152	Mickey Hatcher	.05
153	Bryan Harvey	.05
154	Jay Buhner	.08
155a	Dwight Evans (diamond after 162 G 1982)	.10
155b	Dwight Evans (no diamond after 162 G 1982)	.05
156	Carlos Martinez	.05
157	John Smoltz	.08
158	Jose Uribe	.05
159	Joe Boever	.05
160	Vince Coleman	.05
161	Tim Leary	.05
162	Ozzie Canseco	.08
163	Dave Johnson	.05
164	Edgar Diaz	.05
165	Sandy Alomar	.08
166	Harold Baines	.08
167a	Randy Tomlin ("Harriburg" 1989-90)	.10
167b	Randy Tomlin ("Harrisburg" 1989-90)	.05
168	John Olerud	.15
169	Luis Aquino	.05
170	Carlton Fisk	.10
171	Tony LaRussa	.05
172	Pete Incaviglia	.05
173	Jason Grimsley	.05
174	Ken Caminiti	.10
175	Jack Armstrong	.05
176	John Orton	.05
177	Reggie Harris	.10
178	Dave Valle	.05
179	Pete Harnisch	.05
180	Tony Gwynn	.25
181	Duane Ward	.05
182	Junior Noboa	.05
183	Clay Parker	.05
184	Gary Green	.05
185	Joe Magrane	.05
186	Rod Booker	.05
187	Greg Cadaret	.05
188	Damon Berryhill	.05
189	Daryl Irvine	.10
190	Matt Williams	.15

#	Player	Value
191	*Willie Blair*	.10
192	Rob Deer	.05
193	Felix Fermin	.05
194	Xavier Hernandez	.08
195	Wally Joyner	.08
196	*Jim Vatcher*	.05
197	*Chris Nabholz*	.08
198	R.J. Reynolds	.05
199	Mike Hartley	.05
200	Darryl Strawberry	.10
201	Tom Kelly	.05
202	*Jim Leyritz*	.15
203	Gene Harris	.05
204	Herm Winningham	.05
205	*Mike Perez*	.08
206	Carlos Quintana	.05
207	Gary Wayne	.05
208	Willie Wilson	.05
209	Ken Howell	.05
210	Lance Parrish	.08
211	Brian Barnes (Future Star)	.10
212	Steve Finley	.05
213	Frank Wills	.05
214	Joe Girardi	.05
215	Dave Smith	.05
216	Greg Gagne	.05
217	Chris Bosio	.05
218	*Rick Parker*	.08
219	Jack McDowell	.05
220	Tim Wallach	.05
221	Don Slaught	.05
222	*Brian McRae*	.25
223	Allan Anderson	.05
224	Juan Gonzalez	.60
225	Randy Johnson	.20
226	Alfredo Griffin	.05
227	Steve Avery	.08
228	Rex Hudler	.05
229	Rance Mulliniks	.05
230	Sid Fernandez	.05
231	Doug Rader	.05
232	Jose DeJesus	.05
233	Al Leiter	.05
234	*Scott Erickson*	.10
235	Dave Parker	.10
236a	Frank Tanana (no diamond after 269 SO 1975)	.10
236b	Frank Tanana (diamond after 269 SO 1975)	.05
237	Rick Cerone	.05
238	Mike Dunne	.05
239	*Darren Lewis*	.25
240	Mike Scott	.05
241	Dave Clark	.05
242	Mike LaCoss	.05
243	Lance Johnson	.05
244	Mike Jeffcoat	.05
245	Kal Daniels	.05
246	Kevin Wickander	.05
247	Jody Reed	.05
248	Tom Gordon	.05
249	Bob Melvin	.05
250	Dennis Eckersley	.08
251	Mark Lemke	.05
252	*Mel Rojas*	.10
253	Garry Templeton	.05
254	*Shawn Boskie*	.10
255	Brian Downing	.05
256	Greg Hibbard	.05
257	Tom O'Malley	.05
258	Chris Hammond	.10
259	Hensley Meulens	.05
260	Harold Reynolds	.05
261	Bud Harrelson	.05
262	Tim Jones	.05
263	Checklist 2	.05
264	*Dave Hollins*	.25
265	Mark Gubicza	.05
266	Carmen Castillo	.05
267	Mark Knudson	.05
268	Tom Brookens	.05
269	Joe Hesketh	.05
270a	Mark McGwire (1987 SLG .618)	1.50
270b	Mark McGwire (1987 SLG 618)	1.50
271	*Omar Olivares*	.10
272	Jeff King	.05
273	Johnny Ray	.05
274	Ken Williams	.05
275	Alan Trammell	.08
276	Bill Swift	.05
277	Scott Coolbaugh	.05
278	*Alex Fernandez* (#1 Draft Pick)	.25
279a	Jose Gonzalez (photo of Billy Bean, left-handed batter)	.15
279b	Jose Gonzalez (correct photo, right-handed batter)	.10
280	Bret Saberhagen	.05
281	Larry Sheets	.05
282	Don Carman	.05
283	Marquis Grissom	.10
284	Bill Spiers	.05
285	Jim Abbott	.08
286	Ken Oberkfell	.05
287	Mark Grant	.05
288	Derrick May	.10
289	Tim Birtsas	.05
290	Steve Sax	.05
291	John Wathan	.05
292	Bud Black	.05
293	Jay Bell	.05
294	Mike Moore	.05
295	Rafael Palmeiro	.15
296	Mark Williamson	.05
297	Manny Lee	.05
298	Omar Vizquel	.05
299	*Scott Radinsky*	.15
300	Kirby Puckett	.25
301	Steve Farr	.05
302	Tim Teufel	.05
303	Mike Boddicker	.05
304	Kevin Reimer	.05
305	Mike Scioscia	.05
306a	Lonnie Smith (136 G 1990)	.10
306b	Lonnie Smith (135 G 1990)	.05
307	Andy Benes	.08
308	Tom Pagnozzi	.05
309	Norm Charlton	.05
310	Gary Carter	.08
311	Jeff Pico	.05
312	Charlie Hayes	.05
313	Ron Robinson	.05
314	Gary Pettis	.05
315	Roberto Alomar	.25
316	Gene Nelson	.05
317	Mike Fitzgerald	.05
318	Rick Aguilera	.05
319	Jeff McKnight	.05
320	Tony Fernandez	.05
321	Bob Rodgers	.05
322	*Terry Shumpert*	.05
323	Cory Snyder	.05
324a	Ron Kittle ("6 Home Runs" in career summary)	.10
324b	Ron Kittle ("7 Home Runs" in career summary)	.05
325	Brett Butler	.08
326	Ken Patterson	.05
327	Ron Hassey	.05
328	Walt Terrell	.05
329	Dave Justice	.25
330	Dwight Gooden	.10
331	Eric Anthony	.05
332	Kenny Rogers	.05
333	*Chipper Jones* (#1 Draft Pick)	2.50
334	Todd Benzinger	.05
335	Mitch Williams	.05
336	Matt Nokes	.05
337a	Keith Comstock (Mariners logo)	.05
337b	Keith Comstock (Cubs logo)	.10
338	Luis Rivera	.05
339	Larry Walker	.20
340	Ramon Martinez	.08
341	John Moses	.05
342	*Mickey Morandini*	.10
343	Jose Oquendo	.05
344	Jeff Russell	.05
345	Len Dykstra	.10
346	Jesse Orosco	.05
347	Greg Vaughn	.05
348	Todd Stottlemyre	.05
349	Dave Gallagher	.05
350	Glenn Davis	.05
351	Joe Torre	.05
352	Frank White	.05
353	Tony Castillo	.05
354	Sid Bream	.05
355	Chili Davis	.05
356	Mike Marshall	.05
357	Jack Savage	.05
358	Mark Parent	.05
359	Chuck Cary	.05
360	Tim Raines	.10
361	Scott Garrelts	.05
362	*Hector Villanueva*	.05
363	Rick Mahler	.05
364	Dan Pasqua	.05
365	Mike Schooler	.05
366a	Checklist 3 (Carl Nichols #19)	.05
366b	Checklist 3 (Carl Nichols #119)	.05
367	*Dave Walsh*	.05
368	Felix Jose	.05
369	Steve Searcy	.05
370	Kelly Gruber	.05
371	Jeff Montgomery	.05
372	Spike Owen	.05
373	Darrin Jackson	.05
374	*Larry Casian*	.10
375	Tony Pena	.05
376	Mike Harkey	.05
377	Rene Gonzales	.05
378a	*Wilson Alvarez* (no 1989 Port Charlotte stats)	.30
378b	*Wilson Alvarez* (1989 Port Charlotte stats)	.20
379	Randy Velarde	.05
380	Willie McGee	.08
381	Jim Leyland	.05
382	Mackey Sasser	.05
383	Pete Smith	.05
384	Gerald Perry	.05
385	Mickey Tettleton	.05
386	Cecil Fielder (All-Star)	.08
387	Julio Franco (All-Star)	.05
388	Kelly Gruber (All-Star)	.05
389	Alan Trammell (All-Star)	.05
390	Jose Canseco (All-Star)	.10
391	Rickey Henderson (All-Star)	.10
392	Ken Griffey, Jr. (All-Star)	.40
393	Carlton Fisk (All-Star)	.08
394	Bob Welch (All-Star)	.05
395	Chuck Finley (All-Star)	.05
396	Bobby Thigpen (All-Star)	.05
397	Eddie Murray (All-Star)	.08
398	Ryne Sandberg (All-Star)	.10
399	Matt Williams (All-Star)	.08
400	Barry Larkin (All-Star)	.08
401	Barry Bonds (All-Star)	.15
402	Darryl Strawberry (All-Star)	.08
403	Bobby Bonilla (All-Star)	.05
404	Mike Scoscia (All-Star)	.05
405	Doug Drabek (All-Star)	.05
406	Frank Viola (All-Star)	.05
407	John Franco (All-Star)	.05
408	Ernie Riles	.05
409	Mike Stanley	.05
410	Dave Righetti	.05
411	Lance Blankenship	.05
412	Dave Bergman	.05
413	Terry Mulholland	.05
414	Sammy Sosa	.75
415	Rick Sutcliffe	.05
416	Randy Milligan	.05
417	Bill Krueger	.05
418	Nick Esasky	.05
419	Jeff Reed	.05
420	Bobby Thigpen	.05
421	Alex Cole	.05
422	Rick Rueschel	.05
423	Rafael Ramirez	.05
424	Calvin Schiraldi	.05
425	Andy Van Slyke	.05
426	*Joe Grahe*	.10
427	Rick Dempsey	.05
428	*John Barfield*	.05
429	Stump Merrill	.05
430	Gary Gaetti	.08
431	Paul Gibson	.05
432	Delino DeShields	.05
433	Pat Tabler	.05
434	Julio Machado	.05
435	Kevin Maas	.05
436	Scott Bankhead	.05
437	Doug Dascenzo	.05
438	Vicente Palacios	.05
439	Dickie Thon	.05
440	George Bell	.05
441	Zane Smith	.05
442	Charlie O'Brien	.05
443	Jeff Innis	.05
444	Glenn Braggs	.05
445	Greg Swindell	.05
446	*Craig Grebeck*	.05
447	John Burkett	.05
448	Craig Lefferts	.05
449	Juan Berenguer	.05
450	Wade Boggs	.20
451	Neal Heaton	.05
452	Bill Schroeder	.05
453	Lenny Harris	.05

No.	Name	Price
454a	Kevin Appier (no 1990 Omaha stats)	.20
454b	Kevin Appier (1990 Omaha stats)	.10
455	Walt Weiss	.05
456	Charlie Leibrandt	.05
457	Todd Hundley	.12
458	Brian Holman	.05
459	Tom Trebelhorn	.05
460	Dave Steib	.05
461a	Robin Ventura (gray inner photo frame at left)	.15
461b	Robin Ventura (red inner photo frame at left)	.15
462	Steve Frey	.05
463	Dwight Smith	.05
464	Steve Buechele	.05
465	Ken Griffey	.05
466	Charles Nagy	.10
467	Dennis Cook	.05
468	Tim Hulett	.05
469	Chet Lemon	.05
470	Howard Johnson	.05
471	*Mike Lieberthal* (#1 Draft Pick)	.20
472	Kirt Manwaring	.05
473	Curt Young	.05
474	*Phil Plantier*	.20
475	Teddy Higuera	.05
476	Glenn Wilson	.05
477	Mike Fetters	.05
478	Kurt Stillwell	.05
479	Bob Patterson	.05
480	Dave Magadan	.05
481	Eddie Whitson	.05
482	Tino Martinez	.15
483	Mike Aldrete	.05
484	Dave LaPoint	.05
485	Terry Pendleton	.05
486	Tommy Greene	.10
487	Rafael Belliard	.05
488	Jeff Manto	.10
489	Bobby Valentine	.05
490	Kirk Gibson	.05
491	*Kurt Miller* (#1 Draft Pick)	.15
492	Ernie Whitt	.05
493	Jose Rijo	.05
494	Chris James	.05
495	Charlie Hough	.05
496	Marty Barrett	.05
497	Ben McDonald	.08
498	Mark Salas	.05
499	Melido Perez	.05
500	Will Clark	.20
501	Mike Bielecki	.05
502	Carney Lansford	.05
503	Roy Smith	.05
504	*Julio Valera*	.05
505	Chuck Finley	.05
506	Darnell Coles	.05
507	Steve Jeltz	.05
508	*Mike York*	.05
509	Glenallen Hill	.05
510	John Franco	.05
511	Steve Balboni	.05
512	Jose Mesa	.08
513	Jerald Clark	.05
514	Mike Stanton	.05
515	Alvin Davis	.05
516	*Karl Rhodes*	.10
517	Joe Oliver	.05
518	Cris Carpenter	.05
519	Sparky Anderson	.08
520	Mark Grace	.15
521	Joe Orsulak	.05
522	Stan Belinda	.05
523	*Rodney McCray*	.05
524	Darrel Akerfelds	.05
525	Willie Randolph	.05
526a	Moises Alou (37 R 1990 Pirates)	.20
526b	Moises Alou (0 R 1990 Pirates)	.10
527a	Checklist 4 (Kevin McReynolds #719)	.05
527b	Checklist 4 (Kevin McReynolds #105)	.05
528	Denny Martinez	.08
529	*Mark Newfield* (#1 Draft Pick)	.15
530	Roger Clemens	.25
531	*Dave Rhode*	.10
532	Kirk McCaskill	.05
533	Oddibe McDowell	.05
534	Mike Jackson	.05
535	Ruben Sierra	.08
536	Mike Witt	.05
537	Jose Lind	.05
538	Bip Roberts	.05
539	Scott Terry	.05
540	George Brett	.20
541	Domingo Ramos	.05
542	Rob Murphy	.05
543	Junior Felix	.05
544	Alejandro Pena	.05
545	Dale Murphy	.10
546	Jeff Ballard	.05
547	Mike Pagliarulo	.05
548	Jaime Navarro	.05
549	John McNamara	.05
550	Eric Davis	.08
551	Bob Kipper	.05
552	Jeff Hamilton	.05
553	*Joe Klink*	.08
554	Brian Harper	.05
555	*Turner Ward*	.10
556	Gary Ward	.05
557	Wally Whitehurst	.05
558	Otis Nixon	.05
559	Adam Peterson	.05
560	Greg Smith	.05
561	Tim McIntosh (Future Star)	.10
562	Jeff Kunkel	.05
563	*Brent Knackert*	.10
564	Dante Bichette	.15
565	Craig Biggio	.10
566	*Craig Wilson*	.10
567	Dwayne Henry	.05
568	Ron Karkovice	.05
569	Curt Schilling	.05
570	Barry Bonds	.35
571	Pat Combs	.05
572	Dave Anderson	.05
573	*Rich Rodriguez*	.08
574	John Marzano	.05
575	Robin Yount	.15
576	Jeff Kaiser	.05
577	Bill Doran	.05
578	Dave West	.05
579	Roger Craig	.05
580	Dave Stewart	.05
581	Luis Quinones	.05
582	Marty Clary	.05
583	Tony Phillips	.08
584	Kevin Brown	.05
585	Pete O'Brien	.05
586	Fred Lynn	.05
587	Jose Offerman (Future Star)	.10
588a	Mark Whiten (hand inside left border)	.15
588b	Mark Whiten (hand over left border)	.25
589	*Scott Ruskin*	.10
590	Eddie Murray	.15
591	Ken Hill	.08
592	B.J. Surhoff	.05
593a	*Mike Walker* (No 1990 Canton-Akron stats)	.15
593b	*Mike Walker* (1990 Canton-Akron stats)	.15
594	*Rich Garces* (Future Star)	.10
595	Bill Landrum	.05
596	*Ronnie Walden* (#1 Draft Pick)	.10
597	Jerry Don Gleaton	.05
598	Sam Horn	.05
599a	Greg Myers (no 1990 Syracuse stats)	.10
599b	Greg Myers (1990 Syracuse stats)	.10
600	Bo Jackson	.15
601	Bob Ojeda	.05
602	Casey Candaele	.05
603a	*Wes Chamberlain* (photo of Louie Meadows, no bat)	.25
603b	*Wes Chamberlain* (correct photo, holding bat)	.10
604	Billy Hatcher	.05
605	Jeff Reardon	.05
606	Jim Gott	.05
607	Edgar Martinez	.08
608	Todd Burns	.05
609	Jeff Torborg	.05
610	Andres Galarraga	.08
611	Dave Eiland	.05
612	Steve Lyons	.05
613	Eric Show	.05
614	Luis Salazar	.05
615	Bert Blyleven	.08
616	Todd Zeile	.08
617	Bill Wegman	.05
618	Sil Campusano	.05
619	David Wells	.05
620	Ozzie Guillen	.05
621	Ted Power	.05
622	Jack Daugherty	.05
623	Jeff Blauser	.05
624	Tom Candiotti	.05
625	Terry Steinbach	.05
626	Gerald Young	.05
627	*Tim Layana*	.08
628	Greg Litton	.05
629	Wes Gardner	.05
630	Dave Winfield	.15
631	Mike Morgan	.05
632	Lloyd Moseby	.05
633	Kevin Tapani	.05
634	Henry Cotto	.05
635	Andy Hawkins	.05
636	Geronimo Pena	.05
637	Bruce Ruffin	.05
638	Mike Macfarlane	.05
639	Frank Robinson	.05
640	Andre Dawson	.10
641	Mike Henneman	.05
642	Hal Morris	.08
643	Jim Presley	.05
644	Chuck Crim	.05
645	Juan Samuel	.05
646	*Andujar Cedeno*	.10
647	Mark Portugal	.05
648	Lee Stevens	.08
649	*Bill Sampen*	.08
650	Jack Clark	.05
651	*Alan Mills*	.10
652	Kevin Romine	.05
653	*Anthony Telford*	.15
654	Paul Sorrento	.15
655	Erik Hanson	.05
656a	Checklist 5 (Vincente Palacios #348)	
656b	Checklist 5 (Palacios #433)	.05
656c	Checklist 5 (Palacios #438)	.05
657	Mike Kingery	.05
658	*Scott Aldred*	.05
659	*Oscar Azocar*	.05
660	Lee Smith	.08
661	Steve Lake	.05
662	Rob Dibble	.05
663	Greg Brock	.05
664	John Farrell	.05
665	Mike LaValliere	.05
666	Danny Darwin	.05
667	Kent Anderson	.05
668	Bill Long	.05
669	Lou Pinella	.05
670	Rickey Henderson	.12
671	Andy McGaffigan	.05
672	Shane Mack	.05
673	*Greg Olson*	.05
674a	Kevin Gross (no diamond after 89 BB 1988)	.10
674b	Kevin Gross (diamond after 89 BB 1988)	.10
675	Tom Brunansky	.05
676	*Scott Chiamparino*	.10
677	Billy Ripken	.05
678	Mark Davidson	.05
679	Bill Bathe	.05
680	David Cone	.08
681	*Jeff Schaefer*	.05
682	*Ray Lankford*	.20
683	Derek Lilliquist	.05
684	Milt Cuyler	.05
685	Doug Drabek	.05
686	Mike Gallego	.05
687a	John Cerutti (4.46 ERA 1990)	.05
687b	John Cerutti (4.76 ERA 1990)	.05
688	*Rosario Rodriguez*	.08
689	John Kruk	.05
690	Orel Hershiser	.08
691	Mike Blowers	.05
692a	*Efrain Valdez* (no text below stats)	.15
692b	*Efrain Valdez* (two lines of text below stats)	.15
693	Francisco Cabrera	.05
694	Randy Veres	.05
695	Kevin Seitzer	.05
696	Steve Olin	.05
697	Shawn Abner	.05
698	Mark Guthrie	.05
699	Jim Lefebvre	.05
700	Jose Canseco	.20
701	Pascual Perez	.05
702	*Tim Naehring*	.15

703	Juan Agosto	.05
704	Devon White	.05
705	Robby Thompson	.05
706a	Brad Arnsberg (68.2 IP Rangers 1990)	.05
706b	Brad Arnsberg (62.2 IP Rangers 1990)	.05
707	Jim Eisenreich	.05
708	John Mitchell	.05
709	Matt Sinatro	.05
710	Kent Hrbek	.08
711	Jose DeLeon	.05
712	Ricky Jordan	.05
713	Scott Scudder	.05
714	Marvell Wynne	.05
715	Tim Burke	.05
716	Bob Geren	.05
717	Phil Bradley	.05
718	Steve Crawford	.05
719	Keith Miller	.05
720	Cecil Fielder	.15
721	*Mark Lee*	.05
722	Wally Backman	.05
723	Candy Maldonado	.05
724	*David Segui*	.10
725	Ron Gant	.12
726	Phil Stephenson	.05
727	Mookie Wilson	.05
728	Scott Sanderson	.05
729	Don Zimmer	.05
730	Barry Larkin	.10
731	*Jeff Gray*	.05
732	Franklin Stubbs	.05
733	Kelly Downs	.05
734	John Russell	.05
735	Ron Darling	.05
736	Dick Schofield	.05
737	Tim Crews	.05
738	Mel Hall	.05
739	*Russ Swan*	.05
740	Ryne Sandberg	.20
741	Jimmy Key	.05
742	Tommy Gregg	.05
743	Bryn Smith	.05
744	Nelson Santovenia	.05
745	Doug Jones	.05
746	John Shelby	.05
747	Tony Fossas	.05
748	Al Newman	.05
749	Greg Harris	.05
750	Bobby Bonilla	.08
751	*Wayne Edwards*	.05
752	Kevin Bass	.05
753	*Paul Marak*	.05
754	Bill Pecota	.05
755	Mark Langston	.05
756	Jeff Huson	.05
757	Mark Gardner	.05
758	Mike Devereaux	.05
759	Bobby Cox	.05
760	Benny Santiago	.08
761	Larry Andersen	.05
762	Mitch Webster	.05
763	*Dana Kiecker*	.05
764	Mark Carreon	.08
765	Shawon Dunston	.10
766	Jeff Robinson	.05
767	*Dan Wilson (#1 Draft Pick)*	.15
768	Donn Pall	.05
769	*Tim Sherrill*	.05
770	Jay Howell	.05
771	Gary Redus	.05
772	Kent Mercker	.05
773	Tom Foley	.05
774	Dennis Rasmussen	.05
775	Julio Franco	.08
776	Brent Mayne	.10
777	John Candelaria	.05
778	Danny Gladden	.05
779	Carmelo Martinez	.05
780a	Randy Myers (Career losses 15)	.08
780b	Randy Myers (Career losses 19)	.08
781	Darryl Hamilton	.05
782	Jim Deshaies	.05
783	Joel Skinner	.05
784	Willie Fraser	.05
785	Scott Fletcher	.05
786	Eric Plunk	.05
787	Checklist 6	.05
788	Bob Milacki	.05
789	Tom Lasorda	.10
790	Ken Griffey, Jr.	1.50
791	Mike Benjamin	.08
792	Mike Greenwell	.10

1991 Topps Tiffany

Topps ended its annual run of special collectors edition boxed sets in 1991, producing the glossy sets in considerably more limited quantity than in previous years. Cards are identical to the regular 1991 Topps set except for the use of white cardboard stock and a high-gloss front finish.

	MT
Complete Set (792):	150.00
Common Player:	.10
(Star cards valued at 3X-4X corresponding regular issue Topps cards)	

1991 Topps Box Panel Cards

Styled like the standard 1991 Topps cards, this 16-card set honors milestones of the featured players. The cards were found on the bottom of wax pack boxes. The cards are designated in alphabetical order by (A-P) and are not numbered.

		MT
Complete Set (16):		2.50
Common Player:		.08
A	Bert Blyleven	.08
B	George Brett	.50
C	Brett Butler	.10
D	Andre Dawson	.10
E	Dwight Evans	.08
F	Carlton Fisk	.10
G	Alfredo Griffin	.08
H	Rickey Henderson	.25
I	Willie McGee	.08
J	Dale Murphy	.15
K	Eddie Murray	.25
L	Dave Parker	.08
M	Jeff Reardon	.08
N	Nolan Ryan	1.50
O	Juan Samuel	.08
P	Robin Yount	.25

1991 Topps Traded

"Team USA" players are featured in the 1991 Topps Traded set. The cards feature the same style as the regular 1991 issue, including the 40th anniversary logo. The set includes 132 cards and showcases rookies and traded players along with "Team USA." The cards are numbered with a "T" designation in alphabetical order.

		MT
Complete Set (132):		7.00
Common Player:		.05
1	Juan Agosto	.05
2	Roberto Alomar	.25
3	Wally Backman	.05
4	*Jeff Bagwell*	3.00
5	Skeeter Barnes	.05
6	Steve Bedrosian	.05
7	Derek Bell	.35
8	George Bell	.05
9	Rafael Belliard	.05
10	Dante Bichette	.15
11	Bud Black	.05
12	Mike Boddicker	.05
13	Sid Bream	.05
14	Hubie Brooks	.05
15	Brett Butler	.10
16	Ivan Calderon	.05
17	John Candelaria	.05
18	Tom Candiotti	.05
19	Gary Carter	.10
20	Joe Carter	.15
21	Rick Cerone	.05
22	Jack Clark	.05
23	Vince Coleman	.05
24	Scott Coolbaugh	.05
25	Danny Cox	.05
26	Danny Darwin	.05
27	Chili Davis	.08
28	Glenn Davis	.05
29	Steve Decker	.10
30	Rob Deer	.05
31	Rich DeLucia	.05
32	*John Dettmer (USA)*	.05
33	Brian Downing	.05
34	*Darren Dreifort (USA)*	1.00
35	Kirk Dressendorfer	.15
36	Jim Essian	.05
37	Dwight Evans	.05
38	Steve Farr	.05
39	Jeff Fassero	.10
40	Junior Felix	.05
41	Tony Fernandez	.05
42	Steve Finley	.05
43	Jim Fregosi	.05
44	Gary Gaetti	.08
45	*Jason Giambi (USA)*	.75
46	Kirk Gibson	.05
47	Leo Gomez	.15
48	Luis Gonzalez	.15
49	*Jeff Granger (USA)*	.15
50	*Todd Greene (USA)*	.35
51	*Jeffrey Hammonds (USA)*	.40
52	Mike Hargrove	.05
53	Pete Harnisch	.08
54	*Rick Helling (USA)*	.25
55	Glenallen Hill	.08
56	Charlie Hough	.05
57	Pete Incaviglia	.05
58	Bo Jackson	.20
59	Danny Jackson	.05
60	Reggie Jefferson	.15
61	*Charles Johnson (USA)*	1.50
62	Jeff Johnson	.20
63	*Todd Johnson (USA)*	.20
64	Barry Jones	.05

65	Chris Jones	.05
66	Scott Kamieniecki	.05
67	*Pat Kelly*	.20
68	Darryl Kile	.10
69	Chuck Knoblauch	.40
70	Bill Krueger	.05
71	Scott Leius	.10
72	*Donnie Leshnock* (USA)	.10
73	Mark Lewis	.15
74	Candy Maldonado	.05
75	*Jason McDonald* (USA)	.10
76	Willie McGee	.08
77	Fred McGriff	.25
78	*Billy McMillon* (USA)	.10
79	Hal McRae	.05
80	*Dan Melendez* (USA)	.15
81	Orlando Merced	.15
82	Jack Morris	.05
83	*Phil Nevin* (USA)	.15
84	Otis Nixon	.05
85	Johnny Oates	.05
86	Bob Ojeda	.05
87	Mike Pagliarulo	.05
88	Dean Palmer	.25
89	Dave Parker	.08
90	Terry Pendleton	.05
91	*Tony Phillips* (USA)	.25
92	Doug Piatt	.10
93	Ron Polk (U.S.A.)	.05
94	Tim Raines	.08
95	Willie Randolph	.05
96	Dave Righetti	.05
97	Ernie Riles	.05
98	*Chris Roberts* (USA)	.15
99	Jeff Robinson (Angels)	.05
100	Jeff Robinson (Orioles)	.05
101	*Ivan Rodriguez*	2.00
102	*Steve Rodriguez* (USA)	.10
103	Tom Runnells	.05
104	Scott Sanderson	.05
105	Bob Scanlan	.05
106	Pete Schourek	.15
107	Gary Scott	.05
108	*Paul Shuey* (USA)	.15
109	*Doug Simons*	.10
110	Dave Smith	.05
111	Cory Snyder	.05
112	Luis Sojo	.05
113	*Kennie Steenstra* (USA)	.10
114	Darryl Strawberry	.20
115	Franklin Stubbs	.05
116	*Todd Taylor* (USA)	.10
117	Wade Taylor	.10
118	Garry Templeton	.05
119	Mickey Tettleton	.08
120	Tim Teufel	.05
121	Mike Timlin	.10
122	*David Tuttle* (USA)	.10
123	Mo Vaughn	.75
124	*Jeff Ware* (USA)	.10
125	Devon White	.08
126	Mark Whiten	.08
127	Mitch Williams	.05
128	*Craig Wilson* (USA)	.10
129	Willie Wilson	.05
130	*Chris Wimmer* (USA)	.10
131	*Ivan Zweig* (USA)	.10
132	Checklist	.05

		MT
Complete Set (22):		5.00
Common Player:		.10
1	Tony LaRussa	.10
2	Mark McGwire	1.50
3	Steve Sax	.10
4	Wade Boggs	.40
5	Cal Ripken, Jr.	.90
6	Rickey Henderson	.30
7	Ken Griffey, Jr.	.90
8	Jose Canseco	.40
9	Sandy Alomar, Jr.	.10
10	Bob Welch	.10
11	Al Lopez	.10
12	Roger Craig	.10
13	Will Clark	.25
14	Ryne Sandberg	.45
15	Chris Sabo	.10
16	Ozzie Smith	.30
17	Kevin Mitchell	.10
18	Len Dykstra	.10
19	Andre Dawson	.15
20	Mike Scoscia	.10
21	Jack Armstrong	.10
22	Juan Marichal	.15

1991 Topps All-Star Glossy Set of 22

Continuing the same basic format used since 1984, these glossy-front rack-pak inserts honor the players, manager and honorary captains of the previous year's All-Star Game. Fronts have a league logo in the lower-left corner, a 1990 All-Star banner above the photo and a Topps 40th anniversary logo superimposed over the photo. Backs have a shield and star design and the legend "1990 All-Star Commemorative Set" above the player's name, position and card number. Backs are printed in red and blue.

1991 Topps Desert Shield

As a special treat for U.S. armed services personnel serving in the Persian Gulf prior to and during the war with Iraq, Topps produced a special edition of its 1991 baseball card set featuring a gold-foil overprint honoring the military effort. Enough cards were produced to equal approximately 6,800 sets. While some cards actually reached the troops in the Middle East, many were shortstopped by military supply personnel stateside and sold into the hobby. Many of the cards sent to Saudi Arabia never returned to the U.S., however, making the supply of available cards somewhat scarce. At the peak of their popularity Desert Shield cards sold for price two to three times their current levels. The checklist cards in the set were not overprinted. At least two types of counterfeit overprint have been seen on genuine Topps cards in an attempt to cash in on the scarcity of these war "veterans."

	MT
Complete Set (792):	2000.
Common Player:	1.50

(Star cards valued at 100X corresponding cards in regular 1991 Topps issue)

1991 Topps Glossy Rookies

Similar in format to previous years' glossy rookies sets, this 33-card issue was available one per pack in 100-card jumbo cello packs. Card fronts have a colored "1990 Rookies" banner above the player photo, with the player's name in red in a yellow bar beneath. The Topps 40th anniversary logo appears in one of the upper corners of the photo. Backs are printed in red and blue and feature a "1990 Rookies Commemorative Set" shield logo. The player's name, position, team and card number are printed beneath. Cards are numbered alphabetically.

		MT
Complete Set (33):		11.00
Common Player:		.25
1	Sandy Alomar, Jr.	.25
2	Kevin Appier	.35
3	Steve Avery	.40
4	Carlos Baerga	.25
5	John Burkett	.60
6	Alex Cole	.35
7	Pat Combs	.25
8	Delino DeShields	.25
9	Travis Fryman	.25
10	Marquis Grissom	.50
11	Mike Harkey	.25
12	Glenallen Hill	.25
13	Jeff Huson	.25
14	Felix Jose	.25
15	Dave Justice	.90
16	Jim Leyritz	.30

17	Kevin Maas	.25
18	Ben McDonald	.25
19	Kent Mercker	.25
20	Hal Morris	.30
21	Chris Nabholz	.25
22	Tim Naehring	.25
23	Jose Offerman	.25
24	John Olerud	.50
25	Scott Radinsky	.25
26	Scott Ruskin	.25
27	Kevin Tapani	.25
28	Frank Thomas	3.00
29	Randy Tomlin	.25
30	Greg Vaughn	.30
31	Robin Ventura	.40
32	Larry Walker	.50
33	Todd Zeile	.35

1991 Topps 1990 Major League Debut

This 171-card set features the players who made their Major League debut in 1990. The cards are styled like the 1991 Topps cards and are numbered in alphabetical order. The card backs are printed horizontally and feature information about the player's debut and statistics. The issue was sold only as a boxed set through hobby channels.

		MT
Complete Set (171):		18.00
Common Player:		.05
1	Paul Abbott	.05
2	Steve Adkins	.05
3	Scott Aldred	.05
4	Gerald Alexander	.05
5	Moises Alou	.50
6	Steve Avery	.15
7	Oscar Azocar	.05
8	Carlos Baerga	.60
9	Kevin Baez	.05
10	Jeff Baldwin	.05
11	Brian Barnes	.08
12	Kevin Bearse	.05
13	Kevin Belcher	.10
14	Mike Bell	.05
15	Sean Berry	.10
16	Joe Bitker	.05
17	Willie Blair	.05
18	Brian Bohanon	.05
19	Mike Bordick	.15
20	Shawn Boskie	.15
21	Rod Brewer	.05
22	Kevin Brown	.05
23	Dave Burba	.05
24	Jim Campbell	.05
25	Ozzie Canseco	.10
26	Chuck Carr	.05
27	Larry Casian	.05
28	Andujar Cedeno	.15
29	Wes Chamberlain	.10

30	Scott Chiamparino	.05
31	Steve Chitren	.05
32	Pete Coachman	.05
33	Alex Cole	.05
34	Jeff Conine	.35
35	Scott Cooper	.15
36	Milt Cuyler	.05
37	Steve Decker	.05
38	Rich DeLucia	.05
39	Delino DeShields	.25
40	Mark Dewey	.05
41	Carlos Diaz	.05
42	Lance Dickson	.10
43	Narciso Elvira	.05
44	Luis Encarnacion	.05
45	Scott Erickson	.40
46	Paul Faries	.05
47	Howard Farmer	.05
48	Alex Fernandez	.35
49	Travis Fryman	.45
50	Rich Garces	.05
51	Carlos Garcia	.05
52	Mike Gardiner	.05
53	Bernard Gilkey	.25
54	Tom Gilles	.05
55	Jerry Goff	.05
56	Leo Gomez	.15
57	Luis Gonzalez	.30
58	Joe Grahe	.10
59	Craig Grebeck	.05
60	Kip Gross	.05
61	Eric Gunderson	.05
62	Chris Hammond	.10
63	Dave Hansen	.10
64	Reggie Harris	.05
65	Bill Haselman	.05
66	Randy Hennis	.05
67	Carlos Hernandez	.10
68	Howard Hilton	.05
69	Dave Hollins	.25
70	Darren Holmes	.10
71	John Hoover	.05
72	Steve Howard	.05
73	Thomas Howard	.10
74	Todd Hundley	.35
75	Daryl Irvine	.05
76	Chris Jelic	.05
77	Dana Kiecker	.05
78	Brent Knackert	.05
79	Jimmy Kremers	.05
80	Jerry Kutzler	.05
81	Ray Lankford	.50
82	Tim Layana	.05
83	Terry Lee	.05
84	Mark Leiter	.05
85	Scott Leius	.15
86	Mark Leonard	.05
87	Darren Lewis	.20
88	Scott Lewis	.05
89	Jim Leyritz	.10
90	Dave Liddell	.05
91	Luis Lopez	.05
92	Kevin Maas	.05
93	Bob MacDonald	.05
94	Carlos Maldonado	.05
95	Chuck Malone	.05
96	Ramon Manon	.05
97	Jeff Manto	.05
98	Paul Marak	.05
99	Tino Martinez	.45
100	Derrick May	.05
101	Brent Mayne	.10
102	Paul McClellan	.05
103	Rodney McCray	.05
104	Tim McIntosh	.05
105	Brian McRae	.30
106	Jose Melendez	.05
107	Orlando Merced	.20
108	Alan Mills	.05
109	Gino Minutelli	.05
110	Mickey Morandini	.15
111	Pedro Munoz	.15
112	Chris Nabholz	.05
113	Tim Naehring	.10
114	Charles Nagy	.20
115	Jim Neidlinger	.05
116	Rafael Novoa	.05
117	Jose Offerman	.15
118	Omar Olivares	.05
119	Javier Ortiz	.05
120	Al Osuna	.05
121	Rick Parker	.05
122	Dave Pavlas	.05
123	Geronimo Pena	.10
124	Mike Perez	.05
125	Phil Plantier	.25

126	Jim Poole	.05
127	Tom Quinlan	.05
128	Scott Radinsky	.10
129	Darren Reed	.10
130	Karl Rhodes	.10
131	Jeff Richardson	.05
132	Rich Rodriguez	.08
133	Dave Rohde	.05
134	Mel Rojas	.15
135	Vic Rosario	.05
136	Rich Rowland	.05
137	Scott Ruskin	.05
138	Bill Sampen	.05
139	Andres Santana	.05
140	David Segui	.12
141	Jeff Shaw	.05
142	Tim Sherrill	.05
143	Terry Shumpert	.05
144	Mike Simms	.05
145	Daryl Smith	.05
146	Luis Sojo	.10
147	Steve Springer	.05
148	Ray Stephens	.05
149	Lee Stevens	.10
150	Mel Stottlemyre, Jr.	.05
151	Glenn Sutko	.05
152	Anthony Telford	.08
153	Frank Thomas	3.00
154	Randy Tomlin	.15
155	Brian Traxler	.05
156	Efrain Valdez	.05
157	Rafael Valdez	.05
158	Julio Valera	.05
159	Jim Vatcher	.05
160	Hector Villanueva	.05
161	Hector Wagner	.05
162	Dave Walsh	.05
163	Steve Wapnick	.05
164	Colby Ward	.05
165	Turner Ward	.05
166	Terry Wells	.05
167	Mark Whiten	.20
168	Mike York	.05
169	Cliff Young	.05
170	Checklist	.05
171	Checklist	.05

1992 Topps

This 792-card set features white stock much like the 1991 issue. The card fronts feature full-color action and posed photos with a gray inner frame and the player name and position at bottom. Backs feature biographical information, statistics and stadium photos on player cards where space is available. All-Star cards and #1 Draft Pick cards are once again included. Topps brought back four-player rookie cards in 1992. Nine Top Prospect cards of this nature can be found within the set. "Match the Stats" game cards were inserted into packs of 1992 Topps cards. Special bonus cards were given away to winners of this insert game. This was the first Topps regular-issue baseball card set since 1951 which was sold without bubblegum.

	MT
Complete Set (792):	20.00
Common Player:	.05
Wax Box:	14.00

#	Player	Price
1	Nolan Ryan	.75
2	Rickey Henderson (Record Breaker)	.05
3	Jeff Reardon (Record Breaker)	.05
4	Nolan Ryan (Record Breaker)	.40
5	Dave Winfield (Record Breaker)	.05
6	*Brien Taylor* (Draft Pick)	.25
7	*Jim Olander*	.05
8	*Bryan Hickerson*	.05
9	John Farrell (Draft Pick)	.05
10	Wade Boggs	.15
11	Jack McDowell	.05
12	Luis Gonzalez	.05
13	Mike Scioscia	.05
14	Wes Chamberlain	.05
15	Denny Martinez	.05
16	Jeff Montgomery	.05
17	Randy Milligan	.05
18	Greg Cadaret	.05
19	Jamie Quirk	.05
20	Bip Roberts	.05
21	Buck Rodgers	.05
22	Bill Wegman	.05
23	Chuck Knoblauch	.10
24	Randy Myers	.05
25	Ron Gant	.10
26	Mike Bielecki	.05
27	Juan Gonzalez	.60
28	Mike Schooler	.05
29	Mickey Tettleton	.05
30	John Kruk	.05
31	Bryn Smith	.05
32	Chris Nabholz	.05
33	Carlos Baerga	.15
34	Jeff Juden	.05
35	Dave Righetti	.05
36	*Scott Ruffcorn* (Draft Pick)	.15
37	Luis Polonia	.05
38	Tom Candiotti	.05
39	Greg Olson	.05
40	Cal Ripken, Jr.	1.50
41	Craig Lefferts	.05
42	Mike Macfarlane	.05
43	Jose Lind	.05
44	Rick Aguilera	.05
45	Gary Carter	.08
46	Steve Farr	.05
47	Rex Hudler	.05
48	Scott Scudder	.05
49	Damon Berryhill	.05
50	Ken Griffey, Jr.	1.50
51	Tom Runnells	.05
52	Juan Bell	.05
53	Tommy Gregg	.05
54	David Wells	.05
55	Rafael Palmeiro	.10
56	Charlie O'Brien	.05
57	Donn Pall	.05
58	Top Prospects-Catchers(*Brad Ausmus*), (*Jim Campanis*), (*Dave Nilsson*), (*Doug Robbins*)	.20
59	Mo Vaughn	.30
60	Tony Fernandez	.05
61	Paul O'Neill	.05
62	Gene Nelson	.05
63	Randy Ready	.05
64	Bob Kipper	.05
65	Willie McGee	.05
66	*Scott Stahoviak* (Draft Pick)	.15
67	Luis Salazar	.05
68	Marvin Freeman	.05
69	Kenny Lofton	.75
70	Gary Gaetti	.05
71	Erik Hanson	.05
72	Eddie Zosky	.10
73	Brian Barnes	.05
74	Scott Leius	.05
75	Bret Saberhagen	.05
76	Mike Gallego	.05
77	Jack Armstrong	.05
78	Ivan Rodriguez	.35
79	Jesse Orosco	.05
80	Dave Justice	.25
81	*Ced Landrum*	.05
82	*Doug Simons*	.10
83	Tommy Greene	.05
84	Leo Gomez	.05
85	Jose DeLeon	.05
86	Steve Finley	.05
87	*Bob MacDonald*	.10
88	Darrin Jackson	.05
89	Neal Heaton	.05
90	Robin Yount	.20
91	Jeff Reed	.05
92	Lenny Harris	.05
93	Reggie Jefferson	.05
94	Sammy Sosa	1.00
95	Scott Bailes	.05
96	*Tom McKinnon* (Draft Pick)	.10
97	Luis Rivera	.05
98	Mike Harkey	.05
99	Jeff Treadway	.05
100	Jose Canseco	.15
101	Omar Vizquel	.05
102	*Scott Kamieniecki*	.10
103	Ricky Jordan	.05
104	Jeff Ballard	.05
105	Felix Jose	.05
106	Mike Boddicker	.05
107	Dan Pasqua	.05
108	*Mike Timlin*	.12
109	Roger Craig	.05
110	Ryne Sandberg	.25
111	Mark Carreon	.05
112	Oscar Azocar	.05
113	Mike Greenwell	.05
114	Mark Portugal	.05
115	Terry Pendleton	.05
116	Willie Randolph	.05
117	Scott Terry	.05
118	Chili Davis	.05
119	Mark Gardner	.05
120	Alan Trammell	.10
121	Derek Bell	.10
122	Gary Varsho	.05
123	Bob Ojeda	.05
124	*Shawn Livsey* (Draft Pick)	.10
125	Chris Hoiles	.05
126	Top Prospects-1st Baseman(*Rico Brogna*, John Jaha, Ryan Klesko, Dave Staton)	1.00
127	Carlos Quintana	.05
128	Kurt Stillwell	.05
129	Melido Perez	.05
130	Alvin Davis	.05
131	Checklist 1	.05
132	Eric Show	.05
133	Rance Mulliniks	.05
134	Darryl Kile	.05
135	Von Hayes	.05
136	Bill Doran	.05
137	Jeff Robinson	.05
138	Monty Fariss	.05
139	Jeff Innis	.05
140	Mark Grace	.10
141	Jim Leyland	.05
142	Todd Van Poppel	.05
143	Paul Gibson	.05
144	Bill Swift	.05
145	Danny Tartabull	.05
146	Al Newman	.05
147	Cris Carpenter	.05
148	*Anthony Young*	.25
149	*Brian Bohanon*	.10
150	Roger Clemens	.35
151	Jeff Hamilton	.05
152	Charlie Leibrandt	.05
153	Ron Karkovice	.05
154	Hensley Meulens	.05
155	Scott Bankhead	.05
156	*Manny Ramirez* (Draft Pick)	1.50
157	Keith Miller	.05
158	Todd Frohwirth	.05
159	Darrin Fletcher	.05
160	Bobby Bonilla	.08
161	Casey Candaele	.05
162	Paul Faries	.05
163	Dana Kiecker	.05
164	Shane Mack	.05
165	Mark Langston	.05
166	Geronimo Pena	.05
167	Andy Allanson	.05
168	Dwight Smith	.05
169	Chuck Crim	.05
170	Alex Cole	.05
171	Bill Plummer	.05
172	Juan Berenguer	.05
173	Brian Downing	.05
174	Steve Frey	.05
175	Orel Hershiser	.08
176	*Ramon Garcia*	.10
177	Danny Gladden	.05
178	Jim Acker	.05
179	Top Prospects-2nd Baseman(*Cesar Bernhardt*), (*Bobby DeJardin*), (*Armando Moreno*), *Andy Stankiewicz*)	.25
180	Kevin Mitchell	.08
181	Hector Villanueva	.05
182	Jeff Reardon	.05
183	Brent Mayne	.05
184	Jimmy Jones	.05
185	Benny Santiago	.08
186	*Cliff Floyd* (Draft Pick)	.50
187	Ernie Riles	.05
188	Jose Guzman	.05
189	Junior Felix	.05
190	Glenn Davis	.05
191	Charlie Hough	.05
192	*Dave Fleming*	.10
193	Omar Oliveras	.05
194	Eric Karros	.15
195	David Cone	.05
196	*Frank Castillo*	.05
197	Glenn Braggs	.05
198	Scott Aldred	.05
199	Jeff Blauser	.05
200	Len Dykstra	.08
201	Buck Showalter	.05
202	Rick Honeycutt	.05
203	Greg Myers	.05
204	Trevor Wilson	.05
205	Jay Howell	.05
206	Luis Sojo	.05
207	Jack Clark	.05
208	Julio Machado	.05
209	Lloyd McClendon	.05
210	Ozzie Guillen	.05
211	*Jeremy Hernandez*	.10
212	Randy Velarde	.05
213	Les Lancaster	.05
214	*Andy Mota*	.10
215	Rich Gossage	.05
216	*Brent Gates* (Draft Pick)	.25
217	Brian Harper	.05
218	Mike Flanagan	.05
219	Jerry Browne	.05
220	Jose Rijo	.05
221	Skeeter Barnes	.05
222	Jaime Navarro	.05
223	Mel Hall	.05
224	*Brett Barberie*	.15
225	Roberto Alomar	.25
226	Pete Smith	.05
227	Daryl Boston	.05
228	Eddie Whitson	.05
229	Shawn Boskie	.05
230	Dick Schofield	.05
231	*Brian Drahman*	.10
232	John Smiley	.05
233	Mitch Webster	.05
234	Terry Steinbach	.05
235	Jack Morris	.05
236	Bill Pecota	.05
237	*Jose Hernandez*	.10
238	Greg Litton	.05
239	Brian Holman	.05
240	Andres Galarraga	.08
241	Gerald Young	.05
242	Mike Mussina	.25
243	Alvaro Espinoza	.05
244	Darren Daulton	.05
245	John Smoltz	.08
246	*Jason Pruitt* (Draft Pick)	.10
247	Chuck Finley	.05
248	Jim Gantner	.05
249	Tony Fossas	.05
250	Ken Griffey	.05
251	Kevin Elster	.05
252	Dennis Rasmussen	.05
253	Terry Kennedy	.05
254	*Ryan Bowen*	.15
255	Robin Ventura	.15
256	Mike Aldrete	.05
257	Jeff Russell	.05
258	Jim Lindeman	.05
259	Ron Darling	.05
260	Devon White	.05
261	Tom Lasorda	.10
262	Terry Lee	.10
263	Bob Patterson	.05
264	Checklist 2	.05
265	Teddy Higuera	.05

266	Roberto Kelly	.05
267	Steve Bedrosian	.05
268	Brady Anderson	.12
269	*Ruben Amaro*	.08
270	Tony Gwynn	.35
271	Tracy Jones	.05
272	Jerry Don Gleaton	.05
273	Craig Grebeck	.05
274	*Bob Scanlan*	.10
275	Todd Zeile	.08
276	*Shawn Green* (Draft Pick)	.40
277	Scott Chiamparino	.05
278	Darryl Hamilton	.05
279	Jim Clancy	.05
280	Carlos Martinez	.05
281	Kevin Appier	.05
282	*John Wehner*	.10
283	Reggie Sanders	.15
284	Gene Larkin	.05
285	Bob Welch	.05
286	Gilberto Reyes	.05
287	*Pete Schourek*	.15
288	Andujar Cedeno	.05
289	Mike Morgan	.05
290	Bo Jackson	.15
291	Phil Garner	.05
292	Ray Lankford	.10
293	Mike Henneman	.05
294	Dave Valle	.05
295	Alonzo Powell	.05
296	Tom Brunansky	.05
297	Kevin Brown	.05
298	Kelly Gruber	.05
299	Charles Nagy	.05
300	Don Mattingly	.40
301	Kirk McCaskill	.05
302	Joey Cora	.05
303	Dan Plesac	.05
304	Joe Oliver	.05
305	Tom Glavine	.08
306	*Al Shirley* (Draft Pick)	.10
307	Bruce Ruffin	.05
308	*Craig Shipley*	.08
309	Dave Martinez	.05
310	Jose Mesa	.05
311	Henry Cotto	.05
312	Mike LaValliere	.05
313	Kevin Tapani	.05
314	Jeff Huson	.05
315	Juan Samuel	.05
316	Curt Schilling	.05
317	Mike Bordick	.05
318	Steve Howe	.05
319	Tony Phillips	.08
320	George Bell	.05
321	Lou Pinella	.05
322	Tim Burke	.05
323	Milt Thompson	.05
324	Danny Darwin	.05
325	Joe Orsulak	.05
326	Eric King	.05
327	Jay Buhner	.05
328	*Joel Johnston*	.10
329	Franklin Stubbs	.05
330	Will Clark	.20
331	Steve Lake	.05
332	*Chris Jones*	.10
333	Pat Tabler	.05
334	Kevin Gross	.05
335	Dave Henderson	.05
336	*Greg Anthony* (Draft Pick)	.10
337	Alejandro Pena	.05
338	Shawn Abner	.05
339	Tom Browning	.05
340	Otis Nixon	.05
341	Bob Geren	.05
342	*Tim Spehr*	.10
343	*Jon Vander Wal*	.20
344	Jack Daugherty	.05
345	Zane Smith	.05
346	*Rheal Cormier*	.15
347	Kent Hrbek	.08
348	*Rick Wilkins*	.10
349	Steve Lyons	.05
350	Gregg Olson	.05
351	Greg Riddoch	.05
352	Ed Nunez	.05
353	*Braulio Castillo*	.08
354	Dave Bergman	.05
355	*Warren Newson*	.10
356	Luis Quinones	.05
357	Mike Witt	.05
358	*Ted Wood*	.10
359	Mike Moore	.05
360	Lance Parrish	.05
361	Barry Jones	.05

362	*Javier Ortiz*	.10
363	John Candelaria	.05
364	Glenallen Hill	.05
365	Duane Ward	.05
366	Checklist 3	.05
367	Rafael Belliard	.05
368	Bill Krueger	.05
369	*Steve Whitaker* (Draft Pick)	.10
370	Shawon Dunston	.08
371	Dante Bichette	.10
372	*Kip Gross*	.05
373	Don Robinson	.05
374	Bernie Williams	.30
375	Bert Blyleven	.05
376	*Chris Donnels*	.10
377	*Bob Zupcic*	.05
378	Joel Skinner	.05
379	Steve Chitren	.05
380	Barry Bonds	.35
381	Sparky Anderson	.05
382	Sid Fernandez	.05
383	Dave Hollins	.05
384	Mark Lee	.05
385	Tim Wallach	.05
386	Will Clark (All-Star)	.10
387	Ryne Sandberg (All-Star)	.10
388	Howard Johnson (All-Star)	.05
389	Barry Larkin (All-Star)	.05
390	Barry Bonds (All-Star)	.10
391	Ron Gant (All-Star)	.05
392	Bobby Bonilla (All-Star)	.05
393	Craig Biggio (All-Star)	.05
394	Denny Martinez (All-Star)	.05
395	Tom Glavine (All-Star)	.05
396	Lee Smith (All-Star)	.05
397	Cecil Fielder (All-Star)	.10
398	Julio Franco (All-Star)	.05
399	Wade Boggs (All-Star)	.10
400	Cal Ripken, Jr. (All-Star)	.25
401	Jose Canseco (All-Star)	.10
402	Joe Carter (All-Star)	.05
403	Ruben Sierra (All-Star)	.05
404	Matt Nokes (All-Star)	.05
405	Roger Clemens (All-Star)	.15
406	Jim Abbott (All-Star)	.05
407	Bryan Harvey (All-Star)	.05
408	Bob Milacki	.05
409	Geno Petralli	.05
410	Dave Stewart	.05
411	Mike Jackson	.05
412	Luis Aquino	.05
413	Tim Teufel	.05
414	Jeff Ware (Draft Pick)	.10
415	Jim Deshaies	.05
416	Ellis Burks	.10
417	Allan Anderson	.05
418	Alfredo Griffin	.05
419	Wally Whitehurst	.05
420	Sandy Alomar	.08
421	Juan Agosto	.05
422	Sam Horn	.05
423	*Jeff Fassero*	.10
424	*Paul McClellan*	.10
425	Cecil Fielder	.15
426	Tim Raines	.08
427	*Eddie Taubensee*	.10
428	Dennis Boyd	.05
429	Tony LaRussa	.05
430	Steve Sax	.05
431	Tom Gordon	.05
432	Billy Hatcher	.05
433	Cal Eldred	.05
434	Wally Backman	.05
435	Mark Eichhorn	.05
436	Mookie Wilson	.05
437	*Scott Servais*	.10
438	Mike Maddux	.05
439	*Chico Walker*	.05
440	Doug Drabek	.05
441	Rob Deer	.05
442	Dave West	.05
443	Spike Owen	.05
444	*Tyrone Hill* (Draft Pick)	.10
445	Matt Williams	.20
446	Mark Lewis	.05
447	David Segui	.05
448	Tom Pagnozzi	.05
449	*Jeff Johnson*	.10
450	Mark McGwire	1.50
451	Tom Henke	.05
452	Wilson Alvarez	.05
453	Gary Redus	.05
454	Darren Holmes	.05
455	Pete O'Brien	.05
456	Pat Combs	.05
457	Hubie Brooks	.05

458	Frank Tanana	.05
459	Tom Kelly	.05
460	Andre Dawson	.10
461	Doug Jones	.05
462	Rich Rodriguez	.05
463	*Mike Simms*	.10
464	Mike Jeffcoat	.05
465	Barry Larkin	.12
466	Stan Belinda	.05
467	Lonnie Smith	.05
468	Greg Harris	.05
469	Jim Eisenreich	.05
470	Pedro Guerrero	.05
471	Jose DeJesus	.05
472	*Rich Rowland*	.10
473	Top Prospects-3rd Baseman *(Frank Bolick)*, *(Craig Paquette)*, *(Tom Redington)*, *(Paul Russo)*	.20
474	*Mike Rossiter* (Draft Pick)	.15
475	Robby Thompson	.05
476	Randy Bush	.05
477	Greg Hibbard	.05
478	Dale Sveum	.05
479	*Chito Martinez*	.10
480	Scott Sanderson	.05
481	Tino Martinez	.15
482	Jimmy Key	.05
483	Terry Shumpert	.05
484	Mike Hartley	.05
485	Chris Sabo	.05
486	Bob Walk	.05
487	John Cerutti	.05
488	Scott Cooper	.10
489	Bobby Cox	.05
490	Julio Franco	.05
491	Jeff Brantley	.05
492	Mike Devereaux	.05
493	Jose Offerman	.05
494	Gary Thurman	.05
495	Carney Lansford	.05
496	Joe Grahe	.05
497	*Andy Ashby*	.08
498	Gerald Perry	.05
499	Dave Otto	.05
500	Vince Coleman	.05
501	*Rob Mallicoat*	.05
502	Greg Briley	.05
503	Pascual Perez	.05
504	*Aaron Sele* (Draft Pick)	.40
505	Bobby Thigpen	.05
506	Todd Benzinger	.05
507	Candy Maldonado	.05
508	Bill Gullickson	.05
509	Doug Dascenzo	.05
510	Frank Viola	.05
511	Kenny Rogers	.05
512	Mike Heath	.05
513	Kevin Bass	.05
514	*Kim Batiste*	.10
515	Delino DeShields	.05
516	*Ed Sprague*	.10
517	Jim Gott	.05
518	*Jose Melendez*	.10
519	Hal McRae	.05
520	Jeff Bagwell	.45
521	Joe Hesketh	.05
522	Milt Cuyler	.05
523	Shawn Hillegas	.05
524	Don Slaught	.05
525	Randy Johnson	.20
526	*Doug Piatt*	.10
527	Checklist 4	.05
528	*Steve Foster*	.15
529	Joe Girardi	.05
530	Jim Abbott	.08
531	Larry Walker	.15
532	Mike Huff	.05
533	Mackey Sasser	.05
534	*Benji Gil* (Draft Pick)	.20
535	Dave Stieb	.05
536	Willie Wilson	.05
537	*Mark Leiter*	.05
538	Jose Uribe	.05
539	Thomas Howard	.05
540	Ben McDonald	.08
541	*Jose Tolentino*	.10
542	*Keith Mitchell*	.05
543	Jerome Walton	.05
544	*Cliff Brantley*	.10
545	Andy Van Slyke	.05
546	Paul Sorrento	.05
547	Herm Winningham	.05
548	Mark Guthrie	.05
549	Joe Torre	.05
550	Darryl Strawberry	.12

551	Top Prospects- Shortstops(Manny Alexander, Alex Arias, Wil Cordero, Chipper Jones)	1.00
552	Dave Gallagher	.05
553	Edgar Martinez	.08
554	Donald Harris	.05
555	Frank Thomas	1.50
556	Storm Davis	.05
557	Dickie Thon	.05
558	Scott Garrelts	.05
559	Steve Olin	.05
560	Rickey Henderson	.15
561	Jose Vizcaino	.05
562	*Wade Taylor*	.10
563	Pat Borders	.05
564	*Jimmy Gonzalez* (Draft Pick)	.10
565	Lee Smith	.05
566	Bill Sampen	.05
567	Dean Palmer	.08
568	Bryan Harvey	.05
569	Tony Pena	.05
570	Lou Whitaker	.05
571	Randy Tomlin	.05
572	Greg Vaughn	.05
573	Kelly Downs	.05
574	Steve Avery	.08
575	Kirby Puckett	.35
576	*Heathcliff Slocumb*	.05
577	Kevin Seitzer	.05
578	Lee Guetterman	.05
579	Johnny Oates	.05
580	Greg Maddux	1.00
581	Stan Javier	.05
582	Vicente Palacios	.05
583	Mel Rojas	.05
584	*Wayne Rosenthal*	.10
585	Lenny Webster	.05
586	Rod Nichols	.05
587	Mickey Morandini	.05
588	Russ Swan	.05
589	Mariano Duncan	.05
590	Howard Johnson	.05
591	Top Prospects- Outfielders(*Jacob Brumfield*), (*Jeremy Burnitz*), (*Alan Cockrell*, D.J. Dozier)	.25
592	*Denny Neagle*	.10
593	Steve Decker	.05
594	*Brian Barber* (Draft Pick)	.10
595	Bruce Hurst	.05
596	Kent Mercker	.05
597	*Mike Magnante*	.05
598	Jody Reed	.05
599	Steve Searcy	.05
600	Paul Molitor	.20
601	Dave Smith	.05
602	Mike Fetters	.05
603	*Luis Mercedes*	.10
604	Chris Gwynn	.05
605	Scott Erickson	.05
606	Brook Jacoby	.05
607	Todd Stottlemyre	.05
608	Scott Bradley	.05
609	Mike Hargrove	.05
610	Eric Davis	.08
611	*Brian Hunter*	.05
612	Pat Kelly	.05
613	Pedro Munoz	.10
614	Al Osuna	.05
615	Matt Merullo	.05
616	Larry Andersen	.05
617	Junior Ortiz	.05
618	Top Prospects- Outfielders(*Cesar Hernandez*, Steve Hosey, Dan Peltier), (*Jeff McNeely*)	.20
619	Danny Jackson	.05
620	George Brett	.30
621	*Dan Gakeler*	.10
622	Steve Buechele	.05
623	Bob Tewksbury	.05
624	*Shawn Estes* (Draft Pick)	.75
625	Kevin McReynolds	.05
626	*Chris Haney*	.05
627	Mike Sharperson	.05
628	Mark Williamson	.05
629	Wally Joyner	.08
630	Carlton Fisk	.10
631	*Armando Reynoso*	.10
632	Felix Fermin	.05
633	Mitch Williams	.05
634	Manuel Lee	.05
635	Harold Baines	.08
636	Greg Harris	.05
637	Orlando Merced	.05

638	Chris Bosio	.05
639	*Wayne Housie*	.10
640	Xavier Hernandez	.05
641	*David Howard*	.10
642	Tim Crews	.05
643	Rick Cerone	.05
644	Terry Leach	.05
645	Deion Sanders	.15
646	Craig Wilson	.05
647	Marquis Grissom	.08
648	Scott Fletcher	.05
649	Norm Charlton	.05
650	Jesse Barfield	.05
651	*Joe Slusarski*	.10
652	Bobby Rose	.05
653	Dennis Lamp	.05
654	*Allen Watson* (Draft Pick)	.20
655	Brett Butler	.08
656	Top Prospects- Outfielders(*Rudy Pemberton*, Henry Rodriguez), (*Lee Tinsley*), (*Gerald Williams*)	.25
657	Dave Johnson	.05
658	Checklist 5	.05
659	Brian McRae	.05
660	Fred McGriff	.10
661	Bill Landrum	.05
662	Juan Guzman	.05
663	Greg Gagne	.05
664	Ken Hill	.05
665	*Dave Haas*	.05
666	Tom Foley	.05
667	*Roberto Hernandez*	.10
668	Dwayne Henry	.05
669	Jim Fregosi	.05
670	Harold Reynolds	.05
671	Mark Whiten	.05
672	Eric Plunk	.05
673	Todd Hundley	.10
674	*Mo Sanford*	.10
675	Bobby Witt	.05
676	Top Prospects-Pitchers(*Pat Mahomes*), (*Sam Militello*, Roger Salkeld), (*Turk Wendell*)	.15
677	John Marzano	.05
678	Joe Klink	.05
679	Pete Incaviglia	.05
680	Dale Murphy	.10
681	Rene Gonzales	.05
682	Andy Benes	.08
683	Jim Poole	.05
684	*Trever Miller* (Draft Pick)	.15
685	*Scott Livingstone*	.12
686	Rich DeLucia	.05
687	*Harvey Pulliam*	.10
688	Tim Belcher	.05
689	Mark Lemke	.05
690	John Franco	.05
691	Walt Weiss	.05
692	Scott Ruskin	.05
693	Jeff King	.05
694	Mike Gardiner	.05
695	Gary Sheffield	.15
696	Joe Boever	.05
697	Mike Felder	.05
698	John Habyan	.05
699	Cito Gaston	.05
700	Ruben Sierra	.08
701	Scott Radinsky	.05
702	Lee Stevens	.05
703	*Mark Wohlers*	.10
704	Curt Young	.05
705	Dwight Evans	.05
706	Rob Murphy	.05
707	Gregg Jefferies	.05
708	Tom Bolton	.05
709	Chris James	.05
710	Kevin Maas	.05
711	*Ricky Bones*	.10
712	Curt Wilkerson	.05
713	Roger McDowell	.05
714	*Calvin Reese* (Draft Pick)	.20
715	Craig Biggio	.08
716	*Kirk Dressendorfer*	.10
717	Ken Dayley	.05
718	B.J. Surhoff	.05
719	Terry Mulholland	.05
720	Kirk Gibson	.05
721	Mike Pagliarulo	.05
722	Walt Terrell	.05
723	Jose Oquendo	.05
724	Kevin Morton	.05
725	Dwight Gooden	.12
726	Kirt Manwaring	.05
727	Chuck McElroy	.05

728	Dave Burba	.10
729	Art Howe	.05
730	Ramon Martinez	.08
731	Donnie Hill	.05
732	Nelson Santovenia	.05
733	Bob Melvin	.05
734	*Scott Hatteberg* (Draft Pick)	.10
735	Greg Swindell	.05
736	Lance Johnson	.05
737	Kevin Reimer	.05
738	Dennis Eckersley	.08
739	Rob Ducey	.05
740	Ken Caminiti	.08
741	Mark Gubicza	.05
742	Billy Spiers	.05
743	Darren Lewis	.08
744	Chris Hammond	.05
745	Dave Magadan	.05
746	Bernard Gilkey	.10
747	Willie Banks	.05
748	Matt Nokes	.05
749	Jerald Clark	.05
750	Travis Fryman	.08
751	Steve Wilson	.05
752	Billy Ripken	.05
753	Paul Assenmacher	.05
754	Charlie Hayes	.05
755	Alex Fernandez	.08
756	Gary Pettis	.05
757	Rob Dibble	.05
758	Tim Naehring	.05
759	Jeff Torborg	.05
760	Ozzie Smith	.25
761	Mike Fitzgerald	.05
762	John Burkett	.05
763	Kyle Abbott	.05
764	*Tyler Green* (Draft Pick)	.20
765	Pete Harnisch	.05
766	Mark Davis	.05
767	Kal Daniels	.05
768	Jim Thome	.20
769	Jack Howell	.05
770	Sid Bream	.05
771	*Arthur Rhodes*	.10
772	Garry Templeton	.05
773	Hal Morris	.08
774	Bud Black	.05
775	Ivan Calderon	.05
776	*Doug Henry*	.10
777	John Olerud	.10
778	Tim Leary	.05
779	Jay Bell	.05
780	Eddie Murray	.15
781	Paul Abbott	.05
782	Phil Plantier	.08
783	Joe Magrane	.05
784	Ken Patterson	.05
785	Albert Belle	.30
786	Royce Clayton	.10
787	Checklist 6	.05
788	Mike Stanton	.05
789	Bobby Valentine	.05
790	Joe Carter	.10
791	Danny Cox	.05
792	Dave Winfield	.12

1992 Topps Gold

Topps Gold cards share a checklist and format with the regular-issue 1992 Topps baseball issue except the color bars with the player's name and team printed beneath the photo have been replaced with gold foil. On back the light blue Topps logo printed beneath the stats has been replaced with a gold "ToppsGold" logo. Topps Gold cards were random inserts in all forms of packs. Additionally, factory sets of Gold cards were sold which included an autographed card of Yankees #1 draft pick Brien Taylor, and which had the checklist cards replaced with player cards. Several errors connected with the gold name/team strips are noted; no corrected versions were issued.

		MT
Complete Set (792):		150.00
Complete Factory Set (793):		200.00
Common Player:		.25
	(Star cards valued at 10X-15X corresponding cards in regular 1992 Topps)	
86	Steve Finley (incorrect name, Mark Davidson, on gold strip)	.25
131	Terry Mathews	.25
264	Rod Beck	1.50
288	Andujar Cedeno (incorrect team, Yankees, listed on gold strip)	.60
366	Tony Perezchica	.25
465	Barry Larkin (incorrect team, Astros, listed on gold strip)	2.00
527	Terry McDaniel	.25
532	Mike Huff (incorrect team, Red Sox, listed on gold strip)	.25
658	John Ramos	.25
787	Brian Williams	.25
793	Brien Taylor (autographed edition of 12,000; factory sets only)	35.00

1992 Topps Gold Winners

A second gold-foil enhanced parallel version of the regular 1992 Topps issue was the Gold Winner cards awarded as prizes in a scratch-off contest found in each pack. Winner cards are identical to the Topps Gold cards except for the addition of a gold-foil "Winner" and star added above the team name.

Due to a flaw in the dfesign of the scratch-off game cards, it was easy to win every time and the Winner cards had to be produced in quantities far greater than originally planned, making them rather common. Six checklist cards from the regular issue were replaced with player cards in the Winners edition.

		MT
Complete Set (792):		80.00
Common Player:		.15
	(Star cards valued at 5X-7X corresponding cards in regular 1992 Topps issue)	
131	Terry Mathews	.15
264	Rod Beck	.90
366	Tony Perezchica	.15
465a	Barry Larkin (team name incorrect, Astros)	.90
465b	Barry Larkin (team name correct, Reds)	.35
527	Terry McDaniel	.15
658	John Ramos	.15
787	Brian Williams	.15

1992 Topps Traded

Members of the United States baseball team are featured in this 132-card boxed set released by Topps. The cards are styled after the regular 1992 Topps cards and are numbered alphabetically. Several United States baseball players featured in this set were also featured in the 1991 Topps Traded set.

		MT
Complete Set (132):		70.00
Common Player:		.05
1	*Willie Adams* (USA)	.20
2	Jeff Alkire (USA)	.20
3	Felipe Alou	.05
4	Moises Alou	.35
5	Ruben Amaro	.05
6	Jack Armstrong	.05
7	Scott Bankhead	.05
8	Tim Belcher	.05
9	George Bell	.05
10	Freddie Benavides	.10
11	Todd Benzinger	.05
12	Joe Boever	.05
13	Ricky Bones	.05
14	Bobby Bonilla	.10
15	Hubie Brooks	.05
16	Jerry Browne	.05
17	Jim Bullinger	.05
18	Dave Burba	.05
19	Kevin Campbell	.10
20	Tom Candiotti	.05
21	Mark Carreon	.05
22	Gary Carter	.10
23	Archi Cianfrocco	.05
24	Phil Clark	.05
25	*Chad Curtis*	.75
26	Eric Davis	.08
27	Tim Davis (USA)	.10
28	Gary DiSarcina	.05
29	Darren Dreifort (USA)	.25
30	Mariano Duncan	.05
31	Mike Fitzgerald	.05
32	John Flaherty	.12
33	Darrin Fletcher	.10
34	Scott Fletcher	.05
35	Ron Fraser (USA)	.08
36	Andres Galarraga	.10
37	Dave Gallagher	.05
38	Mike Gallego	.05
39	*Nomar Garciaparra* (USA)	60.00
40	Jason Giambi (USA)	.50
41	Danny Gladden	.05
42	Rene Gonzales	.05
43	Jeff Granger (USA)	.40
44	Rick Greene (USA)	.10
45	Jeffrey Hammonds (USA)	.75
46	Charlie Hayes	.05
47	Von Hayes	.05
48	Rick Helling (USA)	.10
49	Butch Henry	.10
50	Carlos Hernandez	.12
51	Ken Hill	.05
52	Butch Hobson	.05
53	Vince Horsman	.10
54	Pete Incaviglia	.05
55	Gregg Jefferies	.10
56	Charles Johnson (USA)	1.00
57	Doug Jones	.05
58	Brian Jordan	.75
59	Wally Joyner	.08
60	*Daron Kirkreit* (USA)	.20
61	Bill Krueger	.05
62	Gene Lamont	.05
63	Jim Lefebvre	.05
64	*Danny Leon*	.05
65	Pat Listach	.25
66	Kenny Lofton	2.00
67	Dave Martinez	.05
68	Derrick May	.05
69	Kirk McCaskill	.05
70	*Chad McConnell* (USA)	.40
71	Kevin McReynolds	.05
72	Rusty Meacham	.05
73	Keith Miller	.05
74	Kevin Mitchell	.08
75	*Jason Moler* (USA)	.30
76	Mike Morgan	.05
77	Jack Morris	.05
78	*Calvin Murray* (USA)	.25
79	Eddie Murray	.15
80	Randy Myers	.08
81	Denny Neagle	.10
82	Phil Nevin (USA)	.20
83	Dave Nilsson	.10
84	Junior Ortiz	.05
85	Donovan Osborne	.05
86	Bill Pecota	.05
87	Melido Perez	.05
88	Mike Perez	.05
89	Hipolito Pena	.05
90	Willie Randolph	.05
91	Darren Reed	.12
92	Bip Roberts	.05
93	Chris Roberts (USA)	.40
94	Steve Rodriguez (USA)	.12
95	Bruce Ruffin	.05
96	Scott Ruskin	.05
97	Bret Saberhagen	.08
98	Rey Sanchez	.12
99	Steve Sax	.05
100	Curt Schilling	.05
101	Dick Schofield	.05
102	Gary Scott	.05
103	Kevin Seitzer	.05
104	Frank Seminara	.12
105	Gary Sheffield	.20
106	John Smiley	.05
107	Cory Snyder	.05
108	Paul Sorrento	.05
109	Sammy Sosa	3.00
110	Matt Stairs	.12
111	Andy Stankiewicz	.10
112	Kurt Stillwell	.05
113	Rick Sutcliffe	.05
114	Bill Swift	.05
115	Jeff Tackett	.12
116	Danny Tartabull	.05
117	Eddie Taubensee	.12
118	Dickie Thon	.05
119	*Michael Tucker* (USA)	.60
120	Scooter Tucker	.12
121	*Marc Valdes* (USA)	.10
122	Julio Valera	.10
123	*Jason Varitek* (USA)	.75
124	*Ron Villone* (USA)	.20
125	Frank Viola	.05
126	*B.J. Wallace* (USA)	.75
127	Dan Walters	.12
128	Craig Wilson (USA)	.12
129	Chris Wimmer (USA)	.12
130	Dave Winfield	.15
131	Herm Winningham	.05
132	Checklist	.05

1992 Topps Traded Gold

A reported 6,000 sets of 1992 Topps Traded were produced in a gold edition, with gold-foil strips on front bearing the player and team names. The cards are in all other respects identical to the regular boxed Traded issue.

		MT
Complete Set (132):		30.00
Common Player:		.15

(Star cards valued at 2X-3X corresponding cards in regular Topps Traded issue)

1992 Topps 1991 Major League Debut

This 194-card set highlights the debut date of 1991 Major League rookies. Two checklist cards are also included in this boxed set. The card fronts resemble the 1992 Topps cards. A debut banner appears in the lower-right corner of the card front. The set is packaged in an attractive collector box and the cards are numbered alphabetically. This set was available only through hobby dealers.

		MT
Complete Set (194):		18.00
Common Player:		.08
1	Kyle Abbott	.20
2	Dana Allison	.08
3	Rich Amaral	.08
4	Ruben Amaro	.08
5	Andy Ashby	.15
6	Jim Austin	.08
7	Jeff Bagwell	3.00
8	Jeff Banister	.08
9	Willie Banks	.15
10	Bret Barberie	.20
11	Kim Batiste	.08
12	Chris Beasley	.08
13	Rod Beck	.25
14	Derek Bell	.50
15	Esteban Beltre	.08
16	Freddie Benavides	.08
17	Rickey Bones	.10
18	Denis Boucher	.08
19	Ryan Bowen	.10
20	Cliff Brantley	.10
21	John Briscoe	.08
22	Scott Brosius	.08
23	Terry Bross	.08
24	Jarvis Brown	.08
25	Scott Bullett	.10
26	Kevin Campbell	.08
27	Amalio Carreno	.08
28	Matias Carrillo	.08
29	Jeff Carter	.08
30	Vinny Castilla	.45
31	Braulio Castillo	.08
32	Frank Castillo	.08
33	Darrin Chapin	.08
34	Mike Christopher	.08
35	Mark Clark	.10
36	Royce Clayton	.15
37	Stu Cole	.08
38	Gary Cooper	.08
39	Archie Corbin	.08
40	Rheal Cormier	.10
41	Chris Cron	.08
42	Mike Dalton	.08
43	Mark Davis	.08
44	Francisco de la Rosa	.08
45	Chris Donnels	.10
46	Brian Drahman	.10
47	Tom Drees	.08
48	Kirk Dressendorfer	.15
49	Bruce Egloff	.08
50	Cal Eldred	.20
51	Jose Escobar	.08
52	Tony Eusebio	.10
53	Hector Fajardo	.10
54	Monty Farriss	.10
55	Jeff Fassero	.15
56	Dave Fleming	.10
57	Kevin Flora	.08
58	Steve Foster	.08
59	Dan Gakeler	.08
60	Ramon Garcia	.08
61	Chris Gardner	.08
62	Jeff Gardner	.10
63	Chris George	.10
64	Ray Giannelli	.08
65	Tom Goodwin	.12
66	Mark Grater	.08
67	Johnny Guzman	.10
68	Juan Guzman	.30
69	Dave Haas	.08
70	Chris Haney	.10
71	Shawn Hare	.10
72	Donald Harris	.10
73	Doug Henry	.10
74	Pat Hentgen	.20
75	Gil Heredia	.15
76	Jeremy Hernandez	.08
77	Jose Hernandez	.08
78	Roberto Hernandez	.10
79	Bryan Hickerson	.10
80	Milt Hill	.08
81	Vince Horsman	.08
82	Wayne Housie	.08
83	Chris Howard	.08
84	David Howard	.10
85	Mike Humphreys	.08
86	Brian Hunter	.08
87	Jim Hunter	.08
88	Mike Ignasiak	.08
89	Reggie Jefferson	.15
90	Jeff Johnson	.10
91	Joel Johnson	.08
92	Calvin Jones	.08
93	Chris Jones	.15
94	Stacy Jones	.08
95	Jeff Juden	.20
96	Scott Kamieniecki	.15
97	Eric Karros	.60
98	Pat Kelly	.15
99	John Kiely	.08
100	Darryl Kile	.20
101	Wayne Kirby	.10
102	Garland Kiser	.08
103	Chuck Knoblauch	.60
104	Randy Knorr	.08
105	Tom Kramer	.08
106	Ced Landrum	.08
107	Patrick Lennon	.08
108	Jim Lewis	.08
109	Mark Lewis	.20
110	Doug Lindsey	.08
111	Scott Livingstone	.15
112	Kenny Lofton	.75
113	Ever Magallanes	.08
114	Mike Magnante	.10
115	Barry Manuel	.08
116	Josias Manzanillo	.10
117	Chito Martinez	.10
118	Terry Mathews	.08
119	Rob Mauer	.08
120	Tim Mauser	.08
121	Terry McDaniel	.08
122	Rusty Meacham	.08
123	Luis Mercedes	.10
124	Paul Miller	.10
125	Keith Mitchell	.08
126	Bobby Moore	.08
127	Kevin Morton	.10
128	Andy Mota	.08
129	Jose Mota	.08
130	Mike Mussina	.60
131	Jeff Mutis	.08
132	Denny Neagle	.40
133	Warren Newson	.10
134	Jim Olander	.08
135	Erik Pappas	.10
136	Jorge Pedre	.08
137	Yorkis Perez	.10
138	Mark Petkovsek	.10
139	Doug Piatt	.08
140	Jeff Plympton	.08
141	Harvey Pulliam	.08
142	John Ramos	.08
143	Mike Remlinger	.08
144	Laddie Renfroe	.08
145	Armando Reynoso	.10
146	Arthur Rhodes	.20
147	Pat Rice	.10
148	Nikco Riesgo	.08
149	Carlos Rodriguez	.08
150	Ivan Rodriguez	2.00
151	Wayne Rosenthal	.08
152	Rico Rossy	.08
153	Stan Royer	.15
154	Rey Sanchez	.10
155	Reggie Sanders	.40
156	Mo Sanford	.20
157	Bob Scanlan	.10
158	Pete Schourek	.15
159	Gary Scott	.08
160	Tim Scott	.08
161	Tony Scruggs	.08
162	Scott Servais	.10
163	Doug Simons	.08
164	Heathcliff Slocumb	.08
165	Joe Slusarski	.10
166	Tim Spehr	.10
167	Ed Sprague	.12
168	Jeff Tackett	.10
169	Eddie Taubensee	.12
170	Wade Taylor	.10
171	Jim Thome	.45
172	Mike Timlin	.15
173	Jose Tolentino	.08
174	John Vander Wal	.10
175	Todd Van Poppel	.10
176	Mo Vaughn	1.00
177	Dave Wainhouse	.08
178	Don Wakamatsu	.08
179	Bruce Walton	.08
180	Kevin Ward	.08
181	Dave Weathers	.08
182	Eric Wedge	.08
183	John Wehner	.08
184	Rick Wilkins	.15
185	Bernie Williams	1.00
186	Brian Williams	.08
187	Ron Witmeyer	.08
188	Mark Wohlers	.12
189	Ted Wood	.08
190	Anthony Young	.25
191	Eddie Zosky	.20
192	Bob Zupcic	.08
193	Checklist	.08
194	Checklist	.08

1993 Topps

Topps issued in a two-series format in 1993. Series I includes cards #1-396; Series II comprises #397-825. The card fronts feature full-color photos enclosed by a white border. The player's name and team appear at the bottom. The backs feature an additional player photo and biographical information at the top. The bottom box includes statistics and player information. The cards are numbered in red in a yellow flag on the back.

		MT
Complete Set (825):		30.00
Common Player:		.05
Series 1 or 2 Wax Box:		20.00
1	Robin Yount	.15
2	Barry Bonds	.40
3	Ryne Sandberg	.40
4	Roger Clemens	.50
5	Tony Gwynn	.50
6	*Jeff Tackett*	.08
7	Pete Incaviglia	.05
8	Mark Wohlers	.05
9	Kent Hrbek	.08
10	Will Clark	.15
11	Eric Karros	.10
12	Lee Smith	.08
13	Esteban Beltre	.05
14	Greg Briley	.05
15	Marquis Grissom	.08
16	Dan Plesac	.05
17	Dave Hollins	.05
18	Terry Steinbach	.05
19	Ed Nunez	.05
20	Tim Salmon	.45
21	Luis Salazar	.05
22	Jim Eisenreich	.05
23	Todd Stottlemyre	.05
24	Tim Naehring	.05
25	John Franco	.05
26	Skeeter Barnes	.05
27	*Carlos Garcia*	.15
28	Joe Orsulak	.05
29	Dwayne Henry	.05
30	Fred McGriff	.20
31	Derek Lilliquist	.05
32	Don Mattingly	.40
33	B.J. Wallace (1992 Draft Pick)	.15
34	Juan Gonzalez	.50
35	John Smoltz	.15
36	Scott Servais	.05
37	Lenny Webster	.05
38	Chris James	.05
39	Roger McDowell	.05
40	Ozzie Smith	.25
41	Alex Fernandez	.08
42	Spike Owen	.05
43	Ruben Amaro	.05
44	Kevin Seitzer	.05
45	Dave Fleming	.05
46	*Eric Fox*	.08
47	Bob Scanlan	.05
48	Bert Blyleven	.05
49	Brian McRae	.05
50	Roberto Alomar	.30
51	Mo Vaughn	.50
52	Bobby Bonilla	.10
53	Frank Tanana	.05
54	Mike LaValliere	.05
55	Mark McLemore	.05
56	Chad Mottola (1992 Draft Pick)	.15
57	Norm Charlton	.05
58	Jose Melendez	.05
59	Carlos Martinez	.05
60	Roberto Kelly	.05
61	Gene Larkin	.05
62	Rafael Belliard	.05
63	Al Osuna	.05
64	Scott Chiamparino	.05
65	Brett Butler	.05
66	John Burkett	.05
67	Felix Jose	.05
68	Omar Vizquel	.05
69	*John Vander Wal*	.12
70	Roberto Hernandez	.08
71	Ricky Bones	.05
72	*Jeff Grotewold*	.12
73	Mike Moore	.05
74	Steve Buechele	.05
75	Juan Guzman	.05
76	Kevin Appier	.05
77	Junior Felix	.05
78	Greg Harris	.05
79	Dick Schofield	.05
80	Cecil Fielder	.10
81	Lloyd McClendon	.05
82	David Segui	.05
83	Reggie Sanders	.10
84	Kurt Stillwell	.05
85	Sandy Alomar	.10
86	John Habyan	.05
87	Kevin Reimer	.05
88	Mike Stanton	.05
89	Eric Anthony	.05
90	Scott Erickson	.05
91	Craig Colbert	.05
92	Tom Pagnozzi	.05
93	*Pedro Astacio*	.10
94	Lance Johnson	.05
95	Larry Walker	.20
96	Russ Swan	.05
97	Scott Fletcher	.05
98	*Derek Jeter* (1992 Draft Pick)	4.00
99	*Mike Williams*	.05
100	Mark McGwire	2.00
101	*Jim Bullinger*	.12
102	Brian Hunter	.05
103	Jody Reed	.05
104	*Mike Butcher*	.10
105	Gregg Jefferies	.08
106	Howard Johnson	.05
107	*John Kiely*	.12
108	Jose Lind	.05
109	Sam Horn	.05
110	Barry Larkin	.15
111	Bruce Hurst	.05
112	Brian Barnes	.05
113	Thomas Howard	.05
114	Mel Hall	.05
115	Robby Thompson	.05
116	Mark Lemke	.05
117	Eddie Taubensee	.05
118	David Hulse	.05
119	Pedro Munoz	.05
120	Ramon Martinez	.08
121	Todd Worrell	.05
122	Joey Cora	.05
123	Moises Alou	.10
124	Franklin Stubbs	.05
125	Pete O'Brien	.05
126	*Bob Ayrault*	.12
127	Carney Lansford	.05
128	Kal Daniels	.05
129	Joe Grahe	.05
130	Jeff Montgomery	.05
131	Dave Winfield	.10
132	Preston Wilson (1992 Draft Pick)	.15
133	Steve Wilson	.05
134	Lee Guetterman	.05
135	Mickey Tettleton	.05
136	Jeff King	.05
137	Alan Mills	.05
138	Joe Oliver	.05
139	Gary Gaetti	.05
140	Gary Sheffield	.15
141	Dennis Cook	.05
142	Charlie Hayes	.05
143	Jeff Huson	.05
144	Kent Mercker	.05
145	*Eric Young*	.10
146	Scott Leius	.05
147	Bryan Hickerson	.05
148	Steve Finley	.10
149	Rheal Cormier	.05
150	Frank Thomas	1.50
151	*Archi Cianfrocco*	.08
152	Rich DeLucia	.05
153	Greg Vaughn	.05
154	Wes Chamberlain	.05
155	Dennis Eckersley	.10
156	Sammy Sosa	1.00
157	Gary DiSarcina	.05
158	*Kevin Koslofski*	.08
159	*Doug Linton*	.08
160	Lou Whitaker	.05
161	Chad McDonnell (1992 Draft Pick)	.12
162	Joe Hesketh	.05
163	*Tim Mauser*	.08
164	Leo Gomez	.05
165	Jose Rijo	.05
166	*Tim Scott*	.10
167	Steve Olin	.05
168	Kevin Maas	.05
169	Kenny Rogers	.05
170	Dave Justice	.25
171	Doug Jones	.05
172	*Jeff Reboulet*	.10
173	Andres Galarraga	.15
174	Randy Velarde	.05
175	Kirk McCaskill	.05
176	Darren Lewis	.05
177	Lenny Harris	.05
178	Jeff Fassero	.05
179	Ken Griffey, Jr.	1.50
180	Darren Daulton	.05
181	John Jaha	.05
182	Ron Darling	.05
183	Greg Maddux	1.25
184	*Damion Easley*	.10
185	Jack Morris	.05
186	Mike Magnante	.05
187	John Dopson	.05
188	Sid Fernandez	.05
189	Tony Phillips	.05
190	Doug Drabek	.05
191	*Sean Lowe* (1992 Draft Pick)	.10
192	Bob Milacki	.05
193	*Steve Foster*	.08
194	Jerald Clark	.05
195	Pete Harnisch	.05
196	Pat Kelly	.05
197	Jeff Frye	.10
198	Alejandro Pena	.05
199	Junior Ortiz	.05
200	Kirby Puckett	.50
201	Jose Uribe	.05
202	Mike Scioscia	.05
203	Bernard Gilkey	.05
204	Dan Pasqua	.05
205	Gary Carter	.08
206	Henry Cotto	.05
207	Paul Molitor	.40
208	Mike Hartley	.05
209	Jeff Parrett	.05
210	Mark Langston	.05
211	Doug Dascenzo	.05
212	Rick Reed	.05
213	Candy Maldonado	.05
214	Danny Darwin	.05
215	*Pat Howell*	.08
216	Mark Leiter	.05
217	Kevin Mitchell	.08
218	Ben McDonald	.08
219	Bip Roberts	.05
220	Benny Santiago	.08
221	Carlos Baerga	.10
222	Bernie Williams	.40
223	*Roger Pavlik*	.10
224	Sid Bream	.05
225	Matt Williams	.25
226	Willie Banks	.05
227	Jeff Bagwell	.50
228	Tom Goodwin	.05
229	Mike Perez	.05
230	Carlton Fisk	.08
231	John Wetteland	.05
232	Tino Martinez	.15
233	*Rick Greene* (1992 Draft Pick)	.08
234	Tim McIntosh	.05
235	Mitch Williams	.05
236	*Kevin Campbell*	.08
237	Jose Vizcaino	.05
238	Chris Donnels	.05
239	Mike Boddicker	.05
240	John Olerud	.10
241	Mike Gardiner	.05
242	Charlie O'Brien	.05
243	Rob Deer	.05
244	Denny Neagle	.05
245	Chris Sabo	.05
246	Gregg Olson	.05
247	Frank Seminara	.05
248	Scott Scudder	.05
249	Tim Burke	.05
250	Chuck Knoblauch	.20
251	Mike Bielecki	.05
252	Xavier Hernandez	.05
253	Jose Guzman	.05
254	Cory Snyder	.05
255	Orel Hershiser	.08
256	Wil Cordero	.08
257	Luis Alicea	.05
258	Mike Schooler	.05
259	Craig Grebeck	.05
260	Duane Ward	.05
261	Bill Wegman	.05
262	Mickey Morandini	.05
263	*Vince Horsman*	.08
264	Paul Sorrento	.05
265	Andre Dawson	.08
266	Rene Gonzales	.05
267	Keith Miller	.05
268	Derek Bell	.10
269	*Todd Steverson* (1992 Draft Pick)	.15
270	Frank Viola	.05

No.	Name	Value
271	Wally Whitehurst	.05
272	*Kurt Knudsen*	.08
273	*Dan Walters*	.12
274	Rick Sutcliffe	.05
275	Andy Van Slyke	.05
276	Paul O'Neill	.15
277	Mark Whiten	.05
278	Chris Nabholz	.05
279	Todd Burns	.05
280	Tom Glavine	.15
281	*Butch Henry*	.08
282	Shane Mack	.08
283	Mike Jackson	.05
284	Henry Rodriguez	.08
285	Bob Tewksbury	.05
286	Ron Karkovice	.05
287	Mike Gallego	.05
288	Dave Cochrane	.05
289	Jesse Orosco	.05
290	Dave Stewart	.08
291	Tommy Greene	.05
292	Rey Sanchez	.05
293	Rob Ducey	.05
294	Brent Mayne	.05
295	Dave Stieb	.05
296	Luis Rivera	.05
297	Jeff Innis	.05
298	Scott Livingstone	.05
299	Bob Patterson	.05
300	Cal Ripken, Jr.	1.50
301	Cesar Hernandez	.05
302	Randy Myers	.05
303	Brook Jacoby	.05
304	Melido Perez	.05
305	Rafael Palmeiro	.15
306	Damon Berryhill	.05
307	*Dan Serafini* (1992 Draft Pick)	.10
308	Darryl Kile	.05
309	*J.T. Bruett*	.10
310	Dave Righetti	.05
311	Jay Howell	.05
312	Geronimo Pena	.05
313	Greg Hibbard	.05
314	Mark Gardner	.05
315	Edgar Martinez	.10
316	Dave Nilsson	.05
317	Kyle Abbott	.05
318	Willie Wilson	.05
319	Paul Assenmacher	.05
320	*Tim Fortugno*	.08
321	Rusty Meacham	.05
322	Pat Borders	.05
323	Mike Greenwell	.08
324	Willie Randolph	.05
325	Bill Gullickson	.05
326	Gary Varsho	.05
327	Tim Hulett	.05
328	Scott Ruskin	.05
329	Mike Maddux	.05
330	Danny Tartabull	.05
331	Kenny Lofton	.40
332	Geno Petralli	.05
333	Otis Nixon	.05
334	*Jason Kendall* (1992 Draft Pick)	.75
335	Mark Portugal	.05
336	Mike Pagliarulo	.05
337	Kirt Manwaring	.05
338	Bob Ojeda	.05
339	*Mark Clark*	.08
340	John Kruk	.08
341	Mel Rojas	.05
342	Erik Hanson	.05
343	Doug Henry	.05
344	Jack McDowell	.10
345	Harold Baines	.05
346	Chuck McElroy	.05
347	Luis Sojo	.05
348	Andy Stankiewicz	.05
349	*Hipolito Pichardo*	.08
350	Joe Carter	.12
351	Ellis Burks	.05
352	Pete Schourek	.05
353	*Buddy Groom*	.10
354	Jay Bell	.05
355	Brady Anderson	.15
356	Freddie Benavides	.05
357	Phil Stephenson	.05
358	Kevin Wickander	.05
359	Mike Stanley	.05
360	Ivan Rodriguez	.40
361	Scott Bankhead	.05
362	Luis Gonzalez	.05
363	John Smiley	.05
364	Trevor Wilson	.05
365	Tom Candiotti	.05
366	Craig Wilson	.05
367	Steve Sax	.05
368	Delino Deshields	.05
369	Jaime Navarro	.05
370	Dave Valle	.05
371	Mariano Duncan	.05
372	Rod Nichols	.05
373	Mike Morgan	.05
374	Julio Valera	.05
375	Wally Joyner	.08
376	Tom Henke	.05
377	Herm Winningham	.05
378	Orlando Merced	.05
379	Mike Munoz	.05
380	Todd Hundley	.05
381	Mike Flanagan	.05
382	Tim Belcher	.05
383	Jerry Browne	.05
384	Mike Benjamin	.05
385	Jim Leyritz	.05
386	Ray Lankford	.08
387	Devon White	.05
388	Jeremy Hernandez	.05
389	Brian Harper	.05
390	Wade Boggs	.15
391	Derrick May	.08
392	Travis Fryman	.08
393	Ron Gant	.08
394	Checklist 1-132	.05
395	Checklist 133-264	.05
396	Checklist 265-396	.05
397	George Brett	.40
398	Bobby Witt	.05
399	Daryl Boston	.05
400	Bo Jackson	.15
401	Fred McGriff, Frank Thomas (All-Star)	.40
402	Ryne Sandberg, Carlos Baerga (All-Star)	.15
403	Gary Sheffield, Edgar Martinez (All-Star)	.05
404	Barry Larkin, Travis Fryman (All-Star)	.10
405	Andy Van Slyke, Ken Griffey, Jr. (All-Star)	.40
406	Larry Walker, Kirby Puckett (All-Star)	.25
407	Barry Bonds, Joe Carter (All-Star)	.15
408	Darren Daulton, Brian Harper (All-Star)	.05
409	Greg Maddux, Roger Clemens (All-Star)	.25
410	Tom Glavine, Dave Fleming (All-Star)	.10
411	Lee Smith, Dennis Eckersley (All-Star)	.05
412	Jamie McAndrew	.05
413	Pete Smith	.05
414	Juan Guerrero	.05
415	Todd Frohwirth	.05
416	Randy Tomlin	.05
417	B.J. Surhoff	.05
418	Jim Gott	.05
419	Mark Thompson (1992 Draft Pick)	.10
420	Kevin Tapani	.05
421	Curt Schilling	.05
422	*J.T. Snow*	.50
423	Top Prospects 1B(Ryan Klesko, Ivan Cruz, Bubba Smith, Larry Sutton)	.50
424	John Valentin	.05
425	Joe Girardi	.05
426	*Nigel Wilson*	.15
427	Bob MacDonald	.05
428	Todd Zeile	.05
429	Milt Cuyler	.05
430	Eddie Murray	.15
431	Rich Amaral	.05
432	Pete Young	.05
433	Rockies Future Stars(Roger Bailey, Tom Schmidt)	.15
434	Jack Armstrong	.05
435	Willie McGee	.05
436	Greg Harris	.05
437	Chris Hammond	.05
438	*Ritchie Moody* (1992 Draft Pick)	.15
439	Bryan Harvey	.05
440	Ruben Sierra	.10
441	Marlins Future Stars(Don Lemon, Todd Pridy)	.10
442	Kevin McReynolds	.05
443	Terry Leach	.05
444	David Nied	.10
445	Dale Murphy	.08
446	Luis Mercedes	.05
447	*Keith Shepherd*	.10
448	Ken Caminiti	.05
449	James Austin	.05
450	Darryl Strawberry	.10
451	Top Prospects 2B(Ramon Caraballo, Jon Shave, Brent Gates), *(Quinton McCracken)*	.15
452	Bob Wickman	.05
453	Victor Cole	.05
454	*John Johnstone*	.10
455	Chili Davis	.05
456	Scott Taylor	.05
457	Tracy Woodson	.05
458	David Wells	.05
459	*Derek Wallace* (1992 Draft Pick)	.20
460	Randy Johnson	.35
461	*Steve Reed*	.05
462	Felix Fermin	.05
463	Scott Aldred	.05
464	Greg Colbrunn	.05
465	Tony Fernandez	.05
466	Mike Felder	.05
467	Lee Stevens	.05
468	Matt Whiteside	.05
469	Dave Hansen	.05
470	Rob Dibble	.05
471	Dave Gallagher	.05
472	Chris Gwynn	.05
473	Dave Henderson	.05
474	Ozzie Guillen	.05
475	Jeff Reardon	.05
476	Rockies Future Stars(Mark Voisard, Will Scalzitti)	.15
477	Jimmy Jones	.05
478	Greg Cadaret	.05
479	Todd Pratt	.05
480	Pat Listach	.08
481	*Ryan Luzinski* (1992 Draft Pick)	.15
482	Darren Reed	.05
483	*Brian Griffiths*	.10
484	John Wehner	.05
485	Glenn Davis	.05
486	*Eric Wedge*	.10
487	Jesse Hollins	.05
488	Manuel Lee	.05
489	*Scott Fredrickson*	.10
490	Omar Olivares	.05
491	Shawn Hare	.05
492	Tom Lampkin	.05
493	Jeff Nelson	.05
494	Top Prospects 3B(Kevin Young, Adell Davenport, Eduardo Perez, Lou Lucca)	.15
495	Ken Hill	.05
496	Reggie Jefferson	.05
497	Marlins Future Stars(Matt Petersen, Willie Brown)	.10
498	Bud Black	.05
499	Chuck Crim	.05
500	Jose Canseco	.20
501	Major League Managers(Johnny Oates, Bobby Cox)	.05
502	Major League Managers(Butch Hobson, Jim Lefebvre)	.05
503	Major League Managers(Buck Rodgers, Tony Perez)	.05
504	Major League Managers(Gene Lamont, Don Baylor)	.05
505	Major League Managers(Mike Hargrove, Rene Lachemann)	.05
506	Major League Managers(Sparky Anderson, Art Howe)	.05
507	Major League Managers(Hal McRae, Tommy Lasorda)	.20
508	Major League Manager(Phil Garner, Felipe Alou)	.05
509	Major League Managers(Tom Kelly, Jeff Torborg)	.05
510	Major League Managers(Buck Showalter, Jim Fregosi)	.05

511	Major League Managers(Tony LaRussa, Jim Leyland)	.05
512	Major League Managers(Lou Piniella, Joe Torre)	.05
513	Major League Managers(Toby Harrah, Jim Riggleman)	.05
514	Major League Managers(Cito Gaston, Dusty Baker)	.05
515	Greg Swindell	.05
516	Alex Arias	.05
517	Bill Pecota	.05
518	*Benji Grigsby* (1992 Draft Pick)	.15
519	David Howard	.05
520	Charlie Hough	.05
521	Kevin Flora	.05
522	Shane Reynolds	.05
523	*Doug Bochtler*	.10
524	Chris Hoiles	.05
525	Scott Sanderson	.05
526	Mike Sharperson	.05
527	Mike Fetters	.05
528	Paul Quantrill	.05
529	Top Propsects SS(Dave Silvestri, Chipper Jones, Benji Gil, Jeff Patzke)	2.50
530	Sterling Hitchcock	.05
531	Joe Millette	.05
532	Tom Brunansky	.05
533	Frank Castillo	.05
534	Randy Knorr	.05
535	Jose Oquendo	.05
536	Dave Haas	.05
537	Rockies Future Stars(Jason Hutchins, Ryan Turner)	.15
538	Jimmy Baron (1992 Draft Pick)	.10
539	Kerry Woodson	.05
540	Ivan Calderon	.05
541	Denis Boucher	.05
542	Royce Clayton	.08
543	Reggie Williams	.05
544	Steve Decker	.05
545	Dean Palmer	.05
546	Hal Morris	.05
547	*Ryan Thompson*	.10
548	Lance Blankenship	.05
549	Hensley Meulens	.05
550	Scott Radinsky	.05
551	*Eric Young*	.15
552	Jeff Blauser	.05
553	Andujar Cedeno	.05
554	Arthur Rhodes	.05
555	Terry Mulholland	.05
556	Darryl Hamilton	.05
557	Pedro Martinez	.05
558	Marlins Future Stars(Ryan Whitman, Mark Skeels)	.15
559	*Jamie Arnold* (1992 Draft Pick)	.15
560	Zane Smith	.05
561	Matt Nokes	.05
562	Bob Zupcic	.05
563	Shawn Boskie	.05
564	Mike Timlin	.05
565	Jerald Clark	.05
566	Rod Brewer	.05
567	Mark Carreon	.05
568	Andy Benes	.05
569	Shawn Barton	.05
570	Tim Wallach	.05
571	Dave Mlicki	.05
572	Trevor Hoffman	.05
573	John Patterson	.05
574	DeShawn Warren (1992 Draft Pick)	.15
575	Monty Fariss	.05
576	Top Prospects OF(Darrell Sherman, Damon Buford, Cliff Floyd, Michael Moore)	.20
577	Tim Costo	.05
578	Dave Magadan	.05
579	Rockies Future Stars(Neil Garret, Jason Bates)	.15
580	Walt Weiss	.05
581	Chris Haney	.05
582	Shawn Abner	.05
583	Marvin Freeman	.05
584	Casey Candaele	.05
585	Ricky Jordan	.05
586	Jeff Tabaka	.05
587	Manny Alexander	.05

588	Mike Trombley	.05
589	Carlos Hernandez	.05
590	Cal Eldred	.05
591	Alex Cole	.05
592	Phil Plantier	.05
593	Brett Merriman	.05
594	Jerry Nielsen	.05
595	Shawon Dunston	.08
596	Jimmy Key	.05
597	Gerald Perry	.05
598	Rico Brogna	.05
599	Marlins Future Stars(Clemente Nunez, Dan Robinson)	.15
600	Bret Saberhagen	.05
601	Craig Shipley	.05
602	Henry Mercedes	.05
603	Jim Thome	.20
604	Rod Beck	.05
605	Chuck Finley	.05
606	J. Owens	.05
607	Dan Smith	.05
608	Bill Doran	.05
609	Lance Parrish	.05
610	Denny Martinez	.05
611	Tom Gordon	.05
612	Byron Mathews (1992 Draft Pick)	.10
613	Joel Adamson	.05
614	Brian Williams	.05
615	Steve Avery	.15
616	Top Prospects OF(Matt Mieske, Tracy Sanders, Midre Cummings, Ryan Freeburg)	
617	Craig Lefferts	.05
618	Tony Pena	.05
619	Billy Spiers	.05
620	Todd Benzinger	.05
621	Rockies Future Stars(Mike Kotarski, Greg Boyd)	.15
622	Ben Rivera	.05
623	Al Martin	.10
624	Sam Militello	.05
625	Rick Aguilera	.05
626	Danny Gladden	.05
627	Andres Berumen	.05
628	Kelly Gruber	.05
629	Cris Carpenter	.05
630	Mark Grace	.15
631	Jeff Brantley	.05
632	Chris Widger (1992 Draft Pick)	.10
633	Russian Angels(Rodolf Razjigaev, Evgenyi Puchkov, Ilya Bogatyrev)	.10
634	Mo Sanford	.05
635	Albert Belle	.40
636	Tim Teufel	.05
637	Greg Myers	.05
638	Brian Bohanon	.05
639	Mike Bordick	.05
640	Dwight Gooden	.10
641	Marlins Future Stars(Pat Leahy, Gavin Baugh)	.10
642	Milt Hill	.05
643	Luis Aquino	.05
644	Dante Bichette	.15
645	Bobby Thigpen	.05
646	Rich Scheid	.05
647	Brian Sackinsky (1992 Draft Pick)	.10
648	Ryan Hawblitzel	.05
649	Tom Marsh	.05
650	Terry Pendleton	.08
651	*Rafael Bournigal*	.10
652	Dave West	.05
653	Steve Hosey	.05
654	Gerald Williams	.05
655	Scott Cooper	.05
656	Gary Scott	.05
657	Mike Harkey	.05
658	Top Prospects OF(Jeromy Burnitz, Melvin Nieves, Rich Becker, Shon Walker)	.30
659	Ed Sprague	.05
660	Alan Trammell	.08
661	Rockies Future Stars(Garvin Alston, Mike Case)	.15
662	Donovan Osborne	.05
663	Jeff Gardner	.05
664	Calvin Jones	.05
665	Darrin Fletcher	.08
666	Glenallen Hill	.05

667	Jim Rosenbohm (1992 Draft Pick)	.10
668	Scott Lewis	.05
669	Kip Yaughn	.05
670	Julio Franco	.05
671	Dave Martinez	.05
672	Kevin Bass	.05
673	Todd Van Poppel	.10
674	Mark Gubicza	.05
675	Tim Raines	.08
676	Rudy Seanez	.05
677	Charlie Leibrandt	.05
678	Randy Milligan	.05
679	Kim Batiste	.05
680	Craig Biggio	.05
681	Darren Holmes	.05
682	John Candelaria	.05
683	Marlins Future Stars(Jerry Stafford, Eddie Christian)	.15
684	Pat Mahomes	.05
685	Bob Walk	.05
686	Russ Springer	.05
687	Tony Sheffield (1992 Draft Picks)	.10
688	Dwight Smith	.05
689	Eddie Zosky	.05
690	Bien Figueroa	.05
691	Jim Tatum	.05
692	Chad Kreuter	.05
693	Rich Rodriguez	.05
694	Shane Turner	.05
695	Kent Bottenfield	.05
696	Jose Mesa	.05
697	*Darrell Whitmore*	.10
698	Ted Wood	.05
699	Chad Curtis	.05
700	Nolan Ryan	1.00
701	Top Prospects C(Mike Piazza, Carlos Delgado, Brook Fordyce, Donnie Leshnock)	2.00
702	*Tim Pugh*	.12
703	Jeff Kent	.10
704	Rockies Future Stars(Jon Goodrich, Danny Figueroa)	.15
705	Bob Welch	.05
706	Sherard Clinkscales (1992 Draft Pick)	
707	Donn Pall	.05
708	Greg Olson	.05
709	Jeff Juden	.05
710	Mike Mussina	.30
711	Scott Chiamparino	.05
712	Stan Javier	.05
713	John Doherty	.05
714	Kevin Gross	.05
715	Greg Gagne	.05
716	Steve Cooke	.05
717	Steve Farr	.05
718	Jay Buchner	.08
719	Butch Henry	.05
720	David Cone	.05
721	Rick Wilkins	.05
722	Chuck Carr	.05
723	*Kenny Felder* (1992 Draft Pick)	.15
724	Guillermo Velasquez	.05
725	Billy Hatcher	.05
726	Marlins Future Stars(Mike Veneziale, Ken Kendrena)	.15
727	Jonathan Hurst	.05
728	Steve Frey	.05
729	Mark Leonard	.05
730	Charles Nagy	.05
731	Donald Harris	.05
732	Travis Buckley	.05
733	Tom Browning	.05
734	Anthony Young	.05
735	Steve Shifflett	.05
736	Jeff Russell	.05
737	Wilson Alvarez	.05
738	Lance Painter	.05
739	Dave Weathers	.05
740	Len Dykstra	.08
741	Mike Devereaux	.05
742	Top Prospects SP(Rene Arocha, Alan Embree), (*Tim Crabtree*, Brien Taylor)	.20
743	Dave Landaker (1992 Draft Pick)	.05
744	Chris George	.05
745	Eric Davis	.05
746	Rockies Future Stars(Mark Strittmatter, LaMarr Rogers)	.15
747	Carl Willis	.05
748	Stan Belinda	.05

749	Scott Kamieniecki	.05
750	Rickey Henderson	.08
751	Eric Hillman	.05
752	Pat Hentgen	.05
753	Jim Corsi	.05
754	Brian Jordan	.08
755	Bill Swift	.05
756	Mike Henneman	.05
757	Harold Reynolds	.05
758	Sean Berry	.05
759	Charlie Hayes	.05
760	Luis Polonia	.05
761	Darrin Jackson	.05
762	Mark Lewis	.05
763	Rob Maurer	.05
764	Willie Greene	.05
765	Vince Coleman	.05
766	Todd Revenig	.05
767	Rich Ireland (1992 Draft Pick)	.10
768	Mike MacFarlane	.05
769	Francisco Cabrera	.05
770	Robin Ventura	.08
771	Kevin Ritz	.05
772	Chito Martinez	.05
773	Cliff Brantley	.05
774	Curtis Leskanic	.05
775	Chris Bosio	.05
776	Jose Offerman	.05
777	Mark Guthrie	.05
778	Don Slaught	.05
779	Rich Monteleone	.05
780	Jim Abbott	.08
781	Jack Clark	.05
782	Marlins Future Stars(Rafael Mendoza, Dan Roman)	.15
783	Heathcliff Slocumb	.05
784	Jeff Branson	.05
785	Kevin Brown	.05
786	Top Prospects RP(Mike Christopher, Ken Ryan, Aaron Taylor, Gus Gandarillas)	.15
787	Mike Matthews (1992 Draft Pick)	.05
788	Mackey Sasser	.05
789	Jeff Conine	.08
790	George Bell	.05
791	Pat Rapp	.05
792	Joe Boever	.05
793	Jim Poole	.05
794	Andy Ashby	.05
795	Deion Sanders	.20
796	Scott Brosius	.05
797	Brad Pennington (Coming Attraction)	.10
798	Greg Blosser (Coming Attraction)	.10
799	*Jim Edmonds* (Coming Attraction)	1.00
800	Shawn Jeter (Coming Attraction)	.15
801	Jesse Levis (Coming Attraction)	.05
802	Phil Clark (Coming Attraction)	.10
803	Ed Pierce (Coming Attraction)	.05
804	*Jose Valentin* (Coming Attraction)	.20
805	Terry Jorgensen (Coming Attraction)	.05
806	Mark Hutton (Coming Attraction)	.05
807	Troy Neel (Coming Attraction)	.08
808	Bret Boone (Coming Attraction)	.20
809	Chris Colon (Coming Attraction)	.05
810	*Domingo Martinez* (Coming Attraction)	.10
811	Javier Lopez (Coming Attraction)	.30
812	Matt Walbeck (Coming Attraction)	.10
813	Dan Wilson (Coming Attraction)	.10
814	Scooter Tucker (Coming Attraction)	.10
815	*Billy Ashley* (Coming Attraction)	.10
816	*Tim Laker* (Coming Attraction)	.10
817	Bobby Jones (Coming Attraction)	.10
818	Brad Brink (Coming Attraction)	.05
819	William Pennyfeather (Coming Attraction)	.05
820	Stan Royer (Coming Attraction)	.10
821	Doug Brocail (Coming Attraction)	.10
822	Kevin Rogers (Coming Attraction)	.05
823	Checklist 397-528	.05
824	Checklist 541-691	.05
825	Checklist 692-825	.05

1993 Topps Gold

Expanding on the concept begun in 1992, Topps issued a "gold" version of each of its regular 1993 cards as a package insert. One Gold card was found in each wax pack; three per rack-pack and five per jumbo cello pack. Ten Gold cards were included in each factory set. Identical in format to the regular-issue 1993 Topps cards, the Gold version replaces the black or white Topps logo on front with a "ToppsGold" logo in gold-foil. The color bars and angled strips beneath the player photo which carry the player and team ID on regular cards are replaced with a gold-foil version on the insert cards. Backs are identical to the regular cards. The six checklist cards in the regular issue were replaced in the Gold version with cards of players who do not appear in the 1993 Topps set.

		MT
Complete Set (825):		110.00
Common Player:		.25
	(Star cards valued at 3X-4X corresponding cards in regular 1993 Topps issue)	
394	Bernardo Brito	.25
395	Jim McNamara	.25
396	Rich Sauveur	.25
823	Keith Brown	.25
824	Russ McGinnis	.25
825	Mike Walker	.25

1993 Topps Black Gold

Randomly inserted in regular 1993 Topps packs, as well as 10 per factory set, Black Gold cards are found in both single-player ver-

sions and "Winner" cards. The single-player cards feature an action photo set against a black background and highlighted at top and bottom with gold foil. Backs have another player photo at left, again on a black background. A career summary is printed in a blue box at right. A "Topps Black Gold" logo appears at top-left, and the player's name is printed in gold foil in an art deco device at top-right. The Winner cards picture tiny versions of the Black Gold player cards for which they could be redeemed by mail.

JOE OLIVER

		MT
Complete Set (44):		10.00
Common Player:		.25
Winner A (1-11):		.50
Winner B (12-22):		.50
Winner C (23-33):		.50
Winner D (34-44):		.50
Winner AB (1-22):		1.00
Winner CD (23-44):		1.00
Winner ABCD (1-44):		2.00
1	Barry Bonds	.75
2	Will Clark	.30
3	Darren Daulton	.25
4	Andre Dawson	.25
5	Delino DeShields	.25
6	Tom Glavine	.30
7	Marquis Grissom	.25
8	Tony Gwynn	.75
9	Eric Karros	.25
10	Ray Lankford	.25
11	Barry Larkin	.30
12	Greg Maddux	2.00
13	Fred McGriff	.30
14	Joe Oliver	.25
15	Terry Pendleton	.25
16	Bip Roberts	.25
17	Ryne Sandberg	.50
18	Gary Sheffield	.30
19	Lee Smith	.25
20	Ozzie Smith	.40
21	Andy Van Slyke	.25
22	Larry Walker	.40
23	Roberto Alomar	.40
24	Brady Anderson	.35
25	Carlos Baerga	.25
26	Joe Carter	.25
27	Roger Clemens	.65
28	Mike Devereaux	.25
29	Dennis Eckersley	.25
30	Cecil Fielder	.35
31	Travis Fryman	.25
32	Juan Gonzalez	.75
33	Ken Griffey Jr.	3.00
34	Brian Harper	.25
35	Pat Listach	.25
36	Kenny Lofton	.65
37	Edgar Martinez	.25
38	Jack McDowell	.25
39	Mark McGwire	1.50
40	Kirby Puckett	.75
41	Mickey Tettleton	.25

42	Frank Thomas	3.00
43	Robin Ventura	.25
44	Dave Winfield	.25

1993 Topps Traded

The 1993 Topps Traded baseball set features many players in their new uniforms as a result of trades, free agent signings and rookie call-ups. The set also features 35 expansion players from the Colorado Rockies and Florida Marlins, as well as 22 Team USA members exclusive to Topps. The 132-card set is packed in a color deluxe printed box.

		MT
	Complete Set (132):	30.00
	Common Player:	.05
1	Barry Bonds	.50
2	Rich Renteria	.05
3	Aaron Sele	.50
4	*Carlton Loewer* (USA)	.15
5	Erik Pappas	.05
6	*Greg McMichael*	.15
7	Freddie Benavides	.05
8	Kirk Gibson	.05
9	Tony Fernandez	.05
10	*Jay Gainer* (USA)	.20
11	Orestes Destrade	.05
12	*A.J. Hinch* (USA)	6.00
13	Bobby Munoz	.05
14	Tom Henke	.05
15	Rob Butler	.05
16	Gary Wayne	.05
17	David McCarty	.20
18	Walt Weiss	.05
19	*Todd Helton* (USA)	18.00
20	Mark Whiten	.05
21	Ricky Gutierrez	.10
22	*Dustin Hermanson* (USA)	1.00
23	*Sherman Obando*	.10
24	Mike Piazza	3.00
25	Jeff Russell	.05
26	Jason Bere	.10
27	*Jack Voight*	.10
28	Chris Bosio	.05
29	Phil Hiatt	.15
30	*Matt Beaumont* (USA)	.10
31	Andres Galarraga	.20
32	Greg Swindell	.05
33	Vinny Castilla	.05
34	*Pat Clougherty* (USA)	.10
35	Greg Briley	.05
36	Dallas Green, Davey Johnson	.05
37	Tyler Green	.10
38	Craig Paquette	.05
39	Danny Sheaffer	.05
40	Jim Converse	.05
41	Terry Harvey	.05
42	Phil Plantier	.10
43	*Doug Saunders*	.10
44	Benny Santiago	.05
45	*Dante Powell* (USA)	.75
46	Jeff Parrett	.05
47	Wade Boggs	.20
48	Paul Molitor	.30
49	Turk Wendell	.05
50	David Wells	.05
51	Gary Sheffield	.20
52	Kevin Young	.15
53	Nelson Liriano	.05
54	Greg Maddux	2.50
55	Derek Bell	.10
56	*Matt Turner*	.20
57	*Charlie Nelson* (USA)	.10
58	Mike Hampton	.05
59	*Troy O'Leary*	.50
60	Benji Gil	.15
61	*Mitch Lyden*	.15
62	J.T. Snow	.40
63	Damon Buford	.10
64	Gene Harris	.05
65	Randy Myers	.05
66	Felix Jose	.05
67	*Todd Dunn* (USA)	.10
68	Jimmy Key	.05
69	Pedro Castellano	.05
70	*Mark Merila* (USA)	.10
71	Rich Rodriguez	.05

72	Matt Mieske	.05
73	Pete Incaviglia	.05
74	Carl Everett	.10
75	Jim Abbott	.10
76	Luis Aquino	.05
77	*Rene Arocha*	.25
78	*Jon Shave*	.10
79	*Todd Walker* (USA)	6.00
80	Jack Armstrong	.05
81	Jeff Richardson	.05
82	Blas Minor	.05
83	Dave Winfield	.15
84	Paul O'Neill	.15
85	*Steve Reich* (USA)	.10
86	Chris Hammond	.05
87	*Hilly Hathaway*	.15
88	Fred McGriff	.20
89	*Dave Telgheder*	.10
90	*Richie Lewis*	.15
91	Brent Gates	.10
92	Andre Dawson	.05
93	*Andy Barkett* (USA)	.10
94	Doug Drabek	.05
95	Joe Klink	.05
96	Willie Blair	.05
97	*Danny Graves* (USA)	.10
98	Pat Meares	.05
99	Mike Lansing	.10
100	*Marcos Armas*	.15
101	*Darren Grass* (USA)	.10
102	Chris Jones	.05
103	*Ken Ryan*	.15
104	Ellis Burks	.05
105	Bobby Kelly	.05
106	Dave Magadan	.05
107	*Paul Wilson* (USA)	.50
108	Rob Natal	.05
109	Paul Wagner	.05
110	Jeromy Burnitz	.20
111	Monty Fariss	.05
112	Kevin Mitchell	.05
113	*Scott Pose*	.15
114	Dave Stewart	.05
115	*Russ Johnson* (USA)	.50
116	Armando Reynoso	.05
117	Geronimo Berroa	.05
118	*Woody Williams*	.50
119	*Tim Bogar*	.15
120	*Bob Scafa* (USA)	.15
121	Henry Cotto	.05
122	Gregg Jefferies	.10
123	Norm Charlton	.05
124	*Bret Wagner* (USA)	.05
125	David Cone	.15
126	Daryl Boston	.05
127	Tim Wallach	.05
128	*Mike Martin* (USA)	.10
129	*John Cummings*	.15
130	Ryan Bowen	.05
131	*John Powell* (USA)	.20
132	Checklist 1	.05

1994 Topps

Once again released in two series of 396 cards each, Topps' basic baseball issue for 1994 offers a standard mix of regular player cards, Future Stars, multi-player rookie cards and double-header All-Star cards. On most cards the player photo on front is framed in a home-plate shaped design. The player's name appears in script beneath the photo and a team color-coded strip at bottom carries the team name and position designation. On back is a player photo, a red box at top with biographical details and a marbled panel which carries the stats and a career highlight. Cards are UV coated on each side. Inserts include a gold-foil enhanced parallel card in every pack, plus random Black Gold cards.

		MT
	Complete Set (792):	28.00
	Common Player:	.05
	Series 1 or 2 Wax Box:	18.00
1	Mike Piazza (All-Star Rookie)	1.00
2	Bernie Williams	.40
3	Kevin Rogers	.05
4	Paul Carey (Future Star)	.10
5	Ozzie Guillen	.05
6	Derrick May	.05
7	Jose Mesa	.05
8	Todd Hundley	.05
9	Chris Haney	.05
10	John Olerud	.10
11	Andujar Cedeno	.05
12	John Smiley	.05
13	Phil Plantier	.05
14	Willie Banks	.05
15	Jay Bell	.05
16	Doug Henry	.05
17	Lance Blankenship	.05
18	Greg Harris	.05
19	Scott Livingstone	.05
20	Bryan Harvey	.05
21	Wil Cordero (All-Star Rookie)	.05
22	Roger Pavlik	.05
23	Mark Lemke	.05
24	Jeff Nelson	.05
25	Todd Zeile	.05
26	Billy Hatcher	.05
27	Joe Magrane	.05
28	Tony Longmire (Future Star)	.10
29	Omar Daal	.05
30	Kirt Manwaring	.05
31	Melido Perez	.05
32	Tim Hulett	.05
33	Jeff Schwarz	.05
34	Nolan Ryan	1.00
35	Jose Guzman	.05
36	Felix Fermin	.05
37	Jeff Innis	.05
38	Brent Mayne	.05
39	*Huck Flener*	.05
40	Jeff Bagwell	.60
41	Kevin Wickander	.05
42	Ricky Gutierrez	.05
43	Pat Mahomes	.05
44	Jeff King	.05
45	Cal Eldred	.05
46	Craig Paquette	.05
47	Richie Lewis	.05
48	Tony Phillips	.05
49	Armando Reynoso	.05
50	Moises Alou	.08
51	Manuel Lee	.05
52	Otis Nixon	.05
53	Billy Ashley (Future Star)	.10
54	Mark Whiten	.05
55	Jeff Russell	.05
56	Chad Curtis	.05
57	Kevin Stocker	.05
58	Mike Jackson	.05
59	Matt Nokes	.05
60	Chris Bosio	.05
61	Damon Buford	.05
62	Tim Belcher	.05
63	Glenallen Hill	.05
64	Bill Wertz	.05
65	Eddie Murray	.10
66	Tom Gordon	.05
67	Alex Gonzalez (Future Star)	.15

No.	Player	Value
68	Eddie Taubensee	.05
69	Jacob Brumfield	.05
70	Andy Benes	.05
71	Rich Becker (Future Star)	.10
72	Steve Cooke (All-Star Rookie)	.05
73	Billy Spiers	.05
74	Scott Brosius	.05
75	Alan Trammell	.08
76	Luis Aquino	.05
77	Jerald Clark	.05
78	Mel Rojas	.05
79	OF Prospects(Billy Masse, Stanton Cameron, Tim Clark, Craig McClure)	.15
80	Jose Canseco	.30
81	Greg McMichael (All-Star Rookie)	.08
82	Brian Turang	.05
83	Tom Urban	.05
84	Garret Anderson (Future Star)	.30
85	Tony Pena	.05
86	Ricky Jordan	.05
87	Jim Gott	.05
88	Pat Kelly	.05
89	Bud Black	.05
90	Robin Ventura	.10
91	Rick Sutcliffe	.05
92	Jose Bautista	.05
93	Bob Ojeda	.05
94	Phil Hiatt	.05
95	Tim Pugh	.05
96	Randy Knorr	.05
97	Todd Jones (Future Star)	.05
98	Ryan Thompson	.05
99	Tim Mauser	.05
100	Kirby Puckett	.75
101	Mark Dewey	.05
102	B.J. Surhoff	.05
103	Sterling Hitchcock	.05
104	Alex Arias	.05
105	David Wells	.05
106	Daryl Boston	.05
107	Mike Stanton	.05
108	Gary Redus	.05
109a	Delino DeShields (red "Expos, 2B")	.15
109b	Delino DeShields (yellow "Expos, 2B")	.05
110	Lee Smith	.05
111	Greg Litton	.05
112	Frank Rodriguez (Future Star)	.10
113	Russ Springer	.05
114	Mitch Williams	.05
115	Eric Karros	.10
116	Jeff Brantley	.05
117	Jack Voight	.05
118	Jason Bere	.10
119	Kevin Roberson	.08
120	Jimmy Key	.05
121	Reggie Jefferson	.05
122	Jeremy Burnitz	.10
123	Billy Brewer (Future Star)	.05
124	Willie Canate	.05
125	Greg Swindell	.05
126	Hal Morris	.05
127	Brad Ausmus	.05
128	George Tsamis	.05
129	Denny Neagle	.05
130	Pat Listach	.05
131	Steve Karsay	.05
132	Bret Barberie	.05
133	Mark Leiter	.05
134	Greg Colbrunn	.05
135	David Nied	.05
136	Dean Palmer	.05
137	Steve Avery	.10
138	Bill Haselman	.05
139	Tripp Cromer (Future Star)	.10
140	Frank Viola	.05
141	Rene Gonzales	.05
142	Curt Schilling	.05
143	Tim Wallach	.05
144	Bobby Munoz	.05
145	Brady Anderson	.05
146	Rod Beck	.05
147	Mike LaValliere	.05
148	Greg Hibbard	.05
149	Kenny Lofton	.40
150	Dwight Gooden	.10
151	Greg Gagne	.05
152	Ray McDavid (Future Star)	.10
153	Chris Donnels	.05
154	Dan Wilson	.05
155	Todd Stottlemyre	.05
156	David McCarty	.08
157	Paul Wagner	.05
158	SS Prospects(Orlando Miller, Brandon Wilson, Derek Jeter, Mike Neal)	.50
159	Mike Fetters	.05
160	Scott Lydy	.05
161	Darrell Whitmore	.05
162	Bob MacDonald	.05
163	Vinny Castilla	.05
164	Denis Boucher	.05
165	Ivan Rodriguez	.40
166	Ron Gant	.08
167	Tim Davis	.05
168	Steve Dixon	.05
169	Scott Fletcher	.05
170	Terry Mulholland	.05
171	Greg Myers	.05
172	Brett Butler	.05
173	Bob Wickman	.05
174	Dave Martinez	.05
175	Fernando Valenzuela	.05
176	Craig Grebeck	.05
177	Shawn Boskie	.05
178	Albie Lopez	.05
179	Butch Huskey (Future Star)	.15
180	George Brett	.40
181	Juan Guzman	.05
182	Eric Anthony	.05
183	Bob Dibble	.05
184	Craig Shipley	.05
185	Kevin Tapani	.05
186	Marcus Moore	.05
187	Graeme Lloyd	.05
188	Mike Bordick	.05
189	Chris Hammond	.05
190	Cecil Fielder	.15
191	Curtis Leskanic	.05
192	Lou Frazier	.05
193	Steve Dreyer	.05
194	Javier Lopez (Future Star)	.25
195	Edgar Martinez	.08
196	Allen Watson	.10
197	John Flaherty	.05
198	Kurt Stillwell	.05
199	Danny Jackson	.05
200	Cal Ripken, Jr.	1.50
201	Mike Bell (Draft Pick)	.05
202	Alan Benes (Draft Pick)	.75
203	Matt Farner (Draft Pick)	.05
204	Jeff Granger (Draft Pick)	.15
205	Brooks Kieschnick (Draft Pick)	.35
206	Jeremy Lee (Draft Pick)	.05
207	Charles Peterson (Draft Pick)	.05
208	Andy Rice (Draft Pick)	.05
209	Billy Wagner (Draft Pick)	.40
210	Kelly Wunsch (Draft Pick)	.15
211	Tom Candiotti	.05
212	Domingo Jean (Draft Pick)	.10
213	John Burkett	.05
214	George Bell	.05
215	Dan Plesac	.05
216	Manny Ramirez (Future Star)	.75
217	Mike Maddux	.05
218	Kevin McReynolds	.05
219	Pat Borders	.05
220	Doug Drabek	.05
221	Larry Luebbers	.05
222	Trevor Hoffman	.05
223	Pat Meares	.05
224	Danny Miceli (Future Star)	.10
225	Greg Vaughn	.05
226	Scott Hemond	.05
227	Pat Rapp	.05
228	Kirk Gibson	.05
229	Lance Painter	.05
230	Larry Walker	.15
231	Benji Gil (Future Star)	.10
232	Mark Wohlers	.05
233	Rich Amaral	.05
234	Erik Pappas	.05
235	Scott Cooper	.05
236	Mike Butcher	.05
237	OF Prospects(Curtis Pride, Shawn Green, Mark Sweeney, Eddie Davis)	.20
238	Kim Batiste	.05
239	Paul Assenmacher	.05
240	Will Clark	.15
241	Jose Offerman	.05
242	Todd Frohwirth	.05
243	Tim Raines	.08
244	Rick Wilkins	.05
245	Bret Saberhagen	.05
246	Thomas Howard	.05
247	Stan Belinda	.05
248	Rickey Henderson	.10
249	Brian Williams	.05
250	Barry Larkin	.08
251	Jose Valentin (Future Star)	.05
252	Lenny Webster	.05
253	Blas Minor	.05
254	Tim Teufel	.05
255	Bobby Witt	.05
256	Walt Weiss	.05
257	Chad Kreuter	.05
258	Roberto Mejia	.05
259	Cliff Floyd (Future Star)	.15
260	Julio Franco	.05
261	Rafael Belliard	.05
262	Marc Newfield	.10
263	Gerald Perry	.05
264	Ken Ryan	.05
265	Chili Davis	.05
266	Dave West	.05
267	Royce Clayton	.08
268	Pedro Martinez	.05
269	Mark Hutton	.05
270	Frank Thomas	1.50
271	Brad Pennington	.05
272	Mike Harkey	.05
273	Sandy Alomar	.05
274	Dave Gallagher	.05
275	Wally Joyner	.05
276	Ricky Trlicek	.05
277	Al Osuna	.05
278	Calvin Reese (Future Star)	.15
279	Kevin Higgins	.05
280	Rick Aguilera	.05
281	Orlando Merced	.05
282	Mike Mohler	.05
283	John Jaha	.05
284	Robb Nen	.05
285	Travis Fryman	.05
286	Mark Thompson (Future Star)	.05
287	Mike Lansing (All-Star Rookie)	.10
288	Craig Lefferts	.05
289	Damon Berryhill	.05
290	Randy Johnson	.30
291	Jeff Reed	.05
292	Danny Darwin	.05
293	J.T. Snow (All-Star Rookie)	.10
294	Tyler Green	.05
295	Chris Hoiles	.05
296	Roger McDowell	.05
297	Spike Owen	.05
298	Salomon Torres (Future Star)	.10
299	Wilson Alvarez	.05
300	Ryne Sandberg	.40
301	Derek Lilliquist	.05
302	Howard Johnson	.05
303	Greg Cadaret	.05
304	Pat Hentgen	.05
305	Craig Biggio	.05
306	Scott Service	.05
307	Melvin Nieves	.05
308	Mike Trombley	.05
309	Carlos Garcia (All-Star Rookie)	.05
310	Robin Yount	.15
311	Marcos Armas	.05
312	Rich Rodriguez	.05
313	Justin Thompson (Future Star)	.05
314	Danny Sheaffer	.05
315	Ken Hill	.05
316	P Propsects(Chad Ogea), (Duff Brumley), (Terrell Wade), (Chris Michalak)	.25
317	Cris Carpenter	.05
318	Jeff Blauser	.05
319	Ted Power	.05
320	Ozzie Smith	.15
321	John Dopson	.05
322	Chris Turner	.05
323	Pete Incaviglia	.05
324	Alan Mills	.05
325	Jody Reed	.05
326	Rich Monteleone	.05
327	Mark Carreon	.05
328	Donn Pall	.05
329	Matt Walbeck (Future Star)	.05
330	Charles Nagy	.05
331	Jeff McKnight	.05
332	Jose Lind	.05
333	Mike Timlin	.05
334	Doug Jones	.05

#	Player	Price
335	Kevin Mitchell	.05
336	Luis Lopez	.05
337	Shane Mack	.05
338	Randy Tomlin	.05
339	Matt Mieske	.05
340	Mark McGwire	2.00
341	Nigel Wilson (Future Star)	.10
342	Danny Gladden	.05
343	Mo Sanford	.05
344	Sean Berry	.05
345	Kevin Brown	.05
346	Greg Olson	.05
347	Dave Magadan	.05
348	Rene Arocha	.05
349	Carlos Quintana	.05
350	Jim Abbott	.05
351	Gary DiSarcina	.05
352	Ben Rivera	.05
353	Carlos Hernandez	.05
354	Darren Lewis	.05
355	Harold Reynolds	.05
356	Scott Ruffcorn (Future Star)	.15
357	Mark Gubicza	.05
358	Paul Sorrento	.05
359	Anthony Young	.05
360	Mark Grace	.08
361	Rob Butler	.05
362	Kevin Bass	.05
363	Eric Helfand (Future Star)	.05
364	Derek Bell	.05
365	Scott Erickson	.05
366	Al Martin	.05
367	Ricky Bones	.05
368	Jeff Branson	.05
369	3B Prospects(Luis Ortiz, David Bell, Jason Giambi), *(George Arias)*	.15
370a	Benny Santiago	.05
370b	Mark McLemore (originally checklisted as #379)	.05
371	John Doherty	.05
372	Joe Girardi	.05
373	Tim Scott	.05
374	Marvin Freeman	.05
375	Deion Sanders	.25
376	Roger Salkeld	.05
377	Bernard Gilkey	.05
378	Tony Fossas	.05
379	(Not issued, see #370)	
380	Darren Daulton	.05
381	Chuck Finley	.05
382	Mitch Webster	.05
383	Gerald Williams	.05
384	Frank Thomas, Fred McGriff (All Star)	.40
385	Roberto Alomar, Robby Thompson (All Star)	.20
386	Wade Boggs, Matt Williams (All Star)	.10
387	Cal Ripken, Jr., Jeff Blauser (All Star)	.20
388	Ken Griffey, Jr., Len Dykstra (All Star)	.40
389	Juan Gonzalez, Dave Justice (All Star)	.30
390	Albert Belle, Barry Bonds (All Star)	.30
391	Mike Stanley, Mike Piazza (All Star)	.40
392	Jack McDowell, Greg Maddux (All Star)	.25
393	Jimmy Key, Tom Glavine (All Star)	.10
394	Jeff Montgomery, Randy Myers (All Star)	.05
395	Checklist 1	.05
396	Checklist 2	.05
397	Tim Salmon (All-Star Rookie)	.40
398	Todd Benzinger	.05
399	Frank Castillo	.05
400	Ken Griffey, Jr.	1.50
401	John Kruk	.05
402	Dave Telgheder	.05
403	Gary Gaetti	.25
404	Jim Edmonds	.05
405	Don Slaught	.05
406	Jose Oquendo	.05
407	Bruce Ruffin	.05
408	Phil Clark	.05
409	Joe Klink	.05
410	Lou Whitaker	.05
411	Kevin Seitzer	.05
412	Darrin Fletcher	.05
413	Kenny Rogers	.05
414	Bill Pecota	.05
415	Dave Fleming	.05
416	Luis Alicea	.05
417	Paul Quantrill	.05
418	Damion Easley	.05
419	Wes Chamberlain	.05
420	Harold Baines	.05
421	Scott Radinsky	.05
422	Rey Sanchez	.05
423	Junior Ortiz	.05
424	Jeff Kent	.05
425	Brian McRae	.05
426	Ed Sprague	.05
427	Tom Edens	.05
428	Willie Greene	.05
429	Bryan Hickerson	.05
430	Dave Winfield	.08
431	Pedro Astacio	.05
432	Mike Gallego	.05
433	Dave Burba	.05
434	Bob Walk	.05
435	Darryl Hamilton	.05
436	Vince Horsman	.05
437	Bob Natal	.05
438	Mike Henneman	.05
439	Willie Blair	.05
440	Denny Martinez	.05
441	Dan Peltier	.05
442	Tony Tarasco	.05
443	John Cummings	.05
444	Geronimo Pena	.05
445	Aaron Sele	.15
446	Stan Javier	.05
447	Mike Williams	.05
448	1B Prospects(Greg Pirkl, Roberto Petagine, D.J. Boston, Shawn Wooten)	.15
449	Jim Poole	.05
450	Carlos Baerga	.20
451	Bob Scanlan	.05
452	Lance Johnson	.05
453	Eric Hillman	.05
454	Keith Miller	.05
455	Dave Stewart	.05
456	Pete Harnisch	.05
457	Roberto Kelly	.05
458	Tim Worrell	.05
459	Pedro Munoz	.05
460	Orel Hershiser	.05
461	Randy Velarde	.05
462	Trevor Wilson	.05
463	Jerry Goff	.05
464	Bill Wegman	.05
465	Dennis Eckersley	.08
466	Jeff Conine (All-Star Rookie)	.08
467	Joe Boever	.05
468	Dante Bichette	.08
469	Jeff Shaw	.05
470	Rafael Palmeiro	.08
471	*Phil Leftwich*	.10
472	Jay Buhner	.08
473	Bob Tewksbury	.05
474	Tim Naehring	.05
475	Tom Glavine	.08
476	Dave Hollins	.05
477	Arthur Rhodes	.05
478	Joey Cora	.05
479	Mike Morgan	.05
480	Albert Belle	.50
481	John Franco	.05
482	Hipolito Pichardo	.05
483	Duane Ward	.05
484	Luis Gonzalez	.05
485	Joe Oliver	.05
486	Wally Whitehurst	.05
487	Mike Benjamin	.05
488	Eric Davis	.05
489	Scott Kamieniecki	.05
490	Kent Hrbek	.05
491	*John Hope*	.15
492	Jesse Orosco	.05
493	Troy Neel	.05
494	Ryan Bowen	.05
495	Mickey Tettleton	.05
496	Chris Jones	.05
497	John Wetteland	.05
498	David Hulse	.05
499	Greg Maddux	1.50
500	Bo Jackson	.08
501	Donovan Osborne	.05
502	Mike Greenwell	.05
503	Steve Frey	.05
504	Jim Eisenreich	.05
505	Robby Thompson	.05
506	Leo Gomez	.05
507	Dave Staton	.05
508	Wayne Kirby (All-Star Rookie)	.05
509	Tim Bogar	.05
510	David Cone	.05
511	Devon White	.05
512	Xavier Hernandez	.05
513	Tim Costo	.05
514	Gene Harris	.05
515	Jack McDowell	.05
516	Kevin Gross	.05
517	Scott Leius	.05
518	Lloyd McClendon	.05
519	*Alex Diaz*	.08
520	Wade Boggs	.20
521	Bob Welch	.05
522	Henry Cotto	.05
523	Mike Moore	.05
524	Tim Laker	.05
525	Andres Galarraga	.08
526	Jamie Moyer	.05
527	2B Prospects(Norberto Martin, Ruben Santana, Jason Hardtke, Chris Sexton)	.20
528	Sid Bream	.05
529	Erik Hanson	.05
530	Ray Lankford	.05
531	Rob Deer	.05
532	Rod Correia	.05
533	Roger Mason	.05
534	Mike Devereaux	.05
535	Jeff Montgomery	.05
536	Dwight Smith	.05
537	Jeremy Hernandez	.05
538	Ellis Burks	.05
539	Bobby Jones	.15
540	Paul Molitor	.20
541	Jeff Juden	.05
542	Chris Sabo	.05
543	Larry Casian	.05
544	Jeff Gardner	.05
545	Ramon Martinez	.05
546	Paul O'Neill	.05
547	Steve Hosey	.05
548	Dave Nilsson	.05
549	Ron Darling	.05
550	Matt Williams	.25
551	Jack Armstrong	.05
552	Bill Krueger	.05
553	Freddie Benavides	.05
554	Jeff Fassero	.05
555	Chuck Knoblauch	.05
556	Guillermo Velasquez	.05
557	Joel Johnston	.05
558	Tom Lampkin	.05
559	Todd Van Poppel	.05
560	Gary Sheffield	.08
561	Skeeter Barnes	.05
562	Darren Holmes	.05
563	John Vander Wal	.05
564	Mike Ignasiak	.05
565	Fred McGriff	.20
566	Luis Polonia	.05
567	Mike Perez	.05
568	John Valentin	.05
569	Mike Felder	.05
570	Tommy Greene	.05
571	David Segui	.05
572	Roberto Hernandez	.05
573	Steve Wilson	.05
574	Willie McGee	.05
575	Randy Myers	.05
576	Darrin Jackson	.05
577	Eric Plunk	.05
578	Mike MacFarlane	.05
579	Doug Brocail	.05
580	Steve Finley	.05
581	John Roper	.05
582	Danny Cox	.05
583	Chip Hale	.05
584	Scott Bullett	.05
585	Kevin Reimer	.05
586	Brent Gates	.05
587	Matt Turner	.05
588	Rich Rowland	.05
589	Kent Bottenfield	.05
590	Marquis Grissom	.08
591	Doug Strange	.05
592	Jay Howell	.05
593	Omar Vizquel	.05
594	Rheal Cormier	.05
595	Andre Dawson	.08
596	Hilly Hathaway	.05
597	Todd Pratt	.05
598	Mike Mussina	.25
599	Alex Fernandez	.08

600	Don Mattingly	.75
601	Frank Thomas (Measures of Greatness)	.75
602	Ryne Sandberg (Measures of Greatness)	.10
603	Wade Boggs (Measures of Greatness)	.08
604	Cal Ripken, Jr. (Measures of Greatness)	.75
605	Barry Bonds (Measures of Greatness)	.30
606	Ken Griffey, Jr. (Measures of Greatness)	.75
607	Kirby Puckett (Measures of Greatness)	.25
608	Darren Daulton (Measures of Greatness)	.05
609	Paul Molitor (Measures of Greatness)	.10
610	Terry Steinbach	.05
611	Todd Worrell	.05
612	Jim Thome	.10
613	Chuck McElroy	.05
614	John Habyan	.05
615	Sid Fernandez	.05
616	OF Prospects(Eddie Zambrano, Glenn Murray, Chad Mottola), (Jermaine Allensworth)	.50
617	Steve Bedrosian	.05
618	Rob Ducey	.05
619	Tom Browning	.05
620	Tony Gwynn	.30
621	Carl Willis	.05
622	Kevin Young	.05
623	Rafael Novoa	.05
624	Jerry Browne	.05
625	Charlie Hough	.05
626	Chris Gomez	.05
627	Steve Reed	.05
628	Kirk Rueter	.08
629	Matt Whiteside	.05
630	Dave Justice	.25
631	Brad Holman	.05
632	Brian Jordan	.05
633	Scott Bankhead	.05
634	Torey Lovullo	.05
635	Len Dykstra	.08
636	Ben McDonald	.05
637	Steve Howe	.05
638	Jose Vizcaino	.05
639	Bill Swift	.05
640	Darryl Strawberry	.08
641	Steve Farr	.05
642	Tom Kramer	.05
643	Joe Orsulak	.05
644	Tom Henke	.05
645	Joe Carter	.15
646	Ken Caminiti	.05
647	Reggie Sanders	.08
648	Andy Ashby	.05
649	Derek Parks	.05
650	Andy Van Slyke	.05
651	Juan Bell	.05
652	Roger Smithberg	.05
653	Chuck Carr	.05
654	Bill Gullickson	.05
655	Charlie Hayes	.05
656	Chris Nabholz	.05
657	Karl Rhodes	.05
658	Pete Smith	.05
659	Bret Boone	.05
660	Gregg Jefferies	.08
661	Bob Zupcic	.05
662	Steve Sax	.05
663	Mariano Duncan	.05
664	Jeff Tackett	.05
665	Mark Langston	.05
666	Steve Buechele	.05
667	Candy Maldonado	.05
668	Woody Williams	.05
669	Tim Wakefield	.05
670	Danny Tartabull	.05
671	Charlie O'Brien	.05
672	Felix Jose	.05
673	Bobby Ayala	.05
674	Scott Servais	.05
675	Roberto Alomar	.30
676	Pedro Martinez	.05
677	Eddie Guardado	.05
678	Mark Lewis	.05
679	Jaime Navarro	.05
680	Ruben Sierra	.05
681	Rick Renteria	.05
682	Storm Davis	.05
683	Cory Snyder	.05

684	Ron Karkovice	.05
685	Juan Gonzalez	.25
686	C Prospects(Chris Howard, Carlos Delgado, Jason Kendall, Paul Bako)	.60
687	John Smoltz	.05
688	Brian Dorsett	.05
689	Omar Olivares	.05
690	Mo Vaughn	.30
691	Joe Grahe	.05
692	Mickey Morandini	.05
693	Tino Martinez	.05
694	Brian Barnes	.05
695	Mike Stanley	.05
696	Mark Clark	.05
697	Dave Hansen	.05
698	Willie Wilson	.05
699	Pete Schourek	.05
700	Barry Bonds	.40
701	Kevin Appier	.05
702	Tony Fernandez	.05
703	Darryl Kile	.05
704	Archi Cianfrocco	.05
705	Jose Rijo	.05
706	Brian Harper	.05
707	Zane Smith	.05
708	Dave Henderson	.05
709	Angel Miranda	.05
710	Orestes Destrade	.05
711	Greg Gohr	.05
712	Eric Young	.05
713	P Prospects(Todd Williams, Ron Watson, Kirk Bullinger, Mike Welch)	.15
714	Tim Spehr	.05
715	Hank Aaron (20th Anniversary #715)	.50
716	Nate Minchey	.05
717	Mike Blowers	.05
718	Kent Mercker	.05
719	Tom Pagnozzi	.05
720	Roger Clemens	.50
721	Eduardo Perez	.05
722	Milt Thompson	.05
723	Gregg Olson	.05
724	Kirk McCaskill	.05
725	Sammy Sosa	1.00
726	Alvaro Espinoza	.05
727	Henry Rodriguez	.05
728	Jim Leyritz	.05
729	Steve Scarsone	.05
730	Bobby Bonilla	.08
731	Chris Gwynn	.05
732	Al Leiter	.05
733	Bip Roberts	.05
734	Mark Portugal	.05
735	Terry Pendleton	.05
736	Dave Valle	.05
737	Paul Kilgus	.05
738	Greg Harris	.05
739	Jon Ratliff (Draft Pick)	.15
740	Kirk Presley (Draft Pick)	.45
741	Josue Estrada (Draft Pick)	.10
742	Wayne Gomes (Draft Pick)	.15
743	Pat Watkins (Draft Pick)	.20
744	Jamey Wright (Draft Pick)	.15
745	Jay Powell (Draft Pick)	.15
746	Ryan McGuire (Draft Pick)	.25
747	Marc Barcelo (Draft Pick)	.10
748	Sloan Smith (Draft Pick)	.15
749	John Wasdin (Draft Pick)	.40
750	Marc Valdes (Draft Pick)	.10
751	Dan Ehler (Draft Pick)	.10
752	Andre King (Draft Pick)	.30
753	Greg Keagle (Draft Pick)	.20
754	Jason Myers (Draft Pick)	.10
755	Dax Winslett (Draft Pick)	.10
756	Casey Whitten (Draft Pick)	.15
757	Tony Fuduric (Draft Pick)	.12
758	Greg Norton (Draft Pick)	.10
759	Jeff D'Amico (Draft Pick)	.25
760	Ryan Hancock (Draft Pick)	.15
761	David Cooper (Draft Pick)	.12
762	Kevin Orie (Draft Pick)	.50
763	John O'Donoghue, Mike Oquist (Coming Attractions)	.10
764	Cory Bailey, Scott Hatteberg (Coming Attractions)	.12
765	Mark Holzemer, Paul Swingle (Coming Attractions)	.10
766	James Baldwin, Rod Bolton (Coming Attractions)	.40
767	Jerry DiPoto, Julian Tavarez (Coming Attractions)	.40

768	Danny Bautista, Sean Bergman (Coming Attractions)	.10
769	Bob Hamelin, Joe Vitiello (Coming Attractions)	.20
770	Mark Kiefer, Troy O'Leary (Coming Attractions)	.15
771	Denny Hocking, Oscar Munoz (Coming Attractions)	.15
772	Russ Davis, Brien Taylor (Coming Attractions)	.20
773	Kurt Abbott, Miguel Jimenez (Coming Attractions)	.20
774	Kevin King, Eric Plantenberg (Coming Attractions)	.15
775	Jon Shave, Desi Wilson (Coming Attractions)	.15
776	Domingo Cedeno, Paul Spoljaric (Coming Attractions)	.10
777	Chipper Jones, Ryan Klesko (Coming Attractions)	1.50
778	Steve Trachsel, Turk Wendell (Coming Attractions)	.30
779	Johnny Ruffin, Jerry Spradlin (Coming Attractions)	.08
780	Jason Bates, John Burke (Coming Attractions)	.15
781	Carl Everett, Dave Weathers (Coming Attractions)	.15
782	Gary Mota, James Mouton (Coming Attractions)	.25
783	Raul Mondesi, Ben Van Ryn (Coming Attractions)	.50
784	Gabe White, Rondell White (Coming Attractions)	.25
785	Brook Fordyce, Bill Pulsipher (Coming Attractions)	.20
786	Kevin Foster, Gene Schall (Coming Attractions)	.10
787	Rich Aude, Midre Cummings (Coming Attractions)	.15
788	Brian Barber, Richard Batchelor (Coming Attractions)	.10
789	Brian Johnson, Scott Sanders (Coming Attractions)	.10
790	Rikkert Faneyte, J.R. Phillips (Coming Attractions)	.15
791	Checklist 3	.05
792	Checklist 4	.05

1994 Topps Gold

This premium parallel set was issued as inserts in virtually all forms of Topps packaging. Identical in all other ways to the regular Topps cards, the Gold version replaces the white or black Topps logo on front with a gold-foil "Topps Gold" logo, and prints either the player name or card title in gold foil. The four checklist cards from the regular issue are replaced with cards of players not found in the regular Topps set.

	MT
Complete Set (792):	75.00
Common Player:	.15
(Star cards valued at 4X-5X corresponding cards in regular Topps issue)	

1994 Topps Black Gold

The Black Gold insert set returned for 1994 randomly included in all types of Topps packaging.

Single Black Gold cards, as well as cards redeemable by mail for 11, 22 or 44 Black Gold cards, were produced. The basic single-player card features an action photo, the background of which has been almost completely blacked out. At top is the team name in black letters against a gold prismatic foil background. The player name at bottom is in the same gold foil. On back, bordered in white, is a background which fades from black at top to gray at the bottom and is gridded with white lines. To the left is another color player action photo. The Topps Black Gold logo and player name appear in gold foil; the latter printed on a simulated wooden board "hanging" from the top of the card. A second hanging plank has player stats and rankings from the 1993 season. The multi-card redemption cards come in two versions. The type found in packs has all 11, 22 or 44 of the cards pictured on front in miniature and redemption details printed on back. A second version, returned with the single cards won, has on back a checklist and non-redemption notice. Stated odds of winning Black Gold cards were one in 72 packs for single cards; one in 180 packs for 11-card winners and one in 720 packs (one per foil-pack case) for a 22-card winner.

		MT
Complete Set (44):		32.00
Complete Series 1 (22):		20.00
Complete Series 2 (22):		12.50
Common Player:		.25
1	Roberto Alomar	.60
2	Carlos Baerga	.25
3	Albert Belle	.75
4	Joe Carter	.25
5	Cecil Fielder	.30
6	Travis Fryman	.25
7	Juan Gonzalez	.75
8	Ken Griffey, Jr.	4.00
9	Chris Hoiles	.25
10	Randy Johnson	.40
11	Kenny Lofton	1.00
12	Jack McDowell	.25
13	Paul Molitor	.40
14	Jeff Montgomery	.25
15	John Olerud	.25
16	Rafael Palmeiro	.35
17	Kirby Puckett	1.25
18	Cal Ripken, Jr.	4.00
19	Tim Salmon	.50
20	Mike Stanley	.25
21	Frank Thomas	4.00
22	Robin Ventura	.30

23	Jeff Bagwell	1.00
24	Jay Bell	.25
25	Craig Biggio	.35
26	Jeff Blauser	.25
27	Barry Bonds	.75
28	Darren Daulton	.25
29	Len Dykstra	.25
30	Andres Galarraga	.25
31	Ron Gant	.25
32	Tom Glavine	.30
33	Mark Grace	.35
34	Marquis Grissom	.25
35	Gregg Jefferies	.25
36	Dave Justice	.35
37	John Kruk	.25
38	Greg Maddux	2.00
39	Fred McGriff	.40
40	Randy Myers	.25
41	Mike Piazza	2.00
42	Sammy Sosa	1.00
43	Robby Thompson	.25
44	Matt Williams	.30
---	Winner A	.75
---	Winner B	.75
---	Winner C	.75
---	Winner D	.75
---	Winner A/B	1.00
---	Winner C/D	1.00
---	Winner A/B/C/D	1.50

1994 Topps Traded

Topps Traded consists of 132 cards featuring many top prospects and rookies, as well as traded veterans. Also included with this boxed set was an eight-card Topps Finest subset, including six MVPs and two Rookie of the Year cards. Regular cards have the same design as the previously released 1994 Topps set. Players are featured on a white bordered card, with their name across the bottom in white. "Anatomy of a Trade" is a two-card subset that includes Roberto Kelly/Deion Sanders and Pedro Martinez/Delino DeShields on a split, puzzle-like front. There is also a Prospect card, showcasing a top prospect from AAA, AA and A, as well as a top-rated draft pick. In addition, there are 12 Draft Pick cards included in the Topps Traded set. Finally, there are two cards that pay tribute to Ryne Sandberg, one in a Phillies uniform, one with the Cubs.

		MT
Complete Set (132):		70.00
Common Player:		.05
1	Paul Wilson (Draft Pick)	.50
2	Bill Taylor	.05
3	Dan Wilson	.08
4	Mark Smith	.05
5	Toby Borland	.10
6	Dave Clark	.05
7	Denny Martinez	.08
8	Dave Gallagher	.05
9	Josias Manzanillo	.08
10	Brian Anderson	.20
11	Damon Berryhill	.05
12	Alex Cole	.05
13	Jacob Shumate (Draft Pick)	.15
14	Oddibe McDowell	.05
15	Willie Banks	.05
16	Jerry Browne	.05
17	Donnie Elliott	.05
18	Ellis Burks	.10
19	Chuck McElroy	.05
20	Luis Polonia	.05
21	Brian Harper	.05
22	Mark Portugal	.05
23	Dave Henderson	.05
24	Mark Acre	.15
25	Julio Franco	.05
26	Darren Hall	.05
27	Eric Anthony	.05
28	Sid Fernandez	.05

29	Rusty Greer	6.00
30	Riccardo Ingram	.15
31	Gabe White	.10
32	Tim Belcher	.05
33	*Terrence Long* (Draft Pick)	.25
34	Mark Dalesandro	.10
35	Mike Kelly	.05
36	Jack Morris	.05
37	Jeff Brantley	.05
38	Larry Barnes (Draft Pick)	.15
39	Brian Hunter	.10
40	Otis Nixon	.05
41	Bret Wagner (Draft pick)	.15
42	Anatomy of a Trade(Pedro Martinez, Delino DeShields)	.05
43	Heathcliff Slocumb	.05
44	*Ben Grieve* (Draft Pick)	45.00
45	John Hudek	.15
46	Shawon Dunston	.08
47	Greg Colbrunn	.05
48	Joey Hamilton	.40
49	Marvin Freeman	.05
50	Terry Mulholland	.05
51	Keith Mitchell	.05
52	Dwight Smith	.05
53	Shawn Boskie	.05
54	*Kevin Witt* (Draft Pick)	6.00
55	Ron Gant	.05
56	1994 Prospects(Trenidad Hubbard, Jason Schmidt, Larry Sutton, Stephen Larkin)	.45
57	Jody Reed	.05
58	Rick Helling	.10
59	John Powell (Draft Pick)	.10
60	Eddie Murray	.25
61	Joe Hall	.15
62	Jorge Fabregas	.05
63	Mike Mordecai	.25
64	Ed Vosberg	.05
65	Rickey Henderson	.08
66	Tim Grieve (Draft pick)	.15
67	Jon Lieber	.05
68	Chris Howard	.05
69	Matt Walbeck	.05
70	Chan Ho Park	6.00
71	Bryan Eversgerd	.10
72	John Dettmer	.05
73	Erik Hanson	.05
74	Mike Thurman (Draft pick)	.15
75	Bobby Ayala	.05
76	Rafael Palmeiro	.25
77	Bret Boone	.10
78	Paul Shuey (Future Star)	.10
79	Kevin Foster	.10
80	Dave Magadan	.05
81	Bip Roberts	.05
82	Howard Johnson	.05
83	Xavier Hernandez	.05
84	Ross Powell	.08
85	*Doug Million* (Draft Pick)	.05
86	Geronimo Berroa	.08
87	Mark Farris (Draft Pick)	.25
88	Butch Henry	.05
89	Junior Felix	.05
90	Bo Jackson	.10
91	Hector Carrasco	.10
92	Charlie O'Brien	.05
93	Omar Vizquel	.05
94	David Segui	.05
95	Dustin Hermanson (Draft Pick)	1.00
96	Gar Finnvold	.10
97	Dave Stevens	.05
98	Corey Pointer (Draft Pick)	.15
99	Felix Fermin	.05
100	Lee Smith	.05
101	Reid Ryan (Draft Pick)	.15
102	Bobby Munoz	.05
103	Anatomy of a Trade(Deion Sanders, Roberto Kelly)	.10
104	Turner Ward	.05
105	William Van Landingham	.15
106	Vince Coleman	.05
107	Stan Javier	.05
108	Darrin Jackson	.05
109	C.J. Nitkowski (Draft Pick)	.20
110	Anthony Young	.05
111	Kurt Miller	.05
112	*Paul Konerko* (Draft Pick)	15.00
113	Walt Weiss	.05
114	Daryl Boston	.05
115	Will Clark	.25
116	Matt Smith (Draft Pick)	.05
117	Mark Leiter	.05
118	Gregg Olson	.05

119	Tony Pena	.05
120	Jose Vizcaino	.05
121	Rick White	.10
122	Rich Rowland	.05
123	Jeff Reboulet	.08
124	Greg Hibbard	.05
125	Chris Sabo	.05
126	Doug Jones	.05
127	Tony Fernandez	.05
128	Carlos Reyes	.08
129	Kevin Brown (Draft Pick)	.05
130	Commemorative(Ryne Sandberg)	1.00
131	Commemorative(Ryne Sandberg)	1.00
132	Checklist 1-132	.05

1994 Topps Traded Finest Inserts

Eight Topps Finest cards were included in the 1994 Topps Traded set. Cards picture the player on a blue and gold Finest card. Either Rookie of the Year or MVP is printed across the bottom on the opposite side of the player's name, indicating the player's candidacy for such an award in 1994. Backs offer a portrait photo, stats through the All-Star break and comments on the player's season to that point.

		MT
Complete Set (8):		25.00
Common Player:		1.50
1	Greg Maddux	5.00
2	Mike Piazza	4.00
3	Matt Williams	1.50
4	Raul Mondesi	2.50
5	Ken Griffey Jr.	8.00
6	Kenny Lofton	3.00
7	Frank Thomas	6.00
8	Manny Ramirez	3.00

1995 Topps

Topps 1995 baseball arrived offering Cyberstats, which projected full-season statistics for the strike shortened year, as well as League Leaders and Stadium Club First Day Issue preproduction inserts. The entire Series I set was composed of 396 cards, including subsets like 1994 Draft Picks, Star Tracks, a Babe Ruth commemorative card and the Topps All-Stars, featuring two players per card at each position, as selected by Topps. Regular cards have a jagged white border around the

color picture of the player, with his name in gold foil under the picture. Series II concluded the Cyberstats inserts and added 264 cards to the regular set. Subsets in Series II included a continuation of the Draft Picks from Series I, as well as two-player On Deck cards and four-player Prospects cards, arranged by position.

P — CHICAGO WHITE SOX

		MT
Complete Set (660):		40.00
Complete Series 1 (396):		22.00
Complete Series 2 (264):		18.00
Common Player:		.05
Series 1 or 2 Wax Box:		35.00
1	Frank Thomas	2.50
2	Mickey Morandini	.05
3a	Babe Ruth (100th Birthday, no gold "Topps" logo)	1.50
3b	Babe Ruth (100th Birthday, gold "Topps" logo)	1.50
4	Scott Cooper	.05
5	David Cone	.10
6	Jacob Shumate (Draft Pick)	.15
7	Trevor Hoffman	.08
8	Shane Mack	.05
9	Delino DeShields	.05
10	Matt Williams	.25
11	Sammy Sosa	1.00
12	Gary DiSarcina	.05
13	Kenny Rogers	.05
14	Jose Vizcaino	.05
15	Lou Whitaker	.05
16	Ron Darling	.05
17	Dave Nilsson	.05
18	Chris Hammond	.05
19	Sid Bream	.05
20	Denny Martinez	.08
21	Orlando Merced	.05
22	John Wetteland	.05
23	Mike Devereaux	.05
24	Rene Arocha	.05
25	Jay Buhner	.12
26	Darren Holmes	.05
27	Hal Morris	.05
28	*Brian Buchanan* (Draft Pick)	.15
29	Keith Miller	.05
30	Paul Molitor	.30
31	Dave West	.05
32	Tony Tarasco	.05
33	Scott Sanders	.05
34	Eddie Zambrano	.05
35	Ricky Bones	.05
36	John Valentin	.05
37	Kevin Tapani	.05
38	Tim Wallach	.05
39	Darren Lewis	.05
40	Travis Fryman	.10
41	Mark Leiter	.05
42	Jose Bautista	.05
43	Pete Smith	.05
44	Bret Barberie	.05
45	Dennis Eckersley	.08
46	Ken Hill	.05
47	Chad Ogea (Star Track)	.12
48	Pete Harnisch	.05

49	James Baldwin (Future Star)	.15
50	Mike Mussina	.30
51	Al Martin	.05
52	Mark Thompson (Star Track)	.05
53	Matt Smith (Draft Pick)	.08
54	Joey Hamilton (All Star Rookie)	.10
55	Edgar Martinez	.08
56	John Smiley	.05
57	Rey Sanchez	.05
58	Mike Timlin	.05
59	Ricky Bottalico (Star Track)	.10
60	Jim Abbott	.08
61	Mike Kelly	.05
62	Brian Jordan	.15
63	Ken Ryan	.10
64	Matt Mieske	.05
65	Rick Aguilera	.05
66	Ismael Valdes	.08
67	Royce Clayton	.08
68	Junior Felix	.05
69	Harold Reynolds	.05
70	Juan Gonzalez	1.00
71	Kelly Stinnett	.05
72	Carlos Reyes	.05
73	Dave Weathers	.05
74	Mel Rojas	.05
75	Doug Drabek	.05
76	Charles Nagy	.05
77	Tim Raines	.08
78	Midre Cummings	.05
79	1B Prospects(Gene Schall), *(Scott Talanoa), (Harold Williams), (Ray Brown)*	.15
80	Rafael Palmeiro	.10
81	Charlie Hayes	.05
82	Ray Lankford	.15
83	Tim Davis	.05
84	*C.J. Nitkowski* (Draft Pick)	.15
85	Andy Ashby	.05
86	Gerald Williams	.05
87	Terry Shumpert	.05
88	Heathcliff Slocumb	.05
89	Domingo Cedeno	.05
90	Mark Grace	.15
91	*Brad Woodall* (Star Track)	.08
92	Gar Finnvold	.05
93	Jaime Navarro	.05
94	Carlos Hernandez	.05
95	Mark Langston	.05
96	Chuck Carr	.05
97	Mike Gardiner	.05
98	David McCarty	.05
99	Cris Carpenter	.05
100	Barry Bonds	.50
101	David Segui	.05
102	Scott Brosius	.05
103	Mariano Duncan	.05
104	Kenny Lofton	.50
105	Ken Caminiti	.20
106	Darrin Jackson	.05
107	Jim Poole	.05
108	Wil Cordero	.05
109	Danny Miceli	.05
110	Walt Weiss	.05
111	Tom Pagnozzi	.05
112	Terrence Long (Draft Pick)	.05
113	Bret Boone	.05
114	Daryl Boston	.05
115	Wally Joyner	.08
116	Rob Butler	.05
117	Rafael Belliard	.05
118	Luis Lopez	.05
119	Tony Fossas	.05
120	Len Dykstra	.08
121	Mike Morgan	.05
122	Denny Hocking	.05
123	Kevin Gross	.05
124	Todd Benzinger	.05
125	John Doherty	.05
126	Eduardo Perez	.05
127	Dan Smith	.08
128	Joe Orsulak	.05
129	Brent Gates	.05
130	Jeff Conine	.08
131	Doug Henry	.05
132	Paul Sorrento	.05
133	Mike Hampton	.05
134	Tim Spehr	.05
135	Julio Franco	.05
136	Mike Dyer	.05
137	Chris Sabo	.05
138	Rheal Cormier	.05
139	Paul Konerko (Draft Pick)	2.00

140	Dante Bichette	.15
141	Chuck McElroy	.05
142	Mike Stanley	.05
143	Bob Hamelin (All Star Rookie)	.05
144	Tommy Greene	.05
145	John Smoltz	.10
146	Ed Sprague	.05
147	Ray McDavid (Star Track)	.10
148	Otis Nixon	.05
149	Turk Wendell	.05
150	Chris James	.05
151	Derek Parks	.08
152	Jose Offerman	.05
153	Tony Clark (Future Star)	.75
154	Chad Curtis	.05
155	Mark Portugal	.05
156	Bill Pulsipher (Future Star)	.15
157	Troy Neel	.05
158	Dave Winfield	.08
159	Bill Wegman	.05
160	Benny Santiago	.05
161	Jose Mesa	.05
162	Luis Gonzalez	.05
163	Alex Fernandez	.05
164	Freddie Benavides	.05
165	Ben McDonald	.05
166	Blas Minor	.05
167	Bret Wagner (Draft Pick)	.05
168	Mac Suzuki (Future Star)	.10
169	Roberto Mejia	.05
170	Wade Boggs	.20
171	Calvin Reese (Future Star)	.10
172	Hipolito Pichardo	.05
173	Kim Batiste	.05
174	Darren Hall	.05
175	Tom Glavine	.10
176	Phil Plantier	.05
177	Chris Howard	.05
178	Karl Rhodes	.05
179	LaTroy Hawkins (Future Star)	.25
180	Raul Mondesi (All Star Rookie)	.40
181	Jeff Reed	.05
182	Milt Cuyler	.05
183	Jim Edmonds	.15
184	Hector Fajardo	.05
185	Jeff Kent	.05
186	Wilson Alvarez	.05
187	Geronimo Berroa	.05
188	Billy Spiers	.05
189	Derek Lilliquist	.05
190	Craig Biggio	.08
191	Roberto Hernandez	.05
192	Bob Natal	.05
193	Bobby Ayala	.05
194	*Travis Miller* (Draft Pick)	.20
195	Bob Tewksbury	.05
196	Rondell White	.20
197	Steve Cooke	.05
198	Jeff Branson	.05
199	Derek Jeter (Future Star)	1.75
200	Tim Salmon	.25
201	Steve Frey	.05
202	Kent Mercker	.05
203	Randy Johnson	.35
204	Todd Worrell	.05
205	Mo Vaughn	.60
206	Howard Johnson	.05
207	John Wasdin (Future Star)	.10
208	Eddie Williams	.05
209	Tim Belcher	.05
210	Jeff Montgomery	.05
211	Kirt Manwaring	.05
212	Ben Grieve (Draft Pick)	3.00
213	Pat Hentgen	.05
214	Shawon Dunston	.10
215	Mike Greenwell	.05
216	Alex Diaz	.05
217	Pat Mahomes	.05
218	Dave Hanson	.05
219	Kevin Rogers	.05
220	Cecil Fielder	.10
221	Andrew Lorraine (Star Track)	.10
222	Jack Armstrong	.05
223	Todd Hundley	.15
224	Mark Acre	.05
225	Darrell Whitmore	.05
226	Randy Milligan	.05
227	Wayne Kirby	.05
228	Darryl Kile	.05
229	Bob Zupcic	.05
230	Jay Bell	.05

231	Dustin Hermanson (Draft Pick)	.08
232	Harold Baines	.08
233	Alan Benes (Future Star)	.30
234	Felix Fermin	.05
235	Ellis Burks	.10
236	Jeff Brantley	.05
237	OF Prospects(Brian Hunter, Jose Malave, Shane Pullen), *(Karim Garcia)*	2.00
238	Matt Nokes	.05
239	Ben Rivera	.05
240	Joe Carter	.15
241	Jeff Granger (Star Track)	.05
242	Terry Pendleton	.05
243	Melvin Nieves	.05
244	Frank Rodriguez (Future Star)	.10
245	Darryl Hamilton	.05
246	Brooks Kieschnick (Future Star)	.25
247	Todd Hollandsworth (Future Star)	.25
248	Joe Rosselli (Future Star)	.08
249	Bill Gullickson	.05
250	Chuck Knoblauch	.10
251	Kurt Miller (Star Track)	.05
252	Bobby Jones	.10
253	Lance Blankenship	.05
254	Matt Whiteside	.05
255	Darrin Fletcher	.05
256	Eric Plunk	.05
257	Shane Reynolds	.05
258	Norberto Martin	.05
259	Mike Thurman (Draft Pick)	.05
260	Andy Van Slyke	.05
261	Dwight Smith	.05
262	Allen Watson	.10
263	Dan Wilson	.05
264	Brent Mayne	.05
265	Bip Roberts	.05
266	Sterling Hitchcock	.05
267	Alex Gonzalez (Star Track)	.15
268	Greg Harris	.05
269	Ricky Jordan	.05
270	Johnny Ruffin	.05
271	Mike Stanton	.05
272	Rich Rowland	.05
273	Steve Trachsel	.08
274	Pedro Munoz	.05
275	Ramon Martinez	.08
276	Dave Henderson	.05
277	Chris Gomez (All Star Rookie)	.10
278	Joe Grahe	.05
279	Rusty Greer	.08
280	John Franco	.05
281	Mike Bordick	.05
282	Jeff D'Amico (Future Star)	.08
283	Dave Magadan	.05
284	Tony Pena	.05
285	Greg Swindell	.05
286	Doug Million (Draft Pick)	.05
287	Gabe White (Star Track)	.25
288	Trey Beamon (Future Star)	.15
289	Arthur Rhodes	.05
290	Juan Guzman	.05
291	Jose Oquendo	.05
292	Willie Blair	.05
293	Eddie Taubensee	.05
294	Steve Howe	.05
295	Greg Maddux	1.75
296	Mike MacFarlane	.05
297	Curt Schilling	.05
298	Phil Clark	.05
299	Woody Williams	.05
300	Jose Canseco	.25
301	Aaron Sele	.10
302	Carl Willis	.05
303	Steve Buechele	.05
304	Dave Burba	.05
305	Orel Hershiser	.08
306	Damion Easley	.05
307	Mike Henneman	.05
308	Josias Manzanillo	.05
309	Kevin Seitzer	.05
310	Ruben Sierra	.08
311	Bryan Harvey	.05
312	Jim Thome	.10
313	*Ramon Castro* (Draft Pick)	.15
314	Lance Johnson	.05
315	Marquis Grissom	.08
316	SP Prospects(Terrell Wade, Juan Acevedo, Matt Arrandale, Eddie Priest)	.15
317	Paul Wagner	.05

318	Jamie Moyer	.05
319	Todd Zeile	.08
320	Chris Bosio	.05
321	Steve Reed	.05
322	Erik Hanson	.05
323	Luis Polonia	.05
324	Ryan Klesko	.40
325	Kevin Appier	.05
326	Jim Eisenreich	.05
327	Randy Knorr	.05
328	Craig Shipley	.05
329	Tim Naehring	.05
330	Randy Myers	.05
331	Alex Cole	.05
332	Jim Gott	.05
333	Mike Jackson	.05
334	John Flaherty	.05
335	Chili Davis	.05
336	Benji Gil (Star Track)	.08
337a	Jason Jacome (No Diamond Vision logo on back photo)	.15
337b	Jason Jacome (Diamond Vision logo on back photo)	.15
338	Stan Javier	.05
339	Mike Fetters	.05
340	Rick Renteria	.05
341	Kevin Witt (Draft Pick)	.05
342	Scott Servais	.05
343	Craig Grebeck	.05
344	Kirk Rueter	.05
345	Don Slaught	.05
346	*Armando Benitez* (Star Track)	.15
347	Ozzie Smith	.20
348	Mike Blowers	.05
349	Armando Reynoso	.05
350	Barry Larkin	.15
351	Mike Williams	.05
352	Scott Kamieniecki	.05
353	Gary Gaetti	.08
354	Todd Stottlemyre	.05
355	Fred McGriff	.20
356	Tim Mauser	.05
357	Chris Gwynn	.05
358	Frank Castillo	.05
359	Jeff Reboulet	.08
360	Roger Clemens	.60
361	Mark Carreon	.08
362	Chad Kreuter	.05
363	Mark Farris (Draft Pick)	.05
364	Bob Welch	.05
365	Dean Palmer	.05
366	Jeromy Burnitz	.05
367	B.J. Surhoff	.05
368	Mike Butcher	.05
369	RP Prospects(Brad Clontz, Steve Phoenix, Scott Gentile, Bucky Buckles)	.10
370	Eddie Murray	.15
371	Orlando Miller (Star Track)	.05
372	Ron Karkovice	.05
373	Richie Lewis	.05
374	Lenny Webster	.05
375	Jeff Tackett	.05
376	Tom Urbani	.05
377	Tino Martinez	.15
378	Mark Dewey	.08
379	Charlie O'Brien	.05
380	Terry Mulholland	.05
381	Thomas Howard	.05
382	Chris Haney	.05
383	Billy Hatcher	.05
384	Jeff Bagwell, Frank Thomas (All Stars)	1.00
385	Bret Boone, Carlos Baerga (All Stars)	.15
386	Matt Williams, Wade Boggs (All Stars)	.15
387	Wil Cordero, Cal Ripken Jr. (All Stars)	.75
388	Barry Bonds, Ken Griffey Jr. (All Stars)	1.00
389	Tony Gwynn, Albert Belle (All Stars)	.40
390	Dante Bichette, Kirby Puckett (All Stars)	.40
391	Mike Piazza, Mike Stanley (All Stars)	.40
392	Greg Maddux, David Cone (All Stars)	.60
393	Danny Jackson, Jimmy Key (All Stars)	.05
394	John Franco, Lee Smith (All Stars)	.05
395	Checklist 1-198	.05

No.	Player	Price
396	Checklist 199-396	.05
397	Ken Griffey Jr.	2.50
398	*Rick Heiserman* (Draft Pick)	.10
399	Don Mattingly	.75
400	Henry Rodriguez	.05
401	Lenny Harris	.05
402	Ryan Thompson	.05
403	Darren Oliver	.05
404	Omar Vizquel	.05
405	Jeff Bagwell	.60
406	*Doug Webb* (Draft Pick)	.10
407	Todd Van Poppel	.05
408	Leo Gomez	.05
409	Mark Whiten	.05
410	Pedro Martinez	.05
411	Reggie Sanders	.08
412	Kevin Foster	.05
413	Danny Tartabull	.05
414	Jeff Blauser	.05
415	Mike Magnante	.05
416	Tom Candiotti	.05
417	Rod Beck	.05
418	Jody Reed	.05
419	Vince Coleman	.05
420	Danny Jackson	.05
421	*Ryan Nye* (Draft Pick)	.20
422	Larry Walker	.20
423	Russ Johnson (Draft Pick)	.15
424	Pat Borders	.05
425	Lee Smith	.08
426	Paul O'Neill	.08
427	Devon White	.05
428	Jim Bullinger	.05
429	SP Prospects(Greg Hansell, Brian Sackinsky, Carey Paige, Rob Welch)	.10
430	Steve Avery	.08
431	Tony Gwynn	.75
432	Pat Meares	.05
433	Bill Swift	.05
434	David Wells	.05
435	John Briscoe	.05
436	Roger Pavlik	.05
437	*Jayson Peterson* (Draft Pick)	.20
438	Roberto Alomar	.50
439	Billy Brewer	.05
440	Gary Sheffield	.20
441	Lou Frazier	.05
442	Terry Steinbach	.05
443	*Jay Payton* (Draft Pick)	.75
444	Jason Bere	.10
445	Denny Neagle	.05
446	Andres Galarraga	.08
447	Hector Carrasco	.05
448	Bill Risley	.05
449	Andy Benes	.05
450	Jim Leyritz	.05
451	Jose Oliva	.05
452	Greg Vaughn	.05
453	Rich Monteleone	.05
454	Tony Eusebio	.05
455	Chuck Finley	.05
456	Kevin Brown	.05
457	Joe Boever	.05
458	Bobby Munoz	.05
459	Bret Saberhagen	.05
460	Kurt Abbott	.05
461	Bobby Witt	.05
462	Cliff Floyd	.10
463	Mark Clark	.05
464	Andujar Cedeno	.05
465	Marvin Freeman	.05
466	Mike Piazza	1.00
467	Willie Greene	.05
468	Pat Kelly	.05
469	Carlos Delgado	.15
470	Willie Banks	.05
471	Matt Walbeck	.05
472	Mark McGwire	3.00
473	McKay Christensen (Draft Pick)	.15
474	Alan Trammell	.08
475	Tom Gordon	.05
476	Greg Colbrunn	.05
477	Darren Daulton	.05
478	Albie Lopez	.05
479	Robin Ventura	.12
480	C Prospects(*Eddie Perez*, Jason Kendall), (*Einar Diaz*, Bret Hemphill)	.20
481	Bryan Eversgerd	.10
482	Dave Fleming	.05
483	Scott Livingstone	.05
484	Pete Schourek	.05
485	Bernie Williams	.40
486	Mark Lemke	.05
487	Eric Karros	.10
488	Scott Ruffcorn	.05
489	Billy Ashley	.10
490	Rico Brogna	.05
491	John Burkett	.05
492	*Cade Gaspar* (Draft Pick)	.15
493	Jorge Fabregas	.05
494	Greg Gagne	.05
495	Doug Jones	.05
496	Troy O'Leary	.05
497	Pat Rapp	.05
498	Butch Henry	.05
499	John Olerud	.12
500	John Hudek	.05
501	Jeff King	.05
502	Bobby Bonilla	.08
503	Albert Belle	.60
504	Rick Wilkins	.05
505	John Jaha	.05
506	Nigel Wilson	.05
507	Sid Fernandez	.05
508	Deion Sanders	.40
509	Gil Heredia	.05
510	*Scott Elarton* (Draft Pick)	.40
511	Melido Perez	.05
512	Greg McMichael	.05
513	Rusty Meacham	.05
514	Shawn Green	.15
515	Carlos Garcia	.05
516	Dave Stevens	.05
517	Eric Young	.05
518	Omar Daal	.05
519	Kirk Gibson	.05
520	Spike Owen	.05
521	*Jacob Cruz* (Draft Pick)	.75
522	Sandy Alomar	.08
523	Steve Bedrosian	.05
524	Ricky Gutierrez	.05
525	Dave Veres	.05
526	Gregg Jefferies	.08
527	Jose Valentin	.05
528	Robb Nen	.05
529	Jose Rijo	.05
530	Sean Berry	.05
531	Mike Gallego	.05
532	Roberto Kelly	.05
533	Kevin Stocker	.05
534	Kirby Puckett	.75
535	Chipper Jones	1.00
536	Russ Davis	.05
537	Jon Lieber	.05
538	*Trey Moore* (Draft Pick)	.10
539	Joe Girardi	.05
540	2B Prospects(Quilvio Veras, Arquimedez Pozo, Miguel Cairo, Jason Camilli)	.20
541	Tony Phillips	.08
542	Brian Anderson	.15
543	Ivan Rodriguez	.50
544	Jeff Cirillo	.05
545	Joey Cora	.05
546	Chris Hoiles	.05
547	Bernard Gilkey	.10
548	Mike Lansing	.05
549	Jimmy Key	.05
550	Mark Wohlers	.05
551	*Chris Clemons* (Draft Pick)	.15
552	Vinny Castilla	.08
553	Mark Guthrie	.05
554	Mike Lieberthal	.05
555	*Tommy Davis* (Draft Pick)	.15
556	Robby Thompson	.05
557	Danny Bautista	.05
558	Will Clark	.30
559	Rickey Henderson	.20
560	Todd Jones	.05
561	Jack McDowell	.05
562	Carlos Rodriguez	.05
563	Mark Eichhorn	.05
564	Jeff Nelson	.05
565	Eric Anthony	.05
566	Randy Velarde	.05
567	Javy Lopez	.15
568	Kevin Mitchell	.05
569	Steve Karsay	.05
570	*Brian Meadows* (Draft Pick)	.20
571	SS Propects(*Rey Ordonez*, Mike Metcalfe, Ray Holbert, Kevin Orie)	1.00
572	John Kruk	.05
573	Scott Leius	.05
574	John Patterson	.05
575	Kevin Brown	.08
576	Mike Moore	.05
577	Manny Ramirez	.50
578	Jose Lind	.05
579	Derrick May	.05
580	Cal Eldred	.05
581	3B Prospects(David Bell, Joel Chelmis, Lino Diaz), (*Aaron Boone*)	.15
582	J.T. Snow	.10
583	Luis Sojo	.05
584	Moises Alou	.10
585	Dave Clark	.05
586	Dave Hollins	.05
587	Nomar Garciaparra (Draft Pick)	4.00
588	Cal Ripken Jr.	2.50
589	Pedro Astacio	.05
590	J.R. Phillips	.10
591	Jeff Frye	.05
592	Bo Jackson	.10
593	Steve Ontiveros	.05
594	David Nied	.05
595	Brad Ausmus	.05
596	Carlos Baerga	.25
597	James Mouton	.05
598	Ozzie Guillen	.05
599	OF Prospects(Ozzie Timmons, Curtis Goodwin, Johnny Damon), (*Jeff Abbott*)	.30
600	Yorkis Perez	.05
601	Rich Rodriguez	.05
602	Mark McLemore	.05
603	Jeff Fassero	.05
604	John Roper	.05
605	*Mark Johnson* (Draft Pick)	.20
606	Wes Chamberlain	.05
607	Felix Jose	.05
608	Tony Longmire	.05
609	Duane Ward	.05
610	Brett Butler	.10
611	William Van Landingham	.10
612	Mickey Tettleton	.05
613	Brady Anderson	.15
614	Reggie Jefferson	.05
615	Mike Kingery	.05
616	Derek Bell	.10
617	Scott Erickson	.05
618	Bob Wickman	.05
619	Phil Leftwich	.05
620	Dave Justice	.30
621	Paul Wilson (Draft Pick)	.15
622	Pedro Martinez	.08
623	Terry Mathews	.05
624	Brian McRae	.05
625	Bruce Ruffin	.05
626	Steve Finley	.05
627	Ron Gant	.10
628	Rafael Bournigal	.05
629	Darryl Strawberry	.08
630	Luis Alicea	.05
631	Mark Smith, Scott Klingenbeck (On Deck)	.10
632	Cory Bailey, Scott Hatteberg (On Deck)	.15
633	Todd Greene, Troy Percival (On Deck)	.20
634	Rod Bolton, Olmedo Saenz (On Deck)	.15
635	Herb Perry, Steve Kline (On Deck)	.10
636	Sean Bergman, Shannon Penn (On Deck)	.10
637	Joe Vitiello, Joe Randa (On Deck)	.10
638	Jose Mercedes, Duane Singleton (On Deck)	.05
639	Marty Cordova, Marc Barcelo (On Deck)	.15
640	Ruben Rivera, Andy Pettitte (On Deck)	1.00
641	Willie Adams, Scott Spiezio (On Deck)	.10
642	Eddie Diaz, Desi Relaford (On Deck)	.15
643	Jon Shave, Terrell Lowery (On Deck)	.10
644	Paul Spoljaric, Angel Martinez (On Deck)	.05
645	Damon Hollins, Tony Graffanino (On Deck)	.10
646	Darron Cox, Doug Glanville (On Deck)	.10
647	Tim Belk, Pat Watkins (On Deck)	.10
648	Rod Pedraza, Phil Schneider (On Deck)	.10
649	Marc Valdes, Vic Darensbourg (On Deck)	.10

650	Rick Huisman, Roberto Petagine (On Deck)	.05
651	Ron Coomer, Roger Cedeno (On Deck)	.15
652	*Carlos Perez*, Shane Andrews (On Deck)	.30
653	Jason Isringhausen, Chris Roberts (On Deck)	.65
654	Kevin Jordan, Wayne Gomes (On Deck)	.10
655	Esteban Loaiza, Steve Pegues (On Deck)	.20
656	John Frascatore, Terry Bradshaw (On Deck)	.10
657	Bryce Florie, Andres Berumen (On Deck)	.10
658	Keith Williams, Dan Carlson (On Deck)	.10
659	Checklist	.05
660	Checklist	.05

1995 Topps Cyberstats

2B/OF—SAN DIEGO PADRES

Inserted into all type of Topps packaging at the rate of about one per 15 cards, this special series attempted to "complete" the statistics from the strike-shortened 1994 baseball season for nearly 400 players. Topps used computer modeling to predict how each player would have ended the season. Fronts of the cards are the same as found in the regular Topps set, except they have been printed on metallic foil. Backs have a black background.

	MT
Complete Set (396):	80.00
Complete Series 1 (198):	40.00
Complete Series 2 (198):	40.00
Common Player:	.10
1	Frank Thomas	6.00
2	Mickey Morandini	.10
3	Todd Worrell	.10
4	David Cone	.10
5	Trevor Hoffman	.10
6	Shane Mack	.10
7	Delino DeShields	.10
8	Matt Williams	.60
9	Sammy Sosa	4.00
10	Gary DiSarcina	.10
11	Kenny Rogers	.10
12	Jose Vizcaino	.10
13	Lou Whitaker	.10
14	Ron Darling	.10
15	Dave Nilsson	.10
16	Dennis Martinez	.10
17	Orlando Merced	.10
18	John Wetteland	.10
19	Mike Devereaux	.10
20	Rene Arocha	.10
21	Jay Buhner	.30
22	Hal Morris	.10

23	Paul Molitor	.75
24	Dave West	.10
25	Scott Sanders	.10
26	Eddie Zambrano	.10
27	Ricky Bones	.10
28	John Valentin	.10
29	Kevin Tapani	.10
30	Tim Wallach	.10
31	Darren Lewis	.10
32	Travis Fryman	.10
33	Bret Barberie	.10
34	Dennis Eckersley	.10
35	Ken Hill	.10
36	Pete Harnisch	.10
37	Mike Mussina	.75
38	Dave Winfield	.35
39	Joey Hamilton	.10
40	Edgar Martinez	.10
41	John Smiley	.10
42	Jim Abbott	.15
43	Mike Kelly	.10
44	Brian Jordan	.10
45	Ken Ryan	.10
46	Matt Mieske	.10
47	Rick Aguilera	.10
48	Ismael Valdes	.10
49	Royce Clayton	.10
50	Juan Gonzalez	4.00
51	Mel Rojas	.10
52	Doug Drabek	.10
53	Charles Nagy	.10
54	Tim Raines	.10
55	Midre Cummings	.10
56	Rafael Palmeiro	.30
57	Charlie Hayes	.10
58	Ray Lankford	.10
59	Tim Davis	.10
60	Andy Ashby	.10
61	Mark Grace	.25
62	Mark Langston	.10
63	Chuck Carr	.10
64	Barry Bonds	2.50
65	David Segui	.10
66	Mariano Duncan	.10
67	Kenny Lofton	1.50
68	Ken Caminiti	.25
69	Darrin Jackson	.10
70	Wil Cordero	.10
71	Walt Weiss	.10
72	Tom Pagnozzi	.10
73	Bret Boone	.10
74	Wally Joyner	.10
75	Luis Lopez	.10
76	Len Dykstra	.10
77	Pedro Munoz	.10
78	Kevin Gross	.10
79	Eduardo Perez	.10
80	Brent Gates	.10
81	Jeff Conine	.10
82	Paul Sorrento	.10
83	Julio Franco	.10
84	Chris Sabo	.10
85	Dante Bichette	.30
86	Mike Stanley	.10
87	Bob Hamelin	.10
88	Tommy Greene	.10
89	Jeff Brantley	.10
90	Ed Sprague	.10
91	Otis Nixon	.10
92	Chad Curtis	.10
93	Chuck McElroy	.10
94	Troy Neel	.10
95	Benito Santiago	.10
96	Jose Mesa	.10
97	Luis Gonzalez	.10
98	Alex Fernandez	.10
99	Ben McDonald	.10
100	Wade Boggs	.40
101	Tom Glavine	.15
102	Phil Plantier	.10
103	Raul Mondesi	.75
104	Jim Edmonds	.25
105	Jeff Kent	.10
106	Wilson Alvarez	.10
107	Geronimo Berroa	.10
108	Craig Biggio	.10
109	Roberto Hernandez	.10
110	Bobby Ayala	.10
111	Bob Tewksbury	.10
112	Rondell White	.25
113	Steve Cooke	.10
114	Tim Salmon	.45
115	Kent Mercker	.10
116	Randy Johnson	1.00
117	Mo Vaughn	1.50
118	Eddie Williams	.10

119	Jeff Montgomery	.10
120	Kirt Manwaring	.10
121	Pat Hentgen	.10
122	Shawon Dunston	.10
123	Tim Belcher	.10
124	Cecil Fielder	.20
125	Todd Hundley	.10
126	Mark Acre	.10
127	Darrell Whitmore	.10
128	Darryl Kile	.10
129	Jay Bell	.10
130	Harold Baines	.10
131	Felix Fermin	.10
132	Ellis Burks	.10
133	Joe Carter	.20
134	Terry Pendleton	.10
135	Junior Felix	.10
136	Bill Gullickson	.10
137	Melvin Nieves	.10
138	Chuck Knoblauch	.15
139	Bobby Jones	.10
140	Darrin Fletcher	.10
141	Andy Van Slyke	.10
142	Allen Watson	.10
143	Dan Wilson	.10
144	Bip Roberts	.10
145	Sterling Hitchcock	.10
146	Johnny Ruffin	.10
147	Steve Trachsel	.10
148	Ramon Martinez	.10
149	Dave Henderson	.10
150	Chris Gomez	.10
151	Rusty Greer	.10
152	John Franco	.10
153	Mike Bordick	.10
154	Dave Magadan	.10
155	Greg Swindell	.10
156	Arthur Rhodes	.10
157	Juan Guzman	.10
158	Greg Maddux	5.00
159	Mike Macfarlane	.10
160	Curt Schilling	.10
161	Jose Canseco	.50
162	Aaron Sele	.20
163	Steve Buechele	.10
164	Orel Hershiser	.10
165	Mike Henneman	.10
166	Kevin Seitzer	.10
167	Ruben Sierra	.10
168	Alex Cole	.10
169	Jim Thome	.35
170	Lance Johnson	.10
171	Marquis Grissom	.10
172	Jamie Moyer	.10
173	Todd Zeile	.10
174	Chris Bosio	.10
175	Steve Howe	.10
176	Luis Polonia	.10
177	Ryan Klesko	1.00
178	Kevin Appier	.10
179	Tim Naehring	.10
180	Randy Myers	.10
181	Mike Jackson	.10
182	Chili Davis	.10
183	Jason Jacome	.10
184	Stan Javier	.10
185	Scott Servais	.10
186	Kirk Rueter	.10
187	Don Slaught	.10
188	Ozzie Smith	1.50
189	Barry Larkin	.40
190	Gary Gaetti	.10
191	Fred McGriff	.90
192	Roger Clemens	1.50
193	Dean Palmer	.10
194	Jeromy Burnitz	.10
195	Scott Kamieniecki	.10
196	Eddie Murray	.60
197	Ron Karkovice	.10
198	Tino Martinez	.15
199	Ken Griffey Jr.	8.00
200	Don Mattingly	3.00
201	Henry Rodriguez	.10
202	Lenny Harris	.10
203	Ryan Thompson	.10
204	Darren Oliver	.10
205	Omar Vizquel	.10
206	Jeff Bagwell	3.00
207	Todd Van Poppel	.10
208	Leo Gomez	.10
209	Mark Whiten	.10
210	Pedro Martinez	.10
211	Reggie Sanders	.10
212	Kevin Foster	.10
213	Danny Tartabull	.10
214	Jeff Blauser	.10

215	Mike Magnante	.10
216	Tom Candiotti	.10
217	Rod Beck	.10
218	Jody Reed	.10
219	Vince Coleman	.10
220	Danny Jackson	.10
221	Larry Walker	.50
222	Pat Borders	.10
223	Lee Smith	.10
224	Paul O'Neill	.10
225	Devon White	.10
226	Jim Bullinger	.10
227	Steve Avery	.10
228	Tony Gwynn	1.50
229	Pat Meares	.10
230	Bill Swift	.10
231	David Wells	.10
232	John Briscoe	.10
233	Roger Pavlik	.10
234	Roberto Alomar	1.00
235	Billy Brewer	.10
236	Gary Sheffield	.40
237	Lou Frazier	.10
238	Terry Steinbach	.10
239	Omar Daal	.10
240	Jason Bere	.10
241	Denny Neagle	.10
242	Danny Bautista	.10
243	Hector Carrasco	.10
244	Bill Risley	.10
245	Andy Benes	.10
246	Jim Leyritz	.10
247	Jose Oliva	.10
248	Greg Vaughn	.10
249	Rich Monteleone	.10
250	Tony Eusebio	.10
251	Chuck Finley	.10
252	Joe Boever	.10
253	Bobby Munoz	.10
254	Bret Saberhagen	.10
255	Kurt Abbott	.10
256	Bobby Witt	.10
257	Cliff Floyd	.15
258	Mark Clark	.10
259	Andujar Cedeno	.10
260	Marvin Freeman	.10
261	Mike Piazza	5.00
262	Pat Kelly	.10
263	Carlos Delgado	.10
264	Willie Banks	.10
265	Matt Walbeck	.10
266	Mark McGwire	8.00
267	Alan Trammell	.10
268	Tom Gordon	.10
269	Greg Colbrunn	.10
270	Darren Daulton	.10
271	Albie Lopez	.10
272	Robin Ventura	.15
273	Bryan Eversgerd	.10
274	Dave Fleming	.10
275	Scott Livingstone	.10
276	Pete Schourek	.10
277	Bernie Williams	.75
278	Mark Lemke	.10
279	Eric Karros	.15
280	Billy Ashley	.10
281	Rico Brogna	.10
282	John Burkett	.10
283	Jorge Fabregas	.10
284	Greg Gagne	.10
285	Doug Jones	.10
286	Troy O'Leary	.10
287	Pat Rapp	.10
288	Butch Henry	.10
289	John Olerud	.15
290	John Hudek	.10
291	Jeff King	.10
292	Bobby Bonilla	.15
293	Albert Belle	2.00
294	Rick Wilkins	.10
295	John Jaha	.10
296	Sid Fernandez	.10
297	Deion Sanders	.50
298	Gil Heredia	.10
299	Melido Perez	.10
300	Greg McMichael	.10
301	Rusty Meacham	.10
302	Shawn Green	.10
303	Carlos Garcia	.10
304	Dave Stevens	.10
305	Eric Young	.10
306	Kirk Gibson	.10
307	Spike Owen	.10
308	Sandy Alomar	.10
309	Ricky Gutierrez	.10
310	Dave Veres	.10

311	Gregg Jefferies	.10
312	Jose Valentin	.10
313	Robb Nen	.10
314	Jose Rijo	.10
315	Sean Berry	.10
316	Mike Gallego	.10
317	Roberto Kelly	.10
318	Kevin Stocker	.10
319	Kirby Puckett	3.00
320	Jon Lieber	.10
321	Joe Girardi	.10
322	Tony Phillips	.10
323	Brian Anderson	.10
324	Ivan Rodriguez	.50
325	Jeff Cirillo	.10
326	Joey Cora	.10
327	Chris Hoiles	.10
328	Bernard Gilkey	.10
329	Mike Lansing	.10
330	Jimmy Key	.10
331	Vinny Castilla	.10
332	Mark Guthrie	.10
333	Mike Lieberthal	.10
334	Will Clark	.50
335	Rickey Henderson	.20
336	Todd Jones	.10
337	Jack McDowell	.10
338	Carlos Rodriguez	.10
339	Mark Eichhorn	.10
340	Jeff Nelson	.10
341	Eric Anthony	.10
342	Randy Velarde	.10
343	Javier Lopez	.25
344	Kevin Mitchell	.10
345	Steve Bedrosian	.10
346	John Kruk	.10
347	Scott Leius	.10
348	John Patterson	.10
349	Kevin Brown	.10
350	Mike Moore	.10
351	Manny Ramirez	1.25
352	Jose Lind	.10
353	Derrick May	.10
354	Cal Eldred	.10
355	J.T. Snow	.10
356	Luis Sojo	.10
357	Moises Alou	.10
358	Dave Clark	.10
359	Dave Hollins	.10
360	Cal Ripken Jr.	7.00
361	Pedro Astacio	.10
362	Tony Longmire	.10
363	Jeff Frye	.10
364	Bo Jackson	.10
365	Steve Ontiveros	.10
366	David Nied	.10
367	Brad Ausmus	.10
368	Carlos Baerga	.15
369	James Mouton	.10
370	Ozzie Guillen	.10
371	Yorkis Perez	.10
372	Rich Rodriguez	.10
373	Mark McLemore	.10
374	Jeff Fassero	.10
375	John Roper	.10
376	Wes Chamberlain	.10
377	Felix Jose	.10
378	Brett Butler	.10
379	William Van Landingham	.10
380	Mickey Tettleton	.10
381	Brady Anderson	.25
382	Reggie Jefferson	.10
383	Mike Kingery	.10
384	Derek Bell	.10
385	Scott Erickson	.10
386	Bob Wickman	.10
387	Phil Leftwich	.10
388	Dave Justice	.25
389	Pedro Martinez	.10
390	Terry Mathews	.10
391	Brian McRae	.10
392	Bruce Ruffin	.10
393	Steve Finley	.10
394	Rafael Bournigal	.10
395	Darryl Strawberry	.10
396	Luis Alicea	.10

1995 Topps Cyberstat Season in Review

Juan Gonzalez

This special edition of Cyberstat cards was available only in Topps factory sets. Carrying forward the idea of computerized projections to complete the strike-shortened 1994 season, the Season in Review cards speculate on career milestones and the playoffs that never happened. The Season in Review cards have player action photos printed on a foil background resembling the U.S. flag. Names are in gold foil. Backs have a black background and a recap of the computer simulation.

		MT
Complete Set (7):		11.00
Common Player:		2.00
1	Barry Bonds (61 Home Runs)	3.00
2	Jose Canseco (AL West One-Game Playoff)	1.50
3	Juan Gonzalez (AL Divisional Playoffs)	3.00
4	Fred McGriff (NL Divisional Playoffs)	2.00
5	Carlos Baerga (ALCS MVP)	1.50
6	Ryan Klesko (NLCS MVP)	2.50
7	Kenny Lofton (World Series MVP)	2.50

1995 Topps League Leaders

STOLEN BASE LEADER — DEION SANDERS

Modern cards have little collector value in conditions lower than Mint.
Figure NM cards at 75% of values shown;
EX cards at 40%.

League Leaders is a 50-card insert set found in one of every six retail packs only of both Series I and II. The set includes the top five players in each league across 10 statistical categories. Cards featured the statistical category running up the right side, with the player's name across the bottom. Photo backgrounds have been darkened and posterized to make the player action stand out. Backs have the player's stat rankings within his division and league, and a bar graph at bottom gives his performance in that statistical category for the previous five seasons.

		MT
Complete Set (50):		35.00
Complete Series 1 (25):		16.00
Complete Series 2 (25):		20.00
Common Player:		.30
1	Albert Belle	1.00
2	Kevin Mitchell	.30
3	Wade Boggs	.45
4	Tony Gwynn	1.00
5	Moises Alou	.30
6	Andres Galarraga	.35
7	Matt Williams	.60
8	Barry Bonds	1.25
9	Frank Thomas	4.00
10	Jose Canseco	.60
11	Jeff Bagwell	1.50
12	Kirby Puckett	1.50
13	Julio Franco	.30
14	Albert Belle	1.00
15	Fred McGriff	.75
16	Kenny Lofton	1.25
17	Otis Nixon	.30
18	Brady Anderson	.35
19	Deion Sanders	.60
20	Chuck Carr	.30
21	Pat Hentgen	.30
22	Andy Benes	.30
23	Roger Clemens	.90
24	Greg Maddux	3.00
25	Pedro Martinez	.30
26	Paul O'Neill	.30
27	Jeff Bagwell	1.50
28	Frank Thomas	4.00
29	Hal Morris	.30
30	Kenny Lofton	1.25
31	Ken Griffey Jr.	5.00
32	Jeff Bagwell	1.50
33	Albert Belle	1.00
34	Fred McGriff	.75
35	Cecil Fielder	.35
36	Matt Williams	.40
37	Joe Carter	.35
38	Dante Bichette	.45
39	Frank Thomas	4.00
40	Mike Piazza	2.00
41	Craig Biggio	.30
42	Vince Coleman	.30
43	Marquis Grissom	.30
44	Chuck Knoblauch	.45
45	Darren Lewis	.30
46	Randy Johnson	.60
47	Jose Rijo	.30
48	Chuck Finley	.30
49	Bret Saberhagen	.30
50	Kevin Appier	.30

1995 Topps
Opening Day

This 10-card set featuring top performers on the belated opening day of the 1995 season was available exclusively in retail factory sets. Card fronts feature color action photos printed on textured foil in a U.S. flag-like design. A large colorful Opening Day logo appears in an upper corner while the player's key stats from that game appear in a foil box at lower-right. Backs have a portrait photo along with complete details and a stats line of the opening day performance.

		MT
Complete Set (10):		16.00
Common Player:		2.00
1	Kevin Appier	2.00
2	Dante Bichette	3.00
3	Ken Griffey Jr.	8.00
4	Todd Hundley	3.00
5	John Jaha	2.00
6	Fred McGriff	3.00
7	Raul Mondesi	3.00
8	Manny Ramirez	4.00
9	Danny Tartabull	2.00
10	Devon White	2.00

1995 Topps
Total Bases Finest

Printed in Topps Finest technology, including a peel-off plastic protector coating on the front, these cards honor the 1994 statistical leaders in total bases. The cards have a silver waffle-texture background on front as a background to the color action photo. At bottom is a team logo and team-color bar with the player's name. Backs feature a portrait photo and the player's total base stats. These inserts are found in Series II Topps packs at an average rate of one per 36 packs (one box).

		MT
Complete Set (15):		60.00
Common Player:		1.00
1	Jeff Bagwell	4.00
2	Albert Belle	3.00
3	Ken Griffey Jr.	10.00
4	Frank Thomas	8.00
5	Matt Williams	2.00
6	Dante Bichette	2.00
7	Barry Bonds	4.00
8	Moises Alou	1.00
9	Andres Galarraga	1.00
10	Kenny Lofton	3.00
11	Rafael Palmeiro	1.00
12	Tony Gwynn	4.00
13	Kirby Puckett	4.00
14	Jose Canseco	2.00
15	Jeff Conine	1.00

1995 Topps
Traded and Rookies

Traded players, free agents who signed with new teams and all the up-and-coming rookies are the meat of the 1995 Topps Traded and Rookies set, sold for the first time exclusively in foil pack form. Maintaining the same format used in Series 1 and 2 Topps, the updates also reused the Future Star, Draft Pick and Star Track subsets, along with four-player Prospects cards. New subsets included Rookie of the Year Candidates, All-Stars, On Deck and "At the Break," 10 cards chronicling star players' performances through the first half of the 1995 season. A double-thick, foil-printed version of the "At the Break" cards called "Power Boosters" were the only inserts in the Traded/Rookies set.

		MT
Complete Set (165):		25.00
Common Player:		.05
Wax Box:		35.00
1	Frank Thomas (At The Break)	1.00
2	Ken Griffey Jr. (At The Break)	1.00
3	Barry Bonds (At The Break)	.40
4	Albert Belle (At The Break)	.25
5	Cal Ripken Jr. (At The Break)	1.00
6	Mike Piazza (At The Break)	.65
7	Tony Gwynn (At The Break)	.40
8	Jeff Bagwell (At The Break)	.25
9	Mo Vaughn (At The Break)	.15
10	Matt Williams (At The Break)	.15
11	Ray Durham	.10
12	*Juan LeBron* (Draft Pick)	.60
13	Shawn Green (Rookie of the Year Candidate)	.10
14	Kevin Gross	.05
15	Jon Nunnally	.05
16	*Brian Maxcy*	.10
17	Mark Kiefer	.05
18	*Carlos Beltran* (Draft Pick)	3.00

19	Mike Mimbs	.10
20	Larry Walker	.20
21	Chad Curtis	.05
22	Jeff Barry	.05
23	Joe Oliver	.05
24	Tomas Perez	.10
25	Michael Barrett (Draft Pick)	3.00
26	Brian McRae	.05
27	Derek Bell	.05
28	Ray Durham (Rookie of the Year Candidate)	.10
29	Todd Williams	.05
30	Ryan Jaroncyk (Draft Pick)	.20
31	Todd Steverson	.05
32	Mike Devereaux	.05
33	Rheal Cormier	.05
34	Benny Santiago	.05
35	Bobby Higginson	1.00
36	Jack McDowell	.05
37	Mike Macfarlane	.05
38	Tony McKnight (Draft Pick)	.20
39	Brian Hunter (Rookie of the Year Candidate)	.15
40	Hideo Nomo (Star Track)	3.00
41	Brett Butler	.08
42	Donovan Osborne	.05
43	Scott Karl	.05
44	Tony Phillips	.05
45	Marty Cordova (Rookie of the Year Candidate)	.20
46	Dave Mlicki	.05
47	Bronson Arroyo (Draft Pick)	.35
48	John Burkett	.05
49	J.D. Smart (Draft Pick)	.25
50	Mickey Tettleton	.05
51	Todd Stottlemyre	.05
52	Mike Perez	.05
53	Terry Mulholland	.05
54	Edgardo Alfonzo	.05
55	Zane Smith	.05
56	Jacob Brumfield	.05
57	Andujar Cedeno	.05
58	Jose Parra	.05
59	Manny Alexander	.05
60	Tony Tarasco	.05
61	Orel Hershiser	.05
62	Tim Scott	.05
63	Felix Rodriguez	.05
64	Ken Hill	.05
65	Marquis Grissom	.08
66	Lee Smith	.05
67	Jason Bates (Rookie of the Year Candidate)	.08
68	Felipe Lira	.05
69	Alex Hernandez (Draft Pick)	.40
70	Tony Fernandez	.05
71	Scott Radinsky	.05
72	Jose Canseco	.20
73	Mark Grudzielanek	.50
74	Ben Davis (Draft Pick)	4.00
75	Jim Abbott	.05
76	Roger Bailey	.05
77	Gregg Jefferies	.05
78	Erik Hanson	.05
79	Brad Radke	.75
80	Jaime Navarro	.05
81	John Wetteland	.05
82	Chad Fonville	.15
83	John Mabry	.05
84	Glenallen Hill	.05
85	Ken Caminiti	.05
86	Tom Goodwin	.05
87	Darren Bragg	.05
88	1995 Prospects (Pitchers)(Pat Ahearne), (Gary Rath), (Larry Wimberly), (Robbie Bell)	.25
89	Jeff Russell	.05
90	Dave Gallagher	.05
91	Steve Finley	.05
92	Vaughn Eshelman	.05
93	Kevin Jarvis	.05
94	Mark Gubicza	.05
95	Tim Wakefield	.05
96	Bob Tewksbury	.05
97	Sid Roberson	.10
98	Tom Henke	.05
99	Michael Tucker (Future Star)	.15
100	Jason Bates	.05
101	Otis Nixon	.05
102	Mark Whiten	.05
103	Dilson Torres	.05
104	Melvin Bunch	.10
105	Terry Pendleton	.05
106	Corey Jenkins (Draft Pick)	.20
107	On Deck(Glenn Dishman), (Rob Grable)	.15
108	Reggie Taylor (Draft Pick)	1.50
109	Curtis Goodwin (Rookie of the Year Candidate)	.05
110	David Cone	.05
111	Antonio Osuna	.05
112	Paul Shuey	.05
113	Doug Jones	.05
114	Mark McLemore	.05
115	Kevin Ritz	.05
116	John Kruk	.05
117	Trevor Wilson	.05
118	Jerald Clark	.05
119	Julian Tavarez	.05
120	Tim Pugh	.05
121	Todd Zeile	.05
122	1995 Prospects (Fielders)(Mark Sweeney), (George Arias), (Richie Sexson), (Brian Schneider)	6.00
123	Bobby Witt	.05
124	Hideo Nomo (Rookie of the Year Candidate)	1.50
125	Joey Cora	.05
126	Jim Scharrer (Draft Pick)	.10
127	Paul Quantrill	.05
128	Chipper Jones (Rookie of the Year Candidate)	1.00
129	Kenny James (Draft Pick)	.10
130	On Deck(Lyle Mouton, Mariano Rivera)	.05
131	Tyler Green (Rookie of the Year Candidate)	.10
132	Brad Clontz	.05
133	Jon Nunnally (Rookie of the Year Candidate)	.05
134	Dave Magadan	.05
135	Al Leiter	.05
136	Bret Barberie	.05
137	Bill Swift	.05
138	Scott Cooper	.05
139	Roberto Kelly	.05
140	Charlie Hayes	.05
141	Pete Harnisch	.05
142	Rich Amaral	.05
143	Rudy Seanez	.05
144	Pat Listach	.05
145	Quilvio Veras (Rookie of the Year Candidate)	.08
146	Jose Olmeda (Draft Pick)	.10
147	Roberto Petagine	.05
148	Kevin Brown	.05
149	Phil Plantier	.05
150	Carlos Perez (Rookie of the Year Candidate)	.20
151	Pat Borders	.05
152	Tyler Green	.10
153	Stan Belinda	.05
154	Dave Stewart	.05
155	Andre Dawson	.05
156	Frank Thomas, Fred McGriff (All-Star)	.50
157	Carlos Baerga, Craig Biggio (All-Star)	.10
158	Wade Boggs, Matt Williams (All-Star)	.10
159	Cal Ripken Jr., Ozzie Smith (All-Star)	.50
160	Ken Griffey Jr., Tony Gwynn (All-Star)	.50
161	Albert Belle, Barry Bonds (All-Star)	.25
162	Kirby Puckett, Len Dykstra (All-Star)	.25
163	Ivan Rodriguez, Mike Piazza (All-Star)	.25
164	Randy Johnson, Hideo Nomo (All-Star)	1.50
165	Checklist	.05

1995 Topps Traded and Rookies Power Boosters

Virtually identical to the first 10 cards of the 1995 Topps Traded and Rookies issue, the "At the Break" subset is the only insert found in Traded packs. Cards are printed on double-thick cardboard stock on metallized foil. The chase cards are found at an average rate of one per 36 packs.

		MT
Complete Set (10):		100.00
Common Player:		5.00
1	Frank Thomas	25.00
2	Ken Griffey Jr.	30.00
3	Barry Bonds	8.00
4	Albert Belle	8.00
5	Cal Ripken Jr.	25.00
6	Mike Piazza	12.00
7	Tony Gwynn	10.00
8	Jeff Bagwell	10.00
9	Mo Vaughn	7.00
10	Matt Williams	5.00

1995 Topps/DIII

Describing its cards as featuring "infinite depth perspectives" with game-action photos, Topps entered the 3-D card market with its Dimension III product. Utilizing "super thick laminated construction" to provide the illusion of depth, the cards feature borderless action photos on front. Backs are conventionally printed with a color portrait photo and several sets of stats that go beyond the usual to the provide a more in-depth look at the player's performance.

		MT
Complete Set (59):		27.50
Common Player:		.25
Retail Wax Box:		35.00
Hobby Wax Box:		50.00
1	Dave Justice	.40
2	Cal Ripken Jr.	5.00
3	Ruben Sierra	.25
4	Roberto Alomar	1.00
5	Dennis Martinez	.25
6	Todd Zeile	.25
7	Albert Belle	1.50
8	Chuck Knoblauch	.50
9	Roger Clemens	1.00
10	Cal Eldred	.25
11	Dennis Eckersley	.25
12	Andy Benes	.25
13	Moises Alou	.25
14	Andres Galarraga	.25
15	Jim Thome	.50
16	Tim Salmon	.50
17	Carlos Garcia	.25
18	Scott Leius	.25
19	Jeff Montgomery	.25
20	Brian Anderson	.25
21	Will Clark	.50
22	Bobby Bonilla	.25
23	Mike Stanley	.25
24	Barry Bonds	1.50
25	Jeff Conine	.25
26	Paul O'Neill	.25
27	Mike Piazza	2.50
28	Tom Glavine	.35
29	Jim Edmonds	.40

30	Lou Whitaker	.25
31	Jeff Frye	.25
32	Ivan Rodriguez	.50
33	Bret Boone	.25
34	Mike Greenwell	.25
35	Mark Grace	.45
36	Darren Lewis	.25
37	Don Mattingly	2.50
38	Jose Rijo	.25
39	Robin Ventura	.25
40	Bob Hamelin	.25
41	Tim Wallach	.25
42	Tony Gwynn	1.50
43	Ken Griffey Jr.	6.00
44	Doug Drabek	.25
45	Rafael Palmeiro	.25
46	Dean Palmer	.25
47	Bip Roberts	.25
48	Barry Larkin	.25
49	Dave Nilsson	.25
50	Wil Cordero	.25
51	Travis Fryman	.25
52	Chuck Carr	.25
53	Rey Sanchez	.25
54	Walt Weiss	.25
55	Joe Carter	.25
56	Len Dykstra	.25
57	Orlando Merced	.25
58	Ozzie Smith	.75
59	Chris Gomez	.25

1995 Topps DIII Zone

A barrage of baseballs in the background, behind a player action photo, are featured on the front of this DIII chase set. Backs have a blazing baseball across the top and a description and stats of the pictured player's hot streaks of the previous season -- those times when athletes are said to be "in the zone." The inserts are found on average of one per six packs.

		MT
Complete Set (6):		22.00
Common Player:		2.00
1	Frank Thomas	10.00
2	Kirby Puckett	3.50
3	Jeff Bagwell	3.00
4	Fred McGriff	2.50
5	Raul Mondesi	2.00
6	Kenny Lofton	3.00

1995 Topps Embossed

Taking the embossed sports-card idea which Action Packed developed years earlier to a new level, Topps Embossed baseball features the tactile image on both sides of the card. Fronts have a lightly textured border while the central player photo is deeply embossed. The player name is embossed in gold-foil letters at bottom. Backs have another embossed player photo and various levels of embossing around the borders and boxes which contain stats and trivia.

		MT
Complete Set (140):		20.00
Common Player:		.10
Comp. Embossed Gold Set (140):		70.00
Embossed Golds: 2X to 4X		
Wax Box:		40.00
1	Kenny Lofton	.75
2	Gary Sheffield	.20
3	Hal Morris	.10
4	Cliff Floyd	.15
5	Pat Hentgen	.10
6	Tony Gwynn	1.00
7	Jose Valentin	.10
8	Jason Bere	.10
9	Jeff Kent	.10
10	John Valentin	.10
11	Brian Anderson	.10
12	Deion Sanders	.40
13	Ryan Thompson	.10
14	Ruben Sierra	.10
15	Jay Bell	.10
16	Chuck Carr	.10
17	Brent Gates	.10
18	Bret Boone	.10
19	Paul Molitor	.25
20	Chili Davis	.10
21	Ryan Klesko	.50
22	Will Clark	.35
23	Greg Vaughn	.10
24	Moises Alou	.10
25	Ray Lankford	.10
26	Jose Rijo	.10
27	Bobby Jones	.10
28	Rick Wilkins	.10
29	Cal Eldred	.10
30	Juan Gonzalez	1.00
31	Royce Clayton	.10
32	Bryan Harvey	.10
33	Dave Nilsson	.10
34	Chris Hoiles	.10
35	David Nied	.10
36	Javy Lopez	.20
37	Tim Wallach	.10
38	Bobby Bonilla	.10
39	Danny Tartabull	.10
40	Andy Benes	.10
41	Dean Palmer	.10
42	Chris Gomez	.10
43	Kevin Appier	.10
44	Brady Anderson	.20
45	Alex Fernandez	.10
46	Roberto Kelly	.10
47	Dave Hollins	.10
48	Chuck Finley	.10
49	Wade Boggs	.20
50	Travis Fryman	.10
51	Ken Griffey Jr.	3.00
52	John Olerud	.10
53	Delino DeShields	.10
54	Ivan Rodriguez	.15
55	Tommy Greene	.10
56	Tom Pagnozzi	.10
57	Bip Roberts	.10
58	Luis Gonzalez	.10
59	Rey Sanchez	.10
60	Ken Ryan	.10
61	Darren Daulton	.10
62	Rick Aguilera	.10
63	Wally Joyner	.10
64	Mike Greenwell	.10
65	Jay Buhner	.10
66	Craig Biggio	.10
67	Charles Nagy	.10
68	Devon White	.10
69	Randy Johnson	.25
70	Shawon Dunston	.10
71	Kirby Puckett	1.00
72	Paul O'Neill	.10
73	Tino Martinez	.20
74	Carlos Garcia	.10
75	Ozzie Smith	.50
76	Cecil Fielder	.15
77	Mike Stanley	.10
78	Lance Johnson	.10
79	Tony Phillips	.10

80	Bobby Munoz	.10
81	Kevin Tapani	.10
82	William Van Landingham	.10
83	Dante Bichette	.25
84	Tom Candiotti	.10
85	Wil Cordero	.10
86	Jeff Conine	.10
87	Joey Hamilton	.10
88	Mark Whiten	.10
89	Jeff Montgomery	.10
90	Andres Galarraga	.10
91	Roberto Alomar	.50
92	Orlando Merced	.10
93	Mike Mussina	.30
94	Pedro Martinez	.10
95	Carlos Baerga	.20
96	Steve Trachsel	.10
97	Lou Whitaker	.10
98	David Cone	.10
99	Chuck Knoblauch	.15
100	Frank Thomas	2.50
101	Dave Justice	.20
102	Raul Mondesi	.30
103	Rickey Henderson	.20
104	Doug Drabek	.10
105	Sandy Alomar	.10
106	Roger Clemens	.60
107	Mark McGwire	2.00
108	Tim Salmon	.25
109	Greg Maddux	2.00
110	Mike Piazza	1.50
111	Tom Glavine	.10
112	Walt Weiss	.10
113	Cal Ripken Jr.	2.50
114	Eddie Murray	.40
115	Don Mattingly	1.25
116	Ozzie Guillen	.10
117	Bob Hamelin	.10
118	Jeff Bagwell	1.00
119	Eric Karros	.10
120	Barry Bonds	.75
121	Mickey Tettleton	.10
122	Mark Langston	.10
123	Robin Ventura	.10
124	Bret Saberhagen	.10
125	Albert Belle	.75
126	Rafael Palmeiro	.10
127	Fred McGriff	.25
128	Jimmy Key	.10
129	Barry Larkin	.10
130	Tim Raines	.10
131	Len Dykstra	.10
132	Todd Zeile	.10
133	Joe Carter	.10
134	Matt Williams	.25
135	Terry Steinbach	.10
136	Manny Ramirez	.50
137	John Wetteland	.10
138	Rod Beck	.10
139	Mo Vaughn	.50
140	Darren Lewis	.10

1995 Topps Embossed Golden Idols

The only insert in the Topps Embossed baseball set was a parallel set of the 140 cards rendered in gold tones on front and inserted at the rate of one per pack. Backs are identical to the regular version.

	MT
Complete Set (140):	70.00
Common Player:	.25
(Star cards valued at 2X-4X corresponding regular Embossed cards)	

1996 Topps

At 440 cards, the basic Topps set for 1996 was the smallest regular-issue from the company since it adopted the 2-1/2" x 3-1/2" format in 1957. Honoring the late Mickey Mantle on card No. 7, Topps announced it would hereafter retire that card number.

	MT
Complete Set (440):	35.00
Complete Series 1 (220):	20.00
Complete Series 2 (220):	10.00
Common Player:	.05
Unlisted Stars: .20 to .35	
Series 1 Wax Box:	60.00
Series 2 Wax Box:	70.00
1	Tony Gwynn (Star Power)	.25
2	Mike Piazza (Star Power)	.40
3	Greg Maddux (Star Power)	.50
4	Jeff Bagwell (Star Power)	.30
5	Larry Walker (Star Power)	.20
6	Barry Larkin (Star Power)	.10
7	Mickey Mantle (Commemorative)	4.00
8	Tom Glavine (Star Power)	.10
9	Craig Biggio (Star Power)	.05
10	Barry Bonds (Star Power)	.20
11	Heathcliff Slocumb (Star Power)	.05
12	Matt Williams (Star Power)	.15
13	Todd Helton (Draft Pick)	1.00
14	Mark Redman (Draft Pick)	.15
15	Michael Barrett (Draft Pick)	.20
16	Ben Davis (Draft Pick)	.25
17	Juan LeBron (Draft Pick)	.20
18	Tony McKnight (Draft Pick)	.10
19	Ryan Jaroncyk (Draft Pick)	.05
20	Corey Jenkins (Draft Pick)	.15
21	Jim Scharrer (Draft Pick)	.05
22	*Mark Bellhorn (Draft Pick)*	.25
23	*Jarrod Washburn (Draft Pick)*	.40
24	*Geoff Jenkins (Draft Pick)*	.75
25	*Sean Casey (Draft Pick)*	1.50
26	*Brett Tomko (Draft Pick)*	.20
27	Tony Fernandez	.05
28	Rich Becker	.05
29	Andujar Cedeno	.05
30	Paul Molitor	.20
31	Brent Gates	.05
32	Glenallen Hill	.05
33	Mike MacFarlane	.05
34	Manny Alexander	.05
35	Todd Zeile	.05

36	Joe Girardi	.05
37	Tony Tarasco	.05
38	Tim Belcher	.05
39	Tom Goodwin	.05
40	Orel Hershiser	.08
41	Tripp Cromer	.05
42	Sean Bergman	.05
43	Troy Percival	.05
44	Kevin Stocker	.05
45	Albert Belle	.60
46	Tony Eusebio	.05
47	Sid Roberson	.05
48	Todd Hollandsworth	.10
49	Mark Wohlers	.05
50	Kirby Puckett	.65
51	Darren Holmes	.05
52	Ron Karkovice	.05
53	Al Martin	.05
54	Pat Rapp	.05
55	Mark Grace	.15
56	Greg Gagne	.05
57	Stan Javier	.05
58	Scott Sanders	.05
59	J.T. Snow	.05
60	David Justice	.15
61	Royce Clayton	.05
62	Kevin Foster	.05
63	Tim Naehring	.05
64	Orlando Miller	.05
65	Mike Mussina	.30
66	Jim Eisenreich	.05
67	Felix Fermin	.05
68	Bernie Williams	.40
69	Robb Nen	.05
70	Ron Gant	.15
71	Felipe Lira	.05
72	Jacob Brumfield	.05
73	John Mabry	.05
74	Mark Carreon	.05
75	Carlos Baerga	.10
76	Jim Dougherty	.05
77	Ryan Thompson	.05
78	Scott Leius	.05
79	Roger Pavlik	.05
80	Gary Sheffield	.40
81	Julian Tavarez	.05
82	Andy Ashby	.05
83	Mark Lemke	.05
84	Omar Vizquel	.05
85	Darren Daulton	.05
86	Mike Lansing	.05
87	Rusty Greer	.05
88	Dave Stevens	.05
89	Jose Offerman	.05
90	Tom Henke	.05
91	Troy O'Leary	.05
92	Michael Tucker	.05
93	Marvin Freeman	.05
94	Alex Diaz	.05
95	John Wetteland	.05
96	Cal Ripken Jr. (Tribute Card)	2.50
97	Mike Mimbs	.05
98	Bobby Higginson	.05
99	Edgardo Alfonzo	.05
100	Frank Thomas	2.50
101	Steve Gibralter, Bob Abreu (AAA Stars)	.15
102	Brian Givens, T.J. Mathews (AAA Stars)	.05
103	Chris Pritchett, Trenidad Hubbard (AAA Stars)	.10
104	Eric Owens, Butch Huskey (AAA Stars)	.15
105	Doug Drabek	.05
106	Tomas Perez	.05
107	Mark Leiter	.05
108	Joe Oliver	.05
109	Tony Castillo	.05
110	Checklist	
111	Kevin Seitzer	.05
112	Pete Schourek	.05
113	Sean Berry	.05
114	Todd Stottlemyre	.05
115	Joe Carter	.10
116	Jeff King	.05
117	Dan Wilson	.05
118	Kurt Abbott	.05
119	Lyle Mouton	.05
120	Jose Rijo	.05
121	Curtis Goodwin	.05
122	*Jose Valentin*	.05
123	Ellis Burks	.10
124	David Cone	.10
125	Eddie Murray	.25
126	Brian Jordan	.10

127	Darrin Fletcher	.05
128	Curt Schilling	.05
129	Ozzie Guillen	.05
130	Kenny Rogers	.05
131	Tom Pagnozzi	.05
132	Garret Anderson	.05
133	Bobby Jones	.05
134	Chris Gomez	.05
135	Mike Stanley	.05
136	Hideo Nomo	.60
137	Jon Nunnally	.05
138	Tim Wakefield	.05
139	Steve Finley	.05
140	Ivan Rodriguez	.50
141	Quilvio Veras	.05
142	Mike Fetters	.05
143	Mike Greenwell	.05
144	Bill Pulsipher	.15
145	Mark McGwire	3.00
146	Frank Castillo	.05
147	Greg Vaughn	.05
148	Pat Hentgen	.05
149	Walt Weiss	.05
150	Randy Johnson	.30
151	David Segui	.05
152	Benji Gil	.05
153	Tom Candiotti	.05
154	Geronimo Berroa	.05
155	John Franco	.05
156	Jay Bell	.05
157	Mark Gubicza	.05
158	Hal Morris	.05
159	Wilson Alvarez	.05
160	Derek Bell	.10
161	Ricky Bottalico	.05
162	Bret Boone	.05
163	Brad Radke	.05
164	John Valentin	.05
165	Steve Avery	.08
166	Mark McLemore	.05
167	Danny Jackson	.05
168	Tino Martinez	.15
169	Shane Reynolds	.05
170	Terry Pendleton	.05
171	Jim Edmonds	.10
172	Esteban Loaiza	.10
173	Ray Durham	.05
174	Carlos Perez	.05
175	Raul Mondesi	.25
176	Steve Ontiveros	.05
177	Chipper Jones	1.25
178	Otis Nixon	.05
179	John Burkett	.05
180	Gregg Jefferies	.08
181	Denny Martinez	.08
182	Ken Caminiti	.12
183	Doug Jones	.05
184	Brian McRae	.05
185	Don Mattingly	1.00
186	Mel Rojas	.05
187	Marty Cordova	.10
188	Vinny Castilla	.08
189	John Smoltz	.15
190	Travis Fryman	.05
191	Chris Hoiles	.05
192	Chuck Finley	.05
193	Ryan Klesko	.40
194	Alex Fernandez	.05
195	Dante Bichette	.25
196	Eric Karros	.10
197	Roger Clemens	.40
198	Randy Myers	.05
199	Tony Phillips	.08
200	Cal Ripken Jr.	2.00
201	Rod Beck	.05
202	Chad Curtis	.05
203	Jack McDowell	.05
204	Gary Gaetti	.08
205	Ken Griffey Jr.	2.50
206	Ramon Martinez	.08
207	Jeff Kent	.05
208	Brad Ausmus	.05
209	Devon White	.05
210	Jason Giambi (Future Star)	.10
211	Nomar Garciaparra (Future Star)	1.00
212	Billy Wagner (Future Star)	.05
213	Todd Greene (Future Star)	.15
214	Paul Wilson (Future Star)	.15
215	Johnny Damon (Future Star)	.10
216	Alan Benes (Future Star)	.15
217	Karim Garcia (Future Star)	.30
218	Dustin Hermanson (Future Star)	.10
219	Derek Jeter (Future Star)	1.50

220	Checklist	.05
221	Kirby Puckett (Star Power)	.30
222	Cal Ripken Jr. (Star Power)	.75
223	Albert Belle (Star Power)	.30
224	Randy Johnson (Star Power)	.15
225	Wade Boggs (Star Power)	.10
226	Carlos Baerga (Star Power)	.10
227	Ivan Rodriguez (Star Power)	.10
228	Mike Mussina (Star Power)	.15
229	Frank Thomas (Star Power)	1.00
230	Ken Griffey Jr. (Star Power)	1.00
231	Jose Mesa (Star Power)	.05
232	*Matt Morris* (Draft Pick)	.40
233	Craig Wilson (Draft Pick)	.05
234	*Alvie Shepherd* (Draft Pick)	.10
235	Randy Winn (Draft Pick)	.05
236	*David Yocum* (Draft Pick)	.20
237	Jason Brester (Draft Pick)	.10
238	*Shane Monahan* (Draft Pick)	.40
239	Brian McNichol (Draft Pick)	.05
240	Reggie Taylor (Draft Pick)	.05
241	Garrett Long (Draft Pick)	.05
242	*Jonathan Johnson* (Draft Pick)	.20
243	*Jeff Liefer* (Draft Pick)	.40
244	*Brian Powell* (Draft Pick)	.05
245	Brian Buchanan (Draft Pick)	.12
246	Mike Piazza	1.25
247	Edgar Martinez	.05
248	Chuck Knoblauch	.15
249	Andres Galarraga	.10
250	Tony Gwynn	1.00
251	Lee Smith	.08
252	Sammy Sosa	1.50
253	Jim Thome	.30
254	Frank Rodriguez	.05
255	Charlie Hayes	.05
256	Bernard Gilkey	.10
257	John Smiley	.05
258	Brady Anderson	.20
259	Rico Brogna	.05
260	Kirt Manwaring	.05
261	Len Dykstra	.05
262	Tom Glavine	.10
263	Vince Coleman	.05
264	John Olerud	.12
265	Orlando Merced	.05
266	Kent Mercker	.05
267	Terry Steinbach	.05
268	Brian Hunter	.05
269	Jeff Fassero	.05
270	Jay Buhner	.10
271	Jeff Brantley	.05
272	Tim Raines	.05
273	Jimmy Key	.05
274	Mo Vaughn	.60
275	Andre Dawson	.10
276	Jose Mesa	.05
277	Brett Butler	.10
278	Luis Gonzalez	.05
279	Steve Sparks	.05
280	Chili Davis	.05
281	Carl Everett	.05
282	Jeff Cirillo	.05
283	Thomas Howard	.05
284	Paul O'Neill	.08
285	Pat Meares	.05
286	Mickey Tettleton	.05
287	Rey Sanchez	.05
288	Bip Roberts	.05
289	Roberto Alomar	.50
290	Ruben Sierra	.05
291	John Flaherty	.05
292	Bret Saberhagen	.05
293	Barry Larkin	.15
294	Sandy Alomar	.08
295	Ed Sprague	.05
296	Gary DiSarcina	.05
297	Marquis Grissom	.08
298	John Frascatore	.05
299	Will Clark	.25
300	Barry Bonds	.60
301	Ozzie Smith	.25
302	Dave Nilsson	.05
303	Pedro Martinez	.05
304	Joey Cora	.05
305	Rick Aguilera	.05
306	Craig Biggio	.08
307	Jose Vizcaino	.05
308	Jeff Montgomery	.05
309	Moises Alou	.05
310	Robin Ventura	.10
311	David Wells	.05
312	Delino DeShields	.05
313	Trevor Hoffman	.05

314	Andy Benes	.05
315	Deion Sanders	.25
316	Jim Bullinger	.05
317	John Jaha	.05
318	Greg Maddux	1.50
319	Tim Salmon	.20
320	Ben McDonald	.05
321	*Sandy Martinez*	.05
322	Dan Miceli	.05
323	Wade Boggs	.20
324	Ismael Valdes	.05
325	Juan Gonzalez	1.00
326	Charles Nagy	.05
327	Ray Lankford	.10
328	Mark Portugal	.05
329	Bobby Bonilla	.08
330	Reggie Sanders	.10
331	Jamie Brewington	.05
332	Aaron Sele	.05
333	Pete Harnisch	.05
334	Cliff Floyd	.05
335	Cal Eldred	.05
336	Jason Bates (Now Appearing)	.05
337	Tony Clark (Now Appearing)	.50
338	Jose Herrera (Now Appearing)	.05
339	Alex Ochoa (Now Appearing)	.10
340	Mark Loretta (Now Appearing)	.05
341	*Donne Wall* (Now Appearing)	.05
342	Jason Kendall (Now Appearing)	.10
343	Shannon Stewart (Now Appearing)	.10
344	Brooks Kieschnick (Now Appearing)	.20
345	Chris Snopek (Now Appearing)	.20
346	Ruben Rivera (Now Appearing)	.35
347	Jeff Suppan (Now Appearing)	.05
348	Phil Nevin (Now Appearing)	.05
349	John Wasdin (Now Appearing)	.05
350	Jay Payton (Now Appearing)	.10
351	Tim Crabtree (Now Appearing)	.05
352	Rick Krivda (Now Appearing)	.05
353	Bob Wolcott (Now Appearing)	.05
354	Jimmy Haynes (Now Appearing)	.05
355	Herb Perry	.05
356	Ryne Sandberg	.40
357	Harold Baines	.08
358	Chad Ogea	.05
359	Lee Tinsley	.05
360	Matt Williams	.25
361	Randy Velarde	.05
362	Jose Canseco	.25
363	Larry Walker	.25
364	Kevin Appier	.05
365	Darryl Hamilton	.05
366	Jose Lima	.05
367	Javy Lopez	.12
368	Dennis Eckersley	.08
369	Jason Isringhausen	.20
370	Mickey Morandini	.05
371	Scott Cooper	.05
372	Jim Abbott	.08
373	Paul Sorrento	.05
374	Chris Hammond	.05
375	Lance Johnson	.05
376	Kevin Brown	.05
377	Luis Alicea	.05
378	Andy Pettitte	.65
379	Dean Palmer	.05
380	Jeff Bagwell	.75
381	Jaime Navarro	.05
382	Rondell White	.10
383	Erik Hanson	.05
384	Pedro Munoz	.05
385	Heathcliff Slocumb	.05
386	Wally Joyner	.08
387	Bob Tewksbury	.05
388	David Bell	.05
389	Fred McGriff	.25
390	Mike Henneman	.05
391	Robby Thompson	.05

392	Norm Charlton	.05
393	Cecil Fielder	.15
394	Benito Santiago	.05
395	Rafael Palmeiro	.15
396	Ricky Bones	.05
397	Rickey Henderson	.20
398	C.J. Nitkowski	.05
399	Shawon Dunston	.12
400	Manny Ramirez	.75
401	Bill Swift	.05
402	Chad Fonville	.05
403	Joey Hamilton	.05
404	Alex Gonzalez	.05
405	Roberto Hernandez	.05
406	Jeff Blauser	.05
407	LaTroy Hawkins	.05
408	Greg Colbrunn	.05
409	Todd Hundley	.10
410	Glenn Dishman	.05
411	Joe Vitiello	.05
412	Todd Worrell	.05
413	Wil Cordero	.05
414	Ken Hill	.05
415	Carlos Garcia	.05
416	Bryan Rekar	.05
417	Shawn Green (Topps Rookie All-Star)	.10
418	Tyler Green	.05
419	Mike Blowers	.05
420	Kenny Lofton	.60
421	Denny Neagle	.05
422	Jeff Conine	.05
423	Mark Langston	.05
424	Steve Cox, *Jesse Ibarra,* Derrek Lee, *Ron Wright* (Prospects)	1.00
425	*Jim Bonnici,* Billy Owens, Richie Sexson, *Daryle Ward* (Prospects)	.35
426	Kevin Jordan, *Bobby Morris,* Desi Relaford, *Adam Riggs* (Prospects)	.05
427	Tim Harkrider, Rey Ordonez, Neifi Perez, Enrique Wilson (Prospects)	.25
428	Bartolo Colon, Doug Million, Rafael Orellano, *Ray Ricken* (Prospects)	.10
429	Jeff D'Amico, *Marty Janzen,* Gary Rath, Clint Sodowsky (Prospects)	.05
430	Matt Drews, *Rich Hunter, Matt Ruebel,* Bret Wagner (Prospects)	.05
431	Jaime Bluma, *Dave Coggin,* Steve Montgomery, Brandon Reed (Prospects)	.10
432	Mike Figga, *Raul Ibanez,* Paul Konerko, Julio Mosquera (Prospects)	.20
433	Brian Barber, Marc Kroon, Marc Valdes, Don Wengert (Prospects)	.05
434	George Arias, Chris Haas, Scott Rolen, Scott Spiezio (Prospects)	1.00
435	*Brian Banks,* Vladimir Guerrero, Andruw Jones, Billy McMillon (Prospects)	4.00
436	Roger Cedeno, Ben Grieve, *Shane Gibson, Spencer* (Prospects)	3.00
437	Anton French, Demond Smith, *Darond Stovall,* Keith Williams (Prospects)	.05
438	*Michael Coleman,* Jacob Cruz, Richard Hidalgo, Charles Peterson (Prospects)	.25
439	Trey Beamon, Yamil Benitez, Jermaine Dye, Angel Echevarria (Prospects)	.20
440	Checklist	.05

1996 Topps Classic Confrontations

Head-to-head stats among baseball's top pitchers and hitters are featured in this insert set. The cards were seeded one per pack in the special 50-cent packs sold exclusively at Wal-Mart during the T206 Honus Wagner card giveaway promotion. Fronts have player action poses against a granite background and are highlighted in gold foil. Backs have a portrait photo and stats.

		MT
Complete Set (15):		6.00
Common Player:		.25
1	Ken Griffey Jr.	1.50
2	Cal Ripken Jr.	1.00
3	Edgar Martinez	.25
4	Kirby Puckett	.75
5	Frank Thomas	1.00
6	Barry Bonds	.50
7	Reggie Sanders	.25
8	Andres Galarraga	.25
9	Tony Gwynn	.75
10	Mike Piazza	.90
11	Randy Johnson	.35
12	Mike Mussina	.35
13	Roger Clemens	.50
14	Tom Glavine	.25
15	Greg Maddux	.90

1996 Topps 5-Star Mystery Finest

The 5-Star Mystery Finest inserts have an opaque black film over the card front, like the regular Mystery Finest, but has the words "5-Star" in large letters across the background. They are inserted at the average rate of one per 36 packs.

	MT
Complete Set (5):	50.00
Common Player:	2.00
Refractors: 3X to 5X	
M22 Hideo Nomo	6.00
M23 Cal Ripken Jr.	15.00
M24 Mike Piazza	12.00
M25 Ken Griffey Jr.	20.00
M26 Frank Thomas	12.00

1996 Topps Masters of the Game

Appearing at a one per 18 pack rate, these inserts are exclusive to Series 1 hobby packs.

		MT
Complete Set (20):		45.00
Common Player:		1.00
1	Dennis Eckersley	1.00
2	Denny Martinez	1.00
3	Eddie Murray	1.50
4	Paul Molitor	2.00
5	Ozzie Smith	2.00
6	Rickey Henderson	1.50
7	Tim Raines	1.00
8	Lee Smith	1.00
9	Cal Ripken Jr.	8.00
10	Chili Davis	1.00
11	Wade Boggs	1.50
12	Tony Gwynn	3.00
13	Don Mattingly	4.00
14	Bret Saberhagen	1.00
15	Kirby Puckett	3.00
16	Joe Carter	1.00
17	Roger Clemens	2.00
18	Barry Bonds	2.50
19	Greg Maddux	6.00
20	Frank Thomas	8.00

1996 Topps Mickey Mantle Reprint Cards

One of Mickey Mantle's regular-issue Bowman or Topps cards from each year 1951-1969 was reproduced in 2-1/2" x 3-1/2" format as a Series 1 insert. Each card carries a gold-foil commemorative seal in one corner of the front. The reprints are found one per six retail packs and, in hobby, once per nine packs. The 1965-69 reprints were somewhat shortprinted (four 1965-69 cards for each five 1951-1964) and are 20% scarcer.

		MT
Complete Set (19):		120.00
Common Mantle:		6.00
Common SP Mantle (15-19):		12.00
1	1951 Bowman #253	10.00
2	1952 Topps #311	15.00
3	1953 Topps #82	6.00
4	1954 Bowman #65	6.00
5	1955 Bowman #202	6.00
6	1956 Topps #135	6.00
7	1957 Topps #95	6.00
8	1958 Topps #150	6.00
9	1959 Topps #10	6.00
10	1960 Topps #350	6.00
11	1961 Topps #300	6.00
12	1962 Topps #200	6.00
13	1963 Topps #200	6.00
14	1964 Topps #50	6.00
15	1965 Topps #350	10.00
16	1966 Topps #50	10.00
17	1967 Topps #150	10.00
18	1968 Topps #280	10.00
19	1969 Topps #500	10.00

1996 Topps/Finest Mickey Mantle

Nineteen of Mickey Mantle's regular-issue Bowman and Topps cards from 1951-1969 were printed in Finest technology for this Series 2 insert set. Each card's chrome front is protected with a peel-off plastic layer. Average insertion rate for the Mantle Finest reprints is one per 18 packs. The 1965-69 reprints were printed in a ratio of four for every five 1951-64 reprints, making them 20% scarcer.

		MT
Complete Set (19):		140.00
Common Mantle:		6.00
Common Shortprint Mantle (15-19):		10.00
1	1951 Bowman #253	12.00
2	1952 Topps #311	20.00
3	1953 Topps #82	10.00
4	1954 Bowman #65	6.00
5	1955 Bowman #202	6.00
6	1956 Topps #135	6.00
7	1957 Topps #95	6.00
8	1958 Topps #150	6.00
9	1959 Topps #10	6.00
10	1960 Topps #350	6.00
11	1961 Topps #300	6.00
12	1962 Topps #200	6.00

13	1963 Topps #200	6.00
14	1964 Topps #50	6.00
15	1965 Topps #350	10.00
16	1966 Topps #50	10.00
17	1967 Topps #150	10.00
18	1968 Topps #280	10.00
19	1969 Topps #500	10.00

1996 Topps/Finest Mickey Mantle Refractors

Each of the 19 Mickey Mantle Finest reprints in Series 2 can also be found in an unmarked Refractor version. Average insertion rate of these superscarce inserts is one per 144 packs.

		MT
Complete Set (19):		725.00
Common Mantle:		40.00
Common SP Mantle (15-19):		48.00
1	1951 Bowman #253	80.00
2	1952 Topps #311	120.00
3	1953 Topps #82	48.00
4	1954 Bowman #65	40.00
5	1955 Bowman #202	40.00
6	1956 Topps #135	40.00
7	1957 Topps #95	40.00
8	1958 Topps #150	40.00
9	1959 Topps #10	40.00
10	1960 Topps #350	40.00
11	1961 Topps #300	40.00
12	1962 Topps #200	40.00
13	1963 Topps #200	40.00
14	1964 Topps #50	40.00
15	1965 Topps #350	48.00
16	1966 Topps #50	48.00
17	1967 Topps #150	48.00
18	1968 Topps #280	48.00
19	1969 Topps #500	48.00

1996 Topps Mickey Mantle Foundation Card

This black-and-white card was an insert exclusive to specially marked 1996 Topps factory sets. In standard 2-1/2" x 3-1/2" format, the card offers on its back information about the foundation and it work in health care and organ donation causes.

	MT
Mickey Mantle	6.00

1996 Topps Mickey Mantle Redemption

Each of the 19 Mantle reprint cards, minus the commemorative gold-foil stamp on front, was also issued in a sweepstakes set. Seeded one per 108 packs, these cards could be sent in for a chance to win the authentic Mantle card pictured on front. Between one and 10 genuine Mantles were awarded for each of the 19 years. Cards entered in the sweepstakes were not returned when the contest ended Oct. 15, 1996. The sweepstakes cards are a Series 2 exclusive insert.

		MT
Complete Set (19):		300.00
Common Mantle:		16.00
1	1951 Bowman #253	25.00
2	1952 Topps #311	40.00
3	1953 Topps #82	20.00
4	1954 Bowman #65	16.00
5	1955 Bowman #202	16.00
6	1956 Topps #135	16.00
7	1957 Topps #95	16.00
8	1958 Topps #150	16.00
9	1959 Topps #10	16.00
10	1960 Topps #350	16.00
11	1961 Topps #300	16.00
12	1962 Topps #200	16.00
13	1963 Topps #200	16.00
14	1964 Topps #50	16.00
15	1965 Topps #350	16.00
16	1966 Topps #50	16.00
17	1967 Topps #150	16.00
18	1968 Topps #280	16.00
19	1969 Topps #500	16.00

1996 Topps Mickey Mantle Case Inserts

Inserted one per case of Series 2 Topps, these special versions of the 19 Mickey Mantle reprint cards come pre-packaged in a hard plastic holder. The cards are identical to the other reprints except for the inclusion of a foil stamp at bottom-back indicating that it is a case card. Like the other Mantle reprints, the 1965-69 cards are somewhat scarcer due to short-printing.

		MT
Complete Set (19):		850.00
Common Mantle:		40.00
Common SP Mantle (15-19):		50.00
1	1951 Bowman #253	65.00
2	1952 Topps #311	100.00
3	1953 Topps #82	50.00
4	1954 Bowman #65	40.00
5	1955 Bowman #202	40.00
6	1956 Topps #135	40.00
7	1957 Topps #95	40.00
8	1958 Topps #150	40.00
9	1959 Topps #10	40.00

10	1960 Topps #350	40.00
11	1961 Topps #300	40.00
12	1962 Topps #200	40.00
13	1963 Topps #200	40.00
14	1964 Topps #50	40.00
15	1965 Topps #350	50.00
16	1966 Topps #50	50.00
17	1967 Topps #150	50.00
18	1968 Topps #280	50.00
19	1969 Topps #500	50.00

1996 Topps Mystery Finest

Each Mystery Finest insert has an opaque black film over the card front, concealing the identity of the player until removed. The inserts are seeded at the rate of one per 36 packs.

		MT
Complete Set (21)		150.00
Common Player:		3.00
Refractors: 3X to 6X		
M1	Hideo Nomo	6.00
M2	Greg Maddux	12.00
M3	Randy Johnson	4.00
M4	Chipper Jones	12.00
M5	Marty Cordova	3.00
M6	Garret Anderson	3.00
M7	Cal Ripken Jr.	18.00
M8	Kirby Puckett	8.00
M9	Tony Gwynn	8.00
M10	Manny Ramirez	5.00
M11	Jim Edmonds	3.00
M12	Mike Piazza	12.00
M13	Barry Bonds	5.00
M14	Raul Mondesi	3.00
M15	Sammy Sosa	10.00
M16	Ken Griffey Jr.	20.00
M17	Albert Belle	5.00
M18	Dante Bichette	3.00
M19	Mo Vaughn	5.00
M20	Jeff Bagwell	8.00
M21	Frank Thomas	15.00

1996 Topps Power Boosters

This insert set is printed in Topps' "Power Matrix" technology, replacing two regular cards when found on the average of once per 36 packs. The Power Boosters reproduce the Star Power and Draft Picks subsets on a double-thick card.

A player's name in *italic* type indicates a rookie card.

		MT
Complete Set (20):		30.00
Complete Series 1 (10):		20.00
Complete Series 2 (10):		10.00
Common Player:		.50
1	Roberto Alomar	1.50
2	Carlos Baerga	.75
3	Albert Belle	1.50
4	Cecil Fielder	.50
5	Ken Griffey Jr.	6.00
6	Randy Johnson	1.00
7	Paul O'Neill	.50
8	Cal Ripken Jr.	5.00
9	Frank Thomas	5.00
10	Mo Vaughn	2.00
11	Jay Buhner	.75
12	Marty Cordova	.75
13	Jim Edmonds	.75
14	Juan Gonzalez	3.00
15	Kenny Lofton	2.00
16	Edgar Martinez	.50
17	Don Mattingly	3.00
18	Mark McGwire	8.00
19	Rafael Palmeiro	.75
20	Tim Salmon	1.00

1996 Topps Profiles-NL

Projected future stars of the National League are featured in this insert set. Ten players each are found in Series 1 and 2 packs at the rate of one per 12, on average.

		MT
Complete Set (20):		20.00
Complete Series 1 (10):		12.00
Complete Series 2 (10):		8.00
Common Player:		.50
1	Jeff Bagwell	2.50
2	Derek Bell	.50
3	Barry Bonds	2.00
4	Greg Maddux	4.00
5	Fred McGriff	.75
6	Raul Mondesi	.75
7	Mike Piazza	4.00
8	Reggie Sanders	.50
9	Sammy Sosa	4.00
10	Larry Walker	1.00
11	Dante Bichette	.75
12	Andres Galarraga	.75
13	Ron Gant	.50
14	Tom Glavine	.50
15	Chipper Jones	4.00
16	David Justice	.50
17	Barry Larkin	.50
18	Hideo Nomo	1.50
19	Gary Sheffield	1.00
20	Matt Williams	1.00

1996 Topps Wrecking Crew

Printed on foilboard stock, cards of 15 players known for their hitting prowess are featured in this insert set. Found only in Series 2 hobby packs, the inserts are a one per 72 packs find, on average.

		MT
Complete Set (15):		75.00
Common Player:		2.00
WC1	Jeff Bagwell	7.00
WC2	Albert Belle	5.00
WC3	Barry Bonds	5.00
WC4	Jose Canseco	3.00
WC5	Joe Carter	2.00
WC6	Cecil Fielder	2.00
WC7	Ron Gant	2.00
WC8	Juan Gonzalez	8.00
WC9	Ken Griffey Jr.	20.00
WC10	Fred McGriff	3.00
WC11	Mark McGwire	25.00
WC12	Mike Piazza	10.00
WC13	Frank Thomas	15.00
WC14	Mo Vaughn	6.00
WC15	Matt Williams	3.00

1996 Topps Chrome

In conjunction with baseball's postseason, Topps introduced the premiere edition of Chrome Baseball. The set has 165 of the elite players from 1996 Topps Baseball Series I and II. Card #7 is a Mickey Mantle tribute card, similar to Topps' Series I card. There are four insert sets: Masters of the Game and Wrecking Crew, and scarcer Refractor versions for both types.

		MT
Complete Set (165):		75.00
Common Player:		.25
Complete Refractor Set (165):		2500.
Common Refractor:		5.00
Refractors: 10x to 20x		
Wax Box:		100.00
1	Tony Gwynn (Star Power)	2.00
2	Mike Piazza (Star Power)	2.50
3	Greg Maddux (Star Power)	2.50
4	Jeff Bagwell (Star Power)	1.50
5	Larry Walker (Star Power)	.75
6	Barry Larkin (Star Power)	.50
7	Mickey Mantle (Commemorative)	10.00
8	Tom Glavine (Star Power)	.40
9	Craig Biggio (Star Power)	.25
10	Barry Bonds (Star Power)	1.00
11	Heathcliff Slocumb (Star Power)	.25
12	Matt Williams (Star Power)	.50
13	Todd Helton (Draft Pick)	15.00
14	Paul Molitor	1.50
15	Glenallen Hill	.25
16	Troy Percival	.25
17	Albert Belle	2.00
18	Mark Wohlers	.25
19	Kirby Puckett	3.00
20	Mark Grace	.50
21	J.T. Snow	.25
22	David Justice	.50
23	Mike Mussina	1.50
24	Bernie Williams	1.50
25	Ron Gant	.25
26	Carlos Baerga	.25
27	Gary Sheffield	1.00
28	Cal Ripken Jr. (Tribute Card)	8.00
29	Frank Thomas	6.00
30	Kevin Seitzer	.25
31	Joe Carter	.40
32	Jeff King	.25
33	David Cone	.40
34	Eddie Murray	.75
35	Brian Jordan	.25
36	Garret Anderson	.25
37	Hideo Nomo	1.50
38	Steve Finley	.25
39	Ivan Rodriguez	1.50
40	Quilvio Veras	.25
41	Mark McGwire	10.00
42	Greg Vaughn	.25
43	Randy Johnson	1.50
44	David Segui	.25

		MT
Complete Set (26):		75.00
Common Player:		2.50
1	Tony Gwynn (Star Power)	7.50
2	Mike Piazza (Star Power)	12.00
3	Greg Maddux (Star Power)	12.00
4	Jeff Bagwell (Star Power)	8.00
5	Larry Walker (Star Power)	3.00
6	Barry Larkin (Star Power)	3.00
8	Tom Glavine (Star Power)	2.50
9	Craig Biggio (Star Power)	2.50
10	Barry Bonds (Star Power)	4.00
11	Heathcliff Slocumb (Star Power)	2.50
12	Matt Williams (Star Power)	4.00
13	Todd Helton (Draft Pick)	10.00
14	Mark Redman (Draft Pick)	2.50
15	Michael Barrett (Draft Pick)	2.50
16	Ben Davis (Draft Pick)	4.00
17	Juan LeBron (Draft Pick)	2.50
18	Tony McKnight (Draft Pick)	2.50
19	Ryan Jaroncyk (Draft Pick)	2.50
20	Corey Jenkins (Draft Pick)	2.50
21	Jim Scharrer (Draft Pick)	2.50
22	Mark Bellhorn (Draft Pick)	2.50
23	Jarrod Washburn (Draft Pick)	2.50
24	Geoff Jenkins (Draft Pick)	4.00
25	Sean Casey (Draft Pick)	6.00
26	Brett Tomko (Draft Pick)	2.50

1996 Topps Profiles-AL

Ten cards from this insert issue can be found in each of Topps Series 1 and 2. Analyzing an up-and-coming star, the cards are found every 12th pack, on average.

A player's name in *italic* type indicates a rookie card.

45	Derek Bell	.25
46	John Valentin	.25
47	Steve Avery	.25
48	Tino Martinez	.75
49	Shane Reynolds	.25
50	Jim Edmonds	.40
51	Raul Mondesi	.60
52	Chipper Jones	5.00
53	Gregg Jefferies	.25
54	Ken Caminiti	1.00
55	Brian McRae	.25
56	Don Mattingly	2.50
57	Marty Cordova	.25
58	Vinny Castilla	.25
59	John Smoltz	.60
60	Travis Fryman	.25
61	Ryan Klesko	1.00
62	Alex Fernandez	.25
63	Dante Bichette	.50
64	Eric Karros	.25
65	Roger Clemens	2.50
66	Randy Myers	.25
67	Cal Ripken Jr.	6.00
68	Rod Beck	.25
69	Jack McDowell	.25
70	Ken Griffey Jr.	8.00
71	Ramon Martinez	.25
72	Jason Giambi (Future Star)	.50
73	Nomar Garciaparra (Future Star)	5.00
74	Billy Wagner (Future Star)	.50
75	Todd Greene (Future Star)	.25
76	Paul Wilson (Future Star)	.40
77	Johnny Damon (Future Star)	.25
78	Alan Benes (Future Star)	.50
79	Karim Garcia (Future Star)	.75
80	Derek Jeter (Future Star)	2.50
81	Kirby Puckett (Star Power)	1.50
82	Cal Ripken Jr. (Star Power)	3.00
83	Albert Belle (Star Power)	1.00
84	Randy Johnson (Star Power)	.50
85	Wade Boggs (Star Power)	.40
86	Carlos Baerga (Star Power)	.25
87	Ivan Rodriguez (Star Power)	.60
88	Mike Mussina (Star Power)	.75
89	Frank Thomas (Star Power)	3.00
90	Ken Griffey Jr. (Star Power)	4.00
91	Jose Mesa (Star Power)	.25
92	*Matt Morris* (Draft Pick)	3.00
93	Mike Piazza	5.00
94	Edgar Martinez	.25
95	Chuck Knoblauch	.50
96	Andres Galarraga	.50
97	Tony Gwynn	4.00
98	Lee Smith	.25
99	Sammy Sosa	4.00
100	Jim Thome	1.00
101	Bernard Gilkey	.25
102	Brady Anderson	.40
103	Rico Brogna	.25
104	Lenny Dykstra	.40
105	Tom Glavine	.25
106	John Olerud	.25
107	Terry Steinbach	.25
108	Brian Hunter	.25
109	Jay Buhner	.50
110	Mo Vaughn	2.00
111	Jose Mesa	.25
112	Brett Butler	.25
113	Chili Davis	.25
114	Paul O'Neill	.40
115	Roberto Alomar	1.50
116	Barry Larkin	.50
117	Marquis Grissom	.25
118	Will Clark	.50
119	Barry Bonds	2.00
120	Ozzie Smith	1.00
121	Pedro Martinez	.40
122	Craig Biggio	.40
123	Moises Alou	.40
124	Robin Ventura	.25
125	Greg Maddux	5.00
126	Tim Salmon	.50
127	Wade Boggs	.50
128	Ismael Valdes	.25
129	Juan Gonzalez	3.50
130	Ray Lankford	.25
131	Bobby Bonilla	.40
132	Reggie Sanders	.25
133	Alex Ochoa (Now Appearing)	.25
134	Mark Loretta (Now Appearing)	.25

135	Jason Kendall (Now Appearing)	.25
136	Brooks Kieschnick (Now Appearing)	.25
137	Chris Snopek (Now Appearing)	.25
138	Ruben Rivera (Now Appearing)	.50
139	Jeff Suppan (Now Appearing)	.25
140	John Wasdin (Now Appearing)	.25
141	Jay Payton (Now Appearing)	.40
142	Rick Krivda (Now Appearing)	.25
143	Jimmy Haynes (Now Appearing)	.25
144	Ryne Sandberg	1.50
145	Matt Williams	.50
146	Jose Canseco	.50
147	Larry Walker	.75
148	Kevin Appier	.25
149	Javy Lopez	.40
150	Dennis Eckersley	.25
151	Jason Isringhausen	.25
152	Dean Palmer	.25
153	Jeff Bagwell	3.00
154	Rondell White	.40
155	Wally Joyner	.25
156	Fred McGriff	.50
157	Cecil Fielder	.40
158	Rafael Palmeiro	.40
159	Rickey Henderson	.25
160	Shawon Dunston	.25
161	Manny Ramirez	2.00
162	Alex Gonzalez	.25
163	Shawn Green	.25
164	Kenny Lofton	2.00
165	Jeff Conine	.25

1996 Topps Chrome Wrecking Crew

Wrecking Crew insert cards were inserted one per every 24 packs of 1996 Topps Chrome Baseball. Refractor versions were also made for these cards; they are seeded one per every 72 packs.

		MT
Complete Set (15):		90.00
Common Player:		3.00
Refractors: 1.5x to 3x		
WC1	Jeff Bagwell	10.00
WC2	Albert Belle	6.00
WC3	Barry Bonds	6.00
WC4	Jose Canseco	4.00
WC5	Joe Carter	3.00
WC6	Cecil Fielder	3.00
WC7	Ron Gant	3.00
WC8	Juan Gonzalez	12.00
WC9	Ken Griffey Jr.	25.00
WC10	Fred McGriff	4.00
WC11	Mark McGwire	25.00
WC12	Mike Piazza	15.00
WC13	Frank Thomas	15.00
WC14	Mo Vaughn	6.00
WC15	Matt Williams	4.00

1996 Topps Chrome Masters of the Game

These 1996 Topps Chrome inserts were seeded one per every 12 packs. Each of the cards is also reprinted in a Refractor version; these cards are seeded one per every 36 packs.

		MT
Complete Set (20):		75.00
Common Player:		2.00
Refractors: 1.5x to 3x		
1	Dennis Eckersley	2.00

2	Denny Martinez	2.00
3	Eddie Murray	4.00
4	Paul Molitor	5.00
5	Ozzie Smith	5.00
6	Rickey Henderson	2.00
7	Tim Raines	2.00
8	Lee Smith	2.00
9	Cal Ripken Jr.	15.00
10	Chili Davis	2.00
11	Wade Boggs	3.00
12	Tony Gwynn	10.00
13	Don Mattingly	8.00
14	Bret Saberhagen	2.00
15	Kirby Puckett	8.00
16	Joe Carter	3.00
17	Roger Clemens	8.00
18	Barry Bonds	6.00
19	Greg Maddux	12.00
20	Frank Thomas	12.00

1996 Topps Gallery

MARQUIS GRISSOM

This 180-card set is printed on 24-point stock utilizing metallic inks and a high-definition printing process. Then a high-gloss film is applied to each card, followed by foil stamping. The regular set is broken down into five subsets - The Classics, The Modernists, The Futurists, The Masters and New Editions. Each theme has a different design. Gallery also has four insert sets. Player's Private Issue cards are a parallel set to the main issue; these cards are seeded one per every 12 packs. The backs are sequentially numbered from 0-999, with the first 100 cards sent to the players; the rest are inserted into packs. The backs are UV coated on the photo only, to allow for autographing. The other insert sets are Expressionists, Photo Gallery and a Mickey Mantle Masterpiece card.

		MT
Complete Set (180):		35.00
Common Player:		.15
Unlisted Stars: .25 to .50		
Complete Players Private Issue (180): 800.00		
Private Issue: 8X to 15X		
1	Tom Glavine	.40
2	Carlos Baerga	.20
3	Dante Bichette	.30
4	Mark Langston	.15
5	Ray Lankford	.15
6	Moises Alou	.15
7	Marquis Grissom	.15
8	Ramon Martinez	.15
8p	Ramon Martinez (unmarked promo, "Pitcher" spelled out under photo on back)	5.00
9	Steve Finley	.15

10	Todd Hundley	.25
11	Brady Anderson	.25
12	John Valentin	.15
13	Heathcliff Slocumb	.15
14	Ruben Sierra	.15
15	Jeff Conine	.15
16	Jay Buhner	.25
16p	Jay Buhner (unmarked promo; height, weight and "Bats" on same line)	5.00
17	Sammy Sosa	2.00
18	Doug Drabek	.15
19	Jose Mesa	.15
20	Jeff King	.15
21	Mickey Tettleton	.15
22	Jeff Montgomery	.15
23	Alex Fernandez	.25
24	Greg Vaughn	.15
25	Chuck Finley	.15
26	Terry Steinbach	.15
27	Rod Beck	.15
28	Jack McDowell	.20
29	Mark Wohlers	.15
30	Lenny Dykstra	.15
31	Bernie Williams	.75
32	Travis Fryman	.15
33	Jose Canseco	.40
34	Ken Caminiti	.50
35	Devon White	.15
36	Bobby Bonilla	.25
37	Paul Sorrento	.15
38	Ryne Sandberg	1.00
39	Derek Bell	.15
40	Bobby Jones	.15
41	J.T. Snow	.15
42	Denny Neagle	.15
43	Tim Wakefield	.15
44	Andres Galarraga	.40
45	David Segui	.15
46	Lee Smith	.15
47	Mel Rojas	.15
48	John Franco	.15
49	Pete Schourek	.15
50	John Wetteland	.15
51	Paul Molitor	.75
52	Ivan Rodriguez	.75
53	Chris Hoiles	.15
54	Mike Greenwell	.15
55	Orel Hershiser	.15
56	Brian McRae	.15
57	Geronimo Berroa	.15
58	Craig Biggio	.15
59	David Justice	.30
59p	David Justice (unmarked promo; height,weight and "Bats" on same line)	5.00
60	Lance Johnson	.15
61	Andy Ashby	.15
62	Randy Myers	.15
63	Gregg Jefferies	.15
64	Kevin Appier	.15
65	Rick Aguilera	.15
66	Shane Reynolds	.15
67	John Smoltz	.40
68	Ron Gant	.25
69	Eric Karros	.15
70	Jim Thome	.50
71	Terry Pendleton	.15
72	Kenny Rogers	.15
73	Robin Ventura	.15
74	Dave Nilsson	.15
75	Brian Jordan	.20
76	Glenallen Hill	.15
77	Greg Colbrunn	.15
78	Roberto Alomar	1.00
79	Rickey Henderson	.15
80	Carlos Garcia	.15
81	Dean Palmer	.15
82	Mike Stanley	.15
83	Hal Morris	.15
84	Wade Boggs	.25
85	Chad Curtis	.15
86	Roberto Hernandez	.15
87	John Olerud	.15
88	Frank Castillo	.15
89	Rafael Palmeiro	.25
90	Trevor Hoffman	.15
91	Marty Cordova	.25
92	Hideo Nomo	1.00
93	Johnny Damon	.25
94	Bill Pulsipher	.15
95	Garret Anderson	.15
96	Ray Durham	.15
97	Ricky Bottalico	.15
98	Carlos Perez	.15
99	Troy Percival	.15

100	Chipper Jones	2.50
101	Esteban Loaiza	.25
102	John Mabry	.15
103	Jon Nunnally	.15
104	Andy Pettitte	1.25
105	Lyle Mouton	.15
106	Jason Isringhausen	.25
107	Brian Hunter	.15
108	Quilvio Veras	.15
109	Jim Edmonds	.15
110	Ryan Klesko	.60
111	Pedro Martinez	.15
112	Joey Hamilton	.15
113	Vinny Castilla	.15
114	Alex Gonzalez	.15
115	Raul Mondesi	.40
116	Rondell White	.15
117	Dan Miceli	.15
118	Tom Goodwin	.15
119	Bret Boone	.15
120	Shawn Green	.15
121	Jeff Cirillo	.15
122	Rico Brogna	.15
123	Chris Gomez	.15
124	Ismael Valdes	.15
125	Javy Lopez	.15
126	Manny Ramirez	1.00
127	Paul Wilson	.25
128	Billy Wagner	.15
129	Eric Owens	.15
130	Todd Greene	.25
131	Karim Garcia	.75
132	Jimmy Haynes	.15
133	Michael Tucker	.15
134	John Wasdin	.15
135	Brooks Kieschnick	.20
136	Alex Ochoa	.25
137	Ariel Prieto	.15
138	Tony Clark	.75
139	Mark Loretta	.15
140	Rey Ordonez	.75
141	Chris Snopek	.15
142	Roger Cedeno	.20
143	Derek Jeter	2.00
144	Jeff Suppan	.15
145	Greg Maddux	2.50
146	Ken Griffey Jr.	4.00
147	Tony Gwynn	1.50
148	Darren Daulton	.15
149	Will Clark	.30
150	Mo Vaughn	1.00
151	Reggie Sanders	.15
152	Kirby Puckett	1.50
153	Paul O'Neill	.15
154	Tim Salmon	.25
155	Mark McGwire	4.00
156	Barry Bonds	1.00
157	Albert Belle	1.00
158	Edgar Martinez	.15
159	Mike Mussina	.50
160	Cecil Fielder	.25
161	Kenny Lofton	.75
162	Randy Johnson	.40
163	Juan Gonzalez	1.50
164	Jeff Bagwell	1.50
165	Joe Carter	.20
166	Mike Piazza	2.50
167	Eddie Murray	.50
168	Cal Ripken Jr.	3.00
169	Barry Larkin	.25
170	Chuck Knoblauch	.40
171	Chili Davis	.15
172	Fred McGriff	.50
173	Matt Williams	.40
174	Roger Clemens	1.00
175	Frank Thomas	3.00
176	Dennis Eckersley	.15
177	Gary Sheffield	.60
178	David Cone	.20
179	Larry Walker	.50
180	Mark Grace	.25

		MT
Complete Set (20):		100.00
Common Player:		1.50
1	Mike Piazza	18.00
2	J.T. Snow	1.50
3	Ken Griffey Jr.	30.00
4	Kirby Puckett	12.00
5	Carlos Baerga	1.50
6	Chipper Jones	18.00
7	Hideo Nomo	8.00
8	Mark McGwire	30.00
9	Gary Sheffield	6.00
10	Randy Johnson	4.00
11	Ray Lankford	1.50
12	Sammy Sosa	10.00
13	Denny Martinez	1.50
14	Jose Canseco	3.00
15	Tony Gwynn	12.00
16	Edgar Martinez	1.50
17	Reggie Sanders	1.50
18	Andres Galarraga	2.50
19	Albert Belle	8.00
20	Barry Larkin	3.00

1996 Topps Gallery Masterpiece

Topps continues its tribute to Mickey Mantle with this 1996 Topps Gallery insert card. The card, seeded one per every 48 packs, has three photos of Mantle on the front, with his comprehensive career statistics on the back.

		MT
MP1	Mickey Mantle	10.00

1996 Topps Gallery Photo Gallery

Photo Gallery is a collection of 15 cards featuring photography of baseball's biggest stars and greatest moments from the last season. The text on the card includes details of the card's front and back photos. The cards are seeded one per every 30 packs.

1996 Topps Gallery Expressionists

These 1996 Topps Gallery inserts feature 20 team leaders printed on triple foil-stamped and texture-embossed cards. Cards are seeded one per every 24 packs.

		MT
Complete Set (15):		100.00
Common Player:		2.50
PG1	Eddie Murray	6.00
PG2	Randy Johnson	5.00
PG3	Cal Ripken Jr.	25.00
PG4	Bret Boone	2.50
PG5	Frank Thomas	25.00
PG6	Jeff Conine	2.50
PG7	Johnny Damon	3.00
PG8	Roger Clemens	8.00
PG9	Albert Belle	8.00
PG10	Ken Griffey Jr.	30.00
PG11	Kirby Puckett	12.00
PG12	David Justice	3.00
PG13	Bobby Bonilla	2.50
PG14	Larry Walker, Andres	3.00
	Galarraga, Vinny Castilla,	
	Dante Bichette	
PG15	Mark Wohlers, Javier Lopez	2.50

1996 Topps Gallery Players Private Issue

The first 999 examples of each of the base cards in the Gallery issue are designated on the front with a gold-foil stamp as "Players Private Issue." The first 100 of those cards were given to the depicted player, the others are randomly packed. Besides the logo on front, the PPI cards are identified on back with an individual serial number.

	MT
Complete Set (180):	475.00
Common Player:	1.50
(Star cards valued at 8X to	
15X regular Gallery	
versions)	

1996 Topps Laser

Topps' 1996 Laser Baseball is the first set where laser-cut technology is used on every card, creating surgically-precise cutting across the entire card surface. Every card in the 128-card regular issue set features one of four designs, laser-cut into 20-point stock. One card from each of the four different designs is found in a four-card pack. Three different laser-cut insert sets were also produced: Bright Spots, Power Cuts and Stadium Stars. Cards 1-8 from each insert set were in Series I packs; cards 9-16 were seeded in Series II packs.

		MT
Complete Set (128):		120.00
Complete Series I Set (64):		60.00
Complete Series II Set (64):		60.00
Common Player:		.50
Unlisted Stars: .75 to 1.00		
Wax Box:		65.00
1	Moises Alou	.50
2	Derek Bell	.50
3	Joe Carter	.75
4	Jeff Conine	.50
5	Darren Daulton	.50
6	Jim Edmonds	.75
7	Ron Gant	.50
8	Juan Gonzalez	5.00
9	Brian Jordan	.75
10	Ryan Klesko	1.00
11	Paul Molitor	1.50
12	Tony Phillips	.50
13	Manny Ramirez	3.00
14	Sammy Sosa	5.00
15	Devon White	.50
16	Bernie Williams	1.50
17	Garret Anderson	.50
18	Jay Bell	.50
19	Craig Biggio	.50
20	Bobby Bonilla	.75
21	Ken Caminiti	1.00
22	Shawon Dunston	.50
23	Mark Grace	.75
23p	Mark Grace (unmarked photo, plain, rather than brushed, gold foil)	5.00
24	Gregg Jefferies	.50
25	Jeff King	.50
26	Javy Lopez	.75
27	Edgar Martinez	.50
28	Dean Palmer	.50
29	J.T. Snow	.50
30	Mike Stanley	.50
30p	Mike Stanley (unmarked promo; plain, rather than brushed, gold foil)	3.00
31	Terry Steinbach	.50
32	Robin Ventura	.50
33	Roberto Alomar	2.50
34	Jeff Bagwell	4.00
35	Dante Bichette	1.00
36	Wade Boggs	.75
37	Barry Bonds	2.50
38	Jose Canseco	1.00
39	Vinny Castilla	.50
40	Will Clark	1.00
41	Marty Cordova	.50
42	Ken Griffey Jr.	10.00
43	Tony Gwynn	4.00
44	Rickey Henderson	.50
45	Chipper Jones	6.00
46	Mark McGwire	10.00
47	Brian McRae	.50
48	Ryne Sandberg	2.50
49	Andy Ashby	.50
50	Alan Benes	.75
51	Andy Benes	.50
52	Roger Clemens	3.00
53	Doug Drabek	.50
54	Dennis Eckersley	.50
55	Tom Glavine	.75
56	Randy Johnson	1.50
57	Mark Langston	.50

58	Denny Martinez	.50
59	Jack McDowell	.75
60	Hideo Nomo	1.50
61	Shane Reynolds	.50
62	John Smoltz	1.00
63	Paul Wilson	1.00
64	Mark Wohlers	.50
65	Shawn Green	.50
66	Marquis Grissom	.50
67	Dave Hollins	.50
68	Todd Hundley	.75
69	David Justice	.75
70	Eric Karros	.50
71	Ray Lankford	.50
72	Fred McGriff	1.00
73	Hal Morris	.50
74	Eddie Murray	1.50
75	Paul O'Neill	.50
76	Rey Ordonez	1.50
77	Reggie Sanders	.50
78	Gary Sheffield	1.25
79	Jim Thome	1.00
80	Rondell White	.50
81	Travis Fryman	.50
82	Derek Jeter	5.00
83	Chuck Knoblauch	.75
84	Barry Larkin	.75
85	Tino Martinez	.50
86	Raul Mondesi	1.00
87	John Olerud	.50
88	Rafael Palmeiro	.75
89	Mike Piazza	6.00
90	Cal Ripken Jr.	8.00
91	Ivan Rodriguez	1.50
92	Frank Thomas	6.00
93	John Valentin	.50
94	Mo Vaughn	3.00
95	Quilvio Veras	.50
96	Matt Williams	1.00
97	Brady Anderson	.75
98	Carlos Baerga	.50
99	Albert Belle	2.50
100	Jay Buhner	.75
101	Johnny Damon	.75
102	Chili Davis	.50
103	Ray Durham	.50
104	Lenny Dykstra	.50
105	Cecil Fielder	.75
106	Andres Galarraga	.75
107	Brian Hunter	.50
108	Kenny Lofton	2.50
109	Kirby Puckett	3.00
110	Tim Salmon	.75
111	Greg Vaughn	.50
112	Larry Walker	1.00
113	Rick Aguilera	.50
114	Kevin Appier	.50
115	Kevin Brown	.50
116	David Cone	.50
117	Alex Fernandez	.50
118	Chuck Finley	.50
119	Joey Hamilton	.50
120	Jason Isringhausen	.75
121	Greg Maddux	6.00
122	Pedro Martinez	.50
123	Jose Mesa	.50
124	Jeff Montgomery	.50
125	Mike Mussina	1.50
126	Randy Myers	.50
127	Kenny Rogers	.50
128	Ismael Valdes	.50

1996 Topps Laser Bright Spots

Top young stars are featured on these 1996 Topps Laser cards, which use etched silver and gold diffraction foil. The cards are seeded one per every 20 packs. Numbers 1-8 are in Series I packs; cards 9-16 are in Series II packs.

Values shown reflect the market as of January, 1999.

On-field performances of current players in the 1999 baseball season are not factored in.

		MT
Complete Set (8):		160.00
Complete Series I Set (8):		70.00
Complete Series II Set (8):		90.00
Common Player:		6.00
1	Brian Hunter	8.00
2	Derek Jeter	30.00
3	Jason Kendall	6.00
4	Brooks Kieschnick	8.00
5	Rey Ordonez	15.00
6	Jason Schmidt	8.00
7	Chris Snopek	6.00
8	Bob Wolcott	6.00
9	Alan Benes	10.00
10	Marty Cordova	10.00
11	Jimmy Haynes	6.00
12	Todd Hollandsworth	10.00
13	Derek Jeter	25.00
14	Chipper Jones	40.00
15	Hideo Nomo	20.00
16	Paul Wilson	6.00

1996 Topps Laser Power Cuts

This 1996 Topps Laser insert set spotlights 16 of the game's top power hitters on etched foil and gold diffraction foil cards. These cards were seeded one per every 40 packs; numbers 1-8 were in Series I packs; cards 9-16 were in Series II packs.

		MT
Complete Set (8):		300.00
Complete Series I Set (8):		140.00
Complete Series II Set (8):		150.00
Common Player:		10.00
1	Albert Belle	20.00
2	Jay Buhner	10.00
3	Fred McGriff	15.00
4	Mike Piazza	40.00

5	Tim Salmon	15.00
6	Frank Thomas	40.00
7	Mo Vaughn	20.00
8	Matt Williams	15.00
9	Jeff Bagwell	30.00
10	Barry Bonds	20.00
11	Jose Canseco	12.00
12	Cecil Fielder	10.00
13	Juan Gonzalez	30.00
14	Ken Griffey Jr.	70.00
15	Sammy Sosa	40.00
16	Larry Walker	12.00

1996 Topps Laser Stadium Stars

These 1996 Topps Laser cards are the most difficult to find; they are seeded one per every 60 packs. The 16 cards feature a laser-sculpted cover that folds back to reveal striated silver and gold etched diffraction foil on each card front. Cards 1-8 were in Series I packs; numbers 9-16 were Series II inserts.

		MT
Complete Set (8):		225.00
Complete Series I Set (8):		125.00
Complete Series II Set (8):		100.00
Common Player:		5.00
1	Carlos Baerga	5.00
2	Barry Bonds	15.00
3	Andres Galarraga	8.00
4	Ken Griffey Jr.	60.00
5	Barry Larkin	8.00
6	Raul Mondesi	8.00
7	Kirby Puckett	15.00
8	Cal Ripken Jr.	50.00
9	Will Clark	8.00
10	Roger Clemens	20.00
11	Tony Gwynn	30.00
12	Randy Johnson	12.00
13	Kenny Lofton	15.00
14	Edgar Martinez	5.00
15	Ryne Sandberg	15.00
16	Frank Thomas	40.00

1997 Topps

Topps' 1997 set includes the first-ever player cards of the expansion Diamondbacks and Devil

Rays; 16 Mickey Mantle reprints; a special Jackie Robinson tribute card; 27 Willie Mays Topps and Bowman reprints; randomly-inserted Willie Mays autographed reprint cards; and Inter-League Finest and Finest Refractors cards. The base set has 275 cards in each series. Each card front has a gloss coating on the photo and a spot matte finish on the outside border. Gold foil stamping is also used. Card backs have informative text, complete player stats and biographies, and a second photo. The Jackie Robinson card pays tribute to the 50th anniversary of his breaking the color line. This card is #42 in the regular issue. Mantle reprints, seeded one per every 12 packs, feature the 16 remaining Mantle cards which were not reprinted in 1996 Topps baseball. The cards, each stamped with a gold foil logo, are numbered from #21 to #36. Willie Mays has 27 of his cards reprinted and seeded one per every eight packs. Each card also has a gold foil stamp.

		MT
Complete Set (496):		30.00
Complete Series 1 Set (276):		15.00
Complete Series 2 Set (220):		15.00
Common Player:		.05
Series I & II Wax Box:		40.00
1	Barry Bonds	.50
2	Tom Pagnozzi	.05
3	Terrell Wade	.05
4	Jose Valentin	.05
5	Mark Clark	.05
6	Brady Anderson	.15
7	Not issued	
8	Wade Boggs	.20
9	Scott Stahoviak	.05
10	Andres Galarraga	.15
11	Steve Avery	.05
12	Rusty Greer	.05
13	Derek Jeter	1.25
14	Ricky Bottalico	.05
15	Andy Ashby	.05
16	Paul Shuey	.05
17	F.P. Santangelo	.05
18	Royce Clayton	.05
19	Mike Mohler	.05
20	Mike Piazza	1.50
21	Jaime Navarro	.05
22	Billy Wagner	.05
23	Mike Timlin	.05
24	Garret Anderson	.05
25	Ben McDonald	.05
26	Mel Rojas	.05
27	John Burkett	.05
28	Jeff King	.05
29	Reggie Jefferson	.05
30	Kevin Appier	.05
31	Felipe Lira	.05
32	Kevin Tapani	.05
33	Mark Portugal	.05
34	Carlos Garcia	.05
35	Joey Cora	.05
36	David Segui	.05
37	Mark Grace	.20
38	Erik Hanson	.05
39	Jeff D'Amico	.05
40	Jay Buhner	.15
41	B.J. Surhoff	.05
42	Jackie Robinson	3.00
43	Roger Pavlik	.05
44	Hal Morris	.05
45	Mariano Duncan	.05
46	Harold Baines	.08
47	Jorge Fabregas	.05
48	Jose Herrera	.05
49	Jeff Cirillo	.05
50	Tom Glavine	.10
51	Pedro Astacio	.05
52	Mark Gardner	.05
53	Arthur Rhodes	.05
54	Troy O'Leary	.05

No.	Player	Price
55	Bip Roberts	.05
56	Mike Lieberthal	.05
57	Shane Andrews	.05
58	Scott Karl	.05
59	Gary DiSarcina	.05
60	Andy Pettitte	.60
61a	Kevin Elster	.05
61b	Mike Fetters (should be #84)	.05
62	Mark McGwire	3.00
63	Dan Wilson	.05
64	Mickey Morandini	.05
65	Chuck Knoblauch	.12
66	Tim Wakefield	.05
67	Raul Mondesi	.25
68	Todd Jones	.05
69	Albert Belle	.60
70	Trevor Hoffman	.05
71	Eric Young	.05
72	Robert Perez	.05
73	Butch Huskey	.05
74	Brian McRae	.05
75	Jim Edmonds	.10
76	Mike Henneman	.05
77	Frank Rodriguez	.05
78	Danny Tartabull	.05
79	Robby Nen	.05
80	Reggie Sanders	.10
81	Ron Karkovice	.05
82	Benny Santiago	.08
83	Mike Lansing	.05
84	Not issued - see #61b	
85	Craig Biggio	.10
86	Mike Bordick	.05
87	Ray Lankford	.10
88	Charles Nagy	.05
89	Paul Wilson	.05
90	John Wetteland	.05
91	Tom Candiotti	.05
92	Carlos Delgado	.05
93	Derek Bell	.10
94	Mark Lemke	.05
95	Edgar Martinez	.08
96	Rickey Henderson	.20
97	Greg Myers	.05
98	Jim Leyritz	.05
99	Mark Johnson	.05
100	Dwight Gooden (Season Highlights)	.05
101	Al Leiter (Season Highlights)	.05
102a	John Mabry (Season Highlights)(last line on back ends "... Mabry"))	.05
102b	John Mabry (Season Highlights)(last line on back ends "...walked.")	.05
103	Alex Ochoa (Season Highlights)	.05
104	Mike Piazza (Season Highlights)	.60
105	Jim Thome	.30
106	Ricky Otero	.05
107	Jamey Wright	.05
108	Frank Thomas	2.50
109	Jody Reed	.05
110	Orel Hershiser	.08
111	Terry Steinbach	.05
112	Mark Loretta	.05
113	Turk Wendell	.05
114	Marvin Benard	.05
115	Kevin Brown	.05
116	Robert Person	.05
117	Joey Hamilton	.05
118	Francisco Cordova	.10
119	John Smiley	.05
120	Travis Fryman	.05
121	Jimmy Key	.05
122	Tom Goodwin	.05
123	Mike Greenwell	.05
124	Juan Gonzalez	1.00
125	Pete Harnisch	.05
126	Roger Cedeno	.05
127	Ron Gant	.10
128	Mark Langston	.05
129	Tim Crabtree	.05
130	Greg Maddux	1.50
131	William VanLandingham	.05
132	Wally Joyner	.10
133	Randy Myers	.05
134	John Valentin	.10
135	Bret Boone	.05
136	Bruce Ruffin	.05
137	Chris Snopek	.05
138	Paul Molitor	.40
139	Mark McLemore	.05
140	Rafael Palmeiro	.10
141	Herb Perry	.05
142	Luis Gonzalez	.05
143	Doug Drabek	.05
144	Ken Ryan	.05
145	Todd Hundley	.10
146	Ellis Burks	.10
147	Ozzie Guillen	.05
148	Rich Becker	.05
149	Sterling Hitchcock	.05
150	Bernie Williams	.40
151	Mike Stanley	.05
152	Roberto Alomar	.50
153	Jose Mesa	.08
154	Steve Trachsel	.05
155	Alex Gonzalez	.05
156	Troy Percival	.05
157	John Smoltz	.20
158	Pedro Martinez	.05
159	Jeff Conine	.10
160	Bernard Gilkey	.08
161	Jim Eisenreich	.05
162	Mickey Tettleton	.05
163	Justin Thompson	.05
164	Jose Offerman	.05
165	Tony Phillips	.08
166	Ismael Valdes	.05
167	Ryne Sandberg	.50
168	Matt Mieske	.05
169	Geronimo Berroa	.05
170	Otis Nixon	.05
171	John Mabry	.05
172	Shawon Dunston	.10
173	Omar Vizquel	.05
174	Chris Holles	.05
175	Doc Gooden	.10
176	Wilson Alvarez	.05
177	Todd Hollandsworth	.10
178	Roger Salkeld	.05
179	Rey Sanchez	.05
180	Rey Ordonez	.30
181	Denny Martinez	.08
182	Ramon Martinez	.08
183	Dave Nilsson	.05
184	Marquis Grissom	.10
185	Randy Velarde	.05
186	Ron Coomer	.05
187	Tino Martinez	.25
188	Jeff Brantley	.05
189	Steve Finley	.05
190	Andy Benes	.08
191	Terry Adams	.05
192	Mike Blowers	.05
193	Russ Davis	.05
194	Darryl Hamilton	.05
195	Jason Kendall	.08
196	Johnny Damon	.15
197	Dave Martinez	.05
198	Mike Macfarlane	.05
199	Norm Charlton	.05
200	Doug Million, Damian Moss, Bobby Rodgers (Prospect)	.20
201	Geoff Jenkins, Raul Ibanez, Mike Cameron (Prospect)	.25
202	Sean Casey, Jim Bonnici, Dmitri Young (Prospect)	.10
203	Jed Hansen, Homer Bush, Felipe Crespo (Prospect)	.05
204	Kevin Orie, Gabe Alvarez, Aaron Boone (Prospect)	.25
205	Ben Davis, Kevin Brown, Bobby Estalella (Prospect)	.05
206	Billy McMillon, *Bubba Trammell*, Dante Powell (Prospect)	.75
207	Jarrod Washburn, *Marc Wilkins*, Glendon Rusch (Prospect)	.15
208	Brian Hunter	.05
209	Jason Giambi	.08
210	Henry Rodriguez	.05
211	Edgar Renteria	.20
212	Edgardo Alfonzo	.05
213	Fernando Vina	.05
214	Shawn Green	.05
215	Ray Durham	.05
216	Joe Randa	.05
217	Armando Reynoso	.05
218	Eric Davis	.08
219	Bob Tewksbury	.05
220	Jacob Cruz	.05
221	Glenallen Hill	.05
222	Gary Gaetti	.08
223	Donne Wall	.05
224	Brad Clontz	.05
225	Marty Janzen	.05
226	Todd Worrell	.05
227	John Franco	.05
228	David Wells	.05
229	Gregg Jefferies	.10
230	Tim Naehring	.05
231	Thomas Howard	.05
232	Roberto Hernandez	.05
233	Kevin Ritz	.05
234	Julian Tavarez	.05
235	Ken Hill	.05
236	Greg Gagne	.05
237	Bobby Chouinard	.05
238	Joe Carter	.10
239	Jermaine Dye	.15
240	Antonio Osuna	.05
241	Julio Franco	.05
242	Mike Grace	.05
243	Aaron Sele	.05
244	David Justice	.15
245	Sandy Alomar	.10
246	Jose Canseco	.25
247	Paul O'Neill	.05
248	Sean Berry	.05
249	*Nick Bierbrodt,Kevin Sweeney* (Diamond Backs)	.50
250	*Larry Rodriguez,Vladimir Nunez* (Diamond Backs)	.40
251	Ron Hartman, David Hayman (Diamond Backs)	.10
252	Alex Sanchez, Matt Quatraro (Devil Rays)	.10
253	Ronni Seberino,*Pablo Ortega* (Devil Rays)	.40
254	Rex Hudler	.05
255	Orlando Miller	.05
256	Mariano Rivera	.25
257	Brad Radke	.05
258	Bobby Higginson	.05
259	Jay Bell	.05
260	Mark Grudzielanek	.05
261	Lance Johnson	.05
262	Ken Caminiti	.10
263	J.T. Snow	.05
264	Gary Sheffield	.20
265	Darrin Fletcher	.05
266	Eric Owens	.05
267	Luis Castillo	.15
268	Scott Rolen	.75
269	*Todd Noel*, John Oliver (Draft Pick)	.25
270	*Robert Stratton*, Corey Lee (Draft Pick)	.20
271	*Gil Meche,Matt Halloran* (Draft Pick)	.50
272	*Eric Milton*, Dermal Brown (Draft Pick)	1.00
273	*Josh Garrett,Chris Reitsma* (Draft Pick)	.50
274	*A.J. Zapp,Jason Marquis* (Draft Pick)	.25
275	Checklist	.05
276	Checklist	.05
277	Chipper Jones	1.50
278	Orlando Merced	.05
279	Ariel Prieto	.05
280	Al Leiter	.05
281	Pat Meares	.05
282	Darryl Strawberry	.08
283	Jamie Moyer	.05
284	Scott Servais	.05
285	Delino DeShields	.05
286	Danny Graves	.05
287	Gerald Williams	.05
288	Todd Greene	.05
289	Rico Brogna	.05
290	Derrick Gibson	.05
291	Joe Girardi	.05
292	Darren Lewis	.05
293	Nomar Garciaparra	1.00
294	Greg Colbrunn	.05
295	Jeff Bagwell	1.00
296	Brent Gates	.05
297	Jose Vizcaino	.05
298	Alex Ochoa	.05
299	Sid Fernandez	.05
300	Ken Griffey Jr.	2.50
301	Chris Gomez	.05
302	Wendell Magee	.10
303	Darren Oliver	.05
304	Mel Nieves	.05
305	Sammy Sosa	1.50
306	George Arias	.05
307	Jack McDowell	.05
308	Stan Javier	.05
309	Kimera Bartee	.05
310	James Baldwin	.05

311	Rocky Coppinger	.05
312	Keith Lockhart	.05
313	C.J. Nitkowski	.05
314	Allen Watson	.05
315	Darryl Kile	.05
316	Amaury Telemaco	.05
317	Jason Isringhausen	.05
318	Manny Ramirez	.75
319	Terry Pendleton	.05
320	Tim Salmon	.15
321	Eric Karros	.10
322	Mark Whiten	.05
323	Rick Krivda	.05
324	Brett Butler	.10
325	Randy Johnson	.30
326	Eddie Taubensee	.05
327	Mark Leiter	.05
328	Kevin Gross	.05
329	Ernie Young	.05
330	Pat Hentgen	.05
331	Rondell White	.10
332	Bobby Witt	.05
333	Eddie Murray	.30
334	Tim Raines	.08
335	Jeff Fassero	.05
336	Chuck Finley	.05
337	Willie Adams	.05
338	Chan Ho Park	.05
339	Jay Powell	.05
340	Ivan Rodriguez	.30
341	Jermaine Allensworth	.05
342	Jay Payton	.15
343	T.J. Mathews	.05
344	Tony Batista	.05
345	Ed Sprague	.05
346	Jeff Kent	.05
347	Scott Erickson	.05
348	Jeff Suppan	.05
349	Pete Schourek	.05
350	Kenny Lofton	.75
351	Alan Benes	.10
352	Fred McGriff	.30
353	Charlie O'Brien	.05
354	Darren Bragg	.05
355	Alex Fernandez	.05
356	Al Martin	.05
357	Bob Wells	.05
358	Chad Mottola	.05
359	Devon White	.05
360	David Cone	.08
361	Bobby Jones	.05
362	Scott Sanders	.05
363	Karim Garcia	.40
364	Kirt Manwaring	.05
365	Chili Davis	.08
366	Mike Hampton	.05
367	Chad Ogea	.05
368	Curt Schilling	.05
369	Phil Nevin	.05
370	Roger Clemens	.50
371	Willie Greene	.05
372	Kenny Rogers	.05
373	Jose Rijo	.05
374	Bobby Bonilla	.08
375	Mike Mussina	.30
376	Curtis Pride	.05
377	Todd Walker	.40
378	Jason Bere	.05
379	Heathcliff Slocumb	.05
380	Dante Bichette	.20
381	Carlos Baerga	.10
382	Livan Hernandez	.10
383	Jason Schmidt	.05
384	Kevin Stocker	.05
385	Matt Williams	.25
386	Bartolo Colon	.15
387	Will Clark	.25
388	Dennis Eckersley	.08
389	Brooks Kieschnick	.12
390	Ryan Klesko	.40
391	Mark Carreon	.05
392	Tim Worrell	.05
393	Dean Palmer	.05
394	Wil Cordero	.05
395	Javy Lopez	.15
396	Rich Aurilla	.05
397	Greg Vaughn	.05
398	Vinny Castilla	.10
399	Jeff Montgomery	.05
400	Cal Ripken Jr.	2.00
401	Walt Weiss	.05
402	Brad Ausmus	.05
403	Ruben Rivera	.25
404	Mark Wohlers	.05
405	Rick Aguilera	.05
406	Tony Clark	.50

407	Lyle Mouton	.05
408	Bill Pulsipher	.05
409	Jose Rosado	.05
410	Tony Gwynn	1.00
411	Cecil Fielder	.15
412	John Flaherty	.05
413	Lenny Dykstra	.05
414	Ugueth Urbina	.05
415	Brian Jordan	.15
416	Bob Abreu	.05
417	Craig Paquette	.05
418	Sandy Martinez	.05
419	Jeff Blauser	.05
420	Barry Larkin	.25
421	Kevin Seitzer	.05
422	Tim Belcher	.05
423	Paul Sorrento	.05
424	Cal Eldred	.05
425	Robin Ventura	.10
426	John Olerud	.10
427	Bob Wolcott	.05
428	Matt Lawton	.05
429	Rod Beck	.05
430	Shane Reynolds	.05
431	Mike James	.05
432	Steve Wojciechowski	.05
433	Vladimir Guerrero	.75
434	Dustin Hermanson	.10
435	Marty Cordova	.05
436	Marc Newfield	.05
437	Todd Stottlemyre	.05
438	Jeffrey Hammonds	.05
439	Dave Stevens	.05
440	Hideo Nomo	.50
441	Mark Thompson	.05
442	Mark Lewis	.05
443	Quinton McCracken	.05
444	Cliff Floyd	.05
445	Denny Neagle	.05
446	John Jaha	.05
447	Mike Sweeney	.05
448	John Wasdin	.05
449	Chad Curtis	.05
450	Mo Vaughn	.75
451	Donovan Osborne	.05
452	Ruben Sierra	.08
453	Michael Tucker	.05
454	Kurt Abbott	.05
455	Andruw Jones	1.50
456	Shannon Stewart	.05
457	Scott Brosius	.05
458	Juan Guzman	.05
459	Ron Villone	.05
460	Moises Alou	.10
461	Larry Walker	.30
462	Eddie Murray (Season Highlights)	.20
463	Paul Molitor (Season Highlights)	.20
464	Hideo Nomo (Season Highlights)	.25
465	Barry Bonds (Season Highlights)	.40
466	Todd Hundley (Season Highlights)	.05
467	Rheal Cormier	.05
468	*Jason Conti*	.40
469	Rod Barajas	.05
470	Jared Sandberg, Cedric Bowers	.05
471	Paul Wilders, Chie Gunner	.05
472	Mike Decelle, Marcus McCain	.05
473	Todd Zeile	.08
474	Neifi Perez	.05
475	Jeromy Burnitz	.05
476	Trey Beamon	.05
477	John Patterson, Braden Looper (Draft Picks)	.05
478	*Danny Peoples, Jake Westbrook* (Draft Picks)	.25
479	*Eric Chavez*, Adam Eaton (Draft Picks)	1.00
480	*Joe Lawrence*, Pete Tucci (Draft Picks)	.05
481	Kris Benson, Billy Koch (Draft Picks)	.05
482	John Nicholson, Andy Prater (Draft Picks)	.05
483	*Mark Kotsay*, Mark Johnson (Draft Picks)	1.50
484	Armando Benitez	.05
485	Mike Matheny	.05
486	Jeff Reed	.05

487	Mark Bellhorn, Russ Johnson, Enrique Wilson (Prospects)	.05
488	Ben Grieve, Richard Hidalgo, Scott Morgan (Prospects)	1.00
489	Paul Konerko, Derrek Lee, Ron Wright (Prospects)	1.00
490	Wes Helms, *Bill Mueller*, Brad Seitzer (Prospects)	.75
491	Jeff Abbott, Shane Monahan, Edgard Velazquez (Prospects)	.20
492	*Jimmy Anderson*, Ron Blazier, Gerald Witasick, Jr. (Prospects)	.25
493	Darin Blood, Heath Murray, Carl Pavano (Prospects)	.05
494	Mark Redman, *Mike Villano*, Nelson Figueroa (Prospects)	.20
495	Checklist	.05
496	Checklist	.05

1997 Topps All-Stars

Ivan Rodriguez

Topps' 1997 All-Stars insert cards, printed on a dazzling rainbow foilboard, feature the top players from each position. There are 22 cards, 11 from each league, which showcase the top three players from each position as voted by Topps' sports department. On the front of each card is a photo of a "first team" all-star player; the back has a different photo of that player, who appears alongside the "second team" and "third team" selections. These cards are seeded one per every 18 1997 Topps Series I packs.

	MT
Complete Set (22):	75.00
Common Player:	1.50
AS1 Ivan Rodriguez	2.00
AS2 Todd Hundley	1.50
AS3 Frank Thomas	12.00
AS4 Andres Galarraga	2.00
AS5 Chuck Knoblauch	1.50
AS6 Eric Young	1.50
AS7 Jim Thome	3.00
AS8 Chipper Jones	10.00
AS9 Cal Ripken Jr.	12.00
AS10 Barry Larkin	2.00
AS11 Albert Belle	4.00
AS12 Barry Bonds	4.00
AS13 Ken Griffey Jr.	15.00
AS14 Ellis Burks	1.50
AS15 Juan Gonzalez	7.00
AS16 Gary Sheffield	2.50
AS17 Andy Pettitte	4.00
AS18 Tom Glavine	1.50
AS19 Pat Hentgen	1.50
AS20 John Smoltz	2.00

AS21	Roberto Hernandez	1.50
AS22	Mark Wohlers	1.50

1997 Topps Awesome Impact

This flashy insert exclusive to Series 2 retail packaging features young players who have quickly made their mark in the big leagues. Fronts have player action photos against a background of silver primatic geometric shapes. Backs are horizontal with a player portrait photo, recent stats and a few words about the player's current and projected impact. Stated odds of finding this insert are one per 18 packs. Cards are numbered with an "AI" prefix.

		MT
Complete Set (20):		75.00
Common Player:		1.00
1	Jaime Bluma	1.00
2	Tony Clark	2.50
3	Jermaine Dye	1.00
4	Nomar Garciaparra	10.00
5	Vladimir Guerrero	8.00
6	Todd Hollandsworth	3.00
7	Derek Jeter	9.00
8	Andruw Jones	8.00
9	Chipper Jones	12.00
10	Jason Kendall	2.00
11	Brooks Kieschnick	1.00
12	Alex Ochoa	1.00
13	Rey Ordonez	3.00
14	Neifi Perez	3.00
15	Edgar Renteria	2.50
16	Mariano Rivera	1.50
17	Ruben Rivera	1.00
18	Scott Rolen	9.00
19	Billy Wagner	1.50
20	Todd Walker	1.00

1997 Topps Hobby Masters

These 10 cards lead the way as dealers' top selections. The cards, printed on 28-point diffraction foilboard, replace two regular cards in every 36th pack of 1997 Topps Series I product.

		MT
Complete Set (20):		100.00
Complete Series 1 (10):		55.00
Complete Series 2 (10):		45.00
Common Player:		1.50
HM1	Ken Griffey Jr.	15.00
HM2	Cal Ripken Jr.	12.00
HM3	Greg Maddux	10.00
HM4	Albert Belle	4.00

HM5	Tony Gwynn	8.00
HM6	Jeff Bagwell	6.00
HM7	Randy Johnson	3.00
HM8	Raul Mondesi	1.50
HM9	Juan Gonzalez	8.00
HM10	Kenny Lofton	4.00
HM11	Frank Thomas	12.00
HM12	Mike Piazza	10.00
HM13	Chipper Jones	10.00
HM14	Brady Anderson	1.50
HM15	Ken Caminiti	2.00
HM16	Barry Bonds	4.00
HM17	Mo Vaughn	4.00
HM18	Derek Jeter	10.00
HM19	Sammy Sosa	8.00
HM20	Andres Galarraga	1.50

1997 Topps Inter-League Match Ups

The double-sided Inter-League Finest and Inter-League Finest Refracators (seeded one in 36 and one in 216 Topps Series I packs respectively) feature top individual matchups from inter-league rivalries. One player from each major league team is represented, for a total of 28 players on 14 different cards. Each card is covered with a Finest clear protector.

		MT
Complete Set (14):		70.00
Common Player:		3.00
Refractors: 3x to 4x		
ILM1	Mark McGwire, Barry Bonds	20.00
ILM2	Tim Salmon, Mike Piazza	10.00
ILM3	Ken Griffey Jr., Dante Bichette	15.00
ILM4	Juan Gonzalez, Tony Gwynn	8.00
ILM5	Frank Thomas, Sammy Sosa	25.00
ILM6	Albert Belle, Barry Larkin	4.00
ILM7	Johnny Damon, Brian Jordan	3.00
ILM8	Paul Molitor, Jeff King	3.00
ILM9	John Jaha, Jeff Bagwell	6.00
ILM10	Bernie Williams, Todd Hundley	4.00
ILM11	Joe Carter, Henry Rodriguez	3.00
ILM12	Cal Ripken Jr., Gregg Jefferies	12.00
ILM13	Mo Vaughn, Chipper Jones	10.00
ILM14	Travis Fryman, Gary Sheffield	3.00

1997 Topps Mickey Mantle Finest

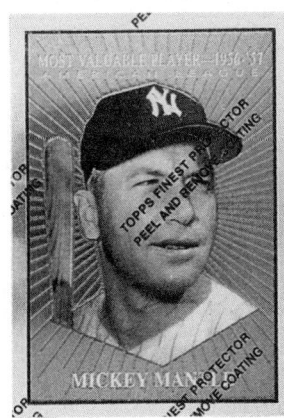

The 16-card Mickey Mantle reprints insert that was found in Series I was re-issued in Series II in the Topps Finest technology. The Finest versions are found on average of every 24 packs.

		MT
Complete Set (16):		90.00
Common Mantle:		7.00
21	1953 Bowman #44	6.00
22	1953 Bowman #59	9.00
23	1957 Topps #407	6.00
24	1958 Topps #418	6.00
25	1958 Topps #487	6.00
26	1959 Topps #461	6.00
27	1959 Topps #564	6.00
28	1960 Topps #160	6.00
29	1960 Topps #563	6.00
30	1961 Topps #406	6.00
31	1961 Topps #475	6.00
32	1961 Topps #578	6.00
33	1962 Topps #18	6.00
34	1962 Topps #318	6.00
35	1962 Topps #471	6.00
36	1964 Topps #331	6.00

1997 Topps Mickey Mantle Finest Refractors

Each of the 16 Mantle Finest reprints from Series II can also be found in a Refractor version. Refractors are found every 216 packs, on average.

		MT
Complete Set (16):		450.00
Common Mantle:		30.00
21	1953 Bowman #44	30.00
22	1953 Bowman #59	50.00
23	1957 Topps #407	30.00
24	1958 Topps #418	30.00
25	1958 Topps #487	30.00
26	1959 Topps #461	30.00
27	1959 Topps #564	30.00
28	1960 Topps #160	30.00
29	1960 Topps #563	30.00
30	1961 Topps #406	30.00
31	1961 Topps #475	30.00
32	1961 Topps #578	30.00
33	1962 Topps #18	30.00
34	1962 Topps #318	30.00
35	1962 Topps #471	30.00
36	1964 Topps #331	30.00

1997 Topps Mickey Mantle Reprints

All 16 remaining Mickey Mantle cards that were not reprinted in 1996 Topps Baseball are found in this insert, seeded every 12 packs of Series I Topps. The set starts off with No. 21 and runs through No. 36 since the '96 reprints were numbered 1-20.

		MT
Complete Set (16):		70.00
Common Card:		6.00
21	1953 Bowman #44	6.00
22	1953 Bowman #59	8.00
23	1957 Topps #407	6.00
24	1958 Topps #418	6.00
25	1958 Topps #487	6.00
26	1959 Topps #461	6.00
27	1959 Topps #564	6.00
28	1960 Topps #160	6.00
29	1960 Topps #563	6.00
30	1961 Topps #406	6.00
31	1961 Topps #475	6.00
32	1961 Topps #578	6.00
33	1962 Topps #18	6.00
34	1962 Topps #318	6.00
35	1962 Topps #471	6.00
36	1964 Topps #331	6.00

1997 Topps Screenplays

(2)	Albert Belle	7.00
(3)	Barry Bonds	6.00
(4)	Andres Galarraga	5.00
(5)	Nomar Garciaparra	12.00
(6)	Juan Gonzalez	10.00
(7)	Ken Griffey Jr.	20.00
(8)	Tony Gwynn	11.00
(9)	Derek Jeter	15.00
(10)	Randy Johnson	5.00
(11)	Andruw Jones	10.00
(12)	Chipper Jones	12.00
(13)	Kenny Lofton	6.00
(14)	Mark McGwire	20.00
(15)	Paul Molitor	5.00
(16)	Hideo Nomo	9.00
(17)	Cal Ripken Jr.	16.00
(18)	Sammy Sosa	12.00
(19)	Frank Thomas	15.00
(20)	Jim Thome	5.00

1997 Topps Screenplays Inserts

		MT
Complete Set (6):		275.00
Common Player:		25.00
1	Larry Walker	25.00
2	Cal Ripken Jr.	60.00
3	Chipper Jones	50.00
4	Frank Thomas	60.00
5	Mike Piazza	50.00
6	Ken Griffey Jr.	80.00

1997 Topps Season's Best

Season's Best features 25 players on prismatic illusion foilboard, and can be found every six packs. The set has the top five players from five statistical categories: home runs, RBIs, batting average, steals, and wins. Season's Best were found in packs of Topps Series II, and later reprinted on chromium stock as part of Topps Chrome.

		MT
Complete Set (25):		30.00
Common Player:		.50
1	Tony Gwynn	3.00
2	Frank Thomas	6.00
3	Ellis Burks	.50
4	Paul Molitor	1.50
5	Chuck Knoblauch	.75
6	Mark McGwire	10.00
7	Brady Anderson	.50
8	Ken Griffey Jr.	8.00
9	Albert Belle	2.00
10	Andres Galarraga	.50
11	Andres Galarraga	.50
12	Albert Belle	2.00

13	Juan Gonzalez	4.00
14	Mo Vaughn	2.00
15	Rafael Palmeiro	.50
16	John Smoltz	.50
17	Andy Pettitte	2.00
18	Pat Hentgen	.50
19	Mike Mussina	1.50
20	Andy Benes	.50
21	Kenny Lofton	2.00
22	Tom Goodwin	.50
23	Otis Nixon	.50
24	Eric Young	.50
25	Lance Johnson	.50

1997 Topps Stars

The premiere version of this product was sold only to hobby shops that were members of the Topps Home Team Advantage program. Each of the 125 regular cards in the set is printed on 20-point stock. Card fronts feature spot UV coating with a textured star pattern running down one side of the card. Inserts include the parallel Always Mint set, as well al '97 All-Stars, Future All-Stars, All-Star memories, and Autographed Rookie Reprints. Cards were sold in seven-card packs for $3 each.

		MT
Complete Set (125):		70.00
Common Player:		.10
Always Mint Stars: 15x to 25x		
Always Mint Yng Stars & RC's:10x to 20x		
Wax Box:		50.00
1	Larry Walker	.40
2	Tino Martinez	.25
3	Cal Ripken Jr.	3.00
4	Ken Griffey Jr.	4.00
5	Chipper Jones	2.50
6	David Justice	.25
7	Mike Piazza	2.50
8	Jeff Bagwell	1.75
9	Ron Gant	.10
10	Sammy Sosa	2.00
11	Tony Gwynn	2.00
12	Carlos Baerga	.10
13	Frank Thomas	3.00
14	Moises Alou	.20
15	Barry Larkin	.20
16	Ivan Rodriguez	.75
17	Greg Maddux	2.50
18	Jim Edmonds	.20
19	Jose Canseco	.25
20	Rafael Palmeiro	.25
21	Paul Molitor	.75
22	Kevin Appier	.10
23	Raul Mondesi	.25
24	Lance Johnson	.10
25	Edgar Martinez	.10
26	Andres Galarraga	.25
27	Mo Vaughn	1.00
28	Ken Caminiti	.25
29	Cecil Fielder	.20

Twenty of the game's top stars were featured in this multi-part collectible. The packaging is a X-x/x" diameter lithographed steel can. The can was shrink-wrapped at the factory with a round checklist disc covering the color player photo on top of the can. The top has a woodgrain border around the photo and a gold facsimile autograph. The back of the topper disc has a career summary of the player. Inside the tin is a 2-1/2" x 3-1/2" plastic motion card with several seconds of game action shown as the angle of view changes. The cards is covered by a peel-off protective layer on front and back. Foam pieces in the package allow both the can and card to be displayed upright. Issue price was about $10 per can. The unnumbered cans are checklisted here alphabetically. Values shown are for can/card combinations.

		MT
Complete Set (20):		150.00
Common Player:		5.00
Box:		90.00
(1)	Jeff Bagwell	8.00

30	Harold Baines	.10
31	Roberto Alomar	.75
32	Shawn Estes	.10
33	Tom Glavine	.20
34	Dennis Eckersley	.20
35	Manny Ramirez	1.00
36	John Olerud	.10
37	Juan Gonzalez	2.00
38	Chuck Knoblauch	.30
39	Albert Belle	1.00
40	Vinny Castilla	.10
41	John Smoltz	.20
42	Barry Bonds	1.00
43	Randy Johnson	.75
44	Brady Anderson	.20
45	Jeff Blauser	.10
46	Craig Biggio	.20
47	Jeff Conine	.10
48	Marquis Grissom	.20
49	Mark Grace	.30
50	Roger Clemens	1.50
51	Mark McGwire	5.00
52	Fred McGriff	.25
53	Gary Sheffield	.40
54	Bobby Jones	.10
55	Eric Young	.10
56	Robin Ventura	.10
57	Wade Boggs	.25
58	Joe Carter	.20
59	Ryne Sandberg	1.00
60	Matt Williams	.30
61	Todd Hundley	.20
62	Dante Bichette	.25
63	Chili Davis	.10
64	Kenny Lofton	1.00
65	Jay Buhner	.20
66	Will Clark	.25
67	Travis Fryman	.10
68	Pat Hentgen	.10
69	Ellis Burks	.10
70	Mike Mussina	.75
71	Hideo Nomo	.75
72	Sandy Alomar	.10
73	Bobby Bonilla	.20
74	Rickey Henderson	.10
75	David Cone	.20
76	Terry Steinbach	.10
77	Pedro Martinez	.25
78	Jim Thome	.75
79	Rod Beck	.10
80	Randy Myers	.10
81	Charles Nagy	.10
82	Mark Wohlers	.10
83	Paul O'Neill	.25
84	Curt Shilling	.20
85	Joey Cora	.10
86	John Franco	.10
87	Kevin Brown	.20
88	Benito Santiago	.10
89	Ray Lankford	.20
90	Bernie Williams	.75
91	Jason Dickson	.10
92	Jeff Cirillo	.10
93	Nomar Garciaparra	2.50
94	Mariano Rivera	.20
95	Javy Lopez	.20
96	Tony Womack	1.50
97	Jose Rosado	.10
98	Denny Neagle	.20
99	Darryl Kile	.10
100	Justin Thompson	.10
101	Juan Encarnacion	.75
102	Brad Fullmer	.10
103	Kris Benson	3.00
104	Todd Helton	1.00
105	Paul Konerko	1.25
106	Travis Lee	15.00
107	Todd Greene	.10
108	Mark Kotsay	4.00
109	Carl Pavano	.50
110	Kerry Wood	30.00
111	Jason Romano	.75
112	Geoff Goetz	.40
113	Scott Hodges	.50
114	Aaron Akin	.40
115	Vernon Wells	5.00
116	Chris Stowe	.40
117	Brett Caradonna	2.00
118	Adam Kennedy	1.00
119	Jayson Werth	4.00
120	Glenn Davis	1.50
121	Troy Cameron	2.00
122	J.J. Davis	3.00
123	Jason Dellaero	.50
124	Jason Standridge	1.00
125	Lance Berkman	8.00

1997 Topps Stars All-Star Memories

This 10-card insert features stars who have had memorable performances in previous All-Star Games. Cards feature a laser-cut cascade of stars on a foilboard stock. Backs have another photo and a description of the All-Star memory. The cards were inserted 1:24 packs.

		MT
Complete Set (10):		75.00
Common Player:		4.00
ASM1	Cal Ripken Jr.	20.00
ASM2	Jeff Conine	4.00
ASM3	Mike Piazza	15.00
ASM4	Randy Johnson	6.00
ASM5	Ken Griffey Jr.	25.00
ASM6	Fred McGriff	5.00
ASM7	Moises Alou	4.00
ASM8	Hideo Nomo	8.00
ASM9	Larry Walker	6.00
ASM10	Sandy Alomar	4.00

1997 Topps Stars Autographed Rookie Reprints

Fifteen different Hall of Famers autographed reprinted versions of their Topps rookie cards. Each card features a special certified stamp.

		MT
Complete Set (15):		300.00
Common Player:		20.00
(1)	Luis Aparicio	25.00
(3)	Jim Bunning	20.00
(4)	Bob Feller	25.00
(5)	Rollie Fingers	25.00
(6)	Monte Irvin	20.00
(7)	Al Kaline	35.00
(8)	Ralph Kiner	20.00
(9)	Eddie Mathews	30.00
(10)	Hal Newhouser	20.00
(11)	Gaylord Perry	25.00
(12)	Robin Roberts	20.00
(13)	Brooks Robinson	40.00
(14)	Enos Slaughter	20.00
(15)	Earl Weaver	25.00

1997 Topps Stars Future All-Stars

This 15-card set showcases the top candidates to make their All-Star Game debut in 1998. Cards

feature a prismatic rainbow foil background and were inserted 1:12 packs.

		MT
Complete Set (15):		50.00
Common Player:		2.50
FAS1	Derek Jeter	8.00
FAS2	Andruw Jones	8.00
FAS3	Vladimir Guerrero	5.00
FAS4	Scott Rolen	6.00
FAS5	Jose Guillen	3.00
FAS6	Jose Cruz, Jr.	10.00
FAS7	Darin Erstad	5.00
FAS8	Tony Clark	3.00
FAS9	Scott Spiezio	2.50
FAS10	Kevin Orie	2.50
FAS11	Calvin Reese	2.50
FAS12	Billy Wagner	2.50
FAS13	Matt Morris	2.50
FAS14	Jeremi Gonzalez	2.50
FAS15	Hideki Irabu	6.00

1997 Topps Stars 1997 All-Stars

This 20-card insert honors participants of the 1997 All-Star Game in Cleveland. Cards were inserted 1:24 packs. Fronts are printed on prismatic foil with hundreds of stars in the background. On back is another player photo and his All-Star Game 1997 and career stats.

		MT
Complete Set (20):		200.00
Common Player:		6.00
AS1	Greg Maddux	30.00
AS2	Randy Johnson	8.00
AS3	Tino Martinez	6.00
AS4	Jeff Bagwell	15.00
AS5	Ivan Rodriguez	12.00
AS6	Mike Piazza	30.00
AS7	Cal Ripken Jr.	40.00
AS8	Ken Caminiti	6.00
AS9	Tony Gwynn	25.00
AS10	Edgar Martinez	6.00
AS11	Craig Biggio	6.00
AS12	Roberto Alomar	10.00
AS13	Larry Walker	8.00
AS14	Brady Anderson	6.00
AS15	Barry Bonds	12.00
AS16	Ken Griffey Jr.	50.00
AS17	Ray Lankford	6.00
AS18	Paul O'Neill	6.00
AS19	Jeff Blauser	6.00
AS20	Sandy Alomar	6.00

1997 Topps Sweet Strokes

These retail-exclusive Sweet Strokes insert cards consist of 15 Power Matrix foil cards of the top hitters in the game. These players have the swings to produce game winning-hits. The cards were seeded one per every 12 1997 Topps Series I retail packs.

		MT
Complete Set (15):		40.00
Common Player:		1.00
SS1	Roberto Alomar	2.00

SS2	Jeff Bagwell	4.00
SS3	Albert Belle	2.50
SS4	Barry Bonds	2.50
SS5	Mark Grace	1.00
SS6	Ken Griffey Jr.	10.00
SS7	Tony Gwynn	4.00
SS8	Chipper Jones	6.00
SS9	Edgar Martinez	1.00
SS10	Mark McGwire	12.00
SS11	Rafael Palmeiro	1.00
SS12	Mike Piazza	6.00
SS13	Gary Sheffield	1.50
SS14	Frank Thomas	8.00
SS15	Mo Vaughn	2.50

1997 Topps Team Timber

Team Timber was a 16-card insert that was exclusive to retail packs and inserted one per 36. The set displays the game's top sluggers on laminated litho wood cards.

		MT
Complete Set (16):		75.00
Common Player:		1.50
TT1	Ken Griffey Jr.	15.00
TT2	Ken Caminiti	2.00
TT3	Bernie Williams	3.00
TT4	Jeff Bagwell	6.00
TT5	Frank Thomas	12.00
TT6	Andres Galarraga	1.50
TT7	Barry Bonds	4.00
TT8	Rafael Palmeiro	1.50
TT9	Brady Anderson	1.50
TT10	Juan Gonzalez	8.00
TT11	Mo Vaughn	4.00
TT12	Mark McGwire	15.00
TT13	Gary Sheffield	2.50
TT14	Albert Belle	4.00
TT15	Chipper Jones	10.00
TT16	Mike Piazza	10.00

1997 Topps Willie Mays Finest

The introduction of Series II Topps offered collectors a chance to find Finest technology versions of each of the 27 commemorative reprint Topps and Bowman cards from throughout Mays' career. The Finest Mays reprints are found one in every 30 packs, on average.

		MT
Complete Set (27):		90.00
Common Card:		4.00
1	1951 Bowman #305	8.00
2	1952 Topps #261	6.00
3	1953 Topps #244	6.00
4	1954 Bowman #89	4.00
5	1954 Topps #90	4.00
6	1955 Bowman #184	4.00
7	1955 Topps #194	4.00
8	1956 Topps #130	4.00
9	1957 Topps #10	4.00
10	1958 Topps #5	4.00
11	1959 Topps #50	4.00
12	1960 Topps #200	4.00
13	1961 Topps #150	4.00
14	1961 Topps #579	4.00
15	1962 Topps #300	4.00
16	1963 Topps #300	4.00
17	1964 Topps #150	4.00
18	1965 Topps #250	4.00
19	1966 Topps #1	4.00
20	1967 Topps #200	4.00
21	1968 Topps #50	4.00
22	1969 Topps #190	4.00
23	1970 Topps #600	4.00
24	1971 Topps #600	4.00
25	1971 Topps #600	4.00
26	1972 Topps #49	4.00
27	1973 Topps #305	4.00

1997 Topps Willie Mays Finest Refractors

A high-end parallel set to the Willie Mays 27-card commemorative reprint issue is the Finest Refractor version issued in Series II. Refractors are found on average of once per 180 packs.

		MT
Complete Set (27):		500.00
Common Card:		20.00
1	1951 Bowman #305	50.00
2	1952 Topps #261	40.00
3	1953 Topps #244	40.00
4	1954 Bowman #89	30.00
5	1954 Topps #90	30.00
6	1955 Bowman #184	30.00
7	1955 Topps #194	30.00
8	1956 Topps #130	30.00
9	1957 Topps #10	30.00
10	1958 Topps #5	30.00
11	1959 Topps #50	30.00
12	1960 Topps #200	30.00
13	1961 Topps #150	30.00
14	1961 Topps #579	30.00
15	1962 Topps #300	30.00
16	1963 Topps #300	30.00
17	1964 Topps #150	30.00
18	1965 Topps #250	30.00
19	1966 Topps #1	30.00
20	1967 Topps #200	30.00
21	1968 Topps #50	30.00
22	1969 Topps #190	30.00
23	1970 Topps #600	30.00
24	1971 Topps #600	30.00
25	1971 Topps #600	30.00
26	1972 Topps #49	30.00
27	1973 Topps #305	30.00

1997 Topps Willie Mays Reprints

There are 27 different Willie Mays cards reprinted in Topps Series I and II and seeded every eight packs. The inserts form a collection of Topps and Bowman cards from throughout Mays' career and each is highlighted by a special commemorative gold foil stamp. Each of the Mays reprints can also be found in an autographed edition, bearing a special "Certified Autograph Issue" gold-foil logo.

A player's name in *italic* type indicates a rookie card.

		MT
Complete Set (27):		80.00
Common Card:		3.00
Autographed Card:		100.00
1	1951 Bowman #305	6.00
2	1952 Topps #261	4.00
3	1953 Topps #244	4.00
4	1954 Bowman #89	3.00
5	1954 Topps #90	3.00
6	1955 Bowman #184	3.00
7	1955 Topps #194	3.00
8	1956 Topps #130	3.00
9	1957 Topps #10	3.00
10	1958 Topps #5	3.00
11	1959 Topps #50	3.00
12	1960 Topps #200	3.00
13	1961 Topps #150	3.00
14	1961 Topps #579	3.00
15	1962 Topps #300	3.00
16	1963 Topps #300	3.00
17	1964 Topps #150	3.00
18	1965 Topps #250	3.00
19	1966 Topps #1	3.00
20	1967 Topps #200	3.00
21	1968 Topps #50	3.00
22	1969 Topps #190	3.00
23	1970 Topps #600	3.00
24	1971 Topps #600	3.00
25	1971 Topps #600	3.00
26	1972 Topps #49	3.00
27	1973 Topps #305	3.00

1997 Topps/Chrome

Chrome Baseball reprinted the top 165 cards from Topps Series I and II baseball on a chromium, metallized stock. Chrome sold in four-card packs and included three insert sets: Diamond Duos, which was created exclusively for this product, Season's Best and Topps All-Stars, which were both reprinted from Topps products. Refractor versions of each card were found every 12 packs.

		MT
Complete Set (165):		70.00
Common Player:		.20
Common Refractors:		5.00
Star Refractors: 12x to 18x		
Young Stars and RC's: 8x to 12x		
Wax Box:		90.00
1	Barry Bonds	2.00
2	Jose Valentin	.20
3	Brady Anderson	.20
4	Wade Boggs	.40
5	Andres Galarraga	.50
6	Rusty Greer	.20
7	Derek Jeter	5.00
8	Ricky Bottalico	.20
9	Mike Piazza	5.00
10	Garret Anderson	.20
11	Jeff King	.20

12	Kevin Appier	.20
13	Mark Grace	.40
14	Jeff D'Amico	.20
15	Jay Buhner	.40
16	Hal Morris	.20
17	Harold Baines	.20
18	Jeff Cirillo	.20
19	Tom Glavine	.40
20	Andy Pettitte	2.00
21	Mark McGwire	10.00
22	Chuck Knoblauch	.40
23	Raul Mondesi	.50
24	Albert Belle	2.00
25	Trevor Hoffman	.20
26	Eric Young	.20
27	Brian McRae	.20
28	Jim Edmonds	.20
29	Robb Nen	.20
30	Reggie Sanders	.20
31	Mike Lansing	.20
32	Craig Biggio	.40
33	Ray Lankford	.20
34	Charles Nagy	.20
35	Paul Wilson	.20
36	John Wetteland	.20
37	Derek Bell	.20
38	Edgar Martinez	.20
39	Rickey Henderson	.20
40	Jim Thome	.75
41	Frank Thomas	6.00
42	Jackie Robinson (Tribute)	6.00
43	Terry Steinbach	.20
44	Kevin Brown	.20
45	Joey Hamilton	.20
46	Travis Fryman	.20
47	Juan Gonzalez	3.50
48	Ron Gant	.40
49	Greg Maddux	5.00
50	Wally Joyner	.20
51	John Valentin	.20
42	Bret Boone	.20
53	Paul Molitor	1.00
54	Rafael Palmeiro	.40
55	Todd Hundley	.50
56	Ellis Burks	.20
57	Bernie Williams	1.50
58	Roberto Alomar	1.50
59	Jose Mesa	.20
60	Troy Percival	.20
61	John Smoltz	.50
62	Jeff Conine	.20
63	Bernard Gilkey	.20
64	Mickey Tettleton	.20
65	Justin Thompson	.20
66	Tony Phillips	.20
67	Ryne Sandberg	1.50
68	Geronimo Berroa	.20
69	Todd Hollandsworth	.20
70	Rey Ordonez	.20
71	Marquis Grissom	.20
72	Tino Martinez	.50
73	Steve Finley	.20
74	Andy Benes	.20
75	Jason Kendall	.20
76	Johnny Damon	.20
77	Jason Giambi	.20
78	Henry Rodriguez	.20
79	Edgar Renteria	.20
80	Ray Durham	.20
81	Gregg Jefferies	.20
82	Roberto Hernandez	.20
83	Joe Carter	.40
84	Jermaine Dye	.20
85	Julio Franco	.20
86	David Justice	.50
87	Jose Canseco	.50
88	Paul O'Neill	.20
89	Mariano Rivera	.40
90	Bobby Higginson	.20
91	Mark Grudzielanek	.20
92	Lance Johnson	.20
93	Ken Caminiti	.60
94	Gary Sheffield	.60
95	Luis Castillo	.25
96	Scott Rolen	3.00
97	Chipper Jones	5.00
98	Darryl Strawberry	.20
99	Nomar Garciaparra	3.00
100	Jeff Bagwell	3.50
101	Ken Griffey Jr.	8.00
102	Sammy Sosa	4.00
103	Jack McDowell	.20
104	James Baldwin	.20
105	Rocky Coppinger	.20
106	Manny Ramirez	1.75
107	Tim Salmon	.40

108	Eric Karros	.20
109	Brett Butler	.20
110	Randy Johnson	1.25
111	Pat Hentgen	.20
112	Rondell White	.20
113	Eddie Murray	.75
114	Ivan Rodriguez	1.50
115	Jermaine Allensworth	.20
116	Ed Sprague	.20
117	Kenny Lofton	2.00
118	Alan Benes	.40
119	Fred McGriff	.50
120	Alex Fernandez	.20
121	Al Martin	.20
122	Devon White	.20
123	David Cone	.40
124	Karim Garcia	.20
125	Chili Davis	.20
126	Roger Clemens	2.50
127	Bobby Bonilla	.20
128	Mike Mussina	1.50
129	Todd Walker	1.25
130	Dante Bichette	.40
131	Carlos Baerga	.20
132	Matt Williams	.60
133	Will Clark	.50
134	Dennis Eckersley	.20
135	Ryan Klesko	1.00
136	Dean Palmer	.20
137	Javy Lopez	.40
138	Greg Vaughn	.20
139	Vinny Castilla	.20
140	Cal Ripken Jr.	6.00
141	Ruben Rivera	.20
142	Mark Wohlers	.20
143	Tony Clark	1.25
144	Jose Rosado	.20
145	Tony Gwynn	3.50
146	Cecil Fielder	.40
147	Brian Jordan	.20
148	Bob Abreu	.20
149	Barry Larkin	.50
150	Robin Ventura	.20
151	John Olerud	.20
152	Rod Beck	.20
153	Vladimir Guerrero	2.50
154	Marty Cordova	.20
155	Todd Stottlemyre	.20
156	Hideo Nomo	1.50
157	Denny Neagle	.20
158	John Jaha	.20
159	Mo Vaughn	2.00
160	Andruw Jones	4.00
161	Moises Alou	.20
162	Larry Walker	.50
163	Eddie Murray (Season Highlights)	.50
164	Paul Molitor (Season Highlights)	.75
165	Checklist	.20

1997 Topps/ Chrome All-Stars

Topps Chrome All-Stars display the same 22 cards found in Topps Series I, however these are reprinted on a Chrome stock. Regular versions are seeded every 24 packs, while Refractor versions arrive every 72 packs.

		MT
Complete Set (22):		90.00
Common Player:		2.00
Refractors: 2.5x to 3x		
AS1	Ivan Rodriguez	5.00
AS2	Todd Hundley	3.00
AS3	Frank Thomas	12.00
AS4	Andres Galarraga	4.00
AS5	Chuck Knoblauch	2.00
AS6	Eric Young	2.00
AS7	Jim Thome	4.00
AS8	Chipper Jones	12.00
AS9	Cal Ripken Jr.	15.00
AS10	Barry Larkin	3.00
AS11	Albert Belle	5.00
AS12	Barry Bonds	5.00
AS13	Ken Griffey Jr.	20.00
AS14	Ellis Burks	2.00
AS15	Juan Gonzalez	10.00
AS16	Gary Sheffield	3.00
AS17	Andy Pettitte	4.00
AS18	Tom Glavine	3.00
AS19	Pat Hentgen	2.00
AS20	John Smoltz	2.00
AS21	Roberto Hernandez	2.00
AS22	Mark Wohlers	2.00

1997 Topps/Chrome Diamond Duos

Diamond Duos is the only one of the three insert sets in Chrome Baseball that was developed exclusively for this product. The set has 10 cards featuring two superstar teammates on double-sided chromium cards. Diamond Duos are found every 36 packs, while Refractor versions are found every 108 packs.

		MT
Complete Set (10):		120.00
Common Player:		3.00
Refractors: 2x to 3x		
DD1	Chipper Jones, Andruw Jones	15.00
DD2	Derek Jeter, Bernie Williams	15.00
DD3	Ken Griffey Jr., Jay Buhner	25.00
DD4	Kenny Lofton, Manny Ramirez	10.00
DD5	Jeff Bagwell, Craig Biggio	10.00
DD6	Juan Gonzalez, Ivan Rodriguez	12.00
DD7	Cal Ripken Jr., Brady Anderson	20.00
DD8	Mike Piazza, Hideo Nomo	15.00
DD9	Andres Galarraga, Dante Bichette	5.00
DD10	Frank Thomas, Albert Belle	20.00

1997 Topps/Chrome Season's Best

Season's Best includes the 25 players found in Topps Series II, but in a chromium version. The top five players from five statistical categories, including Leading Looters, Bleacher Reachers and Kings of Swing. Regular versions are seeded every 18 packs, with Refractors every 54 packs.

		MT
Complete Set (25):		100.00
Common Player:		2.50
Refractors: 2.5x to 3x		
1	Tony Gwynn	10.00

#	Player	Price
2	Frank Thomas	12.00
3	Ellis Burks	2.50
4	Paul Molitor	4.00
5	Chuck Knoblauch	2.50
6	Mark McGwire	25.00
7	Brady Anderson	2.50
8	Ken Griffey Jr.	20.00
9	Albert Belle	5.00
10	Andres Galarraga	4.00
11	Andres Galarraga	4.00
12	Albert Belle	5.00
13	Juan Gonzalez	10.00
14	Mo Vaughn	5.00
15	Rafael Palmeiro	3.00
16	John Smoltz	3.00
17	Andy Pettitte	4.00
18	Pat Hentgen	2.50
19	Mike Mussina	5.00
20	Andy Benes	2.50
21	Kenny Lofton	5.00
22	Tom Goodwin	2.50
23	Otis Nixon	2.50
24	Eric Young	2.50
25	Lance Johnson	2.50

1997 Topps/Gallery

The second year of Gallery features 180 cards printed on extra-thick 24-point stock. Card fronts feature a player photo surrounded by an embossed foil "frame" to give each card the look of a piece of artwork. Backs contain career stats and biographical information on each player. Inserts include Peter Max Serigraphs, Signature Series Serigraphs, Player's Private Issue (parallel set), Photo Gallery and Gallery of Heroes. Cards were sold exclusively in hobby shops in eight-card packs for $4 each.

		MT
Complete Set (180):		50.00
Common Player:		.15
Unlisted Semistars: .30 to .50		
Wax Box:		60.00
1	Paul Molitor	1.00
2	Devon White	.15
3	Andres Galarraga	.30
4	Cal Ripken Jr.	4.00
5	Tony Gwynn	2.00
6	Mike Stanley	.15
7	Orel Hershiser	.15
8	Jose Canseco	.40
9	Chili Davis	.15
10	Harold Baines	.15
11	Rickey Henderson	.15
12	Darryl Strawberry	.15
13	Todd Worrell	.15
14	Cecil Fielder	.30
15	Gary Gaetti	.15
16	Bobby Bonilla	.15
17	Will Clark	.40
18	Kevin Brown	.15
19	Tom Glavine	.30
20	Wade Boggs	.30
21	Edgar Martinez	.15
22	Lance Johnson	.15
23	Gregg Jefferies	.15
24	Bip Roberts	.15
25	Tony Phillips	.15
26	Greg Maddux	3.00
27	Mickey Tettleton	.15
28	Terry Steinbach	.15
29	Ryne Sandberg	1.50
30	Wally Joyner	.15
31	Joe Carter	.25
32	Ellis Burks	.15
33	Fred McGriff	.40
34	Barry Larkin	.40
35	John Franco	.15
36	Rafael Palmeiro	.30
37	Mark McGwire	5.00
38	Ken Caminiti	.40
39	David Cone	.25
40	Julio Franco	.15
41	Roger Clemens	2.00
42	Barry Bonds	1.50
43	Dennis Eckersley	.15
44	Eddie Murray	.50
45	Paul O'Neill	.15
46	Craig Biggio	.15
47	Roberto Alomar	1.00
48	Mark Grace	.30
49	Matt Williams	.50
50	Jay Buhner	.25
51	John Smoltz	.40
52	Randy Johnson	.75
53	Ramon Martinez	.15
54	Curt Schilling	.15
55	Gary Sheffield	.50
56	Jack McDowell	.15
57	Brady Anderson	.15
58	Dante Bichette	.30
59	Ron Gant	.30
60	Alex Fernandez	.30
61	Moises Alou	.15
62	Travis Fryman	.15
63	Dean Palmer	.15
64	Todd Hundley	.30
65	Jeff Brantley	.15
66	Bernard Gilkey	.15
67	Geronimo Berroa	.15
68	John Wetteland	.15
69	Robin Ventura	.15
70	Ray Lankford	.15
71	Kevin Appier	.15
72	Larry Walker	.40
73	Juan Gonzalez	2.50
74	Jeff King	.15
75	Greg Vaughn	.15
76	Steve Finley	.15
77	Brian McRae	.15
78	Paul Sorrento	.15
79	Ken Griffey Jr.	5.00
80	Omar Vizquel	.15
81	Jose Mesa	.15
82	Albert Belle	1.25
83	Glenallen Hill	.15
84	Sammy Sosa	3.00
85	Andy Benes	.15
86	David Justice	.40
87	Marquis Grissom	.15
88	John Olerud	.15
89	Tino Martinez	.30
90	Frank Thomas	3.00
91	Raul Mondesi	.40
92	Steve Trachsel	.15
93	Jim Edmonds	.15
94	Rusty Greer	.15
95	Joey Hamilton	.15
96	Ismael Valdes	.15
97	Dave Nilsson	.15
98	John Jaha	.15
99	Alex Gonzalez	.15
100	Javy Lopez	.30
101	Ryan Klesko	.75
102	Tim Salmon	.30
103	Bernie Williams	1.00
104	Roberto Hernandez	.15
105	Chuck Knoblauch	.30
106	Mike Lansing	.15
107	Vinny Castilla	.15
108	Reggie Sanders	.15
109	Mo Vaughn	1.50
110	Rondell White	.15
111	Ivan Rodriguez	1.00
112	Mike Mussina	1.00
113	Carlos Baerga	.15
114	Jeff Conine	.15
115	Jim Thome	.50
116	Manny Ramirez	1.50
117	Kenny Lofton	1.50
118	Wilson Alvarez	.15
119	Eric Karros	.15
120	Robb Nen	.15
121	Mark Wohlers	.15
122	Ed Sprague	.15
123	Pat Hentgen	.15
124	Juan Guzman	.15
125	Derek Bell	.15
126	Jeff Bagwell	2.00
127	Eric Young	.15
128	John Valentin	.15
129	Al Martin (photo actually Javy Lopez)	.45
130	Trevor Hoffman	.15
131	Henry Rodriguez	.15
132	Pedro Martinez	.40
133	Mike Piazza	3.00
134	Brian Jordan	.15
135	Jose Valentin	.15
136	Jeff Cirillo	.15
137	Chipper Jones	3.00
138	Ricky Bottalico	.15
139	Hideo Nomo	1.00
140	Troy Percival	.15
141	Rey Ordonez	.15
142	Edgar Renteria	.15
143	Luis Castillo	.25
144	Vladimir Guerrero	1.50
145	Jeff D'Amico	.15
146	Andruw Jones	2.50
147	Darin Erstad	2.50
148	Bob Abreu	.15
149	Carlos Delgado	.15
150	Jamey Wright	.15
151	Nomar Garciaparra	2.50
152	Jason Kendall	.15
153	Jermaine Allensworth	.15
154	Scott Rolen	2.50
155	Rocky Coppinger	.15
156	Paul Wilson	.15
157	Garret Anderson	.15
158	Mariano Rivera	.30
159	Ruben Rivera	.40
160	Andy Pettitte	1.50
161	Derek Jeter	2.50
162	Neifi Perez	.15
163	Ray Durham	.15
164	James Baldwin	.15
165	Marty Cordova	.15
166	Tony Clark	.60
167	Michael Tucker	.15
168	Mike Sweeney	.15
169	Johnny Damon	.15
170	Jermaine Dye	.15
171	Alex Ochoa	.15
172	Jason Isringhausen	.15
173	Mark Grudzielanek	.15
174	Jose Rosado	.15
175	Todd Hollandsworth	.15
176	Alan Benes	.30
177	Jason Giambi	.15
178	Billy Wagner	.15
179	Justin Thompson	.15
180	Todd Walker	.75

1997 Topps/Gallery of Heroes

This 10-card die-cut insert features a design resembling stained glass. Cards were inserted 1:36 packs.

Values shown reflect the market as of January, 1999. On-field performances of current players in the 1999 baseball season are not factored in.

		MT
Complete Set (10):		180.00
Common Player:		8.00
GH1	Derek Jeter	20.00
GH2	Chipper Jones	25.00
GH3	Frank Thomas	30.00
GH4	Ken Griffey Jr.	40.00
GH5	Cal Ripken Jr.	30.00
GH6	Mark McGwire	40.00
GH7	Mike Piazza	25.00
GH8	Jeff Bagwell	18.00
GH9	Tony Gwynn	18.00
GH10	Mo Vaughn	10.00

1997 Topps/Gallery Peter Max

Noted artist Peter Max has painted renditions of 10 superstar players and offered his commentary about those players on the backs. Cards were inserted 1:24 packs. In addition, Max-autographed cards signed and numbered from an edition of 40 are inserted 1:1,200 packs.

		MT
Complete Set (10):		100.00
Common Player:		4.00
Complete Autographed Set (10):		2400.00
Common Autographed Player:		150.00
1	Ken Griffey Jr.	20.00
1	Ken Griffey Jr. (autographed)	550.00
2	Frank Thomas	15.00
2	Frank Thomas (autographed)	500.00

3	Albert Belle	6.00
3	Albert Belle (autographed)	150.00
4	Barry Bonds	6.00
4	Barry Bonds (autographed)	150.00
5	Derek Jeter	12.00
5	Derek Jeter (autographed)	250.00
6	Ken Caminiti	4.00
6	Ken Caminiti (autographed)	150.00
7	Mike Piazza	12.00
7	Mike Piazza (autographed)	400.00
8	Cal Ripken Jr.	15.00
8	Cal Ripken Jr. (autographed)	450.00
9	Mark McGwire	20.00
9	Mark McGwire (autographed)	400.00
10	Chipper Jones	12.00
10	Chipper Jones (autographed)	300.00

1997 Topps/Gallery Photo Gallery

This 21-card set features full-bleed, high-gloss action photos of some of the game's top stars. Cards were inserted 1:24 packs.

		MT
Complete Set (16):		150.00
Common Player:		4.00
PG1	World Series	10.00
PG2	Paul Molitor	8.00
PG3	Eddie Murray	7.00
PG4	Ken Griffey Jr.	35.00
PG5	Chipper Jones	20.00
PG6	Derek Jeter	20.00
PG7	Frank Thomas	25.00
PG8	Mark McGwire	35.00
PG9	Kenny Lofton	8.00
PG10	Gary Sheffield	6.00
PG11	Mike Piazza	20.00
PG12	Vinny Castilla	4.00
PG13	Andres Galarraga	4.00
PG14	Andy Pettitte	8.00
PG15	Robin Ventura	4.00
PG16	Barry Larkin	4.00

1997 Topps/Gallery Players Private Issue

A parallel version of the Gallery issue called Players Private Issue was produced as a 1:12 pack insert. The PPI cards differ from trhe regular version in the use of a "PPI-" prefix to the card number on front and the application of a small silver PPI seal in a lower corner. On back, the line "One of 250 Issued" has been added.

		MT
Complete Set (180):		1700.
Common Player:		5.00
Semistars:		10.00
Stars: 25x to 35x		
1	Paul Molitor	35.00
2	Devon White	5.00
3	Andres Galarraga	10.00
4	Cal Ripken Jr.	125.00
5	Tony Gwynn	80.00
6	Mike Stanley	5.00
7	Orel Hershiser	5.00
8	Jose Canseco	10.00
9	Chili Davis	5.00
10	Harold Baines	5.00
11	Rickey Henderson	5.00
12	Darryl Strawberry	5.00
13	Todd Worrell	5.00
14	Cecil Fielder	10.00
15	Gary Gaetti	5.00
16	Bobby Bonilla	5.00
17	Will Clark	10.00

18	Kevin Brown	5.00
19	Tom Glavine	10.00
20	Wade Boggs	10.00
21	Edgar Martinez	5.00
22	Lance Johnson	5.00
23	Gregg Jefferies	5.00
24	Bip Roberts	5.00
25	Tony Phillips	5.00
26	Greg Maddux	90.00
27	Mickey Tettleton	5.00
28	Terry Steinbach	5.00
29	Ryne Sandberg	40.00
30	Wally Joyner	5.00
31	Joe Carter	10.00
32	Ellis Burks	5.00
33	Fred McGriff	12.00
34	Barry Larkin	12.00
35	John Franco	5.00
36	Rafael Palmeiro	10.00
37	Mark McGwire	200.00
38	Ken Caminiti	15.00
39	David Cone	10.00
40	Julio Franco	5.00
41	Roger Clemens	50.00
42	Barry Bonds	50.00
43	Dennis Eckersley	5.00
44	Eddie Murray	30.00
45	Paul O'Neill	5.00
46	Craig Biggio	10.00
47	Roberto Alomar	35.00
48	Mark Grace	10.00
49	Matt Williams	15.00
50	Jay Buhner	10.00
51	John Smoltz	10.00
52	Randy Johnson	35.00
53	Ramon Martinez	5.00
54	Curt Schilling	5.00
55	Gary Sheffield	15.00
56	Jack McDowell	5.00
57	Brady Anderson	5.00
58	Dante Bichette	10.00
59	Ron Gant	10.00
60	Alex Fernandez	8.00
61	Moises Alou	5.00
62	Travis Fryman	5.00
63	Dean Palmer	5.00
64	Todd Hundley	10.00
65	Jeff Brantley	5.00
66	Bernard Gilkey	5.00
67	Geronimo Berroa	5.00
68	John Wetteland	5.00
69	Robin Ventura	5.00
70	Ray Lankford	5.00
71	Kevin Appier	5.00
72	Larry Walker	20.00
73	Juan Gonzalez	80.00
74	Jeff King	5.00
75	Greg Vaughn	5.00
76	Steve Finley	5.00
77	Brian McRae	5.00
78	Paul Sorrento	5.00
79	Ken Griffey Jr.	150.00
80	Omar Vizquel	5.00
81	Jose Mesa	5.00
82	Albert Belle	50.00
83	Glenallen Hill	5.00
84	Sammy Sosa	100.00
85	Andy Benes	5.00
86	David Justice	10.00
87	Marquis Grissom	5.00
88	John Olerud	5.00
89	Tino Martinez	10.00
90	Frank Thomas	125.00
91	Raul Mondesi	10.00
92	Steve Trachsel	5.00
93	Jim Edmonds	5.00
94	Rusty Greer	5.00
95	Joey Hamilton	5.00
96	Ismael Valdes	5.00
97	Dave Nilsson	5.00
98	John Jaha	5.00
99	Alex Gonzalez	5.00
100	Javy Lopez	10.00
101	Ryan Klesko	30.00
102	Tim Salmon	10.00
103	Bernie Williams	35.00
104	Roberto Hernandez	5.00
105	Chuck Knoblauch	10.00
106	Mike Lansing	5.00
107	Vinny Castilla	5.00
108	Reggie Sanders	5.00
109	Mo Vaughn	50.00
110	Rondell White	5.00
111	Ivan Rodriguez	35.00
112	Mike Mussina	35.00
113	Carlos Baerga	5.00

114	Jeff Conine	5.00
115	Jim Thome	20.00
116	Manny Ramirez	40.00
117	Kenny Lofton	50.00
118	Wilson Alvarez	5.00
119	Eric Karros	5.00
120	Robb Nen	5.00
121	Mark Wohlers	5.00
122	Ed Sprague	5.00
123	Pat Hentgen	5.00
124	Juan Guzman	5.00
125	Derek Bell	5.00
126	Jeff Bagwell	80.00
127	Eric Young	5.00
128	John Valentin	5.00
129	Al Martin	5.00
130	Trevor Hoffman	5.00
131	Henry Rodriguez	5.00
132	Pedro Martinez	10.00
133	Mike Piazza	100.00
134	Brian Jordan	5.00
135	Jose Valentin	5.00
136	Jeff Cirillo	5.00
137	Chipper Jones	100.00
138	Ricky Bottalico	5.00
139	Hideo Nomo	35.00
140	Troy Percival	5.00
141	Rey Ordonez	5.00
142	Edgar Renteria	5.00
143	Luis Castillo	8.00
144	Vladimir Guerrero	60.00
145	Jeff D'Amico	5.00
146	Andruw Jones	80.00
147	Darin Erstad	60.00
148	Bob Abreu	5.00
149	Carlos Delgado	5.00
150	Jamey Wright	5.00
151	Nomar Garciaparra	50.00
152	Jason Kendall	5.00
153	Jermaine Allensworth	5.00
154	Scott Rolen	50.00
155	Rocky Coppinger	5.00
156	Paul Wilson	5.00
157	Garret Anderson	5.00
158	Mariano Rivera	10.00
159	Ruben Rivera	10.00
160	Andy Pettitte	50.00
161	Derek Jeter	100.00
162	Neifi Perez	5.00
163	Ray Durham	5.00
164	James Baldwin	5.00
165	Marty Cordova	5.00
166	Tony Clark	40.00
167	Michael Tucker	5.00
168	Mike Sweeney	5.00
169	Johnny Damon	5.00
170	Jermaine Dye	5.00
171	Alex Ochoa	5.00
172	Jason Isringhausen	5.00
173	Mark Grudzielanek	5.00
174	Jose Rosado	5.00
175	Todd Hollandsworth	5.00
176	Alan Benes	10.00
177	Jason Giambi	5.00
178	Billy Wagner	5.00
179	Justin Thompson	5.00
180	Todd Walker	20.00

1998 Topps

Topps was issued in two series in 1998 that totalled 503 cards, with 282 in Series I and 220 in Series ii. Cards featured a gold border instead of the traditional white used in past years and the product featured Roberto Clemente inserts and a tribute card No. 21 in the base set. Series Highlights, Expansion Team Prospects, Interleague Highlights, Season Highlights, Prospects and Draft Picks. Subsets in Series II included: Expansion Teams, InterLeague Preview, Season Highlights, Prospects and Draft Picks. Every card in the set is paralleled in a Minted in Cooperstown insert that was stamped on-site at the Baseball Hall of Fame in Cooperstown. Inserts in Series I include: Roberto Clemente Reprints, Clemente Finest, Clemente Tribute, Memorabililia Madness, Etch a Sketch, Mystery Finest, Flashback and Baby Boomers. Inserts in Series II included: Clemente Reprints, Clemente Finest, 1998 Rookie Class, Mystery Finest, Milestones, Focal Points, and Clout 9.

		MT
Complete Set (503):		40.00
Complete Series I Set (282):		20.00
Complete Series II Set (220):		20.00
Common Player:		.05
Minted: 5x to 10x		
Inserted 1:8		
Wax Box:		45.00
1	Tony Gwynn	1.25
2	Larry Walker	.25
3	Billy Wagner	.05
4	Denny Neagle	.05
5	Vladimir Guerrero	.75
6	Kevin Brown	.10
7	NOT ISSUED	
8	Mariano Rivera	.15
9	Tony Clark	.50
10	Deion Sanders	.15
11	Francisco Cordova	.05
12	Matt Williams	.20
13	Carlos Baerga	.05
14	Mo Vaughn	.60
15	Bobby Witt	.05
16	Matt Stairs	.05
17	Chan Ho Park	.10
18	Mike Bordick	.05
19	Michael Tucker	.05
20	Frank Thomas	2.00
21	Roberto Clemente	2.00
22	Dmitri Young	.05
23	Steve Trachsel	.05
24	Jeff Kent	.05
25	Scott Rolen	1.25
26	John Thomson	.05
27	Joe Vitiello	.05
28	Eddie Guardado	.05
29	Charlie Hayes	.05
30	Juan Gonzalez	1.25
31	Garret Anderson	.05
32	John Jaha	.05
33	Omar Vizquel	.05
34	Brian Hunter	.05
35	Jeff Bagwell	1.00
36	Mark Lemke	.05
37	Doug Glanville	.05
38	Dan Wilson	.05
39	Steve Cooke	.05
40	Chili Davis	.05
41	Mike Cameron	.05
42	F.P. Santangelo	.05
43	Brad Ausmus	.05
44	Gary DiSarcina	.05
45	Pat Hentgen	.05
46	Wilton Guerrero	.05
47	Devon White	.05
48	Danny Patterson	.05
49	Pat Meares	.05
50	Rafael Palmeiro	.15
51	Mark Gardner	.05
52	Jeff Blauser	.05
53	Dave Hollins	.05

54	Carlos Garcia	.05
55	Ben McDonald	.05
56	John Mabry	.05
57	Trevor Hoffman	.05
58	Tony Fernandez	.05
59	Rich Loiselle	.05
60	Mark Leiter	.05
61	Pat Kelly	.05
62	John Flaherty	.05
63	Roger Bailey	.05
64	Tom Gordon	.05
65	Ryan Klesko	.25
66	Darryl Hamilton	.05
67	Jim Eisenreich	.05
68	Butch Huskey	.05
69	Mark Grudzielanek	.05
70	Marquis Grissom	.15
71	Mark McLemore	.05
72	Gary Gaetti	.05
73	Greg Gagne	.05
74	Lyle Mouton	.05
75	Jim Edmonds	.15
76	Shawn Green	.05
77	Greg Vaughn	.05
78	Terry Adams	.05
79	*Kevin Polcovich*	.20
80	Troy O'Leary	.05
81	Jeff Shaw	.05
82	Rich Becker	.05
83	David Wells	.05
84	Steve Karsay	.05
85	Charles Nagy	.05
86	B.J. Surhoff	.05
87	Jamey Wright	.05
88	James Baldwin	.05
89	Edgardo Alfonzo	.05
90	Jay Buhner	.15
91	Brady Anderson	.15
92	Scott Servais	.05
93	Edgar Renteria	.05
94	Mike Lieberthal	.05
95	Rick Aguilera	.05
96	Walt Weiss	.05
97	Deivi Cruz	.05
98	Kurt Abbott	.05
99	Henry Rodriguez	.05
100	Mike Piazza	1.50
101	Bill Taylor	.05
102	Todd Zeile	.05
103	Rey Ordonez	.05
104	Willie Greene	.05
105	Tony Womack	.05
106	Mike Sweeney	.05
107	Jeffrey Hammonds	.05
108	Kevin Orie	.05
109	Alex Gonzalez	.05
110	Jose Canseco	.20
111	Paul Sorrento	.05
112	Joey Hamilton	.05
113	Brad Radke	.05
114	Steve Avery	.05
115	Esteban Loaiza	.05
116	Stan Javier	.05
117	Chris Gomez	.05
118	Royce Clayton	.05
119	Orlando Merced	.05
120	Kevin Appier	.05
121	Mel Nieves	.05
122	Joe Girardi	.05
123	Rico Brogna	.05
124	Kent Mercker	.05
125	Manny Ramirez	.50
126	Jeromy Burnitz	.05
127	Kevin Foster	.05
128	Matt Morris	.05
129	Jason Dickson	.05
130	Tom Glavine	.15
131	Wally Joyner	.05
132	Rick Reed	.05
133	Todd Jones	.05
134	Dave Martinez	.05
135	Sandy Alomar	.05
136	Mike Lansing	.05
137	Sean Berry	.05
138	Doug Jones	.05
139	Todd Stottlemyre	.05
140	Jay Bell	.05
141	Jaime Navarro	.05
142	Chris Hoiles	.05
143	Joey Cora	.05
144	Scott Spiezio	.05
145	Joe Carter	.15
146	Jose Guillen	.50
147	Damion Easley	.05
148	Lee Stevens	.05
149	Alex Fernandez	.05

150	Randy Johnson	.40
151	J.T. Snow	.15
152	Chuck Finley	.05
153	Bernard Gilkey	.05
154	David Segui	.05
155	Dante Bichette	.15
156	Kevin Stocker	.05
157	Carl Everett	.05
158	Jose Valentin	.05
159	Pokey Reese	.05
160	Derek Jeter	1.50
161	Roger Pavlik	.05
162	Mark Wohlers	.05
163	Ricky Bottalico	.05
164	Ozzie Guillen	.05
165	Mike Mussina	.50
166	Gary Sheffield	.20
167	Hideo Nomo	.50
168	Mark Grace	.20
169	Aaron Sele	.05
170	Darryl Kile	.10
171	Shawn Estes	.05
172	Vinny Castilla	.10
173	Ron Coomer	.05
174	Jose Rosado	.05
175	Kenny Lofton	.60
176	Jason Giambi	.10
177	Hal Morris	.05
178	Darren Bragg	.05
179	Orel Hershiser	.05
180	Ray Lankford	.10
181	Hideki Irabu	.75
182	Kevin Young	.05
183	Javy Lopez	.15
184	Jeff Montgomery	.05
185	Mike Holtz	.05
186	George Williams	.05
187	Cal Eldred	.05
188	Tom Candiotti	.05
189	Glenallen Hill	.05
190	Brian Giles	.05
191	Dave Mlicki	.05
192	Garrett Stephenson	.05
193	Jeff Frye	.05
194	Joe Oliver	.05
195	Bob Hamelin	.05
196	Luis Sojo	.05
197	LaTroy Hawkins	.05
198	Kevin Elster	.05
199	Jeff Reed	.05
200	Dennis Eckersley	.15
201	Bill Mueller	.05
202	Russ Davis	.05
203	Armando Benitez	.05
204	Quilvio Veras	.05
205	Tim Naehring	.05
206	Quinton McCracken	.05
207	Raul Casanova	.05
208	Matt Lawton	.05
209	Luis Alicea	.05
210	Luis Gonzalez	.05
211	Allen Watson	.05
212	Gerald Williams	.05
213	David Bell	.05
214	Todd Hollandsworth	.05
215	Wade Boggs	.15
216	Jose Mesa	.05
217	Jamie Moyer	.05
218	Darren Daulton	.10
219	Mickey Morandini	.05
220	Rusty Greer	.15
221	Jim Bullinger	.05
222	Jose Offerman	.05
223	Matt Karchner	.05
224	Woody Williams	.05
225	Mark Loretta	.05
226	Mike Hampton	.05
227	Willie Adams	.05
228	Scott Hatteberg	.05
229	Rich Amaral	.05
230	Terry Steinbach	.05
231	Glendon Rusch	.05
232	Bret Boone	.05
233	Robert Person	.05
234	Jose Hernandez	.05
235	Doug Drabek	.05
236	Jason McDonald	.05
237	Chris Widger	.05
238	*Tom Martin*	.05
239	Dave Burba	.05
240	Pete Rose	.05
241	Bobby Ayala	.05
242	Tim Wakefield	.05
243	Dennis Springer	.05
244	Tim Belcher	.05

245	Jon Garland, Geoff Goetz (Draft Pick)	.15
246	Glenn Davis, Lance Berkman (Draft Pick)	.50
247	Vernon Wells, Aaron Akin (Draft Pick)	.25
248	Adam Kennedy, Jason Romano (Draft Pick)	.10
249	Jason Dellaero, Troy Cameron (Draft Pick)	.20
250	Alex Sanchez, *Jared Sandberg* (Expansion Team Prospects)	.20
251	Pablo Ortega, Jim Manias (Expansion Team Prospects)	.15
252	Jason Conti, *Mike Stoner* (Expansion Team Prospects)	.50
253	John Patterson, Larry Rodriguez (Expansion Team Prospects)	.20
254	Adrian Beltre, *Ryan Minor*, Aaron Boone (Prospect)	1.00
255	Ben Grieve, Brian Buchanan, Dermal Brown (Prospect)	1.00
256	Carl Pavano, Kerry Wood, Gil Meche (Prospect)	3.00
257	David Ortiz, Daryle Ward, Richie Sexson (Prospect)	.35
258	Randy Winn, Juan Encarnacion, Andrew Vessel (Prospect)	.25
259	Kris Benson, Travis Smith, Courtney Duncan (Prospect)	.40
260	Chad Hermansen, Brent Butler, *Warren Morris* (Prospect)	.50
261	Ben Davis, Elieser Marrero, Ramon Hernandez (Prospect)	.05
262	Eric Chavez, Russell Branyan, Russ Johnson (Prospect)	.40
263	Todd Dunwoody, John Barnes, *Ryan Jackson* (Prospect)	.25
264	Matt Clement, Roy Halladay, *Brian Fuentes* (Prospect)	.40
265	Randy Johnson (Season Highlight)	.25
266	Kevin Brown (Season Highlight)	.05
267	Ricardo Rincon, Cordova, Rincon (Season Highlight)	.05
268	Nomar Garciaparra (Season Highlight)	.75
269	Tino Martinez (Season Highlight)	.10
270	Chuck Knoblauch (Interleague)	.15
271	Pedro Martinez (Interleague)	.10
272	Denny Neagle (Interleague)	.05
273	Juan Gonzalez (Interleague)	.60
274	Andres Galarraga (Interleague)	.10
275	Checklist	.05
276	Checklist	.05
277	(World Series)	.05
278	(World Series)	.05
279	(World Series)	.05
280	(World Series)	.05
281	(World Series)	.05
282	(World Series)	.05
283	(World Series)	.05
284	Tino Martinez	.20
285	Roberto Alomar	.50
286	Jeff King	.05
287	Brian Jordan	.05
288	Darin Erstad	.60
289	Ken Caminiti	.20
290	Jim Thome	.40
291	Paul Molitor	.50
292	Ivan Rodriguez	.60
293	Bernie Williams	.50
294	Todd Hundley	.15
295	Andres Galarraga	.20
296	Greg Maddux	1.50
297	Edgar Martinez	.10
298	Ron Gant	.15
299	Derek Bell	.05

300	Roger Clemens	1.00
301	Rondell White	.15
302	Barry Larkin	.15
303	Robin Ventura	.10
304	Jason Kendall	.05
305	Chipper Jones	1.50
306	John Franco	.05
307	Sammy Sosa	1.50
308	Troy Percival	.05
309	Chuck Knoblauch	.25
310	Ellis Burks	.15
311	Al Martin	.05
312	Tim Salmon	.25
313	Moises Alou	.15
314	Lance Johnson	.05
315	Justin Thompson	.15
316	Will Clark	.20
317	Barry Bonds	.60
318	Craig Biggio	.20
319	John Smoltz	.15
320	Cal Ripken Jr.	2.00
321	Ken Griffey Jr.	2.50
322	Paul O'Neill	.15
323	Todd Helton	.60
324	John Olerud	.15
325	Mark McGwire	3.00
326	Jose Cruz Jr.	1.50
327	Jeff Cirillo	.05
328	Dean Palmer	.05
329	John Wetteland	.05
330	Steve Finley	.05
331	Albert Belle	.60
332	Curt Schilling	.15
333	Raul Mondesi	.20
334	Andruw Jones	.75
335	Nomar Garciaparra	1.50
336	David Justice	.20
337	Andy Pettitte	.40
338	Pedro Martinez	.25
339	Travis Miller	.05
340	Chris Stynes	.05
341	Gregg Jefferies	.05
342	Jeff Fassero	.05
343	Craig Counsell	.05
344	Wilson Alvarez	.05
345	Bip Roberts	.05
346	Kelvim Escobar	.05
347	Mark Bellhorn	.05
348	Rickey Henderson	.05
349	Fred McGriff	.15
350	Chuck Carr	.05
351	Bob Abreu	.05
352	Juan Guzman	.05
353	Fernando Vina	.05
354	Andy Benes	.05
355	Dave Nilsson	.05
356	Bobby Bonilla	.10
357	Ismael Valdes	.05
358	Carlos Perez	.05
359	Kirk Rueter	.05
360	Bartolo Colon	.05
361	Mel Rojas	.05
362	Johnny Damon	.05
363	Geronimo Berroa	.05
364	Reggie Sanders	.05
365	Jermaine Allensworth	.05
366	Orlando Cabrera	.05
367	Jorge Fabregas	.05
368	Scott Stahoviak	.05
369	Ken Cloude	.05
370	Donovan Osborne	.05
371	Roger Cedeno	.05
372	Neifi Perez	.05
373	Chris Holt	.05
374	Cecil Fielder	.15
375	Marty Cordova	.05
376	Tom Goodwin	.05
377	Jeff Suppan	.05
378	Jeff Brantley	.05
379	Mark Langston	.05
380	Shane Reynolds	.05
381	Mike Fetters	.05
382	Todd Greene	.05
383	Ray Durham	.05
384	Carlos Delgado	.05
385	Jeff D'Amico	.05
386	Brian McRae	.05
387	Alan Benes	.15
388	Heathcliff Slocumb	.05
389	Eric Young	.05
390	Travis Fryman	.05
391	David Cone	.15
392	Otis Nixon	.05
393	Jeremi Gonzalez	.05
394	Jeff Juden	.05
395	Jose Vizcaino	.05

396	Ugueth Urbina	.05
397	Ramon Martinez	.10
398	Robb Nen	.05
399	Harold Baines	.10
400	Delino DeShields	.05
401	John Burkett	.05
402	Sterling Hitchcock	.05
403	Mark Clark	.05
404	Mariano Duncan	.05
405	Scott Brosius	.05
406	Chad Curtis	.05
407	Brian Johnson	.05
408	Roberto Kelly	.05
409	Rey Sanchez	.05
410	Michael Tucker	.05
411	Mark Kotsay	.20
412	Mark Lewis	.05
413	Ryan McGuire	.05
414	Shawon Dunston	.10
415	Brad Rigby	.05
416	Scott Erickson	.05
417	Bobby Jones	.05
418	Darren Oliver	.05
419	John Smiley	.05
420	T.J. Mathews	.05
421	Dustin Hermanson	.05
422	Mike Timlin	.05
423	Willie Blair	.05
424	Manny Alexander	.05
425	Bob Tewksbury	.05
426	Pete Schourek	.05
427	Reggie Jefferson	.05
428	Ed Sprague	.05
429	Jeff Conine	.05
430	Roberto Hernandez	.05
431	Tom Pagnozzi	.05
432	Jaret Wright	1.50
433	Livan Hernandez	.20
434	Andy Ashby	.05
435	Todd Dunn	.05
436	Bobby Higginson	.05
437	Jack McDowell	.05
438	Jim Leyritz	.05
439	Matt Williams	.20
440	Brett Tomko	.05
441	Joe Randa	.05
442	Chris Carpenter	.05
443	Dennis Reyes	.05
444	Al Leiter	.05
445	Jason Schmidt	.05
446	Ken Hill	.05
447	Shannon Stewart	.05
448	Enrique Wilson	.05
449	Fernando Tatis	.05
450	Jimmy Key	.05
451	Darrin Fletcher	.05
452	John Valentin	.05
453	Kevin Tapani	.05
454	Eric Karros	.05
455	Jay Bell	.05
456	Walt Weiss	.05
457	Devon White	.05
458	Carl Pavano	.05
459	Mike Lansing	.05
460	John Flaherty	.05
461	Richard Hidalgo	.05
462	Quinton McCracken	.05
463	Karim Garcia	.15
464	Miguel Cairo	.05
465	Edwin Diaz	.05
466	Bobby Smith	.05
467	Yamil Benitez	.05
468	*Rich Butler*	.25
469	*Ben Ford*	.05
470	Bubba Trammell	.05
471	Brent Brede	.05
472	Brooks Kieschnick	.05
473	Carlos Castillo	.05
474	Brad Radke (Season Highlight)	.05
475	Roger Clemens (Season Highlight)	.50
476	Curt Schilling (Season Highlight)	.10
477	John Olerud (Season Highlight)	.05
478	Mark McGwire (Season Highlight)	1.50
479	Mike Piazza, Ken Griffey Jr. (Interleague)	1.00
480	Jeff Bagwell, Frank Thomas (Interleague)	1.00
481	Chipper Jones, Nomar Garciaparra (Interleague)	.75
482	Larry Walker, Juan Gonzalez (Interleague)	.60

483	Gary Sheffield, Tino Martinez (Interleague)	.15
484	Derrick Gibson, Michael Coleman, Norm Hutchins (Prospect)	.05
485	Braden Looper, Cliff Politte, Brian Rose (Prospect)	.25
486	Eric Milton, Jason Marquis, Corey Lee (Prospect)	.15
487	A.J. Hinch, Mark Osborne,*Robert Fick* (Prospect)	.50
488	Aramis Ramirez, Alex Gonzalez, Sean Casey (Prospect)	1.00
489	*Donnie Bridges,Tim Drew* (Draft Pick)	.40
490	*Ntema Ndungidi,Darnell McDonald* (Draft Pick)	.50
491	*Ryan Anderson*, Mark Mangum (Draft Pick)	1.50
492	J.J. Davis,*Troy Glaus* (Draft Pick)	1.50
493	Jayson Werth,*Dan Reichert* (Draft Pick)	.25
494	*John Curtice,Mike Cuddyer* (Draft Pick)	.50
495	*Jack Cust*, Jason Standridge (Draft Pick)	.40
496	Brian Anderson (Expansion Team Prospect)	.05
497	Tony Saunders (Expansion Team Prospect)	.05
498	Vladimir Nunez,*Jhensy Sandoval* (Expansion Team Prospect)	.10
499	Brad Penny, Nick Bierbrodt (Expansion Team Prospect)	.05
500	*Dustin Carr,Luis Cruz* (Expansion Team Prospect)	.25
501	*Marcus McCain,Cedrick Bowers* (Expansion Team Prospect)	.40
502	Checklist	.05
503	Checklist	.05
504	Alex Rodriguez	2.00

1998 Topps Baby Boomers

This 15-card retail exclusive insert was seeded one per 36 packs of Series I. It featured some of the top young players in the game and was numbered with a "BB" prefix.

		MT
Complete Set (15):		60.00
Common Player:		2.00
Inserted 1:36 retail		
BB1	Derek Jeter	10.00
BB2	Scott Rolen	8.00
BB3	Nomar Garciaparra	10.00
BB4	Jose Cruz Jr.	6.00
BB5	Darin Erstad	6.00
BB6	Todd Helton	4.00
BB7	Tony Clark	3.00
BB8	Jose Guillen	3.00
BB9	Andruw Jones	8.00
BB10	Vladimir Guerrero	5.00
BB11	Mark Kotsay	3.00
BB12	Todd Greene	2.00
BB13	Andy Pettitte	4.00
BB14	Justin Thompson	2.00
BB15	Alan Benes	2.00

1998 Topps Clout 9

Clout 9 captured nine players known for their statistical supremacy. Cards were numbered with a "C" prefix and inserted one per 72 packs of Series II.

		MT
Complete Set (9):		75.00
Common Player:		3.00
Inserted 1:72		
C1	Edgar Martinez	3.00
C2	Mike Piazza	15.00
C3	Frank Thomas	20.00
C4	Craig Biggio	4.00
C5	Vinny Castilla	4.00
C6	Jeff Blauser	3.00
C7	Barry Bonds	6.00
C8	Ken Griffey Jr.	25.00
C9	Larry Walker	5.00

1998 Topps Etch-A-Sketch

Etch a Sketch featured nine different players depicted by nationally acclaimed artist George Vlosich III. Known as "The Etch a Sketch Kid," Vlosich created each one of these Series I inserts, which were inserted at a rate of one per 36 packs.

		MT
Complete Set (9):		50.00
Common Player:		2.00
Inserted 1:36		
ES1	Albert Belle	4.00
ES2	Barry Bonds	3.00

ES3	Ken Griffey Jr.	12.00
ES4	Greg Maddux	8.00
ES5	Hideo Nomo	2.50
ES6	Mike Piazza	8.00
ES7	Cal Ripken Jr.	10.00
ES8	Frank Thomas	10.00
ES9	Mo Vaughn	3.00

1998 Topps Flashback

This double-sided insert showed "then and now" photos of 10 top major leaguers. One side contained a shot of the player in 1998, while the other side showed him at the beginning of his major league career. Flashback inserts were seeded one per 72 packs and numbered with a "FB" prefix.

		MT
Complete Set (10):		70.00
Common Player:		3.00
Inserted 1:72		
FB1	Barry Bonds	6.00
FB2	Ken Griffey Jr.	25.00
FB3	Paul Molitor	4.00
FB4	Randy Johnson	4.00
FB5	Cal Ripken Jr.	20.00
FB6	Tony Gwynn	12.00
FB7	Kenny Lofton	6.00
FB8	Gary Sheffield	4.00
FB9	Deion Sanders	3.00
FB10	Brady Anderson	3.00

1998 Topps Focal Point

This hobby exclusive insert contained 15 top players and focused on the skills that have made that player great. Focal Point inserts were available in Series II packs and seeded one per 36 packs, and were numbered with a "FP" prefix.

		MT
Complete Set (15):		120.00
Common Player:		2.00
Inserted 1:36		
FP1	Juan Gonzalez	10.00
FP2	Nomar Garciaparra	12.00
FP3	Jose Cruz Jr.	8.00
FP4	Cal Ripken Jr.	15.00
FP5	Ken Griffey Jr.	20.00
FP6	Ivan Rodriguez	5.00
FP7	Larry Walker	4.00
FP8	Barry Bonds	5.00
FP9	Roger Clemens	8.00
FP10	Frank Thomas	15.00
FP11	Chuck Knoblauch	3.00
FP12	Mike Piazza	12.00
FP13	Greg Maddux	12.00
FP14	Vladimir Guerrero	6.00
FP15	Andruw Jones	6.00

1998 Topps Hallbound

Hall Bound featured 15 top players who are considered locks to be inducted into the Hall of Fame when there career is over. This insert was exclusive to Series I hobby packs and seeded one per 36 packs.

		MT
Complete Set (15):		100.00
Common Player:		2.00
HB1	Paul Molitor	3.50
HB2	Tony Gwynn	8.00
HB3	Wade Boggs	2.50
HB4	Roger Clemens	7.00
HB5	Dennis Eckersley	2.00
HB6	Cal Ripken Jr.	14.00
HB7	Greg Maddux	10.00
HB8	Rickey Henderson	2.00
HB9	Ken Griffey Jr.	18.00
HB10	Frank Thomas	15.00
HB11	Mark McGwire	20.00
HB12	Barry Bonds	5.00
HB13	Mike Piazza	10.00
HB14	Juan Gonzalez	8.00
HB15	Randy Johnson	4.00

A player's name in *italic* type indicates a rookie card.

1998 Topps Inter-League Mystery Finest

Five of the 1997 season's most intriguing inter-league matchups are showcased with four cards each in Inter-League Mystery Finest. Regular versions of this Series I insert are seeded one per 36 packs, while Refractor versions are seeded one per 144 packs.

		MT
Complete Set (20):		100.00
Common Player:		2.00
Inserted 1:36		
Refractors: 2x to 3x		
Inserted 1:144		
ILM1	Chipper Jones	12.00
ILM2	Cal Ripken Jr.	15.00
ILM3	Greg Maddux	12.00
ILM4	Rafael Palmeiro	2.50
ILM5	Todd Hundley	2.00
ILM6	Derek Jeter	10.00
ILM7	John Olerud	2.00
ILM8	Tino Martinez	3.00
ILM9	Larry Walker	4.00
ILM10	Ken Griffey Jr.	20.00
ILM11	Andres Galarraga	3.00
ILM12	Randy Johnson	4.00
ILM13	Mike Piazza	12.00
ILM14	Jim Edmonds	2.00
ILM15	Eric Karros	2.00
ILM16	Tim Salmon	3.00
ILM17	Sammy Sosa	10.00
ILM18	Frank Thomas	15.00
ILM19	Mark Grace	3.00
ILM20	Albert Belle	5.00

1998 Topps Milestones

Milestones features 10 records that could be broken during the 1998 season and the player's who have the best shot at breaking them. This retail exclusive insert is seeded one per 36 packs and is numbered with a "MS" prefix.

		MT
Complete Set (10):		60.00
Common Player:		1.50
MS1	Barry Bonds	4.00
MS2	Roger Clemens	5.00
MS3	Dennis Eckersley	1.50
MS4	Juan Gonzalez	7.50
MS5	Ken Griffey Jr.	15.00
MS6	Tony Gwynn	7.50
MS7	Greg Maddux	10.00
MS8	Mark McGwire	15.00
MS9	Cal Ripken Jr.	12.50
MS10	Frank Thomas	12.50

1998 Topps Mystery Finest

This 20-card insert set features top players on bordered and borderless designs, with Refractor versions of each. Exclusive to Series II packs, bordered cards are seeded 1:36 packs, borderless are seeded 1:72 packs, bordered Refractors are 1:108 and borderless Refractors are seeded 1:288 packs. Mystery Finest inserts are numbered with a "M" prefix.

		MT
Complete Set (20):		200.00
Common Player:		2.50
Inserted 1:36		
Borderless 1:72: 1x to 1.5x		
Bordered Refractors 1:108: 2x		
Borderless Refractors 1:288: 4x to 5x		
M1	Nomar Garciaparra	15.00
M2	Chipper Jones	15.00
M3	Scott Rolen	10.00
M4	Albert Belle	6.00
M5	Mo Vaughn	6.00
M6	Jose Cruz Jr.	10.00
M7	Mark McGwire	20.00
M8	Derek Jeter	15.00
M9	Tony Gwynn	12.00
M10	Frank Thomas	20.00
M11	Tino Martinez	4.00
M12	Greg Maddux	15.00
M13	Juan Gonzalez	12.00
M14	Larry Walker	4.00
M15	Mike Piazza	15.00
M16	Cal Ripken Jr.	20.00
M17	Jeff Bagwell	10.00
M18	Andruw Jones	6.00
M19	Barry Bonds	6.00
M20	Ken Griffey Jr.	25.00

1998 Topps 98 Rookie Class

Rookie Class features 10 young stars from 1998 and was exclusive to Series II packs. The cards were inserted one per 12 packs and numbered with a "R" prefix.

		MT
Complete Set (10):		20.00
Common Player:		1.00
Inserted 1:12		
R1	Travis Lee	8.00
R2	Richard Hidalgo	1.00
R3	Todd Helton	3.00
R4	Paul Konerko	3.00
R5	Mark Kotsay	2.00
R6	Derrek Lee	1.50
R7	Eli Marrero	1.00
R8	Fernando Tatis	1.00
R9	Juan Encarnacion	1.00
R10	Ben Grieve	4.00

A player's name in *italic* type indicates a rookie card.

1998 Topps Opening Day

Topps Opening Day was a retail exclusive product included 165 cards, with 110 from Series I and 55 from Series II. The 55 cards from Series II were available in this product prior to the cards being released. Opening Day cards featured a silver border vs. the gold border in the base set, and included a silver Opening Day stamp.

		MT
Complete Set (165):		15.00
Common Player:		.05
1	Tony Gwynn	1.00
2	Larry Walker	.25
3	Billy Wagner	.05
4	Denny Neagle	.15
5	Vladimir Guerrero	.60
6	Kevin Brown	.15
7	Mariano Rivera	.15
8	Tony Clark	.40
9	Deion Sanders	.15
10	Matt Williams	.15
11	Carlos Baerga	.05
12	Mo Vaughn	.50
13	Chan Ho Park	.15
14	Frank Thomas	1.50
15	John Jaha	.05
16	Steve Trachsel	.05
17	Jeff Kent	.05
18	Scott Rolen	.60
19	Juan Gonzalez	1.00
20	Garret Anderson	.05
21	Roberto Clemente	1.50
22	Omar Vizquel	.05
23	Brian Hunter	.05
24	Jeff Bagwell	.75
25	Chili Davis	.05
26	Mike Cameron	.15
27	Pat Hentgen	.15
28	Wilton Guerrero	.05
29	Devon White	.05
30	Rafael Palmeiro	.20
31	Jeff Blauser	.05
32	Dave Hollins	.05
33	Trevor Hoffman	.10
34	Ryan Klesko	.25
35	Butch Huskey	.05
36	Mark Grudzielanek	.05
37	Marquis Grissom	.05
38	Jim Edmonds	.15
39	Greg Vaughn	.05
40	David Wells	.05
41	Charles Nagy	.05
42	B.J. Surhoff	.05
43	Edgardo Alfonzo	.05
44	Jay Buhner	.15
45	Brady Anderson	.15
46	Edgar Renteria	.05
47	Rick Aguilera	.05
48	Henry Rodriguez	.05
49	Mike Piazza	1.25
50	Todd Zeile	.05
51	Rey Ordonez	.05
52	Tony Womack	.05
53	Mike Sweeney	.05
54	Jeffrey Hammonds	.05
55	Kevin Orie	.05
56	Alex Gonzalez	.05
57	Jose Canseco	.20
58	Joey Hamilton	.05
59	Brad Radke	.05
60	Kevin Appier	.05
61	Manny Ramirez	.40
62	Jeromy Burnitz	.05
63	Matt Morris	.05
64	Jason Dickson	.05
65	Tom Glavine	.15
66	Wally Joyner	.05
67	Todd Jones	.05
68	Sandy Alomar	.10
69	Mike Lansing	.05
70	Todd Stottlemyre	.05
71	Jay Bell	.05
72	Joey Cora	.05
73	Scott Spiezio	.05
74	Joe Carter	.10
75	Jose Guillen	.20
76	Damion Easley	.05
77	Alex Fernandez	.05
78	Randy Johnson	.40
79	J.T. Snow	.15
80	Bernard Gilkey	.05
81	David Segui	.05
82	Dante Bichette	.15
83	Derek Jeter	1.25
84	Mark Wohlers	.05
85	Ricky Bottalico	.05
86	Mike Mussina	.40
87	Gary Sheffield	.20
88	Hideo Nomo	.40
89	Mark Grace	.15
90	Darryl Kile	.05
91	Shawn Estes	.15
92	Vinny Castilla	.10
93	Jose Rosado	.05
94	Kenny Lofton	.50
95	Jason Giambi	.05
96	Ray Lankford	.05
97	Hideki Irabu	.25
98	Javy Lopez	.05
99	Jeff Montgomery	.05
100	Dennis Eckersley	.05
101	Armando Benitez	.05
102	Tim Naehring	.05
103	Luis Gonzalez	.05
104	Todd Hollandsworth	.05
105	Wade Boggs	.15
106	Mickey Morandini	.05
107	Rusty Greer	.15
108	Terry Steinbach	.05
109	Pete Rose	.25
110	Checklist	.05
111	Tino Martinez	.25
112	Roberto Alomar	.40
113	Jeff Kent	.05
114	Brian Jordan	.05
115	Darin Erstad	.50
116	Ken Caminiti	.15
117	Jim Thome	.30
118	Paul Molitor	.40
119	Ivan Rodriguez	.50
120	Bernie Williams	.40
121	Todd Hundley	.15
122	Andres Galarraga	.20
123	Greg Maddux	1.25
124	Edgar Martinez	.05
125	Ron Gant	.05
126	Derek Bell	.05
127	Roger Clemens	.75
128	Rondell White	.15
129	Barry Larkin	.15
130	Robin Ventura	.15
131	Jason Kendall	.05
132	Chipper Jones	1.25
133	John Franco	.05
134	Sammy Sosa	1.00
135	Chuck Knoblauch	.20
136	Ellis Burks	.05
137	Al Martin	.05
138	Tim Salmon	.25
139	Moises Alou	.15
140	Lance Johnson	.05
141	Justin Thompson	.05
142	Will Clark	.15
143	Barry Bonds	.50
144	Craig Biggio	.20
145	John Smoltz	.15

146	Cal Ripken Jr.	1.50
147	Ken Griffey Jr.	2.00
148	Paul O'Neill	.15
149	Todd Helton	.60
150	John Olerud	.05
151	Mark McGwire	2.50
152	Jose Cruz Jr.	.75
153	Jeff Cirillo	.05
154	Dean Palmer	.05
155	John Wetteland	.05
156	Eric Karros	.05
157	Steve Finley	.05
158	Albert Belle	.50
159	Curt Schilling	.15
160	Raul Mondesi	.20
161	Andruw Jones	.60
162	Nomar Garciaparra	1.25
163	David Justice	.15
164	Andy Pettitte	.40
165	Pedro Martinez	.25

1998 Topps Roberto Clemente Finest

Clemente Finest inserts were included in both Series I and II at a rate of one per 72 packs. There were a total of 19 different, with odd numbers in Series I and even numbers in Series II. The insert helped honor the memory of the 25th anniversary of his death.

		MT
Complete Set (19):		150.00
Common Clemente:		10.00
Inserted 1:72		
Common Refractor:		25.00
Refractors: 2x to 3x		
Inserted 1:288		
1	(1955)	20.00
2	1956	10.00
3	(1957)	10.00
4	1958	10.00
5	(1959)	10.00
6	1960	10.00
7	(1961)	10.00
8	1962	10.00
9	(1963)	10.00
10	1964	10.00
11	(1965)	10.00
12	1966	10.00
14	1968	10.00
15	(1969)	10.00
16	1970	10.00
17	(1971)	10.00
18	1972()	10.00
19	1973	10.00

1998 Topps Roberto Clemente Reprints

Nineteen different Topps Clemente cards were reprinted with a gold foil stamp and included 1998 Topps. Odd numbers were included in Series I, while even numbers were inserted into Series II, both at a rate of one per 18 packs. The insert was created to honor the memory of the 25th anniversary of Clemente's death.

		MT
Complete Set (19):		70.00
Common Clemente:		4.00
Inserted 1:18		
1	1955	10.00
2	(1956)	4.00
3	1957	4.00
4	(1958)	4.00
5	1959	4.00
6	(1960)	4.00
7	1961	4.00
8	(1962)	4.00
9	1963	4.00
10	(1964)	4.00
11	1965	4.00
12	(1966)	4.00
13	1967	4.00
14	(1968)	4.00
15	1969	4.00
16	(1970)	4.00
17	1971	4.00
18	(1972)	4.00
19	1973	4.00

1998 Topps Roberto Clemente Tribute

Five Clemente Tribute cards were produced for Series I and inserted in one per 12 packs. The set features some classic photos of Clemente and honor his memory in the 25th anniversary of his death. Clemente Tribute cards are numbered with a "RC" prefix.

		MT
Complete Set (5):		12.00
Common Clemente:		3.00
Inserted 1:12		
RC1	Roberto Clemente	3.00
RC2	Roberto Clemente	3.00
RC3	Roberto Clemente	3.00
RC4	Roberto Clemente	3.00
RC5	Roberto Clemente	3.00

1998 Topps Chrome

All 502 cards from Topps Series I and II were reprinted in chromium versions for Topps Chrome. Chrome was released in two series, with Series I containing 282 cards and Series II including 220 cards. Four-card packs were sold for a suggested retail price of $3, while cards included a Topps Chrome logo. Chrome also included a sampling of the inserts from Topps, along with Refractor versions of every card and insert. Series I inserts included: Flashbacks, Baby Boomers and Hall Bound. Series II inserts included: Milestones, '98 Rookie Class and Clout 9.

		MT
Complete Set (502):		250.00
Complete Series I Set (282):		160.00
Complete Series II Set (220):		90.00
Common Player:		.25
Unlisted Stars: 1.00 to 2.00		
Star Refractors: 10x to 15x		
Yng Stars & RC's: 6x to 12x		
Inserted 1:12		
Wax Box:		100.00
1	Tony Gwynn	4.00
2	Larry Walker	1.00
3	Billy Wagner	.25
4	Denny Neagle	.25
5	Vladimir Guerrero	2.50
6	Kevin Brown	.50
8	Mariano Rivera	.75
9	Tony Clark	1.50
10	Deion Sanders	.75
11	Francisco Cordova	.25
12	Matt Williams	1.00
13	Carlos Baerga	.25
14	Mo Vaughn	2.00
15	Bobby Witt	.25
16	Matt Stairs	.25
17	Chan Ho Park	.50
18	Mike Bordick	.25
19	Michael Tucker	.25
20	Frank Thomas	6.00
21	Roberto Clemente (Tribute)	6.00
22	Dmitri Young	.25
23	Steve Trachsel	.25
24	Jeff Kent	.25
25	Scott Rolen	4.00
26	John Thomson	.25
27	Joe Vitiello	.25
28	Eddie Guardado	.25
29	Charlie Hayes	.25
30	Juan Gonzalez	4.00
31	Garret Anderson	.25
32	John Jaha	.25
33	Omar Vizquel	.25
34	Brian Hunter	.25
35	Jeff Bagwell	3.00
36	Mark Lemke	.25
37	Doug Glanville	.25
38	Dan Wilson	.25
39	Steve Cooke	.25
40	Chili Davis	.25
41	Mike Cameron	.25
42	F.P. Santangelo	.25
43	Brad Ausmus	.25
44	Gary DiSarcina	.25
45	Pat Hentgen	.25
46	Wilton Guerrero	.25
47	Devon White	.25
48	Danny Patterson	.25
49	Pat Meares	.25
50	Rafael Palmeiro	.75
51	Mark Gardner	.25
52	Jeff Blauser	.25
53	Dave Hollins	.25
54	Carlos Garcia	.25
55	Ben McDonald	.25
56	John Mabry	.25
57	Trevor Hoffman	.25
58	Tony Fernandez	.25
59	Rich Loiselle	.25
60	Mark Leiter	.25
61	Pat Kelly	.25
62	John Flaherty	.25
63	Roger Bailey	.25
64	Tom Gordon	.25
65	Ryan Klesko	1.00
66	Darryl Hamilton	.25
67	Jim Eisenreich	.25
68	Butch Huskey	.25
69	Mark Grudzielanek	.25
70	Marquis Grissom	.25

No.	Player	Value
71	Mark McLemore	.25
72	Gary Gaetti	.25
73	Greg Gagne	.25
74	Lyle Mouton	.25
75	Jim Edmonds	.25
76	Shawn Green	.25
77	Terry Vaughn	.25
78	Terry Adams	.25
79	*Kevin Polcovich*	.60
80	Troy O'Leary	.25
81	Jeff Shaw	.25
82	Rich Becker	.25
83	David Wells	.25
84	Steve Karsay	.25
85	Charles Nagy	.25
86	B.J. Surhoff	.25
87	Jamey Wright	.25
88	James Baldwin	.25
89	Edgardo Alfonzo	.50
90	Jay Buhner	.75
91	Brady Anderson	.50
92	Scott Servais	.25
93	Edgar Renteria	.25
94	Mike Lieberthal	.25
95	Rick Aguilera	.25
96	Walt Weiss	.25
97	Deivi Cruz	.25
98	Kurt Abbott	.25
99	Henry Rodriguez	.25
100	Mike Piazza	5.00
101	Bill Taylor	.25
102	Todd Zeile	.25
103	Rey Ordonez	.25
104	Willie Greene	.25
105	Tony Womack	.25
106	Mike Sweeney	.25
107	Jeffrey Hammonds	.25
108	Kevin Orie	.25
109	Alex Gonzalez	.25
110	Jose Canseco	.75
111	Paul Sorrento	.25
112	Joey Hamilton	.25
113	Brad Radke	.25
114	Steve Avery	.25
115	Esteban Loaiza	.25
116	Stan Javier	.25
117	Chris Gomez	.25
118	Royce Clayton	.25
119	Orlando Merced	.25
120	Kevin Appier	.25
121	Mel Nieves	.25
122	Joe Girardi	.25
123	Rico Brogna	.25
124	Kent Mercker	.25
125	Manny Ramirez	1.50
126	Jeromy Burnitz	.25
127	Kevin Foster	.25
128	Matt Morris	.50
129	Jason Dickson	.25
130	Tom Glavine	.50
131	Wally Joyner	.25
132	Rick Reed	.25
133	Todd Jones	.25
134	Dave Martinez	.25
135	Sandy Alomar	.50
136	Mike Lansing	.25
137	Sean Berry	.25
138	Doug Jones	.25
139	Todd Stottlemyre	.25
140	Jay Bell	.25
141	Jaime Navarro	.25
142	Chris Hoiles	.25
143	Joey Cora	.25
144	Scott Spiezio	.25
145	Joe Carter	.50
146	Jose Guillen	.75
147	Damion Easley	.25
148	Lee Stevens	.25
149	Alex Fernandez	.25
150	Randy Johnson	1.50
151	J.T. Snow	.50
152	Chuck Finley	.25
153	Bernard Gilkey	.25
154	David Segui	.25
155	Dante Bichette	.75
156	Kevin Stocker	.25
157	Carl Everett	.25
158	Jose Valentin	.50
159	Pokey Reese	.25
160	Derek Jeter	5.00
161	Roger Pavlik	.25
162	Mark Wohlers	.25
163	Ricky Bottalico	.25
164	Ozzie Guillen	.25
165	Mike Mussina	1.50
166	Gary Sheffield	1.00

No.	Player	Value
167	Hideo Nomo	2.00
168	Mark Grace	.75
169	Aaron Sele	.25
170	Darryl Kile	.25
171	Shawn Estes	.25
172	Vinny Castilla	.50
173	Ron Coomer	.25
174	Jose Rosado	.25
175	Kenny Lofton	2.00
176	Jason Giambi	.25
177	Hal Morris	.25
178	Darren Bragg	.25
179	Orel Hershiser	.25
180	Ray Lankford	.25
181	Hideki Irabu	1.00
182	Kevin Young	.25
183	Javy Lopez	.25
184	Jeff Montgomery	.25
185	Mike Holtz	.25
186	George Williams	.25
187	Cal Eldred	.25
188	Tom Candiotti	.25
189	Glenallen Hill	.25
190	Brian Giles	.25
191	Dave Mlicki	.25
192	Garrett Stephenson	.25
193	Jeff Frye	.25
194	Joe Oliver	.25
195	Bob Hamelin	.25
196	Luis Sojo	.25
197	LaTroy Hawkins	.25
198	Kevin Elster	.25
199	Jeff Reed	.25
200	Dennis Eckersley	.50
201	Bill Mueller	.25
202	Russ Davis	.25
203	Armando Benitez	.25
204	Quilvio Veras	.25
205	Tim Naehring	.25
206	Quinton McCracken	.25
207	Raul Casanova	.25
208	Matt Lawton	.25
209	Luis Alicea	.25
210	Luis Gonzalez	.25
211	Allen Watson	.25
212	Gerald Williams	.25
213	David Bell	.25
214	Todd Hollandsworth	.25
215	Wade Boggs	.75
216	Jose Mesa	.25
217	Jamie Moyer	.25
218	Darren Daulton	.25
219	Mickey Morandini	.25
220	Rusty Greer	.50
221	Jim Bullinger	.25
222	Jose Offerman	.25
223	Matt Karchner	.25
224	Woody Williams	.25
225	Mark Loretta	.25
226	Mike Hampton	.25
227	Willie Adams	.25
228	Scott Hatteberg	.25
229	Rich Amaral	.25
230	Terry Steinbach	.25
231	Glendon Rusch	.25
232	Bret Boone	.25
233	Robert Person	.25
234	Jose Hernandez	.25
235	Doug Drabek	.25
236	Jason McDonald	.25
237	Chris Widger	.25
238	*Tom Martin*	.25
239	Dave Burba	.25
240	Pete Rose	.25
241	Bobby Ayala	.25
242	Tim Wakefield	.25
243	Dennis Springer	.25
244	Tim Belcher	.25
245	Jon Garland, Geoff Goetz (Draft Pick)	3.00
246	Glenn Davis, Lance Berkman (Draft Pick)	6.00
247	Vernon Wells, Aaron Akin (Draft Pick)	4.00
248	Adam Kennedy, Jason Romano (Draft Pick)	3.00
249	Jason Dellaero, Troy Cameron (Draft Pick)	3.00
250	Alex Sanchez, *Jared Sandberg* (Expansion)	3.00
251	Pablo Ortega, *James Manias* (Expansion)	2.00
252	Jason Conti, *Mike Stoner* (Expansion)	8.00
253	John Patterson, Larry Rodriguez (Expansion)	1.50

No.	Player	Value
254	Adrian Beltre, *Ryan Minor*, Aaron Boone (Prospect)	12.00
255	Ben Grieve, Brian Buchanan, Dermal Brown (Prospect)	6.00
256	Carl Pavano, Kerry Wood, Gil Meche (Prospect)	15.00
257	David Ortiz, Daryle Ward, Richie Sexson (Prospect)	4.00
258	Randy Winn, Juan Encarnacion, Andrew Vessel (Prospect)	1.00
259	Kris Benson, Travis Smith, Courtney Duncan (Prospect)	2.50
260	Chad Hermansen, Brent Butler, *Warren Morris* (Prospect)	5.00
261	Ben Davis, Elieser Marrero, Ramon Hernandez (Prospect)	2.50
262	Eric Chavez, Russell Branyan, Russ Johnson (Prospect)	4.00
263	Todd Dunwoody, John Barnes, *Ryan Jackson* (Prospect)	2.50
264	Matt Clement, Roy Halladay, Brian Fuentes (Prospect)	4.00
265	Randy Johnson (Season Highlight)	.75
266	Kevin Brown (Season Highlight)	.40
267	Francisco Cordova, Ricardo Rincon (Season Highlight)	.25
268	Nomar Garciaparra (Season Highlight)	3.00
269	Tino Martinez (Season Highlight)	.50
270	Chuck Knoblauch (Inter-League)	.50
271	Pedro Martinez (Inter-League)	.50
272	Denny Neagle (Inter-League)	.25
273	Juan Gonzalez (Inter-League)	2.00
274	Andres Galarraga (Inter-League)	.50
275	Checklist	.25
276	Checklist	.25
277	Moises Alou (World Series)	.25
278	Sandy Alomar (World Series)	.25
279	Gary Sheffield (World Series)	.50
280	Matt Williams (World Series)	.50
281	Livan Hernandez (World Series)	.50
282	Chad Ogea (World Series)	.25
283	Celebration (World Series)	.75
284	Tino Martinez	.75
285	Roberto Alomar	1.50
286	Jeff King	.25
287	Brian Jordan	.25
288	Darin Erstad	2.00
289	Ken Caminiti	1.00
290	Jim Thome	1.50
291	Paul Molitor	1.50
292	Ivan Rodriguez	2.00
293	Bernie Williams	1.50
294	Todd Hundley	.50
295	Andres Galarraga	.75
296	Greg Maddux	5.00
297	Edgar Martinez	.50
298	Ron Gant	.50
299	Derek Bell	.25
300	Roger Clemens	3.00
301	Rondell White	.50
302	Barry Larkin	.75
303	Robin Ventura	.50
304	Jason Kendall	.25
305	Chipper Jones	5.00
306	John Franco	.25
307	Sammy Sosa	5.00
308	Troy Percival	.25
309	Chuck Knoblauch	.75
310	Ellis Burks	.25
311	Al Martin	.25
312	Tim Salmon	.75
313	Moises Alou	.50
314	Lance Johnson	.25
315	Justin Thompson	.25
316	Will Clark	.75

317	Barry Bonds	2.00
318	Craig Biggio	.50
319	John Smoltz	.50
320	Cal Ripken Jr.	6.00
321	Ken Griffey Jr.	8.00
322	Paul O'Neill	.50
323	Todd Helton	2.00
324	John Olerud	.25
325	Mark McGwire	10.00
326	Jose Cruz Jr.	2.00
327	Jeff Cirillo	.25
328	Dean Palmer	.25
329	John Wetteland	.25
330	Steve Finley	.25
331	Albert Belle	2.00
332	Curt Schilling	.50
333	Raul Mondesi	.50
334	Andruw Jones	2.00
335	Nomar Garciaparra	5.00
336	David Justice	.75
337	Andy Pettitte	1.00
338	Pedro Martinez	1.00
339	Travis Miller	.25
340	Chris Stynes	.25
341	Gregg Jefferies	.25
342	Jeff Fassero	.25
343	Craig Counsell	.25
344	Wilson Alvarez	.25
345	Bip Roberts	.25
346	Kelvim Escobar	.25
347	Mark Bellhorn	.25
348	Rickey Henderson	.25
349	Fred McGriff	.50
350	Chuck Carr	.25
351	Bob Abreu	.25
352	Juan Guzman	.25
353	Fernando Vina	.25
354	Andy Benes	.50
355	Dave Nilsson	.25
356	Bobby Bonilla	.50
357	Ismael Valdes	.25
358	Carlos Perez	.25
359	Kirk Rueter	.25
360	Bartolo Colon	.25
361	Mel Rojas	.25
362	Johnny Damon	.25
363	Geronimo Berroa	.25
364	Reggie Sanders	.25
365	Jermaine Allensworth	.25
366	Orlando Cabrera	.25
367	Jorge Fabregas	.25
368	Scott Stahoviak	.25
369	Ken Cloude	.50
370	Donovan Osborne	.25
371	Roger Cedeno	.25
372	Neifi Perez	.25
373	Chris Holt	.25
374	Cecil Fielder	.50
375	Marty Cordova	.25
376	Tom Goodwin	.25
377	Jeff Suppan	.25
378	Jeff Brantley	.25
379	Mark Langston	.25
380	Shane Reynolds	.25
381	Mike Fetters	.25
382	Todd Greene	.25
383	Ray Durham	.25
384	Carlos Delgado	.25
385	Jeff D'Amico	.25
386	Brian McRae	.25
387	Alan Benes	.50
388	Heathcliff Slocumb	.25
389	Eric Young	.25
390	Travis Fryman	.25
391	David Cone	.50
392	Otis Nixon	.25
393	Jeremi Gonzalez	.25
394	Jeff Juden	.25
395	Jose Vizcaino	.25
396	Ugueth Urbina	.25
397	Ramon Martinez	.50
398	Robb Nen	.25
399	Harold Baines	.25
400	Delino DeShields	.25
401	John Burkett	.25
402	Sterling Hitchcock	.25
403	Mark Clark	.25
404	Mariano Duncan	.25
405	Scott Brosius	.25
406	Chad Curtis	.25
407	Brian Johnson	.25
408	Roberto Kelly	.25
409	Rey Sanchez	.25
410	Michael Tucker	.25
411	Mark Kotsay	.75
412	Mark Lewis	.25

413	Ryan McGuire	.25
414	Shawon Dunston	.25
415	Brad Rigby	.25
416	Scott Erickson	.25
417	Bobby Jones	.25
418	Darren Oliver	.25
419	John Smiley	.25
420	T.J. Mathews	.25
421	Dustin Hermanson	.25
422	Mike Timlin	.25
423	Willie Blair	.25
424	Manny Alexander	.25
425	Bob Tewksbury	.25
426	Pete Schourek	.25
427	Reggie Jefferson	.25
428	Ed Sprague	.25
429	Jeff Conine	.25
430	Roberto Hernandez	.25
431	Tom Pagnozzi	.25
432	Jaret Wright	2.50
433	Livan Hernandez	.25
434	Andy Ashby	.25
435	Todd Dunn	.25
436	Bobby Higginson	.25
437	Jack McDowell	.25
438	Jim Leyritz	.25
439	Matt Williams	.75
440	Brett Tomko	.25
441	Joe Randa	.25
442	Chris Carpenter	.25
443	Dennis Reyes	.25
444	Al Leiter	.25
445	Jason Schmidt	.25
446	Ken Hill	.25
447	Shannon Stewart	.25
448	Enrique Wilson	.25
449	Fernando Tatis	.50
450	Jimmy Key	.25
451	Darrin Fletcher	.25
452	John Valentin	.25
453	Kevin Tapani	.25
454	Eric Karros	.50
455	Jay Bell	.25
456	Walt Weiss	.25
457	Devon White	.25
458	Carl Pavano	.50
459	Mike Lansing	.25
460	John Flaherty	.25
461	Richard Hidalgo	.25
462	Quinton McCracken	.25
463	Karim Garcia	.50
464	Miguel Cairo	.25
465	Edwin Diaz	.25
466	Bobby Smith	.25
467	Yamil Benitez	.25
468	*Rich Butler*	1.50
469	*Ben Ford*	.50
470	Bubba Trammell	.25
471	Brent Brede	.25
472	Brooks Kieschnick	.25
473	Carlos Castillo	.25
474	Brad Radke (Season Highlight)	.25
475	Roger Clemens (Season Highlight)	1.50
476	Curt Schilling (Season Highlight)	.25
477	John Olerud (Season Highlight)	.25
478	Mark McGwire (Season Highlight)	5.00
479	Mike Piazza, Ken Griffey Jr. (Interleague)	5.00
480	Jeff Bagwell, Frank Thomas (Interleague)	3.00
481	Chipper Jones, Nomar Garciaparra (Interleague)	3.00
482	Larry Walker, Juan Gonzalez (Interleague)	2.50
483	Gary Sheffield, Tino Martinez (Interleague)	.50
484	Derrick Gibson, Michael Coleman, Norm Hutchins (Prospect)	.50
485	Braden Looper, Cliff Politte, Brian Rose (Prospect)	2.00
486	Eric Milton, Jason Marquis, Corey Lee (Prospect)	1.00
487	A.J. Hinch, Mark Osborne, *Robert Fick* (Prospect)	6.00
488	Aramis Ramirez, Alex Gonzalez, Sean Casey (Prospect)	8.00
489	*Donnie Bridges, Tim Drew* (Draft Pick)	2.00

490	*Ntema Ndungidi, Darnell McDonald* (Draft Pick)	6.00
491	*Ryan Anderson,* Mark Mangum (Draft Pick)	8.00
492	J.J. Davis, *Troy Glaus* (Draft Pick)	6.00
493	Jayson Werth, Dan Reichert (Draft Pick)	2.00
494	*John Curtice,* Mike Cuddyer (Draft Pick)	2.00
495	*Jack Cust,* Jason Standridge (Draft Pick)	1.50
496	Brian Anderson (Expansion Team Prospect)	.25
497	Tony Saunders (Expansion Team Prospect)	.50
498	Vladimir Nunez, *Jhensy Sandoval* (Expansion Team Prospect)	.50
499	Brad Penny, Nick Bierbrodt (Expansion Team Prospect)	.25
500	*Dustin Carr, Luis Cruz* (Expansion Team Prospect)	1.00
501	*Marcus McCain, Cedrick Bowers* (Expansion Team Prospect)	.25
502	Checklist	.25
503	Checklist	.25
504	Alex Rodriguez	5.00
		.25

1998 Topps Chrome Refractors

Each card in the regular Topps Series 1 and Series 2 Chrome issue could also be found in a refractor version seeded approximately one per 12 packs. Refractor versions are so designated above the card number of back.

	MT
Common Player:	4.00
(Stars and rookies valued at 5-15X regular Chrome version)	

1998 Topps Chrome Baby Boomers

This 15-card insert featured players with less than three years of experience. Cards were inserted one per 24 packs, with Refractor versions found every 72 packs of Series I. Cards were numbered with a "BB" prefix.

		MT
Complete Set (15):		90.00
Common Player:		2.00
Inserted 1:24		
Refractors: 2x to 3x		
Inserted 1:72		
BB1	Derek Jeter	15.00
BB2	Scott Rolen	12.00
BB3	Nomar Garciaparra	15.00
BB4	Jose Cruz Jr.	10.00
BB5	Darin Erstad	6.00
BB6	Todd Helton	6.00
BB7	Tony Clark	4.00
BB8	Jose Guillen	4.00
BB9	Andruw Jones	12.00
BB10	Vladimir Guerrero	8.00
BB11	Mark Kotsay	4.00
BB12	Todd Greene	2.00
BB13	Andy Pettitte	4.00
BB14	Justin Thompson	2.00
BB15	Alan Benes	2.00

1998 Topps Chrome Clout 9

This nine-card insert included players for their statistical supremacy. Clout 9 cards were found in

Series II packs at a rate of one per 24 packs, with Refractor versions every 72 packs.

		MT
Complete Set (9):		75.00
Common Player:		3.00
Inserted 1:24		
Refractors: 1.5x to 2x		
Inserted 1:72		
C1	Edgar Martinez	3.00
C2	Mike Piazza	20.00
C3	Frank Thomas	25.00
C4	Craig Biggio	4.00
C5	Vinny Castilla	4.00
C6	Jeff Blauser	3.00
C7	Barry Bonds	8.00
C8	Ken Griffey Jr.	30.00
C9	Larry Walker	6.00

1998 Topps Chrome Flashback

This 10-card double-sided insert features top players as they looked in 1998 on one side, and how they looked when they first appeared in the majors on the other side. Flashback inserts were seeded one per 24 packs of Series I, with Refractors every 72 packs. This insert was numbered with a "FB" prefix.

		MT
Complete Set (10):		60.00
Common Player:		3.00
Inserted 1:24		
Refractors: 2x to 3x		
Inserted 1:72		
FB1	Barry Bonds	5.00
FB2	Ken Griffey Jr.	20.00
FB3	Paul Molitor	4.00
FB4	Randy Johnson	4.00
FB5	Cal Ripken Jr.	15.00
FB6	Tony Gwynn	10.00
FB7	Kenny Lofton	5.00
FB8	Gary Sheffield	4.00
FB9	Deion Sanders	3.00
FB10	Brady Anderson	3.00

1998 Topps Chrome Hallbound

Hall Bound highlighted 15 players destined for the Hall of Fame on die-cut cards. Inserted at a rate of one per 24 packs of Series I, with Refractors every 72 packs, these were numbered with a "HB" prefix.

		MT
Complete Set (15):		125.00
Common Player:		3.00
Inserted 1:24		
Refractors: 2x to 3x		
Inserted 1:72		
HB1	Paul Molitor	5.00
HB2	Tony Gwynn	12.00
HB3	Wade Boggs	4.00
HB4	Roger Clemens	10.00
HB5	Dennis Eckersley	3.00
HB6	Cal Ripken Jr.	20.00
HB7	Greg Maddux	15.00
HB8	Rickey Henderson	3.00
HB9	Ken Griffey Jr.	25.00
HB10	Frank Thomas	20.00
HB11	Mark McGwire	30.00
HB12	Barry Bonds	6.00
HB13	Mike Piazza	15.00
HB14	Juan Gonzalez	12.00
HB15	Randy Johnson	5.00

1998 Topps Chrome Milestones

Ten superstars who were within reach of major records for the 1998 season are featured in Milestones.

This Series II insert was seeded one per 24 packs, with Refractor versions seeded one per 72 packs. Milestones were numbered with a "MS" prefix.

		MT
Complete Set (10):		125.00
Common Player:		3.00
Inserted 1:24		
Refractors: 1.5x to 2x		
Inserted 1:72		
MS1	Barry Bonds	8.00
MS2	Roger Clemens	10.00
MS3	Dennis Eckersley	3.00
MS4	Juan Gonzalez	15.00
MS5	Ken Griffey Jr.	30.00
MS6	Tony Gwynn	15.00
MS7	Greg Maddux	20.00
MS8	Mark McGwire	35.00
MS9	Cal Ripken Jr.	25.00
MS10	Frank Thomas	25.00

1998 Topps Chrome 98 Rookie Class

This insert featured 10 players with less than one year of major league experience. Inserted in Series II packs at a rate of one per 12 packs, with Refractors every 24 packs, '98 Rookie Class inserts were numbered with a "R" prefix.

		MT
Complete Set (10):		30.00
Common Player:		1.50
Inserted 1:12		
Refractors: 1x to 1.5x		
Inserted 1:24		
R1	Travis Lee	12.00
R2	Richard Hidalgo	1.50
R3	Todd Helton	5.00
R4	Paul Konerko	4.00
R5	Mark Kotsay	3.00
R6	Derek Lee	3.00
R7	Eli Marrero	1.50
R8	Fernando Tatis	1.50
R9	Juan Encarnacion	1.50
R10	Ben Grieve	10.00

1998 Topps Gallery

Gallery returned in 1998 with a 150-card set broken up into five different subsets - Exhibitions, Impressions, Expressionists, Portraits and Permanent Collection. The set was paralleled twice - first in a Player's Private Issue set and, second in Gallery Proofs. Gallery cards were made to look like works of art instead of simply a photo of the player on cardboard, and were sold

in six-card packs. Inserts in this single-series product include: Photo Gallery, Gallery of Heroes and Awards Gallery.

		MT
Complete Set (150):		50.00
Common Player:		.20
Wax Box:		65.00
1	Andruw Jones	1.25
2	Fred McGriff	.40
3	Wade Boggs	.40
4	Pedro Martinez	.75
5	Matt Williams	.50
6	Wilson Alvarez	.20
7	Henry Rodriguez	.20
8	Jay Bell	.20
9	Marquis Grissom	.20
10	Darryl Kile	.20
11	Chuck Knoblauch	.50
12	Kenny Lofton	1.25
13	Quinton McCracken	.20
14	Andres Galarraga	.50
15	Brian Jordan	.20
16	Mike Lansing	.20
17	Travis Fryman	.20
18	Tony Saunders	.20
19	Moises Alou	.40
20	Travis Lee	4.00
21	Garret Anderson	.20
22	Ken Caminiti	.40
23	Pedro Astacio	.20
24	Ellis Burks	.20
25	Albert Belle	1.25
26	Alan Benes	.40
27	Jay Buhner	.50
28	Derek Bell	.20
29	Jeromy Burnitz	.20
30	Kevin Appier	.20
31	Jeff Cirillo	.20
32	Bernard Gilkey	.20
33	David Cone	.40
34	Jason Dickson	.20
35	Jose Cruz Jr.	.75
36	Marty Cordova	.20
37	Ray Durham	.20
38	Jaret Wright	1.25
39	Billy Wagner	.20
40	Roger Clemens	2.00
41	Juan Gonzalez	2.50
42	Jeremi Gonzalez	.20
43	Mark Grudzielanek	.20
44	Tom Glavine	.40
45	Barry Larkin	.40
46	Lance Johnson	.20
47	Bobby Higginson	.20
48	Mike Mussina	1.00
49	Al Martin	.20
50	Mark McGwire	6.00
51	Todd Hundley	.20
52	Ray Lankford	.20
53	Jason Kendall	.20
54	Javy Lopez	.40
55	Ben Grieve	2.00
56	Randy Johnson	.75
57	Jeff King	.20
58	Mark Grace	.50
59	Rusty Greer	.40
60	Greg Maddux	3.00
61	Jeff Kent	.20
62	Rey Ordonez	.20
63	Hideo Nomo	.75
64	Charles Nagy	.20
65	Rondell White	.40
66	Todd Helton	1.25
67	Jim Thome	.75
68	Denny Neagle	.20
69	Ivan Rodriguez	1.25
70	Vladimir Guerrero	1.25
71	Jorge Posada	.20
72	J.T. Snow Jr.	.20
73	Reggie Sanders	.20
74	Scott Rolen	2.00
75	Robin Ventura	.40
76	Mariano Rivera	.40
77	Cal Ripken Jr.	4.00
78	Justin Thompson	.20
79	Mike Piazza	3.00
80	Kevin Brown	.20
81	Sandy Alomar	.40
82	Craig Biggio	.40
83	Vinny Castilla	.40
84	Eric Young	.20
85	Bernie Williams	.75
86	Brady Anderson	.20

87	Bobby Bonilla	.20
88	Tony Clark	.75
89	Dan Wilson	.20
90	John Wetteland	.20
91	Barry Bonds	1.25
92	Chan Ho Park	.50
93	Carlos Delgado	.40
94	David Justice	.50
95	Chipper Jones	3.00
96	Shawn Estes	.20
97	Jason Giambi	.20
98	Ron Gant	.40
99	John Olerud	.40
100	Frank Thomas	4.00
101	Jose Guillen	.40
102	Brad Radke	.20
103	Troy Percival	.20
104	John Smoltz	.40
105	Edgardo Alfonzo	.20
106	Dante Bichette	.40
107	Larry Walker	.50
108	John Valentin	.20
109	Roberto Alomar	1.00
110	Mike Cameron	.20
111	Eric Davis	.20
112	Johnny Damon	.20
113	Darin Erstad	1.25
114	Omar Vizquel	.20
115	Derek Jeter	2.50
116	Tony Womack	.20
117	Edgar Renteria	.20
118	Raul Mondesi	.40
119	Tony Gwynn	2.50
120	Ken Griffey Jr.	5.00
121	Jim Edmonds	.20
122	Brian Hunter	.20
123	Neifi Perez	.20
124	Dean Palmer	.20
125	Alex Rodriguez	3.00
126	Tim Salmon	.50
127	Curt Schilling	.40
128	Kevin Orie	.20
129	Andy Pettitte	.75
130	Gary Sheffield	.50
131	Jose Rosado	.20
132	Manny Ramirez	1.25
133	Rafael Palmeiro	.50
134	Sammy Sosa	3.00
135	Jeff Bagwell	2.00
136	Delino DeShields	.20
137	Ryan Klesko	.50
138	Mo Vaughn	1.25
139	Steve Finley	.20
140	Nomar Garciaparra	3.00
141	Paul Molitor	.75
142	Pat Hentgen	.20
143	Eric Karros	.20
144	Bobby Jones	.20
145	Tino Martinez	.50
146	Matt Morris	.20
147	Livan Hernandez	.40
148	Edgar Martinez	.20
149	Paul O'Neill	.40
150	Checklist	.20

		MT
Complete Set (10):		75.00
Common Player:		3.00
Inserted 1:24		
AG1	Ken Griffey Jr.	25.00
AG2	Larry Walker	4.00
AG3	Roger Clemens	8.00
AG4	Pedro Martinez	4.00
AG5	Nomar Garciaparra	15.00
AG6	Scott Rolen	8.00
AG7	Frank Thomas	20.00
AG8	Tony Gwynn	12.00
AG9	Mark McGwire	30.00
AG10	Livan Hernandez	3.00

1998 Topps Gallery of Heroes

Gallery of Heroes was a 15-card insert printed on colored, die-cut plastic that resembled a stained glass window. Cards were inserted one per 24 packs and numbered with a "GH" prefix.

		MT
Complete Set (15):		250.00
Common Player:		3.00
Inserted 1:24		
GH1	Ken Griffey Jr.	40.00
GH2	Derek Jeter	20.00
GH3	Barry Bonds	10.00
GH4	Alex Rodriguez	25.00
GH5	Frank Thomas	30.00
GH6	Nomar Garciaparra	25.00
GH7	Mark McGwire	40.00
GH8	Mike Piazza	25.00
GH9	Cal Ripken Jr.	30.00
GH10	Jose Cruz Jr.	6.00
GH11	Jeff Bagwell	15.00
GH12	Chipper Jones	25.00
GH13	Juan Gonzalez	20.00
GH14	Hideo Nomo	8.00
GH15	Greg Maddux	25.00

1998 Topps Gallery Photo Gallery

This 10-card insert captured unique shots of players on a silver foilboard design. Photo Gallery inserts were seeded one per 24 packs and numbered with a "PG" prefix.

		MT
Complete Set (10):		100.00
Common Player:		3.00
Inserted 1:24		
PG1	Alex Rodriguez	15.00
PG2	Frank Thomas	20.00
PG3	Derek Jeter	12.00
PG4	Cal Ripken Jr.	20.00
PG5	Ken Griffey Jr.	25.00
PG6	Mike Piazza	15.00
PG7	Nomar Garciaparra	15.00
PG8	Tim Salmon	4.00
PG9	Jeff Bagwell	8.00
PG10	Barry Bonds	6.00

1998 Topps Gallery Players Private Issue

Player's Private Issue cards paralleled the 150-card base set with a distinct design and embossing. These parallel cards were inserted one per 12 packs.

	MT
Common Player:	8.00
Semistars:	20.00
Unlisted Stars:	30.00
Production 250 sets	
Gallery Proofs: 1.25x to 2x	
Production 125 sets	
1 Andruw Jones	35.00

1998 Topps Gallery Awards Gallery

Awards Gallery featured 10 players who earned the highest honors in the game on a horizontal design. Fronts featured a shot of the player and the award he won on silver foilboard. These were inserted every 24 packs and numbered with an "AG" prefix.

2	Fred McGriff	15.00
3	Wade Boggs	15.00
4	Pedro Martinez	25.00
5	Matt Williams	20.00
6	Wilson Alvarez	8.00
7	Henry Rodriguez	8.00
8	Jay Bell	8.00
9	Marquis Grissom	8.00
10	Darryl Kile	8.00
11	Chuck Knoblauch	20.00
12	Kenny Lofton	35.00
13	Quinton McCracken	8.00
14	Andres Galarraga	25.00
15	Brian Jordan	8.00
16	Mike Lansing	8.00
17	Travis Fryman	8.00
18	Tony Saunders	8.00
19	Moises Alou	15.00
20	Travis Lee	100.00
21	Garret Anderson	8.00
22	Ken Caminiti	15.00
23	Pedro Astacio	8.00
24	Ellis Burks	8.00
25	Albert Belle	35.00
26	Alan Benes	12.00
27	Jay Buhner	20.00
28	Derek Bell	8.00
29	Jeromy Burnitz	8.00
30	Kevin Appier	8.00
31	Jeff Cirillo	8.00
32	Bernard Gilkey	8.00
33	David Cone	15.00
34	Jason Dickson	8.00
35	Jose Cruz Jr.	30.00
36	Marty Cordova	8.00
37	Ray Durham	8.00
38	Jaret Wright	40.00
39	Billy Wagner	8.00
40	Roger Clemens	50.00
41	Juan Gonzalez	75.00
42	Jeremi Gonzalez	8.00
43	Mark Grudzielanek	8.00
44	Tom Glavine	15.00
45	Barry Larkin	15.00
46	Lance Johnson	8.00
47	Bobby Higginson	8.00
48	Mike Mussina	30.00
49	Al Martin	8.00
50	Mark McGwire	160.00
51	Todd Hundley	8.00
52	Ray Lankford	8.00
53	Jason Kendall	8.00
54	Javy Lopez	12.00
55	Ben Grieve	50.00
56	Randy Johnson	30.00
57	Jeff King	8.00
58	Mark Grace	20.00
59	Rusty Greer	15.00
60	Greg Maddux	90.00
61	Jeff Kent	8.00
62	Rey Ordonez	8.00
63	Hideo Nomo	30.00
64	Charles Nagy	8.00
65	Rondell White	15.00
66	Todd Helton	40.00
67	Jim Thome	30.00
68	Denny Neagle	8.00
69	Ivan Rodriguez	40.00
70	Vladimir Guerrero	40.00
71	Jorge Posada	8.00
72	J.T. Snow Jr.	8.00
73	Reggie Sanders	8.00
74	Scott Rolen	50.00
75	Robin Ventura	15.00
76	Mariano Rivera	15.00
77	Cal Ripken Jr.	120.00
78	Justin Thompson	8.00
79	Mike Piazza	90.00
80	Kevin Brown	8.00
81	Sandy Alomar	15.00
82	Craig Biggio	15.00
83	Vinny Castilla	15.00
84	Eric Young	8.00
85	Bernie Williams	30.00
86	Brady Anderson	8.00
87	Bobby Bonilla	15.00
88	Tony Clark	25.00
89	Dan Wilson	8.00
90	John Wetteland	8.00
91	Barry Bonds	40.00
92	Chan Ho Park	20.00
93	Carlos Delgado	15.00
94	David Justice	20.00
95	Chipper Jones	90.00
96	Shawn Estes	8.00
97	Jason Giambi	8.00

98	Ron Gant	15.00
99	John Olerud	15.00
100	Frank Thomas	120.00
101	Jose Guillen	15.00
102	Brad Radke	8.00
103	Troy Percival	8.00
104	John Smoltz	15.00
105	Edgardo Alfonzo	8.00
106	Dante Bichette	15.00
107	Larry Walker	20.00
108	John Valentin	8.00
109	Roberto Alomar	30.00
110	Mike Cameron	8.00
111	Eric Davis	8.00
112	Johnny Damon	8.00
113	Darin Erstad	40.00
114	Omar Vizquel	8.00
115	Derek Jeter	75.00
116	Tony Womack	8.00
117	Edgar Renteria	8.00
118	Raul Mondesi	15.00
119	Tony Gwynn	75.00
120	Ken Griffey Jr.	150.00
121	Jim Edmonds	8.00
122	Brian Hunter	8.00
123	Neifi Perez	8.00
124	Dean Palmer	8.00
125	Alex Rodriguez	100.00
126	Tim Salmon	20.00
127	Curt Schilling	15.00
128	Kevin Orie	8.00
129	Andy Pettitte	30.00
130	Gary Sheffield	25.00
131	Jose Rosado	8.00
132	Manny Ramirez	40.00
133	Rafael Palmeiro	20.00
134	Sammy Sosa	80.00
135	Jeff Bagwell	50.00
136	Delino DeShields	8.00
137	Ryan Klesko	20.00
138	Mo Vaughn	40.00
139	Steve Finley	8.00
140	Nomar Garciaparra	90.00
141	Paul Molitor	30.00
142	Pat Hentgen	8.00
143	Eric Karros	15.00
144	Bobby Jones	8.00
145	Tino Martinez	20.00
146	Matt Morris	8.00
147	Livan Hernandez	12.00
148	Edgar Martinez	8.00
149	Paul O'Neill	15.00
150	Checklist	8.00

1998 Topps Gold Label

Vladimir Guerrero

Topps debuted its Gold Label Baseball in 1998 with 100 card printed on 30-point "spectral-reflective stock" with gold foil stamping and two shots of the player on each card front. Cards arrived in Gold Label, Black Label and Red Label versions, all with varying levels of insertion. The rarity of the cards was determined by the photo and foil stamping of the cards. In the foreground of each card, the photograph is the same, but in the background one of three shots is featured. Variation 1: fielding are considered base cards, Variation 2: running (inserted 1:4 packs) and Variation 3: hitting (inserted 1:8 packs) are seeded levels. For pitching the levels are: Variation 1: ready (regular), Variation 2: pitch (inserted 1:4 packs) and Variation 3: follow-through (inserted 1:8 packs). Black Label cards are the second-most rare, while Red Label cards are third. Only one insert is issued in Gold Label, called Home Run Race of '98, and it is also available Gold, Red and Black versions.

		MT
Complete Set (100):		90.00
Common Player:		.25
Variation 2: 2x		
Inserted 1:4		
Variation 3: 4x		
Inserted 1:8		
1	Kevin Brown	.50
2	Greg Maddux	4.00
3	Albert Belle	1.50
4	Andres Galarraga	.75
5	Craig Biggio	.40
6	Matt Williams	.75
7	Derek Jeter	3.00
8	Randy Johnson	1.00
9	Jay Bell	.25
10	Jim Thome	.75
11	Roberto Alomar	1.00
12	Tom Glavine	.50
13	Reggie Sanders	.25
14	Tony Gwynn	3.00
15	Mark McGwire	8.00
16	Jeromy Burnitz	.25
17	Andruw Jones	1.50
18	Jay Buhner	.75
19	Robin Ventura	.40
20	Jeff Bagwell	2.00
21	Roger Clemens	2.50
22	*Masato Yoshii*	.75
23	Travis Fryman	.25
24	Rafael Palmeiro	.50
25	Alex Rodriguez	4.00
26	Sandy Alomar	.25
27	Chipper Jones	4.00
28	Rusty Greer	.25
29	Cal Ripken Jr.	5.00
30	Tony Clark	1.00
31	Derek Bell	.25
32	Fred McGriff	.50
33	Paul O'Neill	.75
34	Moises Alou	.50
35	Henry Rodriguez	.25
36	Steve Finley	.25
37	Marquis Grissom	.25
38	Jason Giambi	.25
39	Javy Lopez	.40
40	Damion Easley	.25
41	Mariano Rivera	.50
42	Mo Vaughn	1.50
43	Mike Mussina	1.00
44	Jason Kendall	.25
45	Pedro Martinez	1.50
46	Frank Thomas	4.00
47	Jim Edmonds	.25
48	Hideki Irabu	.75
49	Eric Karros	.40
50	Juan Gonzalez	3.00
51	Ellis Burks	.25
52	Dean Palmer	.25
53	Scott Rolen	1.50
54	Raul Mondesi	.50
55	Quinton McCracken	.25
56	John Olerud	.50
57	Ken Caminiti	.50
58	Brian Jordan	.25
59	Wade Boggs	.50
60	Mike Piazza	4.00
61	Darin Erstad	1.50
62	Curt Schilling	.50
63	David Justice	.75
64	Kenny Lofton	1.50

65	Barry Bonds	1.50
66	Ray Lankford	.25
67	Brian Hunter	.25
68	Chuck Knoblauch	.75
69	Vinny Castilla	.25
70	Vladimir Guerrero	1.50
71	Tim Salmon	.75
72	Larry Walker	.75
73	Paul Molitor	1.00
74	Barry Larkin	.75
75	Edgar Martinez	.25
76	Bernie Williams	1.00
77	Dante Bichette	.75
78	Nomar Garciaparra	4.00
79	Ben Grieve	2.00
80	Ivan Rodriguez	1.50
81	Todd Helton	1.00
82	Ryan Klesko	.50
83	Sammy Sosa	4.00
84	Travis Lee	3.00
85	Jose Cruz	1.50
86	Mark Kotsay	.25
87	Richard Hidalgo	.25
88	Rondell White	.50
89	Greg Vaughn	.50
90	Gary Sheffield	.50
91	Paul Konerko	.50
92	Mark Grace	.50
93	*Kevin Millwood*	4.00
94	Manny Ramirez	1.50
95	Tino Martinez	.75
96	Brad Fullmer	.50
97	Todd Walker	.25
98	Carlos Delgado	.25
99	Kerry Wood	6.00
100	Ken Griffey Jr.	6.00

1998 Topps Gold Label Red

Red Label cards were the third highest tier of Topps Gold Label and featured red foil stamping. Red Label cards were sequentially numbered as follows: Variation 1 cards were numbered to 100 and inserted 1:165 packs, Variation 2 cards were numbered to 50 and inserted 1:330 packs and Variation 3 cards are numbered to 25 and inserted 1:660 packs.

		MT
Common Player:		15.00
Variation 2: 1.5x to 2x		
Production 50 sets		
Variation 3: 3x to 4x		
Production 25 sets		
1	Kevin Brown	30.00
2	Greg Maddux	200.00
3	Albert Belle	80.00
4	Andres Galarraga	40.00
5	Craig Biggio	25.00
6	Matt Williams	30.00
7	Derek Jeter	175.00
8	Randy Johnson	60.00
9	Jay Bell	15.00
10	Jim Thome	50.00
11	Roberto Alomar	60.00
12	Tom Glavine	40.00
13	Reggie Sanders	15.00
14	Tony Gwynn	150.00
15	Mark McGwire	400.00
16	Jeromy Burnitz	15.00
17	Andruw Jones	80.00
18	Jay Buhner	40.00
19	Robin Ventura	25.00
20	Jeff Bagwell	120.00
21	Roger Clemens	140.00
22	Masato Yoshii	40.00
23	Travis Fryman	15.00
24	Rafael Palmeiro	30.00
25	Alex Rodriguez	200.00
26	Sandy Alomar	15.00
27	Chipper Jones	200.00
28	Rusty Greer	15.00
29	Cal Ripken Jr.	250.00
30	Tony Clark	40.00
31	Derek Bell	15.00
32	Fred McGriff	25.00
33	Paul O'Neill	40.00
34	Moises Alou	30.00

35	Henry Rodriguez	15.00
36	Steve Finley	15.00
37	Marquis Grissom	15.00
38	Jason Giambi	15.00
39	Javy Lopez	25.00
40	Damion Easley	15.00
41	Mariano Rivera	30.00
42	Mo Vaughn	80.00
43	Mike Mussina	60.00
44	Jason Kendall	15.00
45	Pedro Martinez	70.00
46	Frank Thomas	200.00
47	Jim Edmonds	15.00
48	Hideki Irabu	30.00
49	Eric Karros	25.00
50	Juan Gonzalez	150.00
51	Ellis Burks	15.00
52	Dean Palmer	15.00
53	Scott Rolen	90.00
54	Raul Mondesi	25.00
55	Quinton McCracken	15.00
56	John Olerud	25.00
57	Ken Caminiti	25.00
58	Brian Jordan	15.00
59	Wade Boggs	30.00
60	Mike Piazza	200.00
61	Darin Erstad	80.00
62	Curt Schilling	30.00
63	David Justice	30.00
64	Kenny Lofton	80.00
65	Barry Bonds	80.00
66	Ray Lankford	15.00
67	Brian Hunter	15.00
68	Chuck Knoblauch	50.00
69	Vinny Castilla	15.00
70	Vladimir Guerrero	80.00
71	Tim Salmon	40.00
72	Larry Walker	50.00
73	Paul Molitor	60.00
74	Barry Larkin	25.00
75	Edgar Martinez	15.00
76	Bernie Williams	60.00
77	Dante Bichette	30.00
78	Nomar Garciaparra	200.00
79	Ben Grieve	100.00
80	Ivan Rodriguez	80.00
81	Todd Helton	40.00
82	Ryan Klesko	25.00
83	Sammy Sosa	200.00
84	Travis Lee	140.00
85	Jose Cruz Jr.	80.00
86	Mark Kotsay	30.00
87	Richard Hidalgo	15.00
88	Rondell White	30.00
89	Greg Vaughn	30.00
90	Gary Sheffield	30.00
91	Paul Konerko	30.00
92	Mark Grace	40.00
93	Kevin Millwood	90.00
94	Manny Ramirez	80.00
95	Tino Martinez	50.00
96	Brad Fullmer	30.00
97	Todd Walker	15.00
98	Carlos Delgado	15.00
99	Kerry Wood	200.00
100	Ken Griffey Jr.	300.00

1998 Topps Gold Label Home Run Race

Home Run Race of '98 was a four-card set containing Mark McGwire, Sammy Sosa, Ken Griffey Jr. and Roger Maris. Each of the current player feature a background photo of Maris, while the fourth card features two shots of Maris. Gold, Black and Red Label versions were identified by the different foil-stamp logos. Gold cards were inserted 1:12 packs, Black Label cards were inserted 1:48 packs and Red Label cards were sequentially numbered to 61 and inserted 1:4,055 packs.

A player's name in *italic* type indicates a rookie card.

		MT
Complete Set (4):		60.00
Common Player:		10.00
Inserted 1:12		
Blacks: 2x to 3x		
Inserted 1:48		
HR1	Roger Maris	10.00
HR2	Mark McGwire	30.00
HR3	Ken Griffey Jr.	20.00
HR4	Sammy Sosa	20.00

1998 Topps Gold Label Home Run Race Red

		MT
Common Player:		150.00
Production 61 sets		
HR1	Roger Maris	150.00
HR2	Mark McGwire	400.00
HR3	Ken Griffey Jr.	300.00
HR4	Sammy Sosa	250.00

1998 Topps Stars

Topps Stars adopted an all-sequential numbering format in 1998 with a 150-card set. Every card was available in a bronze (numbered to 9,799), red (9,799), silver (4,399), gold (2,299) and gold rainbow format (99) with different color foil to distinguish between the groups. Players were each judged in five categories: arm strength, hit for average, power, defense and speed. Inserts in the product include: Galaxy, Luminaries, Supernovas, Rookie Reprints and Rookie Reprint Autographs. All regular-issue cards and inserts were individually numbered except the Rookie Reprints.

		MT
Complete Set (150):		100.00
Common Player:		.25
Production 9,799 sets		
1	Greg Maddux	6.00
2	Darryl Kile	.25
3	Rod Beck	.25
4	Ellis Burks	.25
5	Gary Sheffield	.75
6	David Ortiz	.25
7	Marquis Grissom	.40
8	Tony Womack	.25
9	Mike Mussina	2.00
10	Bernie Williams	2.00
11	Andy Benes	.25
12	Rusty Greer	.50
13	Carlos Delgado	.25
14	Jim Edmonds	.50
15	Raul Mondesi	.75
16	Andres Galarraga	1.00
17	Wade Boggs	.50
18	Paul O'Neill	.75
19	Edgar Renteria	.25
20	Tony Clark	1.50
21	Vladimir Guerrero	2.50
22	Moises Alou	.50
23	Bernard Gilkey	.25
24	Lance Johnson	.25
25	Ben Grieve	3.00
26	Sandy Alomar	.25
27	Ray Durham	.25
28	Shawn Estes	.25
29	David Segui	.25
30	Javy Lopez	.40
31	Steve Finley	.25
32	Rey Ordonez	.25
33	Derek Jeter	5.00
34	Henry Rodriguez	.25
35	Mo Vaughn	2.50
36	Richard Hidalgo	.25
37	Omar Vizquel	.25
38	Johnny Damon	.25
39	Brian Hunter	.25
40	Matt Williams	1.00
41	Chuck Finley	.25
42	Jeromy Burnitz	.25
43	Livan Hernandez	.25
44	Delino DeShields	.25
45	Charles Nagy	.25
46	Scott Rolen	3.00
47	Neifi Perez	.25
48	John Wetteland	.25
49	Eric Milton	.25
50	Mike Piazza	6.00
51	Cal Ripken Jr.	8.00
52	Mariano Rivera	.50
53	Butch Huskey	.25
54	Quinton McCracken	.25
55	Jose Cruz Jr.	2.50
56	Brian Jordan	.25
57	Hideo Nomo	1.50
58	Masato Yoshii	.25
59	Cliff Floyd	.25
60	Jose Guillen	.50
61	Jeff Shaw	.25
62	Edgar Martinez	.25
63	Rondell White	.50
64	Hal Morris	.25
65	Barry Larkin	.75
66	Eric Young	.25
67	Ray Lankford	.25
68	Derek Bell	.25
69	Charles Johnson	.25
70	Robin Ventura	.50
71	Chuck Knoblauch	.75
72	Kevin Brown	.75
73	Jose Valentin	.25
74	Jay Buhner	.75
75	Tony Gwynn	5.00
76	Andy Pettitte	1.50
77	Edgardo Alfonzo	.25
78	Kerry Wood	10.00
79	Darin Erstad	2.50
80	Paul Konerko	.50
81	Jason Kendall	.25
82	Tino Martinez	1.00

No.	Player	Price
83	Brad Radke	.25
84	Jeff King	.25
85	Travis Lee	5.00
86	Jeff Kent	.25
87	Trevor Hoffman	.25
88	David Cone	.50
89	Jose Canseco	1.00
90	Juan Gonzalez	5.00
91	Todd Hundley	.25
92	John Valentin	.25
93	Sammy Sosa	8.00
94	Jason Giambi	.25
95	Chipper Jones	6.00
96	Jeff Blauser	.25
97	Brad Fullmer	.50
98	Derek Lee	.25
99	Denny Neagle	.25
100	Ken Griffey Jr.	10.00
101	David Justice	.75
102	Tim Salmon	.75
103	J.T. Snow	.25
104	Fred McGriff	.50
105	Brady Anderson	.25
106	Larry Walker	1.00
107	Jeff Cirillo	.25
108	Andruw Jones	2.50
109	Manny Ramirez	2.50
110	Justin Thompson	.25
111	Vinny Castilla	.50
112	Chan Ho Park	.50
113	Mark Grudzielanek	.25
114	Mark Grace	.75
115	Ken Caminiti	.50
116	Ryan Klesko	.75
117	Rafael Palmeiro	.75
118	Pat Hentgen	.25
119	Eric Karros	.50
120	Randy Johnson	1.50
121	Roberto Alomar	1.50
122	John Olerud	.75
123	Paul Molitor	1.50
124	Dean Palmer	.25
125	Nomar Garciaparra	6.00
126	Curt Schilling	.50
127	Jay Bell	.25
128	Craig Biggio	.50
129	Marty Cordova	.25
130	Ivan Rodriguez	2.50
131	Todd Helton	2.00
132	Jim Thome	1.50
133	Albert Belle	2.50
134	Mike Lansing	.25
135	Mark McGwire	12.00
136	Roger Clemens	4.00
137	Tom Glavine	.50
138	Ron Gant	.25
139	Alex Rodriguez	8.00
140	Jeff Bagwell	3.00
141	John Smoltz	.50
142	Kenny Lofton	2.50
143	Dante Bichette	.50
144	Pedro Martinez	2.00
145	Barry Bonds	2.50
146	Travis Fryman	.25
147	Bobby Jones	.25
148	Bobby Higginson	.25
149	Reggie Sanders	.25
150	Frank Thomas	8.00

1998 Topps Stars Silver

Silver versions of all 150 Topps Stars cards were available and seeded one per pack. They were distinguished by silver foil on the front and sequentail numbering to 4,399 on the back.

		MT
Complete Set (150):		350.00
Common Player:		.75
Production 4,399 sets		
1	Greg Maddux	15.00
2	Darryl Kile	.75
3	Rod Beck	.75
4	Ellis Burks	.75
5	Gary Sheffield	1.50
6	David Ortiz	.75
7	Marquis Grissom	1.00
8	Tony Womack	.75
9	Mike Mussina	5.00
10	Bernie Williams	5.00
11	Andy Benes	.75
12	Rusty Greer	1.00
13	Carlos Delgado	.75
14	Jim Edmonds	1.00
15	Raul Mondesi	1.50
16	Andres Galarraga	3.00
17	Wade Boggs	1.50
18	Paul O'Neill	1.50
19	Edgar Renteria	.75
20	Tony Clark	4.00
21	Vladimir Guerrero	6.00
22	Moises Alou	1.00
23	Bernard Gilkey	.75
24	Lance Johnson	.75
25	Ben Grieve	8.00
26	Sandy Alomar	1.00
27	Ray Durham	.75
28	Shawn Estes	.75
29	David Segui	.75
30	Javy Lopez	1.00
31	Steve Finley	.75
32	Rey Ordonez	.75
33	Derek Jeter	12.00
34	Henry Rodriguez	.75
35	Mo Vaughn	6.00
36	Richard Hidalgo	.75
37	Omar Vizquel	.75
38	Johnny Damon	.75
39	Brian Hunter	.75
40	Matt Williams	3.00
41	Chuck Finley	.75
42	Jeromy Burnitz	.75
43	Livan Hernandez	.75
44	Delino DeShields	.75
45	Charles Nagy	.75
46	Scott Rolen	8.00
47	Neifi Perez	.75
48	John Wetteland	.75
49	Eric Milton	1.50
50	Mike Piazza	15.00
51	Cal Ripken Jr.	18.00
52	Mariano Rivera	1.00
53	Butch Huskey	.75
54	Quinton McCracken	.75
55	Jose Cruz Jr.	6.00
56	Brian Jordan	.75
57	Hideo Nomo	4.00
58	Masato Yoshii	1.50
59	Cliff Floyd	.75
60	Jose Guillen	1.00
61	Jeff Shaw	.75
62	Edgar Martinez	1.00
63	Rondell White	1.00
64	Hal Morris	.75
65	Barry Larkin	1.50
66	Eric Young	.75
67	Ray Lankford	.75
68	Derek Bell	.75
69	Charles Johnson	.75
70	Robin Ventura	1.00
71	Chuck Knoblauch	1.50
72	Kevin Brown	1.50
73	Jose Valentin	.75
74	Jay Buhner	1.50
75	Tony Gwynn	12.00
76	Andy Pettitte	4.00
77	Edgardo Alfonzo	.75
78	Kerry Wood	25.00
79	Darin Erstad	6.00
80	Paul Konerko	1.00
81	Jason Kendall	.75
82	Tino Martinez	3.00
83	Brad Radke	.75
84	Jeff King	.75
85	Travis Lee	12.00
86	Jeff Kent	.75
87	Trevor Hoffman	.75
88	David Cone	1.00
89	Jose Canseco	3.00
90	Juan Gonzalez	12.00
91	Todd Hundley	.75
92	John Valentin	.75
93	Sammy Sosa	15.00
94	Jason Giambi	.75
95	Chipper Jones	15.00
96	Jeff Blauser	.75
97	Brad Fullmer	1.00
98	Derek Lee	.75
99	Denny Neagle	.75
100	Ken Griffey Jr.	25.00
101	David Justice	1.50
102	Tim Salmon	1.50
103	J.T. Snow	.75
104	Fred McGriff	1.00
105	Brady Anderson	.75
106	Larry Walker	3.00
107	Jeff Cirillo	.75
108	Andruw Jones	6.00
109	Manny Ramirez	6.00
110	Justin Thompson	.75
111	Vinny Castilla	1.00
112	Chan Ho Park	1.00
113	Mark Grudzielanek	.75
114	Mark Grace	1.50
115	Ken Caminiti	1.00
116	Ryan Klesko	1.50
117	Rafael Palmeiro	1.50
118	Pat Hentgen	.75
119	Eric Karros	1.00
120	Randy Johnson	4.00
121	Roberto Alomar	4.00
122	John Olerud	1.50
123	Paul Molitor	4.00
124	Dean Palmer	.75
125	Nomar Garciaparra	15.00
126	Curt Schilling	1.00
127	Jay Bell	.75
128	Craig Biggio	1.00
129	Marty Cordova	.75
130	Ivan Rodriguez	6.00
131	Todd Helton	5.00
132	Jim Thome	4.00
133	Albert Belle	6.00
134	Mike Lansing	.75
135	Mark McGwire	25.00
136	Roger Clemens	10.00
137	Tom Glavine	1.00
138	Ron Gant	.75
139	Alex Rodriguez	18.00
140	Jeff Bagwell	8.00
141	John Smoltz	1.00
142	Kenny Lofton	6.00
143	Dante Bichette	1.00
144	Pedro Martinez	5.00
145	Barry Bonds	6.00
146	Travis Fryman	.75
147	Bobby Jones	.75
148	Bobby Higginson	.75
149	Reggie Sanders	.75
150	Frank Thomas	18.00

1998 Topps Stars Gold

All 150 cards were paralleled in Gold Star versions. This was the second rarest version of each card and was numbered to 2,299. Gold Star versions featured gold foil and were seeded every two packs.

		MT
Complete Set (150):		700.00
Common Player:		2.50
Production 2,299 sets		
1	Greg Maddux	25.00
2	Darryl Kile	2.50
3	Rod Beck	2.50
4	Ellis Burks	2.50
5	Gary Sheffield	5.00
6	David Ortiz	2.50
7	Marquis Grissom	2.50
8	Tony Womack	2.50
9	Mike Mussina	8.00
10	Bernie Williams	8.00
11	Andy Benes	2.50
12	Rusty Greer	4.00
13	Carlos Delgado	2.50
14	Jim Edmonds	4.00
15	Raul Mondesi	5.00
16	Andres Galarraga	6.00
17	Wade Boggs	5.00
18	Paul O'Neill	5.00
19	Edgar Renteria	2.50
20	Tony Clark	6.00
21	Vladimir Guerrero	10.00
22	Moises Alou	4.00
23	Bernard Gilkey	2.50
24	Lance Johnson	2.50
25	Ben Grieve	12.00
26	Sandy Alomar	4.00
27	Ray Durham	2.50
28	Shawn Estes	2.50
29	David Segui	2.50
30	Javy Lopez	4.00
31	Steve Finley	2.50
32	Rey Ordonez	2.50
33	Derek Jeter	20.00
34	Henry Rodriguez	2.50

35	Mo Vaughn	10.00
36	Richard Hidalgo	2.50
37	Omar Vizquel	2.50
38	Johnny Damon	2.50
39	Brian Hunter	2.50
40	Matt Williams	5.00
41	Chuck Finley	2.50
42	Jeromy Burnitz	2.50
43	Livan Hernandez	2.50
44	Delino DeShields	2.50
45	Charles Nagy	2.50
46	Scott Rolen	12.00
47	Neifi Perez	2.50
48	John Wetteland	2.50
49	Eric Milton	5.00
50	Mike Piazza	25.00
51	Cal Ripken Jr.	30.00
52	Mariano Rivera	4.00
53	Butch Huskey	2.50
54	Quinton McCracken	2.50
55	Jose Cruz Jr.	10.00
56	Brian Jordan	2.50
57	Hideo Nomo	6.00
58	Masato Yoshii	5.00
59	Cliff Floyd	2.50
60	Jose Guillen	4.00
61	Jeff Shaw	2.50
62	Edgar Martinez	4.00
63	Rondell White	4.00
64	Hal Morris	2.50
65	Barry Larkin	5.00
66	Eric Young	2.50
67	Ray Lankford	2.50
68	Derek Bell	2.50
69	Charles Johnson	2.50
70	Robin Ventura	4.00
71	Chuck Knoblauch	5.00
72	Kevin Brown	4.00
73	Jose Valentin	2.50
74	Jay Buhner	5.00
75	Tony Gwynn	20.00
76	Andy Pettitte	8.00
77	Edgardo Alfonzo	2.50
78	Kerry Wood	40.00
79	Darin Erstad	10.00
80	Paul Konerko	4.00
81	Jason Kendall	2.50
82	Tino Martinez	5.00
83	Brad Radke	2.50
84	Jeff King	2.50
85	Travis Lee	20.00
86	Jeff Kent	2.50
87	Trevor Hoffman	2.50
88	David Cone	4.00
89	Jose Canseco	6.00
90	Juan Gonzalez	20.00
91	Todd Hundley	2.50
92	John Valentin	2.50
93	Sammy Sosa	25.00
94	Jason Giambi	2.50
95	Chipper Jones	25.00
96	Jeff Blauser	2.50
97	Brad Fullmer	4.00
98	Derrek Lee	2.50
99	Denny Neagle	2.50
100	Ken Griffey Jr.	40.00
101	David Justice	5.00
102	Tim Salmon	5.00
103	J.T. Snow	2.50
104	Fred McGriff	4.00
105	Brady Anderson	2.50
106	Larry Walker	6.00
107	Jeff Cirillo	2.50
108	Andruw Jones	10.00
109	Manny Ramirez	10.00
110	Justin Thompson	2.50
111	Vinny Castilla	4.00
112	Chan Ho Park	4.00
113	Mark Grudzielanek	2.50
114	Mark Grace	5.00
115	Ken Caminiti	4.00
116	Ryan Klesko	5.00
117	Rafael Palmeiro	5.00
118	Pat Hentgen	2.50
119	Eric Karros	4.00
120	Randy Johnson	8.00
121	Roberto Alomar	8.00
122	John Olerud	5.00
123	Paul Molitor	8.00
124	Dean Palmer	2.50
125	Nomar Garciaparra	25.00
126	Curt Schilling	4.00
127	Jay Bell	2.50
128	Craig Biggio	4.00
129	Marty Cordova	2.50
130	Ivan Rodriguez	10.00
131	Todd Helton	8.00
132	Jim Thome	8.00
133	Albert Belle	10.00
134	Mike Lansing	2.50
135	Mark McGwire	40.00
136	Roger Clemens	15.00
137	Tom Glavine	4.00
138	Ron Gant	4.00
139	Alex Rodriguez	30.00
140	Jeff Bagwell	12.00
141	John Smoltz	4.00
142	Kenny Lofton	10.00
143	Dante Bichette	4.00
144	Pedro Martinez	8.00
145	Barry Bonds	10.00
146	Travis Fryman	2.50
147	Bobby Jones	2.50
148	Bobby Higginson	2.50
149	Reggie Sanders	2.50
150	Frank Thomas	30.00

1998 Topps Stars Gold Rainbow

Each card in Topps Stars was available in a Gold Rainbow version. This was the most limited of the five parallels and was numbered to 99. Cards featured gold prismatic foil on the front and were seeded every 46 packs.

		MT
Common Player:		15.00
Semistars:		40.00
Production 99 sets		
1	Greg Maddux	125.00
2	Darryl Kile	15.00
3	Rod Beck	15.00
4	Ellis Burks	15.00
5	Gary Sheffield	25.00
6	David Ortiz	15.00
7	Marquis Grissom	15.00
8	Tony Womack	15.00
9	Mike Mussina	40.00
10	Bernie Williams	40.00
11	Andy Benes	15.00
12	Rusty Greer	20.00
13	Carlos Delgado	15.00
14	Jim Edmonds	20.00
15	Raul Mondesi	25.00
16	Andres Galarraga	30.00
17	Wade Boggs	25.00
18	Paul O'Neill	25.00
19	Edgar Renteria	15.00
20	Tony Clark	30.00
21	Vladimir Guerrero	50.00
22	Moises Alou	20.00
23	Bernard Gilkey	15.00
24	Lance Johnson	15.00
25	Ben Grieve	60.00
26	Sandy Alomar	20.00
27	Ray Durham	15.00
28	Shawn Estes	15.00
29	David Segui	15.00
30	Javy Lopez	20.00
31	Steve Finley	15.00
32	Rey Ordonez	15.00
33	Derek Jeter	100.00
34	Henry Rodriguez	15.00
35	Mo Vaughn	50.00
36	Richard Hidalgo	15.00
37	Omar Vizquel	15.00
38	Johnny Damon	15.00
39	Brian Hunter	15.00
40	Matt Williams	25.00
41	Chuck Finley	15.00
42	Jeromy Burnitz	15.00
43	Livan Hernandez	15.00
44	Delino DeShields	15.00
45	Charles Nagy	15.00
46	Scott Rolen	60.00
47	Neifi Perez	15.00
48	John Wetteland	15.00
49	Eric Milton	20.00
50	Mike Piazza	125.00
51	Cal Ripken Jr.	150.00
52	Mariano Rivera	20.00
53	Butch Huskey	15.00
54	Quinton McCracken	15.00
55	Jose Cruz Jr.	50.00
56	Brian Jordan	15.00
57	Hideo Nomo	30.00
58	Masato Yoshii	20.00
59	Cliff Floyd	15.00
60	Jose Guillen	20.00
61	Jeff Shaw	15.00
62	Edgar Martinez	20.00
63	Rondell White	20.00
64	Hal Morris	15.00
65	Barry Larkin	25.00
66	Eric Young	15.00
67	Ray Lankford	15.00
68	Derek Bell	15.00
69	Charles Johnson	15.00
70	Robin Ventura	20.00
71	Chuck Knoblauch	25.00
72	Kevin Brown	20.00
73	Jose Valentin	15.00
74	Jay Buhner	25.00
75	Tony Gwynn	100.00
76	Andy Pettitte	40.00
77	Edgardo Alfonzo	15.00
78	Kerry Wood	150.00
79	Darin Erstad	50.00
80	Paul Konerko	20.00
81	Jason Kendall	15.00
82	Tino Martinez	25.00
83	Brad Radke	15.00
84	Jeff King	15.00
85	Travis Lee	100.00
86	Jeff Kent	15.00
87	Trevor Hoffman	15.00
88	David Cone	20.00
89	Jose Canseco	30.00
90	Juan Gonzalez	100.00
91	Todd Hundley	15.00
92	John Valentin	15.00
93	Sammy Sosa	125.00
94	Jason Giambi	15.00
95	Chipper Jones	125.00
96	Jeff Blauser	15.00
97	Brad Fullmer	20.00
98	Derrek Lee	15.00
99	Denny Neagle	15.00
100	Ken Griffey Jr.	200.00
101	David Justice	25.00
102	Tim Salmon	25.00
103	J.T. Snow	15.00
104	Fred McGriff	20.00
105	Brady Anderson	15.00
106	Larry Walker	30.00
107	Jeff Cirillo	15.00
108	Andruw Jones	50.00
109	Manny Ramirez	50.00
110	Justin Thompson	15.00
111	Vinny Castilla	20.00
112	Chan Ho Park	20.00
113	Mark Grudzielanek	15.00
114	Mark Grace	25.00
115	Ken Caminiti	20.00
116	Ryan Klesko	25.00
117	Rafael Palmeiro	25.00
118	Pat Hentgen	15.00
119	Eric Karros	20.00
120	Randy Johnson	40.00
121	Roberto Alomar	40.00
122	John Olerud	25.00
123	Paul Molitor	40.00
124	Dean Palmer	15.00
125	Nomar Garciaparra	125.00
126	Curt Schilling	20.00
127	Jay Bell	15.00
128	Craig Biggio	20.00
129	Marty Cordova	15.00
130	Ivan Rodriguez	50.00
131	Todd Helton	40.00
132	Jim Thome	40.00
133	Albert Belle	50.00
134	Mike Lansing	15.00
135	Mark McGwire	250.00
136	Roger Clemens	75.00
137	Tom Glavine	20.00
138	Ron Gant	20.00
139	Alex Rodriguez	150.00
140	Jeff Bagwell	60.00
141	John Smoltz	20.00
142	Kenny Lofton	50.00
143	Dante Bichette	20.00
144	Pedro Martinez	40.00
145	Barry Bonds	50.00
146	Travis Fryman	15.00
147	Bobby Jones	15.00
148	Bobby Higginson	15.00
149	Reggie Sanders	15.00
150	Frank Thomas	125.00

1998 Topps Stars Galaxy

Galaxy featured 10 players who possess all five skills featured in Topps Stars Baseball. Four versions were available and sequentially numbered, including: Bronze (numbered to 100, inserted 1:682 packs), Silver (numbered to 75, inserted 1:910), Gold (numbered to 50, inserted 1:1,364) and Gold Rainbow (numbered to 5, inserted 1:13,643).

		MT
Complete Set (10):		800.00
Common Player:		25.00
Production 100 sets		
Silvers: 1x to 1.5x		
Production 75 sets		
Golds: 1.5x to 2x		
Production 50 sets		
G1	Barry Bonds	50.00
G2	Jeff Bagwell	75.00
G3	Nomar Garciaparra	125.00
G4	Chipper Jones	100.00
G5	Ken Griffey Jr.	200.00
G6	Sammy Sosa	125.00
G7	Larry Walker	40.00
G8	Alex Rodriguez	140.00
G9	Craig Biggio	25.00
G10	Raul Mondesi	25.00

1998 Topps Stars Luminaries

Luminaries featured three top players in each tool group in Topps Stars. The 15-card insert arrived in four different versions and were sequentially numbered. They were inserted as follows: bronze (numbered to 100, inserted 1:455), silver (numbered to 75, inserted 1:606), gold (numbered to 50, inserted 1:910) and gold rainbow (numbered to 5, inserted 1:9,095).

		MT
Complete Set (15):		1000.
Common Player:		25.00
Production 100 sets		
Silvers: 1x to 1.5x		
Production 75 sets		
Golds: 1.5x to 2x		
Production 50 sets		
L1	Ken Griffey Jr.	200.00
L2	Mark McGwire	250.00
L3	Juan Gonzalez	100.00
L4	Tony Gwynn	100.00
L5	Frank Thomas	125.00
L6	Mike Piazza	125.00
L7	Chuck Knoblauch	30.00
L8	Kenny Lofton	50.00
L9	Barry Bonds	50.00
L10	Matt Williams	30.00
L11	Raul Mondesi	25.00
L12	Ivan Rodriguez	50.00
L13	Alex Rodriguez	140.00
L14	Nomar Garciaparra	125.00
L15	Ken Caminiti	25.00

1998 Topps Stars Rookie Reprints

Topps reprinted the rookie cards of five Hall of Famers in Rookie Reprints. The cards are inserted one per 24 packs and have UV coating.

A player's name in *italic* type indicates a rookie card.

		MT
Complete Set (5):		20.00
Common Player:		3.00
	Johnny Bench	6.00
	Whitey Ford	3.00
	Joe Morgan	3.00
	Mike Schmidt	8.00
	Carl Yastrzemski	4.00

1998 Topps Stars Rookie Reprints Autographs

Autographed versions of all five Rookie Reprint inserts were available and seeded one per 273 packs. Each card arrive with a Topps "Certified Autograph Issue" stamp to ensure its authenticity.

		MT
Complete Set (5):		220.00
Common Player:		25.00
	Johnny Bench	60.00
	Whitey Ford	30.00
	Joe Morgan	40.00
	Mike Schmidt	90.00
	Carl Yastrzemski	60.00

1998 Topps Stars Supernovas

Supernovas was a 10-card insert in Topps Stars and included rookies and prospects who either have all five tools focused on in the product, or excel dramatically in one of the five. Four sequentially numbered levels were available, with insert rates as follows: bronze (numbered to 100, inserted 1:682), silver (numbered to 75, inserted 1:910), gold (numbered to 50, inserted 1:1,364) and gold rainbow (numbered to 5, inserted 1:13,643).

		MT
Complete Set (10):		400.00
Common Player:		20.00
Production 100 sets		
Silvers: 1x to 1.5x		
Production 75 sets		
Golds: 1.5x to 2x		
Production 50 sets		
S1	Ben Grieve	60.00
S2	Travis Lee	100.00
S3	Todd Helton	50.00
S4	Adrian Beltre	30.00
S5	Derrek Lee	20.00
S6	David Ortiz	20.00
S7	Brad Fullmer	30.00
S8	Mark Kotsay	20.00
S9	Paul Konerko	20.00
S10	Kerry Wood	120.00

1998 Topps Stars N' Steel

Stars 'N Steel was a 44-card set printed on four-colored textured film laminate bonded to a sheet of 25-gauge metal. Regular cards featured a silver colored border while gold versions were also available and seeded one per 12 packs. Stars 'N Steel was available only to Home Team Advantage members and was packaged in three-card packs that arrived in sturdy, tri-fold stand-up display unit. A second parallel version was also available featuring gold holographic technology and was seeded one per 40 packs.

		MT
Complete Set (44):		150.00
Common Player:		2.00
Golds: 2x to 4x		
Refractors: 6x to 12x		
Wax Box:		100.00
1	Roberto Alomar	5.00
2	Jeff Bagwell	10.00
3	Albert Belle	6.00
4	Dante Bichette	2.00
5	Barry Bonds	6.00
6	Jay Buhner	3.00
7	Ken Caminiti	2.00
8	Vinny Castilla	2.00
9	Roger Clemens	10.00
10	Jose Cruz Jr.	10.00
11	Andres Galarraga	3.00
12	Nomar Garciaparra	15.00
13	Juan Gonzalez	12.00
14	Mark Grace	3.00
15	Ken Griffey Jr.	25.00
16	Tony Gwynn	12.00
17	Todd Hundley	2.00
18	Derek Jeter	12.00
19	Randy Johnson	4.00
20	Andruw Jones	10.00
21	Chipper Jones	15.00
22	David Justice	2.00
23	Ray Lankford	2.00
24	Barry Larkin	3.00
25	Kenny Lofton	6.00
26	Greg Maddux	15.00
27	Edgar Martinez	2.00
28	Tino Martinez	3.00
29	Mark McGwire	30.00
30	Paul Molitor	5.00
31	Rafael Palmeiro	3.00
32	Mike Piazza	15.00
33	Manny Ramirez	5.00
34	Cal Ripken Jr.	18.00
35	Ivan Rodriguez	6.00
36	Scott Rolen	10.00

37	Tim Salmon	3.00
38	Gary Sheffield	3.00
39	Sammy Sosa	20.00
40	Frank Thomas	15.00
41	Jim Thome	4.00
42	Mo Vaughn	6.00
43	Larry Walker	3.00
44	Bernie Williams	4.00

1998 Topps TEK

		MT
Complete Set (90):		125.00
Common Player:		.25
Silvers: 4x to 8x		
Inserted 1:6		
1	Ben Grieve	3.00
2	Kerry Wood	10.00
3	Barry Bonds	2.50
4	John Olerud	.50
5	Ivan Rodriguez	2.50
6	Frank Thomas	6.00
7	Bernie Williams	2.50
8	Dante Bichette	.75
9	Alex Rodriguez	6.00
10	Tom Glavine	.50
11	Eric Karros	.40
12	Craig Biggio	.50
13	Mark McGwire	12.00
14	Derek Jeter	6.00
15	Nomar Garciaparra	6.00
16	Brady Anderson	.25
17	Vladimir Guerrero	3.00
18	David Justice	.75
19	Chipper Jones	6.00
20	Jim Edmonds	.25
21	Roger Clemens	4.00
22	Mark Kotsay	.25
23	Tony Gwynn	5.00
24	Todd Walker	.50
25	Tino Martinez	1.00
26	Andruw Jones	2.50
27	Sandy Alomar	.25
28	Sammy Sosa	8.00
29	Gary Sheffield	.75
30	Ken Griffey Jr.	10.00
31	Aramis Ramirez	.50
32	Curt Schilling	.50
33	Robin Ventura	.40
34	Larry Walker	1.00
35	Darin Erstad	2.00
36	Todd Dunwoody	.25
37	Paul O'Neill	.75
38	Vinny Castilla	.50
39	Randy Johnson	2.00
40	Rafael Palmeiro	.75
41	Pedro Martinez	2.00
42	Derek Bell	.25
43	Carlos Delgado	.25
44	Matt Williams	.75
45	Kenny Lofton	2.50
46	Edgar Renteria	.25
47	Albert Belle	2.50
48	Jeromy Burnitz	.25
49	Adrian Beltre	.75
50	Greg Maddux	6.00
51	Cal Ripken Jr.	8.00
52	Jason Kendall	.25
53	Ellis Burks	.25
54	Paul Molitor	1.50
55	Moises Alou	.50
56	Raul Mondesi	.50
57	Barry Larkin	.50
58	Tony Clark	1.50
59	Travis Lee	5.00
60	Juan Gonzalez	5.00
61	*Troy Glaus*	10.00
62	Jose Cruz Jr.	2.00
63	Paul Konerko	.50
64	Edgar Martinez	.25
65	Javy Lopez	.50
66	Manny Ramirez	2.50
67	Roberto Alomar	1.50
68	Ken Caminiti	.50
69	Todd Helton	2.00
70	Chuck Knoblauch	.75
71	Kevin Brown	.50
72	Tim Salmon	.75
73	*Orlando Hernandez*	15.00
74	Jeff Bagwell	3.00
75	Brian Jordan	.25
76	Derrek Lee	.25
77	Brad Fullmer	.75
78	Mark Grace	.75

79	Jeff King	.25
80	Mike Mussina	2.00
81	Jay Buhner	.75
82	Quinton McCracken	.25
83	A.J. Hinch	.25
84	Richard Hidalgo	.25
85	Andres Galarraga	.75
86	Mike Piazza	6.00
87	Mo Vaughn	2.50
88	Scott Rolen	3.00
89	Jim Thome	1.00
90	Ray Lankford	.25

1992 Triple Play

This set was released only in wax pack form. Cards feature red borders. Boyhood photos, mascots and ballparks are among the featured cards. This set was designed to give collectors an alternative product to the high-end card sets. The cards are standard size.

		MT
Complete Set (264):		11.00
Common Player:		.05
Wax Box:		10.00
1	SkyDome	.05
2	Tom Foley	.05
3	Scott Erickson	.05
4	Matt Williams	.15
5	Dave Valle	.05
6	Andy Van Slyke (Little Hotshot)	.05
7	Tom Glavine	.10
8	Kevin Appier	.08
9	Pedro Guerrero	.05
10	Terry Steinbach	.05
11	Terry Mulholland	.05
12	Mike Boddicker	.05
13	Gregg Olson	.05
14	Tim Burke	.05
15	Candy Maldonado	.05
16	Orlando Merced	.05
17	Robin Ventura	.10
18	Eric Anthony	.05
19	Greg Maddux	.75
20	Erik Hanson	.05
21	Bob Ojeda	.05
22	Nolan Ryan	.50
23	Dave Righetti	.05
24	Reggie Jefferson	.05
25	Jody Reed	.05
26	Awesome Action(Steve Finley, Gary Carter)	.05
27	Chili Davis	.05
28	Hector Villanueva	.05
29	Cecil Fielder	.15
30	Hal Morris	.08
31	Barry Larkin	.15
32	Bobby Thigpen	.05
33	Andy Benes	.08
34	Harold Baines	.08
35	David Cone	.05
36	Mark Langston	.05
37	Bryan Harvey	.05
38	John Kruk	.08

39	Scott Sanderson	.05
40	Lonnie Smith	.05
41	Awesome Action(Rex Hudler)	.05
42	George Bell	.05
43	Steve Finley	.05
44	Mickey Tettleton	.05
45	Robby Thompson	.05
46	Pat Kelly	.05
47	Marquis Grissom	.12
48	Tony Pena	.05
49	Alex Cole	.05
50	Steve Buechele	.05
51	Ivan Rodriguez	.15
52	John Smiley	.05
53	Gary Sheffield	.20
54	Greg Olson	.05
55	Ramon Martinez	.08
56	B.J. Surhoff	.05
57	Bruce Hurst	.05
58	Todd Stottlemyre	.05
59	Brett Butler	.10
60	Glenn Davis	.05
61	Awesome Action(Glenn Braggs, Kirt Manwaring)	.05
62	Lee Smith	.08
63	Rickey Henderson	.15
64	Fun at the Ballpark(David Cone, Jeff Innis, John Franco)	.05
65	Rick Aguilera	.05
66	Kevin Elster	.05
67	Dwight Evans	.05
68	Andujar Cedeno	.05
69	Brian McRae	.08
70	Benito Santiago	.08
71	Randy Johnson	.15
72	Roberto Kelly	.05
73	Awesome Action(Juan Samuel)	.05
74	Alex Fernandez	.05
75	Felix Jose	.05
76	Brian Harper	.05
77	Scott Sanderson (Little Hotshot)	.05
78	Ken Caminiti	.10
79	Mo Vaughn	.20
80	Roger McDowell	.05
81	Robin Yount	.15
82	Dave Magadan	.05
83	Julio Franco	.05
84	Roberto Alomar	.30
85	Steve Avery	.05
86	Travis Fryman	.05
87	Fred McGriff	.15
88	Dave Stewart	.08
89	Larry Walker	.15
90	Chris Sabo	.05
91	Chuck Finley	.05
92	Dennis Martinez	.05
93	Jeff Johnson	.05
94	Len Dykstra	.08
95	Mark Whiten	.05
96	Wade Taylor	.05
97	Lance Dickson	.05
98	Kevin Tapani	.05
99	Awesome Action(Luis Polonia, Tony Phillips)	.05
100	Milt Cuyler	.05
101	Willie McGee	.05
102	Awesome Action(Tony Fernandez, Ryne Sandberg)	.05
103	Albert Belle	.25
104	Todd Hundley	.05
105	Ben McDonald	.05
106	Doug Drabek	.05
107	Tim Raines	.08
108	Joe Carter	.10
109	Reggie Sanders	.10
110	John Olerud	.10
111	Darren Lewis	.05
112	Juan Gonzalez	.25
113	Awesome Action(Andre Dawson)	.05
114	Mark Grace	.15
115	George Brett	.25
116	Barry Bonds	.30
117	Lou Whitaker	.05
118	Jose Oquendo	.05
119	Lee Stevens	.05
120	Phil Plantier	.05
121	Awesome Action(Devon White, Matt Merullo)	.05
122	Greg Vaughn	.05
123	Royce Clayton	.05

124	Bob Welch	.05
125	Juan Samuel	.05
126	Ron Gant	.08
127	Edgar Martinez	.05
128	Andy Ashby	.05
129	Jack McDowell	.05
130	Awesome Action(Dave Henderson, Jerry Browne)	.05
131	Leo Gomez	.05
132	Checklist 1-88	.05
133	Phillie Phanatic	.05
134	Bret Barbarie	.05
135	Kent Hrbek	.08
136	Hall of Fame	.05
137	Omar Vizquel	.05
138	The Famous Chicken	.05
139	Terry Pendleton	.05
140	Jim Eisenreich	.05
141	Todd Zeile	.08
142	Todd Van Poppel	.05
143	Darren Daulton	.05
144	Mike Macfarlane	.05
145	Luis Mercedes	.05
146	Trevor Wilson	.05
147	Dave Steib	.05
148	Andy Van Slyke	.05
149	Carlton Fisk	.08
150	Craig Biggio	.08
151	Joe Girardi	.05
152	Ken Griffey, Jr.	1.25
153	Jose Offerman	.05
154	Bobby Witt	.05
155	Will Clark	.20
156	Steve Olin	.05
157	Greg Harris	.05
158	Dale Murphy (Little Hotshot)	.08
159	Don Mattingly	.35
160	Shawon Dunston	.10
161	Bill Gullickson	.05
162	Paul O'Neill	.08
163	Norm Charlton	.05
164	Bo Jackson	.25
165	Tony Fernandez	.05
166	Dave Henderson	.05
167	Dwight Gooden	.10
168	Junior Felix	.05
169	Lance Parrish	.05
170	Pat Combs	.05
171	Chuck Knoblauch	.15
172	John Smoltz	.08
173	Wrigley Field	.05
174	Andre Dawson	.08
175	Pete Harnisch	.05
176	Alan Trammell	.08
177	Kirk Dressendorfer	.05
178	Matt Nokes	.05
179	Wil Cordero	.05
180	Scott Cooper	.05
181	Glenallen Hill	.05
182	John Franco	.05
183	Rafael Palmeiro	.08
184	Jay Bell	.05
185	Bill Wegman	.05
186	Deion Sanders	.20
187	Darryl Strawberry	.10
188	Jaime Navarro	.05
189	Darren Jackson	.05
190	Eddie Zosky	.05
191	Mike Scioscia	.05
192	Chito Martinez	.05
193	Awesome Action(Pat Kelly, Ron Tingley)	.05
194	Ray Lankford	.05
195	Dennis Eckersley	.08
196	Awesome Action(Ivan Calderon, Mike Maddux)	.05
197	Shane Mack	.05
198	Checklist 89-176	.05
199	Cal Ripken, Jr.	1.00
200	Jeff Bagwell	.45
201	David Howard	.05
202	Kirby Puckett	.30
203	Harold Reynolds	.05
204	Jim Abbott	.08
205	Mark Lewis	.05
206	Frank Thomas	1.25
207	Rex Hudler	.05
208	Vince Coleman	.05
209	Delino DeShields	.05
210	Luis Gonzalez	.05
211	Wade Boggs	.15
212	Orel Hershiser	.08
213	Cal Eldred	.05
214	Jose Canseco	.20
215	Jose Guzman	.05
216	Roger Clemens	.25

217	Dave Justice	.20
218	Tony Phillips	.05
219	Tony Gwynn	.30
220	Mitch Williams	.05
221	Bill Sampen	.05
222	Billy Hatcher	.05
223	Gary Gaetti	.05
224	Tim Wallach	.05
225	Kevin Maas	.05
226	Kevin Brown	.05
227	Sandy Alomar	.08
228	John Habyan	.05
229	Ryne Sandberg	.25
230	Greg Gagne	.05
231	Autographs(Mark McGwire)	1.00
232	Mike LaValliere	.05
233	Mark Gubicza	.05
234	Lance Parrish (Little Hotshot)	.05
235	Carlos Baerga	.10
236	Howard Johnson	.05
237	Mike Mussina	.15
238	Ruben Sierra	.08
239	Lance Johnson	.05
240	Devon White	.05
241	Dan Wilson	.05
242	Kelly Gruber	.05
243	Brett Butler (Little Hotshot)	.05
244	Ozzie Smith	.20
245	Chuck McElroy	.05
246	Shawn Boskie	.05
247	Mark Davis	.05
248	Bill Landrum	.05
249	Frank Tanana	.05
250	Darryl Hamilton	.05
251	Gary DiSarcina	.05
252	Mike Greenwell	.08
253	Cal Ripken, Jr. (Little Hotshot)	.25
254	Paul Molitor	.15
255	Tim Teufel	.05
256	Chris Hoiles	.05
257	Rob Dibble	.05
258	Sid Bream	.05
259	Chito Martinez	.05
260	Dale Murphy	.10
261	Greg Hibbard	.05
262	Mark McGwire	1.00
263	Oriole Park	.05
264	Checklist 177-264	.05

1992 Triple Play Gallery of Stars

DANNY TARTABULL

Two levels of scarcity are represented in this insert issue. Cards #1-6 (all cards have a GS prefix to the card number) feature in their new uniforms players who changed teams for 1993. Those inserts were found in the standard Triple Play foil packs and are somewhat more common than cards #7-12, which were found only in jumbo packs and which feature a better selection of established stars and rookies. All of the inserts feature the artwork of Dick Perez, with player portraits set against a colorful background. Silver-foil accents highlight the front design. Backs are red with a white "tombstone" containing a career summary.

		MT
Complete Set (12):		24.00
Common Player:		1.00
1	Bobby Bonilla	1.50
2	Wally Joyner	1.50
3	Jack Morris	1.00
4	Steve Sax	1.00
5	Danny Tartabull	1.00
6	Frank Viola	1.00
7	Jeff Bagwell	3.00
8	Ken Griffey, Jr.	7.00
9	David Justice	2.00
10	Ryan Klesko	2.50
11	Cal Ripken, Jr.	6.00
12	Frank Thomas	5.00

1993 Triple Play

MARK LEMKE 2B

For the second year, Leaf-Donruss used the "Triple Play" brand name for its base-level card set aimed at the younger collector. The 264-card set was available in several types of retail packaging and included a number of special subsets, such as childhood photos (labeled LH - Little Hotshots - in the checklist) and insert sets. Checklist card #264 incorrectly shows card #129, Joe Robbie Stadium, as #259. There is a second card, "Equipment," which also bears #129. An "Action Baseball" scratch-off game card was included in each foil pack.

		MT
Complete Set (264):		10.00
Common Player:		.05
Wax Box:		14.00
1	Ken Griffey, Jr.	1.00
2	Roberto Alomar	.30
3	Cal Ripken, Jr.	1.00
4	Eric Karros	.15
5	Cecil Fielder	.15
6	Gary Sheffield	.25
7	Darren Daulton	.05
8	Andy Van Slyke	.05
9	Dennis Eckersley	.08
10	Ryne Sandberg	.30
11	Mark Grace (Little Hotshots)	.10
12	Awesome Action #1(Luis Polonia, David Segui)	.05
13	Mike Mussina	.10
14	Vince Coleman	.05
15	Rafael Belliard	.05
16	Ivan Rodriguez	.25
17	Eddie Taubensee	.05

18	Cal Eldred	.05
19	Rick Wilkins	.05
20	Edgar Martinez	.05
21	Brian McRae	.08
22	Darren Holmes	.05
23	Mark Whiten	.05
24	Todd Zeile	.08
25	Scott Cooper	.05
26	Frank Thomas	1.00
27	Wil Cordero	.05
28	Juan Guzman	.05
29	Pedro Astacio	.05
30	Steve Avery	.05
31	Barry Larkin	.12
32	President Clinton	.25
33	Scott Erickson	.05
34	Mike Devereaux	.05
35	Tino Martinez	.10
36	Brent Mayne	.05
37	Tim Salmon	.25
38	Dave Hollins	.08
39	Royce Clayton	.05
40	Shawon Dunston	.08
41	Eddie Murray	.10
42	Larry Walker	.12
43	Jeff Bagwell	.25
44	Milt Cuyler	.05
45	Mike Bordick	.05
46	Mike Greenwell	.05
47	Steve Sax	.05
48	Chuck Knoblauch	.10
49	Charles Nagy	.05
50	Tim Wakefield	.05
51	Tony Gwynn	.15
52	Rob Dibble	.05
53	Mickey Morandini	.05
54	Steve Hosey	.05
55	Mike Piazza	.75
56	Bill Wegman	.05
57	Kevin Maas	.05
58	Gary DiSarcina	.05
59	Travis Fryman	.05
60	Ruben Sierra	.05
61	Awesome Action #2(Ken Caminiti)	.05
62	Brian Jordan	.08
63	Scott Chiamparino	.05
64	Awesome Action #3(Mike Bordick, George Brett)	.08
65	Carlos Garcia	.05
66	Checklist 1-66	.05
67	John Smoltz	.08
68	Awesome Action #4(Mark McGwire, Brian Harper)	1.00
69	Kurt Stillwell	.05
70	Chad Curtis	.10
71	Rafael Palmeiro	.15
72	Kevin Young	.05
73	Glenn Davis	.05
74	Dennis Martinez	.05
75	Sam Militello	.05
76	Mike Morgan	.05
77	Frank Thomas (Little Hotshots)	.75
78	Staying Fit(Bip Roberts, Mike Devereaux)	.05
79	Steve Buechele	.05
80	Carlos Baerga	.08
81	Robby Thompson	.05
82	Kirk McCaskill	.05
83	Lee Smith	.08
84	Gary Scott	.05
85	Tony Pena	.05
86	Howard Johnson	.05
87	Mark McGwire	1.00
88	Bip Roberts	.05
89	Devon White	.08
90	John Franco	.05
91	Tom Browning	.05
92	Mickey Tettleton	.05
93	Jeff Conine	.08
94	Albert Belle	.20
95	Fred McGriff	.12
96	Nolan Ryan	.75
97	Paul Molitor (Little Hotshots)	.15
98	Juan Bell	.05
99	Dave Fleming	.05
100	Craig Biggio	.08
101a	Andy Stankiewicz (white name on front)	.05
101b	Andy Stankiewicz (red name on front)	.25
102	Delino DeShields	.05
103	Damion Easley	.08
104	Kevin McReynolds	.05
105	David Nied	.05
106	Rick Sutcliffe	.05
107	Will Clark	.15
108	Tim Raines	.08
109	Eric Anthony	.05
110	Mike LaValliere	.05
111	Dean Palmer	.08
112	Eric Davis	.08
113	Damon Berryhill	.05
114	Felix Jose	.05
115	Ozzie Guillen	.05
116	Pat Listach	.05
117	Tom Glavine	.08
118	Roger Clemens	.25
119	Dave Henderson	.05
120	Don Mattingly	.50
121	Orel Hershiser	.08
122	Ozzie Smith	.15
123	Joe Carter	.10
124	Bret Saberhagen	.08
125	Mitch Williams	.05
126	Jerald Clark	.05
127	Mile High Stadium	.05
128	Kent Hrbek	.10
129a	Equipment(Curt Schilling, Mark Whiten)	.05
129b	Joe Robbie Stadium	.05
130	Gregg Jefferies	.10
131	John Orton	.05
132	Checklist 67-132	.05
133	Bret Boone	.08
134	Pat Borders	.05
135	Gregg Olson	.05
136	Brett Butler	.10
137	Rob Deer	.05
138	Darrin Jackson	.08
139	John Kruk	.05
140	Jay Bell	.05
141	Bobby Witt	.05
142	New Cubs(Dan Plesac, Randy Myers, Jose Guzman)	.05
143	Wade Boggs (Little Hotshots)	.15
144	Awesome Action #5(Kenny Lofton)	.10
145	Ben McDonald	.05
146	Dwight Gooden	.10
147	Terry Pendleton	.05
148	Julio Franco	.05
149	Ken Caminiti	.08
150	Greg Vaughn	.05
151	Sammy Sosa	.75
152	David Valle	.05
153	Wally Joyner	.08
154	Dante Bichette	.08
155	Mark Lewis	.05
156	Bob Tewksbury	.05
157	Billy Hatcher	.05
158	Jack McDowell	.05
159	Marquis Grissom	.08
160	Jack Morris	.05
161	Ramon Martinez	.08
162	Deion Sanders	.15
163	Tim Belcher	.05
164	Mascots	.10
165	Scott Leius	.05
166	Brady Anderson	.10
167	Randy Johnson	.15
168	Mark Gubicza	.05
169	Chuck Finley	.05
170	Terry Mulholland	.05
171	Matt Williams	.12
172	Dwight Smith	.05
173	Bobby Bonilla	.10
174	Ken Hill	.05
175	Doug Jones	.05
176	Tony Phillips	.05
177	Terry Steinbach	.05
178	Frank Viola	.05
179	Robin Ventura	.10
180	Shane Mack	.05
181	Kenny Lofton	.20
182	Jeff King	.05
183	Tim Teufel	.05
184	Chris Sabo	.05
185	Lenny Dykstra	.05
186	Trevor Wilson	.05
187	Darryl Strawberry	.12
188	Robin Yount	.20
189	Bob Wickman	.05
190	Luis Polonia	.05
191	Alan Trammell	.10
192	Bob Welch	.05
193	Awesome Action #6	.05
194	Tom Pagnozzi	.05
195	Bret Barberie	.05
196	Awesome Action #7(Mike Scioscia)	.05
197	Randy Tomlin	.05
198	Checklist 133-198	.05
199	Ron Gant	.08
200	Awesome Action #8(Roberto Alomar)	.10
201	Andy Benes	.08
202	Pepper	.05
203	Steve Finley	.05
204	Steve Olin	.05
205	Chris Hoiles	.05
206	John Wetteland	.05
207	Danny Tartabull	.05
208	Bernard Gilkey	.08
209	Tom Glavine (Little Hotshots)	.10
210	Benito Santiago	.08
211	Mark Grace	.15
212	Glenallen Hill	.05
213	Jeff Brantley	.05
214	George Brett	.50
215	Mark Lemke	.05
216	Ron Karkovice	.05
217	Tom Brunansky	.05
218	Todd Hundley	.05
219	Rickey Henderson	.20
220	Joe Oliver	.05
221	Juan Gonzalez	.50
222	John Olerud	.08
223	Hal Morris	.05
224	Lou Whitaker	.05
225	Bryan Harvey	.05
226	Mike Gallego	.05
227	Willie McGee	.05
228	Jose Oquendo	.05
229	Darren Daulton (Little Hotshots)	.05
230	Curt Schilling	.05
231	Jay Buhner	.10
232	New Astros(Doug Drabek, Greg Swindell)	.05
233	Jaime Navarro	.05
234	Kevin Appier	.05
235	Mark Langston	.05
236	Jeff Montgomery	.05
237	Joe Girardi	.05
238	Ed Sprague	.05
239	Dan Walters	.05
240	Kevin Tapani	.05
241	Pete Harnisch	.05
242	Al Martin	.05
243	Jose Canseco	.25
244	Moises Alou	.10
245	Mark McGwire (Little Hotshots)	1.00
246	Luis Rivera	.05
247	George Bell	.05
248	B.J. Surhoff	.05
249	Dave Justice	.12
250	Brian Harper	.05
251	Sandy Alomar, Jr.	.10
252	Kevin Brown	.05
253	New Dodgers(Tim Wallach, Jody Reed, Todd Worrell)	.05
254	Ray Lankford	.10
255	Derek Bell	.08
256	Joe Grahe	.05
257	Charlie Hayes	.05
258	New Yankees(Wade Boggs, Jim Abbott)	.25
259	Joe Robbie Stadium	.05
260	Kirby Puckett	.40
261	Fun at the Ballpark(Jay Bell, Vince Coleman)	.05
262	Bill Swift	.05
263	Fun at the Ballpark(Roger McDowell)	.05
264	Checklist 199-264	.05

1993 Triple Play Gallery

The Gallery of Stars cards were found as random inserts in Triple Play jumbo packs. The cards feature Dick Perez painted representations of the players.

A player's name in *italic* type indicates a rookie card.

		MT
Complete Set (10):		24.00
Common Player:		1.00
1	Barry Bonds	3.00
2	Andre Dawson	1.00
3	Wade Boggs	1.50
4	Greg Maddux	7.50
5	Dave Winfield	1.50
6	Paul Molitor	1.50
7	Jim Abbott	1.00
8	J.T. Snow	1.50
9	Benito Santiago	1.00
10	David Nied	1.00

1993 Triple Play League Leaders

These "double-headed" cards feature one player on each side. The six cards were random inserts in Triple Play retail packs.

		MT
Complete Set (6):		15.00
Common Player:		1.00
1	Barry Bonds, Dennis Eckersley	2.50
2	Greg Maddux, Dennis Eckersley	5.00
3	Eric Karros, Pat Listach	1.00
4	Fred McGriff, Juan Gonzalez	3.50
5	Darren Daulton, Cecil Fielder	1.00
6	Gary Sheffield, Edgar Martinez	1.00

> A player's name in *italic* type indicates a rookie card.

1993 Triple Play Nicknames

Popular nicknames of 10 of the game's top stars are featured in silver foil on this insert set found in Triple Play foil packs.

		MT
Complete Set (10):		25.00
Common Player:		1.00
1	Frank Thomas (Big Hurt)	5.00
2	Roger Clemens (Rocket)	2.00
3	Ryne Sandberg (Ryno)	1.50
4	Will Clark (Thrill)	1.50
5	Ken Griffey, Jr. (Junior)	6.00
6	Dwight Gooden (Doc)	1.00
7	Nolan Ryan (Express)	4.50
8	Deion Sanders (Prime Time)	1.50
9	Ozzie Smith (Wizard)	1.50
10	Fred McGriff (Crime Dog)	1.00

1994 Triple Play

Triple Play cards returned for a third year in 1994, this time with a borderless design. According to company officials, production was less than 1994 Donruss Series I baseball, which was roughly 17,500 20-box cases. In the regular-issue 300-card set, 10 players from each team were featured, along with a 17-card Rookie Review subset and several insert sets.

		MT
Complete Set (300):		14.00
Common Player:		.05
Wax Box:		22.00
1	Mike Bordick	.05

2	Dennis Eckersley	.08
3	Brent Gates	.05
4	Rickey Henderson	.15
5	Mark McGwire	1.00
6	Troy Neel	.05
7	Craig Paquette	.05
8	Ruben Sierra	.05
9	Terry Steinbach	.05
10	Bobby Witt	.05
11	Chad Curtis	.08
12	Chili Davis	.05
13	Gary DiSarcina	.05
14	Damion Easley	.05
15	Chuck Finley	.05
16	Joe Grahe	.05
17	Mark Langston	.05
18	Eduardo Perez	.05
19	Tim Salmon	.25
20	J.T. Snow	.10
21	Jeff Bagwell	.60
22	Craig Biggio	.10
23	Ken Caminiti	.10
24	Andujar Cedeno	.05
25	Doug Drabek	.05
26	Steve Finley	.05
27	Luis Gonzalez	.05
28	Pete Harnisch	.05
29	Darryl Kile	.05
30	Mitch Williams	.05
31	Roberto Alomar	.30
32	Joe Carter	.20
33	Juan Guzman	.05
34	Pat Hentgen	.05
35	Paul Molitor	.20
36	John Olerud	.10
37	Ed Sprague	.05
38	Dave Stewart	.05
39	Duane Ward	.05
40	Devon White	.05
41	Steve Avery	.05
42	Jeff Blauser	.05
43	Ron Gant	.08
44	Tom Glavine	.08
45	Dave Justice	.20
46	Greg Maddux	.75
47	Fred McGriff	.20
48	Terry Pendleton	.05
49	Deion Sanders	.25
50	John Smoltz	.08
51	Ricky Bones	.05
52	Cal Eldred	.05
53	Darryl Hamilton	.05
54	John Jaha	.05
55	Pat Listach	.05
56	Jaime Navarro	.05
57	Dave Nilsson	.05
58	B.J. Surhoff	.05
59	Greg Vaughn	.05
60	Robin Yount	.20
61	Bernard Gilkey	.05
62	Gregg Jefferies	.08
63	Brian Jordan	.08
64	Ray Lankford	.05
65	Tom Pagnozzi	.05
66	Ozzie Smith	.20
67	Bob Tewksbury	.05
68	Allen Watson	.05
69	Mark Whiten	.05
70	Todd Zeile	.05
71	Steve Buechele	.05
72	Mark Grace	.15
73	Jose Guzman	.05
74	Derrick May	.05
75	Mike Morgan	.05
76	Randy Myers	.05
77	Ryne Sandberg	.30
78	Sammy Sosa	.75
79	Jose Vizcaino	.05
80	Rick Wilkins	.05
81	Pedro Astacio	.05
82	Brett Butler	.08
83	Delino DeShields	.05
84	Orel Hershiser	.08
85	Eric Karros	.08
86	Ramon Martinez	.08
87	Jose Offerman	.05
88	Mike Piazza	.75
89	Darryl Strawberry	.10
90	Tim Wallach	.05
91	Moises Alou	.08
92	Wil Cordero	.05
93	Jeff Fassero	.05
94	Darrin Fletcher	.05
95	Marquis Grissom	.10
96	Ken Hill	.05
97	Mike Lansing	.05

98	Kirk Rueter	.05
99	Larry Walker	.20
100	John Wetteland	.05
101	Rod Beck	.05
102	Barry Bonds	.40
103	John Burkett	.05
104	Royce Clayton	.05
105	Darren Lewis	.05
106	Kirt Manwaring	.05
107	Willie McGee	.08
108	Bill Swift	.05
109	Robby Thompson	.05
110	Matt Williams	.20
111	Sandy Alomar Jr.	.10
112	Carlos Baerga	.10
113	Albert Belle	.40
114	Wayne Kirby	.05
115	Kenny Lofton	.30
116	Jose Mesa	.05
117	Eddie Murray	.20
118	Charles Nagy	.05
119	Paul Sorrento	.05
120	Jim Thome	.10
121	Rich Amaral	.05
122	Eric Anthony	.05
123	Mike Blowers	.05
124	Chris Bosio	.05
125	Jay Buhner	.08
126	Dave Fleming	.05
127	Ken Griffey, Jr.	1.50
128	Randy Johnson	.15
129	Edgar Martinez	.08
130	Tino Martinez	.15
131	Bret Barberie	.05
132	Ryan Bowen	.05
133	Chuck Carr	.05
134	Jeff Conine	.08
135	Orestes Destrade	.05
136	Chris Hammond	.05
137	Bryan Harvey	.05
138	Dave Magadan	.05
139	Benito Santiago	.05
140	Gary Sheffield	.15
141	Bobby Bonilla	.08
142	Jeromy Burnitz	.05
143	Dwight Gooden	.08
144	Todd Hundley	.08
145	Bobby Jones	.05
146	Jeff Kent	.05
147	Joe Orsulak	.05
148	Bret Saberhagen	.05
149	Pete Schourek	.05
150	Ryan Thompson	.05
151	Brady Anderson	.10
152	Harold Baines	.08
153	Mike Devereaux	.05
154	Chris Hoiles	.05
155	Ben McDonald	.05
156	Mark McLemore	.05
157	Mike Mussina	.10
158	Rafael Palmeiro	.10
159	Cal Ripken, Jr.	1.50
160	Chris Sabo	.05
161	Brad Ausmus	.05
162	Derek Bell	.08
163	Andy Benes	.05
164	Doug Brocail	.05
165	Archi Cianfrocco	.05
166	Ricky Gutierrez	.05
167	Tony Gwynn	.20
168	Gene Harris	.05
169	Pedro Martinez	.08
170	Phil Plantier	.05
171	Darren Daulton	.05
172	Mariano Duncan	.05
173	Len Dykstra	.05
174	Tommy Greene	.05
175	Dave Hollins	.05
176	Danny Jackson	.05
177	John Kruk	.05
178	Terry Mulholland	.05
179	Curt Schilling	.05
180	Kevin Stocker	.05
181	Jay Bell	.05
182	Steve Cooke	.05
183	Carlos Garcia	.05
184	Joel Johnston	.05
185	Jeff King	.05
186	Al Martin	.05
187	Orlando Merced	.05
188	Don Slaught	.05
189	Andy Van Slyke	.05
190	Kevin Young	.05
191	Kevin Brown	.08
192	Jose Canseco	.25
193	Will Clark	.20

194	Juan Gonzalez	.30
195	Tom Henke	.05
196	David Hulse	.05
197	Dean Palmer	.08
198	Roger Pavlik	.05
199	Ivan Rodriguez	.15
200	Kenny Rogers	.05
201	Roger Clemens	.25
202	Scott Cooper	.05
203	Andre Dawson	.08
204	Mike Greenwell	.05
205	Billy Hatcher	.05
206	Jeff Russell	.05
207	Aaron Sele	.08
208	John Valentin	.08
209	Mo Vaughn	.30
210	Frank Viola	.05
211	Rob Dibble	.05
212	Willie Greene	.05
213	Roberto Kelly	.05
214	Barry Larkin	.10
215	Kevin Mitchell	.05
216	Hal Morris	.05
217	Joe Oliver	.05
218	Jose Rijo	.05
219	Reggie Sanders	.10
220	John Smiley	.05
221	Dante Bichette	.10
222	Ellis Burks	.08
223	Andres Galarraga	.08
224	Joe Girardi	.05
225	Charlie Hayes	.05
226	Darren Holmes	.05
227	Howard Johnson	.05
228	Roberto Mejia	.05
229	David Nied	.05
230	Armando Reynoso	.05
231	Kevin Appier	.05
232	David Cone	.05
233	Greg Gagne	.05
234	Tom Gordon	.05
235	Felix Jose	.05
236	Wally Joyner	.08
237	Jose Lind	.05
238	Brian McRae	.05
239	Mike MacFarlane	.05
240	Jeff Montgomery	.05
241	Eric Davis	.08
242	John Doherty	.05
243	Cecil Fielder	.10
244	Travis Fryman	.08
245	Bill Gullickson	.05
246	Mike Henneman	.05
247	Tony Phillips	.08
248	Mickey Tettleton	.05
249	Alan Trammell	.08
250	Lou Whitaker	.08
251	Rick Aguilera	.05
252	Scott Erickson	.05
253	Kent Hrbek	.08
254	Chuck Knoblauch	.10
255	Shane Mack	.05
256	Dave McCarty	.05
257	Pat Meares	.05
258	Kirby Puckett	.40
259	Kevin Tapani	.05
260	Dave Winfield	.15
261	Wilson Alvarez	.05
262	Jason Bere	.08
263	Alex Fernandez	.05
264	Ozzie Guillen	.05
265	Roberto Hernandez	.05
266	Lance Johnson	.05
267	Jack McDowell	.05
268	Tim Raines	.08
269	Frank Thomas	1.50
270	Robin Ventura	.08
271	Jim Abbott	.08
272	Wade Boggs	.15
273	Mike Gallego	.05
274	Pat Kelly	.05
275	Jimmy Key	.05
276	Don Mattingly	.60
277	Paul O'Neill	.10
278	Mike Stanley	.05
279	Danny Tartabull	.05
280	Bernie Williams	.25
281	Chipper Jones	.60
282	Ryan Klesko	.30
283	Javier Lopez	.10
284	Jeffrey Hammonds	.08
285	Jeff McNeely	.05
286	Manny Ramirez	.35
287	Billy Ashley	.10
288	Raul Mondesi	.35
289	Cliff Floyd	.10

290	Rondell White	.15
291	Steve Karsay	.10
292	Midre Cummings	.10
293	Salomon Torres	.05
294	J.R. Phillips	.10
295	Marc Newfield	.10
296	Carlos Delgado	.10
297	Butch Huskey	.10
298	Checklist (Frank Thomas)	.05
299	Checklist (Barry Bonds)	.05
300	Checklist (Juan Gonzalez)	.05

1994 Triple Play Bomb Squad

Ten of the top major league home run hitters are included in this insert set. Fronts feature sepia-toned player photos within a wide brown frame. Gold foil enhances the typography. Backs have a white background with representations of vintage airplanes. A bar chart at left gives the player's home run totals by year. A small color portrait photo is at upper-right. Below are a few words about his homer history.

		MT
Complete Set (10):		20.00
Common Player:		1.00
1	Frank Thomas	6.00
2	Cecil Fielder	1.00
3	Juan Gonzalez	3.00
4	Barry Bonds	2.00
5	Dave Justice	1.00
6	Fred McGriff	1.25
7	Ron Gant	1.00
8	Ken Griffey, Jr.	8.00
9	Albert Belle	1.50
10	Matt Williams	1.00

1994 Triple Play Medalists

Statistical performance over the 1992-93 seasons was used to rank the players appearing in the Medalists insert set. Horizontal format cards have photos of the first, second and third place winners in appropriate boxes of gold, silver and bronze foil. "Medalists," the "medals" and "Triple Play 94" are embossed on the front. Backs have color action photos of each player along with team logos and a few stats.

		MT
Complete Set (15):		12.00
Common Player:		.50
1	A.L. Catchers(Chris Hoiles, Mickey Tettleton, Brian Harper)	.50
2	N.L. Catchers(Darren Daulton, Rick Wilkins, Kirt Manwaring)	.50
3	A.L. First Basemen(Frank Thomas, Rafael Palmeiro, John Olerud)	2.50
4	N.L. First Basemen(Mark Grace, Fred McGriff, Jeff Bagwell)	1.50
5	A.L. Second Basemen(Roberto Alomar, Carlos Baerga, Lou Whitaker)	1.00
6	N.L. Second Basemen(Ryne Sandberg, Craig Biggio, Robby Thompson)	1.00
7	A.L. Shortstops(Tony Fernandez, Cal Ripken, Jr., Alan Trammell)	2.00
8	N.L. Shortstops(Barry Larkin, Jay Bell, Jeff Blauser)	.50
9	A.L. Third Basemen(Robin Ventura, Travis Fryman, Wade Boggs)	.65
10	N.L. Third Basemen(Terry Pendleton, Dave Hollins, Gary Sheffield)	.50
11	A.L. Outfielders(Ken Griffey, Jr., Kirby Puckett, Albert Belle)	2.00
12	N.L. Outfielders(Barry Bonds, Andy Van Slyke, Len Dykstra)	1.00
13	A.L. Starters(Jack McDowell, Kevin Brown, Randy Johnson)	.65
14	N.L. Starters(Greg Maddux, Jose Rijo, Billy Swift)	.90
15	Designated Hitters(Paul Molitor, Dave Winfield, Harold Baines)	.50

1994 Triple Play Nicknames

Eight of baseball's most colorful team nicknames are featured in this insert set. Fronts feature a back-

ground photo representative of the nickname, with a player photo is superimposed over that. Backs have another player photo and a history of the team's nickname.

		MT
Complete Set (8):		15.00
Common Player:		1.50
1	Cecil Fielder	1.00
2	Ryne Sandberg	2.00
3	Gary Sheffield	1.00
4	Joe Carter	1.00
5	John Olerud	1.50
6	Cal Ripken, Jr.	6.00
7	Mark McGwire	6.00
8	Gregg Jefferies	1.50

1991 Ultra

This 400-card set was originally going to be called the Elite set, but Fleer chose to use the Ultra label. The card fronts feature gray borders surrounding full-color action photos. The backs feature three player photos and statistics. Hot Prospects and Great Performers are among the special cards featured within the set.

		MT
Complete Set (400):		25.00
Common Player:		.05
Wax Box:		17.00
1	Steve Avery	.10
2	Jeff Blauser	.05
3	Francisco Cabrera	.05
4	Ron Gant	.20
5	Tom Glavine	.15
6	Tommy Gregg	.05
7	Dave Justice	.25
8	Oddibe McDowell	.05
9	Greg Olson	.05
10	Terry Pendleton	.05
11	Lonnie Smith	.05
12	John Smoltz	.15
13	Jeff Treadway	.05
14	Glenn Davis	.05
15	Mike Devereaux	.05
16	Leo Gomez	.05
17	Chris Hoiles	.05
18	Dave Johnson	.05
19	Ben McDonald	.10
20	Randy Milligan	.05
21	Gregg Olson	.05
22	Joe Orsulak	.05

23	Bill Ripken	.05
24	Cal Ripken, Jr.	2.00
25	David Segui	.05
26	Craig Worthington	.05
27	Wade Boggs	.25
28	Tom Bolton	.05
29	Tom Brunansky	.05
30	Ellis Burks	.15
31	Roger Clemens	.40
32	Mike Greenwell	.05
33	Greg Harris	.05
34	Daryl Irvine	.05
35	Mike Marshall	.05
36	Tim Naehring	.10
37	Tony Pena	.05
38	*Phil Plantier*	.10
39	Carlos Quintana	.05
40	Jeff Reardon	.05
41	Jody Reed	.05
42	Luis Rivera	.05
43	Jim Abbott	.10
44	Chuck Finley	.05
45	Bryan Harvey	.05
46	Donnie Hill	.05
47	Jack Howell	.05
48	Wally Joyner	.10
49	Mark Langston	.05
50	Kirk McCaskill	.05
51	Lance Parrish	.08
52	Dick Schofield	.05
53	Lee Stevens	.05
54	Dave Winfield	.15
55	George Bell	.05
56	Damon Berryhill	.05
57	Mike Bielecki	.05
58	Andre Dawson	.10
59	Shawon Dunston	.05
60	Joe Girardi	.05
61	Mark Grace	.15
62	Mike Harkey	.05
63	Les Lancaster	.05
64	Greg Maddux	1.50
65	Derrick May	.05
66	Ryne Sandberg	.60
67	Luis Salazar	.05
68	Dwight Smith	.05
69	Hector Villanueva	.05
70	Jerome Walton	.05
71	Mitch Williams	.05
72	Carlton Fisk	.08
73	Scott Fletcher	.05
74	Ozzie Guillen	.05
75	Greg Hibbard	.05
76	Lance Johnson	.05
77	Steve Lyons	.05
78	Jack McDowell	.08
79	Dan Pasqua	.05
80	Melido Perez	.05
81	Tim Raines	.05
82	Sammy Sosa	2.00
83	Cory Snyder	.05
84	Bobby Thigpen	.05
85	Frank Thomas	4.00
86	Robin Ventura	.20
87	Todd Benzinger	.05
88	Glenn Braggs	.05
89	Tom Browning	.05
90	Norm Charlton	.05
91	Eric Davis	.10
92	Rob Dibble	.05
93	Bill Doran	.05
94	Mariano Duncan	.05
95	Billy Hatcher	.05
96	Barry Larkin	.15
97	Randy Myers	.05
98	Hal Morris	.10
99	Joe Oliver	.05
100	Paul O'Neill	.08
101a	Jeff Reed	.05
101b	Beau Allred (Should be #104)	.05
102	Jose Rijo	.05
103a	Chris Sabo	.05
103b	Carlos Baerga (Should be #106)	.05
104	(Not issued, see #101b)	.05
105	Sandy Alomar,Jr.	.10
106	(Not issued, see #103b)	.05
107	Albert Belle	.75
108	Jerry Browne	.05
109	Tom Candiotti	.05
110	Alex Cole	.05
111a	John Farrell	.05
111b	Chris James (Should be #114)	.05
112	Felix Fermin	.05

395	Nolan Ryan (Great Performer)	.60
396	Bobby Thigpen (Great Performer)	.05
397	Checklist	.05
398	Checklist	.05
399	Checklist	.05
400	Checklist	.05

1991 Ultra Gold

BO JACKSON
KANSAS CITY ROYALS • OUTFIELD

A pair of action photos flanking and below a portrait in a home plate frame at top-center are featured on these cards. Background is a graduated gold coloring. The Fleer Ultra Team logo is in the upper-left corner. Backs have narrative career information. The Puckett and Sandberg cards feature incorrect historical information on the backs.

		MT
Complete Set (10):		5.00
Common Player:		.25
1	Barry Bonds	1.00
2	Will Clark	.50
3	Doug Drabek	.25
4	Ken Griffey, Jr.	4.00
5	Rickey Henderson	.35
6	Bo Jackson	.50
7	Ramon Martinez	.30
8	Kirby Puckett	1.25
9	Chris Sabo	.25
10	Ryne Sandberg	.90

1991 Ultra Update

RICK WILKINS CUBS CATCHER

This 120-card set was produced as a supplement to the premier Fleer Ultra set. Cards feature

the same style as the regular Fleer Ultra cards. The cards were sold only as complete sets in full color, shrinkwrapped boxes.

		MT
Complete Set (120):		40.00
Common Player:		.15
1	Dwight Evans	.15
2	Chito Martinez	.15
3	Bob Melvin	.15
4	*Mike Mussina*	8.00
5	Jack Clark	.15
6	Dana Kiecker	.15
7	Steve Lyons	.15
8	Gary Gaetti	.25
9	Dave Gallagher	.15
10	Dave Parker	.25
11	Luis Polonia	.15
12	Luis Sojo	.15
13	Wilson Alvarez	2.00
14	Alex Fernandez	2.00
15	Craig Grebeck	.15
16	Ron Karkovice	.15
17	Warren Newson	.15
18	Scott Radinsky	.15
19	Glenallen Hill	.15
20	Charles Nagy	1.00
21	Mark Whiten	.15
22	Milt Cuyler	.15
23	Paul Gibson	.15
24	Mickey Tettleton	.15
25	Todd Benzinger	.15
26	Storm Davis	.15
27	Kirk Gibson	.15
28	Bill Pecota	.15
29	Gary Thurman	.15
30	Darryl Hamilton	.15
31	Jaime Navarro	.15
32	Willie Randolph	.15
33	Bill Wegman	.15
34	Randy Bush	.15
35	Chili Davis	.15
36	Scott Erickson	.25
37	Chuck Knoblauch	4.00
38	Scott Leius	.15
39	Jack Morris	.15
40	John Habyan	.15
41	Pat Kelly	.15
42	Matt Nokes	.15
43	Scott Sanderson	.15
44	Bernie Williams	6.00
45	Harold Baines	.20
46	Brook Jacoby	.15
47	Ernest Riles	.15
48	Willie Wilson	.15
49	Jay Buhner	1.00
50	Rich DeLucia	.15
51	Mike Jackson	.15
52	Bill Krueger	.15
53	Bill Swift	.15
54	Brian Downing	.15
55	Juan Gonzalez	20.00
56	Dean Palmer	1.50
57	Kevin Reimer	.15
58	*Ivan Rodriguez*	10.00
59	Tom Candiotti	.15
60	Juan Guzman	.30
61	Bob MacDonald	.15
62	Greg Myers	.15
63	Ed Sprague	.15
64	Devon White	.30
65	Rafael Belliard	.15
66	Juan Berenguer	.15
67	Brian Hunter	.15
68	Kent Mercker	.15
69	Otis Nixon	.15
70	Danny Jackson	.15
71	Chuck McElroy	.15
72	Gary Scott	.15
73	Heathcliff Slocumb	.15
74	Chico Walker	.15
75	Rick Wilkins	.30
76	Chris Hammond	.15
77	Luis Quinones	.15
78	Herm Winningham	.15
79	*Jeff Bagwell*	15.00
80	Jim Corsi	.15
81	Steve Finley	.15
82	*Luis Gonzalez*	.45
83	Pete Harnisch	.15
84	Darryl Kile	.20
85	Brett Butler	.20
86	Gary Carter	.25
87	Tim Crews	.15

88	Orel Hershiser	.20
89	Bob Ojeda	.15
90	Bret Barberie	.15
91	Barry Jones	.15
92	Gilberto Reyes	.15
93	Larry Walker	4.00
94	Hubie Brooks	.15
95	Tim Burke	.15
96	Rick Cerone	.15
97	Jeff Innis	.15
98	Wally Backman	.15
99	Tommy Greene	.15
100	Ricky Jordan	.15
101	Mitch Williams	.15
102	John Smiley	.15
103	Randy Tomlin	.15
104	Gary Varsho	.15
105	Cris Carpenter	.15
106	Ken Hill	.55
107	Felix Jose	.15
108	*Omar Oliveras*	.15
109	Gerald Perry	.15
110	Jerald Clark	.15
111	Tony Fernandez	.15
112	Darrin Jackson	.15
113	Mike Maddux	.15
114	Tim Teufel	.15
115	Bud Black	.15
116	Kelly Downs	.15
117	Mike Felder	.15
118	Willie McGee	.20
119	Trevor Wilson	.15
120	Checklist	.15

1992 Ultra

JOE CARTER
TORONTO BLUE JAYS • OUTFIELD

Fleer released its second annual Ultra set in 1992. Card fronts feature full-color action photos with a marble accent at the card bottom. The flip sides are horizontal with two additional player photos. Many insert sets were randomly included in foil packs as premiums. These included rookie, All-Star and award winners, among others. A two-card Tony Gwynn send-away set was also available through an offer from Fleer. For $1 and 10 Ultra wrappers, collectors could receive the Gwynn cards. The set is numbered by team; cards #1-300 comprise Series I, cards #301-600 are Series II.

		MT
Complete Set (600):		40.00
Common Player:		.10
Series 1 Wax Box:		40.00
Series 2 Wax Box:		30.00
1	Glenn Davis	.10
2	Mike Devereaux	.10
3	Dwight Evans	.10
4	Leo Gomez	.10
5	Chris Hoiles	.10
6	Sam Horn	.10

#	Player	Value	#	Player	Value	#	Player	Value
7	Chito Martinez	.10	103	Roberto Kelly	.10	199	Craig Biggio	.20
8	Randy Milligan	.10	104	Kevin Maas	.10	200	Ken Caminiti	.15
9	Mike Mussina	.60	105	Don Mattingly	1.00	201	Andujar Cedeno	.10
10	Billy Ripken	.10	106	Hensley Meulens	.10	202	Steve Finley	.10
11	Cal Ripken, Jr.	2.50	107	Matt Nokes	.10	203	Luis Gonzalez	.10
12	Tom Brunansky	.10	108	Steve Sax	.10	204	Pete Harnisch	.10
13	Ellis Burks	.25	109	Harold Baines	.12	205	Xavier Hernandez	.10
14	Jack Clark	.10	110	Jose Canseco	.50	206	Darryl Kile	.10
15	Roger Clemens	.90	111	Ron Darling	.10	207	Al Osuna	.10
16	Mike Greenwell	.10	112	Mike Gallego	.10	208	Curt Schilling	.10
17	Joe Hesketh	.10	113	Dave Henderson	.10	209	Brett Butler	.12
18	Tony Pena	.10	114	Rickey Henderson	.25	210	Kal Daniels	.10
19	Carlos Quintana	.10	115	Mark McGwire	3.00	211	Lenny Harris	.10
20	Jeff Reardon	.10	116	Terry Steinbach	.10	212	Stan Javier	.10
21	Jody Reed	.10	117	Dave Stewart	.12	213	Ramon Martinez	.15
22	Luis Rivera	.10	118	Todd Van Poppel	.10	214	Roger McDowell	.10
23	Mo Vaughn	.75	119	Bob Welch	.10	215	Jose Offerman	.10
24	Gary DiSarcina	.10	120	Greg Briley	.10	216	Juan Samuel	.10
25	Chuck Finley	.10	121	Jay Buhner	.12	217	Mike Scioscia	.10
26	Gary Gaetti	.15	122	Rich DeLucia	.10	218	Mike Sharperson	.10
27	Bryan Harvey	.10	123	Ken Griffey, Jr.	4.00	219	Darryl Strawberry	.15
28	Lance Parrish	.12	124	Erik Hanson	.10	220	Delino DeShields	.15
29	Luis Polonia	.10	125	Randy Johnson	.35	221	Tom Foley	.10
30	Dick Schofield	.10	126	Edgar Martinez	.20	222	Steve Frey	.10
31	Luis Sojo	.10	127	Tino Martinez	.25	223	Dennis Martinez	.10
32	Wilson Alvarez	.10	128	Pete O'Brien	.10	224	Spike Owen	.10
33	Carlton Fisk	.15	129	Harold Reynolds	.10	225	Gilberto Reyes	.10
34	Craig Grebeck	.10	130	Dave Valle	.10	226	Tim Wallach	.10
35	Ozzie Guillen	.10	131	Julio Franco	.10	227	Daryl Boston	.10
36	Greg Hibbard	.10	132	Juan Gonzalez	1.00	228	Tim Burke	.10
37	Charlie Hough	.10	133	Jeff Huson	.10	229	Vince Coleman	.10
38	Lance Johnson	.10	134	Mike Jeffcoat	.10	230	David Cone	.10
39	Ron Karkovice	.10	135	Terry Mathews	.10	231	Kevin Elster	.10
40	Jack McDowell	.12	136	Rafael Palmeiro	.25	232	Dwight Gooden	.15
41	Donn Pall	.10	137	Dean Palmer	.12	233	Todd Hundley	.10
42	Melido Perez	.10	138	Geno Petralli	.10	234	Jeff Innis	.10
43	Tim Raines	.15	139	Ivan Rodriguez	.50	235	Howard Johnson	.10
44	Frank Thomas	3.00	140	Jeff Russell	.10	236	Dave Magadan	.10
45	Sandy Alomar, Jr.	.15	141	Nolan Ryan	3.00	237	Mackey Sasser	.10
46	Carlos Baerga	.12	142	Ruben Sierra	.10	238	Anthony Young	.10
47	Albert Belle	.60	143	Roberto Alomar	.75	239	Wes Chamberlain	.10
48	Jerry Browne	.10	144	Pat Borders	.10	240	Darren Daulton	.10
49	Felix Fermin	.10	145	Joe Carter	.12	241	Len Dykstra	.12
50	Reggie Jefferson	.10	146	Kelly Gruber	.10	242	Tommy Greene	.10
51	Mark Lewis	.10	147	Jimmy Key	.10	243	Charlie Hayes	.10
52	Carlos Martinez	.10	148	Manny Lee	.10	244	Dave Hollins	.12
53	Steve Olin	.10	149	Rance Mulliniks	.10	245	Ricky Jordan	.10
54	Jim Thome	.90	150	Greg Myers	.10	246	John Kruk	.10
55	Mark Whiten	.10	151	John Olerud	.20	247	Mickey Morandini	.10
56	Dave Bergman	.10	152	Dave Stieb	.10	248	Terry Mulholland	.10
57	Milt Cuyler	.10	153	Todd Stottlemyre	.10	249	Dale Murphy	.10
58	Rob Deer	.10	154	Duane Ward	.10	250	Jay Bell	.10
59	Cecil Fielder	.25	155	Devon White	.10	251	Barry Bonds	.75
60	Travis Fryman	.15	156	Eddie Zosky	.10	252	Steve Buechele	.10
61	Scott Livingstone	.10	157	Steve Avery	.10	253	Doug Drabek	.10
62	Tony Phillips	.12	158	Rafael Belliard	.10	254	Mike LaValliere	.10
63	Mickey Tettleton	.10	159	Jeff Blauser	.10	255	Jose Lind	.10
64	Alan Trammell	.20	160	Sid Bream	.10	256	Lloyd McClendon	.10
65	Lou Whitaker	.12	161	Ron Gant	.10	257	Orlando Merced	.10
66	Kevin Appier	.12	162	Tom Glavine	.20	258	Don Slaught	.10
67	Mike Boddicker	.10	163	Brian Hunter	.10	259	John Smiley	.10
68	George Brett	.70	164	Dave Justice	.20	260	Zane Smith	.10
69	Jim Eisenreich	.10	165	Mark Lemke	.10	261	Randy Tomlin	.10
70	Mark Gubicza	.10	166	Greg Olson	.10	262	Andy Van Slyke	.10
71	David Howard	.10	167	Terry Pendleton	.10	263	Pedro Guerrero	.10
72	Joel Johnston	.10	168	Lonnie Smith	.10	264	Felix Jose	.10
73	Mike Macfarlane	.10	169	John Smoltz	.15	265	Ray Lankford	.10
74	Brent Mayne	.10	170	Mike Stanton	.10	266	Omar Olivares	.10
75	Brian McRae	.10	171	Jeff Treadway	.10	267	Jose Oquendo	.10
76	Jeff Montgomery	.10	172	Paul Assenmacher	.10	268	Tom Pagnozzi	.10
77	Terry Shumpert	.10	173	George Bell	.10	269	Bryn Smith	.10
78	Don August	.10	174	Shawon Dunston	.15	270	Lee Smith	.10
79	Dante Bichette	.30	175	Mark Grace	.20	271	Ozzie Smith	.40
80	Ted Higuera	.10	176	Danny Jackson	.10	272	Milt Thompson	.10
81	Paul Molitor	.30	177	Les Lancaster	.10	273	Todd Zeile	.10
82	Jamie Navarro	.10	178	Greg Maddux	1.50	274	Andy Benes	.12
83	Gary Sheffield	.35	179	Luis Salazar	.10	275	Jerald Clark	.10
84	Bill Spiers	.10	180	Rey Sanchez	.10	276	Tony Fernandez	.10
85	B.J. Surhoff	.10	181	Ryne Sandberg	.50	277	Tony Gwynn	.65
86	Greg Vaughn	.10	182	Jose Vizcaino	.10	278	Greg Harris	.10
87	Robin Yount	.30	183	Chico Walker	.10	279	Thomas Howard	.10
88	Rick Aguilera	.10	184	Jerome Walton	.10	280	Bruce Hurst	.10
89	Chili Davis	.12	185	Glenn Braggs	.10	281	Mike Maddux	.10
90	Scott Erickson	.12	186	Tom Browning	.10	282	Fred McGriff	.40
91	Brian Harper	.10	187	Rob Dibble	.10	283	Benito Santiago	.12
92	Kent Hrbek	.12	188	Bill Doran	.10	284	Kevin Bass	.10
93	Chuck Knoblauch	.20	189	Chris Hammond	.10	285	Jeff Brantley	.10
94	Scott Leius	.10	190	Billy Hatcher	.10	286	John Burkett	.10
95	Shane Mack	.10	191	Barry Larkin	.20	287	Will Clark	.40
96	Mike Pagliarulo	.10	192	Hal Morris	.12	288	Royce Clayton	.10
97	Kirby Puckett	1.00	193	Joe Oliver	.10	289	Steve Decker	.10
98	Kevin Tapani	.10	194	Paul O'Neill	.15	290	Kelly Downs	.10
99	Jesse Barfield	.10	195	Jeff Reed	.10	291	Mike Felder	.10
100	Alvaro Espinoza	.10	196	Jose Rijo	.10	292	Darren Lewis	.15
101	Mel Hall	.10	197	Chris Sabo	.10	293	Kirt Manwaring	.10
102	Pat Kelly	.10	198	Jeff Bagwell	1.00	294	Willie McGee	.10

No.	Player	Price	No.	Player	Price	No.	Player	Price
295	Robby Thompson	.10	388	Dan Plesac	.10	484	Dave Martinez	.10
296	Matt Williams	.40	389	Kevin Seitzer	.10	485	Bip Roberts	.10
297	Trevor Wilson	.10	390	Franklin Stubbs	.10	486	Reggie Sanders	.15
298	Checklist 1-108(Sandy Alomar, Jr.)	.10	391	William Suero	.10	487	Greg Swindell	.10
299	Checklist 109-208(Rey Sanchez)	.10	392	Bill Wegman	.10	488	Ryan Bowen	.10
300	Checklist 209-300(Nolan Ryan)	.15	393	Willie Banks	.10	489	Casey Candaele	.10
301	Brady Anderson	.15	394	Jarvis Brown	.10	490	Juan Guerrero	.10
302	Todd Frohwirth	.10	395	Greg Gagne	.10	491	Pete Incaviglia	.10
303	Ben McDonald	.10	396	Mark Guthrie	.10	492	Jeff Juden	.10
304	Mark McLemore	.10	397	Bill Krueger	.10	493	Rob Murphy	.10
305	Jose Mesa	.10	398	*Pat Mahomes*	.25	494	Mark Portugal	.10
306	Bob Milacki	.10	399	Pedro Munoz	.12	495	Rafael Ramirez	.10
307	Gregg Olson	.10	400	John Smiley	.10	496	Scott Servais	.10
308	David Segui	.10	401	Gary Wayne	.10	497	Ed Taubensee	.10
309	Rick Sutcliffe	.10	402	Lenny Webster	.10	498	Brian Williams	.10
310	Jeff Tackett	.10	403	Carl Willis	.10	499	Todd Benzinger	.10
311	Wade Boggs	.35	404	Greg Cadaret	.10	500	John Candelaria	.10
312	Scott Cooper	.10	405	Steve Farr	.10	501	Tom Candiotti	.10
313	John Flaherty	.10	406	Mike Gallego	.10	502	Tim Crews	.10
314	Wayne Housie	.10	407	Charlie Hayes	.10	503	Eric Davis	.15
315	Peter Hoy	.10	408	Steve Howe	.10	504	Jim Gott	.10
316	John Marzano	.10	409	Dion James	.10	505	Dave Hansen	.10
317	Tim Naehring	.10	410	Jeff Johnson	.10	506	Carlos Hernandez	.10
318	Phil Plantier	.10	411	Tim Leary	.10	507	Orel Hershiser	.10
319	Frank Viola	.10	412	Jim Leyritz	.10	508	Eric Karros	.15
320	Matt Young	.10	413	Melido Perez	.10	509	Bob Ojeda	.10
321	Jim Abbott	.15	414	Scott Sanderson	.10	510	Steve Wilson	.10
322	Hubie Brooks	.10	415	Andy Stankiewicz	.10	511	Moises Alou	.15
323	*Chad Curtis*	.30	416	Mike Stanley	.10	512	Bret Barberie	.10
324	Alvin Davis	.10	417	Danny Tartabull	.10	513	Ivan Calderon	.10
325	Junior Felix	.10	418	Lance Blankenship	.10	514	Gary Carter	.15
326	Von Hayes	.10	419	Mike Bordick	.10	515	Archi Cianfrocco	.10
327	Mark Langston	.10	420	Scott Brosius	.10	516	Jeff Fassero	.10
328	Scott Lewis	.10	421	Dennis Eckersley	.15	517	Darrin Fletcher	.10
329	Don Robinson	.10	422	Scott Hemond	.10	518	Marquis Grissom	.20
330	Bobby Rose	.10	423	Carney Lansford	.10	519	Chris Haney	.10
331	Lee Stevens	.10	424	Henry Mercedes	.10	520	Ken Hill	.10
332	George Bell	.10	425	Mike Moore	.10	521	Chris Nabholz	.10
333	Esteban Beltre	.10	426	Gene Nelson	.10	522	Bill Sampen	.10
334	Joey Cora	.10	427	Randy Ready	.10	523	John VanderWal	.10
335	Alex Fernandez	.20	428	Bruce Walton	.10	524	David Wainhouse	.10
336	Roberto Hernandez	.15	429	Willie Wilson	.10	525	Larry Walker	.35
337	Mike Huff	.10	430	Rich Amaral	.10	526	John Wetteland	.12
338	Kirk McCaskill	.10	431	Dave Cochrane	.10	527	Bobby Bonilla	.15
339	Dan Pasqua	.10	432	Henry Cotto	.10	528	Sid Fernandez	.10
340	Scott Radinsky	.10	433	Calvin Jones	.10	529	John Franco	.10
341	Steve Sax	.10	434	Kevin Mitchell	.10	530	Dave Gallagher	.10
342	Bobby Thigpen	.10	435	Clay Parker	.10	531	Paul Gibson	.10
343	Robin Ventura	.25	436	Omar Vizquel	.10	532	Eddie Murray	.25
344	Jack Armstrong	.10	437	Floyd Bannister	.10	533	Junior Noboa	.10
345	Alex Cole	.10	438	Kevin Brown	.10	534	Charlie O'Brien	.10
346	Dennis Cook	.10	439	John Cangelosi	.10	535	Bill Pecota	.10
347	Glenallen Hill	.10	440	Brian Downing	.10	536	Willie Randolph	.10
348	Thomas Howard	.10	441	Monty Fariss	.10	537	Bret Saberhagen	.10
349	Brook Jacoby	.10	442	Jose Guzman	.10	538	Dick Schofield	.10
350	Kenny Lofton	1.00	443	Donald Harris	.10	539	Pete Schourek	.10
351	Charles Nagy	.12	444	Kevin Reimer	.10	540	Ruben Amaro	.10
352	Rod Nichols	.10	445	Kenny Rogers	.10	541	Andy Ashby	.15
353	Junior Ortiz	.10	446	Wayne Rosenthal	.10	542	Kim Batiste	.10
354	Dave Otto	.10	447	Dickie Thon	.10	543	Cliff Brantley	.10
355	Tony Perezchica	.10	448	Derek Bell	.20	544	Mariano Duncan	.10
356	Scott Scudder	.10	449	Juan Guzman	.15	545	Jeff Grotewold	.10
357	Paul Sorrento	.10	450	Tom Henke	.10	546	Barry Jones	.10
358	Skeeter Barnes	.10	451	Candy Maldonado	.10	547	Julio Peguero	.10
359	Mark Carreon	.10	452	Jack Morris	.10	548	Curt Schilling	.10
360	John Doherty	.10	453	David Wells	.10	549	Mitch Williams	.10
361	Dan Gladden	.10	454	Dave Winfield	.20	550	Stan Belinda	.10
362	Bill Gullickson	.10	455	Juan Berenguer	.10	551	Scott Bullett	.10
363	Shawn Hare	.10	456	Damon Berryhill	.10	552	Cecil Espy	.10
364	Mike Henneman	.10	457	Mike Bielecki	.10	553	Jeff King	.10
365	Chad Kreuter	.10	458	Marvin Freeman	.10	554	Roger Mason	.10
366	Mark Leiter	.10	459	Charlie Leibrandt	.10	555	Paul Miller	.10
367	Mike Munoz	.10	460	Kent Mercker	.10	556	Denny Neagle	.15
368	Kevin Ritz	.10	461	Otis Nixon	.10	557	Vocente Palacios	.10
369	Mark Davis	.10	462	Alejandro Pena	.10	558	Bob Patterson	.10
370	Tom Gordon	.10	463	Ben Rivera	.10	559	Tom Prince	.10
371	Chris Gwynn	.10	464	Deion Sanders	.25	560	Gary Redus	.10
372	Gregg Jefferies	.15	465	Mark Wohlers	.10	561	Gary Varsho	.10
373	Wally Joyner	.15	466	Shawn Boskie	.10	562	Juan Agosto	.10
374	Kevin McReynolds	.10	467	Frank Castillo	.10	563	Cris Carpenter	.10
375	Keith Miller	.10	468	Andre Dawson	.15	564	*Mark Clark*	.20
376	Rico Rossy	.10	469	Joe Girardi	.10	565	Jose DeLeon	.10
377	Curtis Wilkerson	.10	470	Chuck McElroy	.10	566	Rich Gedman	.10
378	Ricky Bones	.10	471	Mike Morgan	.10	567	Bernard Gilkey	.15
379	Chris Bosio	.10	472	Ken Patterson	.10	568	Rex Hudler	.10
380	Cal Eldred	.10	473	Bob Scanlan	.10	569	Tim Jones	.10
381	Scott Fletcher	.10	474	Gary Scott	.10	570	Donovan Osborne	.10
382	Jim Gantner	.10	475	Dave Smith	.10	571	Mike Perez	.10
383	Darryl Hamilton	.10	476	Sammy Sosa	1.50	572	Gerald Perry	.10
384	Doug Henry	.10	477	Hector Villanueva	.10	573	Bob Tewksbury	.10
385	*Pat Listach*	.10	478	Scott Bankhead	.10	574	Todd Worrell	.10
386	Tim McIntosh	.10	479	Tim Belcher	.10	575	Dave Eiland	.10
387	Edwin Nunez	.10	480	Freddie Benavides	.10	576	Jeremy Hernandez	.10
			481	Jacob Brumfield	.10	577	Craig Lefferts	.10
			482	Norm Charlton	.10	578	Jose Melendez	.10
			483	Dwayne Henry	.10	579	Randy Myers	.10

580	Gary Pettis	.10
581	Rich Rodriguez	.10
582	Gary Sheffield	.30
583	Craig Shipley	.10
584	Kurt Stillwell	.10
585	Tim Teufel	.10
586	*Rod Beck*	.25
587	Dave Burba	.10
588	Craig Colbert	.10
589	Bryan Hickerson	.10
590	Mike Jackson	.10
591	Mark Leonard	.10
592	Jim McNamara	.10
593	John Patterson	.10
594	Dave Righetti	.10
595	Cory Snyder	.10
596	Bill Swift	.10
597	Ted Wood	.10
598	Checklist 301-403(Scott Sanderson)	.10
599	Checklist 404-498(Junior Ortiz)	.10
600	Checklist 499-600(Mike Morgan)	.10

1992 Ultra All-Rookies

The 10 promising rookies in this set could be found on special cards inserted in Ultra Series 2 foil packs.

		MT
Complete Set (10):		13.00
Common Player:		.50
1	Eric Karros	2.50
2	Andy Stankiewicz	.50
3	Gary DiSarcina	.50
4	Archi Cianfrocco	.50
5	Jim McNamara	.50
6	Chad Curtis	.65
7	Kenny Lofton	7.00
8	Reggie Sanders	1.50
9	Pat Mahomes	.50
10	Donovan Osborne	.50

1992 Ultra All-Stars

An All-Star team from each league, with two pitchers, could be assembled by collecting these inserts from Ultra Series 2 foil packs.

Modern cards have little collector value in conditions lower than Mint. Figure NM cards at 75% of values shown; EX cards at 40%.

Values shown reflect the market as of January, 1999. On-field performances of current players in the 1999 baseball season are not factored in.

		MT
Complete Set (20):		40.00
Common Player:		.50
1	Mark McGwire	6.00
2	Roberto Alomar	1.50
3	Cal Ripken, Jr.	7.50
4	Wade Boggs	1.25
5	Mickey Tettleton	.50
6	Ken Griffey, Jr.	10.00
7	Roberto Kelly	.50
8	Kirby Puckett	6.00
9	Frank Thomas	8.00
10	Jack McDowell	.50
11	Will Clark	1.50
12	Ryne Sandberg	1.50
13	Barry Larkin	.75
14	Gary Sheffield	.75
15	Tom Pagnozzi	.50
16	Barry Bonds	2.50
17	Deion Sanders	1.00
18	Darryl Strawberry	.60
19	David Cone	.50
20	Tom Glavine	.75

1992 Ultra Award Winners

The 25 cards in this insert issue were randomly packaged with Series 1 Ultra. One of the Cal Ripken cards (#21) can be found with a photo made from a reversed negative, as well as with the proper orientation. Neither version carries a premium.

		MT
Complete Set (26):		75.00
Common Player:		.75
1	Jack Morris	.75
2	Chuck Knoblauch	1.50
3	Jeff Bagwell	4.00

4	Terry Pendleton	.75
5	Cal Ripken, Jr.	8.00
6	Roger Clemens	2.00
7	Tom Glavine	1.00
8	Tom Pagnozzi	.75
9	Ozzie Smith	2.50
10	Andy Van Slyke	.75
11	Barry Bonds	3.50
12	Tony Gwynn	4.00
13	Matt Williams	1.00
14	Will Clark	1.00
15	Robin Ventura	.90
16	Mark Langston	.75
18	Devon White	.75
19	Don Mattingly	5.00
20	Roberto Alomar	2.50
21a	Cal Ripken, Jr. (reversed negative)	8.00
21b	Cal Ripken, Jr. (correct)	8.00
22	Ken Griffey, Jr.	12.00
23	Kirby Puckett	5.00
24	Greg Maddux	6.00
25	Ryne Sandberg	2.00

1992 Ultra Tony Gwynn

This 12-card subset of Ultra's spokesman features 10 cards which were available as inserts in Series I foil packs, plus two cards labeled "Special No. 1" and "Special No. 2" which could only be obtained in a send-away offer. Some 2,000 of these cards carry a "certified" Gwynn autograph. Not part of the issue, but similar in format were a pair of extra Tony Gwynn cards. One pictures him with Fleer CEO Paul Mullan, the other shows him with the poster child for Casa de Amparo, a children's shelter in San Diego County.

		MT
Complete Set (12):		12.00
Common Card:		1.00
Certified Autograph Card:		90.00
	INSERT CARDS	
1	Tony Gwynn (fielding)	1.00
2	Tony Gwynn (batting)	1.00
3	Tony Gwynn (fielding)	1.00
4	Tony Gwynn (batting)	1.00
5	Tony Gwynn (base-running)	1.00
6	Tony Gwynn (awards)	1.00
7	Tony Gwynn (bunting)	1.00
8	Tony Gwynn (batting)	1.00
9	Tony Gwynn (running)	1.00
10	Tony Gwynn (batting)	1.00
	SEND-AWAY CARDS	
1	Tony Gwynn (batting)	2.00
2	Tony Gwynn (fielding)	2.00
	SPECIAL CARDS	
---	Tony Gwynn, Paul Mullan	6.00
---	Tony Gwynn (Casa de Amparo)	15.00

1	Tony Gwynn (leaping at outfield wall)	1.00
2	Tony Gwynn (batting in brown warm-up jersey)	1.00
1	Tony Gwynn (batting)	1.00
2	Tony Gwynn (fielding)	1.00
---	Tony Gwynn, Paul Mullan	6.00
---	Casa de Amparo Salute(Tony Gwynn)	15.00

1993 Ultra

The first series of 300 cards retains Fleer's successful features from 1992, including additional gold foil stamping, UV coating, and team color-coded marbled bars on the fronts. The backs feature a stylized ballpark background, which creates a 3-D effect, stats and portrait and an action photo. Dennis Eckersley is featured in a limited-edition "Career Highlights" set and personally autographed more than 2,000 of his cards, to be randomly inserted into both series' packs. A 10-card Home Run Kings subset and 25-card Ultra Awards Winners subset were also randomly inserted in packs. Ultra Rookies cards are included in both series. Ultra's second series has three limited-edition subsets: Ultra All-Stars, Ultra All-Rookie Team, and Strikeout Kings, plus cards featuring Colorado Rockies and Florida Marlins players.

		MT
Complete Set (650):		35.00
Complete Series 1 (300):		15.00
Complete Series 2 (350):		20.00
Common Player:		.10
Series 1 or 2 Wax Box:		45.00
1	Steve Avery	.10
2	Rafael Belliard	.10
3	Damon Berryhill	.10
4	Sid Bream	.10
5	Ron Gant	.20
6	Tom Glavine	.20
7	Ryan Klesko	.75
8	Mark Lemke	.10
9	Javier Lopez	.25
10	Greg Olson	.10
11	Terry Pendleton	.10
12	Deion Sanders	.25
13	Mike Stanton	.10
14	Paul Assenmacher	.10
15	Steve Buechele	.10
16	Frank Castillo	.10
17	Shawon Dunston	.15
18	Mark Grace	.25
19	Derrick May	.10
20	Chuck McElroy	.10
21	Mike Morgan	.10
22	Bob Scanlan	.10
23	Dwight Smith	.10
24	Sammy Sosa	1.50
25	Rick Wilkins	.10
26	Tim Belcher	.10
27	Jeff Branson	.10
28	Bill Doran	.10
29	Chris Hammond	.10
30	Barry Larkin	.20
31	Hal Morris	.10
32	Joe Oliver	.10
33	Jose Rijo	.10
34	Bip Roberts	.10
35	Chris Sabo	.10
36	Reggie Sanders	.15
37	Craig Biggio	.20
38	Ken Caminiti	.20
39	Steve Finley	.10
40	Luis Gonzalez	.10
41	Juan Guerrero	.10
42	Pete Harnisch	.10
43	Xavier Hernandez	.10
44	Doug Jones	.10
45	Al Osuna	.10
46	Eddie Taubensee	.10
47	Scooter Tucker	.10
48	Brian Williams	.10
49	Pedro Astacio	.10
50	Rafael Bournigal	.10
51	Brett Butler	.15
52	Tom Candiotti	.10
53	Eric Davis	.15
54	Lenny Harris	.10
55	Orel Hershiser	.12
56	Eric Karros	.20
57	Pedro Martinez	.40
58	Roger McDowell	.10
59	Jose Offerman	.10
60	Mike Piazza	3.00
61	Moises Alou	.20
62	Kent Bottenfield	.10
63	Archi Cianfrocco	.10
64	Greg Colbrunn	.10
65	Wil Cordero	.15
66	Delino DeShields	.10
67	Darrin Fletcher	.10
68	Ken Hill	.10
69	Chris Nabholz	.10
70	Mel Rojas	.10
71	Larry Walker	.25
72	Sid Fernandez	.10
73	John Franco	.10
74	Dave Gallagher	.10
75	Todd Hundley	.20
76	Howard Johnson	.10
77	Jeff Kent	.15
78	Eddie Murray	.25
79	Bret Saberhagen	.12
80	Chico Walker	.10
81	Anthony Young	.10
82	Kyle Abbott	.10
83	Ruben Amaro Jr.	.10
84	Juan Bell	.10
85	Wes Chamberlain	.10
86	Darren Daulton	.10
87	Mariano Duncan	.10
88	Dave Hollins	.10
89	Ricky Jordan	.10
90	John Kruk	.10
91	Mickey Morandini	.10
92	Terry Mulholland	.10
93	Ben Rivera	.10
94	Mike Williams	.10
95	Stan Belinda	.10
96	Jay Bell	.10
97	Jeff King	.10
98	Mike LaValliere	.10
99	Lloyd McClendon	.10
100	Orlando Merced	.10
101	Zane Smith	.10
102	Randy Tomlin	.10
103	Andy Van Slyke	.10
104	Tim Wakefield	.15
105	John Wehner	.10
106	Bernard Gilkey	.15
107	Brian Jordan	.15
108	Ray Lankford	.15
109	Donovan Osborne	.10
110	Tom Pagnozzi	.10
111	Mike Perez	.10
112	Lee Smith	.12
113	Ozzie Smith	.50
114	Bob Tewksbury	.10
115	Todd Zeile	.10
116	Andy Benes	.15
117	Greg Harris	.10
118	Darrin Jackson	.10
119	Fred McGriff	.25
120	Rich Rodriguez	.10
121	Frank Seminara	.10
122	Gary Sheffield	.25
123	Craig Shipley	.10
124	Kurt Stillwell	.10
125	Dan Walters	.10
126	Rod Beck	.10
127	Mike Benjamin	.10
128	Jeff Brantley	.10
129	John Burkett	.10
130	Will Clark	.25
131	Royce Clayton	.10
132	Steve Hosey	.10
133	Mike Jackson	.10
134	Darren Lewis	.10
135	Kirt Manwaring	.10
136	Bill Swift	.10
137	Robby Thompson	.10
138	Brady Anderson	.20
139	Glenn Davis	.10
140	Leo Gomez	.10
141	Chito Martinez	.10
142	Ben McDonald	.10
143	Alan Mills	.10
144	Mike Mussina	.50
145	Gregg Olson	.10
146	David Segui	.10
147	Jeff Tackett	.10
148	Jack Clark	.10
149	Scott Cooper	.10
150	Danny Darwin	.10
151	John Dopson	.10
152	Mike Greenwell	.10
153	Tim Naehring	.10
154	Tony Pena	.10
155	Paul Quantrill	.10
156	Mo Vaughn	.75
157	Frank Viola	.10
158	Bob Zupcic	.10
159	Chad Curtis	.15
160	Gary DiScarcina	.10
161	Damion Easley	.10
162	Chuck Finley	.10
163	Tim Fortugno	.10
164	Rene Gonzales	.10
165	Joe Grahe	.10
166	Mark Langston	.10
167	John Orton	.10
168	Luis Polonia	.10
169	Julio Valera	.10
170	Wilson Alvarez	.15
171	George Bell	.10
172	Joey Cora	.10
173	Alex Fernandez	.15
174	Lance Johnson	.10
175	Ron Karkovice	.10
176	Jack McDowell	.20
177	Scott Radinsky	.10
178	Tim Raines	.12
179	Steve Sax	.10
180	Bobby Thigpen	.10
181	Frank Thomas	2.50
182	Sandy Alomar Jr.	.20
183	Carlos Baerga	.10
184	Felix Fermin	.10
185	Thomas Howard	.10
186	Mark Lewis	.10
187	Derek Lilliquist	.10
188	Carlos Martinez	.10
189	Charles Nagy	.15
190	Scott Scudder	.10
191	Paul Sorrento	.10
192	Jim Thome	.50
193	Mark Whiten	.10
194	Milt Cuyler	.10
195	Rob Deer	.10
196	John Doherty	.10
197	Travis Fryman	.20
198	Dan Gladden	.10
199	Mike Henneman	.10
200	John Kiely	.10
201	Chad Kreuter	.10
202	Scott Livingstone	.10
203	Tony Phillips	.12
204	Alan Trammell	.15
205	Mike Boddicker	.10
206	George Brett	.75
207	Tom Gordon	.10
208	Mark Gubicza	.10
209	Gregg Jefferies	.15
210	Wally Joyner	.12
211	Kevin Koslofski	.10

#	Player	Price	#	Player	Price	#	Player	Price
212	Brent Mayne	.10	302	Jeff Blauser	.10	398	Tom Goodwin	.10
213	Brian McRae	.10	303	Francisco Cabrera	.10	399	Kevin Gross	.10
214	Kevin McReynolds	.10	304	Marvin Freeman	.10	400	Carlos Hernandez	.10
215	Rusty Meacham	.10	305	Brian Hunter	.10	401	Ramon Martinez	.15
216	Steve Shifflett	.10	306	Dave Justice	.25	402	Raul Mondesi	.75
217	James Austin	.10	307	Greg Maddux	3.00	403	Jody Reed	.10
218	Cal Eldred	.10	308	*Greg McMichael*	.15	404	Mike Sharperson	.10
219	Darryl Hamilton	.10	309	Kent Mercker	.10	405	Cory Snyder	.10
220	Doug Henry	.10	310	Otis Nixon	.10	406	Darryl Strawberry	.15
221	John Jaha	.10	311	Pete Smith	.10	407	*Rick Trlicek*	.10
222	Dave Nilsson	.10	312	John Smoltz	.25	408	Tim Wallach	.10
223	Jesse Orosco	.10	313	Jose Guzman	.10	409	Todd Worrell	.10
224	B.J. Surhoff	.10	314	Mike Harkey	.10	410	Tavo Alvarez	.10
225	Greg Vaughn	.15	315	Greg Hibbard	.10	411	*Sean Berry*	.15
226	Bill Wegman	.10	316	Candy Maldonado	.10	412	Frank Bolick	.10
227	Robin Yount	.25	317	Randy Myers	.10	413	Cliff Floyd	.20
228	Rick Aguilera	.10	318	Dan Plesac	.10	414	Mike Gardiner	.10
229	J.T. Bruett	.10	319	Rey Sanchez	.10	415	Marquis Grissom	.20
230	Scott Erickson	.10	320	Ryne Sandberg	.60	416	*Tim Laker*	.15
231	Kent Hrbek	.12	321	*Tommy Shields*	.10	417	*Mike Lansing*	.25
232	Terry Jorgensen	.10	322	Jose Vizcaino	.10	418	Dennis Martinez	.12
233	Scott Leius	.10	323	*Matt Walbeck*	.15	419	John Vander Wal	.10
234	Pat Mahomes	.10	324	Willie Wilson	.10	420	John Wetteland	.12
235	Pedro Munoz	.15	325	Tom Browning	.10	421	Rondell White	.20
236	Kirby Puckett	1.00	326	Tim Costo	.10	422	Bobby Bonilla	.15
237	Kevin Tapani	.12	327	Rob Dibble	.10	423	Jeromy Burnitz	.15
238	Lenny Webster	.10	328	Steve Foster	.10	424	*Vince Burnitz*	.10
239	Carl Willis	.10	329	Roberto Kelly	.12	425	*Mike Draper*	.10
240	Mike Gallego	.10	330	Randy Milligan	.10	426	Tony Fernandez	.10
241	John Habyan	.10	331	Kevin Mitchell	.12	427	Dwight Gooden	.15
242	Pat Kelly	.10	332	*Tim Pugh*	.15	428	Jeff Innis	.10
243	Kevin Maas	.10	333	Jeff Reardon	.10	429	Bobby Jones	.20
244	Don Mattingly	1.00	334	*John Roper*	.10	430	Mike Maddux	.10
245	Hensley Meulens	.10	335	Juan Samuel	.10	431	Charlie O'Brien	.10
246	Sam Militello	.10	336	John Smiley	.10	432	Joe Orsulak	.10
247	Matt Nokes	.10	337	San Wilson	.10	433	Pete Schourek	.10
248	Melido Perez	.10	338	Scott Aldred	.10	434	Frank Tanana	.10
249	Andy Stankiewicz	.10	339	Andy Ashby	.10	435	*Ryan Thompson*	.20
250	Randy Velarde	.10	340	Freddie Benavides	.10	436	Kim Batiste	.10
251	Bob Wickman	.10	341	Dante Bichette	.20	437	Mark Davis	.10
252	Bernie Williams	.60	342	Willie Blair	.10	438	Jose DeLeon	.10
253	Lance Blankenship	.10	343	Daryl Boston	.10	439	Len Dykstra	.15
254	Mike Bordick	.10	344	Vinny Castilla	.20	440	Jim Eisenreich	.10
255	Jerry Browne	.10	345	Jerald Clark	.10	441	Tommy Greene	.10
256	Ron Darling	.10	346	Alex Cole	.10	442	Pete Incaviglia	.10
257a	Dennis Eckersley	.15	347	Andres Galarraga	.20	443	Danny Jackson	.10
257b	Dennis Eckersley (Wt. 195; no "MLBPA" on back - unmarked sample card)	5.00	348	Joe Girardi	.10	444	Todd Pratt	.10
			349	*Ryan Hawblitzel*	.15	445	Curt Schilling	.10
			350	Charlie Hayes	.10	446	Milt Thompson	.10
257c	Dennis Eckersley (Wt, 195; no "Printed in USA" on back - unmarked sample card)	5.00	351	Butch Henry	.10	447	David West	.10
			352	Darren Holmes	.10	448	Mitch Williams	.10
			353	Dale Murphy	.15	449	Steve Cooke	.10
258	Rickey Henderson	.15	354	David Nied	.10	450	Carlos Garcia	.10
259	Vince Horsman	.10	355	Jeff Parrett	.10	451	Al Martin	.15
260	Troy Neel	.15	356	*Steve Reed*	.15	452	*Blas Minor*	.15
261	Jeff Parrett	.10	357	Bruce Ruffin	.10	453	Dennis Moeller	.10
262	Terry Steinbach	.10	358	*Danny Sheaffer*	.15	454	Denny Neagle	.10
263	Bob Welch	.10	359	Bryn Smith	.10	455	Don Slaught	.10
264	Bobby Witt	.10	360	*Jim Tatum*	.10	456	Lonnie Smith	.10
265	Rich Amaral	.10	361	Eric Young	.15	457	Paul Wagner	.10
266	Bret Boone	.20	362	Gerald Young	.10	458	Bob Walk	.10
267	Jay Buhner	.25	363	Luis Aquino	.10	459	Kevin Young	.20
268	Dave Fleming	.10	364	*Alex Arias*	.10	460	*Rene Arocha*	.25
269	Randy Johnson	.40	365	Jack Armstrong	.10	461	Brian Barber	.10
270	Edgar Martinez	.15	366	Bret Barberie	.10	462	Rheal Cormier	.10
271	Mike Schooler	.10	367	Ryan Bowen	.10	463	Gregg Jefferies	.15
272	Russ Swan	.10	368	Greg Briley	.10	464	Joe Magrane	.10
273	Dave Valle	.10	369	Cris Carpenter	.10	465	Omar Olivares	.10
274	Omar Vizquel	.10	370	Chuck Carr	.10	466	Geronimo Pena	.10
275	Kerry Woodson	.10	371	*Jeff Conine*	.25	467	Allen Watson	.10
276	Kevin Brown	.10	372	Steve Decker	.10	468	Mark Whiten	.15
277	Julio Franco	.10	373	Orestes Destrade	.10	469	Derek Bell	.15
278	Jeff Frye	.10	374	Monty Fariss	.10	470	Phil Clark	.10
279	Juan Gonzalez	1.00	375	Junior Felix	.10	471	*Pat Gomez*	.20
280	Jeff Huson	.10	376	Chris Hammond	.10	472	Tony Gwynn	1.00
281	Rafael Palmeiro	.20	377	Bryan Harvey	.10	473	Jeremy Hernandez	.10
282	Dean Palmer	.15	378	*Trevor Hoffman*	.15	474	Bruce Hurst	.10
283	Roger Pavlik	.10	379	Charlie Hough	.10	475	Phil Plantier	.10
284	Ivan Rodriguez	.75	380	Joe Klink	.10	476	*Scott Sanders*	.25
285	Kenny Rogers	.10	381	*Richie Lewis*	.10	477	*Tim Scott*	.10
286	Derek Bell	.15	382	Dave Magadan	.10	478	*Darrell Sherman*	.10
287	Pat Borders	.10	383	Bob McClure	.10	479	Guillermo Velasquez	.10
288	Joe Carter	.15	384	*Scott Pose*	.15	480	*Tim Worrell*	.10
289	Bob MacDonald	.10	385	Rich Renteria	.15	481	Todd Benzinger	.10
290	Jack Morris	.10	386	Benito Santiago	.12	482	Bud Black	.10
291	John Olerud	.15	387	Walt Weiss	.10	483	Barry Bonds	.75
292	Ed Sprague	.12	388	Nigel Wilson	.15	484	Dave Burba	.10
293	Todd Stottlemyre	.10	389	Eric Anthony	.10	485	Bryan Hickerson	.10
294	Mike Timlin	.10	390	Jeff Bagwell	1.00	486	Dave Martinez	.10
295	Duane Ward	.10	391	Andujar Cedeno	.10	487	Willie McGee	.12
296	David Wells	.10	392	Doug Drabek	.10	488	Jeff Reed	.10
297	Devon White	.10	393	Darryl Kile	.10	489	Kevin Rogers	.15
298	Checklist	.10	394	Mark Portugal	.10	490	Matt Williams	.25
299	Checklist	.10	395	Karl Rhodes	.10	491	Trevor Wilson	.10
300	Checklist	.10	396	Scott Servais	.10	492	Harold Baines	.10
301	Steve Bedrosian	.10	397	Greg Swindell	.10	493	Mike Devereaux	.10

494	Todd Frohwirth	.10
495	Chris Hoiles	.10
496	Luis Mercedes	.10
497	*Sherman Obando*	.15
498	*Brad Pennington*	.15
499	Harold Reynolds	.10
500	Arthur Rhodes	.10
501	Cal Ripken, Jr.	2.50
502	Rick Sutcliffe	.10
503	Fernando Valenzuela	.12
504	Mark Williamson	.10
505	Scott Bankhead	.10
506	Greg Blosser	.10
507	Ivan Calderon	.10
508	Roger Clemens	1.00
509	Andre Clemens	.10
510	Scott Fletcher	.10
511	Greg Harris	.10
512	Billy Hatcher	.10
513	Bob Melvin	.10
514	Carlos Quintana	.10
515	Luis Rivera	.10
516	Jeff Russell	.10
517	*Ken Ryan*	.25
518	Chili Davis	.10
519	*Jim Edmonds*	1.50
520	Gary Gaetti	.12
521	Torey Lovullo	.10
522	*Tony Percival*	.10
523	Tim Salmon	.60
524	Scott Sanderson	.10
525	*J.T. Snow*	.75
526	Jerome Walton	.10
527	Jason Bere	.10
528	*Rod Bolton*	.15
529	Ellis Burks	.15
530	Carlton Fisk	.15
531	Craig Grebeck	.10
532	Ozzie Guillen	.10
533	Roberto Hernandez	.10
534	Bo Jackson	.25
535	Kirk McCaskill	.10
536	Dave Stieb	.10
537	Robin Ventura	.25
538	Albert Belle	.75
539	Mike Bielecki	.10
540	Glenallen Hill	.10
541	Reggie Jefferson	.10
542	Kenny Lofton	.75
543	*Jeff Mutis*	.15
544	Junior Ortiz	.10
545	Manny Ramirez	.75
546	Jeff Treadway	.10
547	Kevin Wickander	.10
548	Cecil Fielder	.25
549	Kirk Gibson	.10
550	*Greg Gohr*	.10
551	David Haas	.10
552	Bill Krueger	.10
553	Mike Moore	.10
554	Mickey Tettleton	.10
555	Lou Whitaker	.10
556	Kevin Appier	.10
557	*Billy Brewer*	.15
558	David Cone	.12
559	Greg Gagne	.10
560	Mark Gardner	.10
561	Phil Hiatt	.10
562	Felix Jose	.10
563	Jose Lind	.10
564	Mike Macfarlane	.10
565	Keith Miller	.10
566	Jeff Montgomery	.10
567	Hipolito Pechardo	.10
568	Ricky Bones	.10
569	Tom Brunansky	.10
570	*Joe Kmak*	.10
571	Pat Listach	.10
572	*Graeme Lloyd*	.10
573	*Carlos Maldonado*	.10
574	Josias Manzanillo	.10
575	Matt Mieske	.15
576	Kevin Reimer	.10
577	Bill Spiers	.10
578	Dickie Thon	.10
579	Willie Banks	.10
580	Jim Deshaies	.10
581	Mark Guthrie	.10
582	Brian Harper	.10
583	Chuck Knoblauch	.25
584	Gene Larkin	.10
585	Shane Mack	.10
586	David McCarty	.15
587	Mike Pagliarulo	.10
588	Mike Trombley	.10
589	Dave Winfield	.15

590	Jim Abbott	.15
591	Wade Boggs	.25
592	*Russ Davis*	.20
593	Steve Farr	.10
594	Steve Howe	.10
595	*Mike Humphreys*	.10
596	Jimmy Key	.10
597	Jim Leyritz	.10
598	*Bobby Munoz*	.15
599	Paul O'Neill	.10
600	Spike Owen	.10
601	Mike Stanley	.10
602	Danny Tartabull	.10
603	Scott Brosius	.10
604	Storm Davis	.10
605	Eric Fox	.10
606	Goose Gossage	.10
607	Scott Hammond	.10
608	Dave Henderson	.10
609	Mark McGwire	4.00
610	*Mike Mohler*	.10
611	Edwin Nunez	.10
612	Kevin Seitzer	.10
613	Ruben Sierra	.15
614	Chris Bosio	.10
615	Norm Charlton	.10
616	*Jim Converse*	.10
617	*John Cummings*	.10
618	Mike Felder	.10
619	Ken Griffey, Jr.	3.00
620	*Mike Hampton*	.10
621	Erik Hanson	.10
622	Bill Haselman	.10
623	Tino Martinez	.10
624	Lee Tinsley	.15
625	*Fernando Vina*	.15
626	*David Wainhouse*	.15
627	Jose Canseco	.25
628	Benji Gil	.15
629	Tom Henke	.10
630	*David Hulse*	.20
631	Manuel Lee	.10
632	Craig Lefferts	.10
633	*Robb Nen*	.15
634	Gary Redus	.10
635	Bill Ripken	.10
636	Nolan Ryan	2.50
637	Dan Smith	.10
638	*Matt Whiteside*	.10
639	Roberto Alomar	.60
640	Juan Guzman	.15
641	Pat Hentgen	.15
642	Darrin Jackson	.10
643	Randy Knorr	.10
644	*Domingo Martinez*	.20
645	Paul Molitor	.40
646	Dick Schofield	.10
647	Dave Stewart	.10
648	Checklist	.10
649	Checklist	.10
650	Checklist	.10

1993 Ultra All-Rookies

MIKE PIAZZA

These insert cards are foil stamped on both sides and were randomly inserted into Series II

packs. The cards have black fronts, with six different colors of type. The player's uniform number and position are located in the upper right-hand corner. The player's name and Ultra logo are gold-foil stamped. Backs have a black background on which is a player photo and a career summary.

		MT
Complete Set (10):		20.00
Common Player:		1.00
1	Rene Arocha	1.00
2	Jeff Conine	1.50
3	Phil Hiatt	1.00
4	Mike Lansing	1.00
5	Al Martin	1.25
6	David Nied	1.00
7	Mike Piazza	12.50
8	Tim Salmon	4.00
9	J.T. Snow	2.50
10	Kevin Young	1.25

1993 Ultra All-Stars

This 20-card set features 10 of the top players from each league. Cards were randomly inserted into Series II packs and are foil stamped on both sides.

		MT
Complete Set (20):		45.00
Common Player:		.75
1	Darren Daulton	.75
2	Will Clark	1.50
3	Ryne Sandberg	3.00
4	Barry Larkin	1.00
5	Gary Sheffield	1.50
6	Barry Bonds	3.00
7	Ray Lankford	.75
8	Larry Walker	1.00
9	Greg Maddux	8.00
10	Lee Smith	.75
11	Ivan Rodriguez	3.00
12	Mark McGwire	6.00
13	Carlos Baerga	.75
14	Cal Ripken, Jr.	10.00
15	Edgar Martinez	.75
16	Juan Gonzalez	4.00
17	Ken Griffey, Jr.	12.00
18	Kirby Puckett	4.00
19	Frank Thomas	10.00
20	Mike Mussina	2.00

1993 Ultra Award Winners

This insert set features 18 Top Glove players (nine from each league), two rookies of the year, three MVPs (both leagues and World Series), both Cy Young

Award winners and one Player of the Year. All cards are UV coated and foil stamped on both sides and were found in Series I packs. Fronts have a black background with "Fleer Ultra Award Winners" splashed around in trendy colors. The Ultra logo, player's name and his award are spelled out in gold foil. The horizontally arranged backs have much the same elements, plus a summary of the season's performance which led to the award. There is a close-up player photo, as well.

		MT
Complete Set (25):		40.00
Common Player:		.75
1	Greg Maddux	6.00
2	Tom Pagnozzi	.75
3	Mark Grace	1.25
4	Jose Lind	.75
5	Terry Pendleton	.75
6	Ozzie Smith	2.00
7	Barry Bonds	3.00
8	Andy Van Slyke	.75
9	Larry Walker	1.50
10	Mark Langston	.75
11	Ivan Rodriguez	1.50
12	Don Mattingly	3.00
13	Roberto Alomar	2.00
14	Robin Ventura	.75
15	Cal Ripken, Jr.	8.00
16	Ken Griffey, Jr.	10.00
17	Kirby Puckett	3.00
18	Devon White	.75
19	Pat Listach	.75
20	Eric Karros	1.00
21	Pat Borders	.75
22	Greg Maddux	6.00
23	Dennis Eckersley	.75
24	Barry Bonds	3.00
25	Gary Sheffield	1.50

1993 Ultra Dennis Eckersley Career Highlights

This limited-edition subset chronicles Dennis Eckersley's illustrious career. Cards, which are UV coated and silver foil-stamped on both sides, were randomly inserted into both series' packs. Eckersley autographed more than 2,000 of the cards, which were also randomly inserted into packs. By sending in 10 Fleer Ultra wrappers plus $1, collectors could receive two additional Eckersley cards which were not available in regular packs. Card fronts have a color action photo, the background of which has been colorized into shades of purple. A black marble strip at bottom has the city name and years he was with the team in silver foil. A large black marble box in one corner has the "Dennis Eckersley Career Highlights" logo in silver foil. On back, a purple box is dropped out of a color photo, and silver-foil typography describes some phrase of Eck's career.

		MT
Complete Set (12):		5.00
Common Card:		.50
Autographed Card:		75.00
1	"Perfection" (A's 1987-92)	.50
2	"The Kid" (Indians 1975-77)	.50
3	"The Warrior" (Indians 1975-77)	.50
4	"Beantown Blazer" (Red Sox 1978-84)	.50
5	"Eckspeak" (Red Sox 1978-84)	.50
6	"Down to Earth" (Red Sox 1978-84)	.50
7	"Wrigley Bound" (Cubs 1984-86)	.50
8	"No Relief" (A's 1987-92)	.50
9	"In Control" (A's 1987-92)	.50
10	"Simply the Best" (A's 1987-92)	.50
11	"Reign of Perfection" (A's 1987-92)	.50
12	"Leaving His Mark" (A's 1987-92)	.50

1993 Ultra Home Run Kings

This insert set features top home run kings. Cards, which are UV coated and have gold foil stamping on both sides, were inserts in Series I packs.

		MT
Complete Set (10):		15.00
Common Player:		1.00
1	Juan Gonzalez	4.00
2	Mark McGwire	8.00
3	Cecil Fielder	1.50
4	Fred McGriff	2.00
5	Albert Belle	3.00
6	Barry Bonds	3.00
7	Joe Carter	1.00
8	Gary Sheffield	2.00
9	Darren Daulton	1.00
10	Dave Hollins	1.00

1993 Ultra Performers

An Ultra Performers set of Fleer Ultra baseball cards was offered directly to collectors in 1993. The set, available only by mail, was limited to 150,000 sets. The cards featured gold-foil stamping and UV coating on each side and a six-photo design, including five on the front of the card. Each card was identified on the back by set serial number jet-printed in black in a strip at bottom.

		MT
Complete Set (10):		18.00
Common Player:		1.00
1	Barry Bonds	2.50
2	Juan Gonzalez	3.00
3	Ken Griffey, Jr.	6.00
4	Eric Karros	.75
5	Pat Listach	.75
6	Greg Maddux	4.00
7	David Nied	.75
8	Gary Sheffield	1.00
9	J.T. Snow	1.00
10	Frank Thomas	5.00

1993 Ultra Strikeout Kings

Five of baseball's top strikeout pitchers are featured in this second-series Ultra insert set. Cards are UV coated and foil stamped on both sides. Each card front has a picture of a pitcher winding up to throw. A baseball is in the background, with the pitcher in the forefront.

		MT
Complete Set (5):		15.00
Common Player:		1.00
1	Roger Clemens	3.00
2	Juan Guzman	1.00
3	Randy Johnson	2.00
4	Nolan Ryan	10.00
5	John Smoltz	2.00

1994 Ultra

Issued in two series of 300 cards each, Ultra for 1994 represented a new highwater mark in production values for a mid-priced brand. Each side of the basic cards is UV coated and gold-foil embossed. Fronts feature full-bleed action photos. At bottom the player name, team, position and Fleer Ultra logo appear in gold foil above a gold-foil strip. Some rookie cards are specially designated with a large gold "ROOKIE" above the Ultra logo. Backs feature a basic background that is team color coordinated. Three more player action photos are featured on the back, along with a team logo and a modicum of stats and personal data. There is a gold stripe along the left edge and the player's name and card number appear in gold in the lower-left corner. The set features seven types of insert cards, packaged one per pack.

		MT
Complete Set (600):		40.00
Common Player:		.10
Series 1 or 2 Wax Box:		45.00
1	Jeffrey Hammonds	.15

2	Chris Hoiles	.10	98	Bobby Munoz	.10
3	Ben McDonald	.10	99	Paul O'Neill	.15
4	Mark McLemore	.10	100	Melido Perez	.10
5	Alan Mills	.10	101	Mike Stanley	.10
6	Jamie Moyer	.10	102	Danny Tartabull	.10
7	Brad Pennington	.10	103	Bernie Williams	.40
8	Jim Poole	.10	104	*Kurt Abbott*	.25
9	Cal Ripken, Jr.	2.50	105	Mike Bordick	.10
10	Jack Voigt	.10	106	Ron Darling	.10
11	Roger Clemens	1.00	107	Brent Gates	.15
12	Danny Darwin	.10	108	Miguel Jimenez	.10
13	Andre Dawson	.15	109	Steve Karsay	.15
14	Scott Fletcher	.10	110	Scott Lydy	.10
15	Greg Harris	.10	111	Mark McGwire	4.00
16	Billy Hatcher	.10	112	Troy Neel	.10
17	Jeff Russell	.10	113	Craig Paquette	.10
18	Aaron Sele	.20	114	Bob Welch	.10
19	Mo Vaughn	.60	115	Bobby Witt	.10
20	Mike Butcher	.10	116	Rich Amaral	.10
21	Rod Correia	.10	117	Mike Blowers	.10
22	Steve Frey	.10	118	Jay Buhner	.12
23	*Phil Leftwich*	.10	119	Dave Fleming	.10
24	Torey Lovullo	.10	120	Ken Griffey, Jr.	3.00
25	Ken Patterson	.10	121	Tino Martinez	.20
26	Eduardo Perez	.15	122	Marc Newfield	.15
27	Tim Salmon	.35	123	Ted Power	.10
28	J.T. Snow	.25	124	Mackey Sasser	.10
29	Chris Turner	.10	125	Omar Vizquel	.10
30	Wilson Alvarez	.10	126	Kevin Brown	.15
31	Jason Bere	.15	127	Juan Gonzalez	1.00
32	Joey Cora	.10	128	Tom Henke	.10
33	Alex Fernandez	.15	129	David Hulse	.10
34	Roberto Hernandez	.10	130	Dean Palmer	.12
35	Lance Johnson	.10	131	Roger Pavlik	.10
36	Ron Karkovice	.10	132	Ivan Rodriguez	.75
37	Kirk McCaskill	.10	133	Kenny Rogers	.10
38	Jeff Schwarz	.10	134	Doug Strange	.10
39	Frank Thomas	2.50	135	Pat Borders	.10
40	Sandy Alomar Jr.	.15	136	Joe Carter	.20
41	Albert Belle	.75	137	Darnell Coles	.10
42	Felix Fermin	.10	138	Pat Hentgen	.15
43	Wayne Kirby	.10	139	Al Leiter	.12
44	Tom Kramer	.10	140	Paul Molitor	.35
45	Kenny Lofton	.75	141	John Olerud	.15
46	Jose Mesa	.10	142	Ed Sprague	.10
47	Eric Plunk	.10	143	Dave Stewart	.12
48	Paul Sorrento	.10	144	Mike Timlin	.10
49	Jim Thome	.35	145	Duane Ward	.10
50	Bill Wertz	.10	146	Devon White	.10
51	John Doherty	.10	147	Steve Avery	.12
52	Cecil Fielder	.20	148	Steve Bedrosian	.10
53	Travis Fryman	.20	149	Damon Berryhill	.10
54	Chris Gomez	.10	150	Jeff Blauser	.10
55	Mike Henneman	.10	151	Tom Glavine	.15
56	Chad Kreuter	.10	152	Chipper Jones	1.50
57	Bob MacDonald	.10	153	Mark Lemke	.10
58	Mike Moore	.10	154	Fred McGriff	.30
59	Tony Phillips	.15	155	Greg McMichael	.10
60	Lou Whitaker	.10	156	Deion Sanders	.40
61	Kevin Appier	.10	157	John Smoltz	.15
62	Greg Gagne	.10	158	Mark Wohlers	.10
63	Chris Gwynn	.10	159	Jose Bautista	.10
64	Bob Hamelin	.10	160	Steve Buechele	.10
65	Chris Haney	.10	161	Mike Harkey	.10
66	Phil Hiatt	.10	162	Greg Hibbard	.10
67	Felix Jose	.10	163	Chuck McElroy	.10
68	Jose Lind	.10	164	Mike Morgan	.10
69	Mike Macfarlane	.10	165	Kevin Roberson	.15
70	Jeff Montgomery	.10	166	Ryne Sandberg	.60
71	Hipolito Pichardo	.10	167	Jose Vizcaino	.10
72	Juan Bell	.10	168	Rick Wilkins	.10
73	Cal Eldred	.10	169	Willie Wilson	.10
74	Darryl Hamilton	.10	170	Willie Greene	.12
75	Doug Henry	.10	171	Roberto Kelly	.10
76	Mike Ignasiak	.10	172	Larry Luebbers	.10
77	John Jaha	.12	173	Kevin Mitchell	.12
78	Graeme Lloyd	.10	174	Joe Oliver	.10
79	Angel Miranda	.10	175	John Roper	.10
80	Dave Nilsson	.12	176	Johnny Ruffin	.10
81	Troy O'Leary	.10	177	Reggie Sanders	.15
82	Kevin Reimer	.10	178	John Smiley	.10
83	Willie Banks	.10	179	Jerry Spradlin	.10
84	Larry Casian	.10	180	Freddie Benavides	.10
85	Scott Erickson	.10	181	Dante Bichette	.30
86	Eddie Guardado	.10	182	Willie Blair	.10
87	Kent Hrbek	.12	183	Kent Bottenfield	.10
88	Terry Jorgensen	.10	184	Jerald Clark	.10
89	Chuck Knoblauch	.25	185	Joe Girardi	.10
90	Pat Meares	.10	186	Roberto Mejia	.10
91	Mike Trombley	.10	187	Steve Reed	.10
92	Dave Winfield	.15	188	Armando Reynoso	.10
93	Wade Boggs	.20	189	Bruce Ruffin	.10
94	Scott Kamieniecki	.10	190	Eric Young	.10
95	Pat Kelly	.10	191	Luis Aquino	.10
96	Jimmy Key	.12	192	Bret Barberie	.10
97	Jim Leyritz	.12	193	Ryan Bowen	.10

#	Player	Value
194	Chuck Carr	.10
195	Orestes Destrade	.10
196	Richie Lewis	.10
197	Dave Magadan	.10
198	Bob Natal	.10
199	Gary Sheffield	.20
200	Matt Turner	.10
201	Darrell Whitmore	.12
202	Eric Anthony	.10
203	Jeff Bagwell	1.00
204	Andujar Cedeno	.10
205	Luis Gonzalez	.10
206	Xavier Hernandez	.10
207	Doug Jones	.10
208	Darryl Kile	.10
209	Scott Servais	.10
210	Greg Swindell	.10
211	Brian Williams	.10
212	Pedro Astacio	.12
213	Brett Butler	.15
214	Omar Daal	.10
215	Jim Gott	.10
216	Raul Mondesi	.50
217	Jose Offerman	.10
218	Mike Piazza	1.50
219	Cory Snyder	.10
220	Tim Wallach	.10
221	Todd Worrell	.10
222	Moises Alou	.10
223	Sean Berry	.10
224	Wil Cordero	.10
225	Jeff Fassero	.10
226	Darrin Fletcher	.10
227	Cliff Floyd	.15
228	Marquis Grissom	.15
229	Ken Hill	.10
230	Mike Lansing	.12
231	Kirk Rueter	.10
232	John Wetteland	.10
233	Rondell White	.30
234	Tim Bogar	.10
235	Jeromy Burnitz	.15
236	Dwight Gooden	.15
237	Todd Hundley	.15
238	Jeff Kent	.10
239	Josias Manzanillo	.10
240	Joe Orsulak	.10
241	Ryan Thompson	.10
242	Kim Batiste	.10
243	Darren Daulton	.12
243a	Darren Daulton (promotional sample)	1.00
244	Tommy Greene	.10
245	Dave Hollins	.10
246	Pete Incaviglia	.10
247	Danny Jackson	.10
248	Ricky Jordan	.10
249	John Kruk	.10
249a	John Kruk (promotional sample)	1.00
250	Mickey Morandini	.10
251	Terry Mulholland	.10
252	Ben Rivera	.10
253	Kevin Stocker	.10
254	Jay Bell	.10
255	Steve Cooke	.10
256	Jeff King	.10
257	Al Martin	.10
258	Danny Micelli	.10
259	Blas Minor	.10
260	Don Slaught	.10
261	Paul Wagner	.10
262	Tim Wakefield	.10
263	Kevin Young	.12
264	Rene Arocha	.12
265	Richard Batchelor	.10
266	Gregg Jefferies	.15
267	Brian Jordan	.15
268	Jose Oquendo	.10
269	Donovan Osborne	.10
270	Erik Pappas	.10
271	Mike Perez	.10
272	Bob Tewksbury	.10
273	Mark Whiten	.10
274	Todd Zeile	.15
275	Andy Ashby	.10
276	Brad Ausmus	.10
277	Phil Clark	.10
278	Jeff Gardner	.10
279	Ricky Gutierrez	.10
280	Tony Gwynn	1.00
281	Tim Mauser	.10
282	Scott Sanders	.10
283	Frank Seminara	.10
284	Wally Whitehurst	.10
285	Rod Beck	.10
286	Barry Bonds	.75
287	Dave Burba	.10
288	Mark Carreon	.10
289	Royce Clayton	.10
290	Mike Jackson	.10
291	Darren Lewis	.10
292	Kirt Manwaring	.10
293	Dave Martinez	.10
294	Billy Swift	.10
295	Salomon Torres	.10
296	Matt Williams	.30
297	Checklist 1-103 (Joe Orsulak)	.10
298	Checklist 104-201 (Pete Incaviglia)	.10
299	Checklist 202-300 (Todd Hundley)	.10
300	Checklist - Inserts (John Doherty)	.10
301	Brady Anderson	.25
302	Harold Baines	.12
303	Damon Buford	.10
304	Mike Devereaux	.10
305	Sid Fernandez	.10
306	Rick Krivda	.10
307	Mike Mussina	.50
308	Rafael Palmeiro	.20
309	Arthur Rhodes	.10
310	Chris Sabo	.10
311	Lee Smith	.12
312	Gregg Zaun	.15
313	Scott Cooper	.10
314	Mike Greenwell	.10
315	Tim Naehring	.10
316	Otis Nixon	.10
317	Paul Quantrill	.10
318	John Valentin	.15
319	Dave Valle	.10
320	Frank Viola	.10
321	Brian Anderson	.15
322	Garret Anderson	.15
323	Chad Curtis	.12
324	Chili Davis	.12
325	Gary DiSarcina	.10
326	Damion Easley	.10
327	Jim Edmonds	.40
328	Chuck Finley	.10
329	Joe Grahe	.10
330	Bo Jackson	.15
331	Mark Langston	.10
332	Harold Reynolds	.10
333	James Baldwin	.15
334	Ray Durham	.60
335	Julio Franco	.10
336	Craig Grebeck	.10
337	Ozzie Guillen	.10
338	Joe Hall	.10
339	Darrin Jackson	.10
340	Jack McDowell	.12
341	Tim Raines	.15
342	Robin Ventura	.15
343	Carlos Baerga	.15
344	Derek Lilliquist	.10
345	Dennis Martinez	.12
346	Jack Morris	.10
347	Eddie Murray	.20
348	Chris Nabholz	.10
349	Charles Nagy	.10
350	Chad Ogea	.10
351	Manny Ramirez	.90
352	Omar Vizquel	.10
353	Tim Belcher	.10
354	Eric Davis	.12
355	Kirk Gibson	.10
356	Rick Greene	.10
357	Mickey Tettleton	.10
358	Alan Trammell	.12
359	David Wells	.10
360	Stan Belinda	.10
361	Vince Coleman	.10
362	David Cone	.10
363	Gary Gaetti	.15
364	Tom Gordon	.10
365	Dave Henderson	.10
366	Wally Joyner	.15
367	Brent Mayne	.10
368	Brian McRae	.10
369	Michael Tucker	.20
370	Ricky Bones	.10
371	Brian Harper	.10
372	Tyrone Hill	.15
373	Mark Kiefer	.10
374	Pat Listach	.10
375	Mike Matheny	.12
376	Jose Mercedes	.10
377	Jody Reed	.10
378	Kevin Seitzer	.10
379	B.J. Surhoff	.10
380	Greg Vaughn	.12
381	Turner Ward	.10
382	Wes Weger	.15
383	Bill Wegman	.10
384	Rick Aguilera	.10
385	Rich Becker	.10
386	Alex Cole	.10
387	Steve Dunn	.10
388	Keith Garagozzo	.15
389	LaTroy Hawkins	.20
390	Shane Mack	.10
391	David McCarty	.15
392	Pedro Munoz	.10
393	Derek Parks	.20
394	Kirby Puckett	1.00
395	Kevin Tapani	.10
396	Matt Walbeck	.10
397	Jim Abbott	.15
398	Mike Gallego	.10
399	Xavier Hernandez	.10
400	Don Mattingly	1.00
401	Terry Mulholland	.10
402	Matt Nokes	.10
403	Luis Polonia	.10
404	Bob Wickman	.10
405	Mark Acre	.10
406	Fausto Cruz	.20
407	Dennis Eckersley	.12
408	Rickey Henderson	.20
409	Stan Javier	.10
410	Carlos Reyes	.10
411	Ruben Sierra	.12
412	Terry Steinbach	.10
413	Bill Taylor	.10
414	Todd Van Poppel	.10
415	Eric Anthony	.10
416	Bobby Ayala	.10
417	Chris Bosio	.10
418	Tim Davis	.10
419	Randy Johnson	.40
420	Kevin King	.10
421	Anthony Manahan	.15
422	Edgar Martinez	.15
423	Keith Mitchell	.10
424	Roger Salkeld	.10
425	Mac Suzuki	.15
426	Dan Wilson	.10
427	Duff Brumley	.15
428	Jose Canseco	.50
429	Will Clark	.35
430	Steve Dreyer	.10
431	Rick Helling	.10
432	Chris James	.10
433	Matt Whiteside	.10
434	Roberto Alomar	.75
435	Scott Brow	.10
436	Domingo Cedeno	.15
437	Carlos Delgado	.25
438	Juan Guzman	.12
439	Paul Spoljaric	.10
440	Todd Stottlemyre	.10
441	Woody Williams	.10
442	Dave Justice	.20
443	Mike Kelly	.10
444	Ryan Klesko	.90
445	Javier Lopez	.20
446	Greg Maddux	2.00
447	Kent Mercker	.10
448	Charlie O'Brien	.10
449	Terry Pendleton	.10
450	Mike Stanton	.10
451	Tony Tarasco	.10
452	Terrell Wade	.30
453	Willie Banks	.10
454	Shawon Dunston	.15
455	Mark Grace	.20
456	Jose Guzman	.10
457	Jose Hernandez	.10
458	Glenallen Hill	.10
459	Blaise Ilsley	.10
460	Brooks Kieschnick	1.00
461	Derrick May	.10
462	Randy Myers	.10
463	Karl Rhodes	.10
464	Sammy Sosa	1.50
465	Steve Trachsel	.35
466	Anthony Young	.10
467	Eddie Zambrano	.15
468	Bret Boone	.10
469	Tom Browning	.10
470	Hector Carrasco	.15
471	Rob Dibble	.10
472	Erik Hanson	.10
473	Thomas Howard	.10

474	Barry Larkin	.20
475	Hal Morris	.12
476	Jose Rijo	.10
477	John Burke	.10
478	Ellis Burks	.20
479	Marvin Freeman	.10
480	Andres Galarraga	.15
481	Greg Harris	.10
482	Charlie Hayes	.10
483	Darren Holmes	.10
484	Howard Johnson	.10
485	*Marcus Moore*	.15
486	David Nied	.10
487	Mark Thompson	.10
488	Walt Weiss	.10
489	Kurt Abbott	.10
490	Matias Carrillo	.10
491	Jeff Conine	.15
492	Chris Hammond	.10
493	Bryan Harvey	.10
494	Charlie Hough	.10
495	*Yorkis Perez*	.15
496	Pat Rapp	.15
497	Benito Santiago	.15
498	David Weathers	.10
499	Craig Biggio	.15
500	Ken Caminiti	.15
501	Doug Drabek	.10
502	*Tony Eusebio*	.20
503	Steve Finley	.10
504	Pete Harnisch	.10
505	Brian Hunter	.25
506	Domingo Jean	.10
507	Todd Jones	.10
508	Orlando Miller	.15
509	James Mouton	.15
510	Roberto Petagine	.10
511	Shane Reynolds	.10
512	Mitch Williams	.10
513	Billy Ashley	.15
514	Tom Candiotti	.10
515	Delino DeShields	.10
516	Kevin Gross	.10
517	Orel Hershiser	.12
518	Eric Karros	.15
519	Ramon Martinez	.12
520	*Chan Ho Park*	.35
521	Henry Rodriguez	.20
522	Joey Eischen	.12
523	Rod Henderson	.10
524	Pedro Martinez	.25
525	Mel Rojas	.10
526	Larry Walker	.40
527	*Gabe White*	.25
528	Bobby Bonilla	.12
529	Jonathan Hurst	.10
530	Bobby Jones	.15
531	Kevin McReynolds	.10
532	Bill Pulsipher	.15
533	Bret Saberhagen	.10
534	David Segui	.10
535	Pete Smith	.10
536	*Kelly Stinnett*	.15
537	Dave Telgheder	.10
538	*Quilvio Veras*	.15
539	Jose Vizcaino	.10
540	Pete Walker	.10
541	Ricky Bottalico	.10
542	Wes Chamberlain	.10
543	Mariano Duncan	.10
544	Len Dykstra	.15
545	Jim Eisenreich	.10
546	*Phil Geisler*	.10
547	*Wayne Gomes*	.12
548	Doug Jones	.10
549	Jeff Juden	.10
550	Mike Lieberthal	.10
551	*Tony Longmire*	.15
552	Tom Marsh	.12
553	Bobby Munoz	.10
554	Curt Schilling	.10
555	Carlos Garcia	.12
556	*Ravelo Manzanillo*	.10
557	Orlando Merced	.10
558	*Will Pennyfeather*	.10
559	Zane Smith	.10
560	Andy Van Slyke	.10
561	Rick White	.10
562	Luis Alicea	.10
563	*Brian Barber*	.15
564	Clint Davis	.10
565	Bernard Gilkey	.15
566	Ray Lankford	.15
567	Tom Pagnozzi	.10
568	Ozzie Smith	.40
569	Rick Sutcliffe	.10

570	Allen Watson	.15
571	Dmitri Young	.15
572	Derek Bell	.15
573	Andy Benes	.15
574	Archi Cianfrocco	.10
575	Joey Hamilton	.25
576	Gene Harris	.10
577	Trevor Hoffman	.12
578	*Tim Hyers*	.15
579	*Brian Johnson*	.15
580	*Keith Lockhart*	.25
581	Pedro Martinez	.25
582	Ray McDavid	.15
583	Phil Plantier	.10
584	Bip Roberts	.10
585	Dave Staton	.10
586	Todd Benzinger	.10
587	John Burkett	.10
588	Bryan Hickerson	.10
589	Willie McGee	.12
590	John Patterson	.10
591	Mark Portugal	.10
592	Kevin Rogers	.10
593	*Joe Rosselli*	.10
594	*Steve Soderstrom*	.10
595	Robby Thompson	.10
596	125th Anniversary card	.15
597	Checklist	.10
598	Checklist	.10
599	Checklist	.10
600	Checklist	.10

1994 Ultra
All-Rookie Team

A stylized sunrise landscape is the background for this insert set featuring top rookies and inserted into Ultra Series II packs at the rate of about one per 10. Backs repeat the motif with an action photo. Both sides are gold-foil enhanced and UV-coated.

		MT
Complete Set (10):		10.00
Common Player:		.60
1	Kurt Abbott	1.00
2	Carlos Delgado	1.50
3	Cliff Floyd	1.00
4	Jeffrey Hammonds	1.00
5	Ryan Klesko	3.00
6	Javier Lopez	1.50
7	Raul Mondesi	3.00
8	James Mouton	.60
9	Chan Ho Park	1.00
10	Dave Staton	.60

1994 Ultra All-Stars

Fleer's opinion of the top 20 players in 1994 are featured in this most common of the Series II Ultra insert sets. Silver-foil highlights enhance the chase cards, found, ac-

cording to stated odds, once per three packs, on average. National Leaguers have purple backgrounds front and back, American Leaguers have red.

		MT
Complete Set (20):		20.00
Common Player:		.50
1	Chris Hoiles	.50
2	Frank Thomas	5.00
3	Roberto Alomar	1.50
4	Cal Ripken, Jr.	6.00
5	Robin Ventura	.75
6	Albert Belle	1.50
7	Juan Gonzalez	2.00
8	Ken Griffey, Jr.	6.00
9	John Olerud	.50
10	Jack McDowell	.50
11	Mike Piazza	3.00
12	Fred McGriff	1.00
13	Ryne Sandberg	1.25
14	Jay Bell	.50
15	Matt Williams	1.00
16	Barry Bonds	1.50
17	Len Dykstra	.50
18	Dave Justice	.75
19	Tom Glavine	.60
20	Greg Maddux	3.00

1994 Ultra
Award Winners

The most common of the Fleer Ultra insert sets for 1994 is the 25-card "Award Winners." Horizontal format cards feature front and back background with a gold-embossed look. A player action photo appears on the front. A gold-foil seal on the front has a symbolic player representation flanked by the pictured player's name and award. A gold Fleer Ultra logo is at top. Backs have a player portrait photo and a write-up about the award. The name of the award and the player's name appear in gold foil at the top. Stated odds of finding an Award Winners card were one in three packs.

		MT
Complete Set (25):		20.00
Common Player:		.40
1	Ivan Rodriguez	1.00
2	Don Mattingly	2.50
3	Roberto Alomar	1.50
4	Robin Ventura	.60
5	Omar Vizquel	.40
6	Ken Griffey, Jr.	6.00
7	Kenny Lofton	1.50
8	Devon White	.50
9	Mark Langston	.40
10	Kirt Manwaring	.40
11	Mark Grace	.75
12	Robby Thompson	.40
13	Matt Williams	.75
14	Jay Bell	.40
15	Barry Bonds	1.50
16	Marquis Grissom	.40
17	Larry Walker	.60
18	Greg Maddux	3.00
19	Frank Thomas	5.00
20	Barry Bonds	1.50
21	Paul Molitor	.75
22	Jack McDowell	.40
23	Greg Maddux	3.00
24	Tim Salmon	.75
25	Mike Piazza	3.00

1994 Ultra Career Achievement Awards

The outstanding careers of five of baseball's top veteran stars are recognized in this chase set, inserted on average once every 21 packs of Ultra Series II. The gold-highlighted horizontal fronts combine a current color photo with a background single-tint photo from the player's earlier days. Backs flip-flop the photo use, with the current photo in the background and the earlier photo in full color in the foreground. The gold Ultra Career Achievement Award seal is repeated on back, as well.

		MT
Complete Set (5):		12.00
Common Player:		1.00
1	Joe Carter	1.00
2	Paul Molitor	2.00
3	Cal Ripken, Jr.	8.00
4	Ryne Sandberg	2.00
5	Dave Winfield	1.00

1994 Ultra Firemen

Ten of the major leagues' leading relief pitchers are featured in this Ultra insert set. Cards have an action photo of the player superimposed over a background photo of a fire truck. A shield at top, in gold foil, has a smoke-eater's helmet, stylized flames and proclaims the player an "Ultra Fireman." Backs are horizontal in format and feature the pumper's control panel in the background photo. A color player

portrait photo appears on one side, with a description of his relief role and successes in a whitened box. Fireman crads are found, on average, once per 11 packs, according to stated odds.

		MT
Complete Set (10):		6.00
Common Player:		.75
1	Jeff Montgomery	.75
2	Duane Ward	.75
3	Tom Henke	.75
4	Roberto Hernandez	.75
5	Dennis Eckersley	1.00
6	Randy Myers	.75
7	Rod Beck	.75
8	Bryan Harvey	.75
9	John Wetteland	.75
10	Mitch Williams	.75

1994 Ultra Hitting Machines

A heavy metal background of gears and iron-letter logo is featured in this insert set honoring the game's top hitters. The cards turn up about once in every five packs of Ultra Series II. Both front and back are highlighted in silver foil.

		MT
Complete Set (10):		12.00
Common Player:		.50
1	Roberto Alomar	1.00
2	Carlos Baerga	1.00
3	Barry Bonds	1.50
4	Andres Galarraga	.50
5	Juan Gonzalez	1.50
6	Tony Gwynn	1.00
7	Paul Molitor	.75
8	John Olerud	.50
9	Mike Piazza	2.50
10	Frank Thomas	4.00

1994 Ultra Home Run Kings

One of two high-end insert sets in '94 Ultra is the 12-card "Home Run Kings" found exclusively in 14-

card foil packs, on an average of once per 36-pack box. Featuring the technology Fleer calls "etched metallization," the cards have a black background with a red and blue foil representation of a batter. An action photo of a player taking a mighty cut or starting his home-run trot is featured. A large gold-foil "Home Run King" crown-and-shield device are in an upper corner, while the Ultra logo and player name are in gold foil at bottom. Backs have a white background with the red and blue batter symbol. The player's name appears in gold foil at the top, along with a portrait photo and a summary of his home run prowess.

		MT
Complete Set (12):		80.00
Common Player:		3.00
1	Juan Gonzalez	8.00
2	Ken Griffey, Jr.	20.00
3	Frank Thomas	15.00
4	Albert Belle	5.00
5	Rafael Palmeiro	3.00
6	Joe Carter	2.00
7	Barry Bonds	5.00
8	Dave Justice	3.00
9	Matt Williams	3.00
10	Fred McGriff	3.00
11	Ron Gant	2.00
12	Mike Piazza	10.00

1994 Ultra League Leaders

Arguably the least attractive of the '94 Fleer Ultra inserts are the 10 "League Leaders." Fronts feature a full-bleed action photo on which the bottom has been re-colored to a team hue giving the effect of teal, purple and magenta miasmas rising from the turf. An Ultra logo appear in gold foil in an upper corner, with the player's name in gold foil at about the dividing line between the natural color and colorized portions of the photo. A large "League Leader" appears in the bottom half of the photo, with the category led printed in the lower-left. Backs repeat the team color at top, fading to white at the bottom. In gold foil are "League Leader" and the category. A portrait-type player photo appears at bottom. Several paragraphs detail the league leading performance of the previous season.

		MT
Complete Set (10):		5.00
Common Player:		.50
1	John Olerud	.50
2	Rafael Palmeiro	.60
3	Kenny Lofton	1.00
4	Jack McDowell	.50
5	Randy Johnson	.75
6	Andres Galarraga	.50
7	Len Dykstra	.50
8	Chuck Carr	.50
9	Tom Glavine	.60
10	Jose Rijo	.50

1994 Ultra On-Base Leaders

One of the lesser-known, but most valuable, stats - on-base percentage - is featured in this subset found exclusively in 17-card packs, at the rate of about one per 37 packs. The fronts feature color photos against a stat-filled printed-foil background.

		MT
Complete Set (12):		175.00
Common Player:		5.00
1	Roberto Alomar	15.00
2	Barry Bonds	20.00
3	Len Dykstra	5.00
4	Andres Galarraga	5.00
5	Mark Grace	10.00
6	Ken Griffey, Jr.	50.00
7	Gregg Jefferies	5.00
8	Orlando Merced	5.00
9	Paul Molitor	12.00
10	John Olerud	5.00
11	Tony Phillips	5.00
12	Frank Thomas	40.00

1994 Ultra Phillies Finest

As a tribute to two of Fleer's home-team heroes, the Philadelphia-based card company created an Ultra insert set featuring 12 cards each of "Phillies Finest," John Kruk and Darren Daulton. Twenty of the cards were issued as Series 1 and 2 inserts, about one in every eight packs, while four were available only by a mail-in offer. Fronts feature action photos with large block letters popping out of the background. The Ultra logo and player name appear in gold foil. Backs have portrait photos and career summaries, with the player's name and card number in gold foil. Daulton and Kruk each autographed 1,000 of the inserts. Stated odds of finding the autographed cards were one in 11,000 packs. Values listed are per card.

		MT
Complete Set (24):		10.00
Common player:		.50
Autographed card:		60.00
1-5	Darren Daulton	.50
6-10	John Kruk	.50
11-15	Darren Daulton	.50
16-20	John Kruk	.50
9a	John Kruk (PROMOTIONAL SAMPLE)	3.00
	MAIL-IN CARDS	
1M, 3M	Darren Daulton	1.50
2M, 4M	John Kruk	1.50
1	Darren Daulton (holding mask and glove)	.50
2	Darren Daulton (power swing, home uniform)	.50
3	Darren Daulton (blocking home plate)	.50
4	Darren Daulton (home run trot, home uniform)	.50
1M	Darren Daulton (standing, throwing)	1.50
2M	John Kruk (ready to field)	1.50
3M	Darren Daulton (awaiting pitch)	1.50
4M	John Kruk (running)	1.50

1994 Ultra RBI Kings

Exclusive to the 19-card jumbo packs of Fleer Ultra are a series of 12 "RBI Kings" insert cards, found, according to stated odds, one per 36 packs. The horizontal-format card front uses Fleer's "etched metallized" technology to produce a sepia-toned background photo, in front of which is a color player photo. An Ultra logo appears in gold foil in an upper corner while a fancy shield-and-scroll "RBI King" logo and the player's name are in gold at the bottom. Backs repeat the basic front motif and include a color player portrait photo, his name in gold foil and a paragraph justifying his selection as an RBI King.

		MT
Complete Set (12):		170.00
Common Player:		6.00
1	Albert Belle	15.00
2	Frank Thomas	50.00
3	Joe Carter	6.00
4	Juan Gonzalez	30.00
5	Cecil Fielder	6.00
6	Carlos Baerga	6.00
7	Barry Bonds	15.00
8	David Justice	6.00
9	Ron Gant	6.00
10	Mike Piazza	30.00
11	Matt Williams	7.50
12	Darren Daulton	6.00

1994 Ultra Rising Stars

An outer space background printed on metallic foil sets this chase set apart from most of the rest of the Ultra Series II inserts. The silver-foil enhanced cards of projected superstars of tomorrow are found on average once every 37 packs.

		MT
Complete Set (12):		95.00
Common Player:		4.00
1	Carlos Baerga	3.00
2	Jeff Bagwell	18.00
3	Albert Belle	15.00
4	Cliff Floyd	4.00
5	Travis Fryman	3.00

6	Marquis Grissom	3.00
7	Kenny Lofton	15.00
8	John Olerud	3.00
9	Mike Piazza	20.00
10	Kirk Rueter	3.00
11	Tim Salmon	10.00
12	Aaron Sele	3.00

1994 Ultra Second Year Standouts

Approximately once every 11 packs, the Ultra insert find is a "Second Year Standout" card. Ten of the game's sophomore stars are featured. Fronts feature a pair of action photos against a team-color background. Gold-foil highlights are the Ultra logo, the player's name and a "Second Year Standout" shield. The shield and player name are repeated in gold foil on the back, as is the team color background. There is a player portrait photo at bottom and a summary of the player's 1993 season.

		MT
Complete Set (10):		12.00
Common Player:		.50
1	Jason Bere	.75
2	Brent Gates	.50
3	Jeffrey Hammonds	.75
4	Tim Salmon	2.50
5	Aaron Sele	.75
6	Chuck Carr	.50
7	Jeff Conine	1.00
8	Greg McMichael	.50
9	Mike Piazza	8.00
10	Kevin Stocker	.50

1994 Ultra Strikeout Kings

A gold-foil "Strikeout Kings" crown-and-shield logo is featured on the front of this chase set. Cards are found on average once per seven packs. Each of the cards features the K-king in sequential action photos. Backs have a larger action photo with a large version of the Strikeout King shield in the background.

A player's name in *italic* type indicates a rookie card.

		MT
Complete Set (5):		5.00
Common Player:		.75
1	Randy Johnson	1.00
2	Mark Langston	.75
3	Greg Maddux	2.50
4	Jose Rijo	.75
5	John Smoltz	1.00

1995 Ultra

A clean design enhanced with three different colors of metallic foil graphics is featured on the basic cards of 1995 Fleer Ultra. Two series of 250 cards each were issued with cards arranged alphabetically within team, also sequenced alphabetically. Fronts have a gold-foil Ultra logo in an upper corner, with the player's name and team logo in a team-color coded foil at bottom. There are no other graphic elements on the borderless photos. Backs have a large photo rendered in a single color, again team-coded. A postage-stamp sized color photo in one corner is flanked by a few vital stats in silver foil. Career and '94 stats are printed at bottom, enhanced by the foil color from the front. Cards were issued in 12-card retail and hobby packs at $1.99 and jumbo pre-priced ($2.69) magazine packs. Each pack contains one of the several insert series from the appropriate series.

		MT
Complete Set (450):		35.00
Complete Series 1 (250):		20.00
Complete Series 2 (200):		15.00
Common Player:		.10

Gold Medallion: 1.5x-2x		
Series 1 or 2 Wax Box:		50.00
1	Brady Anderson	.20
2	Sid Fernandez	.10
3	Jeffrey Hammonds	.10
4	Chris Hoiles	.10
5	Ben McDonald	.10
6	Mike Mussina	.40
7	Rafael Palmeiro	.15
8	Jack Voigt	.10
9	Wes Chamberlain	.10
10	Roger Clemens	.40
11	Chris Howard	.10
12	Tim Naehring	.10
13	Otis Nixon	.10
14	Rich Rowland	.10
15	Ken Ryan	.10
16	John Valentin	.15
17	Mo Vaughn	.50
18	Brian Anderson	.15
19	Chili Davis	.12
20	Damion Easley	.10
21	Jim Edmonds	.20
22	Mark Langston	.10
23	Tim Salmon	.30
24	J.T. Snow	.15
25	Chris Turner	.10
26	Wilson Alvarez	.10
27	Joey Cora	.10
28	Alex Fernandez	.12
29	Roberto Hernandez	.10
30	Lance Johnson	.10
31	Ron Karkovice	.10
32	Kirk McCaskill	.10
33	Tim Raines	.15
34	Frank Thomas	2.50
35	Sandy Alomar	.15
36	Albert Belle	.75
37	Mark Clark	.10
38	Kenny Lofton	.75
39	Eddie Murray	.40
40	Eric Plunk	.10
41	Manny Ramirez	.60
42	Jim Thome	.35
43	Omar Vizquel	.10
44	Danny Bautista	.10
45	Junior Felix	.10
46	Cecil Fielder	.20
47	Chris Gomez	.10
48	Chad Kreuter	.10
49	Mike Moore	.10
50	Tony Phillips	.15
51	Alan Trammell	.15
52	David Wells	.10
53	Kevin Appier	.10
54	Billy Brewer	.10
55	David Cone	.10
56	Greg Gagne	.12
57	Bob Hamelin	.10
58	Jose Lind	.10
59	Brent Mayne	.10
60	Brian McRae	.10
61	Terry Shumpert	.10
62	Ricky Bones	.10
63	Mike Fetters	.10
64	Darryl Hamilton	.10
65	John Jaha	.10
66	Graeme Lloyd	.10
67	Matt Mieske	.10
68	Kevin Seitzer	.10
69	Jose Valentin	.10
70	Turner Ward	.10
71	Rick Aguilera	.10
72	Rich Becker	.10
73	Alex Cole	.10
74	Scott Leius	.10
75	Pat Meares	.10
76	Kirby Puckett	1.00
77	Dave Stevens	.10
78	Kevin Tapani	.10
79	Matt Walbeck	.10
80	Wade Boggs	.30
81	Scott Kamieniecki	.10
82	Pat Kelly	.10
83	Jimmy Key	.10
84	Paul O'Neill	.10
85	Luis Polonia	.10
86	Mike Stanley	.10
87	Danny Tartabull	.10
88	Bob Wickman	.10
89	Mark Acre	.10
90	Geronimo Berroa	.12
91	Mike Bordick	.10
92	Ron Darling	.10
93	Stan Javier	.10
94	Mark McGwire	4.00

95	Troy Neel	.10
96	Ruben Sierra	.15
97	Terry Steinbach	.10
98	Eric Anthony	.10
99	Chris Bosio	.10
100	Dave Fleming	.10
101	Ken Griffey Jr.	3.00
102	Reggie Jefferson	.10
103	Randy Johnson	.40
104	Edgar Martinez	.12
105	Bill Risley	.10
106	Dan Wilson	.10
107	Cris Carpenter	.10
108	Will Clark	.30
109	Juan Gonzalez	1.50
110	Rusty Greer	.10
111	David Hulse	.10
112	Roger Pavlik	.10
113	Ivan Rodriguez	.50
114	Doug Strange	.10
115	Matt Whiteside	.10
116	Roberto Alomar	.50
117	Brad Cornett	.10
118	Carlos Delgado	.12
119	Alex Gonzalez	.10
120	Darren Hall	.10
121	Pat Hentgen	.10
122	Paul Molitor	.25
123	Ed Sprague	.10
124	Devon White	.10
125	Tom Glavine	.15
126	Dave Justice	.20
127	Roberto Kelly	.10
128	Mark Lemke	.10
129	Greg Maddux	2.00
130	Charles Johnson	.10
131	Kent Mercker	.10
132	Charlie O'Brien	.10
133	John Smoltz	.25
134	Willie Banks	.10
135	Steve Buechele	.10
136	Kevin Foster	.10
137	Glenallen Hill	.10
138	Ray Sanchez	.10
139	Sammy Sosa	1.50
140	Steve Trachsel	.10
141	Rick Wilkins	.10
142	Jeff Brantley	.10
143	Hector Carrasco	.10
144	Kevin Jarvis	.10
145	Barry Larkin	.25
146	Chuck McElroy	.10
147	Jose Rijo	.10
148	Johnny Ruffin	.10
149	Deion Sanders	.25
150	Eddie Taubensee	.10
151	Dante Bichette	.25
152	Ellis Burks	.15
153	Joe Girardi	.10
154	Charlie Hayes	.10
155	Mike Kingery	.10
156	Steve Reed	.10
157	Kevin Ritz	.10
158	Bruce Ruffin	.10
159	Eric Young	.10
160	Kurt Abbott	.10
161	Chuck Carr	.10
162	Chris Hammond	.10
163	Bryan Harvey	.10
164	Terry Mathews	.10
165	Yorkis Perez	.10
166	Pat Rapp	.10
167	Gary Sheffield	.35
168	Dave Weathers	.10
169	Jeff Bagwell	.75
170	Ken Caminiti	.20
171	Doug Drabek	.10
172	Steve Finley	.10
173	John Hudek	.10
174	Todd Jones	.10
175	James Mouton	.10
176	Shane Reynolds	.10
177	Scott Servais	.10
178	Tom Candiotti	.10
179	Omar Daal	.10
180	Darren Dreifort	.10
181	Eric Karros	.15
182	Ramon Martinez	.10
183	Raul Mondesi	.35
184	Henry Rodriguez	.12
185	Todd Worrell	.10
186	Moises Alou	.15
187	Sean Berry	.10
188	Wil Cordero	.10
189	Jeff Fassero	.10
190	Darrin Fletcher	.10

191	Butch Henry	.10
192	Ken Hill	.10
193	Mel Rojas	.10
194	John Wetteland	.10
195	Bobby Bonilla	.12
196	Rico Brogna	.10
197	Bobby Jones	.10
198	Jeff Kent	.10
199	Josias Manzanillo	.10
200	Kelly Stinnett	.10

1995 Ultra All-Rookies

Enlarged pieces of the central color action photo, set on a white background, make up the front design on these inserts. The player's name, card title and Ultra logo are printed in silver foil. Horizontal backs have another color photo, which is also repeated in single-color fashion. A career summary is printed over the larger photo. The All-Rookie inserts are found only in 12-card packs, at the rate of about one per four packs.

		MT
Complete Set (10):		8.00
Common Player:		.40
Gold Medallion: 2X		
1	Cliff Floyd	.50
2	Chris Gomez	.40
3	Rusty Greer	.50
4	Bob Hamelin	.50
5	Joey Hamilton	.60
6	John Hudek	.50
7	Ryan Klesko	2.00
8	Raul Mondesi	2.00
9	Manny Ramirez	3.00
10	Steve Trachsel	.40

1995 Ultra All-Stars

Twenty of the top players in the majors were chosen as Ultra All-Stars in this Series II chase set. Fronts have a color player photo at left. At right is a second photo, printed in only one color. A large "ALL-STAR" is at bottom, with the player's name above and team below in silver foil. An Ultra logo is at left. Backs have another color photo, with a '94 season summary printed in a black panel at right. These cards were found one per five packs, on average.

		MT
Complete Set (20):		20.00
Common Player:		.25
Gold Medallion: 2X		
1	Moises Alou	.25
2	Albert Belle	1.25
3	Craig Biggio	.25
4	Wade Boggs	.40
5	Barry Bonds	1.00
6	David Cone	.25
7	Ken Griffey Jr.	5.00
8	Tony Gwynn	1.50
9	Chuck Knoblauch	.40
10	Barry Larkin	.40
11	Kenny Lofton	1.00
12	Greg Maddux	3.00
13	Fred McGriff	.50
14	Paul O'Neill	.25
15	Mike Piazza	2.00
16	Kirby Puckett	1.50
17	Cal Ripken Jr.	4.00
18	Ivan Rodriguez	.60
19	Frank Thomas	4.00
20	Matt Williams	.40

1995 Ultra Award Winners

Various official and unofficial award winners from the 1994 season are featured in this Series I insert set. Horizontal cards have a color player photo on the right side, with a single-color, vertically compressed action photo at left. The player's award is printed in a white strip at top, while his name and team logo, along with the Ultra logo, are at bottom. All front typography is in gold foil. Backs repeat the compressed photo at left, combined with another color photo at right. A season summary is printed over the photo at left. The Award Winners inserts were common to all types of packaging, found at the rate of about one per four packs.

		MT
Complete Set (25):		18.00
Common Player:		.25
Gold Medallion: 2x		
1	Ivan Rodriguez	.75

2	Don Mattingly	2.00
3	Roberto Alomar	1.00
4	Wade Boggs	.40
5	Omar Vizquel	.25
6	Ken Griffey Jr.	5.00
7	Kenny Lofton	1.00
8	Devon White	.25
9	Mark Langston	.25
10	Tom Pagnozzi	.25
11	Jeff Bagwell	2.00
12	Craig Biggio	.25
13	Matt Williams	.50
14	Barry Larkin	.50
15	Barry Bonds	1.25
16	Marquis Grissom	.25
17	Darren Lewis	.25
18	Greg Maddux	3.00
19	Frank Thomas	4.00
20	Jeff Bagwell	1.50
21	David Cone	.25
22	Greg Maddux	3.00
23	Bob Hamelin	.25
24	Raul Mondesi	.50
25	Moises Alou	.25

1995 Ultra Golden Prospects

A hobby-pack exclusive, found at the rate of one per eight packs on average in Series I. Fronts feature a player photo at right, with three horizontally and vertically compressed versions of the same photo at right. The photo's background has been rendered in a single color. All typography - Ultra logo, card title, name and team - is in gold foil. Backs are also horizontal and have a color player photo and career summary.

		MT
Complete Set (10):		15.00
Common Player:		.50
Gold Medallion: 2x		
1	James Baldwin	.75
2	Alan Benes	1.50
3	Armando Benitez	.50
4	Ray Durham	.75
5	LaTroy Hawkins	.50
6	Brian Hunter	1.00
7	Derek Jeter	5.00
8	Charles Johnson	.75
9	Alex Rodriguez	8.00
10	Michael Tucker	.75

1995 Ultra Gold Medallion

Less than 10% of the production run of Fleer Ultra (regular and insert sets) was produced in a special parallel Gold Medallion edition. On these special cards an embossed round gold seal replaces the Fleer Ultra logo in the upper corner. One Gold Medallion card was inserted into each Ultra foil pack.

	MT
Complete Set (450):	125.00
Complete Series I (1-250):	75.00

	MT
Complete Series II (251-450)	50.00
Common Player:	.25
(Star cards valued at 1.5-2X regular Fleer Ultra version)	

1995 Ultra Gold Medallion Rookies Mail-in

This set of 20 was available only by mailing in 10 Fleer Ultra wrappers plus $5.95. A reported 100,000 sets were produced. The cards are in the same format as the regular-issue Fleer Ultra. Each card has a team logo, player name and "ROOKIE" notation in gold foil at bottom, and the round Gold Medallion seal in an upper-corner of the borderless game-action photo front. Backs have two more action photos, a large one in one-color and a small one in full-color. Much of the typography on back is rendered in gold foil. Card numbers have an M prefix.

		MT
Complete Set (20):		9.00
Common Player:		.25
M-1	Manny Alexander	.25
M-2	Edgardo Alfonzo	.50
M-3	Jason Bates	.25
M-4	Andres Berumen	.25
M-5	Darren Bragg	.25
M-6	Jamie Brewington	.25
M-7	Jason Christiansen	.25
M-8	Brad Clontz	.25
M-9	Marty Cordova	1.00
M-10	Johnny Damon	1.00
M-11	Vaughn Eshelman	.25
M-12	Chad Fonville	.35
M-13	Curtis Goodwin	.35
M-14	Tyler Green	.35
M-15	Bob Higginson	.50
M-16	Jason Isringhausen	.75
M-17	Hideo Nomo	4.00
M-18	Jon Nunnally	.50
M-19	Carlos Perez	.50
M-20	Julian Tavarez	.25

1995 Ultra Hitting Machines

Various mechanical devices and dynamics make up the letters of "HITTING MACHINE" behind the color player action photo in this insert set. Both of those elements, along with the gold-foil player name, team and Ultra logo are in UV-coated contrast to the matte-

finish gray background. Backs are also horizontal in format and feature a portrait photo at right, against a gray-streaked background. A career summary is printed at right. The Hitting Machines series is found only in Series II Ultra retail packs, at the rate of one card per eight packs, on average.

		MT
Complete Set (10):		20.00
Common Player:		.50
Gold Medallion: 2x		
1	Jeff Bagwell	2.50
2	Albert Belle	1.50
3	Dante Bichette	.75
4	Barry Bonds	1.50
5	Jose Canseco	1.00
6	Ken Griffey Jr.	6.00
7	Tony Gwynn	3.00
8	Fred McGriff	.75
9	Mike Piazza	4.00
10	Frank Thomas	5.00

1995 Ultra Home Run Kings

Retail packaging of Fleer Ultra Series I was the hiding place for this sluggers' chase set. An average of one out of eight packs yielded a Home Run King insert. Fronts have a photo of the player's home run cut, while large letters "H," "R" and "K" are stacked vertically down one side. All front typography is in gold foil. Backs have another batting photo and a couple of sentences of recent career slugging prowess.

		MT
Complete Set (10):		25.00
Common Player:		.75
Gold Medallion: 2x		
1	Ken Griffey Jr.	10.00
2	Frank Thomas	8.00
3	Albert Belle	2.50
4	Jose Canseco	1.50
5	Cecil Fielder	1.00
6	Matt Williams	1.00

7	Jeff Bagwell	3.00
8	Barry Bonds	2.50
9	Fred McGriff	1.50
10	Andres Galarraga	.75

1995 Ultra League Leaders

Top performers in major statistical categories are featured in this Series I insert. Cards were seeded in all types of Ultra packaging at the rate of about one card per three packs. Cards have a horizontal orientation with a color player action photo printed over a black logo of the appropriate league. American Leaguers' cards have a light brown overall background color, National Leaguers have dark green. The player's name, team and Ultra logos, and box with his league-leading category are printed in silver foil. The background from the front is carried over to the back, where a color portrait photo is at left, and a '94 season summary printed at right.

		MT
Complete Set (10):		4.00
Common Player:		.25
Gold Medallion: 2x		
1	Paul O'Neill	.25
2	Kenny Lofton	1.00
3	Jimmy Key	.25
4	Randy Johnson	.75
5	Lee Smith	.25
6	Tony Gwynn	1.50
7	Craig Biggio	.25
8	Greg Maddux	2.00
9	Andy Benes	.25
10	John Franco	.25

1995 Ultra On-Base Leaders

Numerous smaller versions in several sizes of the central action photo against a graduated color background from the front design of this Series II insert set. The player name, card title and Ultra logo are printed in gold foil down one side. Backs have a horizontal player photo with a large team logo at top, a smaller version at bottom and a 1994 season summary. One out of eight (on average) pre-priced packs yielded an On-Base Leaders insert.

		MT
Complete Set (10):		40.00
Common Player:		2.50
Gold Medallion: 2x		
1	Jeff Bagwell	6.00
2	Albert Belle	5.00
3	Craig Biggio	2.50
4	Wade Boggs	3.00
5	Barry Bonds	5.00
6	Will Clark	3.00
7	Tony Gwynn	8.00
8	Dave Justice	3.00
9	Paul O'Neill	2.50
10	Frank Thomas	12.00

1995 Ultra Power Plus

The scarcest of the Series I Ultra inserts are the Power Plus cards, printed on 100% etched foil and inserted at the rate of less than one per box. Fronts have a player action photo overprinted on a background of "POWER PLUS" logos in various metallic colors. A team logo and player name are at bottom in gold foil, as is the Ultra logo at top. Backs are conventionally printed and have a player photo on one side and season summary on the other.

		MT
Complete Set (6):		40.00
Common Player:		3.00
Gold Medallion: 2x		
1	Albert Belle	4.00
2	Ken Griffey Jr.	16.00
3	Frank Thomas	12.00
4	Jeff Bagwell	6.00
5	Barry Bonds	4.00
6	Matt Williams	4.00

1995 Ultra RBI Kings

A bright aura surrounds the central player action photo on these cards, separating the player image

from an indistinct colored background. At center is a large gold-foil "RBI KING" with the player's name above and team below. Backs have a similar design with a white box at bottom covering the player's RBI abilities. This set is found only in Series I jumbo packs, at an average rate of one per eight packs.

		MT
Complete Set (10):		45.00
Common Player:		2.00
Gold Medallion: 2x		
1	Kirby Puckett	6.00
2	Joe Carter	2.00
3	Albert Belle	5.00
4	Frank Thomas	12.00
5	Julio Franco	2.00
6	Jeff Bagwell	6.00
7	Matt Williams	4.00
8	Dante Bichette	2.50
9	Fred McGriff	3.00
10	Mike Piazza	8.00

1995 Ultra Rising Stars

The top of the line among Series II chase cards is this set printed on 100% etched foil and seeded at the rate of less than one per box, on average. Horizontal-format cards have two player photos on a background of multi-colored rays. The Ultra logo, card title, player name and team are printed in gold foil. Backs repeat the colored rays, have another player photo and a career summary.

		MT
Complete Set (9):		50.00
Common Player:		2.50
Gold Medallion: 2x		
1	Moises Alou	2.50
2	Jeff Bagwell	6.00
3	Albert Belle	5.00
4	Juan Gonzalez	8.00
5	Chuck Knoblauch	2.50
6	Kenny Lofton	5.00
7	Raul Mondesi	3.00
8	Mike Piazza	10.00
9	Frank Thomas	15.00

1995 Ultra Second Year Standouts

Fifteen of the game's sophomore stars are featured in this Series I insert set. Horizontal-format cards have player action photos front and back set against a background of orange and yellow rays. Besides the player name, card title and Ultra logo in gold-foil, the front features a pair of leafed branches flanking a team logo, all in embossed gold-foil. Backs have a career summary. The series was seeded at the average rate of one per six packs.

		MT
Complete Set (15):		10.00
Common Player:		.25
Gold Medallion: 2x		
1	Cliff Floyd	.40
2	Chris Gomez	.25
3	Rusty Greer	.25
4	Darren Hall	.25
5	Bob Hamelin	.25
6	Joey Hamilton	.40
7	Jeffrey Hammonds	.35
8	John Hudek	.25
9	Ryan Klesko	2.00
10	Raul Mondesi	2.00
11	Manny Ramirez	3.00
12	Bill Risley	.25
13	Steve Trachsel	.35
14	William Van Landingham	.45
15	Rondell White	1.00

1995 Ultra Strikeout Kings

A purple background with several types of concentric and overlapping circular designs in white are the background of this Series II chase set. An action color photo of the K-King is at center, while down one side are stacked photos of the

grips used for various pitches. The player name, card title and Ultra logo are in silver foil. Backs have a portrait photo and career summary with purple circles behind and a black background. Stated odds of finding a Strikeout King card are one in five packs, on average.

		MT
Complete Set (6):		5.00
Common Player:		.50
Gold Medallion: 2x		
1	Andy Benes	.50
2	Roger Clemens	1.00
3	Randy Johnson	1.00
4	Greg Maddux	3.00
5	Pedro Martinez	.75
6	Jose Rijo	.50

1996 Ultra

A 40% thicker cardboard stock and silver-foil highlights are featured in this year's edition. Fronts are very basic with a borderless action photo and silver-foil graphics. Backs feature a three-photo montage along with 1995 and career stats. The set was released in two 300-card series; each card is also reprinted as part of a limited-edition Gold Medallion parallel set. One Gold Medallion card is found in every pack. Each series has eight insert sets. Series I inserts are RBI Kings, Home Run Kings, Fresh Foundations, Diamond Producers, Power Plus, Season Crowns, Golden Prospects and Prime Leather. Series II inserts are Call to the Hall, Golden Prospects, Hitting Machines, On-Base Leaders, RESPECT, Rawhide, Rising Stars and Thunderclap. Checklist cards were also randomly inserted into packs from both series.

		MT
Complete Set (600):		40.00
Complete Series 1 Set (300):		25.00
Complete Series 2 Set (300):		18.00
Common Player:		.10
Wax Box:		45.00
1	Manny Alexander	.10
2	Brady Anderson	.20
3	Bobby Bonilla	.15
4	Scott Erickson	.10
5	Curtis Goodwin	.10
6	Chris Hoiles	.10
7	Doug Jones	.10
8	Jeff Manto	.10
9	Mike Mussina	.35
10	Rafael Palmeiro	.15
11	Cal Ripken Jr.	2.50

12	Rick Aguilera	.10
13	Luis Alicea	.10
14	Stan Belinda	.10
15	Jose Canseco	.25
16	Roger Clemens	1.00
17	Mike Greenwell	.10
18	Mike Macfarlane	.10
19	Tim Naehring	.10
20	Troy O'Leary	.10
21	John Valentin	.15
22	Mo Vaughn	.75
23	Tim Wakefield	.10
24	Brian Anderson	.10
25	Garret Anderson	.15
26	Chili Davis	.12
27	Gary DiSarcina	.10
28	Jim Edmonds	.20
29	Jorge Fabregas	.10
30	Chuck Finley	.10
31	Mark Langston	.10
32	Troy Percival	.10
33	Tim Salmon	.25
34	Lee Smith	.12
35	Wilson Alvarez	.10
36	Ray Durham	.10
37	Alex Fernandez	.10
38	Ozzie Guillen	.10
39	Roberto Hernandez	.10
40	Lance Johnson	.10
41	Ron Karkovice	.10
42	Lyle Mouton	.10
43	Tim Raines	.15
44	Frank Thomas	2.50
45	Carlos Baerga	.15
46	Albert Belle	.75
47	Orel Hershiser	.12
48	Kenny Lofton	.75
49	Dennis Martinez	.12
50	Jose Mesa	.12
51	Eddie Murray	.40
52	Chad Ogea	.10
53	Manny Ramirez	.75
54	Jim Thome	.40
55	Omar Vizquel	.10
56	Dave Winfield	.25
57	Chad Curtis	.10
58	Cecil Fielder	.15
59	John Flaherty	.10
60	Travis Fryman	.10
61	Chris Gomez	.10
62	Bob Higginson	.15
63	Felipe Lira	.10
64	Brian Maxcy	.10
65	Alan Trammell	.12
66	Lou Whitaker	.10
67	Kevin Appier	.10
68	Gary Gaetti	.12
69	Tom Goodwin	.10
70	Tom Gordon	.10
71	Jason Jacome	.10
72	Wally Joyner	.15
73	Brent Mayne	.10
74	Jeff Montgomery	.10
75	Jon Nunnally	.10
76	Joe Vitiello	.10
77	Ricky Bones	.10
78	Jeff Cirillo	.10
79	Mike Fetters	.10
80	Darryl Hamilton	.10
81	David Hulse	.10
82	Dave Nilsson	.10
83	Kevin Seitzer	.10
84	Steve Sparks	.10
85	B.J. Surhoff	.10
86	Jose Valentin	.10
87	Greg Vaughn	.10
88	Marty Cordova	.15
89	Chuck Knoblauch	.20
90	Pat Meares	.10
91	Pedro Munoz	.10
92	Kirby Puckett	.75
93	Brad Radke	.10
94	Scott Stahoviak	.10
95	Dave Stevens	.10
96	Mike Trombley	.10
97	Matt Walbeck	.10
98	Wade Boggs	.20
99	Russ Davis	.10
100	Jim Leyritz	.10
101	Don Mattingly	1.00
102	Jack McDowell	.10
103	Paul O'Neill	.10
104	Andy Pettitte	1.00
105	Mariano Rivera	.20
106	Ruben Sierra	.12
107	Darryl Strawberry	.15

#	Player	Price	#	Player	Price	#	Player	Price
108	John Wetteland	.10	204	Quilvio Veras	.10	300	Matt Williams	.25
109	Bernie Williams	.50	205	Jeff Bagwell	1.00	301	Roberto Alomar	.75
110	Geronimo Berroa	.15	206	Derek Bell	.15	302	Armando Benitez	.10
111	Scott Brosius	.10	207	Doug Drabek	.10	303	Mike Devereaux	.10
112	Dennis Eckersley	.12	208	Tony Eusebio	.10	304	Jeffrey Hammonds	.10
113	Brent Gates	.10	209	Mike Hampton	.10	305	Jimmy Haynes	.10
114	Rickey Henderson	.20	210	Brian Hunter	.10	306	Scott McClain	.10
115	Mark McGwire	4.00	211	Todd Jones	.10	307	Kent Mercker	.10
116	Ariel Prieto	.10	212	Orlando Miller	.10	308	Randy Myers	.10
117	Terry Steinbach	.10	213	James Mouton	.10	309	B.J. Surhoff	.10
118	Todd Stottlemyre	.10	214	Shane Reynolds	.10	310	Tony Tarasco	.10
119	Todd Van Poppel	.10	215	Dave Veres	.10	311	David Wells	.10
120	Steve Wojciechowski	.10	216	Billy Ashley	.15	312	Wil Cordero	.10
121	Rich Amaral	.10	217	Brett Butler	.15	313	Alex Delgado	.10
122	Bobby Ayala	.10	218	Chad Fonville	.10	314	Tom Gordon	.10
123	Mike Blowers	.10	219	Todd Hollandsworth	.15	315	Dwayne Hosey	.10
124	Chris Bosio	.10	220	Eric Karros	.15	316	Jose Malave	.10
125	Joey Cora	.10	221	Ramon Martinez	.12	317	Kevin Mitchell	.12
126	Ken Griffey Jr.	3.00	222	Raul Mondesi	.25	318	Jamie Moyer	.10
127	Randy Johnson	.40	223	Hideo Nomo	.75	319	Aaron Sele	.10
128	Edgar Martinez	.15	224	Mike Piazza	2.00	320	Heathcliff Slocumb	.10
129	Tino Martinez	.15	225	Kevin Tapani	.10	321	Mike Stanley	.10
130	Alex Rodriguez	3.00	226	Ismael Valdes	.10	322	Jeff Suppan	.10
131	Dan Wilson	.10	227	Todd Worrell	.10	323	Jim Abbott	.10
132	Will Clark	.25	228	Moises Alou	.15	324	George Arias	.10
133	Jeff Frye	.10	229	Wil Cordero	.10	325	Todd Greene	.10
134	Benji Gil	.10	230	Jeff Fassero	.10	326	Bryan Harvey	.10
135	Juan Gonzalez	1.50	231	Darrin Fletcher	.10	327	J.T. Snow	.15
136	Rusty Greer	.10	232	Mike Lansing	.10	328	Randy Velarde	.10
137	Mark McLemore	.10	233	Pedro Martinez	.25	329	Tim Wallach	.10
138	Roger Pavlik	.10	234	Carlos Perez	.10	330	Harold Baines	.12
139	Ivan Rodriguez	.50	235	Mel Rojas	.10	331	Jason Bere	.10
140	Kenny Rogers	.10	236	David Segui	.10	332	Darren Lewis	.10
141	Mickey Tettleton	.10	237	Tony Tarasco	.10	333	Norberto Martin	.10
142	Roberto Alomar	.75	238	Rondell White	.15	334	Tony Phillips	.15
143	Joe Carter	.20	239	Edgardo Alfonzo	.10	335	Bill Simas	.10
144	Tony Castillo	.10	240	Rico Brogna	.10	336	Chris Snopek	.10
145	Alex Gonzalez	.10	241	Carl Everett	.10	337	Kevin Tapani	.10
146	Shawn Green	.10	242	Todd Hundley	.15	338	Danny Tartabull	.10
147	Pat Hentgen	.15	243	Butch Huskey	.10	339	Robin Ventura	.15
148	Sandy Martinez	.10	244	Jason Isringhausen	.20	340	Sandy Alomar	.15
149	Paul Molitor	.25	245	Bobby Jones	.10	341	Julio Franco	.10
150	John Olerud	.15	246	Jeff Kent	.10	342	Jack McDowell	.10
151	Ed Sprague	.10	247	Bill Pulsipher	.15	343	Charles Nagy	.10
152	Jeff Blauser	.10	248	Jose Vizcaino	.10	344	Julian Tavarez	.10
153	Brad Clontz	.10	249	Ricky Bottalico	.10	345	Kimera Bartee	.10
154	Tom Glavine	.20	250	Darren Daulton	.10	346	Greg Keagle	.10
155	Marquis Grissom	.15	251	Jim Eisenreich	.10	347	Mark Lewis	.10
156	Chipper Jones	2.00	252	Tyler Green	.10	348	Jose Lima	.10
157	David Justice	.20	253	Charlie Hayes	.10	349	Melvin Nieves	.10
158	Ryan Klesko	.50	254	Gregg Jefferies	.15	350	Mark Parent	.10
159	Javier Lopez	.20	255	Tony Longmire	.10	351	Eddie Williams	.10
160	Greg Maddux	2.00	256	Michael Mimbs	.10	352	Johnny Damon	.15
161	John Smoltz	.20	257	Mickey Morandini	.10	353	Sal Fasano	.10
162	Mark Wohlers	.10	258	Paul Quantrill	.10	354	Mark Gubicza	.10
163	Jim Bullinger	.10	259	Heathcliff Slocumb	.10	355	Bob Hamelin	.10
164	Frank Castillo	.10	260	Jay Bell	.10	356	Chris Haney	.10
165	Shawon Dunston	.15	261	Jacob Brumfield	.10	357	Keith Lockhart	.10
166	Kevin Foster	.10	262	Angelo Encarnacion	.15	358	Mike Macfarlane	.10
167	Luis Gonzalez	.10	263	John Ericks	.12	359	Jose Offerman	.10
168	Mark Grace	.20	264	Mark Johnson	.15	360	Bip Roberts	.10
169	Rey Sanchez	.10	265	Esteban Loaiza	.15	361	Michael Tucker	.15
170	Scott Servais	.10	266	Al Martin	.10	362	Chuck Carr	.10
171	Sammy Sosa	1.50	267	Orlando Merced	.10	363	Bobby Hughes	.10
172	Ozzie Timmons	.10	268	Dan Miceli	.10	364	John Jaha	.10
173	Steve Trachsel	.10	269	Denny Neagle	.10	365	Mark Loretta	.10
174	Bret Boone	.10	270	Brian Barber	.10	366	Mike Matheny	.10
175	Jeff Branson	.10	271	Scott Cooper	.10	367	Ben McDonald	.10
176	Jeff Brantley	.10	272	Tripp Cromer	.10	368	Matt Mieske	.10
177	Dave Burba	.10	273	Bernard Gilkey	.15	369	Angel Miranda	.10
178	Ron Gant	.15	274	Tom Henke	.10	370	Fernando Vina	.10
179	Barry Larkin	.25	275	Brian Jordan	.15	371	Rick Aguilera	.10
180	Darren Lewis	.10	276	John Mabry	.10	372	Rich Becker	.10
181	Mark Portugal	.10	277	Tom Pagnozzi	.10	373	LaTroy Hawkins	.10
182	Reggie Sanders	.15	278	Mark Petkovsek	.10	374	Dave Hollins	.10
183	Pete Schourek	.10	279	Ozzie Smith	.40	375	Roberto Kelly	.10
184	John Smiley	.10	280	Andy Ashby	.10	376	Matt Lawton	.10
185	Jason Bates	.10	281	Brad Ausmus	.10	377	Paul Molitor	.25
186	Dante Bichette	.25	282	Ken Caminiti	.20	378	Dan Naulty	.10
187	Ellis Burks	.15	283	Glenn Dishman	.10	379	Rich Robertson	.10
188	Vinny Castilla	.12	284	Tony Gwynn	1.00	380	Frank Rodriguez	.10
189	Andres Galarraga	.20	285	Joey Hamilton	.15	381	David Cone	.10
190	Darren Holmes	.10	286	Trevor Hoffman	.10	382	Mariano Duncan	.10
191	Armando Reynoso	.10	287	Phil Plantier	.10	383	Andy Fox	.10
192	Kevin Ritz	.10	288	Jody Reed	.10	384	Joe Girardi	.10
193	Bill Swift	.10	289	Eddie Williams	.10	385	Dwight Gooden	.15
194	Larry Walker	.35	290	Barry Bonds	.75	386	Derek Jeter	1.50
195	Kurt Abbott	.10	291	Jamie Brewington	.10	387	Pat Kelly	.10
196	John Burkett	.10	292	Mark Carreon	.10	388	Jimmy Key	.10
197	Greg Colbrunn	.10	293	Royce Clayton	.10	389	Matt Luke	.10
198	Jeff Conine	.15	294	Glenallen Hill	.10	390	Tino Martinez	.20
199	Andre Dawson	.20	295	Mark Leiter	.10	391	Jeff Nelson	.10
200	Chris Hammond	.10	296	Kirt Manwaring	.10	392	Melido Perez	.10
201	Charles Johnson	.15	297	J.R. Phillips	.10	393	Tim Raines	.15
202	Robb Nen	.10	298	Deion Sanders	.25	394	Ruben Rivera	.40
203	Terry Pendleton	.10	299	William VanLandingham	.10	395	Kenny Rogers	.10

396	Tony Batista	.10
397	Allen Battle	.10
398	Mike Bordick	.10
399	Steve Cox	.10
400	Jason Giambi	.10
401	Doug Johns	.10
402	Pedro Munoz	.10
403	Phil Plantier	.10
404	Scott Spiezio	.10
405	George Williams	.10
406	Ernie Young	.10
407	Darren Bragg	.10
408	Jay Buhner	.20
409	Norm Charlton	.10
410	Russ Davis	.10
411	Sterling Hitchcock	.10
412	Edwin Hurtado	.10
413	*Raul Ibanez*	.10
414	Mike Jackson	.10
415	Luis Sojo	.10
416	Paul Sorrento	.10
417	Bob Wolcott	.10
418	Damon Buford	.10
419	Kevin Gross	.10
420	Darryl Hamilton	.10
421	Mike Henneman	.10
422	Ken Hill	.10
423	Dean Palmer	.10
424	Bobby Witt	.10
425	Tilson Brito	.10
426	Giovanni Carrara	.10
427	Domingo Cedeno	.10
428	Felipe Crespo	.10
429	Carlos Delgado	.10
430	Juan Guzman	.10
431	Erik Hanson	.10
432	*Marty Janzen*	.10
433	Otis Nixon	.10
434	Robert Perez	.10
435	Paul Quantrill	.10
436	Bill Risley	.10
437	Steve Avery	.10
438	Jermaine Dye	.25
439	Mark Lemke	.10
440	*Marty Malloy*	.10
441	Fred McGriff	.40
442	Greg McMichael	.10
443	Wonderful Monds	.15
444	Eddie Perez	.10
445	Jason Schmidt	.10
446	Terrell Wade	.10
447	Terry Adams	.10
448	Scott Bullett	.10
449	*Robin Jennings*	.10
450	Doug Jones	.10
451	Brooks Kieschnick	.20
452	Dave Magadan	.10
453	*Jason Maxwell*	.10
454	Brian McRae	.10
455	Rodney Myers	.10
456	Jaime Navarro	.10
457	Ryne Sandberg	.75
458	Vince Coleman	.10
459	Eric Davis	.12
460	Steve Gibralter	.10
461	Thomas Howard	.10
462	Mike Kelly	.10
463	Hal Morris	.10
464	Eric Owens	.10
465	Jose Rijo	.10
466	Chris Sabo	.10
467	Eddie Taubensee	.10
468	Trenidad Hubbard	.10
469	Curt Leskanic	.10
470	Quinton McCracken	.10
471	Jayhawk Owens	.10
472	Steve Reed	.10
473	Bryan Rekar	.10
474	Bruce Ruffin	.10
475	Bret Saberhagen	.10
476	Walt Weiss	.10
477	Eric Young	.10
478	Kevin Brown	.10
479	Al Leiter	.10
480	Pat Rapp	.10
481	Gary Sheffield	.50
482	Devon White	.10
483	Bob Abreu	.10
484	Sean Berry	.10
485	Craig Biggio	.10
486	Jim Dougherty	.10
487	Richard Hidalgo	.10
488	Darryl Kile	.10
489	Derrick May	.10
490	Greg Swindell	.10
491	Rick Wilkins	.10

492	Mike Blowers	.10
493	Tom Candiotti	.10
494	Roger Cedeno	.10
495	Delino DeShields	.10
496	Greg Gagne	.10
497	Karim Garcia	.35
498	*Wilton Guerrero*	.30
499	Chan Ho Park	.12
500	Israel Alcantara	.10
501	Shane Andrews	.10
502	Yamil Benitez	.10
503	Cliff Floyd	.10
504	Mark Grudzielanek	.10
505	Ryan McGuire	.10
506	Sherman Obando	.10
507	Jose Paniagua	.10
508	Henry Rodriguez	.15
509	Kirk Rueter	.10
510	Juan Acevedo	.10
511	John Franco	.10
512	Bernard Gilkey	.15
513	Lance Johnson	.10
514	Rey Ordonez	.40
515	Robert Person	.10
516	Paul Wilson	.20
517	Toby Borland	.10
518	*David Doster*	.10
519	Lenny Dykstra	.12
520	Sid Fernandez	.10
521	*Mike Grace*	.40
522	*Rich Hunter*	.10
523	Benito Santiago	.12
524	Gene Schall	.10
525	Curt Schilling	.10
526	*Kevin Sefcik*	.10
527	Lee Tinsley	.10
528	David West	.10
529	Mark Whiten	.10
530	Todd Zeile	.15
531	Carlos Garcia	.10
532	Charlie Hayes	.10
533	Jason Kendall	.15
534	Jeff King	.10
535	Mike Kingery	.10
536	Nelson Liriano	.10
537	Dan Plesac	.10
538	Paul Wagner	.10
539	Luis Alicea	.10
540	David Bell	.10
541	Alan Benes	.15
542	Andy Benes	.15
543	*Mike Busby*	.10
544	Royce Clayton	.10
545	Dennis Eckersley	.12
546	Gary Gaetti	.12
547	Ron Gant	.15
548	Aaron Holbert	.10
549	Ray Lankford	.15
550	T.J. Mathews	.10
551	Willie McGee	.12
552	*Miguel Mejia*	.10
553	Todd Stottlemyre	.10
554	Sean Bergman	.10
555	Willie Blair	.10
556	Andujar Cedeno	.10
557	Steve Finley	.10
558	Rickey Henderson	.20
559	Wally Joyner	.15
560	Scott Livingstone	.10
561	Marc Newfield	.10
562	Bob Tewksbury	.10
563	Fernando Valenzuela	.12
564	Rod Beck	.10
565	Doug Creek	.10
566	Shawon Dunston	.15
567	*Osvaldo Fernandez*	.25
568	Stan Javier	.10
569	Marcus Jensen	.10
570	Steve Scarsone	.10
571	Robby Thompson	.10
572	Allen Watson	.10
573	Roberto Alomar (Ultra Stars)	.35
574	Jeff Bagwell (Ultra Stars)	.50
575	Albert Belle (Ultra Stars)	.40
576	Wade Boggs (Ultra Stars)	.20
577	Barry Bonds (Ultra Stars)	.40
578	Juan Gonzalez (Ultra Stars)	.60
579	Ken Griffey Jr. (Ultra Stars)	1.50
580	Tony Gwynn (Ultra Stars)	.50
581	Randy Johnson (Ultra Stars)	.25
582	Chipper Jones (Ultra Stars)	.75
583	Barry Larkin (Ultra Stars)	.15
584	Kenny Lofton (Ultra Stars)	.40
585	Greg Maddux (Ultra Stars)	1.00

586	Raul Mondesi (Ultra Stars)	.20
587	Mike Piazza (Ultra Stars)	.75
588	Cal Ripken Jr. (Ultra Stars)	1.25
589	Tim Salmon (Ultra Stars)	.20
590	Frank Thomas (Ultra Stars)	1.25
591	Mo Vaughn (Ultra Stars)	.40
592	Matt Williams (Ultra Stars)	.15
593	Marty Cordova (Raw Power)	.10
594	Jim Edmonds (Raw Power)	.10
595	Cliff Floyd (Raw Power)	.10
596	Chipper Jones (Raw Power)	.75
597	Ryan Klesko (Raw Power)	.40
598	Raul Mondesi (Raw Power)	.20
599	Manny Ramirez (Raw Power)	.40
600	Ruben Rivera (Raw Power)	.25

1996 Ultra
Call to the Hall

Ten probable future Hall of Famers are featured on these cards, which use classic style original illustrations of the players. The cards were seeded one per every 24 Series 2 packs.

		MT
Complete Set (10):		80.00
Common Player:		2.50
Gold Medallion Edition: 2X-3X		
1	Barry Bonds	4.50
2	Ken Griffey Jr.	20.00
3	Tony Gwynn	8.00
4	Rickey Henderson	2.50
5	Greg Maddux	12.00
6	Eddie Murray	3.00
7	Cal Ripken Jr.	15.00
8	Ryne Sandberg	6.00
9	Ozzie Smith	4.00
10	Frank Thomas	12.00

1996 Ultra
Checklists

Fleer Ultra featured 10 check-list cards that were inserted every four packs. These cards featured a superstar player on the front and, throughout the set, a full checklist of all cards in the 1996 Ultra set on the back.

		MT
Complete Set (10):		12.00
Common Player:		.25
1	Albert Belle	.75
2	Cecil Fielder	.25
3	Ken Griffey Jr.	3.00
4	Tony Gwynn	1.00
5	Derek Jeter	1.50
6	Jason Kendall	.25
7	Ryan Klesko	.75
8	Greg Maddux	2.00
9	Cal Ripken Jr.	2.50
10	Frank Thomas	2.50

1996 Ultra Diamond Dust

This card commemorates Cal Ripken's history-making 1995 record of playing in 2,131 consecutive regular-season games. Horizontal in format, the front has a color action photo of Ripken on a simulated leather background. Back has a photo of Ripken on the night he set the new record. Sandwiched between front and back is a dime-sized plastic capsule of dirt certified, according to the facsimile autograph on back of the team's head groundskeeper, to have been used on the infield at Oriole Park in Camden Yards during the 1995 season.

	MT
Cal Ripken Jr.	150.00

1996 Ultra Diamond Producers

A horizontal layout and two versions of the same photo printed on holographic foil are featured in this insert set. Stated odds of finding a Diamond Producers card are one per every 20 Series I packs.

		MT
Complete Set (12):		85.00
Common Player:		2.00
Gold Medallions: 2X to 3X		
1	Albert Belle	5.00
2	Barry Bonds	4.00
3	Ken Griffey Jr.	20.00
4	Tony Gwynn	7.00
5	Greg Maddux	12.00
6	Hideo Nomo	5.00
7	Mike Piazza	10.00
8	Kirby Puckett	7.50
9	Cal Ripken Jr.	15.00
10	Frank Thomas	12.00
11	Mo Vaughn	5.00
12	Matt Williams	2.00

1996 Ultra Fresh Foundations

Rising stars who can carry their teams' fortunes into the next century are featured in this foil-printed insert set, found on average of one card per every three Series I foil packs.

		MT
Complete Set (10):		8.00
Common Player:		.50
Gold Medallions: 2X to 3X		
1	Garret Anderson	.50
2	Marty Cordova	.75
3	Jim Edmonds	.75
4	Brian Hunter	.50
5	Chipper Jones	3.00
6	Ryan Klesko	1.00
7	Raul Mondesi	1.00
8	Hideo Nomo	1.50
9	Manny Ramirez	1.00
10	Rondell White	.50

1996 Ultra Golden Prospects, Series 1

A hobby-pack-only insert, these horizontal format cards have rainbow foil ballpark backgrounds and feature 1996's rookie crop. They are found on average of one per every five Series I packs.

		MT
Complete Set (10):		6.00
Common Player:		.25
Gold Medallions: 2X to 3X		
1	Yamil Benitez	.40
2	Alberto Castillo	.25
3	Roger Cedeno	.50
4	Johnny Damon	.50
5	Micah Franklin	.40
6	Jason Giambi	.50
7	Jose Herrera	.25
8	Derek Jeter	4.00
9	Kevin Jordan	.25
10	Ruben Rivera	1.50

1996 Ultra Golden Prospects, Series 2

The Golden Prospects insert series continued with 15 more young stars found exclusively in Series 2 hobby packs, though in much lower numbers than the Series 1 inserts.

		MT
Complete Set (15):		75.00
Common Player:		4.00
Gold Medallions: 2X to 3X		
1	Bob Abreu	6.00
2	Israel Alcantara	4.00
3	Tony Batista	4.00
4	Mike Cameron	4.00
5	Steve Cox	4.00
6	Jermaine Dye	5.00
7	Wilton Guerrero	8.00
8	Richard Hidalgo	5.00
9	Raul Ibanez	5.00
10	Marty Janzen	4.00
11	Robin Jennings	4.00
12	Jason Maxwell	4.00
13	Scott McClain	4.00
14	Wonderful Monds	6.00
15	Chris Singleton	4.00

Values quoted in this guide reflect the retail price of a card — the price a collector can expect to pay when buying a card from a dealer.

The wholesale price — that which a collector can expect to receive from a dealer when selling cards — will be significantly lower, depending on desirability and condition.

1996 Ultra Gold Medallion

Limited to less than 10% of the regular edition's production, the Gold Medallion parallel set replaces the front photo's background with gold foil featuring a large embossed Fleer Ultra Gold Medallion seal at center. One Gold Medallion card is found in each foil pack.

	MT
Complete Set (600):	100.00
Common Player:	.25
(Star cards valued at 2X-3X regular edition Fleer Ultra)	

1996 Ultra Hitting Machines

These die-cut 1996 Fleer Ultra Series II insert cards showcase the heaviest hitters on cards featuring a machine-gear design. The cards were seeded one per every 288 Series II packs.

		MT
Complete Set (10):		250.00
Common Player:		10.00
1	Albert Belle	25.00
2	Barry Bonds	25.00
3	Juan Gonzalez	50.00
4	Ken Griffey Jr.	100.00
5	Edgar Martinez	10.00
6	Rafael Palmeiro	10.00
7	Mike Piazza	60.00
8	Tim Salmon	15.00
9	Frank Thomas	60.00
10	Matt Williams	15.00

1996 Ultra Home Run Kings

Printed on a thin wood veneer, these super-scarce inserts are seeded one per every 75 Series I

packs. Because of quality control problems, the cards were initially released as exchange cards, with instructions on back for a mail-in redemption offer for the actual wooden card.

		MT
Complete Set (12):		60.00
Common Player:		4.00
Gold Medallions: 2X to 3X		
1	Jeff Bagwell	8.00
2	Albert Belle	6.00
3	Dante Bichette	3.00
4	Barry Bonds	6.00
5	Ron Gant	3.00
6	Ken Griffey Jr.	25.00
7	Manny Ramirez	6.00
8	Tim Salmon	4.00
9	Frank Thomas	15.00
10	Mo Vaughn	6.00
11	Larry Walker	4.00
12	Matt Williams	4.00

1996 Ultra Home Run Kings Exchange Cards

Printed on a thin wood veneer, these super-scarce inserts are found at the rate of only one per 75 packs. Because of quality control problems, the cards were initially released as exchange cards, with instructions on back for a mail-in redemption offer for the actual wooden card. The redemption period expired Dec. 1, 1996.

		MT
Complete Set (12):		16.00
Common Player:		.75
Gold Medallions: 2X to 3X		
1	Jeff Bagwell	1.50
2	Albert Belle	1.00
3	Dante Bichette	1.00
4	Barry Bonds	1.50
5	Ron Gant	.75
6	Ken Griffey Jr.	4.00
7	Manny Ramirez	1.00
8	Tim Salmon	1.00
9	Frank Thomas	4.00
10	Mo Vaughn	1.00
11	Larry Walker	1.00
12	Matt Williams	.75

1996 Ultra On-Base Leaders

These 1996 Fleer Ultra Series II inserts feature 10 of the game's top on-base leaders. The cards were seeded one per every four packs.

		MT
Complete Set (10):		10.00
Common Player:		.50
Gold Medallion: 2X to 3X		
1	Wade Boggs	.75
2	Barry Bonds	1.25
3	Tony Gwynn	2.00
4	Rickey Henderson	.75
5	Chuck Knoblauch	.50
6	Edgar Martinez	.50
7	Mike Piazza	3.00
8	Tim Salmon	.75
9	Frank Thomas	4.00
10	Jim Thome	.75

1996 Ultra Power Plus

Etched-foil backgrounds, multiple player photos and a horizontal format are featured in this chase set. Stated odds of finding one of the dozen Power Plus cards are one per every 10 Series I packs.

		MT
Complete Set (12):		30.00
Common Player:		.75
Gold Medallions: 2X to 3X		
1	Jeff Bagwell	4.00
2	Barry Bonds	2.50
3	Ken Griffey Jr.	10.00
4	Raul Mondesi	1.00
5	Rafael Palmeiro	.75
6	Mike Piazza	6.00
7	Manny Ramirez	1.50
8	Tim Salmon	1.00
9	Reggie Sanders	.75
10	Frank Thomas	8.00
11	Larry Walker	1.50
12	Matt Williams	1.00

1996 Ultra Prime Leather

An embossed leather-feel background is featured on these cards of top fielders, seeded one per every eight Series I packs, on average.

		MT
Complete Set (18):		35.00
Common Player:		.75
Gold Medallions: 2X to 3X		
1	Ivan Rodriguez	2.00
2	Will Clark	1.00
3	Roberto Alomar	3.00
4	Cal Ripken Jr.	10.00
5	Wade Boggs	1.00
6	Ken Griffey Jr.	12.00
7	Kenny Lofton	3.00
8	Kirby Puckett	4.00
9	Tim Salmon	1.00
10	Mike Piazza	7.00
11	Mark Grace	1.00
12	Craig Biggio	.75
13	Barry Larkin	1.00
14	Matt Williams	1.00
15	Barry Bonds	2.50
16	Tony Gwynn	4.00
17	Brian McRae	.75
18	Raul Mondesi	1.00

1996 Ultra Rawhide

Ten top fielders are featured on these 1996 Fleer Ultra Series II inserts. The cards were seeded one per every eight packs.

		MT
Complete Set (10):		35.00
Common Player:		1.00
Gold Medallion: 2X to 3X		
1	Roberto Alomar	2.50
2	Barry Bonds	2.50
3	Mark Grace	1.00
4	Ken Griffey Jr.	10.00
5	Kenny Lofton	2.50
6	Greg Maddux	6.00
7	Raul Mondesi	1.25
8	Mike Piazza	6.00
9	Cal Ripken Jr.	8.00
10	Matt Williams	1.00

A player's name in *italic* type indicates a rookie card.

1996 Ultra RBI Kings

Retail packs are the exclusive provenance of this 10-card set of top RBI men. Stated odds of finding an RBI King card are one per every five Series I packs.

		MT
Complete Set (10):		18.00
Common Player:		.40
Gold Medallions: 2X to 3X		
1	Derek Bell	.50
2	Albert Belle	2.50
3	Dante Bichette	.75
4	Barry Bonds	1.75
5	Jim Edmonds	.50
6	Manny Ramirez	1.25
7	Reggie Sanders	.50
8	Sammy Sosa	5.00
9	Frank Thomas	8.00
10	Mo Vaughn	2.00

1996 Ultra R-E-S-P-E-C-T

These cards feature 10 players held in high esteem by their major league peers. The cards were seeded one per every 18 1996 Ultra Series II packs.

		MT
Complete Set (10):		50.00
Common Player:		1.50
Gold Medallion: 2X to 3X		
1	Joe Carter	1.50
2	Ken Griffey Jr.	15.00
3	Tony Gwynn	7.00
4	Greg Maddux	10.00
5	Eddie Murray	2.00
6	Kirby Puckett	7.00
7	Cal Ripken Jr.	12.00

8	Ryne Sandberg	5.00
9	Frank Thomas	10.00
10	Mo Vaughn	4.00

1996 Ultra Rising Stars

Ten of baseball's best young players are spotlighted on these 1996 Fleer Ultra Series II inserts. Cards were seeded one per every four packs.

		MT
Complete Set (10):		8.00
Common Player:		.25
1	Garret Anderson	.35
2	Marty Cordova	.50
3	Jim Edmonds	.40
4	Cliff Floyd	.25
5	Brian Hunter	.35
6	Chipper Jones	2.50
7	Ryan Klesko	1.50
8	Hideo Nomo	1.50
9	Manny Ramirez	2.00
10	Rondell White	.50

1996 Ultra Season Crowns

Large coats-of-arms printed on "Ultra Crystal" clear plastic are the background for player action photos in this insert set. Odds of one per every 10 Series II packs were stated.

		MT
Complete Set (10):		30.00
Common Player:		.75
Gold Medallions: 2X to 3X		
1	Barry Bonds	2.00

2	Tony Gwynn	4.00
3	Randy Johnson	1.00
4	Kenny Lofton	2.00
5	Greg Maddux	6.00
6	Edgar Martinez	.75
7	Hideo Nomo	3.00
8	Cal Ripken Jr.	8.00
9	Frank Thomas	8.00
10	Tim Wakefield	.75

1996 Ultra Thunderclap

The active career home run leaders are featured in this retail-exclusive Ultra insert set. Seeded only one per 72 packs, the Thunderclap cards have action photos on front with simulated lightning in the background and other graphic highlights rendered in holographic foil. Backs have a large portrait photo and career summary. Each of these scarce retail inserts can also be found in an even more elusive Gold Medallion version.

		MT
Complete Set (20):		450.00
Common Player:		8.00
Gold Medallion: 2x to 3x		
1	Albert Belle	25.00
2	Barry Bonds	25.00
3	Bobby Bonilla	8.00
4	Jose Canseco	12.00
5	Joe Carter	8.00
6	Will Clark	8.00
7	Andre Dawson	8.00
8	Cecil Fielder	8.00
9	Andres Galarraga	15.00
10	Juan Gonzalez	45.00
11	Ken Griffey Jr.	90.00
12	Fred McGriff	8.00
13	Mark McGwire	100.00
14	Eddie Murray	15.00
15	Rafael Palmeiro	12.00
16	Kirby Puckett	25.00
17	Cal Ripken Jr.	65.00
18	Ryne Sandberg	25.00
19	Frank Thomas	60.00
20	Matt Williams	12.00

1997 Ultra

Ultra arrived in a 300-card Series I issue with two parallel sets, Gold and Platinum, which featured "G" and "P" prefixes on the card number, respectively. Cards were issued in 10-card packs. Player names and the Ultra logo are in silver holographic foil. Backs contains complete year-by-year statistics, plus two photos of the player. This also marked the first time that the Gold and Platinum parallel sets displayed a different photo than the base cards. Inserts in Ultra included: Rookie Reflections, Double Trouble, Checklists, Season Crowns, RBI Kings, Power Plus, Fielder's Choice, Diamond Producers, HR Kings and Baseball Rules.

		MT
Complete Set (553):		55.00
Complete Series 1 Set (300):		30.00
Complete Series 2 Set (253):		25.00
Common Player:		.10
Series I & II Wax Box:		60.00
1	Roberto Alomar	.75
2	Brady Anderson	.10
3	Rocky Coppinger	.10
4	Jeffrey Hammonds	.10
5	Chris Hoiles	.10
6	Eddie Murray	.40
7	Mike Mussina	.60
8	Jimmy Myers	.10
9	Randy Myers	.10
10	Arthur Rhodes	.10
11	Cal Ripken Jr.	2.50
12	Jose Canseco	.25
13	Roger Clemens	1.00
14	Tom Gordon	.10
15	Jose Malave	.10
16	Tim Naehring	.10
17	Troy O'Leary	.10
18	Bill Selby	.10
19	Heathcliff Slocumb	.10
20	Mike Stanley	.10
21	Mo Vaughn	.75
22	Garret Anderson	.10
23	George Arias	.10
24	Chili Davis	.10
25	Jim Edmonds	.20
26	Darin Erstad	1.25
27	Chuck Finley	.10
28	Todd Greene	.10
29	Troy Percival	.10
30	Tim Salmon	.20
31	Jeff Schmidt	.10
32	Randy Velarde	.10
33	Shad Williams	.10
34	Wilson Alvarez	.10
35	Harold Baines	.10
36	James Baldwin	.10
37	Mike Cameron	.10
38	Ray Durham	.10
39	Ozzie Guillen	.10
40	Roberto Hernandez	.10
41	Darren Lewis	.10
42	Jose Munoz	.10
43	Tony Phillips	.10
44	Frank Thomas	2.50
45	Sandy Alomar Jr.	.10
46	Albert Belle	.75
47	Mark Carreon	.10
48	Julio Franco	.10
49	Orel Hershiser	.10

50	Kenny Lofton	.75
51	Jack McDowell	.15
52	Jose Mesa	.10
53	Charles Nagy	.10
54	Manny Ramirez	.75
55	Julian Tavarez	.10
56	Omar Vizquel	.10
57	Raul Casanova	.10
58	Tony Clark	.60
59	Travis Fryman	.10
60	Bob Higginson	.10
61	Melvin Nieves	.10
62	Curtis Pride	.10
63	Justin Thompson	.10
64	Alan Trammell	.10
65	Kevin Appier	.10
66	Johnny Damon	.30
67	Keith Lockhart	.10
68	Jeff Montgomery	.10
69	Jose Offerman	.10
70	Bip Roberts	.10
71	Jose Rosado	.10
72	Chris Stynes	.10
73	Mike Sweeney	.10
74	Jeff Cirillo	.10
75	Jeff D'Amico	.10
76	John Jaha	.10
77	Scott Karl	.10
78	Mike Matheny	.10
79	Ben McDonald	.10
80	Matt Mieske	.10
81	Marc Newfield	.10
82	Dave Nilsson	.10
83	Jose Valentin	.10
84	Fernando Vina	.10
85	Rick Aguilera	.10
86	Marty Cordova	.10
87	Chuck Knoblauch	.10
88	Matt Lawton	.10
89	Pat Meares	.10
90	Paul Molitor	.25
91	Greg Myers	.10
92	Dan Naulty	.10
93	Kirby Puckett	1.00
94	Frank Rodriguez	.10
95	Wade Boggs	.20
96	Cecil Fielder	.15
97	Joe Girardi	.10
98	Dwight Gooden	.15
99	Derek Jeter	1.50
100	Tino Martinez	.30
101	*Ramiro Mendoza*	.10
102	Andy Pettitte	.75
103	Mariano Rivera	.20
104	Ruben Rivera	.20
105	Kenny Rogers	.10
106	Darryl Strawberry	.10
107	Bernie Williams	.50
108	Tony Batista	.10
109	Geronimo Berroa	.10
110	Bobby Chouinard	.10
111	Brent Gates	.10
112	Jason Giambi	.10
113	*Damon Mashore*	.10
114	Mark McGwire	4.00
115	Scott Spiezio	.10
116	John Wasdin	.10
117	Steve Wojciechowski	.10
118	Ernie Young	.10
119	Norm Charlton	.10
120	Joey Cora	.10
121	Ken Griffey Jr.	3.00
122	Sterling Hitchcock	.10
123	Raul Ibanez	.10
124	Randy Johnson	.50
125	Edgar Martinez	.10
126	Alex Rodriguez	3.00
127	Matt Wagner	.10
128	Bob Wells	.10
129	Dan Wilson	.10
130	Will Clark	.25
131	Kevin Elster	.10
132	Juan Gonzalez	1.25
133	Rusty Greer	.10
134	Darryl Hamilton	.10
135	Mike Henneman	.10
136	Ken Hill	.10
137	Mark McLemore	.10
138	Dean Palmer	.10
139	Roger Pavlik	.10
140	Ivan Rodriguez	.60
141	Joe Carter	.20
142	Carlos Delgado	.10
143	Alex Gonzalez	.10
144	Juan Guzman	.10
145	Pat Hentgen	.10

No.	Name	Price	No.	Name	Price	No.	Name	Price
146	Marty Janzen	.10	242	Lance Johnson	.10	338	Jim Leyritz	.10
147	Otis Nixon	.10	243	Bobby Jones	.10	339	Paul O'Neill	.10
148	Charlie O'Brien	.10	244	Alex Ochoa	.10	340	Bruce Ruffin	.10
149	John Olerud	.10	245	Rey Ordonez	.20	341	Michael Tucker	.10
150	Robert Perez	.10	246	Paul Wilson	.20	342	Andy Benes	.10
151	Jermaine Dye	.15	247	Ron Blazier	.10	343	Craig Biggio	.20
152	Tom Glavine	.15	248	David Doster	.10	344	Rex Hudler	.10
153	Andruw Jones	1.50	249	Jim Eisenreich	.10	345	Brad Radke	.10
154	Chipper Jones	2.00	250	Mike Grace	.30	346	Deion Sanders	.25
155	Ryan Klesko	.50	251	Mike Lieberthal	.10	347	Moises Alou	.10
156	Javier Lopez	.20	252	Wendell Magee	.10	348	Brad Ausmus	.10
157	Greg Maddux	2.00	253	Mickey Morandini	.10	349	Armando Benitez	.10
158	Fred McGriff	.35	254	Ricky Otero	.10	350	Mark Gubicza	.10
159	Wonderful Monds	.10	255	Scott Rolen	1.50	351	Terry Steinbach	.10
160	John Smoltz	.20	256	Curt Schilling	.10	352	Mark Whiten	.10
161	Terrell Wade	.10	257	Todd Zeile	.10	353	Ricky Bottalico	.10
162	Mark Wohlers	.10	258	Jermaine Allensworth	.10	354	Brian Giles	.10
163	Brant Brown	.10	259	Trey Beamon	.10	355	Eric Karros	.10
164	Mark Grace	.20	260	Carlos Garcia	.10	356	Jimmy Key	.10
165	Tyler Houston	.10	261	Mark Johnson	.10	357	Carlos Perez	.10
166	Robin Jennings	.10	262	Jason Kendall	.10	358	Alex Fernandez	.10
167	Jason Maxwell	.10	263	Jeff King	.10	359	J.T. Snow	.10
168	Ryne Sandberg	.75	264	Al Martin	.10	360	Bobby Bonilla	.15
169	Sammy Sosa	1.50	265	Denny Neagle	.10	361	Scott Brosius	.10
170	Amaury Telemaco	.10	266	Matt Ruebel	.10	362	Greg Swindell	.10
171	Steve Trachsel	.10	267	*Marc Wilkins*	.10	363	Jose Vizcaino	.10
172	*Pedro Valdes*	.10	268	Alan Benes	.10	364	Matt Williams	.30
173	Tim Belk	.10	269	Dennis Eckersley	.10	365	Darren Daulton	.10
174	Bret Boone	.10	270	Ron Gant	.10	366	Shane Andrews	.10
175	Jeff Brantley	.10	271	Aaron Holbert	.10	367	Jim Eisenreich	.10
176	Eric Davis	.10	272	Brian Jordan	.10	368	Ariel Prieto	.10
177	Barry Larkin	.25	273	Ray Lankford	.10	369	Bob Tewksbury	.10
178	Chad Mottola	.10	274	John Mabry	.10	370	Mike Bordick	.10
179	Mark Portugal	.10	275	T.J. Mathews	.10	371	Rheal Cormier	.10
180	Reggie Sanders	.10	276	Ozzie Smith	.40	372	Cliff Floyd	.10
181	John Smiley	.10	277	Todd Stottlemyre	.10	373	David Justice	.20
182	Eddie Taubensee	.10	278	Mark Sweeney	.10	374	John Wetteland	.10
183	Dante Bichette	.20	279	Andy Ashby	.10	375	Mike Blowers	.10
184	Ellis Burks	.10	280	Steve Finley	.10	376	Jose Canseco	.30
185	Andres Galarraga	.20	281	John Flaherty	.10	377	Roger Clemens	1.00
186	Curt Leskanic	.10	282	Chris Gomez	.10	378	Kevin Mitchell	.10
187	Quinton McCracken	.10	283	Tony Gwynn	1.25	379	Todd Zeile	.10
188	Jeff Reed	.10	284	Joey Hamilton	.10	380	Jim Thome	.50
189	Kevin Ritz	.10	285	Rickey Henderson	.10	381	Turk Wendell	.10
190	Walt Weiss	.10	286	Trevor Hoffman	.10	382	Rico Brogna	.10
191	Jamey Wright	.10	287	Jason Thompson	.10	383	Eric Davis	.10
192	Eric Young	.10	288	Fernando Valenzuela	.10	384	Mike Lansing	.10
193	Kevin Brown	.10	289	Greg Vaughn	.10	385	Devon White	.10
194	Luis Castillo	.25	290	Barry Bonds	.75	386	Marquis Grissom	.10
195	Jeff Conine	.10	291	Jay Canizaro	.10	387	Todd Worrell	.10
196	Andre Dawson	.10	292	Jacob Cruz	.10	388	Jeff Kent	.10
197	Charles Johnson	.10	293	Shawon Dunston	.10	389	Mickey Tettleton	.10
198	Al Leiter	.10	294	Shawn Estes	.10	390	Steve Avery	.10
199	Ralph Milliard	.10	295	Mark Gardner	.10	391	David Cone	.20
200	Robb Nen	.10	296	Marcus Jensen	.10	392	Scott Cooper	.10
201	Edgar Renteria	.15	297	*Bill Mueller*	.10	393	Lee Stevens	.10
202	Gary Sheffield	.35	298	Chris Singleton	.10	394	Kevin Elster	.10
203	Bob Abreu	.10	299	Allen Watson	.10	395	Tom Goodwin	.10
204	Jeff Bagwell	1.25	300	Matt Williams	.25	396	Shawn Green	.10
205	Derek Bell	.10	301	Rod Beck	.10	397	Pete Harnisch	.10
206	Sean Berry	.10	302	Jay Bell	.10	398	Eddie Murray	.40
207	Richard Hidalgo	.10	303	Shawon Dunston	.10	399	Joe Randa	.10
208	Todd Jones	.10	304	Reggie Jefferson	.10	400	Scott Sanders	.10
209	Darryl Kile	.10	305	Darren Oliver	.10	401	John Valentin	.10
210	Orlando Miller	.10	306	Benito Santiago	.10	402	Todd Jones	.10
211	Shane Reynolds	.10	307	Gerald Williams	.10	403	Terry Adams	.10
212	Billy Wagner	.10	308	Damon Buford	.10	404	Brian Hunter	.10
213	Donne Wall	.10	309	Jeromy Burnitz	.10	405	Pat Listach	.10
214	Roger Cedeno	.10	310	Sterling Hitchcock	.10	406	Kenny Lofton	.75
215	Greg Gagne	.10	311	Dave Hollins	.10	407	Hal Morris	.10
216	Karim Garcia	.35	312	Mel Rojas	.10	408	Ed Sprague	.10
217	Wilton Guerrero	.15	313	Robin Ventura	.10	409	Rich Becker	.10
218	Todd Hollandsworth	.10	314	David Wells	.10	410	Edgardo Alfonzo	.10
219	Ramon Martinez	.10	315	Cal Eldred	.10	411	Albert Belle	.75
220	Raul Mondesi	.20	316	Gary Gaetti	.10	412	Jeff King	.10
221	Hideo Nomo	.60	317	John Hudek	.10	413	Kirt Manwaring	.10
222	Chan Ho Park	.10	318	Brian Johnson	.10	414	Jason Schmidt	.10
223	Mike Piazza	2.00	319	Denny Neagle	.10	415	Allen Watson	.10
224	Ismael Valdes	.10	320	Larry Walker	.35	416	Lee Tinsley	.10
225	Moises Alou	.15	321	Russ Davis	.10	417	Brett Butler	.10
226	Derek Aucoin	.10	322	Delino DeShields	.10	418	Carlos Garcia	.10
227	Yamil Benitez	.10	323	Charlie Hayes	.10	419	Mark Lemke	.10
228	Jeff Fassero	.10	324	Jermaine Dye	.10	420	Jaime Navarro	.10
229	Darrin Fletcher	.10	325	John Ericks	.10	421	David Segui	.10
230	Mark Grudzielanek	.10	326	Jeff Fassero	.10	422	Ruben Sierra	.10
231	Barry Manuel	.10	327	Nomar Garciaparra	2.00	423	B.J. Surhoff	.10
232	Pedro Martinez	.25	328	Willie Greene	.10	424	Julian Tavarez	.10
233	Henry Rodriguez	.10	329	Greg McMichael	.10	425	Billy Taylor	.10
234	Ugueth Urbina	.10	330	Damion Easley	.10	426	Ken Caminiti	.25
235	Rondell White	.10	331	Ricky Bones	.10	427	Chuck Carr	.10
236	Carlos Baerga	.15	332	John Burkett	.10	428	Benji Gil	.10
237	John Franco	.10	333	Royce Clayton	.10	429	Terry Mulholland	.10
238	Bernard Gilkey	.10	334	Greg Colbrunn	.10	430	Mike Stanton	.10
239	Todd Hundley	.10	335	Tony Eusebio	.10	431	Wil Cordero	.10
240	Butch Huskey	.10	336	Gregg Jefferies	.10	432	Chili Davis	.10
241	Jason Isringhausen	.15	337	Wally Joyner	.10	433	Mariano Duncan	.10

434	Orlando Merced	.10
435	Kent Mercker	.10
436	John Olerud	.10
437	Quilvio Veras	.10
438	Mike Fetters	.10
439	Glenallen Hill	.10
440	Bill Swift	.10
441	Tim Wakefield	.10
442	Pedro Astacio	.10
443	Vinny Castilla	.10
444	Doug Drabek	.10
445	Alan Embree	.10
446	Lee Smith	.10
447	Darryl Hamilton	.10
448	Brian McRae	.10
449	Mike Timlin	.10
450	Bob Wickman	.10
451	Jason Dickson	.20
452	Chad Curtis	.10
453	Mark Leiter	.10
454	Damon Berryhill	.10
455	Kevin Orie	.10
456	Dave Burba	.10
457	Chris Holt	.10
458	*Ricky Ledee*	1.50
459	Mike Devereaux	.10
460	Pokey Reese	.10
461	Tim Raines	.10
462	Ryan Jones	.10
463	Shane Mack	.10
464	Darren Dreifort	.10
465	Mark Parent	.10
466	Mark Portugal	.10
467	Dante Powell	.20
468	Craig Grebeck	.10
469	Ron Villone	.10
470	Dmitri Young	.10
471	Shannon Stewart	.10
472	Rick Helling	.10
473	Bill Haselman	.10
474	Albie Lopez	.10
475	Glendon Rusch	.10
476	Derrick May	.10
477	Chad Ogea	.10
478	Kirk Reuter	.10
479	Chris Hammond	.10
480	Russ Johnson	.10
481	James Mouton	.10
482	Mike Macfarlane	.10
483	Scott Ruffcorn	.10
484	Jeff Frye	.10
485	Richie Sexson	.10
486	*Emil Brown*	.20
487	Desi Wilson	.10
488	Brent Gates	.10
489	Tony Graffanino	.10
490	Dan Miceli	.10
491	*Orlando Cabrera*	.50
492	*Tony Womack*	.50
493	Jerome Walton	.10
494	Mark Thompson	.10
495	Jose Guillen	.75
496	Willie Blair	.10
497	T.J. Staton	.10
498	Scott Kamieniecki	.10
499	Vince Coleman	.10
500	Jeff Abbott	.10
501	Chris Widger	.10
502	Kevin Tapani	.10
503	Carlos Castillo	.10
504	Luis Gonzalez	.10
505	Tim Belcher	.10
506	Armando Reynoso	.10
507	Jamie Moyer	.10
508	*Randall Simon*	1.50
509	Vladimir Guerrero	1.00
510	Wady Almonte	.10
511	Dustin Hermanson	.10
512	*Deivi Cruz*	.75
513	Luis Alicea	.10
514	*Felix Heredia*	.25
515	Don Slaught	.10
516	Shigetosi Hasegawa	.10
517	Matt Walbeck	.10
518	David Arias (last name actually Ortiz)	1.00
519	*Brady Raggio*	.10
520	Rudy Pemberton	.10
521	Wayne Kirby	.10
522	Calvin Maduro	.10
523	Mark Lewis	.10
524	Mike Jackson	.10
525	Sid Fernandez	.10
526	Mike Bielecki	.10
527	*Bubba Trammell*	1.00
528	Brent Brede	.10

529	Matt Morris	.15
530	Joe Borowski	.10
531	Orlando Miller	.10
532	Jim Bullinger	.10
533	Robert Person	.10
534	Doug Glanville	.10
535	Terry Pendleton	.10
536	Jorge Posada	.10
537	*Marc Sagmoen*	.10
538	*Fernando Tatis*	1.50
539	Aaron Sele	.10
540	Brian Banks	.10
541	Derrek Lee	.10
542	John Wasdin	.10
543	*Justin Towle*	.40
544	Pat Cline	.10
545	Dave Magadan	.10
546	Jeff Blauser	.10
547	Phil Nevin	.10
548	Todd Walker	.75
549	Elieser Marrero	.10
550	Bartolo Colon	.10
551	*Jose Cruz Jr.*	4.00
552	Todd Dunwoody	.30
553	*Hideki Irabu*	2.50

1997 Ultra Baseball "Rules"!

Baseball Rules was a 10-card insert that was found only in retail packs at a rate of one per 36 packs. The cards are die-cut with a player in front of a mound of baseballs with embossed seams on the front, while each card back explains a baseball term or rule.

		MT
Complete Set (10):		100.00
Common Player:		3.00
1	Barry Bonds	6.00
2	Ken Griffey Jr.	25.00
3	Derek Jeter	10.00
4	Chipper Jones	15.00
5	Greg Maddux	15.00
6	Mark McGwire	30.00
7	Troy Percival	3.00
8	Mike Piazza	15.00
9	Cal Ripken Jr.	20.00
10	Frank Thomas	20.00

1997 Ultra Checklists

There are 10 Checklist cards in each series of Ultra baseball covering all regular-issue cards and inserts. The front of the card features a superstar, while the back contains a portion of the set checklist. The cards have the player's name and "CHECKLIST" in bold, all caps across the bottom in silver foil.

		MT
Complete Set (10):		16.00
Common Player:		.25
	SERIES 1	
1	Dante Bichette	.25
2	Barry Bonds	.50
3	Ken Griffey Jr.	2.00
4	Greg Maddux	1.25
5	Mark McGwire	2.00
6	Mike Piazza	1.25
7	Cal Ripken Jr.	1.50
8	John Smoltz	.25
9	Sammy Sosa	.75
10	Frank Thomas	1.50
	SERIES 2	
1	Andruw Jones	1.00
2	Ken Griffey Jr.	2.00
3	Frank Thomas	1.50
4	Alex Rodriguez	2.00
5	Cal Ripken Jr.	1.50
6	Mike Piazza	1.25
7	Greg Maddux	1.25
8	Chipper Jones	1.25
9	Derek Jeter	1.25
10	Juan Gonzalez	1.00

1997 Ultra Diamond Producers

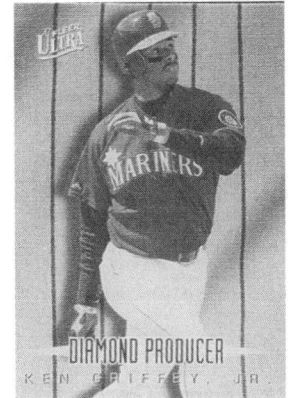

Printed on textured, uniform-like material, this 12-card insert contains some of the most consistent producers in baseball. Horizontal backs are conventionally printed with another color player photo on a pin-striped background and a few words about him. This was the most difficult insert Ultra foil-pack insert, with a ratio of one per 288.

		MT
Complete Set (12):		500.00
Common Player:		15.00
1	Jeff Bagwell	35.00
2	Barry Bonds	25.00
3	Ken Griffey Jr.	100.00
4	Chipper Jones	60.00
5	Kenny Lofton	25.00
6	Greg Maddux	60.00
7	Mark McGwire	100.00
8	Mike Piazza	60.00
9	Cal Ripken Jr.	80.00
10	Alex Rodriguez	60.00
11	Frank Thomas	75.00
12	Matt Williams	15.00

1997 Ultra
Double Trouble

Double Trouble is a 20-card, team color coded set pairing two stars from the same team on a horizontal front. These inserts were found every four packs.

		MT
Complete Set (20):		20.00
Common Player:		.50
1	Roberto Alomar, Cal Ripken Jr.	2.50
2	Mo Vaughn, Jose Canseco	1.00
3	Jim Edmonds, Tim Salmon	.50
4	Harold Baines, Frank Thomas	2.50
5	Albert Belle, Kenny Lofton	1.00
6	Chuck Knoblauch, Marty Cordova	.50
7	Andy Pettitte, Derek Jeter	2.00
8	Jason Giambi, Mark McGwire	3.00
9	Ken Griffey Jr., Alex Rodriguez	4.00
10	Juan Gonzalez, Will Clark	2.00
11	Greg Maddux, Chipper Jones	2.50
12	Mark Grace, Sammy Sosa	1.50
13	Dante Bichette, Andres Galarraga	.50
14	Jeff Bagwell, Derek Bell	1.50
15	Hideo Nomo, Mike Piazza	2.00
16	Henry Rodriguez, Moises Alou	.50
17	Rey Ordonez, Alex Ochoa	.75
18	Ray Lankford, Ron Gant	.50
19	Tony Gwynn, Rickey Henderson	1.50
20	Barry Bonds, Matt Williams	1.00

1997 Ultra
Fame Game

This eight-card hobby-exclusive insert showcases players who have displayed Hall of Fame potential. The player photo on front and Fame Game logo are embossed and highlighted in gold and silver foil. Backs have a color portrait photo and a few words about the player. Cards were inserted 1:8 packs.

		MT
Complete Set (18):		65.00
Common Player:		.75
1	Ken Griffey Jr.	10.00
2	Frank Thomas	8.00
3	Alex Rodriguez	10.00
4	Cal Ripken Jr.	8.00
5	Mike Piazza	6.00
6	Greg Maddux	6.00
7	Derek Jeter	6.00
8	Jeff Bagwell	4.00
9	Juan Gonzalez	4.00
10	Albert Belle	2.50
11	Tony Gwynn	4.00
12	Mark McGwire	12.00
13	Andy Pettitte	2.50
14	Kenny Lofton	2.50
15	Roberto Alomar	2.00
16	Ryne Sandberg	2.50
17	Barry Bonds	2.50
18	Eddie Murray	1.00

1997 Ultra
Fielder's Choice

Fielder's Choice highlights 18 of the top defensive players in baseball. Fronts of the horizontal cards have a leather look and feel and are highlighted in gold foil. Backs are conventionally printed with another player photo and some words about his fielding ability. Fielder's Choice inserts were found every 144 packs.

		MT
Complete Set (18):		300.00
Common Player:		10.00
1	Roberto Alomar	15.00
2	Jeff Bagwell	35.00
3	Wade Boggs	10.00
4	Barry Bonds	20.00
5	Mark Grace	10.00
6	Ken Griffey Jr.	80.00
7	Marquis Grissom	10.00
8	Charles Johnson	10.00
9	Chuck Knoblauch	10.00
10	Barry Larkin	15.00
11	Kenny Lofton	20.00
12	Greg Maddux	50.00
13	Raul Mondesi	15.00
14	Rey Ordonez	15.00

15	Cal Ripken Jr.	60.00
16	Alex Rodriguez	80.00
17	Ivan Rodriguez	12.00
18	Matt Williams	10.00

1997 Ultra
Golden Prospects

This 10-card set was exclusive to hobby shop packs and highlighted the top young players in baseball. Action photos on front and portraits on back are set on a sepia background. Cards were inserted 1:4 packs.

		MT
Complete Set (10):		8.00
Common Player:		.25
1	Andruw Jones	2.50
2	Vladimir Guerrero	1.50
3	Todd Walker	.75
4	Karim Garcia	.25
5	Kevin Orie	.25
6	Brian Giles	.25
7	Jason Dickson	.50
8	Jose Guillen	1.00
9	Ruben Rivera	.50
10	Derrek Lee	.50

1997 Ultra
Gold Medallion
Edition

A new concept in parallel editions was debuted by Ultra in Series I. While sharing the card numbers with regular-issue Ultra cards, the Gold Medallion Edition features a "G" prefix to the card number and gold-foil highlights on front. Unlike past parallels, however, the '97 Ultra Gold Medallion and Platinum Medallion inserts share a photograph which is entirely different from the regular Ultra base cards. Gold Medallion Edition cards are identified as such in the lower-right corner and were inserted at a rate of one per pack.

	MT
Complete Set (553):	80.00
Common Player:	.25
(Gold Medallion Edition stars valued at 3-6X regular Fleer Ultra.)	

1997 Ultra Hitting Machines

This 36-card insert was only found in hobby packs and showcases the game's top hitters. Cards were inserted at a ratio of 1:36 packs.

	MT
Complete Set (18):	220.00
Common Player:	3.00
1 Andruw Jones	15.00
2 Ken Griffey Jr.	30.00
3 Frank Thomas	25.00
4 Alex Rodriguez	30.00
5 Cal Ripken Jr.	25.00
6 Mike Piazza	18.00
7 Derek Jeter	18.00
8 Albert Belle	8.00
9 Tony Gwynn	12.00
10 Jeff Bagwell	12.00
11 Mark McGwire	35.00
12 Kenny Lofton	8.00
13 Manny Ramirez	8.00
14 Roberto Alomar	6.00
15 Ryne Sandberg	8.00
16 Eddie Murray	4.00
17 Sammy Sosa	20.00
18 Ken Caminiti	3.00

1997 Ultra HR Kings

HR Kings are printed on clear plastic with transparent refractive holofoil crowns and other objects in the plastic. Backs contain a white

silhouette of the player with career summary and logos within the figure. Stated odds of finding an HR King card were one per 36 packs.

	MT
Complete Set (12):	100.00
Common Player:	3.00
1 Albert Belle	6.00
2 Barry Bonds	6.00
3 Juan Gonzalez	10.00
4 Ken Griffey Jr.	25.00
5 Todd Hundley	3.00
6 Ryan Klesko	5.00
7 Mark McGwire	30.00
8 Mike Piazza	15.00
9 Sammy Sosa	15.00
10 Frank Thomas	20.00
11 Mo Vaughn	8.00
12 Matt Williams	3.00

1997 Ultra Leather Shop

Baseball's best fielders are honored in this 12-card hobby-exclusive insert. Cards were inserted at a ratio of 1:6 packs and feature an embossed grain-like finish on the fronts.

	MT
Complete Set (12):	20.00
Common Player:	.50
1 Ken Griffey Jr.	5.00
2 Alex Rodriguez	5.00
3 Cal Ripken Jr.	4.00
4 Derek Jeter	3.00
5 Juan Gonzalez	2.00

6	Tony Gwynn	2.00
7	Jeff Bagwell	2.00
8	Roberto Alomar	1.00
9	Ryne Sandberg	1.25
10	Ken Caminiti	.75
11	Kenny Lofton	1.25
12	John Smoltz	.50

1997 Ultra Platinum Medallion Edition

A new concept in parallel editions was debuted by Ultra in Series I. While sharing the card numbers with regular-issue Ultra cards, the Platinum Medallion Edition features a "P" prefix to the card number and holographic-foil highlights on front. Unlike past parallels, however, the '97 Ultra Gold Medallion and Platinum Medallion inserts share a photograph which is entirely different from the regular Ultra base cards are identified as such in the lower-right corner and were inserted at a rate of one per 100 packs.

	MT
Complete Set (553):	1200.
Common Player:	3.00
(Platinum Medallion Edition stars valued at 30-45X regular Fleer Ultra.)	

1997 Ultra Power Plus Series 1

Series 1 Power Plus is a 12-card insert utilizing silver rainbow holofoil in the background, with the featured player in the foreground. Backs another action photo and the player's credentials. The insert captures power hitters that also excel in other areas of the game. Power Plus inserts can be found every 24 packs.

	MT
Complete Set (12):	100.00
Common Player:	2.50
1 Jeff Bagwell	8.00
2 Barry Bonds	5.00
3 Juan Gonzalez	8.00
4 Ken Griffey Jr.	18.00
5 Chipper Jones	12.00
6 Mark McGwire	15.00

7	Mike Piazza	12.00
8	Cal Ripken Jr.	15.00
9	Alex Rodriguez	18.00
10	Sammy Sosa	10.00
11	Frank Thomas	15.00
12	Matt Williams	3.00

1997 Ultra Power Plus Series 2

Similar in design to the Power Plus insert in Series I, this 12-card insert salutes the game's top sluggers and was found only in hobby packs. Cards were inserted at a ratio of 1:8 packs. Front design features gold holographic foil graphics. Backs have another photo and a description of the player's skills.

		MT
Complete Set (12):		40.00
Common Player:		.75
1	Ken Griffey Jr.	7.00
2	Frank Thomas	6.00
3	Alex Rodriguez	7.00
4	Cal Ripken Jr.	5.00
5	Mike Piazza	4.00
6	Chipper Jones	4.00
7	Albert Belle	2.00
8	Juan Gonzalez	3.00
9	Jeff Bagwell	3.00
10	Mark McGwire	8.00
11	Mo Vaughn	1.75
12	Barry Bonds	1.75

1997 Ultra RBI Kings

Ten different players are featured in RBI Kings, which contain a metallic paisley background, with an English shield of armor and latin words in the background. RBI Kings were inserted every 18 packs of Series I.

		MT
Complete Set (10):		50.00
Common Player:		2.00
1	Jeff Bagwell	6.00
2	Albert Belle	4.00
3	Dante Bichette	2.00
4	Barry Bonds	4.00
5	Jay Buhner	2.00
6	Juan Gonzalez	6.00
7	Ken Griffey Jr.	15.00
8	Sammy Sosa	10.00
9	Frank Thomas	12.00
10	Mo Vaughn	5.00

1997 Ultra Rookie Reflections

Rookie Reflections features 10 of the 1996 season's top first-year stars. Cards are inserted every four packs. Front features an action photo on a black-and-silver starburst pattern. Horizontal backs have another photo and a career summary of the prospect.

		MT
Complete Set (10):		10.00
Common Player:		.25
1	James Baldwin	.25
2	Jermaine Dye	.75
3	Darin Erstad	3.00
4	Todd Hollandsworth	.25
5	Derek Jeter	4.00
6	Jason Kendall	.50
7	Alex Ochoa	.25
8	Rey Ordonez	.50
9	Edgar Renteria	.75
10	Scott Rolen	2.00

1997 Ultra Season Crowns

Season Crowns were found at a rate of one per eight packs of Ultra I Baseball. This etched, silver-foil insert contained 12 statistical leaders and award winners from the 1996 season.

		MT
Complete Set (12):		25.00
Common Player:		.75
1	Albert Belle	2.00
2	Dante Bichette	.50
3	Barry Bonds	2.00
4	Kenny Lofton	2.00
5	Edgar Martinez	.50
6	Mark McGwire	10.00
7	Andy Pettitte	2.00
8	Mike Piazza	5.00
9	Alex Rodriguez	8.00
10	John Smoltz	.50
11	Sammy Sosa	5.00
12	Frank Thomas	6.00

1997 Ultra Starring Role

Another hobby-exclusive insert, these 12 cards salute baseball's clutch performers and were found 1:288 packs.

		MT
Complete Set (12):		600.00
Common Player:		15.00
1	Andruw Jones	25.00
2	Ken Griffey Jr.	100.00
3	Frank Thomas	60.00
4	Alex Rodriguez	70.00
5	Cal Ripken Jr.	75.00
6	Mike Piazza	60.00
7	Greg Maddux	60.00
8	Chipper Jones	60.00
9	Derek Jeter	60.00
10	Juan Gonzalez	50.00
11	Albert Belle	25.00
12	Tony Gwynn	50.00

1997 Ultra Thunderclap

This 10-card hobby-exclusive insert showcases hitters who strike fear in opposing pitchers. Cards were inserted 1:18 packs. Fronts are highlighted by streaks of gold prismatic foil lightning in a story sky. Backs have another player photo and a few words about him.

		MT
Complete Set (10):		70.00
Common Player:		2.00
1	Barry Bonds	4.00
2	Mo Vaughn	4.00
3	Mark McGwire	20.00
4	Jeff Bagwell	6.00
5	Juan Gonzalez	6.00
6	Alex Rodriguez	15.00
7	Chipper Jones	9.00
8	Ken Griffey Jr.	15.00
9	Mike Piazza	9.00
10	Frank Thomas	12.00

1997 Ultra Top 30

This 30-card insert was found only in retail store packs and salutes the 30 most collectible players in the game. Cards were inserted one per pack. A Top 30 Gold Medallion parallel set was also produced and inserted 1:18 packs.

		MT
Complete Set (30):		18.00
Common Player:		.25
Gold Medallions: 10x		
1	Andruw Jones	1.00
2	Ken Griffey Jr.	2.50
3	Frank Thomas	2.00
4	Alex Rodriguez	2.50
5	Cal Ripken Jr.	2.00
6	Mike Piazza	1.50
7	Greg Maddux	1.50
8	Chipper Jones	1.50
9	Derek Jeter	1.50
10	Juan Gonzalez	1.00
11	Albert Belle	.75
12	Tony Gwynn	1.00
13	Jeff Bagwell	1.00
14	Mark McGwire	3.00
15	Andy Pettitte	.50
16	Mo Vaughn	.50
17	Kenny Lofton	.50
18	Manny Ramirez	.50
19	Roberto Alomar	.40
20	Ryne Sandberg	.50
21	Hideo Nomo	.40
22	Barry Bonds	.50
23	Eddie Murray	.30
24	Ken Caminiti	.25
25	John Smoltz	.25
26	Pat Hentgen	.25
27	Todd Hollandsworth	.25
28	Matt Williams	.30
29	Bernie Williams	.40
30	Brady Anderson	.25

1998 Ultra

Ultra was released in two series and contained a total of 501 cards, with 250 in Series I and 251 in Series II. The product sold in 10-card packs for an SRP of $2.59 and three parallel sets - Gold Medallion, Platinum Medallion and Masterpieces. Series I has 210 regular cards, 25 Prospects (seeded 1:4 packs), 10 Season's Crowns (seeded 1:12) and five Checklists (1:8). Series II had 202 regular cards, 25 Pizzazz (seeded 1:4), 20 New Horizons and three checklists. Series II also added a Mike Piazza N.Y. Mets cards that was added to the set as card No. 501 and inserted every 20 packs. Inserts in Series I include: Big Shots, Double Trouble, Kid Gloves, Back to the Future, Artistic Talents, Fall Classics, Power Plus, Prime Leather, Diamond Producers, Diamond Ink and Million Dollar Moments. Series II included: Notables, Rocket to Stardom, Millennium Men, Win Now, Ticket Studs, Diamond Immortals, Diamond Ink, Top 30 and 750 sequentially numbered Alex Rodriguez autographed cards.

		MT
Complete Set (501):		150.00
Complete Series I Set (250):		80.00
Complete Series II Set (250):		70.00
Common Player:		.10
A. Rodriguez Auto. Sample (750)		125.00
Wax Box:		55.00
1	Ken Griffey Jr.	3.00
2	Matt Morris	.10
3	Roger Clemens	1.00
4	Matt Williams	.25
5	Roberto Hernandez	.10
6	Rondell White	.10
7	Tim Salmon	.20
8	Brad Radke	.10
9	Brett Butler	.10
10	Carl Everett	.10
11	Chili Davis	.10
12	Chuck Finley	.10
13	Darryl Kile	.10
14	Deivi Cruz	.10
15	Gary Gaetti	.10
16	Matt Stairs	.10
17	Pat Meares	.10
18	Will Cunnane	.10
19	*Steve Woodard*	.30
20	Andy Ashby	.10
21	Bobby Higginson	.20
22	Brian Jordan	.10
23	Craig Biggio	.20
24	Jim Edmonds	.20
25	Ryan McGuire	.10
26	Scott Hatteberg	.10
27	Willie Greene	.10
28	Albert Belle	.75
29	Ellis Burks	.10
30	Hideo Nomo	.60
31	Jeff Bagwell	1.25
32	Kevin Brown	.10
33	Nomar Garciaparra	2.00
34	Pedro Martinez	.25
35	Raul Mondesi	.25
36	Ricky Bottalico	.10
37	Shawn Estes	.10
38	Shawon Dunston	.10
39	Terry Steinbach	.10
40	Tom Glavine	.20
41	Todd Dunwoody	.10
42	Deion Sanders	.25
43	Gary Sheffield	.35
44	Mike Lansing	.10
45	Mike Lieberthal	.10
46	Paul Sorrento	.10
47	Paul O'Neill	.20
48	Tom Goodwin	.10
49	Andruw Jones	1.50
50	Barry Bonds	.75
51	Bernie Williams	.50
52	Jeremi Gonzalez	.20
53	Mike Piazza	2.00
54	Russ Davis	.10
55	Vinny Castilla	.10
56	Rod Beck	.10
57	Andres Galarraga	.20
58	Ben McDonald	.10
59	Billy Wagner	.10
60	Charles Johnson	.10
61	Fred McGriff	.25
62	Dean Palmer	.10
63	Frank Thomas	2.50
64	Ismael Valdes	.10
65	Mark Bellhorn	.10
66	Jeff King	.10
67	John Wetteland	.10
68	Mark Grace	.25
69	Mark Kotsay	.50
70	Scott Rolen	1.50
71	Todd Hundley	.20
72	Todd Worrell	.10
73	Wilson Alvarez	.10
74	Bobby Jones	.10
75	Jose Canseco	.25
76	Kevin Appier	.10
77	Neifi Perez	.10
78	Paul Molitor	.50
79	Quilvio Veras	.10
80	Randy Johnson	.50
81	Glendon Rusch	.10
82	Curt Schilling	.25
83	Alex Rodriguez	2.50
84	Rey Ordonez	.10
85	Jeff Juden	.10
86	Mike Cameron	.10
87	Ryan Klesko	.25
88	Trevor Hoffman	.10
89	Chuck Knoblauch	.25
90	Larry Walker	.30
91	Mark McLemore	.10
92	B.J. Surhoff	.10
93	Darren Daulton	.10
94	Ray Durham	.10
95	Sammy Sosa	2.00
96	Eric Young	.10
97	Gerald Williams	.10
98	Javy Lopez	.15
99	John Smiley	.10
100	Juan Gonzalez	1.50
101	Shawn Green	.10
102	Charles Nagy	.10
103	David Justice	.25
104	Joey Hamilton	.10
105	Pat Hentgen	.10
106	Raul Casanova	.10
107	Tony Phillips	.10
108	Tony Gwynn	1.50
109	Will Clark	.25
110	Jason Giambi	.10
111	Jay Bell	.10
112	Johnny Damon	.10
113	Alan Benes	.10
114	Jeff Suppan	.10
115	*Kevin Polcovich*	.25
116	Shigetosi Hasegawa	.10
117	Steve Finley	.10

#	Player	Value
118	Tony Clark	.40
119	David Cone	.20
120	Jose Guillen	.40
121	*Kevin Millwood*	1.00
122	Greg Maddux	2.00
123	Dave Nilsson	.10
124	Hideki Irabu	.75
125	Jason Kendall	.10
126	Jim Thome	.40
127	Delino DeShields	.10
128	Edgar Renteria	.20
129	Edgardo Alfonzo	.10
130	J.T. Snow	.10
131	Jeff Abbott	.10
132	Jeffrey Hammonds	.10
133	Rich Loiselle	.10
134	Vladimir Guerrero	1.50
135	Jay Buhner	.20
136	Jeff Cirillo	.10
137	Jeromy Burnitz	.10
138	Mickey Morandini	.10
139	Tino Martinez	.25
140	Jeff Shaw	.10
141	Rafael Palmeiro	.20
142	Bobby Bonilla	.20
143	Cal Ripken Jr.	2.50
144	*Chad Fox*	.25
145	Dante Bichette	.20
146	Dennis Eckersley	.20
147	Mariano Rivera	.20
148	Mo Vaughn	.75
149	Reggie Sanders	.10
150	Derek Jeter	1.75
151	Rusty Greer	.20
152	Brady Anderson	.20
153	Brett Tomko	.10
154	Jaime Navarro	.10
155	Kevin Orie	.10
156	Roberto Alomar	.60
157	Edgar Martinez	.10
158	John Olerud	.10
159	John Smoltz	.20
160	Ryne Sandberg	.75
161	Billy Taylor	.10
162	Chris Holt	.10
163	Damion Easley	.10
164	Darin Erstad	.75
165	Joe Carter	.20
166	Kelvim Escobar	.10
167	Ken Caminiti	.25
168	Pokey Reese	.10
169	Ray Lankford	.10
170	Livan Hernandez	.20
171	Steve Kline	.10
172	Tom Gordon	.10
173	Travis Fryman	.10
174	Al Martin	.10
175	Andy Pettitte	.50
176	Jeff Kent	.10
177	Jimmy Key	.10
178	Mark Grudzielanek	.10
179	Tony Saunders	.20
180	Barry Larkin	.25
181	Bubba Trammell	.20
182	Carlos Delgado	.10
183	Carlos Baerga	.10
184	Derek Bell	.10
185	Henry Rodriguez	.10
186	Jason Dickson	.10
187	Ron Gant	.10
188	Tony Womack	.10
189	Justin Thompson	.10
190	Fernando Tatis	.30
191	Mark Wohlers	.10
192	Takashi Kashiwada	.50
193	Garret Anderson	.10
194	Jose Cruz, Jr.	1.00
195	Ricardo Rincon	.10
196	Tim Naehring	.10
197	Moises Alou	.20
198	Eric Karros	.10
199	John Jaha	.10
200	Marty Cordova	.10
201	Travis Lee	3.00
202	Mark Davis	.10
203	Vladimir Nunez	.10
204	Stanton Cameron	.10
205	*Mike Stoner*	1.00
206	*Rolando Arrojo*	.40
207	Rick White	.10
208	Luis Polonia	.10
209	Greg Blosser	.10
210	Cesar Devarez	.10
211	Jeff Bagwell (Season Crown)	4.00
212	Barry Bonds (Season Crown)	2.50
213	Roger Clemens (Season Crown)	4.00
214	Nomar Garciaparra (Season Crown)	7.00
215	Ken Griffey Jr. (Season Crown)	10.00
216	Tony Gwynn (Season Crown)	5.00
217	Randy Johnson (Season Crown)	1.50
218	Mark McGwire (Season Crown)	12.00
219	Scott Rolen (Season Crown)	5.00
220	Frank Thomas (Season Crown)	8.00
221	Matt Perisho (Prospect)	.10
222	Wes Helms (Prospect)	1.00
223	*David Dellucci* (Prospect)	2.00
224	Todd Helton (Prospect)	3.00
225	Brian Rose (Prospect)	1.00
226	Aaron Boone (Prospect)	.25
227	Keith Foulke (Prospect)	.50
228	Homer Bush (Prospect)	.40
229	Shannon Stewart (Prospect)	.25
230	Richard Hidalgo (Prospect)	1.00
231	Russ Johnson (Prospect)	.50
232	*Henry Blanco* (Prospect)	.40
233	Paul Konerko (Prospect)	5.00
234	Antone Williamson (Prospect)	.50
235	*Shane Bowers* (Prospect)	.50
236	Jose Vidro (Prospect)	.25
237	Derek Wallace (Prospect)	.25
238	Ricky Ledee (Prospect)	1.50
239	Kris Benson (Prospect)	5.00
240	Lou Collier (Prospect)	.50
241	Derrek Lee (Prospect)	1.00
242	Ruben Rivera (Prospect)	.50
243	Jorge Velandia (Prospect)	.25
244	Andrew Vessel (Prospect)	.40
245	Chris Carpenter (Prospect)	.50
246	Checklist(Ken Griffey Jr.)	1.50
247	Checklist(Andruw Jones)	.75
248	Checklist(Alex Rodriguez)	1.00
249	Checklist(Frank Thomas)	1.25
250	Checklist(Cal Ripken Jr.)	1.00
251	Carlos Perez	.10
252	Larry Sutton	.10
253	Brad Rigby	.10
254	Wally Joyner	.10
255	Todd Stottlemyre	.10
256	Nerio Rodriguez	.10
257	Jeff Frye	.10
258	Pedro Astacio	.10
259	Cal Eldred	.10
260	Chili Davis	.10
261	Freddy Garcia	.10
262	Bobby Witt	.10
263	Michael Coleman	.10
264	Mike Caruso	.20
265	Mike Lansing	.10
266	Dennis Reyes	.10
267	F.P. Santangelo	.10
268	Darryl Hamilton	.10
269	Mike Fetters	.10
270	Charlie Hayes	.10
271	Royce Clayton	.10
272	Doug Drabek	.10
273	James Baldwin	.10
274	Brian Hunter	.10
275	Chan Ho Park	.20
276	John Franco	.10
277	David Wells	.10
278	Eli Marrero	.10
279	Kerry Wood	5.00
280	Donnie Sadler	.10
281	*Scott Winchester*	.25
282	Hal Morris	.10
283	Brad Fullmer	.25
284	Bernard Gilkey	.10
285	Ramiro Mendoza	.10
286	Kevin Brown	.20
287	David Segui	.10
288	Willie McGee	.10
289	Darren Oliver	.10
290	Antonio Alfonseca	.10
291	Eric Davis	.10
292	Mickey Morandini	.10
293	*Frank Catalanotto*	.20
294	Derrek Lee	.10
295	Todd Zeile	.10
296	Chuck Knoblauch	.25
297	Wilson Delgado	.10
298	Raul Ibanez	.10
299	Orel Hershiser	.10
300	Ozzie Guillen	.10
301	Aaron Sele	.10
302	Joe Carter	.20
303	Darryl Kile	.10
304	Shane Reynolds	.10
305	Todd Dunn	.10
306	Bob Abreu	.10
307	Doug Strange	.10
308	Jose Canseco	.30
309	Lance Johnson	.10
310	Harold Baines	.10
311	Todd Pratt	.10
312	Greg Colbrunn	.10
313	*Masato Yoshii*	.50
314	Felix Heredia	.10
315	Dennis Martinez	.10
316	Geronimo Berroa	.10
317	Darren Lewis	.10
318	Billy Ripken	.10
319	Enrique Wilson	.10
320	Alex Ochoa	.10
321	Doug Glanville	.10
322	Mike Stanley	.10
323	Gerald Williams	.10
324	Pedro Martinez	.10
325	Jaret Wright	1.00
326	Terry Pendleton	.10
327	LaTroy Hawkins	.10
328	Emil Brown	.10
329	Walt Weiss	.10
330	Omar Vizquel	.10
331	Carl Everett	.10
332	Fernando Vina	.10
333	Mike Blowers	.10
334	Dwight Gooden	.20
335	Mark Lewis	.10
336	Jim Leyritz	.10
337	Kenny Lofton	.75
338	*John Halama*	.30
339	Jose Valentin	.10
340	Desi Relaford	.10
341	Dante Powell	.10
342	Ed Sprague	.10
343	Reggie Jefferson	.10
344	Mike Hampton	.10
345	Marquis Grissom	.10
346	Heathcliff Slocumb	.10
347	Francisco Cordova	.10
348	Ken Cloude	.25
349	Benito Santiago	.10
350	Denny Neagle	.10
351	Sean Casey	.25
352	Robb Nen	.10
353	Orlando Merced	.10
354	Adrian Brown	.10
355	Gregg Jefferies	.10
356	Otis Nixon	.10
357	Michael Tucker	.10
358	Eric Milton	.25
359	Travis Fryman	.10
360	Gary DiSarcina	.10
361	Mario Valdez	.10
362	Craig Counsell	.10
363	Jose Offerman	.10
364	Tony Fernandez	.10
365	Jason McDonald	.10
366	Sterling Hitchcock	.10
367	Donovan Osborne	.10
368	Troy Percival	.10
369	Henry Rodriguez	.10
370	Dmitri Young	.10
371	Jay Powell	.10
372	Jeff Conine	.10
373	Orlando Cabrera	.10
374	Butch Huskey	.10
375	*Mike Lowell*	.10
376	Kevin Young	.10
377	Jamie Moyer	.10
378	Jeff D'Amico	.10
379	Scott Erickson	.10
380	*Magglio Ordonez*	.75
381	Melvin Nieves	.10
382	Ramon Martinez	.20
383	A.J. Hinch	.50
384	Jeff Brantley	.10
385	Kevin Elster	.10
386	Allen Watson	.10
387	Moises Alou	.20
388	Jeff Blauser	.10
389	Pete Harnisch	.10
390	Shane Andrews	.10
391	Rico Brogna	.10
392	Stan Javier	.10

393	David Howard	.10
394	Darryl Strawberry	.20
395	Kent Mercker	.10
396	Juan Encarnacion	.25
397	Sandy Alomar	.20
398	Al Leiter	.20
399	Tony Graffanino	.10
400	Terry Adams	.10
401	Bruce Aven	.10
402	Derrick Gibson	.10
403	Jose Cabrera	.10
404	Rich Becker	.10
405	David Ortiz	.40
406	Brian McRae	.10
407	Bobby Estalella	.10
408	Bill Mueller	.10
409	Dennis Eckersley	.20
410	Sandy Martinez	.10
411	Jose Vizcaino	.10
412	Jermaine Allensworth	.10
413	Miguel Tejada	.40
414	Turner Ward	.10
415	Glenallen Hill	.10
416	Lee Stevens	.10
417	Cecil Fielder	.25
418	Ruben Sierra	.10
419	Jon Nunnally	.10
420	Rod Myers	.10
421	Dustin Hermanson	.10
422	James Mouton	.10
423	Dan Wilson	.10
424	Roberto Kelly	.10
425	Antonio Osuna	.10
426	Jacob Cruz	.10
427	Brent Mayne	.10
428	Matt Karchner	.10
429	Damian Jackson	.10
430	Roger Cedeno	.10
431	Rickey Henderson	.10
432	Joe Randa	.10
433	Greg Vaughn	.10
434	Andres Galarraga	.40
435	Rod Beck	.10
436	Curtis Goodwin	.10
437	Brad Ausmus	.10
438	Bob Hamelin	.10
439	Todd Walker	.30
440	Scott Brosius	.10
441	Lenny Dykstra	.10
442	Abraham Nunez	.10
443	Brian Johnson	.10
444	Randy Myers	.10
445	Bret Boone	.10
446	Oscar Henriquez	.10
447	Mike Sweeney	.10
448	Kenny Rogers	.10
449	Mark Langston	.10
450	Luis Gonzalez	.10
451	John Burkett	.10
452	Bip Roberts	.10
453	Travis Lee (New Horizons)	1.00
454	Felix Rodriguez (New Horizons)	.10
455	Andy Benes (New Horizons)	.10
456	Willie Blair (New Horizons)	.10
457	Brian Anderson (New Horizons)	.10
458	Jay Bell (New Horizons)	.10
459	Matt Williams (New Horizons)	.25
460	Devon White (New Horizons)	.10
461	Karim Garcia (New Horizons)	.10
462	Jorge Fabregas (New Horizons)	.10
463	Wilson Alvarez (New Horizons)	.10
464	Roberto Hernandez (New Horizons)	.10
465	Tony Saunders (New Horizons)	.10
466	Rolando Arrojo (New Horizons)	.40
467	Wade Boggs (New Horizons)	.25
468	Fred McGriff (New Horizons)	.25
469	Paul Sorrento (New Horizons)	.10
470	Kevin Stocker (New Horizons)	.10
471	Bubba Trammell (New Horizons)	.25
472	Quinton McCracken (New Horizons)	.10

473	Checklist(Ken Griffey Jr.)	1.00
474	Checklist(Cal Ripken Jr.)	.75
475	Checklist(Frank Thomas)	.60
476	Ken Griffey Jr. (Pizzazz)	6.00
477	Cal Ripken Jr. (Pizzazz)	5.00
478	Frank Thomas (Pizzazz)	5.00
479	Alex Rodriguez (Pizzazz)	4.00
480	Nomar Garciaparra (Pizzazz)	4.00
481	Derek Jeter (Pizzazz)	3.00
482	Andruw Jones (Pizzazz)	1.50
483	Chipper Jones (Pizzazz)	4.00
484	Greg Maddux (Pizzazz)	4.00
485	Mike Piazza (Pizzazz)	4.00
486	Juan Gonzalez (Pizzazz)	3.00
487	Jose Cruz (Pizzazz)	1.00
488	Jaret Wright (Pizzazz)	2.50
489	Hideo Nomo (Pizzazz)	1.00
490	Scott Rolen (Pizzazz)	2.00
491	Tony Gwynn (Pizzazz)	3.00
492	Roger Clemens (Pizzazz)	2.00
493	Darin Erstad (Pizzazz)	1.50
494	Mark McGwire (Pizzazz)	8.00
495	Jeff Bagwell (Pizzazz)	2.00
496	Mo Vaughn (Pizzazz)	1.50
497	Albert Belle (Pizzazz)	1.50
498	Kenny Lofton (Pizzazz)	1.50
499	Ben Grieve (Pizzazz)	2.00
500	Barry Bonds (Pizzazz)	1.50
501	Mike Piazza (mets)	3.00

1998 Ultra Artistic Talents

This 18-card insert featured top players in the game on a canvas-like surface with the insert name in silver holographic letters across the top. The backs are done in black and white and numbered with an "AT" suffix. Artistic Talents are inserted one per eight packs.

		MT
Complete Set (18):		60.00
Common Player:		.75
Inserted 1:8		
1	Ken Griffey Jr.	8.00
2	Andruw Jones	4.00
3	Alex Rodriguez	6.00
4	Frank Thomas	6.00
5	Cal Ripken Jr.	6.00
6	Derek Jeter	5.00
7	Chipper Jones	5.00
8	Greg Maddux	5.00
9	Mike Piazza	5.00
10	Albert Belle	2.50
11	Darin Erstad	3.00
12	Juan Gonzalez	4.00
13	Jeff Bagwell	3.00
14	Tony Gwynn	4.00
15	Mark McGwire	10.00
16	Scott Rolen	4.00
17	Barry Bonds	2.50
18	Kenny Lofton	2.50

1998 Ultra Back to the Future

This 15-card insert was printed in a horizontal format with a base-ball field background. Cards were numbered with a "BF" suffix and seeded one per six packs.

		MT
Complete Set (15):		20.00
Common Player:		.50
Inserted 1:6		
1	Andruw Jones	2.50
2	Alex Rodriguez	4.00
3	Derek Jeter	3.00
4	Darin Erstad	2.00
5	Mike Cameron	.50
6	Scott Rolen	2.50
7	Nomar Garciaparra	3.00
8	Hideki Irabu	1.50
9	Jose Cruz, Jr.	2.00
10	Vladimir Guerrero	1.50
11	Mark Kotsay	1.00
12	Tony Womack	.50
13	Jason Dickson	.50
14	Jose Guillen	.75
15	Tony Clark	1.00

1998 Ultra Big Shots

Big Shots was a 15-card insert displaying some of the top home run hitters in baseball. A generic stadium is pictured across the bottom with the insert name running up the left side. Cards were numbered with a "BS" suffix and inserted one per four Series I packs.

		MT
Complete Set (15):		15.00
Common Player:		.25
Inserted 1:4		
1	Ken Griffey Jr.	4.00
2	Frank Thomas	3.00
3	Chipper Jones	2.50
4	Albert Belle	1.25
5	Juan Gonzalez	2.00
6	Jeff Bagwell	1.50

7	Mark McGwire	5.00
8	Barry Bonds	1.00
9	Manny Ramirez	.75
10	Mo Vaughn	1.00
11	Matt Williams	.25
12	Jim Thome	.50
13	Tino Martinez	.25
14	Mike Piazza	2.50
15	Tony Clark	.75

1998 Ultra Diamond Immortals

This Series II insert showcased 15 top player on an intricate silver holographic foil design that frames each player. Cards were numbered with a "DI" suffix and inserted one per 288 packs.

		MT
Complete Set (15):		850.00
Common Player:		20.00
Inserted 1:288		
1	Ken Griffey Jr.	125.00
2	Frank Thomas	75.00
3	Alex Rodriguez	75.00
4	Cal Ripken Jr.	90.00
5	Mike Piazza	75.00
6	Mark McGwire	140.00
7	Greg Maddux	75.00
8	Andruw Jones	30.00
9	Chipper Jones	75.00
10	Derek Jeter	60.00
11	Tony Gwynn	60.00
12	Juan Gonzalez	60.00
13	Jose Cruz	20.00
14	Roger Clemens	40.00
15	Barry Bonds	30.00

1998 Ultra Diamond Producers

This 15-card insert captured players on a prismatic silver design, with a wood backdrop and a black felt frame around the border. Cards were seeded one per 288 Series I packs and numbered with a "DP" suffix.

		MT
Complete Set (15):		700.00
Common Player:		20.00
Inserted 1:288		
1	Ken Griffey Jr.	100.00
2	Andruw Jones	25.00
3	Alex Rodriguez	60.00
4	Frank Thomas	60.00
5	Cal Ripken Jr.	80.00
6	Derek Jeter	60.00
7	Chipper Jones	60.00
8	Greg Maddux	60.00

9	Mike Piazza	60.00
10	Juan Gonzalez	50.00
11	Jeff Bagwell	35.00
12	Tony Gwynn	50.00
13	Mark McGwire	125.00
14	Barry Bonds	25.00
15	Jose Cruz, Jr.	25.00

1998 Ultra Double Trouble

Double Trouble includes 20 cards and pairs two teammates on a horizontal format with the team's logo and the insert name featured in a silver holographic circle in the middle. These were numbered with a "DT" suffix and exclusive to Series I packs at a rate of one per four.

		MT
Complete Set (20):		20.00
Common Player:		.25
Inserted 1:4		
1	Ken Griffey Jr., Alex Rodriguez	4.00
2	Vladimir Guerrero, Pedro Martinez	1.50
3	Andruw Jones, Kenny Lofton	2.00
4	Chipper Jones, Greg Maddux	2.50
5	Derek Jeter, Tino Martinez	2.00
6	Frank Thomas, Albert Belle	3.00
7	Cal Ripken Jr., Roberto Alomar	2.50
8	Mike Piazza, Hideo Nomo	2.00
9	Darin Erstad, Jason Dickson	1.00
10	Juan Gonzalez, Ivan Rodriguez	1.50
11	Jeff Bagwell, Darryl Kile	1.50
12	Tony Gwynn, Steve Finley	1.50
13	Mark McGwire, Ray Lankford	4.00
14	Barry Bonds, Jeff Kent	.75
15	Andy Pettitte, Bernie Williams	.50
16	Mo Vaughn, Nomar Garciaparra	1.50
17	Matt Williams, Jim Thome	.25
18	Hideki Irabu, Mariano Rivera	1.50
19	Roger Clemens, Jose Cruz, Jr.	1.50
20	Manny Ramirez, David Justice	.50

1998 Ultra Fall Classics

This Series I insert pictures 15 stars over a green holographic bacground that contains the insert name in script. Fall Classics were inserted one per 18 packs and numbered with a "FC" suffix.

		MT
Complete Set (15):		100.00
Common Player:		2.00
Inserted 1:18		
1	Ken Griffey Jr.	15.00
2	Andruw Jones	4.00
3	Alex Rodriguez	12.00

4	Frank Thomas	10.00
5	Cal Ripken Jr.	12.00
6	Derek Jeter	9.00
7	Chipper Jones	9.00
8	Greg Maddux	9.00
9	Mike Piazza	9.00
10	Albert Belle	4.00
11	Juan Gonzalez	7.50
12	Jeff Bagwell	6.00
13	Tony Gwynn	7.50
14	Mark McGwire	20.00
15	Barry Bonds	3.50

1998 Ultra Gold Medallion Edition

This parallel to the basic Ultra set is found seeded on a one per pack ratio. Cards are similar to the regular-issue Ultra except for a gold presentation of the embossed player name on front and a shower of gold specks in the photo background. Backs have a "G" suffix to the card number and a "GOLD MEDALLION EDITION" notation at bottom.

		MT
Complete Set (250):		75.00
Common Player:		.25
Inserted 1:1		
(Star cards 2X-4X regular Ultra)		

1998 Ultra Kid Gloves

Kid Gloves featured top fielders in the game over an embossed glove background. Exclusive to Series I packs, they were inserted in one per eight packs and numbered with a "KG" suffix.

		MT
Complete Set (12):		30.00
Common Player:		.75
Inserted 1:8		
1	Andruw Jones	3.00
2	Alex Rodriguez	5.00
3	Derek Jeter	4.00
4	Chipper Jones	4.00
5	Darin Erstad	2.00
6	Todd Walker	1.00
7	Scott Rolen	3.00
8	Nomar Garciaparra	4.00
9	Jose Cruz, Jr.	3.00
10	Charles Johnson	.75
11	Rey Ordonez	.75
12	Vladimir Guerrero	2.00

1998 Ultra Millennium Men

Millenium Men was a 15-card hobby-only insert exclusive to Series II packs. These tri-fold cards featured an embossed wax seal design and could be unfolded to reveal another shot of the player, team logo and statistics. They were numbered with a "MM" suffix and inserted every 35 packs.

		MT
Complete Set (15):		200.00
Common Player:		4.00
Inserted 1:35		
1	Jose Cruz	6.00
2	Ken Griffey Jr.	30.00
3	Cal Ripken Jr.	25.00
4	Derek Jeter	15.00
5	Andruw Jones	8.00
6	Alex Rodriguez	20.00
7	Chipper Jones	20.00
8	Scott Rolen	10.00
9	Nomar Garciaparra	20.00
10	Frank Thomas	20.00
11	Mike Piazza	20.00
12	Greg Maddux	20.00
13	Juan Gonzalez	15.00
14	Ben Grieve	10.00
15	Jaret Wright	8.00

1998 Ultra Notables

This 20-card insert pictured a player over a holographic background with either an American League or National League logo in

the background. Notables were seeded one per four Series II packs and numbered with a "N" suffix.

		MT
Complete Set (20):		25.00
Common Player:		.25
Inserted 1:4		
1	Frank Thomas	3.00
2	Ken Griffey Jr.	4.00
3	Edgar Renteria	.25
4	Albert Belle	1.00
5	Juan Gonzalez	2.00
6	Jeff Bagwell	1.50
7	Mark McGwire	5.00
8	Barry Bonds	1.00
9	Scott Rolen	1.50
10	Mo Vaughn	1.00
11	Andruw Jones	1.00
12	Chipper Jones	2.50
13	Tino Martinez	.50
14	Mike Piazza	2.50
15	Tony Clark	.50
16	Jose Cruz	.75
17	Nomar Garciaparra	2.50
18	Cal Ripken Jr.	3.00
19	Alex Rodriguez	2.50
20	Derek Jeter	2.00

1998 Ultra Platinum Medallion

Insertion odds on this super-scarce insert set are not given but each card is produced and serially numbered in an edition of only 100. Fronts are similar to regular Ultra cards except the photo is black-and-white and the name is rendered in silver prismatic foil. Backs are in color with the serial number printed in silver foil at bottom.

	MT
Common Player:	30.00
(Star cards 50X-75X regular Ultra)	

1998 Ultra Power Plus

This 10-card insert was exclusive to Series I packs and seeded one per 36 packs. Cards pictured the player over an embossed blue background featuring plus signs. These were numbered with a "PP" suffix.

A player's name in *italic* type indicates a rookie card.

		MT
Complete Set (10):		120.00
Common Player:		3.00
Inserted 1:36		
1	Ken Griffey Jr.	25.00
2	Andruw Jones	6.00
3	Alex Rodriguez	15.00
4	Frank Thomas	15.00
5	Mike Piazza	15.00
6	Albert Belle	6.00
7	Juan Gonzalez	12.00
8	Jeff Bagwell	8.00
9	Barry Bonds	6.00
10	Jose Cruz, Jr.	6.00

1998 Ultra Prime Leather

This 18-card insert features top fielders on a leather-like card stock, with a large baseball in the background. Cards are seeded one per 144 Series I packs and numbered with a "PL" suffix.

		MT
Complete Set (18):		550.00
Common Player:		10.00
Inserted 1:144		
1	Ken Griffey Jr.	75.00
2	Andruw Jones	35.00
3	Alex Rodriguez	50.00
4	Frank Thomas	50.00
5	Cal Ripken Jr.	50.00
6	Derek Jeter	40.00
7	Chipper Jones	40.00
8	Greg Maddux	40.00
9	Mike Piazza	40.00
10	Albert Belle	20.00
11	Darin Erstad	25.00

12	Juan Gonzalez	35.00
13	Jeff Bagwell	30.00
14	Tony Gwynn	35.00
15	Roberto Alomar	15.00
16	Barry Bonds	20.00
17	Kenny Lofton	20.00
18	Jose Cruz, Jr.	25.00

1998 Ultra Rocket to Stardom

This 15-card insert set was exclusive to Series II packs and inserted in one per 20 packs. Cards were in black-and-white and were die-cut and embossed. The insert contained a collection of top young stars and was numbered with a "RS" suffix.

		MT
Complete Set (15):		45.00
Common Player:		2.00
Inserted 1:20		
1	Ben Grieve	8.00
2	Magglio Ordonez	4.00
3	Travis Lee	12.00
4	Carl Pavano	2.00
5	Brian Rose	2.00
6	Brad Fullmer	4.00
7	Michael Coleman	2.00
8	Juan Encarnacion	2.00
9	Karim Garcia	2.00
10	Todd Helton	4.00
11	Richard Hildalgo	2.00
12	Paul Konerko	4.00
13	Rod Myers	2.00
14	Jaret Wright	6.00
15	Miguel Tejada	4.00

1998 Ultra Ticket Studs

Fifteen players are featured on fold-out game ticket-like cards in Ticket Studs. The cards arrived folded across the middle and open to reveal a full-length shot of the player with prismatic team color stripes in over a white background that has section, seat and row numbers. Cards were inserted one per 144 Series II packs and are numbered with a "TS" suffix.

A player's name in *italic* type indicates a rookie card.

		MT
Complete Set (15):		500.00
Common Player:		10.00
Inserted 1:144		
1	Travis Lee	25.00
2	Tony Gwynn	35.00
3	Scott Rolen	25.00
4	Nomar Garciaparra	50.00
5	Mike Piazza	50.00
6	Mark McGwire	100.00
7	Ken Griffey Jr.	75.00
8	Juan Gonzalez	40.00
9	Jose Cruz	15.00
10	Frank Thomas	50.00
11	Derek Jeter	40.00
12	Chipper Jones	50.00
13	Cal Ripken Jr.	60.00
14	Andruw Jones	18.00
15	Alex Rodriguez	50.00

1998 Ultra Top 30

		MT
Complete Set (30):		35.00
Common Player:		.25
Inserted 1:1 R		
1	Barry Bonds	1.00
2	Ivan Rodriguez	1.00
3	Kenny Lofton	1.00
4	Albert Belle	1.00
5	Mo Vaughn	1.00
6	Jeff Bagwell	1.50
7	Mark McGwire	5.00
8	Darin Erstad	1.00
9	Roger Clemens	2.00
10	Tony Gwynn	2.00
11	Scott Rolen	1.00
12	Hideo Nomo	.50

13	Juan Gonzalez	2.00
14	Mike Piazza	2.50
15	Greg Maddux	2.50
16	Chipper Jones	2.50
17	Andruw Jones	1.00
18	Derek Jeter	2.00
19	Nomar Garciaparra	2.50
20	Alex Rodriguez	2.50
21	Frank Thomas	2.50
22	Cal Ripken Jr.	3.00
23	Ken Griffey Jr.	4.00
24	Jose Cruz Jr.	1.00
25	Jaret Wright	1.00
26	Travis Lee	1.50
27	Wade Boggs	.40
28	Chuck Knoblauch	.40
29	Joe Carter	.25
30	Ben Grieve	1.50

1998 Ultra Win Now

This Series II insert has 20 top players printed on plastic card stock, with a color shot of the player on the left side and a close-up shot on the right with black lines through it. Win Now cards were seeded one per 72 packs and numbered with a "WN" suffix.

		MT
Complete Set (20):		425.00
Common Player:		6.00
Inserted 1:72		
1	Alex Rodriguez	30.00
2	Andruw Jones	12.00
3	Cal Ripken Jr.	40.00
4	Chipper Jones	30.00
5	Darin Erstad	15.00
6	Derek Jeter	25.00
7	Frank Thomas	35.00
8	Greg Maddux	30.00
9	Hideo Nomo	10.00
10	Jeff Bagwell	15.00
11	Jose Cruz	10.00
12	Juan Gonzalez	25.00
13	Ken Griffey Jr.	50.00
14	Mark McGwire	60.00
15	Mike Piazza	30.00
16	Mo Vaughn	12.00
17	Nomar Garciaparra	30.00
18	Roger Clemens	15.00
19	Scott Rolen	15.00
20	Tony Gwynn	25.00

1989 Upper Deck

This premiere "Collector's Choice" issue from Upper Deck contains 700 cards (2-1/2" by 3-1/2") with full-color photos on both sides. The first 26 cards feature

Star Rookies. The set also includes 26 special portrait cards with team checklist backs and seven numberical checklist cards. Major 1988 award winners (Cy Young, Rookie of Year, MVP) are honored on 10 cards in the set, in addition to their individual player cards. There are also special cards for the Most Valuable Players in both League Championship series and the World Series. The card fronts feature player photos framed by a white border. A vertical brown and green artist's rendition of the runner's lane that leads from home plate to first base is found along the right margin. Backs carry full-color action poses that fill the card back, except for a compact (yet complete) stats chart. A high-number series, cards 701-800, featuring rookies and traded players, was released in mid-season in foil packs mixed within the complete set, in boxed complete sets and in high number set boxes.

Dale Murphy

		MT
Complete Set (800):		125.00
Complete Low Set (700):		110.00
Complete High Set (100):		15.00
Common Player:		.10
Low Wax Box:		125.00
High Wax Box:		100.00
1	Ken Griffey, Jr.	100.00
2	Luis Medina	.10
3	Tony Chance	.10
4	Dave Otto	.10
5	Sandy Alomar, Jr.	2.00
6	Rolando Roomes	.10
7	David West	.15
8	Cris Carpenter	.15
9	Gregg Jefferies	.50
10	Doug Dascenzo	.10
11	Ron Jones	.10
12	Luis de los Santos	.10
13a	Gary Sheffield ("SS" upside-down)	4.00
13b	Gary Sheffield ("SS" correct)	4.00
14	Mike Harkey	.15
15	Lance Blankenship	.15
16	William Brennan	.15
17	John Smoltz	3.00
18	Ramon Martinez	1.25
19	Mark Lemke	.20
20	Juan Bell	.10
21	Rey Palacios	.10
22	Felix Jose	.15
23	Van Snider	.10
24	Dante Bichette	2.00
25	Randy Johnson	5.00
26	Carlos Quintana	.15
27	Star Rookie Checklist 1-26	.10
28	Mike Schooler	.10
29	Randy St. Claire	.10
30	Jerald Clark	.15
31	Kevin Gross	.10
32	Dan Firova	.10
33	Jeff Calhoun	.10
34	Tommy Hinzo	.10
35	Ricky Jordan	.20
36	Larry Parrish	.10
37	Bret Saberhagen	.15
38	Mike Smithson	.10
39	Dave Dravecky	.10
40	Ed Romero	.10
41	Jeff Musselman	.10
42	Ed Hearn	.10
43	Rance Mulliniks	.10
44	Jim Eisenreich	.10
45	Sil Campusano	.10
46	Mike Krukow	.10
47	Paul Gibson	.10
48	Mike LaCoss	.10
49	Larry Herndon	.10
50	Scott Garrelts	.10
51	Dwayne Henry	.10
52	Jim Acker	.10
53	Steve Sax	.10
54	Pete O'Brien	.10
55	Paul Runge	.10
56	Rick Rhoden	.10
57	John Dopson	.10
58	Casey Candaele	.10
59	Dave Righetti	.10
60	Joe Hesketh	.10
61	Frank DiPino	.10
62	Tim Laudner	.10
63	Jamie Moyer	.10
64	Fred Toliver	.10
65	Mitch Webster	.10
66	John Tudor	.10
67	John Cangelosi	.10
68	Mike Devereaux	.10
69	Brian Fisher	.10
70	Mike Marshall	.10
71	Zane Smith	.10
72a	Brian Holton (ball not visible on card front, photo actually Shawn Hillegas)	1.50
72b	Brian Holton (ball visible, correct photo)	.10
73	Jose Guzman	.10
74	Rick Mahler	.10
75	John Shelby	.10
76	Jim Deshaies	.10
77	Bobby Meacham	.10
78	Bryn Smith	.10
79	Joaquin Andujar	.10
80	Richard Dotson	.10
81	Charlie Lea	.10
82	Calvin Schiraldi	.10
83	Les Straker	.10
84	Les Lancaster	.10
85	Allan Anderson	.10
86	Junior Ortiz	.10
87	Jesse Orosco	.10
88	Felix Fermin	.10
89	Dave Anderson	.10
90	Rafael Belliard	.10
91	Franklin Stubbs	.10
92	Cecil Espy	.10
93	Albert Hall	.10
94	Tim Leary	.10
95	Mitch Williams	.10
96	Tracy Jones	.10
97	Danny Darwin	.10
98	Gary Ward	.10
99	Neal Heaton	.10
100	Jim Pankovits	.10
101	Bill Doran	.10
102	Tim Wallach	.10
103	Joe Magrane	.10
104	Ozzie Virgil	.10
105	Alvin Davis	.10
106	Tom Brookens	.10
107	Shawon Dunston	.15
108	Tracy Woodson	.10
109	Nelson Liriano	.10
110	Devon White	.15
111	Steve Balboni	.10
112	Buddy Bell	.10
113	German Jimenez	.10
114	Ken Dayley	.10
115	Andres Galarraga	.60
116	Mike Scioscia	.10
117	Gary Pettis	.10
118	Ernie Whitt	.10
119	Bob Boone	.10
120	Ryne Sandberg	1.00
121	Bruce Benedict	.10
122	Hubie Brooks	.10
123	Mike Moore	.10
124	Wallace Johnson	.10
125	Bob Horner	.10
126	Chili Davis	.10
127	Manny Trillo	.10
128	Chet Lemon	.10
129	John Cerutti	.10
130	Orel Hershiser	.10
131	Terry Pendleton	.10
132	Jeff Blauser	.10
133	Mike Fitzgerald	.10
134	Henry Cotto	.10
135	Gerald Young	.10
136	Luis Salazar	.10
137	Alejandro Pena	.10
138	Jack Howell	.10
139	Tony Fernandez	.10
140	Mark Grace	.60
141	Ken Caminiti	1.00
142	Mike Jackson	.10
143	Larry McWilliams	.10
144	Andres Thomas	.10
145	Nolan Ryan	3.00
146	Mike Davis	.10
147	DeWayne Buice	.10
148	Jody Davis	.10
149	Jesse Barfield	.10
150	Matt Nokes	.10
151	Jerry Reuss	.10
152	Rick Cerone	.10
153	Storm Davis	.10
154	Marvell Wynne	.10
155	Will Clark	.75
156	Luis Aguayo	.10
157	Willie Upshaw	.10
158	Randy Bush	.10
159	Ron Darling	.10
160	Kal Daniels	.10
161	Spike Owen	.10
162	Luis Polonia	.10
163	Kevin Mitchell	.15
164	Dave Gallagher	.10
165	Benito Santiago	.15
166	Greg Gagne	.10
167	Ken Phelps	.10
168	Sid Fernandez	.10
169	Bo Diaz	.10
170	Cory Snyder	.10
171	Eric Show	.10
172	Robby Thompson	.10
173	Marty Barrett	.10
174	Dave Henderson	.10
175	Ozzie Guillen	.10
176	Barry Lyons	.10
177	Kelvin Torve	.10
178	Don Slaught	.10
179	Steve Lombardozzi	.10
180	Chris Sabo	.20
181	Jose Uribe	.10
182	Shane Mack	.10
183	Ron Karkovice	.10
184	Todd Benzinger	.10
185	Dave Stewart	.10
186	Julio Franco	.10
187	Ron Robinson	.10
188	Wally Backman	.10
189	Randy Velarde	.10
190	Joe Carter	.25
191	Bob Welch	.10
192	Kelly Paris	.10
193	Chris Brown	.10
194	Rick Reuschel	.10
195	Roger Clemens	1.25
196	Dave Concepcion	.10
197	Al Newman	.10
198	Brook Jacoby	.10
199	Mookie Wilson	.10
200	Don Mattingly	1.50
201	Dick Schofield	.10
202	Mark Gubicza	.10
203	Gary Gaetti	.15
204	Dan Pasqua	.10
205	Andre Dawson	.20
206	Chris Speier	.10
207	Kent Tekulve	.10
208	Rod Scurry	.10
209	Scott Bailes	.10
210	Rickey Henderson	.15
211	Harold Baines	.10
212	Tony Armas	.10
213	Kent Hrbek	.10
214	Darrin Jackson	.10
215	George Brett	1.50
216	Rafael Santana	.10

217	Andy Allanson	.10	313	Ken Oberkfell	.10	403	Joey Meyer	.10
218	Brett Butler	.10	314	Jerry Browne	.10	404	Larry Andersen	.10
219	Steve Jeltz	.10	315	R.J. Reynolds	.10	405	Rex Hudler	.10
220	Jay Buhner	.50	316	Scott Bankhead	.10	406	Mike Schmidt	1.50
221	Bo Jackson	.25	317	Milt Thompson	.10	407	John Franco	.10
222	Angel Salazar	.10	318	Mario Diaz	.10	408	Brady Anderson	1.50
223	Kirk McCaskill	.10	319	Bruce Ruffin	.10	409	Don Carman	.10
224	Steve Lyons	.10	320	Dave Valle	.10	410	Eric Davis	.15
225	Bert Blyleven	.10	321a	*Gary Varsho* (batting righty	2.00	411	Bob Stanley	.10
226	Scott Bradley	.10		on card back, photo actually		412	Pete Smith	.10
227	Bob Melvin	.10		Mike Bielecki)		413	Jim Rice	.10
228	Ron Kittle	.10	321b	*Gary Varsho* (batting lefty on	.10	414	Bruce Sutter	.10
229	Phil Bradley	.10		card back, correct photo)		415	Oil Can Boyd	.10
230	Tommy John	.10	322	Paul Mirabella	.10	416	Ruben Sierra	.20
231	Greg Walker	.10	323	Chuck Jackson	.10	417	Mike LaValliere	.10
232	Juan Berenguer	.10	324	Drew Hall	.10	418	Steve Buechele	.10
233	Pat Tabler	.10	325	Don August	.10	419	Gary Redus	.10
234	*Terry Clark*	.10	326	*Israel Sanchez*	.10	420	Scott Fletcher	.10
235	Rafael Palmeiro	.50	327	Denny Walling	.10	421	Dale Sveum	.10
236	Paul Zuvella	.10	328	Joel Skinner	.10	422	Bob Knepper	.10
237	Willie Randolph	.10	329	Danny Tartabull	.10	423	Luis Rivera	.10
238	Bruce Fields	.10	330	Tony Pena	.10	424	Ted Higuera	.10
239	Mike Aldrete	.10	331	Jim Sundberg	.10	425	Kevin Bass	.10
240	Lance Parrish	.15	332	Jeff Robinson	.10	426	Ken Gerhart	.10
241	Greg Maddux	3.00	333	Odibbe McDowell	.10	427	Shane Rawley	.10
242	John Moses	.10	334	Jose Lind	.10	428	Paul O'Neill	.25
243	Melido Perez	.10	335	Paul Kilgus	.10	429	Joe Orsulak	.10
244	Willie Wilson	.10	336	Juan Samuel	.10	430	Jackie Gutierrez	.10
245	Mark McLemore	.10	337	Mike Campbell	.10	431	Gerald Perry	.10
246	Von Hayes	.10	338	Mike Maddux	.10	432	Mike Greenwell	.10
247	Matt Williams	1.00	339	Darnell Coles	.10	433	Jerry Royster	.10
248	John Candelaria	.10	340	Bob Dernier	.10	434	Ellis Burks	.30
249	Harold Reynolds	.10	341	Rafael Ramirez	.10	435	Ed Olwine	.10
250	Greg Swindell	.10	342	Scott Sanderson	.10	436	Dave Rucker	.10
251	Juan Agosto	.10	343	B.J. Surhoff	.10	437	Charlie Hough	.10
252	Mike Felder	.10	344	Billy Hatcher	.10	438	Bob Walk	.10
253	Vince Coleman	.10	345	Pat Perry	.10	439	Bob Brower	.10
254	Larry Sheets	.10	346	Jack Clark	.10	440	Barry Bonds	1.25
255	George Bell	.10	347	Gary Thurman	.10	441	Tom Foley	.10
256	Terry Steinbach	.10	348	*Timmy Jones*	.10	442	Rob Deer	.10
257	*Jack Armstrong*	.10	349	Dave Winfield	.20	443	Glenn Davis	.10
258	Dickie Thon	.10	350	Frank White	.10	444	Dave Martinez	.10
259	Ray Knight	.10	351	Dave Collins	.10	445	Bill Wegman	.10
260	Darryl Strawberry	.15	352	Jack Morris	.15	446	Lloyd McClendon	.10
261	Doug Sisk	.10	353	Eric Plunk	.10	447	Dave Schmidt	.10
262	Alex Trevino	.10	354	Leon Durham	.10	448	Darren Daulton	.20
263	Jeff Leonard	.10	355	Ivan DeJesus	.10	449	Frank Williams	.10
264	Tom Henke	.10	356	*Brian Holman*	.15	450	Don Aase	.10
265	Ozzie Smith	.75	357a	Dale Murphy (reversed	20.00	451	Lou Whitaker	.10
266	Dave Bergman	.10		negative)		452	Goose Gossage	.10
267	Tony Phillips	.10	357b	Dale Murphy (corrected)	.20	453	Ed Whitson	.10
268	Mark Davis	.10	358	Mark Portugal	.10	454	Jim Walewander	.10
269	Kevin Elster	.10	359	Andy McGaffigan	.10	455	Damon Berryhill	.10
270	Barry Larkin	.40	360	Tom Glavine	1.00	456	Tim Burke	.10
271	Manny Lee	.10	361	Keith Moreland	.10	457	Barry Jones	.10
272	Tom Brunansky	.10	362	Todd Stottlemyre	.20	458	Joel Youngblood	.10
273	Craig Biggio	2.50	363	Dave Leiper	.10	459	Floyd Youmans	.10
274	Jim Gantner	.10	364	Cecil Fielder	.30	460	Mark Salas	.10
275	Eddie Murray	.40	365	Carmelo Martinez	.10	461	Jeff Russell	.10
276	Jeff Reed	.10	366	Dwight Evans	.10	462	Darrell Miller	.10
277	Tim Teufel	.10	367	Kevin McReynolds	.10	463	Jeff Kunkel	.10
278	Rick Honeycutt	.10	368	Rich Gedman	.10	464	*Sherman Corbett*	.10
279	Guillermo Hernandez	.10	369	Len Dykstra	.15	465	Curtis Wilkerson	.10
280	John Kruk	.20	370	Jody Reed	.10	466	Bud Black	.10
281	*Luis Alicea*	.20	371	Jose Canseco	.40	467	Cal Ripken, Jr.	2.50
282	Jim Clancy	.10	372	Rob Murphy	.10	468	John Farrell	.10
283	Billy Ripken	.10	373	Mike Henneman	.10	469	Terry Kennedy	.10
284	Craig Reynolds	.10	374	Walt Weiss	.10	470	Tom Candiotti	.10
285	Robin Yount	.50	375	*Rob Dibble*	.15	471	Roberto Alomar	1.50
286	Jimmy Jones	.10	376	Kirby Puckett	1.00	472	Jeff Robinson	.10
287	Ron Oester	.10	377	Denny Martinez	.10	473	Vance Law	.10
288	Terry Leach	.10	378	Ron Gant	.40	474	Randy Ready	.10
289	Dennis Eckersley	.20	379	Brian Harper	.10	475	Walt Terrell	.10
290	Alan Trammell	.10	380	*Nelson Santovenia*	.10	476	Kelly Downs	.10
291	Jimmy Key	.15	381	Lloyd Moseby	.10	477	*Johnny Paredes*	.10
292	Chris Bosio	.10	382	Lance McCullers	.10	478	Shawn Hillegas	.10
293	Jose DeLeon	.10	383	Dave Stieb	.10	479	Bob Brenly	.10
294	Jim Traber	.10	384	Tony Gwynn	1.50	480	Otis Nixon	.10
295	Mike Scott	.10	385	Mike Flanagan	.10	481	Johnny Ray	.10
296	Roger McDowell	.10	386	Bob Ojeda	.10	482	Geno Petralli	.10
297	Garry Templeton	.10	387	Bruce Hurst	.10	483	Stu Cliburn	.10
298	Doyle Alexander	.10	388	Dave Magadan	.10	484	Pete Incaviglia	.10
299	Nick Esasky	.10	389	Wade Boggs	.25	485	Brian Downing	.10
300	Mark McGwire	5.00	390	Gary Carter	.10	486	Jeff Stone	.10
301	*Darryl Hamilton*	.20	391	Frank Tanana	.10	487	Carmen Castillo	.10
302	Dave Smith	.10	392	Curt Young	.10	488	Tom Niedenfuer	.10
303	Rick Sutcliffe	.10	393	Jeff Treadway	.10	489	Jay Bell	.10
304	Dave Stapleton	.10	394	Darrell Evans	.10	490	Rick Schu	.10
305	Alan Ashby	.10	395	Glenn Hubbard	.10	491	*Jeff Pico*	.10
306	Pedro Guerrero	.10	396	Chuck Cary	.10	492	*Mark Parent*	.15
307	Ron Guidry	.10	397	Frank Viola	.10	493	Eric King	.10
308	Steve Farr	.10	398	Jeff Parrett	.10	494	Al Nipper	.10
309	Curt Ford	.10	399	*Terry Blocker*	.10	495	Andy Hawkins	.10
310	Claudell Washington	.10	400	Dan Gladden	.10	496	Daryl Boston	.10
311	Tom Prince	.10	401	*Louie Meadows*	.10	497	Ernie Riles	.10
312	*Chad Kreuter*	.15	402	Tim Raines	.15	498	Pascual Perez	.10

499	Bill Long	.10	592	Pete Stanicek	.10	675	Ryne Sandberg (TC)	.30
500	Kirt Manwaring	.10	593	*Pat Borders*	.20	676	Kirk Gibson (TC)	.10
501	Chuck Crim	.10	594	*Bryan Harvey*	.15	677	Andres Galarraga (TC)	.15
502	Candy Maldonado	.10	595	Jeff Ballard	.10	678	Will Clark (TC)	.20
503	Dennis Lamp	.10	596	Jeff Reardon	.10	679	Cory Snyder (TC)	.10
504	Glenn Braggs	.10	597	Doug Drabek	.10	680	Alvin Davis (TC)	.10
505	Joe Price	.10	598	Edwin Correa	.10	681	Darryl Strawberry (TC)	.10
506	Ken Williams	.10	599	Keith Atherton	.10	682	Cal Ripken, Jr. (TC)	.40
507	Bill Pecota	.10	600	Dave LaPoint	.10	683	Tony Gwynn (TC)	.40
508	Rey Quinones	.10	601	Don Baylor	.10	684	Mike Schmidt (TC)	.25
509	*Jeff Bittiger*	.10	602	Tom Pagnozzi	.10	685	Andy Van Slyke (TC)	.10
510	Kevin Seitzer	.10	603	Tim Flannery	.10	686	Ruben Sierra (TC)	.10
511	Steve Bedrosian	.10	604	Gene Walter	.10	687	Wade Boggs (TC)	.20
512	Todd Worrell	.10	605	Dave Parker	.15	688	Eric Davis (TC)	.10
513	Chris James	.10	606	Mike Diaz	.10	689	George Brett (TC)	.30
514	Jose Oquendo	.10	607	Chris Gwynn	.10	690	Alan Trammell (TC)	.10
515	David Palmer	.10	608	Odell Jones	.10	691	Frank Viola (TC)	.10
516	John Smiley	.10	609	Carlton Fisk	.20	692	Harold Baines (TC)	.10
517	Dave Clark	.10	610	Jay Howell	.10	693	Don Mattingly (TC)	.30
518	Mike Dunne	.10	611	Tim Crews	.10	694	Checklist 1-100	.10
519	Ron Washington	.10	612	Keith Hernandez	.10	695	Checklist 101-200	.10
520	Bob Kipper	.10	613	Willie Fraser	.10	696	Checklist 201-300	.10
521	Lee Smith	.15	614	Jim Eppard	.10	697	Checklist 301-400	.10
522	Juan Castillo	.10	615	Jeff Hamilton	.10	698	Checklist 401-500	.10
523	Don Robinson	.10	616	Kurt Stillwell	.10	699	Checklist 501-600	.10
524	Kevin Romine	.10	617	Tom Browning	.10	700	Checklist 601-700	.10
525	Paul Molitor	.50	618	Jeff Montgomery	.10	701	Checklist 701-800	.10
526	Mark Langston	.15	619	Jose Rijo	.10	702	Jessie Barfield	.10
527	Donnie Hill	.10	620	Jamie Quirk	.10	703	Walt Terrell	.10
528	Larry Owen	.10	621	Willie McGee	.10	704	Dickie Thon	.10
529	Jerry Reed	.10	622	Mark Grant	.10	705	Al Leiter	.10
530	Jack McDowell	.20	623	Bill Swift	.10	706	Dave LaPoint	.10
531	Greg Mathews	.10	624	Orlando Mercado	.10	707	*Charlie Hayes*	.40
532	John Russell	.10	625	*John Costello*	.10	708	Andy Hawkins	.10
533	Don Quisenberry	.10	626	Jose Gonzalez	.10	709	Mickey Hatcher	.10
534	Greg Gross	.10	627a	Bill Schroeder (putting on	1.25	710	Lance McCullers	.10
535	Danny Cox	.10		shin guards on card back,		711	Ron Kittle	.10
536	Terry Francona	.10		photo actually Ronn		712	Bert Blyleven	.10
537	Andy Van Slyke	.10		Reynolds)		713	Rick Dempsey	.10
538	Mel Hall	.10	627b	Bill Schroeder (arms	.10	714	Ken Williams	.10
539	Jim Gott	.10		crossed on card back,		715	Steve Rosenberg	.10
540	Doug Jones	.10		correct photo)		716	Joe Skalski	.10
541	Criag Lefferts	.10	628a	Fred Manrique (throwing on	1.00	717	Spike Owen	.10
542	Mike Boddicker	.10		card back, photo actually		718	Todd Burns	.10
543	Greg Brock	.10		Ozzie Guillen)		719	Kevin Gross	.10
544	Atlee Hammaker	.10	628b	Fred Manrique (batting on	.10	720	Tommy Herr	.10
545	Tom Bolton	.10		card back, correct photo)		721	Rob Ducey	.10
546	*Mike Macfarlane*	.25	629	Ricky Horton	.10	722	Gary Green	.10
547	*Rich Renteria*	.10	630	Dan Plesac	.10	723	*Gregg Olson*	.15
548	John Davis	.10	631	Alfredo Griffin	.10	724	Greg Harris	.15
549	Floyd Bannister	.10	632	Chuck Finley	.15	725	Craig Worthington	.10
550	Mickey Brantley	.10	633	Kirk Gibson	.10	726	Tom Howard	.15
551	Duane Ward	.10	634	Randy Myers	.10	727	Dale Mohorcic	.10
552	Dan Petry	.10	635	Greg Minton	.10	728	Rich Yett	.10
553	Mickey Tettleton	.15	636	Herm Winningham	.10	729	Mel Hall	.10
554	Rick Leach	.10	637	Charlie Leibrandt	.10	730	Floyd Youmans	.10
555	Mike Witt	.10	638	Tim Birtsas	.10	731	Lonnie Smith	.10
556	Sid Bream	.10	639	Bill Buckner	.10	732	Wally Backman	.10
557	Bobby Witt	.10	640	Danny Jackson	.10	733	Trevor Wilson	.10
558	Tommy Herr	.10	641	Greg Booker	.10	734	Jose Alvarez	.10
559	Randy Milligan	.10	642	Jim Presley	.10	735	Bob Milacki	.10
560	*Jose Cecena*	.10	643	Gene Nelson	.10	736	*Tom Gordon*	.20
561	Mackey Sasser	.10	644	Rod Booker	.10	737	Wally Whitehurst	.10
562	Carney Lansford	.10	645	Dennis Rasmussen	.10	738	Mike Aldrete	.10
563	Rick Aguilera	.10	646	Juan Nieves	.10	739	Keith Miller	.10
564	Ron Hassey	.10	647	Bobby Thigpen	.10	740	Randy Milligan	.10
565	Dwight Gooden	.20	648	Tim Belcher	.10	741	Jeff Parrett	.10
566	Paul Assenmacher	.10	649	Mike Young	.10	742	*Steve Finley*	.75
567	Neil Allen	.10	650	Ivan Calderon	.10	743	*Junior Felix*	.15
568	Jim Morrison	.10	651	*Oswaldo Peraza*	.10	744	*Pete Harnisch*	.25
569	Mike Pagliarulo	.10	652a	Pat Sheridan (no position on	30.00	745	Bill Spiers	.15
570	Ted Simmons	.10		front)		746	Hensley Meulens	.10
571	Mark Thurmond	.10	652b	Pat Sheridan (position on	.10	747	Juan Bell	.10
572	Fred McGriff	.40		front)		748	Steve Sax	.10
573	Wally Joyner	.10	653	Mike Morgan	.10	749	Phil Bradley	.10
574	*Jose Bautista*	.10	654	Mike Heath	.10	750	Rey Quinones	.10
575	Kelly Gruber	.10	655	Jay Tibbs	.10	751	Tommy Gregg	.15
576	Cecilio Guante	.10	656	Fernando Valenzuela	.10	752	Kevin Brown	.25
577	Mark Davidson	.10	657	Lee Mazzilli	.10	753	Derek Lilliquist	.10
578	Bobby Bonilla	.25	658	Frank Viola	.10	754	*Todd Zeile*	.40
579	Mike Stanley	.10	659	Jose Canseco	.40	755	Jim Abbott	.15
580	Gene Larkin	.10	660	Walt Weiss	.10	756	*Ozzie Canseco*	.10
581	Stan Javier	.10	661	Orel Hershiser	.10	757	Nick Esasky	.10
582	Howard Johnson	.10	662	Kirk Gibson	.10	758	Mike Moore	.10
583a	Mike Gallego (photo on card	1.00	663	Chris Sabo	.15	759	Rob Murphy	.10
	back reversed)		664	Dennis Eckersley	.10	760	Rick Mahler	.10
583b	Mike Gallego (correct	.10	665	Orel Hershiser	.10	761	Fred Lynn	.10
	photo)		666	Kirk Gibson	.10	762	*Kevin Blankenship*	.10
584	David Cone	.50	667	Orel Hershiser	.10	763	Eddie Murray	.40
585	*Doug Jennings*	.10	668	Wally Joyner (TC)	.10	764	*Steve Searcy*	.10
586	Charlie Hudson	.10	669	Nolan Ryan (TC)	.60	765	*Jerome Walton*	.10
587	Dion James	.10	670	Jose Canseco (TC)	.20	766	*Erik Hanson*	.25
588	Al Leiter	.20	671	Fred McGriff (TC)	.15	767	Bob Boone	.15
589	Charlie Puleo	.10	672	Dale Murphy (TC)	.10	768	Edgar Martinez	.75
590	Roberto Kelly	.15	673	Paul Molitor (TC)	.20	769	*Jose DeJesus*	.10
591	Thad Bosley	.10	674	Ozzie Smith (TC)	.20	770	*Greg Briley*	.10

771	*Steve Peters*	.10
772	Rafael Palmeiro	.60
773	Jack Clark	.10
774	Nolan Ryan	3.00
775	Lance Parrish	.10
776	*Joe Girardi*	.15
777	Willie Randolph	.10
778	Mitch Williams	.10
779	Dennis Cook	.10
780	*Dwight Smith*	.15
781	*Lenny Harris*	.15
782	*Torey Lovullo*	.15
783	*Norm Charlton*	.25
784	Chris Brown	.10
785	Todd Benzinger	.10
786	Shane Rawley	.10
787	*Omar Vizquel*	1.50
788	*LaVel Freeman*	.10
789	Jeffrey Leonard	.10
790	*Eddie Williams*	.15
791	Jamie Moyer	.10
792	Bruce Hurst	.10
793	Julio Franco	.15
794	Claudell Washington	.10
795	Jody Davis	.10
796	Odibbe McDowell	.10
797	Paul Kilgus	.10
798	Tracy Jones	.10
799	Steve Wilson	.20
800	Pete O'Brien	.10

1990 Upper Deck

Tom Gordon

Following the success of its first issue, Upper Deck released another 800-card set in 1990. The cards feature full-color photos on both sides in the standard 2-1/2" x 3-1/2" format. The artwork of Vernon Wells Sr. is featured on the front of all team checklist cards. The 1990 set also introduces two new Wells illustrations - a tribute to Mike Schmidt upon his retirement and one commemorating Nolan Ryan's 5,000 career strikeouts. The cards are similar in design to the 1989 issue. The high-number series (701-800) was released as a boxed set, in factory sets and in foil packs at mid-season. Cards #101-199 can be found either with or without the copyright line on back; no premium attaches to either.

		MT
Complete Set (800):		25.00
Complete Low Set (700):		20.00
Complete High Set (100):		5.00
Common Player:		.05
Low or High Wax Box:		20.00
1	Star Rookie Checklist	.05
2	*Randy Nosek*	.05
3	*Tom Drees*	.05
4	Curt Young	.05

5	Angels checklist(Devon White)	.05
6	Luis Salazar	.05
7	Phillies checklist(Von Hayes)	.05
8	Jose Bautista	.05
9	*Marquis Grissom*	.50
10	Dodgers checklist(Orel Hershiser)	.05
11	Rick Aguilera	.05
12	Padres checklist(Benito Santiago)	.05
13	Deion Sanders	.50
14	Marvell Wynne	.05
15	David West	.05
16	Pirates checklist(Bobby Bonilla)	.05
17	*Sammy Sosa*	12.00
18	Yankees checklist(Steve Sax)	.05
19	Jack Howell	.05
20	Mike Schmidt Retires(Mike Schmidt)	.50
21	Robin Ventura	.40
22	Brian Meyer	.05
23	*Blaine Beatty*	.05
24	Mariners checklist(Ken Griffey, Jr.)	.40
25	Greg Vaughn	.20
26	*Xavier Hernandez*	.10
27	*Jason Grimsley*	.10
28	*Eric Anthony*	.10
29	Expos checklist(Tim Raines)	.05
30	David Wells	.05
31	Hal Morris	.50
32	Royals checklist(Bo Jackson)	.15
33	*Kelly Mann*	.05
34	Nolan Ryan 5000 Strikeouts(Nolan Ryan)	1.00
35	*Scott Service*	.05
36	Athletics checklist(Mark McGwire)	1.00
37	Tino Martinez	.30
38	Chili Davis	.08
39	Scott Sanderson	.05
40	Giants checklist(Kevin Mitchell)	.05
41	Tigers checklist(Lou Whitaker)	.05
42	*Scott Coolbaugh*	.05
43	*Jose Cano*	.05
44	*Jose Vizcaino*	.25
45	*Bob Hamelin*	.15
46	*Jose Offerman*	.15
47	Kevin Blankenship	.05
48	Twins checklist(Kirby Puckett)	.20
49	*Tommy Greene*	.15
50	N.L. Top Vote Getter(Will Clark)	.25
51	Rob Nelson	.05
52	*Chris Hammond*	.15
53	Indians checklist(Joe Carter)	.05
54a	*Ben McDonald* (Orioles Logo)	2.00
54b	*Ben McDonald* (Star Rookie logo)	.30
55	Andy Benes	.50
56	*John Olerud*	.40
57	Red Sox checklist(Roger Clemens)	.15
58	Tony Armas	.05
59	*George Canale*	.05
60a	Orioles checklist(Mickey Tettleton) (#683 Jamie Weston)	4.00
60b	Orioles checklist(Mickey Tettleton) (#683 Mickey Weston)	.08
61	*Mike Stanton*	.15
62	Mets checklist(Dwight Gooden)	.05
63	*Kent Mercker*	.20
64	*Francisco Cabrera*	.05
65	Steve Avery	.15
66	Jose Canseco	.40
67	*Matt Merullo*	.05
68	Cardinals checklist(Vince Coleman)	.05
69	Ron Karkovice	.05
70	*Kevin Maas*	.05
71	Dennis Cook	.05
72	*Juan Gonzalez*	5.00

73	Cubs checklist(Andre Dawson)	.05
74	*Dean Palmer*	.40
75	A.L. Top Vote Getter(Bo Jackson)	.15
76	*Rob Richie*	.05
77	*Bobby Rose*	.05
78	*Brian DuBois*	.05
79	White Sox checklist(Ozzie Guillen)	.05
80	Gene Nelson	.05
81	Bob McClure	.05
82	Rangers checklist(Julio Franco)	.05
83	Greg Minton	.05
84	Braves checklist(John Smoltz)	.10
85	Willie Fraser	.05
86	Neal Heaton	.05
87	*Kevin Tapani*	.30
88	Astros checklist(Mike Scott)	.05
89a	Jim Gott (incorrect photo)	5.00
89b	Jim Gott (correct photo)	.05
90	Lance Johnson	.05
91	Brewers checklist(Robin Yount)	.10
92	Jeff Parrett	.05
93	*Julio Machado*	.05
94	Ron Jones	.05
95	Blue Jays checklist(George Bell)	.05
96	Jerry Reuss	.05
97	Brian Fisher	.05
98	*Kevin Ritz*	.10
99	Reds checklist(Barry Larkin)	.10
100	Checklist 1-100	.05
101	Gerald Perry	.05
102	Kevin Appier	.15
103	Julio Franco	.05
104	Craig Biggio	.20
105	Bo Jackson	.20
106	*Junior Felix*	.05
107	Mike Harkey	.05
108	Fred McGriff	.35
109	Rick Sutcliffe	.05
110	Pete O'Brien	.05
111	Kelly Gruber	.05
112	Pat Borders	.05
113	Dwight Evans	.05
114	Dwight Gooden	.05
115	*Kevin Batiste*	.05
116	Eric Davis	.10
117	Kevin Mitchell	.10
118	Ron Oester	.05
119	Brett Butler	.05
120	Danny Jackson	.05
121	Tommy Gregg	.05
122	Ken Caminiti	.25
123	Kevin Brown	.10
124	George Brett	.50
125	Mike Scott	.05
126	Cory Snyder	.05
127	George Bell	.05
128	Mark Grace	.30
129	Devon White	.05
130	Tony Fernandez	.05
131	Don Aase	.05
132	Rance Mulliniks	.05
133	Marty Barrett	.05
134	Nelson Liriano	.05
135	Mark Carreon	.15
136	Candy Maldonado	.05
137	Tim Birtsas	.05
138	Tom Brookens	.05
139	John Franco	.05
140	Mike LaCoss	.05
141	Jeff Treadway	.05
142	Pat Tabler	.05
143	Darrell Evans	.05
144	Rafael Ramirez	.05
145	Oddibe McDowell	.05
146	Brian Downing	.05
147	Curtis Wilkerson	.05
148	Ernie Whitt	.05
149	Bill Schroeder	.05
150	Domingo Ramos	.05
151	Rick Honeycutt	.05
152	Don Slaught	.05
153	Mitch Webster	.05
154	Tony Phillips	.08
155	Paul Kilgus	.05
156	Ken Griffey, Jr.	6.00
157	Gary Sheffield	.35
158	Wally Backman	.05
159	B.J. Surhoff	.05
160	Louie Meadows	.05

#	Player	Price		#	Player	Price		#	Player	Price
161	Paul O'Neill	.10		257	Tom Brunansky	.05		353	Harold Baines	.05
162	*Jeff McKnight*	.05		258	Mike Davis	.05		354	Mike Greenwell	.05
163	Alvaro Espinoza	.05		259	Jeff Ballard	.05		355	Ruben Sierra	.25
164	*Scott Scudder*	.05		260	Scott Terry	.05		356	Andres Galarraga	.25
165	Jeff Reed	.05		261	Sid Fernandez	.05		357	Andre Dawson	.15
166	Gregg Jefferies	.20		262	Mike Marshall	.05		358	*Jeff Brantley*	.15
167	Barry Larkin	.15		263	Howard Johnson	.05		359	Mike Bielecki	.05
168	Gary Carter	.05		264	Kirk Gibson	.05		360	Ken Oberkfell	.05
169	Robby Thompson	.05		265	Kevin McReynolds	.05		361	Kurt Stillwell	.05
170	Rolando Roomes	.05		266	Cal Ripken, Jr.	1.50		362	Brian Holman	.05
171	Mark McGwire	2.00		267	Ozzie Guillen	.05		363	Kevin Seitzer	.05
172	Steve Sax	.05		268	Jim Traber	.05		364	Alvin Davis	.05
173	Mark Williamson	.05		269	Bobby Thigpen	.05		365	Tom Gordon	.05
174	Mitch Williams	.05		270	Joe Orsulak	.05		366	Bobby Bonilla	.10
175	Brian Holton	.05		271	Bob Boone	.10		367	Carlton Fisk	.25
176	Rob Deer	.10		272	Dave Stewart	.05		368	*Steve Carter*	.05
177	Tim Raines	.10		273	Tim Wallach	.05		369	Joel Skinner	.05
178	Mike Felder	.05		274	Luis Aquino	.05		370	John Cangelosi	.05
179	Harold Reynolds	.05		275	Mike Moore	.05		371	Cecil Espy	.05
180	Terry Francona	.05		276	Tony Pena	.05		372	*Gary Wayne*	.05
181	Chris Sabo	.05		277	Eddie Murray	.30		373	Jim Rice	.05
182	Darryl Strawberry	.10		278	Milt Thompson	.05		374	*Mike Dyer*	.05
183	Willie Randolph	.05		279	Alejandro Pena	.05		375	Joe Carter	.20
184	Billy Ripken	.05		280	Ken Dayley	.05		376	Dwight Smith	.05
185	Mackey Sasser	.05		281	Carmen Castillo	.05		377	*John Wetteland*	.35
186	Todd Benzinger	.05		282	Tom Henke	.05		378	Ernie Riles	.05
187	Kevin Elster	.05		283	Mickey Hatcher	.05		379	Otis Nixon	.05
188	Jose Uribe	.05		284	Roy Smith	.05		380	Vance Law	.05
189	Tom Browning	.05		285	Manny Lee	.05		381	Dave Bergman	.05
190	Keith Miller	.05		286	Dan Pasqua	.05		382	Frank White	.05
191	Don Mattingly	.40		287	Larry Sheets	.05		383	Scott Bradley	.05
192	Dave Parker	.10		288	Garry Templeton	.05		384	Israel Sanchez	.05
193	Roberto Kelly	.10		289	Eddie Williams	.05		385	Gary Pettis	.05
194	Phil Bradley	.05		290	Brady Anderson	.15		386	Donn Pall	.05
195	Ron Hassey	.05		291	Spike Owen	.05		387	John Smiley	.05
196	Gerald Young	.05		292	Storm Davis	.05		388	Tom Candiotti	.05
197	Hubie Brooks	.05		293	Chris Bosio	.05		389	Junior Ortiz	.05
198	Bill Doran	.05		294	Jim Eisenreich	.05		390	Steve Lyons	.05
199	Al Newman	.05		295	Don August	.05		391	Brian Harper	.05
200	Checklist 101-200	.05		296	Jeff Hamilton	.05		392	Fred Manrique	.05
201	Terry Puhl	.05		297	Mickey Tettleton	.05		393	Lee Smith	.05
202	Frank DiPino	.05		298	Mike Scioscia	.05		394	Jeff Kunkel	.05
203	Jim Clancy	.05		299	Kevin Hickey	.05		395	Claudell Washington	.05
204	Bob Ojeda	.05		300	Checklist 201-300	.05		396	John Tudor	.05
205	Alex Trevino	.05		301	Shawn Abner	.05		397	Terry Kennedy	.05
206	Dave Henderson	.05		302	Kevin Bass	.05		398	Lloyd McClendon	.05
207	Henry Cotto	.05		303	Bip Roberts	.05		399	Craig Lefferts	.05
208	Rafael Belliard	.05		304	Joe Girardi	.05		400	Checklist 301-400	.05
209	Stan Javier	.05		305	Danny Darwin	.05		401	Keith Moreland	.05
210	Jerry Reed	.05		306	Mike Heath	.05		402	Rich Gedman	.05
211	Doug Dascenzo	.05		307	Mike Macfarlane	.05		403	Jeff Robinson	.05
212	Andres Thomas	.05		308	Ed Whitson	.05		404	Randy Ready	.05
213	Greg Maddux	1.00		309	Tracy Jones	.05		405	Rick Cerone	.05
214	Mike Schooler	.05		310	Scott Fletcher	.05		406	Jeff Blauser	.05
215	Lonnie Smith	.05		311	Darnell Coles	.05		407	Larry Andersen	.05
216	Jose Rijo	.05		312	Mike Brumley	.05		408	Joe Boever	.05
217	Greg Gagne	.05		313	Bill Swift	.05		409	Felix Fermin	.05
218	Jim Gantner	.05		314	Charlie Hough	.05		410	Glenn Wilson	.05
219	Allan Anderson	.05		315	Jim Presley	.05		411	Rex Hudler	.05
220	Rick Mahler	.05		316	Luis Polonia	.05		412	Mark Grant	.05
221	Jim Deshaies	.05		317	Mike Morgan	.05		413	Dennis Martinez	.05
222	Keith Hernandez	.05		318	Lee Guetterman	.05		414	Darrin Jackson	.05
223	Vince Coleman	.10		319	Jose Oquendo	.05		415	Mike Aldrete	.05
224	David Cone	.25		320	Wayne Tolleson	.05		416	Roger McDowell	.05
225	Ozzie Smith	.25		321	Jody Reed	.05		417	Jeff Reardon	.05
226	Matt Nokes	.05		322	Damon Berryhill	.05		418	Darren Daulton	.05
227	Barry Bonds	.50		323	Roger Clemens	.40		419	Tim Laudner	.05
228	Felix Jose	.05		324	Ryne Sandberg	.40		420	Don Carman	.05
229	Dennis Powell	.05		325	Benito Santiago	.05		421	Lloyd Moseby	.05
230	Mike Gallego	.05		326	Bret Saberhagen	.10		422	Doug Drabek	.05
231	Shawon Dunston	.10		327	Lou Whitaker	.05		423	Lenny Harris	.05
232	Ron Gant	.20		328	Dave Gallagher	.05		424	Jose Lind	.05
233	Omar Vizquel	.05		329	Mike Pagliarulo	.05		425	*Dave Johnson*	.05
234	Derek Lilliquist	.05		330	Doyle Alexander	.05		426	Jerry Browne	.05
235	Erik Hanson	.05		331	Jeffrey Leonard	.05		427	*Eric Yelding*	.05
236	Kirby Puckett	.75		332	Torey Lovullo	.05		428	Brad Komminsk	.05
237	Bill Spiers	.05		333	Pete Incaviglia	.05		429	Jody Davis	.05
238	Dan Gladden	.05		334	Rickey Henderson	.15		430	Mariano Duncan	.05
239	Bryan Clutterbuck	.05		335	Rafael Palmeiro	.25		431	Mark Davis	.05
240	John Moses	.05		336	Ken Hill	.20		432	Nelson Santovenia	.05
241	Ron Darling	.05		337	Dave Winfield	.20		433	Bruce Hurst	.05
242	Joe Magrane	.05		338	Alfredo Griffin	.05		434	*Jeff Huson*	.05
243	Dave Magadan	.05		339	Andy Hawkins	.05		435	Chris James	.05
244	Pedro Guerrero	.05		340	Ted Power	.05		436	*Mark Guthrie*	.05
245	Glenn Davis	.05		341	Steve Wilson	.05		437	Charlie Hayes	.05
246	Terry Steinbach	.05		342	Jack Clark	.05		438	Shane Rawley	.05
247	Fred Lynn	.05		343	Ellis Burks	.15		439	Dickie Thon	.05
248	Gary Redus	.05		344	Tony Gwynn	.40		440	Juan Berenguer	.05
249	Kenny Williams	.05		345	Jerome Walton	.05		441	Kevin Romine	.05
250	Sid Bream	.05		346	Roberto Alomar	.60		442	Bill Landrum	.05
251	Bob Welch	.05		347	*Carlos Martinez*	.05		443	Todd Frohwirth	.05
252	Bill Buckner	.05		348	Chet Lemon	.05		444	Craig Worthington	.05
253	Carney Lansford	.05		349	Willie Wilson	.05		445	Fernando Valenzuela	.09
254	Paul Molitor	.35		350	Greg Walker	.05		446	Albert Belle	1.00
255	Jose DeJesus	.05		351	Tom Bolton	.05		447	*Ed Whited*	.05
256	Orel Hershiser	.05		352	German Gonzalez	.05		448	Dave Smith	.05

#	Player	Price
449	Dave Clark	.05
450	Juan Agosto	.05
451	Dave Valle	.05
452	Kent Hrbek	.05
453	Von Hayes	.05
454	Gary Gaetti	.05
455	Greg Briley	.05
456	Glenn Braggs	.05
457	Kirt Manwaring	.05
458	Mel Hall	.05
459	Brook Jacoby	.05
460	Pat Sheridan	.05
461	Rob Murphy	.05
462	Jimmy Key	.15
463	Nick Esasky	.05
464	Rob Ducey	.05
465	Carlos Quintana	.05
466	*Larry Walker*	1.50
467	Todd Worrell	.05
468	Kevin Gross	.05
469	Terry Pendleton	.05
470	Dave Martinez	.05
471	Gene Larkin	.05
472	Len Dykstra	.10
473	Barry Lyons	.05
474	Terry Mulholland	.10
475	*Chip Hale*	.05
476	Jesse Barfield	.05
477	Dan Plesac	.05
478a	Scott Garrelts (Photo actually Bill Bathe)	3.00
478b	Scott Garrelts (Correct photo)	.05
479	Dave Righetti	.05
480	Gus Polidor	.05
481	Mookie Wilson	.05
482	Luis Rivera	.05
483	Mike Flanagan	.05
484	Dennis "Oil Can" Boyd	.05
485	John Cerutti	.05
486	John Costello	.05
487	Pascual Perez	.05
488	Tommy Herr	.05
489	Tom Foley	.05
490	Curt Ford	.05
491	Steve Lake	.05
492	Tim Teufel	.05
493	Randy Bush	.05
494	Mike Jackson	.05
495	Steve Jeltz	.05
496	Paul Gibson	.05
497	Steve Balboni	.05
498	Bud Black	.05
499	Dale Sveum	.05
500	Checklist 401-500	.05
501	Timmy Jones	.05
502	Mark Portugal	.05
503	Ivan Calderon	.05
504	Rick Rhoden	.05
505	Willie McGee	.08
506	Kirk McCaskill	.05
507	Dave LaPoint	.05
508	Jay Howell	.05
509	Johnny Ray	.05
510	Dave Anderson	.05
511	Chuck Crim	.05
512	Joe Hesketh	.05
513	Dennis Eckersley	.10
514	Greg Brock	.05
515	Tim Burke	.05
516	Frank Tanana	.05
517	Jay Bell	.10
518	Guillermo Hernandez	.05
519	Randy Kramer	.05
520	Charles Hudson	.05
521	Jim Corsi	.05
522	Steve Rosenberg	.05
523	Cris Carpenter	.05
524	*Matt Winters*	.05
525	Melido Perez	.05
526	Chris Gwynn	.05
527	Bert Blyleven	.09
528	Chuck Cary	.05
529	Daryl Boston	.05
530	Dale Mohorcic	.05
531	Geronimo Berroa	.25
532	Edgar Martinez	.15
533	Dale Murphy	.10
534	Jay Buhner	.20
535	John Smoltz	.50
536	Andy Van Slyke	.05
537	Mike Henneman	.08
538	Miguel Garcia	.05
539	Frank Williams	.05
540	R.J. Reynolds	.05
541	Shawn Hillegas	.05
542	Walt Weiss	.05
543	*Greg Hibbard*	.10
544	Nolan Ryan	1.25
545	Todd Zeile	.10
546	Hensley Meulens	.05
547	Tim Belcher	.05
548	Mike Witt	.05
549	Greg Cadaret	.05
550	Franklin Stubbs	.05
551	*Tony Castillo*	.05
552	Jeff Robinson	.05
553	*Steve Olin*	.05
554	Alan Trammell	.10
555	Wade Boggs	.25
556	Will Clark	.40
557	Jeff King	.05
558	Mike Fitzgerald	.05
559	Ken Howell	.05
560	Bob Kipper	.05
561	Scott Bankhead	.05
562a	*Jeff Innis* (Photo actually David West)	3.00
562b	*Jeff Innis* (Correct photo)	.05
563	Randy Johnson	.50
564	*Wally Whithurst*	.05
565	*Gene Harris*	.05
566	Norm Charlton	.05
567	Robin Yount	.50
568	*Joe Oliver*	.05
569	Mark Parent	.05
570	John Farrell	.05
571	Tom Glavine	.40
572	Rod Nichols	.05
573	Jack Morris	.09
574	Greg Swindell	.05
575	Steve Searcy	.05
576	Ricky Jordan	.05
577	Matt Williams	.40
578	Mike LaValliere	.05
579	Bryn Smith	.05
580	Bruce Ruffin	.05
581	Randy Myers	.08
582	*Rick Wrona*	.05
583	Juan Samuel	.05
584	Les Lancaster	.05
585	Jeff Musselman	.05
586	Rob Dibble	.05
587	Eric Show	.05
588	Jesse Orosco	.05
589	Herm Winningham	.05
590	Andy Allanson	.05
591	Dion James	.05
592	Carmelo Martinez	.05
593	Luis Quinones	.05
594	Dennis Rasmussen	.05
595	Rich Yett	.05
596	Bob Walk	.05
597a	Andy McGaffigan (player #48, photo actually Rich Thompson)	.70
597b	Andy McGaffigan (player #27, correct photo)	.05
598	Billy Hatcher	.05
599	Bob Knepper	.05
600	Checklist 501-600	.05
601	Joey Cora	.10
602	*Steve Finley*	.20
603	Kal Daniels	.05
604	Gregg Olson	.05
605	Dave Steib	.05
606	*Kenny Rogers*	.10
607	Zane Smith	.05
608	*Bob Geren*	.05
609	Chad Kreuter	.05
610	Mike Smithson	.05
611	*Jeff Wetherby*	.05
612	*Gary Mielke*	.05
613	Pete Smith	.05
614	*Jack Daugherty*	.05
615	Lance McCullers	.05
616	Don Robinson	.05
617	Jose Guzman	.05
618	Steve Bedrosian	.05
619	Jamie Moyer	.05
620	Atlee Hammaker	.05
621	*Rick Luecken*	.05
622	Greg W. Harris	.05
623	Pete Harnisch	.05
624	Jerald Clark	.05
625	Jack McDowell	.10
626	Frank Viola	.05
627	Ted Higuera	.05
628	*Marty Pevey*	.05
629	Bill Wegman	.05
630	Eric Plunk	.05
631	Drew Hall	.05
632	Doug Jones	.08
633	Geno Petralli	.05
634	Jose Alvarez	.05
635	Bob Milacki	.05
636	Bobby Witt	.05
637	Trevor Wilson	.05
638	Jeff Russell	.05
639	Mike Krukow	.05
640	Rick Leach	.05
641	Dave Schmidt	.05
642	Terry Leach	.05
643	Calvin Schiraldi	.05
644	Bob Melvin	.05
645	Jim Abbott	.25
646	*Jaime Navarro*	.20
647	Mark Langston	.05
648	Juan Nieves	.05
649	Damaso Garcia	.05
650	Charlie O'Brien	.05
651	Eric King	.05
652	Mike Boddicker	.05
653	Duane Ward	.05
654	Bob Stanley	.05
655	Sandy Alomar, Jr.	.05
656	Danny Tartabull	.05
657	Randy McCament	.05
658	Charlie Leibrandt	.05
659	Dan Quisenberry	.05
660	Paul Assenmacher	.05
661	Walt Terrell	.05
662	Tim Leary	.05
663	Randy Milligan	.05
664	Bo Diaz	.05
665	Mark Lemke	.05
666	Jose Gonzalez	.05
667	Chuck Finley	.10
668	John Kruk	.08
669	Dick Schofield	.05
670	Tim Crews	.05
671	John Dopson	.05
672	*John Orton*	.05
673	Eric Hetzel	.05
674	Lance Parrish	.08
675	Ramon Martinez	.20
676	Mark Gubicza	.05
677	Greg Litton	.05
678	Greg Mathews	.05
679	Dave Dravecky	.05
680	Steve Farr	.05
681	Mike Devereaux	.05
682	Ken Griffey, Sr.	.05
683a	Jamie Weston (first name incorrect)	4.00
683b	*Mickey Weston* (corrected)	.05
684	Jack Armstrong	.05
685	Steve Buechele	.05
686	Bryan Harvey	.05
687	Lance Blankenship	.05
688	Dante Bichette	.50
689	Todd Burns	.05
690	Dan Petry	.05
691	*Kent Anderson*	.05
692	Todd Stottlemyre	.10
693	Wally Joyner	.05
694	Mike Rochford	.05
695	Floyd Bannister	.05
696	Rick Reuschel	.05
697	Jose DeLeon	.05
698	Jeff Montgomery	.08
699	Kelly Downs	.05
700a	Checklist 601-700 (#683 Jamie Weston)	.05
700b	Checklist 601-700 (# 683 Mickey Weston)	.05
701	Jim Gott	.05
702	"Rookie Threats"(Delino DeShields, Larry Walker, Marquis Grissom)	.40
703	Alejandro Pena	.05
704	Willie Randolph	.05
705	Tim Leary	.05
706	Chuck McElroy	.05
707	Gerald Perry	.05
708	Tom Brunansky	.05
709	John Franco	.05
710	Mark Davis	.05
711	*Dave Justice*	1.00
712	Storm Davis	.05
713	Scott Ruskin	.05
714	Glenn Braggs	.05
715	Kevin Bearse	.05
716	Jose Nunez	.05
717	Tim Layana	.05
718	Greg Myers	.05
719	Pete O'Brien	.05
720	John Candelaria	.05

721	Craig Grebeck	.05
722	Shawn Boskie	.05
723	Jim Leyritz	.20
724	Bill Sampen	.05
725	Scott Radinsky	.10
726	*Todd Hundley*	.75
727	Scott Hemond	.10
728	Lenny Webster	.05
729	Jeff Reardon	.05
730	Mitch Webster	.05
731	Brian Bohanon	.05
732	Rick Parker	.05
733	Terry Shumpert	.05
734a	Nolan Ryan (300-win stripe on front)	2.00
734b	Nolan Ryan (no stripe)	8.00
735	John Burkett	.20
736	*Derrick May*	.10
737	*Carlos Baerga*	.25
738	Greg Smith	.05
739	Joe Kraemer	.05
740	Scott Sanderson	.05
741	Hector Villanueva	.05
742	Mike Fetters	.10
743	Mark Gardner	.20
744	Matt Nokes	.05
745	Dave Winfield	.20
746	*Delino DeShields*	.15
747	Dann Howitt	.05
748	Tony Pena	.05
749	Oil Can Boyd	.05
750	Mike Benjamin	.05
751	Alex Cole	.05
752	Eric Gunderson	.05
753	Howard Farmer	.05
754	Joe Carter	.35
755	*Ray Lankford*	.75
756	Sandy Alomar,Jr.	.05
757	Alex Sanchez	.05
758	Nick Esasky	.05
759	Stan Belinda	.10
760	Jim Presley	.05
761	Gary DiSarcina	.15
762	Wayne Edwards	.10
763	Pat Combs	.15
764	Mickey Pina	.05
765	*Wilson Alvarez*	.40
766	Dave Parker	.15
767	Mike Blowers	.15
768	Tony Phillips	.05
769	Pascual Perez	.05
770	Gary Pettis	.05
771	Fred Lynn	.10
772	*Mel Rojas*	.15
773	David Segui	.15
774	Gary Carter	.05
775	Rafael Valdez	.05
776	Glenallen Hill	.15
777	Keith Hernandez	.05
778	Billy Hatcher	.05
779	Marty Clary	.05
780	Candy Maldonado	.05
781	Mike Marshall	.05
782	Billy Jo Robidoux	.05
783	Mark Langston	.10
784	*Paul Sorrento*	.25
785	*Dave Hollins*	.20
786	Cecil Fielder	.25
787	Matt Young	.05
788	Jeff Huson	.05
789	Lloyd Moseby	.05
790	Ron Kittle	.05
791	Hubie Brooks	.05
792	Craig Lefferts	.05
793	Kevin Bass	.05
794	Bryn Smith	.05
795	Juan Samuel	.05
796	Sam Horn	.05
797	Randy Myers	.10
798	Chris James	.05
799	Bill Gullickson	.05
800	Checklist 701-800	.05

1990 Upper Deck Reggie Jackson Heroes

This Baseball Heroes set is devoted to Reggie Jackson. The cards, numbered 1-9, are the first in a continuing series of cards issued in subsequent years. An unnumbered cover card that says "Baseball Heroes" was also issued. The Jackson cards were randomly inserted in high number foil packs only. Jackson also autographed 2,500 numbered cards, which were randomly included in high number packs.

		MT
Complete Set (10):		20.00
Common Player:		2.00
Autographed Card:		300.00
1	1969 Emerging Superstar(Reggie Jackson)	2.00
2	1973 An MVP Year(Reggie Jackson)	2.00
3	1977 "Mr. October"(Reggie Jackson)	2.00
4	1978 Jackson vs. Welch(Reggie Jackson)	2.00
5	1982 Under the Halo(Reggie Jackson)	2.00
6	1984 500!(Reggie Jackson)	2.00
7	1986 Moving Up the List(Reggie Jackson)	2.00
8	1987 A Great Career Ends(Reggie Jackson)	2.00
9	Heroes Checklist 1-9(Reggie Jackson)	2.00
----	Header card	2.00

1991 Upper Deck

Shawn Abner

More than 110 rookies are included among the first 700 cards in the 1991 Upper Deck set. A 100-card high-number series was released in late summer. Cards feature top quality white stock and color photos on front and back. A nine-card "Baseball Heroes" bonus set honoring Nolan Ryan, is among the many insert specials in the '91 UD set. Others include a card of Chicago Bulls superstar Michael Jordan. Along with the Ryan bonus cards, 2,500 cards personally autographed and numbered by Ryan were randomly inserted. Upper Deck cards are packaged in tamper-proof foil packs. Each pack contains 15 cards and cards and a 3-1/2" x 2-1/2" 3-D team logo hologram sticker.

		MT
Complete Set (800):		20.00
Complete Low Series (1-700):		15.00
Complete High Series (701-800):		5.00
Common Player:		.05
Low or High Wax Box:		15.00
1	Star Rookie Checklist	.05
2	*Phil Plantier*	.15
3	*D.J. Dozier*	.05
4	Dave Hansen	.05
5	Mo Vaughn	1.50
6	*Leo Gomez*	.10
7	*Scott Aldred*	.05
8	*Scott Chiamparino*	.05
9	*Lance Dickson*	.05
10	*Sean Berry*	.15
11	Bernie Williams	.50
12	*Brian Barnes*	.08
13	*Narciso Elvira*	.05
14	*Mike Gardiner*	.10
15	*Greg Colbrunn*	.15
16	*Bernard Gilkey*	.25
17	Mark Lewis	.10
18	*Mickey Morandini*	.10
19	Charles Nagy	.15
20	Geronimo Pena	.10
21	*Henry Rodriguez*	.25
22	Scott Cooper	.08
23	*Andujar Cedeno*	.10
24	Eric Karros	.75
25	*Steve Decker*	.05
26	*Kevin Belcher*	.10
27	*Jeff Conine*	.50
28	Oakland Athletics checklist(Dave Stewart)	.05
29	Chicago White Sox checklist(Carlton Fisk)	.05
30	Texas Rangers checklist(Rafael Palmeiro)	.10
31	California Angels checklist(Chuck Finley)	.05
32	Seattle Mariners checklist(Harold Reynolds)	.05
33	Kansas City Royals checklist(Bret Saberhagen)	.05
34	Minnesota Twins checklist(Gary Gaetti)	.05
35	Scott Leius	.05
36	Neal Heaton	.05
37	*Terry Lee*	.05
38	Gary Redus	.05
39	Barry Jones	.05
40	Chuck Knoblauch	.40
41	Larry Andersen	.05
42	Darryl Hamilton	.05
43	Boston Red Sox checklist(Mike Greenwell)	.05
44	Toronto Blue Jays checklist(Kelly Gruber)	.05
45	Detroit Tigers checklist(Jack Morris)	.05
46	Cleveland Indians checklist(Sandy Alomar Jr.)	.05
47	Baltimore Orioles checklist(Gregg Olson)	.05
48	Milwaukee Brewers checklist(Dave Parker)	.05
49	New York Yankees checklist(Roberto Kelly)	.05
50	Top Prospect '91 checklist	.05
51	Kyle Abbott (Top Prospect)	.10
52	Jeff Juden (Top Prospect)	.20
53	Todd Van Poppel (Top Prospect)	.15
54	*Steve Karsay* (Top Prospect)	.15
55	*Chipper Jones* (Top Prospect)	4.00

#	Player	Price
56	Chris Johnson (Top Prospect)	.08
57	John Ericks (Top Prospect)	.08
58	Gary Scott (Top Prospect)	.05
59	Kiki Jones (Top Prospect)	.05
60	Wil Cordero (Top Prospect)	.25
61	Royce Clayton (Top Prospect)	.20
62	Tim Costo (Top Prospect)	.08
63	Roger Salkeld (Top Prospect)	.10
64	Brook Fordyce (Top Prospect)	.08
65	Mike Mussina (Top Prospect)	2.00
66	Dave Staton (Top Prospect)	.15
67	Mike Lieberthal (Top Prospect)	.20
68	Kurt Miller (Top Prospect)	.15
69	Dan Peltier (Top Prospect)	.08
70	Greg Blosser (Top Prospect)	.08
71	Reggie Sanders (Top Prospect)	.60
72	Brent Mayne (Top Prospect)	.08
73	Rico Brogna (Top Prospect)	.25
74	Willie Banks (Top Prospect)	.10
75	Len Brutcher (Top Prospect)	.05
76	Pat Kelly (Top Prospect)	.10
77	Cincinnati Reds checklist(Chris Sabo)	.05
78	Los Angeles Dodgers checklist(Ramon Martinez)	.08
79	San Francisco Giants checklist(Matt Williams)	.10
80	San Diego Padres checklist(Roberto Alomar)	.10
81	Houston Astros checklist(Glenn Davis)	.05
82	Atlanta Braves checklist(Ron Gant)	.10
83	"Fielder's Feat"(Cecil Fielder)	.15
84	Orlando Merced	.20
85	Domingo Ramos	.05
86	Tom Bolton	.05
87	Andres Santana	.05
88	John Dopson	.05
89	Kenny Williams	.05
90	Marty Barrett	.05
91	Tom Pagnozzi	.05
92	Carmelo Martinez	.05
93	"Save Master"(Bobby Thigpen)	.05
94	Pittsburgh Pirates checklist(Barry Bonds)	.20
95	New York Mets checklist(Gregg Jefferies)	.05
96	Montreal Expos checklist(Tim Wallach)	.05
97	Philadelphia Phillies checklist(Lenny Dykstra)	.05
98	St. Louis Cardinals checklist(Pedro Guerrero)	.05
99	Chicago Cubs checklist(Mark Grace)	.08
100	Checklist 1-100	.05
101	Kevin Elster	.05
102	Tom Brookens	.05
103	Mackey Sasser	.05
104	Felix Fermin	.05
105	Kevin McReynolds	.05
106	Dave Steib	.05
107	Jeffrey Leonard	.05
108	Dave Henderson	.05
109	Sid Bream	.05
110	Henry Cotto	.05
111	Shawon Dunston	.08
112	Mariano Duncan	.08
113	Joe Girardi	.05
114	Billy Hatcher	.05
115	Greg Maddux	.75
116	Jerry Browne	.05
117	Juan Samuel	.05
118	Steve Olin	.05
119	Alfredo Griffin	.05
120	Mitch Webster	.05
121	Joel Skinner	.05
122	Frank Viola	.05
123	Cory Snyder	.05
124	Howard Johnson	.05
125	Carlos Baerga	.15
126	Tony Fernandez	.05
127	Dave Stewart	.05
128	Jay Buhner	.15
129	Mike LaValliere	.05
130	Scott Bradley	.05
131	Tony Phillips	.05
132	Ryne Sandberg	.30
133	Paul O'Neill	.10
134	Mark Grace	.20
135	Chris Sabo	.05
136	Ramon Martinez	.15
137	Brook Jacoby	.05
138	Candy Maldonado	.05
139	Mike Scioscia	.05
140	Chris James	.05
141	Craig Worthington	.05
142	Manny Lee	.05
143	Tim Raines	.10
144	Sandy Alomar, Jr.	.10
145	John Olerud	.15
146	Ozzie Canseco	.10
147	Pat Borders	.05
148	Harold Reynolds	.05
149	Tom Henke	.05
150	R.J. Reynolds	.05
151	Mike Gallego	.05
152	Bobby Bonilla	.10
153	Terry Steinbach	.05
154	Barry Bonds	.60
155	Jose Canseco	.25
156	Gregg Jefferies	.10
157	Matt Williams	.25
158	Craig Biggio	.15
159	Daryl Boston	.05
160	Ricky Jordan	.05
161	Stan Belinda	.05
162	Ozzie Smith	.50
163	Tom Brunansky	.05
164	Todd Zeile	.10
165	Mike Greenwell	.05
166	Kal Daniels	.05
167	Kent Hrbek	.08
168	Franklin Stubbs	.05
169	Dick Schofield	.05
170	Junior Ortiz	.05
171	Hector Villanueva	.05
172	Dennis Eckersley	.15
173	Mitch Williams	.08
174	Mark McGwire	2.00
175	Fernando Valenzuela	.05
176	Gary Carter	.10
177	Dave Magadan	.05
178	Robby Thompson	.05
179	Bob Ojeda	.05
180	Ken Caminiti	.15
181	Don Slaught	.05
182	Luis Rivera	.05
183	Jay Bell	.05
184	Jody Reed	.05
185	Wally Backman	.05
186	Dave Martinez	.05
187	Luis Polonia	.05
188	Shane Mack	.05
189	Spike Owen	.05
190	Scott Bailes	.05
191	John Russell	.05
192	Walt Weiss	.05
193	Jose Oquendo	.05
194	Carney Lansford	.05
195	Jeff Huson	.05
196	Keith Miller	.05
197	Eric Yelding	.05
198	Ron Darling	.05
199	John Kruk	.05
200	Checklist 101-200	.05
201	John Shelby	.05
202	Bob Geren	.05
203	Lance McCullers	.05
204	Alvaro Espinoza	.05
205	Mark Salas	.05
206	Mike Pagliarulo	.05
207	Jose Uribe	.05
208	Jim Deshaies	.05
209	Ron Karkovice	.05
210	Rafael Ramirez	.05
211	Donnie Hill	.05
212	Brian Harper	.05
213	Jack Howell	.05
214	Wes Gardner	.05
215	Tim Burke	.05
216	Doug Jones	.05
217	Hubie Brooks	.05
218	Tom Candiotti	.05
219	Gerald Perry	.05
220	Jose DeLeon	.05
221	Wally Whitehurst	.05
222	Alan Mills	.10
223	Alan Trammell	.10
224	Dwight Gooden	.10
225	Travis Fryman	.15
226	Joe Carter	.15
227	Julio Franco	.08
228	Craig Lefferts	.05
229	Gary Pettis	.05
230	Dennis Rasmussen	.05
231a	Brian Downing (no position on front)	.50
231b	Brian Downing (DH on front)	.05
232	Carlos Quintana	.05
233	Gary Gaetti	.05
234	Mark Langston	.08
235	Tim Wallach	.05
236	Greg Swindell	.05
237	Eddie Murray	.20
238	Jeff Manto	.05
239	Lenny Harris	.05
240	Jesse Orosco	.05
241	Scott Lusader	.05
242	Sid Fernandez	.05
243	Jim Leyritz	.20
244	Cecil Fielder	.20
245	Darryl Strawberry	.10
246	Frank Thomas	3.00
247	Kevin Mitchell	.05
248	Lance Johnson	.08
249	Rick Rueschel	.05
250	Mark Portugal	.05
251	Derek Lilliquist	.05
252	Brian Holman	.05
253	Rafael Valdez	.05
254	B.J. Surhoff	.05
255	Tony Gwynn	.60
256	Andy Van Slyke	.05
257	Todd Stottlemyre	.08
258	Jose Lind	.05
259	Greg Myers	.05
260	Jeff Ballard	.05
261	Bobby Thigpen	.05
262	Jimmy Kremers	.05
263	Robin Ventura	.20
264	John Smoltz	.20
265	Sammy Sosa	.75
266	Gary Sheffield	.20
267	Len Dykstra	.08
268	Bill Spiers	.05
269	Charlie Hayes	.05
270	Brett Butler	.05
271	Bip Roberts	.05
272	Rob Deer	.05
273	Fred Lynn	.08
274	Dave Parker	.08
275	Andy Benes	.10
276	Glenallen Hill	.10
277	Steve Howard	.10
278	Doug Drabek	.05
279	Joe Oliver	.05
280	Todd Benzinger	.05
281	Eric King	.05
282	Jim Presley	.05
283	Ken Patterson	.05
284	Jack Daugherty	.05
285	Ivan Calderon	.05
286	Edgar Diaz	.05
287	Kevin Bass	.05
288	Don Carman	.05
289	Greg Brock	.05
290	John Franco	.05
291	Joey Cora	.05
292	Bill Wegman	.05
293	Eric Show	.05
294	Scott Bankhead	.05
295	Garry Templeton	.05
296	Mickey Tettleton	.05
297	Luis Sojo	.05
298	Jose Rijo	.05
299	Dave Johnson	.05
300	Checklist 201-300	.05
301	Mark Grant	.05
302	Pete Harnisch	.08
303	Greg Olson	.05
304	Anthony Telford	.10
305	Lonnie Smith	.05
306	Chris Hoiles	.08
307	Bryn Smith	.05
308	Mike Devereaux	.05
309a	Milt Thompson ("86" in stats obscured by "bull's eye")	.50
309b	Milt Thompson ("86" visible)	.05
310	Bob Melvin	.05
311	Luis Salazar	.05
312	Ed Whitson	.05
313	Charlie Hough	.05
314	Dave Clark	.05
315	Eric Gunderson	.05
316	Dan Petry	.05
317	Dante Bichette	.20
318	Mike Heath	.05

#	Player	Price	#	Player	Price	#	Player	Price
319	Damon Berryhill	.05	415	Greg Gagne	.05	511	Casey Candaele	.05
320	Walt Terrell	.05	416	Tom Herr	.05	512	Mookie Wilson	.05
321	Scott Fletcher	.05	417	Jeff Parrett	.05	513	Dave Smith	.05
322	Dan Plesac	.05	418	Jeff Reardon	.05	514	*Chuck Carr*	.08
323	Jack McDowell	.10	419	Mark Lemke	.05	515	Glenn Wilson	.05
324	Paul Molitor	.35	420	Charlie O'Brien	.05	516	Mike Fitzgerald	.05
325	Ozzie Guillen	.05	421	Willie Randolph	.05	517	Devon White	.05
326	Gregg Olson	.05	422	Steve Bedrosian	.05	518	Dave Hollins	.08
327	Pedro Guerrero	.05	423	Mike Moore	.05	519	Mark Eichhorn	.05
328	Bob Milacki	.05	424	Jeff Brantley	.05	520	Otis Nixon	.05
329	John Tudor	.05	425	Bob Welch	.05	521	*Terry Shumpert*	.05
330	Steve Finley	.05	426	Terry Mulholland	.05	522	*Scott Erickson*	.15
331	Jack Clark	.05	427	*Willie Blair*	.10	523	Danny Tartabull	.05
332	Jerome Walton	.05	428	Darrin Fletcher	.10	524	Orel Hershiser	.10
333	Andy Hawkins	.05	429	Mike Witt	.05	525	George Brett	.40
334	Derrick May	.05	430	Joe Boever	.05	526	Greg Vaughn	.05
335	Roberto Alomar	.35	431	Tom Gordon	.05	527	Tim Naehring	.05
336	Jack Morris	.05	432	*Pedro Munoz*	.10	528	Curt Schilling	.10
337	Dave Winfield	.15	433	Kevin Seitzer	.05	529	Chris Bosio	.05
338	Steve Searcy	.05	434	Kevin Tapani	.05	530	Sam Horn	.05
339	Chili Davis	.08	435	Bret Saberhagen	.10	531	Mike Scott	.05
340	Larry Sheets	.05	436	Ellis Burks	.10	532	George Bell	.05
341	Ted Higuera	.05	437	Chuck Finley	.05	533	Eric Anthony	.05
342	*David Segui*	.15	438	Mike Boddicker	.05	534	*Julio Valera*	.05
343	Greg Cadaret	.05	439	Francisco Cabrera	.05	535	Glenn Davis	.05
344	Robin Yount	.25	440	Todd Hundley	.20	536	Larry Walker	.20
345	Nolan Ryan	.80	441	Kelly Downs	.05	537	Pat Combs	.05
346	Ray Lankford	.15	442	*Dann Howitt*	.05	538	*Chris Nabholz*	.05
347	Cal Ripken, Jr.	1.50	443	Scott Garrelts	.05	539	Kirk McCaskill	.05
348	Lee Smith	.05	444	Rickey Henderson	.15	540	Randy Ready	.05
349	Brady Anderson	.15	445	Will Clark	.30	541	Mark Gubicza	.05
350	Frank DiPino	.05	446	Ben McDonald	.08	542	Rick Aguilera	.05
351	Hal Morris	.05	447	Dale Murphy	.10	543	*Brian McRae*	.25
352	Deion Sanders	.20	448	Dave Righetti	.05	544	Kirby Puckett	.45
353	Barry Larkin	.15	449	Dickie Thon	.05	545	Bo Jackson	.20
354	Don Mattingly	.50	450	Ted Power	.05	546	Wade Boggs	.20
355	Eric Davis	.08	451	Scott Coolbaugh	.05	547	Tim McIntosh	.05
356	Jose Offerman	.05	452	Dwight Smith	.05	548	Randy Milligan	.05
357	Mel Rojas	.10	453	Pete Incaviglia	.08	549	Dwight Evans	.05
358	Rudy Seanez	.10	454	Andre Dawson	.10	550	Billy Ripken	.05
359	Oil Can Boyd	.05	455	Ruben Sierra	.05	551	Erik Hanson	.05
360	Nelson Liriano	.05	456	Andres Galarraga	.15	552	Lance Parrish	.05
361	Ron Gant	.08	457	Alvin Davis	.05	553	Tino Martinez	.15
362	*Howard Farmer*	.10	458	Tony Castillo	.05	554	Jim Abbott	.10
363	Dave Justice	.20	459	Pete O'Brien	.05	555	Ken Griffey, Jr.	2.50
364	Delino DeShields	.08	460	Charlie Leibrandt	.05	556	Milt Cuyler	.05
365	Steve Avery	.08	461	Vince Coleman	.05	557	*Mark Leonard*	.05
366	David Cone	.15	462	Steve Sax	.05	558	Jay Howell	.05
367	Lou Whitaker	.05	463	*Omar Oliveras*	.08	559	Lloyd Moseby	.05
368	Von Hayes	.05	464	*Oscar Azocar*	.05	560	Chris Gwynn	.05
369	Frank Tanana	.05	465	Joe Magrane	.05	561	*Mark Whiten*	.15
370	Tim Teufel	.05	466	*Karl Rhodes*	.10	562	Harold Baines	.05
371	Randy Myers	.05	467	Benito Santiago	.10	563	Junior Felix	.05
372	Roberto Kelly	.05	468	*Joe Klink*	.08	564	Darren Lewis	.10
373	Jack Armstrong	.05	469	Sil Campusano	.05	565	Fred McGriff	.20
374	Kelly Gruber	.05	470	Mark Parent	.05	566	Kevin Appier	.10
375	Kevin Maas	.05	471	*Shawn Boskie*	.10	567	*Luis Gonzalez*	.20
376	Randy Johnson	.25	472	Kevin Brown	.10	568	Frank White	.05
377	David West	.05	473	Rick Sutcliffe	.05	569	Juan Agosto	.05
378	*Brent Knackert*	.05	474	Rafael Palmeiro	.15	570	Mike Macfarlane	.05
379	Rick Honeycutt	.05	475	Mike Harkey	.05	571	Bert Blyleven	.08
380	Kevin Gross	.05	476	Jaime Navarro	.05	572	Ken Griffey, Sr.	.10
381	Tom Foley	.05	477	Marquis Grissom	.10	573	Lee Stevens	.05
382	Jeff Blauser	.05	478	Marty Clary	.05	574	Edgar Martinez	.10
383	*Scott Ruskin*	.05	479	Greg Briley	.05	575	Wally Joyner	.08
384	Andres Thomas	.05	480	Tom Glavine	.15	576	Tim Belcher	.05
385	Dennis Martinez	.08	481	Lee Guetterman	.05	577	John Burkett	.05
386	Mike Henneman	.05	482	Rex Hudler	.05	578	Mike Morgan	.05
387	Felix Jose	.05	483	Dave LaPoint	.05	579	Paul Gibson	.05
388	Alejandro Pena	.05	484	Terry Pendleton	.05	580	Jose Vizcaino	.05
389	Chet Lemon	.05	485	Jesse Barfield	.05	581	Duane Ward	.05
390	*Craig Wilson*	.10	486	Jose DeJesus	.05	582	Scott Sanderson	.05
391	Chuck Crim	.05	487	*Paul Abbott*	.05	583	David Wells	.08
392	Mel Hall	.05	488	Ken Howell	.05	584	Willie McGee	.05
393	Mark Knudson	.05	489	Greg W. Harris	.05	585	John Cerutti	.05
394	Norm Charlton	.05	490	Roy Smith	.05	586	Danny Darwin	.05
395	Mike Felder	.05	491	Paul Assenmacher	.05	587	Kurt Stillwell	.05
396	*Tim Layana*	.05	492	Geno Petralli	.05	588	Rich Gedman	.05
397	Steve Frey	.05	493	Steve Wilson	.05	589	Mark Davis	.05
398	Bill Doran	.05	494	Kevin Reimer	.05	590	Bill Gullickson	.05
399	Dion James	.05	495	Bill Long	.05	591	Matt Young	.05
400	Checklist 301-400	.05	496	Mike Jackson	.05	592	Bryan Harvey	.05
401	Ron Hassey	.05	497	Oddibe McDowell	.05	593	Omar Vizquel	.05
402	Don Robinson	.05	498	Bill Swift	.05	594	*Scott Lewis*	.05
403	Gene Nelson	.05	499	Jeff Treadway	.05	595	Dave Valle	.05
404	Terry Kennedy	.05	500	Checklist 401-500	.05	596	Tim Crews	.05
405	Todd Burns	.05	501	Gene Larkin	.05	597	Mike Bielecki	.05
406	Roger McDowell	.05	502	Bob Boone	.05	598	Mike Sharperson	.05
407	Bob Kipper	.05	503	Allan Anderson	.05	599	Dave Bergman	.05
408	Darren Daulton	.05	504	Luis Aquino	.05	600	Checklist 501-600	.05
409	Chuck Cary	.05	505	Mark Guthrie	.05	601	Steve Lyons	.05
410	Bruce Ruffin	.05	506	Joe Orsulak	.05	602	Bruce Hurst	.05
411	Juan Berenguer	.05	507	*Dana Kiecker*	.05	603	Donn Pall	.05
412	Gary Ward	.05	508	Dave Gallagher	.05	604	*Jim Vatcher*	.05
413	Al Newman	.05	509	Greg A. Harris	.05	605	Dan Pasqua	.05
414	Danny Jackson	.05	510	Mark Williamson	.05	606	Kenny Rogers	.05

607	*Jeff Schulz*	.05
608	Brad Arnsberg	.05
609	Willie Wilson	.05
610	Jamie Moyer	.05
611	Ron Oester	.05
612	Dennis Cook	.05
613	Rick Mahler	.05
614	Bill Landrum	.05
615	Scott Scudder	.05
616	*Tom Edens*	.05
617	"1917 Revisited" (Chicago White Sox team photo)	.10
618	Jim Gantner	.05
619	Darrel Akerfelds	.05
620	Ron Robinson	.05
621	Scott Radinsky	.05
622	Pete Smith	.05
623	Melido Perez	.05
624	Jerald Clark	.05
625	Carlos Martinez	.05
626	*Wes Chamberlain*	.10
627	Bobby Witt	.05
628	Ken Dayley	.05
629	*John Barfield*	.05
630	Bob Tewksbury	.05
631	Glenn Braggs	.05
632	*Jim Neidlinger*	.05
633	Tom Browning	.05
634	Kirk Gibson	.05
635	Rob Dibble	.05
636	"Stolen Base Leaders"(Lou Brock, Rickey Henderson)	.15
637	Jeff Montgomery	.05
638	Mike Schooler	.05
639	Storm Davis	.05
640	*Rich Rodriguez*	.05
641	Phil Bradley	.05
642	Kent Mercker	.05
643	Carlton Fisk	.10
644	Mike Bell	.05
645	*Alex Fernandez*	.40
646	Juan Gonzalez	1.00
647	Ken Hill	.10
648	Jeff Russell	.05
649	*Chuck Malone*	.05
650	Steve Buechele	.05
651	Mike Benjamin	.05
652	Tony Pena	.05
653	Trevor Wilson	.05
654	Alex Cole	.05
655	Roger Clemens	.40
656	"The Bashing Years"(Mark McGwire)	1.00
657	*Joe Grahe*	.05
658	Jim Eisenreich	.05
659	Dan Gladden	.05
660	Steve Farr	.05
661	*Bill Sampen*	.05
662	*Dave Rohde*	.05
663	Mark Gardner	.05
664	*Mike Simms*	.05
665	Moises Alou	.15
666	Mickey Hatcher	.05
667	Jimmy Key	.10
668	John Wetteland	.08
669	John Smiley	.05
670	Jim Acker	.05
671	Pascual Perez	.05
672	*Reggie Harris*	.10
673	Matt Nokes	.05
674	*Rafael Novoa*	.05
675	Hensley Meulens	.05
676	Jeff M. Robinson	.05
677	"Ground Breaking" (New Comiskey Park)	.15
678	Johnny Ray	.05
679	Greg Hibbard	.05
680	Paul Sorrento	.05
681	Mike Marshall	.05
682	Jim Clancy	.05
683	Rob Murphy	.05
684	Dave Schmidt	.05
685	*Jeff Gray*	.05
686	Mike Hartley	.05
687	Jeff King	.05
688	Stan Javier	.05
689	Bob Walk	.05
690	Jim Gott	.05
691	Mike LaCoss	.05
692	John Farrell	.05
693	Tim Leary	.05
694	*Mike Walker*	.05
695	Eric Plunk	.05
696	Mike Fetters	.05
697	Wayne Edwards	.05
698	Tim Drummond	.05

699	Willie Fraser	.05
700	Checklist 601-700	.05
701	Mike Heath	.05
702	"Rookie Threats"(Luis Gonzalez, Karl Rhodes, Jeff Bagwell)	.60
703	Jose Mesa	.05
704	Dave Smith	.05
705	Danny Darwin	.05
706	Rafael Belliard	.05
707	Rob Murphy	.05
708	Terry Pendleton	.05
709	Mike Pagliarulo	.05
710	Sid Bream	.05
711	Junior Felix	.05
712	Dante Bichette	.20
713	Kevin Gross	.05
714	Luis Sojo	.05
715	Bob Ojeda	.05
716	Julio Machado	.05
717	Steve Farr	.05
718	Franklin Stubbs	.05
719	Mike Boddicker	.05
720	Willie Randolph	.05
721	Willie McGee	.05
722	Chili Davis	.05
723	Danny Jackson	.05
724	Cory Snyder	.05
725	"MVP Lineup"(Andre Dawson, George Bell, Ryne Sandberg)	.15
726	Rob Deer	.05
727	Rich DeLucia	.05
728	Mike Perez	.05
729	Mickey Tettleton	.05
730	Mike Blowers	.05
731	Gary Gaetti	.10
732	Brett Butler	.05
733	Dave Parker	.10
734	Eddie Zosky	.05
735	Jack Clark	.05
736	Jack Morris	.05
737	Kirk Gibson	.10
738	Steve Bedrosian	.05
739	Candy Maldonado	.05
740	Matt Young	.05
741	Rich Garces	.05
742	George Bell	.05
743	Deion Sanders	.20
744	Bo Jackson	.20
745	Luis Mercedes	.05
746	Reggie Jefferson	.08
747	Pete Incaviglia	.05
748	Chris Hammond	.05
749	Mike Stanton	.05
750	Scott Sanderson	.05
751	Paul Faries	.05
752	Al Osuna	.05
753	Steve Chitren	.05
754	Tony Fernandez	.05
755	*Jeff Bagwell*	3.00
756	Kirk Dressendorfer	.05
757	Glenn Davis	.05
758	Gary Carter	.05
759	Zane Smith	.05
760	Vance Law	.05
761	Denis Boucher	.05
762	Turner Ward	.05
763	Roberto Alomar	.30
764	Albert Belle	.40
765	Joe Carter	.20
766	Pete Schourek	.08
767	Heathcliff Slocumb	.05
768	Vince Coleman	.05
769	Mitch Williams	.05
770	Brian Downing	.05
771	Dana Allison	.05
772	Pete Harnisch	.05
773	Tim Raines	.05
774	Darryl Kile	.15
775	Fred McGriff	.20
776	Dwight Evans	.05
777	Joe Slusarski	.05
778	Dave Righetti	.05
779	Jeff Hamilton	.05
780	Ernest Riles	.05
781	Ken Dayley	.05
782	Eric King	.05
783	Devon White	.05
784	Beau Allred	.05
785	Mike Timlin	.10
786	Ivan Calderon	.05
787	Hubie Brooks	.05
788	Juan Agosto	.05
789	Barry Jones	.05
790	Wally Backman	.05

791	Jim Presley	.05
792	Charlie Hough	.05
793	Larry Andersen	.05
794	Steve Finley	.05
795	Shawn Abner	.05
796	Jeff M. Robinson	.05
797	Joe Bitker	.05
798	Eric Show	.05
799	Bud Black	.05
800	Checklist 701-800	.05
SP1	Michael Jordan	15.00
SP2	"A Day to Remember"(Rickey Henderson, Nolan Ryan)	3.00
HH1	Hank Aaron (hologram)	3.00

1991 Upper Deck Final Edition

Oil Can Boyd

Upper Deck surprised the hobby with the late-season release of this 100-card boxed set. The cards are numbered with an "F" designation. A special "Minor League Diamond Skills" subset (cards #1-21) features several top prospects. An All-Star subset (cards #79-99) is also included in this set. The cards are styled like the regular 1991 Upper Deck issue Special team hologram cards are included with the set.

		MT
Complete Set (100):		5.00
Common Player:		.05
1	Ryan Klesko, Reggie Sanders (Minor League Diamond Skills Checklist)	.50
2	Pedro Martinez	1.50
3	Lance Dickson	.05
4	Royce Clayton	.15
5	Scott Bryant	.05
6	Dan Wilson	.25
7	*Dmitri Young*	.25
8	*Ryan Klesko*	2.00
9	Tom Goodwin	.10
10	*Rondell White*	1.50
11	Reggie Sanders	.20
12	Todd Van Poppel	.05
13	Arthur Rhodes	.05
14	Eddie Zosky	.05
15	Gerald Williams	.08
16	Robert Eenhoorn	.05
17	*Jim Thome*	1.50
18	*Marc Newfield*	.15
19	Kerwin Moore	.05
20	Jeff McNeely	.05
21	Frankie Rodriguez	.10
22	Andy Mota	.05
23	Chris Haney	.05
24	*Kenny Lofton*	2.00
25	Dave Nilsson	.10
26	Derek Bell	.15
27	Frank Castillo	.10

28	Candy Maldonado	.05
29	Chuck McElroy	.05
30	Chito Martinez	.05
31	Steve Howe	.05
32	Freddie Benavides	.05
33	Scott Kamieniecki	.10
34	Denny Neagle	.40
35	Mike Humphreys	.05
36	Mike Remlinger	.05
37	Scott Coolbaugh	.05
38	Darren Lewis	.10
39	Thomas Howard	.10
40	John Candelaria	.05
41	Todd Benzinger	.05
42	Wilson Alvarez	.15
43	Patrick Lennon	.05
44	Rusty Meacham	.05
45	*Ryan Bowen*	.08
46	*Rick Wilkins*	.10
47	*Ed Sprague*	.15
48	*Bob Scanlan*	.05
49	Tom Candiotti	.05
50	Dennis Martinez (Perfecto)	.10
51	Oil Can Boyd	.05
52	Glenallen Hill	.05
53	*Scott Livingstone*	.05
54	Brian Hunter	.20
55	*Ivan Rodriguez*	2.50
56	*Keith Mitchell*	.05
57	Roger McDowell	.05
58	Otis Nixon	.05
59	*Juan Bell*	.05
60	Bill Krueger	.05
61	*Chris Donnels*	.05
62	Tommy Greene	.05
63	Doug Simons	.05
64	*Andy Ashby*	.15
65	*Anthony Young*	.05
66	*Kevin Morton*	.05
67	*Bret Barberie*	.10
68	*Scott Servais*	.15
69	Ron Darling	.05
70	Vicente Palacios	.05
71	*Tim Burke*	.05
72	*Gerald Alexander*	.05
73	Reggie Jefferson	.05
74	Dean Palmer	.10
75	Mark Whiten	.05
76	Randy Tomlin	.05
77	*Mark Wohlers*	.25
78	Brook Jacoby	.05
79	Ken Griffey Jr., Ryne Sandberg (All-Star Checklist)	.40
80	Jack Morris (AS)	.05
81	Sandy Alomar, Jr. (AS)	.05
82	Cecil Fielder (AS)	.10
83	Roberto Alomar (AS)	.20
84	Wade Boggs (AS)	.15
85	Cal Ripken, Jr. (AS)	.50
86	Rickey Henderson (AS)	.10
87	Ken Griffey, Jr. (AS)	.75
88	Dave Henderson (AS)	.05
89	Danny Tartabull (AS)	.05
90	Tom Glavine (AS)	.10
91	Benito Santiago (AS)	.05
92	Will Clark (AS)	.15
93	Ryne Sandberg (AS)	.20
94	Chris Sabo (AS)	.05
95	Ozzie Smith (AS)	.15
96	Ivan Calderon (AS)	.05
97	Tony Gwynn (AS)	.20
98	Andre Dawson (AS)	.05
99	Bobby Bonilla (AS)	.05
100	Checklist	.05

1991 Upper Deck Hank Aaron Heroes

This set devoted to Hank Aaron is numbered 19-27 and includes an unnumbered "Baseball Heroes" cover card. The cards are found in foil and jumbo packs of Upper Deck high-number cards.

A player's name in *italic* type indicates a rookie card.

		MT
Complete Set (10):		7.00
Common Aaron:		.50
Autographed Card:		400.00
Aaron Header:		4.00
19	1954 Rookie Year	.50
20	1957 MVP	.50
21	1966 Move to Atlanta	.50
22	1970 3,000	.50
23	1974 715	.50
24	1975 Return to Milwaukee	.50
25	1976 755	.50
26	1982 Hall of Fame	.50
27	Checklist - Heroes 19-27	.50

1991 Upper Deck Heroes of Baseball

This four-card set features three members of Baseball's Hall of Fame: Harmon Killebrew, Gaylord Perry and Ferguson Jenkins. Each has a card for himself, plus there's a card which features all three players. The cards were found in specially-marked low number foil packs. The cards are numbered H1-H4. Upper Deck also produced 3,000 autographed and numbered cards for each player.

		MT
Complete Set (4):		40.00
Autographed Card:		120.00
1	Harmon Killebrew	15.00
2	Gaylord Perry	15.00
3	Ferguson Jenkins	15.00
4	Gaylord Perry, Ferguson Jenkins, Harmon Killebrew	15.00

1991 Upper Deck Nolan Ryan Heroes

This set devoted to Nolan Ryan is numbered 10-18 and includes an unnumbered "Baseball Heroes" cover card. The cards are found in low-number foil and jumbo boxes.

		MT
Complete Set (10):		6.50
Common Player:		.50
Ryan header Card:		4.00
Autographed Card:		600.00
10	1968 Victory #1	.50
11	1973 A Career Year	.50
12	1975 Double Milestone	.50
13	1979 Back Home	.50
14	1981 All-Time Leader	.50
15	1989 5,000	.50
16	1990 The Sixth	.50
17	1990 ... and Still Counting	.50
18	Checklist - Heroes 10-18	.50

1991 Upper Deck Silver Sluggers

Alan Trammell

Each year the "Silver Slugger" award is presented to the player at each position with the highest batting average in each league. Upper Deck produced special cards in honor of the 1990 season award winners. The cards were randomly inserted in jumbo packs of Upper Deck cards. The cards feature a "SS" designation along with the card number. The cards are designed like the regular issue Upper Deck cards from 1991, but feature a Silver Slugger bat along the left border of the card.

		MT
Complete Set (18):		12.00
Common Player:		.50
1	Julio Franco	.50
2	Alan Trammell	.50
3	Rickey Henderson	.75

4	Jose Canseco	1.00
5	Barry Bonds	2.00
6	Eddie Murray	1.00
7	Kelly Gruber	.50
8	Ryne Sandberg	1.50
9	Darryl Strawberry	.50
10	Ellis Burks	.60
11	Lance Parrish	.50
12	Cecil Fielder	.65
13	Matt Williams	1.00
14	Dave Parker	.50
15	Bobby Bonilla	.60
16	Don Robinson	.50
17	Benito Santiago	.50
18	Barry Larkin	.75

1992 Upper Deck

Upper Deck introduced a new look in 1992. The baseline style was no longer used. The cards feature full-color action photos on white stock, with the player's name and the Upper Deck logo along the top border. The team name is in the bottom-right corner of the photo. Once again a 100-card high number series was released in late summer. Ted Williams autographed 2,500 Baseball Heroes cards which were randomly inserted into Upper Deck packs. Several subsets are also featured in the 1992 issue including Star Rookies and Top Prospects. Cards originating from factory sets have gold-foil holograms on back, rather than silver.

		MT
Complete Set (800):		20.00
Complete Low Series (1-700):		15.00
Complete High Series (701-800):		5.00
Common Player:		.05
Low or High Wax Box:		20.00
1	Star Rookie Checklist(Ryan Klesko, Jim Thome)	.50
2	Royce Clayton (Star Rookie)	.15
3	*Brian Jordan* (Star Rookie)	.25
4	*Dave Fleming* (Star Rookie)	.10
5	Jim Thome (Star Rookie)	.50
6	Jeff Juden (Star Rookie)	.10
7	*Roberto Hernandez* (Star Rookie)	.12
8	Kyle Abbott (Star Rookie)	.10
9	*Chris George* (Star Rookie)	.05
10	*Rob Maurer* (Star Rookie)	.05
11	*Donald Harris* (Star Rookie)	.05
12	*Ted Wood* (Star Rookie)	.05
13	*Patrick Lennon* (Star Rookie)	.05
14	Willie Banks (Star Rookie)	.05
15	Roger Salkeld (Star Rookie)	.10
16	Wil Cordero (Star Rookie)	.20
17	*Arthur Rhodes* (Star Rookie)	.10

18	Pedro Martinez (Star Rookie)	.50
19	*Andy Ashby* (Star Rookie)	.10
20	Tom Goodwin (Star Rookie)	.10
21	*Braulio Castillo* (Star Rookie)	.05
22	Todd Van Poppel (Star Rookie)	.05
23	*Brian Williams* (Star Rookie)	.05
24	Ryan Klesko (Star Rookie)	1.00
25	Kenny Lofton (Star Rookie)	1.50
26	Derek Bell (Star Rookie)	.15
27	Reggie Sanders (Star Rookie)	.15
28	Dave Winfield (Winfield's 400th)	.10
29	Atlanta Braves Checklist(Dave Justice)	.08
30	Cincinnati Reds Checklist(Rob Dibble)	.05
31	Houston Astros Checklist(Craig Biggio)	.08
32	Los Angeles Dodgers Checklist(Eddie Murray)	.10
33	San Diego Padres Checklist(Fred McGriff)	.10
34	San Francisco Giants Checklist(Willie McGee)	.05
35	Chicago Cubs Checklist(Shawon Dunston)	.05
36	Montreal Expos Checklist(Delino DeShields)	.05
37	New York Mets Checklist(Howard Johnson)	.05
38	Philadelphia Phillies Checklist(John Kruk)	.05
39	Pittsburgh Pirates Checklist(Doug Drabek)	.05
40	St. Louis Cardinals Checklist(Todd Zeile)	.05
41	Steve Avery (Playoff Perfection)	.05
42	*Jeremy Hernandez*	.05
43	*Doug Henry*	.10
44	*Chris Donnels*	.05
45	*Mo Sanford*	.05
46	*Scott Kamieniecki*	.15
47	Mark Lemke	.05
48	Steve Farr	.05
49	Francisco Oliveras	.05
50	*Ced Landrum*	.05
51	Top Prospect Checklist(Rondell White, Marc Newfield)	.20
52	*Eduardo Perez* (Top Prospect)	.10
53	*Tom Nevers* (Top Prospect)	.05
54	*David Zancanaro* (Top Prospect)	.05
55	*Shawn Green* (Top Prospect)	.35
56	*Mark Wohlers* (Top Prospect)	.25
57	Dave Nilsson (Top Prospect)	.20
58	Dmitri Young (Top Prospect)	.20
59	*Ryan Hawblitzel* (Top Prospect)	.10
60	Raul Mondesi (Top Prospect)	.50
61	Rondell White (Top Prospect)	.50
62	Steve Hosey (Top Prospect)	.05
63	*Manny Ramirez* (Top Prospect)	2.00
64	Marc Newfield (Top Prospect)	.20
65	Jeromy Burnitz (Top Prospect)	.30
66	*Mark Smith* (Top Prospect)	.05
67	*Joey Hamilton* (Top Prospect)	.50
68	*Tyler Green* (Top Prospect)	.10
69	*John Farrell* (Top Prospect)	.05
70	*Kurt Miller* (Top Prospect)	.10
71	*Jeff Plympton* (Top Prospect)	.05
72	Dan Wilson (Top Prospect)	.25
73	*Joe Vitiello* (Top Prospect)	.10
74	Rico Brogna (Top Prospect)	.15
75	*David McCarty* (Top Prospect)	.10
76	*Bob Wickman* (Top Prospect)	.10
77	*Carlos Rodriguez* (Top Prospect)	.10
78	Jim Abbott (Stay in School)	.10
79	Bloodlines(Pedro Martinez, Ramon Martinez)	.20

80	Bloodlines(Kevin Mitchell, Keith Mitchell)	.05
81	Bloodlines(Sandy Jr. & Roberto Alomar, Sandy Jr. & Roberto Alomar)	.15
82	Bloodlines(Cal Jr. & Billy Ripken, Cal Jr. & Billy Ripken)	.45
83	Bloodlines(Tony & Chris Gwynn, Tony & Chris Gwynn)	.20
84	Bloodlines(Dwight Gooden, Gary Sheffield)	.15
85	Bloodlines(Ken, Sr.; Ken, Jr.; & Craig Griffey, Ken, Jr.; & Craig Griffey, Ken, Sr.; Ken, Jr.; & Craig Griffey)	1.00
86	California Angels Checklist(Jim Abbott)	.05
87	Chicago White Sox Checklist(Frank Thomas)	.50
88	Kansas City Royals Checklist(Danny Tartabull)	.05
89	Minnesota Twins Checklist(Scott Erickson)	.05
90	Oakland Athletics Checklist(Rickey Henderson)	.05
91	Seattle Mariners Checklist(Edgar Martinez)	.05
92	Texas Rangers Checklist(Nolan Ryan)	.40
93	Baltimore Orioles Checklist(Ben McDonald)	.05
94	Boston Red Sox Checklist(Ellis Burks)	.05
95	Cleveland Indians Checklist(Greg Swindell)	.05
96	Detroit Tigers Checklist(Cecil Fielder)	.10
97	Milwaukee Brewers Checklist(Greg Vaughn)	.05
98	New York Yankees Checklist(Kevin Maas)	.05
99	Toronto Blue Jays Checklist(Dave Steib)	.05
100	Checklist 1-100	.05
101	Joe Oliver	.05
102	Hector Villanueva	.05
103	Ed Whitson	.05
104	Danny Jackson	.05
105	Chris Hammond	.05
106	Ricky Jordan	.05
107	Kevin Bass	.05
108	Darrin Fletcher	.05
109	Junior Ortiz	.05
110	Tom Bolton	.05
111	Jeff King	.05
112	Dave Magadan	.05
113	Mike LaValliere	.05
114	Hubie Brooks	.05
115	Jay Bell	.05
116	David Wells	.05
117	Jim Leyritz	.05
118	Manuel Lee	.05
119	Alvaro Espinoza	.05
120	B.J. Surhoff	.05
121	Hal Morris	.08
122	Shawon Dunston	.10
123	Chris Sabo	.05
124	Andre Dawson	.15
125	Eric Davis	.08
126	Chili Davis	.08
127	Dale Murphy	.10
128	Kirk McCaskill	.05
129	Terry Mulholland	.05
130	Rick Aguilera	.05
131	Vince Coleman	.05
132	Andy Van Slyke	.05
133	Gregg Jefferies	.05
134	Barry Bonds	.35
135	Dwight Gooden	.05
136	Dave Steib	.05
137	Albert Belle	.30
138	Teddy Higuera	.05
139	Jesse Barfield	.05
140	Pat Borders	.05
141	Bip Roberts	.05
142	Rob Dibble	.05
143	Mark Grace	.20
144	Barry Larkin	.15
145	Ryne Sandberg	.30
146	Scott Erickson	.05
147	Luis Polonia	.05
148	John Burkett	.05

No.	Name	Price	No.	Name	Price	No.	Name	Price
149	Luis Sojo	.05	245	Ivan Rodriguez	.30	341	Glenn Braggs	.05
150	Dickie Thon	.05	246	Len Dykstra	.10	342	Tom Glavine	.15
151	Walt Weiss	.05	247	Deion Sanders	.25	343	Wally Joyner	.05
152	Mike Scioscia	.05	248	Dwight Evans	.05	344	Fred McGriff	.15
153	Mark McGwire	1.50	249	Larry Walker	.15	345	Ron Gant	.10
154	Matt Williams	.15	250	Billy Ripken	.05	346	Ramon Martinez	.10
155	Rickey Henderson	.10	251	Mickey Tettleton	.05	347	Wes Chamberlain	.05
156	Sandy Alomar, Jr.	.10	252	Tony Pena	.05	348	Terry Shumpert	.05
157	Brian McRae	.05	253	Benito Santiago	.05	349	Tim Teufel	.05
158	Harold Baines	.05	254	Kirby Puckett	.40	350	Wally Backman	.05
159	Kevin Appier	.10	255	Cecil Fielder	.12	351	Joe Girardi	.05
160	Felix Fermin	.05	256	Howard Johnson	.05	352	Devon White	.08
161	Leo Gomez	.15	257	Andujar Cedeno	.05	353	Greg Maddux	.75
162	Craig Biggio	.15	258	Jose Rijo	.05	354	*Ryan Bowen*	.10
163	Ben McDonald	.05	259	Al Osuna	.05	355	Roberto Alomar	.30
164	Randy Johnson	.30	260	Todd Hundley	.12	356	Don Mattingly	.45
165	Cal Ripken, Jr.	1.50	261	Orel Hershiser	.08	357	Pedro Guerrero	.05
166	Frank Thomas	1.50	262	Ray Lankford	.12	358	Steve Sax	.05
167	Delino DeShields	.05	263	Robin Ventura	.15	359	Joey Cora	.05
168	Greg Gagne	.05	264	Felix Jose	.05	360	Jim Gantner	.05
169	Ron Karkovice	.05	265	Eddie Murray	.25	361	Brian Barnes	.05
170	Charlie Leibrandt	.05	266	Kevin Mitchell	.05	362	Kevin McReynolds	.10
171	Dave Righetti	.05	267	Gary Carter	.05	363	*Bret Barberie*	.10
172	Dave Henderson	.05	268	Mike Benjamin	.05	364	David Cone	.15
173	Steve Decker	.05	269	Dick Schofield	.05	365	Dennis Martinez	.05
174	Darryl Strawberry	.10	270	Jose Uribe	.05	366	*Brian Hunter*	.10
175	Will Clark	.25	271	Pete Incaviglia	.05	367	Edgar Martinez	.08
176	Ruben Sierra	.05	272	Tony Fernandez	.05	368	Steve Finley	.05
177	Ozzie Smith	.25	273	Alan Trammell	.10	369	Greg Briley	.05
178	Charles Nagy	.05	274	Tony Gwynn	.40	370	Jeff Blauser	.05
179	Gary Pettis	.05	275	Mike Greenwell	.05	371	Todd Stottlemyre	.08
180	Kirk Gibson	.05	276	Jeff Bagwell	.50	372	Luis Gonzalez	.05
181	Randy Milligan	.05	277	Frank Viola	.05	373	Rick Wilkins	.05
182	Dave Valle	.05	278	Randy Myers	.05	374	*Darryl Kile*	.10
183	Chris Hoiles	.05	279	Ken Caminiti	.12	375	John Olerud	.20
184	Tony Phillips	.05	280	Bill Doran	.05	376	Lee Smith	.05
185	Brady Anderson	.10	281	Dan Pasqua	.05	377	Kevin Maas	.05
186	Scott Fletcher	.05	282	Alfredo Griffin	.05	378	Dante Bichette	.15
187	Gene Larkin	.05	283	Jose Oquendo	.05	379	Tom Pagnozzi	.05
188	Lance Johnson	.05	284	Kal Daniels	.05	380	Mike Flanagan	.05
189	Greg Olson	.05	285	Bobby Thigpen	.05	381	Charlie O'Brien	.05
190	Melido Perez	.05	286	Robby Thompson	.05	382	Dave Martinez	.05
191	Lenny Harris	.05	287	Mark Eichhorn	.05	383	Keith Miller	.05
192	Terry Kennedy	.05	288	Mike Felder	.05	384	Scott Ruskin	.05
193	Mike Gallego	.05	289	Dave Gallagher	.05	385	Kevin Elster	.05
194	Willie McGee	.05	290	Dave Anderson	.05	386	Alvin Davis	.05
195	Juan Samuel	.05	291	Mel Hall	.05	387	Casey Candaele	.05
196	Jeff Huson	.05	292	Jerald Clark	.05	388	Pete O'Brien	.05
197	Alex Cole	.05	293	Al Newman	.05	389	Jeff Treadway	.05
198	Ron Robinson	.05	294	Rob Deer	.05	390	Scott Bradley	.05
199	Joel Skinner	.05	295	Matt Nokes	.05	391	Mookie Wilson	.05
200	Checklist 101-200	.05	296	Jack Armstrong	.05	392	Jimmy Jones	.05
201	Kevin Reimer	.05	297	Jim Deshaies	.05	393	Candy Maldonado	.05
202	Stan Belinda	.05	298	Jeff Innis	.05	394	Eric Yelding	.05
203	Pat Tabler	.05	299	Jeff Reed	.05	395	Tom Henke	.05
204	Jose Guzman	.05	300	Checklist 201-300	.05	396	Franklin Stubbs	.05
205	Jose Lind	.05	301	Lonnie Smith	.05	397	Milt Thompson	.05
206	Spike Owen	.05	302	Jimmy Key	.10	398	Mark Carreon	.05
207	Joe Orsulak	.05	303	Junior Felix	.05	399	Randy Velarde	.05
208	Charlie Hayes	.05	304	Mike Heath	.05	400	Checklist 301-400	.05
209	Mike Devereaux	.05	305	Mark Langston	.05	401	Omar Vizquel	.05
210	Mike Fitzgerald	.05	306	Greg W. Harris	.05	402	Joe Boever	.05
211	Willie Randolph	.05	307	Brett Butler	.05	403	Bill Krueger	.05
212	Rod Nichols	.05	308	Luis Rivera	.05	404	Jody Reed	.05
213	Mike Boddicker	.05	309	Bruce Ruffin	.05	405	Mike Schooler	.05
214	Bill Spiers	.05	310	Paul Faries	.05	406	Jason Grimsley	.05
215	Steve Olin	.05	311	Terry Leach	.05	407	Greg Myers	.05
216	*David Howard*	.05	312	*Scott Brosius*	.10	408	Randy Ready	.05
217	Gary Varsho	.05	313	Scott Leius	.05	409	*Mike Timlin*	.15
218	Mike Harkey	.05	314	Harold Reynolds	.05	410	Mitch Williams	.05
219	Luis Aquino	.05	315	Jack Morris	.08	411	Garry Templeton	.05
220	Chuck McElroy	.05	316	David Segui	.05	412	Greg Cadaret	.05
221	Doug Drabek	.05	317	Bill Gullickson	.05	413	Donnie Hill	.05
222	Dave Winfield	.15	318	Todd Frohwirth	.05	414	Wally Whitehurst	.05
223	Rafael Palmeiro	.15	319	*Mark Leiter*	.08	415	Scott Sanderson	.05
224	Joe Carter	.10	320	Jeff M. Robinson	.05	416	Thomas Howard	.05
225	Bobby Bonilla	.10	321	Gary Gaetti	.05	417	Neal Heaton	.05
226	Ivan Calderon	.05	322	John Smoltz	.15	418	Charlie Hough	.05
227	Gregg Olson	.05	323	Andy Benes	.10	419	Jack Howell	.05
228	Tim Wallach	.05	324	Kelly Gruber	.05	420	Greg Hibbard	.05
229	Terry Pendleton	.05	325	Jim Abbott	.05	421	Carlos Quintana	.05
230	Gilberto Reyes	.05	326	John Kruk	.05	422	*Kim Batiste*	.30
231	Carlos Baerga	.10	327	Kevin Seitzer	.05	423	Paul Molitor	.30
232	Greg Vaughn	.05	328	Darrin Jackson	.05	424	Ken Griffey, Jr.	1.50
233	Bret Saberhagen	.05	329	Kurt Stillwell	.05	425	Phil Plantier	.15
234	Gary Sheffield	.20	330	Mike Maddux	.05	426	Denny Neagle	.15
235	Mark Lewis	.05	331	Dennis Eckersley	.10	427	Von Hayes	.05
236	George Bell	.05	332	Dan Gladden	.05	428	Shane Mack	.05
237	Danny Tartabull	.05	333	Jose Canseco	.25	429	Darren Daulton	.08
238	Willie Wilson	.05	334	Kent Hrbek	.05	430	Dwayne Henry	.05
239	Doug Dascenzo	.05	335	Ken Griffey, Sr.	.05	431	Lance Parrish	.05
240	Bill Pecota	.05	336	Greg Swindell	.05	432	*Mike Humphreys*	.05
241	Julio Franco	.05	337	Trevor Wilson	.05	433	Tim Burke	.05
242	Ed Sprague	.05	338	Sam Horn	.05	434	Bryan Harvey	.05
243	Juan Gonzalez	.50	339	Mike Henneman	.05	435	Pat Kelly	.05
244	Chuck Finley	.05	340	Jerry Browne	.05	436	Ozzie Guillen	.05

437	Bruce Hurst	.05
438	Sammy Sosa	.75
439	Dennis Rasmussen	.05
440	Ken Patterson	.05
441	Jay Buhner	.10
442	Pat Combs	.05
443	Wade Boggs	.15
444	George Brett	.30
445	Mo Vaughn	.25
446	Chuck Knoblauch	.20
447	Tom Candiotti	.05
448	Mark Portugal	.05
449	Mickey Morandini	.05
450	Duane Ward	.05
451	Otis Nixon	.05
452	Bob Welch	.05
453	Rusty Meacham	.05
454	Keith Mitchell	.05
455	Marquis Grissom	.10
456	Robin Yount	.25
457	*Harvey Pulliam*	.05
458	Jose DeLeon	.05
459	Mark Gubicza	.05
460	Darryl Hamilton	.05
461	Tom Browning	.05
462	Monty Fariss	.05
463	Jerome Walton	.05
464	Paul O'Neill	.08
465	Dean Palmer	.08
466	Travis Fryman	.15
467	John Smiley	.05
468	Lloyd Moseby	.05
469	*John Wehner*	.05
470	Skeeter Barnes	.05
471	Steve Chitren	.05
472	Kent Mercker	.05
473	Terry Steinbach	.05
474	Andres Galarraga	.15
475	Steve Avery	.05
476	Tom Gordon	.05
477	Cal Eldred	.05
478	Omar Olivares	.05
479	Julio Machado	.05
480	Bob Milacki	.05
481	Les Lancaster	.05
482	John Candelaria	.05
483	Brian Downing	.05
484	Roger McDowell	.05
485	Scott Scudder	.05
486	Zane Smith	.05
487	John Cerutti	.05
488	Steve Buechele	.05
489	Paul Gibson	.05
490	Curtis Wilkerson	.05
491	Marvin Freeman	.05
492	Tom Foley	.05
493	Juan Berenguer	.05
494	Ernest Riles	.05
495	Sid Bream	.05
496	Chuck Crim	.05
497	Mike Macfarlane	.05
498	Dale Sveum	.05
499	Storm Davis	.05
500	Checklist 401-500	.05
501	Jeff Reardon	.05
502	Shawn Abner	.05
503	Tony Fossas	.05
504	Cory Snyder	.05
505	Matt Young	.05
506	Allan Anderson	.05
507	Mark Lee	.05
508	Gene Nelson	.05
509	Mike Pagliarulo	.05
510	Rafael Belliard	.05
511	Jay Howell	.05
512	Bob Tewksbury	.05
513	Mike Morgan	.05
514	John Franco	.05
515	Kevin Gross	.05
516	Lou Whitaker	.05
517	Orlando Merced	.05
518	Todd Benzinger	.05
519	Gary Redus	.05
520	Walt Terrell	.05
521	Jack Clark	.05
522	Dave Parker	.10
523	Tim Naehring	.05
524	Mark Whiten	.08
525	Ellis Burks	.10
526	*Frank Castillo*	.10
527	Brian Harper	.05
528	Brook Jacoby	.05
529	Rick Sutcliffe	.05
530	Joe Klink	.05
531	Terry Bross	.05
532	Jose Offerman	.05

533	Todd Zeile	.05
534	Eric Karros	.10
535	*Anthony Young*	.05
536	Milt Cuyler	.05
537	Randy Tomlin	.05
538	*Scott Livingstone*	.05
539	Jim Eisenreich	.05
540	Don Slaught	.05
541	Scott Cooper	.05
542	Joe Grahe	.05
543	Tom Brunansky	.05
544	Eddie Zosky	.05
545	Roger Clemens	.40
546	Dave Justice	.30
547	Dave Stewart	.05
548	David West	.05
549	Dave Smith	.05
550	Dan Plesac	.05
551	Alex Fernandez	.10
552	Bernard Gilkey	.05
553	Jack McDowell	.08
554	Tino Martinez	.15
555	Bo Jackson	.15
556	Bernie Williams	.25
557	Mark Gardner	.05
558	Glenallen Hill	.05
559	Oil Can Boyd	.05
560	Chris James	.05
561	*Scott Servais*	.10
562	*Rey Sanchez*	.15
563	*Paul McClellan*	.05
564	*Andy Mota*	.05
565	Darren Lewis	.05
566	*Jose Melendez*	.05
567	Tommy Greene	.05
568	Rich Rodriguez	.05
569	*Heathcliff Slocumb*	.05
570	Joe Hesketh	.05
571	Carlton Fisk	.10
572	Erik Hanson	.05
573	Wilson Alvarez	.05
574	*Rheal Cormier*	.05
575	Tim Raines	.05
576	Bobby Witt	.05
577	Roberto Kelly	.05
578	Kevin Brown	.10
579	Chris Nabholz	.05
580	Jesse Orosco	.05
581	Jeff Brantley	.05
582	Rafael Ramirez	.05
583	Kelly Downs	.05
584	Mike Simms	.05
585	*Mike Remlinger*	.05
586	Dave Hollins	.05
587	Larry Andersen	.05
588	Mike Gardiner	.05
589	Craig Lefferts	.05
590	Paul Assenmacher	.05
591	Bryn Smith	.05
592	Donn Pall	.05
593	Mike Jackson	.05
594	Scott Radinsky	.05
595	Brian Holman	.05
596	Geronimo Pena	.05
597	Mike Jeffcoat	.05
598	Carlos Martinez	.05
599	Geno Petralli	.05
600	Checklist 501-600	.05
601	Jerry Don Gleaton	.05
602	Adam Peterson	.05
603	Craig Grebeck	.05
604	Mark Guthrie	.05
605	Frank Tanana	.05
606	Hensley Meulens	.05
607	Mark Davis	.05
608	Eric Plunk	.05
609	Mark Williamson	.05
610	Lee Guetterman	.05
611	Bobby Rose	.05
612	Bill Wegman	.05
613	Mike Hartley	.05
614	*Chris Beasley*	.05
615	Chris Bosio	.05
616	Henry Cotto	.05
617	*Chico Walker*	.05
618	Russ Swan	.05
619	Bob Walk	.05
620	Billy Swift	.05
621	*Warren Newson*	.05
622	Steve Bedrosian	.05
623	*Ricky Bones*	.08
624	Kevin Tapani	.05
625	*Juan Guzman*	.10
626	*Jeff Johnson*	.05
627	Jeff Montgomery	.05
628	Ken Hill	.05

629	Gary Thurman	.05
630	Steve Howe	.05
631	Jose DeJesus	.05
632	Bert Blyleven	.05
633	Jaime Navarro	.05
634	Lee Stevens	.05
635	Pete Harnisch	.05
636	Bill Landrum	.05
637	Rich DeLucia	.05
638	Luis Salazar	.05
639	Rob Murphy	.05
640	A.L. Diamond Skills Checklist(Rickey Henderson, Jose Canseco)	.05
641	Roger Clemens (Diamond Skills)	.20
642	Jim Abbott (Diamond Skills)	.05
643	Travis Fryman (Diamond Skills)	.05
644	Jesse Barfield (Diamond Skills)	.05
645	Cal Ripken, Jr. (Diamond Skills)	.50
646	Wade Boggs (Diamond Skills)	.10
647	Cecil Fielder (Diamond Skills)	.10
648	Rickey Henderson (Diamond Skills)	.05
649	Jose Canseco (Diamond Skills)	.10
650	Ken Griffey, Jr. (Diamond Skills)	.50
651	Kenny Rogers	.05
652	*Luis Mercedes*	.05
653	Mike Stanton	.05
654	Glenn Davis	.05
655	Nolan Ryan	.75
656	Reggie Jefferson	.05
657	*Javier Ortiz*	.05
658	Greg A. Harris	.05
659	Mariano Duncan	.05
660	Jeff Shaw	.05
661	Mike Moore	.05
662	*Chris Haney*	.05
663	*Joe Slusarski*	.05
664	*Wayne Housie*	.05
665	Carlos Garcia	.05
666	Bob Ojeda	.05
667	*Bryan Hickerson*	.05
668	Tim Belcher	.05
669	Ron Darling	.05
670	Rex Hudler	.05
671	Sid Fernandez	.05
672	*Chito Martinez*	.05
673	Pete Schourek	.15
674	*Armando Renoso*	.05
675	Mike Mussina	.35
676	Kevin Morton	.05
677	Norm Charlton	.05
678	Danny Darwin	.05
679	Eric King	.05
680	Ted Power	.05
681	Barry Jones	.05
682	Carney Lansford	.05
683	Mel Rojas	.05
684	Rick Honeycutt	.05
685	*Jeff Fassero*	.15
686	Cris Carpenter	.05
687	Tim Crews	.05
688	Scott Terry	.05
689	Chris Gwynn	.05
690	Gerald Perry	.05
691	John Barfield	.05
692	Bob Melvin	.05
693	Juan Agosto	.05
694	Alejandro Pena	.05
695	Jeff Russell	.05
696	Carmelo Martinez	.05
697	Bud Black	.05
698	Dave Otto	.05
699	Billy Hatcher	.05
700	Checklist 601-700	.05
701	Clemente Nunez	.15
702	"Rookie Threats"(Donovan Osborne, Brian Jordan, Mark Clark)	.10
703	Mike Morgan	.05
704	Keith Miller	.05
705	Kurt Stillwell	.05
706	Damon Berryhill	.05
707	Von Hayes	.05
708	Rick Sutcliffe	.05
709	Hubie Brooks	.05
710	Ryan Turner	.10

711	N.L. Diamond Skills Checklist(Barry Bonds, Andy Van Slyke)	.15
712	Jose Rijo (Diamond Skills)	.05
713	Tom Glavine (Diamond Skills)	.10
714	Shawon Dunston (Diamond Skills)	.08
715	Andy Van Slyke (Diamond Skills)	.05
716	Ozzie Smith (Diamond Skills)	.10
717	Tony Gwynn (Diamond Skills)	.20
718	Will Clark (Diamond Skills)	.10
719	Marquis Grissom (Diamond Skills)	.08
720	Howard Johnson (Diamond Skills)	.05
721	Barry Bonds (Diamond Skills)	.20
722	Kirk McCaskill	.05
723	Sammy Sosa	.50
724	George Bell	.05
725	Gregg Jefferies	.05
726	Gary DiSarcina	.08
727	Mike Bordick	.05
728	Eddie Murray (400 Home Run Club)	.20
729	Rene Gonzales	.05
730	Mike Bielecki	.05
731	Calvin Jones	.05
732	Jack Morris	.05
733	Frank Viola	.15
734	Dave Winfield	.05
735	Kevin Mitchell	.05
736	Billy Swift	.05
737	Dan Gladden	.05
738	Mike Jackson	.05
739	Mark Carreon	.05
740	Kirt Manwaring	.05
741	Randy Myers	.05
742	Kevin McReynolds	.05
743	Steve Sax	.05
744	Wally Joyner	.05
745	Gary Sheffield	.15
746	Danny Tartabull	.05
747	Julio Valera	.05
748	Denny Neagle	.10
749	Lance Blankenship	.05
750	Mike Gallego	.05
751	Bret Saberhagen	.05
752	Ruben Amaro	.08
753	Eddie Murray	.15
754	Kyle Abbott	.08
755	Bobby Bonilla	.10
756	Eric Davis	.08
757	Eddie Taubensee	.10
758	Andres Galarraga	.15
759	Pete Incaviglia	.05
760	Tom Candiotti	.05
761	Tim Belcher	.05
762	Ricky Bones	.05
763	Bip Roberts	.05
764	Pedro Munoz	.05
765	Greg Swindell	.05
766	Kenny Lofton	.60
767	Gary Carter	.05
768	Charlie Hayes	.05
769	Dickie Thon	.05
770	Diamond Debuts Checklist(Donovan Osborne)	.05
771	Bret Boone (Diamond Debuts)	.20
772	Archi Cianfrocco (Diamond Debuts)	.05
773	Mark Clark (Diamond Debuts)	.05
774	Chad Curtis (Diamond Debuts)	.10
775	Pat Listach (Diamond Debuts)	.05
776	Pat Mahomes (Diamond Debuts)	.05
777	Donovan Osborne (Diamond Debuts)	.08
778	John Patterson (Diamond Debuts)	.05
779	Andy Stankiewicz (Diamond Debuts)	.08
780	Turk Wendell (Diamond Debuts)	.05
781	Bill Krueger	.05
782	Rickey Henderson (Grand Theft)	.10

783	Kevin Seitzer	.05
784	Dave Martinez	.05
785	John Smiley	.05
786	Matt Stairs	.05
787	Scott Scudder	.05
788	John Wetteland	.05
789	Jack Armstrong	.05
790	Ken Hill	.08
791	Dick Schofield	.05
792	Mariano Duncan	.05
793	Bill Pecota	.05
794	*Mike Kelly*	.10
795	Willie Randolph	.05
796	*Butch Henry*	.05
797	*Carlos Hernandez*	.05
798	Doug Jones	.05
799	Melido Perez	.05
800	Checklist	.05
SP3	"Prime Time's Two"(Deion Sanders)	3.00
SP4	"Mr. Baseball"(Tom Selleck, Frank Thomas)	5.00
HH2	(Ted Williams) (hologram)	3.00

1992 Upper Deck Bench/Morgan Heroes

This set is devoted to two of the vital cogs in Cincinnati's Big Red Machine: Hall of Famers Johnny Bench and Joe Morgan. Cards, numbered 37-45, were included in high number packs. An unnumbered cover card was also produced. Both players autographed 2,500 of card #45, the painting of the Reds duo by sports artist Vernon Wells.

		MT
Complete Set (10):		11.00
Common Player:		1.00
Header Card:		6.00
Autographed Card:		300.00
37	1968 Rookie of the Year(Johnny Bench)	1.00
38	1968-77 Ten Straight Gold Gloves(Johnny Bench)	1.00
39	1970 & 1972 MVP(Johnny Bench)	1.00
40	1965 Rookie Year(Joe Morgan)	.50
41	1975-76 Back-to-Back MVP(Joe Morgan)	.50
42	1980-83 The Golden Years(Joe Morgan)	.50
43	1972-79 Big Red Machine(Johnny Bench, Joe Morgan)	.75
44	1989 & 1990 Hall of Fame(Johnny Bench, Joe Morgan)	.75
45	Checklist - Heroes 37-45(Johnny Bench, Joe Morgan)	.75

1992 Upper Deck College POY Holograms

This three-card hologram set features the College Player of the Year winners from 1989-91. Cards

were randomly inserted in high number foil packs and have a CP prefix for numbering.

		MT
Complete Set (3):		.75
Common Player:		.25
1	David McCarty	.25
2	Mike Kelly	.25
3	Ben McDonald	.25

1992 Upper Deck Hall of Fame Heroes

This set features three top players from the 1970s: Vida Blue, Lou Brock and Rollie Fingers. The cards continue from last year's set by using numbers H5-H8. The three players are each on one card; the fourth card features all three. They were found in low-number foil packs and specially-marked jumbo packs. Both types of packs could also contain autographed cards; each player signed 3,000 cards.

		MT
Complete Set (4):		30.00
Common Player:		8.00
Vida Blue Autograph:		75.00
Lou Brock Autograph:		100.00
Rollie Fingers Autograph:		90.00
5	Vida Blue	8.00
6	Lou Brock	10.00
7	Rollie Fingers	9.00
8	Vida Blue, Lou Brock, Rollie Fingers	10.00

1992 Upper Deck Heroes Highlights

Special packaging of 1992 Upper Deck high numbers produced for sales to dealers at its Heroes of Baseball show series included these cards of former players as inserts. Cards have a Heroes Highlights banner including the player's name and the date of his career highlight beneath the photo. In a tombstone frame on back, the highlight is chronicled. Cards are numbered alphabetically by player name, with the card number carrying an HI prefix.

		MT
Complete Set (10):		30.00
Common Player:		2.00
1	Bobby Bonds	2.00
2	Lou Brock	2.00
3	Rollie Fingers	2.00
4	Bob Gibson	2.50
5	Reggie Jackson	4.00
6	Gaylord Perry	2.00
7	Robin Roberts	2.00
8	Brooks Robinson	3.50
9	Billy Williams	2.00
10	Ted Williams	7.00

1992 Upper Deck Home Run Heroes

This 26-card set features a top home run hitter from each major league team. The cards, numbered HR1-HR26, were found in low-number jumbo packs, one per pack.

		MT
Complete Set (26):		16.00
Common Player:		.40
1	Jose Canseco	1.00
2	Cecil Fielder	.60
3	Howard Johnson	.40
4	Cal Ripken, Jr.	4.00
5	Matt Williams	.75
6	Joe Carter	.50
7	Ron Gant	.50
8	Frank Thomas	4.00
9	Andre Dawson	.40
10	Fred McGriff	.75
11	Danny Tartabull	.40
12	Chili Davis	.40
13	Albert Belle	1.25
14	Jack Clark	.40
15	Paul O'Neill	.40
16	Darryl Strawberry	.40
17	Dave Winfield	.50
18	Jay Buhner	.40
19	Juan Gonzalez	2.00
20	Greg Vaughn	.40
21	Barry Bonds	1.25
22	Matt Nokes	.40
23	John Kruk	.40
24	Ivan Calderon	.40
25	Jeff Bagwell	2.00
26	Todd Zeile	.40

1992 Upper Deck Scouting Report

MARK WOHLERS

These cards were randomly inserted in Upper Deck high-number jumbo packs. The set is numbered SR1-SR25 and features 25 top prospects, including 1992 Rookies of the Year Pat Listach and Eric Karros. "Scouting Report" is written down the side on the front in silver lettering. The back features a clipboard which shows a photo, a player profile and a major league scouting report.

		MT
Complete Set (25):		16.00
Common Player:		.25
1	Andy Ashby	.50
2	Willie Banks	.25
3	Kim Batiste	.25
4	Derek Bell	1.00
5	Archi Cianfrocco	.25
6	Royce Clayton	.75
7	Gary DiSarcina	.25
8	Dave Fleming	.25
9	Butch Henry	.25
10	Todd Hundley	1.00
11	Brian Jordan	1.00
12	Eric Karros	1.00
13	Pat Listach	.25
14	Scott Livingstone	.25
15	Kenny Lofton	6.00
16	Pat Mahomes	.25
17	Denny Neagle	1.00
18	Dave Nilsson	.50
19	Donovan Osborne	.25
20	Reggie Sanders	.75
21	Andy Stankiewicz	.25
22	Jim Thome	2.00
23	Julio Valera	.25
24	Mark Wohlers	.75
25	Anthony Young	.25

1992 Upper Deck Ted Williams' Best

Twenty of the best hitters in baseball according to legend Ted Williams are featured in this special insert set from Upper Deck. The cards are styled much like the 1992 FanFest cards and showcase each chosen player. Each card is numbered with a "T" designation.

Modern cards have little collector value in conditions lower than Mint. Figure NM cards at 75% of values shown; EX cards at 40%.

BEST HITTERS OF THE FUTURE
ROBERTO ALOMAR

		MT
Complete Set (20):		24.00
Common Player:		.50
1	Wade Boggs	.75
2	Barry Bonds	1.50
3	Jose Canseco	.75
4	Will Clark	.75
5	Cecil Fielder	.60
6	Tony Gwynn	2.00
7	Rickey Henderson	.50
8	Fred McGriff	.75
9	Kirby Puckett	2.00
10	Ruben Sierra	.50
11	Roberto Alomar	1.25
12	Jeff Bagwell	2.00
13	Albert Belle	1.25
14	Juan Gonzalez	2.50
15	Ken Griffey, Jr.	6.00
16	Chris Hoiles	.50
17	Dave Justice	.75
18	Phil Plantier	.50
19	Frank Thomas	5.00
20	Robin Ventura	.60

1992 Upper Deck Ted Williams Heroes

This Baseball Heroes set devoted to Ted Williams continues where previous efforts left off by numbering it from 28-36. An unnumbered "Baseball Heroes" cover card is also included. Cards were found in low-number foil and jumbo packs. Williams also autographed 2,500 cards, which were numbered and randomly inserted in low-number packs.

	MT
Complete Set (10):	6.50
Common Player:	.50
Autographed Card:	450.00
Williams Header:	4.00

28	1939 Rookie Year	.50
29	1941 .406!	.50
30	1942 Triple Crown Year	.50
31	1946 & 1949 MVP	.50
32	1947 Second Triple Crown	.50
33	1950s Player of the Decade	.50
34	1960 500 Home Run Club	.50
35	1966 Hall of Fame	.50
36	Checklist - Heroes 28-36	.50

1993 Upper Deck

Upper Deck introduced its 1993 set in a two-series format to adjust to expansion. Cards 1-420 make up the first series. Special subsets in series one include rookies, team-mates and community heroes. The card fronts feature full-color player photos surrounded by a white bor-der. "Upper Deck" appears at the top of the photo and the player ID at the bottom. The backs feature ver-tical photos, which is a change from the past, and more complete statis-tics than what Upper Deck has had in the past. The hologram appears in the lower left corner on the card back.

		MT
Complete Set (840):		40.00
Complete Series 1 (420):		20.00
Complete Series 2 (420):		20.00
Common Player:		.05
Series 1 or 2 Wax Box:		25.00
1	Tim Salmon (Checklist)	.25
2	Mike Piazza (Star Rookie)	2.00
3	Rene Arocha (Star Rookie)	.20
4	Willie Greene (Star Rookie)	.15
5	Manny Alexander (Star Rookie)	.10
6	Dan Wilson (Star Rookie)	.12
7	Dan Smith (Star Rookie)	.10
8	Kevin Rogers (Star Rookie)	.10
9	Nigel Wilson (Star Rookie)	.10
10	Joe Vitko (Star Rookie)	.10
11	Tim Costo (Star Rookie)	.15
12	Alan Embree (Star Rookie)	.15
13	Jim Tatum (Star Rookie)	.05
14	Cris Colon (Star Rookie)	.10
15	Steve Hosey (Star Rookie)	.10
16	Sterling Hitchcock (Star Rookie)	.15
17	Dave Mlicki (Star Rookie)	.15
18	Jessie Hollins (Star Rookie)	.10
19	Bobby Jones (Star Rookie)	.40
20	Kurt Miller (Star Rookie)	.15
21	Melvin Nieves (Star Rookie)	.25
22	Billy Ashley (Star Rookie)	.20
23	J.T. Snow (Star Rookie)	.75
24	Chipper Jones (Star Rookie)	1.25
25	Tim Salmon (Star Rookie)	.50
26	Tim Pugh (Star Rookie)	.10
27	David Nied (Star Rookie)	.05
28	Mike Trombley (Star Rookie)	.10

29	Javier Lopez (Star Rookie)	.40
30	Community Heroes Checklist(Jim Abbott)	.05
31	Jim Abbott (Community Heroes)	.10
32	Dale Murphy (Community Heroes)	.10
33	Tony Pena (Community Heroes)	.10
34	Kirby Puckett (Community Heroes)	.40
35	Harold Reynolds (Community Heroes)	.10
36	Cal Ripken, Jr. (Community Heroes)	.75
37	Nolan Ryan (Community Heroes)	.50
38	Ryne Sandberg (Community Heroes)	.25
39	Dave Stewart (Community Heroes)	.10
40	Dave Winfield (Community Heroes)	.10
41	Teammates Checklist(Joe Carter, Mark McGwire)	1.00
42	Blockbuster Trade(Joe Carter, Roberto Alomar)	.15
43	Brew Crew(Pat Listach, Robin Yount, Paul Molitor)	.15
44	Iron and Steal(Brady Anderson, Cal Ripken, Jr.)	.25
45	Youthful Tribe(Albert Belle, Sandy Alomar Jr., Jim Thome, Carlos Baerga, Kenny Lofton)	.25
46	Motown Mashers(Cecil Fielder, Mickey Tettleton)	.10
47	Yankee Pride(Roberto Kelly, Don Mattingly)	.20
48	Boston Cy Sox(Frank Viola, Roger Clemens)	.25
49	Bash Brothers(Ruben Sierra, Mark McGwire)	1.00
50	Twin Titles(Kent Hrbek, Kirby Puckett)	.20
51	Southside Sluggers(Robin Ventura, Frank Thomas)	.50
52	Latin Stars(Jose Canseco, Ivan Rodriguez, Rafael Palmeiro, Juan Gonzalez)	.25
53	Lethal Lefties(Mark Langston, Jim Abbott, Chuck Finley)	.10
54	Royal Family(Gregg Jefferies, George Brett, Wally Joyner)	.20
55	Pacific Sox Exchange(Kevin Mitchell, Jay Buhner, Ken Griffey, Jr.)	.50
56	George Brett	.50
57	Scott Cooper	.05
58	Mike Maddux	.05
59	Rusty Meacham	.05
60	Wil Cordero	.10
61	Tim Teufel	.05
62	Jeff Montgomery	.05
63	Scott Livingstone	.05
64	Doug Dascenzo	.05
65	Bret Boone	.10
66	Tim Wakefield	.10
67	Curt Schilling	.05
68	Frank Tanana	.05
69	Len Dykstra	.08
70	Derek Lilliquist	.05
71	Anthony Young	.05
72	Hipolito Pichardo	.08
73	Rod Beck	.05
74	Kent Hrbek	.05
75	Tom Glavine	.15
76	Kevin Brown	.10
77	Chuck Finley	.05
78	Bob Walk	.05
79	Rheal Cormier	.05
80	Rick Sutcliffe	.05
81	Harold Baines	.08
82	Lee Smith	.05
83	Geno Petralli	.05
84	Jose Oquendo	.05
85	Mark Gubicza	.05
86	Mickey Tettleton	.08
87	Bobby Witt	.05
88	Mark Lewis	.05
89	Kevin Appier	.10
90	Mike Stanton	.05
91	Rafael Belliard	.05
92	Kenny Rogers	.05

93	Randy Velarde	.05
94	Luis Sojo	.05
95	Mark Leiter	.05
96	Jody Reed	.05
97	Pete Harnisch	.05
98	Tom Candiotti	.05
99	Mark Portugal	.05
100	Dave Valle	.05
101	Shawon Dunston	.08
102	B.J. Surhoff	.05
103	Jay Bell	.05
104	Sid Bream	.05
105	Checklist 1-105(Frank Thomas)	.25
106	Mike Morgan	.05
107	Bill Doran	.05
108	Lance Blankenship	.05
109	Mark Lemke	.05
110	Brian Harper	.05
111	Brady Anderson	.15
112	Bip Roberts	.05
113	Mitch Williams	.05
114	Craig Biggio	.15
115	Eddie Murray	.25
116	Matt Nokes	.05
117	Lance Parrish	.05
118	Bill Swift	.05
119	Jeff Innis	.05
120	Mike LaValliere	.05
121	Hal Morris	.08
122	Walt Weiss	.05
123	Ivan Rodriguez	.40
124	Andy Van Slyke	.05
125	Roberto Alomar	.30
126	Robby Thompson	.05
127	Sammy Sosa	.75
128	Mark Langston	.05
129	Jerry Browne	.05
130	Chuck McElroy	.05
131	Frank Viola	.05
132	Leo Gomez	.05
133	Ramon Martinez	.10
134	Don Mattingly	.60
135	Roger Clemens	.75
136	Rickey Henderson	.10
137	Darren Daulton	.10
138	Ken Hill	.05
139	Ozzie Guillen	.05
140	Jerald Clark	.05
141	Dave Fleming	.05
142	Delino DeShields	.08
143	Matt Williams	.20
144	Larry Walker	.25
145	Ruben Sierra	.05
146	Ozzie Smith	.20
147	Chris Sabo	.05
148	Carlos Hernandez	.08
149	Pat Borders	.05
150	Orlando Merced	.05
151	Royce Clayton	.05
152	Kurt Stillwell	.05
153	Dave Hollins	.05
154	Mike Greenwell	.05
155	Nolan Ryan	1.00
156	Felix Jose	.05
157	Junior Felix	.05
158	Derek Bell	.10
159	Steve Buechele	.05
160	John Burkett	.05
161	Pat Howell	.05
162	Milt Cuyler	.05
163	Terry Pendleton	.05
164	Jack Morris	.08
165	Tony Gwynn	.75
166	Deion Sanders	.25
167	Mike Devereaux	.05
168	Ron Darling	.05
169	Orel Hershiser	.05
170	Mike Jackson	.05
171	Doug Jones	.05
172	Dan Walters	.05
173	Darren Lewis	.05
174	Carlos Baerga	.10
175	Ryne Sandberg	.35
176	Gregg Jefferies	.10
177	John Jaha	.05
178	Luis Polonia	.05
179	Kirt Manwaring	.05
180	Mike Magnante	.05
181	Billy Ripken	.05
182	Mike Moore	.05
183	Eric Anthony	.05
184	Lenny Harris	.05
185	Tony Pena	.05
186	Mike Felder	.05
187	Greg Olson	.05

#	Player	Value
188	Rene Gonzales	.05
189	Mike Bordick	.05
190	Mel Rojas	.05
191	Todd Frohwirth	.05
192	Darryl Hamilton	.05
193	Mike Fetters	.05
194	Omar Olivares	.05
195	Tony Phillips	.05
196	Paul Sorrento	.05
197	Trevor Wilson	.05
198	Kevin Gross	.05
199	Ron Karkovice	.05
200	Brook Jacoby	.05
201	Mariano Duncan	.05
202	Dennis Cook	.05
203	Daryl Boston	.05
204	Mike Perez	.05
205	Manuel Lee	.05
206	Steve Olin	.05
207	Charlie Hough	.05
208	Scott Scudder	.05
209	Charlie O'Brien	.05
210	Checklist 106-210(Barry Bonds)	.15
211	Jose Vizcaino	.05
212	Scott Leius	.05
213	Kevin Mitchell	.08
214	Brian Barnes	.05
215	Pat Kelly	.05
216	Chris Hammond	.05
217	Rob Deer	.05
218	Cory Snyder	.05
219	Gary Carter	.10
220	Danny Darwin	.05
221	Tom Gordon	.05
222	Gary Sheffield	.20
223	Joe Carter	.15
224	Jay Buhner	.15
225	Jose Offerman	.05
226	Jose Rijo	.05
227	Mark Whiten	.05
228	Randy Milligan	.05
229	Bud Black	.05
230	Gary DiSarcina	.05
231	Steve Finley	.05
232	Dennis Martinez	.05
233	Mike Mussina	.20
234	Joe Oliver	.05
235	Chad Curtis	.05
236	Shane Mack	.05
237	Jaime Navarro	.05
238	Brian McRae	.05
239	Chili Davis	.08
240	Jeff King	.05
241	Dean Palmer	.05
242	Danny Tartabull	.05
243	Charles Nagy	.05
244	Ray Lankford	.10
245	Barry Larkin	.15
246	Steve Avery	.08
247	John Kruk	.08
248	Derrick May	.05
249	Stan Javier	.05
250	Roger McDowell	.05
251	Dan Gladden	.05
252	Wally Joyner	.08
253	Pat Listach	.05
254	Chuck Knoblauch	.20
255	Sandy Alomar Jr.	.10
256	Jeff Bagwell	.60
257	Andy Stankiewicz	.05
258	Darrin Jackson	.05
259	Brett Butler	.05
260	Joe Orsulak	.05
261	Andy Benes	.10
262	Kenny Lofton	.35
263	Robin Ventura	.10
264	Ron Gant	.10
265	Ellis Burks	.10
266	Juan Guzman	.05
267	Wes Chamberlain	.05
268	John Smiley	.05
269	Franklin Stubbs	.05
270	Tom Browning	.05
271	Dennis Eckersley	.08
272	Carlton Fisk	.10
273	Lou Whitaker	.06
274	Phil Plantier	.05
275	Bobby Bonilla	.10
276	Ben McDonald	.05
277	Bob Zupcic	.05
278	Terry Steinbach	.05
279	Terry Mulholland	.05
280	Lance Johnson	.05
281	Willie McGee	.05
282	Bret Saberhagen	.08
283	Randy Myers	.05
284	Randy Tomlin	.05
285	Mickey Morandini	.05
286	Brian Williams	.05
287	Tino Martinez	.15
288	Jose Melendez	.05
289	Jeff Huson	.05
290	Joe Grahe	.05
291	Mel Hall	.05
292	Otis Nixon	.05
293	Todd Hundley	.15
294	Casey Candaele	.05
295	Kevin Seitzer	.05
296	Eddie Taubensee	.05
297	Moises Alou	.15
298	Scott Radinsky	.05
299	Thomas Howard	.05
300	Kyle Abbott	.05
301	Omar Vizquel	.05
302	Keith Miller	.05
303	Rick Aguilera	.05
304	Bruce Hurst	.05
305	Ken Caminiti	.15
306	Mike Pagiarulo	.05
307	Frank Seminara	.05
308	Andre Dawson	.10
309	Jose Lind	.05
310	Joe Boever	.05
311	Jeff Parrett	.05
312	Alan Mills	.05
313	Kevin Tapani	.05
314	Darryl Kile	.05
315	Checklist 211-315(Will Clark)	.05
316	Mike Sharperson	.05
317	John Orton	.05
318	Bob Tewksbury	.05
319	Xavier Hernandez	.05
320	Paul Assenmacher	.05
321	John Franco	.05
322	Mike Timlin	.05
323	Jose Guzman	.05
324	Pedro Martinez	.20
325	Bill Spiers	.05
326	Melido Perez	.05
327	Mike Macfarlane	.05
328	Ricky Bones	.05
329	Scott Bankhead	.05
330	Rich Rodriguez	.05
331	Geronimo Pena	.05
332	Bernie Williams	.35
333	Paul Molitor	.25
334	Roger Mason	.05
335	David Cone	.15
336	Randy Johnson	.30
337	Pat Mahomes	.05
338	Erik Hanson	.05
339	Duane Ward	.05
340	Al Martin	.05
341	Pedro Munoz	.05
342	Greg Colbrunn	.05
343	Julio Valera	.05
344	John Olerud	.15
345	George Bell	.05
346	Devon White	.05
347	Donovan Osborne	.05
348	Mark Gardner	.05
349	Zane Smith	.05
350	Wilson Alvarez	.10
351	*Kevin Koslofski*	.05
352	Roberto Hernandez	.05
353	Glenn Davis	.05
354	Reggie Sanders	.10
355	Ken Griffey, Jr.	2.00
355a	Ken Griffey Jr. (promo, 1992-dated hologram on back)	6.00
355b	Ken Griffey, Jr. (8-1/2" x 11" limited edition of 1,000)	25.00
356	Marquis Grissom	.10
357	Jack McDowell	.10
358	Jimmy Key	.10
359	Stan Belinda	.05
360	Gerald Williams	.05
361	Sid Fernandez	.05
362	Alex Fernandez	.10
363	John Smoltz	.15
364	Travis Fryman	.10
365	Jose Canseco	.25
366	Dave Justice	.20
367	*Pedro Astacio*	.15
368	Tim Belcher	.05
369	Steve Sax	.05
370	Gary Gaetti	.05
371	Jeff Frye	.10
372	Bob Wickman	.05
373	*Ryan Thompson*	.15
374	*David Hulse*	.15
375	Cal Eldred	.05
376	Ryan Klesko	.75
377	*Damion Easley*	.10
378	*John Kiely*	.10
379	*Jim Bullinger*	.15
380	Brian Bohanon	.05
381	Rod Brewer	.05
382	*Fernando Ramsey*	.08
383	Sam Militello	.05
384	Arthur Rhodes	.05
385	Eric Karros	.10
386	Rico Brogna	.08
387	*John Valentin*	.25
388	*Kerry Woodson*	.05
389	Ben Rivera	.05
390	*Matt Whiteside*	.08
391	Henry Rodriguez	.05
392	John Wetteland	.08
393	Kent Mercker	.05
394	Bernard Gilkey	.05
395	Doug Henry	.05
396	Mo Vaughn	.40
397	Scott Erickson	.05
398	Bill Gullickson	.05
399	Mark Guthrie	.05
400	Dave Martinez	.05
401	*Jeff Kent*	.15
402	Chris Hoiles	.05
403	Mike Henneman	.05
404	Chris Nabholz	.05
405	Tom Pagnozzi	.05
406	Kelly Gruber	.05
407	Bob Welch	.05
408	Frank Castillo	.05
409	John Dopson	.05
410	Steve Farr	.05
411	Henry Cotto	.05
412	Bob Patterson	.05
413	Todd Stottlemyre	.10
414	Greg A. Harris	.05
415	Denny Neagle	.10
416	Bill Wegman	.05
417	Willie Wilson	.08
418	Terry Leach	.05
419	Willie Randolph	.05
420	Checklist 316-420(Mark McGwire)	1.00
421	Calvin Murray (Top Prospects Checklist)	.10
422	*Pete Janicki* (Top Prospect)	.10
423	Todd Jones (Top Prospect)	.08
424	Mike Neill (Top Prospect)	.10
425	Carlos Delgado (Top Prospect)	.30
426	Jose Oliva (Top Prospect)	.05
427	Tyrone Hill (Top Prospect)	.10
428	Dmitri Young (Top Prospect)	.20
429	*Derek Wallace* (Top Prospect)	.15
430	*Michael Moore* (Top Prospect)	.15
431	Cliff Floyd (Top Prospect)	.15
432	Calvin Murray (Top Prospect)	.10
433	Manny Ramirez (Top Prospect)	.75
434	Marc Newfield (Top Prospect)	.15
435	Charles Johnson (Top Prospect)	.30
436	Butch Huskey (Top Prospect)	.15
437	Brad Pennington (Top Prospect)	.10
438	*Ray McDavid* (Top Prospect)	.15
439	Chad McConnell (Top Prospect)	.15
440	*Midre Cummings* (Top Prospect)	.15
441	Benji Gil (Top Prospect)	.15
442	Frank Rodriguez (Top Prospect)	.15
443	*Chad Mottola* (Top Prospect)	.15
444	*John Burke* (Top Prospect)	.15
445	Michael Tucker (Top Prospect)	.20
446	Rick Greene (Top Prospect)	.10
447	Rich Becker (Top Prospect)	.10
448	Mike Robertson (Top Prospect)	.05
449	*Derek Jeter* (Top Prospect)	6.00

450	Checklist 451-470 Inside the Numbers(David McCarty, Ivan Rodriguez)	.15
451	Jim Abbott (Inside the Numbers)	.05
452	Jeff Bagwell (Inside the Numbers)	.40
453	Jason Bere (Inside the Numbers)	.05
454	Delino DeShields (Inside the Numbers)	.05
455	Travis Fryman (Inside the Numbers)	.05
456	Alex Gonzalez (Inside the Numbers)	.05
457	Phil Hiatt (Inside the Numbers)	.05
458	Dave Hollins (Inside the Numbers)	.05
459	Chipper Jones (Inside the Numbers)	.40
460	Dave Justice (Inside the Numbers)	.15
461	Ray Lankford (Inside the Numbers)	.05
462	David McCarty (Inside the Numbers)	.05
463	Mike Mussina (Inside the Numbers)	.20
464	Jose Offerman (Inside the Numbers)	.05
465	Dean Palmer (Inside the Numbers)	.05
466	Geronimo Pena (Inside the Numbers)	.05
467	Eduardo Perez (Inside the Numbers)	.05
468	Ivan Rodriguez (Inside the Numbers)	.20
469	Reggie Sanders (Inside the Numbers)	.05
470	Bernie Williams (Inside the Numbers)	.20
471	Checklist 472-485 Team Stars(Barry Bonds, Matt Williams, Will Clark)	.20
472	Strike Force(John Smoltz, Steve Avery, Greg Maddux, Tom Glavine)	.15
473	Red October(Jose Rijo, Rob Dibble, Roberto Kelly, Reggie Sanders, Barry Larkin)	.08
474	Four Corners(Gary Sheffield, Phil Plantier, Tony Gwynn, Fred McGriff)	.20
475	Shooting Stars(Doug Drabek, Craig Biggio, Jeff Bagwell)	.15
476	Giant Sticks(Will Clark, Barry Bonds, Matt Williams)	.25
477	Boyhood Friends(Darryl Strawberry, Eric Davis)	.05
478	Rock Solid(Dante Bichette, David Nied, Andres Galarraga)	.10
479	Inaugural Catch(Dave Magadan, Orestes Destrade, Bret Barbarie, Jeff Conine)	.05
480	Steel City Champions(Tim Wakefield, Andy Van Slyke, Jay Bell)	.05
481	"Les Grandes Etoiles"(Marquis Grissom, Delino DeShields, Dennis Martinez, Larry Walker)	.10
482	Runnin' Redbirds(Geronimo Pena, Ray Lankford, Ozzie Smith, Bernard Gilkey)	.10
483	Ivy Leaguers(Ryne Sandberg, Mark Grace, Randy Myers)	.15
484	Big Apple Power Switch(Eddie Murray, Bobby Bonilla, Howard Johnson)	.10
485	Hammers & Nails(John Kruk, Dave Hollins, Darren Daulton, Len Dykstra)	.05
486	Barry Bonds (Award Winners)	.15
487	Dennis Eckersley (Award Winners)	.05
488	Greg Maddux (Award Winners)	.35

489	Dennis Eckersley (Award Winners)	.05
490	Eric Karros (Award Winners)	.05
491	Pat Listach (Award Winners)	.05
492	Gary Sheffield (Award Winners)	.15
493	Mark McGwire (Award Winners)	1.00
494	Gary Sheffield (Award Winners)	.10
495	Edgar Martinez (Award Winners)	.08
496	Fred McGriff (Award Winners)	.15
497	Juan Gonzalez (Award Winners)	.25
498	Darren Daulton (Award Winners)	.08
499	Cecil Fielder (Award Winners)	.10
500	Checklist 501-510 Diamond Debuts(Brent Gates)	.10
501	Tavo Alvarez (Diamond Debuts)	.05
502	Rod Bolton (Diamond Debuts)	.05
503	John Cummings (Diamond Debuts)	.10
504	Brent Gates (Diamond Debuts)	.15
505	Tyler Green (Diamond Debuts)	.10
506	Jose Martinez (Diamond Debuts)	.15
507	Troy Percival (Diamond Debuts)	.05
508	Kevin Stocker (Diamond Debuts)	.05
509	Matt Walbeck (Diamond Debuts)	.15
510	Rondell White (Diamond Debuts)	.20
511	Billy Ripken	.05
512	Mike Moore	.05
513	Jose Lind	.05
514	Chito Martinez	.05
515	Jose Guzman	.05
516	Kim Batiste	.05
517	Jeff Tackett	.05
518	Charlie Hough	.05
519	Marvin Freeman	.05
520	Carlos Martinez	.05
521	Eric Young	.05
522	Pete Incaviglia	.05
523	Scott Fletcher	.05
524	Orestes Destrade	.05
525	Checklist 421-525(Ken Griffey, Jr.)	.20
526	Ellis Burks	.10
527	Juan Samuel	.05
528	Dave Magadan	.05
529	Jeff Parrett	.05
530	Bill Krueger	.05
531	Frank Bolick	.05
532	Alan Trammell	.10
533	Walt Weiss	.05
534	David Cone	.15
535	Greg Maddux	1.50
536	Kevin Young	.05
537	Dave Hansen	.05
538	Alex Cole	.05
539	Greg Hibbard	.05
540	Gene Larkin	.05
541	Jeff Reardon	.05
542	Felix Jose	.05
543	Jimmy Key	.10
544	Reggie Jefferson	.05
545	Gregg Jefferies	.05
546	Dave Stewart	.05
547	Tim Wallach	.05
548	Spike Owen	.05
549	Tommy Greene	.05
550	Fernando Valenzuela	.05
551	Rich Amaral	.05
552	Bret Barberie	.05
553	Edgar Martinez	.08
554	Jim Abbott	.05
555	Frank Thomas	2.00
556	Wade Boggs	.20
557	Tom Henke	.05
558	Milt Thompson	.05
559	Lloyd McClendon	.05
560	Vinny Castilla	.05
561	Ricky Jordan	.05

562	Andujar Cedeno	.05
563	Greg Vaughn	.05
564	Cecil Fielder	.15
565	Kirby Puckett	.50
566	Mark McGwire	2.00
567	Barry Bonds	.40
568	Jody Reed	.05
569	Todd Zeile	.05
570	Mark Carreon	.05
571	Joe Girardi	.05
572	Luis Gonzalez	.05
573	Mark Grace	.15
574	Rafael Palmeiro	.15
575	Darryl Strawberry	.10
576	Will Clark	.25
577	Fred McGriff	.20
578	Kevin Reimer	.05
579	Dave Righetti	.05
580	Juan Bell	.05
581	Jeff Brantley	.05
582	Brian Hunter	.05
583	Tim Naehring	.05
584	Glenallen Hill	.05
585	Cal Ripken, Jr.	1.50
586	Albert Belle	.40
587	Robin Yount	.20
588	Chris Bosio	.05
589	Pete Smith	.05
590	Chuck Carr	.05
591	Jeff Blauser	.05
592	Kevin McReynolds	.05
593	Andres Galarraga	.15
594	Kevin Maas	.05
595	Eric Davis	.05
596	Brian Jordan	.10
597	Tim Raines	.05
598	Rick Wilkins	.05
599	Steve Cooke	.05
600	Mike Gallego	.05
601	Mike Munoz	.05
602	Luis Rivera	.05
603	Junior Ortiz	.05
604	Brent Mayne	.05
605	Luis Alicea	.05
606	Damon Berryhill	.05
607	Dave Henderson	.05
608	Kirk McCaskill	.05
609	Jeff Fassero	.05
610	Mike Harkey	.05
611	Francisco Cabrera	.05
612	Rey Sanchez	.05
613	Scott Servais	.05
614	Darrin Fletcher	.05
615	Felix Fermin	.05
616	Kevin Seitzer	.05
617	Bob Scanlan	.05
618	Billy Hatcher	.05
619	John Vander Wal	.05
620	Joe Hesketh	.05
621	Hector Villanueva	.05
622	Randy Milligan	.05
623	Tony Tarasco	.15
624	Russ Swan	.05
625	Willie Wilson	.05
626	Frank Tanana	.05
627	Pete O'Brien	.05
628	Lenny Webster	.05
629	Mark Clark	.05
630	Checklist 526-630(Roger Clemens)	.15
631	Alex Arias	.05
632	Chris Gwynn	.05
633	Tom Bolton	.05
634	Greg Briley	.05
635	Kent Bottenfield	.05
636	Kelly Downs	.05
637	Manuel Lee	.05
638	Al Leiter	.05
639	Jeff Gardner	.05
640	Mike Gardiner	.05
641	Mark Gardner	.05
642	Jeff Branson	.05
643	Paul Wagner	.05
644	Sean Berry	.05
645	Phil Hiatt	.05
646	Kevin Mitchell	.05
647	Charlie Hayes	.05
648	Jim Deshaies	.05
649	Dan Pasqua	.05
650	Mike Maddux	.05
651	Domingo Martinez	.10
652	Greg McMichael	.10
653	Eric Wedge	.05
654	Mark Whiten	.05
655	Bobby Kelly	.05
656	Julio Franco	.05

657	Gene Harris	.05
658	Pete Schourek	.05
659	Mike Bielecki	.05
660	Ricky Gutierrez	.05
661	Chris Hammond	.05
662	Tim Scott	.05
663	Norm Charlton	.05
664	Doug Drabek	.05
665	Dwight Gooden	.10
666	Jim Gott	.05
667	Randy Myers	.05
668	Darren Holmes	.05
669	Tim Spehr	.05
670	Bruce Ruffin	.05
671	Bobby Thigpen	.05
672	Tony Fernandez	.05
673	Darrin Jackson	.05
674	Gregg Olson	.05
675	Rob Dibble	.05
676	Howard Johnson	.05
677	*Mike Lansing*	.15
678	Charlie Leibrandt	.05
679	Kevin Bass	.05
680	Hubie Brooks	.05
681	Scott Brosius	.05
682	Randy Knorr	.05
683	Dante Bichette	.15
684	Bryan Harvey	.05
685	Greg Gohr	.05
686	Willie Banks	.05
687	Robb Nen	.05
688	Mike Scioscia	.05
689	John Farrell	.05
690	John Candelaria	.05
691	Damon Buford	.05
692	Todd Worrell	.05
693	Pat Hentgen	.05
694	John Smiley	.05
695	Greg Swindell	.05
696	Derek Bell	.10
697	Terry Jorgensen	.05
698	Jimmy Jones	.05
699	David Wells	.10
700	Dave Martinez	.05
701	Steve Bedrosian	.05
702	Jeff Russell	.05
703	Joe Magrane	.05
704	Matt Mieske	.05
705	Paul Molitor	.25
706	Dale Murphy	.10
707	Steve Howe	.05
708	Greg Gagne	.05
709	Dave Eiland	.05
710	David West	.05
711	Luis Aquino	.05
712	Joe Orsulak	.05
713	Eric Plunk	.05
714	Mike Felder	.05
715	Joe Klink	.05
716	Lonnie Smith	.05
717	Monty Fariss	.05
718	Craig Lefferts	.05
719	John Habyan	.05
720	Willie Blair	.05
721	Darnell Coles	.05
722	Mark Williamson	.05
723	Bryn Smith	.05
724	Greg W. Harris	.05
725	*Graeme Lloyd*	.10
726	Cris Carpenter	.05
727	Chico Walker	.05
728	Tracy Woodson	.05
729	Jose Uribe	.05
730	Stan Javier	.05
731	Jay Howell	.05
732	Freddie Benavides	.05
733	Jeff Reboulet	.05
734	Scott Sanderson	.05
735	Checklist 631-735(Ryne Sandberg)	.10
736	Archi Cianfrocco	.05
737	Daryl Boston	.05
738	Craig Grebeck	.05
739	Doug Dascenzo	.05
740	Gerald Young	.05
741	Candy Maldonado	.05
742	Joey Cora	.05
743	Don Slaught	.05
744	Steve Decker	.05
745	Blas Minor	.05
746	Storm Davis	.05
747	Carlos Quintana	.05
748	Vince Coleman	.05
749	Todd Burns	.05
750	Steve Frey	.05
751	Ivan Calderon	.05

752	*Steve Reed*	.10
753	Danny Jackson	.05
754	Jeff Conine	.05
755	Juan Gonzalez	.50
756	Mike Kelly	.05
757	John Doherty	.05
758	Jack Armstrong	.05
759	John Wehner	.05
760	Scott Bankhead	.05
761	Jim Tatum	.10
762	*Scott Pose*	.10
763	Andy Ashby	.05
764	Ed Sprague	.05
765	Harold Baines	.05
766	Kirk Gibson	.05
767	Troy Neel	.05
768	Dick Schofield	.05
769	Dickie Thon	.05
770	Butch Henry	.05
771	Junior Felix	.05
772	*Ken Ryan*	.10
773	Trevor Hoffman	.05
774	Phil Plantier	.05
775	Bo Jackson	.15
776	Benito Santiago	.08
777	Andre Dawson	.10
778	Bryan Hickerson	.05
779	Dennis Moeller	.05
780	Ryan Bowen	.05
781	Eric Fox	.05
782	Joe Kmak	.05
783	Mike Hampton	.05
784	*Darrell Sherman*	.10
785	J.T. Snow	.15
786	Dave Winfield	.15
787	Jim Austin	.05
788	Craig Shipley	.05
789	Greg Myers	.05
790	Todd Benzinger	.05
791	Cory Snyder	.05
792	David Segui	.05
793	Armando Reynoso	.05
794	Chili Davis	.08
795	Dave Nilsson	.05
796	Paul O'Neill	.15
797	Jerald Clark	.05
798	Jose Mesa	.05
799	Brian Holman	.05
800	Jim Eisenreich	.05
801	Mark McLemore	.05
802	Luis Sojo	.05
803	Harold Reynolds	.05
804	Dan Plesac	.05
805	Dave Stieb	.05
806	Tom Brunansky	.05
807	Kelly Gruber	.05
808	Bob Ojeda	.05
809	Dave Burba	.05
810	Joe Boever	.05
811	Jeremy Hernandez	.05
812	Angels Checklist(Tim Salmon)	.15
813	Astros Checklist(Jeff Bagwell)	.25
814	Athletics Checklist(Mark McGwire)	.75
815	Blue Jays Checklist(Roberto Alomar)	.15
816	Braves Checklist(Steve Avery)	.05
817	Brewers Checklist(Pat Listach)	.05
818	Cardinals Checklist(Gregg Jefferies)	.05
819	Cubs Checklist(Sammy Sosa)	.50
820	Dodgers Checklist(Darryl Strawberry)	.05
821	Expos Checklist(Dennis Martinez)	.05
822	Giants Checklist(Robby Thompson)	.05
823	Indians Checklist(Albert Belle)	.20
824	Mariners Checklist(Randy Johnson)	.15
825	Marlins Checklist(Nigel Wilson)	.05
826	Mets Checklist(Bobby Bonilla)	.08
827	Orioles Checklist(Glenn Davis)	.05
828	Padres Checklist(Gary Sheffield)	.10
829	Phillies Checklist(Darren Daulton)	.08

830	Pirates Checklist(Jay Bell)	.05
831	Rangers Checklist(Juan Gonzalez)	.25
832	Red Sox Checklist(Andre Dawson)	.08
833	Reds Checklist(Hal Morris)	.05
834	Rockies Checklist(David Nied)	.05
835	Royals Checklist(Felix Jose)	.05
836	Tigers Checklist(Travis Fryman)	.05
837	Twins Checklist(Shane Mack)	.05
838	White Sox Checklist(Robin Ventura)	.05
839	Yankees Checklist(Danny Tartabull)	.05
840	Checklist 736-840(Roberto Alomar)	.15
SP5	3,000 Hits(Robin Yount, George Brett)	2.00
SP6	Nolan Ryan	4.00

1993 Upper Deck Clutch Performers

Reggie Jackson has selected the players who perform the best under pressure for this 20-card insert set. Cards were available only in Series II retail packs and use the prefix R for numbering. Fronts have a black bottom panel with "Clutch Performers" printed in dark gray. Jackson's facsimile autograph is overprinted in gold foil. On back, under a second player photo, is Jackson's picture and his assessment of the player. There are a few lines of stats to support the player's selection to this exclusive company.

		MT
Complete Set (20):		15.00
Common Player:		.25
1	Roberto Alomar	1.00
2	Wade Boggs	.40
3	Barry Bonds	1.25
4	Jose Canseco	.50
5	Joe Carter	.25
6	Will Clark	.50
7	Roger Clemens	1.50
8	Dennis Eckersley	.25
9	Cecil Fielder	.40
10	Juan Gonzalez	1.50
11	Ken Griffey, Jr.	5.00
12	Rickey Henderson	.25
13	Barry Larkin	.40
14	Don Mattingly	1.50
15	Fred McGriff	.50
16	Terry Pendleton	.25
17	Kirby Puckett	1.50
18	Ryne Sandberg	1.00
19	John Smoltz	.25
20	Frank Thomas	4.00

1993 Upper Deck 5th Anniversary

Chipper Jones

This 15-card insert set replicates 15 of Upper Deck's most popular cards from its first five years. Foil stamping and a fifth-anniversary logo appear on the cards, which are otherwise reproductions of the originals. The prefix A appears before each card number. The cards were available in Series II hobby packs only.

		MT
Complete Set (15):		20.00
Common Player:		.50
1	Ken Griffey, Jr.	7.50
2	Gary Sheffield	1.00
3	Roberto Alomar	1.50
4	Jim Abbott	.50
5	Nolan Ryan	4.00
6	Juan Gonzalez	2.00
7	Dave Justice	.75
8	Carlos Baerga	.50
9	Reggie Jackson	.75
10	Eric Karros	.50
11	Chipper Jones	2.50
12	Ivan Rodriguez	1.25
13	Pat Listach	.50
14	Frank Thomas	6.00
15	Tim Salmon	.75

1993 Upper Deck Future Heroes

Kirby Puckett

This insert set includes eight player cards, a checklist and an unnumbered header card. The cards are numbered 55-63 as a continua-

tion of previous Heroes sets, but this one features more than one player; previous sets featured only one player. Card fronts have a Future Heroes logo and a facsimile autograph. The player's name is revealed using a peeled-back paper effect. Cards were randomly inserted in Series II foil packs.

		MT
Complete Set (10):		15.00
Common Player:		1.25
Header Card:		.25
55	Roberto Alomar	1.00
56	Barry Bonds	1.50
57	Roger Clemens	1.50
58	Juan Gonzalez	2.00
59	Ken Griffey, Jr.	5.00
60	Mark McGwire	5.00
61	Kirby Puckett	2.00
62	Frank Thomas	4.00
63	Checklist	.10

1993 Upper Deck Highlights

Bip Roberts

These 20 insert cards commemorate highlights from the 1992 season. Cards, which were randomly inserted in Series II packs, have a '92 Season Highlights logo on the bottom, with the player's name inside a banner trailing from the logo. The date of the significant event is under the player's name. Card backs have the logo at the top and are numbered with an HI prefix. A headline describes what highlight occurred, while the text describes the event.

		MT
Complete Set (20):		130.00
Common Player:		2.00
1	Roberto Alomar	10.00
2	Steve Avery	2.00
3	Harold Baines	2.50
4	Damon Berryhill	2.00
5	Barry Bonds	10.00
6	Bret Boone	2.00
7	George Brett	15.00
8	Francisco Cabrera	2.00
9	Ken Griffey, Jr.	40.00
10	Rickey Henderson	2.50
11	Kenny Lofton	10.00
12	Mickey Morandini	2.00
13	Eddie Murray	4.00
14	David Nied	2.00
15	Jeff Reardon	2.00
16	Bip Roberts	2.00
17	Nolan Ryan	40.00
18	Ed Sprague	2.00
19	Dave Winfield	3.00
20	Robin Yount	5.00

1993 Upper Deck Home Run Heroes

Albert Belle

This 28-card insert set features the top home run hitters from each team for 1992. Cards, inserted in Series I jumbo packs, are numbered with an HR prefix. The card fronts have "Home Run Heroes" printed vertically at the left edge and an embossed bat with the player's name and Upper Deck trademark at bottom. Backs have a purple or pink posterized photo and a few words about the player.

		MT
Complete Set (28):		15.00
Common Player:		.25
1	Juan Gonzalez	2.00
2	Mark McGwire	5.00
3	Cecil Fielder	.50
4	Fred McGriff	.50
5	Albert Belle	1.25
6	Barry Bonds	1.25
7	Joe Carter	.40
8	Darren Daulton	.25
9	Ken Griffey, Jr.	5.00
10	Dave Hollins	.25
11	Ryne Sandberg	1.00
12	George Bell	.25
13	Danny Tartabull	.25
14	Mike Devereaux	.25
15	Greg Vaughn	.25
16	Larry Walker	.75
17	Dave Justice	.50
18	Terry Pendleton	.25
19	Eric Karros	.40
20	Ray Lankford	.25
21	Matt Williams	.75
22	Eric Anthony	.15
23	Bobby Bonilla	.25
24	Kirby Puckett	2.00
25	Mike Macfarlane	.25
26	Tom Brunansky	.25
27	Paul O'Neill	.40
28	Gary Gaetti	.25

1993 Upper Deck Iooss Collection

Sports photographer Walter Iooss Jr. has captured 26 current players in this insert set featuring their candid portraits. Cards have full-bleed photos and gold foil stamping. Backs have biographical sketches and are numbered using a WI prefix. They are available in Series I retail packs.

The Upper Deck Iooss Collection

		MT
Complete Set (27):		18.00
Common Player:		.50
Header Card:		1.00
1	Tim Salmon	.75
2	Jeff Bagwell	2.00
3	Mark McGwire	5.00
4	Roberto Alomar	1.00
5	Steve Avery	.50
6	Paul Molitor	1.00
7	Ozzie Smith	1.00
8	Mark Grace	.75
9	Eric Karros	.50
10	Delino DeShields	.50
11	Will Clark	.75
12	Albert Belle	1.25
13	Ken Griffey, Jr.	5.00
14	Howard Johnson	.50
15	Cal Ripken, Jr.	5.00
16	Fred McGriff	.75
17	Darren Daulton	.50
18	Andy Van Slyke	.50
19	Nolan Ryan	5.00
20	Wade Boggs	.75
21	Barry Larkin	.75
22	George Brett	1.50
23	Cecil Fielder	.50
24	Kirby Puckett	2.00
25	Frank Thomas	4.00
26	Don Mattingly	2.00

1993 Upper Deck On Deck

These UV-coated cards feature 25 of the game's top players. Each card has a full-bleed photo on the front and questions and answers on the back. Available only in Series II jumbo packs, the cards have a D prefix for numbering.

		MT
Complete Set (25):		24.00
Common Player:		.25
1	Jim Abbott	.25
2	Roberto Alomar	1.00
3	Carlos Baerga	.25
4	Albert Belle	1.25
5	Wade Boggs	.40
6	George Brett	1.75
7	Jose Canseco	.50
8	Will Clark	.50
9	Roger Clemens	1.50
10	Dennis Eckersley	.25
11	Cecil Fielder	.40
12	Juan Gonzalez	1.50
13	Ken Griffey, Jr.	5.00
14	Tony Gwynn	1.50
15	Bo Jackson	.50
16	Chipper Jones	2.50
17	Eric Karros	.40
18	Mark McGwire	5.00
19	Kirby Puckett	1.50
20	Nolan Ryan	4.50
21	Tim Salmon	.50
22	Ryne Sandberg	1.00
23	Darryl Strawberry	.25
24	Frank Thomas	4.00
25	Andy Van Slyke	.25

1993 Upper Deck Then And Now

This 18-card lithogram set features both Hall of Famers and current players. The cards feature a combination of four-color player photos and a holographic background. They were random inserts in both Series I and Series II packs. Numbering includes the prefix TN. A limited edition of 2,500 supersize 5" by 7" Mickey Mantle Then and Now cards was created for sale through Upper Deck Authenticated.

		MT
Complete Set (18):		50.00
Complete Series 1 (9):		25.00
Complete Series 2 (9):		25.00
Common Player:		.75
1	Wade Boggs	1.50
2	George Brett	3.00
3	Rickey Henderson	.75
4	Cal Ripken, Jr.	10.00
5	Nolan Ryan	10.00
6	Ryne Sandberg	3.00
7	Ozzie Smith	2.00
8	Darryl Strawberry	.75
9	Dave Winfield	.75
10	Dennis Eckersley	.75
11	Tony Gwynn	4.00
12	Howard Johnson	.75
13	Don Mattingly	4.00
14	Eddie Murray	1.00
15	Robin Yount	2.00
16	Reggie Jackson	1.50
17	Mickey Mantle	15.00
17a	Mickey Mantle (5" x 7")	40.00
18	Willie Mays	6.00

> Values shown reflect the market as of January, 1999. On-field performances of current players in the 1999 baseball season are not factored in.

1993 Upper Deck Triple Crown

These insert cards were available in 1993 Upper Deck Series I foil packs sold by hobby dealers. The set features 10 players who are candidates to win baseball's Triple Crown. Card fronts have a crown and the player's name at the bottom. Backs put that material at the top and explain why the player might lead the league in home runs, batting average and runs batted in.

		MT
Complete Set (10):		24.00
Common Player:		.75
1	Barry Bonds	2.00
2	Jose Canseco	1.00
3	Will Clark	1.00
4	Ken Griffey, Jr.	8.00
5	Fred McGriff	1.00
6	Kirby Puckett	3.00
7	Cal Ripken, Jr.	6.00
8	Gary Sheffield	1.00
9	Frank Thomas	6.00
10	Larry Walker	1.00

1993 Upper Deck Willie Mays Heroes

This 10-card insert set includes eight individually-titled cards, an illustrated checklist and one header card. The set is a continuation of Upper Deck's previous Heroes efforts, honoring greats such as Hank Aaron, Nolan Ryan, and Reggie Jackson, and is numbered 46-54. Cards were randomly inserted into Series I foil packs.

		MT
Complete Set (10):		5.00
Common Mays:		.50
Header Card:		3.00
46	1951 Rookie-of-the-Year	.50
47	1954 The Catch	.50
48	1956-57 30-30 Club	.50

49	1961 Four-Homer Game	.50
50	1965 Most Valuable Player	.50
51	1969 600-Home Run Club	.50
52	1972 New York Homecoming	.50
53	1979 Hall of Fame	.50
54	Checklist - Heroes 46-54	.50
		.15

1994 Upper Deck

Upper Deck's 1994 offering was a typical presentation for the company, combining high-quality regular-issue cards with innovative subsets and high-tech chase cards. Series I, besides the standard player cards, features subsets including 30 Star Rookies, with metallic borders, 10 "Fantasy Team" stars who excelled in Rotisserie League stats, 14 Home Field Advantage cards showcasing National League stadiums and hometeam stars, and, 15 stars under the age of 25 in a subset titled, "The Future is Now." Regular issue cards feature a color photo on front and a second, black-and-white version of the same photo at left in a vertically stretched format. The player's name, team and Upper Deck logo appear on front in copper foil. Backs have a color photo, recent and career major league stats and an infield-shaped hologram. Series II offered, in addition to regular cards, subsets of 14 American League Home Field Advantage cards, a group of "Classic Alumni" minor league players, a selection of "Diamond Debuts" cards and a group of "Top Prospects." Retail packaging contained a special Mickey Mantle/Ken Griffey, Jr. card which could be found bearing either one or both of the players' autographs in an edition of 1,000 each. Series II retail packs offered a chance to find an autographed version of Alex Rodriguez' Classic Alumni card.

		MT
Complete Set (550):		45.00
Complete Series 1 (280):		30.00
Complete Series 2 (270):		18.00
Common Player:		.10
Series 1 E/W Wax Box:		50.00
Series 1 Cen. Wax Box:		70.00
Series 2 E/W Wax Box:		35.00
Series 2 Cen. Wax Box:		45.00
1	Brian Anderson (Star Rookie)	.15

2	Shane Andrews (Star Rookie)	.10
3	James Baldwin (Star Rookie)	.15
4	Rich Becker (Star Rookie)	.10
5	Greg Blosser (Star Rookie)	.10
6	Ricky Bottalico (Star Rookie)	.15
7	Midre Cummings (Star Rookie)	.15
8	Carlos Delgado (Star Rookie)	.20
9	Steve Dreyer (Star Rookie)	.15
10	Joey Eischen (Star Rookie)	.15
11	Carl Everett (Star Rookie)	.10
12	Cliff Floyd (Star Rookie)	.20
13	Alex Gonzalez (Star Rookie)	.20
14	Jeff Granger (Star Rookie)	.10
15	Shawn Green (Star Rookie)	.15
16	Brian Hunter (Star Rookie)	.40
17	Butch Huskey (Star Rookie)	.15
18	Mark Hutton (Star Rookie)	.10
19	Michael Jordan (Star Rookie)	12.00
20	Steve Karsay (Star Rookie)	.15
21	Jeff McNeely (Star Rookie)	.10
22	Marc Newfield (Star Rookie)	.15
23	Manny Ramirez (Star Rookie)	1.00
24	Alex Rodriguez (Star Rookie)	12.00
25	Scott Ruffcorn (Star Rookie)	.15
26	Paul Spoljaric (Star Rookie)	.10
27	Salomon Torres (Star Rookie)	.10
28	Steve Trachsel (Star Rookie)	.15
29	Chris Turner (Star Rookie)	.10
30	Gabe White (Star Rookie)	.10
31	Randy Johnson (Fantasy Team)	.30
32	John Wetteland (Fantasy Team)	.10
33	Mike Piazza (Fantasy Team)	1.00
34	Rafael Palmeiro (Fantasy Team)	.15
35	Roberto Alomar (Fantasy Team)	.35
36	Matt Williams (Fantasy Team)	.20
37	Travis Fryman (Fantasy Team)	.10
38	Barry Bonds (Fantasy Team)	.40
39	Marquis Grissom (Fantasy Team)	.10
40	Albert Belle (Fantasy Team)	.40
41	Steve Avery (Future/Now)	.10
42	Jason Bere (Future/Now)	.10
43	Alex Fernandez (Future/Now)	.15
44	Mike Mussina (Future/Now)	.40
45	Aaron Sele (Future/Now)	.10
46	Rod Beck (Future/Now)	.10
47	Mike Piazza (Future/Now)	1.00
48	John Olerud (Future/Now)	.10
49	Carlos Baerga (Future/Now)	.10
50	Gary Sheffield (Future/Now)	.15
51	Travis Fryman (Future/Now)	.10
52	Juan Gonzalez (Future/Now)	.60
53	Ken Griffey, Jr. (Future/Now)	2.00
54	Tim Salmon (Future/Now)	.25
55	Frank Thomas (Future/Now)	2.00
56	Tony Phillips	.10
57	Julio Franco	.10
58	Kevin Mitchell	.10
59	Raul Mondesi	.50
60	Rickey Henderson	.15
61	Jay Buhner	.20
62	Bill Swift	.10
63	Brady Anderson	.15
64	Ryan Klesko	.55
65	Darren Daulton	.10
66	Damion Easley	.10
67	Mark McGwire	3.00
68	John Roper	.10
69	Dave Telgheder	.10
70	Dave Nied	.10
71	Mo Vaughn	.40
72	Tyler Green	.10
73	Dave Magadan	.10
74	Chili Davis	.10
75	Archi Cianfrocco	.10
76	Joe Girardi	.10
77	Chris Hoiles	.10

78	Ryan Bowen	.10
79	Greg Gagne	.10
80	Aaron Sele	.15
81	Dave Winfield	.15
82	Chad Curtis	.15
83	Andy Van Slyke	.10
84	Kevin Stocker	.10
85	Deion Sanders	.35
86	Bernie Williams	.50
87	John Smoltz	.20
88	Ruben Santana	.10
89	Dave Stewart	.10
90	Don Mattingly	.75
91	Joe Carter	.15
92	Ryne Sandberg	.40
93	Chris Gomez	.10
94	Tino Martinez	.20
95	Terry Pendleton	.10
96	Andre Dawson	.10
97	Wil Cordero	.10
98	Kent Hrbek	.10
99	John Olerud	.15
100	Kirt Manwaring	.10
101	Tim Bogar	.10
102	Mike Mussina	.50
103	Nigel Wilson	.10
104	Ricky Gutierrez	.10
105	Roberto Mejia	.10
106	Tom Pagnozzi	.10
107	Mike Macfarlane	.10
108	Jose Bautista	.10
109	Luis Ortiz	.10
110	Brent Gates	.10
111	Tim Salmon	.25
112	Wade Boggs	.20
113	Tripp Cromer	.10
114	Denny Hocking	.10
115	Carlos Baerga	.15
116	J.R. Phillips	.15
117	Bo Jackson	.15
118	Lance Johnson	.10
119	Bobby Jones	.20
120	Bobby Witt	.10
121	Ron Karkovice	.10
122	Jose Vizcaino	.10
123	Danny Darwin	.10
124	Eduardo Perez	.10
125	Brian Looney	.10
126	Pat Hentgen	.15
127	Frank Viola	.10
128	Darren Holmes	.10
129	Wally Whitehurst	.10
130	Matt Walbeck	.10
131	Albert Belle	.75
132	Steve Cooke	.10
133	Kevin Appier	.15
134	Joe Oliver	.10
135	Benji Gil	.10
136	Steve Buechele	.10
137	Devon White	.10
138	Sterling Hitchcock	.10
139	Phil Leftwich	.10
140	Jose Canseco	.35
141	Rick Aguilera	.10
142	Rod Beck	.10
143	Jose Rijo	.10
144	Tom Glavine	.20
145	Phil Plantier	.10
146	Jason Bere	.10
147	Jamie Moyer	.10
148	Wes Chamberlain	.10
149	Glenallen Hill	.10
150	Mark Whiten	.10
151	Bret Barberie	.10
152	Chuck Knoblauch	.20
153	Trevor Hoffman	.10
154	Rick Wilkins	.10
155	Juan Gonzalez	1.00
156	Ozzie Guillen	.10
157	Jim Eisenreich	.10
158	Pedro Astacio	.10
159	Joe Magrane	.10
160	Ryan Thompson	.10
161	Jose Lind	.10
162	Jeff Conine	.10
163	Todd Benzinger	.10
164	Roger Salkeld	.10
165	Gary DiSarcina	.10
166	Kevin Gross	.10
167	Charlie Hayes	.10
168	Tim Costo	.10
169	Wally Joyner	.10
170	Johnny Ruffin	.10
171	Kirk Rueter	.10
172	Len Dykstra	.10
173	Ken Hill	.10

No.	Player	Price
174	Mike Bordick	.10
175	Billy Hall	.10
176	Rob Butler	.10
177	Jay Bell	.10
178	Jeff Kent	.10
179	David Wells	.10
180	Dean Palmer	.10
181	Mariano Duncan	.10
182	Orlando Merced	.10
183	Brett Butler	.10
184	Milt Thompson	.10
185	Chipper Jones	1.25
186	Paul O'Neill	.15
187	Mike Greenwell	.10
188	Harold Baines	.10
189	Todd Stottlemyre	.15
190	Jeromy Burnitz	.10
191	Rene Arocha	.10
192	Jeff Fassero	.12
193	Robby Thompson	.10
194	Greg W. Harris	.10
195	Todd Van Poppel	.10
196	Jose Guzman	.10
197	Shane Mack	.10
198	Carlos Garcia	.10
199	Kevin Roberson	.10
200	David McCarty	.10
201	Alan Trammell	.15
202	Chuck Carr	.10
203	Tommy Greene	.10
204	Wilson Alvarez	.15
205	Dwight Gooden	.15
206	Tony Tarasco	.15
207	Darren Lewis	.10
208	Eric Karros	.15
209	Chris Hammond	.10
210	Jeffrey Hammonds	.15
211	Rich Amaral	.10
212	Danny Tartabull	.10
213	Jeff Russell	.10
214	Dave Staton	.10
215	Kenny Lofton	.55
216	Manuel Lee	.10
217	Brian Koelling	.10
218	Scott Lydy	.10
219	Tony Gwynn	.75
220	Cecil Fielder	.15
221	Royce Clayton	.10
222	Reggie Sanders	.15
223	Brian Jordan	.10
224	Ken Griffey, Jr.	3.00
224a	Ken Griffey, Jr. (promo card)	4.00
225	Fred McGriff	.35
226	Felix Jose	.10
227	Brad Pennington	.10
228a	Chris Bosio ("ARINERS")	.10
228b	Chris Bosio ("MARINERS")	.10
229	Mike Stanley	.10
230	Willie Greene	.10
231	Alex Fernandez	.15
232	Brad Ausmus	.10
233	Darrell Whitmore	.10
234	Marcus Moore	.10
235	Allen Watson	.15
236	Jose Offerman	.10
237	Rondell White	.25
238	Jeff King	.10
239	Luis Alicea	.10
240	Dan Wilson	.10
241	Ed Sprague	.10
242	Todd Hundley	.20
243	Al Martin	.10
244	Mike Lansing	.10
245	Ivan Rodriguez	.50
246	Dave Fleming	.10
247	John Doherty	.10
248	Mark McLemore	.10
249	Bob Hamelin	.10
250	Curtis Pride	.20
251	Zane Smith	.10
252	Eric Young	.10
253	Brian McRae	.10
254	Tim Raines	.10
255	Javier Lopez	.25
256	Melvin Nieves	.10
257	Randy Myers	.10
258	Willie McGee	.10
259	Jimmy Key	.15
260	Tom Candiotti	.10
261	Eric Davis	.10
262	Craig Paquette	.10
263	Robin Ventura	.15
264	Pat Kelly	.10
265	Gregg Jefferies	.10
266	Cory Snyder	.10
267	Dave Justice (Home Field Advantage)	.25
268	Sammy Sosa (Home Field Advantage)	1.50
269	Barry Larkin (Home Field Advantage)	.15
270	Andres Galarraga (Home Field Advantage)	.15
271	Gary Sheffield (Home Field Advantage)	.15
272	Jeff Bagwell (Home Field Advantage)	.50
273	Mike Piazza (Home Field Advantage)	.75
274	Larry Walker (Home Field Advantage)	.20
275	Bobby Bonilla (Home Field Advantage)	.10
276	John Kruk (Home Field Advantage)	.10
277	Jay Bell (Home Field Advantage)	.10
278	Ozzie Smith (Home Field Advantage)	.25
279	Tony Gwynn (Home Field Advantage)	.40
280	Barry Bonds (Home Field Advantage)	.40
281	Cal Ripken, Jr. (Home Field Advantage)	2.00
282	Mo Vaughn (Home Field Advantage)	.40
283	Tim Salmon (Home Field Advantage)	.25
284	Frank Thomas (Home Field Advantage)	2.00
285	Albert Belle (Home Field Advantage)	.40
286	Cecil Fielder (Home Field Advantage)	.20
287	Wally Joyner (Home Field Advantage)	.10
288	Greg Vaughn (Home Field Advantage)	.10
289	Kirby Puckett (Home Field Advantage)	.75
290	Don Mattingly (Home Field Advantage)	.75
291	Terry Steinbach (Home Field Advantage)	.10
292	Ken Griffey, Jr. (Home Field Advantage)	2.00
293	Juan Gonzalez (Home Field Advantage)	.75
294	Paul Molitor (Home Field Advantage)	.25
295	Tavo Alvarez (Classic Alumni)	.15
296	Matt Brunson (Classic Alumni)	.15
297	Shawn Green (Classic Alumni)	.15
298	Alex Rodriguez (Classic Alumni)	3.00
299	Shannon Stewart (Classic Alumni)	.12
300	Frank Thomas	2.50
301	Mickey Tettleton	.10
302	Pedro Munoz	.10
303	Jose Valentin	.10
304	Orestes Destrade	.10
305	Pat Listach	.10
306	Scott Brosius	.10
307	Kurt Miller	.10
308	Rob Dibble	.10
309	Mike Blowers	.10
310	Jim Abbott	.10
311	Mike Jackson	.10
312	Craig Biggio	.15
313	Kurt Abbott	.20
314	Chuck Finley	.10
315	Andres Galarraga	.20
316	Mike Moore	.10
317	Doug Strange	.10
318	Pedro J. Martinez	.15
319	Kevin McReynolds	.10
320	Greg Maddux	1.60
321	Mike Henneman	.10
322	Scott Leius	.10
323	John Franco	.10
324	Jeff Blauser	.10
325	Kirby Puckett	.75
326	Darryl Hamilton	.10
327	John Smiley	.10
328	Derrick May	.10
329	Jose Vizcaino	.10
330	Randy Johnson	.50
331	Jack Morris	.10
332	Graeme Lloyd	.10
333	Dave Valle	.10
334	Greg Myers	.10
335	John Wetteland	.10
336	Jim Gott	.10
337	Tim Naehring	.10
338	Mike Kelly	.10
339	Jeff Montgomery	.10
340	Rafael Palmeiro	.20
341	Eddie Murray	.25
342	Xavier Hernandez	.10
343	Bobby Munoz	.10
344	Bobby Bonilla	.10
345	Travis Fryman	.15
346	Steve Finley	.10
347	Chris Sabo	.10
348	Armando Reynoso	.10
349	Ramon Martinez	.15
350	Will Clark	.35
351	Moises Alou	.15
352	Jim Thome	.50
353	Bob Tewksbury	.10
354	Andujar Cedeno	.10
355	Orel Hershiser	.10
356	Mike Devereaux	.10
357	Mike Perez	.10
358	Dennis Martinez	.10
359	Dave Nilsson	.10
360	Ozzie Smith	.40
361	Eric Anthony	.05
362	Scott Sanders	.10
363	Paul Sorrento	.10
364	Tim Belcher	.10
365	Dennis Eckersley	.10
366	Mel Rojas	.10
367	Tom Henke	.10
368	Randy Tomlin	.10
369	B.J. Surhoff	.10
370	Larry Walker	.20
371	Joey Cora	.10
372	Mike Harkey	.10
373	John Valentin	.10
374	Doug Jones	.10
375	Dave Justice	.20
376	Vince Coleman	.10
377	David Hulse	.10
378	Kevin Seitzer	.10
379	Pete Harnisch	.10
380	Ruben Sierra	.10
381	Mark Lewis	.10
382	Bip Roberts	.10
383	Paul Wagner	.10
384	Stan Javier	.10
385	Barry Larkin	.15
386	Mark Portugal	.10
387	Roberto Kelly	.10
388	Andy Benes	.15
389	Felix Fermin	.10
390	Marquis Grissom	.15
391	Troy Neel	.10
392	Chad Kreuter	.10
393	Gregg Olson	.10
394	Charles Nagy	.10
395	Jack McDowell	.10
396	Luis Gonzalez	.10
397	Benito Santiago	.10
398	Chris James	.10
399	Terry Mulholland	.10
400	Barry Bonds	.60
401	Joe Grahe	.10
402	Duane Ward	.10
403	John Burkett	.10
404	Scott Servais	.10
405	Bryan Harvey	.10
406	Bernard Gilkey	.10
407	Greg McMichael	.10
408	Tim Wallach	.10
409	Ken Caminiti	.20
410	John Kruk	.10
411	Darrin Jackson	.10
412	Mike Gallego	.10
413	David Cone	.15
414	Lou Whitaker	.10
415	Sandy Alomar Jr.	.10
416	Bill Wegman	.10
417	Pat Borders	.10
418	Roger Pavlik	.10
419	Pete Smith	.10
420	Steve Avery	.10
421	David Segui	.10
422	Rheal Cormier	.10
423	Harold Reynolds	.10
424	Edgar Martinez	.15
425	Cal Ripken, Jr.	3.00

426	Jaime Navarro	.10
427	Sean Berry	.10
428	Bret Saberhagen	.10
429	Bob Welch	.10
430	Juan Guzman	.10
431	Cal Eldred	.10
432	Dave Hollins	.10
433	Sid Fernandez	.10
434	Willie Banks	.10
435	Darryl Kile	.10
436	Henry Rodriguez	.10
437	Tony Fernandez	.10
438	Walt Weiss	.10
439	Kevin Tapani	.10
440	Mark Grace	.15
441	Brian Harper	.10
442	Kent Mercker	.10
443	Anthony Young	.10
444	Todd Zeile	.10
445	Greg Vaughn	.10
446	Ray Lankford	.10
447	David Weathers	.10
448	Bret Boone	.10
449	Charlie Hough	.10
450	Roger Clemens	.75
451	Mike Morgan	.10
452	Doug Drabek	.10
453	Danny Jackson	.10
454	Dante Bichette	.35
455	Roberto Alomar	.55
456	Ben McDonald	.10
457	Kenny Rogers	.10
458	Bill Gullickson	.10
459	Darrin Fletcher	.10
460	Curt Schilling	.15
461	Billy Hatcher	.10
462	Howard Johnson	.10
463	Mickey Morandini	.10
464	Frank Castillo	.10
465	Delino DeShields	.10
466	Gary Gaetti	.10
467	Steve Farr	.10
468	Roberto Hernandez	.10
469	Jack Armstrong	.10
470	Paul Molitor	.30
471	Melido Perez	.10
472	Greg Hibbard	.10
473	Jody Reed	.10
474	Tom Gordon	.10
475	Gary Sheffield	.20
476	John Jaha	.10
477	Shawon Dunston	.15
478	Reggie Jefferson	.10
479	Don Slaught	.10
480	Jeff Bagwell	.75
481	Tim Pugh	.10
482	Kevin Young	.10
483	Ellis Burks	.15
484	Greg Swindell	.10
485	Mark Langston	.10
486	Omar Vizquel	.10
487	Kevin Brown	.15
488	Terry Steinbach	.10
489	Mark Lemke	.10
490	Matt Williams	.30
491	Pete Incaviglia	.10
492	Karl Rhodes	.10
493	*Shawn Green*	.15
494	Hal Morris	.10
495	Derek Bell	.10
496	Luis Polonia	.10
497	Otis Nixon	.10
498	Ron Darling	.10
499	Mitch Williams	.10
500	Mike Piazza	1.50
501	Pat Meares	.10
502	Scott Cooper	.10
503	Scott Erickson	.10
504	Jeff Juden	.10
505	Lee Smith	.10
506	Bobby Ayala	.10
507	Dave Henderson	.10
508	Erik Hanson	.10
509	Bob Wickman	.10
510	Sammy Sosa	1.50
511	Hector Carrasco (Diamond Debuts)	.10
512	Tim Davis (Diamond Debuts)	.10
513	Joey Hamilton (Diamond Debuts)	.40
514	Robert Eenhoorn (Diamond Debuts)	.15
515	Jorge Fabregas (Diamond Debuts)	.10

516	Tim Hyers (Diamond Debuts)	.10
517	John Hudek (Diamond Debuts)	.15
518	*James Mouton* (Diamond Debuts)	.20
519	Herbert Perry (Diamond Debuts)	.10
520	*Chan Ho Park* (Diamond Debuts)	1.00
521	Bill VanLandingham (Diamond Debuts)	.15
522	Paul Shuey (Diamond Debuts)	.15
523	*Ryan Hancock* (Top Prospects)	.20
524	*Billy Wagner* (Top Prospects)	.75
525	Jason Giambi (Top Prospects)	.40
526	*Jose Silva* (Top Prospects)	.15
527	*Terrell Wade* (Top Prospects)	.25
528	Todd Dunn (Top Prospects)	.15
529	*Alan Benes* (Top Prospects)	1.50
530	*Brooks Kieschnick* (Top Prospects)	.75
531	Todd Hollandsworth (Top Prospects)	.25
532	*Brad Fullmer* (Top Prospects)	2.00
533	*Steve Soderstrom* (Top Prospects)	.10
534	Daron Kirkreit (Top Prospects)	.10
535	*Arquimedez Pozo* (Top Prospects)	.15
536	Charles Johnson (Top Prospects)	.20
537	Preston Wilson (Top Prospects)	.15
538	Alex Ochoa (Top Prospects)	.25
539	*Derrek Lee* (Top Prospects)	2.50
540	*Wayne Gomes* (Top Prospects)	.15
541	*Jermaine Allensworth* (Top Prospects)	.50
542	*Mike Bell* (Top Prospects)	.45
543	*Trot Nixon* (Top Prospects)	.20
544	Pokey Reese (Top Prospects)	.15
545	*Neifi Perez* (Top Prospects)	1.00
546	Johnny Damon (Top Prospects)	.25
547	Matt Brunson (Top Prospects)	.15
548	LaTroy Hawkins (Top Prospects)	.25
549	*Eddie Pearson* (Top Prosepcts)	.15
550	Derek Jeter (Top Prospects)	2.00
A298	Alex Rodriguez (autographed)	200.00
MM1	(Mickey Mantle, Ken Griffey Jr.) (Mantle autograph)	400.00
KG1	(Mickey Mantle, Ken Griffey Jr.) (Griffey autograph)	250.00
GM1	(Mickey Mantle, Ken Griffey Jr.) (both autographs)	1000.

1994 Upper Deck Diamond Collection

The premium chase cards in 1994 Upper Deck Diamond Collection cards are a series of Diamond Collection cards issued in regional subsets. Ten cards are found unique to each of three geo-graphic areas of distribution. Western region cards carry a "W" prefix to the card number, Central cards have a "C" prefix and Eastern cards have an "E" prefix. The region is also indicated in silver foil printing on the front of the card, with a large "W, C" or "E" in a compass design. The player's name and team are presented in a foil strip at bottom. A "Diamond Collection" logo is shown in embossed-look typography in the background. Diamond Collection cards are inserted only in hobby packs.

		MT
Complete Set (30):		325.00
Common Player:		3.00
Complete Central (10):		150.00
CENTRAL REGION		
1C	Michael Jordan	50.00
2C	Jeff Bagwell	15.00
3C	Barry Larkin	5.00
4C	Kirby Puckett	18.00
5C	Manny Ramirez	10.00
6C	Ryne Sandberg	10.00
7C	Ozzie Smith	10.00
8C	Frank Thomas	40.00
9C	Andy Van Slyke	3.00
10C	Robin Yount	6.00
Complete East (10):		75.00
EASTERN REGION		
1E	Roberto Alomar	7.00
2E	Roger Clemens	10.00
3E	Len Dykstra	3.00
4E	Cecil Fielder	4.00
5E	Cliff Floyd	3.00
6E	Dwight Gooden	3.00
7E	Dave Justice	5.00
8E	Don Mattingly	15.00
9E	Cal Ripken, Jr.	35.00
10E	Gary Sheffield	7.00
Complete West (10):		100.00
WESTERN REGION		
1W	Barry Bonds	10.00
2W	Andres Galarraga	4.00
3W	Juan Gonzalez	20.00
4W	Ken Griffey, Jr.	50.00
5W	Tony Gwynn	12.00
6W	Rickey Henderson	3.00
7W	Bo Jackson	4.00
8W	Mark McGwire	50.00
9W	Mike Piazza	20.00
10W	Tim Salmon	5.00

1994 Upper Deck Electric Diamond

Each of the regular-issue and subset cards from 1994 Upper Deck was also produced in a limited edition premium pack insert "Electric Diamond" version. Where the regular cards have the Upper Deck logo, player and team name in copper foil, the Electric Diamond version has those elements in silver prismatic foil, along with an "Electric Diamond" identification line next to the UD logo. Backs are identical to the regular cards. (Many of the first series cards can be found with player names on back in either silver or copper.) Electric Diamond cards are found, on average, about every other pack.

	MT
Complete Set (550):	150.00
Complete Series 1 (1-280):	90.00
Complete Series 2 (281-550):	60.00
Common Player:	.20
(Star cards valued at 3X-5X corresponding cards in regular Upper Deck issue)	

1994 Upper Deck Jumbo Checklists

Each hobby foil box of 1994 Upper Deck cards contains one jumbo checklist card. Each of the 5" x 7" cards features Ken Griffey, Jr. There is a large color action photo along with a hologram of the player on front, highlighted by copper-foil printing. Backs have one of four checklists and are numbered with a CL prefix.

		MT
Complete Set (4):		12.00
Common Griffey Jr.:		3.00
1CL	Numerical Checklist(Ken Griffey, Jr.)	3.00
2CL	Alphabetical Checklist(Ken Griffey, Jr.)	3.00
3CL	Team Checklist(Ken Griffey, Jr.)	3.00
4CL	Insert Checklist(Ken Griffey, Jr.)	3.00

1994 Upper Deck Mantle Heroes

Mickey Mantle Baseball Hero is a 10-card set that chronicles his career. The cards, which include an unnumbered header card, were randomly inserted into both hobby and retail packs of Series II Upper Deck Baseball. This set starts with his rookie season in 1951 and concludes with his induction into The Hall of Fame. It is numbered 64-72 and was the eighth in the continuing "Baseball Heroes" series, which began in 1990.

		MT
Complete Set (10):		75.00
Common Mantle:		8.00
64	1951 - The Early Years(Mickey Mantle)	8.00
65	1953 - Tape Measure Home Runs(Mickey Mantle)	8.00

66	1956 - Triple Crown Season(Mickey Mantle)	8.00
67	1957 - 2nd Consecutive MVP(Mickey Mantle)	8.00
68	1961 - Chases The Babe(Mickey Mantle)	8.00
69	1964 - Series Home Run Record(Mickey Mantle)	8.00
70	1967 - 500th Home Run(Mickey Mantle)	8.00
----	Header card(Mickey Mantle)	8.00

1994 Upper Deck Mickey Mantle's Long Shots

Retail packaging was the exclusive venue for this insert set of contemporary long-ball sluggers. Horizontal fronts feature game-action photos with holographic foil rendering of the background. In one of the lower corners appears the logo "1994 Mickey Mantle's Long Shots". Backs have a color player photo at top, with a photo of Mantle beneath and a statement by him about the featured player. Previous season and career stats are included. Cards are numbered with an "MM" prefix. Besides the 20 current player cards there is a Mickey Mantle card and two trade cards which could be redeemed for complete insert card sets.

		MT
Complete Set (21):		50.00
Common Player:		.75
(1)	Mickey Mantle Trade Card (silver): (Redeemable for 21-card Mantle Long Shots set)	4.00
(2)	Mickey Mantle Trade Card (blue): (Redeemable for Electric Diamond version Mantle Long Shots set)	4.00
1MM	Jeff Bagwell	4.00
2MM	Albert Belle	3.00
3MM	Barry Bonds	3.00
4MM	Jose Canseco	1.50
5MM	Joe Carter	1.00
6MM	Carlos Delgado	1.00
7MM	Cecil Fielder	1.00
8MM	Cliff Floyd	.75
9MM	Juan Gonzalez	5.00
10MM	Ken Griffey, Jr.	12.00
11MM	Dave Justice	1.50
12MM	Fred McGriff	1.50
13MM	Mark McGwire	12.00
14MM	Dean Palmer	.75
15MM	Mike Piazza	7.50
16MM	Manny Ramirez	2.50
17MM	Tim Salmon	1.00
18MM	Frank Thomas	10.00
19MM	Mo Vaughn	2.50
20MM	Matt Williams	1.50
21MM	Mickey Mantle (Header)	12.00

A player's name in *italic* type indicates a rookie card.

1994 Upper Deck Next Generation

Next Generation linked 20 of the top current stars with all-time greats, using the HoloView card printing technology. Next Generation trade cards could be redeemed for a complete set matching the cards found in retail packs. This insert set was inserted at a rate of one per 20 packs, while the Trade Card was inserted one per case.

		MT
Complete Set (18):		100.00
Common Player:		1.50
1	Roberto Alomar	8.00
2	Carlos Delgado	2.00
3	Cliff Floyd	2.00
4	Alex Gonzalez	1.50
5	Juan Gonzalez	12.00
6	Ken Griffey, Jr.	30.00
7	Jeffrey Hammonds	1.50
8	Michael Jordan	35.00
9	Dave Justice	3.00
10	Ryan Klesko	6.00
11	Javier Lopez	3.00
12	Raul Mondesi	4.00
13	Mike Piazza	15.00
14	Kirby Puckett	10.00
15	Manny Ramirez	8.00
16	Alex Rodriguez	30.00
17	Tim Salmon	4.00
18	Gary Sheffield	4.00

1994 Upper Deck SP Insert

Fifteen SP Preview cards were inserted into Series II packs of Upper Deck baseball. The cards were inserted with regional distribution and gave collectors a chance to see what the SP super-premium cards would look like. There were five cards available in the East, Central and West and were inserted at a rate of about one per 36 packs. Most of the preview inserts have different front and back photos than the regularly issued SPs, along with other differences in typography and graphics elements.

		MT
Complete Set (15):		130.00
Common Player:		.75
EASTERN REGION		
1	Roberto Alomar	4.00
2	Cliff Floyd	.75
3	Javier Lopez	2.00
4	Don Mattingly	10.00
5	Cal Ripken Jr.	20.00
CENTRAL REGION		
1	Jeff Bagwell	5.00
2	Michael Jordan	25.00
3	Kirby Puckett	7.50
4	Manny Ramirez	3.50
5	Frank Thomas	15.00
WESTERN REGION		
1	Barry Bonds	9.00
2	Juan Gonzalez	10.00
3	Ken Griffey Jr.	25.00
4	Mike Piazza	10.00
5	Tim Salmon	2.50
1	Roberto Alomar	5.75
2	Cliff Floyd	1.50
3	Javier Lopez	3.00
4	Don Mattingly	7.50
5	Cal Ripken, Jr.	22.00
1	Jeff Bagwell	6.75
2	Michael Jordan	28.00
3	Kirby Puckett	6.75
4	Manny Ramirez	6.00
5	Frank Thomas	20.00
1	Barry Bonds	5.25
2	Juan Gonzalez	7.50
3	Ken Griffey, Jr.	24.00
4	Mike Piazza	9.00
5	Tim Salmon	3.00

1995 Upper Deck

Chicago White Sox – OF

Issued in two series of 225 base cards each, with loads of subsets and inserts, the 1995 Upper Deck set was a strong collector favorite from the outset. Basic cards feature a borderless front photo with the player's name and UD logo in bronze foil. Backs have another large color photo, recent stats and career totals and appropriate logos, along with the infield-shaped holo-

gram. Subsets in each series include Star Rookies and Top Prospects, each with special designs highlighting the game's young stars. Series I has a "'90s Midpoint Analysis" subset studying the decade's superstars, and Series II has another hot rookies' subset, Diamond Debuts. The set closes with a five-card "Final Tribute" subset summarizing the careers of five recently retired superstars. Retail and hobby versions were sold with each featuring some unique insert cards. Basic packaging of each type was the 12-card foil pack at $1.99, though several other configurations were also released.

		MT
Complete Set (450):		45.00
Complete Series 1 (225):		20.00
Complete Series 2 (225):		25.00
Common Player:		.10
Series 1 or 2 Wax Box:		55.00
1	Ruben Rivera (Top Prospect)	1.00
2	Bill Pulsipher (Top Prospect)	.20
3	Ben Grieve (Top Prospect)	3.00
4	Curtis Goodwin (Top Prospect)	.15
5	Damon Hollins (Top Prospect)	.10
6	Todd Greene (Top Prospect)	.15
7	Glenn Williams (Top Prospect)	.10
8	Bret Wagner (Top Prospect)	.10
9	*Karim Garcia* (Top Prospect)	2.00
10	Nomar Garciaparra (Top Prospect)	3.00
11	*Raul Casanova* (Top Prospect)	.50
12	Matt Smith (Top Prospect)	.15
13	Paul Wilson (Top Prospect)	.20
14	Jason Isringhausen (Top Prospect)	.40
15	Reid Ryan (Top Prospect)	.25
16	Lee Smith	.10
17	Chili Davis	.10
18	Brian Anderson	.10
19	Gary DiSarcina	.10
20	Bo Jackson	.15
21	Chuck Finley	.10
22	Darryl Kile	.10
23	Shane Reynolds	.10
24	Tony Eusebio	.10
25	Craig Biggio	.15
26	Doug Drabek	.10
27	Brian L. Hunter	.20
28	James Mouton	.10
29	Geronimo Berroa	.10
30	Rickey Henderson	.10
31	Steve Karsay	.10
32	Steve Ontiveros	.10
33	Ernie Young	.10
34	Dennis Eckersley	.10
35	Mark McGwire	4.00
36	Dave Stewart	.10
37	Pat Hentgen	.10
38	Carlos Delgado	.20
39	Joe Carter	.25
40	Roberto Alomar	.75
41	John Olerud	.10
42	Devon White	.10
43	Roberto Kelly	.10
44	Jeff Blauser	.10
45	Fred McGriff	.40
46	Tom Glavine	.20
47	Mike Kelly	.10
48	Javy Lopez	.20
49	Greg Maddux	2.00
50	Matt Mieske	.10
51	Troy O'Leary	.15
52	Jeff Cirillo	.15
53	Cal Eldred	.10
54	Pat Listach	.10
55	Jose Valentin	.15
56	John Mabry	.10
57	Bob Tewksbury	.10
58	Brian Jordan	.15

59	Gregg Jefferies	.10
60	Ozzie Smith	.40
61	Geronimo Pena	.10
62	Mark Whiten	.10
63	Rey Sanchez	.10
64	Willie Banks	.10
65	Mark Grace	.20
66	Randy Myers	.10
67	Steve Trachsel	.15
68	Derrick May	.10
69	Brett Butler	.10
70	Eric Karros	.10
71	Tim Wallach	.10
72	Delino DeShields	.10
73	Darren Dreifort	.10
74	Orel Hershiser	.10
75	Billy Ashley	.15
76	Sean Berry	.10
77	Ken Hill	.10
78	John Wetteland	.10
79	Moises Alou	.10
80	Cliff Floyd	.10
81	Marquis Grissom	.15
82	Larry Walker	.20
83	Rondell White	.25
84	William VanLandingham	.20
85	Matt Williams	.40
86	Rod Beck	.10
87	Darren Lewis	.10
88	Robby Thompson	.10
89	Darryl Strawberry	.10
90	Kenny Lofton	.75
91	Charles Nagy	.10
92	Sandy Alomar Jr.	.10
93	Mark Clark	.10
94	Dennis Martinez	.10
95	Dave Winfield	.15
96	Jim Thome	.40
97	Manny Ramirez	.75
98	Goose Gossage	.10
99	Tino Martinez	.20
100	Ken Griffey Jr.	3.00
100a	Ken Griffey Jr. (overprinted "For Promotional Use Only")	3.00
101	Greg Maddux (Analysis: '90s Midpoint)	1.00
102	Randy Johnson (Analysis: '90s Midpoint)	.20
103	Barry Bonds (Analysis: '90s Midpoint)	.30
104	Juan Gonzalez (Analysis: '90s Midpoint)	.50
105	Frank Thomas (Analysis: '90s Midpoint)	1.50
106	Matt Williams (Analysis: '90s Midpoint)	.20
107	Paul Molitor (Analysis: '90s Midpoint)	.25
108	Fred McGriff (Analysis: '90s Midpoint)	.25
109	Carlos Baerga (Analysis: '90s Midpoint)	.10
110	Ken Griffey Jr. (Analysis: '90s Midpoint)	1.50
111	Reggie Jefferson	.10
112	Randy Johnson	.40
113	Marc Newfield	.15
114	Robb Nen	.10
115	Jeff Conine	.10
116	Kurt Abbott	.10
117	Charlie Hough	.10
118	Dave Weathers	.10
119	Juan Castillo	.10
120	Bret Saberhagen	.10
121	Rico Brogna	.10
122	John Franco	.10
123	Todd Hundley	.20
124	Jason Jacome	.15
125	Bobby Jones	.10
126	Bret Barberie	.10
127	Ben McDonald	.10
128	Harold Baines	.10
129	Jeffrey Hammonds	.15
130	Mike Mussina	.40
131	Chris Hoiles	.10
132	Brady Anderson	.15
133	Eddie Williams	.10
134	Andy Benes	.15
135	Tony Gwynn	1.00
136	Bip Roberts	.10
137	Joey Hamilton	.20
138	Luis Lopez	.10
139	Ray McDavid	.10
140	Lenny Dykstra	.10
141	Mariano Duncan	.10
142	Fernando Valenzuela	.10

#	Player	Price
143	Bobby Munoz	.10
144	Kevin Stocker	.10
145	John Kruk	.10
146	Jon Lieber	.10
147	Zane Smith	.10
148	Steve Cooke	.10
149	Andy Van Slyke	.10
150	Jay Bell	.10
151	Carlos Garcia	.10
152	John Dettmer	.10
153	Darren Oliver	.10
154	Dean Palmer	.10
155	Otis Nixon	.10
156	Rusty Greer	.15
157	Rick Helling	.10
158	Jose Canseco	.40
159	Roger Clemens	1.00
160	Andre Dawson	.10
161	Mo Vaughn	.75
162	Aaron Sele	.10
163	John Valentin	.10
164	Brian Hunter	.10
165	Bret Boone	.10
166	Hector Carrasco	.10
167	Pete Schourek	.10
168	Willie Greene	.10
169	Kevin Mitchell	.10
170	Deion Sanders	.40
171	John Roper	.10
172	Charlie Hayes	.10
173	David Nied	.10
174	Ellis Burks	.15
175	Dante Bichette	.30
176	Marvin Freeman	.10
177	Eric Young	.10
178	David Cone	.20
179	Greg Gagne	.10
180	Bob Hamelin	.10
181	Wally Joyner	.10
182	Jeff Montgomery	.10
183	Jose Lind	.10
184	Chris Gomez	.10
185	Travis Fryman	.15
186	Kirk Gibson	.10
187	Mike Moore	.10
188	Lou Whitaker	.10
189	Sean Bergman	.10
190	Shane Mack	.10
191	Rick Aguilera	.10
192	Denny Hocking	.10
193	Chuck Knoblauch	.20
194	Kevin Tapani	.10
195	Kent Hrbek	.10
196	Ozzie Guillen	.10
197	Wilson Alvarez	.10
198	Tim Raines	.10
199	Scott Ruffcorn	.10
200	Michael Jordan	4.00
201	Robin Ventura	.15
202	Jason Bere	.10
203	Darrin Jackson	.10
204	Russ Davis	.15
205	Jimmy Key	.15
206	Jack McDowell	.15
207	Jim Abbott	.10
208	Paul O'Neill	.15
209	Bernie Williams	.50
210	Don Mattingly	1.00
211	Orlando Miller (Star Rookie)	.10
212	Alex Gonzalez (Star Rookie)	.20
213	Terrell Wade (Star Rookie)	.15
214	Jose Oliva (Star Rookie)	.15
215	Alex Rodriguez (Star Rookie)	3.00
216	Garret Anderson (Star Rookie)	.20
217	Alan Benes (Star Rookie)	.35
218	Armando Benitez (Star Rookie)	.10
219	Dustin Hermanson (Star Rookie)	.10
220	Charles Johnson (Star Rookie)	.20
221	Julian Tavarez (Star Rookie)	.15
222	Jason Giambi (Star Rookie)	.40
223	LaTroy Hawkins (Star Rookie)	.10
224	Todd Hollandsworth (Star Rookie)	.20
225	Derek Jeter (Star Rookie)	1.50
226	*Hideo Nomo* (Star Rookie)	3.00
227	Tony Clark (Star Rookie)	1.00
228	Roger Cedeno (Star Rookie)	.10
229	Scott Stahoviak (Star Rookie)	.10
230	Michael Tucker (Star Rookie)	.15
231	Joe Rosselli (Star Rookie)	.10
232	Antonio Osuna (Star Rookie)	.10
233	*Bobby Higginson* (Star Rookie)	1.50
234	*Mark Grudzielanek* (Star Rookie)	.50
235	Ray Durham (Star Rookie)	.30
236	Frank Rodriguez (Star Rookie)	.10
237	Quilvio Veras (Star Rookie)	.10
238	Darren Bragg (Star Rookie)	.10
239	Ugueth Urbina (Star Rookie)	.10
240	Jason Bates (Star Rookie)	.10
241	David Bell (Diamond Debuts)	.10
242	Ron Villone (Diamond Debuts)	.10
243	Joe Randa (Diamond Debuts)	.10
244	*Carlos Perez* (Diamond Debuts)	.25
245	Brad Clontz (Diamond Debuts)	.10
246	Steve Rodriguez (Diamond Debuts)	.10
247	Joe Vitiello (Diamond Debuts)	.10
248	Ozzie Timmons (Diamond Debuts)	.10
249	Rudy Pemberton (Diamond Debuts)	.10
250	Marty Cordova (Diamond Debuts)	.20
251	Tony Graffanino (Top Prospect)	.10
252	*Mark Johnson* (Top Prospect)	.25
253	*Tomas Perez* (Top Prospect)	.20
254	Jimmy Hurst (Top Prospect)	.10
255	Edgardo Alfonzo (Top Prospect)	.15
256	Jose Malave (Top Prospect)	.10
257	*Brad Radke* (Top Prospect)	.20
258	Jon Nunnally (Top Prospect)	.10
259	Dilson Torres (Top Prospect)	.20
260	Esteban Loaiza (Top Prospect)	.25
261	*Freddy Garcia* (Top Prospect)	.20
262	Don Wengert (Top Prospect)	.10
263	*Robert Person* (Top Prospect)	.10
264	*Tim Unroe* (Top Prospect)	.15
265	Juan Acevedo (Top Prospect)	.10
266	Eduardo Perez	.10
267	Tony Phillips	.10
268	Jim Edmonds	.20
269	Jorge Fabregas	.10
270	Tim Salmon	.25
271	Mark Langston	.10
272	J.T. Snow	.10
273	Phil Plantier	.10
274	Derek Bell	.10
275	Jeff Bagwell	1.00
276	Luis Gonzalez	.10
277	John Hudek	.10
278	Todd Stottlemyre	.15
279	Mark Acre	.10
280	Ruben Sierra	.10
281	Mike Bordick	.10
282	Ron Darling	.10
283	Brent Gates	.10
284	Todd Van Poppel	.10
285	Paul Molitor	.40
286	Ed Sprague	.10
287	Juan Guzman	.10
288	David Cone	.20
289	Shawn Green	.20
290	Marquis Grissom	.10
291	Kent Mercker	.10
292	Steve Avery	.10
293	Chipper Jones	1.75
294	John Smoltz	.25
295	Dave Justice	.20
296	Ryan Klesko	.60
297	Joe Oliver	.10
298	Ricky Bones	.10
299	John Jaha	.10
300	Greg Vaughn	.10
301	Dave Nilsson	.10
302	Kevin Seitzer	.10
303	Bernard Gilkey	.10
304	Allen Battle	.10
305	Ray Lankford	.10
306	Tom Pagnozzi	.10
307	Allen Watson	.10
308	Danny Jackson	.10
309	Ken Hill	.10
310	Todd Zeile	.10
311	Kevin Roberson	.10
312	Steve Buechele	.10
313	Rick Wilkins	.10
314	Kevin Foster	.10
315	Sammy Sosa	1.50
316	Howard Johnson	.10
317	Greg Hansell	.10
318	Pedro Astacio	.10
319	Rafael Bournigal	.10
320	Mike Piazza	1.75
321	Ramon Martinez	.15
322	Raul Mondesi	.40
323	Ismael Valdes	.15
324	Wil Cordero	.10
325	Tony Tarasco	.10
326	Roberto Kelly	.10
327	Jeff Fassero	.10
328	Mike Lansing	.10
329	Pedro J. Martinez	.20
330	Kirk Rueter	.10
331	Glenallen Hill	.10
332	Kirt Manwaring	.10
333	Royce Clayton	.10
334	J.R. Phillips	.10
335	Barry Bonds	.75
336	Mark Portugal	.10
337	Terry Mulholland	.10
338	Omar Vizquel	.10
339	Carlos Baerga	.10
340	Albert Belle	.75
341	Eddie Murray	.30
342	Wayne Kirby	.10
343	Chad Ogea	.10
344	Tim Davis	.10
345	Jay Buhner	.20
346	Bobby Ayala	.10
347	Mike Blowers	.10
348	Dave Fleming	.10
349	Edgar Martinez	.15
350	Andre Dawson	.15
351	Darrell Whitmore	.10
352	Chuck Carr	.10
353	John Burkett	.10
354	Chris Hammond	.10
355	Gary Sheffield	.50
356	Pat Rapp	.10
357	Greg Colbrunn	.10
358	David Segui	.10
359	Jeff Kent	.10
360	Bobby Bonilla	.15
361	Pete Harnisch	.10
362	Ryan Thompson	.10
363	Jose Vizcaino	.10
364	Brett Butler	.10
365	Cal Ripken Jr.	3.00
366	Rafael Palmeiro	.20
367	Leo Gomez	.10
368	Andy Van Slyke	.10
369	Arthur Rhodes	.10
370	Ken Caminiti	.25
371	Steve Finley	.10
372	Melvin Nieves	.10
373	Andujar Cedeno	.10
374	Trevor Hoffman	.10
375	Fernando Valenzuela	.10
376	Ricky Bottalico	.10
377	Dave Hollins	.10
378	Charlie Hayes	.10
379	Tommy Greene	.10
380	Darren Daulton	.15
381	Curt Schilling	.15
382	Midre Cummings	.10
383	Al Martin	.10
384	Jeff King	.10
385	Orlando Merced	.10
386	Denny Neagle	.15
387	Don Slaught	.10
388	Dave Clark	.10
389	Kevin Gross	.10
390	Will Clark	.30
391	Ivan Rodriguez	.60
392	Benji Gil	.10
393	Jeff Frye	.10
394	Kenny Rogers	.10

395	Juan Gonzalez	1.00
396	Mike Macfarlane	.10
397	Lee Tinsley	.10
398	Tim Naehring	.10
399	Tim Vanegmond	.10
400	Mike Greenwell	.10
401	Ken Ryan	.10
402	John Smiley	.10
403	Tim Pugh	.10
404	Reggie Sanders	.15
405	Barry Larkin	.25
406	Hal Morris	.10
407	Jose Rijo	.10
408	Lance Painter	.10
409	Joe Girardi	.10
410	Andres Galarraga	.20
411	Mike Kingery	.10
412	Roberto Mejia	.10
413	Walt Weiss	.10
414	Bill Swift	.10
415	Larry Walker	.25
416	Billy Brewer	.10
417	Pat Borders	.10
418	Tom Gordon	.10
419	Kevin Appier	.15
420	Gary Gaetti	.10
421	Greg Gohr	.10
422	Felipe Lira	.10
423	John Doherty	.10
424	Chad Curtis	.10
425	Cecil Fielder	.20
426	Alan Trammell	.15
427	David McCarty	.10
428	Scott Erickson	.10
429	Pat Mahomes	.10
430	Kirby Puckett	1.00
431	Dave Stevens	.10
432	Pedro Munoz	.10
433	Chris Sabo	.10
434	Alex Fernandez	.15
435	Frank Thomas	2.50
436	Roberto Hernandez	.10
437	Lance Johnson	.10
438	Jim Abbott	.10
439	John Wetteland	.10
440	Melido Perez	.10
441	Tony Fernandez	.10
442	Pat Kelly	.10
443	Mike Stanley	.10
444	Danny Tartabull	.10
445	Wade Boggs	.20
446	Robin Yount (Final Tribute)	.35
447	Ryne Sandberg (Final Tribute)	.50
448	Nolan Ryan (Final Tribute)	2.00
449	George Brett (Final Tribute)	.75
450	Mike Schmidt (Final Tribute)	.50

1995 Upper Deck Autograph Trade Cards

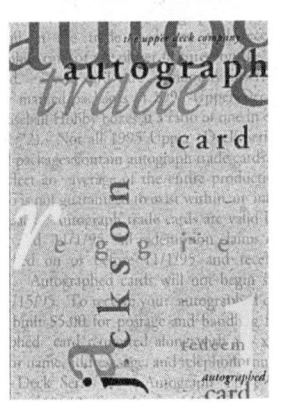

On the average of once every 72 packs (two boxes) of Series II hobby, a trade card good for an autographed player card could be found as an insert. The cards feature the player name, but no picture, on front, while the reverse has instructions for redeeming the card for a $5 fee. The autograph trade cards expired on Nov. 1, 1995.

		MT
Complete Set (5):		10.00
Common Player:		2.00
(1)	Roger Clemens	2.00
(2)	Reggie Jackson	1.00
(3)	Willie Mays	3.00
(4)	Raul Mondesi	2.00
(5)	Frank Robinson	2.00

1995 Upper Deck Autograph Redemption Cards

These cards were sent to collectors who redeemed Autograph Trade cards found in Series II Upper Deck baseball. A certificate of authenticity with a holographic serial number matching that on the card back was issued with each card.

		MT
Complete Set (5):		140.00
Common Player:		25.00
(1)	Roger Clemens	40.00
(2)	Reggie Jackson	25.00
(3)	Willie Mays	50.00
(4)	Raul Mondesi	25.00
(5)	Frank Robinson	25.00

1995 Upper Deck Autographed Jumbos

By sending in quantities of foil wrappers from Upper Deck baseball cards, collectors could receive a jumbo 5" x 7" blow-up of a player's card. The offer was limited to 8,000 Roger Clemens cards (Se-ries I) and 6,000 Alex Rodriguez cards (Series II). Each card bears a serial number hologram on back and comes with a matching Upper Deck Authenticated auhtenticity guarantee card.

		MT
Complete Set (2):		80.00
Common Player:		30.00
(1)	Roger Clemens	40.00
(2)	Alex Rodriguez	50.00

1995 Upper Deck Babe Ruth Baseball Heroes

In the 100th anniversary year of his birth, Babe Ruth was the featured star in Upper Deck continuing "Heroes" insert set. Ten cards, including an unnumbered header, were issued in Series II packs. The cards featured colorized photos printed on metallic foil on the front. Backs have stats and/or biographical data. On average, one Babe Ruth Heroes card is found per 34 packs.

		MT
Complete Set (10):		100.00
Common Player:		10.00
73	1914-18 Pitching Career(Babe Ruth)	10.00
74	1919 - Move to Outfield(Babe Ruth)	10.00
75	1920 - Renaissance Man(Babe Ruth)	10.00
76	1923 - House That Ruth Built(Babe Ruth)	10.00
77	1927 - 60-Homer Season(Babe Ruth)	10.00
78	1928 - Three-homer Game(Babe Ruth)	10.00
79	1932 - The Called Shot(Babe Ruth)	10.00
80	1930-35 - Milestones(Babe Ruth)	10.00
81	1935 - The Last Hurrah(Babe Ruth)	10.00
---	Header card	3.00

1995 Upper Deck Checklists

Upscale checklists for the 1995 UD set were part of the insert card program, seeded about one per 17 packs, on average. Horizontally formatted fronts are printed on metallic foil and include a career highlight of the pictured player. Backs have the checklist data. Five checklists were issued in each of Series I and Series II.

		MT
Complete Set (10):		15.00
Common Player:		
	Series I	
1	Checklist 1-75 (Montreal Expos)	1.00
2	Checklist 76-150(Fred McGriff)	2.00
3	Checklist 151-225(John Valentin) (unassisted triple play)	1.00
4	Special Edition Checklist(Greg Maddux)	4.00
5	Special Edition Checklist 69-135(Kenny Rogers) (perfect game)	1.00
	Series II	
1	Checklist 226-300(Cecil Fielder)	2.00
2	Checklist 301-375(Tony Gwynn)	3.00
3	Checklist 376-450(Greg Maddux)	4.00
4	Special Edition Checklist 136-203(Randy Johnson)	2.50
5	Special Edition Checklist 204-270(Mike Schmidt)	4.00

1995 Upper Deck Electric Diamond

Included as an insert at the rate of one per retail foil pack and two per jumbo pack, this set parallels the regular issue. The only differences are that the Electric Diamond cards utilize silver-foil highlights on front, compared to the copper foil on the regular cards. The Electric Diamond cards also include a home-plate shaped logo printed in silver foil in one of the upper corners.

A player's name in *italic* type indicates a rookie card.

	MT
Complete Set (1-450):	100.00
Complete Series 1 (1-225):	50.00
Complete Series 2 (226-450):	50.00
Common Player:	.25
Veteran Stars: 2X to 4X	
Young Stars and Rookies: 1X to 2X	
(Star cards valued at 1.5-2X regular U.D.)	

1995 Upper Deck Electric Diamond Gold

A parallel set of a parallet set, the Electric Diamond Gold cards were found at an average rate of one per 36 retail packs. They differ from the standard ED inserts in that the home plate-shaped Electric Diamond logo in the upper corner and the player's name at bottom are printed in gold foil, rather than the silver of the ED cards or the copper of the regular-issue UD cards.

	MT
Complete Set (450):	2400.
Common Player:	4.00
Veteran Stars: 15X to 25X	
Young Stars and Rookies: 12X to 20X	
--- (Stars valued at 20-35X corresponding regular-issue 1995 U.D. cards.)	

1995 Upper Deck Hobby Predictors

Candidates for 1995 MVP and Rookie of the Year in each league are featured in the interactive insert series called Predictors. Twenty potential award winners were released in each of Series I and II at the rate of one per 30 packs on average. Cards feature on front a player photo inside a diamond cut-out on a rich looking black and marbled background. In gold foil are his name and team at top, and "PREDICTOR" and the category at bottom. Backs feature game rules and details for redeeming the card if the pictured player wins the specified award. Winners could trade in the card for a foil-enhanced set of Predictor cards. The trade-in offer expired at the end of 1995.

		MT
Complete Set (40):		90.00
Complete Series 1 (20):		50.00
Complete Series 2 (20):		40.00
Common Player:		1.00
H1	Albert Belle	2.50
H2	Juan Gonzalez	4.00
H3	Ken Griffey Jr.	10.00
H4	Kirby Puckett	4.00
H5	Frank Thomas	8.00
H6	Jeff Bagwell	4.00
H7	Barry Bonds	2.50
H8	Mike Piazza	6.00
H9	Matt Williams	1.50
H10	1995 MVP Long Shot	1.00
H11	Armando Benitez	1.00
H12	Alex Gonzalez	1.00
H13	Shawn Green	1.00
H14	Derek Jeter	4.00
H15	Alex Rodriguez	10.00
H16	Alan Benes	1.50
H17	Brian L. Hunter	1.50
H18	Charles Johnson	1.25
H19	Jose Oliva	1.00
H20	1995 ROY Long Shot	1.00
H21	Cal Ripken Jr.	8.00
H22	Don Mattingly	4.00
H23	Roberto Alomar	2.00
H24	Kenny Lofton	3.00
H25	Will Clark	1.50
H26	Mark McGwire	8.00
H27	Greg Maddux	6.00
H28	Fred McGriff	1.50
H29	Andres Galarraga	1.00
H30	Jose Canseco	1.50
H31	Ray Durham	1.00
H32	Mark Grudzielanek	1.00
H33	Scott Ruffcorn	1.00
H34	Michael Tucker	1.00
H35	Garret Anderson	1.00
H36	Darren Bragg	1.00
H37	Quilvio Veras	1.00
H38	Hideo Nomo	3.00
H39	Chipper Jones	6.00
H40	Marty Cordova	1.50

1995 Upper Deck Retail Predictors

Candidates for the Triple Crown categories of league leaders in hits, home runs and RBIs are featured in this retail-only insert set, found at the average rate of one per 30 packs in both Series I and II. If the player pictured on the card front won the category specified on his card, it could be redeemed for a special foil-enhanced version of the subset prior to the Dec. 31, 1995, deadline.

		MT
Complete Set (60):		125.00
Complete Series 1 (30):		75.00
Complete Series 2 (30):		50.00
Common Player:		1.00
R1	Albert Belle	2.50
R2	Jose Canseco	1.50
R3	Juan Gonzalez	4.00
R4	Ken Griffey Jr.	10.00
R5	Frank Thomas	8.00
R6	Jeff Bagwell	4.00
R7	Barry Bonds	2.50
R8	Fred McGriff	1.50
R9	Matt Williams	1.00
R10	1995 Home Run Long Shot	1.00
R11	Albert Belle	2.50
R12	Joe Carter	1.00
R13	Cecil Fielder	1.00
R14	Kirby Puckett	4.00
R15	Frank Thomas	8.00
R16	Jeff Bagwell	4.00
R17	Barry Bonds	2.00
R18	Mike Piazza	6.00
R19	Matt Williams	1.00
R20	1995 RBI Long Shot	1.00
R21	Wade Boggs	1.00
R22	Kenny Lofton	2.50
R23	Paul Molitor	1.50
R24	Paul O'Neill	1.00
R25	Frank Thomas	8.00

R26	Jeff Bagwell	4.00
R27	Tony Gwynn	4.00
R28	Gregg Jefferies	1.00
R29	Hal Morris	1.00
R30	1995 Batting Long Shot	1.00
R31	Joe Carter	1.00
R32	Cecil Fielder	1.00
R33	Rafael Palmeiro	1.00
R34	Larry Walker	1.00
R35	Manny Ramirez	2.50
R36	Tim Salmon	1.50
R37	Mike Piazza	6.00
R38	Andres Galarraga	1.00
R39	Dave Justice	1.00
R40	Gary Sheffield	1.50
R41	Juan Gonzalez	4.00
R42	Jose Canseco	1.50
R43	Will Clark	1.50
R44	Rafael Palmeiro	1.00
R45	Ken Griffey Jr.	10.00
R46	Ruben Sierra	1.00
R47	Larry Walker	1.00
R48	Fred McGriff	1.50
R49	Dante Bichette	1.50
R50	Darren Daulton	1.00
R51	Will Clark	1.50
R52	Ken Griffey Jr.	10.00
R53	Don Mattingly	4.00
R54	John Olerud	1.00
R55	Kirby Puckett	4.00
R56	Raul Mondesi	1.50
R57	Moises Alou	1.00
R58	Bret Boone	1.00
R59	Albert Belle	2.50
R60	Mike Piazza	6.00

1995 Upper Deck Special Edition

Printed on metallic foil on front, and inserted into hobby packs only at the rate of one per pack, this insert series is found in both Series I (#1-135) and Series II (#136-270). A silver stripe at top has the name of the issue and the issuers, while stacked black and silver bars at bottom have the player name, team and position. Backs are conventionally printed and have another color photo, career data and 1994 and lifetime stats.

		MT
Complete Set (270):		150.00
Complete Series 1 (135):		60.00
Complete Series 2 (135):		90.00
Common Player:		.25
1	Cliff Floyd	.25
2	Wil Cordero	.25
3	Pedro J. Martinez	.40
4	Larry Walker	.40
5	Derek Jeter	5.00
6	Mike Stanley	.25
7	Melido Perez	.25
8	Jim Leyritz	.25

9	Danny Tartabull	.25
10	Wade Boggs	.40
11	Ryan Klesko	2.00
12	Steve Avery	.25
13	Damon Hollins	.25
14	Chipper Jones	6.00
15	Dave Justice	.50
16	Glenn Williams	.25
17	Jose Oliva	.25
18	Terrell Wade	.25
19	Alex Fernandez	.40
20	Frank Thomas	8.00
21	Ozzie Guillen	.25
22	Roberto Hernandez	.25
23	Albie Lopez	.25
24	Eddie Murray	1.50
25	Albert Belle	2.50
26	Omar Vizquel	.25
27	Carlos Baerga	.25
28	Jose Rijo	.25
29	Hal Morris	.25
30	Reggie Sanders	.25
31	Jack Morris	.25
32	Raul Mondesi	.75
33	Karim Garcia	2.50
34	Todd Hollandsworth	.50
35	Mike Piazza	6.00
36	Chan Ho Park	.50
37	Ramon Martinez	.35
38	Kenny Rogers	.25
39	Will Clark	.75
40	Juan Gonzalez	4.00
41	Ivan Rodriguez	2.00
42	Orlando Miller	.25
43	John Hudek	.25
44	Luis Gonzalez	.25
45	Jeff Bagwell	4.00
46	Cal Ripken Jr.	8.00
47	Mike Oquist	.25
48	Armando Benitez	.25
49	Ben McDonald	.25
50	Rafael Palmeiro	.40
51	Curtis Goodwin	.25
52	Vince Coleman	.25
53	Tom Gordon	.25
54	Mike Macfarlane	.25
55	Brian McRae	.25
56	Matt Smith	.25
57	David Segui	.25
58	Paul Wilson	2.00
59	Bill Pulsipher	.50
60	Bobby Bonilla	.40
61	Jeff Kent	.25
62	Ryan Thompson	.25
63	Jason Isringhausen	.75
64	Ed Sprague	.25
65	Paul Molitor	1.00
66	Juan Guzman	.25
67	Alex Gonzalez	.40
68	Shawn Green	.40
69	Mark Portugal	.25
70	Barry Bonds	2.50
71	Robby Thompson	.25
72	Royce Clayton	.25
73	Ricky Bottalico	.25
74	Doug Jones	.25
75	Darren Daulton	.25
76	Gregg Jefferies	.25
77	Scott Cooper	.25
78	Nomar Garciaparra	8.00
79	Ken Ryan	.25
80	Mike Greenwell	.25
81	LaTroy Hawkins	.25
82	Rich Becker	.25
83	Scott Erickson	.25
84	Pedro Munoz	.25
85	Kirby Puckett	3.50
86	Orlando Merced	.25
87	Jeff King	.25
88	Midre Cummings	.25
89	Bernard Gilkey	.25
90	Ray Lankford	.25
91	Todd Zeile	.25
92	Alan Benes	1.00
93	Bret Wagner	.25
94	Rene Arocha	.25
95	Cecil Fielder	.50
96	Alan Trammell	.25
97	Tony Phillips	.25
98	Junior Felix	.25
99	Brian Harper	.25
100	Greg Vaughn	.25
101	Ricky Bones	.25
102	Walt Weiss	.25
103	Lance Painter	.25
104	Roberto Mejia	.25

105	Andres Galarraga	.50
106	Todd Van Poppel	.25
107	Ben Grieve	6.00
108	Brent Gates	.25
109	Jason Giambi	.50
110	Ruben Sierra	.25
111	Terry Steinbach	.25
112	Chris Hammond	.25
113	Charles Johnson	.25
114	Jesus Tavarez	.25
115	Gary Sheffield	.75
116	Chuck Carr	.25
117	Bobby Ayala	.25
118	Randy Johnson	1.00
119	Edgar Martinez	.25
120	Alex Rodriguez	10.00
121	Kevin Foster	.25
122	Kevin Roberson	.25
123	Sammy Sosa	5.00
124	Steve Trachsel	.25
125	Eduardo Perez	.25
126	Tim Salmon	.50
127	Todd Greene	.50
128	Jorge Fabregas	.25
129	Mark Langston	.25
130	Mitch Williams	.25
131	Raul Casanova	.50
132	Mel Nieves	.25
133	Andy Benes	.25
134	Dustin Hermanson	.25
135	Trevor Hoffman	.25
136	Mark Grudzielanek	.40
137	Ugueth Urbina	.25
138	Moises Alou	.25
139	Roberto Kelly	.25
140	Rondell White	.40
141	Paul O'Neill	.25
142	Jimmy Key	.25
143	Jack McDowell	.40
144	Ruben Rivera	.75
145	Don Mattingly	4.00
146	John Wetteland	.25
147	Tom Glavine	.50
148	Marquis Grissom	.25
149	Javy Lopez	.50
150	Fred McGriff	1.00
151	Greg Maddux	6.00
152	Chris Sabo	.25
153	Ray Durham	.40
154	Robin Ventura	.25
155	Jim Abbott	.25
156	Jimmy Hurst	.25
157	Tim Raines	.25
158	Dennis Martinez	.25
159	Kenny Lofton	2.00
160	Dave Winfield	.25
161	Manny Ramirez	2.00
162	Jim Thome	1.00
163	Barry Larkin	.50
164	Bret Boone	.25
165	Deion Sanders	.75
166	Ron Gant	.40
167	Benito Santiago	.25
168	Hideo Nomo	5.00
169	Billy Ashley	.25
170	Roger Cedeno	.25
171	Ismael Valdes	.25
172	Eric Karros	.25
173	Rusty Greer	.50
174	Rick Helling	.25
175	Nolan Ryan	8.00
176	Dean Palmer	.25
177	Phil Plantier	.25
178	Darryl Kile	.25
179	Derek Bell	.25
180	Doug Drabek	.25
181	Craig Biggio	.40
182	Kevin Brown	.25
183	Harold Baines	.25
184	Jeffrey Hammonds	.25
185	Chris Hoiles	.25
186	Mike Mussina	1.50
187	Bob Hamelin	.25
188	Jeff Montgomery	.25
189	Michael Tucker	.25
190	George Brett	2.50
191	Edgardo Alfonzo	.25
192	Brett Butler	.25
193	Bobby Jones	.25
194	Todd Hundley	.75
195	Bret Saberhagen	.25
196	Pat Hentgen	.25
197	Roberto Alomar	2.00
198	David Cone	.50
199	Carlos Delgado	.40
200	Joe Carter	.40

201	William Van Landingham	.25
202	Rod Beck	.25
203	J.R. Phillips	.25
204	Darren Lewis	.25
205	Matt Williams	.75
206	Lenny Dykstra	.25
207	Dave Hollins	.25
208	Mike Schmidt	1.50
209	Charlie Hayes	.25
210	Mo Vaughn	2.00
211	Jose Malave	.25
212	Roger Clemens	2.50
213	Jose Canseco	.60
214	Mark Whiten	.25
215	Marty Cordova	.25
216	Rick Aguilera	.25
217	Kevin Tapani	.25
218	Chuck Knoblauch	.50
219	Al Martin	.25
220	Jay Bell	.25
221	Carlos Garcia	.25
222	Freddy Garcia	.25
223	Jon Lieber	.25
224	Danny Jackson	.25
225	Ozzie Smith	1.50
226	Brian Jordan	.25
227	Ken Hill	.25
228	Scott Cooper	.25
229	Chad Curtis	.25
230	Lou Whitaker	.25
231	Kirk Gibson	.25
232	Travis Fryman	.25
233	Jose Valentin	.25
234	Dave Nilsson	.25
235	Cal Eldred	.25
236	Matt Mieske	.25
237	Bill Swift	.25
238	Marvin Freeman	.25
239	Jason Bates	.25
240	Larry Walker	.75
241	David Nied	.25
242	Dante Bichette	.50
243	Dennis Eckersley	.25
244	Todd Stottlemyre	.25
245	Rickey Henderson	.25
246	Geronimo Berroa	.25
247	Mark McGwire	12.00
248	Quilvio Veras	.25
249	Terry Pendleton	.25
250	Andre Dawson	.25
251	Jeff Conine	.25
252	Kurt Abbott	.25
253	Jay Buhner	.50
254	Darren Bragg	.25
255	Ken Griffey Jr.	10.00
256	Tino Martinez	.50
257	Mark Grace	.50
258	Ryne Sandberg	1.50
259	Randy Myers	.25
260	Howard Johnson	.25
261	Lee Smith	.25
262	J.T. Snow	.25
263	Chili Davis	.25
264	Chuck Finley	.25
265	Eddie Williams	.25
266	Joey Hamilton	.25
267	Ken Caminiti	.75
268	Andujar Cedeno	.25
269	Steve Finley	.25
270	Tony Gwynn	3.50

1995 Upper Deck Special Edition Gold

An insert set within an insert set, gold-foil enhanced versions of the Special Edition cards were seeded into hobby packs at the rate of about one per box. The substitution of gold ink for silver is also carried over onto the background of the card back.

	MT
Complete Set (270):	1750.
Complete Series 1 (1-135):	850.00
Complete Series 2 (136-270):	950.00
Common Player:	2.00
(Star cards valued about 5X-10X corresponding cards in silver edition)	

1995 Upper Deck Steal of a Deal

A horizontal format with an action photo printed over a green foil background and a large bronze seal indicating how the player was acquired are featured in this 15-card insert set. The front has a terra-cotta border, which is carried over to the back. A large green box on back details the transaction and describes why it can be categorized as a "steal" for the player's new team. These top-of-the-line chase cards were seeded in both hobby and retail packs of Series I at the average rate of one per 34 packs.

		MT
Complete Set (15):		100.00
Common Player:		2.00
SD1	Mike Piazza	16.00
SD2	Fred McGriff	4.00
SD3	Kenny Lofton	10.00
SD4	Jose Oliva	2.00
SD5	Jeff Bagwell	12.00
SD6	Roberto Alomar, Joe Carter	6.00
SD7	Steve Karsay	2.00
SD8	Ozzie Smith	8.00
SD9	Dennis Eckersley	2.00
SD10	Jose Canseco	5.00
SD11	Carlos Baerga	2.00
SD12	Cecil Fielder	4.00
SD13	Don Mattingly	15.00
SD14	Bret Boone	2.00
SD15	Michael Jordan	40.00

1995 Upper Deck Update Trade Cards

Inserted into Series II at the rate of about one per 11 packs was this five-card series of trade cards. Each card could be mailed in with $2 to receive nine cards from a special UD Update set picturing traded or free agent players in the uniforms of their new teams. The front of each trade card pictures one of

the traded players in his old uniform against a red and blue background. Backs have instructions for redeeming the trade cards. The mail-in offer expired Feb. 1, 1996.

		MT
Complete Set (5):		6.00
Common Player:		1.00
TC1	Orel Hershiser	1.00
TC2	Terry Pendleton	1.00
TC3	Benito Santiago	1.00
TC4	Kevin Brown	1.00
TC5	Gregg Jefferies	1.00

1995 Upper Deck Update

These 45 cards depicting traded and free agent players in the uniforms of their new 1995 teams were available only by redeeming trade-in cards found in Series II packs. Each trade-in card was good for one nine-card segment of the Update series when sent with $2 prior to the Feb. 1, 1996, deadline. Update cards share the same format as the regular 1995 Upper Deck set. The Updates are sequenced according to team nickname.

		MT
Complete Set (45):		8.00
Common Player:		.15
451	Jim Abbott	.25
452	Danny Tartabull	.15
453	Ariel Prieto	.25
454	Scott Cooper	.15
455	Tom Henke	.15
456	Todd Zeile	.30
457	Brian McRae	.25
458	Luis Gonzalez	.15
459	Jaime Navarro	.15
460	Todd Worrell	.15
461	Roberto Kelly	.15
462	Chad Fonville	.20
463	Shane Andrews	.20
464	David Segui	.15
465	Deion Sanders	.50
466	Orel Hershiser	.25
467	Ken Hill	.20
468	Andy Benes	.25
469	Terry Pendleton	.15
470	Bobby Bonilla	.20
471	Scott Erickson	.15
472	Kevin Brown	.25
473	Glenn Dishman	.15
474	Phil Plantier	.15
475	Gregg Jefferies	.30
476	Tyler Green	.15
477	Heathcliff Slocumb	.15
478	Mark Whiten	.15
479	Mickey Tettleton	.15
480	Tim Wakefield	.15

481	Vaughn Eshelman	.15
482	Rick Aguilera	.15
483	Erik Hanson	.15
484	Willie McGee	.20
485	Troy O'Leary	.15
486	Benito Santiago	.15
487	Darren Lewis	.15
488	Dave Burba	.15
489	Ron Gant	.25
490	Bret Saberhagen	.25
491	Vinny Castilla	.20
492	Frank Rodriguez	.15
493	Andy Pettitte	.75
494	Ruben Sierra	.15
495	David Cone	.25

1996 Upper Deck

RUBEN SIERRA — Yankees™ of

Upper Deck Series I consists of 240 regular-issue cards. There are 187 regular player cards plus subsets of Star Rookies, Young at Heart, Beat the Odds, Milestones, Post-season, checklists and expansion logos. The issue was marketed in 10-card foil packs in hobby and retail versions. Hobby packs feature a Special Edition insert while retail packs offer Electric Diamond parallel cards. Series I insert sets are Blue Chip Prospects, Future Shock and Power Driven. Cal Ripken Jr. Collection cards are inserted in both series, as are Retail Predictor (home runs, batting average and RBIs) and Hobby Predictor (Player of the Month, Pitcher of the Month and rookie hits leaders) cards. Series II has 240 cards, including subsets for Star Rookies, Diamond Debuts, Strange But True, Managerial Salutes and Best of a Generation. Additional insert sets include Hot Commodities, Hideo Nomo Highlights, Run Producers and the Lovero Collection.

		MT
Complete Set (480):		60.00
Complete Series 1 (240):		30.00
Complete Series 2 (240):		30.00
Common Player:		.10
Wax Box:		45.00
1	Cal Ripken Jr. (Milestones)	2.50
2	Eddie Murray (Milestones)	.40
3	Mark Wohlers	.10
4	Dave Justice	.20
5	Chipper Jones	2.00
6	Javier Lopez	.20
7	Mark Lemke	.10
8	Marquis Grissom	.10
9	Tom Glavine	.20
10	Greg Maddux	2.00
11	Manny Alexander	.10
12	Curtis Goodwin	.10
13	Scott Erickson	.10

14	Chris Hoiles	.10
15	Rafael Palmeiro	.20
16	Rick Krivda	.10
17	Jeff Manto	.10
18	Mo Vaughn	.75
19	Tim Wakefield	.10
20	Roger Clemens	.75
21	Tim Naehring	.10
22	Troy O'Leary	.10
23	Mike Greenwell	.10
24	Stan Belinda	.10
25	John Valentin	.10
26	J.T. Snow	.10
27	Gary DiSarcina	.10
28	Mark Langston	.10
29	Brian Anderson	.10
30	Jim Edmonds	.15
31	Garret Anderson	.10
32	Orlando Palmeiro	.10
33	Brian McRae	.10
34	Kevin Foster	.10
35	Sammy Sosa	1.50
36	Todd Zeile	.10
37	Jim Bullinger	.10
38	Luis Gonzalez	.10
39	Lyle Mouton	.10
40	Ray Durham	.10
41	Ozzie Guillen	.10
42	Alex Fernandez	.10
43	Brian Keyser	.10
44	Robin Ventura	.10
45	Reggie Sanders	.10
46	Pete Schourek	.10
47	John Smiley	.10
48	Jeff Brantley	.10
49	Thomas Howard	.10
50	Bret Boone	.10
51	Kevin Jarvis	.10
52	Jeff Branson	.10
53	Carlos Baerga	.10
54	Jim Thome	.40
55	Manny Ramirez	.75
56	Omar Vizquel	.10
57	Jose Mesa	.10
58	Julian Tavarez	.10
59	Orel Hershiser	.10
60	Larry Walker	.35
61	Bret Saberhagen	.10
62	Vinny Castilla	.10
63	Eric Young	.10
64	Bryan Rekar	.10
65	Andres Galarraga	.20
66	Steve Reed	.10
67	Chad Curtis	.10
68	Bobby Higginson	.10
69	Phil Nevin	.10
70	Cecil Fielder	.20
71	Felipe Lira	.10
72	Chris Gomez	.10
73	Charles Johnson	.20
74	Quilvio Veras	.10
75	Jeff Conine	.10
76	John Burkett	.10
77	Greg Colbrunn	.10
78	Terry Pendleton	.10
79	Shane Reynolds	.10
80	Jeff Bagwell	1.25
81	Orlando Miller	.10
82	Mike Hampton	.10
83	James Mouton	.10
84	Brian L. Hunter	.10
85	Derek Bell	.10
86	Kevin Appier	.10
87	Joe Vitiello	.10
88	Wally Joyner	.10
89	Michael Tucker	.15
90	Johnny Damon	.15
91	Jon Nunnally	.10
92	Jason Jacome	.10
93	Chad Fonville	.10
94	Chan Ho Park	.10
95	Hideo Nomo	.60
96	Ismael Valdes	.10
97	Greg Gagne	.10
98	Diamondbacks-Devil Rays (Expansion Card)	.25
99	Raul Mondesi	.30
100	Dave Winfield (Young at Heart)	.10
101	Dennis Eckersley (Young at Heart)	.10
102	Andre Dawson (Young at Heart)	.10
103	Dennis Martinez (Young at Heart)	.10

104	Lance Parrish (Young at Heart)	.10
105	Eddie Murray (Young at Heart)	.25
106	Alan Trammell (Young at Heart)	.10
107	Lou Whitaker (Young at Heart)	.10
108	Ozzie Smith (Young at Heart)	.25
109	Paul Molitor (Young at Heart)	.20
110	Rickey Henderson (Young at Heart)	.10
111	Tim Raines (Young at Heart)	.10
112	Harold Baines (Young at Heart)	.10
113	Lee Smith (Young at Heart)	.10
114	Fernando Valenzuela (Young at Heart)	.10
115	Cal Ripken Jr. (Young at Heart)	1.75
116	Tony Gwynn (Young at Heart)	.50
117	Wade Boggs (Young at Heart)	.15
118	Todd Hollandsworth	.15
119	Dave Nilsson	.10
120	*Jose Valentin*	.20
121	Steve Sparks	.10
122	Chuck Carr	.10
123	John Jaha	.10
124	Scott Karl	.10
125	Chuck Knoblauch	.20
126	Brad Radke	.10
127	Pat Meares	.10
128	Ron Coomer	.10
129	Pedro Munoz	.10
130	Kirby Puckett	1.00
131	David Segui	.10
132	Mark Grudzielanek	.10
133	Mike Lansing	.10
134	Sean Berry	.10
135	Rondell White	.15
136	Pedro J. Martinez	.20
137	Carl Everett	.10
138	Dave Mlicki	.10
139	Bill Pulsipher	.10
140	Jason Isringhausen	.20
141	Rico Brogna	.10
142	Edgardo Alfonzo	.10
143	Jeff Kent	.10
144	Andy Pettitte	1.00
145	Mike Piazza (Beat the Odds)	1.00
146	Cliff Floyd (Beat the Odds)	.10
147	Jason Isringhausen (Beat the Odds)	.10
148	Tim Wakefield (Beat the Odds)	.10
149	Chipper Jones (Beat the Odds)	1.00
150	Hideo Nomo (Beat the Odds)	.30
151	Mark McGwire (Beat the Odds)	1.50
152	Ron Gant (Beat the Odds)	.10
153	Gary Gaetti (Beat the Odds)	.10
154	Don Mattingly	1.25
155	Paul O'Neill	.20
156	Derek Jeter	1.50
157	Joe Girardi	.10
158	Ruben Sierra	.10
159	Jorge Posada	.10
160	Geronimo Berroa	.10
161	Steve Ontiveros	.10
162	George Williams	.10
163	Doug Johns	.10
164	Ariel Prieto	.10
165	Scott Brosius	.10
166	Mike Bordick	.10
167	Tyler Green	.10
168	Mickey Morandini	.10
169	Darren Daulton	.10
170	Gregg Jefferies	.10
171	Jim Eisenreich	.10
172	Heathcliff Slocumb	.10
173	Kevin Stocker	.10
174	Esteban Loaiza	.10
175	Jeff King	.10
176	Mark Johnson	.10
177	Denny Neagle	.10
178	Orlando Merced	.10
179	Carlos Garcia	.10
180	Brian Jordan	.10

181	Mike Morgan	.10
182	Mark Petkovsek	.10
183	Bernard Gilkey	.10
184	John Mabry	.10
185	Tom Henke	.10
186	Glenn Dishman	.10
187	Andy Ashby	.10
188	Bip Roberts	.10
189	Melvin Nieves	.10
190	Ken Caminiti	.25
191	Brad Ausmus	.10
192	Deion Sanders	.25
193	Jamie Brewington	.10
194	Glenallen Hill	.10
195	Barry Bonds	.75
196	William VanLandingham	.10
197	Mark Carreon	.10
198	Royce Clayton	.10
199	Joey Cora	.10
200	Ken Griffey Jr.	3.00
201	Jay Buhner	.20
202	Alex Rodriguez	3.00
203	Norm Charlton	.10
204	Andy Benes	.10
205	Edgar Martinez	.10
206	Juan Gonzalez	1.50
207	Will Clark	.25
208	Kevin Gross	.10
209	Roger Pavlik	.10
210	Ivan Rodriguez	.50
211	Rusty Greer	.10
212	Angel Martinez	.10
213	Tomas Perez	.10
214	Alex Gonzalez	.10
215	Joe Carter	.20
216	Shawn Green	.10
217	Edwin Hurtado	.10
218	(Edgar Martinez, Tony Pena) (Post Season Checklist)	.10
219	Chipper Jones, Barry Larkin (Post Season Checklist)	.35
220	Orel Hershiser (Post Season Checklist)	.10
221	Mike Devereaux (Post Season Checklist)	.10
222	Tom Glavine (Post Season Checklist)	.10
223	Karim Garcia (Star Rookies)	.40
224	Arquimedez Pozo (Star Rookies)	.10
225	Billy Wagner (Star Rookies)	.15
226	John Wasdin (Star Rookies)	.10
227	Jeff Suppan (Star Rookies)	.10
228	Steve Gibralter (Star Rookies)	.10
229	Jimmy Haynes (Star Rookies)	.10
230	Ruben Rivera (Star Rookies)	.40
231	Chris Snopek (Star Rookies)	.15
232	Alex Ochoa (Star Rookies)	.10
233	Shannon Stewart (Star Rookies)	.10
234	Quinton McCracken (Star Rookies)	.15
235	Trey Beamon (Star Rookies)	.10
236	Billy McMillon (Star Rookies)	.10
237	Steve Cox (Star Rookies)	.10
238	George Arias (Star Rookies)	.10
239	Yamil Benitez (Star Rookies)	.10
240	Todd Greene (Star Rookies)	.20
241	Jason Kendall (Star Rookie)	.20
242	Brooks Kieschnick (Star Rookie)	.20
243	*Osvaldo Fernandez* (Star Rookie)	.15
244	*Livan Hernandez* (Star Rookie)	2.00
245	Rey Ordonez (Star Rookie)	.30
246	*Mike Grace* (Star Rookie)	.20
247	Jay Canizaro (Star Rookie)	.10
248	Bob Wolcott (Star Rookie)	.20
249	Jermaine Dye (Star Rookie)	.20
250	Jason Schmidt (Star Rookie)	.10
251	*Mike Sweeney* (Star Rookie)	.40
252	Marcus Jensen (Star Rookie)	.10
253	Mendy Lopez (Star Rookie)	.10
254	*Wilton Guerrero* (Star Rookie)	1.25

255	Paul Wilson (Star Rookie)	.20
256	Edgar Renteria (Star Rookie)	.20
257	Richard Hidalgo (Star Rookie)	.10
258	Bob Abreu (Star Rookie)	.10
259	*Robert Smith* (Diamond Debuts)	.30
260	Sal Fasano (Diamond Debuts)	.10
261	Enrique Wilson (Diamond Debuts)	.10
262	*Rich Hunter* (Diamond Debuts)	.10
263	Sergio Nunez (Diamond Debuts)	.10
264	Dan Serafini (Diamond Debuts)	.10
265	*David Doster* (Diamond Debuts)	.10
266	Ryan McGuire (Diamond Debuts)	.10
267	Scott Spiezio (Diamond Debuts)	.20
268	Rafael Orellano (Diamond Debuts)	.10
269	Steve Avery	.10
270	Fred McGriff	.30
271	John Smoltz	.20
272	Ryan Klesko	.60
273	Jeff Blauser	.10
274	Brad Clontz	.10
275	Roberto Alomar	.75
276	B.J. Surhoff	.10
277	Jeffrey Hammonds	.10
278	Brady Anderson	.20
279	Bobby Bonilla	.20
280	Cal Ripken Jr.	2.50
281	Mike Mussina	.60
282	Wil Cordero	.10
283	Mike Stanley	.10
284	Aaron Sele	.10
285	Jose Canseco	.30
286	Tom Gordon	.10
287	Heathcliff Slocumb	.10
288	Lee Smith	.10
289	Troy Percival	.10
290	Tim Salmon	.25
291	Chuck Finley	.10
292	Jim Abbott	.10
293	Chili Davis	.10
294	Steve Trachsel	.10
295	Mark Grace	.20
296	Rey Sanchez	.10
297	Scott Servais	.10
298	Jaime Navarro	.10
299	Frank Castillo	.10
300	Frank Thomas	2.50
301	Jason Bere	.10
302	Danny Tartabull	.10
303	Darren Lewis	.10
304	Roberto Hernandez	.10
305	Tony Phillips	.10
306	Wilson Alvarez	.10
307	Jose Rijo (NEW)	.10
308	Hal Morris	.10
309	Mark Portugal	.10
310	Barry Larkin	.25
311	Dave Burba	.10
312	Eddie Taubensee	.10
313	Sandy Alomar Jr.	.10
314	Dennis Martinez	.10
315	Albert Belle	.75
316	Eddie Murray	.40
317	Charles Nagy	.10
318	Chad Ogea	.10
319	Kenny Lofton	1.00
320	Dante Bichette	.25
321	Armando Reynoso	.10
322	Walt Weiss	.10
323	Ellis Burks	.10
324	Kevin Ritz	.10
325	Bill Swift	.10
326	Jason Bates	.10
327	Tony Clark	.75
328	Travis Fryman	.10
329	Mark Parent	.10
330	Alan Trammell	.10
331	C.J. Nitkowski	.10
332	Jose Lima	.10
333	Phil Plantier	.10
334	Kurt Abbott	.10
335	Andre Dawson (NEW)	.10
336	Chris Hammond	.10
337	Robb Nen	.10
338	Pat Rapp	.10

339	Al Leiter	.10
340	Gary Sheffield	.25
341	Todd Jones	.10
342	Doug Drabek	.10
343	Greg Swindell (NEW)	.10
344	Tony Eusebio	.10
345	Craig Biggio	.20
346	Darryl Kile	.10
347	Mike Macfarlane	.10
348	Jeff Montgomery	.10
349	Chris Haney	.10
350	Bip Roberts	.10
351	Tom Goodwin	.10
352	Mark Gubicza	.10
353	Joe Randa (NEW)	.10
354	Ramon Martinez	.10
355	Eric Karros	.10
356	Delino DeShields	.10
357	Brett Butler	.10
358	Todd Worrell	.10
359	Mike Blowers	.10
360	Mike Piazza	2.00
361	Ben McDonald	.10
362	Ricky Bones	.10
363	Greg Vaughn	.10
364	Matt Mieske	.10
365	Kevin Seitzer	.10
366	Jeff Cirillo	.10
367	LaTroy Hawkins	.10
368	Frank Rodriguez	.10
369	Rick Aguilera	.10
370	Roberto Alomar (Best of a Generation)	.40
371	Albert Belle (Best of a Generation)	.40
372	Wade Boggs (Best of a Generation)	.15
373	Barry Bonds (Best of a Generation)	.40
374	Roger Clemens (Best of a Generation)	.40
375	Dennis Eckersley (Best of a Generation)	.10
376	Ken Griffey Jr. (Best of a Generation)	1.50
377	Tony Gwynn (Best of a Generation)	.50
378	Rickey Henderson (Best of a Generation)	.10
379	Greg Maddux (Best of a Generation)	1.00
380	Fred McGriff (Best of a Generation)	.20
381	Paul Molitor (Best of a Generation)	.20
382	Eddie Murray (Best of a Generation)	.25
383	Mike Piazza (Best of a Generation)	1.00
384	Kirby Puckett (Best of a Generation)	.50
385	Cal Ripken Jr. (Best of a Generation)	1.25
386	Ozzie Smith (Best of a Generation)	.30
387	Frank Thomas (Best of a Generation)	1.25
388	Matt Walbeck	.10
389	Dave Stevens	.10
390	Marty Cordova	.20
391	Darrin Fletcher	.10
392	Cliff Floyd	.10
393	Mel Rojas	.10
394	Shane Andrews	.10
395	Moises Alou	.10
396	Carlos Perez	.10
397	Jeff Fassero	.10
398	Bobby Jones	.10
399	Todd Hundley	.25
400	John Franco	.10
401	Jose Vizcaino	.10
402	Bernard Gilkey	.10
403	Pete Harnisch	.10
404	Pat Kelly	.10
405	David Cone	.20
406	Bernie Williams	.50
407	John Wetteland	.10
408	Scott Kamieniecki	.10
409	Tim Raines	.10
410	Wade Boggs	.20
411	Terry Steinbach	.10
412	Jason Giambi	.10
413	Todd Van Poppel	.10
414	Pedro Rojas	.10
415	Eddie Murray-1990 (Strange But True)	.25

416	Dennis Eckersley-1990 (Strange But True)	.10
417	Bip Roberts-1992 (Strange But True)	.10
418	Glenallen Hill-1992 (Strange But True)	.10
419	John Hudek-1994 (Strange But True)	.10
420	Derek Bell-1995 (Strange But True)	.10
421	Larry Walker-1995 (Strange But True)	.20
422	Greg Maddux-1995 (Strange But True)	1.00
423	Ken Caminiti-1995 (Strange But True)	.20
424	Brent Gates	.10
425	Mark McGwire	4.00
426	Mark Whiten	.10
427	Sid Fernandez	.10
428	Ricky Bottalico	.10
429	Mike Mimbs	.10
430	Lenny Dykstra	.10
431	Todd Zeile	.10
432	Benito Santiago	.10
433	Danny Miceli	.10
434	Al Martin	.10
435	Jay Bell	.10
436	Charlie Hayes	.10
437	Mike Kingery	.10
438	Paul Wagner	.10
439	Tom Pagnozzi	.10
440	Ozzie Smith	.60
441	Ray Lankford	.10
442	Dennis Eckersley	.10
443	Ron Gant	.20
444	Alan Benes	.20
445	Rickey Henderson	.10
446	Jody Reed	.10
447	Trevor Hoffman	.10
448	Andujar Cedeno	.10
449	Steve Finley	.10
450	Tony Gwynn	1.00
451	Joey Hamilton	.10
452	Mark Leiter	.10
453	Rod Beck	.10
454	Kirt Manwaring	.10
455	Matt Williams	.30
456	Robby Thompson	.10
457	Shawon Dunston	.10
458	Russ Davis	.10
459	Paul Sorrento	.10
460	Randy Johnson	.50
461	Chris Bosio	.10
462	Luis Sojo	.10
463	Sterling Hitchcock	.10
464	Benji Gil	.10
465	Mickey Tettleton	.10
466	Mark McLemore	.10
467	Darryl Hamilton	.10
468	Ken Hill	.10
469	Dean Palmer	.10
470	Carlos Delgado	.20
471	Ed Sprague	.10
472	Otis Nixon	.10
473	Pat Hentgen	.10
474	Juan Guzman	.10
475	John Olerud	.10
476	Checklist(Buck Showalter)	.10
477	Checklist(Bobby Cox)	.10
478	Checklist(Tommy Lasorda)	.25
479	Checklist(Jim Leyland)	.10
480	Checklist(Sparky Anderson)	.10

1996 Upper Deck Blue Chip Prospects

Twenty top young stars who could make a major impact in the major leagues in upcoming seasons are featured in this insert set. Each card is highlighted with blue-foil printing and double die-cut technology, which includes a zig-zag pattern around the top and a die-cut around both bottom corners. The cards are found one per 20 packs in Series 1 foil packs.

A player's name in *italic* type indicates a rookie card.

		MT
Complete Set (20):		200.00
Common Player:		6.00
BC1	Hideo Nomo	20.00
BC2	Johnny Damon	8.00
BC3	Jason Isringhausen	6.00
BC4	Bill Pulsipher	6.00
BC5	Marty Cordova	6.00
BC6	Michael Tucker	6.00
BC7	John Wasdin	6.00
BC8	Karim Garcia	10.00
BC9	Ruben Rivera	8.00
BC10	Chipper Jones	40.00
BC11	Billy Wagner	6.00
BC12	Brooks Kieschnick	6.00
BC13	Alex Ochoa	6.00
BC14	Roger Cedeno	6.00
BC15	Alex Rodriguez	60.00
BC16	Jason Schmidt	6.00
BC17	Derek Jeter	40.00
BC18	Brian L. Hunter	6.00
BC19	Garret Anderson	6.00
BC20	Manny Ramirez	12.00

1996 Upper Deck Cal Ripken Collection

Part of a cross-brand insert set, four cards are included as Series I inserts at the rate of one per 24 packs. Five cards are also included in Series II, one per every 23 packs. They chronicle Cal Ripken's career and highlights.

		MT
Complete Set (5-8, 13-17):		60.00
Common Ripken:		8.00
Header:		8.00
5	Cal Ripken Jr.	8.00
6	Cal Ripken Jr.	8.00
7	Cal Ripken Jr.	8.00
8	Cal Ripken Jr.	8.00
13	Cal Ripken Jr.	8.00
14	Cal Ripken Jr.	8.00
15	Cal Ripken Jr.	8.00
16	Cal Ripken Jr.	8.00
17	Cal Ripken Jr.	8.00

1996 Upper Deck Diamond Destiny

This late-season release is found exclusively in retail foil packs labeled "Upper Deck Tech." They are inserted at a rate of one per pack, sold with eight regular 1996 Upper Deck cards at a suggested retail of around $3. The cards have three versions of the same action photo; in color and black-and-white on front, and in black-and-white on back. A large team logo also appears on front and back. In the upper half of the card is a 1-3/16" diameter round color transparency portrait of the player. The basic version of this chase set had bronze foil highlights. Parallel silver and gold versions are found on average of one per 35 and one per 143 packs, respectively.

		MT
Complete Set (Bronze):		150.00
Common Player (Bronze):		2.00
Silver Player: 3x-4x		
Gold Player: 8X-12X		
DD1	Chipper Jones	10.00
DD2	Fred McGriff	2.00
DD3	Ryan Klesko	3.00
DD4	John Smoltz	2.00
DD5	Greg Maddux	10.00
DD6	Cal Ripken Jr.	12.00
DD7	Roberto Alomar	4.00
DD8	Eddie Murray	3.00
DD9	Brady Anderson	2.00
DD10	Mo Vaughn	5.00
DD11	Roger Clemens	6.00
DD12	Darin Erstad	6.00
DD13	Sammy Sosa	10.00
DD14	Frank Thomas	12.00
DD15	Barry Larkin	3.00
DD16	Albert Belle	5.00
DD17	Manny Ramirez	5.00
DD18	Kenny Lofton	5.00
DD19	Dante Bichette	2.00
DD20	Gary Sheffield	3.00
DD21	Jeff Bagwell	6.00
DD22	Hideo Nomo	4.00
DD23	Mike Piazza	10.00
DD24	Kirby Puckett	6.00
DD25	Paul Molitor	4.00
DD26	Chuck Knoblauch	4.00
DD27	Wade Boggs	3.00
DD28	Derek Jeter	8.00
DD29	Rey Ordonez	3.00
DD30	Mark McGwire	15.00

DD31	Ozzie Smith	4.00
DD32	Tony Gwynn	7.00
DD33	Barry Bonds	5.00
DD34	Matt Williams	3.00
DD35	Ken Griffey Jr.	15.00
DD36	Jay Buhner	2.00
DD37	Randy Johnson	3.00
DD38	Alex Rodriguez	10.00
DD39	Juan Gonzalez	8.00
DD40	Joe Carter	2.00

1996 Upper Deck Future Stock

Future Stock inserts are found on average of one per six packs of Series 1, highlighting 20 top young stars on a die-cut design. Each card has a blue border, vertical photo and silver-foil stamping on the front.

		MT
Complete Set (20):		20.00
Common Player:		.75
FS1	George Arias	1.50
FS2	Brian Barnes	1.00
FS3	Trey Beamon	1.00
FS4	Yamil Benitez	.75
FS5	Jamie Brewington	1.00
FS6	Tony Clark	4.00
FS7	Steve Cox	.75
FS8	Carlos Delgado	3.00
FS9	Chad Fonville	1.00
FS10	Steve Gibralter	1.50
FS11	Curtis Goodwin	1.50
FS12	Todd Greene	2.00
FS13	Jimmy Haynes	1.00
FS14	Quinton McCracken	1.00
FS15	Billy McMillon	1.00
FS16	Chan Ho Park	2.50
FS17	Arquimedez Pozo	.75
FS18	Chris Snopek	1.00
FS19	Shannon Stewart	1.00
FS20	Jeff Suppan	1.00

1996 Upper Deck Gameface

		MT
Complete Set (10):		10.00
Common Player:		.25
GF1	Ken Griffey Jr.	2.00
GF2	Frank Thomas	2.00
GF3	Barry Bonds	.50
GF4	Albert Belle	.50
GF5	Cal Ripken Jr.	1.75
GF6	Mike Piazza	1.50
GF7	Chipper Jones	1.50
GF8	Matt Williams	.25
GF9	Hideo Nomo	.50
GF10	Greg Maddux	1.50

A player's name in *italic* type indicates a rookie card.

1996 Upper Deck Hobby Predictor

These inserts depict 60 top players as possible winners in the categories of Player of the Month, Pitcher of the Month and Rookie Hits Leader. If the pictured player won that category any month of the season the card was redeemable for a 10-card set with a different look, action photos and printed on silver-foil stock. Hobby Predictor inserts are found on average once per dozen packs in both series. Winning cards are indicated by (W).

		MT
Complete Set (60):		120.00
Complete Series 1 Set (30):		60.00
Complete Series 2 Set (30):		60.00
Common Player:		1.00
Expired: 11-18-96		
H1	Albert Belle	2.50
H2	Kenny Lofton	3.00
H3	Rafael Palmeiro	1.50
H4	Ken Griffey Jr.	10.00
H5	Tim Salmon	1.00
H6	Cal Ripken Jr.	8.00
H7	Mark McGwire (W)	6.00
H8	Frank Thomas (W)	6.00
H9	Mo Vaughn (W)	3.00
H10	Player of the Month Long Shot (W)	1.00
H11	Roger Clemens	1.50
H12	David Cone	1.50
H13	Jose Mesa	1.00
H14	Randy Johnson	2.00
H15	Steve Finley	1.00
H16	Mike Mussina	2.00
H17	Kevin Appier	1.00
H18	Kenny Rogers	1.00
H19	Lee Smith	1.00

H20	Pitcher of the Month Long Shot (W)	1.00
H21	George Arias	1.00
H22	Jose Herrera	1.00
H23	Tony Clark	1.00
H24	Todd Greene	1.00
H25	Derek Jeter (W)	6.00
H26	Arquimedez Pozo	1.00
H27	Matt Lawton	1.00
H28	Shannon Stewart	1.00
H29	Chris Snopek	1.00
H30	Rookie Hits Long Shot	1.00
H31	Jeff Bagwell (W)	4.00
H32	Dante Bichette	2.00
H33	Barry Bonds (W)	2.50
H34	Tony Gwynn	4.00
H35	Chipper Jones	6.00
H36	Eric Karros	1.00
H37	Barry Larkin	1.00
H38	Mike Piazza	6.00
H39	Matt Williams	1.00
H40	Player of the Month Long Shot (W)	1.00
H41	Osvaldo Fernandez	1.00
H42	Tom Glavine	1.50
H43	Jason Isringhausen	1.00
H44	Greg Maddux	6.00
H45	Pedro J. Martinez	1.00
H46	Hideo Nomo	2.50
H47	Pete Schourek	1.00
H48	Paul Wilson	1.50
H49	Mark Wohlers	1.00
H50	Pitcher of the Month Long Shot	1.00
H51	Bob Abreu	1.00
H52	Trey Beamon	1.00
H53	Yamil Benitez	1.00
H54	Roger Cedeno (W)	2.00
H55	Todd Hollandsworth	1.50
H56	Marvin Benard	1.00
H57	Jason Kendall	1.50
H58	Brooks Kieschnick	1.00
H59	Rey Ordonez (W)	2.00
H60	Rookie Hits Long Shot (W)	1.00

1996 Upper Deck Hobby Predictor Redemption

Persons who redeemed winning cards from UD's interactive Predictor insert series received a 10-card set of the top players in various statistical categories. The redemption cards are similar in format to the Predictor cards, but have fronts printed on silver-foil. In palce of the contest rules found on the backs of Predictor cards, the redemption cards have a career summary.

	MT
Complete Set (30):	12.00
Common Player:	.25
H31 Jeff Bagwell	1.00
H32 Dante Bichette	.40
H33 Barry Bonds	.75
H34 Tony Gwynn	1.00
H35 Chipper Jones	1.50
H36 Eric Karros	.25
H37 Barry Larkin	.25
H38 Mike Piazza	1.50
H39 Matt Williams	.25
H40 Player of the Month Long Shot	.25
H41 Osvaldo Fernandez	.25
H42 Tom Glavine	.40
H43 Jason Isringhausen	.25
H44 Greg Maddux	1.00
H45 Pedro Martinez	.35
H46 Hideo Nomo	.50
H47 Pete Schourek	.25
H48 Paul Wilson	.40
H49 Mark Wohlers	.25
H50 Pitcher of the Month Long Shot	.25
H51 Bob Abreu	.35
H52 Trey Beamon	.25
H53 Yamil Benitez	.25
H54 Roger Cedeno	.25
H55 Todd Hollandsworth	.25
H56 Marvin Benard	.25
H57 Jason Kendall	.35
H58 Brooks Kieschnick	.25
H59 Rey Ordonez	.45
H60 Rookie Hits Long Shot	.25

1996 Upper Deck Hot Commodities

These 20 die-cut cards were seeded one per every 37 1996 Upper Deck Series II packs.

	MT
Complete Set (20):	175.00
Common Player:	4.00
HC1 Ken Griffey Jr.	30.00
HC2 Hideo Nomo	8.00
HC3 Roberto Alomar	8.00
HC4 Paul Wilson	4.00
HC5 Albert Belle	8.00
HC6 Manny Ramirez	8.00
HC7 Kirby Puckett	12.00
HC8 Johnny Damon	4.00
HC9 Randy Johnson	6.00
HC10 Greg Maddux	18.00
HC11 Chipper Jones	18.00
HC12 Barry Bonds	8.00
HC13 Mo Vaughn	8.00
HC14 Mike Piazza	18.00
HC15 Cal Ripken Jr.	25.00
HC16 Tim Salmon	6.00
HC17 Sammy Sosa	15.00
HC18 Kenny Lofton	8.00
HC19 Tony Gwynn	15.00
HC20 Frank Thomas	25.00

1996 Upper Deck Lovero Collection

Every sixth pack of 1996 Upper Deck Series II has a V.J. Lovero insert card. This 20-card set features unique shots from Lovero, one of the most well-known photographers in the country. Some of the cards feature Randy Johnson wearing a conehead, Frank Thomas blowing a bubble while throwing the ball, and Jay Buhner and his child both chewing on a bat.

	MT
Complete Set (20):	35.00
Common Player:	.50
VJ1 Rod Carew	.75
VJ2 Hideo Nomo	2.00
VJ3 Derek Jeter	4.00
VJ4 Barry Bonds	2.00
VJ5 Greg Maddux	5.00
VJ6 Mark McGwire	8.00
VJ7 Jose Canseco	1.00
VJ8 Ken Caminiti	.50
VJ9 Raul Mondesi	1.00
VJ10 Ken Griffey Jr.	8.00
VJ11 Jay Buhner	.50
VJ12 Randy Johnson	1.50
VJ13 Roger Clemens	2.00
VJ14 Brady Anderson	.50
VJ15 Frank Thomas	6.00
VJ16 Angels Outfielders	.50
VJ17 Mike Piazza	4.00
VJ18 Dante Bichette	1.00
VJ19 Tony Gwynn	3.00
VJ20 Jim Abbott	.50

1996 Upper Deck Nomo Highlights

The 1995 rookie season of Los Angeles Dodgers' pitcher Hideo Nomo is recapped in this five-card 1996 Upper Deck insert set. The cards were seeded one per every 23 Series 2 packs. A 5" x 7" version of each card was also issued as a retail box insert. Values are the same as for small cards.

	MT
Complete Set (5):	10.00
Common Nomo:	2.50
1 Hideo Nomo	2.50
2 Hideo Nomo	2.50
3 Hideo Nomo	2.50
4 Hideo Nomo	2.50
5 Hideo Nomo	2.50

1996 Upper Deck Power Driven

Twenty of the game's top power hitters are analyzed in depth by baseball writer Peter Gammons on these Series 1 insert cards. Found once per 36 packs, on average, the cards are printed on an embossed light F/X design.

	MT
Complete Set (20):	140.00
Common Player:	3.00
PD1 Albert Belle	8.00
PD2 Barry Bonds	9.00
PD3 Jay Buhner	4.00
PD4 Jose Canseco	4.00
PD5 Cecil Fielder	3.00
PD6 Juan Gonzalez	12.00
PD7 Ken Griffey Jr.	30.00
PD8 Eric Karros	3.00
PD9 Fred McGriff	5.00
PD10 Mark McGwire	30.00
PD11 Rafael Palmeiro	3.00
PD12 Mike Piazza	18.00
PD13 Manny Ramirez	8.00
PD14 Tim Salmon	4.00
PD15 Reggie Sanders	3.00
PD16 Sammy Sosa	15.00
PD17 Frank Thomas	25.00
PD18 Mo Vaughn	8.00
PD19 Larry Walker	5.00
PD20 Matt Williams	4.00

1996 Upper Deck Retail Predictor

Retail Predictor inserts feature 60 possible winners in the categories of monthly leader in home runs, batting average and RBIs. If the pictured player led a category in any month, his card was redeemable for a 10-card set featuring action photos on silver foil. Retail Predictors are found on average once per 12 packs in each series. Winning cards are indicated by (W).

A player's name in *italic* type indicates a rookie card.

		MT
Complete Set (60):		125.00
Complete Series 1 (30):		75.00
Complete Series 2 (30):		50.00
Common Player:		1.00
Expired: 11-18-96		
R1	Albert Belle (W)	2.50
R2	Jay Buhner (W)	1.00
R3	Juan Gonzalez	4.00
R4	Ken Griffey Jr.	10.00
R5	Mark McGwire (W)	6.00
R6	Rafael Palmeiro	1.50
R7	Tim Salmon	1.00
R8	Frank Thomas	8.00
R9	Mo Vaughn (W)	2.50
R10	Home Run Long Shot (W)	1.00
R11	Albert Belle (W)	2.50
R12	Jay Buhner	1.00
R13	Jim Edmonds	1.00
R14	Cecil Fielder	1.00
R15	Ken Griffey Jr.	10.00
R16	Edgar Martinez	1.00
R17	Manny Ramirez	2.50
R18	Frank Thomas	8.00
R19	Mo Vaughn Win	2.50
R20	RBI Long Shot (W)	1.00
R21	Roberto Alomar (W)	2.00
R22	Carlos Baerga	1.00
R23	Wade Boggs	1.00
R24	Ken Griffey Jr.	10.00
R25	Chuck Knoblauch	1.00
R26	Kenny Lofton	2.50
R27	Edgar Martinez	1.00
R28	Tim Salmon	1.00
R29	Frank Thomas	8.00
R30	Batting Average Long Shot (W)	1.00
R31	Dante Bichette	1.00
R32	Barry Bonds (W)	2.50
R33	Ron Gant	1.00
R34	Chipper Jones	6.00
R35	Fred McGriff	1.50
R36	Mike Piazza	6.00
R37	Sammy Sosa	4.00
R38	Larry Walker	1.00
R39	Matt Williams	1.50
R40	Home Run Long Shot	1.00
R41	Jeff Bagwell (W)	4.00
R42	Dante Bichette	1.00
R43	Barry Bonds (W)	2.50
R44	Jeff Conine	1.00
R45	Andres Galarraga	1.00
R46	Mike Piazza	6.00
R47	Reggie Sanders	1.00
R48	Sammy Sosa	4.00
R49	Matt Williams	1.50
R50	RBI Long Shot	1.00
R51	Jeff Bagwell	4.00
R52	Derek Bell	1.00
R53	Dante Bichette	1.00
R54	Craig Biggio	1.00
R55	Barry Bonds	2.50
R56	Bret Boone	1.00
R57	Tony Gwynn	4.00
R58	Barry Larkin	1.50
R59	Mike Piazza (W)	6.00
R60	AVG Long Shot	1.00

1996 Upper Deck Retail Predictor Redemption

Persons who redeemed winning cards from UD's interactive Predictor insert series received a 10-card set of the top players in various statistical categories. The redemption cards are similar in format to the Predictor cards, but have fronts printed on silver-foil. In palce of the contest rules found on the backs of Predictor cards, the redemption cards have a career summary.

		MT
Complete Set (30):		12.00
Common Player:		.25
R31	Dante Bichette	.25
R32	Barry Bonds	.75
R33	Ron Gant	.25

R34	Chipper Jones	1.50
R35	Fred McGriff	.40
R36	Mike Piazza	1.50
R37	Sammy Sosa	1.50
R38	Larry Walker	.35
R39	Matt Williams	.25
R40	Home Run Long Shot	.25
R41	Jeff Bagwell	1.00
R42	Dante Bichette	.25
R43	Barry Bonds	.75
R44	Jeff Conine	.25
R45	Andres Galarraga	.25
R46	Mike Piazza	1.50
R47	Reggie Sanders	.25
R48	Sammy Sosa	1.50
R49	Matt Williams	.25
R50	RBI Long Shot	.25
R51	Jeff Bagwell	1.00
R52	Derek Bell	.25
R53	Dante Bichette	.25
R54	Craig Biggio	.25
R55	Barry Bonds	.75
R56	Bret Boone	.25
R57	Tony Gwynn	1.00
R58	Barry Larkin	.25
R59	Mike Piazza	1.50
R60	AVG Long Shot	.25

1996 Upper Deck Run Producers

These double die-cut, embossed and color foil-stamped cards feature 20 of the game's top RBI men. The cards were seeded one per every 71 packs of 1996 Upper Deck Series II.

		MT
Complete Set (20):		200.00
Common Player:		4.00
RP1	Albert Belle	10.00
RP2	Dante Bichette	5.00
RP3	Barry Bonds	10.00
RP4	Jay Buhner	4.00
RP5	Jose Canseco	4.00
RP6	Juan Gonzalez	20.00
RP7	Ken Griffey Jr.	50.00
RP8	Tony Gwynn	20.00
RP9	Kenny Lofton	10.00
RP10	Edgar Martinez	4.00
RP11	Fred McGriff	6.00
RP12	Mark McGwire	50.00
RP13	Rafael Palmeiro	4.00
RP14	Mike Piazza	30.00
RP15	Manny Ramirez	8.00
RP16	Tim Salmon	4.00
RP17	Sammy Sosa	25.00
RP18	Frank Thomas	40.00
RP19	Mo Vaughn	10.00
RP20	Matt Williams	5.00

1997 Upper Deck

The 520-card, regular-sized set was available in 12-card packs. The base card fronts feature a full action shot with the player's name near the bottom edge above a bronze-foil, wood-grain stripe. The player's team logo is in the lower left corner in silver foil. Each card front has the date of the game pictured with a brief description. The card backs contain more detailed game highlight descriptions and statistics, along with a small action shot in the upper left quadrant. Subsets are: Jackie Robinson Tribute (1-9), Strike Force (65-72), Defensive Gems (136-153), Global Impact (181-207), Season Highlights Checklist (214-222) and Star Rookies (223-240). Inserts are: Game Jerseys, Ticket To Stardom, Power Package, Amazing Greats and Rock Solid Foundation. A 30-card update to Series I was released early in the season featuring 1996 post-season highlights and star rookies. The card faces had red or purple borders and were numbered 241 to 270. A second update set of 30 was released near the end of the 1997 season, numbered 521-550 and featuring traded players and rookies in a format identical to Series I and II UD. Both of the update sets were available only via a mail-in redemption offer.

		MT
Complete Set (550):		110.00
Complete Series I Set (240):		30.00
Complete Update Set (241-270):		10.00
Complete Series II Set (250):		60.00
Complete Update Set (521-550):		12.00
Common Player:		.10
Hobby Box:		60.00
1	Jackie Robinson	1.00
2	Jackie Robinson	1.00
3	Jackie Robinson	1.00
4	Jackie Robinson	1.00
5	Jackie Robinson	1.00
6	Jackie Robinson	1.00
7	Jackie Robinson	1.00
8	Jackie Robinson	1.00
9	Jackie Robinson	1.00
10	Chipper Jones	2.00
11	Marquis Grissom	.10
12	Jermaine Dye	.20
13	Mark Lemke	.10
14	Terrell Wade	.10
15	Fred McGriff	.30
16	Tom Glavine	.15
17	Mark Wohlers	.10
18	Randy Myers	.10
19	Roberto Alomar	.75
20	Cal Ripken Jr.	2.50
21	Rafael Palmeiro	.15
22	Mike Mussina	.40
23	Brady Anderson	.10
24	Jose Canseco	.25
25	Mo Vaughn	1.00
26	Roger Clemens	1.00
27	Tim Naehring	.10
28	Jeff Suppan	.10
29	Troy Percival	.10
30	Sammy Sosa	1.50
31	Amaury Telemaco	.10
32	Rey Sanchez	.10
33	Scott Servais	.10
34	Steve Trachsel	.10
35	Mark Grace	.20
36	Wilson Alvarez	.10
37	Harold Baines	.10
38	Tony Phillips	.10
39	James Baldwin	.10
40	Frank Thomas (wrong (Ken Griffey Jr.'s) vital data)	2.50
41	Lyle Mouton	.10
42	Chris Snopek	.10
43	Hal Morris	.10
44	Eric Davis	.10
45	Barry Larkin	.25
46	Reggie Sanders	.10
47	Pete Schourek	.10
48	Lee Smith	.10

#	Player	Price
49	Charles Nagy	.10
50	Albert Belle	.75
51	Julio Franco	.10
52	Kenny Lofton	.75
53	Orel Hershiser	.10
54	Omar Vizquel	.10
55	Eric Young	.10
56	Curtis Leskanic	.10
57	Quinton McCracken	.10
58	Kevin Ritz	.10
59	Walt Weiss	.10
60	Dante Bichette	.25
61	Marc Lewis	.10
62	Tony Clark	.50
63	Travis Fryman	.10
64	John Smoltz (Strike Force)	.15
65	Greg Maddux (Strike Force)	1.00
66	Tom Glavine (Strike Force)	.15
67	Mike Mussina (Strike Force)	.20
68	Andy Pettitte (Strike Force)	.40
69	Mariano Rivera (Strike Force)	.15
70	Hideo Nomo (Strike Force)	.30
71	Kevin Brown (Strike Force)	.10
72	Randy Johnson (Strike Force)	.20
73	Felipe Lira	.10
74	Kimera Bartee	.10
75	Alan Trammell	.10
76	Kevin Brown	.10
77	Edgar Renteria	.25
78	Al Leiter	.10
79	Charles Johnson	.10
80	Andre Dawson	.10
81	Billy Wagner	.10
82	Donne Wall	.10
83	Jeff Bagwell	1.25
84	Keith Lockhart	.10
85	Jeff Montgomery	.10
86	Tom Goodwin	.10
87	Tim Belcher	.10
88	Mike Macfarlane	.10
89	Joe Randa	.10
90	Brett Butler	.10
91	Todd Worrell	.10
92	Todd Hollandsworth	.10
93	Ismael Valdes	.10
94	Hideo Nomo	.60
95	Mike Piazza	2.00
96	Jeff Cirillo	.10
97	Ricky Bones	.10
98	Fernando Vina	.10
99	Ben McDonald	.10
100	John Jaha	.10
101	Mark Loretta	.10
102	Paul Molitor	.50
103	Rick Aguilera	.10
104	Marty Cordova	.10
105	Kirby Puckett	.60
106	Dan Naulty	.10
107	Frank Rodriguez	.10
108	Shane Andrews	.10
109	Henry Rodriguez	.10
110	Mark Grudzielanek	.10
111	Pedro J. Martinez	.10
112	Ugueth Urbina	.10
113	David Segui	.10
114	Rey Ordonez	.25
115	Bernard Gilkey	.10
116	Butch Huskey	.10
117	Paul Wilson	.10
118	Alex Ochoa	.10
119	John Franco	.10
120	Dwight Gooden	.10
121	Ruben Rivera	.25
122	Andy Pettitte	.75
123	Tino Martinez	.30
124	Bernie Williams	.50
125	Wade Boggs	.15
126	Paul O'Neill	.10
127	Scott Brosius	.10
128	Ernie Young	.10
129	Doug Johns	.10
130	Geronimo Berroa	.10
131	Jason Giambi	.10
132	John Wasdin	.10
133	Jim Eisenreich	.10
134	Ricky Otero	.10
135	Ricky Bottalico	.10
136	Mark Langston (Defensive Gems)	.10
137	Greg Maddux (Defensive Gems)	1.00
138	Ivan Rodriguez (Defensive Gems)	.20
139	Charles Johnson (Defensive Gems)	.10
140	J.T. Snow (Defensive Gems)	.10
141	Mark Grace (Defensive Gems)	.15
142	Roberto Alomar (Defensive Gems)	.40
143	Craig Biggio (Defensive Gems)	.10
144	Ken Caminiti (Defensive Gems)	.10
145	Matt Williams (Defensive Gems)	.15
146	Omar Vizquel (Defensive Gems)	.10
147	Cal Ripken Jr. (Defensive Gems)	1.25
148	Ozzie Smith (Defensive Gems)	.25
149	Rey Ordonez (Defensive Gems)	.15
150	Ken Griffey Jr. (Defensive Gems)	1.50
151	Devon White (Defensive Gems)	.10
152	Barry Bonds (Defensive Gems)	.50
153	Kenny Lofton (Defensive Gems)	.40
154	Mickey Morandini	.10
155	Gregg Jefferies	.10
156	Curt Schilling	.10
157	Jason Kendall	.10
158	Francisco Cordova	.15
159	Dennis Eckersley	.12
160	Ron Gant	.12
161	Ozzie Smith	.20
162	Brian Jordan	.10
163	John Mabry	.10
164	Andy Ashby	.10
165	Steve Finley	.10
166	Fernando Valenzuela	.10
167	Archi Cianfrocco	.10
168	Wally Joyner	.10
169	Greg Vaughn	.10
170	Barry Bonds	.15
171	William VanLandingham	.10
172	Marvin Benard	.10
173	Rich Aurilia	.10
174	Jay Canizaro	.10
175	Ken Griffey Jr.	3.00
176	Bob Wells	.10
177	Jay Buhner	.20
178	Sterling Hitchcock	.10
179	Edgar Martinez	.10
180	Rusty Greer	.10
181	Dave Nilsson (Global Impact)	.10
182	Larry Walker (Global Impact)	.35
183	Edgar Renteria (Global Impact)	.15
184	Rey Ordonez (Global Impact)	.20
185	Rafael Palmeiro (Global Impact)	.10
186	Osvaldo Fernandez (Global Impact)	.10
187	Raul Mondesi (Global Impact)	.15
188	Manny Ramirez (Global Impact)	.50
189	Sammy Sosa (Global Impact)	.75
190	Robert Eenhoorn (Global Impact)	.10
191	Devon White (Global Impact)	.10
192	Hideo Nomo (Global Impact)	.30
193	Mac Suzuki (Global Impact)	.10
194	Chan Ho Park (Global Impact)	.10
195	Fernando Valenzuela (Global Impact)	.10
196	Andruw Jones (Global Impact)	.75
197	Vinny Castilla (Global Impact)	.10
198	Dennis Martinez (Global Impact)	.10
199	Ruben Rivera (Global Impact)	.20
200	Juan Gonzalez (Global Impact)	.60
201	Roberto Alomar (Global Impact)	.40
202	Edgar Martinez (Global Impact)	.10
203	Ivan Rodriguez (Global Impact)	.20
204	Carlos Delgado (Global Impact)	.10
205	Andres Galarraga (Global Impact)	.15
206	Ozzie Guillen (Global Impact)	.10
207	Midre Cummings (Global Impact)	.10
208	Roger Pavlik	.10
209	Darren Oliver	.10
210	Dean Palmer	.10
211	Ivan Rodriguez	.60
212	Otis Nixon	.10
213	Pat Hentgen	.10
214	Ozzie Smith, Andre Dawson, Kirby Puckett CL (Season Highlights)	.25
215	Barry Bonds, Gary Sheffield, Brady Anderson CL (Season Highlights)	.25
216	Ken Caminiti CL (Season Highlights)	.10
217	John Smoltz CL (Season Highlights)	.10
218	Eric Young CL (Season Highlights)	.10
219	Juan Gonzalez CL (Season Highlights)	.60
220	Eddie Murray CL (Season Highlights)	.20
221	Tommy Lasorda CL (Season Highlights)	.25
222	Paul Molitor CL (Season Highlights)	.15
223	Luis Castillo	.25
224	Justin Thompson	.10
225	Rocky Coppinger	.10
226	Jermaine Allensworth	.10
227	Jeff D'Amico	.10
228	Jamey Wright	.10
229	Scott Rolen	1.25
230	Darin Erstad	1.25
231	Marty Janzen	.10
232	Jacob Cruz	.10
233	Raul Ibanez	.10
234	Nomar Garciaparra	2.00
235	Todd Walker	.60
236	Brian Giles	.10
237	Matt Beech	.10
238	Mike Cameron	.10
239	Jose Paniagua	.10
240	Andruw Jones	1.50
241	Brant Brown (Star Rookies)	.10
242	Robin Jennings (Star Rookies)	.10
243	Willie Adams (Star Rookies)	.10
244	Ken Caminiti (Division Series)	.20
245	Brian Jordan (Division Series)	.10
246	Chipper Jones (Division Series)	2.00
247	Juan Gonzalez (Division Series)	1.50
248	Bernie Williams (Division Series)	.50
249	Roberto Alomar (Division Series)	.50
250	Bernie Williams (Post-Season)	.50
251	David Wells (Post-Season)	.10
252	Cecil Fielder (Post-Season)	.15
253	Darryl Strawberry (Post-Season)	.10
254	Andy Pettitte (Post-Season)	.75
255	Javier Lopez (Post-Season)	.15
256	Gary Gaetti (Post-Season)	.10
257	Ron Gant (Post-Season)	.10
258	Brian Jordan (Post-Season)	.10
259	John Smoltz (Post-Season)	.20
260	Greg Maddux (Post-Season)	2.00
261	Tom Glavine (Post-Season)	.20
262	Chipper Jones (World Series)	2.00
263	Greg Maddux (World Series)	2.00
264	David Cone (World Series)	.15
265	Jim Leyritz (World Series)	.10
266	Andy Pettitte (World Series)	.75

492	Tony Gwynn	1.25
493	Joey Hamilton	.10
494	Rickey Henderson	.10
495	Glenallen Hill	.10
496	Rod Beck	.10
497	Osvaldo Fernandez	.10
498	Rick Wilkins	.10
499	Joey Cora	.10
500	Alex Rodriguez	3.00
501	Randy Johnson	.60
502	Paul Sorrento	.10
503	Dan Wilson	.10
504	Jamie Moyer	.10
505	Will Clark	.25
506	Mickey Tettleton	.10
507	John Burkett	.10
508	Ken Hill	.10
509	Mark McLemore	.10
510	Juan Gonzalez	1.25
511	Bobby Witt	.10
512	Carlos Delgado	.10
513	Alex Gonzalez	.10
514	Shawn Green	.10
515	Joe Carter	.20
516	Juan Guzman	.10
517	Charlie O'Brien	.10
518	Ed Sprague	.10
519	Mike Timlin	.10
520	Roger Clemens	1.00
521	Eddie Murray	.35
522	Jason Dickson	.20
523	Jim Leyritz	.10
524	Michael Tucker	.10
525	Kenny Lofton	1.00
526	Jimmy Key	.10
527	Mel Rojas	.10
528	Deion Sanders	.25
529	Bartolo Colon	.10
530	Matt Williams	.40
531	Marquis Grissom	.10
532	David Justice	.25
533	*Bubba Trammell*	1.00
534	Moises Alou	.10
535	Bobby Bonilla	.10
536	Alex Fernandez	.10
537	Jay Bell	.10
538	Chili Davis	.10
539	Jeff King	.10
540	Todd Zeile	.10
541	John Olerud	.10
542	Jose Guillen	.75
543	Derrek Lee	.10
544	Dante Powell	.10
545	J.T. Snow	.10
546	Jeff Kent	.10
547	*Jose Cruz Jr.*	4.00
548	John Wetteland	.10
549	Orlando Merced	.10
550	*Hideki Irabu*	2.00

1997 Upper Deck Amazing Greats

The 20-card, regular-sized insert set was included every 138 packs of 1997 Upper Deck baseball. The cards include real wood with two player shots imaged on the card front. The team logo appears in the upper right corner of the horizontal card. The cards are numbered with the "AG" prefix.

		MT
Complete Set (20):		500.00
Common Player:		8.00
AG1	Ken Griffey Jr.	60.00
AG2	Roberto Alomar	10.00
AG3	Alex Rodriguez	50.00
AG4	Paul Molitor	10.00
AG5	Chipper Jones	40.00
AG6	Tony Gwynn	30.00
AG7	Kenny Lofton	15.00
AG8	Albert Belle	15.00
AG9	Matt Williams	8.00
AG10	Frank Thomas	40.00
AG11	Greg Maddux	40.00
AG12	Sammy Sosa	40.00
AG13	Kirby Puckett	20.00
AG14	Jeff Bagwell	20.00
AG15	Cal Ripken Jr.	50.00
AG16	Manny Ramirez	15.00
AG17	Barry Bonds	15.00
AG18	Mo Vaughn	15.00
AG19	Eddie Murray	10.00
AG20	Mike Piazza	40.00

1997 Upper Deck Blue Chip Prospects

This 20-card insert was found in packs of Series II and features a die-cut design. Cards appear to have a photo slide attached to them featuring a portrait shot of the promising youngster depicted on the card. A total of 500 of each card were produced.

		MT
Complete Set (20):		600.00
Common Player:		10.00
BC1	Andruw Jones	40.00
BC2	Derek Jeter	60.00
BC3	Scott Rolen	60.00
BC4	Manny Ramirez	25.00
BC5	Todd Walker	25.00
BC6	Rocky Coppinger	10.00
BC7	Nomar Garciaparra	100.00
BC8	Darin Erstad	50.00
BC9	Jermaine Dye	10.00
BC10	Vladimir Guerrero	50.00
BC11	Edgar Renteria	10.00
BC12	Bob Abreu	10.00
BC13	Karim Garcia	15.00
BC14	Jeff D'Amico	10.00
BC15	Chipper Jones	60.00
BC16	Todd Hollandsworth	10.00
BC17	Andy Pettitte	20.00
BC18	Ruben Rivera	10.00
BC19	Jason Kendall	10.00
BC20	Alex Rodriguez	80.00

1997 Upper Deck Game Jersey

The three-card, regular-sized set was inserted every 800 packs of Upper Deck Series I. The cards contained a square of the player's game-used jersey, and carried a "GJ" card number prefix.

		MT
Complete Set (3):		800.00
Common Player:		100.00
GJ1	Ken Griffey Jr.	600.00
GJ2	Tony Gwynn	300.00
GJ3	Rey Ordonez	100.00

1997 Upper Deck Hot Commodities

This 20-card insert from Series II features a flame pattern behind the image of the player depicted on the front of the card. Odds of finding a card were 1:13 packs.

		MT
Complete Set (20):		130.00
Common Player:		2.50
HC1	Alex Rodriguez	10.00
HC2	Andruw Jones	3.00
HC3	Derek Jeter	8.00
HC4	Frank Thomas	8.00
HC5	Ken Griffey Jr.	12.00
HC6	Chipper Jones	8.00
HC7	Juan Gonzalez	6.00
HC8	Cal Ripken Jr.	10.00
HC9	John Smoltz	2.50
HC10	Mark McGwire	15.00
HC11	Barry Bonds	3.00
HC12	Albert Belle	4.00
HC13	Mike Piazza	8.00
HC14	Manny Ramirez	4.00
HC15	Mo Vaughn	4.00
HC16	Tony Gwynn	6.00
HC17	Vladimir Guerrero	4.00
HC18	Hideo Nomo	2.00
HC19	Greg Maddux	8.00
HC20	Kirby Puckett	4.00

1997 Upper Deck Long Distance Connection

This 20-card insert from Series II features the top home run hitters in the game. Odds of finding a card were 1:35 packs.

		MT
Complete Set (20):		200.00
Common Player:		4.00
LD1	Mark McGwire	35.00
LD2	Brady Anderson	4.00
LD3	Ken Griffey Jr.	35.00
LD4	Albert Belle	8.00
LD5	Juan Gonzalez	18.00
LD6	Andres Galarraga	4.00
LD7	Jay Buhner	4.00
LD8	Mo Vaughn	8.00
LD9	Barry Bonds	8.00
LD10	Gary Sheffield	6.00
LD11	Todd Hundley	4.00
LD12	Frank Thomas	25.00
LD13	Sammy Sosa	20.00
LD14	Rafael Palmeiro	4.00
LD15	Alex Rodriguez	30.00
LD16	Mike Piazza	20.00
LD17	Ken Caminiti	6.00

LD18	Chipper Jones	20.00
LD19	Manny Ramirez	8.00
LD20	Andruw Jones	10.00

1997 Upper Deck Memorable Moments

This issue was a one per pack insert in special Series 1 and 2 Collector's Choice six-card retail packs. In standard 2-1/2" x 3-1/2", the cards are die-cut at top and bottom in a wave pattern. Fronts, highlighted in matte bronze foil, have action photos and a career highlight. Backs have another photo and a more complete explanation of the Memorable Moment.

		MT
Complete Set (20):		16.00
Common Player:		.50
		.50
	SERIES 1	
1	Andruw Jones	1.00
2	Chipper Jones	1.50
3	Cal Ripken Jr.	2.00
4	Frank Thomas	2.50
5	Manny Ramirez	.50
6	Mike Piazza	2.00
7	Mark McGwire	3.00
8	Ken Griffey Jr.	3.00
9	Barry Bonds	1.50
10	Alex Rodriguez	2.00
	SERIES 2	
1	Ken Griffey Jr.	3.00
2	Albert Belle	.75
3	Derek Jeter	1.00
4	Greg Maddux	2.00
5	Tony Gwynn	2.00
6	Ryne Sandberg	1.50
7	Juan Gonzalez	1.50
8	Roger Clemens	1.50
9	Jose Cruz Jr.	1.00
10	Mo Vaughn	.50

1997 Upper Deck Power Package

The 20-card, regular-sized, die-cut set was inserted every 23 packs of 1997 Upper Deck baseball. The player's name is printed in gold foil along the top border of the card face, which also features Light F/X. The die-cut cards have a silver-foil border and team-color frame with a "Power Package" logo in gold foil centered on the bottom border. The card backs have a short highlight in a brown box bordered by team colors and are numbered with the "PP" prefix.

		MT
Complete Set (20):		140.00
Common Player:		3.00
PP1	Ken Griffey Jr.	30.00
PP2	Joe Carter	3.00
PP3	Rafael Palmeiro	3.00
PP4	Jay Buhner	3.00
PP5	Sammy Sosa	15.00
PP6	Fred McGriff	3.00
PP7	Jeff Bagwell	12.00
PP8	Albert Belle	8.00
PP9	Matt Williams	3.00
PP10	Mark McGwire	35.00
PP11	Gary Sheffield	5.00
PP12	Tim Salmon	3.00
PP13	Ryan Klesko	4.00
PP14	Manny Ramirez	8.00
PP15	Mike Piazza	20.00
PP16	Barry Bonds	8.00
PP17	Mo Vaughn	8.00
PP18	Jose Canseco	3.00
PP19	Juan Gonzalez	15.00
PP20	Frank Thomas	20.00

1997 Upper Deck Predictor

A new concept in interactive cards was UD's Series II Predictor inserts. Each player's card has four scratch-off baseball bats at the top-right. Under each bat is printed a specific accomplishment - hit for cycle, CG shutout, etc. - If the player attained that goal during the '97 season, and if the collector had scratched off the correct bat among the four, the Predictor card could be redeemed (with $2) for a premium TV cel card of the player. Thus if the player made one of his goals, the collector had a 25% chance of choosing the right bat. Two goals gave a 50% chance, etc. The Predictor cards have color action photos of the players at the left end of the horizontal format. The background at left and bottom is a red scorecard motif. Behind the bats is

a black-and-white stadium scene. Backs repeat the red scorecard design with contest rules printed in white. A (W) in the checklist here indicates the player won one or more of his goals making his cards eligible for redemption. The redemption period ended Nov. 22, 1997. Values shown are for unscratched cards.

		MT
Complete Set (30):		40.00
Common Player:		.50
Prices for Unscratched Cards		
1	Andruw Jones	2.00
2	Chipper Jones	3.00
3	Greg Maddux (W)	3.00
4	Fred McGriff (W)	.75
5	John Smoltz (W)	.75
6	Brady Anderson (W)	.75
7	Cal Ripken Jr. (W)	4.00
8	Mo Vaughn (W)	1.25
9	Sammy Sosa	1.25
10	Albert Belle (W)	1.25
11	Frank Thomas	4.00
12	Kenny Lofton (W)	1.25
13	Jim Thome	.50
14	Dante Bichette (W)	.75
15	Andres Galarraga	.50
16	Gary Sheffield	.50
17	Hideo Nomo (W)	1.00
18	Mike Piazza (W)	3.00
19	Derek Jeter (W)	3.00
20	Bernie Williams	.50
21	Mark McGwire (W)	6.00
22	Ken Caminiti (W)	.75
23	Tony Gwynn (W)	2.50
24	Barry Bonds (W)	1.25
25	Jay Buhner (W)	.65
26	Ken Griffey Jr. (W)	5.00
27	Alex Rodriguez (W)	4.00
28	Juan Gonzalez (W)	2.50
29	Dean Palmer (W)	.65
30	Roger Clemens (W)	2.00

1997 Upper Deck Predictor Prize Cards

Persons who redeemed winning Predictor scratch-off cards prior to the Nov. 22, 1997, deadline received a premium version of that player's card. A $2 per card handling fee was charged. The Predictor prize cards are in a format similar to the scratch-off cards, with a red background on front and back depicting the motif of a baseball score card. The prize cards are printed on plastic in 3-1/2" x 2-1/2"

Modern cards have little collector value in conditions lower than Mint. Figure NM cards at 75% of values shown; EX cards at 40%.

Values shown reflect the market as of January, 1999. On-field performances of current players in the 1999 baseball season are not factored in.

format. Fronts have a player portrait photo at left. At right is a large semi-circular mirrored window with an action photo visible when held to the light. Backs have a few stats, copyright data, logos, etc., with a reverse image in the window. Card fronts were covered with a sheet of peel-off protection plastic. The prize cards are numbered on back with a "P" prefix.

		MT
Complete Set (22):		250.00
Common Player:		3.00
P3	Greg Maddux	16.00
P4	Fred McGriff	4.50
P5	John Smoltz	4.50
P6	Brady Anderson	3.00
P7	Cal Ripken Jr.	24.00
P8	Mo Vaughn	7.50
P11	Frank Thomas	30.00
P12	Kenny Lofton	6.00
P14	Dante Bichette	3.50
P17	Hideo Nomo	9.00
P18	Mike Piazza	18.00
P19	Derek Jeter	16.00
P21	Mark McGwire	9.00
P22	Ken Caminiti	4.50
P23	Tony Gwynn	15.00
P24	Barry Bonds	7.50
P25	Jay Buhner	3.00
P26	Ken Griffey Jr.	30.00
P27	Alex Rodriguez	24.00
P28	Juan Gonzalez	15.00
P29	Dean Palmer	3.00
P30	Roger Clemens	12.00

1997 Upper Deck Rock Solid Foundation

The 20-card, regular-sized set was inserted every seven packs of 1997 Upper Deck baseball. The card fronts feature rainbow foil with the player's name in silver foil along the top border. The team logo appears in gold foil in the lower right corner with "Rock Solid Foundation" also printed in gold foil over a marbled background. The card backs have the same marbled background with a close-up shot on the upper half. A short text is also included and the cards are numbered with the "RS" prefix.

		MT
Complete Set (20):		50.00
Common Player:		2.00
RS1	Alex Rodriguez	15.00
RS2	Rey Ordonez	3.00
RS3	Derek Jeter	10.00
RS4	Darin Erstad	10.00

RS5	Chipper Jones	10.00
RS6	Johnny Damon	3.00
RS7	Ryan Klesko	3.00
RS8	Charles Johnson	2.00
RS9	Andy Pettitte	6.00
RS10	Manny Ramirez	5.00
RS11	Ivan Rodriguez	3.00
RS12	Jason Kendall	2.00
RS13	Rondell White	2.00
RS14	Alex Ochoa	2.00
RS15	Javy Lopez	2.00
RS16	Pedro J. Martinez	2.00
RS17	Carlos Delgado	2.00
RS18	Paul Wilson	3.00
RS19	Alan Benes	2.00
RS20	Raul Mondesi	3.00

1997 Upper Deck Run Producers

A 24-card insert found in Series II, Run Producers salutes the top offensive players in the game. Cards were inserted 1:69 packs. Die-cut into a shield shape, the cards have an action photo in a home-plate shaped center section and several colors of foil highlights. Backs have recent stats and career highlights.

		MT
Complete Set (24):		350.00
Common Player:		8.00
RP1	Ken Griffey Jr.	60.00
RP2	Barry Bonds	15.00
RP3	Albert Belle	15.00
RP4	Mark McGwire	60.00
RP5	Frank Thomas	40.00
RP6	Juan Gonzalez	30.00
RP7	Brady Anderson	8.00
RP8	Andres Galarraga	8.00
RP9	Rafael Palmeiro	8.00
RP10	Alex Rodriguez	50.00
RP11	Jay Buhner	8.00
RP12	Gary Sheffield	10.00
RP13	Sammy Sosa	40.00
RP14	Dante Bichette	8.00
RP15	Mike Piazza	40.00
RP16	Manny Ramirez	15.00
RP17	Kenny Lofton	15.00
RP18	Mo Vaughn	15.00
RP19	Tim Salmon	8.00
RP20	Chipper Jones	40.00
RP21	Jim Thome	12.00
RP22	Ken Caminiti	10.00
RP23	Jeff Bagwell	20.00
RP24	Paul Molitor	12.00

1997 Upper Deck Ticket to Stardom

The 20-card, regular-sized, die-cut set was inserted every 34 packs of 1997 Upper Deck baseball. Card fronts have a gold-foil border on three sides with a portrait and action photo. Half of the player's league emblem appears on either the left or right border of the horizontal cards, as two cards can be placed together to form a "ticket." The card backs feature an in-depth text with the same headshot as the card front and are numbered with the "TS" prefix.

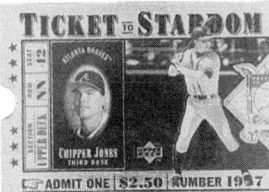

		MT
Complete Set (20):		150.00
Common Player:		4.00
TS1	Chipper Jones	25.00
TS2	Jermaine Dye	3.00
TS3	Rey Ordonez	4.00
TS4	Alex Ochoa	4.00
TS5	Derek Jeter	25.00
TS6	Ruben Rivera	5.00
TS7	Billy Wagner	4.00
TS8	Jason Kendall	4.00
TS9	Darin Erstad	20.00
TS10	Alex Rodriguez	30.00
TS11	Bob Abreu	4.00
TS12	Richard Hidalgo	4.00
TS13	Karim Garcia	5.00
TS14	Andruw Jones	15.00
TS15	Carlos Delgado	4.00
TS16	Rocky Coppinger	4.00
TS17	Jeff D'Amico	4.00
TS18	Johnny Damon	4.00
TS19	John Wasdin	4.00
TS20	Manny Ramirez	8.00

1997 Upper Deck Ticket to Stardom Retail

Double-size "full ticket" versions of Upper Deck's Series 1 Ticket to Stardom inserts were produced as an incentive for collectors to buy a boxed three-pack of Collector's Choice cards in a special retail-only packaging. Unlike the insert Ticket cards which feature only one player and measure 3-1/2" x 2-1/2", the retail version measures 5" x 2-1/2" and features two players. The basic format of the retail cards follows the inserts, with gold-foil background, a vignetted player portrait at one end with an action photo toward center and a league logo at center. Arrangement of graphics on the retail ticket prevent unscrupulous persons from cutting them in half and passing them off as the more valuable insert cards. Backs repeat the player portrait photo and present a career summary. Cards are numbered in the upper-left corner. Seven players were dropped from the original Ticket checklist and replaced in the retail issue with new faces.

		MT
Complete Set (10):		55.00
Common Player:		4.00
TS1	Chipper Jones, Andruw Jones	10.00
TS2	Rey Ordonez, Kevin Orie	4.00
TS3	Derek Jeter, Nomar Garciaparra	7.50
TS4	Billy Wagner, Jason Kendall	4.00
TS5	Darin Erstad, Alex Rodriguez	15.00
TS6	Bob Abreu, Jose Guillen	4.00
TS7	Wilton Guerrero, Vladimir Guerrero	7.50
TS8	Carlos Delgado, Rocky Coppinger	4.00
TS9	Jason Dickson, Johnny Damon	4.00
TS10	Bartolo Colon, Manny Ramirez	6.00

1997 Upper Deck UD3

Released in April, this 60-card set is broken down into three different 20-card subsets, each utilizing a different print technology. There are 20 PROmotion cards (Light F/X cards featuring a special foil stock), 20 Future Impact cards (Cel-Chrome cards that feature a 3-D image on transparent chromium), and 20 Homerun Heroes (Electric Wood cards printed on an embossed wood/paper stock). Cards were sold in three-card packs (with one subset card per pack) for $3.99 each. Inserts include Superb Signatures, Generation Next and Marquee Attraction.

		MT
Complete Set (60):		50.00
Common Player:		.40
Wax Box:		80.00
1	Mark McGwire	6.00
2	Brady Anderson	.50
3	Ken Griffey Jr.	5.00
4	Albert Belle	1.25
5	Andres Galarraga	.60
6	Juan Gonzalez	2.50
7	Jay Buhner	.50
8	Mo Vaughn	1.25
9	Barry Bonds	1.25
10	Gary Sheffield	.75
11	Todd Hundley	.40
12	Ellis Burks	.40
13	Ken Caminiti	.75
14	Vinny Castilla	.40
15	Sammy Sosa	3.00
16	Frank Thomas	4.00
17	Rafael Palmeiro	.60
18	Mike Piazza	3.00
19	Matt Williams	.75
20	Eddie Murray	1.00
21	Roger Clemens	1.50
22	Tim Salmon	.50
23	Robin Ventura	.40
24	Ron Gant	.40
25	Cal Ripken Jr.	4.00
26	Bernie Williams	1.00
27	Hideo Nomo	1.00
28	Ivan Rodriguez	1.00
29	John Smoltz	.60
30	Paul Molitor	1.00
31	Greg Maddux	3.00
32	Raul Mondesi	.60
33	Roberto Alomar	1.00
34	Barry Larkin	.60
35	Tony Gwynn	2.50
36	Jim Thome	.75
37	Kenny Lofton	1.25
38	Jeff Bagwell	2.00
39	Ozzie Smith	.75
40	Kirby Puckett	2.00
41	Andruw Jones	2.50
42	Vladimir Guerrero	2.00
43	Edgar Renteria	.40
44	Luis Castillo	.75
45	Darin Erstad	2.00
46	Nomar Garciaparra	3.50
47	Todd Greene	.40
48	Jason Kendall	.40
49	Rey Ordonez	.50
50	Alex Rodriguez	5.00
51	Manny Ramirez	1.25
52	Todd Walker	1.25
53	Ruben Rivera	.60
54	Andy Pettitte	1.25
55	Derek Jeter	3.00
56	Todd Hollandsworth	.40
57	Rocky Coppinger	.40
58	Scott Rolen	2.50
59	Jermaine Dye	.50
60	Chipper Jones	3.00

1997 Upper Deck UD3 Generation Next

A 20-card insert saluting the game's up-and-coming stars with two different photos of the player on each card front. Odds of finding these cards were 1:11 packs.

		MT
Complete Set (20):		150.00
Common Player:		4.00
GN1	Alex Rodriguez	25.00
GN2	Vladimir Guerrero	10.00
GN3	Luis Castillo	5.00
GN4	Rey Ordonez	6.00
GN5	Andruw Jones	12.00
GN6	Darin Erstad	15.00
GN7	Edgar Renteria	6.00
GN8	Jason Kendall	4.00
GN9	Jermaine Dye	4.00
GN10	Chipper Jones	18.00
GN11	Rocky Coppinger	4.00
GN12	Andy Pettitte	10.00
GN13	Todd Greene	4.00
GN14	Todd Hollandsworth	4.00
GN15	Derek Jeter	15.00
GN16	Ruben Rivera	6.00
GN17	Todd Walker	6.00
GN18	Nomar Garciaparra	15.00
GN19	Scott Rolen	12.00
GN20	Manny Ramirez	10.00

A player's name in *italic* type indicates a rookie card.

1997 Upper Deck UD3 Marquee Attraction

The game's top names are featured in this insert set, inserted 1:144 packs. Cards featured a peel-off protector that would expose a holographic image on the card fronts.

		MT
Complete Set (10):		500.00
Common Player:		15.00
MA1	Ken Griffey Jr.	100.00
MA2	Mark McGwire	120.00
MA3	Juan Gonzalez	40.00
MA4	Barry Bonds	20.00
MA5	Frank Thomas	80.00
MA6	Albert Belle	25.00
MA7	Mike Piazza	60.00
MA8	Cal Ripken Jr.	80.00
MA9	Mo Vaughn	20.00
MA10	Alex Rodriguez	100.00

1997 Upper Deck UD3 Superb Signatures

Autographed cards of Ken Griffey Jr., Ken Caminiti, Vladimir Guerrero and Derek Jeter were inserted 1:1,500 packs.

		MT
Complete Set (4):		1000.
Common Autograph:		100.00
1	Ken Caminiti	100.00
2	Ken Griffey Jr.	500.00
3	Vladimir Guerrero	200.00
4	Derek Jeter	225.00

1998 Upper Deck

Upper Deck Baseball was released in three series. Series One consisted of 270 base cards, with five subsets. Inserts included A Piece of the Action, Amazing Greats, National Pride, Ken Griffey Jr.'s Home Run Chronicles and 10th Anniversary Preview. The 270-card second series also had five subsets. Inserts include Prime Nine, Ken Griffey Jr.'s Home Run Chronicles, Tape Measure Titans, Blue Chip Prospects, Clearly Dominant and A Piece of the Action. The third series, Upper Deck Rookie Edition, had a 210-card base set. Insert sets were Ken Griffey Jr. Game Jersey, Game Jersey Rookie Cards, Unparalleled, Destination Stardom, All-Star Credentials and Retrospectives.

		MT
Complete Set (750):		135.00
Complete Series I Set (270):		25.00
Complete Series II Set (270):		25.00
Complete Series III Set (210):		85.00
Common Emminent Prestige (601-630):		
Common Player:		.10
Series I,II & III Box:		55.00
1	Tino Martinez (History in the Making)	.15
2	Jimmy Key (History in the Making)	.10
3	Jay Buhner (History in the Making)	.15
4	Mark Gardner (History in the Making)	.10
5	Greg Maddux (History in the Making)	1.00
6	Pedro J. Martinez (History in the Making)	.15
7	Hideo Nomo, Shigetosi Hasegawa (History in the Making)	.25
8	Sammy Sosa (History in the Making)	.75
9	Mark McGwire (Griffey Hot List)	2.00
10	Ken Griffey Jr. (Griffey Hot List)	1.50
11	Larry Walker (Griffey Hot List)	.20
12	Tino Martinez (Griffey Hot List)	.15
13	Mike Piazza (Griffey Hot List)	1.00
14	Jose Cruz, Jr. (Griffey Hot List)	.75
15	Tony Gwynn (Griffey Hot List)	.75
16	Greg Maddux (Griffey Hot List)	1.00
17	Roger Clemens (Griffey Hot List)	.50
18	Alex Rodriguez (Griffey Hot List)	1.00
19	Shigetosi Hasegawa	.10
20	Eddie Murray	.25
21	Jason Dickson	.10
22	Darin Erstad	.75
23	Chuck Finley	.10
24	Dave Hollins	.10
25	Garret Anderson	.10
26	Michael Tucker	.10
27	Kenny Lofton	.75
28	Javier Lopez	.20
29	Fred McGriff	.25
30	Greg Maddux	2.00
31	Jeff Blauser	.10
32	John Smoltz	.20
33	Mark Wohlers	.10
34	Scott Erickson	.10
35	Jimmy Key	.10
36	Harold Baines	.10
37	Randy Myers	.10
38	B.J. Surhoff	.10
39	Eric Davis	.10
40	Rafael Palmeiro	.20
41	Jeffrey Hammonds	.10
42	Mo Vaughn	.75
43	Tom Gordon	.10
44	Tim Naehring	.10
45	Darren Bragg	.10
46	Aaron Sele	.10
47	Troy O'Leary	.10
48	John Valentin	.10
49	Doug Glanville	.10
50	Ryne Sandberg	.75
51	Steve Trachsel	.10
52	Mark Grace	.25
53	Kevin Foster	.10
54	Kevin Tapani	.10
55	Kevin Orie	.10
56	Lyle Mouton	.10
57	Ray Durham	.10
58	Jaime Navarro	.10
59	Mike Cameron	.10
60	Albert Belle	.75
61	Doug Drabek	.10
62	Chris Snopek	.10
63	Eddie Taubensee	.10
64	Terry Pendleton	.10
65	Barry Larkin	.20
66	Willie Greene	.10
67	Deion Sanders	.20
68	Pokey Reese	.10
69	Jeff Shaw	.10
70	Jim Thome	.40
71	Orel Hershiser	.10
72	Omar Vizquel	.10
73	Brian Giles	.10
74	David Justice	.25
75	Bartolo Colon	.10
76	Sandy Alomar Jr.	.20
77	Neifi Perez	.10
78	Eric Young	.10
79	Vinny Castilla	.10
80	Dante Bichette	.20
81	Quinton McCracken	.10
82	Jamey Wright	.10
83	John Thomson	.10
84	Damion Easley	.10
85	Justin Thompson	.10
86	Willie Blair	.10
87	Raul Casanova	.10
88	Bobby Higginson	.10
89	Bubba Trammell	.20
90	Tony Clark	.50
91	Livan Hernandez	.20
92	Charles Johnson	.10
93	Edgar Renteria	.10
94	Alex Fernandez	.10
95	Gary Sheffield	.30
96	Moises Alou	.20
97	Tony Saunders	.20
98	Robb Nen	.10
99	Darryl Kile	.10
100	Craig Biggio	.20
101	Chris Holt	.10
102	Bob Abreu	.10
103	Luis Gonzalez	.10
104	Billy Wagner	.10
105	Brad Ausmus	.10
106	Chili Davis	.10
107	Tim Belcher	.10
108	Dean Palmer	.10
109	Jeff King	.10
110	Jose Rosado	.10
111	Mike Macfarlane	.10
112	Jay Bell	.10
113	Todd Worrell	.10
114	Chan Ho Park	.10
115	Raul Mondesi	.25
116	Brett Butler	.10
117	Greg Gagne	.10
118	Hideo Nomo	.50
119	Todd Zeile	.10
120	Eric Karros	.20
121	Cal Eldred	.10
122	Jeff D'Amico	.10
123	Antone Williamson	.10
124	Doug Jones	.10
125	Dave Nilsson	.10
126	Gerald Williams	.10
127	Fernando Vina	.10
128	Ron Coomer	.10
129	Matt Lawton	.10
130	Paul Molitor	.40
131	Todd Walker	.10
132	Rick Aguilera	.10
133	Brad Radke	.10
134	Bob Tewksbury	.10
135	Vladimir Guerrero	1.00
136	Tony Gwynn (Define The Game)	.75
137	Roger Clemens (Define The Game)	.75
138	Dennis Eckersley (Define The Game)	.10
139	Brady Anderson (Define The Game)	.10
140	Ken Griffey Jr. (Define The Game)	1.50
141	Derek Jeter (Define The Game)	1.00
142	Ken Caminiti (Define The Game)	.15
143	Frank Thomas (Define The Game)	1.25
144	Barry Bonds (Define The Game)	.40
145	Cal Ripken Jr. (Define The Game)	1.25
146	Alex Rodriguez (Define The Game)	1.25
147	Greg Maddux (Define The Game)	1.00
148	Kenny Lofton (Define The Game)	.40
149	Mike Piazza (Define The Game)	1.00
150	Mark McGwire (Define The Game)	1.50
151	Andruw Jones (Define The Game)	.75
152	Rusty Greer (Define The Game)	.10
153	F.P. Santangelo (Define The Game)	.10
154	Mike Lansing	.10
155	Lee Smith	.10
156	Carlos Perez	.10
157	Pedro J. Martinez	.20
158	Ryan McGuire	.10
159	F.P. Santangelo	.10
160	Rondell White	.20
161	Takashi Kashiwada	.50
162	Butch Huskey	.10
163	Edgardo Alfonzo	.10
164	John Franco	.10
165	Todd Hundley	.20
166	Rey Ordonez	.10
167	Armando Reynoso	.10
168	John Olerud	.10
169	Bernie Williams	.50
170	Andy Pettitte	.50
171	Wade Boggs	.25
172	Paul O'Neill	.20
173	Cecil Fielder	.20
174	Charlie Hayes	.10
175	David Cone	.20
176	Hideki Irabu	.75
177	Mark Bellhorn	.10
178	Steve Karsay	.10
179	Damon Mashore	.10
180	Jason McDonald	.10
181	Scott Spiezio	.10
182	Ariel Prieto	.10
183	Jason Giambi	.10
184	Wendell Magee	.10
185	Rico Brogna	.10
186	Garrett Stephenson	.10
187	Wayne Gomes	.10
188	Ricky Bottalico	.10
189	Mickey Morandini	.10
190	Mike Lieberthal	.10
191	*Kevin Polcovich*	.25
192	Francisco Cordova	.10
193	Kevin Young	.10
194	Jon Lieber	.10
195	Kevin Elster	.10
196	Tony Womack	.10
197	Lou Collier	.10
198	*Mike Defelice*	.20
199	Gary Gaetti	.10
200	Dennis Eckersley	.10
201	Alan Benes	.10
202	Willie McGee	.10
203	Ron Gant	.10
204	Fernando Valenzuela	.10
205	Mark McGwire	4.00
206	Archi Cianfrocco	.10
207	Andy Ashby	.10
208	Steve Finley	.10
209	Quilvio Veras	.10
210	Ken Caminiti	.25
211	Rickey Henderson	.10
212	Joey Hamilton	.10
213	Derek Lee	.10
214	Bill Mueller	.10
215	Shawn Estes	.10
216	J.T. Snow	.10
217	Mark Gardner	.10
218	Terry Mulholland	.10
219	Dante Powell	.10
220	Jeff Kent	.10
221	Jamie Moyer	.10

No.	Card	Price
456	Larry Walker (Upper Echelon)	.20
457	Alex Rodriguez (Upper Echelon)	1.00
458	Tony Gwynn (Upper Echelon)	.60
459	Frank Thomas (Upper Echelon)	1.25
460	Tino Martinez	.25
461	Chad Curtis	.10
462	Ramiro Mendoza	.10
463	Joe Girardi	.10
464	David Wells	.10
465	Mariano Rivera	.20
466	Willie Adams	.10
467	George Williams	.10
468	Dave Telgheder	.10
469	Dave Magadan	.10
470	Matt Stairs	.10
471	Billy Taylor	.10
472	Jimmy Haynes	.10
473	Gregg Jefferies	.10
474	Midre Cummings	.10
475	Curt Schilling	.20
476	Mike Grace	.10
477	Mark Leiter	.10
478	Matt Beech	.10
479	Scott Rolen	1.25
480	Jason Kendall	.10
481	Esteban Loaiza	.10
482	Jermaine Allensworth	.10
483	Mark Smith	.10
484	Jason Schmidt	.10
485	Jose Guillen	.25
486	Al Martin	.10
487	Delino DeShields	.10
488	Todd Stottlemyre	.10
489	Brian Jordan	.10
490	Ray Lankford	.10
491	Matt Morris	.10
492	Royce Clayton	.10
493	John Mabry	.10
494	Wally Joyner	.10
495	Trevor Hoffman	.10
496	Chris Gomez	.10
497	Sterling Hitchcock	.10
498	Pete Smith	.10
499	Greg Vaughn	.10
500	Tony Gwynn	1.50
501	Will Cunnane	.10
502	Darryl Hamilton	.10
503	Brian Johnson	.10
504	Kirk Rueter	.10
505	Barry Bonds	.75
506	Osvaldo Fernandez	.10
507	Stan Javier	.10
508	Julian Tavarez	.10
509	Rich Aurilia	.10
510	Alex Rodriguez	2.00
511	David Segui	.10
512	Rich Amaral	.10
513	Raul Ibanez	.10
514	Jay Buhner	.20
515	Randy Johnson	.50
516	Heathcliff Slocumb	.10
517	Tony Saunders	.10
518	Kevin Elster	.10
519	John Burkett	.10
520	Juan Gonzalez	1.50
521	John Wetteland	.10
522	Domingo Cedeno	.10
523	Darren Oliver	.10
524	Roger Pavlik	.10
525	Jose Cruz Jr.	1.00
526	Woody Williams	.10
527	Alex Gonzalez	.10
528	Robert Person	.10
529	Juan Guzman	.10
530	Roger Clemens	1.00
531	Shawn Green	.10
532	Cordova, Ricon, Smith (Season Highlights)	.10
533	Nomar Garciaparra (Season Highlights)	1.00
534	Roger Clemens (Season Highlights)	.60
535	Mark McGwire (Season Highlights)	1.50
536	Larry Walker (Season Highlights)	.20
537	Mike Piazza (Season Highlights)	1.00
538	Curt Schilling (Season Highlights)	.10
539	Tony Gwynn (Season Highlights)	.75
540	Ken Griffey Jr. (Season Highlights)	1.50
541	Carl Pavano (Star Rookies)	.10
542	Shane Monahan (Star Rookies)	.10
543	*Gabe Kapler* (Star Rookies)	2.00
544	Eric Milton (Star Rookies)	.25
545	Gary Matthews Jr. (Star Rookies)	.50
546	*Mike Kinkade* (Star Rookies)	.50
547	*Ryan Christenson* (Star Rookies)	.25
548	Corey Koskie (Star Rookies)	.50
549	Norm Hutchins (Star Rookies)	.10
550	Russell Branyan (Star Rookies)	.10
551	*Masato Yoshii* (Star Rookies)	.50
552	*Jesus Sanchez* (Star Rookies)	.25
553	Anthony Sanders (Star Rookies)	.20
554	Edwin Diaz (Star Rookies)	.10
555	Gabe Alvarez (Star Rookies)	.10
556	*Carlos Lee* (Star Rookies)	.75
557	Mike Darr (Star Rookies)	.10
558	Kerry Wood (Star Rookies)	5.00
559	Carlos Guillen (Star Rookies)	.10
560	Sean Casey (Star Rookies)	.30
561	*Manny Aybar* (Star Rookies)	.25
562	Octavio Dotel (Star Rookies)	.10
563	Jarrod Washburn (Star Rookies)	.10
564	Mark L. Johnson (Star Rookies)	.10
565	Ramon Hernandez (Star Rookies)	.10
566	*Rich Butler* (Star Rookies)	.50
567	Mike Caruso (Star Rookies)	.25
568	Cliff Politte (Star Rookies)	.10
569	Scott Elarton (Star Rookies)	.10
570	*Magglio Ordonez* (Star Rookies)	.75
571	*Adam Butler* (Star Rookies)	.25
572	Marlon Anderson (Star Rookies)	.10
573	*Julio Ramirez* (Star Rookies)	.50
574	*Darron Ingram* (Star Rookies)	.20
575	Bruce Chen (Star Rookies)	.10
576	*Steve Woodard* (Star Rookies)	.25
577	Hiram Bocachica (Star Rookies)	.10
578	Kevin Witt (Star Rookies)	.10
579	Javier Vazquez (Star Rookies)	.10
580	Alex Gonzalez (Star Rookies)	.10
581	Brian Powell (Star Rookies)	.10
582	Wes Helms (Star Rookies)	.10
583	Ron Wright (Star Rookies)	.10
584	Rafael Medina (Star Rookies)	.10
585	Daryle Ward (Star Rookies)	.15
586	Geoff Jenkins (Star Rookies)	.10
587	Preston Wilson (Star Rookies)	.10
588	*Jim Chamblee* (Star Rookies)	.25
589	*Mike Lowell* (Star Rookies)	.40
590	A.J. Hinch (Star Rookies)	.50
591	*Francisco Cordero* (Star Rookies)	.25
592	*Rolando Arrojo* (Star Rookies)	1.00
593	Braden Looper (Star Rookies)	.10
594	Sidney Ponson (Star Rookies)	.10
595	Matt Clement (Star Rookies)	.10
596	Carlton Loewer (Star Rookies)	.10
597	Brian Meadows (Star Rookies)	.10
598	Danny Klassen (Star Rookies)	.20
599	Larry Sutton (Star Rookies)	.10
600	Travis Lee (Star Rookies)	2.50
601	Randy Johnson (Eminent Prestige)	2.00
602	Greg Maddux (Eminent Prestige)	6.00
603	Roger Clemens (Eminent Prestige)	3.00
604	Jaret Wright (Eminent Prestige)	2.50
605	Mike Piazza (Eminent Prestige)	6.00
606	Tino Martinez (Eminent Prestige)	1.00
607	Frank Thomas (Eminent Prestige)	8.00
608	Mo Vaughn (Eminent Prestige)	2.50
609	Todd Helton (Eminent Prestige)	2.50
610	Mark McGwire (Eminent Prestige)	12.00
611	Jeff Bagwell (Eminent Prestige)	3.00
612	Travis Lee (Eminent Prestige)	5.00
613	Scott Rolen (Eminent Prestige)	3.00
614	Cal Ripken Jr. (Eminent Prestige)	8.00
615	Chipper Jones (Eminent Prestige)	6.00
616	Nomar Garciaparra (Eminent Prestige)	6.00
617	Alex Rodriguez (Eminent Prestige)	6.00
618	Derek Jeter (Eminent Prestige)	5.00
619	Tony Gwynn (Eminent Prestige)	5.00
620	Ken Griffey Jr. (Eminent Prestige)	10.00
621	Kenny Lofton (Eminent Prestige)	2.50
622	Juan Gonzalez (Eminent Prestige)	5.00
623	Jose Cruz Jr. (Eminent Prestige)	2.00
624	Larry Walker (Eminent Prestige)	1.00
625	Barry Bonds (Eminent Prestige)	2.50
626	Ben Grieve (Eminent Prestige)	3.00
627	Andruw Jones (Eminent Prestige)	2.50
628	Vladimir Guerrero (Eminent Prestige)	2.50
629	Paul Konerko (Eminent Prestige)	1.00
630	Paul Molitor (Eminent Prestige)	2.00
631	Cecil Fielder	.20
632	Jack McDowell	.10
633	Mike James	.10
634	Brian Anderson	.10
635	Jay Bell	.10
636	Devon White	.10
637	Andy Stankiewicz	.10
638	Tony Batista	.10
639	Omar Daal	.10
640	Matt Williams	.25
641	Brent Brede	.10
642	Jorge Fabregas	.10
643	Karim Garcia	.10
644	Felix Rodriguez	.10
645	Andy Benes	.10
646	Willie Blair	.10
647	Jeff Suppan	.10
648	Yamil Benitez	.10
649	Walt Weiss	.10
650	Andres Galarraga	.25
651	Doug Drabek	.10
652	Ozzie Guillen	.10
653	Joe Carter	.10
654	Dennis Eckersley	.10
655	Pedro J. Martinez	.30
656	Jim Leyritz	.10
657	Henry Rodriguez	.10
658	Rod Beck	.10
659	Mickey Morandini	.10
660	Jeff Blauser	.10
661	Ruben Sierra	.10
662	Mike Sirotka	.10
663	Pete Harnisch	.10
664	Damian Jackson	.10
665	Dmitri Young	.10
666	Steve Cooke	.10
667	Geronimo Berroa	.10
668	Shawon Dunston	.10
669	Mike Jackson	.10
670	Travis Fryman	.10

671	Dwight Gooden	.10
672	Paul Assenmacher	.10
673	Eric Plunk	.10
674	Mike Lansing	.10
675	Darryl Kile	.10
676	Luis Gonzalez	.10
677	Frank Castillo	.10
678	Joe Randa	.10
679	Bip Roberts	.10
680	Derrek Lee	.10
681	Mike Piazza	2.00
682	Sean Berry	.10
683	Ramon Garcia	.10
684	Carl Everett	.10
685	Moises Alou	.10
686	Hal Morris	.10
687	Jeff Conine	.10
688	Gary Sheffield LA	.35
689	Jose Vizcaino	.10
690	Charles Johnson	.10
691	Bobby Bonilla LA	.20
692	Marquis Grissom	.10
693	Alex Ochoa	.10
694	Mike Morgan	.10
695	Orlando Merced	.10
696	David Ortiz	.30
697	Brent Gates	.10
698	Otis Nixon	.10
699	Trey Moore	.10
700	Derrick May	.10
701	Rich Becker	.10
702	Al Leiter	.20
703	Chili Davis	.10
704	Scott Brosius	.10
705	Chuck Knoblauch	.30
706	Kenny Rogers	.10
707	Mike Blowers	.10
708	Mike Fetters	.10
709	Tom Candiotti	.10
710	Rickey Henderson	.10
711	Bob Abreu	.10
712	Mark Lewis	.10
713	Doug Glanville	.10
714	Desi Relaford	.10
715	Kent Mercker	.10
716	J. Kevin Brown	.20
717	James Mouton	.10
718	Mark Langston	.10
719	Greg Myers	.10
720	Orel Hershiser	.10
721	Charlie Hayes	.10
722	Robb Nen	.10
723	Glenallen Hill	.10
724	Tony Saunders	.10
725	Wade Boggs	.25
726	Kevin Stocker	.10
727	Wilson Alvarez	.10
728	Albie Lopez	.10
729	Dave Martinez	.10
730	Fred McGriff	.20
731	Quinton McCracken	.10
732	Bryan Rekar	.10
733	Paul Sorrento	.10
734	Roberto Hernandez	.10
735	Bubba Trammell	.10
736	Miguel Cairo	.10
737	John Flaherty	.10
738	Terrell Wade	.10
739	Roberto Kelly	.10
740	Mark Mclemore (McLemore)	.10
741	Danny Patterson	.10
742	Aaron Sele	.10
743	Tony Fernandez	.10
744	Randy Myers	.10
745	Jose Canseco	.30
746	Darrin Fletcher	.10
747	Mike Stanley	.10
748	Marquis Grissom (Season Highlights)	.10
749	Fred McGriff (Season Highlights)	.20
750	Travis Lee (Season Highlights)	1.00

1998 Upper Deck Amazing Greats

The 30-card Amazing Greats insert is printed on acetate. The cards are numbered to 2,000. A die-cut parallel was sequentially numbered to 250. Amazing Greats was an insert in Upper Deck Series One packs.

		MT
Complete Set (30):		550.00
Common Player:		6.00
Die-Cuts (250): 3x to 4x		
AG1	Ken Griffey Jr.	60.00
AG2	Derek Jeter	30.00
AG3	Alex Rodriguez	40.00
AG4	Paul Molitor	12.00
AG5	Jeff Bagwell	20.00
AG6	Larry Walker	8.00
AG7	Kenny Lofton	12.00
AG8	Cal Ripken Jr.	40.00
AG9	Juan Gonzalez	25.00
AG10	Chipper Jones	30.00
AG11	Greg Maddux	30.00
AG12	Roberto Alomar	10.00
AG13	Mike Piazza	30.00
AG14	Andres Galarraga	8.00
AG15	Barry Bonds	12.00
AG16	Andy Pettitte	10.00
AG17	Nomar Garciaparra	30.00
AG18	Hideki Irabu	8.00
AG19	Tony Gwynn	25.00
AG20	Frank Thomas	50.00
AG21	Roger Clemens	20.00
AG22	Sammy Sosa	30.00
AG23	Jose Cruz, Jr.	25.00
AG24	Manny Ramirez	10.00
AG25	Mark McGwire	70.00
AG26	Randy Johnson	10.00
AG27	Mo Vaughn	12.00
AG28	Gary Sheffield	8.00
AG29	Andruw Jones	20.00
AG30	Albert Belle	12.00

1998 Upper Deck A Piece of the Action

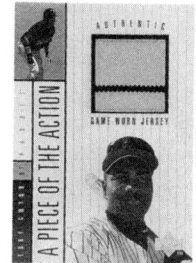

A Piece of the Action was inserted in both Series One and Series Two packs. Series One featured 10 cards: five with a piece of game-used jersey and five with a piece of game-used bat. Series Two offered a piece of game-used bat and jersey on four cards. The cards were inserted one per 2,500 packs in both series.

		MT
Complete Set (14):		2100.
Complete Series 1 Set (10):		1700.
Complete Series 2 Set (4):		450.00
Common Player:		75.00
Inserted 1:2,500		
(1)	Tony Gwynn (Jersey)	300.00
(2)	Tony Gwynn (Bat)	225.00
(3)	Alex Rodriguez (Jersey)	400.00
(4)	Alex Rodriguez (Bat)	300.00
(5)	Gary Sheffield (Jersey)	100.00
(6)	Gary Sheffield (Bat)	75.00
(7)	Todd Hollandsworth (Jersey)	100.00
(8)	Todd Hollandsworth (Bat)	75.00
(9)	Greg Maddux (Jersey)	400.00
(10)	Jay Buhner (Bat)	90.00
(11)	Roberto Alomar	200.00
(12)	Jay Buhner	125.00
(13)	Andruw Jones	250.00
(14)	Gary Sheffield	125.00

1998 Upper Deck Blue Chip Prospects

Inserted in Series Two packs, Blue Chip Prospects is printed on die-cut acetate. The cards are sequentially numbered to 2,000.

		MT
Complete Set (30):		600.00
Common Player:		8.00
BC1	Nomar Garciaparra	60.00
BC2	Scott Rolen	40.00
BC3	Jason Dickson	8.00
BC4	Darin Erstad	20.00
BC5	Brad Fullmer	12.00
BC6	Jaret Wright	40.00
BC7	Justin Thompson	8.00
BC8	Matt Morris	8.00
BC9	Fernando Tatis	8.00
BC10	Alex Rodriguez	60.00
BC11	Todd Helton	25.00
BC12	Andy Pettitte	15.00
BC13	Jose Cruz Jr.	50.00
BC14	Mark Kotsay	15.00
BC15	Derek Jeter	50.00
BC16	Paul Konerko	20.00
BC17	Todd Dunwoody	8.00
BC18	Vladimir Guerrero	20.00
BC19	Miguel Tejada	20.00
BC20	Chipper Jones	60.00
BC21	Kevin Orie	8.00
BC22	Juan Encarnacion	8.00
BC23	Brian Rose	20.00
BC24	Andruw Jones	25.00
BC25	Livan Hernandez	15.00
BC26	Brian Giles	8.00
BC27	Brett Tomko	8.00
BC28	Jose Guillen	12.00
BC29	Aaron Boone	8.00
BC30	Ben Grieve	35.00

1998 Upper Deck Clearly Dominant

Clearly Dominant was an insert in Series Two. Printed on Light F/X plastic stock, the 30-card set is sequentially numbered to 250.

		MT
Common Player:		25.00
Production 250 sets		
CD1	Mark McGwire	250.00
CD2	Derek Jeter	150.00
CD3	Alex Rodriguez	150.00
CD4	Paul Molitor	40.00
CD5	Jeff Bagwell	100.00
CD6	Ivan Rodriguez	60.00
CD7	Kenny Lofton	60.00
CD8	Cal Ripken Jr.	200.00
CD9	Albert Belle	60.00
CD10	Chipper Jones	150.00
CD11	Gary Sheffield	40.00
CD12	Roberto Alomar	50.00
CD13	Mo Vaughn	60.00
CD14	Andres Galarraga	30.00
CD15	Nomar Garciaparra	150.00
CD16	Randy Johnson	40.00
CD17	Mike Mussina	50.00
CD18	Greg Maddux	150.00
CD19	Tony Gwynn	120.00
CD20	Frank Thomas	200.00
CD21	Roger Clemens	80.00
CD22	Dennis Eckersley	25.00
CD23	Juan Gonzalez	120.00
CD24	Tino Martinez	40.00
CD25	Andruw Jones	80.00
CD26	Larry Walker	40.00
CD27	Ken Caminiti	30.00
CD28	Mike Piazza	150.00
CD29	Barry Bonds	60.00
CD30	Ken Griffey Jr.	240.00

1998 Upper Deck Ken Griffey's HR Chronicles

Griffey's Home Run Chronicles was inserted in both Series One and Two packs. Series One had 30 cards, each spotlighting one of Ken Griffey Jr.'s first 30 home runs of the 1997 season. Series Two had 26 cards highlighting the rest of his 1997 home run output. In both series, the cards were inserted one per nine packs.

		MT
Complete Set (56):		190.00
Common Griffey Jr.:		4.00
Inserted 1:9		
KG1	Ken Griffey Jr.	5.00
KG2	Ken Griffey Jr.	5.00
KG3	Ken Griffey Jr.	5.00
KG4	Ken Griffey Jr.	5.00
KG5	Ken Griffey Jr.	5.00
KG6	Ken Griffey Jr.	5.00
KG7	Ken Griffey Jr.	5.00
KG8	Ken Griffey Jr.	5.00
KG9	Ken Griffey Jr.	5.00
KG10	Ken Griffey Jr.	5.00
KG11	Ken Griffey Jr.	5.00
KG12	Ken Griffey Jr.	5.00
KG13	Ken Griffey Jr.	5.00
KG14	Ken Griffey Jr.	5.00
KG15	Ken Griffey Jr.	5.00
KG16	Ken Griffey Jr.	5.00
KG17	Ken Griffey Jr.	5.00
KG18	Ken Griffey Jr.	5.00
KG19	Ken Griffey Jr.	5.00
KG20	Ken Griffey Jr.	5.00
KG21	Ken Griffey Jr.	5.00
KG22	Ken Griffey Jr.	5.00
KG23	Ken Griffey Jr.	5.00
KG24	Ken Griffey Jr.	5.00
KG25	Ken Griffey Jr.	5.00
KG26	Ken Griffey Jr.	5.00
KG27	Ken Griffey Jr.	5.00
KG28	Ken Griffey Jr.	5.00
KG29	Ken Griffey Jr.	5.00
KG30	Ken Griffey Jr.	5.00

1998 Upper Deck National Pride

National Pride is a 42-card insert printed on die-cut rainbow foil. The set honors the nationality of the player with their country's flag in the background. The cards were inserted one per 24 packs.

		MT
Complete Set (42):		350.00
Common Player:		3.00
NP1	Dave Nilsson	3.00
NP2	Larry Walker	5.00
NP3	Edgar Renteria	3.00
NP4	Jose Canseco	4.00
NP5	Rey Ordonez	3.00
NP6	Rafael Palmeiro	4.00
NP7	Livan Hernandez	3.00
NP8	Andruw Jones	20.00
NP9	Manny Ramirez	12.00
NP10	Sammy Sosa	25.00
NP11	Raul Mondesi	5.00
NP12	Moises Alou	3.00
NP13	Pedro J. Martinez	3.00
NP14	Vladimir Guerrero	15.00
NP15	Chili Davis	3.00
NP16	Hideo Nomo	10.00
NP17	Hideki Irabu	8.00
NP18	Shigetosi Hasegawa	3.00
NP19	Takashi Kashiwada	3.00
NP20	Chan Ho Park	3.00
NP21	Fernando Valenzuela	3.00
NP22	Vinny Castilla	3.00
NP23	Armando Reynoso	3.00

NP24	Karim Garcia	4.00
NP25	Marvin Benard	3.00
NP26	Mariano Rivera	3.00
NP27	Juan Gonzalez	25.00
NP28	Roberto Alomar	10.00
NP29	Ivan Rodriguez	10.00
NP30	Carlos Delgado	3.00
NP31	Bernie Williams	10.00
NP32	Edgar Martinez	3.00
NP33	Frank Thomas	50.00
NP34	Barry Bonds	12.00
NP35	Mike Piazza	30.00
NP36	Chipper Jones	30.00
NP37	Cal Ripken Jr.	40.00
NP38	Alex Rodriguez	40.00
NP39	Ken Griffey Jr.	60.00
NP40	Andres Galarraga	4.00
NP41	Omar Vizquel	3.00
NP42	Ozzie Guillen	3.00

1998 Upper Deck Prime Nine

Nine of the most popular players are featured in this insert set. The cards are printed on silver foil stock and inserted 1:5.

	MT
Complete Set (60):	175.00
Common Griffey (PN1-PN7):	6.00
Common Piazza (PN8-PN14):	4.00
Common Thomas (PN15-PN21):	6.00
Common McGwire (PN22-PN28):	3.00
Common Ripken (PN29-PN35):	5.00
Common Gonzalez (PN36-PN42):	3.00
Common Gwynn (PN43-PN49):	3.00
Common Bonds (PN50-PN55):	1.50
Common Maddux (PN56-PN60):	4.00

1998 Upper Deck Tape Measure Titans

Tape Measure Titans is a 30-card insert seeded 1:23. The set honors the game's top home run hitters.

		MT
Complete Set (30):		240.00
Common Player:		2.50
Inserted 1:23		
1	Mark McGwire	35.00
2	Andres Galarraga	4.00
3	Jeff Bagwell	12.00
4	Larry Walker	5.00
5	Frank Thomas	25.00
6	Rafael Palmeiro	4.00
7	Nomar Garciaparra	20.00
8	Mo Vaughn	8.00
9	Albert Belle	8.00
10	Ken Griffey Jr.	30.00
11	Manny Ramirez	6.00
12	Jim Thome	5.00
13	Tony Clark	5.00
14	Juan Gonzalez	15.00
15	Mike Piazza	20.00
16	Jose Canseco	2.50
17	Jay Buhner	3.00
18	Alex Rodriguez	20.00
19	Jose Cruz Jr.	8.00
20	Tino Martinez	4.00
21	Carlos Delgado	2.50
22	Andruw Jones	8.00
23	Chipper Jones	20.00
24	Fred McGriff	4.00
25	Matt Williams	4.00
26	Sammy Sosa	15.00
27	Vinny Castilla	2.50
28	Tim Salmon	5.00
29	Ken Caminiti	4.00
30	Barry Bonds	8.00

1998 Upper Deck 10th Anniversary Preview

10th Anniversary Preview is a 60-card set. The foil cards have the same design as the 1989 Upper Deck base cards. The set was inserted one per five packs.

		MT
Complete Set (60):		120.00
Common Player:		.75
1	Greg Maddux	8.00
2	Mike Mussina	2.50
3	Roger Clemens	4.00
4	Hideo Nomo	2.50
4	David Cone	.75
6	Tom Glavine	.75
7	Andy Pettitte	2.50
8	Jimmy Key	.75
9	Randy Johnson	2.50
10	Dennis Eckersley	.75
11	Lee Smith	.75
12	John Franco	.75

		MT
13	Randy Myers	.75
14	Mike Piazza	8.00
15	Ivan Rodriguez	3.00
16	Todd Hundley	1.00
17	Sandy Alomar Jr.	.75
18	Frank Thomas	10.00
19	Rafael Palmeiro	1.00
20	Mark McGwire	15.00
21	Mo Vaughn	3.00
22	Fred McGriff	1.25
23	Andres Galarraga	1.25
24	Mark Grace	1.25
25	Jeff Bagwell	5.00
26	Roberto Alomar	2.50
27	Chuck Knoblauch	1.50
28	Ryne Sandberg	3.00
29	Eric Young	.75
30	Craig Biggio	1.00
31	Carlos Baerga	.75
32	Robin Ventura	.75
33	Matt Williams	1.25
34	Wade Boggs	1.00
35	Dean Palmer	.75
36	Chipper Jones	8.00
37	Vinny Castilla	.75
38	Ken Caminiti	1.25
39	Omar Vizquel	.75
40	Cal Ripken Jr.	10.00
41	Derek Jeter	8.00
42	Alex Rodriguez	10.00
43	Barry Larkin	1.25
44	Mark Grudzielanek	.75
45	Albert Belle	3.00
46	Manny Ramirez	3.00
47	Jose Canseco	1.25
48	Ken Griffey Jr.	12.00
49	Juan Gonzalez	6.00
50	Kenny Lofton	3.00
51	Sammy Sosa	5.00
52	Larry Walker	1.50
53	Gary Sheffield	1.50
54	Rickey Henderson	.75
55	Tony Gwynn	6.00
56	Barry Bonds	3.00
57	Paul Molitor	2.50
58	Edgar Martinez	.75
59	Chili Davis	.75
60	Eddie Murray	1.25

1998 Upper Deck Rookie Edition Preview

		MT
Complete Set (10):		25.00
Common Player:		1.00
1	Nomar Garciaparra	6.00
2	Scott Rolen	5.00
3	Mark Kotsay	2.00
4	Todd Helton	3.00
5	Paul Konerko	4.00
6	Juan Encarnacion	1.00
7	Brad Fullmer	1.50
8	Miguel Tejada	2.00
9	Richard Hidalgo	1.00
10	Ben Grieve	5.00

1998 Upper Deck Rookie Edition All-Star Credentials

All-Star Credentials is a 30-card insert seeded 1:9. It features the game's top players.

		MT
Complete Set (30):		100.00
Common Player:		.75
Inserted 1:9		
AS1	Ken Griffey Jr.	12.00
AS2	Travis Lee	8.00
AS3	Ben Grieve	4.00
AS4	Jose Cruz Jr.	2.50
AS5	Andruw Jones	3.00
AS6	Craig Biggio	.75
AS7	Hideo Nomo	2.00
AS8	Cal Ripken Jr.	10.00
AS9	Jaret Wright	3.00
AS10	Mark McGwire	10.00
AS11	Derek Jeter	6.00
AS12	Scott Rolen	5.00
AS13	Jeff Bagwell	4.00
AS14	Manny Ramirez	3.00
AS15	Alex Rodriguez	8.00
AS16	Chipper Jones	8.00
AS17	Larry Walker	1.00
AS18	Barry Bonds	3.00
AS19	Tony Gwynn	6.00
AS20	Mike Piazza	8.00
AS21	Roger Clemens	4.00
AS22	Greg Maddux	8.00
AS23	Jim Thome	2.00
AS24	Tino Martinez	1.00
AS25	Nomar Garciaparra	8.00
AS26	Juan Gonzalez	6.00
AS27	Kenny Lofton	3.00
AS28	Randy Johnson	1.50
AS29	Todd Helton	3.00
AS30	Frank Thomas	10.00

1998 Upper Deck Rookie Edition A Piece of the Action

A Piece of the Action consists of five Game Jersey cards. Three rookie Game Jersey cards were sequentially numbered to 200, while a Ken Griffey Jr. Game Jersey card was numbered to 300. Griffey also signed and hand-numbered 24 Game Jersey cards.

		MT
Common Card:		200.00
KG	Ken Griffey Jr. (300)	750.00
KGS	Ken Griffey Jr. (24) (Signed)	3000.
BG	Ben Grieve (200)	300.00
JC	Jose Cruz Jr. (200)	200.00
TL	Travis Lee (200)	400.00

1998 Upper Deck Rookie Edition Destination Stardom

This 60-card insert features top young players. The cards are die-cut and foil-enhanced. The insertion rate was one card per five packs.

		MT
Complete Set (60):		75.00
Common Player:		.50
Inserted 1:5		
DS1	Travis Lee	10.00
DS2	Nomar Garciaparra	10.00
DS3	Alex Gonzalez	.50
DS4	Richard Hidalgo	.50
DS5	Jaret Wright	4.00
DS6	Mike Kinkade	.50
DS7	Matt Morris	.50
DS8	Gary Mathews Jr.	.50
DS9	Brett Tomko	.50
DS10	Todd Helton	3.00
DS11	Scott Elarton	.50
DS12	Scott Rolen	4.00
DS13	Jose Cruz Jr.	2.00
DS14	Jarrod Washburn	.50
DS15	Sean Casey	1.50
DS16	Magglio Ordonez	2.00
DS17	Gabe Alvarez	.50
DS18	Todd Dunwoody	.50
DS19	Kevin Witt	.50
DS20	Ben Grieve	5.00
DS21	Daryle Ward	.60
DS22	Matt Clement	.50
DS23	Carlton Loewer	.50
DS24	Javier Vazquez	.50
DS25	Paul Konerko	2.00
DS26	Preston Wilson	.50
DS27	Wes Helms	.50
DS28	Derek Jeter	6.00
DS29	Corey Koskie	.50
DS30	Russell Branyan	.50
DS31	Vladimir Guerrero	3.00
DS32	Ryan Christenson	.50
DS33	Carlos Lee	.50
DS34	David Dellucci	.50
DS35	Bruce Chen	.50
DS36	Ricky Ledee	1.00
DS37	Ron Wright	.50
DS38	Derrek Lee	.50
DS39	Miguel Tejada	2.00
DS40	Brad Fullmer	2.00
DS41	Rich Butler	2.50
DS42	Chris Carpenter	.50
DS43	Alex Rodriguez	10.00
DS44	Darron Ingram	.50
DS45	Kerry Wood	15.00
DS46	Jason Varitek	.50
DS47	Ramon Hernandez	.50
DS48	Aaron Boone	.50
DS49	Juan Encarnacion	.50
DS50	A.J. Hinch	1.50
DS51	Mike Lowell	.50
DS52	Fernando Tatis	1.00
DS53	Jose Guillen	1.50
DS54	Mike Caruso	.50
DS55	Carl Pavano	.50
DS56	Chris Clemons	.50
DS57	Mark L. Johnson	.50
DS58	Ken Cloude	.50
DS59	Rolando Arrojo	2.50
DS60	Mark Kotsay	2.50

1998 Upper Deck Rookie Edition Retrospectives

Retrospectives is a 30-card insert seeded 1:24. The cards offer a look back at the careers of baseball's top stars.

A player's name in *italic* type indicates a rookie card.

	MT
Complete Set (30):	200.00
Common Player:	2.50
Inserted 1:24	
1 Dennis Eckersley	2.50
2 Rickey Henderson	2.50
3 Harold Baines	2.50
4 Cal Ripken Jr.	25.00
5 Tony Gwynn	15.00
6 Wade Boggs	2.50
7 Orel Hershiser	2.50
8 Joe Carter	2.50
9 Roger Clemens	10.00
10 Barry Bonds	8.00
11 Mark McGwire	35.00
12 Greg Maddux	20.00
13 Fred McGriff	2.50
14 Rafael Palmeiro	3.00
15 Craig Biggio	2.50
16 Brady Anderson	2.50
17 Randy Johnson	5.00
18 Gary Sheffield	4.00
19 Albert Belle	8.00
20 Ken Griffey Jr.	30.00
21 Juan Gonzalez	15.00
22 Larry Walker	4.00
23 Tino Martinez	4.00
24 Frank Thomas	25.00
25 Jeff Bagwell	10.00
26 Kenny Lofton	8.00
27 Mo Vaughn	8.00
28 Mike Piazza	20.00
29 Alex Rodriguez	20.00
30 Chipper Jones	20.00

1998 Upper Deck Rookie Edition Unparalleled

Unparalleled is a 20-card, hobby-only insert. The set consists of holo-pattern foil-stamped cards. They were inserted one per 72 packs.

	MT
Complete Set (20):	400.00
Common Player:	5.00
Inserted 1:72	
1 Ken Griffey Jr.	50.00
2 Travis Lee	30.00
3 Ben Grieve	15.00
4 Jose Cruz Jr.	10.00
5 Nomar Garciaparra	30.00
6 Hideo Nomo	10.00
7 Kenny Lofton	12.00
8 Cal Ripken Jr.	40.00
9 Roger Clemens	20.00
10 Mike Piazza	30.00
11 Jeff Bagwell	20.00
12 Chipper Jones	30.00
13 Greg Maddux	30.00
14 Randy Johnson	10.00
15 Alex Rodriguez	30.00
16 Barry Bonds	12.00
17 Frank Thomas	40.00
18 Juan Gonzalez	25.00
19 Tony Gwynn	25.00
20 Mark McGwire	60.00

A player's name in *italic* type indicates a rookie card.

1998 Upper Deck Special F/X

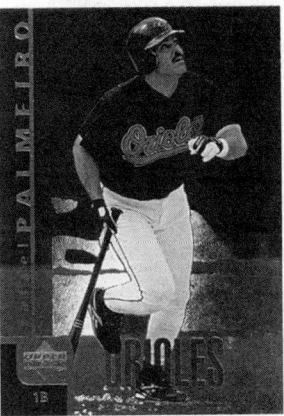

Special F/X is a retail-only product. The 150-card set consists of 125 regular cards, the 15-card Star Rookies subset and a 10-card subset called Ken Griffey Jr.'s Hot List. The base cards are printed on 20-point stock. The only insert is Power Zone which has four levels: Level One, Level Two - October-best, Level Three - Power Driven and Level Four - Superstar Xcitement.

		MT
Complete Set (150):		50.00
Common Player:		.25
Unlisted Stars: .75 to 1.00		
1	Ken Griffey Jr. (Griffey Hot List)	5.00
2	Mark McGwire (Griffey Hot List)	3.00
3	Alex Rodriguez (Griffey Hot List)	3.00
4	Larry Walker (Griffey Hot List)	.75
5	Tino Martinez (Griffey Hot List)	.75
6	Mike Piazza (Griffey Hot List)	3.00
7	Jose Cruz Jr. (Griffey Hot List)	1.00
8	Greg Maddux (Griffey Hot List)	3.00
9	Tony Gwynn (Griffey Hot List)	2.50
10	Roger Clemens (Griffey Hot List)	2.00
11	Jason Dickson	.25
12	Darin Erstad	1.50
13	Chuck Finley	.25
14	Dave Hollins	.25
15	Garret Anderson	.25
16	Michael Tucker	.25
17	Javier Lopez	.40
18	John Smoltz	.40
19	Mark Wohlers	.25
20	Greg Maddux	3.00
21	Scott Erickson	.25
22	Jimmy Key	.25
23	B.J. Surhoff	.25
24	Eric Davis	.25
25	Rafael Palmeiro	.50
26	Tim Naehring	.25
27	Darren Bragg	.25
28	Troy O'Leary	.25
29	John Valentin	.25
30	Mo Vaughn	1.50
31	Mark Grace	.75
32	Kevin Foster	.25
33	Kevin Tapani	.25
34	Kevin Orie	.25
35	Albert Belle	1.50
36	Ray Durham	.25

37	Jaime Navarro	.25
38	Mike Cameron	.25
39	Eddie Taubensee	.25
40	Barry Larkin	.75
41	Willie Greene	.25
42	Jeff Shaw	.25
43	Omar Vizquel	.25
44	Brian Giles	.25
45	Jim Thome	1.00
46	David Justice	.75
47	Sandy Alomar Jr.	.50
48	Neifi Perez	.25
49	Dante Bichette	.50
50	Vinny Castilla	.50
51	John Thomson	.25
52	Damion Easley	.25
53	Justin Thompson	.25
54	Bobby Higginson	.25
55	Tony Clark	1.00
56	Charles Johnson	.25
57	Edgar Renteria	.25
58	Alex Fernandez	.25
59	Gary Sheffield	.75
60	Livan Hernandez	.25
61	Craig Biggio	.75
62	Chris Holt	.25
63	Billy Wagner	.25
64	Brad Ausmus	.25
65	Dean Palmer	.25
66	Tim Belcher	.25
67	Jeff King	.25
68	Jose Rosado	.25
69	Chan Ho Park	.75
70	Raul Mondesi	.50
71	Hideo Nomo	1.00
72	Todd Zeile	.25
73	Eric Karros	.40
74	Cal Eldred	.25
75	Jeff D'Amico	.25
76	Doug Jones	.25
77	Dave Nilsson	.25
78	Todd Walker	.25
79	Rick Aguilera	.25
80	Paul Molitor	1.00
81	Brad Radke	.25
82	Vladimir Guerrero	1.50
83	Carlos Perez	.25
84	F.P. Santangelo	.25
85	Rondell White	.40
86	Butch Huskey	.25
87	Edgardo Alfonzo	.25
88	John Franco	.25
89	John Olerud	.40
90	Todd Hundley	.25
91	Bernie Williams	1.00
92	Andy Pettitte	1.00
93	Paul O'Neill	.50
94	David Cone	.40
95	Jason Giambi	.25
96	Damon Mashore	.25
97	Scott Spiezio	.25
98	Ariel Prieto	.25
99	Rico Brogna	.25
100	Mike Lieberthal	.25
101	Garrett Stephenson	.25
102	Ricky Bottalico	.25
103	Kevin Polcovich	.25
104	Jon Lieber	.25
105	Kevin Young	.25
106	Tony Womack	.25
107	Gary Gaetti	.25
108	Alan Benes	.50
109	Willie McGee	.25
110	Mark McGwire	3.00
111	Ron Gant	.40
112	Andy Ashby	.25
113	Steve Finley	.25
114	Quilvio Veras	.25
115	Ken Caminiti	.50
116	Joey Hamilton	.25
117	Bill Mueller	.25
118	Mark Gardner	.25
119	Shawn Estes	.25
120	J.T. Snow	.25
121	Dante Powell	.25
122	Jeff Kent	.25
123	Jamie Moyer	.25
124	Joey Cora	.25
125	Ken Griffey Jr.	5.00
126	Jeff Fassero	.25
127	Edgar Martinez	.40
128	Will Clark	.50
129	Lee Stevens	.25
130	Ivan Rodriguez	1.50
131	Rusty Greer	.50
132	Ed Sprague	.25

133	Pat Hentgen	.25
134	Shannon Stewart	.25
135	Carlos Delgado	.40
136	Brett Tomko (Star Rookie)	.25
137	Jose Guillen (Star Rookie)	.50
138	Elieser Marrero (Star Rookie)	.25
139	Dennis Reyes (Star Rookie)	.25
140	Mark Kotsay (Star Rookie)	.75
141	Richie Sexson (Star Rookie)	.25
142	Todd Helton (Star Rookie)	1.50
143	Jeremi Gonzalez (Star Rookie)	.25
144	Jeff Abbott (Star Rookie)	.25
145	Matt Morris (Star Rookie)	.25
146	Aaron Boone (Star Rookie)	.25
147	Todd Dunwoody (Star Rookie)	.25
148	Mario Valdez (Star Rookie)	.25
149	Fernando Tatis (Star Rookie)	.25
150	Jaret Wright (Star Rookie)	2.00

1998 Upper Deck Special F/X OctoberBest

OctoberBest is Level Two of the Power Zone insert. This 20-card insert is die-cut and printed on silver foil. Inserted one per 34 packs, the set features the postseason exploits of 20 players from Power Zone Level One.

		MT
Complete Set (15):		160.00
Common Player:		4.00
Inserted 1:34		
PZ1	Frank Thomas	25.00
PZ2	Juan Gonzalez	15.00
PZ3	Mike Piazza	20.00
PZ4	Mark McGwire	40.00
PZ5	Jeff Bagwell	12.00
PZ6	Barry Bonds	8.00
PZ7	Ken Griffey Jr.	30.00
PZ8	John Smoltz	4.00
PZ9	Andruw Jones	8.00
PZ10	Greg Maddux	20.00
PZ11	Sandy Alomar Jr.	4.00
PZ12	Roberto Alomar	6.00
PZ13	Chipper Jones	20.00
PZ14	Kenny Lofton	8.00
PZ15	Tom Glavine	4.00

1998 Upper Deck Special F/X Power Driven

Power Driven is Level Three of the Power Zone insert. Inserted 1:69, the set features the top 10 power hitters from Power Zone Level Two. The cards feature gold Light F/X,

		MT
Complete Set (10):		150.00
Common Player:		6.00
Inserted 1:69		
PZ1	Frank Thomas	30.00
PZ2	Juan Gonzalez	20.00
PZ3	Mike Piazza	25.00
PZ4	Larry Walker	6.00
PZ5	Mark McGwire	50.00
PZ6	Jeff Bagwell	15.00
PZ7	Mo Vaughn	10.00
PZ8	Barry Bonds	10.00
PZ9	Tino Martinez	6.00
PZ10	Ken Griffey Jr.	40.00

1998 Upper Deck Special F/X Power Zone

Power Zone Level One is a 30-card insert seeded one per seven packs. The cards are printed using silver Light F/X technology.

		MT
Complete Set (20):		50.00
Common Player:		.75
Inserted 1:7		
PZ1	Jose Cruz Jr.	2.00
PZ2	Frank Thomas	8.00
PZ3	Juan Gonzalez	5.00
PZ4	Mike Piazza	6.00
PZ5	Mark McGwire	12.00
PZ6	Barry Bonds	2.50
PZ7	Greg Maddux	6.00
PZ8	Alex Rodriguez	6.00
PZ9	Nomar Garciaparra	6.00
PZ10	Ken Griffey Jr.	10.00
PZ11	John Smoltz	.75
PZ12	Andruw Jones	2.50
PZ13	Sandy Alomar Jr.	.75
PZ14	Roberto Alomar	2.00
PZ15	Chipper Jones	6.00
PZ16	Kenny Lofton	2.50
PZ17	Larry Walker	1.50
PZ18	Jeff Bagwell	4.00
PZ19	Mo Vaughn	2.50
PZ20	Tom Glavine	.75

1998 Upper Deck Special F/X Superstar Xcitement

Printed on Light F/X gold foil, this 10-card set features the same players as the Power Driven insert. This set is Power Zone Level Four and is sequentially numbered to 250.

		MT
Complete Set (10):		1000.
Common Player:		20.00
Production 250 sets		
PZ1	Jose Cruz Jr.	40.00
PZ2	Frank Thomas	150.00
PZ3	Juan Gonzalez	100.00
PZ4	Mike Piazza	120.00
PZ5	Mark McGwire	220.00
PZ6	Barry Bonds	50.00
PZ7	Greg Maddux	120.00
PZ8	Alex Rodriguez	120.00
PZ9	Nomar Garciaparra	120.00
PZ10	Ken Griffey Jr.	200.00

1998 Upper Deck UD 3

	MT
Complete Set (270):	700.00
Comm. Fut. Impacts (1-30):	.50
Inserted 1:12	
Die-Cuts: 1x to 1.5x	
Production 2,000 sets	

Grading Guide

Mint (MT): A perfect card. Well-centered with all corners sharp and square. No creases, stains, edge nicks, surface marks, yellowing or fading.

Near Mint (NM): A nearly perfect card. At first glance, a NM card appears to be perfect. May be slightly off-center. No surface marks, creases or loss of gloss.

Excellent (EX): Corners are still fairly sharp with only moderate wear. Borders may be off-center. No creases or stains on fronts or backs, but may show slight loss of surface luster.

Very Good (VG): Shows obvious handling. May have rounded corners, minor creases, major gum or wax stains. No major creases, tape marks, writing, etc.

Good (G): A well-worn card, but exhibits no intentional damage. May have major or multiple creases. Corners may be rounded well beyond card border.

Comm. Pow. Corps (31-60):		.25
Inserted 1:1.5		
Die-Cuts: 3x to 4x		
Production 2,000 sets		
Comm. Establ. (61-90):		.50
Inserted 1:6		
Die-Cuts: 2x to 3x		
Production 2,000 sets		
Comm. Fut. Impact (91-120):		.40
Inserted 1:6		
Die-Cuts: 3x to 5x		
Production 1,000 sets		
Comm. Pow Corps (121-150):		.25
Inserted 1:4		
Die-Cuts: 6x to 10x		
Production 1,000 sets		
Comm. Establ. (151-180):		.25
Inserted 1:1		
Die-Cuts: 12x to 20x		
Production 1,000 sets		
Comm. Fut. Impact (181-210):		.25
Inserted 1:1		
Die-Cuts: 25x to 40x		
Production 100 sets		
Comm. Pow Corps (211-240):		1.50
Inserted 1:12		
Die-Cuts: 8x to 15x		
Production 100 sets		
Comm. Establ. (241-270):		2.00
Inserted 1:24		
Die-Cuts: 5x to 8x		
Production 100 sets		
1	Travis Lee	12.00
2	A.J. Hinch	.50
3	Mike Caruso	.50
4	Miguel Tejada	1.50
5	Brad Fullmer	1.50
6	Eric Milton	.50
7	Mark Kotsay	2.00
8	Darin Erstad	6.00
9	Magglio Ordonez	1.50
10	Ben Grieve	8.00
11	Brett Tomko	.50
12	*Mike Kinkade*	1.00
13	Rolando Arrojo	5.00
14	Todd Helton	1.50
15	Scott Rolen	4.00
16	Bruce Chen	.50
17	Daryle Ward	.50
18	Jaret Wright	4.00
19	Cliff Politte	.50
20	Paul Konerko	.75
21	Kerry Wood	25.00
22	Russell Branyan	.50
23	Gabe Alvarez	.50
24	Juan Encarnacion	.50
25	Andruw Jones	4.00
26	Vladimir Guerrero	5.00
27	Eli Marrero	.25
28	Matt Clement	.25
29	Gary Matthews Jr.	1.00
30	Derek Lee	.50
31	Ken Caminiti	.75
32	Gary Sheffield	1.00
33	Jay Buhner	.75
34	Ryan Klesko	.75
35	Nomar Garciaparra	5.00
36	Vinny Castilla	.25
37	Tony Clark	.75
38	Sammy Sosa	5.00
39	Tino Martinez	.75
40	Mike Piazza	5.00
41	Manny Ramirez	2.00
42	Larry Walker	.75
43	Jose Cruz Jr.	2.00
44	Matt Williams	.75
45	Frank Thomas	5.00
46	Jim Edmonds	.25
47	Raul Mondesi	.50
48	Alex Rodriguez	5.00
49	Albert Belle	2.00
50	Mark McGwire	10.00
51	Tim Salmon	.75
52	Andres Galarraga	.75
53	Jeff Bagwell	3.00
54	Jim Thome	1.00
55	Barry Bonds	2.00
56	Carlos Delgado	.25
57	Mo Vaughn	2.00
58	Chipper Jones	4.00
59	Juan Gonzalez	4.00
60	Ken Griffey Jr.	8.00
61	David Cone	.40
62	Hideo Nomo	3.00
63	Edgar Martinez	.25

64	Fred McGriff	1.00	160	Paul Molitor	1.00	256	Dante Bichette	3.00
65	Cal Ripken Jr.	10.00	161	Eric Karros	.40	257	Brady Anderson	2.00
66	Todd Hundley	.25	162	Rafael Palmeiro	.40	258	Craig Biggio	2.00
67	Barry Larkin	.75	163	Chuck Knoblauch	.75	259	Derek Jeter	25.00
68	Dennis Eckersley	.25	164	Ivan Rodriguez	1.25	260	Roger Clemens	20.00
69	Randy Johnson	3.00	165	Greg Maddux	2.50	261	Roberto Alomar	8.00
70	Paul Molitor	3.00	166	Dante Bichette	.50	262	Wade Boggs	4.00
71	Eric Karros	.25	167	Brady Anderson	.25	263	Charles Johnson	2.00
72	Rafael Palmeiro	.75	168	Craig Biggio	.25	264	Mark Grace	3.00
73	Chuck Knoblauch	2.00	169	Derek Jeter	2.50	265	Kenny Lofton	10.00
74	Ivan Rodriguez	4.00	170	Roger Clemens	2.00	266	Mike Mussina	8.00
75	Greg Maddux	8.00	171	Roberto Alomar	1.00	267	Pedro J. Martinez	8.00
76	Dante Bichette	1.50	172	Wade Boggs	.50	268	Curt Schilling	2.00
77	Brady Anderson	.25	173	Charles Johnson	.25	269	Bernie Williams	6.00
78	Craig Biggio	.75	174	Mark Grace	.50	270	Tony Gwynn	20.00
79	Derek Jeter	7.00	175	Kenny Lofton	1.25			
80	Roger Clemens	6.00	176	Mike Mussina	1.00			
81	Roberto Alomar	2.50	177	Pedro J. Martinez	1.00			
82	Wade Boggs	.75	178	Curt Schilling	.40			
83	Charles Johnson	.25	179	Bernie Williams	.75			
84	Mark Grace	.75	180	Tony Gwynn	2.00			
85	Kenny Lofton	4.00	181	Travis Lee	3.00			
86	Mike Mussina	3.00	182	A.J. Hinch	.25			
87	Pedro J. Martinez	3.00	183	Mike Caruso	.40			
88	Curt Schilling	.50	184	Miguel Tejada	.75			
89	Bernie Williams	2.50	185	Brad Fullmer	.75			
90	Tony Gwynn	6.00	186	Eric Milton	.25			
91	Travis Lee	6.00	187	Mark Kotsay	.75			
92	A.J. Hinch	.50	188	Darin Erstad	1.50			
93	Mike Caruso	.40	189	Magglio Ordonez	1.00			
94	Miguel Tejada	1.00	190	Ben Grieve	2.00			
95	Brad Fullmer	1.50	191	Brett Tomko	.25			
96	Eric Milton	.25	192	Mike Kinkade	.25			
97	Mark Kotsay	1.50	193	Rolando Arrojo	2.00			
98	Darin Erstad	3.00	194	Todd Helton	1.00			
99	Magglio Ordonez	1.50	195	Scott Rolen	1.50			
100	Ben Grieve	5.00	196	Bruce Chen	.25			
101	Brett Tomko	.40	197	Daryle Ward	.25			
102	Mike Kinkade	.40	198	Jaret Wright	1.25			
103	Rolando Arrojo	4.00	199	Cliff Politte	.25			
104	Todd Helton	2.50	200	Paul Konerko	.50			
105	Scott Rolen	4.00	201	Kerry Wood	6.00			
106	Bruce Chen	.40	202	Russell Branyan	.25			
107	Daryle Ward	.40	203	Gabe Alvarez	.25			
108	Jaret Wright	3.00	204	Juan Encarnacion	.25			
109	Sean Casey	.50	205	Andruw Jones	1.00			
110	Paul Konerko	.75	206	Vladimir Guerrero	1.50			
111	Kerry Wood	12.00	207	Eli Marrero	.25			
112	Russell Branyan	.40	208	Matt Clement	.25			
113	Gabe Alvarez	.40	209	Gary Matthews Jr.	.25			
114	Juan Encarnacion	.40	210	Derrek Lee	.25			
115	Andruw Jones	3.00	211	Ken Caminiti	1.50			
116	Vladimir Guerrero	4.00	212	Gary Sheffield	2.50			
117	Eli Marrero	.40	213	Jay Buhner	2.50			
118	Matt Clement	.40	214	Ryan Klesko	2.50			
119	Gary Matthews Jr.	1.00	215	Nomar Garciaparra	15.00			
120	Derrek Lee	.25	216	Vinny Castilla	1.50			
121	Ken Caminiti	.50	217	Tony Clark	4.00			
122	Gary Sheffield	.75	218	Sammy Sosa	15.00			
123	Jay Buhner	.50	219	Tino Martinez	3.00			
124	Ryan Klesko	.50	220	Mike Piazza	15.00			
125	Nomar Garciaparra	5.00	221	Manny Ramirez	6.00			
126	Vinny Castilla	.25	222	Larry Walker	3.00			
127	Tony Clark	1.00	223	Jose Cruz Jr.	6.00			
128	Sammy Sosa	5.00	224	Matt Williams	2.50			
129	Tino Martinez	1.00	225	Frank Thomas	15.00			
130	Mike Piazza	5.00	226	Jim Edmonds	1.50			
131	Manny Ramirez	2.00	227	Raul Mondesi	2.00			
132	Larry Walker	1.00	228	Alex Rodriguez	15.00			
133	Jose Cruz Jr.	2.00	229	Albert Belle	6.00			
134	Matt Williams	.75	230	Mark McGwire	30.00			
135	Frank Thomas	5.00	231	Tim Salmon	2.50			
136	Jim Edmonds	.25	232	Andres Galarraga	3.00			
137	Raul Mondesi	.40	233	Jeff Bagwell	8.00			
138	Alex Rodriguez	5.00	234	Jim Thome	4.00			
139	Albert Belle	2.00	235	Barry Bonds	6.00			
140	Mark McGwire	10.00	236	Carlos Delgado	1.50			
141	Tim Salmon	.50	267	Mo Vaughn	6.00			
142	Andres Galarraga	.75	238	Chipper Jones	12.00			
143	Jeff Bagwell	2.50	239	Juan Gonzalez	12.00			
144	Jim Thome	.75	240	Ken Griffey Jr.	25.00			
145	Barry Bonds	2.00	241	David Cone	2.50			
146	Carlos Delgado	.25	242	Hideo Nomo	6.00			
147	Mo Vaughn	2.00	243	Edgar Martinez	2.00			
148	Chipper Jones	4.00	244	Fred McGriff	2.50			
149	Juan Gonzalez	4.00	245	Cal Ripken Jr.	30.00			
150	Ken Griffey Jr.	8.00	246	Todd Hundley	2.00			
151	David Cone	.40	247	Barry Larkin	2.50			
152	Hideo Nomo	.75	248	Dennis Eckersley	2.00			
153	Edgar Martinez	.25	249	Randy Johnson	8.00			
154	Fred McGriff	.25	250	Paul Molitor	8.00			
155	Cal Ripken Jr.	3.00	251	Eric Karros	2.00			
156	Todd Hundley	.25	252	Rafael Palmeiro	3.00			
157	Barry Larkin	.40	253	Chuck Knoblauch	4.00			
158	Dennis Eckersley	.25	254	Ivan Rodriguez	10.00			
159	Randy Johnson	1.00	255	Greg Maddux	25.00			

1998 UD Retro

	MT
Complete Set (130):	50.00
Common Player:	.15
1	Jim Edmonds	.25
2	Darin Erstad	1.00
3	Tim Salmon	.50
4	Jay Bell	.15
5	Matt Williams	.50
6	Andres Galarraga	.75
7	Andruw Jones	1.00
8	Chipper Jones	2.50
9	Greg Maddux	2.50
10	Rafael Palmeiro	.40
11	Cal Ripken Jr.	2.50
12	Brooks Robinson	.75
13	Nomar Garciaparra	3.00
14	Pedro Martinez	.75
15	Mo Vaughn	1.00
16	Ernie Banks	.75
17	Mark Grace	.40
18	Gary Matthews	.15
19	Sammy Sosa	3.00
20	Albert Belle	1.00
21	Carlton Fisk	.15
22	Frank Thomas	2.50
23	Ken Griffey Sr.	.15
24	Paul Konerko	.30
25	Barry Larkin	.30
26	Sean Casey	.25
27	Tony Perez	.15
28	Bob Feller	.15
29	Kenny Lofton	.75
30	Manny Ramirez	1.00
31	Jim Thome	.60
32	Omar Vizquel	.15
33	Dante Bichette	.40
34	Larry Walker	.50
35	Tony Clark	.50
36	Damion Easley	.15
37	Cliff Floyd	.15
38	Livan Hernandez	.15
39	Jeff Bagwell	1.25
40	Craig Biggio	.25
41	Al Kaline	.25
42	Johnny Damon	.15
43	Dean Palmer	.15
44	Charles Johnson	.15
45	Eric Karros	.15
46	Gaylord Perry	.15

47	Raul Mondesi	.30
48	Gary Sheffield	.30
49	Eddie Mathews	.50
50	Warren Spahn	.75
51	Jeromy Burnitz	.15
52	Jeff Cirillo	.15
53	Marquis Grissom	.15
54	Paul Molitor	.75
55	Kirby Puckett	1.00
56	Brad Radke	.15
57	Todd Walker	.25
58	Vladimir Guerrero	1.50
59	Brad Fullmer	.40
60	Rondell White	.25
61	Bobby Jones	.15
62	Hideo Nomo	.60
63	Mike Piazza	2.50
64	Tom Seaver	.75
65	Frank Thomas (original)	.15
66	Yogi Berra	.75
67	Derek Jeter	2.00
68	Tino Martinez	.40
69	Paul O'Neill	.30
70	Andy Pettitte	.50
71	Rollie Fingers	.15
72	Rickey Henderson	.25
73	Matt Stairs	.15
74	Scott Rolen	1.00
75	Curt Schilling	.25
76	Jose Guillen	.15
77	Jason Kendall	.15
78	Lou Brock	.40
79	Bob Gibson	.50
80	Ray Lankford	.15
81	Mark McGwire	5.00
83	Kevin Brown	.25
84	Ken Caminiti	.25
85	Tony Gwynn	2.00
86	Greg Vaughn	.25
87	Barry Bonds	1.00
88	Willie Stargell	.50
89	Willie McCovey	.40
90	Ken Griffey Jr.	4.00
91	Randy Johnson	.75
92	Alex Rodriguez	2.50
93	Quinton McCracken	.15
94	Fred McGriff	.30
95	Juan Gonzalez	2.00
96	Ivan Rodriguez	1.00
97	Nolan Ryan	4.00
98	Jose Canseco	.60
99	Roger Clemens	1.50
100	Jose Cruz Jr.	.75
101	*Justin Baughman*	.50
102	*David Dellucci* (Futurama)	1.00
103	Travis Lee (Futurama)	1.00
104	*Troy Glaus* (Futurama)	4.00
105	Kerry Wood (Futurama)	4.00
106	Mike Caruso (Futurama)	.15
107	Jim Parque (Futurama)	.15
108	Brett Tomko (Futurama)	.15
109	Russell Branyan (Futurama)	.15
110	Jaret Wright (Futurama)	.75
111	Todd Helton (Futurama)	1.00
112	Gabe Alvarez (Futurama)	.15
113	*Matt Anderson* (Futurama)	.75
114	Alex Gonzalez (Futurama)	.15
115	Mark Kotsay (Futurama)	.30
116	Derrek Lee (Futurama)	.15
117	Richard Hidalgo (Futurama)	.15
118	Adrian Beltre (Futurama)	1.00
119	Geoff Jenkins (Futurama)	.15
120	Eric Milton (Futurama)	.15
121	Brad Fullmer (Futurama)	.25
122	Vladimir Guerrero (Futurama)	1.50
123	Carl Pavano (Futurama)	.15
124	*Orlando Hernandez* (Futurama)	5.00
125	Ben Grieve (Futurama)	1.00
126	A.J. Hinch (Futurama)	.15
127	Matt Clement (Futurama)	.15
128	*Gary Matthews Jr.* (Futurama)	.50
129	Aramis Ramirez (Futurama)	.75
130	Rolando Arrojo (Futurama)	1.50

1998 UD Retro Big Boppers

		MT
Complete Set (30):		600.00
Common Player:		5.00
Production 500 sets		
BB1	Darin Erstad	15.00

BB2	Rafael Palmeiro	8.00
BB3	Cal Ripken Jr.	40.00
BB4	Nomar Garciaparra	40.00
BB5	Mo Vaughn	15.00
BB6	Frank Thomas	40.00
BB7	Albert Belle	15.00
BB8	Jim Thome	10.00
BB9	Manny Ramirez	15.00
BB10	Tony Clark	10.00
BB11	Tino Martinez	8.00
BB12	Ben Grieve	18.00
BB13	Ken Griffey Jr.	60.00
BB14	Alex Rodriguez	40.00
BB15	Jay Buhner	8.00
BB16	Juan Gonzalez	30.00
BB17	Jose Cruz Jr.	12.00
BB18	Jose Canseco	10.00
BB19	Travis Lee	15.00
BB20	Chipper Jones	30.00
BB21	Andres Galarraga	10.00
BB22	Andruw Jones	15.00
BB23	Sammy Sosa	50.00
BB24	Vinny Castilla	5.00
BB25	Larry Walker	10.00
BB26	Jeff Bagwell	15.00
BB27	Gary Sheffield	8.00
BB28	Mike Piazza	40.00
BB29	Mark McGwire	75.00
BB30	Barry Bonds	15.00

1998 UD Retro Groovy Kind of Glove

		MT
Complete Set (30):		125.00
Common Player:		1.50
Inserted 1:7		
G1	Roberto Alomar	3.00
G2	Cal Ripken Jr.	10.00
G3	Nomar Garciaparra	10.00
G4	Frank Thomas	10.00
G5	Robin Ventura	1.50
G6	Omar Vizquel	1.50
G7	Kenny Lofton	4.00
G8	Ben Grieve	5.00
G9	Alex Rodriguez	10.00
G10	Ken Griffey Jr.	15.00
G11	Ivan Rodriguez	4.00
G12	Travis Lee	4.00
G13	Matt Williams	2.00
G14	Greg Maddux	10.00
G15	Andres Galarraga	3.00
G16	Andruw Jones	4.00
G17	Kerry Wood	12.00
G18	Mark Grace	2.00
G19	Craig Biggio	2.00
G20	Charles Johnson	1.50
G21	Raul Mondesi	2.00
G22	Mike Piazza	10.00
G23	Rey Ordonez	1.50
G24	Derek Jeter	8.00
G25	Scott Rolen	4.00
G26	Mark McGwire	20.00
G27	Ken Caminiti	2.00
G28	Tony Gwynn	8.00
G29	J.T. Snow	1.50
G30	Barry Bonds	4.00

1998 UD Retro Lunchbox

		MT
Complete Set (6):		75.00
Common Lunchbox:		8.00
	Nomar Garciaparra	12.00
	Ken Griffey Jr.	20.00
	Chipper Jones	10.00
	Travis Lee	8.00
	Mark McGwire	25.00
	Cal Ripken Jr.	15.00

1998 UD Retro New Frontier

		MT
Complete Set (30):		150.00
Common Player:		2.50
Production 1,000 sets		
NF1	Justin Baughman	2.50
NF2	David Dellucci	4.00
NF3	Travis Lee	12.00
NF4	Troy Glaus	20.00
NF5	Mike Caruso	2.50
NF6	Jim Parque	2.50
NF7	Kerry Wood	30.00
NF8	Brett Tomko	2.50
NF9	Russell Branyan	2.50
NF10	Jaret Wright	8.00
NF11	Todd Helton	8.00
NF12	Gabe Alvarez	2.50
NF13	Matt Anderson	4.00
NF14	Alex Gonzalez	2.50
NF15	Mark Kotsay	3.00
NF16	Derrek Lee	2.50
NF17	Richard Hidalgo	2.50
NF18	Adrian Beltre	8.00
NF19	Geoff Jenkins	2.50
NF20	Eric Milton	2.50
NF21	Brad Fullmer	4.00
NF22	Vladimir Guerrero	15.00
NF23	Carl Pavano	2.50
NF24	Orlando Hernandez	25.00
NF25	Ben Grieve	12.00
NF26	A.J. Hinch	2.50
NF27	Matt Clement	2.50
NF28	Gary Matthews	4.00
NF29	Aramis Ramirez	5.00
NF30	Rolando Arrojo	8.00

A player's name in *italic* type indicates a rookie card.

1998 UD Retro
1990s Time Capsule

		MT
Complete Set (50):		100.00
Common Player:		.75
Inserted 1:2		
TC1	Mike Mussina	2.00
TC2	Rafael Palmeiro	1.00
TC3	Cal Ripken Jr.	6.00
TC4	Nomar Garciaparra	6.00
TC5	Pedro Martinez	2.00
TC6	Mo Vaughn	2.50
TC7	Albert Belle	2.50
TC8	Frank Thomas	6.00
TC9	David Justice	1.00
TC10	Kenny Lofton	2.00
TC11	Manny Ramirez	2.50
TC12	Jim Thome	1.50
TC13	Derek Jeter	5.00
TC14	Tino Martinez	1.50
TC15	Ben Grieve	2.50
TC16	Rickey Henderson	.75
TC17	Ken Griffey Jr.	10.00
TC18	Randy Johnson	2.00
TC19	Alex Rodriguez	6.00
TC20	Wade Boggs	1.00
TC21	Fred McGriff	.75
TC22	Juan Gonzalez	5.00
TC23	Ivan Rodriguez	2.50
TC24	Nolan Ryan	10.00
TC25	Jose Canseco	1.50
TC26	Roger Clemens	4.00
TC27	Jose Cruz Jr.	2.00
TC28	Travis Lee	2.50
TC29	Matt Williams	1.00
TC30	Andres Galarraga	1.50
TC31	Andruw Jones	2.50
TC32	Chipper Jones	5.00
TC33	Greg Maddux	6.00
TC34	Kerry Wood	8.00
TC35	Barry Larkin	1.00
TC36	Dante Bichette	1.00
TC37	Larry Walker	1.50
TC38	Livan Hernandez	.75
TC39	Jeff Bagwell	2.50
TC40	Craig Biggio	.75
TC41	Charles Johnson	.75
TC42	Gary Sheffield	1.00
TC43	Marquis Grissom	.75
TC44	Mike Piazza	6.00
TC45	Scott Rolen	2.50
TC46	Curt Schilling	.75
TC47	Mark McGwire	12.00
TC48	Ken Caminiti	.75
TC49	Tony Gwynn	5.00
TC50	Barry Bonds	2.50

1998 UD Retro
Quantum Leap

	MT
Complete Set (30):	4500.
Common Player:	40.00
Production 50 sets	

Q1	Darin Erstad	100.00
Q2	Cal Ripken Jr.	250.00
Q3	Nomar Garciaparra	250.00
Q4	Frank Thomas	250.00
Q5	Kenny Lofton	100.00
Q6	Ben Grieve	125.00
Q7	Ken Griffey Jr.	400.00
Q8	Alex Rodriguez	250.00
Q9	Juan Gonzalez	200.00
Q10	Jose Cruz Jr.	80.00
Q11	Roger Clemens	150.00
Q12	Travis Lee	100.00
Q13	Chipper Jones	200.00
Q14	Greg Maddux	250.00
Q15	Kerry Wood	250.00
Q16	Jeff Bagwell	125.00
Q17	Mike Piazza	250.00
Q18	Scott Rolen	100.00
Q19	Mark McGwire	500.00
Q20	Tony Gwynn	200.00
Q21	Larry Walker	60.00
Q22	Derek Jeter	200.00
Q23	Sammy Sosa	300.00
Q24	Barry Bonds	100.00
Q25	Mo Vaughn	100.00
Q26	Roberto Alomar	80.00
Q27	Todd Helton	80.00
Q28	Ivan Rodriguez	100.00
Q29	Vladimir Guerrero	150.00
Q30	Albert Belle	100.00

1998 UD Retro
Sign of the Times

	MT
Complete Set (32):	
Common Autograph:	
Inserted 1:36	

EB	Ernie Banks (300)	
YB	Yogi Berra (150)	
RB	Russell Branyan (750)	
LB	Lou Brock (300)	
JC	Jose Cruz Jr. (300)	
RF	Rollie Fingers (600)	
BF	Bob Feller (600)	
CF	Carlton Fisk (600)	
BGi	Bob Gibson (300)	
BGr	Ben Grieve (300)	
KGj	Ken Griffey Jr. (100)	
KGs	Ken Griffey Sr. (600)	
JG	Jose Guillen (300)	
TG	Tony Gwynn (200)	
AK	Al Kaline (600)	
PK	Paul Konerko (750)	
TLe	Travis Lee (300)	
EM	Eddie Mathews (600)	
GMj	Gary Matthews Jr. (750)	
GMs	Gary Matthews (600)	
WM	Willie McCovey (600)	
TP	Tony Perez (600)	
GP	Gaylord Perry (1,000)	
KP	Kirby Puckett (450)	
BR	Brooks Robinson (300)	
SR	Scott Rolen (300)	
NR	Nolan Ryan (500)	
TS	Tom Seaver (300)	
WS	Warren Spahn (600)	
WiS	Willie Stargell (600)	
FT	Frank Thomas (600)	
KW	Kerry Wood (200)	

Z

1995 Zenith

At the top of the pyramid of Pinnacle's baseball card lines for 1995 was Zenith, a super-premium brand utilizing all-foil metallized printing technology on double-thick 24-point cardboard stock to emphasize the quality look and feel. Six-card packs carried a retail price of $3.99. Two styles comprise the 150-card base set. The 110 veteran player cards are curiously arranged in alphabetical order according to the player's first names (with the exception of card #48, a special Japanese-language card of Hideo Nomo). These cards have a color player action photo on a black and gold background that is a view of a pyramid from its pinnacle. One the horizontal back, a portrait photo of the player in a partly-cloudy blue sky overlooks a playing field which offers his hit location preferences versus righty and lefty pitching. A scoreboard has his 1994 and career stats. The Pinnacle anti-counterfeiting optical-variable bar is in the lower-right corner. The rookie cards which comprise the final 40 cards in the set have a color photo at center with a gold-tone version of the same picture in the background. A large gold "ROOKIE" is vertically at right. Backs are similar to those on the veterans' cards except they have a scouting report in place of the hit-location chart.

		MT
Complete Set (150):		50.00
Common Player:		.25
Wax Box:		75.00
1	Albert Belle	1.00
2	Alex Fernandez	.25
3	Andy Benes	.25
4	Barry Larkin	.50
5	Barry Bonds	1.00
6	Ben McDonald	.25

#	Player	Price
7	Bernard Gilkey	.25
8	Billy Ashley	.25
9	Bobby Bonilla	.40
10	Bret Saberhagen	.25
11	Brian Jordan	.25
12	Cal Ripken Jr.	3.00
13	Carlos Baerga	.25
14	Carlos Delgado	.40
15	Cecil Fielder	.40
16	Chili Davis	.25
17	Chuck Knoblauch	.60
18	Craig Biggio	.40
19	Danny Tartabull	.25
20	Dante Bichette	.40
21	Darren Daulton	.25
22	Dave Justice	.40
23	Dave Winfield	.35
24	David Cone	.40
25	Dean Palmer	.25
26	Deion Sanders	.60
27	Dennis Eckersley	.35
28	Derek Bell	.25
29	Don Mattingly	1.50
30	Edgar Martinez	.40
31	Eric Karros	.35
32	Erik Hanson	.25
33	Frank Thomas	3.00
34	Fred McGriff	.50
35	Gary Sheffield	.60
36	Gary Gaetti	.25
37	Greg Maddux	2.50
38	Gregg Jefferies	.25
39	Ivan Rodriguez	1.00
40	Kenny Rogers	.25
41	J.T. Snow	.40
42	Hal Morris	.25
43	Eddie Murray (3,000 hit)	.75
44	Javier Lopez	.40
45	Jay Bell	.25
46	Jeff Conine	.25
47	Jeff Bagwell	1.50
48	Hideo Nomo	3.00
49	Jeff Kent	.25
50	Jeff King	.25
51	Jim Thome	.75
52	Jimmy Key	.25
53	Joe Carter	.40
54	John Valentin	.25
55	John Olerud	.25
56	Jose Canseco	.50
57	Jose Rijo	.25
58	Jose Offerman	.25
59	Juan Gonzalez	2.00
60	Ken Caminiti	.50
61	Ken Griffey Jr.	4.00
62	Kenny Lofton	1.00
63	Kevin Appier	.25
64	Kevin Seitzer	.25
65	Kirby Puckett	1.50
66	Kirk Gibson	.25
67	Larry Walker	.75
68	Lenny Dykstra	.25
69	Manny Ramirez	.75
70	Mark Grace	.50
71	Mark McGwire	5.00
72	Marquis Grissom	.40
73	Jim Edmonds	.40
74	Matt Williams	.40
75	Mike Mussina	.75
76	Mike Piazza	2.50
77	Mo Vaughn	1.00
78	Moises Alou	.40
79	Ozzie Smith	.75
80	Paul O'Neill	.40
81	Paul Molitor	.75
82	Rafael Palmeiro	.50
83	Randy Johnson	.75
84	Raul Mondesi	.50
85	Ray Lankford	.25
86	Reggie Sanders	.25
87	Rickey Henderson	.25
88	Rico Brogna	.25
89	Roberto Alomar	.75
90	Robin Ventura	.25
91	Roger Clemens	1.50
92	Ron Gant	.40
93	Rondell White	.40
94	Royce Clayton	.25
95	Ruben Sierra	.25
96	Rusty Greer	.50
97	Ryan Klesko	.60
98	Sammy Sosa	2.00
99	Shawon Dunston	.25
100	Steve Ontiveros	.25
101	Tim Naehring	.25
102	Tim Salmon	.50

#	Player	Price
103	Tino Martinez	.50
104	Tony Gwynn	2.00
105	Travis Fryman	.25
106	Vinny Castilla	.25
107	Wade Boggs	.75
108	Wally Joyner	.25
109	Wil Cordero	.25
110	Will Clark	.50
111	Chipper Jones	2.50
112	C.J. Nitkowski	.25
113	Curtis Goodwin	.25
114	Tim Unroe	.25
115	Vaughn Eshelman	.25
116	Marty Cordova	.40
117	Dustin Hermanson	.25
118	Rich Becker	.25
119	Ray Durham	.25
120	Shane Andrews	.25
121	Scott Ruffcorn	.25
122	*Mark Grudzielanek*	.75
123	James Baldwin	.25
124	*Carlos Perez*	.50
125	Julian Tavarez	.25
126	Joe Vitiello	.25
127	Jason Bates	.25
128	Edgardo Alfonzo	.40
129	Juan Acevedo	.40
130	Bill Pulsipher	.40
131	*Bob Higginson*	1.50
132	Russ Davis	.25
133	Charles Johnson	.50
134	Derek Jeter	2.50
135	Phil Nevin	.25
136	LaTroy Hawkins	.40
137	Brian Hunter	.25
138	Roberto Petagine	.40
139	Jim Pittsley	.25
140	Garret Anderson	.40
141	Ugueth Urbina	.25
142	Antonio Osuna	.25
143	Michael Tucker	.25
144	Benji Gil	.25
145	Jon Nunnally	.25
146	Alex Rodriguez	4.00
147	Todd Hollandsworth	.25
148	Alex Gonzalez	.40
149	*Hideo Nomo*	3.00
150	Shawn Green	.25
---	Numeric checklist	.25
---	Chase program checklist	.25

		MT
Complete Set (19):		60.00
Common Player:		1.50
1	Cal Ripken Jr.	8.00
2	Frank Thomas	8.00
3	Mike Piazza	6.00
4	Kirby Puckett	5.00
5	Manny Ramirez	3.00
6	Tony Gwynn	4.00
7	Hideo Nomo	5.00
8	Matt Williams	2.00
9	Randy Johnson	3.00
10	Raul Mondesi	2.00
11	Albert Belle	2.50
12	Ivan Rodriguez	2.50
13	Barry Bonds	3.00
14	Carlos Baerga	1.50
15	Ken Griffey Jr.	10.00
16	Jeff Conine	1.50
17	Frank Thomas	8.00
18	Cal Ripken Jr.	8.00
19	Barry Bonds	3.00

1995 Zenith Rookie Roll Call

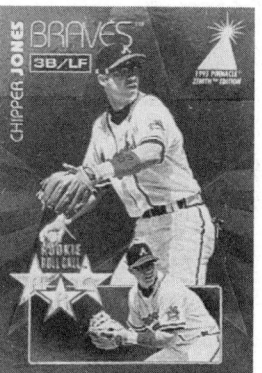

Dufex foil printing technology on both front and back is featured on this insert set. Fronts have a large and a small player photo on a green background dominated by a large star. Backs have another photo on a green and gold background. A prestigious black and gold box at left in the horizontally formatted design has a few good words about the prospect. Stated odds of finding a Rookie Roll Call card are one per 24 packs, on average.

		MT
Complete Set (18):		200.00
Common Player:		5.00
1	Alex Rodriguez	80.00
2	Derek Jeter	40.00
3	Chipper Jones	40.00
4	Shawn Green	12.00
5	Todd Hollandsworth	6.00
6	Bill Pulsipher	6.00
7	Hideo Nomo	35.00
8	Ray Durham	5.00
9	Curtis Goodwin	6.00
10	Brian Hunter	6.00
11	Julian Tavarez	5.00
12	Marty Cordova	5.00
13	Michael Tucker	6.00
14	Edgardo Alfonzo	6.00
15	LaTroy Hawkins	5.00
16	Carlos Perez	6.00
17	Charles Johnson	12.00
18	Benji Gil	5.00

1995 Zenith All-Star Salute

Kirby Puckett
ALL-STAR GAME VETERAN

The most common of the Zenith inserts is a series of 18 All-Star Salute cards. Fronts have action photos printed on foil. Backs have the 1995 All-Star Game logo and a large photo of the player taken at the game, with a few words about his All-Star history. The Salute cards are seeded at the rate of one per six packs, on average.

1995 Zenith Z-Team

The scarcest of the Zenith insert cards are those of 18 "living legends" profiled in the Z-Team series. Found at an average rate of only one per 72 packs, the cards are printed in technology Pinnacle calls 3-D Dufex.

		MT
Complete Set (18):		300.00
Common Player:		8.00
1	Cal Ripken Jr.	40.00
2	Ken Griffey Jr.	50.00
3	Frank Thomas	40.00
4	Matt Williams	8.00
5	Mike Piazza	30.00
6	Barry Bonds	12.00
7	Raul Mondesi	8.00
8	Greg Maddux	30.00
9	Jeff Bagwell	20.00
10	Manny Ramirez	12.00
11	Larry Walker	8.00
12	Tony Gwynn	25.00
13	Will Clark	8.00
14	Albert Belle	12.00
15	Kenny Lofton	12.00
16	Rafael Palmeiro	8.00
17	Don Mattingly	15.00
18	Carlos Baerga	8.00

1996 Zenith

Pinnacle's 1996 Zenith set has 150 cards in the regular set, including 30 Rookies, 20 Honor roll and two checklist cards. Each card in the set has a parallel Artist's Proof version (seeded one per every 35 packs). Insert sets include Z Team, Mozaics and two versions of Diamond Club. Normal Dufex versions of Diamond Club appear one every 24 packs; parallel versions, which have an actual diamond chip incorporated into the card design, were seeded one per every 350 packs.

		MT
Complete Set (150):		40.00
Common Player:		.25
Artist's Proofs Comp. Set (150):		2000.
Common Artist's Proofs:		4.00
Veteran Star Artist's Proofs: 15x to 25x		
Rookies and Young Stars: 8x to 15x		
Unlisted Stars: .40 to .60		
Wax Box:		75.00
1	Ken Griffey Jr.	4.00
2	Ozzie Smith	.75
3	Greg Maddux	2.50
4	Rondell White	.40
5	Mark McGwire	5.00
6	Jim Thome	.75
7	Ivan Rodriguez	.75
8	Marc Newfield	.25
9	Travis Fryman	.25
10	Fred McGriff	.45
11	Shawn Green	.25
12	Mike Piazza	2.50
13	Dante Bichette	.40
14	Tino Martinez	.50
15	Sterling Hitchcock	.25
16	Ryne Sandberg	1.00
17	Rico Brogna	.25
18	Roberto Alomar	.75
19	Barry Larkin	.35
20	Bernie Williams	.75
21	Gary Sheffield	.50
22	Frank Thomas	2.50
23	Gregg Jefferies	.25
24	Jeff Bagwell	1.75
25	Marty Cordova	.25
26	Jim Edmonds	.40
27	Jay Bell	.25
28	Ben McDonald	.25
29	Barry Bonds	1.00
30	Mo Vaughn	1.00
31	Johnny Damon	.25
32	Dean Palmer	.25
33	Ismael Valdes	.25
34	Manny Ramirez	.90
35	Edgar Martinez	.25
36	Cecil Fielder	.35
37	Ryan Klesko	.75
38	Ray Lankford	.25
39	Tim Salmon	.40
40	Joe Carter	.30
41	Jason Isringhausen	.25
42	Rickey Henderson	.25
43	Lenny Dykstra	.25
44	Andre Dawson	.25
45	Paul O'Neill	.40
46	Ray Durham	.25
47	Raul Mondesi	.50
48	Jay Buhner	.40
49	Eddie Murray	.75
50	Henry Rodriguez	.25
51	Hal Morris	.25
52	Mike Mussina	.75
53	Wally Joyner	.25
54	Will Clark	.50
55	Chipper Jones	2.50
56	Brian Jordan	.25
57	Larry Walker	.50
58	Wade Boggs	.40
59	Melvin Nieves	.25
60	Charles Johnson	.25
61	Juan Gonzalez	2.00
62	Carlos Delgado	.25
63	Reggie Sanders	.25
64	Brian Hunter	.25
65	Edgardo Alfonzo	.25
66	Kenny Lofton	.90
67	Paul Molitor	.75
68	Mike Bordick	.25
69	Garret Anderson	.25
70	Orlando Merced	.25
71	Craig Biggio	.40
72	Chuck Knoblauch	.50
73	Mark Grace	.40
74	Jack McDowell	.25
75	Randy Johnson	.75
76	Cal Ripken Jr.	3.00
77	Matt Williams	.50
78	Benji Gil	.25
79	Moises Alou	.40
80	Robin Ventura	.25
81	Greg Vaughn	.25
82	Carlos Baerga	.25
83	Roger Clemens	1.50
84	Hideo Nomo	.75
85	Pedro Martinez	.40
86	John Valentin	.25
87	Andres Galarraga	.40
88	Andy Pettitte	.90
89	Derek Bell	.25
90	Kirby Puckett	1.25
91	Tony Gwynn	2.00
92	Brady Anderson	.30
93	Derek Jeter	2.50
94	Michael Tucker	.25
95	Albert Belle	1.00
96	David Cone	.35
97	J.T. Snow	.25
98	Tom Glavine	.40
99	Alex Rodriguez	3.00
100	Sammy Sosa	2.00
101	Karim Garcia	.60
102	Alan Benes	.30
103	Chad Mottola	.25
104	*Robin Jennings*	.25
105	Bob Abreu	.25
106	Tony Clark	1.00
107	George Arias	.25
108	Jermaine Dye	.25
109	Jeff Suppan	.25
110	*Ralph Milliard*	.25
111	Ruben Rivera	.30
112	Billy Wagner	.25
113	Jason Kendall	.25
114	*Mike Grace*	.50
115	Edgar Renteria	.40
116	Jason Schmidt	.25
117	Paul Wilson	.40
118	Rey Ordonez	.40
119	*Rocky Coppinger*	.40
120	*Wilton Guerrero*	.90
121	Brooks Kieschnick	.25
122	Raul Casanova	.25
123	Alex Ochoa	.25
124	Chan Ho Park	.25
125	John Wasdin	.25
126	Eric Owens	.25
127	Justin Thompson	.25
128	Chris Snopek	.25
129	Terrell Wade	.25
130	*Darin Erstad*	5.00
131	Albert Belle (Honor Roll)	.50
132	Cal Ripken Jr. (Honor Roll)	1.50
133	Frank Thomas (Honor Roll)	1.50
134	Greg Maddux (Honor Roll)	1.25
135	Ken Griffey Jr. (Honor Roll)	2.00
136	Mo Vaughn (Honor Roll)	.50
137	Chipper Jones (Honor Roll)	1.25
138	Mike Piazza (Honor Roll)	1.25
139	Ryan Klesko (Honor Roll)	.35
140	Hideo Nomo (Honor Roll)	.40
141	Roberto Alomar (Honor Roll)	.40
142	Manny Ramirez (Honor Roll)	.50
143	Gary Sheffield (Honor Roll)	.30
144	Barry Bonds (Honor Roll)	.50
145	Matt Williams (Honor Roll)	.25
146	Jim Edmonds (Honor Roll)	.25
147	Derek Jeter (Honor Roll)	1.25
148	Sammy Sosa (Honor Roll)	.75
149	Kirby Puckett (Honor Roll)	.75
150	Tony Gwynn (Honor Roll)	1.00

1996 Zenith Artist's Proofs

Each card in the '96 Zenith base set can also be found in a specially marked Artist's Proof version. The AP cards were found on average of once per 35 packs.

	MT
Complete Set (150):	2000.
Common Player:	4.00

(Veteran stars' Artist's Proofs 20X-30X regular Zenith; young stars and rookies 8X-15X.)

1996 Zenith Diamond Club

Twenty different players are featured on these two 1996 Pinnacle Zenith insert cards. Normal Dufex versions are inserted one per every 24 packs. Parallel versions of these cards, containing an actual diamond chip incorporated into the design, were seeded one per every 350 packs.

		MT
Complete Set (20):		180.00
Common Player:		4.00
Diamond Versions: 2x to 4x		
1	Albert Belle	8.00
2	Mo Vaughn	8.00
3	Ken Griffey Jr.	30.00
4	Mike Piazza	20.00
5	Cal Ripken Jr.	25.00
6	Jermaine Dye	4.00
7	Jeff Bagwell	12.00
8	Frank Thomas	25.00
9	Alex Rodriguez	25.00
10	Ryan Klesko	6.00
11	Roberto Alomar	6.00
12	Sammy Sosa	20.00
13	Matt Williams	4.00
14	Gary Sheffield	6.00
15	Ruben Rivera	4.00
16	Darin Erstad	20.00
17	Randy Johnson	6.00
18	Greg Maddux	20.00
19	Karim Garcia	8.00
20	Chipper Jones	20.00

1996 Zenith Mozaics

Each of these 1996 Pinnacle Zenith cards contains multiple player images for the team represented on the card. The cards were inserted one per every 10 packs.

		MT
Complete Set (25):		175.00
Common Player:		3.00
1	Greg Maddux, Chipper Jones, Ryan Klesko	20.00

2	Juan Gonzalez, Will Clark, Ivan Rodriguez	8.00
3	Frank Thomas, Robin Ventura, Ray Durham	20.00
4	Matt Williams, Barry Bonds, Osvaldo Fernandez	6.00
5	Ken Griffey Jr., Randy Johnson, Alex Rodriguez	25.00
6	Sammy Sosa, Ryne Sandberg, Mark Grace	15.00
7	Jim Edmonds, Tim Salmon, Garret Anderson	3.00
8	Cal Ripken Jr., Roberto Alomar, Mike Mussina	18.00
9	Mo Vaughn, Roger Clemens, John Valentin	8.00
10	Barry Larkin, Reggie Sanders, Hal Morris	3.00
11	Ray Lankford, Brian Jordan, Ozzie Smith	4.00
12	Dante Bichette, Larry Walker, Andres Galarraga	3.00
13	Mike Piazza, Hideo Nomo, Raul Mondesi	15.00
14	Ben McDonald, Greg Vaughn, Kevin Seitzer	3.00
15	Joe Carter, Carlos Delgado, Alex Gonzalez	3.00
16	Gary Sheffield, Charles Johnson, Jeff Conine	3.00
17	Rondell White, Moises Alou, Henry Rodriguez	3.00
18	Albert Belle, Manny Ramirez, Carlos Baerga	10.00
19	Kirby Puckett, Paul Molitor, Chuck Knoblauch	10.00
20	Tony Gwynn, Rickey Henderson, Wally Joyner	10.00
21	Mark McGwire, Mike Bordick, Scott Brosius	15.00
22	Paul O'Neill, Bernie Williams, Wade Boggs	4.00
23	Jay Bell, Orlando Merced, Jason Kendall	3.00
24	Rico Brogna, Paul Wilson, Jason Isringhausen	3.00
25	Jeff Bagwell, Craig Biggio, Derek Bell	12.00

1996 Zenith Z-Team

Pinnacle's 1996 Zenith baseball continues the Z Team insert concept with a new clear plastic treatment that is micro-etched for a see-through design that allows light to shine through etched highlights and a green baseball field background. The 18 cards were seeded one per every 72 packs.

		MT
Complete Set (18):		450.00
Common Player:		10.00
1	Ken Griffey Jr.	75.00
2	Albert Belle	20.00

3	Cal Ripken Jr.	60.00
4	Frank Thomas	60.00
5	Greg Maddux	50.00
6	Mo Vaughn	20.00
7	Chipper Jones	50.00
8	Mike Piazza	50.00
9	Ryan Klesko	10.00
10	Hideo Nomo	20.00
11	Roberto Alomar	15.00
12	Manny Ramirez	20.00
13	Gary Sheffield	15.00
14	Barry Bonds	20.00
15	Matt Williams	15.00
16	Jim Edmonds	10.00
17	Kirby Puckett	25.00
18	Sammy Sosa	40.00

1997 Zenith

This set combines standard size trading cards with cards in an 8" x 10" format. The standard size set consists of 60 cards. Card fronts feature full-bleed photos and the word "Zenith", but no reference to the player's name or team is found on the fronts. Backs have another player photo, a hit location chart and 1996/career stats. There are four inserts in the set, all of which are printed on the larger size format - 8" x 10", 8" x 10" Dufex, 8" x 10" V-2, and Z-Team. Each sale unit contained one pack of five standard-size cards and two larger size cards for a suggested retail price of $9.99.

		MT
Complete Set (50):		50.00
Common Player:		.50
Wax box:		60.00
1	Frank Thomas	5.00
2	Tony Gwynn	3.00
3	Jeff Bagwell	2.50
4	Paul Molitor	1.00
5	Roberto Alomar	1.00
6	Mike Piazza	4.00
7	Albert Belle	1.50
8	Greg Maddux	4.00
9	Barry Larkin	.50
10	Tony Clark	1.50
11	Larry Walker	1.00
12	Chipper Jones	4.00
13	Juan Gonzalez	3.00
14	Barry Bonds	1.50
15	Ivan Rodriguez	1.25
16	Sammy Sosa	2.00
17	Derek Jeter	4.00
18	Hideo Nomo	1.25
19	Roger Clemens	1.50
20	Ken Griffey Jr.	6.00
21	Andy Pettitte	1.50
22	Alex Rodriguez	5.00
23	Tino Martinez	.75

24	Bernie Williams	1.00
25	Ken Caminiti	.75
26	John Smoltz	.50
27	Javier Lopez	.50
28	Mark McGwire	6.00
29	Gary Sheffield	1.00
30	David Justice	.75
30p	David Justice (marked SAMPLE)	3.00
31	Randy Johnson	1.00
32	Chuck Knoblauch	.60
33	Mike Mussina	1.25
34	Deion Sanders	.75
35	Cal Ripken Jr.	5.00
36	Darin Erstad	2.00
37	Kenny Lofton	1.50
38	Jay Buhner	.50
39	Brady Anderson	.50
40	Edgar Martinez	.50
41	Mo Vaughn	1.50
42	Ryne Sandberg	1.50
43	Andruw Jones	3.00
44	Nomar Garciaparra	3.00
45	*Hideki Irabu*	4.00
46	Wilton Guerrero	.50
47	*Jose Cruz Jr.*	4.00
48	Vladimir Guerrero	2.00
49	Scott Rolen	2.50
50	Jose Guillen	1.50

1997 Zenith 8x10

This 24-card insert takes select cards from the standard set and blows them up to an 8" x 10" format. Cards were inserted one per pack. A Dufex version of each 8" x 10" insert card was also available at a rate of one per pack (except in packs which contained either a Z-Team or V-2 card).

		MT
Complete Set (24):		80.00
Common Player:		1.00
Dufex versions: 1x to 1.5x		
1	Frank Thomas	8.00
2	Tony Gwynn	5.00
3	Jeff Bagwell	4.00
4	Ken Griffey Jr.	10.00
5	Mike Piazza	6.00
6	Greg Maddux	6.00
7	Ken Caminiti	1.50
8	Albert Belle	2.50
9	Ivan Rodriguez	2.00
10	Sammy Sosa	5.00
11	Mark McGwire	12.00
12	Roger Clemens	3.00
13	Alex Rodriguez	8.00
14	Chipper Jones	6.00
15	Juan Gonzalez	5.00
16	Barry Bonds	2.50
17	Derek Jeter	6.00
18	Hideo Nomo	2.00
19	Cal Ripken Jr.	8.00
20	Hideki Irabu	4.00
21	Andruw Jones	5.00
22	Nomar Garciaparra	5.00
23	Vladimir Guerrero	3.00
24	Scott Rolen	5.00

1997 Zenith V-2

This eight-card die-cut insert utilizes motion technology as well as foil printing to create a very high-tech 8" x 10" card. Cards were inserted 1:47 packs.

		MT
Complete Set (8):		250.00
Common Player:		20.00
1	Ken Griffey Jr.	60.00
2	Andruw Jones	20.00
3	Frank Thomas	50.00
4	Mike Piazza	40.00
5	Alex Rodriguez	40.00
6	Cal Ripken Jr.	50.00
7	Derek Jeter	30.00
8	Vladimir Guerrero	20.00

1997 Zenith Z-Team

This nine-card 8" x 10" insert is printed on a mirror gold mylar foil stock with each card sequentially numbered to 1,000.

		MT
Complete Set (9):		400.00
Common Player:		25.00
1	Ken Griffey Jr.	100.00
2	Larry Walker	20.00
3	Frank Thomas	75.00
4	Alex Rodriguez	60.00
5	Mike Piazza	60.00
6	Cal Ripken Jr.	75.00
7	Derek Jeter	50.00
8	Andruw Jones	30.00
9	Roger Clemens	30.00

1998 Zenith

Zenith Baseball was part of Pinnacle's "Dare to Tear" program. Sold in three-card packs, the set consisted of 5"-x-7" cards, each with a standard-size card inside. Collectors had to decide whether to keep the large cards or tear them open to get the smaller card inside. Eighty 5"-x-7" cards and 100 regular cards made up the set. The regular, or Z2, cards were paralleled twice - Z-Silver (1:7) and Z-Gold (numbered to 100). The large cards also had two parallels - Impulse (1:7) and Gold Impulse (numbered to 100). Inserts include Raising the Bar, Rookie Thrills, Epix, 5x7 Z Team, Z Team, Gold Z Team, Rookie Z Team and Gold Rookie Z Team.

		MT
Complete Set (100):		75.00
Common Player:		.25
Unlisted Stars: .50 to 1.00		
Silvers: 2x to 4x		
Inserted 1:7		
Wax Box:		80.00
1	Larry Walker	.50
2	Ken Griffey Jr.	6.00
2p	Ken Griffey Jr. (SAMPLE)	.25
3	Cal Ripken Jr.	5.00
4	Sammy Sosa	4.00
5	Andruw Jones	1.50
6	Frank Thomas	5.00
7	Tony Gwynn	3.00
8	Rafael Palmeiro	.40
9	Tim Salmon	.50
10	Randy Johnson	1.00
11	Juan Gonzalez	3.00
12	Greg Maddux	4.00
13	Vladimir Guerrero	2.00
14	Mike Piazza	4.00
15	Andres Galarraga	.50
16	Alex Rodriguez	4.00
17	Derek Jeter	4.00
18	Nomar Garciaparra	4.00
19	Ivan Rodriguez	1.50
20	Chipper Jones	4.00
21	Barry Larkin	.40
22	Mo Vaughn	1.50
23	Albert Belle	1.50
24	Scott Rolen	2.00
25	Sandy Alomar Jr.	.40
26	Roberto Alomar	1.00
27	Andy Pettitte	1.00
28	Chuck Knoblauch	.50
29	Jeff Bagwell	2.50
30	Mike Mussina	1.00
31	Fred McGriff	.40
32	Roger Clemens	2.50
33	Rusty Greer	.25
34	Edgar Martinez	.25
35	Paul Molitor	1.00
36	Mark Grace	.50
37	Darin Erstad	1.50
38	Kenny Lofton	1.50
39	Tom Glavine	.40
40	Javier Lopez	.25
41	Will Clark	.50
42	Tino Martinez	.50
43	Raul Mondesi	.50
44	Brady Anderson	.25
45	Chan Ho Park	.40
46	Jason Giambi	.25
47	Manny Ramirez	1.25
48	Jay Buhner	.50
49	Dante Bichette	.40
50	Jose Cruz Jr.	1.50
51	Charles Johnson	.25
52	Bernard Gilkey	.25
53	Johnny Damon	.25
54	David Justice	.40
55	Justin Thompson	.25
56	Bobby Higginson	.25
57	Todd Hundley	.25
58	Gary Sheffield	.50
59	Barry Bonds	1.50
60	Mark McGwire	8.00
61	John Smoltz	.40
62	Tony Clark	1.00
63	Brian Jordan	.25
64	Jason Kendall	.25
65	Mariano Rivera	.50
66	Pedro Martinez	.75
67	Jim Thome	1.00
68	Neifi Perez	.25
69	Kevin Brown	.25
70	Hideo Nomo	1.25
71	Craig Biggio	.40
72	Bernie Williams	1.00
73	Jose Guillen	.40
74	Ken Caminiti	.40
75	Livan Hernandez	.40
76	Ray Lankford	.25
77	Jim Edmonds	.40
78	Matt Williams	.50
79	Mark Kotsay	1.00
80	Moises Alou	.40
81	Antone Williamson	.25
82	Jaret Wright	3.00
83	Jacob Cruz	.25
84	Abraham Nunez	.25
85	Raul Ibanez	.25
86	Miguel Tejada	.25
87	Derek Lee	.25
88	Juan Encarnacion	.25

89	Todd Helton	1.50
90	Travis Lee	5.00
91	Ben Grieve	2.50
92	Ryan McGuire	.25
93	Richard Hidalgo	.25
94	Paul Konerko	.50
95	Shannon Stewart	.25
96	Homer Bush	.25
97	Lou Collier	.25
98	Jeff Abbott	.25
99	Brett Tomko	.25
100	Fernando Tatis	.25

1998 Zenith Epix

Epix is a cross-brand insert. The set honors the top Plays, Games, Seasons and Moments in the careers of top baseball players. Epix consisted of 24 cards in Zenith, inserted 1:11. The cards have orange, purple and emerald versions.

		MT
Common Orange:		6.00
Purples: 1x to 1.5x		
Emeralds: 2x to 3x		
1	Ken Griffey Jr. S	80.00
2	Juan Gonzalez S	40.00
3	Jeff Bagwell S	25.00
4	Ivan Rodriguez S	20.00
5	Nomar Garciaparra S	50.00
6	Ryne Sandberg S	20.00
7	Frank Thomas M	100.00
8	Derek Jeter M	60.00
9	Tony Gwynn M	60.00
10	Albert Belle M	30.00
11	Scott Rolen M	40.00
12	Barry Larkin M	15.00
13	Alex Rodriguez P	20.00
14	Cal Ripken Jr. P	25.00
15	Chipper Jones P	20.00
16	Roger Clemens P	10.00
17	Mo Vaughn P	8.00
18	Mark McGwire P	40.00
19	Mike Piazza G	30.00
20	Andruw Jones G	15.00
21	Greg Maddux G	30.00
22	Barry Bonds G	15.00
23	Paul Molitor G	10.00
24	Eddie Murray G	8.00

1998 Zenith 5x7

The 80 Zenith 5x7 cards all contained a regular-size card. Collectors could tear open the 5x7 to get at the smaller card inside. The set has two parallels: 5x7 Impulse (1:7) and 5x7 Gold Impulse (1:43).

	MT
Complete Set (80):	100.00
Common Player:	.50
Silvers: 2x to 4x	
Inserted 1:7	

1	Nomar Garciaparra	5.00
2	Andres Galarraga	1.00
3	Greg Maddux	5.00
4	Frank Thomas	6.00
5	Mark McGwire	8.00
6	Rafael Palmeiro	1.00
7	John Smoltz	.50
8	Jeff Bagwell	3.00
9	Andruw Jones	2.00
10	Rusty Greer	.50
11	Paul Molitor	1.50
12	Bernie Williams	1.50
13	Kenny Lofton	2.00
14	Alex Rodriguez	5.00
15	Derek Jeter	4.00
16	Scott Rolen	3.00
17	Albert Belle	2.00
18	Mo Vaughn	2.00
19	Chipper Jones	5.00
20	Chuck Knoblauch	.75
21	Mike Piazza	5.00
22	Tony Gwynn	4.00
23	Juan Gonzalez	4.00
24	Andy Pettitte	1.00
25	Tim Salmon	1.00
26	Brady Anderson	.50
27	Mike Mussina	1.50
28	Edgar Martinez	.50
29	Jose Guillen	.50
30	Hideo Nomo	1.50
31	Jim Thome	1.00
32	Mark Grace	.75
33	Darin Erstad	2.00
34	Bobby Higginson	.50
35	Ivan Rodriguez	2.00
36	Todd Hundley	.50
37	Sandy Alomar Jr.	.50
38	Gary Sheffield	.75
39	David Justice	.75
40	Ken Griffey Jr.	8.00
41	Vladimir Guerrero	2.00
42	Larry Walker	.75
43	Barry Bonds	2.00
44	Randy Johnson	1.00
45	Roger Clemens	3.00
46	Raul Mondesi	.75
47	Tino Martinez	.75
48	Jason Giambi	.50
49	Matt Williams	.75
50	Cal Ripken Jr.	6.00
51	Barry Larkin	.75
52	Jim Edmonds	.50
53	Ken Caminiti	.75
54	Sammy Sosa	3.00
55	Tony Clark	1.00
56	Manny Ramirez	1.50
57	Bernard Gilkey	.50
58	Jose Cruz Jr.	2.00
59	Brian Jordan	.50
60	Kevin Brown	.50
61	Craig Biggio	.75
62	Javier Lopez	.50
63	Jay Buhner	.75
64	Roberto Alomar	1.50
65	Justin Thompson	.50
66	Todd Helton	2.00
67	Travis Lee	6.00
68	Paul Konerko	.75
69	Jaret Wright	4.00
70	Ben Grieve	3.00
71	Juan Encarnacion	.50
72	Ryan McGuire	.50
73	Derrek Lee	.50
74	Abraham Nunez	.50
75	Richard Hidalgo	.50
76	Miguel Tejada	.50
77	Jacob Cruz	.50
78	Homer Bush	.50
79	Jeff Abbott	.50
80	Lou Collier	.50
	Checklist	.50

1998 Zenith 5x7 Gold

The 5x7 Gold Impulse set parallels the 80-card 5x7 base set. The cards were inserted one per 43 packs.

	MT
Common Player:	25.00
Semistars:	50.00

Production 100 sets		
1	Nomar Garciaparra	300.00
2	Andres Galarraga	50.00
3	Greg Maddux	300.00
4	Frank Thomas	400.00
5	Mark McGwire	500.00
6	Rafael Palmeiro	50.00
7	John Smoltz	40.00
8	Jeff Bagwell	200.00
9	Andruw Jones	125.00
10	Rusty Greer	25.00
11	Paul Molitor	100.00
12	Bernie Williams	100.00
13	Kenny Lofton	150.00
14	Alex Rodriguez	300.00
15	Derek Jeter	250.00
16	Scott Rolen	180.00
17	Albert Belle	150.00
18	Mo Vaughn	150.00
19	Chipper Jones	275.00
20	Chuck Knoblauch	50.00
21	Mike Piazza	300.00
22	Tony Gwynn	250.00
23	Juan Gonzalez	250.00
24	Andy Pettitte	100.00
25	Tim Salmon	50.00
26	Brady Anderson	25.00
27	Mike Mussina	100.00
28	Edgar Martinez	25.00
29	Jose Guillen	40.00
30	Hideo Nomo	125.00
31	Jim Thome	80.00
32	Mark Grace	50.00
33	Darin Erstad	125.00
34	Bobby Higginson	25.00
35	Ivan Rodriguez	150.00
36	Todd Hundley	25.00
37	Sandy Alomar Jr.	40.00
38	Gary Sheffield	50.00
39	David Justice	50.00
40	Ken Griffey Jr.	500.00
41	Vladimir Guerrero	125.00
42	Larry Walker	60.00
43	Barry Bonds	150.00
44	Randy Johnson	80.00
45	Roger Clemens	200.00
46	Raul Mondesi	50.00
47	Tino Martinez	50.00
48	Jason Giambi	25.00
49	Matt Williams	60.00
50	Cal Ripken Jr.	400.00
51	Barry Larkin	50.00
52	Jim Edmonds	25.00
53	Ken Caminiti	40.00
54	Sammy Sosa	200.00
55	Tony Clark	100.00
56	Manny Ramirez	125.00
57	Bernard Gilkey	25.00
58	Jose Cruz Jr.	150.00
59	Brian Jordan	25.00
60	Kevin Brown	25.00
61	Craig Biggio	40.00
62	Javier Lopez	25.00
63	Jay Buhner	50.00
64	Roberto Alomar	100.00
65	Justin Thompson	25.00
66	Todd Helton	125.00
67	Travis Lee	250.00
68	Paul Konerko	50.00
69	Jaret Wright	150.00
70	Ben Grieve	150.00
71	Juan Encarnacion	25.00
72	Ryan McGuire	25.00
73	Derrek Lee	25.00
74	Abraham Nunez	25.00
75	Richard Hidalgo	25.00
76	Miguel Tejada	40.00
77	Jacob Cruz	25.00
78	Homer Bush	25.00
79	Jeff Abbott	25.00
80	Lou Collier	25.00
	Checklist	25.00

1998 Zenith 5x7 Z-Team

The 5x7 Z Team insert is a nine-card set seeded one per 35 packs.

	MT
Complete Set (9):	300.00
Common Player:	20.00

Inserted 1:35

1	Frank Thomas	50.00
2	Ken Griffey Jr.	60.00
3	Mike Piazza	40.00
4	Cal Ripken Jr.	50.00
5	Alex Rodriguez	40.00
6	Greg Maddux	40.00
7	Derek Jeter	30.00
8	Chipper Jones	40.00
9	Roger Clemens	25.00

1998 Zenith Gold

The Z-Gold set parallels the Z2 base set. The 100-card set adds gold coloring to the border on the right side of the cards. The parallel is sequentially numbered to 100.

		MT
Common Player:		25.00
Semistars:		50.00
Production 100 sets		
1	Larry Walker	60.00
2	Ken Griffey Jr.	400.00
3	Cal Ripken Jr.	300.00
4	Sammy Sosa	200.00
5	Andruw Jones	100.00
6	Frank Thomas	300.00
7	Tony Gwynn	200.00
8	Rafael Palmeiro	40.00
9	Tim Salmon	40.00
10	Randy Johnson	80.00
11	Juan Gonzalez	200.00
12	Greg Maddux	250.00
13	Vladimir Guerrero	100.00
14	Mike Piazza	250.00
15	Andres Galarraga	40.00
16	Alex Rodriguez	250.00
17	Derek Jeter	200.00
18	Nomar Garciaparra	250.00
19	Ivan Rodriguez	100.00
20	Chipper Jones	225.00
21	Barry Larkin	40.00
22	Mo Vaughn	100.00
23	Albert Belle	100.00
24	Scott Rolen	150.00
25	Sandy Alomar Jr.	40.00
26	Roberto Alomar	80.00
27	Andy Pettitte	80.00
28	Chuck Knoblauch	50.00
29	Jeff Bagwell	150.00
30	Mike Mussina	80.00
31	Fred McGriff	40.00
32	Roger Clemens	150.00
33	Rusty Greer	25.00
34	Edgar Martinez	25.00
35	Paul Molitor	80.00
36	Mark Grace	50.00
37	Darin Erstad	125.00
38	Kenny Lofton	100.00
39	Tom Glavine	40.00
40	Javier Lopez	25.00
41	Will Clark	40.00
42	Tino Martinez	40.00
43	Raul Mondesi	40.00
44	Brady Anderson	25.00
45	Chan Ho Park	40.00
46	Jason Giambi	25.00
47	Manny Ramirez	100.00
48	Jay Buhner	40.00
49	Dante Bichette	40.00
50	Jose Cruz Jr.	90.00
51	Charles Johnson	25.00
52	Bernard Gilkey	25.00
53	Johnny Damon	25.00
54	David Justice	50.00
55	Justin Thompson	25.00
56	Bobby Higginson	25.00
57	Todd Hundley	25.00
58	Gary Sheffield	50.00
59	Barry Bonds	100.00
60	Mark McGwire	400.00
61	John Smoltz	30.00
62	Tony Clark	70.00
63	Brian Jordan	25.00
64	Jason Kendall	25.00
65	Mariano Rivera	40.00
66	Pedro Martinez	80.00
67	Jim Thome	70.00
68	Neifi Perez	25.00
69	Kevin Brown	30.00

70	Hideo Nomo	90.00
71	Craig Biggio	40.00
72	Bernie Williams	80.00
73	Jose Guillen	40.00
74	Ken Caminiti	40.00
75	Livan Hernandez	25.00
76	Ray Lankford	25.00
77	Jim Edmonds	30.00
78	Matt Williams	50.00
79	Mark Kotsay	50.00
80	Moises Alou	40.00
81	Antone Williamson	25.00
82	Jaret Wright	125.00
83	Jacob Cruz	25.00
84	Abraham Nunez	25.00
85	Raul Ibanez	25.00
86	Miguel Tejada	40.00
87	Derek Lee	25.00
88	Juan Encarnacion	25.00
89	Todd Helton	100.00
90	Travis Lee	200.00
91	Ben Grieve	150.00
92	Ryan McGuire	25.00
93	Richard Hidalgo	25.00
94	Paul Konerko	50.00
95	Shannon Stewart	25.00
96	Homer Bush	25.00
97	Lou Collier	25.00
98	Jeff Abbott	25.00
99	Brett Tomko	25.00
100	Fernando Tatis	35.00

1998 Zenith Raising the Bar

Raising the Bar is a 15-card insert seeded 1:25. The set features players who have set high standards for other players to follow.

		MT
Complete Set (15):		350.00
Common Player:		6.00
Inserted 1:25		
1	Ken Griffey Jr.	50.00
2	Frank Thomas	40.00
3	Alex Rodriguez	30.00
4	Tony Gwynn	30.00
5	Mike Piazza	30.00
6	Ivan Rodriguez	15.00
7	Cal Ripken Jr.	40.00
8	Greg Maddux	30.00
9	Hideo Nomo	12.00
10	Mark McGwire	50.00
11	Juan Gonzalez	25.00
12	Andruw Jones	15.00
13	Jeff Bagwell	20.00
14	Chipper Jones	30.00
15	Nomar Garciaparra	30.00

1998 Zenith Rookie Thrills

Rookie Thrills is a 15-card insert seeded 1:25. The set features many of the top rookies of 1998.

		MT
Complete Set (15):		75.00
Common Player:		5.00
Inserted 1:25		
1	Travis Lee	25.00
2	Juan Encarnacion	4.00
3	Derek Lee	4.00
4	Raul Ibanez	4.00
5	Ryan McGuire	4.00
6	Todd Helton	10.00
7	Jacob Cruz	4.00
8	Abraham Nunez	4.00
9	Paul Konerko	8.00
10	Ben Grieve	15.00
11	Jeff Abbott	4.00
12	Richard Hidalgo	4.00
13	Jaret Wright	10.00
14	Lou Collier	4.00
15	Miguel Tejada	6.00

1998 Zenith Z-Team

The Z Team insert was created in 5x7 and standard-size versions. The 5x7 Z Team insert consisted of nine cards and was inserted 1:35. The standard-size Z Team also had nine cards and was inserted 1:35. The nine Rookie Z Team cards were seeded 1:58 and gold versions of both were found 1:175.

		MT
Complete Set (18):		550.00
Common Player:		20.00
#'s 1-9 1:35		
#'s 10-18 1:58		
Golds: 1.5x to 3x		
Inserted 1:175		
1	Frank Thomas	50.00
2	Ken Griffey Jr.	60.00
3	Mike Piazza	40.00
4	Cal Ripken Jr.	50.00
5	Alex Rodriguez	40.00
6	Greg Maddux	40.00
7	Derek Jeter	30.00
8	Chipper Jones	40.00
9	Roger Clemens	20.00
10	Ben Grieve	30.00
11	Derek Lee	8.00
12	Jose Cruz Jr.	15.00
13	Nomar Garciaparra	50.00
14	Travis Lee	50.00
15	Todd Helton	25.00
16	Paul Konerko	15.00
17	Miguel Tejada	15.00
18	Scott Rolen	25.00

A player's name in *italic* type indicates a rookie card.

Bonus Vintage Card Section

1974 Topps

Issued all at once at the beginning of the year, rather than by series throughout the baseball season as had been done since 1952, this 660-card '74 Topps set features a famous group of error cards. At the time the cards were printed, it was uncertain whether the San Diego Padres would move to Washington, D.C., and by the time a decision was made some Padres cards had appeared with a "Washington, Nat'l League" designation on the front. A total of 15 cards were affected, and those with the Washington designation bring prices well in excess of regular cards of the same players (the Washington variations are not included in the complete set prices quoted below). The 2-1/2" x 3-1/2" cards feature color photos (frequently game-action shots) along with the player's name, team and position. Specialty cards abound, starting with a Hank Aaron tribute and running through the usual managers, statistical leaders, playoff and World Series highlights, multiplayer rookie cards and All-Stars.

		NM
Complete Set (660):		550.00
Common Player:		.30
1	Hank Aaron (All-Time Home Run King)	35.00
2	Hank Aaron (Aaron Special 1954-57)	5.00
3	Hank Aaron (Aaron Special 1958-61)	4.00
4	Hank Aaron (Aaron Special 1962-65)	4.00
5	Hank Aaron (Aaron Special 1966-69)	4.00
6	Hank Aaron (Aaron Special 1970-73)	4.00
7	Catfish Hunter	2.50
8	George Theodore	.30
9	Mickey Lolich	.60
10	Johnny Bench	10.00
11	Jim Bibby	.30
12	Dave May	.30
13	Tom Hilgendorf	.30
14	Paul Popovich	.30
15	Joe Torre	.50
16	Orioles Team	2.00
17	Doug Bird	.30
18	Gary Thomasson	.30
19	Gerry Moses	.30
20	Nolan Ryan	60.00
21	Bob Gallagher	.30
22	Cy Acosta	.30
23	Craig Robinson	.30
24	John Hiller	.30
25	Ken Singleton	.30
26	*Bill Campbell*	.30
27	George Scott	.30
28	Manny Sanguillen	.30
29	Phil Niekro	2.00
30	Bobby Bonds	.75
31	Astros Mgr./Coaches(Roger Craig, Preston Gomez, Grady Hatton, Hub Kittle, Bob Lillis)	.50
32a	John Grubb (Washington)	3.50
32b	John Grubb (San Diego)	.30
33	Don Newhauser	.30
34	Andy Kosco	.30
35	Gaylord Perry	2.50
36	Cardinals Team	1.00
37	Dave Sells	.30
38	Don Kessinger	.35
39	Ken Suarez	.30
40	Jim Palmer	5.00
41	Bobby Floyd	.30
42	Claude Osteen	.30
43	Jim Wynn	.30
44	Mel Stottlemyre	.30
45	Dave Johnson	.30
46	Pat Kelly	.30
47	*Dick Ruthven*	.30
48	Dick Sharon	.30
49	Steve Renko	.30
50	Rod Carew	5.00
51	Bobby Heise	.30
52	Al Oliver	.60
53a	Fred Kendall (Washington)	3.50
53b	Fred Kendall (San Diego)	.30
54	*Elias Sosa*	.30
55	Frank Robinson	6.00
56	Mets Team	1.50
57	Darold Knowles	.30
58	Charlie Spikes	.30
59	Ross Grimsley	.30
60	Lou Brock	4.50
61	Luis Aparicio	4.00
62	Bob Locker	.30
63	Bill Sudakis	.30
64	Doug Rau	.30
65	Amos Otis	.30
66	Sparky Lyle	.30
67	Tommy Helms	.30
68	Grant Jackson	.30
69	Del Unser	.30
70	Dick Allen	.75
71	Danny Frisella	.30
72	Aurelio Rodriguez	.30
73	Mike Marshall	.30
74	Twins Team	1.00
75	Jim Colborn	.30
76	Mickey Rivers	.30
77a	Rich Troedson (Washington)	3.50
77b	Rich Troedson (San Diego)	.30
78	Giants Mgr./Coaches(Joe Amalfitano, Charlie Fox, Andy Gilbert, Don McMahon, John McNamara)	.50
79	Gene Tenace	.30
80	Tom Seaver	12.00
81	Frank Duffy	.30
82	Dave Giusti	.30
83	Orlando Cepeda	.75
84	Rick Wise	.30
85	Joe Morgan	4.00
86	Joe Ferguson	.30
87	Fergie Jenkins	3.00
88	Freddie Patek	.30
89	Jackie Brown	.30
90	Bobby Murcer	.40
91	Ken Forsch	.30
92	Paul Blair	.30
93	Rod Gilbreath	.30
94	Tigers Team	1.00
95	Steve Carlton	6.00
96	*Jerry Hairston*	.30
97	Bob Bailey	.30
98	Bert Blyleven	.60
99	Brewers Mgr./Coaches(Del Crandall, Harvey Kuenn, Joe Nossek, Jim Walton, Al Widmar)	.50
100	Willie Stargell	4.50
101	Bobby Valentine	.30
102a	Bill Greif (Washington)	3.50
102b	Bill Greif (San Diego)	.30
103	Sal Bando	.30
104	Ron Bryant	.30
105	Carlton Fisk	10.00
106	Harry Parker	.30
107	Alex Johnson	.30
108	Al Hrabosky	.30
109	Bob Grich	.40
110	Billy Williams	4.00
111	Clay Carroll	.30
112	Dave Lopes	.40
113	Dick Drago	.30
114	Angels Team	1.00
115	Willie Horton	.30
116	Jerry Reuss	.30
117	Ron Blomberg	.30
118	Bill Lee	.30
119	Phillies Mgr./Coaches(Carroll Beringer, Bill DeMars, Danny Ozark, Ray Ripplemeyer, Bobby Wine)	.50
120	Wilbur Wood	.30
121	Larry Lintz	.30
122	Jim Holt	.30
123	Nelson Briles	.30
124	Bob Coluccio	.30
125a	Nate Colbert (Washington)	3.50
125b	Nate Colbert (San Diego)	.30
126	Checklist 1-132	.50
127	Tom Paciorek	.30
128	John Ellis	.30
129	Chris Speier	.30
130	Reggie Jackson	14.00
131	Bob Boone	2.25
132	Felix Millan	.30
133	*David Clyde*	.30
134	Denis Menke	.30
135	Roy White	.30
136	Rick Reuschel	.30
137	Al Bumbry	.30
138	Ed Brinkman	.30
139	Aurelio Monteagudo	.30
140	Darrell Evans	.45
141	Pat Bourque	.30
142	Pedro Garcia	.30
143	Dick Woodson	.30
144	Dodgers Mgr./Coaches(Red Adams, Walter Alston, Monty Basgall, Jim Gilliam, Tom Lasorda) (Mgr.)	1.50
145	Dock Ellis	.30
146	Ron Fairly	.30
147	Bart Johnson	.30
148a	Dave Hilton (Washington)	3.50
148b	Dave Hilton (San Diego)	.30
149	Mac Scarce	.30
150	John Mayberry	.30
151	Diego Segui	.30
152	Oscar Gamble	.30
153	Jon Matlack	.30
154	Astros Team	1.00
155	Bert Campaneris	.30
156	Randy Moffitt	.30
157	Vic Harris	.30
158	Jack Billingham	.30
159	Jim Ray Hart	.30
160	Brooks Robinson	6.00
161	*Ray Burris*	.30
162	Bill Freehan	.30
163	Ken Berry	.30
164	Tom House	.30
165	Willie Davis	.30
166	Royals Mgr./Coaches(Galen Cisco, Harry Dunlop, Charlie Lau, Jack McKeon)	.50
167	Luis Tiant	.40
168	Danny Thompson	.30
169	*Steve Rogers*	.30
170	Bill Melton	.30
171	Eduardo Rodriguez	.30
172	Gene Clines	.30
173a	*Randy Jones* (Washington)	3.50
173b	*Randy Jones* (San Diego)	.30
174	Bill Robinson	.30
175	Reggie Cleveland	.30
176	John Lowenstein	.30
177	Dave Roberts	.30
178	Garry Maddox	.30
179	Mets Mgr./Coaches(Yogi Berra, Roy McMillan, Joe Pignatano, Rube Walker, Eddie Yost)	1.50
180	Ken Holtzman	.30
181	Cesar Geronimo	.30
182	Lindy McDaniel	.30
183	Johnny Oates	.30
184	Rangers Team	1.00
185	Jose Cardenal	.30
186	Fred Scherman	.30
187	Don Baylor	.90
188	Rudy Meoli	.30
189	Jim Brewer	.30
190	Tony Oliva	.50
191	Al Fitzmorris	.30
192	Mario Guerrero	.30

193	Tom Walker	.30
194	Darrell Porter	.30
195	Carlos May	.30
196	Jim Fregosi	.30
197a	Vicente Romo (Washington)	3.50
197b	Vicente Romo (San Diego)	.30
198	Dave Cash	.30
199	Mike Kekich	.30
200	Cesar Cedeno	.30
201	Batting Leaders(Rod Carew, Pete Rose)	4.00
202	Home Run Leaders(Reggie Jackson, Willie Stargell)	3.00
203	RBI Leaders(Reggie Jackson, Willie Stargell)	3.00
204	Stolen Base Leaders(Lou Brock, Tommy Harper)	1.00
205	Victory Leaders(Ron Bryant, Wilbur Wood)	.40
206	Earned Run Average Leaders(Jim Palmer, Tom Seaver)	3.00
207	Strikeout Leaders(Nolan Ryan, Tom Seaver)	15.00
208	Leading Firemen(John Hiller, Mike Marshall)	.30
209	Ted Sizemore	.30
210	Bill Singer	.30
211	Cubs Team	1.00
212	Rollie Fingers	3.00
213	Dave Rader	.30
214	Billy Grabarkewitz	.30
215	Al Kaline	5.00
216	Ray Sadecki	.30
217	Tim Foli	.30
218	Johnny Briggs	.30
219	Doug Griffin	.30
220	Don Sutton	2.25
221	White Sox Mgr./Coaches(Joe Lonnett, Jim Mahoney, Alex Monchak, Johnny Sain, Chuck Tanner)	.50
222	Ramon Hernandez	.30
223	Jeff Burroughs	.30
224	Roger Metzger	.30
225	Paul Splittorff	.30
226a	Washington Nat'l. Team	7.50
226b	Padres Team	2.00
227	Mike Lum	.30
228	Ted Kubiak	.30
229	Fritz Peterson	.30
230	Tony Perez	1.25
231	Dick Tidrow	.30
232	Steve Brye	.30
233	Jim Barr	.30
234	John Milner	.30
235	Dave McNally	.30
236	Cardinals Mgr./Coaches(Vern Benson, George Kissell, Johnny Lewis, Red Schoendienst, Barney Schultz)	.50
237	Ken Brett	.30
238	Fran Healy	.30
239	Bill Russell	.40
240	Joe Coleman	.30
241a	Glenn Beckert (Washington)	3.50
241b	Glenn Beckert (San Diego)	2.50
242	Bill Gogolewski	.30
243	Bob Oliver	.30
244	Carl Morton	.30
245	Cleon Jones	.30
246	A's Team	2.00
247	Rick Miller	.30
248	Tom Hall	.30
249	George Mitterwald	.30
250a	Willie McCovey (Washington)	24.00
250b	Willie McCovey (San Diego)	5.00
251	Graig Nettles	.45
252	*Dave Parker*	11.00
253	John Boccabella	.30
254	Stan Bahnsen	.30
255	Larry Bowa	.30
256	Tom Griffin	.30
257	Buddy Bell	.30
258	Jerry Morales	.30
259	Bob Reynolds	.30
260	Ted Simmons	.40
261	Jerry Bell	.30
262	Ed Kirkpatrick	.30
263	Checklist 133-264	.50

264	Joe Rudi	.30
265	Tug McGraw	.30
266	Jim Northrup	.30
267	Andy Messersmith	.30
268	Tom Grieve	.30
269	Bob Johnson	.30
270	Ron Santo	.50
271	Bill Hands	.30
272	Paul Casanova	.30
273	Checklist 265-396	.50
274	Fred Beene	.30
275	Ron Hunt	.30
276	Angels Mgr./Coaches(Tom Morgan, Salty Parker, Jimmie Reese, John Roseboro, Bobby Winkles)	.50
277	Gary Nolan	.30
278	Cookie Rojas	.30
279	Jim Crawford	.30
280	Carl Yastrzemski	6.00
281	Giants Team	1.00
282	Doyle Alexander	.30
283	Mike Schmidt	50.00
284	Dave Duncan	.30
285	Reggie Smith	.30
286	Tony Muser	.30
287	Clay Kirby	.30
288	*Gorman Thomas*	.30
289	Rick Auerbach	.30
290	Vida Blue	.30
291	Don Hahn	.30
292	Chuck Seelbach	.30
293	Milt May	.30
294	Steve Foucault	.30
295	Rick Monday	.30
296	Ray Corbin	.30
297	Hal Breeden	.30
298	Roric Harrison	.30
299	Gene Michael	.30
300	Pete Rose	15.00
301	Bob Montgomery	.30
302	Rudy May	.30
303	George Hendrick	.30
304	Don Wilson	.30
305	Tito Fuentes	.30
306	Orioles Mgr./Coaches(George Bamberger, Jim Frey, Billy Hunter, George Staller, Earl Weaver)	1.50
307	Luis Melendez	.30
308	Bruce Dal Canton	.30
309a	Dave Roberts (Washington)	3.50
309b	Dave Roberts (San Diego)	.30
310	Terry Forster	.30
311	Jerry Grote	.30
312	Deron Johnson	.30
313	Berry Lersch	.30
314	Brewers Team	1.00
315	Ron Cey	.50
316	Jim Perry	.30
317	Richie Zisk	.30
318	Jim Merritt	.30
319	Randy Hundley	.30
320	Dusty Baker	.40
321	Steve Braun	.30
322	Ernie McAnally	.30
323	Richie Scheinblum	.30
324	Steve Kline	.30
325	Tommy Harper	.30
326	Reds Mgr./Coaches(Sparky Anderson, Alex Grammas, Ted Kluszewski, George Scherger, Larry Shepard)	1.50
327	Tom Timmermann	.30
328	Skip Jutze	.30
329	Mark Belanger	.30
330	Juan Marichal	3.50
331	All-Star Catchers(Johnny Bench, Carlton Fisk)	3.00
332	All-Star First Basemen(Hank Aaron, Dick Allen)	3.50
333	All-Star Second Basemen(Rod Carew, Joe Morgan)	3.00
334	All-Star Third Basemen(Brooks Robinson, Ron Santo)	3.00
335	All-Star Shortstops(Bert Campaneris, Chris Speier)	.40
336	All-Star Left Fielders(Bobby Murcer, Pete Rose)	2.50
337	All-Star Center Fielders(Cesar Cedeno, Amos Otis)	.40

338	All-Star Right Fielders(Reggie Jackson, Billy Williams)	3.00
339	All-Star Pitchers(Catfish Hunter, Rick Wise)	.80
340	Thurman Munson	5.00
341	*Dan Driessen*	.30
342	Jim Lonborg	.30
343	Royals Team	1.00
344	Mike Caldwell	.30
345	Bill North	.30
346	Ron Reed	.30
347	Sandy Alomar	.30
348	Pete Richert	.30
349	John Vukovich	.30
350	Bob Gibson	5.00
351	Dwight Evans	3.00
352	Bill Stoneman	.30
353	Rich Coggins	.30
354	Cubs Mgr./Coaches(Hank Aguirre, Whitey Lockman, Jim Marshall, J.C. Martin, Al Spangler)	.50
355	Dave Nelson	.30
356	Jerry Koosman	.30
357	Buddy Bradford	.30
358	Dal Maxvill	.30
359	Brent Strom	.30
360	Greg Luzinski	.45
361	Don Carrithers	.30
362	Hal King	.30
363	Yankees Team	2.00
364a	Cito Gaston (Washington)	4.50
364b	Cito Gaston (San Diego)	.50
365	Steve Busby	.30
366	Larry Hisle	.30
367	Norm Cash	.45
368	Manny Mota	.30
369	Paul Lindblad	.30
370	Bob Watson	.30
371	Jim Slaton	.30
372	Ken Reitz	.30
373	John Curtis	.30
374	Marty Perez	.30
375	Earl Williams	.30
376	Jorge Orta	.30
377	Ron Woods	.30
378	Burt Hooton	.30
379	Rangers Mgr./Coaches(Art Fowler, Frank Lucchesi, Billy Martin, Jackie Moore, Charlie Silvera)	.50
380	Bud Harrelson	.30
381	Charlie Sands	.30
382	Bob Moose	.30
383	Phillies Team	1.00
384	Chris Chambliss	.30
385	Don Gullett	.30
386	Gary Matthews	.30
387a	Rich Morales (Washington)	3.50
387b	Rich Morales (San Diego)	.30
388	Phil Roof	.30
389	Gates Brown	.30
390	Lou Piniella	.40
391	Billy Champion	.30
392	Dick Green	.30
393	Orlando Pena	.30
394	Ken Henderson	.30
395	Doug Rader	.30
396	Tommy Davis	.30
397	George Stone	.30
398	Duke Sims	.30
399	Mike Paul	.30
400	Harmon Killebrew	4.50
401	Elliott Maddox	.30
402	Jim Rooker	.30
403	Red Sox Mgr./Coaches(Don Bryant, Darrell Johnson, Eddie Popowski, Lee Stange, Don Zimmer)	.50
404	Jim Howarth	.30
405	Ellie Rodriguez	.30
406	Steve Arlin	.30
407	Jim Wohlford	.30
408	Charlie Hough	.35
409	Ike Brown	.30
410	Pedro Borbon	.30
411	Frank Baker	.30
412	Chuck Taylor	.30
413	Don Money	.30
414	Checklist 397-528	.50
415	Gary Gentry	.30
416	White Sox Team	1.00
417	Rich Folkers	.30
418	Walt Williams	.30
419	Wayne Twitchell	.30

420	Ray Fosse	.30
421	Dan Fife	.30
422	Gonzalo Marquez	.30
423	Fred Stanley	.30
424	Jim Beauchamp	.30
425	Pete Broberg	.30
426	Rennie Stennett	.30
427	Bobby Bolin	.30
428	Gary Sutherland	.30
429	Dick Lange	.30
430	Matty Alou	.30
431	*Gene Garber*	.30
432	Chris Arnold	.30
433	Lerrin LaGrow	.30
434	Ken McMullen	.30
435	Dave Concepcion	.50
436	Don Hood	.30
437	Jim Lyttle	.30
438	Ed Herrmann	.30
439	Norm Miller	.30
440	Jim Kaat	.75
441	Tom Ragland	.30
442	Alan Foster	.30
443	Tom Hutton	.30
444	Vic Davalillo	.30
445	George Medich	.30
446	Len Randle	.30
447	Twins Mgr./Coaches(Vern Morgan, Frank Quilici, Bob Rodgers, Ralph Rowe)	.50
448	Ron Hodges	.30
449	Tom McCraw	.30
450	Rich Hebner	.30
451	Tommy John	.60
452	Gene Hiser	.30
453	Balor Moore	.30
454	Kurt Bevacqua	.30
455	Tom Bradley	.30
456	*Dave Winfield*	125.00
457	Chuck Goggin	.30
458	Jim Ray	.30
459	Reds Team	1.00
460	Boog Powell	.75
461	John Odom	.30
462	Luis Alvarado	.30
463	Pat Dobson	.30
464	Jose Cruz	.50
465	Dick Bosman	.30
466	Dick Billings	.30
467	Winston Llenas	.30
468	Pepe Frias	.30
469	Joe Decker	.30
470	A.L. Playoffs(Reggie Jackson)	5.00
471	N.L. Playoffs	.80
472	World Series Game 1(Rollie Fingers)	.80
473	World Series Game 2(Willie Mays)	5.00
474	World Series Game 3	.80
475	World Series Game 4	.80
476	World Series Game 5	.80
477	World Series Game 6(Reggie Jackson)	5.00
478	World Series Game 7	.80
479	World Series Summary (A's Celebrate)	.80
480	Willie Crawford	.30
481	Jerry Terrell	.30
482	Bob Didier	.30
483	Braves Team	1.00
484	Carmen Fanzone	.30
485	Felipe Alou	.50
486	Steve Stone	.30
487	Ted Martinez	.30
488	Andy Etchebarren	.30
489	Pirates Mgr./Coaches(Don Leppert, Bill Mazeroski, Danny Murtaugh, Don Osborn, Bob Skinner)	.75
490	Vada Pinson	.60
491	Roger Nelson	.30
492	Mike Rogodzinski	.30
493	Joe Hoerner	.30
494	Ed Goodson	.30
495	Dick McAuliffe	.30
496	Tom Murphy	.30
497	Bobby Mitchell	.30
498	Pat Corrales	.30
499	Rusty Torres	.30
500	Lee May	.30
501	Eddie Leon	.30
502	Dave LaRoche	.30
503	Eric Soderholm	.30
504	Joe Niekro	.30
505	Bill Buckner	.30

506	Ed Farmer	.30
507	Larry Stahl	.30
508	Expos Team	1.00
509	Jesse Jefferson	.30
510	Wayne Garrett	.30
511	Toby Harrah	.30
512	Joe Lahoud	.30
513	Jim Campanis	.30
514	Paul Schaal	.30
515	Willie Montanez	.30
516	Horacio Pina	.30
517	Mike Hegan	.30
518	Derrel Thomas	.30
519	Bill Sharp	.30
520	Tim McCarver	.45
521	Indians Mgr./Coaches(Ken Aspromonte, Clay Bryant, Tony Pacheco)	.50
522	J.R. Richard	.50
523	Cecil Cooper	.35
524	Bill Plummer	.30
525	Clyde Wright	.30
526	Frank Tepedino	.30
527	Bobby Darwin	.30
528	Bill Bonham	.30
529	Horace Clarke	.30
530	Mickey Stanley	.30
531	Expos Mgr./Coaches(Dave Bristol, Larry Doby, Gene Mauch, Cal McLish, Jerry Zimmerman)	.90
532	Skip Lockwood	.30
533	Mike Phillips	.30
534	Eddie Watt	.30
535	Bob Tolan	.30
536	Duffy Dyer	.30
537	Steve Mingori	.30
538	Cesar Tovar	.30
539	Lloyd Allen	.30
540	Bob Robertson	.30
541	Indians Team	1.00
542	Rich Gossage	2.00
543	Danny Cater	.30
544	Ron Schueler	.30
545	Billy Conigliaro	.30
546	Mike Corkins	.30
547	Glenn Borgmann	.30
548	Sonny Siebert	.30
549	Mike Jorgensen	.30
550	Sam McDowell	.30
551	Von Joshua	.30
552	Denny Doyle	.30
553	Jim Willoughby	.30
554	Tim Johnson	.30
555	Woodie Fryman	.30
556	Dave Campbell	.30
557	Jim McGlothlin	.30
558	Bill Fahey	.30
559	Darrel Chaney	.30
560	Mike Cuellar	.30
561	Ed Kranepool	.30
562	Jack Aker	.30
563	Hal McRae	.40
564	Mike Ryan	.30
565	Milt Wilcox	.30
566	Jackie Hernandez	.30
567	Red Sox Team	1.50
568	Mike Torrez	.30
569	Rick Dempsey	.30
570	Ralph Garr	.30
571	Rich Hand	.30
572	Enzo Hernandez	.30
573	Mike Adams	.30
574	Bill Parsons	.30
575	Steve Garvey	5.00
576	Scipio Spinks	.30
577	Mike Sadek	.30
578	Ralph Houk	.30
579	Cecil Upshaw	.30
580	Jim Spencer	.30
581	Fred Norman	.30
582	*Bucky Dent*	1.50
583	Marty Pattin	.30
584	Ken Rudolph	.30
585	Merv Rettenmund	.30
586	Jack Brohamer	.30
587	*Larry Christenson*	.30
588	Hal Lanier	.30
589	Boots Day	.30
590	Rogelio Moret	.30
591	Sonny Jackson	.30
592	Ed Bane	.30
593	Steve Yeager	.30
594	Leroy Stanton	.30
595	Steve Blass	.30

596	Rookie Pitchers(*Wayne Garland*, Fred Holdsworth), (Mark Littell, Dick Pole)	.30
597	Rookie Shortstops(Dave Chalk, John Gamble, Pete Mackanin), (*Manny Trillo*)	.80
598	Rookie Outfielders(*Dave Augustine*), (Ken Griffey), (*Steve Ontiveros*), (*Jim Tyrone*)	10.00
599a	Rookie Pitchers(Ron Diorio, Dave Freisleben, Frank Riccelli, Greg Shanahan) (Freisleben- Washington)	.80
599b	Rookie Pitchers(Ron Diorio, Dave Freisleben, Frank Riccelli, Greg Shanahan) (Freisleben- San Diego large print)	3.50
599c	Rookie Pitchers(Ron Diorio, Dave Freisleben, Frank Riccelli, Greg Shanahan) (Freisleben- San Diego small print)	6.00
600	Rookie Infielders(*Ron Cash*), (*Jim Cox*), (*Bill Madlock*), (*Reggie Sanders*)	4.00
601	Rookie Outfielders(*Ed Armbrister*), (*Rich Bladt*), (*Brian Downing*), (Bake McBride)	3.00
602	Rookie Pitchers(Glenn Abbott, Rick Henninger, Craig Swan, Dan Vossler)	.30
603	Rookie Catchers(Barry Foote, Tom Lundstedt), (*Charlie Moore*, Sergio Robles)	.30
604	Rookie Infielders(*Terry Hughes*), (*John Knox*), (*Andy Thornton*), (Frank White)	4.00
605	Rookie Pitchers(*Vic Albury*), (Ken Frailing), (Kevin Kobel), (*Frank Tanana*)	3.00
606	Rookie Outfielders(Jim Fuller, Wilbur Howard, Tommy Smith, Otto Velez)	.30
607	Rookie Shortstops(Leo Foster, Tom Heintzelman, Dave Rosello), (*Frank Taveras*)	.30
608a	Rookie Pitchers(Bob Apodaca, Dick Baney, John D'Acquisto, Mike Wallace) (Apodaca incorrect)	2.00
608b	Rookie Pitchers(Bob Apodaca, Dick Baney, John D'Acquisto, Mike Wallace) (corrected)	.30
609	Rico Petrocelli	.30
610	Dave Kingman	.45
611	Rick Stelmaszek	.30
612	Luke Walker	.30
613	Dan Monzon	.30
614	Adrian Devine	.30
615	Johnny Jeter	.30
616	Larry Gura	.30
617	Ted Ford	.30
618	Jim Mason	.30
619	Mike Anderson	.30
620	Al Downing	.30
621	Bernie Carbo	.30
622	Phil Gagliano	.30
623	Celerino Sanchez	.30
624	Bob Miller	.30
625	Ollie Brown	.30
626	Pirates Team	1.00
627	Carl Taylor	.30
628	Ivan Murrell	.30
629	Rusty Staub	.60
630	Tommie Agee	.30
631	Steve Barber	.30
632	George Culver	.30
633	Dave Hamilton	.30
634	Braves Mgr./Coaches(Jim Busby, Eddie Mathews, Connie Ryan, Ken Silvestri, Herm Starrette)	1.00
635	John Edwards	.30
636	Dave Goltz	.30
637	Checklist 529-660	.50
638	Ken Sanders	.30
639	Joe Lovitto	.30
640	Milt Pappas	.30
641	Chuck Brinkman	.30
642	Terry Harmon	.30

643	Dodgers Team	2.50
644	Wayne Granger	.30
645	Ken Boswell	.30
646	George Foster	.75
647	*Juan Beniquez*	.30
648	Terry Crowley	.30
649	Fernando Gonzalez	.30
650	Mike Epstein	.30
651	Leron Lee	.30
652	Gail Hopkins	.30
653	Bob Stinson	.30
654a	Jesus Alou (no position)	8.00
654b	Jesus Alou ("Outfield")	.30
655	Mike Tyson	.30
656	Adrian Garrett	.30
657	Jim Shellenback	.30
658	Lee Lacy	.30
659	Joe Lis	.30
660	Larry Dierker	.30

1975 Topps

What was once seen as the strongest rookie card crop of any modern card set made this a collector favorite from the outset. As several of the superstar prospects faded into merely outstanding ballplayers by the ends of their careers, however, demand has leveled. Featuring the most colorful designs since 1972, which Topps has yet to top into the mid 1990s, cards feature large front photos with facsimile autographs, and red-and-green backs which include a cartoon trivia fact and complete stats. A subset of 1951-74 MVP cards which reproduces or creates contemporary cards of past stars is one of several special features of the set, as are a group of four-on-one rookie cards. While the cards were all issued at one time, the first 132 cards have been discovered to have been printed in noticeably lesser quantities than the rest of the issue. This scarcity is not noted among the mini-version of the set which was produced as a test issue. Team/manager cards are sometimes found on thinner, white cardboard stock; these are a special version produced for a mail-in offer.

		NM
	Complete Set (660):	650.00
	Common Player (1-132):	.35
	Common Player (133-660):	.30
1	Hank Aaron ('74 Highlights)	25.00
2	Lou Brock ('74 Highlights)	2.00
3	Bob Gibson ('74 Highlights)	2.25
4	Al Kaline ('74 Highlights)	2.50
5	Nolan Ryan ('74 Highlights)	28.00
6	Mike Marshall ('74 Highlights)	.35
7	Dick Bosman, Steve Busby, Nolan Ryan ('74 Highlights)	6.00
8	Rogelio Moret	.35
9	Frank Tepedino	.35
10	Willie Davis	.35
11	Bill Melton	.35
12	David Clyde	.35
13	Gene Locklear	.35
14	Milt Wilcox	.35
15	Jose Cardenal	.35
16	Frank Tanana	.35
17	Dave Concepcion	.45
18	Tigers Team (Ralph Houk)	1.00
19	Jerry Koosman	.35
20	Thurman Munson	5.00
21	Rollie Fingers	3.00
22	Dave Cash	.35
23	Bill Russell	.45
24	Al Fitzmorris	.35
25	Lee May	.35
26	Dave McNally	.35
27	Ken Reitz	.35
28	Tom Murphy	.35

29	Dave Parker	3.00
30	Bert Blyleven	.75
31	Dave Rader	.35
32	Reggie Cleveland	.35
33	Dusty Baker	.40
34	Steve Renko	.35
35	Ron Santo	.65
36	Joe Lovitto	.35
37	Dave Freisleben	.35
38	Buddy Bell	.35
39	Andy Thornton	.40
40	Bill Singer	.35
41	Cesar Geronimo	.35
42	Joe Coleman	.35
43	Cleon Jones	.35
44	Pat Dobson	.35
45	Joe Rudi	.40
46	Phillies Team (Danny Ozark)	1.00
47	Tommy John	.90
48	Freddie Patek	.35
49	Larry Dierker	.35
50	Brooks Robinson	5.00
51	*Bob Forsch*	.80
52	Darrell Porter	.35
53	Dave Giusti	.35
54	Eric Soderholm	.35
55	Bobby Bonds	.50
56	Rick Wise	.35
57	Dave Johnson	.35
58	Chuck Taylor	.35
59	Ken Henderson	.35
60	Fergie Jenkins	2.50
61	Dave Winfield	40.00
62	Fritz Peterson	.35
63	Steve Swisher	.35
64	Dave Chalk	.35
65	Don Gullett	.35
66	Willie Horton	.35
67	Tug McGraw	.35
68	Ron Blomberg	.35
69	John Odom	.35
70	Mike Schmidt	45.00
71	Charlie Hough	.35
72	Royals Team (Jack McKeon)	1.00
73	J.R. Richard	.45
74	Mark Belanger	.35
75	Ted Simmons	.35
76	Ed Sprague	.35
77	Richie Zisk	.35
78	Ray Corbin	.35
79	Gary Matthews	.35
80	Carlton Fisk	9.00
81	Ron Reed	.35
82	Pat Kelly	.35
83	Jim Merritt	.35
84	Enzo Hernandez	.35
85	Bill Bonham	.35
86	Joe Lis	.35
87	George Foster	.35
88	Tom Egan	.35
89	Jim Ray	.35
90	Rusty Staub	.45
91	Dick Green	.35
92	Cecil Upshaw	.35
93	Dave Lopes	.35
94	Jim Lonborg	.35
95	John Mayberry	.35
96	Mike Cosgrove	.35
97	Earl Williams	.35
98	Rich Folkers	.35
99	Mike Hegan	.35
100	Willie Stargell	3.50
101	Expos Team (Gene Mauch)	1.00
102	Joe Decker	.35
103	Rick Miller	.35
104	Bill Madlock	.60
105	Buzz Capra	.35
106	*Mike Hargrove*	.45
107	Jim Barr	.35
108	Tom Hall	.35
109	George Hendrick	.35
110	Wilbur Wood	.35
111	Wayne Garrett	.35
112	Larry Hardy	.35
113	Elliott Maddox	.35
114	Dick Lange	.35
115	Joe Ferguson	.35
116	Lerrin LaGrow	.35
117	Orioles Team (Earl Weaver)	2.25
118	Mike Anderson	.35
119	Tommy Helms	.35
120	Steve Busby (photo actually Fran Healy)	.35
121	Bill North	.35
122	Al Hrabosky	.35

123	Johnny Briggs	.35
124	Jerry Reuss	.35
125	Ken Singleton	.35
126	Checklist 1-132	.45
127	Glen Borgmann	.35
128	Bill Lee	.35
129	Rick Monday	.35
130	Phil Niekro	2.00
131	Toby Harrah	.35
132	Randy Moffitt	.35
133	Dan Driessen	.30
134	Ron Hodges	.30
135	Charlie Spikes	.30
136	Jim Mason	.30
137	Terry Forster	.30
138	Del Unser	.30
139	Horacio Pina	.30
140	Steve Garvey	6.00
141	Mickey Stanley	.30
142	Bob Reynolds	.30
143	*Cliff Johnson*	.30
144	Jim Wohlford	.30
145	Ken Holtzman	.30
146	Padres Team (John McNamara)	1.00
147	Pedro Garcia	.30
148	Jim Rooker	.30
149	Tim Foli	.30
150	Bob Gibson	4.50
151	Steve Brye	.30
152	Mario Guerrero	.30
153	Rick Reuschel	.30
154	Mike Lum	.30
155	Jim Bibby	.30
156	Dave Kingman	.45
157	Pedro Borbon	.30
158	Jerry Grote	.30
159	Steve Arlin	.30
160	Graig Nettles	.45
161	Stan Bahnsen	.30
162	Willie Montanez	.30
163	Jim Brewer	.30
164	Mickey Rivers	.30
165	Doug Rader	.30
166	Woodie Fryman	.30
167	Rich Coggins	.30
168	Bill Greif	.30
169	Cookie Rojas	.30
170	Bert Campaneris	.35
171	Ed Kirkpatrick	.30
172	Red Sox Team (Darrell Johnson)	1.50
173	Steve Rogers	.30
174	Bake McBride	.30
175	Don Money	.30
176	Burt Hooton	.30
177	Vic Correll	.30
178	Cesar Tovar	.30
179	Tom Bradley	.30
180	Joe Morgan	4.00
181	Fred Beene	.30
182	Don Hahn	.30
183	Mel Stottlemyre	.30
184	Jorge Orta	.30
185	Steve Carlton	6.00
186	Willie Crawford	.30
187	Denny Doyle	.30
188	Tom Griffin	.30
189	1951-MVPs (Yogi Berra, Roy Campanella)	2.00
190	1952-MVPs (Hank Sauer, Bobby Shantz)	.40
191	1953-MVPs (Roy Campanella, Al Rosen)	1.00
192	1954-MVPs (Yogi Berra, Willie Mays)	3.00
193	1955-MVPs (Yogi Berra, Roy Campanella)	2.50
194	1956-MVPs (Mickey Mantle, Don Newcombe)	10.00
195	1957-MVPs (Hank Aaron, Mickey Mantle)	17.50
196	1958-MVPs (Ernie Banks, Jackie Jensen)	1.00
197	1959-MVPs (Ernie Banks, Nellie Fox)	1.50
198	1960-MVPs (Dick Groat, Roger Maris)	1.50
199	1961-MVPs (Roger Maris, Frank Robinson)	1.50
200	1962-MVPs (Mickey Mantle, Maury Wills)	9.00
201	1963-MVPs (Elston Howard, Sandy Koufax)	1.50
202	1964-MVPs (Ken Boyer, Brooks Robinson)	1.25

203	1965-MVPs(Willie Mays, Zoilo Versalles)	1.50
204	1966-MVPs(Roberto Clemente, Frank Robinson)	3.50
205	1967-MVPs(Orlando Cepeda, Carl Yastrzemski)	1.25
206	1968-MVPs(Bob Gibson, Denny McLain)	1.25
207	1969-MVPs(Harmon Killebrew, Willie McCovey)	1.25
208	1970-MVPs(Johnny Bench, Boog Powell)	1.25
209	1971-MVPs(Vida Blue, Joe Torre)	.50
210	1972-MVPs(Rich Allen, Johnny Bench)	1.25
211	1973-MVPs(Reggie Jackson, Pete Rose)	5.00
212	1974-MVPs(Jeff Burroughs, Steve Garvey)	.60
213	Oscar Gamble	.30
214	Harry Parker	.30
215	Bobby Valentine	.30
216	Giants Team(Wes Westrum)	1.00
217	Lou Piniella	.45
218	Jerry Johnson	.30
219	Ed Herrmann	.30
220	Don Sutton	2.50
221	Aurelio Rodriquez (Rodriguez)	.30
222	Dan Spillner	.30
223	*Robin Yount*	90.00
224	Ramon Hernandez	.30
225	Bob Grich	.30
226	Bill Campbell	.30
227	Bob Watson	.30
228	*George Brett*	125.00
229	Barry Foote	.30
230	Catfish Hunter	2.00
231	Mike Tyson	.30
232	Diego Segui	.30
233	Billy Grabarkewitz	.30
234	Tom Grieve	.30
235	Jack Billingham	.30
236	Angels Team(Dick Williams)	1.00
237	Carl Morton	.30
238	Dave Duncan	.30
239	George Stone	.30
240	Garry Maddox	.30
241	Dick Tidrow	.30
242	Jay Johnstone	.30
243	Jim Kaat	.75
244	Bill Buckner	.30
245	Mickey Lolich	.40
246	Cardinals Team(Red Schoendienst)	1.00
247	Enos Cabell	.30
248	Randy Jones	.30
249	Danny Thompson	.30
250	Ken Brett	.30
251	Fran Healy	.30
252	Fred Scherman	.30
253	Jesus Alou	.30
254	Mike Torrez	.30
255	Dwight Evans	.75
256	Billy Champion	.30
257	Checklist 133-264	.45
258	Dave LaRoche	.30
259	Len Randle	.30
260	Johnny Bench	10.00
261	Andy Hassler	.30
262	Rowland Office	.30
263	Jim Perry	.30
264	John Milner	.30
265	Ron Bryant	.30
266	Sandy Alomar	.30
267	Dick Ruthven	.30
268	Hal McRae	.30
269	Doug Rau	.30
270	Ron Fairly	.30
271	Jerry Moses	.30
272	Lynn McGlothen	.30
273	Steve Braun	.30
274	Vicente Romo	.30
275	Paul Blair	.30
276	White Sox Team(Chuck Tanner)	1.00
277	Frank Taveras	.30
278	Paul Lindblad	.30
279	Milt May	.30
280	Carl Yastrzemski	7.00
281	Jim Slaton	.30
282	Jerry Morales	.30
283	Steve Foucault	.30
284	Ken Griffey	.50

285	Ellie Rodriguez	.30
286	Mike Jorgensen	.30
287	Roric Harrison	.30
288	Bruce Ellingsen	.30
289	Ken Rudolph	.30
290	Jon Matlack	.30
291	Bill Sudakis	.30
292	Ron Schueler	.30
293	Dick Sharon	.30
294	*Geoff Zahn*	.30
295	Vada Pinson	.45
296	Alan Foster	.30
297	Craig Kusick	.30
298	Johnny Grubb	.30
299	Bucky Dent	.30
300	Reggie Jackson	14.00
301	Dave Roberts	.30
302	*Rick Burleson*	.30
303	Grant Jackson	.30
304	Pirates Team(Danny Murtaugh)	1.00
305	Jim Colborn	.30
306	Batting Leaders(Rod Carew, Ralph Garr)	.50
307	Home Run Leaders(Dick Allen, Mike Schmidt)	.90
308	Runs Batted In Leaders(Johnny Bench, Jeff Burroughs)	.75
309	Stolen Base Leaders(Lou Brock, Bill North)	.40
310	Victory Leaders(Jim Hunter, Fergie Jenkins, Andy Messersmith, Phil Niekro)	.75
311	Earned Run Average Leaders(Buzz Capra, Catfish Hunter)	.45
312	Strikeout Leaders(Steve Carlton, Nolan Ryan)	11.00
313	Leading Firemen(Terry Forster, Mike Marshall)	.30
314	Buck Martinez	.30
315	Don Kessinger	.30
316	Jackie Brown	.30
317	Joe Lahoud	.30
318	Ernie McAnally	.30
319	Johnny Oates	.30
320	Pete Rose	24.00
321	Rudy May	.30
322	Ed Goodson	.30
323	Fred Holdsworth	.30
324	Ed Kranepool	.35
325	Tony Oliva	.45
326	Wayne Twitchell	.30
327	Jerry Hairston	.30
328	Sonny Siebert	.30
329	Ted Kubiak	.30
330	Mike Marshall	.30
331	Indians Team(Frank Robinson)	1.50
332	Fred Kendall	.30
333	Dick Drago	.30
334	*Greg Gross*	.30
335	Jim Palmer	4.50
336	Rennie Stennett	.30
337	Kevin Kobel	.30
338	Rick Stelmaszek	.30
339	Jim Fregosi	.30
340	Paul Splittorff	.30
341	Hal Breeden	.30
342	Leroy Stanton	.30
343	Danny Frisella	.30
344	Ben Oglivie	.30
345	Clay Carroll	.30
346	Bobby Darwin	.30
347	Mike Caldwell	.30
348	Tony Muser	.30
349	Ray Sadecki	.30
350	Bobby Murcer	.30
351	Bob Boone	.40
352	Darold Knowles	.30
353	Luis Melendez	.30
354	Dick Bosman	.30
355	Chris Cannizzaro	.30
356	Rico Petrocelli	.30
357	Ken Forsch	.30
358	Al Bumbry	.30
359	Paul Popovich	.30
360	George Scott	.30
361	Dodgers Team(Walter Alston)	1.50
362	Steve Hargan	.30
363	Carmen Fanzone	.30
364	Doug Bird	.30
365	Bob Bailey	.30
366	Ken Sanders	.30

367	Craig Robinson	.30
368	Vic Albury	.30
369	Merv Rettenmund	.30
370	Tom Seaver	12.00
371	Gates Brown	.30
372	John D'Acquisto	.30
373	Bill Sharp	.30
374	Eddie Watt	.30
375	Roy White	.30
376	Steve Yeager	.30
377	Tom Hilgendorf	.30
378	Derrel Thomas	.30
379	Bernie Carbo	.30
380	Sal Bando	.30
381	John Curtis	.30
382	Don Baylor	.75
383	Jim York	.30
384	Brewers Team(Del Crandall)	1.00
385	Dock Ellis	.30
386	Checklist 265-396	.45
387	Jim Spencer	.30
388	Steve Stone	.30
389	Tony Solaita	.30
390	Ron Cey	.30
391	Don DeMola	.30
392	Bruce Bochte	.30
393	Gary Gentry	.30
394	Larvell Blanks	.30
395	Bud Harrelson	.30
396	Fred Norman	.30
397	Bill Freehan	.30
398	Elias Sosa	.30
399	Terry Harmon	.30
400	Dick Allen	.80
401	Mike Wallace	.30
402	Bob Tolan	.30
403	Tom Buskey	.30
404	Ted Sizemore	.30
405	John Montague	.30
406	Bob Gallagher	.30
407	*Herb Washington*	.50
408	Clyde Wright	.30
409	Bob Robertson	.30
410	Mike Cueller (Cuellar)	.30
411	George Mitterwald	.30
412	Bill Hands	.30
413	Marty Pattin	.30
414	Manny Mota	.30
415	John Hiller	.30
416	Larry Lintz	.30
417	Skip Lockwood	.30
418	Leo Foster	.30
419	Dave Goltz	.30
420	Larry Bowa	.30
421	Mets Team(Yogi Berra)	2.00
422	Brian Downing	.30
423	Clay Kirby	.30
424	John Lowenstein	.30
425	Tito Fuentes	.30
426	George Medich	.30
427	Clarence Gaston	.30
428	Dave Hamilton	.30
429	*Jim Dwyer*	.30
430	Luis Tiant	.30
431	Rod Gilbreath	.30
432	Ken Berry	.30
433	Larry Demery	.30
434	Bob Locker	.30
435	Dave Nelson	.30
436	Ken Frailing	.30
437	*Al Cowens*	.30
438	Don Carrithers	.30
439	Ed Brinkman	.30
440	Andy Messersmith	.30
441	Bobby Heise	.30
442	Maximino Leon	.30
443	Twins Team(Frank Quilici)	1.00
444	Gene Garber	.30
445	Felix Millan	.30
446	Bart Johnson	.30
447	Terry Crowley	.30
448	Frank Duffy	.30
449	Charlie Williams	.30
450	Willie McCovey	4.50
451	Rick Dempsey	.30
452	Angel Mangual	.30
453	Claude Osteen	.30
454	Doug Griffin	.30
455	Don Wilson	.30
456	Bob Coluccio	.30
457	Mario Mendoza	.30
458	Ross Grimsley	.30
459	A.L. Championships(Frank Robinson)	.80

460	N.L. Championships(Steve Garvey)	.80
461	World Series Game 1(Reggie Jackson)	1.50
462	World Series Game 2	.80
463	World Series Game 3(Rollie Fingers)	.90
464	World Series Game 4	.80
465	World Series Game 5	.80
466	A's Do It Again!	.80
467	Ed Halicki	.30
468	Bobby Mitchell	.30
469	Tom Dettore	.30
470	Jeff Burroughs	.30
471	Bob Stinson	.30
472	Bruce Dal Canton	.30
473	Ken McMullen	.30
474	Luke Walker	.30
475	Darrell Evans	.45
476	*Ed Figueroa*	.30
477	Tom Hutton	.30
478	Tom Burgmeier	.30
479	Ken Boswell	.30
480	Carlos May	.30
481	*Will McEnaney*	.30
482	Tom McCraw	.30
483	Steve Ontiveros	.30
484	Glenn Beckert	.30
485	Sparky Lyle	.30
486	Ray Fosse	.30
487	Astros Team(Preston Gomez)	1.00
488	Bill Travers	.30
489	Cecil Cooper	.30
490	Reggie Smith	.30
491	Doyle Alexander	.30
492	Rich Hebner	.30
493	Don Stanhouse	.30
494	*Pete LaCock*	.30
495	Nelson Briles	.30
496	Pepe Frias	.30
497	Jim Nettles	.30
498	Al Downing	.30
499	Marty Perez	.30
500	Nolan Ryan	65.00
501	Bill Robinson	.30
502	Pat Bourque	.30
503	Fred Stanley	.30
504	Buddy Bradford	.30
505	Chris Speier	.30
506	Leron Lee	.30
507	Tom Carroll	.30
508	Bob Hansen	.30
509	Dave Hilton	.30
510	Vida Blue	.30
511	Rangers Team(Billy Martin)	1.25
512	Larry Milbourne	.30
513	Dick Pole	.30
514	Jose Cruz	.30
515	Manny Sanguillen	.30
516	Don Hood	.30
517	Checklist 397-528	.45
518	Leo Cardenas	.30
519	Jim Todd	.30
520	Amos Otis	.30
521	Dennis Blair	.30
522	Gary Sutherland	.30
523	Tom Paciorek	.30
524	John Doherty	.30
525	Tom House	.30
526	Larry Hisle	.30
527	Mac Scarce	.30
528	Eddie Leon	.30
529	Gary Thomasson	.30
530	Gaylord Perry	1.75
531	Reds Team(Sparky Anderson)	3.00
532	Gorman Thomas	.30
533	Rudy Meoli	.30
534	Alex Johnson	.30
535	Gene Tenace	.30
536	Bob Moose	.30
537	Tommy Harper	.30
538	Duffy Dyer	.30
539	Jesse Jefferson	.30
540	Lou Brock	3.75
541	Roger Metzger	.30
542	Pete Broberg	.30
543	Larry Biittner	.30
544	Steve Mingori	.30
545	Billy Williams	3.00
546	John Knox	.30
547	Von Joshua	.30
548	Charlie Sands	.30
549	Bill Butler	.30
550	Ralph Garr	.30

551	Larry Christenson	.30
552	Jack Brohamer	.30
553	John Boccabella	.30
554	Rich Gossage	.40
555	Al Oliver	.45
556	Tim Johnson	.30
557	Larry Gura	.30
558	Dave Roberts	.30
559	Bob Montgomery	.30
560	Tony Perez	1.50
561	A's Team(Alvin Dark)	1.00
562	Gary Nolan	.30
563	Wilbur Howard	.30
564	Tommy Davis	.30
565	Joe Torre	.50
566	Ray Burris	.30
567	*Jim Sundberg*	.45
568	Dale Murray	.30
569	Frank White	.30
570	Jim Wynn	.30
571	Dave Lemanczyk	.30
572	Roger Nelson	.30
573	Orlando Pena	.30
574	Tony Taylor	.30
575	Gene Clines	.30
576	Phil Roof	.30
577	John Morris	.30
578	Dave Tomlin	.30
579	Skip Pitlock	.30
580	Frank Robinson	6.50
581	Darrel Chaney	.30
582	Eduardo Rodriguez	.30
583	Andy Etchebarren	.30
584	Mike Garman	.30
585	Chris Chambliss	.30
586	Tim McCarver	.35
587	Chris Ward	.30
588	Rick Auerbach	.30
589	Braves Team(Clyde King)	1.00
590	Cesar Cedeno	.30
591	Glenn Abbott	.30
592	Balor Moore	.30
593	Gene Lamont	.30
594	Jim Fuller	.30
595	Joe Niekro	.30
596	Ollie Brown	.30
597	Winston Llenas	.30
598	Bruce Kison	.30
599	Nate Colbert	.30
600	Rod Carew	6.50
601	Juan Beniquez	.30
602	John Vukovich	.30
603	Lew Krausse	.30
604	Oscar Zamora	.30
605	John Ellis	.30
606	Bruce Miller	.30
607	Jim Holt	.30
608	Gene Michael	.30
609	Ellie Hendricks	.30
610	Ron Hunt	.30
611	Yankees Team(Bill Virdon)	1.50
612	Terry Hughes	.30
613	Bill Parsons	.30
614	Rookie Pitchers(Jack Kucek, Dyar Miller, Vern Ruhle, Paul Siebert)	
615	Rookie Pitchers(Pat Darcy), *(Dennis Leonard), (Tom Underwood, Hank Webb)*	.30
616	Rookie Outfielders(*Dave Augustine), (Pepe Mangual), (Jim Rice), (John Scott)*	10.00
617	Rookie Infielders(*Mike Cubbage), (Doug DeCinces, Reggie Sanders, Manny Trillo)*	1.75
618	Rookie Pitchers(*Jamie Easterly,* Tom Johnson), *(Scott McGregor), (Rick Rhoden)*	2.25
619	Rookie Outfielders(Benny Ayala, Nyls Nyman, Tommy Smith, Jerry Turner)	.30
620	Rookie Catchers-Outfielders(*Gary Carter), (Marc Hill), (Danny Meyer), (Leon Roberts)*	22.00
621	Rookie Pitchers(*John Denny), (Rawly Eastwick), (Jim Kern, Juan Veintidos)*	.60
622	Rookie Outfielders(*Ed Armbrister), (Fred Lynn), (Tom Poquette), (Terry Whitfield)*	6.00

623	Rookie Infielders(*Phil Garner), (Keith Hernandez), (Bob Sheldon), (Tom Veryzer)*	4.00
624	Rookie Pitchers(Doug Konieczny), *(Gary Lavelle,* Jim Otten, Eddie Solomon)	.30
625	Boog Powell	.45
626	Larry Haney	.30
627	Tom Walker	.30
628	*Ron LeFlore*	.80
629	Joe Hoerner	.30
630	Greg Luzinski	.35
631	Lee Lacy	.30
632	Morris Nettles	.30
633	Paul Casanova	.30
634	Cy Acosta	.30
635	Chuck Dobson	.30
636	Charlie Moore	.30
637	Ted Martinez	.30
638	Cubs Team(Jim Marshall)	1.00
639	Steve Kline	.30
640	Harmon Killebrew	4.50
641	Jim Northrup	.30
642	Mike Phillips	.30
643	Brent Strom	.30
644	Bill Fahey	.30
645	Danny Cater	.30
646	Checklist 529-660	.45
647	*Claudell Washington*	.80
648	Dave Pagan	.30
649	Jack Heidemann	.30
650	Dave May	.30
651	John Morlan	.30
652	Lindy McDaniel	.30
653	Lee Richards	.30
654	Jerry Terrell	.30
655	Rico Carty	.30
656	Bill Plummer	.30
657	Bob Oliver	.30
658	Vic Harris	.30
659	Bob Apodaca	.30
660	Hank Aaron	25.00

1975 Topps Mini

This popular set was actually a test issue to see how collectors would react to cards which were 20% smaller than the standard 2-1/2" x 3-1/2". Other than their 2-1/4" x 3-1/8" size, they are exactly the same, front and back as the regular-issue '75 Topps. The experimental cards were sold in Michigan and on the West Coast, where they were quickly gobbled up by collectors, dealers and speculators. While the minis for many years enjoyed a 2X premium over regular 1975 Topps values, that differential has shrunk in recent years.

	NM
Complete Set (660):	995.00
Common Player:	.40
(Stars and rookies valued about 125% to 150% of regular 1975 Topps version)	

1976 Topps

These 2-1/2" x 3-1/2" cards begin a design trend for Topps. The focus was more on the photo quality in past years with a corresponding trend toward simplicity in the borders. The front of the cards has the player's name and team in two strips while his position is in the lower-left corner under a drawing of a player representing that position. The backs have a bat and ball with the card number on the left; statistics and personal information and career highlights on the right. The 660-card set features a number of specialty sets including record-setting performances, statistical leaders, playoff and World Series highlights, the Sporting News All-Time All-Stars and father and son combinations.

		NM
	Complete Set (660):	350.00
	Common Player:	.30
1	Hank Aaron (Record Breaker)	15.00
2	Bobby Bonds (Record Breaker)	.30
3	Mickey Lolich (Record Breaker)	.30
4	Dave Lopes (Record Breaker)	.30
5	Tom Seaver (Record Breaker)	3.00
6	Rennie Stennett (Record Breaker)	.30
7	Jim Umbarger	.30
8	Tito Fuentes	.30
9	Paul Lindblad	.30
10	Lou Brock	3.50
11	Jim Hughes	.30
12	Richie Zisk	.30
13	Johnny Wockenfuss	.30
14	Gene Garber	.30
15	George Scott	.30
16	Bob Apodaca	.30
17	Yankees Team(Billy Martin)	1.25
18	Dale Murray	.30
19	George Brett	60.00
20	Bob Watson	.30
21	Dave LaRoche	.30
22	Bill Russell	.40
23	Brian Downing	.30
24	Cesar Geronimo	.30
25	Mike Torrez	.30
26	Andy Thornton	.30
27	Ed Figueroa	.30
28	Dusty Baker	1.00
29	Rick Burleson	.30
30	*John Montefusco*	.30
31	Len Randle	.30
32	Danny Frisella	.30
33	Bill North	.30
34	Mike Garman	.30
35	Tony Oliva	.40
36	Frank Taveras	.30
37	John Hiller	.30
38	Garry Maddox	.30
39	Pete Broberg	.30
40	Dave Kingman	.35
41	*Tippy Martinez*	.30
42	Barry Foote	.30
43	Paul Splittorff	.30
44	Doug Rader	.30
45	Boog Powell	.35
46	Dodgers Team(Walter Alston)	1.00
47	Jesse Jefferson	.30
48	Dave Concepcion	.35
49	Dave Duncan	.30
50	Fred Lynn	1.50
51	Ray Burris	.30
52	Dave Chalk	.30
53	Mike Beard	.30
54	Dave Rader	.30
55	Gaylord Perry	1.75
56	Bob Tolan	.30
57	Phil Garner	.30
58	Ron Reed	.30
59	Larry Hisle	.30
60	Jerry Reuss	.30
61	Ron LeFlore	.30
62	Johnny Oates	.30
63	Bobby Darwin	.30
64	Jerry Koosman	.30
65	Chris Chambliss	.30
66	Father & Son(Buddy Bell, Gus Bell)	.30
67	Father & Son(Bob Boone, Ray Boone)	.40
68	Father & Son(Joe Coleman, Joe Coleman, Jr.)	.30
69	Father & Son(Jim Hegan, Mike Hegan)	.30
70	Father & Son(Roy Smalley, III, Roy Smalley, Jr.)	.30
71	Steve Rogers	.30
72	Hal McRae	.35
73	Orioles Team(Earl Weaver)	.90
74	Oscar Gamble	.30

75	Larry Dierker	.30
76	Willie Crawford	.30
77	Pedro Borbon	.30
78	Cecil Cooper	.30
79	Jerry Morales	.30
80	Jim Kaat	.75
81	Darrell Evans	.40
82	Von Joshua	.30
83	Jim Spencer	.30
84	Brent Strom	.30
85	Mickey Rivers	.30
86	Mike Tyson	.30
87	Tom Burgmeier	.30
88	Duffy Dyer	.30
89	Vern Ruhle	.30
90	Sal Bando	.30
91	Tom Hutton	.30
92	Eduardo Rodriguez	.30
93	Mike Phillips	.30
94	Jim Dwyer	.30
95	Brooks Robinson	5.00
96	Doug Bird	.30
97	Wilbur Howard	.30
98	*Dennis Eckersley*	35.00
99	Lee Lacy	.30
100	Catfish Hunter	2.00
101	Pete LaCock	.30
102	Jim Willoughby	.30
103	Biff Pocoroba	.30
104	Reds Team(Sparky Anderson)	.90
105	Gary Lavelle	.30
106	Tom Grieve	.30
107	Dave Roberts	.30
108	Don Kirkwood	.30
109	Larry Lintz	.30
110	Carlos May	.30
111	Danny Thompson	.30
112	*Kent Tekulve*	.60
113	Gary Sutherland	.30
114	Jay Johnstone	.30
115	Ken Holtzman	.30
116	Charlie Moore	.30
117	Mike Jorgensen	.30
118	Red Sox Team(Darrell Johnson)	.50
119	Checklist 1-132	.35
120	Rusty Staub	.35
121	Tony Solaita	.30
122	Mike Cosgrove	.30
123	Walt Williams	.30
124	Doug Rau	.30
125	Don Baylor	.60
126	Tom Dettore	.30
127	Larvell Blanks	.30
128	Ken Griffey	.35
129	Andy Etchebarren	.30
130	Luis Tiant	.30
131	Bill Stein	.30
132	Don Hood	.30
133	Gary Matthews	.30
134	Mike Ivie	.30
135	Bake McBride	.30
136	Dave Goltz	.30
137	Bill Robinson	.30
138	Lerrin LaGrow	.30
139	Gorman Thomas	.30
140	Vida Blue	.30
141	*Larry Parrish*	.50
142	Dick Drago	.30
143	Jerry Grote	.30
144	Al Fitzmorris	.30
145	Larry Bowa	.30
146	George Medich	.30
147	Astros Team(Bill Virdon)	.50
148	Stan Thomas	.30
149	Tommy Davis	.30
150	Steve Garvey	3.00
151	Bill Bonham	.30
152	Leroy Stanton	.30
153	Buzz Capra	.30
154	Bucky Dent	.30
155	Jack Billingham	.30
156	Rico Carty	.30
157	Mike Caldwell	.30
158	Ken Reitz	.30
159	Jerry Terrell	.30
160	Dave Winfield	17.50
161	Bruce Kison	.30
162	Jack Pierce	.30
163	Jim Slaton	.30
164	Pepe Mangual	.30
165	Gene Tenace	.30
166	Skip Lockwood	.30
167	Freddie Patek	.30
168	Tom Hilgendorf	.30

169	Graig Nettles	.45
170	Rick Wise	.30
171	Greg Gross	.30
172	Rangers Team(Frank Lucchesi)	.50
173	Steve Swisher	.30
174	Charlie Hough	.30
175	Ken Singleton	.30
176	Dick Lange	.30
177	Marty Perez	.30
178	Tom Buskey	.30
179	George Foster	.45
180	Rich Gossage	.90
181	Willie Montanez	.30
182	Harry Rasmussen	.30
183	Steve Braun	.30
184	Bill Greif	.30
185	Dave Parker	1.50
186	Tom Walker	.30
187	Pedro Garcia	.30
188	Fred Scherman	.30
189	Claudell Washington	.30
190	Jon Matlack	.30
191	N.L. Batting Leaders(Bill Madlock, Manny Sanguillen, Ted Simmons)	.35
192	A.L. Batting Leaders(Rod Carew, Fred Lynn, Thurman Munson)	1.00
193	N.L. Home Run Leaders(Dave Kingman, Greg Luzinski, Mike Schmidt)	1.00
194	A.L. Home Run Leaders(Reggie Jackson, John Mayberry, George Scott)	1.00
195	N.L. RBI Leaders(Johnny Bench, Greg Luzinski, Tony Perez)	1.00
196	A.L. RBI Leaders(Fred Lynn, John Mayberry, George Scott)	.35
197	N.L. Stolen Base Leaders(Lou Brock, Dave Lopes, Joe Morgan)	.40
198	A.L. Stolen Base Leaders(Amos Otis, Mickey Rivers, Claudell Washington)	.30
199	N.L. Victory Leaders(Randy Jones, Andy Messersmith, Tom Seaver)	1.00
200	A.L. Victory Leaders(Vida Blue, Catfish Hunter, Jim Palmer)	.75
201	N.L. ERA Leaders(Randy Jones, Andy Messersmith, Tom Seaver)	1.00
202	A.L. ERA Leaders(Dennis Eckersley, Catfish Hunter, Jim Palmer)	3.50
203	N.L. Strikeout Leaders(Andy Messersmith, John Montefusco, Tom Seaver)	1.00
204	A.L. Strikeout Leaders(Bert Blyleven, Gaylord Perry, Frank Tanana)	.60
205	Major League Leading Firemen(Rich Gossage, Al Hrabosky)	.30
206	Manny Trillo	.30
207	Andy Hassler	.30
208	Mike Lum	.30
209	Alan Ashby	.30
210	Lee May	.30
211	Clay Carroll	.30
212	Pat Kelly	.30
213	Dave Heaverlo	.30
214	Eric Soderholm	.30
215	Reggie Smith	.30
216	Expos Team(Karl Kuehl)	.50
217	Dave Freisleben	.30
218	John Knox	.30
219	Tom Murphy	.30
220	Manny Sanguillen	.30
221	Jim Todd	.30
222	Wayne Garrett	.30
223	Ollie Brown	.30
224	Jim York	.30
225	Roy White	.30
226	Jim Sundberg	.30
227	Oscar Zamora	.30
228	John Hale	.30
229	*Jerry Remy*	.30

#	Player	Price
230	Carl Yastrzemski	5.00
231	Tom House	.30
232	Frank Duffy	.30
233	Grant Jackson	.30
234	Mike Sadek	.30
235	Bert Blyleven	.50
236	Royals Team(Whitey Herzog)	.80
237	Dave Hamilton	.30
238	Larry Biittner	.30
239	John Curtis	.30
240	Pete Rose	15.00
241	Hector Torres	.30
242	Dan Meyer	.30
243	Jim Rooker	.30
244	Bill Sharp	.30
245	Felix Millan	.30
246	Cesar Tovar	.30
247	Terry Harmon	.30
248	Dick Tidrow	.30
249	Cliff Johnson	.30
250	Fergie Jenkins	1.75
251	Rick Monday	.30
252	Tim Nordbrook	.30
253	Bill Buckner	.30
254	Rudy Meoli	.30
255	Fritz Peterson	.30
256	Rowland Office	.30
257	Ross Grimsley	.30
258	Nyls Nyman	.30
259	Darrel Chaney	.30
260	Steve Busby	.30
261	Gary Thomasson	.30
262	Checklist 133-264	.35
263	*Lyman Bostock*	.80
264	Steve Renko	.30
265	Willie Davis	.30
266	Alan Foster	.30
267	Aurelio Rodriguez	.30
268	Del Unser	.30
269	Rick Austin	.30
270	Willie Stargell	2.50
271	Jim Lonborg	.30
272	Rick Dempsey	.30
273	Joe Niekro	.30
274	Tommy Harper	.30
275	*Rick Manning*	.35
276	Mickey Scott	.30
277	Cubs Team(Jim Marshall)	.50
278	Bernie Carbo	.30
279	Roy Howell	.30
280	Burt Hooton	.30
281	Dave May	.30
282	Dan Osborn	.30
283	Merv Rettenmund	.30
284	Steve Ontiveros	.30
285	Mike Cuellar	.30
286	Jim Wohlford	.30
287	Pete Mackanin	.30
288	Bill Campbell	.30
289	Enzo Hernandez	.30
290	Ted Simmons	.30
291	Ken Sanders	.30
292	Leon Roberts	.30
293	Bill Castro	.30
294	Ed Kirkpatrick	.30
295	Dave Cash	.30
296	Pat Dobson	.30
297	Roger Metzger	.30
298	Dick Bosman	.30
299	Champ Summers	.30
300	Johnny Bench	6.00
301	Jackie Brown	.30
302	Rick Miller	.30
303	Steve Foucault	.30
304	Angels Team(Dick Williams)	.50
305	Andy Messersmith	.30
306	Rod Gilbreath	.30
307	Al Bumbry	.30
308	Jim Barr	.30
309	Bill Melton	.30
310	Randy Jones	.30
311	Cookie Rojas	.30
312	Don Carrithers	.30
313	*Dan Ford*	.30
314	Ed Kranepool	.30
315	Al Hrabosky	.30
316	Robin Yount	30.00
317	*John Candelaria*	2.00
318	Bob Boone	.30
319	Larry Gura	.30
320	Willie Horton	.30
321	Jose Cruz	.30
322	Glenn Abbott	.30
323	Rob Sperring	.30
324	Jim Bibby	.30
325	Tony Perez	1.25
326	Dick Pole	.30
327	Dave Moates	.30
328	Carl Morton	.30
329	Joe Ferguson	.30
330	Nolan Ryan	60.00
331	Padres Team(John McNamara)	.50
332	Charlie Williams	.30
333	Bob Coluccio	.30
334	Dennis Leonard	.30
335	Bob Grich	.30
336	Vic Albury	.30
337	Bud Harrelson	.30
338	Bob Bailey	.30
339	John Denny	.30
340	Jim Rice	2.00
341	Lou Gehrig (All Time 1B)	9.00
342	Rogers Hornsby (All Time 2B)	1.00
343	Pie Traynor (All Time 3B)	.30
344	Honus Wagner (All Time SS)	2.25
345	Babe Ruth (All Time OF)	11.00
346	Ty Cobb (All Time OF)	5.00
347	Ted Williams (All Time OF)	8.00
348	Mickey Cochrane (All Time C)	.30
349	Walter Johnson (All Time RHP)	1.00
350	Lefty Grove (All Time LHP)	.35
351	Randy Hundley	.30
352	Dave Giusti	.30
353	*Sixto Lezcano*	.30
354	Ron Blomberg	.30
355	Steve Carlton	5.00
356	Ted Martinez	.30
357	Ken Forsch	.30
358	Buddy Bell	.30
359	Rick Reuschel	.30
360	Jeff Burroughs	.30
361	Tigers Team(Ralph Houk)	.50
362	Will McEnaney	.30
363	*Dave Collins*	.40
364	Elias Sosa	.30
365	Carlton Fisk	4.00
366	Bobby Valentine	.30
367	Bruce Miller	.30
368	Wilbur Wood	.30
369	Frank White	.30
370	Ron Cey	.30
371	Ellie Hendricks	.30
372	Rick Baldwin	.30
373	Johnny Briggs	.30
374	Dan Warthen	.30
375	Ron Fairly	.30
376	Rich Hebner	.30
377	Mike Hegan	.30
378	Steve Stone	.30
379	Ken Boswell	.30
380	Bobby Bonds	.45
381	Denny Doyle	.30
382	Matt Alexander	.30
383	John Ellis	.30
384	Phillies Team(Danny Ozark)	.80
385	Mickey Lolich	.35
386	Ed Goodson	.30
387	Mike Miley	.30
388	Stan Perzanowski	.30
389	Glenn Adams	.30
390	Don Gullett	.30
391	Jerry Hairston	.30
392	Checklist 265-396	.35
393	Paul Mitchell	.30
394	Fran Healy	.30
395	Jim Wynn	.30
396	Bill Lee	.30
397	Tim Foli	.30
398	Dave Tomlin	.30
399	Luis Melendez	.30
400	Rod Carew	4.00
401	Ken Brett	.30
402	Don Money	.30
403	Geoff Zahn	.30
404	Enos Cabell	.30
405	Rollie Fingers	2.00
406	Ed Herrmann	.30
407	Tom Underwood	.30
408	Charlie Spikes	.30
409	Dave Lemanczyk	.30
410	Ralph Garr	.30
411	Bill Singer	.30
412	Toby Harrah	.30
413	Pete Varney	.30
414	Wayne Garland	.30
415	Vada Pinson	.40
416	Tommy John	.60
417	Gene Clines	.30
418	Jose Morales	.30
419	Reggie Cleveland	.30
420	Joe Morgan	4.00
421	A's Team	.50
422	Johnny Grubb	.30
423	Ed Halicki	.30
424	Phil Roof	.30
425	Rennie Stennett	.30
426	Bob Forsch	.30
427	Kurt Bevacqua	.30
428	Jim Crawford	.30
429	Fred Stanley	.30
430	Jose Cardenal	.30
431	Dick Ruthven	.30
432	Tom Veryzer	.30
433	Rick Waits	.30
434	Morris Nettles	.30
435	Phil Niekro	3.50
436	Bill Fahey	.30
437	Terry Forster	.30
438	Doug DeCinces	.30
439	Rick Rhoden	.30
440	John Mayberry	.30
441	Gary Carter	5.00
442	Hank Webb	.30
443	Giants Team	.50
444	Gary Nolan	.30
445	Rico Petrocelli	.30
446	Larry Haney	.30
447	Gene Locklear	.30
448	Tom Johnson	.30
449	Bob Robertson	.30
450	Jim Palmer	3.50
451	Buddy Bradford	.30
452	Tom Hausman	.30
453	Lou Piniella	.35
454	Tom Griffin	.30
455	Dick Allen	.50
456	Joe Coleman	.30
457	Ed Crosby	.30
458	Earl Williams	.30
459	Jim Brewer	.30
460	Cesar Cedeno	.30
461	NL & AL Championships	.50
462	1975 World Series	.50
463	Steve Hargan	.30
464	Ken Henderson	.30
465	Mike Marshall	.30
466	Bob Stinson	.30
467	Woodie Fryman	.30
468	Jesus Alou	.30
469	Rawly Eastwick	.30
470	Bobby Murcer	.30
471	Jim Burton	.30
472	Bob Davis	.30
473	Paul Blair	.30
474	Ray Corbin	.30
475	Joe Rudi	.30
476	Bob Moose	.30
477	Indians Team(Frank Robinson)	.80
478	Lynn McGlothen	.30
479	Bobby Mitchell	.30
480	Mike Schmidt	24.00
481	Rudy May	.30
482	Tim Hosley	.30
483	Mickey Stanley	.30
484	Eric Raich	.30
485	Mike Hargrove	.30
486	Bruce Dal Canton	.30
487	Leron Lee	.30
488	Claude Osteen	.30
489	Skip Jutze	.30
490	Frank Tanana	.30
491	Terry Crowley	.30
492	Marty Pattin	.30
493	Derrel Thomas	.30
494	Craig Swan	.30
495	Nate Colbert	.30
496	Juan Beniquez	.30
497	Joe McIntosh	.30
498	Glenn Borgmann	.30
499	Mario Guerrero	.30
500	Reggie Jackson	13.50
501	Billy Champion	.30
502	Tim McCarver	.40
503	Elliott Maddox	.30
504	Pirates Team(Danny Murtaugh)	.50
505	Mark Belanger	.30
506	George Mitterwald	.30
507	Ray Bare	.30
508	*Duane Kuiper*	.30
509	Bill Hands	.30

No.	Player	Price
510	Amos Otis	.30
511	Jamie Easterly	.30
512	Ellie Rodriguez	.30
513	Bart Johnson	.30
514	Dan Driessen	.30
515	Steve Yeager	.30
516	Wayne Granger	.30
517	John Milner	.30
518	*Doug Flynn*	.30
519	Steve Brye	.30
520	Willie McCovey	2.75
521	Jim Colborn	.30
522	Ted Sizemore	.30
523	Bob Montgomery	.30
524	Pete Falcone	.30
525	Billy Williams	2.00
526	Checklist 397-528	.35
527	Mike Anderson	.30
528	Dock Ellis	.30
529	Deron Johnson	.30
530	Don Sutton	2.50
531	Mets Team(Joe Frazier)	.75
532	Milt May	.30
533	Lee Richard	.30
534	Stan Bahnsen	.30
535	Dave Nelson	.30
536	Mike Thompson	.30
537	Tony Muser	.30
538	Pat Darcy	.30
539	John Balaz	.30
540	Bill Freehan	.30
541	Steve Mingori	.30
542	Keith Hernandez	1.00
543	Wayne Twitchell	.30
544	Pepe Frias	.30
545	Sparky Lyle	.30
546	Dave Rosello	.30
547	Roric Harrison	.30
548	Manny Mota	.30
549	Randy Tate	.30
550	Hank Aaron	18.00
551	Jerry DaVanon	.30
552	Terry Humphrey	.30
553	Randy Moffitt	.30
554	Ray Fosse	.30
555	Dyar Miller	.30
556	Twins Team(Gene Mauch)	.30
557	Dan Spillner	.30
558	Cito Gaston	.30
559	Clyde Wright	.30
560	Jorge Orta	.30
561	Tom Carroll	.30
562	Adrian Garrett	.30
563	Larry Demery	.30
564	Kurt Bevacqua (Bubble Gum Blowing Champ)	.30
565	Tug McGraw	.30
566	Ken McMullen	.30
567	George Stone	.30
568	Rob Andrews	.30
569	Nelson Briles	.30
570	George Hendrick	.30
571	Don DeMola	.30
572	Rich Coggins	.30
573	Bill Travers	.30
574	Don Kessinger	.30
575	Dwight Evans	1.00
576	Maximino Leon	.30
577	Marc Hill	.30
578	Ted Kubiak	.30
579	Clay Kirby	.30
580	Bert Campaneris	.30
581	Cardinals Team(Red Schoendienst)	.50
582	Mike Kekich	.30
583	Tommy Helms	.30
584	Stan Wall	.30
585	Joe Torre	.30
586	Ron Schueler	.30
587	Leo Cardenas	.30
588	Kevin Kobel	.30
589	Rookie Pitchers(Santo Alcala), (*Mike Flanagan*, Joe Pactwa, Pablo Torrealba)	1.00
590	Rookie Outfielders(Henry Cruz), (*Chet Lemon*), (*Ellis Valentine*, Terry Whitfield)	.75
591	Rookie Pitchers(Steve Grilli, Craig Mitchell, Jose Sosa, George Throop)	.30
592	Rookie Infielders(*Dave McKay*), (*Willie Randolph*), (*Jerry Royster*), (*Roy Staiger*)	3.00
593	Rookie Pitchers(Larry Anderson, Ken Crosby, Mark Littell), (*Butch Metzger*)	.30
594	Rookie Catchers & Outfielders(Andy Merchant, Ed Ott, Royle Stillman, Jerry White)	.30
595	Rookie Pitchers(Steve Barr, Art DeFilippis, Randy Lerch, Sid Monge)	.30
596	Rookie Infielders(Lamar Johnson), (*Johnny LeMaster*, Jerry Manuel), (*Craig Reynolds*)	.30
597	Rookie Pitchers(*Don Aase*, Jack Kucek, Frank LaCorte, Mike Pazik)	.30
598	Rookie Outfielders(Hector Cruz), (*Jamie Quirk*, Jerry Turner, Joe Wallis)	.30
599	Rookie Pitchers(*Rob Dressler*), (*Ron Guidry*), (*Bob McClure*), (*Pat Zachry*)	4.00
600	Tom Seaver	6.00
601	Ken Rudolph	.30
602	Doug Konieczny	.30
603	Jim Holt	.30
604	Joe Lovitto	.30
605	Al Downing	.30
606	Brewers Team(Alex Grammas)	.50
607	Rich Hinton	.30
608	Vic Correll	.30
609	Fred Norman	.30
610	Greg Luzinski	.30
611	Rich Folkers	.30
612	Joe Lahoud	.30
613	Tim Johnson	.30
614	Fernando Arroyo	.30
615	Mike Cubbage	.30
616	Buck Martinez	.30
617	Darold Knowles	.30
618	Jack Brohamer	.30
619	Bill Butler	.30
620	Al Oliver	.40
621	Tom Hall	.30
622	Rick Auerbach	.30
623	Bob Allietta	.30
624	Tony Taylor	.30
625	J.R. Richard	.30
626	Bob Sheldon	.30
627	Bill Plummer	.30
628	John D'Acquisto	.30
629	Sandy Alomar	.30
630	Chris Speier	.30
631	Braves Team(Dave Bristol)	.50
632	Rogelio Moret	.30
633	*John Stearns*	.30
634	Larry Christenson	.30
635	Jim Fregosi	.30
636	Joe Decker	.30
637	Bruce Bochte	.30
638	Doyle Alexander	.30
639	Fred Kendall	.30
640	Bill Madlock	.45
641	Tom Paciorek	.30
642	Dennis Blair	.30
643	Checklist 529-660	.35
644	Tom Bradley	.30
645	Darrell Porter	.30
646	John Lowenstein	.30
648	Al Cowens	.30
649	Dave Roberts	.30
650	Thurman Munson	5.00
651	John Odom	.30
652	Ed Armbrister	.30
653	*Mike Norris*	.30
654	Doug Griffin	.30
655	Mike Vail	.30
656	White Sox Team(Chuck Tanner)	.50
657	*Roy Smalley*	.30
658	Jerry Johnson	.30
659	Ben Oglivie	.30
660	Dave Lopes	.30

1977 Topps

The 1977 Topps Set is a 660-card effort featuring front designs dominated by a color photograph on which there is a facsimile autograph. Above the picture are the player's name, team and position. The backs of the 2-1/2" x 3-1/2" cards include personal and career statistics along with newspaper-style highlights and a cartoon. Specialty cards include statistical leaders, record performances, a new "Turn Back The Clock" feature which highlighted great past moments and a "Big League Brothers" feature.

No.	Player	NM
	Complete Set (660):	325.00
	Common Player:	.20
1	Batting Leaders(George Brett, Bill Madlock)	3.00
2	Home Run Leaders(Graig Nettles, Mike Schmidt)	1.00
3	RBI Leaders(George Foster, Lee May)	.20
4	Stolen Base Leaders(Dave Lopes, Bill North)	.20
5	Victory Leaders(Randy Jones, Jim Palmer)	.40
6	Strikeout Leaders(Nolan Ryan, Tom Seaver)	9.00
7	ERA Leaders(John Denny, Mark Fidrych)	.20
8	Leading Firemen(Bill Campbell, Rawly Eastwick)	.20
9	Doug Rader	.20
10	Reggie Jackson	12.00
11	Rob Dressler	.20
12	Larry Haney	.20
13	Luis Gomez	.20
14	Tommy Smith	.20
15	Don Gullett	.20
16	Bob Jones	.20
17	Steve Stone	.25
18	Indians Team(Frank Robinson)	2.00
19	John D'Acquisto	.20
20	Graig Nettles	.25
21	Ken Forsch	.20
22	Bill Freehan	.20
23	Dan Driessen	.20
24	Carl Morton	.20
25	Dwight Evans	.90
26	Ray Sadecki	.20
27	Bill Buckner	.20
28	Woodie Fryman	.20
29	Bucky Dent	.20
30	Greg Luzinski	.25
31	Jim Todd	.20
32	Checklist 1-132	.25
33	Wayne Garland	.20
34	Angels Team(Norm Sherry)	.35
35	Rennie Stennett	.20
36	John Ellis	.20
37	Steve Hargan	.20
38	Craig Kusick	.20
39	Tom Griffin	.20
40	Bobby Murcer	.20
41	Jim Kern	.20
42	Jose Cruz	.20
43	Ray Bare	.20
44	Bud Harrelson	.20
45	Rawly Eastwick	.20
46	Buck Martinez	.20
47	Lynn McGlothen	.20
48	Tom Paciorek	.20
49	Grant Jackson	.20
50	Ron Cey	.35
51	Brewers Team(Alex Grammas)	.35
52	Ellis Valentine	.20
53	Paul Mitchell	.20
54	Sandy Alomar	.20
55	Jeff Burroughs	.20
56	Rudy May	.20
57	Marc Hill	.20
58	Chet Lemon	.20
59	Larry Christenson	.20
60	Jim Rice	1.50
61	Manny Sanguillen	.20
62	Eric Raich	.20
63	Tito Fuentes	.20
64	Larry Biittner	.20
65	Skip Lockwood	.20
66	Roy Smalley	.20
67	*Joaquin Andujar*	.20
68	Bruce Bochte	.20
69	Jim Crawford	.20
70	Johnny Bench	5.00
71	Dock Ellis	.20
72	Mike Anderson	.20

73	Charlie Williams	.20
74	A's Team(Jack McKeon)	.35
75	Dennis Leonard	.20
76	Tim Foli	.20
77	Dyar Miller	.20
78	Bob Davis	.20
79	Don Money	.20
80	Andy Messersmith	.20
81	Juan Beniquez	.20
82	Jim Rooker	.20
83	Kevin Bell	.20
84	Ollie Brown	.20
85	Duane Kuiper	.20
86	Pat Zachry	.20
87	Glenn Borgmann	.20
88	Stan Wall	.20
89	*Butch Hobson*	.20
90	Cesar Cedeno	.20
91	John Verhoeven	.20
92	Dave Rosello	.20
93	Tom Poquette	.20
94	Craig Swan	.20
95	Keith Hernandez	.90
96	Lou Piniella	.30
97	Dave Heaverlo	.20
98	Milt May	.20
99	Tom Hausman	.20
100	Joe Morgan	2.50
101	Dick Bosman	.20
102	Jose Morales	.20
103	Mike Bacsik	.20
104	*Omar Moreno*	.20
105	Steve Yeager	.20
106	Mike Flanagan	.20
107	Bill Melton	.20
108	Alan Foster	.20
109	Jorge Orta	.20
110	Steve Carlton	4.50
111	Rico Petrocelli	.20
112	Bill Greif	.20
113	Blue Jays Mgr./Coaches(Roy Hartsfield, Don Leppert, Bob Miller, Jackie Moore, Harry Warner)	.90
114	Bruce Dal Canton	.20
115	Rick Manning	.20
116	Joe Niekro	.20
117	Frank White	.20
118	Rick Jones	.20
119	John Stearns	.20
120	Rod Carew	6.00
121	Gary Nolan	.20
122	Ben Oglivie	.20
123	Fred Stanley	.20
124	George Mitterwald	.20
125	Bill Travers	.20
126	Rod Gilbreath	.20
127	Ron Fairly	.20
128	Tommy John	.30
129	Mike Sadek	.20
130	Al Oliver	.40
131	Orlando Ramirez	.20
132	Chip Lang	.20
133	Ralph Garr	.20
134	Padres Team(John McNamara)	.35
135	Mark Belanger	.20
136	*Jerry Mumphrey*	.20
137	Jeff Terpko	.20
138	Bob Stinson	.20
139	Fred Norman	.20
140	Mike Schmidt	15.00
141	Mark Littell	.20
142	Steve Dillard	.20
143	Ed Herrmann	.20
144	*Bruce Sutter*	3.00
145	Tom Veryzer	.20
146	Dusty Baker	.25
147	Jackie Brown	.20
148	Fran Healy	.20
149	Mike Cubbage	.20
150	Tom Seaver	6.00
151	Johnnie LeMaster	.20
152	Gaylord Perry	2.00
153	Ron Jackson	.20
154	Dave Giusti	.20
155	Joe Rudi	.20
156	Pete Mackanin	.20
157	Ken Brett	.20
158	Ted Kubiak	.20
159	Bernie Carbo	.20
160	Will McEnaney	.20
161	*Garry Templeton*	.60
162	Mike Cuellar	.20
163	Dave Hilton	.20
164	Tug McGraw	.20
165	Jim Wynn	.20
166	Bill Campbell	.20
167	Rich Hebner	.20
168	Charlie Spikes	.20
169	Darold Knowles	.20
170	Thurman Munson	3.50
171	Ken Sanders	.20
172	John Milner	.20
173	Chuck Scrivener	.20
174	Nelson Briles	.20
175	*Butch Wynegar*	.20
176	Bob Robertson	.20
177	Bart Johnson	.20
178	Bombo Rivera	.20
179	Paul Hartzell	.20
180	Dave Lopes	.20
181	Ken McMullen	.20
182	Dan Spillner	.20
183	Cardinals Team(Vern Rapp)	.35
184	Bo McLaughlin	.20
185	Sixto Lezcano	.20
186	Doug Flynn	.20
187	Dick Pole	.20
188	Bob Tolan	.20
189	Rick Dempsey	.20
190	Ray Burris	.20
191	Doug Griffin	.20
192	Clarence Gaston	.20
193	Larry Gura	.20
194	Gary Matthews	.20
195	Ed Figueroa	.20
196	Len Randle	.20
197	Ed Ott	.20
198	Wilbur Wood	.20
199	Pepe Frias	.20
200	Frank Tanana	.20
201	Ed Kranepool	.20
202	Tom Johnson	.20
203	Ed Armbrister	.20
204	Jeff Newman	.20
205	Pete Falcone	.20
206	Boog Powell	.50
207	Glenn Abbott	.20
208	Checklist 133-264	.25
209	Rob Andrews	.20
210	Fred Lynn	.60
211	Giants Team(Joe Altobelli)	.35
212	Jim Mason	.20
213	Maximino Leon	.20
214	Darrell Porter	.20
215	Butch Metzger	.20
216	Doug DeCinces	.20
217	Tom Underwood	.20
218	*John Wathan*	.20
219	Joe Coleman	.20
220	Chris Chambliss	.20
221	Bob Bailey	.20
222	Francisco Barrios	.20
223	Earl Williams	.20
224	Rusty Torres	.20
225	Bob Apodaca	.20
226	Leroy Stanton	.20
227	*Joe Sambito*	.20
228	Twins Team(Gene Mauch)	.35
229	Don Kessinger	.25
230	Vida Blue	.20
231	George Brett (Record Breaker)	8.00
232	Minnie Minoso (Record Breaker)	.35
233	Jose Morales (Record Breaker)	.20
234	Nolan Ryan (Record Breaker)	20.00
235	Cecil Cooper	.20
236	Tom Buskey	.20
237	Gene Clines	.20
238	Tippy Martinez	.20
239	Bill Plummer	.20
240	Ron LeFlore	.20
241	Dave Tomlin	.20
242	Ken Henderson	.20
243	Ron Reed	.20
244	John Mayberry	.20
245	Rick Rhoden	.20
246	Mike Vail	.20
247	Chris Knapp	.20
248	Wilbur Howard	.20
249	Pete Redfern	.20
250	Bill Madlock	.30
251	Tony Muser	.20
252	Dale Murray	.20
253	John Hale	.20
254	Doyle Alexander	.20
255	George Scott	.20
256	Joe Hoerner	.20
257	Mike Miley	.20
258	Luis Tiant	.20
259	Mets Team(Joe Frazier)	.50
260	J.R. Richard	.25
261	Phil Garner	.20
262	Al Cowens	.20
263	Mike Marshall	.20
264	Tom Hutton	.20
265	*Mark Fidrych*	.90
266	Derrel Thomas	.20
267	Ray Fosse	.20
268	Rick Sawyer	.20
269	Joe Lis	.20
270	Dave Parker	1.50
271	Terry Forster	.20
272	Lee Lacy	.20
273	Eric Soderholm	.20
274	Don Stanhouse	.20
275	Mike Hargrove	.20
276	A.L. Championship (Chambliss' Dramatic Homer Decides It)	.25
277	N.L. Championship (Reds Sweep Phillies 3 In Row)	.25
278	Danny Frisella	.20
279	Joe Wallis	.20
280	Catfish Hunter	1.25
281	Roy Staiger	.20
282	Sid Monge	.20
283	Jerry DaVanon	.20
284	Mike Norris	.20
285	Brooks Robinson	6.00
286	Johnny Grubb	.20
287	Reds Team(Sparky Anderson)	.80
288	Bob Montgomery	.20
289	Gene Garber	.20
290	Amos Otis	.20
291	*Jason Thompson*	.20
292	Rogelio Moret	.20
293	Jack Brohamer	.20
294	George Medich	.20
295	Gary Carter	3.00
296	Don Hood	.20
297	Ken Reitz	.20
298	Charlie Hough	.20
299	Otto Velez	.20
300	Jerry Koosman	.20
301	Toby Harrah	.20
302	Mike Garman	.20
303	Gene Tenace	.20
304	Jim Hughes	.20
305	Mickey Rivers	.20
306	Rick Waits	.20
307	Gary Sutherland	.20
308	Gene Pentz	.20
309	Red Sox Team(Don Zimmer)	.35
310	Larry Bowa	.20
311	Vern Ruhle	.20
312	Rob Belloir	.20
313	Paul Blair	.20
314	Steve Mingori	.20
315	Dave Chalk	.20
316	Steve Rogers	.20
317	Kurt Bevacqua	.20
318	Duffy Dyer	.20
319	Rich Gossage	.25
320	Ken Griffey	.30
321	Dave Goltz	.20
322	Bill Russell	.25
323	Larry Lintz	.20
324	John Curtis	.20
325	Mike Ivie	.20
326	Jesse Jefferson	.20
327	Astros Team(Bill Virdon)	.35
328	Tommy Boggs	.20
329	Ron Hodges	.20
330	George Hendrick	.20
331	Jim Colborn	.20
332	Elliott Maddox	.20
333	Paul Reuschel	.20
334	Bill Stein	.20
335	Bill Robinson	.20
336	Denny Doyle	.20
337	Ron Schueler	.20
338	Dave Duncan	.20
339	Adrian Devine	.20
340	Hal McRae	.25
341	Joe Kerrigan	.20
342	Jerry Remy	.20
343	Ed Halicki	.20
344	Brian Downing	.20
345	Reggie Smith	.20
346	Bill Singer	.20

347	George Foster	.30
348	Brent Strom	.20
349	Jim Holt	.20
350	Larry Dierker	.20
351	Jim Sundberg	.20
352	Mike Phillips	.20
353	Stan Thomas	.20
354	Pirates Team(Chuck Tanner)	.35
355	Lou Brock	2.50
356	Checklist 265-396	.25
357	Tim McCarver	.30
358	Tom House	.20
359	Willie Randolph	.25
360	Rick Monday	.20
361	Eduardo Rodriguez	.20
362	Tommy Davis	.20
363	Dave Roberts	.20
364	Vic Correll	.20
365	Mike Torrez	.20
366	Ted Sizemore	.20
367	Dave Hamilton	.20
368	Mike Jorgensen	.20
369	Terry Humphrey	.20
370	John Montefusco	.20
371	Royals Team(Whitey Herzog)	.90
372	Rich Folkers	.20
373	Bert Campaneris	.20
374	Kent Tekulve	.20
375	Larry Hisle	.20
376	Nino Espinosa	.20
377	Dave McKay	.20
378	Jim Umbarger	.20
379	Larry Cox	.20
380	Lee May	.20
381	Bob Forsch	.20
382	Charlie Moore	.20
383	Stan Bahnsen	.20
384	Darrel Chaney	.20
385	Dave LaRoche	.20
386	Manny Mota	.20
387	Yankees Team(Billy Martin)	1.00
388	Terry Harmon	.20
389	Ken Kravec	.20
390	Dave Winfield	15.00
391	Dan Warthen	.20
392	Phil Roof	.20
393	John Lowenstein	.20
394	Bill Laxton	.20
395	Manny Trillo	.20
396	Tom Murphy	.20
397	*Larry Herndon*	.20
398	Tom Burgmeier	.20
399	Bruce Boisclair	.20
400	Steve Garvey	3.00
401	Mickey Scott	.20
402	Tommy Helms	.20
403	Tom Grieve	.20
404	Eric Rasmussen	.20
405	Claudell Washington	.20
406	Tim Johnson	.20
407	Dave Freisleben	.20
408	Cesar Tovar	.20
409	Pete Broberg	.20
410	Willie Montanez	.20
411	World Series Games 1 & 2(Joe Morgan, Johnny Bench)	.75
412	World Series Games 3 & 4(Johnny Bench)	.75
413	World Series Summary	.45
414	Tommy Harper	.20
415	Jay Johnstone	.20
416	Chuck Hartenstein	.20
417	Wayne Garrett	.20
418	White Sox Team(Bob Lemon)	.35
419	Steve Swisher	.20
420	Rusty Staub	.25
421	Doug Rau	.20
422	Freddie Patek	.20
423	Gary Lavelle	.20
424	Steve Brye	.20
425	Joe Torre	.25
426	Dick Drago	.20
427	Dave Rader	.20
428	Rangers Team(Frank Lucchesi)	.35
429	Ken Boswell	.20
430	Fergie Jenkins	1.75
431	Dave Collins	.20
432	Buzz Capra	.20
433	Nate Colbert (Turn Back The Clock)	.20

434	Carl Yastrzemski (Turn Back The Clock)	.90
435	Maury Wills (Turn Back The Clock)	.35
436	Bob Keegan (Turn Back The Clock)	.20
437	Ralph Kiner (Turn Back The Clock)	.25
438	Marty Perez	.20
439	Gorman Thomas	.20
440	Jon Matlack	.20
441	Larvell Blanks	.20
442	Braves Team(Dave Bristol)	.35
443	Lamar Johnson	.20
444	Wayne Twitchell	.20
445	Ken Singleton	.20
446	Bill Bonham	.20
447	Jerry Turner	.20
448	Ellie Rodriguez	.20
449	Al Fitzmorris	.20
450	Pete Rose	10.00
451	Checklist 397-528	.25
452	Mike Caldwell	.20
453	Pedro Garcia	.20
454	Andy Etchebarren	.20
455	Rick Wise	.20
456	Leon Roberts	.20
457	Steve Luebber	.20
458	Leo Foster	.20
459	Steve Foucault	.20
460	Willie Stargell	2.00
461	Dick Tidrow	.20
462	Don Baylor	.30
463	Jamie Quirk	.20
464	Randy Moffitt	.20
465	Rico Carty	.20
466	Fred Holdsworth	.20
467	Phillies Team(Danny Ozark)	.50
468	Ramon Hernandez	.20
469	Pat Kelly	.20
470	Ted Simmons	.20
471	Del Unser	.20
472	Rookie Pitchers(Don Aase, Bob McClure, Gil Patterson, Dave Wehrmeister)	.20
473	Rookie Outfielders(*Andre Dawson*), (*Gene Richards*), (*John Scott*), (*Denny Walling*)	50.00
474	Rookie Shortstops(Bob Bailor, Kiko Garcia, Craig Reynolds, Alex Taveras)	.20
475	Rookie Pitchers(Chris Batton, Rick Camp, Scott McGregor, Manny Sarmiento)	.20
476	Rookie Catchers(*Gary Alexander*), (*Rick Cerone*), (*Dale Murphy*), (*Kevin Pasley*)	18.00
477	Rookie Infielders(Doug Ault), (*Rich Dauer*), Orlando Gonzalez, Phil Mankowski)	.20
478	Rookie Pitchers(Jim Gideon, Leon Hooten, Dave Johnson, Mark Lemongello)	.20
479	Rookie Outfielders(Brian Asselstine), (*Wayne Gross*), Sam Mejias, Alvis Woods)	.20
480	Carl Yastrzemski	4.50
481	Roger Metzger	.20
482	Tony Solaita	.20
483	Richie Zisk	.20
484	Burt Hooton	.20
485	Roy White	.25
486	Ed Bane	.20
487	Rookie Pitchers(Larry Anderson, Ed Glynn, Joe Henderson, Greg Terlecky)	.20
488	Rookie Outfielders(*Jack Clark*), (*Ruppert Jones*), (*Lee Mazzilli*), (*Dan Thomas*)	4.00
489	Rookie Pitchers(*Len Barker*, Randy Lerch), (*Greg Minton*, Mike Overy)	.40
490	Rookie Shortstops(*Billy Almon*, Mickey Klutts, Tommy McMillan, Mark Wagner)	.20
491	Rookie Pitchers(*Mike Dupree*), (*Dennis Martinez*), (*Craig Mitchell*), (*Bob Sykes*)	10.00
492	Rookie Outfielders(*Tony Armas*), (*Steve Kemp*), (*Carlos Lopez*), (*Gary Woods*)	.80

493	Rookie Pitchers(*Mike Krukow*, Jim Otten, Gary Wheelock, Mike Willis)	.30
494	Rookie Infielders(Juan Bernhardt, Mike Champion), (*Jim Gantner*), (*Bump Wills*)	.35
495	Al Hrabosky	.20
496	Gary Thomasson	.20
497	Clay Carroll	.20
498	Sal Bando	.20
499	Pablo Torrealba	.20
500	Dave Kingman	.30
501	Jim Bibby	.20
502	Randy Hundley	.20
503	Bill Lee	.20
504	Dodgers Team(Tom Lasorda)	1.50
505	Oscar Gamble	.20
506	Steve Grilli	.20
507	Mike Hegan	.20
508	Dave Pagan	.20
509	Cookie Rojas	.20
510	John Candelaria	.20
511	Bill Fahey	.20
512	Jack Billingham	.20
513	Jerry Terrell	.20
514	Cliff Johnson	.20
515	Chris Speier	.20
516	Bake McBride	.20
517	*Pete Vuckovich*	.50
518	Cubs Team(Herman Franks)	.35
519	Don Kirkwood	.20
520	Garry Maddox	.20
521	Bob Grich	.20
522	Enzo Hernandez	.20
523	Rollie Fingers	2.00
524	Rowland Office	.20
525	Dennis Eckersley	8.00
526	Larry Parrish	.20
527	Dan Meyer	.20
528	Bill Castro	.20
529	Jim Essian	.20
530	Rick Reuschel	.20
531	Lyman Bostock	.20
532	Jim Willoughby	.20
533	Mickey Stanley	.20
534	Paul Splittorff	.20
535	Cesar Geronimo	.20
536	Vic Albury	.20
537	Dave Roberts	.20
538	Frank Taveras	.20
539	Mike Wallace	.20
540	Bob Watson	.20
541	John Denny	.20
542	Frank Duffy	.20
543	Ron Blomberg	.20
544	Gary Ross	.20
545	Bob Boone	.30
546	Orioles Team(Earl Weaver)	.90
547	Willie McCovey	2.50
548	*Joel Youngblood*	.20
549	Jerry Royster	.20
550	Randy Jones	.20
551	Bill North	.20
552	Pepe Mangual	.20
553	Jack Heidemann	.20
554	Bruce Kimm	.20
555	Dan Ford	.20
556	Doug Bird	.20
557	Jerry White	.20
558	Elias Sosa	.20
559	Alan Bannister	.20
560	Dave Concepcion	.30
561	Pete LaCock	.20
562	Checklist 529-660	.25
563	Bruce Kison	.20
564	Alan Ashby	.20
565	Mickey Lolich	.25
566	Rick Miller	.20
567	Enos Cabell	.20
568	Carlos May	.20
569	Jim Lonborg	.20
570	Bobby Bonds	.30
571	Darrell Evans	.35
572	Ross Grimsley	.20
573	Joe Ferguson	.20
574	Aurelio Rodriguez	.20
575	Dick Ruthven	.20
576	Fred Kendall	.20
577	Jerry Augustine	.20
578	Bob Randall	.20
579	Don Carrithers	.20
580	George Brett	30.00
581	Pedro Borbon	.20
582	Ed Kirkpatrick	.20

583	Paul Lindblad	.20
584	Ed Goodson	.20
585	Rick Burleson	.20
586	Steve Renko	.20
587	Rick Baldwin	.20
588	Dave Moates	.20
589	Mike Cosgrove	.20
590	Buddy Bell	.20
591	Chris Arnold	.20
592	Dan Briggs	.20
593	Dennis Blair	.20
594	Biff Pocoroba	.20
595	John Hiller	.20
596	*Jerry Martin*	.20
597	Mariners	1.25
	Mgr./Coaches(Don Bryant,	
	Jim Busby, Darrell Johnson,	
	Vada Pinson, Wes Stock)	
598	Sparky Lyle	.20
599	Mike Tyson	.20
600	Jim Palmer	3.00
601	Mike Lum	.20
602	Andy Hassler	.20
603	Willie Davis	.20
604	Jim Slaton	.20
605	Felix Millan	.20
606	Steve Braun	.20
607	Larry Demery	.20
608	Roy Howell	.20
609	Jim Barr	.20
610	Jose Cardenal	.20
611	Dave Lemanczyk	.20
612	Barry Foote	.20
613	Reggie Cleveland	.20
614	Greg Gross	.20
615	Phil Niekro	2.50
616	Tommy Sandt	.20
617	Bobby Darwin	.20
618	Pat Dobson	.20
619	Johnny Oates	.20
620	Don Sutton	3.00
621	Tigers Team(Ralph Houk)	.45
622	Jim Wohlford	.20
623	Jack Kucek	.20
624	Hector Cruz	.20
625	Ken Holtzman	.20
626	Al Bumbry	.20
627	Bob Myrick	.20
628	Mario Guerrero	.20
629	Bobby Valentine	.20
630	Bert Blyleven	.40
631	Big League	5.00
	Brothers(George Brett, Ken	
	Brett)	
632	Big League Brothers(Bob	.20
	Forsch, Ken Forsch)	
633	Big League Brothers(Carlos	.20
	May, Lee May)	
634	Big League Brothers(Paul	.20
	Reuschel, Rick Reuschel)	
	(names switched)	
635	Robin Yount	22.00
636	Santo Alcala	.20
637	Alex Johnson	.20
638	Jim Kaat	.45
639	Jerry Morales	.20
640	Carlton Fisk	3.00
641	Dan Larson	.20
642	Willie Crawford	.20
643	Mike Pazik	.20
644	Matt Alexander	.20
645	Jerry Reuss	.20
646	Andres Mora	.20
647	Expos Team(Dick Williams)	.35
648	Jim Spencer	.20
649	Dave Cash	.20
650	Nolan Ryan	40.00
651	Von Joshua	.20
652	Tom Walker	.20
653	Diego Segui	.20
654	Ron Pruitt	.20
655	Tony Perez	.75
656	Ron Guidry	.50
657	Mick Kelleher	.20
658	Marty Pattin	.20
659	Merv Rettenmund	.20
660	Willie Horton	.20

1978 Topps

At 726 cards, this was the largest issue from Topps since 1972. In design, the color player photo is slightly larger than usual, with the player's name and team at the bottom. In the upper right-hand corner of the 2-1/2" x 3-1/2" cards there is a small white baseball with the player's position. Most of the starting All-Stars from the previous year had a red, white and blue shield instead of the baseball. Backs feature statistics and a baseball situation which made a card game of baseball possible. Specialty cards include baseball records, statistical leaders and the World Series and playoffs. As one row of cards per sheet had to be doubleprinted to accommodate the 726-card set size, some cards are more common, yet that seems to have no serious impact on their prices.

		NM
Complete Set (726):		225.00
Common Player:		.20
1	Lou Brock (Record Breaker)	1.25
2	Sparky Lyle (Record Breaker)	.20
3	Willie McCovey (Record Breaker)	.75
4	Brooks Robinson (Record Breaker)	1.50
5	Pete Rose (Record Breaker)	3.00
6	Nolan Ryan (Record Breaker)	12.50
7	Reggie Jackson (Record Breaker)	2.00
8	Mike Sadek	.20
9	Doug DeCinces	.20
10	Phil Niekro	2.00
11	Rick Manning	.20
12	Don Aase	.20
13	Art Howe	.20
14	Lerrin LaGrow	.20
15	Tony Perez	.45
16	Roy White	.20
17	Mike Krukow	.20
18	Bob Grich	.20
19	Darrell Porter	.20
20	Pete Rose	8.00
21	Steve Kemp	.20
22	Charlie Hough	.20
23	Bump Wills	.20
24	Don Money	.20
25	Jon Matlack	.20
26	Rich Hebner	.20
27	Geoff Zahn	.20
28	Ed Ott	.20
29	Bob Lacey	.20
30	George Hendrick	.20
31	Glenn Abbott	.20
32	Garry Templeton	.20
33	Dave Lemanczyk	.20
34	Willie McCovey	2.50
35	Sparky Lyle	.30
36	*Eddie Murray*	125.00
37	Rick Waits	.20
38	Willie Montanez	.20
39	*Floyd Bannister*	.60
40	Carl Yastrzemski	4.00
41	Burt Hooton	.20
42	Jorge Orta	.20
43	Bill Atkinson	.20
44	Toby Harrah	.20
45	Mark Fidrych	.25
46	Al Cowens	.20
47	Jack Billingham	.20
48	Don Baylor	.30
49	Ed Kranepool	.20
50	Rick Reuschel	.20
51	Charlie Moore	.20
52	Jim Lonborg	.20
53	Phil Garner	.20
54	Tom Johnson	.20
55	Mitchell Page	.20
56	Randy Jones	.20
57	Dan Meyer	.20
58	Bob Forsch	.20
59	Otto Velez	.20
60	Thurman Munson	6.00
61	Larvell Blanks	.20
62	Jim Barr	.20
63	Don Zimmer	.20
64	Gene Pentz	.20

65	Ken Singleton	.20
66	White Sox Team	.25
67	Claudell Washington	.20
68	Steve Foucault	.20
69	Mike Vail	.20
70	Rich Gossage	.20
71	Terry Humphrey	.20
72	Andre Dawson	12.00
73	Andy Hassler	.20
74	Checklist 1-121	.20
75	Dick Ruthven	.20
76	Steve Ontiveros	.20
77	Ed Kirkpatrick	.20
78	Pablo Torrealba	.20
79	Darrell Johnson (DP)	.20
80	Ken Griffey	.25
81	Pete Redfern	.20
82	Giants Team	.25
83	Bob Montgomery	.20
84	Kent Tekulve	.20
85	Ron Fairly	.20
86	Dave Tomlin	.20
87	John Lowenstein	.20
88	Mike Phillips	.20
89	Ken Clay	.20
90	Larry Bowa	.20
91	Oscar Zamora	.20
92	Adrian Devine	.20
93	Bobby Cox	.25
94	Chuck Scrivener	.20
95	Jamie Quirk	.20
96	Orioles Team	.25
97	Stan Bahnsen	.20
98	Jim Essian	.20
99	*Willie Hernandez*	.30
100	George Brett	20.00
101	Sid Monge	.20
102	Matt Alexander	.20
103	Tom Murphy	.20
104	Lee Lacy	.20
105	Reggie Cleveland	.20
106	Bill Plummer	.20
107	Ed Halicki	.20
108	Von Joshua	.20
109	Joe Torre	.25
110	Richie Zisk	.20
111	Mike Tyson	.20
112	Astros Team	.25
113	Don Carrithers	.20
114	Paul Blair	.20
115	Gary Nolan	.20
116	Tucker Ashford	.20
117	John Montague	.20
118	Terry Harmon	.20
119	Denny Martinez	.30
120	Gary Carter	2.00
121	Alvis Woods	.20
122	Dennis Eckersley	5.00
123	Manny Trillo	.20
124	*Dave Rozema*	.20
125	George Scott	.20
126	Paul Moskau	.20
127	Chet Lemon	.20
128	Bill Russell	.25
129	Jim Colborn	.20
130	Jeff Burroughs	.20
131	Bert Blyleven	.30
132	Enos Cabell	.20
133	Jerry Augustine	.20
134	*Steve Henderson*	.20
135	Ron Guidry	.20
136	Ted Sizemore	.20
137	Craig Kusick	.20
138	Larry Demery	.20
139	Wayne Gross	.20
140	Rollie Fingers	2.00
141	Ruppert Jones	.20
142	John Montefusco	.20
143	Keith Hernandez	.80
144	Jesse Jefferson	.20
145	Rick Monday	.20
146	Doyle Alexander	.20
147	Lee Mazzilli	.20
148	Andre Thornton	.20
149	Dale Murray	.20
150	Bobby Bonds	.20
151	Milt Wilcox	.20
152	*Ivan DeJesus*	.20
153	Steve Stone	.20
154	Cecil Cooper	.20
155	Butch Hobson	.20
156	Andy Messersmith	.20
157	Pete LaCock	.20
158	Joaquin Andujar	.20
159	Lou Piniella	.30
160	Jim Palmer	3.00

161	Bob Boone	.20
162	Paul Thormodsgard	.20
163	Bill North	.20
164	Bob Owchinko	.20
165	Rennie Stennett	.20
166	Carlos Lopez	.20
167	Tim Foli	.20
168	Reggie Smith	.20
169	Jerry Johnson	.20
170	Lou Brock	2.50
171	Pat Zachry	.20
172	Mike Hargrove	.20
173	Robin Yount	16.00
174	Wayne Garland	.20
175	Jerry Morales	.20
176	Milt May	.20
177	Gene Garber	.20
178	Dave Chalk	.20
179	Dick Tidrow	.20
180	Dave Concepcion	.25
181	Ken Forsch	.20
182	Jim Spencer	.20
183	Doug Bird	.20
184	Checklist 122-242	.20
185	Ellis Valentine	.20
186	*Bob Stanley*	.20
187	Jerry Royster	.20
188	Al Bumbry	.20
189	Tom Lasorda	.55
190	John Candelaria	.20
191	Rodney Scott	.20
192	Padres Team	.25
193	Rich Chiles	.20
194	Derrel Thomas	.20
195	Larry Dierker	.20
196	Bob Bailor	.20
197	Nino Espinosa	.20
198	Ron Pruitt	.20
199	Craig Reynolds	.20
200	Reggie Jackson	8.00
201	Batting Leaders(Rod Carew, Dave Parker)	.50
202	Home Run Leaders(George Foster, Jim Rice)	.25
203	RBI Leaders(George Foster, Larry Hisle)	.20
204	Stolen Base Leaders(Freddie Patek, Frank Taveras)	.20
205	Victory Leaders(Steve Carlton, Dave Goltz, Dennis Leonard, Jim Palmer)	.65
206	Strikeout Leaders(Phil Niekro, Nolan Ryan)	2.50
207	ERA Leaders(John Candelaria, Frank Tanana)	.20
208	Leading Firemen(Bill Campbell, Rollie Fingers)	.25
209	Dock Ellis	.20
210	Jose Cardenal	.20
211	Earl Weaver (DP)	.50
212	Mike Caldwell	.20
213	Alan Bannister	.20
214	Angels Team	.25
215	Darrell Evans	.35
216	Mike Paxton	.20
217	Rod Gilbreath	.20
218	Marty Pattin	.20
219	Mike Cubbage	.20
220	Pedro Borbon	.20
221	Chris Speier	.20
222	Jerry Martin	.20
223	Bruce Kison	.20
224	Jerry Tabb	.20
225	Don Gullett	.20
226	Joe Ferguson	.20
227	Al Fitzmorris	.20
228	Manny Mota	.20
229	Leo Foster	.20
230	Al Hrabosky	.20
231	Wayne Nordhagen	.20
232	Mickey Stanley	.20
233	Dick Pole	.20
234	Herman Franks	.20
235	Tim McCarver	.30
236	Terry Whitfield	.20
237	Rich Dauer	.20
238	Juan Beniquez	.20
239	Dyar Miller	.20
240	Gene Tenace	.20
241	Pete Vuckovich	.20
242	Barry Bonnell	.20
243	Bob McClure	.20
244	Expos Team	.25
245	Rick Burleson	.20
246	Dan Driessen	.20

247	Larry Christenson	.20
248	Frank White	.20
249	Dave Goltz	.20
250	Graig Nettles	.25
251	Don Kirkwood	.20
252	Steve Swisher	.20
253	Jim Kern	.20
254	Dave Collins	.20
255	Jerry Reuss	.20
256	Joe Altobelli	.20
257	Hector Cruz	.20
258	John Hiller	.20
259	Dodgers Team	.50
260	Bert Campaneris	.20
261	Tim Hosley	.20
262	Rudy May	.20
263	Danny Walton	.20
264	Jamie Easterly	.20
265	Sal Bando	.20
266	*Bob Shirley*	.20
267	Doug Ault	.20
268	Gil Flores	.20
269	Wayne Twitchell	.20
270	Carlton Fisk	4.00
271	Randy Lerch	.20
272	Royle Stillman	.20
273	Fred Norman	.20
274	Freddie Patek	.20
275	Dan Ford	.20
276	Bill Bonham	.20
277	Bruce Boisclair	.20
278	Enrique Romo	.20
279	Bill Virdon	.20
280	Buddy Bell	.20
281	Eric Rasmussen	.20
282	Yankees Team	.75
283	Omar Moreno	.20
284	Randy Moffitt	.20
285	Steve Yeager	.20
286	Ben Oglivie	.20
287	Kiko Garcia	.20
288	Dave Hamilton	.20
289	Checklist 243-363	.20
290	Willie Horton	.20
291	Gary Ross	.20
292	Gene Richard	.20
293	Mike Willis	.20
294	Larry Parrish	.20
295	Bill Lee	.20
296	Biff Pocoroba	.20
297	Warren Brusstar	.20
298	Tony Armas	.20
299	Whitey Herzog	.30
300	Joe Morgan	2.50
301	Buddy Schultz	.20
302	Cubs Team	.25
303	Sam Hinds	.20
304	John Milner	.20
305	Rico Carty	.20
306	Joe Niekro	.20
307	Glenn Borgmann	.20
308	Jim Rooker	.20
309	Cliff Johnson	.20
310	Don Sutton	2.00
311	Jose Baez	.20
312	Greg Minton	.20
313	Andy Etchebarren	.20
314	Paul Lindblad	.20
315	Mark Belanger	.20
316	Henry Cruz	.20
317	Dave Johnson	.30
318	Tom Griffin	.20
319	Alan Ashby	.20
320	Fred Lynn	.40
321	Santo Alcala	.20
322	Tom Paciorek	.20
323	Jim Fregosi (DP)	.20
324	Vern Rapp	.20
325	Bruce Sutter	.25
326	Mike Lum	.20
327	Rick Langford	.20
328	Brewers Team	.25
329	John Verhoeven	.20
330	Bob Watson	.20
331	Mark Littell	.20
332	Duane Kuiper	.20
333	Jim Todd	.20
334	John Stearns	.20
335	Bucky Dent	.20
336	Steve Busby	.20
337	Tom Grieve	.20
338	Dave Heaverlo	.20
339	Mario Guerrero	.20
340	Bake McBride	.20
341	Mike Flanagan	.20
342	Aurelio Rodriguez	.20

343	John Wathan (DP)	.20
344	Sam Ewing	.20
345	Luis Tiant	.20
346	Larry Biittner	.20
347	Terry Forster	.20
348	Del Unser	.20
349	Rick Camp (DP)	.20
350	Steve Garvey	2.50
351	Jeff Torborg	.20
352	Tony Scott	.20
353	Doug Bair	.20
354	Cesar Geronimo	.20
355	Bill Travers	.20
356	Mets Team	.60
357	Tom Poquette	.20
358	Mark Lemongello	.20
359	Marc Hill	.20
360	Mike Schmidt	12.00
361	Chris Knapp	.20
362	Dave May	.20
363	Bob Randall	.20
364	Jerry Turner	.20
365	Ed Figueroa	.20
366	Larry Milbourne (DP)	.20
367	Rick Dempsey	.20
368	Balor Moore	.20
369	Tim Nordbrook	.20
370	Rusty Staub	.25
371	Ray Burris	.20
372	Brian Asselstine	.20
373	Jim Willoughby	.20
374	Jose Morales	.20
375	Tommy John	.30
376	Jim Wohlford	.20
377	Manny Sarmiento	.20
378	Bobby Winkles	.20
379	Skip Lockwood	.20
380	Ted Simmons	.20
381	Phillies Team	.35
382	Joe Lahoud	.20
383	Mario Mendoza	.20
384	Jack Clark	.35
385	Tito Fuentes	.20
386	Bob Gorinski	.20
387	Ken Holtzman	.20
388	Bill Fahey (DP)	.20
389	Julio Gonzalez	.20
390	Oscar Gamble	.20
391	Larry Haney	.20
392	Billy Almon	.20
393	Tippy Martinez	.20
394	Roy Howell	.20
395	Jim Hughes	.20
396	Bob Stinson	.20
397	Greg Gross	.20
398	Don Hood	.20
399	Pete Mackanin	.20
400	Nolan Ryan	35.00
401	Sparky Anderson	.40
402	Dave Campbell	.20
403	Bud Harrelson	.20
404	Tigers Team	.25
405	Rawly Eastwick	.20
406	Mike Jorgensen	.20
407	Odell Jones	.20
408	Joe Zdeb	.20
409	Ron Schueler	.20
410	Bill Madlock	.20
411	A.L. Championships (Yankees Rally To Defeat Royals)	.70
412	N.L. Championships (Dodgers Overpower Phillies In Four)	.50
413	World Series (Reggie & Yankees Reign Supreme)	2.50
414	Darold Knowles (DP)	.20
415	Ray Fosse	.20
416	Jack Brohamer	.20
417	Mike Garman	.20
418	Tony Muser	.20
419	Jerry Garvin	.20
420	Greg Luzinski	.20
421	Junior Moore	.20
422	Steve Braun	.20
423	Dave Rosello	.20
424	Red Sox Team	.45
425	Steve Rogers	.20
426	Fred Kendall	.20
427	*Mario Soto*	.40
428	Joel Youngblood	.20
429	Mike Barlow	.20
430	Al Oliver	.30
431	Butch Metzger	.20
432	Terry Bulling	.20
433	Fernando Gonzalez	.20

#	Name	Price	#	Name	Price	#	Name	Price
434	Mike Norris	.20	530	Dave Winfield	6.00	626	Blue Jays Team	.25
435	Checklist 364-484	.20	531	Tom Underwood	.20	627	Dave Johnson	.20
436	Vic Harris (DP)	.20	532	Skip Jutze	.20	628	Ralph Garr	.20
437	Bo McLaughlin	.20	533	Sandy Alomar	.20	629	Don Stanhouse	.20
438	John Ellis	.20	534	Wilbur Howard	.20	630	Ron Cey	.25
439	Ken Kravec	.20	535	Checklist 485-605	.20	631	Danny Ozark	.20
440	Dave Lopes	.20	536	Roric Harrison	.20	632	Rowland Office	.20
441	Larry Gura	.20	537	Bruce Bochte	.20	633	Tom Veryzer	.20
442	Elliott Maddox	.20	538	Johnnie LeMaster	.20	634	Len Barker	.20
443	Darrel Chaney	.20	539	Vic Davalillo	.20	635	Joe Rudi	.20
444	Roy Hartsfield	.20	540	Steve Carlton	4.00	636	Jim Bibby	.20
445	Mike Ivie	.20	541	Larry Cox	.20	637	Duffy Dyer	.20
446	Tug McGraw	.20	542	Tim Johnson	.20	638	Paul Splittorff	.20
447	Leroy Stanton	.20	543	Larry Harlow	.20	639	Gene Clines	.20
448	Bill Castro	.20	544	Len Randle	.20	640	Lee May	.20
449	Tim Blackwell	.20	545	Bill Campbell	.20	641	Doug Rau	.20
450	Tom Seaver	7.00	546	Ted Martinez	.20	642	Denny Doyle	.20
451	Twins Team	.25	547	John Scott	.20	643	Tom House	.20
452	Jerry Mumphrey	.20	548	Billy Hunter (DP)	.20	644	Jim Dwyer	.20
453	Doug Flynn	.20	549	Joe Kerrigan	.20	645	Mike Torrez	.20
454	Dave LaRoche	.20	550	John Mayberry	.20	646	Rick Auerbach	.20
455	Bill Robinson	.20	551	Braves Team	.25	647	Steve Dunning	.20
456	Vern Ruhle	.20	552	Francisco Barrios	.20	648	Gary Thomasson	.20
457	Bob Bailey	.20	553	*Terry Puhl*	.25	649	*Moose Haas*	.20
458	Jeff Newman	.20	554	Joe Coleman	.20	650	Cesar Cedeno	.20
459	Charlie Spikes	.20	555	Butch Wynegar	.20	651	Doug Rader	.20
460	Catfish Hunter	2.00	556	Ed Armbrister	.20	652	Checklist 606-726	.20
461	Rob Andrews	.20	557	Tony Solaita	.20	653	Ron Hodges	.20
462	Rogelio Moret	.20	558	Paul Mitchell	.20	654	Pepe Frias	.20
463	Kevin Bell	.20	559	Phil Mankowski	.20	655	Lyman Bostock	.20
464	Jerry Grote	.20	560	Dave Parker	.80	656	Dave Garcia	.20
465	Hal McRae	.20	561	Charlie Williams	.20	657	Bombo Rivera	.20
466	Dennis Blair	.20	562	Glenn Burke	.20	658	Manny Sanguillen	.20
467	Alvin Dark	.20	563	Dave Rader	.20	659	Rangers Team	.25
468	*Warren Cromartie*	.20	564	Mick Kelleher	.20	660	Jason Thompson	.20
469	Rick Cerone	.20	565	Jerry Koosman	.20	661	Grant Jackson	.20
470	J.R. Richard	.20	566	Merv Rettenmund	.20	662	Paul Dade	.20
471	Roy Smalley	.20	567	Dick Drago	.20	663	Paul Reuschel	.20
472	Ron Reed	.20	568	Tom Hutton	.20	664	Fred Stanley	.20
473	Bill Buckner	.20	569	*Lary Sorensen*	.20	665	Dennis Leonard	.20
474	Jim Slaton	.20	570	Dave Kingman	.30	666	Billy Smith	.20
475	Gary Matthews	.20	571	Buck Martinez	.20	667	Jeff Byrd	.20
476	Bill Stein	.20	572	Rick Wise	.20	668	Dusty Baker	.25
477	Doug Capilla	.20	573	Luis Gomez	.20	669	Pete Falcone	.20
478	Jerry Remy	.20	574	Bob Lemon	.30	670	Jim Rice	.75
479	Cardinals Team	.25	575	Pat Dobson	.20	671	Gary Lavelle	.20
480	Ron LeFlore	.20	576	Sam Mejias	.20	672	Don Kessinger	.20
481	Jackson Todd	.20	577	A's Team	.25	673	Steve Brye	.20
482	Rick Miller	.20	578	Buzz Capra	.20	674	*Ray Knight*	1.00
483	Ken Macha	.20	579	*Rance Mulliniks*	.25	675	Jay Johnstone	.20
484	Jim Norris	.20	580	Rod Carew	4.00	676	Bob Myrick	.20
485	Chris Chambliss	.20	581	Lynn McGlothen	.20	677	Ed Herrmann	.20
486	John Curtis	.20	582	Fran Healy	.20	678	Tom Burgmeier	.20
487	Jim Tyrone	.20	583	George Medich	.20	679	Wayne Garrett	.20
488	Dan Spillner	.20	584	John Hale	.20	680	Vida Blue	.20
489	Rudy Meoli	.20	585	Woodie Fryman	.20	681	Rob Belloir	.20
490	Amos Otis	.20	586	Ed Goodson	.20	682	Ken Brett	.20
491	Scott McGregor	.20	587	John Urrea	.20	683	Mike Champion	.20
492	Jim Sundberg	.20	588	Jim Mason	.20	684	Ralph Houk	.20
493	Steve Renko	.20	589	*Bob Knepper*	.40	685	Frank Taveras	.20
494	Chuck Tanner	.20	590	Bobby Murcer	.20	686	Gaylord Perry	2.00
495	Dave Cash	.20	591	George Zeber	.20	687	*Julio Cruz*	.25
496	*Jim Clancy*	.20	592	Bob Apodaca	.20	688	George Mitterwald	.20
497	Glenn Adams	.20	593	Dave Skaggs	.20	689	Indians Team	.25
498	Joe Sambito	.20	594	Dave Freisleben	.20	690	Mickey Rivers	.20
499	Mariners Team	.25	595	Sixto Lezcano	.20	691	Ross Grimsley	.20
500	George Foster	.30	596	Gary Wheelock	.20	692	Ken Reitz	.20
501	Dave Roberts	.20	597	Steve Dillard	.20	693	Lamar Johnson	.20
502	Pat Rockett	.20	598	Eddie Solomon	.20	694	Elias Sosa	.20
503	Ike Hampton	.20	599	Gary Woods	.20	695	Dwight Evans	.35
504	Roger Freed	.20	600	Frank Tanana	.20	696	Steve Mingori	.20
505	Felix Millan	.20	601	Gene Mauch	.20	697	Roger Metzger	.20
506	Ron Blomberg	.20	602	Eric Soderholm	.20	698	Juan Bernhardt	.20
507	Willie Crawford	.20	603	Will McEnaney	.20	699	Jackie Brown	.20
508	Johnny Oates	.20	604	Earl Williams	.20	700	Johnny Bench	5.00
509	Brent Strom	.20	605	Rick Rhoden	.20	701	Rookie Pitchers(Tom Hume, Larry Landreth), (Steve McCatty, Bruce Taylor)	.20
510	Willie Stargell	2.50	606	Pirates Team	.25			
511	Frank Duffy	.20	607	Fernando Arroyo	.20			
512	Larry Herndon	.20	608	Johnny Grubb	.20	702	Rookie Catchers(Bill Nahorodny, Kevin Pasley, Rick Sweet, Don Werner)	.20
513	Barry Foote	.20	609	John Denny	.20			
514	Rob Sperring	.20	610	Garry Maddox	.20			
515	Tim Corcoran	.20	611	Pat Scanlon	.20	703	Rookie Pitchers(Larry Andersen), (Tim Jones), (Mickey Mahler), (Jack Morris)	3.50
516	Gary Beare	.20	612	Ken Henderson	.20			
517	Andres Mora	.20	613	Marty Perez	.20			
518	Tommy Boggs (DP)	.20	614	Joe Wallis	.20			
519	Brian Downing	.20	615	Clay Carroll	.20	704	Rookie 2nd Basemen(Garth Iorg, Dave Oliver, Sam Perlozzo), (Lou Whitaker)	15.00
520	Larry Hisle	.20	616	Pat Kelly	.20			
521	Steve Staggs	.20	617	Joe Nolan	.20			
522	Dick Williams	.20	618	Tommy Helms	.20	705	Rookie Outfielders(Dave Bergman, Miguel Dilone), (Clint Hurdle, Willie Norwood)	.20
523	*Donnie Moore*	.20	619	*Thad Bosley*	.20			
524	Bernie Carbo	.20	620	Willie Randolph	.20			
525	Jerry Terrell	.20	621	Craig Swan	.20			
526	Reds Team	.45	622	Champ Summers	.20	706	Rookie 1st Basemen(Wayne Cage, Ted Cox), (Pat Putnam), (Dave Revering)	.20
527	Vic Correll	.20	623	Eduardo Rodriguez	.20			
528	Rob Picciolo	.20	624	Gary Alexander	.20			
529	Paul Hartzell	.20	625	Jose Cruz	.20			

707	Rookie Shortstops(Mickey Klutts), (Paul Molitor), (Alan Trammell), (U.L. Washington)	100.00
708	Rookie Catchers(Bo Diaz, Dale Murphy), (Lance Parrish), (Ernie Whitt)	12.00
709	Rookie Pitchers(Steve Burke), (Matt Keough, Lance Rautzhan), (Dan Schatzeder)	.20
710	Rookie Outfielders(Dell Alston, Rick Bosetti), (Mike Easler, Keith Smith)	.20
711	Rookie Pitchers(Cardell Camper, Dennis Lamp, Craig Mitchell, Roy Thomas)	.20
712	Bobby Valentine	.20
713	Bob Davis	.20
714	Mike Anderson	.20
715	Jim Kaat	.35
716	Cito Gaston	.20
717	Nelson Briles	.20
718	Ron Jackson	.20
719	Randy Elliott	.20
720	Fergie Jenkins	2.00
721	Billy Martin	.45
722	Pete Broberg	.20
723	Johnny Wockenfuss	.20
724	Royals Team	.25
725	Kurt Bevacqua	.20
726	Wilbur Wood	.20

1979 Topps

The size of this issue remained the same as in 1978 with 726 cards making their appearance. Actually, the 2-1/2" x 3-1/2" cards have a relatively minor design change from the previous year. The large color photo still dominates the front, with the player's name, team and position below it. The baseball with the player's position was moved to the lower left and the position replaced by a Topps logo. On the back, the printing color was changed and the game situation was replaced by a quiz called "Baseball Dates". Specialty cards include statistical leaders, major league records set during the season and eight cards devoted to career records. For the first time, rookies were arranged by teams under the heading of "Prospects." The key Ozzie Smith rookie card is usually seen with very poor centering.

		NM
	Complete Set (726):	175.00
	Common Player:	.15
1	Batting Leaders(Rod Carew, Dave Parker)	1.50
2	Home Run Leaders(George Foster, Jim Rice)	.15
3	RBI Leaders(George Foster, Jim Rice)	.15
4	Stolen Base Leaders(Ron LeFlore, Omar Moreno)	.15
5	Victory Leaders(Ron Guidry, Gaylord Perry)	.15
6	Strikeout Leaders(J.R. Richard, Nolan Ryan)	4.00
7	ERA Leaders(Ron Guidry, Craig Swan)	.15
8	Leading Firemen(Rollie Fingers, Rich Gossage)	.20
9	Dave Campbell	.15
10	Lee May	.15
11	Marc Hill	.15
12	Dick Drago	.15
13	Paul Dade	.15
14	Rafael Landestoy	.15
15	Ross Grimsley	.15
16	Fred Stanley	.15
17	Donnie Moore	.15
18	Tony Solaita	.15
19	Larry Gura	.15
20	Joe Morgan	1.25
21	Kevin Kobel	.15
22	Mike Jorgensen	.15

23	Terry Forster	.15
24	Paul Molitor	30.00
25	Steve Carlton	3.00
26	Jamie Quirk	.15
27	Dave Goltz	.15
28	Steve Brye	.15
29	Rick Langford	.15
30	Dave Winfield	12.00
31	Tom House	.15
32	Jerry Mumphrey	.15
33	Dave Rozema	.15
34	Rob Andrews	.15
35	Ed Figueroa	.15
36	Alan Ashby	.15
37	Joe Kerrigan	.15
38	Bernie Carbo	.15
39	Dale Murphy	6.00
40	Dennis Eckersley	4.00
41	Twins Team(Gene Mauch)	.25
42	Ron Blomberg	.15
43	Wayne Twitchell	.15
44	Kurt Bevacqua	.15
45	Al Hrabosky	.15
46	Ron Hodges	.15
47	Fred Norman	.15
48	Merv Rettenmund	.15
49	Vern Ruhle	.15
50	Steve Garvey	.90
51	Ray Fosse	.15
52	Randy Lerch	.15
53	Mick Kelleher	.15
54	Dell Alston	.15
55	Willie Stargell	2.00
56	John Hale	.15
57	Eric Rasmussen	.15
58	Bob Randall	.15
59	John Denny	.15
60	Mickey Rivers	.15
61	Bo Diaz	.15
62	Randy Moffitt	.15
63	Jack Brohamer	.15
64	Tom Underwood	.15
65	Mark Belanger	.15
66	Tigers Team(Les Moss)	.25
67	Jim Mason	.15
68	Joe Niekro	.15
69	Elliott Maddox	.15
70	John Candelaria	.15
71	Brian Downing	.15
72	Steve Mingori	.15
73	Ken Henderson	.15
74	Shane Rawley	.15
75	Steve Yeager	.15
76	Warren Cromartie	.15
77	Dan Briggs	.15
78	Elias Sosa	.15
79	Ted Cox	.15
80	Jason Thompson	.15
81	Roger Erickson	.15
82	Mets Team(Joe Torre)	.50
83	Fred Kendall	.15
84	Greg Minton	.15
85	Gary Matthews	.15
86	Rodney Scott	.15
87	Pete Falcone	.15
88	Bob Molinaro	.15
89	Dick Tidrow	.15
90	Bob Boone	.15
91	Terry Crowley	.15
92	Jim Bibby	.15
93	Phil Mankowski	.15
94	Len Barker	.15
95	Robin Yount	10.00
96	Indians Team(Jeff Torborg)	.25
97	Sam Mejias	.15
98	Ray Burris	.15
99	John Wathan	.15
100	Tom Seaver	3.50
101	Roy Howell	.15
102	Mike Anderson	.15
103	Jim Todd	.15
104	Johnny Oates	.15
105	Rick Camp	.15
106	Frank Duffy	.15
107	Jesus Alou	.15
108	Eduardo Rodriguez	.15
109	Joel Youngblood	.15
110	Vida Blue	.15
111	Roger Freed	.15
112	Phillies Team(Danny Ozark)	.25
113	Pete Redfern	.15
114	Cliff Johnson	.15
115	Nolan Ryan	27.50
116	Ozzie Smith	90.00
117	Grant Jackson	.15
118	Bud Harrelson	.15

119	Don Stanhouse	.15
120	Jim Sundberg	.15
121	Checklist 1-121	.15
122	Mike Paxton	.15
123	Lou Whitaker	3.00
124	Dan Schatzeder	.15
125	Rick Burleson	.15
126	Doug Bair	.15
127	Thad Bosley	.15
128	Ted Martinez	.15
129	Marty Pattin	.15
130	Bob Watson	.15
131	Jim Clancy	.15
132	Rowland Office	.15
133	Bill Castro	.15
134	Alan Bannister	.15
135	Bobby Murcer	.15
136	Jim Kaat	.25
137	Larry Wolfe	.15
138	Mark Lee	.15
139	Luis Pujols	.15
140	Don Gullett	.15
141	Tom Paciorek	.15
142	Charlie Williams	.15
143	Tony Scott	.15
144	Sandy Alomar	.15
145	Rick Rhoden	.15
146	Duane Kuiper	.15
147	Dave Hamilton	.15
148	Bruce Boisclair	.15
149	Manny Sarmiento	.15
150	Wayne Cage	.15
151	John Hiller	.15
152	Rick Cerone	.15
153	Dennis Lamp	.15
154	Jim Gantner	.15
155	Dwight Evans	.35
156	Buddy Solomon	.15
157	U.L. Washington	.15
158	Joe Sambito	.15
159	Roy White	.15
160	Mike Flanagan	.15
161	Barry Foote	.15
162	Tom Johnson	.15
163	Glenn Burke	.15
164	Mickey Lolich	.20
165	Frank Taveras	.15
166	Leon Roberts	.15
167	Roger Metzger	.15
168	Dave Freisleben	.15
169	Bill Nahorodny	.15
170	Don Sutton	1.50
171	Gene Clines	.15
172	Mike Bruhert	.15
173	John Lowenstein	.15
174	Rick Auerbach	.15
175	George Hendrick	.15
176	Aurelio Rodriguez	.15
177	Ron Reed	.15
178	Alvis Woods	.15
179	Jim Beattie	.15
180	Larry Hisle	.15
181	Mike Garman	.15
182	Tim Johnson	.15
183	Paul Splittorff	.15
184	Darrel Chaney	.15
185	Mike Torrez	.15
186	Eric Soderholm	.15
187	Mark Lemongello	.15
188	Pat Kelly	.15
189	Eddie Whitson	.25
190	Ron Cey	.15
191	Mike Norris	.15
192	Cardinals Team(Ken Boyer)	.25
193	Glenn Adams	.15
194	Randy Jones	.15
195	Bill Madlock	.15
196	Steve Kemp	.15
197	Bob Apodaca	.15
198	Johnny Grubb	.15
199	Larry Milbourne	.15
200	Johnny Bench	2.00
201	Mike Edwards (Record Breaker)	.15
202	Ron Guidry (Record Breaker)	.15
203	J.R. Richard (Record Breaker)	.15
204	Pete Rose (Record Breaker)	1.00
205	John Stearns (Record Breaker)	.15
206	Sammy Stewart (Record Breaker)	.15
207	Dave Lemanczyk	.15
208	Cito Gaston	.15

478	Juan Beniquez	.15	
479	Padres Team(Roger Craig)	.25	
480	Fred Lynn	.25	
481	Skip Lockwood	.15	
482	Craig Reynolds	.15	
483	Checklist 364-484	.15	
484	Rick Waits	.15	
485	Bucky Dent	.15	
486	Bob Knepper	.15	
487	Miguel Dilone	.15	
488	Bob Owchinko	.15	
489	Larry Cox (photo actually	.15	
	Dave Rader)		
490	Al Cowens	.15	
491	Tippy Martinez	.15	
492	Bob Bailor	.15	
493	Larry Christenson	.15	
494	Jerry White	.15	
495	Tony Perez	.30	
496	Barry Bonnell	.15	
497	Glenn Abbott	.15	
498	Rich Chiles	.15	
499	Rangers Team(Pat	.25	
	Corrales)		
500	Ron Guidry	.20	
501	Junior Kennedy	.15	
502	Steve Braun	.15	
503	Terry Humphrey	.15	
504	*Larry McWilliams*	.15	
505	Ed Kranepool	.15	
506	John D'Acquisto	.15	
507	Tony Armas	.15	
508	Charlie Hough	.15	
509	Mario Mendoza	.15	
510	Ted Simmons	.15	
511	Paul Reuschel	.15	
512	Jack Clark	.25	
513	Dave Johnson	.15	
514	Mike Proly	.15	
515	Enos Cabell	.15	
516	Champ Summers	.15	
517	Al Bumbry	.15	
518	Jim Umbarger	.15	
519	Ben Oglivie	.15	
520	Gary Carter	1.75	
521	Sam Ewing	.15	
522	Ken Holtzman	.15	
523	John Milner	.15	
524	Tom Burgmeier	.15	
525	Freddie Patek	.15	
526	Dodgers Team(Tom	.60	
	Lasorda)		
527	Lerrin LaGrow	.15	
528	Wayne Gross	.15	
529	Brian Asselstine	.15	
530	Frank Tanana	.15	
531	Fernando Gonzalez	.15	
532	Buddy Schultz	.15	
533	Leroy Stanton	.15	
534	Ken Forsch	.15	
535	Ellis Valentine	.15	
536	Jerry Reuss	.15	
537	Tom Veryzer	.15	
538	Mike Ivie	.15	
539	John Ellis	.15	
540	Greg Luzinski	.15	
541	Jim Slaton	.15	
542	Rick Bosetti	.15	
543	Kiko Garcia	.15	
544	Fergie Jenkins	1.50	
545	John Stearns	.15	
546	Bill Russell	.15	
547	Clint Hurdle	.15	
548	Enrique Romo	.15	
549	Bob Bailey	.15	
550	Sal Bando	.15	
551	Cubs Team(Herman	.25	
	Franks)		
552	Jose Morales	.15	
553	Denny Walling	.15	
554	Matt Keough	.15	
555	Biff Pocoroba	.15	
556	Mike Lum	.15	
557	Ken Brett	.15	
558	Jay Johnstone	.15	
559	Greg Pryor	.15	
560	John Montefusco	.15	
561	Ed Ott	.15	
562	Dusty Baker	.25	
563	Roy Thomas	.15	
564	Jerry Turner	.15	
565	Rico Carty	.15	
566	Nino Espinosa	.15	
567	Rich Hebner	.15	
568	Carlos Lopez	.15	
569	Bob Sykes	.15	

570	Cesar Cedeno	.15	
571	Darrell Porter	.15	
572	Rod Gilbreath	.15	
573	Jim Kern	.15	
574	Claudell Washington	.15	
575	Luis Tiant	.15	
576	Mike Parrott	.15	
577	Brewers Team(George	.25	
	Bamberger)		
578	Pete Broberg	.15	
579	Greg Gross	.15	
580	Ron Fairly	.15	
581	Darold Knowles	.15	
582	Paul Blair	.15	
583	Julio Cruz	.15	
584	Jim Rooker	.15	
585	Hal McRae	.15	
586	*Bob Horner*	.90	
587	Ken Reitz	.15	
588	Tom Murphy	.15	
589	Terry Whitfield	.15	
590	J.R. Richard	.15	
591	Mike Hargrove	.15	
592	Mike Krukow	.15	
593	Rick Dempsey	.15	
594	Bob Shirley	.15	
595	Phil Niekro	1.50	
596	Jim Wohlford	.15	
597	Bob Stanley	.15	
598	Mark Wagner	.15	
599	Jim Spencer	.15	
600	George Foster	.15	
601	Dave LaRoche	.15	
602	Checklist 485-605	.15	
603	Rudy May	.15	
604	Jeff Newman	.15	
605	Rick Monday	.15	
606	Expos Team(Dick Williams)	.25	
607	Omar Moreno	.15	
608	Dave McKay	.15	
609	Silvio Martinez	.15	
610	Mike Schmidt	8.00	
611	Jim Norris	.15	
612	*Rick Honeycutt*	.25	
613	Mike Edwards	.15	
614	Willie Hernandez	.15	
615	Ken Singleton	.15	
616	Billy Almon	.15	
617	Terry Puhl	.15	
618	Jerry Remy	.15	
619	*Ken Landreaux*	.15	
620	Bert Campaneris	.15	
621	Pat Zachry	.15	
622	Dave Collins	.15	
623	Bob McClure	.15	
624	Larry Herndon	.15	
625	Mark Fidrych	.15	
626	Yankees Team(Bob Lemon)	.50	
627	Gary Serum	.15	
628	Del Unser	.15	
629	Gene Garber	.15	
630	Bake McBride	.15	
631	Jorge Orta	.15	
632	Don Kirkwood	.15	
633	Rob Wilfong	.15	
634	Paul Lindblad	.15	
635	Don Baylor	.25	
636	Wayne Garland	.15	
637	Bill Robinson	.15	
638	Al Fitzmorris	.15	
639	Manny Trillo	.15	
640	Eddie Murray	25.00	
641	*Bobby Castillo*	.15	
642	Wilbur Howard	.15	
643	Tom Hausman	.15	
644	Manny Mota	.15	
645	George Scott	.15	
646	Rick Sweet	.15	
647	Bob Lacey	.15	
648	Lou Piniella	.20	
649	John Curtis	.15	
650	Pete Rose	8.00	
651	Mike Caldwell	.15	
652	Stan Papi	.15	
653	Warren Brusstar	.15	
654	Rick Miller	.15	
655	Jerry Koosman	.15	
656	Hosken Powell	.15	
657	George Medich	.15	
658	Taylor Duncan	.15	
659	Mariners Team(Darrell	.25	
	Johnson)		
660	Ron LeFlore	.15	
661	Bruce Kison	.15	
662	Kevin Bell	.15	
663	Mike Vail	.15	

664	Doug Bird	.15	
665	Lou Brock	2.00	
666	Rich Dauer	.15	
667	Don Hood	.15	
668	Bill North	.15	
669	Checklist 606-726	.15	
670	Catfish Hunter	1.50	
671	Joe Ferguson	.15	
672	Ed Halicki	.15	
673	Tom Hutton	.15	
674	Dave Tomlin	.15	
675	Tim McCarver	.25	
676	Johnny Sutton	.15	
677	Larry Parrish	.15	
678	Geoff Zahn	.15	
679	Derrel Thomas	.15	
680	Carlton Fisk	1.50	
681	*John Henry Johnson*	.15	
682	Dave Chalk	.15	
683	Dan Meyer	.15	
684	Jamie Easterly	.15	
685	Sixto Lezcano	.15	
686	Ron Schueler	.15	
687	Rennie Stennett	.15	
688	Mike Willis	.15	
689	Orioles Team(Earl Weaver)	.60	
690	Buddy Bell	.15	
691	Dock Ellis	.15	
692	Mickey Stanley	.15	
693	Dave Rader	.15	
694	Burt Hooton	.15	
695	Keith Hernandez	.40	
696	Andy Hassler	.15	
697	Dave Bergman	.15	
698	Bill Stein	.15	
699	Hal Dues	.15	
700	Reggie Jackson	4.00	
701	Orioles Prospects(Mark	.15	
	Corey, John Flinn), (*Sammy		
	Stewart*)		
702	Red Sox Prospects(Joel	.15	
	Finch, Garry Hancock, Allen		
	Ripley)		
703	Angels Prospects(Jim	.15	
	Anderson, Dave Frost, Bob		
	Slater)		
704	White Sox Prospects(Ross	.15	
	Baumgarten, Mike Colbern),		
	(*Mike Squires*)		
705	Indians Prospects(*Alfredo*	.25	
	Griffin, Tim Norrid, Dave		
	Oliver)		
706	Tigers Prospects(Dave	.15	
	Stegman, Dave Tobik, Kip		
	Young)		
707	Royals Prospects(Randy	.15	
	Bass, Jim Gaudet, Randy		
	McGilberry)		
708	Brewers Prospects(*Kevin	.25	
	Bass*), (*Eddie Romero*, Ned		
	Yost)		
709	Twins Prospects(Sam	.15	
	Perlozzo, Rick Sofield,		
	Kevin Stanfield)		
710	Yankees Prospects(Brian	.20	
	Doyle), (*Mike Heath*, Dave		
	Rajsich)		
711	A's Prospects(*Dwayne	.15	
	Murphy*, Bruce Robinson,		
	Alan Wirth)		
712	Mariners Prospects(Bud	.15	
	Anderson, Greg Biercevicz,		
	Byron McLaughlin)		
713	Rangers Prospects(*Danny	.25	
	Darwin*, Pat Putnam), (*Billy		
	Sample*)		
714	Blue Jays Prospects(Victor	.15	
	Cruz, Pat Kelly, Ernie Whitt)		
715	Braves Prospects(*Bruce	.25	
	Benedict*), (*Glenn Hubbard*,		
	Larry Whisenton)		
716	Cubs Prospects(Dave	.15	
	Geisel, Karl Pagel), (*Scot		
	Thompson*)		
717	Reds Prospects(*Mike	.15	
	LaCoss*), (*Ron Oester*), (*Harry		
	Spilman*)		
718	Astros Prospects(Bruce	.15	
	Bochy, Mike Fischlin, Don		
	Pisker)		
719	Dodgers Prospects(*Pedro	2.00	
	Guerrero*), (*Rudy Law*, Joe		
	Simpson)		
720	Expos Prospects(*Jerry Fry*),	.90	
	(*Jerry Pirtle*), (*Scott		
	Sanderson*)		

721	Mets Prospects(*Juan Berenguer*, Dwight Bernard, Dan Norman)	.15
722	Phillies Prospects(*Jim Morrison*), (*Lonnie Smith*), (*Jim Wright*)	.50
723	Pirates Prospects(*Dale Berra*, Eugenio Cotes, Ben Wiltbank)	.15
724	Cardinals Prospects(Tom Bruno), (*George Frazier*), (*Terry Kennedy*)	.20
725	Padres Prospects(Jim Beswick, Steve Mura, Broderick Perkins)	.15
726	Giants Prospects(Greg Johnston, Joe Strain, John Tamargo)	.15

1980 Topps

Again numbering 726 cards measuring 2-1/2" x 3-1/2", Topps did make some design changes in 1980. Fronts have the usual color picture with a facsimile autograph. The player's name appears above the picture, while his position is on a pennant at the upper left and his team on another pennant in the lower right. Backs no longer feature games, returning instead to statistics, personal information, a few headlines and a cartoon about the player. Specialty cards include statistical leaders, and previous season highlights. Many rookies again appear in team threesomes.

		NM
Complete Set (726):		175.00
Common Player:		.12
Wax Box:		
1	Lou Brock, Carl Yastrzemski (Highlights)	1.00
2	Willie McCovey (Highlights)	.40
3	Manny Mota (Highlights)	.12
4	Pete Rose (Highlights)	2.00
5	Garry Templeton (Highlights)	.12
6	Del Unser (Highlights)	.12
7	Mike Lum	.12
8	Craig Swan	.12
9	Steve Braun	.12
10	Denny Martinez	.20
11	Jimmy Sexton	.12
12	John Curtis	.12
13	Ron Pruitt	.12
14	Dave Cash	.12
15	Bill Campbell	.12
16	Jerry Narron	.12
17	Bruce Sutter	.12
18	Ron Jackson	.12
19	Balor Moore	.12
20	Dan Ford	.12
21	Manny Sarmiento	.12
22	Pat Putnam	.12
23	Derrel Thomas	.12
24	Jim Slaton	.12
25	Lee Mazzilli	.12
26	Marty Pattin	.12
27	Del Unser	.12
28	Bruce Kison	.12
29	Mark Wagner	.12
30	Vida Blue	.12
31	Jay Johnstone	.12
32	Julio Cruz	.12
33	Tony Scott	.12
34	Jeff Newman	.12
35	Luis Tiant	.15
36	Rusty Torres	.12
37	Kiko Garcia	.12
38	Dan Spillner	.12
39	Rowland Office	.12
40	Carlton Fisk	3.00
41	Rangers Team(Pat Corrales)	.25
42	*Dave Palmer*	.12
43	Bombo Rivera	.12
44	Bill Fahey	.12
45	Frank White	.12

46	Rico Carty	.12
47	Bill Bonham	.12
48	Rick Miller	.12
49	Mario Guerrero	.12
50	J.R. Richard	.20
51	Joe Ferguson	.12
52	Warren Brusstar	.12
53	Ben Oglivie	.12
54	Dennis Lamp	.12
55	Bill Madlock	.15
56	Bobby Valentine	.12
57	Pete Vuckovich	.12
58	Doug Flynn	.12
59	Eddy Putman	.12
60	Bucky Dent	.15
61	Gary Serum	.12
62	Mike Ivie	.12
63	Bob Stanley	.12
64	Joe Nolan	.12
65	Al Bumbry	.12
66	Royals Team(Jim Frey)	.25
67	Doyle Alexander	.12
68	Larry Harlow	.12
69	Rick Williams	.12
70	Gary Carter	1.50
71	John Milner	.12
72	Fred Howard	.12
73	Dave Collins	.12
74	Sid Monge	.12
75	Bill Russell	.15
76	John Stearns	.12
77	*Dave Stieb*	1.00
78	Ruppert Jones	.12
79	Bob Owchinko	.12
80	Ron LeFlore	.12
81	Ted Sizemore	.12
82	Astros Team(Bill Virdon)	.25
83	*Steve Trout*	.15
84	Gary Lavelle	.12
85	Ted Simmons	.12
86	Dave Hamilton	.12
87	Pepe Frias	.12
88	Ken Landreaux	.12
89	Don Hood	.12
90	Manny Trillo	.12
91	Rick Dempsey	.12
92	Rick Rhoden	.12
93	Dave Roberts	.12
94	*Neil Allen*	.12
95	Cecil Cooper	.12
96	A's Team(Jim Marshall)	.25
97	Bill Lee	.12
98	Jerry Terrell	.12
99	Victor Cruz	.12
100	Johnny Bench	3.00
101	Aurelio Lopez	.12
102	Rich Dauer	.12
103	*Bill Caudill*	.15
104	Manny Mota	.12
105	Frank Tanana	.12
106	*Jeff Leonard*	.25
107	Francisco Barrios	.12
108	Bob Horner	.12
109	Bill Travers	.12
110	Fred Lynn	.20
111	Bob Knepper	.12
112	White Sox Team(Tony LaRussa)	.40
113	Geoff Zahn	.12
114	Juan Beniquez	.12
115	Sparky Lyle	.12
116	Larry Cox	.12
117	Dock Ellis	.12
118	Phil Garner	.12
119	Sammy Stewart	.12
120	Greg Luzinski	.20
121	Checklist 1-121	.12
122	Dave Rosello	.12
123	Lynn Jones	.12
124	Dave Lemanczyk	.12
125	Tony Perez	.25
126	Dave Tomlin	.12
127	Gary Thomasson	.12
128	Tom Burgmeier	.12
129	Craig Reynolds	.12
130	Amos Otis	.12
131	Paul Mitchell	.12
132	Biff Pocoroba	.12
133	Jerry Turner	.12
134	Matt Keough	.12
135	Bill Buckner	.15
136	Dick Ruthven	.12
137	*John Castino*	.12
138	Ross Baumgarten	.12
139	*Dane Iorg*	.12
140	Rich Gossage	.15

141	Gary Alexander	.12
142	Phil Huffman	.12
143	Bruce Bochte	.12
144	Steve Comer	.12
145	Darrell Evans	.20
146	Bob Welch	.25
147	Terry Puhl	.12
148	Manny Sanguillen	.12
149	Tom Hume	.12
150	Jason Thompson	.12
151	Tom Hausman	.12
152	John Fulgham	.12
153	Tim Blackwell	.12
154	Lary Sorensen	.12
155	Jerry Remy	.12
156	Tony Brizzolara	.12
157	Willie Wilson	.12
158	Rob Picciolo	.12
159	Ken Clay	.12
160	Eddie Murray	10.00
161	Larry Christenson	.12
162	Bob Randall	.12
163	Steve Swisher	.12
164	Greg Pryor	.12
165	Omar Moreno	.12
166	Glenn Abbott	.12
167	Jack Clark	.12
168	Rick Waits	.12
169	Luis Gomez	.12
170	Burt Hooton	.12
171	Fernando Gonzalez	.12
172	Ron Hodges	.12
173	John Henry Johnson	.12
174	Ray Knight	.12
175	Rick Reuschel	.12
176	Champ Summers	.12
177	Dave Heaverlo	.12
178	Tim McCarver	.15
179	*Ron Davis*	.15
180	Warren Cromartie	.12
181	Moose Haas	.12
182	Ken Reitz	.12
183	Jim Anderson	.12
184	Steve Renko	.12
185	Hal McRae	.20
186	Junior Moore	.12
187	Alan Ashby	.12
188	Terry Crowley	.12
189	Kevin Kobel	.12
190	Buddy Bell	.15
191	Ted Martinez	.12
192	Braves Team(Bobby Cox)	.40
193	Dave Goltz	.12
194	Mike Easler	.12
195	John Montefusco	.12
196	Lance Parrish	.25
197	Byron McLaughlin	.12
198	Dell Alston	.12
199	Mike LaCoss	.12
200	Jim Rice	.25
201	Batting Leaders(Keith Hernandez, Fred Lynn)	.10
202	Home Run Leaders(Dave Kingman, Gorman Thomas)	.10
203	Runs Batted In Leaders(Don Baylor, Dave Winfield)	.45
204	Stolen Base Leaders(Omar Moreno, Willie Wilson)	.10
205	Victory Leaders(Mike Flanagan, Joe Niekro, Phil Niekro)	.25
206	Strikeout Leaders(J.R. Richard, Nolan Ryan)	3.00
207	ERA Leaders(Ron Guidry, J.R. Richard)	.25
208	Wayne Cage	.12
209	Von Joshua	.12
210	Steve Carlton	3.00
211	Dave Skaggs	.12
212	Dave Roberts	.12
213	Mike Jorgensen	.12
214	Angels Team(Jim Fregosi)	.35
215	Sixto Lezcano	.12
216	Phil Mankowski	.12
217	Ed Halicki	.12
218	Jose Morales	.12
219	Steve Mingori	.12
220	Dave Concepcion	.12
221	Joe Cannon	.12
222	*Ron Hassey*	.25
223	Bob Sykes	.12
224	Willie Montanez	.12
225	Lou Piniella	.15
226	Bill Stein	.12
227	Len Barker	.12

228	Johnny Oates	.12
229	Jim Bibby	.12
230	Dave Winfield	8.00
231	Steve McCatty	.12
232	Alan Trammell	2.00
233	LaRue Washington	.12
234	Vern Ruhle	.12
235	Andre Dawson	3.00
236	Marc Hill	.12
237	Scott McGregor	.12
238	Rob Wilfong	.12
239	Don Aase	.12
240	Dave Kingman	.15
241	Checklist 122-242	.12
242	Lamar Johnson	.12
243	Jerry Augustine	.12
244	Cardinals Team(Ken Boyer)	.25
245	Phil Niekro	1.50
246	Tim Foli	.12
247	Frank Riccelli	.12
248	Jamie Quirk	.12
249	Jim Clancy	.12
250	Jim Kaat	.30
251	Kip Young	.12
252	Ted Cox	.12
253	John Montague	.12
254	Paul Dade	.12
255	Dusty Baker	.12
256	Roger Erickson	.12
257	Larry Herndon	.12
258	Paul Moskau	.12
259	Mets Team(Joe Torre)	.50
260	Al Oliver	.15
261	Dave Chalk	.12
262	Benny Ayala	.12
263	Dave LaRoche	.12
264	Bill Robinson	.12
265	Robin Yount	9.00
266	Bernie Carbo	.12
267	Dan Schatzeder	.12
268	Rafael Landestoy	.12
269	Dave Tobik	.12
270	Mike Schmidt	4.00
271	Dick Drago	.12
272	Ralph Garr	.12
273	Eduardo Rodriguez	.12
274	Dale Murphy	3.00
275	Jerry Koosman	.12
276	Tom Veryzer	.12
277	Rick Bosetti	.12
278	Jim Spencer	.12
279	Rob Andrews	.12
280	Gaylord Perry	1.50
281	Paul Blair	.12
282	Mariners Team(Darrell Johnson)	.25
283	John Ellis	.12
284	Larry Murray	.12
285	Don Baylor	.20
286	Darold Knowles	.12
287	John Lowenstein	.12
288	Dave Rozema	.12
289	Bruce Bochy	.12
290	Steve Garvey	1.25
291	Randy Scarbery	.12
292	Dale Berra	.12
293	Elias Sosa	.12
294	Charlie Spikes	.12
295	Larry Gura	.12
296	Dave Rader	.12
297	Tim Johnson	.12
298	Ken Holtzman	.12
299	Steve Henderson	.12
300	Ron Guidry	.25
301	Mike Edwards	.12
302	Dodgers Team(Tom Lasorda)	.60
303	Bill Castro	.12
304	Butch Wynegar	.12
305	Randy Jones	.12
306	Denny Walling	.12
307	Rick Honeycutt	.12
308	Mike Hargrove	.12
309	Larry McWilliams	.12
310	Dave Parker	.60
311	Roger Metzger	.12
312	Mike Barlow	.12
313	Johnny Grubb	.12
314	*Tim Stoddard*	.12
315	Steve Kemp	.12
316	Bob Lacey	.12
317	Mike Anderson	.12
318	Jerry Reuss	.12
319	Chris Speier	.12
320	Dennis Eckersley	2.00
321	Keith Hernandez	.25

322	Claudell Washington	.12
323	Mick Kelleher	.12
324	Tom Underwood	.12
325	Dan Driessen	.12
326	Bo McLaughlin	.12
327	Ray Fosse	.12
328	Twins Team(Gene Mauch)	.25
329	Bert Roberge	.12
330	Al Cowens	.12
331	Rich Hebner	.12
332	Enrique Romo	.12
333	Jim Norris	.12
334	Jim Beattie	.12
335	Willie McCovey	2.00
336	George Medich	.12
337	Carney Lansford	.12
338	Johnny Wockenfuss	.12
339	John D'Acquisto	.12
340	Ken Singleton	.12
341	Jim Essian	.12
342	Odell Jones	.12
343	Mike Vail	.12
344	Randy Lerch	.12
345	Larry Parrish	.12
346	Buddy Solomon	.12
347	*Harry Chappas*	.12
348	Checklist 243-363	.12
349	Jack Brohamer	.12
350	George Hendrick	.12
351	Bob Davis	.12
352	Dan Briggs	.12
353	Andy Hassler	.12
354	Rick Auerbach	.12
355	Gary Matthews	.12
356	Padres Team(Jerry Coleman)	.25
357	Bob McClure	.12
358	Lou Whitaker	.90
359	Randy Moffitt	.12
360	Darrell Porter	.12
361	Wayne Garland	.12
362	Danny Goodwin	.12
363	Wayne Gross	.12
364	Ray Burris	.12
365	Bobby Murcer	.20
366	Rob Dressler	.12
367	Billy Smith	.12
368	*Willie Aikens*	.20
369	Jim Kern	.12
370	Cesar Cedeno	.12
371	Jack Morris	.50
372	Joel Youngblood	.12
373	*Dan Petry*	.20
374	Jim Gantner	.12
375	Ross Grimsley	.12
376	Gary Allenson	.12
377	Junior Kennedy	.12
378	Jerry Mumphrey	.12
379	Kevin Bell	.12
380	Garry Maddox	.12
381	Cubs Team(Preston Gomez)	.25
382	Dave Freisleben	.12
383	Ed Ott	.12
384	Joey McLaughlin	.12
385	Enos Cabell	.12
386	Darrell Jackson	.12
387a	Fred Stanley (name in red)	.12
387b	Fred Stanley (name in yellow)	3.00
388	Mike Paxton	.12
389	Pete LaCock	.12
390	Fergie Jenkins	1.50
391	Tony Armas	.12
392	Milt Wilcox	.12
393	Ozzie Smith	20.00
394	Reggie Cleveland	.12
395	Ellis Valentine	.12
396	Dan Meyer	.12
397	Roy Thomas	.12
398	Barry Foote	.12
399	Mike Proly	.12
400	George Foster	.15
401	Pete Falcone	.12
402	Merv Rettenmund	.12
403	Pete Redfern	.12
404	Orioles Team(Earl Weaver)	.50
405	Dwight Evans	.25
406	Paul Molitor	12.00
407	Tony Solaita	.12
408	Bill North	.12
409	Paul Splittorff	.12
410	Bobby Bonds	.20
411	Frank LaCorte	.12
412	Thad Bosley	.12
413	Allen Ripley	.12

414	George Scott	.12
415	Bill Atkinson	.12
416	*Tom Brookens*	.12
417	Craig Chamberlain	.12
418	Roger Freed	.12
419	Vic Correll	.12
420	Butch Hobson	.12
421	Doug Bird	.12
422	Larry Milbourne	.12
423	Dave Frost	.12
424	Yankees Team(Dick Howser)	.45
425	Mark Belanger	.12
426	Grant Jackson	.12
427	Tom Hutton	.12
428	Pat Zachry	.12
429	Duane Kuiper	.12
430	Larry Hisle	.12
431	Mike Krukow	.12
432	Willie Norwood	.12
433	Rich Gale	.12
434	Johnnie LeMaster	.12
435	Don Gullett	.12
436	Billy Almon	.12
437	Joe Niekro	.12
438	Dave Revering	.12
439	Mike Phillips	.12
440	Don Sutton	1.50
441	Eric Soderholm	.12
442	Jorge Orta	.12
443	Mike Parrott	.12
444	Alvis Woods	.12
445	Mark Fidrych	.20
446	Duffy Dyer	.12
447	Nino Espinosa	.12
448	Jim Wohlford	.12
449	Doug Bair	.12
450	George Brett	15.00
451	Indians Team(Dave Garcia)	.25
452	Steve Dillard	.12
453	Mike Bacsik	.12
454	Tom Donohue	.12
455	Mike Torrez	.12
456	Frank Taveras	.12
457	Bert Blyleven	.25
458	Billy Sample	.12
459	Mickey Lolich	.12
460	Willie Randolph	.12
461	Dwayne Murphy	.12
462	Mike Sadek	.12
463	Jerry Royster	.12
464	John Denny	.12
465	Rick Monday	.12
466	Mike Squires	.12
467	Jesse Jefferson	.12
468	Aurelio Rodriguez	.12
469	Randy Niemann	.12
470	Bob Boone	.20
471	Hosken Powell	.12
472	Willie Hernandez	.12
473	Bump Wills	.12
474	Steve Busby	.12
475	Cesar Geronimo	.12
476	Bob Shirley	.12
477	Buck Martinez	.12
478	Gil Flores	.12
479	Expos Team(Dick Williams)	.25
480	Bob Watson	.12
481	Tom Paciorek	.12
482	*Rickey Henderson*	40.00
483	Bo Diaz	.12
484	Checklist 364-484	.12
485	Mickey Rivers	.12
486	Mike Tyson	.12
487	Wayne Nordhagen	.12
488	Roy Howell	.12
489	Preston Hanna	.12
490	Lee May	.12
491	Steve Mura	.12
492	Todd Cruz	.12
493	Jerry Martin	.12
494	Craig Minetto	.12
495	Bake McBride	.12
496	Silvio Martinez	.12
497	Jim Mason	.12
498	Danny Darwin	.12
499	Giants Team(Dave Bristol)	.25
500	Tom Seaver	3.00
501	Rennie Stennett	.12
502	Rich Wortham	.12
503	Mike Cubbage	.12
504	Gene Garber	.12
505	Bert Campaneris	.12
506	Tom Buskey	.12
507	Leon Roberts	.12
508	U.L. Washington	.12

#	Player	Price
509	Ed Glynn	.12
510	Ron Cey	.15
511	Eric Wilkins	.12
512	Jose Cardenal	.12
513	Tom Dixon	.12
514	Steve Ontiveros	.12
515	Mike Caldwell	.12
516	Hector Cruz	.12
517	Don Stanhouse	.12
518	Nelson Norman	.12
519	Steve Nicosia	.12
520	Steve Rogers	.12
521	Ken Brett	.12
522	Jim Morrison	.12
523	Ken Henderson	.12
524	Jim Wright	.12
525	Clint Hurdle	.12
526	Phillies Team(Dallas Green)	.60
527	Doug Rau	.12
528	Adrian Devine	.12
529	Jim Barr	.12
530	Jim Sundberg	.12
531	Eric Rasmussen	.12
532	Willie Horton	.12
533	Checklist 485-605	.12
534	Andre Thornton	.12
535	Bob Forsch	.12
536	Lee Lacy	.12
537	*Alex Trevino*	.12
538	Joe Strain	.12
539	Rudy May	.12
540	Pete Rose	9.00
541	Miguel Dilone	.12
542	Joe Coleman	.12
543	Pat Kelly	.12
544	*Rick Sutcliffe*	2.00
545	Jeff Burroughs	.12
546	Rick Langford	.12
547	John Wathan	.12
548	Dave Rajsich	.12
549	Larry Wolfe	.12
550	Ken Griffey	.15
551	Pirates Team(Chuck Tanner)	.25
552	Bill Nahorodny	.12
553	Dick Davis	.12
554	Art Howe	.12
555	Ed Figueroa	.12
556	Joe Rudi	.12
557	Mark Lee	.12
558	Alfredo Griffin	.12
559	Dale Murray	.12
560	Dave Lopes	.15
561	Eddie Whitson	.12
562	Joe Wallis	.12
563	Will McEnaney	.12
564	Rick Manning	.12
565	Dennis Leonard	.12
566	Bud Harrelson	.12
567	Skip Lockwood	.12
568	*Gary Roenicke*	.12
569	Terry Kennedy	.12
570	Roy Smalley	.12
571	Joe Sambito	.12
572	Jerry Morales	.12
573	Kent Tekulve	.12
574	Scot Thompson	.12
575	Ken Kravec	.12
576	Jim Dwyer	.12
577	Blue Jays Team(Bobby Mattick)	.25
578	Scott Sanderson	.12
579	Charlie Moore	.12
580	Nolan Ryan	20.00
581	Bob Bailor	.12
582	Brian Doyle	.12
583	Bob Stinson	.12
584	Kurt Bevacqua	.12
585	Al Hrabosky	.12
586	Mitchell Page	.12
587	Garry Templeton	.12
588	Greg Minton	.12
589	Chet Lemon	.12
590	Jim Palmer	3.00
591	Rick Cerone	.12
592	Jon Matlack	.12
593	Jesus Alou	.12
594	Dick Tidrow	.12
595	Don Money	.12
596	Rick Matula	.12
597	Tom Poquette	.12
598	Fred Kendall	.12
599	Mike Norris	.12
600	Reggie Jackson	7.00
601	Buddy Schultz	.12
602	Brian Downing	.12
603	Jack Billingham	.12
604	Glenn Adams	.12
605	Terry Forster	.12
606	Reds Team(John McNamara)	.35
607	Woodie Fryman	.12
608	Alan Bannister	.12
609	Ron Reed	.12
610	Willie Stargell	2.00
611	Jerry Garvin	.12
612	Cliff Johnson	.12
613	Randy Stein	.12
614	John Hiller	.12
615	Doug DeCinces	.20
616	Gene Richards	.12
617	Joaquin Andujar	.12
618	Bob Montgomery	.12
619	Sergio Ferrer	.12
620	Richie Zisk	.12
621	Bob Grich	.20
622	Mario Soto	.12
623	Gorman Thomas	.12
624	Lerrin LaGrow	.12
625	Chris Chambliss	.12
626	Tigers Team(Sparky Anderson)	.50
627	Pedro Borbon	.12
628	Doug Capilla	.12
629	Jim Todd	.12
630	Larry Bowa	.15
631	Mark Littell	.12
632	Barry Bonnell	.12
633	Bob Apodaca	.12
634	Glenn Borgmann	.12
635	John Candelaria	.12
636	Toby Harrah	.12
637	Joe Simpson	.12
638	*Mark Clear*	.12
639	Larry Biittner	.12
640	Mike Flanagan	.12
641	Ed Kranepool	.12
642	Ken Forsch	.12
643	John Mayberry	.12
644	Charlie Hough	.12
645	Rick Burleson	.12
646	Checklist 606-726	.12
647	Milt May	.12
648	Roy White	.12
649	Tom Griffin	.12
650	Joe Morgan	2.00
651	Rollie Fingers	1.50
652	Mario Mendoza	.12
653	Stan Bahnsen	.12
654	Bruce Boisclair	.12
655	Tug McGraw	.15
656	Larvell Blanks	.12
657	Dave Edwards	.12
658	Chris Knapp	.12
659	Brewers Team(George Bamberger)	.25
660	Rusty Staub	.15
661	Orioles Future Stars(Mark Corey, Dave Ford, Wayne Krenchicki)	.12
662	Red Sox Future Stars(Joel Finch, Mike O'Berry, Chuck Rainey)	.12
663	Angels Future Stars(Ralph Botting, Bob Clark), *(Dickie Thon)*	.25
664	White Sox Future Stars(Mike Colbern, *(Guy Hoffman*, Dewey Robinson)	.12
665	Indians Future Stars(Larry Andersen, Bobby Cuellar, Sandy Wihtol)	.12
666	Tigers Future Stars(Mike Chris, Al Greene, Bruce Robbins)	.12
667	Royals Future Stars(Renie Martin, Bill Paschall), *(Dan Quisenberry)*	1.50
668	Brewers Future Stars(Danny Boitano, Willie Mueller, Lenn Sakata)	.12
669	Twins Future Stars(Dan Graham, Rick Sofield), *(Gary Ward)*	.25
670	Yankees Future Stars(Bobby Brown, Brad Gulden, Darryl Jones)	.12
671	A's Future Stars(Derek Bryant, Brian Kingman), *(Mike Morgan)*	.60
672	Mariners Future Stars(Charlie Beamon, Rodney Craig, Rafael Vasquez)	.12
673	Rangers Future Stars(Brian Allard, Jerry Don Gleaton, Greg Mahlberg)	.12
674	Blue Jays Future Stars(Butch Edge, Pat Kelly, Ted Wilborn)	.12
675	Braves Future Stars(Bruce Benedict, Larry Bradford, Eddie Miller)	.12
676	Cubs Future Stars(Dave Geisel, Steve Macko, Karl Pagel)	.12
677	Reds Future Stars(Art DeFreites), *(Frank Pastore*, Harry Spilman)	.12
678	Astros Future Stars(Reggie Baldwin, Alan Knicely), *(Pete Ladd)*	.12
679	Dodgers Future Stars(Joe Beckwith), *(Mickey Hatcher*, Dave Patterson)	.25
680	Expos Future Stars*(Tony Bernazard*, Randy Miller, John Tamargo)	.12
681	Mets Future Stars(Dan Norman), *(Jesse Orosco*, *(Mike Scott)*	1.00
682	Phillies Future Stars(Ramon Aviles), *(Dickie Noles*, Kevin Saucier)	.12
683	Pirates Future Stars(Dorian Boyland, Alberto Lois, Harry Saferight)	.12
684	Cardinals Future Stars(George Frazier), *(Tom Herr*, Dan O'Brien)	.30
685	Padres Future Stars(Tim Flannery, Brian Greer, Jim Wilhelm)	.12
686	Giants Future Stars(Greg Johnston, Dennis Littlejohn, Phil Nastu)	.12
687	Mike Heath	.12
688	Steve Stone	.12
689	Red Sox Team(Don Zimmer)	.25
690	Tommy John	.40
691	Ivan DeJesus	.12
692	Rawly Eastwick	.12
693	Craig Kusick	.12
694	Jim Rooker	.12
695	Reggie Smith	.15
696	Julio Gonzalez	.12
697	David Clyde	.12
698	Oscar Gamble	.12
699	Floyd Bannister	.12
700	Rod Carew	2.00
701	*Ken Oberkfell*	.12
702	Ed Farmer	.12
703	Otto Velez	.12
704	Gene Tenace	.12
705	Freddie Patek	.12
706	Tippy Martinez	.12
707	Elliott Maddox	.12
708	Bob Tolan	.12
709	Pat Underwood	.12
710	Graig Nettles	.15
711	Bob Galasso	.12
712	Rodney Scott	.12
713	Terry Whitfield	.12
714	Fred Norman	.12
715	Sal Bando	.12
716	Lynn McGlothen	.12
717	Mickey Klutts	.12
718	Greg Gross	.12
719	Don Robinson	.12
720	Carl Yastrzemski	2.00
721	Paul Hartzell	.12
722	Jose Cruz	.15
723	Shane Rawley	.12
724	Jerry White	.12
725	Rick Wise	.12
726	Steve Yeager	.12

A player's name in *italic* type indicates a rookie card.

TABLE OF CONTENTS

L

S

Z